WHITMAN ENCYCLOPEDIA OF U.S. PAPER MONEY

Q. David Bowers

Foreword by
Fred Reed

Valuations Editor
Tom Denly

Research Consultants
Peter Huntoon
Don C. Kelly
Doug Murray

Whitman
Publishing, LLC
PUBLISHING SINCE 1934

WHITMAN ENCYCLOPEDIA
OF
U.S. PAPER MONEY

© 2009 Whitman Publishing, LLC
3101 Clairmont Road • Suite C • Atlanta, GA 30329

Correspondence concerning this book may be directed to the publisher, Attn: Whitman Encyclopedia of U.S. Paper Money, at the address above.

ISBN: 0794827039
Printed in the United States of America

Unless otherwise indicated, all notes illustrated with front and back are the actual two sides of a single note (not composites), so that every detail is correct.

Disclaimer: No warranty or representation of any kind is made concerning the accuracy or completeness of the information presented, or its usefulness in numismatic purchases or sales. The opinions of others may vary. The author and consultants may buy, sell, and sometimes hold certain of the items discussed in this book.

Caveat: The price estimates given are subject to variation and differences of opinion. Certain rare notes, encased postage stamps, and other items trade infrequently, and an estimate or past auction price may have little relevance to future transactions. Before making decisions to buy or sell, consult the latest information. Grading of currency is subject to wide interpretation, and opinions can differ, sometimes widely, even with notes certified by grading services. Past performance of any item in the market is not necessarily an indication of future performance, as the future is unknown. Such factors as changing demand, popularity, grading interpretations, emergence of hoards, new discoveries, strength of the overall market, and economic conditions will continue to be influences.

Valuations: Estimated market prices are given in various grades with information derived from multiple sources. These are given simply as an opinion and guide at the time of compilation in 2009. Certain actual transactions may take place at higher or lower figures, especially in the case of particularly rare or high-grade notes.

Advertisements within this book: Whitman Publishing, LLC, does not endorse, warrant, or guarantee any of the products or services of its advertisers. All warranties and guarantees are the sole responsibility of the advertiser.

About the cover: Collectors have nicknamed the large-size $1 Legal Tender Note, Series of 1869, the "Rainbow Note" because of its beautiful colors. Its vignettes show Christopher Columbus making sight of land, and a portrait of George Washington. The small-size $10,000 Federal Reserve Note, Series of 1934, meanwhile, has just a splash of color in its green seal and serial numbers. The stern portrait in the center is of Salmon P. Chase, the secretary of the Treasury who introduced the modern federal banknote system.

If you enjoy the *Whitman Encyclopedia of U.S. Paper Money*, you'll also enjoy these books: *A Guide Book of United States Paper Money, 100 Greatest American Currency Notes, A Guide Book of Southern States Currency, United States Currency,* and *A Guide Book of Counterfeit Confederate Currency. Obsolete Paper Money Issued by Banks in the United States 1782–1866* explores the colorful, ornate paper money that first circulated in the 13 colonies, and served American commerce up through the Civil War. *America's Money, America's Story* has much to offer the student of American paper currency, as does *Abraham Lincoln: The Image of His Greatness.*

For a complete catalog of numismatic reference books, supplies, and storage products, visit Whitman Publishing online at www.whitmanbooks.com.

CONTENTS

ABOUT THE AUTHOR

Q. David Bowers became a professional numismatist as a teenager in 1953, later (1960) earning a B.A. in finance from the Pennsylvania State University, which in 1976 bestowed its Distinguished Alumni Award on him. He served as president of the Professional Numismatists Guild from 1977 to 1979 and president of the American Numismatic Association from 1983 to 1985. He is a recipient of the Founder's and Farran Zerbe awards, the highest honors of the PNG and the ANA, and is a fellow of the American Antiquarian Society and the American Numismatic Society. He is the author of over 50 books and has received more honors from the Numismatic Literary Guild than has any other person. His column, "The Joys of Collecting," has been a feature of *Coin World* since 1961 and is the longest-running column by any author in the history of numismatics. His monthly column in *The Numismatist* has received many honors. He is also an award-winning columnist for *Paper Money* magazine. His *Obsolete Paper Money Issued by Banks in the United States 1782–1866* received three national awards, including the Wismer Literary Award from the Society of Paper Money Collectors. *100 Greatest American Currency Notes*, co-authored with David M. Sundman, has been widely honored. As chairman of Stack's LLC in New York City and Wolfeboro, New Hampshire, and as numismatic director for Whitman Publishing, LLC, he is also in the forefront of current events in the hobby.

Foreword author Fred Reed is a lifelong journalist, is the author or editor of more than a dozen books, and has written hundreds of articles. His work has won him numerous literary awards from the American Numismatic Association, the Society of Paper Money Collectors, the Numismatic Literary Guild, and other organizations. Reed has been editor-publisher of the Society of Paper Money Collectors' award-winning bimonthly journal *Paper Money* since 1999, and he is a regular columnist for *Coin World*, *Bank Note Reporter*, and *Coins* magazine. His groundbreaking research on Abraham Lincoln has been published in the *Lincoln Herald*, *The Numismatist*, and *Paper Money*, among other publications. Among his most recent publications is *Abraham Lincoln: The Image of His Greatness* (Book of the Year, Numismatic Literary Guild, 2009).

HOW TO USE THIS BOOK

Chapters 1 to 5 include information about grading, pricing, the market, popularity, how notes were made and distributed, and other information that is relevant to all later chapters. I recommend that you read this information first. This should give you a good foundation to be an informed, indeed smart buyer.

For individual note listings within the same series, identifying information (e.g., signature combination, seal color) has been omitted where it remains unchanged from one note to another. Throughout the book, the notation "Unknown" in a note's listing means that no notes are known to exist today.

Prices in this book are estimates based on the opinions of contributors, including the pricing panel coordinated by Tom Denly. In the marketplace prices can vary, often widely, especially for scarce, rare, and high-grade notes. Auction data for star notes and mules can be very erratic, making estimates especially tentative. In practice this is no different from the market fluctuations seen in certain *coin* series, such as colonial coins and die varieties of early United States copper and silver coins. Selected auction records cited for certain notes may not include the highest or lowest prices recorded, and in any event, auction activity and price movements are ongoing. Grades given in auction citations may be different from grades assigned to the same notes in earlier offerings. In all instances, consult current information available on the Internet or in the marketplace before making buying or selling decisions.

Grading is a matter of opinion, and opinions can vary. See chapter 4 for grading information. Price estimates for Uncirculated notes are for those certified by either Professional Coin Grading Service (PCGS) or Paper Money Guaranty (PMG), as at present these two services have the widest acceptance in the marketplace. Some valuable notes that are uncertified or that are certified by other services may be worth as much, or less, or more, and should be evaluated on their own merits before buying.

Printages (quantities of notes printed) that are estimates appear with the notation (est.); many of these estimates were calculated by Doug Murray. Some other printages, including those from Treasury reports, may be approximate as well (reports can be incomplete or subject to change). In many instances, especially for large-size notes, printages are often irrelevant to the number of notes surviving today.

Research concerning paper money is part of an evolving scenario, and the marketplace changes as well. The present book contains much information not available elsewhere in a single source. Corrections, additions, and comments for future editions are welcome.

CREDITS AND ACKNOWLEDGMENTS

Q. David Bowers and Whitman Publishing express appreciation to the many collectors, dealers, and scholars in the field of paper money who helped in various ways, a veritable "Who's Who" of paper-money scholarship.

Tom Denly, the valuations editor, holds membership number 1 in the Society of Paper Money Collectors. He has been a director of that society, of the Professional Currency Dealers Association, and of the Professional Numismatists Guild, among other offices. While in the business for over 30 years, he has studied prices, markets, and varieties.

Peter Huntoon has over a period of years shared much information concerning National Bank Notes, plate variations, history, and more. His research at the Smithsonian Institution and the National Archives, in cooperation with other scholars, has made available much information not available to past generations. His book *United States Large Size National Bank Notes* (1995) and a digitized later update have provided much information.

Don C. Kelly has made available his data on National Bank Note history and census numbers, continuing the John Hickman Project. He has studied in detail each of the 12,636 note-issuing National Banks, and his *National Bank Note Census* (compiled with James Kelly) lists known recorded notes by variety and offers, where available, specific information about serial numbers, plate letters, and grade.

Doug Murray has provided technical information concerning the sequence of printing notes, plate letters and numbers, star notes, and mules, and has helped in many other ways. He also provided historical as well as estimated printages, based on many years of groundbreaking research. These figures are usually based upon Treasury data but interpolated to reflect signature combinations or varieties within those figures, based upon the proportion of the number of notes known today. Doug's contributions also include data from the Bureau of Engraving and Printing (BEP) proof sheets studied at the Smithsonian Institution, information from the National Archives, and images of important notes. Doug worked with the author on an almost daily basis during the final months of manuscript preparation for this book.

Special thanks to **Martin Gengerke,** who provided extensive market data and rarity information from his data base, plus illustrations of certain very rare notes. His contributions form the base of much of the auction and rarity information given for large-size notes.

Appreciation is extended to the following:

Mike Abramson of Executive Currency provided images of unusual serial numbers and other information. **Sandy Bashover** of Track & Price provided auction information and price data. **Ashley Billingsley** provided images of various notes, including rarities. **Robert Bishop** provided images. **Wynn Bowers** provided copyediting and suggestions. **Jason W. Bradford** of Professional Coin Grading Service (PCGS) provided information on grading standards and interpretations, and reviewed pricing. **Lane Brunner** provided suggestions.

Murray Clark provided notes for illustration. **Edward A. and Joanne Dauer** provided images of various notes, including rarities. **Jennifer Donley** of the Smithsonian Institution provided images of rare currency. **Richard Doty,** senior curator of numismatics at the Smithsonian Institution, helped with information and images, including from their collection and the BEP archives.

Jeff Fisher provided notes for illustration. **Jerry Fochtman** helped with historical and numismatic aspects of Fractional Currency and in other ways. **Roberta A. French,** longtime research associate, helped in many ways over a long period of time.

Stephen Goldsmith provided market information. **Bruce Hagen** provided market information and consultation. **Warren S. Henderson** provided notes for illustration. **Heritage Auctions, Dustin Johnston, Len Glazer,** and **Allen Mincho** provided currency images including rarities, and reviewed parts of the manuscript; Johnston also helped with pricing. **Frank Hezmall** provided images. **Wayne Homren** helped publicize the search for needed images.

Harry E. Jones provided information and illustrations regarding error notes. **Glen Jorde** of Paper Money Guaranty (PMG) provided information on grading standards and interpretations.

Donald H. Kagin provided images and information. **Laura A. Kessler** reviewed pricing. **Lyn F. Knight** provided notes for illustration, including rarities. **David Koble** provided many small-size notes for illustration and helped in other ways.

Karen Lee of the Smithsonian Institution helped with information and images, including from their collection and the BEP archives. **Dana Linett** assisted with pricing. **Jess Lipka** provided notes for illustration.

Derek Moffitt provided much information on printing quantities and distribution of small-size notes and information on star notes. **Priscilla Moore** provided copyediting and suggestions. **Douglas Mudd,** curator of the ANA Edward C. Rochette Money Museum, provided information including images from the Aubrey and Adeline Bebee Collection. **Susan Novak** helped with extensive correspondence and transcriptions.

Alex Perakis provided notes for illustration. **The San Francisco Federal Reserve Bank Museum** provided images of various notes, including rarities. **Sergio Sanchez** provided images of notes and reviewed pricing. **The Smithsonian Institution** provided information and proof impressions of National Bank Notes. **Stack's, Christine Karstedt,** and **Lawrence Stack** provided information, many images including some from the John J. Ford Jr. collection, and the sharing of staff expertise. **Greg Stiles** suggested several improvements for the book. **David M. Sundman** of Littleton Coin Co. made generous contributions to the book's historical and technical information, and provided many illustrations.

Jamie Yakes provided images of scarce and rare small-size bank notes, information about mules, and review of sections of the text. **William Youngerman** provided an illustration.

Finally, to **Gene Hessler** goes much credit for identifying and gathering into one place information concerning the identities of artists and engravers for various types of federal currency from 1861 onward. His published books are a marvelous resource.

FOREWORD
by Fred Reed

For author Q. David Bowers, U.S. federal paper money is a banquet—and he insists on dining heartily on every course. With this new *Whitman Encyclopedia of U.S. Paper Money*, Dave invites the rest of us to share a menu of stupendous proportions.

What we know today as Federal Reserve Notes—small in size and with face values of $1 to $100—offer just a hint of the rich and varied history of U.S. paper money. Older notes, some workmanlike in appearance, others wondrously ornate, reflect the expansion, economics, and wars that have shaped U.S. history. These notes are evidences of the times, sometimes turbulent, from which they came.

The historical context of the various classes of U.S. paper money is important, and this work relates in an engaging manner the backgrounds out of which these notes came. A collector's interests might lie among the silver and gold certificates spawned by Western mineral deposits, or "America's hometown currency" of National Bank Notes, or the Federal Reserve Notes that have proliferated in the last century. All the types and varieties are succinctly described and cataloged here, with a great many illustrations of notes ranging from typical to exceedingly rare. Closeup details of significant and interesting features are shown as well, all in full color.

Collecting U.S. federal paper money is today a hobby and a business pursued by tens of thousands of adherents in a more or less organized fashion. A century ago, however, that number was surely only in the low hundreds. The reason for this growth is partly due to the availability of more notes to collect, but even more so to the growth in syngraphic research during that time.

Information on paper money in the 19th century was sparse. The first paper-money enthusiasts gravitated to colonial and Continental notes, Confederate currency, and Fractional Currency. It wasn't until much later that hobbyists took up the pursuit of federal notes proper. Research followed slowly, and cataloging was haphazard. Collectors were frequently rebuffed by official sources, and paper-money articles in the hobby's periodicals were spotty and often filled with errors. For decades it was illegal to even *picture* paper money in a guidebook. Catalogs of important collections omitted signatures, descriptions of seals, and other important details.

Over the second half of the 20th century, however, improved U.S. paper-money references began to appear with some frequency. The complexity and nuances of U.S. federal paper money would be daunting if it were not for researcher-authors like my longtime colleague Q. David Bowers. Dave has become the most prolific popularizer of the entire U.S. numismatic field, from coppers to gold, from soup to nuts. Those of us who have followed his career over the years knew it was only a matter of time until his interest in paper-money collecting spilled over into the pages of well-researched and

elaborately illustrated volumes like the *Whitman Encyclopedia.* And here again, we find that wherever Dave Bowers shines his light, enlightenment is sure to follow. Over decades and scores of numismatic books, Bowers has become the most cited and quoted numismatic author of all time.

The panorama of U.S. federal paper money is broad and Q. David Bowers surveys it in its entirety. He packs this *Whitman Encyclopedia* with years of personal investigation, observations, and the research of specialists in the field. He knew personally Amon Carter, John Hickman, William A. Philpott, Herman K. Crofoot, and other legends in the field. For this work Bowers has explored a vast shelf of sources ranging from Treasury and congressional documents to numismatic publications of all kinds and eras. He serves up choice bite-size morsels that are understandable to the novice and an intellectual delight to the experienced collector. Even collectors with years of study will find much that is new, novel, and neat in Bowers's very readable text.

The book is a large reference to be sure, but Bowers intends it to be a practical guide for the collector, too. He opens with important collector-oriented information on grading, buying practices, and market conditions. As a professional numismatic dealer for a half century, Bowers knows well whereof he speaks. His teachings, if understood and applied, will make the reader a more astute purchaser of paper money.

The scope of this book is truly encyclopedic. From the earliest issues of the unified colonies during the Revolutionary era, through the small-size Treasury notes that financed the War of 1812, to antebellum interest-bearing Treasury notes, to National Gold Bank Notes, Bowers telescopes a great deal of history and lore into digest entries that provide historical context, catalog varieties, and illustrate representative examples.

The meat of this work is its extensive coverage of U.S. federal issues from the Civil War era to the present. Bowers explains how notes have evolved over time, how they are made and distributed. Then follows a comprehensive summary of all classes of U.S. paper money from 3¢ Fractional Currency to $100,000 bills. Chapters on U.S. encased postage stamps and paper-money errors, and appendices on Treasury terms and signatures found on federal notes, round out the presentation.

When the scholars of the Enlightenment and their predecessors invented the "encyclopedia" what they had in mind was a comprehensive compendium of knowledge, organized systematically in narrative segments. Such compendia can be general or specific. Among the former, one thinks readily of the *Encyclopedia Britannica;* among the latter, medical or religious works are typical. With the publication of this *Whitman Encyclopedia* all fans of U.S. paper money have a worthy claim to a handy, one-volume encyclopedia of their own.

INTRODUCTION AND OVERVIEW

Paper money furnishes an interesting—indeed, fascinating—field of numismatic pursuit. Most collectors, dealers, and scholars who have been involved for a few years or more wouldn't trade this specialty for any other.

And yet, there are many complexities to paper money, as well as aspects that are little understood. In this book many of these are addressed specifically. They may or may not be vital, or even slightly necessary, to the purchase or sale of a note, but they will contribute to buyers' understanding. It has been my experience that the more information that can be gained, the better. If examined closely, the face or back of even an "ordinary" note, say a $1 Legal Tender Note of 1862, will reveal a veritable panorama of interesting features. Such aspects as signatures, series imprints, plate letters and numbers, the appearance of the Treasury seal, patent information, variations in typography, style of serial numbers, and more will become evident and will invite even closer inspection. This can be a numismatic delight.

On the other hand, many if not most readers of this book will be more interested in two basic aspects: grade and price. This is fine and is another part of numismatics. That is no different from the marketplace for rare coins. Some collectors and dealers examining a variety of large copper cent, say a 1794 Starred Reverse Sheldon-48 variety, will be interested only in grade and price. Others may want to join the Early American Coppers Club, read the dozens of pages that have been printed about the various aspects of this variety (including a *poem* that was written about it in the 19th century), and to learn as much as possible.

I daresay that the owner of an 1862 $1 Legal Tender Note who learns as much as possible about the history and tradition of the variety, like the 1794 Starred Reverse copper cent owners, will appreciate and savor its possession far more than someone who is interested only in grade and price. Moreover, prices always change, and whether we like it or not, assigned grades sometimes change as well. Art, history, romance, and numismatic appeal will last forever; these are the prime aspects of interest for anyone who enjoys numismatics.

No one has to collect either an 1862 note or a 1794 cent. They are not essential to life. However, they can certainly contribute to well-being, in the sense that numismatics is a world into itself, with many pleasures, challenges, and nice experiences in the offing. Also, I like to think that numismatists are fine people, a cut above average citizens.

SCOPE OF THE BOOK

This book begins here with general information. Historical and basic type information for federal paper money from 1861 to date is given in chapters 2 and 3. Chapters 4 and 5 include techniques of grading, how to be a smart buyer, and other information I believe you will find to be very useful. Following are chapters in denomination order from $1 to $100,000. (Yes, Virginia, there are $100,000 notes. Only the Treasury department has them, including one on loan to the ANA Edward C. Rochette Money Museum. Another is shown now and again at Bureau of Engraving and Printing—BEP—displays at numismatic conventions.) While chapter 2 gives basic information on the different series, from the Interest-Bearing Notes of early 1861 down to the latest Federal Reserve Notes currently available from banks, it is in the specialized chapters that most historical, technical, and numismatic facts are presented, along with prices.

Bringing up the rear are chapters on Postage and Fractional Currency, paper-money errors, Continental Currency, early 19th-century Treasury Notes, and encased postage stamps. In the appendices you will find information about signatures as well as paper-money terms and definitions.

ORGANIZATION

In this book, notes in the federal series are listed in order of denomination from 1861 to the present, although now with some slight modifications.

The first notes in the federal series are of the $1 types, progressing in order to $10,000, plus, for a touch of whimsy perhaps, the aforementioned $100,000 note.

Within those categories the various classes—such as Legal Tender Notes, National Bank Notes, Silver Certificates, or whatever—are arranged, followed by series and signature combinations listed chronologically, punctuated with different varieties. This layout is similar to what has been used in coin reference books for a long time. As an example, in coin references, sections on dollars begin with early large silver varieties, continuing through Liberty Seated, Morgan, and Peace issues, then clad Eisenhower dollars, and finally the "mini" dollars, including the Sacagawea and Presidential issues of today. Certain of these types are vastly different from each other in size, metallic content, and appearance,

$1 Legal Tender Note, Series of 1862, an early "greenback" issue (Whitman-6). The portrait at the upper left is of Salmon P. Chase, who was appointed as Lincoln's secretary of the Treasury in 1861.

such as a 1794 Flowing Hair silver dollar and the modern Presidential "golden dollars."

Regarding federal notes, they can be considered in different ways. Arthur and Ira Friedberg's text *Paper Money of the United States*, launched in 1953, is arranged by legislation that affected notes, such as Silver Certificates in one section, National Bank Notes in another section, Legal Tender Notes elsewhere, and National Gold Bank Notes in still a different place. Small-size notes are treated separately, and some small-size notes (such as the HAWAII and Yellow Seal issues for World War II) are in other sections. The *Comprehensive Catalog of U.S. Paper Money*, by Gene Hessler and Carlson Chambliss, arranges by denomination from $1 to $10,000, but presents large notes in one part of the book and small notes in another. Each arrangement can have its advantages.

This prompted some thinking with regard to the present text. I picked a layout continuous from $1 to $10,000 (oops, make that $100,000!), as I feel an item can be found easily that way. Also, certain front matter, such as information about the Bureau of Engraving and Printing, serial numbers, star notes, Treasury seals, and the like, is equally applicable to large-size and small-size paper.

HISTORY AND TECHNICALITIES

To me, the history of a given series or note can be just as interesting as the note itself. I have derived immense enjoyment

from reading *Banker's Magazine*, annual reports of the Treasury department and its divisions, articles in numismatic periodicals (the *Essay-Proof Journal*, *Paper Money*, and the *Bank Note Reporter* are the most important), reports of congressional committees, newspaper and other popular press articles, and more.

Bank notes are closely intertwined with financial history, as well as with elements of politics. Silver Certificates resulted from one of the greatest boondoggles of all time, the Bland-Allison Act of February 28, 1878. Probably not many readers know that the reason for erratic production of small-size Legal Tender Notes made in the 1950s and 1960s was another piece of legislation in 1878, the Act of May 3, which provided that the total amount of Legal Tender Notes in circulation was to be maintained at precisely $346,861,016. The rule was never changed. Curious artifacts from this are the Series of 1966 and 1966-A $100 bills, printed in quantity to maintain this archaic amount, which was apparently easier than turning out a flood of low-denomination bills.

The Panic of 1907 resulted in a design change for National Bank Notes of all denominations. The very curious Series of 1929 Federal Reserve Bank Notes would not have been produced had not Franklin Delano Roosevelt, in office for just two days, decreed a "Bank Holiday" beginning on March 6, 1933, during which every financial institution

Although the printage was relatively low, the $100 Federal Reserve Bank Note, Series of 1929, from the Federal Reserve Bank of Cleveland is readily available in Uncirculated grade on the market today. Although these notes are dated 1929, they were printed in 1933 and mostly released in the 1940s. Such information is interesting to contemplate across various notes and series.

locked its doors. These notes were literally made in the blink of an eye, the first ones in just two days.

An early Treasury seal with a "spiked border" has 34 projections. Why 34? Because this was the number of states in the Union when the seal was devised.

If there are rocket scientists in paper-money research, two nominees would have to be Peter Huntoon and Doug Murray. Their depth of research into proofs, documents, account books, and other information at the National Archives and at the Smithsonian Institution is absolutely incredible. They have analyzed printing techniques, distribution, technical points of design, and more. Much of the information they provided for this book has never been available in any single source before.

"You can see a lot by just looking," observed Yogi Berra. As curious as it may seem, many discoveries have been made in recent years, including by Huntoon and Murray, simply by closely viewing various notes. Others had not thought to do it before. Along the way, many interesting varieties have been discovered. This technique is old news to *coin* collectors, who, ever since the publication of books and monographs on die varieties by Édouard Frossard, J.W. Haseltine, Frank W. Andrews, and others in the 19th century, have studied and collected varieties through the aid of a looking glass. Not so with paper money. If you are the slightest bit skeptical, just look through paper-money catalogs and reference books of the 1930s and 1940s, and you will see that in many instances, it is impossible to classify them today because of the lack of information about dates, signatures, seals, and the like, even for rarities. There were no pictures back then, as this was against Treasury regulations. Accordingly, research and the transmission of useful information were stifled.

In the January 1934 issue of *The Numismatist*, Robert H. Lloyd, in "Cataloguing Paper Money," took issue with contemporary auction catalogs, which often gave few details of the notes being offered. For example, he cited a listing of a note described as "$1 bill, red seal, Unc." The signature combination, date of issue, and other information was not provided! Lloyd reminded prospective catalogers: "Signature combinations are of major importance and run throughout the series. Comparatively few issues are found with only one set of signatures, while some issues have a dozen or so." He further stated that currency should be described as "United States Notes," "Silver Certificates," or in some other appropriate manner. This seems basic today, but back then there was hardly any interest in such things.

As to populations and market appearances of notes, the Hickman Project, a census of National Bank Note serial numbers begun by John Hickman decades ago, has been continued by Don C. Kelly and his son James, the latest iteration being their book, *National Bank Notes*, and the accompanying *National Bank Note Census* CD. This effort continues to capture information about every individual National Bank Note observed or reported. Hickman, who often worked closely with currency specialist Dean Oakes, was a marvelous fellow. At a convention in the early 1980s I mentioned to him that I had located a Series of 1882 Brown Back $5 on the Lake National Bank of Wolfborough, New Hampshire (the town name of Wolfeborough, per the old style, was misspelled by the bank in its title and all of its printed material). He paused to think a moment, perhaps contemplating the 12,636 national banks that issued notes from 1863 onward and the data he had compiled on them, and then said, "That is the first note I have heard of on that bank." Unforgettable!

Martin Gengerke has been compiling market appearances of large-size notes for many years. His information has been very useful for me. In more recent times, Sandy Bashhover's "Track & Price" database, largely based on market appearances and citations since 1990, has become essential as well.

Many mysteries remain to be solved, or at least investigated. The Second Issue of Fractional Currency is quite the enigma—different varieties of paper were used, as were three different printing processes, in combination with erratic and inconsistent published records and printage figures. Trying to unravel the puzzle of Gold Certificates made under the Act of March 3, 1863, was a pleasant exercise in cooperation with

Doug Murray during research for the book, but not all has been answered. Who engraved this or that design can be uncertain, as at least two early artists at the National Currency Bureau billed the government for "their" work, but subcontracted privately to outsiders. Certain Interest-Bearing Notes yielding 7.3% interest for three years and other issues of the mid-1860s were a playground for mischief and pilfering within the bureau, again with inconsistent records. And so on.

In some instances, large quantities of notes were printed, but none were ever distributed, at least, not to the knowledge of Peter Huntoon and Doug Murray, who have checked archival records. In other instances, large quantities were issued, but notes are scarce to rare today. Why, for example, is the Series of 1929 $5 Federal Reserve Bank Note from San Francisco, of which 360,000 were printed, a great rarity in Uncirculated condition and worth many thousands of dollars, when in the same series a $100 note from Cleveland, of which 276,000 were printed, can be purchased in Uncirculated grade for just a few hundred dollars?

Even when we *do* know something, it can be difficult to understand. I defy just about anyone to state with accuracy when the issuance of certain series of notes began and when it ended. Why in the National Bank Notes field were Series of 1882 Value Back notes issued into the 1920s, when in the meantime there had been new designs—three different designs for the Series of 1902 alone? Why could a bank chartered in 1863 end up with a higher charter number than one formed in 1880? Congress authorized the addition of the motto "In God We Trust" to paper money in 1955, so why do certain Series of *1875* notes have it? Why, in 1873, would the holder of a Legal Tender Note be unable to spend it in San Francisco, while the holder of a National Gold Bank Note could easily spend it there, but would not consider spending it in New York City? The answers are in this book, and it is interesting to delve into them.

Continental Currency notes have their own fascination, such as the curious mottoes on each denomination, often imparting object lessons or philosophy to those who could understand them. A good knowledge of Latin helped. If today the Treasury department were to issue a note prominently inscribed POST NUBILA PHOEBUS or DEUS REGNAT EXULTET TERRA, there would be howls of protest. The present era of designs is rather dumbed down. In 1969 the Treasury seal, which had been inscribed THESAUR. AMER. SEPTENT. SIGIL. for over a century, was revised to read, THE DEPARTMENT OF THE TREASURY. Regardless, we can all (or at least some of us can) be grateful that old-time paper money richly reflects tradition.

Further on the subject of Continental Currency, why are bills imprinted "York-Town" (today's York, Pennsylvania, at one time the capital of the new United States) rarer than the others, even though York-Town notes were made in larger quantities than for any earlier issue?

On encased postage stamps, what is the product *Cocoaine*, and what is *Kalliston?* Owning an encasement advertising these, put out by Joseph Burnett in Boston, is worthwhile, but it is also worthwhile to learn what the inscriptions mean. Ditto for "S.T. 1860.X" on another encased postage stamp, a cabalistic notation that aroused much public speculation in the 1860s.

Just as is true for other numismatic series, while simple ownership of a Legal Tender Note, or piece of Postage Currency, or a Continental Currency $55 note (how unusual!), or an encased postage stamp can be pleasurable, knowing its story can double that enjoyment.

GRADE

The preceding said, I'll now offer a few more words on grade and price. First, about grade: The value of a note in

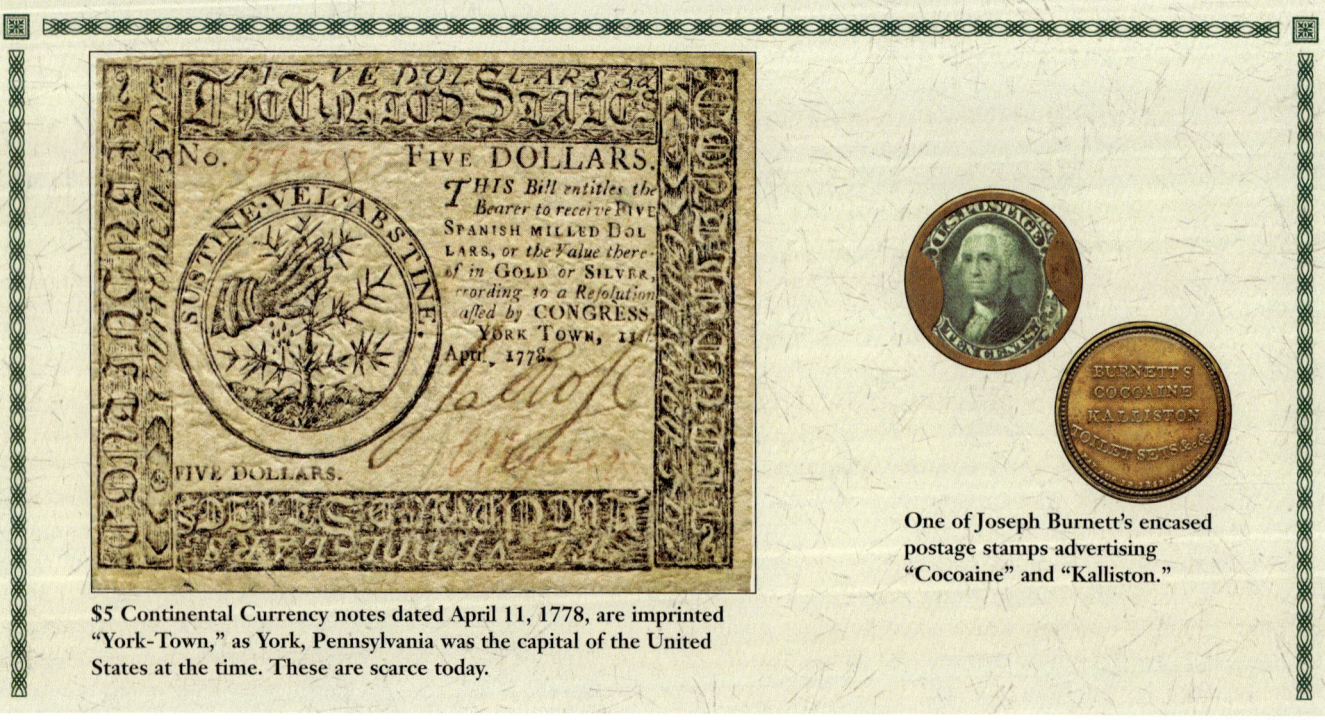

$5 Continental Currency notes dated April 11, 1778, are imprinted "York-Town," as York, Pennsylvania was the capital of the United States at the time. These are scarce today.

One of Joseph Burnett's encased postage stamps advertising "Cocoaine" and "Kalliston."

the marketplace is generally dependent on its grade. The higher the state of preservation, the more valuable a note will be. A bill in tattered Fair grade can be valued at a low figure and may not be wanted by everyone. An unused, crisp and bright note graded as Unc-65 is apt to be widely desired and, often, very expensive.

In paper money as well as in other areas of numismatics, one rule does not fit all. For certain Continental Currency notes (see chapter 20), an Uncirculated note printed on special blue paper may be valued at less than an About Uncirculated note of the same variety, but signed and used in commerce.

While hardly anyone would want a tattered, Fair-grade example of a federal note that is readily available in higher grades, should a $20 Demand Note be found with the words "for the" hand-signed, it would likely bring thousands of dollars, even if in a low grade, as only a single example is known to exist. Similarly, there are *many* rare varieties of early National Bank Notes that have been graded from Fair to Good or Very Good and have sold for many thousands of dollars. These, of course, are the exceptions.

The grading of paper money is an art, not a science, and different dealers and collectors, as well as commercial grading services, often have interpretations that vary, often widely. More than just a few notes have been improved by professional conservation, as in the illustrated Arkansas $1 note, a practice common and well respected in the field of manuscripts, autographs, and prints (as with the National Archives and Library of Congress, for example). In the field of paper money, such conservation is viewed differently, is hardly ever mentioned in retail price listings, and when revealed is apt to cause a problem. Interestingly, *auction* descriptions are apt to mention conservation if the cataloger is aware of it.

Chapter 4 addresses paper-money grading. The codification of grade levels is in its beginning stages, at least as far as trying to reduce practices to a set of readable and understandable guidelines. As yet there is no *Official American Numismatic Association Grading Standards for Paper Money* book, nor have any standards been published by the Society of Paper Money Collectors or the Professional Currency Dealers Association. Although you are on your own, it is easy to get assistance in the way of opinions and suggestions from dealers and other collectors.

If it is any help, I mention that within numismatics there are no "official" grading standards for tokens or medals either, and that in other fields of collecting and connoisseurship there are none for modern art or old masters, none for autographs and manuscripts, none for antique furniture, none for etchings and prints, none for ancient Greek and Roman artifacts, and none for old books. This is just a short list. In fact, *very few* collecting fields have standards agreed upon by everyone. However, *enjoyment* is the operative word for nearly everyone in those specialties. I should mention that the establishment of grading standards for coins has made a lot of people unhappy and has been a detriment to enjoyment for these individuals.

Think positively. Grading standards will become increasingly well defined in years to come. In the field of paper money, don't let grading or any other aspect take away from your happiness.

PRICE

What is it worth? How much does it cost? What will lot number 154 sell for in an upcoming Lyn Knight sale, or lot number 12025 in the next Heritage sale? Or what will I have to bid for notes I would like to buy that are to cross the

A unique note from the low end of the grading scale, a $1 note of the National Bank of Western Arkansas at Fort Smith. From a 2003 Lyn Knight sale, described in part as "Very Good. The condition is well used and restored. . . . Never before has a $1 first charter [of Arkansas] been offered for sale. . . . In fact, there are only four Arkansas first charters known to exist in any denomination, making it one of the top rarities of first charters. . . . This note is unique for bank title as well." ("First charter" is a nickname, in this instance for what is properly called an Original Series note.)

No matter what the grade, this Arkansas "ace" (as $1 notes are often called) is a trophy note deluxe, as it is the only known such note from the entire state. The price paid was $44,000, plus a 15% buyer's fee, plus 5% to the dealer-agent who bid, for a total cost of $52,800.

The beautiful and popular $1 Series of 1896 "Educational Note" (W-59). This variety is available in just about any grade desired and is in demand all across the board.

block at Stack's, Spink-Smythe, or some other auction event?

With the possible exception of current notes you can get for face value at a bank, prices are hardly standard. For a popular $1 Series of 1896 Silver Certificate "Educational Note" in a given grade, one dealer might ask $1,400, and another $1,700. It could be that the $1,400 note is more attractive. Or it could have problems.

Was a certain Series of 1929 Federal Reserve Bank Note certified as Unc-65 really worth the more than $3,000 it sold for recently, if an uncertified Unc-63 note of that variety was offered by the same well-respected dealer for $625? Visually, there did not seem to be much difference between the two. This is a real-life question that came up when this book was in preparation.

As you become more and more involved with paper money, you will find that prices vary, sometimes widely, among sellers and in auction sales. Although each section of this book lists prices for various currency items, often in a wide selection of grades, by no means are they precise in terms of going into the marketplace and acquiring a note for exactly that figure. Nor is any other price guide for coins, tokens, medals, or paper money precise either. At best, these are general guides, a distillation of expert opinion at the time the guide is published. And what a great lineup of market experts valuations editor Tom Denly has enlisted for this book!

To the above add the subjective nature of grading a note, and you have a situation in which there can be many variables. In many ways this is an *advantage* for you, although at first glance it may not seem to be so. The secret is that if you gain knowledge, learn to evaluate notes for grade and quality, and look around in the marketplace, you can make very profitable buys. Most advanced collectors and dealers would not have it any other way!

COLLECTING CONSIDERATIONS

When it comes to actually acquiring notes, collectors and dealers have a number of ways of thinking. Typically, a spe-

cialist in National Bank Notes thinks first of *location*, and cares very little about the signature combination, with a very few exceptions (such as the rare Jeffries-Spinner pair in the Original Series). In fact, signature combinations are so unimportant for the class that most collectors of National Bank Notes don't seem to notice them at all. And if a note has a special signature, such as a $1 "ace" with Jeffries-Spinner from a certain town, this can actually be an annoyance to anyone wanting to buy it for its location, such as in a Heritage sale on September 26, 2003, where lot 3218, an Original Series $1 note from the First National Bank of Mankato, Minnesota, in Fine grade, was described in part as follows:

> This note possesses the very rarest of Treasury signature combinations. . . . Only a handful of Jeffries-Spinner notes are known from all banks combined, with this example the only such note we've ever seen or heard of from Mankato, and the only $1 reported from this bank.

The successful bidder paid $8,500, plus a 15% buyer's fee, plus 5% to the agent for doing the bidding, or $10,200. If the note had had Treasury signatures such as the often-seen Colby-Spinner combination, likely the price would have been a third of that. (This note is illustrated in chapter 6.)

Moreover, if you ask a specialist in, say, National Bank Notes of Iowa as to how many of his or her notes have Lyons-Roberts signatures, or those of Vernon-Treat, the answer might be, "I have never checked." On the other hand, a collector of small-size $1 notes take signature combinations very seriously, ditto for variations in the plates. An Uncirculated Series 1928-D Silver Certificate with the Julian-Woodin signatures costs in the hundreds of dollars, while a comparable 1928-E note imprinted Julian-Morgenthau runs into the thousands. In the current series, Federal Reserve Bank locations are of prime importance, as is the location of printing, either in Washington, D.C., or Fort Worth, Texas. Even the *size* of a plate number can mean a large difference in value in certain small-size notes. A collector of large-size National Bank Notes would not notice such number variations.

Again I mention that there are exceptions to just about every paper-money rule. While a collector of small-size $1 or

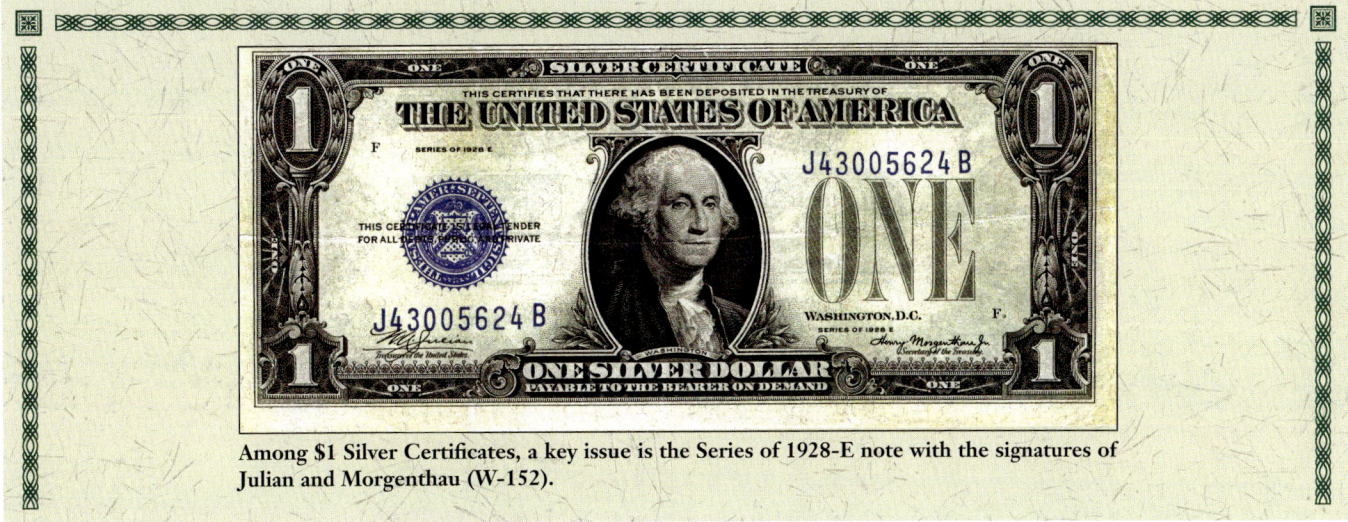

Among $1 Silver Certificates, a key issue is the Series of 1928-E note with the signatures of Julian and Morgenthau (W-152).

$2 notes would pay close attention to signatures or even minor plate differences, this would not be true, at least not even close to the same extent, for a typical numismatist buying a small-size $5,000 or other high-denomination note. These are "trophy notes" and play to a fairly narrow audience of those who can afford them. Not much attention is paid the details on such pieces. A collector will usually be content with a single note, not an array of different bills arranged by signature combinations and Federal Reserve Banks.

In still other instances, collectors and dealers think of notes in related groups. For example, the $1, $2, and $5 "Educational Notes" are often collected as a group, never mind that they are Silver Certificates. They could be Legal Tender Notes or anything else. There are signature variations for these notes, but scarcely anyone cares at all. It is the design that counts. Similarly, we have the "Rainbow Notes," the $1 to $10 Series of 1869 Legal Tender Notes with beautiful colors on their faces. Again, they could be Silver Certificates or Treasury Notes or something else, and they still would have the same degree of popularity.

Come to think of it, this may be like contemplating a hand during a card game. Sometimes one thinks of a straight—everything in a row, say 7, 8, 9, 10, and jack. Other times a flush, or all of the same suit, such as clubs or spades, will

come to mind, and then who cares about whether they are aces, deuces, or 10s? Still other times, in groups such as two of one number, such as a pair of 7s, and three of another, such as a trio of queens, will be a winner, and a stray ace will be of no interest at all. There is no one best way to evaluate cards, except in certain special games.

More than a few collectors use the "I like it" method when compiling a want list. Such a person might collect a $5 Series of 1882 Brown Back note with the flashy "circus poster" layout of the bank name and address, and a colorful back, but would have no interest at all in acquiring a much rarer Series of 1882 Value Back. I have more to say about the "I like it" factor in chapter 5.

Bills with nicknames such as the "Battleship Note," "Silver Dollar Note," "Technicolor Note," "Bison Note," and "Porthole Note" play to a good audience, as do many others. For a round-up of these, you may want to borrow or buy a copy of *100 Greatest American Currency Notes*, by David Sundman and me. Paper-money enthusiasts comprised of collectors, dealers, and scholars voted for their favorites, Whitman Publishing compiled the results, and the authors gathered pictures and wrote the descriptions.

All of these factors are interesting to contemplate as you consider building your collection.

HISTORY AND OVERVIEW OF FEDERAL NOTES

This chapter discusses each of the major types of regular currency from 1861 to date, including information on when they debuted and what monetary purpose they were intended to meet. However, to understand some of the distinctions among the types of currency produced, as well as the variations within a certain type, you must first become familiar with the basic characteristics and vocabulary of paper money.

CHARACTERISTICS OF FEDERAL NOTES

Beyond gaining a general knowledge of the various series and types of paper money, it is important to become familiar with characteristics that can lend value or interest to currency. Perhaps the best known of such features is the addition of a star to a serial number to create a "star note." Many of these, especially those printed prior to the 1950s, can be worth many multiples of the price of a regular note. Similarly, the size, color, and placement of the Treasury seal can affect value, sometimes dramatically. Ditto for signature combinations—on an early National Bank Note, the Jeffries-Spinner pair can make a note worth *much* more than, say, one imprinted Colby-Spinner.

SIZE OF NOTES

The sizes of most federal notes from 1861 to date can be divided into two categories, large and small. Large-size bills measure about 7 inches by 3 inches, although there are variations. An Original Series National Bank Note is slightly smaller than an Interest-Bearing Note or a Federal Reserve Bank Note, for example. The width of the margins can vary considerably, especially among National Bank bills, and that affects the size. Virtually nothing has appeared in print concerning proper margin sizes. Most large-size currency sheets, nearly always with four subjects, were trimmed by one machine and cut apart by another. Accordingly, if a note of a given variety is smaller than others of that variety, it has probably been trimmed by a numismatist, perhaps to make it appear better centered or to remove a stain or other problem.

National Bank Notes are exceptions to the foregoing. These were shipped to banks in uncut sheets, which cashiers or other employees cut apart with shears or scissors, often carelessly. Most were in four-subject sheets, but some large denominations were arranged as two subjects, such as $50-$100.

Small-size bills, issued since 1929, measure slightly more than 6 inches by 2.5 inches. Small-size bills have been printed in sheets of 6, 12, and (starting in 1952) 18 subjects, and today 32 subjects.

COLORED INKS

The majority of bills from the 1861 Demand Note "greenbacks" to the present day are printed in green on the back. This practice arose from the promotion of this color by the American Bank Note Co., proprietors of the "Patent Green Tint" introduced in 1857 on state-bank bills, and the assertion that of all colors it was most resistant to counterfeiting by photographic means. Although this was not true (red was a better deterrent), green became the "color of money." Today, the term *greenback* remains part of the American idiom.

On April 28, 1863, Asahel K. Eaton of New York City was granted patent number 32,298 for "improvement in ink for printing bank notes." This imprint appeared on a few note plates of the era, generally replacing the 1857 patent.

Certain large-size Gold Certificates were printed in yellow or orange on the back, some Silver Certificates were in brown, as were the first Series of 1882 National Bank Notes, and there are other scattered exceptions. The backs of Fractional Currency notes of the Second Issue were made in a variety of colors, including purple and carmine.

Beginning in 1869 and continuing into the late 1870s, a special paper with a blue-tinted streak was used for printing notes of many kinds. Most National Gold Bank Notes were produced on a yellow-tinted paper. Today's colorized notes have various pastel shades on the face, as well as some brighter colors.

SIGNATURES ON PAPER MONEY

The signatures of the register of the Treasury and the Treasurer of the United States were added to paper money from the earliest Interest-Bearing Notes of 1861. At first these officers signed the notes personally, but it quickly became evident that this was an impossible task. When Demand Notes were introduced in August 1861, 70 clerks were kept

$5 Series of 1882 Brown Back Note issued by the National Granite State Bank of Exeter, New Hampshire, with the vanity signature of Warren F. Putnam. He had been named to the post of cashier in 1873 after the previous cashier, N.A. Shute, had absconded with the bank's funds. Putnam followed suit, fleeing with a large amount of money, and was arrested on November 5, 1893, after which the bank failed.

busy adding their own signatures for the Treasury officers. In 1862, printed signatures became standard. Today, the printed signatures are those of the Treasurer of the United States and the secretary of the Treasury.

On some early federal notes extending into the 1880s, there are autographed countersignatures of other Treasury officials, such as assistant Treasurers. These are found on certain Gold Certificates, many Silver Certificates of Deposit of the Series of 1878 and 1880, and on some high-denomination bills. Signing these became a tiring task, and countersignatures were often added to the printing plates. This, of course, eliminated any security checks that personally autographed countersignatures may have had.

Large-size Federal Reserve Notes and Federal Reserve Bank Notes of both sizes have printed signatures of Federal Reserve officers in addition to the federal names. Sometimes these were hastily or clumsily printed, as on some of the larger-denomination large-size notes and many of the Series of 1929 Federal Reserve Bank Notes.

National Bank Notes from 1863 through the early 20th century have a space at the bottom for the cashier and president of the issuing bank to sign in ink. This led to many variations. Some officers were so proud that they created "vanity signatures," large and with flourishes. Others made the task as simple as possible by using one or two initials and a hastily written surname.

The president of a national bank, particularly of a small one, had as his (rarely her) main duty the conducting of meetings of the board of directors and the annual meeting of shareholders. He was at the bank only occasionally. Salaries for bank presidents were often of a token nature, just a fraction of that paid to cashiers. It was not unusual for a bank president to live at a distance, or to serve in the state or national capital as an elected official. In such instances, others signed for him, usually adding "v," "vp," or "vice" in ink after their signatures. At other times the president would sign a pile of sheets first, and then leave them with the cashier for the latter to sign when they were paid out.

The cashier of a small or medium-size bank was the chief operating officer and the highest paid by far. It was the cashier's duty to be sure that accounts were kept properly, security was in place, and the bank was operated according to accepted principles. Most National Bank Notes were personally signed by the cashier. Only rarely is a note seen today with "asst." or some similar notation to indicate that another person did the work. It was widely thought that a bill did not become "money" until both officers signed. Notes signed by just one officer and then stolen would thus have no value. In reality, thieves simply added their own version of the signatures to notes and spent them. The bank was still responsible for the loss, as court decisions determined.

The practice of having bank officers' signatures added to National Bank Note printing plates began in 1921, an accommodation to banks that paid a premium for this service. Earlier, some large banks had signatures overprinted once they received sheets of notes, typically done by a commercial printer. Rubber-stamped signatures became very common as well, sometimes applied separately in colored ink. These stamps often faded, rendering the names illegible.

CLASS OF NOTE

Federal currency has been issued in well-defined classes; however, nomenclature for a given class can vary widely.

As an example, consider the $5 denomination. What we call the Demand Notes of 1861 had no particular title. The inscription read, "The United States promise to pay to the bearer five dollars on demand," causing these to be called Demand Notes in Treasury records.

Similarly, the first of what we call Legal Tender Notes, the Series of 1862, have no title, but on the back there is the imprint, "This note is a legal tender for. . . . " Then in 1869, the imprint TREASURY NOTE was used. The title of the same class was changed to UNITED STATES NOTE with the Series of 1875, a designation retained through the small-size series. Numismatists call them all Legal Tender Notes.

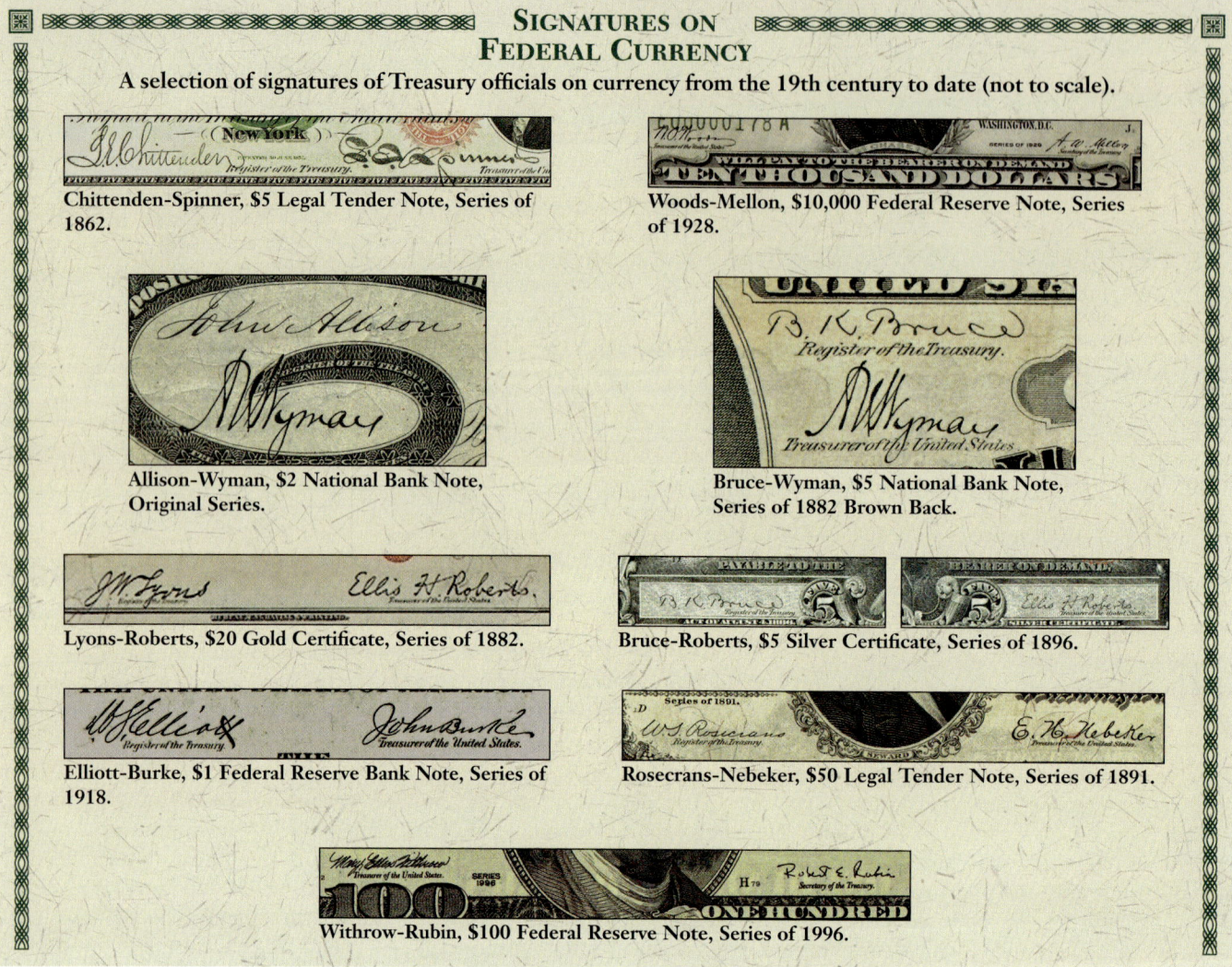

SIGNATURES ON FEDERAL CURRENCY

A selection of signatures of Treasury officials on currency from the 19th century to date (not to scale).

Chittenden-Spinner, $5 Legal Tender Note, Series of 1862.

Woods-Mellon, $10,000 Federal Reserve Note, Series of 1928.

Allison-Wyman, $2 National Bank Note, Original Series.

Bruce-Wyman, $5 National Bank Note, Series of 1882 Brown Back.

Lyons-Roberts, $20 Gold Certificate, Series of 1882.

Bruce-Roberts, $5 Silver Certificate, Series of 1896.

Elliott-Burke, $1 Federal Reserve Bank Note, Series of 1918.

Rosecrans-Nebeker, $50 Legal Tender Note, Series of 1891.

Withrow-Rubin, $100 Federal Reserve Note, Series of 1996.

National Bank Notes are actually titled NATIONAL CURRENCY, but no collector today would say, "I collect National Currency Notes." Instead, *National Bank Notes* is the term used, although this exact term was never printed on currency. National Gold Bank Notes of the 1870s have no particular title at all, but REDEEMABLE IN GOLD COIN is lettered at the top border.

Silver Certificates were lettered SILVER CERTIFICATE from the outset in 1878, continuing through the small-size series in the 20th century.

The imprint TREASURY NOTE (which had also been used on Series of 1869 Legal Tender Notes) is seen on the Series of 1890 Treasury or Coin Notes.

What we call Federal Reserve Notes (such as the large-size Series of 1914) are titled just that, FEDERAL RESERVE NOTE, as are small-size notes today. However, what we call Federal Reserve Bank Notes are instead titled NATIONAL CURRENCY.

The study of illustrations in the text will reveal the inscriptions used by a particular series in its era.

INSCRIPTIONS AND OBLIGATIONS

The promise to pay or the "will pay" on a note is called the *obligation*. There have been wide variations in wording in different series over the years. Legal Tender Notes began in

1862 with "promises to pay," but by 1869 it was changed to the definite "will pay." Perhaps the government had become more confident by then.

At one time or another, certain notes were payable in silver dollars in particular or silver coins in general, and others in gold coins. As only Uncle Sam can do, the gold obligation was repudiated in 1933 and the silver obligation in the late 1960s. Today, all bills are simply legal tender for all debts, with nothing else said.

Certain notes beginning in the 1860s have the obligation printed out in detail, sometimes mentioning debts, customs duties, and even convertibility into bonds. The counterfeiting clause, as it is sometimes called, is also printed in detail on certain early notes, outlining the penalties for such an offense.

SERIES

Most currency bears a designation as to the dated series within its type. Generally, a series designation or date was made when there was a change in design or some other aspect of a note, such as Series of 1875 or Series of 1880. The series is stated somewhere on most notes, but sometimes not. In some instances, such as for early Gold Certificates, the date of the enabling act is printed on the note, but no specific series designation. These are called Act of 1863 or Series of 1863 notes by numismatists.

OBLIGATIONS ON FEDERAL CURRENCY

A selection of obligation or promise to pay inscriptions on United States paper money (not to scale).

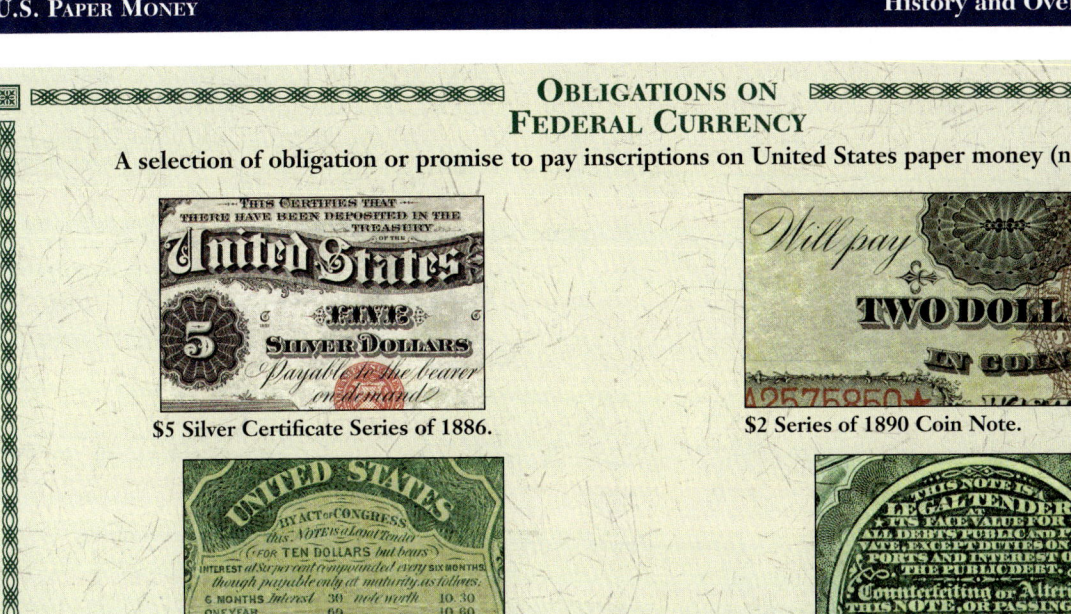

$5 Silver Certificate Series of 1886.

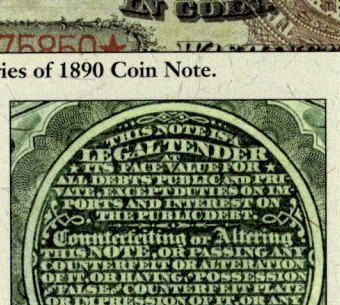

$2 Series of 1890 Coin Note.

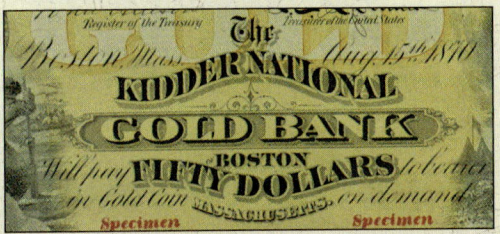

$10 Compound Interest Treasury Note.

$20 Legal Tender Note, Series of 1869.

$50 Kidder National Gold Bank, proof impression.

$20 Compound Interest Treasury Note.

$10,000 Federal Reserve Note, Series of 1928.

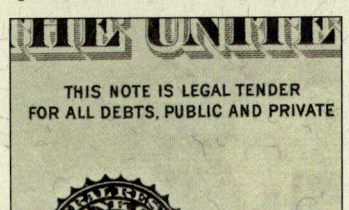

$1 Federal Reserve Note, Series of 1969.

$10 Federal Reserve Note, Series of 1914.

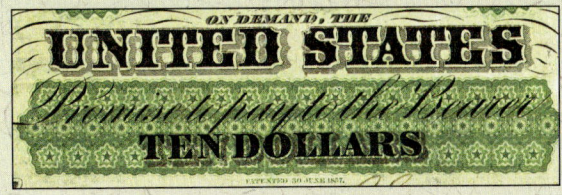

$10 Demand Note, Series of 1861.

Among small-size bills, the series designation was at first changed only when there was a significant alteration or revision of the design. A change in signatures resulted in the addition of an alphabetic suffix (e.g., Series of 1935-A, 1935-B, 1935-C, and so on). Beginning in 1974, the series year changed with the appointment of a new secretary of the Treasury. Commencing with the Series of 1990, a new series year has begun each time there is a change in either of the two printed signatures.

The series year date remains constant and is sometimes used over a span of succeeding years until a new series is instituted. Accordingly, the actual year a bill is issued is usually later than the series date printed on it. As an example, Series of 1901 Legal Tender Notes (the famous "Bison Notes") were issued into the 1920s. Series of 1875 National Bank Notes were issued as late as 1902.

DENOMINATIONS

The face value or denomination of a note is prominent, usually expressed in some or all corners as a numeral (such as 5 or 10), with added lettering (such as FIVE or TEN), and sometimes with one or more roman numerals (such as V or X). These value designations are called *counters* by banknote engravers. The dollar sign ($) is rarely used.

On some bills, the denomination appears many times—for example, in small letters and numbers as part of the bor-

der design. Modern Federal Reserve Notes with new security features include some repeated denomination information in a hidden or hard-to-see manner as well as in numbers scattered in the field.

SEALS

The Treasury seal, featuring the scales of justice and a key, is a standard feature of notes and appears in various sizes and colors. The Latin inscription THESAUR. AMER. SEPTENT. SIGIL. surrounded the seal until the Series of 1969 small-size notes, when it was changed to THE DEPARTMENT OF THE TREASURY.

The Treasury seal has been imprinted in many different colors over a long span of years and series, including red

SEALS ON FEDERAL CURRENCY

A selection of Treasury seals on notes from the 1860s to date, illustrating the diversity of colors, sizes, and styles (not to scale).

$1 Legal Tender Note, Series of 1869.

$20 Legal Tender Note, Series of 1869.

$2 National Bank Note, Original Series.

$5,000 Gold Certificate, Series of 1878.

$5 Legal Tender Note, Series of 1880.

$50 National Bank Note, 1902 Red Seal.

$1 National Bank Note, Series of 1875.

$5 Silver Certificate, Series of 1899.

$100 Gold Certificate, Series of 1928.

$5 Series of 1934-A with HAWAII.

$50 Federal Reserve Note, Series of 2004.

$500 Federal Reserve Note, Series of 1928.

$100 Legal Tender Note, Series of 1966.

(from bright red to light pink), various shades of green, gold, yellow, brown, and blue. Often the intensity of a particular seal color varied within a given series or variety depending on the amount and quality of ink used.

Certain small-size notes from 1928 through the mid-1930s have the Treasury seal printed in either a light yellow-green or a purer light to medium or even dark green. Over a period of time these shades have been given different designations, at first "light green" and "dark green," sometimes "blue-green"; in this text, they are referred to as "light yellow-green" and simply "green." The differences can be subtle.

The face of the Great Seal of the United States (an unfinished pyramid with an all-seeing eye) appears to the left on the back of most small-size $1 bills. The reverse of the Great Seal, with an eagle grasping an olive branch and arrows, has been used on many denominations and types, including current $1 notes.

State and territorial seals are on the backs of National Bank Notes of the Original Series, Series of 1875, and Series of 1882 Brown Backs.

Federal Reserve seals were first used on Federal Reserve Notes of the Series of 1914. Styles varied, but until modern times they included both the name (city location) of the bank and its number, 1 to 12, and sometimes the bank's letter, A to L. Currently, the Treasury Seal is generic.

VIGNETTES OR ILLUSTRATIONS

Illustrations on bills, called *vignettes*, range from the marvelously ornate, such as the faces of the Series of 1896 "Educational series" Silver Certificates and the backs of the Series of 1890 Coin Notes, to simple portraits and buildings, as on small-size bills. Some vignettes and portraits found on currency were also used elsewhere, such as on postage stamps and fiscal paper.

Gene Hessler has done much research on the artists and engravers of early vignettes (see the bibliography). Often, several vignettes by different engravers were used to create the face and back of a given note. In some instances, paintings hanging in the Rotunda of the United States Capitol were used, such as on the backs of Original Series and Series of 1875 National Bank Notes. One of these, the *Declaration of Independence*, is currently used on $2 Federal Reserve Notes (copied from but not credited to a vignette created by the American Bank Note Company for the $100 National Bank Notes).

Beginning in the 1920s, paper-money designs became commoditized, fine art was abandoned, and simplification became the rule. All $1 notes henceforth depicted Washington, all $2 notes Jefferson, all $5 notes Lincoln, and so on. Beginning with the small-size notes issued in 1929, most

backs became generic within a denomination as well. Accordingly, the Great Seal is seen on the back of all $1 bills, the Lincoln Memorial on $5 bills, and so on.

PLATE LETTERS AND NUMBERS

Letters identify the plate position of a note on the face of large-size bills, and for most types from the late 19th century onward a tiny numeral designates the back plate position. On the face of a four-subject plate with four notes of the same denominations, letters are in order, such as A, B, C, and D. On further plates, such as for National Bank Notes, the next sequence is used, as E, F, G, and H. There are other variations.

Even within a given denomination and type, the location of plate letters and numbers can differ. On some notes a letter in upper case (usually) or lower case can have a plate number before it, following, above, or below, or even at some distance. Beginning in 1917 it was standard to have a capital letter with a number following immediately, such as C12, the number often much smaller than its companion letter.[1] On a few 19th-century notes, the Treasury seals, separately imprinted on notes, were also tagged with a tiny number.

Small-size bills have a combination letter and number on the face, such as H22, and a number on the back, such as 178. Beginning in the late 1980s, when the Western Facility or branch of the Bureau of Engraving and Printing was opened in Fort Worth, Texas, the letters "FW" were included as part of the plate letter and number.

Face and back numbers can also vary in size among notes of the same denomination and series.

The Rotunda of the United States Capitol. The heroic-size paintings on view furnished the motifs for certain early National Bank Notes. (J.F. Jarvis, *Views of Washington*, 1890)

PLATE LETTERS & NUMBERS ON FEDERAL CURRENCY

A selection of front and back plate letters and numbers on currency from the 19th century to date (not to scale).

$1 Legal Tender Note, Series of 1862. Face: Plate number and letter 36C.

$1 Silver Certificate, Series of 1896. Face: Plate number and letter D3.

$5 Silver Certificate, Series of 1896. Face: Plate letter B and number 35 (at bottom of V) not near each other.

$20 Series of 1882 Brown Back. Back: Plate number 3 in microscopic numerals.

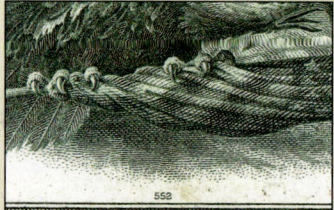

$1 Federal Reserve Bank Note. Back: Plate number 552 below eagle.

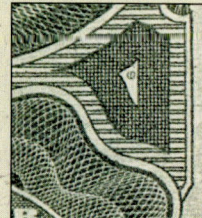

$1 Coin Note, Series of 1890. Back: Plate number 6 horizontal in tiny triangular area near upper right.

$20 Coin Note, Series of 1891. Back: Plate number 1 on inside of right border.

$1 Silver Certificate, Series of 1886. Face: Plate number and letter 131D left of center.

$10 Legal Tender Note, Series of 1901. Face: Plate letter and number H166.

$5 Legal Tender Note, Series of 1875. Face: Plate letter and number B20.

SERIAL NUMBERS

Serial numbers were printed separately, in two places (except on very early notes), and in different colors for different classes and series. Serial numbers can be found in black and in various shades of red, blue, brown, gold, yellow, and green. Today, green is used. One number was printed high on the note and the other low. In the olden days when worn notes were redeemed, they were bundled face-up and cut apart lengthwise prior to being destroyed. The serial number placement allowed each half to have the same number.[2] The placement tradition has continued to the present.

Certain early notes have a series number in addition to a serial number, the popular Legal Tender Notes of 1862 and 1863 being examples, with

Cutting redeemed bills in half lengthwise at the Treasury department, seemingly a dangerous procedure. (Bosselman & Co., circa 1903)

SERIAL NUMBERS
ON FEDERAL CURRENCY
A selection of serial numbers on currency from the 19th century to date (not to scale).

$10 Gold Certificate, Series of 1922-F.

$10 Federal Reserve Note, Series 1934-A HAWAII.

$20 Gold Certificate, Series of 1863.

$20 Federal Reserve Note, Series of 1996.

$50 Gold Certificate, Series of 1882.

$50 Interest-Bearing Note, Series of 1861.

$100 Interest-Bearing Note, Series of 1865.

$1 Legal Tender Note, Series of 1869.

$1 Legal Tender Note, Series of 1923.

SERIES and NEW SERIES followed by a number; this number was not related to the separate plate letter or number.

Many serial numbers were given a letter prefix, a letter suffix, or both. Large-size notes used just the number itself, sometimes with a prefix letter, such as K1 (for the first note in a K series), or C12234. Typographical ornaments, including stars, Maltese crosses, and other characters were sometimes added as decorations, with no other significance (but see the section on Star Notes).

Small-size notes have eight numbers plus a letter prefix and, on most, a suffix. Exceptions are 1929 National Bank Notes, which for Type 1 have a prefix letter, six numbers, and a suffix, and for Type 2, a prefix letter, six digits, and no suffix. The most recent Federal Reserve Notes ($5 and above) have two letters as a prefix, eight numbers, and a suffix letter. These added letters permit the numbers to be lower.

STAR NOTES

On April 14, 1910, BEP director J.T. Ralph wrote to Treasurer Lee McClung suggesting that

the Bureau be authorized to prepare a stock of notes, numbered in sequence. . . . distinguished from all other notes by a special letter or character printed before and/or after the serial number [and] that these notes be

substituted in place of any defective specimens. . . . a notation being made on a package of currency, indicating that said package contained such substituted note or notes.[3]

The first star notes were created on June 21, 1910, for the $1 and $5 Silver Certificates, star serials ★1B to ★100B for each denomination. In time the procedure was adapted to other series (but not National Bank Notes), in instances in which some notes in a series were misprinted or otherwise had to be destroyed and replaced. The serial numbers on the face of the replacement notes are preceded or followed by a star. These are called *star notes* today and form a separate specialty for many numismatists. *The Complete Catalog of United States Large Size Star Notes, 1910–1929* by Doug Murray is essential, as is the *Standard Guide to Small-Size U.S. Paper Money, 1928 to Date*, by John Schwartz and Scott Lindquist, for star notes among later issues.

Earlier, stars were often added as a decoration, with no other meaning. Examples of decorative stars include Series of 1869 Legal Tender Notes and Series of 1890 and 1891 Treasury or Coin Notes. There are no star notes among National Bank Notes. In the early times, before stars were used on replacements, if a note was misprinted and destroyed, another note with the same serial numbers was created with no special identification. This numbering was often done on another machine, sometimes with a slightly

Star replacement. $2 Federal Reserve Bank Note, Series of 1918.

Star replacement. $1 Silver Certificate, Series of 1935-B.

different type font, so that the sequence in the regular machine did not have to be reset or interrupted.

On a few 19th-century replacement *plates* for National Bank Notes, a tiny star was added on the plate (not at the serial number) to designate this. These are detailed by Peter Huntoon in *Large Size United States National Bank Notes*.

PRINTERS' NAMES

Certain early federal bills bore the names of the private companies that printed them, including the American, Continental, and National bank-note companies in New York City beginning in the 1860s, joined by the Columbian Bank Note Company in Washington, D.C., in the 1870s. Later large-size bills have the imprint of the Bureau of Engraving and Printing (in several forms). On small-size bills the bureau is not mentioned, but since the opening of the Fort Worth branch printing plant (Western Facility), starting with the Series of 1988-A, a small FW appears on notes printed there.

Vignettes, even by the most prominent of engravers, are not signed, although attributions can be made by using Treasury documents and published information. Sometimes staff engravers, such as George W. Casilear, farmed out work to private artists and did not disclose the arrangement. Accordingly, the true authorship of some vignettes may be unknown.

DIFFERENT ISSUES, TYPES, AND SERIES

Interest-Bearing Notes
AUTHORIZED 1861 TO 1865 • LARGE-SIZE

Uncertainty in Early 1861

In early 1861 the United States Treasury was running low on funds. With Southern states seceding and with the Union in threat of dissolution, the matter required resolution. There was uncertainty nationwide, as revealed in this letter from a banker, E. Clark, dated January 9, 1861. In Chicago for a visit, he wrote to an acquaintance, S.J. Kirkwood, in Des Moines City, Iowa:

> I arrived here this day and find the money market in a bad or feverish condition. I have met some Indiana bankers who say to me confidentially that they must suspend unless they get relief by N. York resuming specie payment. Their money is returning on them rapidly notwithstanding the demand for money [to be paid out].
>
> I find our branch has run down in coin $310,000 in ten days. Gold advances here 2% today. You may judge

yourself what will be our condition in case this state of things continues. Ohio [banks] must suspend as they cannot weather the storm. This is the opinion of the best bankers here.[4]

The Panic of 1861, little remembered today, caused 5,935 companies in the North to fail, at a loss of $178,632,170, and 1,058 in the South for $8,577,830.[5] Money was in short supply. The Act of February 8, 1861, provided for a new issue of bonds denominated from $1,000 up to be sold to augment the Treasury coffers.

John Sherman, who two years later was the senator and author of the 1863 act that created national banks, recalled this:

> On the eighth of February, 1861, a bill became a law providing for the sale of $20,000,000 six percent bonds, and these were sold at the rate of $89.10 for $100, yielding $18,415,000. Such was the humiliating financial condition of the government of the United States at the close of Mr. Buchanan's administration.
>
> The expenditures of the government for the fiscal year ending June 30, 1861, were $84,577,258.60, of which $42,064,082.95 was procured from loans and Treasury notes, leaving a balance in the Treasury, at the close of the fiscal year 1861, of $2,395,635.21. This condition still existed when Congress subsequently met in special session.[6]

The Act of March 2, 1861

The Act of March 2, 1861, was the next important legislation and inaugurated what paper-money collectors consider federal currency in a new era or setting. These are the first notes (or bonds) generally listed in popular numismatic references. An issue of 60-day notes, bearing interest equal to 6% annualized, was authorized, to the amount of $10,000,000, with each bond having a face value of $1,000 or more. An additional, larger amount (of which $25,364,450 was subsequently sold) had a two-year maturity. Advertisements were placed to entice brokers, banks, and exchange houses to bid for them, at a minimum of face value, after which the buyers would resell them to investors.

If buyers could not be found at par, the Treasury was authorized to produce a large quantity of smaller-denomination bonds—we call them *notes* today—of $50 and higher, to be sold to the public. A space for the interest rate was left blank on the face of each note, to be filled in by hand. Other notes bore printing stating a 6% annual interest rate for a two-year term. These were sold at a discount to securities houses and banks to reflect the interest at maturity. The buyers then retailed them to individual customers. Payment and receipt of Interest-Bearing Notes was done in the office of L.E. Chittenden, register of the Treasury. The notes were printed under contract by the National Bank Note Company in New York City and did not bear the Treasury seal. Soon afterward the Civil War commenced. More demands were placed on Treasury funds, and reserves were further depleted. Financial help was desperately needed.

The acts of July 17 and August 5, 1861, which also created Demand Notes (see the next section), provided for Interest-Bearing Treasury Notes at 7.3% with a maturity of three years. Secretary of the Treasury Salmon P. Chase met in New York City with leading bankers from that city, Boston, and Philadelphia to plan for their distribution. The financiers agreed to take up the whole of the notes then under consideration, and then to market them to others. The first arrangement was negotiated on August 19. It was an easy sale, as such notes seemed to be a safe investment in that time of uncertainty—at least in the North, where most citizens were confident their side would win the war. In border areas such as southern Ohio and the state of Maryland, loyalties and outlooks were mixed.

Irregularities

Under acts passed from 1861 to 1865, Interest-Bearing Notes of $10 to $5,000 were authorized in large total amounts, for periods of one and two years, at 6% interest, and three-year notes at 7.3%, the latter issued in denominations from $50 up. Beginning in 1863, many (but not all) Interest-Bearing Notes were printed by the National Currency Bureau. Plates were made by the bureau using vignettes and certain other elements provided by bank-note companies in New York.

An investigation of the National Currency Bureau that commenced in 1867 and was published in 1869 revealed many irregularities in record keeping for the Series of June 30, 1864, 7.3% Interest-Bearing Notes, including double printing of notes with the same serial numbers, the private serial numbering of notes by hand stamping, the apparent theft of some sheets, and more—a sorry affair.[7] As stated, most of the 7.3% notes were printed by the National Currency Bureau, but others were printed on contract. No clear delineation of where specific notes were made has been located. Some printing plates were made by George D. Baldwin in New York City, but most were created within the department. Some letters and counters were made by James Conner's Sons in New York, but most were fashioned in Washington. Treasury reports are inconsistent as to what work was accomplished and where.

The 7.3% notes had daily interest printed on them, computed at 1¢ per day for the $50 denomination, rising proportionately for higher values. This rate was devised by secretary of the Treasury Salmon P. Chase "because it was equitable to both borrower and lender, and peculiarly convenient of calculation."[8]

For certain of the Interest-Bearing Note series there were two ways for banks and other bulk purchasers to sell them: at a discount, the note to be redeemable for face value at maturity; or at face value, with coupons attached that could be redeemed at six-month intervals. These were generally called "maturity notes" and "coupon notes." Each type had no redemption value until the maturity date one, two, or three years after the issue date imprinted on the face of the note.

The redemption of coupons caused no end of problems. Holders of notes had to detach the coupons in the presence of either an officer of a national bank or of the Treasury department. Coupons detached otherwise could not be redeemed unless held to the note's maturity and turned in at that time. In the meantime, the note was no longer considered legal tender until the redemption of the *next* coupon.[9] Each coupon was sent by a bank to Washington, where clerks dutifully entered each in a ledger, with separate accounts for each serially numbered note.

As the printing details and the redemption provisions were different on each of these two classes, maturity notes and coupon notes are listed with separate reference numbers in the present book. All issues after the 1861 series had the Treasury seal. Red, blue, and possibly other colors for serial numbers were used from time to time, with no specific record kept as to the numbers of imprints for each hue.[10]

The one-year Interest-Bearing Notes of 1863 were issued from February 4, 1864, to June 1, 1864. The two-year maturity notes were issued from March 16, 1864, to May 30, 1864, and the coupon notes from January 12, 1864, to April 20, 1864.

The quantities issued for many of the Interest-Bearing Notes were prodigious. The 7.3% notes dated August 15, 1864, alone numbered in the millions: $50, 363,952; $100, 566,039; $500, 171,666; $1,000, 118,528; and $5,000, 4,166; for a total face value of $299,992,500. By June 30, 1868, $299,217,850 had been redeemed, leaving just $744,650 outstanding. As noted, due to irregularities within the department, certain of these figures are approximate, but are probably substantially correct.

Distribution

Newspapers and magazines of the day carried many advertisements of banks and brokers that traded in Interest-Bearing Notes. Jay Cooke & Co., headquartered in Philadelphia, was the most active selling agent for these, advertising them as bonds and emphasizing their unique character. All told, 148 agents were appointed, who could earn a commission of one-fifth of one percent on the first $500,000 of subscriptions obtained, and one-eighth of one percent on any higher amount. For one particular issue, subscriptions aggregated $24,678,86.84, of which Cooke accounted for $5,224,500.[11]

Interest-Bearing Notes were a widespread financial sensation in the North, in a time when many standard investments were uncertain. National banks used them as backing for the issuance of paper money and as reserves. These were not used in general circulation or commerce.

An effort was made to sell certain high-denomination notes in Europe, but agents and friends of the Confederacy in England in particular put out much unfavorable publicity about the finances of the Union, and sales abroad were minimal. Maturity notes (without coupons) were used for overseas sales.

Nearly all Interest-Bearing Notes were redeemed in due course, with the result that any example is a great rarity today. Certain types of the large denominations are not known to exist, and even the designs of some of them are uncertain, although extant proof impressions provide information. For numismatic purposes, viewing pictures of notes and reading about them will have to suffice, for actual examples are almost impossible to find.

Advertisement by Jay Cooke selling Interest-Bearing Notes and government bonds, February 11, 1865. Featured are 7.3% Interest-Bearing Notes with a three-year term.

Demand Notes
AUTHORIZED IN 1861 • LARGE-SIZE

Act of July 17, 1861

Following the onset of the Civil War and with continuing financial stringency, a partial solution was provided by the earlier-mentioned Act of July 17, 1861, amended on August 5, which authorized a new $250,000,000 loan, comprising mostly Interest-Bearing Notes and bonds, but also including $50,000,000 in currency to be known as Demand Notes. In contrast to Interest-Bearing Notes, Demand Notes were made in lower denominations for widespread popular distribution. As these bore no interest, they were in effect a free loan to the government. The Confederacy's unexpected victory at the Battle of Bull Run on July 17 contributed to overall uncertainty, giving a cloudy outlook as to whether such notes would be a success.

Plates were engraved and notes were printed by the American Bank Note Company in New York City under a contract signed on July 25, 1861. The Act of August 5, 1861, added details, including the convertibility, if desired by the holder, of the Demand Notes into long-term bonds paying 6% annual interest.

The main legislative provision authorizing these notes declared that

> the Secretary of the Treasury may also issue, in exchange for coin, and as part of the above loan, or may pay for salaries or other dues from the United States, Treasury notes of a less denomination than fifty dollars, not bearing interest, but payable on demand by the assistant Treasurer of the United States, at Philadelphia, New York or Boston.

Demand Notes were printed on 20-pound bank-note paper (1,000 sheets weighed 20 pounds) made by J.M. Willcox & Co., of Glen Mills, Pennsylvania.

Resistance to the Notes

The first Demand Notes were paid out in August 1861 and used to pay government salaries in Washington. Soon thereafter, notes were given to Union soldiers, defense contractors, and others to whom the government was obligated. This form of payment was not welcomed by the recipients, who preferred "hard money" in the form of coins, as this narrative in a biography of secretary of the Treasury Salmon P. Chase demonstrates:

> There was on their first appearance a genuine reluctance on the part even of loyal people to receive them, and as a matter of securing their credit, the Secretary and his assistant (George Harrington), and other leading officers of the Treasury . . . signed a paper agreeing to accept them in payment of their salaries; all of this notwithstanding the fact that the notes were convertible at will into gold, and actually were so converted until the suspension of cash payments the following December.
>
> The merchants and shopkeepers in Washington sought to discredit them, and railroad officers and banks

and bankers in some instances at any rate, and in different parts of the country, refused to receive them at all. But they soon established themselves in the public confidence, and were everywhere preferred to the state bank currency.[12]

A circular letter was sent by the Treasury department to the assistant U.S. Treasurers at the aforementioned depositories, directing them to redeem Demand Notes in gold coins, if requested. In actuality, the Treasury was depleted and had little in the way of gold reserves. However, the illusion that gold coins were on hand for redemption seemed to settle the situation, and from then until December 28, 1861, paper Demand Notes and gold $5, $10, and $20 coins had equivalent values in banking and the general marketplace.

This circular letter was to become very important after December 28, after which time banks stopped paying out gold coins at par, and the bills of state-chartered banks began to depreciate in terms of gold. By then, $33,460,000 in Demand Notes had been paid out. This issue was supplemented on February 12, 1862, by an additional $10,000,000 in Demand Notes redeemable in gold. By early March, the entire $60,000,000 amount had been printed and issued.

The Demand Notes were payable at five different federal depositories, known as Sub-Treasuries, located in New York City, Philadelphia, Boston, Cincinnati, and St. Louis. The New York office under the authority of assistant Treasurer John J. Cisco was by far the most important.

Demand Notes were made in denominations of $5, $10, and $20 to promote popular distribution. The backs were printed in green ink, quickly giving rise to the term *greenback*, although this was more widely applied to the later Legal Tender Notes (see the next section), which were issued in far greater quantities. Even today in popular parlance, green is the "color of money." The Demand Notes do *not* bear the Treasury seal, as there was no requirement for this in the amended legislation of August 5, 1861.

The earliest bills were personally signed in ink by L(ucius) E. Chittenden, register of the Treasury, and F(rancis) E(lias) Spinner, Treasurer. None of these are known to numismatists today. Soon a corps of 70 clerks was on hand to add their own names and the notation "for the" in place of the Treasury officers. Later issues, constituting the majority, had "for the" printed by the plate, but still were signed by clerks. As no recipients of the bills had any idea who these people were or what their signatures should look like, the signatures had no security value.[13] Demand Notes were issued from August 26, 1861, to March 5, 1862.

Notes Highly Prized

Demand Notes became highly prized, and after Legal Tender Notes were first paid out in April 1862 and *not* redeemable in gold or usable at par for customs duties, Demand Notes sold for a sharp premium, especially after the coin-hoarding panic of July 1862.

Almost immediately after the Legal Tender Notes were circulated, the Treasury department began retiring as many Demand Notes as it could. Within a year after they were issued, Demand Notes, still exchangeable at par for gold, were seldom seen in financial circles, and none were in general circulation, as they were worth more than the Legal Tender Notes. By early August 1862, it took $115.25 in Legal Tender bills to buy $100 in gold coins or Demand Notes.

By July 1, 1880, all but $60,535 of the Demand Notes had been redeemed. Today, Demand Notes range from scarce to very rare. Varieties with "for the" handwritten are especially elusive. Most were issued in New York.

Legal Tender or United States Notes
SERIES OF 1862 TO 1923 • LARGE-SIZE

Notes Not Redeemable in Coin

Legal Tender Notes, as they are generally called, were mostly imprinted with UNITED STATES NOTE at the border. These were born of necessity, for after December 28, 1861, gold coins disappeared from circulation, and a widely accepted paper money medium was needed, other than the high-denomination Interest-Bearing Notes, which did not circulate. Short of funds, the government did not have enough gold coins to act as backing for more Demand Notes. The situation was becoming increasingly uncomfortable.

No prospect of victory was in sight for the Union, and losses in the various military campaigns escalated each month. Banks, manufacturers, and merchants became increasingly worried. On January 15, 1862, the *London Post* commented:

> The monetary intelligence from America is of the most important kind. National bankruptcy is not an agreeable prospect, but it is the only one presented by the existing state of American finance. What a strange tale does not the history of the United States for the past twelve months unfold? What a striking moral does it not point? Never before was the world dazzled by a career of more reckless extravagance. Never before did a flourishing and prosperous state make such gigantic strides towards affecting its own ruin.

On January 29, 1862, in a letter to the Committee of Ways and Means, secretary of the Treasury Salmon P. Chase stated in part:

> It is not unknown to the Committee that I have felt, nor do I wish to conceal, that I now feel a great aversion to making anything but coin legal tender in payment of debts. It has been my anxious wish to avoid the necessity of such legislation. It is, however, at present impossible, in consequence of the large expenditures entailed by the war, and the suspension [of the payment of gold coins] of the banks, to procure sufficient coin for disbursement; and it has, therefore, become indispensably necessary that we should resort to the issue of United States Notes.

> Making them a legal tender might, however, still be avoided, if the willingness manifested by the people gen-

erally, the railroad companies, and by many of the banking institutions, to receive and pay them as money in all transactions, were absolutely or practically universal; but, unfortunately there are some people and some institutions which refuse to receive and pay them. Such discriminations would, if possible, be prevented; and the provision making the notes a legal tender, in a great measure at least, prevented it by putting all citizens in this respect on the same level, both of rights and of duties.

Chase went on to say that such was a temporary measure, and that he hoped to "secure the earliest possible return to a sound currency of coin and promptly convertible notes," the last referring to the success enjoyed by the Demand Notes redeemable in gold coins. The Legal Tender Notes were backed only by the credit of the federal government, the status of which was very uncertain in the minds of many, although by that time the finances of the Confederacy were in even worse shape.

Legal Tender Notes Issued

The first Legal Tender Notes were dated March 10, 1862, and were issued in denominations from $5 to $1,000, followed by those dated August 1, 1862, of the values of $1 and $2. It was the two smaller denominations to which the National Currency Bureau, with Spencer M. Clark as chief (although he also tended to his "acting engineer in charge" duties), affixed Treasury seals with newly acquired machinery. Clark designed the seals, and the dies for them were made by the American Bank Note Company, at first in three versions. Another sealing machine had been in use earlier for the higher denominations and was probably continued in operation. A $3 Legal Tender Note was contemplated, this being a popular denomination with state banks, but was never issued. However, the American Bank Note Company prepared Legal Tender Note plates for this denomination in July 1862.[14] Most circulation of Legal Tender Notes consisted of the lower denominations of $1, $2, $5, $10, and $20.

These were printed on 18-pound bank-note paper made by J.M. Willcox & Co. This stock, thinner than the 20-pound paper used for Demand Notes, became the general weight used for the next several years, with exceptions.

The order for $5, $10, $20, $500, and $1,000 printing plates went to American and the contract for $1, $2, $50, and $100 plates went to National.[15] Some of the lower-denomination American plates were altered from those used earlier to print Demand Notes. The printer added the Treasury signatures by using special ink on a separate plate and also applied the serial numbers. In some instances, plates made by American were used for printing by National, and vice versa. Some plates made by one company have the imprints of both. Legal Tender Notes of the series of 1862 and 1863 were issued from April 2, 1862, to April 19, 1869, after which they were replaced with the new Series of 1869 designs.

These notes were legal tender for all debts, public and private, except for import duties and payment on the public debt. As they were not exchangeable at par for silver or gold coins, the prospect for these paper bills was uncertain, and memories of failed and broken banks from the financial

$100 Legal Tender Note issued under the Act of February 25, 1862, and dated March 10, 1862. Notes of varying denominations came into wide use, including in payments to government and military personnel. These had no backing in coin.

panics of 1837 and 1857 remained in the minds of many citizens. Someone with a $100 Legal Tender Note in 1863 could get two $50 Legal Tender Notes or a fistful of ones and twos, but not Demand Notes, Interest-Bearing Notes, or silver or gold coins.[16] Soldiers and government personnel continued to receive their pay in Legal Tender Notes. An account in the *Worcester* (Massachusetts) *Daily Spy*, August 6, 1863, datelined Cairo, Illinois, reflects this:

> The steamer *Ruth*, valued at $10,000, was burned at midnight at the foot of Island No. 1. She was bound for Helena, and had on board eight paymasters and their clerks, with $2,600,000 in greenbacks to pay Gen. Grant's army. . . . The fire broke out in the aft part of the boat, some saying between the decks and others in a nursery room. As soon as the fire was discovered the boat headed toward the shore on the Missouri side, and struck the bank with full force. The engines were still operating as the engineers left, the boat swung around, and the boat headed downstream with about 30 people who must have perished.
>
> In the meantime, soldiers aboard were said "to have stood by the boxes containing the money till it was certain that all was consumed." The boxes were iron-bound and too heavy to be removed; besides, the flames spread all over the boat in less than five minutes. There is nothing satisfactory as to how the fire originated. It is believed, however, to have been the work of an incendiary in the interest of the rebel government.

Legal Tender bills depreciated from the very beginning. Soon, a double system of pricing arose in the marketplace—a higher price if paid in Legal Tender bills, a lower one if coins were tendered in payment. Indeed, at the outset, there were many merchants who would not accept Legal Tender Notes at all and demanded coins. Not even the Philadelphia Mint would accept Legal Tender Notes in payment at par for the Proof coins it struck for collectors, a situation that endured for many years. To buy such pieces, numismatists had to buy older silver and gold coins from an exchange broker and submit them to the Mint in payment.

In 1877, John Jay Knox, the comptroller of the Currency, reported the exchange rates for Legal Tender Notes in terms of gold coins as of July 1 each year, dating back to the Civil War:

1863: 76.6¢	**1871:** 89.0¢
1864: 38.7¢	**1872:** 87.5¢
1865: 70.4¢	**1873:** 86.4¢
1866: 66.0¢	**1874:** 91.0¢
1867: 71.7¢	**1875:** 87.2¢
1868: 70.1¢	**1876:** 89.2¢
1869: 73.5¢	**1877:** 94.5¢
1870: 85.6¢	**1877:** 97.3¢[17]

In other words, in 1864 it took $1,000 in Legal Tender Notes to buy $387 (face value) in gold coins.

In the Confederacy, the situation was even worse, and toward the end of 1864 it took $2,174 in Confederate bills to buy $100 in federal coins (which remained highly regarded in the South).

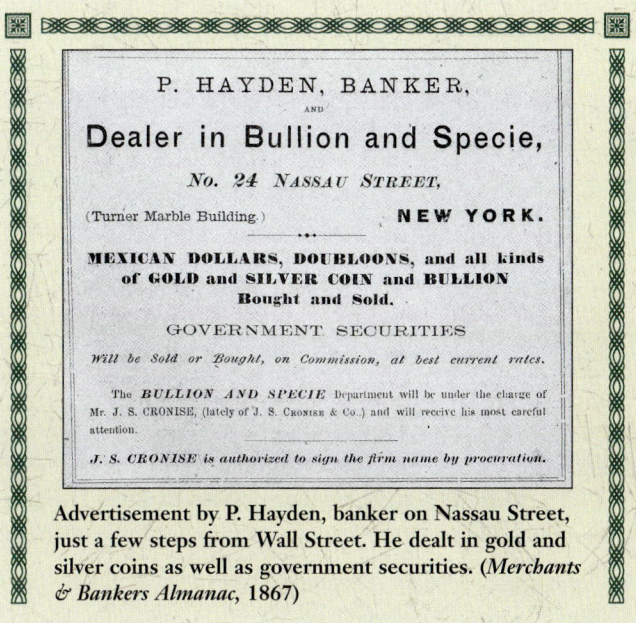

Advertisement by P. Hayden, banker on Nassau Street, just a few steps from Wall Street. He dealt in gold and silver coins as well as government securities. (*Merchants & Bankers Almanac*, 1867)

Technical Aspects

The $1, $2, $10, and $50 Legal Tender Notes have imprinted on their faces a *series* number, beginning with 1. On the $5, $20, $100, $500, and $1,000 the first series was unnumbered, and the imprint began with 2. Each new series inaugurated a restart in the *serial* number sequence.

As the numbering machine for serial numbers contained only five digits, with a maximum number of 99,999, the serial number 100,000 was set by hand. The next note had a new series number and also started a new serial-number run with 1. As an example, series 1 went from 1 to 99,999, plus the number 100,000 hand set, after which series 2 started anew at 1 and continued to 99,999, and so on. Accordingly, a low serial number for a Legal Tender Note may be very important in series 1 or an unnumbered first series, but it is less so in later series. The study of these notes today is complicated by numismatic data that have captured serial numbers but not series numbers. It can be seen that a series 1 note with a serial number of 75,000 was printed earlier than a series 2 note with serial number 1, or 10, or 25,000. Two different payable provisions were printed on the backs of the issues of 1862 and 1863, of the denominations $5 upward: the First Obligation, which permitted exchange of the notes for U.S. interest-bearing long-term bonds, and the Second Obligation, which did not include this provision.

Of possible interest to specialists is that the early Legal Tender Notes can be divided into three general groups:

1. Denominations of $5 to $1,000 with First Obligation backs, identified using the SERIES designations (signifying print runs and not the same as *serial* numbers) and one company imprint, showing who made the plates and did the face, back, and tint printing. In all instances the Treasury seals were added by the National Currency Bureau in Washington.
2. Denominations of $1 to $1,000 with the Second Obligation backs. The denominations of $5 to $1,000 had NEW SERIES imprinted and added the name of a second bank-note company, implying a division of work. At the time, the processes in New York included printing the tint on the front, the back, the black vignettes and inscriptions on the front, then separately the Treasury signatures in one process and the serial numbering in another.
3. In early 1864, while continuing the printing of Second Obligation notes, the previously-added second bank-note company name was dropped. Some denominations went back to just the first company imprint and others changed to double mentions of either National or American.

Sometimes plates printed by one company were used by another, and at other times work was shared for different aspects. On October 10, 1867, Fitch Shepard, president of the National Bank Note Company, stated this to a congressional committee:

> We engraved the $50s and $100s of the Legal Tenders, and American Company the $5s, $10s, and $20s. We printed the $10s and the American Company the $5s, I think. We made the engravings for both the ones and twos, but the printing was divided between our company and the American Company. The Legal Tenders were complete except sealing and cutting up. . . . We put both numbers on the Legal Tenders here. . . . By looking at a Legal Tender note you will see that there are two numbers on different corners of the note, so that when the notes are canceled by being split in two a number is left on each part. The $5s and $20s were numbered by us [National].[18]

A close reading of the above reflects such sharing, such as National printing $10 notes from American plates and both companies printing $1 and $2 notes from plates made by National, as well as, in some instances, printing by one company and serial numbering by another.

Different System in the West

On the West Coast, the state legislature of California had decreed in 1850 that paper money of any kind was illegal for use in commerce. This would prevent problems with unsound banks, such as many forty-niners had experienced back East before heading into the sunset to seek their fortunes. Accordingly, in 1862, when Legal Tender bills were first issued, and continuing for years afterward, they were of no use at face value in commerce in such places as San Francisco or Sacramento. Instead, silver and gold coins were the medium of exchange, and anyone wanting to spend a Legal Tender bill had to accept a deep discount equal to the premium charged for gold and silver in the East.

The federal government did not countenance this arrangement and in the West paid the wages of Army and Navy personnel and other federal employees in Legal Tender bills. The recipients had no choice but to take large losses when they spent the notes. For a long time, it took $20 in such bills to buy merchandise priced at $12 to $15 in terms of gold coins. On August 25, 1864, employees in the San Francisco office of the Assessor of Internal Revenue went on strike, seeking payment of their wages in gold coins or, alternatively, higher wages if they continued to be paid in Legal Tender Notes.[19]

Parity Achieved in 1876 and 1878

In 1869, new designs were introduced for Legal Tender Notes. All were printed on paper with a band of tinted blue from embedded microscopic fibers. The $1 to $10 denominations are now called "Rainbow Notes," from the light green, dark green, and red overprints. All of the Series of 1869 notes have a tiny circular imprint, "Patented 1866 July 24," which refers to James M. Willcox's patent for adding fibers as a security feature.[20] This was produced at Willcox's factory in Glen Mills, Pennsylvania. Series of 1869 notes were issued from October 19, 1869, to July 25, 1874.

Legal Tender Notes beginning with the Series of 1874—issued from July 13, 1874, to Sept. 13, 1875—included mention (in microprinting) of George W. Casilear's November 24, 1868, patent for adding a colored serial number over a finely detailed engraving.[21] Casilear had been an engraver

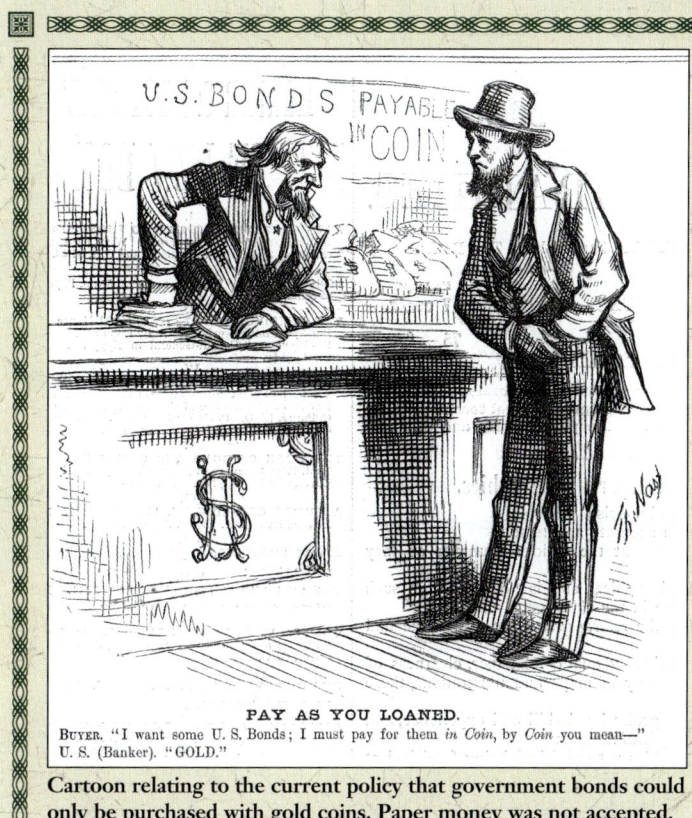

PAY AS YOU LOANED.

BUYER. "I want some U. S. Bonds; I must pay for them *in Coin*, by *Coin* you mean—"
U. S. (Banker). "GOLD."

Cartoon relating to the current policy that government bonds could only be purchased with gold coins. Paper money was not accepted. ("Pay As You Loaned," by Thomas Nast, *Harper's Weekly*, 1877)

RESUMPTION.
The Dance of the Dollars, January 1st, 1879.

Cartoon, "The Dance of the Dollars, January 1, 1879," celebrating the availability of gold coins at par for the first time since December 28, 1861. (*Harper's Weekly*, January 11, 1879)

with the National Currency Bureau since 1862, although he had secretly outsourced some of his work to other artists. Next were Series of 1875 notes issued from July 20, 1875, to June 20, 1879.

After the Civil War the difference in value of gold and silver coins versus paper money began to narrow, and finally, on April 20, 1876, silver coins were released in quantity and traded at par with Legal Tender Notes. The sudden availability of half dimes, dimes, quarters, and half dollars ended the need for Fractional Currency.

On December 17, 1878, gold coins and paper finally achieved parity. Although the Treasury expected that a great demand for gold coins would arise, this did not happen. With the assurance that Legal Tender Notes could be redeemed for gold, just about everyone was content to keep using paper.

SERIES OF 1928 TO 1966
SMALL-SIZE

Red Seals and Serial Numbers

Small-size Legal Tender Notes were made for the Series of 1928 (issued in 1929) to 1966. Printed with a distinctive bright red Treasury seal and serial numbers, denominations are $1, $2, $5, and $100, the last being a latecomer, first produced in the Series of 1966. The designs follow closely those of the small-size Silver Certificates.

Interestingly, the only $1 bills in this class are the Series of 1928. The others, including the not particularly popular $2

note, were made in larger quantities through the 1960s. Under the Act of May 3, 1878, circulation of Legal Tender Notes was to be maintained at $346,861,016, which the Treasury later adhered to through the use of an adequate supply of Series 1966 and 1966-A $100 bills (a technical and legislative curiosity). No new Legal Tender Notes have been printed for many years.

Compound Interest Treasury Notes
AUTHORIZED IN 1863 AND 1864 • LARGE-SIZE

New Loan Issue

Authorized by acts of Congress on March 3, 1863, and June 30, 1864, Compound Interest Treasury Notes were, in essence, loans to the federal government. The designs are closely related to those of the Interest-Bearing Notes. Made in denominations of $10, $20, $50, $100, $500, and $1,000, they featured on the back a schedule of the accumulating interest, compounded at 6% annually. These bills were to be held for three years, at the end of which the principal and interest would be paid. For a $10 note, this amounted to a total of $11.94.

Interest began to accrue on the imprinted date on the face of the note, known to be as early as June 10, 1864, and as late as October 16, 1865. Each bill had "gold" lettering in bronzing powder (also used on certain Fractional Currency bills) stating COMPOUND INTEREST TREASURY NOTE and the numerals of the denomination, applied on a blank sheet as the first step by women working in a special room in the Treasury Building, after which later printing sequences took place. The size of each note was 3.5 inches by 7.5 inches, or slightly larger than a Legal Tender Note. These were issued from June 9, 1864, to July 24, 1866, according to Treasury records, the first and last of these dates a day earlier and months later than the imprints on notes that survive today.

As these bills did not accrue interest after the expiration date, most were redeemed at the end of three years. Interest on the bills authorized in 1863 ceased on June 10, 1867, and interest on those authorized in 1864 ceased on May 16, 1868, although any bill issued after May 16, 1865, would still have some time to run. Today, such bills are very rare, and issued examples of $500 and $1,000 values are unknown.

National Bank Notes
AUTHORIZED 1863
ORIGINAL SERIES TO SERIES OF 1902 • LARGE-SIZE

The National Banking Act

In 1861, John Sherman of Ohio, who had served in Congress since 1854, took Salmon P. Chase's seat in the Senate when the latter was named by president Abraham Lincoln to be secretary of the Treasury. Later, Sherman served as 32nd secretary of the Treasury from 1877 to 1881. Back in the Senate after his Treasury term, he was the author of the 1890 Sherman Silver Purchase Act, which provided most of the silver to coin Morgan dollars through 1904 and also spawned the Coin or Treasury Notes of 1890. By any reckoning he is one of the most important American political figures in the annals of federal paper money.[22]

Sherman realized that the banks of the United States could be a great asset in financing the war effort. At the time, most of them issued their own currency, primarily from the presses of the American Bank Note Company. Sherman envisioned a National Currency, as it was to be called, backed by interest-bearing bonds of the United States, to be issued by the various banks. His proposal was introduced in the Senate on January 26, 1863.

Under the proposal, which was subsequently modified, millions of dollars in new bonds could be sold. The bills were to have the name of the bank and its location, and also the seal, authorization, and appropriate printed signatures of Treasury department officials. The state-chartered banks could *convert* (the term used in much of the Treasury department's correspondence) into a national bank (or banking) association through forming a new corporate entity. *Reorganize* is a better term.

Sherman felt that a bond-backed currency was far preferable to seemingly limitless issues of paper money without backing, such as more Legal Tender Notes. Should a national bank fail, its bills would still be good, as the Treasury department would have securities to redeem them. There would be no uncertainty. State banks were not forced to convert, merely given the opportunity to do so, providing they were in sound financial condition.

Sherman met with strong opposition from his fellow legislators. In the various states, officers and directors of banks were nearly always men of means and importance, often

John Sherman in the library of his Washington, D.C., home in 1885. (*John Sherman's Recollections*, 1895)

Sherman as depicted on a Series of 1902 National Bank Note.

with strong political connections. The idea of the government regulating banks was viewed very unfavorably.

However, after much discussion and modification, on February 25, 1863, the "Loan Bill," better known as the National Banking Act, passed Congress. Under its provisions, all banks granted charters by the national government were allowed to deposit government bonds with the Treasurer of the United States, after which they could issue notes in an amount limited to 90% of the par value of the bonds so given. The banks would earn interest on the bonds and would also have the cachet of issuing paper money with their own imprints. Even if a bank failed, the notes would still be good, as the deposited bonds could be cashed in to redeem the bills. In time, most bankers came to realize that it was an ideal situation for all involved. This arrangement expedited the sale of many Interest-Bearing Notes as well as long-term bonds and brought millions of dollars into the Treasury.

New Designs Solicited

Secretary Chase sent out a notice soliciting designs for National Bank bills for the denominations of $5 up (it was not until later that the $1 and $2 denominations were considered):

To Artists, Engravers, and Others

Designs for National Currency Notes are hereby invited, of the denominations of $5, $10, $20, $50, $100, $500, and $1,000, to be issued under the Act of Congress authorizing a National Currency, approved February 25, 1863.

The designs must be national in their character: and none will be considered that have been used, in whole or in part, upon any currency, bond, certificate, or other representative of value, and completed bills must all be of the uniform size of seven inches by three inches.

Designs must be for both the obverse and reverse of the note, and be susceptible of receiving upon their obverse the following legend: "National Currency, secured by the Bonds of the United States, deposited with the Treasurer of the United States," as well as the signatures of the Treasurer of the United States and the Register of the Treasury, together with the promise to pay of the association issuing the notes, signed by the President and Cashier thereof, and their place of redemption.[23]

The reverse must be susceptible of receiving the following legend: "This note is receivable at par in all parts of the United States in payment of taxes, excises, and all other dues to the United States, except for duties on imports; and also for all salaries and other debts and demands owing by the United States to individuals, corporations, and associations, within the United States, except interest on public debt."

And, also, to have suitable tablets for imprinting the following synopsis of Sec. 57 and 58 of the Act authorizing a National Currency, approved February 25, 1863 [the counterfeiting clause]:

"Every person making or engraving, or aiding to make or engrave, or passing or attempting to pass,

any imitation or alteration of this note; and every person having in possession a plate or impression made in imitation of it, or any paper made in imitation of that on which the note is printed, is, by the Act of Congress approved 25th February, 1863, guilty of felony, and subject to fine not exceeding one thousand dollars, or imprisonment not exceeding fifteen years at hard labor, or both."

Designs will be received until the 28th day of March, 1863, and must in all cases be accompanied by models or illustrative drawings, and the Department reserves the right to reject any or all that may be offered. For such designs or parts of designs as may be accepted, suitable compensation will be paid, not exceeding in the aggregate two hundred dollars for each note; and the accepted designs will then become the exclusive property of the United States. The designs not accepted will be returned to the parties submitting them.

Proposals will also be received for furnishing dies in accordance with the designs; stating the cost of the completed dies, and the date at which they can be furnished; the Secretary reserving the right to accept designs or parts of designs, and causing them to be engraved by other parties than those submitting the designs, if he deems it for the interest of the government to do so. In all cases the dies, and all transfers or copies thereof, are to be the exclusive property of the United States. In the selection of designs, special attention will be given to security against counterfeiting, and against alterations, as well as to suitableness for use as currency.

Proposals and designs must be enclosed in sealed envelopes, and directed to the Secretary of the Treasury, and plainly endorsed, "Designs and Proposals for National Currency," and will be opened on the 28th day of March, 1863, at 12 o'clock, M.

Clark's Plan for Designs

Spencer M. Clark, chief of the National Currency Bureau (but still with his title of engineer as well), advanced his own ideas in a letter to Secretary Chase, March 28, 1863:

I respectfully suggest as a design for a National Currency the engraving of national historic pictures of the full size of the note to be issued, and submit, as "a model of illustrative drawing," a two-dollar note, made up of a copy of Weir's painting of the "Embarkation of the Pilgrims," with a suitable reverse.

I claim that this style of note possesses greater security against counterfeiting and alteration than any device yet in use.

First. If the note be engraved in the highest style of art, its different portions, such as etching, portraits, lettering, drapery, etc., executed by those who have made these portions respective specialties. It will present an amount of artistic labor to be accomplished by the burin which would appall and stagger counterfeiters in the outset, even if they possessed the requisite talent and skill to counterfeit it. As there is a peculiarity in the engraving of every proficient of high art, (as easily detected by an expert as different styles of hand writing), such a note, properly executed, could not be counterfeited so as not to be readily detected by the skillful. The notes now in use, made up of separate dies, actually afford facilities for counterfeiting, from their patchwork composition, while a note made from a single die, of its whole size, and not repeated in parts, presents difficulties of counterfeiting almost in geometric ratio to its increased size from a mere vignette.

To make a note's genuineness apparent to the unskilled, additional methods are suggested. To counterfeit it by photography, which is the readiest way to deceive the masses who handle notes, particularly those who most receive and pay small notes, a non-photographic material should be introduced into, and be inseparable from, the paper, so that a photograph or phototype should present a defaced or mottled appearance, easily distinguished by all. A sample of paper thus prepared is submitted for the Secretary's inspection.

Second. I claim that my suggestion would, if carried into effect, be a complete protection against alterations. Alterations, as the Secretary is aware, are the most numerous, as well as the most dangerous of frauds, far exceeding in number and danger all counterfeits; and in the multiform issues which now fill the channels of circulation, comparatively no protection is given except to those who are skilled in the art, and make their detection a study. But if a two-dollar bill is always the picture of the "Embarkation of the Pilgrims," and a ten-dollar bill is always the picture of "Washington Crossing the Delaware," the public, even those who cannot read, as well as those who do not understand our language, or who cannot distinguish its numerals, will soon educate themselves to these facts in handling the money, so that they could never be deceived into taking one denomination for another, though the figures or letters denoting the denomination of the note, were ever so cleverly altered. The skillful can protect themselves, but the unskillful require something plain and patent to the senses. I claim that my National Picture Currency furnishes this desideratum.

Third. A lesser but not unimportant advantage of such a currency would be, that a series properly selected, with their subject titles imprinted on the notes, would tend to teach the masses the prominent periods in our country's history. The laboring man, who should receive every Saturday night a copy of the "Surrender of Burgoyne" for his weekly wages, would soon inquire who General Burgoyne was, and to whom he surrendered. His curiosity would be aroused, and he would learn the facts from a fellow laborer or from his employer. The same would be true of other national pictures, and in time many would be taught leading incidents in our country's history; so that they would soon be familiar to those who would never read them in books, teaching them history, and imbuing them with a national feeling.

Thus a series of pictures of full note size might be selected, beginning with the earliest scenes of savage life, and terminating in the advanced stages of civilization, which would be an illuminated history of the country's progress; or a series beginning at bow and arrow warfare, and terminating in a perfected iron-clad; or a series beginning at the earliest modes of journeying in the birch-bark canoe, and terminating in the present perfection of steam craft: or a series illustrating methods of payment, beginning at exchanges of values by shells and wampum in uncivilized tribes, and terminating in Coupon and Registered Bonds and Treasury Notes, as dealt from a modern banking-house.

The reverse of the note, as exhibited on the model, possesses, as now drawn, no distinctive merit, except that it is "national in its character," and is an appropriate design, and there are intended to be as many circular counters as the note represents dollars-one counter on a one-dollar, two on a two-dollar, five on a five-dollar, etc. It should be executed in the highest style of art similar to the obverse. I design to fill the counters now in blank with a non-counterfeit composition, which cannot well be exhibited in drawing, and can only be clearly manifest in actual execution. But I have prepared a photographic approximation of it for the Secretary's inspection. A blank tablet is left for the legend, which can be differently filled for the different issues, as the acts of Congress may require.

I propose, also, to print upon the obverse of the note its denomination, date of issue, and Treasury seal, with the coat-of-arms of the states where the association is located, in gold characters, peculiarly attached, so as to be absolutely irremovable, before printing the note proper. This is an additional safeguard against photography and alteration, makes the denomination, of the note more discernible in a dim light, and when held between the eye and light appears in bold black characters, vastly more discernible and more enduring than any water-mark. A specimen thus prepared is ready for the Secretary's inspection.

There has not been time to prepare a full series of notes, but I have made preparations for them, which can be easily completed if the Secretary should adopt my suggestions.

Modifications and Provisions

Provision was made under the 1863 legislation for issuing National Bank Notes in denominations of $5 to $1,000. A secondary act of June 3, 1864, included revisions and additions, allowing the issuance of $1, $2, and $3 denominations, but with no more than one-sixth of a bank's bills being of these low values. The $3 denomination was never employed, but the others were, beginning in 1865.

Banks could not use their former names but were required to take a numerical designation, the First National Bank for the first application approved from a town or city, Second National Bank for the next, and so on. This worked well for

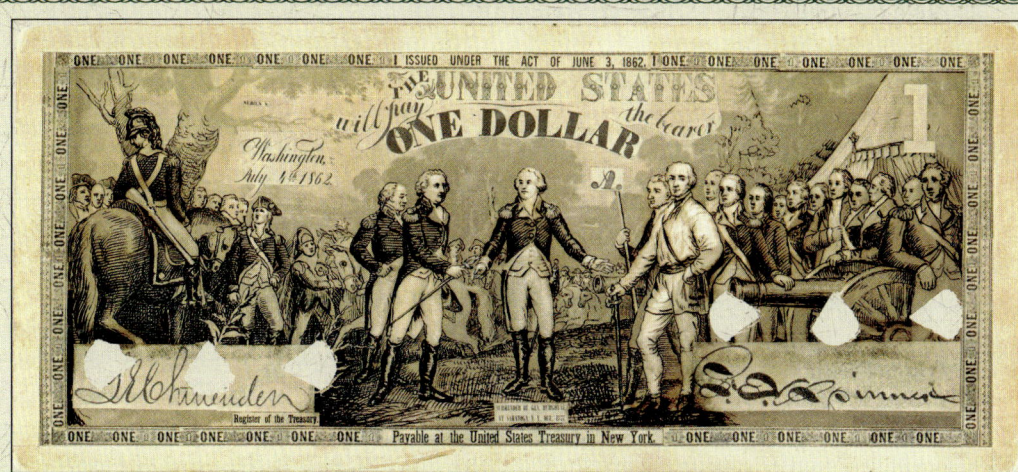

A Treasury department paste-up proof, unique, mounted on cardboard, of a proposed design for a $1 note, August 4, 1862. This illustrates Clark's point that "the laboring man, who should receive every Saturday night a copy of the 'Surrender of Burgoyne' for his weekly wages, would soon inquire who General Burgoyne was, and to whom he surrendered. His curiosity would be aroused, and he would learn the facts from a fellow laborer or from his employer."

The artwork, *Surrender of General Burgoyne at Saratoga, New York, October 17th, 1777*, by John Murdoch, is from a John Trumbull painting of the same name (now in the Frick Museum). General John Burgoyne is shown surrendering his sword to General Horatio Gates on October 17, 1777.

The concept of a "scenic" note that would be difficult to alter was hardly new. Although earlier examples could be cited, the main proponent of this was W.L. Ormsby, author of *Bank Note Engraving* (1852), which advanced what he called the "unit" system.

A few notes were made by Ormsby and his New York Bank Note Company (which in 1862 was combined into the new Continental Bank Note Company) for state-chartered banks, such as the $1 of the Carroll County Bank of Sandwich, New Hampshire, shown here. The idea proved impractical for Ormsby, as different banks preferred to have custom designs that could be made quickly by combining various stock vignettes and counters. In contrast, a unit or scenic printing plate would involve much special engraving.

First National Banks, but in the larger cities, many bank officers balked at becoming second, third, fourth, or any other later number, as these might reflect a lower status than being named "First." This was particularly frustrating to larger banks that had not rushed to send in applications when smaller ones did.

Many banks complied with this registration system, however, and in New York City, the Tenth National Bank was a reality before Congress changed the rules in 1864 to permit other designations as long as National was a part of the title. Soon after, the Irving National Bank, Central National Bank, National Currency Bank, and other institutions were formed in the same city. The only exception to the "National" word requirement was the Bank of North America in Philadelphia,

for which Congress granted an exemption, as it was the oldest commercial bank in the United States.

The capitalized word *The* was included in the bank name of most bills, such as The National Bank of Commerce of New London, Connecticut. In most instances it was small and hardly noticeable. Sometimes it was in large type and the same font as that of the bank name. In descriptions of bills in numismatic texts, however, *the* is usually not capitalized. Other title variations seen on notes are many. Some banks are given as being located in New York City, others in the City of New York. Some are "in" a location, others are "at" or "of" a certain place.[24] Punctuation can vary, and a bank might use such variations as Citizen's, Citizens', or simply Citizens on its notes and stationery. For the sake of consistency, most numismatists omit apostrophes when mentioning titles. Similarly, some years ago the United States Post Office directed that apostrophes be deleted from place names.

Each bank was given a charter number, awarded in sequence. By the end of the National Bank Note–issuing era, in late spring 1935, the numbers had reached 14,348. Not all of these banks exercised the privilege to issue currency, but 12,636 did.

"Firsts" in the Series

The First National Bank of Portsmouth, New Hampshire, was first to submit an application to the comptroller of the Currency, but due to an omission in the form it was returned, after which it was sent back in proper order, and charter 19 was awarded. Number 1 went to the First National Bank of Philadelphia, controlled by financier Jay Cooke, who had endeared himself to the Treasury department by selling many Interest-Bearing Notes and government bonds. Cooke would remain prominent in government securities until his company collapsed in the Panic of 1873.

Not by intention, but by mistake, the First National Bank of Davenport, Iowa, became the first to open for business. The Treasury department had instructed new banks to commence trade on Monday, July 1, 1863, but the notice arrived in Davenport on the preceding Saturday, June 29th, and was not read carefully, so the doors were immediately opened to the public.

Still another "first" was claimed by the First National Bank of Washington, D.C., charter number 26, which was the first to issue currency. Bills were delivered to the bank on December 21, 1863, in the form of four-subject $5-$5-$5-$5 sheets, made in New York by the Continental Bank Note Company, and with Treasury seals imprinted in red by the National Currency Bureau.

The Act of March 3, 1873, provided for replacing worn and mutilated circulating National Bank Notes, and "for engraving and preparing in such manner and on such paper and of such design as the Secretary of the Treasury may prescribe, new circulation notes for such associations to replace notes of a design and denomination now successfully counterfeited." A new plate for $10 notes was produced, and some paper money was printed. However, the secretary of the Treasury thereupon countermanded the Act, stating that no change in design would be made.[25]

Denominations, Series, and Printing

In time, national banks were chartered in all states and in several territories that later became states. One of these, Alaska, was known as a *district* from 1884 to 1912, then as a territory from 1912 until it achieved statehood in 1959.

The First National Bank of Davenport, Iowa, which opened for business two days before any other National Bank did. Years later, three more stories were added to the building shown here.

This photograph dates from 1883 and shows a lady draped in sheets of $5 Series of 1882 Brown Back notes from the First National Bank of Meridian, Mississippi, with additional sheets behind her and on the ground. Although over 38,000 such bills were released by the bank, just two are known today, per the Don C. Kelly and James M. Kelly census.

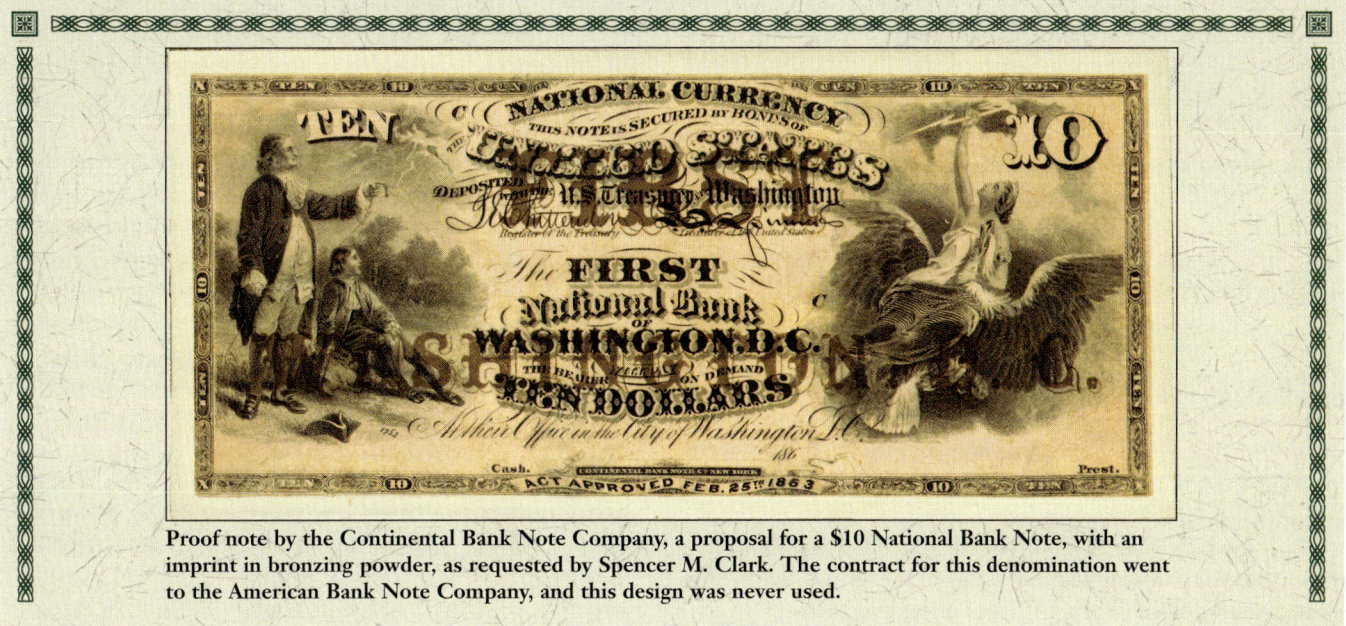

Proof note by the Continental Bank Note Company, a proposal for a $10 National Bank Note, with an imprint in bronzing powder, as requested by Spencer M. Clark. The contract for this denomination went to the American Bank Note Company, and this design was never used.

However, all currency issued there, including after 1912, has the district address on the notes.

Bills of the large-size format were issued in denominations of $1, $2, $5, $10, $20, $50, $100, $500, and $1,000. The $1 and $2 issues were discontinued on January 1, 1879, and some years later the $500 and $1,000 values were also dropped.

From the first bills of 1863 through July 1875 (known as the Original Series), National Bank Notes were printed in New York City by the American, National, and Continental bank-note companies. In these times, the face of each note required one printing while the back, with black and green ink, required two. The contractors added the bank serial numbers in red ink.

Spencer M. Clark had wanted an imprint of bronzing powder to be used as the first impression on the sheets. In November 1863, the first contractor to have notes ready, Continental, prepared proofs with and without bronzing powder. On December 1, Edward E. Dunbar and W.D. Wilson of the firm took these samples to Washington for review. The bronzing-powder idea was dropped.[26]

The bills were then sent to the National Currency Bureau First Division in sheets of four subjects (two for certain high denominations). There they were imprinted with the Treasury seal in red, the bank charter number in red (for bills issued after the implementation of the Act of June 20, 1874), and the Treasury serial number in red ink (in blue on certain earlier notes).

The sheets were then forwarded to the banks, where they were signed by the officers and then cut apart, usually by the use of shears. The $5 bills, printed by Continental, had closer spacing between the notes than did those of other denominations printed elsewhere and thus, when cut apart, had very tight margins.

The Act of March 3, 1875, provided that only part of the three-part printing (black face and separate black and green impressions for the back) be done privately, and the balance be done by the Treasury department. A vertical red imprint

on the face to the left of the center, SERIES 1875, identifies notes of the new series.

In 1877, the Treasury department solicited new bids for the printing of National Bank and Legal Tender notes. On September 25, 1877, submissions were reviewed from seven private companies as well as the Bureau of Engraving and Printing. The contract went to the bureau, which, after a period of transition, produced all notes. Certain old plates bearing the names of private companies were reentered with the bureau's imprint. In other instances, the names of the private companies were retained on the plates, and a printed notation in the field that the work had been done at the bureau was added.

Keeping Accounts

In Washington, a corps of clerks maintained ledgers on every national bank that issued paper money. When a note was redeemed, an appropriate entry was made. This involved taking a $1 bill, turning it face up, determining which bank issued it, finding the appropriate ledger page, and deleting it from the total. The clerks were often careless, and by mistake or intention added false figures. Determining where a bill came from could take time, as names such as First National Bank were used by many institutions, city and town names were often not prominently printed, and state names were usually in very small italic type. Beginning in 1874, the charter number of the bank was printed twice, prominently, on the face of each note, greatly aiding the ease of sorting for redemption.

The number of notes listed as outstanding on Treasury records is a useful guide for collectors today. However, figures can be approximate or misleading. After the disastrous Chicago Fire of 1871, the Treasury deducted $1,000,000 in outstanding notes from its records, estimating that this represented the amount of currency destroyed.

As an example of useful Treasury data, the Bank of the Commonwealth at Manchester, New Hampshire (which was not a commonwealth, by the way), organized on January 28,

1892, had an authorized capital of $100,000. Economic conditions were poor, the Panic of 1893 struck, and on August 7, 1893, the bank suspended operations. By that time it had issued $67,500 in paper money. A Treasury report of 1913 stated that all but $280 had been redeemed, but no notes are known to exist today. Similarly, none are known of the Carroll County National Bank of Sandwich, New Hampshire, which issued $48,000 worth, with $487 reported outstanding. Although there is no way to determine if these numbers are accurate, they do provide hope that—at least in theory—a few such notes may be found someday.

All large-size National Bank Notes include a day, month, and year date on the face, which refers to when the plate was prepared. It has no relation to the establishment of the bank. In instances of charter extensions, subsequent plates were often given a date of 20 years later.

An 1877 View of Issuance and Status

John Jay Knox, comptroller of the Currency, gave this report on National Bank Notes as of July 1, 1877:

$1: Issued, 20,616,024 notes • Redeemed, 16,815,568 notes • Outstanding, 3,800,456 notes

$2: Issued, 6,896,968 • Redeemed, 5,755,526 • Outstanding, 1,141,442

$5: Issued, 56,816,848 • Redeemed, 28,115,868 • Outstanding, 28,700,980

$10: Issued, 22,266,064 • Redeemed, 12,434,779 • Outstanding, 9,831,285

$20: Issued, 6,776,253 • Redeemed, 3,503,528 • Outstanding, 3,272,725

$50: Issued, 1,079,781 • Redeemed, 634,679 • Outstanding, 445,102

$100: Issued, 767,317 • Redeemed, 479,317 • Outstanding, 288,000

$500: Issued, 20,022 • Redeemed, 17,615 • Outstanding, 2,407

$1,000: Issued, 5,668 • Redeemed, 5,411 • Outstanding, 257[27]

Changes

Series of 1882 National Bank Notes, which featured new back designs, were made in the denominations of $5, $10, $20, $50, and $100 beginning in that year. Eventually, three different back designs were made for each denomination.

Regional letters were introduced in 1902. These facilitated the sorting of worn and redeemed notes into categories. Printed in color, these included N (for North), M (Midwest), S (South), W (West), and P (Pacific). This practice began in early 1902 and continued until early 1924.

The Series of 1902 inaugurated yet another set of designs for all denominations from $5 to $100. Including face and back variations, this series came to include the Red Seal, Blue Seal Date Back, and Blue Seal Plain Back varieties. The Aldrich-Vreeland Act of 1908 changed the requirement for bonds backing the issuance of notes, necessitating a revision of the imprint on the face of currency. Other evolutions and

changes included discontinuing the federal serial number and using only the bank serial, and allowing the names of bank officers to be included in the original printing plate.

National Bank Charter Dates

This chart lists each year that national bank charters were granted during the note-issuing period from 1863 to 1935. In many instances banks that were chartered in 1863 and 1864 had their charters expire in 1882, forcing them to reincorporate, at least on paper, and get a new, later charter number. Not all national banks issued currency, but the vast majority did.

Year	Charter Number	Year	Charter Number
1863	1 to 179	1900	5241 to 5662
1864	180 to 682	1901	5663 to 6074
1865	683 to 1626	1902	6075 to 6566
1866	1627 to 1665	1903	6567 to 7081
1867	1666 to 1675	1904	7082 to 7541
1868	1676 to 1688	1905	7542 to 8027
1869	1689 to 1696	1906	8028 to 8489
1870	1697 to 1759	1907	8490 to 8979
1871	1760 to 1912	1908	8980 to 9302
1872	1913 to 2073	1909	9303 to 9622
1873	2074 to 2131	1910	9623 to 9913
1874	2132 to 2214	1911	9914 to 10119
1875	2215 to 2315	1912	10120 to 10305
1876	2316 to 2344	1913	10306 to 10472
1877	2345 to 2375	1914	10473 to 10672
1878	2376 to 2405	1915	10673 to 10810
1879	2406 to 2445	1916	10811 to 10932
1880	2446 to 2498	1917	10933 to 11126
1881	2499 to 2606	1918	11127 to 11282
1882	2607 to 2849	1919	11283 to 11570
1883	2850 to 3101	1920	11571 to 11903
1884	3102 to 3281	1921	11904 to 12082
1885	3282 to 3427	1922	12083 to 12287
1886	3428 to 3612	1923	12288 to 12481
1887	3613 to 3832	1924	12482 to 12615
1888	3833 to 3954	1925	12616 to 12866
1889	3955 to 4190	1926	12867 to 13022
1890	4191 to 4494	1927	13023 to 13159
1891	4495 to 4673	1928	13160 to 13269
1892	4674 to 4832	1929	13270 to 13412
1893	4833 to 4934	1930	13413 to 13516
1894	4935 to 4983	1931	13517 to 13586
1895	4984 to 5029	1932	13587 to 13654
1896	5030 to 5054	1933	13655 to 13920
1897	5055 to 5108	1934	13921 to 14217
1898	5109 to 5165	1935	14318 to 14348
1899	5166 to 5240		

Review of Large-Size National Bank Note Types

Original Series National Bank Notes

Banks that were chartered from 1863 until mid-1875 received what numismatists call Original Series notes. The slang term for these and also for Series of 1875 notes, in use since the early 20th century, is *First Charter*, but as longtime student of the series Peter Huntoon states, this term has absolutely no

$1 National Bank Note, Original Series. Winchester (New Hampshire) National Bank, charter number 887.

Winchester National Bank and Michigan St., Winchester, N.H.

Constructed in the Greek Revival style in the late 1840s, this brick building housed the Winchester Bank, and later the Winchester National Bank. The view is from a Metropolitan News Co. postcard of 1908.

basis in either history or imprints on the notes. Perhaps it is similar to calling a federal one-cent piece a *penny.*

Notes in the Original Series include the $1, $2, $5, $10, $20, $50, $100, $500, and $1,000 denominations. Each bears the printed signatures of two Treasury officers and a space at the bottom of the note for the cashier and president to affix their autographed signatures. Sometimes, assistant cashiers and vice presidents signed, usually making an inked notation such as "asst," "v," or "vp."

The Act of June 20, 1874, provided that the charter number in red ink be added to the face of each note. While a few notes were imprinted with just one number, most have two: one horizontal at the right and the other vertical to the left of the center. This was intended to facilitate the sorting of currency when it became worn and was returned to the Treasury department for redemption. The charter numbers in two positions permitted the bills to be separated by holding them either horizontally or on end vertically. Although styles and locations varied, charter numbers were used on all National Bank Notes of all later series, including small-size currency printed from 1929 through 1935.

The face designs of an Original Series note typically included vignettes from American history and/or representations of Miss Liberty and other allegorical figures. A bright red Treasury seal is on each, with a border of 34 spikes. The backs were printed in black at the center, with a scenic vignette from history. The border was printed in green. To the left a state or territorial seal reflecting the issuing bank's location was placed. For some territories a generic eagle was used instead.

In the planning stages, it seemed that the Continental Bank Note Company would provide most of the large scenic vignettes for the backs of the notes. This did not come to pass.

When matters were settled, Secretary Chase, acting on the advice of assistant Treasurer John J. Cisco, awarded the American Bank Note Co. the $10, $20, $50, and $100 issues, Continental the $5 (which, it turned out, was the denomination made in the largest quantity), and National the $500 and $1,000, although contracts reveal that the first plan was to have Continental print the $10 notes. Spencer M. Clark, chief of the National Currency Bureau, viewed Continental's quality of work to be below that of American and National. However, it turned out that its National Bank Notes were very well done.

There is no record of *any* numismatic interest in Original Series notes during the time they were issued. Survival of higher-grade examples is a matter of chance or the deliberate retention of notes as souvenirs by bank officers.

National Bank Note Company vignettes for use on high-denomination National Bank Notes. (Proof impressions from the Banking House and Counting Room edition of *Heath's Infallible Counterfeit Detector*)

Series of 1875 National Bank Notes

Banks that were chartered from mid-1875 to July 11, 1882, received Series of 1875 notes when they ordered currency, as did earlier banks when they reordered. These were printed from the same plates used for Original Series notes, but with an imprint added to the face noting that production was now at the Bureau of Engraving and Printing in Washington. The signature of the private contractor who made the Original Series plate, these being the American, National, and Continental companies, was retained. In other instances, the plate was reentered and the company name removed, and in still other instances the bureau made new plates using the old designs.

The first order for an 1875 $10-$10-$10-$20 to be made entirely at the BEP was entered in the ledgers on June 18, 1875, although the plate may not have been made until November. It was for the Citizens National Bank of Keene, New Hampshire, charter 2299, and had a plate date of September 25, 1875. Likely, the very first plate made for any notes was for a sheet of $5-$5-$5-$5 for the same bank, an example of which is illustrated here.

The imprint SERIES 1875 is in red on each, vertically left of center. The small red Treasury seal now has a scalloped border. No change was made in the back design or arrangement.

For Treasury signatures, care was taken to try to match signatures with the engraved date on the plate. There were exceptions, however. When an Original Series plate was converted to become a Series of 1875 plate, the signatures and dates were left unchanged. In other instances current Treasury signatures were used but the date was not changed on the plate. In a few instances, new plates with dates have later Treasury combinations, such as one mentioned by Doug Walcutt for $5, $10, and $20 plates for the First National Bank of Huntington, Pennsylvania (charter 31) with an engraved date of July 21, 1882, but with the Bruce-

Wyman signature combination, although these two were not in office together until April 1, 1883.[28]

A bank chartered from 1875 through early July 1882 received Series of 1875 notes for the next 20 years. An institution chartered in, say, January 1882 would receive Series of 1875 notes until January 1902. In the meantime, new designs were made—such as the Series of 1882—and new banks or ones with charter extensions from mid-1882 onward would receive notes of the new designs. This arrangement, difficult to understand and with many exceptions, is explained in detail under the various denominations studied and priced in chapters 6 through 14.

By July 1, 1882, Original Series and Series of 1875 notes in circulation totaled $358,742,034. After that time, production diminished, but (as noted) for some banks, it continued as late as 1902.

In practice, most banks issuing Original Series and Series of 1875 notes ordered currency of the $1 denomination through $20 from the Treasury department, with $5 notes being the most popular. The issuance of $1 and $2 notes was limited to a third of the face value of currency ordered, as the government desired to have higher denominations used. In practice, values above $20 were not made in quantity. Today, any $50 or $100 note is rare, those of $500 are so rare as to be uncollectible, and none of the $1,000 value are known.

The bills of the Original Series and Series of 1875 era are much more ornate than are later issues, with historical scenes and other motifs. Today, they are the crème de la crème of the National Bank Note series.

The elusive quality of certain Western and territorial notes with these designs has given some of them an aura of fame and great value. Only a tiny fraction of the Original Series and Series of 1875 notes originally issued still exist at the present time. For many issues, especially from smaller banks, such grades as Good, Very Good, or Fine may represent the

$5 Series of 1875 note from the Citizens National Bank of Keene, New Hampshire. This bank was incorporated on September 18, 1875, and began business on October 1 of the same year. Accordingly, it did not order any Original Series notes. A communication from Peter Huntoon underscores the significance of the illustrated example:

"The BEP plate history ledgers at the Smithsonian clearly reveal that the Series of 1875 $5-$5-$5-$5 face plate for Keene was the first such plate made entirely at the BEP following the transfer of dies, rolls, and plates to the BEP from the bank-note companies beginning in mid-1875. This particular plate was made from transfer rolls prepared by the Continental Bank Note Company. It appears that the title block die was prepared at the BEP."

highest condition known for some varieties. Margins are often tight or even cut into the border on some bills, as the sheets were separated by hand using shears or scissors. These notes are eagerly sought. For some banks that in their day issued thousands of bills, none are known today of these or any later series.

National Gold Bank Notes

As described earlier, on the West Coast such Legal Tender Notes did not trade at par; merchants, banks, and others would accept them only at deep discounts. National Bank Notes, issued in the East since 1863, were traded at similar reductions and were not wanted.

Samuel Bowles, a newspaper editor from Springfield, Massachusetts, was on the West Coast shortly after the Civil War and wrote:

> Paper money has been kept out [of California] by the force of a very obstinate public opinion and the instrumentality of state legislation. Our national currency of greenbacks are seen here simply as merchandise; you buy and sell them at the brokers. . . .
>
> Of course, being made a "legal tender" by United States law, it is competent to pay a debt here with them, but no man who should do this once . . . could henceforth have any credit in the mercantile community. All large and long credits are now coupled with an express stipulation that they are on a specie footing, and a law of the state, known as the "Specific Contract Act," protects such arrangements.[29]

This unusual East Coast–versus–West Coast arrangement is very significant in the history of American paper money, although not widely known to historians, and is directly responsible for a special class of currency, authorized in 1870, known as National Gold Bank Notes.

By 1870, no national banks had been established in California, as their bills would not have been useful in commerce. To remedy this, Congress took an unusual step. The Act of July 12, 1870, provided for the establishment of special institutions, to be known as national gold banks, to issue bills redeemable at par in gold coins.

Nine such institutions were established in California and issued bills from $5 to $500, although not all denominations were utilized by each bank. These found immediate acceptance in commerce in California and were equal in value to gold coins. Indeed, they were literally as good as gold. Bills of the First National Gold Bank of San Francisco, the National Gold Bank of D.O. Mills & Co., Sacramento, and others traded at a premium in terms of Legal Tender bills or National Bank bills from the Midwest and East.

Worthy of special mention is the Kidder National Gold Bank of Boston, organized and chartered in August 1870, apparently with the thought that its notes, redeemable in gold coins, would be of special interest to the commercial community in the Northeast. In actuality the idea seems to have been flawed, as such notes would have been unfamiliar to bankers as well as the general public, and they would have required special handling. National Gold Bank Notes did not circulate outside of California, and the Easterners had

no knowledge of them. The story is told by Peter Huntoon in *Large Size United States National Bank Notes*: "The Kidder National Gold Bank of Boston (charter 1699) was the first national gold bank chartered, and holds the distinction of being the only one to utilize the $500-$1,000 combination. Its history is brief."

On August 15, 1870, bonds worth $50,000 were deposited to secure the circulation for the bank. This was followed on November 5, 1870, with an additional $100,000 bond deposit. The first shipment of notes was made to the bank on March 11, 1871, when 50 sheets of the $50-$100 combination were sent. The comptroller received 75 sheets of its $500-$1,000 combination on April 5, 1871, and sent them to the bank three days later. The high-denomination shipment boosted the Kidder circulation to a total of $120,000, the 80% legal limit, special for this series of notes, for the $150,000 in bonds that the bank deposited as security. These two shipments accounted for all the notes ever printed for the bank. All were Original Series notes, and the $1,000 bills were the only $1,000 National Gold Bank Notes made.

None of the Kidder notes reached circulation. All were returned and redeemed by the comptroller on December 4, 1871. The bonds for the bank were sold on December 9 and 19 in $140,000 and $10,000 increments, and the bank was liquidated on November 8, 1872. Proofs remain of the $50 and $100 denominations, but none seem to remain of the $500 and $1,000 denominations.

The record of high and low exchange rates for the year 1873 reveals that the exchange value of Legal Tender bills in terms of gold coins or National Gold Bank Notes ranged from a low of $106.12 in November to a high of $119.12 in April. This means that in April 1873 it would have taken over $1,190 in Legal Tender bills, plus an exchange fee, to buy $1,000 in federal gold coins or National Gold Bank Notes.

The face designs of the National Gold Bank issues are similar to those used on regular Original Series and Series of 1875 National Bank Notes. The back vignette differs

A faro game in progress in California. National Bank Notes and other federal currency did not circulate in California, where commerce and banking were conducted in coins, mostly gold. That changed in the 1870s when national gold banks were formed.

greatly, though, and is a collage printed in black, almost photographic in its clarity, of a large group of various United States gold coins, with the obverse of an 1871 double eagle being the most prominent. The borders of the back are in brown. A special light yellow-gold paper was used to print most (but not all) of the bills. The obligation stated that the issuing bank, not the federal government, would pay gold coins to the bearer on demand, an interesting distinction.

As time passed, the difference in exchange value between Legal Tender Notes and gold coins narrowed. Congress mandated that they be exchangeable at par beginning on January 1, 1879. The market anticipated this, and parity was achieved on December 17, 1878. Afterward, National Gold Bank Notes became redundant. On February 14, 1880, an act of Congress allowed the national gold banks to adopt new titles as national banks and keep their charter numbers.

National Gold Bank Notes, typically showing extensive use in circulation, were withdrawn in an era in which no numismatic attention is known to have been paid to them. Today, all range from scarce to very rare. When seen, they are nearly always in lower grades such as Very Good. Those issued by the First National Gold Bank of San Francisco survive in larger numbers than those of all others combined.

Series of 1882 National Bank Notes

After passage of the Act of July 12, 1882, which provided for the extension for a further 20 years of the charters of banks formed earlier, a new series of notes was created. These constituted the types distributed at and after that time to newly formed banks as well as older banks at the time of their charter extensions. Sometimes these are nicknamed *Second Charter* notes, but such use has no basis in history.

The first official issue of Series of 1882 bills for banks extended from July 12, 1882, to April 11, 1902, but notes of these designs were issued as late as 1922. The scenario for the later date is provided by banks chartered close to but before April 11, 1902. Accordingly, a bank chartered very early in 1902 would have been given the current Series of 1882 designs, and would be provided with that series for the next 20 years. Again, this overlap can be confusing to numismatists. Complicating matters, there are many exceptions to general rules and policies. The aforementioned book by Peter Huntoon clarifies these and other complex situations.

The basic face designs were continued from the Original Series and Series of 1875 notes, except for the $5 denomination. The $5 note was redesigned at the Bureau of Engraving and Printing under the direction of George W. Casilear, chief of the engraving department, who had been on the staff since December 1, 1862. Much experimentation was done with the lettering at the center of the $5 plates, including the bank name, town, and state, creating some highly interesting varieties from the viewpoint of today's numismatists. Plates for $10, $20, $50, and $100 notes have the Bureau of Engraving and Printing imprint as part of the design at the center within the bottom border. Some plates were reentered (altered) from those used for the Series of 1875 notes.

Denominations produced for the Series of 1882 were $5, $10, $20, $50, and $100. Designs varied and fell into three classifications:

Brown Back notes have the back printed in brown, with the bank's charter number in large blue-green numerals at the center. Each Brown Back note depicts the appropriate state or territorial seal of its issuing bank or a generic seal for a territory. This necessarily involved the preparation of many different plates. The policy was discontinued on later types, at which time a standard plate was used for all.

Date Back notes were issued under the provisions of the Aldrich-Vreeland Act of May 30, 1908, which permitted securities other than government bonds to be deposited against issuing paper money. Under this legislation Congress loosened the deposit requirements to encourage banks to order more currency, an effort to combat the shortage of circulating paper caused by the Panic of 1907. The back of each note has the dates 1882–1908. Accordingly, we have bills that are imprinted on the face with the Act of 1882 but that were not issued until a generation later. The provisions of the Act expired in 1915, but some bills continued to be printed into 1916.

Value Back notes succeeded the Date Backs beginning in 1915, although issues overlapped. Again, the 1882 date on the face must have been confusing to the public. These have the denomination spelled out at the center, such as TWENTY DOLLARS.

As a class, Series of 1882 notes are more plentiful than the earlier series bills, as the economy had expanded by that era, and more banks had been chartered. As is the case with other National Bank Notes, they are collected by types, states, or towns within states. The most often seen are the Brown Back notes. As a class, Date Back notes are scarce (although there are exceptions), and Value Backs are scarcer yet. The $50 and $100 Value Backs are extremely rare, as only two banks issued them, one in Ohio and the other in Louisiana.

Series of 1902 National Bank Notes

The Act of April 12, 1902, provided 20-year extensions of expiring bank charters. Accordingly, new legislation would have been required by April 11, 1922, for still further extensions. By that later time Congress provided that 99-year extensions could be made, later followed by legislation that charters were permanent as long as a bank remained financially solid.

In 1902, new designs were prepared and issued to banks extending their charters as well as to newly formed banks. Sometimes these are nicknamed *Third Charter* notes, but as before, such use has no basis in history. Denominations continued as previously: $5, $10, $20, $50, and $100. Several variations of seals and imprints were made:

Series of 1902 Red Seal notes were issued from 1902 until 1908, when the Aldrich-Vreeland Act changed the deposit requirement for securities, thus necessitating a new imprint on the face. The Banking Act of 1900 had lowered the capital requirement for new banks from $50,000 to just $25,000. Older banks that had no need to renew their charters continued receiving Series of 1882 Brown Back notes from the Bureau of Engraving and Printing, this again being somewhat confusing unless studied carefully. Today, the Red Seals, with the Treasury seal, bank charter numbers, and district letters in bright red, are numismatic favorites.

Series of 1902 Blue Seal Date Back notes, with 1902 and 1908 on the back, were issued under the provisions of the Aldrich-Vreeland Act of May 30, 1908, and had "and other securities" lettered on the face, in addition to the mention of United States bonds. New banks, as well as banks extending their charters after May 1908, received notes of this type. Otherwise, banks received the Series of 1882 Date Backs (with 1882–1908 on the back).

Series of 1902 Blue Seal Plain Back notes were issued after the Aldrich-Vreeland Act expired on June 30, 1915. Newly created as well as reentered plates mentioned United States bonds only. However, some older face plates with "and other securities" were continued in use. Plain Back bills are by far the most plentiful today as a type.

SERIES OF 1929 SMALL-SIZE

Series of 1929 National Bank Notes

National Bank Notes in small-size format were issued in sheets of six notes. These are all Series of 1929, with the Treasury signatures of E.E. Jones and W.O. Woods, who served together from January 22, 1929, to May 31, 1933. Such bills continued to be issued until May 1935. Each also bore the name and location of each bank and the printed signatures of that bank's cashier and president. These were produced in denominations of $5, $10, $20, $50, and $100, with the $50 and $100 values usually made in small quantities. The back designs are the same as used for other small-size currency of the same denominations, such as Legal Tender Notes, Silver Certificates, and Federal Reserve Notes.

There are two types:

1929 Type 1 (printed from May 1929 to May 1933): These have the bank charter number twice on the face in black. The six notes on each sheet had the same serial number, six digits, with prefixes A through F, and each with the suffix A. Accordingly, the first sheet printed for a given bank would have serials A000001A, B000001A, C000001A, D000001A, E000001A, and F000001A. The second sheet would have these serials: A000002A, B000002A, C000002A, D000002A, E000002A, and F000002A, and so on.

1929 Type 2 (printed from May 1933 to May 1935): These have the bank charter number twice on the face in black, *and also twice in brown* (a quick way to identify the bills at a glance). The six notes on each sheet had different serial numbers, in sequence, each with the prefix A but with no suffix. Accordingly, the first sheet printed for a given bank would have these serials: A000001, A000002, A000003, A000004, A000005, and A000006. The second sheet would have these serials: A000007, A000008, A000009, A0000010, A0000011, and A0000012, and so on.

On March 11, 1935, the printing of National Bank currency was abruptly halted at about eleven o'clock in the morning. Orders still on the presses were not completed, per research by Peter Huntoon. The last regular shipment took place from the comptroller's office on May 31, 1935, plus two later shipments for "bond adjustments" because of an error; these stragglers were sent to the First National Bank of Chillicothe, Ohio.

Today, bills of Type 1 are typically much more plentiful in numismatic hands than are those of Type 2, and are therefore less expensive. There are exceptions among certain banks. While most banks issued both types, some issued just Type 1 and others just Type 2.

As to values, those from more populous states are relatively inexpensive, while those from such states as Arizona and Nevada are considerably more costly. Within any state, there can be "rare banks" for which the bills are very valuable.

Peter Huntoon has calculated that during the period of large-size notes, the face value released was $14,081,185,225. For small-size National Bank Notes the amount was $2,845,191,970. The number of banks that applied for and received notes during the period from 1863 to 1935 was 12,636. At any given time, only a small percentage of that amount was in circulation, as bills—particularly in small denominations—tended to wear out quickly and then were redeemed, to be exchanged for other issues.

By October 31, 1935, only a few months after the issuance of small-size National Bank Notes had ceased, $14,035,682,565 in large-size notes and $2,358,689,700 in small-size notes had been redeemed, or nearly 97% of all that had been issued since 1863.

Gold Certificates AUTHORIZED 1863 SERIES OF 1863 TO 1922 • LARGE-SIZE

Act of March 3, 1863

The class of paper money known as Gold Certificates has a rich history. Bills under this heading were issued in nine different series or authorizations, beginning under the Act of March 3, 1863. With the exception of the $20 bill, most of these early bills were of higher denominations, $100 to $10,000.

These were printed by the National Currency Bureau. A paper with a slight yellow tint was used to emulate a gold color. Of the first series, denominations of $20, $100, $500, $1,000, $5,000, and $10,000 were made. The first were paid out on November 13, 1865, according to Treasury reports, by which time the Civil War had been over for six months. Gold still sold at a premium, however, and would do so until December 17, 1878. The issuance of Gold Certificates under the Act of 1863 was ended on December 1, 1878.[30]

In 1882 a new series was inaugurated. The intent was that those who paid gold coins into the Treasury could receive gold certificates in exchange. The Treasury would then hold a similar sum of gold as backing.

Counting $20 gold coins at the Philadelphia Mint in 1894. In this era Treasury reserves were very low, and there was concern that gold coins would disappear from circulation. Many of these were kept by the Treasury as backing for Gold Certificates.

Gold Certificates were used in banking and commercial transactions, not in general trade. Import duties were payable in gold, and these notes created a convenient way to do it. It seems that gold coins were not always required to receive these notes, as in this account of an exception:

> The Department, in order to protect importers from the fluctuations of the gold market, and at the same time measurably to repress the advance in price, supplied Gold Certificates upon deposits of Legal Tender Notes, in the Sub-Treasury, at one-quarter of one percent less than the current rate for coin. These certificates were receivable in payment of duties upon imports. They were issued directly to the importer making the deposit and were unassignable.[31]

The Gold Panic of 1869 resulted when certain speculators endeavored to corner the market on the metal, driving the price up and causing great financial distress to those who were caught short. A subsequent investigation produced testimony from leading Eastern banks, including statements of their gold holdings. In most instances, Gold Certificates were kept on hand in addition to or in lieu of gold coins.[32]

The designs of the 1863 Gold Certificates were standard across the denominations. Each featured at the left an eagle perched on a shield with flag, and to the right the denomination in lacy, light green lathework. Today, these early bills range in availability from extremely rare to unknown. Notes were made with imprints of Boston, New York, Philadelphia, and Washington. Nearly all were issued in New York, with only a small amount in Washington. No record of issuance has been found for Boston or Philadelphia. Printage and distribution quantities vary in official reports.

Series of 1870, 1871 ($100 only), and 1875 Gold Certificates were issued under the same act, but seem to have seen even more limited use than the first series. These are exceedingly rare today, and relatively little is known about

them. Many news reports and other accounts of the 1870s mention such certificates, but not with sufficient detail to numismatically differentiate them today.

Later Issues

It was not until the Series of 1882 that Gold Certificates were issued in large quantities for wide use by the general public. By this time gold coins were once again readily available at banks and were used in commerce. Appropriate quantities of gold coins were held by the Treasury as backing. Such certificates were also produced as the Series of 1900, 1905, 1906, 1913, and 1922. Later series included denominations of $10, $20, $50, $100, $500, $1,000, $5,000, and $10,000, but not all values were issued in each series. Bills were "payable in gold coin." The backs were printed in bright yellow-orange ink.

The plates for the 1882 notes in some instances have "shingle style" lettering, familiar from certain of the Series of 1882 $5 National Bank Notes (these being the first of the Nationals with bureau-created designs).

Today, large-size Gold Certificates are collected mostly by types, and only of the Series of 1882 and onward. Most are scarce or rare, but some are affordable, particularly those issued in the 20th century.

SERIES OF 1928 TO 1934 SMALL-SIZE

Gold Certificates of 1928 to 1934

Small-size Gold Certificates were made only for a short time, in the Series of 1928, 1928-A, and some of 1934. The last two were not issued, but some of the 1928-A notes may have been used to a very limited extent for internal transactions within the Federal Reserve Banks and Treasury system. The gold policies of President Franklin D. Roosevelt's new administration underwent many transitions in 1933 and early 1934. Finally, in 1934, the Gold Reserve Act of January 30 summarized previous legislation and decrees, revalued gold bullion from $20.67 per ounce to $35, and apparently ended the use of gold as money. However, some gold coins were later paid out, and the Series of 1934 Gold Certificates were printed (but never used).

Unfortunately, beginning in 1933 the Treasury department took the position that Gold Certificates of any sort could not be legally held by anyone, including numismatists. Banks were directed to turn in any that they received, and notes were seized from collectors who displayed them.[33] There was an underground trade in such currency by collectors and dealers who considered the regulations to be unfair. Finally—through the intervention of paper-money collector Amon G. Carter Jr.—on April 24, 1964, secretary of the Treasury C. Douglas Dillon removed all restrictions. Notes came out of hiding from all directions, and since then they have been openly bought and sold. Numismatic research is hampered by these notes having been "underground" from 1933 until 1964, resulting in hardly anything appearing in print concerning them. Before 1933, hardly anyone was interested.

Denominations of small-size Gold Certificates include $10, $20, $50, $100, $500, $1,000, $5,000, and $10,000, each with a distinctive yellow seal and yellow serial numbers. Some have the backs printed in green, but a few were printed in gold. Examples of the $10 to $100 denominations are readily collectible as types. The $500 and $1,000 denominations are rare but available, and higher values are essentially noncollectible.

Silver Certificates
AUTHORIZED 1878
SERIES OF 1878 TO 1923 • LARGE-SIZE

Silver Certificates of Deposit

Silver Certificates were born under the Bland-Allison Act of February 28, 1878, the same legislation that created what we now know as the Morgan silver dollar. Soon afterward, Silver Certificates of Deposit (as identified on the face) were made, but in relatively small numbers, in denominations from $10 to $1,000. Boldly emblazoned on the back of each was the word SILVER, in letters so large that it could be read from across the room, with CERTIFICATE below it. This was a strong signal to the silver-mining interests of the West that, indeed, their senators and congressmen were acting in the interests of this important industry.

The distribution and use of the Series of 1878 and 1880, the earliest Silver Certificates of Deposit (generally called simply Silver Certificates), is curious to contemplate today. It seems that these were not intended to be widely circulated. Instead, they were held by banks. There was special interest in them on the West Coast, and it is said that some were exported to China, where silver was a favorite metal with the citizenry and gold was in no particular demand. In any event, distribution seems to have been limited. Most

were redeemed. As a class these range from scarce to extremely rare today. On the Series of 1878 notes with red Treasury seals and added countersignatures, the key faces to the *right* (with the handle at the left), an engraving error.

The earliest Silver Certificates were not officially legal tender, but were specifically payable in silver dollars and were considered "lawful money." (Later Silver Certificates were legal tender.) This was no problem, for from the beginning of Morgan dollar coinage, large quantities piled up in government storage facilities. The silver dollars were legal tender, so in a way the bills were also, de facto. The government was very precise in the wording of its various note issues and what they represented. That is why so many different classes of paper money were created, often circulating in commerce at the same time.

Silver Certificates

Beginning with the Series of 1886 these notes were designated only as Silver Certificates, and on the face instead of the back. The Act of August 4, 1886, authorized these, after which this class of note was made in very large quantities, including the new $1, $2, and $5 denominations. Vast quantities of Morgan dollars, put up in cloth bags of 1,000 coins each, continued to accumulate as backing for these bills. The Series of 1886 notes were popular, as were the various later series, some of which had very beautiful designs.

In 1918 the Pittman Act provided for the melting of over 350,000,000 of the stored silver dollars, not even close to the entire supply in existence, but enough to sharply deplete stocks held by the government. In October 1921 *The Numismatist* included this item:

> When all those dollars were melted the United States had to call in all the Silver Certificates—the $1, $2, and $5 bills, to speak in common lingo—representing the dollars that were deposited in the vaults of the mints. Under the law of the land the Treasury must hold a silver dollar for each dollar Silver Certificate issued. So with the melting of the silver dollars the Silver Certificates had to be recalled.
>
> To cover that loss in currency, the government issued short-term certificates of indebtedness bearing 2% interest. The silver dollars now being coined [the new Morgan dollars of 1921] allow for the issuance of new Silver Certificates, which are being used in calling in those certificates of indebtedness.

This was an exaggeration, as *all* were not called in. However, many were. The Series of 1918 Federal Reserve Bank Notes (see listing) were issued to replace many of the Silver Certificates. The silver dollar situation eased, and in the 1920s many more Silver Certificates were issued, but only in lower denominations. By that time nearly all of the earlier notes had disappeared from circulation.

Popular Issues

Today, Silver Certificates are very popular to collect. It is delightful that many beautiful designs can be found on the smaller $1, $2, and $5 denominations, which were also the values made in the largest quantities. In particular, the Series of 1896 "Educational Notes" are elegant, with the faces depicting allegorical scenes of goddesses known as *History Instructing Youth* ($1), *Science Presenting Steam and Electricity to Commerce and Manufacture* ($2), and *Electricity as the Dominant Force in the World* ($5). This was indeed the age of electricity, and the world was changing as a result. On the back of each Educational bill are portraits of two prominent Americans.

As much as they are appreciated today, at the time they were made they were roundly criticized by certain key BEP employees. In 1897 an intensive congressional investigation of the BEP included this testimony from George W. Casilear, engraver and superintendent, who had been with the bureau since 1862, although not continuously:

> *Question by Congressman Lyman:* Do you know, Mr. Casilear, the history of the designs that are now used for Silver Certificates?
>
> *Answer by Mr. Casilear:* I know they employed Mr. Will Low, and he is more of a scenic painter than a designer. The way he came into the Bureau, or was brought to the notice of the Bureau, was in this way: They advertised for proposals. I got up a design—that is, I didn't get it up personally myself, because I was very busy at that time getting up some Treasury notes and one thing and another, but I suggested how to get it up, and it was in this way that Will Low came there, through Mr. Thatcher, of Albany. He was a sort of pet of his, and we had a meeting at the Fifth Avenue Hotel to submit our designs, and Mr. Thatcher submitted Will Low's—that is, a mere sketch of it—as he proposed it.
>
> It was very poorly drawn—all of the drawing, in fact—and Mr. Thatcher wanted to get it up as a woodcut. He thought it would be an elegant thing to get a Boston wood engraver, who had some style in drawing for their magazine articles, and I said if they used it as a woodcut it would be an abomination to the whole country at large. I went and fought him before the Assistant Secretary, who had charge of that matter, and Thatcher and I finally agreed to have it done in legitimate style, as plate work, and it was gotten up in that way.
>
> Well, they employed an engraver on it. He wanted me to do it, and I couldn't do it, because the engravers I wanted I couldn't get; and they were the best that I could get my eye upon at the time. There were three that I had in view; but he went and brought on a German by the name of Schlecht. I never liked his work. Well, [bureau chief Claude] Johnson, showed me his work. Johnson said he didn't want any of that engraving; but I suppose he did the best he could, and he brought this man on. Well, they made a great botch of it. It is the worst thing I ever saw in my life. The certificates have been criticized abroad and everywhere. Sir Sidney Waterloo said it was a disgrace to America. He is in the company that does the bank-note work for South American states; that is, Argentina, etc.
>
> Then they employed Mr. Low to get up some of these designs, and also employed Shirlaw, and a man by the name of Beckwith. I don't know it to be a fact, but I

am told he put them on at salaries of $6,000 a year; that is, he did Shirlaw, so it was announced in the papers afterwards; and Will Low. What he did with Beckwith, whether he took any more designs by him or not, I don't know, but he is the best artist of the three.

> I can say as regards the merit of the engraving, it is the poorest work that I ever saw on a bank note. Since the history of Jacob Perkins, the inventor of transferring, it is the poorest work I ever saw. As regards the designs, they are an outrage. Prior to the rebellion the bank note companies did just as good engraving. Bank-note engraving was a specialty among engravers. They sent out and picked up the very best talent . . .
>
> That is about the history of it. The public will say the rest.[34]

Other testimony varied, but was generally negative, due in large part to the decision to have outside artists create designs that were traditionally the duty of in-house talent. In addition, there was a tremendous amount of infighting and bickering among bureau artists, supervisors, and others, which seems to have colored many of their comments in what developed into book-length testimony.

Once the Series of 1896 Silver Certificates reached circulation, some bankers complained that the ink smudged easily, and their complicated designs made them hard to count. Seemingly, they did not have honor in their own time, within either the Treasury department or the banking community. Only the public loved them!

Elsewhere in the Silver Certificate series, the Series of 1886 $1 bills depict Martha Washington; the Series of 1886 $5 bill shows on the back five Morgan silver dollars; the Series of 1899 $5 bill has a realistic portrait of an Indian chief; the Series of 1923 $5 bill has Abraham Lincoln within a "porthole" (a heavy circular frame); and the Series of 1886 $10 bill has the image of vice president Thomas A. Hendricks (who died on November 25, 1885) in a distinctively shaped frame, creating what today is known as the "Tombstone Note."

SERIES OF 1928 TO 1953 SMALL-SIZE

Later Low-Denomination Silver Certificates

Silver Certificates of the small size were produced in denominations of $1, $5, and $10. The earliest, the $1 bills, were imprinted as the Series of 1928, although the small-size format was not actually introduced until 1929. The Series of 1928 alone is payable in "one silver dollar." Later, $1 bills as well as Silver Certificates of all other denominations are payable "in silver" or in "silver coin," but make no mention of dollar coins. Beginning with Series 1928-E, Silver Certificates were legal tender and stated this on their face. Save for certain World War II issues, all have the Treasury seal in blue.

On June 4, 1963, with the market price of silver rising, Congress prohibited any further issuance of Silver Certificates. They continued to be redeemed in unspecified silver coins. In

March 1964, secretary of the Treasury C. Douglas Dillon decreed that Silver Certificates could no longer be redeemed for silver coins. *The Numismatist* printed this in May:

> In providing for Silver Certificate redemption in bullion only, the secretary ruled that holders of Silver Certificates may exchange them for silver bullion at the rate of $1.292929292 an ounce at the New York and San Francisco assay offices—not at the Treasury. The certificate holder will get, in lieu of a silver dollar, a little paper envelope containing some gray, powdered silver. It will weigh just what the silver in a dollar weighed.

A nationwide scramble to buy the notes ensued, as silver was selling for more than this on the open market. Redemption in silver ceased on June 24, 1968, after which circulated modern notes had no value above that printed on their faces.

Except for the backs of the $1 bills of Series 1928 through 1934, the small-size notes appear quite similar to bills of the same denomination in other series. Similar to the practice for Legal Tender Notes and Federal Reserve Notes, most series were given letter suffixes, which were changed whenever the signature combination changed. The series date was changed only when there was a modification of the design, these revisions sometimes being of a trivial nature.

Varieties

The panorama of small-size Silver Certificates is strewn with interesting varieties with "stories," including Series of 1935-A $1 notes with bright red R and S surcharges on the face, others overprinted HAWAII, and Yellow Seal notes meant for distribution in World War II to Allied troops in Sicily and North Africa. *The History of the Bureau of Engraving and Printing*, published in 1962, tells the story:

> The first order for the Hawaii overprint notes was given on June 28, 1942, and the first bills were delivered on the same day. These were put into circulation in Hawaii in July. A decree was given that no other paper money could be used in the islands after August 15, 1942, unless a special permit was obtained. Another directive stated that no notes should be sent to the mainland, but they should all remain in Hawaii.
>
> In 1944 when American forces invaded Japanese-held islands in the Pacific they brought Hawaiian overprint paper money with them, for use by the soldiers and also by the residents of the areas taken over. On October 21, 1944, the Treasury Department decreed that the need for the Hawaiian currency had ended. No other notes were made, and examples on hand were allowed to be distributed on the mainland as well as in Hawaii.
>
> Special notes with yellow seals were made for use in the North Africa Campaign, and were given to the troops there in November 1942, the directive for them having been given two months earlier. These were also used in Sicily. About this time, Military Payment Certificates were originated and widely used, replacing the Yellow Seal notes.

Certain of the above World War II issues were also made in the Federal Reserve Note series.

Treasury Notes (Coin Notes)
AUTHORIZED 1890
SERIES OF 1890 AND 1891 • LARGE-SIZE

Silver Dollars and Gold Coins

The Series of 1890 and 1891 Treasury Notes were issued to buy silver bullion under the Sherman Silver Purchase Act of 1890, authored by Senator John Sherman. This was another nod to the all-powerful silver-mining interests in the West. For a short time before this point, it seemed that Morgan silver dollars would no longer be made, because the supply had run out as authorized by the Bland-Allison Act of February 28, 1878.

The new legislation provided for more silver bullion to be purchased by the government and coined into dollars. Payments to suppliers were to be made by these Treasury Notes, also called Coin Notes. The production of Silver Certificates was halted, and these bills took their place for a time.

Additional paper money was anathema to hard-money advocates and conservative financiers, as this was viewed as inflationary. Simultaneously, the Treasury reserve of gold coins was sharply reduced by exports, because overseas banks and merchants (except in China and India) detested silver. It was not at all certain what types of coins would be available to redeem the new notes.

As only "coin" was specified, it was left to the discretion of the secretary of the Treasury whether gold or silver should be exchanged for these notes. In practice, most people wanted gold, causing some anxiety among Treasury officials, who nonetheless paid out double eagles and other coins as requested.

Soon, silver dollars were again plentiful in current production. A new gold rush was ignited in Cripple Creek, Colorado, in 1891, and later in the decade the Klondike furnished additional supplies. This resulted in increased

Cartoon urging repeal of the Sherman Silver Purchase Act of 1890, showing despair, but with the bright hope of gold, in the form of a double eagle as the sun in the distance. ("Out of the Silver Flood," by Louis Dalrymple, *Puck*, September 13, 1893)

coinage of gold, but the export demand was still so great that supplies held by the Treasury were often dangerously low, especially in the years before "Silverite" William Jennings Bryan lost the 1896 election. After that time, Treasury reserves increased dramatically.

Later in the 1890s, Silver Certificates were issued in large quantities, and production of Coin Notes slowed, then stopped. Contemporary reports and documents reveal that Coin Notes were a particular annoyance to the Treasury department, perhaps because of the uncertainty as to the class of coins needed to be held in reserve for their redemption. A special effort was made to retire them quickly.

Ornate Backs

The Treasury or Coin Notes of the first type, or Series of 1890, are considered to be among the most beautiful of all United States currency due to the ornate engraving on the back of each. The entire area is filled with designs and lettering, with no open or white space. Each of the denominations is delightful to behold. In particular, the $100 "Watermelon Note" is held in high esteem, with the zeros resembling the fruit. Even better is the very rare $1,000 "Grand Watermelon Note," one example of which was the first note of any kind to cross the auction block for over $1 million. This variety holds the number-one spot in *100 Greatest American Currency Notes* (Q. David Bowers and David M. Sundman, Whitman Publishing, 2006).

As gorgeous as these may seem to viewers today, in 1890 they were viewed as susceptible to counterfeiting, and their use was discontinued soon afterward. This premise was based on the old theory (prominent in the history of the Bank of England, for example) that bills should have open areas, as they would be less confusing to the public, and counterfeits could be more easily detected. New security paper was introduced for the Series of 1891, with two vertical columns of distributed fibers (previously two horizontal threads had been used).

The Series of 1891 bills, with ample open spaces on the back, solved the supposed problem. Their plain appearance motivated bureau chief Claude Johnson in 1894 to hire outside artists to make the notes more artistic, thus reversing the open-back policy recently instituted. As related, the new issues in the Silver Certificate series caused a new set of problems and precipitated a congressional investigation.

Federal Reserve Bank Notes
AUTHORIZED 1913
SERIES OF 1915 AND 1918 • LARGE-SIZE

The Federal Reserve Act

The Federal Reserve Act of December 23, 1913, set up a system of 12 regional banks that is still in operation today. These are located in Boston (identification letter A and number 1), New York City (B-2), Philadelphia (C-3), Cleveland (D-4), Richmond (E-5), Atlanta (F-6), Chicago (G-7), St. Louis (H-8), Minneapolis (I-9), Kansas City (J-10), Dallas (K-11), and San Francisco (L-12).

A shortage of paper money was envisioned, as credit was tight, and it seemed likely that many national banks would have their notes redeemed by the Treasury department but not issue new notes as replacements. A new class of currency was devised under the provisions of the Act, the Federal Reserve Bank Note. These notes could be issued in amounts not limited in any way to the capital of the Federal Reserve Bank, a provision quite unlike that for national banks. The title NATIONAL CURRENCY was included on each, similar to that on National Bank Notes. These became the Series of 1915 notes. The first of these were issued in 1916. Maximum circulation was achieved in October 1917 when $12,970,425 in these bills was outstanding.

Series of 1918 Notes

The Series of 1918 Federal Reserve Bank Notes were also the result of a special monetary situation. The Pittman Act of April 23, 1918, provided for the melting of silver dollars that had been stored as backing for Silver Certificates:

> To conserve the gold supply of the United States; to permit the settlement in silver of trade balances adverse to the United States; to provide silver for subsidiary coinage and for commercial use; to assist foreign governments at war with the enemies of the United States; and for the above purposes to stabilize the price and encourage the production of silver. Be it enacted by the Senate and House of Representatives of the United States of America in Congress assembled, That the secretary of the Treasury is hereby authorized from time to time to melt or break up and to sell as bullion not in excess of 350,000,000 standard silver dollars now or hereafter held in the Treasury of the United States.
>
> Any Silver Certificates which may be outstanding against such standard silver dollars so melted or broken up shall be retired at the rate of $1 face amount of such certificates for each standard silver dollar melted or broken up. Sales of such bullion shall be made at such prices not less than $1 per ounce of silver one thousand fine and upon such terms as shall be established from time to time by the secretary of the Treasury.

At the time, gold was selling for more on international markets than the $20.67 price pegged by the Treasury department. Gold coins disappeared from cashiers' drawers and became scarce. It was feared that the nation's gold reserves would be depleted. As silver was in strong demand in parts of the British Empire, especially India, this legislation served in part for international payments that would otherwise have been made in gold. Eventually, 270,232,722 silver dollars of earlier dates were converted to bullion.

Many Silver Certificates were called in and replaced in large part by Series of 1918 Federal Reserve Bank Notes. The high point in circulation of these was $236,597,570 in a report dated January 1, 1921. Millions more silver dollars were coined in 1921 to replenish Treasury reserves and to allow quantities of Silver Certificates to be issued once again. In 1922 the large-scale retirement of Federal Reserve Bank Notes was underway, and within a few years most had disappeared from circulation.[35]

Issues and Imprints

Among Federal Reserve Bank Notes, the Series of 1915 includes $5, $10, and $20 denominations, and the Series of 1918 includes these, plus the $1, $2, and $50 values.

On the face the banks are named by city and also by a letter and number, assigned sequentially from Boston (number 1) to San Francisco (number 12). Each note bears the appropriate letter as the serial number prefix, as described above.

With one exception, all Federal Reserve Bank Notes of all denominations and series bear the date of September 18, 1914, the date placed on the organization certificate of each bank. However, "since there was no air mail in those days, the Secretary of the Federal Reserve Bank Organization Committee in Washington allowed two extra days (to September 20) to the San Francisco District."[36] Accordingly, the Series of 1915 San Francisco notes are dated September 20, 1914, as are Series of 1918 issues, except for an "error" plate (W-928-L) that is dated September 18, 1914.

Federal Reserve Bank Notes closely follow the concept of Series of 1914 Federal Reserve Notes (but without "Bank" in the title), as described in the following section. The major difference, a technical but important one, was that Federal Reserve Bank Notes were obligations of the particular Federal Reserve Bank, while Federal Reserve Notes were obligations of the Federal Reserve as a whole and thus do not have individual Federal Reserve Bank officers' signatures. Additionally, Federal Reserve Bank Notes were receivable in payment of all taxes, excises, and other dues to the United States *except* duties on imports (customs) and interest on the public debt, while Federal Reserve Notes were receivable for customs and also had a gold clause.

The $50 note was made only for the St. Louis Federal Reserve Bank and is a numismatic classic. Treasury records show that only 70 of these are outstanding. In numismatic hands over 50 have been recorded, due to scouting by Texas banker William A. Philpott Jr., who contemplated the low printage of 4,000 notes and commenced contacting various banks to find them.

Designs and Varieties

Each Federal Reserve Bank Note has the city name boldly at the center, as, for example, BOSTON. The back designs of the $1 note, with an eagle clutching a flag, and the $2 note, with a dreadnought-type battleship, have been collectors' favorites for a long time. The denominations of $5 to $50 use the same back motifs as on the Federal Reserve Notes, Series of 1914 (see the following section).

Federal Reserve Bank Notes were produced with two Treasury signatures and two Federal Reserve Bank officers' signatures. Sometimes this can significantly expand the number of collectible varieties. For example, the San Francisco Federal Reserve Bank $1 bills are found with Teehee and Burke of the Treasury and in two varieties of bank signatures, Clerk-Lynch and Clerk-Calkins. Then for the same bank come the Elliott-Burke Treasury combination with Clerk-Lynch and Ambrose-Calkins, for a total of four varieties. Across the various denominations, such combinations can be interesting to collect. Some of the higher denominations have rubber-stamped or casually applied signatures of bank officers that have faded to near illegibility.[37]

Of nearly $762,000,000 in Federal Reserve Bank Notes issued, only about two million dollars' worth remains outstanding. Indeed, most were redeemed by the mid-1920s. The issuance quantities and the number of notes outstanding as of January 15, 1951, are as follows:

$1: Issued, 478,892,000 notes • Outstanding, 1,504,962 notes

$2: Issued, 67,596,000 • Outstanding, fewer than 10,000

$5: Issued, 24,292,000 • Outstanding, 41,033

$10: Issued, 1,655,000 • Outstanding, 3,649

$20: Issued, 488,000 • Outstanding, 1,252

$50: Issued, 4,000 • Outstanding, 70

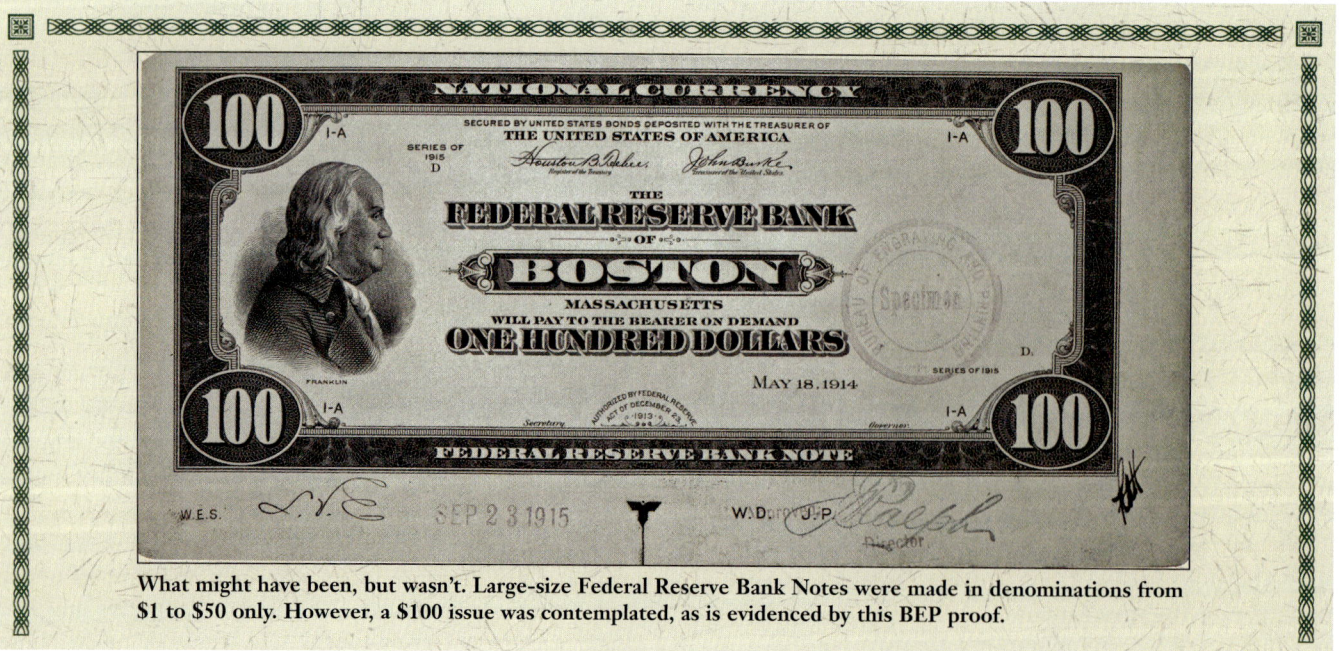

What might have been, but wasn't. Large-size Federal Reserve Bank Notes were made in denominations from $1 to $50 only. However, a $100 issue was contemplated, as is evidenced by this BEP proof.

This reflects once again that while gold coins were often kept as souvenirs in the early 20th century, paper money did not have the same attraction. Accordingly, in proportion, many paper issues are quite scarce today.

SERIES OF 1929
SMALL-SIZE

The Bank Holiday of March 1933

Federal Reserve Bank Notes in small-size format were printed in sheets of six notes, all Series of 1929, with the Treasury signatures of E.E. Jones and W.O. Woods, who served together from January 22, 1929, to May 31, 1933. These are similar in many respects to National Bank Notes but have the name of the Federal Reserve Bank, its location and district letter (A to L), the printed signatures of Treasury officials Jones and Woods, and the separately imprinted signatures of two Federal Reserve Bank officers. Not all 12 banks issued notes of every denomination.

These have a very curious history and in Treasury annals are often called *emergency notes*. Soon after Franklin D. Roosevelt was inaugurated (on March 4, 1933), he took action to preserve the integrity of banks, many of which were experiencing great difficulties in the Depression. Over 5,000 had already failed. The Bank Holiday was declared, and all banks were closed beginning on Monday, March 6. Examinations were made quickly, and those that met strong requirements of capital and liquidity were allowed to reopen after Thursday, March 9. Others remained closed and were either liquidated over a period of time or merged into stronger banks. Many new charters were granted in 1933 and early 1934.

Emergency Notes

The Treasury anticipated that after the "good" banks reopened there would be a rush by the public to convert their savings and checking accounts to paper money as security should anything happen to the bank. Roosevelt had prohibited the payout of gold coins, the traditional haven of safety.

To provide for this sudden need for large quantities of paper money, sheets of National Bank Notes already partially printed except for the name of the issuing bank, serial numbers, and bank signatures, and available in quantity at the Bureau of Engraving and Printing, were overprinted with *Federal Reserve Bank* names! The CASHIER and PRESIDENT notations already printed at the bottom of each note were blanked out, sometimes carelessly (with parts of the original words remaining), and overprinted with new designations, such as GOVERNOR or another title, and the names of Federal Reserve Bank officers.

Printing commenced, and within two days the first bills were ready. The expected rush did not occur, however, although the BEP shipped notes to the banks for months afterward, into February 1934. By that time 7,317 packages containing about 29 million notes remained in Treasury vaults. These were paid out years later during World War II when there was a sharp demand for paper money.[38] Such bills, especially of the $50 and $100 denominations, were common in circulation into the early 1960s.

Today, small-size Federal Reserve Bank Notes are easily enough collected by type, with one of each denomination. Specialists pursue bank locations as well, among which there are several that are scarce or rare. Average grades tend to be high, and many varieties are available at the Uncirculated level. The key issue is the San Francisco $5 note, which is usually seen with evidence of extensive use, suggesting that most must have been paid out in 1933. Relatively little has ever been published about how these notes were specifically distributed or about the biographies of the Federal Reserve officers whose names appear on them.

Federal Reserve Notes
AUTHORIZED 1913
SERIES OF 1914 AND 1918 • LARGE-SIZE

Large-size Federal Reserve Notes, authorized in 1913 and first printed in 1914, were redeemable in dollars, including "in gold on demand at the Treasury Department of the United States in the City of Washington, District of Columbia, or in gold or lawful money at any Federal Reserve Bank." They were backed specifically by 40% gold on deposit. Thus, in a way, these can be considered as gold coin notes.

Denominations of $5, $10, $20, $50, $100, $500, $1,000, $5,000, and $10,000 were produced with different combinations of bank and Treasury officials' signatures. Rarest are the Series of 1914 Red Seal notes, all of which bear the signatures of Burke and McAdoo. The BEP imported the red ink, and after World War I started in August 1914, the supply was cut off. When the inventory of ink of this color was exhausted, a change was made to blue, by which time Red Seals had been printed for only four months, ending in December.[39] The 1914 Blue Seal notes went on to be produced for 13 years afterward.

The face designs feature portraits of government officials in history, Federal Reserve Bank identification letters A to L and numbers 1 to 12, plus other inscriptions, while the backs have scenic motifs. Today, examples of the values from $5 to $100 of the Blue Seal variety are easily found on the market as types, but certain signature combinations are rare, as are all higher denominations. All Red Seals range from scarce to rare, especially in higher grades. Interest in these elusive issues is growing rapidly, in contrast to the situation a decade ago, when few people desired them.

Doug Murray, for one, has reviewed archival data and has delisted certain signature combinations and varieties that were routinely included in certain past reference books upon learning that no plates were ever made to print them.

SERIES OF 1928 TO DATE
SMALL-SIZE

Modern Federal Reserve Notes

Small-size Federal Reserve Notes are the bills of our current era, today taking the place of other classes. Each bears a seal with the name, location, and identifying letter or number (or, in recent times, letter code with the serial number) of one of the 12 Federal Reserve Banks. These notes constitute the foundation of modern collecting of current issues and varieties, a field that attracts many enthusiasts.

Federal Reserve Notes are printed in denominations of $1, $2 (occasionally), $5, $10, $20, $50, and $100. In the Series of 1928 to the Series of 1934-C, values of $500, $1,000, $5,000, and $10,000 were made, but not every denomination in every series. It is likely that the Series 1934-B and C were never released, as none are known in numismatic hands today.

These higher denominations are all collectors' items. There is a surprising demand even for the $10,000 bills due to their novelty as a trophy notes. The Series of 1928 notes were payable in gold, a provision later removed. Certain of the earlier issues were made with either light yellow-green or green (in various shades called dark green, blue-green, light green, etc.) Treasury seals.

In 1963, Congress ended the production of Silver Certificates due to the rising price of that metal. Their place was taken by Federal Reserve Notes. In the $1 series there had been no small-size issues of this type before. Such notes were first released on November 26, 1963, and have been numismatic favorites ever since. Nathan Goldstein II told of the passion launched in 1963, which has continued to today:

> Serial number collecting has taken a large number of collectors by storm. Unusual runs, identical digits, repeating numbers, etc.—all make a most interesting showing. Low serials or those with the large number of 0s seem to be of great interest, and there is much activity in matching identical numbers between districts or other series. There is truly a great wide-open world of paper money collecting, and the very elaborate or just simple collections can be as interesting as anything you have ever attempted to accomplish.[40]

In the 1990s the Western Facility was established in Fort Worth, Texas, a fully equipped printing plant, the first branch of the Bureau of Engraving and Printing. Notes printed there have FW as part of the face plate letter and number designation.

The designs of Federal Reserve Notes are fairly similar to those of other small-size bills until the late 1990s, when significant changes began to be made to the portraits on the face and the buildings on the back of each denomination of $5 and higher. Improvements were added for security, including microscopic printing and anticopying features. Bills printed before the design revision featured eight-digit serials, prefixed by a letter (A to L) for the bank, plus various letter suffixes to expand the number of notes beyond the limit imposed by eight digits. The redesigned bills omit printed mention of specific Federal Reserve Bank branches, but have a designation indicating the Federal Reserve district—for example, G7 for Chicago or L12 for San Francisco. The next stage in their evolution was "colorized" notes, featuring additional security provisions and various hues and shades not earlier used on small-size notes.

A BEP commentary told of the changes made for the $20 note in the Series of 2004 and is reflective of modern anti-counterfeiting practices (adapted):

> The new $20 bills are safer, smarter and more secure. . . . Look at the number "20" in the lower right corner on the face of the bill. When you tilt the bill up and down, the color-shifting ink changes from copper to green. The color shift is more dramatic in the redesigned currency making it even easier for people to check their money. Hold the bill up to the light and look for the watermark, or faint image, similar to the large portrait. The watermark is part of the paper itself and it can be seen from both sides of the bill.
>
> A security thread, or plastic strip, is embedded in the paper and runs vertically up one side of the bill. If you look closely, the words "USA TWENTY" and a small flag are visible along the thread from both sides of the bill. The security thread also glows green under ultraviolet light. The most noticeable difference in the redesigned $20 bill is the addition of subtle background colors of green, peach and blue to both sides of the bill. This marked the first time in modern American history that U.S. cash included colors other than black and green. The words "TWENTY USA" are printed in blue in the background to the right of the portrait and small yellow numeral "20"s are printed in the background on the back of the bill. Different background colors will be used for the different denominations. This will help everyone to tell denominations apart.
>
> The oval borders and fine lines surrounding the portrait on the face and the White House vignette on the back of the bill are removed. The portrait is moved up and shoulders are extended into the border. Additional engraving details were added to the vignette background. The redesigned $20 bill features microprinting on the face of the bill in two new areas: bordering the first three letters of the "TWENTY USA" ribbon to the right of the portrait, the inscription "USA20" is printed in blue. And "THE UNITED STATES OF AMERICA 20 USA 20" appears in black on the border below the Treasurer's signature.

Today, Federal Reserve Notes, especially the smaller denominations, are very popular. The smaller values are generally readily available and quite affordable in Uncirculated grade. They are widely collected on a systematic basis, by bank and by Treasury signature combinations: each bill has two printed signatures, the secretary of the Treasury (instead of the register, beginning in 1933), and the Treasurer.

Transitions: face of a $20 Federal Reserve Note, Series of 1988-A, with the general face style used since the early days of small-size notes of this denomination.

Face of a $20 Federal Reserve Note, the style introduced with the Series of 1996. A larger portrait of Jackson is used, and other changes were made.

Face of a $20 Federal Reserve Note, Series of 2004, with "colorized" printing and enhanced security features. This is the latest version.

3

THE DEVELOPMENT AND FEDERALIZATION OF PAPER MONEY

OVERVIEW

As discussed in the previous chapter, the production of standard issues of federal paper money commenced with the Interest-Bearing Notes and Demand Notes of 1861, issued to finance the Civil War. In later years, many different series of currency were produced, based upon their backing or stated obligation, with face values from $1 to $10,000. Even $100,000 bills were made, but for internal Treasury use only, not for circulation.

Interest-Bearing Notes were issued early in 1861, followed by Demand Notes in the summer. Legal Tender Notes made their debut in early 1862, but were not specifically redeemable in specie (gold or silver coins), and thus depreciated rapidly in terms of coins. Other classes of paper money made over time included Gold Certificates, Silver Certificates, Treasury Notes (also called Coin Notes), National Bank Notes, and two types of Federal Reserve Notes, among others. Large-size currency was issued until 1929, in which year the transition was made to the small size still in use today, although some small-size currency is of the Series of 1928, as this was the release year originally planned.

In the 20th century, Federal Reserve Notes were introduced, and over time the other classes of currency were discontinued. Today, only the Federal Reserve Notes remain, in denominations of $1, $2, $5, $10, $20, $50, and $100. Recently, the designs of most bills have undergone changes, with modification of the portraits to larger sizes and the addition of colorizing and new security features.

THE FIRST FEDERAL PAPER MONEY

The first notes in the series of federal paper money from 1861 to date were the Interest-Bearing Notes issued under the Act of March 2, 1861. This legislation provided that notes, also called bonds, pay 6% annual interest prorated to a term of 60 days. Other bonds paid the same rate over a term of two years. The 60-day notes were a quick sellout,

and two-year notes were very popular as well. Although these and later types of Interest Bearing Notes are considered to be currency by modern numismatists, they did not see extensive hand-to-hand circulation. Instead, they were sold at a discount from face value to represent the interest, held by most of the purchasers, then redeemed for face value at the expiration date. These usually were bid on in bulk by banks and security dealers, not by individual citizens here and there. Only a few remained unredeemed, making all notes of this class very rare today. In fact, not a single one of the 60-day notes is known to have survived.

Interest-Bearing Notes were printed by the National Bank Note Company in New York City, a firm that began business in 1859 and was a main supplier of paper money to state-chartered banks across the United States. National was widely admired for the artistic quality of its paper money, often made with ornate vignettes, especially the "counters" or denomination imprints. Ostensibly, its main competitor was the larger American Bank Note Company formed in 1858 in the same city. However, the two firms quickly realized it was better to work together than to really compete. Charges of collusion later flew about, in which rumors abounded but facts were scarce. More about this later.

Bundles of the notes were shipped from New York City to the Loan Branch, a department in the immense Treasury Building in Washington, where in several rooms trimming, record-keeping, and other aspects of distribution took place. The same Greek Revival–style structure, located adjacent to the White House, remains the center of Treasury management today. It was extensively enlarged in the early 1860s.

THE NEEDS OF WAR

The bombardment of federal Fort Sumter in the harbor of Charleston, South Carolina, by Confederate shore batteries on April 11 precipitated what became known as the War of the Rebellion (later *Civil War* became the general term).

It would be an easy win for the North, Lincoln and his cabinet thought. Most industry and financial operations were concentrated there, while the Confederacy was viewed

The Treasury Building, Washington, D.C., as it appeared in the 1860s. Within this Greek Revival structure in 1862 the National Currency Bureau, First Division, directed by Spencer M. Clark, imprinted red Treasury seals on currency printed in New York City by the American and National bank-note companies. Beginning in 1863, Fractional Currency notes were printed in their entirety here. In the same year the bureau set up its own paper factory on the premises. Treasury officials, including secretary Salmon P. Chase, had their offices in the same structure.

The National Bank Note Company was located upstairs at No. 1 Wall Street in New York City. Shown here is a street view from the era and a detail of the NBNCo sign.

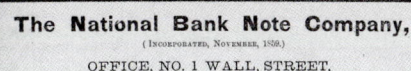

Advertisement by National Bank Note Company.

Wall Street in the 1860s, with the United States Sub-Treasury to the left. (W.L. Ormsby for *Eighty Years' Progress*, 1867)

as having an agricultural base with cotton, rice, corn, and tobacco, called "the wealth of the South" on a popular token issued in 1860. The president called for 75,000 men to enlist for three months—surely enough time to conclude the secession and restore national unity. In New York City and elsewhere, festive parties and gala parades were held as soldiers prepared to head off to war.

In early 1861, cash reserves in the Treasury were very low, a result of a combination of poor planning by the James Buchanan administration, confusion caused by the secession of Southern states from the Union (beginning with South Carolina on December 20, 1860), and, simply, lack of revenue. The earlier-mentioned Interest-Bearing Notes helped raise funds, but financial problems continued.

THE DEMAND FOR DEMAND NOTES

The outlook for the economy remained uncertain in 1861, as it had been for nearly a year. The Treasury needed further infusions of money. Congress met in an extra session on July 4. Secretary of the Treasury Salmon P. Chase estimated that the government would require more than $318,519,581.87 for the current fiscal year ending on June 30, 1862, to quell the rebellion and for other purposes.[1] Lincoln requested the authority to borrow $400,000,000.

The Act of July 17, 1861, was the result. However, just $250,000,000 was authorized. Part of the "loan" was to be in the form of Demand Notes to be issued in denominations of $5, $10, and $20. The Act of August 5 added and modified certain provisions and provided for convertibility of the Demand Notes into 20-year, 6% bonds in denominations of $500 and more.

These notes were authorized for up to a total of $60 million. The new currency was redeemable in gold or silver coins on demand. With the war in progress, conditions in Washington were anything but stable, as recalled by Senator John Sherman:

> We had to appeal to the patriotism of bankers to accept the Demand Notes of the United States as money, with no prospect of being able to pay them. Our regular army was practically disbanded by the disloyalty of many of its leading officers.
>
> Washington was then practically in a state of siege, forcing me, in May 1861, to go there at the heels of the 7th regiment of New York Militia, avoiding the regular channels of travel. The city of Baltimore was decked under the flag of rebellion. Through the state of Mary-

$10 Demand Note of 1861 depicting president Abraham Lincoln, printed by the American Bank Note Company in New York City on special 20-pound paper. The "Patent Green Tint" used by the American Bank Note Company, as seen on this note, was said to deter counterfeiting by photography. In practice, it was ineffective. No matter; the Treasury department paid ABNCo royalties for its use.

Uncut sheets of four notes were sent by mail to the Treasury department in Washington, where clerks used shears to cut them apart. These early notes did not have the Treasury seal. Demand Notes were the first federal paper money to circulate widely since the Continental Currency issues of the 1780s.

The American Bank Note Co., located in the Merchants' Exchange, New York City, as it appeared in 1861. Formed by a consolidation of eight private bank-note engraving and printing companies in March 1858, the firm printed the lion's share of federal currency on contract from 1861 through the mid-1870s, after which the Treasury did all of its own work at the Bureau of Engraving and Printing.

The printing room at the American Bank Note Co. in 1861. Artisans inked the steel plates with rollers, then printed sheets of Demand Notes, four to a sheet, on hand-operated roller presses, or *spider* presses, using dampened paper. Afterward, serial numbers were added and the notes were dried, bundled, and shipped to the Treasury department in Washington, where the sheets were cut apart.

land, loyal citizens passed in disguise, except by a single route opened and defended by military power.[2]

A few days after the Act of July 17, 1861, was signed, Confederate troops won a decisive victory at Bull Run, in Manassas, Virginia, not far from Washington. Federal soldiers became scattered in disarray, some of them making their way back to the capital. In the words of Hugh McCulloch, "Members of Congress and other civilians who had gone out to witness a Union victory had returned stricken with terror. If the Confederates had known the real condition of Washington and the character of its defenses, they might have captured the city and placed their banners upon its public buildings."[3] All of a sudden, the outlook changed. The war would last not three months, but several years. (Details of Demand Notes are given in chapter 2, as are details of all other series.)

THE RISE OF FRACTIONAL CURRENCY

In late 1861 and early 1862, a severe shortage of circulating coins took place. Uncertain whether the Union would prevail in the War of the Rebellion, as had been widely expected by Northerners, or whether the Confederacy would be the victor, citizens hoarded every form of hard money. Even one-cent pieces disappeared from circulation. This spawned many substitutes, including copper tokens, printed tickets, scrip notes, encased postage stamps (see chapter 22), and Postage Currency, later followed by Fractional Currency.

Beginning in August 1862, Postage Currency notes were issued to take the place of the vanished coins. These notes carried denominations of 5¢, 10¢, 25¢, and 50¢, and bore the designs of current postage stamps. Printing was accomplished in New York City by the National and American bank-note companies. In 1863, Postage Currency was succeeded by redesigned Fractional Currency notes, which

were printed by the government. Fractional Currency notes continued to be produced through the war, and were not discontinued until 1876. (See chapter 18 for more on the emergence and history of Postage and Fractional Currency.)

REBEL REQUIREMENTS

In the meantime, the Confederate States of America, with its capital in Montgomery, Alabama, formulated plans to operate as a new nation. Prior to the bombardment of Fort Sumter, warm relations with the Union were hoped for, and it was anticipated that the anti-slavery / pro-slavery question would be put to rest. The United States of America would not allow slavery, while the Confederate States of America would. That controversy settled, business between the two separate nations could flourish. At least that was the desire of many leaders in the South.

Seeking its own paper money, the Confederacy contracted with the National Bank Note Company in New York to make an issue of $50, $100, $500, and $1,000 notes. An order for bonds was also placed with the American Bank Note Company (ABNCo). G.B. Lamar, a banker and entrepreneur with interests in Savannah and New York City, facilitated the arrangements. In Philadelphia, Robert Lovett Jr. prepared patterns for Confederate one-cent pieces.

The Confederacy had its own financial problems, even more acute than those of the Union. Coins quickly disappeared from circulation. It was hoped that its bonds would attract many investors, particularly in England, a prime destination for exports of cotton, and a highly successful effort was mounted to sell securities in London.

Abraham Lincoln, who had won the presidency on the Republican ticket the past November, was inaugurated on March 4th. Differences between the North and the South intensified, but he hoped that reunification would take place, even though the Confederacy had no interest in reconciliation.

$1,000 Interest-Bearing Note printed by the National Bank Note Company for the Confederate States of America in March 1861, just prior to the onset of the Civil War. Depicted are two famous sons of the South, Senator John C. Calhoun to the left and president Andrew Jackson to the right. Twelve months after the date of issue the CSA promised to pay interest at the rate of 10¢ per day. The denomination letter, M, is part of a rich kaleidograph counter, a masterpiece of engraving. Today, notes of this variety are numismatic classics. Slightly over 100 are known to exist.

United States $50 Interest-Bearing Note, 1861, paying 6% interest annually and redeemable in two years, printed by the National Bank Note Company. The same Jackson portrait used on the CSA note is seen at the lower left, while secretary of the Treasury Salmon P. Chase is depicted at the right.

One of 12 pattern cents made in early 1861 by Robert Lovett Jr. of Philadelphia for the new Confederate States of America. In early 1861 the Confederacy hoped for normal business relationships with the Union (the North). (Enlarged 1.5x)

DEVELOPING PAPER MONEY AT THE TREASURY DEPARTMENT

FROM PRIVATE SECTOR TO PUBLIC WORKS

The production of paper money was originally contracted out, with the government supplying printing plates to private-sector printers. In 1861 the National and American bank-note companies in New York City carried out the printing of paper money; later they were joined by the Continental Bank Note Company, formed in January 1863. Within the Treasury Building in Washington, D.C., notes received from the contractors were trimmed, separated, and distributed. Signatures were also applied at this point.

Over time, more of the process was removed from the private sector: the Department of the Treasury installed equipment for imprinting the Treasury seal, and in 1863 added presses to print certain types of paper money to supplement that done by contractors. In 1880 the Bureau of Engraving and Printing moved into its own building and was able to print paper money of all kinds in addition to security documents and, some years later, postage and other stamps. The production of paper money was thus moved entirely to the public sector.

SPENCER MORTON CLARK'S FIRST STEPS

Spencer Morton Clark's early work at the Treasury department laid the groundwork for the eventual establishment of the First Division of the National Currency Bureau within the Treasury department. His subsequent actions drove the department's ever-expanding involvement and control over the manufacture of U.S. paper money.

In early 1856, Clark, who hailed from Brattleboro, Vermont, but more recently had been situated in Hartford, Connecticut, was hired as a clerk in the Bureau of Construction, a division of the Treasury department. In August of the same year he was named as chief clerk, a position he held until May 1860, when he was appointed "acting engineer in charge." In the 1860 *Annual Report of the Secretary of the Treasury* he prepared meticulous accounts of construction and repairs to customs houses, post offices, warehouses, government hospitals, courthouses, and other facilities, including a major extension underway at the Treasury Building in Washington, for secretary of the Treasury Howell Cobb, who resigned in December of that year.[4]

In the winter of 1861–1862, Clark contemplated the designs of Demand Notes and suggested to Treasury secretary Salmon P. Chase that "scenic" motifs would be more appropriate than the current designs. His specific recommendation, to use the scenes from American history depicted in the murals in the Rotunda of the Capitol, was eventually adopted for the National Bank Notes of the Original Series and the Series of 1875. It was Clark's idea that viewing paper money could be instructive to citizens.[5] The notes that were ultimately produced with these designs were described years later in a numismatic account as "the most beautiful of any ever issued by the Treasury department."[6] The Demand Notes catalyzed the formation of what later became known as the National Currency Bureau, First Division.

EARLY ACTIVITY AND GROWTH

Clark's responsibilities at the Treasury department expanded, and soon he was involved in various aspects of receiving and processing paper money. Various names were assigned to the premises where currency operations took place, including *Note Room, Note Bureau,* and *Small Note Department,* among others.[7] In the summer of 1862 he designed a machine for cutting and separating the four-subject sheets of the new $1 and $2 Legal Tender Notes, which heretofore had been cut apart by shears. The success of the machine impressed Secretary Chase, who encouraged Clark to suggest other efficiencies.

As this occurred in Washington, the American Bank Note Company in New York City secured a lucrative contract for printing Legal Tender Notes, and the National Bank Note Company perfected an agreement to produce notes in the same series. The early history of the operation, as penned by Clark in an 1864 retrospective, is given below. By this time the term *Civil War* was used to describe the ongoing conflict:

Origin of the Division

This Division had its origin in an attempt to trim and separate Treasury Notes [Legal Tender Notes] by machinery. This work, up to the summer of 1862, had been executed by hand labor. The first paper issues of the government, made necessary by the existing civil war, were manufactured by the New York bank-note companies, and sent to this Department in sheets of four notes each. After they were received here, the signatures of the proper officers were attached, and they were then trimmed and separated by hand labor with shears.

It soon became apparent that the officers whose signatures were necessary—the Treasurer and the Register of the Treasury—were physically unable to write their names as rapidly and as many times as the necessities of the public service required. The authority of Congress was therefore obtained to employ other persons to sign for these officers, and a corps of seventy clerks was ultimately employed for this purpose, at salaries of $1,200 each per annum, and placed under the care of the clerk then in charge of the Loan Branch of the Secretary's office.[8]

It soon became obvious that so many different signatures to notes of the same issue afforded very little security to the public. The cost of so many signers also largely increased the expense of the issue. The propriety and economy of printing the signatures, by a peculiar process and with peculiar ink, and of dispensing with written signatures, then suggested itself, and I reported to the then Secretary of the Treasury, Mr. Chase, my belief that if the signatures were thus mechanically attached they would offer greater security against counterfeiting than so many different written signatures; and that an additional evidence of lawful issue might be made with a copy of the Treasury seal, printed in the Treasury building, on each note, bond, or coupon issued.

I urged this view to him, orally, at different times, and endeavored to prove that it would prevent losses, both to the government and the people, and largely lessen the cost to adopt it. Mr. Chase was favorably impressed with the plan, and opened a correspondence with the assistant treasurer at New York [John J. Cisco], and with other gentlemen of large experience, in reference to the propriety and safety of printed signatures in connection with a printed copy of the seal.

This resulted in his approval of the scheme, and an application to Congress for the necessary authority to carry it into operation. This authority was given by act approved February 25, 1862.[9]

He then orally directed me to procure the necessary machinery to seal the notes, and to design a suitable copy of the seal. I complied with this order by procuring presses, specially made for the purpose, on approved models, and by designing the copy of the seal now in use. This design has for its interior a *fac simile* of the seal adopted by the Treasury Department for its documents on a ground of geometric lathe work, the exterior being composed of thirty-four points, similarly executed. These points were designed to be typical of the thirty-four States, and to simulate the appearance of seals ordinarily affixed to public documents. It was difficult of execution, and it was believed that counterfeiters could not readily make a successful imitation of it. So far the belief has seemed well founded, for it has not, that I am aware of, been successfully imitated.

The American Bank Note Company of New York was employed to make the original dies for seals of three sizes, which were satisfactorily executed and paid for, as appears by their bills on file of September 30, October 13, and November 9, 1862. They have since refused to surrender these dies to the Government, though they have been formally demanded, and any additional price proffered that they might require. Only duplicates made from these dies are now used in the Department, the originals being still retained by the Company.[10]

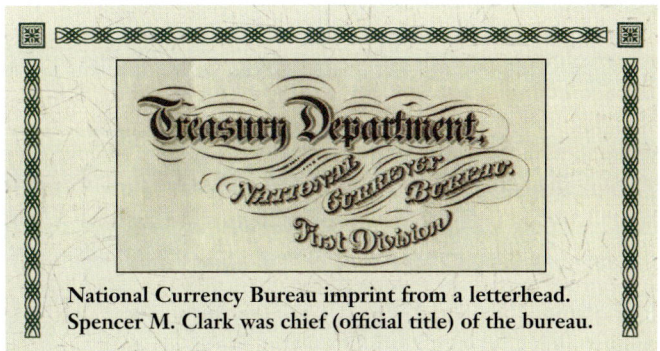

**National Currency Bureau imprint from a letterhead.
Spencer M. Clark was chief (official title) of the bureau.**

SOURCING PAPER

In early 1862, Clark implemented his plan to do more paper-money work within the Treasury Building. Seeking efficiencies, he reviewed current operations, including contracts with the bank-note companies in New York City. On July 7, 1862, he reported to Secretary Chase that paper should be manufactured on Treasury premises. The bank-note companies in New York City were charging $22.50 per thousand sheets "for a paper inferior to that which I can buy in the open market for $12."

An advertisement was sent out, and the American and National bank-note companies in New York City sent samples of sheets at $18 per thousand from a well-known maker, while the maker himself submitted identical sheets for $12.50 per thousand. Clark soon deduced that American and National, while ostensibly competitors, colluded with each other on matters of pricing in proposals and contracts with the government. On July 28, 1862, Clark filed a detailed report, stating that paper of 14 pounds specification would be ideal:

> The use of the "green tint" has forced the Department into the use of heavy paper to sustain it—the first 22 pounds, now 18 pounds. If a million dollars in *ones* is to be transmitted, they will weigh one thousand pounds more (less difference of weight in clippings which is fractional) if printed on 18 pound paper than on 14 pound. In my judgment (which was confirmed by the expertise of banks), the thinner the paper within a given limit, of a good quality, the better it is for all purposes. I have issued bills on paper (printed on one side only) of 11 pounds, which is the most satisfactory issue of bills I ever made.

Further comments were made, including on the use of watermarks on paper, of which all samples were found to be unsatisfactory.[11] Throughout this period Clark seemed to always have the best interests of the bureau at heart, and when possibilities for economy and efficiency were demonstrated to Secretary Chase, they were nearly always approved. However, Clark incurred the wrath of the American and National companies, who continued to profit greatly from Treasury work.

In the early autumn of 1862, Dr. Stuart Gwynn of Boston, Massachusetts, submitted to the Treasury paper samples "of most extraordinary character and excellence," composed of a vegetable membrane of his own invention.[12] Secretary Chase was very impressed. On October 13, 1862, a contract was perfected with Gwynn for the production of this paper for the Treasury department. The agreement provided that a secret mark "of such size and device as may be directed by the secretary," was to be placed on the web of the paper (to this day, numismatists do not know what this mark was, or if the idea was even implemented).

With just six days' notice by telegram from Chase, Gwynn went to Washington. He was given capacious rooms in the Treasury Building, under his own lock and key, to engage in experiments with new membrane and other types of paper, and with a group of helpers to produce the paper used in the printing processes.

The first membrane paper that Gwynn produced at the Treasury department was unsatisfactory, as it was susceptible to splitting. The process was revised, generating a paper which "cannot be dissolved in hot or cold water, which cannot be split, and which has an irremovable non-photographic tint in its spider-like fiber, which takes ink more readily, retains it longer, and wears better than the paper heretofore manufactured by currency of any country," according to a contemporary report. Although details of the process are not known today, it is believed that Gwynn introduced tinted fibers between two sheets of specially pre-manufactured paper which were chemically treated and pressed together to form a single sheet.[13]

From October 7 to December 21, 1863, Gwynn delivered 98,562 sheets of special paper for use on hydraulic presses, the first of which (press number 1) commenced operation on October 6 using paper not part of the above accounting. Press number 6 began printing on October 23.

SIGNATURES AND SEALS

The first actual printing operations within the Treasury Building, though limited in their scope, seem to have begun in March 1862. Two presses were put into operation to add the signatures of Treasury officials on notes, using a specially compounded ink recommended by S.M. Clark. It seems that this operation was conducted only for a short time. Little is known about it today.[14] Early in the same year a press was obtained to imprint red Treasury seals on notes.

Secretary Chase directed that expanded imprinting of seals take place, as per this letter sent to Clark on August 22, 1862:

> You are hereby instructed to take charge of the preparation for the issue of the one and two dollar Treasury Notes [Legal Tender Notes]. . . . This order is not issued as a permanency. It is my intention to give the experiment of machinery a full and fair trial. . . . If it is not more economical and better than the present method, its use will not be continued.
>
> You will therefore, on and after Monday next, receive from the mail [from the New York printer] the one and two dollar notes, making the customary receipt therefore, and after sealing and trimming, deliver them to the treasurer and take his receipt. . . .
>
> The sealing press in the hall, which has been ordered up stairs, you will now remove below, together with the new counter shafts and pulleys designed for the new presses, and place them with the two presses ordered, in the room below, adjacent to the cutters.[15]

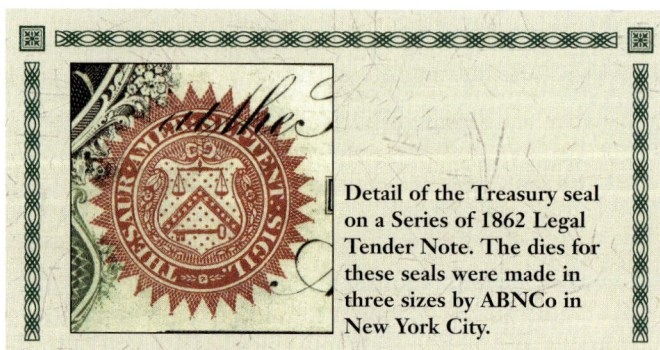

Detail of the Treasury seal on a Series of 1862 Legal Tender Note. The dies for these seals were made in three sizes by ABNCo in New York City.

The "sealing press in the hall" had been used by employees in the Loan Department to affix the Treasury seal, ever since the press arrived in early 1862. Clark had not been involved.[16] Nothing was said about the addition of serial numbers, and this operation continued to be done in New York City. The American and National bank-note companies each printed various Legal Tender Notes in denominations of $1, $2, $5, $10, $20, $50, $100, $500, and $1,000.

The expanded operation of seal printing began within a week of Chase's directive. A steam engine and boiler were put in place in the southwest room in the basement of the south wing of the Treasury Building. "On the 29th day of August, 1862, I commenced the work with one male assistant and four female operatives," Clark stated.[17]

GOVERNMENT ENGRAVERS

As of that time no plate engravers had been employed. Just as the actual printing of paper money was initially carried out by private-sector companies, before this point the Treasury department had contracted out plate engraving rather than hiring government-employed engravers. In August 1862, however, Clark hired James Duthie, a skilled engraver of bank-note plates, on a temporary basis at $1,600 per year, with the agreement that as the operation expanded he would "be advanced to fair engraver's wages if the work should be continued."[18] Duthie commenced work on new designs for the $1 and $2 Legal Tender Notes, these incorporating some of the "scenic" designs favored by Clark, but no change was made from those currently in use, printed from plates made by the National Bank Note Company.[19]

Hiring Duthie initiated a shift toward government-employed engravers rather than outside contractors. Duthie went to New York City and arranged for Joseph P. Ourdan, a well-known portrait engraver, and Archibald McLees, an engraver who specialized in letters, to come to the bureau as well.[20] Work of the new engraving staff began on November 20, 1862.[21] Among Ourdan's early work for the bureau, he designed the head of Washington used on Second Issue Fractional Currency (which commenced in 1863).

THE NATIONAL CURRENCY BUREAU IS BORN

The positive outcome of the early operations of Clark and his employees emboldened them to greater goals, as is evident from a letter written by Clark to Chase on January 5, 1863. In this letter Clark discusses the affixing of Treasury seals to Legal Tender Notes:

> I have the honor to report that the engravers have reached their proposed maximum delivery of one and two dollar notes, say thirty-six thousand impressions (or $192,000) per day, and I take occasion to report the present condition of trimming and sealing them.
>
> We now trim, seal, and separate, each day, the same quantity as received from the engravers, viz., thirty-six thousand impressions. . . . I stated in the original programme that the pay-roll for thirty thousand impres-

sions would not exceed $1,700 per month. It has not yet in any month amounted to $1,000. . . . The operatives now work "by the piece," as it is technically termed—*i.e.*, a given price per thousand impressions for each operator. They earn from $1.20 to $1.80 per day, depending upon their skill and industry.[22]

Imbued with the success of his operations and the cost savings effected, Clark envisioned that a department to be known as the National Currency Bureau would be best suited to conduct *all* operations of making paper money, rendering the services of the American, National, and the then new (formed in 1862) Continental bank-note companies unnecessary. Secretary Chase was very impressed with what he observed, and encouraged Clark to expand.

While historians generally agree that the motives of Chase and Clark were honest and directed to benefit the government, the same cannot be said for some others in the Lincoln administration, or the clever John J. Cisco, who headed the important Sub-Treasury in New York City and was the key person in the awarding of currency printing contracts.

PRODUCTION BEGINS

The Act of March 3, 1863, provided for a new series of "small notes," now named Fractional Currency, to be printed at the National Currency Bureau, as the division came to be designated. Clark's wishes had come true, at least in part, for this was an auspicious beginning. Meanwhile, in New York City the larger-denomination bills continued to be made by American and National. Actual production of Fractional Currency in Washington seems to have begun in late 1863, although by that time certain Interest-Bearing Notes had been printed for nearly a year using paper obtained from outside sources.[23] Other Interest-Bearing Notes were printed by contractors.

A statement given on July 1, 1863, does give details of the production of notes by that time but seems to relate only to the office of Hugh McCulloch, an Indiana banker who had been appointed as comptroller of the Currency on May 9th. The listing is for salaried employees and does not include the piece-work operatives, nor are any engravers mentioned. This exchange includes a conversation between McCulloch and Chase:

> I said to him that I had but one request to make, which was that I was to be responsible for the proper organization and management of the Bureau, which might become a very important one, I should have the selection of my clerks. To this he readily assented.
>
> "Manage," said he, "the Bureau in your own way. When you need clerks, and as you need them, send their names to me and they will be appointed." . . .
>
> The organization of the bureau was undertaken with Samuel T. Howard, Deputy Comptroller, who proved to be by his executive abilities, intelligence, and industry admirably suited for the place; and two young ladies, Miss John [*sic*], who died early, and Miss Wilson.[24]

The Sub-Treasury Building on the corner of Wall and Nassau streets, New York City, was supervised by assistant United States Treasurer John J. Cisco. The American and National bank-note companies were located nearby.

"The Sub-Treasury, Counting the Gold." Sub-Treasury facilities, established in several cities during the administration of Andrew Jackson, were vital to the distribution of coins and paper money. The office in New York was by far the most important. (*Harper's Weekly*, February 16, 1859)

John J. Cisco as depicted on a vignette in an 1876 presentation album issued by the Bureau of Engraving and Printing.

In his autobiography, McCulloch credited himself and others with conceptualizing the bureau, although his importance in this regard is not substantiated by contemporary Treasury and congressional records. It is most likely that he was more involved with national banks and their paper money than with other currency. The 1863 citation is given here just for the record, as engravers, Clark's staff, and others were not part of this particular accounting (as later noted):

Expenses of the National Currency Bureau

The expenses of the National Currency Bureau to the 1st day of July, A.D. 1863, were nineteen hundred and ninety-one dollars and seventeen cents, ($1,991.17), at which time nothing had been paid for the engraving of dies or for any purpose other than salaries, and stationery. The following is a statement of the persons employed in this bureau and the compensation of each, per annum.

H. Baldwin, clerk: $1,600
J.C. Hopper, clerk: $1,600[25]
O.W. Comstock, clerk: $1,200
J.J. Edson, messenger: $840[26]
Miss M. Johns, copyist: $600
Miss M.L. Wilson, copyist: $600[27]

Employees concerned with Interest-Bearing Notes and certain other paper money were in another division, the Loan Department. Spencer M. Clark was still situated as acting engineer in charge, Treasury department, Bureau of Construction, by the time of this report. Further evidence of this is a letter by Clark dated July 28, 1863, on Treasury department, Bureau of Construction letterhead, signed with his old title, "acting engineer in charge," although by that time the National Currency Bureau and his title as chief had been used in various Treasury correspondence. It seems that he held the two titles simultaneously. As more than a few modern-day historians and researchers have discovered, Treasury records can be confusing and contradictory. Sometimes the study of the printing details on existing notes can clarify—numismatic forensics, so to speak.

Clark ordered traditional hand-operated presses, which printed one sheet at a time, as well as 77 or 78 hydrostatic "dry presses" that operated under great pressure. Other machines were built to order or bought.

The first distribution of Fractional Currency printed at the bureau took place on October 10, 1863.[28] (Postage and Fractional Currency are studied in chapter 18.) The paper was made by Gwynn.

A room filled with hydrostatic presses in operation in 1863 at the National Currency Bureau, likely a publicity illustration and not representative of reality. These powerful machines permitted full sheets of currency to be printed quickly, without the usual process of dampening the paper beforehand. Although 77 or 78 of these machines were purchased, faulty metal caused problems, and by early summer 1864 only seven or eight were in operation. (Engraving included in the *History of the Bureau of Engraving and Printing*)

Operators printing Fractional Currency on hydrostatic presses, as photographed circa 1863. Again, this could not have represented a large number of presses actually in service, as it is unlikely that even as many as a dozen operated at a given time.

The Bronzing Room at the National Currency Bureau. Platen-type Howell presses with rotating beds were used to apply adhesive ink to blank sheets of paper, after which the young female employees would dust the sheets with bronzing powder, then brush off the excess. At the right the girls at floor level and also on the upper level are wearing hoods. In actuality, these employees also covered their faces with paper masks in an attempt to minimize the effects of the microscopic bronze particles in the atmosphere, which caused great respiratory distress. The process was later modified whereby the ink and bronzing powder were combined before application, but the unhealthy conditions remained.

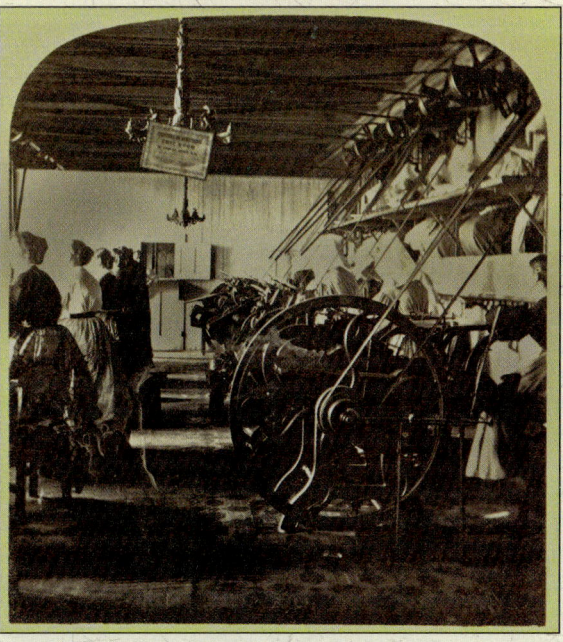

Actual photograph of the Bronzing Room.

Ladies checking freshly-printed sheets of paper money.

Cutting machines in use. These separated pre-trimmed sheets into four separate notes with plate letters A, B, C, and D. All had the same serial number. They were packaged in piles by plate letters, separated so that each bundle contained one of each serial.

Another view of a cutting machine. Sheets of $1 and $2 Legal Tender Notes are being processed. (*Frank Leslie's Illustrated Newspaper*, May 1867)

PRIVATE INDUSTRY RESPONDS

Amidst all this enthusiasm within the National Currency Bureau, Clark did not reckon with the immense power that the American (in particular), National, and Continental bank-note companies wielded. They had close connections to assistant U.S. Treasurer John J. Cisco at the Sub-Treasury in New York City. This was by far the most important branch of the Treasury department, and it engaged in large-scale transactions with the movement and storage of gold coins and paper money, among other activities. It was also the most important office for the distribution and redemption of currency, including the new Gold Certificates.

Secretary Chase relied upon Cisco for many important decisions relating to currency, seemingly without investigation or question. In turn, Cisco seems to have feathered his own financial nest in various ways that are difficult to analyze today. Among other things, he controlled the building at 144 Greenwich Street in which the Continental Bank Note Company rented premises. During this era he rose from running a store in New York City, to being the focal point of Treasury activities in the same city, to becoming a man of great wealth.[29]

The bank-note companies wrote a stream of disparaging letters to Treasury department officers, men in the Lincoln administration, and to senators and congressmen. They insisted that the government get out of the currency-printing business, fabricating stories of inefficiencies, thefts, and mismanagement by the pesky Spencer M. Clark and the National Currency Bureau. Meanwhile, Clark did a lot of field work and advised Secretary Chase and others of vast overcharges made by the private companies. Winning the Civil War was the prime focus of attention for Chase and others in the Lincoln administration. Accusations and charges involving many different contractors, including munitions and other military suppliers, were regularly sent to Chase and others and also published in newspapers. There simply was not enough time to check into most of them, although Congress held hearings now and then.

Dr. Gwynn's in-house factory could not make enough paper to satisfy the demand, so bids were sought from outside suppliers. Both American and National contacted private mills, bringing a new round of "paper profits." Printing charges by the New York–based companies continued to be viewed as outrageous, but paper money was needed in large quantities, and there were few practical alternatives.

Clark found that while the New York companies charged $104 to print 1,000 four-subject sheets of paper money, the cost for his bureau to do it was just $34. The contractors had charged $58.77 to print 1,000 sheets of Fractional Currency, while in-house it could be done for only $20.37-1/2. It was learned that Tracy Edson, president of the American Bank Note Company, in consultation with officers of the National and Continental companies, had tried to buy Clark off, reportedly offering $50,000 cash, but had been spurned in the effort. They were perplexed by this, as Clark was a man of modest means. Everything in Washington was for sale for a price, they thought.

A veritable battle ensued. Charges ranging from dishonesty to incompetence to immorality were made against Clark. Alexander C. Wilson, president of the Continental Bank Note Company, the least important of the three New York City contractors, took the lead, backed by American and National, in researching Clark's past activities. On August 27, 1863, Wilson wrote to Secretary Chase that the head of the bureau had gone bankrupt years earlier, was dishonest, had been arrested as a customer during a raid on a house of prostitution in New York City, and was not worthy of the public trust.[30]

A Scandal Erupts

At the same time, in the office of the Redemption Department, which processed worn and retired paper money, a clerk named Charles Cornwell absconded with notes worth about $31,000. These were later recovered during a search of his home by register L.E. Chittenden and Treasury solicitor Edward Jordan.

Separately, G.A. Henderson in the Requisition Warrant Department, who entered the files of invoices to be paid, "misplaced" certain of them, for which maneuvers he received money from outside sources. With these gains he bought a fine house, furnished it elegantly, and acquired two or three horses, appearing to live far beyond his means.[31]

Accusations of Lafayette C. Baker

These revelations prompted Secretary Chase to write to secretary of war Edwin M. Stanton on December 23, 1863, requesting that a detective officer be assigned to the Treasury department to investigate the security of the entire operation, and to report his findings. Lafayette C. Baker, a provost marshal in the War department, received the commission. On the 24th, Chase wrote to Stanton:

> Sir: Will you oblige me by directing Colonel Baker to make such investigations and arrests, and exercise such custody of persons arrested, as I may find needful for the detection and punishment of frauds on the government committed by persons in this department.
> Yours truly, S.P. Chase

Baker soon learned of the controversy surrounding Clark, although neither Chase nor anyone else in the Treasury department had suggested that Clark was under suspicion. The accusations made by the New York bank-note companies might have some merit, so Baker thought, and he determined to get to the bottom of it. Secretary Chase continued to admire Clark's work and unstinting energy, but did not impede the investigation.

Baker focused upon Clark as the root of much evil, and considered Dr. Gwynn to be a charlatan. Possibly sensing an opportunity for glory, on January 6, 1864, Baker summarily arrested Gwynn and on the next day had him locked up in the Old Capitol Prison. Baker then took the opportunity to rummage through Gwynn's papers and personal effects, both in the Treasury Building and at his home in Georgetown, and reported that these furnished unequivocal evidence of fraud. Gwynn would soon be making a full confession, the investigator said.

When the matter was investigated by others, nothing of an incriminating nature was found. On February 5 he was set free, by which time no charges of any kind had been preferred against him. Baker continued to insist that the truth would come to light, and that Gwynn would tell all. In April 1864 Baker submitted a detailed report to Secretary Chase, stating that fraud, immorality, and corruption pervaded the entire National Currency Bureau. Secretary Chase was not impressed and asked the secretary of war to terminate Baker's assignment.

The matter did not end there: on April 30 Congress instigated an investigation.[32] Hundreds of pages of testimony and records were gathered. Baker contacted some young women with loose morals who had worked in the bureau, and apparently persuaded them to testify that at night Clark had plied them with liquor and seduced them, even bedding one young lady in his home while his wife was out of town on a trip. Sloppy and unsupervised accounting in the National Currency Bureau allowed Clark to steal what he wanted to, Baker's accusations continued. Gwynn could make paper and Clark could print money, with records falsified and no one the wiser, it was alleged. The lurid accounts were widely distributed in newspapers nationwide; they made spicy reading then, and they still do today.

Findings of the Investigation

Among other documents presented to the congressional investigating committee, a letter was shown from Secretary Chase dated June 3, 1864, which stated that Baker had proved nothing and that Clark's work had been very beneficial to the government.

The congressional investigation disclosed that one of the women who Clark had allegedly seduced roomed with Ada Thompson (an actress at a local theater) and with another Treasury employee. Baker slipped into their apartment, found a diary and personal items of the woman, and, working through Miss Thompson, known in testimony as the "Special Female Friend," threatened to expose certain questionable or illegal actions of the young lady and send her to the Old Capitol Prison unless she signed a statement that he had fabricated.

It was revealed that "nearly every witness summoned to prove the alleged immoralities in the Treasury Department was previously manipulated by him," and in some instances Baker completely composed their testimony. Further from the record:

> In one instance, with a barbarity rarely surpassed, he arrested a funeral procession, took from the coffin the corpse of a young lady, late an employee in the Treasury Department, charging that she had died in an attempt the procure an abortion, the result of immoralities in the Treasury Department. The case was examined by a justice in the city, and a post mortem examination held, which resulted in a decision that the young lady died of pulmonary consumption. The physicians reported that the post mortem investigation afforded incontestible evidence of the unsullied virtue of the deceased.[33]

The committee exonerated Clark completely and commended him on his integrity and the great service he had rendered to the Treasury department. All was not ideal, however, and in 1867 his activities were the subject of another investigation, this time by the Treasury itself in cooperation with Congress.

As to Baker, in 1867 he self-published the *History of the United States Secret Service*, which detailed the lurid testimony of 1864 and left the reader with the impression that Clark was a scoundrel. (There was no follow-up in the book detailing what happened to Clark or noting that Baker had been dismissed from the investigation.) Baker seems to have had a personal relationship with one of the prostitutes who testified against Clark, for he called her a "long time" friend and included her as a beneficiary in a codicil to his will.[34]

A SNAPSHOT OF OPERATIONS IN 1864

Fortunate by-products of the investigation were Clark's multiple sessions of testimony in May 1864. His responses provide us with a detailed description of some of the minutiae and inner workings of the National Currency Bureau at that time.

Clark stated that after the uncalled-for arrest of Dr. Stuart Gwynn and his subsequent resignation, the making of paper ceased, but only for a short time.

> I buy it in open market, where I can get it best and cheapest. I have bought some of one of the bank note companies of New York, some of E. Goodwin, Scotland, Connecticut, and some of Mr. [P.W.] Hudson, of Manchester, Connecticut; more of Mr. Hudson than of anybody else. I have bought some from the cargoes of blockade-runners in Boston, English manufactured paper, sold at the marshal's sale, and also some from blockade-runners taken into Philadelphia.[35] I have paid for it from eight to twelve dollars per thousand sheets— mostly about ten dollars. We formerly paid the bank note companies for paper about twenty-two dollars.

Soon after the investigation concluded, the production of paper recommenced in the bureau without Gwynn. At first,

paper was made for stationery, envelopes, bonds, paper money, and other work. Soon, its use became limited to currency and certain revenue stamps.

Perhaps the earliest-dated reference to the use of the name *Bureau of Engraving and Printing* (as the National Currency Bureau came to be called) is in Clark's printed testimony of May 19, 1864:

> In answer to the committee's inquiry as to the amount expended in printing in the Treasury Department, as compared with the amount expended by the bank note company, I have to say that the entire amount expended for all purposes since the Bureau of Engraving and Printing was first started, a period of twenty-one months, is $555,297.57.

Various other designations continued in use, mostly the *National Currency Bureau*, but also the *Printing Bureau*, and the *Bureau, Engraving and Printing*, sometimes with an ampersand instead of the word *and*.

Clark's 1864 report also included this:

> An inventory showed 2 steam engines, one four horsepower and one thirty horsepower; 7 engine lathes; 2 planing machines; 15 transfer presses; 72 hydraulic presses; 4 hydraulic receivers; 25 hydraulic pumps; 96 roller presses; 5 paper presses; 6 Hoe & Company cylinder presses; one Washington press; one Ready Proof press; 22 numbering machines; 9 trimming machines; 7 separating machines; 14 sealing presses; 4 double-acting separators for Fractional Currency; and other equipment, for a total of 324 devices. Operating this machinery were 237 males and 288 females, but the number varies. The production included other federal imprints besides paper money.

At the time only six to eight of the 77 or 78 hydraulic (hydrostatic) presses in the department were running. Most had never been put into operation, and others were broken. The main cause was poor iron used by the manufacturer, Woodruff, Beach & Co., of Hartford, Connecticut. The machines, which cost $1,000 or more each ($1,700 including peripheral equipment and installation, with steam engines and pumps furnished by Poole & Hunt of Baltimore), were unable to withstand the pressures involved, and the pumps associated with them often failed.[36] As to the speed of the presses, "I timed them to-day, while they were printing, by my watch. At most of the presses they averaged three-quarters of a minute for inking and taking an impression. I have seen an impression taken where the plate was inked in two and a half seconds."

In contrast, a hand press of the roller type, printing on dampened paper, took about four times as long. Some of the problems with faulty hydrostatic presses were corrected. On June 3, 1864, Secretary Chase wrote that they "are now in daily use, producing dry-printed impressions of unexcelled perfection and beauty."[37] Both Clark and Chase continued to insist that they were a vital part of the bureau's equipment. In actuality, the new presses never worked well and were never important in production after 1863.[38]

At the National Currency Bureau, notes printed from 1864 onward were numbered in series from 1 to 100,000, although the stamps were capable of going to 999,999. Legal Tender Notes and National Bank Notes continued to be printed and numbered by the New York contractors, who used machines that went up to 99,999, although 100,000 could be set by hand. Seals were applied in Washington, as had been done since early 1862. Fractional Currency (beginning in 1863), some Interest-Bearing Notes (1864), Compound Interest Treasury Notes (1864), and Gold Certificates (1865) were printed, numbered, and sealed by the National Currency Bureau.

STATE BANKS GO FEDERAL

Meanwhile, Secretary Chase was left "almost friendless" in another controversy. The National Banking Act (popularly called the Loan Bill), which was passed by Congress on February 25, 1863, provided for state-chartered banks to re-incorporate under a special program to become national banks and to issue paper money. Engineered by Senator John Sherman, this was a brilliant move, which would have

the newly formed institutions invest in Treasury bonds, against which the banks could issue paper money.

Most officers and directors of the state-chartered banks were hostile to this federal intervention in the banking business, and relayed their anger to representatives, senators, and others in Washington.[39] Chase was criticized, his motives were called into question, and he was subject to continuing humiliation. In time Chase was vindicated by history; the national banks became immensely successful and raised hundreds of millions of dollars for the Treasury. Chase, who had his own political agenda, including seeking the presidency, resigned his Treasury post on June 30, 1864, by which time Lincoln had secured the nomination for a second term. A few months later, following the death of Roger Taney, Lincoln appointed Chase as chief justice of the Supreme Court. Chase remained in the post until his death in 1873.

William P. Fessenden took his place as secretary of the Treasury, serving only until March 3, 1865. The following secretary was Hugh McCulloch, who had earlier served as comptroller of the Currency.

A traditional hand-operated roller press in use. This method was used from the earliest days until well into the 20th century. (*Harper's Weekly*, February 16, 1890)

Transfer press used for taking imprints on roller dies (also called *cylinder dies*) and transferring their impressions to a bank-note printing plate. This was called *siderography*, a process invented by Jacob Perkins earlier in the century. Multiplication of engravings could be done mechanically. Great skill was required, enabling siderographers to be among the mostly highly paid professionals in the engraving industry. (*Scientific American*, December 1872)

THE ROLLER DIE.

Roller die for the denomination on a "Lazy Two" National Bank Note. (*Scientific American*, December 1872)

Engraving vignette dies for images to be used on bank-note plates. The work was tedious and required a high level of artistic skill. (*Scientific American*, December 1872)

"THE BIOGRAPHY OF A GREENBACK"

A reporter for the *New York Tribune* visited the bureau on several occasions in 1864, after the investigation had concluded, and filed a lengthy story concerning the technical aspects of operation. By this time the bureau was printing some Interest-Bearing Notes and all Compound Interest Treasury Notes in addition to Fractional Currency. Beyond these, various types of bonds and security items were made. The story lacked coverage of the printing part of the enterprise; it also made no mention of the investigation or the fact that Gwynn was no longer employed. Nevertheless, "Our National Treasury (Number One), The Biography of a Greenback," is the most extensive view of the bureau found:[40]

THE TREASURY BUILDING

Conspicuous among the many prominent and costly public buildings which adorn the otherwise unimposing city of Washington, stands the United States Treasury. It has always been an object of much interest to strangers and visitors, and now that the splendid west wing is completed, and the whole vast and often complex machinery of the entire department— extended and remodeled as it has been, in order to meet the increased and daily increasing demands of the government service—is in perfect working order, it has become the principal object of attraction to all who have occasion to visit the city either on business or pleasure.

The national currency, thanks to the good credit of the government and the loyalty of the people, is now so extensively circulated, and greenbacks, if not quite "as good as gold," are everywhere held in such high esteem that any other kind of money is seldom seen in the current transactions of the day. Familiar as these promises to pay are, however, there are few who know any thing about the several processes through which they pass, preparatory to their issue and circulation among the people.

Among the numerous biographies of the day, the biography of a bank note, or rather a United States Treasury note, cannot, therefore, but be read with interest and profit.

THE NATIONAL CURRENCY BUREAU

Prior to 1862 the money issues of the government were executed by the bank note engravers and companies of New York. The difficulties which grew out of printing the public securities at a point distant from the seat of government, and allowing plates and dies of such great value to remain in the hands of the parties only commercially connected with the government, and the monopoly power which these companies were thus enabled to exercise, giving them power to control prices and dictate terms to the government, induced the late Secretary of the Treasury to seek some means of bringing the whole business more immediately under his control.

The printing of the public money in the Treasury was begun in the autumn of 1862. New presses and new machinery have been added, from time to time, until now the whole enormous aggregate of the national currency, with the exception of the notes issued by the National banks, which are prepared in New York, are engraved, printed, sealed, separated and trimmed in the Treasury building.[41] We desire to give a brief description of the different processes through which these notes pass in their course through the various divisions of this department.

Here the printing of the government paper money, and other work incidental to the preparation of the vast issues of the department, is carried on. It occupies the whole or greater portion of the basement, sub-basement and upper floors of the building, an area, the proportions of which will be better realized, when it is remembered that the ground upon which the building stands exceeds three acres in extent. The building is composed of five stories, exclusive of the sub-basement. Its entire length is 520 feet, and its width, 288 feet.

Armed with the necessary pass, which the courteous attention of the Secretary has supplied on short notice, we enter the vast building at the southeast basement door, touch our hat to the captain of the day watch, note the hour on the clock just inside the entrance, and pass on through a long hall dimly lighted by the door we have just entered, to another entrance or rather screen, with an aperture in the centre, through which the employees of the bureau daily enter and leave their several divisions of labor. . . .

CHIEF CLARK AS GUIDE

Pursuing our way through a small group of large-hooped women who throng the entrance, we reach the office of the Superintendent, or Chief of the first division of the National Note Bureau, situated in the southeast corner of the west wing of the building. This is by no means our first visit, and after having our pass viséd by Mr. Clark, who hands it to an assistant for record, we start, in company with that gentleman, on our tour of investigation.

Our first visit is to the forging room. This apartment, or rather subterranean chamber, could not fail to have pleased the Cyclopean giants, Brontes, Stereopes and Argos, who constructed the artillery of the thunder-darting Jove, so admirably adapted is it to the purposes to which it is devoted. It is located in the sub-basement of the building, equally removed from the various other divisions of the bureau, and where the noise from the work is completely deadened. In the forge room, or blacksmith's shop, as it is more familiarly known, all the forging required in the department is done. The forges, of which there are two, are driven by one of Alden's patent blow fans, and one or other of them is kept in constant operation.

Between the forging and the machine shops is located the engine-room, where are found one of Poole & Hunt's, Baltimore, upright engines, working away like a young Titan. This engine is nominally of four horsepower; but, by keeping it under a strong pressure of steam, a power of six horses is obtained, and by an ingeniously contrived economy, it is made to drive not only the machinery in the basement, but also that on the floor above, which we shall have occasion to describe soon.

THE MACHINE SHOP

From the forging room we pass readily to the machine shop, with which the former is immediately connected, the whole forming one main division of the sub-basement, 90 feet long and 25 feet wide. This apartment is furnished with lathes, planes, drills, adapted to the construction of all the new, and the repair of all the old, machinery required or used in the building. Without this important auxiliary, troublesome and frequently dangerous delays would be submitted to. Experience has taught the very efficient chief of this bureau that even government printing offices are not exempt from the accidents which sometimes befall the best regulated families, and he has provided against the consequences of their too frequent recurrence by this timely provision. With this machine room in operation he is, to a great extent, if not wholly, independent of outside manufacturers and dealers. If a machine of which, as we shall presently see, there are over 300 in operation in different parts of the building, is broken or otherwise out of order, the injured or refractory member is brought here, and, to use a departmentism, is adjusted in "due course," and reassigned to its appropriate work.

Formerly all the elaborate and costly machinery necessary in the manufacture of the paper money and other issues of the department had to be purchased in New York and other cities of the East, and brought to Washington at an enormous outlay of time and money. The saving in cost of freight, and the delay necessary to its safe transmission, has already saved an immense outlay to the government.

There are six turning-lathes, one grinding machine, one drill-press, and three planing-machines at present in operation in this room. On our last visit we noticed a trimming machine intended for use in the separating and trimming of Treasury notes which had just been completed, and would be ready for use in a day or two. The work and general appearance of this machine will compare favorably with that of machines made by the best establishments elsewhere.

There being no foundry connected with the department, the casting necessary for the several machines constructed here is done at the United States Navy Yard and other places outside the building. Connected with the machine shop are commodious store-rooms, supplied with iron, oil, tools, and the numerous other articles required in the prosecution of its numerous details.

THE PAPER-MAKING ROOM

We now mount a flight of stone stairs to the basement floor, and enter the Paper Making Room.

Until within a comparatively recent period, the paper necessary for the use of the bureau has been made and supplied by manufacturers in Connecticut, Philadelphia and elsewhere. Ernest efforts were made during the first two years to secure a peculiar kind of paper, the manufacture of which should be known only to the government, and exclusively used by it.

A committee of the American Academy of Science was appointed by the late Secretary of the Treasury to make investigations and report upon the feasibility of obtaining such a fabric. In October, 1862, a new description of paper, known as "membrane" paper, was presented to the Secretary, which seemed to satisfy the required conditions. Arrangements were at once perfected for its manufacture in the building, and after a series of experiments by Dr. Stuart Gwynn, its inventor, and the present chief of the bureau, Mr. Spencer M. Clark, a successful result was thought to have been achieved. About half a million dollars of the fractional currency had been printed on this paper, when it was found that numerous and counterfeit issues of this money were being circulated. Many of these imitations were so admirably executed as almost to defy detection, and a change was at once deemed necessary.

The manufacture of a paper combining the qualities necessary for plate printing, as well as being anti-photographic and not liable to split, was at once a desideratum and a necessity. It was accordingly resolved to make further experiments, which were again entrusted to Dr. Gwynn. This gentleman, to whom, in conjunction with Mr. Clark, the government is largely indebted for their persistent efforts in the teeth of determined and continued opposition from almost every quarter, has at last succeeded in producing a paper which we have every reason to think will baffle the energies of counterfeiters for some time to come. . . .

The experiments of Messrs. Gwynn and Clark resulted in the production of a paper at once firm in texture, smooth of surface, and of the required density, with the all-important additional advantage of being completely anti-photographic. This great and essential feature is gained by introducing into the pulp of which the paper is composed a fibre which mingles with the pulp in the process of manufacture, and which cannot be photographed without discoloring the paper to which it is desired to transfer impressions, giving it the appearance of a coarse black spider-web. As this fibre is made in the paper, and not merely attached to the surface, it cannot be removed without destroying the paper. Thus all attempts to counterfeit money printed on it will be baffled.

The room we are now visiting is fitted with the necessary mills and machinery to make this paper, driven by a 20-horsepower engine of the most elaborate manufacture, and, as we have already said, is most jealously and securely guarded, not one, not even the Secretary himself, being allowed to enter. A considerable amount of this fibrous paper is already made, and about the first of October the printing of the Fractional Currency on it will commence.[42]

The balance of the national securities have been hitherto printed on the common bank-note paper, which, being a commercial commodity, does not itself furnish any special guard against counterfeiting or fraudulent issues. The paper is purchased of the manufacturers, delivered to the department by the express company in boxes, containing ten packages of a thousand sheets each, which are deposited in the paper room. The receipts of the express company, the invoices of the manufacturers, their bills presented to the auditor for settlement, the books of the paper room, and the amount of currency issued, furnish the data from which it may be ascertained whether any unauthorized paper passes through the department.

From the paper room the packages are delivered to the superintendent of the counting room, where they are counted, and whence they are delivered to the various subdivisions of the bureau.

THE INK ROOM

Another phase in the biography of our Treasury note or bond, is the manufacture of the ink with which it is printed. The transition from paper to ink is at once natural and easy, and we accordingly find it carried on in a small adjoining room on the opposite side of the hall. The mills, six in number, driven by a small engine similar to that in the machine room, are grinding away upon as many different colored inks, which are supplied to the various press-rooms as fast as they are required for printing. That mill in the corner of the room, and furthest from you, as you enter the door, is grinding the green ink so well known, and so much esteemed, on the back of our uniform national currency, and from which they take their distinctive and familiar name of "greenback."

The mill next to it has a "batch" of purple in it. Look how smooth and bright it is. It has been "going through the mill" for the last four hours, and the superintendent says it will require two hours more grinding before the process will be complete. It is one of the most valuable inks in use, and is used in backing the twenty-five cent currency notes.

The colors are not made in the building, but are received dry from the manufacturer, and the proper quantity of oil having been added, the dough or paste is then ready for the mill. Some thirty different pigments are used, as many as eight being sometimes used to effect one combination. The six mills are in constant operation, and the daily produce is about 400 pounds, or over a ton per week. A row of large cans, twelve in number, are ranged on a platform on the side of the room as you enter. Each of these cans is capable of holding between five and six hundred pounds of ink. As each "bath" of ink is ground, it is put in one or the other of these cans, and supplied thence to the press-rooms above. Inks made here are all of the very finest quality, and this said, the subject of ink-making, in this connection, is exhausted; for any one who has visited a paint shop has seen the whole process, on, perhaps, a smaller scale. Mr. William McClure has charge of the ink room.

THE PICTORIAL ENGRAVING ROOMS

We have now got the machine, the paper and the ink—the materiel with which to print the note or other issue desired to be made. It is now necessary to produce the impression which is to impart the desired value—and this brings us somewhat abruptly—for we have to pass other adjoining rooms and minor details to reach it—to the Engraving Rooms. . . . You see that oblong room at the end of the long hall, through the windows of which the strong light is shining. That is one of the art or Pictorial Engraving Rooms.

The Superintendent is absent today, but a gentlemanly, obliging workman who comes toward us with his graver in his hand, kindly offers to show us round the room. Five picture engravers are usually employed in the art department. Sometimes a single workman executes the whole of a vignette or picture, but more frequently several engravers are in turn engaged upon it; one engraving the figures, another the landscape, another the animals, another the border which surrounds it, and so on, each performing the part in which he is most proficient. In this way the utmost excellence of work is attained. Two of the five seats are occupied. Let us see what the occupants are at work on.

You notice that square-built man with long hair and decidedly Teutonic aspect, with his glass in his eye and his plate before him. It is rather too late in the day, or, perhaps, without scrutinizing him too closely, you might suppose he was eating his dinner; but he has neither lager in one nor káse and brod in the other. These are his tools, and he is simply and soberly at work. That glass, metaphorically speaking, is always in his eye; and that plate is a standing dish with him, for it is always before him. More valuable than Porcelain,

Sevres or Majolica, or even than the fabled dish of Apollo, for it has cost him a whole year's labor and the government nearly three thousand dollars. It is not finished yet, and may not be for six months to come.

It is only a small plate, not more than seven inches long by three wide, about the size of a National bank note, and is intended, when finished, to replace the original greenbacks. The drawing represents the discovery of the Mississippi river by De Soto, and is copied from the large painting by Powell, in the rotunda of the Capitol [apparently for a $1,000 Interest-Bearing Note, March 3, 1863, 5% interest, 2 years]. A similar picture, but of smaller dimensions, representing the landing of Columbus, also taken from the Capitol collection, and engraved by another artist, has also become familiar to us on the back of the National Bank notes now in circulation.

You still think the plate is a small one, and marvel at the cost. Let us examine it closely. Count the number of lines in that stalwart figure seated on the ground, leaning on his mattock, or in that of the burly, well-fed priest who, with his opened breviary in one hand, seems with the other to be in the act of consecrating the Cross which is being raised on the bank of the river. Multiply the aggregate number of lines in these two figures by that in the twenty-four principal figures which compose the entire group; add to this the almost countless number of lines which enter into the composition of the other figures and auxiliaries of the picture—consider that the position, shape and size of every one of these lines, from the heaviest indentation to the fine hair line—so fine that it is scarcely observable to the naked eye—have been carefully considered, and then cut in the hard metal, and then, and not till then, my friend, unless you are an artist or engraver yourself, can you properly estimate the amount of time and labor requisite to make such a plate as that which lays there before that patient, painstaking workman, with the long hair, the broad shoulders and the sunken eye.

"Three thousand dollars expended in the engraving of a single plate!" You still marvel at the cost, and add, "But it will pay for itself handsomely by and by." We shall see.

At another desk in the Pictorial Engraving Room we find an engraver putting the finishing touches on a fine portrait of Hon. Wm. Pitt Fessenden, the new Secretary [of the Treasury, succeeding Chase], which will, when finished, embellish one or another, perhaps all of the Department issues.[43] In the room is a pentograph [sic] for reducing letters and letter ornamentation used in note engraving. This machine was constructed and put up in the machine shop of the building.

THE GEOMETRIC LATHE ROOM

We now go to the Geometric Lathe Room, where certain parts of a note are executed by machinery with a delicacy and precision altogether unattainable by the human eye and hand. By this machine all the elaborate work which forms so noticeable a feature on almost all of the Department money issues is done. It is a most admirable and ingeniously contrived machine and was built by Albert Tichenor, of Newark, aided by other expert mechanics, and is now owned by the government.[44]

The machine work of the die having been executed, the letters and figures which represent the description and denomination of the note, and which are necessary to designate its value, are next engraved upon it by hand.

The original plate or bed-piece having now been prepared, it must now go through the process of hardening in order to fit it for the purposes of a "transfer." . . .

THE TEMPERING ROOM

We next go to the Tempering Room in the sub-basement of the building. It is a small apartment with a furnace occupying one entire side of it. On the top of the furnace are placed a number of crucibles fitted with sliding covers, which by means of a rope and pulley can be adjusted to the desired temperature.

The die or bed-piece, whether engraved by hand or machinery, is made of softened steel. It is then placed in one of these crucibles, fitted up with animal carbon, and hermetically closed. The carbon volatilized by the intense heat combines with the steel and completely hardens it. From three to four hours are ordinarily required to accomplish this operation.

THE TRANSFER ROOMS

We now look into the Transfer Rooms where the hardened plate is ready for the transfer process. There are two rooms devoted to this. In one we found 14, in the other three presses, built by Poole & Hunt of Baltimore—large imposing machines, some of them fitted with lever wheels.

The plate or die of softened steel of the size required is put in the press immediately under a roller. The lever is then applied, and the roller revolves slowly over the hardened die and thus receives the impress of every line. It is frequently necessary to repeat the process several times in order to obtain an impression of the requisite depth. It is absolutely necessary that the machine be worked with perfect accuracy. The slightest deviation, either in the bed plate or in the roller, would destroy its efficiency for printing.

The impression on the roller is, of course, in a raised form. This roller is, in turn, hardened. Then any number of flat plates similar to the original are prepared, and receive in a like manner the impressions from the roller. They thus become perfect facsimiles of the original die, and we have thus produced, by the aid of this machine, in a few minutes, what it was taken months and probably years with graver and eyeglass to execute. This process is technically called "laying down a plate." Upwards of 750 plates have been thus prepared in the last 12 months.[45]

THE PLATE ROOM

The finished plates are now deposited in the Plate Room, from which they can be removed only when actually wanted for printing. The dimensions of this vault are 20 feet long by 12 feet wide. The door is constructed of chilled iron and fitted with a burglar-proof lock. The sides of the vault are fitted with cases, with numbered compartments, in which the several kinds and denominations of issue are kept.

In the room outside the vault is one of Cady's Patent Chilled Iron Safes in which the rolls and dies are kept. The number of rolls amounts to 700 and the dies to about 500. There are two keys to this safe, one of which is in the charge of Mr. George A. Casilear, custodian of the plates, and the other in the custody of the appointee of the United States Treasurer. . . .

Impressions are taken of every plate in use in the Bureau, and filed in this office in books kept for that purpose, so that in case any of the plates are lost or missing, by a reference to this book the necessary clue may be obtained.

THE LETTERING ROOM

We now go to the Lettering Room and see what becomes of the plate after it leaves the transfer press. The portraits, checks, counters, &c., have now all been put on the face of the plate by the "transfer," and the lettering in the body of the note or bond is wanted to complete it.

The main object sought to be attained by reserving the lettering to the last is that by so doing, the fine lines which are required to be made in engraving the script letters are secured from the liability to breakage to which they would be exposed were they subjected to the heavy pressure of the transfer press.

There are seven engravers employed in the Lettering Room. The room itself is about 120 feet long by 30 feet in width, and well lighted by nine windows, as indeed are all the rooms in this floor of the building.

We have now the paper, ink, and plate in readiness for printing. It is next in order to bring the three together and produce from their combination the notes. This is done on the 4th or attic floor of the building. . . .

THE PAPER ROOM

There are two processes of printing money carried out in the National Note Bureau [*sic*]. These are the wet and dry processes. We will endeavor briefly to explain each of them, but before we enter the printers' rooms, let us glance into the Paper Room. This is a branch of the principal Paper Store-room downstairs, from which the stock necessary for the use of the printers is supplied. Here we find large quantities of government paper money in almost every stage of process, from the one thousand dollar bonds down to the five cent notes all stacked on shelves convenient for access. . . .

The method of conducting the daily routine of business in this room is very simple. Currently, but one kind of paper is made in the building. This is the fibrous paper. The other descriptions of paper, of which there are several, are supplied to the Department by manufacturers.

As fast as the orders for the different issues are received from the Secretary's office the paper is cut and given out to the printers. Each Treasury, or Demand Note, or bond passes through this room three times, and each Fractional Currency note twice.

The two other impressions or printings upon the Fractional Currency are made upon the bronzing machine downstairs. You see that tall pile of paper stacked up on that shelf, with the gilt oval ring on its face. That has been through the first process and is now ready for the numeral on its back. After it passes through that operation it will come back here again, to be again given out to the printers successively for the face and back printing, after which it will be complete and ready for the Sorting and Examining Room.

In this room the plates for daily use in the printing room are kept under charges of the superintendent, who is personally responsible for them. When a certain plate is wanted, a printed order is filled out for it, which is charged directly to the printer in a register kept for this purpose, and labeled "Plate printers daily receipt for deliveries of plates to journeymen." As the sheets leave the printers they are taken to a Drying Room and thoroughly dried, after which they are again taken to the Paper Room.

EXAMINING AND SORTING ROOM

From the Paper Room we now pass to the Examining and Sorting Room, which is immediately adjoining on the opposite of the passage. Here a similar scene presents itself to that just witnessed in the Paper Room. The sheets, as they leave the Drying Room are brought here to be counted, examined, and packed preparatory to delivery in the chief's office downstairs. Women, most frequently young girls, are employed in this work, as they are quicker and more accurate than men. Six are employed in this room, and their aggregate daily count is about 40,000 sheets.

Here also and in the Paper Room the work is given out to the printers. In the morning each man receives the plate which he is to print, and the necessary paper to fill the order. At night, when his day's work is finished, he brings back the plate with the printed sheets, which are credited to him in the book. . . .

HYDROSTATIC PRESS OR DRY PRINTING ROOM

A few steps further bring us to the Hydrostatic Press or Dry Printing Room. This is a splendid apartment, 100 feet long by 30 wide, and contains over 50 presses, which have been supplied to the Department at an aggregate cost of $75,000. It was suggested to the late Secretary of the Treasury that much greater security and economy would be attained if notes could be printed without wetting, thus securing the paper from irregular shrinkage and also give in the engraving a clearer and more perfect impression.

To effect this, much greater pressure was necessary than could be obtained by the common roller presses then in use. Requisite machinery was therefore obtained, and the impressions taken by hydraulic pressure. The experiments to secure this end have been applied only to a part of the Fractional Currency. Though many objections were made by experts to the practicality of this plan, still it is pleased to have proved successful, and over a million dollars of Fractional Currency have already been produced by this process. The work is of a very superior quality, and the sheets thus printed are separated by machinery. . . . Specimen sheets show a clearer impression and a remarkable distinction with which the faintest water-line is made to stand boldly out.

All sorts of stories were circulated of the building being crushed down, of their being an impossibility to take with a machine more than 75 impressions per day, and a hundred others of a similar character. But, inviting men of judgment and skill in machinery to test the plan, Mr. Chase went on and instructed Mr. Clark to continue the experiments and perfect the system. The first tests were made by hand pumps. Machine pumps have now been rigged, and the whole is in motion. By a very ingenious contrivance and outside of the building, a reservoir of hydraulic power is created from which these presses are fed.

WET PRINTING

The wet printing which is carried on in a similar apartment in the adjoining wing of the building may thus been briefly described. The wetting is done by cloths instead of by dipping or sprinkling as in newspaper printing. A room is prepared especially for this with iron weights for pressing.

Each man has his own particular place assigned him, and all work in harmony, and with precision and celerity. The printing is now done on the old-fashioned engraver's press, which is nothing more than a simple pin roller, covered with cloth and paper, to press the printing paper into the indentures, placed in a strong frame and turned back and forth by hand, by spokes placed in the end of the roller.

Two persons work at each press, a man and a woman, the former attending the plate, the latter the paper. The plate is kept warm while working by a gas heater. The sheets, when printed, are each laid between other sheets of thin brown paper, to keep them from blurring, and sent in hundreds to the Drying Room. The first process of bond print is numbering the coupons and the denomination with a yellow mordant, and as they fly from the press are bronzed as they appear when issued. Yellow is used because it cannot be photographed without showing too plainly to be mistaken. . . .

There are upwards of 100 presses at this in the adjoining room, the whole employing about 200 hands. At the time of our visit the whole of this large force as at work, and the scene presented was very interesting and not a little exciting. Three rows of presses are ranged parallel with each other, with sufficient space allowed between each row to allow workmen to operate the press.

Each note, as now produced, requires at least three separate printings. 1st, the black; 2d, the green on the face; and 3d, the green on the back. This is independent of the numbering and the sealing which follows. . . . The number of impressions which a good workman can take in a day by this process is about 500. . . . At the end of each day's work the sheets are delivered to the superintendent of the Drying Room, dried, again counted, pressed, and then delivered to the superintendent of the Sorting and Examining Room, where they are inspected, the mutilated or imperfect sheets being placed by themselves, and the whole sent to the superintendent of the Counting Room in the basement.

After completing the printing and intermediate processes, the sheets are re-counted, packed in bundles, and finally delivered to the United States Treasurer, who receipts for them. . . . We have now got our precious Greenback, upon which has been expended so much time and attention, back to where it first started from, in the principal basement office.

NUMBERING ROOM

Here it remains under lock and key until it goes to the Numbering Room. You have noticed the row of red figures on the Treasury Notes, near the right hand upper corner. These figures constitute the serial numbers of the note, and afford a sort of index to their whole history.

The numbers are printed by a very ingenious little press, so arranged that the action by which one number is printed, changes the type for the next impression, with no possibility of error. The figures are placed in the edges of six discs, placed side by side, and fastened to an arm worked by the treadle. The discs are turned by ratchet, and will number from 1 to 999,999. For consecutive numbering, a small hook is attached to the ratchet, and the machine shifts itself. Otherwise, the discs are turned by the number.

No two notes with the same "letter" can have the same number, so that a record of the letter and number is sufficient to identify any note numbered by the machine. . . . About 30 girls are employed in this room, and the noise they make with their machines is deafening. However much disposed they may be to talk, they have certainly no opportunity for it here.

On the basement floor and adjoining the Numbering Room are located cylinder presses and bronzing machines, where the Compound Interest Treasury Notes and other issues requiring bronzed letters on their face are operated upon.

This was formerly a very dirty and unhealthy process requiring great care on the part of the operatives engaged in this work, but new machines have been lately introduced to obviate this difficulty. Before their introduction the bronze had to be added letter by letter, by means of a brush in the hands of the operator. This bronze is used in a powder, and the small particles in the process of application would fly off and fill the atmosphere, thus causing great injury to the health of the women engaged in the work. This evil has been obviated to a great extent by the machine now in use, but the girls still find it necessary to encase their heads and a great portion of the face in unsightly paper caps which give them a grotesque and not altogether pleasing appearance. If any female readers are ambitious to become bronze statues, let them apply at this room and take my word for it that they will be accommodated.

TRIMMING, SEALING, AND CUTTING

Our Greenback has now received its distinctive serial number and is now ready for trimming, sealing, and cutting. This was formerly done by hand, and of course very imperfectly and laboriously. There were two things sought to be overcome in cutting by machinery—the inequality of the registry and the shrinkage. It was desirable that the edges should be trimmed, so they would wear well. If cut with a straight knife they would be beveled one way. As they are now cut, with circular knives running pinchingly, they have an edge beveled both ways. The sheets are registered in the center and the shrinkage between the two edges. As fast as they are trimmed, the sheets are taken to the sealing presses, of which there are 14, worked entirely by girls. The red figure known as the seal is imprinted upon the note, and then it is ready for the separator.

The notes of the value of one dollar and upward are printed four on a sheet.[46] One machine trims the margins, and another separates them. The separating machine is an ingenious contrivance. It slits them very fast and lays them with regularity in a box, each series of numbers separately. The notes are lettered A, B, C, and D, and the numbers on each are the same. Therefore, it is essential that they should be kept carefully apart. Each of the boxes that receives them has a movable bottom.

When the cutting for the day first commences this bottom is near the top of the box, but as the cutting progresses and the number of the bills increases, a ratchet lets the bottom drop the thickness of a bill, so the box is kept just so full all the time, to make the bills slide in without doubling. It is intended that the cutting should be a criterion by which to judge the genuineness of the bills, for every one must be of the same width and length.

Attached to the Numbering, Sealing, and Separating Rooms are Counting Rooms, where each day's work of each employee in the several rooms is counted and passed to the office record. . . . We have now completed our tour of inspection in the Note Printing Bureau.

THE BUREAU MATURES AND GROWS

From the last years of the Civil War through the turn of the century, developments in monetary policy and technology, accompanied by political machinations, played a hand in the bureau's production of various paper-money devices. Such circumstances were the agents of change—and, sometimes, the lack thereof—in paper-money production.

FROM THE CIVIL WAR TO THE TURN OF THE CENTURY

Concluding the War

By early 1865 the finances of the Confederate States of America were in shambles. Its paper money, produced by Southern printers and issued in large quantities, had depreciated to near-worthlessness. Bond sales, including to investors in England and other European countries, had slowed to a trickle. The production of distinctive coins for the Confederacy never came to pass, and it was chronically short of specie.

In the North this year Gold Certificates, full-sized currency authorized under the Act of March 3, 1863, were first printed at the National Currency Bureau in denominations of $20, $100, $500, $1,000, $5,000, and $10,000, from plates engraved on the premises. A standard design with an eagle and shield to the left and the counter to the right in lacy, green printing was used for all denominations in that series. These were issued beginning in November through John J. Cisco at the Sub-Treasury in New York City, where at first they were countersigned in ink by H.H. Van Dyck and later issued with his printed signature. While most were paid out in New York City, a small quantity was issued at the Treasury in Washington. Some notes were printed for Boston and Philadelphia, but there is no record of their use.

The National Currency Bureau limited use of plates as well as printing elements made by the electrotyping process circa 1864 to 1865. At first these were made by contract with James Conner's Sons of New York City. Later the bureau experimented with making its own plates. Products included a back for $10 and $100 Compound Interest Treasury Notes, and plates for at least two types of Fractional Currency and for bonds.[47]

In the United States, national banks, first formed in 1863, were a dynamic part of commerce by 1865. National Bank Notes, issued by banks that bought and deposited government bonds as security, were common in circulation. All were printed in New York by the American, National, and Continental bank-note companies, then shipped to Washington by Adams Express (an exclusive carrier on this specific route, other than the Post Office), where the Treasury seals and certain of the serial numbers were applied. Afterward, the notes, in uncut sheets, were shipped to various banks.

Bond sales augmented the cash reserves of the Treasury, while providing a good investment for the banks involved, a continuously brilliant scenario. Compound Interest Treasury Notes and Interest-Bearing Notes remained popular with bankers and men of wealth and found ready sale. Secure investment alternatives were few, as uncertainty as to the economy prevailed.

The war ended on April 9, 1865, when Confederate General Robert E. Lee surrendered to Union General Ulysses S. Grant at Appomattox Court House in Virginia. Citizens and soldiers on both sides of the conflict were exhausted. At last it was over. Peace and restored relations between the North and South were in the offing.

The postwar economy remained uncertain; there was wild speculation in gold and stocks, and hoarded silver and gold coins remained securely held. In fact, it was not until April 20, 1876, that silver coins were again seen in quantity in circulation and could be exchanged at par for gold, and not until December 17, 1878, that gold coins and paper achieved parity.

Optimism for the future ended quickly when President Lincoln, attending Ford's Theatre on the evening of the 14th to see Laura Keene on the boards in *Our American Cousin*, was shot by John Wilkes Booth. He lingered into the early hours, then died.

Vice president Andrew Johnson assumed the presidency. Reconstruction, as it was termed, took place in the next several years, although *retribution* against the South was preferred by many Northerners.

New Controversies Arise

On April 7, 1866, Congress passed legislation prohibiting the portrait of any living person on any United States currency or bond. This came about after Spencer M. Clark, without consulting anyone, placed his own portrait on a 5¢ Fractional Currency note. The visage was described as that of "Clark," logically assumed to be William Clark of Lewis and Clark expedition fame. When the true identity was revealed, legislators took action. Before then, Salmon P. Chase in particular had been featured on notes, and some other paper money had depicted President Lincoln. No prohibition was made the depiction of living people on *coins*, nor is there any such restriction today.

On December 17, 1866, Treasury secretary Hugh McCulloch directed that a committee composed of S.W. Marsh (of the secretary of the Treasury's office), H.G. Root (the Treasurer's office), and L.D. Moore of the register's office be appointed to examine the records of all securities prepared by the National Currency Bureau and to take an inventory of plates, dies, and transfer rolls, to advise what should be kept for further use and what should be destroyed. By this time former secretary Salmon P. Chase had been gone for more than two years, serving as chief justice of the Supreme Court. He was no longer involved in any way with Treasury matters.

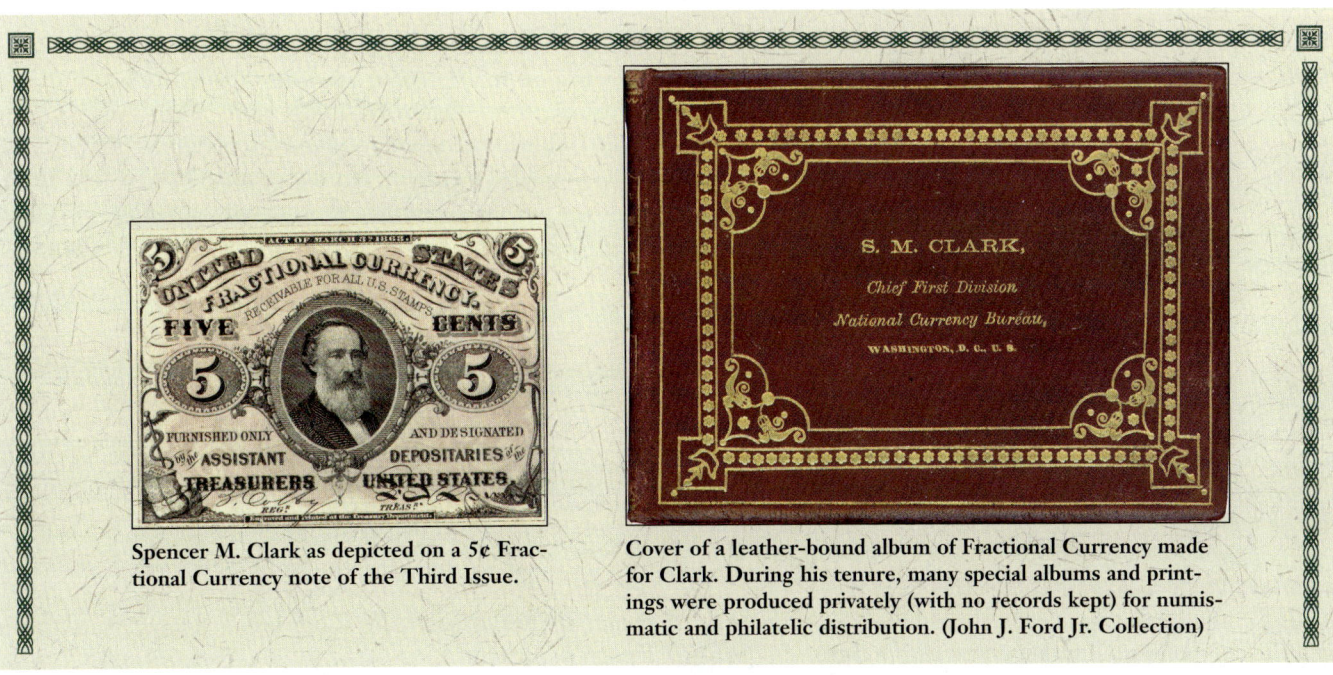

Spencer M. Clark as depicted on a 5¢ Fractional Currency note of the Third Issue.

Cover of a leather-bound album of Fractional Currency made for Clark. During his tenure, many special albums and printings were produced privately (with no records kept) for numismatic and philatelic distribution. (John J. Ford Jr. Collection)

There had been continuing rumors and comments of careless record-keeping and other sloppy procedures within the National Currency Bureau. In the wake of Clark's exoneration by the 1864 congressional committee, subsequent complaints had been ignored. However, there did seem to be problems. Soon, the Treasury's own inquiry expanded far beyond its intended scope. In 1867 both houses of Congress resolved to establish a committee to examine the official conduct of the bureau and learn the extent of possible frauds and mistakes.

The first committee within the Treasury department convened on January 24, 1867. In March another group, the Joint Select Committee on Retrenchment, began its work. Much supporting evidence was introduced; although there was no indication of criminal wrongdoing by Clark, gross negligence and improper record-keeping were found. As the inquiry progressed and alarming things were found, George B. McCartee was appointed in September 1868 as chief pro tem, so that employees could testify without fear of reprisal.[48]

Many curious facts came to light. It was revealed that Clark had been receiving royalties each month on the machines that separated sheets into bank notes, although all of these devices had either been constructed on the premises by Treasury employees other than Clark or had been purchased from outside suppliers.

The printage records of the Second Issue of Fractional Currency were found to be in such disarray and so contradictory that it was completely impossible to determine how many had been produced and distributed, and the same could be said for the Third Issue. In some instances, records indicated that more had been paid out than the face value of notes that had been printed! Scarcely any record was kept of the security paper used. Some Series of 1864 Interest-Bearing Notes disappeared now and then, and no one seemed to have been concerned at the time. Among other unusual revelations, notes totaling $5,790 were found in a closet, and 1,000 sheets of notes were found hidden under a coat, not recorded and seemingly forgotten![49]

The committee asked Clark to resign, and he did so on November 17, 1868. McCartee was appointed as chief on March 11, 1869. Clark went to the Department of Agriculture, where he remained until he was placed in charge of the Bureau of Vital Statistics in 1890, where he served until his passing on December 10 of that year.

Soon, McCartee experienced a reprise of Clark's travails, when the New York City bank-note companies began assailing his morals, motives, and honesty. An anonymous leaflet signed by an "employee" asserted that the new chief was conducting an affair with a local widow and engaging in other improprieties. This time it had no lasting effect. Such harassment would continue unrelentingly for years afterward, however. Congressmen in particular lent a ready ear to private contractors, then harangued officials at the Treasury department and elsewhere on their behalf.

Finalizing Paper Procurement

By 1869, the bureau occupied about 60,000 square feet of space in the Treasury Building, from the basement to the top floor. In the lowest level, the large paper-making plant recycled redeemed notes and also used linen stock to make paper for bank notes and whisky revenue stamps.[50] At the same time, extensive supplies of paper were purchased from outside suppliers.

On March 31, 1869, secretary of the Treasury George S. Boutwell formed a contract with J.M. Willcox & Co. of Glen Mills, Pennsylvania, for the manufacture of a special paper for Fractional Currency and Legal Tender Notes. It was specified that silk fibers of two different colors be introduced, and a watermark consisting of the letters *U.S.* be used as well. The firm had been a source of paper earlier in the decade.

It was later found that this paper had fibers of just one color, red, rather than two as specified. This particular paper was used only to print Fractional Currency and no other notes. In September 1869 a new agreement provided for a paper that would have fibers and also a "band or bands of dark-blue jute fiber, two or three inches in width, traversing one face of the sheets."

This paper, patented in 1866 and today recognizable for its blue-tinted streak (from the tiny fibers), was used on Fractional Currency as well as many other notes and added considerable beauty to all of them. It was delivered by Willcox until August 31, 1877, when the bureau decided that it already had enough stock on hand to last for a long time and ceased to order supplies. During the paper's use, it was found that, while attractive and ideal for money, the paper was not good for securities in which signatures or endorsements had to be added.[51]

New proposals for supplying paper were solicited in 1879, and in June of that year Crane & Company, of Dalton, Massachusetts, landed a contract, which involved adding more colored silk fibers for security.[52] This ended the long-term arrangement with Willcox. Although other firms were later used on occasion, Crane remained an important supplier and even today furnishes security paper for Federal Reserve Notes.

Financial Crises and a Snapshot of the Time

Effective on July 1, 1866, a federal tax of 10% was imposed on transactions that used notes issued by state-chartered banks. This effectively ended the circulation of that class of paper money, yielding the field to federal issues alone. National banks continued to open, and by 1867 the total authorized capital permitted by Congress in 1863, amounting to $300,000,000, was reached. The number of new incorporations slowed to a trickle.

In 1869 a new series of Legal Tender Notes was issued, some of them in brilliant colors with red and green hues on blue-tinted paper. In 1870, National Gold Bank Notes were authorized, a new class of paper money backed by gold coins in an era in which other types of currency could be exchanged at par only for other paper. These notes traded at a sharp premium in the West. In the same year the authorized capital for national banks was increased by $54,000,000, and $25,000,000 of unused earlier assigned capital was redistributed, after which time there was a flurry of new bank incorporations.

On September 24, 1869, "Black Friday," a short-lived financial panic, took place when the price of gold collapsed after having been driven up by speculators James Fisk and Jay Gould, who had attempted to corner the market. They had colluded with President Grant's brother-in-law, Abel Corbin, who was engaged in banking. Corbin was to secretly inform Fisk and Gould if the government decided to act and sell gold, as rumored, to stop the speculation. According to some accounts, Grant was tipped off and ordered the Treasury to dump gold. Whatever happened—as accounts varied widely—Fisk and Gould were largely unharmed, but many speculators who had gone along for the ride, including Corbin, were ruined.

Silver and gold coins continued to be hoarded by the public. Gold Certificates were printed and issued by the Treasury department, but were sold at a premium and thus were freely exchangeable with gold coins. The value of double eagles, as well as Gold Certificates, had risen about 30% in the half year of gold speculation prior to the collapse. Even after Black Friday, gold still sold at a strong premium in relation to Legal Tender Notes.

September 8, 1873, is sometimes given as the starting date of the most widespread peacetime financial crisis since the Hard Times era that began in 1837. It commenced with the collapse on this day of the Warehouse Security Company, a financier of railroad enterprises. This triggered a failure of many banks and brokerage houses. The New York Stock Exchange closed down for 10 days to reconsider its position, the first such event in its history. Jay Cooke & Company, which had been the main commercial marketer of Interest-Bearing Notes and bonds in the 1860s, failed on September 18, 1873, and on September 19 the related First National Bank of Washington, D.C. (first to issue National Bank Notes, in December 1863), went into receivership.

In the same year, the book *Ten Years in Washington: Life and Scenes in the National Capital, as a Woman Sees Them,* by Mary Clemmer Ames, was published. This book included a tour of the BEP and its operations. At the time J.M. Willcox & Co. was the exclusive supplier of bank note paper. No mention was made of manufacturing paper within the bureau. According to Ames, paper with "localized blue fibre" was produced by Willcox under the watchful eye of a government superintendent in residence, "who, with a corps of assistants, receives the paper from the contractors, counts, examines, holds it carefully guarded night and day, until delivered to the Treasury of the United States."

At the BEP itself, she described the adding of Treasury seals and serial numbers to currency:

> After coming forth from the presses, softly polished, every exquisite line and figure embossed in keen relief, the note sheets pass to the surface-sealing division. The process of seal-printing is the same as the first, and each sheet has to go through the same process the second time. Under the superintendence of Mr. Gray, six Gordon and six Campbell presses print the beautiful pink surface-seals. . . .[53]
>
> Having been sealed, the sheet must now be numbered, and for that purpose passes into the numbering division,

where it receives the last touch of printing from machines attended solely by women and girls. This machine works on the same principle as the famous paging machine. The numbers are set on the surface of a small wheel, and with every stroke of the stamp the next consecutive number flies up into its place; with the same stroke, a small roller, taking the red ink from the plate and feeding it to the type. These machines are regulated to change the numbers for a whole series. Two red numbers on each bill are put on by these machines. Intense care is necessary in this work, to prevent mistakes, and each bill is critically examined to ascertain its correctness. If mistakes are discovered at once, they can be rectified; but the red ink soon hardens and becomes indelible. If the mistake is discovered too late to correct it, it is charged to the lady who made it.[54] This has been found to be the only way to secure adequate care on the part of the numberers.

Ames had this to say about the bureau chief:

> Mr. George B. McCartee, the present Chief of the Bureau of Printing and Engraving of the United States Treasury, is so utterly the master of the momentous machinery which he "runs," that you cannot ask him a question concerning the labor in detail of his eleven hundred employees that he cannot answer more perfectly than the person doing the work.
>
> The responsibilities and mental anxieties of its chief are so inexorable, that he must be at his post by a little past seven in the morning, and remain till five P.M. He must return about seven P.M., and remain until ten at night.

The Bureau of Engraving and Printing Takes Over

The Banking Act of January 14, 1875, removed limits to capitalization and allowed banks to circulate whatever amount of paper money they wished. The American economy was regaining strength, especially in the prairie states, and many new national banks were formed.

Despite continuing intense political pressure brought by contractors, year by year the Bureau of Engraving and Printing, as it was now generally designated, became stronger and did more of its own work.

Through mid-1875, all National Bank Notes continued to be printed by the American, Continental, and National bank-note companies in New York City. American and National also printed Legal Tender Notes, joined in the 1870s by the Columbian Bank Note Company of Washington, D.C., which printed the backs. On the National Bank Notes, the National Currency Bureau in Washington added the Treasury seals and federal serial numbers.

The Act of March 3, 1875, provided that one or even both sides of the notes could be printed by private establishments, but no one contractor could print more than one side, and the final printing was to be done at the Treasury department in Washington. This translated into the Treasury acquiring plates from the contractors, entering its own imprint, and printing one side of most notes—soon both sides of all notes. This move was strongly resisted by the bank-note companies in New York City, which made the transfers drag out.

In 1876 Congress mandated that all printing of currency except National Bank Notes should be done by the Bureau of Engraving and Printing but that the cost should "not exceed the price paid under existing contracts."[55] Private companies continued to print one side or the other on National Bank Notes for a few years afterward.

Although Fractional Currency of the second and third issues was printed in-house, the fourth and fifth issues were a combination of private contracts and Treasury work. The series was discontinued in 1876, when the reappearance of silver coins made these minor denomination bills unnecessary. These little notes were very popular with stamp collectors and numismatists, who also bought large quantities of specimen and proof impressions, some earlier examples of which bore the supposed autographed signatures of Treasury officials (most of which had been nicely imitated by clerks).

As might be expected, this expansion at the bureau further enraged the private contractors, who had been reaping large profits. This culminated in 1877, when political pressure became so intense that discussions were held in Congress about completely terminating the bureau! Undaunted, the bureau continued to add to its operations.

The Banking Act of July 12, 1882, provided for the charters of national banks to be extended. This furnished the occasion for new series of related paper money, including $5 issues with innovative typography, notably titles set in what collectors call the "circus poster" and "shingle" styles.[56] A new series of Gold Certificates was launched as well. What might be termed the Golden Age of bank-note artistry was underway, in which bureau artists engraved dies with especially ornate and attractive designs, a practice that was continued until the very early 1890s, when plainness and simplicity became the rule.

The Appropriations Act for fiscal year 1884 mandated that all work for bank note plates, except for certain face plates of National Bank Notes, be done by the bureau. Two years later the related act for 1886 provided that *all* currency issued by or under the authority of the United States of America was to be printed entirely at the bureau and that all new plates be made there.[57]

Silver Policy and Its Effects on Notes

In the meantime, the price of silver bullion had been falling on world markets since about 1870, when it was demonetized by several European countries. Times became tough in the American West, where silver mining was a key element to prosperity. In 1878 the Bland-Allison Act provided for the government to buy two to four million of dollars' worth of silver each month and coin it into dollars. Silver Certificates of Deposit (later called simply Silver Certificates) were authorized, backed by these coins. These were receivable for customs duties, taxes, and public dues, but could not be used as reserves by national banks. These were made in limited quantities and in higher denominations, $10 and above, beginning in that year. Then in 1886, production increased dramatically, and $1, $2, and $5 notes were added.

This was a political boondoggle deluxe. While the price of silver had been falling on international markets, new discoveries were made and new mines opened in Nevada, Utah, Colorado (in particular), and elsewhere. Silver dollars had not been minted since 1873. Western mining interests gave momentum to "Silverites," who applied great pressure to senators and representatives in the West and Midwest to have the government support the price of the metal. At the time the government would convert to coin all of the *gold* submitted to the mints, but silver was taken in only if there was a need for it. Silverites proposed that the right of unlimited coinage be given to silver interests as well. The Bland-

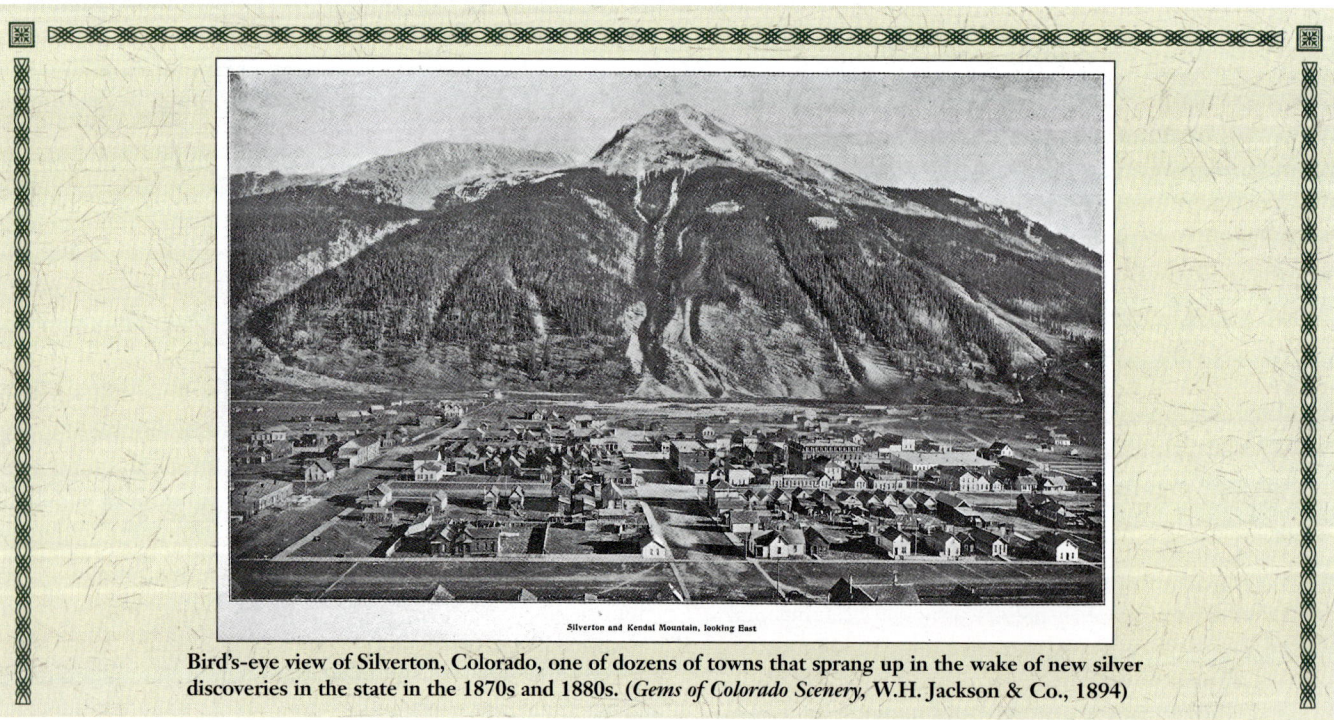

Silverton and Kendal Mountain, looking East

Bird's-eye view of Silverton, Colorado, one of dozens of towns that sprang up in the wake of new silver discoveries in the state in the 1870s and 1880s. (*Gems of Colorado Scenery*, W.H. Jackson & Co., 1894)

Allison Act helped absorb some silver, but untold additional amounts of the metal found no buyers.

In politics this became known as the *silver question*, and the continuing petition to monetize the metal was called the *free silver movement.* Speeches were given and books were written on the subject. Indeed, enough remain today that a bookshelf could be filled with different titles. In the meantime, foreign banks and merchants viewed the silver situation in America with fear, lest the United States settle its exchange bills with silver dollars instead of gold. This precipitated a drain of gold from the Treasury. The outlook was sufficiently precarious that in 1890 when Treasury or Coin Notes, a new class of paper money, were issued and were to be redeemable in coin, the Treasury reserved the right not to pay in gold if supplies were low.

A Building of Its Own

As operations increased and more paper money was printed by the bureau, in addition to bonds, certificates, and other security paper, it outgrew its space in the Treasury Building. A local health department report found unhealthy conditions in the attic, where many men and women worked under a low ceiling and in cramped spaces. It was time for a change. Work commenced on a new building, at 14th and B streets SW. Romanesque in style, it was designed by James G. Hill, supervising architect of the Treasury. It measured 220 feet long by 135 feet wide, and cost about $300,000 to construct.

The first space was occupied there in 1879, and by July 1, 1880, all important work was completed, and operations were relocated. In time, more space was needed. Paper making was not part of the new operation, but all other facilities and activities made the move. On August 30, 1890, Congress appropriated $80,000 for the building of a new wing at the southeast corner. This provided 13,000 square feet of additional space. Another wing was added following an appropriation on June 6, 1900.

Following the move to the new building, new Series of 1880 plates in the Legal Tender series bore the bureau's name exclusively, with no mention of the private contractors who had created many of the first examples of the design plates that were still in use, although some work was still done by outside suppliers. In the same year $1 and $2 National Bank Notes were discontinued, as gold coins of small denominations were now available at face value at tellers' windows of banks, the first time since December 1861.

Power presses, strongly resisted by the work force, were managed under the Steam Plate Branch, set up this year.[58] However, most printing continued to be done on roller or "spider" presses, which were operated by hand. On these presses, four-subject sheets were turned out one at a time. The process continued to be tedious. Paper was wetted, then wrapped in damp cloth and aged for up to a week

or slightly more, because moist paper took ink impressions better. The backs were printed first. The sheets were then dried so that the ink would set. Then they were dampened again, wrapped in cloth, and in time used to print the faces. Afterward they were placed in racks to dry, then put in bundles to "season," since a seasoned note lasted longer in circulation and was less susceptible to becoming soiled. Treasury officials stated that an experienced banker or merchant could quickly tell an unseasoned note from one that had been through the normal process.

For many years employees had grudgingly accepted the use of hydrostatic (in the 1860s) and, on a limited basis, steam-powered presses. The hydrostatic devices were idled when Spencer M. Clark left the bureau in 1868, but steam presses continued. These became a particular bone of contention in the 1870s and 1880s.

In 1877 the bureau tested a new printing press invented by James Milligan of Brooklyn, New York.[59] The trial was extended from its introduction in May 1877 to actual use in January 1878, but the inventor, who was shepherding the device carefully, did not consider it to be fully operative until August 1, 1878. In December 1877 a committee was formed of Representative Hiram P. Bell of the House Committee on Banking and Currency and four qualified people from the Treasury department. They evaluated the Milligan press as well as another steam press, the Neal-Appleton. They concluded that these presses "did not attain as high a standard as that done by the hand-roller presses," but they were suitable for saving money in printing other items, the Milligan being preferable to the Neal-Appleton. The matter was complex, as press manufacturers not only sold equipment to the bureau, but they demanded a royalty on all notes and security paper printed by the presses.

A proposal was made that Milligan make five other presses at $500 each, and receive a royalty of $1 for each 1,000 impressions printed. In August 1881, another type of steam

The Bureau of Engraving and Printing Building was partially occupied in 1879. By the summer of 1880, operations had been completely transferred from the Treasury Building to within its walls. After this time the Series of 1880 notes were printed in the facility from new or modified old plates. (J.F. Jarvis, *Views of Washington,* 1890)

press, the Homer Lee, was tested. Although there was dissension among committee members, it was felt that the Homer Lee press could print securities as well as the Milligan press could, and at a lesser expense. However, problems arose, and consideration for it was dropped. The Milligan presses printed the green backs of certain Legal Tender Notes as well as tobacco tax stamps in large quantities without significant problems.

The Appropriations Act for 1884 was the first to provide that sums equal to the wages formerly paid to plate printers could be used in part to pay royalties on steam plate printing machines. No more than 26 printers' assistants were allowed on these high-speed devices, a restriction that continued for many years, sharply limiting the numbers of such presses. A union representing the printers vigorously opposed any power presses and fought to have them stopped. The matter continued for years in congressional discussions and political maneuvering.

After July 1, 1887, the demand for tax stamps for tobacco, cigars, and cigarettes required more Milligan presses to be installed, bringing the total to 18. *The Bureau of Engraving and Printing Report for Fiscal Year 1888* noted: "The steam-presses are now printing much more than one third of the work of the Bureau with a great economy of room, labor, and expense. The cost of printing done by them is less than $80,000. To print the same work by hand would cost $180,000."

In the meantime, printers using roller presses of the old type at the BEP continued to be concerned that they would no longer have work to do. The Knights of Labor of North America, in a gathering held in Minneapolis, Minnesota, in August 1887, passed a resolution that "all government securities, notes, bonds, checks, and stamps shall be printed in the highest style of the art of plate printing, from hand-roller presses."[60]

Hope did not change to reality. However, the old-time tradition continued to be maintained for many operations. For years afterward, Congress placed strict limits on power-press use, not wanting to alienate bureau workers or the powerful union that organized them. A visitor to the bureau in 1890 could see notes printed in exactly the same manner that they were produced in, say, an engraving shop of 1820.

In 1886 the process of adding Treasury seals was moved from the BEP to the Treasury Building, where it continued until 1910, when sealing returned to the bureau.

GOLD, SILVER, AND WESTERN PROSPERITY

The late 1880s were years of great growth and prosperity, especially in the Midwest. New cities were laid out, banks organized, and buildings erected. Interest rates of 8% to 10% or more were paid on bonds, collectively known as "Western paper," issued by various municipalities and other interests in the prairie states—Illinois, Kansas, Iowa, Nebraska, and others. Bankers in the East, who were accustomed to earning 5% to 6%, if that, could easily buy Western bonds in large quantities through brokers, with little if any work or investigation done by the bank cashier or the directors. One banker in New England, annoyed by federal restrictions that no more than 10% of a bank's investments could be in a single security, was aided by a broker and another bank in devising a roundabout way to set up separate accounts that permitted much larger investments. Such opportunities were not to be missed.[61]

For a time, these investments proved to be good on balance, and interest was paid regularly. In the meantime, large tracts of land in the prairie states were being laid out as new towns and cities; other developments were also planned, exciting expansion that drew much interest and even more investment attention.

STEAM PRINTING-PRESS.

Steam-powered printing press. These labor-saving devices turned out notes of high quality but were strongly resisted by BEP employees and their union. (*Scientific American*, February 1890)

NUMBERING MACHINE

Currency numbering machine in use in 1890 at the Bureau of Engraving and Printing. (*Scientific American*, February 1890)

Take, for example, Sioux City, Iowa—a growing community whose expansion required large amounts of cash. Its promoters were willing to pay high interest rates to obtain it.[62] Four daily and 13 weekly newspapers kept residents abreast of current events, and money was kept flowing by 13 "good banks in successful operation," with plans for two more. Municipal improvements in Sioux City reached $16,000,000 by 1890. A transportation system that in 1884 consisted of five horse-drawn street cars on three miles of track had expanded by 1890 to 66 electric cars on 16 miles of track, plus a cable car system with 16 cars on three and one-half miles of track ("this is the only cable line in Iowa today and was built by men who have faith in the future of Sioux City"). The most grandiose project was an elevated railway, 22 feet above the ground, built by the King Bridge & Iron Company of Cleveland. This impressed all who saw it and rode upon its rails. Clearly, everything was up to date in Sioux City.

This scenario was repeated in Midwestern towns and cities in all directions. Money poured in from the East, causing some tightness of funds available for loans in that section of the country. The free silver movement continued to be the burning political question of the day. Frightened that American debtors might repay their loans in silver dollars instead of double eagles, foreign banks and merchants continued to demand gold. Federal stocks of the precious metal continued to dwindle.

Soon, there was trouble with this idyllic scenario. The turning point was the summer of 1890.[63] Growth slowed in the Midwest, banks closed, and municipal construction was halted and projects abandoned. Bonds and other obligations went into default, causing distress with Eastern banks and investors. European buyers of Midwest securities became sellers, precipitating more problems. Bank failures increased.

On April 15, 1893, the gold reserves of the United States, largely stored in the Sub-Treasury in New York City, fell below the legal minimum of $100 million. The Treasury halted the payment of Gold Certificates, setting off widespread fear as far away as Europe. Demands were made for more gold coins, and supplies fell further.

Silverites and the silver movement made things worse. Creditors, including foreign banks and merchants, were afraid that their debts would be paid in silver dollars instead of double eagles. The run on gold continued.

On Wall Street, stocks dropped precipitately on May 5, and the market collapsed on June 27. The Panic of 1893 was underway. Ultimately, more than 600 banks and 15,000 businesses failed, 74 railroads went into receivership, and millions of workers became unemployed.

Before this uncertainty and continuing into the panic, the Treasury issued a new class of paper money, Treasury or Coin Notes, used to buy more silver bullion, in a continuing effort to support that still-sagging market. These could be redeemed in *coin*, which should have meant gold or silver coins. However, legislation provided that only silver coins could be paid out—at the discretion of the Treasurer of the United States—in case the vault reserves ran low on gold. Matters continued to decline. (For more about the scenario, see the sections on Treasury or Coin Notes and Silver Certificates in chapter 2).

In early February of 1895 the federal gold reserves dipped below $40 million, causing great concern in the Treasury department and financial circles. On the 5th of that month J.P. Morgan and other bankers from New York City went to the White House to meet with president Grover Cleveland.[64] After Morgan left, the cabinet went into session for the rest of the day to discuss the crisis. Morgan's proposal to form a syndicate that would buy 3,500,000 ounces of gold was accepted. The metal was to be purchased abroad at slightly more than $21 an ounce, as it was not available anywhere at the current standard price of $20.67 per ounce. Thirty-year gold bonds paying a high interest rate were issued. Disaster was averted, but it caused great dissention among members of Cleveland's Democratic Party, most of whom wanted gold to be eliminated and silver to be the metal of choice for paper-money backing and national finance.

The silver question had its culmination in the presidential election of 1896, when the greatest Silverite of them all, Democratic candidate William Jennings Bryan, opposed

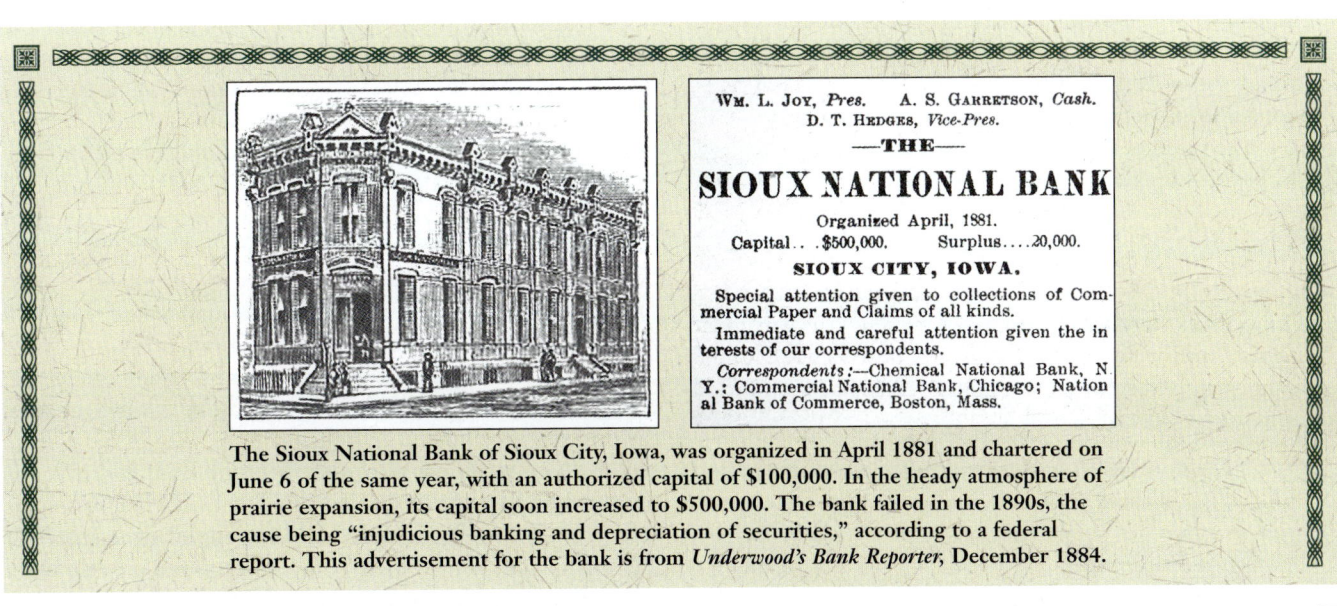

WM. L. JOY, *Pres.*   A. S. GARRETSON, *Cash.*
D. T. HEDGES, *Vice-Pres.*

—THE—

SIOUX NATIONAL BANK

Organized April, 1881.

Capital.. .$500,000.   Surplus....20,000.

SIOUX CITY, IOWA.

Special attention given to collections of Commercial Paper and Claims of all kinds.

Immediate and careful attention given the interests of our correspondents.

Correspondents:—Chemical National Bank, N.Y.; Commercial National Bank, Chicago; National Bank of Commerce, Boston, Mass.

The Sioux National Bank of Sioux City, Iowa, was organized in April 1881 and chartered on June 6 of the same year, with an authorized capital of $100,000. In the heady atmosphere of prairie expansion, its capital soon increased to $500,000. The bank failed in the 1890s, the cause being "injudicious banking and depreciation of securities," according to a federal report. This advertisement for the bank is from *Underwood's Bank Reporter*, December 1884.

Republican William McKinley, who maintained that gold was the only proper standard for coinage.[65] At the Democratic National Foundation meeting held on July 8, Bryan gave his famous "Cross of Gold" speech, stating that if cities were torn down they would spring up again as if by magic, but if farms were torn down, grass would grow in the city streets. He concluded with the ringing statement, "You shall not press down upon the brow of labor this crown of thorns, you shall not crucify mankind upon a cross of gold."

Riding on a platform of free and unlimited coinage of silver, Bryan was swept into the Democratic nomination for president. McKinley, governor of Ohio, gained the Republican nomination and in November won the election easily, famously campaigning while hardly leaving the front porch of his house. The defeat of the Silverites was a body blow to the most important political issue of the era, but the movement lived on to play a diminished but still important part in the 1900 election.

STEPS FORWARD, STEPS BACK

Attempts to improve note designs and to upgrade technology were made in the 1890s, only to be met with resistance by Congress and forces within the bureau itself.

In the second administration of president Grover Cleveland, Claude M. Johnson was appointed as chief of the BEP. Currency designs, some of which were very elegant in the 1880s and in the Coin Notes of the Series of 1890, had changed to simple vignettes with large areas of open space on the back. This was said to deter counterfeiting, although there was no real evidence to support such claims. Dissatisfied with the state of artistry on paper money, Johnson stated as much in 1894 in a report to secretary of the Treasury John G. Carlisle:

> Artistic skill applicable to the production of bank notes, bonds, etc., has not advanced with time. Bank notes prepared twenty-five years ago are as finely engraved as these of to-day, but the designs, as a rule, are weak and meaningless. The conventional design for bank notes which has been used for many years appears to be wholly lacking in artistic merit, consisting as it does of a patchwork of engraving, including portrait, title and the lathe work counters, having no connection with each other. I consider the artistic beauty of a design for a bank note to be as essential to protection against counterfeiting as the manner in which either the engraving or printing is executed.[66]

Determined to make changes, Johnson went to New York City, where he hired Thomas F. Morris, a skilled artist and designer who had worked with many well-known engravers. The object was to redesign American currency, in particular the Silver Certificates. What happened next was recounted years later by Morris's son, Thomas II, an accomplished numismatic historian:

> Chief Johnson believed that the primary object in the production of these new certificates was to gain beauty, and in order to obtain this he considered that the stereotyped lathe and scroll work upon the face of the

plate was somewhat unimportant. It was his idea that the United States notes of issue should in each denomination represent in their designs some ideal typical of the Republic, to illustrate its growth, power, history and resources.

> Mr. Morris thereupon set down certain ideas to be created, which were to be the following: The $1 certificate was to represent steam and electricity, the $2 our navy, the $5 our postal service, the $10 our press; the $20 old and new, and the $50 North, South, East and West.

> Preliminary designs were drawn, but there was but one design actually executed and finished, on May 21st, 1894, for the $2 note. This represented the new American Navy. Two white cruisers were seen upon the ocean, one coming bow on at the left of the note and the other showing her port side in the centre background. A large sitting figure leaning upon a hammer at the right hand corner represented the shipbuilders. Two infantile Neptunes with tridents, dolphins and shellfish graced the lower left-hand corner of the note.

> To further crystallize his own ideas, which were diametrically opposed to the views of his Engraving Division Chief, Mr. Johnson called upon certain well-known artists of the country to submit designs for the $1, $2, $5, $10, and $50 Silver Certificates. These were to be followed by the $100, $500 and $1,000 pieces.

> Mr. Johnson came to New York and interviewed, among others, Will Low, who at that time was commissioned to paint certain friezes and murals for the new Library of Congress at Washington; Walter Shirlaw, the allegorical painter; Edwin H. Blashfield, a mural painter of note who had just completed important work at the Columbian Exposition; and C.S. Rhinehart, better known as an illustrator, was asked to submit sketches, but there is no record that any of his designs were accepted or used in the preparation of this series.

In the early part of 1894 these artists went about their tasks with much fervor, but it must be borne in mind that the original designs as submitted by the artists were not used in their final development. Morris was therefore compelled to rework his designs into presentable bank notes from the standpoint of security and character of design, it being understood that the bureau was privileged to change any designs that were found to be unsuitable for reproduction into bank notes. Will Low was commissioned to execute the $1 and $2 notes; Walter Shirlaw, the $5 and $10 notes; and Blashfield, the $50 design of Silver Certificate.[67]

The result was the creation of three new designs for the Series of 1896 Silver Certificates, today known by numismatists as the $1, $2, and $5 "Educational Notes" (the $10 and $50 notes were never made). These caused a major uproar at the Bureau of Engraving and Printing, as the engravers on staff resented that outside artists had created the designs. As talented as they may have been in the private sector, the interlopers were perceived by BEP engravers as totally incompetent to design bank notes. Other problems arose concerning the bureau and the general atmosphere of the workplace. There were complaints about quality, work practices, discrimination, and more. In 1897, Congress launched a full-scale investigation. A lengthy report by a Senate committee went into every aspect of operations. Employees from the cleaning crew to top administrators were questioned, and their answers transcribed.[68]

Afterward, business continued much as usual. The 1896 high point in artistry was never again approached, however, as designs fell once again to the BEP staff (with a few exceptions).

By the late 1890s the economy was on a rebound, employment was rising, and good times seemed to be in the offing. In 1898 the United States went to war against Spain. William Randolph Hearst and other publishers stirred up public sentiment after the mysterious sinking of the USS *Maine* in the harbor of Havana, Cuba (probably an accident, and still unexplained). It was a one-sided affair; Spain capitulated, and the United States took possession of the Philippine Islands, Cuba, and some other places. All of this helped stimulate commerce and profits, as war usually does.

Printing efficiency at the BEP was increased when new flat-bed power presses were introduced in 1898, though again, not without complaints and controversy. The Act of July 1, 1898, shut down these units and related presses and directed that all bank notes and certain other security items be printed from hand-roller presses. This rule was later changed, and the backs of some notes were printed with steam power. The quantity of currency in circulation was less than the Treasury department desired, but the bureau had no practical way of increasing production as long as it had to rely on archaic methods.

INTO THE TWENTIETH CENTURY

As was the case in the bureau's early years, politics, monetary policy, and technological advances were the drivers of change at the bureau through the 20th century. Added to the mix was a drive for marketing and profit opportunities. New laws led to new-size notes, and the variety of note types settled on the single Federal Reserve Note we are familiar with today.

The Rise and Fall of National Banks

The Act of March 14, 1900, generally known as the Gold Standard Act as it officially placed America on that basis, was pivotal in the field of banking and paper money as well,

The Bureau of Engraving and Printing building as it appeared in the early 20th century. (American Pearl-101)

Main press room at the BEP. Over 500 hand-operated roller presses were in place, as union work rules stifled the widespread use of power equipment. (Copyright by Waldon Fawcett, 1904)

In the foreground pressmen are inking four-subject printing plates by using rollers in the main press room, circa 1903. This time-honored process had been used since the early 19th century.

Numbering printed sheets of currency. An exception to the general rule of manual labor, power equipment had been used for this process since the early 1860s. (Copyright by Waldon Fawcett, 1904)

Counting and packing paper money at the BEP. (Copyright by Waldon Fawcett, 1904)

Finished notes were taken by horse-drawn wagon from the BEP to the Treasury Building where they were stored in vaults, awaiting distribution. (Detroit Publishing Co., 1906)

Boxes of currency in a Treasury vault. The $5 Silver Certificate boxes each contained 4,000 notes, a total face value of $20,000. At the center left are two bundles of Series of 1882 $5,000 Gold Certificates next to an unopened box marked that it contains 3,000 Gold Certificates serially numbered 3001 to 6000, with a total face value of $30,000,000.

although this was unrelated to the title subject. It provided that, in towns with fewer than 3,000 citizens, a national bank could be capitalized for a figure as low as $25,000—half the amount required before this. At the same time, National Bank Notes could be ordered for an amount up to 100% of the bonds deposited, but banks were allowed to request as little as 25%, or $6,250 face value. This resulted in what historian Don C. Kelly calls a lot of "mom and pop banks," or small institutions, often run by families, that went into business in rural areas.

In his book *National Bank Notes,* Kelly observed that in the five years prior to the Act, just 257 national banks were formed, but in the next five years, 2,300 were organized. A numismatic benefit was that certain of these "moms and pops" in the hinterlands saved first sheets with number 1 serial numbers as souvenirs or mementos, including more than a few of the 1902 Red Seal issues. As might be expected, most bills ordered by these little banks were of lower denominations, with the values of $5 and $10 the most popular, the $20 notes less so, and not much interest at all in the $50 or $100 notes.

The Knickerbocker Trust Company in New York City. ("Bank Buildings," *Architectural Review,* March 1905)

J.P. Morgan, preeminent banker of the early 20th century. Morgan also had an interest in numismatics. Today his collection of gold Proof sets is in the American Numismatic Society, New York.

The Banking Act of April 12, 1902, provided for extension of certain bank charters and furnished the opportunity for a new series of currency designs from $5 to $100. In the meantime, the controversial Series of 1896 Silver Certificates had been replaced by new designs for the $1, $2, and $5 denominations. Never mind that numismatists today consider them to be among the most beautiful ever issued.

Prosperity returned in full force to America in the early years of the new century. It was the age of the invention of the airplane, the popularization of the automobile, and the teddy bear. President Theodore Roosevelt sent the Great White Fleet of battleships around the world in a show of American military might, and at home he worked with Augustus Saint-Gaudens in the creation of the beautiful MCMVII double eagle. All seemed to be well.

Some of the prosperity proved to be an illusion. Many banks and investors borrowed unwisely to finance expansion and new business ideas. One of them was bank president Charles T. Barney, who headed the Knickerbocker Trust Company, housed in a showcase Greek Revival–style building designed by New York's most famous architectural firm, McKim, Mead, and White.[69] The institution stood tall and proud on Fifth Avenue as one of the largest banks in the country. Deposits and transfers for many municipalities, corporations, other banks, and institutions came and went, and profits mounted. Not satisfied with this success, Barney invested large amounts of bank funds in an effort to corner the market in copper, perceived as a sure bet. The plan failed when huge quantities of the metal were dumped on the market. The bank sustained huge losses.

News of the bank's disaster spread, and the National Bank of Commerce, another large institution in the city, refused to accept Knickerbocker checks. A quick audit revealed that the bank was utterly insolvent. When this was realized on October 23, there was a run on the bank by depositors to withdraw their money.

This excitement was followed by other runs across the United States, even in distant Butte, Montana. J.P. Morgan called an emergency meeting, and on the night of November 3 locked himself and leading New York City bankers in his new library on East 36th Street. Finally, in the wee hours of the next morning, they agreed to cooperate in a bailout. John D. Rockefeller pledged $10 million. Following telegraphed instructions, a similar amount in gold coins was shipped to New York on board the new luxury passenger liner *Lusitania,* and Morgan himself loaned $30 million to the city (at 6% interest) to prevent it from defaulting on its bonds.

Even Hetty Green, the wealthy stock investor nicknamed the "Witch of Wall Street," got into the act. She had predicted a collapse and had sold most of her stocks beforehand and, for good measure, had marketed much real estate. Now with a good reserve of cash she loaned money to retailers, brokers, and to the city of New York (soon her son, Colonel E.H.R. Green, would develop an interest in numismatics and begin to build a large collection of coins and paper money). None of this helped Knickerbocker depositors. Barney shot himself on November 14th.

The Dow Jones Industrial Average, which had stood at 94.35 when the market closed in 1906, had fallen to 58.75 by December 31, 1907. Gloom was pervasive as citizens recalled the Panic of 1893.

New Designs, New Facilities, Old Controversies

Times remained difficult in 1908. Thus, it was a show of good faith when on May 27, Congress authorized construction of a new building to house the Bureau of Engraving and Printing. Appropriations amounting to $2,929,999.60 were made for the building and the interior vaults, and $681,107 for furniture, equipment, and moving expenses. The new structure was occupied following a ceremony held on March 19, 1914.

On May 30, 1908, the Emergency Currency Act (Aldrich-Vreeland Act) sought to increase liquidity and the money supply by allowing bankers to deposit commercial bonds, commercial paper, and other securities in addition to government bonds, for the issuance of notes.[70] Two new types of National Bank Notes were issued, the 1882 Date Back bills with 1882–1908 on the reverse side, and the Series of 1902 Date Back bills with 1902–1908.

In 1908, B. Max Mehl, of Fort Worth, Texas, was rapidly expanding his rare coin business, including publishing *Mehl's Numismatic Monthly*. The February issue included a feature article on the BEP, where most of the 3,000 workers were women. Security measures were discussed, including this scenario:

> In those departments of the Bureau such as the Examining Division, where it would be difficult to fix the blame for the loss of a sheet of notes or certificates upon one employee, all the workers must share in the responsibility.
>
> On one occasion a large force of men and women money counters were kept prisoners at the Bureau from 6 o'clock in the evening until 2 o'clock the next morning while a search was made for a missing security. Finally, after eight hours' search, the recreant paper was located in one of the funnels of the ventilating system, whence it had been blown by the fans which are used to create a current of air in the work rooms.

In 1909 the Treasury department proposed that in the future, standard portraits would be used on Silver Certificates. The $1 note was to portray Washington; the $2, Jefferson; the $5, Lincoln; the $10, Cleveland; the $20, Jackson; the $50, Grant; the $100, Franklin; the $500, Chase; and the $1,000, Hamilton. Some such portraits had already been used; however, it was not until years later that, for example, the Indian Chief on the $5 note was replaced by Lincoln.

During the printing of currency, many sheets were spoiled. Except for National Bank Notes, these were replaced with *star notes* beginning with $1 and $5 Silver Certificates on June 21, 1910. Star notes were sheets of paper money printed to take their place, but with a star placed adjacent to the serial number.[71] Over a period of time, star replacements were made in other series. Earlier, stars had been used as decorations with serials, such as on the Legal Tender Notes of the Series of 1869 and the Coin Notes of 1890, among others. Now they had a meaning.

Reviving a controversial topic, the Act of August 24, 1912, provided that

> Should the Secretary of the Treasury decide to print on the . . . power plate printing presses any of the classes of work hereinbefore permitted to be printed on such presses, not more than one fifth of the total number of hand-roller presses required to produce the estimated quantity of such work in any fiscal year shall be deplaned in each fiscal year. *Provided further,* That the Secretary of the Treasury may in his discretion apply motors to hand-roller presses that are now, or may hereafter be, operated at the Bureau of Engraving and Printing, but such presses, if equipped with motors, shall be regarded as hand-roller presses within the meaning of this Act.

By this time, electricity had replaced steam as the motive force.

The Federal Reserve Act of December 23, 1913, provided for the establishment of the Federal Reserve System, with banks in 12 cities from Boston to San Francisco. This led to the production of Federal Reserve Notes in 1914, and, afterward, Federal Reserve Bank Notes.

In 1914 the bureau moved into its new building, where it was able to utilize more space, modern facilities, and many improvements. In the same year, World War I began in Europe, catalyzing a vigorous period for the American economy as factories supplied equipment and goods to the Allies. Memories of the Panic of 1907 faded. All was well. Onward and upward. This enthusiasm and activity eventually fueled a greater demand for coins and paper money.

"During the bumper year ending October 31, 1914, a staggering $818,227,830 in national bank notes was issued to somewhat fewer than 7,600 different banks," wrote historian Peter Huntoon.

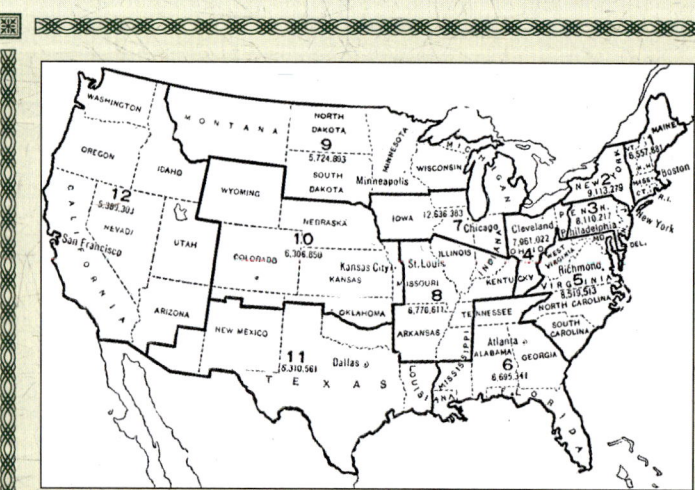

Federal Reserve District map. Each of the 12 districts is identified by a number and sequential letter. Hence, 1, or the Boston district, is also A, while 12, or San Francisco, is L. On the notes such are expressed as A-1, B-2, C-3, etc., to L-12. (*American Monthly Review of Reviews*, December 1914)

The new Bureau of Engraving and Printing building, first occupied in 1914. This remained the center for most activities until it was supplemented by the Annex Building in 1938.

The task of printing and stocking these sheets was astonishing. . . . Redemptions were also a bookkeeping nightmare. Redeemed National Bank Notes had to be sorted by bank, series, and denomination. The scale of this problem can be appreciated when you consider that, for the peak year ending October 31, 1914, over $700 million was redeemed and sorted. This amounts to a numbing average of $2.7 million per working day.[72]

All was not well in this procedure. The process was conducted by the Treasury department, not the BEP. Lee Lofthus wrote this in 2008:

> New research in Treasury records at the National Archives demonstrates that the outstanding circulation data for individual national banks . . . is inaccurate and cannot be relied upon as an indicator of rarity.
>
> Errors in the massive process required to count and sort tens of millions of pieces of unfit National Bank Notes each year made their way into the Comptroller of the Currency redemption ledgers, rendering the final entries unreliable. The reference catalogs [quoted in modern numismatic texts] accurately reflect the ledgers, but the ledgers themselves are inaccurate.
>
> A review of a representative sample of the Comptroller's National Currency and Bond Ledgers has identified widespread redemption entry errors where certain denominations of National Bank Notes were redeemed in excess of the numbers of notes issued to the bank.[73]

Other problems were caused by redemption clerks stealing the notes—probably not a widespread practice, but one that had caused concerns dating back to the early 1860s.

The problem of power presses would not go away. On October 6, 1917, the secretary of the Treasury was authorized "during the continuance of the war with Germany" to have paper money (and certain other items) "printed in such manner and by whatever process and on any style of presses

that he may consider to be suitable." At the end of the war, provisions of earlier applicable acts were to be in effect once again. However, the Act of July 11, 1919, extended the authority of the secretary. The Act of January 3, 1923, made the use of powered presses permanent.

In 1917, gold coins disappeared from circulation, and silver rose in price. There was concern that Silver Certificates and Gold Certificates might not be issued again. Federal Reserve Bank Notes of the Series of 1918 were issued to replace Silver Certificates, which were being rapidly retired as the federal stock of silver dollars became depleted. But by 1920, normal conditions resumed.

In 1918 the BEP began printing currency on eight-subject sheets instead of four, except for National Bank Notes, which retained the traditional format.

On September 26, 1918, president Woodrow Wilson signed authorization to allow national banks to open trust departments. Subsequently some added the word "trust" or a variation to their notes. This necessitated a change in the title, meaning new plates. Eventually 393 different banks in 35 states had the word "trust" in their names. As there are exceptions everywhere in the annals of paper money, finance, and banking, it may be appropriate to mention that the National Gold Bank and Trust Company of San Francisco was chartered in *1872*.

Into the 1920s

The National Bank Act of March 3, 1919, contained an amendment permitting engraved bank officers' signatures on National Bank Notes. This was expanded in an amendment of January 13, 1920. Use of engraved signatures began in 1921. Many bank presidents and cashiers were too busy to laboriously sign thousands of notes. By this time, rubber stamps, sometimes using brightly colored ink, were employed by many institutions.

In April 1920 a new type of electrolytic process developed by George U. Rose, superintendent of the engraving

Clerks in the Treasury Building in the early 20th century, shown counting, identifying, and sorting redeemed notes. This was done by women, each of whom worked at a separate roll-top desk and was responsible for the notes given to her. Counterfeits were rejected, and good notes were arranged by series. National Bank Notes had to be sorted by charter numbers, after which other clerks entered redemption quantities in separate accounts kept for each bank. (Mrs. John A. Logan, *Thirty Years in Washington*, 1901)

The end of the line: A committee watches as $570,000 worth of redeemed, worn paper money is fed into a macerating machine for destruction. In the early days the National Currency Bureau destroyed worn notes by burning them. After the BEP was situated it is own building in 1880, notes were macerated and reduced to pulp in boiling water. The pulp was then sold.

department at the BEP, used electrolytic deposition of metal instead of the old siderographic transfer process to create printing plates (although electrotyping of currency printing plates had been done as an experiment in the bureau in the mid-1860s). A department was set up for their manufacture. However, this timesaving process met with resistance from siderographers, was discontinued, then reactivated; by the late 1920s it was the standard method. In the early times the electrolytic plates yielded about 48,000 satisfactory impressions, or fewer than the 50,000 to 100,000 typical of a roller-press plate.[74] By 1930 the number was 100,000. By 1962 about 98% of the paper money was printed from electrolytic plates, with about 500,000 impressions per plate.[75]

In 1921 a nationwide economic recession reduced the price of certain goods, lessened the demand for new coins and paper money, and precipitated many business failures. Wartime prosperity became history. Hard times lingered for several years, and many banks and businesses failed.

Eventually the "Roaring Twenties," as the era came to be called, saw a new era of prosperity beginning about 1924. A land boom in Florida flared up, caused great excitement, but it petered out in 1925. Elsewhere business was good and getting even better. Expansion was the plan of the day. Money flowed freely, Ford Model T's were everywhere, national banks erected new buildings, most homes had radios, bathtub gin and smuggled whisky livened up speakeasies, Gatsby-esque magnates commissioned ever-larger mansions, jazz music drew millions to cabarets, and all seemed to be well.

On Wall Street, turkeys became swans, and there was no direction except up and up some more. Profits multiplied, and on Main Street the local barbershop was a good place to get stock market tips on United States Steel, or an under-valued railroad stock, or one of entrepreneur Samuel Insull's dynamic public utilities. The prices of securities continued to rise, bringing even more investors into the fold.

During the joint administration of register of the Treasury Harley V. Speelman and Treasurer Frank White, which began on January 25, 1922, and lasted until September 30, 1927, record quantities of paper money were printed in various series, including Legal Tender Notes, Silver Certificates, Gold Certificates, and National Bank Notes, a reflection of posterity.

The Banking Act of February 25, 1927, provided that bank charters could extend to perpetuity, as long as an institution remained financially sound, as indeed nearly all were.

Small-Size Notes

Changing the size of paper money was a subject investigated multiple times in the early 20th century, including a vigorous study by Franklin MacVeagh, who served as secretary of the Treasury from March 9, 1909, until March 5, 1913, under president Howard Taft. Philippine Islands paper money of small size served as the inspiration. Current notes measuring 3.04 inches high by 7.2 inches wide would be replaced by those measuring 2.625 inches by 6.25 inches, saving an estimated $600,000 in production cost, according to the proposal.[76] No action was taken.

MacVeagh revived the idea in 1913, just before leaving office. His successor, William McAdoo, did not pursue it aggressively, although discussions continued. Other government officials addressed the matter in ensuing years. Finally, on August 20, 1925, secretary of the Treasury Andrew W. Mellon appointed a committee of 25 people to study the matter. This group reported favorably, and in May 1927 Mellon approved the change to a new, small size. It was agreed that standard portraits should be continued on the different denominations, as had been proposed in 1909, and the Treasury seals and serial numbers should be of a distinctive color on each of the classes or types. Silver Certificates were to be overprinted in blue, Legal Tender Notes in red, Gold Certificates in yellow, Federal Reserve Notes in green, and National Bank Notes in brown. Backs for a given denomination were to be of standard designs, rather than different for each class, and printed in green, except, perhaps, for Gold Certificates. New notes designed as Series of 1928 were scheduled to be released that year.

Delays occurred at the BEP, and commercial interests also wanted more time to prepare. It was not until June 22, 1929, that the first small-size bills were delivered to the comptroller of the Currency. Actual distribution to the public through Federal Reserve Banks began on July 10, with some of the issues still marked "Series of 1928." Printing of National Bank Notes called the Series of 1929 began in mid-July, with orders filled in succession by charter numbers, the lowest numbers first. Denominations of $5, $10, $20, $50, and $100 were made.

The Treasury stated that it would distribute a large quantity of the new notes and quickly redeem an equal number of the large-size bills. There was an overlap of the old and the new, with the final large-size National Bank Notes leaving the Treasury on August 17, by which time small-size notes were common in wallets, cash drawers, and bank vaults.

Paper-money collector Robert H. Lloyd contributed "The New Currency in Review" to *The Numismatist* for its July issue. In it he wrote:

> The $1, $2, $5, and $10 have been sent out as samples to all banks, so that the public may become a little more familiar with them when they arrive in quantity.
>
> The serial numbers are a big disappointment. In the first place, they lack the individuality of the old numbers, since the new numbers look more like a coupon number found so often on cigar stores' script. . . . Unfortunately, the new numbers will all have two letters and eight or nine figures. This will lessen the novelty of low numbers and render their detection more difficult.
>
> For example, note A222B of the 1923 series would be noticeable for the shortness of the serial number. Now the Series of 1928 will correspond by having cipher letters precede, as follows, A0000222A. It is probable that only letters will be used as prefixes and suffixes to the serial numbers. The many forms of symbols used in the past, such as are still found on the $5 U.S. note and the $10 Gold Certificate will be discontinued. . . .
>
> The quantity of new notes ready is sufficient for a time. The $1 will immediately appear numbered A00000001A

to A10000000A and B00000001A to B100000000A; the $2, A00000001A to A10000000A, while the Federal Reserve Notes will have their respective district letter prefixed with numbers that will soon be in the millions, but which are counted in the thousands on all samples seen so far.

All in all, the new notes are acceptable and it is hoped that they will eliminate the "confusing" and "variable" types of the past which have seemed to bother bankers and financial men more than the public. However, there is nothing confusing in the present currency system to one who knows something of the financial history of this country.

Redemptions of old-style notes became intense. Within a few years, nearly all had disappeared from circulation. The public liked the new size of the bills, and no significant complaints were made about them. Numismatists regretted the sameness of the new issues, with each class sharing the same back design within a given denomination. The small-size currency included Legal Tender Notes, Gold Certificates, Silver Certificates, National Bank Notes, and Federal Reserve Notes. Federal Reserve Bank Notes were to come in 1933.

By early 1929, 50 hand-operated presses remained in operation at the BEP. With the advent of the small-size bills, they were idled. At the peak in earlier years there were as many as 585 in operation, making notes of all kinds. Now these were sold for scrap, and only a few were kept on hand for test printings of plates and for special orders.[77]

The Great Depression Hits

Storm clouds were now rising on the economic horizon. Speculation in stocks continued to be intense, often on easy credit whereby investors could put up just 10% margin, allowing $1,000 to buy $10,000 worth of shares. This was fine if the market value increased. If the shares doubled in value to $20,000, a profit of $10,000 was realized, or 10 times the $1,000 investment.

However, if the stock went down just a small percent, from $10,000 to $9,000, the entire investment would be wiped out. No problem if the market went up; disaster if it didn't. Happily, this scenario was theoretical, not factual. Stocks kept rising. Nearly everyone was an investment genius. Personal financial statements reflected wealth where earlier there were modest amounts entered.

In late 1928 and early 1929 new money for investing became "tight," causing some worries. Most investors had spent what they had available, and few sources remained to be tapped. No one wanted to be a naysayer, and to all outward appearances Wall Street was still paved with gold.

Not far away, on New York City's Coenties Alley near Stone Street, the investment house of Guttag Brothers had its own building. Julius and Henry Guttag were also active numismatists. In fact, it was Julius who in 1923 dreamed up the idea of "National Coin Week," which the American Numismatic Association promoted vigorously. Profits from the securities business poured in, allowing the brothers to produce a fine new reference work on New Jersey coppers of 1786 to 1788, to issue *Guttag's Coin Bulletin*, and to adver-

tise that they had sufficient funds to handle any coin deal offered. In 1928, the Guttags had experienced a chill, and in 1929 they were among the first securities firms to become illiquid, despite trying to wholesale much of their coin inventory. The summer of 1929 was difficult for them. Not to worry. All would be well soon. All eyes were on the stock market as prices kept rising.

Then disaster. In October the market crashed. Speculators who had bought on margin were wiped out, and those who had earned fortunes on paper were now broke. The house of Guttag collapsed, and a reported $9 million was lost—an immense fortune in those days.[78] Waldo C. Newcomer, president of the National Exchange Bank of Baltimore, saw his fortune dwindle to a fraction of its former worth. His collection of rare coins, one of the finest in the country, was shipped off to dealer B. Max Mehl in Texas, who proceeded to offer it for sale. As coins had not been the object of speculation in the twenties, they held their values reasonably well.

Matters went from bad to worse. Herbert Hoover, a gentleman of wealth used to upper-class perquisites, was in the White House. The slump, which quickly turned into the Great Depression, was temporary, he said. In the meantime, the elaborate dinners served to his guests stood in stark contrast to unemployed workers in the street. Prosperity was just around the corner, he promised.

In the 1932 presidential election, Hoover campaigned on his expectation that all would soon be well. Few Americans shared his confidence. Most thought he had done a downright poor job as chief executive. Franklin D. Roosevelt, more of a realist, and with no need to defend his past record, declared that the country's finances were disastrous, and pledged new programs to make it better. He won by a landslide.

The crisis deepened. By January 1933, over 5,000 banks had failed, and there was no relief in sight. The demand for paper money had slowed considerably. The BEP laid off all temporary and part-time workers and required others to take days off without pay or to be furloughed.

The Roosevelt Changes

Roosevelt was inaugurated on March 4, 1933. By that time he had many plans in place, including those formulated with secretary of the Treasury William H. Woodin (a numismatist of renown). A "New Deal" was promised, and it was not long in coming.

Woodin drafted and Roosevelt announced a "complete bank holiday in the United States for the period Monday March 6th to Thursday, March 9, 1933, both inclusive." The payment of Gold Certificates and gold coins was suspended, and the scene was set for a panic or rush on banks afterward, as depositors were expected to scramble to convert their accounts into paper money. An emergency was in the offing. Within two days, printing of special Federal Reserve Bank Notes commenced, and large quantities were made.

Banks that were found by the Treasury to be sound were permitted to reopen for business. Many others were liquidated. By December 31, 1933, over 9,000 were out of business.[79] The expected demand for the new paper money did not materialize, as the banks that reopened were considered to be on firm ground.

81

The California National Bank of Sacramento, shown here soon after it was chartered in 1906, failed during the Depression and went into receivership in 1933.

The Scranton (Pennsylvania) National Bank was chartered on January 22, 1934, number 13947, by the Reconstruction Finance Corporation set up by the Roosevelt administration. It took over troubled assets of another bank. It was late in the story of National Bank Notes, but did manage to issue $325,000, face value, in $5, $10, and $20 notes. This is stock certificate number 1 for 4,000 shares taken by the RFC.

The Annex Building of the Bureau of Engraving and Printing was first occupied in 1938, providing expanded facilities for nearly all phases of operation. Authorized by Congress in 1936, construction began in the same year. Comprising more than 600,000 square feet, the cost was reckoned as $5,667,000, exclusive of equipment and certain other features. (*History of the Bureau of Engraving and Printing*)

Investigation of other banks continued for a long time afterward, during which time many reopened, while others went into involuntary liquidation. Still other banks underwent reorganization (usually under a similar-appearing but slightly different name) or were forced to merge with stronger banks. Many of these banks issued Series of 1929 Type 2 National Bank Notes, which were first made in May 1933.

On January 30, 1934, the Gold Reserve Act demonetized that metal. Its price had been $20.67 per ounce since the early 19th century. Roosevelt raised it to $35, in effect stealing the profit from citizens who had surrendered their gold coins at face value in 1933, a fact widely ignored by historians, although banker-numismatist Louis E. Eliasberg often talked about it in later years.

The distribution of Gold Certificates stopped in 1933, although some were printed into early 1934. The wording of the obligation on certain other notes, stating they could be redeemed in gold, was changed to state that the bills were legal tender, but not otherwise convertible. Silver Certificates remained payable in silver.

In May 1935 the last National Bank Notes were printed. By that time charter number 14348 had been reached, with

12,636 banks actually issuing paper money since December 1863.

The Depression prompted the government to launch many new construction and public works projects. These boosted employment, bolstered the economy, and had other beneficial effects. Among the many new government structures erected was a large and impressive Annex Building for the BEP. On May 17, 1938, it was officially occupied, providing extensive facilities that are still in use today.

LATER YEARS

World War II, which began in Europe in 1939, lasted until August 1945. The demand for wartime goods and matériel spurred the economy, the Depression ended quickly, and there was an unprecedented demand for more coins and paper money. In the 1940s, Federal Reserve Bank Notes that had been made in 1933 but not used were brought out of storage and placed in circulation, as were some undistributed Legal Tender Notes from the same era.

By April 1942, the world's supply of silk was interrupted by Japanese actions in the Pacific. Nylon fibers were substituted for silk in the manufacture of paper. By April 1943, nylon was in short supply as well, and the government switched to colored cotton threads. Cotton continued to be used until it was replaced by a synthetic fiber in 1950. Various experiments with paper were conducted during the war and afterward, and changes in printing techniques were made as well.

One improvement in printing and plate-making consisted of adding the signatures to the sheets after the faces were printed, rather than having the signatures in the plates. This way, every time there was a change of administration, new plates did not have to be made, and revised currency could be issued quickly. This change was first done with Series of 1935 $1 notes and was applied to all denominations in 1953. For most denominations, printing was made more efficient when the signatures were added to the numbering presses beginning in 1950. The first so imprinted were the $5, $10, and $20 bills for the Federal Reserve Bank of Richmond, delivered on November 3 of that year. These notes were distributed in the Washington area to test the public reaction to a slight change in appearance, but no one noticed the difference, and so the process was universally adopted.[80]

In 1955, rotary presses were tested for the production of paper money. Two years later, in 1957, the bureau ordered eight rotary presses, in addition to the test press that had been used. Now 32-subject plates became the standard.

For the new presses, which did not require the complicated process of dampening the paper, the paper content was changed. Linen content was reduced to 25% from the 50% in use at that time (even higher in earlier years). A sheet-fed rotary press could produce about 2,400 impressions per hour, as compared to 900 from a flat-bed press. It was the policy to print the backs first, store them for about 24 hours to let the green ink set and dry, then print the other side. Various types of transfer-resistant inks were adapted, so that impressions from one side would not leave traces on the other when the notes were tightly packaged.

The BEP and Collectors

Although the United States Mint had catered to collectors for many years with the issuance of Proof sets, commemoratives, and the like, the Bureau of Engraving and Printing had moved at a slower pace in its dealings with the numismatic community.

In 1967, Robert Conlon became director of the BEP. His administration ushered in a new era of dynamic change. Special souvenir cards were introduced, featuring vignettes and impressions from historical plates. Questions about paper-money production, errors, and other aspects were answered promptly and with enthusiasm, and other advances were made.[81] In 1968 the bureau set up a dazzling display at the ANA Convention in San Diego. Notes with a face value totaling over $1 *billion* were displayed, and visitors could watch paper money being printed on an antique hand press.

During the Bicentennial year of 1976, special offers were made to collectors. Other products were introduced as the years went by. In October 1981, uncut 32-subject sheets and 16-subject half-sheets were placed on sale. In 1982, half-sheets of Bicentennial $2 notes were made available. Earlier, currency sheets of any kind were given out sparingly, often only to those with special connections to the Treasury department.

In the late 20th century, many experiments toward printing efficiency were made, including one trial run of 10,000 sheets of $1 bills printed on Tyvek, a translucent plastic sheeting often used as insulation in building construction. This was done under the suggestion of Ed Weitzman, who had seen bills on Tyvek that were being used in Haiti and the Isle of Man. The American versions did not have Treasury seals or numbers. The idea was dropped when it was found that dirt and grease clung to the notes and soon made them unattractive. Later, other plastic polymer substrate materials came into wide use in many countries. In the United States the political friends of the Crane Paper Company, longtime contract supplier of paper to the BEP, scuttled any such proposals.[82]

In 1979, Robert J. Leuver was made assistant director of the BEP, and on January 1, 1983, he was named as the director. Interface with the numismatic community accelerated. In October 1984, then president of the American Numismatic Association, I wrote in my monthly column in *The Numismatist*:

> Robert Leuver, director of the Bureau of Engraving and Printing, has made great strides in numismatic relations since he assumed his position. At the BEP's facilities in Washington, D.C., a gift shop has been opened where collectors can view and purchase vignettes, uncut sheets and other printed delicacies. Who would have believed 10 years ago that collectors would be able to order full uncut sheets of currency at affordable prices? Such an opportunity would have been nonexistent. However, now not only are uncut sheets available, but sheets also are offered in different formats and from various Federal Reserve districts.
>
> Under the direction of Leuver, the BEP has coordinated printing demonstrations at conventions sponsored by the ANA and other hobby organizations, and its traveling exhibits of high-denomination notes have attracted much attention. Not to be overlooked is the permanent BEP exhibit at ANA Headquarters that was arranged by Mr. Leuver's predecessor.

He also worked with different types of printing processes, including an experiment in which web-fed presses were used to produce $1 bills, and which various types of inks were produced. Seeking new career directions, in 1988 Leuver accepted the executive directorship of the American Numismatic Association, a position he held until 1997, the year of his 70th birthday.

The excellent relations between the BEP and collectors have continued and expanded since then. Perhaps the ultimate gesture of good faith has been the printing of "error" notes, star notes ordinarily made to replace defective notes, but now made in limited printings for sale at a premium to numismatists. These products have been widely appreciated, and typically the sale of a limited edition product, including unusual serial numbers, star notes, and the like, is a quick sellout. Today, the BEP exhibits are drawing crowds at numismatic conventions, and employees assigned to those programs are very knowledgeable and ever willing to answer questions and be helpful, while nearby displays of interesting notes for sale beckon.

PAPER-MONEY GRADING

THE DEVELOPMENT AND HISTORY OF GRADING

CONTROVERSIAL AND EMOTIONAL

If there is any one subject that stirs collectors' passions, it is grading. The present chapter is devoted to it, as comments about grading are important in many of the following sections of the book.

As author of the longest-running column in American numismatic history, I've been communicating with *Coin World* readers since 1961. If I were to write an article about varieties of Treasury seals found on paper money, I might receive two or three letters from readers (nearly all by e-mail these days). Even if I went into *fascinating* detail (personal opinion here), such as mentioning that four seals on certain $2 Legal Tender Notes were incorrectly inserted upside down, or that a later historian mused that in 1862 Spencer M. Clark, then head of the National Currency Bureau, should have removed seven of the 34 projections on the Treasury seal because that number of states had seceded from the Union, I might get a mere three or four letters. If I were to write about grading, I would get dozens!

In 1949 in *Early American Cents*, Dr. William H. Sheldon created one of the finest numismatic texts ever. The subject was large copper one-cent pieces dated from 1793 to 1814. He devised the Sheldon Grading Scale of 70 points, a numerical system specifically designed for the topic at hand, but later extended with unintended consequences to cover everything from Hard Times tokens of 1837, to Iowa (and other) statehood quarters , to paper money. More about this later.

For now, his comment that *ownership* of a coin was worth five points in its grade was and is poignant. I have seen time and again that a dealer or collector holding a large cent or an 1890 Coin Note or a Lesher "dollar" will often grade it as high as he or she can, without incurring too much criticism, while a buyer will point out its problems and grade it lower: "See that flaw on the bottom edge? A magnifying glass will help. Use mine."

NUMERICAL GRADING IN 1977

Perhaps following in the footsteps of Dr. Sheldon, in 1977, William P. Koster proposed a numerical scale for grading paper money, comprising these categories: 5, Fair; 10, Good;

15, Very Good; 20 to 30, Fine; 35 to 40, Fine to Very Fine; 45 to 55, Very Fine; 55 to 60, Very Fine to Extremely Fine; 70 to 80, Extremely Fine; 85, Extremely Fine to About Uncirculated; 90, About Uncirculated; 95 to 113, Uncirculated.

Koster offered the following discussion of standards for high grades:

> In current practice it seems to me that Uncirculated defines a condition distinguishable from the new. It describes a note which never saw circulation, but which may have a teller's crease from counting or a pinhole or two or in general very faint signs of handling. An Uncirculated note is just a trace lower than a new note in quality. It would contain no folds, wrinkles, or stains . . . .
>
> 100: new or crisp Uncirculated. A new note is the one which is in the average condition in which it was distributed by the Treasury Department. National Bank Notes could have irregular trimming if cut apart by hand. Poor centering or close trimming, an occasional grain in the paper, red smear on the back of the note from a wet seal, could be included on nationals, a new note would contain no pinholes and must be free of folds, counting creases, and even the faintest sign of aging.
>
> 110 to 113, superb, Gem. Notes that are perfectly printed and well centered, with good impression of serial numbers, bright signature in the case of National Bank Notes. The Gem category would only be used for notes that clearly exceed the then-current production standards.[1]

Nothing came of the proposal. The adaptation of numerical grading to paper money would await the next generation, and then the old Sheldon system would be used.

THE 70-POINT GRADING SCALE

The nomenclature for grades of federal paper money evolved years ago, embracing terms used for rare coins. What used to be called *New* grade by many collectors and dealers is now generally referred to as Uncirculated (not Mint State, as bills are printed, not minted). The designation *CU* was popular years ago, for Crisp Uncirculated; at the same time *BU*, or Brilliant Uncirculated, represented the epitome for a coin. The designation *CU* is still used by some today, such as in the *National Bank Note Census*, by Don C. Kelly and James M. Kelly.

In recent times—*very* recent times, that is, not until the 21st century—the 70-point Sheldon Scale, which is generally known as the American Numismatic Association Grading Standards for Coins, has been used widely for paper money. This is particularly true for currency certification services, which are now only a few years old.

A 70-point scale is illogical for coins, as the system was created in 1949 to be a *market formula* for grading copper cents of 1793 to 1814. Dr. Sheldon devised this as part of a system that included a *basal value* for each cent. If a variety of 1796 had a basal value of $2, then in EF-40 grade it would have a market value of $2 times 40, or $80. Grade numbers could be multiplied as well. According to Sheldon, an MS-60 cent was worth three times the price of a VF-20 cent of the same variety. Back in 1949 there was not as much emphasis on the Mint State or Uncirculated grade.

The utility of his formula in calculating market values died at the starting gate. However, it appeared to have scientific accuracy to casual observers, and in any event, it offered a convenient shorthand, so it lived on in another context. We continue to use it today, although basal values are no longer considered.

The shorthand feature is indeed very convenient, making numbers very useful. If a newcomer to the field of paper money were told a note graded *Good*, what would this mean? Would the note be good in the sense of *desirable?* What about a note called *Fine?* Would that mean *satisfactory*, or *exquisite*; would it be as nice as *Good?*

Abbreviated and with numbers attached, we have such designations as G-4 (Good-4), F-12 (Fine-12), VF-20 (Very Fine-20), AU-50 (About Uncirculated-50), and so on.

At quick glance, a newcomer will know that an F-12 note is better than a G-4 note, and that an AU-50 is better yet, but not as desirable as an Unc-60. Very useful, most would agree. Beyond this, the numbers have no significance of any kind. An Unc-60 note is not three times better or three times more valuable than a VF-20 note. The grade of Very Fine begins at VF-20 and stops short of EF-40, thus covering 20 points. However, just *one* point is allowed for each of the Uncirculated categories, such as Unc-60, Unc-61, and so on—11 points for as many grades, up to Unc-70. There is only a slight difference in value between a VF-20 note and one graded VF-25, five points higher, but there can be a *huge* difference between the price of an Unc-60 and an Unc-65 note, also a five-point spread.

In various dealers' catalogs and elsewhere, there are comments and standards given for grading, as in *Paper Money of the United States*, by Arthur and Ira Friedberg, or *The Comprehensive Catalog of U.S. Currency*, by Gene Hessler and Carlson Chambliss, to mention just two. Catalogs issued by Spink-Smythe have grading guidelines expressed, and some other offerings do as well.

Currency has experienced "gradeflation" over the years. In the 1960s and early 1970s, for a bill to qualify as Uncirculated it had to be crisp and without a hint of a fold or stain. In the

1970s my company was the largest wholesale customer of Lyn F. Knight. A lot of time would be spent by both parties, examining notes under light, discussing margins, and more. Notes that had even a hint of a crease or had a smudge simply did not qualify as Uncirculated. No argument.

Today, U.S. paper money with some such evidences of circulation is often called Uncirculated, and those without such traces have graduated to choice and gem Uncirculated. Even Unc-65 and higher notes can have problems when a connoisseur describes them, although the notations on holders are silent on such aspects. This may be okay, if we all play by the same rules. Besides, no one cares much about how Dave Bowers or Lyn Knight or Len Glazer or Art Kagin would have graded a note in, say, 1975. Today is today, and yesterday is history.

As will be discussed in the next chapter, a smart buyer will realize that the assigned grade or number is only one factor in the desirability of a note. To me, an Unc-60 note with the Treasury seal remaining bright red is more desirable than an Unc-64 with the seal faded. In fact, if I were buying a note this would be a no-brainer, to use a popular term. For an *investor* who has money but not knowledge, buying the Unc-64 would be also a no-brainer. For *you*, seeking to carefully form a fine collection with excellent value in every purchase, it is important to consider what grade numbers mean and what they don't mean.

Refinements and changes in grading interpretations are sure to come as the market adjusts. This is a *sport*—but a serious one, as grading can involve large differences in the prices paid.

GRADE CATEGORIES USED IN THIS BOOK

When I began work on the first draft of this section, I corresponded and spoke with many people, seeking input. I quickly learned that no two professionals had the same opinion. Most were fairly liberal in that they accepted that 21st-century grading interpretations had to be used. Among those consulted were experts at PCGS and Paper Money Guaranty (PMG, a division of NGC), Dr. Lane Brunner (who at the time was working on the possible creation of currency grading standards to be adopted by the American Numismatic Association), and many collectors and dealers. Equally important, as a professional in the field, I saw what was being bought, sold, and traded, and the grades used.

Although just about everyone agreed that grading was more conservative a generation ago, I had little choice except to embrace modern interpretations. If I were to give guidelines that I used in 1955, 1965, 1975, or some other time years ago, you would find them to be useless in the market today. They would be of no value when you viewed notes in a dealer's stock or in an auction catalog. For one thing, we didn't use numbers at all back then.

Numbers became popular in the 1990s, with Uncirculated-65 (abbreviated as Unc-65) at about the top of the scale. Few notes merited a designation that high. Today, notes graded as Unc-65 are common, but with no particular uniformity that I have been able to observe. Unc-68, 69, and the ultimate, 70, can now be found.

The term *Exceptional Paper Quality* has been added to some grades, often with meaning, especially among recently graded notes, but not consistently. So far as I am aware, within a given variety of note, the same paper was used (exceptions are minor). The term has not been defined in print, or if it has, I have not seen it. I recently saw an Unc-65 "Exceptional Paper Quality" note that to my eyes was faded and yellowed overall. I wonder if it was actually *limp?* Not being able to take it out of its holder, I could not tell.

In summary, I have not tried to *create* grading guidelines, but to simply interpret what I view as current use. It is to be expected that others' perspectives may differ, and perhaps with good cause. Accordingly, accept these comments as my current view. Seek other information elsewhere, and factor that into your grading decisions and evaluations. And, if assigning numerical grades to notes is not your cup of tea, just ignore the entire matter and use adjectives!

GRADING GUIDELINES

Gem Uncirculated (Unc-65 through Unc-68): A note that is flawless, with the same freshness, crispness, and bright color as when first printed. In theory, it must be perfectly centered, with full margins, and free of any marks, blemishes, or traces of handling. In practice some require the use of negative adjectives when connoisseurs describe them, although holders are nearly always silent concerning negatives.

Choice Uncirculated (Unc-63): An Uncirculated note that is fresher and brighter than the norm for its particular issue. Almost as nice as Gem Uncirculated but not quite there. Must be reasonably well centered.

Uncirculated (Unc-60): A note that shows no trace of circulation. It might not have perfect centering and might have one or more pinholes, counting smudges, or other evidence of improper handling, but it still retains its original crispness.[2] Such imperfections do not generally impair the choice appearance of a new note, and such notes are to be regarded as being in Uncirculated condition, although they generally command slightly lower prices than notes in perfect condition. With this grade there are many differences of opinion, especially between buyers and sellers.

About Uncirculated (AU-50, AU-53, AU-55, and AU-58): A bright, crisp note that appears to be new, but upon close examination shows a trace of very light use, such as a corner fold or faint crease. About Uncirculated is a borderline condition, applied to a note that may not be quite Uncirculated but is still obviously better than an average Extremely Fine note. Such notes command prices only slightly below those of Unc-60 notes and can be highly desirable.

Extremely Fine (EF-40 and EF-45): A note that shows some faint evidence of circulation, although it will still be bright and retain nearly full crispness. It may have two or three minor folds or creases, but no tears or stains and no discolorations. The abbreviation *XF* is often used, but is not one I prefer.

Very Fine (VF-20, VF-25, VF-30, and VF-35): A note that has been in circulation, but not actively or for long. It still retains some crispness and is still choice enough in its condition to be desirable overall. It may show folds or creases, or some light smudges from the hands of a past generation. Sometimes, Very Fine notes are the best available in certain rare issues, and they should be cherished accordingly. Currently there are a lot of really *nice* notes certified at these levels.

Fine (Fine-12 and Fine-15): A note that shows evidence of much more circulation. The note has lost its crispness and very fine detail, and creases are more pronounced, although it still is not seriously soiled or stained.

Very Good (VG-8 and VG-10): A note that has had considerable wear or circulation and may be limp, soiled, or dark in appearance and might even have a small tear or two on an edge.

Good (Good-4): A note that is badly worn, with margin or body tears, frayed margins, and missing corners.

Lower grades: Poor-1, Fair-2, and About Good-3 (AG-3) describe notes that are fillers at best, but they can still be desirable if of an extremely rare or previously unknown variety.

GRADING AND THE MARKETPLACE

OPINION, NOT SCIENCE

Although numbers attached to grades of coins, paper money, and other numismatic items may appear to be scientific, they are not. Numbers can be very useful, however, as will be explained.

As grading was, is, and always will be a matter of opinion, and as even the most expert of connoisseurs can differ, there is ample room for emotion, controversy, and other nonscientific elements to be included in a transaction. This seems to be normal and takes place in other venues—in buying or selling a used automobile, rating a stock or bond, evaluating a house or condominium, or, for that matter, grading a wine. This is a *sport* here.

The best preparation is to gain an understanding of the nature of grading. As it is not scientific, a certified note graded as Unc-65 may or may not be called that if taken out of the holder and examined in a blind test by another grading service or even the same service used in the first place. Perhaps it will be AU-58?

This type of scenario is familiar to you, of course, if you've been involved in rare *coins* for any length of time. Many are the instances in which a coin certified as AU-58 has "graduated" to MS-65 or some other, higher grade.

As can be readily seen, the above descriptions, as well as those found elsewhere, are highly subjective, and their interpretations can vary. Some dealers are strict graders, and a VF-20 note obtained from them may be as nice as an EF-40 note from others. Experience is the best teacher, and no amount of words can replace experience in the field and consultation with others. Be aware. Look around. Compare. I cannot overemphasize the importance of this.

Today the standards for grading paper money are in transition. Such terms as *exceptional paper quality*, *great embossing*, and others are used by some of the grading services, but often not by those who buy and sell, such as in auction catalogs of leading currency sellers (unless they are quoting information on a certified holder).

Perhaps more important—indeed, *much more* important to old-time collectors as well as anyone seeking to be a smart buyer today—are the margins and centering and the overall brightness of a note. Some aspects of these are discussed in the next chapter. Many notes have faded over a period of years, with the Treasury seal (if pink or red) being one of the first areas to be affected. Paper exposed to light for a long period of time can take on a yellow hue or appear washed out.

A few years ago David Sundman and I made the joint purchase of a rare Series of 1902 Red Seal note with the serial number 1 from the First National Bank of Portsmouth, New Hampshire. For many decades it had hung in a frame on the wall of the bank, a display to be admired. The once-red seal had faded to a light yellow, and yet the note was otherwise in gem Uncirculated condition. A proper description would tell of all of its features in detail, not simply assign a number and let it go at that. If this note were described as Unc-65 with no mention of the seal, that would not be correct. If it were lowered to Unc-63 to compensate for the problem, that would not be cricket either. Probably a description such as "Crispness and preservation fully Unc-65, but with the red seal faded to a light yellow" would be necessary. In that way a buyer would know what to expect. As the note is *unique*, the price might not be affected at all. If it were a common note, it might sell at, say, the Unc-60 price level.

COMMERCIAL GRADING SERVICES

Third-party commercial grading services for paper money are operated under the names PCGS (not affiliated with the coin service of the same name) and PMG, as well as several other entities, some of which are owned by currency dealers. These services place notes in holders and add information as to their opinions concerning the grade.

Important: *The Uncirculated price estimates in this book apply only to notes certified by PCGS or PMG.* This is not intended to mean or infer that notes that are not certified at all, or that are certified by other services, are in any way inferior. Some may be better, some may be the same, and others may be subpar. Instead, this is a reality of the marketplace. PCGS and PMG notes generally (but not always) bring higher prices than do those certified by other services, in the experience of valuations editor Tom Denly. If notes certified by another service ever command the same average prices of PCGS and PMG notes, that service will be recognized in a future edition.

In any event, it is the note itself that counts, not what is printed on a holder. Moreover, a professional with longtime experience can likely grade a note just as well as any service you can name. Lyn F. Knight, whose experience goes back many years, states this clearly in the introductions to his auction catalogs. His terms of sale (per a recent offering) state:

Descriptions and Grading. Bidder acknowledges as follows: Grading and evaluation is an art and not a science. The grade, quality, designation, variety, rarity, provenance, and historic relevance of any items in this sale are qualified statements of good faith opinion of Knight or its consignor(s). It is possible that two people will not always grade the same item alike. Also, as market conditions change, grading standards change, and will most likely continue to do so in the future. Each bidder's own examination of the item(s) is the criterion and not the grade represented by another. Every effort is made by Knight to determine provenance and authenticity. It is the bidder's responsibility to arrive at a final conclusion prior to bidding. In any purchase or sale, the value of the item(s) is determined by the price. *The bidder hereby assumes all risks of value concerning any and all purchases. . . .*

Grading or condition or other attributes of the lots may have a material effect on the value of the item(s) purchased, and the opinion of others (including independent grading services) may differ with the independent grading services opinion or interpretation of Knight. Knight shall not be bound by any prior or subsequent opinion, determination or certification by any independent grading service. . . .

Notwithstanding anything to the contrary in these Terms and Conditions of Auction Sale, *lots listed in this catalogue graded by any third party grading service may not be returned for any reason whatsoever.*

While the preceding policy may seem to be harsh, I agree with it. There is absolutely no way that Lyn F. Knight, or I, or you, can tell if a note certified as Unc-65 or some other high grade and sealed in a holder has been starched, or is limp, or has a subtle fold, or was offered at a lower grade earlier, perhaps even described with stains, pinholes, or other defects. The imprint on the holder simply states what an employee or employees of a particular grading service considered the note to be graded at a particular time.

During the course of preparation of this book, one of America's leading dealers in paper money made this suggestion:

Where serial numbers are available and where cataloguers have noted tears, folds, etc., this information should go into a public data base for all to see. Once a note is registered and its serial number recorded, it would be made available to the public and at that point the consumer would have the right to buy it or refuse to buy it.

A lot of this information is available should anyone want to compile a comprehensive database to include it. It would probably be a sensation in the marketplace! Until then, the current mind set seems to be: what the certified holder says is the grade *is indeed the grade*. Period.

The grading game played by collectors and dealers is generally that any adjectives that seem to be negative should be applied sparingly, and for high grade items, not at all. To make you feel better, here is a reality check for coins.

Silver, to take an example, naturally tones over a period of time. Except for silver dollars stored in bulk in Mint bags, all

$1 Legal Tender Note, Series of 1928, in a PCGS holder certified as Gem New 65 (Unc-65). Photographed against a black background.

$2 Legal Tender Note, Series of 1928, in an NGC holder certified as 65 Gem Uncirculated (Unc-65). Photographed against a black background.

silver coins dating prior to the 20th century have acquired natural toning. This includes *all* silver Proofs made for collectors. Yet Capped Bust silver coins of the early 19th century, Liberty Seated coins, and others that are *fully bright and brilliant* are very plentiful today, including in PCGS, NGC, and other holders issued by respective grading services.

A fully brilliant 1825 half dollar, for example, is simply certified as MS-66 (or 67, or whatever). A fuller description would be, "MS-65, dipped to restore the full brightness it had when it was minted." Similarly, some Series of 1899 $1 Silver Certificates graded as, for example, as Unc-63, could be more fully described as, "Unc-63, lightly washed and pressed to restore brightness."

Such a half dollar and Silver Certificate are each highly desirable. I am simply endeavoring you to understand reality.

Once again, this is a *sport*—not that we all want it to be such.

"IMPROVING" CURRENCY

If a note has been trimmed to make the margins uniform or to remove a defect, this should be mentioned, at least if we were in an ideal world. Once again, reality is usually different.

Martin Gengerke described in a letter to *Coin World* an instance in which a rare $100 note had been auctioned by one of America's leading houses, carefully described as being in a circulated grade, and with pinholes in the border. The buyer or some other later owner conserved (or *doctored*, or you supply another word) the note, then put in a certified holder and offered it again at auction as gem Uncirculated.

This unique $20 Series of 1861 Demand Note has "for the" handwritten on the face. Sold as part of the Harry W. Bass, Jr. Collection in 1999, lot 17, it was described as "Good-6. Damaged (CGA). Variety with 'For the' handwritten. Body of a VG or perhaps Fine note, though extensive edge repairs are visible around the back margins. The lower right corner, relative to the face, is missing."

Although it had already had "extensive" repairs when Harry Bass acquired it, the note was further restored, as shown here when it appeared on the market again in 2008. (Courtesy of Martin Gengerke)

Although things like this *should* be mentioned, often they are not, either by intent or by lack of knowledge. If you buy a note certified as, say, Unc-63 today, and then see a picture in an old auction catalog in which it is graded Extremely Fine with a tear in the margin, that would seem to be *your* problem, not someone else's, although I realize that opinions can differ.

As quoted earlier, Lyn F. Knight, for one, states that if a problem later arises with a certified note, that is your concern, not his. Most other sellers, perhaps *all* other sellers (I have never met an exception) would likely agree. On the other hand, *buyers* might not. Likely the twain will never meet in complete agreement.

Similarly, in the world of rare *coins*, it is today's grade that counts, never mind that there are abundant instances of coins being illustrated and offered at lower grades earlier. In an instance related by Saul Teichman, a leading expert in United States pattern coins, *many* (not just a few) copper patterns that had been cleaned and polished by the late King Farouk of Egypt, and had been illustrated and described as

such in later American catalogs, have now been conserved (or use your own word) and are certified as Proof-63, 64, or 65, without further notations that they were once cleaned to death.

I don't mean to be difficult here, but simply to make you aware of current practices in the marketplace. Such practices are even more common in such fields as fine art, antiques, prints, and relics from ancient Greece and Rome. I recently received a beautiful catalog of Greek and Roman antiquities for sale, each item pictured in full color and nearly all very beautiful to behold. Not a single word told of any conservation or restoration having been done to the objects, yet it is likely that nearly all had been professionally improved in one way or another.

Generally, if you buy it, you own it. Sorry about that, but the realities of the marketplace cannot be ignored. Again, this is no different in other fields. If you buy a Monet painting and later find it has been restored or conserved, and you are not happy with the news, that is your problem, unless you discover the situation immediately after the sale took place (even then, getting a refund may have complications). The good news is that with education and field work—for instance, personally examining many notes—you can become more expert than perhaps 90% of your competitors at a convention or in an auction room.

Many bills have been improved, some desirably so, by "laundering" to remove dirt and grease, then drying between pieces of tissue paper. The late William A. Philpott Jr., a leading currency collector and dealer by the time I met him in the 1950s, told me that he often took a note that was in a high grade, say what we would call Extremely Fine or About Uncirculated today, and wet it with warm water. He would then gently use a paste made of Ivory soap to rub over both sides while the note was on a china plate or other hard surface. It would then be rinsed, patted with tissue paper, then carefully placed between two sheets of tissue and put into a book to dry. I tried this myself on some current notes, and it worked well. Given a choice I'd rather have a clean, bright note than a dirty, dingy one. I see no harm in doing this. In fact, I have a few dingy Series of 1902 Blue Seal, Plain Back notes in a bank vault, as part of my collection of New Hampshire Nationals, that I will do this to someday.

Some collectors and dealers have added starch in an effort to restore crispness. Spraying with Krylon or another fixative has been tried by others. I would be hesitant about applying any chemicals or sprays, but that is my opinion. Still other bills have had holes or tears repaired. Small-size Red Seal Legal Tender Notes, if laundered or processed, often bleed through, with the seal appearing as a pink spot on the back, a point of observation known to some experts but not to the general collecting community. Certification services seem to ignore such processing.

Such improvements are generally accepted, but, if the seller is aware of them, they should be mentioned when the note is offered for sale. Again, this is in an ideal world.

In the early 20th century the Treasury department used paper-laundering machines to clean and brighten notes that had seen circulation. These were then dried on racks, bundled, and placed back in circulation. This was an extensive program, and countless bills were thus processed.

There is no conclusion I wish you to draw on the subject of conserving or restoring paper money. I simply mention it to make you aware of the issues it raises.

Currency-laundering machine in operation at the Treasury department in 1912. Such devices used yellow soap, warm water, and light acid and are said to have worked very well. Thousands of soiled notes could be processed each hour. (Bureau of Engraving and Printing, courtesy of Michael Beck)

HOW TO BE
A SMART BUYER

This chapter explores some of the characteristics of paper money—technical aspects as well as elements that may affect grading and value in a larger sense. I first outline basic ideas, then go on to discuss some different ways to form a collection, and then give four steps that I consider to be useful for smart buying. Later chapters will be useful in connection with the present one, as they will give more specifics as to why some notes (or cncased postage stamps or other related items) are rare and why some are common, why some can be found only in low grades while high grades are the rule for others.

If you know more than the other fellow (or gal) does, you will spend your money more wisely, you will obtain better-quality items, and you will have more confidence in what you do. You will be smarter than 90% of the others who collect paper money. And, not to overuse the word, you will *enjoy* the pursuit immensely.

$20 Gold Certificate, Series of 1905 (W-2226), popularly called the "Technicolor Note" by collectors.

WAYS TO COLLECT
CONSIDERING THE POSSIBILITIES

What should I collect?

The possibilities are many.

Most large-size U.S. bills from 1861 to 1929 and small-size bills from 1929 to date are relatively easy to acquire. Even so, notes in high grades from a given era are often much harder to find than are comparable coins. It is a common reaction for a coin collector who discovers paper money to marvel at how reasonable the prices of bank notes are in comparison.

Most types of lower-denomination bills in the more extensive categories (Legal Tender Notes, Silver Certificates, and various Federal Reserve Bank issues are examples) are plentiful in relation to the demand for them, although certain varieties and signature combinations can be rare. Because the Treasury department did not grant permission to illustrate bills until William A. Philpott Jr., prominent currency specialist, successfully petitioned for them to do this in 1951, old auction catalogs that listed notes were sadly lacking in technical features useful today for studying the bills. As a result, most older publications are next to useless for research today, beyond the most basic information. The first comprehensive book with illustrations was Robert Friedberg's *Paper Money of the United States*, which was published in 1953. It created a sensation and paved the way for thousands of numismatists to take up this specialty. More useful articles and references have been published in the past 50 years than in the century before that.

Today, with reference books, databases, and illustrations of notes, you will have no problem learning what various bills look like. Counterfeits and alterations are not much of a problem in collecting federal currency, for it has always been a federal offense to issue false notes, with severe penalties, and few false bills have remained in circulation for very long.

After surveying the field and considering the possibilities you may decide to specialize in a particular area of paper money, such as National Bank Notes, Silver Certificates, large-size $1 bills by types, small-size Federal Reserve Notes by bank and signature combinations, star notes, or something else of interest.

LARGE-SIZE NOTES

A "type" collection of one each of the different basic designs makes a very nice display. A good place to start is with the $1 and $2 denominations, for certain of the rare series (Demand Notes, Interest-Bearing Notes, and Gold Certificates are examples) were not made of these denominations, and thus the quest is simplified. Afterward, your collection can be expanded to include $5 bills. This is an ideal way to acquaint yourself with the panorama of designs, denominations, and changes over the years. Starting with lower values is an excellent path to gaining familiarity with grading, quality, and the printed characteristics of the notes themselves.

This plan can be expanded later to include higher denominations such as $10 and $20, after which point the going becomes difficult, especially for the earlier types. Perhaps selected types of $50 and $100 bills can be included. As to $500, $1,000, or even higher values, these are so rare and so expensive that only a few people have been fortunate enough to collect them over the years, and then only by scattered examples. The late Amon Carter Jr. of Fort Worth, Texas, was an exception. He loved high-denomination notes and sought them for many years, backed by his family's business success (with holdings that included in American Airlines, the Fort Worth *Star-Telegram*, and other entities).

Building a systematic collection by varieties involves going beyond basic types and collecting, for example, different signature combinations or Treasury seal variations. Not many people do this for large-size bills, with the result that such popular types as the 1890 Coin Notes, 1899 Indian Chief $5 Silver Certificates, and others are sometimes priced generically—with little premium added for elusive signature or seal varieties unless the rarity is extreme.

Just as die varieties can be collected for early coins, there are many plate variations among early paper money issues. The Legal Tender Series of 1862 and 1863 are a playground in this regard. Although even specialists will probably opt to get just one of each basic type and signature combination, there are differences in whether a note has one or two serial numbers, the location of the seal, imprints of the bank-note companies, absence or presence of patent dates, and notations as to SERIES or NEW SERIES. This book contains much new information in this regard.[1]

On the other hand, some may dismiss such technicalities, as indeed was done in the field of rare coins in 1881 when *A Description of 268 Varieties of U.S. Cents, 1816–1857, in the Collection of Frank D. Andrews* was published. At the time, some observers thought that this paying attention to die varieties was beyond ridiculous. Today, however, a rare-die copper cent that requires a magnifying glass to discern can bring thousands of dollars more than a common one.

Collecting paper money is a matter of preference, and you or anyone can collect whatever is of interest. There is no one "best" way.

Federal Reserve Bank Notes, Series of 1915 to 1918, can be collected with different combinations of Federal Reserve Banks, each of the two Treasury signatures, and each of two bank signatures, offering many variables. Lower denominations, especially the $1 bills, are quite inexpensive and include many different varieties.

Across all types, certain terms of combined service for the register of the Treasury and the Treasurer of the United States were very short, the briefest being just 18 days, from June 1 to June 18, 1893, for William S. Rosecrans and Daniel N. Morgan. While at first it might seem that short terms together would have created extremely rare and valuable bills, this is not necessarily the case, as printing quantities were sometimes extensive during a short term and sparse during a long one, and in other instances plates with certain signatures were used long after one or both persons left office.

National Bank Notes are a dynamic field, with most numismatists seeking examples from a particular location, such as New York City, or their home town, or paper money issued in territories before they became states. Collecting Nationals by design types is also a challenge, with the Series of 1882 $50 and $100 Value Backs being almost impossible

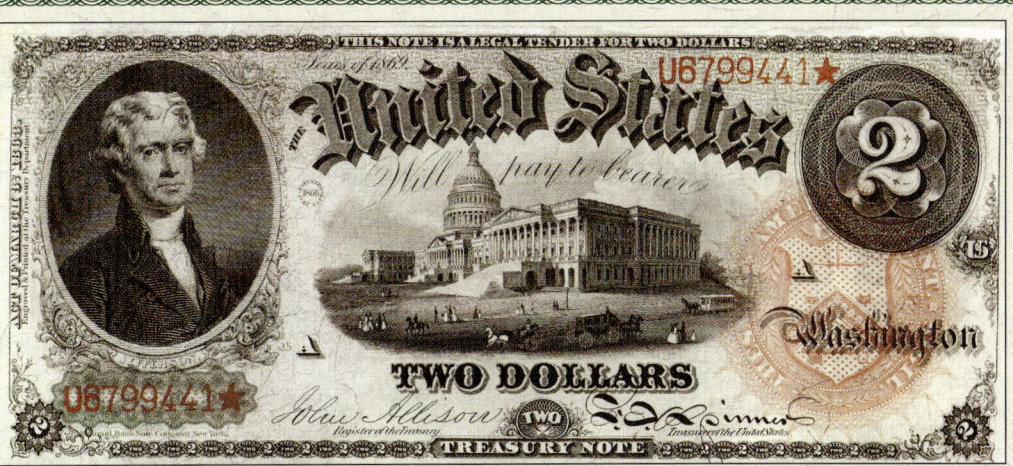

$2 Legal Tender Note, Series of 1869 (W-310). Known as the "Rainbow Note" from the multiple colors on the face, and printed on paper with a blue-tinted streak, this has always been a popular addition to a type set of lower denomination large-size notes. The ornate engraving on the back is typical of federal notes of the era.

An example of a rare variety is this $1 Treasury or Coin Note, Series of 1890, with signatures of Rosecrans and Nebeker (W-81). Only about 50 to 55 are known, of which very few can match the Uncirculated grade of the illustrated note. Indeed, Martin Gengerke in his U.S. Paper Money Records census of 2008 records only six examples coming to market over a period of many years. A collector seeking an example of this *type* would likely choose a W-80 with Rosecrans-Huston signatures instead, as an estimated 450 to 500 are known. High-grade examples come on the market with regularity. All of the Series of 1890 notes are remarkable for their richly engraved reverse designs.

An example of a rare variety of Fractional Currency, W-6363, with brown surcharges M/2/6/5 at the corners of the back, and with a tiny position letter "a" at the lower left of the face. The surcharges lend extreme value and make the note worth many times the price of an otherwise identical note without the surcharges.

$5 National Bank Note, Original Series, issued by the First National Bank of Portland, Connecticut (W-681), printed as part of a four-subject sheet, $5-$5-$5-$5, on contract by the Continental Bank Note Company of New York City. These were spaced very closely together on the sheet, with the result that all the notes are closely trimmed, as seen here. Beginning in 1875, such notes were made by the Bureau of Engraving and Printing in Washington, D.C.

Large-size Nationals were issued from 1863 to 1929 in seven major types: Original Series;

Series of 1875; Series of 1882 Brown Back, Date Back, and Value Back; and Series of 1902 Red Seal, Blue Seal Date Back, and Blue Seal Plain Back. Over 10,000 different banks issued such notes, but not necessarily of all types and denominations, providing a wide and dynamic field of collecting interest.

to find, and ditto for $50 Original Series and any National Gold Bank Note of the Series of 1875. However, for denominations from $1 to $20, a type set is feasible.

SMALL-SIZE NOTES

While few people have the money or the desire to collect small-size bills from $1 to $100 by all combinations—or, for that matter, any of the rare $500, $1,000, $5,000, and $10,000 bills—quite a few collectors desire to get one each of as many different design types as they can, especially of the denominations from $1 to $5, or even up to $100. Changes in type

were not frequent, and except for the higher values, such a display can be acquired in high grades at a modest cost.

Small-size bills can be collected systematically as well, by denomination, signature, and Federal Reserve Bank. Lower denominations, especially the $1 notes, are quite inexpensive and furnish many different varieties. Such a collection can be kept current by adding new bills each time there is a new signature combination or some other change. Today, such notes are printed in two locations—the BEP in Washington, D.C., and the Western Facility in Fort Worth, Texas—and for 12 different Federal Reserve Banks, yielding 24 possible vari-

$10,000 Federal Reserve Note, Series of 1928 (W-5670-E). The number 5 in four places and the letter E in the seal to the left designate that it was printed for and issued by the Federal Reserve Bank of Richmond. The portrait is of secretary of the Treasury Salmon P. Chase, who was appointed by Lincoln in 1861 and served until 1864, later becoming chief justice of the U.S. Supreme Court.

Although the high face value and the even higher numismatic value preclude these from being popular, they are in great demand as trophy notes by those who can afford them. The late Amon Carter Jr. often carried several in the pocket of his suit jacket, as conversation pieces to show off to restaurant, airline, and other personnel—hardly any of whom had ever seen such notes or even knew they existed.

$2 Federal Reserve Note, Series of 2003, with a star following the serial number (W-552-L★). The number 12 in four places and the letter L in the seal to the left designated that it was printed for and issued by the Federal Reserve Bank of San Francisco. The back has the vignette *Signing of the Declaration, 1776,* engraved for the American Bank Note Company in the early 1860s for use on the Original Series $100 National Bank Notes, and later copied for use on the $2 note as here, but with the credit line removed. The original painting the vignette is based on, by John Trumbull, hangs in the Rotunda of the Capitol in Washington.

eties. However, it is often the case that the bills for the different banks are split between the facilities, with some are printed by one and some by the other. Just as a dedicated collector of early copper cents will seek die varieties, many who pursue small-denomination notes will pay premiums for certain *blocks* (ranges of serial numbers), *mules* (unusual combinations of face and back plates), and other bills with interesting technical aspects. Small-size notes are very popular and have been the focus of interest for many collectors.

From time to time the Bureau of Engraving and Printing offers current notes, including special serial numbers, sheets, and other items of interest. Star notes, which are supposed to be replacements for error notes, are sometimes deliberately printed for collectors. (So far the United States

Mint has not been creating deliberate misstrikes and errors in *coins* for resale to numismatists.) Star notes are very popular and form a specialty in themselves. Some early star notes are extremely rare and, consequently, expensive when and if they are located. Some plate number and letter combinations are also rare and can be valuable.

Within the $10 to $100 denominations' series and signature varieties from the 1920s to the 1960s, there are many notes with modest values that are very difficult to find in Uncirculated grade. Little attention was paid to them at the time of issue, and now they are elusive. During the course of gathering illustrations for this book, some such supposedly common notes proved to be anything but! I must admit that I was very surprised.

Small-size National Bank Notes of the Series of 1929 are enthusiastically collected, again by location, similar to the discipline for large-size Nationals. Enough exist that a specialized collection can be made for most states, although some are scarcer than others.

INTERESTING SERIAL NUMBERS

This is a particularly popular pursuit, especially for small-size bills of small denominations. The eight serial numbers can yield all sorts of possibilities. The beginning and ending letters are of interest as well, especially if both are A, but most

attention is paid to the numerals. Low serial numbers such as 00000001 (especially), 00001492, 00001776, and others sell for premiums. "Lucky" 7s are popular; a note numbered 77777777 would be worth passing around at a show for collectors to see, while having a bunch of 7s together but mixed with other numbers is interesting, too, such as 83777779. This would be ideal for "liar's poker," a game played at coin shows in which the winner has the best "poker hand" as reflected in the serial number on a bill taken from random (hopefully!) examples in the players' wallets.

Some time ago the BEP issued sets of notes with "lucky" 8s in the serial numbers, this being an auspicious digit for Chinese people, a tradition that has extended elsewhere.

Numbers that are symmetrical are called *radar notes* (reading the same way in each direction) or, more formally, palindromes, such as 12344321 or 44888844. Ascending or descending runs or *ladders*, such as 12345678 or 98765432, are desirable. *Repeaters* are interesting and usually inexpensive, such as 20202020 or 88778877, and so on.

Bills with the serial number 00000001 are in great demand and have been for a long time. In general such notes are elusive, and fortunate is the collector who (over a period of years) can obtain several examples in any class other than the National Bank Note series, where they are more often seen.

A SELECTION OF NOTES WITH INTERESTING AND UNUSUAL SERIAL NUMBERS

A SELECTION OF NOTES WITH INTERESTING AND UNUSUAL SERIAL NUMBERS (*continued*)

SPECIMENS, PROOFS, AND VIGNETTES

Specimen impressions of Fractional Currency bills were printed by the tens of thousands. These are special impressions, printed on one side only, made for collectors or for study. These can be collected as a specialty in their own right and are studied in chapter 18. Specimens of regular large-size and small-size bills have been made over the years for limited distribution, but they are not currently available to collectors.

Proofs of regular U.S. bills, often printed on heavy paper or cardboard and with wide margins, have been made in very small quantities and are not widely distributed, but examples become available from time to time. These are usually made to demonstrate a new design, perhaps with the intention of modifying it. Others are made for presentation or display

A SELECTION OF SPECIMENS AND PROOFS

$5 Legal Tender Note, Series of 1926-F, with A00000000A serial number and marked SPECIMEN.

$1 Silver Certificate, Series of 1899 (W-62), proof impression of the face on heavy stock with wide margins.

$2 Silver Certificate, Series of 1899 (W-369), proof impression of the face on heavy stock with wide margins.

purposes. The delineation between proof and specimen notes is not clear in numismatic practice. Some such notes have SPECIMEN printed on them, or punched in tiny holes by a cancellation machine, and have all zeros in the serial number. Most are rare and expensive.

Scattered, individually printed vignettes from large-size National Bank Notes and other 19th-century bills are on the market, these showing portraits, battle scenes, or other topics on light cardstock. These are interesting to collect in connection with the bills themselves and are usually inexpensive. Some are pages from large presentation books with nicely imprinted covers, containing specimen vignettes distributed by the Treasury department in the 1870s and 1880s. Much rarer are specially made books of Fractional Currency specimens. Souvenir cards issued in modern times by the BEP reproduce many classic vignettes as well as face and back plates, and are interesting and inexpensive to collect. These have been made for and sold at numismatic conventions and for other occasions.

"BECAUSE I LIKE IT"

Within the field of paper money, many numismatists use the "because I like it" method to acquire notes. I made passing mention of this in chapter 1. In a way, this is an ideal way to maintain your interest in collecting. Attracted by the beauty of the Series of 1896 Silver Certificates, the well-known "Educational Notes," you or someone else might buy only these, but have no interest in other Silver Certificates. A few years ago a basketball star, who did not collect currency before and has not since, bought a Series of 1890 $1,000 "Grand Watermelon Note," when his agent, Dwight Manley, a numismatist, casually told him about it and piqued his interest. After a while he sold it at a profit. A New England *coin* collector saw an "Indian Chief Note," a $5 Silver Certificate of the Series of 1899, bought one, and then went on to collect Gold Certificates, as these were interesting to him as well. Morey Perlmutter contributed an article, "The Quintessential Quintet," to the March 1974 issue of *Paper Money*, in which he enumerated the "five most popular United States notes": the Series of 1896 "Educational" $1, $2, and $5 Silver Certificates; the 1899 Indian Chief $5 Silver Certificate; and the 1901 $10 Legal Tender Bison Note.

Currency errors, the subject of a separate chapter in this book, are fascinating and popular. During the Bicentennial, a California coin collector was offered several $2 bills with upside-down serial numbers by dealer Harry J. Forman for $200 each; he bought them and gave one to each of his two sons. Today they would sell for far more.

Notes with so-called courtesy autographs by Treasury officials form an interesting pursuit. Among 19th-century bills, those autographed by Daniel N. Morgan (register of the Treasury from June 1, 1893, to June 30, 1897) are particularly numerous, as he often signed them for visitors to his office in Washington. Treasury officials who visit conventions today are usually happy to sign notes. *Mint* directors are often asked for their autographs on dollar bills, although this does not seem logical, as they make *coins*.

While uncut sheets of large-size bills are sometimes seen, especially for National Bank Notes of the Series of 1902, they

are not common and cannot be collected systematically. Six-subject sheets of small-size Series of 1929 Nationals are more available but are still scarce. Today, the BEP sells sheets, making them easy to collect, but a bit clumsy to store or display.

Browsing through this book, reviewing auction catalogs, or poking around on the Internet can give you other ideas for which notes you might like to own.

WHAT MAKES A NOTE COMMON OR RARE?

"What is it worth?" and "What is its grade?" are the two questions most frequently asked by newcomers to the hobby, and less often by old-timers. "How rare is it?" is probably third.

Some notes are common, and others are hard to find. Popular price guides list printing quantities and prices, but usually do not go beyond that. As you contemplate the notes listed in the following chapters you may wonder why some are rare in high grades, while others are frequently seen at the Uncirculated level. Sometimes certain notes from the same era, such as Fractional Currency of the mid-1860s, can be common in Uncirculated grade, while *years* may pass before an equivalent-quality Original Series $50 National Bank Note from the same era crosses the auction block.

The following sections give some reasons why there are such differences, plus aspects of availability overall and determinants of availability in certain grades.

DENOMINATION

In any series, it is a general rule that the lower denominations are more available than are the higher ones. In the federal series of notes from 1861 to date, the lower values such as $1, $2, and $5 are also more often seen in Uncirculated and other high grades than are higher values. Certain varieties of $50 or $100 bills might be rare or unknown in such preservation.

Today, many more people collect currently-issued varieties of $1 Federal Reserve Notes than those of the $100 denomination. Because of that, a generation from now many of the $1 notes will be common, but certain of the $100 will range from scarce to even rare. During the search for photographs for this book, I found that quite a few small-size $20 to $100 notes, with modest catalog values, were very difficult to find in Uncirculated grade.

Similarly, among encased postage stamps, which were issued in values of 1¢, 3¢, 5¢, 10¢, 12¢, 24¢, 30¢, and 90¢, those of the 1¢ to 10¢ values are generally common, while higher denominations range from scarce to rare and very rare.

PRINTAGES

Printing quantities, called *printages* here, can be a guide to availability, but only in part; such factors as redemption policies, distribution areas, and hoard discoveries affect the equation. In many instances, the published quantities of notes printed are different from the quantities of notes actually distributed. Many Treasury records for early notes, particularly those of the 1860s, are inconsistent, erratic, or incomplete. Two reports on the same series and issue can have two different printages. That having been said, certainly most are at least approximate.

Listings of known notes by serial number and plate information, published by Martin Gengerke, Don C. Kelly, and Track & Price, are useful guides to actual rarity of scarcer and more expensive notes that have made public appearances in catalogs or have been reported to the compilers.

Printages are interesting to contemplate. Generally, within a given series and era, if one note has a printage of 50,000 and another has 200,000, the first is the rarer of the two. However, there are many low-printage notes that are readily available, and some high-printage notes can range from extremely rare to unknown. We can only marvel at the large quantities of Interest-Bearing Notes and Gold Certificates printed in the 1860s, which are of legendary rarity today.

Redemption Provisions

Continental Currency notes, issued from 1775 to 1779, were repudiated by the government, not an auspicious start for the United States of America. Today, a note of $1 face value or of $80 (the highest issue) is worth absolutely nothing if presented to the Treasury department. Large quantities of unwanted notes remained in the hands of citizens after the Revolutionary War, accounting for the generous supply available today.

In contrast, nearly all Interest-Bearing Notes, Compound Interest Treasury Notes, Gold Certificates, Silver Certificates of Deposit, Coin Notes, and other 19th-century federal paper money types were redeemed by the Treasury department at par once they were worn or became obsolete. Notes that were once common can be great rarities today. With 21,000 issued under the Act of 1863, $10,000 Gold Certificates were once plentiful, but as they were mostly held by banks and then redeemed, not a single example is known today.

The life of notes was often short. Today, it is estimated that a new $1 bill will last about 18 months. Likely, for most 19th-century denominations, a given variety, such as a particular signature combination, was largely redeemed within a decade of its issue, this being most true of the smaller denominations.

Hoards

Every once in a while, in an old bank vault or other location, a cache of bills comes to light. Often, these are Uncirculated and have sequential serial numbers. Although details are rarely announced, the existence of such can be deduced if a series of Uncirculated, sequentially numbered bills is published. Often, hoard notes are particularly choice and, further, offer the opportunity to acquire examples that might not otherwise be available, at least not easily. The Series of 1886 $5 Silver Certificate (the "Silver Dollar Note") is readily available in Uncirculated grade due to hoards. Conversely, $5 Original Series National Gold Bank Notes are unknown in that grade, as no hoards have ever been found.

While most hoards are dispersed quietly, perhaps from fear of disturbing the market, others have created a lot of attention in print.[2] A hoard from the First National Bank of Davenport, Iowa, was dispersed from the late 1950s until 1994, when the remainder, valued at about $600,000, was sold through Dean Oakes, a well-known currency specialist. From the 1860s onward, that bank saved thousands of dollars' face value of its own notes, storing them as "vault cash." Denominations ranged from $1 to $100.[3] There were many Original Series and Series of 1875 "Lazy 2" notes and even a Series of 1890 $100 "Watermelon Note." As if these was not enough, the hoard also included $2 Red Seal Legal Tender Notes from 1928 to 1953 with a face value of $18,000; 50 $500 bills; 50 $1,000 bills with consecutive serial numbers; one $5,000 bill; a type set of Original Series and Series of 1875 notes; and a group of Series of 1902, Red Seal $100 notes with the bank's imprint.

There was still more, including 10 bundles of the $5 Legal Tender Notes of 1862, 1863, and 1869, totaling 1,000 notes, with bank straps on them dated 1868 and 1871, these representing 10% of the $50,000 the bank was required to keep on hand to satisfy the requirements of its charter. Silver Certificates of 1880 and 1891 through the $100 value were also well represented, plus Legal Tender Notes of all series through the $100 denomination and $500 notes of the Series of 1880. National Bank Notes were there from all over the country. Several serial number 1 notes from the First National Bank of Davenport were on hand, as were other serial 1 notes from other Iowa banks. What a treasure trove!

The so-called Oat Bin Hoard ranks as another significant find.[4] In 1966 Dr. Howard Carter of Leawood, Kansas, purchased a fabulous cache of paper money comprising over $28,000 in face value that had been "brought to the Midwest from Virginia shortly after the War Between the States; they were later found in an oat bin that had not been emptied for many years."[5] Other notes were probably acquired at a later date. One of the foremost treasures in the cache was a $1,000 Legal Tender Note of the early 1860s. Dean Oakes and Don Jensen bought them all, a holding particularly rich in National Bank Notes, and over a period of time sold them to numismatists, with some of the rarer items offered in an auction by Hickman & Oakes (John Hickman and Dean Oakes) on November 24, 1979.

On May 31, 1971, R.W. Kirkland of Carrollton, Texas, was operating a backhoe as part of a storm sewer construction project, with two men assisting him. As a bucket load of earth was dumped, a jar tumbled out. Upon inspection it was found to contain a staggering $47,400 face value in Gold Certificates!

The databases compiled by Martin Gengerke, Don C. Kelly, and Track & Price list many notes that are close together in serial numbers, usually evidence of some hoard dispersed quietly years ago. Everyone benefits from the availability of such currency.

NUMISMATIC POPULARITY

Certain currency types and series have been popular for a long time, and in such instances, many Uncirculated notes exist from the early days. Nowhere is this more true than with Fractional Currency, which was avidly collected in the 1860s and 1870s, in an era when no one collected large-size notes. These were widely publicized in the *American Journal of Numismatics*, dealers' catalogs, and also in publications intended for stamp collectors. The last became interested as the first Postage Currency issued, predecessors to Fractional Currency, bore designs of current postage stamps. Accordingly, most standard varieties and proofs of Fractional Currency are plentiful today. Ironically, Confederate States of America notes, including large denominations, were avidly collected from the 1870s onward, when large-size federal notes were almost totally neglected!

Most lower-denomination small-size bills issued from the Series of 1928 (first issued in 1929) through the 1940s were saved by collectors and dealers, including bundles of popular varieties such as the $1 notes with HAWAII overprints and the special R and S red overprints (publicized in the *Numismatic Scrapbook Magazine* and other places). In the 1940s Aubrey and Adeline Bebee, dealers in Chicago who moved to Omaha in the 1950s, bought and sold large quantities of Uncirculated small-size notes when other professional numismatists did not stock them. Numismatists can be grateful for their foresight.

After about 1953, the collecting of small-size notes became very popular. As a result, even larger quantities of most lower-denomination bills from that time forward exist now. Bill Donlon, a Utica, New York, numismatist and theater operator, popularized small-size bills in the 1950s and 1960s and helped expand the market, especially for $1 to $10 notes. In sharp contrast, certain higher-denomination varieties of modern issues, such as $20, $50, and $100 notes, can range from scarce to rare in Uncirculated grades as the Bebees, Donlon, and others did not specialize in these values.

Today the Bureau of Engraving and Printing sells notes with special serial numbers and even star notes, charging a premium for them. It can be expected that these will remain easily available in the marketplace for years to come.

In summary, if a series was popular at the time of its issue, chances are excellent that high-grade examples will be plentiful on the market for years afterward. If a series was ignored in its time, unless there have been hoards, such notes can be extremely rare in high grades today.

POPULARITY WITH THE GENERAL PUBLIC

Apart from numismatic activity, some notes with particularly attractive designs were saved as souvenirs by the general public, such as the Series of 1896 Silver Certificate, the $1, $2, and $5 "Educational Notes." For any currency from any era, serial number 1 notes were attractive to bank tellers, bank officers, and others and were often retrieved and saved when recognized in circulation.

In early 1969 a rumor swept the country that new $1 Federal Reserve Notes with the signature combination of Granahan and Barr would become rare and valuable, as Treasurer Kathryn O'Hay Granahan and secretary of the Treasury Joseph Barr were in office together only from December 23, 1968, to January 20, 1969, or less than a month. A wild scramble ensued to get these notes, which, alas, kept being printed from old plates well after January 20. Today, such bills are extremely common.

"HARD MONEY" HIDDEN AS A PRECAUTION

This aspect mitigates *against* the survival of paper money. In all known historical scenarios, someone with a $20 note in one hand and a gold $20 double eagle in the other would spend the paper money first. Today, gold coins survive in much higher proportions to their mintages than notes do their printages. Consider that for the Series of 1878 $20 Silver Certificate of Deposit varieties the printage was about 174,000, from which only six notes are known today. For the 1878 Philadelphia Mint double eagle coins, 543,625 were minted, of which an estimated 8,000 to 11,000 exist today. This calculates to just 1 note in 29,000 known today, while 1 coin in about 54 or so remains for the double eagle. Stated another way, the note is over 500 times rarer!

Similarly, more people kept 1886 silver dollars than they did of Series of 1886 Silver Certificates. Many other examples could be cited. To be sure, there are some famous hoards of paper money, but their total numismatic value is less than 0.1% of the value of gold and silver coins that have been found hidden away.

A PLAN FOR SUCCESS
GETTING STARTED

If you are entering the field of paper money today and want to obtain the best quality and value for the money spent, here is what you might do:

First, get your bearings. Go through the front matter of this book and then look through the illustrations and read their captions. Chapters 1 to 5 are the most important. Then read the narrative before each denomination in the following chapters, such as the text at the start of the $1 listings, $2 listings, and so on. Even if you do not contemplate adding a certain note to your collection, read about it, examine the illustration, and gain familiarity with its aspects. There is no such thing as too much knowledge in the field of paper money or, for that matter, in most other walks of life. As you contemplate the appearance of the various notes, ask yourself these questions: Are there some that are particularly appealing? Are there curious aspects, such as a high-printage note described as a rarity? What do the different words, terms, and phrases on the note mean? With your budget in mind, review the prices to see if a nice note is affordable. Is there a series you might like to collect—such as all of the signature combinations in small-size $1 bills, or do you like star notes? Ask yourself two questions: "What can I learn that will *add value* to my purchases the next time I am at a convention or auction?" and "How can I be more aware?"

Start small. Visit a show or a dealer's shop. Review advertisements in numismatic magazines and newspapers and seek further information via catalogs and Internet listings. Buy one, two, or three notes by direct sale (not by auction or other bidding), being sure in advance that you can return the notes within a short time (say a week) if you don't like them or simply change your mind. Most dealers will allow this.

Subscribe to the monthly *Bank Note Reporter* (F+W Publications, Iola, Wisconsin), sign on for the bimonthly *Paper*

Money Values (Amos Press, Sidney, Ohio), and join the Society of Paper Money Collectors (publisher of *Paper Money* magazine, issued bimonthly). This will give you a lot of current reading material at low cost. This is the "wind" that will either fan your flame of interest into a blaze or snuff it out. Hopefully it will be the former.

A few weeks or a month or two later, consider if you like the currency you have already bought. Given the chance to start anew, with your present knowledge, would you buy the same things? If not, why not? Determine the extent of your interest—is it casual or do you find paper money to be really fascinating? Think of *collecting*, and don't let the word *investment* enter your mind! Old timers will tell you that if you go in as an investor in this or any other numismatic field, and do not take the time or effort to gain *knowledge*, likely you will have an unsatisfactory experience, even if you buy "choice" or "gem" examples. On the other hand, if you enter as a collector and buy slowly and carefully, the investment angle will take care of itself. This is a time-proven rule that is very hard for beginning buyers to understand.

Take stock of where you are. If you are not fascinated by paper money yet, then stop now. Try Morgan silver dollars, medals, Civil War tokens, or something else instead. However, if you have enjoyed yourself to this point, then by all means go further, but with caution.

Welcome to the field of collecting paper money! Enjoy the hobby, the notes you acquire, and the friendship of dealers and collectors who share your enthusiasm. Find out when and where shows are held. Go on the Internet and poke around on auction and direct-sale sites and other places. View, read, absorb.

Now is the time to build a small library. Check the bibliography section of this book and review the titles that interest you the most. Those in print can usually be bought from a dealer or members of the Professional Currency Dealers Association, or be found elsewhere on the Internet. Chain bookstores such as Barnes & Noble, Books-A-Million, and Borders are apt to have some paper money books in their hobby section, and you can browse through them.

FOUR STEPS TO SUCCESS
STEP 1: GRADE ASSIGNED

You are holding a piece of paper money in your hand. Or perhaps you see a note on the Internet. Should you buy it? Your first step is to look at the assigned grade of the note, which dealers usually provide by a label on the holder. The designation may be adjectival, such as Very Fine, or a combination of adjectival and numerical, such as EF-40 or Unc-63.

The assigned grade is simply the starting point in the buying process. This is one of the most important concepts for success. By this time you will have familiarized yourself with the grading of paper money (see chapter 4).

When you visit a dealer's shop or a convention or contemplate a catalog offering, have an approximate grade in mind for each note you are seeking. If you are looking for a

Series of 1896 $1 "Educational Note" (W-59 and W-60 in chapter 6), look up the market price, consider your budget, and then seek an example at the price level you have in mind. If you have $1,000 to spend, consider a high-grade circulated note. There is no sense looking at Unc-65 or higher pieces that you cannot afford (except to gain knowledge). On the other hand, if you have the inclination and can afford it, by all means, check out an example certified as Unc-65. In time you can make up a "want list" with the varieties and grades you are seeking.

No matter what grades you want, reject any notes that seem to be overgraded. This comment is with the realization that you will need some experience, for lacking this you will not know any better. The best way to gain experience is to visit a convention or a dealer's shop and look through as many notes as you can. This might range from only a few to several dozen or more. Indeed, I recommend this as *essential* before you spend a lot of money. Few dealers have deep inventories of the scarcer issues. At a convention the possibilities are greater. On the Internet you can see many notes offered, and it can be useful to learn by viewing those images, although photographs can be manipulated and often do not reveal problems that can be seen in person.

You will find that at a convention or visiting a coin shop, some dealers are happy to let you learn by examining notes in stock. Others may make it known that unless you are a "big buyer," they are wasting their time with you. Fortunately, more dealers are in the former class. If a dealer spends significant time with you, it is good policy to buy something—perhaps a book or two, or an album, or an inexpensive note. If at a later time you do become a buyer of scarcer notes, give that dealer some of your business. Building a good relationship with several favorite dealers will repay your effort in spades. This is a quid pro quo, or tit for tat, proposition. If a dealer keeps you happy by selling you nice notes for reasonable prices, you will keep the dealer happy by becoming a steady customer. A win-win situation for all involved.

Again, take your time. There will always be notes available for you to buy. An 1896 $1 "Educational Note" will be available next year at this time if you don't buy it now. To be sure, there are exceptions galore, such as among rare National Bank Notes. If a note is one of a kind in Don C. Kelly and James M. Kelly's *National Bank Note Census*, it may be a now-or-never opportunity. However, before leaping it would be a good idea to ask a dealer or two about an estimated market value.

In less time than you realize, you will learn the fundamentals of grading, how prices can vary, and other information. This advice may be repetitive, but revisiting an experience is always worthwhile. I absolutely guarantee that if you spend next weekend curled up with this book in your favorite easy chair, and then read through it again a month from now, there will be many new things to capture your attention the second time around.

With Step 1, with a note offered in the grade you are seeking, you have a candidate *for your further consideration*.

STEP 2: EYE APPEAL AT FIRST GLANCE

Now, the process becomes easier! At this point take closer look at the note you are thinking of buying. Is it "pretty"? Unless it is a rarity, it is virtually certain that if this note is not attractive, you will find another that is. Even a note at a circulated level such as VF-20 should be attractive within its grade. There are many really beautiful Very Fine notes. I promise!

Check the margins on both sides. The margins should be *parallel* to the design of the note—simply put, the margin should have the same width along its length, and not be distant from the design in one spot and close to it on another. Slanted margins should be avoided. The top and bottom margins can be of different sizes, as can the left and right margins. Each should have an ample amount of white space. There are exceptions, such as on $5 Original Series and Series of 1875 National Bank Notes, which were placed very close together on the printing plate (this was not done with other denominations in this series). Many such exceptions are mentioned under specific listings in this book. Again, there is no such thing as having too much knowledge.

Brightness is another extremely important aspect of the attractiveness of a note. The first thing to fade on an older note is the Treasury seal, especially if it is printed in red. It is important to know what the correct color should be. A good way to do this is to view multiple examples of the same type. Other colors, such as serial numbers and decorative overprints, can fade as well. Both sunlight and artificial light (particularly fluorescent) cause fading. With a few exceptions, notes were printed on bright white paper stock. Faded notes often have a yellowish cast, even if classified in high gem Uncirculated grades.

Among notes graded as Uncirculated, even at high numbers, there are some in which the ink used to print the green back has permeated through the paper to create the appearance of smudging on the face. Try to avoid these and acquire notes with completely bright paper, if notes in a particular series can be found thus. On many notes, especially small-size notes, it is common for extra specks and spatters of green ink to be in the white borders of the back, called offsets or transfers. Avoid these as well.

Even if the price of an offered note seems to be a super-bargain, cast it aside if it is not "pretty" or presents some doubt in your mind or is described with some mitigating conditions. A rule told to me by Tom Denly has guided me well, and it will be of equal value to you: If you have to say *but* when describing the appearance of a note, don't buy it.

Examples:

"It is a nice Unc-63 Silver Certificate, *but* the margins are uneven."

"This Continental Currency $5 note is as bright as I have ever seen, *but* the border is cut into the edge of the design."

"I've been looking for an nice About Uncirculated Series of 1902 Blue Seal, Plain Back note for my type set, and this one certainly is priced to be a bargain, *but* the signatures are faded."

"This 'Martha Washington' Silver Certificate is beautiful, and the grade of Unc-65 is what I want, *but* it is rather yellowish overall and seems to be somewhat faded."

If you hear yourself describing the note this way, stop right here. Stop considering this note, and go back to Step 1 and pick another note. You are acting the part of a connoisseur. Congratulations!

A defective note (poor margins, faded seal, etc.) graded as Unc-63, or with "exceptional paper quality," or with any other modifier, is still defective even if it is priced at *half* of the current market price! Do not be tempted by overgraded or ugly notes offered at "below wholesale" prices. Keep your checkbook in your pocket.

The good news is that with some exceptions among rare early notes and among National Bank Notes from a particular location, in time the market will offer many very nice notes for your contemplation. Also good news for those who own notes that do not pass the Step 2 test is that the majority of buyers don't care about eye appeal, and there is a ready market for such bills. As is true for coins, many buyers would rather acquire an Unc-65 note with a problem than a problem-free Unc-63 note. Not I. Hopefully not you either.

If the note is attractive to your eye and passes the first two tests with no *but*s needed, then in some distant year when time comes to sell it, the piece will be attractive to the eyes of other buyers too, an important aspect.

Now, with an attractive piece of currency in your hand, you have a candidate *for your further consideration.*

STEP 3: A CLOSER LOOK

At this point you have a note that you believe to be more or less in the adjectival or numerical grade assigned by the seller or, if you are in the fast lane, that is verified in that grade by your own experience. You also have for consideration one that has passed your test for excellent eye appeal, including good margins, bright paper (except for well-circulated notes), and original color.

The next step is to take out a magnifying glass and evaluate the details of the note. Hold the note up to the light, such as an incandescent bulb (but never the sun). See if there are any tiny holes (pinholes) or thin areas. Check also for areas of the paper that do not transmit light evenly. A dark or heavy area can indicate a repair, such as an expertly closed pinhole or added paper.

Examine the margins, especially the four corners of a note. On Uncirculated examples the corners should be sharp, not rounded. Although the state of the numismatic art has not yet progressed to the point at which information is available, if you can compare the margins to another note of the same variety, you may be able to discern if it has been trimmed. For National Bank Notes that were trimmed by cashiers using shears or other paper cutters, allowance has to be made for some differences. However, even on an early large-size National note the margins should not be trimmed into the border of the design.

Check the paper for other problems. If it is not in a certified holder you can do as experts do: for a note offered as

Uncirculated, hold it by each end, the note horizontal, and push one end about 25% toward the other, so the note gently bends upward. If a fold has been pressed out, the curve will not be even, but will show a slight peak. Also by gently handling the note you can tell if the note has been laundered so as to make the paper somewhat limp, or starched so as to make it slightly heavier and less flexible. If you have a friend who is an expert, ask him or her to evaluate the note. However, many professionals do not consider it to be their business to pass judgment on the grading and pricing of their competitors' offerings. They are busy enough with their own clientele, and, besides, the easiest way to alienate another dealer is to degrade his or her merchandise.

Remember that grade is important, but other factors can be equally or more important. There are many great notes out there that are assigned such grades as F-12, VF-20, EF-40, and other designations than Uncirculated. These are well worth investigating and sometimes offer exceptional value for the price paid. Besides, in some series you can buy *five* problem-free EF-40 notes, attractive and bright, for the same cost as a single Unc-63.

Now, after you have closely examined the note you are considering, give it the *but* test again!

If the note has passed this and the two preceding tests, it is ready *for further consideration*. Chances are very good that you are holding a very nice example in your hands!

STEP 4: ESTABLISHING A FAIR MARKET PRICE

If you've done everything right, you have a note that is correctly graded, of excellent eye appeal, and is a poster example of its assigned grade, whether it be VG-8, VF-30, EF-45, or Unc-65. Now how to determine the price you should pay?

For starters, use one or several handy market guides for a ballpark estimate, starting with this book. *The Bank Note Reporter* publishes market values each month, and *Paper Money Values* appears bimonthly, both giving suggestions and price updates. The *Currency Dealer Newsletter* offers valuable data for certified notes. Other reference books, such as the Friedberg, Hessler-Chambliss, Schwartz-Lindquist, and other guides (see the bibliography) are valuable. The Martin Gengerke study and Track & Price both give historical prices for notes identified by their serial numbers and plate letters, often revealing how a particular note was graded when it was sold years ago. Again, there is no such thing as too much information. If you are thinking of spending, say, $1,000 or more for notes each year, then spending a couple hundred dollars total on subscriptions and books simply has to be the bargain of a lifetime.

Dealers can often provide insights as to overall market strength for a given variety, its availability, and more. Consult with them (but don't forget to put some business their way). A dealer with a good reputation (you can ask around about this) can be a very valuable asset. Auction estimates and prices can be useful. For most of the more available types in this book, current market information is readily available.

If the note in your hands is not a rarity, then buy it if it is at or near the market price. It is often the situation that very strong prices are asked for bills in grades above Unc-65. Upon inspection there may be very little difference in appearance from that of, say, a Unc-63 or 64 note. Be very careful about paying big premiums for small differences in grade, bearing in mind that grading is simply an opinion. Don't hesitate to ask a collector or dealer friend about any stiff premium, to see if there is a logical explanation, or if the added premium is worthwhile.

Ideally, you will now be able to buy a piece of paper money that is a first-class example of its assigned grade, is attractive to own, has no *but* exceptions, and costs a fair market price.

Congratulations! You are a smart buyer! You own a great note!

PATIENCE AND PRACTICE

If you follow each of these steps, not only will you become a smart buyer, but you will also gain confidence and be well on your way to truly enjoying your paper-money-collecting experience.

At the outset, buy notes that are less expensive. In that way, if you make a mistake, it will be a small one. Even if you can afford it, there is no sense starting your collection by buying a Watermelon Note (W-3630) or other classic rarity. Every collection has common notes as well as scarce ones. Buy common notes first.

Connoisseurship takes time. This is desirable, as it adds to the enjoyment of collecting. Buyers who rush into the market and buy willy-nilly soon burn out. Their interest fades, and they leave the hobby. The more time you take, the more you read, the more you learn, the more you will benefit.

PAPER MONEY AS AN INVESTMENT

Over a long period of time, a carefully formed collection of high-quality U.S. paper money has nearly always yielded an excellent financial return. Ample verification of this can be obtained by reviewing auction catalogs from 10 or more years ago or checking retail listings in magazines or the valuations in back numbers of reference books.

Given here are a series of vignettes—not the bank-note kind, but glimpses of history. Selected offerings from a generation or two ago are cross-referenced with Whitman and Friedberg numbers. Values of the older time are given together with updated, current prices.

While the primary emphasis of collecting paper money should always be enjoyment, the fact remains that a collection gathered with connoisseurship and care and held for the long term has usually proved to be a superb financial investment upon its sale, as mentioned. To many currency specialists, this is the icing on the cake. At the same time, it is important to be aware that not all notes have gone up in value; some have decreased. However, the overall trend has been upward in the past.

A 1966 OFFERING OF SERIAL NUMBER 1 NOTES

A dramatic example of price appreciation is provided by the full-page advertisement of William A. Philpott Jr. in *The Numismatist* from January 1966. This Texas collector and dealer usually priced his paper money aggressively, but delivered rarity and quality. This particular offering was of large-size National Bank Notes with serial number 1. This excerpt from a much longer listing includes notes from many different states in different grades. Valuations are not particularly related to signature combinations (per Whitman and Friedberg numbers), but to location. The rare Mississippi note provides an excellent illustration. Modern prices provided by Lyn F. Knight illustrate the advance in values since 1966:

California, Colton: First National Bank, serial number 1 • Whitman-767, Friedberg-597 • $5 Series of 1902, Date Back • *1966:* F $30 • *Today:* $35,000

Connecticut, Meriden: Meriden National Bank, serial number 1 • W-765, F-595 • $5 Series of 1902, Date Back • *1966:* EF $70 • *Today:* $9,000

Illinois, Lincoln: First National Bank, serial number 1 • W-2863, F-515 • $50 Series of 1882, Brown Back • *1966:* Unc $500 • *Today:* $75,000

Indiana, Fowler: First National Bank, serial number 1 • W-1371, F-490 • $10 Series of 1882, Brown Back • *1966:* Unc $150 • *Today:* $5,000

Iowa, Chariton: Lucas County National Bank, serial number 1 • W-2119, F-649 • $20 National Bank Note, Series of 1902, Blue Seal, Date Back • *1966:* EF $300 • *Today:* $12,000

Kansas, Wichita: 4th National Bank, serial number 1 • W-757, F-589 • $5 Series of 1902, Red Seal • *1966:* Unc $75 • *Today:* $10,000

Massachusetts, Fitchburg: Safety Fund National Bank, serial number 1 • W-765, F-595 • $5 Series of 1902, Date Back • *1966:* Unc $75 • *Today:* $12,000

Michigan, St. Johns: St. Johns National Bank, serial number 1 • W-2117, F-621 • $20 National Bank Note, Series of 1902, Blue Seal, Date Back • *1966:* Unc $225 • *Today:* $12,500

Mississippi, Gulfport: First National Bank, serial number 1 • W-1413, F-621 • $10 Series of 1902, Blue Seal, Date Back • *1966:* Unc $150 • *Today:* $65,000

New Jersey, Metuchen: Metuchen National Bank, serial number 1 • W-1413, F-621 • $10 Series of 1902, Blue Seal, Date Back • *1966:* Unc $175 • *Today:* $8,000

Pennsylvania, Mount Pleasant: First National Bank, serial number 1 • W-1360, F-479 • $10 Series of 1882, Brown Back • *1966:* VF $90 • *Today:* $6,000

Vermont, Lyndonville: Lyndonville National Bank, serial number 1 • W-765, F-595 • $5 Series of 1902, Date Back • *1966:* Unc $150 • *Today:* $17,000

West Virginia, Cameron: First National Bank, serial number 1 • W-1371, F-490 • $10 Series of 1882, Brown Back • *1966:* EF $100 • *Today:* $11,000

Wisconsin, Manitowoc: First National Bank, serial number 1 • W-1427, F-631 • $10 Series of 1902, Blue Seal, Plain Back • *1966:* Unc $75 • *Today:* $4,500

THE DONLON COLLECTION SALE OF 1971

On May 22, 1971, William P. Donlon, a well-known collector, dealer, researcher, and to me a fine friend, sold his personal reference collection in a mail-bid offering. *New* was the term he used to describe what has been changed to *Unc* here, the two being the same. Given below are prices realized and modern values. Whitman and Friedberg numbers are cross-referenced, so you can find them quickly if you want to look them up for more information.

Large-Size Notes

$1 1874 Legal Tender Note • W-14, F-19 • *1971:* Unc $125 • *Today:* $1,350

$1 1917 Legal Tender Note • Purchased from Abe Kosoff in 1931, the first year Donlon collected notes • W-38, F-38 • *1971:* Unc $38.50 • *Today:* $325

$1 1896 Silver Certificate • "Educational Note" • W-59, F-224 • *1971:* Unc $110 • *Today:* $2,250

$1 1890 Treasury or Coin Note • W-81, F-348 • *1971:* Unc $385 • *Today:* $6,200

$2 1869 Legal Tender Note • "Rainbow Note" • W-310, F-42 • *1971:* Unc $275 • *Today:* $6,300

$2 1896 Silver Certificate • "Educational Note" • W-368, F-248 • *1971:* Unc $155 • *Today:* $6,250

$2 1918 Federal Reserve Bank Note • Minneapolis • W-425-I, F-772 • *1971:* Unc $145 • *Today:* $3,400

$5 1861 Demand Note • W-606, F-1a • Payable in New York, "for the" handwritten • *1971:* VG–F $700 • *Today:* $40,000

$5 1861 Demand Note • W-607, F-1 • Payable in New York, "for the" printed • *1971:* VF–EF $750 • *2007:* $138,000 in CAA sale

$5 1875 Legal Tender Note • W-661, F-75 • "Mr. Grinnell said, 'You will be proud to own this note, in mint condition.'" • *1971:* Unc $160 • *Today:* $35,000

$5 1896 Silver Certificate • "Educational Note" • W-800, F-269 • *1971:* Unc $460 • *Today:* $10,500

$5 National Gold Bank Note • First National Gold Bank of San Francisco, Original Series • W-690, F-1136 • *1971:* EF $850 • *Today:* $45,000

$10 1861 Demand Note • W-1211, F-8a • Payable in Boston, "for the" handwritten • *1971:* G–VG, estimated at $750; unsold as there was "no bid" • *1990:* $17,600 in Stack's sale

$10 1864 Compound Interest Treasury Note • W-1230, F-190 • *1971:* EF $1,875 • *Today:* $17,500

$10 1890 Treasury or Coin Note • W-1521, F-367 • *1971:* Unc $550 • *Today:* $8,500

$10 1901 Legal Tender Note • "Bison Note" • W-1294, F-114 • *1971:* Unc $155 • *Today:* $5,250

$20 1864 Compound Interest Treasury Note • W-1950, F-191 • *1971:* F $1,650 • *2007:* $29,900 in CAA sale

$20 1878 Silver Certificate • W-2153, F-307 • Autographed signature of A.U. Wyman • *1971:* VG $1,000 • *2005:* $10,925 in CAA sale

$20 1880 Silver Certificate • W-2170, F-309 • *1971:* EF $155 • *Today:* $17,000

$50 1869 Legal Tender Note • W-2800, F-151 • *1971:* Unc $3,500 • *2005:* $149,500 in Knight sale

$50 1880 Legal Tender Note • W-2810, F-161 • *1971:* Unc $560 • *Today:* $20,000

$50 1918 Federal Reserve Bank Note • St. Louis • W-3030, F-831 • *1971:* Unc $2,850 • *Today:* $35,000

$100 1863 Legal Tender Note • Cover note on the Donlon book, *United States Large Size Paper Money 1861 to 1923* • W-3436, F-167a • *1971:* AU $2,350 • *2006:* Unc-63 $184,000 in CAA sale

$100 1869 Legal Tender Note • W-3480, F-168 • *1971:* Unc $3,100 • *1998:* $44,000 in Knight sale

$100 1890 Treasury or Coin Note • Famous "Watermelon Note" • W-3630, F-377 • *1971:* VF–EF $3,200 • *Today:* $95,000

$100 1902 Red Seal, National Bank Note • First National Bank of Porto Rico; "Unique!" territorial • W-3570, F-686 • *1971:* VF–EF $8,750 • *Today:* $16,000

Small-Size Notes

$1 Series of 1928 Legal Tender Note • Woods-Woodin • W-140, F-1500 • *1971:* Unc $152.50 • *Today:* $400

$1 Series of 1935-A Silver Certificate, red R surcharge • W-159, F-1609 • *1971:* Unc $73.50 • *Today:* $750

$1 Series of 1935-A Silver Certificate, red S surcharge • W-160, F-1610 • *1971:* Unc $62 • *Today:* $675

$1 Series of 1935-A Silver Certificate, Yellow Seal • Star note • W-162★, F-2306★ • *1971:* Unc $200 • *Today:* $3,250

$2 Series of 1928 Legal Tender Note • Tate-Mellon • W-500, F-1501 • *1971:* Unc $175 • *Today:* $140

$5 Series of 1928 Legal Tender Note • Woods-Mellon, trophy note with serial B10000000A • W-1000, F-1525 • *1971:* Unc $156 • *Today:* $125

$5 Series of 1929 Federal Reserve Bank Note • New York • W-1050-B, F-1850B • *1971:* Unc $22.50 • *Today:* $350

$5 Series of 1953-A Silver Certificate • Priest-Humphrey, repeating serial F02020202A • W-1108, F-1656 • *1971:* Unc $55 • *Today:* $30

$5 Series of 1928 Federal Reserve Note • Philadelphia • W-1118-C, F-1950C • *1971:* Unc $37.50 • *Today:* $275

$5 Series of 1934 Federal Reserve Note with HAWAII overprint • W-1140-L, F-2301 • *1971:* Unc $70 • *Today:* $750

$5 Series of 1950-D Federal Reserve Note • New York • W-1166-B, F-1965B • *1971:* Unc $6 • *Today:* $25

$10 Series of 1928 Gold Certificate • Chicago • W-1710, F-2400 • *1971:* Unc $73 • *Today:* $750

$10 Series of 1933 Silver Certificate • Julian-Woodin, low serial A00000444A • W-1745, F-1700 • *1971:* Unc $1,400 • *Today:* $20,000

$10 Series of 1928 Federal Reserve Note • Cleveland • W-1800-D, F-2000D • *1971:* Unc $21 • *Today:* $350

$10 Series of 1950-A Federal Reserve Note • Dallas, star note • W-1815-K★, F-2011K★ • *1971:* Unc $32 • *Today:* $300

$10 Series of 1963 Federal Reserve Note • Chicago • W-1820-G, F-2016G • *1971:* Unc $20 • *Today:* $45

$20 Series of 1928 Gold Certificate • Chicago • W-2450, F-2402 • *1971:* Unc $47 • *Today:* $825

$20 Series of 1929 Federal Reserve Bank Note • Minneapolis • W-2438-I, F-1870I • *1971:* Unc $62 • *Today:* $300

$20 Series of 1928 Federal Reserve Note • Cleveland, star note • W-2500-D★, F-2050D★ • *1971:* Unc $42 • *Today:* $1,750

$20 Series of 1928-A Federal Reserve Note • Boston • W-2501-A, F-2051A • *1971:* Unc $75 • *Today:* $800

$20 Series of 1950-A Federal Reserve Note • New York • W-2531-B, F-2060B • *1971:* Unc $30 • *Today:* $55

$50 Series of 1928 Gold Certificate • Chicago • W-3050, F-2404 • *1971:* Unc $104 • *Today:* $2,500

$50 Series of 1929 Federal Reserve Bank Note • Cleveland • W-3043-D, F-1880D • *1971:* Unc $80 • *Today:* $350

$50 Series of 1928 Federal Reserve Note • St. Louis • W-3060-H, F-2100H • *1971:* Unc $60 • *Today:* $700

$100 Series of 1928 Gold Certificate • Chicago • W-3818, F-2405 • *1971:* AU $120 • *Today:* $2,750

$100 Series of 1966 Legal Tender Note • Granahan-Fowler, trophy note with serial A00000016A; cover note for Donlon book on small-size currency • W-3800, F-1550 • *1971:* Unc $190 • *Today:* $450

$100 Series of 1928-A Federal Reserve Note • Chicago • W-3821-G, F-2151G • *1971:* Unc $120 • *Today:* $325

6

$1 NOTES

LARGE SIZE

Made in large quantities ever since the first Legal Tender Notes of the summer of 1862, bills of the $1 denomination have been plentiful in commerce through to the present day. Every once in a while a movement starts to eliminate the paper dollar and create a coin substitute. The theory is that a dollar bill, which may last only 18 months in active circulation, could be replaced with a metal dollar that would last 10 years or more. The Susan B. Anthony dollars launched in 1979 were not a success in commerce, nor were the Sacagawea dollars of 2000 or the Presidential dollars commencing in 2007. In the meantime, the paper dollar continues to be as useful and popular as ever; even vending machines include bill acceptors.

From a collecting viewpoint, large-size $1 bills are wonderfully diverse in their designs and, for most early types, are quite affordable. The main collecting emphasis is on basic designs and types, although signature combinations, Treasury seal variations, and other changes can be fascinating to explore.

LEGAL TENDER NOTES
(Also Known as United States Notes)

The early $1 bills of the Legal Tender type bear the portrait of secretary of the Treasury Salmon P. Chase, who was living at the time. The total printage of the $1 denomination amounted to 28,351,348 notes. Smaller quantities were printed of other denominations in the Legal Tender series, but their total face value was higher.

On Legal Tender Notes, the portrait of George Washington was selected for the $1 bill beginning with the Series of 1869, this also being one of the famous "Rainbow Notes." After that time, the father of our country was featured intermittently on large-size notes of this denomination issued in different series.

Series of 1862

The first federal $1 bills were the Legal Tender Notes, Series of 1862, each with a bright green back (illus. on p. 108ff.). The face, back, and tint plates for the $1 Series of 1862 Legal

Tender Notes were engraved by the National Bank Note Company. Printing was shared by American and National.[1]

Treasury signatures of Chittenden and Spinner were printed on the face by using a separate plate and a special ink. Treasury seals were added by the National Currency Bureau in Washington, D.C. The PATENTED APRIL 23RD 1860 imprint refers to the "cycloidal configurations" patent granted to James MacDonough, which was supposed to deter counterfeiting.

The face has the portrait of then-secretary of the Treasury Salmon P. Chase at the left, a counter at the lower center with spaces for the denomination, 1, 2, or 3, to be highlighted (here the 1; the inclusion of the 3 indicates that the Treasury considered issuing a $3 note, a popular denomination at the time with state-chartered banks, but this did not come to pass).

The back is printed in green, another in the greenback series, and has the denomination and redemption information. The last is the so-called Second Obligation: "This note is a Legal Tender for all debts public and private, except for duties on imports and interest on the public debt, and is receivable in payment of all loans made to the United States."

There is a general uniformity of color and appearance, but differences in motifs, across all denominations in the Series of 1862 and 1863 Legal Tender bills. The $1 notes were made in large quantities and are readily collectible as a basic type today. The bold signature of F.E. Spinner printed on the notes—the most dramatic of any Treasury individual—has always been popular. The paper quality of these bills was excellent, and many bright white notes survive today. Each note has a printed series number on the face as well as a serial number. These notes were issued in 284 numbered series, all but the incomplete final one running from serial 1 to 100,000, as clearly shown in correspondence between the Treasury department and the American and National banknote companies. Research by Doug Murray on the various denominations of early Legal Tender Notes is included here, the first time this has been available in a single source. Several scarcities and rarities are included in the $1 listings.

The size of the red serial numbers can vary; most are large, but some are small.

SERIES OF 1862

$1 Legal Tender Note, Series of 1862 (W-2). Featured is a portrait of Treasury secretary Salmon P. Chase, as on all in this series. NATIONAL BANK NOTE COMPANY and AMERICAN BANK NOTE COMPANY are printed above the lower border. W-2 is the second variety printed. The lower left serial number was later overprinted by the Treasury seal, as also seen on W-1. This note is imprinted SERIES 1.

Detail of the SERIES 1 imprint on W-2.

Detail of the variant seal (W-2) without the closely spaced radial lines.

Whitman-1 • Friedberg-17 • First Legal Tender $1 notes printed; NATIONAL BANK NOTE CO. and AMERICAN BANK NOTE CO. N.Y. above lower border; left serial number overprinted on Treasury seal; earliest part of Series 1 • 5,000 (estimated printage)

Recorded population: 5 • *Highest graded:* VF-20 • *Commentary:* The first issued note, serial 1, series 1, plate a, VF, survives and for many years was in the Chase Manhattan Bank Money Museum. These are very rare today; the relatively few examples known are in circulated grades. • *Selected information:* Smythe (3/1991), series 1, serial 39, plate C (given hereafter as S1/39/C), F–VF, $600. Heritage (4/2008), S1/1684/D, VF–EF, $48,875.

VG-8	F-12	VF-20
$12,000	$17,000	$25,000

W-2 • F-17b • As preceding, but with ABNCo monogram added near the right border; left serial number overprinted on Treasury seal; Treasury seal without inner border of radial parallel lines; early part of Series 1 • 7,000 (est.)

Recorded population: 6 • *Highest graded:* EF-40 • *Commentary:* Very scarce in all grades • *Selected information:* Heritage (4/2006), S1/2818/B, VF, $6,325, resold for $12,011 by buyer. Denly offering (2007), S1/10341/A, VG, $14,500.

VG-8	F-12	VF-20	EF-40
$8,500	$12,000	$16,000	—

W-3 • F-17b • As preceding; Treasury seal with inner border of radial parallel lines; Early part of Series 1 • 12,000 (est.)

Recorded population: 1 • *Selected information:* Very scarce in all grades. The known note grades VF–EF.

W-4 • F-17a • As W-3, but with left serial number overprinted on denomination; Series 1 to 166 • 16,512,000 (est.)

Estimated population: 450 to 600 • *Highest graded:* Unc.

VG-8	F-12	VF-20	EF-40	AU-50	Unc-60	Unc-63	Unc-65
$220	$400	$700	$980	$1,600	$1,850	$2,350	$5,000

W-5 • F-16 • NATIONAL BANK NOTE COMPANY twice above lower border; no ABNCo monogram; with 1857 patent date; left serial number overprinted on denomination; SERIES printed to the left of center; Series 166 to 174 • 813,224 (est.)

Estimated population: 150 to 180 • *Highest graded:* Unc.

VG-8	F-12	VF-20	EF-40	AU-50	Unc-60	Unc-63	Unc-65
$350	$500	$900	$1,250	$2,200	$2,800	$3,300	$6,000

W-6 • F-16 • NATIONAL BANK NOTE COMPANY twice above lower border; no ABNCo monogram; without 1857 patent date; left serial number overprinted on denomination; SERIES printed to the left of center; Series 174 to 234 • 5,850,776 (est.)

Estimated population: 500 to 700 • *Highest graded:* Unc.

VG-8	F-12	VF-20	EF-40	AU-50	Unc-60	Unc-63	Unc-65
$220	$400	$700	$980	$1,600	$1,850	$2,350	$5,000

SERIES OF 1862,
continued

$1 Legal Tender Note, Series of 1862, another variety (W-9). NATIONAL BANK NOTE COMPANY is imprinted twice above the lower border.

Detail of the SERIES 251 and serial number imprints on a W-9 note. With each series the serial numbering sequence began anew at 1.

Detail of the standard Treasury seal (W-9 and others) with a border of tiny, closely spaced radial lines outside of the shield, but inside of the circle with the inscription.

Back of a $1 Legal Tender Note, Series of 1862, with the Second Obligation wording, as used on all.

W-7 • F-17a • Printed within the production of W-6, Series 199 to 204; NATIONAL BANK NOTE CO. and AMERICAN BANK NOTE CO. N.Y. above lower border; ABNCo monogram near center at right edge of face; no. 1857 patent date; left serial number over denomination; SERIES printed; face plate numbers 17-19-20-22-24 only • 50,000 (est.)

Estimated population: 20 to 25 • *Highest graded:* VF-35.

VG-8	F-12	VF-20
$350	$500	$900

W-8 • F-16a • Printed within the production of W-6, Series 204 to 219; NATIONAL BANK NOTE CO. twice above lower border; ABNCo monogram at right end;

left serial number over denomination; face plate numbers 17-19-20-22-24 only • 150,000 (est.)

Estimated population: 60 to 65 • *Highest graded:* Unc.

VG-8	F-12	VF-20	EF-40	AU-50	Unc-60	Unc-63	Unc-65
$350	$500	$900	$1,250	$2,200	$2,800	$3,300	$7,500

W-9 • F-16 • NATIONAL BANK NOTE COMPANY twice above lower border; left serial number overprinted on denomination; SERIES printed to the right of center; Series 235 to 284 • 4,946,000

Estimated population: 800 to 1,000 • *Highest graded:* Unc.

VG-8	F-12	VF-20	EF-40	AU-50	Unc-60	Unc-63	Unc-65
$220	$400	$700	$980	$1,600	$1,850	$2,350	$5,000

Series of 1869

The next major type, the Series of 1869 Legal Tender Note, features George Washington at the center of the face, the first appearance on federal note of an image that still greets us on $1 bills today. His portrait was very common on notes of state-chartered banks, dating back to at least 1803. To the left is a vignette of Christopher Columbus sighting land, "discovering" America.

The star at the serial number is a decoration (not a designation for a replacement note, as stars indicated on most later issues). The portrait was engraved by Alfred Sealey from the famous painting by Gilbert Stuart (the standard source for other Washington images on federal paper money, including the portrait used on $1 notes today).

This issue is famously known as the "Rainbow Note," named for its blue-tinted paper and colorful overprinting of red and green. A large pink Treasury seal is at the right. Serial numbers have A, B, K, V, and Z prefixes. Other of the lower denominations in the Series of 1869, the $2, $5, and $10, are also known as "Rainbow Notes."

The back is printed in green and has the NATIONAL BANK NOTE CO. N.Y. imprint at the bottom center. As a class, Series of 1869 notes were issued from October 19, 1869, to July 25, 1874.

$1 Legal Tender Note, Series of 1869 (W-11), the famous "Rainbow Note." This colorful type is distinguished by the light green overprint at the top of the note and the green frame around the serial number at the lower left.

Detail of the left side of the face. No one is sure what the Great Discoverer actually looked like. Accordingly, representations of him on paper money, medals, and coins vary widely. The 1866 patent to the right of the D plate letter refers to the J.M. Willcox & Co. patent for security bank-note paper with fibers.

Detail of the right side of the Treasury seal, with the tiny seal number 26 in pink, and, above it, the plate letter and number D2. Plate identification letters and numbers are varied among 19th-century issues and have not been widely published.

Back of a $1 Legal Tender Note, Series of 1869, the only use of this design.

W-11 • F-18 • Allison-Spinner (1869–1875) • Large pink seal with scalloped border • 41,868,000

Estimated population: 1,000 to 1,400 • *Highest graded:* Unc • *Commentary:* These are plentiful on the market today, although the demand for higher-grade examples has made them somewhat elusive at those levels. The "Rainbow Note" is one of the most sought-after 19th-century issues.

VG-8	F-12	VF-20	EF-40	AU-50	Unc-60	Unc-63	Unc-65
$300	$600	$950	$1,850	$2,700	$3,100	$3,400	$8,000

Series of 1874

The Series of 1869 designs evolved into the later series issued from 1874 through the Series of 1917, which retained the same face motifs but a completely new back. These notes from W-14 onward display variations in the Treasury seal, signature combinations, and other elements, and lack green on the face (therefore they are not as colorful as W-11 and are not called "Rainbow Notes"). Notes W-14 to W-22 have a small pink Treasury seal to the left of the portrait and a large oval pink cartouche in the field to the right, with DOLLAR superimposed over ONE. All have a small red Treasury seal with a spiked border.

The back is printed in green, with an open space to the left (usually with prominent silk fibers) and the obligation and counterfeiting clause to the right. Near the bottom border COLUMBIAN BANK NOTE CO. appears twice. As a class, Series of 1874 notes were issued from July 13, 1874, to Sept. 13, 1875.

Generally only a single note of the later large-size Legal Tender bills (the 1874 to 1917 issues) is collected to illustrate the type. The specialist can go further and have a field day seeking over 20 varieties of Treasury seals, overprints, serial number colors, and signature combinations. Certain of these range from scarce to rare, but the premium charged is modest, as this method of collecting by systematic acquisition is not presently in the limelight.

W-14 • F-19 • Allison-Spinner (1869–1875) • Small pink seal with spiked border • 18,988,000

Estimated population: 225 to 250 • *Highest graded:* Unc • *Commentary:* Readily collectible, and worth considering for its distinctive 1874 imprint, although this and others are usually collected as a design type.

VG-8	F-12	VF-20	EF-40	AU-50	Unc-60	Unc-63	Unc-65
$140	$195	$325	$660	$900	$1,100	$1,350	$2,400

SERIES OF 1874

$1 Legal Tender Note, Series of 1874 (W-14). This is the only variety within this short-lived series.

Back design of the $1 Legal Tender Note, Series of 1874, a motif used through the Series of 1917 (with imprint variations).

Series of 1875

The Series of 1875 notes W-15 to W-19 with the Allison-New signature combination were first printed with a pink series letter on the face at the border in a circle at the lower right, as SERIES / A / 1875. Serial numbers are red, and the small spiked Treasury seal is pink. The back is as in the previous issue, with COLUMBIAN BANK NOTE CO. imprinted twice. As a class, Series of 1875 notes were issued from July 20, 1875, to June 20, 1879. The order of issuance of the varieties, which is different from certain other texts, is from research by Doug Murray.

The "Doubled Plate at OF 1875" error was first published by Currency Auctions of America in their sale of October 27, 1995, lot 1354. It is found on plate 35, position B. The estimate of known specimens is from the Martin Gengerke census. These will likely change as more people become aware of the variety and inspect their notes.

W-15 • F-21 • Allison-New (1875–1876) • SERIES / A / 1875 imprint in pink • 1,000,000

Estimated population: 30 to 35 • *Highest graded:* Unc • *Commentary:* Somewhat scarce overall, especially so in Uncirculated grades.

VG-8	F-12	VF-20	EF-40	AU-50	Unc-60	Unc-63	Unc-65
$850	$1,400	$2,100	$2,900	$3,400	$4,100	$4,650	$10,000

W-16 • F-22 • SERIES / B / 1875 imprint in pink • 1,000,000

Estimated population: 26 to 32 • *Highest graded:* Unc • *Commentary:* Same comment as preceding.

VG-8	F-12	VF-20	EF-40	AU-50	Unc-60	Unc-63
$1,000	$1,550	$2,500	$3,400	$4,000	$5,500	$6,500

W-16 Doubled Plate, Series B • Doubled Plate at OF 1875; plate 35, position B

Recorded population: 5 • *Highest graded:* CU • *Commentary:* Very rare at present, but it is likely that many notes of this general type have not been checked for this feature.

W-17 • F-23 • SERIES / C / 1875 imprint in pink • 1,000,000

Estimated population: 42 to 46 • *Highest graded:* Unc • *Commentary:* Scarce, but collectible, including in high grades.

VG-8	F-12	VF-20	EF-40	AU-50	Unc-60	Unc-63	Unc-65
$800	$1,275	$1,850	$2,600	$3,100	$3,750	$4,400	$5,000

W-17 Doubled Plate, Series C • Doubled Plate at OF 1875; plate 35, position B • Likely printed, none seen

W-18 • F-24 • SERIES / D / 1875 imprint in pink • 1,000,000

Estimated population: 18 to 20 • *Highest graded:* Unc • *Commentary:* Very scarce in all grades, rare in Uncirculated.

VG-8	F-12	VF-20	EF-40	AU-50	Unc-60	Unc-63
$1,000	$1,750	$2,700	$3,750	$4,400	$6,000	$10,000

W-18 Doubled Plate, Series D • Doubled Plate at OF 1875; plate 35, position B • Likely printed, none seen

W-19 • F-25 • SERIES / E / 1875 imprint in pink • 1,000,000

Estimated population: 26 to 30 • *Highest graded:* Unc • *Commentary:* Very scarce in all grades, rare in Uncirculated.

VG-8	F-12	VF-20	EF-40	AU-50	Unc-60	Unc-63
$900	$1,450	$2,300	$3,250	$4,000	$5,500	$6,500

W-19 Doubled Plate, Series E • Doubled Plate at OF 1875; plate 35, position B

Recorded population: 2 • *Highest graded:* AU • *Commentary:* Exceedingly rare, but not widely recognized.

SERIES OF 1875

$1 Legal Tender Note, Series of 1875 (W-15), with Series / A / 1875 printed in pink ink.

Detail of the "Doubled Plate, series B" error on the face of a variety of W-16. All with this error are from face plate 35, position B.

W-20 • F-20 • No pink series letter imprint • 9,000,000

Estimated population: 225 to 250 • *Highest graded:* Unc • *Commentary:* Plentiful in all grades.

VG-8	F-12	VF-20	EF-40	AU-50	Unc-60	Unc-63	Unc-65
$125	$175	$275	$500	$800	$975	$1,100	$2,150

W-20 Doubled Plate, No Series Imprint • Doubled Plate at OF 1875; plate 35, position B

Recorded population: 4 • *Highest graded:* CU.

W-21 • F-26 • Allison-Wyman (1876–1877) • 12,212,000

Estimated population: 450 to 550 • *Highest graded:* Unc • *Commentary:* Plentiful in all grades.

VG-8	F-12	VF-20	EF-40	AU-50	Unc-60	Unc-63	Unc-65
$135	$180	$250	$450	$675	$925	$1,050	$2,100

Series of 1878

The face and back designs are as previously described, but with SERIES OF 1878 added at the top border of the back and PRINTED AT THE BUREAU, ENGRAVING & PRINTING at the bottom. The Columbian imprints remain. The serial numbers are in red.

W-22 • F-27 • Allison-Gilfillan (1877–1878) • Small pink spiked seal; very last printed had a security paper

change from a vertical to a horizontal blue stain with fibers across entire length • 12,512,000

Estimated population: 350 to 400 • *Highest graded:* Unc • *Commentary:* Plentiful in all grades.

VG-8	F-12	VF-20	EF-40	AU-50	Unc-60	Unc-63	Unc-65
$115	$170	$250	$425	$650	$900	$1,100	$2,250

Series of 1880

The face design (illus. on p. 114) is similar to the preceding. There are three back imprint styles:

Back Style 1: With COLUMBIAN BANK NOTE CO. imprinted twice at the bottom edge of the design (style used on Series 1874, 1875, and 1878). Now with SERIES OF 1880 in the top margin and PRINTED AT THE BUREAU, ENGRAVING AND PRINTING in the bottom margin. Used on W-23 Back Style 1.

Back Style 2: As preceding, but now with SERIES OF 1880 vertically in the left margin and PRINTED AT THE BUREAU, ENGRAVING AND PRINTING vertically in the right margin. Used on W-23 Back Style 2 to W-26.

$1 Legal Tender Note, Series of 1878 (W-22).

Back of the same note.

SERIES OF 1880

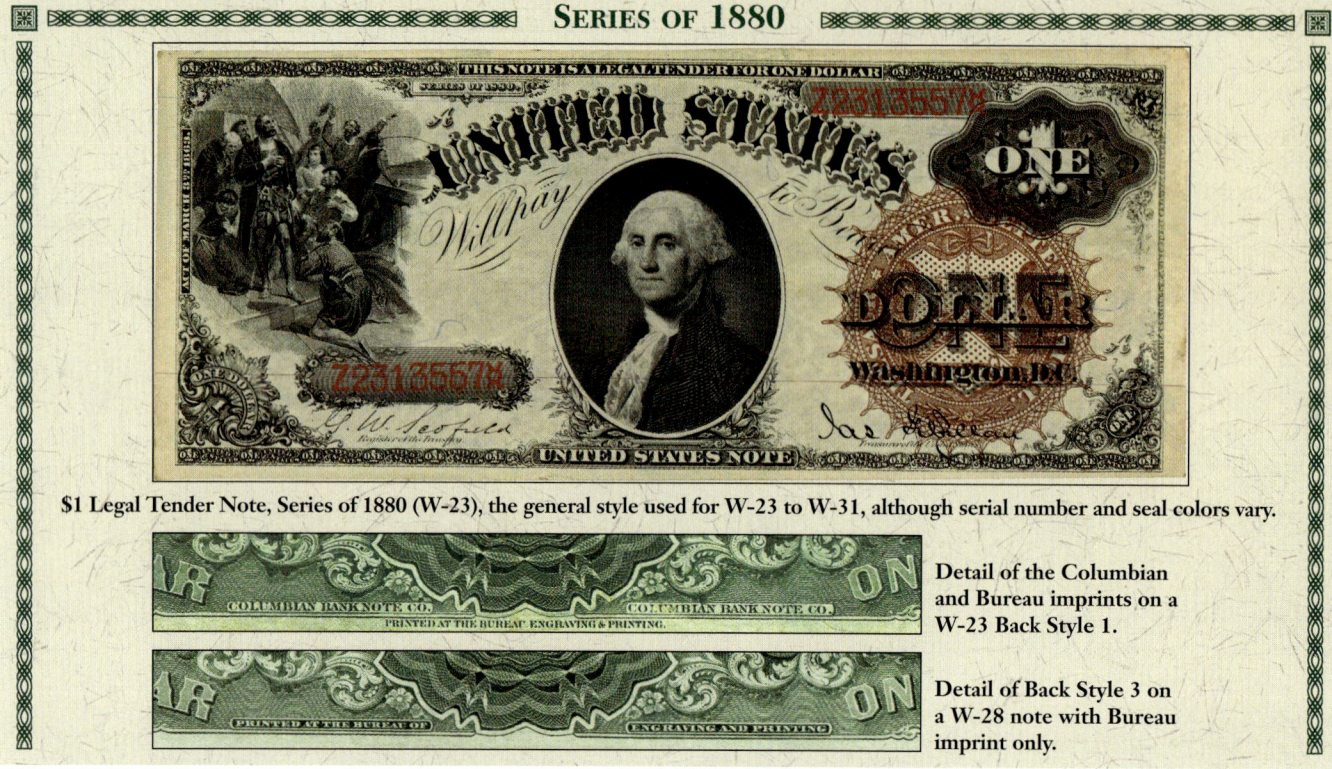

$1 Legal Tender Note, Series of 1880 (W-23), the general style used for W-23 to W-31, although serial number and seal colors vary.

Detail of the Columbian and Bureau imprints on a W-23 Back Style 1.

Detail of Back Style 3 on a W-28 note with Bureau imprint only.

Back Style 3: PRINTED AT THE BUREAU OF and ENGRAVING AND PRINTING where the two Columbian imprints were on earlier plates. Vertically in the open field at the left, SERIES OF 1880. Used on W-27 to W-31.

Notes W-23 to W-25 have red serial numbers; W-26 to W-31 have blue serial numbers. While the seals on some are often called *red*, they are distinctly pink.

W-23a Back Style 1 • F-28 • Scofield-Gilfillan (1878–1881) • Large brown seal • 2,000,000 (est.)
Estimated population: 5 to 10 • *Commentary:* Very scarce in all grades. As this variety becomes known and studied, more information will be learned.

W-23b Back Style 2 • F-28 • 17,964,000 (est.)
Estimated population: 250 to 290 • *Highest graded:* Unc • *Commentary:* Readily available in all grades.

VG-8	F-12	VF-20	EF-40	AU-50	Unc-60	Unc-63	Unc-65
$125	$175	$275	$450	$575	$750	$950	$1,850

W-24 • F-29 • Bruce-Gilfillan (1881–1883) • 17,036,000 (est.)
Estimated population: 250 to 290 • *Highest graded:* Unc • *Commentary:* Readily available in all grades.

VG-8	F-12	VF-20	EF-40	AU-50	Unc-60	Unc-63	Unc-65
$125	$175	$275	$450	$575	$750	$950	$1,850

W-25 • F-30 • Bruce-Wyman (1883–1885) • Large brown seal, red serial numbers • 18,208,000 (est.)
Estimated population: 600 to 700 • *Highest graded:* Unc • *Commentary:* Readily available in all grades.

VG-8	F-12	VF-20	EF-40	AU-50	Unc-60	Unc-63	Unc-65
$125	$175	$275	$450	$575	$750	$950	$1,850

W-26 • F-30a • Large red seal, blue serial numbers • 1,636,000 printed, but never released (none in numismatic hands[2])

W-27 • F-31 • Rosecrans-Huston (1889–1891) • Large red spiked seal • 704,000 (est.)
Estimated population: 140 to 150 • *Highest graded:* Unc • *Commentary:* A scarce variety, particularly in higher grades.

VG-8	F-12	VF-20	EF-40	AU-50	Unc-60	Unc-63	Unc-65
$400	$525	$1,000	$1,500	$2,000	$2,500	$3,200	$6,750

W-28 • F-32 • Large brown seal • 432,000 (est.)
Estimated population: 70 to 80 • *Highest graded:* Unc • *Commentary:* Scarce, especially so in Uncirculated grades.

VG-8	F-12	VF-20	EF-40	AU-50	Unc-60	Unc-63	Unc-65
$525	$700	$1,400	$1,950	$2,600	$3,000	$5,000	$7,750

W-29 • F-33 • Rosecrans-Nebeker (1891–1893) • 56,000 (est.)
Estimated population: 35 to 38 • *Highest graded:* Unc • *Commentary:* Recognized as a rarity for a long time. With only a few exceptions, examples are in circulated grades. Key to the Series of 1880 $1 notes.

VG-8	F-12	VF-20	EF-40	AU-50	Unc-60	Unc-63	Unc-65
$800	$1,250	$2,400	$3,000	$4,750	$5,500	$7,000	$11,500

W-30 • F-34 • Small pink seal with scalloped border • 1,488,000 (est.)
Estimated population: 120 to 140 • *Highest graded:* Unc • *Commentary:* Two security paper types. Early type 1 has two horizontal threads the entire width of note. Later type 2 has two vertical bands of distributed red and blue fibers.

VG-8	F-12	VF-20	EF-40	AU-50	Unc-60	Unc-63	Unc-65
$100	$165	$250	$450	$700	$850	$1,150	$2,100

SERIES OF 1917

$1 Legal Tender Note, Series of 1917 (W-33), the general style used for W-33 to W-37.

Detail of Legal Tender Note, Series of 1917, with transposed signatures (W-35).

Back Plate Location 1.

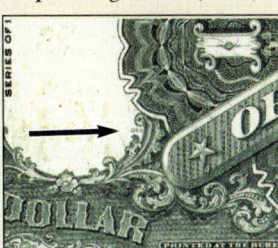

Back Plate Location 2.

Back of a $1 Legal Tender Note, Series of 1917.

W-31 • F-35 • Tillman-Morgan (1893–1897) • 1,996,000 (est.)

Estimated population: 170 to 185 • *Highest graded:* Unc • *Commentary:* Although the printage is low in this context, quite a few have survived, including some at the Uncirculated level.

VG-8	F-12	VF-20	EF-40	AU-50	Unc-60	Unc-63	Unc-65
$100	$150	$225	$400	$650	$750	$1,025	$1,800

Series of 1917

Notes W-33 to W-37 have a small pink Treasury seal with a scalloped border to the left and red serial numbers. One type has the plate number within a scroll at the lower right of the open space, and the other has the plate number centered above the decoration at the bottom of the open space.[3]

The overall back design is the same as on earlier notes, but now the Columbian Bank Note Company identification has been replaced with PRINTED AT THE BUREAU ENGRAVING AND PRINTING near the bottom center.

This series introduces the first star replacement notes in the present text (although star notes were printed in the Silver Certificate class before this). These each have a star as part of the serial number and represent replacement notes made for sheets printed in error or with some problem that were later destroyed.

Mules: Back plate numbers can be in one of two locations (information from Doug Murray on this and certain other large-size note variations):

Back Plate Location 1 (regular use): W-33 to W-37 (available on all in this sequence)

Back Plate Location 2 (regular use): W-36 and W-37. Back Plate Location 2 was introduced as the new standard partway through the production of W-36. Accordingly, a W-36 note with a Location 1 number can be considered a mule.

W-33 • F-36 • Teehee-Burke (1915–1919) • 269,684,000 (est.)

Estimated population: 2,000 to 2,500 • *Highest graded:* Unc • *Commentary:* Plentiful in all grades.

VG-8	F-12	VF-20	EF-40	AU-50	Unc-60	Unc-63	Unc-65
$90	$105	$125	$150	$195	$250	$325	$600

W-33★ • F-36★

Estimated population: 200 to 250 • *Highest graded:* Unc • *Selected information:* Heritage (9/2007), ★5137B/A, Unc-65 (PMG), $2,530. Heritage (1/2007), ★17439B/C, Unc-64 (PCGS), $1,800. Heritage (10/2007), ★1609164B/D, VG-10 (PMG), $212.75. Knight (3/2005), ★1691750B/B, F–VF, $345. Heritage (11/2007), ★1748812B/D, F-12 (PMG), $345. Heritage (1/2007), ★4178642B/B, AU-53 (PMG), $632.50.

W-34 • F-37 • Elliott-Burke (1919–1921) • 299,032,000 (est.)

Estimated population: 3,000 to 4,000 • *Highest graded:* Unc • *Commentary:* Plentiful in all grades.

VG-8	F-12	VF-20	EF-40	AU-50	Unc-60	Unc-63	Unc-65
$90	$105	$125	$150	$195	$250	$325	$600

W-34★ • F-37★

Estimated population: 275 to 325 • *Highest graded:* Unc • *Selected information:* Heritage (4/2008), ★4870369B/A, F-15 (PCGS), $345; ★4910142B/B, VF-20 (PCGS), $373.75. Heritage (1/2008), ★5481932B, EF-40 (PCGS), $805; ★5915949B/A, VF–EF, $546.25. Knight (3/2007), ★7664871B/C, EF-40 (PCGS), $575. Knight (3/2008), ★10296285B/A, VF, $431.25. B&M (11/2007), ★10904367B/C, EF-40 (PCGS), B&M $1,265.

W-35 • F-37a • Burke-Elliott (transposed signatures) • 100,000 (est.)

Estimated population: 130 to 160 • *Highest graded:* Unc • *Commentary:* From face plate 1519 only. First reported by George H. Blake in *The Numismatist*, February 1921.

VG-8	F-12	VF-20	EF-40	AU-50	Unc-60	Unc-63	Unc-65
$400	$500	$650	$850	$1,000	$1,200	$1,800	$3,500

W-36 • F-38 • Elliott-White (1921–1922) • 20,000,000, or about 20% regular (est.)

Estimated population: 200 to 300 • *Highest graded:* Unc • *Selected information:* Rarer than the mule below.

VG-8	F-12	VF-20	EF-40	AU-50	Unc-60	Unc-63	Unc-65
$90	$105	$125	$150	$195	$250	$325	$600

W-36★ • F-38★

Estimated population: 80 to 90 • *Highest graded:* Unc • *Selected information:* Heritage (1/2008), ★11053778B, VF, pinholes, $402.50. Heritage (1/2006), ★11496264B/D, VF–EF, $632.50. Knight (6/2007), ★12301255B/C, VF-30 (PMG), $488.75; later in Knight (6/2008), EF-40 (PCGS), $805.

W-36 Mule • F-38 • 81,176,000, or about 80% mules (est.)

Estimated population: 650 to 800 • *Highest graded:* Unc.

VG-8	F-12	VF-20	EF-40	AU-50	Unc-60	Unc-63	Unc-65
$90	$105	$125	$150	$195	$250	$325	$600

W-36 Mule★ • F-38★

Estimated population: 65 to 70 • *Highest graded:* AU • *Selected information:* CAA (1/2004), ★10589165B/A, AU, $862.50; ★10589166B/B, AU, $977.50. Smythe (9/2002), ★10825263B/C, VF, $345. Knight (6/2008), ★10912144B/D, VF-35 (PCGS), $805.

W-37 • F-39 • Speelman-White (1922–1927) • 289,376,000, or about 98% regular (est.)

Estimated population: 5,000 to 8,000 • *Highest graded:* Unc • *Commentary:* Plentiful in all grades. Into the 1950s it was not uncommon for bank tellers to accumulate quantities of low-grade examples of this variety from deposits turned in by customers.

VG-8	F-12	VF-20	EF-40	AU-50	Unc-60	Unc-63	Unc-65
$85	$100	$120	$145	$185	$235	$300	$550

W-37★ • F-39★

Estimated population: 300 to 325 • *Highest graded:* Unc • *Selected information:* Knight (3/2007), ★12462491B/C, EF-40 (PCGS), $747.50. Smythe (9/2000), ★13449147B/C, Unc, $660. Knight (6/2007), ★13475978B/B, VF-25 (PMG), $316.25. Smythe (4/2007), ★13600816B/D, VF–EF, $431.25. Knight (6/2008), ★13784552B, Unc-64 (PMG), $1,840. Heritage (4/2007), ★13787282B/F, G–VG, $92.

W-37 Mule • F-39 • 7,000,000, or about 2% mules (est.)

Estimated population: 90 to 120 • *Highest graded:* Unc • *Selected information:* Heritage (7/2006), N45179667A/C, Mule, EF, $235.75. Heritage (9/2007), N50442785A/A, Unc-64 (PMG), $373.75. Knight (3/2007), R30A/F, Unc-67 (PMG), $3,162.50. Heritage (9/2007), R44A/H, Unc-65 (PMG), $1,150.

W-37 Mule★ • F-39★

Estimated population: 20 to 25 • *Highest graded:* Unc • *Selected information:* Hickman & Oakes (5/1984), ★12379519B/G, AU, $126.

SERIES OF 1923

$1 Legal Tender Note, Series of 1923 (W-38★). Low-number star note. Portrait of Washington engraved by G.F.C. Smillie.

Back of a Legal Tender Note, Series of 1923.

Series of 1923

The Series of 1923 features a redesign of the face, with Washington looking toward the viewer's right (rather than toward the left, as before). At the Treasury seal is this imprint: "This note is a legal tender at its face value for all debts public and private except duties on imports and interest on the national debt." Bright red overprints are used for the small Treasury seal with a scalloped border, the serial numbers, and the denomination design in the right field.

The back is new as well, with the denomination and embellishments at the center, surrounded by a large open field inside of the border. The Treasury department believed that large open areas on notes made it easier to detect counterfeits. In contrast, complex designs were apt to be scrutinized less carefully by holders of such bills.

W-38 • F-40 • Speelman-White (1922–1927) • 81,872,000
Estimated population: 3,500 to 5,000 • *Highest graded:* Unc.

VG-8	F-12	VF-20	EF-40	AU-50	Unc-60	Unc-63	Unc-65
$130	$185	$310	$390	$580	$650	$750	$1,300

W-38★ • F-40★
Estimated population: 180 to 220 • *Highest graded:* Unc •
Selected information: Knight (10/2006), ★4307D/G, Unc

(PCGS), $3,450. B&M (3/2007), Unc-64 (PMG), $5,175. Heritage (1/2008), ★408972D/D, F-12 (PMG), $632.50. Heritage (1/2006), ★492260D/D, EF, $1,725. Knight (11/2005), ★537552D/D, EF-45, $1,265.

NATIONAL BANK NOTES

Original Series
(Authorized Issue 1865 to 1875)

These notes (illus. on p. 119) were printed by the American and National bank-note companies in New York City. These were usually (but not always) printed in four-subject sheets of $1-$1-$1-$2, with the American Bank Note Company imprint on the bottom border of the $1 notes and the National Bank Note Company imprint on the $2 notes. Plate letters in sequence are A, B, and C on the $1 notes and A on the $2. By definition, three times as many $1 notes were printed as were those of the $2 denomination. All have a small red Treasury seal with a spiked border.

These were printed with red (usually) or blue Treasury serial numbers. The first group with red serials had no prefix or suffix letter. Printing began on March 28, 1865, with Treasury serial number 9 and ended on October 4, 1865, with Treasury number 999413. The next set of red serials began on March 23, 1866, with letter A as a prefix, followed by B, C, D, and E. Set E ended on August 19, 1875. A set with blue serials was started on October 4, 1865, with Treasury serial number 9 and ended on March 23, 1866, with Treasury serial number 999693. Blue serials with prefix letter A seem to have been used by only four banks from September 28, 1866, to July 10, 1875: Washington County National Bank of Greenwich, New York; West Chester County National Bank of Peekskill, New York; Merchants National Bank of Bangor, Maine; and City National Bank of Manchester, New Hampshire. These last notes were all printed on anomalous plates laid out as $1-$1-$2-$2.[4]

The Act of June 20, 1874, provided for the imprinting of the bank's charter number. This was done in red ink, one number vertically left of center and the other horizontally on the right.

Original Series $1 National Bank Notes were first made in 1865, although the $5 denomination was distributed as early as December 1863. On $1 and $2 Original Series Notes, the earliest date seen on a plate is January 2, 1865, with a large group in this category, indicating batch production. Other often-seen dates include July 1, 1865, and August 15, 1865, also for batches. The $1 notes are popularly designated as "aces" by numismatists.

At the center of the face is a medium-size motif, *Concordia*, also known as *Maidens Before the Altar*, created by T.A. Liebler and engraved by Charles Burt (who worked privately in the 1860s, then later for the Treasury department). Depicted are two women standing by an altar of peace, an allusion to the ongoing war. On the back is *The Landing of the Pilgrims*, engraved by Edwin White. On the left side of the back is a state seal representing the location of the issuing bank, and to the right is an eagle (on some notes issued in territories, an eagle is at both ends).

The total number of $1 National Bank Notes issued was 23,169,677, of which about 80% were of the Original Series.

Original Series and Series of 1875 $1 bills play to a very wide audience and are usually collected by the place of issue, sometimes by state and other times by towns and cities within a state. Only rarely are these or other National Bank Notes collected by signature combinations. Most Original Series bills have the Colby-Spinner signatures; fewer have Allison-Spinner. Those with the Jeffries-Spinner pairing (W-41) are exceedingly rare and valuable. In archival research Peter Huntoon has learned that fewer than two dozen banks issued notes with this signature combination.

The most extreme price differences are seen when the issuing location is uncommon—for example, such states as South Carolina and Wyoming, whose bills of this denomination are so rare as to be non-collectible. Those from Utah Territory, Alabama, Montana Territory, West Virginia, and a few other places are quite scarce and bring strong premiums as well. Most plentiful are those from the Eastern states with large populations, such as New York, Pennsylvania, and Massachusetts. A crisp, bright Unc-60 Series of 1875 $1 bill from a New York City bank for which many examples exist will be valued at just a fraction of the price of a F-12 bill from a "rare bank" in a Western territory.

Banks of Issue and Rarity of Notes

Based upon census information from Don C. Kelly and James M. Kelly (*National Bank Note Census*, Version 4.0) and with some information from other sources, this listing gives each location, the number of banks issuing this series of notes within each, and a commentary.[5] The census describes 3,100 notes. The presence of serial number 1 notes is specifically indicated for locations where they exist; if no number 1 notes are mentioned for a given state, there are none.

Alabama • 4 banks of issue • 5 notes reported • National Bank of Birmingham (2), Gainesville National Bank (1), First National Bank of Mobile (2). Grades from G (2) to F (1) reported.

Arkansas • 2 banks of issue • 1 note reported • A rarest of the rare, landmark state, a numismatic icon; National Bank of Western Arkansas (VG). No Series of 1875 $1 notes were issued by this state, adding market pressure to Original Series notes.

Colorado Territory • 6 banks of issue • 22 notes reported • For a territory Colorado has an exceptionally generous population of Original Series notes. The majority of these are Unc and from the First National Bank of Pueblo. A single serial number 1 note is from the First National Bank of Denver (Unc).

Connecticut • 66 banks of issue • 152 notes reported • Notes are available from many banks. Typical grades range from G to F, with AU or Unc very rare.

Dakota Territory (combining what became North and South Dakota) • 1 bank of issue • 10 reported • All are from the First National Bank of Yankton, including several in AU and Unc grades. No Series of 1875 $1 notes were issued by this territory, adding to the desirability of the few known Original Series notes.

Delaware • 5 banks of issue • 9 notes reported • Grades range from G to EF. Most are from the New Castle County National Bank of Odessa.

District of Columbia • 4 banks of issue • 4 notes reported • One is from the National Bank of the Republic (F), and three are from the Citizens National Bank (G and VF, one not graded).

Georgia • 5 banks of issue • 3 notes reported • First National Bank of Americus (Poor), National Bank of Athens (F), First National Bank of Newnan (VG).

Idaho Territory • 1 bank of issue • None reported.

Illinois • 98 banks of issue • 322 notes reported • One of the more collectible states, with many different banks available. Over 110 Unc notes survive from the First National Bank of Kansas (Illinois) and the First National Bank of Lincoln combined, the last always a popular title, with over 75 such notes. There are nine serial number 1 notes, a remarkably large population.

Indiana • 66 banks of issue • 131 notes reported • A popular and readily collectible state. Unc examples from the First National Bank of Lebanon are plentiful in this context. There are two serial number 1 notes, one of which is Unc (Richmond National Bank).

ORIGINAL SERIES

$1 National Bank Note, Original Series (W-42). First National Bank of Lincoln, Illinois, charter 2126. Bank serial 1198, federal serial D642470, plate A. Dated on the plate Sept. 15th 1873. Chartered on August 24, 1873, with Harrison B. Schuler as the founding cashier and John D. Gillett as the first president. The face is similar in style to other notes W-40 to W-42. The imprint of the American Bank Note Co. is at the bottom center. The federal serial number is in red at the left and the bank serial number is at the upper right. The bank officers signed in ink at the bottom.

Back of the First National Bank of Lincoln, Illinois, note, the style used on the Original Series and Series of 1875 $1 notes. At the left is the Illinois state seal, representing the state in which the First National Bank of Lincoln was located.

Iowa • 57 banks of issue • 76 notes reported • This state is generally thought of as scarce or rare, but a surprising number of different notes still survive, with most graded from VG to VF. There are six serial number 1 notes, the three highest graded at EF. Iowa was in a rapid growth stage in this era and many banks were formed. However, the survival rate of notes is much lower than for most Northeastern states.

Kansas • 22 banks of issue • 35 notes reported • Somewhat scarce as a state. Most notes show extensive wear. There are four serial number 1 notes, First National Banks of Emporia (F), Manhattan (Unc), and Parsons (Fair and F).

Kentucky • 32 banks of issue • 30 notes reported • Most are from either the German National Bank of Covington or the similarly-named bank in Louisville. Grades vary, but a fair number of AU notes exist.

Louisiana • 3 banks of issue • 7 notes reported • Notes are from three different banks in New Orleans. Grades range from G–VG to F. No Series of 1875 $1 notes were issued by this state, adding market pressure to the few known Original Series notes.

Maine • 41 banks of issue • 77 notes reported • A nice selection of banks is represented, but most notes are from either the Lincoln National Bank of Bath or the Belfast National Bank. Only one Unc note is listed (First National Bank of Portland), but a number of notes in the census are not graded.

Maryland • 13 banks of issue • 16 notes reported • A well-known rare state. Notes are from a wide selection of banks.

Massachusetts • 182 banks of issue • 374 notes reported • A highly collectible state with notes from many banks. Most are in circulated grades, although Unc notes are from several banks. There are seven serial number 1 notes, including two Unc notes from the Hampshire County National Bank of Northampton.

Michigan • 55 banks of issue • 94 notes reported • The selection is from quite a few different banks, with the Southern Michigan National Bank of Coldwater being the most populous, with a handful of Unc notes. There are six serial number 1 notes, the highest listed as AU.

Minnesota • 28 banks of issue • 55 notes reported • Somewhat scarce as a state, but a wide number of banks are represented. More than a dozen Unc notes are listed from the Merchants National Bank of Winona, all in a tight range of serial numbers, reflecting a hoard. There are three serial number 1 notes reported, one from the State National Bank of Minneapolis (F) and two VF from the First National Bank of Northfield.

Missouri • 28 banks of issue • 115 notes reported • The roster is including the Unc notes from the Moniteau National Bank of California (Missouri), a hoard that is familiar to anyone who has studied auction offerings over a period of time. There are two serial number 1 notes reported, both from that bank, one EF, the other not graded.

Montana Territory • 2 banks of issue • 13 notes reported • These are nearly evenly distributed between the First National Bank of Helena and the Missoula National Bank. Grades range from VG to EF. No Series of 1875 $1 notes were issued by this territory, placing additional pressure on the Original Series notes. Any territorial ace is a showpiece and an auction highlight.

Nebraska • 8 banks of issue • 11 notes reported • Several different banks are represented. Grades range from G to VF. Scarce and desirable in any grade. One serial number 1 note is from the Nebraska City National Bank (VF).

Nebraska Territory • 2 banks of issue • 4 reported • All are from the First National Bank of Omaha, grades from G to F. These classics are among the most desirable of all Original Series aces. Years can elapse between offerings.

New Hampshire • 31 banks of issue • 88 notes reported • Notes are from a wide variety of banks, with most from the First National Bank of Portsmouth and the Kearsarge National Bank of Warner. Most show extensive circulation.[6]

New Jersey • 41 banks of issue • 89 notes reported • A nice selection of banks is represented, including several with a half dozen or more. Grades range from well worn to Unc, the last being scarce. There are two serial number 1 notes, both on the First National Bank of Trenton (EF and ungraded).

New Mexico Territory • 2 banks of issue • 14 notes reported • There are 11 from the First National Bank of Santa Fe, and three from the Second National Bank of the same city. All are circulated. Any of these would be a great attraction in an auction sale.

New York • 223 banks of issue • 629 notes reported • This is far and away the most "common" state; notes are widely distributed across many different banks. Unc notes are few and far between, with no hoards or runs. An amazing 13 serial number 1 notes are reported, a record, but only one is graded Unc.

North Carolina • 5 banks of issue • 6 notes reported • A famously rare state, with market offerings few and far between. Grades range from VG to EF–AU from three banks.

Ohio • 106 banks of issue • 220 notes reported • Many different banks are represented. A hoard of nearly three dozen Unc notes is listed for the First National Bank of Newark, affording ample opportunity to acquire a high-grade example

of the type. There are seven serial number 1 notes, one of which is listed as Unc (First National Bank of East Liverpool, for which an EF example is also given).

Pennsylvania • 86 banks of issue • 174 notes reported • Notes are widely distributed, with no hoards. Unc examples are rare, although two are listed for the First National Bank of Clearfield. There are six serial number 1 notes from as many different banks, none listed as Unc.

Rhode Island • 52 banks of issue • 158 notes reported • A plentiful state, but with many repetitions from the same banks. Most show extensive circulation. There is one serial number 1 note from the Woonsocket National Bank (F).

South Carolina • 4 banks of issue • 2 notes reported • An incredibly challenging state, one of the very rarest. Both are from the Bank of Charleston National Banking Association (F and VF), chartered in 1872, and with the largest capital in the state. An offering of such a note would be a market sensation.

Tennessee • 15 banks of issue • 8 notes reported • A well-known, rare state. Notes are in the spotlight whenever offered. Grades range from G to F. Three are from the First National Bank of Memphis.

Texas • 4 banks of issue • 11 notes reported • Fairly rare as a state and in strong demand. VF is the highest reported grade. Five are from the National Bank of Texas in Galveston.

Utah Territory • 4 banks of issue • 27 notes reported • There are two serial number 1 notes, both on the Deseret National Bank of Salt Lake City, the source of all but six notes known from the territory. Mormon leader Brigham Young signed as president, making the notes distinctive souvenirs for those of Mormon faith and no doubt accounting for the number surviving. No Series of 1875 $1 notes were issued by this territory, adding desirability to the Originals.

Vermont • 33 banks of issue • 71 notes reported • Slightly scarce as a state. A selection of banks is represented, with notes of the Lamoille County National Bank of Hyde Park, the National Bank of Rutland, and the Woodstock National Bank being the most populous. Don C. Kelly lists no Unc notes.

Virginia • 1 bank of issue • 1 note reported • Serial 1794 on the Exchange National Bank of Norfolk (F), a holy grail note for the specialist. No Series of 1875 $1 notes were issued by this state, making the sole Original Series note all the more important.

West Virginia • 5 banks of issue • 5 notes reported • Three are from the National Exchange Bank of Weston and the others from the Peoples National Bank of Martinsburg and the First National Bank of Wheeling. One graded VG, the others F. No Series of 1875 $1 notes were issued by this state, adding market pressure to Original Series notes.

Wisconsin • 29 banks of issue • 20 notes reported • Scarce as a state. Distributed over various banks, with none reported as Unc. There are three serial number 1 notes, from the First National Bank of Boscobel (F) and the First National Bank of Chippewa Falls (VF and ungraded).

Wyoming Territory • 1 bank of issue • 2 notes reported • Rarest of the rare notes, combining absolute rarity with territorial status. Both are from the Wyoming National Bank of

Laramie City (F and VF–EF). No Series of 1875 $1 notes were issued by this territory, making these even more important than would otherwise be the case.

Generic prices for a typical note from a state from which notes range from plentiful to just slightly scarce:

VG-8	F-12	VF-20	EF-40	AU-50	Unc-60	Unc-63	Unc-65
$550	$900	$1,200	$1,800	$2,250	$2,750	$3,700	$5,250

W-40 • F-380 • Colby-Spinner (1864–1867)

Estimated population: 2,500 to 3,000 • *Highest graded:* Unc.

VG-8	F-12	VF-20	EF-40	AU-50	Unc-60	Unc-63	Unc-65
$550	$900	$1,200	$1,800	$2,250	$2,750	$3,700	$5,250

W-41 • F-381 • Jeffries-Spinner (1867–1869)

Estimated population: 9 or 10 • *Highest graded:* VF-30 • *Commentary:* This signature combination is exceedingly rare in this and other denominations. • *Selected information:* Heritage (4/2008), B556859/371/A, Union Square NB of New York, NY, the only extant note of any denomination on this bank, VF, $25,300. CAA (9/2003), 4010-E269960/A, First NB of Mankato, MN, only $1 note extant, F, $9,775.

VG-8	F-12	VF-20
$2,500	$4,000	$7,000

W-42 • F-382 • Allison-Spinner (1869–1875)

Estimated population: 800 to 1,000 • *Highest graded:* Unc.

VG-8	F-12	VF-20	EF-40	AU-50	Unc-60	Unc-63	Unc-65
$550	$900	$1,200	$1,800	$2,250	$2,750	$3,700	$5,250

Series of 1875
(Authorized Issue 1875 to 1878)

These (illus. on p. 124) continued the use of plates signed by the American Bank Note Company ($1 notes) and the National Bank Note Company (the single $2 note). The printing was done by the Treasury department in Washington. An imprint was entered into the plate, which on the $1 bill is vertically inside the right border: PRINTED AT THE BUREAU, ENGRAVING & PRINTING, TREASURY DEPT. The small red Treasury seal has a scalloped rather than a spiked border. All have SERIES 1875 imprinted vertically in red left of center, near the bank charter number.[7] The Treasury and bank serial numbers and two charter numbers are also in red. A small percentage of these notes are printed on paper with a vertical blue tint streak of the type most familiarly used on the Legal Tender Notes beginning with the Series of 1869 (paper made under the James M. Willcox patent of July 24, 1866). These are especially colorful and attractive.

Beginning with the Series of 1875, banks could order unusual combinations of plate arrangements. On March 21, 1865, 500 sheets of $1-$1-$1-$1 were sent to the First National Bank of Philadelphia, charter 1. This was the only bank for which such a combination was issued, meaning that the plate letter D on a $1 note from this bank would be unusual, except that all 500 sheets delivered were cancelled and not issued.[8]

In nearly all instances, Series of 1875 notes are rarer than those of the Original Series, as they were issued only from 1875 until distribution was halted on January 1, 1879. However, most numismatists consider one of either series as sufficient to illustrate the type. If the acquisition of such notes becomes more sophisticated, perhaps Series of 1875 notes will be appreciated for their rarity.

Average grades of surviving examples are higher than for Original Series notes. As this design was not a novelty when it was used on the Series of 1875, and as many bank officers had already saved Original Series notes as souvenirs, serial number 1 notes are very rare.

Banks of Issue and Rarity of Notes

Based upon census information from Don C. Kelly and James M. Kelly (*National Bank Note Census*, Version 4.0) and with some information from other sources, this listing gives each state or territory, the number of banks issuing this series of notes within it, and a commentary.[9] The census describes 1,129 notes, or about a third of the number registered for Original Series notes.

Fewer banks issued Series of 1875 notes, as the era for this type was only from 1875 to the end of 1878. In addition, the rush to form national banks, so intense during the Original Series period, had diminished. Locations with serial number 1 notes are specifically identified; otherwise, there are none.

Alabama • 1 bank of issue • No notes reported.

Colorado Territory • 2 banks of issue • No notes reported.

Connecticut • 34 banks of issue • 91 notes reported • One of the more collectible states for this series. Notes are distributed over various banks, with the National Exchange Bank of Hartford, the Farmers and Mechanics Bank of Hartford, and the First National Bank of West Killingly having more than any of the others. Grades are mostly circulated, punctuated with a few Unc notes.

Delaware • 1 bank of issue • 4 notes reported • A rare state. All notes are from the New Castle National Bank of Odessa. Grades are Fair (2), VG, and F.

District of Columbia • 1 bank of issue • 2 notes reported • Both of these showpieces are from the German-American National Bank.

Georgia • 1 bank of issue • 1 note reported • Rarest of the rare. First National Bank of Americus (VG).

Idaho Territory • 1 bank of issue • No notes reported.

Illinois • 14 banks of issue • 9 notes reported • This is a rare state by any evaluation, although the easy availability of Original Series notes, including over 110 Unc examples, softens the market price. Still, any Series of 1875 note is a prize, but it takes a specialist to appreciate this. Don C. Kelly reports just one Unc (First National Bank of Macomb).

Indiana • 19 banks of issue • 44 notes reported • A collectible state as a type, but most notes are clustered under just a few banks, including the First National Bank of Indianapolis, the National State Bank of Lafayette, First National Bank of Marshall County at Plymouth, and the Richmond National Bank. The one serial number 1 note is from the Richmond National Bank (AU).

Iowa • 11 banks of issue • 10 notes reported • A rare state for sure, but the availability of Original Series notes helps ameliorate the market price. Four are from the First National Bank of Dubuque and three from the Commercial National Bank of the same city. One is Unc.

Kansas • 8 banks of issue • 60 notes reported • One of the more collectible states in this series, due to rapid growth and speculation in the prairie states at the time, leading to the establishment of new banks and the issuance of a lot of paper money. Most are circulated, typically VF to AU, spaced with a few Unc examples. The one serial number 1 note is from the First National Bank of Parsons (VF).

Kentucky • 10 banks of issue • 28 notes reported • Slightly scarce as a state. Fifteen notes, including several Unc, are from the German National Bank of Covington.

Maine • 11 banks of issue • 24 notes reported • Collectible as a state, just slightly on the scarce side. Five notes are from the Belfast National Bank and seven are from the First National Bank of Waterville. Don C. Kelly reports no Unc examples. There is one serial number 1 note from the Union National Bank of Phillips (AU).

Massachusetts • 116 banks of issue • 332 notes reported • A common state for this series. Of these, 44, mostly Unc, are from the Home National Bank of Milford. Otherwise, grades are as you find them, mostly with evidence of wear, including from five to a dozen or more from some banks. There is one serial number 1 note, of the National Bank of North America of Boston (EF).

Michigan • 13 banks of issue • 14 notes reported • A scarce state. Notes are from just a few banks, including the First National Bank of Lapeer, which also has the only Unc example in the Kelly census.

Minnesota • 6 banks of issue • 4 notes reported • A rare state by any reckoning, with two notes from the First National Bank of Owatonna and two from the Farmers National Bank in the same city, grades from VG to VF. However, as Original Series notes are often seen (in the context of this series, that is), the appreciation of the rarity of a Series of 1875 note is mainly by specialists.

Missouri • 5 banks • 6 notes reported • Three from the Exchange National Bank of Columbia, one from the Bates County National Bank of Butler, and two from the First National Bank of Paris, G to EF. Again, as Original Series notes from this state are plentiful, not much attention is paid to the rarity of Series of 1875 notes.

Nebraska • 3 banks of issue • 2 notes reported • Rarity to the fore. First National Bank of Lincoln (VG–F) and the Nebraska City National Bank (EF).

Nebraska Territory • 1 bank of issue • No notes reported.

New Hampshire • 18 banks of issue • 18 notes reported • This is a scarce state for this particular series, not so for Original Series notes. Most are from the Laconia National Bank and the Manchester National Bank. Grades from Fair to EF.

New Jersey • 10 banks of issue • 21 notes reported • A scarce state. From a selection of banks. Grades from G to EF.

New Mexico Territory • 1 bank of issue • 4 notes reported • Both rare and additionally desirable as a territory. All from the First National Bank of Santa Fe. Grades from G to F.

New York • 77 banks of issue • 179 notes reported • A common state in this context, although many notes are from the same handful of large banks. Most are circulated, but a few Unc examples are reported. There are three serial number 1 notes, all from the Tradesmens National Bank of New York City, each showing wear.

North Carolina • 4 banks of issue • 7 notes reported • A rare state for which auction offerings are infrequent. Four different banks are represented, with grades from Poor to EF, although three are not graded.

Ohio • 25 banks of issue • 34 notes reported • Scarce as a state. No Unc examples are in the Kelly census.

Pennsylvania • 17 banks of issue • 47 notes reported • Almost common the context of this series. Several banks each account for clusters of notes. No Unc examples are in the Kelly census.

Rhode Island • 34 banks of issue • 101 notes reported • A common state for this series, although several banks each account for clusters of notes. Several Unc notes are in the Kelly census. There are two serial number 1 notes, both from the Newport National Bank (EF and EF–AU).

South Carolina • 1 bank of issue • No notes reported.

Tennessee • 2 banks of issue • 1 note reported • A holy grail state. The solo note is from the German National Bank of Memphis (VG).

Texas • 1 bank of issue • No notes reported.

Vermont • 27 banks of issue • 31 notes reported • Eleven are from the National Bank of Lyndon. Only one Unc note is listed by Don C. Kelly, from the First National Bank of Orwell.

Wisconsin • 4 banks of issue • 54 notes reported • A common state, or nearly so in this context. However, as 49 notes are from the LaCrosse National Bank (just one Unc), others are very rare. There are two serial number 1 notes, each from the previously mentioned bank (F).

Generic prices for a typical note from a state in which notes range from plentiful to just slightly scarce:

VG-8	F-12	VF-20	EF-40	AU-50	Unc-60	Unc-63	Unc-65
$550	$900	$1,200	$1,800	$2,250	$2,750	$3,700	$6,000

W-43 • F-383 • Allison-New (1875–1876)
Estimated population: 500 to 600 • *Highest graded:* Unc.

VG-8	F-12	VF-20	EF-40	AU-50	Unc-60	Unc-63	Unc-65
$550	$900	$1,200	$1,800	$2,250	$2,750	$3,700	$6,000

W-44 • F-384 • Allison-Wyman (1876–1877)
Estimated population: 475 to 550 • *Highest graded:* Unc.

VG-8	F-12	VF-20	EF-40	AU-50	Unc-60	Unc-63	Unc-65
$550	$900	$1,200	$1,800	$2,250	$2,750	$3,700	$6,000

REPRESENTATIVE STATE SEALS
USED ON $1 NATIONAL BANK NOTES
Original Series and Series of 1875

Seal of Alabama   Seal of Colorado   Seal of Connecticut   Seal of Delaware

Seal of Illinois   Seal of Iowa   Seal of Indiana   Seal of Kansas

Seal of Kentucky   Seal of Louisiana   Seal of Maine   Seal of Maryland

Seal of Massachusetts   Seal of Michigan   Seal of Minnesota   Seal of Missouri

Seal of Nebraska   Seal of New Hampshire   Seal of New Jersey   Seal of New York

Seal of Ohio   Seal of Pennsylvania   Seal of Rhode Island   Seal of Texas

Seal of Utah Territory   Seal of Vermont   Seal of Virginia   Seal of West Virginia

SERIES OF 1875

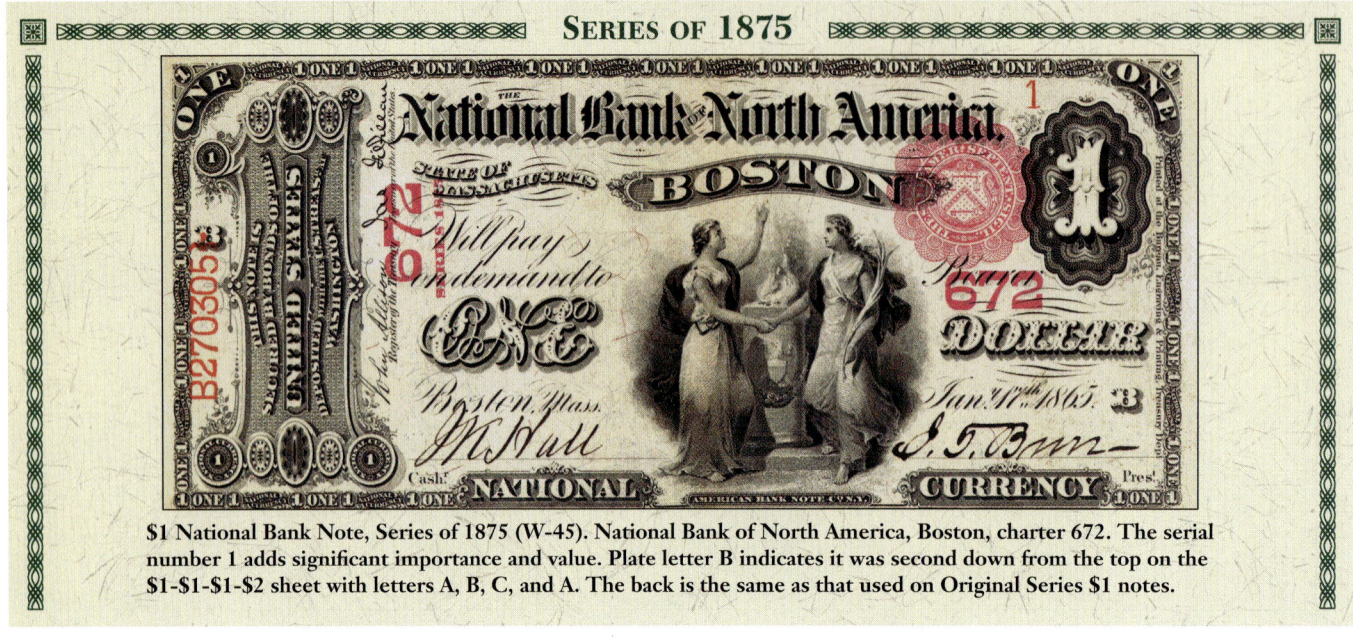

$1 National Bank Note, Series of 1875 (W-45). National Bank of North America, Boston, charter 672. The serial number 1 adds significant importance and value. Plate letter B indicates it was second down from the top on the $1-$1-$1-$2 sheet with letters A, B, C, and A. The back is the same as that used on Original Series $1 notes.

W-45 • F-385 • Allison-Gilfillan (1877–1878)
Estimated population: 200 to 225 • *Highest graded:* Unc.

VG-8	F-12	VF-20	EF-40	AU-50	Unc-60	Unc-63
$550	$900	$1,200	$1,800	$2,250	$2,750	$3,700

W-46 • F-386 • Scofield-Gilfillan (1878–1881)
Estimated population: 80 to 90 • *Highest graded:* Unc.

VG-8	F-12	VF-20	EF-40	AU-50	Unc-60	Unc-63
$550	$900	$1,200	$1,800	$2,250	$2,750	$3,700

SILVER CERTIFICATES

Series of 1886

Silver Certificates of the $1 denomination commence with the Series of 1886. By this time tens of millions of newly minted Morgan-designed silver dollars had piled up in Treasury vaults and other storage. Such coins provided the backing for Silver Certificates, which were specifically redeemable in one silver dollar.

This initial type depicts Martha Washington—the first time that a First Lady of the United States appeared on federal paper money. Charles Burt was the engraver. Numismatists often call these "Martha notes." (Females of various kinds, ranging from allegorical goddesses to women in historical panoramas, had been used for a long time, including on currency issued by state-chartered banks and in certain of the state seals on the backs of Original Series and Series of 1875 National Bank Notes.) The same portrait of Mrs. Washington was used on the Series of 1891 Silver Certificates, followed by the Series of 1896 "Educational Note." All Series of 1886 notes have blue serial numbers beginning with B. Sizes and colors of the Treasury seal vary.

The back, ornately engraved, includes redemption information at the center, essentially stating that it could be spent for any purpose.

W-50 • F-215 • Rosecrans-Jordan (1885–1887) • Small red seal with plain border • 13,660,000 (est.)
Estimated population: 650 to 800 • *Highest graded:* Unc.

VG-8	F-12	VF-20	EF-40	AU-50	Unc-60	Unc-63	Unc-65
$280	$390	$525	$775	$1,250	$1,400	$1,800	$4,000

W-51 • F-216 • Rosecrans-Hyatt (1887–1889) • 7,380,000 (est.)
Estimated population: 250 to 300 • *Highest graded:* Unc.

VG-8	F-12	VF-20	EF-40	AU-50	Unc-60	Unc-63	Unc-65
$280	$390	$525	$775	$1,250	$1,400	$1,800	$4,000

W-52 • F-217 • Large red seal • 18,780,000 (est.)
Estimated population: 500 to 600 • *Highest graded:* Unc.

VG-8	F-12	VF-20	EF-40	AU-50	Unc-60	Unc-63	Unc-65
$280	$390	$525	$775	$1,250	$1,400	$1,800	$4,500

W-53 • F-218 • Rosecrans-Huston (1889–1891) • 13,760,000 (est.)
Estimated population: 275 to 325 • *Highest graded:* Unc.

VG-8	F-12	VF-20	EF-40	AU-50	Unc-60	Unc-63	Unc-65
$280	$390	$525	$775	$1,250	$1,400	$1,800	$4,500

W-54 • F-219 • Large brown seal • 10,300,000 (est.)
Estimated population: 325 to 375 • *Highest graded:* Unc.

VG-8	F-12	VF-20	EF-40	AU-50	Unc-60	Unc-63	Unc-65
$280	$390	$525	$775	$1,250	$1,400	$1,800	$4,500

W-55 • F-220 • Rosecrans-Nebeker (1891–1893) • Large brown seal with spiked border • 4,400,000 (est.)
Estimated population: 150 to 165 • *Highest graded:* Unc.

VG-8	F-12	VF-20	EF-40	AU-50	Unc-60	Unc-63	Unc-65
$280	$390	$525	$775	$1,250	$1,400	$1,800	$5,500

SERIES OF 1886

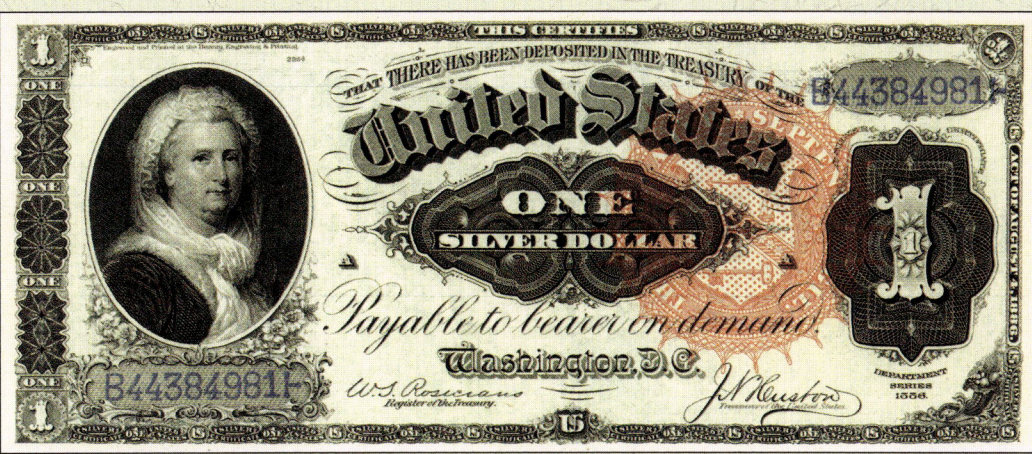

$1 Silver Certificate, Series of 1886 (W-53), similar to all notes W-50 to W-56 except for Treasury seal and signature variations. These are often called "Martha Notes."

Detail of the portrait (W-50). Face plate letters and numbers can vary widely in location among $1 notes of the late 19th century. Here the tiny number 1972 is near the top border and the medium-size letter B is at a distance to the lower right of the portrait.

Detail of the plate letter and number, 21B, close to each other on the face of another note (W-55).

Back of a Silver Certificate, Series of 1886.

W-56 • F-221 • Small red seal with scalloped border • 4,204,000 (est.)

Estimated population: 145 to 175 • Highest graded: Unc.

VG-8	F-12	VF-20	EF-40	AU-50	Unc-60	Unc-63	Unc-65
$320	$440	$550	$800	$1,300	$1,400	$1,800	$3,750

Series of 1891

For the Series of 1891 notes (illus. on p. 126), the designation MARTHA WASHINGTON was added in tiny letters below the portrait, and the back was redesigned. The new back features open spaces, to deter counterfeiting. Notes of this type have a serial number beginning with letter E.

W-57 • F-222 • Rosecrans-Nebeker (1891–1893) • Small red seal with scalloped border • 13,320,000 (est.)

Estimated population: 250 to 300 • Highest graded: Unc.

VG-8	F-12	VF-20	EF-40	AU-50	Unc-60	Unc-63	Unc-65
$320	$440	$500	$625	$875	$1,100	$1,275	$3,750

W-58 • F-223 • Tillman-Morgan (1893) • 52,088,000 (est.)

Estimated population: 1,100 to 1,400 • Highest graded: Unc.

VG-8	F-12	VF-20	EF-40	AU-50	Unc-60	Unc-63	Unc-65
$280	$360	$450	$575	$825	$1,000	$1,200	$2,800

SERIES OF 1891

$1 Silver Certificate, Series of 1891 (W-58).

Back of a Silver Certificate, Series of 1891.

Detail of the plate number 37 on the back of a W-58 note.

Series of 1896

The $1 note is the lowest and most available denomination in the 1896 "Educational Note" series, a high-water mark in bank-note artistry. On the face is *History Instructing Youth*, with the goddess and her pupil positioned approximately where the Lee mansion is, across the Potomac River from Washington, D.C. She points to the Washington Monument. The District of Columbia spreads before them, with the Capitol, the Washington Monument, and more. To the right a book is opened to reveal the beginning text of the Constitution. Around the border at the left, top, and right, within wreaths, are the names of famous people in American history: Longfellow, Sherman (presumably William Tecumseh, not John), Lincoln, Irving, Cooper, Fulton, Calhoun, Clay, Jackson, Adams (either John or John Quincy), Jefferson, Washington (within a wreath larger than the others'), Franklin, Hamilton, Perry, Marshall, Webster, Morse, Hawthorne, Bancroft, Grant, Farragut, and Emerson. All notes have a small red seal with a spiked border. The design is by Will H. Low, a talented artist in the private sector, with engraving by Charles Schlecht and some changes by Thomas F. Morris.

On the back of the note George and Martha Washington appear in separate portraits with ornate borders, designed by Morris and engraved by Alfred Sealey and Charles Burt.

An article by Morris's son, Thomas Jr., "U.S. Silver Certificates, Series of 1896," in the June 1934 *Numismatist*, included the following about the $1 certificates:[10]

> Certain changes were made of the original design as submitted by the artist and after weeks of toil by the engraver, Charles Schlecht, who had just previously finished the government's beautiful Columbian Diploma (also designed by Will Low) and who did the figures and the balance of the featured design, the lettering and scroll work was entrusted to Mr. Kennedy. Certain changes in the style of lettering were, however, made and one or two minor changes were also effected.

W-59 • F-224 • Tillman-Morgan (1893–1897) • Small red seal with spiked border • 33,952,000 (est.)
Estimated population: 3,500 to 5,000 • Highest graded: Unc.

VG-8	F-12	VF-20	EF-40	AU-50	Unc-60	Unc-63	Unc-65
$350	$450	$630	$1,200	$1,700	$1,900	$2,250	$4,200

W-60 • F-225 • Bruce-Roberts (1897) • 23,392,000 (est.)
Estimated population: 1,500 to 2,000 • Highest graded: Unc.

VG-8	F-12	VF-20	EF-40	AU-50	Unc-60	Unc-63	Unc-65
$350	$450	$630	$1,200	$1,700	$1,900	$2,250	$4,500

SERIES OF 1896

$1 Silver Certificate, Series of 1896 (W-59). The famous "Educational Note" with the ornate vignette *History Instructing Youth*. A vista of Washington, D.C., is in the distance. This design is considered by many to be the high point of artistry in the $1 denomination.

Detail of the plate letter and number B9 at the lower left of the face of a W-59 note.

Location of the plate number 2 at the lower right of the open space to the left of the portraits on the back of a W-59 note.

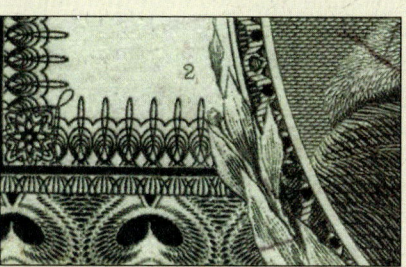

Back of a $1 Series of 1896 note with portraits of Martha and George Washington.

Series of 1899

The Series of 1896 bills were replaced by the Series of 1899 issues (illus. on p. 129), with a bold image of the national bird on the face, officially known as the *Eagle of the Capitol*, also officially as *Eagle and the Capitol* (earlier used on $10 Interest Bearing Notes of 1863 and $10 Compound Interest Treasury Notes). At the bottom border of the face, flanking SILVER CERTIFICATE, are small portraits of Lincoln and Grant, evoking memories of the Civil War. Grant was one of quite a few Union generals to be showcased on federal paper money, an honor not accorded to any

heroes of the Confederacy (although they were well represented on CSA paper). All have a blue Treasury seal with a scalloped border.

These were made in many signature combinations and produced until the advent of the Series of 1923. Collectors call these "Black Eagle Notes." More than just a few such bills with low serial numbers were saved, furnishing an interesting opportunity to collect them today. Two varieties exist bearing the Vernon-McClung signature combination: the usual, with the series date below the serial number (W-65); and a rarity, with the date to the right of the Treasury seal (W-66).

Mules: Back plate numbers can be in one of two locations.[11] On May 14, 1921, with the new Elliott-White signature combination starting, all Legal Tender, Silver Certificate, and Gold Certificate back plates were given numbers beginning with 1 and in a new location, although no notice was given of the change.

Back Plate Location 1 (regular use): W-61 to W-71. This was the standard location until May 14, 1921. Also used to create a mule of W-72 and W-73.

Back Plate Location 2 (regular use): W-72 and W-73. Also used to create a mule of W-71.

W-61 • F-226 • Lyons-Roberts (1898–1905) • Series date above serial number • 100,000,000

Estimated population: 425 to 475 • *Highest graded:* Unc.

VG-8	F-12	VF-20	EF-40	AU-50	Unc-60	Unc-63	Unc-65
$115	$145	$185	$270	$325	$425	$675	$1,250

W-62 • F-226a • Series date below serial number • 350,900,000 (est.)

Estimated population: 900 to 1,100 • *Highest graded:* Unc.

VG-8	F-12	VF-20	EF-40	AU-50	Unc-60	Unc-63	Unc-65
$100	$132	$170	$230	$300	$400	$500	$700

W-63 • F-227 • Lyons-Treat (1905–1906) • 108,900,000 (est.)

Estimated population: 300 to 350 • *Highest graded:* Unc.

VG-8	F-12	VF-20	EF-40	AU-50	Unc-60	Unc-63	Unc-65
$110	$132	$160	$225	$300	$375	$525	$900

W-64 • F-228 • Vernon-Treat (1906–1909) • 374,199,600 (est.)

Estimated population: 1,000 to 1,200 • *Highest graded:* Unc.

VG-8	F-12	VF-20	EF-40	AU-50	Unc-60	Unc-63	Unc-65
$110	$132	$160	$225	$300	$375	$525	$675

W-65 • F-229 • Vernon-McClung (1909–1911) • 224,792,000 (est.)

Estimated population: 700 to 850 • *Highest graded:* Unc • *Commentary:* Deliveries began on July 1, 1910, and ended on July 25, 1911. The first sheet of these, serials V1 to V4, was presented to Yale University.[12]

VG-8	F-12	VF-20	EF-40	AU-50	Unc-60	Unc-63	Unc-65
$110	$132	$160	$225	$300	$375	$525	$675

W-65★ • F-229★

Estimated population: 35 to 40 • *Highest graded:* Unc • *Commentary:* On June 21, 1910, star replacement notes were made of this and the related $5 Silver Certificates (W-805★); these became the first of their kind in any series. Earlier, stars had been used as decorations on some notes, without any specific purpose.

VG-8	F-12	VF-20	EF-40	AU-50	Unc-60	Unc-63	Unc-65
$280	$475	$700	$950	$1,200	$2,000	$3,000	$5,000

W-66 • F-229a • Vernon-McClung (1909–1911) • Series date vertical at right border • 26,612,000 (est.)

Estimated population: 150 to 165 • *Highest graded:* Unc • *Commentary:* This is a well-known rarity within the context of this series and always attracts attention when offered at auction.

VG-8	F-12	VF-20	EF-40	AU-50	Unc-60	Unc-63	Unc-65
$1,100	$2,400	$4,000	$5,000	$5,750	$6,500	$8,000	$14,000

W-66★ • F-229a★

Recorded population: 2 • *Highest graded:* Unc • *Selected information:* Smythe (1998), CU, $4,070.

W-67 • F-230 • Napier-McClung (1911–1912) • 469,020,000 (est.)

Estimated population: 1,300 to 1,600 • *Highest graded:* Unc • *Commentary:* Deliveries began on July 26, 1911, and ended on December 29, 1913.

VG-8	F-12	VF-20	EF-40	AU-50	Unc-60	Unc-63	Unc-65
$100	$125	$155	$215	$280	$360	$500	$650

W-67★ • F-230★

Estimated population: 45 to 48 • *Highest graded:* Unc • *Selected information:* CAA (9/2006), ★1285369B/A, Unc-65 (PCGS), $3,450. CAA (5/2005), ★1885544B/D, CU-65 (PCGS), $2,185. Knight (11/2007), ★2183091B/C, EF-40 (PCGS), $1,335.15. Heritage (9/2007), ★2742462B/B, Unc-68 (PCGS), $23,000.

W-68 • F-231 • Napier-Thompson (1912–1913) • 6,740,000

Estimated population: 150 to 160 • *Highest graded:* Unc • *Commentary:* Printing of this signature combination (without regard to varieties) began on December 14, 1912, and ended on May 31, 1913.

VG-8	F-12	VF-20	EF-40	AU-50	Unc-60	Unc-63	Unc-65
$300	$475	$625	$1,000	$1,800	$1,900	$2,500	$3,500

W-69 • F-232 • Parker-Burke (1913–1914) • 354,268,000 (est.)

Estimated population: 1,200 to 1,400 • *Highest graded:* Unc.

VG-8	F-12	VF-20	EF-40	AU-50	Unc-60	Unc-63	Unc-65
$90	$120	$150	$210	$270	$350	$500	$650

W-69★ • F-232★

Estimated population: 53 to 55 • *Highest graded:* Unc • *Selected information:* CAA (5/2005), ★4480606B/B, AU, $1,495. Knight (11/2007), ★4858393B/A, AU-58 (PCGS), $2,070. Knight (3/2008), ★5180333B/A, F, $373.75.

W-70 • F-233 • Teehee-Burke (1915–1919) • 790,444,000 (est.)

Estimated population: 5,000 to 7,000 • *Highest graded:* Unc.

VG-8	F-12	VF-20	EF-40	AU-50	Unc-60	Unc-63	Unc-65
$90	$120	$150	$210	$270	$350	$500	$650

W-70★ • F-233★

Estimated population: 185 to 200 • *Highest graded:* Unc • *Selected information:* CAA (9/2006), ★6955479B/C, VF-20 (PMG), $402.50. Stack's (3/2007), ★7838030B/B, VF, $506.

SERIES OF 1899

$1 Silver Certificate, Series of 1899. The popular "Black Eagle Note" (W-70). These were issued over a long period of years in over a dozen different varieties.

Detail of date above serial number on W-61.

Detail of date below serial number on W-62 to W-65.

Detail of date to right of seal on W-66 to W-73.

Back of a "Black Eagle Note."

Back Plate Location 1. The tiny plate number 5891 is hardly visible in the open space far above the M (AMERICA).

Back Plate Location 2. The tiny plate number 1005 is in the lower right of the open space.

Heritage (10/2007), ★8203600B/D, G, $195.50. Knight (3/2007), ★8779695B/C, AU-58 (PCGS), $1,725. Knight (6/2008), ★10400064B/D, VF-35 (PCGS), $690.

W-71 • F-234 • Elliott-Burke (1919–1921) • 60,320,000, or about 97% regular (est.)

Estimated population: 1,000 to 1,200 • *Highest graded:* Unc.

VG-8	F-12	VF-20	EF-40	AU-50	Unc-60	Unc-63	Unc-65
$90	$120	$150	$210	$270	$350	$500	$650

W-71★ • F-234★

Estimated population: 55 to 60 • *Highest graded:* Unc • *Selected information:* Knight (6/2007), ★14202485B/A, F-12 (PMG), $402.50.

W-71 Mule • F-234 • 2,000,000, or about 3% mules (est.)

Estimated population: 55 to 65 • *Highest graded:* Unc • *Selected information:* Knight (12/1998), E46179206A/F, Unc, $165. Heritage (1/2007), E89453078A/B, Unc, $546.25. Heritage (10/2007), M90306259A/G, VF, $184.

W-71 Mule★ • F-234★

Estimated population: 9 to 11 • *Highest graded:* AU • *Selected information:* CAA (5/2005), ★13436316B/D, VG–F, $1,035.

W-72 • F-235 • Elliott-White (1921–1922) • 174,460,000, or about 75% regular (est.)

Estimated population: 1,600 to 2,000 • *Highest graded:* Unc.

VG-8	F-12	VF-20	EF-40	AU-50	Unc-60	Unc-63	Unc-65
$90	$120	$150	$210	$270	$350	$500	$650

W-72★ • F-235★

Estimated population: 150 to 200 • *Highest graded:* Unc.

VG-8	F-12	VF-20	EF-40	AU-50	Unc-60	Unc-63
$175	$250	$500	$900	$1,800	$2,800	$3,800

W-72 Mule • F-235 • 58,000,000, or about 25% mules (est.)

Estimated population: 500 to 600 • *Highest graded:* Unc • *Selected information:* Knight (11/2007), E9402062A/B, VF-25 (PMG), $149.50. Heritage (5/2007), E40373365A/A, Unc, $632.50. Knight (11/2005), E42790298A/B, Unc, $632.50. Heritage (1/2007), F.62709223A/C, Unc, $575. CAA (9/2004), H75A/C, Unc-64 (PMG), $2,300. Knight (11/2006), H80A/D, Unc-64 (PCGS), $1,610. Heritage (1/2006), N20718567A/G, F, $109.25. Heritage (8/2007), N38202697A/E, EF-40 (PCGS), $276.

W-72 Mule★ • F-235★

Estimated population: 30 to 35 • *Highest graded:* Unc.

VG-8	F-12	VF-20	EF-40	AU-50	Unc-60	Unc-63
$700	$1,000	$1,700	$3,000	$5,500	$7,750	$10,000

W-73 • F-236 • Speelman-White (1922–1927) • 588,200,000, or about 99% regular (est.)

Estimated population: 6,000 to 9,000 • *Highest graded:* Unc.

VG-8	F-12	VF-20	EF-40	AU-50	Unc-60	Unc-63	Unc-65
$90	$120	$150	$210	$270	$350	$500	$650

W-73★ • F-236★

Estimated population: 225 to 235 • *Highest graded:* Unc • *Selected information:* CAA (5/2005), ★16190945B/A, Unc, $2,300. Knight (11/2007), ★16485924B/D, Unc, $3,680. CAA (9/2005), ★18188381B/E, Unc, $3,105. Knight (10/2006), ★18842378B/B, VF-35 (PCGS), $402.50. CAA (9/2006), ★18870929B/A, Unc-63 (PMG), $1,495.

W-73 Mule • F-236 • 5,000,000, or about 1% mules (est.)

Estimated population: 60 to 90 • *Highest graded:* Unc • *Selected information:* Heritage (7/2007), N67290651A/G, Mule, VF, $172.50. Knight (3/2005), N82866860A/D, Mule, Unc, $747.50. Stack's (6/2005), N100000000A/D, Mule, George H. Blake, AU-58 (PMG), $23,000 (value based on serial number); R1A/A, Unc-64, $29,900 (value based on serial 1). CAA (4/2006), R3A/C, Unc-63, $3,220 (value based on low serial number). CAA (9/2006), R49027462A/B, Unc-67 (PMG), $1,725.

W-73 Mule★ • F-236★

Recorded population: 6 • *Highest graded:* VF or finer • *Selected information:* CAA (6/1995), ★17894942B/F, VF, $121.

Series of 1923

Series of 1923 Silver Certificates, with Washington in a encore appearance on the face, were made in three signature combinations, with Woods-Tate being much scarcer than the others. All have the Treasury seal, an ornate counter to the right, and serial numbers in blue.

Variety W-74, with over two billion notes, is the most prodigious issue among all large-size notes by a large margin. Gene Hessler states that 8,353 face plates were required to do the printing. This computes to an average quantity of 291,128 notes printed from each plate.

W-74 • F-237 • Speelman-White (1922–1927) • 2,431,800,000 (est.)

Estimated population: 16,000 to 22,000 • *Highest graded:* Unc • *Commentary:* The record-breaking production of these notes resulted in these being very common today.

VG-8	F-12	VF-20	EF-40	AU-50	Unc-60	Unc-63	Unc-65
$20	$30	$40	$55	$70	$85	$110	$225

W-74★ • F-237★

Estimated population: 1,400 to 1,500 • *Highest graded:* Unc.

VG-8	F-12	VF-20	EF-40	AU-50	Unc-60	Unc-63	Unc-65
$70	$100	$200	$350	$600	$900	$1,200	—

W-75 • F-238 • Woods-White (1927–1928) • 223,496,000 (est.)

Estimated population: 5,000 to 6,000 • *Highest graded:* Unc.

VG-8	F-12	VF-20	EF-40	AU-50	Unc-60	Unc-63	Unc-65
$20	$30	$40	$55	$70	$85	$110	$235

W-75★ • F-238★

Estimated population: 425 to 450 • *Highest graded:* Unc.

VG-8	F-12	VF-20	EF-40	AU-50	Unc-60	Unc-63	Unc-65
$100	$150	$350	$550	$850	$1,200	$1,500	—

W-76 • F-239 • Woods-Tate (1928–1929) • 4,700,000 (est.)

Estimated population: 400 to 450 • *Highest graded:* Unc.

VG-8	F-12	VF-20	EF-40	AU-50	Unc-60	Unc-63	Unc-65
$120	$200	$350	$450	$600	$1,300	$1,400	$2,000

W-76★ • F-239★

Estimated population: 12 to 14 • *Highest graded:* AU-50 • *Selected information:* Hickman & Oakes (6/1985), ★21148750D/F, AU, $525. Stack's (12/1992), ★21148751D/G, EF, $850. NASCA (4/1982), ★21197999D/G, EF, $625. CAA (1/2000), ★21561952D/D, VG–F $605. CAA (1/2005), ★21812864D/H, VG, $2,415. Knight (11/2003), ★23040605D/E, EF–AU, $2,875.

SERIES OF 1923

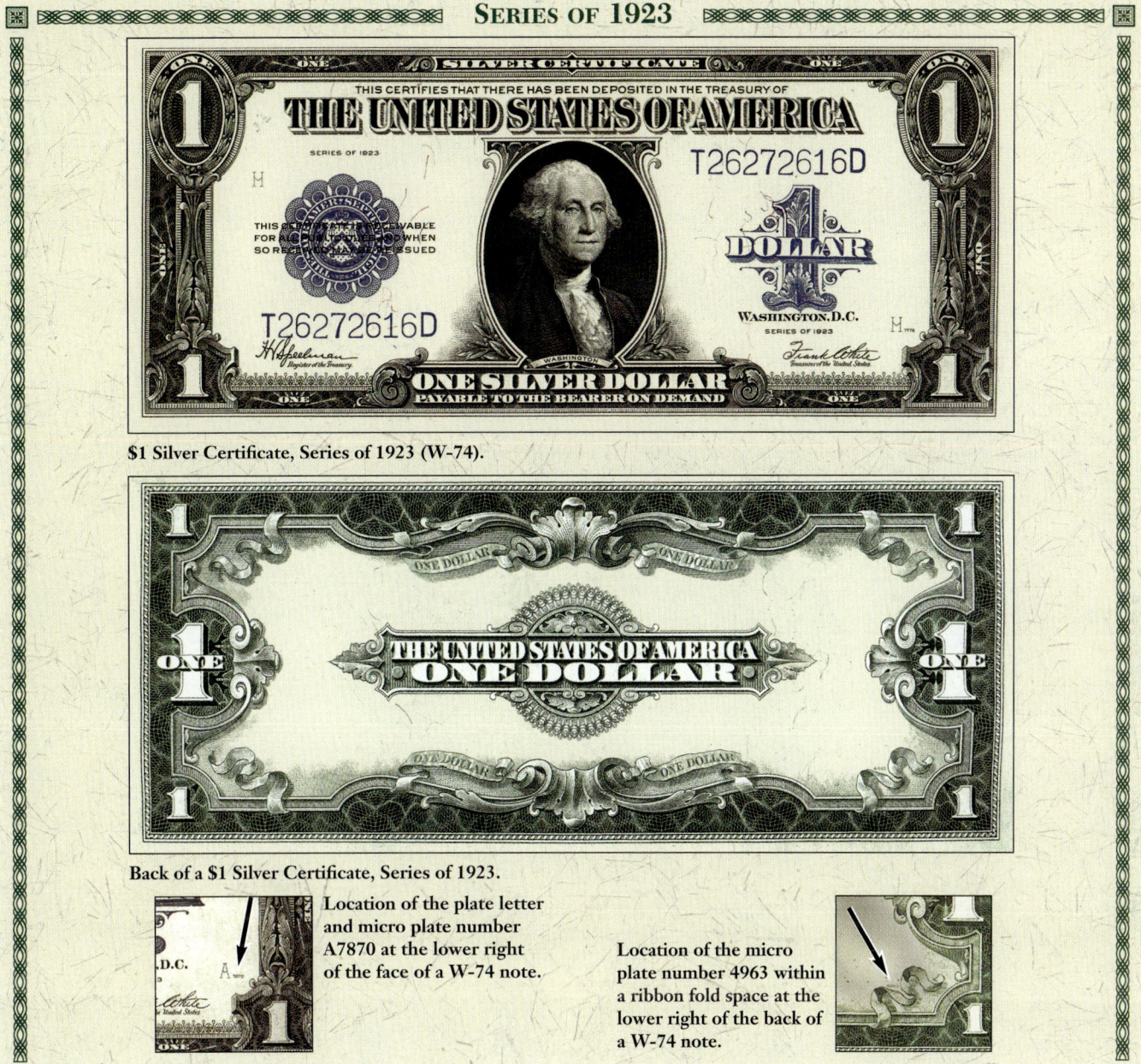

$1 Silver Certificate, Series of 1923 (W-74).

Back of a $1 Silver Certificate, Series of 1923.

Location of the plate letter and micro plate number A7870 at the lower right of the face of a W-74 note.

Location of the micro plate number 4963 within a ribbon fold space at the lower right of the back of a W-74 note.

TREASURY OR COIN NOTES

Series of 1890

The face of each of the $1 Coin or Treasury Note, Series of 1890 and the subsequent Series of 1891 (illus. on pp. 132–133), features the portrait of Edwin M. Stanton, secretary of war under presidents Lincoln and Johnson—one of many individuals once prominent but little remembered today who can be seen on large-size federal paper money.

The focus and admiration of numismatists is on the back, where the word ONE is in large and intricately engraved letters against an extremely rich green background. At the Bureau of Engraving and Printing, this was a team effort in the strictest sense, and involved the combined talents of D.M. Cooper, W.A. Coppenhaver, W.H. Douglas, E.M. Hall, E.E. Myers, and George U. Rose Jr., according to Gene Hessler.

All Treasury or Coin Notes, across all denominations, have a star next to the serial number, an artistic touch and not indicating a replacement note (as it does today). These are beautiful to behold, especially on high-grade examples. As a class these bills are scarce, creating one of the more elusive types within the $1 denomination; W-81 is the rarest, with Uncirculated examples being especially so.

W-80 • F-347 • Rosecrans-Huston (1889–1891) • Large brown seal • 4,288,000 (est.)

Estimated population: 400 to 500 • *Highest graded:* Unc.

VG-8	F-12	VF-20	EF-40	AU-50	Unc-60	Unc-63	Unc-65
$250	$475	$900	$1,800	$2,500	$2,900	$4,500	$12,000

W-81 • F-348 • Rosecrans-Nebeker (1891–1893) • Large brown seal • 552,000 (est.)

Estimated population: 50 to 55 • *Highest graded:* Unc.

VG-8	F-12	VF-20	EF-40	AU-50	Unc-60	Unc-63	Unc-65
$250	$575	$1,500	$3,500	$4,000	$5,000	$6,200	$16,000

SERIES OF 1890

$1 Treasury or Coin Note, Series of 1890 (W-80), the first of three varieties of this type. Depicted is Edwin M. Stanton, Lincoln's secretary of war during the Civil War. The distinctive large (very large!) brown Treasury seal adds color to the face of this and W-81, while W-82 has a small red seal. The star at the serial number is an ornament.

$1 Treasury or Coin Note, Series of 1890 (W-82), showing a smaller Treasury seal in red.

Back of a Treasury or Coin Note, Series of 1890, with ornate detailed features, making this a numismatic favorite today. This is the lowest denomination in the Series of 1890 Treasury or Coin Notes, all of which have rich engraving on the back, culminating with the famous "Watermelon Note" ($100) and "Grand Watermelon Note" ($1,000).

Detail showing the plate letter and number D21 on the lower left face of a W-82 note.

Detail showing the plate number 10, oriented sideways, in a triangular white space near the right edge of the back of a W-80 note. The number is near the lower right of this image. During this decade the bureau engravers seemed to play hide-and-seek, often putting the back plate numbers in unusual places. In this series in the case of horizontal figures, sometimes the digit 6 was underlined to differentiate it from a 9, and vice versa. Otherwise a 6 or a 9 on its side would have been hard to identify positively.

SERIES OF 1891

$1 Treasury or Coin Note, Series of 1891 (W-85), one of three varieties with the new back type. The face is essentially the same as that of the preceding type. A small red Treasury seal was used on all varieties.

Back of a Treasury or Coin Note, Series of 1891, with the new "open" design.

Detail showing the tiny plate number 58 on a W-85 note, located just above the flower in a decoration near the left edge.

W-82 • F-349 • Small red seal with scalloped border • 2,320,000 (est.)

Estimated population: 160 to 180 • *Highest graded:* Unc.

VG-8	F-12	VF-20	EF-40	AU-50	Unc-60	Unc-63	Unc-65
$250	$475	$900	$1,800	$2,500	$2,900	$3,600	$10,000

Series of 1891

After considering the Series of 1890 and its use in circulation, the Treasury department wanted open areas on the back, feeling that the old design was too "busy" and that filling the entire space made counterfeiting easier. Accordingly, the Series of 1891 was created.

W-83 • F-350 • Rosecrans-Nebeker (1891–1893) • Small red seal with scalloped border • 13,160,000

Estimated population: 325 to 375 • *Highest graded:* Unc.

VG-8	F-12	VF-20	EF-40	AU-50	Unc-60	Unc-63	Unc-65
$200	$360	$400	$575	$800	$900	$1,125	$2,000

W-84 • F-351 • Tillman-Morgan (1893–1897) • 35,940,000 (est.)

Estimated population: 1,200 to 1,400 • *Highest graded:* Unc.

VG-8	F-12	VF-20	EF-40	AU-50	Unc-60	Unc-63	Unc-65
$200	$360	$400	$575	$800	$900	$1,125	$1,800

W-85 • F-352 • Bruce-Roberts (1897–1898) • 8,444,000 (est.)

Estimated population: 500 to 750 • *Highest graded:* Unc.

VG-8	F-12	VF-20	EF-40	AU-50	Unc-60	Unc-63	Unc-65
$200	$360	$400	$575	$800	$900	$1,125	$1,800

FEDERAL RESERVE BANK NOTES

Series of 1918

The $1 Federal Reserve Bank Notes, Series of 1918 (illus. on p. 135), are sometimes called "Green Eagle Notes." These feature the city location of the issuing Federal Reserve Bank on the face and a patriotic eagle grasping a flag on the back. Such currency was produced in many different combinations, yielding a series that is quite popular today. All bear the date of May 18, 1914, except the San Francisco notes, which are dated May 20, 1914. All have a blue Treasury seal.

Notes of this type can be collected either as a single example to illustrate the type, by acquiring one note from each of the 12 banks, or by signature combinations.

Star notes are known for all of the varieties except W-101-A and in all instances are rare. A generation ago such star notes were curious, but not in the mainstream of interest. Today, Doug Murray's research in combination with population estimates has changed that, and a star note at auction, particularly a scarce variety, will make everyone sit up straight and pay attention.

W-100-A • F-708 • Boston • Teehee-Burke (1915–1919) • Bullen-Morss • 14,776,000 (est.)

Estimated population: 300 to 275 • *Highest graded:* Unc.

VG-8	F-12	VF-20	EF-40	AU-50	Unc-60	Unc-63	Unc-65
$105	$135	$165	$200	$275	$325	$400	$850

W-100-A★ • F-708★

Estimated population: 12 to 14 • *Highest graded:* Unc • *Selected information:* Stack's (9/1992), A41★/A, Unc, $500 (low serial). Heritage (4/2008), A33603★/G, VF-25 (PMG), $1,495. CAA (10/195), A70431★/C, G, $77. Knight (2/2002), A86570★/B, VG, $161. Stack's (3/1991), A160665★/A, F–VF, $170.

W-101-A • F-709 • Willett-Morss • 4,924,000 (est.)

Estimated population: 80 to 90 • *Highest graded:* Unc • *Commentary:* In his 1951 study of these notes (see the bibliography), W.A. Philpott Jr. commented: "The $1 Teehee & Burke, Willett & Morss, is rare in Uncirculated state, and seldom found better than Very Fine. The other Boston $1's can be found Uncirculated without too much of a hunt."

VG-8	F-12	VF-20	EF-40	AU-50	Unc-60	Unc-63	Unc-65
$140	$190	$240	$300	$375	$400	$550	$1,200

W-102-A • F-710 • Elliott-Burke (1919–1921) • 19,900,000 (est.)

Estimated population: 500 to 600 • *Highest graded:* Unc.

VG-8	F-12	VF-20	EF-40	AU-50	Unc-60	Unc-63	Unc-65
$105	$135	$165	$200	$275	$325	$400	$850

W-102-A★ • F-710★

Estimated population: 19 to 21 • *Highest graded:* Unc.

VG-8	F-12	VF-20	EF-40	AU-50	Unc-60	Unc-63
$350	$500	$1,000	$1,800	$3,100	$4,300	$5,500

W-104-B • F-711 • New York • Teehee-Burke (1915–1919) • Sailer-Strong • 8,616,000 (est.)

Estimated population: 300 to 350 • *Highest graded:* Unc.

VG-8	F-12	VF-20	EF-40	AU-50	Unc-60	Unc-63	Unc-65
$105	$135	$165	$200	$275	$325	$400	$850

W-104-B★ • F-711★

Estimated population: 11 to 13 • *Highest graded:* Unc.

VG-8	F-12	VF-20	EF-40	AU-50	Unc-60	Unc-63
$500	$700	$1,400	$2,500	$4,400	$6,000	$7,500

W-105-B • F-712 • Hendricks-Strong • 60,528,000 (est.)

Estimated population: 800 to 950 • *Highest graded:* Unc.

VG-8	F-12	VF-20	EF-40	AU-50	Unc-60	Unc-63	Unc-65
$105	$135	$165	$200	$275	$325	$400	$850

W-105-B★ • F-712★

Estimated population: 28 to 32 • *Highest graded:* Unc • *Selected information:* Knight (3/2007), B5442★/B, Unc-65 (PMG), $4,370. Knight (9/2007), B308498★/B, EF-40 (PCGS), $1,495. Heritage (5/2007), B343495★/C, G–VG, $218.50.

W-106-B • F-713 • Elliott-Burke (1919–1921) • 37,580,000 (est.)

Estimated population: 600 to 700 • *Highest graded:* Unc.

VG-8	F-12	VF-20	EF-40	AU-50	Unc-60	Unc-63	Unc-65
$105	$135	$165	$200	$275	$325	$400	$850

W-106-B★ • F-713★

Estimated population: 37 to 42 • *Highest graded:* Unc • *Selected information:* Knight (3/2007), B682652/★D, Unc-65 (PMG), $4,830. Knight (2/2004), B842639★/C, VF–EF, $575. CAA (9/2000), B914398★/B, VF, $352. Knight (6/2000), B942915★/C, EF, $440. Knight (6/2002), B982904★/D, VG, $230. Heritage (1/2006), B1094982★/B, AU-55 (PCGS), $2,070.

W-107-C • F-714 • Philadelphia • Teehee-Burke (1915–1919) • Hardt-Passmore • 2,504,000 (est.)

Estimated population: 120 to 135 • *Highest graded:* Unc.

VG-8	F-12	VF-20	EF-40	AU-50	Unc-60	Unc-63	Unc-65
$105	$135	$165	$200	$275	$325	$400	$850

W-107-C★ • F-714★

Estimated population: 9 or 10 • *Highest graded:* AU-50 • *Selected information:* Heritage (5/2001), C10049★/A, VF, $282. Heritage (1/2006), C104963★, VF, $1,495.

W-108-C • F-715 • Dyer-Passmore • 19,364,000 (est.)

Estimated population: 325 to 375 • *Highest graded:* Unc.

VG-8	F-12	VF-20	EF-40	AU-50	Unc-60	Unc-63	Unc-65
$105	$135	$165	$200	$275	$325	$400	$850

W-108-C★ • F-715★

Estimated population: 16 to 18 • *Highest graded:* Unc • *Selected information:* Knight (2/2002), C208616★/D, EF–AU, $748. Knight (6/2008), C214916★/D, VF-20 (PCGS, now VF-30 PCGS), $1,207.50. Heritage (9/2008), C235792★/D, F–VF, $402.50. Knight (2/2002), C244533★/A, EF–AU, $690. Heritage (1/2008), C270286★/B, F-12 (PMG), $546.25. Knight (3/2005), C270813★/A, F–VF, $920.

W-109-C • F-716 • Elliott-Burke (1919–1921) • 9,696,000 (est.)

Estimated population: 85 to 90 • *Highest graded:* Unc • *Commentary:* In his 1951 study of these notes (see the bibliography), W.A. Philpott Jr. observed that this variety is considered to be scarce.

VG-8	F-12	VF-20	EF-40	AU-50	Unc-60	Unc-63	Unc-65
$110	$150	$180	$225	$300	$375	$460	$900

SERIES OF 1918

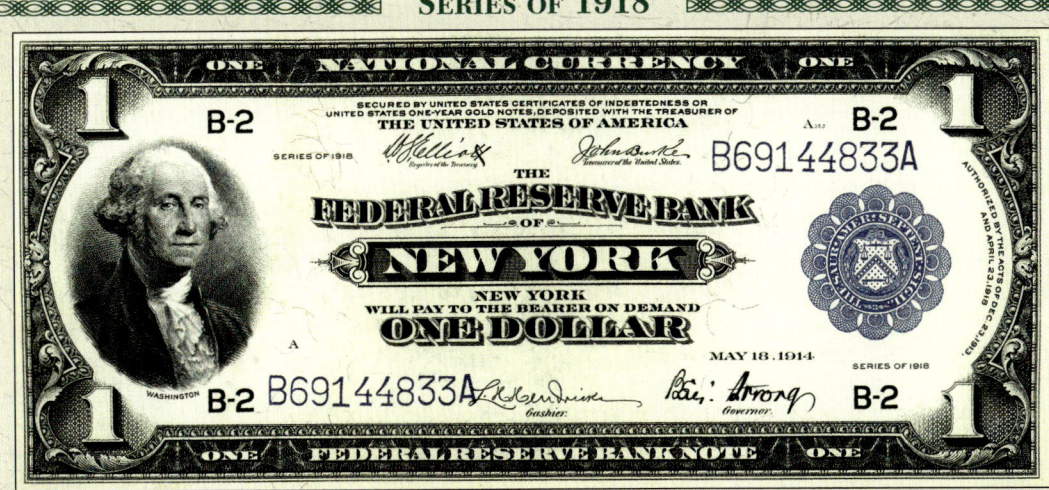

$1 Federal Reserve Bank Note, Series of 1918 (W-106-B), one of many varieties within this type. The letter B (for the New York district) is repeated in various places, including as a prefix to the serial numbers.

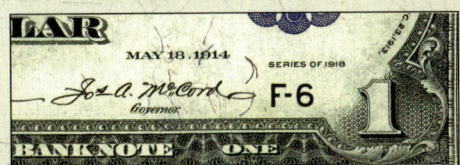

Shown is a detail from W-116-F, an Atlanta note; the F is the district letter. The usual date of May 18, 1914, is seen, as on all other notes in this series except for San Francisco issues.

Shown is a detail of the variant date May 20, 1914, from W-137-L, a San Francisco note; the L is the district letter.

Standard back of a Federal Reserve Bank Note, Series of 1918. This is familiarly known as the "Green Eagle Note."

W-109-C★ • F-716★

Recorded population: 2 • *Highest graded:* VF-20 • *Selected information:* Knight (2/2002), C310914★/B, F, $690. Stack's (9/1996), C312403★/C, VF, $880.

W-110-C • F-717 • Dyer-Norris • 19,492,000 (est.)

Estimated population: 450 to 550 • *Highest graded:* Unc.

VG-8	F-12	VF-20	EF-40	AU-50	Unc-60	Unc-63	Unc-65
$105	$135	$165	$200	$275	$325	$400	$850

W-110-C★ • F-717★

Estimated population: 28 to 30 • *Highest graded:* Unc • *Selected information:* Knight (10/2006), C393056★/D, VG-10 (PMG), $356.50. Knight (6/2008), C393093★/A, VF-35 (PCGS), $1,150. Knight (3/2008), C409592★/D, EF-40 (PCGS), $1,667.50. Knight (11/2007), C416163★/C, EF-45 (PCGS),

$1,092.50. Knight (9/2007), C438257★/A, VF-30 (PCGS), $1,092.50.

W-111-D • F-718 • Cleveland • Teehee-Burke (1915–1919) • Baxter-Fancher • 8,828,000 (est.)

Estimated population: 400 to 500 • *Highest graded:* Unc.

VG-8	F-12	VF-20	EF-40	AU-50	Unc-60	Unc-63	Unc-65
$105	$135	$165	$200	$275	$325	$400	$850

W-111-D★ • F-718★

Estimated population: 15 to 17 • *Highest graded:* Unc • *Selected information:* B&M (4/1997), D106★/B, Unc, $700. B&M (8/1987), D112★/C, Unc, $209. Knight (2/2002), D16270★/B, VG–F (later F), $115; later seen in Knight (6/2004), VF, $747.50. Frank Martinelli (10/1995), D32416★/H, F–VF, price list $450.

W-112-D • F-719 • Davis-Fancher • 11,448,000 (est.)
Estimated population: 150 to 165 • Highest graded: Unc.

VG-8	F-12	VF-20	EF-40	AU-50	Unc-60	Unc-63	Unc-65
$105	$135	$165	$200	$275	$325	$400	$850

W-112-D★ • F-719★
Recorded population: 7 • Highest graded: Unc • Selected information: CAA (2008), VF-25 (PCGS), $1,150. Stack's (1991), CU, $700.

W-113-D • F-720 • Elliott-Burke (1919–1921) • 22,608,000 (est.)
Estimated population: 350 to 400 • Highest graded: Unc.

VG-8	F-12	VF-20	EF-40	AU-50	Unc-60	Unc-63	Unc-65
$105	$135	$165	$200	$275	$325	$400	$850

W-113-D★ • F-720★
Estimated population: 18 to 20 • Highest graded: Unc • Selected information: Knight (11/2006), D255719★/C, VG, $632.50. Stack's (5/2006), D306111★/C, Unc, $3,450. Knight (2/2002), D306113★/A, Unc, $1,438. Knight (6/2008), D316909★/A, EF-40 (PCGS), $1,840. Heritage (9/2008), D366626★/B, F, $575. Heritage (5/2007), D391474★/B, G–VG, $322.

W-114-E • F-721 • Richmond • Teehee-Burke (1915–1919) • Keesee-Seay • 14,040,000 (est.)
Estimated population: 250 to 300 • Highest graded: Unc.

VG-8	F-12	VF-20	EF-40	AU-50	Unc-60	Unc-63	Unc-65
$105	$135	$165	$200	$275	$325	$400	$850

W-114-E★ • F-721★
Estimated population: 9 or 10 • Highest graded: EF-40 • Selected information: Knight (6/2008), E31037★/E, EF-45 (PCGS), $2,559. Herbert I. Melnick (6/1983), E101109★, VF, $140; later seen in Knight (2/2002), EF/AU, $805. CAA (5/1999), E114764★/H, VG–F, $220.

W-115-E • F-722 • Elliott-Burke (1919–1921) • 14,344,000 (est.)
Estimated population: 160 to 180 • Highest graded: Unc.

VG-8	F-12	VF-20	EF-40	AU-50	Unc-60	Unc-63	Unc-65
$110	$150	$180	$225	$300	$360	$475	$1,000

W-115-E★ • F-722★
Estimated population: 9 or 10 • Highest graded: Unc • Selected information: Knight (11/2007), E273524★/D, VF-35 (PMG), $1,265. Knight (3/2008), E296391★/C, VF-35 (PCGS), $1,380.

W-116-F • F-723 • Atlanta • Teehee-Burke (1915–1919) • Pike-McCord • 8,204,000 (est.)
Estimated population: 175 to 190 • Highest graded: Unc.

VG-8	F-12	VF-20	EF-40	AU-50	Unc-60	Unc-63	Unc-65
$110	$150	$180	$225	$300	$360	$460	$900

W-116-F★ • F-723★
Recorded population: 2 • Highest graded: F-12 • Selected information: Knight (2/2002) F32967★/C, VF/F, $978. CAA (10/1995), F49286★/B, F, $825.

W-117-F • F-724 • Bell-McCord • 2,656,000 (est.)
Estimated population: 35 to 40 • Highest graded: Unc.

VG-8	F-12	VF-20	EF-40	AU-50	Unc-60	Unc-63
$120	$175	$225	$400	$800	$1,200	$1,600

W-117-F★ • F-724★
Recorded population: 4 • Highest graded: AU-50 • Selected information: CAA (6/1995), F89238★/B, F+, $1,050. Knight (6/2008), F99405★/A, Net-10 (PCGS), $747.

W-118-F • F-725 • Bell-Wellborn • 5,240,000 (est.)
Estimated population: 50 to 60 • Highest graded: Unc.

VG-8	F-12	VF-20	EF-40	AU-50	Unc-60	Unc-63	Unc-65
$110	$160	$200	$250	$350	$425	$575	$1,200

W-118-F★ • F-725★
Recorded population: 3 • Highest graded: AU-50 • Commentary: No meaningful recent auction records • *Selected information:* CAA (5/1993), F117332★/D, AU, $616. Smythe (6/1990), F139829★/A, VG–F, $180.

W-119-F • F-726 • Elliott-Burke (1919–1921) • 18,524,000 (est.)
Estimated population: 150 to 165 • Highest graded: Unc.

VG-8	F-12	VF-20	EF-40	AU-50	Unc-60	Unc-63	Unc-65
$105	$135	$165	$200	$275	$325	$400	$850

W-119-F★ • F-726★
Recorded population: 4 • Highest graded: EF-40 • Selected information: Knight (6/2008), F264561★/A, F-15 (PCGS), $920.

W-120-G • F-727 • Chicago • Teehee-Burke (1915–1919) • McCloud-McDougal • 22,300,000 (est.)
Estimated population: 500 to 700 • Highest graded: Unc • Commentary: In his 1951 study of these notes (see the bibliography), W.A. Philpott Jr. stated, "There are still 222,583 Chicago $1s (three different signatures) outstanding, even though 64,432,000 were issued." This was considered by Philpott to be an exceptionally large quantity.

VG-8	F-12	VF-20	EF-40	AU-50	Unc-60	Unc-63	Unc-65
$105	$135	$165	$200	$275	$325	$400	$850

W-120-G★ • F-727★
Estimated population: 22 to 24 • Highest graded: Unc • Selected information: Knight (2/2002), G6063★/C, Unc, $1,150. CAA (5/2000), G8034★/B, F–VF, $247.50. Knight (9/2007), G31006★/B, AU-50 (PCGS), $1,725. Stack's (3/2002), G109558★/F, Choice EF, $345. Knight (11/2001), G132424★/D, VG, $132.

W-121-G • F-728 • Cramer-McDougal • 13,388,000 (est.)
Estimated population: 140 to 150 • Highest graded: Unc.

VG-8	F-12	VF-20	EF-40	AU-50	Unc-60	Unc-63	Unc-65
$105	$135	$165	$200	$275	$325	$400	$850

W-121-G★ • F-728★
Recorded population: 5 • Highest graded: VF-30 • Selected information: Knight (6/2008), G231997★/A, F-12 (PMG), $920. Knight (10/2006), G247337★/A, VF, $2,760. Knight (6/2004), G253660★/D, VF, $3,450.

W-122-G • F-729 • Elliott-Burke (1919–1921) • 28,744,000 (est.)

Estimated population: 550 to 700 • *Highest graded:* Unc.

VG-8	F-12	VF-20	EF-40	AU-50	Unc-60	Unc-63	Unc-65
$105	$135	$165	$200	$275	$325	$400	$850

W-122-G★ • F-729★

Estimated population: 17 to 19 • *Highest graded:* AU-50 • *Selected information:* CAA (1/2002), G551104★/D, VF, $414. Knight (3/2005), G634918★/B, VF, $862.50. Stack's (11/2007), G653187★/C, VF, $805. Knight (6/2008), G666441★, VF-30 (PCGS, later EF-40 PCGS), $1,610.

W-123-H • F-730 • St. Louis • Teehee-Burke (1915–1919) • Attebery-Wells • 9,728,000 (est.)

Estimated population: 160 to 170 • *Highest graded:* Unc • *Commentary:* In his 1951 study of these notes (see the bibliography), W.A. Philpott Jr. stated, "The St. Louis $1s are the second scarcest of the 12 banks, there only being fewer Minneapolis $1s than St. Louis $1s. St. Louis $1's outstanding as of October 30, 1944, were 82,511 for four different signatures, or about 20,626 for each." This comment refers to all St. Louis varieties, not just W-123-H.

VG-8	F-12	VF-20	EF-40	AU-50	Unc-60	Unc-63	Unc-65
$105	$135	$165	$200	$275	$325	$400	$950

W-123-H★ • F-730★

Estimated population: 10 to 12 • *Highest graded:* Unc • *Selected information:* Knight (2/2002), H2509★/A, F, $719. Heritage (1/2006), H3742★/B, EF–AU, $2,185. Knight (6/2008), H68388★/H, F-15 (PCGS), $1,380.

W-124-H • F-731 • Attebery-Biggs • 4,472,000 (est.)

Estimated population: 60 to 70 • *Highest graded:* Unc.

VG-8	F-12	VF-20	EF-40	AU-50	Unc-60	Unc-63
$110	$160	$200	$250	$350	$425	$575

W-124-H★ • F-731★

Recorded population: 5 • *Highest graded:* VF-30 • *Selected information:* Heritage (1/2006), H124125★/A, VG–F, $2,760.

W-125-H • F-732 • Elliott-Burke (1919–1921) • 5,100,000 (est.)

Estimated population: 55 to 65 • *Highest graded:* Unc.

VG-8	F-12	VF-20	EF-40	AU-50	Unc-60	Unc-63	Unc-65
$110	$160	$200	$250	$350	$425	$575	$1,200

W-125-H★ • F-732★

Recorded population: 1 • *Selected information:* Smythe (3/2005), H163950★/B, VF, $3,163.

W-126-H • F-733 • White-Biggs • 8,608,000 (est.)

Estimated population: 115 to 130 • *Highest graded:* Unc.

VG-8	F-12	VF-20	EF-40	AU-50	Unc-60	Unc-63	Unc-65
$105	$135	$165	$200	$275	$325	$400	$950

W-126-H★ • F-733★

Recorded population: 5 • *Highest graded:* VF-30 • *Selected information:* Knight (6/2008), H241508★/D, F-12 (PCGS), $1,265. CAA (9/2005), H272609★/A, F, $2,760.

W-127-I • F-734 • Minneapolis • Teehee-Burke (1915–1919) • Cook-Wold • 9,120,000 (est.)

Estimated population: 150 to 165 • *Highest graded:* Unc.

VG-8	F-12	VF-20	EF-40	AU-50	Unc-60	Unc-63	Unc-65
$105	$135	$165	$200	$275	$325	$400	$1,000

W-127-I★ • F-734★

Recorded population: 5 • *Highest graded:* F-12 • *Selected information:* Knight (3/2005), I101052★/D, VG, problems, $845.

W-128-I • F-735 • Cook-Young • 600,000 (est.)

Estimated population: 55 to 65 • *Highest graded:* Unc • *Commentary:* In his 1951 study of these notes (see the bibliography), W.A. Philpott Jr. stated, "The rarest of the six notes of various denominations issued by Minneapolis is the $1 Teehee & Burke, Cook & Young. In Uncirculated state it is very rare and difficult to find. On October 30, 1944, there were 59,777 $1's out [of the various Minneapolis $1 issues]."

VG-8	F-12	VF-20	EF-40	AU-50	Unc-60	Unc-63	Unc-65
$120	$160	$500	$750	$1,200	$1,300	$1,800	$2,400

W-128-I★ • F-735★

Recorded population: 3 • *Highest graded:* VF-25 • *Selected information:* Smythe (2005), VG-8, $2,415.

W-129-I • F-736 • Elliott-Burke (1919–1921) • 7,092,000 (est.)

Estimated population: 150 to 160 • *Highest graded:* Unc.

VG-8	F-12	VF-20	EF-40	AU-50	Unc-60	Unc-63	Unc-65
$110	$150	$200	$250	$400	$500	$800	$1,250

W-129-I★ • F-736★

Recorded population: 6 • *Highest graded:* EF–AU • *Selected information:* Knight (2/2002), I126572★/D, EF–AU, $1,179. Knight (2/2004), I128190★/B, VG, $1,208.

W-130-J • F-737 • Kansas City • Teehee-Burke (1915–1919) • Anderson-Miller • 12,000,000 (est.)

Estimated population: 225 to 275 • *Highest graded:* Unc.

VG-8	F-12	VF-20	EF-40	AU-50	Unc-60	Unc-63	Unc-65
$105	$135	$165	$200	$275	$325	$400	$850

W-130-J★ • F-737★

Estimated population: 9 or 10 • *Highest graded:* F-12 • *Selected information:* DBR Currency (10/2007), J69157★/E, G, web site price listing $1,495.

W-131-J • F-738 • Elliott-Burke (1919–1921) • 2,700,000 (est.)

Estimated population: 220 to 240 • *Highest graded:* Unc.

VG-8	F-12	VF-20	EF-40	AU-50	Unc-60	Unc-63	Unc-65
$105	$135	$165	$200	$275	$325	$400	$850

W-131-J★ • F-738★

Recorded population: 6 • *Highest graded:* Unc • *Selected information:* Knight (6/2008), J112553★/A, Unc-63 (PCGS), $4,830. Knight (11/2003), J135184★/D, F, $862.50.

W-132-J • F-739 • Helm-Miller • 10,120,000 (est.)
Estimated population: 220 to 240 • *Highest graded:* Unc.

VG-8	F-12	VF-20	EF-40	AU-50	Unc-60	Unc-63	Unc-65
$105	$135	$165	$200	$275	$325	$400	$850

W-132-J★ • F-739★
Recorded population: 5 • *Highest graded:* VF-30 • *Selected information:* Heritage (1/2006), J147564★/D, VF, $1,495. Heritage (1/2008), J222306★/B, VG-8 (PMG), $920.

W-133-K • F-740 • Dallas • Teehee-Burke (1915–1919) • Talley-Van Zandt • 8,600,000 (est.)
Estimated population: 180 to 200 • *Highest graded:* Unc.

VG-8	F-12	VF-20	EF-40	AU-50	Unc-60	Unc-63	Unc-65
$110	$150	$180	$225	$300	$375	$550	$1,200

W-133-K★ • F-740★
Estimated population: 10 to 12 • *Highest graded:* Unc • *Selected information:* Knight (2/2002), K2995★/C, VF, $1,064. Smythe (4/2007), K16866★/B, G–VG, problems, $690. Knight (3/2005), K38483★/C, G–VG, $518. Knight (6/2008), K94213★/A, VF-20 (PCGS), $1,553.

W-134-K • F-741 • Elliott-Burke (1919–1921) • 2,632,000 (est.)
Estimated population: 55 to 60 • *Highest graded:* Unc • *Commentary:* In his 1951 study of these notes (see the bibliography), W.A. Philpott Jr. stated, "The most difficult note to get Uncirculated of the Dallas Bank's 14 notes in various series is the $1 Elliott & Burke, Talley & Van Zandt. The writer has seen many Extremely Fine—but has never seen an Uncirculated one."

VG-8	F-12	VF-20	EF-40	AU-50	Unc-60	Unc-63
$120	$165	$200	$250	$300	—	$2,100

W-134-K★ • F-741★
Recorded population: 5 • *Highest graded:* VF-30 • *Selected information:* Heritage (1/2006), K126749★/A, VG, $1,495.

W-135-K • F-742 • Lawder-Van Zandt • 6,632,000 (est.)
Estimated population: 115 to 130 • *Highest graded:* Unc.

VG-8	F-12	VF-20	EF-40	AU-50	Unc-60	Unc-63	Unc-65
$120	$165	$200	$240	$280	$350	$1,450	$2,300

W-135-K★ • F-742★
Estimated population: 10 to 12 • *Highest graded:* Unc • *Selected information:* CAA (5/2004), K165339★/C, Unc, $3,680. Knight (6/2008), K165342★/B, Unc-62 (PCGS), $4,370.

W-136-L • F-743 • San Francisco • Teehee-Burke (1915–1919) • Clerk-Lynch • 12,260,000 (est.)
Estimated population: 275 to 325 • *Highest graded:* Unc.

VG-8	F-12	VF-20	EF-40	AU-50	Unc-60	Unc-63	Unc-65
$105	$135	$165	$200	$275	$350	$500	$1,250

W-136-L★ • F-743★
Estimated population: 15 to 17 • *Highest graded:* Unc • *Selected information:* Knight (3/2008), L32949★/A, VF-25 (PCGS), $1,495. Stack's (3/1991), L37210★/B, Unc, $220. Hickman &

Oakes (6/1987), L61252★/D, VG, $110. Smythe (6/1990), L62678★/B, F, $149. Smythe (11/1993), L67853★/A, F, $120. Knight (6/2008), L90839★/C, VF-30 (PMG), $1,265. Knight (2/2002), L112441★/A, VG–F, $299. CAA (10/1995), L123961★/A, VG–F, $132.

W-137-L • F-744 • Clerk-Calkins • 2,140,000 (est.)
Estimated population: 45 to 50 • *Highest graded:* Unc.

VG-8	F-12	VF-20	EF-40	AU-50	Unc-60	Unc-63	Unc-65
$120	$165	$185	$225	$275	$350	$500	$1,450

W-137-L★ • F-744★
Recorded population: 3 • *Highest graded:* VG–F • *Selected information:* L125502★/B, VG–F; L126801★/E, VG. Federal Reserve Bank of San Francisco Exhibit, L140157★/E, G.

W-138-L • F-745 • Elliott-Burke (1919–1921) • 3,376,000 (est.)
Estimated population: 60 to 70 • *Highest graded:* Unc.

VG-8	F-12	VF-20	EF-40	AU-50	Unc-60	Unc-63	Unc-65
$120	$165	$185	$225	$275	$350	$500	$1,350

W-138-L★ • F-745★
Recorded population: 4 • *Highest graded:* EF-40 • *Selected information:* Smythe (6/2000), L165079★/C, VF, $2,475.

W-139-L • F-746 • Ambrose-Calkins • 6,008,000 (est.)
Estimated population: 130 to 150 • *Highest graded:* Unc.

VG-8	F-12	VF-20	EF-40	AU-50	Unc-60	Unc-63	Unc-65
$120	$165	$185	$225	$275	$350	$500	$1,250

W-139-L★ • F-746★
Recorded population: 2 • *Highest graded:* VF-30 • *Selected information:* Knight (6/2008), L202433★/A, VG-8 (PCGS), $1,840. CAA (5/1997), L211975★, VF (later EF), $715.

SMALL SIZE

Small-size $1 notes are the most widely collected federal issues today. The face value is low, and most were made in sufficient quantities that examples are readily available, although certain early issues are scarce in Uncirculated grade. This class of notes begins with a single Legal Tender Note issue with a curious history, and continues to include an extensive run of Silver Certificates. Among these are several special issues, including those made for Hawaii and North Africa during World War II and experimental notes with R and S overprints. The portrait engraver for all Washington face styles through the early 21st century was George F.C. Smillie, after the famous Gilbert Stuart portrait. Joachim C. Benzing created the backs (in two styles, first with ONE DOLLAR and later with the obverse and reverse of the Great Seal).

Beginning on September 22, 1949, new $1 back plates were made slightly smaller by subtly removing details of the design, narrowing the printed area. This created "Wide Back" (early style) and "Narrow Back" (later style) varieties. We can be thankful to Aubrey and Adeline Bebee, professional numismatists from Chicago who relocated to Omaha in the 1950s, for preserving large quantities of early issues, including sheets when they could find them, and selling them to collectors. In Fort Worth, Texas, Amon G. Carter Jr. saved many thousands of small-size notes, often ordering them in "bricks" of 4,000. Even so, the number preserved was small in comparison to the large number of collectors seeking them today.

The new era of small-size $1 Federal Reserve Notes commenced with the Series of 1963, with most series issued by all of the 12 different Federal Reserve Banks and bearing appropriate designations. This was by default; the popular Silver Certificates were discontinued at that time, due to the rising market price of the metal, which made it impossible to continue to redeem them for silver coins at face value. For some Federal Reserve Note series, not all banks participated. Each note has a green Treasury seal. All these notes are highly collectible today and are available in approximate proportion to the numbers actually printed. Star notes are scarcer.

With the completion of a second printing facility, a branch in Fort Worth, Texas (known as the Western Facility), some bills were produced there. These are identified by a small FW on the face, a new element. In theory, for each new signature combination there could be 12 different varieties from the Bureau of Engraving and Printing in Washington, D.C., 12 star-note varieties, and the same number of varieties from Fort Worth, yielding up to a theoretical 48 different in total! In fact, not all banks and printing locations (Washington and Fort Worth) issued bills for every series. It is readily appreciated that $1 bills furnish an affordable denomination for such comprehensive collecting—to collect $50 or $100 bills by all varieties would be beyond the reach of most numismatists.

For a time, beginning with certain printings of the Series of 1988-A, $1 notes were printed in Washington on a web-fed press that took paper from a large roll, rather than in individual sheets, and used a cylinder plate with 96 notes. This experiment lasted for eight years, was limited only to the $1 denomination, and was finally terminated as a failure. These notes have small differences in the plate letters and numbers and are described in the listings. Some experiments with ink were conducted during the same time period.

As recently as the early 1960s the collection and maintenance of a full set of the currently-issued date and signature combinations of $1 notes was easy enough to do, but since then, the advent of the Federal Reserve Bank and FW (Fort Worth) varieties has extended the panorama from horizon to horizon, and hundreds of varieties beckon. What fun!

In the pages that follow, a star beside a small-sized note refers to a star note—one printed to replace another made in error and destroyed. Collecting small-size star notes has become a passion in its own right, and certain of these command substantial premiums. The collecting of mules, or face-plate varieties combined with back plates from a slightly earlier or later series, is another specialty. For this and other small-sized notes, the regularly updated book by John Schwartz and Scott Lindquist, *The Standard Guide to Small-Size U.S. Paper Money 1928 to Date*, is essential, and gives detailed information about serial number "blocks" and sequences and other useful information.

LEGAL TENDER NOTES

Series of 1928, Red Seal
Woods-Woodin (1933)

Small-size $1 Legal Tender Notes consist only of the Series of 1928 (illus. on p. 140). This is because of an obscure provision in the Bland-Allison Act of February 28, 1878, which limited the total face value of Legal Tender Notes to precisely $346,861,016. Accordingly, they were not produced regularly in the small-size series. Issues were erratic, minimal in the $1 series, much more extensive in the $2 and $5 values, and with curious issues in the $100 denomination, Series of 1966 and 1966-A.

The $1 notes have the combined signatures of W.O. Woods and W.H. Woodin. Woodin was president Franklin D. Roosevelt's first secretary of the Treasury. He was one of the most prominent numismatists of his era, specializing in gold coins. At one time he hoped to write a book on early half eagles by die varieties, but never did. Thomas L. Elder sold certain of Woodin's coins at auction in 1911. Soon thereafter, his article in *The Numismatist* extolling the rewards of investing in coins was published. Woodin became ill with cancer of the throat and died before completing even a year in office. Had he lived, it is certain that the history of gold coins and paper money in the era beginning in 1933 would be different from that we know today.

The obligation is to pay the bearer "one dollar," but not specified as to coin or paper. Such bills were issued on the good faith and credit of the government, without metallic backing, this being true of Legal Tender Notes back to their inception in 1862. The imprint on the Treasury seal reads: "This note is a legal tender at its face value for all debts public and private except duties on imports and interest on the public debt."

Often, collectors simply call these bills "1928 Red Seals." The series date of 1928 reflects a curious Treasury department practice and is not related to the time of issue. Roosevelt was inaugurated on March 4, 1933, and these bills were made after that date. Logically, they should have been designated Series of 1933.

These notes with red Treasury seal and red serial numbers were printed in April and May of 1933, but only $8,012 were released at the time.[13] Years later, from November 1948 to February 1949, the rest from the printage of 1,872,012 were released in Puerto Rico. This location was chosen because the distinctive red seals would become common in circulation there. If released on the mainland, such notes would have been mixed with other notes, seen only occasionally, and might have raised questions.

In *The Numismatist* issue of September 1967 (see the bibliography), William A. Philpott Jr. singled out seven small-size star notes, including this one, that he considered to be "excessively rare and hard to come by."

W-140 • F-1500 • 1,872,012

VG-8	F-12	VF-20	EF-40	AU-50	Unc-60	Unc-63	Unc-65
$95	$160	$240	$275	$300	$325	$400	$550

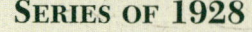

SERIES OF 1928

$1 Legal Tender Note, Series of 1928 (W-140). Portrait of Washington. The distinctive bright red serial numbers and Treasury seal are unique to this numismatically popular but short-lived small-size type.

Detail of the obligation area of the face.

Back of $1 Legal Tender Note, Series of 1928. Also used on $1 Silver Certificates of Series 1928 to 1934.

W-140★ • F-1500★ • 8,000

VG-8	F-12	VF-20	EF-40	AU-50	Unc-60	Unc-63	Unc-65
$2,500	$4,000	$7,000	$11,000	$15,000	$19,000	$25,000	$40,000

SILVER CERTIFICATES

Silver Certificates in the $1 denomination were the basic currency unit in American life until the rising price of silver made it impossible to redeem the notes at par for coins (see the small-size introductory material), ending the series. All varieties are readily collectible, with the Series of 1928-E being the key. Early star notes range from scarce to rare, particularly in Uncirculated grades.

All have the Treasury seal and serial numbers in blue, except for the W-161 (HAWAII overprint) and W-162 (yellow seal for World War II actions in Sicily and North Africa).

Series of 1928, Blue Seal
Tate-Mellon (1928–1929)

This series had the earliest obligation, the ONE SILVER DOLLAR PAYABLE TO THE BEARER ON DEMAND imprint, specifically mentioning a silver dollar. In keeping with tradition, specific quantities of these coins were stored by the Treasury department as backing for these notes.

W-141 • F-1600 • 638,296,908

VG-8	F-12	VF-20	EF-40	AU-50	Unc-60	Unc-63	Unc-65
$25	$30	$40	$45	$55	$75	$95	$160

W-141★ • F-1600★

VG-8	F-12	VF-20	EF-40	AU-50	Unc-60	Unc-63	Unc-65
$45	$80	$125	$300	$450	$550	$750	$1,200

Series of 1928-A, Blue Seal
Woods-Mellon (1929–1932)

This series continued with the ONE SILVER DOLLAR PAYABLE TO THE BEARER ON DEMAND imprint.

Notes with serials beginning with X and Y and each ending in B were made on special experimental paper with different rag content, while Z to B notes were on regular paper and used as a control. Notes with these serials are worth a premium and are listed below as W-143 to W-145. These same serial numbers were used on Series 1928-B notes as part of the experiment.[14]

W-142 • F-1601 • 2,267,809,500

VG-8	F-12	VF-20	EF-40	AU-50	Unc-60	Unc-63	Unc-65
$25	$30	$40	$45	$55	$70	$90	$150

SERIES OF 1928, BLUE SEAL

$1 Silver Certificate, Series of 1928 (W-141).

Detail of the obligation ONE SILVER DOLLAR.

Back of the $1 Silver Certificate, Series of 1938. Type also used on $1 Legal Tender Notes, Series of 1928.

SERIES OF 1928-A, BLUE SEAL

Detail of the signatures and the series imprints of a $1 Silver Certificate, Series of 1928-A (W-142). The back is the standard type of the $1 Legal Tender Notes, Series of 1928, and $1 Silver Certificates, Series of 1928 to 1934.

W-142★ • F-1601★

VG-8	F-12	VF-20	EF-40	AU-50	Unc-60	Unc-63	Unc-65
$45	$80	$100	$250	$350	$475	$650	$900

W-143 • F-unlisted • Experimental paper made of 50% linen and 50% cotton; serials starting with X and ending with B

VG-8	F-12	VF-20	EF-40	AU-50	Unc-60	Unc-63	Unc-65
$30	$50	$75	$115	$160	$225	$300	$425

W-144 • F-unlisted • Experimental paper made of 75% linen and 25% cotton; serials starting with Y and ending with B

VG-8	F-12	VF-20	EF-40	AU-50	Unc-60	Unc-63	Unc-65
$30	$50	$75	$100	$135	$180	$250	$350

W-145 • F-unlisted • Regular paper used as a control; serials starting with Z and ending with B

VG-8	F-12	VF-20	EF-40	AU-50	Unc-60	Unc-63	Unc-65
$40	$60	$90	$125	$175	$250	$325	$450

Series of 1928-B, Blue Seal
Woods-Mills (1932–1933)

This series (illus. on p. 142) continued the ONE SILVER DOLLAR PAYABLE TO THE BEARER ON DEMAND obligation.

Experimental paper varieties with X-B and Y-B serials and control notes with Z-B serials were also made in this series and command a premium.

141

W-146 • F-1602 • 674,597,808

VG-8	F-12	VF-20	EF-40	AU-50	Unc-60	Unc-63	Unc-65
$25	$30	$40	$45	$55	$75	$100	$170

W-146★ • F-1602★

VG-8	F-12	VF-20	EF-40	AU-50	Unc-60	Unc-63	Unc-65
$50	$120	$250	$450	$775	$1,000	$1,400	$2,200

W-147 • F-unlisted • Experimental paper made of 50% linen and 50% cotton; serials starting with X and ending with B

VG-8	F-12	VF-20	EF-40	AU-50	Unc-60	Unc-63	Unc-65
$30	$50	$75	$125	$175	$250	$325	$450

W-148 • F-unlisted • Experimental paper made of 75% linen and 25% cotton; serials starting with Y and ending with B

VG-8	F-12	VF-20	EF-40	AU-50	Unc-60	Unc-63	Unc-65
$30	$50	$75	$125	$175	$250	$325	$450

W-149 • F-unlisted • Regular paper used as a control; serials starting with Z and ending with B

VG-8	F-12	VF-20	EF-40	AU-50	Unc-60	Unc-63	Unc-65
$40	$60	$90	$145	$200	$270	$350	$475

Series of 1928-C, Blue Seal
Woods-Woodin (1933)

This series continued the ONE SILVER DOLLAR PAYABLE TO THE BEARER ON DEMAND imprint.

W-150 • F-1603 • 5,364,348

VG-8	F-12	VF-20	EF-40	AU-50	Unc-60	Unc-63	Unc-65
$100	$150	$200	$300	$400	$475	$625	$1,200

W-150★ • F-1603★ • 12 to 16 known (est.)

VG-8	F-12	VF-20	EF-40	AU-50	Unc-60	Unc-63	Unc-65
$1,800	$4,500	$7,500	$12,500	$17,500	$21,000	$28,000	$50,000

Series of 1928-D, Blue Seal
Julian-Woodin (1933)

This series continued the ONE SILVER DOLLAR PAYABLE TO THE BEARER ON DEMAND imprint.

W-151 • F-1604 • 14,451,372

VG-8	F-12	VF-20	EF-40	AU-50	Unc-60	Unc-63	Unc-65
$40	$55	$100	$160	$210	$275	$450	$750

W-151★ • F-1604★ • 12 to 16 known (est.)

VG-8	F-12	VF-20	EF-40	AU-50	Unc-60	Unc-63	Unc-65
$1,400	$3,500	$5,500	$9,500	$14,000	$17,000	$22,500	$45,000

Series of 1928-E, Blue Seal
Julian-Morgenthau (1934–1945)

This series continued the ONE SILVER DOLLAR PAYABLE TO THE BEARER ON DEMAND imprint. These were printed only for a short time and were succeeded by Series of 1935 with a different imprint. For many years the 1928-E Silver Certificate has been recognized as a key

SERIES OF 1928-B, BLUE SEAL

Detail of the signatures and the series imprints of a $1 Silver Certificate, Series of 1928-B (W-146).

SERIES OF 1928-C, BLUE SEAL

Detail of the signatures and the series imprints of a $1 Silver Certificate, Series of 1928-C (W-150).

SERIES OF 1928-D, BLUE SEAL

Detail of the signatures and the series imprints of a $1 Silver Certificate, Series of 1928-D (W-151).

SERIES OF 1928-E, BLUE SEAL

Detail of the signatures and the series imprints of a $1 Silver Certificate, Series of 1928-E (W-152).

The backs of all the notes shown are the standard type of $1 Legal Tender Notes, Series of 1928, and $1 Silver Certificates, Series of 1928 to 1934.

issue among lower-denomination small-size notes. It therefore comes as no surprise to learn that in *The Numismatist* in September 1967 (see the bibliography), William A. Philpott Jr. included this among seven small-size star notes that he considered to be "excessively rare and hard to come by."

W-152 • F-1605 • 3,519,324

VG-8	F-12	VF-20	EF-40	AU-50	Unc-60	Unc-63	Unc-65
$325	$450	$700	$1,000	$1,200	$1,400	$2,100	$3,100

W-152★ • F-1605★ • 9 to 11 known (est.)

VG-8	F-12	VF-20	EF-40	AU-50	Unc-60	Unc-63	Unc-65
$5,600	$9,000	$15,000	$29,000	$38,000	$50,000	$70,000	$100,000

Series of 1934, Blue Seal
Julian-Morgenthau (1934–1945)

The obligation on Series 1934 notes was changed to ONE DOLLAR IN SILVER PAYABLE. After this time it was not necessary for the Treasury department to specifically store silver dollars as a guaranty. Any other silver coins could be used. The face design was changed in other ways, including the relocation of the Treasury seal to the right, now with ONE printed over it. SERIES OF 1934 appears under WASHINGTON, D.C.

W-153 • F-1606 • 682,176,000

VG-8	F-12	VF-20	EF-40	AU-50	Unc-60	Unc-63	Unc-65
$23	$28	$35	$39	$55	$85	$120	$200

W-153★ • F-1606★ • 7,680,000

VG-8	F-12	VF-20	EF-40	AU-50	Unc-60	Unc-63	Unc-65
$70	$110	$170	$250	$375	$500	$900	$1,500

Series of 1935, Blue Seal
Julian-Morgenthau (1934–1945)

This series (illus. on p. 144) continued the ONE DOLLAR IN SILVER PAYABLE imprint. SERIES 1935 is printed at the upper left and lower right of the face. The Treasury seal no longer has the ONE overprint.

Series of 1935 notes introduce Silver Certificates in the style used for the rest of the series, with an unfinished pyramid and all-seeing eye to the left (the obverse of the Great Seal of the United States) and a heraldic eagle to the right (the reverse of the Great Seal). Originally these emblems were transposed, but President Roosevelt personally directed that they be placed in the positions finally used. The *History of the Bureau of Engraving 1862–1962* gives illustrations of the first proposal and tells of the process.

Mules: Most backs have the plate number in small or "micro" letters, but mules have the larger, "macro"-size serials, as used on Series 1935-A (the "macro" plates are numbered 930 and higher). These are worth a premium. Star-note mules are very rare and worth considerably more.[15]

Special notes were printed in 1937 as an experiment, with serials A-B and B-B on new paper, and C-B notes as a control.

W-154 • F-1607 • 1,681,552,000

VG-8	F-12	VF-20	EF-40	AU-50	Unc-60	Unc-63	Unc-65
$4	$6	$7	$8	$9	$13	$30	$65

W-154★ • F-1607★

VG-8	F-12	VF-20	EF-40	AU-50	Unc-60	Unc-63	Unc-65
$50	$95	$150	$225	$300	$400	$500	$800

W-154 Mule • F-1607

VG-8	F-12	VF-20	EF-40	AU-50	Unc-60	Unc-63	Unc-65
$18	$30	$45	$60	$80	$140	$180	$225

SERIES OF 1934, BLUE SEAL

$1 Silver Certificate, Series of 1934 (W-153), redesigned from the preceding, including a new obligation statement below the portrait. The back is the standard type of $1 Legal Tender Notes, Series of 1928, and also $1 Silver Certificates, Series of 1928 to 1934.

Detail of the obligation area, now revised to ONE DOLLAR IN SILVER.

SERIES OF 1935, BLUE SEAL

$1 Silver Certificate, Series of 1935 (W-154).

Back of W-154. This inaugurated the standard back type used on all regular $1 Silver Certificates, Series of 1935 to 1935-F.

Detail of micro plate number on back of a note, plate number 165.

Detail of macro plate number on back of a note.

W-154 Mule★ • F-1607★

VG-8	F-12	VF-20	EF-40	AU-50	Unc-60	Unc-63	Unc-65
$500	$900	$1,400	$2,000	$2,500	$3,750	$4,500	$7,000

W-155 • F-unlisted • Experimental paper; serials starting with A and ending with B

VG-8	F-12	VF-20	EF-40	AU-50	Unc-60	Unc-63	Unc-65
$15	$30	$50	$75	$100	$150	$175	$295

W-156 • F-unlisted • Experimental paper; serials starting and ending with B

VG-8	F-12	VF-20	EF-40	AU-50	Unc-60	Unc-63	Unc-65
$40	$75	$125	$250	$325	$500	$600	$750

W-157 • F-unlisted • Regular paper used as a control; serials starting with C and ending with B

VG-8	F-12	VF-20	EF-40	AU-50	Unc-60	Unc-63	Unc-65
$40	$75	$125	$250	$375	$500	$600	$750

Series of 1935-A, Blue Seal
Julian-Morgenthau (1934–1945)

The ONE DOLLAR IN SILVER PAYABLE obligation continued. SERIES 1935 A is printed on face below and slightly left of the Treasury seal (just once, instead of twice,

and in a different location than earlier). On the back, the plate number is of a larger standard, called "macro" by collectors (as compared to micro size for earlier issues).

Mules: Some Series of 1935-A notes, W-158 and W-158★, called mules, have the earlier micro plate numbers (back plate numbers 2 and 436 to 829). These are worth a premium. Star-note mules are scarcer yet.

The notes with distinctive bright red R and S surcharges were made to test regular (R) paper in comparison to special (S) paper, the latter impregnated with chemicals in an effort to increase their durability. Placed into circulation in June 1944, they attracted considerable numismatic notice, and many were saved by collectors and dealers from publicity in the *Numismatic Scrapbook Magazine* and elsewhere. It seems that not enough worn examples were recovered from circulation and tested, and thus no conclusions were made as to the durability of each class of paper stock. There are some notes with forged overprints, but the serial numbers are wrong on these. For the R overprint, the serials are S70884001C to S72068000C, and for the S overprint, they are S73884001C to S75068000C. Star notes of both styles have no prefix letter and end with A.

W-158 • F-1608 • 6,111,832,000

VG-8	F-12	VF-20	EF-40	AU-50	Unc-60	Unc-63	Unc-65
$2	$3	$3	$4	$5	$9	$13	$30

SERIES OF 1935-A, BLUE SEAL

$1 Silver Certificate, Series of 1935-A (W-158). The back is the standard for all Series of 1935 and related notes.

$1 Silver Certificate, Series of 1935-A (W-159) with bright R (for regular paper) surcharge at lower right.

$1 Silver Certificate, Series of 1935-A (W-160) with bright S (for special paper) surcharge at lower right.

W-158★ • F-1608★

VG-8	F-12	VF-20	EF-40	AU-50	Unc-60	Unc-63	Unc-65
$10	$20	$35	$55	$80	$100	$150	$225

W-158 Mule • F-1608

VF-20	EF-40	AU-50	Unc-60	Unc-63	Unc-65
$5	$15	$28	$38	$45	$70

W-158 Mule★ • F-1608★

VG-8	F-12	VF-20	EF-40	AU-50	Unc-60	Unc-63	Unc-65
$40	$75	$120	$200	$375	$475	$525	$750

W-159 • F-1609 • Bright red R surcharge • 1,184,000

VG-8	F-12	VF-20	EF-40	AU-50	Unc-60	Unc-63	Unc-65
$90	$115	$145	$180	$270	$525	$750	$1,150

W-159★ • F-1609★ • 12,000

VG-8	F-12	VF-20	EF-40	AU-50	Unc-60	Unc-63	Unc-65
$600	$1,500	$2,250	$3,700	$5,250	$5,900	$7,750	$10,000

W-160 • F-1610 • Bright red S surcharge • 1,184,000

VG-8	F-12	VF-20	EF-40	AU-50	Unc-60	Unc-63	Unc-65
$90	$110	$130	$165	$225	$450	$675	$1,000

W-160★ • F-1610★ • 12,000

VG-8	F-12	VF-20	EF-40	AU-50	Unc-60	Unc-63	Unc-65
$600	$1,350	$2,000	$3,400	$5,100	$5,600	$7,250	$10,000

Series of 1935-A, Brown Seal, HAWAII Overprint
Julian-Morgenthau (1934–1945)

The obligation ONE DOLLAR IN SILVER PAYABLE is continued.

These notes, with HAWAII overprinted on the face and the back and with a special brown Treasury seal and brown serial numbers were used from 1942 to 1944 in the Hawaiian Islands, then under threat of Japanese invasion. If the islands had fallen into the hands of the enemy, such notes could be repudiated and would have no value on world markets. The Japanese were scoring great success in the South Pacific at the time.

Citizens of the islands were commanded to exchange all older notes and receive these, which resulted in many collectible large-size National Bank Notes being quietly preserved when attention was called to them (although most were indeed redeemed and destroyed). Although the HAWAII overprint notes were distributed as intended, after 1944 large quantities remained in Treasury stocks and were put into general circulation on the mainland.

W-161 • F-2300 • 35,052,000

VG-8	F-12	VF-20	EF-40	AU-50	Unc-60	Unc-63	Unc-65
$25	$38	$50	$70	$90	$120	$150	$350

W-161★ • F-2300★ • 204,000

VG-8	F-12	VF-20	EF-40	AU-50	Unc-60	Unc-63	Unc-65
$100	$200	$425	$750	$1,400	$2,000	$3,000	$5,000

Series of 1935-A, Yellow Seal, for North Africa
Julian-Morgenthau (1934–1945)

This series continued the ONE DOLLAR IN SILVER PAYABLE obligation.

These notes, with a special, light-yellow seal, but with no distinctive overprint, were produced for use by Allied forces in the Mediterranean Sea and North Africa. They were used from 1942 to 1944 when the Allies were battling Nazi forces in that area. Similar to the Hawaiian issues, if the area was lost by the Allies and the notes fell into the hands of the enemy, they could be repudiated and would have no value on world markets.

At the time, United States currency maintained solid value in underground markets in Nazi-held European countries and also in the Union of Soviet Socialist Republics during the dictatorship of Josef Stalin.

W-162 • F-2306 • 26,916,000

VG-8	F-12	VF-20	EF-40	AU-50	Unc-60	Unc-63	Unc-65
$25	$62	$75	$85	$105	$145	$195	$500

W-162★ • F-2306★ • 144,000

VG-8	F-12	VF-20	EF-40	AU-50	Unc-60	Unc-63	Unc-65
$120	$250	$500	$850	$1,600	$2,200	$3,250	$5,600

Series of 1935-B, Blue Seal
Julian-Vinson (1945–1946)

This series (illus. on p. 148) continued the standard obligation, ONE DOLLAR IN SILVER PAYABLE.

W-163 • F-1611 • 806,612,000

VG-8	F-12	VF-20	EF-40	AU-50	Unc-60	Unc-63	Unc-65
$2	$3	$3	$4	$5	$14	$18	$35

W-163★ • F-1611★

VG-8	F-12	VF-20	EF-40	AU-50	Unc-60	Unc-63	Unc-65
$20	$45	$60	$90	$115	$190	$275	$400

Series of 1935-C, Blue Seal
Julian-Snyder (1946–1949)

This series (illus. on p. 148) continued the standard obligation, ONE DOLLAR IN SILVER PAYABLE.

W-164 • F-1612 • 3,088,108,000

VG-8	F-12	VF-20	EF-40	AU-50	Unc-60	Unc-63	Unc-65
$2	$3	$3	$4	$4	$9	$12	$22

W-164★ • F-1612★

VG-8	F-12	VF-20	EF-40	AU-50	Unc-60	Unc-63	Unc-65
$6	$13	$20	$35	$45	$65	$85	$125

Series of 1935-D, Blue Seal, Wide Back
Clark-Snyder (1949–1953)

This series (illus. on p. 148) continued the standard obligation, ONE DOLLAR IN SILVER PAYABLE. There are two varieties of back design for this series: the "W" (wide) is about 1/16th of an inch taller than the "N" (narrow). The back plate numbers on the "W" notes are 5015 and lower. Back plate numbers for the "N" notes are 5017 and higher. On the "N" notes there is less space between the border at top and bottom and the lettering and numerals near the border.

Beginning partway through Series 1935-D, the 18-subject sheet was introduced to replace the 12-subject sheet used for small-size Silver Certificates. The Wide Back notes were only printed on 12-subject sheets; Narrow Back notes were printed on both 12- and 18-subject sheets.

W-165 • F-1613W • 4,656,968,000

VG-8	F-12	VF-20	EF-40	AU-50	Unc-60	Unc-63	Unc-65
$2	$3	$3	$4	$4	$8	$13	$28

W-165★ • F-1613W★

VG-8	F-12	VF-20	EF-40	AU-50	Unc-60	Unc-63	Unc-65
$5	$10	$20	$60	$75	$100	$140	$195

W-166 • F-1613N • Part of W-165 printage

VG-8	F-12	VF-20	EF-40	AU-50	Unc-60	Unc-63	Unc-65
$2	$3	$3	$4	$4	$8	$11	$22

Series of 1935-D, Blue Seal, Narrow Back
Clark-Snyder (1949–1953)

W-166★ • F-1613N★

VG-8	F-12	VF-20	EF-40	AU-50	Unc-60	Unc-63	Unc-65
$5	$10	$15	$20	$30	$35	$50	$95

See the preceding listing for an overview of the differences between Wide Back and Narrow Back notes.

SERIES OF 1935-A, BROWN SEAL, HAWAII OVERPRINT

$1 Silver Certificate, Series of 1935-A (W-161), with HAWAII overprinted at the left and right ends and with Treasury seal and serial numbers in brown.

Special back of the $1 Silver Certificate, Series of 1935-A issue, with large HAWAII overprint used only on this type.

SERIES OF 1935-A, YELLOW SEAL FOR NORTH AFRICA

$1 Silver Certificate, Series of 1935-A (W-162), with Treasury seal printed in yellow, to signify its use in the Mediterranean and North African war theaters. The back of the North Africa note is not distinctive and is the standard design of the era.

Series of 1935-E, Blue Seal
Priest-Humphrey (1953–1957)

This series continued the standard obligation, ONE DOLLAR IN SILVER PAYABLE.

W-167 • F-1614 • 5,134,056,000

VG-8	F-12	VF-20	EF-40	AU-50	Unc-60	Unc-63	Unc-65
$2	$3	$3	$4	$4	$6	$10	$16

W-167★ • F-1614★ • 225,000,000 (est.)

VG-8	F-12	VF-20	EF-40	AU-50	Unc-60	Unc-63	Unc-65
$3	$4	$6	$8	$10	$28	$35	$70

Series of 1935-F, Blue Seal
Priest-Anderson (1957–1961)

This series continued the standard obligation, ONE DOLLAR IN SILVER PAYABLE. No motto is on the back.

Notes with IN GOD WE TRUST were first released on October 1, 1957. The Priest-Anderson era began on September 27, 1957. It is surprising that so many without-motto $1 notes were printed with their signatures.

W-168 • F-1615 • 1,173,360,000

VG-8	F-12	VF-20	EF-40	AU-50	Unc-60	Unc-63	Unc-65
$2	$3	$3	$4	$4	$6	$10	$16

SERIES OF 1935-B, BLUE SEAL

Detail of the signatures and the series imprint of a $1 Silver Certificate, Series of 1935-B (W-163). No series imprint at upper left.

SERIES OF 1935-C, BLUE SEAL

Detail of the signatures and the series imprint of a $1 Silver Certificate, Series of 1935-C (W-164). No series imprint at upper left.

SERIES OF 1935-D, BLUE SEAL

Detail of the signatures and the series imprint of a $1 Silver Certificate, Series of 1935-D (W-165). No series imprint at upper left.

Detail of the top border of the "Wide Back" style. The amount of space between the top and bottom border and the nearby lettering is wider or larger on this style.

Detail of the top border of the "Narrow Back" style (W-166).

SERIES OF 1935-E, BLUE SEAL

Detail of the signatures and the series imprint of a $1 Silver Certificate, Series of 1935-E (W-167). No series imprint at upper left.

SERIES OF 1935-F, BLUE SEAL

Detail of the signatures and the series imprint of a $1 Silver Certificate, Series of 1935-F (W-168). No series imprint at upper left.

SERIES OF 1935-G, BLUE SEAL, NO MOTTO

Detail of the signatures and the series imprint of a $1 Silver Certificate, Series of 1935-G (W-169). No series imprint at upper left.

The backs of all the notes shown are the standard for all Series of 1935 and related notes, except as noted.

W-168★ • F-1615★ • 53,200,000

VG-8	F-12	VF-20	EF-40	AU-50	Unc-60	Unc-63	Unc-65
$3	$4	$6	$8	$10	$25	$32	$60

Series of 1935-G, Blue Seal, No Motto
Smith-Dillon (1961–1962)

This series continued the standard obligation, ONE DOL-LAR IN SILVER PAYABLE. No motto is on the back.

These notes are anachronistic, as the IN GOD WE TRUST imprint on the back had been in use since 1957 (see the notes on the Series of 1957 following the Series of 1935-H). The Bureau of Engraving and Printing was using up its supply of old back plates.

W-169 • F-1616 • 194,600,000

VG-8	F-12	VF-20	EF-40	AU-50	Unc-60	Unc-63	Unc-65
$2	$3	$3	$4	$4	$8	$12	$20

W-169★ • F-1616★ • 8,640,000

VG-8	F-12	VF-20	EF-40	AU-50	Unc-60	Unc-63	Unc-65
$3	$5	$7	$10	$17	$40	$55	$95

Series of 1935-G, Blue Seal, With Motto
Smith-Dillon (1961–1962)

This series continued the standard obligation, ONE DOL-LAR IN SILVER PAYABLE. The motto is included on the back.

Although the Series of 1935-G notes have IN GOD WE TRUST and are listed earlier numerically per the series number and letter, the Series of 1957 notes were actually released several years earlier. Accordingly, this issue could be called a mule. The situation is somewhat confusing until studied. Notes of the Series of 1935-G have back plates numbered 6787 or higher.

W-170 • F-1617 • 31,320,000

VG-8	F-12	VF-20	EF-40	AU-50	Unc-60	Unc-63	Unc-65
$4	$8	$10	$12	$15	$35	$50	$80

W-170★ • F-1617★ • 1,080,000

VG-8	F-12	VF-20	EF-40	AU-50	Unc-60	Unc-63	Unc-65
$20	$35	$60	$85	$120	$175	$250	$400

Series of 1935-H, Blue Seal
Granahan-Dillon (1963–1965)

This series continued the standard obligation, ONE DOL-LAR IN SILVER PAYABLE. The motto is included on the back. The last 18-subject sheets made at the BEP were Series of 1935-H notes ending at serial number E1080000J, delivered on October 4, 1963.[16]

W-171 • F-1618 • 30,520,000

VG-8	F-12	VF-20	EF-40	AU-50	Unc-60	Unc-63	Unc-65
$2	$3	$4	$5	$8	$11	$20	$35

SERIES OF 1935-G, BLUE SEAL, WITH MOTTO

Detail of the signatures and the series imprint of a $1 Silver Certificate, Series of 1935-G (W-170), identical to the No Motto type.

Back of a $1 Silver Certificate, Series of 1935-G, type with IN GOD WE TRUST above ONE (W-170). This same type was used for Silver Certificates, Series 1935-G (With Motto, here) to Series of 1957 (which was issued before Series of 1935-G), and Federal Reserve Notes, Series of 1963 on.

SERIES OF 1935-H, BLUE SEAL

Detail of the signatures and the series imprint of a $1 Silver Certificate, Series of 1935-H (W-171). The back is the now-standard With Motto type. There is no series imprint in the upper left.

W-171★ • F-1618★ • 1,436,000

VG-8	F-12	VF-20	EF-40	AU-50	Unc-60	Unc-63	Unc-65
$6	$9	$14	$20	$30	$45	$60	$95

Series of 1957, Blue Seal
Priest-Anderson (1957–1961)

This series continued the standard obligation, ONE DOLLAR IN SILVER PAYABLE.

These notes were delivered on September 9, 1957, and released into circulation on October 1. Ivy Baker Priest and Robert B. Anderson had been in office together only since September 29, although the combination had been anticipated early enough to allow the notes to be printed. At later times, some of the Series of 1935-G and all of the Series of 1935-H (see preceding listings) were printed with IN GOD WE TRUST backs.

The addition of the motto to all paper money was the idea of Matt Rothert of Camden, Arkansas, a numismatist and currency specialist who later served a distinguished term as president of the American Numismatic Association. This was not the first use of the motto, as IN GOD WE TRUST is the inscription on the state seal of Florida and had been used on Original Series, Series of 1875, and 1882 Brown Back notes for national banks, and the $5 Series of 1886 Silver Certificates had displayed the reverses of four Morgan silver dollars, of which the motto was part of the design. The motto was first used in coinage on the bronze two-cent piece of 1864.

W-172 • F-1619 • 2,609,600,000

VG-8	F-12	VF-20	EF-40	AU-50	Unc-60	Unc-63	Unc-65
$2	$3	$3	$4	$4	$7	$11	$20

W-172★ • F-1619★ • 307,640,000

VG-8	F-12	VF-20	EF-40	AU-50	Unc-60	Unc-63	Unc-65
$3	$4	$4	$5	$8	$12	$19	$30

Series of 1957-A, Blue Seal
Smith-Dillon (1961–1962)

This series continued the standard obligation, ONE DOLLAR IN SILVER PAYABLE.

W-173 • F-1620 • 1,594,080,000

VG-8	F-12	VF-20	EF-40	AU-50	Unc-60	Unc-63	Unc-65
$2	$3	$3	$4	$4	$7	$11	$20

W-173★ • F-1620★ • 94,720,000

VG-8	F-12	VF-20	EF-40	AU-50	Unc-60	Unc-63	Unc-65
$3	$4	$4	$5	$8	$12	$19	$30

Series of 1957-B, Blue Seal
Granahan-Dillon (1963–1965)

This series continued the standard obligation, ONE DOLLAR IN SILVER PAYABLE. These are the last of the $1 Silver Certificates. The last 32-subject sheets made at the

$1 Silver Certificate, Series of 1957, star note (W-172★).

Back of a $1 Silver Certificate, Series of 1957. These were the first to be printed with IN GOD WE TRUST on the back.

SERIES OF 1957-A, BLUE SEAL

Detail of the signatures and the series imprint of a $1 Silver Certificate, Series of 1957-A (W-173).

SERIES OF 1957-B, BLUE SEAL

Detail of the signatures and the series imprint of a $1 Silver Certificate, Series of 1957-B (W-174).

The backs of all the notes shown are the standard type with the motto, as introduced in the Series of 1957.

BEP of Series of 1957-B notes, ending at Y12480000A, were delivered on November 6, 1963.[17]

In March 1964 the Treasury department stopped paying out silver dollars, and in 1965 the traditional 90% silver alloy for the dime, quarter, and half dollar was discontinued. The market price of silver was rising sharply. After a time, the Treasury stopped redeeming Silver Certificates in silver coins of any kind, but the department continued to exchange them for bullion (granules of silver in envelopes) until July 24, 1968, by which time the buying and selling of such notes was a large business with great profits to be made. Long lines of people waited their turn in coin shops and other stores, where clerks paid a premium for the certificates. These in turn were sold to wholesalers who redeemed them at the Treasury. One entrepreneur was handling so much bulk in these notes that he bought his own airplane to haul them (a vintage DC-3). After 1968, Silver Certificates had no special redemption value. More than a few "smart" citizens, who invested in the certificates believing they would increase further in value, were left holding notes worth only the face value.

W-174 • F-1621 • 718,400,000

VG-8	F-12	VF-20	EF-40	AU-50	Unc-60	Unc-63	Unc-65
$2	$3	$3	$4	$4	$7	$11	$20

W-174★ • F-1621★ • 49,280,000

VG-8	F-12	VF-20	EF-40	AU-50	Unc-60	Unc-63	Unc-65
$3	$4	$4	$5	$8	$12	$22	$35

FEDERAL RESERVE NOTES

By 1963 the price of silver bullion had risen on world markets to the point at which Congress prohibited the further issue of Silver Certificates. Federal Reserve Notes, already standard in other denominations, were used instead. This engendered a new series of $1 notes, the first of which were released on November 23, 1963, to the delight of collectors.[18] A new vista of inexpensive issues beckoned, with varieties from each of the 12 Federal Reserve Banks. This later included additional varieties from the new Western Facility in Fort Worth, Texas (designated by FW on the face of the notes), and some experimental notes printed by web presses (newspaper style) at the main BEP plant in Washington. Star notes add to the possibilities.

Today small-size Federal Reserve Notes are front row center in collecting enthusiasm and activities, with some dealers specializing in them.

Series of 1963, Green Seal
Granahan-Dillon (1963–1965)

The face (illus. on p. 153) featured Washington and the frame design, as in the preceding classes. On this issue the Federal Reserve seal is in the left field. Above it is the obligation "This note is legal tender for all debts, public and private." The motto IN GOD WE TRUST appears on the back.

Prices for a typical note for this series, unless listed otherwise, are as follows:

Unc-60	Unc-63	Unc-65
$5	$6	$8

Prices for a typical star note for this series, unless listed otherwise, are as follows:

Unc-60	Unc-63	Unc-65
$6	$7	$10

W-175-A • F-1900A • Boston • 87,680,000

W-175-A★ • F-1900A★ • 6,400,000

W-175-B • F-1900B • New York • 219,200,000

W-175-B★ • F-1900B★ • 15,360,000

W-175-C • F-1900C • Philadelphia • 123,680,000

W-175-C★ • F-1900C★ • 10,880,000

W-175-D • F-1900D • Cleveland • 108,320,000

W-175-D★ • F-1900D★ • 8,320,000

W-175-E • F-1900E • Richmond • 159,520,000

W-175-E★ • F-1900E★ • 12,160,000

W-175-F • F-1900F • Atlanta • 221,120,000

W-175-F★ • F-1900F★ • 19,200,000

W-175-G • F-1900G • Chicago • 279,360,000

W-175-G★ • F-1900G★ • 19,840,000

W-175-H • F-1900H • St. Louis • 99,840,000

W-175-H★ • F-1900H★ • 9,600,000

W-175-I • F-1900I • Minneapolis • 44,800,000

W-175-I★ • F-1900I★ • 5,120,000

Unc-60	Unc-63	Unc-65
$7	$9	$13

W-175-J • F-1900J • Kansas City • 88,960,000

W-175-J★ • F-1900J★ • 8,960,000

W-175-K • F-1900K • Dallas • 85,760,000

W-175-K★ • F-1900K★ • 8,960,000

Unc-60	Unc-63	Unc-65
$7	$9	$13

W-175-L • F-1900L • San Francisco • 1,999,999,999

W-175-L★ • F-1900L★ • 14,720,000

AU-50	Unc-60	Unc-63	Unc-65
$10	$19	$25	$40

Series of 1963-A, Green Seal
Granahan-Fowler (1965–1966)

Prices for a typical note for this series, unless listed otherwise, are as follows:

Unc-60	Unc-63	Unc-65
$4	$5	$7

Prices for a typical star note for this series, unless listed otherwise, are as follows:

Unc-60	Unc-63	Unc-65
$6	$8	$11

W-176-A • F-1901A • Boston • 319,840,000

W-176-A★ • F-1901A★ • 19,840,000

W-176-B • F-1901B • New York • 657,600,000

W-176-B★ • F-1901B★ • 47,680,000

W-176-C • F-1901C • Philadelphia • 375,520,000

W-176-C★ • F-1901C★ • 26,240,000

W-176-D • F-1901D • Cleveland • 337,120,000

W-176-D★ • F-1901D★ • 21,120,000

W-176-E • F-1901E • Richmond • 532,000,000

W-176-E★ • F-1901E★ • 41,600,000

W-176-F • F-1901F • Atlanta • 636,480,000

W-176-F★ • F-1901F★ • 40,960,000

W-176-G • F-1901G • Chicago • 784,480,000

W-176-G★ • F-1901G★ • 52,640,000

W-176-H • F-1901H • St. Louis • 264,000,000

W-176-H★ • F-1901H★ • 17,920,000

W-176-I • F-1901I • Minneapolis • 112,160,000

W-176-I★ • F-1901I★ • 7,040,000

Unc-60	Unc-63	Unc-65
$8	$11	$15

W-176-J • F-1901J • Kansas City • 219,200,000

W-176-J★ • F-1901J★ • 14,720,000

W-176-K • F-1901K • Dallas • 288,960,000

W-176-K★ • F-1901K★ • 19,184,000

Unc-60	Unc-63	Unc-65
$8	$11	$15

W-176-L • F-1901L • San Francisco • 576,800,000

W-176-L★ • F-1901L★ • 43,040,000

Series of 1963-B, Green Seal
Granahan-Barr (1968–1969)

Katherine O'Hay Granahan and Joseph Barr were in office together only from December 23, 1968, to January 20, 1969. When $1 notes with their signatures began to appear in circulation there was a nationwide rush to obtain what surely would become highly-prized rarities. However, the Bureau of Engraving and Printing kept using the plates after their joint term had ended. By the time production was completed, 458,880,000 had been printed. Although other series of $1 notes of the era typically had larger printages, so many "Barr notes," as they were called, were saved that they will probably be very common for generations to come. The Bureau of Engraving and Printing does not acknowledge this hoarding, but states: "There are fewer notes bearing his facsimile signature than notes imprinted with signatures of other Secretaries of the Treasury because of his short tenure in that office."

Prices for a typical note for this series, unless listed otherwise, are as follows:

Unc-60	Unc-63	Unc-65
$4	$5	$7

Prices for a typical star note for this series, unless listed otherwise, are as follows:

Unc-60	Unc-63	Unc-65
$10	$13	$17

W-177-B • F-1902B • New York • 123,040,000

W-177-B★ • F-1902B★ • 3,680,000

W-177-E • F-1902E • Richmond • 93,600,000

W-177-E★ • F-1902E★ • 3,200,000

W-177-G • F-1902G • Chicago • 91,040,000

W-177-G★ • F-1902G★ • 2,400,000

W-177-J • F-1902J • Kansas City • 44,800,000

W-177-L • F-1902L • San Francisco • 106,400,000

W-177-L★ • F-1902L★ • 3,040,000

Series of 1969, Green Seal
Elston-Kennedy (1969–1970)

The Series of 1969 (illus. on p. 155) featured a redesigned Treasury seal with the inscription THE DEPARTMENT OF THE TREASURY 1789, replacing the earlier style with the Latin wording THESAUR. AMER. SEPTENT. SIGIL. The design in the interior of the seal was modified as well.

SERIES OF 1963, GREEN SEAL

$1 Federal Reserve Note, Series of 1963 (W-175-A). This is the general type of Series 1963 to 1969. The Treasury seal is in green. The Federal Reserve Bank name and letter are part of the seal at the left—here, Boston, with a letter A.

Back of a $1 Federal Reserve Note, Series of 1963. Standard With Motto type introduced in the Silver Certificate Series of 1957.

SERIES OF 1963-A, GREEN SEAL

Detail of the signatures and the series imprint of a $1 Federal Reserve Note, Series of 1963-A (W-176). The back is the standard With Motto type.

SERIES OF 1963-B, GREEN SEAL

Detail of the signatures and the series imprint of a $1 Federal Reserve Note, Series of 1963-B (W-177). The back is the standard With Motto type.

Prices for a typical note for this series, unless listed otherwise, are as follows:

Unc-60	Unc-63	Unc-65
$3	$4	$6

Prices for a typical star note for this series, unless listed otherwise, are as follows:

Unc-60	Unc-63	Unc-65
$6	$8	$11

W-178-A • F-1903A • Boston • 99,200,000

W-178-A★ • F-1903A★ • 5,120,000

W-178-B • F-1903B • New York • 269,120,000

W-178-B★ • F-1903B★ • 14,080,000

W-178-C • F-1903C • Philadelphia • 68,480,000

W-178-C★ • F-1903C★ • 3,776,000

Unc-60	Unc-63	Unc-65
$5	$6	$8

W-178-D • F-1903D • Cleveland • 120,480,000

W-178-D★ • F-1903D★ • 5,760,000

W-178-E • F-1903E • Richmond • 250,560,000

W-178-E★ • F-1903E★ • 10,880,000

W-178-F • F-1903F • Atlanta • 185,120,000

W-178-F★ • F-1903F★ • 7,680,000

W-178-G • F-1903G • Chicago • 359,520,000

W-178-G★ • F-1903G★ • 12,160,000

W-178-H • F-1903H • St. Louis • 74,880,000

W-178-H★ • F-1903H★ • 3,840,000

W-178-I • F-1903I • Minneapolis • 48,000,000

W-178-I★ • F-1903I★ • 1,920,000

Unc-60	Unc-63	Unc-65
$13	$18	$26

W-178-J • F-1903J • Kansas City • 95,360,000

W-178-J★ • F-1903J★ • 5,760,000

W-178-K • F-1903K • Dallas • 113,440,000

W-178-K★ • F-1903K★ • 5,120,000

W-178-L • F-1903L • San Francisco • 226,240,000

W-178-L★ • F-1903L★ • 9,600,000

Series of 1969-A, Green Seal
Kabis-Kennedy (1970–1971)

Dorothy Andrews Elson married Walter L. Kabis during her term in office, thus becoming Mrs. Kabis. The Series of 1969-A $1 notes are the only currency with the Kabis-Kennedy signature combination, an interesting distinction.

Prices for a typical note for this series, unless listed otherwise, are as follows:

Unc-60	Unc-63	Unc-65
$3	$4	$6

Prices for a typical star note for this series, unless listed otherwise, are as follows:

Unc-60	Unc-63	Unc-65
$6	$8	$11

W-179-A • F-1904A • Boston • 40,480,000

W-179-A★ • F-1904A★ • 1,120,000

W-179-B • F-1904B • New York • 122,400,000

W-179-B★ • F-1904B★ • 6,240,000

W-179-C • F-1904C • Philadelphia • 44,960,000

W-179-C★ • F-1904C★ • 1,760,000

W-179-D • F-1904D • Cleveland • 30,080,000

W-179-D★ • F-1904D★ • 1,280,000

W-179-E • F-1904E • Richmond • 66,080,000

W-179-E★ • F-1904E★ • 3,200,000

W-179-F • F-1904F • Atlanta • 70,560,000

W-179-F★ • F-1904F★ • 2,400,000

W-179-G • F-1904G • Chicago • 75,680,000

W-179-G★ • F-1904G★ • 4,480,000

W-179-H • F-1904H • St. Louis • 41,420,000

W-179-H★ • F-1904H★ • 1,280,000

W-179-I • F-1904I • Minneapolis • 21,760,000

W-179-I★ • F-1904I★ • 640,000

AU-50	Unc-60	Unc-63	Unc-65
$10	$22	$35	$55

W-179-J • F-1904J • Kansas City • 40,480,000

W-179-J★ • F-1904J★ • 1,120,000

Unc-60	Unc-63	Unc-65
$8	$11	$17

W-179-K • F-1904K • Dallas • 27,520,000

W-179-L • F-1904L • San Francisco • 51,840,000

W-179-L★ • F-1904L★ • 3,840,000

Series of 1969-B, Green Seal
Kabis-Connally (1971)

Most currency with Kabis's signature is combined with John B. Connally, as here. Just one issue, the preceding 1969-A $1 notes, have the Kabis-Kennedy signature combination.

Prices for a typical note for this series, unless listed otherwise, are as follows:

Unc-60	Unc-63	Unc-65
$3	$4	$6

Prices for a typical star note for this series, unless listed otherwise, are as follows:

Unc-60	Unc-63	Unc-65
$6	$8	$11

W-180-A • F-1905A • Boston • 94,720,000

W-180-A★ • F-1905A★ • 1,920,000

W-180-B • F-1905B • New York • 329,440,000

W-180-B★ • F-1905B★ • 7,040,000

W-180-C • F-1905C • Philadelphia • 133,280,000

W-180-C★ • F-1905C★ • 3,200,000

W-180-D • F-1905D • Cleveland • 91,520,000

W-180-D★ • F-1905D★ • 4,480,000

W-180-E • F-1905E • Richmond • 180,000,000

W-180-E★ • F-1905E★ • 3,480,000

W-180-F • F-1905F • Atlanta • 200,000,000

W-180-F★ • F-1905F★ • 3,840,000

W-180-G • F-1905G • Chicago • 204,480,000

W-180-G★ • F-1905G★ • 4,480,000

W-180-H • F-1905H • St. Louis • 59,520,000

W-180-H★ • F-1905H★ • 1,920,000

W-180-I • F-1905I • Minneapolis • 33,920,000

W-180-I★ • F-1905I★ • 640,000

AU-50	Unc-60	Unc-63	Unc-65
$10	$22	$35	$55

W-180-J • F-1905J • Kansas City • 67,200,000

W-180-J★ • F-1905J★ • 2,560,000

W-180-K • F-1905K • Dallas • 116,640,000

W-180-K★ • F-1905K★ • 5,120,000

W-180-L • F-1905L • San Francisco • 208,960,000

W-180-L★ • F-1905L★ • 5,760,000

Series of 1969-C, Green Seal
Banuelos-Connally (1971–1972)

Prices for a typical note for this series, unless listed otherwise, are as follows:

Unc-60	Unc-63	Unc-65
$4	$5	$7

W-181-B • F-1906B • New York • 49,920,000

W-181-D • F-1906D • Cleveland • 15,520,000

W-181-D★ • F-1906D★ • 480,000

AU-50	Unc-60	Unc-63	Unc-65
$12	$24	$42	$60

W-181-E • F-1906E • Richmond • 61,600,000

W-181-E★ • F-1906E★ • 480,000

AU-50	Unc-60	Unc-63	Unc-65
$12	$25	$45	$65

W-181-F • F-1906F • Atlanta • 60,960,000

W-181-F★ • F-1906F★ • 3,680,000

AU-50	Unc-60	Unc-63	Unc-65
$6	$15	$20	$29

W-181-G • F-1906G • Chicago • 137,120,000

$1 Federal Reserve Note, Series of 1969 (W-178-J). Federal Reserve Bank of Kansas City.

Detail of old-type Treasury seal with wording in Latin.

Detail of new-type Treasury seal with wording in English, as introduced on Series of 1969 notes.

SERIES OF 1969-A, GREEN SEAL

Detail of the signatures and the series imprint of a $1 Federal Reserve Note, Series of 1969-A (W-179-H).

SERIES OF 1969-B, GREEN SEAL

Detail of the signatures and the series imprint of a $1 Federal Reserve Note, Series of 1969-B (W-180-E).

SERIES OF 1969-C, GREEN SEAL

Detail of the signatures and the series imprint of a $1 Federal Reserve Note, Series of 1969-C (W-181-J).

The backs of all the notes shown are the standard type with the motto, as introduced in the Series of 1957.

W-181-G★ • F-1906G★ • 1,748,000

AU-50	Unc-60	Unc-63	Unc-65
$8	$18	$25	$35

W-181-H • F-1906H • St. Louis • 23,680,000

W-181-H★ • F-1906H★ • 640,000

AU-50	Unc-60	Unc-63	Unc-65
$6	$15	$20	$29

W-181-I • F-1906I • Minneapolis • 25,600,000

W-181-I★ • F-1906I★ • 640,000

AU-50	Unc-60	Unc-63	Unc-65
$12	$24	$30	$48

W-181-J • F-1906J • Kansas City • 38,560,000

W-181-J★ • F-1906J★ • 1,120,000

Unc-60	Unc-63	Unc-65
$13	$18	$26

W-181-K • F-1906K • Dallas • 29,440,000

W-181-K★ • F-1906K★ • 640,000

AU-50	Unc-60	Unc-63	Unc-65
$12	$24	$40	$60

W-181-L • F-1906L • San Francisco • 101,280,000

W-181-L★ • F-1906L★ • 2,400,000

VF-20	EF-40	AU-50	Unc-60	Unc-63	Unc-65
$55	$75	$95	$130	$200	$325

Series of 1969-D, Green Seal
Banuelos-Shultz (1972–1974)

Prices for a typical note for this series, unless listed otherwise, are as follows:

Unc-60	Unc-63	Unc-65
$3	$4	$6

Prices for a typical star note for this series, unless listed otherwise, are as follows:

Unc-60	Unc-63	Unc-65
$7	$9	$12

W-182-A • F-1907A • Boston • 187,040,000

W-182-A★ • F-1907A★ • 1,120,000

AU-50	Unc-60	Unc-63	Unc-65
$6	$15	$20	$29

W-182-B • F-1907B • New York • 468,480,000

W-182-B★ • F-1907B★ • 4,480,000

W-182-C • F-1907C • Philadelphia • 218,560,000

W-182-C★ • F-1907C★ • 4,320,000

W-182-D • F-1907D • Cleveland • 161,440,000

W-182-D★ • F-1907D★ • 2,400,000

W-182-E • F-1907E • Richmond • 374,240,000

W-182-E★ • F-1907E★ • 8,480,000

W-182-F • F-1907F • Atlanta • 377,440,000

W-182-F★ • F-1907F★ • 5,280,000

W-182-G • F-1907G • Chicago • 378,080,000

W-182-G★ • F-1907G★ • 5,270,000

W-182-H • F-1907H • St. Louis • 168,480,000

W-182-H★ • F-1907H★ • 1,760,000

W-182-I • F-1907I • Minneapolis • 83,200,000

W-182-J • F-1907J • Kansas City • 185,760,000

Unc-60	Unc-63	Unc-65
$4	$5	$7

W-182-J★ • F-1907J★ • 3,040,000

W-182-K • F-1907K • Dallas • 158,240,000

Unc-60	Unc-63	Unc-65
$4	$5	$7

W-182-K★ • F-1907K★ • 6,240,000

W-182-L • F-1907L • San Francisco • 400,640,000

W-182-L★ • F-1907L★ • 6,400,000

Series of 1974, Green Seal
Neff-Simon (1974–1977)

Prices for a typical note for this series, unless listed otherwise, are as follows:

Unc-60	Unc-63	Unc-65
$3	$4	$6

Prices for a typical star note for this series, unless listed otherwise, are as follows:

Unc-60	Unc-63	Unc-65
$6	$8	$11

W-183-A • F-1908A • Boston • 269,760,000

W-183-A★ • F-1908A★ • 2,400,000

W-183-B • F-1908B • New York • 740,320,000

SERIES OF 1969-D, GREEN SEAL

Detail of the signatures and the series imprint of a $1 Federal Reserve Note, Series of 1969-D (W-182-L). The back is the standard With Motto type.

W-183-B★ • F-1908B★ **• 8,800,000**

W-183-C • F-1908C **• Philadelphia • 308,800,000**

W-183-C★ • F-1908C★ **• 1,600,000**

W-183-D • F-1908D **• Cleveland • 240,960,000**

W-183-D★ • F-1908D★ **• 960,000**

AU-50	Unc-60	Unc-63	Unc-65
$7	$17	$22	$32

W-183-E • F-1908E **• Richmond • 644,000,000**

W-183-E★ • F-1908E★ **• 4,960,000**

W-183-F • F-1908F **• Atlanta • 599,680,000**

W-183-F★ • F-1908F★ **• 5,632,000**

W-183-G • F-1908G **• Chicago • 473,600,000**

W-183-G★ • F-1908G★ **• 4,992,000**

W-183-H • F-1908H **• St. Louis • 291,520,000**

W-183-H★ • F-1908H★ **• 2,880,000**

W-183-I • F-1908I **• Minneapolis • 144,160,000**

W-183-I★ • F-1908I★ **• 480,000**

Unc-60	Unc-63	Unc-65
$8	$10	$14

W-183-J • F-1908J **• Kansas City • 223,520,000**

W-183-J★ • F-1908J★ **• 2,144,000**

W-183-K • F-1908K **• Dallas • 330,560,000**

W-183-K★ • F-1908K★ **• 1,216,000**

W-183-L • F-1908L **• San Francisco • 736,960,000**

W-183-L★ • F-1908L★ **• 3,520,000**

Series of 1977, Green Seal
Morton-Blumenthal (1977–1979)

Prices for a typical note for this series (illus. on p. 158), unless listed otherwise, are as follows:

Unc-60	Unc-63	Unc-65
$3	$4	$6

Prices for a typical star note for this series, unless listed otherwise, are as follows:

Unc-60	Unc-63	Unc-65
$6	$8	$11

W-184-A • F-1909A **• Boston • 188,160,000**

W-184-A★ • F-1909A★ **• 3,072,000**

AU-50	Unc-60	Unc-63	Unc-65
$5	$15	$20	$29

W-184-B • F-1909B **• New York • 635,520,000**

W-184-B★ • F-1909B★ **• 10,112,000**

W-184-C • F-1909C **• Philadelphia • 216,960,000**

W-184-C★ • F-1909C★ **• 4,480,000**

W-184-D • F-1909D **• Cleveland • 213,120,000**

W-184-D★ • F-1909D★ **• 3,328,000**

W-184-E • F-1909E **• Richmond • 418,560,000**

W-184-E★ • F-1909E★ **• 640,000**

W-184-F • F-1909F **• Atlanta • 565,120,000**

W-184-F★ • F-1909F★ **• 8,960,000**

W-184-G • F-1909G **• Chicago • 615,680,000**

W-184-G★ • F-1909G★ **• 9,472,000**

W-184-H • F-1909H **• St. Louis • 199,680,000**

W-184-H★ • F-1909H★ **• 2,048,000**

W-184-I • F-1909I **• Minneapolis • 115,200,000**

W-184-I★ • F-1909I★ **• 2,944,000**

W-184-J • F-1909J **• Kansas City • 223,360,000**

W-184-J★ • F-1909J★ **• 3,840,000**

W-184-K • F-1909K **• Dallas • 289,280,000**

W-184-K★ • F-1909K★ **• 4,608,000**

W-184-L • F-1909L **• San Francisco • 516,480,000**

W-184-L★ • F-1909L★ **• 8,320,000**

SERIES OF 1974, GREEN SEAL

$1 Federal Reserve Note, Series of 1974 (W-183-B). Federal Reserve Bank of New York. The back is the standard With Motto type.

Series of 1977-A, Green Seal
Morton-Miller (1979–1981)

Philadelphia notes of serial blocks C-D can be found with faded backs, as the BEP was experimenting with a new type of green ink that "later developed unacceptable wear and characteristics which resulted in a faded appearance," noted a letter from the BEP to Bob Waszilycsak in March 1985, when he was investigating the matter. The problem was much more severe on Series of 1981 notes.[19]

Prices for a typical note for this series, unless listed otherwise, are as follows:

Unc-60	Unc-63	Unc-65
$3	$4	$6

Prices for a typical star note for this series, unless listed otherwise, are as follows:

Unc-60	Unc-63	Unc-65
$6	$8	$11

W-185-A • F-1910A • Boston • 204,800,000

W-185-A★ • F-1910A★ • 2,432,000

AU-50	Unc-60	Unc-63	Unc-65
$8	$18	$25	$35

W-185-B • F-1910B • New York • 592,000,000

W-185-B★ • F-1910B★ • 9,472,000

W-185-C • F-1910C • Philadelphia • 196,480,000

W-185-C★ • F-1910C★ • 2,688,000

W-185-D • F-1910D • Cleveland • 174,720,000

W-185-D★ • F-1910D★ • 2,560,000

W-185-E • F-1910E • Richmond • 377,600,000

W-185-E★ • F-1910E★ • 6,400,000

W-185-F • F-1910F • Atlanta • 396,160,000

W-185-F★ • F-1910F★ • 5,376,000

W-185-G • F-1910G • Chicago • 250,680,000

W-185-G★ • F-1910G★ • 2,560,000

W-185-H • F-1910H • St. Louis • 103,680,000

W-185-H★ • F-1910H★ • 1,664,000

W-185-I • F-1910I • Minneapolis • 38,400,000

W-185-I★ • F-1910I★ • 384,000

W-185-J • F-1910J • Kansas City • 266,880,000

W-185-J★ • F-1910J★ • 4,864,000

W-185-K • F-1910K • Dallas • 313,600,000

W-185-K★ • F-1910K★ • 6,016,000

W-185-L • F-1910L • San Francisco • 432,280,000

W-185-L★ • F-1910L★ • 5,888,000

Series of 1981, Green Seal
Buchanan-Regan (1981–1983)

Back plate number 129 is located at the lower left of the reverse, just to the right of the projecting beaded area. This is quite different from the normal location at the lower right. This variety is also found on $1 Series 1985 Federal Reserve Notes.[20]

Many notes can be found with faded backs, as the BEP was experimenting with a new type of green ink, which "later developed unacceptable wear and characteristics which resulted in a faded appearance" on many in this series and some of the Series of 1977-A.[21]

SERIES OF 1977, GREEN SEAL

$1 Federal Reserve Note, Series of 1977 (W-184-D). Federal Reserve Bank of Cleveland. The back is the standard With Motto type.

SERIES OF 1977-A, GREEN SEAL

Detail of the signatures and the series imprint of a $1 Federal Reserve Note, Series of 1977-A (W-185-F). The back is the standard With Motto type.

Prices for a typical note for this series, unless listed otherwise, are as follows:

Unc-60	Unc-63	Unc-65
$3	$4	$6

Prices for a typical star note for this series, unless listed otherwise, are as follows:

Unc-60	Unc-63	Unc-65
$8	$10	$14

W-186-A • F-1911A • Boston • 308,480,000

W-186-A★ • F-1911A★ • 3,200,000

Unc-60	Unc-63	Unc-65
$8	$12	$18

W-186-B • F-1911B • New York • 963,840,000

W-186-B★ • F-1911B★ • 11,776,000

W-186-C • F-1911C • Philadelphia • 359,680,000

W-186-C★ • F-1911C★ • 1,536,000

VF-20	EF-40	AU-50	Unc-60	Unc-63	Unc-65
$25	$50	$80	$110	$140	$200

W-186-D • F-1911D • Cleveland • 295,680,000

W-186-D★ • F-1911D★ • 1,792,000

W-186-E • F-1911E • Richmond • 603,520,000

W-186-E★ • F-1911E★ • 3,840,000

Unc-60	Unc-63	Unc-65
$10	$15	$25

W-186-F • F-1911F • Atlanta • 741,760,000

W-186-F★ • F-1911F★ • 3,200,000

Unc-60	Unc-63	Unc-65
$10	$15	$25

W-186-G • F-1911G • Chicago • 629,760,000

W-186-G★ • F-1911G★ • 5,184,000

Unc-60	Unc-63	Unc-65
$10	$15	$25

W-186-H • F-1911H • St. Louis • 163,840,000

W-186-H★ • F-1911H★ • 1,056,000

W-186-I • F-1911I • Minneapolis • 105,600,000

W-186-I★ • F-1911I★ • 1,152,000

W-186-J • F-1911J • Kansas City • 302,080,000

W-186-J★ • F-1911J★ • 3,216,000

W-186-K • F-1911K • Dallas • 385,920,000

W-186-K★ • F-1911K★ • 1,920,000

Unc-60	Unc-63	Unc-65
$10	$15	$25

W-186-L • F-1911L • San Francisco • 677,760,000

W-186-L★ • F-1911L★ • 4,992,000

Series of 1981-A, Green Seal
Ortega-Regan (1983–1985)

The first $1 notes with this signature combination (illus. on p. 160) came off a press at the BEP on January 9, 1984. Director Bob Leuver arranged a special ceremony with both signatories on hand.[22]

Prices for a typical note for this series, unless listed otherwise, are as follows:

Unc-60	Unc-63	Unc-65
$3	$4	$6

Prices for a typical star note for this series, unless listed otherwise, are as follows:

Unc-60	Unc-63	Unc-65
$10	$15	$25

W-187-A • F-1912A • Boston • 204,800,000

W-187-B • F-1912B • New York • 537,600,000

W-187-B★ • F-1912B★ • 9,216,000

W-187-C • F-1912C • Philadelphia • 99,200,000

W-187-D • F-1912D • Cleveland • 188,800,000

W-187-E • F-1912E • Richmond • 441,600,000

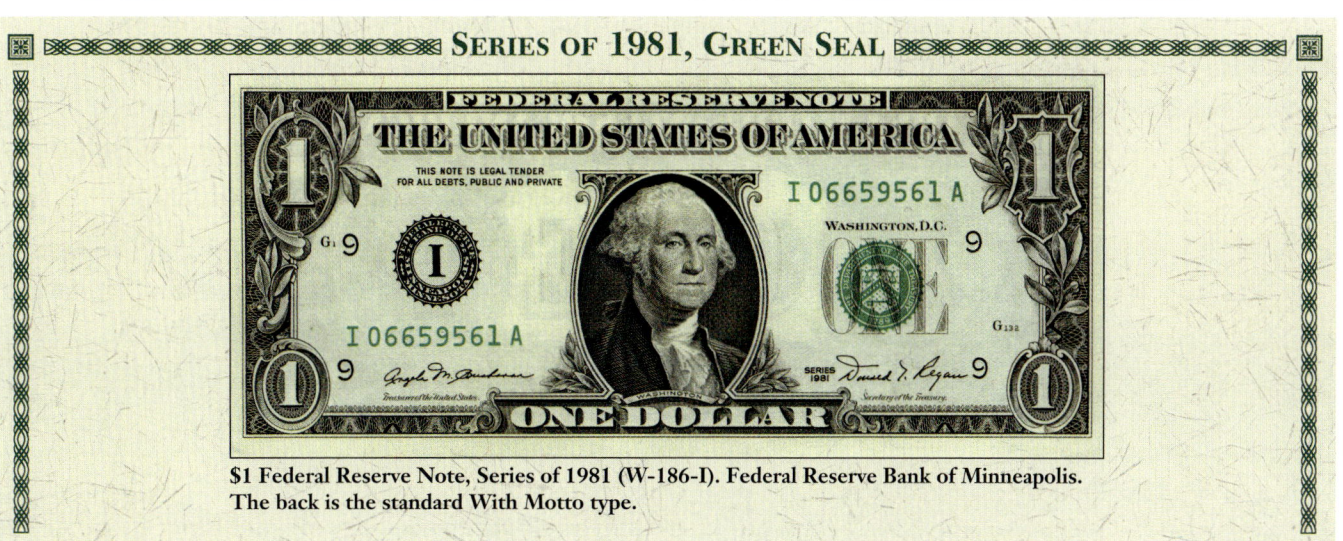

SERIES OF 1981, GREEN SEAL

$1 Federal Reserve Note, Series of 1981 (W-186-I). Federal Reserve Bank of Minneapolis. The back is the standard With Motto type.

W-187-E★ • F-1912E★ • 6,400,000

W-187-F • F-1912F • Atlanta • 483,200,000

W-187-G • F-1912G • Chicago • 482,000,000

W-187-G★ • F-1912G★ • 3,200,000

W-187-H • F-1912H • St. Louis • 182,400,000

W-187-I • F-1912I • Minneapolis • 122,400,000

W-187-J • F-1912J • Kansas City • 176,000,000

W-187-K • F-1912K • Dallas • 188,800,000

W-187-K★ • F-1912K★ • 3,200,000

VG-8	F-12	VF-20	EF-40	AU-50	Unc-60	Unc-63	Unc-65
$125	$200	$300	$400	$500	$700	$1,000	$1,500

W-187-L • F-1912L • San Francisco • 659,000,000

W-187-L★ • F-1912L★ • 3,200,000

Series of 1985, Green Seal
Ortega-Baker (1985–1988)

Prices for a typical note for this series, unless listed otherwise, are as follows:

Unc-60	Unc-63	Unc-65
$3	$4	$6

W-188-A • F-1913A • Boston • 553,600,000

W-188-B • F-1913B • New York • 1,795,200,000

W-188-C • F-1913C • Philadelphia • 422,400,000

W-188-D • F-1913D • Cleveland • 636,800,000

W-188-E • F-1913E • Richmond • 1,190,400,000

W-188-E★ • F-1913E★ • 6,400,000

Unc-60	Unc-63	Unc-65
$8	$10	$14

W-188-F • F-1913F • Atlanta • 1,414,400,000

W-188-G • F-1913G • Chicago • 1,190,400,000

W-188-G★ • F-1913G★ • 5,120,000

Unc-60	Unc-63	Unc-65
$8	$10	$14

W-188-H • F-1913H • St. Louis • 400,000,000

W-188-H★ • F-1913H★ • 640,000

VG-8	F-12	VF-20	EF-40	AU-50	Unc-60	Unc-63	Unc-65
$125	$250	$400	$500	$650	$850	$1,250	$1,650

W-188-I • F-1913I • Minneapolis • 246,400,000

W-188-I★ • F-1913I★ • 3,200,000

Unc-60	Unc-63	Unc-65
$8	$12	$18

W-188-J • F-1913J • Kansas City • 390,400,000

W-188-K • F-1913K • Dallas • 697,600,000

W-188-K★ • F-1913K★ • 3,200,000

Unc-60	Unc-63	Unc-65
$10	$15	$25

W-188-L • F-1913L • San Francisco • 1,881,600,000

W-188-L★ • F-1913L★ • 9,600,000

Unc-60	Unc-63	Unc-65
$8	$10	$14

Series of 1988, Green Seal
Ortega-Brady (1988–1989)

Prices for a typical note for this series, unless listed otherwise, are as follows:

Unc-60	Unc-63	Unc-65
$5	$7	$10

Prices for a typical star note for this series, unless listed otherwise, are as follows:

Unc-60	Unc-63	Unc-65
$10	$15	$25

W-189-A • F-1914A • Boston • 214,400,000

Unc-60	Unc-63	Unc-65
$6	$8	$11

W-189-A★ • F-1914A★ • 3,200,000

Unc-60	Unc-63	Unc-65
$15	$20	$29

W-189-B • F-1914B • New York • 921,600,000

W-189-B★ • F-1914B★ • 2,560,000

W-189-C • F-1914C • Philadelphia • 96,000,000

W-189-D • F-1914D • Cleveland • 195,200,000

W-189-E • F-1914E • Richmond • 728,800,000

W-189-E★ • F-1914E★ • 2,688,000

W-189-F • F-1914F • Atlanta • 390,400,000

SERIES OF 1981-A, GREEN SEAL

Detail of the signatures and the series imprint of a $1 Federal Reserve Note, Series of 1981-A (W-187-F). The back is the standard With Motto type.

W-189-F★ • F-1914F★ • 3,840,000

VG-8	F-12	VF-20	EF-40	AU-50	Unc-60	Unc-63	Unc-65
$125	$250	$400	$500	$650	$850	$1,250	$1,700

W-189-G • F-1914G • Chicago • 416,400,000

W-189-H • F-1914H • St. Louis • 396,800,000

W-189-I • F-1914I • Minneapolis • 246,400,000

W-189-J • F-1914J • Kansas City • 390,400,000

W-189-J★ • F-1914J★ • 3,200,000

W-189-K • F-1914K • Dallas • 80,000,000

W-189-K★ • F-1914K★ • 1,248,000

AU-50	Unc-60	Unc-63	Unc-65
$10	$22	$35	$55

W-189-L • F-1914L • San Francisco • 585,600,000

W-189-L★ • F-1914L★ • 3,200,000

Series of 1988-A, Green Seal, Washington Sheet-Fed Presses
Villalpando-Brady (1989–1993)

Notes in this series (illus. on p. 162) were printed on standard sheet-fed presses, parallel with others that were printed on experimental web-fed presses (see the next section), with slightly different characteristics to the plates.

Prices for a typical note for this series, unless listed otherwise, are as follows:

Unc-60	Unc-63	Unc-65
$3	$4	$6

Prices for a typical star note for this series, unless listed otherwise, are as follows:

Unc-60	Unc-63	Unc-65
$6	$8	$11

W-190-A • F-1915A • Boston • 582,400,000

W-190-B • F-1915B • New York • 2,161,344,000

W-190-B★ • F-1915B★ • 12,800,000

W-190-C • F-1915C • Philadelphia • 472,320,000

W-190-D • F-1915D • Cleveland • 454,400,000

W-190-D★ • F-1915D★ • 6,400,000

W-190-E • F-1915E • Richmond • 1,593,600,000

W-190-E★ • F-1915E★ • 10,880,000

W-190-F • F-1915F • Atlanta • 1,747,200,000

W-190-F★ • F-1915F★ • 12,800,000

SERIES OF 1985, GREEN SEAL

$1 Federal Reserve Note, Series of 1985 (W-188-G). Federal Reserve Bank of Chicago. The back is the standard With Motto type.

SERIES OF 1988, GREEN SEAL

$1 Federal Reserve Note, Series of 1988 (W-189-L). Federal Reserve Bank of San Francisco. The back is the standard With Motto type.

W-190-G • F-1915G • Chicago • 1,728,000,000

W-190-G★ • F-1915G★ • 19,200,000

Unc-60	Unc-63	Unc-65
$10	$15	$25

W-190-H • F-1915H • St. Louis • 410,400,000

W-190-H★ • F-1915H★ • 3,200,000

Unc-60	Unc-63	Unc-65
$10	$15	$25

W-190-I • F-1915I • Minneapolis • 76,800,000

W-190-I★ • F-1915I★ • 5,760,000

Unc-60	Unc-63	Unc-65
$10	$15	$25

W-190-J • F-1915J • Kansas City • 96,000,000

W-190-K • F-1915K • Dallas • 211,200,000

W-190-L • F-1915L • San Francisco • 280,600,000

Series of 1988-A, Green Seal, Washington Web-Fed Presses
Villalpando-Brady (1989–1993)

Beginning with this series, the Bureau of Engraving and Printing used web-fed presses to print some $1 notes, while at the same time the traditional sheet-fed presses were also used. The web-fed presses used a large roll of paper, similar in concept to a newspaper press but with a higher-quality finish. Face and back images for 96 notes were on the surface of each cylinder, which imprinted the web or roll as the paper fed through.

Changes on the web-fed issues include the elimination of the face plate letter, leaving a face plate number only. On the back of web-fed notes the plate number is in the field to the right of the motto; on sheet-fed notes the number is at the inside border below the lower right corner of E (ONE). These were produced beginning in May 1992. Six different Federal Reserve Bank imprints were used. The experiment did not prove to be satisfactory, and the use of these presses

was discontinued a few years later. In the meantime, the runs included signature combinations in several $1 series. No other denominations were produced.

The Atlanta star note is the only star note among the several series of web-press production and thus is highly valued.

W-191-A • F-1917A • Boston • 64,000,000

EF-40	AU-50	Unc-60	Unc-63	Unc-65
$6	$12	$24	$40	$60

W-191-B • F-1917B • New York • 1,920,000

VG-8	F-12	VF-20	EF-40	AU-50	Unc-60	Unc-63	Unc-65
$80	$175	$325	$500	$650	$850	$1,250	$1,700

W-191-C • F-1917C • Philadelphia • 12,800,000

EF-40	AU-50	Unc-60	Unc-63	Unc-65
$8	$16	$30	$50	$70

W-191-E • F-1917E • Richmond • 38,400,000

EF-40	AU-50	Unc-60	Unc-63	Unc-65
$6	$12	$24	$40	$60

W-191-F • F-1917F • Atlanta • 89,600,000

EF-40	AU-50	Unc-60	Unc-63	Unc-65
$5	$10	$22	$35	$55

W-191-F★ • F-1917F★ • 640,000

VG-8	F-12	VF-20	EF-40	AU-50	Unc-60	Unc-63	Unc-65
$250	$400	$600	$800	$1,000	$1,500	$1,750	$2,000

W-191-G • F-1917G • Chicago • 19,200,000

VF-20	EF-40	AU-50	Unc-60	Unc-63	Unc-65
$20	$30	$45	$75	$100	$140

Series of 1988-A, Green Seal, Fort Worth
Villalpando-Brady (1989–1993)

This series commenced the supplemental printing of $1 notes at the Western Facility, as it is called, in Fort Worth, Texas. Although Western Facility has the initials WF and Fort

SERIES OF 1988-A, GREEN SEAL

Detail of the signatures and the series imprint of a sheet-fed, Washington-printed $1 Federal Reserve Note, Series of 1988-A (W-191-B). The back is the standard With Motto type.

Detail of the removal of face plate letters, showing the minor face changes on only the web-fed, Washington-printed issues.

Detail of the back of a web-fed press note showing location of the plate number 8 on this web-fed issue.

Detail of plate letter and serial on a Fort Worth printing of a Series of 1988-A note (W-192-G).

Worth has FW, it is the FW initials that are always used by numismatists. Notes printed at this location may be identified by a small FW on the right of the face, to the left of the plate letter and number. On the back the plate number of Fort Worth issues is in the field to the lower right of IN GOD WE TRUST.

Prices for a typical note for this series, unless listed otherwise, are as follows:

Unc-60	Unc-63	Unc-65
$3	$4	$6

W-192-F • F-1916F • Atlanta • 533,000,000

W-192-G • F-1916G • Chicago • 748,800,000

W-192-G★ • F-1916G★ • 6,400,000

Unc-60	Unc-63	Unc-65
$6	$8	$11

W-192-H • F-1916H • St. Louis • 326,400,000

W-192-I • F-1916I • Minneapolis • 844,800,000

W-192-I★ • F-1916I★ • 7,680,000

Unc-60	Unc-63	Unc-65
$10	$15	$25

W-192-J • F-1916J • Kansas City • 300,800,000

W-192-K • F-1916K • Dallas • 761,000,000

W-192-K★ • F-1916K★ • 3,200,000

Unc-60	Unc-63	Unc-65
$10	$15	$25

W-192-L • F-1916L • San Francisco • 2,009,600,000

W-192-L★ • F-1916L★ • 19,200,000

Unc-60	Unc-63	Unc-65
$6	$8	$11

Series of 1993, Green Seal, Washington Sheet-Fed Presses
Withrow-Bentsen (1994)

On $1 notes with front plate number 1 and back plate number 8, the back plate number is located on the back to the right of TRUST.[23]

Prices for a typical note for this series, unless listed otherwise, are as follows:

Unc-60	Unc-63	Unc-65
$3	$4	$6

W-193-A • F-1918A • Boston • 140,800,000

W-193-B • F-1918B • New York • 716,800,000

W-193-B★ • F-1918B★ • 2,240,000

Unc-60	Unc-63	Unc-65
$6	$8	$11

W-193-C • F-1918C • Philadelphia • 70,400,000

Unc-60	Unc-63	Unc-65
$15	$20	$29

W-193-C★ • F-1918C★ • 640,000

Unc-60	Unc-63	Unc-65
$140	$200	$270

W-193-D • F-1918D • Cleveland • 108,800,000

W-193-E • F-1918E • Richmond • 524,800,000

W-193-F • F-1918F • Atlanta • 787,200,000

W-193-F★ • F-1918F★ • 16,000,000

Unc-60	Unc-63	Unc-65
$6	$8	$11

W-193-G • F-1918G • Chicago • 96,000,000

W-193-L • F-1918L • San Francisco • 128,000,000

Series of 1993, Green Seal, Washington Web-Fed Presses
Withrow-Bentsen (1994)

Only two imprints, New York and Philadelphia, were used on this short series. These were first printed in May 1995.[24]

W-194-B • F-1920B • New York • 12,800,000

Unc-60	Unc-63	Unc-65
$15	$20	$29

W-194-C • F-1920C • Philadelphia • 12,800,000

Unc-60	Unc-63	Unc-65
$15	$20	$29

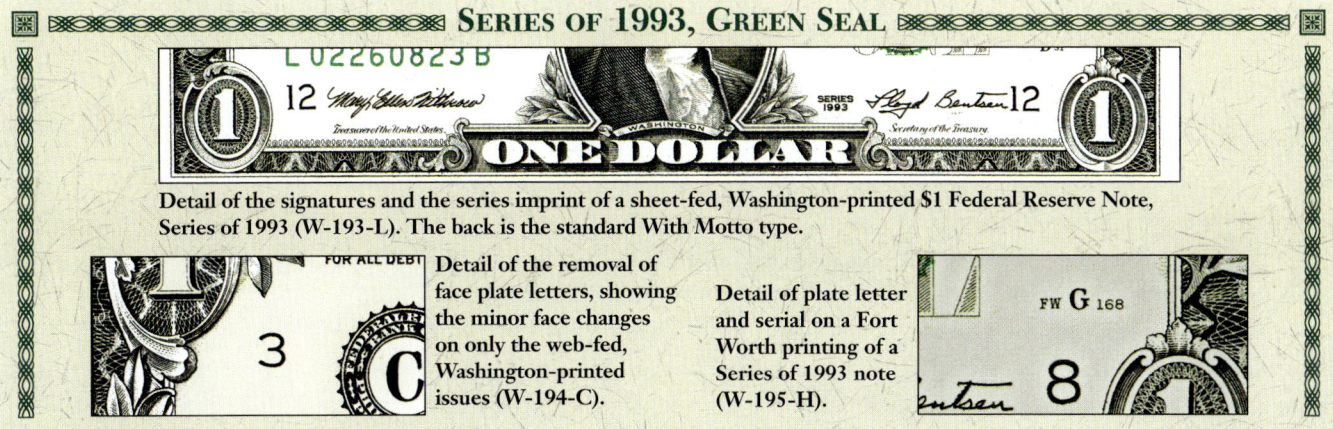

SERIES OF 1993, GREEN SEAL

L 02260823 B

Detail of the signatures and the series imprint of a sheet-fed, Washington-printed $1 Federal Reserve Note, Series of 1993 (W-193-L). The back is the standard With Motto type.

Detail of the removal of face plate letters, showing the minor face changes on only the web-fed, Washington-printed issues (W-194-C).

Detail of plate letter and serial on a Fort Worth printing of a Series of 1993 note (W-195-H).

Series of 1993, Green Seal, Fort Worth
Withrow-Bentsen (1994)

Prices for a typical note for this series, unless listed otherwise, are as follows:

Unc-60	Unc-63	Unc-65
$3	$4	$6

W-195-G • F-1919G • **Chicago** 646,400,000

W-195-G★ • F-1919G★ • 8,960,000

Unc-60	Unc-63	Unc-65
$6	$8	$11

W-195-H • F-1919H • **St. Louis** • 121,600,000

W-195-I • F-1919I • **Minneapolis** • 25,600,000

VF-20	EF-40	AU-50	Unc-60	Unc-63	Unc-65
$35	$50	$80	$120	$150	$200

W-195-K • F-1919K • **Dallas** • 620,800,000

W-195-K★ • F-1919K★ • 19,200,000

Unc-60	Unc-63	Unc-65
$6	$8	$11

W-195-L • F-1919L • **San Francisco** • 1,171,200,000

Series of 1995, Green Seal, Washington Sheet-Fed Presses
Withrow-Rubin (1995–1999)

W-196-B★ notes were printed in sheets of 32 subjects, as normal, one run with 10,000 sheets and the other with 20,000 sheets. However, a duplicate run of the same numbers was made. These differ very slightly in the location of certain plate features, as described by Francis X. Klaes in "Series 1995 $1 'B' Star Notes with Duplicate Serial Numbers," *Paper Money*, July–August 2005.

On notes with face plate number F1 and back plate number 129, the back plate number is located at the lower left of the reverse, just to the right of the projecting beaded area. This quite different from the normal location at the lower right. This variety is also found on Series 1981-A Federal Reserve Notes.[25]

Prices for a typical note for this series, unless listed otherwise, are as follows:

Unc-60	Unc-63	Unc-65
$2	$3	$5

Prices for a typical star note for this series, unless listed otherwise, are as follows:

Unc-60	Unc-63	Unc-65
$4	$5	$7

W-196-A • F-1921A • **Boston** • 1,134,745,600

W-196-A★ • F-1921A★ • 12,160,000

W-196-B • F-1921B • **New York** • 2,062,080,000

W-196-B★ • F-1921B★ • 9,600,000

Unc-60	Unc-63	Unc-65
$8	$10	$14

W-196-C • F-1921C • **Philadelphia** • 428,800,000

W-196-C★ • F-1921C★ • 9,600,000

W-196-D • F-1921D • **Cleveland** • 1,452,800,000

W-196-D★ • F-1921D★ • 7,040,000

W-196-E • F-1921E • **Richmond** • 1,831,400,000

W-196-E★ • F-1921E★ • 7,040,000

W-196-F • F-1921F • **Atlanta** • 1,279,360,000

W-196-F★ • F-1921F★ • 19,840,000

W-196-G • F-1921G • **Chicago** • 38,400,000

W-196-I • F-1921I • **Minneapolis** • 76,800,000

W-196-J • F-1921J • **Kansas City** • 83,200,000

W-196-L • F-1921L • **San Francisco** • 44,800,000

Unc-60	Unc-63	Unc-65
$8	$10	$14

Series of 1995, Green Seal, Washington Web-Fed Presses
Withrow-Rubin (1995–1999)

Printing on this series began in September 1995 and was completed in July 1996, by which time 50,560,000 had been produced.[26] This issue was the end of the web-fed press

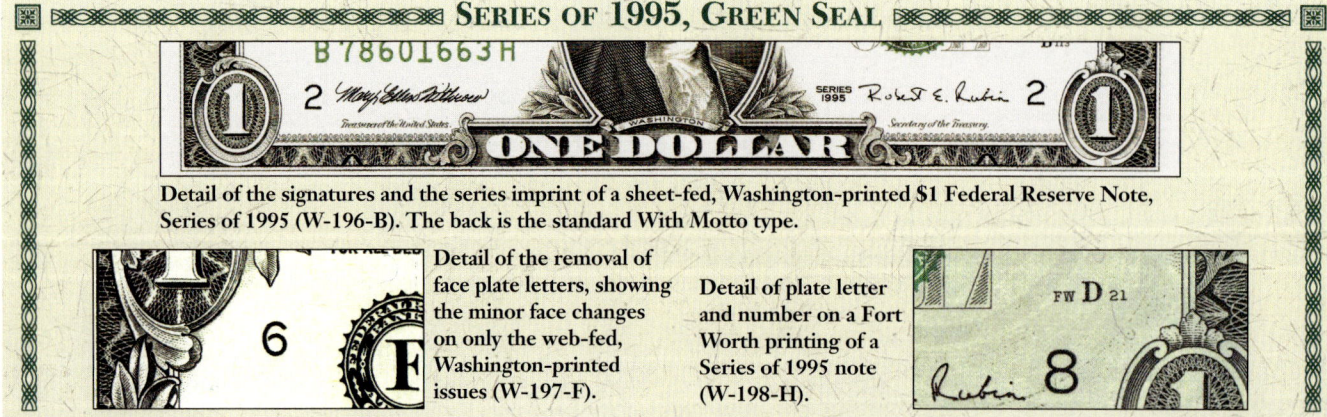

SERIES OF 1995, GREEN SEAL

Detail of the signatures and the series imprint of a sheet-fed, Washington-printed $1 Federal Reserve Note, Series of 1995 (W-196-B). The back is the standard With Motto type.

Detail of the removal of face plate letters, showing the minor face changes on only the web-fed, Washington-printed issues (W-197-F).

Detail of plate letter and number on a Fort Worth printing of a Series of 1995 note (W-198-H).

experiment, which did not prove to be worthwhile. Notes were printed for only four Federal Reserve districts.

W-197-A • F-1923A • Boston • 18,560,000

EF-40	AU-50	Unc-60	Unc-63	Unc-65
—	$6	$10	$14	$20

W-197-B • F-1923B • New York • 12,800,000

EF-40	AU-50	Unc-60	Unc-63	Unc-65
$5	$8	$15	$20	$29

W-197-D • F-1923D • Cleveland • 6,400,000

EF-40	AU-50	Unc-60	Unc-63	Unc-65
$5	$8	$15	$20	$29

W-197-F • F-1923F • Atlanta • 12,800,000

EF-40	AU-50	Unc-60	Unc-63	Unc-65
$5	$8	$15	$20	$29

Series of 1995, Green Seal, Fort Worth
Withrow-Rubin (1995–1999)

Prices for a typical note for this series, unless listed otherwise, are as follows:

Unc-60	Unc-63	Unc-65
$2	$3	$5

Prices for a typical star note for this series, unless listed otherwise, are as follows:

Unc-60	Unc-63	Unc-65
$4	$5	$7

W-198-C • F-1922C • Philadelphia • 76,800,000

W-198-C★ • F-1922C★ • 3,200,000

W-198-D • F-1922D • Cleveland • 134,400,000

W-198-F • F-1922F • Atlanta • 452,480,000

W-198-F★ • F-1922F★ • 3,584,000

W-198-G • F-1922G • Chicago • 1,459,200,000

W-198-G★ • F-1922G★ • 10,240,000

W-198-H • F-1922H • St. Louis • 921,600,000

W-198-I • F-1922I • Minneapolis • 1,310,720,000

W-198-I★ • F-1922I★ • 14,080,000

W-198-J • F-1922J • Kansas City • 262,400,000

W-198-J★ • F-1922J★ • 6,400,000

W-198-K • F-1922K • Dallas • 1,273,600,000

W-198-K★ • F-1922K★ • 1,440,000

Unc-60	Unc-63	Unc-65
$19	$25	$39

W-198-L • F-1922L • San Francisco • 2,252,800,000

W-198-L★ • F-1922L★ • 6,400,000

Series of 1999, Green Seal, Washington
Withrow-Summers (1999–2001)

This and all later issues have been printed on regular sheet-fed presses.

Prices for a typical note for this series, unless listed otherwise, are as follows:

Unc-60	Unc-63	Unc-65
$2	$3	$4

Prices for a typical star note for this series, unless listed otherwise, are as follows:

Unc-60	Unc-63	Unc-65
$4	$5	$7

W-199-A • F-1924A • Boston • 556,800,000

W-199-A★ • F-1924A★ • 3,840,000

W-199-B • F-1924B • New York • 1,497,600,000

W-199-B★ • F-1924B★ • 9,600,000

W-199-C • F-1924C • Philadelphia • 1,062,400,000

W-199-C★ • F-1924C★ • 13,760,000

W-199-D • F-1924D • Cleveland • 268,800,000

W-199-D★ • F-1924D★ • 640,000

EF-40	AU-50	Unc-60	Unc-63	Unc-65
$8	$20	$35	$42	$55

W-199-E • F-1924E • Richmond • 748,800,000

W-199-E★ • F-1924E★ • 7,040,000

W-199-F • F-1924F • Atlanta • 780,800,000

Series of 1999, Green Seal, Fort Worth
Withrow-Summers (1999–2001)

Prices for a typical note for this series, unless listed otherwise, are as follows:

Unc-60	Unc-63	Unc-65
$2	$3	$4

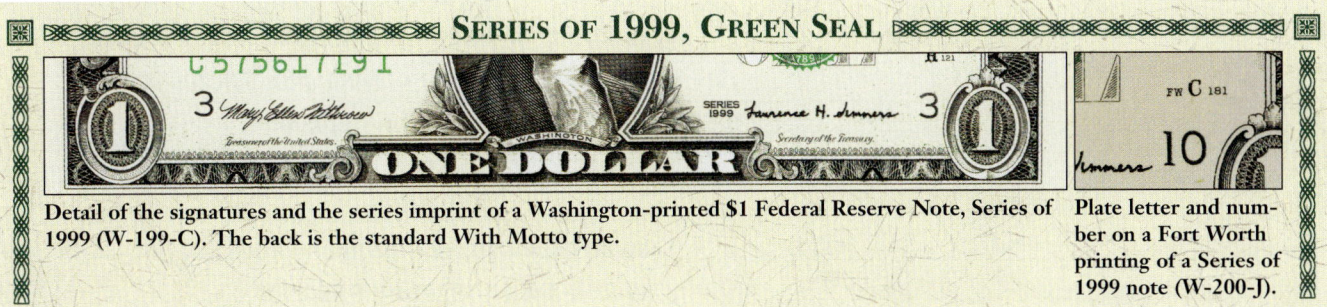

SERIES OF 1999, GREEN SEAL

Detail of the signatures and the series imprint of a Washington-printed $1 Federal Reserve Note, Series of 1999 (W-199-C). The back is the standard With Motto type.

Plate letter and number on a Fort Worth printing of a Series of 1999 note (W-200-J).

Prices for a typical star note for this series, unless listed otherwise, are as follows:

Unc-60	Unc-63	Unc-65
$4	$5	$7

W-200-F • F-1925F • Atlanta • 1,062,400,000

W-200-F★ • F-1925F★ • 640,000

EF-40	AU-50	Unc-60	Unc-63	Unc-65
$24	$40	$75	$100	$130

W-200-G • F-1925G • Chicago • 864,400,000

W-200-H • F-1925H • St. Louis • 89,600,000

W-200-H★ • F-1925H★ • 7,040,000

W-200-I • F-1925I • Minneapolis • 12,800,000

Unc-60	Unc-63	Unc-65
$4	$5	$7

W-200-J • F-1925J • Kansas City • 339,200,000

W-200-K • F-1925K • Dallas • 934,400,000

W-200-L • F-1925L • San Francisco • 1,920,000,000

W-200-L★ • F-1925L★ • 19,840,000

Series of 2001, Green Seal, Washington
Marin-O'Neill (2001–2002)

Prices for a typical note for this series, unless listed otherwise, are as follows:

Unc-60	Unc-63	Unc-65
$2	$3	$4

Prices for a typical star note for this series, unless listed otherwise, are as follows:

Unc-60	Unc-63	Unc-65
$4	$5	$7

W-201-A • F-1926A • Boston • 448,000,000

W-201-A★ • F-1926A★ • 3,520,000

W-201-B • F-1926B • New York • 678,400,000

W-201-C • F-1926C • Philadelphia • 550,400,000

W-201-C★ • F-1926C★ • 6,400,000

W-201-D • F-1926D • Cleveland • 307,200,000

W-201-E • F-1926E • Richmond • 70,400,000

W-201-F • F-1926F • Atlanta • 499,200,000

W-201-F★ • F-1926F★ • 3,520,000

W-201-H • F-1926H • St. Louis • 147,200,000

W-201-H★ • F-1926H★ • 640,000

EF-40	AU-50	Unc-60	Unc-63	Unc-65
$14	$25	$55	$75	$100

W-201-I • F-1926I • Minneapolis • 6,400,000

Unc-60	Unc-63	Unc-65
$8	$10	$14

W-201-J • F-1926J • Kansas City • 19,200,000

Unc-60	Unc-63	Unc-65
$8	$10	$14

Series of 2001, Green Seal, Fort Worth
Marin-O'Neill (2001–2002)

Prices for a typical note for this series, unless listed otherwise, are as follows:

Unc-60	Unc-63	Unc-65
$2	$3	$4

Prices for a typical star note for this series, unless listed otherwise, are as follows:

Unc-60	Unc-63	Unc-65
$4	$5	$7

W-202-F★ • F-1927F★ • Atlanta • 3,840,000

W-202-G • F-1927G • Chicago • 358,400,000

W-202-G★ • F-1927G★ • 4,480,000

W-202-H • F-1927H • St. Louis • 128,000,000

W-202-I • F-1927I • Minneapolis • 57,600,000

W-202-J • F-1927J • Kansas City • 160,000,000

W-202-K • F-1927K • Dallas • 300,800,000

W-202-K★ • F-1927K★ • 3,200,000

W-202-L • F-1927L • San Francisco • 1,152,000,000

W-202-L★ • F-1927L★ • 3,200,000

Series of 2003, Green Seal, Washington
Marin-Snow (2003)

Prices for a typical note for this series, unless listed otherwise, are as follows:

Unc-60	Unc-63	Unc-65
$2	$3	$4

Prices for a typical star note for this series, unless listed otherwise, are as follows:

Unc-60	Unc-63	Unc-65
$4	$5	$7

W-203-A • F-1928A • Boston • 384,000,000

W-203-A★ • F-1928A★ • 3,200,000

W-203-B • F-1928B • New York • 610,600,000

W-203-B★ • F-1928B★ • 5,760,000

W-203-C • F-1928C • Philadelphia • 460,800,000

W-203-D • F-1928D • Cleveland • 326,400,000

W-203-D★ • F-1928D★ • 320,000

AU-50	Unc-60	Unc-63	Unc-65
$25	$55	$80	$105

W-203-E • F-1928E • Richmond • 953,600,000

W-203-E★ • F-1928E★ • 6,880,000

W-203-F • F-1928F • Atlanta • 153,600,000

W-203-F★ • F-1928F★ • 320,000

AU-50	Unc-60	Unc-63	Unc-65
$25	$55	$75	$100

Series of 2003, Green Seal, Fort Worth
Marin-Snow (2003)

Prices for a typical note for this series, unless listed otherwise, are as follows:

Unc-60	Unc-63	Unc-65
$2	$3	$4

Prices for a typical star note for this series, unless listed otherwise, are as follows:

Unc-60	Unc-63	Unc-65
$4	$5	$7

W-204-F • F-1929F • Atlanta • 140,800,000

W-204-F★ • F-1929F★ • 3,200,000

W-204-G • F-1929G • Chicago • 742,400,000

W-204-G★ • F-1929G★ • 10,240,000

W-204-H • F-1929H • St. Louis • 268,800,000

W-204-I • F-1929I • Minneapolis • 147,200,000

W-204-J • F-1929J • Kansas City • 179,200,000

W-204-K • F-1929K • Dallas • 704,000,000

W-204-K★ • F-1929K★ • Dallas • 3,200,000

W-204-L • F-1929L • San Francisco • 1,267,200,000

W-204-L★ • F-1929L★ • 3,200,000

Series of 2003-A, Green Seal, Washington
Cabral-Snow (2004–2006)

Prices for a typical note for this series, unless listed otherwise, are as follows:

Unc-60	Unc-63	Unc-65
$2	$3	$4

Prices for a typical star note for this series, unless listed otherwise, are as follows:

Unc-60	Unc-63	Unc-65
$4	$5	$7

W-205-A • F-1930A • Boston • 300,800,000

W-205-B • F-1930B • New York • 966,400,000

W-205-B★ • F-1930B★ • 7,360,000

AU-50	Unc-60	Unc-63	Unc-65
$25	$55	$80	$105

W-205-C • F-1930C • Philadelphia • 224,000,000

W-205-D • F-1930D • Cleveland • 236,800,000

W-205-E • F-1930E • Richmond • 147,200,000

W-205-E★ • F-1930E★

SERIES OF 2001, GREEN SEAL

Detail of the signatures and the series imprint of a Washington-printed $1 Federal Reserve Note, Series of 2001 (W-201-K). The back is the standard With Motto type.

Plate letter and number on a Fort Worth printing of a Series of 2001 note (W-202-F).

SERIES OF 2003, GREEN SEAL

Detail of the signatures and the series imprint of a Washington-printed $1 Federal Reserve Note, Series of 2003 (W-203-A). The back is the standard With Motto type.

Plate letter and number on a Fort Worth printing of a Series of 2003 note (W-204-I).

SERIES OF 2003-A, GREEN SEAL

Detail of the signatures and the series imprint of a Washington-printed $1 Federal Reserve Note, Series of 2003-A (W-205-C). The back is the standard With Motto type.

Plate letter and number on a Fort Worth printing of a Series of 2003-A note (W-206-F).

W-205-F • F-1930F • Atlanta • 940,800,000

W-205-F★ • F-1930F★ • 3,520,000

Series of 2003-A, Green Seal, Fort Worth
Cabral-Snow (2004–2006)

Prices for a typical note for this series, unless listed otherwise, are as follows:

Unc-60	Unc-63	Unc-65
$2	$3	$4

W-206-F • F-1931F • Atlanta

W-206-G • F-1931G • Chicago • 441,600,000

W-206-H • F-1931H • St. Louis • 166,400,000

W-206-I • F-1931I • Minneapolis • 76,800,000

W-206-J • F-1931J • Kansas City • 294,400,000

W-206-J★ • F-1931J★

Unc-60	Unc-63	Unc-65
$7	$10	$13

W-206-K • F-1931K • Dallas • 364,800,000

W-206-K★ • F-1931K★ • 640,000

Unc-60	Unc-63	Unc-65
$40	$60	$80

W-206-L • F-1931L • San Francisco • 1,024,000,000

Series of 2006, Green Seal, Washington
Cabral-Paulson (2006–2009)

The information given here is accurate as of press time. No valuation charts are provided, as notes in this series can be had in top condition for face value at banks or from dealers (with a nominal handling charge).

W-207-A • F-1932A • Boston

W-207-B • F-1932B • New York

W-207-B★ • F-1932B★

W-207-C • F-1932C • Philadelphia

W-207-D • F-1932D • Cleveland

W-207-E • F-1932E • Richmond

W-207-F • F-1932F • Atlanta

W-207-F★ • F-1932F★

Series of 2006, Green Seal, Fort Worth
Cabral-Paulson (2006–2009)

The information given here is accurate as of press time. No valuation charts are provided, as notes in this series can be had in top condition for face value at banks or from dealers (with a nominal handling charge).

W-208-B • F-1933B • New York

W-208-B★ • F-1933B★

W-208-C • F-1933C • Philadelphia

W-208-F • F-1933F • Atlanta

W-208-F★ • F-1933F★

W-208-G • F-1933G • Chicago

W-208-G★ • F-1933G★

W-208-H • F-1933H • St. Louis

W-208-I • F-1933I • Minneapolis

W-208-J • F-1933J • Kansas City

W-208-J★ • F-1933J★

W-208-K • F-1933K • Dallas

W-208-L • F-1933L • San Francisco

W-208-L★ • F-1933L★

Series of 2009, Green Seal
Rios-Geithner (2009–)

No printing information available as of press time.

SERIES OF 2006, GREEN SEAL

Detail of the signatures and the series imprint of a Washington-printed $1 Federal Reserve Note, Series of 2006 (W-207-E). The back is the standard With Motto type.

Plate letter and number on a Fort Worth printing of a Series of 2006 note (W-208-L).

$2 NOTES

LARGE SIZE

Collecting $2 bills is a short and interesting pursuit. While there are some scarce issues, the overall number of varieties is rather small. There is no $2 equivalent to the lengthy runs of $1 notes, especially in the late 20th century. Across the board, $2 notes are more difficult to find than those of the $1 denomination. Although some varieties are scarce and a few are rare, most large-size $2 notes are very collectible, although for some, finding an Uncirculated example may be a challenge. Dealers' stocks and auction rooms are prime sources. Among National Bank Notes, the Original Series and Series of 1875 "Lazy Deuce" or "Lazy Two" is eagerly sought. The Series of 1896 "Educational Note" is another long-standing favorite, as is the "Battleship Note" in the Federal Reserve Bank Note series.

Did you know that in the 1920s a $2 bill was considered to be a jinx? They were not allowed in some card games, and certain race tracks forbade their being paid out across the counter.[1] Later, some factories paid their employees in $2 bills to be spent locally, to impress local merchants of the importance of those industries.

For a long time the $2 bill was considered to be as extinct as a dodo bird, but as part of the 1976 Bicentennial celebration the Treasury department brought the denomination out of hiding and modified an old stock vignette by the American Bank Note Company of John Trumbull's well-known painting, *The Declaration of Independence* (now with six of the signers removed), to place on the back. The $100 National Bank Notes of the First Charter Period had used the same illustration.

Small-size $2 notes are eminently collectible and form a very interesting set, with the red-overprint Legal Tender Notes being especially colorful.

LEGAL TENDER NOTES
(Also Known as United States Notes)

Series of 1862

The first $2 bills printed were Legal Tender Notes, part of the "greenback" issues launched in 1862. The face, back, and tint plates for the $2 Series of 1862 Legal Tender Notes (illus. on p. 170) were engraved by the National Bank Note

Company, with responsibility for printing shared with American.[2] Treasury signatures of Chittenden and Spinner were printed on the face by using a separate plate and a special ink.

On the face is the portrait of Alexander Hamilton engraved by Joseph P. Ourdan. Two imprint versions of the American and National bank-note companies are found. Similar to the $1 notes of this series, at the bottom center is a 1-2-3 design, with the denomination highlighted with a drop-out white background, in this case a 2 (a $3 bill was considered, which is why the number was featured, but none were ever printed). All have a small red Treasury seal with a spiked border (applied by the National Currency Bureau in Washington). There are two patent imprints, 1860 at the lower left and 1857 at the center right.

The back is printed in green and has the denomination and redemption information. The last is the so-called Second Obligation: "This note is a Legal Tender for all debts public and private, except for duties on imports and interest on the public debt, and is receivable in payment of all loans made to the United States."

These notes are very popular and readily collectible as a type, although they are seen far less frequently than are the $1 bills of the same issue.

W-303 was discovered by Doug Murray in 2002. For this book, he commented:

> This is the only known case in all of federal currency notes, large and small sizes, for which the Treasury seal was applied upside down, in the proper location. This is not a case of having the sheet fed into the sealing press upside down, as are all other upside-down seal errors, where the seal always appears on the wrong side of the note. They apparently locked the gang of four seals in the sealing press upside down! It is from Series 1, where most of the interesting finds are.

W-301 • F-41a • NATIONAL BANK NOTE COMPANY horizontally at bottom border, AMERICAN BANK NOTE CO. NEW YORK vertically at left border; Treasury seal without inner border of radial parallel lines; no face plate number on left; early part of Series 1 • 10,000 (est.)

Recorded population: 6.

W-302 • F-41a • Treasury seal with inner border of radial parallel lines; Series 1 and 2 • 178,000 (est.)
Recorded population: 5.

W-303 • F-41a • As preceding, but with red Treasury seal inverted; last part of Series 1 • 12,000 (est.)
Recorded population: 3 • *Commentary:* This would have been done in the early process of applying seals at the National Currency Bureau. The three known to exist are in a range of

about 10,000 serials, from series 1, plate positions A and B. One of these, in low grade, was cherrypicked on eBay in September 2008.

W-304 • F-41a • Plate number on left; Series 3 to 88 • 8,511,160 (est.)
Estimated population: 225 to 275 • *Highest graded:* Unc.

VG-8	F-12	VF-20	EF-40	AU-50	Unc-60	Unc-63	Unc-65
$460	$740	$1,375	$2,350	$3,000	$3,450	$4,200	$9,000

SERIES OF 1862

$2 Legal Tender Note, Series of 1862 (W-305). Portrait of Alexander Hamilton, first secretary of the Treasury.

Detail of the kaleidograph-style denomination counter, plate letter, and plate number on an example of W-305, serial 44055.

Detail of the series number on the serial 44055 note. "Patented 30 June 1857" below the kaleidograph counter refers to the "Green Tint" or "Canada Green" patent held by the American Bank Note Company for green overprinting.

Detail of the inverted Treasury seal on W-303, a printing process error that is the only such instance known among large-size notes. Series 1, serial 88190, plate B, a spectacular production setup (not printing) error discovered by Doug Murray.

Back of a $2 Legal Tender Note, Series of 1862.

W-305 • F-41 • NATIONAL BANK NOTE COMPANY horizontally at bottom border and NATIONAL BANK NOTE Co. N.Y. vertically at left border; Series 88 to 171 • 8,318,840 (est.)

Estimated population: 700 to 900 • *Highest graded:* Unc.

VG-8	F-12	VF-20	EF-40	AU-50	Unc-60	Unc-63	Unc-65
$460	$740	$1,375	$2,350	$3,000	$3,450	$4,200	$9,000

Series of 1869

Thomas Jefferson made his debut on the $2 bill in the Series of 1869, establishing what proved to be an enduring connection lasting to today. Later, his was the iconic portrait on small-size $2 notes. An Edinburgh Scotsman named Charles Burt created the Jefferson portrait in his capacity as one of the chief engravers for the Treasury department. Engraving of the Capitol scene was done by Louis Delnoce and William Chorlton.

The Series of 1869 $2 note (W-310) is popularly known as the "Rainbow Deuce." The coloration includes green and red printing on blue-tinted paper and a large pink Treasury seal with a spiked border. The face bears the notation ENGRAVED & PRINTED AT THE TREASURY DEPARTMENT and under the left serial number NATIONAL BANK NOTE COMPANY NEW YORK, while the back has AMERICAN BANK NOTE COMPANY, NEW YORK at the bottom left and again at the bottom right. National created the face plate and American the back. Series of 1869 notes were issued from October 19, 1869, to July 25, 1874.

$2 Legal Tender Note, Series of 1869, popularly known as the "Rainbow Deuce" (W-310). Bust of Jefferson, view of the U.S. Capitol.

Detail of the green microprinting at the upper right of the face.

Detail of the serial number, 35A plate designation, and National imprint with bright green frame at the lower left of the face.

Back of the "Rainbow Deuce" note.

This the scarcest issue in the "Rainbow Note" set, which also includes the $1, $5, and $10 notes in the Series of 1869. The star after the serial number is an ornament, is found on all notes, and has no special significance. It is not unusual for the face to be well margined on this issue but the back to be off-center.

W-310 • F-42 • Allison-Spinner (1869–1875) • Large red seal • 24,796,000

Estimated population: 600 to 750 • *Highest graded:* Unc.

VG-8	F-12	VF-20	EF-40	AU-50	Unc-60	Unc-63	Unc-65
$550	$800	$1,800	$3,350	$4,700	$5,250	$6,300	$19,000

Series of 1874

The Legal Tender Notes, Series of 1874 continue the same face design as the Series of 1869, but without the green printing on the face. The Treasury seal (small red with a spiked border) is now at the left, and a large pink scalloped ornament is to the right. The back is a new design, more ornate than the preceding. On the face, below the top border is ENGRAVED AND PRINTED AT THE BUREAU, ENGRAVING & PRINTING. Red serial numbers are continued. The notations COLUMBIAN BANK NOTE CO. and WASHINGTON, D.C. are at the top and bottom of the back. Series of 1874 notes were issued from July 13, 1874, to September 13, 1875.

W-311 • F-43 • Allison-Spinner (1869–1875) • 8,260,000

Estimated population: 125 to 150 • *Highest graded:* Unc.

VG-8	F-12	VF-20	EF-40	AU-50	Unc-60	Unc-63	Unc-65
$200	$400	$700	$1,200	$1,350	$1,450	$1,700	$3,300

$2 Legal Tender Note, Series of 1874 (W-311). (ANA Edward C. Rochette Money Museum)

Detail from another note, the upper left of the face showing the series imprint and plate A/1 information.

Back of a $2 Legal Tender Note, Series of 1874 (W-311).

Series of 1875

The face design of the previous series is continued. Serial numbers are red, and the small, spiked Treasury seal is pink. The first two groups printed had SERIES A 1875 or SERIES B 1875 in pink at the bottom order right of center.

The back is as preceding, with COLUMBIAN BANK NOTE CO. and WASHINGTON, D.C. at the top and bottom of the back, now with SERIES OF 1875 in the top margin and PRINTED AT THE BUREAU, ENGRAVING AND PRINTING, TREASURY DEPT. in the lower margin. Series of 1875 notes were issued from July 20, 1875, to June 20, 1879.

The sequence given here represents the time of release of the notes, as determined by the research of Doug Murray, and is ordered differently from that in certain other texts.

The centering on the back can be too high or too low when the face of the note is well centered. This point should be checked, as some are well aligned.

W-312 • F-45 • Allison-New (1875–1876) • SERIES / A / 1875 imprint in pink • 1,000,000

Estimated population: 30 to 40 • *Highest graded:* Unc.

VG-8	F-12	VF-20	EF-40	AU-50	Unc-60	Unc-63	Unc-65
$800	$1,300	$1,800	$2,500	$3,500	$4,500	$6,000	$14,000

W-313 • F-46 • SERIES / B / 1875 imprint in pink • 1,000,000

Estimated population: 40 to 50 • *Highest graded:* Unc.

VG-8	F-12	VF-20	EF-40	AU-50	Unc-60	Unc-63	Unc-65
$600	$1,000	$1,500	$2,500	$3,400	$4,250	$6,500	$10,000

W-314 • F-44 • No series imprint • 4,160,000

Estimated population: 75 to 85 • *Highest graded:* Unc.

VG-8	F-12	VF-20	EF-40	AU-50	Unc-60	Unc-63
$250	$450	$650	$950	$1,200	$1,300	$1,900

W-315 • F-47 • Allison-Wyman (1876–1877) • 5,358,000

Estimated population: 90 to 120 • *Highest graded:* Unc.

VG-8	F-12	VF-20	EF-40	AU-50	Unc-60	Unc-63	Unc-65
$200	$400	$700	$1,200	$1,350	$1,450	$1,700	$3,300

Series of 1878

The Legal Tender Notes in the Series of 1878 (illus. on p. 174) have the Treasury seal (small, red with a scalloped border) at the left. The large pink ornament is no longer present. The backs are imprinted the same as the Series of 1875 notes. Face plate number 52 has a plate engraving error. Evidence suggests that new Series of 1878 Allison-Gilfillan plates were being made simultaneously with the new Series of 1880 Scofield-Gilfillan plates. The Series of 1878 notes were using up the last of the old Willcox Company security paper with the distributed fibers and a blue-tinted band, while the Series of 1880 notes were introducing the new Crane Company paper, which had two horizontal threads running completely across the note, plus a sprinkling throughout of short blue and red fibers. Inadvertently, the 1878 plate number 52 had the 1880 Scofield signature added to all four plate positions rather than the correct 1878 Allison signature.[3]

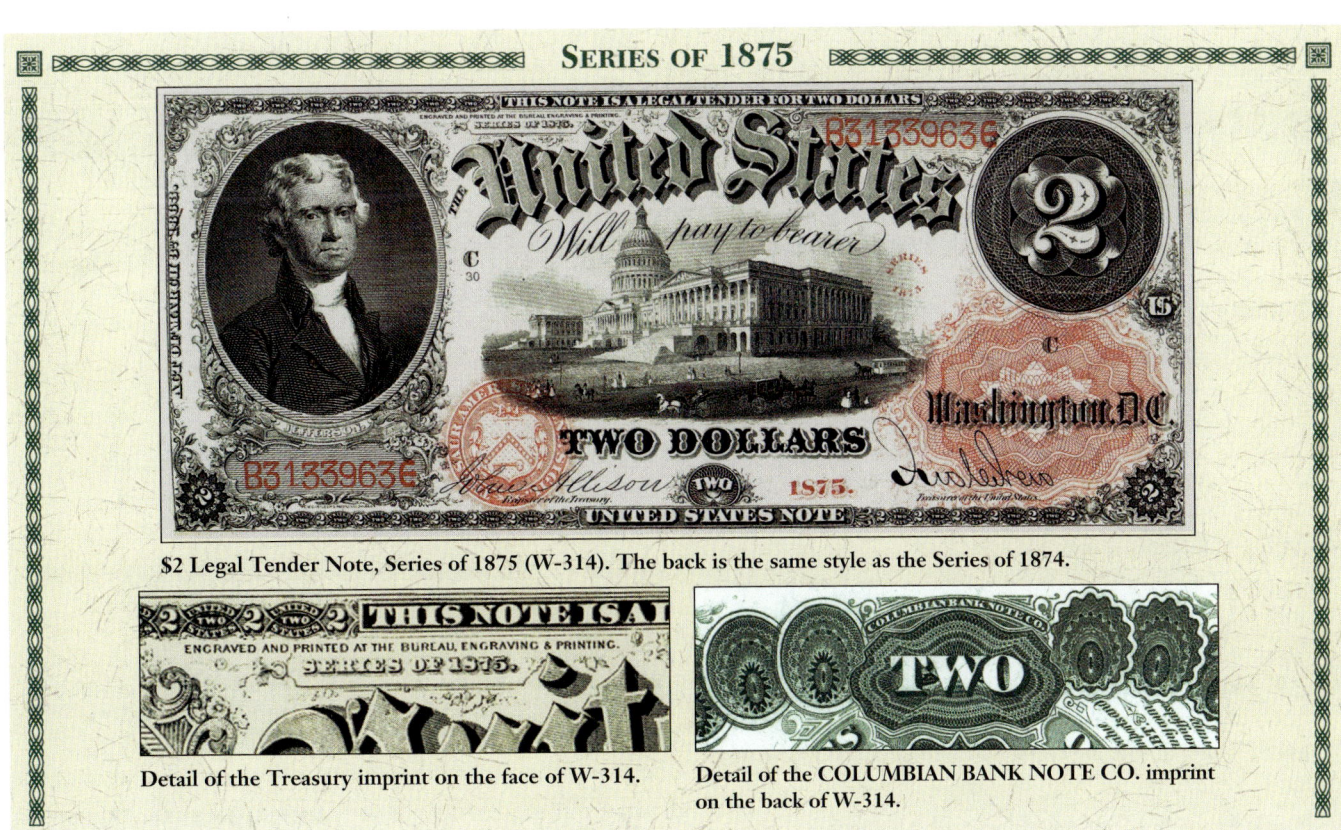

SERIES OF 1875

$2 Legal Tender Note, Series of 1875 (W-314). The back is the same style as the Series of 1874.

Detail of the Treasury imprint on the face of W-314.

Detail of the COLUMBIAN BANK NOTE CO. imprint on the back of W-314.

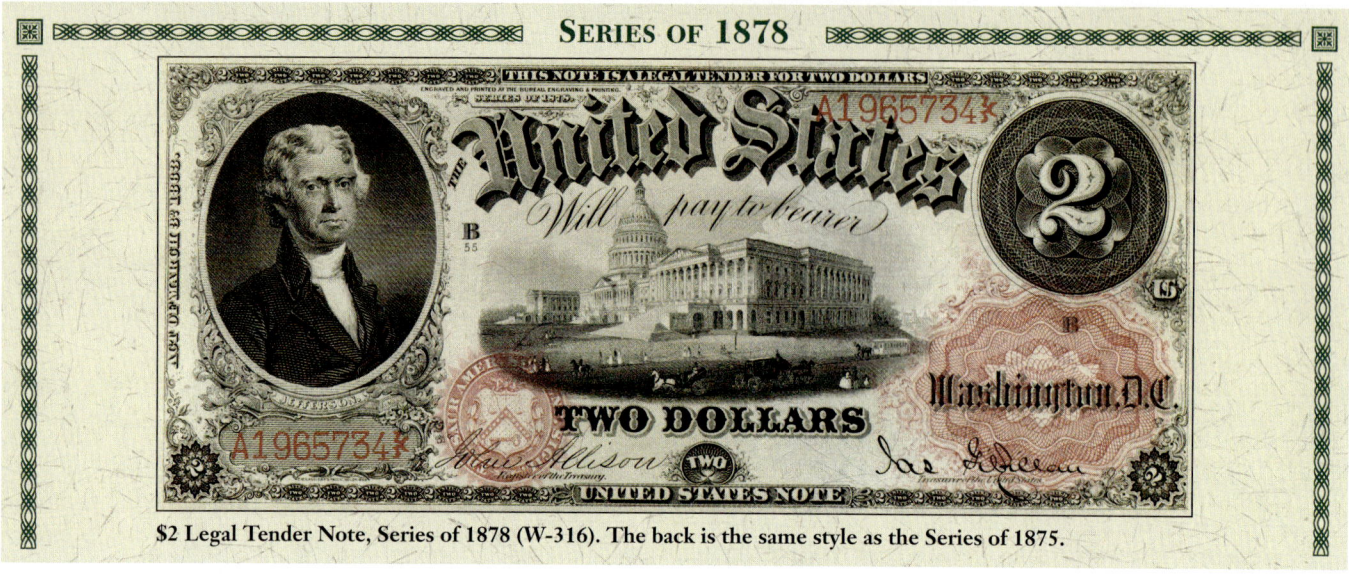

SERIES OF 1878

$2 Legal Tender Note, Series of 1878 (W-316). The back is the same style as the Series of 1875.

W-316 • F-48 • Allison-Gilfillan (1877–1878) • 4,576,000 (est.)

Estimated population: 190 to 225 • *Highest graded:* Unc • *Commentary:* The very last printed had a security paper change from a vertical to a horizontal blue stain with fibers across entire length.

VG-8	F-12	VF-20	EF-40	AU-50	Unc-60	Unc-63	Unc-65
$185	$380	$625	$800	$1,050	$1,300	$1,600	$3,700

W-317 • F-49 • Scofield-Gilfillan (1878–1881) • 100,000 (est.)

Estimated population: 16 to 18 • *Highest graded:* Unc • *Commentary:* From face plate 52 only.

VG-8	F-12	VF-20	EF-40	AU-50	Unc-60	Unc-63
$2,900	$5,750	$12,000	$20,000	—	—	—

Series of 1880

At the right a Treasury seal (colors and sizes vary) replaces the pink scalloped ornament. Red serial numbers are continued from W-318 to W-320 and then changed to blue from W-321 to W-326.

There are three different back imprint styles:

Back Style 1: With COLUMBIAN BANK NOTE CO. and WASHINGTON, D.C. at the top and bottom of the back. SERIES OF 1880 is in the top margin and PRINTED AT THE BUREAU, ENGRAVING AND PRINTING, TREASURY DEPT. in the lower margin. Used on W-318 and W-319, and a very few W-320.

Back Style 2: With COLUMBIAN BANK NOTE CO. and WASHINGTON, D.C., at the top and bottom of the back. SERIES OF 1880 and PRINTED AT THE BUREAU OF ENGRAVING & PRINTING are each in curved lines oriented vertically in the open space at the inside left. Used on most W-320 and W-321.

Back Style 3: Mention of Columbian and Washington is removed. SERIES OF 1880 and PRINTED AT THE BUREAU OF ENGRAVING & PRINTING are each in curved lines oriented vertically in the open space at the inside left. Used from W-322 to W-326.

W-318 • F-50 • Scofield-Gilfillan (1878–1881) • Large brown seal • Back Style 1 • 8,400,000 (est.)

Estimated population: 135 to 160 • *Highest graded:* Unc.

VG-8	F-12	VF-20	EF-40	AU-50	Unc-60	Unc-63	Unc-65
$145	$190	$300	$450	$750	$950	$1,150	$2,350

W-319 • F-51 • Bruce-Gilfillan (1881–1883) • 7,540,000 (est.)

Estimated population: 155 to 175 • *Highest graded:* Unc.

VG-8	F-12	VF-20	EF-40	AU-50	Unc-60	Unc-63	Unc-65
$150	$200	$300	$450	$750	$950	$1,150	$2,350

W-320a Back Style 1 • F-52 • Bruce-Wyman (1883–1885) • Large brown seal, red serial numbers • 520,000 (est.)

Recorded population: 3 • *Highest graded:* AU.

W-320b Back Style 2 • F-52 • 8,064,000 (est.)

Estimated population: 240 to 280 • *Highest graded:* Unc.

VG-8	F-12	VF-20	EF-40	AU-50	Unc-60	Unc-63	Unc-65
$145	$190	$300	$450	$750	$950	$1,150	$2,350

W-321 • F-52a • Large red seal, blue serial numbers • 984,000 printed, but never released • None in numismatic hands[4]

W-322 • F-52b • Rosecrans-Jordan (1885–1887) • 68,000 printed, but never released • None in numismatic hands[5]

W-323 • F-53 • Rosecrans-Huston (1889–1891) • Large red seal • Back Style 3 for this and later notes • 348,000 (est.)

Estimated population: 55 to 65 • *Highest graded:* Unc.

VG-8	F-12	VF-20	EF-40	AU-50	Unc-60	Unc-63	Unc-65
$800	$1,200	$2,000	$4,750	$6,000	$6,750	$10,000	$37,000

SERIES OF 1880

$2 Legal Tender Note, Series of 1880 (W-319).

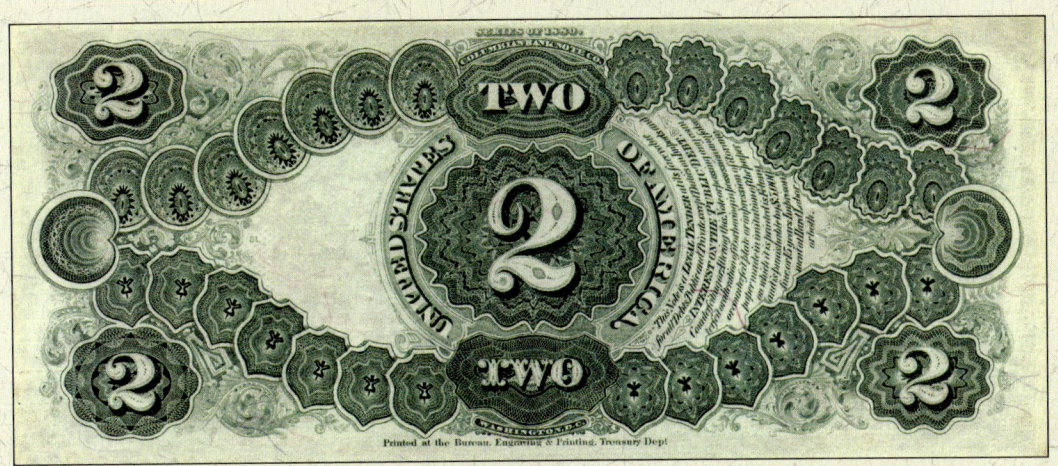

Back of a $2 Legal Tender Note, Series of 1880 (W-319).

Detail of top of Back Style 1 with SERIES and COLOMBIAN imprints (W-319).

Detail of bottom of Back Style 1 with WASHINGTON and BUREAU imprints (W-319).

Detail of left side of Back Styles 2 and 3 (W-323).

Detail of top of Back Style 3, with imprints removed (W-323).

Detail of bottom of Back Style 3, with imprints removed (W-323).

W-324 • F-54 • Large brown seal • 316,000 (est.)

Estimated population: 25 to 30 • *Highest graded:* Unc.

VG-8	F-12	VF-20	EF-40	AU-50	Unc-60	Unc-63
$4,000	$6,500	$9,500	$15,000	$18,000	$22,000	$30,000

W-325 • F-55 • Rosecrans-Nebeker (1891–1893) • Small red seal with scalloped border • 740,000 (est.)

Estimated population: 60 to 70 • *Highest graded:* Unc • *Commentary:* Two security paper types. Early type 1 has two

horizontal threads the entire width of note. Later type 2 has two vertical bands of distributed red and blue fibers.

VG-8	F-12	VF-20	EF-40	AU-50	Unc-60	Unc-63	Unc-65
$150	$190	$250	$375	$575	$950	$1,150	$3,000

W-326 • F-56 • Tillman-Morgan (1893–1897) • 1,232,000 (est.)

Estimated population: 220 to 250 • *Highest graded:* Unc.

VG-8	F-12	VF-20	EF-40	AU-50	Unc-60	Unc-63	Unc-65
$140	$180	$230	$350	$540	$900	$1,100	$1,875

Series of 1917

Designs are as in the previous series, but with a Series of 1917 imprint and red serial numbers. All have a small red Treasury seal with a scalloped border. On the back, SERIES OF 1917 is positioned vertically in the left field.

Gene Hessler and Carlson Chambliss report that notes of this type are notorious for having very little space at the top or bottom margin, except for notes at the top or bottom of the sheet, which often resulted in the margins being trimmed into the design. These were spaced together very closely on the original four-subject sheets. Accordingly, a "tight" margin, but not cut into the border, would be acceptable for a high-grade note.

Mules: Back plate numbers can be in one of two locations.[6] On May 14, 1921, with the new Elliott-White signature combination starting, all Legal Tender, Silver Certificate, and Gold Certificate back plates were given numbers in a new location and beginning with 1, although no notice was given of the change.

> **Back Plate Location 1** (regular use): W-327 and W-328. This was the standard location until May 14, 1921. It was also used to create a mule for W-329 and W-330.

> **Back Plate Location 2** (regular use): W-329 and W-330 (introduced without notice as the new style on May 14, 1921, with the Elliott-White combination). This was also used to create a mule for W-328, which continued being printed midway into W-329 production.

W-327 • F-57 • Teehee-Burke (1915–1919) • Back Plate Location 1 • 69,072,000 (est.)
Estimated population: 700 to 850 • Highest graded: Unc.

VG-8	F-12	VF-20	EF-40	AU-50	Unc-60	Unc-63	Unc-65
$110	$135	$180	$235	$300	$360	$650	$1,000

W-327★ • F-57★
Estimated population: 63 to 67 • Highest graded: Unc.

VG-8	F-12	VF-20	EF-40	AU-50	Unc-60	Unc-63	Unc-65
$175	$250	$500	$750	$1,500	$2,250	$3,000	—

W-328 • F-58 • Elliott-Burke (1919–1921) • 47,246,000, or about 99.9% regular (est.)
Estimated population: 425 to 525 • Highest graded: Unc.

VG-8	F-12	VF-20	EF-40	AU-50	Unc-60	Unc-63	Unc-65
$110	$135	$180	$235	$300	$360	$650	$1,000

W-328★ • F-58★
Estimated population: 50 to 55 • Highest graded: Unc.

VG-8	F-12	VF-20	EF-40	AU-50	Unc-60	Unc-63
$190	$275	$550	$850	$1,700	$2,750	$3,800

W-328 Mule • F-58 • Back Plate Location 2 • 50,000, or about 0.1% mules (est.)
Recorded population: 3 • Highest graded: EF • Commentary: From face plate 315 only.

$2 Legal Tender Note, Series of 1917 (W-329). The back is similar to the preceding style.

Back Plate Location 1.

Back Plate Location 2.

W-329 • F-59 • Elliott-White (1921–1922) • 14,060,000, or about 58% regular (est.)

Estimated population: 350 to 500 for this and the related mule combined • *Highest graded:* Unc.

VG-8	F-12	VF-20	EF-40	AU-50	Unc-60	Unc-63	Unc-65
$110	$135	$180	$235	$300	$360	$650	$1,000

W-329★ • F-59★

Estimated population: 20 to 24 • *Highest graded:* AU-50 • *Selected information:* No recent market data.

VG-8	F-12	VF-20	EF-40	AU-50
$225	$500	$850	$1,300	$2,400

W-329 Mule • F-59 • Back Plate Location 1 • 10,000,000, or about 42% mules (est.)

Estimated population: 70 to 80 • *Highest graded:* Unc • *Selected information:* Hickman Auctions (6/1992), B24329194A, VF, $44. Knight (12/2000), B24360809A, Unc-62 (CGA), $247.50. Heritage (7/2008), B31026892A/D, Unc-64 (PCGS), $690.

VG-8	F-12	VF-20	EF-40
$110	$135	$180	$235

W-329 Mule★ • F-59★

Estimated population: 16 to 18 • *Highest graded:* EF.

VG-8	F-12	VF-20	EF-40
$275	$650	$1,000	$1,500

W-330 • F-60 • Speelman-White (1922–1927) • Back Plate Location 2 • 175,388,000, or about 99% regular (est.)

Estimated population: 6,000 to 8,000 • *Selected information:* CAA (1/2000), 2405796B/D, VG–F, problems, $330. Knight (11/2007), 2486862B/B, F-12 (PCGS), $517.50.

VG-8	F-12	VF-20	EF-40	AU-50	Unc-60	Unc-63	Unc-65
$100	$125	$170	$210	$270	$325	$575	$700

W-330★ • F-60★

Estimated population: 300 to 320 • *Highest graded:* Unc.

VG-8	F-12	VF-20	EF-40	AU-50	Unc-60	Unc-63	Unc-65
$125	$175	$325	$600	$1,500	$2,250	$3,000	—

W-330 Mule • F-60 • Back Plate Location 1 • 1,600,000, or about 1% mules (est.)

Estimated population: 28 to 32 • *Highest graded:* Unc • *Commentary:* As this is a new listing, there is no market history.

NATIONAL BANK NOTES

Original Series
(Authorized Issue 1865 to 1875)

These notes (illus. on p. 179) were printed by the American and National bank-note companies in New York City, possibly with one firm printing one side and the second firm doing the other, but arrangements are not known. These were usually (but not always) printed in four-subject sheets of $1-$1-$1-$2, with the American Bank Note Company imprint on the bottom border of the $1 notes and the National Bank Note Company signature on the $2 notes. Plate letters in sequence were A, B, and C on the $1 notes and A on the $2. By definition, three times as many $1 notes were printed as were those of the $2 denomination. All have a small red Treasury seal with a spiked border.

These were printed with red (usually) or blue Treasury serial numbers. The first group with red serials had no prefix or suffix letter and began on March 28, 1865, with serial number 9 and ended on October 4, 1865, with serial number 999413. The next set of red serials began on March 23, 1866, with letter A as a prefix followed by B, C, D, and E. Set E ended on August 19, 1875. A set with blue serials began on October 4, 1865, with serial number 9 and ended on March 23, 1866, with Treasury serial number 999693. A set of blue serials with prefix letter A seems to have been used by only four banks from September 28, 1866, to July 10, 1875: Washington County National Bank of Greenwich, New York; West Chester County National Bank of Peekskill, New York; Merchants National Bank of Bangor, Maine; and City National Bank of Manchester, New Hampshire. These last notes were all printed on anomalous plates laid out as $1-$1-$2-$2.[7]

The total number of $2 National Bank Notes issued was 7,747,519, of which about 82% were of the Original Series. The Act of June 20, 1874, provided for the imprinting of the bank's charter number.

These have one of the most famous of all designs from a numismatic viewpoint, the so-called "Lazy Deuce" or "Lazy Two." The large numeral 2 is seen on its side. The concept of a "lazy" numeral was not new to paper money, and several antecedents can be found on obsolete currency issued by state banks. On the left of the face is vignette of a female goddess designated as *Stars and Stripes*. At the center of the back is the vignette *Sir Walter Raleigh, 1585*, which is also known as *Sir Walter Raleigh Introducing Corn and Tobacco to the English* (and variations). On the left side of the back is a state or territorial seal representing the issuing location of the bank, and to the right is an eagle (on some notes issued in territories an eagle is at both ends).

Although 6,447,090 Original and 1,410,150 Series of 1875 notes were printed, only a tiny fraction of this survives today, with fewer than 1,900 recorded by Don C. Kelly. Today, all range from scarce to rare, and some are very rare. Distribution of $1 and $2 National Bank bills ceased on January 1, 1879. Typical collectible conditions run from Fair to Fine. Generally, any example that is nice VF or better is an exception to the rule, although now and again some Unc pieces come to light, including a few notes from hoards.

Similar to the situation for $1 National Bank bills, the $2 issues are valued today not as much by signature combinations (although the Jeffries-Spinner pair is exceedingly rare), but by issuing locations. Thus $2 notes from the territories, such as Utah, Montana, or New Mexico, are worth many multiples of what a comparable-condition $2 bill might sell for if issued in Boston, New York, or Philadelphia. Within any state, populous or sparsely settled, there are some "rare banks." A Lazy Deuce that is one of a kind or one of just a handful can bring a sharp premium.

The values given are for common states with larger populations of $2 notes, generally more than 30 or so, and especially the several states for which over 100 are known.

Banks of Issue and Rarity of Notes

Based upon census information from Don C. Kelly and James M. Kelly (*National Bank Note Census*, Version 4.0) and some information from other sources, this listing gives each location, the number of banks issuing this series of notes within each, and a commentary.[8] As a class the Lazy Twos are far rarer than the $1 notes in this series. The census describes 1,263 notes. These are specifically listed below. Fortunately, several states offer a nice selection, and enough Unc notes exist, mostly in clusters, that securing one for a type set will present no problem, although such notes are expensive.

Alabama • 4 banks of issue • No notes reported.

Arkansas • 2 banks of issue • No notes reported.

Colorado Territory • 6 banks of issue • 10 notes reported • Similar to the situation for Original Series $1 bills, for a territory Colorado has an exceptionally generous population of Original Series $2 notes. There are three Unc notes listed by Don C. Kelly, two of which are among the six notes reported from the Colorado National Bank of Denver and the other from the First National Bank of Pueblo. A single serial number 1 note is from the First National Bank of Denver (VF).

Connecticut • 66 banks of issue • 47 notes reported • Fairly widely distributed, with many banks represented. Just one Unc note is listed, this from the Union National Bank of New London. There is one serial number 1 note, from the Ansonia National Bank (EF).

Dakota Territory (combining what became North and South Dakota) • 1 bank of issue • 2 reported • Both are from the First National Bank of Yankton (VF and Unc). No Series of 1875 $2 notes were issued by this territory, making the two Original Series notes all the more important. An auction offering might be worthy of a catalog cover position. No serial number 1 notes.

Delaware • 5 banks of issue • 4 notes reported • Grades range from VG–F to VF. Three are from the Citizens National Bank of Middleton, the other from the New Castle County National Bank of Odessa. No serial number 1 notes.

District of Columbia • 4 banks of issue • 3 notes listed • All are from the National Bank of the Metropolis (G–VG, VG, and ungraded). No serial number 1 notes.

Georgia • 5 banks of issue • No notes reported.

Idaho Territory • 1 bank of issue • 1 note reported • First National Bank of Idaho, Boise City, serial 2 (G). A first-class rarity.

Illinois • 98 banks of issue • 151 notes reported • One of the more collectible states, even common within the context of Lazy Two notes. The Alton National Bank accounts for 41 of these, all of which are in circulated grades. The First National Bank of Kansas (Illinois) has 13, 10 of which are Unc. Thirty are from the First National Bank of Lincoln, most of which are Unc (the same hoard contained $1 notes). Illinois is a prime candidate to locate a Lazy Two for a type set of notes.

Indiana • 66 banks of issue • 67 notes reported • A collectible state with the supply spread across many different banks, although 16 are from the First National Bank of Lebanon, including seven Unc. There is one serial number 1 note, from the First National Bank of Monticello (Fair).

Iowa • 57 banks of issue • 37 notes reported • A readily collectible state with a wide representation of banks. All the notes listed by Don C. Kelly are in circulated grades. There are five serial number 1 notes from as many different banks (VG to EF). Iowa and other prairie states were experiencing boom times after the Civil War, and many banks were formed.

Kansas • 22 banks of issue • 15 notes reported • Scarce to rare as a state. Three are from the First National Bank of Manhattan and a like number are from the Topeka National Bank. Most notes show extensive wear. One Unc reported (First National Bank of Paola, serial not listed[9]). No serial number 1 notes, but a number 2 is given for the Emporia National Bank (AU).

Kentucky • 32 banks of issue • 17 notes reported • A scarce but collectible state. Six are from the German National Bank of Louisville. Grades range from a low of G to a high of AU. There is one serial number 1 note from the German National Bank of Louisville (VF).

Louisiana • 3 banks of issue • 2 notes reported • A prime rarity as a state. Both are from the State National Bank of New Orleans (VG and ungraded). No Series of 1875 $2 notes were issued by this state, placing additional focus on the Original Series notes.

Maine • 41 banks of issue • 24 notes reported • Slightly scarce state, bordering on rare. A nice selection of banks is represented, but the Belfast National Bank accounts for seven of these. The only Unc reported is from the First National Bank of Augusta.

Maryland • 13 banks of issue • 8 notes reported • A rare state with the population well distributed among seven banks. Grades range from VG to VF. No Series of 1875 $2 notes were issued by this state, making these all the more important for the specialist.

Massachusetts • 182 banks of issue • 130 notes reported • A highly collectible state with notes from many different banks, similar to the situation for $1 notes of the Original Series. Most are in circulated grades, although Unc notes are from several banks. There is one serial number 1 note, from the Central National Bank of Boston (AU).

Michigan • 55 banks of issue • 32 notes reported • Slightly scarce state in the context of Lazy Twos. The selection is spread among quite a few banks. Grades range from G to AU.

Minnesota • 28 banks of issue • 21 notes reported • Somewhat scarce as a state, seven are from the Merchants National Bank of Winona, including five Unc (the only other note in this grade is from the Northwestern National Bank of Minneapolis).

Missouri • 28 banks of issue • 44 notes reported • The roster includes the 30 notes from the Moniteau National Bank of California, Missouri, of which at least 20 are Unc. There are three serial number 1 notes reported from the Moniteau

National Bank (VF), First National Bank of St. Louis (F), and Second National Bank of St. Louis (F).

Montana Territory • 2 banks of issue • 2 notes listed • First National Bank of Helena (EF) and the Missoula National Bank (VF, part of an uncut sheet).

Nebraska • 8 banks of issue • 3 notes reported • First National Bank of Brownville (F), First National Bank of Lincoln (G), and Otoe County National Bank of Nebraska City (F).

Nebraska Territory • 2 banks of issue • 3 notes listed • All are from the Otoe County National Bank of Nebraska City, grades from G to VG.

New Hampshire • 31 banks of issue • 31 notes reported • Slightly scarce state in the context of the series. Notes are from a wide variety of banks, with six from the First National Bank of Portsmouth and three from the Monadnock National Bank of East Jaffrey. All are circulated.[10] No serial number 1 notes.

New Jersey • 41 banks of issue • 35 notes reported • A narrow selection of banks includes several with a half dozen or more. Most are well-worn, averaging VG or F. There is one serial number 1 note, the First National Bank of Trenton (Unc). There is another Unc note, from the First National Bank of Jersey City.

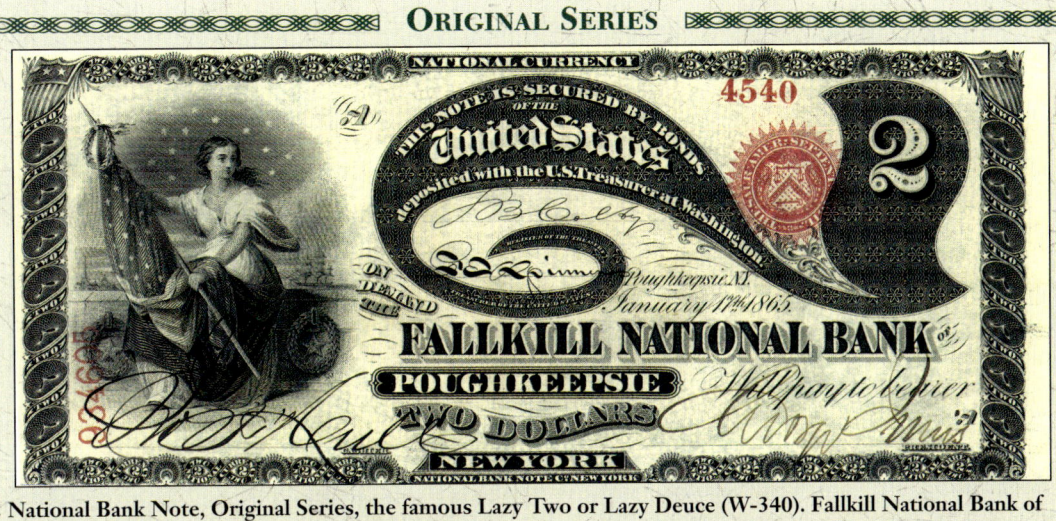

ORIGINAL SERIES

$2 National Bank Note, Original Series, the famous Lazy Two or Lazy Deuce (W-340). Fallkill National Bank of Poughkeepsie, New York. *Stars and Stripes* vignette at the left. This is the general type of W-340 to W-342.

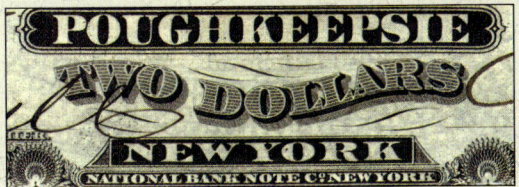

Detail of the NATIONAL BANK NOTE CO. imprint.

Detail of the printed Treasury signatures and part of the ornate 2 design. The National Bank Note Company excelled in the ornateness and intricacies of its vignettes.

Back of W-340, showing the New York state seal reflecting the location of this bank. Except for variations in state and territorial seals, this general design was used on all backs from W-340 to W-346.

New Mexico Territory • 2 banks of issue • 6 notes reported • A very rare but collectible (with some patience) territorial issue. Four are from the First National Bank of Santa Fe, and two are from the Second National Bank of the same city. All are circulated.

New York • 223 banks of issue • 256 notes reported[11] • This is far and away the most "common" state for this type. Unc notes are readily available within the context of this type, with 11 from the Fallkill National Bank of Poughkeepsie. There are three serial number 1 notes reported, Merchants National Bank of Binghamton (EF), National Bank of the Republic, New York City (EF), and the Wilber National Bank of Oneonta (VG).

North Carolina • 5 banks of issue • 6 notes reported • A rare state. Three different banks are represented. All listed notes are in circulated grades. There is one serial number 1 note, from the Commercial National Bank of Charlotte (EF).

Ohio • 106 banks of issue • 106 notes reported • Many different banks are reported. The only Unc notes are seven of the First National Bank of Newark. There are three serial number 1 notes, Piqua National Bank (VG), First National Bank of Washington (AU), and Fayette County National Bank of Washington (EF).

Pennsylvania • 86 banks of issue • 71 notes reported • Plentiful in the context of this type. The distribution is wide. Two Unc notes are listed, the Second National Bank of Mauch Chunk and the First National Bank of Newtown. There is one serial number 1 note, First National Bank of Newtown (VG).

Rhode Island • 52 banks of issue • 46 notes reported • A plentiful state, but with some repetitions from the same banks. All in the census are in circulated grades. There are no number 1 notes.

South Carolina • 4 banks of issue • No notes reported.

Tennessee • 15 banks of issue • 8 notes reported • A rare state. Grades range from G to F. Three are from the First National Bank of Memphis.

Texas • 4 banks of issue • No notes reported.

Utah Territory • 4 banks of issue • 5 notes reported • Two from the Salt Lake City National Bank and three from the Deseret National Bank of Salt Lake City. Grades from G to VF. No Series of 1875 $2 notes were issued by this territory, placing additional demand on the relatively few Original Series notes remaining.

Vermont • 33 banks of issue • 41 notes reported • One of the more collectible states. Two Unc notes are reported, both from the National Bank of Newbury at Wells River.

Virginia • 1 bank of issue • No notes reported.

West Virginia • 5 banks of issue • 1 note reported • First National Bank of Wheeling (VF, serial not listed). A landmark note of incredible importance, especially as no Series of 1875 $2 notes were issued by this state.

Wisconsin • 29 banks of issue • 10 notes reported • Rare as a state. Distributed over 10 different banks, with no notes reported as Unc.

Wyoming Territory • 1 bank of issue • 1 note reported • Rarest-of-the-rare note, in a low grade but unique, combining absolute rarity with territorial status. Wyoming National Bank of Laramie City (Fair, serial 907). No Series of 1875 $2 notes were issued by this territory, making this note even more important than would otherwise be the case.

Generic prices for a typical note from a state from which notes range from plentiful to just slightly scarce:

VG-8	F-12	VF-20	EF-40	AU-50	Unc-60	Unc-63	Unc-65
$3,300	$3,950	$5,100	$6,400	$8,500	$9,750	$11,500	$20,000

W-340 • F-387 • Colby-Spinner (1864–1867)
Estimated population: 1,000 to 1,100 • *Highest graded:* Unc.

VG-8	F-12	VF-20	EF-40	AU-50	Unc-60	Unc-63
$3,300	$3,950	$5,100	$6,400	$8,500	$9,750	$11,500

W-341 • F-388 • Jeffries-Spinner (1867–1869)
Recorded population: 5 • *Highest graded:* AU-50 • *Selected information:* Heritage (1/2008), 705-B447303/A, First NB of Mankato, MN, only $2 on the bank; only modern sale of any W-341, VG, $19,550. Donlon (6/1974), 2071-E454458/A, First NB of Hillsborough, NH, only $2 on the bank, F, $1,650.

W-342 • F-389 • Allison-Spinner (1869–1875)
Estimated population: 320 to 350 • *Highest graded:* Unc.

VG-8	F-12	VF-20	EF-40	AU-50	Unc-60	Unc-63	Unc-65
$3,300	$3,950	$5,100	$6,400	$8,500	$9,575	$11,500	$20,000

Series of 1875
(Authorized Issue 1875 to 1878)

These continued the use of plates designed by the National Bank Note Company for this denomination (American made the $1 notes). The printing was done by the Treasury department in Washington. An imprint was entered into the plate, horizontally below the upper left border on the $2 note: PRINTED AT THE BUREAU, ENGRAVING & PRINTING, TREASURY DEPT. The small red Treasury seal now has a scalloped rather than a spiked border. All have SERIES 1875 imprinted vertically in red left of the center near the bank charter number. The Treasury and bank serial numbers and two charter numbers are also in red. A small percentage of these notes are printed on paper with a vertical blue tint streak. It seems that this paper was used at least into 1878, although the vast majority of notes printed during this time were on white paper.

The values given are for states with populations of 30 or so notes, using the figures above combined with populations for Original Series $2 notes. To date, there is little price differential between Original Series and Series of 1875 notes, as many collectors combine them as a type. In nearly all instances, Series of 1875 notes are rarer, for they were issued only from 1875 until distribution was halted on January 1, 1879. However, when they are found, notes of the Series of

1875 tend to be in higher average grades. As this design was not a novelty when it was used on the Series of 1875, and as many bank officers had already saved Original Series notes as souvenirs, serial number 1 notes are exceedingly rare. For Uncirculated notes we can be grateful for a hoard from the La Crosse (Wisconsin) National Bank.

Banks of Issue and Rarity of Notes

Based upon census information from Don C. Kelly and James M. Kelly (*National Bank Note Census*, Version 4.0) and with some information from other sources, this listing gives each location, the number of banks issuing this series of notes within each, and a brief commentary.[12] The census describes 595 notes, or less than half the quantity of the Original Series Lazy Twos.

Fewer banks issued Series of 1875 notes, as the era for this type was only from 1875 to the end of 1878. Locations with serial number 1 notes are specifically identified; otherwise there are none.

Alabama • 1 bank of issue • No notes reported.

Colorado Territory • 2 banks of issue • No notes reported.

Connecticut • 34 banks of issue • 34 notes reported • One of the more collectible states for this series. Notes are distributed over various banks. The only Unc note is from the National Exchange Bank of Hartford.

Delaware • 1 bank of issue • 1 note reported • New Castle National Bank of Odessa (VG, serial 509). A numismatic prize.

District of Columbia • 1 bank of issue • No notes reported.

Georgia • 1 bank of issue • No notes reported.

Illinois • 14 banks of issue • 6 notes reported • A very rare state. Notes from five banks. The Kelly census lists one Unc note, from the National Bank of Galena.

Indiana • 19 banks of issue • 18 notes reported • A collectible state as a type, but most notes are clustered under just a few titles, including the National State Bank of Lafayette, the First National Bank of Marshall County at Plymouth, and the Richmond National Bank. All are circulated.

Iowa • 11 banks of issue • 3 notes reported • Very rare state; indeed, notes are almost impossible to find. Marion County National Bank of Knoxville (VG–F), First National Bank of Pella (VG–F), and the First National Bank of Tama City (F).

Kansas • 8 banks of issue • 42 notes reported • Of this surprisingly large quantity from a prairie state, 40 are from the First National Bank of Emporia, including two Unc. The others are from the Burlington National Bank (G–VG) and the National Bank of Lawrence (Fair).

Kentucky • 10 banks of issue • 15 notes reported • Slightly scarce as a state. Six notes, including three Unc from the German National Bank of Covington.

$2 National Bank Note, Series of 1875 (W-344). Continental National Bank of Boston, charter 524. This is the general type of W-343 to W-346. The back is the same as that on the Original Series.

Detail of the upper right corner of the same note showing three shades of red, from three separate printing processes: the bank serial number, the Treasury seal, and the bank's charter number.

The *Sir Walter Raleigh* vignette on the back of all Original Series and Series of 1875 $2 National Bank Notes. Raleigh demonstrates the pleasures of smoking tobacco from Virginia to English onlookers.

Maine • 11 banks of issue • 3 notes reported • Very rare state for this series. Cumberland National Bank (VG), Richmond National Bank (G–VG), and Merchants National Bank of Waterville (ungraded).

Massachusetts • 116 banks of issue • 174 notes reported • A common state for this series, although any Lazy Two note, especially in a high grade, is in demand. Of these, 25 (mostly Unc notes) are from the Home National Bank of Milford. Otherwise, grades are as you find them, mostly with evidence of wear, including clusters of five or more from some banks. There is one serial number 1 note, of the National Bank of North America of Boston (AU).

Michigan • 13 banks of issue • 4 notes reported • A very rare state. First National Bank of Houghton (VG), First National Bank of Lepeer (EF), and the First National Bank of Three Rivers (G, VF).

Minnesota • 6 banks of issue • 2 notes reported • A very rare state. One note each from the First National Bank of Owatonna (VG) and the Farmers National Bank in the same city (VG).

Missouri • 5 banks • 1 note reported • Bates County National Bank of Butler (F). A landmark rarity.

Nebraska • 3 banks of issue • No notes reported.

Nebraska Territory • 1 bank of issue • No notes reported.

New Hampshire • 18 banks of issue • 6 notes reported • Rare state. First National Bank of Gonic (F), Manchester National Bank (EF), Indian Head National Bank of Nashua (VG), the First National Bank of Newport (G), and Laconia National Bank (VG–F). There is one serial number 1 note, also of the Laconia National Bank, which is also the only Unc note on record.

New Jersey • 10 banks of issue • 10 notes reported • Scarce state. From a selection of banks. Grades from G to EF.

New Mexico Territory • 1 bank of issue • No notes reported.

New York • 77 banks of issue • 88 notes reported[13] • A common state in this context, although many notes are from the same handful of large banks. Most are circulated, but a few Unc examples are reported. There is one serial number 1 note, from the Tradesmens National Bank of New York (VG).

North Carolina • 4 banks of issue • 1 note reported • Raleigh National Bank (VG). An incredible rarity.

Ohio • 25 banks of issue • 14 notes reported • Scarce to rare as a state. No Unc examples are in the Kelly census. There is one serial number 1 note, First National Bank of Coshocton (EF).

Pennsylvania • 17 banks of issue • 13 notes reported • Rare state. Five are from the Pittsburgh National Bank of Commerce. No Unc examples are in the Kelly census.

Rhode Island • 34 banks of issue • 75 notes reported • A common state for this series, although several banks each account for clusters of notes, including 31 from the Newport National Bank, 6 from the Slater National Bank of North Providence, and 10 from the Manufacturers National Bank

of Providence. Several Unc notes are in the census. There is one serial number 1 note, Newport National Bank (EF).

South Carolina • 1 bank of issue • No notes reported.

Tennessee • 2 banks of issue • No notes reported.

Texas • 1 bank of issue • 1 note reported • Exchange National Bank of Houston (G, serial 97). As the only "Lazy Two" from the Lone Star State (there being no Original Series notes), this is an icon.

Vermont • 27 banks of issue • 9 notes reported • From nine banks. Grades from Fair to AU.

Wisconsin • 4 banks of issue • 64 notes reported • A common state or nearly so in this context. An ideal possibility for a note for a type set. However, as all but one, the majority of which are Unc, are from the La Crosse National Bank, the First National Bank of Appleton note (VG) is a rarity. There is one serial number 1 note reported, and it is from the La Crosse National Bank (F).

Generic prices for a typical note from a state from which notes range from plentiful to just slightly scarce:

VG-8	F-12	VF-20	EF-40	AU-50	Unc-60	Unc-63	Unc-65
$3,300	$3,950	$5,100	$6,400	$8,500	$9,750	$11,500	$20,000

W-343 • F-390 • Allison-New (1875–1876)
Estimated population: 220 to 240 • *Highest graded:* Unc.

VG-8	F-12	VF-20	EF-40	AU-50	Unc-60	Unc-63	Unc-65
$3,300	$3,950	$5,100	$6,400	$8,500	$9,575	$11,500	$20,000

W-344 • F-391 • Allison-Wyman (1876–1877)
Estimated population: 290 to 320 • *Highest graded:* Unc.

VG-8	F-12	VF-20	EF-40	AU-50	Unc-60	Unc-63	Unc-65
$3,300	$3,950	$5,100	$6,400	$8,500	$9,575	$11,500	$20,000

W-345 • F-392 • Allison-Gilfillan (1877–1878)
Estimated population: 70 to 85 • *Highest graded:* Unc.

VG-8	F-12	VF-20	EF-40	AU-50	Unc-60	Unc-63	Unc-65
$3,450	$4,150	$5,350	$6,725	$8,925	$10,050	$12,075	$22,000

W-346 • F-393 • Scofield-Gilfillan (1878–1881)
Estimated population: 50 to 55 • *Highest graded:* Unc.

VG-8	F-12	VF-20	EF-40	AU-50	Unc-60	Unc-63	Unc-65
$3,625	$4,350	$5,600	$7,050	$9,350	$10,550	$12,650	$24,000

SILVER CERTIFICATES

Series of 1886

This is the first of the $2 Silver Certificates, the initial entry in what became an illustrious series of designs. Earlier Silver Certificates, dating back to 1878, had been made only in large denominations, $10 and up, and did not circulate widely. The Series of 1886 bills, produced in large quantities, were intended for extensive use in commerce. Each was backed by two silver dollars held by the Treasury department, which by that time was holding tens of millions of these coins. The portrait of the recently deceased

SERIES OF 1886

$2 Silver Certificate, Series of 1886 (W-362). Depicted is Civil War General Winfield Scott Hancock.

Detail of the plate letter and microprint number on the face of a W-360 note.

Back of a $2 Silver Certificate, Series of 1886 (W-362).

(1886) General Winfield Scott Hancock is at the left. The denomination is enclosed in design work of an ornate counter.

The back of the note is an intricate interweaving of geometric designs, numerals, and lettering, with UNITED STATES SILVER CERTIFICATE in a gentle serpentine curve at the center.

Examples of this type are plentiful in the marketplace, usually in well-circulated grades. Several hoards of Uncirculated notes have made that grade generally available as well, but by now most have been dispersed into collections.

W-360 • F-240 • Rosecrans-Jordan (1885–1887) • Small red seal, circular border • 4,280,000 (est.)

Estimated population: 170 to 190 • *Highest graded:* Unc.

VG-8	F-12	VF-20	EF-40	AU-50	Unc-60	Unc-63	Unc-65
$325	$600	$1,100	$1,700	$2,200	$2,400	$3,100	$6,250

W-361 • F-241 • Rosecrans-Hyatt (1887–1889) • 2,020,000 (est.)

Estimated population: 115 to 130 • *Highest graded:* Unc.

VG-8	F-12	VF-20	EF-40	AU-50	Unc-60	Unc-63	Unc-65
$325	$600	$1,100	$1,700	$2,200	$2,400	$3,100	$6,250

W-362 • F-242 • Large red seal • 6,960,000 (est.)

Estimated population: 475 to 600 • *Highest graded:* Unc.

VG-8	F-12	VF-20	EF-40	AU-50	Unc-60	Unc-63	Unc-65
$325	$600	$1,100	$1,700	$2,200	$2,400	$3,100	$5,500

W-363 • F-243 • Rosecrans-Huston (1889–1891) • 4,480,000 (est.)

Estimated population: 130 to 150 • *Highest graded:* Unc.

VG-8	F-12	VF-20	EF-40	AU-50	Unc-60	Unc-63	Unc-65
$325	$600	$1,100	$1,700	$2,200	$2,400	$3,100	$6,250

W-364 • F-244 • Large brown seal • 3,260,000 (est.)
Estimated population: 165 to 195 • *Highest graded:* Unc.

VG-8	F-12	VF-20	EF-40	AU-50	Unc-60	Unc-63	Unc-65
$325	$600	$1,100	$1,700	$2,200	$2,400	$3,100	$7,500

Series of 1891

For this new series the portrait of General Winfield Scott Hancock was replaced by that of another obscure individual (at least from today's viewpoint): William Windom, a native of Ohio, who later served as a senator from Minnesota, then as secretary of the Treasury for two nonconsecutive terms (1881–1884 and 1889–1891). All of the notes in this series have a small red Treasury seal with scalloped border. The back is completely redesigned in a bowtie-like configuration to furnish more "open space," which the Treasury department felt was a deterrent to counterfeiting.

W-365 • F-245 • Rosecrans-Nebeker (1891–1893) • 6,560,000 (est.)
Estimated population: 330 to 400 • *Highest graded:* Unc.

VG-8	F-12	VF-20	EF-40	AU-50	Unc-60	Unc-63	Unc-65
$300	$550	$1,000	$1,900	$2,700	$3,250	$3,750	$8,000

W-366 • F-246 • Tillman-Morgan (1893–1897) • 14,428,000 (est.)
Estimated population: 450 to 550 • *Highest graded:* Unc.

VG-8	F-12	VF-20	EF-40	AU-50	Unc-60	Unc-63	Unc-65
$300	$550	$1,000	$1,900	$2,700	$3,250	$3,750	$8,000

Series of 1896

The Series of 1896 did away with Windom and introduced one of the most elegant of all American designs, *Science Presenting Steam and Electricity to Commerce and Manufacture.* Illustrated are a goddess representing Science, two other goddesses (Commerce and Manufacture), and two youths (Steam and Electricity), representative of ornate art, architecture, and design in the fading years of the Victorian era. The artist was Edwin H. Blashfield. This motif was originally made for the proposed $50 denomination, but that value was never issued. Instead, it was adopted for the $2, replacing a design by Will H. Low showing two figures: Peace, a woman, and War, a man (also called Defense). Blashfield was roundly criticized by engravers within the BEP, especially by Thomas Morris, as part of an overall dislike for the Series of 1896 notes, in which

$2 Silver Certificate, Series of 1891 (W-366).

Back of a $2 Silver Certificate, Series of 1891 (W-366).

three outside artists encroached on what they believed was in-house prerogative to create new paper money designs.

Roso Marston, a girl about 13 years of age, modeled three of the figures for Blashfield—all except Steam and Electricity, who were modeled by young boys. By that that time she had spent much of her life on the legitimate stage, including in the title role of the popular play *Editha's Burglar*. When Blashfield had her pose, she was currently appearing as Eunice in *Quo Vadis* at the New York Academy of Music. Among other commissions, she had posed for Augustus Saint-Gaudens.[14]

On the back two prominent Americans are depicted: Robert Fulton of steamboat fame, and Samuel F.B. Morse, highly accomplished as an artist but better known as inven-

tor of the telegraph. The face engraving is the work of Charles Schlecht and G.F.C. Smillie. Thomas F. Morris engraved the back as well as some details on the face. Morris passed away in 1898, a great loss to the BEP.[15]

These bills are part of the $1-$2-$5 suite of "Educational Notes" that are often collected as a set. In *100 Greatest American Currency Notes*, whose rankings are based on a survey of collectors and dealers, each of these was ranked high by voters. Although many numismatists consider these to be the epitome of ornate design in the $2 series, the Treasury department felt that such a complicated motif aided counterfeiters because the public would not be likely to scrutinize the notes carefully. In 1897 a congressional inquiry was made

SERIES OF 1896

$2 Silver Certificate, Series of 1896 (W-367), the famous "Educational Note" with the vignette of *Science Presenting Steam and Electricity to Industry and Commerce*.

Detail of the leftmost figure, one of three modeled by Roso Marston.

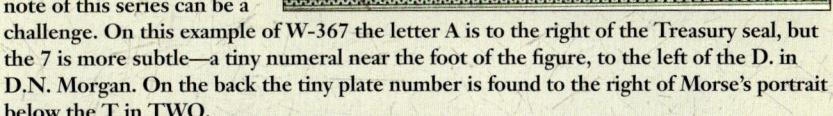

Finding both the plate letter and number on the face of a note of this series can be a challenge. On this example of W-367 the letter A is to the right of the Treasury seal, but the 7 is more subtle—a tiny numeral near the foot of the figure, to the left of the D. in D.N. Morgan. On the back the tiny plate number is found to the right of Morse's portrait below the T in TWO.

Back of the $2 Silver Certificate, Series of 1896 (W-367).

into the production of these notes.[16] Bankers complained that the design was so elaborate that the denomination could not be instantly identified, making such bills difficult to count quickly. Moreover, they tended to smudge when handled.

W-367 • F-247 • Tillman-Morgan (1893–1897) • Small red seal with spiked border • 9,400,000 (est.)

Estimated population: 1,000 to 1,200 • *Highest graded:* Unc.

VG-8	F-12	VF-20	EF-40	AU-50	Unc-60	Unc-63	Unc-65
$625	$1,100	$2,200	$4,200	$5,000	$5,600	$6,250	$9,500

W-368 • F-248 • Bruce-Roberts (1897–1898) • 11,252,000 (est.)

Estimated population: 900 to 1,100 • *Highest graded:* Unc.

VG-8	F-12	VF-20	EF-40	AU-50	Unc-60	Unc-63	Unc-65
$625	$1,100	$2,200	$4,200	$5,000	$5,600	$6,250	$9,500

Series of 1899

The Series of 1899 $2 note has a portrait of George Washington at the lower center of the face, flanked by allegorical figures representing Mechanics and Agriculture. The denomination, serial numbers, and Treasury seal are all printed in blue. These and related bills were specifically backed by silver dollars held by the Treasury department, these being the vast store of Morgan dollars struck since 1878.

The back of the Series 1899 $2 bill has ample open space to the left and right of center, reflecting the view of the Treasury department that plain areas were a deterrent to counterfeiting and also made the notes more distinguishable at a glance. In contrast, complex ornate designs were said to be confusing and easier to counterfeit, although the record does not seem to reflect that.

SERIES OF 1899

$2 Silver Certificate, Series of 1899 (W-378). Notes of the Series of 1899 were produced until the late 1920s.

Back of a $2 Silver Certificate, Series of 1899 (W-378).

Back Plate Location 1.

Back Plate Location 2.

Mules: Back plate numbers can be in one of two locations.[17] On May 14, 1921, with the new Elliott-White signature combination starting, all Legal Tender, Silver Certificate, and Gold Certificate back plates were given numbers beginning with 1 and in a new location, although no notice was given of the change.

Back Plate Location 1 (regular use): W-369 to W-377. This was the standard location until May 14, 1921. Also used to create a mule for W-378.

Back Plate Location 2 (regular use): W-378 introduced without notice as the new style (adopted in certain other series on May 14, 1921) with the Speelman-White signature combination at a later time.

W-369 • F-249 • Lyons-Roberts (1898–1905) • 111,000,000 (est.)

Estimated population: 400 to 450 • *Highest graded:* Unc.

VG-8	F-12	VF-20	EF-40	AU-50	Unc-60	Unc-63	Unc-65
$225	$300	$400	$560	$925	$1,100	$1,450	$3,200

W-370 • F-250 • Lyons-Treat (1905–1906) • 20,000,000 (est.)

Estimated population: 110 to 130 • *Highest graded:* Unc.

VG-8	F-12	VF-20	EF-40	AU-50	Unc-60	Unc-63	Unc-65
$225	$300	$400	$560	$925	$1,100	$1,450	$3,200

W-371 • F-251 • Vernon-Treat (1906–1909) • 76,326,000 (est.)

Estimated population: 380 to 450 • *Highest graded:* Unc.

VG-8	F-12	VF-20	EF-40	AU-50	Unc-60	Unc-63	Unc-65
$225	$330	$400	$560	$925	$1,100	$1,450	$3,200

W-372 • F-252 • Vernon-McClung (1909–1911) • 45,852,000

Estimated population: 225 to 275 • *Highest graded:* Unc • *Commentary:* Deliveries began on July 1, 1910, and ended on June 20, 1911.

VG-8	F-12	VF-20	EF-40	AU-50	Unc-60	Unc-63	Unc-65
$225	$330	$400	$560	$925	$1,100	$1,450	$3,200

W-372★ • F-252★

Estimated population: 12 to 14 • *Highest graded:* Unc • *Selected information:* Knight (6/2008), ★9113B/A, AU-58 (PMG), $7,475; ★9114B/B, AU-58 (PMG) $7,475; ★9115B/C, AU-58 (PMG), $7,475; ★24959B/C, EF-40 (PCGS), $4,025. CAA (9/2005), ★28131B/C, Unc, $5,520.

W-373 • F-253 • Napier-McClung (1911–1912) • 78,936,000

Estimated population: 450 to 550 • *Highest graded:* Unc • *Commentary:* Deliveries began on June 20, 1911, and ended on December 29, 1913.

VG-8	F-12	VF-20	EF-40	AU-50	Unc-60	Unc-63	Unc-65
$225	$330	$400	$560	$925	$1,100	$1,450	$3,200

W-373★ • F-253★

Estimated population: 11 to 13 • *Highest graded:* Unc • *Selected information:* Stack's (12/1992), ★298207B/C, VF, $300. Knight (11/2007), ★324503B/C, F-12 (PCGS), $1,679. Stack's (3/1993), ★434518B/B, Unc, $600. CAA (5/2002), ★498141B/A, Unc, $2,990. CAA (5/1997), ★498144B/D, Unc, $1,650.

W-374 • F-254 • Napier-Thompson (1912–1913) • 1,816,000

Estimated population: 95 to 120 • *Highest graded:* Unc.

VG-8	F-12	VF-20	EF-40	AU-50	Unc-60	Unc-63	Unc-65
$375	$600	$900	$1,250	$1,800	$2,500	$3,400	$5,000

W-375 • F-255 • Parker-Burke (1913–1914) • 61,600,000

Estimated population: 600 to 800 • *Highest graded:* Unc.

VG-8	F-12	VF-20	EF-40	AU-50	Unc-60	Unc-63	Unc-65
$225	$330	$400	$560	$925	$1,100	$1,450	$2,800

W-375★ • F-255★

Recorded population: 8 • *Highest graded:* EF-45 • *Selected information:* Knight (6/2008), ★571900B/D, EF-40 (PCGS), $4,370. Knight (11/2007), ★763954B/B, VF-20 (PCGS), $2,243.

W-376 • F-256 • Teehee-Burke (1915–1919) • 91,816,000

Estimated population: 800 to 1,000 • *Highest graded:* Unc.

VG-8	F-12	VF-20	EF-40	AU-50	Unc-60	Unc-63	Unc-65
$225	$330	$400	$560	$925	$1,100	$1,450	$3,200

W-376★ • F-256★

Estimated population: 45 to 50 • *Highest graded:* Unc.

VG-8	F-12	VF-20	EF-40	AU-50	Unc-60	Unc-63	Unc-65
$525	$750	$1,500	$2,500	$5,000	$7,500	$10,000	—

W-377 • F-257 • Elliott-Burke (1919–1921) • 4,488,000, or about 90% regular (est.)

Estimated population: 210 to 230 • *Highest graded:* Unc.

VG-8	F-12	VF-20	EF-40	AU-50	Unc-60	Unc-63	Unc-65
$225	$330	$400	$560	$925	$1,100	$1,450	$4,000

W-377★ • F-257★

Estimated population: 18 to 20 • *Highest graded:* Unc.

VG-8	F-12	VF-20	EF-40	AU-50	Unc-60	Unc-63
$1,000	$1,500	$3,000	$5,000	$7,500	$11,000	$15,000

W-377 Mule • F-257 • 500,000, or about 10% mules (est.)

Estimated population: 20 to 25 • *Highest graded:* Unc • *Commentary:* As this is a new listing, there is no market history.

W-377 Mule★ • F-257★

Recorded population: 3 • *Highest graded:* F.

W-378 • F-258 • Speelman-White (1922–1927) • 41,800,000, or about 90% regular (est.)

Estimated population: 1,400 to 1,700 • *Highest graded:* Unc.

VG-8	F-12	VF-20	EF-40	AU-50	Unc-60	Unc-63	Unc-65
$225	$330	$400	$560	$925	$1,100	$1,450	$2,800

W-378★ • F-258★

Estimated population: 50 to 55 • *Highest graded:* Unc.

VG-8	F-12	VF-20	EF-40	AU-50	Unc-60	Unc-63	Unc-65
$325	$450	$1,000	$2,000	$4,000	$6,500	$9,000	—

W-378 Mule • F-258 • 4,600,000, or about 10% mules (est.)

Estimated population: 65 to 75 • *Highest graded:* Unc • *Commentary:* As this is a new listing, there is no market history.

W-378 Mule★ • F-258★

Recorded population: 2 • *Highest graded:* F–VF • *Selected information:* Heritage (1/2007), ★1721625B/A, F–VF, $6,900.

TREASURY OR COIN NOTES

Series of 1890

The Series of 1890 Treasury Notes or Coin Notes follow suit with others in the series. These were issued under provisions in the Sherman Silver Purchase Act of 1890, a time that the Silverite political faction was advocating a silver standard, much to the fear of most financiers and nearly all institutions in Europe. There was a run on gold coins in the Treasury. These notes were accordingly made payable in "coin," but without specifying silver or gold. The secretary of the Treasury reserved the right to redeem them in silver instead of gold, if supplies of the latter ran short. As it turned out, although gold reached a critical low, redemptions of Coin Notes in gold were never denied.

The face depicts General James McPherson, a vignette engraved by Charles Burt, portrait specialist at the BEP. Serial numbers are in red, with a decorative star following.

SERIES OF 1890

$2 Treasury or Coin Note, Series of 1890 (W-390).

Back plate number 7 on an example of W-390, within a star near the right edge.

Ornate back of a $2 Treasury or Coin Note, Series of 1890 (W-390).

The back of the Series of 1890 Treasury or Coin Note is completely filled with ornate engraving, in this case including the large word TWO gracefully curved.

The Series of 1890 Treasury notes are scarce today in all grades, particularly in Unc. The Rosecrans-Nebeker signature combination is the key to the series.

W-390 • F-353 • Rosecrans-Huston (1889–1891) • Large brown seal • 2,600,000 (est.)

Estimated population: 190 to 210 • *Highest graded:* Unc.

VG-8	F-12	VF-20	EF-40	AU-50	Unc-60	Unc-63	Unc-65
$425	$950	$2,100	$4,200	$8,000	$8,600	$11,000	$30,000

W-391 • F-354 • Rosecrans-Nebeker (1891–1893) • 500,000 (est.)

Estimated population: 40 to 45 • *Highest graded:* Unc.

VG-8	F-12	VF-20	EF-40	AU-50	Unc-60	Unc-63	Unc-65
$1,000	$2,200	$4,500	$7,500	$13,000	$15,000	$20,000	—

W-392 • F-355 • Small red seal with spiked border • 1,832,000 (est.)

Estimated population: 90 to 100 • *Highest graded:* Unc.

VG-8	F-12	VF-20	EF-40	AU-50	Unc-60	Unc-63	Unc-65
$425	$950	$2,100	$4,200	$8,000	$8,600	$11,000	$20,000

Series of 1891

The Series of 1891 Treasury Notes or Coin Notes represent a modification with generous amounts of open space on the back. The face motifs remain the same. All have a small red seal with scalloped border.

W-393 • F-356 • Rosecrans-Nebeker (1891–1893) • 4,660,000 (est.)

Estimated population: 125 to 150 • *Highest graded:* Unc.

VG-8	F-12	VF-20	EF-40	AU-50	Unc-60	Unc-63	Unc-65
$300	$550	$950	$1,500	$2,250	$2,650	$3,000	$6,250

W-394 • F-357 • Tillman-Morgan (1893–1897) • 12,300,000 (est.)

Estimated population: 500 to 650 • *Highest graded:* Unc.

VG-8	F-12	VF-20	EF-40	AU-50	Unc-60	Unc-63	Unc-65
$300	$550	$950	$1,500	$2,250	$2,650	$3,000	$5,750

W-395 • F-358 • Bruce-Roberts (1897–1898) • 3,012,000

Estimated population: 150 to 165 • *Highest graded:* Unc.

VG-8	F-12	VF-20	EF-40	AU-50	Unc-60	Unc-63	Unc-65
$300	$550	$950	$1,500	$2,250	$2,650	$3,000	$6,000

$2 Treasury or Coin Note, Series of 1891 (W-394). Motifs are basically similar to those used on the preceding type.

Back of a $2 Treasury or Coin Note, Series of 1891, with the new, open design (W-394).

FEDERAL RESERVE BANK NOTES

Series of 1918

Next in the large-size $2 series is the famous and very popular "Battleship Note," descriptive of the design on Federal Reserve Bank Notes of the $2 denomination issued in the Series of 1918. The face has a vignette of Thomas Jefferson to the left. At the center is a title block giving the Federal Reserve city in large letters. Similar to the $1 bills, the $2 notes were released through the Federal Reserve Banks, 12 total, each further identified on the face by a letter (A through L) and related number (1 through 12), and each collectible separately for that reason. All have a blue Treasury seal with a scalloped border.

On the back is what was intended to be a generic dreadnaught fighting ship—that is, not a specific vessel. Named after states, dreadnaughts were objects of great pride. While it was felt best not to show a specific one or reveal the name, the image was taken from the 27,000-ton USS *New York*, commissioned in April 1914.

Most collectors acquire a single "Battleship Note" for type. Those who want to go further with a systematic collection can try to assemble signature combinations. W-408-C is generally regarded as having the rarest signature combination variety within the series. Certain others range from scarce to rare. Star notes are known for certain of the issues and in all instances are rare and valuable.

W-400-A • F-747 • Boston • Teehee-Burke (1915–1919) • Bullen-Morss • 4,012,000 (est.)

Estimated population: 125 to 140 • *Highest graded:* Unc.

VG-8	F-12	VF-20	EF-40	AU-50	Unc-60	Unc-63	Unc-65
$375	$550	$700	$1,000	$1,450	$2,200	$3,000	$4,300

SERIES OF 1918

$2 Federal Reserve Bank Note, Series of 1918 (W-420-G). Federal Reserve Bank of Chicago.

Detail of a W-409-C★ note showing the star serial number and the imprinted signatures of Federal Reserve Bank officers.

Back of the $2 Federal Reserve Bank Note, Series of 1918, or "Battleship Note," showing the USS *New York*.

W-400-A★ • F-747★

Recorded population: 3 • *Highest graded:* EF • *Selected information:* Stanley Morycz price list (1993), A422★/B, EF, $2,700. Listed by Doug Murray, A33565★/A, A43779★/C, VF, $1,210.

W-401-A • F-748 • Willett-Morss • 2,388,000 (est.)

Estimated population: 40 to 50 • *Highest graded:* Unc.

VG-8	F-12	VF-20	EF-40	AU-50	Unc-60	Unc-63
$400	$650	$850	$1,200	$1,800	$2,400	$3,400

W-401-A★ • F-748★

Recorded population: 2 • *Highest graded:* VG • *Selected information:* Steinmetz FPL (1980), A49376★/D, VG–F. CAA (9/2000), A6031★/C, VG, $467.50.

W-402-A • F-749 • Elliott-Burke (1919–1921) • 6,068,000 (est.)

Estimated population: 220 to 240 • *Highest graded:* Unc.

VG-8	F-12	VF-20	EF-40	AU-50	Unc-60	Unc-63	Unc-65
$375	$550	$700	$1,000	$1,450	$2,200	$3,000	$4,300

W-402-A★ • F-749★

Estimated population: 10 to 12 • *Highest graded:* Unc • *Selected information:* Heritage (1/2006), A68494★/B, EF–AU, $6,900.

W-403-B • F-750 • New York • Teehee-Burke (1915–1919) • Sailer-Strong • 1,400,000 (est.)

Estimated population: 125 to 150 • *Highest graded:* Unc.

VG-8	F-12	VF-20	EF-40	AU-50	Unc-60	Unc-63	Unc-65
$375	$550	$700	$1,000	$1,450	$2,200	$3,000	$4,300

W-403-B★ • F-750★

Recorded population: 6 • *Highest graded:* Unc • *Selected information:* Knight (11/2006), B22★/B, Unc, $10,925. Knight (6/2008), B6948★/D, Unc-64 (PCGS), $11,040.

W-404-B • F-751 • Hendricks-Strong • 7,800,000 (est.)

Estimated population: 140 to 160 • *Highest graded:* Unc.

VG-8	F-12	VF-20	EF-40	AU-50	Unc-60	Unc-63	Unc-65
$375	$550	$700	$1,000	$1,450	$2,200	$3,000	$4,300

W-404-B★ • F-751★

Recorded population: 4 • *Highest graded:* AU-50 • *Selected information:* Knight (2/1999), B34002★/B, G, $275. Smythe (6/1990), B36853★/A, AU, $600. Doug Murray listing, B63618★/B, G. Knight (2/1999), B67672★/D, VG or F, $385.

W-405-B • F-752 • Elliott-Burke (1919–1921) • 6,016,000 (est.)

Estimated population: 210 to 230 • *Highest graded:* Unc.

VG-8	F-12	VF-20	EF-40	AU-50	Unc-60	Unc-63	Unc-65
$375	$550	$700	$1,000	$1,450	$2,200	$3,000	$4,300

W-405-B★ • F-752★

Recorded population: 1 • *Selected information:* Smythe (3/2001), B115589★/A, VG, $990.

W-406-C • F-753 • Philadelphia • Teehee-Burke (1915–1919) • Hardt-Passmore • 284,000 (est.)

Estimated population: 90 to 100 • *Highest graded:* Unc.

VG-8	F-12	VF-20	EF-40	AU-50	Unc-60	Unc-63	Unc-65
$375	$550	$700	$1,000	$1,450	$2,200	$3,000	$4,300

W-406-C★ • F-753★

Recorded population: 1 • *Selected information:* CAA (5/2005), C172★/D, VG–F, problems, $6,037.

W-407-C • F-754 • Dyer-Passmore • 3,356,000 (est.)

Estimated population: 100 to 110 • *Highest graded:* Unc.

VG-8	F-12	VF-20	EF-40	AU-50	Unc-60	Unc-63	Unc-65
$375	$550	$700	$1,000	$1,450	$2,200	$3,000	$4,300

W-408-C • F-755 • Philadelphia • Elliott-Burke (1919–1921) • 660,000 (est.)

Estimated population: 20 to 24 • *Highest graded:* Unc • *Commentary:* In his 1951 study of these notes (see the bibliography), W.A. Philpott Jr. stated, "The rarest of the Philadelphia notes is the $2, Elliott & Burke, Dyer & Passmore."

VG-8	F-12	VF-20	EF-40	AU-50	Unc-60	Unc-63
$500	$900	$1,800	$2,750	$6,500	$8,000	$10,000

W-409-C • F-756 • Dyer-Norris • 3,704,000 (est.)

Estimated population: 125 to 140 • *Highest graded:* Unc.

VG-8	F-12	VF-20	EF-40	AU-50	Unc-60	Unc-63	Unc-65
$375	$550	$700	$1,000	$1,450	$2,200	$3,000	$4,300

W-409-C★ • F-756★

Estimated population: 9 or 10 • *Highest graded:* Unc • *Selected information:* Knight (6/2007), C56496★/D, F-12 (PCGS), $1,207.50. Smithsonian Institution, C60203★/C, Unc. Knight (3/2008), C63860★/D, F-15 (PMG), $3,335. Knight (6/2008), C72218★/B, F-12 (PMG), $1,380.

W-410-D • F-757 • Cleveland • Teehee-Burke (1915–1919) • Baxter-Fancher • 1,420,000 (est.)

Estimated population: 340 to 380 • *Highest graded:* Unc.

VG-8	F-12	VF-20	EF-40	AU-50	Unc-60	Unc-63	Unc-65
$375	$550	$700	$1,000	$1,450	$2,200	$3,000	$4,300

W-410-D★ • F-757★

Recorded population: 4 • *Highest graded:* Unc • *Selected information:* Heritage (1/2006), D9172★/D, F; D13752★/D, AU, $9,600. Stack's (9/1992), D13753★/A, Unc, $910. Kagin's (2/1980), D13787★/C, Unc, $2,250.

W-411-D • F-758 • Davis-Fancher • 1,156,000 (est.)

Estimated population: 45 to 55 • *Highest graded:* Unc • *Commentary:* In his 1951 study of these notes (see the bibliography), W.A. Philpott Jr. stated, "All of $2's of the Cleveland Bank are now scarce—less than $3,000,000 of each signature combination having been issued, and less than $23,000 (1,150 pieces) of all three signatures now outstanding. . . . Notes of the Cleveland Bank come in low numbers on all the nine different varieties [across all denominations] for this simple reason: the late Charles Bickford was assistant cashier of the Cleveland Bank and head of the Cash Department at the time these notes were issued. He was a paper money collector himself. As these notes were issued he held back the first 1,000 notes of each signature combination. Hence, today notes on the Cleveland Bank with serial numbers under 1,000 are more common than those with higher serial numbers. Total outstanding on Cleveland, all denominations, on October 30, 1944, was $194,668."

VG-8	F-12	VF-20	EF-40	AU-50	Unc-60	Unc-63	Unc-65
$450	$700	$1,000	$1,450	$2,100	$2,800	$4,300	$5,250

W-411-D★ • F-758★
Recorded population: 1 • *Selected information:* D26468★/D, VF.

W-412-D • F-759 • Elliott-Burke (1919–1921) • 2,072,000 (est.)
Estimated population: 90 to 100 • *Highest graded:* Unc.

VG-8	F-12	VF-20	EF-40	AU-50	Unc-60	Unc-63	Unc-65
$375	$550	$700	$1,000	$1,450	$2,200	$3,000	$4,300

W-412-D★ • F-759★
Recorded population: 1 • *Selected information:* D31433★, AU.

W-413-E • F-760 • Richmond • Teehee-Burke (1915–1919) • Keesee-Seay • 1,700,000 (est.)
Estimated population: 50 to 60 • *Highest graded:* Unc.

VG-8	F-12	VF-20	EF-40	AU-50	Unc-60	Unc-63	Unc-65
$400	$600	$750	$1,150	$1,600	$2,400	$3,400	$4,700

W-413-E★ • F-760★
Recorded population: 5 • *Highest graded:* VF-20 • *Selected information:* CAA (9/2006), E1815★/C, VF–EF, $5,750. Heritage (1/2006), E16415★/C, VG–F, problems, $6,900.

W-414-E • F-761 • Elliott-Burke (1919–1921) • 2,036,000 (est.)
Estimated population: 58 to 62 • *Highest graded:* Unc.

VG-8	F-12	VF-20	EF-40	AU-50	Unc-60	Unc-63
$400	$600	$750	$1,150	$1,600	$2,400	$3,400

W-415-F • F-762 • Atlanta • Teehee-Burke (1915–1919) • Pike-McCord • 780,000 (est.)
Estimated population: 70 to 80 • *Highest graded:* Unc • *Commentary:* In his 1951 study of these notes (see the bibliography), W.A. Philpott Jr. stated, "Of all banks Atlanta $2's are second scarcest (Dallas $2's are rarer) for two reasons: only 2,300,000 were issued, and superstitious Negroes (and maybe white folks too) in the Atlanta District tore off the corners. The author has seen several hundred Atlanta $2s with two and three corners gone!"

VG-8	F-12	VF-20	EF-40	AU-50	Unc-60	Unc-63	Unc-65
$400	$600	$750	$1,150	$1,600	$2,400	$3,400	$4,700

W-416-F • F-763 • Bell-McCord • 1,276,000 (est.)
Estimated population: 40 to 35 • *Highest graded:* EF-40.

VG-8	F-12	VF-20	EF-40
$1,000	$1,800	$2,700	$7,000

W-416-F★ • F-763★
Recorded population: 1 • *Selected information:* CAA (10/1995), F13290★/B, F, $2,420.

W-417-F • F-764 • Elliott-Burke (1919–1921) • Bell-Wellborn • 1,212,000 (est.)
Estimated population: 35 to 40 • *Highest graded:* AU-50.

VG-8	F-12	VF-20	EF-40	AU-50
$500	$900	$1,500	$4,500	$7,900

W-418-G • F-765 • Chicago • Teehee-Burke (1915–1919) • McCloud-McDougal • 2,400,000 (est.)
Estimated population: 135 to 150 • *Highest graded:* Unc • *Commentary:* In his 1951 study of these notes (see the bibliography), W.A. Philpott Jr. stated that the various Chicago $2s are fairly common, with 28,627 remaining outstanding.

VG-8	F-12	VF-20	EF-40	AU-50	Unc-60	Unc-63	Unc-65
$375	$550	$700	$1,000	$1,450	$2,200	$3,000	$4,300

W-418-G★ • F-765★
Recorded population: 5 • *Commentary:* Includes two Unc, G19182★/B and G19206★/B.

W-419-G • F-766 • Cramer-McDougal • 2,200,000 (est.)
Estimated population: 50 to 60 • *Highest graded:* Unc.

VG-8	F-12	VF-20	EF-40	AU-50	Unc-60	Unc-63
$375	$600	$800	$1,100	$1,600	$2,400	$4,200

W-420-G • F-767 • Elliott-Burke (1919–1921) • 4,928,000 (est.)
Estimated population: 160 to 180 • *Highest graded:* Unc.

VG-8	F-12	VF-20	EF-40	AU-50	Unc-60	Unc-63	Unc-65
$375	$550	$700	$1,000	$1,450	$2,200	$3,000	$4,300

W-420-G★ • F-767★
Recorded population: 3 • *Highest graded:* F-12 • *Selected information:* G56980★/D, VG–F. G63763★/C, F. Knight (3/2005), G87217★/A, $1,495.

W-421-H • F-768 • St. Louis • Teehee-Burke (1915–1919) • Attebery-Wells • 1,160,000 (est.)
Estimated population: 60 to 70 • *Highest graded:* Unc.

VG-8	F-12	VF-20	EF-40	AU-50	Unc-60	Unc-63	Unc-65
$450	$700	$1,000	$1,450	$2,100	$2,800	$4,300	$5,250

W-422-H • F-769 • Attebery-Biggs • 660,000 (est.)
Estimated population: 20 to 24 • *Highest graded:* AU-50.

VG-8	F-12	VF-20	EF-40	AU-50
$450	$750	$2,200	$3,800	$4,800

W-423-H • F-770 • Elliott-Burke (1919–1921) • 560,000 (est.)
Estimated population: 27 to 32 • *Highest graded:* AU-50.

VG-8	F-12	VF-20	EF-40	AU-50
$450	$750	$2,100	$3,800	$4,800

W-424-H • F-771 • White-Biggs • 920,000 (est.)
Estimated population: 38 to 47 • *Highest graded:* Unc.

VG-8	F-12	VF-20	EF-40	AU-50	Unc-60	Unc-63	Unc-65
$450	$750	$1,300	$1,800	$2,150	$2,400	$4,500	—

W-425-I • F-772 • Minneapolis • Teehee-Burke (1915–1919) • Cook-Wold • 1,236,000 (est.)

Estimated population: 140 to 160 • *Highest graded:* Unc.

VG-8	F-12	VF-20	EF-40	AU-50	Unc-60	Unc-63	Unc-65
$400	$600	$800	$1,200	$1,700	$2,200	$3,400	$4,800

W-425-I★ • F-772★

Recorded population: 2 • *Selected information:* I6192★/D, VF–EF. I7986★/B, VG–F.

W-426-I • F-773 • Elliott-Burke (1919–1921) • Cook-Young • 440,000 (est.)

Estimated population: 60 to 70 • *Highest graded:* Unc.

VG-8	F-12	VF-20	EF-40	AU-50	Unc-60	Unc-63
$400	$600	$800	$1,200	$1,700	$2,200	$3,750

W-427-J • F-774 • Kansas City • Teehee-Burke (1915–1919) • Anderson-Miller • 1,460,000 (est.)

Estimated population: 120 to 140 • *Highest graded:* Unc.

VG-8	F-12	VF-20	EF-40	AU-50	Unc-60	Unc-63	Unc-65
$375	$550	$700	$1,000	$1,450	$2,200	$3,000	$4,300

W-427-J★ • F-774★

Recorded population: 3 • *Highest graded:* Unc • *Selected information:* J1818★/B, F. J11181★/A, F. Knight (2/2004), $2,300. Knight (11/2006), J18160★/D, Unc, $7,475.

W-428-J • F-775 • Elliott-Burke (1919–1921) • Helm-Miller • 1,192,000 (est.)

Estimated population: 70 to 90 • *Highest graded:* Unc.

VG-8	F-12	VF-20	EF-40	AU-50	Unc-60	Unc-63	Unc-65
$450	$700	$850	$1,200	$2,000	$2,500	$3,400	$4,800

W-429-K • F-776 • Dallas • Teehee-Burke (1915–1919) • Talley-Van Zandt • 1,100,000 (est.)

Estimated population: 120 to 140 • *Highest graded:* Unc • *Commentary:* In his 1951 study of these notes (see the bibliography), W.A. Philpott Jr. stated, "The Dallas Bank's $2 (referring to all varieties) is scarcest of all Federal Reserve Bank Note $2s, there only being 4,017 outstanding (two signatures) on October 30, 1944. Total $2's issued by Dallas Bank were a good half million dollars below any other of the 11 Banks ($2,424,000)."

VG-8	F-12	VF-20	EF-40	AU-50	Unc-60	Unc-63	Unc-65
$450	$700	$1,000	$1,450	$2,100	$2,400	$3,250	$4,750

W-429-K★ • F-776★

Recorded population: 2 • *Highest graded:* Unc • *Selected information:* CAA (9/2006), K741★/A, Unc, $56,350. Knight (6/2008), K2274★/B, VG-8 (PCGS), not sold.

W-431-K • F-777 • Elliott-Burke (1919–1921) • 112,000 (est.)

Estimated population: 38 to 47 • *Highest graded:* Unc.

VG-8	F-12	VF-20	EF-40	AU-50	Unc-60	Unc-63	Unc-65
$450	$700	$1,000	$1,450	$2,100	$2,400	$3,250	$4,750

W-432-L • F-778 • San Francisco • Teehee-Burke (1915–1919) • Clerk-Lynch • 1,812,000 (est.)

Estimated population: 62 to 66 • *Highest graded:* Unc.

VG-8	F-12	VF-20	EF-40	AU-50	Unc-60	Unc-63	Unc-65
$375	$550	$700	$1,000	$1,450	$2,200	$5,000	$14,000

W-432-L★ • F-778★

Recorded population: 1 • *Selected information:* CAA (5/2002), L3777★/A, Unc, $12,650.

W-433-L • F-779 • Elliott-Burke (1919–1921) • Clerk-Calkins • 572,000 (est.)

Estimated population: 38 to 47 • *Highest graded:* Unc.

VG-8	F-12	VF-20	EF-40	AU-50	Unc-60	Unc-63	Unc-65
$450	$700	$1,000	$1,450	$1,700	$2,000	$5,000	$14,000

W-433-L★ • F-779★

Recorded population: 7 • *Highest graded:* Unc • *Selected information:* CAA (5/2002), L29812★/D, Unc-65 (CGA), $3,910. Knight (6/2008), L29816★/D AU-58 (PCGS), $5,520. Heritage (4/2008), L29818★/B, MS-65 (PCGS), $9,200. CAA (1/1999), L29831★/C, Unc, $3,080.

W-434-L • F-780 • Ambrose-Calkins • 804,000 (est.)

Estimated population: 60 to 70 • *Highest graded:* Unc.

VG-8	F-12	VF-20	EF-40	AU-50	Unc-60	Unc-63	Unc-65
$450	$700	$1,000	$1,450	$1,700	$2,200	$3,250	$4,800

SMALL SIZE

Rounding out the $2 denomination are small-size bills, commencing with the bright red–imprinted Legal Tender Notes (Series of 1928 through 1963). The Jefferson portrait by Charles Burt dates to the 19th century. Joachim C. Benzing created Monticello on the back.

Never made in large quantities and never popular with the public, today $2 Legal Tender Notes are much scarcer than are their $1 counterparts. Star notes in particular are elusive, as this specialty was not widely popular until recent decades, by which time many early bills had become lost. Large and small plate numbers were used, though, and some combinations can be valuable. The final issuance of Legal Tender $2 notes was the Series of 1963-A.

The $2 bill seemed dead. Then came the Series of 1976 Federal Reserve Notes with green Treasury seals and serial numbers. These were followed by the Series of 1995 and the Series of 2003 Federal Reserve Notes with green Treasury seals and serial numbers. Of the latter, all were printed at the Western Facility (Fort Worth, Texas), and there are over 10 varieties of star notes deliberately created for collectors. Only 8,000 were printed of each. This inspired some numismatists to suggest that the mints start making mint-error coins to sell. In 2008 another numismatic series of $2 notes was made.

Although in commerce the use of a single $2 bill would be more efficient in terms of printing and distribution than two $1 bills, they have not been popular in circulation, simply because cash register drawers do not have a space for them, and they must be tucked in another location—an annoyance for those involved. No matter; collectors love them dearly, and it is likely that they will remain popular for a long time.

The Bureau of Engraving and Printing enjoys a nice business with collectors by supplying $2 notes and other modern issues, including (in some instances) full sheets and the earlier-mentioned star notes.

This series is compact in comparison to most other small-size denominations and offers interesting collecting possibilities. There are no impossible rarities among the regular issues from 1928 to date. The splash of red color on the Legal Tender Notes adds appeal.

LEGAL TENDER NOTES

Series of 1928, Red Seal
Tate-Mellon (1928–1929)

These notes have red Treasury seal and red serial numbers. Series of 1928 to 1928-B notes have the four-line notation, overprinted by the Treasury seal, "This note is a Legal Tender at its face value for all debts public and private except duties on imports and interest on the public debt."

Some examples of regular (as well as star) notes have no plate number on the back.

W-500 • F-1501 • 55,889,424

VG-8	F-12	VF-20	EF-40	AU-50	Unc-60	Unc-63	Unc-65
$8	$15	$20	$35	$70	$80	$140	$550

W-500★ • F-1501★

VG-8	F-12	VF-20	EF-40	AU-50	Unc-60	Unc-63	Unc-65
$125	$225	$400	$900	$1,250	$1,750	$2,100	$3,000

Series of 1928-A, Red Seal
Woods-Mellon (1929–1932)

W-501 • F-1502 • 46,859,136

VG-8	F-12	VF-20	EF-40	AU-50	Unc-60	Unc-63	Unc-65
$10	$17	$45	$65	$150	$275	$400	$800

W-501★ • F-1502★

VG-8	F-12	VF-20	EF-40	AU-50	Unc-60	Unc-63
$400	$850	$1,700	$3,500	$5,300	$7,000	$9,000

Series of 1928-B, Red Seal
Woods-Mills (1932–1933)

In *The Numismatist* in September 1967 (see the bibliography), William A. Philpott Jr. singled out seven small-size star notes, including this series, that he considered to be "excessively rare and hard to come by."

W-502 • F-1503 • 9,001,632

VG-8	F-12	VF-20	EF-40	AU-50	Unc-60	Unc-63	Unc-65
$55	$110	$225	$500	$675	$900	$1,750	$3,500

W-502★ • F-1503★

VG-8	F-12	VF-20	EF-40	AU-50	Unc-60	Unc-63	Unc-65
$8,500	$15,000	$25,000	$35,000	$45,000	—	—	$100,000

$2 Legal Tender Note, Series of 1928 (W-500).

Back of W-500, with angular view of Monticello, the standard type used through the 1950s.

Series of 1928-C, Red Seal
Julian-Morgenthau (1934–1945)

Beginning with 1928-C, $2 bills have the three-line notation, overprinted by the Treasury seal, "This note is a Legal Tender at its face value for all debts public and private."

Mules: Most backs have the plate number in small or "micro" letters, but mules have the larger or "macro"-size serials as used on Series 1928-D (the macro plates have numbers 289 and higher). These are worth a strong premium.[18]

W-503 • F-1504 • 86,584,008

VG-8	F-12	VF-20	EF-40	AU-50	Unc-60	Unc-63	Unc-65
$9	$12	$17	$22	$35	$75	$135	$295

W-503★ • F-1504★

VG-8	F-12	VF-20	EF-40	AU-50	Unc-60	Unc-63
$275	$450	$650	$1,000	$1,650	$2,000	$3,000

W-503 Mule • F-1504

VG-8	F-12	VF-20	EF-40	AU-50
$850	$1,500	$2,500	$4,000	$6,500

Series of 1928-D, Red Seal
Julian-Morgenthau (1934–1945)

Mules: Most backs have the plate number in macro numbers, but mules have the micro-size numbers as used on Series 1928-C (the micro plates have numbers 288 and lower).

W-504 • F-1505 • 146,381,364

VG-8	F-12	VF-20	EF-40	AU-50	Unc-60	Unc-63	Unc-65
$9	$12	$17	$20	$28	$55	$80	$195

W-504★ • F-1505★

VG-8	F-12	VF-20	EF-40	AU-50	Unc-60	Unc-63	Unc-65
$35	$60	$90	$225	$375	$550	$700	$1,000

SERIES OF 1928-A, RED SEAL

Signatures and series imprints of a $2 Federal Reserve Note, Series of 1928-A (W-501). The back is the standard type of the era.

SERIES OF 1928-B, RED SEAL

Signatures and series imprints of a $2 Federal Reserve Note, Series of 1928-B (W-502). The back is the standard type of the era.

SERIES OF 1928-C, RED SEAL

Detail of "micro" plate number on back of a $2 note of the era.

Detail of "macro" plate number on back of a $2 note of the era.

$2 Legal Tender Note, Series of 1928-C (W-503), with the new imprint over the Treasury seal. The back is the standard type used on all $2 Legal Tender Notes, Series 1928 to 1953-C.

SERIES OF 1928-D, RED SEAL

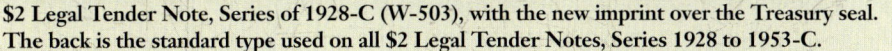

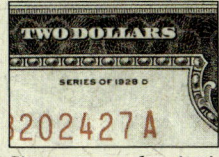

Signatures and series imprints of a $2 Federal Reserve Note, Series of 1928-D (W-504). The back is the standard type of the era.

W-504 Mule • F-1505

VG-8	F-12	VF-20	EF-40	AU-50	Unc-60	Unc-63	Unc-65
$9	$12	$17	$22	$40	$70	$85	$130

W-504 Mule★ • F-1505★

VG-8	F-12	VF-20	EF-40	AU-50	Unc-60	Unc-63	Unc-65
$140	$200	$325	$575	$1,000	$1,300	$1,500	$2,200

Series of 1928-E, Red Seal
Julian-Vinson (1945–1946)

W-505 • F-1506 • 5,261,016

VG-8	F-12	VF-20	EF-40	AU-50	Unc-60	Unc-63	Unc-65
$9	$12	$17	$20	$28	$55	$80	$195

W-505★ • F-1506★

VG-8	F-12	VF-20	EF-40	AU-50	Unc-60	Unc-63
$1,000	$1,800	$2,750	$3,700	$6,000	$7,500	$10,000

Series of 1928-F, Red Seal
Julian-Snyder (1946–1949)

W-506 • F-1507 • 43,349,292

VG-8	F-12	VF-20	EF-40	AU-50	Unc-60	Unc-63	Unc-65
$9	$12	$17	$20	$28	$55	$125	$425

W-506★ • F-1507★

VG-8	F-12	VF-20	EF-40	AU-50	Unc-60	Unc-63	Unc-65
$35	$65	$100	$140	$250	$400	$650	$1,150

Series of 1928-G, Red Seal
Clark-Snyder (1949–1953)

Beginning on December 6, 1949, new $2 Legal Tender Note face plates were made slightly smaller by narrowing the printed area horizontally by subtly removing part of the design. This created "Wide Face" (early style) and "Narrow Face" (later style) varieties. The Narrow style began with the Series of 1928-G, as here. As the changeover occurred after Series 1928-F, all of Series 1928-F are Wide Face and all Series 1928-G and later are Narrow Face.

W-507 • F-1508 • 52,208,000

VG-8	F-12	VF-20	EF-40	AU-50	Unc-60	Unc-63	Unc-65
$9	$12	$17	$20	$28	$55	$125	$425

W-507★ • F-1508★

VG-8	F-12	VF-20	EF-40	AU-50	Unc-60	Unc-63	Unc-65
$35	$65	$100	$140	$250	$400	$600	$1,000

Series of 1953, Red Seal
Priest-Humphrey (1953–1957)

The face of the $2 note was redesigned for this series. The red Treasury seal is now to the right. A gray 2 counter is on the left, and on the right TWO is under the Treasury seal. WASHINGTON, DC is above the seal. The series notation is now in the field to the lower right of the portrait.

W-508 • F-1509 • 45,360,000

VG-8	F-12	VF-20	EF-40	AU-50	Unc-60	Unc-63	Unc-65
$4	$6	$8	$10	$12	$17	$24	$50

W-508★ • F-1509★ • 2,160,000

VG-8	F-12	VF-20	EF-40	AU-50	Unc-60	Unc-63	Unc-65
$9	$15	$22	$27	$40	$95	$120	$190

SERIES OF 1928-E, RED SEAL

Signatures and series imprints of a $2 Federal Reserve Note, Series of 1928-E (W-505). The back is the standard type of the era.

SERIES OF 1928-F, RED SEAL

Signatures and series imprints of a $2 Federal Reserve Note, Series of 1928-F (W-506). The back is the standard type of the era.

SERIES OF 1928-G, RED SEAL

Signatures and series imprints of a $2 Federal Reserve Note, Series of 1928-G (W-507). The back is the standard type of the era.

Series of 1953-A, Red Seal
Priest-Anderson (1957–1961)

W-509 • F-1510 • 18,000,000

VG-8	F-12	VF-20	EF-40	AU-50	Unc-60	Unc-63	Unc-65
$4	$6	$8	$10	$12	$17	$24	$50

W-509★ • F-1510★ • 720,000

VG-8	F-12	VF-20	EF-40	AU-50	Unc-60	Unc-63	Unc-65
$7	$13	$20	$24	$36	$90	$120	$170

Series of 1953-B, Red Seal
Smith-Dillon (1961–1962)

W-510 • F-1511 • 10,800,000

VG-8	F-12	VF-20	EF-40	AU-50	Unc-60	Unc-63	Unc-65
$4	$6	$8	$9	$11	$15	$20	$37

W-510★ • F-1511★ • 720,000

VG-8	F-12	VF-20	EF-40	AU-50	Unc-60	Unc-63	Unc-65
$7	$13	$20	$24	$26	$80	$100	$140

Series of 1953-C, Red Seal
Granahan-Dillon (1963–1965)

W-511 • F-1512 • 5,760,000

VG-8	F-12	VF-20	EF-40	AU-50	Unc-60	Unc-63	Unc-65
$4	$6	$8	$9	$11	$15	$20	$37

W-511★ • F-1512★ • 360,000

VG-8	F-12	VF-20	EF-40	AU-50	Unc-60	Unc-63	Unc-65
$7	$13	$25	$35	$45	$90	$110	$150

Series of 1963, Red Seal
Granahan-Dillon (1963–1965)

The Series of 1963 (illus. on p. 198) has the motto IN GOD WE TRUST added to the back above Monticello. The face now has the two-line obligation "This note is legal tender for all debts, public and private."

W-512 • F-1513 • 15,360,000

VG-8	F-12	VF-20	EF-40	AU-50	Unc-60	Unc-63	Unc-65
$4	$6	$7	$9	$10	$13	$18	$24

SERIES OF 1953, RED SEAL

$2 Legal Tender Note, Series of 1953 (W-508★). The back is the standard type used on all Legal Tender Notes, Series 1928 to 1953-C.

SERIES OF 1953-A, RED SEAL

Signatures and series imprint of a $2 Federal Reserve Note, Series of 1953-A (W-509). The back is the standard type of the era.

SERIES OF 1953-B, RED SEAL

Signatures and series imprint of a $2 Federal Reserve Note, Series of 1953-B (W-510). The back is the standard type of the era.

SERIES OF 1953-C, RED SEAL

Signatures and series imprint of a $2 Federal Reserve Note, Series of 1953-C (W-511). The back is the standard type of the era.

SERIES OF 1963, RED SEAL

$2 Legal Tender Note, Series of 1963 (W-512).

Detail showing the motto.

Back of W-512, with the motto IN GOD WE TRUST added above the dome of Monticello.

SERIES OF 1963-A, RED SEAL

Detail of the signatures and the series imprint of a $2 Federal Reserve Note, Series of 1963-A (W-513). The back is the same as the Series of 1963 with motto.

W-512★ • F-1513★ • 640,000

VG-8	F-12	VF-20	EF-40	AU-50	Unc-60	Unc-63	Unc-65
$7	$10	$12	$16	$24	$45	$60	$80

Series of 1963-A, Red Seal
Granahan-Fowler (1965–1966)

W-513 • F-1514 • 3,200,000

VG-8	F-12	VF-20	EF-40	AU-50	Unc-60	Unc-63	Unc-65
$4	$6	$8	$10	$13	$20	$25	$40

W-513★ • F-1514★ • 640,000

VG-8	F-12	VF-20	EF-40	AU-50	Unc-60	Unc-63	Unc-65
$11	$15	$18	$32	$75	$95	$110	$140

FEDERAL RESERVE NOTES

Series of 1976, Green Seal
Neff-Simon (1974–1977)

Federal Reserve Notes of the Series of 1976 inaugurated this type, although there was absolutely no call for this denomination for use in commerce.

The face layout parallels in concept that used for other Federal Reserve Note denominations of the era. On the $2 note, the portrait of Thomas Jefferson is at the center, the vignette used earlier. To the left is the seal of the Federal Reserve System, with the name of each bank and the bank's letter, A (Boston) through L (San Francisco). The corresponding number of the Federal Reserve Bank, 1 to 12, is given four times on the face, near each corner. The Treasury seal to the right is the modern version, THE DEPART-

SERIES OF 1976, GREEN SEAL

$2 Federal Reserve Note, Series of 1976 (W-550-F).

Back of W-550-F, the new Series of 1976 note made for the Bicentennial, with the vignette *Declaration of Independence, 1776.*

MENT OF THE TREASURY 1789. This seal and the serial numbers are in bright green.

The back has the panoramic vignette *Declaration of Independence, 1776,* based on the famous painting by John Trumbull in the Rotunda of the United States Capitol. The engraving was done by John Girsch for the American Bank Note Company and earlier used on $100 National Bank Notes, Original Series and Series of 1875. In the 1976 $2 reprise it was slightly cropped and altered to the left and right, removing six delegates (including one from New Hampshire). The credit line for the American Bank Note Company was deleted, and no credit was given to Girsch.

For a time they provided some excitement and interest in the Bicentennial year. It was great sport to seek $2 notes cancelled in various states and on the first day of issue, these called B$2C issues (Bicentennial $2 Cancellations). In 1980, Andrew J. Vero published a book, *Price Guide for Bicentennial $2 Bill Cancellations.* Today, this specialty is largely forgotten.

In June 1982 the BEP announced that 16-subject sheets of notes would be available for sale to collectors.[19]

W-550-A • F-1935A • Boston • 29,440,000

Unc-63	Unc-65
$8	$11

W-550-A★ • F-1935A★ • 1,280,000

AU-50	Unc-60	Unc-63	Unc-65
$8	$12	$17	$27

W-550-B • F-1935B • New York • 67,200,000

Unc-63	Unc-65
$7	$10

W-550-B★ • F-1935B★ • 2,560,000

AU-50	Unc-60	Unc-63	Unc-65
$9	$14	$20	$30

W-550-C • F-1935C • Philadelphia • 33,280,000

Unc-63	Unc-65
$7	$10

W-550-C★ • F-1935C★ • 1,280,000

AU-50	Unc-60	Unc-63	Unc-65
$8	$12	$17	$27

W-550-D • F-1935D • Cleveland • 31,360,000

Unc-63	Unc-65
$8	$11

W-550-D★ • F-1935D★ • 1,280,000

AU-50	Unc-60	Unc-63	Unc-65
$12	$18	$24	$30

W-550-E • F-1935E • Richmond • 56,960,000

Unc-63	Unc-65
$8	$11

W-550-E★ • F-1935E★ • 640,000

EF-40	AU-50	Unc-60	Unc-63	Unc-65
$20	$28	$50	$70	$100

W-550-F • F-1935F • Atlanta • 60,800,000

Unc-63	Unc-65
$7	$10

W-550-F★ • F-1935F★ • 1,280,000

AU-50	Unc-60	Unc-63	Unc-65
$10	$15	$22	$26

W-550-G • F-1935G • Chicago • 84,480,000

Unc-63	Unc-65
$7	$10

W-550-G★ • F-1935G★ • 1,280,000

EF-40	AU-50	Unc-60	Unc-63	Unc-65
$14	$22	$35	$50	$70

W-550-H • F-1935H • St. Louis • 39,040,000

Unc-63	Unc-65
$8	$11

W-550-H★ • F-1935H★ • 1,280,000

AU-50	Unc-60	Unc-63	Unc-65
$6	$10	$14	$20

W-550-I • F-1935I • Minneapolis • 23,680,000

AU-50	Unc-60	Unc-63	Unc-65
$5	$12	$14	$17

W-550-I★ • F-1935I★ • 640,000

VF-20	EF-40	AU-50	Unc-60	Unc-63	Unc-65
$60	$95	$160	$220	$280	$350

W-550-J • F-1935J • Kansas City • 24,960,000

AU-50	Unc-60	Unc-63	Unc-65
$9	$14	$18	$23

W-550-J★ • F-1935J★ • 640,000

VF-20	EF-40	AU-50	Unc-60	Unc-63	Unc-65
$45	$70	$120	$160	$200	$250

W-550-K • F-1935K • Dallas • 41,600,000

Unc-60	Unc-63	Unc-65
$7	$11	$14

W-550-K★ • F-1935K★ • 1,280,000

EF-40	AU-50	Unc-60	Unc-63	Unc-65
$6	$9	$17	$25	$35

W-550-L • F-1935L • San Francisco • 82,560,000

Unc-63	Unc-65
$7	$10

W-550-L★ • F-1935L★ • 1,920,000

EF-40	AU-50	Unc-60	Unc-63	Unc-65
$10	$15	$25	$35	$50

Series of 1995, Green Seal
Withrow-Rubin (1995–1999)

Except for Atlanta notes, these were especially printed for sale to the numismatic trade. At the time they were designated as "Millennium Notes," in view of the coming 21st century. These are said to have been all printed in Fort Worth, but see the Series of 2003 comments.

Prices for a typical star note for this series, unless listed otherwise, are as follows:

Unc-65
$55

W-551-A★ • F-1936A★ • Boston • 9,999

W-551-B★ • F-1936B★ • New York • 9,999

W-551-C★ • F-1936C★ • Philadelphia • 9,999

W-551-D★ • F-1936D★ • Cleveland • 9,999

W-551-E★ • F-1936E★ • Richmond • 9,999

W-551-F • F-1936F • Atlanta • 153,600,000

Unc-63	Unc-65
$5	$8

W-551-F★ • F-1936F★ • 9,999 singly, plus 1,280,000 sold as part of sheets[20]

Unc-63	Unc-65
$8	$11

W-551-G★ • F-1936G★ • Chicago • 9,999

W-551-H★ • F-1936H★ • St. Louis • 9,999

W-551-I★ • F-1936I★ • Minneapolis • 9,999

Unc-65
$60

W-551-J★ • F-1936J★ • Kansas City • 9,999

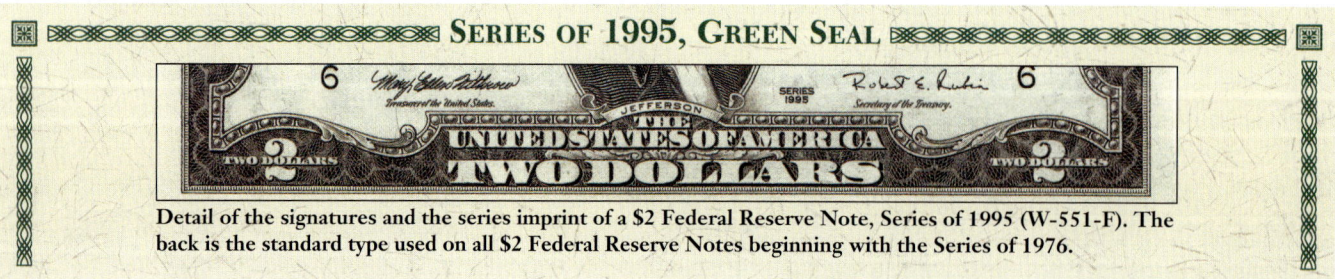

SERIES OF 1995, GREEN SEAL

Detail of the signatures and the series imprint of a $2 Federal Reserve Note, Series of 1995 (W-551-F). The back is the standard type used on all $2 Federal Reserve Notes beginning with the Series of 1976.

W-551-K★ • F-1936K★ • Dallas • 9,999

W-551-L★ • F-1936L★ • San Francisco • 9,999

Series of 2003, Green Seal, Star Notes, Washington and Fort Worth Shared Numismatic Printing
Marin-Snow (2003)

According to Derek Moffitt,

> The 2003 $2 star notes from all 12 districts, sold by the BEP as collector products, were listed in the BEP production reports as having been printed in Washington, D.C. However, the notes themselves carry the "FW" facility mark. When asked, the Bureau of Engraving and Printing said that these notes had been intaglio-printed at Fort Worth, then shipped to Washington for overprinting. By the Bureau of Engraving and Printing's thinking, that apparently makes them "officially" Washington products, but I think it better to list them as Fort Worth products because that is what's printed on the notes. I am not aware of any 2003 or 2003A $2 notes lacking the "FW" mark.

Each of these star notes was printed to the extent of 16,000 examples, the serial numbers beginning with the Federal Reserve letter and continuing to 00016000★. The first 2,000 sets of these were issued as part of "Premium Federal Reserve Set, Series 2003, $2," a booklet that included historical sketches and illustrations of the 12 different Federal Reserve Banks.

Prices for a typical star note for this series, unless listed otherwise, are as follows:

Unc-65
$35

W-552-A★ • F-1937A★ • Boston • 16,000

W-552-B★ • F-1937B★ • New York • 16,000

W-552-C★ • F-1937C★ • Philadelphia • 16,000

W-552-D★ • F-1937D★ • Cleveland • 16,000

W-552-E★ • F-1937E★ • Richmond • 16,000

W-552-F★ • F-1937F★ • Atlanta • 16,000

W-552-G★ • F-1937G★ • Chicago • 16,000

W-552-H★ • F-1937H★ • St. Louis • 16,000

W-552-I★ • F-1937I★ • Minneapolis • 16,000 (see next listing for additional Minneapolis notes of this series)

Unc-63	Unc-65
$30	$35

W-552-J★ • F-1937J★ • Kansas City • 16,000

W-552-K★ • F-1937K★ • Dallas • 16,000

W-552-L★ • F-1937L★ • San Francisco • 16,000

Series of 2003, Green Seal, Fort Worth, Regular Production
Marin-Snow (2003)

These notes (illus. on p. 202) were printed entirely in Fort Worth without the involvement of Washington. W-553-I notes have no star, and W-553-I★ notes, being replacement notes rather than special issues for collectors, are serially numbered above 00016000★.

W-553-I • F-1937I • Minneapolis • 121,600,000

Unc-63	Unc-65
$5	$6

W-553-I★ • F-1937I★ • Regular (not numismatic) printing • 3,840,000

Unc-60	Unc-63	Unc-65
$15	$20	$25

Series of 2003-A, Green Seal, Fort Worth
Cabral-Snow (2004–2006)

In 2008 the BEP announced that in addition to notes printed in quantity for circulation, a special issue of 10,000 notes (illus. on p. 202) would be marketed, commencing with the Richmond Federal Reserve Bank. Each note has a serial

SERIES OF 2003, GREEN SEAL, STAR NOTES, WASHINGTON AND FORT WORTH SHARED NUMISMATIC PRINTING

$2 Federal Reserve Note, Series of 2003 (W-552-L★). Federal Reserve Bank of San Francisco. Part of a series of star notes created for sale at a premium to collectors, not for circulation-note replacement purposes. The back is the standard type used on all $2 Federal Reserve Notes beginning with the Series of 1976.

beginning with 2008, followed by four more digits and a letter. These were offered in an acid-free polymer sleeve. Single notes were priced at $7.95 each. Richmond notes were the first to go on sale on July 30, followed by Philadelphia issues and others, typically selling out on the first day offered.

In August 2009 a new signature combination (Rios-Geithner) was authorized. As of press time it is not known if the $2 denomination will be produced with these signatures.

Prices for a typical note for this series, unless listed otherwise, are as follows:

Unc-63	Unc-65
$4	$6

W-554-A • F-1938A • Boston

W-554-B • F-1938B • New York

W-554-C • F-1938C • Philadelphia

Unc-63	Unc-65
$10	$14

W-554-D • F-1938D • Cleveland

W-554-E • F-1938E • Richmond

W-554-F • F-1938F • Atlanta • 12,800,000

W-554-F★ • F-1938F★

Unc-63	Unc-65
$140	$175

W-554-G • F-1938G • Chicago

W-554-H • F-1938H • St. Louis

W-554-I • F-1938I • Minneapolis

W-554-J • F-1938J • Kansas City

W-554-K • F-1938K • Dallas

W-554-L • F-1938L • San Francisco

SERIES OF 2003, GREEN SEAL, FORT WORTH, REGULAR PRODUCTION

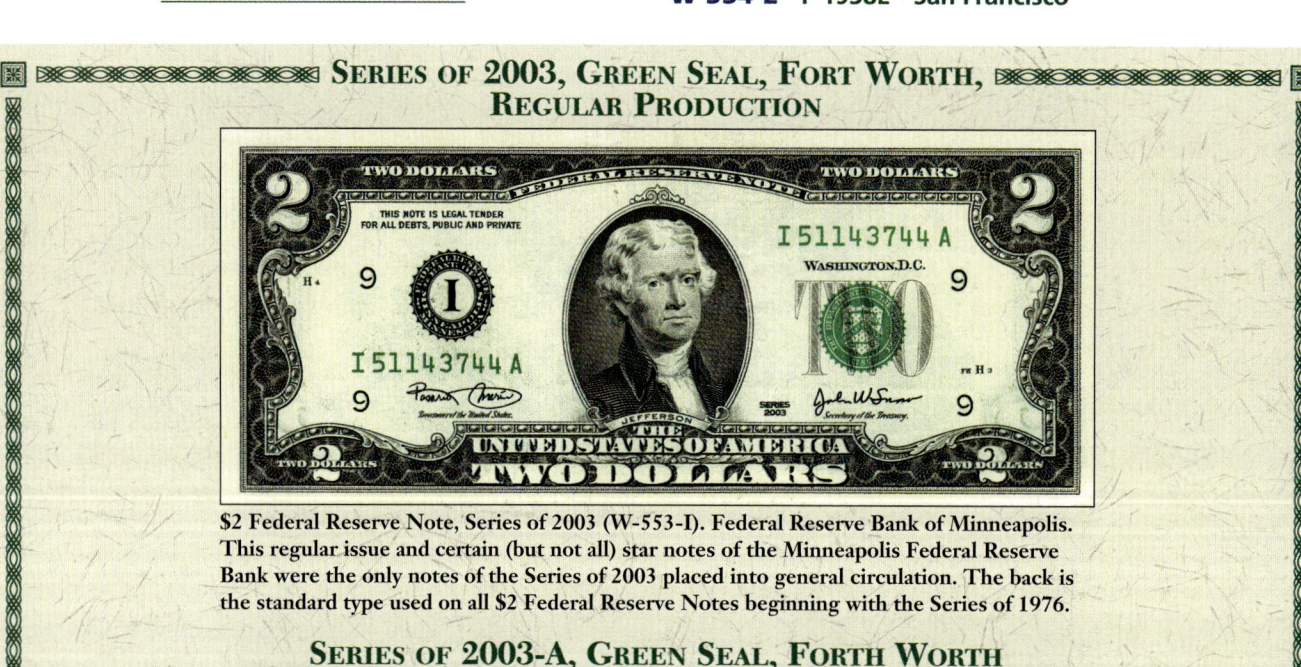

$2 Federal Reserve Note, Series of 2003 (W-553-I). Federal Reserve Bank of Minneapolis. This regular issue and certain (but not all) star notes of the Minneapolis Federal Reserve Bank were the only notes of the Series of 2003 placed into general circulation. The back is the standard type used on all $2 Federal Reserve Notes beginning with the Series of 1976.

SERIES OF 2003-A, GREEN SEAL, FORTH WORTH

$2 Federal Reserve Note, Series of 2003-A (W-554-A). Federal Reserve Bank of Boston. The back is the standard type used on all $2 Federal Reserve Notes beginning with the Series of 1976.

$5 NOTES

LARGE SIZE

Of all large-currency series, few denominations can equal the appeal, beauty, and collecting possibilities of $5 notes. This denomination introduces rare and important Demand Notes. Among National Bank Notes, the Series of 1882 issues are remarkable for their wonderful typographical diversity, and later Nationals are likewise interesting—series that have no counterparts in the lower-denomination $1 and $2 notes. The National Gold Bank Notes, circulated only in California, also make their debut with this denomination.

The $5 Silver Certificate types stand tall and proud with regard to artistry and include issues that have been numismatic favorites for a long time, with the 1896 "Educational Note" considered by some to be the epitome of art on paper money. Further, large-size $5 bills were a very popular denomination in their time, resulting in a fairly good supply of bills today, although there are many exceptions among the varieties.

DEMAND NOTES

Series of 1861

Printed by the American Bank Note Co., the Demand Notes (illus. on p. 204) were the first federal "greenbacks." Authorized by the Act of July 17, 1861, and dated August 10, 1861, bills of this type were rushed into production. These were made in denominations of $5, $10, and $20. Although this is not indicated on the bills, they were redeemable in gold coins, a provision added after the original legislation was passed. Because of this, in 1862 Demand Notes traded at a premium compared to Legal Tender Notes. Demand Notes were issued from August 26, 1861, to March 5, 1862.

The face shows the statue *Freedom* (later, in 1863, this was mounted on top of the United States Capitol, where it remains today) by Thomas Crawford and a portrait of Alexander Hamilton by Archibald Robertson, which bears little resemblance to the Hamilton portrait on the Series of 1862 $2 Legal Tender Notes. There is no Treasury seal.

The cities of the several Sub-Treasury offices—Boston, Cincinnati, New York, Philadelphia, and St. Louis—are imprinted near the bottom center, below which is lettered in green, PATENTED 30 JUNE 1857, referring to the "patent green tint" or "Canada green" promoted by the American Bank Note Company and used on certain other series and denominations in the early 1860s.

The original intent was for these bills to be hand-signed by the Treasurer of the United States and by the secretary of the Treasury. This procedure proved to be impractical at the start, and probably only a few were ever personally autographed by these officials. None have been seen by numismatists. In actuality 70 government clerks did the signing, with the added notation "for the," to reflect that they were acting on behalf of the senior officials. Early varieties have "for the" added in ink, a procedure soon changed to printing the words. The inked "for the" versions are all extreme rarities today. Having dozens of other signature styles and names by upward of 70 employees negated any security benefit, and this practice was discontinued on later types of notes. As a basic class, $5 Demand Notes are scarce, but they are much more available than are the higher denominations. Certain varieties range from extremely rare to unknown.

W-601 • F-3a • Boston • "for the" handwritten; no SERIES imprint • 2,000 (est.)
Recorded population: 1 • *Selected information:* 1804/D, VF-30.

W-602 • F-3 • "for the" printed • 98,000 (est.)
Estimated population: 7 to 9 • *Commentary:* In many instances the absence or presence of SERIES was not given in listings. It may be assumed that this variety is about 13 times rarer than the following.

W-603 • F-3 • Series 2 to 14 • 1,240,000
Estimated population: 105 to 115 • *Highest graded:* EF-45.

VG-8	F-12	VF-20	EF-40
$1,900	$3,200	$5,000	$19,000

W-604 • F-4a • Cincinnati • "for the" handwritten • 1,000 (est.) • Unknown

W-605 • F-4 • "for the" printed • 43,000 (est.)
Recorded population: 5 • *Highest graded:* Unc.

VG-8	F-12	VF-20	EF-40	AU-50	Unc-60	Unc-63
$8,000	$20,000	$45,000	—	—	—	—

W-606 • F-1a • New York • "for the" handwritten; no SERIES imprint • 10,000 (est.)
Recorded population: 9 • *Highest graded:* EF-40.

VG-8	F-12	VF-20	EF-40
$18,000	$40,000	$75,000	$100,000

W-607 • **F-1** • **"for the" printed; no SERIES imprint** • **90,000 (est.)**

Estimated population: 8 to 12 • *Commentary:* In many instances the absence or presence of SERIES was not given in listings. It may be assumed that this variety is about 14 times rarer than the following.

W-608 • **F-1** • **Series 2 to 15** • **1,400,000**

Estimated population: 120 to 130 • *Highest graded:* AU-58 • *Commentary:* AU examples are owned by the ANA Museum and the Federal Reserve Bank of Atlanta.

VG-8	F-12	VF-20	EF-40	AU-50
$1,500	$3,000	$4,000	$19,000	$35,000

W-609 • **F-2** • **Philadelphia** • **"for the" printed; no SERIES imprint** • **100,000**

Estimated population: 8 to 12 • *Commentary:* In many instances the absence or presence of SERIES was not given in listings. It may be assumed that this variety is 13 times rarer than the following.

W-610 • **F-2** • **Series 2 to 14** • **1,300,000**

Estimated population: 120 to 130 • *Highest graded:* Unc • *Commentary:* The plate had "for the" engraved on it before production began, as evidenced by the first note having "for the" printed. Accordingly, there was never a Philadelphia

SERIES OF 1861

$5 Demand Note of 1861 payable at New York and with "for the" handwritten (W-606). There is no series imprint on this note.

Detail of W-606 showing "for the" handwritten plus a Treasury clerk's name.

Detail from another note, W-610, showing "for the" printed. Payable at Philadelphia.

Detail of the serial number on a W-610 note with SERIES 4 below it.

Back of the $5 Demand Note, Series of 1861 (W-606). These were the first federal "greenback" notes.

note with "for the" added in ink. The 1/A note is ex Donlon 9/6/72 $790 (with historical information).

VG-8	F-12	VF-20	EF-40	AU-50	Unc-60	Unc-63
$1,750	$3,000	$5,500	$20,000	$35,000	$60,000	—

W-611 • F-5a • St. Louis • "for the" handwritten • 1,000 (est.) • Unknown

W-612 • F-5 • "for the" printed • 75,000 (est.)
Estimated population: 9 or 10 • *Highest graded:* VF-35.

VG-8	F-12	VF-20
$7,500	$20,000	$30,000

LEGAL TENDER NOTES
(Also Known as United States Notes)

Series of 1862, First Obligation

The earliest readily collectible bills of the $5 denomination are the United States Notes, or Legal Tender Notes, of the Series of 1862 and 1863. These "greenbacks," with the same general face motifs as the $5 Demand Notes (including the 1857 patent notice), exist in several varieties. The face, back, and tint plates for the $5 Series of 1862 and 1863 Legal Tender Notes were engraved by the American Bank Note Company. American also printed most (or possibly all) of the First Obligation notes. American and National shared the printing for the Second Obligation notes.[1] The Chittenden and Spinner Treasury signatures were printed on the face using a separate plate and a special ink.

The numbering was done in "series," each of which started with serial number 1. The addition of the word SERIES begins with SERIES 2 on W-632 (series 1 is not numbered for this denomination). For series 2 through 72, this designation is at the upper left of the note. Series 73 to 119 have the notation at the lower left. All bear the address of the Sub-Treasury in New York City, this being the most important of such facilities. All have a small red Treasury seal.

SERIES OF 1862, FIRST OBLIGATION

$5 Legal Tender Note, Series of 1862 (W-632). The vignettes are similar to those used on the $5 Demand Notes of 1861.

The series number notation varied in location on these notes. This has SERIES high to the left, a detail of a W-632 note from series 48, serial number 1710, plate C. In addition the number 2 is at the lower right corner of the face (not pictured).

Detail of a W-634 note showing SERIES low to the left. From series 78, serial number 1, plate A. In addition, the number 4 is at the lower right corner of the face (not pictured).

Back of a $5 Legal Tender Note, Series of 1862, with the First Obligation imprint.

There are two different styles for the obligation on the back of the notes, with slight differences in the wording as to the debts that can be paid with these notes.

First Obligation: This wording, with different typography on various denominations, states the note is exchangeable for bonds (a provision dropped from the Second Obligation), quoted here with erratic capitalization preserved:

> This Note is a Legal Tender for all debts Public and Private, except Duties on Imports and Interest on the Public Debt and is exchangeable for U.S. Six per cent Twenty Years Bonds redeemable at the pleasure of the U. States after Five Years.

These "6-20" bonds, as they were known, were a popular investment for banks and the public and were heavily advertised by Jay Cooke & Co. and others.

Most numismatists endeavor to acquire a single Series of 1862 or Series of 1863 note type, though there are differences, including the design and wording of the lettering on the face. For these and other Legal Tender denominations of the early 1860s, the various face letters and imprints have not been widely studied.

W-631 • F-61 • Printed on plate: "Act of Feb'y 25th 1862 / March 10, 1862" • AMERICAN BANK NOTE CO. N.Y. at top border; no SERIES imprint • 100,000
Recorded population: 10 • *Highest graded:* VF-30.

VG-8	F-12	VF-20
$3,000	$5,500	$20,000

W-632 • F-61a • As preceding, but now with SERIES printed at upper left; Treasury seal without inner border of radial parallel lines; Series 2 to 59 • 5,750,000 (est.)
Estimated population: 400 to 500 • *Highest graded:* Unc.

VG-8	F-12	VF-20	EF-40	AU-50	Unc-60	Unc-63	Unc-65
$450	$600	$825	$1,000	$1,450	$1,750	$2,450	$3,750

W-633 • F-61a • Treasury seal with inner border of radial parallel lines; Series 59 to 72 • 1,350,000 (est.)
Estimated population: 50 to 100 • *Highest graded:* Unc • *Commentary:* As this is a new listing, there is no market history.

W-634 • F-61a • SERIES printed at lower left; Series 73 to 119 • 4,700,000
Estimated population: 300 to 400.

VG-8	F-12	VF-20	EF-40	AU-50	Unc-60	Unc-63	Unc-65
$450	$600	$825	$1,000	$1,450	$1,750	$2,600	$4,000

Series of 1862 and 1863, Second Obligation

The face is the same design as the preceding. The series numbers are now prefaced with NEW SERIES, as is true with all Second Obligation bank notes of various denominations. The Second Obligation notice is printed on the back. The wording, with different typography on various denominations, does not mention exchanging the notes for 6-20 bonds and thus is different from the First Obligation: "This note is a

Legal Tender for all debts public and private, except for duties on imports and interest on the public debt, and is receivable in payment of all loans made to the United States."

W-635 • F-62 • Printed on plate: Act of Feb'y 25th 1862 / March 10th 1862 • With AMERICAN BANK NOTE CO. N.Y. and NATIONAL BANK NOTE COMPANY above the lower border; one serial number; Second Obligation back; New Series 1 to 23 • 2,300,000
Estimated population: 70 to 80 • *Highest graded:* Unc.

VG-8	F-12	VF-20	EF-40	AU-50	Unc-60	Unc-63
$450	$600	$825	$1,000	$1,450	$1,600	$3,000

W-636 • F-63 • Printed on plate: Act of March 3d 1863 / March 10th 1863 • New Series 24 to 65 • 4,132,764
Estimated population: 190 to 210 • *Highest graded:* Unc.

VG-8	F-12	VF-20	EF-40	AU-50	Unc-60	Unc-63	Unc-65
$500	$700	$925	$1,100	$1,500	$1,750	$3,250	$5,500

W-637 • F-63a • AMERICAN BANK NOTE CO. NEW YORK twice above bottom border; New Series 65 to 75 • 1,000,000
Estimated population: 180 to 200 • *Highest graded:* Unc.

VG-8	F-12	VF-20	EF-40	AU-50	Unc-60	Unc-63	Unc-65
$450	$600	$825	$1,000	$1,450	$1,750	$2,450	$4,000

W-638 • F-63b • Two serial numbers; New Series 75 to 83 • 867,236
Estimated population: 130 to 150 • *Highest graded:* Unc.

VG-8	F-12	VF-20	EF-40	AU-50	Unc-60	Unc-63	Unc-65
$450	$600	$825	$1,000	$1,450	$1,750	$2,450	$4,000

Series of 1869

The Series of 1869 $5 note (illus. on p. 208) is another in the "Rainbow Note" series, featuring blue-tinted paper with green and red printing; the others include the $1, $2, and $10 denominations. The portrait of Andrew Jackson on the face of the $5 note is by Philadelphia artist Thomas Sully, engraved for currency use by Alfred Sealey. *The Pioneer Family* is the engraving work of Henry Gugler. While *Pioneer Family* is the standard term, "Woodchopper" is a popular nickname, referring to the man standing at the center holding an axe with a loyal dog nearby. Serial numbers are in red and begin with A (unknown today) and K (the usual). A decorative star is at the end. As a class, Series of 1869 notes were issued from October 19, 1869, to July 25, 1874.

Examples are plentiful in the marketplace, and thousands exist. Some of the higher-grade pieces that have been illustrated or described in auction catalogs and other public appearances have been recorded in *U.S. Paper Money Records*, to the extent of about 500 notes.

W-650 • F-64 • Allison-Spinner (1869–1875) • Large pink seal • 10,068,000
Estimated population: 700 to 900 • *Highest graded:* Unc.

VG-8	F-12	VF-20	EF-40	AU-50	Unc-60	Unc-63	Unc-65
$265	$475	$1,050	$1,575	$2,400	$3,200	$4,000	$7,000

SERIES OF 1862 AND 1863, SECOND OBLIGATION

$5 Legal Tender Note, Series of 1862 (W-635). Serial number 87974, Plate B. Also type of Series of 1863.

Detail of a W-635 note, NEW SERIES 13 (under the Treasury seal) with a tiny 14 in lower right corner.

Detail of a W-636 note, NEW SERIES 7 with a tiny 43 in lower right corner. Serial number 61062, Plate B.

Back of a $5 Legal Tender Note, Series of 1863 (W-637), with the Second Obligation imprint. Also type of Series of 1862.

Series of 1875

The Series of 1875 notes (illus. on p. 209) continue the *Pioneer Family* type with various signature combinations. The seal is small, with spikes, and is to the left. To the right is a large pink ornament. No longer is there a star after the serial number, and the green overprint has been eliminated. The first two groups printed had SERIES / A / 1875 or SERIES / B / 1875 in pink at the bottom border right of center. The third group, W-654, had the imprint SERIES 1875, with no series letter.

The back was completely redesigned. The signature of the COLUMBIAN BANK NOTE is at the top in two panels and COMPANY WASHINGTON, D.C. is in two panels at the bottom. As a class, Series of 1875 notes were issued from July 20, 1875, to June 20, 1879.

W-651 • F-66 • Allison-New (1875–1876) • SERIES / A / 1875 imprint in pink • Small red seal with scalloped border • 1,000,000

Estimated population: 35 to 40 • Highest graded: Unc.

VG-8	F-12	VF-20	EF-40	AU-50	Unc-60	Unc-63
$1,100	$2,500	$4,000	$6,500	$13,000	$19,000	$30,000

W-652 • F-67 • SERIES / B / 1875 imprint in pink • 1,000,000

Estimated population: 135 to 150 • Highest graded: Unc.

VG-8	F-12	VF-20	EF-40	AU-50	Unc-60	Unc-63	Unc-65
$140	$190	$325	$550	$650	$900	$1,300	$2,500

W-653 • F-65 • 3,800,000

Estimated population: 70 to 80 • Highest graded: Unc.

VG-8	F-12	VF-20	EF-40	AU-50	Unc-60	Unc-63	Unc-65
$140	$250	$425	$675	$850	$1,000	$1,500	$3,000

SERIES OF 1869

$5 Legal Tender Note, Series of 1869 (W-650). The famous $5 "Rainbow Note," long a numismatic favorite.

Detail of the lower left serial number and the C plate letter on a "Rainbow Note."

Detail of the 14C plate number and letter and pink seal number 10.

Back of a $5 Legal Tender Note, Series of 1869 (W-650).

W-654 • F-68 • Allison-Wyman (1876–1877) • SERIES 1875 imprint in pink • 3,436,000

Estimated population: 140 to 160 • *Highest graded:* Unc.

VG-8	F-12	VF-20	EF-40	AU-50	Unc-60	Unc-63	Unc-65
$130	$180	$300	$500	$625	$950	$1,300	$2,550

Series of 1878

The face (illus. on p. 210) is similar to the preceding, except for the series imprint. On the back the Columbian Bank Note Company information is retained. SERIES OF 1880 is now in the top margin, and PRINTED AT THE BUREAU ENGRAVING & PRINTING is in the bottom margin.

W-655 • F-69 • Allison-Gilfillan (1877–1878) • Small red seal with scalloped border • 6,032,000

Estimated population: 165 to 180 • *Highest graded:* Unc • *Commentary:* The very last printed had a security paper change

from a vertical to a horizontal blue stain with fibers across entire length.

VG-8	F-12	VF-20	EF-40	AU-50	Unc-60	Unc-63	Unc-65
$140	$240	$450	$700	$850	$1,200	$1,400	$2,600

Series of 1880

Series of 1880 notes (illus. on p. 211) have the Treasury seal to the right, in several sizes and colors. Notes W-656 to W-658 have the serial numbers in red, while W-659 to W-668 have the serial numbers in blue. There are two back styles for this series.

Back Style 1: With COLUMBIAN and BANK NOTE as part of the design at the top, and COMPANY and WASHINGTON, D.C. in the design at the bottom, as in the preceding series. Now with SERIES OF 1880 added to the top margin, and

SERIES OF 1875

$5 Legal Tender Note, Series of 1875 (W-654).

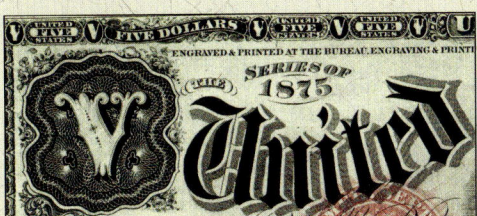

Detail of a Series of 1875 note (W-654) showing the series imprint.

Back of a $5 Legal Tender Note, Series of 1875 (W-654). Standard back for the series.

PRINTED AT THE BUREAU, ENGRAVING & PRINTING added to the bottom margin. This is the same style used in 1878, except for the addition of a plate number at the top of the open space on the left. Used on W-656 to W-659.

Back Style 2: BUREAU OF, ENGRAVING, & PRINTING, and WASHINGTON, D.C. in the four places where Columbian imprints were on earlier plates. SERIES OF 1880 is positioned vertically in the open field at the left. Used on W-660 to W-668.

W-656 • F-70 • Scofield-Gilfillan (1878–1881) • Large brown seal, red serial numbers • 4,100,000 (est.)

Estimated population: 100 to 140 • *Highest graded:* Unc.

VG-8	F-12	VF-20	EF-40	AU-50	Unc-60	Unc-63	Unc-65
$800	$2,200	$2,800	$3,500	$4,000	$4,300	$5,250	$6,500

W-657 • F-71 • Bruce-Gilfillan (1881–1883) • 7,400,000 (est.)

Estimated population: 115 to 125 • *Highest graded:* Unc.

VG-8	F-12	VF-20	EF-40	AU-50	Unc-60	Unc-63	Unc-65
$225	$300	$500	$700	$900	$1,000	$1,500	$3,250

W-658 • F-72 • Bruce-Wyman (1883–1885) • 7,760,000 (est.)

Estimated population: 145 to 160 • *Highest graded:* Unc.

VG-8	F-12	VF-20	EF-40	AU-50	Unc-60	Unc-63	Unc-65
$220	$390	500	$700	$875	$1,000	$1,500	$3,250

W-659 • F-73 • Large red seal, blue serial numbers • 2,504,000 (est.)

Estimated population: 220 to 235 • *Highest graded:* Unc.

VG-8	F-12	VF-20	EF-40	AU-50	Unc-60	Unc-63	Unc-65
$145	$275	$440	$650	$850	$950	$1,400	$2,900

SERIES OF 1878

$5 Legal Tender Note, Series of 1878 (W-655).

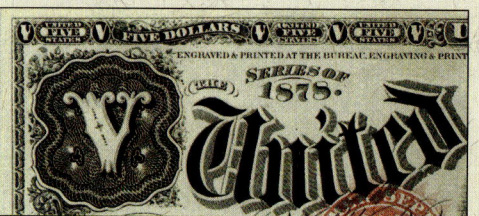

Detail of a Series of 1878 note showing the series imprint.

Back of a $5 Legal Tender Note, Series of 1878 (W-655).

W-660 • F-74 • Rosecrans-Jordan (1885–1887) • Large red seal • 6,196,000 (est.)

Estimated population: 148 to 155 • *Highest graded:* Unc.

VG-8	F-12	VF-20	EF-40	AU-50	Unc-60	Unc-63	Unc-65
$165	$350	$550	$1,050	$1,300	$1,400	$1,700	$2,400

W-661 • F-75 • Rosecrans-Hyatt (1887–1889) • 1,508,000 (est.)

Estimated population: 32 to 36 • *Highest graded:* Unc.

VG-8	F-12	VF-20	EF-40	AU-50	Unc-60	Unc-63
$450	$1,050	$1,800	$5,000	$9,000	$24,000	$35,000

W-662 • F-76 • Rosecrans-Huston (1889–1891) • 4,592,000 (est.)

Estimated population: 75 to 85 • *Highest graded:* Unc.

VG-8	F-12	VF-20	EF-40	AU-50	Unc-60	Unc-63	Unc-65
$275	$575	$1,250	$2,200	$4,500	$8,500	$11,000	$20,000

W-663 • F-77 • Large brown seal • 4,200,000 (est.)

Estimated population: 90 to 100 • *Highest graded:* Unc.

VG-8	F-12	VF-20	EF-40	AU-50	Unc-60	Unc-63	Unc-65
$275	$600	$1,000	$2,500	$4,500	$10,000	$15,000	$25,000

W-664 • F-78 • Rosecrans-Nebeker (1891–1893) • 700,000 (est.)

Estimated population: 45 to 55 • *Highest graded:* Unc.

VG-8	F-12	VF-20	EF-40	AU-50	Unc-60	Unc-63	Unc-65
$275	$750	$1,250	$2,000	$3,000	$4,000	$6,750	$15,000

W-665 • F-79 • Small red seal with scalloped border • 7,000,000 (est.)

Estimated population: 105 to 120 • *Highest graded:* Unc • *Commentary:* Two security paper types used—early type 1 has two

SERIES OF 1880

$5 Legal Tender Note, Series of 1880 (W-657).

Red serial number on W-657 with Geo. W. Casilear's patent information in microprint below it. The supposed innovation regarded printing the serial on an engraved background, said to offer more security.

Blue serial number on W-662.

Back Style 1 with series imprint in the top margin and BUREAU in the bottom margin (W-657).

Back Style 2 with BUREAU imprints and no mention of the Columbian Bank Note Company (W-666).

horizontal threads the entire width of note; later type 2 has two vertical bands of distributed red and blue fibers.

VG-8	F-12	VF-20	EF-40	AU-50	Unc-60	Unc-63	Unc-65
$140	$170	$225	$375	$500	$625	$800	$1,550

W-666 • F-80 • Tillman-Morgan (1893–1897) • 16,400,000 (est.)

Estimated population: 325 to 425 • *Highest graded:* Unc.

VG-8	F-12	VF-20	EF-40	AU-50	Unc-60	Unc-63	Unc-65
$140	$170	$225	$400	$525	$650	$870	$1,725

W-667 • F-81 • Bruce-Roberts (1897–1898) • 6,100,000 (est.)

Estimated population: 125 to 150 • *Highest graded:* Unc.

VG-8	F-12	VF-20	EF-40	AU-50	Unc-60	Unc-63	Unc-65
$170	$200	$300	$550	$650	$820	$1,050	$2,200

W-668 • F-82 • Lyons-Roberts (1898–1905) • 4,532,000 (est.)

Estimated population: 60 to 70 • *Highest graded:* Unc.

VG-8	F-12	VF-20	EF-40	AU-50	Unc-60	Unc-63	Unc-65
$170	$220	$340	$600	$750	$900	$1,450	$2,900

Series of 1907

The face of the Series of 1907 is slightly redesigned, now with a large V DOLLARS in the left field. Serial numbers are red. All have a small red Treasury seal with scalloped border.

Star notes are known as replacements beginning with W-670. Examples for type can be easily obtained, although certain varieties are rare.

An interesting variety, common to many back plates in Series of 1907 Legal Tender Notes, has the first word on the back, PUBLIC, spelled PCBLIC.[2] Doug Murray reports that apparently during the siderographic process a transfer roll or cylinder acquired a small unnoticed nick in the "U," causing all subsequent plates to have PCBLIC. In 2006, Murray examined notes from 224 different back plates and found that about 38%, including many star notes, had this defect, which some call an "error."

Mules: Back plate numbers can be in one of two locations.[3] On May 14, 1921, with the new Elliott-White signature combination starting, *all* Legal Tender, Silver Certificate, and Gold Certificate back plates were given numbers beginning with 1 and in a *new location*, although no notice was given of the change.

> **Back Plate Location 1** (regular use): W-669 to W-675. This was the standard location until May 14, 1921. Also used to create a *mule* for W-676 and W-677.

> **Back Plate Location 2** (regular use): W-676 to W-678 (introduced without notice as the new style on May 14, 1921, with the Elliott-White combination). Also used to create a *mule* for W-675.

W-669 • F-83 • Vernon-Treat (1906–1909) • 36,010,000

Estimated population: 165 to 180 • *Highest graded:* Unc.

VG-8	F-12	VF-20	EF-40	AU-50	Unc-60	Unc-63	Unc-65
$140	$220	$295	$500	$600	$675	$800	$2,000

W-670 • F-84 • Vernon-McClung (1909–1911) • 32,120,000

Estimated population: 140 to 170 • *Highest graded:* Unc • *Commentary:* Deliveries began on July 1, 1910, and ended on September 19, 1911.

VG-8	F-12	VF-20	EF-40	AU-50	Unc-60	Unc-63	Unc-65
$140	$220	$295	$500	$600	$675	$800	$1,750

W-670★ • F-84★

Recorded population: 5 • *Highest graded:* Unc • *Commentary:* Thomas F. Morris II had two in Uncirculated grade, serials ★164535B/C and ★164537B/A. • *Selected information:* Knight (6/2007), ★86626B/B, G-4 (PCGS), $316.

W-671 • F-85 • Napier-McClung (1911–1912) • 54,004,000

Estimated population: 325 to 425 • *Highest graded:* Unc • *Commentary:* Deliveries began on September 19, 1911, and ended on March 9, 1914.

VG-8	F-12	VF-20	EF-40	AU-50	Unc-60	Unc-63	Unc-65
$140	$220	$295	$500	$600	$675	$800	$1,250

W-672 • F-86 • Napier-Thompson (1912–1913) • 1,596,000

Estimated population: 75 to 85 • *Highest graded:* Unc • *Commentary:* Deliveries began on December 26, 1912, and ended on May 23, 1913.

VG-8	F-12	VF-20	EF-40	AU-50	Unc-60	Unc-63	Unc-65
$500	$750	$950	$1,300	$1,450	$1,600	$1,800	$3,750

W-673 • F-87 • Parker-Burke (1913–1914) • 47,116,000

Estimated population: 350 to 425 • *Highest graded:* Unc • *Commentary:* Deliveries began on March 9, 1914, and ended on October 18, 1915.

VG-8	F-12	VF-20	EF-40	AU-50	Unc-60	Unc-63	Unc-65
$125	$190	$265	$440	$500	$550	$680	$1,150

W-673★ • F-87★

Reported population: 8 • *Highest graded:* Unc • *Selected information:* Heritage (1/2006), ★511083B/C, VF–EF, $2,530. Knight (3/2008), ★717297B/A, EF-45 (PCGS), $2,875.

W-674 • F-88 • Teehee-Burke (1915–1919) • 97,268,000 (est.)

Estimated population: 550 to 600 • *Highest graded:* Unc • *Commentary:* Deliveries began on November 22, 1916, and ended on July 28, 1920.

VG-8	F-12	VF-20	EF-40	AU-50	Unc-60	Unc-63	Unc-65
$125	$190	$265	$440	$500	$550	$680	$1,150

W-674★ • F-88★

Estimated population: 52 to 55 • *Highest graded:* Unc.

VF-20	EF-40	AU-50	Unc-60	Unc-63
$800	$1,200	$2,000	$3,000	—

W-675 • F-89 • Elliott-Burke (1919–1921) • 2,300,000, or about 91% regular (est.)

Estimated population: 80 to 90 • *Highest graded:* Unc • *Commentary:* Deliveries began on July 28, 1920.

VG-8	F-12	VF-20	EF-40	AU-50	Unc-60	Unc-63	Unc-65
$125	$190	$265	$440	$500	$550	$680	$1,495

W-675★ • F-89★

Estimated population: 11 to 13 • *Highest graded:* EF-45 • *Selected information:* CAA (9/2000), ★1611752B/D, F, $687.50. CAA (5/2001), ★1669632B/D, F–VF, $825; bought back and later reoffered but unsold.

W-675 Mule • F-89 • Back Plate Location 2 • 240,000, or about 9% mules (est.)

Recorded population: 6 • *Highest graded:* VF.

W-675 Mule★ • F-89★

Recorded population: 1 • *Graded:* EF.

W-676 • F-90 • Elliott-White (1921–1922) • 13,000,000, or about 80% regular (est.)

Estimated population: 250 to 325 • *Highest graded:* Unc.

VG-8	F-12	VF-20	EF-40	AU-50	Unc-60	Unc-63	Unc-65
$190	$275	$400	$620	$750	$875	$1,200	$2,500

W-676★ • F-90★

Estimated population: 11 to 13 • *Highest graded:* EF-45 • *Selected information:* Knight (6/2002), ★1765800B/D, VG-10 (CGA), $748. Don C. Kelly (1980), ★1766130B/B, VF, price listed as $150. DBR Currency Web site (5/2007), ★1790240B/D, VG–F. $1,495. Knight (6/2008), ★1793535B/C, VF-30 (PMG), $1,725. Smythe (6/2005), ★1808587B/C, F, $402.50.

W-676 Mule • F-90 • Back Plate Location 1 • 3,228,000, or about 20% mules (est.)

Estimated population: 23 to 26 • *Highest graded:* Unc • *Commentary:* As this is a new listing, there is no market history.

SERIES OF 1907

$5 Legal Tender Note, Series of 1907 (W-677).

Face plate number location variations on two different W-674 notes. These differences have not been widely studied.

Back of a $5 Legal Tender Note, Series of 1907 (W-677).

Back Plate Location 1.

Back Plate Location 2.

W-676 Mule★ • F-90★

Recorded population: 5 • *Highest graded:* VF • *Selected information:* CAA (1/1999), ★1799398B/B, F, $1,320.

W-677 • F-91 • Speelman-White (1922–1927) • Back Plate Location 2 • 160,160,000, or about 99.94% regular (est.)

Estimated population: 4,000 to 5,500 • *Highest graded:* Unc.

VG-8	F-12	VF-20	EF-40	AU-50	Unc-60	Unc-63	Unc-65
$115	$175	$240	$400	$500	$560	$640	$1,100

W-677★ • F-91★

Estimated population: 155 to 170 • *Highest graded:* Unc.

F-12	VF-20	EF-40	AU-50	Unc-60	Unc-63	Unc-65
$200	$450	$750	$1,850	—	—	$3,500

W-677 Mule • F-91 • Back Plate Location 1 • 100,000, or about 0.06% mules (est.) (back plate 606 only)

Estimated population: 6 to 8 • *Highest graded:* AU.

W-677 Mule★ • F-91★

Recorded population: 1 • *Graded:* VF.

W-678 • F-92 • Woods-White (1927–1928) • Back Plate Location 2 • 14,892,000 (est.)

Estimated population: 200 to 230 • *Highest graded:* Unc.

VG-8	F-12	VF-20	EF-40	AU-50	Unc-60	Unc-63	Unc-65
$190	$275	$400	$620	$750	$875	$1,200	$2,000

W-678★ • F-92★

Recorded population: 6 • *Highest graded:* Unc • *Commentary:* Four are Uncirculated: ★3099139B/C (earlier called AU), ★3231778B/B, ★3231779B/C, and ★3231780B/D.

NATIONAL BANK NOTES

Although it is easy to collect large-size $5 National Bank bills by type, most collectors desire to acquire examples from a favorite state or region. Don C. Kelly's *National Bank Notes* is an essential guide to specific issues.

Prices are for states from which a larger number of notes survive. Notes with territorial imprints, from "rare states," or from "rare banks" often command much more. As reflected in the delineation, certain types and varieties can bring strong premiums, such as the rare "Black Charter" notes, the rare and popular National Gold Bank issues, the ornate 1882 Brown Backs, the elusive 1882 Value Backs, and very popular 1902 Red Seal issues.

Original Series
(Authorized Issue 1863 to 1875)

These notes (illus. on p. 217) were printed by the Continental Bank Note Company of New York, which had been formed in January 1863, and joined the larger American and smaller National bank-note companies in the fulfillment of federal contracts. The contract for $5 *and $10* notes is dated July 30, 1863. The agreed cost to the Treasury was to be $2,250 for "the bed-plates or dies, rolls, and one transferred plate of the five-dollar ($5)' note."[4] Although most contract work for notes of various denominations in the National Bank Note series went to the American and National bank-note companies, Continental scored a coup in that more were printed of the $5 denomination than of any other value. The same firm produced $500 and $1,000 notes.

This was not without its difficulties. Spencer M. Clark, head of the National Currency Bureau, viewed Continental as "a new concern with inferior facilities," and the contract matter was in disarray. Initial proofs of the $5 *and $10* notes were received by Clark on September 25, 1863, and reviewed, mainly with regard to the hardening of the plates. "Subsequently it was ascertained that the *American* Bank Note Company was preparing, without any authority or contract therefore, the work for the $5 and $10 notes from the same designs and for the same issue, as were being prepared by the Continental Company under contract."[5]

Clark continually remonstrated against the bank-note companies in New York City, which caused them, in turn, to mount an indirect attack on Clark, accusing him of moral turpitude and many other offenses. These matters passed, and Continental continued under its contract for $5 notes (but the $10 notes went to American, which printed them as part of $10-$10-$10-$20 sheets).

Continental printed the front, back, and the bank serial number (at the lower left, sometimes difficult to discern as it is over part of the vignette). The sheets, arranged $5-$5-$5-$5, were shipped to the National Currency Bureau, in the basement of the Treasury Building in Washington, where they were imprinted with the Treasury seal and government serial number. From there they went to the banks, where they were cut apart. The spacing between notes was very tight on the $5 denomination, with the result that all notes today are closely cropped at top and bottom, except, sometimes, for notes cut from the top of plate A and the bottom of plate D. This fact is not widely known.

The face depicts two different vignettes, unrelated in concept. To the left is *Columbus in Sight of Land*, from art by Charles Fenton, engraved by Louis Delnoce. To the right is *America Presented to the Old World*, art by T.A. Liebler, engraved by W.W. Rice. The Treasury department designated the two motifs as *Discovery of Land by Columbus* and *Introduction of the Old World to the New*. The latter shows an allegorical scene of a Native American princess, presumably representing America, being presented to female figures representing Europe, Asia, and Africa.

These were printed with red (usually) or blue Treasury serial numbers. The first group, which had red serials with no prefix or suffix letter, began printing on December 18, 1863, with serial number 9, and ended on July 28, 1864, with serial number 999152. After this, a set with blue serial numbers and no prefix commenced printing on July 29, 1864, with Treasury serial number 9 and ended on January 21, 1865, with number 999870. Afterward, red serial numbers with prefixes A, B, C, D, E, H, K, L, N, P, and U were issued. The A set began on January 24, 1865, and the U set ended on August 11, 1875.[6]

All Original Series notes have a small red Treasury seal with a spiked border. The Act of June 20, 1874, provided for the imprinting of the bank's charter number. This was done in red ink, one number vertically left of center and the other horizontally on the right.[7]

The back of the note features *The Landing of Columbus*, art by John Vanderlyn, from a painting in the United States Capitol. Gene Hessler and Carlson Chambliss note that Louis Delnoce and Walter Shirlaw each prepared engravings of this scene for use by the Continental Bank Note Company. On the left side is a state or territorial seal representing the issuing location of the bank, and to the right is an eagle (on some notes issued in territories, an eagle is at both ends).

The first National Bank Notes of any denomination paid out were $5 bills issued by the First National Bank of Washington, D.C., on Monday, December 21, 1863. Each bore federal serial 9 (probably arbitrarily selected so as not to be confused with the bank serial number) and bank serial 1, each imprinted on plates lettered A, B, C, and D. The first notes were saved as souvenirs. Three from this sheet, including plate A, survive today.[8]

Peter Huntoon mentions that the first half dozen or so Original Series $5 plates have the security clause on the plates to the left relative to the words UNITED STATES, most notably on the line that says "This note is secured by bonds of," which on the very first plate is positioned so that the T in *The* is over the N in UNITED STATES, whereas on later plates it is over the I. There are also differences in the flourishes.

Black Charter Notes

As an early experiment in adding charter numbers to the faces of $5 National Bank Notes to aid in sorting them when they were returned to the Treasury department, the Continental Bank Note Company was directed to enter numbers directly onto certain printing plates. Peter Huntoon found that this procedure was used from November 15, 1873, to May 15, 1874. This was prior to the Act of June 20, 1874, which required that charter numbers be overprinted on National Bank Notes. All of these issues have Allison-Spinner (1869–1875) signatures, except as noted below. Huntoon found 10 banks that used Black Charter notes and a possible four more that may have.

Huntoon states that although the idea of having charter numbers entered into the plate, to be printed in black at the same time the rest of the face was produced, was discontinued, the experimental plates remained in use. Some of these were altered to become Series of 1875 plates, still with the Black Charter numbers.

The following Black Charter note banks are listed in order of charter number (including Series of 1875 information). For notes existing today, see "Banks of Issue and Rarity of Notes" for each series.

Charter 1644: First National Bank of Houston, Texas; new plate ordered by an earlier-chartered bank • Scofield-Gilfillan (1878–1881).

Charter 1830: Merchants National Bank of Minneapolis, Minnesota; new plate ordered by an earlier-chartered bank when it changed its title.

Charter 2129: First National Bank of Central City, Colorado Territory, later with a Colorado state address. The first plate had letters A, B, C, and D. This was replaced by another, the Continental name was removed, and new let-

ters were given, E, F, G, and H. This plate was later reentered to give the state address (deleting the mention of the territory), entering the arbitrary date of February 1, 1890, and reentering the Treasury signatures to replace Allison-Spinner with Rosecrans-Huston. Peter Huntoon gives further details of the plates for this issue:

The A-B-C-D territorial plate was an Original Series plate made in 1873 with Allison-Spinner signatures. 2,475 sheets of Original Series notes were printed from it. Next it was altered into an 1875 territorial face with Allison-New signatures during 1875–6. The plate letters stayed the same because the plate was altered.

In 1889 a replacement plate was made, letters E-F-G-H, inscribed "Territory" (although Colorado had achieved statehood in 1876). Obviously no one cared about the obsolete territory then either. In 1890 the E-F-G-H territorial plate was altered into the E-F-G-H state plate by deleting "Territory." Notice that the plate letters did not change. The Series of 1875 printings commenced from it at least as early as 1878 based on the lowest reported serial number for a Series of 1875 note from the plate. Probably, all except the 1890 alteration are mules, combining a territorial front with a state seal back.[9]

Charter 2130: First National Bank of Red Oak, Iowa.

Charter 2131: Green Lane National Bank, Green Lane, Pennsylvania[10]

Charter 2132: Kellogg National Bank, Green Bay, Wisconsin • *Original Series:* No notes reported • *Series of 1875:* Three notes reported.

Charter 2133: First National Bank of De Pere, De Pere, Wisconsin.

Charter 2134: Peoples National Bank, Pueblo, Colorado.

Charter 2135: Commercial National Bank, Charlotte, North Carolina.

Charter 2137: National Bank of Boyertown, Pennsylvania.

Charter 2138: Rochester National Bank, Rochester, New Hampshire.

Charter 2140: First National Bank, Golden, Colorado Territory.

Charter 2141: National Bank of Pontiac, Illinois.

Charter 2142: National Bank of Schwenksville, Pennsylvania • This is the highest number among Black Charter notes.[11]

Banks of Issue and Rarity of Notes

Based upon census information from Don C. Kelly and James M. Kelly (*National Bank Note Census*, Version 4.0) and with some information from other sources, this listing gives each location, the number of banks issuing this series of notes within each, and a commentary.[12]

Of the Original Series of $5 notes the Kelly census records 950 examples, far fewer than for $1 notes of this series (3,100) or even $2 notes (1,263), but far more than the 275 $10 notes reported. Just eight serial number 1 notes are recorded, making any one of these a rare prize. Although many more National Banks issued $5 notes than issued the lower denominations, the face value of the $5 bills seems to have played against significant numbers being saved as souvenirs. While Original Series $5 notes often range from scarce to rare to very rare, most banks also issued Series of 1875 notes of similar motifs, with nearly twice as many of these surviving as a class. Accordingly, the demand for a very rare Original Series $5 bill may be softened if a Series of 1875 note from the same bank is not as rare.

Alabama • 4 banks of issue • 56 notes reported • This is a very common state from the standpoint of surviving notes in high grades, but all except two are from the City National Bank of Selma, and nearly all of these are in AU and Unc grades. The others are from the First National Bank of Huntsville (VG–F) and the First National Bank of Selma (not graded). For *other* Original Series denominations, and even for the Series of 1875 $5 notes, here, indeed, is an extremely rare state.

Arkansas • 4 banks of issue • 1 note reported • Merchants National Bank of Little Rock (F). A numismatic treasure.

Colorado Territory • 9 banks of issue • 4 notes reported • A rare territory from which notes are very desirable, although the availability of *Series of 1875* notes softens the demand for Originals. A single serial number 1 note is from the First National Bank of Denver, Unc. The other three notes are each VG and from the Colorado National Bank of Denver, Miners National Bank of Georgetown, and the First National Bank of Pueblo.

Connecticut • 82 banks of issue • 27 notes reported • Notes are available from a nice selection of different banks. Typical grades range from VG to VF, with higher-grade notes very scarce. The Kelly census lists just three Unc.

Dakota Territory (combining what became North and South Dakota) • 1 bank of issue • No notes reported.

Delaware • 11 banks of issue • 1 note reported • Delaware City National Bank, serial 2073, VF. A landmark note.

District of Columbia • 9 banks of issue • 7 notes reported • Five (including one not listed by Kelly) are from the First National Bank of Washington, including three serial number 1 notes from the first sheet delivered. The Unc example is the serial number 1 note from the plate A position. Two are from the Second National Bank of Washington (EF and AU).

Georgia • 14 banks of issue • 2 notes reported • Georgia National Bank of Atlanta (VG), First National Bank of Newnan (VG). These are classic rarities.

Idaho Territory • 1 bank of issue • None reported.

Illinois • 140 banks of issue • 64 notes reported[13] • One of the more collectible states, with many different banks available. Most are in lower grades, with just a handful of Unc examples reported. Three serial number 1 notes are from the National Bank of Illinois in Chicago (VF–EF), First National Bank of Jacksonville (AU), and the Grundy County National Bank of Morris (VF). It is generally thought that large numbers of Original Series notes across various denominations were destroyed in the Chicago fire of October 8, 1871.

Indiana • 110 banks of issue • 40 notes reported • A readily collectible state. Six Unc notes are listed in the Kelly census, including four from the First National Bank of Shelbyville. Eight notes are from the First National Bank of Rochester, including one Unc. There are two serial number 1 notes, from the Citizens National Bank of Jeffersonville (VG) and the Lafayette National Bank (F).

Iowa • 84 banks of issue • 42 notes reported • This state is generally thought of as scarce or rare, but a nice selection is available. All listed by Don C. Kelly are in worn grades. There are three serial number 1 notes, from the First National Bank of Albia (two) and the First National Bank of Red Oak. *Black Charter notes* (included in preceding total): First National Bank of Red Oak. Two reported, serial number 1 (VG, minor splits[14]) and serial 1888 (F).

Kansas • 27 banks of issue • 8 notes reported • Somewhat rare as a state. Most notes show extensive wear. One is the only Unc note, from the First National Bank of Wyandotte, and another is the only serial number 1 note for the state, from the First National Bank of Manhattan.

Kentucky • 47 banks of issue • 17 notes reported • These are from a wide distribution of banks. All are circulated.

Louisiana • 10 banks of issue • 4 notes reported • Louisiana National Bank of New Orleans (not graded), and three from the New Orleans National Bank (F, VF, and ungraded).

Maine • 68 banks of issue • 19 notes reported • Fifteen banks are represented. Only one Unc note is listed, from the First National Bank of Wiscasset. There is one serial number 1 note, from the Norway National Bank (not graded).

Maryland • 36 banks of issue • 26 notes reported • Eleven of these are from the First National Bank of Westminster, most of which are Unc. There is one serial number 1 note reported from the Central National Bank of Frederick (VF).

Massachusetts • 226 banks of issue • 77 notes reported[15] • Notes from this state are somewhat scarcer than might be expected, considering the large number of issuing banks. Most survivors are in worn grades, VG to F or so, but a few Unc notes are reported. There are three serial number 1 notes from as many banks, Franklin National Bank (EF), Hadley Falls National Bank of Holyoke (Fair), and the Marblehead National Bank (VF).

Michigan • 80 banks of issue • 46 notes reported[16] • The selection is wide and covers many banks. Just one Unc example has been reported, from the First National Bank of Decatur. There are two serial number 1 notes, from the Lumbermans National Bank of Muskegon (EF) and the First National Bank of South Haven (VF–EF).

Minnesota • 37 banks of issue • 23 notes reported • Typical grades range from G to EF, some higher and some lower. The only Unc note is listed from the First National Bank of Saint Peter. One serial number 1 note is from the Citizens National Bank of Faribault (EF–AU). *Black Charter note* (included in preceding total): One reported from the Merchants National Bank of Minneapolis (VG).

Mississippi • 1 bank of issue • No notes reported.

Missouri • 40 banks of issue • 20 notes reported[17] • This is a scarce but collectible state. The highest grade in the Kelly census is a solitary AU. There are four serial number 1 notes reported, all from the Moniteau National Bank of California; all are in circulated grades.

Montana Territory • 6 banks of issue • 2 notes reported • First National Bank of Helena (VG) and the Montana National Bank of the same city (VF). Both are great prizes.

No Series of 1875 $1 notes were issued by this territory, making these Originals even more desirable.

Nebraska • 7 banks of issue • 2 notes reported • One is from the First National Bank of Brownville, the only serial 1 note from the state (AU), and the other note is from the Nebraska City National Bank (AU). Both are exceedingly important.

Nebraska Territory • 3 banks of issue • None reported.

Nevada • 1 bank of issue • No notes reported.

ORIGINAL SERIES

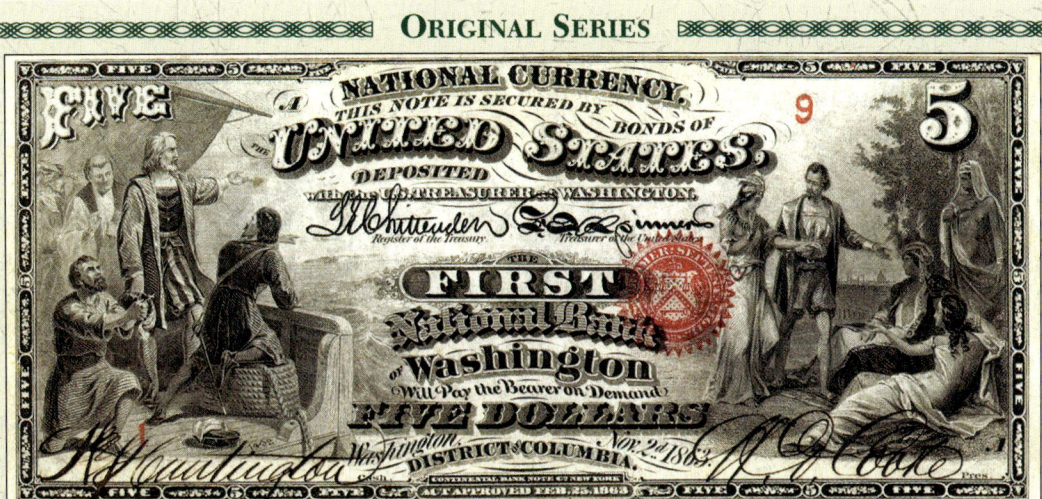

The very first National Bank Note of any kind issued, the plate position A, bank serial number 1 (lower left), and federal serial 9 (the starting number), issued on Monday, December 21, 1863, by the First National Bank of Washington (W-680).

Title block, Continental Bank Note Co. imprint, and other details of an Original Series $5 note.

Detail of the security statement on the face of the first $5 note, with THIS NOTE IS SECURED BY in a slightly different position relative to UNITED STATES OF AMERICA, an early style used only on the first half dozen or so plates, per the research of Peter Huntoon. Note the position of the S (THIS) to the letters above and below. Compare to the following.

Detail of a later plate showing the slightly different position.

Back of the first $5 National Bank Note (W-680), the general style used on all Original Series and Series of 1875 $5 National Bank Notes. To the left is the seal of the District of Columbia, reflective of the bank's location.

New Hampshire • 45 banks of issue • 3 notes reported • These are from the First National Bank of Francestown (VG), the First National Bank of Portsmouth (VF), and the National Mechanics and Traders Bank of Portsmouth (VG–F), a remarkably low showing.

New Jersey • 68 banks of issue • 35 notes reported • These are fairly widely distributed, save for four each from the First National Bank of Newark and the First National Bank of Somerville. All notes listed in the Kelly census are in circulated grades.

New Mexico Territory • 2 banks of issue • 3 notes listed • All are from the Second National Bank of Santa Fe (an F and two VF notes).

New York • 328 banks of issue • 158 notes reported • This is far and away the most "common" state. There is a wide distribution among banks. Most are in circulated grades, but exceptions include 14 Unc notes from the Tradesmens National Bank of the City of New York. Just two serial number 1 notes are reported, the National Bank of Commerce in New York (not graded) and the National State Bank of Troy (Unc).

North Carolina • 10 banks of issue • 8 notes reported • A rare state. Grades range from G to VF–EF, from five banks.

Ohio • 184 banks of issue • 87 notes reported • From many different banks. Unc notes are scarce, with just a handful reported. There are two serial number 1 notes, from the Second National Bank of Akron (F) and the First National Bank of Cadiz (Fair).

Oregon • 1 bank of issue • No notes reported.

Pennsylvania • 228 banks of issue • 63 notes reported[18] • Notes are widely distributed. Surprisingly, the Kelly census lists just one Unc, this from the Farmers National Bank of Reading. There are four serial number 1 notes from as many different banks, with grades from VF to AU.

Rhode Island • 62 banks of issue • 28 notes reported • The notes are fairly widely distributed. The census lists four Unc examples.

South Carolina • 11 banks of issue • 1 note reported • This is a prize serial number 1 note from the National Bank of Chester, a numismatic icon and certainly one of the most important of all Original Series notes across the various denominations.

Tennessee • 27 banks of issue • 4 notes reported • A rare state. Grades are Fair and F with two ungraded. Two are from the State National Bank of Memphis, the others from the German National Bank of Memphis and the first National Bank of Nashville.

Texas • 14 banks of issue • No notes reported.

Utah Territory • 3 banks of issue • 1 note reported • First National Bank of Utah at Salt Lake City (EF). A numismatic treasure.

Vermont • 43 banks of issue • 16 notes reported • Slightly scarce as a state. A selection of banks is represented. The only Unc note is from the National Bank of Poultney.

Virginia • 29 banks of issue • 8 notes reported • Grades range from G–VG to EF. Two are from the National Bank of Vir-ginia of Richmond and three are from the Shenandoah Valley National Bank of Winchester.

West Virginia • 20 banks of issue • 8 notes reported • Grades range from G to EF. Seven different banks are represented.

Wisconsin • 56 banks of issue • 14 notes reported • Scarce as a state. Mostly different banks are represented, with notes graded from Poor to AU, typically VG to F. There is one serial number 1 note, from the Beloit National Bank (AU).

Wyoming Territory • 2 banks of issue • No notes reported.

Generic prices for a typical note, charter in red, from a state from which notes range from plentiful to just slightly scarce:

VG-8	F-12	VF-20	EF-40	AU-50	Unc-60	Unc-63	Unc-65
$1,200	$1,425	$1,750	$2,400	$3,250	$3,800	$4,600	$7,250

W-680 • F-394 • Chittenden-Spinner (1861–1864)
Estimated population: 200 to 225 • *Highest graded:* Unc.

VG-8	F-12	VF-20	EF-40	AU-50	Unc-60	Unc-63
$1,200	$1,425	$1,750	$2,400	$3,250	$3,800	$4,600

W-681 • F-397 • Colby-Spinner (1864–1867)
Estimated population: 360 to 420 • *Highest graded:* Unc.

VG-8	F-12	VF-20	EF-40	AU-50	Unc-60	Unc-63	Unc-65
$1,200	$1,425	$1,750	$2,400	$3,250	$3,800	$4,600	$7,250

W-682 • F-398 • Jeffries-Spinner (1867–1869)
Estimated population: 11 to 13 • *Highest graded:* EF-40.

VG-8	F-12	VF-20	EF-40
$2,500	$3,200	$4,000	$4,800

W-683 • F-399 • Allison-Spinner (1869–1875)
Estimated population: 205 to 220 • *Highest graded:* Unc.

VG-8	F-12	VF-20	EF-40	AU-50	Unc-60	Unc-63
$2,500	$3,200	$4,000	$4,800	$5,500	$8,500	$10,000

National Gold Bank Notes, Original Series

Produced only in the Series of 1872, 1873, and 1874 and distributed only by banks in California, all National Gold Bank Notes are rare today. They circulated extensively, with none known to have been saved by collectors at the time of issue. Interestingly, the *American Journal of Numismatics*, the authoritative publication of the hobby at the time, took no particular notice of them (or of other large-size federal currency, except in passing).

The National Gold Bank Notes depict on the face the same design used for National Bank Notes of the Original Series. The distinctive feature on this new series is the obligation, "Payable to Bearer on Demand FIVE DOLLARS GOLD COIN." The back is entirely different from the regular Original Series notes and displays a montage of United States gold coins of different denominations, with an 1871 double eagle prominent. This same design was used on all denominations of National Gold Bank Notes from $5 to $100. All have the printed signatures of Allison and Spinner plus autographed signatures of bank officials. Nearly all were printed on yellow-tinted paper.

There are 409 $5 notes recorded by Don C. Kelly, these constituting the overwhelming majority of 579 Original Series National Gold Bank Notes of all denominations combined (Kelly figures are used in the listings below). For the $5 bills, the highest grade recorded is EF, and there are hardly any of these. Typical grades are G, VG, and F. Any note in VF grade is a prize indeed. Treasury records indicate a total of 3,451 of the $5 value unredeemed. Thus there is the potential for new discoveries, although most are probably lost forever.

W-690 • F-1136 • Dated 1870 • San Francisco • First National Gold Bank • 33,000

Estimated population: 400 to 600 • *Highest graded:* AU-50 • *Commentary:* This is far and away the most available issue among National Gold Bank Notes.

VG-8	F-12	VF-20	EF-40	AU-50
$2,600	$5,500	$12,500	$45,000	—

NATIONAL GOLD BANK NOTES, ORIGINAL SERIES

$5 National Gold Bank Note, Original Series (W-691), of the National Gold Bank of D.O. Mills & Co. Printed on yellow-tinted paper. This institution was founded by Darius Ogden Mills, who was originally a Sacramento shopkeeper during the Gold Rush. Mills College is named after him.

Title block of the D.O. Mills note, including the promise to pay or obligation to pay in gold.

Back of W-691. The same gold-coin montage was used on other National Gold Bank Note denominations.

W-691 • F-1138 • Dated 1872 • Sacramento • National Gold Bank of D.O. Mills & Co. • 7,960

Estimated population: 42 to 46 • *Highest graded:* AU-50.

VG-8	F-12	VF-20	EF-40	AU-50
$3,200	$8,500	$60,000	—	—

W-692 • F-1137 • San Francisco • National Gold Bank and Trust Co. • 17,840

Estimated population: 9 or 10 • *Highest graded:* VF-20 • *Commentary:* The "and Trust Company" is very rare title wording for that era.

VG-8	F-12	VF-20
$3,200	$8,500	$45,000

W-693 • F-1139 • Dated 1873 • Santa Barbara • First National Gold Bank • 4,000

Estimated population: 10 to 12 • *Highest graded:* VG-10.

VG-8
$8,000

W-694 • F-1140 • Stockton • First National Gold Bank • 2,000

Estimated population: 15 to 17 • *Highest graded:* VF-30.

VG-8	F-12	VF-20
$6,500	$15,000	—

W-695 • F-1141 • Dated 1874 • San Jose • Farmers National Gold Bank • 8,028

Estimated population: 50 to 60 • *Highest graded:* EF-40.

VG-8	F-12	VF-20	EF-40
$4,500	$6,000	$45,000	—

Series of 1875
(Authorized Issue 1875 to 1902)

These continued the use of plates created by the Continental Bank Note Company. The printing was done by the Treasury department in Washington. A tiny logotype with the lettering arranged around a circle was entered into the face plate, centered between the signatures of the two Treasury officials: PRINTED AT THE BUREAU ENGRAVING & PRINTING TREASURY DEPT. On some plates the CONTINENTAL BANK NOTE CO. imprint above the bottom border was removed. The small red Treasury seal now has a scalloped rather than a spiked border. All have SERIES 1875 imprinted vertically in red left of center, near the bank charter number. The Treasury and bank serial numbers and two charter numbers are also in red. A small percentage of these notes are printed on paper with a vertical blue tint streak. These are especially attractive.

Black Charter Notes

For more detail, see the historical information above concerning Black Charter Notes of the Original Series. For notes still existing today, see "Banks of Issue and Rarity of Notes" for the Series of 1875. Listed here are possible banks of issue, based on existing notes or potential from plates ordered, in order of charter number:

Charter 1830: Merchants National Bank of Minneapolis, Minnesota

Charter 2129: First National Bank of Central City, Colorado Territory, later with Colorado state address

Charter 2130: First National Bank of Red Oak, Iowa

Charter 2131:[19] Green Lane National Bank, Green Lane, Pennsylvania

Charter 2132: Kellogg National Bank, Green Bay, Wisconsin

Charter 2133: First National Bank of De Pere, Wisconsin

Charter 2134: Peoples National Bank, Pueblo, Colorado

Charter 2135: Commercial National Bank, Charlotte, North Carolina

Charter 2141: National Bank of Pontiac, Illinois

Charter 2142: National Bank of Schwenksville, Pennsylvania

Peter Huntoon refers to the CONTINENTAL BANK NOTE CO. imprint being removed from a Series of 1875 $5 plate for the Citizens National Bank of Washington City, District of Columbia, charter 1893. Both original and reentered Proofs exist. He observed that this was made as an original plate in 1874 with Allison-Spinner signatures and with an entered date of June 15, 1874. Then it was converted to a Series of 1875 plate by putting in Wyman's signature instead of Spinner's and adding the Bureau imprint. The plate date was not changed. In 1888 the CONTINENTAL BANK NOTE CO. imprint was removed. The Treasury signatures were not changed. Several signature combinations range from extremely rare to unique. As is true for other National Bank Notes, numismatic emphasis is mainly on bank location. Series of 1875 notes are rare as a class. Average grades encountered in the marketplace are higher than for the Original Series.

Banks of Issue and Rarity of Notes

Based upon census information from Don C. Kelly and James M. Kelly (*National Bank Note Census*, Version 4.0) and with some information from other sources, this listing gives each location, the number of banks issuing this series of notes within each, and a commentary.[20] Locations with serial number 1 notes are specifically identified; otherwise there are none.

The Kelly census records 1,791 notes of this series, in contrast with 950 of the Original Series. More states are represented. Interestingly, more banks issued Series of 1875 notes than issued those of the Series of 1882. One reason for this is that banks formed after the Act of July 11, 1882, or that extended their charters after this time, received Series of 1882 Brown Back notes instead. While the Original Series notes were issued only from 1863 to 1875, the Series of 1875 notes continued to be sent to banks that were formed or extended their charters before the 1882 legislation went into effect. Hence, a bank that received a charter extension or was formed in early 1882 would receive Series of 1875 notes for the next 20 years, or into early 1902. Again, this and related scenarios can be confusing unless studied carefully.

Alabama • 6 banks of issue • 4 notes reported • Eufaula National Bank (EF, ungraded), National Bank of Huntsville (ungraded), First National Bank of Tuskaloosa (F). Alabama is a very rare state for Series of 1875 notes, although many Original Series $5 bills exist from the Selma cache.

Arizona Territory • 1 bank of issue • 3 notes listed • All are from the First National Bank of Tucson (VG–F, VF–EF, EF). The VG–F note has serial number 1.

Arkansas • 2 banks of issue • No notes reported.

California • 3 banks of issue • 1 note reported • First National Bank of Alameda (VG). An incredible rarity.

Colorado • 13 banks of issue • 15 notes listed • All notes are circulated. Colorado attained statehood in 1876, near the beginning of the Series of 1875 issuance period. *Black Charter note* (included in preceding total): First National Bank of Central City. One reported (VF).[21]

Colorado Territory • 8 banks of issue • 29 notes reported • A single serial number 1 note is from the First National Bank of Denver (Unc). *Black Charter notes* (included in preceding total): 18 reported (VG to AU, average VF). These are from a small hoard and are the showcase Black Charter notes, the only territorial issues with this distinctive feature. Enough are available that they come on the market with some frequency, always attracting attention. Six of these are from the original plate, letters A to D, and 12 are from the replacement plate, letters E to H without CONTINENTAL BANK NOTE CO.

Connecticut • 81 banks of issue • 51 notes reported • Notes are available from a nice selection of banks. Typical grades range from VG to VF, with higher-grade notes being very scarce. Don C. Kelly records just one Unc note, from the Middletown National Bank.

Dakota Territory (combining what became North and South Dakota) • 12 banks of issue • 15 notes reported • Four of these are from what would become North Dakota, including a serial number 1 note on the Bismarck National Bank (EF), a Citizens National Bank of Grand Forks note (G), and two on the First National Bank of Valley City (F, VF–EF). Eleven of these are from what would become South Dakota, these including four serial number 1 notes, all from the first sheet of the First National Bank of Deadwood, one graded EF–AU, the others Unc. Among other circulated notes two are from the Merchants National Bank of Deadwood and three are from the First National Bank of Yankton.

Delaware • 9 banks of issue • 1 note reported • First National Bank of Milford, serial 3997, G. A rare prize, even with the low grade.

District of Columbia • 5 banks of issue • 4 notes reported • Four different banks (VG to VF). Rare and desirable.

$5 National Bank Note, Series of 1875 (W-700). Chase National Bank of the City of New York, which grew to become one of that city's most important financial institutions. The back is the same as that used on $5 National Bank Note, Original Series, notes.

Title block and bottom border of the Chase National Bank Note showing the retained signature of the Continental Bank Note Co.

Detail of the Bureau imprint on an Original Series plate, now used to print Series of 1875 notes.

Florida • 1 bank of issue • 3 notes listed • All from the First National Bank of Pensacola (G, VG, F–VF). Of added interest, as IN GOD WE TRUST appears on the state emblem on the back, the first use of this motto on a federal note. This seal appears on all Florida-issued Series of 1875 and 1882 Brown Back notes of all denominations, but is not often seen, as such notes are generally elusive. No serial number 1 notes have been reported.

Georgia • 8 banks of issue • 3 notes reported • First National Bank of Americus (ungraded), City National Bank of Griffin (VF–EF), and Merchants National Bank of Savannah (VF). Each is of great importance.

Idaho Territory • 1 bank of issue • 1 note reported • First National Bank of Idaho in Boise City, serial 1772, VF. A landmark note.

Illinois • 102 banks of issue • 132 notes reported • Readily collectible as a type, but the census is including hoards from several banks: Greene County National Bank of Carrollton (39 notes found, including 16 Unc, among which is the only serial number 1 note from the state), National Bank of Illinois in Chicago (six circulated notes), Merchants National Bank of Galena (26, including two Unc), First National Bank of Lincoln (six, including two Unc), and Ricker National Bank of Quincy (11, including one Unc). *Black Charter notes* (included in preceding total): National Bank of Pontiac. Five reported (VG, EF–AU, two punch-canceled G, and a washed F[22]).

Indiana • 87 banks of issue • 72 notes reported • While various banks are represented, special mention is made of the National Bank of Rockville (eight circulated) and, especially, the First National Bank of Vincennes (26, including two Unc). The only other Unc note is from the Hamilton National Bank of Fort Wayne, which is also the only serial number 1 note.

Iowa • 68 banks of issue • 88 notes reported • A very collectible state. Unc notes would be rare were it not for the First National Bank of Charles City, from which five have been recorded, with only a handful from others. There is one serial number 1 note, the First National Bank of Storm Lake (EF). *Black Charter notes* (included in preceding total): Two from the First National Bank of Red Oak (both VG).

Kansas • 19 banks of issue • 25 notes reported • The only Unc note is from the First National Bank of Topeka, which also accounts for 12 other notes, graded mostly VG and F.

Kentucky • 13 banks of issue • 37 notes reported • These are from a wide distribution of banks and are all in circulated grades.

Louisiana • 4 banks of issue • 4 notes reported • Louisiana National Bank of New Orleans (not graded), State National Bank of New Orleans (VG–F), and New Orleans National Bank (VF and EF).

Maine • 56 banks of issue • 20 notes reported • Four Unc notes have been reported, two each from the Lincoln National Bank of Bath and the First National Bank of Wiscasset.

Maryland • 27 banks of issue • 36 notes reported • The only Unc note reported is from the National Union Bank of Maryland of Baltimore. Fourteen circulated notes are listed from the Third National Bank of Cumberland.

Massachusetts • 232 banks of issue • 158 notes reported • A wide variety of banks is represented. Seven Unc notes are listed in the Kelly census. There are two serial number 1 notes, Winthrop National Bank of Boston (VF) and the Hudson National Bank (AU).

Michigan • 69 banks of issue • 63 notes reported • The selection is wide and covers many banks. Just five Unc notes are listed in the census, two from the First National Bank of Decatur and one from the First National Bank of Holly. There are two serial number 1 notes, from the First National Bank of Manistee (G) and the First National Bank of Quincy (EF).

Minnesota • 30 banks of issue • 26 notes reported • There are three Unc notes in the census, each from the Farmers National Bank of Owatonna.

Mississippi • 1 bank of issue • No notes reported.

Missouri • 25 banks of issue • 21 notes reported • The three Unc notes in the census are from the National Bank of Rolla.

Montana • 1 bank of issue • 3 notes reported • All are from the First National Bank of Miles City; each is graded F.

Montana Territory • 8 banks of issue • 10 notes reported • The three Unc notes in the census are from the First National Bank of Butte. From a rare but collectible territory, the notes always attract a lot of attention when auctioned.

Nebraska • 12 banks of issue • 15 notes reported • Grades range from VG to EF. Six banks are represented.

Nebraska Territory • 1 bank of issue • No notes reported.

New Hampshire • 45 banks of issue • 19 notes reported • Five notes are from the Second National Bank of Manchester and a like number are from the Rochester National Bank (Black Charter Notes). There are three serial number 1 notes reported, each Unc, plate positions A, B, and D, from the Mechanicks (quaint spelling) National Bank of Concord. These also stand as the only notes in that grade that have been recorded. Eight circulated notes are also listed from this bank. *Black Charter notes* (included in preceding total): Rochester National Bank, six reported (VG to VF[23]).

New Jersey • 55 banks of issue • 55 notes reported • Save for one Unc note from the First National Bank of Newark, all are in worn grades.

New Mexico Territory • 4 banks of issue • 5 notes reported • Three are from the First National Bank of Albuquerque (F, G–VG, F), one is from the San Miguel National Bank of Las Vegas (F), and the last is from the Second National Bank of Santa Fe (AU). Rare and desirable, with the territorial status creating additional appeal.

New York • 288 banks of issue • 349 notes reported • Many different banks are represented. For this state, finding an Unc example will not be difficult. A cluster of 42 notes from the Chase National Bank of the City of New York largely comprises the notes in that grade, and among the 18 notes of the Bank of New York National Banking Association there are seven such. There are five serial number 1 notes reported from as many different banks, and all are in circulated grades.

North Carolina • 8 banks of issue • 18 notes reported • Notes of this state, none of which have been recorded as Unc (although some are ungraded, as with most other states), include 11 from the National Bank of Greensboro, without which North Carolina bills would be rarities. *Black Charter*

note (included in preceding total): Commercial National Bank of Charlotte. One reported[24] (not graded).

North Dakota • 3 banks of issue • 4 notes reported • Three from the First National Bank of Mandan (two AU, one ungraded), plus one from the First National Bank of Valley City (VG–F; a Dakota *Territory* $5 note of this bank is separately listed above).

SERIES OF 1875, BLACK CHARTER NOTES

$5 National Bank Note, Series of 1875, of the "Black Charter" type (W-698), First National Bank of Central City, Colorado, with the charter number (in this case 2129) entered twice in the plate. This is from the plate in its first state with CONTINENTAL BANK NOTE Co. NEW YORK above the bottom border. Signed by F.C. Messinger as cashier (Otto Sauer as president). Messinger was announced as the new cashier in *Banker's Magazine*, February 1881, indicating this note was not issued before that time.

Detail of the title block on plate position A. First-state plate with the CONTINENTAL BANK NOTE CO. imprint.

Detail of the title block from the reentered plate with letters E to H (this is G), without the CONTINENTAL BANK NOTE CO. imprint.

Detail of the charter number at the upper left on the reentered plate.

Back of a First National Bank of Central City, Colorado note (W-698), similar in design to that used on Original Series notes. This particular note shows the Colorado seal at the left, reflecting the bank's location.

Ohio • 144 banks of issue • 117 notes reported • Many different banks are reported. Unc notes are comprised of two from the Metropolitan National Bank of Cincinnati, one from the First National Bank of Monroeville, and three from the First National Bank of Upper Sandusky. There are three serial number 1 notes, from Peoples National Bank of Bellefontaine (EF), the City National Bank of Canton (VF), and the Potters National Bank of East Liverpool (VG).

Pennsylvania • 183 banks of issue • 177 notes reported • Notes are widely distributed. An Unc note is listed from each of these: First National Bank of Altoona, First National Bank of McKeesport, First National Bank of Montrose, Farmers and Mechanics National Bank of Philadelphia, and Merchants National Bank of Philadelphia. There are two serial number 1 notes from the Merchants National Bank of Philadelphia (Unc) and the Fort Pitt National Bank of Pittsburgh (AU). *Black Charter notes* (included in preceding total): National Bank of Boyertown, five reported (VG to EF). National Bank of Schwenksville, one note reported (VF).

Rhode Island • 60 banks of issue • 58 notes reported • The notes are fairly widely distributed and are all described as being in circulated grades.

South Carolina • 9 banks of issue • 4 notes reported • National Bank of Anderson (VG, VG–F), National Bank of Chester (VG), and Merchants and Planters National Bank of Union (F).

South Dakota • 2 banks of issue • No notes reported.[25]

Tennessee • 15 banks of issue • 20 notes reported • Just five different banks are represented. Two Unc notes are listed, from the State National Bank of Memphis and the Stones River National Bank of Murfreesboro.

Texas • 11 banks of issue • 21 notes reported • Just six different banks are represented. The only Unc note is listed from the City National Bank of Dallas.

Utah Territory • 2 banks of issue • 1 note reported • Deseret National Bank of Salt Lake City, serial 247, VG. A territorial prize.

Vermont • 42 banks of issue • 24 notes reported • Ten different banks are represented, with five notes from the Allen National Bank of Fair Haven. The only Unc note listed is from the National Bank of Barre.

Virginia • 11 banks of issue • 6 notes listed • All are in circulated grades, from the Loudon National Bank of Leesburg, Lynchburg National Bank, Exchange National Bank of Norfolk, Farmers National Bank of Salem, and two from the National Valley Bank of Staunton.

Washington • 1 bank of issue • 2 notes reported • Both are from the First National Bank of Walla Walla (VG, F–VF). Equally rare but perhaps not as dramatic as the two related territorial notes from the same bank.

Washington Territory • 2 banks of issue • 2 notes reported • Both are from the First National Bank of Walla Walla (VG, EF). Highly important and desirable territorial rarities.

West Virginia • 11 banks of issue • 10 notes reported • Five banks are represented. Grades range from VG to EF.

Wisconsin • 43 banks of issue • 28 notes listed • All are in circulated grades, including seven from the Manufacturers National Bank of Neenah. There are two serial number 1 notes, from the First National Bank of Chippewa Falls (AU) and the National Exchange Bank of Waukesha (F). *Black Charter notes* (included in preceding total): Kellogg National Bank of Green Bay (a VF and two AU).

Wyoming • 2 banks of issue • 15 notes listed • All are in circulated grades, from the Stock Growers National Bank of Cheyenne (14) and the Wyoming National Bank of Laramie City (one).

Wyoming Territory • 3 banks of issue • 6 notes reported • One each from the First National Bank of Cheyenne (VG) and the Stock Growers National Bank of Cheyenne (F), plus four from the Wyoming National Bank of Laramie City, including the one Unc note from the territory. No serial number 1 notes listed.

Generic prices for a typical note, charter in red, from a state from which notes range from plentiful to just slightly scarce:

VG-8	F-12	VF-20	EF-40	AU-50	Unc-60	Unc-63	Unc-65
$1,200	$1,425	$1,750	$2,400	$3,250	$3,800	$4,600	$7,250

W-698 • F-401 • Allison-New (1875–1876)
Estimated population: 800 to 1,200 • *Highest graded:* Unc.

VG-8	F-12	VF-20	EF-40	AU-50	Unc-60	Unc-63	Unc-65
$1,200	$1,425	$1,750	$2,400	$3,250	$3,800	$4,600	$7,250

W-699 • F-402 • Allison-Wyman (1876–1877)
Estimated population: 170 to 190 • *Highest graded:* Unc.

VG-8	F-12	VF-20	EF-40	AU-50	Unc-60	Unc-63
$1,200	$1,425	$1,750	$2,400	$3,250	$3,800	$4,600

W-700 • F-403 • Allison-Gilfillan (1877–1878)
Estimated population: 135 to 150 • *Highest graded:* Unc.

VG-8	F-12	VF-20	EF-40	AU-50	Unc-60	Unc-63
$1,200	$1,425	$1,750	$2,400	$3,250	$3,800	$4,600

W-701 • F-404 • Scofield-Gilfillan (1878–1881)
Estimated population: 450 to 550 • *Highest graded:* Unc.

VG-8	F-12	VF-20	EF-40	AU-50	Unc-60	Unc-63
$1,200	$1,425	$1,750	$2,400	$3,250	$3,800	$4,600

W-702 • F-405 • Bruce-Gilfillan (1881–1883)
Estimated population: 300 to 400 • *Highest graded:* Unc.

VG-8	F-12	VF-20	EF-40	AU-50	Unc-60	Unc-63
$1,200	$1,425	$1,750	$2,400	$3,250	$3,800	$4,600

W-703 • F-406 • Bruce-Wyman (1883–1885)
Recorded population: 4 • *Highest graded:* VF-30.

VG-8	F-12	VF-20
$1,200	$1,425	$1,750

W-704 • F-406a • Bruce-Jordan (1885)
Recorded population: 4 • *Highest graded:* EF-40 • *Selected information:* Heritage (4/2008), 2369-Z875937/B, Farmers and Mechanics NB of Mercer, PA, F, $16,100.

W-705 • F-408 • Rosecrans-Jordan (1885–1887)

Recorded population: 7 • *Highest graded:* Unc.

VG-8	F-12	VF-20	EF-40	AU-50	Unc-60	Unc-63
$1,200	$1,425	$1,750	$2,400	$3,250	$3,800	$4,600

W-706 • F-407 • Rosecrans-Huston (1889–1891)

Estimated population: 36 to 42 • *Highest graded:* AU-53.

VG-8	F-12	VF-20	EF-40	AU-50
$1,200	$1,425	$1,750	$2,400	$3,250

W-707 • F-408a • Rosecrans-Nebeker (1891–1893)

Recorded population: 2 • *Selected information:* Heritage (5/2007), 2887-Y453830/C, Western NB of Pueblo, CO (only $5 of this series on the bank), F, damaged, $8,912.50. Knight (8/2003), 2892-Z769750/D, United States NB of New York, NY (only $5 and one of just three notes overall on this bank), VG, $7,475.

W-708 • F-408b • Tillman-Morgan (1893–1897)

Recorded population: 2 • *Selected information:* Knight (3/2006), 197-Y185800/C, Westminster NB of Gardner, MA (only $5 of this series on the bank), G (Fair in Kelly census), $7,188.

Series of 1882, Brown Back
(Authorized Issue 1882 to 1908)

These notes (illus. on p. 227) were the result of the charter expirations of the earliest national banks and the formation of new ones, as provided by the Act of July 11, 1882. By then the Bureau of Engraving had been printing notes for seven years and had been fully operating in its new building for two years. The Treasury department decided not to use the face and back plates created earlier by the Continental Bank Note Company for the Original Series and Series of 1875 notes, and allowed its own engravers to come up with new ideas. This procedure was quite unlike what was done with the other National Bank Notes in the Series of 1882, which simply copied the face designs used earlier and in many instances were printed from old plates that had been altered.

Charter numbers were overprinted in brown on the face from the outset, horizontally at the upper right. The Treasury seal was in brown as well. Beginning in September 1890, the position of the charter numbers was changed to horizontal at the upper right. Peter Huntoon states that fewer than 14% of the plates had the vertical position, and as these were some of the first printed, even fewer survive today. Regional letters N, E, M, S, W, and P were overprinted twice in brown on the face of notes starting with shipments received on March 17, 1902.

For the Series of 1882 $5 bills, the portrait of recently assassinated President James A. Garfield, engraved by Lorenzo Hatch, formed the illustration for the left side of the face, with the bank title block at the center. The decorative border of the notes was changed from the style used on Original Series and Series of 1875 notes to include the serial number of the bank six times, said to have been of use if a fragment of a note was sent to the Treasury department for redemption. The reverse was completely redesigned to create the Brown Back style. On the left was a state or territo-

rial seal representing the issuing bank's location, as had been done on earlier series. This necessitated making sets of plates for each state or territory. On the right was a perched eagle. At the center, a greenish-blue impression was applied with the bank's charter number in large figures, enabling the bills to be easily sorted when they were redeemed. These bills were first issued in 1882. From that time until the Series of 1902 bills were made, any bank with its charter extended in mid-1882 or later, and any newly chartered bank, received notes of this type, and continued to receive them for the next 20 years, even though the new Series of 1902 notes were introduced during that time. Series of 1882 Brown Backs were printed into March 1908, at which time the Aldrich-Vreeland Act mandated new wording, and production stopped.

Peter Huntoon writes that early Series of 1882 Brown Back notes had the Treasury signatures "stacked," one over the other.[26] Beginning in December 1886 and continuing into the early 20th century, new plates had an "in-line" or side-by-side arrangement, and some old plates were reentered in this format. Accordingly, for reference these can be called:

Signature Layout a: Treasury signatures one over the other, or "stacked."

Signature Layout b: Treasury signatures side by side, or "in line."

The possibility of creating imprints provided a rich panorama of artistic expression at the BEP, and today certain of the styles used for title blocks have been given interesting nicknames, such as "circus poster" and "shingle." Peter Huntoon has studied these variations extensively and has published much concerning them, some of this incorporating the research of the late Doug Walcutt. The wide variety of layouts, in combination with notes being plentiful in the marketplace, has made this series a numismatic favorite. At the Memphis Paper Money Show in 2006, Lyn F. Knight displayed a large, specialized collection devoted to this series, the prelude to an auction sale of what was titled the Power Collection.

For the condition-conscious buyer Unc notes are easy to find, at least for a basic "type" note and for many states as well.

Banks of Issue and Rarity of Notes

Based upon census information from Don C. Kelly and James M. Kelly (*National Bank Note Census*, Version 4.0) and with some information from other sources, this listing gives each location, the number of banks issuing this series of notes within each, and a commentary.[27]

The survey records 6,141 Series of 1882 Brown Back $5 notes, the largest population by far of any 19th-century National Bank Note type. These are readily collectible by states, and many different towns and banks are available as well. Wide diversity in typography and the two-color back add to the appeal of these notes. For the well-financed specialist there are 276 serial number 1 notes to contemplate, a very strong showing. Locations with serial number 1 notes are specifically identified; otherwise there are none.

Alabama • 16 banks of issue • 18 notes reported • One Unc, First National Bank of Opelika.

Arizona Territory • 2 banks of issue • 3 notes reported • Prescott National Bank (one VG and two VG–F).

Arkansas • 6 banks of issue • 14 notes reported • One Unc, Gate City National Bank of Texarkana.

California • 33 banks of issue • 262 notes reported • Mostly circulated, but there are dozens of Unc as well. Seven serial number 1 notes are recorded.

Colorado • 27 banks of issue • 46 notes reported • Five Unc, including four serial number 1 notes from the Mercantile National Bank of Pueblo. Seven serial number 1 notes are known total, a strong showing considering that only 46 notes are known overall.

Connecticut • 75 banks of issue • 172 notes reported • A wide selection of banks and grades. Ten serial number 1 notes are recorded.

Dakota Territory • 35 banks of issue • 13 notes reported • Two Unc, First National Bank of Aberdeen and the Sioux Falls National Bank. Five serial number 1 notes are known, these considered "trophy notes," as are any serial 1 territorials.

Delaware • 8 banks of issue • 5 notes listed • All are circulated. One serial number 1 note is from the Lewes National Bank (VF).

District of Columbia • 5 banks of issue • 26 notes listed • All are circulated.

Florida • 20 banks of issue • 27 notes listed • All are circulated. One serial number 1 note is from the First National Bank of Tampa (AU). Thus, there is a nice supply of these, each with IN GOD WE TRUST as part of the state seal, an early use of the motto on a federal note.

Georgia • 27 banks of issue • 51 notes reported • One Unc, Third National Bank of Atlanta, and from the same bank as the only serial number 1 note (VF).

Hawaii Territory • 2 banks of issue • 24 notes reported • One Unc, First National Bank of Hawaii, from which all but two of the other notes, all circulated, originated.

Idaho Territory • 4 banks of issue • 3 notes reported • First National Bank of Ketchum (AU), First National Bank of Pocatello (EF), and the only serial number 1 note, First National Bank of Pocatello (VF).

Idaho • 8 banks of issue • 5 notes reported • From four different banks, all in circulated grades. One serial number 1 note is from the First National Bank of Wallace (EF).

Illinois • 105 banks of issue • 239 notes reported • Various grades, including a small percentage of Unc notes. The census lists 16 serial number 1 notes, including four Unc from three banks.

Indian Territory • 15 banks of issue • 43 notes reported • Four Unc from the First National Bank of Marlow. Eight serial number 1 notes are known, including four Unc notes from the First National Bank of Marlow. Although the Indian Territory existed into the 20th century and the notes are not extreme rarities, their territorial status has made them everlastingly in demand.

Indiana • 71 banks of issue • 146 notes reported • Mostly circulated grades. Four serial number 1 notes are known, including one Unc from the Rockville National Bank.

Iowa • 96 banks of issue • 108 notes reported • Various grades, including a handful of Unc notes. Seven serial number 1 notes are known, including three Unc from the City National Bank of Clinton.

Kansas • 113 banks of issue • 107 notes reported • Mostly circulated, but with some Unc notes, including four from the First National Bank of Hutchinson. The census lists 14 serial number 1 notes, including one Unc note from the First National Bank of Holton—overall, a very strong showing for any state.

Kentucky • 36 banks of issue • 91 notes reported • Two Unc from the State National Bank of Frankfort and the Union National Bank of Louisville. Two serial number 1 notes are known, of the First National Bank of Hopkinsville (VF) and Citizens National Bank of Lebanon (EF–AU).

Louisiana • 18 banks of issue • 39 notes reported • One Unc, First National Bank of Shreveport. Four serial number 1 notes are available from as many banks.

Maine • 48 banks of issue • 114 notes reported • Circulated grades, plus a handful of Unc notes. Four serial number 1 notes are available from as many banks.

Maryland • 43 banks of issue • 80 notes reported • Two serial number 1 notes are known, Merchants National Bank of Baltimore (VF) and the First National Bank of Catonville (VG).

Massachusetts • 239 banks of issue • 512 notes reported • Most are circulated, but a cluster of 13 Unc notes from the First National Bank of Attleboro is memorable. Nine serial number 1 notes are known, including Unc examples from the First National Bank of Fall River and the Pacific National Bank of Nantucket (the seemingly out-of-place name of this bank is from Nantucket being a prime whaling port for ships outward bound to the Pacific Ocean).

Michigan • 68 banks of issue • 17 notes reported • Various grades up to Unc. The census lists 12 serial number 1 notes, including Unc notes from the First National Bank of Bay City, Third National Bank of Detroit, Grand Rapids National Bank, and Fifth National Bank of Grand Rapids.

Minnesota • 64 banks of issue • 66 notes reported • Includes a handful of Unc notes. The census lists 10 serial number 1 notes, including Unc notes from the National Bank of Winona and the First National Bank of Winona.

Mississippi • 11 banks of issue • 15 notes reported • One Unc note from the First National Bank of Meridian. One serial number 1 note is from the First National Bank of Starkville (VF–EF).

Missouri • 59 banks of issue • 307 notes reported • Wide selection, mostly circulated, but ample Unc, including 23 from the State National Bank of St. Louis. Five serial number 1 notes are known, including one Unc from the Grundy County National Bank of Trenton.

Montana • 15 banks of issue • 11 notes reported • Five serial number 1 notes are known, two from the Globe National Bank of Kalispell and three from the Conrad National Bank

SERIES OF 1882, BROWN BACK

$5 National Bank Note, Series of 1882, Brown Back, First National Bank of Attleboro, Massachusetts (W-718), the type used from W-710 to W-723. At the left is a portrait of President James A. Garfield, recently assassinated. A large brown Treasury seal is on all. The title blocks (bank names and addresses) vary widely in style within this type. The 2232 overprint is this bank's charter number, and the regional letter N represents North, the area in which this bank was located. Such letters helped with the sorting of notes when they were redeemed by the Treasury department.

Signature Layout a, or the "stacked" layout, on the face of a W-467 note, Bruce-Wyman.

Signature Layout b, or the "in-line" layout, on the face of a W-467 note, Bruce-Wyman.

Back of the First National Bank Attleboro note, the type used from W-710 to W-723. The bank's charter number is at the center. At the left is the state seal of Massachusetts, reflecting this bank's location.

Detail of the back of a $5 National Bank Note, Series of 1882, Brown Back, with no plate number showing.

Detail of the back of a $5 National Bank Note, Series of 1882, Brown Back, showing the tiny plate number 145 at the center of the blank space.

of Kalispell, the last including the only two Unc notes from the state.

Montana Territory • 9 banks of issue • 6 notes reported • Circulated grades from three banks. One serial number 1 note is from the First National Bank of Billings (VF).

Nebraska • 112 banks of issue • 240 notes reported • A remarkable hoard of 89 Unc notes is from the Saint Paul National Bank. The census lists 13 serial number 1 notes, all in circulated grades.

Nevada • 1 bank of issue • No notes reported.

New Hampshire • 49 banks of issue • 101 notes reported • Mostly in circulated grades. Three serial number 1 notes are from the Peoples National Bank of Laconia (F–VF), Citizens National Bank of Newport (EF), and National Mechanics and Traders Bank of Portsmouth (EF).

New Jersey • 90 banks of issue • 217 notes reported[28] • Nine serial number 1 notes are known, including Unc notes from the Second National Bank of Atlantic City and the Carlstadt National Bank.

New Mexico Territory • 7 banks of issue • 11 notes reported • Circulated grades from three banks, including eight notes from the First National Bank of Raton.

New York • 274 banks of issue • 1,142 notes reported • Various grades. Unc hoards from the National Bank of Commerce (mainly) and the First National Bank of Utica comprise well over 100 notes. The census lists 38 serial number 1 notes in various grades up to Unc. This state takes the prize.

North Carolina • 18 banks of issue • 41 notes reported • Mostly circulated, except for seven Unc from the First National Bank of Salisbury.

North Dakota • 14 banks of issue • 2 notes reported • Capital National Bank of Bismarck (EF) and Fargo National Bank (VG).

Ohio • 147 banks of issue • 390 notes reported • Dozens of Unc notes from several clusters. The census reports 16 serial number 1 notes in circulated grades.

Oklahoma • 13 banks of issue • 7 notes reported • All are in circulated grades.

Oklahoma Territory • 16 banks of issue • 15 notes reported • Two Unc from the Stillwater National Bank.

Oregon • 11 banks of issue • 9 notes reported • Five banks. All are in circulated grades. Two serial number 1 notes are known, First National Bank of Hopkinsville (VF) and Citizens National Bank of Lebanon (EF–AU).

Pennsylvania • 274 banks of issue • 574 notes reported • Wide selection of grades. Among Unc notes are six from the First National Bank of Milford. The census lists 26 serial number 1 notes, including 11 Unc, a very strong showing.

Rhode Island • 62 banks of issue • 138 notes reported • Unc notes include several from the First National Bank of Smithfield of Slaterville and the First National Bank of Warren.

South Carolina • 12 banks of issue • 9 notes reported • Circulated notes from four banks.

South Dakota • 33 banks of issue • 18 notes reported • Circulated grades. One serial number 1 note is known from the First National Bank of Lead (EF).

Tennessee • 30 banks of issue • 30 notes reported • One Unc, First National Bank of Jackson.

Texas • 74 banks of issue • 98 notes reported • Circulated except for a hoard of 22 Unc from the First National Bank of Shiner. Six serial number 1 notes are known in circulated grades.

Utah • 7 banks of issue • 17 notes reported • Circulated grades. Mostly from the Deseret National Bank of Salt Lake City. One serial number 1 note is from the First National Bank of Brigham City (AU).

Utah Territory • 5 banks of issue • 2 notes reported • First National Bank of Park City (both AU).

Vermont • 38 banks of issue • 82 notes reported • Five Unc from four banks. Four serial number 1 notes are known in circulated grades.

Virginia • 30 banks of issue • 47 notes reported • Two Unc, from the National Bank of Petersburg and the Citizens National Bank of Roanoke. One serial number 1 note is from the Norfolk National Bank (VF).

Washington • 32 banks of issue • 16 notes reported • One Unc, from the Seattle National Bank.

Washington Territory • 13 banks of issue • 5 notes reported • Circulated notes from four banks.

West Virginia • 27 banks of issue • 59 notes reported • Six Unc notes. Three serial number 1 notes are known. Traders National Bank of Clarksburg (Unc), First National Bank of Sistersville (Unc), and National Exchange Bank of Wheeling (VF).

Wisconsin • 58 banks of issue • 134 notes reported • Two Unc, one from the First National Bank of Berlin. The census lists 14 serial number 1 notes, including one Unc note from the First National Bank of Stoughton.

Wyoming • 3 banks of issue • 4 notes reported • Circulated grades, all from the Stock Growers National Bank of Cheyenne.

Wyoming Territory • 2 banks of issue • 1 note reported • This is a serial number 1 note from the First National Bank of Douglas (VF), a landmark item to be sure.

Generic prices for a typical note from a state from which notes range from plentiful to just slightly scarce:

VG-8	F-12	VF-20	EF-40	AU-50	Unc-60	Unc-63	Unc-65
$450	$650	$750	$1,000	$1,425	$1,900	$2,300	$3,700

W-710 • F-466 • Bruce-Gilfillan (1881–1883)
Estimated population: 600 to 900 • Highest graded: Unc.

VG-8	F-12	VF-20	EF-40	AU-50	Unc-60	Unc-63	Unc-65
$450	$650	$750	$1,000	$1,425	$1,900	$2,300	$3,700

W-711 • F-467 • Bruce-Wyman (1883–1885)
Estimated population: 1,600 to 2,200 • Highest graded: Unc.

VG-8	F-12	VF-20	EF-40	AU-50	Unc-60	Unc-63	Unc-65
$450	$650	$750	$1,000	$1,425	$1,900	$2,300	$3,700

W-712 • F-468 • Bruce-Jordan (1885)
Estimated population: 350 to 500 • Highest graded: Unc.

VG-8	F-12	VF-20	EF-40	AU-50	Unc-60	Unc-63	Unc-65
$450	$650	$750	$1,000	$1,425	$1,900	$2,300	$3,700

W-713 • F-469 • Rosecrans-Jordan (1885–1887)
Estimated population: 800 to 950 • Highest graded: Unc.

VG-8	F-12	VF-20	EF-40	AU-50	Unc-60	Unc-63	Unc-65
$450	$650	$750	$1,000	$1,425	$1,900	$2,300	$3,700

W-714 • F-470 • Rosecrans-Hyatt (1887–1889)
Estimated population: 300 to 350 • *Highest graded:* Unc.

VG-8	F-12	VF-20	EF-40	AU-50	Unc-60	Unc-63	Unc-65
$450	$650	$750	$1,000	$1,425	$1,900	$2,300	$3,700

W-715 • F-471 • Rosecrans-Huston (1889–1891)
Estimated population: 700 to 800 • *Highest graded:* Unc.

VG-8	F-12	VF-20	EF-40	AU-50	Unc-60	Unc-63
$450	$650	$750	$1,000	$1,425	$1,900	$2,300

W-716 • F-472 • Rosecrans-Nebeker (1891–1893)
Estimated population: 600 to 700 • *Highest graded:* Unc.

VG-8	F-12	VF-20	EF-40	AU-50	Unc-60	Unc-63	Unc-65
$450	$650	$750	$1,000	$1,425	$1,900	$2,300	$3,700

W-717 • F-473 • Rosecrans-Morgan (1893)
Estimated population: 23 to 26 • *Highest graded:* Unc.

VG-8	F-12	VF-20	EF-40	AU-50	Unc-60	Unc-63
$550	$800	$950	$1,250	$1,800	$2,400	$3,000

W-718 • F-474 • Tillman-Morgan (1893–1897)
Estimated population: 650 to 750 • *Highest graded:* Unc.

VG-8	F-12	VF-20	EF-40	AU-50	Unc-60	Unc-63	Unc-65
$450	$650	$750	$1,000	$1,425	$1,900	$2,300	$3,700

W-719 • F-475 • Tillman-Roberts (1897)
Estimated population: 125 to 140 • *Highest graded:* Unc.

VG-8	F-12	VF-20	EF-40	AU-50	Unc-60	Unc-63	Unc-65
$450	$650	$750	$1,000	$1,425	$1,900	$2,300	$3,700

W-720 • F-476 • Bruce-Roberts (1897–1898)
Estimated population: 60 to 70 • *Highest graded:* Unc.

VG-8	F-12	VF-20	EF-40	AU-50	Unc-60	Unc-63
$450	$650	$750	$1,000	$1,425	$1,900	$2,300

W-721 • F-477 • Lyons-Roberts (1898–1905)
Estimated population: 15 to 18 • *Highest graded:* Unc.

VG-8	F-12	VF-20	EF-40	AU-50	Unc-60	Unc-63	Unc-65
$450	$650	$750	$1,000	$1,425	$1,900	$2,300	$3,700

W-722 • F-477a • Lyons-Treat (1905–1906) • Unknown

W-723 • F-478 • Vernon-Treat (1906–1909)
Recorded population: 7 • *Highest graded:* AU-50.

VG-8	F-12	VF-20	EF-40	AU-50
$450	$650	$750	$1,000	$1,425

Series of 1882, Date Back
(Authorized Issue 1908–1915, Some 1916)

This unexpected issue (illus. on p. 231) was created to reflect a change in the security or backing of the notes authorized by the Aldrich-Vreeland Act of May 30, 1908. Notes were issued starting in that year. Production of 1882 Brown Backs ceased, and new orders were filled by the Date Back type.

In order to make it easier to fund the notes, banks were allowed to deposit good securities and/or government bonds, while earlier only U.S. government bonds had been allowed. All have the inscription on the face, THIS NOTE IS SECURED BY BONDS OF THE UNITED STATES OR OTHER SECURITIES. This was often done by altering face plates of the same design used for earlier series. Although the Act expired on June 30, 1915, marking the end of the official use of this imprint and the related back, some plates continued to be used into 1916. Otherwise, the face motifs were the same as on the Series of 1882 Brown Backs, but no longer with a wide variety of innovative typography. The serial numbers, charter number, two regional letters, and the Treasury seal were now all in blue.

The back was redesigned completely. At the center is a large open space with the dates 1882 and 1908 and an ornament between them. Above, near the border, is the obligation or redemption clause, and below near the border is the counterfeiting clause. At the left is a portrait of Washington, after Gilbert Stuart's painting. At the right is an angular view of the United States Capitol. Gone are the state seals, making plate preparation a much easier task.

As a class, Date Backs are scarce. Systematic acquisition of these is nearly impossible, but representative examples can be added to collections of many different states. Uncirculated notes are available for type due to some clusters, but for many states no such notes have surfaced.

Only three examples are known of the Rosecrans-Morgan signature combination (W-732) and none of Vernon-McClung (W-738). Although federal signatures are not front row center in numismatic interest in National Bank Notes, when a truly rare combination comes to market there is always a lot of attention paid to it. For a combination that is only slightly rarer than others, not much notice is taken.

Banks of Issue and Rarity of Notes

Based upon census information from Don C. Kelly and James M. Kelly (*National Bank Note Census*, Version 4.0) and with some information from other sources, this listing gives each location, the number of banks issuing this series of notes within each, and a commentary.[29]

The survey records 1,614 Series of 1882 Date Back notes, or less than a third of the 6,141 Series of 1882 Brown Back $5 notes listed. Territorial notes from the continental United States number just 8, including 2 from Arizona and 2 from New Mexico, both of which achieved statehood in 1912. The First National Bank of Hawaii at Honolulu has 24 notes on the roster. There are 18 serial number 1 notes listed, anchored by a cluster of Unc notes from the Rocky Mountain silver mining town of Central City, Colorado. Locations with serial number 1 notes are specifically identified; otherwise there are none.

Alabama • 9 banks of issue • 15 notes reported • Only five different banks are represented, including the First National Bank of Dothan (seven) and the Dothan National Bank (five). All are circulated.

Arizona • 1 bank of issue • No notes reported • This is the only issuing state for which this is true.

Arizona Territory • 1 bank of issue • 2 notes reported • Both are from the Prescott National Bank (F, VF).

California • 20 banks of issue • 123 notes reported • Only two are listed as Unc, one from the Western National Bank of San Francisco and one from the First National Bank of Whittier.

Colorado • 9 banks of issue • 12 notes reported • Five circulated notes from the First National Bank of Sterling, three from other banks, and four serial number 1 notes, all Unc, from the First National Bank of Central City.

Connecticut • 8 banks of issue • 7 notes reported • Circulated notes from four banks.

Delaware • 3 banks of issue • 3 notes reported • First National Bank of Frederick (VF) and the Lewes National Bank (two EF).

District of Columbia • 2 banks of issue • 15 notes reported • Two from the Second National Bank and 13 from the Riggs National Bank, the last including four Unc.

Florida • 7 banks of issue • 16 notes reported • Six different banks, all circulated except three Unc notes from the Exchange National Bank of Tampa.

Georgia • 16 banks of issue • 27 notes reported • Nine banks. Two Unc notes, from the Third National Bank of Atlanta and the Cordele National Bank. One serial number 1 note is from the First National Bank of Valdosta (VG).

Hawaii Territory • 2 banks of issue • 24 notes listed • All from the First National Bank of Honolulu at Honolulu, G to AU.

Idaho • 3 banks of issue • 4 notes reported • Circulated notes from three banks.

Illinois • 68 banks of issue • 83 notes reported • Two Unc from the Citizens National Bank of Alton and the Corn Exchange National Bank of Chicago.

Indiana • 36 banks of issue • 41 notes reported • The only Unc note is from the Peoples National Bank of Lawrenceburgh. One serial number 1 note is from the First National Bank of Vincennes (not graded).

Iowa • 54 banks of issue • 62 notes reported • Four Unc notes, including two serial number 1 notes, the First National Bank of Denison and the Citizens National Bank of Des Moines, both Unc.

Kansas • 15 banks of issue • 11 notes reported • Circulated notes from six banks.

Kentucky • 18 banks of issue • 106 notes reported • Anchored by 74 notes from the National Bank of Kentucky of Louisville, mostly Unc. A rare opportunity for "type" notes, as Date Backs of this quality are very elusive.

Louisiana • 7 banks of issue • 14 notes reported • Circulated grades, including nine from the Commercial National Bank of New Orleans.

Maine • 12 banks of issue • 4 notes reported • Circulated grades from the Manufacturers National Bank of Lewiston (three) and the Searsport National Bank.

Maryland • 19 banks of issue • 28 notes reported • Circulated notes from various banks.

Massachusetts • 41 banks of issue • 111 notes reported • Several clusters, including 36 (all but three in circulated grades) from the National Shawmut Bank of Boston and 25 (including 16 Unc) from the First National Bank of Webster, the last a cache of wide importance for anyone seeking a "type" note. Two serial number 1 notes are from Park National Bank of Holyoke (VF) and the First National Bank of Webster (Unc).

Michigan • 18 banks of issue • 44 notes reported • Four Unc notes.

Minnesota • 34 banks of issue • 36 notes reported • Includes 10 Unc notes from the Farmers National Bank of Alexandria, plus some ungraded and possibly high-quality notes from the same institution.

Mississippi • 1 bank of issue • 4 notes reported • Circulated notes from the First National Bank of Commerce of Hattiesburg.

Missouri • 23 banks of issue • 83 notes reported • This generous population, mostly circulated notes, includes clusters from several banks.

Montana • 3 banks of issue • 2 notes reported • Conrad National Bank of Kalispell (VF) and the State National Bank of Miles City (EF).

Nebraska • 17 banks of issue • 15 notes reported • Circulated notes from nine banks. One serial number 1 note is listed from the Custer National Bank of Broken Bow (VG).

New Hampshire • 14 banks of issue • 17 notes reported • Includes three Unc from the First National Bank of Nashua.

New Jersey • 36 banks of issue • 33 notes reported • Various banks, including several clusters. The only Unc note is from the Second National Bank of Red Bank.

New Mexico • 5 banks of issue • 6 notes reported • Five are from the First National Bank of Albuquerque and one is from the First National Bank of Carlsbad, all in circulated grades.

New Mexico Territory • 6 banks of issue • 6 notes reported • Circulated notes from four different banks. One serial number 1 note is from the First National Bank of Alamogordo (G).

New York • 70 banks of issue • 11 notes reported • Various banks, including six Unc notes. One serial number 1 note is recorded from the Citizens National Bank of Albion (Unc).

North Carolina • 11 banks of issue • 38 notes reported • Circulated notes. Just seven different banks are represented. Many notes are not graded.

North Dakota • 5 banks of issue • 5 notes reported • Circulated notes from the First National Bank of Fargo.

Ohio • 58 banks of issue • 112 notes reported • Circulated notes from various banks. One is Unc, from the Clinton County National Bank of Wilmington.

Oklahoma • 31 banks of issue • 31 notes reported • Circulated notes from various banks, including clusters.

Oregon • 3 banks of issue • 2 notes reported • First National Bank of Ontario (VG) and the United States National Bank of Portland (F–VF).

Pennsylvania • 124 banks of issue • 141 notes reported • Two Unc notes, First National Bank of New Bethlehem and the First National Bank of New Bloomfield. Three serial number

1 notes are known, United States National Bank of Johnstown (AU) and the First National Bank of Bloomfield (AU, Unc).

Rhode Island • 2 banks of issue • 11 notes reported • One circulated note from the Union National Bank of Newport and 10 from the United National Bank of Providence.

South Carolina • 8 banks of issue • 10 notes reported • Circulated notes from three banks.

South Dakota • 5 banks of issue • 1 note reported • First National Bank of Lead, serial 571, G.

Tennessee • 13 banks of issue • 25 notes reported • Eight Unc notes, all from the First National Bank of Jackson.

Texas • 40 banks of issue • 59 notes reported • Mostly circulated notes in clusters. Two are Unc, from the State National Bank of Austin and City National Bank of Dallas.

Utah • 7 banks of issue • 11 notes reported • Circulated notes from five banks.

Vermont • 9 banks of issue • 10 notes reported • Circulated notes from six banks.

Virginia • 18 banks of issue • 14 notes reported • Circulated notes from eight banks.

Washington • 4 banks of issue • 5 notes reported • Circulated notes from the Seattle National Bank (one) and the First National Bank of Walla Walla (four).

West Virginia • 14 banks of issue • 17 notes reported • Circulated notes from seven different banks, including nine from the National Exchange Bank of Wheeling.

Wisconsin • 25 banks of issue • 56 notes reported • Mostly circulated notes from various banks, some in clusters. Three are Unc. One serial number 1 note is listed from the National Bank of Manitowoc (Unc).

Wyoming • 1 bank of issue • 1 note reported • Stock Growers National Bank of Cheyenne, serial 6515, F–VF.

Generic prices for a typical note from a state from which notes range from plentiful to just slightly scarce:

VG-8	F-12	VF-20	EF-40	AU-50	Unc-60	Unc-63	Unc-65
$450	$600	$700	$900	$1,300	$1,800	$2,100	$3,500

W-730 • F-532 • Rosecrans-Huston (1889–1891)
Estimated population: 48 to 55 • *Highest graded:* Unc.

VG-8	F-12	VF-20	EF-40	AU-50	Unc-60	Unc-63
$450	$600	$700	$900	$1,300	$1,800	$2,100

SERIES OF 1882, DATE BACK

$5 National Bank Note, Series of 1882, Date Back, Fourth National Bank of Boston (W-733), the type used from W-730 to W-739 as well as W-745 to W-752. Blue Treasury seal. The 2277 overprint is the charter number; N represents North, the area in which the bank was located.

Back of W-733, the type used from W-730 to W-739, the Date Back.

W-731 • F-533 • Rosecrans-Nebeker (1891–1893)
Estimated population: 120 to 130 • *Highest graded:* Unc.

VG-8	F-12	VF-20	EF-40	AU-50	Unc-60	Unc-63
$450	$600	$700	$900	$1,300	$1,800	$2,100

W-732 • F-533a • Rosecrans-Morgan (1893)
Recorded population: 3 • *Highest graded:* EF-40.

VG-8	F-12	VF-20	EF-40
$450	$600	$700	$900

W-733 • F-534 • Tillman-Morgan (1893–1897)
Estimated population: 325 to 400 • *Highest graded:* Unc.

VG-8	F-12	VF-20	EF-40	AU-50	Unc-60	Unc-63	Unc-65
$450	$600	$700	$900	$1,300	$1,800	$2,100	$3,500

W-734 • F-535 • Tillman-Roberts (1897)
Estimated population: 36 to 42 • *Highest graded:* AU-50.

VG-8	F-12	VF-20	EF-40	AU-50
$450	$600	$700	$900	$1,300

W-735 • F-536 • Bruce-Roberts (1897–1898)
Estimated population: 28 to 32 • *Highest graded:* Unc.

VG-8	F-12	VF-20	EF-40	AU-50	Unc-60	Unc-63
$450	$600	$700	$900	$1,300	$1,800	$2,100

W-736 • F-537 • Lyons-Roberts (1898–1905)
Estimated population: 1,100 to 1,250 • *Highest graded:* Unc.

VG-8	F-12	VF-20	EF-40	AU-50	Unc-60	Unc-63	Unc-65
$450	$600	$700	$900	$1,300	$1,800	$2,100	$3,500

W-737 • F-538 • Vernon-Treat (1906–1909)
Estimated population: 32 to 36 • *Highest graded:* EF-40.

VG-8	F-12	VF-20	EF-40
$450	$600	$700	$900

W-738 • F-538a • Vernon-McClung (1909–1911) • Unknown

W-739 • F-538b • Napier-McClung (1911–1912)
Recorded population: 7 • *Highest graded:* EF-40.

VG-8	F-12	VF-20	EF-40
$1,000	$2,000	$2,600	$3,300

Series of 1882, Value Back
(Authorized Issue 1915+)

When the Aldrich-Vreeland act expired on June 20, 1915, the BEP created the Value Back, spelling out the denomination, to replace the Date Back type. Henceforth the security of the notes reverted to bonds only, as it had been before the implementation of the Aldrich-Vreeland Act of May 30, 1908.

> **Plate Style a:** Some old face plates remained in use from the earlier series, these with the inscription on the face, THIS NOTE IS SECURED BY BONDS OF THE UNITED STATES OR OTHER SECURITIES. Notes from this plate were made in large quantities and can be called *mules.*

> **Plate Style b:** A "new" plate style was created, a copy of that used for all 1882 Brown Backs, with the security stated, SECURED BY UNITED STATES BONDS DEPOSITED WITH THE TREASURER OF THE UNITED STATES. This is the correct or proper plate intended for use on Value Back notes.

Otherwise the face was similar to that used for the Series of 1882 Date Back, with the serial numbers, charter number, two regional letters, and the Treasury seal all in blue. The back continued the same vignettes as the preceding type, but now with FIVE DOLLARS in large letters at the center.

Except for three hoards from Illinois, Pennsylvania, and Wisconsin, Unc notes are very rare. At the time they were issued these attracted hardly any notice from numismatists. Accordingly, the survival of any note in any grade is largely a matter of chance. New discoveries are always being made, though. In the offing are possibilities for notes to be found from states known to have issued notes, but for which none have been reported or for which the population is very small (see below). The Lyons-Treat signature combination (W-749) is unknown, and W-752 notes are rare. Although Plate Styles a and b are well described in the specialized texts by Gene Hessler, Carlson Chambliss, Peter Huntoon, and Don C. Kelly, to this point they have scarcely been recognized in auction catalogs or other offerings.

Banks of Issue and Rarity of Notes
Based upon census information from Don C. Kelly and James M. Kelly (*National Bank Note Census*, Version 4.0) and with some information from other sources, this listing gives each location, the number of banks issuing this series of notes within each, and a commentary.[30]

The Kelly survey records 880 Value Back notes, or about half the number traced for Date Back notes (1,614) and about one-seventh of the 6,141 Brown Backs surveyed. Territorial notes, 34 in number, are all from the same bank in Hawaii. The single serial number 1 note recorded by the Kelly team is from the Lincoln National Bank of Cincinnati.

Alabama • 5 banks of issue • 9 notes reported • Circulated grades, eight from the Dothan National Bank and one from the First National Bank of Greensboro.

California • 9 banks of issue • 57 notes reported • Circulated notes from just five banks, including quantities from the First National Bank of Los Angeles, the Citizens National Bank of Los Angeles, and the Wells Fargo Nevada National Bank of San Francisco.

Colorado • 2 banks of issue • 4 notes reported • Circulated notes from the Fort Collins National Bank (one) and the First National Bank of Sterling (three).

Connecticut • 5 banks of issue • 11 notes reported • Circulated notes from five banks.

Delaware • 2 banks of issue • No notes reported • One of just a few such states not recorded.

District of Columbia • 1 bank of issue • 4 notes reported • Circulated notes from the Riggs National Bank.

SERIES OF 1882, VALUE BACK

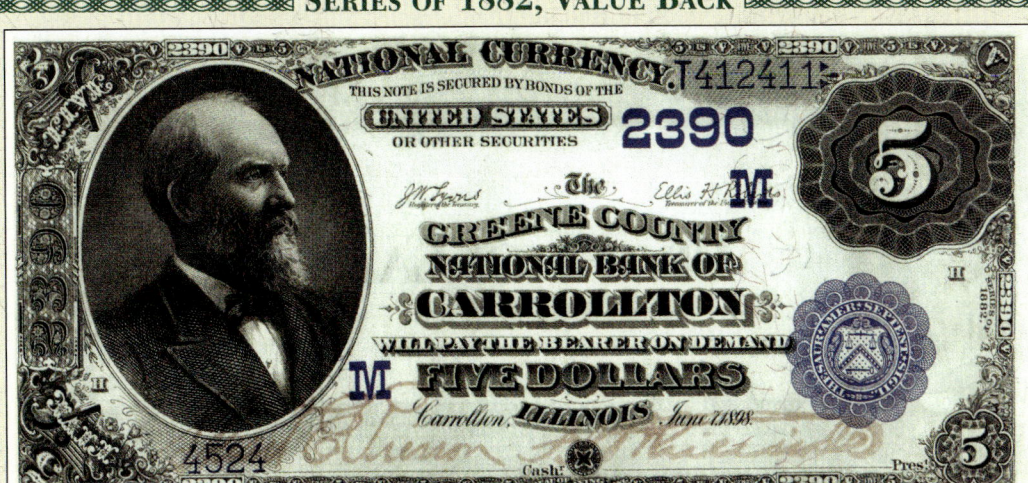

$5 National Bank Note, Series of 1882, Value Back (W-748), a scarce type. Greene County National Bank of Carrollton, Illinois, from a small hoard. The type was used from W-745 to W-752, as well as for the earlier W-730 to W-739. Blue Treasury seal. The 2390 overprint is the bank's charter number, and M represents Midwest, the area in which the bank was located. Rubber-stamped signatures of bank officers are somewhat faded.

The backing of the typical W-748 note is in bonds OR OTHER SECURITIES as seen here on the Greene County National Bank Note.

This $5 of the First National Bank of Los Angeles is backed only in bonds, the typical security used on Series of 1882 *Brown Back* notes and, here, on a Value Back.

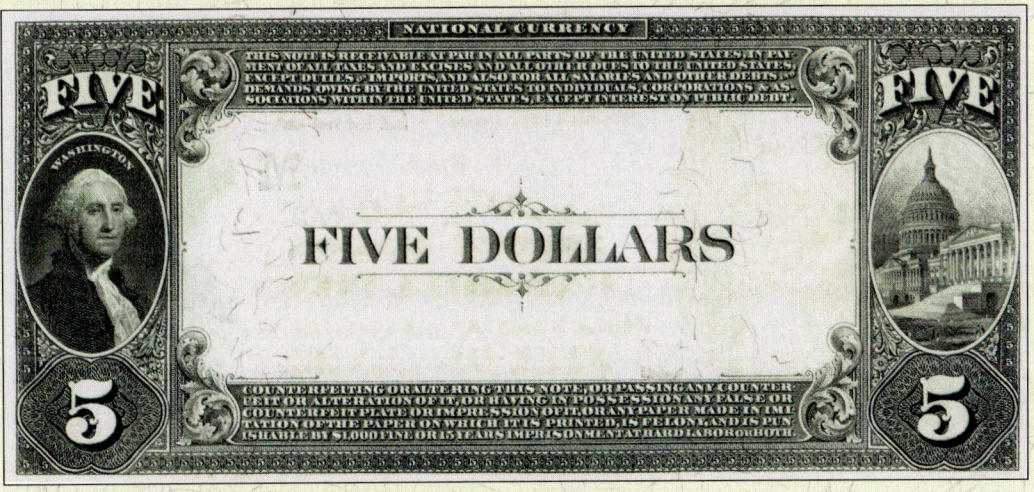

Back of W-748, the type used from W-745 to W-752, the Value Back.

Florida • 3 banks of issue • 11 notes reported • These are from three different banks, with eight—including one Unc— from the American National Bank of Pensacola.

Georgia • 3 banks of issue • 10 notes reported • Circulated notes from the Lowry National Bank of Atlanta.

Hawaii Territory • 1 bank of issue • 35 notes reported • All, including one Unc, are from the First National Bank of Hawaii at Honolulu. These are the only territorial notes of this type, as none were issued in Alaska.

Idaho • 2 banks of issue • 1 note reported • First National Bank of Saint Anthony (F).

Illinois • 23 banks of issue • 80 notes reported • Of the reported notes, 19 (all but three Unc) are from the Greene County National Bank of Carrollton—the mother lode for type notes (but also see Wisconsin).

Indiana • 13 banks of issue • 22 notes reported • Various banks. The two Unc are from the Citizens National Bank of Bedford and the People's National Bank of Lawrenceburgh.

Iowa • 21 banks of issue • 68 notes reported • Circulated notes mostly in clusters. Three Unc.

Kansas • 5 banks of issue • 10 notes reported • Circulated notes from six banks.

Kentucky • 6 banks of issue • 30 notes reported • Dominated by 21 notes from the National Bank of Kentucky of Louisville, including an Unc note.

Maine • 2 banks of issue • 2 notes reported • Searsport National Bank (G, not graded)

Maryland • 9 banks of issue • 16 notes reported • Circulated notes from just four banks.

Massachusetts • 7 banks of issue • 9 notes reported • From three banks. The only Unc is from the Hudson National Bank. A sparse count from a state which typically produced many notes.

Michigan • 6 banks of issue • 28 notes reported • Circulated notes from just six banks.

Minnesota • 19 banks of issue • 34 notes reported • From 12 banks. The only Unc is from the First National Bank of Redwood Falls.

Mississippi • 1 bank of issue • No notes reported • One of just a few such states not recorded.

Missouri • 4 banks of issue • 2 notes reported • First National Bank of Monett (F) and the Peoples National Bank of Warrensburg (F).

Nebraska • 4 banks of issue • 7 notes reported • High-grade circulated notes from three banks.

New Hampshire • 6 banks of issue • 4 notes reported • Circulated notes from the Mechanicks National Bank of Concord (two) and the Lancaster National Bank (two).

New Jersey • 14 banks of issue • 23 notes reported • Circulated notes from 11 banks.

New Mexico • 4 banks of issue • 11 notes reported • Lower-grade circulated notes from three different banks, including eight from the First National Bank of Albuquerque.

New York • 48 banks of issue • 61 notes reported • Mostly from different banks. The only Unc is from the National Bank of Ogdensburg.

North Carolina • 5 banks of issue • 7 notes reported • Circulated notes from the National Bank of Fayetteville (five) and the Murchison National Bank of Wilmington (two).

North Dakota • 3 banks of issue • 2 notes reported • First National Bank of Cooperstown (F, not graded)

Ohio • 27 banks of issue • 78 notes reported • Mostly circulated notes in clusters, but a handful of Unc examples is notable. One number 1 note is from the Lincoln National Bank of Cincinnati (Unc). This is the only such Value Back note recorded in the Kelly census!

Oklahoma • 21 banks of issue • 23 notes reported • These come from 11 banks. The only Unc is from the Shawnee National Bank.

Oregon • 1 bank of issue • No notes reported • One of just a few such states not recorded.

Pennsylvania • 46 banks of issue • 83 notes reported • Some clusters of banks. Unc notes include eight from the First National Bank of New Bloomfield.

South Carolina • 2 banks of issue • No notes reported • One of just a few such states not recorded.

South Dakota • 3 banks of issue • 1 note reported • First National Bank of Arlington (VG).

Tennessee • 2 banks of issue • 1 note reported • First National Bank of Dyersburg (VG).

Texas • 18 banks of issue • 50 notes reported • Mostly circulated notes and mostly in clusters, but several Unc notes are listed.

Utah • 3 banks of issue • 1 note reported • First National Bank of Price (VF).

Vermont • 3 banks of issue • 1 note reported • Bennington County National Bank of Bennington (VF).

Virginia • 9 banks of issue • 24 notes reported • Circulated notes from six banks.

Washington • 2 banks of issue • 1 note reported • First National Bank of Walla (VG).

West Virginia • 6 banks of issue • 13 notes reported • From three banks. The two Unc are from the First National Bank of New Martinsville and the National Exchange Bank of Wheeling.

Wisconsin • 11 banks of issue • 44 notes reported • Dominated by 26 from the Marine National Bank of Milwaukee, including 13 Unc.

Wyoming • 1 bank of issue • 1 note reported • Stock Growers National Bank of Cheyenne (VF–EF).

Generic prices for a typical note from a state from which notes range from plentiful to just slightly scarce:

VG-8	F-12	VF-20	EF-40	AU-50	Unc-60	Unc-63	Unc-65
$550	$675	$800	$1,050	$1,600	$2,200	$2,600	$3,750

W-745 • F-573 • Tillman-Morgan (1893–1897)
Estimated population: 10 to 12 • Highest graded: VF-30.

VG-8	F-12	VF-20
$550	$675	$800

W-746 • F-573a • Tillman-Roberts (1897)
Recorded population: 6 • Highest graded: EF-40.

VG-8	F-12	VF-20	EF-40
$550	$675	$800	$1,050

W-747 • F-574a • Bruce-Roberts (1897–1898)
Estimated population: 8 or 9 • Highest graded: Unc.

VG-8	F-12	VF-20	EF-40	AU-50	Unc-60	Unc-63
$550	$675	$800	$1,050	$1,600	$2,200	$2,600

W-748 • F-574 • Lyons-Roberts (1898–1905)
Estimated population: 800 to 900 • Highest graded: Unc.

VG-8	F-12	VF-20	EF-40	AU-50	Unc-60	Unc-63	Unc-65
$550	$675	$800	$1,050	$1,600	$2,200	$2,600	$3,750

W-749 • F-574b • Lyons-Treat (1905–1906) • Unknown

W-750 • F-575 • Vernon-Treat (1906–1909)
Estimated population: 28 to 32 • Highest graded: VF-30.

VG-8	F-12	VF-20
$550	$675	$800

W-751 • F-575a • Napier-McClung (1911–1912)

Estimated population: 11 to 13 • *Highest graded:* AU-50.

VG-8	F-12	VF-20	EF-40	AU-50
$550	$675	$800	$1,050	$1,600

W-752 • F-575b • Teehee-Burke (1915–1919)

Recorded population: 6 • *Highest graded:* Unc • *Selected information:* Heritage (9/2007), 317-T647929/C, German NB of Cincinnati, OH, VG–F, $1,006. Heritage (4/2008), 2372-T651984/B, German NB of Cincinnati, OH, EF, $1,955.

Series of 1902, Red Seal
(Authorized Issue From 1902 to 1908)

The Act of April 12, 1902, provided that established banks of good reputation could extend their charters for another 40 years and new banks could gain a 60-year charter. New designs were prepared, known today as 1902 Red Seal notes (illus. on p. 237), though older series were still being issued. All were secured by federal government bonds deposited with the Treasurer of the United States. During the life span of the 1902 Red Seal notes, certain banks continued to receive Series of 1882 Brown Back notes, depending on the date of their charter extension or founding.

Faces and backs were redesigned for the new Series of 1902 notes. These continued to be issued until the Aldrich-Vreeland Act of May 30, 1908, went into effect, after which time the Red Seal notes were abruptly replaced by the 1902 to 1908 Date Backs, which were guaranteed in bonds "and other securities." Accordingly, this series was very short-lived.

The Red Seal notes are distinguished by the Treasury seal, two charter numbers, and two regional letters printed in bright red, with the serial numbers in blue. The face has the portrait of president Benjamin Harrison (in office 1889–1893, between the two non-consecutive terms of Grover Cleveland). The back depicts *The Landing of the Pilgrims*, the same motif used on $1 Original Series National Bank Notes. The same design was also used for the Series of 1902 Date Back (but with 1902 and 1908 added) and Plain Back issues. Both sides were engraved by G.F.C. Smillie.

Many of these were issued by banks with capital as low as $25,000, permitted under federal rules in the early 20th century. Some of these were what Don C. Kelly calls "mom and pop" banks, slimly financed, with just $25,000 capital and permitted to issue as little as $6,250 face value in notes, but carefully tended by their owners. Serial number 1 notes are fairly plentiful in this series, as many were saved as souvenirs by bank officials.

This is one of the most popular of all National Bank Note types. The market demand is never-ending, for rare states and banks as well as common ones.

Banks of Issue and Rarity of Notes

Based upon census information from Don C. Kelly and James M. Kelly (*National Bank Note Census*, Version 4.0) and with some information from other sources, this listing gives each location, the number of banks issuing this series of notes within each, and a commentary.[31]

The Kelly survey records 1,761 of this series, a large enough number to satisfy a wide audience of numismatists, but fewer Red Seal notes than are recorded for the $10 denomination. Serial number 1 notes abound, with 217 accounted for. Many were kept as souvenirs from low-capital startups. These are specifically listed below. Territorial notes number 43, from several different places—most prominently Alaska. Unc notes are easily enough found, but always attract attention when offered at auction, due to the appeal of this series.

Alabama • 22 banks of issue • 20 notes reported • Including 12 from the First National Bank of Oxford, four of which are Unc. The two serial number 1 notes are from the First National Bank of Alexander City (not graded) and the First National Bank of Oxford (Unc, included in preceding count).

Alaska Territory • 1 bank of issue • 33 notes listed • All from the First National Bank of Fairbanks, mostly Unc, including two serial number 1 notes (AU, Unc). Alaska was a district from 1884 until it became a territory on August 24, 1912, which it remained until statehood in 1959. *All* large-size Alaska notes in all series have the "district" address. Regardless, numismatists call all "territorials."

Arizona Territory • 1 bank of issue • No notes reported • An unusual situation.

Arkansas • 22 banks of issue • 6 notes reported • Circulated notes from five banks. One serial number 1 note is recorded, from the American National Bank of Fort Smith.

California • 62 banks of issue • 74 notes reported • Various banks. The only Unc is from the American National Bank of Los Angeles. The census lists 14 serial number 1 notes, all circulated.

Colorado • 27 banks of issue • 11 notes reported • Various banks. The only Unc is from the First National Bank of Denver. Two serial number 1 notes are from the First National Bank of Ault and the First National Bank of Brush, neither graded.

Connecticut • 48 banks of issue • 74 notes reported • Mostly circulated, but with over 20 Unc. Seven serial number 1 notes are known, including two Unc.

Delaware • 5 banks of issue • 3 notes reported • Newcastle County National Bank of Odessa (F–VF, VF) and the National Bank of Wilmington & Brandywine (F). A scarce state.

District of Columbia • 4 banks of issue • 14 notes reported • Circulated grades, including nine from the National Metropolitan Bank.

Florida • 21 banks of issue • 7 notes reported • Circulated from six banks. A scarce state relative to the strong demand.

Georgia • 27 banks of issue • 11 notes reported • Circulated grades. The single serial number 1 note is from the Atkins National Bank of Maysville (AU).

Hawaii Territory • 1 bank of issue • No notes reported • What a find a note would be!

Idaho • 15 banks of issue • 8 notes reported • Circulated notes from four banks. Three serial number 1 notes are known, all AU from the First National Bank of Rexburg.

Illinois • 72 banks of issue • 76 notes reported • Various banks. Five Unc. Five serial number 1 notes are known, including three of the Unc notes included in the preceding count.

Indian Territory • 15 banks of issue • 7 notes reported • Circulated from six banks. One serial number 1 note is known from the First National Bank of Hartshorne (F).

Indiana • 65 banks of issue • 49 notes reported • Various banks. The census lists 10 Unc. Six serial number 1 notes are known, including three Unc.

Iowa • 28 banks of issue • 18 notes reported • Four Unc. Four serial number 1 notes are known, including two Unc.

Kansas • 35 banks of issue • 19 notes reported • Circulated grades. Two number 1 notes are from the National State Bank of Stockton (VF–EF) and the First National Bank of Waverly (EF).

Kentucky • 24 banks of issue • 25 notes reported • Circulated grades from various banks, including seven from the First National Bank of Louisa. Eight serial number 1 notes are known, all in circulated grades.

Louisiana • 10 banks of issue • 15 notes reported • Circulated grades from five different banks, including seven from the Whitney-Central National Bank of New Orleans.

Maine • 31 banks of issue • 26 notes reported • Circulated grades from various banks.

Maryland • 34 banks of issue • 32 notes reported • The only Unc is from the First National Bank of Hyattsville. One serial number 1 note is from the First National Bank of Union Bridge (F).

Massachusetts • 127 banks of issue • 100 notes reported • A diversity of banks. Many Unc notes. The census lists 11 serial number 1 notes, mostly Unc.

Michigan • 24 banks of issue • 35 notes reported • Six Unc. One serial number 1 note is from the First National Bank of Lewistown (VG).

Minnesota • 50 banks of issue • 23 notes reported • Two Unc are from the First National Bank of Chisholm. Three serial number 1 notes are known, all circulated.

Mississippi • 14 banks of issue • 8 notes reported • Circulated notes from five banks.

Missouri • 34 banks of issue • 54 notes reported • Circulated notes from various banks, including several clusters. Six serial number 1 notes are known, in circulated grades.

Montana • 8 banks of issue • 6 notes reported • Circulated grades from four banks. One serial number 1 note is from the First National Bank of Lewistown (VG).

Nebraska • 28 banks of issue • 20 notes reported • Eight banks. Seven Unc including the following. Eight serial number 1 notes are known, including four Unc from the First National Bank of York.

Nevada • 6 banks of issue • 5 notes reported • Circulated notes from three banks.

New Hampshire • 29 banks of issue • 18 notes reported • Circulated notes from 12 banks. Four serial number 1 notes are from the Laconia National Bank, each EF.

New Jersey • 59 banks of issue • 73 notes reported • Includes 17 Unc from the Cumberland National Bank of Bridgeton. The census lists 13 serial number 1 notes, including some Unc.

New Mexico Territory • 4 banks of issue • No notes reported.

New York • 177 banks of issue • 352 notes reported • Various banks. Many Unc notes. The census lists 38 serial number 1 notes, many of which are Unc.

North Carolina • 22 banks of issue • 3 notes reported • National Bank of Greenville (not graded), Commercial National Bank of Raleigh (VG), and a serial number 1 note from the American National Bank of Asheville (F–VF).

North Dakota • 17 banks of issue • 3 notes reported • First National Bank of Finley (VG) plus two serial number 1 notes from the Merchant's National Bank of Dickinson and the Merchants National Bank of Fargo, each AU.

Ohio • 77 banks of issue • 114 notes reported • Seven Unc notes. The census lists 11 serial number 1 notes, including one Unc from the Third National Bank of Dayton.

Oklahoma • 7 banks of issue • 1 note reported • This is a serial number 1 note from the Farmers National Bank of Lexington (F).

Oklahoma Territory • 13 banks of issue • 3 notes reported • Enid National Bank (both VG) and the First National Bank of Hollis (VG). No serial number 1 notes known.

Oregon • 11 banks of issue • 18 notes reported • Circulated except for eight serial number 1 notes, four each from the Citizens National Bank of Baker City and the First National Bank of Burns, all Unc. An unusual lineup.

Pennsylvania • 210 banks of issue • 279 notes reported • Mostly circulated, but with 78 mostly Unc notes from the Mellon National Bank of Pittsburgh, the largest cache of any 1902 Red Seal $5 note. The census lists 33 serial number 1 notes.

Rhode Island • 16 banks of issue • 17 notes reported • The only Unc is from the Atlantic National Bank of Providence.

South Carolina • 9 banks of issue • 3 notes reported • Circulated grades from the Planters National Bank of Bennettsville, Peoples National Bank of Charleston, and Palmetto National Bank of Columbia.

South Dakota • 8 banks of issue • 4 notes reported • Circulated notes from three banks. One serial number 1 note is from the First National Bank of Springfield (AU).

Tennessee • 23 banks of issue • 9 notes reported • Circulated notes from six banks.

Texas • 56 banks of issue • 17 notes reported • Circulated notes from 12 banks. Two serial number 1 notes are known, from the Caldwell National Bank (VF) and the First National Bank of Whitney (EF).

SERIES OF 1902, RED SEAL

$5 National Bank Note, Series of 1902, Red Seal, First National Bank of Fairbanks, Alaska Territory (DISTRICT imprinted on notes). W-755, the same style used on W-755 to W-757. To the left is a portrait of president Benjamin Harrison. The red Treasury seal, charter numbers, and regional letters (P for Pacific) are vivid. Although this particular note is not a rarity, it is highly desired for its territorial imprint.

Back of the $5 National Bank Note, Series of 1902, Red Seal (W-755), the style used on W-755 to W-757 and also W-760 to W-768.

Utah • 2 banks of issue • No notes reported.

Vermont • 23 banks of issue • 15 notes reported • Three Unc notes. One serial number 1 note is from the First National Bank of North Bennington.

Virginia • 31 banks of issue • 19 notes listed.

Washington • 12 banks of issue • 10 notes reported • Two Unc, from the Peoples National Bank of Abington and the First National Bank of Richmond. Two serial number 1 notes are known, First National Bank of Kelso (AU) and the Pioneer National Bank of Ritzville (AU).

West Virginia • 23 banks of issue • 15 notes reported • Circulated notes from various banks. One serial number 1 note is from the West Virginia National Bank of Huntington (VF).

Wisconsin • 26 banks of issue • 92 notes reported • Three Unc notes from the Germania National Bank of Milwaukee and a like number from the Merchants National Bank of Watertown. Six serial number 1 notes are known, including three Unc.

Wyoming • 1 bank of issue • 1 note reported • First National Bank of Meeteetse, serial 339, VG.

Generic prices for a typical note from a state from which notes range from plentiful to just slightly scarce:

VG-8	F-12	VF-20	EF-40	AU-50	Unc-60	Unc-63	Unc-65
$575	$675	$750	$1,000	$1,400	$1,850	$2,100	$2,600

W-755 • F-587 • Lyons-Roberts (1898–1905)
Estimated population: 1,400 to 1,550 • *Highest graded:* Unc.

VG-8	F-12	VF-20	EF-40	AU-50	Unc-60	Unc-63	Unc-65
$575	$675	$750	$1,000	$1,400	$1,850	$2,100	$2,600

W-756 • F-588 • Lyons-Treat (1905–1906)
Estimated population: 155 to 165 • *Highest graded:* Unc.

VG-8	F-12	VF-20	EF-40	AU-50	Unc-60	Unc-63	Unc-65
$575	$675	$750	$1,000	$1,400	$1,850	$2,100	$2,600

W-757 • F-589 • Vernon-Treat (1906–1909)
Estimated population: 185 to 205 • *Highest graded:* Unc.

VG-8	F-12	VF-20	EF-40	AU-50	Unc-60	Unc-63
$575	$675	$750	$1,000	$1,400	$1,850	$2,100

Series of 1902, Blue Seal, Date Back
(Authorized Issue 1908–1915, Some 1916)

Parallel to the situation for Series of 1882 Date Back notes, the unexpected 1902 Blue Seal, Date Back type was created to reflect a change in the security or backing of the notes authorized by the Aldrich-Vreeland Act of May 30, 1908. Notes of the new type were issued beginning in that year. Production of 1902 Red Seals ceased, and new orders were filled by the Date Back type.

In order to make it easier to fund the notes, banks were allowed to deposit good securities and/or government bonds, while earlier only U.S. government bonds had been allowed. All have the inscription in two lines on the face below the top left border, SECURED BY UNITED STATES BONDS OR OTHER SECURITIES. This was often done by altering face plates of the same design used for the Series of 1902 Red Seal notes. Although the Act expired on June 30, 1915, marking the end of the official use of this imprint and the related back, some plates were continued in use into 1916. Otherwise, the face motifs are the same as on the Series of 1902 Red Seal notes, but now with the serial numbers, two charter numbers, two regional letters, and the Treasury seal in blue. The back is the same as used for the 1902 Red Seals, except that the date is printed at the top of the field, 1902 to the left of center and 1908 to the right.

Prices are for states from which a larger number of notes survive. Although the 1902 Blue Seal, Date Back notes are scarce as a class, not much attention has been paid to them in this regard. Many are priced for little more than the much more plentiful 1902 Blue Seal, Plain Backs. High-grade notes are scarcer. The Teehee-Burke signature combination (W-768) is unique.

Banks of Issue and Rarity of Notes

Based upon census information from Don C. Kelly and James M. Kelly (*National Bank Note Census*, Version 4.0) and with some information from other sources, this listing gives each location, the number of banks issuing this series of notes within each, and a commentary.[32]

The Kelly survey records 3,675 notes, or about twice as many as the 1,761 Red Seals listed. Serial number 1 notes are more elusive, however, with only 110 for this type, as compared to 217 for the Red Seals. These are specifically listed below. As a class, Unc notes are scarce, if not rare, especially regarding certain states, towns, or banks. The seemingly inevitable clusters are found here and there, affording an easy opportunity to acquire a type example.

Alabama • 40 banks of issue • 39 notes reported • Circulated notes from various banks, including several clusters. Four serial number 1 notes are from three banks.

Alaska Territory • 1 bank of issue • 1 note reported • First National Bank of Fairbanks (VG), a trophy note par excellence! Alaska was a district from 1884 until it became a territory on August 24, 1912, which it remained until statehood in 1959. *All* large-size Alaska notes in all series have the "district" address. Regardless, numismatists call all "territorials."

Arizona • 3 banks of issue • 1 note reported • Prescott National Bank (G–VG). A classic.

Arizona Territory • 2 banks of issue • No notes reported.

Arkansas • 35 banks of issue • 22 notes reported • Circulated notes from various banks. Two serial number 1 notes are known, both from the National Bank of Commerce of Paragould (VF, EF).

California • 156 banks of issue • 255 notes reported • Many banks. Mostly circulated grades with a few exceptions. Six serial number 1 notes are known, including one Unc from the United States National Bank of San Diego.

Colorado • 43 banks of issue • 37 notes reported • Two Unc, from the First National Bank of Denver and the Denver National Bank. One serial number 1 note is from the First National Bank of Gill (VF).

Connecticut • 53 banks of issue • 106 notes reported • Mostly circulated, with a few exceptions.

Delaware • 8 banks of issue • 8 notes reported • Circulated notes from five banks.

District of Columbia • 6 banks of issue • 16 notes reported • Circulated notes from six banks.

Florida • 35 banks of issue • 33 notes reported • Circulated grades from various banks including several clusters. Two serial number 1 notes are known, both from the Atlantic National Bank of Jacksonville (both VF).

Georgia • 47 banks of issue • 42 notes reported • Circulated grades from various banks including clusters. One serial number 1 note is from the Cohen National Bank of Sandersville (F).

Hawaii Territory • 1 bank of issue • 1 note reported • Baldwin National Bank of Kahului, serial 781, VG–F. A trophy note to be sure!

Idaho • 28 banks of issue • 10 notes reported • Circulated notes from seven banks. One serial number 1 note is from the First National Bank of Driggs (AU).

Illinois • 132 banks of issue • 209 notes reported • Includes several Unc. Six serial number 1 notes are from five banks.

Indiana • 105 banks of issue • 105 notes reported • Several Unc. One serial number 1 notes are known, including the three Unc from the Peoples State National Bank of Anderson and one from the First National Bank of Brazil.

Iowa • 57 banks of issue • 72 notes reported • Mostly circulated notes, four Unc. Five serial number 1 notes are from four banks, including one Unc from the First National Bank of Woodbine.

Kansas • 51 banks of issue • 50 notes reported • Various banks. Mostly circulated grades. Seven serial number 1 notes are known, including Unc notes from the Peoples National Bank of Kansas City and the Fourth National Bank of Wichita.

Kentucky • 45 banks of issue • 60 notes reported • Circulated notes from various banks.

Louisiana • 14 banks of issue • 28 notes reported • Two Unc, from the Whitney-Central National Bank of New Orleans and the Hibernia National Bank of New Orleans.

SERIES OF 1902, BLUE SEAL, DATE BACK

$5 National Bank Note, Series of 1902, Blue Seal, Date Back (W-760), style used on W-760 to W-768. National Bank of Vergennes, Vermont. Blue Treasury seal, charter numbers, and regional letters (N for North).

Back of the $5 National Bank Note, Series of 1902, Blue Seal, Date Back (W-760), as used on W-760 to W-768.

Maine • 41 banks of issue • 37 notes reported • Circulated notes from various banks. One serial number 1 note is from the First National Bank of Portland (F).

Maryland • 47 banks of issue • 98 notes reported • Unc notes comprise four from the Western National Bank of Baltimore and nine from the National Bank of Baltimore.

Massachusetts • 143 banks of issue • 155 notes reported • Mostly circulated, with scattered exceptions. Many different banks, but a few clusters. Seven serial number 1 notes are known, including Unc notes from the Safety Fund National Bank of Fitchburg and the First National Bank of Haverhill.

Michigan • 46 banks of issue • 80 notes reported • Mostly circulated with scattered exceptions. Three serial number 1 notes are known, including one Unc from the Hastings National Bank.

Minnesota • 77 banks of issue • 108 notes reported • Fewer than 10 Unc. Two serial number 1 notes are from the First National Bank of Deerwood (VG) and the First National Bank of Starbuck (EF–AU).

Mississippi • 24 banks of issue • 19 notes reported • Circulated notes from mostly different banks.

Missouri • 58 banks of issue • 235 notes reported • Strong showing, but with many clusters. Scattered Unc. Two serial number 1 notes are from the Southwest National Bank of Kansas City (AU) and the Gate City National Bank of Kansas City (VF).

Montana • 17 banks of issue • 19 notes reported • Circulated notes from mostly different banks.

Nebraska • 52 banks of issue • 73 notes reported • Mostly circulated notes with scattered Unc. Two serial number 1 notes are known, Stock Yards National Bank of South Omaha (Unc) and the Tilden National Bank (F).

Nevada • 7 banks of issue • 9 notes reported • Circulated notes from three banks.

New Hampshire • 33 banks of issue • 46 notes reported • Six Unc from as many banks. Two serial number 1 notes are from the Laconia National Bank (VF, VF–EF).

New Jersey • 108 banks of issue • 101 notes reported • Six Unc notes are from the Cumberland National Bank of Bridgeton. Seven serial number 1 notes are from six banks.

New Mexico • 4 banks of issue • 2 notes reported • First National Bank of Raton (F) and the First National Bank of Santa Fe (F).

New Mexico Territory • 4 banks of issue • 4 notes reported • Circulated notes from three banks.

New York • 234 banks of issue • 466 notes reported • Mostly circulated notes, some clusters, scattered Unc plus eight from the First National Bank of Yonkers. The census lists 14 serial number 1 notes, including three Unc.

North Carolina • 48 banks of issue • 35 notes reported • Circulated notes from various banks. One serial number 1 note is from the First National Bank of Gastonia (VF).

North Dakota • 29 banks of issue • 7 notes reported • Circulated notes from six banks.

Ohio • 110 banks of issue • 203 notes reported • Scattered Unc plus eight from the First National Bank of Cincinnati. Three serial number 1 notes are from three banks.

Oklahoma • 50 banks of issue • 28 notes reported • Three Unc notes from the Oklahoma Stock Yards Bank of Oklahoma City. Two serial number 1 notes are from the Farmers and Merchants National Bank of Fairview and the Oklahoma Stock Yards National Bank of Oklahoma City, neither graded.

Oregon • 25 banks of issue • 20 notes reported • One Unc, from the United States National Bank of Portland.

Pennsylvania • 310 banks of issue • 329 notes reported • Many banks. Several small clusters of Unc notes, plus scattered examples. A plentiful state. The census lists 11 serial number 1 notes, including six Unc, four from the First National Bank of Philadelphia (charter 1, giving these notes an additional special cachet).

Rhode Island • 14 banks of issue • 34 notes reported • The only Unc from the Merchants National Bank of Providence.

South Carolina • 38 banks of issue • 31 notes reported • Circulated grades from various banks, some clusters. One serial number 1 note is from the City National Bank of Sumter (VF).

South Dakota • 16 banks of issue • 6 notes reported • The only Unc note is from the First National Bank of Pukwana; this is also the only serial number 1 note.

Tennessee • 44 banks of issue • 58 notes reported • One Unc, from the Union National Bank of Knoxville. One serial number 1 note is from the Broadway National Bank of Nashville (VF).

Texas • 116 banks of issue • 128 notes reported • Wide selection of banks. Handful of Unc notes. Four serial number 1 notes are from the Groos National Bank of San Antonio, including two Unc.

Utah • 8 banks of issue • 8 notes reported • One Unc, from the Utah National Bank of Salt Lake City.

Vermont • 28 banks of issue • 32 notes reported • Circulated notes from various banks, including several clusters.

Virginia • 29 banks of issue • 56 notes reported • The only Unc from the First National Bank of Richmond. One serial number 1 note is from the Planters National Bank of Fredericksburg (G).

Washington • 27 banks of issue • 15 notes reported • Circulated notes from seven banks.

West Virginia • 53 banks of issue • 34 notes reported • Circulated notes, including scattered clusters.

Wisconsin • 46 banks of issue • 96 notes reported • Two Unc, one each from the First National Bank of Dodgeville and the First National Bank of Martinette. Four serial number 1 notes are known, three from the National Bank of Manitowoc (G, VF, not graded) and one from the First National Bank of Neillsville (not graded).

Wyoming • 6 banks of issue • 7 notes reported • Circulated notes from three banks.

Generic prices for a typical note from a state from which notes range from plentiful to just slightly scarce:

VG-8	F-12	VF-20	EF-40	AU-50	Unc-60	Unc-63	Unc-65
$125	$170	$240	$375	$500	$600	$725	$1,100

W-760 • F-590 • Lyons-Roberts (1898–1905)
Estimated population: 1,650 to 1,900 • Highest graded: Unc.

VG-8	F-12	VF-20	EF-40	AU-50	Unc-60	Unc-63	Unc-65
$125	$170	$240	$375	$500	$600	$725	$1,100

W-761 • F-591 • Lyons-Treat (1905–1906)
Estimated population: 250 to 300 • Highest graded: Unc.

VG-8	F-12	VF-20	EF-40	AU-50	Unc-60	Unc-63
$125	$170	$240	$375	$500	$600	$725

W-762 • F-592 • Vernon-Treat (1906–1909)
Estimated population: 700 to 900 • Highest graded: Unc.

VG-8	F-12	VF-20	EF-40	AU-50	Unc-60	Unc-63	Unc-65
$125	$170	$240	$375	$500	$600	$725	$1,100

W-763 • F-593 • Vernon-McClung (1909–1911)
Estimated population: 600 to 750 • Highest graded: Unc.

VG-8	F-12	VF-20	EF-40	AU-50	Unc-60	Unc-63
$125	$170	$240	$375	$500	$600	$725

W-764 • F-594 • Napier-McClung (1911–1912)
Estimated population: 240 to 280 • Highest graded: Unc.

VG-8	F-12	VF-20	EF-40	AU-50	Unc-60	Unc-63
$125	$170	$240	$375	$500	$600	$725

W-765 • F-595 • Napier-Thompson (1912–1913)
Estimated population: 52 to 60 • Highest graded: Unc.

VG-8	F-12	VF-20	EF-40	AU-50	Unc-60	Unc-63
$150	$200	$270	$420	$550	$675	$800

W-766 • F-596 • Napier-Burke (1913)
Estimated population: 34 to 40 • Highest graded: Unc.

VG-8	F-12	VF-20	EF-40	AU-50	Unc-60	Unc-63
$125	$170	$240	$375	$500	$600	$725

W-767 • F-597 • Parker-Burke (1913–1914)
Estimated population: 70 to 85 • Highest graded: Unc.

VG-8	F-12	VF-20	EF-40	AU-50	Unc-60	Unc-63	Unc-65
$125	$170	$240	$375	$500	$600	$725	$1,100

W-768 • F-597a • Teehee-Burke (1915–1919)

Recorded population: 1 • *Selected information:* The known note is serial 1-K974338B/A, Unc, sold by CAA (5/2000) for $6,050—a premium serial 1 note in high grade from the Citizens NB in Albion, NY.

Series of 1902, Blue Seal, Plain Back
(Authorized Issue 1908–1929)

After the Aldrich-Vreeland Act expired on June 30, 1915, the phrase "or other securities" was no longer added to the face of new printing plates. Henceforth, the style reverted to that of years earlier, secured only by United States bonds. Old plates continued in use, creating two face plate styles for 1902 Plain Back notes (illus. on p. 243).

> **Plate Style a:** This is the old style of 1902 (used on the face of the Date Backs) with the inscription in two lines on the face below the top left border: SECURED BY UNITED STATES BONDS OR OTHER SECURITIES.

> **Plate Style b:** This is the new style introduced in 1908 with the inscription as part of the top border on the face: SECURED BY UNITED STATES BONDS DEPOSITED WITH THE TREAS-URER OF THE UNITED STATES OF AMER-ICA (the last in tiny letters).

For both Plate Style a and Plate Style b notes, the two regional letters (only on certain issues, later deleted), two charter numbers (on all), and serial numbers (on all) are in blue. These were issued into 1929.

Moreover, within the two plate styles there are possibilities for three overprint styles.

> **Overprint Style 1:** Two regional letters, a Treasury serial number, and a bank serial number, 1908 to 1924.

> **Overprint Style 2:** No regional letters with a Treasury serial number and a bank serial number, 1924 and 1925. Notes of this class are somewhat scarce.

> **Overprint Style 3:** No regional letters and no Treasury serial number, but with two bank serial numbers, 1925 to 1929. Notes of this style are very rare as a class.

As a type, surviving examples are plentiful, second only to the $10 notes in this series. The typical note is apt to be well circulated and, if rubber stamped, to have the signatures faded. Uncirculated notes are in the minority among known examples, but many survive, and they come on the market frequently. At present there is little interest in plate styles or overprint varieties, yielding opportunities to acquire rarities while paying no premium.

Banks of Issue and Rarity of Notes

Based upon census information from Don C. Kelly and James M. Kelly (*National Bank Note Census*, Version 4.0) and with some information from other sources, this listing gives each location, the number of banks issuing this series within each, and a commentary.[33]

The Kelly survey records 27,208 notes, a quantity overwhelming anything else among large-size bills of this denomination. In fact, more are known of these than for all other large-size types combined. Serial number 1 notes are more elusive, however, with only 185 known for this type. These are specifically listed below.

Alabama • 69 banks of issue • 409 notes reported • Mostly circulated. Two serial number 1 notes are known, Ensley National Bank of Birmingham (VG–F) and the First National Bank of Monroeville (VG).

Alaska Territory • 1 bank of issue • 20 notes reported • First National Bank of Fairbanks is the source for all, of which five are Unc. Alaska was a district from 1884 until it became a territory on August 24, 1912, which it remained until statehood in 1959. *All* large-size Alaska notes in all series have the district address. Regardless, numismatists call all "territorials."

Arizona • 8 banks of issue • 57 notes reported • Six Unc. One serial number 1 note is from the Commercial National Bank of Phoenix (EF–AU).

Arkansas • 46 banks of issue • 186 notes reported • Mostly circulated. One serial number 1 note is recorded, from the First National Bank of Guerdon.

California • 237 banks of issue • 1,432 notes reported • Relatively few Unc notes available. Six serial number 1 notes are from four banks.

Colorado • 44 banks of issue • 188 notes reported • Unc notes are mostly scattered, but a cluster of four is from the Fort Collins National Bank. One serial number 1 note is from the First National Bank of Dolores (VF).

Connecticut • 55 banks of issue • 742 notes reported • Scattered Unc. Five serial number 1 notes are known, including three from the First National Bank and Trust Co. of New Haven.

Delaware • 7 banks of issue • 48 notes reported • Three Unc.

District of Columbia • 4 banks of issue • 83 notes reported • Mostly circulated, with a handful of exceptions. One serial number 1 note is from the Farmers and Mechanics National Bank of Washington (Unc).

Florida • 45 banks of issue • 250 notes reported • Scattered Unc. Three serial number 1 notes are from as many banks, one Unc (First National Bank & Trust Co. in Orlando).

Georgia • 59 banks of issue • 263 notes reported • Unc notes are rare. One serial number 1 note is from the Atlanta & Lowry National Bank of Atlanta (VF).

Hawaii Territory • 2 banks of issue • 78 notes reported • One from the First National Bank of Kahului (EF), all others from the First National Bank of Hawaii at Honolulu. Mostly circulated.

Idaho • 33 banks of issue • 98 notes reported • The only Unc note is from the American National Bank of Idaho Falls.

Illinois • 180 banks of issue • 1,147 notes reported • Many are Unc, but most are in lower grades. The census lists 12 serial number 1 notes, including two Unc.

Indiana • 123 banks of issue • 863 notes reported • Scattered Unc notes are in the distinct minority. Two serial number 1 notes are known, from the United States National Bank of Indiana Harbor and the Terre Haute National Bank & Trust Co., both Unc.

Iowa • 82 banks of issue • 721 notes reported • Four Unc from the Live Stock National Bank of Sioux City and a few scattered others. Two serial number 1 notes are known, Chariton & Lucas County National Bank of Chariton (Unc) and the Pioneer National Bank of Waterloo (VF).

Kansas • 66 banks of issue • 356 notes reported • Mostly circulated notes, as expected, but a cache of 16 Unc notes from the Thomas County National Bank of Colby is notable. One serial number 1 note is from the First National Bank of Richmond (EF).

Kentucky • 53 banks of issue • 425 notes reported • Unc notes are scarce, save for nine of the Citizens National Bank of Lebanon. Two serial number 1 notes are from the Day & Night National Bank of Pikeville (EF) and the First National Bank of Stone.

Louisiana • 14 banks of issue • 112 notes reported • A remarkable group of 19 Unc notes from the Whitney-Central National Bank of New Orleans.

Maine • 41 banks of issue • 371 notes reported • Scattered Unc notes. One serial number 1 note is from the Searsport National Bank (F–VF).

Maryland • 49 banks of issue • 342 notes reported • Unc notes are well represented due to several hoards, but they are still in the distinct minority.

Massachusetts • 145 banks of issue • 1,111 notes reported • Unc notes include several small groups. Six serial number 1 notes are from as many banks. All are circulated.

Michigan • 79 banks of issue • 808 notes reported • Several caches provide a good supply of Unc notes, but they are scarce in comparison to worn notes. The census lists 12 serial number 1 notes, including Unc notes from the First National Bank of Iron Mountain (1) and the First National Bank in Mount Clemens (4).

Minnesota • 133 banks of issue • 715 notes reported • Unc notes are scattered through the listings. Five serial number 1 notes are from three different banks.

Mississippi • 26 banks of issue • 160 notes reported • Grades are generally low, and Unc notes are scarce.

Missouri • 80 banks of issue • 990 notes reported • Unc notes are well distributed among many banks. The census lists 13 serial number 1 notes, including three Unc from as many banks.

Montana • 26 banks of issue • 101 notes reported • A few Unc notes are well distributed. One serial number 1 note is from the Security National Bank of Lima (AU).

Nebraska • 43 banks of issue • 213 notes reported • Very few are Unc.

Nevada • 6 banks of issue • 70 notes reported • The only Unc is from the Reno National Bank.

New Hampshire • 37 banks of issue • 292 notes reported • Unc notes are scarce and widely distributed, save for seven from the Citizens National Bank of Newport.

New Jersey • 179 banks of issue • 1,314 notes reported • Plentiful circulated notes and enough Unc, including 13 from the First National Bank of Jersey City, to make a type note easy to find. The census lists 15 serial number 1 notes, including eight Unc.

New Mexico • 9 banks of issue • 129 notes reported • Unc notes are rare. One serial number 1 note is from the Albuquerque National Bank (Unc).

New York • 344 banks of issue • 3,400 notes reported • Unc notes are in the minority, but include some clusters. Enough New York notes exist that a specialty can be made in collecting different towns and banks. The census lists 41 serial number 1 notes, including many graded Unc.

North Carolina • 57 banks of issue • 390 notes reported • Most are in low grades. Many notes are not graded. Unc notes are scarce.

North Dakota • 41 banks of issue • 114 notes reported • Only a few Unc notes are among the listings.

Ohio • 146 banks of issue • 1,494 notes reported • One of the more common states. Unc notes are easily available as a type, but can be rare or unknown for specific locations. Four serial number 1 notes are from the Ohio National Bank of Columbus, Unc.

Oklahoma • 72 banks of issue • 158 notes reported • Mostly circulated. Unc notes are very rare. Two serial number 1 notes are from the Oklahoma Stock Yards National Bank of Omaha City (not graded) and the Producers National Bank of Tulsa (F).

Oregon • 28 banks of issue • 120 notes reported • Unc notes are very rare. Four serial number 1 notes are listed from three banks.

Pennsylvania • 375 banks of issue • 2,665 notes reported • A common state with many opportunities. There are 15 circulated notes from the First National Bank of Intercourse, always a premium novelty title in the marketplace. Unc notes are scattered throughout the listing. The census lists 11 serial number 1 notes, including one Unc note from the Glen Lyon National Bank.

Rhode Island • 11 banks of issue • 283 notes reported • Mostly circulated. Circulated notes include clusters from two banks.

South Carolina • 49 banks of issue • 321 notes reported • Unc notes are very elusive. Two serial number 1 notes are available from the South Carolina National Bank of Charleston (EF–AU) and the Woodside National Bank of Greenville (AU).

South Dakota • 27 banks of issue • 98 notes reported • Most Unc notes are from a group of seven from the Home National Bank of Dell Rapids.

Tennessee • 57 banks of issue • 450 notes reported • Mostly circulated, mainly in clumps from a few banks. Unc notes are very scarce.

Texas • 160 banks of issue • 1,297 notes reported • Mostly circulated, many in clumps. Among Unc notes are 19 from the Fort Worth National Bank. The census lists 18 serial number 1 notes, including 10 Unc.

Utah • 11 banks of issue • 111 notes reported • Mostly circulated, in clumps.

SERIES OF 1902, BLUE SEAL, PLAIN BACK

$5 National Bank Note, Series of 1902, Blue Seal, Plain Back (W-770). The Webster and Atlas National Bank of Boston. Early signature combination of Lyons and Roberts. With blue Treasury seal, charter numbers, regional letters, and bank and Treasury serial numbers. Plate Style a, Overprint Style 1.

Detail of Plate Style a, with the security phrase including OR OTHER SECURITIES.

Detail of Plate Style b, the security phrase on an example of W-774, noting the backing only in bonds. Later plates in the Series of 1902 Plain Back series were of this style.

Back of the $5 National Bank Note, Series of 1902, Blue Seal, Plain Back (W-770). Same type as Series of 1902, Red Seal notes.

Vermont • 30 banks of issue • 210 notes reported • Various banks, with the vast majority of notes in circulated grades.

Virginia • 93 banks of issue • 454 notes reported • Unc notes are rarities.

Washington • 34 banks of issue • 173 notes reported • Mostly in clumps. Unc notes are rare. Two serial number 1 notes are from Grays Harbor National Bank of Aberdeen (F, EF).

West Virginia • 63 banks of issue • 346 notes reported • Unc notes are scarce and often from small groups. One serial number 1 note is from the First National Bank of Romney (not graded).

Wisconsin • 82 banks of issue • 682 notes reported • Mostly circulated notes, often in clusters. Unc notes include 13 from the Northwestern National Bank of Milwaukee.

Wyoming • 7 banks of issue • 48 notes reported • Mostly circulated notes. The only Unc is from the American National Bank of Cheyenne. One serial number 1 note is from the American National Bank of Cheyenne.

Generic prices for a typical note from a state from which notes range from plentiful to just slightly scarce:

VG-8	F-12	VF-20	EF-40	AU-50	Unc-60	Unc-63	Unc-65
$110	$130	$170	$330	$425	$600	$675	$900

W-770 • F-598 • Lyons-Roberts (1898–1905)

Estimated population: 10,000 to 12,000 • *Highest graded:* Unc.

VG-8	F-12	VF-20	EF-40	AU-50	Unc-60	Unc-63	Unc-65
$110	$130	$170	$330	$425	$600	$675	$900

W-771 • F-599 • Lyons-Treat (1905–1906)
Estimated population: 1,300 to 1,600 • Highest graded: Unc.

VG-8	F-12	VF-20	EF-40	AU-50	Unc-60	Unc-63	Unc-65
$110	$130	$170	$330	$425	$600	$675	$900

W-772 • F-600 • Vernon-Treat (1906–1909)
Estimated population: 3,800 to 4,500 • Highest graded: Unc.

VG-8	F-12	VF-20	EF-40	AU-50	Unc-60	Unc-63	Unc-65
$110	$130	$170	$330	$425	$600	$675	$900

W-773 • F-601 • Vernon-McClung (1909–1911)
Estimated population: 2,600 to 3,200 • Highest graded: Unc.

VG-8	F-12	VF-20	EF-40	AU-50	Unc-60	Unc-63	Unc-65
$110	$130	$170	$330	$425	$600	$675	$900

W-774 • F-602 • Napier-McClung (1911–1912)
Estimated population: 1,900 to 2,400 • Highest graded: Unc.

VG-8	F-12	VF-20	EF-40	AU-50	Unc-60	Unc-63	Unc-65
$110	$130	$170	$330	$425	$600	$675	$900

W-775 • F-603 • Napier-Thompson (1912–1913)
Estimated population: 350 to 425 • Highest graded: Unc.

VG-8	F-12	VF-20	EF-40	AU-50	Unc-60	Unc-63
$125	$150	$190	$375	$480	$660	$725

W-776 • F-604 • Napier-Burke (1913)
Estimated population: 250 to 300 • Highest graded: Unc.

VG-8	F-12	VF-20	EF-40	AU-50	Unc-60	Unc-63
$110	$130	$170	$330	$425	$600	$675

W-777 • F-605 • Parker-Burke (1913–1914)
Estimated population: 900 to 1,100 • Highest graded: Unc.

VG-8	F-12	VF-20	EF-40	AU-50	Unc-60	Unc-63
$110	$130	$170	$330	$425	$600	$675

W-778 • F-606 • Teehee-Burke (1915–1919)
Estimated population: 3,800 to 4,500 • Highest graded: Unc.

VG-8	F-12	VF-20	EF-40	AU-50	Unc-60	Unc-63	Unc-65
$110	$130	$170	$330	$425	$600	$675	$900

W-779 • F-607 • Elliott-Burke (1919–1921)
Estimated population: 2,800 to 3,500 • Highest graded: Unc.

VG-8	F-12	VF-20	EF-40	AU-50	Unc-60	Unc-63	Unc-65
$110	$130	$170	$330	$425	$600	$675	$900

W-780 • F-608 • Elliott-White (1921–1922)
Estimated population: 1,200 to 1,400 • Highest graded: Unc.

VG-8	F-12	VF-20	EF-40	AU-50	Unc-60	Unc-63	Unc-65
$110	$130	$170	$330	$425	$600	$675	$900

W-781 • F-609 • Speelman-White (1922–1927)
Estimated population: 3,000 to 3,800 • Highest graded: Unc.

VG-8	F-12	VF-20	EF-40	AU-50	Unc-60	Unc-63	Unc-65
$110	$130	$170	$330	$425	$600	$675	$900

W-782 • F-610 • Woods-White (1927–1928)
Estimated population: 120 to 130 • Highest graded: Unc.

VG-8	F-12	VF-20	EF-40	AU-50	Unc-60	Unc-63
$110	$130	$170	$330	$425	$600	$675

W-783 • F-611 • Woods-Tate (1928–1929)
Estimated population: 185 to 205 • Highest graded: Unc.

VG-8	F-12	VF-20	EF-40	AU-50	Unc-60	Unc-63
$110	$130	$170	$330	$425	$600	$675

W-784 • F-612 • Jones-Woods (1929–1933)
Estimated population: 24 to 28 • Highest graded: Unc.

VG-8	F-12	VF-20	EF-40	AU-50	Unc-60	Unc-63	Unc-65
$400	$600	$800	$1,250	$1,600	$1,900	$2,400	$3,200

SILVER CERTIFICATES

Series of 1886

Large-size $5 Silver Certificates began with the Series of 1886, the famous "Silver Dollar Note," as numismatists have designated it. On the face is the portrait of Ulysses S. Grant, hero of the Civil War and former president, who served two terms and died in 1885.

The back of the note displays at the center the obverse of an 1886 Morgan silver dollar, reflecting the series date, flanked by two reverses on each side. Interestingly, the reverses differ slightly in detail among themselves, indicating that they were entered individually, not by doing one and then utilizing the transfer process to copy it. The motto IN GOD WE TRUST, illustrated on the coins, appears in Old English letters. An ornate background and border complete the arrangement.

This use of IN GOD WE TRUST represents a new appearance of the motto on federal paper money (the first was on the Florida state seal of Original Series through Series of 1882 Brown Back bills). This and the Florida uses were inadvertent, it seems, for it was not until 1957 that the Treasury department made the inscription a mandatory part of currency issues.

An early account said that one variety existed with at least one of the notes having TRUST spelled as TRVST, but in many years of looking, I have not encountered an example. This note should have special appeal to *coin* collectors, but this has not happened to any extent. Some long runs of serial numbers for Uncirculated hoard notes are known, making top-grade examples readily collectible for type.

These and other large-size Silver Certificates are specifically payable in five silver dollars. A suitable quantity of silver dollars held by the Treasury department was specifically earmarked as backing for these notes. W-792 was printed in especially large quantities and, as might be expected, is the variety most often seen.

W-790 • F-259 • Rosecrans-Jordan (1885–1887) • Small red seal with plain border • 1,500,000 (est.)
Estimated population: 40 to 45 • Highest graded: Unc.

VG-8	F-12	VF-20	EF-40	AU-50	Unc-60	Unc-63	Unc-65
$900	$1,900	$3,750	$8,000	$10,000	$12,000	$15,000	$32,000

SERIES OF 1886

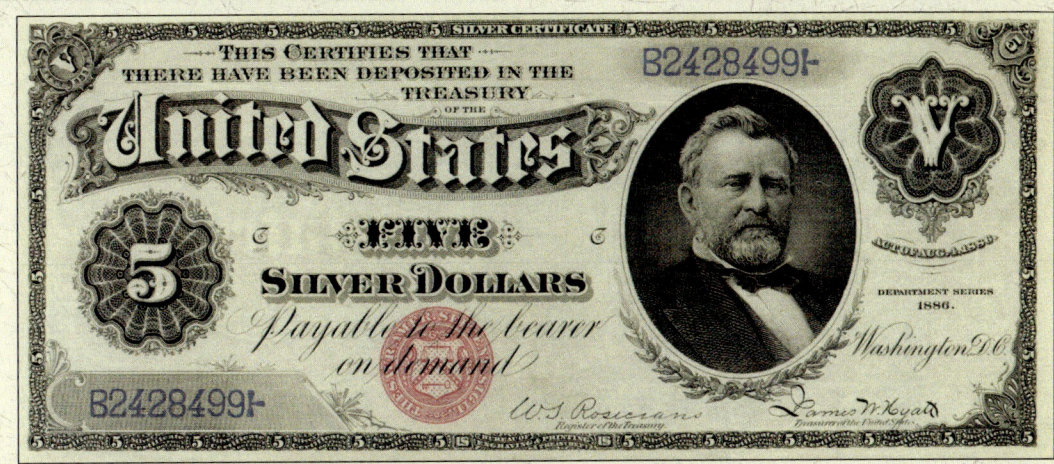

$5 Silver Certificate, Series of 1886 (W-791), the type of W-790 to W-796 and also the general type of W-797 and W-798. Seal placements vary. Portrait of President Grant.

Back of the $5 Silver Certificate, Series of 1886 (W-791), the "Silver Dollar Note." The center coin shows the series date.

W-791 • F-260 • Rosecrans-Hyatt (1887–1889) • 7,440,000 (est.)

Estimated population: 140 to 155 • *Highest graded:* Unc.

VG-8	F-12	VF-20	EF-40	AU-50	Unc-60	Unc-63	Unc-65
$800	$1,600	$3,250	$6,500	$8,000	$9,500	$12,000	$25,000

W-792 • F-261 • Large red seal • 12,172,000 (est.)

Estimated population: 240 to 275 • *Highest graded:* Unc.

VG-8	F-12	VF-20	EF-40	AU-50	Unc-60	Unc-63
$800	$1,600	$3,250	$6,500	$8,000	$9,500	$12,000

W-793 • F-262 • Rosecrans-Huston (1889–1891) • 3,388,000 (est.)

Estimated population: 75 to 90 • *Highest graded:* Unc.

VG-8	F-12	VF-20	EF-40	AU-50	Unc-60	Unc-63	Unc-65
$800	$1,600	$3,250	$6,500	$8,000	$9,500	$12,000	$25,000

W-794 • F-263 • Large brown seal • 6,800,000 (est.)

Estimated population: 310 to 360 • *Highest graded:* Unc.

VG-8	F-12	VF-20	EF-40	AU-50	Unc-60	Unc-63	Unc-65
$800	$1,600	$3,250	$6,500	$8,000	$9,500	$12,000	$20,000

W-795 • F-264 • Rosecrans-Nebeker (1891–1893) • 1,840,000 (est.)

Estimated population: 60 to 70 • *Highest graded:* Unc.

VG-8	F-12	VF-20	EF-40	AU-50	Unc-60	Unc-63	Unc-65
$800	$1,600	$3,250	$6,500	$8,000	$9,500	$12,000	$28,000

W-796 • F-265 • Small red seal with scalloped border • 740,000 (est.)

Estimated population: 36 to 42 • *Highest graded:* Unc.

VG-8	F-12	VF-20	EF-40	AU-50	Unc-60	Unc-63
$1,250	$3,900	$5,700	$8,000	$10,500	$13,000	$18,000

Series of 1891

The Series of 1891 notes continued the face design from the preceding series but had a redesigned back, with two large open spaces, thought to be a deterrent to counterfeiting. Two signature combinations exist. All serial numbers begin with E.

W-797 • F-266 • Rosecrans-Nebeker (1891–1893) • Small red seal with scalloped border • 7,100,000 (est.)

Estimated population: 75 to 85 • *Highest graded:* Unc • *Commentary:* This issue is especially scarce in Uncirculated grades.

VG-8	F-12	VF-20	EF-40	AU-50	Unc-60	Unc-63	Unc-65
$875	$1,400	$1,700	$2,500	$2,900	$3,500	$5,000	$8,000

SERIES OF 1891

$5 Silver Certificate, Series of 1891 (W-797).

Back of the $5 Silver Certificate, Series of 1891 (W-797).

W-798 • F-267 • Tillman-Morgan (1893–1897) • 24,456,000 (est.)

Estimated population: 330 to 360 • *Highest graded:* Unc.

VG-8	F-12	VF-20	EF-40	AU-50	Unc-60	Unc-63	Unc-65
$875	$1,350	$1,600	$2,300	$2,700	$3,100	$4,400	$6,500

Series of 1896

Completing the "Educational" series of bills is the $5 design for the Series of 1896, illustrating an allegorical motif, *Electricity Presenting Light to the World*, sometimes called *Electricity as the Dominant Force in the World*. Adapted from a painting by Walter Shirlaw, this allegory perhaps outdoes any others seen on a federal note.

At the center, Liberty (or perhaps Electricity) holds aloft an Edison bulb, which casts rays on the scene below. To the left, a god in the clouds uses bolts of lightning to urge fiery steeds onward. At the right a flying goddess attracts a dove, with the U.S. Capitol in the distance. This was the era of electricity, as epitomized by the "White City" at the World's Columbian Exposition in 1893, with brilliant illumination at night. New uses for this power were constantly being discovered, and across America homes and businesses were being wired for current, especially in large and medium-size towns. Thomas F. Morris engraved certain of the details, while the main allegory was engraved by G.F.C. Smillie.

This is Neoclassicism at its height: an elegant scene that stands as one of the most popular currency motifs in the view of collectors today, with more than a few considering it to be the ultimate in federal paper-money artistry. The uncovered bosoms of certain of the figures in the scene caused several Boston society ladies to rally against the design, and some banks to resist taking them—the origin of the term *banned in Boston*, according to some. Facts are scarce, and this may be more folklore than anything else. Whatever the combination of circumstances, these beautiful bills were produced for a relatively short period of time, and were replaced by the Series of 1899 (which was also very popular).

The back was conceived by Thomas F. Morris and mostly engraved by G.F.C. Smillie, with portraits of Civil War heroes Ulysses S. Grant and Philip H. Sheridan engraved by Lorenzo Hatch. It is interesting to contemplate that Grant, a great general but considered to be a poor president, is well represented on United States currency. In contrast, the highly regarded Theodore Roosevelt has never been depicted.

This design and the two others in the "Educational" series were greatly criticized by the engravers at the BEP, who resisted bureau chief Claude Johnson's hiring of outside artists. It also hurt when Morris's concept of a naval design was discarded and replaced by Shirlaw's art. At a congressional inquiry in 1897, Chief Johnson testified concerning the $5 note (excerpted):

Series of 1896

$5 Silver Certificate, Series of 1896 (W-800), the famous "Educational Note" with *Electricity Presenting Light to the World*. Many numismatists consider this to be the epitome of art on an American bank note.

Back of the $5 Silver Certificate, Series of 1896 (W-800), with portraits of president Ulysses S. Grant and General Philip Sheridan. The face and back designs were criticized by Thomas F. Morris and some others within the BEP, including the charge that portraits belong on the face of a note, not the back.

The plate letter D (high above the Treasury seal) and number 47 (at the bottom of the V numeral) are widely separated on the face of this W-800 note.

Mr. Morris, since his own design was rejected, was indignant, had a disagreement with all the artists, and there was pulling between the artists and Mr. Morris all the time, to such an extent that in several cases I started to recommend Mr. Morris's dismissal. He aggravated me so. That was the especial policy of that administration; the Secretary of the Treasury had ordered this Bureau to do certain work, and it was Mr. Morris's duty to carry into effect whatever policy was adopted by the Treasury's Office and being executed through this office.

I went to New York and met Mr. Shirlaw, who had been in his early life a bank-note engraver. He was also an artist of some note; had studied in Europe ten years. I suggested to him to make a design, which he did. . . . Of course, that character of work took better engraving than ever had been done in this Bureau before. Naturally, we would employ the best talent. Mr. Smillie was employed, and Mr. Schlecht, for the purpose of executing that work, and adding to the stock of the Bureau generally. Mr. Schlecht had engraved the Columbian Exposition diploma. Mr. Smillie was considered one of the five first-class engravers in the country; had done work for the American and the Hamilton, the Western, and the Canadian bank-note companies.

I will say that, in my opinion, if both designs had been properly transferred, and Mr. Morris had made the counter numbers distinct, as he should have done, that they would have been very successful. [The Shirlaw counter or denomination designs were rejected by Morris.] Now, this is a photograph of Mr. Shirlaw's border. Mr. Morris would not use that border, and put this other border in. You see that the 5 is very distinct. I do not mean to say that that border is altogether satisfactory. The 5 shows that it was intended to have a very plain 5, and Mr. Morris changed it.[34]

Series of 1896 Silver Certificates were produced with three signature combinations, but are mainly collected as a single note for type. Enough survive that finding one will present no difficulty, but the great demand has made choice examples expensive. The $5 note was voted as number 5 in *100 Greatest American Currency Notes*, with the other two "Educational Note" denominations not far behind, the $1 note as number 7 and the $2 note as number 11.

W-799 • F-268 • Tillman-Morgan (1893–1897) • Small red seal with spiked border • 17,300,000 (est.)

Estimated population: 800 to 1,000 • *Highest graded:* Unc.

VG-8	F-12	VF-20	EF-40	AU-50	Unc-60	Unc-63	Unc-65
$1,000	$1,750	$2,750	$5,200	$8,000	$8,500	$10,500	$15,000

W-800 • F-269 • Bruce-Roberts (1897–1898) • 10,700,000 (est.)

Estimated population: 500 to 650 • *Highest graded:* Unc.

VG-8	F-12	VF-20	EF-40	AU-50	Unc-60	Unc-63	Unc-65
$1,000	$1,750	$2,750	$5,200	$8,000	$8,500	$10,500	$15,000

W-801 • F-270 • Lyons-Roberts (1898–1905) • 6,932,000 (est.)

Estimated population: 300 to 350 • *Highest graded:* Unc.

VG-8	F-12	VF-20	EF-40	AU-50	Unc-60	Unc-63	Unc-65
$1,000	$1,750	$2,750	$5,200	$8,000	$8,500	$11,000	$17,000

Series of 1899

The next entry in the chronology of $5 Silver Certificates is the Series of 1899 type. The face for this series featured the portrait of a Sioux Indian chief, commonly called by the name "Running Antelope," and more formally "Ta-to-ka-in-yan-ka." He was depicted in natural style, quite unlike the Indian Head cent of the time, which showed a female wearing a war bonnet (a male type of headdress). Study by experts such as Gene Hessler has revealed that the bonnet is of the Pawnee rather than the Sioux style, a design error.

The face was engraved by G.F.C. Smillie, who also did much of the back. Star notes were issued as replacements beginning with W-805 and are rare today. Notes in this series are specifically payable in five silver dollars, as are other large-size $5 Silver Certificates. All have a blue Treasury seal.

These "Indian Chief" notes, as they are called, were produced for a long period, through the early 1920s, and to the extent of 566,054,000 examples. They are very popular to collect today. In fact, this is one type that appeals to a wide audience beyond numismatic circles.

Mules: Back plate numbers can be in one of two locations.[35] On May 14, 1921, with the new Elliott-White signature combination starting, all Legal Tender, Silver Certificate, and Gold Certificate back plates were given numbers beginning with 1 and in a new location, although no notice was given of the change.

Back Plate Location 1 (regular use): W-802 to W-810. This was the standard location until May 14, 1921. Also used to create a mule for W-811 and W-812.

Back Plate Location 2 (regular use): W-811 and W-812 (introduced without notice as the new style on May 14, 1921, with the Elliott-White combination).

W-802 • F-271 • Lyons-Roberts (1898–1905) • 172,500,000 (est.)

Estimated population: 800 to 950 • *Highest graded:* Unc.

VG-8	F-12	VF-20	EF-40	AU-50	Unc-60	Unc-63	Unc-65
$470	$570	$825	$1,500	$2,350	$2,700	$3,450	$5,750

W-803 • F-272 • Lyons-Treat (1905–1906) • 29,500,000 (est.)

Estimated population: 225 to 275 • *Highest graded:* Unc.

VG-8	F-12	VF-20	EF-40	AU-50	Unc-60	Unc-63	Unc-65
$470	$570	$825	$1,500	$2,350	$2,700	$3,450	$5,750

W-804 • F-273 • Vernon-Treat (1906–1909) • 82,870,000 (est.)

Estimated population: 375 to 450 • *Highest graded:* Unc.

VG-8	F-12	VF-20	EF-40	AU-50	Unc-60	Unc-63	Unc-65
$470	$570	$825	$1,500	$2,350	$2,700	$3,450	$6,750

W-805 • F-274 • Vernon-McClung (1909–1911) • 46,020,000

Estimated population: 225 to 275 • *Highest graded:* Unc.

VG-8	F-12	VF-20	EF-40	AU-50	Unc-60	Unc-63	Unc-65
$470	$570	$825	$1,500	$2,350	$2,700	$3,450	$5,750

W-805★ • F-274★

Estimated population: 11 to 13 • *Highest graded:* Unc • *Commentary:* On June 21, 1910, star replacement notes were made of this and the related $1 Silver Certificates (W-65★). These became the first of their kind in any series. Earlier, stars had been used as decorations on some notes, without any specific purpose. • *Selected information:* CAA (1/2005), ★3815B/C, VG, $3,105. CAA (1/1999), ★54130B/B, Unc, $6,380. Knight (6/2007), ★67886B/B, VG-10 (PCGS), $1,265. CAA (1/2005), ★117466B/B, EF, $2,990. Knight (3/2006), ★120449B/A, VF, $5,750. Knight (6/2007), ★182902B/B, Unc-64 (PCGS, later graded Unc-65 by PMG), $44,850.

W-806 • F-275 • Napier-McClung (1911–1912) • 62,780,000

Estimated population: 550 to 700 • *Highest graded:* Unc.

VG-8	F-12	VF-20	EF-40	AU-50	Unc-60	Unc-63	Unc-65
$470	$570	$825	$1,500	$2,350	$2,700	$3,450	$5,750

SERIES OF 1899

$5 Silver Certificate, Series of 1899 (W-803), the well-known and highly admired "Indian Chief" note.

Detail of a serial number 1 note (W-806), from plate A1724.

Back of the $5 Silver Certificate, Series of 1899 (W-803).

Back Plate Location 1.

Back Plate Location 2.

W-806★ • F-275★

Recorded population: 4 • *Highest graded:* EF-40 • *Selected information:* CAA (1/2000), ★343094B/B, VG+, problems, $633. CAA (1/2005), ★428130B/B, EF+, $4,140.

W-807 • F-276 • Napier-Thompson (1912–1913) • 2,324,000

Estimated population: 60 to 70 • *Highest graded:* Unc.

VG-8	F-12	VF-20	EF-40	AU-50	Unc-60	Unc-63	Unc-65
$525	$700	$950	$1,725	$2,700	$3,100	$3,800	$12,000

W-808 • F-277 • Parker-Burke (1913–1914) • 46,100,000

Estimated population: 500 to 650 • *Highest graded:* Unc.

VG-8	F-12	VF-20	EF-40	AU-50	Unc-60	Unc-63	Unc-65
$470	$570	$825	$1,500	$2,350	$2,700	$3,450	$5,750

W-808★ • F-277★

Estimated population: 10 to 12 • *Highest graded:* Unc • *Selected information:* Knight (10/2000), ★450196B/D, F, $880. Knight (11/2007), ★453569B/A, VF-30 (PCGS), $4,600. CAA (1/2005), ★468871B/C, AU, $14,375.

W-809 • F-278 • Teehee-Burke (1915–1919) • 42,276,000

Estimated population: 500 to 650 • *Highest graded:* Unc.

VG-8	F-12	VF-20	EF-40	AU-50	Unc-60	Unc-63	Unc-65
$470	$570	$825	$1,500	$2,350	$2,700	$3,450	$5,750

W-809★ • F-278★

Estimated population: 16 to 18 • *Highest graded:* Unc.

VF-20	EF-40	AU-50	Unc-60	Unc-63
$2,200	$3,500	$4,500	$6,000	—

W-810 • F-279 • Elliott-Burke (1919–1921) • Back Plate Location 2 • 9,036,000 (est.)

Estimated population: 275 to 350 • *Highest graded:* Unc.

VG-8	F-12	VF-20	EF-40	AU-50	Unc-60	Unc-63	Unc-65
$470	$570	$825	$1,500	$2,350	$2,700	$3,450	$5,750

W-810★ • F-279★

Estimated population: 18 to 20 • *Highest graded:* EF-45.

VF-20	EF-40
$2,200	$3,200

W-811 • F-280 • Elliott-White (1921–1922) • Back Plate Location 2 • 2,500,000, or about 9% regular (est.)

Estimated population: 100 to 120 • *Highest graded:* Unc • *Commentary:* Part of the data for W-811 Mule below; the Back Plate Location 2 is not generally described in auction catalogs. Because this note is rarer than its mule counterpart, its previous pricing is now assigned to the new mule listing. The non-mule note will be monitored for expected pricing upswings due to its increased rarity.

W-811 Mule • F-280 • Back Plate Location 1 • 24,568,000, or about 91% mules (est.)

Estimated population: 800 to 1,200 • *Highest graded:* Unc.

VG-8	F-12	VF-20	EF-40	AU-50	Unc-60	Unc-63	Unc-65
$470	$570	$825	$1,500	$2,350	$2,700	$3,450	$5,750

W-811 Mule★ • F-280★ • Non-mule star not seen

Estimated population: 32 to 36 • *Highest graded:* Unc • *Commentary:* Doug Murray states that all star notes of W-811 are mules, although they are usually not cataloged as such.

VG-8	F-12	VF-20	EF-40	AU-50	Unc-60	Unc-63
$500	$600	$875	$1,600	$2,500	$3,000	$3,700

W-812 • F-281 • Speelman-White (1922–1927) • Back Plate Location 2 • 41,080,000, or about 90% regular (est.)

Estimated population: 1,200 to 1,500 • *Highest graded:* Unc.

VG-8	F-12	VF-20	EF-40	AU-50	Unc-60	Unc-63	Unc-65
$450	$550	$800	$1,450	$2,250	$2,600	$3,300	$5,750

W-812★ • F-281★

Estimated population: 9 or 10 • *Highest graded:* VF-30 • *Selected information:* Knight (6/2007), ★1309415B/C, F-12 (PCGS), $1,150. Knight (6/2008), ★1316576B/D, F-15 (PCGS), $2,875. CAA (1/2005), ★1323302B/F, VF, $2,415. CAA (9/1999), ★1339074B/F, "Pig, profoundly ugly, truly filthy," $220 (included here for its whimsy).

W-812 Mule • F-281 • Back Plate Location 1 • 4,500,000, or about 10% mules (est.)

Estimated population: 45 to 50 • *Highest graded:* Unc • *Commentary:* As this is a new listing, there is no market history.

$5 Silver Certificate, Series of 1923 (W-813), the ever-popular "Porthole Note." Portrait of Abraham Lincoln.

Back of the $5 Silver Certificate, Series of 1923 (W-813), with the Great Seal of the United States.

Series of 1923

The last design type among large-size $5 Silver Certificates is another numismatic favorite. Abraham Lincoln is depicted at the center, surrounded by a heavy circular frame, giving rise to the nickname "Porthole Note." The portrait is from a photograph by Anthony Berger and was engraved by Charles Burt, a contract engraver for the Bureau of Engraving and Printing. The same image was also used on the Federal Reserve Note Series of 1914. With this issue, Lincoln became the standard portrait subject for the $5 denomination; this was continued on all small-size notes of various series.

The back of the Series of 1923 note shows the *reverse* of the Great Seal of the United States (the face of the seal, as used on most small-size $1 notes, shows a pyramid, all-seeing eye, and other Masonic emblems). The engraving was done by Robert Ponickau. By this time the era of elegance was gone, and it was Treasury policy to feature large amounts of white space.

This note is specifically payable in five silver dollars. The blue Treasury seal at the left is over a three-line inscription:

"This certificate is receivable for all public dues and when so received may be reissued." All have the Treasury seal and serial numbers in blue.

W-813 • F-282 • Speelman-White (1922–1927) • 6,316,000
Estimated population: 1,300 to 1,600 • Highest graded: Unc.

VG-8	F-12	VF-20	EF-40	AU-50	Unc-60	Unc-63	Unc-65
$700	$925	$1,475	$2,300	$3,200	$3,600	$4,250	$8,500

W-813★ • F-282★
Estimated population: 43 to 45 • Highest graded: Unc.

VF-20	EF-40	AU-50	Unc-60	Unc-63	Unc-65
$2,000	$4,500	$6,500	$10,000	—	$20,000

TREASURY OR COIN NOTES

Series of 1890

The Treasury Notes, or Coin Notes, Series of 1890, are considered to be a high spot in artistry. The face depicts General

SERIES OF 1890

$5 Treasury or Coin Note, Series of 1890 (W-822), the type of W-820 to W-822. Portrait of Civil War general George H. Thomas.

Detail of the serial number and plate letter and number on face of a W-822 note.

Location of the plate number 7, horizontally at the center of a small floral ornament on the right edge of the back of a W-822 note.

Back of the $5 Treasury or Coin Note, Series of 1890 (W-822), ornately engraved.

George H. Thomas, little remembered today, but one of several Civil War heroes shown on currency in the late 19th century. At quick glance his portrait resembles that of Grant. Serial numbers of these notes begin with the letter A and end with a decorative star. As is true of other notes in the series, the Rosecrans-Nebeker signature combination with large brown Treasury seal is significantly rarer than the others.

The beauty of the note is on the back, where the word FIVE appears in very ornate green letters, with appropriate decorations surrounding. These notes, while scarce, are available today, especially in circulated grades, and are usually collected by type. The Rosecrans-Nebeker signature combination is the key to the series, with only a dozen or so reported.

W-820 • F-359 • Rosecrans-Huston (1889–1891) • Large brown seal • 3,520,000 (est.)

Estimated population: 130 to 145 • *Highest graded:* Unc.

VG-8	F-12	VF-20	EF-40	AU-50	Unc-60	Unc-63	Unc-65
$400	$600	$1,250	$1,950	$4,600	$5,200	$7,700	$15,000

W-821 • F-360 • Rosecrans-Nebeker (1891–1893) • 280,000 (est.)

Estimated population: 15 to 17 • *Highest graded:* Unc.

VG-8	F-12	VF-20	EF-40	AU-50	Unc-60	Unc-63	Unc-65
$2,200	—	$10,000	$50,000	—	$100,000	—	—

W-822 • F-361 • Small red seal with scalloped border • 3,400,000 (est.)

Estimated population: 140 to 155 • *Highest graded:* Unc.

VG-8	F-12	VF-20	EF-40	AU-50	Unc-60	Unc-63	Unc-65
$400	$600	$1,250	$1,950	$4,600	$5,200	$7,700	$13,000

Series of 1891

With the Treasury department preference for more open space on the back of the notes, the Series of 1891 was created to replace the preceding issue. The face continues the same format as earlier, with a small red Treasury seal with scalloped border (as earlier used on W-822) and red serial numbers (now commencing with B and ending with a decorative star). SERIES OF 1891, in upper and lower case letters, is at the top right of the field.

The back is styled differently from that on the Series of 1890 notes, and, in the opinion of most numismatists, not as attractively. These notes were continued in production through the early 20th century. The last signature combination in the series is that of Lyons and Roberts, two men who were in office jointly from 1898 to 1905.

$5 Treasury or Coin Note, Series of 1891 (W-823). The basic features are the same as on the Series of 1890 notes.

Back of the $5 Treasury or Coin Note, Series of 1891 (W-823), with new design featuring open spaces.

W-823 • F-362 • Rosecrans-Nebeker (1891–1893) • 2,800,000 (est.)

Estimated population: 145 to 160 • *Highest graded:* Unc.

VG-8	F-12	VF-20	EF-40	AU-50	Unc-60	Unc-63	Unc-65
$325	$450	$750	$1,075	$1,600	$1,800	$2,500	$4,800

W-824 • F-363 • Tillman-Morgan (1893–1897) • 11,840,000 (est.)

Estimated population: 275 to 350 • *Highest graded:* Unc.

VG-8	F-12	VF-20	EF-40	AU-50	Unc-60	Unc-63	Unc-65
$325	$450	$750	$1,075	$1,600	$1,800	$2,500	$4,800

W-825 • F-364 • Bruce-Roberts (1897–1898) • 1,920,000 (est.)

Estimated population: 165 to 180 • *Highest graded:* Unc.

VG-8	F-12	VF-20	EF-40	AU-50	Unc-60	Unc-63	Unc-65
$325	$450	$750	$1,075	$1,600	$1,800	$2,500	$4,800

W-826 • F-365 • Lyons-Roberts (1898–1905) • 700,000 (est.)

Estimated population: 30 to 40 • *Highest graded:* Unc.

VG-8	F-12	VF-20	EF-40	AU-50	Unc-60	Unc-63
$400	$660	$1,800	$3,500	$5,500	$8,000	$15,000

FEDERAL RESERVE NOTES

Series of 1914, Red Seal

The Federal Reserve Notes, Series of 1914, with red Treasury seal and serial numbers and with the Burke-McAdoo signature combination (illus. on p. 254), are rather simple in their appearance. A portrait of Lincoln is at the center, the Federal Reserve seal is to the left, and the Treasury seal is to the right. The number, 1 to 12, and the large letter, A to L, on the seal at the left indicate the Federal Reserve Bank that issued the note. The back has the vignette *Columbus in Sight of Land* to the left and *Landing of the Pilgrims* to the right.

Collectors usually only buy one $5 Federal Reserve Note to illustrate the type, although it is possible to acquire them by Federal Reserve Bank and plate style as well. These are considerably scarcer as a group than the Blue Seal notes listed subsequently. After World War I commenced in Europe in August 1914, the BEP could not import red ink, so it switched to blue after less than a year of printing Red Seals.

Plate Style a (on Red Seals only): In certain of the following listings, the lowercase a indicates large bank district letter and numeral at bottom left and top right. At the upper left is a small plate letter, but no bank district letter and number.

Plate Style b (on Red and Blue Seals): In certain of the following listings the small letter b indicates a note similar to the preceding, but now with small bank district letter and numeral added above the plate letter at the top left and a small bank district letter and number at the lower right.

W-830-A-a • F-832A • Boston • 1,300,000

Estimated population: 30 to 35 • *Highest graded:* EF-40.

VG-8	F-12	VF-20	EF-40
$225	$425	$650	$1,100

W-830-A-b • F-832B • 2,300,000

Estimated population: 60 to 70 • *Highest graded:* Unc.

VG-8	F-12	VF-20	EF-40	AU-50	Unc-60	Unc-63
$200	$375	$575	$1,000	$1,300	$2,000	$2,950

W-830-B-a • F-833A • New York • 5,200,000

Estimated population: 60 to 70 • *Highest graded:* Unc.

VG-8	F-12	VF-20	EF-40	AU-50	Unc-60	Unc-63	Unc-65
$200	$375	$575	$1,000	$1,300	$2,000	$2,950	$4,750

W-830-B-b • F-833B • 16,392,000

Estimated population: 225 to 275 • *Highest graded:* Unc.

VG-8	F-12	VF-20	EF-40	AU-50	Unc-60	Unc-63	Unc-65
$200	$375	$575	$1,000	$1,300	$2,000	$2,950	$4,750

W-830-C-a • F-834A • Philadelphia • 780,000

Estimated population: 28 to 32 • *Highest graded:* Unc.

VG-8	F-12	VF-20	EF-40	AU-50	Unc-60	Unc-63	Unc-65
$225	$425	$650	$1,100	$1,450	$2,250	$3,100	$5,000

W-830-C-b • F-834B • 3,220,000

Estimated population: 100 to 120 • *Highest graded:* Unc.

VG-8	F-12	VF-20	EF-40	AU-50	Unc-60	Unc-63
$200	$375	$575	$1,000	$1,300	$2,000	$2,950

W-830-D-a • F-835A • Cleveland • 520,000

Estimated population: 20 to 23 • *Highest graded:* Unc.

VG-8	F-12	VF-20	EF-40	AU-50	Unc-60	Unc-63
$250	$450	$700	$1,200	$1,600	$2,500	$3,500

W-830-D-b • F-835B • 3,016,000

Estimated population: 70 to 80 • *Highest graded:* Unc.

VG-8	F-12	VF-20	EF-40	AU-50	Unc-60	Unc-63	Unc-65
$200	$375	$575	$1,000	$1,300	$2,000	$2,950	$4,750

W-830-E-a • F-836A • Richmond • 520,000

Estimated population: 20 to 23 • *Highest graded:* Unc.

VG-8	F-12	VF-20	EF-40	AU-50	Unc-60	Unc-63
$250	$450	$700	$1,200	$1,600	$2,500	$3,500

W-830-E-b • F-836B • 1,480,000

Estimated population: 32 to 36 • *Highest graded:* Unc.

VG-8	F-12	VF-20	EF-40	AU-50	Unc-60	Unc-63
$250	$450	$700	$1,200	$1,600	$2,500	$3,500

W-830-F-a • F-837A • Atlanta • 520,000

Estimated population: 28 to 32 • *Highest graded:* Unc.

VG-8	F-12	VF-20	EF-40	AU-50	Unc-60	Unc-63	Unc-65
$225	$425	$650	$1,100	$1,450	$2,250	$3,100	$5,000

SERIES OF 1914, RED SEAL

$5 Federal Reserve Note, Series of 1914, Red Seal (W-830-C-a). Plate Style a, issued by the Federal Reserve Bank of Philadelphia, with bank identification 3-C at the lower left and top right (in addition to the Federal Reserve Bank seal).

Plate Style a: Detail of the plate letter at upper left, without bank number imprint (W-830-C-a).

Plate Style b: Detail of the bank number (3-C) above the plate letter (in this instance B) at the upper left (W-830-C-b).

Back of the $5 Federal Reserve Note, Series of 1914, Red Seal (W-830-A-a). Also used for $5 Federal Reserve Notes, Series of 1914, Blue Seal. The motifs are the same as used on $5 Federal Reserve Bank Notes, Series of 1915 and 1918, W-900-A to W-929-L.

W-830-F-b • F-837B • 1,080,000
Estimated population: 46 to 52 • *Highest graded:* Unc.

VG-8	F-12	VF-20	EF-40	AU-50	Unc-60	Unc-63
$200	$375	$575	$1,000	$1,300	$2,000	$2,950

W-830-G-a • F-838A • Chicago • 1,300,000
Estimated population: 70 to 80 • *Highest graded:* Unc.

VG-8	F-12	VF-20	EF-40	AU-50	Unc-60	Unc-63
$200	$375	$575	$1,000	$1,300	$2,000	$2,950

W-830-G-b • F-838B • 3,500,000
Estimated population: 135 to 145 • *Highest graded:* Unc.

VG-8	F-12	VF-20	EF-40	AU-50	Unc-60	Unc-63	Unc-65
$200	$375	$575	$1,000	$1,300	$2,000	$2,950	$4,750

W-830-H-a • F-839A • St. Louis • 780,000
Estimated population: 40 to 45 • *Highest graded:* Unc.

VG-8	F-12	VF-20	EF-40	AU-50	Unc-60	Unc-63
$225	$425	$650	$1,100	$1,450	$2,250	$3,100

W-830-H-b • F-839B • 1,612,000
Estimated population: 135 to 145 • *Highest graded:* Unc.

VG-8	F-12	VF-20	EF-40	AU-50	Unc-60	Unc-63	Unc-65
$225	$425	$650	$1,100	$1,450	$2,250	$3,100	$5,000

W-830-I-a • F-840A • Minneapolis • 520,000
Estimated population: 35 to 40 • *Highest graded:* Unc.

VG-8	F-12	VF-20	EF-40	AU-50	Unc-60	Unc-63
$225	$425	$650	$1,100	$1,450	$2,250	$3,100

W-830-I-b • F-840B • 1,088,000
Estimated population: 60 to 70 • *Highest graded:* Unc.

VG-8	F-12	VF-20	EF-40	AU-50	Unc-60	Unc-63	Unc-65
$225	$425	$650	$1,100	$1,450	$2,250	$3,100	$6,000

W-830-J-a • F-841A • Kansas City • 520,000
Estimated population: 38 to 47 • *Highest graded:* Unc.

VG-8	F-12	VF-20	EF-40	AU-50	Unc-60	Unc-63
$225	$425	$650	$1,100	$1,450	$2,400	$3,500

W-830-J-b • F-841B • 1,080,000
Estimated population: 34 to 40 • *Highest graded:* AU-50.

VG-8	F-12	VF-20	EF-40	AU-50
$350	$575	$1,250	$1,750	$2,500

W-830-K-a • F-842A • Dallas • 520,000
Recorded population: 6 • *Highest graded:* EF-40 • *Commentary:* K1A was once owned by William G. McAdoo. K125010A, VG, is in the Federal Reserve Bank of San Francisco. K349013A, VF, is in the Federal Reserve Bank of Chicago.

VG-8	F-12	VF-20	EF-40
$850	$1,500	$2,250	$3,500

W-830-K-b • F-842B • 1,080,000
Estimated population: 36 to 42 • *Highest graded:* Unc.

VG-8	F-12	VF-20	EF-40	AU-50	Unc-60	Unc-63
$350	$575	$1,250	$1,750	$2,500	$4,000	$7,000

W-830-L-a • F-843A • San Francisco • 520,000
Estimated population: 11 to 13 • *Highest graded:* Unc.

VG-8	F-12	VF-20	EF-40	AU-50	Unc-60	Unc-63
$750	$2,100	$3,800	$4,100	$4,400	$4,800	$6,000

W-830-L-b • F-843B • 2,280,000
Estimated population: 40 to 45 • *Highest graded:* Unc.

VG-8	F-12	VF-20	EF-40	AU-50	Unc-60	Unc-63
$225	$425	$650	$1,450	—	—	—

Series of 1914, Blue Seal

As a class the 1914 Blue Seal notes (illus. on p. 257) are much more available than the Red Seal type. These can be collected by bank as well as by signature combination. As they are not in the mainstream of popularity, scarce and rare varieties are priced lower than might otherwise be the case.

In all of the following listings the number 1 to 12 and the large letter A to L on the seal at the left indicate the Federal Reserve Bank that issued the note.

Plate Style b (on Red and Blue Seals): In certain of the following listings the small letter b indicates a note in the format of the Style b also used on Red Seal notes. A large district number and letter are at the lower left and top right, and at the top left a small bank district letter and numeral are added above the plate letter, and a small bank district letter and number are at the lower right. In the Blue Seal series, all Burke-McAdoo, Burke-Glass, and Burke-Houston notes are of this style.

Plate Style c (on Blue Seals only): In certain of the following listings the small letter c indicates large bank district letter and numeral at top right and small district letters and numerals in the other three corners. The letter and numeral at the upper left corner are over a plate letter. Only some late White-Mellon notes are of this style.

Plate Style d (on Blue Seals only): In certain of the following listings the small letter d indicates a note similar to Style b, but positioned both vertically, more

toward the center of the note and closer to the outside edge. Also, the seals to the sides of the portrait are closer than on the b and c issues. White-Mellon (1921–1928) notes are found in b, c, and d styles.

W-840-A-b • F-844 • Boston • Burke-McAdoo (1913–1918) • 10,000,000 (est.)
Estimated population: 60 to 70 • *Highest graded:* Unc.

VG-8	F-12	VF-20	EF-40	AU-50	Unc-60	Unc-63	Unc-65
$70	$85	$105	$140	$180	$200	$375	$750

W-840-A-b★ • F-844★
Recorded population: 4 • *Highest graded:* Unc • *Selected information:* CAA (1/2005), A20861★/E, AU, $3,910.

W-841-A-b • F-845 • Burke-Glass (1918–1920) • 9,000,000 (est.)
Estimated population: 65 to 75 • *Highest graded:* Unc.

VG-8	F-12	VF-20	EF-40	AU-50	Unc-60	Unc-63	Unc-65
$75	$95	$120	$160	$200	$225	$400	$850

W-841-A-b★ • F-845★
Recorded population: 4 • *Highest graded:* AU-53 • *Selected information:* CAA (5/2005), A106215★/C, F+, $4,888. CAA (9/2006), A114231★/C, AU, $5,175.

W-842-A-b • F-846 • Burke-Houston (1920–1921) • 14,376,000 (est.)
Estimated population: 120 to 130 • *Highest graded:* Unc.

VG-8	F-12	VF-20	EF-40	AU-50	Unc-60	Unc-63
$70	$85	$105	$140	$180	$200	$375

W-842-A-b★ • F-846★
Estimated population: 10 to 12 • *Highest graded:* EF-40.

VF-20	EF-40
$500	$1,000

W-843-A-b • F-847A • White-Mellon (1921–1928) • 48,024,000 (est.)
Estimated population: 475 to 550 • *Highest graded:* Unc.

VG-8	F-12	VF-20	EF-40	AU-50	Unc-60	Unc-63	Unc-65
$70	$85	$105	$140	$180	$200	$375	$750

W-843-A-b★ • F-847A★
Estimated population: 25 to 30 • *Highest graded:* Unc.

VF-20	EF-40	AU-50	Unc-60	Unc-63
$400	$800	$1,400	$2,500	—

W-843-A-c • F-847B • 5,716,000 (est.)
Estimated population: 70 to 80 • *Highest graded:* Unc.

VG-8	F-12	VF-20	EF-40	AU-50	Unc-60	Unc-63	Unc-65
$80	$100	$125	$165	$225	$250	$450	$925

W-843-A-d • F-847C • 1,292,000[36] • Printed but not issued

W-844-B-b • F-848 • New York • Burke-McAdoo (1913–1918) • 50,140,000 (est.)
Estimated population: 175 to 190 • *Highest graded:* Unc.

VG-8	F-12	VF-20	EF-40	AU-50	Unc-60	Unc-63	Unc-65
$70	$85	$105	$140	$180	$200	$375	$750

W-844-B-b★ • F-848★

Recorded population: 6 • *Highest graded:* AU-50 • *Commentary:* B1073★/A in the Federal Reserve Bank of New York • *Selected information:* CAA (1/2005), B5472★/D, EF, $1,293.

W-845-B-b • F-849 • Burke-Glass (1918–1920) • 17,268,000 (est.)

Estimated population: 95 to 105 • *Highest graded:* Unc.

VG-8	F-12	VF-20	EF-40	AU-50	Unc-60	Unc-63	Unc-65
$75	$95	$120	$160	$200	$225	$400	$850

W-845-B-b★ • F-849★

Recorded population: 5 • *Highest graded:* Unc • *Selected information:* CAA (5/2002), B249279★/C, Unc, $1,380. Heritage (9/2007), B294971★/C, VG, $748.

W-846-B-b • F-850 • Burke-Houston (1920–1921) • 37,012,000 (est.)

Estimated population: 280 to 340 • *Highest graded:* Unc.

VG-8	F-12	VF-20	EF-40	AU-50	Unc-60	Unc-63	Unc-65
$70	$85	$105	$140	$180	$200	$375	$750

W-846-B-b★ • F-850★

Estimated population: 30 to 35 • *Highest graded:* AU-58.

VF-20	EF-40	AU-50
$300	$650	$1,100

W-847-B-b • F-851A • White-Mellon (1921–1928) • 130,760,000 (est.)

Estimated population: 1,100 to 1,300 • *Highest graded:* Unc.

VG-8	F-12	VF-20	EF-40	AU-50	Unc-60	Unc-63	Unc-65
$70	$85	$105	$140	$180	$200	$375	$750

W-847-B-b★ • F-851A★

Estimated population: 90 to 95 • *Highest graded:* Unc.

VF-20	EF-40	AU-50	Unc-60	Unc-63
$150	$300	$500	$900	—

W-847-B-c • F-851B • 16,568,000 (est.)

Estimated population: 115 to 125 • *Highest graded:* Unc.

VG-8	F-12	VF-20	EF-40	AU-50	Unc-60	Unc-63	Unc-65
$75	$100	$125	$165	$225	$250	$450	$925

W-847-B-c★ • F-851B★

Recorded population: 5 • *Highest graded:* Unc • *Selected information:* Heritage (9/2007), B2165381★/E, F, $2,530.

W-847-B-d • F-851C • 24,512,000 (est.)

Estimated population: 325 to 375 • *Highest graded:* Unc.

VG-8	F-12	VF-20	EF-40	AU-50	Unc-60	Unc-63	Unc-65
$70	$85	$105	$140	$180	$200	$375	$750

W-847-B-d★ • F-851C★

Estimated population: 19 to 22 • *Highest graded:* Unc.

VF-20	EF-40	AU-50	Unc-60	Unc-63
$450	$600	$1,000	$1,800	—

W-848-C-b • F-852 • Philadelphia • Burke-McAdoo (1913–1918) • 8,808,000 (est.)

Estimated population: 60 to 70 • *Highest graded:* Unc.

VG-8	F-12	VF-20	EF-40	AU-50	Unc-60	Unc-63
$70	$85	$105	$140	$180	$200	$375

W-848-C-b★ • F-852★

Recorded population: 5 • *Highest graded:* EF-40 • *Selected information:* Knight (6/2008), C42133★/E, EF-45 (PCGS), $2,990. CAA (5/2005), C71198★/B, G–VG, $1,035.

W-849-C-b • F-853 • Burke-Glass (1918–1920) • 8,316,000 (est.)

Estimated population: 70 to 80 • *Highest graded:* Unc.

VG-8	F-12	VF-20	EF-40	AU-50	Unc-60	Unc-63	Unc-65
$75	$95	$120	$160	$200	$225	$400	$850

W-849-C-b★ • F-853★

Recorded population: 1 • *Commentary:* The known note is serial C128303★/C, F–VF. Listed by Doug Murray.

W-850-C-b • F-854 • Burke-Houston (1920–1921) • 14,168,000 (est.)

Estimated population: 120 to 135 • *Highest graded:* Unc.

VG-8	F-12	VF-20	EF-40	AU-50	Unc-60	Unc-63	Unc-65
$70	$85	$105	$140	$180	$200	$375	$750

W-850-C-b★ • F-854★

Estimated population: 11 to 13 • *Highest graded:* Unc • *Selected information:* Knight (3/2008), C192789★/A, VF-20 (PMG), $1,092.50. Knight (8/2003), C269049★/A, Unc, $1,380. CAA (1/1997), C317210★/B, EF, $250. Heritage (1/2008), C345258★/B, VF-35 (PCGS), $1,265.

W-851-C-b • F-855A • White-Mellon (1921–1928) • 55,160,000 (est.)

Estimated population: 750 to 900 • *Highest graded:* Unc.

VG-8	F-12	VF-20	EF-40	AU-50	Unc-60	Unc-63	Unc-65
$70	$85	$105	$140	$180	$200	$375	$750

W-851-C-b★ • F-855A★

Estimated population: 55 to 65 • *Highest graded:* Unc.

VF-20	EF-40	AU-50	Unc-60	Unc-63
$200	$400	$600	$1,000	—

W-851-C-c • F-855B • 8,088,000 (est.)

Estimated population: 75 to 85 • *Highest graded:* Unc.

VG-8	F-12	VF-20	EF-40	AU-50	Unc-60	Unc-63	Unc-65
$75	$100	$125	$165	$225	$250	$450	$925

W-851-C-c★ • F-855B★

Recorded population: 3 • *Highest graded:* Unc • *Selected information:* CAA (10/1995), C9328675★/E, EF, $1,155. CAA (5/1999), C944834★/B, Unc-66 (PMG), $1,760; later seen in Heritage (9/2008), not sold. Knight (8/2000), C944835★/C, Unc, $2,228.

W-851-C-d • F-855C • 5,284,000 (est.)

Estimated population: 225 to 275 • *Highest graded:* Unc.

VG-8	F-12	VF-20	EF-40	AU-50	Unc-60	Unc-63	Unc-65
$70	$85	$105	$140	$180	$200	$375	$750

SERIES OF 1914, BLUE SEAL

$5 Federal Reserve Note, Series of 1914, Blue Seal. Face of W-851-C-b showing the "b" format, the same as used on "b" style Red Seal notes. The back is the standard back found on Series of 1914 Federal Reserve Notes.

$5 Federal Reserve Note, Series of 1914, Blue Seal. Face of W-851-C-c showing the "c" style of face plate. The back is the standard back found on Series of 1914 Federal Reserve Notes.

$5 Federal Reserve Note, Series of 1914, Blue Seal. Face of W-851-C-d showing the "d" style of face plate. The back is the standard back found on Series of 1914 Federal Reserve Notes.

W-851-C-d★ • F-855C★

Recorded population: 7 • *Highest graded:* VF-30 • *Selected information:* Knight (3/2008) C997306★/B, F, damaged (later graded Net VF-25 by PMG), $920. Heritage (1/2007), C998934★/F, F, $1,495.

W-852-D-b • F-856 • Cleveland • Burke-McAdoo (1913–1918) • 6,324,000 (est.)

Estimated population: 60 to 70 • *Highest graded:* Unc.

VG-8	F-12	VF-20	EF-40	AU-50	Unc-60	Unc-63
$70	$85	$105	$140	$180	$200	$375

W-852-D-b★ • F-856★

Recorded population: 2 • *Highest graded:* Unc • *Commentary:* The known notes include serials D48428★/D, Unc, listed by Doug Murray, and D76622★/F, G–VG, sold in a Knight auction (11/2006) for $1,092.50.

W-853-D-b • F-857 • Burke-Glass (1918–1920) • 3,340,000 (est.)

Estimated population: 42 to 46 • *Highest graded:* Unc.

VG-8	F-12	VF-20	EF-40	AU-50	Unc-60	Unc-63	Unc-65
$85	$115	$200	$275	$360	$500	$800	$1,900

W-853-D-b★ • F-857★

Recorded population: 3 • *Highest graded:* F-15 • *Commentary:* Known notes include serials D90476★/D, VG, sold in a Heritage auction (9/2007) for $1,380; D93195★/C, F–VF; and D98814★/B, VG.

W-854-D-b • F-858 • Burke-Houston (1920–1921) • 12,296,000 (est.)

Estimated population: 100 to 110 • *Highest graded:* Unc.

VG-8	F-12	VF-20	EF-40	AU-50	Unc-60	Unc-63	Unc-65
$70	$85	$105	$140	$180	$200	$375	$750

W-854-D-b★ • F-858★

Estimated population: 11 to 13 • *Highest graded:* Unc • *Selected information:* Heritage (1/2007), D140266★/B, VG, $287.50. CAA (9/2002), D144251★/C, F, $345. CAA (5/2000), D207795★/C, VF, $522.50. Knight (3/2008), D269865★/A, VG-8 (PCGS), $517.50. Knight (2/1997), D295412★/D, Unc, $880. Heritage (1/2008), D308610★/B, F-15 (PCGS), $488.75.

W-855-D-b • F-859A • White-Mellon (1921–1928) • 36,184,000 (est.)

Estimated population: 350 to 425 • *Highest graded:* Unc.

VG-8	F-12	VF-20	EF-40	AU-50	Unc-60	Unc-63	Unc-65
$70	$85	$105	$140	$180	$200	$375	$750

W-855-D-b★ • F-859A★

Estimated population: 30 to 35 • *Highest graded:* Unc.

VF-20	EF-40	AU-50	Unc-60	Unc-63
$450	$600	$1,100	$1,500	—

W-855-D-c • F-859B • 4,432,000 (est.)

Estimated population: 90 to 95 • *Highest graded:* Unc.

VG-8	F-12	VF-20	EF-40	AU-50	Unc-60	Unc-63
$85	$95	$120	$160	$180	$200	$375

W-855-D-c★ • F-859B★

Recorded population: 2 • *Highest graded:* Unc • *Commentary:* The known notes are serial D628232★/H, VF, per Doug Murray, and D628578★/B, Unc.

W-855-D-d • F-859C • 7,104,000 (est.)

Estimated population: 185 to 200 • *Highest graded:* Unc.

VG-8	F-12	VF-20	EF-40	AU-50	Unc-60	Unc-63	Unc-65
$70	$85	$105	$140	$180	$200	$375	$750

W-855-D-d★ • F-859C★

Recorded population: 5 • *Highest graded:* EF-40 • *Selected information:* Heritage (1/2007), D699922★/F, F, $1,825. Heritage (9/2007), D702818★/B, EF (PCGS), $4,313. Knight (11/2005), D707552★/H, EF, $4,313.

W-856-E-b • F-860 • Richmond • Burke-McAdoo (1913–1918) • 6,684,000 (est.)

Estimated population: 60 to 70 • *Highest graded:* Unc.

VG-8	F-12	VF-20	EF-40	AU-50	Unc-60	Unc-63	Unc-65
$70	$85	$105	$140	$180	$200	$375	$750

W-857-E-b • F-861 • Burke-Glass (1918–1920) • 4,616,000 (est.)

Estimated population: 35 to 40 • *Highest graded:* Unc.

VG-8	F-12	VF-20	EF-40	AU-50	Unc-60	Unc-63
$150	$300	$400	$450	$550	$750	$1,200

W-858-E-b • F-862 • Burke-Houston (1920–1921) • 11,452,000 (est.)

Estimated population: 105 to 120 • *Highest graded:* Unc.

VG-8	F-12	VF-20	EF-40	AU-50	Unc-60	Unc-63	Unc-65
$70	$85	$105	$140	$180	$200	$375	$750

W-858-E-b★ • F-862★

Estimated population: 12 to 14 • *Highest graded:* VF-30 • *Selected information:* CAA (5/2003), E162678★/B, F, $258.75. CAA (5/1999), E217992★/D, F, $275. Heritage (9/2007), E228321★/A, F, $580.75. CAA (5/1997), E233562★/B, G–VG, $176. Stack's (3/1991), E246683★/C, VF, $400. Heritage (1/2006), E252514★/B, VF, $977.50. CAA (5/2003), E260713★/A, F-12 (PCGS), $402.50.

W-859-E-b • F-863A • White-Mellon (1921–1928) • 20,140,000 (est.)

Estimated population: 275 to 350 • *Highest graded:* Unc.

VG-8	F-12	VF-20	EF-40	AU-50	Unc-60	Unc-63
$70	$85	$105	$140	$180	$200	$375

W-859-E-b★ • F-863A★

Estimated population: 10 to 12 • *Highest graded:* EF-40 • *Selected information:* CAA (1/2002), E292854★/B, VG, $253. CAA (9/2003), E320318★/B, VF, $661.25. H.I. Melnick (11/1983), E385422★/F, VG, $125. Smythe (6/2003), E427207★/C, EF, $1,495. CAA (5/2005), E432772★/H, F–VF, $920.

W-859-E-c • F-863B • 3,316,000 (est.)

Recorded population: 4 • *Highest graded:* EF-40.

VG-8	F-12	VF-20	EF-40
$300	$800	$1,750	$3,000

W-859-E-d • F-863C • 1,236,000 (est.) • Printed but not issued

W-860-F-b • F-864 • Atlanta • Burke-McAdoo (1913–1918) • 8,700,000 (est.)

Estimated population: 60 to 65 • *Highest graded:* Unc.

VG-8	F-12	VF-20	EF-40	AU-50	Unc-60	Unc-63
$70	$85	$105	$140	$180	$200	$375

W-860-F-b★ • F-864★

Recorded population: 1 • *Selected information:* CAA (1/1997), F1452★/D, F, $1,073.

W-861-F-b • F-865 • Burke-Glass (1918–1920) • 5,200,000 (est.)

Estimated population: 40 to 45 • *Highest graded:* Unc.

VG-8	F-12	VF-20	EF-40	AU-50	Unc-60	Unc-63
$100	$150	$225	$300	$400	$450	$700

W-861-F-b★ • F-865★

Recorded population: 1 • *Selected information:* CAA (5/2005), F34698★/B, G–VG, problems, $5,463.

W-862-F-b • F-866 • Burke-Houston (1920–1921) • 9,200,000 (est.)

Estimated population: 62 to 66 • *Highest graded:* Unc.

VG-8	F-12	VF-20	EF-40	AU-50	Unc-60	Unc-63	Unc-65
$75	$90	$115	$150	$200	$225	$400	$825

W-862-F-b★ • F-866★

Estimated population: 11 to 13 • *Highest graded:* VF-30 • *Selected information:* Heritage (9/2007), F120593★/A, F, $575. CAA (9/2002), F230977★/A, AG–G, $149.50.

W-863-F-b • F-867A • White-Mellon (1921–1928) • 28,092,000 (est.)

Estimated population: 215 to 230 • *Highest graded:* Unc.

VG-8	F-12	VF-20	EF-40	AU-50	Unc-60	Unc-63	Unc-65
$70	$85	$105	$140	$180	$200	$375	$750

W-863-F-b★ • F-867A★

Estimated population: 11 to 13 • *Highest graded:* VF-30 • *Selected information:* Heritage (1/2006), F365873★/A, F–VF, $1,380. Knight (2/1997), F382654★/B, F–VF, $253. CAA (1/2005), F443821★/A, VG, $632.50.

W-863-F-c • F-867B • 2,112,000 (est.)

Estimated population: 9 or 10 • *Highest graded:* Unc.

F-12	VF-20	EF-40	AU-50	Unc-60	Unc-63	Unc-65
$475	$600	$800	$950	$1,100	$1,400	—

W-863-F-d • F-867C • 96,000 (est.) • Printed but not issued

W-864-G-b • F-868 • Chicago • Burke-McAdoo (1913–1918) • 19,020,000 (est.)

Estimated population: 110 to 130 • *Highest graded:* Unc.

VG-8	F-12	VF-20	EF-40	AU-50	Unc-60	Unc-63	Unc-65
$70	$85	$105	$140	$180	$200	$375	$750

W-864-G-b★ • F-868★

Recorded population: 2 • *Highest graded:* F-15 • *Commentary:* The serial numbers for the known notes are G31647★/C, F-15 (PCGS), sold in a Heritage auction (9/2007) for $5,750, and G58630★/B, VG.

W-865-G-b • F-869 • Burke-Glass (1918–1920) • 10,380,000 (est.)

Estimated population: 95 to 105 • *Highest graded:* Unc.

VG-8	F-12	VF-20	EF-40	AU-50	Unc-60	Unc-63	Unc-65
$75	$95	$120	$160	$200	$225	$400	$850

W-865-G-b★ • F-869★

Recorded population: 6 • *Highest graded:* AU-55 (Amon Carter specimen) • *Selected information:* Knight (2/2004), G202138★/B, F-12 (CGA), $1,093.

W-866-G-b • F-870 • Burke-Houston (1920–1921) • 17,484,000 (est.)

Estimated population: 180 to 200 • *Highest graded:* Unc.

VG-8	F-12	VF-20	EF-40	AU-50	Unc-60	Unc-63	Unc-65
$70	$85	$105	$140	$180	$200	$375	$750

W-866-G-b★ • F-870★

Estimated population: 25 to 28 • *Highest graded:* Unc.

F-12	VF-20	EF-40	AU-50	Unc-60	Unc-63
$300	$600	$1,100	$1,800	$2,500	$3,200

W-867-G-b • F-871A • White-Mellon (1921–1928) • 90,376,000 (est.)

Estimated population: 800 to 1,000 • *Highest graded:* Unc.

VG-8	F-12	VF-20	EF-40	AU-50	Unc-60	Unc-63	Unc-65
$70	$85	$105	$140	$180	$200	$375	$750

W-867-G-b★ • F-871A★

Estimated population: 70 to 80 • *Highest graded:* Unc.

F-12	VF-20	EF-40	AU-50	Unc-60	Unc-63
$175	$350	$600	$1,200	$1,600	$2,000

W-867-G-c • F-871B • 16,472,000 (est.)

Estimated population: 300 to 400 • *Highest graded:* Unc.

VG-8	F-12	VF-20	EF-40	AU-50	Unc-60	Unc-63	Unc-65
$70	$85	$105	$140	$180	$200	$375	$750

W-867-G-c★ • F-871B★

Recorded population: 2 • *Highest graded:* VF-30 • *Commentary:* The serials for the known notes are G1384256★/H, VG–F, sold in a Hickman & Oakes auction (11/1988) for $350; and G1395330★/B, VF, listed by Doug Murray.

W-867-G-d • F-871C • 6,344,000 (est.)

Estimated population: 145 to 155 • *Highest graded:* Unc.

VG-8	F-12	VF-20	EF-40	AU-50	Unc-60	Unc-63	Unc-65
$70	$85	$105	$140	$180	$200	$375	$750

W-867-G-d★ • F-871C★

Recorded population: 4 • *Highest graded:* Unc • *Commentary:* The serials for the known notes are G1478429★/A, Unc, offered by Dennis Forgue (6/1998); G1479314★/B, Unc, sold in a Heritage auction (1/2007) for $6,325; G1489429★/A, G–VG, sold in a Heritage auction (9/2007) for $863; and G1491069★/E, VG.

W-868-H-b • F-872 • St. Louis • Burke-McAdoo (1913–1918) • 7,356,000 (est.)

Estimated population: 85 to 95 • *Highest graded:* Unc.

VG-8	F-12	VF-20	EF-40	AU-50	Unc-60	Unc-63	Unc-65
$70	$85	$105	$140	$180	$200	$375	$750

W-868-H-b★ • F-872★

Recorded population: 4 • *Highest graded:* VF-25 • *Selected information:* Heritage (9/2007), H5451★/G, VF-25 (PCGS), $4,313.

W-869-H-b • F-873 • Burke-Glass (1918–1920) • 6,552,000 (est.)

Estimated population: 75 to 85 • *Highest graded:* Unc.

VG-8	F-12	VF-20	EF-40	AU-50	Unc-60	Unc-63
$100	$140	$190	$210	$240	$300	$500

W-869-H-b★ • F-873★

Estimated population: 9 or 10 • *Highest graded:* Unc • *Selected information:* H134710★/B, Unc, Federal Reserve Bank of San Francisco. Heritage (1/2008), H88506★/B, VG-10 (PMG), $431. Heritage (9/2007), H97110★/B, VF-35 (PCGS), $1,265.

W-870-H-b • F-874 • Burke-Houston (1920–1921) • 15,500,000 (est.)

Estimated population: 165 to 180 • *Highest graded:* Unc.

VG-8	F-12	VF-20	EF-40	AU-50	Unc-60	Unc-63	Unc-65
$70	$85	$105	$140	$180	$200	$375	$750

W-870-H-b★ • F-874★

Estimated population: 14 to 16 • *Highest graded:* AU-58.

VF-20	EF-40	AU-50
$550	$1,100	$1,900

W-871-H-b • F-875A • White-Mellon (1921–1928) • 8,060,000 (est.)

Estimated population: 155 to 165 • *Highest graded:* Unc.

VG-8	F-12	VF-20	EF-40	AU-50	Unc-60	Unc-63	Unc-65
$70	$85	$105	$140	$180	$200	$375	$750

W-871-H-b★ • F-875A★

Recorded population: 5 • *Highest graded:* EF-40 • *Selected information:* CAA (1/2000), H426410★/B, VG, $303.

W-871-H-c • F-875B • 1,844,000 (est.)

Estimated population: 75 to 85 • *Highest graded:* Unc.

VG-8	F-12	VF-20	EF-40	AU-50	Unc-60	Unc-63	Unc-65
$75	$90	$110	$150	$170	$220	$395	$800

W-872-I-b • F-876 • Minneapolis • Burke-McAdoo (1913–1918) • 7,612,000 (est.)

Estimated population: 95 to 105 • *Highest graded:* Unc.

VG-8	F-12	VF-20	EF-40	AU-50	Unc-60	Unc-63	Unc-65
$75	$100	$120	$160	$190	$250	$450	$900

W-872-I-b★ • F-876★

Recorded population: 1 • *Commentary:* The known note is serial I27205★/A, VF.

W-873-I-b • F-877 • Burke-Glass (1918–1920) • 3,080,000 (est.)

Estimated population: 55 to 65 • *Highest graded:* Unc.

VG-8	F-12	VF-20	EF-40	AU-50	Unc-60	Unc-63
$90	$115	$150	$200	$300	$475	$750

W-873-I-b★ • F-877★

Recorded population: 3 • *Highest graded:* Unc • *Commentary:* The serials for the known notes include I71161★/A, Unc, owned by the Federal Reserve Bank of San Francisco, and I70419★/C, VG, per Doug Murray. • *Selected information:* CAA (5/1996), I49417★/A, F, $715.

W-874-I-b • F-878 • Burke-Houston (1920–1921) • 3,640,000 (est.)

Estimated population: 58 to 64 • *Highest graded:* Unc.

VG-8	F-12	VF-20	EF-40	AU-50	Unc-60	Unc-63
$75	$100	$120	$160	$190	$250	$450

W-874-I-b★ • F-878★

Estimated population: 11 to 13 • *Highest graded:* VF-20 • *Selected information:* Heritage (9/2007), I83837★/A, F-12 (PCGS), $833.75. CAA (5/1993), I96797★/A, F–VF, $605. Hickman Auctions (6/1991), I112989★/A, "Poor . . . one of the worse looking notes ever," Poor, repaired, $68. Smythe (2/2000), I125599★/C, VG, pinholes, $198. CAA (5/2005), I135443★/C, VF, $2,012.50. CAA (9/2005), I138857★/A, F, damaged, $1,092.50.

W-875-I-b • F-879A • White-Mellon (1921–1928) • 14,068,000 (est.)

Estimated population: 350 to 425 • *Highest graded:* Unc.

VG-8	F-12	VF-20	EF-40	AU-50	Unc-60	Unc-63	Unc-65
$75	$100	$120	$160	$190	$250	$450	$900

W-875-I-b★ • F-879A★

Estimated population: 10 to 12 • *Highest graded:* Unc • *Selected information:* Knight (11/2004), I168304★/D, F, $1,265. Heritage (1/2006), I196060★/D, EF, $2,185.

W-875-I-c • F-879B • 108,000 (est.) • Printed but not issued

W-876-J-b • F-880 • Kansas City • Burke-McAdoo (1913–1918) • 11,108,000 (est.)

Estimated population: 100 to 115 • *Highest graded:* Unc.

VG-8	F-12	VF-20	EF-40	AU-50	Unc-60	Unc-63	Unc-65
$70	$85	$105	$140	$180	$200	$375	$750

W-876-J-b★ • F-880★

Recorded population: 2 • *Highest graded:* F-12 • *Selected information:* CAA (9/2005), J6933★/A, VG, $1,495. CAA (5/1999), J23354★/B, F, $1,320.

W-877-J-b • F-881 • Burke-Glass (1918–1920) • 5,192,000 (est.)

Estimated population: 46 to 52 • *Highest graded:* Unc.

VG-8	F-12	VF-20	EF-40	AU-50	Unc-60	Unc-63	Unc-65
$90	$115	$150	$200	$300	$475	$750	—

W-877-J-b★ • F-881★

Recorded population: 3 • *Highest graded:* EF-40 • *Selected information:* CAA (1/2000), J28215★/G, F–VF, $605. Heritage (9/2007), J82754★/B, F-15 (PCGS), $3,910. CAA (5/2005), J87801★/A, EF, $6,900.

W-878-J-b • F-882 • Burke-Houston (1920–1921) • 2,888,000 (est.)

Estimated population: 130 to 150 • *Highest graded:* Unc.

VG-8	F-12	VF-20	EF-40	AU-50	Unc-60	Unc-63
$70	$85	$105	$140	$180	$200	$375

W-878-J-b★ • F-882★

Estimated population: 10 to 12 • *Highest graded:* AU-50 • *Selected information:* Knight (4/2003), J134754★/B, VG, $259.

Knight (6/2008), J180397★/A, VF-30 (PCGS, later graded EF-40 by PCGS), $1,495. Heritage (1/2006), J195999★/C, F, $1,093.

W-879-J-b • F-883A • White-Mellon (1921–1928) • 22,728,000 (est.)

Estimated population: 375 to 450 • *Highest graded:* Unc.

VG-8	F-12	VF-20	EF-40	AU-50	Unc-60	Unc-63	Unc-65
$70	$85	$105	$140	$180	$200	$375	$750

W-879-J-b★ • F-883A★

Estimated population: 15 to 17 • *Highest graded:* AU-50.

F-12	VF-20	EF-40	AU-50
$550	$1,100	$1,700	$2,500

W-879-J-c • F-883B • 880,000 (est.)

Estimated population: 23 to 27 • *Highest graded:* AU-55.

VG-8	F-12	VF-20	EF-40	AU-50
$100	$200	$400	$650	$950

W-880-K-b • F-884 • Dallas • Burke-McAdoo (1913–1918) • 4,500,000 (est.)

Estimated population: 36 to 42 • *Highest graded:* Unc.

VG-8	F-12	VF-20	EF-40	AU-50	Unc-60	Unc-63	Unc-65
$90	$150	$275	$450	$750	$950	$1,200	$1,600

W-881-K-b • F-885 • Burke-Glass (1918–1920) • 4,700,000 (est.)

Estimated population: 35 to 40 • *Highest graded:* AU-58.

VG-8	F-12	VF-20	EF-40	AU-50
$275	$500	$800	$1,400	$2,000

W-881-K-b★ • F-885★

Recorded population: 2 • *Highest graded:* F-12 • *Commentary:* The serials for the known notes are K35114★/B, F, and K70673★/A, F.

W-882-K-b • F-886 • Burke-Houston (1920–1921) • 3,904,000 (est.)

Estimated population: 48 to 54 • *Highest graded:* Unc.

VG-8	F-12	VF-20	EF-40	AU-50	Unc-60	Unc-63	Unc-65
$90	$115	$150	$200	$300	$475	$750	—

W-882-K-b★ • F-886★

Recorded population: 4 • *Highest graded:* VG-8 • *Commentary:* The serials for the known notes are K93134★/B, G; K117242★/B, VG; K120158★/B, VG, sold in a CAA auction (1/2003) for $920; and K159142★/B, G–VG, sold in a CAA auction (1/1994) for $347.

W-883-K-b • F-887A • White-Mellon (1921–1928) • 12,996,000 (est.)

Estimated population: 185 to 205 • *Highest graded:* Unc.

VG-8	F-12	VF-20	EF-40	AU-50	Unc-60	Unc-63	Unc-65
$70	$85	$105	$140	$180	$200	$375	$750

W-883-K-b★ • F-887A★

Recorded population: 8 • *Highest graded:* VF-30 • *Selected information:* CAA (5/2005), K231110★/B, VG–F, $1,495.

W-883-K-c • F-887B • 1,554,000 (est.)

Estimated population: 30 to 35 • *Highest graded:* Unc.

VG-8	F-12	VF-20	EF-40	AU-50	Unc-60	Unc-63	Unc-65
$90	$115	$150	$200	$300	$475	$750	—

W-883-K-d • F-887C • 172,000 (est.) • Printed but not issued

W-884-L-b • F-888 • San Francisco • Burke-McAdoo (1913–1918) • 10,600,000 (est.)

Estimated population: 55 to 65 • *Highest graded:* AU-50.

VG-8	F-12	VF-20	EF-40	AU-50
$75	$90	$115	$150	$200

W-884-L-b★ • F-888★

Recorded population: 1 • *Commentary:* L29142★/B, VG.

W-885-L-b • F-889 • Burke-Glass (1918–1920) • 4,200,000 (est.)

Estimated population: 18 to 20 • *Highest graded:* AU-50.

VG-8	F-12	VF-20	EF-40	AU-50
$130	$200	$300	$550	$1,200

W-886-L-b • F-890 • Burke-Houston (1920–1921) • 12,628,000 (est.)

Estimated population: 55 to 65 • *Highest graded:* Unc.

VG-8	F-12	VF-20	EF-40	AU-50	Unc-60	Unc-63
$75	$90	$115	$150	$200	$225	$400

W-886-L-b★ • F-890★

Recorded population: 4 • *Highest graded:* EF-40 • *Commentary:* The serials for the known notes are L218058★/B, EF, sold in a CAA auction (10/1995) for $638; L288002★, F; L298782★/B, VF; and L306406★/B, VG–F, sold in a CAA auction (5/1996) for $198.

W-887-L-b • F-891A • White-Mellon (1921–1928) • 54,596,000 (est.)

Estimated population: 300 to 350 • *Highest graded:* Unc.

VG-8	F-12	VF-20	EF-40	AU-50	Unc-60	Unc-63
$70	$85	$105	$140	$180	$200	$375

W-887-L-b★ • F-891a★

Estimated population: 23 to 26 • *Highest graded:* Unc.

F-12	VF-20	EF-40	AU-50	Unc-60	Unc-63
$400	$800	$1,200	$1,800	$2,250	$2,700

W-887-L-c • F-891B • 5,576,000 (est.)

Estimated population: 65 to 70 • *Highest graded:* Unc.

VG-8	F-12	VF-20	EF-40	AU-50	Unc-60	Unc-63
$75	$90	$115	$150	$200	$225	$400

W-887-L-c★ • F-891b★

Recorded population: 1 • *Commentary:* The known note is serial L841502★/F, Unc, ex James M. Wade, ex Aubrey Bebee, now in the ANA Museum.

W-887-L-d • F-891C • 1,768,000 (est.)

Estimated population: 24 to 28 • *Highest graded:* Unc.

VG-8	F-12	VF-20	EF-40	AU-50	Unc-60	Unc-63
$130	$200	$400	$500	$900	$1,200	$2,300

FEDERAL RESERVE BANK NOTES, SERIES OF 1915 AND 1918

Federal Reserve Bank Notes, Series of 1915 and 1918, feature the bank's location spelled out in large letters on the face. The series date is at the upper left and also the lower right. The back is the same general design as seen on the Series of 1914 Federal Reserve Notes, but with different wording. These notes can be acquired by Federal Reserve district as well as by signature combinations. None were issued by the Richmond Federal Reserve Bank.

Series of 1915 and 1918 notes have the signatures of the register of the Treasury and the Treasurer of the United States at the top, and at the bottom the signatures of cashier and governor of the particular Federal Reserve Bank. Their overprinted signatures are on most notes, but some of the Series of 1915 have the signatures separately applied by rubber stamping, sometimes resulting in differences in crispness as well as location. Very early Kansas City $10 notes have autographed signatures, and others may be found.

Series of 1915

Series of 1915 notes have SERIES OF 1915, the date MAY 18, 1914, and in two curved lines vertically at the right border, AUTHORIZED BY THE FEDERAL RESERVE ACT OF DECEMBER 23, 1913. (This notice appears in different formats on higher denominations of this series.)

At the top center of the Series of 1915 notes is the security provision: "Secured by United States bonds deposited with the Treasurer of the United States of America."

These notes are popular, but not in the same league as the $1 (Green Eagle) and $2 (Battleship) bills in the same series, perhaps because the back design is less distinctive.

W-896-F • F-789 • Atlanta • Teehee-Burke (1915–1919) • Pike-McCord • 60,000 (est.)

Estimated population: 32 to 36 • *Highest graded:* AU-58 • *Commentary:* In his 1951 study of these notes (see the bibliography), W.A. Philpott Jr. stated, "All Atlanta $5's are scarce, the 1915, Teehee & Burke, Pike & McCord, being rare." Serial numbers recorded by Martin Gengerke range from F1A to F-56460A.

VG-8	F-12	VF-20	EF-40	AU-50
$150	$325	$500	$700	$900

W-898-F • F-788a • Bell-McCord • No estimate

Recorded population: 1 • *Commentary:* The known note is serial F54748A, face plate D1. This serial is deep within the range recorded by Martin Gengerke for W-896-F, F-789. Rubber-stamped signatures are somewhat faded but legible. Reported in autumn 2008.

W-901-F • F-788 • Bell-Wellborn • 68,000 (est.)

Estimated population: 16 to 18 • *Highest graded:* AU-58 • *Commentary:* Serial numbers recorded by Martin Gengerke range from F63592A (slightly overlapping the range for W-896-F, F-789) to F-120148A.

VG-8	F-12	VF-20	EF-40	AU-50
$200	$400	$1,200	$2,500	$3,500

W-902-G • F-793 • Chicago • Teehee-Burke (1915–1919) • McLallen-McDougal • 320,000

Estimated population: 40 to 45 • *Highest graded:* Unc.

VG-8	F-12	VF-20	EF-40	AU-50	Unc-60	Unc-63	Unc-65
$150	$325	$500	$700	$900	$1,200	$1,650	$2,500

W-903-J • F-801 • Kansas City • Teehee-Burke (1915–1919) • Cross (acting)-Miller • 160,000 (est.)

Estimated population: 12 to 14 • *Highest graded:* Unc.

VG-8	F-12	VF-20	EF-40	AU-50	Unc-60	Unc-63	Unc-65
$450	$1,000	$1,800	$3,000	$4,500	$8,000	$11,000	$15,000

W-904-J • F-800 • Anderson-Miller • 688,000 (est.)

Estimated population: 70 to 80 • *Highest graded:* Unc.

VG-8	F-12	VF-20	EF-40	AU-50	Unc-60	Unc-63
$150	$325	$500	$700	$900	$1,200	$1,650

W-905-J • F-802 • Helm (acting cashier)-Miller • 24,000 (est.)

Recorded population: 5 • *Highest graded:* Unc • *Commentary:* In his 1951 study of these notes (see the bibliography), W.A. Philpott Jr. stated, "The rarest of the Kansas City notes are the 1915 series, Helm & Miller $5 and $10, in Uncirculated condition." The serial numbers known are J855605A/A, VF-25 (PMG), sold at a Heritage auction (4/2008) for $4,312.50; J857077A/A, VF-25 (PMG), sold at a Heritage auction (4/2008) for $7,475; J860111A/C, VG, error with bank signatures stamped across center of note, sold at a Coin Galleries auction (2/1994) for $150; J862559A, Unc, per Mike Crabb (2/1997); and J862567A/C, VF–EF, sold at a Stack's auction (3/1991) for $240.

W-906-K • F-805 • Dallas • Teehee-Burke (1915–1919) • Hoopes-Van Zandt • 208,000 (est.)

Estimated population: 20 to 24 • *Highest graded:* Unc.

VG-8	F-12	VF-20	EF-40	AU-50	Unc-60	Unc-63	Unc-65
$210	$425	$700	$900	$1,200	$1,450	$2,000	—

W-907-K • F-806 • Talley (cashier)-Van Zandt • 120,000 (est.)

Estimated population: 13 to 15 • *Highest graded:* AU-50.

VG-8	F-12	VF-20	EF-40	AU-50
$400	$900	$1,600	$3,000	$4,500

W-908-L • F-808 • San Francisco • Teehee-Burke (1915–1919) • Clerk-Lynch • 336,000

Estimated population: 35 to 40 • *Highest graded:* Unc • *Commentary:* Dated May 20, 1914, instead of May 18 as on all notes of other districts.

VG-8	F-12	VF-20	EF-40	AU-50	Unc-60	Unc-63	Unc-65
$250	$500	$800	$1,000	$1,400	$1,750	$2,600	$4,000

Series of 1918

Series of 1918 notes (illus. on p. 264) have SERIES OF 1918, the date MAY 18, 1914, and at the right border, "Authorized by the acts of December 23, 1913, and April 23, 1918." One

SERIES OF 1915

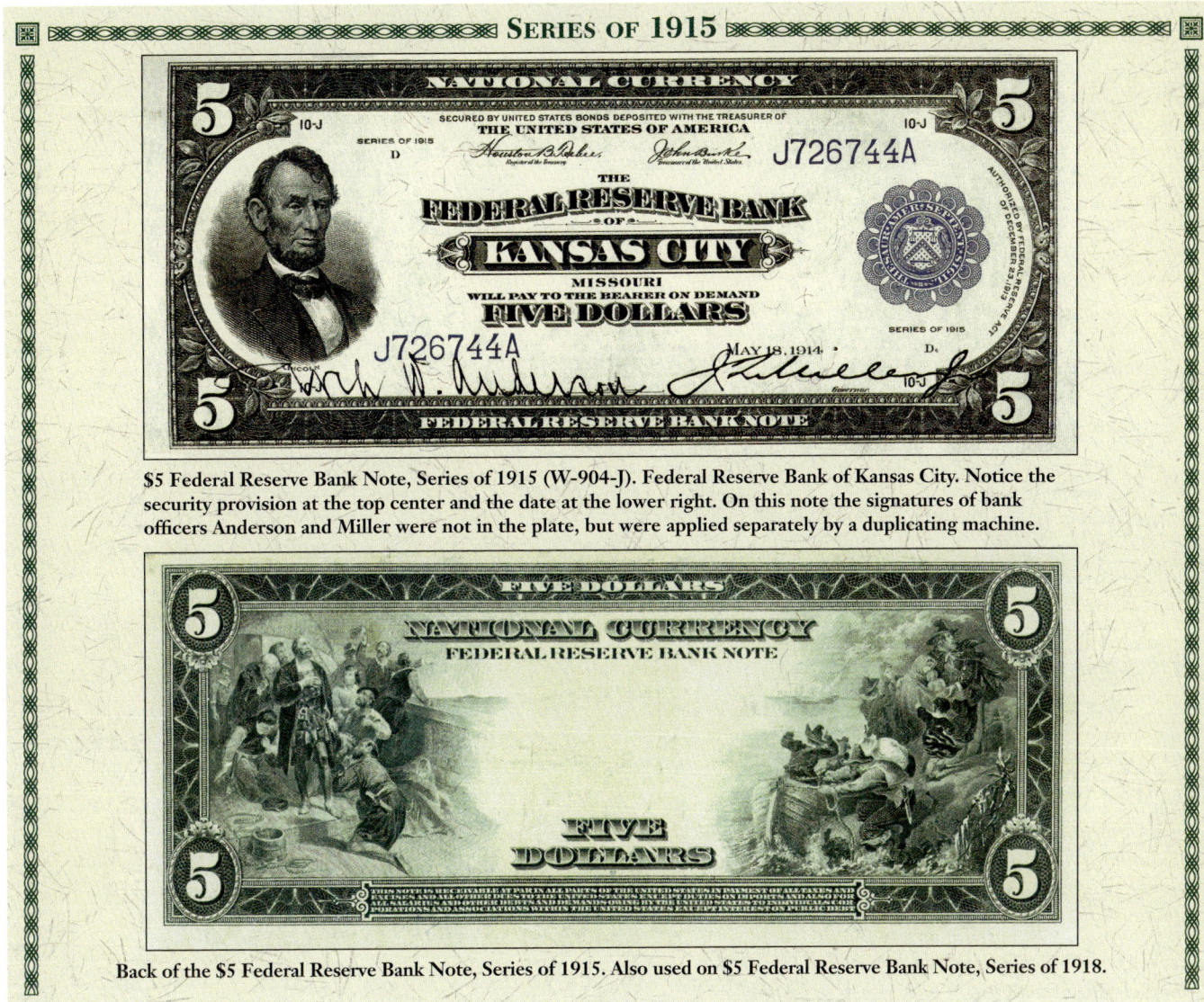

$5 Federal Reserve Bank Note, Series of 1915 (W-904-J). Federal Reserve Bank of Kansas City. Notice the security provision at the top center and the date at the lower right. On this note the signatures of bank officers Anderson and Miller were not in the plate, but were applied separately by a duplicating machine.

Back of the $5 Federal Reserve Bank Note, Series of 1915. Also used on $5 Federal Reserve Bank Note, Series of 1918.

anomalous variety, W-929, San Francisco, is a Series of 1918 with the May 20, 1914, date (this bank also comes with the usual May 18, 1914, date, as W-928).

At the top center is the security provision: "Secured by United States bonds or United States certificates of indebtedness or United States one-year Gold Notes, deposited with the Treasurer of the United States of America."

W-909-A • F-781 • Boston • Teehee-Burke (1915–1919) • Bullen-Morss • 440,000

Estimated population: 40 to 45 • *Highest graded:* Unc • *Commentary:* In his 1951 study of these notes (see the bibliography), W.A. Philpott Jr. commented that the $5 notes of Boston were the rarest of all denominations issued by that bank. As of October 30, 1944, only 375 notes were outstanding.

VG-8	F-12	VF-20	EF-40	AU-50	Unc-60	Unc-63
$200	$400	$600	$900	$1,200	$1,500	$3,250

W-909-A★ • F-781★

Recorded population: 2 • *Highest graded:* VF-20 • *Selected information:* Knight (3/2005), A548★/D, F, $9,200. Dean Oakes (1975), A3925★/A, VF (earlier graded F+), $1,050.

W-910-B • F-782 • New York • Teehee-Burke (1915–1919) • Hendricks-Strong • 6,400,000

Estimated population: 185 to 205 • *Highest graded:* Unc.

VG-8	F-12	VF-20	EF-40	AU-50	Unc-60	Unc-63	Unc-65
$150	$325	$500	$700	$900	$1,200	$1,650	$2,500

W-910-B★ • F-782★

Recorded population: 3 • *Highest graded:* EF-40 • *Selected information:* B&M (4/1997), B4092★/D, EF, $7,150. Heritage (9/2008), B18023★/C, EF-40 (PMG), $18,400.

W-911-C • F-783 • Philadelphia • Teehee-Burke (1915–1919) • Hardt-Passmore • 516,000 (est.)

Estimated population: 48 to 54 • *Highest graded:* Unc.

VG-8	F-12	VF-20	EF-40	AU-50	Unc-60	Unc-63	Unc-65
$150	$325	$500	$700	$900	$1,200	$1,650	$4,000

W-912-C • F-784 • Dyer-Passmore • 1,084,000 (est.)

Estimated population: 40 to 45 • *Highest graded:* Unc.

VG-8	F-12	VF-20	EF-40	AU-50	Unc-60	Unc-63
$165	$350	$550	$750	$950	$1,250	$1,800

SERIES OF 1918

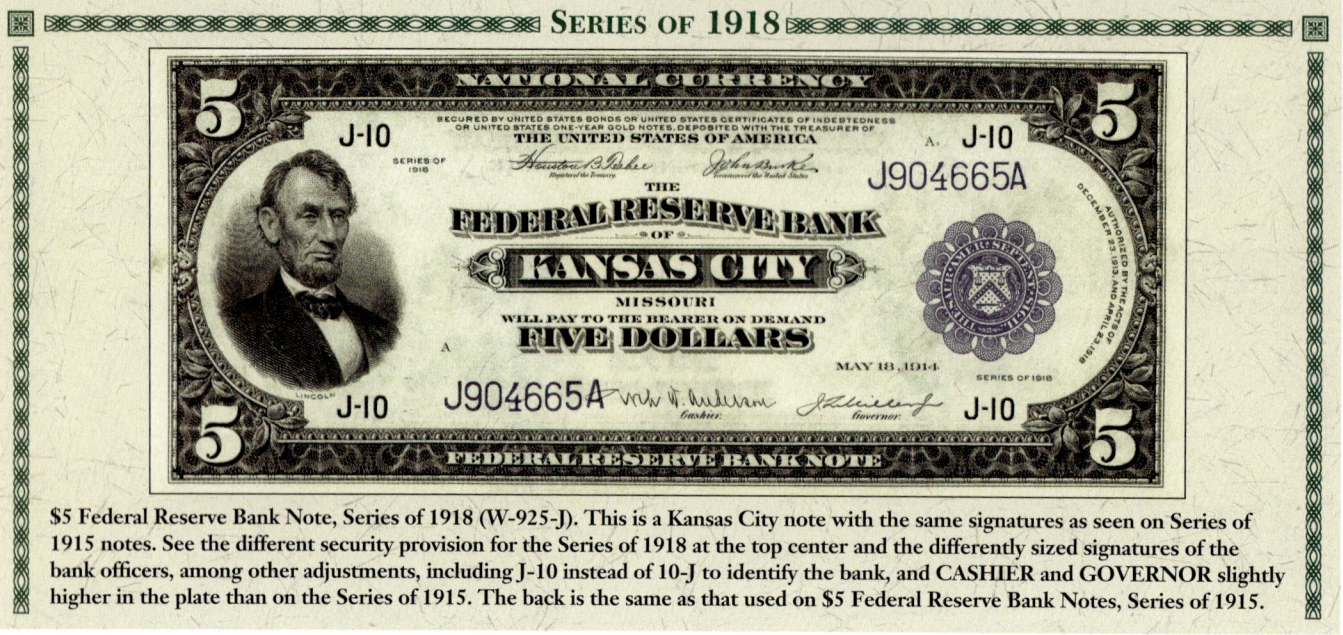

$5 Federal Reserve Bank Note, Series of 1918 (W-925-J). This is a Kansas City note with the same signatures as seen on Series of 1915 notes. See the different security provision for the Series of 1918 at the top center and the differently sized signatures of the bank officers, among other adjustments, including J-10 instead of 10-J to identify the bank, and CASHIER and GOVERNOR slightly higher in the plate than on the Series of 1915. The back is the same as that used on $5 Federal Reserve Bank Notes, Series of 1915.

W-913-D • F-785 • Cleveland • Teehee-Burke (1915–1919) • Baxter-Fancher • 1,376,000 (est.)

Estimated population: 275 to 350 • *Highest graded:* Unc.

VG-8	F-12	VF-20	EF-40	AU-50	Unc-60	Unc-63	Unc-65
$150	$325	$500	$700	$900	$1,200	$1,650	$2,500

W-913-D★ • F-785★

Recorded population: 3 • *Highest graded:* EF-40 • *Commentary:* The known serial numbers are D4781★/A, VG; D4781★/D, EF, sold at a Stack's auction (9/1992) for $1,500; and D8230★/B, G, sold at a CAA auction (6/1994) for $358.

W-914-D • F-786 • Davis-Fancher • 376,000 (est.)

Estimated population: 19 to 22 • *Highest graded:* Unc.

VG-8	F-12	VF-20	EF-40	AU-50	Unc-60	Unc-63
$200	$400	$600	$900	$1,200	$1,900	$3,250

W-915-D • F-787 • Elliott-Burke (1919–1921) • 848,000 (est.)

Estimated population: 54 to 58 • *Highest graded:* Unc.

VG-8	F-12	VF-20	EF-40	AU-50	Unc-60	Unc-63	Unc-65
$150	$325	$500	$700	$900	$1,200	$1,650	$2,500

W-916-F • F-790 • Atlanta • Teehee-Burke (1915–1919) • Pike-McCord • 832,000 (est.)

Estimated population: 70 to 80 • *Highest graded:* Unc.

VG-8	F-12	VF-20	EF-40	AU-50	Unc-60	Unc-63
$150	$325	$500	$700	$900	$1,200	$1,650

W-917-F • F-791 • Bell-Wellborn • 200,000 (est.)

Estimated population: 19 to 22 • *Highest graded:* Unc.

VG-8	F-12	VF-20	EF-40	AU-50	Unc-60	Unc-63
$200	$400	$1,200	$2,500	$3,000	$3,600	$4,500

W-918-F • F-792 • Elliott-Burke (1919–1921) • 168,000 (est.)

Estimated population: 13 to 15 • *Highest graded:* Unc.

VG-8	F-12	VF-20	EF-40	AU-50	Unc-60	Unc-63
$200	$400	$1,200	$2,500	$3,000	$3,600	$4,500

W-919-G • F-794 • Chicago • Teehee-Burke (1915–1919) • McCloud-McDougal • 2,848,000 (est.)

Estimated population: 190 to 210 • *Highest graded:* Unc.

VG-8	F-12	VF-20	EF-40	AU-50	Unc-60	Unc-63	Unc-65
$150	$325	$500	$700	$900	$1,200	$1,650	$2,500

W-919-G★ • F-794★

Recorded population: 3 • *Highest graded:* EF-40 • *Commentary:* The known serial numbers are G6712★/D, VG–F, damaged, sold by Frank Martinelli (10/1995) for $1,750; G10179★/C, EF; and G18661★/A, F, sold at a Heritage auction (1/2006) for $6,325.

W-920-G • F-795 • Cramer-McDougal • 152,000 (est.)

Estimated population: 9 or 10 • *Highest graded:* AU-50 • *Commentary:* In his 1951 study of these notes (see the bibliography), W.A. Philpott Jr. stated, "The rarest of all Chicago notes is the $5 with Teehee & Burke, Cramer & McDougal."

VG-8	F-12	VF-20	EF-40	AU-50
$500	$1,250	$2,500	$3,500	$4,500

W-921-H • F-796 • St. Louis • Teehee-Burke (1915–1919) • Attebery-Wells • 920,000 (est.)

Estimated population: 100 to 110 • *Highest graded:* Unc.

VG-8	F-12	VF-20	EF-40	AU-50	Unc-60	Unc-63
$150	$325	$500	$700	$900	$1,200	$1,650

W-922-H • F-797 • Attebery-Biggs • 272,000 (est.)
Estimated population: 35 to 40 • Highest graded: Unc.

VG-8	F-12	VF-20	EF-40	AU-50	Unc-60	Unc-63
$165	$350	$550	$800	$1,100	$1,500	$2,300

W-923-H • F-798 • Elliott-Burke (1919–1921) • White-Biggs • 332,000 (est.)
Estimated population: 30 to 35 • Highest graded: Unc.

VG-8	F-12	VF-20	EF-40	AU-50	Unc-60	Unc-63
$170	$375	$550	$825	$1,000	$1,300	$2,000

W-924-I • F-799 • Minneapolis • Teehee-Burke (1915–1919) • Cook-Wold • 828,000
Estimated population: 70 to 80 • Highest graded: Unc.

VG-8	F-12	VF-20	EF-40	AU-50	Unc-60	Unc-63
$150	$325	$500	$700	$900	$1,200	$1,650

W-925-J • F-803 • Kansas City • Teehee-Burke (1915–1919) • Anderson-Miller • 1,660,000 (est.)
Estimated population: 65 to 75 • Highest graded: Unc.

VG-8	F-12	VF-20	EF-40	AU-50	Unc-60	Unc-63
$150	$325	$500	$700	$900	$1,200	$1,650

W-925-J★ • F-803★
Recorded population: 2 • Highest graded: VG-8 • Selected information: CAA (5/2005), J9321★/A, VG–F, problems, $4,888. CAA (10/1995), J19915★/C, VG, $578.

W-926-J • F-804 • Elliott-Burke (1919–1921) • Helm-Miller • 2,340,000 (est.)
Estimated population: 120 to 130 • Highest graded: Unc.

VG-8	F-12	VF-20	EF-40	AU-50	Unc-60	Unc-63
$150	$325	$500	$700	$900	$1,200	$1,650

W-927-K • F-807 • Dallas • Teehee-Burke (1915–1919) • Talley-Van Zandt • 500,000
Estimated population: 28 to 33 • Highest graded: Unc.

VG-8	F-12	VF-20	EF-40	AU-50	Unc-60	Unc-63
$250	$500	$800	$1,000	$1,400	$1,750	$2,600

W-928-L • F-809A • San Francisco • Teehee-Burke (1915–1919) • Clerk-Lynch • May 18, 1914, error date • 300,000 (est.)
Estimated population: 23 to 28 • Highest graded: Unc • Commentary: In his 1951 study of these notes (see the bibliography), W.A. Philpott Jr. stated, "There is a $5 note, series 1918 Teehee & Burke, Clerk & Lunch which has the 'regulation' date, May 18, 1914, on its face, evidently an engraver's error in making the first [?] plate for the San Francisco $5, series 1918. The writer considers the May 20, 1914, $5 to be the later one, after the error was discovered and corrected. This May 18, 1914, San Francisco $5 note is not too plentiful." All other San Francisco plates of all denominations are dated May 20, 1914, an authorized exception to the May 18 date used by all other Federal Reserve Banks.

VG-8	F-12	VF-20	EF-40	AU-50	Unc-60
$250	$500	$800	$1,000	$1,400	$1,750

W-929-L • F-809 • May 20, 1914 • 896,000 (est.)
Estimated population: 19 to 22 • Highest graded: Unc.

VG-8	F-12	VF-20	EF-40	AU-50	Unc-60	Unc-63
$210	$425	$700	$900	$1,200	$1,500	$2,000

SMALL SIZE

Small-size $5 notes are very popular today. The face value is relatively low, and most were made in sufficient quantities that examples are readily available, although certain early issues are scarce in Uncirculated grades. On all varieties a portrait of Abraham Lincoln appears on the face, and the back shows a front view of the Lincoln Memorial. The Lincoln portrait by Charles Burt dates from the 19th century and was copied from a Mathew Brady photograph. Joachim C. Benzing created the back. These designs were used up to the advent of modern security notes.

Some artistic license has been taken with the state names on the architrave. In instances in which on the original the state name occupied two lines on the building, such as SOUTH / CAROLINA and NEW / HAMPSHIRE, the modifier was dropped on the currency image, leaving just CAROLINA and HAMPSHIRE. These omissions continue on notes currently being printed.

More varieties of $5 notes are being made now than ever before—a rather interesting situation in this and other modern series. All the Federal Reserve Banks have entered into the equation, as have notes printed at the Western Facility in Fort Worth (identified by FW at the face plate letter and number), creating many different varieties each time there is a signature change or other difference. Mules, Hawaii and North Africa issues, and others add interest.

LEGAL TENDER NOTES

The $5 Legal Tender Notes with their vivid red Treasury seal and serial numbers have been stand-out favorites with numismatists for a long time. While some are scarcer than others, all are available in Uncirculated condition through dealers and auction houses. Early star notes are rare as there was little interest in collecting them at the time.

Series of 1928, Red Seal
Woods-Mellon (1929–1932)

This series (illus. on p. 267) was imprinted with UNITED STATES NOTE, an alternate designation for a Legal Tender Note. The obligation states that it can be redeemed for five dollars, payable on demand; it does not specify what form payment may take.

Series of 1928 and 1928-A notes (W-1000 and W-1002) have the four-line notation, overprinted on the Treasury seal, "This note is a Legal Tender at its face value for all debts public and private except duties on imports and interest on the public debt."

W-1000 • F-1525 • 267,209,616

VG-8	F-12	VF-20	EF-40	AU-50	Unc-60	Unc-63	Unc-65
$14	$18	$24	$34	$60	$95	$125	$180

W-1000★ • F-1525★ • 3,150,000 (est.)

VG-8	F-12	VF-20	EF-40	AU-50	Unc-60	Unc-63	Unc-65
$160	$300	$425	$550	$950	$1,500	$2,000	$4,000

Series of 1928-A, Red Seal
Woods-Mills (1932–1933)

This series continued the design and imprints of the preceding. In *The Numismatist* in September 1967 (see the bibliography), William A. Philpott Jr. singled out seven small-size star notes, including this one, that he considered to be "excessively rare and hard to come by."

W-1002 • F-1526 • 58,194,600

VG-8	F-12	VF-20	EF-40	AU-50	Unc-60	Unc-63	Unc-65
$16	$20	$30	$50	$90	$125	$175	$550

W-1002★ • F-1526★

VG-8	F-12	VF-20	EF-40	AU-50	Unc-60	Unc-63
$600	$1,000	$1,650	$3,000	$4,000	$6,000	$8,000

Series of 1928-B, Red Seal
Julian-Morgenthau (1934–1945)

Beginning with the Series of 1928-B, continuing through the Series of 1953-C, $5 Legal Tender bills have the three-line notation, overprinted on the Treasury seal, "This note is a Legal Tender at its face value for all debts public and private."

Mules: Most backs have the plate number in small or "micro" numbers, but mules have the larger or "macro"-size serials as used on Series 1928-C (the macro plates have numbers 939 and higher). See illustrations under Series of 1928-C. Similar varieties occur in other series, as all used the same backs.

W-1004 • F-1527 • 147,827,340

VG-8	F-12	VF-20	EF-40	AU-50	Unc-60	Unc-63	Unc-65
$14	$16	$20	$40	$65	$100	$120	$200

W-1004★ • F-1527★ • 1,600,000 (est.)

VG-8	F-12	VF-20	EF-40	AU-50	Unc-60	Unc-63	Unc-65
$125	$180	$275	$475	$700	$1,000	$1,400	$2,500

W-1004 Mule • F-1527

VG-8	F-12	VF-20	EF-40	AU-50	Unc-60	Unc-63	Unc-65
$16	$20	$30	$90	$140	$190	$225	$325

W-1004 Mule★ • F-1527★

VG-8	F-12	VF-20	EF-40	AU-50	Unc-60	Unc-63	Unc-65
$750	$1,500	$2,500	$4,000	$5,750	$8,000	$10,000	$13,500

Series of 1928-C, Red Seal
Julian-Morgenthau (1934–1945)

This series continued the design and imprints of the preceding.

Mules: Most backs have the plate number in macro numbers, but mules have the micro-size numbers as used on Series

---

1928-B (the micro plates have numbers 938 and lower; those with number 637 are worth an additional premium). Face plate numbers for these range from 288 to 522. These are worth a strong premium, with star notes bringing even more.

W-1006 • F-1528 • 214,735,765

VG-8	F-12	VF-20	EF-40	AU-50	Unc-60	Unc-63	Unc-65
$14	$16	$20	$35	$45	$60	$85	$200

W-1006★ • F-1528★ • 2,050,000 (est.)

VG-8	F-12	VF-20	EF-40	AU-50	Unc-60	Unc-63	Unc-65
$90	$140	$200	$325	$500	$625	$900	$2,000

W-1006 Mule • F-1528

VG-8	F-12	VF-20	EF-40	AU-50	Unc-60	Unc-63	Unc-65
$15	$18	$25	$45	$55	$90	$130	$175

W-1006 Mule★ • F-1528★

VG-8	F-12	VF-20	EF-40	AU-50	Unc-60	Unc-63	Unc-65
$280	$500	$900	$1,400	$2,000	$3,200	$4,000	$5,400

Series of 1928-D, Red Seal
Julian-Vinson (1945–1946)

This series (illus. on p. 268) continued the design and imprints of the preceding.

Mules: Most backs have the plate number in macro numbers, but mules have the micro-size numbers as used on Series 1928-B (the single micro back plate for this combination has serial number 637). Face plate numbers for these range from 524 to 550. These are seldom seen and are highly valued.

W-1008 • F-1529 • 9,297,120

VG-8	F-12	VF-20	EF-40	AU-50	Unc-60	Unc-63	Unc-65
$30	$45	$90	$120	$200	$260	$375	$600

W-1008★ • F-1529★

VG-8	F-12	VF-20	EF-40	AU-50	Unc-60	Unc-63
$450	$900	$1,500	$2,000	$3,250	$4,500	$6,000

W-1008 Mule • F-1529

VG-8	F-12	VF-20	EF-40	AU-50	Unc-60	Unc-63
$170	$300	$550	$1,100	$1,750	$2,800	$3,700

Series of 1928-E, Red Seal
Julian-Snyder (1946–1949)

This series (illus. on p. 268) continued the design and imprints of the preceding.

Mules: Most backs have the plate number in macro numbers, but mules have the micro-size numbers as used on Series 1928-B (the micro plates for this combination are serial numbers 629 and 637). Face plate numbers for these range from 566 to 627. These are seldom seen and are highly valued if with back plate 629. Back plate 637 is a star note and so is exceedingly rare.

SERIES OF 1928, RED SEAL

Detail of the printing at the Treasury seal.

$5 Legal Tender Note, Series of 1928 (W-1000★). Star note.

Back of the $5 Legal Tender Note, Series of 1928. Standard type of the era.

SERIES OF 1928-A, RED SEAL

Signatures and series imprints of a $5 Legal Tender Note, Series of 1928-A (W-1002). The back is the standard type of the era.

SERIES OF 1928-B, RED SEAL

Detail of the signatures and the series imprints of a $5 Legal Tender Note, Series of 1928-B (W-1004), as well as of the revised three-line imprint over the Treasury seal. The back is the standard type of the era.

SERIES OF 1928-C, RED SEAL

Signatures and series imprints of a $5 Legal Tender Note, Series of 1928-C (W-1006). The back is the standard type of the era.

Detail of macro plate numbers.

Detail of micro plate numbers.

W-1010 • F-1530 • 109,952,760

VG-8	F-12	VF-20	EF-40	AU-50	Unc-60	Unc-63	Unc-65
$14	$16	$20	$35	$50	$70	$90	$175

W-1010★ • F-1530★ • 1,550,000 (est.)

VG-8	F-12	VF-20	EF-40	AU-50	Unc-60	Unc-63	Unc-65
$120	$160	$250	$370	$500	$600	$750	$1,250

W-1010 Mule • F-1530

VG-8	F-12	VF-20	EF-40	AU-50	Unc-60	Unc-63	Unc-65
$140	$215	$375	$550	$850	$1,100	$1,350	$1,800

W-1010 Mule★ • F-1530★ • Unique

Series of 1928-F, Red Seal, Wide Back 1
Clark-Snyder (1949–1953)

This series continued the design and imprints of the preceding, except that beginning on March 8, 1950, new $5 Legal Tender Note face plates were made slightly smaller by narrowing the printed area horizontally by subtly removing part of the design. This created "Wide Face" (early style; face plates up to Series 1928-E) and "Narrow Face" (later style; Series 1928-F face plates) varieties. On November 7, 1951, the back (generic for all $5 series) was made "Narrow" as well.

Series of 1928-F notes are found in Wide and Narrow (scarcer) back varieties. The Wide issues have plate numbers up to 2007, called Wide Back 1, and again with serial numbers 2067 to 2096, called Wide Back 2, with notes in the second range being much scarcer. The Narrow Back numbers are from 2008 to 2066. Such differences have gained notice only in recent years. Similar varieties exist for $5 Silver Certificates, Series of 1934-D.

W-1012 • F-1531 • 104,194,704

VG-8	F-12	VF-20	EF-40	AU-50	Unc-60	Unc-63	Unc-65
$14	$16	$20	$30	$40	$60	$80	$175

W-1012★ • F-1531★ • 1,250,000 (est.)

VG-8	F-12	VF-20	EF-40	AU-50	Unc-60	Unc-63	Unc-65
$85	$130	$190	$300	$500	$700	$900	$1,400

Series of 1928-F, Red Seal, Narrow Back
Clark-Snyder (1949–1953)

This series continued the preceding face design, but had the Narrow Back style. See the information under Wide Back 1 for a description.

W-1013 • F-1531 • Part of W-1012 printage

VG-8	F-12	VF-20	EF-40	AU-50	Unc-60	Unc-63	Unc-65
$16	$20	$25	$35	$50	$90	$140	$225

W-1013★ • F-1531★

VG-8	F-12	VF-20	EF-40	AU-50	Unc-60	Unc-63
$275	$525	$900	$1,450	$2,250	$3,000	$3,600

Series of 1928-F, Red Seal, Wide Back 2
Clark-Snyder (1949–1953)

See the information under Wide Back 1 for a description.

W-1014 • F-1531 • Part of W-1012 printage

VG-8	F-12	VF-20	EF-40	AU-50	Unc-60	Unc-63	Unc-65
$20	$30	$40	$65	$90	$140	$185	$250

W-1014★ • F-1531★

VG-8	F-12	VF-20	EF-40	AU-50	Unc-60	Unc-63
$500	$950	$1,700	$2,500	$3,750	$6,200	$7,500

Series of 1953, Red Seal
Priest-Humphrey (1953–1957)

The face of the $5 note was redesigned for this series. The red Treasury seal is now to the right. A gray counter is on the

SERIES OF 1928-D, RED SEAL

Signatures and series imprints of a $5 Legal Tender Note, Series of 1928-D (W-1008). The back is the standard type of the era.

SERIES OF 1928-E, RED SEAL

Signatures and series imprints of a $5 Legal Tender Note, Series of 1928-E (W-1010). The back is the standard type of the era.

SERIES OF 1928-F, RED SEAL

Signatures and series imprints of a $5 Legal Tender Note, Series of 1928-F (W-1012). The back is the standard type of the era.

Detail of feature on Wide Back notes. This is the style of back plate numbers up to 2007 (Wide Back 1) and 2067 to 2096 (Wide Back 2).

Detail of feature on Narrow Back notes, back plate numbers 2008 to 2066.

left, and on the right FIVE is under the Treasury seal. WASHINGTON, DC is above the seal. The series notation is now in the field to the lower right of the portrait. The plate letter at the upper left is now in a different position. The obligation in three lines is unchanged: "This note is a Legal Tender at its face value for all debts public and private."

W-1016 • F-1532 • 120,880,000

VG-8	F-12	VF-20	EF-40	AU-50	Unc-60	Unc-63	Unc-65
$11	$14	$16	$19	$25	$30	$35	$50

W-1016★ • F-1532★ • 5,760,000

VG-8	F-12	VF-20	EF-40	AU-50	Unc-60	Unc-63	Unc-65
$25	$40	$60	$110	$150	$200	$275	$450

Series of 1953-A, Red Seal
Priest-Anderson (1957–1961)

This series continued the design and imprints of the preceding.

W-1018 • F-1533 • 90,280,000

VG-8	F-12	VF-20	EF-40	AU-50	Unc-60	Unc-63	Unc-65
$10	$14	$16	$19	$24	$30	$35	$50

W-1018★ • F-1533★ • 5,400,000

VG-8	F-12	VF-20	EF-40	AU-50	Unc-60	Unc-63	Unc-65
$10	$15	$25	$50	$75	$150	$200	$300

Series of 1953-B, Red Seal
Smith-Dillon (1961–1962)

This series continued the design and imprints of the preceding.

W-1020 • F-1534 • 44,640,000

VG-8	F-12	VF-20	EF-40	AU-50	Unc-60	Unc-63	Unc-65
$10	$14	$16	$19	$24	$30	$35	$50

W-1020★ • F-1534★ • 2,160,000

VG-8	F-12	VF-20	EF-40	AU-50	Unc-60	Unc-63	Unc-65
$10	$15	$25	$50	$75	$150	$200	$300

Series of 1953-C, Red Seal
Granahan-Dillon (1963–1965)

This series (illus. on p. 270) continued the design and imprints of the preceding.

W-1022 • F-1535 • 8,640,000

VG-8	F-12	VF-20	EF-40	AU-50	Unc-60	Unc-63	Unc-65
$10	$14	$16	$19	$24	$30	$35	$50

W-1022★ • F-1535★ • 320,000

VG-8	F-12	VF-20	EF-40	AU-50	Unc-60	Unc-63	Unc-65
$10	$15	$30	$60	$100	$200	$250	$400

$5 Legal Tender Note, Series of 1953 (W-1016). The back is the standard type of the era.

Signatures and series imprint of a $5 Legal Tender Note, Series of 1953-A (W-1018). The back is the standard type of the era.

Signatures and series imprint of a $5 Legal Tender Note, Series of 1953-B (W-1020). The back is the standard type of the era.

Series of 1963, Red Seal
Granahan-Dillon (1963–1965)

This series was redesigned slightly. On the face the obligation is now "This note is Legal Tender for all debts, public and private." The motto IN GOD WE TRUST now appears on the back.

W-1030 • F-1536 • 63,360,000

VG-8	F-12	VF-20	EF-40	AU-50	Unc-60	Unc-63	Unc-65
$10	$12	$14	$17	$20	$25	$35	$45

W-1030★ • F-1536★ • 3,840,000

VG-8	F-12	VF-20	EF-40	AU-50	Unc-60	Unc-63	Unc-65
$10	$15	$20	$30	$45	$75	$90	$175

NATIONAL BANK NOTES

The Series of 1929 National Bank Notes, first printed in 1929, remained in use through early 1935. There are two styles, Type 1 (1929 to 1933) and Type 2 (1933 to 1935), each issued in six-subject sheets. At the right the brown Treasury seal is overprinted on the obligation, "Redeemable in lawful money of the United States, at United States Treasury or at the bank of issue."

As a class, 1929 Type 1 notes are much more plentiful than Type 2 notes, although for specific national banks the situation can be the reverse. Some banks issued just Type 1 bills, many issued both, and some late-chartered banks, including consolidations and mergers of necessity during the Depression, issued only Type 2 notes. The issues of many different banks are available to collectors.

Prices are for states from which many notes survive. The large population of these notes has stimulated many numismatists to collect as many banks or towns as possible within a given state. Most are in grades of F to VF or so, although quite a few Uncirculated notes exist, many of which have low serial numbers.

Series of 1929, Type 1, Brown Seal
Jones-Woods (1929–1933)

Sheets of Type 1 bills each had the same serial number on a given sheet, prefixed by a letter, A through F, such as A000001A to F000001A. This gives six times more serial number 1 notes than on a sheet of 1929 Type 2 bills. Signa-

SERIES OF 1953-C, RED SEAL

Signatures and series imprint of a $5 Legal Tender Note, Series of 1953-C (W-1022). The back is the standard type of the era.

SERIES OF 1963, RED SEAL

$5 Legal Tender Note, Series of 1963 (W-1030).

Back of W-1030. The motto IN GOD WE TRUST has been added.

Detail of the motto.

tures of the bank cashier and president were printed directly on each note at the BEP. The charter number appears *four times* on the face, twice in black and twice in brown.

Collecting small-size notes by state and location did not become widely popular until the late 20th century, when the Hickman Project and other studies became available. By that time, many choice notes had been lost. There are enough in numismatic hands, however, to make specialized collecting by state or bank a reality.

Banks of Issue and Rarity of Notes

Based upon census information from Don C. Kelly and James M. Kelly (*National Bank Note Census*, Version 4.0) and with some information from other sources, this listing gives each location, the number of banks issuing this series of notes within each, and a commentary.[37]

The Kelly survey records 24,716 notes, slightly fewer than the 27,208 listed for the 1902 Plain Back notes of this denomination. Uncirculated notes are plentiful, including six-subject sheets—these are often serial number 1. The census lists 2,038 serial number 1 notes, including those remaining in sheets. In nearly all scenarios, most serial number 1 notes are Uncirculated. These are specifically listed below. The Kelly listing gives details bank by bank. Grades of notes in collection are higher, on average, than the large-size issues.

Alabama • 62 banks of issue • 425 notes reported • Mostly circulated, but with some clusters of Unc notes. The census lists 29 serial number 1 notes, all Unc.

Alaska • 2 banks of issue • 10 notes reported • VG to VF. Alaska was a territory at the time, but the notes simply say Alaska.

Arizona • 5 banks of issue • 206 notes reported • Seven serial number 1 notes are known, all but one Unc.

Arkansas • 43 banks of issue • 206 notes reported • Mostly circulated, but Unc notes are readily available, including a large hoard from the National Bank of Eastern Arkansas of Forrest City. The census lists 26 serial number 1 notes, nearly all Unc.

California • 111 banks of issue • 1,395 notes reported • Mostly circulated grades. A very popular state for specialized collecting. The census lists 110 serial number 1 notes, nearly all Unc.

Colorado • 33 banks of issue • 256 notes reported • Mostly circulated. The census lists 45 serial number 1 notes, all Unc.

Connecticut • 39 banks of issue • 610 notes reported • Mostly circulated, but with some notable clusters of Unc notes. The census lists 52 serial number 1 notes, nearly all Unc.

Delaware • 6 banks of issue • 71 notes reported • Unc notes are scarce. One serial number 1 note exists, from the New Castle National Bank of Odessa (Unc).

District of Columbia • 4 banks of issue • 71 notes reported • Unc notes are inexplicably elusive. One serial number 1 note exists, from the Second National Bank of Washington (Unc).

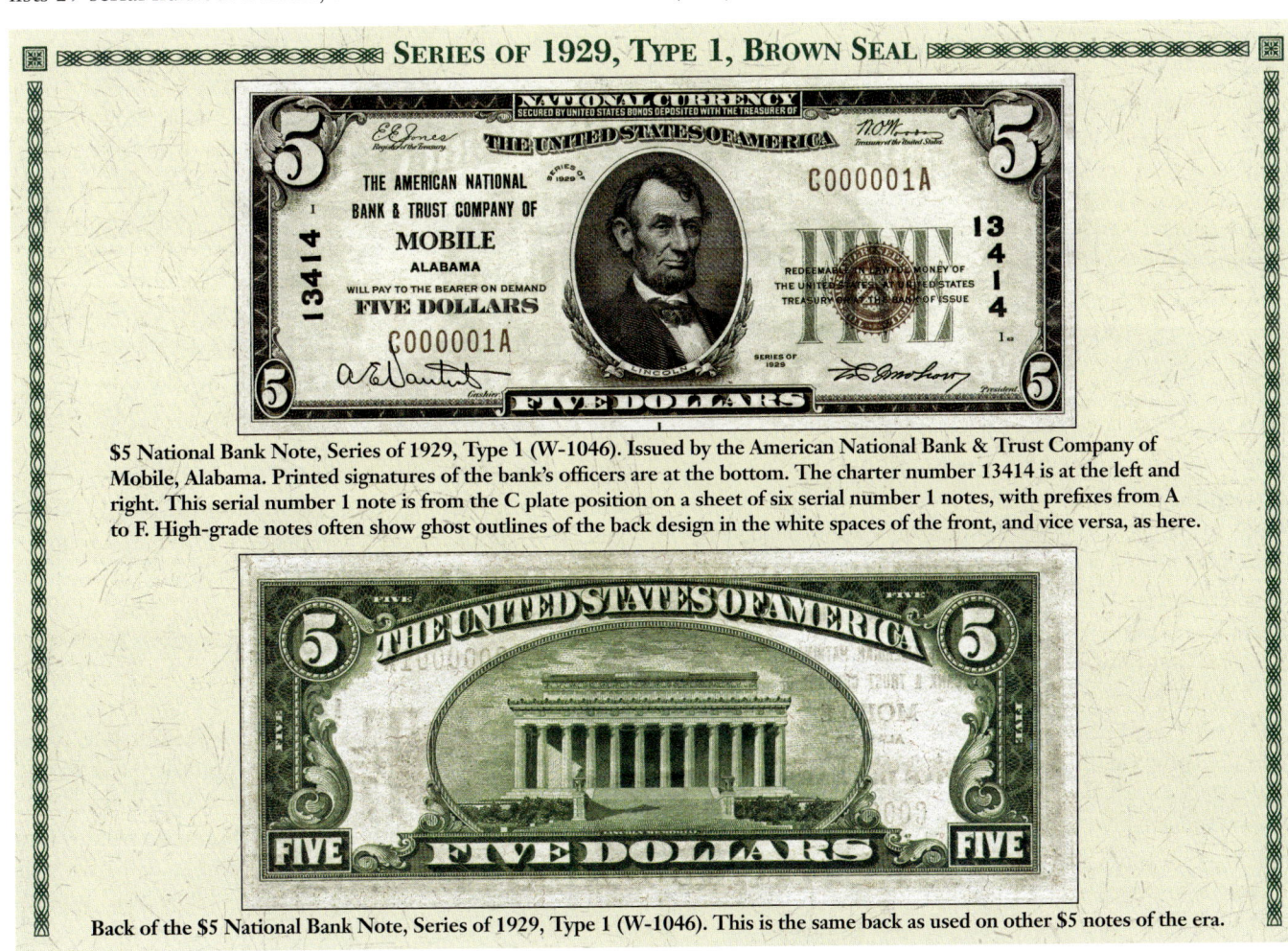

SERIES OF 1929, TYPE 1, BROWN SEAL

$5 National Bank Note, Series of 1929, Type 1 (W-1046). Issued by the American National Bank & Trust Company of Mobile, Alabama. Printed signatures of the bank's officers are at the bottom. The charter number 13414 is at the left and right. This serial number 1 note is from the C plate position on a sheet of six serial number 1 notes, with prefixes from A to F. High-grade notes often show ghost outlines of the back design in the white spaces of the front, and vice versa, as here.

Back of the $5 National Bank Note, Series of 1929, Type 1 (W-1046). This is the same back as used on other $5 notes of the era.

Florida • 39 banks of issue • 306 notes reported • Uncirculated notes are in several clusters, but are otherwise scarce. The census lists 25 serial number 1 notes, nearly all Unc.

Georgia • 45 banks of issue • 208 notes reported • The percentage of Unc notes is very low, although a cache of six from the First National Bank of Waynesboro is important. The census lists 19 serial number 1 notes, all Unc.

Hawaii • 1 bank of issue • 38 notes listed • All from the Bishop First National Bank of Honolulu. Circulated grades exclusively, a remarkable situation. Hawaii was a territory at the time, but the notes simply say Hawaii.

Idaho • 14 banks of issue • 59 notes reported • Mostly circulated. Eight serial number 1 notes are known, all Unc, these constituting the main quantity of notes in this grade from the state.

Illinois • 175 banks of issue • 905 notes reported • Mostly circulated, but with a respectable supply of higher-grade notes, highlighted by 13 from the Quincy-Ricker National Bank of Quincy. The census lists 76 serial number 1 notes, nearly all Unc.

Indiana • 108 banks of issue • 872 notes reported • Unc notes are mostly from a hoard of over 130 from the City National Bank of Goshen. The census lists 69 serial number 1 notes, nearly all Unc.

Iowa • 74 banks of issue • 557 notes reported • Unc notes are scarce, but are mostly in small clusters. The census lists 27 serial number 1 notes, all Unc, but for this state many are not graded.

Kansas • 77 banks of issue • 472 notes reported • Unc notes are scarce, but there are several small clusters. The census lists 49 serial number 1 notes, nearly all Unc.

Kentucky • 44 banks of issue • 261 notes reported • Unc notes are rare, except for nearly all of the 19 serial number 1 notes from the state. Six are from the First National Bank of Wilmore.

Louisiana • 15 banks of issue • 164 notes reported • Unc notes are very scarce. The census lists 12 serial number 1 notes, six AU and six Unc.

Maine • 29 banks of issue • 334 notes reported • Unc notes are in the minority, but several caches are reported. The census lists 43 serial number 1 notes, all but one Unc.

Maryland • 40 banks of issue • 258 notes reported • Unc notes are scarce as a class, but the supply includes a few small groups. The census lists 21 serial number 1 notes, nearly all Unc.

Massachusetts • 122 banks of issue • 958 notes reported • Unc notes include several clusters, most notably from the First National Bank of Haverhill. The census lists 70 serial number 1 notes are known, nearly all Unc.

Michigan • 73 banks of issue • 1,467 notes reported • Unc notes are common, thanks to a huge hoard of over 550 from the First National Bank of Cassopolis. The census lists 54 serial number 1 notes, nearly all Unc.

Minnesota • 106 banks of issue • 754 notes reported • Unc notes are fairly well distributed, save for a few clusters. The census lists 33 serial number 1 notes, nearly all Unc.

Mississippi • 22 banks of issue • 229 notes reported • Mostly in circulated grades. The census lists 12 serial number 1 notes, all Unc.

Missouri • 61 banks of issue • 580 notes reported • Unc notes are mainly in clusters but are scarce as a class. The census lists 31 serial number 1 notes; all graded ones are Unc, but many are not graded yet.

Montana • 15 banks of issue • 113 notes reported • A scarce state. Several clusters of Unc notes make these collectible. The census lists 18 serial number 1 notes, all Unc.

Nebraska • 45 banks of issue • 255 notes reported • The census lists 66 serial number 1 notes, nearly all Unc.

Nevada • 7 banks of issue • 66 notes reported • Unc notes are very rare according to the census, but quite a few notes have not been graded. The only serial number 1 note is from the First National Bank of Elko (Unc). A trophy note deluxe.

New Hampshire • 38 banks of issue • 270 notes reported • The census lists 15 serial number 1 notes, all but one Unc.

New Jersey • 163 banks of issue • 1,124 notes reported • Mostly circulated, but there are several clusters of higher-grade notes. The census lists 98 serial number 1 notes, nearly all Unc.

New Mexico • 7 banks of issue • 149 notes reported • The census lists 13 Unc notes from the First National Bank of Belen, which make up the main supply in this grade. Four of the 12 serial number 1 notes from this state (all Unc) are from this bank.

New York • 320 banks of issue • 2,496 notes reported • The census lists 216 serial number 1 notes, nearly all Unc.

North Carolina • 39 banks of issue • 256 notes reported • Large numbers are not graded. Among those that are graded, Unc notes are few. The census lists 14 serial number 1 notes; all graded are Unc, but seven are not graded.

North Dakota • 32 banks of issue • 136 notes reported • Many are not graded. Several clusters of Unc notes are listed. The census lists 31 serial number 1 notes, nearly all Unc.

Ohio • 132 banks of issue • 1,127 notes reported • Unc notes are in the distinct minority, although several clusters are delineated. The census lists 81 serial number 1 notes, nearly all Unc.

Oklahoma • 47 banks of issue • 199 notes reported • Several clusters of Unc notes account for most of the supply of this grade. The census lists 18 serial number 1 notes, all Unc.

Oregon • 34 banks of issue • 230 notes reported • Several small clusters make Unc notes collectible. Otherwise, most are circulated. The census lists 26 serial number 1 notes, all but one Unc.

Pennsylvania • 387 banks of issue • 2,824 notes reported • From scarce banks to clusters, many notes are available, making specialized collecting of this state a popular pursuit. The census lists 183 serial number 1 notes, nearly all Unc.

Rhode Island • 9 banks of issue • 185 notes reported • The roster is clustered due to the small number of banks that issued these notes. Most are circulated. The census lists 12 serial number 1 notes, all Unc.

South Carolina • 28 banks of issue • 281 notes reported • Several clusters of Unc notes make this grade readily available. The census lists 18 serial number 1 notes, all Unc.

South Dakota • 20 banks of issue • 92 notes reported • The census lists 18 serial number 1 notes, nearly all Unc, accounting for the vast majority of notes in this grade from the state.

Tennessee • 53 banks of issue • 275 notes reported • Unc notes are quite scarce, although there are several small groups. The census lists 14 serial number 1 notes, all but one Unc.

Texas • 164 banks of issue • 1,085 notes reported • Mostly circulated listings punctuated by several clusters of Unc notes. The census lists 185 serial number 1 notes, nearly all Unc.

Utah • 11 banks of issue • 165 notes reported • Three clusters make Unc notes collectible. The census lists 13 serial number 1 notes, all but one Unc.

Vermont • 26 banks of issue • 153 notes reported • Several clusters of Unc notes are listed, otherwise these are scarce. The census lists 22 serial number 1 notes, all but two Unc.

Virginia • 74 banks of issue • 259 notes reported • Several clusters of Unc notes account for most of the supply in this grade. The census lists 24 serial number 1 notes, nearly all Unc.

Washington • 40 banks of issue • 172 notes reported • Unc notes are mainly from several clusters, but are in the distinct minority. The census lists 32 serial number 1 notes, all but one Unc.

West Virginia • 71 banks of issue • 260 notes reported • Mostly circulated. The census lists 21 serial number 1 notes, nearly all Unc; these account for most of the Unc notes from this state.

Wisconsin • 79 banks of issue • 1,091 notes reported • Unc notes include a run from the First National Bank of Wausau. The census lists 45 serial number 1 notes, nearly all Unc.

Wyoming • 4 banks of issue • 41 notes reported • Six serial number 1 notes are known, all Unc from the First National

Bank of Lovell. These also constitute the majority of notes in this grade from this state.

Generic prices for a typical note from a state from which notes range from available to just slightly scarce:

VG-8	F-12	VF-20	EF-40	AU-50	Unc-60	Unc-63	Unc-65
$35	$45	$55	$65	$100	$150	$180	$245

W-1046 • F-1800-1
Estimated population: 28,000 to 30,000 • *Highest graded:* Unc.

VG-8	F-12	VF-20	EF-40	AU-50	Unc-60	Unc-63	Unc-65
$35	$40	$50	$60	$150	$175	$225	$400

Series of 1929, Type 2, Brown Seal
Jones-Woods (1929–1933)

Sheets of Type 2 bills were numbered continuously, with the first sheet from a given bank starting with A000001 and ending with A000006, yielding a single number 1 note, in contrast to 6 on the first Series of 1929 Type 1 sheet. Signatures of the bank cashier and president were printed directly on each note at the BEP.

The average grade of surviving notes is higher than for the earlier series, with EF, AU, and Uncirculated being common as a class. Many Uncirculated notes are in groups or clusters, often extensive, a situation which occurs for most of the states. There are, however, many rare states, cities, and banks. Prices are for states from which a larger number of notes survive. Type 2 notes are much scarcer than Type 1 notes, and are consequently harder to find in the marketplace. Included are issues of many new banks chartered from 1933 to 1935, often consolidations of two or more banks that experienced difficulties during the Depression.

Banks of Issue and Rarity of Notes

Based upon census information from Don C. Kelly and James M. Kelly (*National Bank Note Census,* Version 4.0) and with some information from other sources, this listing gives

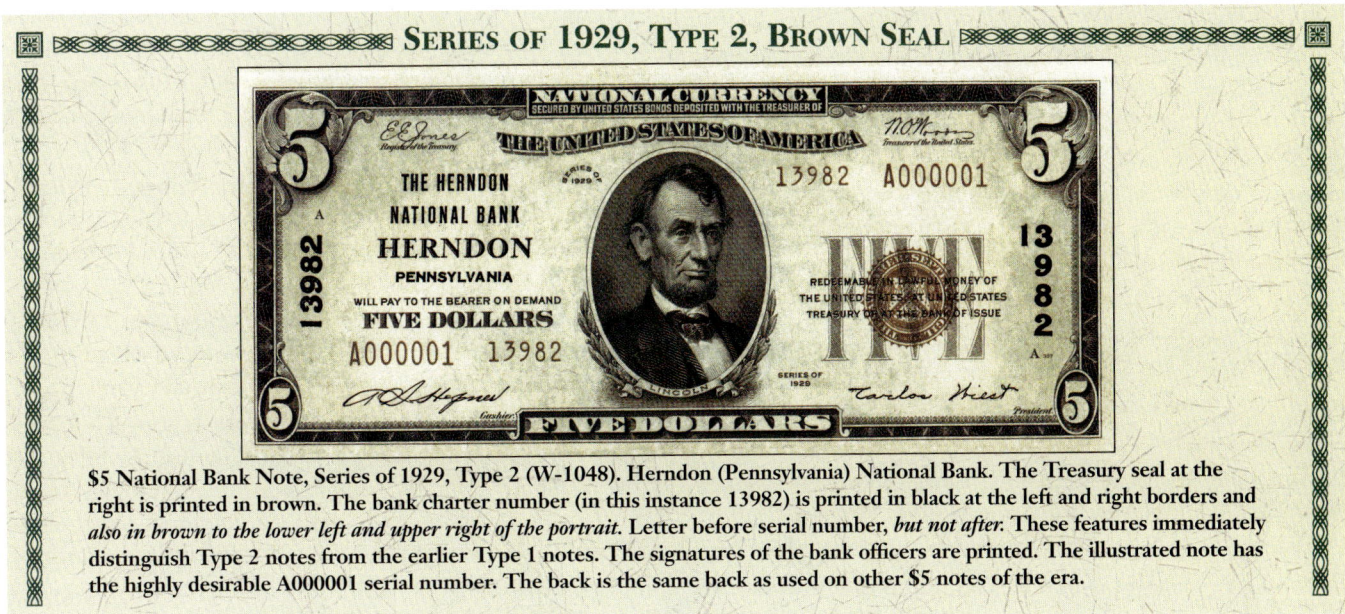

SERIES OF 1929, TYPE 2, BROWN SEAL

$5 National Bank Note, Series of 1929, Type 2 (W-1048). Herndon (Pennsylvania) National Bank. The Treasury seal at the right is printed in brown. The bank charter number (in this instance 13982) is printed in black at the left and right borders and *also in brown to the lower left and upper right of the portrait.* Letter before serial number, *but not after.* These features immediately distinguish Type 2 notes from the earlier Type 1 notes. The signatures of the bank officers are printed. The illustrated note has the highly desirable A000001 serial number. The back is the same back as used on other $5 notes of the era.

each location, the number of banks issuing this series of notes within each, and a commentary.[38]

The Kelly survey records 14,883 notes, about 10,000 fewer than are known for the Type 1 issue. Serial number 1 notes are far fewer of this type, 303 as compared to 2,038 for Type 1, mainly due to the sheet arrangement. These are specifically listed below.

Alabama • 51 banks of issue • 247 notes reported • Most are circulated, but several clusters of Unc notes are recorded. Five serial number 1 notes are known, three of which are Unc.

Alaska • 2 banks of issue • 13 notes reported • Three Unc. Alaska was a territory at the time, but the notes simply say Alaska.

Arizona • 3 banks of issue • 10 notes listed • All are circulated.

Arkansas • 31 banks of issue • 216 notes reported • Circulated notes are augmented by clusters of Unc examples, the most important being more than 100 from the First National Bank in Lake Village. Two serial number 1 notes are known, graded VG and Unc.

California • 90 banks of issue • 746 notes reported • Notes are abundant, including many Unc examples, but most are in clumps. Relatively few different banks are involved. The census lists 16 serial number 1 notes, nearly all Unc.

Colorado • 28 banks of issue • 187 notes reported • Unc notes are plentiful. Relatively few different banks are involved. One serial number 1 note is from the First National Bank in Eads (AU).

Connecticut • 36 banks of issue • 208 notes reported • Circulated notes predominate. Many clusters. Four serial number 1 notes are known, including two Unc.

Delaware • 5 banks of issue • 54 notes listed • All banks are represented, with the most by far from the First National Bank of Dover, mostly Unc.

District of Columbia • 3 banks of issue • 45 notes reported • Four circulated notes are from the Second National Bank of Washington; the balance, a mixture from worn to Unc, are from the Hamilton National Bank of Washington.

Florida • 40 banks of issue • 204 notes reported • Mostly circulated, but some clusters of Unc notes. Five serial number 1 notes are known, including one AU, three Unc, and one not graded.

Georgia • 38 banks of issue • 118 notes reported • Mostly circulated, but with three clusters of Unc notes. Three serial number 1 notes are known, two Unc.

Hawaii • 2 banks of issue • 77 notes reported • Mostly circulated. Both banks are represented. Hawaii was a territory at the time, but the notes simply say Hawaii.

Idaho • 11 banks of issue • 35 notes reported • Five Unc notes.

Illinois • 117 banks of issue • 381 notes reported • Mixture of grades, including several Unc clusters. Nine serial number 1 notes are known, nearly all Unc.

Indiana • 71 banks of issue • 822 notes reported • Many are Unc, including over 275 from the National City Bank of Evansville and additional examples from smaller clusters. Five serial number 1 notes are known, three Unc and two not graded.

Iowa • 44 banks of issue • 200 notes reported • Many are Unc, including over 60 from the Okey-Vernon National Bank of Corning. Five serial number 1 notes are known, one AU and four Unc.

Kansas • 68 banks of issue • 728 notes reported • A mixture of grades including several Unc clusters. Six serial number 1 notes are known, one VG and five Unc.

Kentucky • 40 banks of issue • 498 notes reported • Includes nearly 400 Unc from the First National Bank and Trust Co. of Lexington. Four serial number 1 notes are known, one VG and three Unc.

Louisiana • 20 banks of issue • 226 notes reported • Includes a cluster of 80 mostly Unc notes from the Commercial National Bank in Shreveport. Four serial number 1 notes are known, all Unc.

Maine • 27 banks of issue • 153 notes reported • Mixed grades, including several clusters of Unc notes. Three serial number 1 notes are known, two Unc and one ungraded.

Maryland • 31 banks of issue • 178 notes reported • Mixed grades including dozens of Unc notes. Three serial number 1 notes are known, VG, Unc, and not graded.

Massachusetts • 107 banks of issue • 347 notes reported • Mixed grades, including several clusters of Unc notes. The census lists 10 serial number 1 notes, nine Unc.

Michigan • 54 banks of issue • 200 notes reported • Many circulated punctuated by small clusters of Unc notes. Three serial number 1 notes are known, one Unc.

Minnesota • 93 banks of issue • 286 notes reported • Many circulated plus clusters of Unc notes. Three serial number 1 notes are known, two Unc.

Mississippi • 16 banks of issue • 161 notes reported • Circulated notes plus several extensive clusters of Unc notes. Three serial number 1 notes are known, two Unc and one not graded.

Missouri • 47 banks of issue • 244 notes reported • Many circulated examples are interspersed with clusters of Unc notes. Three serial number 1 notes are known, two Unc and one not graded.

Montana • 17 banks of issue • 76 notes reported • Mostly circulated or ungraded notes, plus several small clusters of Unc notes. Four serial number 1 notes are known, three Unc and one not graded.

Nebraska • 36 banks of issue • 143 notes reported • Circulated notes, plus many Unc notes, mostly in clusters. Six serial number 1 notes are known, one Fair and five Unc.

Nevada • 4 banks of issue • 443 notes reported • Overwhelmed by 435 from the First National Bank in Reno, nearly all of which are Unc or not graded (but presumably Unc). Absent these, Nevada would be a rare state. One serial number 1 note is from the First National Bank of Ely (Unc).

New Hampshire • 38 banks of issue • 176 notes reported • Circulated notes plus many Unc, the last mostly in clusters, including 36 from the First National Bank of Peterborough. Six serial number 1 notes are known, all Unc.

New Jersey • 155 banks of issue • 948 notes reported • Circulated plus several large clusters of Unc notes. The census lists 12 serial number 1 notes, three Unc and two not graded.

New Mexico • 7 banks of issue • 47 notes reported • Mostly circulated, except for a cluster of 14 Unc from the First National Bank of Belen. One serial number 1 note is from the Albuquerque National Trust & Savings Bank (F).

New York • 274 banks of issue • 1,135 notes reported • Mostly circulated plus some clusters of Unc notes. The census lists 35 serial number 1 notes, nearly all Unc.

North Carolina • 31 banks of issue • 53 notes reported • Mostly circulated or ungraded notes, with a few Unc.

North Dakota • 22 banks of issue • 53 notes reported • Mixture of grades, plus many not graded. Four serial number 1 notes are known, two Unc and two not graded.

Ohio • 114 banks of issue • 447 notes reported • Mostly circulated notes, but with clusters of Unc interspersed. The census lists 14 serial number 1 notes, nearly all Unc.

Oklahoma • 54 banks of issue • 153 notes reported • Mostly circulated grades, but with singles and groups of Unc scattered here and there. Four serial number 1 notes are known, three AU and one Unc.

Oregon • 24 banks of issue • 85 notes reported • Mixture of circulated notes and clusters of Unc notes. Five serial number 1 notes are known, four Unc.

Pennsylvania • 370 banks of issue • 2,727 notes reported • Many circulated, plus clusters of Unc, including nearly 1,000 from the Harrisburg National Bank. The census lists 43 serial number 1 notes, nearly all Unc.

Rhode Island • 11 banks of issue • 113 notes reported • Mostly circulated with some Unc notes interspersed. One serial number 1 note is from the Blackstone Canal National Bank (Unc).

South Carolina • 14 banks of issue • 110 notes reported • Mostly circulated, with some clusters of Unc notes. Two serial number 1 notes are known, South Carolina National Bank of Charleston and the Commercial National Bank of Spartanburg, both Unc.

South Dakota • 16 banks of issue • 56 notes reported • Various grades including many Unc from the Rapid City National Bank. One serial number 1 note is from the First National Bank in Mobridge (Unc).

Tennessee • 35 banks of issue • 186 notes reported • Mostly circulated, but with enough clusters of Unc notes to create a good supply. Three serial number 1 notes are known, two Unc and one not graded.

Texas • 178 banks of issue • 644 notes reported • Mostly circulated, but with several clusters of Unc notes. The census lists 38 serial number 1 notes, nearly all Unc, an exceptional number from this state in relation to the more populous states of the East.

Utah • 8 banks of issue • 72 notes reported • Mostly circulated, but with two clusters of Unc notes. Two serial number 1 notes are known, First National Bank and Continental National Bank and Trust Company, both of Salt Lake City and both Unc.

Vermont • 30 banks of issue • 60 notes reported • Mostly circulated plus two clusters of Unc notes. Five serial number 1 notes are known, one Unc and two not graded.

Virginia • 68 banks of issue • 170 notes reported • Mostly circulated plus several clusters of Unc notes. Six serial number 1 notes are known, three Unc.

Washington • 27 banks of issue • 49 notes reported • Mostly circulated, plus two clusters of Unc notes. Two serial number 1 notes are known, First National Bank of Bellingham and the First National Bank of Okanogan, both Unc.

West Virginia • 55 banks of issue • 191 notes reported • Circulated plus several clusters of Unc notes. Four serial number 1 notes are known, all Unc.

Wisconsin • 52 banks of issue • 149 notes reported • Many circulated, plus a few clusters and single Unc notes. Six serial number 1 notes are known, three Unc.

Wyoming • 6 banks of issue • 15 notes reported • A rare state. Two Unc.

Generic prices for a typical note from a state from which notes range from available to just slightly scarce:

VG-8	F-12	VF-20	EF-40	AU-50	Unc-60	Unc-63	Unc-65
$40	$50	$60	$70	$110	$160	$200	$270

W-1048 • F-1800-2
Estimated population: 15,000 to 17,000 • *Highest graded:* Unc.

VG-8	F-12	VF-20	EF-40	AU-50	Unc-60	Unc-63	Unc-65
$35	$40	$50	$60	$150	$175	$225	$400

FEDERAL RESERVE BANK NOTES

Series of 1929, Brown Seal
Jones-Woods (1929–1933)

Federal Reserve Bank Notes of the Series of 1929, Brown Seal (illus. on p. 276), exist from each of the Federal Reserve districts except Richmond. These bills, different from the later Federal Reserve Notes, have NATIONAL CURRENCY at the top margin of the face and were intended to be National Bank Notes (of the 1929 Type 1 style). Production lasted for only a short time in March 1933, when already printed but incomplete National Bank Note sheets were filled in with Federal Reserve Bank information.

The printed signatures on these and other notes include two Treasury officials and two Federal Reserve Bank officials, such as the deputy governor (or assistant deputy governor) and governor, or the cashier and governor. Sometimes "Cashier," and always "President," if already printed on the notes, was blocked out with a black rectangle. Added to the security information already printed at the top center of National Bank Notes was a new line, "or by like deposit of other securities." Sometimes the registration of this added line caused the printing to slightly overlap the printing of SERIES OF below.

SERIES OF 1929, BROWN SEAL

$5 Federal Reserve Bank Note, Series of 1929 (W-1050-G). Federal Reserve Bank of Chicago. This note is imprinted with "Asst. Deputy Governor" and "Governor," with "Cashier" and "President" blanked out.

Back of W-1050-G, also used on other small-size $5 notes of the era.

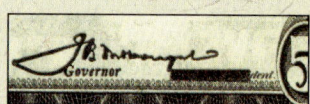

Detail of the lower right of the face of a W-1050-G note.

The $5 note from San Francisco is *the* rarity in the small-size Federal Reserve Bank Note series from $5 to $100. It is likely that these were mostly paid out by the bank in 1933, unlike many other locations, which had remainder quantities on hand that were distributed during World War II. No $5 notes were printed for Richmond.

W-1050-A • F-1850A • Boston • 3,180,000

VG-8	F-12	VF-20	EF-40	AU-50	Unc-60	Unc-63	Unc-65
$26	$38	$50	$85	$125	$200	$300	$450

W-1050-A★ • F-1850A★

VG-8	F-12	VF-20	EF-40	AU-50	Unc-60	Unc-63
$250	$375	$500	$900	$1,600	$3,000	$4,500

W-1050-B • F-1850B • New York • 2,100,000

VG-8	F-12	VF-20	EF-40	AU-50	Unc-60	Unc-63
$26	$35	$45	$100	$140	$225	$350

W-1050-B★ • F-1850B★

VG-8	F-12	VF-20	EF-40	AU-50	Unc-60	Unc-63
$250	$375	$500	$900	$1,600	$3,000	$4,500

W-1050-C • F-1850C • Philadelphia • 3,096,000

VG-8	F-12	VF-20	EF-40	AU-50	Unc-60	Unc-63	Unc-65
$26	$35	$45	$85	$125	$200	$300	$450

W-1050-C★ • F-1850C★

VG-8	F-12	VF-20	EF-40	AU-50	Unc-60	Unc-63
$250	$375	$500	$900	$1,600	$3,000	$4,500

W-1050-D • F-1850D • Cleveland • 4,236,000

VG-8	F-12	VF-20	EF-40	AU-50	Unc-60	Unc-63	Unc-65
$26	$35	$45	$85	$125	$200	$300	$450

W-1050-D★ • F-1850D★

VG-8	F-12	VF-20	EF-40	AU-50	Unc-60	Unc-63
$250	$375	$500	$900	$1,600	$3,000	$4,500

W-1050-F • F-1850F • Atlanta • 1,884,000

VG-8	F-12	VF-20	EF-40	AU-50	Unc-60	Unc-63	Unc-65
$26	$38	$50	$100	$180	$300	$500	$650

W-1050-F★ • F-1850F★

VG-8	F-12	VF-20	EF-40	AU-50	Unc-60	Unc-63
$250	$375	$500	$900	$1,600	$3,000	$4,500

W-1050-G • F-1850G • Chicago • 5,988,000

VG-8	F-12	VF-20	EF-40	AU-50	Unc-60	Unc-63	Unc-65
$26	$35	$45	$85	$125	$200	$275	$425

W-1050-G★ • F-1850G★

VG-8	F-12	VF-20	EF-40	AU-50	Unc-60	Unc-63
$250	$375	$500	$900	$1,600	$3,000	$4,500

W-1050-H • F-1850H • St. Louis • 276,000

VG-8	F-12	VF-20	EF-40	AU-50	Unc-60	Unc-63
$375	$600	$1,000	$1,900	$3,000	$5,000	$6,500

W-1050-H★ • F-1850H★

VG-8	F-12	VF-20	EF-40	AU-50	Unc-60	Unc-63
$250	$375	$500	$900	$1,600	$3,000	$4,500

W-1050-I • F-1850I • Minneapolis • 684,000

VG-8	F-12	VF-20	EF-40	AU-50	Unc-60	Unc-63
$50	$85	$125	$250	$400	$1,000	$1,500

W-1050-I★ • F-1850I★

VG-8	F-12	VF-20	EF-40	AU-50	Unc-60	Unc-63
$250	$375	$500	$900	$1,600	$3,000	$4,500

W-1050-J • F-1850J • Kansas City • 2,460,000

VG-8	F-12	VF-20	EF-40	AU-50	Unc-60	Unc-63	Unc-65
$26	$38	$50	$100	$140	$225	$350	$525

W-1050-J★ • F-1850J★

VG-8	F-12	VF-20	EF-40	AU-50	Unc-60	Unc-63
$250	$375	$500	$900	$1,600	$3,000	$4,500

W-1050-K • F-1850K • Dallas • 996,000

VG-8	F-12	VF-20	EF-40	AU-50	Unc-60	Unc-63	Unc-65
$32	$50	$70	$125	$190	$265	$400	$600

W-1050-K★ • F-1850K★

VG-8	F-12	VF-20	EF-40	AU-50	Unc-60	Unc-63
$250	$375	$500	$900	$1,600	$3,000	$4,500

W-1050-L • F-1850L • San Francisco • 360,000

VG-8	F-12	VF-20	EF-40	AU-50	Unc-60	Unc-63
$2,000	$2,500	$3,000	$5,000	$7,800	$11,000	$15,000

W-1050-L★ • F-1850L★ • Printed, but none located today

SILVER CERTIFICATES

Series of 1934, Blue Seal
Julian-Morgenthau (1934–1945)

FIVE DOLLARS IN SILVER PAYABLE is the obligation on this series (illus. on p. 278), without mention of coins. Printed in blue are the counter in the left field, both serial numbers, and the Treasury seal in the right field. FIVE is printed in large letters to the right, at the seal. SERIES OF 1934 is above the blue counter. At the lower right SERIES OF 1934 is above WASHINGTON, D.C.

Mules: Most backs have the plate number in micro numbers, but mules have the macro-size serials as used on Series 1934-A (the macro plates have numbers 939 and higher).

W-1078 • F-1650 • 393,088,368

VG-8	F-12	VF-20	EF-40	AU-50	Unc-60	Unc-63	Unc-65
$11	$14	$16	$22	$30	$40	$50	$110

W-1078★ • F-1650★ • 3,960,000 (est.)

VG-8	F-12	VF-20	EF-40	AU-50	Unc-60	Unc-63	Unc-65
$30	$50	$75	$150	$300	$400	$600	$1,500

W-1078 Mule • F-1650

VG-8	F-12	VF-20	EF-40	AU-50	Unc-60	Unc-63	Unc-65
$70	$120	$200	$400	$600	$775	$1,000	$1,650

Series of 1934-A, Blue Seal
Julian-Morgenthau (1934–1945)

This series (illus. on p. 278) continued the preceding design.

Mules: Most backs starting with 1934-A have the plate number in macro numbers, but mules have the micro-size numbers as used on Series 1934 (the micro plates have numbers 938 and lower). Mules with micro back plate number 637 are worth a strong premium, with star notes bringing even more.

W-1083 • F-1651 • 656,265,948

VG-8	F-12	VF-20	EF-40	AU-50	Unc-60	Unc-63	Unc-65
$11	$14	$16	$22	$30	$40	$50	$100

W-1083★ • F-1651★ • 7,320,000 (est.)

VG-8	F-12	VF-20	EF-40	AU-50	Unc-60	Unc-63	Unc-65
$30	$50	$75	$125	$190	$280	$375	$600

W-1083 Mule • F-1651

VG-8	F-12	VF-20	EF-40	AU-50	Unc-60	Unc-63	Unc-65
$11	$14	$17	$25	$35	$50	$70	$125

W-1083 Mule★ • F-1651★

VG-8	F-12	VF-20	EF-40	AU-50	Unc-60	Unc-63	Unc-65
$35	$60	$100	$200	$350	$500	$600	$750

Series of 1934-A, Yellow Seal, for North Africa
Julian-Morgenthau (1934–1945)

This series (illus. on p. 278) continued the preceding design. These notes, with a special, light yellow seal but with no distinctive overprint, were produced for use by Allied forces in the Mediterranean and North Africa from 1942 to 1944.

W-1086 • F-2307 • 16,710,000

VG-8	F-12	VF-20	EF-40	AU-50	Unc-60	Unc-63	Unc-65
$45	$70	$90	$135	$190	$300	$375	$775

W-1086★ • F-2307★ • 100,000

VG-8	F-12	VF-20	EF-40	AU-50	Unc-60	Unc-63	Unc-65
$175	$300	$450	$750	$1,500	$2,750	$3,500	$5,500

Series of 1934-B, Blue Seal
Julian-Vinson (1945–1946)

This series (illus. on p. 278) continued the preceding design, now returning to the standard blue Treasury seal.

Series of 1934, Blue Seal

$5 Silver Certificate, Series of 1934, Blue Seal (W-1078).

Back of the $5 Silver Certificate, Series of 1934, Blue Seal (W-1078). Standard back of $5 notes of the era.

Series of 1934-A, Blue Seal

Signatures and series imprints of a $5 Silver Certificate, Series of 1934-A (W-1083). The back is the standard type of the era.

Series of 1934-A, Yellow Seal, for North Africa

$5 Silver Certificate, Series of 1934-A, Yellow Seal (W-1086). With distinctive yellow Treasury seal. Made for use in North Africa during World War II. The back is standard for $5 notes of the era, with no special indication of its use in North Africa.

Series of 1934-B, Blue Seal

Signatures and series imprints of a $5 Silver Certificate, Series of 1934-B (W-1090). The back is the standard type of the era.

Mules: Most backs have the plate number in macro numbers, but mules have the micro-size numbers as used on Series 1934 (the single micro plate for this combination has number 637). These are seldom seen and are highly valued.

W-1090 • F-1652 • 59,128,500

VG-8	F-12	VF-20	EF-40	AU-50	Unc-60	Unc-63	Unc-65
$14	$20	$25	$35	$40	$50	$60	$200

W-1090★ • F-1652★ • 700,000 (est.)

VG-8	F-12	VF-20	EF-40	AU-50	Unc-60	Unc-63	Unc-65
$100	$170	$250	$475	$1,350	$1,750	$2,250	$4,000

W-1090 Mule • F-1652

VG-8	F-12	VF-20	EF-40	AU-50	Unc-60	Unc-63	Unc-65
$60	$115	$175	$300	$500	$700	$900	$1,350

W-1090 Mule★ • F-1652★

VG-8	F-12	VF-20	EF-40	AU-50	Unc-60	Unc-63
$500	$900	$1,500	$2,150	$3,000	$4,800	$6,000

Series of 1934-C, Blue Seal, Wide Face
Julian-Snyder (1946–1949)

Beginning on August 1, 1948, new $5 Silver Certificate face plates were made slightly smaller by narrowing the printed area horizontally by subtly removing part of the design. This created "Wide Face" (early style) and "Narrow Face" (later style) varieties. On November 7, 1951, the back (generic for all $5 series) was made "Narrow" as well.

The face of this series is found with both varieties, the Wide Face here and the Narrow Face listed next. Among the minor differences, the left end of the curved ornament near the 5 at the lower right can have either three double vertical lines (Wide Face) or two (Narrow Face). Such differences, largely overlooked a generation ago, have attracted buyers who have read about them in the Schwartz-Lindquist *Standard Catalogue of Small-Size U.S. Paper Money 1928 to Date*. Related varieties are found with 1934-C Federal Reserve notes, but are slightly differently defined.

Wide Face plate numbers range from 1875 to 2026.

Mules: Most backs starting with 1934-A have the plate number in macro numbers, but mules have the micro-size numbers as used on Series 1934; the micro plates for this particular mule include numbers 629 and 637. These are an early part of the Wide Face style shown here. These have a counterpart in Series of 1934-C Federal Reserve Notes.[39]

W-1100 • F-1653 • 403,146,148

VG-8	F-12	VF-20	EF-40	AU-50	Unc-60	Unc-63	Unc-65
$11	$14	$16	$22	$30	$40	$45	$100

W-1100★ • F-1653★ • 5,210,000 (est.)

VG-8	F-12	VF-20	EF-40	AU-50	Unc-60	Unc-63	Unc-65
$20	$35	$50	$100	$150	$200	$375	$575

W-1100 Mule • F-1653

VG-8	F-12	VF-20	EF-40	AU-50	Unc-60	Unc-63	Unc-65
$30	$45	$70	$100	$140	$200	$250	$450

W-1100 Mule★ • F-1653★

VG-8	F-12	VF-20	EF-40	AU-50	Unc-60	Unc-63	Unc-65
$270	$450	$750	$975	$1,250	$1,550	$2,000	$3,000

Series of 1934-C, Blue Seal, Narrow Face
Julian-Snyder (1946–1949)

This is the Narrow Face style, plates 2028 to 2031. For details see the preceding listing.

Mules: Most backs starting with 1934-A have the plate number in macro numbers, but mules have the micro-size numbers as used on Series 1934 (the micro plates combined with the 1934-C Narrow Face is number 637, which was canceled in June 1949). Printing of these began in August 1948.

W-1102 • F-1653 • Part of W-1100 printage

VG-8	F-12	VF-20	EF-40	AU-50	Unc-60	Unc-63	Unc-65
$20	$35	$50	$115	$170	$240	$300	$450

W-1102★ • F-1653★

Commentary: 2 known, ★17012311A and one in a New Jersey collection.

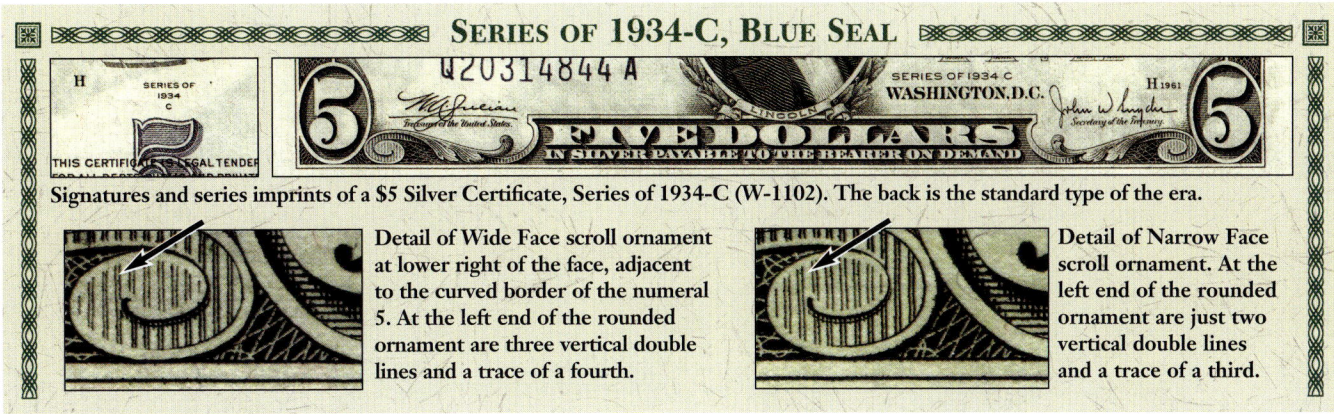

SERIES OF 1934-C, BLUE SEAL

Signatures and series imprints of a $5 Silver Certificate, Series of 1934-C (W-1102). The back is the standard type of the era.

Detail of Wide Face scroll ornament at lower right of the face, adjacent to the curved border of the numeral 5. At the left end of the rounded ornament are three vertical double lines and a trace of a fourth.

Detail of Narrow Face scroll ornament. At the left end of the rounded ornament are just two vertical double lines and a trace of a third.

W-1102 Mule • F-1653

VG-8	F-12	VF-20	EF-40	AU-50	Unc-60	Unc-63	Unc-65
$95	$175	$300	$500	$750	$900	$1,200	$1,800

W-1102 Mule★ • F-1653★
Commentary: 1 known, ★14984863A.

Series of 1934-D, Blue Seal, Wide Back
Clark-Snyder (1949–1953)

This series continued the preceding design.

Series of 1934-D notes are found in Wide and Narrow (scarcer) Back varieties. The Wide issues have plate numbers up to 2007 (Wide Back 1), and plate numbers 2067 to 2096 (Wide Back 2), with notes in the second range being much scarcer. The Narrow Back numbers are from 2008 to 2066. Such differences have gained notice only in recent years. Similar varieties exist for $5 Legal Tender Notes, Series of 1928-F.

W-1104 • F-1654 • 486,146,148

VG-8	F-12	VF-20	EF-40	AU-50	Unc-60	Unc-63	Unc-65
$11	$14	$16	$22	$30	$40	$45	$100

W-1104★ • F-1654★ • 5,800,000 (est.)

VG-8	F-12	VF-20	EF-40	AU-50	Unc-60	Unc-63	Unc-65
$25	$35	$50	$100	$150	$200	$250	$375

Series of 1934-D, Blue Seal, Narrow Back
Clark-Snyder (1949–1953)

This series continued the preceding design.

Narrow Back plate numbers are from 2008 to 2066. See the information in the previous section.

W-1105 • F-1654 • Part of W-1104 printage

VG-8	F-12	VF-20	EF-40	AU-50	Unc-60	Unc-63	Unc-65
$12	$16	$20	$30	$40	$50	$65	$95

W-1105★ • F-1654★

VG-8	F-12	VF-20	EF-40	AU-50	Unc-60	Unc-63	Unc-65
$37	$55	$75	$150	$225	$400	$500	$750

Series of 1953, Blue Seal
Priest-Humphrey (1953–1957)

The face layout was modified. To the right is the Treasury seal printed in blue. The counter left of center is now gray. FIVE is to the right of center, overprinted with the Treasury seal. WASHINGTON, D.C. is printed above the Treasury seal. Back type is the same for all $5 notes through the 1950s.

W-1106 • F-1655 • 339,600,000

VG-8	F-12	VF-20	EF-40	AU-50	Unc-60	Unc-63	Unc-65
$11	$14	$16	$20	$24	$27	$30	$60

SERIES OF 1934-D, BLUE SEAL

Signatures and series imprints of a $5 Silver Certificate, Series of 1934-D (W-1104). The back is the standard type of the era.

SERIES OF 1953, BLUE SEAL

$5 Silver Certificate, Series of 1953 (W-1106). The Series of 1953 continues the standard back of $5 notes of the era.

SERIES OF 1953-A, BLUE SEAL

Signatures and series imprint of a $5 Silver Certificate, Series of 1953-A (W-1108). The back is the standard type of the era.

W-1106★ • F-1655★ • 15,120,000

VG-8	F-12	VF-20	EF-40	AU-50	Unc-60	Unc-63	Unc-65
$16	$22	$35	$45	$65	$110	$150	$275

Series of 1953-A, Blue Seal
Priest-Anderson (1957–1961)

This series continued the preceding design.

W-1108 • F-1656 • 232,400,000

VG-8	F-12	VF-20	EF-40	AU-50	Unc-60	Unc-63	Unc-65
$11	$14	$16	$20	$23	$26	$30	$50

W-1108★ • F-1656★ • 12,960,000

VG-8	F-12	VF-20	EF-40	AU-50	Unc-60	Unc-63	Unc-65
$16	$20	$30	$40	$60	$80	$100	$150

Series of 1953-B, Blue Seal
Smith-Dillon (1961–1962)

This series continued the preceding design.

Most Series of 1953-B notes were never released, due to the rising price of silver (see next). Only 14,196,000 were put into circulation; the final notes were delivered to the Treasury on April 25, 1962. Very few star notes were released, making these a key in the small-size $5 series.

W-1110 • F-1657 • 73,000,000

VG-8	F-12	VF-20	EF-40	AU-50	Unc-60	Unc-63	Unc-65
$11	$14	$16	$20	$23	$26	$30	$50

W-1110★ • F-1657★ • 3,240,000

VG-8	F-12	VF-20	EF-40	AU-50	Unc-60	Unc-63	Unc-65
$2,000	$3,000	$4,000	$7,500	$10,000	$15,000	$17,000	$22,000

Series of 1953-C, Blue Seal
Granahan-Dillon (1963–1965)

Notes of the 1953-C issue were never released, as the price of silver was rising rapidly on the international market, and it was no longer practical to guarantee payment in this metal. The Bureau of Engraving and Printing has exhibited an uncut sheet of star notes at numismatic conventions.

The Treasury kept redeeming older Silver Certificates in bullion until July 24, 1968. After this date, Silver Certificates had no special premium value, except slight advances for those in higher grades sought by numismatists.

W-1112 • F-1658 • None released

W-1112★ • F-1658★ • None released

FEDERAL RESERVE NOTES

Small-size $5 Federal Reserve Notes start with the Series of 1928. Such bills have been issued by the 12 Federal Reserve Banks ever since, but not always for each series. Each note bears identification as to the bank letter and number, such as 7-G for Chicago. Each has a green Treasury seal. In addition to the regular issues, certain Series of 1934 and 1934-A notes have the HAWAII overprint and a brown seal, used during World War II (see related commentary under Small-Size $1 Silver Certificates). Series of 1950 notes from various districts occur in both Wide and Narrow styles. All are collectible, although some are scarcer than others. Beginning with the Series of 1963, the motto IN GOD WE TRUST is on the back.

Commencing with the Series of 1988-A, the Western Facility in Fort Worth, Texas, printed $5 notes in addition to the main plant in Washington. For the Series of 1999, the face and back designs were modified. Lincoln's portrait was changed and enlarged, and anti-counterfeiting security features were added to the design and paper. By this time the widespread use of color copying machines had spawned a new generation of note imitations. In 2006 the face and back were further modified.

Although the $5 denomination is not as widely collected as the $1 or $2 issues, there is still a large group of collectors who seek the different Federal Reserve bank and signature combinations as they are released. Star or replacement notes form a specialty as well.

Series of 1928, Green Seal
Tate-Mellon (1928–1929)

The obligation of this series (illus. on p. 282) is in four lines in the field at the upper left: "Redeemable in gold on demand at the United States Treasury, or in gold or lawful money at any Federal Reserve Bank." On the Series of 1928 and 1928-A notes the seal is in the left field and features the number of the issuing Federal Reserve Bank, 1 to 12. The series imprint appears twice—at the upper left of Lincoln's portrait and above WASHINGTON at the lower right.

W-1118-A • F-1950A • Boston • 8,025,300

VG-8	F-12	VF-20	EF-40	AU-50	Unc-60	Unc-63	Unc-65
$35	$50	$75	$125	$200	$325	$500	$1,000

W-1118-A★ • F-1950A★

VG-8	F-12	VF-20	EF-40	AU-50	Unc-60	Unc-63
$550	$900	$1,450	$1,850	$2,250	$3,000	$5,000

SERIES OF 1953-B, BLUE SEAL

Signatures and series imprint of a $5 Silver Certificate, Series of 1953-B (W-1110). The back is the standard type of the era.

W-1118-B • F-1950 B • New York • 14,701,884

VG-8	F-12	VF-20	EF-40	AU-50	Unc-60	Unc-63	Unc-65
$22	$35	$50	$80	$120	$200	$275	$400

W-1118-B★ • F-1950B★

VG-8	F-12	VF-20	EF-40	AU-50	Unc-60	Unc-63	Unc-65
$200	$300	$400	$575	$750	$900	$1,150	$1,900

W-1118-C • F-1950C • Philadelphia • 11,819,712

VG-8	F-12	VF-20	EF-40	AU-50	Unc-60	Unc-63	Unc-65
$22	$35	$50	$80	$120	$200	$275	$400

W-1118-C★ • F-1950C★

VG-8	F-12	VF-20	EF-40	AU-50	Unc-60	Unc-63
$300	$450	$700	$1,100	$1,500	$2,250	$3,000

W-1118-D • F-1950D • Cleveland • 9,049,500

VG-8	F-12	VF-20	EF-40	AU-50	Unc-60	Unc-63	Unc-65
$22	$35	$45	$75	$110	$180	$250	$350

W-1118-D★ • F-1950D★

VG-8	F-12	VF-20	EF-40	AU-50	Unc-60	Unc-63
$200	$325	$475	$625	$1,100	$1,600	$2,000

W-1118-E • F-1950E • Richmond • 6,027,600

VG-8	F-12	VF-20	EF-40	AU-50	Unc-60	Unc-63	Unc-65
$35	$50	$80	$125	$400	$650	$800	$1,350

W-1118-E★ • F-1950E★

VG-8	F-12	VF-20	EF-40	AU-50	Unc-60	Unc-63
$475	$700	$1,000	$1,750	$2,400	$3,800	$5,000

W-1118-F • F-1950F • Atlanta • 10,964,400

VG-8	F-12	VF-20	EF-40	AU-50	Unc-60	Unc-63	Unc-65
$30	$45	$60	$100	$175	$300	$440	$675

W-1118-F★ • F-1950F★

VG-8	F-12	VF-20	EF-40	AU-50	Unc-60	Unc-63
$475	$700	$1,000	$1,750	$2,400	$3,800	$5,000

W-1118-G • F-1950G • Chicago • 12,320,052

VG-8	F-12	VF-20	EF-40	AU-50	Unc-60	Unc-63	Unc-65
$22	$35	$50	$80	$120	$200	$275	$400

W-1118-G★ • F-1950G★

VG-8	F-12	VF-20	EF-40	AU-50	Unc-60	Unc-63	Unc-65
$85	$125	$200	$525	$700	$900	$1,200	$2,000

W-1118-H • F-1950H • St. Louis • 4,675,200

VG-8	F-12	VF-20	EF-40	AU-50	Unc-60	Unc-63	Unc-65
$30	$45	$60	$100	$175	$275	$350	$500

W-1118-H★ • F-1950H★

VG-8	F-12	VF-20	EF-40	AU-50	Unc-60	Unc-63
$350	$450	$600	$1,450	$2,100	$2,900	$3,500

SERIES OF 1928, GREEN SEAL

$5 Federal Reserve Note, Series of 1928 (W-1118-B). Federal Reserve Bank of New York. (Smithsonian Institution)

Detail of the redemption notice and Federal Reserve seal on this Series of 1928 note.

Back of the $5 Federal Reserve Note, Series of 1928. Standard back of $5 notes of the era.

W-1118-I • F-1950I • Minneapolis • 4,284,300

VG-8	F-12	VF-20	EF-40	AU-50	Unc-60	Unc-63	Unc-65
$125	$165	$225	$550	$850	$1,100	$1,500	$2,250

W-1118-I★ • F-1950I★

VG-8	F-12	VF-20	EF-40	AU-50	Unc-60	Unc-63
$1,100	$1,500	$2,000	$2,750	$3,500	$5,000	$6,000

W-1118-J • F-1950J • Kansas City • 4,480,800

VG-8	F-12	VF-20	EF-40	AU-50	Unc-60	Unc-63	Unc-65
$35	$50	$75	$150	$275	$425	$550	$750

W-1118-J★ • F-1950J★

VG-8	F-12	VF-20	EF-40	AU-50	Unc-60	Unc-63
$350	$550	$800	$1,250	$1,800	$2,750	$3,500

W-1118-K • F-1950K • Dallas • 8,137,824

VG-8	F-12	VF-20	EF-40	AU-50	Unc-60	Unc-63	Unc-65
$35	$50	$60	$100	$180	$290	$375	$525

W-1118-K★ • F-1950K★

VG-8	F-12	VF-20	EF-40	AU-50	Unc-60	Unc-63
$550	$900	$1,300	$1,800	$2,400	$3,350	$4,000

W-1118-L • F-1950L • San Francisco • 9,792,000

VG-8	F-12	VF-20	EF-40	AU-50	Unc-60	Unc-63	Unc-65
$40	$60	$75	$150	$240	$310	$400	$600

W-1118-L★ • F-1950L★

VG-8	F-12	VF-20	EF-40	AU-50	Unc-60	Unc-63
$700	$1,250	$1,700	$2,400	$3,500	$4,800	$6,000

Series of 1928-A, Green Seal
Woods-Mellon (1929–1932)

The "redeemable in gold" provision and the Federal Reserve Bank number at the center of the Federal Reserve seal are similar to the Series of 1928 notes.

W-1120-A • F-1951A • Boston • 9,404,352

VG-8	F-12	VF-20	EF-40	AU-50	Unc-60	Unc-63	Unc-65
$45	$80	$115	$250	$450	$675	$800	$1,250

W-1120-A★ • F-1951A★

VG-8	F-12	VF-20	EF-40	AU-50	Unc-60	Unc-63	Unc-65
$450	$750	$1,000	$1,500	$2,250	$3,200	$5,000	$10,000

W-1120-B • F-1951B • New York • 42,878,196

VG-8	F-12	VF-20	EF-40	AU-50	Unc-60	Unc-63	Unc-65
$25	$30	$40	$65	$125	$190	$250	$400

W-1120-B★ • F-1951B★

VG-8	F-12	VF-20	EF-40	AU-50	Unc-60	Unc-63	Unc-65
$375	$550	$800	$1,250	$1,500	$1,900	$2,500	$3,500

W-1120-C • F-1951C • Philadelphia • 10,806,012

VG-8	F-12	VF-20	EF-40	AU-50	Unc-60	Unc-63	Unc-65
$30	$40	$50	$75	$125	$190	$250	$400

W-1120-C★ • F-1951C★

VG-8	F-12	VF-20	EF-40	AU-50	Unc-60	Unc-63
$450	$750	$1,000	$1,500	$2,250	$2,800	$3,250

W-1120-D • F-1951D • Cleveland • 6,822,000

VG-8	F-12	VF-20	EF-40	AU-50	Unc-60	Unc-63	Unc-65
$30	$40	$50	$75	$125	$190	$250	$325

W-1120-D★ • F-1951D★

VG-8	F-12	VF-20	EF-40	AU-50	Unc-60	Unc-63	Unc-65
$150	$275	$450	$750	$1,250	$1,800	$2,250	$3,000

W-1120-E • F-1951E • Richmond • 2,409,900

VG-8	F-12	VF-20	EF-40	AU-50	Unc-60	Unc-63	Unc-65
$40	$50	$65	$110	$200	$325	$400	$650

W-1120-E★ • F-1951E★

VG-8	F-12	VF-20	EF-40	AU-50	Unc-60	Unc-63
$800	$1,750	$2,400	$3,400	$4,500	$6,000	$7,500

W-1120-F • F-1951F • Atlanta • 3,537,600

VG-8	F-12	VF-20	EF-40	AU-50	Unc-60	Unc-63	Unc-65
$45	$70	$110	$180	$290	$400	$500	$750

W-1120-F★ • F-1951F★

VG-8	F-12	VF-20	EF-40	AU-50	Unc-60	Unc-63
$800	$1,425	$2,000	$3,000	$4,400	$5,800	$7,000

W-1120-G • F-1951G • Chicago • 37,882,176

VG-8	F-12	VF-20	EF-40	AU-50	Unc-60	Unc-63	Unc-65
$35	$45	$65	$80	$125	$180	$235	$325

W-1120-G★ • F-1951G★

VG-8	F-12	VF-20	EF-40	AU-50	Unc-60	Unc-63
$125	$200	$325	$950	$1,500	$1,800	$2,500

W-1120-H • F-1951H • St. Louis • 2,731,824

VG-8	F-12	VF-20	EF-40	AU-50	Unc-60	Unc-63	Unc-65
$25	$30	$40	$75	$120	$170	$250	$350

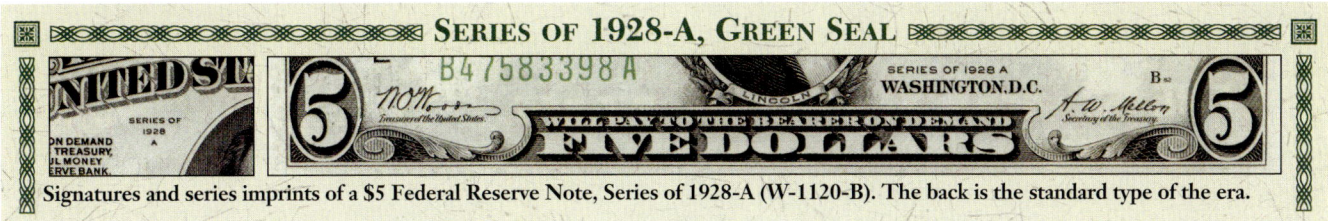

SERIES OF 1928-A, GREEN SEAL

Signatures and series imprints of a $5 Federal Reserve Note, Series of 1928-A (W-1120-B). The back is the standard type of the era.

W-1120-H★ • F-1951H★

VG-8	F-12	VF-20	EF-40	AU-50	Unc-60	Unc-63	Unc-65
$125	$200	$325	$500	$850	$1,000	$1,400	$2,500

W-1120-I • F-1951I • Minneapolis • 652,800

VG-8	F-12	VF-20	EF-40	AU-50	Unc-60	Unc-63	Unc-65
$35	$45	$60	$95	$150	$225	$300	$450

W-1120-J • F-1951J • Kansas City • 3,572,400

VG-8	F-12	VF-20	EF-40	AU-50	Unc-60	Unc-63	Unc-65
$30	$40	$50	$110	$170	$240	$325	$500

W-1120-K • F-1951K • Dallas • 2,564,400

VG-8	F-12	VF-20	EF-40	AU-50	Unc-60	Unc-63	Unc-65
$30	$40	$50	$110	$170	$200	$275	$450

W-1120-K★ • F-1951K★

VF-20
$2,500

W-1120-L • F-1951L • San Francisco • 6,565,500

VG-8	F-12	VF-20	EF-40	AU-50	Unc-60	Unc-63	Unc-65
$30	$40	$50	$75	$125	$190	$250	$400

W-1120-L★ • F-1951L★

VG-8	F-12	VF-20	EF-40	AU-50	Unc-60	Unc-63
$275	$425	$600	$850	$1,300	$1,600	$2,000

Series of 1928-B, Green Seal
Woods-Mellon (1929–1932)

The "redeemable in gold" provision is the same as on Series of 1928 and Series of 1928-A notes. The Federal Reserve seal now has the bank letter at the center, instead of the number.

W-1122-A • F-1952A • Boston • 28,430,724

VF-20	EF-40	AU-50	Unc-60	Unc-63	Unc-65
$20	$28	$38	$60	$100	$160

W-1122-A★ • F-1952A★

VG-8	F-12	VF-20	EF-40	AU-50	Unc-60	Unc-63	Unc-65
$180	$300	$500	$725	$1,000	$1,600	$2,000	$3,000

W-1122-B • F-1952B • New York • 51,157,536

VF-20	EF-40	AU-50	Unc-60	Unc-63	Unc-65
$20	$28	$38	$60	$100	$150

W-1122-B★ • F-1952B★

VG-8	F-12	VF-20	EF-40	AU-50	Unc-60	Unc-63
$180	$300	$500	$725	$900	$1,200	$1,500

W-1122-C • F-1952C • Philadelphia • 25,698,396

VF-20	EF-40	AU-50	Unc-60	Unc-63	Unc-65
$20	$25	$35	$50	$80	$140

W-1122-C★ • F-1952C★

VG-8	F-12	VF-20	EF-40	AU-50	Unc-60	Unc-63	Unc-65
$120	$200	$325	$425	$500	$700	$900	$1,400

W-1122-D • F-1952D • Cleveland • 24,874,272

VF-20	EF-40	AU-50	Unc-60	Unc-63	Unc-65
$20	$28	$38	$60	$100	$160

W-1122-D★ • F-1952D★

VG-8	F-12	VF-20	EF-40	AU-50	Unc-60	Unc-63	Unc-65
$180	$300	$500	$725	$1,000	$1,600	$2,000	$3,000

W-1122-E • F-1952E • Richmond • 15,151,932

VF-20	EF-40	AU-50	Unc-60	Unc-63	Unc-65
$20	$28	$38	$60	$100	$160

W-1122-E★ • F-1952E★

VG-8	F-12	VF-20	EF-40	AU-50	Unc-60	Unc-63	Unc-65
$180	$300	$500	$725	$1,000	$1,600	$2,000	$3,000

W-1122-F • F-1952F • Atlanta • 13,386,420

VF-20	EF-40	AU-50	Unc-60	Unc-63	Unc-65
$20	$28	$38	$60	$100	$160

W-1122-F★ • F-1952F★

VG-8	F-12	VF-20	EF-40	AU-50	Unc-60	Unc-63
$120	$200	$325	$600	$900	$1,400	$1,700

W-1122-G • F-1952G • Chicago • 17,157,036

VF-20	EF-40	AU-50	Unc-60	Unc-63	Unc-65
$20	$28	$38	$60	$100	$160

W-1122-G★ • F-1952G★

Commentary: Current market information unavailable.

W-1122-H • F-1952H • St. Louis • 20,251,716

VF-20	EF-40	AU-50	Unc-60	Unc-63	Unc-65
$20	$25	$35	$50	$80	$140

W-1122-H★ • F-1952H★

VG-8	F-12	VF-20	EF-40	AU-50	Unc-60	Unc-63	Unc-65
$120	$200	$325	$600	$900	$1,200	$1,400	$2,100

W-1122-I • F-1952I • Minneapolis • 6,954,060

F-12	VF-20	EF-40	AU-50	Unc-60	Unc-63	Unc-65
$30	$50	$60	$70	$125	$175	$275

Detail of the signatures and the series imprints of a $5 Federal Reserve Note, Series of 1928-B (W-1122-H), as well as the new style of Federal Reserve seal. The back is the standard type of the era.

W-1122-I★ • F-1952I★

VG-8	F-12	VF-20	EF-40	AU-50	Unc-60	Unc-63
$400	$650	$1,200	$2,000	$3,200	$4,800	$6,000

W-1122-J • F-1952J • Kansas City • 10,677,636

F-12	VF-20	EF-40	AU-50	Unc-60	Unc-63	Unc-65
$25	$40	$70	$100	$200	$275	$400

W-1122-K • F-1952K • Dallas • 4,334,400

F-12	VF-20	EF-40	AU-50	Unc-60	Unc-63	Unc-65
$25	$40	$50	$65	$100	$150	$260

W-1122-L • F-1952L • San Francisco • 28,840,000

VF-20	EF-40	AU-50	Unc-60	Unc-63	Unc-65
$20	$28	$38	$60	$100	$160

W-1122-L★ • F-1952L★

VG-8	F-12	VF-20	EF-40	AU-50	Unc-60	Unc-63	Unc-65
$180	$300	$500	$725	$1,000	$1,600	$2,000	$3,000

Series of 1928-B, Light Yellow-Green Seal
Woods-Mellon (1929–1932)

This series continued the previous design and "redemption in gold" provision.

There is often confusion here for collectors as far as the seal color change. This series introduces a seal color of a bright yellow-green tint, the same that was used on 1928-C and D notes and similar to that used on the 1934 yellow-green seals. In actuality, hues vary. Jamie Yakes commented, "I and a few other specialists have only seen true yellow-green seals on Cleveland, Atlanta, St. Louis, and San Francisco notes in this series."[40]

Where pricing is not given for notes in this series, current market information was unavailable at press time.

W-1125-A • F-1952A • Boston

W-1125-A★ • F-1952A★

W-1125-B • F-1952B • New York

W-1125-B★ • F-1952B★

W-1125-C • F-1952C • Philadelphia

VG-8	F-12	VF-20	EF-40
$50	$90	$125	$250

W-1125-C★ • F-1952C★

VG-8	F-12	VF-20	EF-40	AU-50	Unc-60	Unc-63	Unc-65
$125	$250	$350	$450	$550	$750	$850	$1,200

W-1125-D • F-1952D • Cleveland

VG-8	F-12	VF-20	EF-40
$50	$90	$125	$250

W-1125-D★ • F-1952D★

F-12
$500

W-1125-E • F-1952E • Richmond

W-1125-E★ • F-1952E★

W-1125-F • F-1952F • Atlanta

VG-8	F-12	VF-20	EF-40	AU-50	Unc-60	Unc-63	Unc-65
$20	$35	$50	$75	$125	$200	$275	$400

W-1125-F★ • F-1952F★

VG-8	F-12	VF-20	EF-40
$375	$600	$900	$1,500

W-1125-G • F-1952G • Chicago

W-1125-G★ • F-1952G★

W-1125-H • F-1952H • St. Louis

VG-8	F-12	VF-20	EF-40	AU-50	Unc-60	Unc-63	Unc-65
$20	$35	$50	$75	$125	$200	$275	$400

W-1125-H★ • F-1952H★

VG-8	F-12	VF-20	EF-40	AU-50	Unc-60	Unc-63
$275	$475	$700	$1,400	$2,200	$2,900	$3,500

W-1125-I • F-1952I • Minneapolis

VG-8	F-12	VF-20	EF-40	AU-50	Unc-60	Unc-63	Unc-65
$20	$40	$60	$90	$150	$230	$300	$500

SERIES OF 1928-B, LIGHT YELLOW-GREEN SEAL

$5 Federal Reserve Note, Series of 1928-B (W-1125-D). With light yellow-green Treasury seal. Federal Reserve Bank of Cleveland. Standard back of $5 notes of the era.

W-1125-I★ • F-1952I★

W-1125-J • F-1952J • Kansas City

VG-8	F-12	VF-20	EF-40	AU-50	Unc-60	Unc-63	Unc-65
$20	$35	$50	$75	$125	$200	$275	$400

W-1125-J★ • F-1952J★

W-1125-K • F-1952K • Dallas

W-1125-K★ • F-1952K★

W-1125-L • F-1952L • San Francisco

VG-8	F-12	VF-20	EF-40	AU-50	Unc-60	Unc-63	Unc-65
$20	$35	$50	$75	$125	$200	$275	$400

W-1125-L★ • F-1952L★

VG-8	F-12	VF-20	EF-40
$375	$600	$900	$1,500

Series of 1928-C, Light Yellow-Green Seal
Woods-Mills (1932–1933)

This series continued the previous design and "redemption in gold" provision. This is a very brief series with just three banks of issue.

W-1128-D • F-1953D • Cleveland • 3,293,640 • Unknown

W-1128-F • F-1953F • Atlanta • 2,056,200

VG-8	F-12	VF-20	EF-40	AU-50	Unc-60	Unc-63	Unc-65
$400	$575	$850	$1,500	$2,400	$2,900	$3,750	$6,000

W-1128-F★ • F-1953F★ • Unknown

W-1128-L • F-1953L • San Francisco • 266,304 • Unknown

Series of 1928-D, Light Yellow-Green Seal
Woods-Woodin (1933)

This issue continued the previous design and "redemption in gold" provision. This was an abbreviated series, with just one bank of issue, released in a small quantity. After March 6, 1933, the Treasury stopped putting Gold Certificates and gold coins into normal commercial channels and stopped redeeming currency in gold coins, although some exceptions were made.

W-1131-F • F-1954F • Atlanta • 1,281,600

VG-8	F-12	VF-20	EF-40	AU-50	Unc-60	Unc-63
$1,000	$1,900	$2,400	$3,000	$4,000	$5,750	$7,000

W-1131-F★ • F-1954F★ • Unknown

Series of 1934, Light Yellow-Green Seal
Julian-Morgenthau (1934–1945)

The Series of 1934 continued the same general configuration as the preceding series, but now with a change in the redemption inscription, eliminating mention of gold: "This note is Legal Tender for all debts, public and private, and is redeemable in lawful money of the United States Treasury, or at any Federal Reserve Bank."

SERIES OF 1928-C, LIGHT YELLOW-GREEN SEAL

Signatures and series imprints of a $5 Federal Reserve Note, Series of 1928-C (W-1128-F). The back is the standard type of the era.

SERIES OF 1928-D, LIGHT YELLOW-GREEN SEAL

Signatures and series imprints of a $5 Federal Reserve Note, Series of 1928-D (W-1131-F). The back is the standard type of the era.

SERIES OF 1934, LIGHT YELLOW-GREEN SEAL

$5 Federal Reserve Note, Series of 1934 (W-1134-G). Light yellow-green Treasury seal.
Federal Reserve Bank of Chicago. Standard back of $5 notes of the era.

This issue has a light yellow-green seal, which is light green with a tinge of yellow.

W-1134-A • F-1955A • Boston • 30,510,036

VF-20	EF-40	AU-50	Unc-60	Unc-63	Unc-65
$15	$30	$55	$80	$100	$135

W-1134-A★ • F-1955A★

VG-8	F-12	VF-20	EF-40	AU-50	Unc-60	Unc-63	Unc-65
$40	$75	$100	$240	$400	$750	$1,000	$1,500

W-1134-B • F-1955B • New York • 47,888,760

VF-20	EF-40	AU-50	Unc-60	Unc-63	Unc-65
$15	$20	$40	$70	$100	$140

W-1134-B★ • F-1955B★

VG-8	F-12	VF-20	EF-40	AU-50	Unc-60	Unc-63	Unc-65
$40	$75	$100	$200	$350	$600	$750	$1,100

W-1134-C • F-1955C • Philadelphia • 47,327,760

VF-20	EF-40	AU-50	Unc-60	Unc-63	Unc-65
$15	$20	$35	$50	$75	$100

W-1134-C★ • F-1955C★

VG-8	F-12	VF-20	EF-40	AU-50	Unc-60	Unc-63	Unc-65
$75	$100	$200	$425	$600	$900	$1,250	$1,900

W-1134-D • F-1955D • Cleveland • 62,273,508

VF-20	EF-40	AU-50	Unc-60	Unc-63	Unc-65
$15	$20	$35	$60	$100	$125

W-1134-D★ • F-1955D★ • Unknown

W-1134-E • F-1955E • Richmond • 62,128,452

VF-20	EF-40	AU-50	Unc-60	Unc-63	Unc-65
$15	$20	$35	$60	$100	$125

W-1134-E★ • F-1955E★

VG-8	F-12	VF-20	EF-40	AU-50	Unc-60	Unc-63
$60	$90	$150	$225	$475	$750	$1,250

W-1134-F • F-1955F • Atlanta • 50,548,608

VF-20	EF-40	AU-50	Unc-60	Unc-63	Unc-65
$15	$20	$40	$70	$100	$150

W-1134-F★ • F-1955F★

VG-8	F-12	VF-20	EF-40	AU-50	Unc-60	Unc-63	Unc-65
$75	$135	$220	$400	$650	$900	$1,250	$1,900

W-1134-G • F-1955G • Chicago • 31,299,156

VF-20	EF-40	AU-50	Unc-60	Unc-63	Unc-65
$15	$20	$35	$50	$80	$100

W-1134-G★ • F-1955G★

VG-8	F-12	VF-20	EF-40	AU-50	Unc-60	Unc-63
$40	$75	$100	$200	$350	$600	$750

W-1134-H • F-1955H • St. Louis • 48,737,280

VF-20	EF-40	AU-50	Unc-60	Unc-63	Unc-65
$15	$20	$35	$50	$80	$120

W-1134-H★ • F-1955H★

VG-8	F-12	VF-20	EF-40	AU-50	Unc-60	Unc-63
$65	$100	$175	$240	$575	$850	$1,100

W-1134-I • F-1955I • Minneapolis • 16,795,392

VF-20	EF-40	AU-50	Unc-60	Unc-63	Unc-65
$25	$40	$75	$120	$150	$225

W-1134-I★ • F-1955I★

VG-8	F-12	VF-20	EF-40	AU-50	Unc-60	Unc-63
$60	$90	$150	$225	$475	$750	$1,300

W-1134-J • F-1955J • Kansas City • 31,854,432

VF-20	EF-40	AU-50	Unc-60	Unc-63	Unc-65
$15	$20	$35	$50	$80	$120

W-1134-J★ • F-1955J★

VG-8	F-12	VF-20	EF-40	AU-50	Unc-60	Unc-63
$60	$90	$150	$225	$475	$750	$1,300

W-1134-K • F-1955K • Dallas • 33,332,208

VF-20	EF-40	AU-50	Unc-60	Unc-63	Unc-65
$15	$20	$40	$70	$100	$150

W-1134-K★ • F-1955K★

VG-8	F-12	VF-20	EF-40
$90	$150	$250	$500

W-1134-L • F-1955L • San Francisco • 39,324,168

VF-20	EF-40	AU-50	Unc-60	Unc-63	Unc-65
$15	$20	$35	$50	$90	$125

W-1134-L★ • F-1955L★

VG-8	F-12	VF-20	EF-40	AU-50	Unc-60	Unc-63
$40	$75	$100	$300	$550	$775	$1,000

Series of 1934, Blue-Green Seal
Julian-Morgenthau (1934–1945)

These notes (illus. on p. 288) are similar to the preceding except for the slightly different hue of the Treasury seal. Non-mules are much scarcer than mules for this series.

Mules: Most backs have the plate number in micro numbers, but mules have the macro-size serials as used on Series 1934-A (the macro plates have numbers 939 and higher).

W-1137-A • F-1956A • Boston • Part of W-1134-A printage

VF-20	EF-40	AU-50	Unc-60	Unc-63	Unc-65
$50	$100	$180	$280	$375	$525

SERIES OF 1934, BLUE-GREEN SEAL

$5 Federal Reserve Note, Series of 1934 (W-1137-D). Blue-green Treasury seal. Federal Reserve Bank of Cleveland. Standard back of $5 notes of the era.

W-1137-A★ • F-1956A★

VG-8	F-12	VF-20	EF-40	AU-50	Unc-60	Unc-63	Unc-65
$90	$160	$250	$350	$475	$650	$800	$1,150

W-1137-A Mule • F-1956A • Part of W-1134-A printage

VF-20	EF-40	AU-50	Unc-60	Unc-63	Unc-65
$15	$25	$35	$45	$55	$90

W-1137-A Mule★ • F-1956A★

VG-8	F-12	VF-20	EF-40	AU-50	Unc-60	Unc-63	Unc-65
$25	$50	$80	$140	$210	$280	$350	$450

W-1137-B • F-1956B • New York • Part of W-1134-B printage

VF-20	EF-40	AU-50	Unc-60	Unc-63	Unc-65
$35	$60	$140	$190	$240	$325

W-1137-B★ • F-1956B★

VG-8	F-12	VF-20	EF-40	AU-50	Unc-60	Unc-63	Unc-65
$60	$120	$180	$260	$350	$475	$650	$900

W-1137-B Mule • F-1956B • Part of W-1134-B printage

VF-20	EF-40	AU-50	Unc-60	Unc-63	Unc-65
$15	$25	$35	$45	$55	$90

W-1137-B Mule★ • F-1956B★

VG-8	F-12	VF-20	EF-40	AU-50	Unc-60	Unc-63	Unc-65
$25	$50	$80	$125	$10	$260	$325	$425

W-1137-C • F-1956C • Philadelphia • Part of W-1134-C printage

VF-20	EF-40	AU-50	Unc-60	Unc-63	Unc-65
$35	$60	$140	$190	$240	$325

W-1137-C★ • F-1956C★

VG-8	F-12	VF-20	EF-40	AU-50	Unc-60	Unc-63	Unc-65
$60	$120	$180	$260	$350	$475	$650	$900

W-1137-C Mule • F-1956C • Part of W-1134-C printage

VF-20	EF-40	AU-50	Unc-60	Unc-63	Unc-65
$15	$25	$35	$45	$55	$90

W-1137-C Mule★ • F-1956C★

VG-8	F-12	VF-20	EF-40	AU-50	Unc-60	Unc-63	Unc-65
$25	$50	$80	$140	$210	$280	$350	$450

W-1137-D • F-1956D • Cleveland • Part of W-1134-D printage

VG-8	F-12	VF-20	EF-40	AU-50	Unc-60	Unc-63	Unc-65
$200	$280	$380	$525	$700	$950	$1,200	$1,650

W-1137-D★ • F-1956D★

VG-8	F-12	VF-20	EF-40	AU-50	Unc-60	Unc-63	Unc-65
$80	$150	$225	$325	$500	$700	$950	$1,450

W-1137-D Mule • F-1956D • Part of W-1134-D printage

VF-20	EF-40	AU-50	Unc-60	Unc-63	Unc-65
$15	$25	$35	$45	$55	$90

W-1137-D Mule★ • F-1956D★

VG-8	F-12	VF-20	EF-40	AU-50	Unc-60	Unc-63	Unc-65
$25	$50	$80	$140	$210	$280	$350	$450

W-1137-E • F-1956E • Richmond • Part of W-1134-E printage

VF-20	EF-40	AU-50	Unc-60	Unc-63	Unc-65
$50	$100	$180	$280	$375	$450

W-1137-E★ • F-1956E★

VG-8	F-12	VF-20	EF-40	AU-50	Unc-60	Unc-63
$200	$275	$375	$525	$700	$950	$1,200

W-1137-E Mule • F-1956E • Part of W-1134-E printage

VF-20	EF-40	AU-50	Unc-60	Unc-63	Unc-65
$15	$25	$35	$50	$60	$95

W-1137-E Mule★ • F-1956E★

VG-8	F-12	VF-20	EF-40	AU-50	Unc-60	Unc-63	Unc-65
$25	$50	$80	$140	$210	$280	$350	$450

W-1137-F • F-1956F • Atlanta • Part of W-1134-F printage

VF-20	EF-40	AU-50	Unc-60	Unc-63	Unc-65
$50	$100	$180	$280	$375	$450

W-1137-F★ • F-1956F★

VG-8	F-12	VF-20	EF-40	AU-50	Unc-60	Unc-63
$80	$150	$225	$325	$500	$600	$750

W-1137-F Mule • F-1956F • Part of W-1134-F printage

VF-20	EF-40	AU-50	Unc-60	Unc-63	Unc-65
$15	$25	$35	$45	$55	$90

W-1137-F Mule★ • F-1956F★

VG-8	F-12	VF-20	EF-40	AU-50	Unc-60	Unc-63	Unc-65
$25	$60	$90	$160	$240	$320	$400	$500

W-1137-G • F-1956G • Chicago • Part of W-1134-G printage

VF-20	EF-40	AU-50	Unc-60	Unc-63	Unc-65
$35	$60	$140	$190	$240	$325

W-1137-G★ • F-1956G★

VG-8	F-12	VF-20	EF-40	AU-50	Unc-60	Unc-63	Unc-65
$60	$120	$180	$260	$350	$475	$650	$900

W-1137-G Mule • F-1956G • Part of W-1134-G printage

VF-20	EF-40	AU-50	Unc-60	Unc-63	Unc-65
$15	$25	$35	$45	$55	$90

W-1137-G Mule★ • F-1956G★

VG-8	F-12	VF-20	EF-40	AU-50	Unc-60	Unc-63	Unc-65
$25	$50	$80	$125	$190	$260	$325	$425

W-1137-H • F-1956H • St. Louis • Part of W-1134-H printage

VG-8	F-12	VF-20	EF-40	AU-50	Unc-60	Unc-63	Unc-65
$50	$100	$180	$260	$350	$425	$500	$650

W-1137-H★ • F-1956H★

VG-8	F-12	VF-20	EF-40	AU-50	Unc-60	Unc-63
$120	$200	$300	$500	$700	$800	$950

W-1137-H Mule • F-1956H • Part of W-1134-H printage

VF-20	EF-40	AU-50	Unc-60	Unc-63	Unc-65
$15	$25	$35	$45	$55	$90

W-1137-H Mule★ • F-1956H★

VG-8	F-12	VF-20	EF-40	AU-50	Unc-60	Unc-63	Unc-65
$25	$50	$80	$125	$190	$260	$325	$425

W-1137-I • F-1956I • Minneapolis • Part of W-1134-I printage

VG-8	F-12	VF-20	EF-40	AU-50	Unc-60	Unc-63	Unc-65
$40	$60	$85	$125	$180	$245	$300	$475

W-1137-I★ • F-1956I★

VG-8	F-12	VF-20	EF-40	AU-50	Unc-60	Unc-63
$80	$150	$225	$325	$500	$700	$950

W-1137-I Mule • F-1956I • Part of W-1134-I printage

VF-20	EF-40	AU-50	Unc-60	Unc-63	Unc-65
$15	$30	$45	$60	$80	$115

W-1137-I Mule★ • F-1956I★

VG-8	F-12	VF-20	EF-40	AU-50	Unc-60	Unc-63	Unc-65
$75	$125	$170	$260	$400	$550	$800	$1,050

W-1137-J • F-1956J • Kansas City • Part of W-1134-J printage

VG-8	F-12	VF-20	EF-40	AU-50	Unc-60	Unc-63
$125	$195	$250	$360	$550	$675	$800

W-1137-J★ • F-1956J★

VG-8	F-12	VF-20	EF-40	AU-50
$140	$250	$350	$600	$850

W-1137-J Mule • F-1956J • Part of W-1134-J printage

VF-20	EF-40	AU-50	Unc-60	Unc-63	Unc-65
$15	$25	$35	$45	$55	$90

W-1137-J Mule★ • F-1956J★

Recorded population: 2.

W-1137-K • F-1956K • Dallas • Part of W-1134-K printage

VG-8	F-12	VF-20	EF-40	AU-50	Unc-60	Unc-63
$125	$195	$250	$360	$550	$675	$950

W-1137-K★ • F-1956K★

VG-8	F-12	VF-20	EF-40	AU-50
$140	$250	$350	$600	$850

W-1137-K Mule • F-1956K • Part of W-1134-K printage

VF-20	EF-40	AU-50	Unc-60	Unc-63	Unc-65
$15	$30	$45	$60	$80	$115

W-1137-K Mule★ • F-1956K★

VG-8	F-12	VF-20	EF-40	AU-50	Unc-60	Unc-63	Unc-65
$25	$60	$90	$160	$240	$320	$400	$500

W-1137-L • F-1956L • San Francisco • Part of W-1134-L printage

VG-8	F-12	VF-20	EF-40	AU-50	Unc-60	Unc-63
$40	$60	$85	$125	$180	$245	$350

W-1137-L★ • F-1956L★

VG-8	F-12	VF-20	EF-40	AU-50	Unc-60	Unc-63
$125	$195	$250	$360	$550	$675	$850

W-1137-L Mule • F-1956L • Part of W-1134-L printage

VF-20	EF-40	AU-50	Unc-60	Unc-63	Unc-65
$15	$25	$35	$45	$55	$90

W-1137-L Mule★ • F-1956L★

VG-8	F-12	VF-20	EF-40	AU-50	Unc-60	Unc-63	Unc-65
$25	$60	$90	$160	$240	$320	$400	$500

Series of 1934, Brown Seal, HAWAII Overprint
Julian-Morgenthau (1934–1945)

These notes, with HAWAII overprinted on the face and the back and with a special brown Treasury seal and brown serial numbers, were used from 1942 to 1944 in the Hawaiian Islands, then under threat of Japanese invasion. If the islands had fallen into the hands of the enemy, such notes could be repudiated and would have no value on world markets.

Mules: Most backs have the plate number in micro numbers, but mules have the larger or macro size serials as used on Series 1934-A (the macro plates have numbers 939 and higher).

W-1140-L • F-2301 • 9,416,000

VG-8	F-12	VF-20	EF-40	AU-50	Unc-60	Unc-63	Unc-65
$80	$100	$125	$260	$450	$600	$750	$1,800

W-1140-L★ • F-2301★ • 80,000

VG-8	F-12	VF-20	EF-40	AU-50	Unc-60	Unc-63
$1,500	$2,600	$3,500	$5,500	$7,500	$9,500	$14,000

Series of 1934-A, Brown Seal, HAWAII Overprint
Julian-Morgenthau (1934–1945)

This series continues the special imprints and purposes as preceding.

SERIES OF 1934, BROWN SEAL, HAWAII OVERPRINT

$5 Federal Reserve Note, Series of 1934, Brown Seal (W-1140-L). With HAWAII overprinted at the left and right ends and with Treasury seal and serial numbers in brown.

Back of the $5 Federal Reserve Note, Series of 1934, Brown Seal, with HAWAII overprinted.

SERIES OF 1934-A, BROWN SEAL, HAWAII OVERPRINT

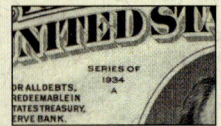

Detail of the signatures and the series imprints of a $5 Federal Reserve Note, Series of 1934-A, HAWAII overprint (W-1142-L). The back is the standard type of the era with the same HAWAII overprint as the Series of 1934 note.

W-1142-L • F-2302 • Included in printage above

VG-8	F-12	VF-20	EF-40	AU-50	Unc-60	Unc-63	Unc-65
$80	$100	$120	$250	$450	$640	$800	$2,000

W-1142-L★ • F-2302★ • Included in printage above

VG-8	F-12	VF-20
$5,000	$7,000	$9,250

Series of 1934-A, Green Seal
Julian-Morgenthau (1934–1945)

This series continued the standard design with green Treasury seal. No notes were printed for St. Louis, Minneapolis, and Kansas City.

Mules: Most backs have the plate number in macro numbers, but mules have the micro-size numbers as used on Series 1934 (the micro plates have serial number 637). Mules in this series are very elusive. While they are hardly inexpensive, the price would be higher if more collectors knew about them.

W-1144-A • F-1957A • Boston • 23,231,568

VF-20	EF-40	AU-50	Unc-60	Unc-63	Unc-65
$15	$20	$25	$30	$40	$60

W-1144-A★ • F-1957A★

F-12	VF-20	EF-40	AU-50	Unc-60	Unc-63	Unc-65
$40	$65	$140	$260	$400	$500	$750

W-1144-B • F-1957B • New York • 143,199,336

VF-20	EF-40	AU-50	Unc-60	Unc-63	Unc-65
$15	$20	$25	$30	$40	$60

W-1144-B★ • F-1957B★

F-12	VF-20	EF-40	AU-50	Unc-60	Unc-63	Unc-65
$30	$50	$110	$225	$350	$450	$650

W-1144-B Mule • F-1957B

VG-8	F-12	VF-20	EF-40	AU-50	Unc-60	Unc-63	Unc-65
$150	$250	$340	$450	$550	$700	$850	$1,100

W-1144-C • F-1957C • Philadelphia • 30,691,632

VF-20	EF-40	AU-50	Unc-60	Unc-63	Unc-65
$15	$20	$25	$30	$40	$60

W-1144-C★ • F-1957C★

F-12	VF-20	EF-40	AU-50	Unc-60	Unc-63	Unc-65
$35	$60	$125	$250	$350	$475	$700

W-1144-C Mule • F-1957C

VG-8	F-12	VF-20	EF-40	AU-50	Unc-60	Unc-63	Unc-65
$175	$290	$400	$475	$575	$725	$1,000	$1,225

W-1144-D • F-1957D • Cleveland • 1,610,676

F-12	VF-20	EF-40	AU-50	Unc-60	Unc-63	Unc-65
$35	$50	$100	$150	$250	$325	$500

W-1144-D★ • F-1957D★

F-12	VF-20	EF-40	AU-50	Unc-60	Unc-63	Unc-65
$70	$125	$225	$350	$475	$600	$900

W-1144-E • F-1957E • Richmond • 6,555,168

VF-20	EF-40	AU-50	Unc-60	Unc-63	Unc-65
$15	$30	$50	$90	$125	$175

W-1144-E★ • F-1957E★

F-12	VF-20	EF-40	AU-50	Unc-60	Unc-63	Unc-65
$45	$75	$200	$350	$475	$600	$900

W-1144-F • F-1957F • Atlanta • 22,811,916

F-12	VF-20	EF-40	AU-50	Unc-60	Unc-63	Unc-65
$30	$45	$75	$125	$170	$225	$390

W-1144-F★ • F-1957F★

F-12	VF-20	EF-40	AU-50	Unc-60	Unc-63	Unc-65
$65	$100	$225	$375	$500	$700	$1,000

W-1144-G • F-1957G • Chicago • 88,376,376

VF-20	EF-40	AU-50	Unc-60	Unc-63	Unc-65
$15	$20	$25	$30	$50	$75

W-1144-G★ • F-1957G★

F-12	VF-20	EF-40	AU-50	Unc-60	Unc-63	Unc-65
$30	$50	$80	$200	$325	$450	$700

W-1144-G Mule • F-1957G

VG-8	F-12	VF-20	EF-40	AU-50	Unc-60	Unc-63	Unc-65
$150	$250	$340	$450	$550	$700	$850	$1,100

W-1144-G Mule★ • F-1957G★

VG-8	F-12	VF-20	EF-40	AU-50	Unc-60	Unc-63
$425	$600	$850	$1,100	$1,400	$2,100	$2,500

W-1144-H • F-1957H • St. Louis • 7,843,452

VF-20	EF-40	AU-50	Unc-60	Unc-63	Unc-65
$15	$20	$25	$35	$60	$90

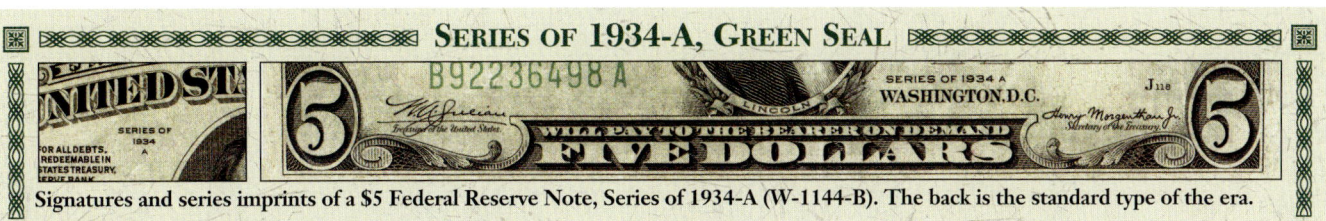

SERIES OF 1934-A, GREEN SEAL

Signatures and series imprints of a $5 Federal Reserve Note, Series of 1934-A (W-1144-B). The back is the standard type of the era.

W-1144-H★ • F-1957H★

F-12	VF-20	EF-40	AU-50	Unc-60	Unc-63	Unc-65
$45	$75	$135	$225	$350	$475	$750

W-1144-H Mule • F-1957H

VG-8	F-12	VF-20	EF-40	AU-50	Unc-60	Unc-63	Unc-65
$175	$290	$400	$475	$575	$725	$1,000	$1,225

W-1144-L • F-1957L • San Francisco • 72,118,452

VF-20	EF-40	AU-50	Unc-60	Unc-63	Unc-65
$15	$20	$25	$30	$40	$65

W-1144-L★ • F-1957L★

F-12	VF-20	EF-40	AU-50	Unc-60	Unc-63	Unc-65
$30	$50	$80	$200	$325	$450	$700

W-1144-L Mule • F-1957L

VG-8	F-12	VF-20	EF-40	AU-50	Unc-60	Unc-63	Unc-65
$175	$290	$400	$475	$575	$725	$1,000	$1,225

W-1144-L Mule★ • F-1957L★

VG-8	F-12	VF-20	EF-40	AU-50	Unc-60	Unc-63
$425	$600	$850	$1,100	$1,400	$2,100	$2,500

Series of 1934-B, Green Seal
Julian-Vinson (1945–1946)

Beginning with the Series of 1934-B notes, there is a change in the wording in the Federal Reserve seal. THE is omitted, leaving just FEDERAL RESERVE.

No 1934-B notes were printed for Dallas (letter K).

Mules: Most backs have the plate number in macro numbers, but mules have the micro-size numbers as used on Series 1934 (the micro plates have serial number 637). Mules are significantly rarer than regular notes.

W-1147-A • F-1958A • Boston • 3,457,800

VF-20	EF-40	AU-50	Unc-60	Unc-63	Unc-65
$15	$40	$75	$100	$140	$225

W-1147-A★ • F-1958A★

VG-8	F-12	VF-20	EF-40	AU-50	Unc-60	Unc-63
$70	$120	$200	$400	$575	$850	$1,100

W-1147-A Mule • F-1958A

VG-8	F-12	VF-20	EF-40	AU-50	Unc-60	Unc-63	Unc-65
$40	$70	$125	$210	$300	$440	$500	$700

W-1147-B • F-1958B • New York • 14,099,580

VF-20	EF-40	AU-50	Unc-60	Unc-63	Unc-65
$15	$35	$55	$75	$95	$135

W-1147-B★ • F-1958B★

VG-8	F-12	VF-20	EF-40	AU-50	Unc-60	Unc-63	Unc-65
$50	$80	$25	$275	$450	$600	$775	$1,000

W-1147-B Mule • F-1958B

VG-8	F-12	VF-20	EF-40	AU-50	Unc-60	Unc-63	Unc-65
$30	$60	$100	$170	$250	$325	$400	$600

W-1147-C • F-1958C • Philadelphia • 8,306,820

VF-20	EF-40	AU-50	Unc-60	Unc-63	Unc-65
$15	$35	$55	$75	$95	$135

W-1147-C★ • F-1958C★

F-12	VF-20	EF-40	AU-50	Unc-60	Unc-63	Unc-65
$160	$250	$400	$525	$675	$800	$1,250

W-1147-C Mule • F-1958C

VG-8	F-12	VF-20	EF-40	AU-50	Unc-60	Unc-63	Unc-65
$40	$70	$125	$210	$300	$440	$500	$700

W-1147-D • F-1958D • Cleveland • 11,348,184

VF-20	EF-40	AU-50	Unc-60	Unc-63	Unc-65
$15	$35	$55	$75	$95	$135

W-1147-D★ • F-1958D★

VG-8	F-12	VF-20	EF-40	AU-50	Unc-60	Unc-63
$60	$100	$150	$300	$475	$680	$800

W-1147-D Mule • F-1958D

VG-8	F-12	VF-20	EF-40	AU-50	Unc-60	Unc-63	Unc-65
$30	$60	$100	$200	$280	$360	$480	$675

W-1147-D Mule★ • F-1958D★

VG-8	F-12	VF-20	EF-40	AU-50	Unc-60	Unc-63
$200	$375	$550	$750	$1,100	$1,400	$1,750

W-1147-E • F-1958E • Richmond • 5,902,848

VF-20	EF-40	AU-50	Unc-60	Unc-63	Unc-65
$15	$45	$80	$100	$140	$200

W-1147-E★ • F-1958E★

VG-8	F-12	VF-20	EF-40	AU-50	Unc-60	Unc-63
$60	$100	$175	$350	$525	$750	$1,100

W-1147-F • F-1958F • Atlanta • 4,314,048

F-12	VF-20	EF-40	AU-50	Unc-60	Unc-63	Unc-65
$25	$45	$90	$165	$250	$350	$600

W-1147-F★ • F-1958F★

VG-8	F-12	VF-20	EF-40	AU-50	Unc-60	Unc-63
$70	$120	$200	$400	$575	$850	$1,100

W-1147-G • F-1958G • Chicago • 9,070,932

VF-20	EF-40	AU-50	Unc-60	Unc-63	Unc-65
$15	$35	$55	$75	$100	$140

W-1147-G★ • F-1958G★

VG-8	F-12	VF-20	EF-40	AU-50	Unc-60	Unc-63
$70	$120	$200	$400	$575	$850	$1,100

W-1147-G Mule • F-1958G

VG-8	F-12	VF-20	EF-40	AU-50	Unc-60	Unc-63	Unc-65
$30	$60	$100	$170	$250	$325	$400	$600

W-1147-H • F-1958H • St. Louis • 4,307,712

VF-20	EF-40	AU-50	Unc-60	Unc-63	Unc-65
$20	$40	$65	$90	$120	$175

W-1147-H★ • F-1958H★

VG-8	F-12	VF-20	EF-40	AU-50	Unc-60	Unc-63	Unc-65
$60	$100	$150	$300	$475	$680	$800	$1,250

W-1147-H Mule • F-1958H

VG-8	F-12	VF-20	EF-40	AU-50	Unc-60	Unc-63
$80	$125	$175	$340	$500	$650	$800

W-1147-I • F-1958I • Minneapolis • 2,482,500

F-12	VF-20	EF-40	AU-50	Unc-60	Unc-63	Unc-65
$15	$25	$60	$95	$140	$175	$275

W-1147-I★ • F-1958I★

VG-8	F-12	VF-20	EF-40	AU-50	Unc-60	Unc-63	Unc-65
$60	$100	$150	$375	$560	$775	$900	$1,350

W-1147-I Mule • F-1958I

VG-8	F-12	VF-20	EF-40	AU-50	Unc-60	Unc-63
$100	$175	$250	$375	$550	$700	$850

W-1147-J • F-1958J • Kansas City • 73,800

VG-8	F-12	VF-20	EF-40
$600	$950	$1,500	$2,300

W-1147-J★ • F-1958J★ • Unknown

W-1147-L • F-1958L • San Francisco • 9,910,296

VF-20	EF-40	AU-50	Unc-60	Unc-63	Unc-65
$15	$25	$40	$70	$100	$135

W-1147-L★ • F-1958L★

VG-8	F-12	VF-20	EF-40	AU-50	Unc-60	Unc-63
$300	$575	$900	$1,125	$1,350	$1,900	$2,500

W-1147-L Mule • F-1958L

VG-8	F-12	VF-20	EF-40	AU-50	Unc-60	Unc-63	Unc-65
$30	$60	$100	$200	$280	$360	$480	$675

W-1147-L Mule★ • F-1958L★

VG-8	F-12	VF-20	EF-40	AU-50	Unc-60	Unc-63	Unc-65
$200	$375	$550	$750	$1,100	$1,400	$1,750	$2,250

Series of 1934-C, Green Seal, Wide Face
Julian-Snyder (1946–1949)

Beginning on May 6, 1949, new $5 Federal Reserve face plates were made slightly smaller by narrowing the printed area horizontally by subtly removing part of the design. This created Wide Face (early style) and Narrow Face (later style) varieties. On November 7, 1951, the back (generic for all $5 series) was made Narrow as well.

The face of this series is found with both, the Wide Face here and the Narrow Face in the next. Among the minor differences: the loop inside the ornament near the 5 at the lower right can have either five double vertical lines (Wide Face) or four (Narrow Face). Related varieties are found with 1934-C Silver Certificates, but are slightly differently defined.

Mules: Most backs starting with 1934-A have the plate number in macro numbers, but mules have the micro-size numbers as used on Series 1934 (the micro plates for this particular mule include numbers 629 and 637). These are an early part of the Wide Face style shown here. These have a counterpart in Series of 1934-C Silver Certificates. There are no mule star notes in the presently-described series.

W-1150-A • F-1959A • Boston • 14,463,600

VF-20	EF-40	AU-50	Unc-60	Unc-63	Unc-65
$15	$30	$45	$60	$85	$110

SERIES OF 1934-B, GREEN SEAL

Detail of the signatures and the series imprints of a $5 Federal Reserve Note, Series of 1934-B (W-1147-D), as well as the new style of Federal Reserve seal. The back is the standard type of the era.

SERIES OF 1934-C, GREEN SEAL

Signatures and series imprints of a $5 Federal Reserve Note, Series of 1934-C (W-1150-A). The back is the standard type of the era.

Detail of Wide Face showing ornament near the 5 at the lower right corner. With five larger double vertical lines at and to the right of the top of the curlicue, plus a tiny line.

Detail of Narrow Face with just four larger double vertical lines at and to the right of the top of the curlicue, plus a tiny line.

W-1150-A★ • F-1959A★

F-12	VF-20	EF-40	AU-50	Unc-60	Unc-63	Unc-65
$60	$100	$325	$600	$800	$1,000	$1,450

W-1150-A Mule • F-1959A

VG-8	F-12	VF-20	EF-40	AU-50	Unc-60	Unc-63	Unc-65
$60	$110	$170	$250	$400	$550	$750	$900

W-1150-B • F-1959B • New York • 74,383,248

VF-20	EF-40	AU-50	Unc-60	Unc-63	Unc-65
$15	$30	$45	$60	$85	$110

W-1150-B★ • F-1959B★

F-12	VF-20	EF-40	AU-50	Unc-60	Unc-63	Unc-65
$60	$100	$225	$425	$600	$750	$1,000

W-1150-B Mule • F-1959B

VG-8	F-12	VF-20	EF-40	AU-50	Unc-60	Unc-63	Unc-65
$60	$110	$170	$250	$400	$550	$750	$900

W-1150-C • F-1959C • Philadelphia • 22,879,212

VF-20	EF-40	AU-50	Unc-60	Unc-63	Unc-65
$15	$30	$45	$60	$85	$110

W-1150-C★ • F-1959C★

F-12	VF-20	EF-40	AU-50	Unc-60	Unc-63	Unc-65
$60	$100	$325	$600	$800	$1,000	$1,450

W-1150-C Mule • F-1959C

VG-8	F-12	VF-20	EF-40	AU-50	Unc-60	Unc-63	Unc-65
$60	$110	$170	$250	$400	$550	$750	$900

W-1150-D • F-1959D • Cleveland • 19,898,256

VF-20	EF-40	AU-50	Unc-60	Unc-63	Unc-65
$15	$30	$45	$60	$85	$110

W-1150-D★ • F-1959D★

F-12	VF-20	EF-40	AU-50	Unc-60	Unc-63	Unc-65
$50	$90	$250	$400	$640	$800	$1,100

W-1150-D Mule • F-1959D

VG-8	F-12	VF-20	EF-40	AU-50	Unc-60	Unc-63	Unc-65
$60	$110	$170	$250	$400	$550	$750	$900

W-1150-E • F-1959E • Richmond • 23,800,524

VF-20	EF-40	AU-50	Unc-60	Unc-63	Unc-65
$15	$30	$45	$60	$80	$110

W-1150-E★ • F-1959E★

F-12	VF-20	EF-40	AU-50	Unc-60	Unc-63	Unc-65
$60	$100	$325	$650	$850	$1,100	$1,500

W-1150-E Mule • F-1959E

VG-8	F-12	VF-20	EF-40	AU-50	Unc-60	Unc-63	Unc-65
$60	$110	$170	$250	$400	$550	$750	$900

W-1150-F • F-1959F • Atlanta • 23,572,968

VF-20	EF-40	AU-50	Unc-60	Unc-63	Unc-65
$15	$30	$45	$60	$80	$110

W-1150-F★ • F-1959F★

F-12	VF-20	EF-40	AU-50	Unc-60	Unc-63	Unc-65
$60	$100	$325	$650	$850	$1,100	$1,500

W-1150-G • F-1959G • Chicago • 60,598,812

VF-20	EF-40	AU-50	Unc-60	Unc-63	Unc-65
$15	$30	$45	$60	$80	$110

W-1150-G★ • F-1959G★

F-12	VF-20	EF-40	AU-50	Unc-60	Unc-63	Unc-65
$60	$100	$250	$400	$640	$800	$1,150

W-1150-G Mule • F-1959G

VG-8	F-12	VF-20	EF-40	AU-50	Unc-60	Unc-63	Unc-65
$60	$110	$170	$250	$400	$550	$750	$900

W-1150-H • F-1959H • St. Louis • 20,393,340

VF-20	EF-40	AU-50	Unc-60	Unc-63	Unc-65
$15	$30	$45	$60	$80	$110

W-1150-H★ • F-1959H★

F-12	VF-20	EF-40	AU-50	Unc-60	Unc-63	Unc-65
$60	$100	$275	$475	$700	$900	$1,250

W-1150-H Mule • F-1959H

VG-8	F-12	VF-20	EF-40	AU-50	Unc-60	Unc-63	Unc-65
$60	$110	$170	$250	$400	$550	$750	$900

W-1150-I • F-1959I • Minneapolis • 5,089,200

F-12	VF-20	EF-40	AU-50	Unc-60	Unc-63	Unc-65
$20	$30	$55	$95	$135	$170	$240

W1150-I★ • F-1959I★

F-12	VF-20	EF-40	AU-50	Unc-60	Unc-63	Unc-65
$100	$200	$475	$850	$1,100	$1,400	$2,100

W-1150-I Mule • F-1959I

VG-8	F-12	VF-20	EF-40	AU-50	Unc-60	Unc-63	Unc-65
$125	$180	$260	$340	$500	$650	$850	$1,000

W-1150-J • F-1959J • Kansas City • 8,313,504

VF-20	EF-40	AU-50	Unc-60	Unc-63	Unc-65
$15	$30	$45	$60	$95	$145

W-1150-J★ • F-1959J★

F-12	VF-20	EF-40	AU-50	Unc-60	Unc-63	Unc-65
$60	$100	$275	$475	$700	$900	$1,250

W-1150-J Mule • F-1959J

VG-8	F-12	VF-20	EF-40	AU-50	Unc-60	Unc-63	Unc-65
$60	$110	$170	$250	$400	$550	$750	$900

W-1150-K • F-1959K • Dallas • 5,107,800

F-12	VF-20	EF-40	AU-50	Unc-60	Unc-63	Unc-65
$15	$25	$45	$65	$90	$120	$190

W-1150-K★ • F-1959K★

F-12	VF-20	EF-40	AU-50	Unc-60	Unc-63	Unc-65
$100	$200	$475	$850	$1,100	$1,400	$2,100

W-1150-L • F-1959L • San Francisco • 9,451,944

VF-20	EF-40	AU-50	Unc-60	Unc-63	Unc-65
$15	$30	$45	$60	$95	$140

W-1150-L★ • F-1959L★

F-12	VF-20	EF-40	AU-50	Unc-60	Unc-63	Unc-65
$60	$100	$275	$475	$700	$900	$1,250

W-1150-L Mule • F-1959L

VG-8	F-12	VF-20	EF-40	AU-50	Unc-60	Unc-63	Unc-65
$60	$110	$170	$250	$400	$550	$750	$900

Series of 1934-C, Green Seal, Narrow Face
Julian-Snyder (1946–1949)

This is the Narrow Face variety (plate numbers 298 to 303). See description in the previous section.

W-1152-B • F-1959B • New York • Part of W-1150-B printage

Commentary: Fewer than eight are known. No auction sales are recorded.

W-1152-B★ • F-1959B★

Recorded population: 2.

Series of 1934-D, Green Seal
Clark-Snyder (1949–1953)

This series continued the preceding design.

W-1155-A • F-1960A • Boston • 12,660,552

VF-20	EF-40	AU-50	Unc-60	Unc-63	Unc-65
$15	$30	$45	$70	$90	$120

W-1155-A★ • F-1960A★

F-12	VF-20	EF-40	AU-50	Unc-60	Unc-63	Unc-65
$75	$135	$210	$325	$475	$600	$900

W-1155-B • F-1960B • New York • 50,976,576

VF-20	EF-40	AU-50	Unc-60	Unc-63	Unc-65
$12	$25	$40	$60	$80	$100

W-1155-B★ • F-1960B★

F-12	VF-20	EF-40	AU-50	Unc-60	Unc-63	Unc-65
$65	$110	$190	$270	$375	$500	$750

W-1155-C • F-1960C • Philadelphia • 12,106,740

VF-20	EF-40	AU-50	Unc-60	Unc-63	Unc-65
$12	$25	$35	$55	$75	$90

W-1155-C★ • F-1960C★

F-12	VF-20	EF-40	AU-50	Unc-60	Unc-63	Unc-65
$75	$135	$210	$325	$475	$600	$900

W-1155-D • F-1960D • Cleveland • 8,969,052

VF-20	EF-40	AU-50	Unc-60	Unc-63	Unc-65
$12	$25	$35	$55	$75	$100

W-1155-D★ • F-1960D★

VG-8	F-12	VF-20	EF-40	AU-50	Unc-60	Unc-63
$65	$140	$250	$400	$550	$900	$1,250

W-1155-E • F-1960E • Richmond • 13,333,032

VF-20	EF-40	AU-50	Unc-60	Unc-63	Unc-65
$12	$25	$40	$65	$85	$110

W-1155-E★ • F-1960E★

VG-8	F-12	VF-20	EF-40	AU-50	Unc-60	Unc-63
$65	$140	$250	$400	$550	$900	$1,250

W-1155-F • F-1960F • Atlanta • 9,599,352

VG-8	F-12	VF-20	EF-40	AU-50	Unc-60	Unc-63
$180	$275	$400	$550	$700	$800	$1,000

W-1155-F★ • F-1960F★

VG-8	F-12	VF-20	EF-40	AU-50	Unc-60	Unc-63
$200	$300	$500	$1,200	$1,600	$2,000	$2,750

W-1155-G • F-1960G • Chicago • 36,601,680

VF-20	EF-40	AU-50	Unc-60	Unc-63	Unc-65
$12	$25	$35	$55	$70	$95

W-1155-G★ • F-1960G★

F-12	VF-20	EF-40	AU-50	Unc-60	Unc-63	Unc-65
$60	$100	$175	$250	$350	$450	$700

SERIES OF 1934-D, GREEN SEAL

Signatures and series imprints of a $5 Federal Reserve Note, Series of 1934-D (W-1155-A). The back is the standard type of the era.

W-1155-H • F-1960H • St. Louis • 8,093,412

VF-20	EF-40	AU-50	Unc-60	Unc-63	Unc-65
$12	$25	$40	$65	$80	$100

W-1155-H★ • F-1960H★

F-12	VF-20	EF-40	AU-50	Unc-60	Unc-63	Unc-65
$75	$135	$210	$325	$475	$600	$900

W-1155-I • F-1960I • Minneapolis • 3,594,900

VG-8	F-12	VF-20	EF-40	AU-50	Unc-60	Unc-63	Unc-65
$35	$65	$100	$175	$250	$325	$400	$750

W-1155-I★ • F-1960I★

VG-8	F-12	VF-20	EF-40	AU-50	Unc-60	Unc-63
$65	$140	$250	$400	$550	$900	$1,250

W-1155-J • F-1960J • Kansas City • 6,538,740

VF-20	EF-40	AU-50	Unc-60	Unc-63	Unc-65
$12	$25	$40	$65	$85	$110

W-1155-J★ • F-1960J★

VG-8	F-12	VF-20	EF-40	AU-50	Unc-60	Unc-63	Unc-65
$60	$100	$170	$250	$375	$500	$700	$1,000

W-1155-K • F-1960K • Dallas • 4,139,016

F-12	VF-20	EF-40	AU-50	Unc-60	Unc-63	Unc-65
$20	$45	$70	$110	$160	$225	$350

W-1155-K★ • F-1960K★

VG-8	F-12	VF-20	EF-40	AU-50	Unc-60	Unc-63	Unc-65
$60	$100	$170	$250	$375	$500	$700	$1,000

W-1155-L • F-1960L • San Francisco • 11,704,200

VF-20	EF-40	AU-50	Unc-60	Unc-63	Unc-65
$12	$25	$40	$65	$80	$100

W-1155-L★ • F-1960L★

VG-8	F-12	VF-20	EF-40	AU-50	Unc-60	Unc-63	Unc-65
$60	$100	$170	$250	$375	$500	$700	$1,000

Series of 1950, Green Seal, Wide Back 1
Clark-Snyder (1949–1953)

The face was modified in this series. The Federal Reserve seal is smaller and has a spiked border. The wording above that seal reads, "This note is Legal Tender for all debts, public and private, and is redeemable in lawful money at the United States Treasury or at any Federal Reserve Bank." The series designation is at the lower right of the portrait. WASHINGTON, D.C. is now above the Treasury seal.

The back of the Series of 1950 notes is found in both Narrow Back and Wide Back varieties. Differences include the number of vertical double lines in the ornament next to the denomination at the lower right. The Wide Back, here, has three vertical double lines in the area indicated (see detail). The Narrow Back has two.

Series of 1928-F notes are also found in Wide and Narrow (scarcer) Back varieties, somewhat similar in concept to the Legal Tender Series of 1928-F, and they share the same back plates. The Wide issues have plate numbers up to 2007, called Wide Back 1, and plate numbers 2067 to 2096 (Wide Back 2), notes in the second range being much scarcer. The Narrow Back numbers are from 2008 to 2066. Such differences have gained notice only in recent years.

W-1157-A • F-1961A • Boston • 30,672,000

VF-20	EF-40	AU-50	Unc-60	Unc-63	Unc-65
$10	$20	$32	$40	$60	$85

W-1157-A★ • F-1961A★ • 408,000

VF-20	EF-40	AU-50	Unc-60	Unc-63	Unc-65
$50	$75	$125	$275	$400	$650

W-1157-B • F-1961B • New York • 106,768,000

VF-20	EF-40	AU-50	Unc-60	Unc-63	Unc-65
$10	$20	$30	$38	$50	$75

W-1157-B★ • F-1961B★ • 1,464,000

VF-20	EF-40	AU-50	Unc-60	Unc-63	Unc-65
$50	$75	$125	$250	$350	$600

W-1157-C • F-1961C • Philadelphia • 44,784,000

VF-20	EF-40	AU-50	Unc-60	Unc-63	Unc-65
$10	$20	$30	$38	$50	$75

W-1157-C★ • F-1961C★ • 600,000

VF-20	EF-40	AU-50	Unc-60	Unc-63	Unc-65
$50	$75	$125	$250	$350	$600

W-1157-D • F-1961D • Cleveland • 54,000,000

VF-20	EF-40	AU-50	Unc-60	Unc-63	Unc-65
$10	$20	$30	$40	$60	$85

W-1157-D★ • F-1961D★ • 744,000

VF-20	EF-40	AU-50	Unc-60	Unc-63	Unc-65
$50	$75	$125	$275	$400	$650

W-1157-E • F-1961E • Richmond • 47,088,000

VF-20	EF-40	AU-50	Unc-60	Unc-63	Unc-65
$15	$25	$40	$60	$80	$110

W-1157-E★ • F-1961E★ • 684,000

VF-20	EF-40	AU-50	Unc-60	Unc-63	Unc-65
$50	$75	$125	$275	$400	$650

W-1157-F • F-1961F • Atlanta • 52,416,000

VF-20	EF-40	AU-50	Unc-60	Unc-63	Unc-65
$30	$65	$100	$125	$175	$275

W-1157-F★ • F-1961F★ • 696,000

VF-20	EF-40	AU-50	Unc-60	Unc-63	Unc-65
$50	$75	$125	$275	$400	$650

SERIES OF 1950, GREEN SEAL

$5 Federal Reserve Note, Series of 1950 (W-1157-A). Federal Reserve Bank of Boston. The back is the standard back design of $5 notes of the era, but in both Wide Back and Narrow Back varieties.

Detail of feature on Wide Back notes. This is the style of back plate numbers up to 2007 (Wide Back 1) and 2067 to 2096 (Wide Back 2). (Illustrations the same as $5 Legal Tender Notes, Series of 1928-F varieties, page 267.)

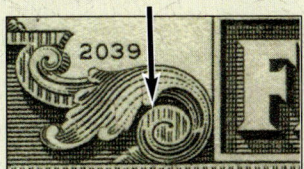

Detail of feature on Narrow Back notes, back plate numbers 2008 to 2066.

W-1157-G • F-1961G • Chicago • 85,104,000

VF-20	EF-40	AU-50	Unc-60	Unc-63	Unc-65
$10	$20	$30	$40	$60	$85

W-1157-G★ • F-1961G★ • 1,176,000

VF-20	EF-40	AU-50	Unc-60	Unc-63	Unc-65
$50	$75	$125	$275	$400	$650

W-1157-H • F-1961H • St. Louis • 36,864,000

VF-20	EF-40	AU-50	Unc-60	Unc-63	Unc-65
$15	$25	$40	$60	$80	$110

W-1157-H★ • F-1961H★ • 552,000

VF-20	EF-40	AU-50	Unc-60	Unc-63	Unc-65
$40	$70	$120	$250	$450	$600

W-1157-I • F-1961I • Minneapolis • 11,796,000

VF-20	EF-40	AU-50	Unc-60	Unc-63	Unc-65
$15	$30	$50	$70	$90	$120

W-1157-I★ • F-1961I★ • 144,000

F-12	VF-20	EF-40	AU-50	Unc-60	Unc-63	Unc-65
$90	$150	$250	$400	$575	$700	$850

W-1157-J • F-1961J • Kansas City • 25,428,000

VF-20	EF-40	AU-50	Unc-60	Unc-63	Unc-65
$10	$20	$30	$40	$60	$85

W-1157-J★ • F-1961J★ • 360,000

VF-20	EF-40	AU-50	Unc-60	Unc-63	Unc-65
$50	$75	$125	$275	$400	$650

W-1157-K • F-1961K • Dallas • 22,848,000

VF-20	EF-40	AU-50	Unc-60	Unc-63	Unc-65
$15	$25	$40	$60	$80	$110

W-1157-K★ • F-1961K★ • 372,000

VF-20	EF-40	AU-50	Unc-60	Unc-63	Unc-65
$40	$70	$120	$250	$450	$600

W-1157-L • F-1961L • San Francisco • 55,008,000

VF-20	EF-40	AU-50	Unc-60	Unc-63	Unc-65
$15	$25	$35	$50	$70	$95

W-1157-L★ • F-1961L★ • 744,000

VF-20	EF-40	AU-50	Unc-60	Unc-63	Unc-65
$50	$75	$125	$275	$400	$600

Series of 1950, Green Seal, Narrow Back
Clark-Snyder (1949–1953)

This series continued the preceding face design, with the Narrow Back style. See the Wide Back 1 listing for a description.

W-1159-A • F-1961A • Boston • Part of W-1157-A printage

VF-20	EF-40	AU-50	Unc-60	Unc-63	Unc-65
$15	$25	$35	$45	$60	$85

W-1159-B • F-1961B • New York • Part of W-1157-B printage

VF-20	EF-40	AU-50	Unc-60	Unc-63	Unc-65
$12	$20	$25	$30	$40	$60

W-1159-B★ • F-1961B★

VG-8	F-12	VF-20	EF-40	AU-50	Unc-60	Unc-63	Unc-65
$25	$40	$60	$100	$175	$275	$375	$525

W-1159-C • F-1961C • Philadelphia • Part of W-1157-C printage

VF-20	EF-40	AU-50	Unc-60	Unc-63	Unc-65
$12	$20	$25	$30	$40	$60

W-1159-C★ • F-1961C★

VG-8	F-12	VF-20	EF-40	AU-50	Unc-60	Unc-63	Unc-65
$25	$40	$60	$100	$160	$250	$350	$475

W-1159-D • F-1961D • Cleveland • Part of W-1157-D printage

VF-20	EF-40	AU-50	Unc-60	Unc-63	Unc-65
$12	$20	$25	$30	$40	$60

W-1159-D★ • F-1961D★

VG-8	F-12	VF-20	EF-40	AU-50	Unc-60	Unc-63	Unc-65
$25	$40	$60	$100	$160	$250	$350	$475

W-1159-E • F-1961E • Richmond • Part of W-1157-E printage

VF-20	EF-40	AU-50	Unc-60	Unc-63	Unc-65
$12	$20	$30	$40	$50	$70

W-1159-E★ • F-1961E★

VG-8	F-12	VF-20	EF-40	AU-50	Unc-60	Unc-63	Unc-65
$25	$40	$60	$100	$175	$275	$375	$525

W-1159-F • F-1961F • Atlanta • Part of W-1157-F printage

VF-20	EF-40	AU-50	Unc-60	Unc-63	Unc-65
$12	$20	$40	$65	$95	$140

W-1159-G • F-1961G • Chicago • Part of W-1157-G printage

VF-20	EF-40	AU-50	Unc-60	Unc-63	Unc-65
$12	$20	$25	$30	$40	$60

W-1159-G★ • F-1961G★

VG-8	F-12	VF-20	EF-40	AU-50	Unc-60	Unc-63	Unc-65
$25	$40	$60	$100	$175	$275	$375	$525

W-1159-H • F-1961H • St. Louis • Part of W-1157-H printage

VF-20	EF-40	AU-50	Unc-60	Unc-63	Unc-65
$12	$20	$30	$40	$50	$70

W-1159-H★ • F-1961H★

VG-8	F-12	VF-20	EF-40	AU-50	Unc-60	Unc-63	Unc-65
$25	$40	$60	$100	$175	$275	$375	$525

W-1159-I • F-1961I • Minneapolis • Part of W-1157-I printage

VF-20	EF-40	AU-50	Unc-60	Unc-63	Unc-65
$12	$20	$40	$65	$95	$140

W-1159-J • F-1961J • Kansas City • Part of W-1157-J printage

VF-20	EF-40	AU-50	Unc-60	Unc-63	Unc-65
$12	$20	$30	$40	$50	$70

W-1159-K • F-1961K • Dallas • Part of W-1157-K printage

VF-20	EF-40	AU-50	Unc-60	Unc-63	Unc-65
$12	$20	$40	$65	$95	$140

W-1159-L • F-1961L • San Francisco • Part of W-1157-L printage

VF-20	EF-40	AU-50	Unc-60	Unc-63	Unc-65
$12	$20	$40	$65	$95	$140

W-1159-L★ • F-1961L★

VG-8	F-12	VF-20	EF-40	AU-50	Unc-60	Unc-63	Unc-65
$25	$40	$60	$100	$175	$275	$375	$525

Series of 1950, Green Seal, Wide Back 2
Clark-Snyder (1949–1953)

See the Wide Back 1 listing for explanation of the variety.

W-1160-A • F-1961A • Boston • Part of W-1157-A printage

VF-20	EF-40	AU-50	Unc-60	Unc-63	Unc-65
$15	$25	$35	$60	$80	$100

W-1160-B • F-1961B • New York • Part of W-1157-B printage

VF-20	EF-40	AU-50	Unc-60	Unc-63	Unc-65
$15	$25	$35	$50	$70	$90

W-1160-B★ • F-1961B★

VG-8	F-12	VF-20	EF-40
$275	$550	$800	$1,250

W-1160-C • F-1961C • Philadelphia • Part of W-1157-C printage

VF-20	EF-40	AU-50	Unc-60	Unc-63	Unc-65
$15	$25	$35	$60	$80	$100

W-1160-C★ • F-1961C★

VG-8	F-12	VF-20	EF-40	AU-50	Unc-60	Unc-63
$190	$350	$500	$750	$1,250	$2,000	$2,600

W-1160-D • F-1961D • Cleveland • Part of W-1157-D printage

VF-20	EF-40	AU-50	Unc-60	Unc-63	Unc-65
$15	$25	$35	$60	$80	$100

W-1160-D★ • F-1961D★

VG-8	F-12	VF-20	EF-40	AU-50	Unc-60	Unc-63	Unc-65
$225	$425	$700	$1,000	$1,700	$2,500	$3,500	$4,500

W-1160-E • F-1961E • Richmond • Part of W-1157-E printage

VF-20	EF-40	AU-50	Unc-60	Unc-63	Unc-65
$15	$25	$35	$60	$80	$100

W-1160-F • F-1961F • Atlanta • Part of W-1157-F printage

VF-20	EF-40	AU-50	Unc-60	Unc-63	Unc-65
$15	$30	$45	$70	$90	$130

W-1160-G • F-1961G • Chicago • Part of W-1157-G printage

VF-20	EF-40	AU-50	Unc-60	Unc-63	Unc-65
$15	$25	$35	$60	$80	$100

W-1160-H • F-1961H • St. Louis • Part of W-1157-H printage

VF-20	EF-40	AU-50	Unc-60	Unc-63	Unc-65
$15	$25	$35	$50	$70	$90

W-1160-I • F-1961I • Minneapolis • Part of W-1157-I printage

VF-20	EF-40	AU-50	Unc-60	Unc-63	Unc-65
$20	$40	$60	$90	$110	$180

W-1160-J • F-1961J • Kansas City • Part of W-1157-J printage

VF-20	EF-40	AU-50	Unc-60	Unc-63	Unc-65
$15	$25	$35	$50	$70	$90

W-1160-K • F-1961K • Dallas • Part of W-1157-K printage

VF-20	EF-40	AU-50	Unc-60	Unc-63	Unc-65
$15	$25	$35	$50	$70	$90

W-1160-L • F-1961L • San Francisco • Part of W-1157-L printage

VF-20	EF-40	AU-50	Unc-60	Unc-63	Unc-65
$15	$25	$35	$60	$80	$100

W-1160-L★ • F-1961L★

VG-8	F-12	VF-20	EF-40	AU-50	Unc-60	Unc-63
$190	$350	$500	$750	$1,250	$2,000	$2,600

Series of 1950-A, Green Seal
Priest-Humphrey (1953–1957)

This series continued the preceding design.

Prices for a typical note for this series, unless listed otherwise, are as follows:

Unc-60	Unc-63	Unc-65
$25	$30	$40

Prices for a typical star note for this series, unless listed otherwise, are as follows:

VF-20	EF-40	AU-50	Unc-60	Unc-63	Unc-65
$30	$45	$60	$70	$80	$110

W-1161-A • F-1962A • Boston • 53,568,000

W-1161-A★ • F-1962A★ • 2,808,000

VF-20	EF-40	AU-50	Unc-60	Unc-63	Unc-65
$30	$45	$55	$65	$75	$100

W-1161-B • F-1962B • New York • 186,472,000

Unc-60	Unc-63	Unc-65
$20	$25	$35

W-1161-B★ • F-1962B★ • 9,216,000

VF-20	EF-40	AU-50	Unc-60	Unc-63	Unc-65
$25	$40	$50	$60	$65	$90

W-1161-C • F-1962C • Philadelphia • 79,616,000

W-1161-C★ • F-1962C★ • 4,320,000

VF-20	EF-40	AU-50	Unc-60	Unc-63	Unc-65
$30	$45	$55	$65	$75	$100

W-1161-D • F-1962D • Cleveland • 45,360,000

W-1161-D★ • F-1962D★ • 2,376,000

W-1161-E • F-1962E • Richmond • 76,672,000

W-1161-E★ • F-1962E★ • 5,400,000

W-1161-F • F-1962F • Atlanta • 86,464,000

W-1161-F★ • F-1962F★ • 5,040,000

W-1161-G • F-1962G • Chicago • 129,296,000

Unc-60	Unc-63	Unc-65
$20	$25	$35

W-1161-G★ • F-1962G★ • 6,284,000

VF-20	EF-40	AU-50	Unc-60	Unc-63	Unc-65
$25	$40	$50	$60	$65	$90

W-1161-H • F-1962H • St. Louis • 54,936,000

W-1161-H★ • F-1962H★ • 3,384,000

W-1161-I • F-1962I • Minneapolis • 11,232,000

Unc-60	Unc-63	Unc-65
$20	$25	$35

W-1161-I★ • F-1962I★ • 864,000

F-12	VF-20	EF-40	AU-50	Unc-60	Unc-63	Unc-65
$40	$70	$125	$200	$290	$350	$475

W-1161-J • F-1962J • Kansas City • 29,952,000

Unc-60	Unc-63	Unc-65
$25	$35	$45

W-1161-J★ • F-1962J★ • 2,088,000

SERIES OF 1950-A, GREEN SEAL

Signatures and series imprint of a $5 Federal Reserve Note, Series of 1950-A (W-1161-A). The back is the standard type of the era.

W-1161-K • F-1962K • Dallas • 24,984,000

W-1161-K★ • F-1962K★ • 1,368,000

W-1161-L • F-1962L • San Francisco • 90,712,000

W-1161-L★ • F-1962L★ • 6,336,000

Series of 1950-B, Green Seal
Priest-Anderson (1957–1961)

This series continued the preceding design.

W-1163-A • F-1963A • Boston • 30,880,000

Unc-60	Unc-63	Unc-65
$25	$35	$45

W-1163-A★ • F-1963A★ • 2,520,000

AU-50	Unc-60	Unc-63	Unc-65
$35	$60	$75	$100

W-1163-B • F-1963B • New York • 85,960,000

Unc-60	Unc-63	Unc-65
$25	$35	$45

W-1163-B★ • F-1963B★ • 4,680,060

AU-50	Unc-60	Unc-63	Unc-65
$25	$50	$65	$90

W-1163-C • F-1963C • Philadelphia • 43,560,000

Unc-60	Unc-63	Unc-65
$25	$35	$45

W-1163-C★ • F-1963C★ • 2,880,000

AU-50	Unc-60	Unc-63	Unc-65
$35	$60	$75	$100

W-1163-D • F-1963D • Cleveland • 38,800,000

Unc-60	Unc-63	Unc-65
$25	$35	$45

W-1163-D★ • F-1963D★ • 2,880,000

AU-50	Unc-60	Unc-63	Unc-65
$35	$60	$75	$100

W-1163-E • F-1963E • Richmond • 52,920,000

Unc-60	Unc-63	Unc-65
$20	$30	$40

W-1163-E★ • F-1963E★ • 2,080,000

AU-50	Unc-60	Unc-63	Unc-65
$55	$80	$100	$130

W-1163-F • F-1963F • Atlanta • 80,560,000

Unc-60	Unc-63	Unc-65
$20	$30	$40

W-1163-F★ • F-1963F★ • 3,960,000

AU-50	Unc-60	Unc-63	Unc-65
$55	$80	$100	$130

W-1163-G • F-1963G • Chicago • 104,320,000

Unc-60	Unc-63	Unc-65
$25	$35	$45

W-1163-G★ • F-1963G★ • 6,120,000

AU-50	Unc-60	Unc-63	Unc-65
$25	$50	$65	$90

W-1163-H • F-1963H • St. Louis • 25,840,000

Unc-60	Unc-63	Unc-65
$25	$35	$45

W-1163-H★ • F-1963H★ • 1,440,000

AU-50	Unc-60	Unc-63	Unc-65
$45	$70	$85	$120

W-1163-I • F-1963I • Minneapolis • 20,880,000

Unc-60	Unc-63	Unc-65
$30	$40	$50

W-1163-I★ • F-1963I★ • 792,000

EF-40	AU-50	Unc-60	Unc-63	Unc-65
$55	$90	$125	$150	$215

W-1163-J • F-1963J • Kansas City • 32,400,000

Unc-60	Unc-63	Unc-65
$20	$30	$40

W-1163-J★ • F-1963J★ • 2,520,000

AU-50	Unc-60	Unc-63	Unc-65
$35	$60	$75	$100

W-1163-K • F-1963K • Dallas • 52,120,000

Unc-60	Unc-63	Unc-65
$20	$30	$40

W-1163-K★ • F-1963K★ • 3,240,000

AU-50	Unc-60	Unc-63	Unc-65
$45	$70	$85	$120

SERIES OF 1950-B, GREEN SEAL

Signatures and series imprint of a $5 Federal Reserve Note, Series of 1950-B (W-1163-K). The back is the standard type of the era.

W-1163-L • F-1963L • San Francisco • 56,080,000

Unc-60	Unc-63	Unc-65
$20	$30	$40

W-1163-L★ • F-1963L★ • 3,600,000

AU-50	Unc-60	Unc-63	Unc-65
$45	$70	$85	$120

Series of 1950-C, Green Seal
Smith-Dillon (1961–1962)

This series continued the preceding design.

Prices for a typical note for this series, unless listed otherwise, are as follows:

Unc-60	Unc-63	Unc-65
$20	$25	$35

W-1165-A • F-1964A • Boston • 20,880,000

W-1165-A★ • F-1964A★ • 720,000

F-12	VF-20	EF-40	AU-50	Unc-60	Unc-63
$45	$75	$110	$150	$190	$225

W-1165-B • F-1964B • New York • 47,440,000

W-1165-B★ • F-1964B★ • 2,880,000

EF-40	AU-50	Unc-60	Unc-63	Unc-65
$35	$45	$50	$60	$80

W-1165-C • F-1964C • Philadelphia • 29,520,000

W-1165-C★ • F-1964C★ • 1,800,000

EF-40	AU-50	Unc-60	Unc-63	Unc-65
$45	$55	$80	$100	$135

W-1165-D • F-1964D • Cleveland • 33,840,000

W-1165-D★ • F-1964D★ • 1,800,000

EF-40	AU-50	Unc-60	Unc-63	Unc-65
$45	$55	$80	$100	$160

W-1165-E • F-1964E • Richmond • 33,480,000

W-1165-E★ • F-1964E★ • 2,160,000

EF-40	AU-50	Unc-60	Unc-63	Unc-65
$50	$65	$110	$130	$200

W-1165-F • F-1964F • Atlanta • 54,360,000

W-1165-F★ • F-1964F★ • 3,240,000

EF-40	AU-50	Unc-60	Unc-63	Unc-65
$45	$55	$80	$100	$135

W-1165-G • F-1964G • Chicago • 56,880,000

W-1165-G★ • F-1964G★ • 3,240,000

EF-40	AU-50	Unc-60	Unc-63	Unc-65
$45	$55	$80	$100	$135

W-1165-H • F-1964H • St. Louis • 22,680,000

Unc-60	Unc-63	Unc-65
$25	$35	$50

W-1165-H★ • F-1964H★ • 720,000

VF-20	EF-40	AU-50	Unc-60	Unc-63	Unc-65
$35	$60	$90	$125	$150	$225

W-1165-I • F-1964I • Minneapolis • 12,960,000

Unc-60	Unc-63	Unc-65
$45	$60	$80

W-1165-I★ • F-1964I★ • 720,000

VF-20	EF-40	AU-50	Unc-60	Unc-63	Unc-65
$50	$80	$120	$170	$225	$300

W-1165-J • F-1964J • Kansas City • 24,760,000

W-1165-J★ • F-1964J★ • 1,800,000

EF-40	AU-50	Unc-60	Unc-63	Unc-65
$45	$55	$80	$100	$135

W-1165-K • F-1964K • Dallas • 3,960,000

AU-50	Unc-60	Unc-63	Unc-65
$35	$60	$80	$100

W-1165-K★ • F-1964K★ • 360,000

VF-20	EF-40	AU-50	Unc-60	Unc-63	Unc-65
$50	$80	$120	$170	$225	$300

W-1165-L • F-1964L • San Francisco • 25,920,000

W-1165-L★ • F-1964L★ • 1,440,000

VF-20	EF-40	AU-50	Unc-60	Unc-63	Unc-65
$40	$65	$100	$135	$160	$240

Series of 1950-D, Green Seal
Granahan-Dillon (1963–1965)

This series (illus. on p. 302) continued the preceding design.

Prices for a typical note for this series, unless listed otherwise, are as follows:

Unc-60	Unc-63	Unc-65
$20	$25	$35

SERIES OF 1950-C, GREEN SEAL

Signatures and series imprint of a $5 Federal Reserve Note, Series of 1950-C (W-1165-A). The back is the standard type of the era.

Prices for a typical star note for this series, unless listed otherwise, are as follows:

AU-50	Unc-60	Unc-63	Unc-65
$55	$80	$100	$130

W-1166-A • F-1965A • Boston • 25,200,000

Unc-60	Unc-63	Unc-65
$25	$30	$40

W-1166-A★ • F-1965A★ • 1,080,000

W-1166-B • F-1965B • New York • 102,160,000

W-1166-B★ • F-1965B★ • 5,040,000

AU-50	Unc-60	Unc-63	Unc-65
$30	$55	$70	$100

W-1166-C • F-1965C • Philadelphia • 21,520,000

W-1166-C★ • F-1965C★ • 1,080,000

AU-50	Unc-60	Unc-63	Unc-65
$35	$60	$80	$110

W-1166-D • F-1965D • Cleveland • 23,400,000

W-1166-D★ • F-1965D★ • 1,080,000

W-1166-E • F-1965E • Richmond • 42,490,000

Unc-60	Unc-63	Unc-65
$25	$30	$40

W-1166-E★ • F-1965E★ • 1,080,000

W-1166-F • F-1965F • Atlanta • 35,200,000

Unc-60	Unc-63	Unc-65
$25	$30	$40

W-1166-F★ • F-1965F★ • 1,800,000

W-1166-G • F-1965G • Chicago • 67,240,000

W-1166-G★ • F-1965G★ • 3,600,000

AU-50	Unc-60	Unc-63	Unc-65
$30	$55	$70	$100

W-1166-H • F-1965H • St. Louis • 20,160,000

W-1166-H★ • F-1965H★ • 720,000

W-1166-I • F-1965I • Minneapolis • 7,920,000

Unc-60	Unc-63	Unc-65
$35	$40	$55

W-1166-I★ • F-1965I★ • 360,000

VF-20	EF-40	AU-50	Unc-60	Unc-63	Unc-65
$40	$60	$100	$145	$180	$260

W-1166-J • F-1965J • Kansas City • 11,160,000

W-1166-J★ • F-1965J★ • 720,000

W-1166-K • F-1965K • Dallas • 7,200,000

Unc-60	Unc-63	Unc-65
$28	$35	$45

W-1166-K★ • F-1965K★ • 360,000

EF-40	AU-50	Unc-60	Unc-63	Unc-65
$55	$100	$160	$200	$270

W-1166-L • F-1965L • San Francisco • 53,280,000

W-1166-L★ • F-1965L★ • 3,600,000

Series of 1950-E, Green Seal
Granahan-Fowler (1965–1966)

This series continued the preceding design. This series is worth noting for having been issued by just three Federal Reserve Banks, similar to the $10 notes of this series.

W-1168-B • F-1966B • New York • 82,000,000

Unc-60	Unc-63	Unc-65
$25	$40	$60

W-1168-B★ • F-1966B★ • 6,678,000

AU-50	Unc-60	Unc-63	Unc-65
$55	$80	$100	$160

W-1168-G • F-1966G • Chicago • 14,760,000

AU-50	Unc-60	Unc-63	Unc-65
$35	$55	$70	$100

W-1168-G★ • F-1966G★ • 1,080,000

EF-40	AU-50	Unc-60	Unc-63	Unc-65
$75	$150	$230	$280	$400

Signatures and series imprint of a $5 Federal Reserve Note, Series of 1950-D (W-1166-C). The back is the standard type of the era.

Signatures and series imprint of a $5 Federal Reserve Note, Series of 1950-E (W-1168-L). The back is the standard type of the era.

W-1168-L • F-1966L • San Francisco • 24,400,000

Unc-60	Unc-63	Unc-65
$39	$55	$75

W-1168-L★ • F-1966L★ • 1,800,000

EF-40	AU-50	Unc-60	Unc-63	Unc-65
$60	$125	$210	$250	$350

Series of 1963, Green Seal
Granahan-Dillon (1963–1965)

The Series of 1963 introduced a new back with IN GOD WE TRUST on a ribbon above the Lincoln Memorial. This addition was also made to Legal Tender Notes, Series of 1963.

The face displays some changes as well. The redemption feature above the Federal Reserve seal to the left now is in two lines: "This note is Legal Tender for all debts, public and private." The lower right plate letter and number are in a slightly higher position.

This series was not issued by the Richmond (E) or Minneapolis (I) banks.

Prices for a typical note for this series, unless listed otherwise, are as follows:

Unc-60	Unc-63	Unc-65
$20	$24	$30

Prices for a typical star note for this series, unless listed otherwise, are as follows:

Unc-60	Unc-63	Unc-65
$45	$60	$80

W-1170-A • F-1967A • Boston • 4,480,000

Unc-60	Unc-63	Unc-65
$24	$30	$40

W-1170-A★ • F-1967A★ • 640,000

Unc-60	Unc-63	Unc-65
$80	$100	$130

W-1170-B • F-1967B • New York • 12,160,000

W-1170-B★ • F-1967B★ • 1,280,000

W-1170-C • F-1967C • Philadelphia • 8,320,000

W-1170-C★ • F-1967C★ • 1,920,000

W-1170-D • F-1967D • Cleveland • 10,240,000

W-1170-D★ • F-1967D★ • 1,920,000

W-1170-F • F-1967F • Atlanta • 17,920,000

W-1170-F★ • F-1967F★ • 2,560,000

W-1170-G • F-1967G • Chicago • 22,400,000

W-1170-G★ • F-1967G★ • 3,200,000

$5 Federal Reserve Note, Series of 1963 (W-1170-J). Federal Reserve Bank of Kansas City. Some changes in the face layout.

Back of the $5 Federal Reserve Note, Series of 1963, introducing IN GOD WE TRUST.   Detail of the motto.

W-1170-H • F-1967H • St. Louis • 14,080,000

W-1170-H★ • F-1967H★ • 1,920,000

W-1170-J • F-1967J • Kansas City • 1,920,000

Unc-60	Unc-63	Unc-65
$24	$30	$40

W-1170-J★ • F-1967J★ • 640,000

Unc-60	Unc-63	Unc-65
$60	$75	$95

W-1170-K • F-1967K • Dallas • 5,760,000

Unc-60	Unc-63	Unc-65
$24	$30	$40

W-1170-K★ • F-1967K★ • 1,920,000

Unc-60	Unc-63	Unc-65
$50	$65	$85

W-1170-L • F-1967L • San Francisco • 18,560,000

W-1170-L★ • F-1967L★ • 1,920,000

Series of 1963-A, Green Seal
Granahan-Fowler (1965–1966)

This series continued the previous design.

W-1171-A • F-1968A • Boston • 77,440,000

Unc-63	Unc-65
$20	$30

W-1171-A★ • F-1968A★ • 5,760,000

Unc-60	Unc-63	Unc-65
$25	$35	$50

W-1171-B • F-1968B • New York • 98,080,000

Unc-63	Unc-65
$15	$25

W-1171-B★ • F-1968B★ • 7,680,000

Unc-60	Unc-63	Unc-65
$22	$30	$45

W-1171-C • F-1968C • Philadelphia • 106,400,000

Unc-63	Unc-65
$15	$25

W-1171-C★ • F-1968C★ • 10,240,000

Unc-60	Unc-63	Unc-65
$20	$30	$45

W-1171-D • F-1968D • Cleveland • 83,840,000

Unc-63	Unc-65
$15	$25

W-1171-D★ • F-1968D★ • 7,040,000

Unc-60	Unc-63	Unc-65
$15	$25	$35

W-1171-E • F-1968E • Richmond • 18,560,000

Unc-63	Unc-65
$20	$30

W-1171-E★ • F-1968E★ • 10,880,000

Unc-60	Unc-63	Unc-65
$20	$30	$45

W-1171-F • F-1968F • Atlanta • 117,920,000

Unc-63	Unc-65
$15	$25

W-1171-F★ • F-1968F★ • 9,600,000

Unc-60	Unc-63	Unc-65
$30	$40	$55

W-1171-G • F-1968G • Chicago • 213,440,000

Unc-63	Unc-65
$15	$25

W-1171-G★ • F-1968G★ • 16,640,000

Unc-60	Unc-63	Unc-65
$20	$30	$45

W-1171-H • F-1968H • St. Louis • 56,960,000

Unc-63	Unc-65
$20	$30

W-1171-H★ • F-1968H★ • 5,120,000

Unc-60	Unc-63	Unc-65
$30	$40	$55

W-1171-I • F-1968I • Minneapolis • 32,640,000

Unc-63	Unc-65
$25	$35

SERIES OF 1963-A, GREEN SEAL

Detail of the signatures and the series imprint of a $5 Federal Reserve Note, Series of 1963-A (W-1171-A). The back is the standard type of the era, with motto.

W-1171-I★ • F-1968I★ • 3,200,000

AU-50	Unc-60	Unc-63	Unc-65
$30	$50	$70	$95

W-1171-J • F-1968J • Kansas City • 55,040,000

Unc-63	Unc-65
$25	$35

W-1171-J★ • F-1968J★ • 5,760,000

Unc-60	Unc-63	Unc-65
$30	$40	$55

W-1171-K • F-1968K • Dallas • 64,000,000

Unc-63	Unc-65
$25	$35

W-1171-K★ • F-1968K★ • 3,840,000

Unc-60	Unc-63	Unc-65
$30	$40	$55

W-1171-L • F-1968L • San Francisco • 128,900,000

Unc-63	Unc-65
$15	$25

W-1171-L★ • F-1968L★ • 12,153,000

Unc-60	Unc-63	Unc-65
$20	$30	$45

Series of 1969, Green Seal
Elston-Kennedy (1969–1970)

The Series of 1969 features a redesigned Treasury seal with the inscription THE DEPARTMENT OF THE TREASURY 1789, replacing the earlier style with the Latin wording, THESAUR. AMER. SEPTENT. SIGIL. The design in the interior of the seal was modified as well.

Prices for a typical note for this series, unless listed otherwise, are as follows:

Unc-60	Unc-63	Unc-65
$13	$16	$22

W-1172-A • F-1969A • Boston • 51,200,000

Unc-60	Unc-63	Unc-65
$16	$20	$28

W-1172-A★ • F-1969A★ • 1,920,000

Unc-60	Unc-63	Unc-65
$35	$50	$70

W-1172-B • F-1969B • New York • 198,560,000

W-1172-B★ • F-1969B★ • 8,960,000

Unc-60	Unc-63	Unc-65
$20	$30	$45

W-1172-C • F-1969C • Philadelphia • 69,120,000

W-1172-C★ • F-1969C★ • 2,560,000

Unc-60	Unc-63	Unc-65
$20	$30	$45

W-1172-D • F-1969D • Cleveland • 56,320,000

W-1172-D★ • F-1969D★ • 2,560,000

Unc-60	Unc-63	Unc-65
$20	$30	$45

W-1172-E • F-1969E • Richmond • 84,480,000

SERIES OF 1969, GREEN SEAL

$5 Federal Reserve Note, Series of 1969 (W-1172-B). Federal Reserve Bank of New York. Standard back of $5 notes of the era, with motto.

Detail of the old-type Treasury seal with wording in Latin.

Detail of the new Treasury seal, with the English wording, as introduced on Series of 1969 notes.

W-1172-E★ • F-1969E★ • 3,200,000

Unc-60	Unc-63	Unc-65
$20	$30	$45

W-1172-F • F-1969F • Atlanta • 84,480,000

W-1172-F★ • F-1969F★ • 3,840,000

Unc-60	Unc-63	Unc-65
$55	$75	$100

W-1172-G • F-1969G • Chicago • 125,600,000

W-1172-G★ • F-1969G★ • 5,120,000

Unc-60	Unc-63	Unc-65
$22	$30	$45

W-1172-H • F-1969H • St. Louis • 27,520,000

Unc-60	Unc-63	Unc-65
$16	$20	$28

W-1172-H★ • F-1969H★ • 1,280,000

Unc-60	Unc-63	Unc-65
$45	$60	$80

W-1172-I • F-1969I • Minneapolis • 16,640,000

Unc-60	Unc-63	Unc-65
$20	$25	$34

W-1172-I★ • F-1969I★ • 640,000

Unc-60	Unc-63	Unc-65
$55	$75	$100

W-1172-J • F-1969J • Kansas City • 48,640,000

W-1172-J★ • F-1969J★ • 3,192,000

Unc-60	Unc-63	Unc-65
$40	$55	$75

W-1172-K • F-1969K • Dallas • 39,680,000

W-1172-K★ • F-1969K★ • 1,920,000

Unc-60	Unc-63	Unc-65
$45	$60	$80

W-1172-L • F-1969L • San Francisco • 103,840,000

W-1172-L★ • F-1969L★ • 4,480,000

Unc-60	Unc-63	Unc-65
$45	$60	$80

Series of 1969-A, Green Seal
Kabis-Connally (1971)

This series continued the previous design. Dorothy Andrews Elson married Walter L. Kabis during her term in office, and became Mrs. Kabis.

Prices for a typical note for this series, unless listed otherwise, are as follows:

Unc-60	Unc-63	Unc-65
$16	$20	$28

W-1173-A • F-1970A • Boston • 23,040,000

W-1173-A★ • F-1970A★ • 1,280,000

Unc-60	Unc-63	Unc-65
$50	$70	$95

W-1173-B • F-1970B • New York • 62,240,000

W-1173-B★ • F-1970B★ • 1,760,000

Unc-60	Unc-63	Unc-65
$45	$60	$80

W-1173-C • F-1970C • Philadelphia • 41,160,000

W-1173-C★ • F-1970C★ • 1,920,000

Unc-60	Unc-63	Unc-65
$45	$60	$80

W-1173-D • F-1970D • Cleveland • 21,120,000

W-1173-D★ • F-1970D★ • 640,000

Unc-60	Unc-63	Unc-65
$60	$80	$110

W-1173-E • F-1970E • Richmond • 37,920,000

W-1173-E★ • F-1970E★ • 1,120,000

Unc-60	Unc-63	Unc-65
$50	$70	$95

W-1173-F • F-1970F • Atlanta • 25,120,000

W-1173-F★ • F-1970F★ • 480,000

Unc-60	Unc-63	Unc-65
$80	$100	$125

W-1173-G • F-1970G • Chicago • 60,800,000

W-1173-G★ • F-1970G★ • 1,920,000

Unc-60	Unc-63	Unc-65
$45	$60	$80

SERIES OF 1969-A, GREEN SEAL

Detail of the signatures and the series imprint of a $5 Federal Reserve Note, Series of 1969-A (W-1173-F). The back is the standard type of the era, with motto.

W-1173-H • F-1970H • St. Louis • 15,360,000

W-1173-H★ • F-1970H★ • 640,000

Unc-60	Unc-63	Unc-65
$60	$80	$110

W-1173-I • F-1970I • Minneapolis • 8,960,000

Unc-60	Unc-63	Unc-65
$28	$35	$48

W-1173-I★ • F-1970I★ • 640,000

Unc-60	Unc-63	Unc-65
$70	$90	$115

W-1173-J • F-1970J • Kansas City • 17,920,000

Unc-60	Unc-63	Unc-65
$20	$25	$35

W-1173-J★ • F-1970J★ • 640,000

Unc-60	Unc-63	Unc-65
$60	$80	$110

W-1173-K • F-1970K • Dallas • 21,120,000

Unc-60	Unc-63	Unc-65
$24	$30	$40

W-1173-K★ • F-1970K★ • 640,000

Unc-60	Unc-63	Unc-65
$60	$80	$110

W-1173-L • F-1970L • San Francisco • 44,800,000

Unc-60	Unc-63	Unc-65
$20	$25	$35

W-1173-L★ • F-1970L★ • 1,920,000

Unc-60	Unc-63	Unc-65
$50	$70	$95

Series of 1969-B, Green Seal
Banuelos-Connally (1971–1972)

This series continued the previous design. Although each of the 12 Federal Reserve Banks issued regular Series of 1969-B notes, three did not issue star notes.

Prices for a typical star note for this series, unless listed otherwise, are as follows:

Unc-60	Unc-63	Unc-65
$150	$200	$265

W-1174-A • F-1971A • Boston • 5,760,000

Unc-60	Unc-63	Unc-65
$70	$90	$115

W-1174-B • F-1971B • New York • 34,560,000

Unc-60	Unc-63	Unc-65
$50	$65	$80

W-1174-B★ • F-1971B★ • 634,000

W-1174-C • F-1971C • Philadelphia • 5,120,000

Unc-60	Unc-63	Unc-65
$60	$75	$95

W-1174-D • F-1971D • Cleveland • 12,160,000

Unc-60	Unc-63	Unc-65
$50	$65	$80

W-1174-E • F-1971E • Richmond • 15,360,000

Unc-60	Unc-63	Unc-65
$50	$65	$80

W-1174-E★ • F-1971E★ • 640,000

W-1174-F • F-1971F • Atlanta • 18,560,000

Unc-60	Unc-63	Unc-65
$50	$65	$80

W-1174-F★ • F-1971F★ • 640,000

W-1174-G • F-1971G • Chicago • 27,040,000

Unc-60	Unc-63	Unc-65
$50	$65	$80

W-1174-G★ • F-1971G★ • 480,000

Unc-60	Unc-63	Unc-65
$170	$210	$295

W-1174-H • F-1971H • St. Louis • 5,120,000

Unc-60	Unc-63	Unc-65
$70	$90	$115

W-1174-I • F-1971I • Minneapolis • 8,320,000

Unc-60	Unc-63	Unc-65
$70	$90	$115

W-1174-J • F-1971J • Kansas City • 8,320,000

Unc-60	Unc-63	Unc-65
$70	$90	$115

W-1174-J★ • F-1971J★ • 640,000

SERIES OF 1969-B, GREEN SEAL

Detail of the signatures and the series imprint of a $5 Federal Reserve Note, Series of 1969-B (W-1174-B). The back is the standard type of the era, with motto.

W-1174-K • F-1971K • Dallas • 12,160,000

Unc-60	Unc-63	Unc-65
$60	$80	$105

W-1174-L • F-1971L • San Francisco • 23,160,000

Unc-60	Unc-63	Unc-65
$50	$65	$80

W-1174-L★ • F-1971L★ • 640,000

Series of 1969-C, Green Seal
Banuelos-Shultz (1972–1974)

This series continued the previous design. All Federal Reserve Banks issued regular Series 1969-C notes, and all but Minneapolis issued star notes.

Prices for a typical note for this series, unless listed otherwise, are as follows:

Unc-60	Unc-63	Unc-65
$16	$20	$28

W-1175-A • F-1972A • Boston • 50,720,000

W-1175-A★ • F-1972A★ • 1,920,000

Unc-60	Unc-63	Unc-65
$45	$60	$80

W-1175-B • F-1972B • New York • 120,000,000

W-1175-B★ • F-1972B★ • 2,400,000

Unc-60	Unc-63	Unc-65
$35	$45	$60

W-1175-C • F-1972C • Philadelphia • 53,760,000

W-1175-C★ • F-1972C★ • 1,280,000

Unc-60	Unc-63	Unc-65
$35	$45	$60

W-1175-D • F-1972D • Cleveland • 43,680,000

W-1175-D★ • F-1972D★ • 1,120,000

Unc-60	Unc-63	Unc-65
$60	$75	$95

W-1175-E • F-1972E • Richmond • 73,760,000

W-1175-E★ • F-1972E★ • 640,000

Unc-60	Unc-63	Unc-65
$45	$60	$80

W-1175-F • F-1972F • Atlanta • 81,440,000

W-1175-F★ • F-1972F★ • 3,200,000

Unc-60	Unc-63	Unc-65
$35	$45	$60

W-1175-G • F-1972G • Chicago • 54,400,000

W-1175-H • F-1972H • St. Louis • 37,760,000

W-1175-H★ • F-1972H★ • 1,280,000

Unc-60	Unc-63	Unc-65
$40	$50	$70

W-1175-I • F-1972I • Minneapolis • 14,080,000

Unc-60	Unc-63	Unc-65
$28	$35	$50

W-1175-J • F-1972J • Kansas City • 41,120,000

W-1175-J★ • F-1972J★ • 1,920,000

Unc-60	Unc-63	Unc-65
$40	$50	$70

W-1175-K • F-1972K • Dallas • 41,120,000

W-1175-K★ • F-1972K★ • 1,920,000

Unc-60	Unc-63	Unc-65
$45	$60	$80

W-1175-L • F-1972L • San Francisco • 80,800,000

W-1175-L★ • F-1972L★ • 3,680,000

Unc-60	Unc-63	Unc-65
$40	$50	$70

Series of 1974, Green Seal
Neff-Simon (1974–1977)

This series continued the previous design. This is unusual in that up to this point a new series date often signaled a change in layout.

Prices for a typical note for this series, unless listed otherwise, are as follows:

Unc-63	Unc-65
$15	$25

Prices for a typical star note for this series, unless listed otherwise, are as follows:

Unc-60	Unc-63	Unc-65
$35	$45	$60

SERIES OF 1969-C, GREEN SEAL

Detail of the signatures and the series imprint of a $5 Federal Reserve Note, Series of 1969-C (W-1175-B). The back is the standard type of the era, with motto.

W-1177-A • F-1973A • Boston • 58,240,000

Unc-63	Unc-65
$15	$22

W-1177-A★ • F-1973A★ • 1,408,000

Unc-60	Unc-63	Unc-65
$40	$50	$70

W-1177-B • F-1973B • New York • 153,120,000

Unc-63	Unc-65
$15	$22

W-1177-B★ • F-1973B★ • 2,656,000

W-1177-C • F-1973C • Philadelphia • 52,920,000

Unc-63	Unc-65
$15	$22

W-1177-C★ • F-1973C★ • 3,040,000

W-1177-D • F-1973D • Cleveland • 78,080,000

Unc-63	Unc-65
$15	$22

W-1177-D★ • F-1973D★ • 1,920,000

W-1177-E • F-1973E • Richmond • 135,200,000

Unc-63	Unc-65
$15	$22

W-1177-E★ • F-1973E★ • 1,760,000

W-1177-F • F-1973F • Atlanta • 127,520,000

W-1177-F★ • F-1973F★ • 3,040,000

W-1177-G • F-1973G • Chicago • 95,520,000

W-1177-G★ • F-1973G★ • 1,760,000

Unc-60	Unc-63	Unc-65
$30	$40	$55

W-1177-H • F-1973H • St. Louis • 64,800,000

W-1177-H★ • F-1973H★ • 1,760,000

Unc-60	Unc-63	Unc-65
$65	$80	$100

W-1177-I • F-1973I • Minneapolis • 41,600,000

W-1177-I★ • F-1973I★ • 2,560,000

W-1177-J • F-1973J • Kansas City • 42,240,000

W-1177-J★ • F-1973J★ • 2,176,000

W-1177-K • F-1973K • Dallas • 57,600,000

W-1177-K★ • F-1973K★ • 1,408,000

Unc-60	Unc-63	Unc-65
$40	$50	$65

W-1177-L • F-1973L • San Francisco • 139,680,000

W-1177-L★ • F-1973L★ • 5,088,000

Series of 1977, Green Seal
Morton-Blumenthal (1977–1979)

This series continued the previous design. All Federal Reserve Banks issued regular Series 1977 notes, and all but Minneapolis issued star notes.

Prices for a typical note for this series, unless listed otherwise, are as follows:

Unc-63	Unc-65
$15	$25

W-1178-A • F-1974A • Boston • 60,800,000

W-1178-A★ • F-1974A★ • 1,664,000

Unc-60	Unc-63	Unc-65
$80	$100	$130

W-1178-B • F-1974B • New York • 183,040,000

W-1178-B★ • F-1974B★ • 3,072,000

Unc-60	Unc-63	Unc-65
$30	$40	$55

W-1178-C • F-1974C • Philadelphia • 78,720,000

W-1178-C★ • F-1974C★ • 1,280,000

Unc-60	Unc-63	Unc-65
$35	$45	$60

W-1178-D • F-1974D • Cleveland • 72,960,000

SERIES OF 1974, GREEN SEAL

Detail of the signatures and the series imprint of a $5 Federal Reserve Note, Series of 1974 (W-1177-D). The back is the standard type of the era, with motto.

SERIES OF 1977, GREEN SEAL

Detail of the signatures and the series imprint of a $5 Federal Reserve Note, Series of 1977 (W-1178-F). The back is the standard type of the era, with motto.

W-1178-D★ • F-1974D★ • 1,152,000

Unc-60	Unc-63	Unc-65
$45	$55	$70

W-1178-E • F-1974E • Richmond • 110,720,000

W-1178-E★ • F-1974E★ • 2,816,000

Unc-60	Unc-63	Unc-65
$35	$45	$60

W-1178-F • F-1974F • Atlanta • 127,360,000

W-1178-F★ • F-1974F★ • 1,920,000

Unc-60	Unc-63	Unc-65
$35	$45	$60

W-1178-G • F-1974G • Chicago • 177,920,000

W-1178-G★ • F-1974G★ • 2,816,000

Unc-60	Unc-63	Unc-65
$30	$40	$55

W-1178-H • F-1974H • St. Louis • 46,080,000

W-1178-H★ • F-1974H★ • 128,000

Unc-60	Unc-63	Unc-65
$125	$150	$225

W-1178-I • F-1974I • Minneapolis • 21,760,000

W-1178-J • F-1974J • Kansas City • 78,080,000

W-1178-J★ • F-1974J★ • 1,408,000

Unc-60	Unc-63	Unc-65
$35	$45	$60

W-1178-K • F-1974K • Dallas • 60,800,000

W-1178-K★ • F-1974K★ • 2,408,000

Unc-60	Unc-63	Unc-65
$30	$40	$55

W-1178-L • F-1974L • San Francisco • 135,040,000

W-1178-L★ • F-1974L★ • 2,432,000

Unc-60	Unc-63	Unc-65
$35	$45	$60

Series of 1977-A, Green Seal
Morton-Miller (1979–1981)

This series continued the previous design.

Prices for a typical note for this series, unless listed otherwise, are as follows:

Unc-63	Unc-65
$15	$25

W-1179-A • F-1975A • Boston • 48,000,000

W-1179-A★ • F-1975A★ • 512,000

EF-40	AU-50	Unc-60	Unc-63	Unc-65
$50	$90	$160	$200	$270

W-1179-B • F-1975B • New York • 113,920,000

W-1179-B★ • F-1975B★ • 2,304,000

Unc-60	Unc-63	Unc-65
$45	$60	$80

W-1179-C • F-1975C • Philadelphia • 55,680,000

W-1179-C★ • F-1975C★ • 640,000

Unc-60	Unc-63	Unc-65
$70	$90	$115

W-1179-D • F-1975D • Cleveland • 85,880,000

W-1179-D★ • F-1975D★ • 1,280,000

Unc-60	Unc-63	Unc-65
$65	$80	$100

W-1179-E • F-1975E • Richmond • 77,440,000

Unc-63	Unc-65
$12	$17

W-1179-E★ • F-1975E★ • 768,000

VF-20	EF-40	AU-50	Unc-60	Unc-63	Unc-65
$45	$80	$150	$220	$300	$400

W-1179-F • F-1975F • Atlanta • 76,160,000

Unc-63	Unc-65
$12	$17

W-1179-F★ • F-1975F★ • 1,152,000

Unc-60	Unc-63	Unc-65
$65	$80	$100

W-1179-G • F-1975G • Chicago • 80,640,000

SERIES OF 1977-A, GREEN SEAL

Detail of the signatures and the series imprint of a $5 Federal Reserve Note, Series of 1977-A (W-1179-I). The back is the standard type of the era, with motto.

W-1179-G★ • F-1975G★ • 1,408,000

Unc-60	Unc-63	Unc-65
$55	$70	$90

W-1179-H • F-1975H • St. Louis • 42,240,000

W-1179-H★ • F-1975H★ • 640,000

Unc-60	Unc-63	Unc-65
$45	$60	$80

W-1179-I • F-1975I • Minneapolis • 10,240,000

Unc-63	Unc-65
$20	$30

W-1179-I★ • F-1975I★ • 256,000

Unc-60	Unc-63	Unc-65
$160	$200	$270

W-1179-J • F-1975J • Kansas City • 52,480,000

W-1179-J★ • F-1975J★ • 1,024,000

Unc-60	Unc-63	Unc-65
$80	$100	$130

W-1179-K • F-1975K • Dallas • 76,160,000

W-1179-K★ • F-1975K★ • 1,408,000

Unc-60	Unc-63	Unc-65
$65	$80	$100

W-1179-L • F-1975L • San Francisco • 106,880,000

W-1179-L★ • F-1975L★ • 1,152,000

Unc-60	Unc-63	Unc-65
$70	$90	$115

Series of 1981, Green Seal
Buchanan-Regan (1981–1983)

All Federal Reserve Banks issued regular Series 1981 notes, and all but Boston issued star notes.

Prices for a typical note for this series, unless listed otherwise, are as follows:

Unc-60	Unc-63	Unc-65
$20	$25	$35

W-1181-A • F-1976A • Boston • 109,000,000

Unc-60	Unc-63	Unc-65
$25	$30	$40

W-1181-B • F-1976B • New York • 250,880,000

W-1181-B★ • F-1976B★ • 4,464,000

Unc-60	Unc-63	Unc-65
$100	$125	$170

W-1181-C • F-1976C • Philadelphia • 112,640,000

W-1181-C★ • F-1976C★ • 640,000

Unc-60	Unc-63	Unc-65
$140	$175	$250

W-1181-D • F-1976D • Cleveland • 122,240,000

W-1181-D★ • F-1976D★ • 1,268,000

Unc-60	Unc-63	Unc-65
$140	$175	$250

W-1181-E • F-1976E • Richmond • 234,880,000

W-1181-E★ • F-1976E★ • 640,000

Unc-60	Unc-63	Unc-65
$120	$150	$200

W-1181-F • F-1976F • Atlanta • 234,880,000

W-1181-F★ • F-1976F★ • 1,644,000

Unc-60	Unc-63	Unc-65
$140	$175	$250

W-1181-G • F-1976G • Chicago • 241,280,000

W-1181-G★ • F-1976G★ • 768,000

Unc-60	Unc-63	Unc-65
$70	$90	$115

W-1181-H • F-1976H • St. Louis • 199,680,000

Unc-60	Unc-63	Unc-65
$25	$30	$40

W-1181-H★ • F-1976H★ • 628,000

Unc-60	Unc-63	Unc-65
$170	$225	$300

W-1181-I • F-1976I • Minneapolis • 109,440,000

Unc-60	Unc-63	Unc-65
$35	$45	$60

W-1181-I★ • F-1976I★ • 640,000

Unc-60	Unc-63	Unc-65
$230	$300	$400

SERIES OF 1981, GREEN SEAL

Detail of the signatures and the series imprint of a $5 Federal Reserve Note, Series of 1981 (W-1181-D). The back is the standard type of the era, with motto.

W-1181-J • F-1976J • Kansas City • 125,440,000

Unc-60	Unc-63	Unc-65
$25	$30	$40

W-1181-J★ • F-1976J★ • 960,000

Unc-60	Unc-63	Unc-65
$140	$175	$250

W-1181-K • F-1976K • Dallas • 138,240,000

Unc-60	Unc-63	Unc-65
$25	$30	$40

W-1181-K★ • F-1976K★ • 640,000

Unc-60	Unc-63	Unc-65
$100	$125	$170

W-1181-L • F-1976L • San Francisco • 263,680,000

W-1181-L★ • F-1976L★ • 1,792,000

Unc-65
$100

Series of 1981-A, Green Seal
Ortega-Regan (1983–1985)

This series continued the previous design. Although all Federal Reserve Banks issued regular Series of 1981-A notes, only New York (B) and San Francisco (L) issued star notes.

W-1182-A • F-1977A • Boston • 192,000,000

Unc-60	Unc-63	Unc-65
$40	$50	$65

W-1182-B • F-1977B • New York • 448,000,000

Unc-60	Unc-63	Unc-65
$30	$40	$55

W-1182-B★ • F-1977B★ • 3,200,000

Unc-60	Unc-63	Unc-65
$120	$150	$200

W-1182-C • F-1977C • Philadelphia • 169,600,000

Unc-60	Unc-63	Unc-65
$40	$50	$70

W-1182-D • F-1977D • Cleveland • 214,400,000

Unc-60	Unc-63	Unc-65
$40	$50	$70

W-1182-E • F-1977E • Richmond • 332,800,000

Unc-60	Unc-63	Unc-65
$35	$45	$60

W-1182-F • F-1977F • Atlanta • 352,000,000

Unc-60	Unc-63	Unc-65
$35	$45	$60

W-1182-G • F-1977G • Chicago • 345,600,000

Unc-60	Unc-63	Unc-65
$35	$45	$60

W-1182-H • F-1977H • St. Louis • 128,000,000

Unc-60	Unc-63	Unc-65
$35	$45	$60

W-1182-I • F-1977I • Minneapolis • 73,800,000

Unc-60	Unc-63	Unc-65
$40	$50	$70

W-1182-J • F-1977J • Kansas City • 134,400,000

Unc-60	Unc-63	Unc-65
$40	$50	$70

W-1182-K • F-1977K • Dallas • 176,000,000

Unc-60	Unc-63	Unc-65
$60	$75	$95

W-1182-L • F-1977L • San Francisco • 150,400,000

Unc-60	Unc-63	Unc-65
$45	$55	$70

W-1182-L★ • F-1977L★ • 3,200,000

AU-50	Unc-60	Unc-63	Unc-65
$60	$100	$130	$175

Series of 1985, Green Seal
Ortega-Baker (1985–1988)

This series continued the previous design. Although all Federal Reserve Banks issued regular Series of 1985 notes, several did not issue star notes.

Prices for a typical note for this series, unless listed otherwise, are as follows:

Unc-60	Unc-63	Unc-65
$16	$20	$28

W-1183-A • F-1978A • Boston • 192,000,000

SERIES OF 1981-A, GREEN SEAL

Detail of the signatures and the series imprint of a $5 Federal Reserve Note, Series of 1981-A (W-1182-A). The back is the standard type of the era, with motto.

W-1183-B • F-1978B • New York • 451,200,000

W-1183-B★ • F-1978B★ • 3,200,000

AU-50	Unc-60	Unc-63	Unc-65
$60	$100	$125	$170

W-1183-C • F-1978C • Philadelphia • 170,400,000

W-1183-C★ • F-1978C★ • 6,400,000

Unc-60	Unc-63	Unc-65
$65	$80	$100

W-1183-D • F-1978D • Cleveland • 216,000,000

W-1183-E • F-1978E • Richmond • 335,200,000

W-1183-E★ • F-1978E★ • 3,200,000

AU-50	Unc-60	Unc-63	Unc-65
$40	$80	$100	$125

W-1183-F • F-1978F • Atlanta • 354,400,000

W-1183-F★ • F-1978F★ • 6,400,000

Unc-60	Unc-63	Unc-65
$50	$65	$85

W-1183-G • F-1978G • Chicago • 348,000,000

W-1183-G★ • F-1978G★ • 6,400,000

Unc-60	Unc-63	Unc-65
$50	$65	$85

W-1183-H • F-1978H • St. Louis • 128,000,000

W-1183-I • F-1978I • Minneapolis • 173,600,000

W-1183-J • F-1978J • Kansas City • 135,200,000

W-1183-K • F-1978K • Dallas • 176,800,000

W-1183-K★ • F-1978K★ • 3,200,000

Unc-60	Unc-63	Unc-65
$70	$90	$115

W-1183-L • F-1978L • San Francisco • 460,800,000

W-1183-L★ • F-1978L★ • 3,200,000

AU-50	Unc-60	Unc-63	Unc-65
$40	$80	$100	$135

Series of 1988, Green Seal
Ortega-Brady (1988–1989)

This series continued the previous design. Although all Federal Reserve Banks issued regular Series of 1988 notes, only a few issued star notes.

Prices for a typical note for this series, unless listed otherwise, are as follows:

Unc-63	Unc-65
$20	$30

W-1184-A • F-1979A • Boston • 86,400,000

W-1184-A★ • F-1979A★ • 768,000

AU-50	Unc-60	Unc-63	Unc-65
$35	$80	$100	$130

W-1184-B • F-1979B • New York • 185,600,000

W-1184-B★ • F-1979B★ • 3,200,000

AU-50	Unc-60	Unc-63	Unc-65
$25	$50	$65	$90

W-1184-C • F-1979C • Philadelphia • 54,400,000

W-1184-D • F-1979D • Cleveland • 111,200,000

W-1184-E • F-1979E • Richmond • 131,200,000

W-1184-F • F-1979F • Atlanta • 137,200,000

W-1184-F★ • F-1979F★ • 6,400,000

AU-50	Unc-60	Unc-63	Unc-65
$20	$40	$60	$80

W-1184-G • F-1979G • Chicago • 134,400,000

W-1184-H • F-1979H • St. Louis • 51,200,000

W-1184-I • F-1979I • Minneapolis • 9,600,000

SERIES OF 1985, GREEN SEAL

Detail of the signatures and the series imprint of a $5 Federal Reserve Note, Series of 1985 (W-1183-H). The back is the standard type of the era, with motto.

SERIES OF 1988, GREEN SEAL

Detail of the signatures and the series imprint of a $5 Federal Reserve Note, Series of 1988 (W-1184-C). The back is the standard type of the era, with motto.

W-1184-J • F-1979J • Kansas City • 44,800,000

W-1184-K • F-1979K • Dallas • 54,500,000

W-1184-L • F-1979L • San Francisco • 70,400,000

Series of 1988-A, Green Seal, Washington
Villalpando-Brady (1989–1993)

This series continued the previous design. The Bureau of Engraving and Printing in Washington printed a full run of Federal Reserve Bank notes, but not all had star issues.

Prices for a typical note for this series, unless listed otherwise, are as follows:

Unc-63	Unc-65
$15	$20

W-1185-A • F-1980A • Boston • 140,800,000

W-1185-A★ • F-1980A★ • 3,200,000

Unc-60	Unc-63	Unc-65
$30	$40	$60

W-1185-B • F-1980B • New York • 640,000,000

W-1185-B★ • F-1980B★ • 4,608,000

Unc-60	Unc-63	Unc-65
$30	$40	$60

W-1185-C • F-1980C • Philadelphia • 70,400,000

W-1185-D • F-1980D • Cleveland • 166,000,000

W-1185-D★ • F-1980D★ • 4,864,000

Unc-60	Unc-63	Unc-65
$25	$35	$50

W-1185-E • F-1980E • Richmond • 486,400,000

W-1185-E★ • F-1980E★ • 3,020,000

Unc-60	Unc-63	Unc-65
$35	$45	$60

W-1185-F • F-1980F • Atlanta • 192,000,000

W-1185-F★ • F-1980F★ • 2,640,000

Unc-60	Unc-63	Unc-65
$35	$45	$60

W-1185-G • F-1980G • Chicago • 633,600,000

W-1185-G★ • F-1980G★

AU-50	Unc-60	Unc-63	Unc-65
$20	$35	$50	$70

W-1185-H • F-1980H • St. Louis • 185,600,000

W-1185-H★ • F-1980H★ • 1,280,000

AU-50	Unc-60	Unc-63	Unc-65
$20	$35	$50	$70

W-1185-I • F-1980I • Minneapolis • 73,600,000

W-1185-I★ • F-1980I★ • 3,200,000

EF-40	AU-50	Unc-60	Unc-63	Unc-65
$50	$90	$160	$225	$300

W-1185-J • F-1980J • Kansas City • 115,200,000

W-1185-K • F-1980K • Dallas • 128,000,000

W-1185-L • F-1980L • San Francisco • 492,800,000

Series of 1988-A, Green Seal, Fort Worth
Villalpando-Brady (1989–1993)

The Western Facility of the Bureau of Engraving and Printing, located in Fort Worth, Texas, commenced issuing $5 notes with this series. Notes printed there have FW as part of the face plate letter and number. Generally, the Western Facility printed notes for Federal Reserve Banks in the Midwest and West, but there have been many exceptions.

Prices for a typical note for this series, unless listed otherwise, are as follows:

Unc-63	Unc-65
$15	$20

W-1186-C • F-1981C • Philadelphia • 25,600,000

W-1186-F • F-1981F • Atlanta • 282,400,000

W-1186-F★ • F-1981F★ • 640,000

AU-50	Unc-60	Unc-63	Unc-65
$20	$30	$40	$60

W-1186-G • F-1981G • Chicago • 76,800,000

W-1186-G★ • F-1981G★ • 1,280,000

AU-50	Unc-60	Unc-63	Unc-65
$20	$35	$45	$65

SERIES OF 1988-A, GREEN SEAL

Detail of the signatures and the series imprint of a Washington-printed $5 Federal Reserve Note, Series of 1988-A (W-1185-B). The back is the standard With Motto type.

Plate letter and number on a Fort Worth printing of a Series of 1988-A note (W-1186-K).

W-1186-J • F-1981J • Kansas City • 25,600,000

W-1186-K • F-1981K • Dallas • 44,800,000

W-1186-L • F-1981L • San Francisco • 179,200,000

W-1186-L★ • F-1981L★ • 3,200,000

AU-50	Unc-60	Unc-63	Unc-65
$20	$30	$40	$60

Series of 1993, Green Seal, Washington
Withrow-Bentsen (1994)

This series continued the previous design.

Prices for a typical note for this series, unless listed otherwise, are as follows:

Unc-63	Unc-65
$15	$20

W-1187-A • F-1982A • Boston • 38,400,000

W-1187-B • F-1982B • New York • 102,400,000

W-1187-B★ • F-1982B★ • 2,816,000

AU-50	Unc-60	Unc-63	Unc-65
$15	$25	$30	$40

W-1187-C • F-1982C • Philadelphia • 38,400,000

W-1187-E • F-1982E • Richmond • 76,800,000

W-1187-E★ • F-1982E★ • 1,920,000

AU-50	Unc-60	Unc-63	Unc-65
$20	$35	$45	$65

W-1187-F • F-1982F • Atlanta • 70,400,000

Series of 1993, Green Seal, Fort Worth
Withrow-Bentsen (1994)

This series continued the previous design.

Prices for a typical note for this series, unless listed otherwise, are as follows:

Unc-63	Unc-65
$15	$20

W-1188-G • F-1983G • Chicago • 64,000,000

W-1188-G★ • F-1983G★ • 1,280,000

EF-40	AU-50	Unc-60	Unc-63	Unc-65
$20	$40	$65	$85	$110

W-1188-H • F-1983H • St. Louis • 64,000,000

W-1188-H★ • F-1983H★ • 2,560,000

AU-50	Unc-60	Unc-63	Unc-65
$20	$30	$40	$55

W-1188-I • F-1983I • Minneapolis • 6,400,000

VF-20	EF-40	AU-50	Unc-60	Unc-63	Unc-65
$45	$80	$140	$250	$325	$425

W-1188-J • F-1983J • Kansas City • 32,000,000

W-1188-K • F-1983K • Dallas • 57,600,000

W-1188-L • F-1983L • San Francisco • 185,600,000

W-1188-L★ • F-1983L★ • 2,560,000

Unc-60	Unc-63	Unc-65
$25	$35	$45

Series of 1995, Green Seal, Washington
Withrow-Rubin (1995–1999)

This series (illus. on p. 316) continued the previous design.

Prices for a typical note for this series, unless listed otherwise, are as follows:

Unc-60	Unc-63	Unc-65
$12	$20	$30

W-1189-A • F-1984A • Boston • 160,000,000

W-1189-A★ • F-1984A★ • 640,000

EF-40	AU-50	Unc-60	Unc-63	Unc-65
$20	$40	$85	$125	$160

W-1189-B • F-1984B • New York • 390,040,444

W-1189-B★ • F-1984B★ • 3,840,000

AU-50	Unc-60	Unc-63	Unc-65
$15	$25	$40	$60

W-1189-C • F-1984C • Philadelphia • 128,000,000

W-1189-D • F-1984D • Cleveland • 89,600,000

W-1189-E • F-1984E • Richmond • 300,800,000

W-1189-F • F-1984F • Atlanta • 179,200,000

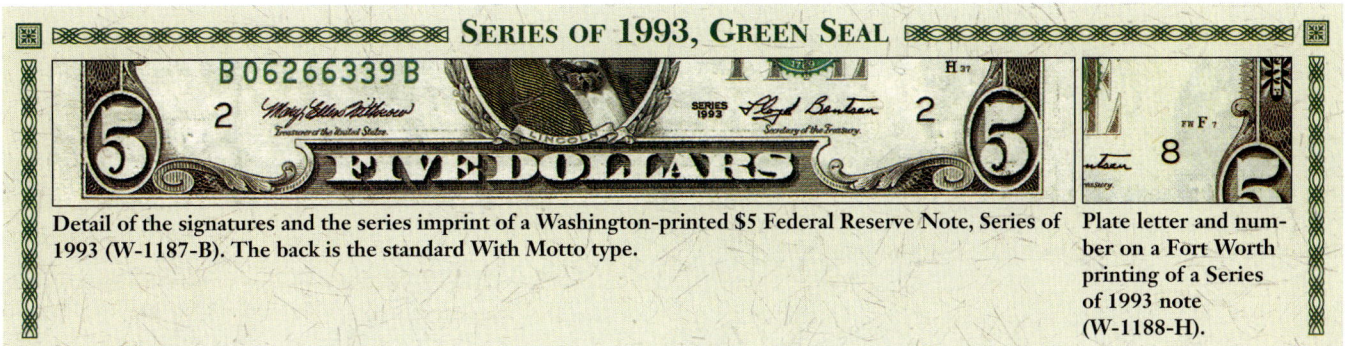

SERIES OF 1993, GREEN SEAL

Detail of the signatures and the series imprint of a Washington-printed $5 Federal Reserve Note, Series of 1993 (W-1187-B). The back is the standard With Motto type.

Plate letter and number on a Fort Worth printing of a Series of 1993 note (W-1188-H).

Series of 1995, Green Seal, Fort Worth
Withrow-Rubin (1995–1999)

The Western Facility printed a full run of 12 varieties in the Series of 1995, but only a few were accompanied by star notes.

Prices for a typical note for this series, unless listed otherwise, are as follows:

Unc-63	Unc-65
$20	$30

W-1190-A • F-1985A • Boston • 57,600,000

W-1190-B • F-1985B • New York • 76,800,000

W-1190-C • F-1985C • Philadelphia • 38,000,000

W-1190-D • F-1985D • Cleveland • 64,000,000

W-1190-D★ • F-1985D★ • 3,200,000

AU-50	Unc-60	Unc-63	Unc-65
$20	$35	$45	$60

W-1190-E • F-1985E • Richmond • 108,000,000

W-1190-F • F-1985F • Atlanta • 448,000,000

W-1190-F★ • F-1985F★ • 70,400,000

EF-40	AU-50	Unc-60	Unc-63	Unc-65
$15	$35	$65	$85	$110

W-1190-G • F-1985G • Chicago • 524,800,000

W-1190-G★ • F-1985G★ • 9,600,000

AU-50	Unc-60	Unc-63	Unc-65
$12	$25	$35	$45

W-1190-H • F-1985H • St. Louis • 204,800,000

W-1190-I • F-1985I • Minneapolis • 64,000,000

Unc-60	Unc-63	Unc-65
$20	$25	$35

W-1190-J • F-1985J • Kansas City • 160,000,000

W-1190-K • F-1985K • Dallas • 204,800,000

W-1190-L • F-1985L • San Francisco • 706,800,000

Series of 1999, Green Seal, Washington
Withrow-Summers (1999–2001)

Both sides of the $5 note were redesigned for the Series of 1999. To the left is a new Federal Reserve seal without any indication of which of the 12 banks issued the note. A letter and number printed below the serial number at the upper left gives that information, such as A1 for Boston, B2 for New York, etc. The redemption phrase is now below the modernized Federal Reserve seal. Lincoln's portrait is modified and enlarged. THE UNITED STATES OF AMERICA appears in microprint lettering on part of the frame, so tiny that the letters cannot be read with the naked eye. THE UNITED STATES OF AMERICA is also in two lines in the upper right field. Other changes are as depicted.

The new back retains the same general features as earlier, but with a dark area around the Lincoln Memorial, which is placed lower in the field. The bottom left and right corner denomination counters are now 5 instead of FIVE. Other changes are as depicted.

Prices for a typical note for this series, unless listed otherwise, are as follows:

Unc-63	Unc-65
$15	$20

W-1191-A • F-1986A • Boston • 19,200,000

W-1191-B • F-1986B • New York • 76,800,000

W-1191-C • F-1986C • Philadelphia • 57,600,000

W-1191-D • F-1986D • Cleveland • 25,600,000

W-1191-E • F-1986E • Richmond • 96,000,000

W-1191-E★ • F-1986E★ • 739,200

Unc-60	Unc-63	Unc-65
$35	$45	$60

Series of 1999, Green Seal, Fort Worth
Withrow-Summers (1999–2001)

This series was redesigned, as described above.

Prices for a typical note for this series, unless listed otherwise, are as follows:

Unc-63	Unc-65
$15	$20

Prices for a typical star note for this series, unless listed otherwise, are as follows:

AU-50	Unc-60	Unc-63	Unc-65
$15	$30	$40	$60

W-1192-A • F-1987A • Boston • 70,400,000

SERIES OF 1995, GREEN SEAL

Detail of the signatures and the series imprint of a Washington-printed $5 Federal Reserve Note, Series of 1995 (W-1189-A). The back is the standard With Motto type. Plate letter and number on a Fort Worth printing of a Series of 1995 note (W-1190-D).

W-1192-A★ • F-1987A★ • 3,200,000

W-1192-B • F-1987B • New York • 256,000,000

W-1192-B★ • F-1987B★ • 3,840,000

W-1192-C • F-1987C • Philadelphia • 89,600,000

W-1192-D • F-1987D • Cleveland • 12,800,000

W-1192-E • F-1987E • Richmond • 185,600,000

W-1192-E★ • F-1987E★ • 3,200,000

W-1192-F • F-1987F • Atlanta • 211,200,000

W-1192-F★ • F-1987F★ • 10,915,200

AU-50	Unc-60	Unc-63	Unc-65
$12	$25	$35	$55

W-1192-G • F-1987G • Chicago • 140,800,000

W-1192-G★ • F-1987G★ • 3,200,000

W-1192-H • F-1987H • St. Louis • 44,800,000

W-1192-I • F-1987I • Minneapolis • 12,800,000

Unc-63	Unc-65
$20	$30

W-1192-J • F-1987J • Kansas City • 32,000,000

W-1192-J★ • F-1987J★ • 3,200,000

AU-50	Unc-60	Unc-63	Unc-65
$18	$35	$45	$65

W-1192-K • F-1987K • Dallas • 121,600,000

W-1192-K★ • F-1987K★ • Listed in BEP reports, but may be an error; none verified[41]

W-1192-L • F-1987L • San Francisco • 243,200,000

Series of 2001, Green Seal, Fort Worth
Marin-O'Neill (2001–2002)

No Series of 2001 $5 notes were printed in Washington.

Prices for a typical note for this series (illus. on p. 318), unless listed otherwise, are as follows:

Unc-63	Unc-65
$15	$20

Prices for a typical star note for this series, unless listed otherwise, are as follows:

AU-50	Unc-60	Unc-63	Unc-65
$18	$30	$40	$55

W-1193-A • F-1988A • Boston • 128,000,000

W-1193-B • F-1988B • New York • 121,600,000

W-1193-C • F-1988C • Philadelphia • 64,000,000

W-1193-D • F-1988D • Cleveland • 83,200,000

W-1193-E • F-1988E • Richmond • 51,200,000

W-1193-F • F-1988F • Atlanta • 224,000,000

W-1193-G • F-1988G • Chicago • 185,600,000

SERIES OF 1999, GREEN SEAL

$5 Federal Reserve Note, Series of 1999 (W-1191-A). Federal Reserve Bank of Boston. Printed in Washington. The face is redesigned, and new security features are added.

Detail of the microprinting at the lower left of the portrait frame.

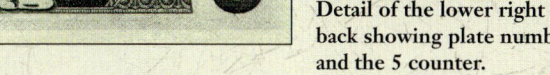

Detail of the lower right of the face showing the imprint of a Fort Worth-printed note.

Back of the $5 Federal Reserve Note, Series of 1999.

Detail of the lower right of the back showing plate number 11 and the 5 counter.

W-1193-H • F-1988H • St. Louis • 102,400,000

W-1193-I • F-1988I • Minneapolis • 32,000,000

Unc-63	Unc-65
$18	$24

W-1193-J • F-1988J • Kansas City • 76,800,000

W-1193-K • F-1988K • Dallas • 211,200,000

W-1193-K★ • F-1988K★

W-1193-L • F-1988L • San Francisco • 281,600,000

W-1193-L★ • F-1988L★ • 5,120,000

Series of 2003, Green Seal, Washington
Marin-Snow (2003)

This series was issued by six Federal Reserve banks.

Prices for a typical note for this series, unless listed otherwise, are as follows:

Unc-63	Unc-65
$15	$20

W-1194-A • F-1989A • Boston • 32,000,000

W-1194-C • F-1989C • Philadelphia • 32,000,000

W-1194-D • F-1989D • Cleveland • 32,000,000

W-1194-F • F-1989F • Atlanta • 89,600,000

W-1194-G • F-1989G • Chicago • 32,000,000

W-1194-G★ • F-1989G★ • 3,200,000

Unc-63	Unc-65
$40	$55

Series of 2003, Green Seal, Fort Worth
Marin-Snow (2003)

This series was issued by all 12 Federal Reserve banks.

Prices for a typical note for this series, unless listed otherwise, are as follows:

Unc-63	Unc-65
$15	$20

W-1195-A • F-1990A • Boston • 25,600,000

W-1195-B • F-1990B • New York • 147,200,000

W-1195-C • F-1990C • Philadelphia • 38,400,000

W-1195-C★ • F-1990C★

Commentary: Current market information not available.

W-1195-D • F-1990D • Cleveland • 32,000,000

W-1195-E • F-1990E • Richmond • 108,800,000

W-1195-F • F-1990F • Atlanta • 96,000,000

W-1195-G • F-1990G • Chicago • 89,600,000

W-1195-H • F-1990H • St. Louis • 51,200,000

W-1195-I • F-1990I • Minneapolis • 32,000,000

Unc-63	Unc-65
$20	$25

W-1195-J • F-1990J • Kansas City • 51,200,000

W-1195-K • F-1990K • Dallas • 96,000,000

W-1195-L • F-1990L • San Francisco • 243,200,000

W-1195-L★ • F-1990L★ • 3,520,000

AU-50	Unc-60	Unc-63	Unc-65
$15	$25	$35	$50

Series of 2003-A, Green Seal, Fort Worth
Cabral-Snow (2004–2006)

All Series of 2003-A notes were printed in Fort Worth.

Prices for a typical note for this series, unless listed otherwise, are as follows:

Unc-63	Unc-65
$15	$20

W-1197-A • F-1991A • Boston • 38,400,000

W-1197-B • F-1991B • New York • 96,000,000

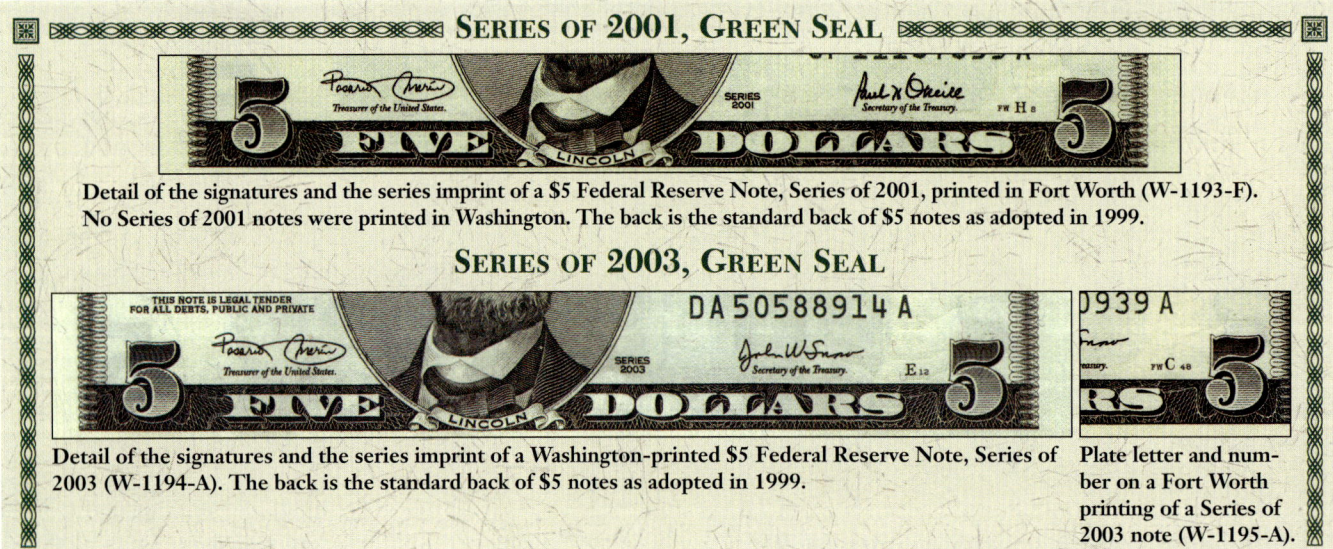

SERIES OF 2001, GREEN SEAL

Detail of the signatures and the series imprint of a $5 Federal Reserve Note, Series of 2001, printed in Fort Worth (W-1193-F). No Series of 2001 notes were printed in Washington. The back is the standard back of $5 notes as adopted in 1999.

SERIES OF 2003, GREEN SEAL

Detail of the signatures and the series imprint of a Washington-printed $5 Federal Reserve Note, Series of 2003 (W-1194-A). The back is the standard back of $5 notes as adopted in 1999.

Plate letter and number on a Fort Worth printing of a Series of 2003 note (W-1195-A).

W-1197-B★ • F-1991B★

EF-40	AU-50	Unc-60	Unc-63	Unc-65
$12	$25	$50	$65	$85

W-1197-C • F-1991C • Philadelphia • 44,800,000

W-1197-D • F-1991D • Cleveland • 38,400,000

W-1197-E • F-1991E • Richmond • 70,400,000

W-1197-F • F-1991F • Atlanta • 134,400,000

W-1197-F★ • F-1991F★ • 52,000

AU-50	Unc-60	Unc-63	Unc-65
$20	$40	$50	$70

W-1197-G • F-1991G • Chicago • 83,200,000

W-1197-G★ • F-1991G★ • 40,000

EF-40	AU-50	Unc-60	Unc-63	Unc-65
$15	$35	$60	$75	$95

W-1197-H • F-1991H • St. Louis • 6,400,000

W-1197-I • F-1991I • Minneapolis • 19,200,000

Unc-63	Unc-65
$20	$25

W-1197-J • F-1991J • Kansas City • 102,400,000

W-1197-K • F-1991K • Dallas • 172,800,000

W-1197-L • F-1991L • San Francisco • 57,600,000

Series of 2006, Green Seal, Fort Worth (Not Colorized, Old Style)
Cabral-Paulson (2006–2009)

Notes of the preceding style were printed for only three Federal Reserve Banks, and only from June to October 2007. These were for Atlanta, Chicago, and Minneapolis. There were no star notes. The Series of 2006 designation is compatible with the nomenclature for the non-colorized $1 and $100 notes. When colorized notes were made (see the following listing), a new series should have been created, per tradition, but was not. Serial numbers begin with H. No valuation charts are provided, as notes in this series can be had in top condition for face value at banks or from dealers (with a nominal handling charge).

W-1198-F • F-1992F • Atlanta • 275,200,000

W-1198-G • F-1992G • Chicago • 108,800,000

W-1198-I • F-1992I • Minneapolis • 25,600,000

Series of 2006, Green Seal, Fort Worth (Colorized)
Cabral-Paulson (2006–2009)

These notes (illus. on p. 320) are the first of the colorized $5 notes, with added security features. These were first released into circulation on March 13, 2008. As noted in the preceding section, had tradition been followed, this series would have had a new designation, such as 2006-A, as non-colorized notes had already been made under the Series of 2006.

The face of the note was modified. The frame is gone from the Lincoln portrait. Added color includes a twilight pink-blue background to the note, except for the edges of the left and right fields. An arc of stars is to the left of the portrait and gold 05 denomination counters are in the left field. Left of the Federal Reserve Bank seal, the background color changes from pink to blue. To the right of the portrait is a heraldic eagle holding an olive branch (the end of which is missing) and arrows. Farther right is an arc of stars and white field areas. The Treasury seal is dark green or black. The Federal Reserve Bank location is not printed, but is identified by the usual code, A1 (Boston), B2 (New York), etc., at the upper left. The paper includes an embedded security strip.

The back of the plate retains the essential typographical elements of the preceding design, but with security features added. This include a twilight pink-blue at the center, many gold 05 denomination counters in the upper right field, and a bright purple 5 at the lower right. The plate number is immediately to the right of the top of the foliage, near the frame for the purple 5.

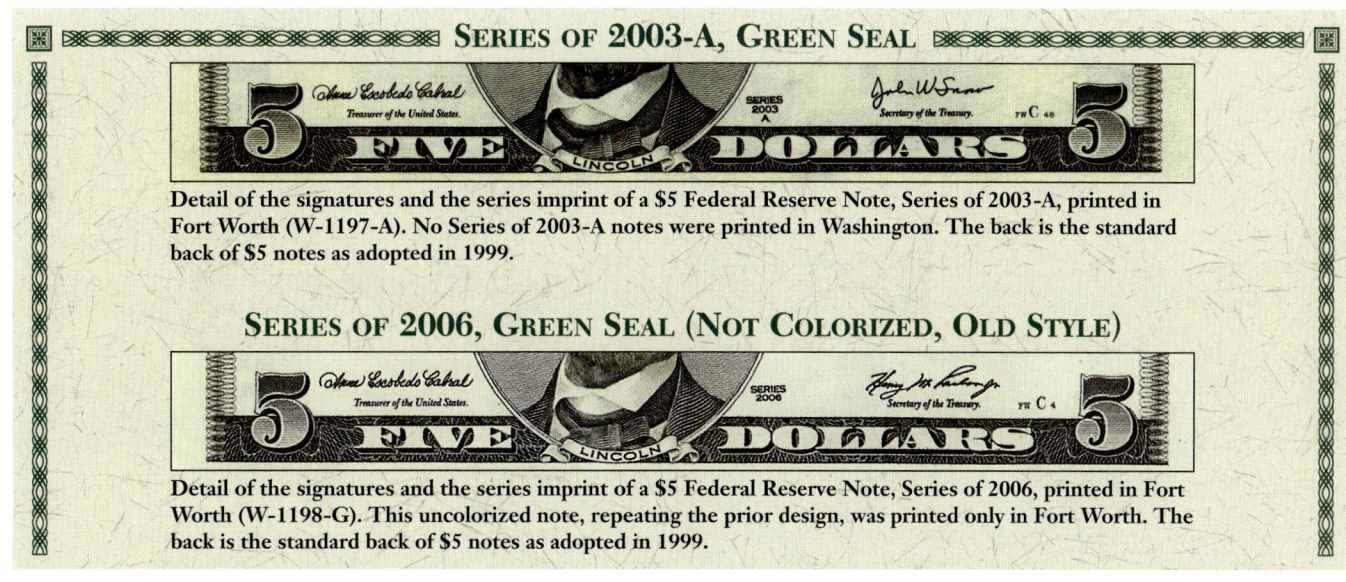

SERIES OF 2003-A, GREEN SEAL

Detail of the signatures and the series imprint of a $5 Federal Reserve Note, Series of 2003-A, printed in Fort Worth (W-1197-A). No Series of 2003-A notes were printed in Washington. The back is the standard back of $5 notes as adopted in 1999.

SERIES OF 2006, GREEN SEAL (NOT COLORIZED, OLD STYLE)

Detail of the signatures and the series imprint of a $5 Federal Reserve Note, Series of 2006, printed in Fort Worth (W-1198-G). This uncolorized note, repeating the prior design, was printed only in Fort Worth. The back is the standard back of $5 notes as adopted in 1999.

Serial numbers begin with I.

All Series of 2006 notes have been printed in Fort Worth. The information given here is accurate as of press time. No valuation charts are provided, as notes in this series can be had in top condition for face value at banks or from dealers (with a nominal handling charge).

W-1199-A • F-1993A • Boston

W-1199-A★ • F-1993A★

W-1199-B • F-1993B • New York

W-1199-C • F-1993C • Philadelphia

W-1199-D • F-1993D • Cleveland

W-1199-E • F-1993E • Richmond

W-1199-F • F-1993F • Atlanta

W-1199-F★ • F-1993F★

W-1199-G • F-1993G • Chicago

W-1199-H • F-1993H • St. Louis

W-1199-I • F-1993I • Minneapolis

W-1199-J • F-1993J • Kansas City

W-1199-K • F-1993K • Dallas

W-1199-L • F-1993L • San Francisco

W-1199-L★ • F-1993L★

Series of 2009, Green Seal
Rios-Geithner (2009–)

No printing information as of press time.

SERIES OF 2006, GREEN SEAL (COLORIZED)

$5 Federal Reserve Note, Series of 2006 (W-1199-E). Federal Reserve Bank of Richmond. Printed in Fort Worth.

Detail of the left field.

Detail of the right field.

Back of the $5 Federal Reserve Note, Series of 2006 (W-1199-E). The frame has been removed from around the Lincoln Memorial. A hint of pink-blue is now at the center, gold 05 denomination counters are in the upper right field, and a bright purple 5 is at the lower right.

Detail of the lower right side of the back, showing 05 denomination counters, plate number 23, and the purple counter.

$10 NOTES

LARGE SIZE

Large-size $10 notes offer an especially wide variety of types; this denomination introduced the Interest-Bearing Notes of 1863 and the Compound Interest Treasury Notes of 1863 and 1864, which were not seen on lower denominations. The Demand Notes of 1861 were continued. The $10 denomination also includes the curious and unique Refunding Certificates of 1879 (actually loan documents and not bank notes, but they are widely sought by currency specialists). In keeping with the general rule that the higher the denomination, the scarcer the note, currency of the $10 denomination is generally scarcer than $1, $2, and $5 notes. This is caused by a combination of two circumstances. First, in many instances fewer notes were printed of a given series or signature combination. Beyond that, due to the high face value, fewer were saved as souvenirs.

Today, most emphasis is on collecting by design type, followed by collecting series within that type, and then the ultimate of specialties—collecting by signature combinations and seal variations. Along the way there are many interesting things to contemplate, including different imprints for payable and guaranty provisions, star notes, and interesting plate characteristics, including mules.

DEMAND NOTES

Series of 1861

The face of the $10 Demand Note (illus. on p. 322) features the portrait of Abraham Lincoln, his first depiction on a federal note. The engraving was by Charles Burt, who utilized a photograph taken by C.S. German.[1] At the top is a stock vignette of an American eagle created by Toppan, Carpenter and Company for use on state bank notes, which was passed to the American Bank Note Company when the companies merged in 1858. To each side is a green "10" counter. To the right is a standing woman, an artist with a palette and drawing board, variously called Art or Painting. Patent imprints of 1857 and 1860, similar to those used on other Demand Notes, Legal Tender Notes, and certain other issues, refer respectively to the Patent Green Tint franchise held by the American Bank Note Company and the cycloidal configurations technique of the National Bank Note Company; both claimed to deter counterfeiting. Whether they did or not

can be argued, but these designs certainly made the notes more colorful. As a class, Demand Notes were issued from August 26, 1861, to March 5, 1862.

The locations of several Sub-Treasury offices—Boston, Cincinnati, New York, Philadelphia, and St. Louis—are printed near the bottom center. The original intent was for these bills to be hand-signed by the Treasurer of the United States and by the secretary of the Treasury. It is likely that some were, but no such examples are known today. This procedure proved to be impractical at the start, and a corps of 70 clerks was hired to do the signing, with the added notation "for the," to reflect that they were acting on behalf of the senior officials. Early varieties have "for the" added in ink, a procedure soon changed to printing the words. The inked "for the" versions are all extreme rarities today. Having dozens of other signature styles and names by upward of 70 employees negated any security benefit, and this routine was discontinued later. There is no Treasury seal. Today, all Demand Notes are very rare. Six of the seven face plates made for this series were later altered to print Series of 1862 Legal Tender Notes.

On the back the "greenback" design is largely geometrical and includes the counters X repeated many times and nearly three dozen TEN imprints.

W-1211 • F-8a • Boston • "for the" handwritten • No SERIES imprint • 29,000 (est.)
Recorded population: 2 • *Highest graded:* VG-8 • *Selected information:* Stack's (10/1990), 28329/A, VG, $17,600. CAA (10/1998), 28848/D, VG, $20,900.

W-1212 • F-8 • "for the" printed • 71,000 (est.)
Recorded population: 1 • *Selected information:* Heritage (9/2007), 55708/D, VG, pinholes, $3,737.

W-1213 • F-8 • Series 2 to 7 • 560,000
Estimated population: 42 to 45 • *Highest graded:* EF-45.

VG-8	F-12	VF-20	EF-40
$3,500	$6,500	$18,000	$35,000

W-1214 • F-9a • Cincinnati • "for the" handwritten • 11,000 (est.)
Recorded population: 1 • *Selected information:* B&M (5/1999), 10070/B, VF-30 (PMG), $86,250; 20183/C, VF-25, problems (PMG), sold in a Heritage auction (1/2008) for $172,500.

W-1215 • F-9 • "for the" printed • 64,000 (est.)

Recorded population: 6 • *Highest graded:* VF-25 • *Commentary:* This face plate was altered into New York plate number 2. • *Selected information:* The known notes are serials 20034/B, VG–F; 32357/A, Fine, sold in 1/1997 for $12,000; 34615/C, F–VF; 41910/B, part of the ANA Museum collection; 53647, Net VF-20 (PMG), sold in a Stack's auction (10/1990) for $10,450.

W-1216 • F-6a • New York • "for the" handwritten • No SERIES imprint • 28,000 (est.)

Recorded population: 5 • *Highest graded:* EF-45 • *Selected information:* The known notes are serials 18436/E, EF, sold in a Kreisberg & Schulman auction (3/1965) for $3,250; 21316/D, VF-20, damaged (PMG), sold in a Heritage auction (9/2008) for $54,625; 25606/B, a part of the ANA Museum collection; 27570/B, Fair; and 27927/C, VF, sold in a Knight auction (8/2005) for $36,800.

W-1217 • F-6 • "for the" printed • 72,000 (est.)

Recorded population: 4 • *Highest graded:* VF-20 • *Selected information:* The known notes are serials 45743/C, VF, sold in a Stack's auction (5/1992) for $2,400; 46479/C, VG–F, from the Robert Schermerhorn Collection in the 1950s; 62412/D, VG–F, sold in a Knight auction (6/1996) for $2,420; and 83647/C, VG, repaired, sold in a Spink auction (7/2007) for $1,260.

W-1218 • F-6 • Series 2 to 7 • 540,000

Estimated population: 45 to 50 • *Highest graded:* VF-30.

VG-8	F-12	VF-20
$3,500	$6,500	$18,000

W-1219 • F-7a • Philadelphia • "for the" handwritten • No SERIES imprint • 7,000 (est.)

Recorded population: 3 • *Selected information:* The known notes are serials 1/A, offered by New Netherlands in *The Numis-*

SERIES OF 1861

$10 Demand Note, Series of 1861, with rare handwritten "for the" (W-1216). Payable at New York. This is the general style used for W-1211 to W-1222. Most others were issued with "for the" printed.

Detail of W-1216 showing "for the" handwritten. $10 Demand Note of 1861 with "for the" printed (W-1212).

Back of the $10 Demand Note, Series of 1861 (W-1216).

matist (1/1971) as the first piece of U.S. currency issued, for $4,000; 5/A, AU, writing on the back, sold in a Knight auction (12/1998) for $64,500; and 6523/C, F-15 (PMG), sold in a Heritage auction (9/2008) for $97,750.

W-1220 • F-7 • "for the" printed • 93,000 (est.)

Recorded population: 4 • *Highest graded:* F-12 • *Commentary:* Population is uncertain, as the recording of series data was usually not done in the past. • *Selected information:* The known notes are serials 37495/C, VG, sold in a Hickman & Oakes auction (11/1982) for $766; 42841/A, Fine, part of the Smithsonian Institution collection; 68414/B, VG, sold in a Donlon auction (6/1974) for $875; and 85073/A, VG–F, sold in a Christie's auction (9/1994) as "VG" for $1,210, later sold in a Knight auction (2/1995) as VF for $1,870.

W-1221 • F-7 • Series 2 to 6 • 480,000

Estimated population: 50 to 55 • *Highest graded:* EF-45.

VG-8	F-12	VF-20	EF-40
$3,500	$6,500	$18,000	—

W-1222 • F-10a • St. Louis • "for the" handwritten • 1,000 (est.) • Unknown

W-1222 • F-10 • "for the" printed • 47,000 (est.)

Recorded population: 4 • *Highest graded:* VG-8 • *Commentary:* This face plate altered into Boston plate number 2. A deceptive counterfeit of this issue was made.[2] • *Selected information:* The known notes are serials 31133/A, in the ANA Museum collection; 35202/B, VG, repaired, sold in a B&M auction (5/1999) for $46,000; 41122/B, VG, sold in a Hickman & Oakes auction (9/1989) for $24,000; and 47760/D.

INTEREST-BEARING NOTES

March 3, 1863, 5% Interest, 1 Year

Interest-Bearing Notes (illus. on p. 324) were issued under the Act of March 3, 1863, and entitled the bearer to interest for one year at the rate of 5%. The face has a portrait of Salmon P. Chase at the left, an eagle at the center (here titled *Eagle, Flag, and Capitol*, though it was also called *Eagle and the Capitol* and later known as the *Eagle of the Capitol* vignette used on the $1 Silver Certificates, Series of 1899), and a standing woman, Peace. The same motifs were used on $10 Compound Interest Treasury Notes.

Starting dates for the interest clock were imprinted on the face, and seem to commence on February 1, 1864, with W-1226, continuing to April 1 of the same year, while notes of W-1228 overlap and are known with dates ranging from March 9, 1864, to May 30, 1864. These were sold at a discount, to reflect the interest, and redeemed at face value upon maturity.

From the 620,000 issued, only slightly more than 500 are outstanding today per Treasury records. There are two varieties, one imprinted by the American Bank Note Company (W-1226) and the other bearing the imprint of the Treasury department (W-1228). The Treasury imprint reflects that the plates were made in Washington, but using transfer rolls supplied by American. All bear a red Treasury seal and the printed signatures of Chittenden and Spinner.

These were popular investments at the time, even bought by state-chartered banks, who added these and other interest-bearing federal obligations to their portfolio, thought to be a safe haven in times of economic uncertainty. In due course, nearly all interest-bearing notes were redeemed and destroyed. Today, fewer than 50 remain. Most show extensive wear.

W-1226 • F-196 • AMERICAN BANK NOTE COMPANY, N.Y. imprint • 620,000

Estimated population: 9 or 10 • *Highest graded:* EF-40 • *Commentary:* Dates of issuance vary within the year 1864. • *Selected information:* CAA (5/2005), 979/D, EF, $19,550. Knight (11/2006), 5442/B, VF, $14,950. Knight (10/2006), 72459/C, F–VF, $10,925.

W-1228 • F-196a • ENGRAVED AND PRINTED IN THE TREASURY DEPARTMENT • Included in printage above

Estimated population: 35 to 40 • *Highest graded:* Unc.

VG-8	F-12	VF-20	EF-40	AU-50	Unc-60
$4,200	$8,000	$20,000	$33,000	$50,000	—

COMPOUND INTEREST TREASURY NOTES OF 1864

Similar to certain other currency, Compound Interest Treasury Notes (illus. on p. 325) were intended to raise money to fight the Civil War. They were printed by the National Currency Bureau in the Treasury Building and were made in denominations up to $1,000. The face has the same motifs as the $10 Interest-Bearing Notes of 1863, with Salmon P. Chase, *Eagle of the Capitol*, and Peace.

Compound Interest Treasury Notes of the $10 denomination were issued under the Acts of March 3, 1863, and June 30, 1864. W-1234 has an erroneous act date entered on it, July 2, 1864. Notes bore interest at the rate of 6% a year, for three years. When each note was given out it had the issue date stamped on it in red. Accordingly, these vary among notes examined today. All notes in this series were printed on four-subject plates lettered A to D, each with the same serial number. The highest-issued, provable printage can be calculated by multiplying the highest known serial by four. These are slightly larger than Legal Tender Notes and measure 3.5 inches by 7.5 inches.

The face is similar in design to the Interest-Bearing Notes of 1863, except for the imprint COMPOUND INTEREST TREASURY NOTE in bronzing powder, thought to be a deterrent to counterfeiting, but very difficult to apply. In the Treasury Building a special room was set aside for this purpose. This was the first impression to be made on the sheet, although it is sometimes referred to as an "overprint."[3] The bronzing powder, most familiarly used on Fractional Currency, tended to flake and deteriorate, with the result that many extant notes have imperfect imprints.

On the back, printed in green, is a schedule of redemption; the bill's value would total $11.94 if it were held for the full three years. Bills of this type were mostly bought as investments by financiers and banking institutions, not used in general commerce by the public. As these bills did not accrue interest after the expiration date, most were redeemed at the

MARCH 3, 1863, 5% INTEREST, 1 YEAR

$10 Interest-Bearing Note of 1863 with AMERICAN BANK NOTE COMPANY imprinted (W-1226). Dated February 29, 1864 (dates vary among notes). Serial 3979, plate D. This style was also used for W-1228, except that the latter was imprinted ENGRAVED AND PRINTED IN THE TREASURY DEPARTMENT. The portrait of secretary of the Treasury Salmon P. Chase is to the left, *Eagle of the Capitol* is at the center, and the goddess of Peace is to the right.

Detail of W-1226 showing the AMERICAN BANK NOTE COMPANY imprint, partially covered by the Treasury seal, and the day and month date. The Treasury seal is of an unusual style, without closely spaced radial lines inside the inner border.

Back of the $10 Interest-Bearing Note of 1863 (W-1226).

end of three years. Interest on the bills authorized in 1863 ceased on June 10, 1867, and interest on those authorized in 1864 ceased on May 16, 1868, although any bill issued after May 16, 1865, would still have some time to run.

At the expiration of the interest period, nearly all were turned in to the Treasury department. Of the 677,940 issued—a truly incredible quantity—only 2,171 remain unredeemed today. Fewer than 150 of these have been identified in numismatic hands. Most extant examples show extensive wear, which invites further investigation, as one would think that most such notes were put away and saved.

W-1230 • F-190 • Chittenden-Spinner (1861–1864) • "Act of March 3d 1864" • Red overprint, JUNE 10, 1864 • 2,328,520

Estimated population: 16 to 18 • Highest graded: EF-40.

VG-8	F-12	VF-20	EF-40
$2,200	$4,300	$10,000	$17,500

COMPOUND INTEREST TREASURY NOTE OF 1864

$10 Compound Interest Treasury Note of 1864 (W-1236). The $10 Interest-Bearing Notes of the same era have a related design. The special imprint was made by applying bronzing powder to blank sheets as the first step in the printing process. Such bronzing was also used on certain Fractional Currency. Serial 84617, plate C9. Issued on August 15, 1864.

Details on the face of W-1236. In the Treasury seal the inscription is punctuated with stars, as usual, but without tiny radial lines within the inner border.

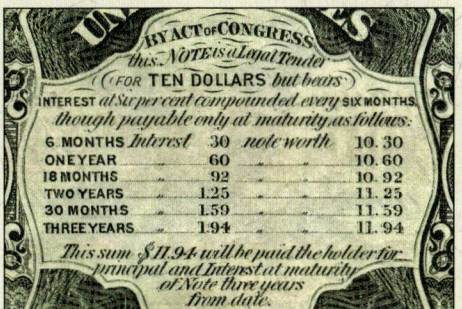

Interest payment schedule on the back of W-1236.

Back of the $10 Compound Interest Treasury Note of 1864 (W-1236).

W-1232 • F-190a • "Act of June 10th 1864" • Red overprint, JULY 15, 1864 • Included in printage above
Estimated population: 21 to 24 • *Highest graded:* AU-50.

VG-8	F-12	VF-20	EF-40	AU-50
$2,000	$4,000	$11,000	—	—

W-1234 • F-190a • "Act of July 2d 1864" (error date) • Red overprint, JULY 15, 1864 • Included in printage above
Recorded population: 4 • *Highest graded:* VF-20 • *Commentary:* Discovered by Mark Hotz in 1990 (8275/B, VF). A similar error was made for $50 notes and perhaps $20s.[4] • *Selected information:* Heritage (1/2008), 9592/C VF (PMG), $13,800.

W-1236 • F-190b • Colby-Spinner (1864–1867) • "Act of June 10th 1864" • Included in printage above

Estimated population: 110 to 120 • *Highest graded:* Unc • *Commentary:* Red overprint dates reported include Aug. 15, 1864; Oct. 15, 1864; and Dec. 15, 1864.

VG-8	F-12	VF-20	EF-40	AU-50	Unc-60
$2,000	$4,000	$10,500	$16,500	—	—

LEGAL TENDER NOTES
(Also Known as United States Notes)

Series of 1862, First Obligation

The Series of 1862 $10 Legal Tender Notes, also called United States Notes, were made in substantial quantities and were first issued on April 2 of that year. The face motifs are similar to those used on the 1861 Demand Notes, but Legal Tender Notes have a red Treasury seal, and imprints differ. The face, back, and tint plates for the $10 Series of 1862 and 1863 Legal Tender Notes were engraved by the American Bank Note Company. National Bank Note Company printed most (if not all) of the First Obligation notes. American and National shared the printing for the Second Obligation notes.[5] Chittenden and Spinner's signatures were printed on the face using a separate plate and a special ink.

Various differences exist, including face arrangements and First Obligation and Second Obligation backs.

First Obligation: This wording, with different typography on various denominations, states the note is exchangeable for bonds (a provision dropped from the Second Obligation): "This note is a Legal Tender for all debts public and private, except for duties on imports and interest on the public debt, and is exchangeable for U.S. six percent twenty years bonds redeemable at the pleasure of the U. States after five years." These "6-20" bonds or "six twenties," as they were known, were a popular investment for banks and the public.

These were issued in 63 series, numbered on the face from 1 to 63, with each series beginning with serial 1 and going up to 100,000. AMERICAN BANK NOTE CO. NEW YORK is in the top border, and at lower left in italic letters is PRINTED BY THE NATIONAL BANK NOTE CO.

Technical note: Six of the seven $10 Demand Note face plates were reworked into $10 1862 Legal Tender Note face plates, numbered 1 through 6. These plates lack the starburst in the bottom border.

Today examples are easily collected in circulated grades, although they are hardly common. While the imprint varieties are interesting to contemplate, most numismatists simply seek one example to illustrate the type.

W-1251 • F-93a • *Printed on plate:* "Act of Feb'y 25th 1862 / March 10, 1862" • AMERICAN BANK NOTE CO. N.Y. at top border, PRINTED BY THE NATIONAL BANK NOTE CO at lower left • Treasury seal at upper right corner • No starburst ornament in bottom border • Series 1 • 78,000 (est.)

Recorded population: 5 • *Highest graded:* F-12 • *Selected information:* No modern auction sales.

W-1252 • F-93b • Treasury seal nearly centered at far right • PATENTED 30 JUNE 1857 at lower center below large green imprint • Series 1 to 9 • 120,000 (est.)

Recorded population: 9 • *Highest graded:* VF-25 • *Commentary:* New listing without market history. Future editions will give pricing information to the extent that it becomes available.

W-1253 • F-93b • As W-1252, but without patent date, overprint plate error • Printed within the production of W-1252, Series 5 to 7 • Small percentage of above printage

Recorded population: 4 • *Highest graded:* VG–F • *Commentary:* New listing without market history. Future editions will give pricing information to the extent that it becomes available.

W-1254 • F-93 • With patent date • Starburst ornament in bottom border • Series 1 to 25 (number after) • 2,302,000 (est.)

Estimated population: 80 to 100 • *Highest graded:* Unc.

VG-8	F-12	VF-20	EF-40	AU-50	Unc-60	Unc-63	Unc-65
$775	$1,175	$1,650	$2,700	$3,700	$4,650	$5,500	$18,000

W-1255 • F-93 • As W-1254 but without patent date

Recorded population: 1 • *Graded:* Fine • *Commentary:* Discovered Memphis 2009.

W-1256 • F-93 • With patent date • Treasury seal without inner border of radial parallel lines • Series 26 to 28 (number above) • 220,000 (est.)

Estimated population: 15 to 25 • *Commentary:* New listing without market history. Future editions will give pricing information to the extent that it becomes available.

W-1257 • F-93 • Treasury seal with inner border of radial parallel lines • Series 28 to 63 • 3,580,000 (est.)

Estimated population: 130 to 150 • *Highest graded:* Unc.

VG-8	F-12	VF-20	EF-40	AU-50	Unc-60	Unc-63	Unc-65
$775	$1,175	$1,650	$2,700	$3,700	$4,650	$5,500	$18,000

Series of 1862 and 1863, Second Obligation

All Legal Tender Notes of the early 1860s, $5 to $1,000 denominations, with Second Obligation backs (illus. on p. 328) have NEW SERIES printed on the face.

Second Obligation: "This note is a Legal Tender for all debts public and private, except for duties on imports and interest on the public debt, and is receivable in payment of all loans made to the United States." This wording, with different typography on the various denominations, does not mention exchanging the notes for 6-20 bonds and thus is different from the First Obligation.

W-1260 • F-94 • *Printed on plate:* "Act of Feb'y 25th 1862 / March 10th 1862" • AMERICAN BANK NOTE CO. NEW YORK at top border, and NATIONAL BANK NOTE CO. above bottom border • Second Obligation back • New Series 1 to 14 • 1,400,000

Estimated population: 50 to 60 • *Highest graded:* Unc.

VG-8	F-12	VF-20	EF-40	AU-50	Unc-60	Unc-63	Unc-65
$1,000	$1,500	$2,100	$3,300	$4,400	$5,600	$7,250	—

SERIES OF 1862, FIRST OBLIGATION

$10 Legal Tender Note, Series of 1862 (W-1256). Portrait of President Lincoln at the left, an eagle and shield at the center, and a goddess representing Art at the right, similar to the motifs on Demand Notes. On the illustrated example the Treasury seal is pink, probably from slight fading.

Detail of W-1256 showing serial number, series information, and plate identification.

Starburst ornament in bottom border of W-1256.

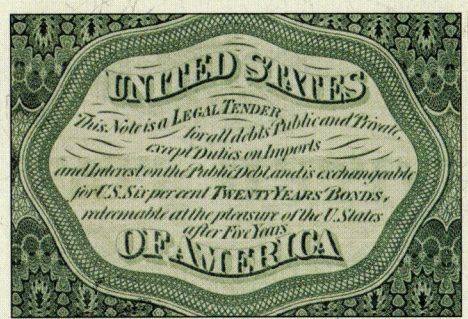

Detail of the First Obligation imprint.

Back of the $10 Legal Tender Note, Series of 1862 (W-1256), with First Obligation wording and style.

W-1261 • *F-95* • *Printed on plate:* "Act of March 3d 1863 / March 10th 1863" • 1857 patent date • New Series 15 to 40 • 2,530,504
Estimated population: 55 to 60 • *Highest graded:* Unc.

VG-8	F-12	VF-20	EF-40	AU-50	Unc-60	Unc-63
$1,000	$1,500	$2,100	$3,300	—	—	$10,000

W-1262 • *F-95* • *Printed on plate:* "March 10th 1863" • 1863 patent date • New Series 40 to 44 • 370,000
Estimated population: 11 to 15 • *Highest graded:* Unc • *Commentary:* New listing without market history. Future editions will give pricing information to the extent that it becomes available.

SERIES OF 1862 AND 1863, SECOND OBLIGATION

$10 Legal Tender Note, Series of 1863 (W-1264), a design similar to that used on the preceding type and on W-1260 to W-1264. New Series 54, plate A-11, serial 62893.

Detail of stylistic "n" on the face of W-1264, for the National Bank Note Company.

Detail of the Second Obligation imprint.

Back of the $10 Legal Tender Note, Series of 1863 (W-1264), with Second Obligation wording and style.

W-1263 • F-95a • AMERICAN BANK NOTE CO. NEW YORK above bottom border • One serial number • New Series 44 to 48 • 400,000

Estimated population: 35 to 40 • *Highest graded:* Unc.

VG-8	F-12	VF-20	EF-40	AU-50	Unc-60	Unc-63
$1,000	$1,500	$2,100	$3,300	$4,400	$6,000	$10,000

W-1264 • F-95b • Stylized "n" for National Bank Note Company • Two serial numbers • New Series 48 to 56 • 800,496

Estimated population: 165 to 180 • *Highest graded:* Unc.

VG-8	F-12	VF-20	EF-40	AU-50	Unc-60	Unc-63	Unc-65
$775	$1,175	$1,650	$2,700	$3,700	$4,600	$5,500	$16,000

Series of 1869

This is the highest denomination in the "Rainbow Note" series, completing a suite that also includes the $1, $2, and $5 notes. The "Rainbow" feature is caused by the green overprint, in addition to the other colors, not found on

SERIES OF 1869

$10 Legal Tender Note, Series of 1869 (W-1275). This is the highest denomination in the "Rainbow Note" series. Vignettes depict Daniel Webster to the left, and to the right, Indian princess Pocahontas being presented to European and other dignitaries. At the lower center is an eagle, which if viewed upside down resembles a jackass. Notes of this issue, as well as those of the next type (with a different back), are often called "Jackass Notes."

The eagle on the Series of 1869 note when viewed upside down resembles the head of a jackass. This eagle also appeared on certain later notes and on Fractional Currency Shields, among other places.

Back of the $10 Legal Tender Note, Series of 1869 (W-1275), with extensive engraving.

higher denominations in the Series of 1869. Tinted blue paper (1866 Willcox patent) adds to the color.

On the left of the face of the $10 obverse is a portrait, engraved by Alfred Sealey, of Daniel Webster, a New Hampshire native who gained prominence as an orator and statesman, holding a number of public offices, including senator and secretary of state. To the right is a vignette of the Indian maiden Pocahontas, her face modestly turned slightly down, being introduced to an assemblage of Europeans, ranging from a princess or queen in a large chair, to a Turk sitting on the ground smoking a long pipe. This motif has been vari-

ously titled *Introduction of the Old World to the New* (Treasury department nomenclature), or *Pocahontas Presented at Court*. A related depiction, also called *Introduction of the Old World to the New*, was used on the face of $5 National Bank Notes of the Original and Series of 1875. *The Baptism of Pocahontas*, entirely different from either of the preceding, is the vignette on the back of the $20 Original and Series of 1875 National Bank Notes.

At the center bottom is a perched American eagle, the same design as used on the top of Fractional Currency Shields. When turned upside down it resembles the head of a donkey, giving this the popular name of "Jackass Note." This particular bird was used on Legal Tender Notes through the Series of 1880.

The eye-pleasing back of the Series of 1869 notes consists of three sections in rich green. At the center is a lot of technical wording. Such inscriptions, common to other notes as well, generally tell what such bills can and cannot be used for—not all were legal tender for everything. As a class, Series of 1869 notes were issued from October 19, 1869, to July 25, 1874.

W-1275 • F-96 • Allison-Spinner (1869–1875) • Large pink seal • 8,376,000

Estimated population: 500 to 600 • *Highest graded:* Unc.

VG-8	F-12	VF-20	EF-40	AU-50	Unc-60	Unc-63	Unc-65
$500	$800	$1,150	$1,700	$2,750	$3,400	$5,300	$14,000

Series of 1875

The face is nearly the same as the Series of 1869 notes, but without the green overprint. Serial numbers are no longer followed by a decorative star (an E-shaped element now appears).

The Series of 1875 notes have a redesigned back. COLUMBIAN BANK NOTE is part of top border design, and COMPANY WASHINGTON, D.C. is part of the bottom border. As a class, Series of 1875 notes were issued from July 20, 1875, to June 20, 1879.

Regarding the curious insertion of Series of 1875-A before Series of 1875, Doug Murray commented:

In theory, the first 1,000,000 were to be Series A, the next 1,000,000 Series B, as in the lower denominations. The $10's have this anomaly where they either forgot to change at one million, or the concept of identifying each

SERIES OF 1875

$10 Legal Tender Note, Series of 1875 with A imprint (W-1276).

Details of the A imprint near the top and bottom borders. At the top, above D (UNITED) is a light pink SERIES A 1875 in a circular arrangement. At the bottom below the eagle is SERIES A 1875.

Back of the $10 Legal Tender Note, Series of 1875 (W-1276).

million was abandoned and they went into the second million as Series A. The whole concept was eventually scrapped, as the notes were continually printed without the Series designation, starting at 1.5 million. This serial numbering oddity has always puzzled me as it is the only case where the one million serial rule was not followed.

Accordingly, the A is simply a designation within a numbering system and is not a series in the normal sense.

W-1276 • F-98 • Allison-New (1875–1876) • SERIES A 1875 imprint in pink • Small pink seal with spiked border • 1,500,000

Estimated population: 35 to 40 • *Highest graded:* Unc.

VG-8	F-12	VF-20	EF-40	AU-50	Unc-60	Unc-63	Unc-65
$670	$1,200	$2,000	$2,400	$3,100	$3,600	$6,800	$25,000

W-1277 • F-97 • 866,000 • No series designation

Estimated population: 12 to 14 • *Highest graded:* AU-50.

VG-8	F-12	VF-20	EF-40	AU-50
$4,000	$6,750	$10,000	$15,000	$30,000

Series of 1878

General designs as the preceding. The back now has PRINTED AT THE BUREAU ENGRAVING AND PRINTING at the center bottom border. SERIES OF 1878 vertically at the left border. COLUMBIAN BANK NOTE as part of top border design and COMPANY WASHINGTON, D.C. as part of the bottom still remain.

W-1278 • F-99 • Allison-Gilfillan (1877–1878) • Small red seal with spiked border • 2,600,000 (est.)

Estimated population: 85 to 95 • *Highest graded:* Unc • *Commentary:* The very last printed had a security paper change from a vertical to a horizontal blue stain with fibers across entire length.

VG-8	F-12	VF-20	EF-40	AU-50	Unc-60	Unc-63	Unc-65
$450	$750	$1,050	$1,500	$2,400	$3,600	$6,750	$12,000

Series of 1880

Notes W-1279 to W-1282 have red serial numbers; those in this range with a large brown Treasury seal have serial numbers beginning with Z. Beginning with W-1283 all serial numbers in the Series of 1880 (illus. on p. 332) begin with A. W-1283 to W-1293 have blue serial numbers.

Back Style 1: With COLUMBIAN BANK NOTE CO. imprinted twice at the bottom edge of the design (style used on Series 1874, 1875, and 1878). Now with SERIES OF 1880 in the left margin and repeated

SERIES OF 1878

$10 Legal Tender Note, Series of 1878 (W-1278).

Back of the $10 Legal Tender Note, Series of 1878 (W-1278), similar in overall design to the preceding.

SERIES OF 1880

$10 Legal Tender Note, Series of 1880 (W-1283), with blue serial numbers.

$10 Legal Tender Note, Series of 1880 (W-1286), showing later style with spiked border on Treasury seal.

vertically in the right margin. In the bottom margin is PRINTED AT THE BUREAU, ENGRAVING AND PRINTING. Used on W-1279 to W-1282 (partial).

Back Style 2: As preceding, but now with SERIES OF 1880 vertically in the open space on the left and no wording in either the right or the left margin. Used on W-1282 (partial) and W-1283.

Back Style 3: PRINTED AT THE BUREAU OF ENGRAVING AND PRINTING curved at the top within the open space to the left, and SERIES OF 1880 curved at the bottom. Used on W-1284 to W-1293.

W-1279 • F-100 • Scofield-Gilfillan (1878–1881) • Large brown seal, red serial numbers • 1,800,000 (est.)

Estimated population: 100 to 140 • *Highest graded:* Unc.

VG-8	F-12	VF-20	EF-40	AU-50	Unc-60	Unc-63	Unc-65
$310	$550	$800	$1,100	$1,550	$1,800	$2,350	$4,500

W-1281 • F-101 • Bruce-Gilfillan (1881–1883) • 1,700,000 (est.)

Estimated population: 50 to 55 • *Highest graded:* Unc.

VG-8	F-12	VF-20	EF-40	AU-50	Unc-60	Unc-63	Unc-65
$310	$550	$800	$1,100	$1,550	$1,800	$2,350	$4,500

W-1282 Back Style 1 • F-102 • Bruce-Wyman (1883–1885) • 2,664,000 (est.)

Estimated population: 110 to 120 • *Highest graded:* Unc.

VG-8	F-12	VF-20	EF-40	AU-50	Unc-60	Unc-63	Unc-65
$310	$550	$800	$1,100	$1,550	$1,800	$2,350	$4,000

W-1282 Back Style 2 • F-102 • Part of W-1282 Back Style 1 printage

Estimated population: Included above • *Highest graded:* Included above • *Commentary:* New listing without market history. Future editions will give pricing information to the extent that it becomes available.

W-1283 • F-103 • Large light red or pink seal with plain border, blue serial numbers • 972,000

Estimated population: 115 to 125 • *Highest graded:* Unc.

VG-8	F-12	VF-20	EF-40	AU-50	Unc-60	Unc-63	Unc-65
$375	$625	$900	$1,200	$1,650	$1,900	$2,600	$3,900

W-1284 • F-104 • Rosecrans-Jordan (1885–1887) • Large light red or pink seal with plain border • Back Style 3 begins • 1,288,000 (est.)

Estimated population: 48 to 54 • *Highest graded:* Unc.

VG-8	F-12	VF-20	EF-40	AU-50	Unc-60	Unc-63	Unc-65
$475	$750	$1,100	$1,600	$2,000	$2,400	$3,000	$5,000

SERIES OF 1880,
continued

$10 Legal Tender Note, Series of 1880, Back Style 1 (W-1282).

$10 Legal Tender Note, Series of 1880, Back Style 2 (W-1283).

$10 Legal Tender Note, Series of 1880, Back Style 3 (W-1286).

W-1285 • F-105 • Rosecrans-Hyatt (1887–1889) • Large peach or pink seal with plain border • 1,440,000 (est.)

Estimated population: 65 to 70 • *Highest graded:* Unc.

VG-8	F-12	VF-20	EF-40	AU-50	Unc-60	Unc-63	Unc-65
$500	$800	$1,175	$1,750	$2,250	$2,600	$3,300	$5,800

W-1286 • F-106 • Large light red or pink seal with spiked border • 2,540,000 (est.)

Estimated population: 110 to 120 • *Highest graded:* Unc.

VG-8	F-12	VF-20	EF-40	AU-50	Unc-60	Unc-63	Unc-65
$310	$525	$800	$1,100	$1,600	$2,000	$2,500	$4,000

W-1287 • F-107 • **Large red seal with spiked border** • **2,652,000 (est.)**

Estimated population: 135 to 150 • *Highest graded:* Unc.

VG-8	F-12	VF-20	EF-40	AU-50	Unc-60	Unc-63	Unc-65
$310	$525	$800	$1,100	$1,600	$2,000	$2,500	$4,000

W-1288 • F-108 • **Large brown seal** • **1,708,000 (est.)**

Estimated population: 115 to 125 • *Highest graded:* Unc.

VG-8	F-12	VF-20	EF-40	AU-50	Unc-60	Unc-63	Unc-65
$310	$525	$800	$1,100	$1,600	$2,000	$2,500	$4,000

W-1289 • F-109 • **Rosecrans-Nebeker (1891–1893)** • **100,000 (est.)**

Recorded population: 2 • *Highest graded:* EF-45 • *Selected information:* CAA (9/2006), A10663929/A, VF, $184,000. Knight (6/1999), A10689887/C, EF-AU, $74,800.

W-1290 • F-110 • **Small red seal with scalloped border** • **3,500,000 (est.)**

Estimated population: 110 to 120 • *Highest graded:* Unc • *Commentary:* Two security paper types were used. Early type 1 has two horizontal threads the entire width of note. Later type 2 has two vertical bands of distributed red and blue fibers.

VG-8	F-12	VF-20	EF-40	AU-50	Unc-60	Unc-63	Unc-65
$300	$520	$750	$1,150	$1,450	$1,800	$2,150	$3,800

W-1291 • F-111 • **Tillman-Morgan (1893–1897)** • **9,200,000 (est.)**

Estimated population: 220 to 235 • *Highest graded:* Unc.

VG-8	F-12	VF-20	EF-40	AU-50	Unc-60	Unc-63	Unc-65
$300	$520	$750	$1,150	$1,450	$1,800	$2,150	$3,400

W-1292 • F-112 • **Bruce-Roberts (1897–1898)** • **1,900,000 (est.)**

Estimated population: 45 to 50 • *Highest graded:* Unc.

VG-8	F-12	VF-20	EF-40	AU-50	Unc-60	Unc-63
$400	$700	$1,000	$2,000	$4,000	$5,000	$6,000

W-1293 • F-113 • **Lyons-Roberts (1898–1905)** • **11,876,000 (est.)**

Estimated population: 325 to 375 • *Highest graded:* Unc.

VG-8	F-12	VF-20	EF-40	AU-50	Unc-60	Unc-63	Unc-65
$300	$520	$750	$1,150	$1,450	$1,800	$2,150	$3,400

Series of 1901

The Series of 1901 "Bison Note," as it is known, is sometimes humorously called the "Buffalo Bill." The animal was sketched by Charles Knight and engraved by M.S. Baldwin. Knight was well known for his talents in sketching and painting wildlife as well as representations of prehistoric animals. A depiction of this particular bison can be found on a 30¢ postage stamp of 1923, among other places. Pablo, the bison pictured, was officially known as National Zoological Park Bison no. 2926. This animal, which arrived on October 23, 1897,[6] was purchased for $500 from Michael Pablo, a rancher from Ronan, Montana. Pablo the bison died on October 3, 1914. To each side are portraits of explorers Meriwether Lewis and William Clark To the right of the

portrait on the left side of the face is a large red X with TEN superimposed. All have small red seals with scalloped borders and red serial numbers.

The back of the note, titled *Progress*, shows Columbia, seemingly representative of agriculture, standing flanked by two mostly open blank panes. The vignette was the work of G.F.C. Smillie.

W-1294 • F-114 • **Lyons-Roberts (1898–1905)** • **47,140,000 (est.)**

Estimated population: 400 to 500 • *Highest graded:* Unc.

VG-8	F-12	VF-20	EF-40	AU-50	Unc-60	Unc-63	Unc-65
$575	$775	$1,275	$2,450	$3,600	$4,400	$5,250	$10,000

W-1295 • F-115 • **Lyons-Treat (1905–1906)** • **11,060,000 (est.)**

Estimated population: 130 to 150 • *Highest graded:* Unc.

VG-8	F-12	VF-20	EF-40	AU-50	Unc-60	Unc-63	Unc-65
$575	$775	$1,275	$2,450	$3,600	$4,400	$5,250	$11,500

W-1296 • F-116 • **Vernon-Treat (1906–1909)** • **15,330,000 (est.)**

Estimated population: 165 to 180 • *Highest graded:* Unc.

VG-8	F-12	VF-20	EF-40	AU-50	Unc-60	Unc-63	Unc-65
$575	$775	$1,275	$2,450	$3,600	$4,400	$5,250	$12,000

W-1297 • F-117 • **Vernon-McClung (1909–1911)** • **5,760,000**

Estimated population: 95 to 115 • *Highest graded:* Unc • *Commentary:* Printing ended on July 26, 1911.

VG-8	F-12	VF-20	EF-40	AU-50	Unc-60	Unc-63	Unc-65
$575	$775	$1,275	$2,450	$4,800	$6,200	$7,900	$20,000

W-1297★ • F-117★

Recorded population: 3 • *Highest graded:* AU-50 • *Selected information:* The known notes are serials ★1664B/D, EF, sold in a Stack's auction (9/1992) for $1,500; ★3685B/A, Fine, sold in a CAA auction (9/2006) for $6,900; and ★9231B/C, AU, listed by Doug Murray.

W-1298 • F-118 • **Napier-McClung (1911–1912)** • **8,476,000**

Estimated population: 120 to 130 • *Highest graded:* Unc • *Commentary:* Deliveries began on July 26, 1911, and ended on January 3, 1914.

VG-8	F-12	VF-20	EF-40	AU-50	Unc-60	Unc-63	Unc-65
$575	$775	$1,275	$2,450	$3,600	$4,400	$5,250	$14,000

W-1298★ • F-118★

Recorded population: 3 • *Highest graded:* Unc • *Selected information:* CAA (1/1999), ★30990B/B, Unc, $13,200. CAA (1/2005), ★62574B/B, AU, $9,775. CAA (4/2006), ★63655B/C, VF-20 (PCGS), $14,950.

W-1299 • F-119 • **Parker-Burke (1913–1914)** • **11,592,000**

Estimated population: 275 to 325 • *Highest graded:* Unc • *Commentary:* Deliveries began on January 4, 1914, and ended on April 28, 1917.

VG-8	F-12	VF-20	EF-40	AU-50	Unc-60	Unc-63	Unc-65
$575	$775	$1,275	$2,450	$3,600	$4,400	$5,250	$12,000

W-1299★ • F-119★

Recorded population: 2 • *Highest graded:* EF-45 • *Selected information:* Knight (6/2008), ★87519B/C, F-12, $7,475. CAA (11/1992), ★138836B/D, EF–AU, $1,705.

W-1300 • F-120 • Teehee-Burke (1915–1919) • 4,776,000 (est.)

Estimated population: 225 to 250 • *Highest graded:* Unc.

VG-8	F-12	VF-20	EF-40	AU-50	Unc-60	Unc-63	Unc-65
$525	$725	$1,175	$2,250	$3,450	$4,150	$5,000	$10,000

W-1300★ • F-120★

Estimated population: 10 to 12 • *Highest graded:* Unc • *Selected information:* CAA (1/2004), ★142916B/D, Unc, $16,100. Knight (6/2008), ★148004B/D, F-12 (PMG), $2,645. Hickman & Oakes (11/1986), ★179619B/C, VG, $291. Knight (11/2007), ★180214B/B, F-12 (PCGS), $3,221.15. Knight (6/2008), ★205575B, EF-40 (PCGS), $9,200. CAA (5/2005), ★232096B/D, VG, $3,450.

W-1301 • F-121 • Elliott-White (1921–1922) • 500,000, or about 6% regular (est.)

Estimated population: 30 to 36 • *Highest graded:* Possibly included in W-1201 mule below • *Commentary:* Because this note is rarer than its mule counterpart, its previous pricing is now assigned to the new mule listing. The non-mule note will be monitored for expected pricing upswings due to its increased rarity.

W-1301 Mule • F-121 • 7,636,000, or about 94% mules (est.)

Estimated population: 550 to 650 • *Highest graded:* Unc.

VG-8	F-12	VF-20	EF-40	AU-50	Unc-60	Unc-63	Unc-65
$575	$775	$1,250	$2,400	$3,650	$4,350	$5,350	$11,000

SERIES OF 1901

$10 Legal Tender Note, Series of 1901, the "Bison Note" (W-1295). Illustrated is a numismatic prize, a serial number 1 note with plate letter A.

Back of the $10 Legal Tender Note, Series of 1901 (W-1295). The standing figure of Columbia is at the center.

Back Plate Location 1.

Back Plate Location 2.

W-1301 Mule★ • F-121★

Estimated population: 35 to 40 • *Highest graded:* Unc • *Commentary:* All stars are mule stars.

F-12	VF-20	EF-40	AU-50	Unc-60	Unc-63
$2,500	$4,000	$6,000	$8,500	—	$15,000

W-1302 • F-122 • Speelman-White (1922–1927) • 34,688,000, or about 95% regular (est.)

Estimated population: 1,500 to 1,700 • *Highest graded:* Unc.

VG-8	F-12	VF-20	EF-40	AU-50	Unc-60	Unc-63	Unc-65
$525	$725	$1,175	$2,250	$3,450	$4,150	$5,000	$10,000

W-1302★ • F-122★

Estimated population: 55 to 58 • *Highest graded:* Unc.

F-12	VF-20	EF-40	AU-50	Unc-60	Unc-63
$2,200	$3,700	$5,800	$8,200	—	$15,500

W-1302 Mule • F-122 • 2,000,000, or about 5% mules (est.)

Estimated population: 90 to 110 • *Highest graded:* Unc • *Commentary:* New listing without market history. Future editions will give pricing information.

W-1302 Mule★ • F-122★

Estimated population: 11 to 13 • *Highest graded:* Unc.

Series of 1923

The Series of 1923 $10 note was printed in relatively small numbers compared to the predecessor design. Featured at the center of the face is a familiar portrait of Andrew Jackson, engraved by Alfred Sealey. At the right of the face is a large red X with TEN superimposed. A small red Treasury seal with a scalloped border is to the left, overprinted on the four-line inscription, "This note is a Legal Tender at its face value for all debts public and private except duties on exports and interest on the public debt." Serial numbers are in red.

The back of the note is composed of numbers without any allegory or personification in a vignette. The two circular counters, one on each side, have given rise to the nickname "Poker Chip Note" for this issue.

W-1303 • F-123 • Speelman-White (1922–1927) • 696,000

Estimated population: 450 to 550 • *Highest graded:* Unc.

VG-8	F-12	VF-20	EF-40	AU-50	Unc-60	Unc-63	Unc-65
$700	$1,600	$3,400	$5,000	$7,000	$7,800	$9,250	$19,000

W-1303★ • F-123★

Recorded population: 2 • *Selected information:* Stack's (9/1992), ★135D/G, EF, $8,500. Heritage (1/2006), ★3330D/F, VG, $83,375.

SERIES OF 1923

$10 Legal Tender Note, Series of 1923 (W-1303), with portrait of Andrew Jackson. This $10 type was issued only in one signature combination, Speelman-White.

Back of the $10 Legal Tender Note, Series of 1923 (W-1303), called the "Poker Chip Note" due to the style of the counters.

NATIONAL BANK NOTES

The various series of $10 National Bank Notes were released parallel with the $5 denomination. Generally, large-size $10 National Bank Notes of all types were issued in four-subject sheets. There were some infrequent variations, including sheets with four $10 bills using plate letters A-B-C-D, instead of the normal A-B-C and then a $20 note with letter A. *United States Large Size National Bank Notes* by Peter Huntoon gives exceptions to this and other rules. Across the entire field of denominations there are many anomalies and curious issues.

Large-size $10 National Bank Notes are collected in several ways—by design type, by state, city, or bank, and so on. The Series of 1902 bills are quite plentiful, especially the Plain Backs, but the earlier types, such as Original Series and 1882 Value Back issues, can be elusive. Generally, those of large banks in Eastern cities are more common, while territorial notes are elusive.

Original Series
(Authorized Issue 1863 to 1875)

These notes (illus. on p. 338) were printed by the American Bank Note Company (imprint at the bottom border). All have a small red Treasury seal with a spiked border.

The first sheets of $10 notes were arranged $10-$10-$10-$10. The first series had red serial numbers, which began with Treasury number 9 on December 24, 1863, and continued to 624556 on April 1, 1869; the prefix letter Z was added to number 624557 and the series continued through number 999303 on March 11, 1875. This was followed by a set with the same plate arrangements and the prefix letter W, beginning on March 12, 1875, and ending on August 13, 1875, with number 153039. The $10-$10-$10-$20 Originals without prefix letter, printed in red ink, began on April 2, 1864, with federal number 22 and ended on June 15, 1865, with federal number 999288. In the same arrangement, blue serial numbers began without a prefix on June 19, 1865, with federal number 22 and ended on October 1, 1867, with number 999446. The same arrangement for $10-$10-$10-$20 was followed with issues in red ink with prefix letters A, B, and D. The A set began on November 21, 1867, and the D set ended on August 13, 1875.[7]

The Act of June 20, 1874, provided for the imprinting of the bank's charter number. This was done in red ink, one number vertically left of center and the other horizontally on the right.

The face of the notes depicts on the left side Benjamin Franklin flying a kite (officially, *Franklin and Electricity*). On the right side is the patriotic arrangement *America Seizing the Lightning*, of a goddess and an eagle. The back shows *De Soto Discovering the Mississippi*, from a painting by W.H. Powell, a vignette later trimmed and altered and used on large-size $500 Federal Reserve Notes. One numismatist described it thus:

> De Soto is pictured with his men on a promontory in a clearing overlooking the Mississippi. De Soto sits on a giant prancing white horse with his men in a large circle around him. He has his regalia on with a white plume in his hat, and is sitting up straight on his horse gazing out across the waters of the Mississippi. His large company of men are busily engaged in the interest of their camp duties. Over to the right of this circle three men are raising a large crucifix.[8]

On the left side is a state or territorial seal representing the issuing location of the bank, and to the right is an eagle (on some notes issued in territories an eagle is at both ends).

The Jeffries-Spinner signature combination is the rarity in the Original Series, with just one reported to exist. As a class these notes are quite scarce, particularly in higher grades. The price pressure for rare states is softened slightly by the greater availability of the Series of 1875 notes, which had the same basic design and have survived in larger numbers.

Banks of Issue and Rarity of Notes

Based upon census information from Don C. Kelly and James M. Kelly (*National Bank Note Census*, Version 4.0) and with some information from other sources, this listing gives each location, the number of banks issuing this series of notes within each, and a commentary.[9]

Don C. Kelly records 275 of these notes, or less than a third of the later Series of 1875 bills. These were issued for less than 11 years. Relatively few were saved. There are many states for which notes are unknown or are great rarities. These are specifically listed below.

Alabama • 7 banks of issue • 1 note reported • First National Bank of Mobile (VG).

Arkansas • 2 banks of issue • No notes reported.

Colorado Territory • 5 banks of issue • 4 notes reported • Three are from the Colorado National Bank of Denver (F, VF, AU). The other is a serial number 1 note from the First National Bank of Denver (VF).

Connecticut • 84 banks of issue • 10 notes reported • Circulated grades from eight banks.

Delaware • 10 banks of issue • No notes reported.

District of Columbia • 9 banks of issue • 5 notes reported • The distribution is among four banks. Grades are F to EF.

Florida • 1 bank of issue • No notes reported.

Georgia • 12 banks of issue • No notes reported.

Idaho Territory • 1 bank of issue • No notes reported.

Illinois • 108 banks of issue • 14 notes reported • Remarkably, all are from different banks. All are in circulated grades, although, as is often the case with a given state, some are ungraded. There are two serial number 1 notes in the Kelly census, from Fourth National Bank of Chicago (VF) and the First National Bank of Jacksonville (AU).

Indiana • 82 banks of issue • 13 notes reported[10] • Circulated notes from mostly different banks. One serial number 1 note exists, from the Lafayette National Bank (ungraded).

Iowa • 51 banks of issue • 4 notes reported • National State Bank of Burlington (F–VF), Clinton National Bank (F), Citizens National Bank of Davenport (F), and Fort Madison National Bank (AU).

Kansas • 10 banks of issue • 1 note reported • First National Bank of Junction City, serial 504, F.

Kentucky • 40 banks of issue • 13 notes reported • There are 11 different banks represented. Grades range from G to F–VF, a low average.

Louisiana • 11 banks of issue • 1 note reported • New Orleans National Bank, serial 1031, VG.

Maine • 69 banks of issue • 6 notes reported • Three are from the First National Bank of Bangor, and one each is from the Second National Bank of Bangor, Marine National Bank of Bath, and Waterville National Bank. Grades from VG to AU.

Maryland • 37 banks of issue • 4 notes reported • From as many different banks, all in Baltimore. VG to EF.

Massachusetts • 224 banks of issue • 26 notes reported • From a wide selection of banks. Several Unc notes. One serial number 1 note in the Kelly census, from the First National Bank of Fall River, which also is the only serial number 1 note in Unc grade from any state.

Michigan • 48 banks of issue • 9 notes reported • From six banks. Grades range from VG to VF–EF.

Minnesota • 21 banks of issue • No notes reported.

Mississippi • 2 banks of issue • No notes reported.

Missouri • 27 banks of issue • 11 notes reported • From six different banks, with the Central National Bank of Boonville accounting for five. Grades from VG to AU.

Montana Territory • 2 banks of issue • No notes reported.

Nebraska • 2 banks of issue • No notes reported.

Nebraska Territory • 2 banks of issue • No notes reported.

Nevada • 1 bank of issue • No notes reported.

New Hampshire • 42 banks of issue • 4 notes reported • Dover National Bank (F), Monadnock National Bank of East Jaffrey (G), First National Bank of Francestown (VG), and Citizens National Bank of Sanbornton (EF).

New Jersey • 62 banks of issue • 8 notes reported • From seven banks. Grades VG to F–VF.

New Mexico Territory • 2 banks of issue • No notes reported.

New York • 295 banks of issue • 39 notes reported[11] • A common state, if it can be called that, with notes from many banks. Remarkably, the highest grade listed is EF. There are two serial number 1 notes listed, both from the Fallkill National Bank of Poughkeepsie (G–VG, VG).

$10 National Bank Note, Original Series (W-1312). Citizens National Bank of Sanbornton, New Hampshire. This particular bank did not move, but changed its address to Tilton when the town was renamed. This type was used for W-1310 to W-1316 of the Original Series. On this early note the Treasury serial number is in blue.

Back of the $10 National Bank Note, Original Series (W-1312), with New Hampshire state seal, reflective of the issuing bank's location.

North Carolina • 9 banks of issue • 3 notes reported • Raleigh National Bank of North Carolina (F), State National Bank of Raleigh (F), and the one serial number 1 note listed, National Bank of New Berne (AU).

Ohio • 154 banks of issue • 25 notes reported • From many banks. The only Unc note from the First National Bank of Lebanon.

Oregon • 1 bank of issue • No notes reported.

Pennsylvania • 210 banks of issue • 27 notes reported[12] • One Unc, from the Bank of North America of Philadelphia.

Rhode Island • 62 banks of issue • 7 notes reported • From as many banks. One Unc, of the Third National Bank of Providence.

South Carolina • 11 banks of issue • 1 note reported • First National Bank of Charleston, serial 10818, EF–AU.

Tennessee • 25 banks of issue • 2 notes reported • First National Bank of Knoxville (Fair) and the First National Bank of Murfreesboro (VF).

Texas • 8 banks of issue • 1 note reported • First National Bank of Houston, serial 2717, F.

Utah Territory • 4 banks of issue • No notes reported.

Vermont • 46 banks of issue • 7 notes reported • Three are from the National Bank of Barre, the others from four different banks. Grades from Fair to EF.

Virginia • 26 banks of issue • 2 notes reported • Loudon National Bank of Leesburg (VF) and Merchants National Bank of Richmond (F).

West Virginia • 18 banks of issue • No notes reported.

Wisconsin • 20 banks of issue • 2 notes reported • First National Bank of Janesville (VF) and the Manufacturers National Bank of Racine (EF).

Wyoming Territory • 1 bank of issue • No notes reported.

Generic prices for a typical note from a state from which notes range from plentiful to just slightly scarce:

VG-8	F-12	VF-20	EF-40	AU-50	Unc-60	Unc-63	Unc-65
$1,450	$1,750	$2,200	$2,750	$3,800	$5,250	$5,800	$9,500

W-1310 • F-409 • Chittenden-Spinner (1861–1864)

Estimated population: 65 to 70 • *Highest graded:* Unc.

VG-8	F-12	VF-20	EF-40	AU-50	Unc-60	Unc-63	Unc-65
$1,450	$1,750	$2,200	$2,750	$3,800	$5,250	$5,800	$9,500

W-1312 • F-412 • Colby-Spinner (1864–1867)

Estimated population: 115 to 125 • *Highest graded:* Unc.

VG-8	F-12	VF-20	EF-40	AU-50	Unc-60	Unc-63	Unc-65
$1,450	$1,750	$2,200	$2,750	$3,800	$5,250	$5,800	$9,500

W-1314 • F-413 • Jeffries-Spinner (1867–1869)

Recorded population: 1 • *Graded:* F-15 • *Selected information:* Heritage (5/2007), 308-A77519/C, State NB of Raleigh, NC, Fine+, $57,500.

W-1316 • F-414 • Allison-Spinner (1869–1875)

Estimated population: 24 to 28 • *Highest graded:* EF-40.

VG-8	F-12	VF-20	EF-40
$1,450	$1,750	$2,200	$2,750

National Gold Bank Notes, Original Series

The National Gold Bank Notes of the early 1870s (illus. on p. 340) also used the face from the Original Series. The back features a montage of gold coins. To the left is the state seal of California. All have the printed signatures of Allison and Spinner, plus hand-signed signatures of local bank officials. For the $10 denomination in the Original Series, each of the National Gold Banks in California issued examples. Although across the series, gold-tinted paper was used for nearly all of these notes, in the $10 denomination there are exceptions among certain bills from Oakland and Petaluma.

Although thousands of these $10 bills were produced, most were redeemed, and today all range from scarce to rare. The Kelly census records just 95, the highest grade being Very Fine–Extremely Fine, exceptional for the series. Treasury records state that 2,481 are outstanding, most of which are no doubt lost for all time. Most numismatists desire to have a single example to illustrate the type. As is the case with National Gold Bank notes of all denominations, most show extensive wear, as James and Don C. Kelly demonstrate in their note-by-note listings in their *National Bank Note Census* CD.

W-1320 • F-1142 • Dated 1870 • San Francisco • First National Gold Bank • 18,004

Estimated population: 35 to 40 • *Highest graded:* VF-30.

VG-8	F-12	VF-20
$5,000	$13,000	$45,000

W-1321 • F-1144 • Dated 1872 • Sacramento • National Gold Bank of D.O. Mills & Co. • 3,823

Recorded population: 5 • *Highest graded:* VF-20 • *Commentary:* One is laminated. There are no modern auction sales.

W-1322 • F-1143 • San Francisco • National Gold Bank and Trust Co. • 12,669

Estimated population: 13 to 15 • *Highest graded:* VF-25.

VG-8	F-12	VF-20
$5,500	$20,000	$50,000

W-1323 • F-1145 • Dated 1873 • Santa Barbara • First National Gold Bank • 2,400

Recorded population: 3 • *Highest graded:* VG-10 • *Selected information:* Serials for existing notes are 543-B302025/B, VG, sold in a Knight auction (8/2003) for $20,450; 609-B302081/B, Fine; and 638-B302110/B, Good, damaged, sold in a CAA auction (5/2005) for $48,875.

W-1324 • F-1146 • Stockton • First National Gold Bank • 15,000

Estimated population: 18 to 20 • *Highest graded:* VF-30.

VG-8	F-12	VF-20
$7,500	$25,000	$60,000

W-1325 • F-1149 • Dated 1874 • Petaluma • First National Gold Bank • 6,000

Recorded population: 7 • *Highest graded:* F-12 • *Selected information:* CAA (5/2005), 797-B568106/A, Fair, $13,800. Knight (6/1995), 847-B568156/B, variously VG to VF+, $4,235. CAA (4/2006), 955-B568264/A, Good, $18,400.

NATIONAL GOLD BANK NOTES, ORIGINAL SERIES

$10 National Gold Bank Note, Original Series, First National Gold Bank of San Francisco (W-1320). The date entered on the plate at the left of the Treasury seal is NOV'R 30TH 1870.

Back of a $10 National Gold Bank Note, Original Series (W-1320). The same montage of gold coins was used on other denominations from $5 to $100.

W-1326 • F-1148 • San Jose • Farmers National Gold Bank • 8,547

Estimated population: 12 to 14 • *Highest graded:* F-12.

VG-8	F-12
$5,500	$20,000

W-1327 • F-1151 • Dated 1875 (but Original Series) • Oakland • First National Gold Bank • 1,500

Recorded population: 7 • *Highest graded:* F-12 • *Selected information:* Spink (7/2007), 12-D396074/C, Fair, $5,760.

W-1328 • F-1151a • Union National Gold Bank • 1,500

Recorded population: 3 • *Highest graded:* G-6 perhaps • *Selected information:* Serials for existing notes are 75-D524862/A, VG, repaired, sold in a Knight auction (2/1996) for $9,900; 133-D524920/C, Good, repaired (Good in the Kelly census); B. Max Mehl (11/1944), 205-D524992/A, About Good (graded VG in 2007 and in the Kelly census), $50.

Series of 1875

These notes (illus. on p. 342) continued the use of plates signed by American Bank Note Company, though the printing was done by the Bureau of Engraving and Printing in

Washington. Vertically near the border at the upper left is PRINTED AT THE BUREAU, ENGRAVING & PRINTING U.S. TREASURY DEPt. For some banks for which there had been no Original Series plates made, the Bureau made new plates with BUREAU OF ENGRAVING & PRINTING TREASURY DEPt. at the bottom border, and no mention of the American Bank Note Company. This could be considered a subtype or even a different type, but has attracted virtually no notice. These seem to be rare.

The small red Treasury seal now has a scalloped rather than a spiked border. All have SERIES 1875 imprinted vertically in red to the left of center, near the bank charter number. The Treasury and bank serial numbers and two charter numbers are also in red. A small percentage of these notes are printed on paper with a vertical streak of blue, the type most familiarly used on the Legal Tender Notes beginning with the Series of 1869 (paper made under the James M. Willcox patent of July 24, 1866). These are especially colorful and attractive.

The first order for $10-$10-$10-$20 sheets of the Series of 1875 from plates made entirely at the BEP was entered in the ledgers on June 18, 1875, although the plate may not have been made until November.[13] It was for the Citizens

National Bank of Keene, New Hampshire, charter 2299, and had a plate date of September 25, 1875.

Although these are easier to find than Original Series notes and tend to be in significantly higher average grades, there are many scarcities and rarities among the listings. Several clusters of Uncirculated notes offer possibilities for acquiring one for type.

Banks of Issue and Rarity of Notes

Based upon census information from Don C. Kelly and James M. Kelly (*National Bank Note Census*, Version 4.0) and with some information from other sources, this listing gives each location, the number of banks issuing this series of notes within each, and a commentary.[14]

The Kelly survey records 959 of these notes, or more than three times the existing Original Series notes. However, they are still rare. These are specifically listed below.

Alabama • 7 banks of issue • 1 note reported • Gainesville National Bank, serial 1119, F.

Arkansas • 1 bank of issue • 1 note reported • Merchants National Bank of Little Rock, serial 4468, F–VF.

California • 7 banks of issue • 18 notes reported • This impressive showing is from just six banks, including six from the First National Bank of Los Angeles and five from the Union National Bank of Oakland. Grades from Fair to AU.

Colorado • 8 banks of issue • 6 notes reported • Five banks. There is one Unc, which is also the only serial number 1 note, from the Merchants National Bank of Denver.

Colorado Territory • 3 banks of issue • 2 notes reported • City National Bank of Denver (F) plus the only serial number 1 note known, from the First National Bank of Denver (Unc).

Connecticut • 81 banks of issue • 30 notes reported • The three Unc notes are all from the Second National Bank of New Haven. Otherwise there is a wide selection of banks for circulated notes.

Dakota Territory • 9 banks of issue • 4 notes reported • From the Fargo National Bank, Citizens National Bank of Grand Forks, First National Bank of Wahpeton (two), in grades G to F–VF.

Delaware • 13 banks of issue • 18 notes reported • There are 12 from the First National Bank of Milford, including eight Unc, making this state a good possibility for acquiring a note for type.

District of Columbia • 7 banks of issue • 14 notes reported • Seven from the Farmers and Mechanics National Bank of Georgetown, including six Unc. Five are from the Central National Bank of Washington, including one Unc.

Florida • 1 bank of issue • No notes reported.

Georgia • 10 banks of issue • 8 notes reported • Circulated notes from four banks.

Idaho Territory • 1 bank of issue • No notes reported.

Illinois • 99 banks of issue • 68 notes reported • A remarkable 28 are from the First National Bank of Paris, with all but one Unc—a highlight situation regarding availability of Series of 1875 notes in this grade. There are two serial number 1

notes, DeKalb National Bank (AU) and Farmers National Bank of Springfield (not graded).

Indiana • 76 banks of issue • 47 notes reported • There are 20 from the First National Bank of Vincennes, with 14 of these Unc, another remarkable opportunity. Otherwise there are many circulated notes, plus three other Unc bills from as many banks.

Iowa • 55 banks of issue • 36 notes reported • Six are Unc, including five from the City National Bank of Clinton.

Kansas • 14 banks of issue • 7 notes reported.

Kentucky • 44 banks of issue • 7 notes reported • Six circulated bills and one Unc, from the First National Bank of Topeka.

Louisiana • 8 banks of issue • 4 notes reported • Circulated notes from three different New Orleans banks.

Maine • 72 banks of issue • 13 notes reported • Selection from various banks, grades G–VG to EF.

Maryland • 38 banks of issue • 22 notes reported • Circulated grades from various banks, plus one Unc from the National Marine Bank of Baltimore.

Massachusetts • 231 banks of issue • 68 notes reported • Eight Unc, including four from the Monument National Bank of Charlestown.

Michigan • 59 banks of issue • 28 notes reported • Six from the Fourth National Bank of Grand Rapids. Circulated grades except for one Unc from the First National Bank of Milford.

Minnesota • 19 banks of issue • 4 notes reported • First National Bank of Brainerd (AU), Fergus Falls National Bank (VF, EF), and the Citizens National Bank of Mankato (VF).

Missouri • 19 banks of issue • 7 notes reported • Circulated notes from five banks.

Montana • 6 banks of issue • 4 notes reported • First National Bank of Butte (F), Northwestern National Bank of Great Falls (VG–F, F), and Merchants National Bank of Helena (VG).

Montana Territory • 6 banks of issue • No notes reported.

Nebraska • 10 banks of issue • 8 notes reported • Circulated notes from five different banks, including four from the Nebraska National Bank of Omaha.

Nebraska Territory • 2 banks of issue • No notes reported.

New Hampshire • 44 banks of issue • 20 notes reported • Circulated notes from 10 banks. One is Unc, from the First National Bank of Portsmouth.

New Jersey • 63 banks of issue • 23 notes reported • Circulated notes from a selection of banks, with some duplication.

New Mexico Territory • 5 banks of issue • 7 notes reported • Circulated notes from the First National Bank of Albuquerque (four) and the First National Bank of Las Vegas (three).

New York • 260 banks of issue • 103 notes reported • Circulated notes except three Unc from the Merchants National Bank of Dunkirk, First National Bank of Ithaca, and the First National Bank of Rondout. There are three serial number 1 notes, all AU from the Wilber National Bank of Oneonta.

North Carolina • 12 banks of issue • 8 notes reported • Circulated notes from the First National Bank of Charlotte (three), First National Bank of Wilson (four), First National Bank of Winston (two), and Wachovia National Bank of Winston (one, the only serial number 1 note from the state, not graded).

North Dakota • 7 banks of issue • 7 notes reported • Two Unc from the First National Bank of Grand Forks.

Ohio • 156 banks of issue • 140 notes reported • Includes 35 Unc notes from the First National Bank of Newark, a remarkable group. Seven others in this grade are from other banks.

Oregon • 2 banks of issue • 3 notes reported • First National Bank of Pendleton (VF–EF) and the First National Bank of Portland (G–VG, F–VF).

Pennsylvania • 221 banks of issue • 99 notes reported[15] • Various banks. 10 Unc notes.

Rhode Island • 59 banks of issue • 24 notes reported • One Unc, from the Roger Williams National Bank of Providence.

South Carolina • 11 banks of issue • 2 notes reported • First National Bank of Charleston (F) and National Bank of Greenville (F).

South Dakota • 2 banks of issue • 1 note reported • First National Bank of Mitchell, serial 1239, EF.

Tennessee • 24 banks of issue • 7 notes reported • Circulated grades from six banks.

Texas • 20 banks of issue • 18 notes reported • Circulated grades, including seven from the State National Bank of Austin.

Utah • 2 banks of issue • No notes reported.

Utah Territory • 3 banks of issue • No notes reported.

Vermont • 45 banks of issue • 9 notes reported • Seven banks. One Unc, from the National Bank of Newbury of Wells River.

Virginia • 19 banks of issue • 15 notes reported • Circulated notes from seven banks.

West Virginia • 15 banks of issue • No notes reported.

Wisconsin • 19 banks of issue • 12 notes reported • Circulated notes from seven banks.

Wyoming • 4 banks of issue • 5 notes reported • Stock Growers National Bank of Cheyenne (F and three F–VF) and the Laramie National Bank (F).

Wyoming Territory • 3 banks of issue • 2 notes reported • Stock Growers National Bank of Cheyenne (VG, F).

SERIES OF 1875

$10 National Bank Note, Series of 1875 (W-1330). First National Bank of Paris, Illinois. From a remarkable hoard of 27 Uncirculated notes, as recorded by Don C. Kelly. Vignettes as on the preceding, but now with SERIES 1875 overprinted in red vertically to left of center and with three-line BUREAU OF ENGRAVING AND PRINTING imprint vertically at border at upper left. The back is the same as that used on $10 National Bank Notes, Original Series.

Detail of the Treasury imprint on W-1330, vertically at the upper left corner of the face, an alteration to an American Bank Note Co. face plate. The bright red SERIES 1875 is also shown.

Generic prices for a typical note from a state from which notes range from plentiful to just slightly scarce:

VG-8	F-12	VF-20	EF-40	AU-50	Unc-60	Unc-63	Unc-65
$1,450	$1,750	$2,200	$2,750	$3,800	$5,250	$5,800	$9,500

W-1330 • F-416 • Allison-New (1875–1876)

Estimated population: 300 to 325 • *Highest graded:* Unc.

VG-8	F-12	VF-20	EF-40	AU-50	Unc-60	Unc-63	Unc-65
$1,450	$1,750	$2,200	$2,750	$3,800	$5,250	$5,800	$9,500

W-1332 • F-417 • Allison-Wyman (1876–1877)

Estimated population: 75 to 85 • *Highest graded:* Unc.

VG-8	F-12	VF-20	EF-40	AU-50	Unc-60	Unc-63	Unc-65
$1,450	$1,750	$2,200	$2,750	$3,800	$5,250	$5,800	$9,500

W-1334 • F-418 • Allison-Gilfillan (1877–1878)

Estimated population: 46 to 50 • *Highest graded:* AU-50.

VG-8	F-12	VF-20	EF-40	AU-50
$1,450	$1,750	$2,200	$2,750	$3,800

W-1336 • F-419 • Scofield-Gilfillan (1878–1881)

Estimated population: 225 to 250 • *Highest graded:* Unc.

VG-8	F-12	VF-20	EF-40	AU-50	Unc-60	Unc-63	Unc-65
$1,600	$1,850	$2,300	$2,850	$3,900	$5,350	$6,000	$9,800

W-1338 • F-420 • Bruce-Gilfillan (1881–1883)

Estimated population: 180 to 200 • *Highest graded:* Unc.

VG-8	F-12	VF-20	EF-40	AU-50	Unc-60	Unc-63	Unc-65
$1,600	$1,850	$2,300	$2,850	$3,900	$5,350	$6,000	$9,800

W-1340 • F-421 • Bruce-Wyman (1883–1885)

Recorded population: 5 • *Highest graded:* AU-50 • *Selected information:* Smythe (2/1999), 2138-K106572/2138/B, NB of D.O. Mills & Co., Sacramento, CA, VG, problems, $4,000. CAA (1/1998), 2168-K857116/B, Citizens & Manufacturers NB of Waterbury, CT, VF, $1,320. No recent sales.

W-1342 • F-422 • Rosecrans-Huston (1889–1891)

Estimated population: 18 to 20 • *Highest graded:* Unc.

VG-8	F-12	VF-20	EF-40	AU-50	Unc-60	Unc-63	Unc-65
$1,800	$2,050	$2,500	$3,050	$4,100	$5,500	$6,250	$10,000

W-1344 • F-423 • Rosecrans-Nebeker (1891–1893)

Estimated population: 11 to 13 • *Highest graded:* EF-40.

VG-8	F-12	VF-20	EF-40
$1,800	$2,050	$2,500	$3,050

W-1346 • F-423a • Tillman-Morgan (1893–1897)

Recorded population: 1 • *Graded:* EF-40.

National Gold Bank Notes, Series of 1875

These have the same face vignettes as other Series of 1875 $10 notes. The inscriptions vary and include the obligation, REDEEMABLE IN GOLD COIN. Now with vertical red SERIES 1875 red overprint to the left of center. The back is similar to the Original Series National Gold Bank Notes of this denomination.

All have the printed signatures of Allison and Spinner and the autographed signatures of the bank cashier and president. Some notes were printed on white instead of yellow paper. The Kelly census records 14 of these notes from just two banks. The highest grade is Fine. As a class the Series of 1875 notes are exceedingly rare. As most numismatists seek examples by location, and an Original Series bill will often suffice, the price for Series of 1875 notes is less than would otherwise be the case.

W-1351 • F-unlisted • Oakland • First National Gold Bank • 36 • Unknown

W-1352 • F-1150 • Petaluma • First National Gold Bank • 4,800

Recorded population: 6 • *Highest graded:* VF-20 • *Commentary:* The finest is 34-D241806/C, sold in a Knight auction (2/2003) for $40,250.

NATIONAL GOLD BANK NOTES, SERIES OF 1875

$10 National Gold Bank Note, Series of 1875, First National Gold Bank of Stockton (charter 2077) with SERIES 1875 imprint (W-1353). REDEEMABLE IN GOLD COIN. Printed on yellow-tint paper. The back is the same as that used on $10 National Gold Bank Notes, Original Series.

W-1353 • F-1147 • Stockton • First National Gold Bank • 879

Recorded population: 8 • *Highest graded:* F-12 • *Commentary:* One is held by the Richmond Federal Reserve Bank. The finest is 285/D8437/A, sold in a CAA auction (5/2005) for $14,950.

Series of 1882, Brown Back
(Authorized Issue 1882 to 1908)

This series was printed for the use of banks that extended their charters and for banks chartered after passage of the Act of July 11, 1882. Once adopted, the series was used by a given bank for the next 20 years. By 1882 the bureau had been printing notes for seven years. To create distinctively new notes, changes were made. The earlier face designs for the $10 through $100 were used, but new plates were made, with the charter number repeated six times around the border. As with the Series of 1875, Series of 1882 $10 and higher notes came with both the American Bank Note Company or BEP imprint, depending on when the plates were made. Plates were typically laid out as $10-$10-$10-$20. In September 1906, the $10-$10-$10-$10 configuration was introduced.

From the outset charter numbers were overprinted in brown on the face, vertically to the left of center on the $10 to $100 issues. The Treasury seal is in brown as well. Beginning in September 1890, the position was changed to horizontal at the upper right. Peter Huntoon states that fewer than 14% of the plates had the vertical position, and as these were earlier, even fewer survive today. Regional letters N, E, M, S, W, and P were overprinted twice in brown on the face of notes starting with shipments received on March 17, 1902. This yields two face varieties: with and without regional letters. Peter Huntoon records two border styles for the face:

Face Style 1: This is most often seen and can be quickly identified as having 10-TEN-10-(charter number)-TEN-10 in the top margin to the left of NATIONAL CURRENCY.

Face Style 2: The rarer style can be quickly identified as having 10-TEN-(charter number)-10-TEN-10 in that location.[16]

The reverse was completely redesigned to create the Brown Back style, printed in ink of that color. On the left is a state or territorial seal representing the issuing bank's location, as had been done on earlier series. This necessitated making a set of plates for each state or territory. On the right is a perched eagle. At the center is a greenish-blue impression of the bank's charter number in large figures, enabling the bills to be easily sorted when they were redeemed.

The average note is apt to be in a grade from Good to Fine, but there are enough Very Fine, Extremely Fine, and About Uncirculated notes around that finding one for type will be easy enough. Uncirculated notes range from the scarce to rare, with the supply augmented by clusters here and there.

Banks of Issue and Rarity of Notes

Based upon census information from Don C. Kelly and James M. Kelly (*National Bank Note Census*, Version 4.0) and with some information from the other sources, this listing gives each location, the number of banks issuing this series of notes within each, and a commentary.[17]

The Kelly survey records 5,480 notes, not a great difference from the 6,141 $5 Brown Back notes of the same type. The $5 notes get more attention, however, due to their often distinctive face typography, which has no counterpart on other denominations. Serial number 1 notes total 146, resulting in occasional auction appearances. These notes are specifically listed below.

Alabama • 16 banks of issue • 54 notes reported • Five Unc, including three from the First National Bank of Montgomery. Two serial number 1 notes are from the First National Bank of Jackson (AU) and the Isbell National Bank of Talladega (EF).

Alaska Territory • 1 bank of issue • No notes reported • Alaska was a district from 1884 until it became a territory on August 24, 1912, which it remained until statehood in 1959. All large-size Alaska notes in all series have the "district" address. Regardless, numismatists call all "territorials."

Arizona Territory • 2 banks of issue • 7 notes reported • Five are from the National Bank of Arizona at Phoenix. All known notes are in circulated grades.

Arkansas • 9 banks of issue • 3 notes reported • All are in circulated grades: First National Bank of DeQueen (F–VF), American National Bank of Fort Smith (F), and the Exchange National Bank of Little Rock (F).

California • 55 banks of issue • 149 notes reported • Two Unc notes are from the First National Bank of Bakersfield and the First National Bank of San Francisco. Four serial number 1 notes are recorded.

Colorado • 47 banks of issue • 26 notes reported • The only Unc note is from the First National Bank of Fort Collins.

Connecticut • 89 banks of issue • 102 notes reported • Most are circulated. Two serial number 1 notes are from the Clinton National Bank (EF–AU, AU).

Dakota Territory • 27 banks of issue • 1 note known • Known note is from the First National Bank of Casselton (G), serial number 482.

Delaware • 18 banks of issue • 28 notes reported • Three Unc notes are from the First National Bank of Milford.

District of Columbia • 13 banks of issue • 46 notes reported • Most are circulated. Two serial number 1 notes are from the National Metropolitan Bank of Washington (Unc) and the Riggs National Bank of Washington (AU).

Florida • 16 banks of issue • 13 notes reported • Two serial number 1 notes are from the First National Bank of Key West (AU, the only Unc note reported for the state) and the Citizens National Bank of Pensacola (VF).

Georgia • 44 banks of issue • 44 notes reported • All are circulated.

Hawaii Territory • 2 banks of issue • 6 notes reported • All are from the First National Bank of Hawaii at Honolulu, all circulated.

Idaho • 12 banks of issue • 5 notes reported • All are circulated.

SERIES OF 1882, BROWN BACK

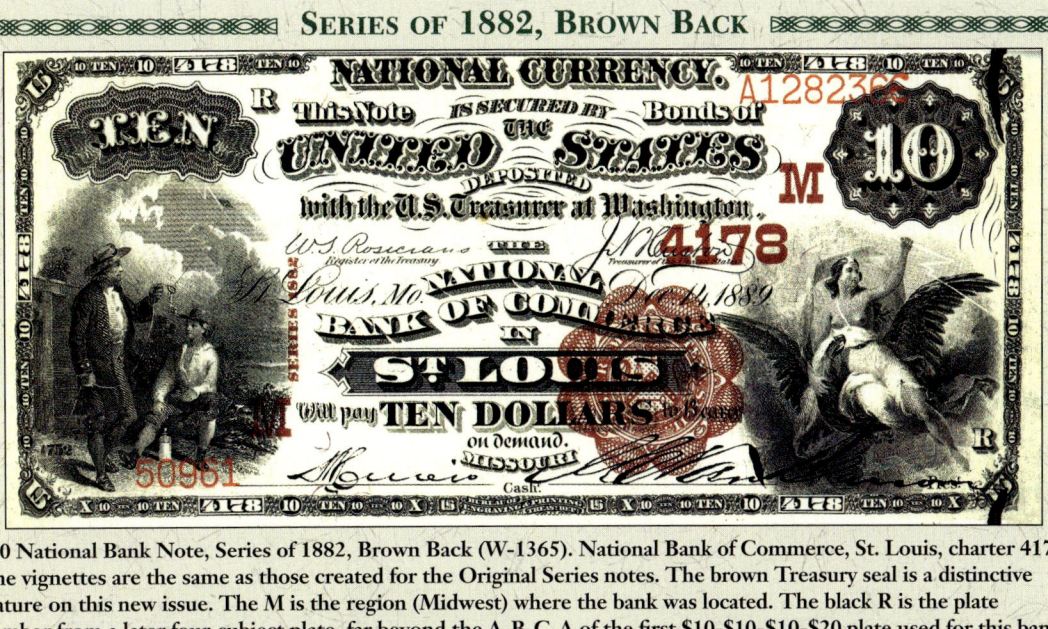

$10 National Bank Note, Series of 1882, Brown Back (W-1365). National Bank of Commerce, St. Louis, charter 4178. The vignettes are the same as those created for the Original Series notes. The brown Treasury seal is a distinctive feature on this new issue. The M is the region (Midwest) where the bank was located. The black R is the plate number from a later four-subject plate, far beyond the A-B-C-A of the first $10-$10-$10-$20 plate used for this bank.

Detail of Face Style 1 showing the upper left margin. National Bank of Commerce, St. Louis, charter 4178 (W-1365).

Detail of Face Style 2 showing the upper left margin. First National Bank of Litchfield, Illinois, charter 3962 (W-1364).

Back of the $10 National Bank Note, Series of 1882, Brown Back (W-1365). National Bank of Commerce, St. Louis, with the charter number and Missouri state seal.

Idaho Territory • 4 banks of issue • 1 note reported • This is serial number 1 from the First National Bank of Lewiston (VF–EF). A trophy note deluxe.

Illinois • 221 banks of issue • 274 notes reported • Most are circulated. The census lists 12 serial number 1 notes.

Indian Territory • 56 banks of issue • 41 notes listed • Two Unc notes are from the Choctaw National Bank of Caddo and the Eufala National Bank of Eufala. There are also two serial number 1 notes, from Eufala National Bank and Purcell National Bank.

Indiana • 133 banks of issue • 146 notes reported • Most are circulated. Three serial number 1 notes are from the Hamil-

ton National Bank of Fort Wayne (Unc), First National Bank of Fowler (EF), and the Greensburg National Bank (Unc).

Iowa • 217 banks of issue • 246 notes reported • Most are circulated. The census lists 12 serial number 1 notes.

Kansas • 142 banks of issue • 102 notes reported • The census lists 10 Unc notes. There are 11 serial number 1 notes recorded.

Kentucky • 82 banks of issue • 156 notes reported • The census lists 10 Unc notes, including nine from the Citizens National Bank of Bowling Green.

Louisiana • 26 banks of issue • 42 notes reported • The only Unc note is from New Orleans National Bank.

Maine • 81 banks of issue • 72 notes reported • Two Unc notes are from the First National Bank of Bangor and the First National Bank of Madison.

Maryland • 73 banks of issue • 112 notes reported • The only Unc note is from Third National Bank of Baltimore. The only serial number 1 note is from the First National Bank of Midland (EF).

Massachusetts • 272 banks of issue • 212 notes reported • The census lists 20 Unc notes. The only serial number 1 note is from the Northampton National Bank (AU).

Michigan • 97 banks of issue • 120 notes reported • Eight Unc notes are listed. Two serial number 1 notes are from the First National Bank of Escanaba (F) and the Saint Johns National Bank (VF).

Minnesota • 112 banks of issue • 82 notes reported • The only Unc note is from Rochester National Bank, Rochester. Two serial number 1 notes are from Albert Lea National Bank (AU) and the First National Bank of Elbow Lake (EF).

Mississippi • 11 banks of issue • 6 notes reported • All are in circulated grades, four of which are from the First National Bank of Vicksburg.

Missouri • 89 banks of issue • 266 notes reported • Most are circulated. Seven serial number 1 notes are recorded.

Montana • 32 banks of issue • 22 notes reported • All are circulated.

Montana Territory • 7 banks of issue • 3 notes reported • All are circulated. The only serial number 1 note is from the Montana National Bank of Helena (VF).

Nebraska • 121 banks of issue • 82 notes reported • The only Unc note is from the City National Bank of Kearney.

Nevada • 1 bank of issue • 1 note reported • From the First National Bank of Winnemucca (F–VF), serial 524.

New Hampshire • 64 banks of issue • 73 notes reported • Nine Unc notes are known.

New Jersey • 122 banks of issue • 179 notes reported • Most reported examples are in circulated grades. Four serial number 1 notes are known, all VF; three are from the First National Bank of Ocean City.

New Mexico Territory • 17 banks of issue • 18 notes reported • The only Unc note is from the First National Bank of Roswell.

New York • 367 banks of issue • 725 notes reported • The census lists 13 serial number 1 notes; 63 of the known Unc notes are from the National Bank of Commerce of New York.

North Carolina • 37 banks of issue • 59 notes reported • All are circulated.

North Dakota • 45 banks of issue • 14 notes reported • All are circulated. Two serial number 1 notes are from the First National Bank of Cando (EF) and the First National Bank of Harvey (not graded).

Ohio • 288 banks of issue • 412 notes reported • Most reported examples are in circulated grades. The only serial number 1 note is from the German National Bank of Cincinnati.

Oklahoma • 52 banks of issue • 14 notes reported • Most are circulated.

Oklahoma Territory • 53 banks of issue • 17 notes reported • Two Unc notes are from the First National Bank of Norman and the First National Bank of Kingfisher. Three serial number 1 notes are recorded.

Oregon • 38 banks of issue • 24 notes reported • All reported notes are in circulated grades.

Pennsylvania • 503 banks of issue • 539 notes reported • Most are circulated. The census lists 21 serial number 1 notes.

Rhode Island • 55 banks of issue • 67 notes reported • Three Unc notes are known.

South Carolina • 30 banks of issue • 28 notes reported • Two Unc notes are from the First National Bank of Charleston.

South Dakota • 41 banks of issue • 30 notes reported • All are circulated. Two serial number 1 notes are from the First National Bank of Canton (EF) and the American National Bank of Deadwood (not graded).

Tennessee • 53 banks of issue • 87 notes reported • All notes are reported are in circulated grades.

Texas • 314 banks of issue • 302 notes reported • Most are in circulated grades. The census lists 18 serial number 1 notes.

Utah • 12 banks of issue • 22 notes reported • Three Unc notes are known.

Utah Territory • 9 banks of issue • 6 notes reported • Three banks are represented. One Unc note is from the Commercial National Bank of Ogden.

Vermont • 51 banks of issue • 39 notes reported • Three Unc notes are known. The only serial number 1 note is from the First National Bank of Fair Haven.

Virginia • 57 banks of issue • 65 notes reported • Two Unc notes are from the National Exchange Bank of Lynchburg and the American National Bank of Richmond. The only serial number 1 note is from the Rockingham National Bank of Harrisonburg (not graded).

Washington • 60 banks of issue • 28 notes reported • One Unc note is from the Washington National Bank of Seattle. Two serial number 1 notes are from the First National Bank of Hoquiam (AU) and the First National Bank of Slaughter (Fine).

Washington Territory • 26 banks of issue • 2 notes reported • From the First National Bank of Colfax (F–VF) and the Citizens National Bank of Tacoma (G–VG).

West Virginia • 51 banks of issue • 49 notes reported • The only Unc note is from the First National Bank of Grafton. Two serial number 1 notes are from the First National Bank of Cameron (F, EF).

Wisconsin • 97 banks of issue • 179 notes reported • The census lists 12 Unc notes. The three serial number 1 notes are from the Lumberman's National Bank of Chippewa Falls (EF), First National Bank of Darlington (VF) and the South Milwaukee National Bank (VF).

Wyoming • 18 banks of issue • 20 notes reported • The only Unc note is from the First National Bank of Lander. Three serial number 1 notes are from the First National Bank of Lander (Unc), First National Bank of Laramie (F), and the Rawlins National Bank of Rawlins (F).

Wyoming Territory • 7 banks of issue • 1 note reported • The only known note is a serial number 1 from the First National Bank of Rawlins (VF–EF). A prize note.

Generic prices for a typical note from a state from which notes range from plentiful to just slightly scarce:

VG-8	F-12	VF-20	EF-40	AU-50	Unc-60	Unc-63	Unc-65
$550	$750	$1,000	$1,350	$1,800	$2,400	$2,750	$4,800

W-1360 • F-479 • Bruce-Gilfillan (1881–1883)
Estimated population: 400 to 500 • *Highest graded:* Unc.

VG-8	F-12	VF-20	EF-40	AU-50	Unc-60	Unc-63	Unc-65
$550	$750	$1,000	$1,350	$1,800	$2,400	$2,750	$4,500

W-1361 • F-480 • Bruce-Wyman (1883–1885)
Estimated population: 900 to 1,100 • *Highest graded:* Unc.

VG-8	F-12	VF-20	EF-40	AU-50	Unc-60	Unc-63	Unc-65
$550	$750	$1,000	$1,350	$1,800	$2,400	$2,750	$4,500

W-1362 • F-481 • Bruce-Jordan (1885)
Estimated population: 225 to 275 • *Highest graded:* Unc.

VG-8	F-12	VF-20	EF-40	AU-50	Unc-60	Unc-63	Unc-65
$600	$800	$1,075	$1,450	$1,900	$2,500	$2,900	$4,800

W-1363 • F-482 • Rosecrans-Jordan (1885–1887)
Estimated population: 450 to 550 • *Highest graded:* Unc.

VG-8	F-12	VF-20	EF-40	AU-50	Unc-60	Unc-63	Unc-65
$550	$750	$1,000	$1,350	$1,800	$2,400	$2,750	$4,800

W-1364 • F-483 • Rosecrans-Hyatt (1887–1889)
Estimated population: 200 to 240 • *Highest graded:* Unc.

VG-8	F-12	VF-20	EF-40	AU-50	Unc-60	Unc-63	Unc-65
$550	$750	$1,000	$1,350	$1,800	$2,400	$2,750	$4,800

W-1365 • F-484 • Rosecrans-Huston (1889–1891)
Estimated population: 800 to 1,000 • *Highest graded:* Unc.

VG-8	F-12	VF-20	EF-40	AU-50	Unc-60	Unc-63	Unc-65
$550	$750	$1,000	$1,350	$1,800	$2,400	$2,750	$4,800

W-1366 • F-485 • Rosecrans-Nebeker (1891–1893)
Estimated population: 600 to 750 • *Highest graded:* Unc.

VG-8	F-12	VF-20	EF-40	AU-50	Unc-60	Unc-63	Unc-65
$550	$750	$1,000	$1,350	$1,800	$2,400	$2,750	$4,800

W-1367 • F-486 • Rosecrans-Morgan (1893)
Estimated population: 11 to 13 • *Highest graded:* EF-40.

VG-8	F-12	VF-20	EF-40
$1,500	$2,000	$2,750	$3,500

W-1368 • F-487 • Tillman-Morgan (1893–1897)
Estimated population: 575 to 700 • *Highest graded:* Unc.

VG-8	F-12	VF-20	EF-40	AU-50	Unc-60	Unc-63	Unc-65
$550	$750	$1,000	$1,350	$1,800	$2,400	$2,750	$4,800

W-1369 • F-488 • Tillman-Roberts (1897)
Estimated population: 65 to 75 • *Highest graded:* Unc.

VG-8	F-12	VF-20	EF-40	AU-50	Unc-60	Unc-63	Unc-65
$550	$750	$1,000	$1,350	$1,800	$2,400	$2,750	$4,800

W-1370 • F-489 • Bruce-Roberts (1897–1898)
Estimated population: 55 to 65 • *Highest graded:* Unc.

VG-8	F-12	VF-20	EF-40	AU-50	Unc-60	Unc-63	Unc-65
$550	$750	$1,000	$1,350	$1,800	$2,400	$2,750	$4,800

W-1371 • F-490 • Lyons-Roberts (1898–1905)
Estimated population: 1,200 to 1,400 • *Highest graded:* Unc.

VG-8	F-12	VF-20	EF-40	AU-50	Unc-60	Unc-63	Unc-65
$550	$750	$1,000	$1,350	$1,800	$2,400	$2,750	$4,800

W-1372 • F-491 • Lyons-Treat (1905–1906)
Estimated population: 11 to 13 • *Highest graded:* VF-25.

VG-8	F-12	VF-20
$700	$1,100	$1,600

W-1373 • F-492 • Vernon-Treat (1906–1909)
Estimated population: 15 to 17 • *Highest graded:* EF-40.

VG-8	F-12	VF-20	EF-40
$850	$1,300	$1,600	$1,950

Series of 1882, Date Back
(Authorized Issue 1908–1915, Some 1916)

This unexpected issue (illus. on p. 349) was created to reflect a change in the security or backing of the notes authorized by the Aldrich-Vreeland Act of May 30, 1908. Notes of the new type were issued beginning in that year. Production of 1882 Brown Backs ceased, and new orders were filled by the Date Back type.

In order to make it easier to fund the notes, banks were allowed to deposit good securities as well as government bonds, while earlier only U.S. government bonds had been allowed. All have the inscription on the face, "This note is secured by bonds of the United States or other securities." This was often done by altering face plates of the same design used for earlier series. Although the Act expired on June 30, 1915, marking the end of the official use of this imprint and the related back, some plates were continued in use into 1916. Otherwise the face motifs are the same as on the Series of 1882 Brown Backs (continued from the Original Series and Series of 1875). The serial numbers, charter number, two regional letters, and the Treasury seal were all in blue.

The back was redesigned completely. At the center is a large open space with the dates 1882 and 1908 and an ornament between them. Above, near the border, is the obligation or redemption clause, and below near the border is the counterfeiting clause. At the left is the portrait of secretary of the Treasury William P. Fessenden, who held the post during the last two years of the Civil War. The engraving was done by Charles Skinner. To the right is a seated mechanic. Gone are the state and territorial seals used, making plate preparation a much easier task.

These were normally issued in sheets of $10-$10-$10-$20, but some sheets were entirely of the $10 denomination, giving the otherwise unusual situation of having a D face plate letter on notes from such a sheet. Probably, in the marketplace only the most sophisticated cataloger or dealer would even notice.

Two face styles exist, similar to the Series of 1882 Brown Back notes, here with the plate amended to add "and other securities." The distribution and extent of these styles among 1882 Date Back notes have not been studied.

> **Face Style 1:** This is most often seen and can be quickly identified as having 10-TEN-10-(charter number)-TEN-10 in the top margin to the left of NATIONAL CURRENCY.
>
> **Face Style 2:** The rarer style can be quickly identified as having 10-TEN-(charter number)-10-TEN-10 in that location.[18]

A rarity to be aware of: "Series of 1882 Date Backs had just begun to be sent to the First National Bank of Bastrop, Texas, when its first 20 years of corporate life expired. Only one of those sheets was sent, a $10-$10-$10-$20 from this plate!"[19]

The average note is apt to be in a grade from Very Good to Very Fine, but there are enough Extremely Fine and About Uncirculated notes around that finding one for type will be easy enough. Uncirculated notes are scarce as a class.

Banks of Issue and Rarity of Notes

Based upon census information from Don C. Kelly and James M. Kelly (*National Bank Note Census*, Version 4.0) and with some information from the other sources, this listing gives each location, the number of banks issuing this series of notes within each, and a commentary.[20]

The Kelly survey records 2,356 notes, far fewer than the 5,480 $10 Brown Back notes. No matter—the Date Backs have always been overlooked, with no particular attention paid to the type, although specific locations are in demand. Serial number 1 notes total 145, resulting in occasional auction appearances. These are specifically listed below.

Alabama • 17 banks of issue • 26 notes reported • Nine different banks are represented, including many from the Fourth National Bank of Montgomery (eight). All are circulated.

Alaska Territory • 1 bank of issue • No notes reported • Alaska was a district from 1884 until it became a territory on August 24, 1912, which it remained until statehood in 1959. All large-size Alaska notes in all series have the "district" address. Regardless, numismatists call all "territorials."

Arizona • 3 banks of issue • 2 notes reported • Both are from the First National Bank of Clifton (F, VF).

Arizona Territory • 5 banks of issue • 1 note reported • From the First National Bank of Clifton (VF).

Arkansas • 3 banks of issue • 1 note reported • The only note reported is from the First National Bank of DeQueen (VF).

California • 25 banks of issue • 165 notes reported • There are 19 banks represented, led by the Wells-Fargo Bank of San Francisco (110, three Unc) and the First National Bank of Los Angeles (18).

Colorado • 22 banks of issue • 20 notes reported • Eight banks are represented, including the Fort Collins National Bank (six). All are circulated.

Connecticut • 10 banks of issue • 11 notes reported • Six banks represented, including the Central National Bank of Norwalk (four). All are circulated.

Delaware • 6 banks of issue • 6 notes reported • Four banks are represented, including the National Bank of Smyrna (three). One Unc, from the Fruit Growers National Bank of Smyrna.

District of Columbia • 5 banks of issue • 18 notes reported • Three banks represented, including the Riggs National Bank of Washington (11). All are circulated.

Florida • 8 banks of issue • 21 notes reported • Five banks represented, including the First National Bank of Pensacola (nine), and the American National Bank of Pensacola (eight). All are circulated.

Georgia • 24 banks of issue • 37 notes reported • There are 12 banks represented, including the Lowry National Bank of Atlanta (11) and the Fourth National Bank of Atlanta (eight). All are circulated.

Hawaii Territory • 2 banks of issue • 13 notes reported • All are from the First National Bank of Hawaii at Honolulu. All are circulated.

Idaho • 4 banks of issue • 1 note reported • From the First National Bank of St. Anthony (VG).

Illinois • 133 banks of issue • 127 notes reported • There are 64 banks represented, including the Corn Exchange of Chicago (eight) and the Ricker National Bank of Quincy (nine). One Unc note, from the Second National Bank of Charleston.

Indiana • 65 banks of issue • 77 notes reported • Including the Citizens National Bank of Evansville (six), Hamilton National Bank of Fort Wayne (six), American National Bank of Indianapolis (five), and the Peoples National Bank of Lawrenceburgh (seven). All are circulated.

Iowa • 130 banks of issue • 176 notes reported • Seven are Unc. There are 61 banks represented, including the Des Moines National Bank (43). Only one serial number 1 note is known, from the First National Bank of Denison (AU).

Kansas • 43 banks of issue • 28 notes reported • There are 18 banks represented, including the Citizens National Bank of Emporia (five) and the First National Bank of Hiawatha (four). One Unc, from the National Bank of Parsons.

Kentucky • 45 banks of issue • 58 notes reported • There are 21 banks represented, including the National Bank of Kentucky in Louisville (16). All are circulated.

Louisiana • 12 banks of issue • 20 notes reported • Eight banks are represented, including the Commercial National Bank of New Orleans (seven). All are circulated.

Maine • 20 banks of issue • 5 notes reported • Four banks are represented; two notes are from the North National Bank of Rockland. All are circulated.

Maryland • 29 banks of issue • 37 notes reported • There are 16 banks represented, including the Drovers & Mechan-

SERIES OF 1882, DATE BACK

$10 National Bank Note, Series of 1882, Date Back (W-1380). The National Security Bank of Philadelphia, charter 1743. The design is the same as the preceding. Now with blue overprints.

Back of the $10 National Bank Note, Series of 1882, Date Back (W-1380). At the left is the portrait of secretary of the Treasury William P. Fessenden, successor in the post to Salmon P. Chase. At the right a mechanic is shown.

ics National Bank of Baltimore (nine) and the Citizens National Bank of Cumberland (six). The only Unc is from the Drovers & Mechanics National Bank of Baltimore.

Massachusetts • 48 banks of issue • 75 notes reported • Four Unc notes are known, two from the National Shawmut Bank of Boston and two from the First National Bank of Webster. There are 22 banks represented, including the National Shawmut Bank of Boston (35).

Michigan • 29 banks of issue • 35 notes reported • There are 14 banks represented, including the Grand Rapids National Bank (11) and the Miners National Bank of Ishpeming (seven). The census lists 12 Unc notes. One serial number 1 note is known, Hastings National Bank of Hastings (F).

Minnesota • 67 banks of issue • 70 notes reported • There are 35 banks represented, including the Northwestern National Bank of Minneapolis (seven) and the Merchants National Bank of St. Paul (nine). All are circulated.

Mississippi • 3 banks of issue • 15 notes reported • The census lists 11 from the First National Bank of Commerce of Hattiesburg. All are circulated.

Missouri • 37 banks of issue • 97 notes reported • There are 14 banks represented, including the National Bank of Commerce of St. Louis (28) and the State National Bank of St. Louis (31). Four Unc notes are from three different banks.

Montana • 13 banks of issue • 14 notes reported • Eight banks are represented, including the National Bank of Montana at Helena (seven). All are circulated.

Nebraska • 43 banks of issue • 47 notes reported • There are 21 banks represented, including the First National Bank of Hastings (seven) and the First National Bank of Beatrice (six). The only Unc note is from the Fullerton National Bank.

New Hampshire • 19 banks of issue • 25 notes reported • There are 10 banks represented, including 10 notes from the National Bank of Franklin, one of which is the state's only Unc note.

New Jersey • 52 banks of issue • 55 notes reported • There are 23 banks represented, including the Merchants National Bank of Newark (five) and the Chelsea National Bank of Atlantic City (five). All are circulated.

New Mexico • 7 banks of issue • 4 notes reported • Two banks are represented, including the First National Bank of Las Vegas (two) and the San Miguel National Bank of Las Vegas (two). All are circulated.

New Mexico Territory • 8 banks of issue • 8 notes reported • Three banks are represented, including the San Miguel National Bank of Las Vegas (four). All are circulated.

New York • 105 banks of issue • 136 notes reported • There are 53 banks represented, including the Chase National Bank of New York (13) and the Lincoln National Bank of New York (15). Three Unc notes are from the Columbia National Bank of Buffalo, Rye National Bank, and the First National Bank of Walton. Three serial number 1 notes are from the Wilber National Bank of Oneonta (all AU).

North Carolina • 27 banks of issue • 24 notes reported • The only Unc note from the First National Bank of Morganton. There are 11 banks represented, including the Commercial National Bank of Charlotte (five) and the National Bank of Fayetteville (five).

North Dakota • 26 banks of issue • 20 notes reported • All are circulated.

Ohio • 112 banks of issue • 138 notes reported • There are 59 banks represented, including the Citizens National Bank of Cincinnati (18) and the Bank of Commerce, Cleveland (12). Three Unc notes are from the First National Bank of Ada, Citizens National Bank of Cincinnati, and the German National Bank of Marietta.

Oklahoma • 85 banks of issue • 59 notes reported • There are 32 banks represented, including the First National Bank of Chickasha (five) and the Durant National Bank (five). All are circulated.

Oregon • 10 banks of issue • 9 notes reported • Four banks are represented, including the First National Bank of Pendleton (five). All are circulated.

Pennsylvania • 250 banks of issue • 207 notes reported • There are 107 banks represented, including the Duquesne National Bank (nine). The census lists 11 notes as Unc. Four serial number 1 notes are known, two from the First National Bank of New Bloomfield (Unc), one from the Farmers National Bank of Athens (EF), and one from the First National Bank of Canton (EF).

Rhode Island • 2 banks of issue • 8 notes reported • Two banks are represented, including the United National Bank of Providence (seven). All are circulated.

South Carolina • 11 banks of issue • 10 notes reported • Six banks are represented, including the First National Bank of Spartanburg (four). All are circulated.

South Dakota • 21 banks of issue • 12 notes reported • Seven banks are represented, including the First National Bank of Mitchell (five). All are circulated.

Tennessee • 24 banks of issue • 22 notes reported • There are 13 banks represented, including the First National Bank of Jackson (six, all Unc, the state's entire population).

Texas • 171 banks of issue • 184 notes reported • There are 78 banks represented, including the City National Bank of Dallas (14), First National Bank of El Paso (10), First National Bank of Fort Worth (10), and the First National Bank of Jacksonville (eight). The census lists 10 Unc notes. The only serial number 1 note is from the Nocana National Bank (Unc).

Utah • 9 banks of issue • 5 notes reported • Four banks are represented, including two from the First National Bank of Price. All are circulated.

Vermont • 12 banks of issue • 4 notes reported • Three banks are represented, including two notes from the Bennington County National Bank. All are circulated.

Virginia • 33 banks of issue • 66 notes reported • The only Unc note is from the Culpeper National Bank, Culpeper. There are 19 banks represented, including the National Bank of Commerce of Norfolk (13) and the American National Bank of Richmond (18).

Washington • 12 banks of issue • 15 notes reported • Six banks are represented, including the Old National Bank of Spokane (five). All are circulated.

West Virginia • 28 banks of issue • 32 notes reported • There are 14 banks represented, including the National Exchange Bank of Wheeling (five). All are circulated.

Wisconsin • 47 banks of issue • 95 notes reported • There are 32 banks represented, including the Wisconsin National Bank of Milwaukee (17) and the Marine National Bank of Wisconsin (10). Five Unc notes are from two different banks, one from the Wisconsin National Bank of Milwaukee and four from the Kellogg National Bank of Green Bay.

Wyoming • 10 banks of issue • 16 notes reported • Seven banks are represented, including the Rawlins National Bank of Rawlins (five). All are circulated.

Generic prices for a typical note from a state from which notes range from plentiful to just slightly scarce:

VG-8	F-12	VF-20	EF-40	AU-50	Unc-60	Unc-63	Unc-65
$550	$720	$900	$1,250	$1,700	$2,300	$2,600	$4,200

W-1380 • F-539 • Rosecrans-Huston (1889–1891)
Estimated population: 90 to 100 • *Highest graded:* Unc.

VG-8	F-12	VF-20	EF-40	AU-50	Unc-60	Unc-63	Unc-65
$550	$720	$900	$1,250	$1,700	$2,300	$2,600	$4,200

W-1381 • F-540 • Rosecrans-Nebeker (1891–1893)
Estimated population: 220 to 240 • *Highest graded:* Unc.

VG-8	F-12	VF-20	EF-40	AU-50	Unc-60	Unc-63	Unc-65
$550	$720	$900	$1,250	$1,700	$2,300	$2,600	$4,200

W-1382 • F-541 • Rosecrans-Morgan (1893)
Recorded population: 2 • *Highest graded:* F-15.

VG-8	F-12
$1,100	$1,350

W-1383 • F-542 • Tillman-Morgan (1893–1897)
Estimated population: 360 to 400 • *Highest graded:* Unc.

VG-8	F-12	VF-20	EF-40	AU-50	Unc-60	Unc-63	Unc-65
$550	$720	$900	$1,250	$1,700	$2,300	$2,600	$4,200

W-1384 • F-543 • Tillman-Roberts (1897)
Estimated population: 48 to 54 • *Highest graded:* AU-50.

VG-8	F-12	VF-20	EF-40	AU-50
$550	$720	$900	$1,250	$1,700

W-1385 • F-544 • Bruce-Roberts (1897–1898)
Estimated population: 40 to 45 • *Highest graded:* EF-40.

VG-8	F-12	VF-20	EF-40
$550	$720	$900	$1,250

W-1386 • F-545 • Lyons-Roberts (1898–1905)
Estimated population: 1,400 to 1,500 • *Highest graded:* Unc.

VG-8	F-12	VF-20	EF-40	AU-50	Unc-60	Unc-63	Unc-65
$550	$720	$900	$1,250	$1,700	$2,300	$2,600	$4,200

W-1387 • F-546 • Vernon-Treat (1906–1909)
Estimated population: 75 to 85 • *Highest graded:* AU-50.

VG-8	F-12	VF-20	EF-40	AU-50
$550	$720	$900	$1,250	$1,700

W-1388 • F-547 • Vernon-McClung (1909–1911)
Recorded population: 2 • *Highest graded:* G-6.

W-1389 • F-548 • Napier-McClung (1911–1912)
Recorded population: 7 • *Highest graded:* VF-20 • *Selected information:* Superior (9/2005), 711-N35289/D, First NB of Las Vegas, NM, VG, $2,875. No other modern sales.

W-1390 • F-548a • Parker-Burke (1913–1914)
Recorded population: 1 • *Selected information:* Knight (6/1995), 142-R346710/142/A, First NB of Gaffney, SC, VF+, $7,975; later seen in Knight (4/2003), $6,900.

Series of 1882, Value Back
(Authorized Issue 1915+)

When the Aldrich-Vreeland Act expired on June 20, 1915, the BEP created the Value Back (illus. on p. 353), spelling out the denomination, to replace the Date Back design. The security of the notes reverted to bonds only, as it had been before the implementation of the Aldrich-Vreeland Act of May 30, 1908.

> **Plate Style a:** Some old face plates remained in use from the earlier series, with the inscription on the face reading, "This note is secured by bonds of the United States or other securities."

> **Plate Style b:** A "new" plate style was created, a copy of that used for all 1882 Brown Backs, with the security stated as "This note is secured by bonds of the United States deposited with the U.S. Treasurer at Washington." This is the correct or proper plate intended for use on Value Back notes.

Otherwise the face was similar to that used for the Series of 1882 Date Back, with the serial numbers, charter number, two regional letters, and the Treasury seal all in blue. The back reused the vignettes of the preceding type, but now with TEN DOLLARS in large letters at the center.

Two face styles exist among Plate Style b notes, a carry-over from the Series of 1882 Brown Back notes, here with information reentered into the plate to add "and other securities." The distribution and extent of these styles among 1882 Value Back notes have not been studied.

> **Face Style 1:** This is most often seen and can be quickly identified as having 10-TEN-10-(charter number)-TEN-10 in the top margin to the left of NATIONAL CURRENCY.

> **Face Style 2:** The rarer style can be quickly identified as having 10-TEN-(charter number)-10-TEN-10 in that location.[21]

Value Backs are far and away the rarest of the three types of 1882 notes, although in the past the market price for some offerings of this type has often been no more than for the plentiful Brown Back, the latter being the most attractive design. The average Value Back note is apt to grade Fine to Very Fine or so, higher than the earlier 1882 series. Uncirculated notes are particularly scarce and are from scattered banks, with no hoards reported. As buyers learn more and become increasingly sophisticated, it is likely that the rarity of this type will be reflected in the auction room. Although Plate Styles a and b are well described in the specialized texts by Gene Hessler, Carlson Chambliss, Peter Huntoon, and Don C. Kelly, to this point they have been nearly completely ignored in auction catalogs and other offerings.

Banks of Issue and Rarity of Notes

Based upon census information from Don C. Kelly and James M. Kelly (*National Bank Note Census*, Version 4.0) and with some information from the other sources, this listing gives each location, the number of banks issuing this series of notes within each, and a commentary.[22]

The Kelly survey records 1,226, or about half of the number of Date Backs and a fifth of the number of Brown Backs; this pattern holds true for other Value Back denominations as well. Remarkably, not a single serial number 1 note is listed. Should one appear it would furnish the opportunity for an enthusiastic write-up in an auction catalog.

Alabama • 8 banks of issue • 20 notes reported • Six banks represented, with the First National Bank of Montgomery having eight notes and the Dothan National Bank having five. The only Unc note is from the Dothan National Bank.

Arizona • 2 banks of issue • 3 notes reported • All are from the First National Bank of Clifton (F, VF–EF, EF).

Arkansas • 2 banks of issue • 1 note reported • From the First National Bank of DeQueen (VG).

California • 14 banks of issue • 61 notes reported • Nine banks are represented, including the Wells-Fargo National Bank of San Francisco (36). All are circulated.

Colorado • 11 banks of issue • 15 notes reported • Eight banks are represented. All are circulated.

Connecticut • 6 banks of issue • 5 notes reported • Three are from the First National Bank of Wallingford. All are circulated.

Delaware • 2 banks of issue • No notes reported.

Florida • 3 banks of issue • No notes reported.

Georgia • 7 banks of issue • 11 notes reported • The Lowry National Bank of Atlanta has most (seven).

Hawaii Territory • 1 bank of issue • 11 notes reported • All are from the First National Bank of Hawaii at Honolulu, circulated.

Idaho • 2 banks of issue • 4 notes reported • Three from the First National Bank of Payette. All are circulated.

Illinois • 133 banks of issue • 141 notes reported • Including the LaSalle National Bank (71, most of which are Unc).

Indiana • 30 banks of issue • 36 notes reported • Four Unc notes are from two different banks.

Iowa • 65 banks of issue • 55 notes reported • Two Unc notes are from the First National Bank of Mason City and the First National Bank of Prescott.

Kansas • 19 banks of issue • 19 notes reported • There are 10 banks represented. All notes are circulated.

Kentucky • 16 banks of issue • 46 notes reported • Clusters include holdings from the National Bank of Kentucky at Louisville (18) and the First Hardin National Bank of Elizabethtown (12, including five Unc).

Louisiana • 1 bank of issue • 2 notes reported • Both are VG–F from the First National Bank of Abbeville.

Maine • 4 banks of issue • 4 notes reported • Two are from the Peoples National Bank of Farmington. All are circulated.

Maryland • 16 banks of issue • 23 notes reported • All are circulated.

Massachusetts • 9 banks of issue • 17 notes reported • Including the Union National Bank of Lowell (eight). All are circulated.

Michigan • 11 banks of issue • 15 notes reported • The one Unc note is from the Citizens National Bank of Houghton.

Minnesota • 36 banks of issue • 36 notes reported • There are 18 banks represented. All notes are circulated.

Mississippi • 2 banks of issue • 1 note reported • First National Bank of Hattiesburg (F), serial 79.

Missouri • 12 banks of issue • 16 notes reported • Including six from the Paris National Bank. One Unc note, from the same bank.

Montana • 2 banks of issue • 6 notes reported • All are from the National Bank of Montana at Helena. All are circulated.

Nebraska • 20 banks of issue • 31 notes reported • Including the First National Bank of Hastings (nine) and the City National Bank of Lincoln (eight). One Unc note, from the Fullerton National Bank of Fullerton, serial 2847.

New Hampshire • 10 banks of issue • 6 notes reported • From six different banks; all notes are circulated.

New Jersey • 26 banks of issue • 26 notes reported • Including the First National Bank of Madison (four) and the Second National Bank of Phillipsburg (four). The only Unc note is from the Citizens National Bank of Long Branch.

New Mexico • 6 banks of issue • 7 notes reported • Four banks are represented, with First National Bank of Las Vegas having four.

New York • 64 banks of issue • 60 notes reported • There are 31 banks represented. Two Unc notes are from the Peoples National Bank of Hoosick Falls and National Bank of Skaneateles.

North Carolina • 12 banks of issue • 14 notes reported • Seven banks are represented. All are circulated.

North Dakota • 20 banks of issue • 15 notes reported • Nine banks are represented. All are circulated.

Ohio • 61 banks of issue • 106 notes reported • There are 34 banks represented, including the Citizens National Bank of Cincinnati (18) and the Old Citizens National Bank of Zanesville (10, including the only Unc).

Oklahoma • 60 banks of issue • 43 notes reported • There are 28 banks represented. Three notes are Unc, from the Shawnee National Bank.

Oregon • 4 banks of issue • 4 notes reported • Three banks are represented. All are circulated.

Pennsylvania • 123 banks of issue • 108 notes reported • There are 53 banks represented, with the Bank of Pittsburgh in Pittsburgh having eight. Four Unc notes are known.

South Carolina • 2 banks of issue • 4 notes reported • Two banks are represented, with the First National Bank of Batesburg having three notes.

South Dakota • 14 banks of issue • 12 notes reported • Six banks are represented. All are in circulated grades.

Tennessee • 8 banks of issue • 14 notes reported • Eight banks are represented. All are circulated.

Texas • 84 banks of issue • 79 notes reported • There are 38 banks represented, including the First National Bank of El Paso (nine) and the Nocona National Bank (seven). Five Unc notes are reported.

Utah • 3 banks of issue • 5 notes reported • Two banks are represented. All are circulated.

Vermont • 3 banks of issue • 2 notes reported • Notes are from the Bennington County National Bank and the First National Bank of Poultney, both EF.

Virginia • 17 banks of issue • 50 notes reported • There are 14 banks represented, including the First National Bank of Clifton Forge (10) and the National Bank of Commerce of Norfolk (13). Three Unc notes reported, two from the First National Bank of Clifton Forge and one from the American National Bank of Richmond.

Washington • 6 banks of issue • 6 notes reported • Three banks are represented, including the Vancouver National Bank of Vancouver (three). All are circulated.

West Virginia • 16 banks of issue • 31 notes reported • There are 12 banks represented, including the Montgomery National Bank of Montgomery (five) and the National Exchange Bank of Wheeling (five). The only Unc note is from the First National Bank of Grafton.

Wisconsin • 21 banks of issue • 46 notes reported • There are 15 banks represented, including the Marine National Bank of Milwaukee (15). Two Unc notes are from the Farmers National Bank of Lake Geneva and the National Exchange Bank of Waukesha.

SERIES OF 1882, VALUE BACK

$10 National Bank Note, Series of 1882, Value Back (W-1397). The Fullerton (Nebraska) National Bank, charter 5384. Regional letter W (for West). This type was used for W-1394 to W-1402. The design is the same as the preceding with blue Treasury overprints.

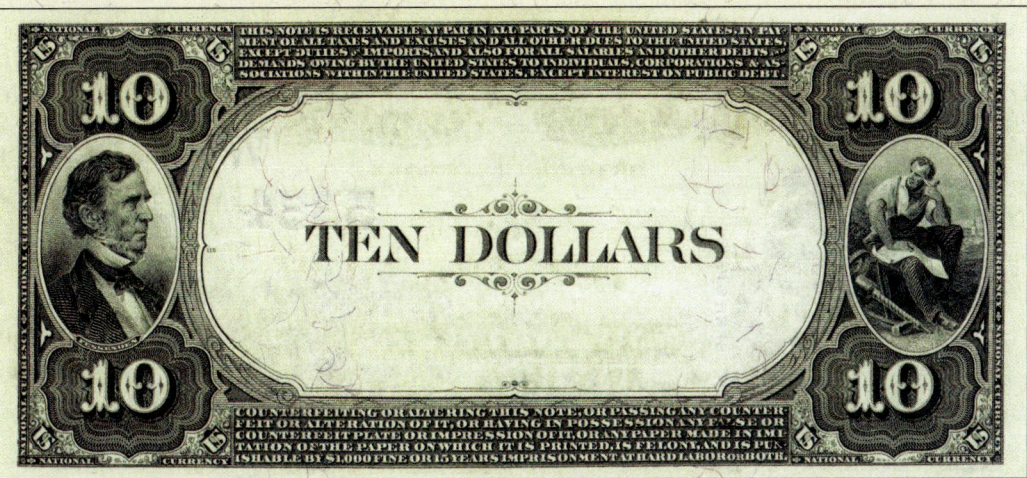

Back of the $10 National Bank Note, Series of 1882, Value Back (W-1397). As a class these are the rarest of the Series of 1882 notes. The vignettes are similar to the preceding.

Wyoming • 4 banks of issue • 9 notes reported • Four banks are represented, including the First National Bank of Kemmerer (three). The only Unc note is from the same bank.

Generic prices for a typical note from a state from which notes range from available to just slightly scarce:

VG-8	F-12	VF-20	EF-40	AU-50	Unc-60	Unc-63	Unc-65
$700	$900	$1,100	$1,400	$1,800	$2,500	$2,950	$3,400

W-1394 • F-576 • Tillman-Morgan (1893–1897)

Recorded population: 7 • *Highest graded:* VF-25 • *Selected information:* Heritage (1/2008), 11609-T787287/D, Southern Illinois NB of East St. Louis, IL, VG, $805. Knight (2/2003), 15199-5076/IN/T636687/D, City NB of Logansport, IN, Fine, $749.

W-1395 • F-576a • Tillman-Roberts (1897)

Recorded population: 6 • *Highest graded:* AU-50 • *Selected information:* Heritage (4/2008), 6225-T488623/D, Peoples NB of Waynesburg, PA, VF-EF, $13,800. Knight (8/2006), 3181-T510809/D, Woodsville NB, NH, VG–F, $4,140.

W-1396 • F-576b • Bruce-Roberts (1897–1898)

Recorded population: 5 • *Highest graded:* F-12 • *Selected information:* CAA (5/2004), 3809-U27047/F, Coshocton NB, OH, Fine, $10,063. Only modern sale recorded.

W-1397 • F-577 • Lyons-Roberts (1898–1905)

Estimated population: 1,100 to 1,300 • *Highest graded:* Unc.

VG-8	F-12	VF-20	EF-40	AU-50	Unc-60	Unc-63	Unc-65
$700	$900	$1,100	$1,400	$1,800	$2,500	$2,950	$3,400

W-1398 • F-577a • Lyons-Treat (1905-1906) • Unknown

W-1399 • F-578 • Vernon-Treat (1906–1909)

Estimated population: 40 to 45 • *Highest graded:* AU-55.

VG-8	F-12	VF-20	EF-40	AU-50	Unc-60	Unc-63	Unc-65
$700	$900	$1,100	$1,400	$1,800	$2,500	$3,000	$3,500

W-1400 • F-579 • Napier-McClung (1911–1912)

Estimated population: 30 to 35 • *Highest graded:* Unc.

VG-8	F-12	VF-20	EF-40	AU-50	Unc-60	Unc-63	Unc-65
$700	$900	$1,100	$1,400	$1,800	$2,500	$3,000	$3,500

W-1401 • F-579a • Parker-Burke (1913–1914) • Unknown

W-1402 • F-579b • Teehee-Burke (1915–1919)

Estimated population: 13 to 15 • *Highest graded:* VF-20.

VG-8	F-12	VF-20
$875	$1,125	$1,500

Series of 1902, Red Seal
(Authorized Issue 1902–1908)

The Act of April 12, 1902, provided for established banks of good reputation to extend their charters for another 40 years and for new banks to gain a 60-year charter. New designs were prepared, known today as 1902 Red Seal Notes, though older series were still being issued. All were secured by federal government bonds deposited with the Treasurer of the United States. During the life span of the 1902 Red Seals, certain banks continued to receive Series of 1882 Brown Back notes, depending on the date of their charter extension or founding.

Faces and backs were redesigned for the new Series of 1902 notes. These continued to be issued until the Aldrich-Vreeland Act of May 30, 1908, went into effect, after which time the Red Seals were abruptly replaced by the 1902 to 1908 Date Backs which were guaranteed in bonds "and other securities." Accordingly, this series was very short-lived.

The Red Seal notes are distinguished by the Treasury seal, two charter numbers, and two regional letters, which are printed in bright red, with the serial numbers in blue. The face illustrates the late president William McKinley; the president was assassinated in September 1901 while greeting visitors to the Temple of Music at the Pan-American Exposition in Buffalo, New York.[23]

The back of the note, *Liberty and Progress*, depicts a standing goddess between two bodies of water, a motif popular in other forms at the recent 1901 Exposition. G.F.C. Smillie engraved the art created by Walter Shirlaw. This design was copied later for use on the back of the $50 St. Louis Federal Reserve Bank Note, with some details altered and retitled as *Panama*.

A rarity to be aware of: "The minimally capitalized First National Bank of Wewoka, Oklahoma, had just started to issue state Red Seals when it was liquidated April 13, 1909. A shipment of 100 $5-$5-$5-$5 sheets went out, but only one sheet of the $10-$10-$10-$20s."[24]

The 1902 Red Seal notes are everlastingly popular with numismatists. Any scarce location is apt to draw a lot of attention. The average note is graded Fine to Very Fine or so, although Extremely Fine and About Uncirculated examples are easily found. Uncirculated notes are quite scarce.

Banks of Issue and Rarity of Notes

Based upon census information from Don C. Kelly and James M. Kelly (*National Bank Note Census*, Version 4.0) and with some information from the other sources, this listing gives each location, the number of banks issuing this series of notes within each, and a commentary.[25]

The Kelly survey records 2,628 notes, significantly more than the 1,781 Red Seals of the $5 denomination and 1,143

of the $20 value. Serial number 1 notes total 280, making them plentiful in the context of the era. These are specifically listed below.

Alabama • 59 banks of issue • 33 notes reported • Eight Unc notes are from three different banks. Five serial number 1 notes are known, three from the First National Bank of Oxford (AU), one from the Houston National Bank of Dothan (Unc) and one from the First National Bank of Evergreen (AU).

Alaska Territory • 1 bank of issue • 1 note reported • First National Bank of Fairbanks (AU), serial 702. Alaska was a district from 1884 until it became a territory on August 24, 1912, which it remained until statehood in 1959. All large-size Alaska notes in all series have the "district" address. Regardless, numismatists call all "territorials."

Arizona Territory • 9 banks of issue • 7 notes reported • Includes the Sandoval National Bank of Nogales (three). The only serial number 1 note is from the Sandoval National Bank of Nogales (VF).

Arkansas • 37 banks of issue • 16 notes reported • There are 10 banks represented, including the State National Bank of Little Rock (four). All are circulated grades. Three serial number 1 notes are from the Merchants National Bank of Fort Smith (not graded), the First National Bank of Springdale (not graded), and from the National Bank of Mena (F).

California • 108 banks of issue • 58 notes reported • There are 27 banks represented, including the Farmers & Mechanics National Bank of Los Angeles (11). All examples are in circulated grades. The census lists 12 serial number 1 notes.

Colorado • 84 banks of issue • 27 notes reported • There are 22 banks represented. Three Unc notes, one from the Denver National Bank, and two from the Trinidad National Bank of Trinidad. Three serial number 1 notes are from the First National Bank of Brighton (not graded), First National Bank of Brush (not graded), and the Trinidad National Bank of Trinidad (Unc).

Connecticut • 69 banks of issue • 58 notes reported • There are 29 banks represented. The census lists 10 Unc notes. Four serial number 1 notes are known, three from the Clinton National Bank of Clinton (Unc, EF–AU, AU) and one from the Phoenix National Bank of Hartford (Unc).

Delaware • 19 banks of issue • 3 notes reported • Three banks are represented. All notes are circulated.

District of Columbia • 7 banks of issue • 14 notes reported • Five banks are represented. All are circulated.

Florida • 30 banks of issue • 12 notes reported • Seven banks are represented, including the First National Bank of Madison (four). All are circulated.

Georgia • 69 banks of issue • 23 notes reported • There are 18 banks represented. The state's only serial number 1 note is from the First National Bank of Fort Valley (EF).

Hawaii Territory • 2 banks of issue • No notes are reported.

Idaho • 29 banks of issue • 7 notes reported • Five banks are represented. The only Unc note is from the First National Bank of Cottonwood. Four serial number 1 notes are listed.

SERIES OF 1902, RED SEAL

$10 National Bank Note, Series of 1902, Red Seal (W-1404). National Black River Bank of Proctorsville, Vermont. The overdone name of the cashier Charles W. Whitcomb is called a *vanity signature*. Many bank officers sought to create attention with such flourishes.

Back of the $10 National Bank Note, Series of 1902, Red Seal (W-1404). Also used on $10 National Bank Note, Series of 1902, Blue Seal, Plain Back notes. A standing figure is on an island or perhaps on land dividing two oceans (this general theme was later copied for the back of the $50 Federal Reserve Notes).

Illinois • 232 banks of issue • 164 notes reported • There are 83 banks are represented. Seven Unc notes are from the various banks. The census lists 15 serial number 1 notes.

Indian Territory • 121 banks of issue • 27 notes listed • Seven serial number 1 notes are recorded.

Indiana • 151 banks of issue • 88 notes reported • There are 45 banks represented. The census lists 13 Unc notes and 19 serial number 1 notes.

Iowa • 163 banks of issue • 79 notes reported • There are 46 banks represented. Seven Unc notes are listed. Four serial number 1 notes are recorded.

Kansas • 139 banks of issue • 76 notes reported • There are 34 banks represented, including the First National Bank of Clifton (24). The census lists 12 Unc notes. Nine serial number 1 notes are available from six different banks.

Kentucky • 88 banks of issue • 61 notes reported • There are 39 banks represented. One Unc note is reported from the Louisa National Bank. Five serial number 1 notes are recorded.

Louisiana • 24 banks of issue • 12 notes reported • All are circulated. Nine banks are represented. Two serial number 1 notes are from German-American National Bank of New Orleans (AU) and the American National Bank of Shreveport (not graded).

Maine • 59 banks of issue • 21 notes reported • There are 16 banks represented. Two Unc notes are from the National Traders Bank of Portland. The census lists four serial number 1 notes.

Maryland • 58 banks of issue • 38 notes reported • There are 21 banks represented. Four Unc notes are from three different banks. Five serial number 1 notes are recorded.

Massachusetts • 164 banks of issue • 53 notes reported • There are 32 banks represented. Six Unc notes are known. Two serial number 1 notes are from the New England National Bank of Boston and the First National Bank of Clinton, both Unc.

Michigan • 56 banks of issue • 55 notes reported • There are 20 banks represented, including the First National Bank of

Marquette (nine). The census lists 12 Unc notes. Three serial number 1 notes are known, all Unc from the Saint Johns National Bank.

Minnesota • 189 banks of issue • 103 notes reported • There are 59 banks represented. The census lists 13 Unc notes and 10 serial number 1 notes.

Mississippi • 25 banks of issue • 23 notes reported, all are circulated • There are 10 banks represented. Two serial number 1 notes are from the First National Bank of Gulfport (EF–AU) and the First National Bank of Vicksburg (not graded).

Missouri • 79 banks of issue • 83 notes reported • There are 32 banks represented, including the Mechanics-American National Bank of St. Louis (15). Four Unc notes are known. The census lists nine serial number 1 notes.

Montana • 24 banks of issue • 5 notes reported • Five banks are represented. All are circulated.

Nebraska • 143 banks of issue • 43 notes reported • There are 29 banks represented. The only Unc note is from the Exchange National Bank of Hastings. The census lists 10 serial number 1 notes.

Nevada • 9 banks of issue • 6 notes reported • Three banks are represented. All are circulated.

New Hampshire • 35 banks of issue • 15 notes reported • There are 13 banks represented. All are circulated.

New Jersey • 114 banks of issue • 62 notes reported • There are 38 banks represented. Two Unc notes are from the Bridgeton National Bank and the Closter National Bank. The census lists 12 serial number 1 notes.

New Mexico Territory • 31 banks of issue • 22 notes reported • There are 14 banks represented. Three serial number 1 notes are known, all from the Citizens National Bank of Roswell (F, VF–EF, Unc). The last is the only Unc example known.

New York • 313 banks of issue • 391 notes reported • Mostly Unc examples. The census lists 26 serial number 1 notes.

North Carolina • 39 banks of issue • 12 notes reported • Nine banks are represented. Two serial number 1 notes are known, both from the National Bank of Kinston (VF, Unc). One is the only Unc example known.

North Dakota • 107 banks of issue • 20 notes reported • There are 20 banks represented. Three Unc notes are known. The census lists eight serial number 1 notes.

Ohio • 230 banks of issue • 255 notes reported • Most are circulated. The census lists 15 serial number 1 notes.

Oklahoma • 96 banks of issue • 3 notes reported • First National Bank of Olustee (VG–F), City National Bank of McAlester (F–VF), and Peoples National Bank of Wapanucka (EF).

Oklahoma Territory • 103 banks of issue • 34 notes reported • The only Unc note is from the First National Bank of Pond Creek. Five serial number 1 notes are recorded.

Oregon • 44 banks of issue • 11 notes reported • Seven banks are represented. Three Unc notes are from the Citizens National Bank of Baker City, First National Bank of Coquille, and the First National Bank of Forest Grove. Four serial number 1 notes are recorded.

Pennsylvania • 485 banks of issue • 222 notes reported • Most are circulated. The census lists 35 serial number 1 notes.

Porto Rico Territory • 1 bank of issue • 7 notes reported • All are circulated examples. Spelled *Porto* in the bank title; address: Island of Porto Rico. Called a "territorial" note by numismatists.

Rhode Island • 25 banks of issue • 11 notes reported • Eight banks are represented. All are circulated.

South Carolina • 22 banks of issue • 14 notes reported • There are 12 banks represented. All are circulated. The only serial number 1 note is from the Citizens National Bank of Anderson (EF).

South Dakota • 67 banks of issue • 20 notes reported • There are 18 banks represented. The only Unc note is from the Dakota National Bank of Aberdeen. Four serial number 1 notes are recorded.

Tennessee • 52 banks of issue • 34 notes reported • There are 20 banks represented. All are circulated. Two serial number 1 notes are known, both F–VF, from the First National Bank of Polk City at Copperhill and the First National Bank of Lenoir City.

Texas • 323 banks of issue • 131 notes reported • The census lists 12 Unc notes. Six serial number 1 notes are recorded.

Utah • 9 banks of issue • 3 notes reported • Two banks are represented. All are circulated.

Vermont • 35 banks of issue • 11 notes reported • Eight banks are represented. All are circulated. The only serial number 1 note is from the First National Bank of Fair Haven (EF).

Virginia • 70 banks of issue • 23 notes reported • There are 14 banks represented, including the National State Bank of Richmond (five) and the First National Bank of Richmond (four). All known examples are in circulated grades. The only serial number 1 note is from the Peoples National Bank of Manassas (AU).

Washington • 41 banks of issue • 9 notes reported • Eight banks are represented. The only serial number 1 note is from the First National Bank of Colfax (Unc, the only one in this grade).

West Virginia • 68 banks of issue • 39 notes reported • There are 23 banks represented. All reported notes are in circulated grades. Seven serial number 1 notes are recorded.

Wisconsin • 69 banks of issue • 74 notes reported • There are 30 banks represented, including the First National Bank of Wisconsin (17). Five Unc notes are known. The census lists three serial number 1 notes, from the First National Bank of Grantsburg (Unc), Ladysmith National Bank (Unc), and the First National Bank of West Allis (VF).

Wyoming • 19 banks of issue • 9 notes reported • Six banks are represented, including the First National Bank of Saratoga (four). Four Unc notes are known. The only serial number 1 note is from the First National Bank of Worland (AU).

Generic prices for a typical note from a state from which notes range from plentiful to just slightly scarce:

VG-8	F-12	VF-20	EF-40	AU-50	Unc-60	Unc-63	Unc-65
$675	$850	$1,100	$1,450	$1,900	$2,250	$2,600	$3,500

W-1404 • F-613 • Lyons-Roberts (1898–1905)
Estimated population: 1,750 to 1,900 • *Highest graded:* Unc.

VG-8	F-12	VF-20	EF-40	AU-50	Unc-60	Unc-63	Unc-65
$675	$850	$1,100	$1,450	$1,900	$2,250	$2,600	$3,500

W-1405 • F-614 • Lyons-Treat (1905–1906)
Estimated population: 250 to 300 • *Highest graded:* Unc.

VG-8	F-12	VF-20	EF-40	AU-50	Unc-60	Unc-63	Unc-65
$675	$850	$1,100	$1,450	$1,900	$2,250	$2,600	$3,500

W-1406 • F-615 • Vernon-Treat (1906–1909)
Estimated population: 275 to 325 • *Highest graded:* Unc.

VG-8	F-12	VF-20	EF-40	AU-50	Unc-60	Unc-63	Unc-65
$675	$850	$1,100	$1,450	$1,900	$2,250	$2,600	$3,500

Series of 1902, Blue Seal, Date Back
(Authorized Issue 1908–1915, Some 1916)

Parallel to the situation for Series of 1882 Date Back notes, the unexpected 1902 Blue Seal, Date Back type (illus. on p. 359) was created to reflect a change in the security or backing of the notes authorized by the Aldrich-Vreeland Act of May 30, 1908. Notes of the new type were issued beginning in that year. Production of 1902 Red Seals ceased, and new orders were filled by the Date Back type.

In order to make it easier to fund the notes, banks were allowed to deposit good securities in addition to government bonds, while earlier only U.S. government bonds had been allowed. All have the inscription as part of the top border on the face, SECURED BY UNITED STATES BONDS OR OTHER SECURITIES. This was often done by altering face plates used for the Series of 1902 Red Seal notes. Although the Act expired on June 30, 1915, marking the end of the official use of this imprint and the related back, some plates were used into 1916. Otherwise the face motifs are the same as on the Series of 1902 Red Seals, but now with the serial numbers, two charter numbers, two regional letters, and the Treasury seal in blue. The back is the same as used for the 1902 Red Seals, except that the dates are printed in the top of the field, 1902 to the left of center and 1908 to the right.

These were printed on sheets arranged as $10-$10-$10-$20. The first sheets of this type were delivered on August 1, 1908—$5 and $10 notes for the First National Bank of Beaver City, Idaho, charter 9119.[26]

Prices are for states from which a larger number of notes survive. Although the 1902 Blue Seal, Date Back notes are slightly scarcer as a class than the Plain Backs, not much attention has been paid to them in this regard. High-grade notes are elusive.

Rarities to be aware of: "The First National Bank of Fort Gibson, Oklahoma, was liquidated March 19, 1909, just after the No. 1 sheet of state notes was sent to the bank. The state printing happened to be from this $10-$10-$10-$20

Series of 1902 Date Back plate. Similarly, exactly one sheet of Series of 1902 Date Backs was sent to the Caldwell (Kansas) National Bank before it was liquidated on June 15, 1909. The Comptroller's office had just run out of Red Seals, and had just gotten into the new stock of $10-$10-$10-$20 Date Backs when the bank liquidated."[27]

Banks of Issue and Rarity of Notes
Based upon census information from Don C. Kelly and James M. Kelly (*National Bank Note Census*, Version 4.0) and with some information from other sources, this listing gives each location, the number of banks issuing this series of notes within each location, the number of notes recorded, and a commentary.[28]

The Kelly survey records 6,610 notes, yielding a wide field of opportunity for seekers of particular locations. Serial number 1 notes total 121, making them scarce as a class. These are specifically listed below. The average note is graded Very Good to Fine or so, although Extremely Fine and About Uncirculated examples are easily found. Uncirculated notes are quite scarce.

Alabama • 87 banks of issue • 85 notes reported • There are 41 banks represented. All are circulated. The only serial number 1 note is from the City National Bank of Selma (AU).

Alaska Territory • 2 banks of issue • 1 note reported • First National Bank of Fairbanks, VG, serial 1914. Alaska was a district from 1884 until it became a territory on August 24, 1912, which it remained until statehood in 1959. All large-size Alaska notes in all series have the "district" address. Regardless, numismatists call all "territorials."

Arizona • 11 banks of issue • 4 notes reported • One Unc note is known, the only serial number 1 note, from the Yuma National Bank.

Arizona Territory • 10 banks of issue • 7 notes reported • Five banks are represented. All are circulated.

Arkansas • 61 banks of issue • 57 notes reported • There are 27 banks represented, including the First National Bank of Batesville (eight) and the Exchange National Bank of Little Rock (seven). Two Unc notes are known. The only serial number 1 note is from the First National Bank of Cotton Plant (VF).

California • 247 banks of issue • 262 notes reported • Three Unc notes are known. The census lists nine serial number 1 notes.

Colorado • 113 banks of issue • 82 notes reported • Two Unc notes are known. The only serial number 1 note is from the Burns National Bank of Durango (EF–AU).

Connecticut • 76 banks of issue • 105 notes reported • The census lists 11 Unc notes. Two serial number 1 notes are from the Clinton National Bank. (Unc, AU).

Delaware • 21 banks of issue • 9 notes reported • Seven banks are represented. All are circulated.

District of Columbia • 12 banks of issue • 39 notes reported • Nine banks are represented. The only Unc note is from the National Bank of Washington. The only serial number 1 note is from the Federal National Bank of Washington (EF).

Florida • 54 banks of issue • 51 notes reported • 26 banks are represented. The only Unc note is from the First National Bank of Saint Petersburg. Three serial number 1 notes are from the First National Bank of Brooksville (all F).

Georgia • 106 banks of issue • 104 notes reported • Four Unc notes are known.

Hawaii Territory • 3 banks of issue • 1 note reported • Baldwin National Bank of Kahului, serial 124 (AU).

Idaho • 54 banks of issue • 37 notes reported • There are 22 banks represented, all circulated examples.

Illinois • 368 banks of issue • 401 notes reported • The census lists 23 notes in Unc grade. Six serial number 1 notes are recorded.

Indiana • 228 banks of issue • 192 notes reported • The census lists 11 Unc notes. Seven serial number 1 notes are recorded.

Iowa • 262 banks of issue • 418 notes reported • The census lists 52 Unc notes. Six serial number 1 notes are recorded.

Kansas • 183 banks of issue • 168 notes reported • The census lists 33 Unc notes, 15 from the First National Bank of Clifton, and 13 serial number 1 notes.

Kentucky • 132 banks of issue • 128 notes reported • Three Unc notes are known. The two serial number 1 notes are from the First National Bank of Lexington (VF) and the United States National Bank of Owensboro (VF).

Louisiana • 29 banks of issue • 26 notes reported • There are 13 banks represented. All are circulated.

Maine • 72 banks of issue • 33 notes reported • There are 25 banks represented. All are circulated. The only serial number 1 note is from the First National Bank of Van Buren (VG).

Maryland • 82 banks of issue • 104 notes reported • There are 35 banks represented. One Unc example is known, from the First National Bank of Baltimore.

Massachusetts • 174 banks of issue • 147 notes reported • Eight Unc notes are known.

Michigan • 95 banks of issue • 157 notes reported • Banks include the First National Bank of Cassopolis (22) and the National Bank of Commerce of Detroit (15). The census lists 21 Unc notes. Three serial number 1 notes are from the Gogebic National Bank of Ironwood (VF), National Lumbermans Bank of Muskegon (Unc), and the First National Bank of Rochester (not graded).

Minnesota • 249 banks of issue • 302 notes reported • The census lists 10 Unc notes. The only serial number 1 note is from the American National Bank of St. Paul (not graded).

Mississippi • 42 banks of issue • 26 notes reported • One Unc note is known, from the First National Bank of Corinth.

Missouri • 127 banks of issue • 336 notes reported • The census lists 18 Unc notes. Three serial number 1 notes are known, all AU, from the Moniteau National Bank of California.

Montana • 58 banks of issue • 35 notes reported • There are 24 banks represented. All are circulated.

Nebraska • 209 banks of issue • 284 notes reported • The census lists 18 Unc notes. The only serial number 1 note is from the Nebraska City National Bank (AU).

Nevada • 12 banks of issue • 13 notes reported • Six banks are represented, including the Nixon National Bank of Reno (five). The only Unc note is from the Nixon National Bank of Reno.

New Hampshire • 47 banks of issue • 27 notes reported • There are 18 banks represented. All are circulated.

New Jersey • 176 banks of issue • 116 notes reported • Four Unc notes are known. The two serial number 1 notes are from the First National Bank of Blackwood and the Califon National Bank.

New Mexico • 33 banks of issue • 11 notes reported • There are 10 banks represented. Two Unc notes are known, from the State National Bank of Albuquerque and the First National Bank of Lake Arthur.

New Mexico Territory • 35 banks of issue • 15 notes reported • There are 10 banks represented, including the State National Bank of Albuquerque (five). Two Unc examples are reported, from the First National Bank of Lake Arthur and the State National Bank of Albuquerque (the only serial number 1 note).

New York • 420 banks of issue • 529 notes reported • The census lists 40 Unc examples, with 10 from the First National Bank of Saratoga Springs. There are 18 serial number 1 notes recorded.

North Carolina • 70 banks of issue • 52 notes reported • All are in circulated grades.

North Dakota • 132 banks of issue • 54 notes reported • One Unc note is from the First National Bank of Northwood. The only serial number 1 note is from the First National Bank of Plaza (not graded).

Ohio • 302 banks of issue • 335 notes reported • Six Unc notes are reported from the First National Bank of Boswell.

Oklahoma • 311 banks of issue • 104 notes reported • One Unc note is from the State National Bank of Boswell. Four serial number 1 notes are from the First National Bank of Allen (EF), Farmers National Bank of Oklahoma City (VF), and the Oklahoma Stock National Bank of Oklahoma City (two, both AU).

Oregon • 78 banks of issue • 55 notes reported • There are 35 banks represented. All are circulated. Three serial number 1 notes are recorded, all EF, from the First National Bank of Junction City, United States National Bank of Newburgh, and the Douglas National Bank of Roseburg.

Pennsylvania • 698 banks of issue • 428 notes reported • The census lists 14 Unc notes. Eight serial number 1 notes are recorded.

Porto Rico Territory • 1 bank of issue • 1 note reported • First National Bank of Porto Rico, San Juan (VG), serial 515. Spelled *Porto* in the bank title; address: Island of Porto Rico. Called a "territorial" note by numismatists.

Rhode Island • 23 banks of issue • 70 notes reported • There are 18 banks represented. Two Unc notes are from the Blackstone Canal National Bank.

South Carolina • 64 banks of issue • 39 notes reported • There are 24 banks represented. The only Unc example is from the Peoples National Bank of Charleston.

SERIES OF 1902, BLUE SEAL, DATE BACK

$10 National Bank Note, Series of 1902, Blue Seal, Date Back (W-1415). The Edwards National Bank of Edwards, New York, charter 10569. A serial number 1 note from plate position C. Blue Treasury seal and other overprints.

Back of the $10 National Bank Note, Series of 1902, Blue Seal, Date Back (W-1415).

South Dakota • 85 banks of issue • 91 notes reported • All are circulated. Three serial number 1 notes are from the First National Bank of Custer City (VF–EF), First National Bank of Pierre (not graded), and First National Bank of Pukwana (VF).

Tennessee • 108 banks of issue • 124 notes reported • Two Unc notes are known.

Texas • 462 banks of issue • 384 notes reported • The census lists 19 Unc notes. Two serial number 1 notes are known, from the First National Bank of Bagwell (Unc) and the Houston National Exchange Bank (F).

Utah • 20 banks of issue • 24 notes reported • There are 12 banks represented. All are circulated.

Vermont • 45 banks of issue • 22 notes reported • There are 14 banks represented. All are circulated. The only serial number 1 note is from the First National Bank of Fair Haven (EF).

Virginia • 122 banks of issue • 96 notes reported • Two Unc examples are reported, from the First National Bank of Richmond and the National City and State Bank of Richmond.

Washington • 79 banks of issue • 40 notes reported • There are 26 banks represented. The only Unc note is from the Pacific National Bank of Tacoma. Three serial number 1 notes are from the Pacific National Bank of Tacoma (one Unc, two AU).

West Virginia • 104 banks of issue • 66 notes reported • The one Unc note is from the National Bank of West Virginia in Wheeling. The only serial number 1 note is from the National Bank of Commerce in Williamson (VF–EF).

Wisconsin • 107 banks of issue • 291 notes reported • Eight Unc examples are reported. Five serial number 1 notes are known from the Commerce National Bank of Manitowoc (EF), National Bank of Manitowoc (F), Citizens National Bank of Merrill (EF, AU, Unc).

Wyoming • 30 banks of issue • 22 notes reported • There are 13 banks represented. All are circulated. One serial number 1 note is from the First National Bank of Laramie (AU).

Generic prices for a typical note from a state from which notes range from plentiful to just slightly scarce:

VG-8	F-12	VF-20	EF-40	AU-50	Unc-60	Unc-63	Unc-65
$150	$175	$250	$400	$575	$725	$800	$1,250

W-1408 • F-616 • Lyons-Roberts (1898–1905)
Estimated population: 2,600 to 3,000 • Highest graded: Unc.

VG-8	F-12	VF-20	EF-40	AU-50	Unc-60	Unc-63	Unc-65
$150	$175	$250	$400	$575	$725	$800	$1,250

W-1409 • F-617 • Lyons-Treat (1905–1906)
Estimated population: 400 to 450 • *Highest graded:* Unc.

VG-8	F-12	VF-20	EF-40	AU-50	Unc-60	Unc-63	Unc-65
$150	$175	$250	$400	$575	$725	$800	$1,250

W-1410 • F-618 • Vernon-Treat (1906–1909)
Estimated population: 1,300 to 1,450 • *Highest graded:* Unc.

VG-8	F-12	VF-20	EF-40	AU-50	Unc-60	Unc-63	Unc-65
$150	$175	$250	$400	$575	$725	$800	$1,250

W-1411 • F-619 • Vernon-McClung (1909–1911)
Estimated population: 700 to 800 • *Highest graded:* Unc.

VG-8	F-12	VF-20	EF-40	AU-50	Unc-60	Unc-63	Unc-65
$150	$175	$250	$400	$575	$725	$800	$1,250

W-1412 • F-620 • Napier-McClung (1911–1912)
Estimated population: 400 to 500 • *Highest graded:* Unc.

VG-8	F-12	VF-20	EF-40	AU-50	Unc-60	Unc-63	Unc-65
$150	$175	$250	$400	$575	$725	$800	$1,250

W-1413 • F-621 • Napier-Thompson (1912–1913)
Estimated population: 64 to 68 • *Highest graded:* Unc.

VG-8	F-12	VF-20	EF-40	AU-50	Unc-60	Unc-63	Unc-65
$175	$200	$275	$430	$625	$775	$875	$1,500

W-1414 • F-622 • Napier-Burke (1913)
Estimated population: 48 to 52 • *Highest graded:* Unc.

VG-8	F-12	VF-20	EF-40	AU-50	Unc-60	Unc-63	Unc-65
$150	$175	$250	$400	$575	$725	$800	$1,250

W-1415 • F-623 • Parker-Burke (1913–1914)
Estimated population: 100 to 110 • *Highest graded:* Unc.

VG-8	F-12	VF-20	EF-40	AU-50	Unc-60	Unc-63	Unc-65
$150	$175	$250	$400	$575	$725	$800	$1,250

W-1416 • F-623a • Teehee-Burke (1915–1919)
Estimated population: 18 to 20 • *Highest graded:* Unc.

VG-8	F-12	VF-20	EF-40	AU-50	Unc-60	Unc-63	Unc-65
$165	$200	$280	$430	$610	$760	$840	$1,325

Series of 1902, Blue Seal, Plain Back
(Authorized Issue 1908 to 1929)

After the Aldrich-Vreeland Act expired on June 30, 1915, the phrase "or other securities" was no longer added to the face of new printing plates. The style reverted to that of years earlier, secured only by United States bonds. Old plates continued in use, creating two face plate styles for 1902 Plain Back notes:

Plate Style a: This is the old style of 1902 (used on the face of the Date Backs), with the inscription—part of the top border on the face—reading, SECURED BY UNITED STATES BONDS OR OTHER SECURITIES.

Plate Style b: This is the new style introduced in 1908, with the inscription—part of the top border on the face—reading, SECURED BY UNITED STATES

BONDS DEPOSITED WITH THE TREASURER OF THE UNITED STATES OF AMERICA.

For both Plate Style a and Plate Style b notes, the two regional letters (used only on certain issues), two charter numbers (on all), and serial numbers (on all) are in blue. These were issued into 1929.

Moreover, within the two plate styles there are possibilities for three overprint styles:

Overprint Style 1: Two regional letters, a Treasury serial number, and a bank serial number, used from 1908 to 1924.

Overprint Style 2: No regional letters; with a Treasury serial number and a bank serial number, used in 1924 and 1925. Notes of this class are somewhat scarce.

Overprint Style 3: No regional letters and no Treasury serial number, but with two bank serial numbers, used from 1925 to 1929. Notes of this style are very rare as a class.

Notes of Plate Style b are much scarcer than those of Plate Style a. As a type, surviving examples (the vast majority being of Plate Style a) are plentiful, indeed the most often seen denomination of this type. Grades encountered are typically Fine or so, often soiled. Bank signatures, often rubber-stamped, are sometimes faded completely. A degree of connoisseurship helps if you want to acquire choice notes. Within a given grade quality can vary widely, even for certified notes. At present there is little interest in plate styles or overprint varieties, yielding opportunities to acquire rarities without paying a premium.

Banks of Issue and Rarity of Notes

Based upon census information from Don C. Kelly and James M. Kelly (*National Bank Note Census*, Version 4.0) and with some information from the other sources, this listing gives each location, the number of banks issuing this series of notes within each, and a commentary.[29]

The Kelly survey records 35,093 notes, which is more than all other large-size $10 notes combined. Among these there are only 121 serial number 1 notes, however. These are specifically listed below.

Alabama • 106 banks of issue • 543 notes reported • The census lists 13 Unc notes.

Alaska Territory • 2 banks of issue • 10 notes reported • No Unc notes are listed. Alaska was a district from 1884 until it became a territory on August 24, 1912, which it remained until statehood in 1959. All large-size Alaska notes in all series have the "district" address. Regardless, numismatists call all "territorials."

Arizona • 20 banks of issue • 115 notes reported • Two Unc examples are reported. The only serial number 1 note is from the First National Bank of Mesa (VG–F).

Arkansas • 70 banks of issue • 307 notes reported • Banks anchored by the First National Bank of Batesville (27). The census lists 15 Unc notes, 14 from Batesville. The only serial number 1 note is from the First National Bank of Paris (VF).

SERIES OF 1902, BLUE SEAL, PLAIN BACK

$10 National Bank Note, Series of 1902, Blue Seal, Plain Back (W-1420). Strafford National Bank of Dover, New Hampshire, charter 1353, regional letter N (North). The charter number and regional letter are in darker blue ink than are the serials and Treasury seals. This note has rubber-stamped signatures—in this case, fairly well preserved, but these are often faded.

Back of the $10 National Bank Note, Series of 1902, Blue Seal, Plain Back (W-1420). Also used on Series of 1902 Red Seal notes.

California • 331 banks of issue • 1,301 notes reported • The census lists 21 Unc examples scattered throughout the state, and 10 serial number 1 notes are recorded.

Colorado • 115 banks of issue • 316 notes reported • The census lists 20 Unc examples.

Connecticut • 78 banks of issue • 502 notes reported • The census lists 48 Unc examples, with 16 from Capitol National Bank of Hartford and 12 from First National Bank of Litchfield. Two serial number 1 notes are from the First National Bank of Bridgeport (F) and the First Stamford National Bank (F).

Delaware • 22 banks of issue • 70 notes reported • There are 15 banks represented. All notes are circulated. The only serial number 1 note is from the First National Bank and the Trust Company of Milford (Fine).

District of Columbia • 13 banks of issue • 296 notes reported • The census lists 32 Unc examples, including 12 from Commercial National Bank of Washington.

Florida • 64 banks of issue • 254 notes reported • Seven Unc notes are listed.

Georgia • 114 banks of issue • 459 notes reported • The census lists 11 Unc notes.

Hawaii Territory • 2 banks of issue • 42 notes reported • First National Bank of Hawaii at Honolulu (40) and the Baldwin National Bank (two). Two Unc examples are reported.

Idaho • 62 banks of issue • 140 notes reported • Banks include the Pacific National Bank of Boise (28). One Unc example is known, from the First National Bank of Jerome.

Illinois • 430 banks of issue • 2,165 notes reported • The census lists 139 Unc examples, including 18 from First National Bank of Peoria. The only serial number 1 note is from the Central National Bank and the Trust Company of Peoria (AU).

Indiana • 261 banks of issue • 1,222 notes reported • The census lists 57 Unc notes, including 16 from First National Bank of Fowler. Two serial number 1 notes are from the United States National Bank of East Chicago (Unc) and the American National Bank of Rushville (F).

Iowa • 332 banks of issue • 2,002 notes reported • The census lists 149 Unc notes from various banks.

Kansas • 220 banks of issue • 891 notes reported • The census lists 46 Unc notes from various banks. Three serial number 1 notes are from the Union National Bank of Manhattan

(Unc), First National Bank of Oswego (F), and the First National Bank in Pratt (EF).

Kentucky • 140 banks of issue • 790 notes reported • The census lists 20 Unc examples, located here and there.

Louisiana • 33 banks of issue • 148 notes reported • Banks include the First National Bank of Shreveport (30). Four Unc notes are reported. The only serial number 1 note is from the First National Bank of Shreveport (not graded).

Maine • 69 banks of issue • 223 notes reported • Five Unc notes are listed.

Maryland • 89 banks of issue • 423 notes reported • The census lists 21 Unc examples.

Massachusetts • 157 banks of issue • 493 notes reported • The census lists 31 Unc notes. Three serial number 1 notes are from the Methuen National Bank (EF), Safe Deposit National Bank of New Bedford (VF), Tanners National Bank of Woburn (AU).

Michigan • 128 banks of issue • 920 notes reported • The census lists 90 Unc examples from various banks and 10 serial number 1 notes.

Minnesota • 306 banks of issue • 1,263 notes reported • The census lists 77 Unc examples scattered throughout the state. Three serial number 1 notes are from the National Bank of Grey Eagle (all Unc).

Mississippi • 35 banks of issue • 192 notes reported • No Unc notes are listed.

Missouri • 140 banks of issue • 1,089 notes reported • The census lists 59 Unc examples scattered throughout the state. Five serial number 1 notes are recorded.

Montana • 84 banks of issue • 261 notes reported • The census lists 14 Unc examples, mostly from the First National Bank of Geyser. Three serial number 1 notes are known, all from the First National Bank of Lima (not graded, Unc, EF).

Nebraska • 186 banks of issue • 952 notes reported • The census lists 96 Unc examples, especially from the Otoe County National Bank of Nebraska City. Four serial number 1 notes are known, three from the First National Bank of York (all Unc) and one from the Union National Bank of Fremont (AU).

Nevada • 9 banks of issue • 55 notes reported • Six banks are represented, including the Farmers & Merchants National Bank of Reno (17), and the Reno National Bank (18). One Unc example is from the Copper National Bank of East Ely (Unc).

New Hampshire • 58 banks of issue • 210 notes reported • There are 51 banks represented. Eight Unc notes are listed.

New Jersey • 250 banks of issue • 918 notes reported • The census lists 14 Unc notes. Eight serial number 1 notes are recorded.

New Mexico • 38 banks of issue • 202 notes reported • Eight Unc examples are reported. The only serial number 1 note is from the Albuquerque National Bank (EF).

New York • 528 banks of issue • 2,459 notes reported • The census lists 239 Unc notes and 19 serial number 1 notes.

North Carolina • 87 banks of issue • 593 notes reported • The census lists 61 Unc specimens, especially from the First National Bank of Dunn (53).

North Dakota • 162 banks of issue • 353 notes reported • Eight Unc specimens are reported. The only serial number 1 note is from the Liberty National Bank of Dickinson (EF).

Ohio • 358 banks of issue • 1,785 notes reported • The census lists 93 Unc scattered throughout the state. Six serial number 1 notes are recorded.

Oklahoma • 341 banks of issue • 709 notes reported • Six Unc examples are reported. Four serial number 1 notes are from the First National Bank of Davis (VF), Citizens National Bank of Okmulgee (AU, Unc), and the First National Bank of Vian (AU).

Oregon • 85 banks of issue • 207 notes reported • Banks include the United States National Bank of Portland (34). Five Unc notes are listed.

Pennsylvania • 872 banks of issue • 3,218 notes reported • The census lists 194 Unc examples. Nine serial number 1 notes are recorded.

Rhode Island • 15 banks of issue • 162 notes reported • The census lists 16 Unc examples.

South Carolina • 77 banks of issue • 415 notes reported • The census lists 22 Unc notes. The only serial number 1 note is from the South Carolina National Bank of Charleston (EF).

South Dakota • 112 banks of issue • 398 notes reported • The census lists 21 Unc examples, including nine from the Home National Bank of Dell Rapids. The only serial number 1 note is from the First National Bank of Onida (not graded).

Tennessee • 124 banks of issue • 675 notes reported • The census lists 59 Unc examples, including many from the First National Bank of Bristol and even more from the First Citizens National Bank of Dyersburg.

Texas • 522 banks of issue • 2,193 notes reported • The census lists 166 Unc specimens. Eight serial number 1 notes are recorded.

Utah • 29 banks of issue • 181 notes reported • Seven Unc notes are listed.

Vermont • 46 banks of issue • 153 notes reported • There are 42 banks reported. One Unc note is from the Montpelier National Bank.

Virginia • 174 banks of issue • 723 notes reported • The census lists 18 Unc notes. The only serial number 1 note is from the First National Bank of Flint Hill (EF).

Washington • 87 banks of issue • 263 notes reported • Five Unc notes are known.

West Virginia • 128 banks of issue • 538 notes reported • The census lists 24 Unc notes, including 19 from the Union National Bank of Sistersville. The only serial number 1 note is from the Matoka National Bank (AU).

Wisconsin • 144 banks of issue • 1,102 notes reported • The census lists 91 Unc examples. Two serial number 1 notes are from the First National Bank in Manitowoc (both AU).

Wyoming • 41 banks of issue • 192 notes reported • Seven Unc examples are reported. The only serial number 1 note is from the First National Bank of Lusk (F–VF).

Generic prices for a typical note from a state from which notes range from plentiful to just slightly scarce:

VG-8	F-12	VF-20	EF-40	AU-50	Unc-60	Unc-63	Unc-65
$110	$135	$170	$325	$525	$625	$700	$1,000

W-1420 • F-624 • Lyons-Roberts (1898–1905)
Estimated population: 10,000 to 12,000 • *Highest graded:* Unc.

VG-8	F-12	VF-20	EF-40	AU-50	Unc-60	Unc-63	Unc-65
$110	$135	$170	$325	$525	$625	$700	$1,000

W-1421 • F-625 • Lyons-Treat (1905–1906)
Estimated population: 2,000 to 2,300 • *Highest graded:* Unc.

VG-8	F-12	VF-20	EF-40	AU-50	Unc-60	Unc-63	Unc-65
$110	$135	$170	$325	$525	$625	$700	$1,000

W-1422 • F-626 • Vernon-Treat (1906–1909)
Estimated population: 5,500 to 6,000 • *Highest graded:* Unc.

VG-8	F-12	VF-20	EF-40	AU-50	Unc-60	Unc-63	Unc-65
$110	$135	$170	$325	$525	$625	$700	$1,000

W-1423 • F-627 • Vernon-McClung (1909–1911)
Estimated population: 3,400 to 3,800 • *Highest graded:* Unc.

VG-8	F-12	VF-20	EF-40	AU-50	Unc-60	Unc-63	Unc-65
$110	$135	$170	$325	$525	$625	$700	$1,000

W-1424 • F-628 • Napier-McClung (1911–1912)
Estimated population: 2,700 to 3,100 • *Highest graded:* Unc.

VG-8	F-12	VF-20	EF-40	AU-50	Unc-60	Unc-63	Unc-65
$110	$135	$170	$325	$525	$625	$700	$1,000

W-1425 • F-629 • Napier-Thompson (1912–1913)
Estimated population: 475 to 525 • *Highest graded:* Unc.

VG-8	F-12	VF-20	EF-40	AU-50	Unc-60	Unc-63	Unc-65
$250	$300	$370	$500	$675	$775	$950	$1,250

W-1426 • F-630 • Napier-Burke (1913)
Estimated population: 400 to 450 • *Highest graded:* Unc.

VG-8	F-12	VF-20	EF-40	AU-50	Unc-60	Unc-63	Unc-65
$110	$135	$170	$325	$525	$625	$700	$1,000

W-1427 • F-631 • Parker-Burke (1913–1914)
Estimated population: 1,500 to 1,700 • *Highest graded:* Unc.

VG-8	F-12	VF-20	EF-40	AU-50	Unc-60	Unc-63	Unc-65
$110	$135	$170	$325	$525	$625	$700	$1,000

W-1428 • F-632 • Teehee-Burke (1915–1919)
Estimated population: 3,500 to 4,000 • *Highest graded:* Unc.

VG-8	F-12	VF-20	EF-40	AU-50	Unc-60	Unc-63	Unc-65
$110	$135	$170	$325	$525	$625	$700	$1,000

W-1429 • F-633 • Elliott-Burke (1919–1921)
Estimated population: 2,750 to 3,000 • *Highest graded:* Unc.

VG-8	F-12	VF-20	EF-40	AU-50	Unc-60	Unc-63	Unc-65
$110	$135	$170	$325	$525	$625	$700	$1,000

W-1430 • F-634 • Elliott-White (1921–1922)
Estimated population: 1,200 to 1,600 • *Highest graded:* Unc.

VG-8	F-12	VF-20	EF-40	AU-50	Unc-60	Unc-63	Unc-65
$110	$135	$170	$325	$525	$625	$700	$1,000

W-1431 • F-635 • Speelman-White (1922–1927)
Estimated population: 1,450 to 1,650 • *Highest graded:* Unc.

VG-8	F-12	VF-20	EF-40	AU-50	Unc-60	Unc-63	Unc-65
$110	$135	$170	$325	$525	$625	$700	$1,000

W-1432 • F-636 • Woods-White (1927–1928)
Estimated population: 60 to 70 • *Highest graded:* Unc.

VG-8	F-12	VF-20	EF-40	AU-50	Unc-60	Unc-63	Unc-65
$110	$135	$170	$325	$525	$625	$700	$1,000

W-1433 • F-637 • Woods-Tate (1928–1929)
Estimated population: 55 to 60 • *Highest graded:* Unc.

VG-8	F-12	VF-20	EF-40	AU-50	Unc-60	Unc-63	Unc-65
$135	$160	$200	$350	$550	$650	$750	$1,050

W-1434 • F-638 • Jones-Woods (1929–1933)
Estimated population: 12 to 14 • *Highest graded:* Unc.

VG-8	F-12	VF-20	EF-40	AU-50	Unc-60	Unc-63	Unc-65
$350	$425	$600	$825	$1,000	$1,350	$1,900	$2,750

SILVER CERTIFICATES

Series of 1878

Silver Certificates of Deposit commence with the Series of 1878 (illus. on p. 364). Each is specifically designated CERTIFICATE OF DEPOSIT on the face and SILVER CERTIFICATE on the back. This series depicts Robert Morris, who served as secretary of finance from 1781 to 1784 in the formative years of the Republic. The inscription SILVER DOLLARS is done in a series of patterns, one for each letter, connected together in a straight row in the "shingle" style. The ASSISTANT TREASURER OF THE U.S. inscription is followed by the location of a Sub-Treasury where silver dollars backing the note were stored. Imprints are known for New York, San Francisco, and the Department of the Treasury in Washington, D.C.

Series of 1878 notes bear two printed Treasury signatures plus either a hand-signed or printed countersignature of another Treasury official. This extra signature proved to be a cumbersome idea. Series of 1880 countersigned notes for New York had the printed signature of Thos. Hillhouse, made before the idea was dropped entirely. No 1880 Washington countersigned notes were printed. All have a large red Treasury seal at top center. On this seal, for this denomination and other countersigned notes in this series, the key faces to the right (with the handle at the left).

On the back the word SILVER is in immense letters, surely pleasing to Silverites, who were quite prominent in politics at the time, and who exerted great pressure on the government to support the market price of that metal. Dark brown ink was used to print this side on paper with a blue tint streak.

Nearly all of these in existence today are in low grades.

W-1460 • F-283 • New York • *Countersigned:* Maxwell White[30] (autographed) • 500 (est.)

Recorded population: 1 • *Selected information:* Heritage (2005), $253,000.

W-1463 • F-284 • *Countersigned:* J.C. Hopper (autographed) • 19,500 (est.)

Recorded population: 4 • *Highest graded:* EF-45 • *Selected information:* CAA (6/1994), A766/B, VF–EF, $18,000. Spink America (5/1995), A767/C, EF, $27,500. CAA (1/2005), A4249/A, EF, $89,125. Hickman & Oakes (11/1986), A18758/B, VG, problems, $4,200.

W-1469 • F-284b[31] • *Countersigned:* Thos. Hillhouse (printed) • 40,000 (est.)

Recorded population: 2 • *Highest graded:* F-15 • *Selected information:* Spink America (5/1995), A30744/D, Fine+, $18,700. Knight (8/2005), A33567/C, Fine, $80,500.

W-1472 • F-284c • San Francisco • *Countersigned:* R.M. Anthony (autographed) • 8,000 (est.) • Unknown

W-1475 • F-285 • Washington • *Countersigned:* A.U. Wyman (autographed) • 4,000 (est.)

Recorded population: 2 • *Highest graded:* Unc • *Selected information:* Spink America (5/1995), A50/B, Uncirculated,

SERIES OF 1878

$10 Silver Certificate of Deposit, Series of 1878 (W-1463), the type of W-1460 to W-1478. The illustrated note is countersigned by J.C. Hopper and is payable in New York. Notes of this type are extremely rare today. Sometimes they are referred to as "triple signed."

Detail of the face of W-1463 showing autographed signature of J.C. Hopper, the printed signatures of Treasury officials, and SILVER DOLLARS in the shingle style layout.

Back of the $10 Silver Certificate of Deposit, Series of 1878 (W-1463), the type of W-1460 to W-1478. Also used on the Series of 1880 notes. Printed on blue-tinted paper, as were other Series of 1878 varieties.

$35,200. Mayflower (11/1956), A51/C, Choice Uncirculated, $1,800; later seen in Stack's (12/1992), VF–EF, $21,000; later seen in CAA (1/1995), regraded EF, $29,700.

W-1478 • F-285a • Countersigned: A.U. Wyman (printed) • 196,000 (est.)

Recorded population: 8 • *Highest graded:* Unc • *Selected information:* Existing notes include A12506/B, Unc, in the ANA Museum collection; A12509/A, VF–EF, in the Smithsonian Institution collection; A26406/B, Good, repaired, sold in a CAA auction (11/1990) for $3,190; A33844/D, EF, sold in a Kagin's auction (6/1981) for $15,600; A94657/A, VG, sold in a Donlon auction (5/1971) for $1,000; A129703/C, VF, problems, sold in a CAA auction (9/2006) for $34,500; A134535/C, F–VF, sold in a CAA auction (1/1995) for $8,360; and A166541/A, VG-10 (PCGS), sold in a Heritage auction (4/2008) for $9,775.

Series of 1880, Countersigned

The designs are similar to the previous series, except that all in the Series of 1880 have a large brown Treasury seal at top center with a brown X below and are printed on white (not blue-tinted) paper. Countersignatures are printed.

W-1480 • F-286 • New York • Countersigned: Thos. Hillhouse (printed) • 400,000

Estimated population: 20 to 23 • *Highest graded:* Unc.

VG-8	F-12	VF-20	EF-40	AU-50	Unc-60	Unc-63
$5,000	$8,600	$17,500	$35,000	$75,000	—	$125,000

W-1482 • F-286a • Washington • Countersigned: A.U. Wyman (printed) • No evidence of printing

Series of 1880, Not Countersigned

The motifs (illus. on p. 356) continue from the preceding. Now there is no countersignature, and in that space is SERIES OF 1880. A counter, X, is at the bottom border on W-1490 to W-1492, but not on W-1493. The back is the same as the preceding.

W-1490 • F-287 • Scofield-Gilfillan (1878–1881) • Large brown seal with brown X below • 3,000,000 (est.)

Estimated population: 95 to 115 • *Highest graded:* Unc.

VG-8	F-12	VF-20	EF-40	AU-50	Unc-60	Unc-63	Unc-65
$1,500	$2,200	$3,200	$5,500	$7,000	$7,800	$9,500	$25,000

W-1491 • F-288 • Bruce-Gilfillan (1881–1883) • 1,300,000 (est.)

Estimated population: 90 to 100 • *Highest graded:* Unc.

VG-8	F-12	VF-20	EF-40	AU-50	Unc-60	Unc-63	Unc-65
$1,500	$2,200	$3,200	$5,500	$7,000	$7,800	$9,500	$25,000

W-1492 • F-289 • Bruce-Wyman (1883–1885) • 3,596,000 (est.)

Estimated population: 190 to 210 • *Highest graded:* Unc.

VG-8	F-12	VF-20	EF-40	AU-50	Unc-60	Unc-63	Unc-65
$1,500	$2,200	$3,200	$5,500	$7,000	$7,800	$9,500	$22,000

W-1493 • F-290 • Large reddish-brown seal without X below • 304,000

Estimated population: 50 to 55 • *Highest graded:* Unc.

VG-8	F-12	VF-20	EF-40	AU-50	Unc-60	Unc-63
$2,500	$3,800	$6,000	$10,000	$20,000	$45,000	$125,000

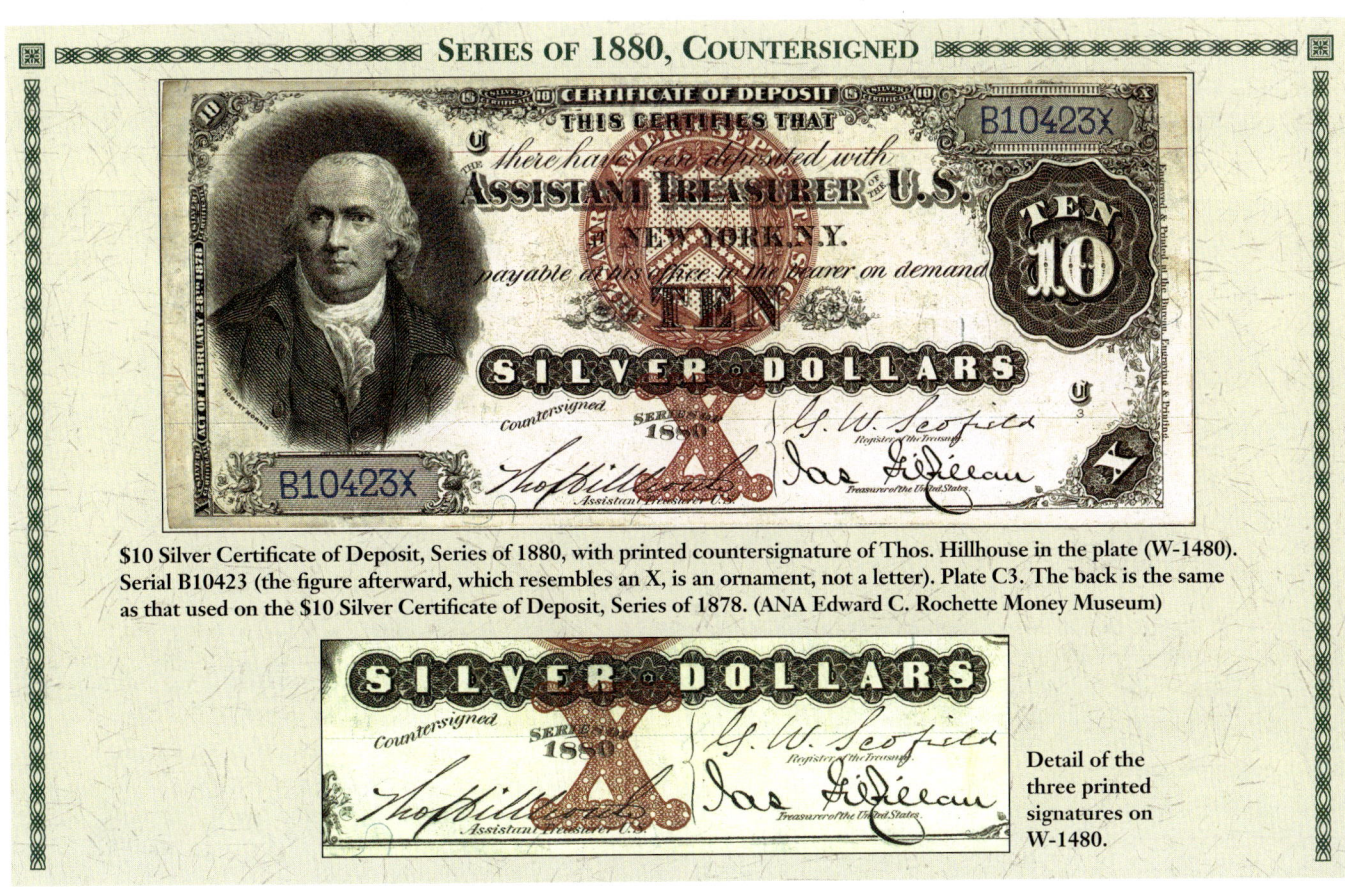

SERIES OF 1880, COUNTERSIGNED

$10 Silver Certificate of Deposit, Series of 1880, with printed countersignature of Thos. Hillhouse in the plate (W-1480). Serial B10423 (the figure afterward, which resembles an X, is an ornament, not a letter). Plate C3. The back is the same as that used on the $10 Silver Certificate of Deposit, Series of 1878. (ANA Edward C. Rochette Money Museum)

Detail of the three printed signatures on W-1480.

SERIES OF 1880, NOT COUNTERSIGNED

$10 Silver Certificate of Deposit, Series of 1880, Not Countersigned (W-1492). Bruce-Wyman. Large brown seal with brown X below. Serial B5647125, plate A18.

$10 Silver Certificate of Deposit, Series of 1880, Not Countersigned (W-1493). Also with signatures of Bruce-Wyman, but with large reddish-brown Treasury seal in a lower position and without the large X at bottom center.

Back of the $10 Silver Certificate of Deposit, Series of 1880, Not Countersigned (W-1492), the type of W-1490 to W-1493, also used on the preceding types of Series of 1878 and 1880 Silver Certificates of Deposit.

Series of 1886

The Series of 1886 Silver Certificates illustrate Thomas A. Hendricks, vice president of the United States for a few months in 1885, during which term he died. The frame for his portrait, curved at the top, led to the name "Tombstone Note."

The back is a richly detailed, complex engraving with the obligation in the center. Such notes were printed for a long time and include seven different signature combinations and Treasury seal variations. They are far scarcer than $10 Legal Tender Notes of the same era.

SERIES OF 1886

$10 Silver Certificate, Series of 1886 (W-1496). Known as the "Tombstone Note," this depicted the recently deceased (1885) vice president Thomas A. Hendricks.

Detail of the lower left of the face of an example of W-1494.

Back of the $10 Silver Certificate, Series of 1886 (W-1496), with ornate engraving filling most of the surface.

W-1494 • F-291 • Rosecrans-Jordan (1885–1887) • Small red seal with plain border • 400,000

Estimated population: 25 to 30 • *Highest graded:* Unc.

VG-8	F-12	VF-20	EF-40	AU-50	Unc-60	Unc-63	Unc-65
$700	$1,100	$2,750	$4,400	$7,500	$8,500	$11,000	$40,000

W-1495 • F-292 • Rosecrans-Hyatt (1887–1889) • 2,500,000 (est.)

Estimated population: 75 to 85 • *Highest graded:* Unc.

VG-8	F-12	VF-20	EF-40	AU-50	Unc-60	Unc-63
$700	$1,100	$2,750	$4,400	$7,500	$8,500	$15,000

W-1496 • F-293 • Large red seal • 5,700,000 (est.)

Estimated population: 148 to 155 • *Highest graded:* Unc.

VG-8	F-12	VF-20	EF-40	AU-50	Unc-60	Unc-63	Unc-65
$700	$1,100	$2,450	$4,400	$7,000	$8,500	$11,000	$35,000

W-1497 • F-294 • Rosecrans-Huston (1889–1891) • 2,200,000 (est.)

Estimated population: 75 to 85 • *Highest graded:* Unc.

VG-8	F-12	VF-20	EF-40	AU-50	Unc-60	Unc-63	Unc-65
$700	$1,100	$2,450	$4,400	$7,000	$8,500	$11,000	$35,000

W-1498 • F-295 • Large brown seal • 1,500,000 (est.)
Estimated population: 55 to 60 • *Highest graded:* Unc.

VG-8	F-12	VF-20	EF-40	AU-50	Unc-60	Unc-63
$700	$1,100	$2,450	$4,400	$7,000	$8,500	$15,000

W-1499 • F-296 • Rosecrans-Nebeker (1891–1893) • 1,500,000 (est.)
Estimated population: 63 to 68 • *Highest graded:* Unc.

VG-8	F-12	VF-20	EF-40	AU-50	Unc-60	Unc-63	Unc-65
$700	$1,100	$2,450	$4,400	$7,000	$8,500	$11,000	$35,000

W-1500 • F-297 • Small red seal with scalloped border • 404,000 (est.)
Estimated population: 15 to 17 • *Highest graded:* Unc.

VG-8	F-12	VF-20	EF-40	AU-50	Unc-60	Unc-63
$1,200	$2,000	$5,000	$9,000	$12,000	$16,000	$30,000

Series of 1891

The Series of 1891 continues the Series of 1886 motifs, with some slight differences in the imprints. The back is entirely new, with large, open spaces, reflecting the Treasury department's preference for simplified designs. This was thought to deter counterfeiting.

W-1501 • F-298 • Rosecrans-Nebeker (1891–1893) • Small red seal with scalloped border • 3,400,000 (est.)
Estimated population: 72 to 76 • *Highest graded:* Unc.

VG-8	F-12	VF-20	EF-40	AU-50	Unc-60	Unc-63	Unc-65
$300	$650	$1,200	$1,800	$2,400	$3,500	$3,900	$15,000

W-1502 • F-299 • Tillman-Morgan (1893–1897) • 19,460,000 (est.)
Estimated population: 280 to 320 • *Highest graded:* Unc.

VG-8	F-12	VF-20	EF-40	AU-50	Unc-60	Unc-63	Unc-65
$275	$600	$1,150	$1,700	$2,300	$3,400	$3,800	$10,000

W-1503 • F-300 • Bruce-Roberts (1897–1898) • 4,940,000 (est.)
Estimated population: 100 to 110 • *Highest graded:* Unc.

VG-8	F-12	VF-20	EF-40	AU-50	Unc-60	Unc-63	Unc-65
$275	$600	$1,150	$1,700	$2,300	$3,400	$3,800	$10,000

W-1504 • F-301 • Lyons-Roberts (1898–1905) • 6,620,000 (est.)
Estimated population: 155 to 165 • *Highest graded:* Unc.

VG-8	F-12	VF-20	EF-40	AU-50	Unc-60	Unc-63	Unc-65
$275	$600	$1,150	$1,700	$2,300	$3,400	$3,800	$10,000

$10 Silver Certificate, Series of 1891 (W-1502), continuing the "Tombstone Note" style.

Back of the $10 Silver Certificate, Series of 1891 (W-1502). New back design with open spaces.

Series of 1908

The face motifs are similar to the preceding, except that a large blue X, with TEN superimposed, has been added to the left field. Serial numbers and the Treasury seal are in blue.

W-1505 • F-302 • Vernon-Treat (1906–1909) • Small blue seal with scalloped border • 4,828,000

Estimated population: 150 to 160 • *Highest graded:* Unc.

VG-8	F-12	VF-20	EF-40	AU-50	Unc-60	Unc-63	Unc-65
$400	$650	$1,000	$1,500	$1,950	$2,350	$3,100	$9,500

W-1506 • F-303 • Vernon-McClung (1909–1911) • 1,756,000

Estimated population: 120 to 130 • *Highest graded:* Unc.

VG-8	F-12	VF-20	EF-40	AU-50	Unc-60	Unc-63	Unc-65
$400	$650	$1,000	$1,500	$1,950	$2,350	$3,100	$9,500

W-1506★ • F-303★

Recorded population: 1 • *Graded:* VG–F • *Commentary:* In his 1951 study of these notes (see the bibliography), W.A. Philpott Jr. stated that the first replacement star notes in any series were $10 notes delivered on June 20, 1910. However, later research by Doug Murray proved this incorrect, and although the $10 certificates were early, the first were $1 and $5 certificates delivered on June 21, 1910. • *Selected information:* CAA (11/1990), ★9668B/D, VG–F, $3,080.

W-1507 • F-304 • Parker-Burke (1913–1914) • Small blue seal with scalloped border • 3,624,000

Estimated population: 275 to 325 • *Highest graded:* Unc.

VG-8	F-12	VF-20	EF-40	AU-50	Unc-60	Unc-63	Unc-65
$400	$650	$1,000	$1,500	$1,950	$2,350	$3,100	$9,000

W-1507★ • F-304★

Recorded population: 1 • *Graded:* EF-40.

REFUNDING CERTIFICATES OF 1879

The Refunding Certificates of 1879 (illus. on p. 370ff.) were popular in their time and were sold through United States post offices. The $10 denomination was thought to be high enough to raise considerable funds for the Treasury, yet low enough to create a popular demand. The strategy worked, and the issue sold out.

Although these are collected as currency, they are actually "baby" bonds. Whether many ever passed hand to hand as money is not known, but the situation is not likely, as most today are in higher grades. The very first issue, W-1510, had a space for the signature of the buyer on the back, but this idea was soon changed in favor of a generic certificate without this feature. Each has the printed signatures of Scofield-Gilfillan (1878–1881) with Gilfillan above Scofield. All were printed on blue-tinted paper.

W-1510 • F-213 • Small red seal with spiked border • 25,000

Recorded population: 2 • *Highest graded:* AU-58 • *Selected information:* Knight (10/2005), A287/C, AU-58 (PCGS), $425,500. Bluestone's Grinnell Sale (11/1944), A3793/A, AU, canceled and with two corners cut off, Bureau of Public Debt.

W-1511 • F-214 • Small red seal with scalloped border • 4,000,000

Estimated population: 165 to 180 • *Highest graded:* Unc.

VG-8	F-12	VF-20	EF-40	AU-50	Unc-60	Unc-63	Unc-65
$1,750	$2,750	$4,000	$5,000	$6,600	$7,500	$10,000	$22,000

TREASURY OR COIN NOTES

Series of 1890

The $10 Treasury or Coin Notes (illus. on p. 372) continue the ornate backs seen on lower denominations of this era, and most of the higher denominations as well. As such, these have been the object of intense interest from the numismatic community for a long time.

The face features the portrait of General Philip Henry Sheridan, one of many Union heroes depicted on late 19th-century federal notes. The portrait was engraved by Lorenzo Hatch, a Bureau of Engraving and Printing specialist in this

SERIES OF 1908

$10 Silver Certificate, Series of 1908 (W-1507). Large blue X in the left field. The back continues the preceding style.

REFUNDING CERTIFICATES OF 1879

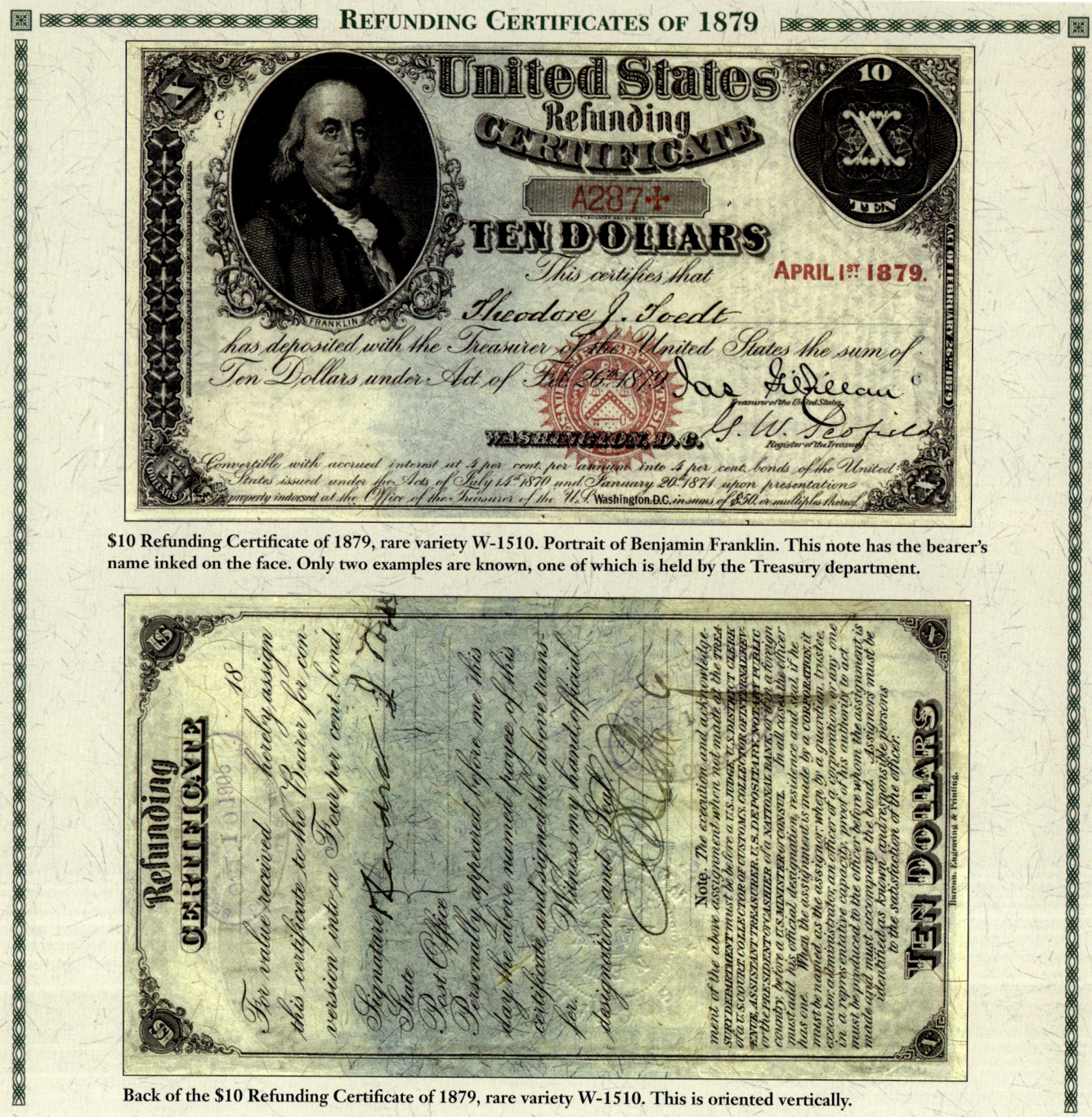

$10 Refunding Certificate of 1879, rare variety W-1510. Portrait of Benjamin Franklin. This note has the bearer's name inked on the face. Only two examples are known, one of which is held by the Treasury department.

Back of the $10 Refunding Certificate of 1879, rare variety W-1510. This is oriented vertically.

field. The Series of 1890 Notes all have serial numbers beginning with A and ending with a decorative star.

The back is filled edge to edge with rich green engraving, with a large TEN at the center. Each letter is ornamented with leaves.

Similar to other issues, the variety with the Rosecrans-Nebeker signature combination and large brown seal was made in smaller quantities and today is a prime rarity. However, a hoard of over two dozen Uncirculated notes, consecutively numbered, has augmented the supply, a situation with no counterpart among the other Series of 1890 Notes with this combination and seal. The other $10 varieties are fairly scarce as well, and can be called rare if Uncirculated.

W-1520 • F-366 • Rosecrans-Huston (1889–1891) • Large brown seal • 2,900,000 (est.)

Estimated population: 120 to 130 • *Highest graded:* Unc.

VG-8	F-12	VF-20	EF-40	AU-50	Unc-60	Unc-63	Unc-65
$700	$1,000	$1,675	$3,300	$4,100	$4,600	$6,500	$22,000

W-1521 • F-367 • Rosecrans-Nebeker (1891–1893) • 240,000 (est.)

Estimated population: 35 to 40 • *Highest graded:* Unc • *Commentary:* A key rarity in any grade.

VG-8	F-12	VF-20	EF-40	AU-50	Unc-60	Unc-63	Unc-65
$875	$1,200	$1,925	$3,600	$4,500	$5,200	$8,500	$28,000

REFUNDING CERTIFICATES OF 1879, continued

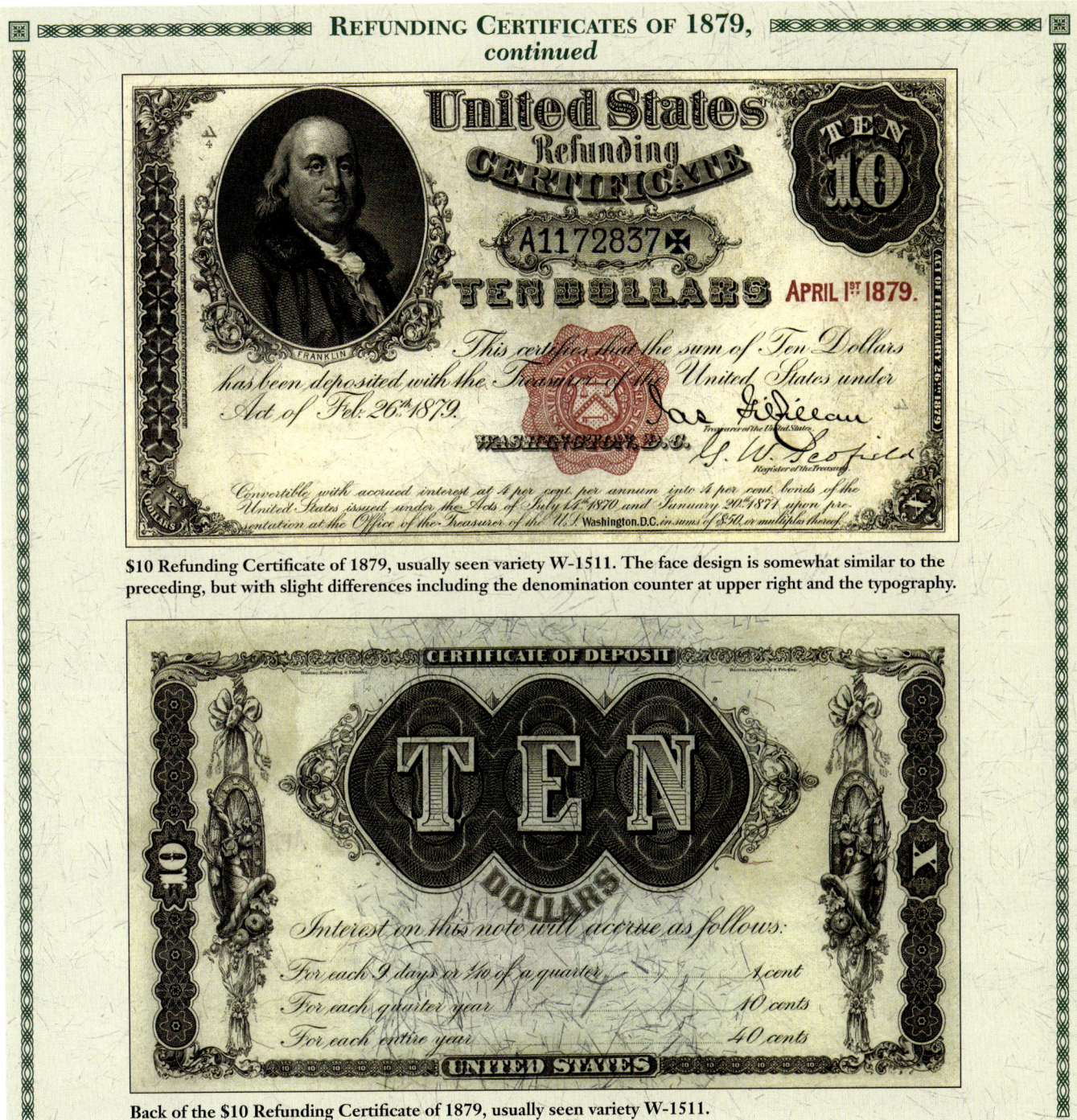

$10 Refunding Certificate of 1879, usually seen variety W-1511. The face design is somewhat similar to the preceding, but with slight differences including the denomination counter at upper right and the typography.

Back of the $10 Refunding Certificate of 1879, usually seen variety W-1511.

W-1522 • F-368 • Small red seal with scalloped border • 1,460,000 (est.)

Estimated population: 145 to 153 • *Highest graded:* Unc.

VG-8	F-12	VF-20	EF-40	AU-50	Unc-60	Unc-63	Unc-65
$700	$1,000	$1,675	$3,300	$4,100	$4,600	$6,500	$18,000

Series of 1891

The face of the Series of 1891 Notes (illus. on p. 373) is similar to the preceding and still features General Sheridan, together with a small red Treasury seal with a scalloped border. Serial numbers begin with the letter B and include a decorative star.

The back has been simplified to create large areas of open space, in keeping with the Treasury opinion that this helped prevent counterfeiting. This notion was hardly new and, in fact, had been discussed in the early 19th century in regard to Bank of England currency. Most examples in numismatic hands show evidence of extensive circulation.

W-1523 • F-369 • Rosecrans-Nebeker (1891–1893) • 1,100,000 (est.)

Estimated population: 135 to 145 • *Highest graded:* Unc.

VG-8	F-12	VF-20	EF-40	AU-50	Unc-60	Unc-63	Unc-65
$450	$750	$1,150	$1,700	$2,000	$2,550	$3,750	$7,600

SERIES OF 1890

$10 Treasury or Coin Note, Series of 1890 (W-1520). This general design was also used for the Series of 1891 notes. The portrait is of General Philip D. Sheridan. The star at the serial number is an ornament and has no meaning.

Detail of the back of an example of W-1520, tiny plate number 9 within a triangle near the lower right border.

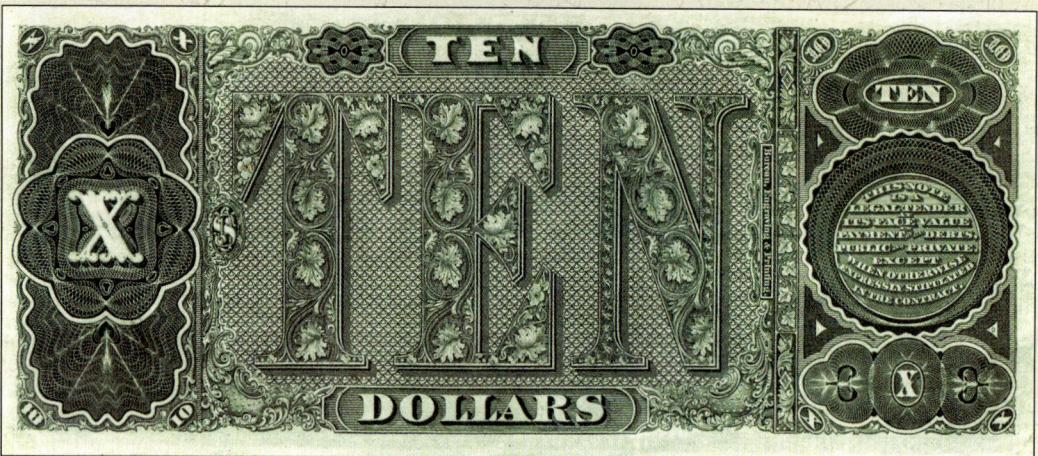

Back type used for the three varieties of Series of 1890 $10 Treasury or Coin Notes, one of the most ornate designs in the $10 series.

W-1524 • F-370 • Tillman-Morgan (1893–1897) • 4,000,000 (est.)

Estimated population: 120 to 130 • *Highest graded:* Unc.

VG-8	F-12	VF-20	EF-40	AU-50	Unc-60	Unc-63	Unc-65
$450	$750	$1,150	$1,700	$2,000	$2,550	$3,750	$7,600

W-1525 • F-371 • Bruce-Roberts (1897–1898) • 928,000 (est.)

Estimated population: 55 to 60 • *Highest graded:* Unc.

VG-8	F-12	VF-20	EF-40	AU-50	Unc-60	Unc-63	Unc-65
$450	$750	$1,150	$1,700	$2,000	$2,550	$3,750	$9,500

GOLD CERTIFICATES

Gold Certificates of the $10 denomination, with a bright yellow-orange back, commence with the Series of 1907. They were made in different signature combinations through the Series of 1922, the last being particularly numerous.

Series of 1907

The face of this type (illus. on p. 375) bears the portrait of Michael Hillegas (Treasurer of the United States 1775–1789), engraved by G.F.C. Smillie from a painting by A.M. Archambault. The inscription on the face states that $10 in gold coin has been deposited in the Treasury as backing for the note and is payable on demand. Large quantities of $10 and, in partic-

SERIES OF 1891

$10 Treasury or Coin Note, Series of 1891 (W-1523), the same design as used for the Series of 1890 notes. In the Series of 1891 all have a small red Treasury seal with a scalloped border.

Back of the $10 Treasury or Coin Note, Series of 1891 (W-1523), an open design said to deter counterfeiting.

ular, $20 gold coins were stored in bags by the Treasury as security for Gold Certificates of various denominations.

Hillegas was important in finances during the American Revolution and was charged with the distribution of Continental Currency during that time. In the early 20th century his descendants successfully petitioned the Treasury department to include his image on paper money. All have a gold Treasury seal with a scalloped border and serial numbers in small digits (compared to the later W-1541 of the Series of 1922). The back, printed in bright orange-gold, includes the Great Seal within a scalloped border.

These first appeared in circulation on July 1, 1907. It was reported that bankers were confused by the gold backs, which were difficult to evaluate at quick glance, making counting difficult.[32]

The orange-gold color tended to fade. Today, notes with a bright back are worth more than those with faded color, regardless of the grade.

W-1530 • F-1167 • Vernon-Treat (1906–1909) • Act of July 12, 1882 • 21,366,800

Estimated population: 155 to 165 • *Highest graded:* Unc.

VG-8	F-12	VF-20	EF-40	AU-50	Unc-60	Unc-63	Unc-65
$200	$275	$350	$700	$950	$1,400	$1,700	$4,500

W-1531 • F-1168 • Vernon-McClung (1909–1911) • 17,476,000

Estimated population: 100 to 115 • *Highest graded:* Unc • *Commentary:* Printing ended on August 23, 1912.

VG-8	F-12	VF-20	EF-40	AU-50	Unc-60	Unc-63	Unc-65
$200	$300	$375	$750	$950	$1,400	$2,000	$4,400

W-1531★ • F-1168★

Recorded population: 4 • *Highest graded:* EF-45 • *Selected information:* Existing examples include ★13810B/B, VG–F; ★35643B/C, VG–F; ★88925B/A, EF, sold in a Stack's auction (3/1993) for $1,800; and ★101378B/B, Fine.

W-1532 • F-1169 • Napier-McClung (1911–1912) • 23,348,000 (est.)

Estimated population: 180 to 200 • *Highest graded:* Unc • *Commentary:* Deliveries began on August 23, 1911, and ended in January 1914.

VG-8	F-12	VF-20	EF-40	AU-50	Unc-60	Unc-63	Unc-65
$200	$275	$350	$700	$1,025	$1,300	$1,670	$4,200

W-1532★ • F-1169★

Recorded population: 3 • *Highest graded:* AU-50 • *Selected information:* Existing examples are ★201522B/B, EF, sold in a

CAA auction (10/1995) for $2,200; ★206424B/D, VG–F; and ★218148B/D, AU, sold in a Stack's auction (3/1993) for $1,800.

W-1533 • F-1169a • Act of March 4, 1907 • 10,086,000 (est.)

Estimated population: 120 to 140 • *Highest graded:* Unc.

VG-8	F-12	VF-20	EF-40	AU-50	Unc-60	Unc-63	Unc-65
$200	$275	$350	$700	$950	$1,300	$1,670	$4,200

W-1534 • F-1170 • Napier-Thompson (1912–1913) • Act of July 12, 1882 • 720,000 (est.)

Estimated population: 25 to 35 • *Highest graded:* Unc • *Commentary:* Deliveries of notes with the Napier-Thompson signatures began on December 31, 1912, and ended on May 19, 1913 (without distinction as to this variety or the next).

VG-8	F-12	VF-20	EF-40	AU-50	Unc-60	Unc-63	Unc-65
$300	$450	$600	$1,500	$1,700	$2,000	$3,000	—

W-1535 • F-1170a • Act of March 4, 1907 • 1,556,000 (est.)

Estimated population: 55 to 65 • *Highest graded:* Unc.

VG-8	F-12	VF-20	EF-40	AU-50	Unc-60	Unc-63	Unc-65
$250	$375	$525	$1,350	$2,200	$3,250	$4,500	$7,500

W-1536 • F-1171 • Parker-Burke (1913–1914) • Back Plate Location 1 (see discussion of Series of 1922) • 20,200,000 (est.)

Estimated population: 250 to 350 • *Highest graded:* Unc • *Commentary:* Deliveries began on December 5, 1913, and ended on May 15, 1914.

VG-8	F-12	VF-20	EF-40	AU-50	Unc-60	Unc-63	Unc-65
$190	$260	$330	$650	$925	$1,250	$1,600	$3,900

W-1536★ • F-1171★

Recorded population: 6 • *Highest graded:* Unc • *Selected information:* Hickman & Oakes (11/1988), ★314055B/C, Unc, $1,650. CAA (5/2000), ★339392B/D, VF, $4,125, CAA (9/2006), ★378094B/B, VG-10 (PMG), $3,737.50.

W-1537 • F-1172 • Teehee-Burke (1915–1919) • 40,340,000 (est.)

Estimated population: 600 to 800 • *Highest graded:* Unc.

VG-8	F-12	VF-20	EF-40	AU-50	Unc-60	Unc-63	Unc-65
$190	$260	$330	$650	$925	$1,250	$1,600	$3,900

W-1537★ • F-1172★

Estimated population: 15 to 17 • *Highest graded:* Unc • *Selected information:* Knight (11/2007), ★395356B/D, F-12 (PMG), $1,955. Knight (3/2007), ★458978B/B, VF-20 (PCGS), $2,530. CAA (5/2001) ★462301B/A, Unc, $7,150. Knight (6/2002), ★524368B/D, EF-40 (CGA), $2,990. CAA (1/2003), ★528024B/D, F–VF, $920.

Series of 1922

Partway through the Series of 1922, the serial numbers on the face of the $10 Gold Certificates were set in significantly larger type, creating a collectible variation. The Series of 1922 Notes also have an inscription in the left field, not present on the earlier issues, which reads, "This certificate is a legal tender in the amount thereof in payment of all debts and dues, public and private acts of March 14, 1900, as amended and December 24, 1919."

These notes were made in an immense quantity, eclipsing the total production of the Series of 1907. As a result, examples are seen frequently today. As recently as the 1950s, these were often available for face value in numismatic circles; there was only limited collecting interest in them, due to Treasury restrictions on holding gold notes.

Mules: Back plate numbers can be in one of two locations.[33] On May 14, 1921, with the new Elliott-White signature combination starting, all Legal Tender, Silver Certificate, and Gold Certificate back plates were given numbers beginning with 1 and in a new location, although no notice was given of the change.

> **Back Plate Location 1** (regular use): W-1530 to W-1537 on the Series of 1907 issues. This was the standard location until May 14, 1921. Also used to create a mule for W-1540 and W-1541 in the Series of 1922.

> **Back Plate Location 2** (regular use): W-1540 and W-1541 in the Series of 1922 (introduced without notice as the new style on May 14, 1921, with the Elliott-White combination).

W-1540 • F-1173a • Speelman-White (1922–1927) • Small serial numbers • Back Plate Location 2 • 9,480,000, or about 70% regular (est.)

Estimated population: 110 to 130 • *Highest graded:* Unc.

VG-8	F-12	VF-20	EF-40	AU-50	Unc-60	Unc-63	Unc-65
$200	$250	$320	$525	$850	$1,400	$1,750	$3,600

W-1540★ • F-1173a★

Recorded population: 2 • *Highest graded:* VF-20 • *Selected information:* Jess Peters (8/1973), ★64987D, Fine, $17.50.

W-1540 Mule • F-1173a • Back Plate Location 1 • 4,024,000, or about 30% mules (est.)

Estimated population: 25 to 30 • *Highest graded:* Unc • *Commentary:* New listing without market history. Future editions will give pricing information to the extent that it becomes available.

W-1540 Mule★ • F-1173a★

Recorded population: 7 • *Highest graded:* VF-30 • *Selected information:* CAA (5/2001), ★10899D/C, Fine, $2,090.

W-1541 • F-1173 • Large serial numbers • Back Plate Location 2 • 144,100,000, or about 98% regular

Estimated population: 3,800 to 4,300 • *Highest graded:* Unc.

VG-8	F-12	VF-20	EF-40	AU-50	Unc-60	Unc-63	Unc-65
$140	$210	$270	$450	$750	$1,000	$1,500	$2,700

W-1541★ • F-1173★

Estimated population: 240 to 280 • *Highest graded:* Unc.

F-12	VF-20	EF-40	AU-50	Unc-60	Unc-63
$750	$1,100	$1,600	$3,500	$4,500	$6,000

SERIES OF 1907

Detail of the style with ACT OF JULY 12, 1882 above the X in left field (W-1530). To the left is plate letter C and micro-print number 41.

$10 Gold Certificate, Series of 1907 (W-1530).

Detail of the style with ACT OF MARCH 4, 1907 above the X in left field (W-1535). To the left is plate letter A and micro-print number 297.

Back of the $10 Gold Certificate, Series of 1907 (W-1530). Also used for the $10 Gold Certificate, Series of 1922. Printed in gold-orange ink. This color is said to have been confusing to bankers.

SERIES OF 1922

Back Plate Location 1. Microprint number at upper right of note.

Back Plate Location 2. Microprint number at upper left of note.

$10 Gold Certificate, Series of 1922 (W-1541). This variety has larger serial numbers than the earlier Gold Certificates.

W-1541 Mule • F-1173 • Back Plate Location 1 • 3,000,000, or about 2% mules (est.)

Estimated population: 80 to 95 • *Highest graded:* Unc • *Selected information:* Heritage (8/2006), H19923354/B, Fine, $288. CAA (5/2005), H30595228/D, Unc, $1,380; H33659876/D, AU-55, $690. Superior (9/2005), H35285138/B, EF, $345. CAA (5/2004), H39496203/C, AU, $553.15; later seen in CAA (9/2004), Unc-67 (CGA), $1,955. CAA (1/2003), H41355895/C, Unc-64 (CGA), $575. Knight (2/2004), H41355896/D, Unc-67 (CGA), $2,041.25. Heritage (1/2007), H42191293/A, EF–AU, $373.75.

W-1541 Mule★ • F-1173★

Recorded population: 6 • *Highest graded:* Unc.

FEDERAL RESERVE NOTES

Federal Reserve Notes of the Series of 1914 depict President Andrew Jackson on the face and have separate illustrations of a farming scene and factories on the back. Some were printed with red seals (by far the rarer class), others with blue. All Red Seal notes have Treasury signatures of Burke and McAdoo. Blue Seal notes exist with several different signature combinations. For both colors of seals, varieties can be collected by Federal Reserve districts.

Series of 1914, Red Seal

Similar to the situation for other notes in this series, the $10 Federal Reserve Notes, Series of 1914, with red Treasury seal and serial numbers and with the Burke-McAdoo signature combination, are rather simple in their appearance and are usually collected singly for the type, although it is possible to acquire them by Federal Reserve Banks and plate styles as well. These are considerably scarcer as a group than the Blue Seal notes listed subsequently. After World War I commenced in Europe in August 1914, the BEP could not import red ink, so switched to blue after less than a year of printing Red Seals.

In all of the following listings the number (1 to 12) and the large letter (A to L) on the seal at the left indicate the Federal Reserve Bank that issued the note.

Plate Style a (on Red Seals only): In certain of the following listings, the small letter a in the Whitman number indicates a large bank district letter and numeral at bottom left and top right. At the upper left is a small plate letter, but no bank district letter and number.

Plate Style b (on Red and Blue Seals): In certain of the following listings, the small letter b in the Whitman number indicates a note similar to the preceding, but with a small bank district letter and numeral added above the plate letter at top left and a small bank district letter and number at the lower right.

W-1550-A-a • F-892A • Boston • 1,000,000
Estimated population: 33 to 36 • *Highest graded:* Unc.

VG-8	F-12	VF-20	EF-40	AU-50	Unc-60	Unc-63	Unc-65
$275	$550	$900	$1,600	$2,100	$2,600	$3,500	$10,000

W-1550-A-b • F-892B • 360,000
Recorded population: 8 • *Highest graded:* VF-30 • *Selected information:* DBR Currency Web site (10/2005), A1051892A/F, VG–F, $2,395. CAA (5/2000), A1113798A/B, VF–EF, $5,225. Knight (11/2006), A1199038A/B, VF, $1,840.

W-1550-B-a • F-893A • New York • 4,000,000
Estimated population: 75 to 85 • *Highest graded:* Unc.

VG-8	F-12	VF-20	EF-40	AU-50	Unc-60	Unc-63	Unc-65
$250	$450	$700	$1,100	$1,700	—	$2,750	$6,000

W-1550-B-b • F-893B • 8,900,000
Estimated population: 180 to 200 • *Highest graded:* Unc.

VG-8	F-12	VF-20	EF-40	AU-50	Unc-60	Unc-63	Unc-65
$250	$450	$700	$1,100	$1,700	$2,250	$2,750	$6,000

W-1550-C-a • F-894A • Philadelphia • 600,000
Estimated population: 28 to 32 • *Highest graded:* Unc.

VG-8	F-12	VF-20	EF-40	AU-50	Unc-60	Unc-63	Unc-65
$300	$550	$1,000	$1,700	$2,400	$3,200	$4,500	$10,000

W-1550-C-b • F-894B • 900,000
Estimated population: 55 to 65 • *Highest graded:* Unc.

VG-8	F-12	VF-20	EF-40	AU-50	Unc-60	Unc-63
$250	$450	$700	$1,100	$1,700	$2,250	$3,200

W-1550-D-a • F-895A • Cleveland • 400,000
Estimated population: 13 to 15 • *Highest graded:* Unc.

VG-8	F-12	VF-20	EF-40	AU-50	Unc-60
$425	$900	$1,700	$2,400	$4,500	—

W-1550-D-b • F-895B • 1,112,000
Estimated population: 45 to 55 • *Highest graded:* AU-50.

VG-8	F-12	VF-20	EF-40	AU-50
$250	$450	$700	$1,100	$1,800

W-1550-E-a • F-896A • Richmond • 400,000
Estimated population: 18 to 20 • *Highest graded:* Unc.

VG-8	F-12	VF-20	EF-40	AU-50	Unc-60	Unc-63	Unc-65
$375	$750	—	—	$3,750	—	—	$10,000

W-1550-E-b • F-896B • 352,000
Estimated population: 20 to 23 • *Highest graded:* EF-45.

VG-8	F-12	VF-20	EF-40
$425	$800	$2,000	$3,000

W-1550-F-a • F-897A • Atlanta • 400,000
Estimated population: 20 to 24 • *Highest graded:* Unc.

VG-8	F-12	VF-20	EF-40	AU-50	Unc-60	Unc-63	Unc-65
$325	$500	$900	$1,900	$2,600	—	$4,000	$10,000

W-1550-F-b • F-897B • 140,000
Recorded population: 7 • *Highest graded:* Unc • *Selected information:* Existing examples include F402705A/A, VF, sold in a Knight auction (6/2008) for $2,185; F492821A/A, Unc, sold in a CAA auction (10/1998) for $1,760; and F500768A/D, AU-53 (PCGS), earlier graded "Gem CU."

W-1550-G-a • F-898A • Chicago • 1,000,000
Estimated population: 75 to 85 • *Highest graded:* Unc.

VG-8	F-12	VF-20	EF-40	AU-50	Unc-60	Unc-63	Unc-65
$250	$450	$700	$1,100	$1,700	$2,250	$2,750	$6,000

W-1550-G-b • F-898B • 804,000
Estimated population: 60 to 70 • *Highest graded:* Unc.

VG-8	F-12	VF-20	EF-40	AU-50	Unc-60	Unc-63	Unc-65
$250	$450	$700	$1,100	$1,700	$2,250	$2,750	$6,000

W-1550-H-a • F-899A • St. Louis • 600,000
Estimated population: 55 to 65 • *Highest graded:* Unc.

VG-8	F-12	VF-20	EF-40	AU-50	Unc-60	Unc-63	Unc-65
$250	$450	$700	$1,100	$1,700	$2,100	$2,750	$6,000

SERIES OF 1914, RED SEAL

$10 Federal Reserve Note, Series of 1914, Red Seal, with Plate Style a (W-1550-C-a). Federal Reserve Bank of Philadelphia.

$10 Federal Reserve Note, Series of 1914, Red Seal, with Plate Style b (W-1550-G-b). Federal Reserve Bank of Chicago.

Back type used on all $10 Federal Reserve Notes, Series of 1914, Red Seal, as well as Series of 1914 Blue Seal varieties. The vignettes depict *Agriculture* to the left and *Commerce* to the right.

W-1550-H-b • F-899B • 296,000
Estimated population: 19 to 22 • *Highest graded:* Unc.

VG-8	F-12	VF-20	EF-40	AU-50	Unc-60	Unc-63	Unc-65
$275	$500	$900	$2,000	$3,000	—	$4,500	—

W-1550-I-a • F-900A • Minneapolis • 400,000
Estimated population: 55 to 65 • *Highest graded:* Unc.

VG-8	F-12	VF-20	EF-40	AU-50	Unc-60	Unc-63	Unc-65
$250	$450	$700	$1,100	$1,700	$2,250	$2,750	$6,000

W-1550-I-b • F-900B • 212,000
Estimated population: 20 to 23 • *Highest graded:* Unc.

VG-8	F-12	VF-20	EF-40	AU-50	Unc-60
$325	$500	$950	—	—	—

W-1550-J-a • F-901A • Kansas City • 400,000
Estimated population: 35 to 40 • *Highest graded:* AU-50.

VG-8	F-12	VF-20	EF-40	AU-50
$275	$500	$775	$1,250	$2,000

W-1550-J-b • F-901B • 216,000
Estimated population: 16 to 18 • *Highest graded:* Unc.

VG-8	F-12	VF-20	EF-40	AU-50	Unc-60	Unc-63	Unc-65
$275	$450	$750	$1,250	—	$3,500	—	$12,000

W-1550-K-a • F-902A • Dallas • 400,000
Estimated population: 20 to 24 • *Highest graded:* Unc.

VG-8	F-12	VF-20	EF-40	AU-50	Unc-60	Unc-63	Unc-65
$325	$500	$1,300	$2,700	$5,000	—	—	$12,000

W-1550-K-b • F-902B • 180,000
Estimated population: 10 to 12 • *Highest graded:* AU-50.

VG-8	F-12	VF-20	EF-40	AU-50
$450	$850	$1,800	$4,000	$6,500

W-1550-L-a • F-903A • San Francisco • 400,000
Estimated population: 23 to 25 • *Highest graded:* EF-45.

VG-8	F-12	VF-20	EF-40
$325	$500	$1,300	$3,250

W-1550-L-b • F-903B • 660,000
Estimated population: 20 to 24 • *Highest graded:* Unc.

VG-8	F-12	VF-20	EF-40	AU-50	Unc-60	Unc-63	Unc-65
$325	$500	$1,300	$2,500	$3,400	—	—	$9,000

Series of 1914, Blue Seal

As a class the $10 Series of 1914 Blue Seal notes are much more plentiful than those with red seals. These can be collected by bank as well as by signature combination. As they are not in the mainstream of popularity, scarce and rare varieties are priced lower than might otherwise be the case.

In all of the following listings the number (1 to 12) and the large letter (A to L) on the seal at the left indicate the Federal Reserve Bank that issued the note.

Plate Style b (on Red and Blue Seals): In certain of the following listings, the small letter b in the Whitman number indicates a note with the same layout as Style b used on Red Seal notes. A large district number and letter are at the lower left and top right, and at the top left a small bank district letter and numeral are added above the plate letter, and a small bank district letter and number are at the lower right. In the Blue Seal series, all Burke-McAdoo, Burke-Glass, and Burke-Houston notes are of this style.

Plate Style c (on Blue Seals only): In certain of the following listings, the small letter c in the Whitman

number indicates large bank district letter and number at the top right and small district letters and numerals in the other three corners. The letter and number at the upper left corner are over a plate letter. Only late White-Mellon notes are of this style.

Plate Style d (on Blue Seals only): In certain of the following listings, the small letter d in the Whitman number indicates a note similar to Style b, but moved in, closer to the center of the note, and up, closer to the outside edge. Also, the seals to the sides of the portrait are closer than on the b and c issues. Only White-Mellon (1921–1928) notes are found in all three styles.

W-1560-A-b • F-904 • Boston • Burke-McAdoo (1913–1918) • 10,552,000 (est.)
Estimated population: 105 to 115 • *Highest graded:* Unc.

VG-8	F-12	VF-20	EF-40	AU-50	Unc-60	Unc-63
$65	$75	$100	$140	$175	$250	$325

W-1560-A-b★ • F-904★
Recorded population: 1 • *Selected information:* Knight (4/1996), A22425★/E, VF–EF, $413.

W-1561-A-b • F-905 • Burke-Glass (1918–1920) • 9,088,000 (est.)
Estimated population: 65 to 70 • *Highest graded:* Unc.

VG-8	F-12	VF-20	EF-40	AU-50	Unc-60	Unc-63
$70	$85	$110	$165	$205	$280	$400

W-1561-A-b★ • F-905★
Recorded population: 1 • *Selected information:* The existing note is serial A73070★/B, VG.

W-1562-A-b • F-906 • Burke-Houston (1920–1921) • 16,284,000 (est.)
Estimated population: 120 to 130 • *Highest graded:* Unc.

VG-8	F-12	VF-20	EF-40	AU-50	Unc-60	Unc-63
$65	$75	$100	$140	$175	$250	$325

W-1562-A-b★ • F-906★
Estimated population: 15 to 17 • *Highest graded:* EF-45 • *Selected information:* Smythe (2/2000), A224185★/A, Fine, $275. Heritage (1/2008), A259561★/A, F-15 (PCGS), $632.50. Knight (11/2001), A284902★/B, VG–F, $248. CAA (5/2004), A290661★/A, VF, $862.50. B&M (11/2007), A306795★/C, VF-25 (PCGS), $633.

W-1563-A-b • F-907A • White-Mellon (1921–1928) • 28,008,000 (est.)
Estimated population: 310 to 340 • *Highest graded:* Unc.

VG-8	F-12	VF-20	EF-40	AU-50	Unc-60	Unc-63	Unc-65
$65	$75	$100	$140	$175	$250	$325	$750

W-1563-A-b★ • F-907A★
Estimated population: 13 to 15 • *Highest graded:* AU-50 • *Selected information:* Heritage (1/2008), A397465★/A, VF-25 (PCGS), $983.25. Knight (3/2008), A401713★/A, F-15 (PCGS), $862.50. CAA (5/1997), A460946★/F, VG, $110. Heritage (1/2006), A528907★/C, Fine, $575.

SERIES OF 1914, BLUE SEAL

$10 Federal Reserve Note, Series of 1914, Blue Seal, with Plate Style b (W-1587-G-b). Federal Reserve Bank of Chicago.

$10 Federal Reserve Note, Series of 1914, Blue Seal, with Plate Style c (W-1587-G-c). Federal Reserve Bank of Chicago.

$10 Federal Reserve Note, Series of 1914, Blue Seal, with Plate Style d (W-1587-G-d). Federal Reserve Bank of Chicago.

W-1563-A-c • F-907B • 4,464,000 (est.)

Estimated population: 90 to 100 • *Highest graded:* Unc.

VG-8	F-12	VF-20	EF-40	AU-50	Unc-60	Unc-63	Unc-65
$70	$90	$110	$165	$205	$280	$350	$800

W-1563-A-c★ • F-907B★

Recorded population: 1 • *Graded:* Unc • *Selected information:* Martinelli (5/1995), A558090★/B, Unc, $2,850.

W-1564-B-b • F-908 • New York • Burke-McAdoo (1913–1918) • 35,368,000 (est.)

Estimated population: 130 to 140 • *Highest graded:* Unc.

VG-8	F-12	VF-20	EF-40	AU-50	Unc-60	Unc-63	Unc-65
$65	$75	$100	$140	$175	$250	$325	$750

W-1564-B-b★ • F-908★

Recorded population: 3 • *Highest graded:* AU-58 • *Selected information:* Existing specimens include B2515★/C, AU;

B4698★/B, Ch AU, sold in a Stack's auction (3/1991) for $525; and B96090★/F, Fine.

W-1565-B-b • F-909 • Burke-Glass (1918–1920) • 24,332,000 (est.)

Estimated population: 115 to 125 • *Highest graded:* Unc.

VG-8	F-12	VF-20	EF-40	AU-50	Unc-60	Unc-63	Unc-65
$70	$85	$110	$165	$205	$280	$400	$875

W-1565-B-b★ • F-909★

Estimated population: 9 or 10 • *Highest graded:* EF-45 • *Selected information:* CAA (1/2005), B117389★/A, VF–EF, $1,035. Heritage (9/2007), B183802★/B, F-12 (PMG), $863. Knight (2/2004), B198381★/A, VG, $575. Knight (6/2007), B361698★/B, VG (later graded F-12 by PMG), $1,092.50.

W-1566-B-b • F-910 • Burke-Houston (1920–1921) • 29,904,000 (est.)

Estimated population: 300 to 350 • *Highest graded:* Unc.

VG-8	F-12	VF-20	EF-40	AU-50	Unc-60	Unc-63	Unc-65
$65	$75	$100	$140	$175	$250	$325	$750

W-1566-B-b★ • F-910★

Estimated population: 25 to 28 • *Highest graded:* AU-50.

F-12	VF-20	EF-40	AU-50
$800	$1,000	$1,400	$1,900

W-1567-B-b • F-911A • White-Mellon (1921–1928) • 42,696,000 (est.)

Estimated population: 600 to 800 • *Highest graded:* Unc.

VG-8	F-12	VF-20	EF-40	AU-50	Unc-60	Unc-63	Unc-65
$65	$75	$100	$140	$175	$250	$325	$750

W-1567-B-b★ • F-911A★

Estimated population: 22 to 24 • *Highest graded:* VF-25.

VG-8	F-12	VF-20
$200	$350	$700

W-1567-B-c • F-911B • 13,184,000 (est.)

Estimated population: 170 to 190 • *Highest graded:* Unc.

VG-8	F-12	VF-20	EF-40	AU-50	Unc-60	Unc-63	Unc-65
$70	$90	$110	$165	$205	$280	$350	$800

W-1567-B-c★ • F-911B★

Recorded population: 6 • *Highest graded:* VF-20 • *Selected information:* CAA (5/1998), B1165562★/F, VF–F, $880. Heritage (1/2008), B1176010★/F, F-15 (PCGS), $1,380. CAA (1/2000), B1202384★/D, Fine, $385.

W-1567-B-d • F-911C • 18,344,000 (est.)

Estimated population: 250 to 300 • *Highest graded:* Unc.

VG-8	F-12	VF-20	EF-40	AU-50	Unc-60	Unc-63	Unc-65
$65	$75	$100	$140	$175	$250	$325	$775

W-1567-B-d★ • F-911C★

Estimated population: 13 to 15 • *Highest graded:* Unc • *Selected information:* Heritage (1/2006), B1305529★/E, VF-25 (PCGS), $1,495. Heritage (9/2007), B1318894★/B, Fine+, $575. Heritage (1/2007), B1330180★/H, Fine, $780. Her-

itage (1/2008), B1331856★/H, VF-30 (PCGS), $1,035. CAA (10/1995), B1366670★/F, Fine, $242. Stack's (4/1996), B1387503★/C, VF, pinholes, $330.

W-1568-C-b • F-912 • Philadelphia • Burke-McAdoo (1913–1918) • 11,112,000 (est.)

Estimated population: 110 to 125 • *Highest graded:* Unc.

VG-8	F-12	VF-20	EF-40	AU-50	Unc-60	Unc-63
$65	$75	$100	$140	$175	$250	$325

W-1568-C-b★ • F-912★

Recorded population: 2 • *Highest graded:* EF-40 • *Selected information:* CAA (1/2003), C13538★/B, EF, $2,185. CAA (4/2006), C68235★/C, VG, $2,070.

W-1569-C-b • F-913 • Burke-Glass (1918–1920) • 5,088,000 (est.)

Estimated population: 60 to 70 • *Highest graded:* Unc.

VG-8	F-12	VF-20	EF-40	AU-50	Unc-60	Unc-63	Unc-65
$80	$100	$120	$165	$255	$400	$650	$1,000

W-1569-C-b★ • F-913★

Recorded population: 3 • *Highest graded:* EF-40 • *Selected information:* Existing examples include serials C80875★/C, EF; C85115★/C, Fine; and C90146★/B, VG, sold in a CAA auction (10/1995) for $798.

W-1570-C-b • F-914 • Burke-Houston (1920–1921) • 9,300,000 (est.)

Estimated population: 90 to 100 • *Highest graded:* Unc.

VG-8	F-12	VF-20	EF-40	AU-50	Unc-60	Unc-63
$70	$85	$110	$165	$205	$280	$700

W-1570-C-b★ • F-914★

Estimated population: 10 or 11 • *Highest graded:* EF-45 • *Selected information:* Heritage (1/2008), C218030★/B, F-15 (PCGS), $863. Stack's (1/2003), C222963★/C, VF, $690. Knight (6/2007), C255731★/C, G-6 (PMG), VF, $259.

W-1571-C-b • F-915A • White-Mellon (1921–1928) • 27,140,000 (est.)

Estimated population: 320 to 340 • *Highest graded:* Unc.

VG-8	F-12	VF-20	EF-40	AU-50	Unc-60	Unc-63	Unc-65
$65	$75	$100	$140	$175	$250	$325	$750

W-1571-C-b★ • F-915A★

Estimated population: 18 to 20 • *Highest graded:* AU-50.

F-12	VF-20	EF-40	AU-50
$600	$1,000	$1,600	$3,000

W-1571-C-d • F-915C • 2,476,000 (est.)

Estimated population: 100 to 110 • *Highest graded:* Unc.

VG-8	F-12	VF-20	EF-40	AU-50	Unc-60	Unc-63	Unc-65
$70	$90	$110	$165	$205	$280	$350	$800

W-1571-C-d★ • F-915C★

Recorded population: 2 • *Selected information:* Existing examples include serials C448155★/G, F–VF, and C453121★/A, VG–F, sold in a Knight auction (2/2002) for $805.

W-1572-D-b • F-916 • Cleveland • Burke-McAdoo (1913–1918) • 6,720,000 (est.)

Estimated population: 75 to 85 • *Highest graded:* Unc.

VG-8	F-12	VF-20	EF-40	AU-50	Unc-60	Unc-63	Unc-65
$70	$90	$110	$165	$205	$280	$400	$1,250

W-1572-D-b★ • F-916★

Recorded population: 3 • *Highest graded:* F-12 • *Selected information:* Existing examples include serials D2486★/B, Fine, sold in a Heritage auction (11/2000) for $525; D3554★, Fine; and D33030★/F, VG.

W-1573-D-b • F-917 • Burke-Glass (1918–1920) • 4,628,000 (est.)

Estimated population: 65 to 75 • *Highest graded:* Unc.

VG-8	F-12	VF-20	EF-40	AU-50	Unc-60	Unc-63
$70	$85	$110	$165	$205	$280	$700

W-1573-D-b★ • F-917★

Recorded population: 5 • *Highest graded:* AU-50 • *Selected information:* Knight (2/2000), D74011★/C, F–VF, $770. Listed by Doug Murray, D75905★/A, AU.

W-1574-D-b • F-918 • Burke-Houston (1920–1921) • 7,940,000 (est.)

Estimated population: 95 to 115 • *Highest graded:* Unc.

VG-8	F-12	VF-20	EF-40	AU-50	Unc-60	Unc-63	Unc-65
$65	$75	$100	$140	$175	$250	$325	$750

W-1574-D-b★ • F-918★

Estimated population: 10 to 12 • *Highest graded:* Unc • *Selected information:* CAA (1/2005), D117455★/C, Unc, $2,415. Heritage (1/2008), D190516★/D, VG-10 (PCGS), $575.

W-1575-D-b • F-919A • White-Mellon (1921–1928) • 18,692,000 (est.)

Estimated population: 320 to 340 • *Highest graded:* Unc.

VG-8	F-12	VF-20	EF-40	AU-50	Unc-60	Unc-63	Unc-65
$65	$75	$100	$140	$175	$250	$325	$750

W-1575-D-b★ • F-919A★

Estimated population: 16 to 18 • *Highest graded:* EF-45.

F-12	VF-20	EF-40
$400	$800	$1,400

W-1575-D-c • F-919B • 2,676,000 (est.)

Estimated population: 60 to 70 • *Highest graded:* Unc.

VG-8	F-12	VF-20	EF-40	AU-50	Unc-60	Unc-63
$70	$85	$110	$165	$205	$280	$700

W-1575-D-d • F-919C • 1,688,000 (est.)

Estimated population: 70 to 80 • *Highest graded:* Unc.

VG-8	F-12	VF-20	EF-40	AU-50	Unc-60	Unc-63
$70	$85	$110	$165	$205	$280	$700

W-1575-D-d★ • F-919C★

Recorded population: 1 • *Selected information:* Heritage (9/2007), D347843★/C, VG, $2,990.

W-1576-E-b • F-920 • Richmond • Burke-McAdoo (1913–1918) • 5,600,000 (est.)

Estimated population: 80 to 90 • *Highest graded:* Unc.

VG-8	F-12	VF-20	EF-40	AU-50	Unc-60	Unc-63
$70	$85	$110	$175	$230	$400	$1,000

W-1576-E-b★ • F-920★

Recorded population: 1 • Reported; no further information.

W-1577-E-b • F-921 • Burke-Glass (1918–1920) • 4,148,000 (est.)

Estimated population: 44 to 48 • *Highest graded:* Unc.

VG-8	F-12	VF-20	EF-40	AU-50	Unc-60	Unc-63
$75	$100	$160	$280	$525	$1,750	$4,000

W-1577-E-b★ • F-921★

Recorded population: 2 • *Highest graded:* VF-20 • *Selected information:* Existing examples include serials E31998★/B, VF, and E58660★/D, F-12 (PCGS), sold in a Heritage auction (9/2007) for $3,220.

W-1578-E-b • F-922 • Burke-Houston (1920–1921) • 6,560,000 (est.)

Estimated population: 110 to 120 • *Highest graded:* Unc.

VG-8	F-12	VF-20	EF-40	AU-50	Unc-60	Unc-63
$80	$100	$120	$165	$205	$300	$600

W-1578-E-b★ • F-922★

Estimated population: 13 or 14 • *Highest graded:* VF-20.

VG-8	F-12	VF-20
$450	$700	$1,200

W-1579-E-b • F-923 • White-Mellon (1921–1928) • 10,468,000 (est.)

Estimated population: 200 to 220 • *Highest graded:* Unc.

VG-8	F-12	VF-20	EF-40	AU-50	Unc-60	Unc-63	Unc-65
$65	$75	$100	$140	$175	$250	$325	$750

W-1579-E-b • F-923★

Recorded population: 3 • *Highest graded:* F-12 • *Selected information:* Existing examples include serials E198969★/A, Fine; E213070★/B, Fine, sold in a CAA auction (9/2001) for $1,045; and E216277★/E, VG.

W-1580-F-b • F-924 • Atlanta • Burke-McAdoo (1913–1918) • 7,560,000 (est.)

Estimated population: 70 to 80 • *Highest graded:* Unc.

VG-8	F-12	VF-20	EF-40	AU-50	Unc-60	Unc-63
$80	$100	$120	$165	$205	$300	$600

W-1580-F-b★ • F-924★

Recorded population: 2 • *Highest graded:* EF-45 • *Selected information:* Existing examples include serials F841★/A, EF, and F7173★/A, VF-20 (PCGS), sold in a Heritage auction (9/2007) for $4,600.

W-1581-F-b • F-925 • Burke-Glass (1918–1920) • 4,500,000 (est.)

Estimated population: 48 to 54 • *Highest graded:* Unc.

VG-8	F-12	VF-20	EF-40	AU-50	Unc-60	Unc-63	Unc-65
$70	$95	$110	$165	$205	$300	$550	$1,250

W-1581-F-b★ • F-925★

Recorded population: 5 • *Highest graded:* VF-25 • *Selected information:* Heritage (9/2007), F40593★/A, VF-25 (PCGS), $2,760.

W-1582-F-b • F-926 • Burke-Houston (1920–1921) • 5,140,000 (est.)

Estimated population: 95 to 115 • *Highest graded:* Unc.

VG-8	F-12	VF-20	EF-40	AU-50	Unc-60	Unc-63	Unc-65
$70	$90	$110	$165	$205	$280	$350	$800

W-1582-F-b★ • F-926★

Recorded population: 2 • *Highest graded:* VF-30 • *Selected information:* Existing examples include serials F108926★, VG–F, and F110450★/B, VF–EF.

W-1583-F-b • F-927A • White-Mellon (1921–1928) • 9,392,000 (est.)

Estimated population: 130 to 150 • *Highest graded:* Unc.

VG-8	F-12	VF-20	EF-40	AU-50	Unc-60
$65	$75	$100	$140	$175	$250

W-1583-F-b★ • F-927A★

Recorded population: 4 • *Highest graded:* EF-40 • *Selected information:* Existing examples include serials F160688★/D, VF–EF; F169299★/G, Fine; F172531★/C, EF, sold in a CAA auction (9/1999) for $3,080; and F182495★/G, F–VF.

W-1583-F-c • F-927B • 4,268,000 (est.)

Estimated population: 75 to 85 • *Highest graded:* Unc.

VG-8	F-12	VF-20	EF-40	AU-50	Unc-60
$80	$100	$120	$180	$450	$800

W-1584-G-b • F-928 • Chicago • Burke-McAdoo (1913–1918) • 20,896,000 (est.)

Estimated population: 220 to 240 • *Highest graded:* Unc.

VG-8	F-12	VF-20	EF-40	AU-50	Unc-60	Unc-63	Unc-65
$65	$75	$100	$140	$175	$250	$325	$750

W-1584-G-b★ • F-928★

Recorded population: 2 • *Highest graded:* Unc • *Selected information:* Spink America (5/1995), G1002★/B, Unc, $5,280. CAA (4/2006), G33070★/B, VF, repaired, $2,990.

W-1585-G-b • F-929 • Burke-Glass (1918–1920) • 9,300,000 (est.)

Estimated population: 130 to 145 • *Highest graded:* Unc.

VG-8	F-12	VF-20	EF-40	AU-50	Unc-60	Unc-63	Unc-65
$65	$75	$100	$160	$205	$300	$550	$850

W-1585-G-b★ • F-929★

Recorded population: 7 • *Highest graded:* VF-30 • *Selected information:* CAA (10/1995), G103538★/B, VF, $770. Heritage (9/2007), G107662★/B, VG, $632.50.

W-1586-G-b • F-930 • Burke-Houston (1920–1921) • 19,512,000 (est.)

Estimated population: 210 to 230 • *Highest graded:* Unc.

VG-8	F-12	VF-20	EF-40	AU-50	Unc-60	Unc-63	Unc-65
$65	$75	$100	$140	$175	$250	$325	$750

W-1586-G-b★ • F-930★

Estimated population: 35 to 37 • *Highest graded:* Unc.

F-12	VF-20	EF-40	AU-50	Unc-60	Unc-63
$400	$600	$900	$1,200	—	$2,200

W-1587-G-b • F-931A • White-Mellon (1921–1928) • 19,692,000 (est.)

Estimated population: 320 to 360 • *Highest graded:* Unc.

VG-8	F-12	VF-20	EF-40	AU-50	Unc-60	Unc-63	Unc-65
$65	$75	$100	$140	$175	$250	$325	$750

W-1587-G-b★ • F-931A★

Estimated population: 28 to 32 • *Highest graded:* Unc.

F-12	VF-20	EF-40	AU-50	Unc-60	Unc-63
$400	$600	$900	$1,300	—	$2,600

W-1587-G-c • F-931B • 11,116,000 (est.)

Estimated population: 225 to 250 • *Highest graded:* Unc.

VG-8	F-12	VF-20	EF-40	AU-50	Unc-60	Unc-63	Unc-65
$70	$90	$110	$165	$205	$300	$375	$850

W-1587-G-c★ • F-931B★

Recorded population: 4 • *Highest graded:* VF-25 • *Selected information:* Existing examples include serials G580969★/E, G–VG; G599339★/G, VF; G605939★/G, Fine, sold in a Heritage auction (1/2007) for $1,610; and G619159★/G, VG–F.

W-1587-G-d • F-931C • 2,484,000 (est.)

Estimated population: 70 to 80 • *Highest graded:* Unc.

VG-8	F-12	VF-20	EF-40	AU-50	Unc-60	Unc-63	Unc-65
$70	$85	$110	$165	$205	$280	$450	$900

W-1587-G-d★ • F-931C★

Recorded population: 2 • *Highest graded:* F-12 • *Selected information:* Existing examples include serials G641808★/D, Fine, and G648456★/H, Fine.

W-1588-H-b • F-932 • St. Louis • Burke-McAdoo (1913–1918) • 6,404,000 (est.)

Estimated population: 75 to 85 • *Highest graded:* Unc.

VG-8	F-12	VF-20	EF-40	AU-50	Unc-60
$75	$90	$140	$230	$400	$700

W-1589-H-b • F-933 • Burke-Glass (1918–1920) • 4,312,000 (est.)

Estimated population: 75 to 85 • *Highest graded:* Unc.

VG-8	F-12	VF-20	EF-40	AU-50	Unc-60	Unc-63	Unc-65
$70	$85	$110	$165	$205	$280	$400	$800

W-1589-H-b★ • F-933★

Recorded population: 3 • *Highest graded:* EF-45 • *Selected information:* Existing examples include serials H89177★/A, EF;

H105034★/B, VG–F, sold in a CAA auction (5/1997) for $770; and H106083★/C, F–VF, sold in a Smythe auction (6/2001) for $1,595.

W-1590-H-b • F-934 • Burke-Houston (1920–1921) • 7,336,000 (est.)

Estimated population: 170 to 190 • *Highest graded:* Unc.

VG-8	F-12	VF-20	EF-40	AU-50	Unc-60	Unc-63	Unc-65
$65	$75	$100	$140	$175	$250	$325	$750

W-1590-H-b★ • F-934★

Estimated population: 15 or 16 • *Highest graded:* EF-45.

F-12	VF-20	EF-40
$850	$1,100	$1,800

W-1591-H-b • F-935 • St. Louis • White-Mellon (1921–1928) • 2,560,000 (est.)

Estimated population: 70 to 80 • *Highest graded:* Unc.

VG-8	F-12	VF-20	EF-40	AU-50	Unc-60	Unc-63
$70	$85	$110	$165	$205	$280	$450

W-1592-I-b • F-936 • Minneapolis • Burke-McAdoo (1913–1918) • 4,940,000 (est.)

Estimated population: 90 to 105 • *Highest graded:* Unc.

VG-8	F-12	VF-20	EF-40	AU-50	Unc-60	Unc-63	Unc-65
$70	$85	$110	$165	$205	$280	$350	$800

W-1592-I-b★ • F-936★

Recorded population: 2 • *Highest graded:* EF-40 • *Selected information:* Existing examples include serials I14496★/D, EF, and I19441★/A, Fine.

W-1593-I-b • F-937 • Burke-Glass (1918–1920) • 1,348,000 (est.)

Estimated population: 40 to 45 • *Highest graded:* Unc.

VG-8	F-12	VF-20	EF-40	AU-50	Unc-60	Unc-63
$75	$90	$140	$180	$250	$400	$800

W-1593-I-b★ • F-937★

Recorded population: 7 • *Highest graded:* VF-20.

W-1594-I-b • F-938 • Burke-Houston (1920–1921) • 2,660,000 (est.)

Recorded population: 7 • *Highest graded:* EF-45 • *Selected information:* CAA (1/2005), I32101/A, VF–EF (later EF–AU), $2,530.

W-1594-I-b★ • F-938★

Estimated population: 10 to 12 • *Highest graded:* EF-40 • *Selected information:* Heritage (1/2006), I53688★/D, Fine, $1,265. Stack's (3/1991), I61517★/A, EF, $400.

W-1595-I-b • F-939 • White-Mellon (1921–1928) • 4,816,000 (est.)

Estimated population: 235 to 255 • *Highest graded:* Unc.

VG-8	F-12	VF-20	EF-40	AU-50	Unc-60	Unc-63	Unc-65
$65	$75	$100	$140	$175	$250	$325	$775

W-1595-I-b★ • F-939★

Recorded population: 6 • *Highest graded:* AU-50 • *Selected information:* CAA (11/1990), I80739★/C, AU, $375. Knight (2/2004), I81855★/C, VG–F, $805.

W-1596-J-b • F-940 • Kansas City • Burke-McAdoo (1913–1918) • 6,684,000 (est.)

Estimated population: 120 to 130 • *Highest graded:* Unc.

VG-8	F-12	VF-20	EF-40	AU-50	Unc-60	Unc-63	Unc-65
$65	$75	$100	$140	$175	$250	$325	$775

W-1596-J-b★ • F-940★

Recorded population: 4 • *Highest graded:* EF-45 • *Selected information:* Existing examples include serials J1347★/C, VG; J14484★/D, EF, sold in a CAA auction (9/2002) for $1,150; J17152★/D, VF; and J17683★/C, VG–F.

W-1597-J-b • F-941 • Burke-Glass (1918–1920) • 1,000,000 (est.)

Estimated population: 20 to 23 • *Highest graded:* Unc.

VG-8	F-12	VF-20	EF-40	AU-50	Unc-60	Unc-63	Unc-65
$130	$240	$420	$580	$750	$1,000	$1,200	$1,400

W-1598-J-b • F-942 • Burke-Houston (1920–1921) • 4,276,000 (est.)

Estimated population: 115 to 125 • *Highest graded:* Unc.

VG-8	F-12	VF-20	EF-40	AU-50	Unc-60	Unc-63	Unc-65
$65	$75	$100	$140	$175	$250	$325	$750

W-1598-J-b★ • F-942★

Estimated population: 14 to 16 • *Highest graded:* Unc.

F-12	VF-20	EF-40	AU-50	Unc-60	Unc-63
$600	$1,200	$2,100	$2,500	—	$3,500

W-1599-J-b • F-943A • White-Mellon (1921–1928) • 3,868,000 (est.)

Estimated population: 145 to 160 • *Highest graded:* Unc.

VG-8	F-12	VF-20	EF-40	AU-50	Unc-60	Unc-63	Unc-65
$65	$75	$100	$140	$175	$250	$325	$750

W-1599-J-d • F-943C • 4,000 (est.) • Printed but not issued

W-1600-K-b • F-944 • Dallas • Burke-McAdoo (1913–1918) • 5,956,000 (est.)

Estimated population: 95 to 115 • *Highest graded:* Unc.

VG-8	F-12	VF-20	EF-40	AU-50	Unc-60	Unc-63	Unc-65
$65	$75	$100	$140	$175	$250	$325	$750

W-1600-K-b★ • F-944★

Recorded population: 3 • *Highest graded:* EF-40 • *Selected information:* Existing examples include serials K23983★/C, EF-40 (PCGS), sold in a Heritage auction (9/2008) for $11,500; K27194★/F, VG–F; and K49911★/G, VG–F, sold in a CAA auction (10/1995) for $330.

W-1601-K-b • F-945 • Burke-Glass (1918–1920) • 1,324,000 (est.)

Estimated population: 20 to 24 • *Highest graded:* EF-45.

VG-8	F-12	VF-20	EF-40
$525	$850	$1,300	$3,500

W-1602-K-b • F-946 • Burke-Houston (1920–1921) • 2,204,000 (est.)

Estimated population: 70 to 80 • *Highest graded:* Unc.

VG-8	F-12	VF-20	EF-40	AU-50	Unc-60	Unc-63
$75	$90	$145	$210	$275	$400	$1,000

W-1602-K-b★ • F-946★

Recorded population: 6 • *Highest graded:* EF-40 • *Selected information:* Heritage (4/2008), K69111★/C, Fine, $2,012.50. CAA (5/2004), K69596★/D, VG–F, problems, $1,150. Heritage (9/2008), K71204★/D, VF-30 (PCGS), $8,625. Stack's (3/1991), K82485★/A, EF, $425.

W-1603-K-b • F-947 • White-Mellon (1921–1928) • 3,336,000 (est.)

Estimated population: 75 to 85 • *Highest graded:* Unc.

VG-8	F-12	VF-20	EF-40	AU-50	Unc-60	Unc-63	Unc-65
$75	$90	$145	$210	$275	$400	$500	$900

W-1604-L-b • F-948 • San Francisco • Burke-McAdoo (1913–1918) • 5,440,000 (est.)

Estimated population: 35 to 42 • *Highest graded:* AU-50.

VG-8	F-12	VF-20	EF-40	AU-50
$110	$180	$275	$575	$1,250

W-1605-L-b • F-949 • Burke-Glass (1918–1920) • 4,200,000 (est.)

Estimated population: 35 to 42 • *Highest graded:* AU-50.

VG-8	F-12	VF-20	EF-40	AU-50
$110	$180	$275	$575	$1,250

W-1605-L-b★ • F-949★

Recorded population: 2 • *Selected information:* Existing examples include serials L41210★/F, Fine, and L50749★/A, VF–EF, sold in a Knight auction (8/2000) $2,310.

W-1606-L-b • F-950 • Burke-Houston (1920–1921) • 9,540,000 (est.)

Estimated population: 60 to 70 • *Highest graded:* AU-55.

VG-8	F-12	VF-20	EF-40	AU-50
$90	$135	$175	$240	$380

W-1607-L-b • F-951A • White-Mellon (1921–1928) • 16,020,000 (est.)

Estimated population: 200 to 225 • *Highest graded:* Unc.

VG-8	F-12	VF-20	EF-40	AU-50	Unc-60	Unc-63	Unc-65
$65	$75	$100	$140	$175	$250	$325	$750

W-1607-L-b★ • F-951A★

Recorded population: 8 • *Highest graded:* VF-20 • *Selected information:* CAA (9/1996), L239443★/G, VG, $203.50. CAA (9/1999), L260727★/G, Fine, damaged, $1,210. CAA (6/1995), L280678★/D, VF, $550. Heritage (1/2007), L323109★/E, VG–F, $862.50.

W-1607-L-c • F-951B • 3,272,000 (est.)

Estimated population: 45 to 50 • *Highest graded:* Unc.

VG-8	F-12	VF-20	EF-40	AU-50	Unc-60
$90	$135	$175	$240	$400	—

W-1607-L-d • F-951C • 1,900,000 (est.)

Estimated population: 75 to 85 • *Highest graded:* Unc.

VG-8	F-12	VF-20	EF-40	AU-50	Unc-60
$75	$115	$135	$180	$400	—

W-1607-L-d★ • F-951C★

Recorded population: 1 • *Selected information:* The existing example is serial L339191★/G, F–VF.

FEDERAL RESERVE BANK NOTES

Large-size Federal Reserve Bank Notes of 1915 and 1918 are similar to the Federal Reserve Notes of 1914, but the city and bank name were made more prominent. These feature the Federal Reserve city spelled out in large letters on the face. The series date is at the far left and the upper right on the 1915 issues, and at the far left and lower right on the 1918 issues. The back is the same general design as seen on the Series of 1914 Federal Reserve Notes, but with different wording.

While signature varieties exist, these are usually collected by district or singly for type. Only half of the 12 districts issued this class of notes in the $10 denomination. As of January 15, 1951, only 3,649 notes of this series remained outstanding.

Series of 1915 and 1918 notes have the signatures of the register of the Treasury and the Treasurer of the United States at the top, and at the bottom the signatures of cashier and governor of the particular Federal Reserve Bank. Their overprinted signatures are on most notes, but some of the Series of 1915 have the signatures separately applied by rubber-stamping, which could result in differences in crispness and location. Very early Kansas City $10 notes have autographed signatures, and others may be found.

Series of 1915

Series of 1915 notes have SERIES OF 1915, the date MAY 18, 1914, and in one curved and three straight lines vertically at the right border, "Authorized by the Federal Reserve Act of December 23, 1913."

At the top center of the Series of 1915 notes is the security provision: "Secured by United States bonds deposited with the Treasurer of the United States of America."

W-1620-F • F-811 • Atlanta • 1915 • Teehee-Burke • Bell-Wellborn • 48,000

Recorded population: 6 • *Highest graded:* EF-40 • *Commentary:* In his 1951 study of these notes (see the bibliography), W.A. Philpott Jr. stated that of the two varieties of Atlanta $10 notes, Series of 1915 and 1918, only 270 notes remained outstanding. • *Selected information:* Existing notes include serials F437A/A, Fine, sold in a CAA auction (1/2000) for $4,180; F3776A, EF-40 (PMG), sold in a Heritage auction (4/2008) for $28,750; F14819A/C, EF, problems, sold in a CAA auction (9/2006) for $9,775; F17841A, EF, strengthened, sold in a CAA auction (1/1998) for $358; F18295A/C, Fine; and F35474A, VG, owned by the Federal Reserve Bank of San Francisco.

SERIES OF 1915

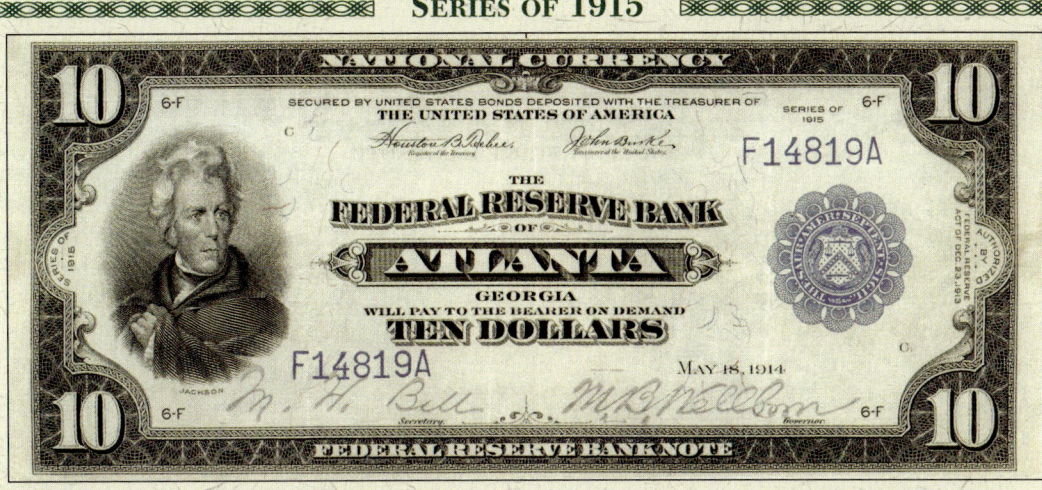

$10 Federal Reserve Bank Note, Series of 1915 (W-1620-F), issued by the Atlanta Federal Reserve Bank. Stamped signatures of bank officials.

Detail of the authorization notice at the right side of the face. (shown rotated 90° counterclockwise)

Back of W-1620-F, the design used on all $10 Federal Reserve Bank Notes, Series of 1915 and 1918. The vignettes, *Agriculture* and *Commerce*, are the same as on the Series of 1914 $10 Federal Reserve Notes, but the lettering is different.

W-1621-G • F-813 • Chicago • McLallen-McDougal • 180,000

Estimated population: 58 to 62 • *Highest graded:* Unc • *Commentary:* In his 1951 study of these notes (see the bibliography), W.A. Philpott Jr. stated that of the two varieties of Chicago $10 notes, Series of 1915 and 1918, only 847 notes remained outstanding.

VG-8	F-12	VF-20	EF-40	AU-50	Unc-60	Unc-63	Unc-65
$1,400	$2,300	$4,000	$6,500	$7,500	$8,500	$10,000	$17,000

W-1622-J • F-817b • Kansas City • Cross (acting)-Miller • Federal Reserve autographed signatures, with "Acting" before Cross's title • 500 (est.)

Recorded population: 2 • *Selected information:* Existing examples include serials J7A, Unc, and J109A/A, AU-58 (PMG).

W-1623-J • F-817a • Federal Reserve signatures stamped in red, with "Acting" before Cross's title • 3,500 (est.)

Recorded population: Unknown • *Selected information:* Among the existing examples are serials J741A, EF, and J1111A/C, Unc (PCGS).

W-1624-J • F-817 • Signatures overprinted, with "Acting" before Cross's title • 276,000 (est.)

Estimated population: 100 to 110 • *Highest graded:* Unc • *Commentary:* This is the most commonly seen issue.

VG-8	F-12	VF-20	EF-40	AU-50	Unc-60	Unc-63	Unc-65
$1,400	$2,300	$4,000	$5,000	$6,000	$7,000	$8,500	$12,000

W-1625-J • F-816 • Anderson-Miller • 208,000 (est.)

Estimated population: 38 to 47 • *Highest graded:* AU-50.

VG-8	F-12	VF-20	EF-40	AU-50
$1,400	$2,450	$4,000	$6,750	$9,000

W-1626-J • F-818 • Helm (acting cashier)-Miller • 16,000

Recorded population: 7 • *Highest graded:* AU-50 • *Commentary:* In his 1951 study of these notes (see the bibliography), W.A. Philpott Jr. stated, "The rarest of the Kansas City notes are the 1915 series, Helm & Miller $5 and $10, in Uncirculated condition." • *Selected information:* CAA (5/2004), J495700A/D, EF, $21,850; Heritage (4/2008), J496936A/D, VF-35 (PMG), $43,125. Stack's (3/1991), J501416A/D, AU, center fold (later graded "Choice Unc"), $880.

W-1627-K • F-819 • Dallas • Hoopes-Van Zandt • 204,000 (est.)

Estimated population: 55 to 60 • *Highest graded:* Unc.

VG-8	F-12	VF-20	EF-40	AU-50	Unc-60	Unc-63	Unc-65
$1,400	$2,300	$4,000	$6,500	$8,000	$10,000	$12,000	$19,000

W-1628-K • F-821 • Talley (cashier)-Van Zandt • 28,000 (est.)

Estimated population: 9 or 10 • *Highest graded:* EF-45 • *Selected information:* Smythe (2/1999), K222157A/A, EF, $3,500. Knight (3/2005), K222392A/D, EF, $2,300. Heritage (4/2008), K223581A, VF-30 (PMG), $14,950.

VG-8	F-12	VF-20	EF-40
$2,750	$4,750	$7,000	$9,000

W-1629-K • F-820 • Gilbert (cashier)-Van Zandt • 8,000 (est.)

Recorded population: 6 • *Highest graded:* VF-30 • *Selected information:* Hickman & Oakes (6/1987), K233368A/D, VF, error with bank signatures too low, $550. Knight (8/2002), K234052A/D, Fine, $2,760. Knight (8/2000), K237566A/B, VF+, $3,740.

Series of 1918

Series of 1918 notes have SERIES OF 1918, the date MAY 18, 1914, and in two curved and two straight lines vertically at the right border, "Authorized by the Acts of December 23, 1913, and April 23, 1918."

At the top center of the Series of 1918 notes is the security provision: "Secured by United States bonds or United States certificates of indebtedness or United States one-year gold notes deposited with the Treasurer of the United States of America."

W-1630-B • F-810 • New York • 1918 • Teehee-Burke • Hendricks-Strong • 200,000

Estimated population: 30 to 35 • *Highest graded:* Unc • *Commentary:* In his 1951 study of these notes (see the bibliography), W.A. Philpott Jr. commented on the great rarity of this variety, noting that only 343 were outstanding as of October 30, 1944.

VG-8	F-12	VF-20	EF-40	AU-50	Unc-60	Unc-63	Unc-65
$1,400	$2,750	$5,000	$7,000	$8,000	$9,000	$10,000	$17,000

W-1631-F • F-812 • Atlanta • Elliott-Burke • Bell-Wellborn • 184,000

Estimated population: 36 to 42 • *Highest graded:* Unc.

VG-8	F-12	VF-20	EF-40	AU-50	Unc-60	Unc-63
$1,400	$2,450	$4,000	$6,500	—	—	$12,000

W-1632-G • F-814 • Chicago • Teehee-Burke • McCloud-McDougal • 200,000

Estimated population: 24 to 48 • *Highest graded:* Unc.

VG-8	F-12	VF-20	EF-40	AU-50	Unc-60	Unc-63	Unc-65
$1,400	$2,300	$4,000	$6,500	$7,500	$8,500	$10,000	$17,000

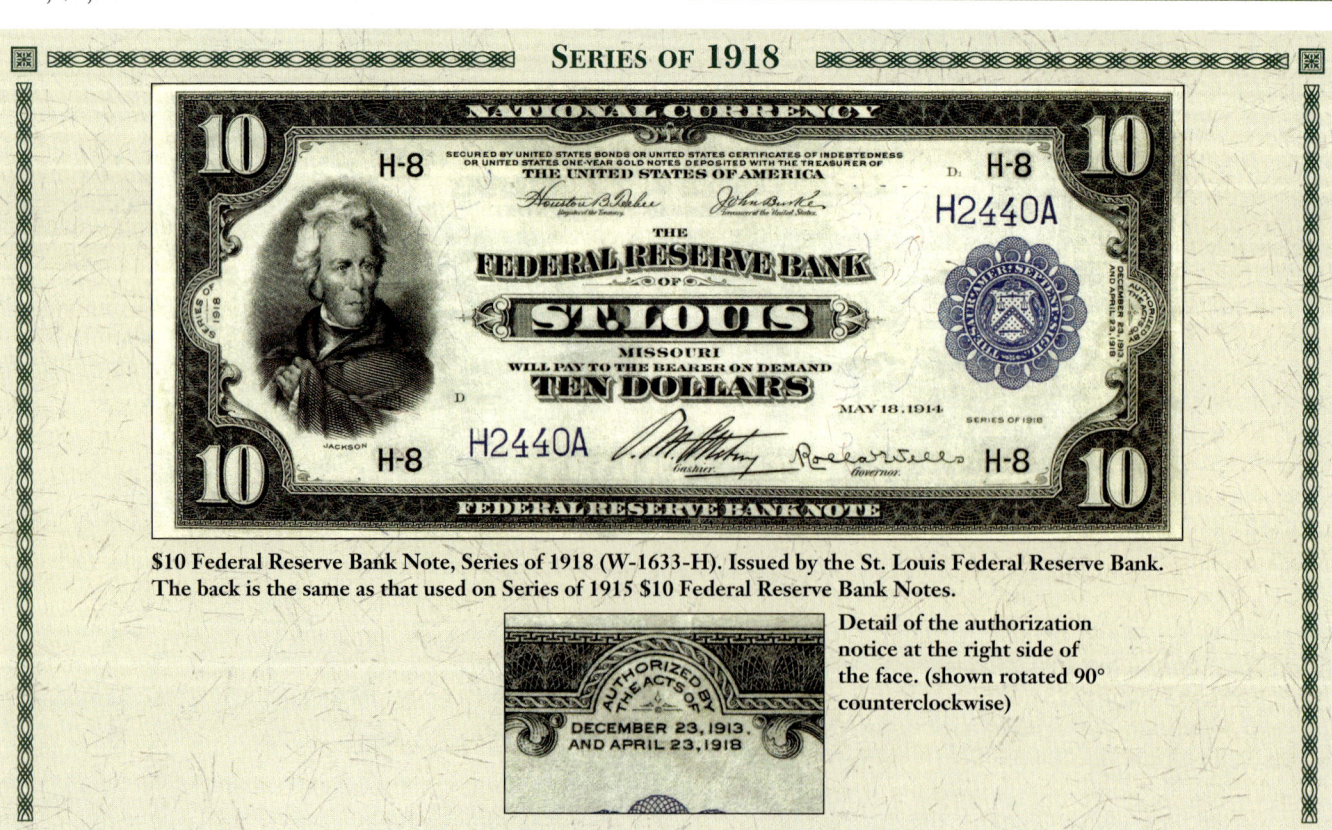

$10 Federal Reserve Bank Note, Series of 1918 (W-1633-H). Issued by the St. Louis Federal Reserve Bank. The back is the same as that used on Series of 1915 $10 Federal Reserve Bank Notes.

Detail of the authorization notice at the right side of the face. (shown rotated 90° counterclockwise)

W-1633-H • F-815 • St. Louis • Attebery-Wells • 100,000

Estimated population: 35 to 40 • *Commentary:* In his 1951 study of these notes (see the bibliography), W.A. Philpott Jr. stated that $10 notes from St. Louis are scarcer than those of any other Federal Reserve bank, with only 237 outstanding as of October 30, 1944.

VG-8	F-12	VF-20	EF-40
$1,500	$2,750	$5,000	$7,750

W-1633-H★ • F-815★

Recorded population: 1 • *Selected information:* Stack's (9/1992), H938★/B, AU, $10,500.

SMALL SIZE

Small-size $10 notes are often collected by variety or, alternatively, by type. Some early issues range from scarce to rare, and some early star notes are exceedingly rare.

All depict Alexander Hamilton on the face and the Treasury Building on the back. The portrait, engraved by George F.C. Smillie, is taken from a painting by John Trumbull and dates to the 19th century. Joachim C. Benzing created the back. These were used up to the advent of modern security notes.

As a class, $10 notes are scarcer than are those of lower denominations. The continuing parade of Federal Reserve Notes, in recent years from the Fort Worth (FW) plant as well as the main facility in Washington, has provided many collectible varieties.

LEGAL TENDER NOTES

Legal Tender Notes of the Series of 1928 were planned, but none of the $10 value were issued, as the total face value of this class of notes, authorized by Congress in the Act of February 28, 1878 (Bland-Allison Act), was filled by other denominations.

Series of 1928, Red Seal
Woods-Woodin (1933)

These were payable in "ten dollars on demand," not specified as to what form, but not necessarily coins. To the left is the four-line notation, overprinted by the Treasury seal, "This note is a legal tender at its face value for all debts public and private except duties on imports and interest on the public debt." In the right field TEN is printed in large letters. Although plates were prepared, there is no record of these notes being issued for general circulation. Some were printed, however, as $10 and $20 notes were exhibited by the Treasury department at the Century of Progress Exposition in Chicago in 1933.

W-1700 • F-unlisted

GOLD CERTIFICATES

The $10 Series of 1928 Gold Certificates with gold Treasury seal are the smallest denomination of bills of this class. The notes were immediately popular. For 1928-A over 100 million were printed, but these were never released.

SERIES OF 1928, GOLD SEAL

$10 Gold Certificate, Series of 1928 (W-1710).

Back of the $10 Gold Certificate, Series of 1928 (W-1710). The type was the standard design used on all small-size $10 notes in various series through the 1950s.

Series of 1928, Gold Seal
Woods-Mellon (1929–1932)

The obligation or payable notice reads: "Ten dollars in gold coin payable to the bearer on demand." At the left the Treasury seal is overprinted on a more standard commentary, with GOLD above and CERTIFICATE below, and three lines between: "This certificate is a legal tender in the amount thereof in payment of all debts and dues public and private." In addition to the yellow (usually called gold) seal, the serial numbers were printed in yellow. An ambitious program was launched, with at least 290 face plates prepared. Well over 100 million were printed. As it turned out, these had a short life in circulation.

W-1710 • F-2400 • 130,812,000

VG-8	F-12	VF-20	EF-40	AU-50	Unc-60	Unc-63	Unc-65
$105	$125	$170	$275	$550	$585	$750	$1,600

W-1710★ • F-2400★

VG-8	F-12	VF-20	EF-40	AU-50	Unc-60	Unc-63	Unc-65
$175	$300	$600	$1,000	$1,350	$2,000	$3,000	$6,000

Series of 1928-A, Gold Seal
Woods-Mills (1929–1932)

Bearing the printed signatures of Woods and Mills, 2,544,000 examples of these notes were shipped. However, shortly after his March 4, 1933, inauguration, president Franklin D. Roosevelt suspended the issuance of gold coins and Gold Certificates to the general public through regular channels. It seems that all of the Series of 1928-A Gold Certificates remained in the hands of the Treasury department. John Schwartz and Scott Lindquist in their *Standard Guide to Small-Size U.S. Paper Money 1928 to Date* state that these are believed to be in existence today, stored in the cellar of the Treasury Building in Washington, D.C.

W-1711 • F-2401 • Not issued

NATIONAL BANK NOTES

Series of 1929 National Bank Notes, first circulated in that year, remained in use through early 1935. There are two styles, Type 1 and Type 2, which were issued in six-subject sheets. Each has a brown Treasury seal and brown serial numbers. Type 1 bills each had the same serial number on a given sheet, prefixed by a letter, A through F (such as A000001A to F000001A). Type 2 bills were numbered continuously, with the first sheet from a given bank starting with A000001 and ending with A000006, yielding a single number 1 note, in contrast to six on the first Series of 1929 Type 1 sheet.

At the right the brown Treasury seal is overprinted on "Redeemable in lawful money of the United States, at United States Treasury or at the bank of issue."

As a class, 1929 Type 1 notes are much more plentiful than Type 2 notes, although for specific national banks the situation can be reversed. Some banks issued just Type 1 bills, many issued both, and some late-chartered banks, including those made in the consolidations and mergers of necessity

during the Depression, issued only Type 2 notes, which commenced printing in May 1933. Collecting small-size $10 Nationals can be a rewarding pursuit, as examples from many different banks are available. Higher denominations are much scarcer.

Prices are for states from which a larger number of notes survive. The large populations of these notes have stimulated many numismatists to collect as many banks or towns as possible within a given state. Most are in grades of Fine to Very Fine or so, although quite a few Uncirculated notes exist, many of which have low serial numbers. Above the $10 denomination, the $20 notes are scarce as a class, and the $50 and $100 notes are rare.

Series of 1929, Type 1, Brown Seal
Jones-Woods (1929–1933)

Type 1 bills each had the same serial number on a given sheet, prefixed by a letter, A through F, such as A000001A to F000001A. This gives six times more number 1 notes than the 1929 Type 2 bills. Signatures of the bank cashier and president were printed directly on each note at the BEP.

While Uncirculated notes are plentiful, the average grade is often Fine or so, as these were not plucked from circulation in quantity until collecting them became popular in the 1940s and, especially, the 1950s. The value chart shows generic prices for a typical note from a state from which notes range from available to just slightly scarce.

Banks of Issue and Rarity of Notes

Based upon census information from Don C. Kelly and James M. Kelly (*National Bank Note Census*, Version 4.0) and with some information from the other sources, this listing gives each location, the number of banks issuing this series of notes within each, and a commentary.[34]

The Kelly survey records 58,715 notes, an immense quantity. This furnishes ample examples to collect, from many states, cities, or favorite banks. As 1,651 serial number 1 notes are recorded, these too are highly collectible. These are specifically listed below. The A plate letter would seem to be more desirable than the others on a number 1 note, but not much mention is made of this.

Alabama • 92 banks of issue • 937 notes reported • Mostly circulated, with a nice run from Leeth National Bank of Cullman (43). The census lists 14 serial number 1 notes.

Alaska • 3 banks of issue • No notes reported • Alaska was a territory at the time, but the notes simply say Alaska.

Arizona • 10 banks of issue • 124 notes reported • Includes the First National Bank of Mesa (22), Consolidated National Bank of Tucson (21) and the First National Bank at Phoenix (33). Six Unc notes are listed. Eight serial number 1 notes are recorded.

Arkansas • 50 banks of issue • 409 notes reported • Mostly circulated, except for a nice run of Unc notes from the National Bank of Eastern Arkansas in Forrest City (31).

California • 156 banks of issue • 2,178 notes reported • Mostly circulated with some scattered Unc examples. The census lists 43 serial number 1 notes.

SERIES OF 1929, TYPE 1, BROWN SEAL

$10 National Bank Note, Series of 1929, Type 1 (W-1720). Gap National Bank and Trust Company, Gap, Pennsylvania. The words "and Trust Company" appeared in relatively few national bank names. The Treasury seal at the right is printed in brown. The bank charter number 2864 is in black at left and right borders.

Back of the $10 National Bank Note, Series of 1929, Type 1 (W-1720). Shown is an angular view of the Treasury Building in Washington, D.C. The automobile in the foreground is generic but has some aspects of a Model A Ford.

Colorado • 81 banks of issue • 662 notes reported • Includes the First National Bank of Denver (56). The census lists 48 serial number 1 notes.

Connecticut • 54 banks of issue • 884 notes reported • Includes the First National Bank of Hartford (63), Hartford National Bank & Trust (49) and the First National Bank & Trust Company of New Haven (53). The census lists 40 serial number 1 notes.

Delaware • 16 banks of issue • 155 notes reported • The census lists 18 Unc notes. Nine serial number 1 notes are recorded.

District of Columbia • 10 banks of issue • 381 notes reported • Many Unc notes are reported, including a run of 33 from the Lincoln National Bank of Washington. Two serial number 1 notes are from National Metropolitan Bank of Washington (VF) and the Lincoln National Bank of Washington (Unc).

Florida • 48 banks of issue • 540 notes reported • Includes the Atlantic National Bank of Jacksonville (86), Florida National Bank of Jacksonville (39) and the Barnett National Bank of Jacksonville (29). Mostly circulated notes with some Unc examples interspersed. The census lists 31 serial number 1 notes.

Georgia • 71 banks of issue • 476 notes reported • Includes the First National Bank of Atlanta (104). Many Unc notes are listed. The census lists 12 serial number 1 notes.

Hawaii • 1 bank of issue • 69 notes reported • Hawaii was a territory at the time, but the notes simply say Hawaii. All are from the Bishop National Bank of Honolulu, including one Unc.

Idaho • 24 banks of issue • 139 notes reported • There are 22 banks represented. Seven Unc notes are known. Six serial number 1 notes are recorded.

Illinois • 394 banks of issue • 2,974 notes reported • Mostly circulated, with a run of 17 Unc Old Second National Bank of Aurora notes. The census lists 63 serial number 1 notes.

Indiana • 203 banks of issue • 1,897 notes reported • Mostly circulated but with a few Unc notes scattered here and there. The census lists 28 serial number 1 notes.

Iowa • 219 banks of issue • 2,109 notes reported • Mostly circulated notes with a few Unc notes scattered here and there. The census lists 50 serial number 1 notes.

Kansas • 191 banks of issue • 1,417 notes reported • Mostly circulated notes are reported, except for 41 serial number 1 notes, which are almost all Unc.

Kentucky • 124 banks of issue • 997 notes reported • Mostly circulated with a few Unc notes scattered here and there. The census lists 14 serial number 1 notes.

Louisiana • 28 banks of issue • 291 notes reported • Seven Unc notes are known.

Maine • 51 banks of issue • 354 notes reported • The census lists 26 Unc notes and 13 serial number 1 notes.

Maryland • 73 banks of issue • 615 notes reported • The census lists 50 Unc notes, including 43 from the National Bank of Rising Sun. Six serial number 1 notes are recorded.

Massachusetts • 128 banks of issue • 1,010 notes reported • Mostly circulated, with a few Unc notes interspersed. The census lists 32 serial number 1 notes.

Michigan • 120 banks of issue • 2,237 notes reported • Mostly circulated notes with some Unc notes throughout. The census lists 49 serial number 1 notes.

Minnesota • 219 banks of issue • 2,524 notes reported • Mostly circulated with many Unc notes throughout. The census lists 28 serial number 1 notes.

Mississippi • 30 banks of issue • 272 notes reported • The census lists 13 Unc notes. Seven serial number 1 notes are recorded.

Missouri • 106 banks of issue • 1,296 notes reported • About half are Unc. The census lists 38 serial number 1 notes.

Montana • 37 banks of issue • 388 notes reported • The census lists 39 Unc notes and 31 serial number 1 notes.

Nebraska • 140 banks of issue • 1,911 notes reported • Includes the Albion National Bank of Albion with over 230 Unc notes. The census lists 78 serial number 1 notes.

Nevada • 9 banks of issue • 93 notes reported • The census lists 20 Unc notes, 14 of them from the First National Bank of Winnemucca. The only serial number 1 note is from the Nevada First National Bank of Tonopah (Unc).

New Hampshire • 54 banks of issue • 477 notes reported • Mostly circulated examples. The census lists 15 serial number 1 notes.

New Jersey • 207 banks of issue • 1,869 notes reported • Mostly circulated; however, there is a large section of Unc notes from the Carlstadt National Bank. The census lists 70 serial number 1 notes.

New Mexico • 19 banks of issue • 237 notes reported • Includes the First National Bank of Albuquerque, Albuquerque National Bank, and the First National Bank of Santa Fe. Three serial number 1 notes are from Albuquerque National Bank (two, both AU) and the First National Bank of Roswell (VG).

New York • 472 banks of issue • 4,686 notes reported • Mostly circulated, except for those from the Chase National Bank of New York. The census lists 175 serial number 1 notes.

North Carolina • 60 banks of issue • 648 notes reported • Includes the First National Bank & Trust Company of Asheville, Commercial National Bank of Charlotte, First National Bank of Durham, and the Charlotte National Bank, the last of which has many Unc notes; otherwise mainly circulated examples are recorded. The census lists 13 serial number 1 notes.

North Dakota • 105 banks of issue • 570 notes reported • Most are circulated. The census lists 21 serial number 1 notes.

Ohio • 302 banks of issue • 3,956 notes reported • Mostly circulated examples, except for those from the First National

Bank of Kent and the First National Bank of Toledo. The census lists 64 serial number 1 notes.

Oklahoma • 193 banks of issue • 1,123 notes reported • Mostly circulated but with some Unc notes scattered here and there. The census lists 33 serial number 1 notes.

Oregon • 74 banks of issue • 524 notes reported • The majority are circulated examples. The census lists 37 serial number 1 notes.

Pennsylvania • 803 banks of issue • 7102 notes reported • Mostly circulated, except for many from the Denver National Bank and the Gap National Bank and Trust Company. The census lists 149 serial number 1 notes; all but five of these are Unc.

Rhode Island • 10 banks of issue • 210 notes reported • Most are circulated. Six serial number 1 notes are recorded.

South Carolina • 36 banks of issue • 197 notes reported • Includes the South Carolina National Bank of Charleston. Most are circulated. The census lists 14 serial number 1 notes, all but one Unc.

South Dakota • 65 banks of issue • 476 notes reported • Most are circulated. The census lists 22 serial number 1 notes, all Unc.

Tennessee • 99 banks of issue • 754 notes reported • Most are circulated. The census lists 24 serial number 1 notes.

Texas • 439 banks of issue • 2,757 notes reported • Clusters of Unc notes are from several different banks. The census lists 187 serial number 1 notes.

Utah • 20 banks of issue • 321 notes reported • The census lists 24 Unc notes and 13 serial number 1 notes.

Vermont • 43 banks of issue • 278 notes reported • Most are circulated. The census lists 19 serial number 1 notes, all Unc.

Virginia • 140 banks of issue • 779 notes reported • Mostly circulated notes are known, except for many from the National Bank of Norton. The census lists 13 serial number 1 notes.

Washington • 81 banks of issue • 680 notes reported • Most are circulated. The census lists 20 serial number 1 notes.

West Virginia • 123 banks of issue • 738 notes reported • Most are circulated. The census lists 22 serial number 1 notes.

Wisconsin • 123 banks of issue • 2,620 notes reported • Most are circulated. The census lists 38 serial number 1 notes.

Wyoming • 23 banks of issue • 370 notes reported • There are 22 banks represented. The census lists 11 Unc notes.

W-1720 • F-1801-1

VG-8	F-12	VF-20	EF-40	AU-50	Unc-60	Unc-63	Unc-65
$40	$45	$60	$85	$125	$135	$175	$270

Series of 1929, Type 2, Brown Seal
Jones-Woods (1929–1933)

Type 2 bills were numbered continuously on a sheet, with the first sheet from a given bank starting with A000001 and ending with A000006, yielding a single number 1 note, in contrast to six on the first Series of 1929 Type 1 sheet. Signatures

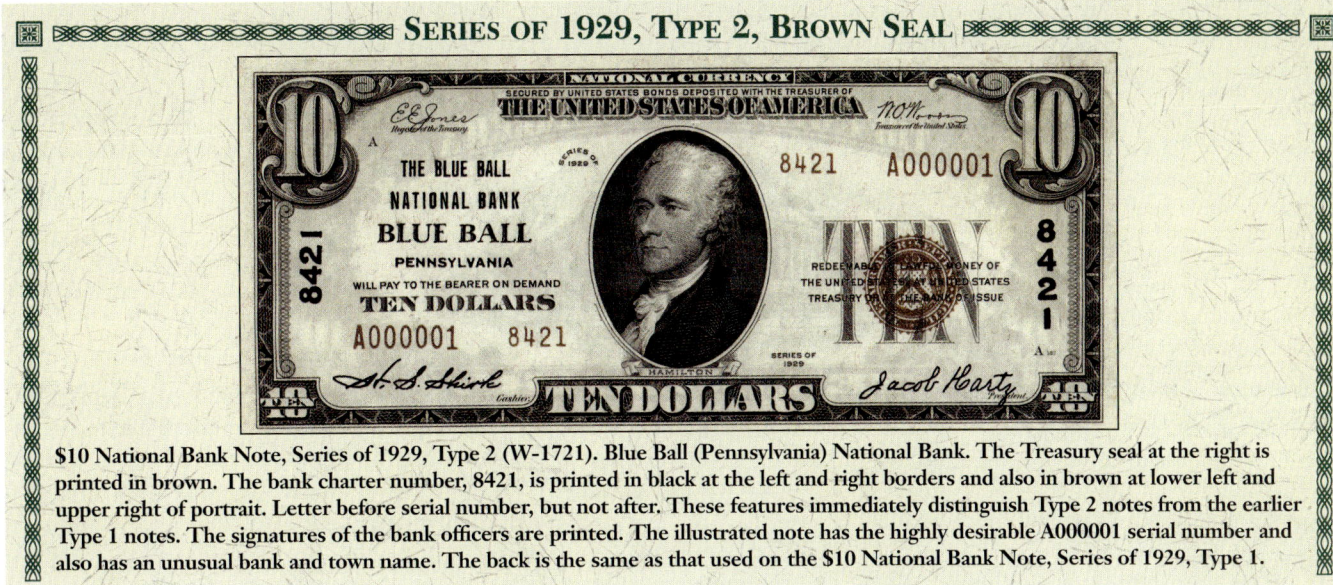

SERIES OF 1929, TYPE 2, BROWN SEAL

$10 National Bank Note, Series of 1929, Type 2 (W-1721). Blue Ball (Pennsylvania) National Bank. The Treasury seal at the right is printed in brown. The bank charter number, 8421, is printed in black at the left and right borders and also in brown at lower left and upper right of portrait. Letter before serial number, but not after. These features immediately distinguish Type 2 notes from the earlier Type 1 notes. The signatures of the bank officers are printed. The illustrated note has the highly desirable A000001 serial number and also has an unusual bank and town name. The back is the same as that used on the $10 National Bank Note, Series of 1929, Type 1.

of the bank cashier and president were printed directly on each note at the BEP. The charter number appears four times on the face, twice in black and twice in brown.

The average grade of a circulated note is apt to be Very Fine or finer, although many lower grades have been recorded. Uncirculated notes are plentiful. The value chart shows generic prices for a typical note from a state from which notes range from available to just slightly scarce.

Banks of Issue and Rarity of Notes

Based upon census information from Don C. Kelly and James M. Kelly (*National Bank Note Census*, Version 4.0) and with some information from the other sources, this listing gives each location, the number of banks issuing this series of notes within each, and a commentary.[35]

The Kelly survey records 19,270, a large quantity, but just a third of the Type 1 notes for this denomination. Just 338 serial number 1 notes are recorded, mostly because sheets of this series have just one such note, instead of six (with different plate letters) found on the Series of 1929 Type 1 bills. These are specifically listed below.

Alabama • 67 banks of issue • 358 notes reported • Mostly circulated examples reported, but there is a run of Unc notes from the First National Bank of Alexander City. Five serial number 1 notes are recorded.

Alaska • 3 banks of issue • No notes reported • Alaska was a territory at the time, but the notes simply say Alaska.

Arizona • 5 banks of issue • 15 notes reported • All are circulated.

Arkansas • 38 banks of issue • 156 notes reported • The census lists 25 Unc notes. Five serial number 1 notes are recorded.

California • 105 banks of issue • 806 notes reported • Many are Unc. The census lists 15 serial number 1 notes.

Colorado • 55 banks of issue • 253 notes reported • Includes the Colorado National Bank of Denver, and the First National Bank of Paonia; the latter has a large selection of Unc notes. Four serial number 1 notes are from the First

National Bank of Cedaredge (AU), First National Bank in Eads (AU), First National Bank of Paonia (Unc) and the Western National Bank of Pueblo (Unc).

Connecticut • 47 banks of issue • 306 notes reported • Most are circulated. Five serial number 1 notes are recorded.

Delaware • 13 banks of issue • 127 notes reported • There are 12 banks represented. About half of the notes are Unc. Two serial number 1 notes are from the First National Bank of Dagsboro (AU) and the Central National Bank of Wilmington (EF).

District of Columbia • 6 banks of issue • 69 notes reported • Nine Unc notes are listed. Five banks are represented, including the Hamilton National Bank of Washington.

Florida • 41 banks of issue • 242 notes reported • Mostly circulated notes are reported, but several banks have many Unc notes. Seven serial number 1 notes are recorded.

Georgia • 54 banks of issue • 215 notes reported • Many Unc notes are listed. Four serial number 1 notes are reported.

Hawaii • 2 banks of issue • 32 notes reported • Hawaii was a territory at the time, but the notes simply say Hawaii. Both banks are represented, but more are from the Bishop National Bank of Hawaii at Honolulu. Two Unc notes are from Bishop National Bank.

Idaho • 17 banks of issue • 49 notes reported • There are 14 banks represented. Seven Unc notes are listed. The only serial number 1 note is from the First National Bank of Bonners Ferry (Unc).

Illinois • 223 banks of issue • 638 notes reported • Many Unc notes from the Lawndale National Bank of Chicago, otherwise most are circulated. The census lists 11 serial number 1 notes.

Indiana • 110 banks of issue • 520 notes reported • Many Unc notes from the National City Bank of Evansville, otherwise mostly circulated notes are listed. Four serial number 1 notes are from Citizens National Bank of Linton (Unc), National Bank of Logansport (AU), Seymour National Bank (Unc), and the Merchants National Bank of South Bend (VF–EF).

Iowa • 84 banks of issue • 440 notes reported • Many Unc notes are from the Live Stock National Bank of Sioux City, otherwise mostly circulated. Four serial number 1 notes are recorded.

Kansas • 142 banks of issue • 346 notes reported • Many Unc notes are from the Chandler National Bank of Lyons, otherwise most are circulated. The census lists 14 serial number 1 notes.

Kentucky • 92 banks of issue • 393 notes reported • Many Unc notes are from the First National Bank & Trust Company of Lexington. Four serial number 1 notes are listed.

Louisiana • 27 banks of issue • 193 notes reported • Mostly circulated notes are listed. Three serial number 1 notes are known, all Unc, from the First National Bank of Jefferson in Gretna, Ouachita National Bank in Monroe, and the First National Bank Lake Providence in Providence.

Maine • 38 banks of issue • 181 notes reported • All are circulated. Two serial number 1 notes are from the First National Granite Bank of Augusta (Unc) and the First National Bank of Bar Harbor (Unc).

Maryland • 57 banks of issue • 251 notes reported • Mostly circulated examples are known, except for from the Second National Bank of Cumberland (29 Unc).

Massachusetts • 105 banks of issue • 1,260 notes reported • Over 1,000 Unc notes from the First National Bank of Easthampton are listed. Three serial number 1 notes are from Manufacturers National Bank of Lynn (Unc), Old Colony National Bank of Plymouth (Unc), First National Bank of Yarmouthport, Yarmouth Port (VF).

Michigan • 80 banks of issue • 302 notes reported • The census lists 16 Unc notes. The only serial number 1 note is from the Escanaba National Bank (VG–F).

Minnesota • 152 banks of issue • 584 notes reported • Unc notes are listed from the various banks. Four serial number 1 notes are from City National Bank of Duluth (Unc), Peoples National Bank of Long Prairie (Unc), Klein National Bank of Madison (EF–AU), and Citizens National Bank of Park Rapids (EF).

Mississippi • 18 banks of issue • 153 notes reported • Many Unc notes are listed, especially from the National Bank of Commerce of Columbus and the First-Columbus National Bank. The only serial number 1 note is from the First National Bank of Laurel (not graded).

Missouri • 62 banks of issue • 232 notes reported • Many Unc notes are from the Lafayette National Bank & Trust Company of Luxemburg. Four serial number 1 notes are recorded.

Montana • 26 banks of issue • 103 notes reported • Most are circulated. Three serial number 1 notes are from the First National Bank of Glasgow, First National Bank of Missoula, and the First National Bank of Whitefish, all Unc.

Nebraska • 95 banks of issue • 504 notes reported • Many Unc notes are from the First National Bank of Cambridge. The census lists 10 serial number 1 notes.

Nevada • 7 banks of issue • 77 notes reported • Six banks are represented. Mostly Unc notes are listed. Three serial

number 1 notes are from the First National Bank of Ely (Unc), Ely National Bank (not graded), and the McGill National Bank (Unc).

New Hampshire • 53 banks of issue • 210 notes reported • Most are circulated, except for the First National Bank of Peterborough (43 Unc). Six serial number 1 notes are recorded.

New Jersey • 180 banks of issue • 847 notes reported • Many Unc notes are known, especially from the Perth Amboy National Bank and the First National Bank & Trust Company of Ramsey. The census lists 10 serial number 1 notes.

New Mexico • 16 banks of issue • 65 notes reported • There are 13 banks represented. Mostly circulated examples are listed. Two serial number 1 notes are from Albuquerque National Trust & Savings Bank (F) and the American National Bank of Silver City (Unc).

New York • 371 banks of issue • 1,294 notes reported • Many Unc notes are interspersed throughout. The census lists 42 serial number 1 notes.

North Carolina • 37 banks of issue • 132 notes reported • Most are circulated.

North Dakota • 51 banks of issue • 74 notes reported • The census lists 10 Unc notes. The only serial number 1 note is from the Dakota National Bank & Trust Company of Bismarck (not graded).

Ohio • 225 banks of issue • 1,030 notes reported • Most are circulated. The census lists 18 serial number 1 notes.

Oklahoma • 136 banks of issue • 335 notes reported • Most are circulated. Six serial number 1 notes are recorded.

Oregon • 43 banks of issue • 128 notes reported • Most are circulated. Six serial number 1 notes are recorded.

Pennsylvania • 686 banks of issue • 2,962 notes reported • Most are circulated, except those from the National Bank of Topton. The census lists 57 serial number 1 notes.

Rhode Island • 10 banks of issue • 149 notes reported • There are 10 banks, including the Rhode Island Hospital National Bank of Providence (88). The census lists 11 Unc notes.

South Carolina • 15 banks of issue • 324 notes reported • There are 12 banks represented, including many Unc examples from the Commercial National Bank of Spartanburg and the National Bank of South Carolina of Sumter.

South Dakota • 40 banks of issue • 127 notes reported • Rapid City National Bank has 59 Unc notes listed.

Tennessee • 70 banks of issue • 356 notes reported • Many Unc notes are known, especially from the Hamilton National Bank of Chattanooga and the Union Planters National Bank & Trust Company of Memphis. Three serial number 1 notes are from Farmers National Bank of Fayetteville (EF), Union Planters National Bank & Trust Company (Unc), and the First National Bank of Savannah (Unc).

Texas • 313 banks of issue • 975 notes reported • Many Unc notes known from various banks. The census lists 37 serial number 1 notes.

Utah • 12 banks of issue • 66 notes reported • Most are circulated. The only serial number 1 note is from the First National Bank of Price (AU).

Vermont • 42 banks of issue • 79 notes reported • Most are circulated. Two serial number 1 notes are from Bradford National Bank (not graded) and the First National Bank of North Bennington (Unc).

Virginia • 116 banks of issue • 331 notes reported • Known notes are mostly circulated, but with several banks offering numerous Unc examples. Eight serial number 1 notes are recorded.

Washington • 50 banks of issue • 230 notes reported • Most are circulated, except for First National Bank of Seattle, with 28 Unc specimens. Five serial number 1 notes are recorded.

West Virginia • 79 banks of issue • 277 notes reported • The census lists 94 Unc notes, including Central National Bank of Buckhannon, with 49. Seven serial number 1 notes are recorded.

Wisconsin • 82 banks of issue • 379 notes reported • The census lists 45 Unc notes, with the Farmers-Merchants National Bank in Princeton having 21. Eight serial number 1 notes are recorded.

Wyoming • 22 banks of issue • 86 notes reported • Five Unc notes are listed. There are 11 banks represented.

W-1721 • F-1801-2

VG-8	F-12	VF-20	EF-40	AU-50	Unc-60	Unc-63	Unc-65
$40	$45	$60	$85	$125	$135	$175	$270

FEDERAL RESERVE BANK NOTES

Series of 1929, Brown Seal
Jones-Woods (1929–1933)

Similar to other issues in this short-lived series, the Federal Reserve Bank Notes of the Series of 1929 were made in a hurry, in March 1933, when it was thought that there would be a rush on banks following President Franklin D. Roosevelt's "bank holiday." Partially printed sheets of $10 National Bank Notes in the Series of 1929 were overprinted with the name and letter of each Federal Reserve Bank. The printed identification of national bank officers, cashier and president, was blanked out with a black rectangle, and titles inserted for Federal Reserve officers, these including the governor or, sometimes, deputy governor, assistant deputy governor, or cashier.

SERIES OF 1929, BROWN SEAL

$10 Federal Reserve Bank Note, Series of 1929 (W-1730-A). Federal Reserve Bank of Boston.

Back of the $10 Federal Reserve Bank Note, Series of 1929 (W-1730-A). The type was used on all small-size $10 series through the 1950s.

Detail of a W-1734-E note with "President" only partially blocked out.

Today among regular notes, those of Dallas are considered to be the most elusive, probably a combination of the low printage (504,000) and, apparently, many held back from release. The Minneapolis notes, of which 58,000 were printed, are quite plentiful by comparison. Star notes were produced for each bank and range from rare to very rare.

Prices for a typical star note for this series, unless listed otherwise, are as follows:

VG-8	F-12	VF-20	EF-40	AU-50	Unc-60	Unc-63	Unc-65
$125	$180	$275	$400	$600	$1,400	$2,200	$3,600

W-1730-A • F-1860A • Boston • 1,680,000

VG-8	F-12	VF-20	EF-40	AU-50	Unc-60	Unc-63	Unc-65
$35	$45	$52	$65	$80	$110	$250	$400

W-1730-A★ • F-1860A★

W-1731-B • F-1860B • New York • 5,556,000

VG-8	F-12	VF-20	EF-40	AU-50	Unc-60	Unc-63	Unc-65
$35	$45	$52	$65	$80	$110	$225	$350

W-1731-B★ • F-1860B★

W-1732-C • F-1860C • Philadelphia • 1,416,000

VG-8	F-12	VF-20	EF-40	AU-50	Unc-60	Unc-63	Unc-65
$35	$45	$52	$65	$80	$110	$250	$400

W-1732-C★ • F-1860C★

W-1733-D • F-1860D • Cleveland • 2,412,000

VG-8	F-12	VF-20	EF-40	AU-50	Unc-60	Unc-63	Unc-65
$35	$45	$52	$65	$80	$110	$250	$400

W-1733-D★ • F-1860D★

W-1734-E • F-1860E • Richmond • 1,356,000

VG-8	F-12	VF-20	EF-40	AU-50	Unc-60	Unc-63	Unc-65
$35	$45	$70	$100	$135	$275	$450	$800

W-1734-E★ • F-1860E★

W-1735-F • F-1860F • Atlanta • 1,056,000

VG-8	F-12	VF-20	EF-40	AU-50	Unc-60	Unc-63	Unc-65
$35	$45	$60	$90	$120	$240	$375	$600

W-1735-F★ • F-1860F★

W-1736-G • F-1860G • Chicago • 3,156,000

VG-8	F-12	VF-20	EF-40	AU-50	Unc-60	Unc-63	Unc-65
$35	$45	$52	$65	$80	$110	$225	$350

W-1736-G★ • F-1860G★

W-1737-H • F-1860H • St. Louis • 1,584,000

VG-8	F-12	VF-20	EF-40	AU-50	Unc-60	Unc-63	Unc-65
$35	$45	$52	$65	$80	$110	$225	$350

W-1737-H★ • F-1860H★

W-1738-I • F-1860I • Minneapolis • 58,000

VG-8	F-12	VF-20	EF-40	AU-50	Unc-60	Unc-63	Unc-65
$35	$50	$70	$100	$135	$275	$375	$750

W-1738-I★ • F-1860I★

W-1739-J • F-1860J • Kansas City • 1,284,000

VG-8	F-12	VF-20	EF-40	AU-50	Unc-60	Unc-63	Unc-65
$35	$45	$52	$65	$80	$110	$250	$400

W-1739-J★ • F-1860J★

W-1740-K • F-1860K • Dallas • 504,000

VG-8	F-12	VF-20	EF-40	AU-50	Unc-60	Unc-63
$150	$250	$400	$800	$1,250	$2,000	$3,000

W-1740-K★ • F-1860K★

W-1741-L • F-1860L • San Francisco • 1,080,000

VG-8	F-12	VF-20	EF-40	AU-50	Unc-60	Unc-63
$70	$100	$150	$275	$600	$1,000	$1,500

W-1741-L★ • F-1860L★

SILVER CERTIFICATES

Silver Certificates begin with the Series of 1933. The text of their obligation mentions that they are payable "in silver coin"—a rarity. Many of these were destroyed, to be replaced with the differently worded Series of 1934 payable "in silver dollars." Later Series of 1953 Silver Certificates were continued through the Series 1953-B and are simply "in silver payable." Variations are delineated below.

Series of 1933, Blue Seal
Julian-Woodin (1933)

The obligation reads TEN DOLLARS PAYABLE IN SILVER COIN on this and the Series of 1933-A, but not on later series. There is a blue Treasury seal at the left, overprinted on four lines of text: "This certificate is issued pursuant to section 56 of the act of May 12, 1933, and is Legal Tender at face value for all debts public and private." This imprint was also used on the Series of 1933-A. The serial numbers are printed in blue. In the right field is TEN in tall letters; SERIES OF 1933 is at the upper left of the portrait of Hamilton, and again at the lower right beneath WASHINGTON.

In *The Numismatist* in September 1967 (see the bibliography), William A. Philpott Jr. singled out seven small-size star notes, including this one, that he considered to be "excessively rare and hard to come by."

W-1745 • F-1700 • 216,000

VG-8	F-12	VF-20	EF-40	AU-50	Unc-60	Unc-63	Unc-65
$3,500	$5,000	$6,000	$7,000	$8,500	$10,000	$20,000	$27,500

W-1745★ • F-1700★ • Unique

Series of 1933-A, Blue Seal
Julian-Morgenthau (1934–1945)

This series continued the obligation TEN DOLLARS PAYABLE IN SILVER COIN. Regarding the 1933-A Blue Seal, although 336,000 were printed, with serial numbers ranging from A00216001A to A00552000A, none have ever been seen in numismatic circles. Apparently they were destroyed, or perhaps they are still in storage.

W-1748 • F-1700a • 336,000 • None issued

Series of 1934, Blue Seal
Julian-Morgenthau (1934–1945)

The obligation reads TEN DOLLARS IN SILVER PAYABLE on this and later notes, without mention of coins. At the right is the Treasury seal printed in blue. The counter, 10, to the left of center is in blue, with TEN in large letters to the right of center. WASHINGTON, D.C., is printed below the Treasury seal. SERIES OF 1934 is at the upper left of the portrait. At the lower right, SERIES OF 1934 is below WASHINGTON.

Mules: Most backs have the plate number in small or "micro" letters, but mules have the larger or "macro"-size serials as used on Series 1934-A (the macro plates are numbered 585 and higher). These are worth a premium. Star note mules are very rare and worth considerably more. Related mules are found among Federal Reserve Notes using the same backs.

SERIES OF 1933, BLUE SEAL

$10 Silver Certificate, Series of 1933 (W-1745). Blue Treasury seal at the left. Large TEN in open field at right. This and the Series of 1933-A are the only issues with "Payable in Silver Coin."

Back of the $10 Silver Certificate, Series of 1933 (W-1745). The type was used on all small-size $10 series through the 1950s.

SERIES OF 1934, BLUE SEAL

$10 Silver Certificate, Series of 1934 (W-1750). Blue Treasury seal at right, with large TEN printed over it. The back is the same as used on other $10 notes through the 1950s.

Example of the normal micro plate number used on the back of a Series of 1934 note.

Example of the later macro plate number used on the back of regular and North Africa Series of 1934 notes.

W-1750 • F-1701 • 88,692,864

VG-8	F-12	VF-20	EF-40	AU-50	Unc-60	Unc-63	Unc-65
$35	$40	$45	$55	$75	$110	$190	$325

W-1750★ • F-1701★

VG-8	F-12	VF-20	EF-40	AU-50	Unc-60	Unc-63	Unc-65
$80	$140	$200	$450	$700	$950	$1,400	$2,000

W-1750 Mule • F-1701

VG-8	F-12	VF-20	EF-40	AU-50	Unc-60	Unc-63	Unc-65
$35	$40	$45	$55	$75	$110	$190	$325

W-1750 Mule★ • F-1701★

VG-8	F-12	VF-20	EF-40	AU-50	Unc-60	Unc-63	Unc-65
$100	$160	$250	$500	$800	$1,100	$1,800	$2,500

Series of 1934, Yellow Seal, for North Africa
Julian-Morgenthau (1934–1945)

Similar to certain other denominations, these "emergency notes," as some call them, were distinguished by having a yellow Treasury seal. Other overprint features remained in blue, similar to other Silver Certificates of the era. These special notes were issued for distribution to Allied forces in the Mediterranean and North African campaigns, with the thought that, if the notes fell into enemy hands, they could be repudiated, and would have no exchange value on the world market. At the time, the American dollar was useful just about everywhere, including in Nazi- and Japanese-held territories.

All have the macro back plate numbers 585 and higher. This note is one of the most famous small-size rarities. Yellow seal notes were also made in the Series of 1934-A, and these are readily available.

In *The Numismatist* in September 1967 (see the bibliography), William A. Philpott Jr. singled out seven small-size star notes, including this one, that he considered to be "excessively rare and hard to come by." He must have seen the single example known today.

W-1752 • F-2308

VG-8	F-12	VF-20	EF-40	AU-50	Unc-60	Unc-63	Unc-65
$2,500	$4,000	$5,250	$9,000	$11,000	$15,000	$27,000	$40,000

W-1752★ • F-2308★ • 1 reported

Series of 1934-A, Blue Seal
Julian-Morgenthau (1934–1945)

Mules: Most backs have the plate number in macro letters, but mules have the smaller, micro-size numbers as used on Series 1934 (the micro plates have numbers lower than 939).

W-1753 • F-1702 • 42,346,428

VG-8	F-12	VF-20	EF-40	AU-50	Unc-60	Unc-63	Unc-65
$35	$40	$45	$60	$85	$140	$275	$400

W-1753★ • F-1702★ • 310,000 (est.)

VG-8	F-12	VF-20	EF-40	AU-50	Unc-60	Unc-63	Unc-65
$125	$200	$300	$500	$850	$1,750	$2,300	$2,900

W-1753 Mule • F-unlisted

VG-8	F-12	VF-20	EF-40	AU-50	Unc-60	Unc-63
$60	$95	$140	$250	$375	$550	$700

W-1753 Mule★ • F-unlisted • Unknown

SERIES OF 1934, YELLOW SEAL, FOR NORTH AFRICA

$10 Silver Certificate, Series of 1934 (W-1752), with distinctive yellow Treasury seal for the North Africa campaign of World War II. The back is the same as used on other $10 notes through the 1950s. (ANA Edward C. Rochette Money Museum)

SERIES OF 1934-A, BLUE SEAL

Signatures and series imprints of a $10 Silver Certificate, Series of 1934-A (W-1753). The back is the standard type of the era.

Series of 1934-A, Yellow Seal, for North Africa
Julian-Morgenthau (1934–1945)

This series was issued for use by Allied forces in the Mediterranean Sea and in the North African campaign in World War II. See the section on Series of 1934 Yellow Seal notes.

W-1754 • F-2309 • 21,860,000

VG-8	F-12	VF-20	EF-40	AU-50	Unc-60	Unc-63	Unc-65
$50	$65	$80	$115	$150	$250	$330	$900

W-1754★ • F-2309★

VG-8	F-12	VF-20	EF-40	AU-50	Unc-60	Unc-63
$125	$200	$340	$525	$900	$2,000	$3,000

Series of 1934-B, Blue Seal
Julian-Vinson (1945–1946)

This series continued the obligation TEN DOLLARS IN SILVER PAYABLE. Face plate number 211 is printed on all. In *The Numismatist* in September 1967 (see the bibliography), William A. Philpott Jr. singled out seven small-size star notes, including this one, that he considered to be "excessively rare and hard to come by."

W-1755 • F-1703 • 337,740

VF-20	EF-40	AU-50	Unc-60	Unc-63
$225	$500	$850	$1,500	$2,500

W-1755★ • F-1703★ • 9,000 (est.)

VG-8	F-12	VF-20	EF-40	AU-50	Unc-60	Unc-63
$1,200	$1,750	$2,500	$4,000	$6,000	$10,000	$16,000

Series of 1934-C, Blue Seal
Julian-Snyder (1946–1949)

This series continued previous the design and the obligation TEN DOLLARS IN SILVER PAYABLE.

W-1756 • F-1704 • 20,032,632

VG-8	F-12	VF-20	EF-40	AU-50	Unc-60	Unc-63	Unc-65
$35	$40	$45	$55	$75	$110	$150	$250

W-1756★ • F-1704★ • 350,000 (est.)

VG-8	F-12	VF-20	EF-40	AU-50	Unc-60	Unc-63	Unc-65
$65	$100	$145	$225	$400	$600	$800	$1,200

Series of 1934-D, Blue Seal, Wide Back
Clark-Snyder (1949–1953)

This series (illus. on p. 398) continued the obligation TEN DOLLARS IN SILVER PAYABLE. The Wide Back notes have back plate numbers 1389 or lower. The Wide Back has slightly more separation between the edge of the ribbon with TEN inscribed and the nearby border.

W-1757 • F-1705 • 11,801,112

VG-8	F-12	VF-20	EF-40	AU-50	Unc-60	Unc-63	Unc-65
$35	$40	$45	$55	$75	$130	$240	$325

W-1757★ • F-1705★ • 160,000 (est.)

VG-8	F-12	VF-20	EF-40	AU-50	Unc-60	Unc-63	Unc-65
$180	$275	$400	$850	$1,250	$2,100	$3,500	$5,500

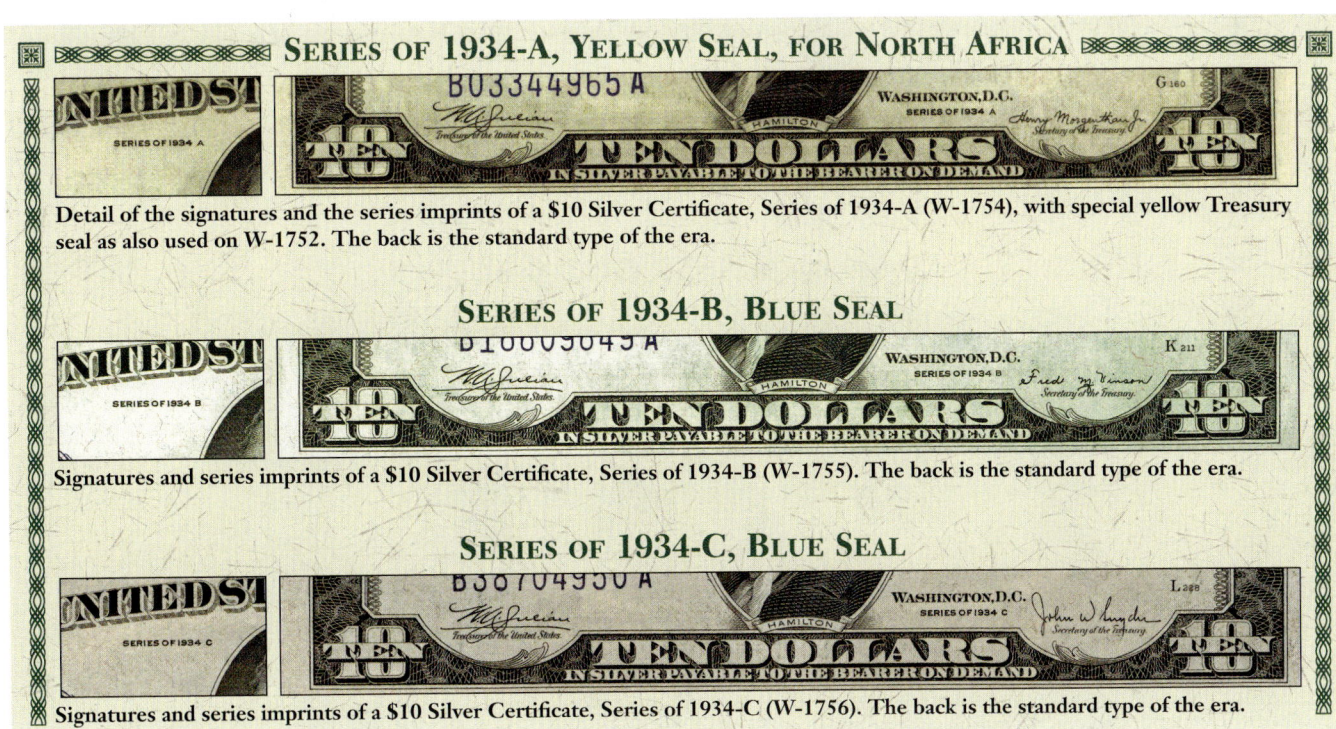

SERIES OF 1934-A, YELLOW SEAL, FOR NORTH AFRICA

Detail of the signatures and the series imprints of a $10 Silver Certificate, Series of 1934-A (W-1754), with special yellow Treasury seal as also used on W-1752. The back is the standard type of the era.

SERIES OF 1934-B, BLUE SEAL

Signatures and series imprints of a $10 Silver Certificate, Series of 1934-B (W-1755). The back is the standard type of the era.

SERIES OF 1934-C, BLUE SEAL

Signatures and series imprints of a $10 Silver Certificate, Series of 1934-C (W-1756). The back is the standard type of the era.

Series of 1934-D, Blue Seal, Narrow Back
Clark-Snyder (1949–1953)

This continued the obligation TEN DOLLARS IN SILVER PAYABLE. The Narrow Back notes have back plate numbers 1390 to 1456. The Narrow Back has a slightly smaller separation between the edge of the ribbon with TEN inscribed and the nearby border.

W-1758 • F-1705

VG-8	F-12	VF-20	EF-40	AU-50	Unc-60	Unc-63	Unc-65
$35	$60	$90	$250	$475	$700	$900	$1,250

W-1758★ • F-1705★

VG-8	F-12	VF-20	EF-40	AU-50	Unc-60	Unc-63	Unc-65
$1,750	$2,750	$4,000	$4,800	$6,000	$7,500	$9,500	$12,500

Series of 1953, Blue Seal
Priest-Humphrey (1953–1957)

This series continued the obligation TEN DOLLARS IN SILVER PAYABLE. The face layout is modified: to the right is the Treasury seal printed in blue. The counter, 10, to the left of center is now gray. The TEN right of center, overprinted with a Treasury seal, is smaller. WASHINGTON,

D.C., is now printed above the Treasury seal. The back is the same type on all $10 note series through the 1950s.

W-1759 • F-1706 • 10,440,000

VG-8	F-12	VF-20	EF-40	AU-50	Unc-60	Unc-63	Unc-65
$40	$50	$60	$75	$90	$145	$250	$430

W-1759★ • F-1706★ • 576,000

VG-8	F-12	VF-20	EF-40	AU-50	Unc-60	Unc-63	Unc-65
$60	$80	$110	$300	$400	$525	$650	$1,000

Series of 1953-A, Blue Seal
Priest-Anderson (1957–1961)

This continued the obligation TEN DOLLARS IN SILVER PAYABLE. At the right is the Treasury seal printed in blue. The counter, 10, to the left of center is gray; TEN is to the right of center, overprinted with a Treasury seal. WASHINGTON, D.C., is above the Treasury seal. The back is the same type used on all $10 note series through the 1950s.

W-1760 • F-1707 • 1,080,000

VG-8	F-12	VF-20	EF-40	AU-50	Unc-60	Unc-63	Unc-65
$50	$65	$80	$125	$170	$270	$395	$600

SERIES OF 1934-D, BLUE SEAL

$10 Silver Certificate, Series of 1934-D (W-1757). The back is the same as used on other $10 notes through the 1950s but is of the Wide Back variety.

Detail of the Wide Back on W-1757.

Detail of the Narrow Back on W-1758.

SERIES OF 1953, BLUE SEAL

$10 Silver Certificate, Series of 1953 (W-1759★). Star note. At the left, 10 is higher and lighter than on the preceding. The overprint TEN on the Treasury seal is smaller. The back is the same as used on other $10 notes through the 1950s.

SERIES OF 1953-A, BLUE SEAL

Signatures and series imprint of a $10 Silver Certificate, Series of 1953-A (W-1760). The back is the standard type of the era.

SERIES OF 1953-B, BLUE SEAL

Signatures and series imprint of a $10 Silver Certificate, Series of 1953-B (W-1761). The back is the standard type of the era.

W-1760★ • F-1707★ • 144,000

VG-8	F-12	VF-20	EF-40	AU-50	Unc-60	Unc-63	Unc-65
$80	$130	$175	$400	$800	$1,500	$2,000	$2,500

Series of 1953-B, Blue Seal
Smith-Dillon (1961–1962)

This series continued the design of the previous and the obligation TEN DOLLARS IN SILVER PAYABLE. No star notes were printed for this series. By the early 1960s the price of silver was rising on the world markets. Silver Certificates were discontinued, and Federal Reserve Notes became the class of notes in general use.

W-1761 • F-1708 • 720,000

VG-8	F-12	VF-20	EF-40	AU-50	Unc-60	Unc-63	Unc-65
$40	$50	$60	$75	$90	$145	$250	$400

FEDERAL RESERVE NOTES

Small-size $10 Federal Reserve Notes began with the Series of 1928, which were first distributed in 1929. Since that time, such bills have been issued by the 12 different Federal Reserve Banks, although not all banks issued notes for all series. Each bears identification by bank letter and number, such as 1-A for Boston. Each has a green Treasury seal. Some variations in Treasury seal tint (light yellow-green or green) exist. On some notes the difference in hues is not immediately obvious, except to those familiar with them. Certain of the Series of 1934-A Federal Reserve Notes were made with brown seals and HAWAII overprints for use in that territory from 1942 to 1944.

Starting with Series 1999 the face and back designs were modified, with Hamilton given a larger and different portrait. Other improvements to the design and paper were largely intended to deter counterfeiting. The Treasury Building, earlier shown in a corner view, was redone, with a front-facing view.

Certain early varieties are very scarce in higher grades, but the demand for them is limited. Although the $10 denomination is not as widely collected as are $1, $2, and $5 bills, many collectors seek the different bank and signature combinations as they are issued. Star or replacement notes form a specialty and are highly prized.

Series of 1928, Green Seal
Tate-Mellon (1928–1929)

The obligation is in four lines in the upper-left field: "Redeemable in gold on demand at the United States Treasury, or in gold or lawful money at any Federal Reserve Bank." On the Series of 1928 notes (illus. on p. 400) the seal in the left field features the number of the issuing Federal Reserve Bank (1 to 12). The series imprint appears twice—at the upper left of Hamilton's portrait and above WASHINGTON at the lower right.

W-1800-A • F-2000A • Boston • 9,804,552

VG-8	F-12	VF-20	EF-40	AU-50	Unc-60	Unc-63	Unc-65
$30	$40	$50	$75	$95	$150	$250	$400

W-1800-A★ • F-2000A★

VG-8	F-12	VF-20	EF-40	AU-50	Unc-60	Unc-63
$200	$350	$500	$800	$1,200	$1,750	$2,800

W-1800-B • F-2000B • New York • 11,295,796

VG-8	F-12	VF-20	EF-40	AU-50	Unc-60	Unc-63	Unc-65
$30	$40	$50	$70	$90	$135	$225	$325

W-1800-B★ • F-2000B★

VG-8	F-12	VF-20	EF-40	AU-50	Unc-60	Unc-63	Unc-65
$100	$175	$300	$450	$700	$850	$1,100	$1,750

W-1800-C • F-2000C • Philadelphia • 8,114,412

VG-8	F-12	VF-20	EF-40	AU-50	Unc-60	Unc-63	Unc-65
$30	$40	$50	$75	$95	$150	$250	$400

W-1800-C★ • F-2000C★

VG-8	F-12	VF-20	EF-40	AU-50	Unc-60	Unc-63	Unc-65
$100	$175	$300	$525	$800	$1,100	$1,500	$2,250

W-1800-D • F-2000D • Cleveland • 7,570,812

VG-8	F-12	VF-20	EF-40	AU-50	Unc-60	Unc-63	Unc-65
$30	$40	$50	$70	$90	$210	$350	$500

W-1800-D★ • F-2000D★

VG-8	F-12	VF-20	EF-40	AU-50	Unc-60	Unc-63	Unc-65
$100	$175	$300	$475	$750	$900	$1,250	$2,000

W-1800-E • F-2000E • Richmond • 4,534,800

VG-8	F-12	VF-20	EF-40	AU-50	Unc-60	Unc-63	Unc-65
$35	$50	$70	$125	$200	$350	$650	$1,000

W-1800-E★ • F-2000E★

VG-8	F-12	VF-20	EF-40	AU-50	Unc-60	Unc-63
$400	$750	$1,200	$1,750	$2,250	$3,500	$5,000

W-1800-F • F-2000F • Atlanta • 6,807,720

VG-8	F-12	VF-20	EF-40	AU-50	Unc-60	Unc-63	Unc-65
$30	$45	$65	$100	$175	$210	$350	$500

W-1800-F★ • F-2000F★

VG-8	F-12	VF-20	EF-40	AU-50	Unc-60	Unc-63
$175	$300	$500	$750	$1,400	$2,000	$3,500

W-1800-G • F-2000G • Chicago • 8,130,000

VG-8	F-12	VF-20	EF-40	AU-50	Unc-60	Unc-63	Unc-65
$30	$40	$50	$70	$90	$135	$225	$325

W-1800-G★ • F-2000G★

VG-8	F-12	VF-20	EF-40	AU-50	Unc-60	Unc-63	Unc-65
$100	$175	$300	$525	$800	$1,100	$1,500	$2,250

W-1800-H • F-2000H • St. Louis • 4,124,100

VG-8	F-12	VF-20	EF-40	AU-50	Unc-60	Unc-63	Unc-65
$30	$45	$65	$100	$175	$210	$300	$450

W-1800-H★ • F-2000H★

VG-8	F-12	VF-20	EF-40	AU-50	Unc-60	Unc-63	Unc-65
$100	$170	$250	$525	$800	$1,100	$1,500	$2,250

W-1800-I • F-2000I • Minneapolis • 3,874,440

VG-8	F-12	VF-20	EF-40	AU-50	Unc-60	Unc-63	Unc-65
$35	$50	$75	$150	$250	$400	$600	$900

W-1800-I★ • F-2000I★

VG-8	F-12	VF-20	EF-40	AU-50	Unc-60	Unc-63
$200	$350	$500	$800	$1,400	$2,000	$3,000

W-1800-J • F-2000J • Kansas City • 3,620,400

VG-8	F-12	VF-20	EF-40	AU-50	Unc-60	Unc-63	Unc-65
$30	$45	$60	$75	$100	$150	$250	$400

W-1800-J★ • F-2000J★

VG-8	F-12	VF-20	EF-40	AU-50	Unc-60	Unc-63	Unc-65
$140	$210	$300	$500	$850	$1,200	$1,800	$3,000

SERIES OF 1928, GREEN SEAL

$10 Federal Reserve Note, Series of 1928 (W-1800-H). St. Louis Federal Reserve Bank, as also indicated by bank number 8.

Back of the $10 Federal Reserve Note, Series of 1928 (W-1800-H). The type was used on all small-size $10 series through the 1950s.

REDEEMABLE IN GOLD ON DEMAND AT THE UNITED STATES TREASURY, OR IN GOLD OR LAWFUL MONEY AT ANY FEDERAL RESERVE BANK.

Detail of the redeemable provision on $10 Federal Reserve Notes, Series of 1928. This wording was continued on later series through early 1933.

W-1800-K • F-2000K • Dallas • 4,855,500

VG-8	F-12	VF-20	EF-40	AU-50	Unc-60	Unc-63	Unc-65
$35	$50	$70	$175	$300	$450	$650	$1,000

W-1800-K★ • F-2000K★

VG-8	F-12	VF-20	EF-40	AU-50	Unc-60	Unc-63	Unc-65
$500	$1,000	$1,500	$2,000	$2,500	$3,000	$4,000	$5,800

W-1800-L • F-2000L • San Francisco • 7,086,900

VG-8	F-12	VF-20	EF-40	AU-50	Unc-60	Unc-63	Unc-65
$30	$40	$50	$70	$90	$135	$225	$325

W-1800-L★ • F-2000L★

VG-8	F-12	VF-20	EF-40	AU-50	Unc-60	Unc-63
$500	$800	$1,200	$1,800	$2,400	$3,000	$4,000

Series of 1928-A, Green Seal
Woods-Mellon (1929–1932)

The "redeemable in gold" provision and the Federal Reserve Bank number at the center of the Federal Reserve seal are similar to the Series of 1928 notes.

W-1801-A • F-2001A • Boston • 2,893,440

VG-8	F-12	VF-20	EF-40	AU-50	Unc-60	Unc-63	Unc-65
$50	$90	$125	$275	$450	$600	$900	$1,500

W-1801-A★ • F-2001A★

VG-8	F-12	VF-20	EF-40
$1,250	$2,300	$4,000	$6,000

W-1801-B • F-2001B • New York • 18,631,056

VG-8	F-12	VF-20	EF-40	AU-50	Unc-60	Unc-63	Unc-65
$35	$50	$70	$100	$150	$200	$300	$500

W-1801-B★ • F-2001B★

VG-8	F-12	VF-20	EF-40	AU-50	Unc-60	Unc-63	Unc-65
$200	$350	$500	$750	$1,000	$1,400	$2,000	$3,000

W-1801-C • F-2001C • Philadelphia • 2,710,680

VG-8	F-12	VF-20	EF-40	AU-50	Unc-60	Unc-63	Unc-65
$30	$40	$50	$110	$190	$300	$500	$700

W-1801-C★ • F-2001C★

VG-8	F-12	VF-20	EF-40	AU-50	Unc-60	Unc-63	Unc-65
$750	$1,250	$2,000	$2,500	$3,000	$4,000	$5,000	$7,500

W-1801-D • F-2001D • Cleveland • 5,610,000

VG-8	F-12	VF-20	EF-40	AU-50	Unc-60	Unc-63	Unc-65
$30	$40	$50	$95	$150	$210	$300	$450

W-1801-D★ • F-2001D★

VG-8	F-12	VF-20	EF-40	AU-50	Unc-60	Unc-63	Unc-65
$200	$350	$500	$750	$1,000	$1,400	$2,000	$3,000

W-1801-E • F-2001E • Richmond • 552,300

VG-8	F-12	VF-20	EF-40	AU-50	Unc-60	Unc-63	Unc-65
$50	$90	$125	$400	$675	$1,050	$1,500	$2,150

W-1801-E★ • F-2001E★

VG-8	F-12	VF-20	EF-40	AU-50
$400	$750	$1,000	$2,000	$2,750

W-1801-F • F-2001F • Atlanta • 3,033,480

VG-8	F-12	VF-20	EF-40	AU-50	Unc-60	Unc-63	Unc-65
$30	$40	$50	$95	$170	$275	$450	$700

W-1801-F★ • F-2001F★

VG-8	F-12	VF-20	EF-40
$700	$1,000	$1,500	$2,250

W-1801-G • F-2001G • Chicago • 8,715,000

VG-8	F-12	VF-20	EF-40	AU-50	Unc-60	Unc-63	Unc-65
$30	$40	$50	$95	$150	$200	$350	$500

W-1801-G★ • F-2001G★

VG-8	F-12	VF-20	EF-40	AU-50	Unc-60	Unc-63	Unc-65
$175	$275	$400	$700	$1,000	$1,250	$1,600	$2,300

W-1801-H • F-2001H • St. Louis • 531,600

VG-8	F-12	VF-20	EF-40	AU-50	Unc-60	Unc-63	Unc-65
$40	$55	$75	$125	$175	$250	$400	$600

W-1801-H★ • F-2001H★

VG-8	F-12	VF-20	EF-40	AU-50	Unc-60	Unc-63
$190	$325	$500	$700	$900	$1,200	$1,500

W-1801-I • F-2001I • Minneapolis • 102,600

VG-8	F-12	VF-20	EF-40	AU-50	Unc-60	Unc-63
$375	$700	$1,000	$1,700	$2,500	$3,800	$5,000

W-1801-J • F-2001J • Kansas City • 410,400

Commentary: Current market information unavailable.

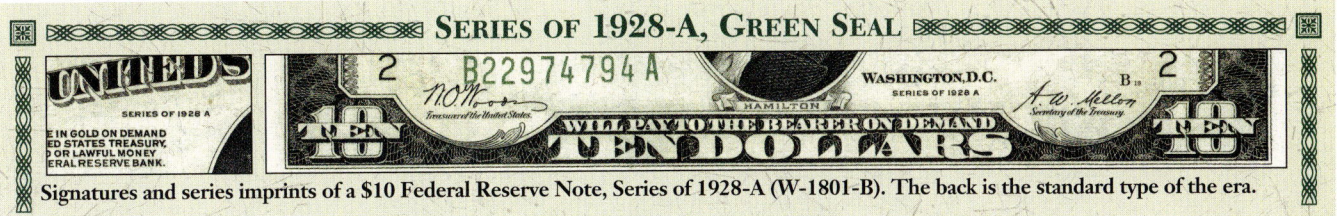

Signatures and series imprints of a $10 Federal Reserve Note, Series of 1928-A (W-1801-B). The back is the standard type of the era.

W-1801-K • F-2001K • Dallas • 961,800

VG-8	F-12	VF-20	EF-40	AU-50
$350	$500	$750	$1,400	$3,000

W-1801-L • F-2001L • San Francisco • 2,547,900

VG-8	F-12	VF-20	EF-40	AU-50	Unc-60	Unc-63	Unc-65
$40	$70	$100	$225	$375	$550	$750	$1,150

W-1801-L★ • F-2001L★

VG-8	F-12	VF-20	EF-40	AU-50	Unc-60	Unc-63	Unc-65
$175	$275	$400	$750	$1,000	$1,250	$1,600	$2,300

Series of 1928-B, Dark Green Seal
Woods-Mellon (1929–1932)

The "redeemable in gold" provision is the same as on Series of 1928 and 1928-A notes. Now the Federal Reserve seal has the bank letter at the center, instead of the number.

W-1802-A • F-2002A • Boston • 33,218,088

VF-20	EF-40	AU-50	Unc-60	Unc-63	Unc-65
$20	$30	$40	$60	$90	$150

W-1802-A★ • F-2002A★

VG-8	F-12	VF-20	EF-40	AU-50	Unc-60	Unc-63	Unc-65
$45	$75	$120	$290	$450	$650	$900	$1,400

W-1802-B • F-2002B • New York • 44,808,308

VF-20	EF-40	AU-50	Unc-60	Unc-63	Unc-65
$20	$30	$40	$55	$80	$125

W-1802-B★ • F-2002B★

VG-8	F-12	VF-20	EF-40	AU-50	Unc-60	Unc-63	Unc-65
$55	$90	$150	$310	$475	$700	$1,000	$1,500

W-1802-C • F-2002C • Philadelphia • 22,689,216

VF-20	EF-40	AU-50	Unc-60	Unc-63	Unc-65
$20	$30	$40	$55	$80	$125

W-1802-C★ • F-2002C★

VG-8	F-12	VF-20	EF-40	AU-50	Unc-60	Unc-63	Unc-65
$55	$90	$150	$310	$475	$700	$1,000	$1,500

W-1802-D • F-2002D • Cleveland • 17,418,024

VF-20	EF-40	AU-50	Unc-60	Unc-63	Unc-65
$20	$30	$40	$55	$80	$125

W-1802-D★ • F-2002D★

VG-8	F-12	VF-20	EF-40	AU-50	Unc-60	Unc-63	Unc-65
$45	$75	$120	$275	$450	$650	$900	$1,400

W-1802-E • F-2002E • Richmond • 12,714,504

VF-20	EF-40	AU-50	Unc-60	Unc-63	Unc-65
$20	$35	$50	$75	$110	$190

W-1802-E★ • F-2002E★

VG-8	F-12	VF-20	EF-40	AU-50	Unc-60	Unc-63	Unc-65
$75	$125	$200	$325	$500	$700	$1,000	$1,500

W-1802-F • F-2002F • Atlanta • 5,246,700

VF-20	EF-40	AU-50	Unc-60	Unc-63	Unc-65
$20	$35	$55	$90	$130	$250

W-1802-F★ • F-2002F★

VG-8	F-12	VF-20	EF-40	AU-50	Unc-60	Unc-63	Unc-65
$55	$90	$150	$310	$500	$750	$1,100	$1,650

W-1802-G • F-2002G • Chicago • 38,035,000

VF-20	EF-40	AU-50	Unc-60	Unc-63	Unc-65
$20	$30	$40	$55	$80	$125

W-1802-G★ • F-2002G★

VG-8	F-12	VF-20	EF-40	AU-50	Unc-60	Unc-63	Unc-65
$45	$70	$100	$200	$300	$450	$600	$1,000

W-1802-H • F-2002H • St. Louis • 10,814,664

VF-20	EF-40	AU-50	Unc-60	Unc-63	Unc-65
$20	$30	$40	$60	$90	$150

SERIES OF 1928-B, DARK GREEN SEAL

$10 Federal Reserve Note, Series of 1928-B (W-1802-D). Federal Reserve Bank of Cleveland. Dark green Treasury seal. Now with the bank letter at the center of the Federal Reserve seal.

W-1802-H★ • F-2002H★

VG-8	F-12	VF-20	EF-40	AU-50	Unc-60	Unc-63	Unc-65
$55	$90	$150	$310	$500	$750	$1,100	$1,650

W-1802-I • F-2002I • Minneapolis • 5,294,460

VF-20	EF-40	AU-50	Unc-60	Unc-63	Unc-65
$20	$35	$50	$75	$110	$190

W-1802-I★ • F-2002I★

VG-8	F-12	VF-20	EF-40	AU-50	Unc-60	Unc-63	Unc-65
$55	$90	$150	$310	$500	$750	$1,100	$1,650

W-1802-J • F-2002J • Kansas City • 7,748,040

VF-20	EF-40	AU-50	Unc-60	Unc-63	Unc-65
$20	$30	$40	$55	$80	$125

W-1802-J★ • F-2002J★

VG-8	F-12	VF-20	EF-40	AU-50	Unc-60	Unc-63	Unc-65
$110	$180	$325	$700	$1,100	$1,800	$2,700	$4,250

W-1802-K • F-2002K • Dallas • 3,396,096

VG-8	F-12	VF-20	EF-40	AU-50	Unc-60	Unc-63	Unc-65
$25	$40	$70	$100	$135	$180	$220	$400

W-1802-L • F-2002L • San Francisco • 22,695,300

VF-20	EF-40	AU-50	Unc-60	Unc-63	Unc-65
$20	$30	$40	$55	$80	$125

W-1802-L★ • F-2002L★

VG-8	F-12	VF-20	EF-40	AU-50	Unc-60	Unc-63	Unc-65
$45	$75	$120	$375	$600	$850	$1,100	$1,750

Series of 1928-B, Light Yellow-Green Seal
Woods-Mellon (1929–1932)

This type is as the preceding, except for the color of the Treasury seal.

Prices for a typical note for this series, unless listed otherwise, are as follows:

VF-20	EF-40	AU-50	Unc-60	Unc-63	Unc-65
$25	$35	$45	$65	$115	$140

W-1803-A • F-2002A • Boston • Part of W-1802-A printage

VF-20	EF-40	AU-50	Unc-60	Unc-63	Unc-65
$25	$35	$45	$80	$150	$180

W-1803-A★ • F-2002A★

VG-8	F-12	VF-20	EF-40	AU-50	Unc-60	Unc-63	Unc-65
$55	$85	$145	$315	$475	$700	$1,000	$1,550

W-1803-B • F-2002B • New York • Part of W-1802-B printage

W-1803-B★ • F-2002B★

VG-8	F-12	VF-20	EF-40	AU-50	Unc-60	Unc-63	Unc-65
$55	$85	$145	$250	$400	$525	$750	$950

W-1803-C • F-2002C • Philadelphia • Part of W-1802-C printage

W-1803-C★ • F-2002C★

VG-8	F-12	VF-20	EF-40	AU-50	Unc-60	Unc-63	Unc-65
$55	$85	$145	$315	$475	$700	$1,000	$1,550

W-1803-D • F-2002D • Cleveland • Part of W-1802-D printage

W-1803-D★ • F-2002D★

VG-8	F-12	VF-20	EF-40	AU-50	Unc-60	Unc-63	Unc-65
$40	$65	$110	$250	$390	$600	$900	$1,400

W-1803-E • F-2002E • Richmond • Part of W-1802-E printage

W-1803-E★ • F-2002E★

VG-8	F-12	VF-20	EF-40	AU-50	Unc-60	Unc-63	Unc-65
$90	$150	$210	$300	$450	$675	$1,000	$1,450

W-1803-F • F-2002F • Atlanta • Part of W-1802-F printage

VF-20	EF-40	AU-50	Unc-60	Unc-63	Unc-65
$25	$35	$45	$80	$150	$180

SERIES OF 1928-B, LIGHT YELLOW-GREEN SEAL

$10 Federal Reserve Note, Series of 1928-B (W-1803-G). Federal Reserve Bank of Chicago. Light yellow-green Treasury seal. The back is the same as used on other $10 notes through the 1950s.

W-1803-F★ • F-2002F★

VG-8	F-12	VF-20	EF-40	AU-50	Unc-60	Unc-63	Unc-65
$90	$150	$210	$300	$450	$675	$1,000	$1,450

W-1803-G • F-2002G • Chicago • Part of W-1802-G printage

VF-20	EF-40	AU-50	Unc-60	Unc-63	Unc-65
$25	$35	$45	$60	$80	$100

W-1803-G★ • F-2002G★

VG-8	F-12	VF-20	EF-40	AU-50	Unc-60	Unc-63	Unc-65
$35	$60	$90	$150	$280	$410	$550	$750

W-1803-H • F-2002H • St. Louis • Part of W-1802-H printage

W-1803-H★ • F-2002H★

VG-8	F-12	VF-20	EF-40	AU-50	Unc-60	Unc-63	Unc-65
$55	$85	$145	$315	$475	$700	$1,000	$1,550

W-1803-I • F-2002I • Minneapolis • Part of W-1802-I printage

VF-20	EF-40	AU-50	Unc-60	Unc-63	Unc-65
$25	$35	$45	$80	$150	$180

W-1803-I★ • F-2002I★

VG-8	F-12	VF-20	EF-40	AU-50	Unc-60	Unc-63	Unc-65
$90	$150	$210	$300	$450	$675	$1,000	$1,450

W-1803-J • F-2002J • Kansas City • Part of W-1802-J printage

W-1803-J★ • F-2002J★

VG-8	F-12	VF-20	EF-40	AU-50	Unc-60	Unc-63	Unc-65
$90	$150	$210	$300	$450	$675	$1,000	$1,450

W-1803-K • F-2002K • Dallas • Part of W-1802-K printage • Printed but unreported

W-1803-L • F-2002L • San Francisco • Part of W-1802-L printage

W-1803-L★ • F-2002L★

VG-8	F-12	VF-20	EF-40	AU-50	Unc-60	Unc-63	Unc-65
$55	$85	$145	$315	$475	$700	$1,000	$1,550

Series of 1928-C, Light Yellow-Green Seal
Woods-Mills (1932–1933)

The "redeemable in gold" provision is the same as on Series of 1928 notes. The Federal Reserve seal at the left has the bank letter at the center. All have a light green Treasury seal.

This is a very truncated series, no doubt because the notes were payable in gold. Shortly after Franklin D. Roosevelt was inaugurated on March 4, 1933, the Treasury stopped putting Gold Certificates and gold coins into normal commercial channels and stopped redeeming currency in gold coins. This had been planned in advance with William H. Woodin, who was named as secretary of the Treasury. It was reported that 688,380 notes were printed for Atlanta, but none have been seen in numismatic hands.

W-1804-B • F-2003B • New York • 2,902,678

VG-8	F-12	VF-20	EF-40	AU-50	Unc-60	Unc-63	Unc-65
$50	$75	$100	$180	$280	$425	$550	$950

W-1804-D • F-2003D • Cleveland • 4,230,428

VG-8	F-12	VF-20	EF-40	AU-50	Unc-60	Unc-63	Unc-65
$250	$450	$600	$900	$1,250	$2,500	$3,500	$4,500

W-1804-D★ • F-2003D★

VG-8	F-12	VF-20
$7,000	$10,000	$15,000

W-1804-E • F-2003E • Richmond • 304,800

VG-8	F-12	VF-20	EF-40	AU-50	Unc-60	Unc-63	Unc-65
$1,250	$2,000	$3,000	$4,500	$6,000	$8,000	$10,500	$16,500

W-1804-F • F-2003F • Atlanta • 688,380 • Unknown

W-1804-G • F-2003G • Chicago • 2,423,400

VG-8	F-12	VF-20	EF-40	AU-50	Unc-60	Unc-63	Unc-65
$50	$75	$100	$180	$280	$425	$550	$950

Series of 1934, Light Yellow-Green Seal
Julian-Morgenthau (1934–1945)

The Series of 1934 continued the same general configuration as the preceding series, but with a change in the obligation, eliminating any mention of gold: "This note is legal tender for all debts, public and private, and is redeemable in lawful money at the United States Treasury, or at any Federal Reserve Bank."

Circulated notes are scarce but seen often enough.

W-1805-A • F-2004A • Boston • 46,276,152

VF-20	EF-40	AU-50	Unc-60	Unc-63	Unc-65
$20	$35	$45	$65	$90	$135

W-1805-A★ • F-2004A★

VG-8	F-12	VF-20	EF-40	AU-50	Unc-60	Unc-63	Unc-65
$30	$55	$80	$175	$375	$575	$800	$1,400

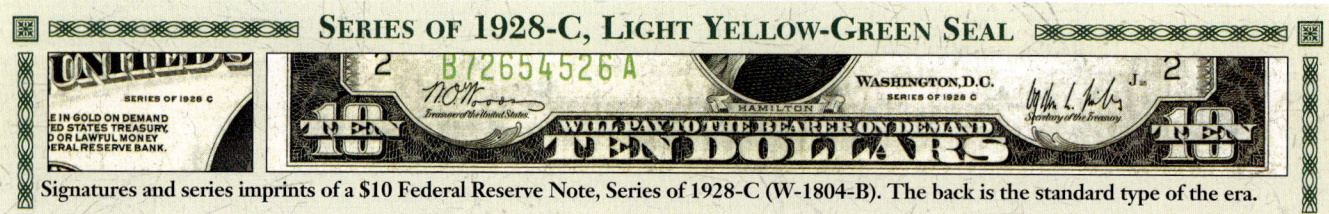

SERIES OF 1928-C, LIGHT YELLOW-GREEN SEAL

Signatures and series imprints of a $10 Federal Reserve Note, Series of 1928-C (W-1804-B). The back is the standard type of the era.

W-1805-B • F-2004B • New York • 117,298,008

VF-20	EF-40	AU-50	Unc-60	Unc-63	Unc-65
$20	$30	$40	$60	$75	$110

W-1805-B★ • F-2004B★

VG-8	F-12	VF-20	EF-40	AU-50	Unc-60	Unc-63	Unc-65
$40	$60	$100	$175	$375	$575	$800	$1,250

W-1805-C • F-2004C • Philadelphia • 34,770,768

VF-20	EF-40	AU-50	Unc-60	Unc-63	Unc-65
$20	$35	$45	$65	$90	$135

W-1805-C★ • F-2004C★

VG-8	F-12	VF-20	EF-40	AU-50	Unc-60	Unc-63	Unc-65
$40	$60	$100	$175	$375	$575	$800	$1,250

W-1805-D • F-2004D • Cleveland • 28,764,108

VF-20	EF-40	AU-50	Unc-60	Unc-63	Unc-65
$20	$35	$45	$65	$90	$135

W-1805-D★ • F-2004D★

VG-8	F-12	VF-20	EF-40	AU-50	Unc-60	Unc-63	Unc-65
$40	$60	$100	$175	$375	$575	$800	$1,250

W-1805-E • F-2004E • Richmond • 16,437,252

VF-20	EF-40	AU-50	Unc-60	Unc-63	Unc-65
$20	$35	$45	$75	$110	$160

W-1805-E★ • F-2004E★

VG-8	F-12	VF-20	EF-40	AU-50	Unc-60	Unc-63	Unc-65
$75	$160	$275	$425	$875	$1,250	$1,650	$2,400

W-1805-F • F-2004F • Atlanta • 20,656,872

VF-20	EF-40	AU-50	Unc-60	Unc-63	Unc-65
$25	$40	$55	$85	$135	$200

W-1805-F★ • F-2004F★

VG-8	F-12	VF-20	EF-40	AU-50	Unc-60	Unc-63	Unc-65
$60	$125	$200	$350	$550	$750	$1,000	$1,500

W-1805-G • F-2004G • Chicago • 69,962,064

VF-20	EF-40	AU-50	Unc-60	Unc-63	Unc-65
$20	$35	$45	$65	$90	$125

W-1805-G★ • F-2004G★

VG-8	F-12	VF-20	EF-40	AU-50	Unc-60	Unc-63	Unc-65
$25	$50	$75	$175	$325	$470	$700	$1,200

W-1805-H • F-2004H • St. Louis • 22,593,204

VF-20	EF-40	AU-50	Unc-60	Unc-63	Unc-65
$20	$35	$45	$75	$110	$160

W-1805-H★ • F-2004H★

VG-8	F-12	VF-20	EF-40	AU-50	Unc-60	Unc-63	Unc-65
$40	$60	$100	$175	$375	$575	$800	$1,250

W-1805-I • F-2004I • Minneapolis • 16,840,980

VF-20	EF-40	AU-50	Unc-60	Unc-63	Unc-65
$20	$40	$55	$85	$135	$200

W-1805-I★ • F-2004I★

VG-8	F-12	VF-20	EF-40	AU-50	Unc-60	Unc-63	Unc-65
$75	$160	$275	$425	$875	$1,250	$1,650	$2,400

W-1805-J • F-2004J • Kansas City • 22,627,824

VF-20	EF-40	AU-50	Unc-60	Unc-63	Unc-65
$20	$35	$45	$65	$90	$135

W-1805-J★ • F-2004J★

VG-8	F-12	VF-20	EF-40	AU-50	Unc-60	Unc-63	Unc-65
$40	$60	$100	$175	$375	$575	$850	$1,250

W-1805-K • F-2004K • Dallas • 21,403,488

VF-20	EF-40	AU-50	Unc-60	Unc-63	Unc-65
$20	$50	$115	$200	$350	$600

W-1805-K★ • F-2004K★

VG-8	F-12	VF-20	EF-40	AU-50	Unc-60	Unc-63	Unc-65
$75	$160	$275	$425	$875	$1,250	$1,650	$2,400

SERIES OF 1934, LIGHT YELLOW-GREEN SEAL

$10 Federal Reserve Note, Series of 1934 (W-1805-I). Federal Reserve Bank of Minneapolis. Light yellow-green Treasury seal. The mention of gold no longer appears. The back of the note is the standard design of the era.

W-1805-L • F-2004L • San Francisco • 37,402,308

VF-20	EF-40	AU-50	Unc-60	Unc-63	Unc-65
$20	$35	$45	$65	$90	$135

W-1805-L★ • F-2004L★

VG-8	F-12	VF-20	EF-40	AU-50	Unc-60	Unc-63	Unc-65
$50	$110	$175	$270	$600	$900	$1,400	$2,000

Series of 1934, Green Seal
Julian-Morgenthau (1934–1945)

This series shares the general characteristics as preceding, except with a green Treasury seal.

Mules: Most backs have the plate number in micro letters, but mules have the larger, macro-size serials as used on Series 1934-A (the macro plates have numbers 585 and higher). These are worth a premium. Star note mules are very rare and worth considerably more. Related mules are found among Silver Certificates using the same backs.

Prices for a typical mule note for this series, unless listed otherwise, are as follows:

VF-20	EF-40	AU-50	Unc-60	Unc-63	Unc-65
$15	$20	$30	$40	$50	$70

Prices for a typical star mule note for this series, unless listed otherwise, are as follows:

VG-8	F-12	VF-20	EF-40	AU-50	Unc-60	Unc-63	Unc-65
$25	$40	$60	$100	$200	$350	$450	$650

W-1806-A • F-2005A • Boston • Part of W-1805-A printage

VF-20	EF-40	AU-50	Unc-60	Unc-63	Unc-65
$20	$30	$45	$60	$90	$125

W-1806-A★ • F-2005A★

VG-8	F-12	VF-20	EF-40	AU-50	Unc-60	Unc-63	Unc-65
$25	$45	$80	$135	$200	$340	$450	$725

W-1806-A Mule • F-2005A • Part of W-1805-A printage

W-1806-A Mule★ • F-2005A★

W-1806-B • F-2005B • New York • Part of W-1805-B printage

VF-20	EF-40	AU-50	Unc-60	Unc-63	Unc-65
$15	$25	$40	$50	$75	$100

W-1806-B★ • F-2005B★

VG-8	F-12	VF-20	EF-40	AU-50	Unc-60	Unc-63	Unc-65
$25	$45	$80	$135	$200	$340	$450	$725

W-1806-B Mule • F-2005B • Part of W-1805-B printage

F-12	VF-20	EF-40	AU-50	Unc-60	Unc-63	Unc-65
$40	$60	$75	$95	$140	$180	$260

W-1806-B Mule★ • F-2005B★

VG-8	F-12	VF-20	EF-40	AU-50	Unc-60	Unc-63	Unc-65
$30	$50	$80	$180	$300	$475	$600	$825

W-1806-C • F-2005C • Philadelphia • Part of W-1805-C printage

VF-20	EF-40	AU-50	Unc-60	Unc-63	Unc-65
$15	$25	$40	$50	$75	$100

W-1806-C★ • F-2005C★

VG-8	F-12	VF-20	EF-40	AU-50	Unc-60	Unc-63	Unc-65
$25	$45	$80	$135	$200	$340	$450	$725

W-1806-C Mule • F-2005C • Part of W-1805-C printage

W-1806-C Mule★ • F-2005C★

VG-8	F-12	VF-20	EF-40	AU-50	Unc-60	Unc-63	Unc-65
$25	$40	$60	$200	$370	$500	$700	$900

W-1806-D • F-2005D • Cleveland • Part of W-1805-D printage

VF-20	EF-40	AU-50	Unc-60	Unc-63	Unc-65
$15	$25	$35	$45	$70	$95

$10 Federal Reserve Note, Series of 1934 (W-1806-B). Federal Reserve Bank of New York. Dark green Treasury seal. The back is the same as used on other $10 notes through the 1950s.

W-1806-D★ • F-2005D★

VG-8	F-12	VF-20	EF-40	AU-50	Unc-60	Unc-63	Unc-65
$35	$65	$100	$175	$280	$380	$525	$850

W-1806-D Mule • F-2005D • Part of W-1805-D printage

W-1806-D Mule★ • F-2005D★

W-1806-E • F-2005E • Richmond • Part of W-1805-E printage

VF-20	EF-40	AU-50	Unc-60	Unc-63	Unc-65
$15	$30	$50	$65	$90	$125

W-1806-E★ • F-2005E★

VG-8	F-12	VF-20	EF-40	AU-50	Unc-60	Unc-63	Unc-65
$50	$95	$140	$275	$400	$560	$700	$1,000

W-1806-E Mule • F-2005E • Part of W-1805-E printage

W-1806-E Mule★ • F-2005E★

VG-8	F-12	VF-20	EF-40	AU-50	Unc-60	Unc-63	Unc-65
$30	$50	$80	$180	$300	$475	$600	$825

W-1806-F • F-2005F • Atlanta • Part of W-1805-F printage

VF-20	EF-40	AU-50	Unc-60	Unc-63	Unc-65
$15	$25	$35	$45	$70	$95

W-1806-F★ • F-2005F★

VG-8	F-12	VF-20	EF-40	AU-50	Unc-60	Unc-63	Unc-65
$50	$95	$140	$275	$400	$560	$700	$1,000

W-1806-F Mule • F-2005F • Part of W-1805-F printage

W-1806-F Mule★ • F-2005F★

W-1806-G • F-2005G • Chicago • Part of W-1805-G printage

VF-20	EF-40	AU-50	Unc-60	Unc-63	Unc-65
$15	$25	$35	$45	$70	$95

W-1806-G★ • F-2005G★

VG-8	F-12	VF-20	EF-40	AU-50	Unc-60	Unc-63	Unc-65
$25	$40	$75	$135	$200	$300	$425	$700

W-1806-G Mule • F-2005G • Part of W-1805-G printage

VF-20	EF-40	AU-50	Unc-60	Unc-63	Unc-65
$15	$20	$25	$30	$40	$50

W-1806-G Mule★ • F-2005G★

W-1806-H • F-2005H • St. Louis • Part of W-1805-H printage

VF-20	EF-40	AU-50	Unc-60	Unc-63	Unc-65
$15	$30	$45	$60	$85	$115

W-1806-H★ • F-2005H★

VG-8	F-12	VF-20	EF-40	AU-50	Unc-60	Unc-63	Unc-65
$35	$60	$95	$150	$275	$400	$525	$850

W-1806-H Mule • F-2005H • Part of W-1805-H printage

W-1806-H Mule★ • F-2005H★

VG-8	F-12	VF-20	EF-40	AU-50	Unc-60	Unc-63	Unc-65
$25	$40	$60	$200	$370	$500	$700	$900

W-1806-I • F-2005I • Minneapolis • Part of W-1805-I printage

VF-20	EF-40	AU-50	Unc-60	Unc-63	Unc-65
$20	$35	$50	$75	$110	$160

W-1806-I★ • F-2005I★

VG-8	F-12	VF-20	EF-40	AU-50	Unc-60	Unc-63	Unc-65
$40	$75	$125	$200	$250	$375	$475	$750

W-1806-I Mule • F-2005I • Part of W-1805-I printage

W-1806-I Mule★ • F-2005I★

VG-8	F-12	VF-20	EF-40	AU-50	Unc-60	Unc-63	Unc-65
$30	$50	$80	$180	$300	$475	$600	$825

W-1806-J • F-2005J • Kansas City • Part of W-1805-J printage

VF-20	EF-40	AU-50	Unc-60	Unc-63	Unc-65
$15	$25	$40	$50	$75	$100

W-1806-J★ • F-2005J★

VG-8	F-12	VF-20	EF-40	AU-50	Unc-60	Unc-63	Unc-65
$25	$45	$80	$125	$175	$275	$400	$675

W-1806-J Mule • F-2005J • Part of W-1805-J printage

W-1806-J Mule★ • F-2005J★

W-1806-K • F-2005K • Dallas • Part of W-1805-K printage

VF-20	EF-40	AU-50	Unc-60	Unc-63	Unc-65
$15	$30	$45	$70	$100	$140

W-1806-K★ • F-2005K★

VG-8	F-12	VF-20	EF-40	AU-50	Unc-60	Unc-63	Unc-65
$20	$35	$60	$150	$275	$400	$550	$825

W-1806-K Mule • F-2005K • Part of W-1805-K printage

W-1806-K Mule★ • F-2005K

Commentary: Schwartz and Lindquist list a star mule for Dallas but not a regular star note.

W-1806-L • F-2005L • San Francisco • Part of W-1805-L printage

VF-20	EF-40	AU-50	Unc-60	Unc-63	Unc-65
$15	$25	$40	$50	$75	$100

W-1806-L★ • F-2005L★

VG-8	F-12	VF-20	EF-40	AU-50	Unc-60	Unc-63	Unc-65
$25	$45	$80	$125	$175	$275	$400	$675

W-1806-L Mule • F-2005L • Part of W-1805-L printage

W-1806-L Mule★ • F-2005L★

Series of 1934-A, Green Seal
Julian-Morgenthau (1934–1945)

This series continued the preceding design.

Mules: Most backs have the plate number in macro letters, but mules have the smaller, micro-size numbers as used on Series 1934 (the micro plates have numbers lower than 585).

Prices for a typical note for this series, unless listed otherwise, are as follows:

EF-40	AU-50	Unc-60	Unc-63	Unc-65
$15	$20	$30	$40	$65

W-1807-A • F-2006A • Boston • 104,540,088

W-1807-A★ • F-2006A★

F-12	VF-20	EF-40	AU-50	Unc-60	Unc-63	Unc-65
$25	$40	$85	$125	$175	$250	$425

W-1807-A Mule • F-2006A

VF-20	EF-40	AU-50	Unc-60	Unc-63	Unc-65
$20	$55	$95	$135	$175	$225

W-1807-A Mule★ • F-2006A★ • Unknown

W-1807-B • F-2006B • New York • 281,940,996

W-1807-B★ • F-2006B★

F-12	VF-20	EF-40	AU-50	Unc-60	Unc-63	Unc-65
$25	$40	$80	$120	$160	$225	$375

W-1807-B Mule • F-2006B

VF-20	EF-40	AU-50	Unc-60	Unc-63	Unc-65
$20	$35	$55	$75	$90	$125

W-1807-B Mule★ • F-2006B★

VG-8	F-12	VF-20	EF-40	AU-50	Unc-60	Unc-63	Unc-65
$70	$140	$225	$350	$500	$700	$850	$1,100

W-1807-C • F-2006C • Philadelphia • 95,338,032

W-1807-C★ • F-2006C★

F-12	VF-20	EF-40	AU-50	Unc-60	Unc-63	Unc-65
$25	$40	$80	$125	$175	$250	$425

W-1807-C Mule • F-2006C

VF-20	EF-40	AU-50	Unc-60	Unc-63	Unc-65
$20	$35	$55	$75	$90	$125

W-1807-C Mule★ • F-2006C★

VG-8	F-12	VF-20	EF-40	AU-50	Unc-60	Unc-63	Unc-65
$70	$140	$225	$350	$500	$750	$925	$1,200

W-1807-D • F-2006D • Cleveland • 93,332,004

W-1807-D★ • F-2006D★

F-12	VF-20	EF-40	AU-50	Unc-60	Unc-63	Unc-65
$25	$40	$80	$125	$175	$250	$425

W-1807-D Mule • F-2006D

VF-20	EF-40	AU-50	Unc-60	Unc-63	Unc-65
$25	$40	$60	$80	$100	$135

W-1807-D Mule★ • F-2006D★ • Unknown

W-1807-E • F-2006E • Richmond • 101,037,912

W-1807-E★ • F-2006E★

F-12	VF-20	EF-40	AU-50	Unc-60	Unc-63	Unc-65
$25	$40	$80	$125	$175	$250	$425

W-1807-E Mule • F-2006E

VF-20	EF-40	AU-50	Unc-60	Unc-63	Unc-65
$25	$45	$80	$150	$240	$325

W-1807-E Mule★ • F-2006E★ • Unknown

W-1807-F • F-2006F • Atlanta • 85,478,160

W-1807-F★ • F-2006F★

F-12	VF-20	EF-40	AU-50	Unc-60	Unc-63	Unc-65
$25	$40	$95	$170	$225	$350	$550

W-1807-F Mule • F-2006F

VF-20	EF-40	AU-50	Unc-60	Unc-63	Unc-65
$25	$45	$80	$150	$240	$325

W-1807-F Mule★ • F-2006F★ • Unknown

W-1807-G • F-2006G • Chicago • 177,285,960

EF-40	AU-50	Unc-60	Unc-63	Unc-65
$15	$20	$25	$35	$55

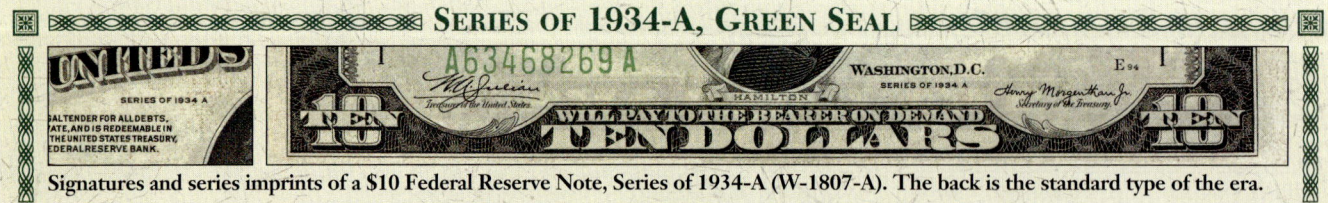

Signatures and series imprints of a $10 Federal Reserve Note, Series of 1934-A (W-1807-A). The back is the standard type of the era.

W-1807-G★ • F-2006G★

F-12	VF-20	EF-40	AU-50	Unc-60	Unc-63	Unc-65
$25	$40	$75	$100	$160	$275	$460

W-1807-G Mule • F-2006G

VF-20	EF-40	AU-50	Unc-60	Unc-63	Unc-65
$20	$35	$55	$75	$90	$125

W-1807-G Mule★ • F-2006G★

VG-8	F-12	VF-20	EF-40	AU-50	Unc-60	Unc-63	Unc-65
$70	$140	$225	$350	$500	$700	$850	$1,100

W-1807-H • F-2006H • St. Louis • 50,694,312

W-1807-H★ • F-2006H★

F-12	VF-20	EF-40	AU-50	Unc-60	Unc-63	Unc-65
$25	$40	$80	$125	$175	$250	$425

W-1807-H Mule • F-2006H • Unknown

W-1807-H Mule★ • F-2006H★ • Unknown

W-1807-I • F-2006I • Minneapolis • 16,340,016

EF-40	AU-50	Unc-60	Unc-63	Unc-65
$20	$32	$45	$50	$75

W-1807-I★ • F-2006I★

F-12	VF-20	EF-40	AU-50	Unc-60	Unc-63	Unc-65
$25	$45	$100	$170	$225	$375	$525

W-1807-I Mule • F-2006I

VF-20	EF-40	AU-50	Unc-60	Unc-63	Unc-65
$25	$60	$110	$160	$210	$270

W-1807-I Mule★ • F-2006I★ • Unknown

W-1807-J • F-2006J • Kansas City • 31,069,978

W-1807-J★ • F-2006J★

F-12	VF-20	EF-40	AU-50	Unc-60	Unc-63	Unc-65
$25	$40	$80	$125	$175	$250	$425

W-1807-J Mule • F-2006J • Unknown

W-1807-J Mule★ • F-2006J★ • Unknown

W-1807-K • F-2006K • Dallas • 28,263,156

EF-40	AU-50	Unc-60	Unc-63	Unc-65
$15	$25	$35	$45	$75

W-1807-K★ • F-2006K★

F-12	VF-20	EF-40	AU-50	Unc-60	Unc-63	Unc-65
$35	$60	$110	$170	$225	$375	$525

W-1807-K Mule • F-2006K • Unknown

W-1807-K Mule★ • F-2006K★ • Unknown

W-1807-L • F-2006L • San Francisco • 125,537,592

EF-40	AU-50	Unc-60	Unc-63	Unc-65
$15	$25	$35	$45	$70

W-1807-L★ • F-2006L★

F-12	VF-20	EF-40	AU-50	Unc-60	Unc-63	Unc-65
$30	$55	$90	$135	$190	$275	$450

W-1807-L Mule • F-2006L

VF-20	EF-40	AU-50	Unc-60	Unc-63	Unc-65
$25	$60	$110	$160	$210	$270

W-1807-L Mule★ • F-2006L★ • Unknown

Series of 1934-A, Brown Seal, HAWAII Overprint
Julian-Morgenthau (1934–1945)

These notes (illus. on p. 410), with the HAWAII overprint on the face and back and a special brown Treasury seal and brown serial numbers, were used from 1942 to 1944 in the Hawaiian Islands, then under threat of Japanese invasion. If the islands had fallen into the hands of the enemy, such notes could be repudiated and would have no value on world markets.

W-1808-L • F-2303 • 10,424,000

VG-8	F-12	VF-20	EF-40	AU-50	Unc-60	Unc-63	Unc-65
$75	$95	$115	$180	$400	$650	$1,250	$3,000

W-1808-L★ • F-2303★

VG-8	F-12	VF-20	EF-40	AU-50	Unc-60	Unc-63	Unc-65
$900	$1,200	$1,500	$3,000	$5,250	$7,000	$10,000	$17,500

Series of 1934-B, Green Seal
Julian-Vinson (1945–1946)

Beginning with the Series of 1934-B notes, there is a change in the wording in the Federal Reserve seal. THE is omitted, leaving just FEDERAL RESERVE (illus. on p. 410).

W-1809-A • F-2007A • Boston • 3,999,600

EF-40	AU-50	Unc-60	Unc-63	Unc-65
$40	$70	$100	$140	$200

W-1809-A★ • F-2007A★

VG-8	F-12	VF-20	EF-40	AU-50	Unc-60	Unc-63	Unc-65
$45	$80	$120	$210	$325	$450	$650	$900

W-1809-B • F-2007B • New York • 34,815,948

EF-40	AU-50	Unc-60	Unc-63	Unc-65
$30	$45	$60	$75	$125

W-1809-B★ • F-2007B★

VG-8	F-12	VF-20	EF-40	AU-50	Unc-60	Unc-63	Unc-65
$30	$50	$80	$125	$185	$250	$400	$650

W-1809-C • F-2007C • Philadelphia • 10,339,020

EF-40	AU-50	Unc-60	Unc-63	Unc-65
$30	$45	$60	$85	$135

W-1809-C★ • F-2007C★

VG-8	F-12	VF-20	EF-40	AU-50	Unc-60	Unc-63	Unc-65
$35	$60	$100	$170	$250	$400	$550	$775

W-1809-D • F-2007D • Cleveland • 1,394,700

EF-40	AU-50	Unc-60	Unc-63	Unc-65
$35	$60	$100	$150	$225

W-1809-D★ • F-2007D★

VG-8	F-12	VF-20	EF-40	AU-50	Unc-60	Unc-63	Unc-65
$650	$110	$175	$300	$475	$700	$1,000	$1,500

W-1809-E • F-2007E • Richmond • 4,018,272

EF-40	AU-50	Unc-60	Unc-63	Unc-65
$40	$60	$90	$140	$210

W-1809-E★ • F-2007E★

VG-8	F-12	VF-20	EF-40	AU-50	Unc-60	Unc-63	Unc-65
$45	$95	$145	$250	$400	$600	$800	$1,300

W-1809-F • F-2007F • Atlanta • 6,746,076

EF-40	AU-50	Unc-60	Unc-63	Unc-65
$30	$45	$65	$90	$145

W-1809-F★ • F-2007F★

VG-8	F-12	VF-20	EF-40	AU-50	Unc-60	Unc-63	Unc-65
$60	$110	$175	$300	$475	$700	$1,000	$1,500

W-1809-G • F-2007G • Chicago • 18,130,836

EF-40	AU-50	Unc-60	Unc-63	Unc-65
$25	$45	$60	$75	$125

W-1809-G★ • F-2007G★

VG-8	F-12	VF-20	EF-40	AU-50	Unc-60	Unc-63	Unc-65
$30	$50	$85	$130	$195	$265	$425	$680

W-1809-H • F-2007H • St. Louis • 6,849,348

EF-40	AU-50	Unc-60	Unc-63	Unc-65
$30	$60	$65	$90	$145

SERIES OF 1934-A, BROWN SEAL, HAWAII OVERPRINT

$10 Federal Reserve Note, Series of 1934-A (W-1808-L), with HAWAII overprinted at the left and right ends and brown Treasury seal and serial numbers.

Back of the $10 Federal Reserve Note, Series of 1934-A (W-1808-L), with large HAWAII overprint.

SERIES OF 1934-B, GREEN SEAL

Detail of the signatures and the series imprints of a $10 Federal Reserve Note, Series of 1934-B (W-1809-K), as well as the new style of Federal Reserve seal. The back is the standard type of the era.

W-1809-H★ • F-2007H★

VG-8	F-12	VF-20	EF-40	AU-50	Unc-60	Unc-63	Unc-65
$40	$65	$110	$180	$265	$425	$600	$850

W-1809-I • F-2007I • Minneapolis • 2,254,800

EF-40	AU-50	Unc-60	Unc-63	Unc-65
$45	$65	$95	$140	$215

W-1809-I★ • F-2007I★

VG-8	F-12	VF-20	EF-40	AU-50	Unc-60	Unc-63	Unc-65
$100	$140	$200	$275	$525	$800	$1,250	$2,000

W-1809-J • F-2007J • Kansas City • 3,835,764

EF-40	AU-50	Unc-60	Unc-63	Unc-65
$35	$50	$85	$120	$160

W-1809-J★ • F-2007J★

VG-8	F-12	VF-20	EF-40	AU-50	Unc-60	Unc-63	Unc-65
$40	$90	$135	$240	$380	$575	$775	$1,225

W-1809-K • F-2007K • Dallas • 3,085,200

EF-40	AU-50	Unc-60	Unc-63	Unc-65
$45	$65	$95	$140	$215

W-1809-K★ • F-2007K★

VG-8	F-12	VF-20	EF-40	AU-50	Unc-60	Unc-63	Unc-65
$50	$100	$150	$325	$600	$850	$1,250	$2,000

W-1809-L • F-2007L • San Francisco • 9,076,800

EF-40	AU-50	Unc-60	Unc-63	Unc-65
$30	$45	$65	$90	$145

W-1809-L★ • F-2007L★

VG-8	F-12	VF-20	EF-40	AU-50	Unc-60	Unc-63	Unc-65
$30	$50	$85	$150	$275	$425	$600	$900

Series of 1934-C, Green Seal, Wide Face
Julian-Snyder (1946–1949)

This issue continued the preceding design. Beginning on August 25, 1949, face plates were made slightly smaller, narrowing the printed area horizontally by subtly removing part of the design. This created Wide Face (early style) and Narrow Face (later style) varieties. On December 20, 1951, the back (generic for all $10 series) was made Narrow as well.

Wide Face style: The spaces between the design elements at the left and right and the nearby border are slightly wider on this issue.

W-1810-A • F-2008A • Boston • 42,431,404

EF-40	AU-50	Unc-60	Unc-63	Unc-65
$15	$25	$35	$50	$80

W-1810-A★ • F-2008A★

VG-8	F-12	VF-20	EF-40	AU-50	Unc-60	Unc-63	Unc-65
$20	$40	$65	$100	$150	$225	$325	$550

W-1810-B • F-2008B • New York • 115,675,644

EF-40	AU-50	Unc-60	Unc-63	Unc-65
$15	$25	$32	$40	$70

W-1810-B★ • F-2008B★

VG-8	F-12	VF-20	EF-40	AU-50	Unc-60	Unc-63	Unc-65
$20	$35	$55	$90	$145	$225	$300	$450

W-1810-C • F-2008C • Philadelphia • 46,874,760

EF-40	AU-50	Unc-60	Unc-63	Unc-65
$15	$25	$32	$40	$70

W-1810-C★ • F-2008C★

VG-8	F-12	VF-20	EF-40	AU-50	Unc-60	Unc-63	Unc-65
$20	$40	$60	$100	$140	$210	$300	$450

W-1810-D • F-2008D • Cleveland • 33,240,000

EF-40	AU-50	Unc-60	Unc-63	Unc-65
$15	$25	$32	$40	$70

W-1810-D★ • F-2008D★

VG-8	F-12	VF-20	EF-40	AU-50	Unc-60	Unc-63	Unc-65
$20	$40	$60	$100	$140	$210	$300	$450

W-1810-E • F-2008E • Richmond • 37,422,600

EF-40	AU-50	Unc-60	Unc-63	Unc-65
$15	$25	$35	$50	$80

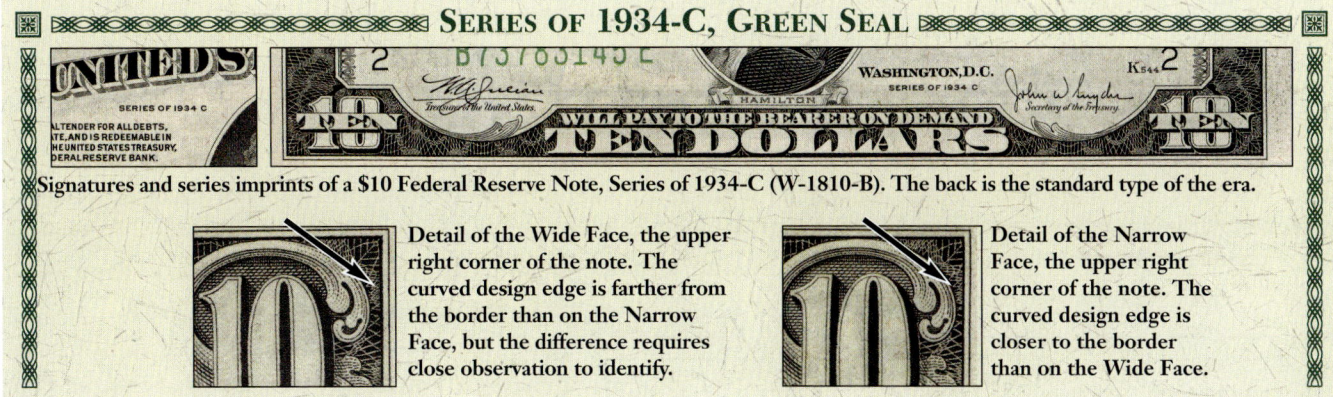

SERIES OF 1934-C, GREEN SEAL

Signatures and series imprints of a $10 Federal Reserve Note, Series of 1934-C (W-1810-B). The back is the standard type of the era.

Detail of the Wide Face, the upper right corner of the note. The curved design edge is farther from the border than on the Narrow Face, but the difference requires close observation to identify.

Detail of the Narrow Face, the upper right corner of the note. The curved design edge is closer to the border than on the Wide Face.

W-1810-E★ • F-2008E★

VG-8	F-12	VF-20	EF-40	AU-50	Unc-60	Unc-63	Unc-65
$20	$40	$65	$110	$150	$225	$300	$450

W-1810-F • F-2008F • Atlanta • 44,838,264

EF-40	AU-50	Unc-60	Unc-63	Unc-65
$15	$25	$35	$55	$90

W-1810-F★ • F-2008F★

VG-8	F-12	VF-20	EF-40	AU-50
$50	$100	$175	$375	$600

W-1810-G • F-2008G • Chicago • 105,875,412

EF-40	AU-50	Unc-60	Unc-63	Unc-65
$15	$25	$32	$40	$70

W-1810-G★ • F-2008G★

VG-8	F-12	VF-20	EF-40	AU-50	Unc-60	Unc-63	Unc-65
$15	$35	$50	$85	$135	$200	$250	$400

W-1810-H • F-2008H • St. Louis • 36,541,404

EF-40	AU-50	Unc-60	Unc-63	Unc-65
$15	$25	$35	$45	$75

W-1810-H★ • F-2008H★

VG-8	F-12	VF-20	EF-40	AU-50	Unc-60	Unc-63	Unc-65
$20	$40	$65	$100	$150	$225	$300	$525

W-1810-I • F-2008I • Minneapolis • 11,944,848

EF-40	AU-50	Unc-60	Unc-63	Unc-65
$15	$25	$50	$80	$125

W-1810-I★ • F-2008I★

VG-8	F-12	VF-20	EF-40	AU-50	Unc-60	Unc-63	Unc-65
$45	$95	$160	$350	$550	$700	$850	$1,250

W-1810-J • F-2008J • Kansas City • 20,874,072

EF-40	AU-50	Unc-60	Unc-63	Unc-65
$15	$25	$35	$55	$90

W-1810-J★ • F-2008J★

VG-8	F-12	VF-20	EF-40	AU-50	Unc-60	Unc-63	Unc-65
$20	$40	$65	$100	$150	$225	$300	$525

W-1810-K • F-2008K • Dallas • 25,642,620

EF-40	AU-50	Unc-60	Unc-63	Unc-65
$15	$25	$35	$55	$90

W-1810-K★ • F-2008K★

VG-8	F-12	VF-20	EF-40	AU-50	Unc-60	Unc-63	Unc-65
$20	$40	$65	$100	$170	$250	$350	$575

W-1810-L • F-2008L • San Francisco • 49,164,480

EF-40	AU-50	Unc-60	Unc-63	Unc-65
$15	$25	$35	$45	$75

W-1810-L★ • F-2008L★

VG-8	F-12	VF-20	EF-40	AU-50	Unc-60	Unc-63	Unc-65
$25	$50	$75	$120	$190	$300	$400	$650

Series of 1934-C, Green Seal, Narrow Face, Kansas City
Julian-Snyder (1946–1949)

The later, Narrow Face style is seen only on Federal Reserve Bank of Kansas City notes in the Series of 1934-C, this being the general style used widely in later series. The space between the design elements at the left and right and the nearby border is slightly tighter on this issue. These are only from face plates numbered 86 to 89.

W-1811-J • F-2008J • Kansas City • Part of W-1810-J printage
Commentary: Current market information unavailable.

W-1811-J★ • F-2008J★ • Unknown

Series of 1934-D, Green Seal
Clark-Snyder (1949–1953)

This series continued the preceding design.

W-1812-A • F-2009A • Boston • 19,917,900

VF-20	EF-40	AU-50	Unc-60	Unc-63	Unc-65
$15	$20	$30	$45	$60	$85

W-1812-A★ • F-2009A★

VG-8	F-12	VF-20	EF-40	AU-50	Unc-60	Unc-63	Unc-65
$25	$50	$75	$130	$200	$300	$400	$575

W-1812-B • F-2009B • New York • 64,067,904

EF-40	AU-50	Unc-60	Unc-63	Unc-65
$15	$25	$40	$55	$80

W-1812-B★ • F-2009B★

VG-8	F-12	VF-20	EF-40	AU-50	Unc-60	Unc-63	Unc-65
$20	$40	$65	$115	$175	$250	$350	$525

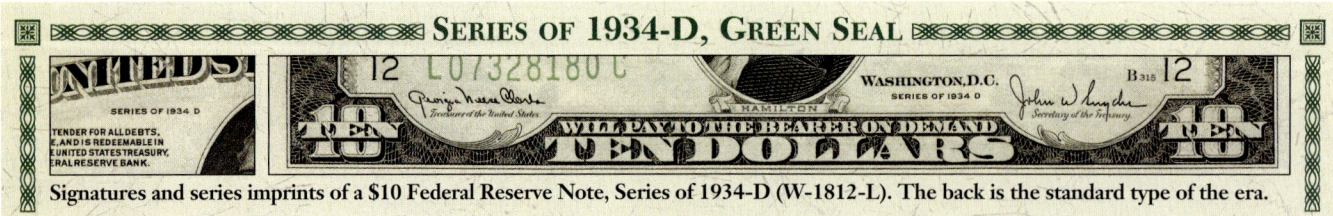

SERIES OF 1934-D, GREEN SEAL

Signatures and series imprints of a $10 Federal Reserve Note, Series of 1934-D (W-1812-L). The back is the standard type of the era.

W-1812-C • F-2009C • Philadelphia • 18,432,000

VF-20	EF-40	AU-50	Unc-60	Unc-63	Unc-65
$15	$20	$30	$45	$60	$85

W-1812-C★ • F-2009C★

VG-8	F-12	VF-20	EF-40	AU-50	Unc-60	Unc-63	Unc-65
$20	$40	$65	$115	$175	$250	$350	$525

W-1812-D • F-2009D • Cleveland • 20,291,316

VF-20	EF-40	AU-50	Unc-60	Unc-63	Unc-65
$15	$20	$30	$45	$60	$85

W-1812-D★ • F-2009D★

VG-8	F-12	VF-20	EF-40	AU-50	Unc-60	Unc-63	Unc-65
$20	$40	$65	$115	$175	$250	$350	$525

W-1812-E • F-2009E • Richmond • 18,090,312

EF-40	AU-50	Unc-60	Unc-63	Unc-65
$20	$30	$45	$60	$80

W-1812-E★ • F-2009E★

VG-8	F-12	VF-20	EF-40	AU-50	Unc-60	Unc-63	Unc-65
$50	$100	$150	$200	$275	$375	$500	$700

W-1812-F • F-2009F • Atlanta • 17,064,816

EF-40	AU-50	Unc-60	Unc-63	Unc-65
$20	$30	$45	$60	$85

W-1812-F★ • F-2009F★

VG-8	F-12	VF-20	EF-40	AU-50	Unc-60	Unc-63	Unc-65
$25	$50	$75	$200	$275	$375	$400	$575

W-1812-G • F-2009G • Chicago • 55,943,844

EF-40	AU-50	Unc-60	Unc-63	Unc-65
$20	$30	$40	$55	$80

W-1812-G★ • F-2009G★

VG-8	F-12	VF-20	EF-40	AU-50	Unc-60	Unc-63	Unc-65
$20	$40	$65	$115	$175	$250	$350	$525

W-1812-H • F-2009H • St. Louis • 15,828,048

VF-20	EF-40	AU-50	Unc-60	Unc-63	Unc-65
$15	$25	$40	$60	$75	$110

W-1812-H★ • F-2009H★

VG-8	F-12	VF-20	EF-40	AU-50	Unc-60	Unc-63	Unc-65
$25	$50	$75	$130	$200	$325	$450	$650

W-1812-I • F-2009I • Minneapolis • 5,237,220

VF-20	EF-40	AU-50	Unc-60	Unc-63	Unc-65
$15	$20	$50	$70	$95	$130

W-1812-I★ • F-2009I★

VG-8	F-12	VF-20	EF-40	AU-50	Unc-60	Unc-63	Unc-65
$35	$70	$110	$130	$200	$325	$450	$650

W-1812-J • F-2009J • Kansas City • 7,992,000

EF-40	AU-50	Unc-60	Unc-63	Unc-65
$20	$30	$45	$60	$95

W-1812-J★ • F-2009J★

VG-8	F-12	VF-20	EF-40	AU-50	Unc-60	Unc-63	Unc-65
$25	$50	$75	$130	$200	$325	$500	$700

W-1812-K • F-2009K • Dallas • 7,178,196

VF-20	EF-40	AU-50	Unc-60	Unc-63	Unc-65
$15	$20	$40	$60	$75	$110

W-1812-K★ • F-2009K★

VG-8	F-12	VF-20	EF-40	AU-50	Unc-60	Unc-63	Unc-65
$25	$50	$75	$130	$200	$325	$500	$700

W-1812-L • F-2009L • San Francisco • 23,956,584

EF-40	AU-50	Unc-60	Unc-63	Unc-65
$20	$40	$60	$75	$110

W-1812-L★ • F-2009L★

VG-8	F-12	VF-20	EF-40	AU-50	Unc-60	Unc-63	Unc-65
$35	$70	$110	$130	$200	$325	$500	$700

Series of 1950, Green Seal, Wide Back
Clark-Snyder (1949–1953)

The Federal Reserve seal is smaller on these notes (illus. on p. 414) and has a spiked border. The wording above that seal reads, "This note is legal tender for all debts, public and private, and is redeemable in lawful money at the United States Treasury, or at any Federal Reserve Bank." The series designation is at the lower right of the portrait.

Back plates are serially numbered 1389 and lower.

W-1813-A • F-2010A • Boston • 70,992,000

EF-40	AU-50	Unc-60	Unc-63	Unc-65
$15	$25	$45	$75	$100

W-1813-A★ • F-2010A★ • 1,008,000

F-12	VF-20	EF-40	AU-50	Unc-60	Unc-63	Unc-65
$30	$55	$120	$200	$300	$450	$600

W-1813-B • F-2010B • New York • 218,576,000

EF-40	AU-50	Unc-60	Unc-63	Unc-65
$15	$25	$45	$70	$95

W-1813-B★ • F-2010B★ • 2,586,000

F-12	VF-20	EF-40	AU-50	Unc-60	Unc-63	Unc-65
$25	$50	$115	$175	$250	$400	$550

W-1813-C • F-2010C • Philadelphia • 76,320,000

EF-40	AU-50	Unc-60	Unc-63	Unc-65
$15	$25	$45	$70	$95

W-1813-C★ • F-2010C★ • 1,008,000

F-12	VF-20	EF-40	AU-50	Unc-60	Unc-63	Unc-65
$30	$55	$120	$200	$300	$450	$600

W-1813-D • F-2010D • Cleveland • 76,032,000

EF-40	AU-50	Unc-60	Unc-63	Unc-65
$15	$25	$45	$70	$95

W-1813-D★ • F-2010D★ • 1,008,000

F-12	VF-20	EF-40	AU-50	Unc-60	Unc-63	Unc-65
$30	$55	$120	$200	$300	$450	$600

W-1813-E • F-2010E • Richmond • 61,776,000

EF-40	AU-50	Unc-60	Unc-63	Unc-65
$15	$25	$45	$70	$95

W-1813-E★ • F-2010E★ • 876,000

F-12	VF-20	EF-40	AU-50	Unc-60	Unc-63	Unc-65
$35	$65	$125	$215	$300	$450	$600

W-1813-F • F-2010F • Atlanta • 63,792,000

EF-40	AU-50	Unc-60	Unc-63	Unc-65
$15	$25	$45	$70	$95

W-1813-F★ • F-2010F★ • 864,000

F-12	VF-20	EF-40	AU-50	Unc-60	Unc-63	Unc-65
$45	$100	$160	$240	$375	$550	$750

W-1813-G • F-2010G • Chicago • 161,056,000

EF-40	AU-50	Unc-60	Unc-63	Unc-65
$15	$25	$45	$70	$95

W-1813-G★ • F-2010G★ • 2,088,000

F-12	VF-20	EF-40	AU-50	Unc-60	Unc-63	Unc-65
$35	$65	$125	$215	$300	$450	$600

W-1813-H • F-2010H • St. Louis • 47,808,000

EF-40	AU-50	Unc-60	Unc-63	Unc-65
$15	$25	$45	$70	$95

W-1813-H★ • F-2010H★ • 648,000

F-12	VF-20	EF-40	AU-50	Unc-60	Unc-63	Unc-65
$40	$75	$140	$230	$350	$500	$700

W-1813-I • F-2010I • Minneapolis • 18,864,000

EF-40	AU-50	Unc-60	Unc-63	Unc-65
$15	$30	$50	$85	$125

W-1813-I★ • F-2010I★ • 552,000

VG-8	F-12	VF-20	EF-40	AU-50	Unc-60	Unc-63	Unc-65
$40	$65	$125	$200	$375	$500	$750	$1,100

W-1813-J • F-2010J • Kansas City • 36,332,000

EF-40	AU-50	Unc-60	Unc-63	Unc-65
$15	$25	$50	$75	$100

W-1813-J★ • F-2010J★ • 456,000

VG-8	F-12	VF-20	EF-40	AU-50	Unc-60	Unc-63	Unc-65
$25	$45	$90	$150	$250	$375	$550	$800

W-1813-K • F-2010K • Dallas • 33,264,000

EF-40	AU-50	Unc-60	Unc-63	Unc-65
$15	$25	$50	$75	$100

W-1813-K★ • F-2010K★ • 480,000

F-12	VF-20	EF-40	AU-50	Unc-60	Unc-63	Unc-65
$40	$80	$135	$225	$350	$500	$700

W-1813-L • F-2010L • San Francisco • 76,896,000

EF-40	AU-50	Unc-60	Unc-63	Unc-65
$15	$25	$50	$75	$100

SERIES OF 1950, GREEN SEAL

$10 Federal Reserve Note, Series of 1950 (W-1813-I). Federal Reserve Bank of Minneapolis. The back is the same as used on other $10 notes through the 1950s.

Detail of the Wide Back style used on the W-1813 group. Similar differences can be found with W-1757 and W-1758.

Detail of the Narrow Back style used on the W-1814 group. Similar differences can be found with W-1757 and W-1758.

W-1813-L★ • F-2010L★ • 1,152,000

F-12	VF-20	EF-40	AU-50	Unc-60	Unc-63	Unc-65
$35	$70	$130	$225	$350	$500	$700

Series of 1950, Green Seal, Narrow Back
Clark-Snyder (1949–1953)

This series continued the preceding design. Plates of the Narrow Back style are serially numbered 1390 to 1456.

Prices for a typical note for this series, unless listed otherwise, are as follows:

VF-20	EF-40	AU-50	Unc-60	Unc-63	Unc-65
$22	$45	$70	$100	$135	$175

Prices for a typical star note for this series, unless listed otherwise, are as follows:

VG-8	F-12	VF-20	EF-40	AU-50	Unc-60	Unc-63	Unc-65
$45	$95	$150	$275	$400	$600	$750	$900

W-1814-A • F-2010A • Boston • Part of W-1813-A printage

W-1814-A★ • F-2010A★

W-1814-B • F-2010B • New York • Part of W-1813-B printage

W-1814-B★ • F-2010B★

W-1814-C • F-2010C • Philadelphia • Part of W-1813-C printage

W-1814-C★ • F-2010C★

W-1814-D • F-2010D • Cleveland • Part of W-1813-D printage

W-1814-D★ • F-2010D★

W-1814-E • F-2010E • Richmond • Part of W-1813-E printage

W-1814-E★ • F-2010E★

W-1814-F • F-2010F • Atlanta • Part of W-1813-F printage

W-1814-G • F-2010G • Chicago • Part of W-1813-G printage

W-1814-G★ • F-2010G★

W-1814-H • F-2010H • St. Louis • Part of W-1813-H printage

W-1814-H★ • F-2010H★

W-1814-I • F-2010I • Minneapolis • Part of W-1813-I printage

VF-20	EF-40	AU-50	Unc-60	Unc-63	Unc-65
$25	$55	$100	$140	$200	$250

W-1814-I★ • F-2010I★

W-1814-J • F-2010J • Kansas City • Part of W-1813-J printage

W-1814-J★ • F-2010J★

W-1814-K • F-2010K • Dallas • Part of W-1813-K printage

VF-20	EF-40	AU-50	Unc-60	Unc-63	Unc-65
$25	$50	$80	$115	$150	$200

W-1814-K★ • F-2010K★

W-1814-L • F-2010L • San Francisco • Part of W-1813-L printage

W-1814-L★ • F-2010L★

Series of 1950-A, Green Seal
Priest-Humphrey (1953–1957)

This series continued the preceding design.

Prices for a typical note for this series, unless listed otherwise, are as follows:

EF-40	AU-50	Unc-60	Unc-63	Unc-65
$15	$25	$45	$65	$100

W-1815-A • F-2011A • Boston • 104,248,000

W-1815-A★ • F-2011A★ • 5,112,000

F-12	VF-20	EF-40	AU-50	Unc-60	Unc-63	Unc-65
$25	$45	$90	$140	$190	$225	$300

W-1815-B • F-2011B • New York • 356,664,000

W-1815-B★ • F-2011B★ • 16,992,000

F-12	VF-20	EF-40	AU-50	Unc-60	Unc-63	Unc-65
$25	$45	$70	$95	$130	$175	$240

W-1815-C • F-2011C • Philadelphia • 71,920,000

W-1815-C★ • F-2011C★ • 3,672,000

F-12	VF-20	EF-40	AU-50	Unc-60	Unc-63	Unc-65
$25	$45	$100	$160	$205	$260	$350

W-1815-D • F-2011D • Cleveland • 75,088,000

W-1815-D★ • F-2011D★ • 3,672,000

F-12	VF-20	EF-40	AU-50	Unc-60	Unc-63	Unc-65
$25	$45	$120	$200	$270	$350	$450

W-1815-E • F-2011E • Richmond • 82,144,000

W-1815-E★ • F-2011E★ • 4,392,000

F-12	VF-20	EF-40	AU-50	Unc-60	Unc-63	Unc-65
$25	$45	$100	$160	$205	$260	$350

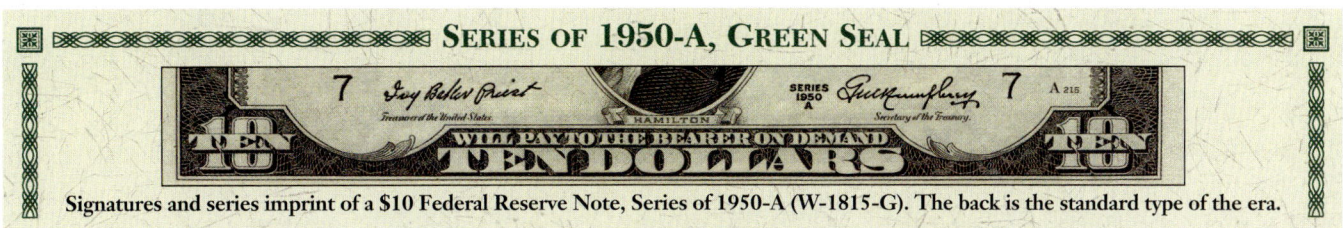

SERIES OF 1950-A, GREEN SEAL

Signatures and series imprint of a $10 Federal Reserve Note, Series of 1950-A (W-1815-G). The back is the standard type of the era.

W-1815-F • F-2011F • Atlanta • 73,288,000

W-1815-F★ • F-2011F★ • 3,816,000

F-12	VF-20	EF-40	AU-50	Unc-60	Unc-63	Unc-65
$25	$45	$125	$220	$300	$425	$600

W-1815-G • F-2011G • Chicago • 235,064,000

EF-40	AU-50	Unc-60	Unc-63	Unc-65
$15	$25	$40	$60	$95

W-1815-G★ • F-2011G★ • 11,160,000

F-12	VF-20	EF-40	AU-50	Unc-60	Unc-63	Unc-65
$25	$45	$120	$200	$270	$350	$500

W-1815-H • F-2011H • St. Louis • 46,512,000

EF-40	AU-50	Unc-60	Unc-63	Unc-65
$15	$25	$40	$60	$95

W-1815-H★ • F-2011H★ • 2,880,000

F-12	VF-20	EF-40	AU-50	Unc-60	Unc-63	Unc-65
$25	$45	$95	$175	$245	$325	$450

W-1815-I • F-2011I • Minneapolis • 8,136,000

EF-40	AU-50	Unc-60	Unc-63	Unc-65
$15	$35	$60	$95	$140

W-1815-I★ • F-2011I★ • 432,000

F-12	VF-20	EF-40	AU-50	Unc-60	Unc-63	Unc-65
$35	$65	$95	$175	$245	$325	$450

W-1815-J • F-2011J • Kansas City • 25,488,000

W-1815-J★ • F-2011J★ • 2,304,000

F-12	VF-20	EF-40	AU-50	Unc-60	Unc-63	Unc-65
$35	$60	$120	$200	$270	$350	$450

W-1815-K • F-2011K • Dallas • 21,816,000

W-1815-K★ • F-2011K★ • 1,584,000

F-12	VF-20	EF-40	AU-50	Unc-60	Unc-63	Unc-65
$35	$60	$120	$170	$225	$300	$400

W-1815-L • F-2011L • San Francisco • 101,584,000

W-1815-L★ • F-2011L★ • 6,408,000

F-12	VF-20	EF-40	AU-50	Unc-60	Unc-63	Unc-65
$35	$60	$100	$145	$185	$225	$300

Series of 1950-B, Green Seal
Priest-Anderson (1957–1961)

This series continued the preceding design.

W-1816-A • F-2012A • Boston • 49,240,000

AU-50	Unc-60	Unc-63	Unc-65
$15	$25	$40	$55

W-1816-A★ • F-2012A★ • 2,880,000

EF-40	AU-50	Unc-60	Unc-63	Unc-65
$35	$70	$100	$135	$200

W-1816-B • F-2012B • New York • 170,840,000

AU-50	Unc-60	Unc-63	Unc-65
$15	$20	$35	$50

W-1816-B★ • F-2012B★ • 8,280,000

EF-40	AU-50	Unc-60	Unc-63	Unc-65
$25	$60	$90	$125	$190

W-1816-C • F-2012C • Philadelphia • 66,880,000

AU-50	Unc-60	Unc-63	Unc-65
$15	$25	$40	$55

W-1816-C★ • F-2012C★ • 3,240,000

EF-40	AU-50	Unc-60	Unc-63	Unc-65
$45	$80	$110	$145	$215

W-1816-D • F-2012D • Cleveland • 55,360,000

AU-50	Unc-60	Unc-63	Unc-65
$15	$20	$35	$50

W-1816-D★ • F-2012D★ • 2,880,000

VF-20	EF-40	AU-50	Unc-60	Unc-63	Unc-65
$30	$50	$85	$115	$150	$225

W-1816-E • F-2012E • Richmond • 51,120,000

AU-50	Unc-60	Unc-63	Unc-65
$15	$20	$35	$50

W-1816-E★ • F-2012E★ • 2,880,000

VF-20	EF-40	AU-50	Unc-60	Unc-63	Unc-65
$40	$80	$125	$200	$300	$440

W-1816-F • F-2012F • Atlanta • 66,520,000

AU-50	Unc-60	Unc-63	Unc-65
$15	$20	$35	$50

SERIES OF 1950-B, GREEN SEAL

Signatures and series imprint of a $10 Federal Reserve Note, Series of 1950-B (W-1816-D). The back is the standard type of the era.

W-1816-F★ • F-2012F★ • 2,880,000

VF-20	EF-40	AU-50	Unc-60	Unc-63	Unc-65
$30	$50	$85	$115	$150	$225

W-1816-G • F-2012G • Chicago • 165,080,000

AU-50	Unc-60	Unc-63	Unc-65
$15	$20	$35	$50

W-1816-G★ • F-2012G★ • 6,480,000

EF-40	AU-50	Unc-60	Unc-63	Unc-65
$25	$60	$90	$125	$190

W-1816-H • F-2012H • St. Louis • 33,040,000

AU-50	Unc-60	Unc-63	Unc-65
$15	$20	$35	$50

W-1816-H★ • F-2012H★ • 1,800,000

VF-20	EF-40	AU-50	Unc-60	Unc-63	Unc-65
$35	$60	$95	$130	$175	$275

W-1816-I • F-2012I • Minneapolis • 13,320,000

AU-50	Unc-60	Unc-63	Unc-65
$15	$25	$40	$55

W-1816-I★ • F-2012I★ • 720,000

VF-20	EF-40	AU-50	Unc-60	Unc-63	Unc-65
$40	$80	$125	$200	$300	$440

W-1816-J • F-2012J • Kansas City • 33,480,000

AU-50	Unc-60	Unc-63	Unc-65
$15	$25	$40	$55

W-1816-J★ • F-2012J★ • 2,520,000

VF-20	EF-40	AU-50	Unc-60	Unc-63	Unc-65
$30	$50	$85	$115	$150	$225

W-1816-K • F-2012K • Dallas • 26,280,000

AU-50	Unc-60	Unc-63	Unc-65
$15	$25	$40	$55

W-1816-K★ • F-2012K★ • 1,440,000

VF-20	EF-40	AU-50	Unc-60	Unc-63	Unc-65
$35	$60	$100	$165	$250	$340

W-1816-L • F-2012L • San Francisco • 55,000,000

AU-50	Unc-60	Unc-63	Unc-65
$15	$25	$40	$55

W-1816-L★ • F-2012L★ • 2,880,000

VF-20	EF-40	AU-50	Unc-60	Unc-63	Unc-65
$35	$60	$95	$130	$175	$275

Series of 1950-C, Green Seal
Smith-Dillon (1961–1962)

This series continued the preceding design. After this time the use of Silver Certificates was diminished, then terminated. Federal Reserve Notes became the mainstay of the currency.

W-1817-A • F-2013A • Boston • 51,120,000

AU-50	Unc-60	Unc-63	Unc-65
$15	$30	$45	$60

W-1817-A★ • F-2013A★ • 2,160,000

EF-40	AU-50	Unc-60	Unc-63	Unc-65
$40	$75	$150	$275	$400

W-1817-B • F-2013B • New York • 126,520,000

AU-50	Unc-60	Unc-63	Unc-65
$15	$30	$45	$60

W-1817-B★ • F-2013B★ • 6,840,000

AU-50	Unc-60	Unc-63	Unc-65
$35	$70	$175	$260

W-1817-C • F-2013C • Philadelphia • 25,200,000

AU-50	Unc-60	Unc-63	Unc-65
$15	$30	$45	$60

W-1817-C★ • F-2013C★ • 720,000

EF-40	AU-50	Unc-60	Unc-63	Unc-65
$45	$90	$175	$300	$450

W-1817-D • F-2013D • Cleveland • 33,120,000

AU-50	Unc-60	Unc-63	Unc-65
$15	$40	$60	$85

W-1817-D★ • F-2013D★ • 1,800,000

EF-40	AU-50	Unc-60	Unc-63	Unc-65
$45	$90	$175	$300	$450

W-1817-E • F-2013E • Richmond • 45,640,000

AU-50	Unc-60	Unc-63	Unc-65
$15	$35	$50	$65

SERIES OF 1950-C, GREEN SEAL

Signatures and series imprint of a $10 Federal Reserve Note, Series of 1950-C (W-1817-I). The back is the standard type of the era.

W-1817-E★ • F-2013E★ • 1,800,000

EF-40	AU-50	Unc-60	Unc-63	Unc-65
$55	$100	$200	$350	$500

W-1817-F • F-2013F • Atlanta • 38,880,000

AU-50	Unc-60	Unc-63	Unc-65
$15	$30	$45	$60

W-1817-F★ • F-2013F★ • 2,880,000

EF-40	AU-50	Unc-60	Unc-63	Unc-65
$40	$85	$175	$300	$450

W-1817-G • F-2013G • Chicago • 69,400,000

AU-50	Unc-60	Unc-63	Unc-65
$15	$30	$45	$60

W-1817-G★ • F-2013G★ • 3,600,000

AU-50	Unc-60	Unc-63	Unc-65
$35	$70	$175	$260

W-1817-H • F-2013H • St. Louis • 23,040,000

AU-50	Unc-60	Unc-63	Unc-65
$20	$45	$65	$90

W-1817-H★ • F-2013H★ • 1,080,000

EF-40	AU-50	Unc-60	Unc-63	Unc-65
$25	$50	$100	$225	$350

W-1817-I • F-2013I • Minneapolis • 9,000,000

AU-50	Unc-60	Unc-63	Unc-65
$30	$55	$75	$100

W-1817-I★ • F-2013I★ • 720,000

EF-40	AU-50	Unc-60	Unc-63	Unc-65
$50	$100	$200	$350	$500

W-1817-J • F-2013J • Kansas City • 23,320,000

AU-50	Unc-60	Unc-63	Unc-65
$20	$45	$65	$90

W-1817-J★ • F-2013J★ • 800,000

EF-40	AU-50	Unc-60	Unc-63	Unc-65
$30	$60	$120	$250	$375

W-1817-K • F-2013K • Dallas • 17,640,000

AU-50	Unc-60	Unc-63	Unc-65
$15	$40	$60	$85

W-1817-K★ • F-2013K★ • 720,000

EF-40	AU-50	Unc-60	Unc-63	Unc-65
$30	$60	$120	$250	$350

W-1817-L • F-2013L • San Francisco • 35,640,000

AU-50	Unc-60	Unc-63	Unc-65
$20	$45	$65	$90

W-1817-L★ • F-2013L★ • 1,800,000

EF-40	AU-50	Unc-60	Unc-63	Unc-65
$30	$60	$125	$225	$350

Series of 1950-D, Green Seal
Granahan-Dillon (1963–1965)

This series continued the preceding design. None were printed for Minneapolis.

W-1818-A • F-2014A • Boston • 38,800,000

Unc-60	Unc-63	Unc-65
$30	$45	$65

W-1818-A★ • F-2014A★ • 1,800,000

EF-40	AU-50	Unc-60	Unc-63	Unc-65
$40	$90	$120	$175	$280

W-1818-B • F-2014B • New York • 150,320,000

Unc-60	Unc-63	Unc-65
$25	$40	$60

W-1818-B★ • F-2014B★ • 6,840,000

EF-40	AU-50	Unc-60	Unc-63	Unc-65
$30	$60	$100	$150	$225

W-1818-C • F-2014C • Philadelphia • 19,080,000

Unc-60	Unc-63	Unc-65
$35	$50	$75

W-1818-C★ • F-2014C★ • 1,080,000

EF-40	AU-50	Unc-60	Unc-63	Unc-65
$40	$90	$120	$175	$275

W-1818-D • F-2014D • Cleveland • 24,120,000

Unc-60	Unc-63	Unc-65
$35	$50	$75

W-1818-D★ • F-2014D★ • 360,000

EF-40	AU-50	Unc-60	Unc-63	Unc-65
$40	$90	$120	$175	$275

SERIES OF 1950-D, GREEN SEAL

Signatures and series imprint of a $10 Federal Reserve Note, Series of 1950-D (W-1818-F). The back is the standard type of the era.

W-1818-E • F-2014E • Richmond • 33,840,000

Unc-60	Unc-63	Unc-65
$35	$50	$75

W-1818-E★ • F-2014E★ • 720,000

EF-40	AU-50	Unc-60	Unc-63	Unc-65
$50	$100	$150	$225	$325

W-1818-F • F-2014F • Atlanta • 36,000,000

Unc-60	Unc-63	Unc-65
$30	$45	$65

W-1818-F★ • F-2014F★ • 1,440,000

EF-40	AU-50	Unc-60	Unc-63	Unc-65
$50	$100	$150	$225	$325

W-1818-G • F-2014G • Chicago • 115,480,000

Unc-60	Unc-63	Unc-65
$25	$40	$60

W-1818-G★ • F-2014G★ • 5,040,000

EF-40	AU-50	Unc-60	Unc-63	Unc-65
$40	$90	$120	$175	$280

W-1818-H • F-2014H • St. Louis • 10,440,000

Unc-60	Unc-63	Unc-65
$35	$50	$75

W-1818-H★ • F-2014H★ • 720,000

EF-40	AU-50	Unc-60	Unc-63	Unc-65
$65	$120	$175	$250	$375

W-1818-J • F-2014J • Kansas City • 15,480,000

Unc-60	Unc-63	Unc-65
$30	$45	$65

W-1818-J★ • F-2014J★ • 1,080,000

EF-40	AU-50	Unc-60	Unc-63	Unc-65
$65	$120	$150	$225	$350

W-1818-K • F-2014K • Dallas • 18,280,000

Unc-60	Unc-63	Unc-65
$35	$50	$75

W-1818-K★ • F-2014K★ • 800,000

EF-40	AU-50	Unc-60	Unc-63	Unc-65
$50	$100	$150	$225	$325

W-1818-L • F-2014L • San Francisco • 62,560,000

Unc-60	Unc-63	Unc-65
$30	$45	$65

W-1818-L★ • F-2014L★ • 3,600,000

EF-40	AU-50	Unc-60	Unc-63	Unc-65
$50	$100	$150	$225	$325

Series of 1950-E, Green Seal
Granahan-Fowler (1965–1966)

The Series of 1950-E continued the preceding design. This series is remarkable for having been issued by just three Federal Reserve Banks, similar to the $5 notes of this issue.

W-1819-B • F-2015B • New York • 12,600,000

AU-50	Unc-60	Unc-63	Unc-65
$35	$70	$95	$125

W-1819-B★ • F-2015B★ • 2,621,000

VF-20	EF-40	AU-50	Unc-60	Unc-63	Unc-65
$60	$125	$185	$250	$325	$450

W-1819-G • F-2015G • Chicago • 65,080,000

AU-50	Unc-60	Unc-63	Unc-65
$40	$75	$100	$140

W-1819-G★ • F-2015G★ • 4,320,000

VF-20	EF-40	AU-50	Unc-60	Unc-63	Unc-65
$60	$125	$165	$220	$275	$400

W-1819-L • F-2015L • San Francisco • 17,280,000

AU-50	Unc-60	Unc-63	Unc-65
$40	$80	$110	$160

W-1819-L★ • F-2015L★ • 720,000

VF-20	EF-40	AU-50	Unc-60	Unc-63	Unc-65
$85	$150	$220	$275	$375	$525

Series of 1963, Green Seal
Granahan-Dillon (1963–1965)

The Series of 1963 (illus. on p. 420) introduces a new back with the motto IN GOD WE TRUST curved in the field above the Treasury Building. The face displays some changes as well. The redemption feature above the Federal Reserve seal to the left now is in two lines: "This note is legal tender for all debts, public and private." The lower right plate letter and number are in a slightly higher position.

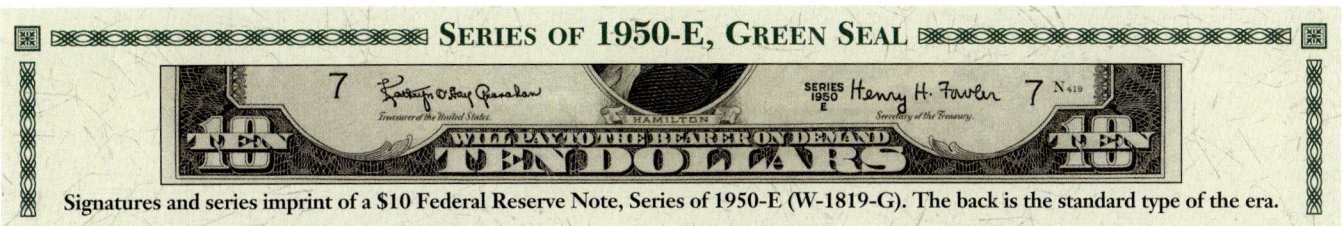

SERIES OF 1950-E, GREEN SEAL

Signatures and series imprint of a $10 Federal Reserve Note, Series of 1950-E (W-1819-G). The back is the standard type of the era.

This series was not issued by Minneapolis (I).

Prices for a typical note for this series, unless listed otherwise, are as follows:

AU-50	Unc-60	Unc-63	Unc-65
$15	$35	$45	$65

W-1820-A • F-2016A • Boston • 5,760,000

W-1820-A★ • F-2016A★ • 640,000

AU-50	Unc-60	Unc-63	Unc-65
$40	$85	$120	$160

W-1820-B • F-2016B • New York • 24,960,000

W-1820-B★ • F-2016B★ • 1,920,000

AU-50	Unc-60	Unc-63	Unc-65
$35	$65	$100	$135

W-1820-C • F-2016C • Philadelphia • 6,400,000

W-1820-C★ • F-2016C★ • 1,280,000

AU-50	Unc-60	Unc-63	Unc-65
$35	$65	$100	$135

W-1820-D • F-2016D • Cleveland • 7,040,000

W-1820-D★ • F-2016D★ • 640,000

AU-50	Unc-60	Unc-63	Unc-65
$40	$75	$110	$145

W-1820-E • F-2016E • Richmond • 4,480,000

W-1820-E★ • F-2016E★ • 640,000

AU-50	Unc-60	Unc-63	Unc-65
$70	$120	$150	$190

W-1820-F • F-2016F • Atlanta • 10,880,000

W-1820-F★ • F-2016F★ • 1,280,000

AU-50	Unc-60	Unc-63	Unc-65
$35	$65	$100	$135

W-1820-G • F-2016G • Chicago • 35,200,000

W-1820-G★ • F-2016G★ • 2,560,000

AU-50	Unc-60	Unc-63	Unc-65
$35	$65	$100	$135

W-1820-H • F-2016H • St. Louis • 13,440,000

AU-50	Unc-60	Unc-63	Unc-65
$20	$50	$65	$90

W-1820-H★ • F-2016H★ • 1,280,000

AU-50	Unc-60	Unc-63	Unc-65
$60	$100	$140	$180

W-1820-J • F-2016J • Kansas City • 3,840,000

AU-50	Unc-60	Unc-63	Unc-65
$20	$45	$60	$80

SERIES OF 1963, GREEN SEAL

$10 Federal Reserve Note, Series of 1963 (W-1820-G★). Federal Reserve Bank of Chicago. Star note.

Back of $10 Federal Reserve Note, Series of 1963 (W-1820-G★), introducing new back design, with IN GOD WE TRUST.

W-1820-J★ • F-2016J★ • 640,000

EF-40	AU-50	Unc-60	Unc-63	Unc-65
$50	$90	$140	$175	$225

W-1820-K • F-2016K • Dallas • 5,120,000

AU-50	Unc-60	Unc-63	Unc-65
$15	$40	$55	$75

W-1820-K★ • F-2016K★ • 640,000

EF-40	AU-50	Unc-60	Unc-63	Unc-65
$35	$70	$115	$150	$195

W-1820-L • F-2016L • San Francisco • 14,080,000

AU-50	Unc-60	Unc-63	Unc-65
$15	$40	$50	$70

W-1820-L★ • F-2016L★ • 1,280,000

AU-50	Unc-60	Unc-63	Unc-65
$45	$85	$125	$160

Series of 1963-A, Green Seal
Granahan-Fowler (1965–1966)

This series continued the preceding design.

Prices for a typical note for this series, unless listed otherwise, are as follows:

Unc-60	Unc-63	Unc-65
$30	$40	$55

Prices for a typical star note for this series, unless listed otherwise, are as follows:

Unc-60	Unc-63	Unc-65
$50	$70	$100

W-1821-A • F-2017A • Boston • 131,360,000

W-1821-A★ • F-2017A★ • 6,400,000

W-1821-B • F-2017B • New York • 199,360,000

W-1821-B★ • F-2017B★ • 9,600,000

W-1821-C • F-2017C • Philadelphia • 100,000,000

W-1821-C★ • F-2017C★ • 4,480,000

W-1821-D • F-2017D • Cleveland • 72,960,000

W-1821-D★ • F-2017D★ • 3,840,000

W-1821-E • F-2017E • Richmond • 114,720,000

W-1821-E★ • F-2017E★ • 5,120,000

W-1821-F • F-2017F • Atlanta • 80,000,000

Unc-60	Unc-63	Unc-65
$30	$40	$50

W-1821-F★ • F-2017F★ • 3,840,000

Unc-60	Unc-63	Unc-65
$55	$75	$110

W-1821-G • F-2017G • Chicago • 195,520,000

W-1821-G★ • F-2017G★ • 9,600,000

W-1821-H • F-2017H • St. Louis • 43,520,000

W-1821-H★ • F-2017H★ • 1,920,000

W-1821-I • F-2017I • Minneapolis • 16,640,000

W-1821-I★ • F-2017I★ • 640,000

Unc-60	Unc-63	Unc-65
$80	$100	$125

W-1821-J • F-2017J • Kansas City • 31,360,000

W-1821-J★ • F-2017J★ • 1,920,000

Unc-60	Unc-63	Unc-65
$55	$75	$110

W-1821-K • F-2017K • Dallas • 51,200,000

W-1821-K★ • F-2017K★ • 1,920,000

Unc-60	Unc-63	Unc-65
$55	$75	$110

W-1821-L • F-2017L • San Francisco • 87,200,000

W-1821-L★ • F-2017L★ • 5,120,000

Series of 1969, Green Seal
Elston-Kennedy (1969–1970)

The Series of 1969 notes (illus. on p. 422) feature a redesigned Treasury seal with the inscription, THE DEPARTMENT OF THE TREASURY 1789, replacing the earlier style with the Latin wording, THESAUR. AMER. SEPTENT. SIGIL. The design in the interior of the seal was modified as well.

Prices for a typical note for this series, unless listed otherwise, are as follows:

Unc-60	Unc-63	Unc-65
$20	$35	$50

W-1822-A • F-2018A • Boston • 71,880,000

W-1822-A★ • F-2018A★ • 2,560,000

Unc-60	Unc-63	Unc-65
$50	$65	$85

W-1822-B • F-2018B • New York • 247,360,000

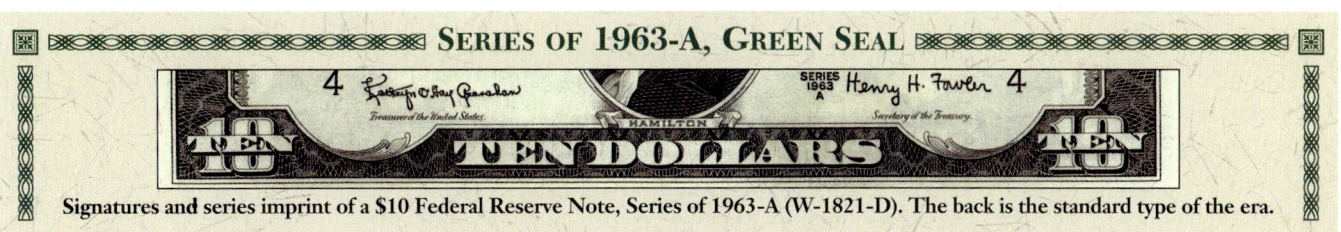

SERIES OF 1963-A, GREEN SEAL

Signatures and series imprint of a $10 Federal Reserve Note, Series of 1963-A (W-1821-D). The back is the standard type of the era.

W-1822-B★ • F-2018B★ • 10,240,000

Unc-60	Unc-63	Unc-65
$50	$65	$85

W-1822-C • F-2018C • Philadelphia • 56,960,000

W-1822-C★ • F-2018C★ • 2,560,000

Unc-60	Unc-63	Unc-65
$50	$65	$85

W-1822-D • F-2018D • Cleveland • 57,600,000

W-1822-D★ • F-2018D★ • 2,560,000

Unc-60	Unc-63	Unc-65
$70	$95	$120

W-1822-E • F-2018E • Richmond • 56,960,000

W-1822-E★ • F-2018E★ • 2,560,000

Unc-60	Unc-63	Unc-65
$70	$95	$120

W-1822-F • F-2018F • Atlanta • 53,760,000

W-1822-F★ • F-2018F★ • 2,560,000

Unc-60	Unc-63	Unc-65
$50	$65	$85

W-1822-G • F-2018G • Chicago • 142,240,000

W-1822-G★ • F-2018G★ • 6,400,000

Unc-60	Unc-63	Unc-65
$50	$65	$85

W-1822-H • F-2018H • St. Louis • 22,400,000

W-1822-H★ • F-2018H★ • 640,000

Unc-60	Unc-63	Unc-65
$140	$200	$325

W-1822-I • F-2018I • Minneapolis • 12,800,000

W-1822-I★ • F-2018I★ • 1,280,000

Unc-60	Unc-63	Unc-65
$55	$70	$90

W-1822-J • F-2018J • Kansas City • 31,360,000

W-1822-J★ • F-2018J★ • 1,280,000

Unc-60	Unc-63	Unc-65
$55	$70	$90

W-1822-K • F-2018K • Dallas • 30,080,000

W-1822-K★ • F-2018K★ • 1,280,000

Unc-60	Unc-63	Unc-65
$55	$70	$90

W-1822-L • F-2018L • San Francisco • 56,320,000

W-1822-L★ • F-2018L★ • 3,185,000

Unc-60	Unc-63	Unc-65
$55	$70	$90

Series of 1969-A, Green Seal
Kabis-Connally (1971)

Treasurer Dorothy Andrews Elson married Walter L. Kabis during her term in office, and became Mrs. Kabis.

This series continued the preceding design. No star notes were printed for Minneapolis (I).

W-1823-A • F-2019A • Boston • 41,120,000

Unc-60	Unc-63	Unc-65
$20	$30	$40

SERIES OF 1969, GREEN SEAL

$10 Federal Reserve Note, Series of 1969 (W-1822-B). Federal Reserve Bank of New York. The back is the same as used on other $10 notes of the era, with IN GOD WE TRUST.

Old (top) and new Treasury seals. W-1822 introduced the new style.

SERIES OF 1969-A, GREEN SEAL

Signatures and series imprint of a $10 Federal Reserve Note, Series of 1969-A (W-1823-G). The back is the standard type of the era.

W-1823-A★ • F-2019A★ • 1,920,000

Unc-60	Unc-63	Unc-65
$35	$50	$70

W-1823-B • F-2019B • New York • 111,840,000

Unc-60	Unc-63	Unc-65
$20	$30	$40

W-1823-B★ • F-2019B★ • 3,840,000

Unc-60	Unc-63	Unc-65
$40	$55	$75

W-1823-C • F-2019C • Philadelphia • 24,320,000

Unc-60	Unc-63	Unc-65
$25	$35	$45

W-1823-C★ • F-2019C★ • 1,920,000

Unc-60	Unc-63	Unc-65
$40	$55	$75

W-1823-D • F-2019D • Cleveland • 23,680,000

Unc-60	Unc-63	Unc-65
$28	$40	$50

W-1823-D★ • F-2019D★ • 1,276,000

Unc-60	Unc-63	Unc-65
$40	$55	$75

W-1823-E • F-2019E • Richmond • 25,600,000

Unc-60	Unc-63	Unc-65
$25	$35	$45

W-1823-E★ • F-2019E★ • 640,000

AU-50	Unc-60	Unc-63	Unc-65
$45	$80	$110	$160

W-1823-F • F-2019F • Atlanta • 13,440,000

Unc-60	Unc-63	Unc-65
$25	$35	$45

W-1823-F★ • F-2019F★ • 640,000

AU-50	Unc-60	Unc-63	Unc-65
$45	$80	$110	$160

W-1823-G • F-2019G • Chicago • 80,160,000

Unc-60	Unc-63	Unc-65
$20	$30	$40

W-1823-G★ • F-2019G★ • 3,560,000

Unc-60	Unc-63	Unc-65
$40	$55	$75

W-1823-H • F-2019H • St. Louis • 15,360,000

Unc-60	Unc-63	Unc-65
$28	$40	$50

W-1823-H★ • F-2019H★ • 640,000

Unc-60	Unc-63	Unc-65
$50	$65	$90

W-1823-I • F-2019I • Minneapolis • 8,320,000

Unc-60	Unc-63	Unc-65
$28	$40	$50

W-1823-J • F-2019J • Kansas City • 10,880,000

Unc-60	Unc-63	Unc-65
$28	$40	$50

W-1823-K • F-2019K • Dallas • 20,480,000

Unc-60	Unc-63	Unc-65
$28	$40	$50

W-1823-K★ • F-2019K★ • 640,000

AU-50	Unc-60	Unc-63	Unc-65
$45	$80	$110	$160

W-1823-L • F-2019L • San Francisco • 23,840,000

Unc-60	Unc-63	Unc-65
$28	$40	$50

W-1823-L★ • F-2019L★ • 640,000

Unc-60	Unc-63	Unc-65
$50	$65	$85

Series of 1969-B, Green Seal
Banuelos-Connally (1971–1972)

This series continued the preceding design. Although each of the 12 Federal Reserve Banks issued regular Series of 1969-B notes, five did not issue star notes.

Prices for a typical note for this series, unless listed otherwise, are as follows:

EF-40	AU-50	Unc-60	Unc-63	Unc-65
$30	$50	$95	$135	$170

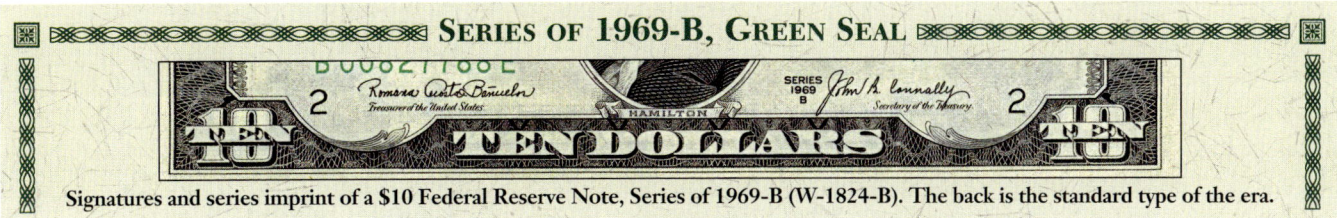

SERIES OF 1969-B, GREEN SEAL

Signatures and series imprint of a $10 Federal Reserve Note, Series of 1969-B (W-1824-B). The back is the standard type of the era.

W-1824-A • F-2020A • Boston • 16,640,000

EF-40	AU-50	Unc-60	Unc-63	Unc-65
$30	$60	$110	$160	$200

W-1824-B • F-2020B • New York • 60,320,000

EF-40	AU-50	Unc-60	Unc-63	Unc-65
$30	$60	$100	$150	$195

W-1824-B★ • F-2020B★ • 1,920,000

VF-20	EF-40	AU-50	Unc-60	Unc-63	Unc-65
$30	$60	$90	$135	$175	$275

W-1824-C • F-2020C • Philadelphia • 16,000,000

W-1824-D • F-2020D • Cleveland • 12,800,000

W-1824-E • F-2020E • Richmond • 12,160,000

W-1824-E★ • F-2020E★ • 640,000

VF-20	EF-40	AU-50	Unc-60	Unc-63	Unc-65
$45	$80	$125	$190	$275	$375

W-1824-F • F-2020F • Atlanta • 13,440,000

W-1824-F★ • F-2020F★ • 640,000

VF-20	EF-40	AU-50	Unc-60	Unc-63	Unc-65
$35	$65	$110	$175	$250	$360

W-1824-G • F-2020G • Chicago • 32,640,000

W-1824-G★ • F-2020G★ • 1,268,000

VF-20	EF-40	AU-50	Unc-60	Unc-63	Unc-65
$25	$50	$100	$160	$225	$325

W-1824-H • F-2020H • St. Louis • 8,960,000

W-1824-H★ • F-2020H★ • 1,280,000

VF-20	EF-40	AU-50	Unc-60	Unc-63	Unc-65
$50	$95	$145	$210	$300	$400

W-1824-I • F-2020I • Minneapolis • 3,200,000

EF-40	AU-50	Unc-60	Unc-63	Unc-65
$60	$100	$140	$185	$290

W-1824-J • F-2020J • Kansas City • 5,120,000

W-1824-J★ • F-2020J★ • 640,000

VF-20	EF-40	AU-50	Unc-60	Unc-63	Unc-65
$45	$80	$125	$190	$275	$375

W-1824-K • F-2020K • Dallas • 5,760,000

EF-40	AU-50	Unc-60	Unc-63	Unc-65
$40	$60	$105	$150	$195

W-1824-L • F-2020L • San Francisco • 23,840,000

EF-40	AU-50	Unc-60	Unc-63	Unc-65
$30	$60	$110	$160	$200

W-1824-L★ • F-2020L★ • 640,000

VF-20	EF-40	AU-50	Unc-60	Unc-63	Unc-65
$45	$80	$125	$190	$275	$375

Series of 1969-C, Green Seal
Banuelos-Shultz (1972–1974)

This series continued the preceding design.

Prices for a typical note for this series, unless listed otherwise, are as follows:

Unc-60	Unc-63	Unc-65
$25	$40	$55

W-1825-A • F-2021A • Boston • 44,800,000

W-1825-A★ • F-2021A★ • 640,000

EF-40	AU-50	Unc-60	Unc-63	Unc-65
$30	$60	$135	$160	$200

W-1825-B • F-2021B • New York • 203,200,000

W-1825-B★ • F-2021B★ • 7,040,000

AU-50	Unc-60	Unc-63	Unc-65
$30	$50	$70	$100

W-1825-C • F-2021C • Philadelphia • 69,920,000

Unc-60	Unc-63	Unc-65
$30	$45	$60

W-1825-C★ • F-2021C★ • 1,280,000

AU-50	Unc-60	Unc-63	Unc-65
$40	$60	$80	$110

W-1825-D • F-2021D • Cleveland • 46,880,000

W-1825-D★ • F-2021D★ • 2,400,000

AU-50	Unc-60	Unc-63	Unc-65
$40	$60	$80	$110

W-1825-E • F-2021E • Richmond • 45,600,000

W-1825-E★ • F-2021E★ • 1,120,000

AU-50	Unc-60	Unc-63	Unc-65
$35	$70	$90	$120

W-1825-F • F-2021F • Atlanta • 46,240,000

SERIES OF 1969-C, GREEN SEAL

Detail of the signatures and the series imprint of a $10 Federal Reserve Note, Series of 1969-C (W-1825-D).
The back is the standard type of the era, with motto.

W-1825-F★ • F-2021F★ • 1,920,000

AU-50	Unc-60	Unc-63	Unc-65
$35	$70	$90	$120

W-1825-G • F-2021G • Chicago • 55,200,000

W-1825-G★ • F-2021G★ • 880,000

AU-50	Unc-60	Unc-63	Unc-65
$40	$60	$80	$110

W-1825-H • F-2021H • St. Louis • 29,800,000

W-1825-H★ • F-2021H★ • 1,280,000

AU-50	Unc-60	Unc-63	Unc-65
$35	$70	$90	$120

W-1825-I • F-2021I • Minneapolis • 11,520,000

W-1825-I★ • F-2021I★ • 640,000

AU-50	Unc-60	Unc-63	Unc-65
$35	$70	$100	$120

W-1825-J • F-2021J • Kansas City • 23,040,000

W-1825-J★ • F-2021J★ • 640,000

EF-40	AU-50	Unc-60	Unc-63	Unc-65
$20	$45	$85	$120	$160

W-1825-K • F-2021K • Dallas • 24,960,000

W-1825-K★ • F-2021K★ • 640,000

EF-40	AU-50	Unc-60	Unc-63	Unc-65
$20	$45	$85	$120	$160

W-1825-L • F-2021L • San Francisco • 56,960,000

W-1825-L★ • F-2021L★ • 640,000

AU-50	Unc-60	Unc-63	Unc-65
$35	$70	$100	$125

Series of 1974, Green Seal
Neff-Simon (1974–1977)

This series continued the preceding design.

Prices for a typical note for this series, unless listed otherwise, are as follows:

Unc-60	Unc-63	Unc-65
$20	$30	$40

W-1826-A • F-2022A • Boston • 104,480,000

W-1826-A★ • F-2022A★ • 2,560,000

Unc-60	Unc-63	Unc-65
$40	$60	$75

W-1826-B • F-2022B • New York • 239,040,000

W-1826-B★ • F-2022B★ • 4,460,000

Unc-60	Unc-63	Unc-65
$40	$60	$75

W-1826-C • F-2022C • Philadelphia • 69,280,000

W-1826-C★ • F-2022C★ • 2,560,000

Unc-60	Unc-63	Unc-65
$40	$60	$75

W-1826-D • F-2022D • Cleveland • 82,080,000

W-1826-D★ • F-2022D★ • 1,920,000

Unc-60	Unc-63	Unc-65
$50	$70	$85

W-1826-E • F-2022E • Richmond • 105,760,000

Unc-60	Unc-63	Unc-65
$25	$35	$45

W-1826-E★ • F-2022E★ • 1,920,000

Unc-60	Unc-63	Unc-65
$35	$55	$70

W-1826-F • F-2022F • Atlanta • 75,520,000

W-1826-F★ • F-2022F★ • 3,200,000

Unc-60	Unc-63	Unc-65
$30	$50	$65

W-1826-G • F-2022G • Chicago • 104,320,000

W-1826-G★ • F-2022G★ • 4,480,000

Unc-60	Unc-63	Unc-65
$30	$50	$65

W-1826-H • F-2022H • St. Louis • 46,240,000

W-1826-H★ • F-2022H★ • 1,280,000

Unc-60	Unc-63	Unc-65
$55	$80	$100

W-1826-I • F-2022I • Minneapolis • 27,520,000

Unc-60	Unc-63	Unc-65
$30	$45	$65

SERIES OF 1974, GREEN SEAL

Detail of the signatures and the series imprint of a $10 Federal Reserve Note, Series of 1974 (W-1826-B). The back is the standard type of the era, with motto.

W-1826-I★ • F-2022I★ • 2,560,000

Unc-60	Unc-63	Unc-65
$80	$105	$130

W-1826-J • F-2022J • Kansas City • 24,320,000

W-1826-J★ • F-2022J★ • 640,000

Unc-60	Unc-63	Unc-65
$35	$55	$70

W-1826-K • F-2022K • Dallas • 39,840,000

W-1826-K★ • F-2022K★ • 1,920,000

Unc-60	Unc-63	Unc-65
$35	$55	$70

W-1826-L • F-2022L • San Francisco • 1,920,000

W-1826-L★ • F-2022L★ • 1,760,000

Unc-60	Unc-63	Unc-65
$35	$55	$70

Series of 1977, Green Seal
Morton-Blumenthal (1977–1979)

This series continued the preceding design.

Prices for a typical note for this series, unless listed otherwise, are as follows:

Unc-60	Unc-63	Unc-65
$25	$35	$45

W-1827-A • F-2023A • Boston • 96,640,000

W-1827-A★ • F-2023A★ • 2,688,000

Unc-60	Unc-63	Unc-65
$65	$85	$115

W-1827-B • F-2023B • New York • 277,120,000

Unc-60	Unc-63	Unc-65
$30	$40	$50

W-1827-B★ • F-2023B★ • 7,168,000

Unc-60	Unc-63	Unc-65
$50	$65	$80

W-1827-C • F-2023C • Philadelphia • 83,200,000

Unc-60	Unc-63	Unc-65
$30	$40	$50

W-1827-C★ • F-2023C★ • 896,000

Unc-60	Unc-63	Unc-65
$75	$100	$130

W-1827-D • F-2023D • Cleveland • 83,200,000

W-1827-D★ • F-2023D★ • 768,000

Unc-60	Unc-63	Unc-65
$75	$100	$130

W-1827-E • F-2023E • Richmond • 71,040,000

W-1827-E★ • F-2023E★ • 1,920,000

Unc-60	Unc-63	Unc-65
$85	$105	$140

W-1827-F • F-2023F • Atlanta • 88,960,000

W-1827-F★ • F-2023F★ • 1,536,000

Unc-60	Unc-63	Unc-65
$60	$80	$110

W-1827-G • F-2023G • Chicago • 174,720,000

W-1827-G★ • F-2023G★ • 3,968,000

Unc-60	Unc-63	Unc-65
$60	$80	$110

W-1827-H • F-2023H • St. Louis • 46,720,000

W-1827-H★ • F-2023H★ • 896,000

Unc-60	Unc-63	Unc-65
$65	$85	$115

W-1827-I • F-2023I • Minneapolis • 10,240,000

Unc-60	Unc-63	Unc-65
$35	$45	$55

W-1827-I★ • F-2023I★ • 256,000

Unc-60	Unc-63	Unc-65
$95	$140	$175

W-1827-J • F-2023J • Kansas City • 50,560,000

W-1827-J★ • F-2023J★ • 896,000

Unc-60	Unc-63	Unc-65
$65	$85	$115

W-1827-K • F-2023K • Dallas • 53,760,000

SERIES OF 1977, GREEN SEAL

Detail of the signatures and the series imprint of a $10 Federal Reserve Note, Series of 1977 (W-1827-D). The back is the standard type of the era, with motto.

W-1827-K★ • F-2023K★ • 640,000

AU-50	Unc-60	Unc-63	Unc-65
$40	$70	$90	$120

W-1827-L • F-2023L • San Francisco • 73,600,000

W-1827-L★ • F-2023L★ • 1,792,000

AU-50	Unc-60	Unc-63	Unc-65
$30	$60	$80	$110

Series of 1977-A, Green Seal
Morton-Miller (1979–1981)

This series continued the preceding design.

Prices for a typical note for this series, unless listed otherwise, are as follows:

Unc-60	Unc-63	Unc-65
$25	$35	$45

W-1828-A • F-2024A • Boston • 83,840,000

Unc-60	Unc-63	Unc-65
$30	$40	$50

W-1828-A★ • F-2024A★ • 1,664,000

AU-50	Unc-60	Unc-63	Unc-65
$35	$75	$95	$115

W-1828-B • F-2024B • New York • 259,280,000

W-1828-B★ • F-2024B★ • 5,248,000

Unc-60	Unc-63	Unc-65
$40	$55	$75

W-1828-C • F-2024C • Philadelphia • 96,000,000

W-1828-C★ • F-2024C★ • 2,048,000

Unc-60	Unc-63	Unc-65
$45	$60	$80

W-1828-D • F-2024D • Cleveland • 44,800,000

W-1828-D★ • F-2024D★ • 2,048,000

Unc-60	Unc-63	Unc-65
$45	$60	$80

W-1828-E • F-2024E • Richmond • 104,320,000

W-1828-E★ • F-2024E★ • 3,072,000

Unc-60	Unc-63	Unc-65
$55	$70	$90

W-1828-F • F-2024F • Atlanta • 33,920,000

W-1828-F★ • F-2024F★ • 640,000

AU-50	Unc-60	Unc-63	Unc-65
$55	$100	$125	$150

W-1828-G • F-2024G • Chicago • 108,160,000

W-1828-G★ • F-2024G★ • 3,200,000

Unc-60	Unc-63	Unc-65
$45	$60	$80

W-1828-H • F-2024H • St. Louis • 27,520,000

W-1828-H★ • F-2024H★ • 640,000

Unc-60	Unc-63	Unc-65
$65	$80	$100

W-1828-I • F-2024I • Minneapolis • 7,680,000

Unc-60	Unc-63	Unc-65
$30	$40	$50

W-1828-I★ • F-2024I★ • 128,000

AU-50	Unc-60	Unc-63	Unc-65
$60	$105	$130	$155

W-1828-J • F-2024J • Kansas City • 40,320,000

Unc-60	Unc-63	Unc-65
$30	$40	$50

W-1828-J★ • F-2024J★ • 2,136,000

AU-50	Unc-60	Unc-63	Unc-65
$35	$70	$85	$105

W-1828-K • F-2024K • Dallas • 60,160,000

W-1828-K★ • F-2024K★ • 4,224,000

Unc-60	Unc-63	Unc-65
$40	$55	$75

W-1828-L • F-2024L • San Francisco • 59,520,000

W-1828-L★ • F-2024L★ • 2,048,000

Unc-60	Unc-63	Unc-65
$45	$60	$80

Series of 1981, Green Seal
Buchanan-Regan (1981–1983)

This series (illus. on p. 428) continued the preceding design. All Federal Reserve Banks issued regular Series 1981 notes, but three did not issue star notes.

SERIES OF 1977-A, GREEN SEAL

Detail of the signatures and the series imprint of a $10 Federal Reserve Note, Series of 1977-A (W-1828-F). The back is the standard type of the era, with motto.

Prices for a typical note for this series, unless listed otherwise, are as follows:

Unc-60	Unc-63	Unc-65
$30	$40	$50

Prices for a typical star note for this series, unless otherwise, are as follows:

AU-50	Unc-60	Unc-63	Unc-65
$35	$85	$110	$145

W-1829-A • F-2025A • Boston • 172,160,000

W-1829-A★ • F-2025A★ • 1,280,000

AU-50	Unc-60	Unc-63	Unc-65
$40	$85	$110	$140

W-1829-B • F-2025B • New York • 434,560,000

W-1829-B★ • F-2025B★ • 1,920,000

W-1829-C • F-2025C • Philadelphia • 131,840,000

W-1829-C★ • F-2025C★ • 632,000

AU-50	Unc-60	Unc-63	Unc-65
$50	$100	$130	$170

W-1829-D • F-2025D • Cleveland • 122,240,000

W-1829-D★ • F-2025D★ • 1,268,000

AU-50	Unc-60	Unc-63	Unc-65
$45	$95	$120	$160

W-1829-E • F-2025E • Richmond • 131,840,000

W-1829-E★ • F-2025E★ • 2,576,000

W-1829-F • F-2025F • Atlanta • 131,840,000

W-1829-F★ • F-2025F★ • 1,908,000

W-1829-G • F-2025G • Chicago • 254,080,000

W-1829-G★ • F-2025G★ • 1,280,000

W-1829-H • F-2025H • St. Louis • 55,280,000

Unc-60	Unc-63	Unc-65
$35	$45	$55

W-1829-I • F-2025I • Minneapolis • 23,680,000

Unc-60	Unc-63	Unc-65
$40	$50	$60

W-1829-I★ • F-2025I★ • 256,000

AU-50	Unc-60	Unc-63	Unc-65
$50	$105	$125	$160

W-1829-J • F-2025J • Kansas City • 53,120,000

W-1829-K • F-2025K • Dallas • 50,560,000

W-1829-L • F-2025L • San Francisco • 144,000,000

W-1829-L★ • F-2025L★ • 1,280,000

Series of 1981-A, Green Seal
Ortega-Regan (1983–1985)

This series continued the preceding design. Although all Federal Reserve Banks issued regular Series of 1981-A notes, only New York (B), Richmond (E), and Atlanta (F) issued star notes.

Prices for a typical note for this series, unless listed otherwise, are as follows:

Unc-60	Unc-63	Unc-65
$25	$35	$45

W-1830-A • F-2026A • Boston • 112,000,000

Unc-60	Unc-63	Unc-65
$30	$40	$50

W-1830-B • F-2026B • New York • 259,000,000

W-1830-B★ • F-2026B★ • 3,200,000

EF-40	AU-50	Unc-60	Unc-63	Unc-65
$45	$95	$195	$275	$400

W-1830-C • F-2026C • Philadelphia • 48,000,000

W-1830-D • F-2026D • Cleveland • 80,000,000

W-1830-E • F-2026E • Richmond • 92,800,000

SERIES OF 1981, GREEN SEAL

Detail of the signatures and the series imprint of a $10 Federal Reserve Note, Series of 1981 (W-1829-F). The back is the standard type of the era, with motto.

SERIES OF 1981-A, GREEN SEAL

Detail of the signatures and the series imprint of a $10 Federal Reserve Note, Series of 1981-A (W-1830-D). The back is the standard type of the era, with motto.

W-1830-E★ • F-2026E★ • 3,200,000

AU-50	Unc-60	Unc-63	Unc-65
$40	$80	$100	$125

W-1830-F • F-2026F • Atlanta • 83,200,000

W-1830-F★ • F-2026F★ • 4,736,000

AU-50	Unc-60	Unc-63	Unc-65
$40	$80	$100	$125

W-1830-G • F-2026G • Chicago • 183,600,000

W-1830-H • F-2026H • St. Louis • 25,600,000

W-1830-I • F-2026I • Minneapolis • 19,200,000

Unc-60	Unc-63	Unc-65
$45	$60	$75

W-1830-J • F-2026J • Kansas City • 48,000,000

W-1830-K • F-2026K • Dallas • 48,000,000

W-1830-L • F-2026L • San Francisco • 115,200,000

Series of 1985, Green Seal
Ortega-Baker (1985–1988)

This series continued the preceding design. Although all Federal Reserve Banks issued regular Series of 1985 notes, several did not issue star notes.

Prices for a typical note for this series, unless listed otherwise, are as follows:

Unc-60	Unc-63	Unc-65
$20	$30	$40

W-1831-A • F-2027A • Boston • 380,800,000

W-1831-A★ • F-2027A★ • 7,296,000

Unc-60	Unc-63	Unc-65
$40	$55	$75

W-1831-B • F-2027B • New York • 1,027,200,000

W-1831-B★ • F-2027B★ • 3,200,000

Unc-60	Unc-63	Unc-65
$40	$55	$75

W-1831-C • F-2027C • Philadelphia • 163,200,000

W-1831-D • F-2027D • Cleveland • 304,000,000

W-1831-D★ • F-2027D★ • 3,200,000

AU-50	Unc-60	Unc-63	Unc-65
$35	$65	$85	$115

W-1831-E • F-2027E • Richmond • 211,200,000

W-1831-F • F-2027F • Atlanta • 297,600,000

W-1831-F★ • F-2027F★ • 3,200,000

AU-50	Unc-60	Unc-63	Unc-65
$50	$85	$125	$160

W-1831-G • F-2027G • Chicago • 358,400,000

W-1831-H • F-2027H • St. Louis • 131,200,000

W-1831-H★ • F-2027H★ • 3,200,000

Unc-60	Unc-63	Unc-65
$55	$75	$100

W-1831-I • F-2027I • Minneapolis • 64,000,000

W-1831-J • F-2027J • Kansas City • 86,400,000

W-1831-K • F-2027K • Dallas • 115,200,000

W-1831-K★ • F-2027K★ • 3,136,000

Unc-60	Unc-63	Unc-65
$50	$65	$85

W-1831-L • F-2027L • San Francisco • 300,800,000

W-1831-L★ • F-2027L★ • 3,200,000

Unc-60	Unc-63	Unc-65
$50	$65	$85

Series of 1988-A, Green Seal
Villalpando-Brady (1989–1993)

This series continued the preceding design. No Series of 1988 $10 Federal Reserve Notes were printed, the first gap after a long sequence of following suit with $5 notes. All Federal Reserve Banks issued regular notes, but most did not issue star notes.

SERIES OF 1985, GREEN SEAL

Detail of the signatures and the series imprint of a $10 Federal Reserve Note, Series of 1985 (W-1831-B). The back is the standard type of the era, with motto.

SERIES OF 1988-A, GREEN SEAL

Detail of the signatures and the series imprint of a $10 Federal Reserve Note, Series of 1988-A (W-1832-H). The back is the standard type of the era, with motto.

Prices for a typical note for this series, unless listed otherwise, are as follows:

Unc-60	Unc-63	Unc-65
$20	$30	$40

Prices for a typical star note for this series, unless listed otherwise, are as follows:

AU-50	Unc-60	Unc-63	Unc-65
$35	$65	$95	$125

W-1832-A • F-2028A • Boston • 198,400,000

W-1832-A★ • F-2028A★ • 6,400,000

W-1832-B • F-2028B • New York • 339,200,000

W-1832-B★ • F-2028B★ • 3,200,000

W-1832-C • F-2028C • Philadelphia • 57,600,000

W-1832-D • F-2028D • Cleveland • 128,000,000

W-1832-D★ • F-2028D★ • Cleveland • 3,200,000

W-1832-E • F-2028E • Richmond • 105,600,000

W-1832-F • F-2028F • Atlanta • 236,800,000

W-1832-G • F-2028G • Chicago • 236,800,000

W-1832-H • F-2028H • St. Louis • 70,400,000

W-1832-I • F-2028I • Minneapolis • 19,200,000

W-1832-J • F-2028J • Kansas City • 51,200,000

W-1832-K • F-2028K • Dallas • 115,200,000

W-1832-L • F-2028L • San Francisco • 217,600,000

W-1832-L★ • F-2028L★ • 3,200,000

Series of 1990, Green Seal
Villalpando-Brady (1989–1993)

This series introduced new security features. Colored threads were added to the paper. On the face THE UNITED STATES OF AMERICA was added in microprint around part of the outside of the portrait frame.

All Federal Reserve Banks issued regular notes, but most did not issue star notes. All were printed in Washington, D.C., although the Western Facility in Fort Worth was in operation by this time.

Prices for a typical note for this series, unless listed otherwise, are as follows:

Unc-63	Unc-65
$20	$30

W-1833-A • F-2029A • Boston • 128,000,000

W-1833-B • F-2029B • New York • 742,400,000

W-1833-B★ • F-2029B★ • 16,874,000

Unc-63
$50

W-1833-C • F-2029C • Philadelphia • 19,200,000

W-1833-C★ • F-2029C★ • 2,560,000

Unc-63
$50

W-1833-D • F-2029D • Cleveland • 89,600,000

W-1833-E • F-2029E • Richmond • 105,600,000

W-1833-F • F-2029F • Atlanta • 160,000,000

W-1833-G • F-2029G • Chicago • 307,200,000

W-1833-G★ • F-2029G★ • 2,560,000

Unc-63
$55

W-1833-H • F-2029H • St. Louis • 70,400,000

W-1833-H★ • F-2029H★ • 1,920,000

Unc-63
$60

W-1833-I • F-2029I • Minneapolis • 12,800,000

W-1833-J • F-2029J • Kansas City • 70,400,000

W-1833-K • F-2029K • Dallas • 57,600,000

W-1833-L • F-2029L • San Francisco • 83,200,000

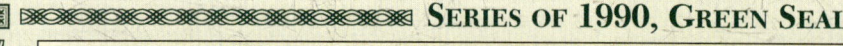

$10 Federal Reserve Note, Series of 1990 (W-1833-B). Federal Reserve Bank of New York. The back is the same as used on other $10 notes of the era.

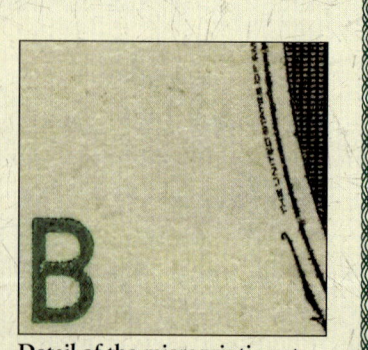

Detail of the microprinting at the portrait frame (at upper right of image).

Series of 1993, Green Seal
Withrow-Bentsen (1994)

This series continued the preceding design. Nine banks issued regular Series of 1993 notes, and three issued star notes. All were produced at the Bureau of Engraving and Printing in Washington, D.C.

Prices for a typical note for this series, unless listed otherwise, are as follows:

Unc-63	Unc-65
$20	$30

W-1834-A • F-2030A • Boston • 147,200,000

W-1834-B • F-2030B • New York • 480,000,000

W-1834-B★ • F-2030B★ • 5,120,000

Unc-63	Unc-65
$60	$75

W-1834-C • F-2030C • Philadelphia • 83,200,000

W-1834-C★ • F-2030C★ • 1,920,000

Unc-60	Unc-63	Unc-65
$40	$60	$75

W-1834-D • F-2030D • Cleveland • 115,200,000

W-1834-F • F-2030F • Atlanta • 121,600,000

W-1834-G • F-2030G • Chicago • 128,000,000

W-1834-G★ • F-2030G★ • 2,176,000

Unc-63	Unc-65
$55	$75

W-1834-H • F-2030H • St. Louis • 89,600,000

W-1834-J • F-2030J • Kansas City • 19,200,000

W-1834-L • F-2030L • San Francisco • 192,000,000

Series of 1995, Green Seal, Washington
Withrow-Rubin (1995–1999)

This series continued the preceding design. Beginning with this series, $10 notes were printed at Washington, D.C., and also at the Western Facility in Fort Worth. The Fort Worth issues have FW as part of the face letters and plate.

Prices for a typical note for this series, unless listed otherwise, are as follows:

Unc-63	Unc-65
$20	$30

W-1835-A • F-2031A • Boston • 192,000,000

W-1835-B • F-2031B • New York • 358,400,000

W-1835-C • F-2031C • Philadelphia • 57,600,000

W-1835-D • F-2031D • Cleveland • 108,000,000

W-1835-E • F-2031E • Richmond • 153,600,000

W-1835-E★ • F-2031E★ • 1,280,000

Unc-63	Unc-65
—	—

W-1835-F • F-2031F • Atlanta • 70,400,000

W-1835-F★ • F-2031F★ • 640,000

Unc-63	Unc-65
—	—

Series of 1995, Green Seal, Fort Worth
Withrow-Rubin (1995–1999)

This series continued the preceding design. This is the first printing of a $10 Federal Reserve issue at the Western Facility in Fort Worth. The face plate has FW as part of the plate letters and number. Generally, the Fort Worth plant emphasized production for Federal Reserve Banks in the Midwest and West. For San Francisco, only star notes were printed.

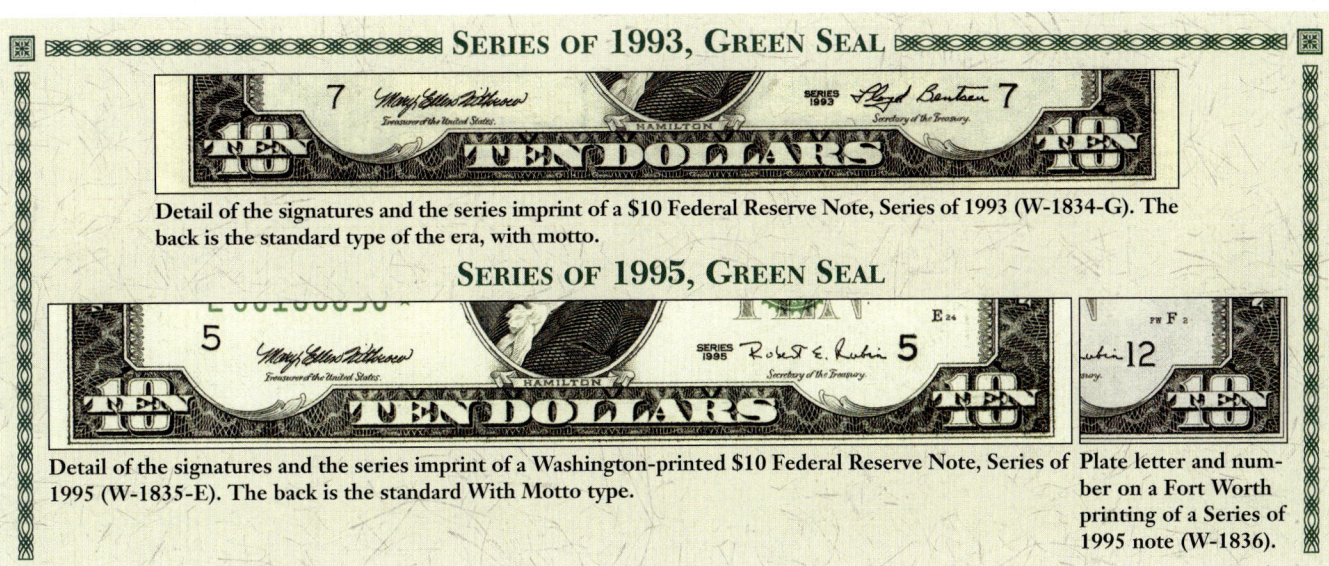

SERIES OF 1993, GREEN SEAL

Detail of the signatures and the series imprint of a $10 Federal Reserve Note, Series of 1993 (W-1834-G). The back is the standard type of the era, with motto.

SERIES OF 1995, GREEN SEAL

Detail of the signatures and the series imprint of a Washington-printed $10 Federal Reserve Note, Series of 1995 (W-1835-E). The back is the standard With Motto type.

Plate letter and number on a Fort Worth printing of a Series of 1995 note (W-1836).

Prices for a typical note for this series, unless listed otherwise, are as follows:

Unc-63	Unc-65
$20	$30

W-1836-B • F-2032B • New York • 76,800,000

W-1836-C • F-2032C • Philadelphia • 89,600,000

W-1836-D • F-2032D • Cleveland • 70,400,000

W-1836-D★ • F-2032D★ • 1,920,000

Unc-63
$50

W-1836-E • F-2032E • Richmond • 134,400,000

W-1836-F • F-2032F • Atlanta • 377,600,000

W-1836-F★ • F-2032F★ • 320,000

EF-40	AU-50	Unc-60	Unc-63	Unc-65
$25	$50	$80	$100	$135

W-1836-G • F-2032G • Chicago • 448,000,000

W-1836-G★ • F-2032G★ • 3,200,000

Unc-60	Unc-63	Unc-65
$35	$45	$60

W-1836-H • F-2032H • St. Louis • 153,600,000

W-1836-H★ • F-2032H★ • 6,400,000

Unc-60	Unc-63	Unc-65
$35	$45	$60

W-1836-I • F-2032I • Minneapolis • 70,400,000

W-1836-J • F-2032J • Kansas City • 147,200,000

W-1836-K • F-2032K • Dallas • 166,400,000

W-1836-L • F-2032L • San Francisco • 275,000,000

W-1836-L★ • F-2032L★ • 3,200,000

Unc-60	Unc-63	Unc-65
$35	$50	$70

Series of 1999, Green Seal, Washington
Withrow-Summers (1999–2001)

Both sides of the $10 note were redesigned for the Series of 1999. To the left is a new Federal Reserve seal without any indication of which of the 12 banks issued the note. A letter and number printed below the serial number at the upper left give that information, such as A1 for Boston, B2 for New York, and so on. The redemption phrase is now below a modernized Federal Reserve seal. Hamilton's portrait is

$10 Federal Reserve Note, Series of 1999 (W-1837-C). Federal Reserve Bank of Philadelphia. Printed in Washington, D.C. On the Series of 1999 notes the name of the Federal Reserve Bank was omitted as part of the extensive redesign. Identification is only by bank letter and number, such as A1 (Boston), B2 (New York), C3 (Philadelphia, shown here), and so on, at the upper left.

The modernized Federal Reserve seal.

Micro-lettering over HAMILTON.

Detail of the counter at the lower right, different from the other three counters, and the tiny plate number above it.

Back of the $10 Federal Reserve Note, Series of 1999 (W-1837-C). Although the elements are similar in concept to the earlier back, the style and arrangement are different.

Detail of the top center of the face showing the imprint of a Fort Worth–printed note.

modified and enlarged. THE UNITED STATES OF AMERICA is in two lines in the upper right field. Other changes are as depicted. Above HAMILTON on the portrait is micro-lettering: THE UNITED STATES OF AMERICA three times consecutively.

The new back retains the some elements that are familiar, but with extensive changes. The Treasury Building is shown in a front or plan view, without the people and automobile depicted in the earlier corner perspective. Series of 1999 notes were printed at both Washington and Fort Worth.

Prices for a typical note for this series, unless listed otherwise, are as follows:

Unc-63	Unc-65
$20	$30

W-1837-A • F-2033A • Boston • 83,200,000

Unc-60	Unc-63	Unc-65
$15	$25	$35

W-1837-A★ • F-2033A★ • 3,200,000

Unc-60	Unc-63	Unc-65
$35	$45	$60

W-1837-B • F-2033B • New York • 300,800,000

W-1837-C • F-2033C • Philadelphia • 64,000,000

W-1837-C★ • F-2033C★ • 3,520,000

Unc-60	Unc-63	Unc-65
$30	$40	$55

W-1837-D • F-2033D • Cleveland • 51,520,000

W-1837-D★ • F-2033D★ • 2,240,000

Unc-60	Unc-63	Unc-65
$35	$45	$60

W-1837-E • F-2033E • Richmond • 112,800,000

W-1837-E★ • F-2033E★ • 675,200

AU-50	Unc-60	Unc-63	Unc-65
$40	$75	$95	$120

W-1837-F • F-2033F • Atlanta • 96,000,000

W-1837-G • F-2033G • Chicago • 83,200,000

W-1837-H • F-2033H • St. Louis • 38,400,000

W-1837-I • F-2033I • Minneapolis • 6,400,000

AU-50	Unc-60	Unc-63	Unc-65
$35	$60	$80	$115

W-1837-J • F-2033J • Kansas City • 12,800,000

W-1837-K • F-2033K • Dallas • 44,800,000

W-1837-L • F-2033L • San Francisco • 32,000,000

Series of 1999, Green Seal, Fort Worth
Withrow-Summers (1999–2001)

This series used the new design, described above.

Prices for a typical note for this series, unless listed otherwise, are as follows:

Unc-60	Unc-63	Unc-65
$15	$25	$35

W-1838-A★ • F-2034A★ • Boston • 3,200,000

Unc-60	Unc-63	Unc-65
$35	$45	$60

W-1838-B★ • F-2034B★ • New York • 3,200,000

Unc-60	Unc-63	Unc-65
$35	$45	$60

W-1838-F • F-2034F • Atlanta • 83,200,000

W-1838-F★ • F-2034F★ • 7,715,200

Unc-60	Unc-63	Unc-65
$25	$35	$45

W-1838-G • F-2034G • Chicago • 44,800,000

W-1838-J • F-2034J • Kansas City • 51,200,000

W-1838-K • F-2034K • Dallas • 128,000,000

W-1838-K★ • F-2034K★ • 12,800,000

Unc-60	Unc-63	Unc-65
$25	$35	$45

W-1838-L • F-2034L • San Francisco • 76,800,000

Series of 2001, Green Seal, Washington
Marin-O'Neill (2001–2002)

This series continued the preceding design.

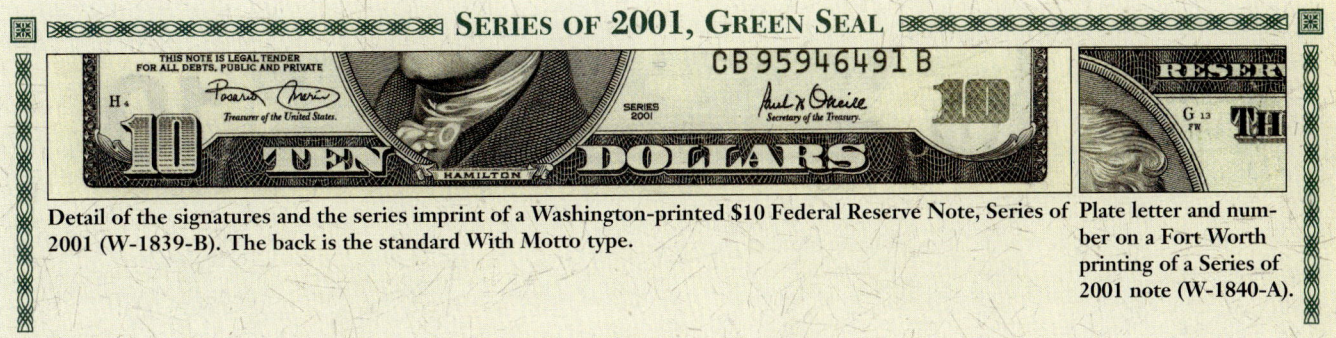

SERIES OF 2001, GREEN SEAL

Detail of the signatures and the series imprint of a Washington-printed $10 Federal Reserve Note, Series of 2001 (W-1839-B). The back is the standard With Motto type.

Plate letter and number on a Fort Worth printing of a Series of 2001 note (W-1840-A).

Prices for a typical note for this series, unless listed otherwise, are as follows:

Unc-63	Unc-65
$20	$30

W-1839-A • F-2035A • Boston • 19,200,000

W-1839-B • F-2035B • New York • 121,600,000

W-1839-B★ • F-2035B★ • 320,000

AU-50	Unc-60	Unc-63	Unc-65
$50	$95	$120	$155

W-1839-C • F-2035C • Philadelphia • 108,800,000

W-1839-D • F-2035D • Cleveland • 57,600,000

W-1839-D★ • F-2035D★ • 1,280,000

Unc-60	Unc-63	Unc-65
$25	$35	$55

W-1839-E • F-2035E • Richmond • 117,760,000

W-1839-F • F-2035F • Atlanta • 38,400,000

W-1839-G★ • F-2035G★ • Chicago • 640,000

EF-40	AU-50	Unc-60	Unc-63	Unc-65
$25	$40	$60	$80	$120

W-1839-H • F-2035H • St. Louis • 12,800,000

W-1839-I • F-2035I • Minneapolis • 6,400,000

Unc-60	Unc-63	Unc-65
$15	$25	$35

Series of 2001, Green Seal, Fort Worth
Marin-O'Neill (2001–2002)

This series continued the preceding design.

Prices for a typical note for this series, unless listed otherwise, are as follows:

Unc-63	Unc-65
$20	$30

W-1840-A • F-2036A • Boston • 147,200,000

W-1840-B • F-2036B • New York • 121,600,000

W-1840-E • F-2036E • Richmond • 44,800,000

W-1840-F • F-2036F • Atlanta • 76,800,000

W-1840-G • F-2036G • Chicago • 160,000,000

W-1840-H • F-2036H • St. Louis • 64,000,000

W-1840-I • F-2036I • Minneapolis • 32,000,000

W-1840-K • F-2036K • Dallas • 38,400,000

Unc-63	Unc-65
$25	$35

W-1840-K★ • F-2036K★ • 3,200,000

Unc-60	Unc-63	Unc-65
$25	$40	$60

W-1840-L★ • F-2036L★ • San Francisco • 3,200,000

Unc-60	Unc-63	Unc-65
$25	$40	$60

Series of 2003, Green Seal, Washington
Marin-Snow (2003)

This series continued the preceding design.

Prices for a typical note for this series, unless listed otherwise, are as follows:

Unc-63	Unc-65
$20	$30

W-1841-A • F-2037A • Boston • 32,000,000

W-1841-A★ • F-2037A★ • 416,000

Unc-60	Unc-63	Unc-65
$110	$150	$180

W-1841-B • F-2037B • New York • 57,600,000

W-1841-C • F-2037C • Philadelphia • 32,000,000

W-1841-D • F-2037D • Cleveland • 38,400,000

W-1841-D★ • F-2037D★ • 1,280,000

Unc-60	Unc-63	Unc-65
$60	$75	$100

W-1841-E • F-2037E • Richmond • 38,400,000

W-1841-F • F-2037F • Atlanta • 57,600,000

W-1841-G • F-2037G • Chicago • 140,800,000

W-1841-H • F-2037H • St. Louis • 38,400,000

W-1841-H★ • F-2037H★ • 768,000

AU-50	Unc-60	Unc-63	Unc-65
$40	$80	$100	$135

SERIES OF 2003, GREEN SEAL

DB 23466159 A

Detail of the signatures and the series imprint of a Washington-printed $10 Federal Reserve Note, Series of 2003 (W-1841-B). The back is the standard With Motto type.

Plate letter and number on a Fort Worth printing of a Series of 2003 note (W-1842-D).

W-1841-I • F-2037I • Minneapolis • 6,400,000

Unc-60	Unc-63	Unc-65
$25	$35	$45

W-1841-J • F-2037J • Kansas City • 51,200,000

W-1841-J★ • F-2037J★ • 2,920,000

AU-50	Unc-60	Unc-63	Unc-65
$20	$45	$60	$85

W-1841-K • F-2037K • Dallas • 76,800,000

W-1841-K★ • F-2037K★ • 320,000

EF-40	AU-50	Unc-60	Unc-63	Unc-65
$30	$55	$95	$125	$165

W-1841-L • F-2037L • San Francisco • 108,800,000

Series of 2003, Green Seal, Fort Worth
Marin-Snow (2003)

This series continued the preceding design. This is the first run of small-size $10 Federal Reserve Notes for which no star notes were printed.

Prices for a typical note for this series, unless listed otherwise, are as follows:

Unc-63
$20

W-1842-A • F-2038A • Boston • 32,000,000

W-1842-B • F-2038B • New York • 89,600,000

W-1842-C • F-2038C • Philadelphia • 44,800,000

W-1842-D • F-2038D • Cleveland • 32,000,000

W-1842-E • F-2038E • Richmond • 44,800,000

W-1842-F • F-2038F • Atlanta • 76,800,000

W-1842-G • F-2038G • Chicago • 6,400,000

W-1842-I • F-2038I • Minneapolis • 6,400,000

Unc-63
$30

Series of 2004-A, Green Seal, Fort Worth
Cabral-Snow (2004–2006)

No Series of 2004 (without suffix) notes were made.

This series (illus. on p. 436) introduced "colorization" to the $10 series. Security features include a red torch (of the Statue of Liberty) in the field to the left of the portrait on the face, and a smaller torch emblem to the right of the portrait. Right of the portrait, in ornate letters, is WE THE PEOPLE. At the lower right of the face is the denomination 10 in gold ink. Microprinting is retained above the HAMILTON label under the portrait, which under high-powered magnification reveals the inscription THE UNITED STATES OF AMERICA TEN DOLLARS THE UNITED STATES OF AMERICA. The denomination 10 is arrayed on the face in unobtrusive gold ink multiple times. The paper includes an embedded security strip.

On the reverse, the denomination 10 in gold ink, very subtle, is seen multiple times in the right field.

All Series of 2004-A notes were printed in Fort Worth.

Prices for a typical note for this series, unless listed otherwise, are as follows:

Unc-63	Unc-65
$20	$30

W-1843-A • F-2039A • Boston • 51,200,000

W-1843-A★ • F-2039A★ • 3,200,000

Unc-60	Unc-63	Unc-65
$35	$50	$65

W-1843-B • F-2039B • New York • 153,600,000

W-1843-B★ • F-2039B★ • 640,000

Unc-60	Unc-63	Unc-65
$70	$90	$115

W-1843-C • F-2039C • Philadelphia • 64,000,000

W-1843-D • F-2039D • Cleveland • 44,800,000

W-1843-E • F-2039E • Richmond • 70,400,000

W-1843-F • F-2039F • Atlanta • 134,400,000

W-1843-F★ • F-2039F★ • 96,000

Unc-63	Unc-65
$200	$225

W-1843-G • F-2039G • Chicago • 96,000,000

W-1843-H • F-2039H • St. Louis • 38,400,000

W-1843-I • F-2039I • Minneapolis • 12,800,000

W-1843-J • F-2039J • Kansas City • 25,600,000

W-1843-K • F-unlisted • Dallas • 57,600,000

W-1843-L • F-unlisted • San Francisco • 89,600,000

W-1843-L★ • F-2039L★ • 640,000

Unc-63	Unc-65
$50	$65

Series of 2006, Green Seal, Fort Worth
Cabral-Paulson (2006–2009)

This series (illus. on p. 436) continued the preceding design. All Series of 2006 notes have been printed in Fort Worth.

This information is accurate as of press time. No valuation charts are provided, as notes in this series can be had in top condition for face value at banks or from dealers (with a nominal handling charge).

W-1844-A • F-2040A • Boston

W-1844-B • F-2040B • New York

W-1844-C • F-2040C • Philadelphia

W-1844-C★ • F-2040C★

W-1844-D • F-2040D • Cleveland

W-1844-E • F-2040E • Richmond

SERIES OF 2004-A, GREEN SEAL

$10 Federal Reserve Note, Series of 2004-A (W-1843-E). Federal Reserve Bank of Richmond, with the E5 at upper left providing the attribution. Printed in Fort Worth, Texas.

Detail of the left field showing the Federal Reserve System seal, part of the torch, and scattered counters.

Detail of the right field showing the black Treasury seal, "We the People," and the gold-colored counter.

Back of the $10 Federal Reserve Note, Series of 2004-A (W-1843-E). Federal Reserve Bank of Richmond. Printed in Fort Worth, Texas.

SERIES OF 2006, GREEN SEAL

Detail of the signatures and the series imprint of a $10 Federal Reserve Note, Series of 2006 (W-1844-G). Printed in Fort Worth, Texas. The back is the standard With Motto type.

Plate letter and number on a Series of 2006 note (W-1844-G).

W-1844-F • F-2040F • Atlanta

W-1844-G • F-2040G • Chicago

W-1844-G★ • F-2040G★

W-1844-H • F-2040H • St. Louis

W-1844-I • F-2040I • Minneapolis

W-1844-J • F-2040J • Kansas City

W-1844-K • F-2040K • Dallas

W-1844-L • F-2040L • San Francisco

Series of 2009, Green Seal
Rios-Geithner (2009–)

No printing information as of press time.

$20 Notes

LARGE SIZE

Pursuing the $20 denomination is a step further into an elite area of collecting. Large-size $20 notes, while available for some types, can be rare in higher grades and extremely rare for certain varieties. Their high face value resulted in few being saved. Over the years most numismatists have sought examples of type, not signature combinations, although there have been some impressive exceptions. This denomination introduces a new class, the Gold Certificates of the 1860s. Relatively little is known about them today.

Researchers such as Doug Murray (plate varieties and star notes) and Peter Huntoon (National Bank Notes) have made many important discoveries in recent years through searches of Treasury department records in the National Archives and examination of proof sheets in the National Numismatic Collection at the Smithsonian Institution. Examination of notes in the field is difficult, as most early issues range from scarce to rare to extremely rare.

DEMAND NOTES

Series of 1861

The Demand Notes of 1861 (illus. on p. 438), printed by the American Bank Note Company, were issued to be payable at Sub-Treasury offices in Boston, Cincinnati, New York, Philadelphia, and St. Louis. The most active depository was in New York City and was managed by John J. Cisco, an entrepreneur whose interesting and somewhat mysterious business career invites biographical study today.

These exist with "for the" handwritten (the early style) and printed (the most available style); all are extremely rare. Certain other Demand Notes of the $20 denomination are not known to have survived, although they were printed and issued. Similar to other Demand Notes, these do not have the Treasury seal.

There were five $20 Demand Note face plates made, one for each Sub-Treasury. Four of the face plates had decorative flourishes around the plate position letters (A, B, C, and D) on the left side. However, the Boston face plate lacks these flourishes around the A-B-C-D plate letters. The $20 St. Louis face plate was later reworked into a second $20 Boston face plate, numbered 2. That number is just to the right of U.S. AT BOSTON. Accordingly, Boston notes come both without and with the flourishes and can be described that way

when listing them. As a class, Demand Notes were issued from August 26, 1861, to March 5, 1862.

W-1900 • F-13a • Boston • "for the" handwritten • No SERIES imprint • 1,000 (est.) • Unknown

W-1901 • F-13 • "for the" printed • 99,000 (est.)
Recorded population: Not specifically recorded • *Commentary:* "Without Flourishes at plate position letter at left."

W-1902 • F-13 • Series 2 to 3 • 200,000
Recorded population: 4 • *Highest graded:* VF-20 • *Commentary:* Two varieties for plate letters A, B, C, and D, "Without Flourishes" and "With Flourishes, plate number 2, ex-St. Louis" (see introduction above) • *Selected information:* Existing examples include serials 20227/C, VG; 2/21180/D, Good, damaged (later graded Fine, damaged), sold in a Knight auction (11/2006) for $92,000; 35993/Am, G–F, sold by Robert F. Schermerhorn (12/1955) to Dean Oakes and later sold in a Stack's auction (10/1990) for $13,750; and 2/79388/D, VF-20 (PMG), sold in a Heritage auction (9/2008) for $74,750.

W-1903 • F-14a • Cincinnati • "for the" handwritten • 1,000 (est.) • Unknown

W-1904 • F-14 • "for the" printed • 24,000 (est.)
Recorded population: 1 • *Graded:* G-6 • *Commentary:* This face plate was altered into New York plate number 2. • *Selected information:* B&M (5/1999), 20447/C, VG/F, repaired, $55,200.

W-1905 • F-11a • New York • "for the" handwritten • No SERIES imprint • 8,000 (est.)
Recorded population: 1 • *Graded:* VF-25 • *Selected information:* Grinnell Collection (11/1944), 7216/D, Good, lower right section missing, $240. Bass Collection, B&M (5/1999), $55,200.

W-1906 • F-11 • "for the" printed • 92,000 (est.)
Recorded population: 8 • *Highest graded:* F–VF • *Selected information:* Existing examples include CAA (6/1994), 24476/D, VG–F, damaged, $4,200; Knight (10/2005), 30973/A, Fine, problems, $92,000; Knight (8/2005), 36843/C, Fine, problems, $39,100; recorded by Martin Gengerke, 39422/B, Fine; CAA (1/2005), 42668/D, Fine, $26,450; Knight (10/1991), 44018/B, EF, damaged, $21,000; Stack's (10/1990), 47314/B, F–VF, $13,200; B&M (5/1999), 74206/B, Good, repaired, $12,650.

W-1907 • F-11 • Series 2 to 4 • 220,000

Recorded population: 8 • Highest graded: F-15 • Selected information: Knight (10/2005), 30973/A, Fine, repaired, $92,000. Knight (8/2005), 36843/C, Fine, problems, $39,100. CAA (1/2005), 42668/D, Fine, $26,450. Knight (10/1991), 3/44018/B, EF, damaged, $21,000.

W-1908 • F-12a • Philadelphia • "for the" handwritten • No SERIES imprint • 1,000 (est.) • Unknown

W-1909 • F-12 • "for the" printed • 99,000 (est.)

Recorded population: 6 • Highest graded: EF • Selected information: Existing examples include Stack's (3/1993), 7204/D, Fine, $13,000; ANA Museum, 14715/C, Fine, repaired; Stack's (10/1990), 19012/D, EF, $19,250; B&M (7/1999), 19056/D, VG–F, $23,000; Smithsonian Institution, 36687/C, Fine, problems; Mayflower (7/1974), 98787/C, VF, $6,750.

SERIES OF 1861

$20 Demand Note, Series of 1861 (W-1907), also payable in New York. The second style with "for the" printed. Series 3, serial 30973, plate A.

Detail of the lower left of W-1905, showing "for the" handwritten.   Detail of the lower left of W-1907, showing "for the" printed.

Detail of the lower right of W-1907, showing the series, serial number, and other features.

Detail of the plate letter D without flourishes surrounding it (W-1902 Without Flourishes).

Detail of the D on the With Flourishes plate.

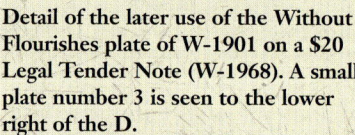

Detail of the later use of the Without Flourishes plate of W-1901 on a $20 Legal Tender Note (W-1968). A small plate number 3 is seen to the lower right of the D.

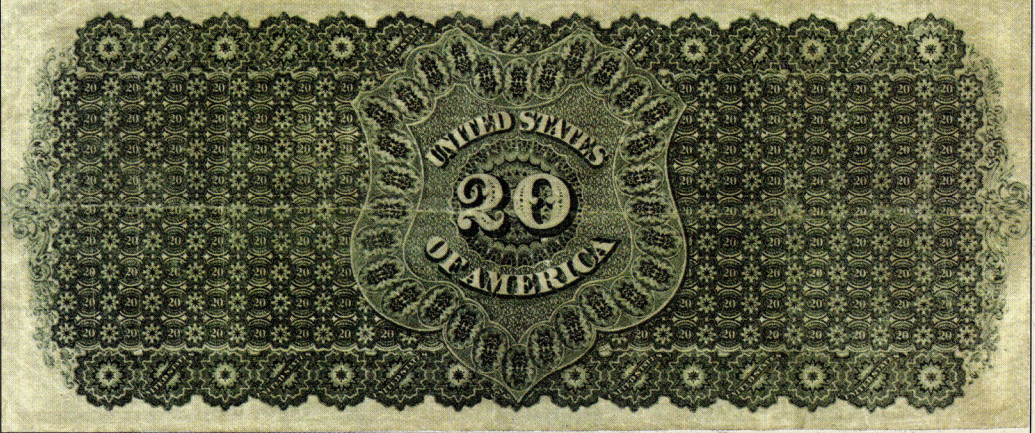

Back of a $20 Demand Note, Series of 1861.

W-1910 • F-12 • Series 2 to 3 • 140,000
Recorded population: 6 • Highest graded: VF-20.

VG-8	F-12	VF-20
$25,000	$50,000	$95,000

W-1911 • F-15a • St. Louis • "for the" handwritten • 1,000 (est.) • Unknown

W-1912 • F-15 • St. Louis • "for the" printed • 24,000 (est.) • Unknown

Commentary: This face plate was altered into Boston plate number 2.

INTEREST-BEARING NOTES

March 3, 1863, 5% Interest, 1 Year

Interest-Bearing Notes for certain high denominations, $50 to $5,000, were issued as early as 1861. It was not until the passage of the Act of March 3, 1863, that the $20 bill was made. These bore interest at the rate of 5% for one year, as determined by a date overprinted in red at the lower right face of the note. These were sold at a discount to reflect the interest, and redeemed at face value upon maturity. More than 20 different starting dates have been recorded, from

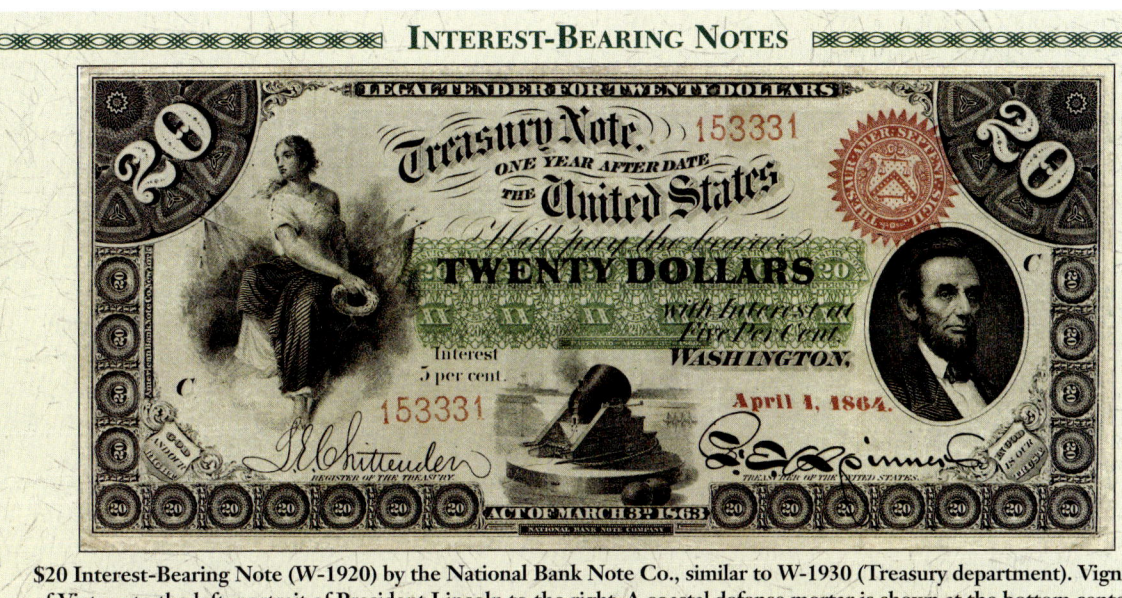

$20 Interest-Bearing Note (W-1920) by the National Bank Note Co., similar to W-1930 (Treasury department). Vignette of Victory to the left, portrait of President Lincoln to the right. A coastal defense mortar is shown at the bottom center.

Detail of the lower center and right of the face of W-1920.

Detail of the green "cycloidal configuration" imprint at the center of the note, an arrangement patented by James MacDonough on April 23, 1860, and promoted as an anti-counterfeiting technique. The patent also referred to ornate counters.

Back of a $20 Interest-Bearing Note (W-1920).

February 13, 1864, to May 25, 1864.[1] As there are so many dates, numismatists have not listed them as separate varieties.

Depicted on the face of the $20 note are a standing goddess with a wreath (*Victory*), a mortar of the type in wide use at coastal forts (*Mortar Firing*), and a portrait of Abraham Lincoln (also used on certain $10 notes of the era) engraved by Frederick Girsch from a photograph by C.S. German. The shields at the lower inside left and right are respectively inscribed GOD AND OUR RIGHT and IN GOD IS OUR TRUST. At this time, various experiments with a motto mentioning God were conducted on pattern coins, culminating with IN GOD WE TRUST (first used in circulation on the two-cent piece of 1864). The same motifs, with different typography, were used on the Compound Interest Treasury Notes of 1864 and 1865. The Treasury imprint on certain notes reflects that the plates were made in Washington, but using transfer rolls supplied by the National Bank Note Company.

The Treasury issued 822,000 of these notes; more than 500 are recorded as still outstanding in Treasury department records. Likely most of these were lost in fires, shipwrecks, thefts, and other mishaps. Today, the number known is fewer than three dozen. Some of these were printed by the National Bank Note Co., and others were printed by the National Currency Bureau (before it became known as the Bureau of Engraving and Printing). All have the printed signatures of Chittenden and Spinner.

W-1920 • F-197 • NATIONAL BANK NOTE CO. imprint • 822,000

Estimated population: 9 or 10 • *Highest graded:* VF-20 • *Selected information:* CAA (2/2005), 2669/B, VF–EF, $63,250. Heritage (1/2007), 8445/C, Fine, $32,200. Knight (3/2008), 113583/B, F–VF, $33,350. CAA (9/2006), 153331/C, VF–EF, $74,750.

W-1930 • F-197a • TREASURY DEPARTMENT imprint • Part of W-1920 printage

Estimated population: 25 to 28 • *Highest graded:* EF-45.

VG-8	F-12	VF-20	EF-40
$9,000	$17,500	$25,000	$52,000

March 3, 1863, 5% Interest, 2 Years

Little is known today about the two-year notes in this series. Although no record has been found of their having been issued, some may have been made, as per this account by Spencer M. Clark, chief of the National Currency Bureau:

> The first loss of Treasury Notes occurred on April 14th or 15th, 1864, in the plate-printers drying room. A parcel of eight hundred unfinished sheets of twenty-dollar five per cent two-year notes, printed on the 14th of April, 1864, when returned from the drying room on the 15th, counted by seven hundred and ninety-nine sheets. Thorough search was made without finding the notes.[2]

On the other hand, an inventory compiled by George W. Casilear of existing plates, dies, counters, etc., held by the bureau as of October 1, 1864, is very specific as to denominations, designs, etc., and makes no mention of a $20 two-

year Interest-Bearing Note. The 1868 *Annual Report of the Treasurer of the United States*, by F.E. Spinner, lists only $50 and $100 March 3, 1863, two-year 5% notes (although see W-3790 and W-4450, as these were made at one time). The comprehensive Annual Report for 1869 (p. 242) does not mention the $20 notes.

W-1940 • F-unlisted • TREASURY DEPARTMENT imprint • 3,200 (if indeed any at all) • Unknown

COMPOUND INTEREST TREASURY NOTES OF 1864 AND 1865

Similar to certain other currency, Compound Interest Treasury Notes were intended to raise money to fight the Civil War. They were printed by the National Currency Bureau and were made in denominations from $10 to $1,000. The highest-issued provable printage can be calculated by multiplying the highest known serial by four. These are slightly larger than Legal Tender Notes and measure 3.5 inches by 7.5 inches.

Compound Interest Treasury Notes of the $20 denomination may have been issued under the Act of March 3, 1863, although no such imprint is known today. All have ACT OF JUNE 30th 1864 at the bottom border. Different starting dates are printed in red on the face. As to whether they should be considered separate varieties is probably moot, although Gene Hessler and Carlson Chambliss do in their *Comprehensive Catalog of U.S. Paper Money*.

The motifs on face are similar in design to the Interest-Bearing Notes of 1863, except for changes in the wording, the omission of the cycloidal configurations, and the imprint COMPOUND INTEREST TREASURY NOTE in bronzing powder. On this series TREASURY DEPARTMENT is near the top border (where the National Bank Note Company imprint is on the Interest-Bearing Notes).

The back, in green, has an interest table that gives the value of the note for six-month periods up to three years after issue. Similar to the situation for Interest-Bearing Notes, the Compound Interest Treasury Notes were a very popular investment for state chartered banks as well as people of wealth. Today, fewer than 70 notes exist from an original printage of 390,000, as nearly all were redeemed when the interest schedule expired.

W-1950 • F-191 • Chittenden-Spinner • 822,000

Recorded population: 4 • *Highest graded:* VF-20 • *Commentary:* Overprinted in red is the date JULY 15, 1864 • *Selected information:* Existing examples include serials 2727/B, VF, sold in a Knight auction (10/2006) for $29,900; 4247/C, VG; 7031/D, VF-35, repaired (PMG), sold in a Heritage auction (9/2007) for $92,000; and 7957/B, Poor.

W-1953 • F-191a • Colby-Spinner • Part of W-1950 printage

Estimated population: 62 to 66 • *Highest graded:* AU-50 • *Commentary:* Red overprint dates reported include AUG. 15, 1864; OCT. 15, 1864; DEC. 15, 1864; AUG. 1, 1865; and SEPT. 15, 1865.

VG-8	F-12	VF-20	EF-40	AU-50
$2,750	$5,500	$19,000	$34,000	—

COMPOUND INTEREST TREASURY NOTES OF 1864 AND 1865

$20 Compound Interest Treasury Note (W-1953). With red overprint of Aug. 15, 1864, the starting date for computing interest.

Interest table on the back of W-1953.

Back of the $20 Compound Interest Treasury Note (W-1953).

LEGAL TENDER NOTES
(Also Known as United States Notes)

Series of 1862, First Obligation

The Series of 1862 $20 Legal Tender Notes (illus. on p. 442), also called United States Notes, were made in substantial quantities and were first issued in March of that year. The face motifs are similar to those used on the 1861 Demand Notes, but a red Treasury seal was added to the Legal Tender Notes, and imprints differ.

The face, back, and tint plates for the $20 Series of 1862 and 1863 Legal Tender Notes were engraved by the American Bank Note Company. American also printed most (if not all) of the First Obligation notes. American and National shared responsibility for printing the Second Obligation notes.[3] Treasury signatures of Chittenden and Spinner were printed on the face using a separate plate and a special ink.

These were issued in 24 series, numbered on the face (except for the unnumbered first series), 2 to 24, with each series beginning with serial 1. All have ACT OF FEB'Y

SERIES OF 1862, FIRST OBLIGATION

$20 Legal Tender Note, Series of 1862 (W-1962). Liberty standing with sword and shield. SERIES 10 at top center. (ANA Edward C. Rochette Money Museum)

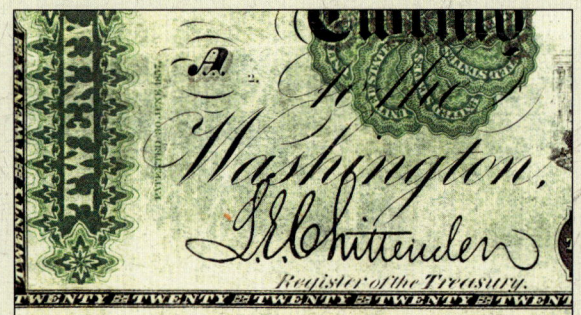

Detail of lower left corner of face with plate A2 identification and vertically in green ink to its left, PATENTED 30 JUNE 1857 (this refers to the "Patent Green Tint," said to deter counterfeiting).

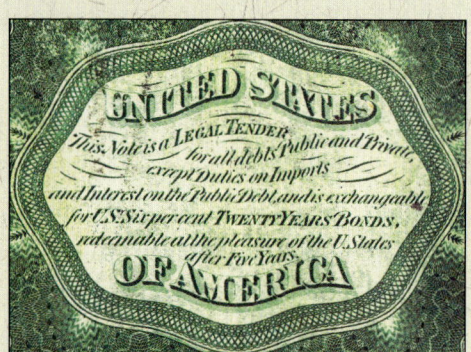

Detail of the First Obligation wording. The 6-20 bonds, as they were called, mentioned in the inscription, were very widely advertised by securities brokers.

Back of the $20 Legal Tender Note, Series of 1862 (W-1962), with First Obligation wording and arrangement as used only on this variety.

25TH 1862 and MARCH 10TH 1862 printed on the plate. All have a small red Treasury seal with a spiked border.

First Obligation: This wording, with different typography on various denominations, states the note is exchangeable for bonds (a provision dropped from the Second Obligation): "This note is a Legal Tender for all debts public and private, except duties on imports and interest on the public debt, and is exchangeable for U.S. six percent twenty years bonds, redeemable at the pleasure of the U. States after five years."

All five $20 Demand Note face plates were reworked into $20 1862 Legal Tender Note face plates, numbered 1 through 5. The Boston Demand Note plate number 1, without the flourishes (see W-1901), became the $20 1862 Legal Tender Note face plate number 3. This face plate was used all the way through the 1862–1863 Legal Tender Notes, and likely can be found for all of the 1862–1863 varieties. Only the W-1961 (First Obligation) and the W-1967 (Second Obligation) notes without flourishes have yet to be confirmed, due to a lack of these notes. In describing any one of these notes with the anomalous A, B, C, or D, the term *Without Flourishes* and the plate letter would be appropriate.

W-1961 • F-124a • **Printed signatures of Chittenden and Spinner** • **AMERICAN BANK NOTE CO. NEW YORK at bottom border** • **Treasury seal nearly at far right and slightly low** • **One red serial number at upper right** • **SERIES not at top center** • **100,000**

Recorded population: 2 • *Highest graded:* VG-8 • *Commentary:* This was for the first run of notes. • *Selected information:* Existing notes include serials 68368/D, Poor, sold in a Superior auction (2/1975) for $32, and 95718/B, VG.

W-1962 • F-124 • **SERIES at top center, beginning with Series 2** • **Treasury seal without inner border of radial parallel lines** • **Series 2 to 12** • **1,050,000 (est.)**

Estimated population: 40 to 50 • *Highest graded:* AU-50 • *Commentary:* This note is seen with and without (plate 3) flourishes around plate letter.

VG-8	F-12	VF-20	EF-40	AU-50
$1,500	$3,000	$5,000	$7,800	—

W-1963 • F-124 • **Treasury seal with inner border of radial parallel lines** • **Series 12 to 24** • **1,250,000 (est.)**

Estimated population: 45 to 55 • *Highest graded:* AU-50 • *Commentary:* This note is seen with and without (plate 3) flourishes around plate letter.

VG-8	F-12	VF-20	EF-40	AU-50
$1,500	$3,000	$5,000	$7,800	—

Series of 1862 and 1863, Second Obligation

The face design (illus. on p. 444ff.) is similar to the preceding. NEW SERIES, with the series number, is printed at the top of the face. Series 1 to 8 make up W-1964; 9 to 18, W-1965; 18 to 20, W-1966; and 20 to 28, W-1967 and 1968.

Second Obligation: "This note is a Legal Tender for all debts public and private, except duties on imports and interest on the public debt, and is receivable in payment of all loans made to the United States." This wording, with different typography on the various denominations, does not mention exchanging the notes for 6-20 bonds and thus is different from the First Obligation.

W-1967 is an especially interesting variety, with two serial numbers high at the left and right, instead of the left one low. In October 1868, George B. McCartee, acting chief of the bureau, wrote to C.S. Van Zandt, secretary of the American Bank Note Company in New York: "I perceive that the twenty dollars Legal Tender Notes are improperly numbered—viz: both numbers are on the upper end of the note. They should be numbered as the one-dollar notes—one set of numbers on the lower left hand corner. Please remedy this at once."[4] This communication places a date on when W-1967 was issued. It was necessary to have one high and one low serial number so that when the bills were redeemed and cut apart lengthwise prior to destruction, each half would have a serial number.

W-1964 • F-125 • *Printed on plate:* ACT OF FEB'Y 25TH 1862 / MARCH 10, 1862 • **Printed signatures Chittenden-Spinner** • **AMERICAN BANK NOTE CO. NEW YORK at bottom border, NATIONAL BANK NOTE COMPANY above** • **Treasury seal nearly at far right and slightly low** • **Red serial number at upper right** • **Second Obligation back** • **New Series 1 to 8** • **800,000**

Estimated population: 40 to 45 • *Highest graded:* AU-50 • *Commentary:* This note is found with and without (plate 3) flourishes around plate letter.

VG-8	F-12	VF-20	EF-40	AU-50
$1,500	$3,000	$5,000	—	—

W-1965 • F-126 • *Printed on plate:* ACT OF MARCH 3D 1863 / MARCH 10, 1863 • **1857 patent date** • **New Series 9 to 18** • **920,984**

Estimated population: 32 to 38 • *Highest graded:* Unc • *Commentary:* This note is found with and without (plate 3) flourishes around plate letter.

VG-8	F-12	VF-20	EF-40	AU-50	Unc-60
$1,500	$3,000	$5,000	$8,000	$12,500	—

W-1966 • F-126a • *Printed on plate:* MARCH 10, 1863 • **AMERICAN BANK NOTE CO. NEW YORK at bottom border** • **No patent date** • **New Series 18 to 20** • **225,000**

Estimated population: 11 to 13 • *Highest graded:* VF-25 • *Commentary:* This note is found with and without (plate 3) flourishes around plate letter.

VG-8	F-12	VF-20
$1,500	$4,000	$9,000

W-1967 • F-126c • **Red serial numbers at upper left and upper right, an error** • **New Series 20 to 21** • **66,016 (est.)**

Recorded population: 6 • *Highest graded:* AU-50 • *Selected information:* No recent auction sales.

W-1968 • F-126b • **Red serial numbers at lower left and upper right** • **New Series 21 to 28** • **734,000 (est.)**

Estimated population: 155 to 165 • *Highest graded:* Unc • *Commentary:* This note is found with and without (plate 3) flourishes around plate letter.

VG-8	F-12	VF-20	EF-40	AU-50	Unc-60	Unc-63	Unc-65
$1,500	$2,500	$4,000	$5,500	$7,000	$9,000	$13,000	$25,000

Series of 1869

Depicted on the face of the Series of 1869 $20 Legal Tender Note (illus. on p. 446) is a profile portrait of Alexander Hamilton, styled differently from that on the $2 Legal Tender Note, Series of 1862. On the right side is the standing goddess Liberty, holding a shield aloft with her left arm, with a walking stick in her right, and wearing a helmet topped with an eagle. The allegorical image was taken from a drawing by John W. Casilear, who studied art under Asher B. Durand and Peter Maverick, and who was a partner in the bank-note engraving and printing firm of Toppan, Carpenter, Casilear &

SERIES OF 1862 AND 1863, SECOND OBLIGATION

$20 Legal Tender Note, Series of 1862 (W-1964). Single serial number at the upper right. NEW SERIES 1, plate D6, serial 67508. Also used on the Series of 1863. (ANA Edward C. Rochette Money Museum)

Detail of the Second Obligation.

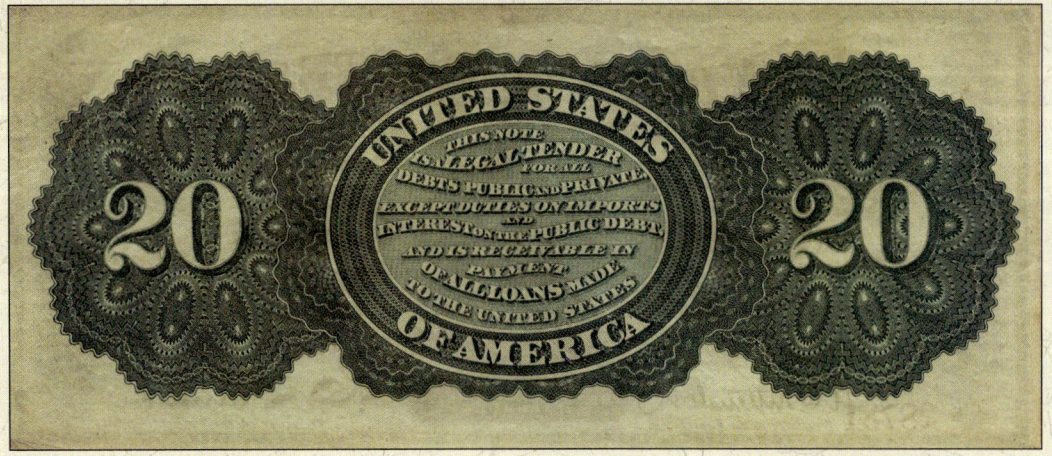

Back of the $20 Legal Tender Note, Series of 1862 (W-1964), with Second Obligation wording and arrangement. Also used on the Series of 1863.

Co. in the 1850s. His nephew George W. Casilear joined the National Currency Bureau in 1862 and later held the post of chief engraver of the BEP. During this era there were many different representations of a goddess representing America, sometimes called Liberty (often with a liberty pole), Columbia, America, or another designation.

The large red Treasury seal, blue serial numbers, and a streak of blue tint in the paper make the face of this issue rather colorful. However, the $20 and higher values in the Series of 1869 lack the green overprint used on the $1 to $10 "Rainbow Notes."

The back is somewhat Egyptian in appearance, bold and geometric, with the Roman numeral XX used 103 times and the standard 20 employed 105 times. Of this type, 3,648,000 notes were printed. Today, more than 150 examples are have been listed by Martin Gengerke in *U.S. Paper Money Records*. As a class, Series of 1869 notes were issued from October 19, 1869, to July 25, 1874.

SERIES OF 1862 AND 1863, SECOND OBLIGATION, *continued*

Face of W-1967. Left serial number at the top. NEW SERIES 21 imprinted near the top border.

Face of W-1968. Serial numbers at lower left and upper right.

W-2000 • F-127 • Allison-Spinner (1869–1875) • Small red seal with scalloped border • 3,648,000

Estimated population: 185 to 205 • *Highest graded:* Unc.

VG-8	F-12	VF-20	EF-40	AU-50	Unc-60	Unc-63	Unc-65
$1,500	$2,900	$4,000	$6,000	$10,000	$12,500	$19,000	$32,000

Series of 1875

The face (illus. on p. 447) has the same motifs as the preceding, but now has XX in red to the left. The Treasury seal has been relocated to the right of the counter, and other changes can be seen. The back is new, by the Columbian Bank Note Company, with the obligation and counterfeiting clauses at the left and an open area at the right. As a class, Series of 1875 notes were issued from July 20, 1875, to June 20, 1879.

W-2001 • F-128 • Allison-New (1875–1876) • Small red seal with spiked border • 1,250,000

Estimated population: 65 to 70 • *Highest graded:* Unc.

VG-8	F-12	VF-20	EF-40	AU-50	Unc-60	Unc-63	Unc-65
$850	$1,600	$2,300	$3,000	$3,700	$4,500	$6,000	$9,000

Series of 1878

The designs (illus. on p. 448) show minor differences in imprints. In the lower margin on the back there is the imprint "Bureau, Engraving and Printing."

W-2002 • F-129 • Allison-Gilfillan (1877–1878) • Small red seal with spiked border • 1,740,000

Estimated population: 210 to 230 • *Highest graded:* Unc • *Commentary:* The very last printed had a security paper change from a vertical to a horizontal blue stain with fibers across entire length.

VG-8	F-12	VF-20	EF-40	AU-50	Unc-60	Unc-63	Unc-65
$650	$850	$1,250	$1,500	$2,000	$2,350	$3,500	$6,850

Series of 1880

Samples of $20 Series of 1880 notes (illus. on p. 449) are available as for type, although Uncirculated examples can be rare. Signature combinations are not often collected, but for the specialist the Series of 1880 with a brown Treasury seal and the Rosecrans-Nebeker signature combination (W-2012) represents a key issue. Serial numbers were printed in blue for W-2003 through W-2018; red serials were used afterward.

SERIES OF 1869

$20 Legal Tender Note, Series of 1869 (W-2000). Portrait of Alexander Hamilton to the left, goddess Victory with helmet to the right. Printed on blue-tinted paper. The star at the serial number is ornamental.

Detail of plate 7b identification at the upper right of the face.

Back of the $20 Legal Tender Note, Series of 1869 (W-2000), a bold geometric motif used only on this issue.

Back Style 1: With COLUMBIAN BANK NOTE CO. WASHINGTON D.C. in three curved lines in the bottom center of the design. SERIES OF 1880 vertically in the left margin and repeated vertically in the right margin. PRINTED AT THE BUREAU, ENGRAVING AND PRINTING in the bottom margin. Used on W-2003 to W-2006.

Back Style 2: No mention of Columbian. In that space in three lines is PRINTED AT THE BUREAU OF ENGRAVING & PRINTING WASHINGTON D.C., with the bottom two lines being the same as on Back Style 1. SERIES OF 1880 is in a curved line at the bottom of the large open space at the right side. Used on W-2007 to W-2020.

Mules: Back plate numbers can be in one of two locations.[5] On May 14, 1921, with the new Elliott-White signature combination starting, all Legal Tender, Silver Certificate, and Gold Certificate back plates were given numbers beginning with 1 and in a new location, although no notice was given of the change.

Back Plate Location 1 (regular use): W-2003 to W-2019. This was the standard location until May 14, 1921. Also used to create a mule for W-2020.

Back Plate Location 2 (regular use): W-2020. Introduced without notice as the new style on May 14, 1921, with the Elliott-White combination.

W-2003 • F-130 • Scofield-Gilfillan (1878–1881) • Large brown seal, blue serial numbers • 360,000 (est.)
Estimated population: 12 to 14 • *Highest graded:* EF-45.

VG-8	F-12	VF-20	EF-40
$1,800	$3,000	$6,000	$12,000

SERIES OF 1875

$20 Legal Tender Note, Series of 1875 (W-2001). (ANA Edward C. Rochette Money Museum)

Detail of the COLUMBIAN BANK NOTE COMPANY imprint.

Back of the $20 Legal Tender Note, Series of 1875 (W-2001).

W-2004 • F-131 • Bruce-Gilfillan (1881–1883) • 360,000 (est.)

Estimated population: 24 to 27 • *Highest graded:* Unc.

VG-8	F-12	VF-20	EF-40
$750	$2,000	$3,000	$5,000

W-2005 • F-132 • Bruce-Wyman (1883–1885) • 776,000 (est.)

Estimated population: 53 to 57 • *Highest graded:* Unc.

VG-8	F-12	VF-20	EF-40	AU-50	Unc-60	Unc-63
$500	$750	$1,400	$2,800	$4,000	$6,800	$10,000

W-2006 • F-133 • Large pink seal with plain border • 380,000 (est.)

Estimated population: 27 to 32 • *Highest graded:* AU-50.

VG-8	F-12	VF-20	EF-40	AU-50
$450	$750	$1,400	$2,800	$4,000

W-2007 • F-134 • Rosecrans-Jordan (1885–1887) • Large pink seal with plain border • Back Style 2 begins • 668,000 (est.)

Estimated population: 54 to 58 • *Highest graded:* Unc.

VG-8	F-12	VF-20	EF-40	AU-50	Unc-60	Unc-63
$375	$725	$1,300	$2,600	$3,800	$5,250	$8,000

W-2008 • F-135 • Rosecrans-Hyatt (1887–1889) • 832,000 (est.)

Estimated population: 62 to 66 • *Highest graded:* Unc.

VG-8	F-12	VF-20	EF-40	AU-50	Unc-60	Unc-63	Unc-65
$325	$600	$900	$1,600	$2,000	$2,100	$2,750	$5,500

W-2009 • F-136 • Large pink seal with spiked border • 1,760,000 (est.)

Estimated population: 135 to 150 • *Highest graded:* Unc.

VG-8	F-12	VF-20	EF-40	AU-50	Unc-60	Unc-63	Unc-65
$325	$600	$900	$1,600	$2,000	$2,100	$2,750	$4,500

SERIES OF 1878

$20 Legal Tender Note, Series of 1878 (W-2002). Plate a2, serial A1013696.

Detail of the face showing Geo. W. Casilear's patent in microprint below the serial number at lower left.

Detail of the back of a Series of 1878 note, showing the only change from the Series of 1875. Plate made by the Columbian Bank Note Company, as with the Series of 1875, but now with BEP imprint in the margin.

W-2010 • F-137 • Rosecrans-Huston (1889–1891) • 1,840,000 (est.)

Estimated population: 90 to 95 • *Highest graded:* Unc.

VG-8	F-12	VF-20	EF-40	AU-50	Unc-60	Unc-63	Unc-65
$325	$600	$950	$1,650	$2,100	$2,250	$2,900	$4,700

W-2011 • F-138 • Large brown seal • 956,000 (est.)

Estimated population: 60 to 65 • *Highest graded:* Unc.

VG-8	F-12	VF-20	EF-40	AU-50	Unc-60	Unc-63	Unc-65
$350	$650	$1,000	$1,700	$2,150	$2,350	$3,050	$10,000

W-2012 • F-139 • Rosecrans-Nebeker (1891–1893) • 184,000 (est.)

Estimated population: 20 to 23 • *Highest graded:* AU-55.

VG-8	F-12	VF-20	EF-40	AU-50
$600	$1,250	$2,500	$4,500	$7,000

W-2013 • F-140 • Small red seal with scalloped border • 1,580,000 (est.)

Estimated population: 95 to 105 • *Highest graded:* Unc • *Commentary:* This variety has two security paper types. Early type 1 has two horizontal threads the entire width of note. Later type 2 has two vertical bands of distributed red and blue fibers.

VG-8	F-12	VF-20	EF-40	AU-50	Unc-60	Unc-63	Unc-65
$300	$450	$700	$1,000	$1,300	$1,475	$2,000	$4,000

W-2014 • F-141 • Tillman-Morgan (1893–1897) • 2,300,000 (est.)

Estimated population: 135 to 145 • *Highest graded:* Unc.

VG-8	F-12	VF-20	EF-40	AU-50	Unc-60	Unc-63	Unc-65
$300	$450	$700	$1,000	$1,300	$1,475	$2,000	$4,000

W-2015 • F-142 • Bruce-Roberts (1897–1898) • 1,440,000 (est.)

Estimated population: 120 to 130 • *Highest graded:* Unc.

VG-8	F-12	VF-20	EF-40	AU-50	Unc-60	Unc-63	Unc-65
$300	$450	$700	$1,000	$1,300	$1,475	$2,000	$4,000

W-2016 • F-143 • Lyons-Roberts (1898–1905) • 1,564,000 (est.)

Estimated population: 90 to 100 • *Highest graded:* Unc.

VG-8	F-12	VF-20	EF-40	AU-50	Unc-60	Unc-63
$270	$400	$625	$900	$1,200	$1,350	$1,800

W-2017 • F-144 • Vernon-Treat (1906–1909) • 404,000

Estimated population: 48 to 52 • *Highest graded:* Unc.

VG-8	F-12	VF-20	EF-40	AU-50	Unc-60	Unc-63	Unc-65
$270	$400	$625	$900	$1,200	$1,350	$1,800	$4,500

W-2018 • F-145 • Vernon-McClung (1909–1911) • 408,000

Estimated population: 70 to 80 • *Highest graded:* Unc.

VG-8	F-12	VF-20	EF-40	AU-50	Unc-60	Unc-63
$270	$400	$625	$900	$1,200	$1,350	$1,800

SERIES OF 1880

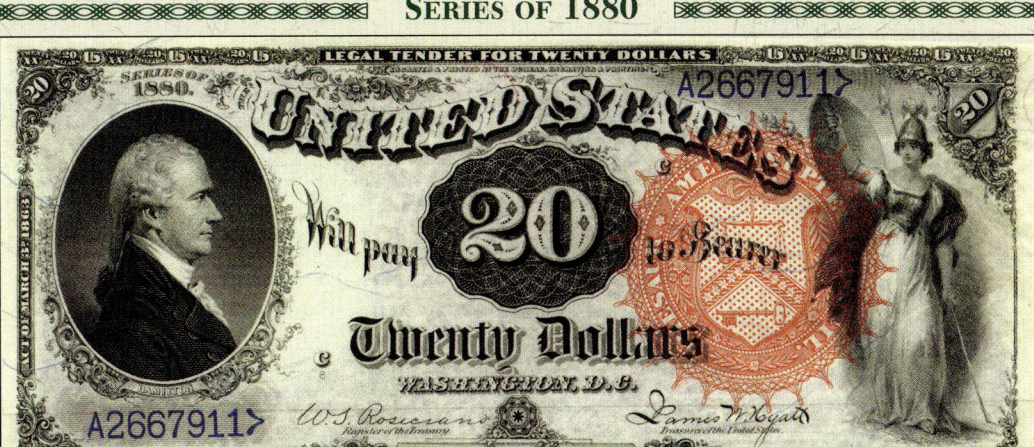

$20 Legal Tender Note, Series of 1880 (W-2009).

Detail of Back Style 1 (W-2006).

Detail of Back Style 2 (W-2009).

Back of the $20 Legal Tender Note, Series of 1880 (W-2009).

Back Plate Location 1.

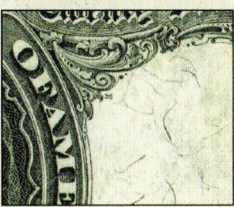

Back Plate Location 2.

W-2019 • F-146 • Teehee-Burke (1915–1919) • Red serial numbers • 400,000

Estimated population: 55 to 60 • *Highest graded:* Unc.

VG-8	F-12	VF-20	EF-40	AU-50	Unc-60	Unc-63	Unc-65
$270	$400	$625	$900	$1,200	$1,350	$1,800	$3,750

W-2019★ • F-146★

Recorded population: 4 • *Highest graded:* Unc • *Selected information:* Existing examples include serials ★450B/B, Unc, in the ANA Museum collection; ★1371B/C, VF; ★1813B/A, VF, sold in a Heritage auction (1/2006) for $14,375; and ★3477B/A, EF, sold in a CAA auction (1/1992) for $1,050.

W-2020 • F-147 • Elliott-White (1921–1922) • 4,000,000, or about 87% regular (est.)

Estimated population: 700 to 800 • *Highest graded:* Unc.

VG-8	F-12	VF-20	EF-40	AU-50	Unc-60	Unc-63	Unc-65
$250	$375	$600	$900	$1,200	$1,350	$1,800	$2,700

W-2020★ • F-147★

Estimated population: 38 to 47 • *Highest graded:* Unc.

F-12	VF-20	EF-40	AU-50	Unc-60	Unc-63
$1,000	$1,800	$3,000	$5,000	$6,000	$8,000

W-2020 Mule • F-147 • 580,000, or about 13% mules (est.)

Estimated population: 50 to 60 • *Highest graded:* Unc • *Commentary:* As this is a new listing, there is no market history.

W-2020 Mule★ • F-147★

Estimated population: 32 to 36 • *Highest graded:* Unc.

F-12	VF-20	EF-40	AU-50	Unc-60	Unc-63
$1,200	$2,000	$3,500	$5,500	$7,000	$10,000

NATIONAL BANK NOTES

Large-size $20 National Bank Notes follow the styles used for other denominations. The Original Series and Series of 1875 were made first, then the Series of 1882 Brown Back, Date Back, and Value Back types, followed by the Series of 1902 Red Seal, Date Back and Plain Back issues. The first three of these types, Original Series through the Series of 1882 Brown Back, illustrate a state or territorial seal on the left of the back.

Large-size $20 National Bank bills are scarcer than the $5 and $10 issues, but enough exist that it is possible to obtain examples to illustrate each type. The quest for specific states, towns, and individual banks is much more daunting; there are quite a few banks for which lower values are known, where none exist of the $20 or higher denominations.

Original Series
(Authorized Issue 1863 to 1875)

Notes of this denomination were printed by the American Bank Note Company, whose imprint appears at the bottom border. The contract, dated July 20, 1863, specified the designs for both sides, separately, of the $20, $50, and $100 denominations, the cost to be charged for the work, and other matters.[6] These were usually printed in four-subject sheets of $10-$10-$10-$20 with plate letters A, B, and C for the $10, and A for the $20. All have a small red Treasury seal with a spiked border.

The printing of $10-$10-$10-$20 Originals, with red ink and no prefix letter, began on April 2, 1864, with federal number 22 and ended on June 15, 1865, with federal number 999288. In the same arrangement blue serial numbers began without a prefix on June 19, 1865, with federal number 22 and ended October 1, 1867, with number 999446. The same arrangement for $10-$10-$10-$20 was followed with issues in red ink with prefix letters A, B, and D. The A set began on November 21, 1867, and the D set ended on August 13, 1875.[7] The Act of June 20, 1874, provided for the imprinting of the bank's charter number. This was done in red ink, one number vertically to the left of center and the other horizontally on the right.

Original Series and Series of 1875 notes depict on the left side of the face a scene, *Battle of Lexington, 1775*, by F.O.C. Darley (the most famous of the American Bank Note Company artists at the time[8]), attributed by Gene Hessler as being engraved by Joseph I. Pease. On the right is an image of the goddess Loyalty, by Alfred Jones. Peter Huntoon describes

three versions of the *Battle of Lexington*, each with differences in certain details, although the design remained the same.

On the back is *The Baptism of Pocahontas*, engraved by Charles Burt. This and other vignettes relating to American history were used on Original Series paper money per the wishes of Spencer M. Clark, chief of the National Currency Bureau, who sought to present a panorama of motifs that would be educational and informative. On the left side is a state or territorial seal representing the issuing location of the bank, and to the right is an eagle (some notes issued in territories have an eagle at both ends).

The unique Jeffries-Spinner federal signature combination is a notable rarity and a great prize, but numismatic emphasis is mainly on the issuing location.

Most notes are well worn, with Fine and Very Fine being the best usually available. For some states there are no notes known, and for others just a scant handful. Attractive Extremely Fine and About Uncirculated examples are rare. Finding one to illustrate the type will not be difficult, but tracking down a particular city or bank can be challenging. Rarity is the key word for this series.

Banks of Issue and Rarity of Notes

Based upon census information from Don C. Kelly and James M. Kelly (*National Bank Note Census*, Version 4.0) and with some information from other sources, this listing gives each location, the number of banks issuing this series of notes within each, and a commentary.[9]

The Kelly survey records only 155 of these notes, a generous amount in the context of the original printage, as only 275 of the related (printed on $10-$10-$10-$20 sheets) $10 notes are reported, although about three times as many $10 bills were made. Of serial number 1 notes three have been recorded for these series and are described below.

Alabama • 7 banks • No notes reported.

Arkansas • 2 banks of issue • 1 note reported • Merchants National Bank of Little Rock (F).

Colorado Territory • 5 banks of issue • 5 notes reported • Colorado National Bank of Denver (Unc, VF, F), and the state's only serial number 1 note, and the First National Bank of Denver (VF, F). The VF note is the only territorial serial number 1 listed by Don C. Kelly.

Connecticut • 84 banks of issue • 6 notes reported • Circulated notes from eight banks.

Delaware • 10 banks of issue • 1 note reported • National Bank of Wilmington, serial 2126, Fine.

District of Columbia • 9 banks of issue • No notes reported.

Georgia • 12 banks of issue • 1 note reported • National Bank of Augusta (G).

Idaho Territory • 1 bank of issue • No notes reported.

Illinois • 100 banks • 6 notes reported • Circulated notes from four different banks, the finest being the only serial number 1, from the First National Bank of Jacksonville (AU).

Indiana • 75 banks of issue • 5 notes reported • Circulated notes from as many banks.

Iowa • 50 banks of issue • 1 note reported • Pella National Bank (VG).

Kansas • 8 banks of issue • No notes reported.

Kentucky • 42 banks of issue • 4 notes reported • Second National Bank of Louisville (VG) and the First National Bank of Richmond (one EF–AU and two AU).

Louisiana • 11 banks of issue • No notes reported.

Maine • 67 banks of issue • 8 notes reported • Circulated notes from seven banks.

Maryland • 37 banks of issue • 7 notes reported • Circulated notes from as many banks.

Massachusetts • 224 banks of issue • 17 notes reported • Circulated notes from 15 banks.

Michigan • 46 banks of issue • 4 notes reported • Circulated notes from as many banks.

Minnesota • 20 banks of issue • No notes reported.

Mississippi • 2 banks of issue • No notes reported.

Missouri • 25 banks of issue • 3 notes reported • Third National Bank of St. Louis (VG–F), Valley National Bank of St. Louis (not graded), and Greene County National Bank of Springfield (F).

Montana Territory • 2 banks of issue • No notes reported.

Nebraska • 3 banks of issue • 2 notes reported • Omaha National Bank (both F).

Nebraska Territory • 2 banks of issue • No notes reported.

Nevada • 1 bank of issue • No notes reported.

New Hampshire • 41 banks of issue • 1 note reported • Rockingham National Bank of Portsmouth, VF–EF, serial not recorded.

New Jersey • 59 banks of issue • 7 notes reported • Circulated notes from five banks.

New Mexico Territory • 2 banks of issue • No notes reported.

New York • 271 banks of issue • 23 notes listed.[10]

ORIGINAL SERIES

$20 National Bank Note, Original Series (W-2031). National White River Bank of Bethel, Vermont. Early Original Series note, Colby-Spinner printed signatures, with blue Treasury serial number at upper right. Serial 41692, plate A. The bank serial 632 is in red at the lower left. This note has seen extensive circulation, a characteristic of nearly all extant examples of this type.

Back of the $20 National Bank Note, Original Series (W-2031). National White River Bank with the state seal of Vermont at the left.

North Carolina • 10 banks of issue • 3 notes reported • First National Bank of Charlotte, Commercial National Bank of Charlotte, and one serial number 1 note, National Bank of New Berne. None are graded.

Ohio • 134 banks of issue • 11 notes reported • From as many different banks, in grades G to F.

Oregon • 1 bank of issue • No notes reported.

Pennsylvania • 200 banks of issue • 19 notes reported[11] • Circulated notes from 16 banks.

Rhode Island • 61 banks of issue • 2 notes reported • Weybosset National Bank of Providence (VG) and American National Bank of Providence (not graded).

South Carolina • 10 banks of issue • No notes reported.

Tennessee • 26 banks of issue • 5 notes reported.

Texas • 9 banks of issue • 3 notes reported • First National Bank of Galveston (not graded), National Exchange Bank of Waco (VF), and the Waco National Bank (not graded).

Utah Territory • 5 banks of issue • No notes reported.

Vermont • 42 banks of issue • 3 notes reported • National Bank of Barre (not graded), National White River Bank of Bethel (F), and Vermont National Bank of St. Albans (not graded).

Virginia • 26 banks of issue • 3 notes reported • Planters National Bank of Richmond (G) and National Valley Bank of Staunton (both VG).

West Virginia • 18 banks of issue • 3 notes reported • National Exchange Bank of Weston (F, EF) and National Bank of West Virginia of Wheeling (F).

Wisconsin • 19 banks of issue • 1 note reported • National Exchange Bank of Milwaukee, serial 1262, G.

Wyoming Territory • 1 bank of issue • No notes reported.

Generic prices for a typical note from a state from which notes range from available to just slightly scarce:

VG-8	F-12	VF-20	EF-40	AU-50	Unc-60	Unc-63	Unc-65
$2,500	$3,000	$3,900	$5,000	$7,200	$8,500	$11,000	$14,000

W-2030 • F-424 • Chittenden-Spinner (1861–1864)
Estimated population: 33 to 36 • *Highest graded:* AU-50.

VG-8	F-12	VF-20	EF-40	AU-50
$2,500	$3,000	$3,900	$5,000	$7,200

W-2031 • F-427 • Colby-Spinner (1864–1867)
Estimated population: 70 to 80 • *Highest graded:* AU-50.

VG-8	F-12	VF-20	EF-40	AU-50
$2,500	$3,000	$3,900	$5,000	$7,200

W-2032 • F-428 • Jeffries-Spinner (1867–1869)
Recorded population: 1.

W-2033 • F-429 • Allison-Spinner (1869–1875)
Estimated population: 20 to 24 • *Highest graded:* AU-50.

VG-8	F-12	VF-20	EF-40	AU-50
$2,500	$3,000	$3,900	$5,000	$7,200

National Gold Bank Notes, Original Series

The $20 National Gold Bank notes of the early 1870s continue the same face as used on the Original and 1875 Series bills of the same denomination, with the vignettes *Battle of Lexington, 1775* and *Loyalty*. The back has the montage of gold coins, including an 1871 double eagle, used on other values in this series.

Although across the series gold-tinted paper was used for nearly all of these notes, in the $20 denomination there are exceptions among certain bills from Petaluma and San Francisco. The Kelly census records 62 examples, of which 32 are from the First National Gold Bank of San Francisco. Martin Gengerke gives specific data on 60 notes. As is the case with National Gold Bank notes of all denominations, most show extensive wear. The $20 bill is the highest denomination in the National Gold Bank Note series that comes on the market with some frequency; $50 and $100 notes are extreme rarities. Of the $20 notes, 506 are reported as outstanding on Treasury records:

W-2040 • F-1152 • Dated 1870 • San Francisco • First National Gold Bank • 11,248
Estimated population: 35 to 40 • *Highest graded:* EF-40 • *Commentary:* Both yellow-tinted (normal for this series) and white paper was used for this issue.

VG-8	F-12	VF-20	EF-40
$15,000	$40,000	$65,000	$115,000

W-2041 • F-1154 • Dated 1872 • Sacramento • National Gold Bank of D.O. Mills & Co. • 3,641
Recorded population: 3 • *Highest graded:* VF-20 • *Selected information:* Stack's (5/1992), 225-A895487/A, VF, $5,250. Knight (11/2003), 1137-B302368/A, G–VG, $34,500. Kagin's (1979), 532-X35863/C, Fair earlier, later listed as VG, $3,950.

W-2042 • F-1159b • San Francisco • National Gold Bank and Trust Co. • 4,223 • Unknown

W-2043 • F-1159a • Dated 1873 • Santa Barbara • First National Gold Bank • 800
Recorded population: 1 • *Selected information:* Knight (6/2001), 795-B302267/A, VG, $231,000.

W-2044 • F-1155 • Dated 1873 • Stockton • First National Gold Bank • 5,000
Recorded population: 8 • *Highest graded:* Fine • *Selected information:* CAA (1/1997), 4730-D809899/A, VG, pinholes, $5,750. CAA (5/2005), 4966-D810135/A, Fine, $25,300.

W-2045 • F-1156 • Dated 1874 • San Jose • Farmers National Gold Bank • 2,849
Recorded population: 8 • *Highest graded:* VG-10 • *Selected information:* CAA (5/2005), 244-B389198/A, VG–F, $25,300. No other modern sales.

W-2046 • F-unlisted • Petaluma • First National Gold Bank • 2,000 • Unknown
Commentary: Both yellow-tinted and white paper was used for this issue.

NATIONAL GOLD BANK NOTES, ORIGINAL SERIES

$20 National Gold Bank Note, Original Series (W-2040). First National Gold Bank of San Francisco, the most prolific issuer of notes in this series. Most were printed on yellow-tinted paper.

Back of W-2040. The same montage of gold coins was used on other National Gold Bank Notes of other denominations.

W-2047 • F-1158 • San Jose • Farmers National Gold Bank • 1,600

Recorded population: 8 • *Highest graded:* F-12 • *Selected information:* Examples of this variety are owned by the Smithsonian Institution and the Federal Reserve Bank of Richmond. Other examples include 58-D396120/A, G–VG, sold in a CAA auction (1/2003) for $12,075, and 1330-D810699/A, Fine (stolen).

W-2048 • F-1159 • Dated 1875 (but Original Series) • Oakland • Union National Gold Bank • 500

Recorded population: 2 • *Highest graded:* VG-8 • *Selected information:* Examples include serials 82-D524869/A, VG, and 82-D524869/A, G–VG, in the Smithsonian Institution collection.

Series of 1875
(Authorized Issue 1875 to 1902)

These notes (illus. on p. 455) continued the use of plates signed by the American Bank Note Company. The printing was done by the BEP in Washington. Vertically, near the border at the upper right is the imprint, PRINTED AT THE BUREAU, ENGRAVING & PRINTING U.S. TREASURY DEPt." For some banks for which there had

been no Original Series plates made, the bureau made new plates with BUREAU OF ENGRAVING & PRINTING TREASURY DEPt. at the bottom border, and no additional imprint or mention of the American Bank Note Company. This could be considered a subtype or even a different type, but has attracted virtually no notice. These seem to be rare.

The small red Treasury seal now has a scalloped rather than a spiked border. All have SERIES 1875 imprinted vertically in red to the left of center, near the bank charter number. The Treasury and bank serial numbers and two charter numbers are also in red. A small percentage of these notes are printed on paper with a vertical blue-tinted streak, the type used on the Legal Tender Notes beginning with the Series of 1869 (paper made under the James M. Willcox patent of July 24, 1866). These are especially colorful and attractive.

There are several very rare Treasury signature combinations in this series. Finding one to illustrate the type will not be difficult, but tracking down a particular city or bank can be challenging, although easier than for the Original Series.

Banks of Issue and Rarity of Notes

Based upon census information from Don C. Kelly and James M. Kelly (*National Bank Note Census*, Version 4.0) and with some information from other sources, this listing gives each location, the number of banks issuing this series of notes within each, and a commentary.[12]

The Kelly survey records 466 of the Series of 1875 notes, or about three times as many as the Original Series. There are only three serial number 1 notes, specifically listed below.

Alabama • 7 banks of issue • 1 note reported • Merchants and Planters National Bank of Montgomery, serial 997, VF.

Arkansas • 1 bank of issue • No notes reported.

California • 7 banks of issue • 5 notes reported • Circulated notes from four banks.

Colorado • 8 banks of issue • 2 notes reported • First National Bank of Fort Collins (VF) and Western National Bank of South Pueblo (EF).

Colorado Territory • 3 banks of issue • No notes reported.

Connecticut • 81 banks of issue • 13 notes reported • From 11 banks. The state's only Unc note is from the Yale National Bank of New Haven.

Dakota Territory • 9 banks of issue • 1 note reported • James River National Bank of Jamestown (AU), serial number 1. This is also the highest graded of any of the six different territorial notes reported for the Series of 1875; the runners-up are all VF. A fantastic trophy note.

Delaware • 13 banks of issue • 1 note reported • New Castle County National Bank of Odessa, serial 1528, F.

District of Columbia • 7 banks of issue • 6 notes reported • Circulated grades, four from the Farmers and Mechanics Bank of Georgetown and two from the Central National Bank of Washington.

Georgia • 9 banks of issue • 1 note reported • National Bank of Augusta, serial 1390, Fine.

Idaho Territory • 1 bank of issue • No notes reported.

Illinois • 96 banks of issue • 34 notes reported • From various banks, some duplication. Nine Unc known (including seven from the First National Bank of Paris). A good state for a type note.

Indiana • 69 banks of issue • 16 notes reported • Circulated grades from various banks plus one Unc from the First National Bank of Vincennes.

Iowa • 55 banks of issue • 14 notes reported • Eight different banks. The only Unc note is from the City National Bank of Clinton.

Kansas • 12 banks of issue • 2 notes reported • First National Bank of Hiawatha (F, Unc).

Kentucky • 45 banks of issue • 18 notes reported • Circulated notes from 14 banks.

Louisiana • 8 banks of issue • 4 notes reported • First National Bank of Baton Rouge (VG), Germania National Bank of New Orleans (EF), Louisiana National Bank of New Orleans (F), and New Orleans National Bank (F).

Maine • 69 banks of issue • 6 notes reported • Circulated notes from as many banks.

Maryland • 38 banks of issue • 8 notes reported • Circulated notes from four different banks, including four from the Manufacturers National Bank of Baltimore.

Massachusetts • 225 banks of issue • 25 notes reported • Circulated notes from a wide selection of banks.

Michigan • 57 banks of issue • 14 notes reported • Circulated notes from 10 banks.

Minnesota • 18 banks of issue • 1 note reported • Merchants National Bank of St. Paul, serial 8822, G.

Missouri • 19 banks of issue • 2 notes reported • Citizens National Bank of Kansas City (both F).

Montana • 6 banks of issue • 3 notes reported • First National Bank of Butte (not graded), Northwestern National Bank of Great Falls (VG), and the Merchants National Bank of Helena (VG).

Montana Territory • 6 banks of issue • No notes reported.

Nebraska • 11 banks of issue • 7 notes reported • Circulated notes from four banks.

Nebraska Territory • 1 bank of issue • 1 note reported • First National Bank of Omaha, serial 1027, VG–F.

Nevada • 1 bank of issue • 2 notes reported • First National Bank of Reno (F, AU).

New Hampshire • 42 banks of issue • 10 notes reported • Circulated notes from eight banks.

New Jersey • 59 banks of issue • 16 notes reported • From 10 different banks, including two Unc notes. A serial number 1 note is from the First National Bank of Madison (VF).

New Mexico Territory • 4 banks of issue • 3 notes reported • First National Bank of Albuquerque (VG, VF) and the Second National Bank of Santa Fe (VF).

New York • 237 banks of issue • 56 notes reported • Seven Unc notes, including the First National Bank of Greenwich (six) and the Lincoln National Bank of the City of New York (one). The only serial number 1 note is from the Wilber National Bank of Oneonta (AU).

North Carolina • 13 banks of issue • 3 notes reported • Commercial National Bank of Charlotte (not graded), First National Bank of Wilson (EF–AU), and Wachovia National Bank of Winston (F).

North Dakota • 7 banks of issue • 1 note reported • First National Bank of Bismarck (VG).

Ohio • 136 banks of issue • 76 notes reported • Various banks. Unc notes include eight from the First National Bank of Newark.

Oregon • 2 banks of issue • 2 notes reported • First National Bank of Pendleton (VG, AU).

Pennsylvania • 212 banks of issue • 64 notes reported • Various banks. Three Unc notes.

Rhode Island • 59 banks of issue • 11 notes reported • Circulated notes from eight banks.

South Carolina • 10 banks of issue • 1 note reported • National Bank of Spartanburg, serial 2804, VG–F.

South Dakota • 2 banks of issue • 1 note reported • Merchants National Bank of Deadwood, serial 692, AU. Popular town name.

Tennessee • 26 banks of issue • 4 notes reported • Circulated notes from as many banks.

SERIES OF 1875

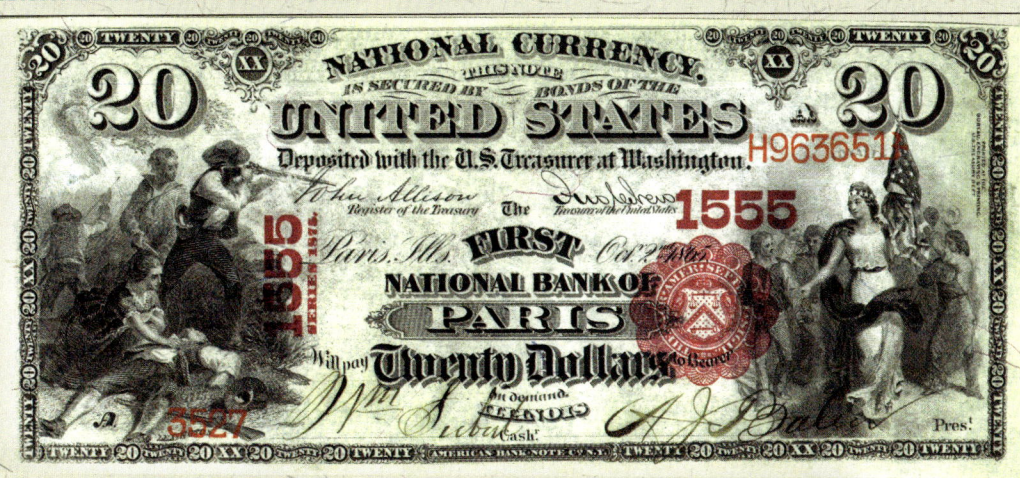

$20 National Bank Note, Series of 1875 (W-2050). The First National Bank of Paris, Illinois. SERIES 1875 overprinted vertically to the left of center. With AMERICAN BANK NOTE Co. N.Y. at the bottom border. At the upper right is the added bureau imprint.

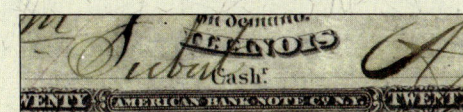

Detail of the AMERICAN BANK NOTE Co. N.Y. notation at the bottom of the face on the First National Bank of Paris note.

The First National Bank of Paris was chartered in 1865 and issued Original Series notes. Later, when Series of 1875 notes were printed by the Bureau of Engraving and Printing, the old plate was used, but with an added bureau imprint at the upper right, shown here.

Detail of the bureau imprint at the bottom of the face of W-2055, Franklin (New Hampshire) National Bank. This bank was organized on November 22, 1879. Therefore there was no Original Series plate on hand to use. The new plate was made by the Bureau of Engraving and Printing.

Back of the $20 National Bank Note, Series of 1875 (W-2050). First National Bank of Paris, with the Kentucky state seal at the left.

Texas • 19 banks of issue • 6 notes reported • Circulated notes from three banks.

Utah • 2 banks of issue • 1 note reported • First National Bank of Ogden, serial 1366, AU.

Utah Territory • 2 banks of issue • No notes reported.

Vermont • 41 banks of issue • 2 notes reported • First National Bank of Fair Haven (F) and National Bank of Rutland (VF).

Virginia • 19 banks of issue • 6 notes reported • Circulated notes from three banks.

West Virginia • 15 banks of issue • 10 notes reported • Three different banks, with six notes from the Citizens National Bank of Parkersburg.

Wisconsin • 18 banks of issue • 6 notes reported • Circulated notes from three different banks, including four from the Commercial National Bank of Appleton.

Wyoming • 4 banks of issue • No notes reported.

Wyoming Territory • 3 banks of issue • 1 note reported • First National Bank of Cheyenne, serial 350, F.

Generic prices for a typical note from a state from which notes range from available to just slightly scarce:

VG-8	F-12	VF-20	EF-40	AU-50	Unc-60	Unc-63	Unc-65
$2,350	$2,900	$3,750	$4,800	$7,000	$8,300	$10,600	$14,000

W-2050 • F-431 • Allison-New (1875–1876)
Estimated population: 130 to 140 • *Highest graded:* Unc.

VG-8	F-12	VF-20	EF-40	AU-50	Unc-60	Unc-63	Unc-65
$2,350	$2,900	$3,750	$4,800	$7,000	$8,300	$10,600	$14,000

W-2051 • F-432 • Allison-Wyman (1876–1877)
Estimated population: 45 to 50 • *Highest graded:* AU-50.

VG-8	F-12	VF-20	EF-40	AU-50
$2,350	$2,900	$3,750	$4,800	$7,000

W-2052 • F-433 • Allison-Gilfillan (1877–1878)
Recorded population: 7 • *Highest graded:* F-12 • *Selected information:* Heritage (4/2008), 776-A457591/A, Second NB of New Haven, CT, Fine, $4,888. Knight (3/2007), 1915-H504278/A, First NB of Milford, MI, Good, $10,350. Knight (10/2006), 6970/A, Quakertown NB, PA, Fine, $3,106.

W-2053 • F-434 • Scofield-Gilfillan (1878–1881)
Estimated population: 125 to 135 • *Highest graded:* Unc.

VG-8	F-12	VF-20	EF-40	AU-50	Unc-60	Unc-63	Unc-65
$2,350	$2,900	$3,750	$4,800	$7,000	$8,300	$10,600	$14,000

W-2054 • F-435 • Bruce-Gilfillan (1881–1883)
Estimated population: 120 to 130 • *Highest graded:* Unc.

VG-8	F-12	VF-20	EF-40	AU-50	Unc-60	Unc-63	Unc-65
$2,350	$2,900	$3,750	$4,800	$7,000	$8,300	$10,600	$14,000

W-2055 • F-436 • Bruce-Wyman (1883–1885)
Recorded population: 3 • *Highest graded:* F-15 • *Selected information:* B&M (3/2002), 25715-K785724/A, City NB of Springfield, MA, F–VF, $8,050. Hickman Auctions (3/1990), 3365-K4739/A, First NB of San Francisco, CA, VG, $2,200.

W-2056 • F-437 • Rosecrans-Huston (1889–1891)
Recorded population: 5 • *Highest graded:* AU-50 • *Selected information:* Heritage (9/2007), 3703-K546521/A, Merchants NB

of Helena, MT, VG, problems, $11,500. Knight (11/2004), 1479-K635966/A, Northwestern NB of Great Falls, MT, VG, problems, $6,325. Knight (11/1997), 2439-K542467/A, First NB of Bismarck, ND, VG, $1,900.

W-2057 • F-438 • Rosecrans-Nebeker (1891–1893)
Recorded population: 7 • *Highest graded:* AU-50 • *Selected information:* Heritage (4/2008), 444-K418949/A, First NB of Greensburg, PA, VF, problems, $5,175. No other modern records.

W-2058 • F-439 • Tillman-Morgan (1893–1897)
Recorded population: 1 • *Graded:* EF-40.

National Gold Bank Notes, Series of 1875

Notes from the First National Gold Bank of San Francisco, charter 1741, are apparently from two plates, with reentering of information on the printing plate changing it to a Series of 1875 plate and changing the signatures from Allison-Spinner to Bruce-Gilfillan. This was the only instance of a reentered national gold bank plate found by Peter Huntoon. In the process of removing John Allison's signature, the J of which extended across the end of the rifle barrel, the barrel tip was removed and replaced with a thick, shorter version.

National Gold Bank Notes of this type have SERIES 1875 printed vertically in red, to the left of center. The entered date on the notes is from the plate-making process and is not related to the Series of 1875. Some notes were printed on white instead of yellow paper. As a class, notes of this series are exceedingly rare. However, very little attention has been paid in comparing Original Series and Series of 1875 notes over the years, so that when an example comes on the market, its premium is less than might be expected. For the $20 note the Kelly census lists just 11 notes, eight of which are from the First National Gold Bank of San Francisco. The highest reported grade is Fine.

W-2060 • F-1153 • Dated 1875 • San Francisco • First National Gold Bank • 3,600
Recorded population: 7 • *Highest graded:* F-15 • *Selected information:* Knight (8/2003), 117-A57253/C, VG, $14,030. Knight

$20 National Gold Bank Note, Series of 1875 (W-2060). First National Gold Bank of San Francisco with SERIES 1875 imprint. Printed on white paper stock. The back design is the same as on the Original Series $20 National Gold Bank Notes.

(11/2006), 768-A60254/C, Fine, $40,250. CAA (5/2005), 893-A60379/A, Fine, $74,750.

W-2061 • F-1155a • Stockton • First National Gold Bank • 293

Recorded population: 1 • *Selected information:* This note is serial 140-D8292/A, Poor, repaired, and is owned by the Federal Reserve Bank of Chicago.

W-2062 • F-1157 • Petaluma • First National Gold Bank • 363

Recorded population: 2 • *Highest graded:* VF-20 • *Selected information:* Existing examples are serials 57-D241829/A, VF, normal paper, sold in a Knight auction (2/2003) for $143,750, and 283-H215229/A, Good, white paper.

W-2063 • F-unlisted • Oakland • First National Gold Bank • 12 • Unknown

Series of 1882, Brown Back
(Authorized Issue 1882 to 1908)

This series (illus. on p. 458) was the result of the expirations of the earliest national banks' charters and the formation of new chartered banks as provided by the Act of July 11, 1882. By then the Bureau of Engraving had been printing notes for seven years. To create distinctively new notes, the backs of the $10, $20, $50, and $100 denominations were changed, though many of the face plates created by the American Bank Note Company for the Original Series and Series of 1875 continued to be used. This was accomplished by either leaving the AMERICAN BANK NOTE COMPANY imprint at the bottom of the face and adding a printed notice in the field that this was a BEP product, or by reentering BUREAU OF ENGRAVING AND PRINTING where the earlier wording had been. In still other instances new plates were created using the old designs. The decorative border of the notes was changed to include the serial number of the bank six times, said to have been of use if a fragment of a note was sent to the Treasury department for redemption. Plates were typically laid out as $10-$10-$10-$20, with plate letters A, B, and C for the $10 and A for the $20. Vertically in brown to the left of the title block is SERIES 1882 on all notes. Charter numbers were overprinted in brown on the face from the outset, positioned vertically to the left of center on the issues from $10 to $100. Beginning in September 1890, the position of the charter number was changed to horizontal at the upper right. Peter Huntoon states that less than 14% of the plates had the vertical position, and as these were earlier, an even smaller percentage survives today. The Treasury seal is in brown as well. Regional letters N, E, M, S, W, and P were overprinted twice in brown on the face of notes starting with shipments received on March 17, 1902.

The reverse was completely redesigned to create the Brown Back style, printed in ink of that color. On the left is a state or territorial seal representing the issuing bank's location, as on earlier series. This necessitated making a separate set of plates for each state or territory. On the right is a perched eagle. At the center, a large, greenish-blue impression of the bank's charter number was applied, enabling the bills to be easily sorted when they were redeemed. These bills were first issued in 1882. Any bank with its charter extended between mid-1882 and 1902, and any new bank, received notes of this type and continued to receive them for the next 20 years, even though the new Series of 1902 notes were introduced during that time. Series of 1882 Brown Backs were printed into March 1908, at which time the Aldrich-Vreeland Act mandated new wording, and production stopped.

Most examples show circulation. Finding one to illustrate the type will not be difficult, but tracking down a particular city or bank can be challenging.

Banks of Issue and Rarity of Notes

Based upon census information from Don C. Kelly and James M. Kelly (*National Bank Note Census*, Version 4.0) and with some information from other sources, this listing gives each location, the number of banks issuing this series of notes within each, and a commentary.[13]

The Kelly survey records 2,456 of the Series of 1882 Brown Back notes, or more than the population of Date Backs and Value Backs combined. Serial number 1 notes are elusive but collectible, with 25 reported. These are specifically listed below.

Alabama • 42 banks of issue • 19 notes reported • The only Unc note is from the First National Bank of Geneva.

Alaska Territory • 1 bank of issue • No notes reported • Alaska was a district from 1884 until it became a territory on August 24, 1912, which it remained until statehood in 1959. All large-size Alaska notes in all series have the "district" address. Regardless, numismatists call all "territorials."

Arizona Territory • 7 banks of issue • 4 notes reported • All are circulated examples.

Arkansas • 9 banks of issue • 2 notes reported • American National Bank of Fort Smith (VG) and the First National Bank of Waldron (F).

California • 55 banks of issue • 72 notes reported • Two serial number 1 notes are from the First National Bank of Hanford (only Unc example) and Consolidated National Bank of San Diego (VF).

Colorado • 47 banks of issue • 16 notes reported • All are circulated examples.

Connecticut • 88 banks of issue • 49 notes reported • All are circulated. The only serial number 1 note is from the Clinton National Bank (EF).

Dakota Territory • 24 banks of issue • No notes reported.

Delaware • 18 banks of issue • 9 notes listed • Circulated notes exist from eight different banks.

District of Columbia • 13 banks of issue • 18 notes reported • All are circulated. One serial number 1 note is known from Riggs National Bank, Washington (not graded).

Florida • 15 banks of issue • 11 notes reported • The only serial number 1 note is from the First National Bank of Key West (AU). The only Unc note is from the American National Bank of Pensacola.

Georgia • 44 banks of issue • 31 notes reported • All are circulated examples.

SERIES OF 1882, BROWN BACK

$20 National Bank Note, Series of 1882, Brown Back (W-2071). National Bank of Commerce in New York, charter 733. Later style, with charter number horizontally at the upper right. This series is similar to the preceding in motifs, but with different overprints. AMERICAN BANK NOTE Co. N.Y. is imprinted in the frame at bottom center, and at the right border there is a three-line imprint in the field relating to the Bureau of Engraving and Printing. This reflects that the plate was first used for printing Original Series notes.

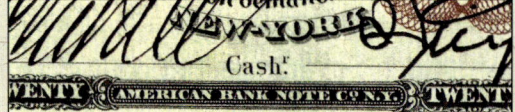

Detail of the American Bank Note Company imprint.

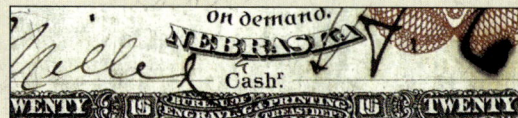

Detail of the BEP imprint on the new City National Bank of Kearney plate.

Back of the $20 National Bank Note, Series of 1882, Brown Back (W-2071). National Bank of Commerce in New York, charter 733. At the left is the state seal of New York, reflecting the location of the bank.

Hawaii Territory • 2 banks of issue • 5 notes reported • All are from the First National Bank of Hawaii, all in circulated grades.

Idaho • 12 banks of issue • 3 notes reported • Boise City National Bank, First National Bank of Hailey, and the First National Bank of Saint Anthony, all circulated.

Idaho Territory • 4 banks of issue • No notes reported.

Illinois • 221 banks of issue • 156 notes reported • The census lists 11 Unc notes. Three serial number 1 notes are from the Old Second National Bank of Aurora (not graded), Southern Illinois National Bank of East St. Louis (EF), and the First National Bank of Jacksonville (Unc).

Indian Territory • 56 banks of issue • 25 notes reported • All are circulated.

Indiana • 133 banks of issue • 80 notes reported • Three Unc notes are listed.

Iowa • 216 banks of issue • 115 notes reported • Seven Unc notes are listed. The only serial number 1 note is from the City National Bank of Clinton (Unc).

Kansas • 142 banks of issue • 50 notes reported • Six Unc notes reported. Two serial number 1 notes are from the Stock Growers National Bank of Ashland (Unc) and the First National Bank of Hutchinson (not graded).

Kentucky • 81 banks of issue • 85 notes reported • Three Unc notes are known.

SERIES OF 1882, BROWN BACK,
continued

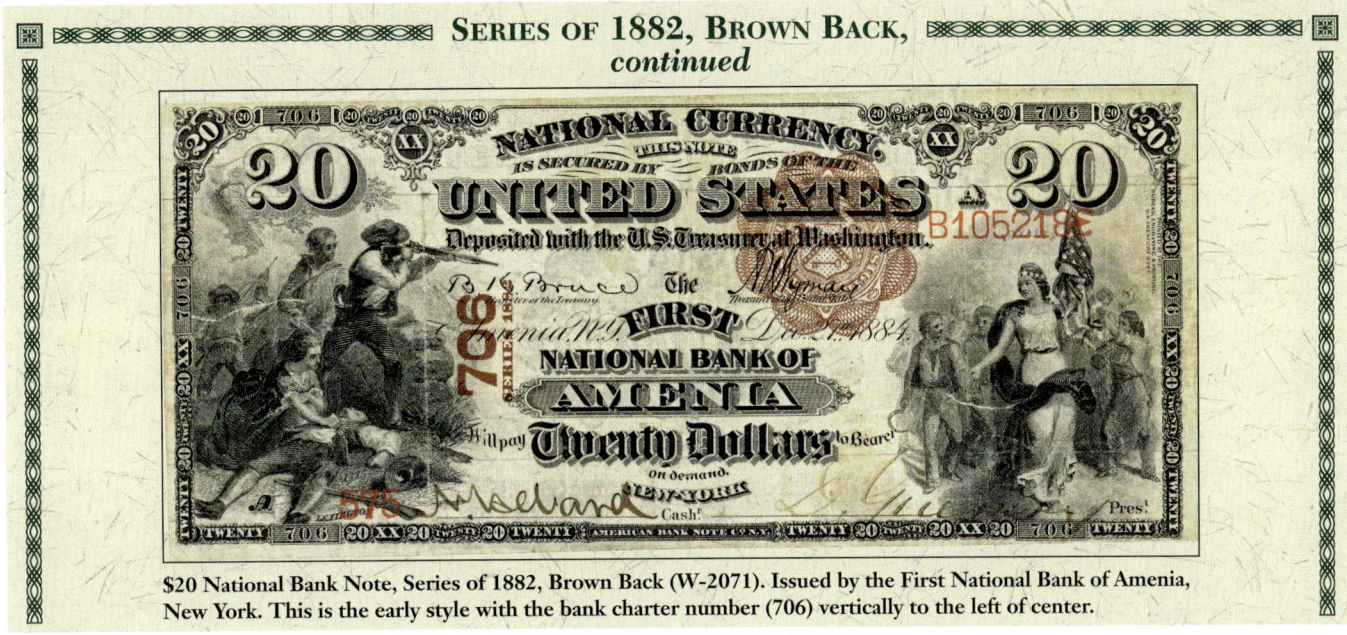

$20 National Bank Note, Series of 1882, Brown Back (W-2071). Issued by the First National Bank of Amenia, New York. This is the early style with the bank charter number (706) vertically to the left of center.

Louisiana • 25 banks of issue • 20 notes reported • All are circulated. Nine banks are represented.

Maine • 81 banks of issue • 28 notes reported • Two Unc notes are from the Lime Rock National Bank of Rockland and the Georges National Bank of Thomaston.

Maryland • 72 banks of issue • 34 notes reported • The only Unc note is from the First National Bank of Cumberland.

Massachusetts • 257 banks of issue • 68 notes reported • The only Unc note is from Middleborough National Bank of Middleborough.

Michigan • 97 banks of issue • 69 notes reported • Eight Unc notes are known.

Minnesota • 110 banks of issue • 44 notes reported • The only Unc note is from the First National Bank of Ceylon.

Mississippi • 11 banks of issue • 3 notes reported • Two are from the First National Bank of Hattiesburg (both F) and one from the First National Bank Lumberton (AU).

Missouri • 88 banks of issue • 86 notes reported • All are circulated. The only serial number 1 note is from the Moniteau National Bank of California (not graded).

Montana • 30 banks of issue • 12 notes listed.

Montana Territory • 7 banks of issue • No notes reported.

Nebraska • 121 banks of issue • 42 notes reported • Four Unc notes are reported, three from City National Bank of Kearney.

Nevada • 1 bank of issue • No notes reported.

New Hampshire • 64 banks of issue • 48 notes reported • Seven Unc notes are listed.

New Jersey • 122 banks of issue • 58 notes reported • Three are Unc, from Mount Holly National Bank, Union National Bank of Newark, and Second National Bank of Red Bank. The only serial number 1 note is from the First National Bank of Ocean City.

New Mexico Territory • 17 banks of issue • 6 notes reported • All are circulated, from four different banks.

New York • 363 banks of issue • 303 notes reported • Circulated for the most part, except 39 Unc notes from the National Bank of Commerce of New York. Three serial number 1 notes are from the New Amsterdam National Bank of New York (EF), Wilber National Bank of Oneonta (EF–AU), and the Peoples National Bank of Sandy Hill (F).

North Carolina • 37 banks of issue • 20 notes listed.

North Dakota • 45 banks of issue • 6 notes reported • From six different banks: one F, one VG, the other four not graded.

Ohio • 287 banks of issue • 197 notes reported • Many Unc notes are from the various banks. Two serial number 1 notes are from the Western Reserve National Bank of Cleveland (VF) and the First National Bank of Newcomerstown (Unc).

Oklahoma • 52 banks of issue • 6 notes reported • All are circulated.

Oklahoma Territory • 52 banks of issue • 14 notes reported • All are circulated examples. The only serial number 1 note is from the First National Bank of Newkirk (AU).

Oregon • 38 banks of issue • 14 notes reported • All are circulated examples. Seven banks are represented.

Pennsylvania • 485 banks of issue • 211 notes reported • Mostly circulated examples. Four serial number 1 notes are recorded.

Rhode Island • 55 banks of issue • 19 notes reported • Three Unc notes are from Ashaway National Bank (one) and Old National Bank of Providence (two).

South Carolina • 30 banks of issue • 14 notes reported • Two are Unc, from the National Bank of Greenville and the First National Bank of Spartanburg.

South Dakota • 41 banks of issue • 13 notes reported • All are circulated examples. Six banks are represented.

Tennessee • 53 banks of issue • 37 notes reported • One Unc note is from the First National Bank of Brownsville.

Texas • 311 banks of issue • 141 notes reported • The census lists 12 Unc notes. Two serial number 1 notes are known,

459

from the Goldwaithe National Bank (VF) and the Itasca National Bank (Unc).

Utah • 12 banks of issue • 7 notes reported • All are circulated, from six different banks.

Utah Territory • 9 banks of issue • No notes reported.

Vermont • 51 banks of issue • 8 notes reported • All are circulated. Seven different banks are represented.

Virginia • 57 banks of issue • 34 notes reported • All are circulated examples.

Washington • 60 banks of issue • 8 notes reported • Seven banks are represented.

Washington Territory • 26 banks of issue • 1 note reported • From the Merchants National Bank of Tacoma, serial 1070, VG–F.

West Virginia • 51 banks of issue • 29 notes reported • All are circulated examples.

Wisconsin • 97 banks of issue • 99 notes reported • The census lists 10 Unc notes.

Wyoming • 18 banks of issue • 7 notes reported • All are circulated examples. Four banks are represented.

Wyoming Territory • 7 banks of issue • No notes reported.

Generic prices for a typical note from a state from which notes range from available to just slightly scarce:

VG-8	F-12	VF-20	EF-40	AU-50	Unc-60	Unc-63	Unc-65
$900	$1,050	$1,600	$2,250	$2,800	$4,200	$6,000	$7,500

W-2070 • F-493 • Bruce-Gilfillan (1881–1883)
Estimated population: 145 to 153 • *Highest graded:* Unc.

VG-8	F-12	VF-20	EF-40	AU-50	Unc-60	Unc-63	Unc-65
$900	$1,050	$1,600	$2,250	$2,800	$4,200	$6,000	$7,500

W-2071 • F-494 • Bruce-Wyman (1883–-1885)
Estimated population: 370 to 410 • *Highest graded:* Unc.

VG-8	F-12	VF-20	EF-40	AU-50	Unc-60	Unc-63	Unc-65
$900	$1,050	$1,600	$2,250	$2,800	$4,200	$6,000	$7,500

W-2072 • F-495 • Bruce-Jordan (1885)
Estimated population: 60 to 65 • *Highest graded:* Unc.

VG-8	F-12	VF-20	EF-40	AU-50	Unc-60	Unc-63	Unc-65
$950	$1,100	$1,700	$2,400	$3,000	$4,400	$6,250	$8,000

W-2073 • F-496 • Rosecrans-Jordan (1885–1887)
Estimated population: 200 to 220 • *Highest graded:* Unc.

VG-8	F-12	VF-20	EF-40	AU-50	Unc-60	Unc-63	Unc-65
$900	$1,050	$1,600	$2,250	$2,800	$4,200	$6,000	$7,500

W-2074 • F-497 • Rosecrans-Hyatt (1887–1889)
Estimated population: 90 to 100 • *Highest graded:* Unc.

VG-8	F-12	VF-20	EF-40	AU-50	Unc-60	Unc-63	Unc-65
$900	$1,050	$1,600	$2,250	$2,800	$4,200	$6,000	$7,500

W-2075 • F-498 • Rosecrans-Huston (1889–1891)
Estimated population: 250 to 275 • *Highest graded:* Unc.

VG-8	F-12	VF-20	EF-40	AU-50	Unc-60	Unc-63	Unc-65
$900	$1,050	$1,600	$2,250	$2,800	$4,200	$6,000	$7,500

W-2076 • F-499 • Rosecrans-Nebeker (1891–1893)
Estimated population: 300 to 350 • *Highest graded:* Unc.

VG-8	F-12	VF-20	EF-40	AU-50	Unc-60	Unc-63	Unc-65
$900	$1,050	$1,600	$2,250	$2,800	$4,200	$6,000	$7,500

W-2077 • F-500 • Rosecrans-Morgan (1893)
Recorded population: 3 • *Highest graded:* EF-40 • *Selected information:* Hickman & Oakes (4/1978), 509-U968950/A, Griggsville NB, IL, EF, problems, $770.

W-2078 • F-501 • Tillman-Morgan (1893–1897)
Estimated population: 230 to 260 • *Highest graded:* Unc.

VG-8	F-12	VF-20	EF-40	AU-50	Unc-60	Unc-63	Unc-65
$900	$1,050	$1,600	$2,250	$2,800	$4,200	$6,000	$7,500

W-2079 • F-502 • Tillman-Roberts (1897)
Estimated population: 40 to 45 • *Highest graded:* AU-50.

VG-8	F-12	VF-20	EF-40	AU-50
$950	$1,100	$1,700	$2,400	$3,000

W-2080 • F-503 • Bruce-Roberts (1897–1898)
Estimated population: 25 to 28 • *Highest graded:* AU-50.

VG-8	F-12	VF-20	EF-40	AU-50
$900	$1,050	$1,600	$2,250	$2,800

W-2081 • F-504 • Lyons-Roberts (1898–1905)
Estimated population: 550 to 650 • *Highest graded:* Unc.

VG-8	F-12	VF-20	EF-40	AU-50	Unc-60	Unc-63	Unc-65
$900	$1,050	$1,600	$2,250	$2,800	$4,200	$6,000	$7,500

W-2082 • F-505 • Lyons-Treat (1905–1906)
Recorded population: 5 • *Highest graded:* F-12 • *Selected information:* Heritage (4/2008), 772-R37183R/A, N Exchange B of Dallas, TX, Fine, $3,737.50. Knight (3/2008), 8343-R122994R/A, N Exchange B of Dallas, TX, Fine, $1,092.50. Knight (8/2001), 238-T310975T/A, First NB of McAlester, Oklahoma Territory, VG, $2,860.

W-2083 • F-506 • Vernon-Treat (1906–1909)
Recorded population: 7 • *Highest graded:* VF-25 • *Selected information:* Smythe (7/2007), 85-T898729T/A, NB of Waupaca, WI, F–VF, $2,760. This is the only modern auction record.

Series of 1882, Date Back
(Authorized Issue 1908 to 1915, Some 1916)

This unexpected issue was created to reflect a change in the backing of the notes authorized by the Aldrich-Vreeland Act of May 30, 1908. Notes of the new type were issued beginning in that year. Brown Back production ceased, and new orders were filled by the Date Back type.

In order to make it easier to fund the notes, banks were allowed to deposit good securities in addition to government bonds, while earlier only U.S. government bonds had been allowed. All have the inscription on the face, "This note is secured by bonds of the United States or other securities." This was often added by altering face plates with the same design that were used for earlier series. Although the Act expired on June 30, 1915, marking the end of the official use of this imprint and the related back, some plates continued

SERIES OF 1882, DATE BACK

$20 National Bank Note, Series of 1882, Date Back (W-2096). The Grand Rapids (Michigan) National Bank, charter 2460. The face layout is generally similar to the Series of 1875 notes, but with "or other securities" added to the backing. BUREAU OF ENGRAVING & PRINTING imprint at lower border. The regional letter M in blue is for "Midwest," a key to help clerks at the Treasury department sort worn notes when they were redeemed.

Back of the $20 National Bank Note, Series of 1882, Date Back (W-2096), with 1882 and 1908 dates.

to be used into 1916. Otherwise, the face motifs are the same as on the Series of 1882 Brown Backs (continued from the Original Series and Series of 1875). The serial numbers, charter number, two regional letters, and the Treasury seal are all in blue.

The back was redesigned completely. At the center is a large open space with the dates 1882 and 1908 with an ornament between them. Above, near the border, is the obligation, and below near the border is the counterfeiting clause. At the left is an eagle perched on a shield, wings upraised. At the right is an eagle with folded wings perched on an olive branch. Gone are the state and territorial seals used in earlier series, making plate preparation a much easier task.

Although the 1882 Date Backs are nearly twice as scarce as Brown Backs, collector interest in them has been lower. As a result, notes from rare states can be surprisingly affordable. Finding one to illustrate the type will not be difficult, but tracking down a particular city or bank can be challenging. Except for a Pennsylvania cache, Uncirculated notes are very rare as a class.

Banks of Issue and Rarity of Notes

Based upon census information from Don C. Kelly and James M. Kelly (*National Bank Note Census*, Version 4.0) and with some information from other sources, this listing gives each location, the number of banks issuing this series of notes within each, and a commentary.[14]

The Kelly survey records 1,440 of the Series of 1882 Date Back notes. Serial number 1 notes are exceedingly rare, with just two recorded (noted specifically below under Montana and New York).

Alabama • 17 banks of issue • 21 notes reported • Nine banks are represented. All are circulated.

Alaska Territory • 1 bank • 1 note reported • The only note reported is from the First National Bank of Juneau (VG), serial 813. Alaska was a district from 1884 until it became a territory on August 24, 1912, which it remained until statehood in 1959. All large-size Alaska notes in all series have the "district" address. Regardless, numismatists call all "territorials."

Arizona • 3 banks of issue • 2 notes reported • Both are from the First National Bank of Clifton (G, F).

Arizona Territory • 5 banks of issue • 1 note reported • The only note reported is from the Prescott National Bank (F), serial 2436.

Arkansas • 3 banks of issue • 3 notes reported • All are from the First National Bank of DeQueen (VF, not graded, VG).

California • 24 banks of issue • 50 notes reported • All are circulated examples.

Colorado • 22 banks of issue • 15 notes reported • Seven banks are represented. The only Unc example is from the First National Bank of Fort Collins.

Connecticut • 10 banks of issue • 5 notes reported • Four banks are represented. All notes are circulated.

Delaware • 6 banks of issue • 5 notes reported • All are circulated, from the Lewes National Bank.

District of Columbia • 5 banks of issue • 8 notes reported • Seven of these are from the Riggs National Bank of Washington. All notes are circulated.

Florida • 8 banks of issue • 10 notes reported • All are circulated, from four different banks.

Georgia • 22 banks of issue • 48 notes reported • All notes are circulated.

Hawaii Territory • 2 banks of issue • 8 notes reported • All are from the First National Bank of Hawaii at Honolulu, all VG.

Idaho • 4 banks of issue • 3 notes reported • First National Bank of Payette (two, both F) and the First National Bank of Saint Anthony (VG–F).

Illinois • 132 banks of issue • 97 notes reported • Nine Unc notes are listed.

Indiana • 64 banks of issue • 36 notes reported • The only Unc example reported from the Citizens National Bank of Peru.

Iowa • 129 banks of issue • 85 notes reported • Two Unc notes are from the First National Bank of Lenox and the First National Bank of Oelwein.

Kansas • 42 banks of issue • 22 notes reported • All known notes are circulated.

Kentucky • 45 banks of issue • 45 notes reported • Three Unc notes are from the First National Bank of Carlisle.

Louisiana • 11 banks of issue • 14 notes reported • Five banks are represented. The only Unc note is from the Commercial National Bank of New Orleans.

Maine • 20 banks of issue • 8 notes reported • Six banks are represented. All notes are circulated.

Maryland • 29 banks of issue • 18 notes reported • Seven banks are represented. Two Unc notes are from the Drovers & Mechanics National Bank of Baltimore.

Massachusetts • 48 banks of issue • 15 notes reported • There are 11 banks represented. Two Unc notes are from the Winthrop National Bank of Boston and the Union National Bank of Lowell.

Michigan • 29 banks of issue • 15 notes reported • Nine banks are represented. The census lists five Unc notes.

Minnesota • 66 banks of issue • 37 notes reported • The only Unc note is from the First National Bank of Winnebago.

Mississippi • 3 banks of issue • 6 notes reported • Three banks are represented. All are circulated.

Missouri • 37 banks of issue • 52 notes reported • All notes are circulated.

Montana • 13 banks of issue • 8 notes reported • Four banks are represented. All are circulated examples. A serial number 1 note is from the National Bank of Helena (EF), a prize rarity. One of just two such notes among all states (the other is from New York).

Nebraska • 43 banks of issue • 28 notes reported • All are circulated.

New Hampshire • 19 banks of issue • 5 notes reported • Four banks are represented. All are circulated.

New Jersey • 51 banks of issue • 20 notes reported • All are circulated.

New Mexico • 7 banks of issue • 6 notes reported • All are circulated.

New Mexico Territory • 8 banks of issue • 1 note reported • From the San Miguel National Bank of Las Vegas (VF).

New York • 105 banks of issue • 50 notes reported • Four Unc notes are known. A serial number 1 note is from the Wilber National Bank of Oneonta (AU). One of just two such notes among all states (the other is from Montana).

North Carolina • 27 banks of issue • 19 notes reported • All are circulated.

North Dakota • 26 banks of issue • 15 notes reported • All are circulated.

Ohio • 112 banks of issue • 110 notes reported • Four Unc notes are listed.

Oklahoma • 84 banks of issue • 48 notes reported • All are circulated.

Oregon • 10 banks of issue • 10 notes reported • Five banks are represented. All are circulated.

Pennsylvania • 247 banks of issue • 180 notes reported • Many Unc notes are listed, especially from the Duquesne National Bank of Pittsburgh.

Rhode Island • 2 banks of issue • 3 notes reported • All are from the United National Bank of Providence, and all are VF.

South Carolina • 11 banks of issue • 10 notes reported • The only Unc note is from the City National Bank of Greenville.

South Dakota • 21 banks of issue • 22 notes reported • All are circulated.

Tennessee • 24 banks of issue • 17 notes reported • Two Unc notes are from the First National Bank of Jackson.

Texas • 169 banks of issue • 132 notes reported • Seven Unc notes are known.

Utah • 8 banks of issue • 3 notes reported • First National Bank of Ogden (two, both VF) and the Utah National Bank of Salt Lake City (VG).

Vermont • 12 banks of issue • 1 note reported • Peoples National Bank of Brattleboro (VG–F).

Virginia • 33 banks of issue • 29 notes reported • Four Unc notes are listed.

Washington • 12 banks of issue • 6 notes reported • Three banks are represented. All are circulated.

West Virginia • 28 banks of issue • 18 notes reported • All are circulated.

Wisconsin • 47 banks of issue • 56 notes reported • Two Unc specimens are from the National Bank of La Crosse.

Wyoming • 10 banks of issue • 14 notes reported • The census lists 12 Unc notes from the First National Bank of Kemmerer.

Generic prices for a typical note from a state from which notes range from available to just slightly scarce:

VG-8	F-12	VF-20	EF-40	AU-50	Unc-60	Unc-63	Unc-65
$900	$1,050	$1,600	$2,200	$2,800	$4,000	$5,800	$8,000

W-2090 • F-549 • Rosecrans-Huston (1889–1891)

Estimated population: 23 to 25 • *Highest graded:* EF-40.

VG-8	F-12	VF-20	EF-40
$900	$1,050	$1,600	$2,200

W-2091 • F-550 • Rosecrans-Nebeker (1891–1893)

Estimated population: 115 to 125 • *Highest graded:* Unc.

VG-8	F-12	VF-20	EF-40	AU-50	Unc-60	Unc-63	Unc-65
$900	$1,050	$1,700	$2,300	$3,000	$4,200	$6,000	$8,500

W-2092 • F-551 • Rosecrans-Morgan (1893)

Recorded population: 2 • *Highest graded:* EF-40 • *Selected information:* Stack's (3/1990), 443-M113721/B, First NB of Marshall County at Plymouth, IN, EF, $550.

W-2093 • F-552 • Tillman-Morgan (1893–1897)

Estimated population: 290 to 320 • *Highest graded:* Unc.

VG-8	F-12	VF-20	EF-40	AU-50	Unc-60	Unc-63	Unc-65
$900	$1,050	$1,600	$2,200	$2,800	$4,000	$5,800	$8,000

W-2094 • F-553 • Tillman-Roberts (1897)

Estimated population: 31 to 34 • *Highest graded:* AU-50.

VG-8	F-12	VF-20	EF-40	AU-50
$900	$1,050	$1,600	$2,200	$2,800

W-2095 • F-554 • Bruce-Roberts (1897–1898)

Estimated population: 28 to 32 • *Highest graded:* EF-40.

VG-8	F-12	VF-20	EF-40
$925	$1,080	$1,650	$2,300

W-2096 • F-555 • Lyons-Roberts (1898–1905)

Estimated population: 800 to 900 • *Highest graded:* Unc.

VG-8	F-12	VF-20	EF-40	AU-50	Unc-60	Unc-63	Unc-65
$900	$1,050	$1,600	$2,200	$2,800	$4,000	$5,800	$8,000

W-2097 • F-556 • Vernon-Treat (1906–1909)

Estimated population: 55 to 60 • *Highest graded:* AU-50.

VG-8	F-12	VF-20	EF-40	AU-50
$900	$1,050	$1,600	$2,200	$2,800

W-2098 • F-556a • Vernon-McClung (1909–1911)

Recorded population: 1 • *Selected information:* CAA (1/1992), 3486-H38004/A, McCartney NB of Fort Howard, WI, Fine, $1,350.

W-2099 • F-557 • Napier-McClung (1911–1912)

Estimated population: 10 to 12 • *Highest graded:* AU-50.

VG-8	F-12	VF-20	EF-40	AU-50
$1,000	$1,150	$1,700	$2,300	$3,000

Series of 1882, Value Back
(Authorized Issue 1915+)

When the Aldrich-Vreeland Act expired on June 20, 1915, the BEP created the Value Back (illus. on p. 465), spelling out the denomination, to replace the Date Back type. The security of the notes reverted to bonds only, as it had been before the implementation of the Aldrich-Vreeland Act of May 30, 1908.

> **Plate Style a:** Some old face plates remained in use from the earlier series, with the inscription on the face that reads, "This note is secured by bonds of the United States or other securities."

> **Plate Style b:** A "new" plate style was created, a copy of that used for all 1882 Brown Backs, with the security stated as, "This note is secured by bonds of the United States deposited with the U.S. Treasurer at Washington." This is the correct or proper plate intended for use on Value Back notes.

Otherwise the face was similar to that used for the Series of 1882 Date Back, with the serial numbers, charter number, two regional letters, and the Treasury seal all in blue. The back used the same vignettes as the preceding type, but now with TWENTY DOLLARS in large letters at the center.

Similar to other denominations, the $20 Value Back outclasses in rarity the other Series of 1882 notes and, for that matter, Series of 1902 notes. Although Plate Styles a and b are well described in specialized texts by Gene Hessler, Carlson Chambliss, Peter Huntoon, and Don C. Kelly, thus far they have scarcely been recognized in auction catalogs or other offerings.

Banks of Issue and Rarity of Notes

Based upon census information from Don C. Kelly and James M. Kelly (*National Bank Note Census*, Version 4.0) and with some information from other sources, this listing gives each location, the number of banks issuing this series of notes within each, and a commentary.[15]

The Kelly survey records just 701 of the Series of 1882 Value Back notes, revealing that these are far rarer than the other two 1882 classes. Uncirculated notes are very rare. No serial number 1 notes are recorded.

Alabama • 8 banks of issue • 13 notes reported • Four banks are represented. All are circulated.

Arizona • 2 banks of issue • 3 notes reported • All are from the First National Bank of Clifton (F, VG, VF).

Arkansas • 2 banks of issue • No notes reported.

California • 13 banks of issue • 15 notes reported • Four banks are represented. All are circulated.

Colorado • 11 banks of issue • 10 notes reported • Six banks are represented. All are circulated.

Connecticut • 6 banks of issue • 5 notes reported • Three banks are represented. All are circulated.

Delaware • 2 banks of issue • No notes reported.

Florida • 2 banks of issue • No notes reported.

Georgia • 7 banks of issue • 13 notes reported • The only Unc note is from the Lowry National Bank of Atlanta.

Hawaii Territory • 1 bank of issue • 2 notes reported • Both are from the First National Bank of Hawaii at Honolulu (F, EF).

Idaho • 2 banks of issue • 1 note reported • First National Bank of Payette (VG).

Illinois • 58 banks of issue • 54 notes reported • Three Unc notes are available, from the Farmers National Bank of Barry, Ricker National Bank of Quincy, and Farmers National Bank of Taylorville.

Indiana • 30 banks of issue • 14 notes reported • All are circulated.

Iowa • 63 banks of issue • 47 notes listed • Four Unc notes are listed.

Kansas • 19 banks of issue • 12 notes reported • All are circulated.

Kentucky • 16 banks of issue • 27 notes reported • The only Unc note is from the First National Bank of Carlisle.

Louisiana • 1 bank of issue • No notes reported.

Maine • 4 banks of issue • 2 notes reported • North National Bank of Rockport (VF) and the Searsport National Bank of Searsport (F).

Maryland • 15 banks of issue • 14 notes reported • All are circulated.

Massachusetts • 8 banks of issue • 5 notes reported • Three banks are represented. All are circulated.

Michigan • 11 banks of issue • 14 notes reported • All are circulated.

Minnesota • 36 banks of issue • 16 notes reported • All are circulated.

Mississippi • 2 banks of issue • No notes reported.

Missouri • 12 banks of issue • 17 notes reported • The only Unc note is from the Paris National Bank.

Montana • 2 banks of issue • 3 notes reported • First National Bank of Chinook (F), National Bank of Montana, Helena (not graded, VF).

Nebraska • 20 banks of issue • 21 notes reported • All are circulated.

New Hampshire • 10 banks of issue • 4 notes reported • Three banks are represented. All are circulated.

New Jersey • 26 banks of issue • 12 notes reported • All are circulated.

New Mexico • 6 banks of issue • 2 notes reported • First National Bank of Las Vegas (EF) and the First National Bank of Roswell (VF).

New York • 64 banks of issue • 25 notes reported • All are circulated.

North Carolina • 12 banks of issue • 6 notes reported • Four different banks. All are circulated.

North Dakota • 12 banks of issue • 3 notes reported • First National Bank of Bottineau (not graded), First National Bank of Cooperstown (VG–F), First National Bank of Hope (F).

Ohio • 61 banks of issue • 72 notes reported • Three Unc notes are from the Citizens National Bank of Chillicothe, Commercial National Bank of Columbus, and the Old Citizens National Bank of Zanesville.

Oklahoma • 59 banks of issue • 41 notes reported • The only Unc note is from the Shawnee National Bank.

Oregon • 4 banks of issue • 3 notes reported • First National Bank of Ashland (VG), La Grande National Bank (VG–F), and the First National Bank of Pendleton (VG).

Pennsylvania • 123 banks of issue • 79 notes reported • Six Unc notes are listed.

South Carolina • 2 banks of issue • 4 notes reported • Three different banks. All are circulated.

South Dakota • 14 banks of issue • 12 notes reported • Five banks. All are circulated.

Tennessee • 8 banks of issue • 3 notes reported • Peoples National Bank of Gallatin (F), and the Unaka National Bank of Johnson City (VF, VG).

Texas • 83 banks of issue • 70 notes reported • The census lists 11 Unc notes.

Utah • 3 banks of issue • No notes reported.

Vermont • 3 banks of issue • No notes reported.

Virginia • 17 banks of issue • 18 notes reported • All are circulated.

Washington • 6 banks of issue • 3 notes reported • All from the Vancouver National Bank (not graded, VF, VG).

West Virginia • 16 banks of issue • 10 notes reported • Seven different banks. All are circulated.

Wisconsin • 21 banks of issue • 22 notes reported • All are circulated.

Wyoming • 4 banks of issue • 4 notes reported • Rawlins National Bank (G–VG), First National Bank of Thermopolis (Fair, F–VF, VF).

Generic prices for a typical note from a state from which notes range from available to just slightly scarce:

VG-8	F-12	VF-20	EF-40	AU-50	Unc-60	Unc-63	Unc-65
$950	$1,250	$1,900	$2,600	$3,400	$4,300	$6,750	$9,000

W-2100 • F-580 • Tillman-Morgan (1893–1897)

Recorded population: 6 • Highest graded: VF-25 • Selected information: CAA (9/2003), 3307-T523605/B, Citizens NB of Tionesta, PA, G–VG, damaged, $1,121. Knight (9/1997), 1345-T787023/B, Southern Illinois NB of East St. Louis, IL, Fine, $413.

SERIES OF 1882, VALUE BACK

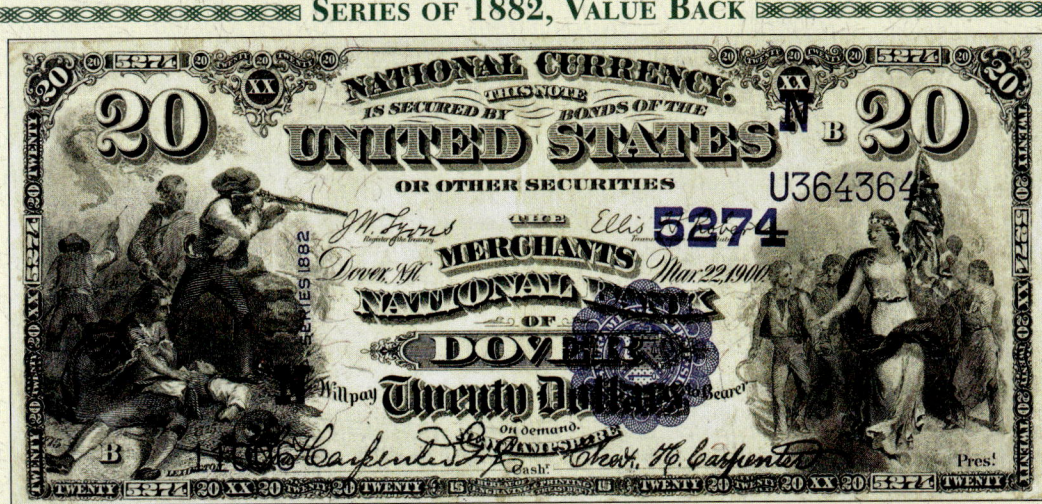

$20 National Bank Note, Series of 1882, Value Back (W-2103). Merchants National Bank of Dover, New Hampshire, charter 5274. With BUREAU OF ENGRAVING & PRINTING imprint at the bottom border and "or other securities" added to the warranty at the top. At the upper right the blue overprint N is for North, the bank's region.

Back of the $20 National Bank Note, Series of 1882, Value Back, with TWENTY DOLLARS.

W-2101 • F-580a • Tillman-Roberts (1897)

Recorded population: 4 • *Highest graded:* VF-25 • *Selected information:* Heritage (4/2008), 11797-U118575/B, Millikin NB of Decatur, IL, VF, $21,850. Smythe (6/2005), 6415-T488813/B, Peoples NB of Waynesburg, PA, VG–F, $2,990. Knight (6/2001), 6643-U103901/B, Citizens NB of East Liverpool, OH, VG–F, $440.

W-2102 • F-580b • Bruce-Roberts (1897–1898)

Recorded population: 3 • *Highest graded:* EF-40 • *Selected information:* Heritage (4/2008), 8925T530023/B, Northampton NB of Easton, PA, F–VF, $19,550. Knight (3/2006), 8418-U210116/B, Nyack NB, NY, EF, $14,950.

W-2103 • F-581 • Lyons-Roberts (1898–1905)

Estimated population: 530 to 550 • *Highest graded:* Unc.

VG-8	F-12	VF-20	EF-40	AU-50	Unc-60	Unc-63	Unc-65
$950	$1,250	$1,900	$2,600	$3,400	$4,300	$6,750	$9,000

W-2104 • F-582 • Lyons-Treat (1905–1906)

Recorded population: 1 • *Graded:* F-12.

W-2105 • F-583 • Vernon-Treat (1906–1909)

Estimated population: 42 to 46 • *Highest graded:* EF-45.

VG-8	F-12	VF-20	EF-40
$950	$1,250	$1,900	$2,600

W-2106 • F-584 • Napier-McClung (1911–1912)

Estimated population: 10 to 12 • *Highest graded:* EF-40.

VG-8	F-12	VF-20	EF-40
$950	$1,250	$1,900	$2,600

W-2107 • F-584a • Parker-Burke (1913–1914)

Recorded population: 2 • *Highest graded:* EF-40 • *Selected information:* Stack's (9/1996), 1042-U156000/A, First NB of Woonsocket, SD, EF, $4,400. Heritage (4/2008), 1101-U156059/A, First NB of Woonsocket, SD, EF, $35,650.

W-2108 • F-585 • Teehee-Burke (1915–1919)

Recorded population: 5 • *Highest graded:* EF-40 • *Selected information:* Existing examples include serials 200-U601388/A, EF, and 375-U601563/A, VF–EF, both from the German NB of Marietta, OH.

Series of 1902, Red Seal
(Authorized Issue 1902 to 1908)

The Act of April 12, 1902, provided for reputable, established banks to extend their charters for another 40 years and for new banks to gain a 60-year charter. New designs were prepared, known today as 1902 Red Seal Notes, though older series were still being issued. All were secured by federal government bonds deposited with the Treasurer of the United States. During the life span of the 1902 Red Seals, certain banks continued to receive Series of 1882 Brown Back notes, depending on the date of their charter extension or founding. These continued to be issued until the Aldrich-Vreeland Act of May 30, 1908, went into effect, after which time the Red Seals were abruptly replaced by the 1902 to 1908 Date Backs which were guaranteed in bonds "and other securities." Accordingly, this series was very short-lived.

The Red Seal notes are distinguished by the bright red Treasury seal, two charter numbers, and two regional letters, with the serial numbers in blue. Both sides were redesigned. At the left side of the face is the portrait of Hugh McCulloch, a highly talented Indiana banker who served two terms as the secretary of the Treasury. Gene Hessler attributes this engraving to Alfred Sealey. The back is a mostly open design with Columbia at the left, the work of G.F.C. Smillie, with the Capitol done by Marcus W. Baldwin. The center and right of the back are blank, a very unusual arrangement among United States currency designs. This is perhaps the ultimate open layout.

The Red Seal notes of all denominations are everlastingly popular with collectors. Examples can range from scarce to impossible for a given state or city, but finding a nice example for type will be no problem. Uncirculated notes are rare, but enough exist that they come on the market with some frequency.

Banks of Issue and Rarity of Notes
Based upon census information from Don C. Kelly and James M. Kelly (*National Bank Note Census*, Version 4.0) and with some information from other sources, this listing gives each location, the number of banks issuing this series of notes within each, and a commentary.[16]

The Kelly survey records 1,143 of these, enough to make them collectible. The census lists 49 serial number 1 notes; these are specifically listed below.

Alabama • 57 banks of issue • 24 notes reported • The only serial number 1 note is from the First National Bank of Oxford.

Alaska Territory • 1 bank of issue • 1 note reported • The only note is from the First National Bank of Fairbanks (VG), serial 738. Alaska was a district from 1884 until it became a territory on August 24, 1912, which it remained until statehood in 1959. All large-size Alaska notes in all series have the "district" address. Regardless, numismatists call all "territorials."

Arizona Territory • 9 banks of issue • 1 note reported • The only note is from the Globe National Bank (F).

Arkansas • 35 banks of issue • 3 notes reported • Three different banks (F, not graded, EF).

California • 106 banks of issue • 23 notes reported • All are circulated.

Colorado • 81 banks of issue • 8 notes reported • All are circulated.

Connecticut • 68 banks of issue • 23 notes reported • Two Unc notes are reported, one each from the Phoenix National Bank of Hartford and the Middlesex County National Bank of Middletown. Three serial number 1 notes are from the Clinton National Bank (AU), Phoenix National Bank of Hartford (Unc), Middlesex City National Bank of Middletown (Unc).

Delaware • 18 banks of issue • No notes reported.

District of Columbia • 7 banks of issue • 4 notes reported • All are circulated.

Florida • 26 banks of issue • 7 notes reported • All are circulated.

Georgia • 65 banks of issue • 5 notes reported • All are circulated.

Hawaii Territory • 2 banks of issue • No notes reported.

Idaho • 27 banks of issue • 1 note reported • First National Bank of Montpelier (F), serial number 78.

Illinois • 231 banks of issue • 99 notes reported • Six Unc notes are listed. Four serial number 1 notes are recorded.

Indian Territory • 117 banks of issue • 12 notes listed • Circulated notes exist from mostly different banks.

Indiana • 143 banks of issue • 42 notes reported • Three Unc notes are reported, Rushville National Bank (one) and the McKeen National Bank of Terre Haute (two). Three serial number 1 notes are from the National Brookville Bank, Brookville (AU), American National Bank of Lafayette (EF), McKeen National Bank of Terre Haute (Unc).

Iowa • 159 banks of issue • 48 notes reported • The only Unc note is from the Clinton National Bank of Clinton. Two serial number 1 notes are from the Lucas County National Bank of Charlton (AU), Clinton National Bank (Unc).

Kansas • 135 banks of issue • 47 notes reported • Most are circulated. The only serial number 1 note is from the First National Bank of Hutchinson (not graded).

Kentucky • 85 banks of issue • 18 notes reported • All are circulated.

Louisiana • 18 banks of issue • 11 notes reported • Two Unc notes are from the Whitney-Central National Bank of New Orleans.

Maine • 59 banks of issue • 14 notes reported • All are circulated. The only serial number 1 note is from the First National Bank of Bar Harbor.

Maryland • 56 banks of issue • 16 notes reported • Two serial number 1 notes are from the First National Bank of Cumberland (Unc) and the Sykesville National Bank (AU). Except for the first, all of the notes from this state are circulated examples.

SERIES OF 1902, RED SEAL

$20 National Bank Note, Series of 1902, Red Seal (W-2109). First National Bank of Enterprise (Alabama), charter 6319. The regional letter S, for South, is at the upper right.

Back of the $20 National Bank Note, Series of 1902, Red Seal (W-2109), the type also used on $20 National Bank Note, Series of 1902, Blue Seal, Plain Back notes. The large amount of open area is quite unusual among U.S. currency designs.

Massachusetts • 163 banks of issue • 24 notes reported • The only serial number 1 note is from the New England National Bank of Boston (AU).

Michigan • 50 banks of issue • 34 notes reported • The census lists 11 Unc examples. Two serial number 1 notes are from the First National Bank of Ontonagon and the Saint Johns National Bank (both Unc).

Minnesota • 185 banks of issue • 34 notes reported • The only Unc note is from the Citizens National Bank of Ortonville.

Mississippi • 23 banks of issue • 6 notes reported • Four are graded F; two are not graded.

Missouri • 69 banks of issue • 30 notes reported • All are circulated. The only serial number 1 note is from the Clinton National Bank (AU).

Montana • 24 banks of issue • 4 notes reported • All are circulated.

Nebraska • 138 banks of issue • 37 notes reported • All are circulated. Two serial number 1 notes are from the Creighton National Bank (EF), First National Bank of York (EF).

Nevada • 9 banks of issue • 2 notes reported • Both are from the Nixon National Bank of Reno (G–VG, VG).

New Hampshire • 35 banks of issue • 11 notes reported • The only Unc note is from the Citizens National Bank of Newport.

New Jersey • 109 banks of issue • 21 notes reported • Two Unc notes are known, from the First National Bank of Beverly and Bridgeton National Bank, Bridgeton. Eight serial number 1 notes are recorded.

New Mexico Territory • 28 banks of issue • 5 notes reported • All are circulated.

New York • 300 banks of issue • 118 notes reported • The census lists 12 Unc notes. Four serial number 1 notes are recorded.

North Carolina • 29 banks of issue • 6 notes reported • All are circulated.

North Dakota • 105 banks of issue • 6 notes reported • The only Unc note is from the First National Bank of Mylo.

Ohio • 226 banks of issue • 124 notes reported • The census lists 12 Unc examples. Five serial number 1 notes are recorded.

Oklahoma • 92 banks of issue • 4 notes reported • All are circulated.

Oklahoma Territory • 99 banks of issue • 9 notes reported • All are circulated.

Oregon • 44 banks of issue • 3 notes reported • First National Bank of Albany (F), Citizens National Bank (AU) and the First National Bank of Portland (G).

Pennsylvania • 474 banks of issue • 92 notes reported • The only Unc note is from the First National Bank of Coalport. Two serial number 1 notes are from the First National Bank of Philadelphia (AU) and the Bituminous National Bank of Winburne (EF).

Porto Rico Territory • 1 bank of issue • 2 notes reported • First National Bank of Porto Rico in San Juan (F–VF, F). Spelled *Porto* in the bank title; address: Island of Porto Rico. Called a "territorial" note by numismatists.

Rhode Island • 25 banks of issue • 6 notes reported • Five different banks. All are circulated.

South Carolina • 20 banks of issue • 3 notes reported • First National Bank of Clinton (Fair), Norwood National Bank of Greenville (VF–EF), American National Bank of Spartanburg (not graded).

South Dakota • 62 banks of issue • 13 notes reported • The only serial number 1 note is from the First National Bank of Belle Fourche (G).

Tennessee • 43 banks of issue • 7 notes reported • Five banks are represented. All are circulated.

Texas • 315 banks of issue • 61 notes reported • Most are circulated. Two serial number 1 notes are from the Bay City National Bank (VF) and the National City Bank of Waco (Unc).

Utah • 8 banks of issue • The only note is from the First National Bank of Murray (G), serial 710.

Vermont • 35 banks of issue • No notes reported.

Virginia • 63 banks of issue • 14 notes reported • All are circulated.

Washington • 39 banks of issue • 5 notes reported • All are circulated.

West Virginia • 68 banks of issue • 20 notes reported • The only Unc note is from the Empire National Bank of Clarksburg. Two serial number 1 notes are from the Ansted National Bank (AU) and the Flat Top National Bank of Bluefield (not graded).

Wisconsin • 65 banks of issue • 27 notes reported • All are circulated.

Wyoming • 18 banks of issue • 7 notes reported • All are circulated, from seven different banks.

Generic prices for a typical note from a state from which notes range from available to just slightly scarce:

VG-8	F-12	VF-20	EF-40	AU-50	Unc-60	Unc-63	Unc-65
$950	$1,200	$1,425	$2,100	$2,800	$3,500	$4,700	$7,400

W-2109 • F-639 • Lyons-Roberts (1898–1905)
Estimated population: 800 to 1,000 • *Highest graded:* Unc.

VG-8	F-12	VF-20	EF-40	AU-50	Unc-60	Unc-63	Unc-65
$950	$1,200	$1,425	$2,100	$2,800	$3,500	$4,700	$7,400

W-2110 • F-640 • Lyons-Treat (1905–1906)
Estimated population: 125 to 140 • *Highest graded:* Unc.

VG-8	F-12	VF-20	EF-40	AU-50	Unc-60	Unc-63	Unc-65
$950	$1,200	$1,425	$2,100	$2,800	$3,500	$4,700	$7,400

W-2111 • F-641 • Vernon-Treat (1906–1909)
Estimated population: 100 to 110 • *Highest graded:* Unc.

VG-8	F-12	VF-20	EF-40	AU-50	Unc-60	Unc-63	Unc-65
$950	$1,200	$1,425	$2,100	$2,800	$3,500	$4,700	$7,400

Series of 1902, Blue Seal, Date Back
(Authorized Issue 1908 to 1915, Some 1916)

Paralleling the Series of 1882 Date Back notes situation, the unexpected 1902 Blue Seal, Date Back type was created to reflect a change in the backing of the notes authorized by the Aldrich-Vreeland Act of May 30, 1908. New notes were issued beginning in that year. Production of 1902 Red Seals ceased, and new orders were filled by the Date Back type.

In order to make it easier to fund the notes, banks were allowed to deposit good securities in addition to government bonds, while earlier only U.S. government bonds had been allowed. All have the inscription as part of the top border on the face, SECURED BY UNITED STATES BONDS OR OTHER SECURITIES. This was often done by altering face plates used for the Series of 1902 Red Seal notes. Although the Act expired on June 30, 1915, marking the end of the official use of this imprint and the related back, some plates continued to be used into 1916. Otherwise the face motifs are the same as on the Series of 1902 Red Seals, but with the serial numbers, two charter numbers, two regional letters, and the Treasury seal in blue. The back is the same as used for the 1902 Red Seals, except that the date is printed in the upper center of the field. These were printed on sheets arranged as $10-$10-$10-$20.

Series of 1902 Date Backs are collectible from most states, although there are rarities for individual locations and banks. Most are in worn grades, often soiled and with the rubber-stamped signatures faded.

Banks of Issue and Rarity of Notes
Based upon census information from Don C. Kelly and James M. Kelly (*National Bank Note Census*, Version 4.0) and with some information from other sources, this listing gives each location, the number of banks issuing this series of notes within each, and a commentary.[17]

The Kelly survey records 3,288 of these, giving a wide field to purchase from. They are rare in comparison to the Plain Backs (18,030 in the census), but little attention has been paid to anything other than bank location, so Date Backs are priced reasonably in the marketplace. The census lists 22 serial number 1 notes, which are specifically listed below.

Alabama • 79 banks of issue • 34 notes reported • The only Unc example is from the First National Bank of Florala.

SERIES OF 1902, BLUE SEAL, DATE BACK

$20 National Bank Note, Series of 1902, Blue Seal, Date Back (W-2112). Ashuelot National Bank of Keene, New Hampshire. Blue Treasury seal and other overprints, including the charter number, 946, and the regional letter, N.

Back of the $20 National Bank Note, Series of 1902, Blue Seal, Date Back (W-2112).

Alaska Territory • 2 banks of issue • No notes reported • Alaska was a district from 1884 until it became a territory on August 24, 1912, which it remained until statehood in 1959. All large-size Alaska notes in all series have the "district" address. Regardless, numismatists call all "territorials."

Arizona • 11 banks of issue • 4 notes reported • Three different banks. All are circulated.

Arizona Territory • 10 banks of issue • 2 notes reported • The only serial number 1 note is from the National Bank of Arizona at Phoenix (VF).

Arkansas • 52 banks of issue • 24 notes reported • All are circulated.

California • 240 banks of issue • 208 notes reported • Seven Unc notes are known, one from the First National Bank of Orange and six from the Bank of California N.A. (National Association). The only serial number 1 note is from the First National Bank of Banning (VF).

Colorado • 107 banks of issue • 39 notes reported • The only Unc note is from the First National Bank of Denver.

Connecticut • 73 banks of issue • 32 notes reported • All are circulated.

Delaware • 21 banks of issue • 5 notes reported • From five different banks, all circulated.

District of Columbia • 11 banks of issue • 25 notes reported • All are circulated.

Florida • 46 banks of issue • 17 notes reported • Two Unc notes are from the Ocala National Bank. The only serial number 1 note is from the First National Bank of Brooksville (F).

Georgia • 85 banks of issue • 34 notes reported • All are circulated.

Hawaii Territory • 3 banks of issue • 1 note reported • The only note is from the Lahaina National Bank (F–VF).

Idaho • 50 banks of issue • 19 notes reported • All are circulated.

Illinois • 338 banks of issue • 187 notes reported • Four Unc notes are listed.

Indiana • 213 banks of issue • 145 notes reported • The only Unc note is from the First National Bank of Medaryville. The only serial number 1 note is from the Peoples State National Bank of Anderson (AU).

Iowa • 255 banks of issue • 200 notes reported • The census lists 10 Unc notes. The only serial number 1 note is from the National Bank of Bloomfield (not graded).

Kansas • 176 banks of issue • 103 notes reported • The census lists 11 Unc notes. Four serial number 1 notes are listed.

Kentucky • 127 banks of issue • 74 notes reported • Two Unc notes are from the First National Bank of Greenup and the Bank of Maysville, National Banking Association.

Louisiana • 24 banks of issue • 18 notes reported • All are circulated examples.

Maine • 71 banks of issue • 35 notes reported • All are circulated.

Maryland • 81 banks of issue • 61 notes reported • Two Unc notes are from the First National Bank of Cumberland; one is the only serial number 1 from the state.

Massachusetts • 168 banks of issue • 48 notes reported • The only Unc note is from the First National Bank of Hyannis.

Michigan • 88 banks of issue • 45 notes reported • Seven Unc notes are listed.

Minnesota • 234 banks of issue • 141 notes reported • All are circulated.

Mississippi • 34 banks of issue • 15 notes reported • All are circulated.

Missouri • 122 banks of issue • 95 notes reported • Four Unc notes are known. The only serial number 1 note is from the Moniteau National Bank of California (AU).

Montana • 55 banks of issue • 19 notes reported • All are circulated.

Nebraska • 203 banks of issue • 156 notes reported • Five Unc notes are listed.

Nevada • 12 banks of issue • 8 notes reported • All are circulated. Four banks are represented.

New Hampshire • 43 banks of issue • 21 notes reported • The only Unc note is from the First National Bank of Newport and is also the only serial number 1 note from the state.

New Jersey • 157 banks of issue • 42 notes reported • All are circulated.

New Mexico • 30 banks of issue • 9 notes reported • The only Unc note is from the First National Bank of Hagerman.

New Mexico Territory • 31 banks of issue • 7 notes reported • Five banks are represented. The only Unc note is from the First National Bank of Portales.

New York • 387 banks of issue • 147 notes reported • The census lists 10 Unc notes. Three serial number 1 notes are from the Canandaigua National Bank (not graded), First National Bank of Lindenhurst (F–VF), and the Wilber National Bank of Oneonta (AU).

North Carolina • 51 banks of issue • 21 notes reported • All are circulated.

North Dakota • 118 banks of issue • 26 notes reported • All are circulated.

Ohio • 390 banks of issue • 204 notes reported • The census lists 28 Unc notes, including 11 from the Central National Bank of Saint Paris.

Oklahoma • 294 banks of issue • 58 notes reported • Two Unc notes are from the Lawton National Bank and the Nowata National Bank. The census lists two serial number 1 notes, from the Oklahoma Stock National Bank of Oklahoma City (not graded) and the Exchange National Bank of Okmulgee (F).

Oregon • 73 banks of issue • 23 notes reported • All are circulated.

Pennsylvania • 694 banks of issue • 248 notes reported • The census lists 23 Unc notes. The only serial number 1 note is from the Union National Bank of Huntington (AU).

Porto Rico Territory • 1 bank of issue • No notes reported • Spelled *Porto* in the bank title; address: Island of Porto Rico. Called a "territorial" note by numismatists.

Rhode Island • 23 banks of issue • 20 notes reported • All are circulated. Seven banks are represented.

South Carolina • 51 banks of issue • 31 notes reported • Two Unc notes are from the First National Bank of Sumter.

South Dakota • 79 banks of issue • 45 notes reported • Three Unc notes are from the Security National Bank of Sioux Falls.

Tennessee • 90 banks of issue • 60 notes reported • Two Unc notes are from the Citizens National Bank of Chattanooga and the First National Bank of Covington.

Texas • 434 banks of issue • 256 notes reported • Five Unc notes are known.

Utah • 19 banks of issue • 17 notes reported • All are circulated.

Vermont • 42 banks of issue • 8 notes reported • Seven different banks. All are circulated.

Virginia • 120 banks of issue • 41 notes reported • The only Unc note is from the Fauquier National Bank of Warrenton.

Washington • 75 banks of issue • 33 notes reported • All are circulated. The only serial number 1 note is from the Pacific National Bank of Tacoma (AU).

West Virginia • 97 banks of issue • 27 notes reported • All are circulated.

Wisconsin • 104 banks of issue • 129 notes reported • Five Unc notes are known. The only serial number 1 note is from the Citizens National Bank of Merrill (EF).

Wyoming • 29 banks of issue • 15 notes reported • All are circulated.

Generic prices for a typical note from a state from which notes range from available to just slightly scarce:

VG-8	F-12	VF-20	EF-40	AU-50	Unc-60	Unc-63	Unc-65
$140	$175	$225	$350	$500	$600	$725	$925

W-2112 • F-642 • Lyons-Roberts (1898–1905)
Estimated population: 1,350 to 1,500 • Highest graded: Unc.

VG-8	F-12	VF-20	EF-40	AU-50	Unc-60	Unc-63	Unc-65
$140	$175	$225	$350	$500	$600	$725	$925

W-2113 • F-643 • Lyons-Treat (1905–1906)
Estimated population: 250 to 280 • Highest graded: Unc.

VG-8	F-12	VF-20	EF-40	AU-50	Unc-60	Unc-63	Unc-65
$140	$175	$225	$350	$500	$600	$725	$925

W-2114 • F-644 • Vernon-Treat (1906–1909)
Estimated population: 575 to 650 • *Highest graded:* Unc.

VG-8	F-12	VF-20	EF-40	AU-50	Unc-60	Unc-63	Unc-65
$140	$175	$225	$350	$500	$600	$725	$925

W-2115 • F-645 • Vernon-McClung (1909–1911)
Estimated population: 325 to 350 • *Highest graded:* Unc.

VG-8	F-12	VF-20	EF-40	AU-50	Unc-60	Unc-63	Unc-65
$140	$175	$225	$350	$500	$600	$725	$925

W-2116 • F-646 • Napier-McClung (1911–1912)
Estimated population: 210 to 230 • *Highest graded:* Unc.

VG-8	F-12	VF-20	EF-40	AU-50	Unc-60	Unc-63	Unc-65
$140	$175	$225	$350	$500	$600	$725	$925

W-2117 • F-647 • Napier-Thompson (1912–1913)
Estimated population: 35 to 40 • *Highest graded:* Unc.

VG-8	F-12	VF-20	EF-40	AU-50	Unc-60	Unc-63	Unc-65
$140	$175	$225	$350	$500	$600	$725	$925

W-2118 • F-648 • Napier-Burke (1913)
Estimated population: 20 to 24 • *Highest graded:* AU-50.

VG-8	F-12	VF-20	EF-40	AU-50
$140	$175	$225	$350	$500

W-2119 • F-649 • Parker-Burke (1913–1914)
Estimated population: 48 to 52 • *Highest graded:* Unc.

VG-8	F-12	VF-20	EF-40	AU-50	Unc-60	Unc-63	Unc-65
$140	$175	$225	$350	$500	$600	$725	$925

W-2120 • F-649a • Teehee-Burke (1915–1919)
Recorded population: 6 • *Highest graded:* VF-20 • *Selected information:* Heritage (4/2008), 2843-N601391B/A, Metropolitan NB of Pittsburgh, PA, VG–F, $1,495. Goldbergs (9/2005), 154-N583302B/A, Merchants-Laclede NB of St. Louis, MO, Fine, $342.

Series of 1902, Blue Seal, Plain Back
(*Authorized Issue 1908 to 1929*)

After the Aldrich-Vreeland Act expired on June 30, 1915, the phrase "or other securities" was no longer added to the face of new printing plates. The style reverted to that of years earlier, secured only by U.S. bonds. Old plates continued in use, creating two face plate styles for 1902 Plain Back notes (Plate Style a is illustrated on p. 473):

> **Plate Style a:** The old style of 1902 notes (used on the face of the Date Backs) with the inscription in the top border on the face reading, SECURED BY UNITED STATES BONDS OR OTHER SECURITIES.

> **Plate Style b:** The new style introduced in 1908, with the inscription in the top border on the face reading, SECURED BY UNITED STATES BONDS DEPOSITED WITH THE TREASURER OF THE UNITED STATES OF AMERICA.

For both Plate Style a and Plate Style b notes, the two regional letters (which were used on certain early issues, then deleted), two charter numbers (on all), and serial numbers (on all) are in blue. These were issued into 1929.

Within the two plate styles there are possibilities for three overprint styles:

> **Overprint Style 1:** Two regional letters, a Treasury serial number, and a bank serial number, printed from 1908 to 1924.

> **Overprint Style 2:** No regional letters; with a Treasury serial number and a bank serial number, printed in 1924 and 1925. Notes of this class are somewhat scarce.

> **Overprint Style 3:** No regional letters and no Treasury serial number, but with two bank serial numbers, printed from 1925 to 1929. Notes of this style are very rare as a class.

Plain Back $20 notes are readily available as a type. As is always the case, certain states, towns, and banks can be rare. The typical note is apt to be well circulated. Uncirculated notes are fairly plentiful in this series, both scattered across several banks and in clusters. Bank signatures are often faded. At present there is little interest in plate styles or overprint varieties, yielding opportunities to acquire rarities while paying no premium.

Banks of Issue and Rarity of Notes

Based upon census information from Don C. Kelly and James M. Kelly (*National Bank Note Census*, Version 4.0) and with some information from other sources, this listing gives each location, the number of banks issuing this series of notes within each, and a commentary.[18]

The Kelly survey records 18,030 of these, a number greater than the total of all $20 notes in all other large-size series combined. The census lists 28 serial number 1 notes; these are specifically listed below.

Alabama • 99 banks of issue • 320 notes reported • Most are circulated.

Alaska Territory • 2 banks of issue • 5 notes reported • All are circulated, from two different banks. Alaska was a district from 1884 until it became a territory on August 24, 1912, which it remained until statehood in 1959. All large-size Alaska notes in all series have the "district" address. Regardless, numismatists call all "territorials."

Arizona • 19 banks of issue • 44 notes reported • The only Unc note is from the Consolidated National Bank of Tucson.

Arkansas • 59 banks of issue • 177 notes reported • The census lists 16 Unc notes.

California • 318 banks of issue • 871 notes reported • Most are circulated. Five serial number 1 notes are recorded.

Colorado • 108 banks of issue • 196 notes reported • Three Unc notes are from the United States National Bank of Denver.

Connecticut • 72 banks of issue • 196 notes reported • Seven Unc notes are known.

Delaware • 22 banks of issue • 36 notes reported • All are circulated.

District of Columbia • 13 banks of issue • 161 notes reported • Nine Unc notes are known.

Florida • 54 banks of issue • 175 notes reported • Six Unc notes are known.

Georgia • 99 banks of issue • 306 notes reported • Most are in circulated grades.

Hawaii Territory • 1 bank of issue • No notes reported.

Idaho • 58 banks of issue • 100 notes reported • Two Unc notes are from the Pacific National Bank of Boise and the Lewiston National Bank.

Illinois • 402 banks of issue • 1,082 notes reported • Most notes are in circulated condition. The only serial number 1 note is from the First National Bank of Cobden (VG).

Indiana • 247 banks of issue • 634 notes reported • The census lists 27 Unc notes. The only serial number 1 note is from the United States National Bank of East Chicago.

Iowa • 320 banks of issue • 1,004 notes reported • Most are circulated.

Kansas • 214 banks of issue • 512 notes reported • Most are circulated. The only serial number 1 note is from the First National Bank of Oswego (G).

Kentucky • 134 banks of issue • 342 notes reported • Seven Unc notes are listed.

Louisiana • 28 banks of issue • 87 notes reported • Six Unc specimens are listed.

Maine • 66 banks of issue • 134 notes reported • Five Unc notes are known.

Maryland • 89 banks of issue • 197 notes reported • Four Unc notes are known.

Massachusetts • 137 banks of issue • 231 notes reported • The census lists 16 Unc notes. The only serial number 1 note is from the Methuen National Bank (VF).

Michigan • 118 banks of issue • 451 notes reported • Most are circulated. Two serial number 1 notes are from the City National Bank of Battle Creek (AU) and the First National Bank of Flint (EF).

Minnesota • 295 banks of issue • 723 notes reported • Most are circulated. The only serial number 1 note is from the National Bank of Grey Eagle (Unc).

Mississippi • 28 banks of issue • 118 notes reported • Five Unc notes are known.

Missouri • 135 banks of issue • 406 notes reported • Most are circulated. One serial number 1 note is from the National Bank of Unionville (Unc).

Montana • 79 banks of issue • 134 notes reported • Two Unc notes are known, from the First National Bank of Geyser and First National Bank of Lima. The only serial number 1 note is from the First National Bank of Lima (AU).

Nebraska • 181 banks of issue • 547 notes reported • Most are circulated. The only serial number 1 note is from the First National Bank of York (Unc).

Nevada • 9 banks of issue • 64 notes reported • The only Unc notes are from the Reno National Bank.

New Hampshire • 52 banks of issue • 86 notes reported • Two Unc notes are from the Citizens National Bank of Newport.

New Jersey • 220 banks of issue • 385 notes reported • Seven Unc notes are known. The only serial number 1 note is from the Labor National Bank of Jersey City (F).

New Mexico • 36 banks of issue • 99 notes reported • The only Unc note is from the American National Bank of Silver City.

New York • 470 banks of issue • 902 notes reported • Most are circulated. Five serial number 1 notes are recorded.

North Carolina • 72 banks of issue • 286 notes reported • Many Unc notes are from the First & Citizens National Bank of Elizabeth City.

North Dakota • 152 banks of issue • 196 notes reported • Two Unc notes are from the Grafton National Bank and the First National Bank of Hankinson.

Ohio • 348 banks of issue • 954 notes reported • Most are circulated. Two serial number 1 notes are from the Union Commercial National Bank of Cleveland (not graded) and the American-First National Bank of Findlay (Unc).

Oklahoma • 320 banks of issue • 417 notes reported • Most are circulated. The only serial number 1 note is from the Citizens National Bank of Okmulgee (AU).

Oregon • 80 banks of issue • 137 notes reported • Two Unc notes are from Condon National Bank and the United States National Bank of Portland.

Pennsylvania • 834 banks of issue • 1,565 notes reported • Most are circulated. The only serial number 1 note is from the Tradesmens National Bank of Philadelphia (Unc).

Rhode Island • 15 banks of issue • 67 notes reported • All are circulated.

South Carolina • 62 banks of issue • 137 notes reported • Three Unc notes are from the First National Bank of Camden, Bank of Charleston National Banking Association, and the Home National Bank of Lexington. The only serial number 1 note is from the National Bank of Honea Path (VG).

South Dakota • 103 banks of issue • 212 notes reported • The census lists 11 Unc notes. The only serial number 1 note is from the First National Bank of Salem (VG–F).

Tennessee • 109 banks of issue • 337 notes reported • Most are circulated.

Texas • 489 banks of issue • 1,347 notes reported • Most are circulated. The only serial number 1 note is from the Dallas National Bank (Unc).

Utah • 28 banks of issue • 100 notes reported • All are circulated.

Vermont • 40 banks of issue • 43 notes reported • Two Unc notes are from the Factory Point National Bank of Manchester Center.

SERIES OF 1902, BLUE SEAL, PLAIN BACK

$20 National Bank Note, Series of 1902, Plain Back (W-2121). The Keene (New Hampshire) National Bank, charter 877. The federal serial number is at the top right; the bank serial number is at the lower left. The regional letter, N, is imprinted twice. Plate Style a, Overprint Style 1.

$20 National Bank Note, Series of 1902, Plain Back (W-2121). The type also used on Series of 1902, Red Seal notes.

Virginia • 162 banks of issue • 377 notes reported • The census lists 35 Unc notes, 22 from the Seaboard Citizens National Bank of Norfolk.

Washington • 81 banks of issue • 179 notes reported • Two Unc notes are from the First National Bank of Everett and the Pacific National Bank of Seattle.

West Virginia • 119 banks of issue • 283 notes reported • The census lists 20 Unc notes, 13 from the Huntington National Bank.

Wisconsin • 132 banks of issue • 546 notes reported • The census lists 29 Unc notes.

Wyoming • 39 banks of issue • 122 notes reported • All are circulated.

Generic prices for a typical note from a state from which notes range from available to just slightly scarce:

VG-8	F-12	VF-20	EF-40	AU-50	Unc-60	Unc-63	Unc-65
$115	$135	$175	$300	$420	$575	$700	$900

W-2121 • F-650 • Lyons-Roberts (1898–1905)

Estimated population: 5,500 to 6,000 • *Highest graded:* Unc.

VG-8	F-12	VF-20	EF-40	AU-50	Unc-60	Unc-63	Unc-65
$115	$135	$175	$300	$420	$575	$700	$900

W-2122 • F-651 • Lyons-Treat (1905–1906)

Estimated population: 1,200 to 1,400 • *Highest graded:* Unc.

VG-8	F-12	VF-20	EF-40	AU-50	Unc-60	Unc-63	Unc-65
$115	$135	$175	$300	$420	$575	$700	$900

W-2123 • F-652 • Vernon-Treat (1906–1909)

Estimated population: 2,750 to 3,500 • *Highest graded:* Unc.

VG-8	F-12	VF-20	EF-40	AU-50	Unc-60	Unc-63	Unc-65
$115	$135	$175	$300	$420	$575	$700	$900

W-2124 • F-653 • Vernon-McClung (1909–1911)

Estimated population: 1,700 to 2,100 • *Highest graded:* Unc.

VG-8	F-12	VF-20	EF-40	AU-50	Unc-60	Unc-63	Unc-65
$115	$135	$175	$300	$420	$575	$700	$900

W-2125 • F-654 • Napier-McClung (1911–1912)

Estimated population: 1,400 to 1,600 • *Highest graded:* Unc.

VG-8	F-12	VF-20	EF-40	AU-50	Unc-60	Unc-63	Unc-65
$115	$135	$175	$300	$420	$575	$700	$900

W-2126 • F-655 • Napier-Thompson (1912–1913)

Estimated population: 225 to 250 • *Highest graded:* Unc.

VG-8	F-12	VF-20	EF-40	AU-50	Unc-60	Unc-63	Unc-65
$115	$135	$175	$300	$420	$575	$700	$900

W-2127 • F-656 • Napier-Burke (1913)

Estimated population: 220 to 245 • *Highest graded:* Unc.

VG-8	F-12	VF-20	EF-40	AU-50	Unc-60	Unc-63	Unc-65
$115	$135	$175	$300	$420	$575	$700	$900

W-2129 • F-657 • Parker-Burke (1913–1914)

Estimated population: 700 to 800 • *Highest graded:* Unc.

VG-8	F-12	VF-20	EF-40	AU-50	Unc-60	Unc-63	Unc-65
$115	$135	$175	$300	$420	$575	$700	$900

W-2130 • F-658 • Teehee-Burke (1915–1919)

Estimated population: 1,700 to 1,900 • *Highest graded:* Unc.

VG-8	F-12	VF-20	EF-40	AU-50	Unc-60	Unc-63	Unc-65
$115	$135	$175	$300	$420	$575	$700	$900

W-2131 • F-659 • Elliott-Burke (1919–1921)

Estimated population: 1,500 to 1,700 • *Highest graded:* Unc.

VG-8	F-12	VF-20	EF-40	AU-50	Unc-60	Unc-63	Unc-65
$115	$135	$175	$300	$420	$575	$700	$900

W-2132 • F-660 • Elliott-White (1921–1922)

Estimated population: 450 to 550 • *Highest graded:* Unc.

VG-8	F-12	VF-20	EF-40	AU-50	Unc-60	Unc-63	Unc-65
$115	$135	$175	$300	$420	$575	$700	$900

W-2133 • F-661 • Speelman-White (1922–1927)

Estimated population: 700 to 800 • *Highest graded:* Unc.

VG-8	F-12	VF-20	EF-40	AU-50	Unc-60	Unc-63	Unc-65
$115	$135	$175	$300	$420	$575	$700	$900

W-2134 • F-662 • Woods-White (1927–1928)

Estimated population: 15 to 17 • *Highest graded:* EF-40.

VG-8	F-12	VF-20	EF-40
$200	$300	$350	$500

W-2135 • F-663 • Woods-Tate (1928–1929)

Estimated population: 19 to 22 • *Highest graded:* Unc.

VG-8	F-12	VF-20	EF-40	AU-50	Unc-60	Unc-63	Unc-65
$300	$400	$500	$625	$800	$1,450	$2,000	$2,750

W-2136 • F-663a • Jones-Woods (1929–1933)

Recorded population: 2 • *Highest graded:* AU-50 • *Selected information:* Heritage (4/2008), 49-13292/A, Brooklyn NB of New York, NY, AU, $20,700.

SILVER CERTIFICATES

Series of 1878

Silver Certificates of Deposit commence with the Series of 1878, depicting naval commander Stephen Decatur on the face. These are specifically designated CERTIFICATE OF DEPOSIT on the face, SILVER CERTIFICATE on the back. On the face the inscription SILVER DOLLARS is done inside a series of patterns, one for each letter, connected together in a straight row. This is the "shingle" style. These notes were printed on blue-tinted paper made under the Willcox patent of 1866. Engraved and printed by the BEP. Notes of this type were payable in cities including New York, San Francisco, and Washington, D.C.

Series of 1878 notes bear two printed Treasury signatures plus either a hand-signed or printed countersignature of another Treasury official. This extra signature proved to be a cumbersome idea. Series of 1880 countersigned notes for New York had the printed signature of Thos. Hillhouse, made before the idea was dropped entirely. No 1880 Washington countersigned notes were printed. There is no specific record of countersignatures, and there is always the possibility for new discoveries. All have a large red Treasury seal at top center. On this seal, for this denomination and other countersigned notes in this series, the key faces to the right (with the handle at the left). These are often called "triple signed notes."

On the back the word SILVER is very prominent, with shingle-style, connected letters, but is much smaller than the same word on the back of the related $10 note.

W-2140 • F-unlisted • New York • *Countersigned:* W.G. White (autographed) • 500 (est.) • Unknown

W-2143 • F-305 • *Countersigned:* J.C. Hopper (autographed) • 19,500 (est.)

Recorded population: 3 • *Highest graded:* F-15 • *Selected information:* Superior (3/1971), A976/D, Fine, $750. Knight (8/2005), A3196/D, VF, $51,750. Stack's (1/1989), A19354/B, Fine, $19,500.

W-2146 • F-306 • *Countersigned:* Thos. Hillhouse (printed) • 38,000 (est.)

Recorded population: 3 • *Highest graded:* F-15 • *Selected information:* Existing examples include serials A21804/D, Fine, sold in a Stack's auction (1/1989) for $27,500; A28862/B, Fine+, part of the Smithsonian Institution collection; and A28958/B, Fine, owned by the Federal Reserve Bank of Chicago.

W-2149 • F-306a • San Francisco • *Countersigned:* R.M. Anthony (autographed) • 8,000 (est.) • Unknown

W-2152 • F-306b • Washington • *Countersigned:* A.U. Wyman (autographed) • 4,000 (est.)

Recorded population: 2 • *Highest graded:* VF-25 • *Selected information:* CAA (5/2005), A1/A, first serial number and plate position, VF, large cigarette burn hole in portrait repaired, $175,375; later seen in Knight (10/2006), $184,000. Spink America (5/1995), A1763/C, VF, $35,200.

W-2153 • F-307 • *Countersigned:* A.U. Wyman (printed) • 104,000 (est.)

Estimated population: 18 to 20 • *Highest graded:* AU-50.

VG-8	F-12	VF-20	EF-40	AU-50
$8,000	$17,000	$38,000	$50,000	$80,000

SERIES OF 1878

$20 Silver Certificate of Deposit, Series of 1878 (W-2153). Standard Treasury department signatures are above each other at the right. To the left of center is space for a countersignature to be added in ink by another official. The illustrated note is countersigned by A.U. Wyman (who before and after this point served as register of the Treasury; at the time he signed this note he was assistant Treasurer) and is payable in Washington.

Back of the $20 Silver Certificate of Deposit, Series of 1878 (W-2153). Printed on blue-tinted paper, as were other Series of 1878 varieties. On this example the coloring is more obvious on the back than on the front.

Series of 1880, Countersigned

The basic motifs of the preceding are continued, but now with changes in the color print. On the face the word TWENTY has been replaced with XX, among other modifications. The back is the same. Printed on white (not blue-tinted) paper (illus. on p. 476).

W-2160 • F-308 • New York • *Countersigned:* Thos. Hillhouse (printed) • 200,000

Estimated population: 11 to 13 • *Highest graded:* EF-45.

VG-8	F-12	VF-20	EF-40
$8,000	$17,000	$38,000	$50,000

Series of 1880, Not Countersigned

The motifs (illus. on p. 477) continue from the preceding. Now there is no countersignature or provision for the same. SERIES OF 1880 is in a slightly different position. The counter, XX, is at the bottom border on W-2170 to W-2172, but not on W-2173. The back is the same as the preceding.

W-2170 • F-309 • Scofield-Gilfillan (1878–1881) • Large brown seal • 1,240,000 (est.)

Estimated population: 58 to 62 • *Highest graded:* AU-50.

VG-8	F-12	VF-20	EF-40	AU-50
$3,000	$5,000	$8,000	$17,000	—

W-2171 • F-310 • Bruce-Gilfillan (1881–1883) • 660,000 (est.)

Estimated population: 46 to 50 • *Highest graded:* Unc.

VG-8	F-12	VF-20	EF-40	AU-50	Unc-60
$3,000	$5,000	$8,000	$17,000	$30,000	—

W-2172 • F-311 • Bruce-Wyman (1883–1885) • 1,814,000 (est.)

Estimated population: 150 to 160 • *Highest graded:* Unc.

VG-8	F-12	VF-20	EF-40	AU-50	Unc-60	Unc-63	Unc-65
$3,000	$5,000	$8,000	$15,000	$22,000	$27,500	$32,000	$50,000

SERIES OF 1880, COUNTERSIGNED

$20 Silver Certificate of Deposit, Series of 1880 (W-2160). Serial B150416, plate D. Printed countersignature of Thos. Hillhouse at left.

Back of the $20 Silver Certificate of Deposit, Series of 1880 (W-2160).

W-2173 • F-312 • Without XX at bottom border • Small red seal • 124,000

Estimated population: 40 to 45 • *Highest graded:* AU-50.

VG-8	F-12	VF-20	EF-40	AU-50
$4,500	$8,000	$15,000	$30,000	$60,000

Series of 1886

The Series of 1886 Silver Certificates (illus. on p. 478), which were first printed in 1887, have at the center a portrait of the late Daniel Manning, who served as secretary of the Treasury from 1885 to 1887 and died in office. Similar to the depiction of the then-recently deceased Thomas A. Hendricks on the related $10 Silver Certificate, the $20 bill honored a man whose memory was still fresh when the notes were first issued. The portrait was engraved by Lorenzo Hatch. To the left a seated woman holds a (cherry?) tree branch, with a cornucopia overflowing with agricultural products at her feet, a vignette named *Science* by the BEP. To the right a seated mechanic holds a sledgehammer.

The back is filled with rich, green engravings and dropout white letters. There is a bow-tie design near the center,

the last emblem suggesting the sobriquet "Diamond Back Note" to some. D.M. Cooper and George U. Rose were the engravers.

For this entire series Uncirculated notes are exceedingly elusive, this including varieties with high printages. As noted elsewhere, there was virtually no numismatic interest in collecting large-size federal paper money during the 19th century. Notes that were common at one time became rare as the years passed, the notes became worn, and eventually the vast majority was redeemed.

W-2174 • F-313 • Rosecrans-Hyatt (1887–1889) • Large pink seal • 12,000

Estimated population: 18 to 20 • *Highest graded:* Unc.

VG-8	F-12	VF-20	EF-40	AU-50	Unc-60	Unc-63	Unc-65
$2,300	$5,000	$9,000	$30,000	$60,000	—	—	$100,000

W-2175 • F-314 • Rosecrans-Huston (1889–1891) • Large brown seal with spiked border • 1,068,000

Estimated population: 75 to 85 • *Highest graded:* AU-50.

VG-8	F-12	VF-20	EF-40	AU-50
$2,000	$4,500	$7,500	$24,000	$40,000

SERIES OF 1880, NOT COUNTERSIGNED

$20 Silver Certificate of Deposit, Series of 1880, Not Countersigned (W-2171).

Back of the $20 Silver Certificate of Deposit, Series of 1880, Not Countersigned (W-2171).

W-2176 • F-315 • Rosecrans-Nebeker (1891–1893) • 280,000 (est.)

Estimated population: 29 to 33 • *Highest graded:* Unc.

VG-8	F-12	VF-20	EF-40	AU-50	Unc-60	Unc-63	Unc-65
$2,000	$4,500	$7,500	$24,000	$40,000	—	—	$75,000

W-2177 • F-316 • Small red seal with scalloped border • 352,000 (est.)

Estimated population: 29 to 33 • *Highest graded:* Unc.

VG-8	F-12	VF-20	EF-40	AU-50	Unc-60	Unc-63	Unc-65
$2,300	$5,000	$9,000	$30,000	$60,000	—	—	$100,000

Series of 1891

The face of the Series of 1891 notes (illus. on p. 479) continues the same motifs, though with some changes in typography and other minor differences. Treasury seals were printed in red from W-2178 to W-2181. Serials are prefixed by the letter E. The back is completely new, in the open style then thought by the BEP to be an aid against counterfeiting. Beginning with W-2182 a large blue XX was added

to the left field, and the seal color was changed to blue, after which the prefix letter H was used on the serial numbers.

On W-2183 the signature of register of the Treasury Houston B. Teehee is smaller. This is found on face plates 19 to 24. The bottom left side of the H (Houston) is just at the right edge of the border ornament below it. On W-2184 the signature is larger. This is found on face plates 25 to 30. The bottom left side of the H (Houston) is over and slightly to the left of the border ornament below it.[19]

In strictly Uncirculated grade, all of the notes are rare. Collecting has mainly been by type rather than signature combinations, with the result that rarer issues do not reflect this in terms of market value.

W-2178 • F-317 • Rosecrans-Nebeker (1891–1893) • Medium-size red seal with scalloped border • 1,300,000 (est.)

Estimated population: 57 to 61 • *Highest graded:* Unc.

VG-8	F-12	VF-20	EF-40	AU-50	Unc-60	Unc-63	Unc-65
$700	$1,250	$2,500	$4,000	$6,000	$7,000	$8,000	$20,000

SERIES OF 1886

$20 Silver Certificate, Series of 1886 (W-2176).

Back of the $20 Silver Certificate, Series of 1886 (W-2176), sometimes called the "Diamond Back Note."

W-2179 • F-318 • Tillman-Morgan (1893–1897) • 6,088,000 (est.)

Estimated population: 190 to 210 • *Highest graded:* Unc.

VG-8	F-12	VF-20	EF-40	AU-50	Unc-60	Unc-63	Unc-65
$700	$1,250	$2,500	$4,000	$6,000	$7,000	$8,000	$20,000

W-2180 • F-319 • Bruce-Roberts (1897–1898) • 1,212,000 (est.)

Estimated population: 65 to 75 • *Highest graded:* Unc.

VG-8	F-12	VF-20	EF-40	AU-50	Unc-60	Unc-63	Unc-65
$700	$1,250	$2,500	$4,000	$6,000	$7,000	$8,000	$20,000

W-2181 • F-320 • Lyons-Roberts (1898–1905) • 504,000 (est.)

Estimated population: 65 to 75 • *Highest graded:* Unc.

VG-8	F-12	VF-20	EF-40	AU-50	Unc-60	Unc-63	Unc-65
$700	$1,250	$2,500	$4,000	$6,000	$7,000	$8,000	$20,000

W-2182 • F-321 • Parker-Burke (1913–1914) • XX in blue in left field • Medium-size blue seal with scalloped border begins • 1,520,000 (est.)

Estimated population: 300 to 350 • *Highest graded:* Unc.

VG-8	F-12	VF-20	EF-40	AU-50	Unc-60	Unc-63	Unc-65
$700	$1,250	$2,500	$4,000	$6,000	$7,000	$8,000	$18,000

W-2182★ • F-321★

Recorded population: 5 • *Highest graded:* EF-45 • *Selected information:* Existing examples include serials ★311B/C, G–VG; ★1144B/D, VG; ★3102B/B, VF, sold in a CAA auction (10/1995) for $3,300; ★4232B/D, EF, sold in a Knight (FL) auction (12/1998) for $8,800; and ★5265B/A, F–VF, sold in a Hickman auction (6/1993) for $2,860.

W-2183 • F-322 • Teehee-Burke (1915–1919) • Small Houston B. Teehee signature; face plates 19 to 24 • 220,000 (est.)

Estimated population: 140 to 180 (includes the following) • *Highest graded:* Unc • *Commentary:* Star notes are not known to have been printed, despite some mentions to the contrary.[20]

VG-8	F-12	VF-20	EF-40	AU-50	Unc-60	Unc-63
$700	$1,250	$2,500	$4,000	$6,000	$7,000	$8,000

W-2184 • F-322 • Large Houston B. Teehee signature; face plates 25 to 30 • 184,000 (est.)

Commentary: Auction data do not recognize the difference between W-2183 and W-2184, as both have the same Friedberg number. The estimated population above combines both varieties.

SERIES OF 1891

$20 Silver Certificate, Series of 1891, earlier style with red Treasury seal (W-2178).

$20 Silver Certificate, Series of 1891, later style with blue XX and Treasury seal (W-2182).

Smaller Houston B. Teehee signature on a W-2183 note.

Larger Houston B. Teehee signature on a W-2184 note.

Back of the $20 Silver Certificate, Series of 1891 (W-2178).

TREASURY OR COIN NOTES

Series of 1890

Depicted on the face of the $20 Treasury Note (illus. on p. 480) is the portrait of John Marshall, fourth chief justice of the Supreme Court. The serial numbers are followed by a decorative star. On the back the word TWENTY is in large ornate letters, gently curved, across the center of the back, against a background with so much intricate engraving that scarcely an open space remains. This has made it a numismatic favorite for a long time.

Following the general pattern of other Series of 1890 notes, the Rosecrans-Nebeker issue with large brown seal, made in small quantities, stands today as being an elusive, formidable rarity.

W-2190 • F-372 • Rosecrans-Huston (1889–1891) • Large brown seal with spiked border • 500,000 (est.)
Estimated population: 70 to 80 • *Highest graded:* Unc.

VG-8	F-12	VF-20	EF-40	AU-50	Unc-60	Unc-63	Unc-65
$2,000	$4,750	$6,750	$10,000	$14,000	$18,000	$25,000	$60,000

SERIES OF 1890

$20 Treasury or Coin Note, Series of 1890 (W-2190). The star at the serial number is ornamental.

Back of the $20 Treasury or Coin Note, Series of 1890 (W-2190), with ornate engraving.

Plate number 1 on the back of W-2190, at the lower right corner of the note.

W-2191 • F-373 • Rosecrans-Nebeker (1891–1893) • 84,000 (est.)

Estimated population: 11 to 13 • *Highest graded:* EF-45.

VG-8	F-12	VF-20	EF-40
$5,500	$14,000	$28,000	$42,000

W-2192 • F-374 • Small pink seal with scalloped border • 708,000

Estimated population: 110 to 120 • *Highest graded:* Unc.

VG-8	F-12	VF-20	EF-40	AU-50	Unc-60	Unc-63	Unc-65
$2,000	$4,750	$6,750	$10,000	$14,000	$18,000	$25,000	$75,000

Series of 1891

The Series of 1891 Treasury Notes retain the face style of the preceding, but the back has been completely redesigned. Now it has an open configuration, with blank spaces to the left and right of the center. For a long time it was thought that Tillman-Morgan was the extent of the signature combinations in the Series of 1891 $20 notes; however, a Bruce-Roberts example was discovered, joined by another, giving a population today of two, only one of which is in private hands. The serial numbers are followed by a decorative star.

W-2193 • F-375 • Tillman-Morgan (1893–1897) • Small pink seal with scalloped border • 492,000 (est.)

Estimated population: 200 or more • *Highest graded:* Unc • *Commentary:* According to Doug Murray, "these notes were in two batches. There were 332,000 delivered in fiscal years 1894 and 1895. The second batch was delivered in FY-1898, exact amount unknown, but I estimate 160,000, based on the highest known serial. The two amounts together would be 492,000."

VG-8	F-12	VF-20	EF-40	AU-50	Unc-60	Unc-63	Unc-65
$2,000	$3,500	$5,250	$8,000	$9,700	$11,000	$15,000	$25,000

W-2194 • F-375a • Bruce-Roberts (1897–1898) • 656,000 (est.) • Mostly destroyed

Recorded population: 2 • *Highest graded:* Unc • *Commentary:* According to Doug Murray, "the two known notes are from five new plates approved for use in February 1898. Because the five earlier-made Tillman-Morgan plates were still being used to print the second batch of 160,000 Tillman-Morgan notes in FY-1898, it is very likely that both the Tillman-Morgan and Bruce-Roberts notes were being made simultaneously, but supposedly being kept separate from each other. Somehow, at least one Bruce-Roberts sheet got into the Tillman-Morgan pile and was given Tillman-Morgan serials of B412709 to B412712. I believe that the Bruce-

$20 Treasury or Coin Note, Series of 1891 (W-2193).

Back of the $20 Treasury or Coin Note, Series of 1891 (W-2193), with the new, open design.

Roberts notes likely had serial numbers B492001 to B820000 (FY-1898), and the remaining amount delivered in FY-1899 had serials B820001 to B1148000. This would be 656,000 Bruce-Roberts notes. The second Bruce-Roberts serial known (B1147901 at the Smithsonian) is 100 notes from the official high, probably saved for the BEP collection before the full amount of the Bruce-Roberts notes (656,000) were destroyed, these notes not being issued." • *Selected information:* There is one note in private hands, serial B412709, which was sold in a CAA auction (9/2006) for $155,250.

GOLD CERTIFICATES

Act of March 3, 1863

Gold Certificates of the $20 denomination (illus. on p. 482) were issued under the Act of March 3, 1863. "Engraved and Printed at the Treasury Department" is imprinted near the top of the note, as at that time Spencer M. Clark was experimenting with different printing techniques at the National Currency Bureau. This class was not specifically designated as "Certificates of Deposit." Rather, on the New York imprint, "It is hereby certified that Twenty Dollars have been deposited with the Assistant Treasurer of the U.S. in New York payable in Gold at his office to the bearer."

At the left of the face is a patriotic depiction of the American eagle on a shield, with arrows, an olive branch, and a flag as part of the suite and E PLURIBUS UNUM lettered above. A printed green latticework is on the center and right of the face. This same motif is seen on other denominations of this early series.

The back illustrates the reverse of a $20 gold double eagle at the center, with geometric lathe work in orange extending to cover most of the rest of the space. This is the first example of federal currency to specifically illustrate a coin of this denomination (followed later by the $5 to $100 National Gold Bank Notes, each of which illustrates the obverse of an 1871 double eagle).

Bills were printed for Boston, New York, Philadelphia, and Washington. Most were issued in New York, with just a tiny fraction in Washington. No record has been found of issuance in Boston or Philadelphia. At the time, gold coins were worth a strong premium in terms of Legal Tender Notes. These did not circulate hand to hand, but were usually bought by paying for them in gold coins, although there were exceptions to this practice. Most of the larger denominations were used as clearing-house certificates, bank reserves, or in payment of import duties, and it is likely that many of the $20 notes saw similar service.[21]

ACT OF MARCH 3, 1863

$20 Gold Certificate issued under the Act of March 3, 1863 (W-2200). New York imprint. Serial 416, plate D1. This note is ink-dated Nov. 2, 1865, and hand-signed by H.H. Van Dyck. Notes of this type were issued from 1865 to 1869. The first official date of issue was November 13, 1865, per Treasury records. Perhaps this note was pre-dated in anticipation of release.

Detail of the top border showing the Treasury department imprint. This class was among the very first printed in its entirety by the National Currency Bureau.

Back of the $20 Gold Certificate issued under the Act of March 3, 1863 (W-2200). The double eagle vignette on the back is not sharply defined on this or any other surviving example, due to the low contrast of the ink color.

W-2196 • F-1166b • Boston imprint • Colby-Spinner (1864–1867) • Autographed countersignature of assistant Treasurer of the United States on all • Small red seal with spiked border • 20,000 printed • None delivered to Treasurer

W-2200 • F-1166b • New York imprint • 36,000 (est.[22])
Recorded population: 2 • Highest graded: VF-20 • Selected information: CAA (1/1999), 416/D, EF, repaired, $357,500; later seen in CAA (9/2001), $154,000; later in CAA (5/2005) $195,500—an interesting price record. Knight (3/2007), 4069/A, VF-20 (CGA), $345,000.

W-2202 • F-1166b • With printed signature of H.H. Van Dyck (allowed on $20 and $100 denominations only) • 168,000 (est.)
Recorded population: 4 • Highest graded: AU-50 • Selected information: Existing examples include serials 36621/A, canceled, now owned by the Bureau of the Public Debt, Washington

D.C.; 41146/B, VF, sold in a Stack's auction (10/1990) for $88,000; 45149/A, VF, pinholes, sold in a Knight auction (6/2000) for $528,000; and 48545/A, canceled, once owned by Robert F. Schermerhorn, but confiscated and canceled by U.S. Secret Service (though under what authority?), now a part of the Smithsonian Institution collection.

W-2204 • F-1166b • Philadelphia imprint • 20,000 printed • None delivered to Treasurer

W-2206 • F-1166b • Washington imprint • 40,000 printed • 17,800 delivered • Unknown

Series of 1882

The face depicts the then-recently assassinated president James Garfield, while the back shows an eagle clutching a lightning bolt, with two cable-laying ships in the distance. This vignette, titled *Ocean Telegraph*, was engraved by

SERIES OF 1882

$20 Gold Certificate, Series of 1882 (W-2220), with the portrait of the late president James Garfield, assassinated in 1881, at the right.

Back of the $20 Gold Certificate, Series of 1882 (W-2220), with the dynamic *Ocean Telegraph* motif.

George D. Baldwin. A portrait of Garfield also appears on the $5 National Bank Notes of 1882, almost a mirror image of this portrait. The inscription GOLD COIN is in the shingle-style lettering layout. Gold coins, absent from commerce since the waning days of December 1861, achieved parity with Legal Tender and other paper on December 17, 1878. Accordingly, the Series of 1882 Gold Certificates could be exchanged at par.

The Atlantic telegraph, as it was best known, was completed in the summer of 1858 amidst great celebrations on both sides of the Atlantic. In New York City a grand display was held in the streets and within the Crystal Palace.[23] Projected by Cyrus W. Field, the connection made possible fast connections between Europe and America, with great implications for news and financial information. The transmission was not instantaneous. A message of 99 words from Queen Victoria to president James Buchanan took 67 minutes to transmit. This was deemed satisfactory, far eclipsing the sending of news by steamship. There was trouble, though; signals were often interrupted or incomplete, and the last clear message was received on September 1. Soon afterward, the project was abandoned. Not until after the Civil War was an effective connection made. In 1866 the SS *Great Eastern* laid new cable and repaired some cable laid in 1865, achieving lasting success.[24]

The orange-gold color on the notes tended to fade. Today notes with a bright back are worth more than those with faded color, regardless of the grade. This is an exceedingly rare class of currency, and surviving examples are greatly treasured.

W-2210 • F-1175 • Bruce-Gilfillan (1881–1883) • Autographed countersignature of Thomas C. Acton • Medium-size brown seal with scalloped border • 14,000

Recorded population: 2 • *Highest graded:* VF-25 • *Selected information:* Existing examples include serials A1/A (first serial number and plate position), F-15, repaired (PMG), sold in a Knight auction (11/2007) for $546,250 and A2205/A, VF.

W-2212 • F-1175a • Printed countersignature of Thomas C. Acton • 586,000

Estimated population: 29 to 33 • *Highest graded:* Unc.

VG-8	F-12	VF-20	EF-40	AU-50	Unc-60
$4,000	$8,000	$14,000	$30,000	—	—

W-2214 • F-1174 • No countersignature • 448,000

Estimated population: 16 to 18 • *Highest graded:* Unc.

VG-8	F-12	VF-20	EF-40	AU-50	Unc-60
$3,500	$10,000	$15,000	$20,000	$33,000	$50,000

W-2216 • F-1176 • Bruce-Wyman (1883–1885) • 232,000
Estimated population: 21 to 23 • *Highest graded:* Unc.

VG-8	F-12	VF-20	EF-40	AU-50	Unc-60	Unc-63
$2,000	$4,500	$6,500	$15,000	$25,000	—	$45,000

W-2218 • F-1177 • Rosecrans-Huston (1889–1891) • 200,000
Estimated population: 35 to 40 • *Highest graded:* Unc.

VG-8	F-12	VF-20	EF-40	AU-50	Unc-60
$2,000	$4,500	$6,500	$15,000	$35,000	—

W-2220 • F-1178 • Lyons-Roberts (1898–1905) • Small red seal with scalloped border • 16,344,000
Estimated population: 525 to 550 • *Highest graded:* Unc.

VG-8	F-12	VF-20	EF-40	AU-50	Unc-60	Unc-63	Unc-65
$600	$950	$2,350	$5,500	$7,500	$9,000	$12,000	$20,000

Series of 1905

Series of 1905 Gold Certificates have a portrait of George Washington, engraved by Alfred Sealey, and a bright red Treasury seal and serial numbers on the face. The field includes a $20 emblem and is gold. This splash of color has prompted these to be called "Technicolor Notes," although color film process had not been invented by 1905 (however, color images were hardly novel, and Thomas Edison used color in his first films of 1894).[25]

On the back the Heraldic Eagle reverse of the Great Seal of the United States is depicted at the center, with ornately engraved borders. The entire design was printed in orange-gold and engraved by Robert Ponickau. This back was continued in the later large-size Gold Certificate series.

The orange-gold color tended to fade. Today notes with a bright back are worth more than those with faded color, regardless of the grade.

W-2225 • F-1179 • Lyons-Roberts (1898–1905) • 1,664,000
Estimated population: 130 to 140 • *Highest graded:* Unc.

VG-8	F-12	VF-20	EF-40	AU-50	Unc-60	Unc-63	Unc-65
$1,400	$2,800	$7,000	$14,000	$20,000	$23,000	$30,000	$50,000

W-2226 • F-1180 • Lyons-Treat (1905–1906) • 3,012,000
Estimated population: 200 to 220 • *Highest graded:* Unc.

VG-8	F-12	VF-20	EF-40	AU-50	Unc-60	Unc-63	Unc-65
$1,400	$2,800	$7,000	$14,000	$20,000	$23,000	$30,000	$50,000

$20 Gold Certificate, Series of 1905 (W-2225), the "Technicolor Note," an anachronistic nickname given many years later for the bright red and gold color on the face. The serial number 1 makes this one of the greatest trophy notes in existence.

Back of the $20 Gold Certificate, Series of 1905 (W-2225), printed in orange-gold.

Series of 1906

The same motifs of the Series of 1905 notes were used on the Series of 1906 notes, but the red color was replaced with gold for the Treasury seal and serial numbers. The emblem $20 was replaced with XX in large, gold letters, and the yellow-gold background was removed, leaving a plain white field. The back used the same design and inks as the preceding.

The orange-gold color tended to fade. Today notes with a bright back are worth more than those with faded color, regardless of the grade.

W-2228 • F-1181 • Vernon-Treat (1906–1909) • 12,176,000

Estimated population: 145 to 160 • *Highest graded:* Unc.

VG-8	F-12	VF-20	EF-40	AU-50	Unc-60	Unc-63	Unc-65
$250	$380	$475	$675	$1,250	$1,900	$2,200	$6,000

W-2229 • F-1182 • Vernon-McClung (1909–1911) • 6,924,000

Estimated population: 115 to 125 • *Highest graded:* Unc • *Commentary:* Deliveries began on July 15, 1910, and ended on November 16, 1911.

VG-8	F-12	VF-20	EF-40	AU-50	Unc-60	Unc-63	Unc-65
$250	$380	$475	$675	$1,250	$1,900	$2,200	$7,000

W-2229★ • F-1182★

Recorded population: 1 • *Selected information:* Smythe (6/1999), ★15038B/B, F–VF, $9,900.

W-2230 • F-1183 • Napier-McClung (1911–1912) • 8,248,000

Estimated population: 180 to 200 • *Highest graded:* Unc • *Commentary:* Deliveries began on November 24, 1911, and ended on May 26, 1913.

VG-8	F-12	VF-20	EF-40	AU-50	Unc-60	Unc-63	Unc-65
$250	$380	$475	$675	$1,250	$1,900	$2,200	$6,500

W-2230★ • F-1183★

Recorded population: 8 • *Highest graded:* EF-45 • *Selected information:* No recent auction sales.

W-2231 • F-1184 • Napier-Thompson (1912–1913) • 1,480,000

Estimated population: 95 to 115 • *Highest graded:* Unc • *Commentary:* Deliveries began on January 3, 1913, and ended on May 23, 1913.

VG-8	F-12	VF-20	EF-40	AU-50	Unc-60	Unc-63	Unc-65
$750	$1,000	$1,300	$1,900	$3,000	$3,500	$4,000	$8,500

SERIES OF 1906

$20 Gold Certificate, Series of 1906 (W-2228), with gold serial numbers and Treasury seal. An XX denomination marker has been added to the left field.

Back of the $20 Gold Certificate, Series of 1906 (W-2228), printed in orange. The type also used on Series of 1922 notes.

W-2232 • F-1185 • Parker-Burke (1913–1914) • 10,200,000

Estimated population: 275 to 300 • *Highest graded:* Unc • *Commentary:* Deliveries began on December 19, 1913.

VG-8	F-12	VF-20	EF-40	AU-50	Unc-60	Unc-63	Unc-65
$250	$380	$475	$675	$1,250	$1,900	$2,200	$6,500

W-2232★ • F-1185★

Estimated population: 10 to 12 • *Highest graded:* EF-45 • *Selected information:* Knight (11/2007), ★125014B/B, VG-10 (PCGS), $2,243. CAA (9/2005), ★150011B/C, VF, $3,220. Knight (6/2008), ★159269B/A, G-6, damaged (PMG), $1,093.

W-2233 • F-1186 • Teehee-Burke (1915–1919) • 8,180,000 (est.)

Estimated population: 310 to 340 • *Highest graded:* Unc.

VG-8	F-12	VF-20	EF-40	AU-50	Unc-60	Unc-63	Unc-65
$235	$360	$450	$650	$1,150	$1,750	$2,000	$6,500

W-2233★ • F-1186★

Recorded population: 8 • *Highest graded:* EF-40 • *Selected information:* Existing examples include serials ★165335B/C, EF-40 (PMG), sold in a Heritage auction (9/2008) for $12,075; ★167750B/B, Fine; ★174297B/A, F–VF; ★176498B/B, G–VG; ★177125B/A, VG, sold in a Coin Galleries auction (2/1990) for $475; ★181267B/C, VG; ★183582B/B, Fine, sold in a Heritage auction (9/2004) for $1,553; and ★186113B/A, AG.

Series of 1922

The Series of 1922 notes use the same motifs as the foregoing. The XX is moved slightly to the right of its former position. In the left field is the imprint "This certificate is a legal tender in the amount thereof in payment of all debts and dues public and private. Acts of March 14, 1900, as amended and December 24, 1919." The back is the same as used on the preceding series.

Mules: Back plate numbers can be in one of two locations.[26] On May 14, 1921, with the new Elliott-White signature combination starting, all Legal Tender, Silver Certificate, and Gold Certificate back plates were given numbers beginning with 1 and in a new location, although no notice was given of the change. In the instance of the $20 Gold Certificates there was no Elliott-White combination, and the new location started with W-2235, the Speelman-White combination.

> **Back Plate Location 1** (regular use): W-2228 to W-2233. This was the standard location until May 14, 1921. Also used to create a mule for W-2235.

> **Back Plate Location 2** (regular use): W-2235. Introduced without notice as the new style on May 14, 1921, with the Elliott-White (Speelman-White, in this case) combination.

The orange-gold color tended to fade. Today notes with a bright back are worth more than those with faded color, regardless of the grade.

W-2235 • F-1187 • Speelman-White (1922–1927) • 75,120,000, or about 86% regular (est.)

Estimated population: 3,500 to 4,000 • *Highest graded:* Unc.

VG-8	F-12	VF-20	EF-40	AU-50	Unc-60	Unc-63	Unc-65
$235	$275	$380	$600	$1,050	$1,400	$1,800	$4,000

W-2235★ • F-1187★

Estimated population: 125 to 135 • *Highest graded:* Unc.

F-12	VF-20	EF-40	AU-50	Unc-60	Unc-63
$800	$1,700	$2,300	$3,000	—	$4,500

SERIES OF 1922

$20 Gold Certificate, Series of 1922 (W-2235). The back is the same as that used on Series of 1906 $20 Gold Certificates.

Back Plate Location 1.

Back Plate Location 2.

W-2235 Mule • F-1187 • 12,000,000, or about 14% mules (est.)

Estimated population: 500 to 650 • *Highest graded:* Unc. *Commentary:* New listing without market history. Future editions will give pricing information to the extent that it becomes available.

W-2235 Mule★ • F-1187★

Estimated population: 16 to 18 • *Highest graded:* Unc.

F-12	VF-20	EF-40	AU-50	Unc-60	Unc-63
$1,000	$1,800	$3,000	$4,500	—	$8,000

FEDERAL RESERVE NOTES

Series of 1914, Red Seal

Federal Reserve Notes of the Series of 1914 (first with red seals, later with blue) illustrate president Grover Cleveland on the face. The back features two vignettes. On the left a locomotive is rushing toward the center, with an automobile nearby and a biplane barely visible in the sky. On the right is a steamship running full speed ahead out of New York Harbor (with the Statue of Liberty visible in the background). This engraving by Marcus W. Baldwin was designated as *Land, Sea, and Air*.

Red Seal notes (illus. on p. 488) all have Treasury signatures of Burke and McAdoo and red serial numbers. As a class Red Seal notes are elusive. After World War I commenced in Europe in August 1914, the BEP could not import red ink, and so switched to blue after less than a year of printing Red Seals.

Similar to the situation for other notes in this Red Seal series, the $20 notes are rather simple in their appearance and are usually collected singly for the type, although it is possible to acquire them by Federal Reserve Bank and plate style as well. These are considerably scarcer as a group than the Blue Seal notes listed subsequently.

In all of the following listings the number (1 to 12) and the large letter (A to L) on the seal at the left indicates the Federal Reserve Bank that issued the note.

> **Plate Style a** (on Red Seals only): In certain of the following listings the small letter a in the Whitman number indicates large bank district letter and numeral at bottom left and top right. At the upper left is a small plate letter, but no bank district letter and number.
>
> **Plate Style b** (on Red and Blue Seals): In certain of the following listings the small letter b in the Whitman number indicates a note similar to the preceding, but now with small bank district letter and numeral added at top left above the plate letter and at the lower right.

W-2240-A-a • F-952A • Boston • 300,000

Estimated population: 20 to 23 • *Highest graded:* Unc.

VG-8	F-12	VF-20	EF-40	AU-50	Unc-60
$300	$700	$2,500	$3,400	$8,000	—

W-2240-A-b • F-952B • 40,000

Recorded population: 3 • *Highest graded:* EF-40 • *Selected information:* Existing examples include serials A319035A/C, EF-40 (PMG), sold in a Heritage auction (4/2008) for $138,000; A330314A (not graded); and A333643A/C.

W-2240-B-a • F-953A • New York • 1,200,000

Estimated population: 20 to 30 • *Highest graded:* Unc.

VG-8	F-12	VF-20	EF-40	AU-50	Unc-60	Unc-63	Unc-65
$300	$600	$1,000	$1,500	$2,300	$3,500	$6,000	$15,000

W-2240-B-b • F-953B • 1,352,000

Estimated population: 95 to 105 • *Highest graded:* Unc.

VG-8	F-12	VF-20	EF-40	AU-50	Unc-60	Unc-63	Unc-65
$300	$600	$1,000	$1,500	$2,300	$3,500	$6,000	$15,000

W-2240-C-a • F-954A • Philadelphia • 180,000

Estimated population: 16 to 18 • *Highest graded:* Unc.

VG-8	F-12	VF-20	EF-40	AU-50	Unc-60	Unc-63
$300	$600	$1,200	$2,100	—	—	$7,200

W-2240-C-b • F-954B • 180,000

Estimated population: 18 to 20 • *Highest graded:* EF-45.

VG-8	F-12	VF-20	EF-40
$375	$750	$1,300	$2,400

W-2240-D-a • F-955A • Cleveland • 120,000

Recorded population: 5 • *Highest graded:* Unc • *Selected information:* Existing examples include serials D2A/B, Uncirculated; D1030A, VG, sold in a Knight auction (2/2003) for $690; D32189A/A, F–VF; and D73547A, Uncirculated, owned by the Federal Reserve Bank of San Francisco.

W-2240-D-b • F-955B • 380,000

Estimated population: 33 to 36 • *Highest graded:* AU-55.

VG-8	F-12	VF-20	EF-40	AU-50
$300	$600	$1,000	$1,500	$3,500

W-2240-E-a • F-956A • Richmond • 120,000

Recorded population: 8 • *Highest graded:* AU-55 • *Selected information:* Existing examples include serials E10622A, VF-20 (PMG), sold in a Knight auction (6/2008) for $5,462.50; E21088A, VF, owned by the Federal Reserve Bank of San Francisco; E44753A, EF, owned by the Federal Reserve Bank of San Francisco; E48434A/B, AU+; E51849A, Good, sold in a Knight auction (8/2003) for $161; E76321A/A, VF–EF; E76747A, Fair, "washed to death," sold in a New Netherlands Coin Co. auction (4/1954); and E103759A/C, VG, sold in a CAA auction (9/2006) for $862.50.

W-2240-E-b • F-956B • 64,000

Recorded population: 6 • *Highest graded:* VF-20 • *Selected information:* Existing examples include serials E127813A, VF–EF, sold in a Stack's auction (3/1991) for $225; E134397A/A, VF–EF; E143955A, VF-30 (PMG), sold in a Knight auction (6/2008) for $5,463; E148904A/D, VF, sold in a Knight auction (10/2006) for $1,955; E164553A/A, VF-30 (PMG), sold in a Heritage auction (4/2008) for $32,200; and E172724A, VF, sold in a CAA auction (1/1997) for $310.

W-2240-F-a • F-957A • Atlanta • 160,000
Estimated population: 15 to 17 • *Highest graded:* Unc.

VG-8	F-12	VF-20	EF-40	AU-50	Unc-60
$500	$1,000	$1,750	$3,800	—	—

W-2240-G-a • F-958A • Chicago • 300,000
Estimated population: 54 to 58 • *Highest graded:* Unc.

VG-8	F-12	VF-20	EF-40	AU-50	Unc-60
$300	$600	$1,000	$1,500	$2,500	—

SERIES OF 1914, RED SEAL

$20 Federal Reserve Note, Series of 1914, Red Seal, Plate Style a (W-2240-G-a). Issued by the Federal Reserve Bank of Chicago, with bank identification 7-G at the lower left and top right (in addition to the Federal Reserve Bank seal). Portrait of president Grover Cleveland as on all 1914 Red Seal and Blue Seal notes.

$20 Federal Reserve Note, Series of 1914, Red Seal, Plate Style b (W-2240-G-b). Similar to Plate Style a, but now with small bank number and letter 7-G above the plate letter (in this instance A) at the upper left and again at the lower right.

Back of the $20 Federal Reserve Note, Series of 1914, Red Seal, the type also used on Series of 1914 Blue Seal $20 Federal Reserve Notes.

W-2240-G-b • F-958B • 148,000

Estimated population: 20 to 23 • Highest graded: Unc.

VG-8	F-12	VF-20	EF-40	AU-50	Unc-60	Unc-63
$300	$600	$1,000	$1,500	$2,300	$3,900	$7,200

W-2240-H-a • F-959A • St. Louis • 180,000

Estimated population: 40 to 45 • Highest graded: Unc.

VG-8	F-12	VF-20	EF-40	AU-50	Unc-60	Unc-63
$300	$600	$1,000	$1,500	$2,500	$4,000	$7,200

W-2240-H-b • F-959B • 44,000

Estimated population: 13 to 15 • Highest graded: Unc.

VG-8	F-12	VF-20	EF-40	AU-50	Unc-60
$500	$1,000	$1,750	$2,500	$3,500	—

W-2240-I-a • F-960A • Minneapolis • 120,000

Estimated population: 21 to 23 • Highest graded: Unc.

VG-8	F-12	VF-20	EF-40	AU-50	Unc-60
$800	$1,500	$3,000	—	—	—

W-2240-I-b • F-960B • 32,000

Recorded population: 5 • Highest graded: EF-45 • Selected information: Existing examples include serials I124844A/D, VG, sold in a Knight auction (11/2003) for $863; I128694A, stolen; I136872A, VG, problems; I142867A; and I151537A, EF, sold in a CAA auction (1/2003) for $2,990.

W-2240-J-a • F-961A • Kansas City • 120,000

Estimated population: 24 to 27 • Highest graded: Unc.

VG-8	F-12	VF-20	EF-40	AU-50	Unc-60
$400	$700	$1,000	$1,500	—	—

W-2240-J-b • F-961B • 32,000

Recorded population: 4 • Highest graded: VF-25 • Selected information: Existing examples include serials J120129A/A, VG, problems, sold in a Knight auction (11/20003) for $2,070; J120516A/D, VF, damaged, sold in a CAA auction (1/2004) for $4,370; J136240A/D, VG–F, problems, sold in a Smythe auction (6/1998) for $440; and J148150A, VF.

W-2240-K-a • F-962A • Dallas • 160,000

Estimated population: 30 to 35 • Highest graded: AU-50.

VG-8	F-12	VF-20	EF-40	AU-50
$500	$1,000	$1,750	$2,500	$4,500

W-2240-L-a • F-963A • San Francisco • 120,000

Recorded population: 7 • Highest graded: EF-45 • Selected information: Existing examples include serials L2458A/B, F-12 (PCGS), sold in a Knight auction (6/2008) for $920; L10878A/B, Fine; L24770A, VG; L27597A/A, EF, sold in a Knight auction (4/2003) for $4,600; L33113A, Fine; L59955A, VG, owned by the Federal Reserve Bank of San Francisco; and L61843A/C, VF, sold in a Knight auction (11/2006) for $3,450.

W-2240-L-b • F-963B • 140,000

Recorded population: 7 • Highest graded: VF-35 • Selected information: Existing examples include serials L125603A/C, VF+,

part of the Smithsonian Institution collection; L127502A/B; L166335A/C, VF-35 (PMG), sold in a Heritage auction (4/2008) for $34,500; L186540A, F-12 (PCGS), sold in a Knight auction (6/2008) for $3,680; L201633A/A, VF-20, repaired (PMG), sold in a Heritage auction (1/2007) for $3,105; L250865A, VF, owned by the Federal Reserve Bank of San Francisco; and L256966A/B, VF, sold in a CAA auction (4/2006) for $4,025.

Series of 1914, Blue Seal

The $20 Blue Seal notes (illus. on p. 490) are much more available than those with Red Seals. These can be collected by bank as well as by signature combination. As they are not in the mainstream of popularity, scarce and rare varieties are priced less than might otherwise be the case.

In all of the following listings the number (1 to 12) and the large letter (A to L) on the seal at the left indicate the Federal Reserve Bank that issued the note.

Plate Style b (on Red and Blue Seals): In certain of the following listings the small letter b in the Whitman number indicates a note with the same layout of the Plate Style b used on Red Seal notes. A large district number and letter are at the lower left and top right, and at the top left a small bank district letter and numeral are added above the plate letter, and a small bank district letter and number are at the lower right. In the Blue Seal series all Burke-McAdoo, Burke-Glass, and Burke-Houston notes are of this style.

Plate Style c (on Blue Seals only): In certain of the following listings the small letter c in the Whitman number indicates a large bank district letter and numeral at the top right and small district letters and numerals in the other three corners. The letter and numeral at the upper left corner are over a plate letter. Only some late White-Mellon notes are of this style.

Plate Style d (on Blue Seals only): The small letter d in the Whitman number indicates a note similar to Plate Style b, but the seals on the left and right are closer to the portrait than on the b and c issues. Also, the larger bank number-letter combinations are vertically closer to the center of the note, but also closer to the left and right outer edges. White-Mellon (1921–1928) notes are found in b, c, and d styles.

W-2250-A-b • F-964 • Boston • Burke-McAdoo (1913–1918) • 4,660,000 (est.)

Estimated population: 65 to 75 • Highest graded: Unc.

VG-8	F-12	VF-20	EF-40	AU-50	Unc-60
$90	$110	$140	$200	$250	$325

W-2250-A-b★ • F-964★

Recorded population: 3 • Highest graded: EF-45 • Selected information: Knight (11/2003), A13696★/H, G–VG, $604. Stack's (9/1996), A32651★/C, EF, $770. Smythe (2/2000), A44180★/H, VF, $688.

SERIES OF 1914, BLUE SEAL

$20 Federal Reserve Note, Series of 1914, Blue Seal, Plate Style b (W-2277-G-b).

$20 Federal Reserve Note, Series of 1914, Blue Seal, Plate Style c (W-2277-G-c).

$20 Federal Reserve Note, Series of 1914, Blue Seal, Plate Style d (W-2277-G-d).

W-2251-A-b • F-965 • Burke-Glass (1918–1920) • 2,780,000 (est.)

Estimated population: 20 to 24 • *Highest graded:* Unc.

VG-8	F-12	VF-20	EF-40	AU-50	Unc-60
$120	$250	$350	$500	—	—

W-2251-A-b★ • F-965★

Recorded population: 3 • *Highest graded:* VF-20 • *Selected information:* Existing examples include serials A48628★/H, F-12

(PCGS), sold in a Heritage auction (4/2008) for $4,025; A57382★/B, VG, problems; and A59777★/A, VF, sold in a CAA auction (5/2005) for $7,475.

W-2252-A-b • F-966 • Burke-Houston (1920–1921) • 8,476,000 (est.)

Estimated population: 130 to 145 • *Highest graded:* Unc.

VG-8	F-12	VF-20	EF-40	AU-50	Unc-60	Unc-63	Unc-65
$90	$110	$140	$200	$250	$325	$400	$850

W-2252-A-b★ • F-966★

Estimated population: 9 or 10 • *Highest graded:* VF-25 • *Selected information:* Knight (11/2004), A131649★/A, VG–F, $690. Heritage (1/2006), A131890★/B, Fine+, $978.

W-2253-A-b • F-967 • White-Mellon (1921–1928) • 9,768,000 (est.)

Estimated population: 150 to 160 • *Highest graded:* Unc.

VG-8	F-12	VF-20	EF-40	AU-50	Unc-60	Unc-63	Unc-65
$90	$110	$140	$200	$250	$325	$400	$850

W-2254-B-b • F-968 • Burke-McAdoo (1913–1918) • 16,172,000 (est.)

Estimated population: 120 to 130 • *Highest graded:* Unc.

VG-8	F-12	VF-20	EF-40	AU-50	Unc-60	Unc-63	Unc-65
$90	$110	$140	$200	$250	$325	$400	$850

W-2254-B-b★ • F-968★

Recorded population: 3 • *Highest graded:* F-12 • *Selected information:* Existing examples include serials B1309★/A, VG; B1381★/A, G–VG, sold in a Heritage auction (1/2006) for $1,208; and B10112★/D, Fine.

W-2255-B-b • F-969 • Burke-Glass (1918–1920) • 10,712,000 (est.)

Estimated population: 120 to 130 • *Highest graded:* Unc.

VG-8	F-12	VF-20	EF-40	AU-50	Unc-60
$100	$125	$170	$250	$400	—

W-2255-B-b★ • F-969★

Recorded population: 5 • *Highest graded:* VF-20 • *Selected information:* Existing examples include serials B59972★/H, VG; B70786★/B, VG; B118898★/B, F-15 (CGA), sold in a Knight auction (11/2004) for $2,990; B125907★, F–VF; B149271★/C, VF-20 (PCGS), sold in a Heritage auction (9/2007) for $1,897.50.

W-2256-B-b • F-970 • Burke-Houston (1920–1921) • 10,908,000 (est.)

Estimated population: 140 to 150 • *Highest graded:* Unc.

VG-8	F-12	VF-20	EF-40	AU-50	Unc-60	Unc-63	Unc-65
$90	$110	$140	$200	$250	$325	$400	$850

W-2256-B-b★ • F-970★

Estimated population: 12 to 14 • *Highest graded:* VF-25.

VG-8	F-12	VF-20
$300	$600	$1,200

W-2257-B-b • F-971A • White-Mellon (1921–1928) • 14,252,000 (est.)

Estimated population: 200 to 210 • *Highest graded:* Unc.

VG-8	F-12	VF-20	EF-40	AU-50	Unc-60	Unc-63	Unc-65
$90	$110	$140	$200	$250	$325	$400	$850

W-2257-B-b★ • F-971A★

Estimated population: 19 to 22 • *Highest graded:* Unc.

F-12	VF-20	EF-40	AU-50	Unc-60	Unc-63
$400	$800	$1,400	$2,200	$2,900	$4,200

W-2257-B-c • F-971B • 4,224,000 (est.)

Estimated population: 70 to 80 • *Highest graded:* Unc.

VG-8	F-12	VF-20	EF-40	AU-50	Unc-60	Unc-63	Unc-65
$120	$150	$180	$270	$400	$500	$650	$1,100

W-2257-B-d • F-971C • 1,028,000 (est.) • Printed but not issued

W-2258-C-b • F-972 • Philadelphia • Burke-McAdoo (1913–1918) • 7,740,000 (est.)

Estimated population: 100 to 110 • *Highest graded:* Unc.

VG-8	F-12	VF-20	EF-40	AU-50	Unc-60	Unc-63	Unc-65
$90	$110	$140	$200	$250	$325	$400	$850

W-2258-C-b★ • F-972★

Estimated population: 9 or 10 • *Highest graded:* EF-45 • *Selected information:* Knight (3/2001), C55241★/A, Fine, $440. CAA (1/2000), C57079★/G, VG-10 (PCGS), $330.

W-2259-C-b • F-973 • Burke-Glass (1918–1920) • 3,160,000 (est.)

Estimated population: 44 to 48 • *Highest graded:* Unc.

VG-8	F-12	VF-20	EF-40	AU-50	Unc-60	Unc-63	Unc-65
$100	$125	$175	$275	$500	$750	$1,200	$2,200

W-2260-C-b • F-974 • Burke-Houston (1920–1921) • 7,824,000 (est.)

Estimated population: 100 to 110 • *Highest graded:* Unc.

VG-8	F-12	VF-20	EF-40	AU-50	Unc-60	Unc-63	Unc-65
$90	$110	$140	$200	$250	$325	$400	$850

W-2260-C-b★ • F-974★

Estimated population: 16 to 18 • *Highest graded:* AU-50.

F-12	VF-20	EF-40	AU-50
$800	$1,000	$1,300	$2,500

W-2261-C-b • F-975 • White-Mellon (1921–1928) • 11,004,000 (est.)

Estimated population: 240 to 260 • *Highest graded:* Unc.

VG-8	F-12	VF-20	EF-40	AU-50	Unc-60	Unc-63	Unc-65
$90	$110	$140	$200	$250	$325	$400	$850

W-2261-C-b★ • F-975★

Estimated population: 10 to 12 • *Highest graded:* EF-45 • *Selected information:* CAA (9/2001), C169070★/B, VF, $550. CAA (5/2004), C169485★/E, EF, $2,185. Smythe (9/2003), C172496★/H, F-12 (PMG), $431. CAA (1/1995), C180118★/F, Fine, $253; later seen in Martinelli (5/1995), $280; later seen in Martinelli (10/1995), $240; later seen in CAA (5/1999), $248. Heritage (1/2008), C186181★/A, F-15 (PMG), $920. CAA (5/2003), C192146★/B, VG, $345.

W-2262-D-b • F-976 • Cleveland • Burke-McAdoo (1913–1918) • 7,560,000 (est.)

Estimated population: 150 to 160 • *Highest graded:* Unc.

VG-8	F-12	VF-20	EF-40	AU-50	Unc-60	Unc-63
$90	$110	$140	$200	$250	$325	$500

W-2262-D-b★ • F-976★

Recorded population: 2 • *Highest graded:* Unc • *Commentary:* No market history available.

W-2263-D-b • F-977 • Burke-Glass (1918–1920) • 3,996,000 (est.)

Estimated population: 90 to 100 • *Highest graded:* Unc.

VG-8	F-12	VF-20	EF-40	AU-50	Unc-60	Unc-63
$120	$150	$180	$270	$400	$500	$650

W-2263-D-b★ • F-977★

Recorded population: 3 • *Highest graded:* VF-25 • *Selected information:* Existing examples include serials D68300★/D, Fine; D70176★/D, VF, sold in a Knight auction (11/2004) for $7,590; and D83138★/B, F-12 (PCGS), sold in a CAA auction (5/2003) for $1,754.

W-2264-D-b • F-978 • Burke-Houston (1920–1921) • 6,308,000 (est.)

Estimated population: 120 to 130 • *Highest graded:* Unc.

VG-8	F-12	VF-20	EF-40	AU-50	Unc-60	Unc-63	Unc-65
$90	$110	$140	$200	$250	$325	$400	$850

W-2264-D-b★ • F-978★

Estimated population: 14 to 16 • *Highest graded:* AU-50.

F-12	VF-20	EF-40	AU-50
$900	$1,200	$2,000	$3,000

W-2265-D-b • F-979A • White-Mellon (1921–1928) • 19,208,000 (est.)

Estimated population: 370 to 390 • *Highest graded:* Unc.

VG-8	F-12	VF-20	EF-40	AU-50	Unc-60	Unc-63	Unc-65
$90	$110	$140	$200	$250	$325	$400	$850

W-2265-D-b★ • F-979A★

Estimated population: 10 to 12 • *Highest graded:* AU-50 • *Selected information:* Knight (3/2008), D204333★/A, F-12 (PCGS), $748. Heritage (4/2008), D227009★/A, F-15 (PCGS), $546. Smythe (10/2004), D245723★/G, Fine, $488.75.

W-2265-D-c • F-979B • 972,000 (est.)

Estimated population: 55 to 60 • *Highest graded:* Unc.

VG-8	F-12	VF-20	EF-40	AU-50	Unc-60	Unc-63	Unc-65
$120	$150	$180	$270	$350	$450	$600	$1,000

W-2266-E-b • F-980 • Richmond • Burke-McAdoo (1913–1918) • 4,216,000 (est.)

Estimated population: 55 to 60 • *Highest graded:* EF-45.

VG-8	F-12	VF-20	EF-40
$90	$110	$165	$300

W-2266-E-b★ • F-980★

Recorded population: 2 • *Highest graded:* VG-8 • *Selected information:* Existing examples include serials E10483★/C, VG, and E30630★/B, VG, sold in a Heritage auction (1/2006) for $2,195.

W-2267-E-b • F-981 • Burke-Glass (1918–1920) • 2,100,000 (est.)

Estimated population: 55 to 60 • *Highest graded:* Unc.

VG-8	F-12	VF-20	EF-40	AU-50	Unc-60
$150	$220	$300	$700	$1,000	—

W-2268-E-b • F-982 • Burke-Houston (1920–1921) • 3,040,000 (est.)

Estimated population: 75 to 85 • *Highest graded:* Unc.

VG-8	F-12	VF-20	EF-40	AU-50	Unc-60
$90	$110	$180	$250	$300	$450

W-2268-E-b★ • F-982★

Estimated population: 10 to 12 • *Highest graded:* VF-25 • *Selected information:* Heritage (9/2007), E69463★/C, Fine, $1,265. Knight (6/2002), E78292★/D, VG–F, $431. Heritage (5/2007), E109921★/A, Fine, $3,220. Heritage (1/2006), E113048★/D, Fine, $1,725. Knight (6/2007), E118090★/B, VF-25 (PMG), $1,265.

W-2269-E-b • F-983A • White-Mellon (1921–1928) • 7,788,000 (est.)

Estimated population: 185 to 200 • *Highest graded:* Unc.

VG-8	F-12	VF-20	EF-40	AU-50	Unc-60	Unc-63	Unc-65
$90	$110	$140	$200	$250	$325	$400	$850

W-2269-E-b★ • F-983A★

Recorded population: 5 • *Highest graded:* VF-20 • *Selected information:* Existing examples include serials E99998★/B, VG–F; E119046★/D, Fine, sold in a CAA auction (1/2001) for $440; E121528★/D, Fine; E122160★/D, VF–EF, sold in a CAA auction (9/2000) for $2,420. and E122582★/B, Fine.

W-2269-E-c • F-983B • 8,000 (est.) • Printed but not issued

W-2270-F-b • F-984 • Atlanta • Burke-McAdoo (1913–1918) • 8,580,000 (est.)

Estimated population: 155 to 165 • *Highest graded:* Unc.

VG-8	F-12	VF-20	EF-40	AU-50	Unc-60	Unc-63	Unc-65
$90	$110	$140	$200	$250	$325	$400	$850

W-2270-F-b★ • F-984★

Estimated population: 11 to 13 • *Highest graded:* Unc.

F-12	VF-20	EF-40	AU-50	Unc-60	Unc-63
$650	$1,200	$2,000	$3,000	—	$5,000

W-2271-F-b • F-985 • Burke-Glass (1918–1920) • No plates made. Listed here for the record.[27]

W-2272-F-b • F-986 • Burke-Houston (1920–1921) • 3,552,000 (est.)

Estimated population: 115 to 125 • *Highest graded:* Unc.

VG-8	F-12	VF-20	EF-40	AU-50	Unc-60	Unc-63	Unc-65
$90	$110	$140	$200	$250	$325	$400	$850

W-2272-F-b★ • F-986★

Recorded population: 5 • *Highest graded:* VF-30 • *Selected information:* Existing examples include serials F75634★/B, F-15 (CGA), sold in a Knight auction (11/2005) for $3,738; F83934★/B, VG–F, sold in a CAA auction (5/2005) for $2,530; F91277★/A, VF+; F95132★/D, VG–F, sold in a CAA auction (5/1999) for $522.50, later sold in a Knight auction (11/2003) for $604; and F95969★/A, VG–F.

W-2273-F-b • F-987A • White-Mellon (1921–1928) • 3,660,000 (est.)

Estimated population: 110 to 120 • *Highest graded:* Unc.

VG-8	F-12	VF-20	EF-40	AU-50	Unc-60	Unc-63	Unc-65
$90	$110	$140	$200	$250	$325	$400	$850

W-2273-F-c • F-987B • 432,000 (est.) • Printed but not issued

W-2274-G-b • F-988 • Chicago • Burke-McAdoo (1913–1918) • 12,812,000 (est.)

Estimated population: 190 to 210 • *Highest graded:* Unc.

VG-8	F-12	VF-20	EF-40	AU-50	Unc-60	Unc-63	Unc-65
$90	$110	$140	$200	$250	$325	$400	$850

W-2275-G-b • F-989 • Burke-Glass (1918–1920) • 5,140,000 (est.)

Estimated population: 100 to 110 • *Highest graded:* Unc.

VG-8	F-12	VF-20	EF-40	AU-50	Unc-60	Unc-63
$100	$125	$170	$250	$400	$600	$1,000

W-2275-G-b★ • F-989★

Recorded population: 6 • *Highest graded:* Unc • *Selected information:* Heritage (1/2007), G55019★/C, VG–F, $1,553. Heritage (9/2007), G70141★/A, VG–F, $805. Stack's (3/1993), G84051★/C, Uncirculated, $750. CAA (10/1995), G90090★/B, VG, $198.

W-2276-G-b • F-990 • Burke-Houston (1920–1921) • 14,620,000 (est.)

Estimated population: 220 to 240 • *Highest graded:* Unc.

VG-8	F-12	VF-20	EF-40	AU-50	Unc-60	Unc-63	Unc-65
$90	$110	$140	$200	$250	$325	$400	$850

W-2276-G-b★ • F-990★

Estimated population: 35 to 40 • *Highest graded:* AU-58.

F-12	VF-20	EF-40	AU-50
$600	$1,200	$1,800	$2,500

W-2277-G-b • F-991A • White-Mellon (1921–1928) • 9,952,000 (est.)

Estimated population: 275 to 300 • *Highest graded:* Unc.

VG-8	F-12	VF-20	EF-40	AU-50	Unc-60	Unc-63	Unc-65
$90	$110	$140	$200	$250	$325	$400	$850

W-2277-G-b★ • F-991A★

Estimated population: 11 to 13 • *Highest graded:* AU-50 • *Selected information:* Heritage (1/2006), G327702★/B, Fine, $1,150. DBR Currency Web site (11/2007), G337928★/D, Fine, $1,495. CAA (9/2006), G342341★/A, Fine, damaged, $632.50.

W-2277-G-c • F-991B • 3,488,000 (est.)

Estimated population: 148 to 155 • *Highest graded:* Unc.

VG-8	F-12	VF-20	EF-40	AU-50	Unc-60	Unc-63	Unc-65
$90	$110	$150	$225	$300	$425	$600	$1,050

W-2277-G-d • F-991C • 316,000

Estimated population: 25 to 35 • *Highest graded:* Unc.

VG-8	F-12	VF-20	EF-40	AU-50	Unc-60
$300	$450	$700	$900	$1,400	$2,200

W-2278-H-b • F-992 • St. Louis • Burke-McAdoo (1913–1918) • 5,272,000 (est.)

Estimated population: 130 to 140 • *Highest graded:* Unc.

VG-8	F-12	VF-20	EF-40	AU-50	Unc-60	Unc-63	Unc-65
$90	$110	$140	$200	$250	$325	$400	$850

W-2278-H-b★ • F-992★

Recorded population: 8 • *Highest graded:* VF-25 • *Selected information:* Heritage (1/2006), H2681★/A, VG, $1,150. Smythe (6/2000), H19356★/D, VG, $297. Heritage (9/2007), H46053★/A, VG, $546. Heritage (1/2008), H48778★/F, VG-8 (PMG), $1,093.

W-2279-H-b • F-993 • Burke-Glass (1918–1920) • 904,000 (est.)

Estimated population: 20 to 24 • *Highest graded:* AU-50.

VG-8	F-12	VF-20	EF-40	AU-50
$120	$250	$400	$600	—

W-2279-H-b★ • F-993★

Recorded population: 1 • *Graded:* VF • *Selected information:* Smythe (6/2001), H57650★/B, VF, $1,980.

W-2280-H-b • F-994 • Burke-Houston (1920–1921) • 3,000,000 (est.)

Estimated population: 95 to 115 • *Highest graded:* Unc.

VG-8	F-12	VF-20	EF-40	AU-50	Unc-60
$90	$110	$140	$250	$400	—

W-2280-H-b★ • F-994★

Estimated population: 18 to 20 • *Highest graded:* Unc.

F-12	VF-20	EF-40	AU-50	Unc-60	Unc-63
$700	$1,100	$1,400	$2,500	—	$4,500

W-2281-H-b • F-995 • White-Mellon (1921–1928) • 1,348,000 (est.)

Estimated population: 95 to 105 • *Highest graded:* Unc.

VG-8	F-12	VF-20	EF-40	AU-50	Unc-60	Unc-63	Unc-65
$90	$110	$140	$200	$250	$325	$400	$850

W-2282-I-b • F-996 • Minneapolis • Burke-McAdoo (1913–1918) • 2,828,000 (est.)

Estimated population: 95 to 115 • *Highest graded:* Unc.

VG-8	F-12	VF-20	EF-40	AU-50	Unc-60	Unc-63	Unc-65
$100	$120	$150	$220	$275	$350	$450	$950

W-2282-I-b★ • F-996★

Recorded population: 6 • *Highest graded:* AU-50 • *Selected information:* Existing examples include serials I2272★/D, Fine, problems, sold in a Smythe auction (7/2007) for $1,955; I3014★/B, Fine; I6190★/B, VF; I6651★/C, VG–F, sold in a Heritage auction (9/2007) for $1,610; and I10424/H, AU.

W-2283-I-b • F-997 • Burke-Glass (1918–1920) • 160,000 (est.)

Estimated population: 18 to 20 • *Highest graded:* Unc.

VG-8	F-12	VF-20	EF-40	AU-50	Unc-60
$150	$275	$425	$1,000	$2,000	—

W-2284-I-b • F-998 • Burke-Houston (1920–1921) • 1,764,000 (est.)

Estimated population: 145 to 160 • *Highest graded:* Unc.

VG-8	F-12	VF-20	EF-40	AU-50	Unc-60	Unc-63	Unc-65
$100	$120	$150	$220	$275	$350	$450	$950

W-2284-I-b★ • F-998★

Recorded population: 4 • *Highest graded:* EF-45 • *Selected information:* Existing examples include serials I22374★/B, VF, owned by Kurt Krueger; I26909★/A, VF, sold in a CAA auction (9/2003) for $2,530; I28674★/B, EF, sold in a CAA auction (10/1998) for $880; and I29697★/A, EF, owned by the Federal Reserve Bank of San Francisco.

W-2285-I-b • F-999 • White-Mellon (1921–1928) • 1,968,000 (est.)

Estimated population: 155 to 165 • *Highest graded:* Unc.

VG-8	F-12	VF-20	EF-40	AU-50	Unc-60	Unc-63	Unc-65
$100	$120	$150	$220	$275	$350	$450	$950

W-2286-J-b • F-1000 • Kansas City • Burke-McAdoo (1913–1918) • 4,808,000 (est.)

Estimated population: 105 to 115 • *Highest graded:* Unc.

VG-8	F-12	VF-20	EF-40	AU-50	Unc-60	Unc-63	Unc-65
$90	$110	$150	$220	$275	$350	$450	$950

W-2287-J-b • F-1001 • Burke-Glass (1918–1920) • No plates made; listed here for the record[28]

W-2288-J-b • F-1002 • Burke-Houston (1920–1921) • 2,412,000 (est.)

Estimated population: 115 to 125 • *Highest graded:* Unc.

VG-8	F-12	VF-20	EF-40	AU-50	Unc-60	Unc-63	Unc-65
$90	$110	$140	$200	$250	$325	$400	$850

W-2288-J-b★ • F-1002★

Estimated population: 11 to 13 • *Highest graded:* VF-25.

VG-8	F-12	VF-20
$500	$900	$1,400

W-2289-J-b • F-1003 • White-Mellon (1921–1928) • 1,800,000 (est.)

Estimated population: 115 to 125 • *Highest graded:* Unc.

VG-8	F-12	VF-20	EF-40	AU-50	Unc-60	Unc-63	Unc-65
$90	$110	$140	$200	$250	$325	$400	$850

W-2290-K-b • F-1004 • Dallas • Burke-McAdoo (1913–1918) • 3,212,000 (est.)

Estimated population: 75 to 85 • *Highest graded:* Unc.

VG-8	F-12	VF-20	EF-40	AU-50	Unc-60	Unc-63	Unc-65
$100	$120	$150	$220	$300	$400	$500	$950

W-2290-K-b★ • F-1004★

Estimated population: 12 to 14 • *Highest graded:* AU-50.

VG-8	F-12	VF-20	EF-40	AU-50
$1,100	$1,800	$2,400	$3,300	$4,500

W-2291-K-b • F-1005 • Burke-Glass (1918–1920) • 468,000 (est.)

Estimated population: 15 to 17 • *Highest graded:* Unc.

VG-8	F-12	VF-20	EF-40	AU-50	Unc-60
$250	$500	$1,250	$4,000	—	—

W-2292-K-b • F-1006 • Burke-Houston (1920–1921) • 1,460,000 (est.)

Estimated population: 75 to 85 • *Highest graded:* Unc.

VG-8	F-12	VF-20	EF-40	AU-50	Unc-60
$110	$150	$200	$400	$700	$1,000

W-2293-K-b • F-1007 • White-Mellon (1921–1928) • 1,764,000 (est.)

Estimated population: 120 to 130 • *Highest graded:* Unc.

VG-8	F-12	VF-20	EF-40	AU-50	Unc-60	Unc-63	Unc-65
$100	$120	$150	$220	$300	$400	$500	$950

W-2294-L-b • F-1008 • San Francisco • Burke-McAdoo (1913–1918) • 6,860,000 (est.)

Estimated population: 90 to 100 • *Highest graded:* Unc.

VG-8	F-12	VF-20	EF-40	AU-50	Unc-60	Unc-63
$90	$110	$140	$200	$250	$325	$500

W-2294-L-b★ • F-1008★

Recorded population: 3 • *Highest graded:* VG-10 • *Selected information:* Existing examples include serials L56896★/D, VG–F; L58188★/D, VG–F; and L71284★/H, VG–F, sold in a Heritage auction (1/2006) for $2,645.

W-2295-L-b • F-1009 • Burke-Glass (1918–1920) • 3,220,000 (est.)

Estimated population: 45 to 50 • *Highest graded:* Unc.

VG-8	F-12	VF-20	EF-40	AU-50	Unc-60
$120	$170	$250	$375	$500	—

W-2295-L-b★ • F-1009★

Recorded population: 2 • *Highest graded:* VF-25 • *Selected information:* Existing examples include serials L81523★/C, Fine, sold in a Knight auction (3/2005) for $3,105, and L86858★/B, VF.

W-2296-L-b • F-1010 • Burke-Houston (1920–1921) • 4,464,000 (est.)

Estimated population: 70 to 80 • *Highest graded:* Unc.

VG-8	F-12	VF-20	EF-40	AU-50	Unc-60	Unc-63
$100	$120	$150	$220	$300	$400	$500

W-2296-L-b★ • F-1010★

Recorded population: 8 • *Highest graded:* EF-45 • *Selected information:* CAA (5/2005), L88702★/B, EF, $3,105. Knight (6/2006), L115058★/B, Fine, $1,265; Heritage (9/2007), L125202★/B, F-12 (PCGS), $920.

W-2297-L-b • F-1011A • White-Mellon (1921–1928) • 14,668,000 (est.)

Estimated population: 240 to 260 • *Highest graded:* Unc.

VG-8	F-12	VF-20	EF-40	AU-50	Unc-60	Unc-63	Unc-65
$90	$110	$140	$200	$250	$325	$400	$850

W-2297-L-b★ • F-1011A★

Estimated population: 16 to 18 • *Highest graded:* Unc.

F-12	VF-20	EF-40	AU-50	Unc-60	Unc-63
$900	$1,400	$1,600	$2,700	—	$5,000

W-2297-L-c • F-1011B • 4,400,000 (est.)

Estimated population: 110 to 120 • *Highest graded:* Unc.

VG-8	F-12	VF-20	EF-40	AU-50	Unc-60	Unc-63
$100	$120	$150	$220	$300	$550	$1,000

W-2297-L-c★ • F-1011b★

Recorded population: 1 • *Graded:* VF-20 • *Selected information:* CAA (1/1995), L269270★/F, VF, $1,045.

W-2297-L-d • F-1011c • 1,884,000 (est.)

Estimated population: 35 to 40 • *Highest graded:* Unc.

VG-8	F-12	VF-20	EF-40	AU-50	Unc-60
$250	$400	$600	$800	$1,250	$2,000

FEDERAL RESERVE BANK NOTES

Series of 1915

Series of 1915 and Series of 1918 notes are similar to the preceding, but with Cleveland's portrait repositioned at the far left to allow room for the imprint of the Federal Reserve Bank and city. The back remains the same. Certain of these have overprinted signatures of the bank officers. Only six of the 12 districts issued notes of this denomination.

Series of 1915 notes have SERIES OF 1915, the date MAY 20, 1914, and in two curved lines above the center of the bottom border, AUTHORIZED BY FEDERAL RESERVE ACT OF DECEMBER 23, 1913.

At the top center of the Series of 1915 notes is the security provision: "Secured by United States bonds deposited with the Treasurer of the United States of America."

$20 Federal Reserve Bank Note, Series of 1915 (W-2315-K). Federal Reserve Bank of Dallas. The illustrated note has the signatures of the bank officers overprinted at the bottom.

Detail of the authorization notice above the lower border on the face (W-2306-G).

Back of the $20 Federal Reserve Bank Note, Series of 1915 (W-2315-K). The design is similar to $20 Federal Reserve Note, Series of 1914, notes, but with different lettering. The type also used on Series of 1918 $20 Federal Reserve Bank Notes.

W-2300-F • F-822a • Atlanta • Teehee-Burke (1915–1919) • Pike (cashier)-McCord • No estimate

Recorded population: 1 • *Graded:* EF-40 • *Commentary:* Said by a leading Texas currency specialist to have been created as a whimsy by W.A. Philpott Jr., who was well known for "improving" paper money. Other specialists have accepted it as a unique authentic note. In any event, its serial number F1233A falls in the middle of serial numbers for W-2302-F which the Gengerke census lists from F245A to F1293A. • *Selected information:* This note is from the Philpott Collection, sold in a Stack's auction (3/1991) for $5,775; later seen in CAA (1/2002), $43,700; later seen in Heritage (4/2008), $161,000.

W-2302-F • F-822 • Bell (cashier)-Wellborn • 4,000 (est.)

Recorded population: 5 • *Highest graded:* AU-50 • *Commentary:* One is held by the Federal Reserve Bank of San Francisco Museum; four are in private hands. • *Selected information:* Knight (2/2004), F1257A/A, AU, $11,500. Heritage (4/2008), F-1293A, $92,000.

W-2304-F • F-822-1 • Bell (secretary)-Wellborn • 20,000 (est.)

Recorded population: 5 • *Highest graded:* EF-45 • *Selected information:* Heritage (4/2008), F4213A, VF-25 (PMG), $43,125. Knight (2/2004), F7733A, AU, problems, $488. Stack's (3/1991), F7822A/B, VF–EF, $770. Stack's (3/1990), F7826A/B, EF, $770.

W-2306-G • F-824 • Chicago • McLallen-McDougal • 80,000

Estimated population: 38 to 47 • *Highest graded:* Unc.

VG-8	F-12	VF-20	EF-40	AU-50	Unc-60	Unc-63	Unc-65
$1,600	$3,500	$6,000	$12,500	$14,000	$15,000	$18,000	$25,000

W-2311-J • F-827 • Kansas City • Cross (acting)-Miller • 100,000

Estimated population: 36 to 42 • *Highest graded:* AU-55.

VG-8	F-12	VF-20	EF-40	AU-50
$2,000	$4,000	$8,000	$15,000	—

W-2312-J • F-826 • Anderson-Miller • 80,000

Estimated population: 32 to 36 • *Highest graded:* EF-40 • *Commentary:* In his 1951 study of these notes (see the bibliography), W.A. Philpott Jr. stated that of the Kansas City $20 notes, only 674 total, or 337 for each signature, remained outstanding as of October 30, 1944. "Of these the Anderson & Miller note seems scarcer than the Cross & Miller."

VG-8	F-12	VF-20	EF-40
$1,600	$3,500	$6,000	$12,500

W-2315-K • F-828 • Dallas • Hoopes-Van Zandt • 88,000

Estimated population: 35 to 40 • *Highest graded:* Unc.

VG-8	F-12	VF-20	EF-40	AU-50	Unc-60
$2,000	$4,000	$8,000	$15,000	—	—

W-2317-K • F-830 • Talley (cashier)-Van Zandt • 8,000

Recorded population: 3 • *Highest graded:* AU-50 • *Selected information:* Existing examples include serials K88623A/C, VF, sold in a Smythe auction (6/1998) for $4,400; K90564A, AU; K95077A, F-15 (PMG).

W-2319-K • F-829 • Gilbert (cashier)-Van Zandt • 4,000

Recorded population: 6 • *Highest graded:* EF-45 • *Selected information:* Smythe (6/1998), K96195A/C, VF, $3,575. Kagin's (1/1979), K96199A, VF–EF, $3,600. Hickman & Oakes (11/1986), K97052A/D, Fine, $1,254. Heritage (4/2008), K97555A, Net VF-25 (PMG), $23,000. CAA (11/1992), K98100A/D, VF, $650. Knight (6/1992), K98583A/C, EF, $1,045.

Series of 1918

Series of 1918 notes have SERIES OF 1918, the date MAY 18, 1914, and in three straight lines vertically at the right border, AUTHORIZED BY THE ACTS OF DECEMBER 23, 1913, AND APRIL 23, 1918.

At the top center of the Series of 1918 notes is the security provision: "Secured by United States bonds or United States Certificates of Indebtedness or United States One-Year Gold Notes, deposited with the Treasurer of the United States of America."

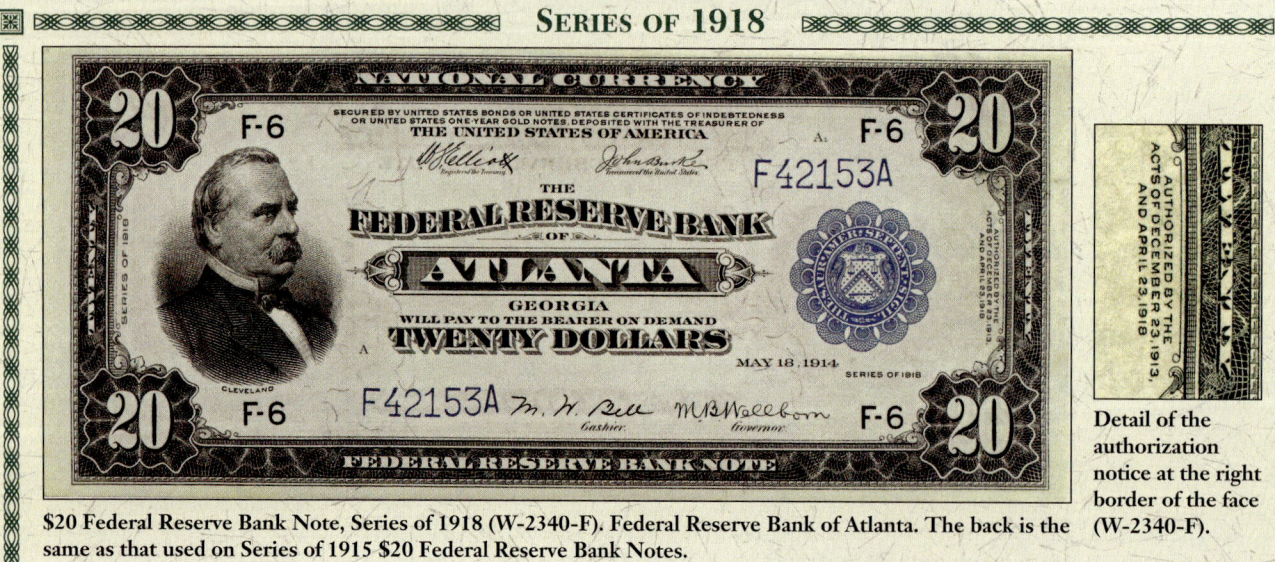

$20 Federal Reserve Bank Note, Series of 1918 (W-2340-F). Federal Reserve Bank of Atlanta. The back is the same as that used on Series of 1915 $20 Federal Reserve Bank Notes.

Detail of the authorization notice at the right border of the face (W-2340-F).

W-2340-F • F-823 • Atlanta • Elliott-Burke (1919–1921) • Bell-Wellborn • 96,000

Estimated population: 50 to 60 • *Highest graded:* Unc • *Selected information:* Nearly all are in circulated grades. Note F1A ex Grinnell as AU (6/1949), $45; various intermediate appearances, including certification as Choice Unc. (not by PCGS or PMG); listed as AU in Knight sale (10/2004), $29,000. Note F85620A/D, currently EF-40 (PMG) was cataloged as high as "Choice Crisp Unc."

VG-8	F-12	VF-20	EF-40	AU-50	Unc-60	Unc-63	Unc-65
$1,600	$3,500	$6,000	$12,500	$14,000	$15,000	$18,000	$25,000

W-2342-H • F-825 • St. Louis • Teehee-Burke (1915–1919) • Attebery-Wells • 24,000

Estimated population: 25 to 35 • *Highest graded:* AU-50 • *Commentary:* In his 1951 study of these notes (see the bibliography), W.A. Philpott Jr. stated that $20 notes from St. Louis are scarcer than those of any other Federal Reserve bank, with only 92 outstanding as of October 30, 1944.

VG-8	F-12	VF-20	EF-40	AU-50
$1,600	$3,500	$6,000	$12,500	$14,000

SMALL SIZE

Small-size $20 notes are usually collected by type. All depict Andrew Jackson on the face and the White House on the back. The portrait, by Alfred Sealey, is taken from a painting by Thomas Sully and dates to the 19th century. E. Hein created the back used until the late 1940s, after which a revised view was made by Charles A. Brooks. These were used until the advent of modern security notes.

Generally, examples issued up to about the 1950s range from scarce to very rare in Uncirculated grade, and star notes are rarer still. Currently, the BEP in Washington and the Fort Worth (FW) plant both produce Federal Reserve Notes, usually in an arrangement in which one facility handles one group of banks and the other takes the remainder, but sometimes there is an overlap. Varieties abound with every change in signatures.

Just keeping up with the face value can be expensive for many numismatists, most of whom do not wish to lay out the amount needed to keep up with current varieties, never mind all of the varieties dating back to 1929. Accordingly, notes of a given rarity are apt to be relatively less expensive in the $20 series than for a lower denomination.

LEGAL TENDER NOTES

Legal Tender Notes of the Series of 1928 were planned, but none of the $20 value were issued, as the total face value of this class of notes (as authorized by Congress under the Act of February 28, 1878) was filled by other denominations.

Series of 1928, Red Seal
Woods-Woodin (1933)

These were payable in "twenty dollars on demand," not specified as to what form, but not necessarily coins. To the left is the four-line notation, overprinted by the Treasury seal, "This note is a legal tender at its face value for all debts public and private except duties on imports and interest on the public debt." In the right field TWENTY is printed in large letters. Although plates were prepared, there is no record of these notes having been issued. Some were printed, however, and $10 and $20 notes were exhibited by the Treasury department at the Century of Progress Exposition in Chicago.

W-2400 • F-unlisted • Unknown in private hands

NATIONAL BANK NOTES

As a class, 1929 Type 1 notes are much more plentiful than Type 2 notes, although for specific national banks the situation can be reversed. Some banks issued just Type 1 bills, many issued both, and some late-chartered banks, including those created in the consolidations and mergers of necessity during the Depression, issued only Type 2 notes, which commenced in May 1933.

At the right the brown Treasury seal is overprinted on "Redeemable in lawful money of the United States, at United States Treasury or at the bank of issue."

Series of 1929, Type 1, Brown Seal
Jones-Woods (1929–1933)

Sheets of Type 1 bills (illus. on p. 499) each had the same serial number on a given sheet, prefixed by a letter, A through F, such as A000001A to F000001A. This gave six times more number 1 notes than on a sheet of 1929 Type 2 bills. The signatures of the bank cashier and president were printed directly on each note at the BEP.

As a class, $20 notes are much harder to find than are the $5 or $10 denominations. Prices are for states from which a larger number of notes survive. Most are in grades of Fine to Very Fine or so, although scattered Uncirculated notes exist. The value chart shows generic prices for a typical note from a state from which notes range from available to just slightly scarce.

Banks of Issue and Rarity of Notes

Based upon census information from Don C. Kelly and James M. Kelly (*National Bank Note Census*, Version 4.0) and with some information from other sources, this listing gives each location, the number of banks issuing this series of notes within each, and a commentary.[29]

The Kelly survey records 45,431 of these notes, a very large number in terms of any National Bank Note series. Uncirculated notes are fairly plentiful, both from scattered banks and several clusters. The census lists 991 number 1 notes, mainly because there were six for each series. These are specifically listed below.

Alabama • 76 banks of issue • 639 notes reported • The census lists 17 Unc notes from various banks. Seven serial number 1 notes are recorded.

Alaska • 3 banks of issue • No notes reported.

Arizona • 10 banks of issue • 153 notes reported • All known examples are in circulated grades.

497

Arkansas • 42 banks of issue • 268 notes reported • The census lists 14 Unc notes, with many from the First National Bank of Fort Smith. Two serial number 1 notes are known, from the First National Bank of Lewisville (F–VF) and the National Bank of Mansfield (VG).

California • 143 banks of issue • 2,070 notes reported • Most examples are in circulated grades. The census lists 60 serial number 1 notes.

Colorado • 75 banks of issue • 605 notes reported • Most are circulated. The census lists 29 serial number 1 notes.

Connecticut • 45 banks of issue • 451 notes reported • Most are circulated. Eight serial number 1 notes are recorded.

Delaware • 14 banks of issue • 92 notes reported • The only Unc note is from the First National Bank & Trust Company of Milford.

District of Columbia • 10 banks of issue • 463 notes reported • The census lists 95 Unc notes, with 31 from the Riggs National Bank of Washington. Seven serial number 1 notes are known, six from the National Metropolitan Bank of Washington.

Florida • 40 banks of issue • 498 notes reported • Many Unc notes are clustered. The census lists 30 serial number 1 notes, all Unc.

Georgia • 65 banks of issue • 370 notes reported • Most are circulated. Nine serial number 1 notes are recorded.

Idaho • 21 banks of issue • 131 notes reported • The census lists 13 notes in Unc grade. Six serial number 1 notes are from the First National Bank Coeur D'Alene, all Unc.

Illinois • 364 banks of issue • 2,508 notes reported • Most are circulated. The census lists 39 serial number 1 notes.

Indiana • 189 banks of issue • 1,804 notes reported • Many Unc notes are from the First National Bank of Elkhart, and the many AU notes are from the Holland National Bank. The census lists 29 serial number 1 notes.

Iowa • 206 banks of issue • 1,820 notes reported • Most are circulated. The census lists 33 serial number 1 notes, mostly Unc.

Kansas • 183 banks of issue • 1,122 notes reported • Most are circulated. The census lists 25 serial number 1 notes.

Kentucky • 117 banks of issue • 740 notes reported • Most are circulated. The census lists 12 serial number 1 notes.

Louisiana • 24 banks of issue • 226 notes reported • The census lists 11 Unc notes.

Maine • 46 banks of issue • 227 notes reported • The census lists 16 Unc notes. Eight serial number 1 notes are recorded.

Maryland • 70 banks of issue • 454 notes reported • Most are circulated. Eight serial number 1 notes are recorded.

Massachusetts • 114 banks of issue • 454 notes reported • Most are circulated. Eight serial number 1 notes are recorded.

Michigan • 111 banks of issue • 1,984 notes reported • Many Unc notes are from the City National Bank & Trust Co. of Battle Creek. The census lists 38 serial number 1 notes.

Minnesota • 206 banks of issue • 1,818 notes reported • Includes the First National Bank of Saint Paul. Most are circulated. The census lists 16 serial number 1 notes.

Mississippi • 23 banks of issue • 208 notes reported • The census lists 19 Unc notes. Six serial number 1 notes are recorded.

Missouri • 95 banks of issue • 967 notes reported • Most are circulated. The census lists 31 serial number 1 notes.

Montana • 31 banks of issue • 258 notes reported • The census lists 15 notes in Unc grade and 12 serial number 1 notes.

Nebraska • 134 banks of issue • 1,497 notes reported • The majority are in circulated grades. The census lists 52 serial number 1 notes.

Nevada • 10 banks of issue • 67 notes reported • The two Unc notes are from the Farmers & Merchants National Bank of Eureka and the Reno National Bank.

New Hampshire • 47 banks of issue • 320 notes reported • The census lists 42 Unc notes, including 14 from the First National Bank of Peterborough. Eight serial number 1 notes are recorded.

New Jersey • 192 banks of issue • 1,268 notes reported • Most are in circulated grades. The census lists 17 serial number 1 notes.

New Mexico • 19 banks of issue • 174 notes reported • Eight Unc notes are known. Six serial number 1 notes are known, all Unc, from the Albuquerque National Bank.

New York • 416 banks of issue • 2,278 notes reported • Most are circulated. The census lists 95 serial number 1 notes.

North Carolina • 47 banks of issue • 329 notes reported • Nine Unc notes are listed. Six serial number 1 notes are recorded.

North Dakota • 96 banks of issue • 439 notes reported • The census lists 19 Unc notes and 10 serial number 1 notes.

Ohio • 294 banks of issue • 2,754 notes reported • Most are circulated. The census lists 33 serial number 1 notes.

Oklahoma • 181 banks of issue • 908 notes reported • Many Unc examples known from the Citizens National Bank of El Reno. The census lists 15 serial number 1 notes.

Oregon • 68 banks of issue • 440 notes reported • The census lists 48 Unc notes, with 16 from the United States National Bank of Portland, and 25 serial number 1 notes.

Pennsylvania • 772 banks of issue • 5,209 notes reported • Most are circulated. The census lists 67 serial number 1 notes.

Rhode Island • 10 banks of issue • 141 notes reported • The census lists 28 Unc notes, with 15 from the Providence National Bank.

South Carolina • 27 banks of issue • 136 notes reported • The census lists 26 Unc notes, including 13 Unc from the Central National Bank of Spartanburg.

South Dakota • 58 banks of issue • 410 notes reported • The census lists 17 Unc notes. Three serial number 1 notes are known, from the First National Bank & Trust Company, Lake Norden (VG–F), Oldham National Bank (F) and the First National Bank of Parkston (F).

SERIES OF 1929, TYPE 1, BROWN SEAL

$20 National Bank Note, Series of 1929, Type 1 (W-2410). The Lakeport National Bank of Laconia, New Hampshire. The Treasury seal at the right is printed in brown as are the serial numbers. The bank charter number, 4740, is in black at the left and right borders. Letters appear before and after the serial number. The signatures of the bank officers are printed. Although this is a low serial number, such are not unusual on National Bank Notes and do not bring a great premium unless they are number 1. However, any low serial number merits some extra value.

Back of the $20 National Bank Note, Series of 1929, Type 1 (W-2410), with a view of the White House. This type was used on all small-size $20 notes of the era.

Tennessee • 81 banks of issue • 669 notes reported • Many Unc notes are from the East Tennessee National Bank of Knoxville. The census lists 12 serial number 1 notes.

Texas • 421 banks of issue • 2,496 notes reported • Most are in circulated grades. The census lists 134 serial number 1 notes.

Utah • 19 banks of issue • 198 notes reported • The census lists 14 notes in Unc condition. The only serial number 1 note is from the First National Bank of Morgan (F).

Vermont • 36 banks of issue • 115 notes reported • Nine notes are in Unc grade.

Virginia • 130 banks of issue • 581 notes reported • Mostly circulated examples are reported, but the Seaboard National Bank of Norfolk has 13 Unc notes. The census lists 13 serial number 1 notes.

Washington • 74 banks of issue • 685 notes reported • Most are circulated. The census lists 15 serial number 1 notes.

West Virginia • 114 banks of issue • 607 notes reported • Three serial number 1 notes are from the First National Bank of Belington (F) and the Central National Bank of Buckhannon (both VF).

Wisconsin • 121 banks of issue • 2,051 notes reported • Over 150 Unc notes are listed. The census records 27 serial number 1 notes.

Wyoming • 22 banks of issue • 284 notes reported • The census lists 15 notes in Unc grade. Seven serial number 1 notes are known, six of which are Unc from the First National Bank of Kemmerer.

W-2410 • F-1802-1
Estimated population: 50,000 to 55,000 • *Highest graded:* Unc.

VG-8	F-12	VF-20	EF-40	AU-50	Unc-60	Unc-63	Unc-65
$40	$45	$50	$65	$80	$105	$125	$160

Series of 1929, Type 2, Brown Seal
Jones-Woods (1929–1933)

Sheets of Type 2 bills were numbered continuously, with the first sheet from a given bank starting with A000001 and ending with A000006, yielding a single number 1 note, in contrast to six on the first Series of 1929 Type 1 sheet. Signatures of the bank cashier and president were printed directly on each note at the BEP. The charter number appears four times on the face, twice in black and twice in brown (illus. on p. 501).

Uncirculated notes are fairly plentiful, as is true of other denominations in this series. The value chart shows generic prices for a typical note from a state from which notes range from available to just slightly scarce.

Banks of Issue and Rarity of Notes

Based upon census information from Don C. Kelly and James M. Kelly (*National Bank Note Census*, Version 4.0) and with some information from other sources, this listing gives each location, the number of banks issuing this series of notes within each, and a commentary.[30]

The Kelly survey records 11,891 of these, a large population. The census lists 293 serial number 1 notes, a fairly high survival ratio considering that the first sheet had only one with this number. These are specifically listed below.

Alabama • 53 banks of issue • 360 notes reported • The census lists 74 Unc notes. Five serial number 1 notes are recorded.

Alaska • 3 banks of issue • No notes reported.

Arizona • 5 banks of issue • 45 notes reported • The census lists 23 Unc notes, including 22 from the Consolidated National Bank of Tucson.

Arkansas • 29 banks of issue • 88 notes reported • The census lists 26 Unc notes from just a few different banks. Four serial number 1 notes are recorded.

California • 92 banks of issue • 543 notes reported • Most are circulated examples. The census lists 18 serial number 1 notes.

Colorado • 48 banks of issue • 124 notes reported • 21 Unc notes are listed. Four serial number 1 notes are recorded.

Connecticut • 37 banks of issue • 105 notes reported • Of the notes reported, 12 are Unc. Three serial number 1 notes are from the Clinton National Bank (EF), Home National Bank of Meriden (EF–AU), and the Plainfield National Bank (F).

Delaware • 11 banks of issue • 60 notes reported • The census lists 25 Unc notes.

District of Columbia • 6 banks of issue • 51 notes reported • Seven Unc notes are listed.

Florida • 31 banks of issue • 842 notes reported • Over 475 Unc notes are reported for American National Bank of Pensacola, a remarkable hoard. Five serial number 1 notes are recorded.

Georgia • 48 banks of issue • 104 notes reported • 18 notes are reported in Unc grades. Two serial number 1 notes are from the Jackson National Bank (Unc) and the La Grange National Bank (Unc).

Idaho • 13 banks of issue • 19 notes reported • The only Unc note is from the First National Bank of Wallace.

Illinois • 193 banks of issue • 375 notes reported • Many Unc notes are from the Lawndale National Bank of Chicago. The census lists 13 serial number 1 notes.

Indiana • 94 banks of issue • 208 notes reported • 29 notes are reported in Unc grade. The only serial number 1 note is from the Old Town First National Bank & Trust Company of Fort Wayne (not graded).

Iowa • 74 banks of issue • 152 notes reported • 36 examples are known in Unc grades. Six serial number 1 notes are recorded.

Kansas • 127 banks of issue • 239 notes reported • Mostly circulated examples are reported but several banks have five or more Unc notes. The census lists 10 serial number 1 notes.

Kentucky • 87 banks of issue • 241 notes reported • 113 Unc notes are reported, including 101 from the First National Bank & Trust Company of Lexington. Three serial number 1 notes are from the Citizens National Bank of Lebanon (not graded), First National Bank of Paintsville (AU), and the Pikesville National Bank (Unc).

Louisiana • 22 banks of issue • 169 notes reported • 57 Unc notes are reported, including 22 from the Hibernia National Bank in New Orleans. Two serial number 1 notes are from the Ouachita National Bank in Monroe (Unc) and the First National Bank of Lake Providence in Providence (Unc).

Maine • 29 banks of issue • 75 notes reported • Five Unc notes are known. The only serial number 1 note is from the First National Bank of Bar Harbor (AU).

Maryland • 54 banks of issue • 139 notes reported • 15 Unc notes are listed. The only serial number 1 note is from the Second National Bank of Hagerstown (Unc).

Massachusetts • 92 banks of issue • 119 notes reported • Eight Unc notes are known. The only serial number 1 note is from the Woburn National Bank (Unc).

Michigan • 69 banks of issue • 223 notes reported • 30 notes are in Unc grade. Four serial number 1 notes are recorded.

Minnesota • 141 banks of issue • 339 notes reported • Most are circulated. Two serial number 1 notes are from the Northwestern National Bank of Litchfield (Unc) and the Klein National Bank of Madison (Unc).

Mississippi • 14 banks of issue • 68 notes reported • Six Unc notes are listed. The only serial number 1 note is from the First National Bank (not graded).

Missouri • 55 banks of issue • 138 notes reported • 47 Unc notes are known from the several different banks. Four serial number 1 notes are recorded.

Montana • 23 banks of issue • 94 notes reported • 13 Unc notes are known. Three serial number 1 notes are from the First National Bank of Great Falls (not graded), First National Bank of Missoula (Unc), and the First National Bank of Whitefish (Unc).

Nebraska • 91 banks of issue • 317 notes reported • Most are circulated. The census lists 11 serial number 1 notes.

Nevada • 6 banks of issue • 39 notes reported • Of the notes reported, 12 are Unc. Two serial number 1 notes are from the Ely National Bank (not graded) and the McGill National Bank (Unc).

New Hampshire • 43 banks of issue • 57 notes reported • Of the reported notes, 10 are Unc. Three serial number 1 notes are from the Merchants National Bank of Dover (EF), First National Bank of Peterborough (Unc) and the Wilton National Bank (EF).

New Jersey • 159 banks of issue • 439 notes reported • Mostly circulated notes are reported, except many Unc

SERIES OF 1929, TYPE 2, BROWN SEAL

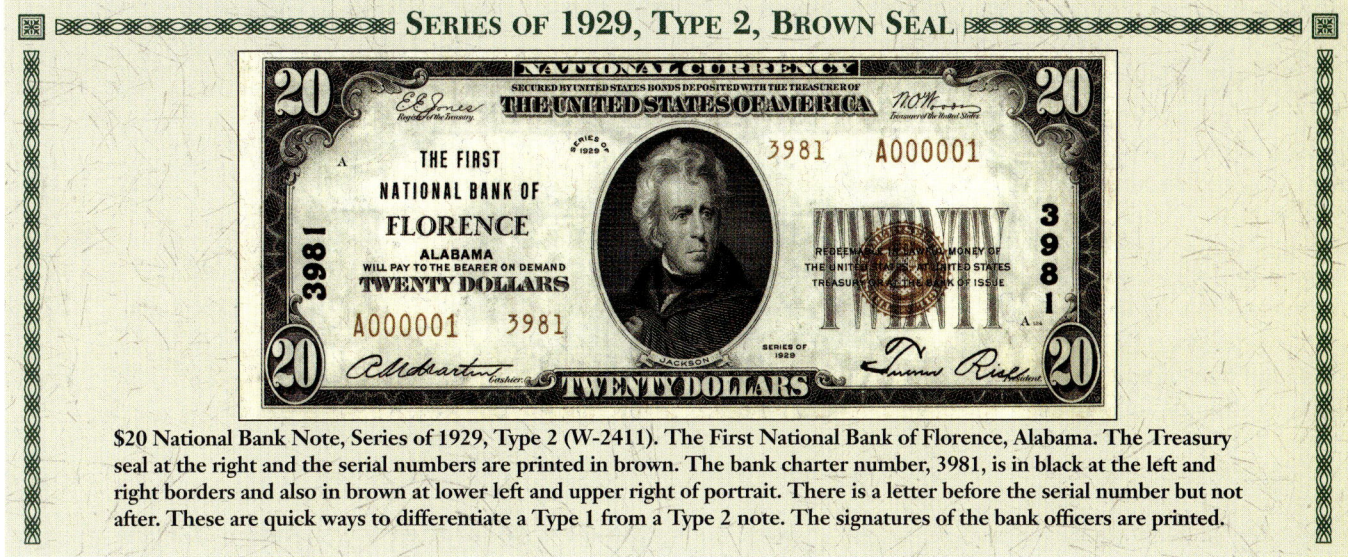

$20 National Bank Note, Series of 1929, Type 2 (W–2411). The First National Bank of Florence, Alabama. The Treasury seal at the right and the serial numbers are printed in brown. The bank charter number, 3981, is in black at the left and right borders and also in brown at lower left and upper right of portrait. There is a letter before the serial number but not after. These are quick ways to differentiate a Type 1 from a Type 2 note. The signatures of the bank officers are printed.

notes from the First National Bank of Vincentown. Six serial number 1 notes are recorded.

New Mexico • 15 banks of issue • 56 notes reported • Two Unc notes are from the Albuquerque Trust & Savings Bank, and the First National Bank of Roswell. The only serial number 1 note is from the Albuquerque National Bank (VF).

New York • 325 banks of issue • 744 notes reported • Many Unc notes are known. 39 serial number 1 notes are recorded.

North Carolina • 30 banks of issue • 89 notes reported • The only Unc note is from the National Bank of Burlington.

North Dakota • 47 banks of issue • 52 notes reported • The only Unc note is from the Merchants National Bank & Trust Company of Fargo. Three serial number 1 notes are from the Dakota National Bank & Trust Company of Bismarck (not graded), First National Bank of Dickinson (F–VF), and the First National Bank of Mott (not graded).

Ohio • 221 banks of issue • 738 notes reported • Many Unc notes are from the Citizens National Bank of Norwalk. 20 serial number 1 notes are recorded.

Oklahoma • 132 banks of issue • 274 notes reported • 39 Unc notes are listed. Four serial number 1 notes are recorded.

Oregon • 36 banks of issue • 96 notes reported • The census lists 39 Unc notes from several different banks. Six serial number 1 notes are recorded.

Pennsylvania • 643 banks of issue • 1,937 notes reported • Many Unc notes are from several different banks. 44 serial number 1 notes are recorded.

Rhode Island • 10 banks of issue • 53 notes reported • Six Unc notes are known.

South Carolina • 11 banks of issue • 134 notes reported • Mostly Unc notes are reported, with 113 from the National Bank of South Carolina of Sumter; one of these is the only serial number 1 note of the state.

South Dakota • 34 banks of issue • 44 notes reported • The only Unc note is from the First National Bank in Pierre.

Tennessee • 59 banks of issue • 285 notes reported • 110 Unc notes are known, with 45 from the First National Bank of Memphis. Eight serial number 1 notes are recorded.

Texas • 288 banks of issue • 720 notes reported • Mostly circulated notes are reported, but with several banks offering six to eight Unc notes. Three serial number 1 notes are recorded.

Utah • 12 banks of issue • 46 notes reported • Six known examples are reported in Unc grade. The only serial number 1 note is from the First National Bank of Price (Unc).

Vermont • 36 banks of issue • 30 notes reported • Seven are Unc. Two serial number 1 notes are from the Merchants National Bank of Burlington (AU) and the First National Bank of Bennington (Unc).

Virginia • 108 banks of issue • 143 notes reported • 28 are known in Unc grade. Three serial number 1 notes are known, all Unc, from the Planters National Bank of Fredericksburg, National Bank of Commerce in Norfolk, and the Massanutton National Bank.

Washington • 45 banks of issue • 165 notes reported • 24 notes are known in Unc grade. Six serial number 1 notes are recorded.

West Virginia • 68 banks of issue • 152 notes reported • The census lists 27 notes in Unc grade. Three serial number 1 notes are from the Union National Bank of Clarksburg (EF), First National Bank of Saint Albans (Unc), and the First National Bank of Terra Alta (Unc).

Wisconsin • 65 banks of issue • 285 notes reported • The census lists 23 Unc notes. Six serial number 1 notes are recorded.

Wyoming • 21 banks of issue • 73 notes reported • 27 Unc notes are listed.

W-2411 • F-1802-2

Estimated population: 13,000 to 14,000 • *Highest graded:* Unc.

VG-8	F-12	VF-20	EF-40	AU-50	Unc-60	Unc-63	Unc-65
$45	$50	$55	$75	$100	$125	$155	$190

FEDERAL RESERVE BANK NOTES

Series of 1929, Brown Seal
Jones-Woods (1929–1933)

Federal Reserve Bank Notes of the Series of 1929, different from the later Federal Reserve Notes, have the inscription NATIONAL CURRENCY at the top margin of the face and were intended to be Type 1 National Bank Notes. Production lasted for only a short time in March 1933, when already printed but incomplete National Bank Note sheets were filled in with Federal Reserve Bank information.

Printed signatures on these and other notes include two of Treasury officials and two of Federal Reserve Bank officials, such as the deputy governor (or assistant deputy governor) and governor, or the cashier and governor. Sometimes "Cashier" and always "President," already printed on the notes, were blocked out with a black rectangle. Added to the security information already printed at the top center of National Bank Notes was a new line, "or by like deposit of other securities." Sometimes the registration of this added line caused the printing to slightly overlap the printing of SERIES OF below.

For the $20 denomination each of the 12 Federal Reserve Banks issued regular notes and, in much smaller quantities, star notes. Dallas issues are scarcer and more expensive than the others.

W-2430-A • F-1870A • Boston • 972,000

VG-8	F-12	VF-20	EF-40	AU-50	Unc-60	Unc-63	Unc-65
$35	$45	$65	$100	$125	$200	$400	$600

W-2430-A★ • F-1870A★

VG-8	F-12	VF-20	EF-40	AU-50	Unc-60	Unc-63
$190	$325	$450	$900	$1,750	$2,000	$2,400

W-2431-B • F-1870B • New York • 2,568,000

VG-8	F-12	VF-20	EF-40	AU-50	Unc-60	Unc-63	Unc-65
$35	$45	$60	$90	$115	$160	$225	$350

W-2431-B★ • F-1870B★

VG-8	F-12	VF-20	EF-40	AU-50	Unc-60	Unc-63
$190	$325	$450	$900	$1,750	$2,000	$2,400

W-2432-C • F-1870C • Philadelphia • 1,008,000

VG-8	F-12	VF-20	EF-40	AU-50	Unc-60	Unc-63	Unc-65
$35	$45	$60	$90	$115	$160	$275	$400

W-2432-C★ • F-1870C★

VG-8	F-12	VF-20	EF-40	AU-50	Unc-60	Unc-63
$190	$325	$450	$900	$1,750	$2,000	$2,400

W-2433-D • F-1870D • Cleveland • 1,020,000

VG-8	F-12	VF-20	EF-40	AU-50	Unc-60	Unc-63	Unc-65
$35	$45	$60	$90	$115	$175	$370	$550

SERIES OF 1929, BROWN SEAL

$20 Federal Reserve Bank Note, Series of 1929 (W-2430-A). Federal Reserve Bank of Boston.

Back of the $20 Federal Reserve Bank Note, Series of 1929 (W-2430-A). This type was used on all small-size $20 notes of the era.

W-2433-D★ • F-1870D★

VG-8	F-12	VF-20	EF-40	AU-50	Unc-60	Unc-63
$190	$325	$450	$900	$1,750	$2,000	$2,400

W-2434-E • F-1870E • Richmond • 1,632,000

VG-8	F-12	VF-20	EF-40	AU-50	Unc-60	Unc-63	Unc-65
$35	$45	$65	$100	$125	$200	$400	$550

W-2434-E★ • F-1870E★

VG-8	F-12	VF-20	EF-40	AU-50	Unc-60	Unc-63
$190	$325	$450	$900	$1,750	$2,000	$2,400

W-2435-F • F-1870F • Atlanta • 960,000

VG-8	F-12	VF-20	EF-40	AU-50	Unc-60	Unc-63	Unc-65
$35	$50	$70	$110	$155	$225	$450	$750

W-2435-F★ • F-1870F★

VG-8	F-12	VF-20	EF-40	AU-50	Unc-60	Unc-63
$190	$325	$450	$900	$1,750	$2,000	$2,400

W-2436-G • F-1870G • Chicago • 2,028,000

VG-8	F-12	VF-20	EF-40	AU-50	Unc-60	Unc-63	Unc-65
$35	$45	$60	$90	$115	$160	$225	$350

W-2436-G★ • F-1870G★

VG-8	F-12	VF-20	EF-40	AU-50	Unc-60	Unc-63
$190	$325	$450	$900	$1,750	$2,000	$2,400

W-2437-H • F-1870H • St. Louis • 444,000

VG-8	F-12	VF-20	EF-40	AU-50	Unc-60	Unc-63	Unc-65
$35	$50	$70	$110	$150	$160	$275	$425

W-2437-H★ • F-1870H★

VG-8	F-12	VF-20	EF-40	AU-50	Unc-60	Unc-63
$190	$325	$450	$900	$1,750	$2,000	$2,400

W-2438-I • F-1870I • Minneapolis • 864,000

VG-8	F-12	VF-20	EF-40	AU-50	Unc-60	Unc-63	Unc-65
$35	$45	$65	$100	$125	$200	$300	$450

W-2438-I★ • F-1870I★

VG-8	F-12	VF-20	EF-40	AU-50	Unc-60	Unc-63
$190	$325	$450	$900	$1,750	$2,000	$2,400

W-2439-J • F-1870J • Kansas City • 612,000

VG-8	F-12	VF-20	EF-40	AU-50	Unc-60	Unc-63	Unc-65
$35	$50	$70	$110	$170	$300	$550	$800

W-2439-J★ • F-1870J★

VG-8	F-12	VF-20	EF-40	AU-50	Unc-60	Unc-63
$190	$325	$450	$900	$1,750	$2,000	$2,400

W-2440-K • F-1870K • Dallas • 468,000

VG-8	F-12	VF-20	EF-40	AU-50	Unc-60	Unc-63
$250	$360	$500	$900	$1,400	$2,000	$2,750

W-2440-K★ • F-1870K★

VG-8	F-12	VF-20	EF-40	AU-50	Unc-60	Unc-63
$190	$325	$450	$900	$1,750	$2,000	$2,400

W-2441-L • F-1870L • San Francisco • 888,000

VG-8	F-12	VF-20	EF-40	AU-50	Unc-60	Unc-63	Unc-65
$40	$70	$135	$250	$375	$575	$800	$1,150

W-2441-L★ • F-1870L★

VG-8	F-12	VF-20	EF-40	AU-50	Unc-60	Unc-63
$190	$325	$450	$900	$1,750	$2,000	$2,400

GOLD CERTIFICATES

Series of 1928, Gold Seal
Woods-Mellon (1929–1932)

On these notes (illus. on p. 504) the obligation reads: "Twenty Dollars in gold coin payable to the bearer on demand." At the left the Treasury seal is overprinted on a more standard commentary, with GOLD above and CERTIFICATE below, with three lines between: "This certificate is a legal tender in the amount thereof in payment of all debts and dues public and private." In addition to the yellow (usually called gold) seal, the serial numbers were printed in yellow. An ambitious program was launched, with at least 174 face plates prepared. Over 60 million notes were printed, short of the production of $10 notes of this series, but still generous. As it turned out, small-size Gold Certificates had a short life.

W-2450 • F-2402 • 66,204,000

VG-8	F-12	VF-20	EF-40	AU-50	Unc-60	Unc-63	Unc-65
$105	$125	$160	$300	$425	$560	$825	$1,800

W-2450★ • F-2402★

VG-8	F-12	VF-20	EF-40	AU-50	Unc-60	Unc-63
$200	$425	$900	$1,900	$2,400	$3,500	$9,000

Series of 1928-A, Gold Seal
Woods-Mills (1932–1933)

These were printed, but none are known to have been issued. By that time the Treasury was no longer paying out Gold Certificates, due to restrictions imposed two days after president Franklin D. Roosevelt's inauguration, beginning on March 6, 1933.

W-2451 • F-2403 • 1,500,000 • None issued

FEDERAL RESERVE NOTES

Small-size Federal Reserve Notes, each with a green Treasury seal, have been produced continually since the Series of 1928. Many different varieties exist, with combinations of Federal Reserve Banks and Treasury signatures. Certain of the Series of 1934 $20 bills were made with brown seals and HAWAII overprints. Most early notes seen today are in circulated grades.

The Series of 1934-C introduced a modified view of the Executive Mansion on the back, now with THE added to

SERIES OF 1928, GOLD SEAL

$20 Gold Certificate, Series of 1928 (W-2450). This design was also used on W-2451 (not released). General style as preceding, but with gold Treasury seal and serial numbers and different lettering.

Back of the $20 Gold Certificate, Series of 1928 (W-2450). This type was used on all small-size $20 notes of the era. Accordingly, there is no way to determine at quick glance if a note is a Gold Certificate unless the face is observed.

the label, to read THE WHITE HOUSE, and with the trees and shrubbery more dense. Both styles were made in the Series of 1934-C.

Commencing with Series of 1996 the face and back designs were modified, with Hamilton given a larger, different portrait. Improvements to the design and paper were largely intended to deter counterfeiting. Another view of the White House, the north portico, appears on the restyled notes. The Series of 2004 notes added more security features, including subtle color.

Series of 1928, Green Seal
Tate-Mellon (1928–1929)

The obligation is in four lines in the upper left field: "Redeemable in gold on demand at the United States Treasury, or in gold or lawful money at any Federal Reserve Bank." On the Series of 1928 and 1928-A notes, the seal is in the left field and features the number of the issuing Federal Reserve Bank, 1 to 12. The series imprint appears twice—at the upper left of Jackson's portrait and below WASHINGTON, D.C., at the lower right.

W-2500-A • F-2050A • Boston • 3,790,880

VG-8	F-12	VF-20	EF-40	AU-50	Unc-60	Unc-63	Unc-65
$50	$120	$200	$275	$500	$950	$1,500	$2,500

W-2500-A★ • F-2050A★

VG-8	F-12	VF-20	EF-40	AU-50	Unc-60	Unc-63	Unc-65
$125	$215	$375	$875	$1,350	$2,400	$3,500	$5,500

W-2500-B • F-2050B • New York • 12,797,200

VG-8	F-12	VF-20	EF-40	AU-50	Unc-60	Unc-63	Unc-65
$35	$50	$65	$90	$130	$190	$250	$400

W-2500-B★ • F-2050B★

VG-8	F-12	VF-20	EF-40	AU-50	Unc-60	Unc-63	Unc-65
$90	$140	$225	$375	$700	$1,200	$1,650	$2,400

W-2500-C • F-2050C • Philadelphia • 3,797,200

VG-8	F-12	VF-20	EF-40	AU-50	Unc-60	Unc-63	Unc-65
$35	$50	$65	$90	$130	$190	$250	$400

W-2500-C★ • F-2050C★

VG-8	F-12	VF-20	EF-40	AU-50	Unc-60	Unc-63	Unc-65
$125	$215	$350	$575	$850	$1,250	$1,650	$2,400

W-2500-D • F-2050D • Cleveland • 10,626,900

VG-8	F-12	VF-20	EF-40	AU-50	Unc-60	Unc-63	Unc-65
$30	$40	$55	$80	$115	$160	$200	$340

W-2500-D★ • F-2050D★

VG-8	F-12	VF-20	EF-40	AU-50	Unc-60	Unc-63	Unc-65
$90	$140	$225	$375	$750	$1,250	$1,750	$2,600

SERIES OF 1928, GREEN SEAL

$20 Federal Reserve Note, Series of 1928 (W-2500-D). Federal Reserve Bank of Cleveland. Type of Series 1928 and 1928-A. The face printing notes that the bill is payable "in gold." The bank location at left is represented by the district number.

REDEEMABLE IN GOLD ON DEMAND AT THE UNITED STATES TREASURY, OR IN GOLD OR LAWFUL MONEY AT ANY FEDERAL RESERVE BANK.

Detail of the gold redemption imprint at the upper left of the face. This wording was used on the Series of 1928 through the Series of 1928-C.

Back of the $20 Federal Reserve Note, Series of 1928 (W-2500-D). This type was used on all small-size $20 notes of the era.

W-2500-E • F-2050E • Richmond • 4,119,600

VG-8	F-12	VF-20	EF-40	AU-50	Unc-60	Unc-63	Unc-65
$35	$50	$65	$90	$125	$175	$225	$370

W-2500-E★ • F-2050E★

VG-8	F-12	VF-20	EF-40	AU-50	Unc-60	Unc-63	Unc-65
$130	$250	$475	$750	$1,100	$1,850	$2,600	$3,500

W-2500-F • F-2050F • Atlanta • 3,842,388

VG-8	F-12	VF-20	EF-40	AU-50	Unc-60	Unc-63	Unc-65
$40	$55	$70	$95	$130	$190	$250	$400

W-2500-F★ • F-2050F★

VG-8	F-12	VF-20	EF-40	AU-50	Unc-60	Unc-63	Unc-65
$115	$240	$450	$750	$1,100	$1,850	$2,600	$3,500

W-2500-G • F-2050G • Chicago • 10,891,740

VG-8	F-12	VF-20	EF-40	AU-50	Unc-60	Unc-63	Unc-65
$30	$40	$55	$80	$115	$160	$200	$340

W-2500-G★ • F-2050G★

VG-8	F-12	VF-20	EF-40	AU-50	Unc-60	Unc-63	Unc-65
$100	$175	$300	$500	$800	$1,300	$1,700	$2,300

W-2500-H • F-2050H • St. Louis • 2,523,300

VG-8	F-12	VF-20	EF-40	AU-50	Unc-60	Unc-63	Unc-65
$30	$40	$55	$80	$125	$175	$225	$370

W-2500-H★ • F-2050H★

VG-8	F-12	VF-20	EF-40	AU-50	Unc-60	Unc-63	Unc-65
$100	$210	$375	$600	$900	$1,400	$2,225	$3,000

W-2500-I • F-2050I • Minneapolis • 2,633,100

VG-8	F-12	VF-20	EF-40	AU-50	Unc-60	Unc-63	Unc-65
$30	$40	$55	$80	$125	$175	$225	$370

W-2500-I★ • F-2050I★

VG-8	F-12	VF-20	EF-40	AU-50	Unc-60	Unc-63	Unc-65
$150	$290	$450	$750	$1,100	$1,850	$2,400	$3,500

W-2500-J • F-2050J • Kansas City • 2,584,500

VG-8	F-12	VF-20	EF-40	AU-50	Unc-60	Unc-63	Unc-65
$30	$40	$55	$80	$115	$160	$200	$340

W-2500-J★ • F-2050J★

VG-8	F-12	VF-20	EF-40	AU-50	Unc-60	Unc-63	Unc-65
$100	$210	$375	$600	$900	$1,400	$2,000	$3,000

W-2500-K • F-2050K • Dallas • 1,568,500

VG-8	F-12	VF-20	EF-40	AU-50	Unc-60	Unc-63	Unc-65
$40	$60	$80	$135	$250	$400	$650	$900

W-2500-K★ • F-2050K★

VG-8	F-12	VF-20	EF-40	AU-50	Unc-60	Unc-63
$550	$925	$1,500	$2,350	$3,000	$4,400	$6,000

W-2500-L • F-2050L • San Francisco • 8,404,800

VG-8	F-12	VF-20	EF-40	AU-50	Unc-60	Unc-63	Unc-65
$30	$40	$55	$80	$130	$190	$250	$375

W-2500-L★ • F-2050L★

VG-8	F-12	VF-20	EF-40	AU-50	Unc-60	Unc-63	Unc-65
$135	$240	$400	$700	$1,000	$1,250	$1,750	$2,300

Series of 1928-A, Green Seal
Woods-Mellon (1929–1932)

The obligation notice, "redeemable in gold," and Federal Reserve seal (with a number in the center) are the same style as preceding. No Minneapolis (I) or San Francisco (L) notes were printed.

W-2501-A • F-2051A • Boston • 1,293,900

VG-8	F-12	VF-20	EF-40	AU-50	Unc-60	Unc-63
$50	$85	$150	$275	$425	$600	$800

W-2501-A★ • F-2051A★

VG-8	F-12	VF-20	EF-40	AU-50	Unc-60	Unc-63	Unc-65
$275	$450	$750	$1,000	$1,350	$1,950	$2,600	$4,000

W-2501-B • F-2051B • New York • 1,055,800

VG-8	F-12	VF-20	EF-40	AU-50	Unc-60	Unc-63	Unc-65
$50	$80	$120	$200	$280	$400	$500	$750

W-2501-B★ • F-2051B★

VG-8	F-12	VF-20	EF-40
$600	$1,000	$1,650	$2,500

W-2501-C • F-2051C • Philadelphia • 1,717,200

VG-8	F-12	VF-20	EF-40	AU-50	Unc-60	Unc-63	Unc-65
$35	$50	$80	$150	$225	$350	$450	$675

W-2501-C★ • F-2051C★

VG-8	F-12	VF-20	EF-40	AU-50
$650	$1,100	$1,750	$2,750	$4,000

W-2501-D • F-2051D • Cleveland • 625,200

VG-8	F-12	VF-20	EF-40	AU-50	Unc-60	Unc-63	Unc-65
$65	$125	$200	$250	$290	$325	$450	$675

W-2501-D★ • F-2051D★

VG-8	F-12	VF-20	EF-40
$650	$1,100	$1,750	$2,750

W-2501-E • F-2051E • Richmond • 1,534,500

VG-8	F-12	VF-20	EF-40	AU-50	Unc-60	Unc-63	Unc-65
$35	$50	$80	$150	$200	$275	$400	$600

W-2501-E★ • F-2051E★

VG-8	F-12	VF-20	EF-40	AU-50	Unc-60
$500	$950	$1,450	$2,000	$3,100	$4,000

W-2501-F • F-2051F • Atlanta • 1,442,400

VG-8	F-12	VF-20	EF-40	AU-50	Unc-60	Unc-63	Unc-65
$32	$45	$60	$115	$160	$200	$300	$500

W-2501-F★ • F-2051F★

VG-8	F-12	VF-20
$700	$1,200	$2,000

W-2501-G • F-2051G • Chicago • 822,000

VG-8	F-12	VF-20	EF-40	AU-50	Unc-60	Unc-63	Unc-65
$32	$45	$60	$110	$160	$200	$300	$500

W-2501-G★ • F-2051G★

VG-8	F-12	VF-20	EF-40	AU-50
$650	$1,100	$1,750	$2,750	$4,000

W-2501-H • F-2051H • St. Louis • 573,300

VG-8	F-12	VF-20	EF-40	AU-50	Unc-60	Unc-63	Unc-65
$35	$55	$80	$150	$200	$275	$400	$600

W-2501-H★ • F-2051H★

VG-8	F-12	VF-20
$700	$1,200	$2,000

W-2501-J • F-2051J • Kansas City • 113,900

VG-8	F-12	VF-20	EF-40	AU-50	Unc-60	Unc-63	Unc-65
$35	$55	$80	$150	$200	$275	$400	$600

W-2501-J★ • F-2051J★

VG-8	F-12	VF-20
$700	$1,200	$2,000

W-2501-K • F-2051K • Dallas • 1,032,000

VG-8	F-12	VF-20	EF-40	AU-50	Unc-60	Unc-63	Unc-65
$45	$75	$100	$175	$230	$300	$400	$600

W-2501-K★ • F-2051K★

VG-8	F-12	VF-20	EF-40	AU-50	Unc-60
$400	$750	$1,150	$1,750	$2,500	$3,250

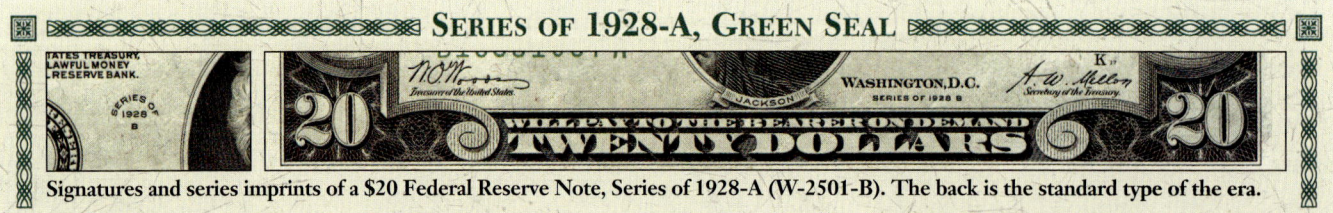

SERIES OF 1928-A, GREEN SEAL

Signatures and series imprints of a $20 Federal Reserve Note, Series of 1928-A (W-2501-B). The back is the standard type of the era.

Series of 1928-B, Green Seal
Woods-Mellon (1929–1932)

The obligation in four lines in the field at the upper left is, as before, "Redeemable in gold on demand at the United States Treasury, or in gold or lawful money at any Federal Reserve Bank."

Now the Federal Reserve seal has the letter (instead of the number) prominent at the center, A (Boston) to L (San Francisco). The series imprint appears twice—at the upper left of Jackson's portrait and below WASHINGTON at the lower right.

The green seal has been called by other designations over the years, including dark green, medium green, blue-green, etc. The distinction between this and the yellow-green variety can best be ascertained by comparing two notes or buying from a knowledgeable dealer. The differences are not great at first glance.

W-2502-A • F-2052A • Boston • 7,749,636

F-12	VF-20	EF-40	AU-50	Unc-60	Unc-63	Unc-65
$30	$45	$50	$65	$85	$110	$135

W-2502-A★ • F-2052A★

VG-8	F-12	VF-20	EF-40	AU-50	Unc-60	Unc-63
$70	$140	$225	$400	$600	$850	$1,100

W-2502-B • F-2052B • New York • 19,448,436

F-12	VF-20	EF-40	AU-50	Unc-60	Unc-63	Unc-65
$30	$45	$50	$65	$80	$100	$120

W-2502-B★ • F-2052B★

VG-8	F-12	VF-20	EF-40	AU-50	Unc-60	Unc-63
$65	$140	$225	$375	$575	$800	$1,000

W-2502-C • F-2052C • Philadelphia • 8,095,548

F-12	VF-20	EF-40	AU-50	Unc-60	Unc-63	Unc-65
$30	$45	$50	$65	$85	$110	$135

W-2502-C★ • F-2052C★

VG-8	F-12	VF-20	EF-40	AU-50	Unc-60	Unc-63
$360	$550	$900	$1,150	$1,500	$2,200	$2,750

W-2502-D • F-2052D • Cleveland • 11,684,196

F-12	VF-20	EF-40	AU-50	Unc-60	Unc-63	Unc-65
$30	$45	$50	$65	$80	$100	$120

W-2502-D★ • F-2052D★

VG-8	F-12	VF-20	EF-40	AU-50	Unc-60	Unc-63
$80	$160	$250	$500	$725	$975	$1,250

W-2502-E • F-2052E • Richmond • 4,413,900

F-12	VF-20	EF-40	AU-50	Unc-60	Unc-63	Unc-65
$30	$45	$60	$90	$145	$200	$290

W-2502-E★ • F-2052E★

VG-8	F-12	VF-20	EF-40	AU-50	Unc-60	Unc-63	Unc-65
$80	$150	$225	$400	$600	$850	$1,100	$1,450

W-2502-F • F-2052F • Atlanta • 2,390,240

VG-8	F-12	VF-20	EF-40	AU-50	Unc-60	Unc-63	Unc-65
$40	$70	$135	$200	$275	$375	$500	$750

W-2502-F★ • F-2052F★

VG-8	F-12	VF-20	EF-40	AU-50	Unc-60	Unc-63	Unc-65
$80	$150	$225	$475	$675	$950	$1,250	$1,600

W-2502-G • F-2052G • Chicago • 17,220,276

F-12	VF-20	EF-40	AU-50	Unc-60	Unc-63	Unc-65
$30	$45	$50	$60	$70	$90	$135

W-2502-G★ • F-2052G★

VG-8	F-12	VF-20	EF-40	AU-50	Unc-60	Unc-63	Unc-65
$65	$135	$200	$350	$500	$750	$1,000	$1,350

W-2502-H • F-2052H • St. Louis • 3,834,600

F-12	VF-20	EF-40	AU-50	Unc-60	Unc-63	Unc-65
$30	$45	$50	$60	$70	$90	$135

W-2502-H★ • F-2052H★

VG-8	F-12	VF-20	EF-40	AU-50	Unc-60	Unc-63	Unc-65
$80	$150	$225	$350	$500	$750	$1,000	$1,400

W-2502-I • F-2052I • Minneapolis • 3,298,920

F-12	VF-20	EF-40	AU-50	Unc-60	Unc-63	Unc-65
$32	$45	$70	$90	$115	$140	$175

W-2502-I★ • F-2052I★

VG-8	F-12	VF-20	EF-40	AU-50	Unc-60	Unc-63	Unc-65
$145	$240	$325	$600	$950	$1,300	$1,600	$2,000

W-2502-J • F-2052J • Kansas City • 4,941,252

F-12	VF-20	EF-40	AU-50	Unc-60	Unc-63	Unc-65
$30	$45	$50	$65	$80	$100	$120

W-2502-J★ • F-2052J★

VG-8	F-12	VF-20	EF-40	AU-50	Unc-60	Unc-63	Unc-65
$80	$150	$225	$400	$600	$850	$1,100	$1,500

SERIES OF 1928-B, GREEN SEAL

Detail of the signatures and the series imprints, as well as the redesigned Federal Reserve seal showing a letter instead of a numeral, of a $20 Federal Reserve Note, Series of 1928-B (W-2502-A). The back is the standard type of the era.

W-2502-K • F-2052K • Dallas • 2,406,060

F-12	VF-20	EF-40	AU-50	Unc-60	Unc-63	Unc-65
$32	$45	$75	$100	$125	$160	$200

W-2502-K★ • F-2052K★

VG-8	F-12	VF-20	EF-40	AU-50	Unc-60	Unc-63	Unc-65
$80	$150	$225	$400	$675	$950	$1,250	$1,600

W-2502-L • F-2052L • San Francisco • 9,689,124

F-12	VF-20	EF-40	AU-50	Unc-60	Unc-63	Unc-65
$30	$45	$50	$65	$85	$110	$135

W-2502-L★ • F-2052L★

VG-8	F-12	VF-20	EF-40	AU-50	Unc-60	Unc-63	Unc-65
$65	$135	$200	$375	$600	$850	$1,100	$1,450

Series of 1928-B, Light Yellow-Green Seal
Woods-Mellon (1929–1932)

This series continued the preceding design. No notes have been reported for Atlanta (F) and Dallas (K).

Prices for a typical note for this series, unless listed otherwise, are as follows:

VG-8	F-12	VF-20	EF-40	AU-50	Unc-60	Unc-63	Unc-65
$30	$35	$38	$40	$43	$55	$80	$125

W-2503-A • F-2052A • Boston • Part of W-2502-A printage

W-2503-A★ • F-2052A★

VG-8	F-12	VF-20	EF-40	AU-50	Unc-60	Unc-63
$70	$125	$175	$250	$485	$700	$900

W-2503-B • F-2052B • New York • Part of W-2502-B printage

W-2503-B★ • F-2052B★

VG-8	F-12	VF-20	EF-40	AU-50	Unc-60	Unc-63
$70	$125	$175	$225	$425	$650	$850

W-2503-C • F-2052C • Philadelphia • Part of W-2502-C printage

W-2503-C★ • F-2052C★

VG-8	F-12	VF-20	EF-40	AU-50	Unc-60	Unc-63
$90	$175	$275	$325	$525	$750	$950

W-2503-D • F-2052D • Cleveland • Part of W-2502-D printage

W-2503-D★ • F-2052D★

VG-8	F-12	VF-20	EF-40	AU-50	Unc-60	Unc-63
$80	$150	$225	$300	$550	$775	$975

W-2503-E • F-2052E • Richmond • Part of W-2502-E printage

VG-8	F-12	VF-20	EF-40	AU-50	Unc-60	Unc-63	Unc-65
$35	$40	$43	$45	$48	$60	$85	$135

W-2503-E★ • F-2052E★

VG-8	F-12	VF-20	EF-40	AU-50	Unc-60	Unc-63
$100	$215	$325	$375	$700	$1,000	$1,300

W-2503-G • F-2052G • Chicago • Part of W-2502-G printage

VG-8	F-12	VF-20	EF-40	AU-50	Unc-60	Unc-63	Unc-65
$30	$35	$38	$40	$43	$55	$75	$115

W-2503-G★ • F-2052G★

VG-8	F-12	VF-20	EF-40	AU-50	Unc-60	Unc-63
$70	$125	$175	$225	$400	$625	$825

W-2503-H • F-2052H • St. Louis • Part of W-2502-H printage

VG-8	F-12	VF-20	EF-40	AU-50	Unc-60	Unc-63	Unc-65
$35	$40	$43	$45	$48	$60	$80	$120

W-2503-H★ • F-2052H★

VG-8	F-12	VF-20	EF-40	AU-50	Unc-60	Unc-63
$90	$175	$275	$315	$475	$700	$900

SERIES OF 1928-B, LIGHT YELLOW-GREEN SEAL

$20 Federal Reserve Note, Series of 1928-B (W-2503-G). Light yellow-green Treasury seal. Federal Reserve Bank of Chicago. Standard back of the era, without motto.

W-2503-I • F-2052I • Minneapolis • Part of W-2502-I printage

VG-8	F-12	VF-20	EF-40	AU-50	Unc-60	Unc-63	Unc-65
$35	$40	$43	$45	$55	$65	$90	$140

W-2503-I★ • F-2052I★

VG-8	F-12	VF-20	EF-40	AU-50	Unc-60	Unc-63
$115	$250	$375	$475	$900	$1,250	$1,600

W-2503-J • F-2052J • Kansas City • Part of W-2502-J printage

W-2503-J★ • F-2052J★

VG-8	F-12	VF-20	EF-40	AU-50	Unc-60	Unc-63
$100	$215	$325	$375	$700	$1,000	$1,300

W-2503-L • F-2052L • San Francisco • Part of W-2502-L printage

W-2503-L★ • F-2052L★

VG-8	F-12	VF-20	EF-40	AU-50	Unc-60	Unc-63
$70	$125	$175	$245	$450	$675	$875

Series of 1928-C, Light Yellow-Green Seal
Woods-Mills (1932–1933)

This series continued the preceding design. The Series of 1928-C was a very short issue, for only two banks and without any star notes. In the 1930s there was hardly any numismatic interest in saving current $20 notes. Therefore, Uncirculated notes are very rare today.

W-2504-G • F-2053G • Chicago • 3,363,300

VG-8	F-12	VF-20	EF-40	AU-50	Unc-60	Unc-63	Unc-65
$125	$200	$300	$675	$1,050	$1,750	$2,500	$5,500

W-2504-L • F-2053L • San Francisco • 1,420,200

VG-8	F-12	VF-20	EF-40	AU-50	Unc-60	Unc-63
$285	$390	$500	$1,000	$1,550	$2,900	$6,000

Series of 1934, Light Yellow-Green Seal
Julian-Morgenthau (1934–1945)

The Series of 1934 continued the same layout as the preceding series, but with a change in the obligation that eliminated the mention of gold: "This note is legal tender for all debts, public and private, and is redeemable in lawful money at the United States Treasury, or at any Federal Reserve Bank."

This issue's Treasury seal is also a slightly different hue than previous issues.

Prices for a typical note for this series, unless listed otherwise, are as follows:

VF-20	EF-40	AU-50	Unc-60	Unc-63	Unc-65
$30	$35	$40	$45	$60	$95

W-2505-A • F-2054A • Boston • 37,673,068

VF-20	EF-40	AU-50	Unc-60	Unc-63	Unc-65
$30	$35	$40	$48	$63	$100

W-2505-A★ • F-2054A★

VG-8	F-12	VF-20	EF-40	AU-50	Unc-60	Unc-63	Unc-65
$65	$90	$125	$200	$325	$425	$675	$1,275

W-2505-B • F-2054B • New York • 37,573,264

VF-20	EF-40	AU-50	Unc-60	Unc-63	Unc-65
$30	$35	$40	$52	$65	$120

W-2505-B★ • F-2054B★

VG-8	F-12	VF-20	EF-40	AU-50
$50	$80	$100	$225	$350

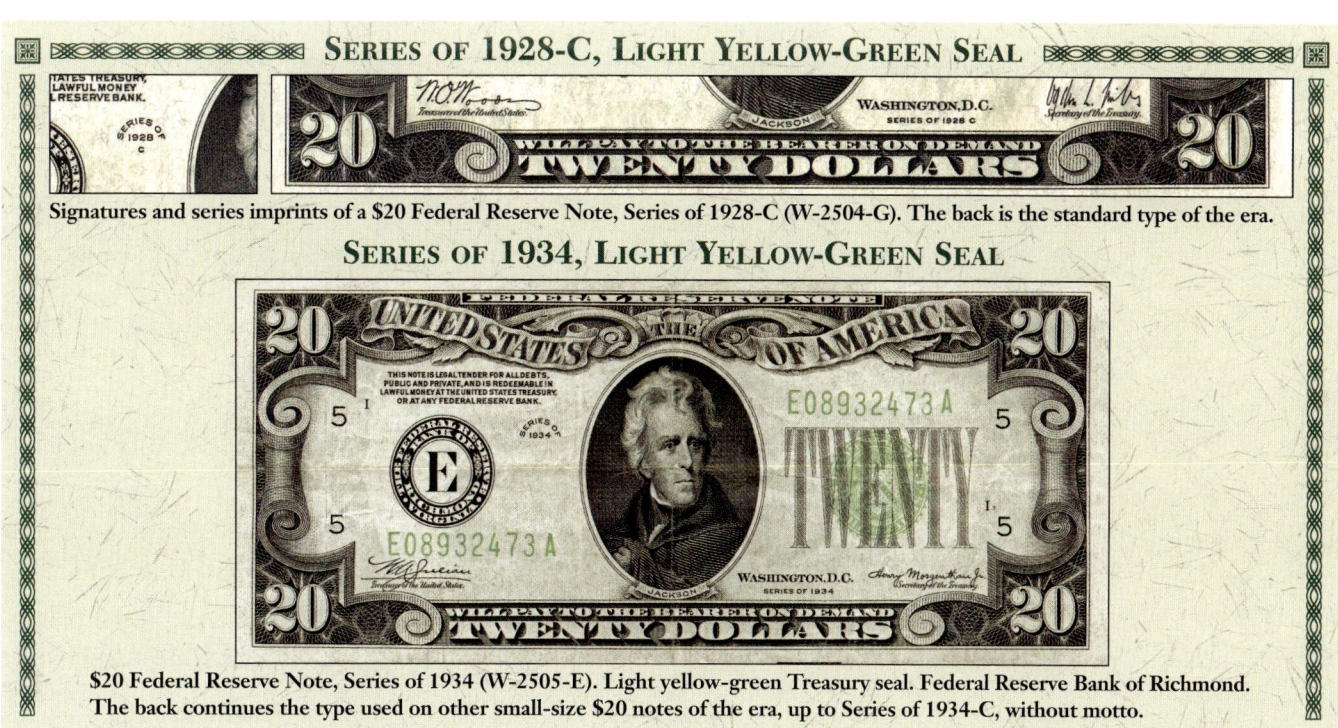

SERIES OF 1928-C, LIGHT YELLOW-GREEN SEAL

Signatures and series imprints of a $20 Federal Reserve Note, Series of 1928-C (W-2504-G). The back is the standard type of the era.

SERIES OF 1934, LIGHT YELLOW-GREEN SEAL

$20 Federal Reserve Note, Series of 1934 (W-2505-E). Light yellow-green Treasury seal. Federal Reserve Bank of Richmond. The back continues the type used on other small-size $20 notes of the era, up to Series of 1934-C, without motto.

W-2505-C • F-2054C • Philadelphia • 53,209,968

W-2505-C★ • F-2054C★

VG-8	F-12	VF-20	EF-40	AU-50	Unc-60	Unc-63	Unc-65
$50	$80	$90	$160	$210	$360	$550	$950

W-2505-D • F-2054D • Cleveland • 48,301,416

W-2505-D★ • F-2054D★

VG-8	F-12	VF-20	EF-40	AU-50	Unc-60	Unc-63	Unc-65
$40	$80	$90	$160	$220	$375	$600	$1,100

W-2505-E • F-2054E • Richmond • 36,259,224

W-2505-E★ • F-2054E★

VG-8	F-12	VF-20	EF-40
$65	$100	$150	$300

W-2505-F • F-2054F • Atlanta • 41,547,660

W-2505-F★ • F-2054F★

VG-8	F-12	VF-20	EF-40	AU-50	Unc-60	Unc-63	Unc-65
$40	$55	$85	$150	$265	$450	$775	$1,375

W-2505-G • F-2054G • Chicago • 20,777,832

W-2505-G★ • F-2054G★

VG-8	F-12	VF-20	EF-40	AU-50	Unc-60	Unc-63	Unc-65
$40	$60	$90	$160	$285	$500	$800	$1,600

W-2505-H • F-2054H • St. Louis • 21,174,552

W-2505-H★ • F-2054H★

VG-8	F-12	VF-20	EF-40	AU-50	Unc-60	Unc-63	Unc-65
$45	$60	$95	$185	$300	$600	$1,000	$1,850

W-2505-I • F-2054I • Minneapolis • 16,795,116

F-12	VF-20	EF-40	AU-50	Unc-60	Unc-63	Unc-65
$25	$35	$40	$50	$65	$85	$175

W-2505-I★ • F-2054I★

VG-8	F-12	VF-20	EF-40	AU-50	Unc-60	Unc-63
$100	$150	$200	$350	$475	$675	$1,450

W-2505-J • F-2054J • Kansas City • 28,865,304

W-2505-J★ • F-2054J★

VG-8	F-12	VF-20	EF-40	AU-50	Unc-60	Unc-63	Unc-65
$50	$90	$140	$200	$300	$600	$1,300	$2,500

W-2505-K • F-2054K • Dallas • 20,852,160

VF-20	EF-40	AU-50	Unc-60	Unc-63	Unc-65
$30	$35	$45	$50	$75	$110

W-2505-K★ • F-2054K★

VG-8	F-12	VF-20	EF-40	AU-50	Unc-60	Unc-63	Unc-65
$65	$100	$150	$235	$325	$675	$1,400	$2,600

W-2505-L • F-2054L • San Francisco • 32,203,956

W-2505-L★ • F-2054L★

VG-8	F-12	VF-20	EF-40	AU-50	Unc-60	Unc-63	Unc-65
$40	$55	$75	$135	$275	$450	$600	$1,050

Series of 1934, Green Seal
Julian-Morgenthau (1934–1945)

This series continued the preceding design. This issue's Treasury seal was a slightly different hue than the previous issue.

Mules: Most backs have the plate number in small or "micro" numbers, but mules have the larger or "macro"-size serials, as used on Series 1934-A (the macro plates are numbers 318 and higher). Mules are not particularly scarce. Uncirculated star notes of the normal, micro reverse and the mule, macro reverse are all rare.

Prices for a typical note for this series, unless listed otherwise, are as follows:

VF-20	EF-40	AU-50	Unc-60	Unc-63	Unc-65
$28	$30	$35	$40	$50	$85

W-2506-A • F-2054A • Boston • Part of W-2505-A printage

VF-20	EF-40	AU-50	Unc-60	Unc-63	Unc-65
$28	$30	$35	$42	$63	$85

SERIES OF 1934, GREEN SEAL

$20 Federal Reserve Note, Series of 1934 (W-2506-F). Dark green Treasury seal. Federal Reserve Bank of Atlanta. The back continues the type used on other small-size $20 notes of the era up to Series of 1934-C.

W-2506-A★ • F-2054A★

VG-8	F-12	VF-20	EF-40
$50	$100	$125	$200

W-2506-A Mule • F-2054A • Part of W-2505-A printage

VF-20	EF-40	AU-50	Unc-60	Unc-63	Unc-65
$25	$28	$30	$33	$40	$75

W-2506-A Mule★ • F-2054A★

VG-8	F-12	VF-20	EF-40	AU-50	Unc-60	Unc-63	Unc-65
$37	$48	$70	$130	$185	$275	$350	$700

W-2506-B • F-2054B • New York • Part of W-2505-B printage

W-2506-B★ • F-2054B★

VG-8	F-12	VF-20	EF-40
$50	$100	$125	$200

W-2506-B Mule • F-2054B • Part of W-2505-B printage

Commentary: Current market information not available.

W-2506-C • F-2054C • Philadelphia • Part of W-2505-C printage

W-2506-C★ • F-2054C★

VG-8	F-12	VF-20	EF-40	AU-50	Unc-60	Unc-63
$35	$42	$60	$110	$175	$225	$300

W-2506-C Mule • F-2054C • Part of W-2505-C printage

VF-20	EF-40	AU-50	Unc-60	Unc-63	Unc-65
$25	$28	$30	$33	$40	$75

W-2506-C Mule★ • F-2054C★

VG-8	F-12	VF-20	EF-40	AU-50	Unc-60	Unc-63	Unc-65
$35	$42	$55	$95	$150	$250	$385	$650

W-2506-D • F-2054D • Cleveland • Part of W-2505-D printage

W-2506-D★ • F-2054D★

VG-8	F-12	VF-20	EF-40	AU-50	Unc-60	Unc-63
$35	$42	$65	$125	$200	$240	$315

W-2506-D Mule • F-2054D • Part of W-2505-D printage

VF-20	EF-40	AU-50	Unc-60	Unc-63	Unc-65
$25	$28	$30	$33	$40	$75

W-2506-D Mule★ • F-2054D★

VG-8	F-12	VF-20	EF-40	AU-50	Unc-60	Unc-63	Unc-65
$35	$42	$60	$100	$190	$275	$425	$900

W-2506-E • F-2054E • Richmond • Part of W-2505-E printage

W-2506-E★ • F-2054E★

VG-8	F-12	VF-20	EF-40	AU-50	Unc-60	Unc-63	Unc-65
$40	$55	$70	$125	$200	$320	$440	$875

W-2506-E Mule • F-2054E • Part of W-2505-E printage

VF-20	EF-40	AU-50	Unc-60	Unc-63	Unc-65
$25	$28	$30	$33	$40	$75

W-2506-E Mule★ • F-2054E★

VG-8	F-12	VF-20	EF-40	AU-50	Unc-60
$35	$42	$85	$140	$235	$325

W-2506-F • F-2054F • Atlanta • Part of W-2505-F printage

W-2506-F★ • F-2054F★

VG-8	F-12	VF-20	EF-40	AU-50	Unc-60	Unc-63
$35	$42	$70	$135	$200	$250	$325

W-2506-F Mule • F-2054F • Part of W-2505-F printage

VF-20	EF-40	AU-50	Unc-60	Unc-63	Unc-65
$25	$28	$30	$33	$40	$75

W-2506-F Mule★ • F-2054F★

VG-8	F-12	VF-20	EF-40	AU-50	Unc-60	Unc-63
$40	$50	$70	$135	$225	$285	$425

W-2506-G • F-2054G • Chicago • Part of W-2505-G printage

W-2506-G★ • F-2054G★

VG-8	F-12	VF-20	EF-40	AU-50	Unc-60	Unc-63
$35	$42	$60	$125	$200	$260	$315

W-2506-H • F-2054H • St. Louis • Part of W-2505-H printage

W-2506-H★ • F-2054H★

VG-8	F-12	VF-20	EF-40	AU-50	Unc-60	Unc-63
$35	$42	$70	$140	$235	$325	$425

W-2506-H Mule • F-2054H • Part of W-2505-H printage

VF-20	EF-40	AU-50	Unc-60	Unc-63	Unc-65
$25	$28	$30	$33	$40	$75

W-2506-H Mule★ • F-2054H★

VG-8	F-12	VF-20	EF-40	AU-50	Unc-60	Unc-63	Unc-65
$35	$42	$55	$95	$150	$250	$350	$700

W-2506-I • F-2054I • Minneapolis • Part of W-2505-I printage

VF-20	EF-40	AU-50	Unc-60	Unc-63	Unc-65
$35	$40	$45	$50	$65	$125

W-2506-I★ • F-2054I★

VG-8	F-12	VF-20	EF-40	AU-50	Unc-60	Unc-63	Unc-65
$45	$55	$75	$150	$240	$310	$385	$725

W-2506-I Mule • F-2054I • Part of W-2505-I printage

VF-20	EF-40	AU-50	Unc-60	Unc-63	Unc-65
$32	$35	$40	$45	$60	$115

W-2506-I Mule★ • F-2054I★

VG-8	F-12	VF-20	EF-40	AU-50
$45	$60	$80	$170	$250

W-2506-J • F-2054J • Kansas City • Part of W-2505-J printage

W-2506-J★ • F-2054J★

VG-8	F-12	VF-20	EF-40	AU-50	Unc-60	Unc-63
$35	$45	$70	$110	$175	$275	$350

W-2506-J Mule • F-2054J • Part of W-2505-J printage

VF-20	EF-40	AU-50	Unc-60	Unc-63	Unc-65
$25	$28	$30	$33	$45	$75

W-2506-J Mule★ • F-2054J★

VG-8	F-12	VF-20	EF-40	AU-50	Unc-60	Unc-63
$60	$75	$100	$150	$250	$375	$575

W-2506-K • F-2054K • Dallas • Part of W-2505-K printage

VF-20	EF-40	AU-50	Unc-60	Unc-63	Unc-65
$28	$30	$35	$45	$55	$95

W-2506-K★ • F-2054K★

VG-8	F-12	VF-20	EF-40
$70	$100	$165	$275

W-2506-K Mule • F-2054K • Part of W-2505-K printage

VF-20	EF-40	AU-50	Unc-60	Unc-63	Unc-65
$30	$35	$40	$45	$55	$85

W-2506-K Mule★ • F-2054K★

VG-8	F-12	VF-20	EF-40	AU-50	Unc-60	Unc-63
$60	$90	$160	$225	$325	$425	$600

W-2506-L • F-2054L • San Francisco • Part of W-2505-L printage

VF-20	EF-40	AU-50	Unc-60	Unc-63	Unc-65
$28	$30	$35	$40	$60	$105

W-2506-L★ • F-2054L★

VG-8	F-12	VF-20	EF-40	AU-50	Unc-60	Unc-63
$35	$45	$70	$125	$200	$310	$400

W-2506-L Mule • F-2054L • Part of W-2505-L printage

VF-20	EF-40	AU-50	Unc-60	Unc-63	Unc-65
$25	$28	$30	$35	$55	$90

W-2506-L Mule★ • F-2054L★

Commentary: Current market information not available.

Series of 1934, Brown Seal, HAWAII Overprint
Julian-Morgenthau (1934–1945)

These notes, with HAWAII overprinted on the face and the back and with a special brown Treasury seal and brown serial numbers, were used from 1942 to 1944 in the Hawaiian Islands, then under threat of Japanese invasion. If the islands had fallen into the hands of the enemy, such notes could be repudiated and would have no value on world markets. This is the largest of the four denominations issued.

Mules: Most backs have the plate number in micro numbers, but mules have larger, macro-size numbers, as used on Series 1934-A (the macro plates are numbers 318 and higher).

W-2510-L • F-2304 • San Francisco • 11,246,000

VG-8	F-12	VF-20	EF-40	AU-50	Unc-60	Unc-63	Unc-65
$50	$80	$200	$1,250	$3,250	$5,000	$6,500	$10,000

W-2510-L★ • F-2304★ • 52,000

VG-8	F-12	VF-20	EF-40	AU-50	Unc-60	Unc-63
$1,200	$2,000	$4,000	$7,500	$13,000	$18,000	$22,500

W-2510-L Mule • F-2304

VG-8	F-12	VF-20	EF-40	AU-50	Unc-60	Unc-63	Unc-65
$45	$65	$110	$250	$550	$1,150	$2,000	$6,500

W-2510-L Mule★ • F-2304★

VG-8	F-12	VF-20	EF-40
$750	$1,300	$2,500	$3,750

Series of 1934-A, Brown Seal, HAWAII Overprint
Julian-Morgenthau (1934–1945)

The design is similar to the HAWAII issue of the Series of 1934.

Mules: Most backs have the plate number in macro numbers, but mules have smaller, micro-size numbers, as used on Series 1934 (the micro plates are numbers 317 and lower).

W-2520-L • F-2305 • San Francisco • Part of W-2510-L printage

VG-8	F-12	VF-20	EF-40	AU-50	Unc-60	Unc-63	Unc-65
$50	$70	$100	$350	$775	$1,100	$1,300	$1,675

W-2520-L★ • F-2305★ • 2,500

VG-8	F-12	VF-20	EF-40	AU-50	Unc-60	Unc-63	Unc-65
$700	$1,300	$1,800	$4,200	$7,000	$11,000	$15,000	$23,000

W-2520-L Mule • F-2305

VG-8	F-12	VF-20	EF-40	AU-50	Unc-60	Unc-63	Unc-65
$85	$150	$250	$500	$850	$1,400	$1,750	$4,000

W-2520-L Mule★ • F-2305★

VG-8	F-12	VF-20	EF-40	AU-50	Unc-60	Unc-63	Unc-65
$1,200	$2,000	$3,300	$5,000	$8,500	$16,500	$22,000	—

Series of 1934-A, Green Seal
Julian-Morgenthau (1934–1945)

This series continued the traditional design.

Mules: Most backs have the plate number in macro numbers, but mules have smaller, micro-size numbers, as used on Series 1934 (the micro plates are numbers 317 and lower).

W-2522-A • F-2055A • Boston • 3,302,416

VF-20	EF-40	AU-50	Unc-60	Unc-63	Unc-65
$30	$35	$40	$55	$65	$90

W-2522-A★ • F-2055A★

VG-8	F-12	VF-20	EF-40	AU-50	Unc-60	Unc-63	Unc-65
$35	$55	$85	$135	$220	$375	$475	$700

W-2522-A Mule • F-2055A

VG-8	F-12	VF-20	EF-40	AU-50	Unc-60	Unc-63	Unc-65
$30	$35	$40	$45	$50	$70	$90	$140

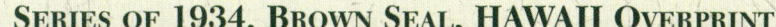

SERIES OF 1934, BROWN SEAL, HAWAII OVERPRINT

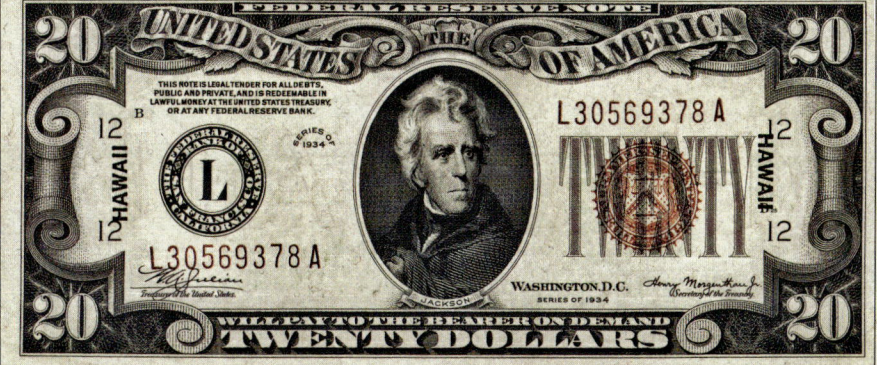

$20 Federal Reserve Note, Series of 1934, Brown Seal, with HAWAII overprint (W-2510-L).

The back of the $20 HAWAII note is the standard design, but with a special overprint.

SERIES OF 1934-A, BROWN SEAL, HAWAII OVERPRINT

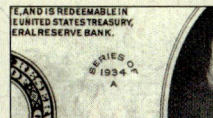 

Detail of the signatures and the series imprints of a $20 Federal Reserve Note, Series of 1934-A, HAWAII overprint (W-2520-L). The back is the standard type of the era with the same HAWAII overprint as the Series of 1934 note.

SERIES OF 1934-A, GREEN SEAL

Signatures and series imprints of a $20 Federal Reserve Note, Series of 1934-A (W-2522-G). The back is the standard type of the era.

W-2522-B • F-2055B • New York • 102,555,538

VF-20	EF-40	AU-50	Unc-60	Unc-63	Unc-65
$25	$30	$35	$45	$55	$80

W-2522-B★ • F-2055B★

VG-8	F-12	VF-20	EF-40	AU-50	Unc-60	Unc-63	Unc-65
$35	$50	$65	$120	$200	$375	$475	$700

W-2522-B Mule • F-2055B

F-12	VF-20	EF-40	AU-50	Unc-60	Unc-63	Unc-65
$25	$30	$35	$38	$48	$65	$90

W-2522-B Mule★ • F-2055B★

VG-8	F-12	VF-20	EF-40
$75	$125	$250	$425

W-2522-C • F-2055C • Philadelphia • 3,371,316

VF-20	EF-40	AU-50	Unc-60	Unc-63	Unc-65
$30	$35	$40	$55	$65	$90

W-2522-C★ • F-2055C★

VG-8	F-12	VF-20	EF-40	AU-50	Unc-60	Unc-63	Unc-65
$35	$50	$70	$125	$220	$375	$475	$700

W-2522-D • F-2055D • Cleveland • 23,475,108

VF-20	EF-40	AU-50	Unc-60	Unc-63	Unc-65
$30	$35	$40	$55	$65	$100

W-2522-D★ • F-2055D★

VG-8	F-12	VF-20	EF-40	AU-50	Unc-60	Unc-63	Unc-65
$35	$50	$65	$120	$220	$375	$475	$700

W-2522-D Mule • F-2055D

VG-8	F-12	VF-20	EF-40	AU-50	Unc-60	Unc-63	Unc-65
$30	$35	$40	$45	$50	$55	$80	$125

W-2522-D Mule★ • F-2055D★

VG-8	F-12	VF-20	EF-40	AU-50
$45	$75	$100	$225	$325

W-2522-E • F-2055E • Richmond • 46,816,224

VF-20	EF-40	AU-50	Unc-60	Unc-63	Unc-65
$30	$35	$40	$55	$65	$90

W-2522-E★ • F-2055E★

VG-8	F-12	VF-20	EF-40	AU-50	Unc-60	Unc-63	Unc-65
$35	$50	$70	$135	$220	$375	$475	$700

W-2522-E Mule • F-2055E

VG-8	F-12	VF-20	EF-40	AU-50	Unc-60	Unc-63	Unc-65
$30	$35	$40	$45	$50	$65	$80	$125

W-2522-F • F-2055F • Atlanta • 6,756,816

VF-20	EF-40	AU-50	Unc-60	Unc-63	Unc-65
$30	$35	$40	$55	$65	$100

W-2522-F★ • F-2055F★

VG-8	F-12	VF-20	EF-40	AU-50	Unc-60	Unc-63	Unc-65
$35	$50	$70	$135	$220	$375	$475	$700

W-2522-G • F-2055G • Chicago • 91,141,452

VF-20	EF-40	AU-50	Unc-60	Unc-63	Unc-65
$25	$30	$40	$48	$60	$80

W-2522-G★ • F-2055G★

VG-8	F-12	VF-20	EF-40	AU-50	Unc-60	Unc-63	Unc-65
$35	$50	$65	$120	$200	$375	$475	$700

W-2522-G Mule • F-2055G

VF-20	EF-40	AU-50	Unc-60	Unc-63	Unc-65
$27	$32	$40	$45	$55	$75

W-2522-G Mule★ • F-2055G★

VG-8	F-12	VF-20	EF-40	AU-50	Unc-60	Unc-63	Unc-65
$45	$60	$85	$150	$200	$250	$325	$1,350

W-2522-H • F-2055H • St. Louis • 3,701,568

VF-20	EF-40	AU-50	Unc-60	Unc-63	Unc-65
$30	$35	$40	$55	$65	$100

W-2522-H★ • F-2055H★

VG-8	F-12	VF-20	EF-40	AU-50	Unc-60	Unc-63	Unc-65
$35	$50	$70	$135	$220	$375	$475	$700

W-2522-H Mule • F-2055H

VG-8	F-12	VF-20	EF-40	AU-50	Unc-60	Unc-63
$45	$60	$85	$170	$225	$275	$350

W-2522-I • F-2055I • Minneapolis • 1,162,500

VF-20	EF-40	AU-50	Unc-60	Unc-63	Unc-65
$35	$43	$50	$65	$75	$115

W-2522-I★ • F-2055I★

VG-8	F-12	VF-20	EF-40	AU-50	Unc-60	Unc-63	Unc-65
$40	$65	$95	$180	$300	$450	$550	$825

W-2522-I Mule • F-2055I

VG-8	F-12	VF-20	EF-40	AU-50	Unc-60
$55	$75	$100	$200	$275	$415

W-2522-J • F-2055J • Kansas City • 3,221,184

VF-20	EF-40	AU-50	Unc-60	Unc-63	Unc-65
$30	$35	$40	$55	$65	$100

W-2522-J★ • F-2055J★

VG-8	F-12	VF-20	EF-40	AU-50	Unc-60	Unc-63	Unc-65
$35	$50	$70	$135	$220	$375	$475	$700

W-2522-J Mule • F-2055J

VG-8	F-12	VF-20	EF-40	AU-50	Unc-60
$45	$60	$85	$170	$250	$300

W-2522-K • F-2055K • Dallas • 2,531,700

VF-20	EF-40	AU-50	Unc-60	Unc-63	Unc-65
$30	$35	$40	$55	$65	$100

W-2522-K★ • F-2055K★

VG-8	F-12	VF-20	EF-40	AU-50	Unc-60	Unc-63	Unc-65
$35	$55	$80	$150	$255	$410	$525	$775

W-2522-K Mule • F-2055K

VG-8	F-12	VF-20	EF-40	AU-50	Unc-60
$50	$70	$90	$185	$260	$400

W-2522-L • F-2055L • San Francisco • 94,454,112

VF-20	EF-40	AU-50	Unc-60	Unc-63	Unc-65
$25	$30	$40	$48	$60	$80

W-2522-L★ • F-2055L★

VG-8	F-12	VF-20	EF-40	AU-50	Unc-60	Unc-63	Unc-65
$35	$50	$70	$135	$220	$375	$475	$700

W-2522-L Mule • F-2055L

VF-20	EF-40	AU-50	Unc-60	Unc-63	Unc-65
$25	$30	$35	$65	$80	$110

W-2522-L Mule★ • F-2055L★

VG-8	F-12	VF-20	EF-40	AU-50
$90	$185	$275	$450	$600

Series of 1934-B, Green Seal
Julian-Vinson (1945–1946)

Beginning with the Series of 1934-B notes, there was a change in the wording in the Federal Reserve seal. THE is omitted, leaving FEDERAL RESERVE.

W-2524-A • F-2056A • Boston • 3,904,800

VF-20	EF-40	AU-50	Unc-60	Unc-63	Unc-65
$30	$35	$45	$70	$85	$125

W-2524-A★ • F-2056A★

VG-8	F-12	VF-20	EF-40	AU-50	Unc-60	Unc-63	Unc-65
$55	$95	$150	$290	$425	$600	$775	$1,100

W-2524-B • F-2056B • New York • 14,876,436

VF-20	EF-40	AU-50	Unc-60	Unc-63	Unc-65
$25	$30	$40	$55	$70	$100

W-2524-B★ • F-2056B★

VG-8	F-12	VF-20	EF-40	AU-50	Unc-60	Unc-63	Unc-65
$40	$65	$105	$190	$275	$450	$600	$850

W-2524-C • F-2056C • Philadelphia • 3,271,452

VF-20	EF-40	AU-50	Unc-60	Unc-63	Unc-65
$30	$35	$45	$70	$85	$125

W-2524-C★ • F-2056C★

VG-8	F-12	VF-20	EF-40	AU-50	Unc-60	Unc-63	Unc-65
$50	$80	$125	$250	$375	$500	$675	$975

W-2524-D • F-2056D • Cleveland • 2,814,600

VF-20	EF-40	AU-50	Unc-60	Unc-63	Unc-65
$30	$35	$45	$75	$100	$150

W-2524-D★ • F-2056D★

VG-8	F-12	VF-20	EF-40	AU-50	Unc-60	Unc-63	Unc-65
$50	$80	$135	$270	$390	$500	$675	$975

W-2524-E • F-2056E • Richmond • 9,451,632

VF-20	EF-40	AU-50	Unc-60	Unc-63	Unc-65
$30	$35	$45	$65	$85	$125

W-2524-E★ • F-2056E★

VG-8	F-12	VF-20	EF-40	AU-50	Unc-60	Unc-63	Unc-65
$50	$80	$125	$190	$275	$450	$675	$955

W-2524-F • F-2056F • Atlanta • 6,887,640

VF-20	EF-40	AU-50	Unc-60	Unc-63	Unc-65
$30	$35	$45	$65	$85	$125

W-2524-F★ • F-2056F★

VG-8	F-12	VF-20	EF-40	AU-50	Unc-60	Unc-63	Unc-65
$50	$80	$125	$250	$375	$560	$750	$1,100

W-2524-G • F-2056G • Chicago • 9,084,600

VF-20	EF-40	AU-50	Unc-60	Unc-63	Unc-65
$25	$30	$40	$55	$70	$100

W-2524-G★ • F-2056G★

VG-8	F-12	VF-20	EF-40	AU-50	Unc-60	Unc-63	Unc-65
$40	$65	$105	$190	$275	$450	$600	$850

W-2524-H • F-2056H • St. Louis • 5,817,300

VF-20	EF-40	AU-50	Unc-60	Unc-63	Unc-65
$30	$35	$45	$65	$85	$125

SERIES OF 1934-B, GREEN SEAL

Detail of the signatures and the series imprints of a $20 Federal Reserve Note, Series of 1934-B (W-2524-I), as well as the new style of Federal Reserve seal. The back is the standard type of the era.

W-2524-H★ • F-2056H★

VG-8	F-12	VF-20	EF-40	AU-50	Unc-60	Unc-63	Unc-65
$50	$80	$125	$190	$275	$450	$675	$975

W-2524-I • F-2056I • Minneapolis • 2,304,800

VF-20	EF-40	AU-50	Unc-60	Unc-63	Unc-65
$30	$35	$45	$75	$100	$150

W-2524-I★ • F-2056I★

VG-8	F-12	VF-20	EF-40	AU-50	Unc-60	Unc-63	Unc-65
$60	$95	$150	$285	$460	$650	$825	$1,175

W-2524-J • F-2056J • Kansas City • 3,524,244

VF-20	EF-40	AU-50	Unc-60	Unc-63	Unc-65
$30	$35	$45	$75	$100	$150

W-2524-J★ • F-2056J★

VG-8	F-12	VF-20	EF-40	AU-50	Unc-60	Unc-63	Unc-65
$60	$95	$150	$290	$470	$650	$825	$1,175

W-2524-K • F-2056K • Dallas • 2,807,388

VF-20	EF-40	AU-50	Unc-60	Unc-63	Unc-65
$30	$35	$45	$65	$85	$125

W-2524-K★ • F-2056K★

VG-8	F-12	VF-20	EF-40	AU-50	Unc-60	Unc-63	Unc-65
$60	$95	$150	$300	$500	$680	$875	$1,300

W-2524-L • F-2056L • San Francisco • 5,289,540

VF-20	EF-40	AU-50	Unc-60	Unc-63	Unc-65
$30	$35	$45	$65	$80	$115

W-2524-L★ • F-2056L★

VG-8	F-12	VF-20	EF-40	AU-50	Unc-60	Unc-63	Unc-65
$60	$95	$150	$285	$460	$650	$825	$1,175

Series of 1934-C, Green Seal, Old Back
Julian-Snyder (1946–1949)

This series continued the preceding design.

On July 3, 1950, the back was redesigned, introducing the "New Back" style.

The Old Back style was used on all small-size $20 notes up to this point. Beneath the vignette is the title WHITE HOUSE. Compare to the New Back design described in the next section.

Prices for a typical note for this series, unless listed otherwise, are as follows:

EF-40	AU-50	Unc-60	Unc-63	Unc-65
$25	$35	$60	$85	$120

W-2525-A • F-2057A • Boston • 7,397,352
W-2525-A★ • F-2057A★

F-12	VF-20	EF-40	AU-50	Unc-60	Unc-63	Unc-65
$60	$100	$200	$325	$525	$750	$1,000

W-2525-B • F-2057B • New York • 18,668,148

AU-50	Unc-60	Unc-63	Unc-65
$30	$45	$60	$80

W-2525-B★ • F-2057B★

F-12	VF-20	EF-40	AU-50	Unc-60	Unc-63	Unc-65
$40	$65	$100	$200	$350	$500	$750

W-2525-C • F-2057C • Philadelphia • 11,590,752
W-2525-C★ • F-2057C★

F-12	VF-20	EF-40	AU-50	Unc-60	Unc-63	Unc-65
$50	$90	$170	$280	$460	$625	$875

W-2525-D • F-2057D • Cleveland • 17,912,424
W-2525-D★ • F-2057D★

F-12	VF-20	EF-40	AU-50	Unc-60	Unc-63	Unc-65
$50	$90	$170	$280	$460	$625	$875

W-2525-E • F-2057E • Richmond • 22,526,568
W-2525-E★ • F-2057E★

F-12	VF-20	EF-40	AU-50	Unc-60	Unc-63	Unc-65
$50	$90	$170	$280	$460	$625	$875

W-2525-F • F-2057F • Atlanta • 18,858,876

EF-40	AU-50	Unc-60	Unc-63	Unc-65
$32	$50	$80	$110	$145

W-2525-F★ • F-2057F★

F-12	VF-20	EF-40	AU-50	Unc-60	Unc-63	Unc-65
$50	$90	$170	$280	$460	$625	$875

W-2525-G • F-2057G • Chicago • 26,031,660

AU-50	Unc-60	Unc-63	Unc-65
$30	$45	$60	$80

W-2525-G★ • F-2057G★

F-12	VF-20	EF-40	AU-50	Unc-60	Unc-63	Unc-65
$40	$65	$100	$200	$325	$480	$725

SERIES OF 1934-C, GREEN SEAL, OLD BACK

Signatures and series imprints of a $20 Federal Reserve Note, Series of 1934-C (W-2525-A). The back is the standard type of the era.

W-2525-H • F-2057H • St. Louis • 13,276,984

W-2525-H★ • F-2057H★

F-12	VF-20	EF-40	AU-50	Unc-60	Unc-63	Unc-65
$50	$90	$170	$280	$460	$625	$875

W-2525-I • F-2057I • Minneapolis • 3,490,200

EF-40	AU-50	Unc-60	Unc-63	Unc-65
$30	$45	$70	$100	$135

W-2525-I★ • F-2057I★

VG-8	F-12	VF-20	EF-40	AU-50	Unc-60	Unc-63	Unc-65
$50	$100	$175	$275	$450	$675	$900	$1,150

W-2525-J • F-2057J • Kansas City • 9,675,468

W-2525-J★ • F-2057J★

F-12	VF-20	EF-40	AU-50	Unc-60	Unc-63	Unc-65
$60	$100	$200	$325	$525	$750	$1,000

W-2525-K • F-2057K • Dallas • 10,205,364

EF-40	AU-50	Unc-60	Unc-63	Unc-65
$30	$45	$70	$100	$135

W-2525-K★ • F-2057K★

F-12	VF-20	EF-40	AU-50	Unc-60	Unc-63	Unc-65
$60	$100	$200	$325	$525	$750	$1,000

W-2525-L • F-2057L • San Francisco • 20,580,000

W-2525-L★ • F-2057L★

F-12	VF-20	EF-40	AU-50	Unc-60	Unc-63	Unc-65
$60	$100	$200	$325	$525	$750	$1,000

Series of 1934-C, Green Seal, New Back
Julian-Snyder (1946–1949)

This issue used the New Back style. The vignette is titled THE WHITE HOUSE, with THE added. The foliage is larger and richer than on the Old Back style. The BEP wanted to change the currency to reflect a new porch that had been added to the building.[31]

Prices for a typical note for this series, unless listed otherwise, are as follows:

VF-20	EF-40	AU-50	Unc-60	Unc-63	Unc-65
$24	$30	$40	$50	$65	$85

W-2526-A • F-2057A • Boston • Part of W-2525-A printage

VF-20	EF-40	AU-50	Unc-60	Unc-63	Unc-65
$24	$30	$40	$50	$65	$90

W-2526-A★ • F-2057A★

VG-8	F-12	VF-20	EF-40	AU-50	Unc-60	Unc-63	Unc-65
$35	$60	$100	$160	$260	$400	$550	$750

W-2526-B • F-2057B • New York • Part of W-2525-B printage

VF-20	EF-40	AU-50	Unc-60	Unc-63	Unc-65
$24	$30	$35	$45	$60	$80

W-2526-B★ • F-2057B★

VG-8	F-12	VF-20	EF-40	AU-50	Unc-60	Unc-63	Unc-65
$30	$55	$85	$140	$225	$300	$425	$625

W-2526-C • F-2057C • Philadelphia • Part of W-2525-C printage

W-2526-C★ • F-2057C★

VG-8	F-12	VF-20	EF-40	AU-50	Unc-60	Unc-63	Unc-65
$30	$55	$85	$140	$225	$325	$450	$650

W-2526-D • F-2057D • Cleveland • Part of W-2525-D printage

W-2526-D★ • F-2057D★

VG-8	F-12	VF-20	EF-40	AU-50	Unc-60	Unc-63	Unc-65
$35	$60	$100	$140	$225	$325	$450	$650

W-2526-E • F-2057E • Richmond • Part of W-2525-E printage

W-2526-E★ • F-2057E★

VG-8	F-12	VF-20	EF-40	AU-50	Unc-60	Unc-63	Unc-65
$35	$60	$100	$140	$225	$325	$450	$650

SERIES OF 1934-C, GREEN SEAL, NEW BACK

Back of the $20 Federal Reserve Note, Series of 1934-C, New Back, with more foliage and THE added to the title. This type was used through the Series of 1950-E. The face is indistinguishable from that used for Series of 1934-C Old Back notes.

W-2526-F • F-2057F • Atlanta • Part of W-2525-F printage

W-2526-F★ • F-2057F★

VG-8	F-12	VF-20	EF-40	AU-50	Unc-60	Unc-63	Unc-65
$35	$60	$100	$140	$225	$350	$525	$750

W-2526-G • F-2057G • Chicago • Part of W-2525-G printage

W-2526-G★ • F-2057G★

VG-8	F-12	VF-20	EF-40	AU-50	Unc-60	Unc-63	Unc-65
$35	$60	$100	$140	$225	$300	$425	$625

W-2526-H • F-2057H • St. Louis • Part of W-2525-H printage

W-2526-H★ • F-2057H★

VG-8	F-12	VF-20	EF-40	AU-50	Unc-60	Unc-63	Unc-65
$35	$65	$110	$150	$250	$325	$450	$650

W-2526-I • F-2057I • Minneapolis • Part of W-2525-I printage

VF-20	EF-40	AU-50	Unc-60	Unc-63	Unc-65
$30	$40	$60	$75	$100	$130

W-2526-I★ • F-2057I★

VG-8	F-12	VF-20	EF-40	AU-50	Unc-60	Unc-63	Unc-65
$35	$60	$100	$150	$250	$325	$450	$650

W-2526-J • F-2057J • Kansas City • Part of W-2525-J printage

W-2526-J★ • F-2057J★

VG-8	F-12	VF-20	EF-40	AU-50	Unc-60	Unc-63	Unc-65
$30	$50	$80	$150	$250	$325	$450	$650

W-2526-K • F-2057K • Dallas • Part of W-2525-K printage

W-2526-K★ • F-2057K★

VG-8	F-12	VF-20	EF-40	AU-50	Unc-60	Unc-63	Unc-65
$45	$75	$125	$170	$270	$350	$450	$650

W-2526-L • F-2057L • San Francisco • Part of W-2525-L printage

W-2526-L★ • F-2057L★

VG-8	F-12	VF-20	EF-40	AU-50	Unc-60	Unc-63	Unc-65
$35	$60	$100	$150	$250	$325	$450	$650

Series of 1934-D, Green Seal, Wide Back
Clark-Snyder (1949–1953)

This series continued the preceding design.

The difference between the Wide Back and the Narrow Back styles is almost microscopic. On the Wide Back the foliage does not touch the ornament below the plate number. On the Narrow Back it does touch. The Wide Back plate numbers are up to 669. The Narrow Back plate numbers are 670 and higher.

Prices for a typical note for this series, unless listed otherwise, are as follows:

EF-40	AU-50	Unc-60	Unc-63	Unc-65
$30	$40	$55	$75	$100

W-2527-A • F-2058A • Boston • 4,520,000

EF-40	AU-50	Unc-60	Unc-63	Unc-65
$30	$45	$70	$90	$125

W-2527-A★ • F-2058A★

VG-8	F-12	VF-20	EF-40	AU-50	Unc-60	Unc-63	Unc-65
$50	$95	$185	$300	$500	$775	$1,000	$1,450

W-2527-B • F-2058B • New York • 27,894,260

EF-40	AU-50	Unc-60	Unc-63	Unc-65
$30	$40	$50	$65	$85

W-2527-B★ • F-2058B★

VG-8	F-12	VF-20	EF-40	AU-50	Unc-60	Unc-63
$60	$110	$225	$400	$700	$925	$1,300

W-2527-C • F-2058C • Philadelphia • 6,022,428

W-2527-C★ • F-2058C★

VG-8	F-12	VF-20	EF-40	AU-50	Unc-60	Unc-63
$60	$110	$225	$400	$700	$975	$1,300

W-2527-D • F-2058D • Cleveland • 8,981,688

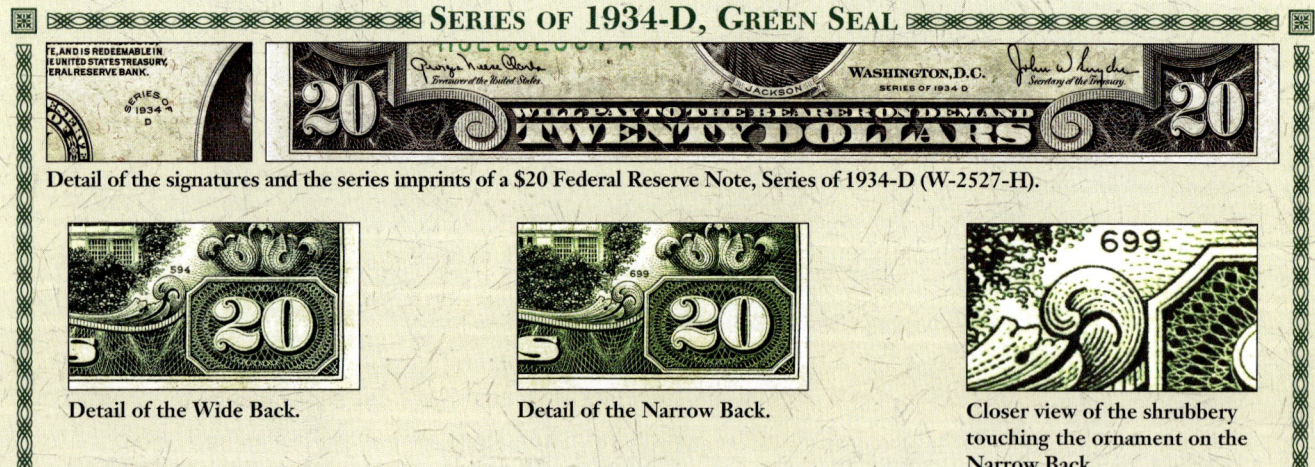

SERIES OF 1934-D, GREEN SEAL

Detail of the signatures and the series imprints of a $20 Federal Reserve Note, Series of 1934-D (W-2527-H).

Detail of the Wide Back.

Detail of the Narrow Back.

Closer view of the shrubbery touching the ornament on the Narrow Back.

W-2527-D★ • F-2058D★

VG-8	F-12	VF-20	EF-40	AU-50	Unc-60	Unc-63	Unc-65
$40	$80	$140	$300	$500	$775	$1,000	$1,500

W-2527-E • F-2058E • Richmond • 17,055,984

W-2527-E★ • F-2058E★

VG-8	F-12	VF-20	EF-40	AU-50	Unc-60	Unc-63	Unc-65
$35	$75	$125	$300	$500	$725	$1,000	$1,500

W-2527-F • F-2058F • Atlanta • 7,495,440

W-2527-F★ • F-2058F★

VG-8	F-12	VF-20	EF-40	AU-50	Unc-60	Unc-63
$60	$110	$225	$400	$700	$975	$1,300

W-2527-G • F-2058G • Chicago • 15,187,596

EF-40	AU-50	Unc-60	Unc-63	Unc-65
$30	$40	$50	$65	$85

W-2527-G★ • F-2058G★

VG-8	F-12	VF-20	EF-40	AU-50	Unc-60	Unc-63	Unc-65
$35	$60	$100	$175	$280	$450	$650	$1,000

W-2527-H • F-2058H • St. Louis • 5,923,248

W-2527-H★ • F-2058H★

VG-8	F-12	VF-20	EF-40	AU-50	Unc-60	Unc-63
$60	$110	$225	$400	$700	$975	$1,300

W-2527-I • F-2058I • Minneapolis • 2,422,416

EF-40	AU-50	Unc-60	Unc-63	Unc-65
$35	$50	$75	$100	$135

W-2527-I★ • F-2058I★ • Not located

W-2527-J • F-2058J • Kansas City • 4,211,904

W-2527-J★ • F-2058J★

VG-8	F-12	VF-20	EF-40	AU-50	Unc-60	Unc-63
$90	$190	$300	$525	$850	$1,200	$1,500

W-2527-K • F-2058K • Dallas • 3,707,364

W-2527-K★ • F-2058K★ • Not located

W-2527-L • F-2058L • San Francisco • 12,015,228

W-2527-L★ • F-2058L★

VG-8	F-12	VF-20	EF-40	AU-50	Unc-60	Unc-63	Unc-65
$35	$75	$125	$300	$500	$750	$950	$1,400

Series of 1934-D, Green Seal, Narrow Back
Clark-Snyder (1949–1953)

This series continued the preceding design.

See the preceding listing for description of back differences. This is a very interesting variety, with only star notes known from Boston (A), and only regular notes from the other Federal Reserve Banks. John Schwartz and Scott Lindquist report that printing of the Narrow Back notes began in July 1950, with plate numbers of 670 and higher.

Prices for a typical note for this series, unless listed otherwise, are as follows:

VF-20	EF-40	AU-50	Unc-60	Unc-63	Unc-65
$35	$55	$80	$130	$180	$225

W-2529-A★ • F-2058A★ • Boston

VG-8	F-12	VF-20	EF-40	AU-50	Unc-60	Unc-63	Unc-65
$85	$150	$250	$375	$500	$800	$1,000	$1,500

W-2529-B • F-2058B • New York • Part of W-2527-B printage

VF-20	EF-40	AU-50	Unc-60	Unc-63	Unc-65
$35	$55	$80	$100	$125	$160

W-2529-C • F-2058C • Philadelphia • Part of W-2527-C printage

W-2529-D • F-2058D • Cleveland • Part of W-2527-D printage

W-2529-E • F-2058E • Richmond • Part of W-2527-E printage

W-2529-F • F-2058F • Atlanta • Part of W-2527-F printage

W-2529-G • F-2058G • Chicago • Part of W-2527-G printage

VF-20	EF-40	AU-50	Unc-60	Unc-63	Unc-65
$35	$55	$80	$100	$125	$160

W-2529-H • F-2058H • St. Louis • Part of W-2527-H printage

W-2529-I • F-2058I • Minneapolis • Part of W-2527-I printage

VF-20	EF-40	AU-50	Unc-60	Unc-63	Unc-65
$50	$70	$100	$175	$225	$300

W-2529-J • F-2058J • Kansas City • Part of W-2527-J printage

W-2529-K • F-2058K • Dallas • Part of W-2527-K printage

W-2529-L • F-2058L • San Francisco • Part of W-2527-L printage

Series of 1950, Green Seal
Clark-Snyder (1949–1953)

Beginning with this issue (illus. on p. 520) the Federal Reserve seal is smaller and has a spiked border. The wording above that seal reads, "This note is legal tender for all debts, public and private, and is redeemable in lawful money at the United States Treasury, or at any Federal Reserve Bank." The only series designation is at the lower right of the portrait.

Prices for a typical note for this series, unless listed otherwise, are as follows:

EF-40	AU-50	Unc-60	Unc-63	Unc-65
$30	$38	$50	$60	$80

W-2530-A • F-2059A • Boston • 23,184,000

W-2530-A★ • F-2059A★

VG-8	F-12	VF-20	EF-40	AU-50	Unc-60	Unc-63	Unc-65
$35	$65	$120	$150	$190	$240	$350	$550

W-2530-B • F-2059B • New York • 80,064,000

W-2530-B★ • F-2059B★

VG-8	F-12	VF-20	EF-40	AU-50	Unc-60	Unc-63	Unc-65
$30	$50	$85	$125	$175	$215	$300	$500

W-2530-C • F-2059C • Philadelphia • 29,520,000

W-2530-C★ • F-2059C★

VG-8	F-12	VF-20	EF-40	AU-50	Unc-60	Unc-63	Unc-65
$35	$60	$100	$140	$185	$250	$375	$550

W-2530-D • F-2059D • Cleveland • 51,120,000

W-2530-D★ • F-2059D★

VG-8	F-12	VF-20	EF-40	AU-50	Unc-60	Unc-63	Unc-65
$30	$50	$85	$125	$200	$280	$400	$650

W-2530-E • F-2059E • Richmond • 67,536,000

W-2530-E★ • F-2059E★

VG-8	F-12	VF-20	EF-40	AU-50	Unc-60	Unc-63	Unc-65
$30	$50	$85	$140	$250	$375	$500	$725

W-2530-F • F-2059F • Atlanta • 39,312,000

W-2530-F★ • F-2059F★

VG-8	F-12	VF-20	EF-40	AU-50	Unc-60	Unc-63	Unc-65
$35	$65	$120	$200	$320	$460	$625	$850

W-2530-G • F-2059G • Chicago • 70,464,000

W-2530-G★ • F-2059G★

VG-8	F-12	VF-20	EF-40	AU-50	Unc-60	Unc-63	Unc-65
$30	$50	$85	$140	$185	$250	$375	$550

W-2530-H • F-2059H • St. Louis • 27,352,000

W-2530-H★ • F-2059H★

VG-8	F-12	VF-20	EF-40	AU-50	Unc-60	Unc-63	Unc-65
$30	$50	$85	$140	$250	$375	$500	$725

W-2530-I • F-2059I • Minneapolis • 9,216,000

EF-40	AU-50	Unc-60	Unc-63	Unc-65
$35	$50	$65	$80	$180

W-2530-I★ • F-2059I★

VG-8	F-12	VF-20	EF-40	AU-50	Unc-60	Unc-63	Unc-65
$35	$65	$120	$220	$340	$485	$650	$875

W-2530-J • F-2059J • Kansas City • 22,752,000

W-2530-J★ • F-2059J★

VG-8	F-12	VF-20	EF-40	AU-50	Unc-60	Unc-63	Unc-65
$30	$50	$85	$180	$300	$400	$550	$775

W-2530-K • F-2059K • Dallas • 22,656,000

EF-40	AU-50	Unc-60	Unc-63	Unc-65
$30	$40	$55	$70	$95

W-2530-K★ • F-2059K★

VG-8	F-12	VF-20	EF-40	AU-50	Unc-60	Unc-63	Unc-65
$35	$60	$100	$200	$320	$460	$625	$850

W-2530-L • F-2059L • San Francisco • 70,272,000

W-2530-L★ • F-2059L★

VG-8	F-12	VF-20	EF-40	AU-50	Unc-60	Unc-63	Unc-65
$35	$60	$100	$150	$225	$300	$425	$675

Series of 1950-A, Green Seal
Priest-Humphrey (1953–1957)

This series continued the preceding design.

Prices for a typical note for this series, unless listed otherwise, are as follows:

EF-40	AU-50	Unc-60	Unc-63	Unc-65
$30	$35	$50	$60	$85

SERIES OF 1950, GREEN SEAL

$20 Federal Reserve Note, Series of 1950 (W-2530-B★). Federal Reserve Bank of New York. Star note. Standard back of the era, without motto.

W-2531-A • F-2060A • Boston • 19,656,000

W-2531-A★ • F-2060A★

VG-8	F-12	VF-20	EF-40	AU-50	Unc-60	Unc-63	Unc-65
$35	$60	$90	$125	$150	$200	$250	$375

W-2531-B • F-2060B • New York • 82,568,000

EF-40	AU-50	Unc-60	Unc-63	Unc-65
$30	$35	$45	$55	$75

W-2531-B★ • F-2060B★

VG-8	F-12	VF-20	EF-40	AU-50	Unc-60	Unc-63	Unc-65
$30	$45	$70	$100	$140	$190	$250	$375

W-2531-C • F-2060C • Philadelphia • 16,560,000

W-2531-C★ • F-2060C★

VG-8	F-12	VF-20	EF-40	AU-50	Unc-60	Unc-63	Unc-65
$30	$45	$70	$100	$140	$190	$250	$375

W-2531-D • F-2060D • Cleveland • 50,320,000

W-2531-D★ • F-2060D★

VG-8	F-12	VF-20	EF-40	AU-50	Unc-60	Unc-63	Unc-65
$30	$45	$70	$100	$140	$190	$250	$375

W-2531-E • F-2060E • Richmond • 69,544,000

W-2531-E★ • F-2060E★

VG-8	F-12	VF-20	EF-40	AU-50	Unc-60	Unc-63	Unc-65
$30	$45	$70	$100	$140	$190	$250	$375

W-2531-F • F-2060F • Atlanta • 27,648,000

W-2531-F★ • F-2060F★

VG-8	F-12	VF-20	EF-40	AU-50	Unc-60	Unc-63	Unc-65
$30	$45	$70	$100	$140	$190	$250	$375

W-2531-G • F-2060G • Chicago • 73,720,000

EF-40	AU-50	Unc-60	Unc-63	Unc-65
$30	$35	$45	$55	$75

W-2531-G★ • F-2060G★

VG-8	F-12	VF-20	EF-40	AU-50	Unc-60	Unc-63	Unc-65
$30	$45	$70	$100	$140	$180	$225	$340

W-2531-H • F-2060H • St. Louis • 22,680,000

W-2531-H★ • F-2060H★

VG-8	F-12	VF-20	EF-40	AU-50	Unc-60	Unc-63	Unc-65
$30	$45	$70	$100	$140	$190	$250	$375

W-2531-I • F-2060I • Minneapolis • 5,544,000

EF-40	AU-50	Unc-60	Unc-63	Unc-65
$30	$50	$60	$75	$100

W-2531-I★ • F-2060I★

VG-8	F-12	VF-20	EF-40	AU-50	Unc-60	Unc-63	Unc-65
$30	$45	$70	$100	$165	$220	$300	$430

W-2531-J • F-2060J • Kansas City • 22,968,000

W-2531-J★ • F-2060J★

VG-8	F-12	VF-20	EF-40	AU-50	Unc-60	Unc-63	Unc-65
$30	$45	$70	$100	$150	$200	$275	$400

W-2531-K • F-2060K • Dallas • 10,728,000

W-2531-K★ • F-2060K★

VG-8	F-12	VF-20	EF-40	AU-50	Unc-60	Unc-63	Unc-65
$30	$45	$70	$100	$150	$200	$275	$400

W-2531-L • F-2060L • San Francisco • 85,528,000

EF-40	AU-50	Unc-60	Unc-63	Unc-65
$30	$35	$45	$55	$75

W-2531-L★ • F-2060L★

VG-8	F-12	VF-20	EF-40	AU-50	Unc-60	Unc-63	Unc-65
$30	$45	$70	$100	$140	$200	$275	$400

Series of 1950-B, Green Seal
Priest-Anderson (1957–1961)

This series continued the preceding design.

W-2532-A • F-2061A • Boston • 5,040,000

AU-50	Unc-60	Unc-63	Unc-65
$30	$45	$60	$80

W-2532-A★ • F-2061A★

VF-20	EF-40	AU-50	Unc-60	Unc-63	Unc-65
$100	$145	$200	$300	$400	$550

SERIES OF 1950-A, GREEN SEAL

Signatures and series imprint of a $20 Federal Reserve Note, Series of 1950-A (W-2531-B). The back is the standard type of the era.

SERIES OF 1950-B, GREEN SEAL

Signatures and series imprint of a $20 Federal Reserve Note, Series of 1950-B (W-2532-B). The back is the standard type of the era.

W-2532-B • F-2061B • New York • 49,960,000

AU-50	Unc-60	Unc-63	Unc-65
$25	$35	$50	$70

W-2532-B★ • F-2061B★

VF-20	EF-40	AU-50	Unc-60	Unc-63	Unc-65
$75	$90	$125	$165	$225	$300

W-2532-C • F-2061C • Philadelphia • 7,920,000

AU-50	Unc-60	Unc-63	Unc-65
$25	$40	$55	$75

W-2532-C★ • F-2061C★

VF-20	EF-40	AU-50	Unc-60	Unc-63	Unc-65
$75	$90	$125	$165	$225	$300

W-2532-D • F-2061D • Cleveland • 38,160,000

AU-50	Unc-60	Unc-63	Unc-65
$25	$40	$55	$75

W-2532-D★ • F-2061D★

VF-20	EF-40	AU-50	Unc-60	Unc-63	Unc-65
$80	$95	$135	$185	$250	$325

W-2532-E • F-2061E • Richmond • 42,120,000

AU-50	Unc-60	Unc-63	Unc-65
$25	$40	$55	$75

W-2532-E★ • F-2061E★

VF-20	EF-40	AU-50	Unc-60	Unc-63	Unc-65
$100	$145	$200	$300	$400	$550

W-2532-F • F-2061F • Atlanta • 40,240,000

AU-50	Unc-60	Unc-63	Unc-65
$25	$40	$55	$75

W-2532-F★ • F-2061F★

VF-20	EF-40	AU-50	Unc-60	Unc-63	Unc-65
$90	$115	$150	$225	$300	$375

W-2532-G • F-2061G • Chicago • 80,560,000

AU-50	Unc-60	Unc-63	Unc-65
$25	$35	$50	$70

W-2532-G★ • F-2061G★

VF-20	EF-40	AU-50	Unc-60	Unc-63	Unc-65
$75	$90	$125	$165	$225	$300

W-2532-H • F-2061H • St. Louis • 19,440,000

AU-50	Unc-60	Unc-63	Unc-65
$30	$40	$55	$75

W-2532-H★ • F-2061H★

VF-20	EF-40	AU-50	Unc-60	Unc-63	Unc-65
$80	$100	$135	$185	$250	$325

W-2532-I • F-2061I • Minneapolis • 12,240,000

AU-50	Unc-60	Unc-63	Unc-65
$30	$45	$60	$80

W-2532-I★ • F-2061I★

VF-20	EF-40	AU-50	Unc-60	Unc-63	Unc-65
$80	$95	$135	$185	$250	$325

W-2532-J • F-2061J • Kansas City • 28,440,000

AU-50	Unc-60	Unc-63	Unc-65
$25	$40	$55	$75

W-2532-J★ • F-2061J★

VF-20	EF-40	AU-50	Unc-60	Unc-63	Unc-65
$90	$115	$150	$225	$300	$375

W-2532-K • F-2061K • Dallas • 11,880,000

AU-50	Unc-60	Unc-63	Unc-65
$25	$40	$55	$75

W-2532-K★ • F-2061K★

VF-20	EF-40	AU-50	Unc-60	Unc-63	Unc-65
$90	$115	$150	$225	$300	$375

W-2532-L • F-2061L • San Francisco • 51,040,000

AU-50	Unc-60	Unc-63	Unc-65
$25	$35	$50	$70

W-2532-L★ • F-2061L★

VF-20	EF-40	AU-50	Unc-60	Unc-63	Unc-65
$90	$115	$150	$225	$300	$375

Series of 1950-C, Green Seal
Smith-Dillon (1961–1962)

This series continued the preceding design.

W-2533-A • F-2062A • Boston • 7,200,000

Unc-60	Unc-63	Unc-65
$45	$60	$80

W-2533-A★ • F-2062A★

VF-20	EF-40	AU-50	Unc-60	Unc-63	Unc-65
$60	$85	$120	$170	$225	$300

W-2533-B • F-2062B • New York • 43,200,000

Unc-60	Unc-63	Unc-65
$35	$50	$70

W-2533-B★ • F-2062B★

VF-20	EF-40	AU-50	Unc-60	Unc-63	Unc-65
$50	$70	$100	$150	$200	$275

W-2533-C • F-2062C • Philadelphia • 7,560,000

Unc-60	Unc-63	Unc-65
$40	$60	$80

W-2533-C★ • F-2062C★

VF-20	EF-40	AU-50	Unc-60	Unc-63	Unc-65
$50	$70	$100	$150	$200	$275

W-2533-D • F-2062D • Cleveland • 28,440,000

Unc-60	Unc-63	Unc-65
$40	$60	$80

W-2533-D★ • F-2062D★

VF-20	EF-40	AU-50	Unc-60	Unc-63	Unc-65
$50	$70	$100	$150	$200	$275

W-2533-E • F-2062E • Richmond • 37,000,000

Unc-60	Unc-63	Unc-65
$35	$55	$75

W-2533-E★ • F-2062E★

VF-20	EF-40	AU-50	Unc-60	Unc-63	Unc-65
$60	$85	$120	$170	$225	$300

W-2533-F • F-2062F • Atlanta • 19,080,000

Unc-60	Unc-63	Unc-65
$35	$55	$75

W-2533-F★ • F-2062F★

VF-20	EF-40	AU-50	Unc-60	Unc-63	Unc-65
$50	$70	$100	$150	$200	$275

W-2533-G • F-2062G • Chicago • 29,160,000

Unc-60	Unc-63	Unc-65
$35	$50	$70

W-2533-G★ • F-2062G★

VF-20	EF-40	AU-50	Unc-60	Unc-63	Unc-65
$40	$60	$90	$130	$175	$250

W-2533-H • F-2062H • St. Louis • 12,960,000

Unc-60	Unc-63	Unc-65
$35	$55	$70

W-2533-H★ • F-2062H★

VF-20	EF-40	AU-50	Unc-60	Unc-63	Unc-65
$60	$85	$120	$170	$225	$300

W-2533-I • F-2062I • Minneapolis • 6,480,000

Unc-60	Unc-63	Unc-65
$40	$60	$80

W-2533-I★ • F-2062I★

VF-20	EF-40	AU-50	Unc-60	Unc-63	Unc-65
$150	$200	$275	$425	$550	$750

W-2533-J • F-2062J • Kansas City • 18,360,000

Unc-60	Unc-63	Unc-65
$35	$55	$75

W-2533-K • F-2062K • Dallas • 9,000,000

Unc-60	Unc-63	Unc-65
$35	$55	$75

W-2533-K★ • F-2062K★

VF-20	EF-40	AU-50	Unc-60	Unc-63	Unc-65
$50	$70	$100	$150	$200	$275

W-2533-L • F-2062L • San Francisco • 45,360,000

Unc-60	Unc-63	Unc-65
$35	$55	$75

W-2533-L★ • F-2062L★

VF-20	EF-40	AU-50	Unc-60	Unc-63	Unc-65
$50	$70	$100	$150	$200	$275

Series of 1950-D, Green Seal
Granahan-Dillon (1963–1965)

This series continued the preceding design.

Prices for a typical star note for this series, unless listed otherwise, are as follows:

VF-20	EF-40	AU-50	Unc-60	Unc-63	Unc-65
$60	$85	$130	$200	$275	$375

W-2534-A • F-2063A • Boston • 9,320,000

AU-50	Unc-60	Unc-63	Unc-65
$35	$50	$65	$85

SERIES OF 1950-C, GREEN SEAL

Signatures and series imprint of a $20 Federal Reserve Note, Series of 1950-C (W-2533-D). The back is the standard type of the era.

SERIES OF 1950-D, GREEN SEAL

Signatures and series imprint of a $20 Federal Reserve Note, Series of 1950-D (W-2534-G). The back is the standard type of the era.

W-2534-A★ • F-2063A★

VF-20	EF-40	AU-50	Unc-60	Unc-63	Unc-65
$60	$85	$130	$200	$275	$360

W-2534-B • F-2063B • New York • 64,280,000

AU-50	Unc-60	Unc-63	Unc-65
$25	$40	$55	$75

W-2534-B★ • F-2063B★

VF-20	EF-40	AU-50	Unc-60	Unc-63	Unc-65
$55	$75	$110	$175	$225	$300

W-2534-C • F-2063C • Philadelphia • 5,400,000

AU-50	Unc-60	Unc-63	Unc-65
$35	$45	$60	$80

W-2534-C★ • F-2063C★

W-2534-D • F-2063D • Cleveland • 23,760,000

AU-50	Unc-60	Unc-63	Unc-65
$25	$35	$50	$70

W-2534-D★ • F-2063D★

F-12	VF-20	EF-40	AU-50	Unc-60	Unc-63	Unc-65
$70	$100	$140	$190	$270	$350	$475

W-2534-E • F-2063E • Richmond • 30,240,000

AU-50	Unc-60	Unc-63	Unc-65
$25	$35	$50	$70

W-2534-E★ • F-2063E★

W-2534-F • F-2063F • Atlanta • 22,680,000

AU-50	Unc-60	Unc-63	Unc-65
$25	$35	$50	$70

W-2534-F★ • F-2063F★

W-2534-G • F-2063G • Chicago • 67,960,000

AU-50	Unc-60	Unc-63	Unc-65
$25	$35	$50	$70

W-2534-G★ • F-2063G★

VF-20	EF-40	AU-50	Unc-60	Unc-63	Unc-65
$45	$70	$100	$150	$225	$325

W-2534-H • F-2063H • St. Louis • 6,120,000

AU-50	Unc-60	Unc-63	Unc-65
$35	$45	$60	$80

W-2534-H★ • F-2063H★

W-2534-I • F-2063I • Minneapolis • 3,240,000

AU-50	Unc-60	Unc-63	Unc-65
$35	$50	$65	$85

W-2534-I★ • F-2063I★

W-2534-J • F-2063J • Kansas City • 8,200,000

AU-50	Unc-60	Unc-63	Unc-65
$25	$35	$50	$70

W-2534-J★ • F-2063J★

W-2534-K • F-2063K • Dallas • 6,480,000

AU-50	Unc-60	Unc-63	Unc-65
$35	$50	$65	$85

W-2534-K★ • F-2063K★

W-2534-L • F-2063L • San Francisco • 69,400,000

AU-50	Unc-60	Unc-63	Unc-65
$35	$45	$60	$80

W-2534-L★ • F-2063L★

Series of 1950-E, Green Seal
Granahan-Fowler (1965–1966)

This series continued the preceding design.

W-2535-B • F-2064B • New York • 8,640,000

VF-20	EF-40	AU-50	Unc-60	Unc-63	Unc-65
$45	$60	$70	$80	$100	$145

W-2535-B★ • F-2064B★

F-12	VF-20	EF-40	AU-50	Unc-60	Unc-63	Unc-65
$110	$185	$270	$350	$500	$650	$850

W-2535-G • F-2064G • Chicago • 9,360,000

VF-20	EF-40	AU-50	Unc-60	Unc-63	Unc-65
$55	$70	$85	$110	$140	$175

W-2535-G★ • F-2064G★

F-12	VF-20	EF-40	AU-50	Unc-60	Unc-63	Unc-65
$200	$325	$500	$690	$840	$1,100	$1,450

W-2535-L • F-2064L • San Francisco • 8,640,000

VF-20	EF-40	AU-50	Unc-60	Unc-63	Unc-65
$55	$70	$85	$110	$140	$175

SERIES OF 1950-E, GREEN SEAL

Signatures and series imprint of a $20 Federal Reserve Note, Series of 1950-E (W-2535-L). The back is the standard type of the era.

W-2535-L★ • F-2064L★

F-12	VF-20	EF-40	AU-50	Unc-60	Unc-63	Unc-65
$140	$200	$300	$375	$530	$680	$900

Series of 1963, Green Seal
Granahan-Dillon (1963–1965)

This series was redesigned slightly. The obligation now reads, "This note is legal tender for all debts, public and private." The motto IN GOD WE TRUST appears on the back.

Prices for a typical note for this series, unless listed otherwise, are as follows:

Unc-60	Unc-63	Unc-65
$60	$85	$120

W-2536-A • F-2065A • Boston • 2,560,000

W-2536-A★ • F-2065A★

VF-20	EF-40	AU-50	Unc-60	Unc-63	Unc-65
$55	$80	$105	$160	$210	$285

W-2536-B • F-2065B • New York • 16,640,000

Unc-60	Unc-63	Unc-65
$50	$70	$105

W-2536-B★ • F-2065B★

VF-20	EF-40	AU-50	Unc-60	Unc-63	Unc-65
$25	$30	$50	$85	$135	$190

W-2536-D • F-2065D • Cleveland • 7,680,000

W-2536-D★ • F-2065D★

VF-20	EF-40	AU-50	Unc-60	Unc-63	Unc-65
$60	$95	$130	$200	$250	$325

W-2536-E • F-2065E • Richmond • 4,480,000

W-2536-E★ • F-2065E★

VF-20	EF-40	AU-50	Unc-60	Unc-63	Unc-65
$45	$65	$90	$130	$175	$250

W-2536-F • F-2065F • Atlanta • 10,240,000

W-2536-F★ • F-2065F★

VF-20	EF-40	AU-50	Unc-60	Unc-63	Unc-65
$45	$65	$90	$130	$175	$250

W-2536-G • F-2065G • Chicago • 2,560,000

W-2536-G★ • F-2065G★

VF-20	EF-40	AU-50	Unc-60	Unc-63	Unc-65
$40	$60	$95	$140	$190	$270

W-2536-H • F-2065H • St. Louis • 3,200,000

W-2536-H★ • F-2065H★

VF-20	EF-40	AU-50	Unc-60	Unc-63	Unc-65
$50	$70	$95	$150	$200	$280

$20 Federal Reserve Note, Series of 1963 (W-2536-B★). Federal Reserve Bank of New York. Star note.

Back of the $20 Federal Reserve Note, Series of 1963, which introduces the motto IN GOD WE TRUST high above the White House. This became the new standard.

Detail showing the motto.

W-2536-J • F-2065J • Kansas City • 3,840,000

Unc-60	Unc-63	Unc-65
$70	$95	$130

W-2536-J★ • F-2065J★

VF-20	EF-40	AU-50	Unc-60	Unc-63	Unc-65
$50	$70	$95	$150	$200	$280

W-2536-K • F-2065K • Dallas • 2,560,000

W-2536-K★ • F-2065K★

VF-20	EF-40	AU-50	Unc-60	Unc-63	Unc-65
$50	$70	$95	$150	$200	$280

W-2536-L • F-2065L • San Francisco • 7,040,000

W-2536-L★ • F-2065L★

VF-20	EF-40	AU-50	Unc-60	Unc-63	Unc-65
$30	$50	$65	$100	$150	$210

Series of 1963-A, Green Seal
Granahan-Fowler (1965–1966)

This series continued the preceding design.

Prices for a typical note for this series, unless listed otherwise, are as follows:

Unc-60	Unc-63	Unc-65
$45	$60	$80

Prices for a typical star note for this series, unless listed otherwise, are as follows:

EF-40	AU-50	Unc-60	Unc-63	Unc-65
$40	$65	$100	$140	$175

W-2537-A • F-2066A • Boston • 32,680,000

W-2537-A★ • F-2066A★ • 1,280,000

W-2537-B • F-2066B • New York • 93,600,000

W-2537-B★ • F-2066B★ • 3,840,000

W-2537-C • F-2066C • Philadelphia • 17,920,000

W-2537-C★ • F-2066C★ • 640,000

W-2537-D • F-2066D • Cleveland • 68,480,000

W-2537-D★ • F-2066D★ • 2,560,000

W-2537-E • F-2066E • Richmond • 128,800,000

W-2537-E★ • F-2066E★ • 5,760,000

W-2537-F • F-2066F • Atlanta • 42,880,000

W-2537-F★ • F-2066F★ • 1,920,000

W-2537-G • F-2066G • Chicago • 156,320,000

W-2537-G★ • F-2066G★ • 7,040,000

W-2537-H • F-2066H • St. Louis • 34,560,000

W-2537-H★ • F-2066H★ • 1,920,000

W-2537-I • F-2066I • Minneapolis • 10,240,000

W-2537-I★ • F-2066I★ • 640,000

W-2537-J • F-2066J • Kansas City • 37,120,000

W-2537-J★ • F-2066J★ • 1,920,000

W-2537-K • F-2066K • Dallas • 38,400,000

W-2537-K★ • F-2066K★ • 1,280,000

W-2537-L • F-2066L • San Francisco • 169,120,000

W-2537-L★ • F-2066L★ • 8,320,000

Series of 1969, Green Seal
Elston-Kennedy (1969–1970)

The Series of 1969 features a redesigned Treasury seal with the inscription THE DEPARTMENT OF THE TREASURY 1789, replacing the earlier style with the Latin wording, THESAUR. AMER. SEPTENT. SIGIL. The design in the interior of the seal was modified as well.

Prices for a typical note for this series, unless listed otherwise, are as follows:

Unc-60	Unc-63	Unc-65
$40	$55	$75

Prices for a typical star note for this series, unless listed otherwise, are as follows:

EF-40	AU-50	Unc-60	Unc-63	Unc-65
$40	$65	$100	$140	$175

W-2538-A • F-2067A • Boston • 19,200,000

W-2538-A★ • F-2067A★ • 1,280,000

W-2538-B • F-2067B • New York • 106,400,000

W-2538-B★ • F-2067B★ • 5,106,000

EF-40	AU-50	Unc-60	Unc-63	Unc-65
$35	$55	$90	$130	$160

W-2538-C • F-2067C • Philadelphia • 10,880,000

W-2538-C★ • F-2067C★ • 1,280,000

W-2538-D • F-2067D • Cleveland • 60,160,000

W-2538-D★ • F-2067D★ • 2,560,000

W-2538-E • F-2067E • Richmond • 66,560,000

W-2538-E★ • F-2067E★ • 2,560,000

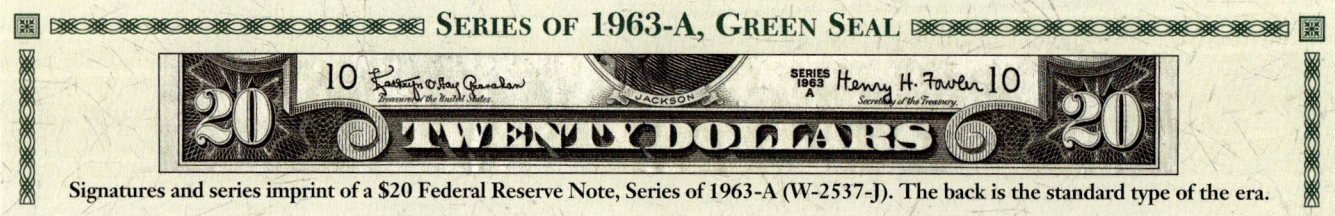

SERIES OF 1963-A, GREEN SEAL

Signatures and series imprint of a $20 Federal Reserve Note, Series of 1963-A (W-2537-J). The back is the standard type of the era.

W-2538-F • F-2067F • Atlanta • 36,480,000

W-2538-F★ • F-2067F★ • 1,280,000

W-2538-G • F-2067G • Chicago • 107,680,000

Unc-60	Unc-63	Unc-65
$35	$50	$65

W-2538-G★ • F-2067G★ • 3,200,000

EF-40	AU-50	Unc-60	Unc-63	Unc-65
$35	$55	$90	$130	$160

W-2538-H • F-2067H • St. Louis • 19,200,000

W-2538-H★ • F-2067H★ • 640,000

W-2538-I • F-2067I • Minneapolis • 12,160,000

W-2538-I★ • F-2067I★ • 640,000

W-2538-J • F-2067J • Kansas City • 39,040,000

W-2538-J★ • F-2067J★ • 1,280,000

W-2538-K • F-2067K • Dallas • 25,600,000

W-2538-K★ • F-2067K★ • 640,000

W-2538-L • F-2067L • San Francisco • 103,840,000

W-2538-L★ • F-2067L★ • 5,120,000

EF-40	AU-50	Unc-60	Unc-63	Unc-65
$35	$55	$90	$130	$160

Series of 1969-A, Green Seal
Kabis-Connally (1971)

Dorothy Andrews Elson married Walter L. Kabis during her term in office, and became Mrs. Kabis. This series (illus. on p. 528) continued the preceding design.

Prices for a typical note for this series, unless listed otherwise, are as follows:

Unc-60	Unc-63	Unc-65
$50	$65	$85

Prices for a typical star note for this series, unless listed otherwise, are as follows:

EF-40	AU-50	Unc-60	Unc-63	Unc-65
$35	$65	$100	$140	$175

W-2539-A • F-2068A • Boston • 13,440,000

W-2539-B • F-2068B • New York • 69,760,000

Unc-60	Unc-63	Unc-65
$45	$60	$80

W-2539-B★ • F-2068B★ • 2,460,000

EF-40	AU-50	Unc-60	Unc-63	Unc-65
$35	$55	$90	$115	$140

W-2539-C • F-2068C • Philadelphia • 13,440,000

W-2539-D • F-2068D • Cleveland • 29,440,000

W-2539-D★ • F-2068D★ • 640,000

W-2539-E • F-2068E • Richmond • 42,400,000

W-2539-E★ • F-2068E★ • 1,920,000

W-2539-F • F-2068F • Atlanta • 13,440,000

W-2539-G • F-2068G • Chicago • 81,640,000

Unc-60	Unc-63	Unc-65
$45	$60	$80

W-2539-G★ • F-2068G★ • 1,920,000

W-2539-H • F-2068H • St. Louis • 14,080,000

W-2539-H★ • F-2068H★ • 640,000

SERIES OF 1969, GREEN SEAL

$20 Federal Reserve Note, Series of 1969 (W-2538-B). Federal Reserve Bank of New York. The back is the standard for the era, with motto.

The old Treasury seal (this example has a yellow-green hue) with Latin wording (from an earlier series note).

The new Treasury seal with English wording (green hue).

W-2539-I • F-2068I • Minneapolis • 7,040,000

Unc-60	Unc-63	Unc-65
$60	$75	$100

W-2539-J • F-2068J • Kansas City • 16,040,000

W-2539-K • F-2068K • Dallas • 14,720,000

W-2539-K★ • F-2068K★ • 640,000

W-2539-L • F-2068L • San Francisco • 50,560,000

Unc-60	Unc-63	Unc-65
$45	$60	$80

W-2539-L★ • F-2068L★ • 1,280,000

EF-40	AU-50	Unc-60	Unc-63	Unc-65
$35	$55	$90	$115	$140

Series of 1969-B, Green Seal
Banuelos-Connally (1971–1972)

This series continued the preceding design.

W-2540-B • F-2069B • New York • 39,200,000

Unc-60	Unc-63	Unc-65
$155	$210	$260

W-2540-B★ • F-2069B★ • 480,000

F-12	VF-20	EF-40	AU-50	Unc-60	Unc-63	Unc-65
$45	$70	$110	$210	$400	$625	$875

W-2540-D • F-2069D • Cleveland • 6,400,000

Unc-60	Unc-63	Unc-65
$210	$275	$325

W-2540-E • F-2069E • Richmond • 27,520,000

Unc-60	Unc-63	Unc-65
$155	$210	$260

W-2540-F • F-2069F • Atlanta • 14,080,000

Unc-60	Unc-63	Unc-65
$155	$210	$260

W-2540-F★ • F-2069F★ • 640,000

F-12	VF-20	EF-40	AU-50	Unc-60	Unc-63	Unc-65
$55	$105	$235	$435	$750	$900	$1,150

W-2540-G • F-2069G • Chicago • 14,240,000

Unc-60	Unc-63	Unc-65
$155	$210	$260

W-2540-G★ • F-2069G★ • 1,112,000

F-12	VF-20	EF-40	AU-50	Unc-60	Unc-63	Unc-65
$50	$80	$175	$345	$600	$775	$1,000

W-2540-H • F-2069H • St. Louis • 5,120,000

Unc-60	Unc-63	Unc-65
$210	$275	$325

W-2540-I • F-2069I • Minneapolis • 2,560,000

Unc-60	Unc-63	Unc-65
$375	$450	$545

W-2540-J • F-2069J • Kansas City • 3,840,000

Unc-60	Unc-63	Unc-65
$250	$325	$385

W-2540-J★ • F-2069J★ • 640,000

F-12	VF-20	EF-40	AU-50	Unc-60	Unc-63	Unc-65
$65	$125	$275	$500	$775	$1,000	$1,250

W-2540-K • F-2069K • Dallas • 12,160,000

Unc-60	Unc-63	Unc-65
$150	$210	$260

W-2540-L • F-2069L • San Francisco • 26,000,000

Unc-60	Unc-63	Unc-65
$135	$175	$215

W-2540-L★ • F-2069L★ • 640,000

F-12	VF-20	EF-40	AU-50	Unc-60	Unc-63	Unc-65
$65	$125	$275	$500	$775	$1,000	$1,250

Series of 1969-C, Green Seal
Banuelos-Shultz (1972–1974)

This series continued the preceding design.

SERIES OF 1969-A, GREEN SEAL

Signatures and series imprint of a $20 Federal Reserve Note, Series of 1969-A (W-2539-E). The back is the standard type of the era.

SERIES OF 1969-B, GREEN SEAL

Signatures and series imprint of a $20 Federal Reserve Note, Series of 1969-B (W-2540-D). The back is the standard type of the era.

Prices for a typical note for this series, unless listed otherwise, are as follows:

Unc-60	Unc-63	Unc-65
$35	$50	$65

W-2541-A • F-2070A • Boston • 17,280,000

W-2541-A★ • F-2070A★ • 640,000

EF-40	AU-50	Unc-60	Unc-63	Unc-65
$30	$45	$90	$115	$145

W-2541-B • F-2070B • New York • 135,200,000

W-2541-B★ • F-2070B★ • 1,640,000

EF-40	AU-50	Unc-60	Unc-63	Unc-65
$25	$40	$75	$100	$130

W-2541-C • F-2070C • Philadelphia • 40,960,000

W-2541-C★ • F-2070C★ • 640,000

EF-40	AU-50	Unc-60	Unc-63	Unc-65
$30	$45	$90	$115	$145

W-2541-D • F-2070D • Cleveland • 57,760,000

W-2541-D★ • F-2070D★ • 480,000

EF-40	AU-50	Unc-60	Unc-63	Unc-65
$35	$50	$95	$120	$150

W-2541-E • F-2070E • Richmond • 80,160,000

W-2541-E★ • F-2070E★ • 1,920,000

EF-40	AU-50	Unc-60	Unc-63	Unc-65
$25	$40	$75	$100	$130

W-2541-F • F-2070F • Atlanta • 35,840,000

W-2541-F★ • F-2070F★ • 640,000

EF-40	AU-50	Unc-60	Unc-63	Unc-65
$30	$45	$90	$115	$145

W-2541-G • F-2070G • Chicago • 78,720,000

W-2541-G★ • F-2070G★ • 640,000

EF-40	AU-50	Unc-60	Unc-63	Unc-65
$30	$45	$90	$115	$145

W-2541-H • F-2070H • St. Louis • 33,920,000

W-2541-H★ • F-2070H★ • 640,000

EF-40	AU-50	Unc-60	Unc-63	Unc-65
$45	$70	$120	$150	$190

W-2541-I • F-2070I • Minneapolis • 14,080,000

Unc-60	Unc-63	Unc-65
$50	$65	$80

W-2541-I★ • F-2070I★ • 640,000

EF-40	AU-50	Unc-60	Unc-63	Unc-65
$30	$45	$90	$115	$145

W-2541-J • F-2070J • Kansas City • 32,000,000

W-2541-J★ • F-2070J★ • 640,000

EF-40	AU-50	Unc-60	Unc-63	Unc-65
$45	$70	$120	$150	$190

W-2541-K • F-2070K • Dallas • 31,360,000

W-2541-K★ • F-2070K★ • 1,920,000

EF-40	AU-50	Unc-60	Unc-63	Unc-65
$30	$45	$75	$100	$130

W-2541-L • F-2070L • San Francisco • 82,080,000

W-2541-L★ • F-2070L★ • 1,120,000

EF-40	AU-50	Unc-60	Unc-63	Unc-65
$35	$50	$95	$120	$150

Series of 1974, Green Seal
Neff-Simon (1974–1977)

This series continued the preceding design.

Prices for a typical note for this series, unless listed otherwise, are as follows:

Unc-60	Unc-63	Unc-65
$40	$55	$75

W-2542-A • F-2071A • Boston • 56,960,000

W-2542-A★ • F-2071A★ • 768,000

Unc-60	Unc-63	Unc-65
$70	$95	$125

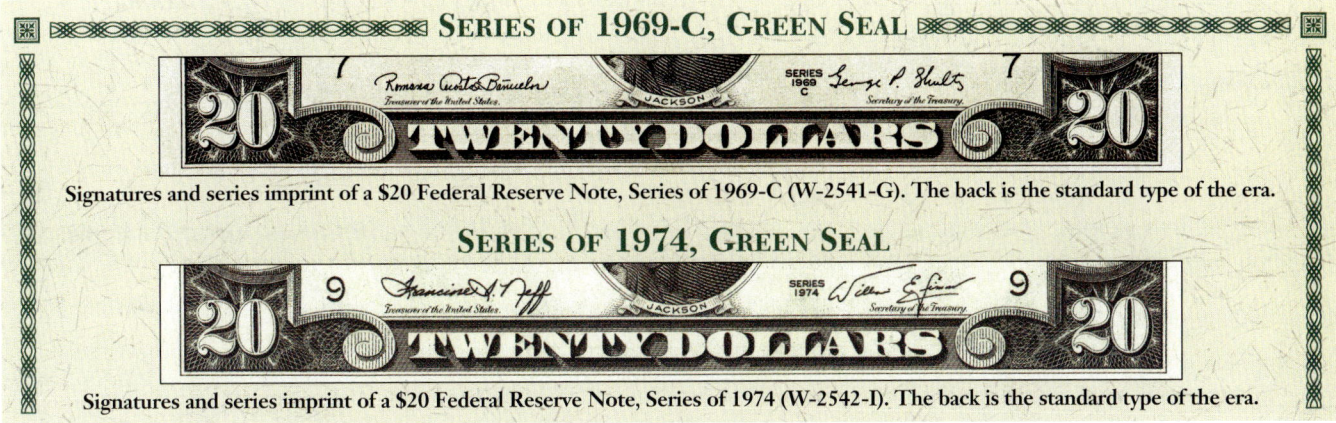

SERIES OF 1969-C, GREEN SEAL

Signatures and series imprint of a $20 Federal Reserve Note, Series of 1969-C (W-2541-G). The back is the standard type of the era.

SERIES OF 1974, GREEN SEAL

Signatures and series imprint of a $20 Federal Reserve Note, Series of 1974 (W-2542-I). The back is the standard type of the era.

W-2542-B • F-2071B • New York • 296,640,000

Unc-60	Unc-63	Unc-65
$30	$45	$65

W-2542-B★ • F-2071B★ • 7,616,000

Unc-60	Unc-63	Unc-65
$35	$60	$90

W-2542-C • F-2071C • Philadelphia • 59,680,000

W-2542-C★ • F-2071C★ • 1,760,000

Unc-60	Unc-63	Unc-65
$80	$105	$135

W-2542-D • F-2071D • Cleveland • 148,000,000

W-2542-D★ • F-2071D★ • 3,296,000

Unc-60	Unc-63	Unc-65
$80	$105	$135

W-2542-E • F-2071E • Richmond • 149,920,000

Unc-60	Unc-63	Unc-65
$30	$45	$65

W-2542-E★ • F-2071E★ • 3,040,000

Unc-60	Unc-63	Unc-65
$80	$105	$135

W-2542-F • F-2071F • Atlanta • 53,280,000

W-2542-F★ • F-2071F★ • 480,000

Unc-60	Unc-63	Unc-65
$90	$115	$145

W-2542-G • F-2071G • Chicago • 249,920,000

Unc-60	Unc-63	Unc-65
$30	$45	$65

W-2542-G★ • F-2071G★ • 4,608,000

Unc-60	Unc-63	Unc-65
$35	$60	$90

W-2542-H • F-2071H • St. Louis • 73,120,000

W-2542-H★ • F-2071H★ • 1,120,000

Unc-60	Unc-63	Unc-65
$65	$90	$120

W-2542-I • F-2071I • Minneapolis • 39,040,000

W-2542-I★ • F-2071I★ • 1,280,000

Unc-60	Unc-63	Unc-65
$65	$90	$120

W-2542-J • F-2071J • Kansas City • 74,400,000

W-2542-J★ • F-2071J★ • 736,000

Unc-60	Unc-63	Unc-65
$65	$90	$120

W-2542-K • F-2071K • Dallas • 68,640,000

W-2542-K★ • F-2071K★ • 608,000

Unc-60	Unc-63	Unc-65
$65	$90	$120

W-2542-L • F-2071L • San Francisco • 128,800,000

Unc-60	Unc-63	Unc-65
$30	$45	$65

W-2542-L★ • F-2071L★ • 4,320,000

Unc-60	Unc-63	Unc-65
$65	$90	$125

Series of 1977, Green Seal
Morton-Blumenthal (1977–1979)

This series continued the preceding design.

Prices for a typical note for this series, unless listed otherwise, are as follows:

Unc-60	Unc-63	Unc-65
$35	$50	$70

Prices for a typical star note for this series, unless listed otherwise, are as follows:

Unc-60	Unc-63	Unc-65
$60	$85	$115

W-2543-A • F-2072A • Boston • 94,720,000

W-2543-A★ • F-2072A★ • 2,688,000

W-2543-B • F-2072B • New York • 569,600,000

W-2543-B★ • F-2072B★ • 12,416,000

W-2543-C • F-2072C • Philadelphia • 117,760,000

W-2543-C★ • F-2072C★ • 2,176,000

W-2543-D • F-2072D • Cleveland • 189,440,000

W-2543-D★ • F-2072D★ • 5,632,000

W-2543-E • F-2072E • Richmond • 257,280,000

W-2543-E★ • F-2072E★ • 6,272,000

W-2543-F • F-2072F • Atlanta • 70,400,000

W-2543-F★ • F-2072F★ • 2,698,000

W-2543-G • F-2072G • Chicago • 358,400,000

SERIES OF 1977, GREEN SEAL

Signatures and series imprint of a $20 Federal Reserve Note, Series of 1977 (W-2543-D). The back is the standard type of the era.

W-2543-G★ • F-2072G★ • 7,552,000

W-2543-H • F-2072H • St. Louis • 98,560,000

W-2543-H★ • F-2072H★ • 1,792,000

W-2543-I • F-2072I • Minneapolis • 15,360,000

W-2543-I★ • F-2072I★ • 512,000

Unc-60	Unc-63	Unc-65
$80	$100	$135

W-2543-J • F-2072J • Kansas City • 148,480,000

W-2543-J★ • F-2072J★ • 4,864,000

W-2543-K • F-2072K • Dallas • 163,840,000

W-2543-K★ • F-2072K★ • 6,656,000

W-2543-L • F-2072L • San Francisco • 263,680,000

W-2543-L★ • F-2072L★ • 6,528,000

Series of 1981, Green Seal
Buchanan-Regan (1981–1983)

This series continued the preceding design.

Prices for a typical note for this series, unless listed otherwise, are as follows:

Unc-60	Unc-63	Unc-65
$50	$65	$85

Prices for a typical star note for this series, unless listed otherwise, are as follows:

Unc-60	Unc-63	Unc-65
$120	$150	$185

W-2544-A • F-2073A • Boston • 191,360,000

W-2544-A★ • F-2073A★ • 1,024,000

W-2544-B • F-2073B • New York • 559,360,000

Unc-60	Unc-63	Unc-65
$35	$50	$70

W-2544-B★ • F-2073B★ • 5,312,000

W-2544-C • F-2073C • Philadelphia • 146,560,000

W-2544-C★ • F-2073C★ • 1,280,000

W-2544-D • F-2073D • Cleveland • 146,560,000

W-2544-D★ • F-2073D★ • 1,280,000

W-2544-E • F-2073E • Richmond • 296,320,000

W-2544-E★ • F-2073E★ • 1,280,000

W-2544-F • F-2073F • Atlanta • 93,440,000

W-2544-F★ • F-2073F★ • 3,200,000

W-2544-G • F-2073G • Chicago • 361,600,000

W-2544-G★ • F-2073G★ • 2,688,000

W-2544-H • F-2073H • St. Louis • 76,160,000

W-2544-H★ • F-2073H★ • 1,536,000

W-2544-I • F-2073I • Minneapolis • 23,040,000

Unc-60	Unc-63	Unc-65
$70	$90	$125

W-2544-I★ • F-2073I★ • 256,000

AU-50	Unc-60	Unc-63	Unc-65
$95	$175	$230	$275

W-2544-J • F-2073J • Kansas City • 147,840,000

W-2544-J★ • F-2073J★ • 1,280,000

W-2544-K • F-2073K • Dallas • 95,360,000

W-2544-K★ • F-2073K★ • 896,000

W-2544-L • F-2073L • San Francisco • 404,480,000

W-2544-L★ • F-2073L★ • 1,424,000

Series of 1981-A, Green Seal
Ortega-Regan (1983–1985)

This series continued the preceding design.

Prices for a typical note for this series, unless listed otherwise, are as follows:

Unc-60	Unc-63	Unc-65
$40	$55	$75

Prices for a typical star note for this series, unless listed otherwise, are as follows:

Unc-60	Unc-63	Unc-65
$65	$90	$125

W-2545-A • F-2074A • Boston • 156,800,000

SERIES OF 1981, GREEN SEAL

Signatures and series imprint of a $20 Federal Reserve Note, Series of 1981 (W-2544-C). The back is the standard type of the era.

SERIES OF 1981-A, GREEN SEAL

Signatures and series imprint of a $20 Federal Reserve Note, Series of 1981-A (W-2545-F). The back is the standard type of the era.

W-2545-B • F-2074B • New York • 352,000,000

Unc-60	Unc-63	Unc-65
$30	$45	$65

W-2545-C • F-2074C • Philadelphia • 57,600,000

W-2545-D • F-2074D • Cleveland • 160,000,000

W-2545-D★ • F-2074D★ • 3,840,000

W-2545-E • F-2074E • Richmond • 214,400,000

W-2545-F • F-2074F • Atlanta • 140,800,000

W-2545-F★ • F-2074F★ • 3,200,000

W-2545-G • F-2074G • Chicago • 211,200,000

W-2545-H • F-2074H • St. Louis • 73,600,000

W-2545-I • F-2074I • Minneapolis • 19,200,000

W-2545-J • F-2074J • Kansas City • 86,400,000

W-2545-K • F-2074K • Dallas • 99,200,000

W-2545-L • F-2074L • San Francisco • 457,600,000

W-2545-L★ • F-2074L★ • 6,400,000

Series of 1985, Green Seal
Ortega-Baker (1985–1988)

This series continued the preceding design.

Prices for a typical note for this series, unless listed otherwise, are as follows:

Unc-60	Unc-63	Unc-65
$30	$40	$60

Prices for a typical star note for this series, unless listed otherwise, are as follows:

Unc-60	Unc-63	Unc-65
$50	$70	$100

W-2546-A • F-2075A • Boston • 416,000,000

W-2546-A★ • F-2075A★ • 3,200,000

W-2546-B • F-2075B • New York • 1,728,000,000

Unc-60	Unc-63	Unc-65
$25	$35	$55

W-2546-B★ • F-2075B★ • 5,760,000

W-2546-C • F-2075C • Philadelphia • 224,000,000

Unc-60	Unc-63	Unc-65
$40	$50	$70

W-2546-C★ • F-2075C★ • 6,400,000

W-2546-D • F-2075D • Cleveland • 585,600,000

W-2546-D★ • F-2075D★ • 6,400,000

W-2546-E • F-2075E • Richmond • 864,000,000

Unc-60	Unc-63	Unc-65
$40	$50	$70

W-2546-E★ • F-2075E★ • 6,400,000

W-2546-F • F-2075F • Atlanta • 313,600,000

W-2546-G • F-2075G • Chicago • 729,600,000

Unc-60	Unc-63	Unc-65
$25	$35	$55

W-2546-G★ • F-2075G★ • 5,760,000

W-2546-H • F-2075H • St. Louis • 203,400,000

W-2546-I • F-2075I • Minneapolis • 112,000,000

Unc-60	Unc-63	Unc-65
$40	$50	$70

W-2546-J • F-2075J • Kansas City • 204,800,000

W-2546-J★ • F-2075J★ • 3,200,000

W-2546-K • F-2075K • Dallas • 192,000,000

W-2546-K★ • F-2075K★ • 3,200,000

W-2546-L • F-2075L • San Francisco • 1,129,600,000

W-2546-L★ • F-2075L★ • 3,200,000

Series of 1988-A, Green Seal
Villalpando-Brady (1989–1993)

No Series of 1988 $20 notes were printed; the series designation skipped to 1988-A. This series continued the preceding design.

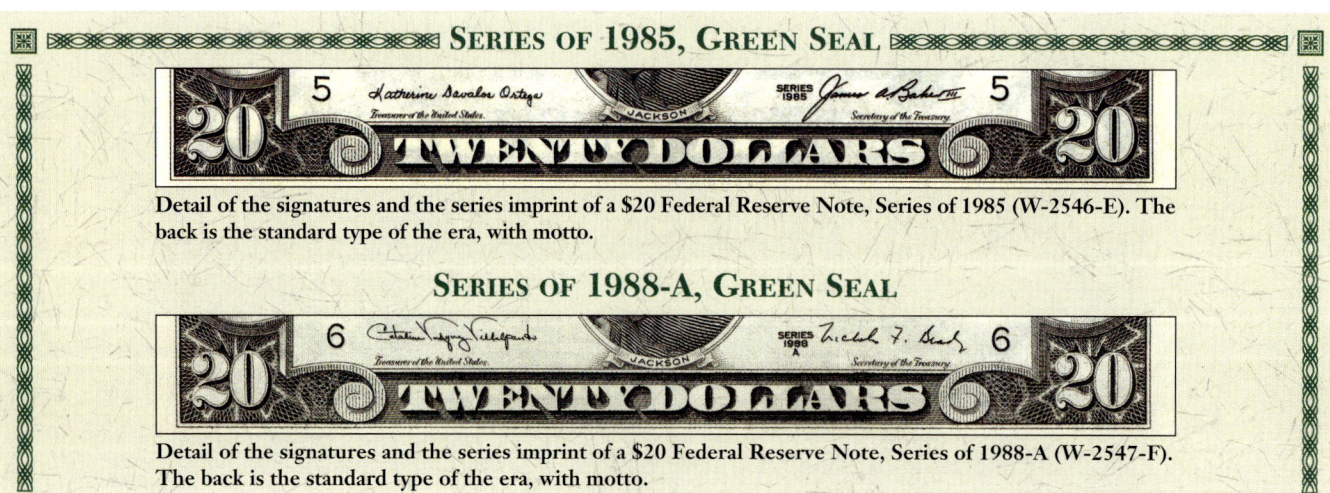

SERIES OF 1985, GREEN SEAL

Detail of the signatures and the series imprint of a $20 Federal Reserve Note, Series of 1985 (W-2546-E). The back is the standard type of the era, with motto.

SERIES OF 1988-A, GREEN SEAL

Detail of the signatures and the series imprint of a $20 Federal Reserve Note, Series of 1988-A (W-2547-F). The back is the standard type of the era, with motto.

Prices for a typical note for this series, unless listed otherwise, are as follows:

Unc-60	Unc-63	Unc-65
$45	$55	$75

Prices for a typical star note for this series, unless listed otherwise, are as follows:

Unc-60	Unc-63	Unc-65
$70	$90	$115

W-2547-A • F-2076A • Boston • 313,600,000

W-2547-B • F-2076B • New York • 979,200,000

Unc-60	Unc-63	Unc-65
$35	$45	$65

W-2547-B★ • F-2076B★ • 6,560,000

W-2547-C • F-2076C • Philadelphia • 96,000,000

W-2547-C★ • F-2076C★ • 3,200,000

W-2547-D • F-2076D • Cleveland • 307,200,000

W-2547-E • F-2076E • Richmond • 281,600,000

W-2547-F • F-2076F • Atlanta • 288,000,000

W-2547-F★ • F-2076F★ • 3,200,000

W-2547-G • F-2076G • Chicago • 563,200,000

Unc-60	Unc-63	Unc-65
$35	$45	$65

W-2547-G★ • F-2076G★ • 3,200,000

W-2547-H • F-2076H • St. Louis • 108,800,000

W-2547-I • F-2076I • Minneapolis • 25,600,000

W-2547-J • F-2076J • Kansas City • 137,200,000

W-2547-K • F-2076K • Dallas • 51,200,000

W-2547-K★ • F-2076K★ • 3,200,000

W-2547-L • F-2076L • San Francisco • 729,600,000

Series of 1990, Green Seal, Washington
Villalpando-Brady (1989–1993)

New security features were added to this issue. Around the outside of most of the portrait frame THE UNITED STATES OF AMERICA is repeated in micro printing. A security thread was added to the paper.

Prices for a typical note for this series, unless listed otherwise, are as follows:

Unc-63	Unc-65
$40	$55

Prices for a typical star note for this series, unless listed otherwise, are as follows:

Unc-60	Unc-63	Unc-65
$60	$80	$110

W-2548-A • F-2077A • Boston • 345,600,000

Unc-63	Unc-65
$35	$50

W-2548-A★ • F-2077A★ • 3,200,000

W-2548-B • F-2077B • New York • 1,446,400,000

Unc-63	Unc-65
$35	$50

W-2548-B★ • F-2077B★ • 16,640,000

W-2548-C • F-2077C • Philadelphia • 96,000,000

W-2548-D • F-2077D • Cleveland • 281,600,000

W-2548-D★ • F-2077D★ • 3,200,000

W-2548-E • F-2077E • Richmond • 307,200,000

W-2548-E★ • F-2077E★ • 3,200,000

W-2548-F • F-2077F • Atlanta • 460,800,000

Unc-63	Unc-65
$35	$50

SERIES OF 1990, GREEN SEAL

$20 Federal Reserve Note, Series of 1990 (W-2548-E★). Federal Reserve Bank of Richmond. Star note. Printed in Washington. The back is the standard for the era, with motto.

Detail of the micro-printing introduced with the Series of 1990.

Detail of the lower right of the face showing the imprint of a Fort Worth-printed note.

W-2548-G • F-2077G • Chicago • 652,800,000

Unc-63	Unc-65
$35	$50

W-2548-H • F-2077H • St. Louis • 172,800,000

W-2548-H★ • F-2077H★ • 3,200,000

W-2548-I • F-2077I • Minneapolis • 70,400,000

W-2548-J • F-2077J • Kansas City • 83,200,000

W-2548-K • F-2077K • Dallas • 25,600,000

W-2548-L • F-2077L • San Francisco • 416,000,000

Unc-63	Unc-65
$35	$50

Series of 1990, Green Seal, Fort Worth
Villalpando-Brady (1989–1993)

This series continued the preceding design. It also introduced notes printed at the Western Facility in Fort Worth, Texas. Imprints include FW as part of the face plate designation.

W-2549-F★ • F-2078F★ • Atlanta • 1,280,000

Unc-60	Unc-63	Unc-65
$60	$80	$110

W-2549-G★ • F-2078G★ • Chicago • 13,400,000

Unc-60	Unc-63	Unc-65
$60	$80	$110

W-2549-I★ • F-2078I★ • Minneapolis • 5,120,000

Unc-60	Unc-63	Unc-65
$70	$90	$120

W-2549-L • F-2078L • San Francisco • Included in printage above

Unc-63	Unc-65
$35	$50

Series of 1993, Green Seal, Washington
Withrow-Bentsen (1994)

This series continued the preceding design.

Prices for a typical note for this series, unless listed otherwise, are as follows:

Unc-63	Unc-65
$35	$50

Prices for a typical star note for this series, unless listed otherwise, are as follows:

Unc-63	Unc-65
$60	$75

W-2550-A • F-2079A • Boston • 288,000,000

W-2550-A★ • F-2079A★ • 2,560,000

W-2550-B • F-2079B • New York • 640,000,000

W-2550-B★ • F-2079B★ • 4,920,000

Unc-63	Unc-65
$55	$70

W-2550-C • F-2079C • Philadelphia • 147,200,000

W-2550-D • F-2079D • Cleveland • 329,600,000

W-2550-D★ • F-2079D★ • 1,920,000

W-2550-E • F-2079E • Richmond • 656,000,000

W-2550-E★ • F-2079E★ • 8,960,000

W-2550-F • F-2079F • Atlanta • 300,800,000

W-2550-H • F-2079H • St. Louis • 19,200,000

Series of 1993, Green Seal, Fort Worth
Withrow-Bentsen (1994)

This series continued the preceding design.

Prices for a typical note for this series, unless listed otherwise, are as follows:

Unc-63	Unc-65
$35	$50

Prices for a typical star note for this series, unless listed otherwise, are as follows:

Unc-60	Unc-63	Unc-65
$45	$70	$100

W-2551-F • F-2080F • Atlanta • 51,200,000

W-2551-F★ • F-2080F★ • 3,200,000

W-2551-G • F-2080G • Chicago • 390,400,000

W-2551-H • F-2080H • St. Louis • 166,400,000

W-2551-J • F-2080J • Kansas City • 102,400,000

W-2551-L • F-2080L • San Francisco • 806,400,000

W-2551-L★ • F-2080L★ • 7,680,000

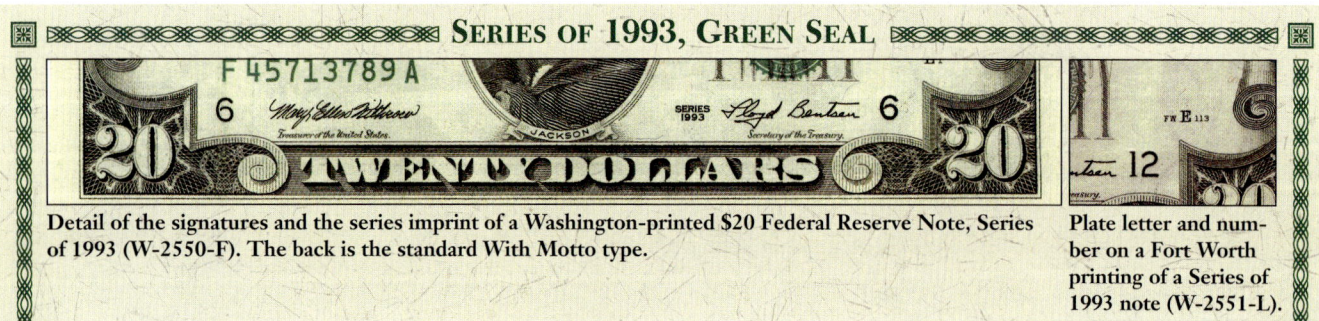

SERIES OF 1993, GREEN SEAL

Detail of the signatures and the series imprint of a Washington-printed $20 Federal Reserve Note, Series of 1993 (W-2550-F). The back is the standard With Motto type.

Plate letter and number on a Fort Worth printing of a Series of 1993 note (W-2551-L).

Series of 1995, Green Seal, Washington
Withrow-Rubin (1995–1999)

This series continued the preceding design.

Prices for a typical note for this series, unless listed otherwise, are as follows:

Unc-63	Unc-65
$40	$55

W-2552-B • F-2081B • New York • 403,200,000

W-2552-B★ • F-2081B★ • 5,760,000

Unc-60	Unc-63	Unc-65
$40	$60	$80

W-2552-C • F-2081C • Philadelphia • 70,400,000

W-2552-D • F-2081D • Cleveland • 140,800,000

W-2552-D★ • F-2081D★ • 640,000

Unc-60	Unc-63	Unc-65
$50	$80	$100

W-2552-E • F-2081E • Richmond • 166,400,000

Series of 1995, Green Seal, Fort Worth
Withrow-Rubin (1995–1999)

This series continued the preceding design.

Prices for a typical note for this series, unless listed otherwise, are as follows:

Unc-63	Unc-65
$35	$50

W-2553-F • F-2082F • Atlanta • 307,200,000

W-2553-F★ • F-2082F★ • 3,200,000

Unc-60	Unc-63	Unc-65
$45	$70	$90

W-2553-G • F-2082G • Chicago • 492,800,000

W-2553-H • F-2082H • St. Louis • 140,800,000

W-2553-I • F-2082I • Minneapolis • 44,800,000

Unc-63	Unc-65
$40	$55

W-2553-J • F-2082J • Kansas City • 230,400,000

W-2553-K • F-2082K • Dallas • 249,600,000

W-2553-L • F-2082L • San Francisco • 614,400,000

Series of 1996, Green Seal, Washington
Withrow-Rubin (1995–1999)

Both sides of the $20 note were redesigned for the Series of 1996 (illus. on p. 536). To the left is a new Federal Reserve seal, with no indication of which of the 12 banks issued the note. That information is given below the serial number at the upper left, where the bank's letter and number are printed, such as A1 for Boston, B2 for New York, etc. The obligation or redemption statement is printed below the modernized Federal Reserve seal. Jackson's portrait is modified and enlarged. THE UNITED STATES OF AMERICA is in three lines in the upper right field. Other changes were also made. To the left and right of the ribbon ends under the portrait there is micro-lettering, THE UNITED STATES OF AMERICA, twice on each side.

The new back retains some elements that are familiar, but with extensive changes. The White House foliage is less extensive than on the previous design, and the counter at the lower right is larger than the others and is surrounded by white. Other changes are illustrated. Series of 1996 notes were printed at both Washington and Fort Worth.

Prices for a typical note for this series, unless listed otherwise, are as follows:

Unc-63	Unc-65
$30	$40

Prices for a typical star note for this series, unless listed otherwise, are as follows:

Unc-60	Unc-63	Unc-65
$30	$40	$50

W-2554-A • F-2083A • Boston • 883,200,000

W-2554-A★ • F-2083A★ • 10,880,000

W-2554-B • F-2083B • New York • 896,000,000

W-2554-B★ • F-2083B★ • 3,200,000

W-2554-C • F-2083C • Philadelphia • 506,400,000

W-2554-C★ • F-2083C★ • 364,000,000

W-2554-D • F-2083D • Cleveland • 483,200,000

W-2554-D★ • F-2083D★

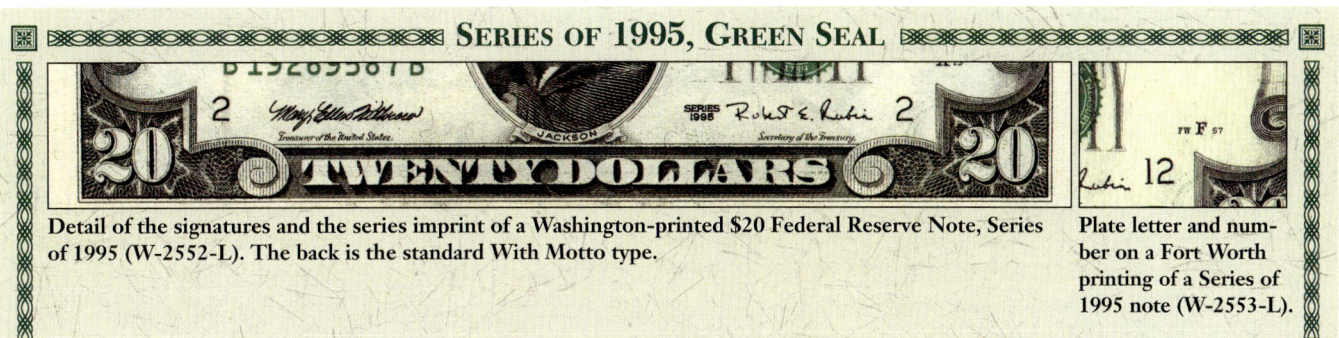

SERIES OF 1995, GREEN SEAL

Detail of the signatures and the series imprint of a Washington-printed $20 Federal Reserve Note, Series of 1995 (W-2552-L). The back is the standard With Motto type.

Plate letter and number on a Fort Worth printing of a Series of 1995 note (W-2553-L).

W-2554-E • F-2083E • Richmond • 925,600,000

W-2554-F • F-2083F • Atlanta • 460,800,000

Series of 1996, Green Seal, Fort Worth
Withrow-Rubin (1995–1999)

This series continued the preceding design.

Prices for a typical note for this series, unless listed otherwise, are as follows:

Unc-63	Unc-65
$30	$40

Prices for a typical star note for this series, unless listed otherwise, are as follows:

Unc-60	Unc-63	Unc-65
$30	$40	$50

W-2555-E • F-2084E • Richmond • 243,200,000

W-2555-E★ • F-2084E★ • 3,200,000

W-2555-F • F-2084F • Atlanta • 925,600,000

W-2555-F★ • F-2084F★ • 3,200,000

W-2555-G • F-2084G • Chicago • 1,151,200,000

W-2555-G★ • F-2084G★ • 12,800,000

W-2555-H • F-2084H • St. Louis • 257,600,000

W-2555-H★ • F-2084H★ • 640,000

AU-50	Unc-60	Unc-63	Unc-65
$75	$125	$170	$220

W-2555-I • F-2084I • Minneapolis • 112,800,000

W-2555-J • F-2084J • Kansas City • 276,800,000

W-2555-K • F-2084K • Dallas • 276,800,000

W-2555-L • F-2084L • San Francisco • 457,600,000

W-2555-L★ • F-2084L★ • 7,040,000

Series of 1999, Green Seal, Washington
Withrow-Summers (1999–2001)

This series continued the preceding design.

Prices for a typical note for this series, unless listed otherwise, are as follows:

Unc-63	Unc-65
$30	$40

Prices for a typical star note for this series, unless listed otherwise, are as follows:

Unc-60	Unc-63	Unc-65
$30	$40	$50

W-2556-A • F-2085A • Boston • 57,600,000

W-2556-A★ • F-2085A★ • 1,920,000

$20 Federal Reserve Note, Series of 1996 (W-2554-D). Federal Reserve Bank of Cleveland. Printed in Washington. The face has been redesigned.

Back of the $20 Federal Reserve Note, Series of 1996 (W-2554-D), with the new design.

Detail of the left field of the face showing the serial number, the district identification (D4), the black Federal Reserve System seal, and other features.

Detail of the lower center of the face showing the imprint of a Fort Worth-printed note.

Detail of the back of a Series of 1996 note showing the bottom right counter, the plate number (15), and other features.

W-2556-B • F-2085B • New York • 608,000,000

W-2556-B★ • F-2085B★ • 1,920,000

W-2556-C • F-2085C • Philadelphia • 192,000,000

W-2556-D • F-2085D • Cleveland • 268,800,000

W-2556-D★ • F-2085D★ • 5,760,000

W-2556-E • F-2085E • Richmond • 492,800,000

Series of 1999, Green Seal, Fort Worth
Withrow-Summers (1999–2001)

This series continued the preceding design.

Prices for a typical note for this series, unless listed otherwise, are as follows:

Unc-63	Unc-65
$30	$40

Prices for a typical star note for this series, unless listed otherwise, are as follows:

Unc-60	Unc-63	Unc-65
$30	$40	$50

W-2557-B★ • F-2086B★ • 3,200,000

W-2557-D • F-2086D • Cleveland • 12,800,000

W-2557-F • F-2086F • Atlanta • 409,600,000

W-2557-G • F-2086G • Chicago • 704,000,000

W-2557-G★ • F-2086G★ • 7,040,000

W-2557-H • F-2086H • St. Louis • 102,400,000

W-2557-I • F-2086I • Minneapolis • 25,600,000

W-2557-J • F-2086J • Kansas City • 70,400,000

W-2557-L • F-2086L • San Francisco • 32,000,000

W-2557-L★ • F-2086L★ • 3,200,000

Unc-60	Unc-63	Unc-65
$40	$50	$60

Series of 2001, Green Seal, Washington
Marin-O'Neill (2001–2002)

This series continued the preceding design.

Prices for a typical note for this series, unless listed otherwise, are as follows:

Unc-63	Unc-65
$30	$40

W-2558-B • F-2087B • New York • 403,200,000

W-2558-B★ • F-2087B★ • 320,000

AU-50	Unc-60	Unc-63	Unc-65
$70	$135	$180	$225

W-2558-D • F-2087D • Cleveland • 83,200,000

W-2558-E • F-2087E • Richmond • 140,800,000

Series of 2001, Green Seal, Fort Worth
Marin-O'Neill (2001–2002)

This series continued the preceding design.

Prices for a typical note for this series, unless listed otherwise, are as follows:

Unc-63	Unc-65
$30	$40

Prices for a typical star note for this series, unless listed otherwise, are as follows:

Unc-60	Unc-63	Unc-65
$30	$40	$50

W-2559-B • F-2088B • New York • 249,600,000

W-2559-E • F-2088E • Richmond • 153,600,000

W-2559-F • F-2088F • Atlanta • 313,600,000

W-2559-G • F-2088G • Chicago • 224,000,000

W-2559-G★ • F-2088G★ • 3,200,000

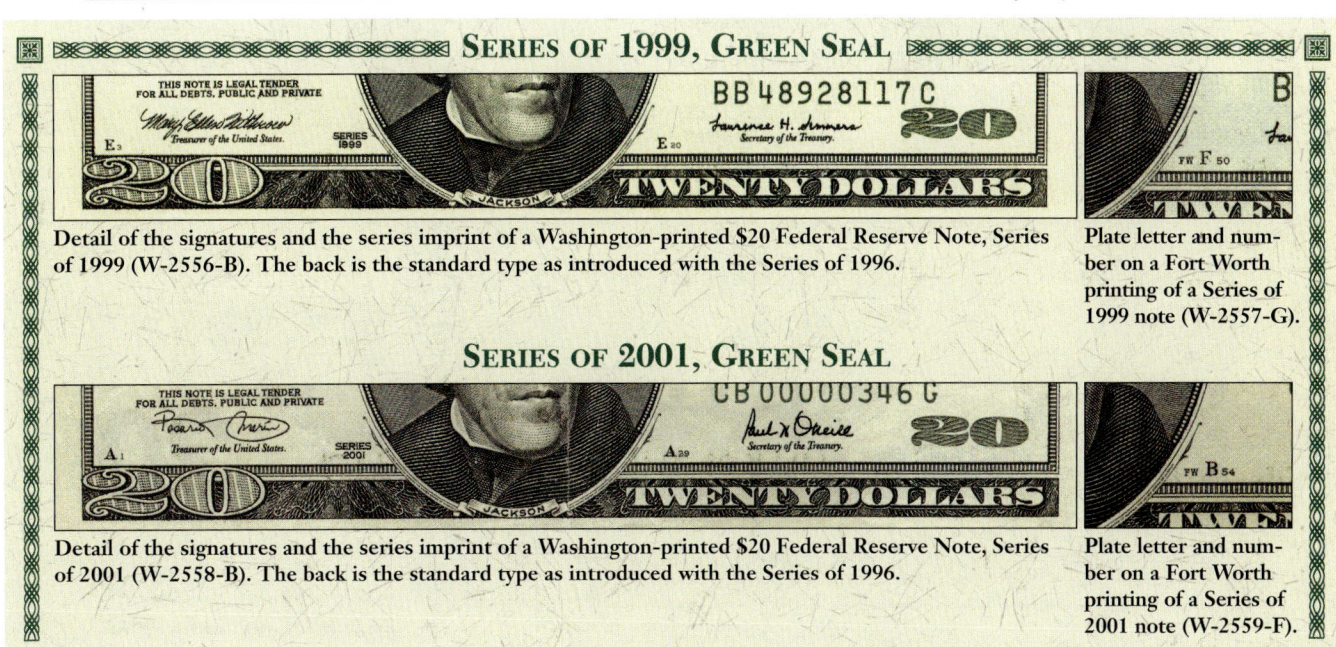

SERIES OF 1999, GREEN SEAL

Detail of the signatures and the series imprint of a Washington-printed $20 Federal Reserve Note, Series of 1999 (W-2556-B). The back is the standard type as introduced with the Series of 1996.

Plate letter and number on a Fort Worth printing of a Series of 1999 note (W-2557-G).

SERIES OF 2001, GREEN SEAL

Detail of the signatures and the series imprint of a Washington-printed $20 Federal Reserve Note, Series of 2001 (W-2558-B). The back is the standard type as introduced with the Series of 1996.

Plate letter and number on a Fort Worth printing of a Series of 2001 note (W-2559-F).

W-2559-H • F-2088H • St. Louis • 44,800,000

W-2559-I • F-2088I • Minneapolis • 57,600,000

W-2559-J • F-2088J • Kansas City • 112,000,000

W-2559-J★ • F-2088J★ • 3,200,000

W-2559-K • F-2088K • Dallas • 166,400,000

W-2559-L • F-2088L • San Francisco • 384,000,000

W-2559-L★ • F-2088L★ • 3,200,000

Series of 2004, Green Seal, Washington
Marin-Snow (2003)

These are the first of the colorized $20 notes, with added security features. Indeed, they were the first of any denomination in the colorized series. The series was introduced on October 9, 2003.

The face of the note was modified. The frame is gone from the Jackson portrait. Added color includes a twilight pink-blue background at the center of note, which changes to blue and blue-green to each side. A light blue heraldic eagle, subtly printed, appears in the left field of the note's face. The eagle holds arrows in the talon to the observer's left and olive branches to the observer's right. To the right TWENTY USA and USA TWENTY are printed in two wavy lines, with the Treasury seal printed over it. The Treasury seal is green. The Federal Reserve Bank location is not printed, but is identified by the usual code—A1 (Boston), B2 (New York), etc.—at the upper left. In the lower right corner, the denomination, 20, is given in gold lettering. The paper includes an embedded security strip. Other features are illustrated.

SERIES OF 2004, GREEN SEAL

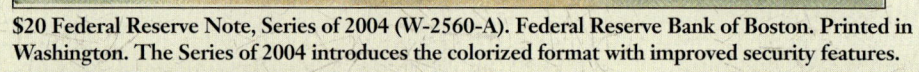

Imprint at upper right face of a Fort Worth–printed note (W-2561-L).

$20 Federal Reserve Note, Series of 2004 (W-2560-A). Federal Reserve Bank of Boston. Printed in Washington. The Series of 2004 introduces the colorized format with improved security features.

Detail of the left side of the face showing the blue eagle and other features.

Detail of the right side of the face showing TWENTY USA and USA TWENTY, and other features.

Back of a Series of 2004 note, illustrating the improved security features.

Detail of the back of a Series of 2004 note showing the lower right counter, the plate number 185, gold 20 imprints, and other features.

The back of the plate retains the essential typographical elements of the preceding design, but with security features added. These include a background color tint similar to the face and many gold denomination counters in the left and right fields.

The BEP offered sets of low-serial-number notes to collectors, priced at $45 each singly, or $40 in groups of 50 or more.

Prices for a typical note for this series, unless listed otherwise, are as follows:

Unc-63	Unc-65
$30	$40

W-2560-A • F-2089A • Boston

W-2560-A★ • F-2089A★

Unc-60	Unc-63	Unc-65
$35	$50	$65

W-2560-B • F-2089B • New York

W-2560-B★ • F-2089B★

AU-50	Unc-60	Unc-63	Unc-65
$65	$115	$170	$210

W-2560-C • F-2089C • Philadelphia

W-2560-C★ • F-2089C★

Unc-60	Unc-63	Unc-65
$35	$50	$65

W-2560-D • F-2089D • Cleveland

W-2560-E • F-2089E • Richmond

W-2560-E★ • F-2089E★

AU-50	Unc-60	Unc-63	Unc-65
$40	$75	$100	$125

W-2560-F • F-2089EF • Atlanta

Series of 2004, Green Seal, Fort Worth
Marin-Snow (2003)

This series continued the preceding design.

Prices for a typical note for this series, unless listed otherwise, are as follows:

Unc-63	Unc-65
$30	$40

Prices for a typical star note for this series, unless listed otherwise, are as follows:

Unc-60	Unc-63	Unc-65
$30	$40	$50

W-2561-D • F-2090D • Cleveland

W-2561-E • F-2090E • Richmond

W-2561-F • F-2090F • Atlanta

W-2561-F★ • F-2090F★

W-2561-G • F-2090G • Chicago

W-2561-G★ • F-2090G★

W-2561-H • F-2090H • St. Louis

W-2561-I • F-2090I • Minneapolis

W-2561-J • F-2090J • Kansas City

W-2561-J★ • F-2090J★

W-2561-K • F-2090K • Dallas

W-2561-K★ • F-2090K★
Commentary: Current pricing information unavailable.

W-2561-L • F-2090L • San Francisco

W-2561-L★ • F-2090L★

Series of 2004-A, Green Seal, Washington
Cabral-Snow (2004–2006)

This series continued the preceding design.

Prices for a typical note for this series, unless listed otherwise, are as follows:

Unc-63	Unc-65
$30	$40

Prices for a typical star note for this series, unless listed otherwise, are as follows:

Unc-60	Unc-63	Unc-65
$35	$45	$60

W-2562-A • F-2091A • Boston • 76,000,000

W-2562-A★ • F-2091A★ • 384,000

W-2562-B • F-2091B • New York • 192,000,000

W-2562-B★ • F-2091B★ • 2,880,000

SERIES OF 2004-A, GREEN SEAL

Detail of the signatures and the series imprint of a Washington-printed $20 Federal Reserve Note, Series of 2004-A (W-2562-A). The back is the standard type with improved security features, as introduced with the Series of 2004.

Plate letter and number on a Fort Worth printing of a Series of 2004-A note (W-2563-L).

W-2562-C • F-2091C • Philadelphia • 96,000,000

W-2562-D • F-2091D • Cleveland • 121,600,000

W-2562-E • F-2091E • Richmond • 364,800,000

W-2562-E★ • F-2091E★ • 3,200,000

W-2562-F • F-2091F • Atlanta • 76,800,000

W-2562-G • F-2091G • Chicago • 38,400,000

W-2562-I • F-2091I • Minneapolis • 25,600,000

W-2562-J • F-2091J • Kansas City • 57,600,000

Series of 2004-A, Green Seal, Fort Worth
Cabral-Snow (2004–2006)

This series continued the preceding design.

Prices for a typical note for this series, unless listed otherwise, are as follows:

Unc-63	Unc-65
$30	$40

W-2563-F • F-2092F • Atlanta • 288,000,000

W-2563-H • F-2092H • St. Louis • 76,800,000

W-2563-I • F-2092I • Minneapolis • 64,000,000

W-2563-J • F-2092J • Kansas City • 134,400,000

W-2563-K • F-2092K • Dallas • 275,200,000

W-2563-K★ • F-2092K★ • 2,304,000

Unc-60	Unc-63	Unc-65
$45	$60	$70

W-2563-L • F-2092L • San Francisco • 185,600,000

Series of 2006, Green Seal, Washington
Cabral-Paulson (2006–2009)

This series continued the preceding design. The information given here is accurate as of press time.

No valuation charts are provided, as notes in this series can be had in top condition for face value at banks or from dealers (with a nominal handling charge).

W-2564-A • F-2093A • Boston

W-2564-B • F-2093B • New York

W-2564-C • F-2093C • Philadelphia

W-2564-D • F-2093D • Cleveland

W-2564-E • F-2093E • Richmond

W-2564-F • F-2093F • Atlanta

W-2564-F★ • F-2093F★

W-2564-G • F-2093G • Chicago

W-2564-G★ • F-2093G★

W-2564-H • F-2093H • St. Louis

W-2564-I • F-2093I • Minneapolis

W-2564-J • F-2093J • Kansas City

W-2564-K • F-2093K • Dallas

W-2564-L • F-2093L • San Francisco

Series of 2006, Green Seal, Fort Worth
Cabral-Paulson (2006–2009)

This series continued the preceding design. The information given here is accurate as of press time.

No valuation charts are provided, as notes in this series can be had in top condition for face value at banks or from dealers (with a nominal handling charge).

W-2565-F • F-2094F • Atlanta

W-2565-G • F-2094G • Chicago

W-2565-H • F-2094H • St. Louis

W-2565-I • F-2094I • Minneapolis

W-2565-J • F-2094J • Kansas City

W-2565-K • F-2094K • Dallas

W-2565-L • F-2094L • San Francisco

Series of 2009, Green Seal
Rios-Geithner (2009–)

No printing information as of press time.

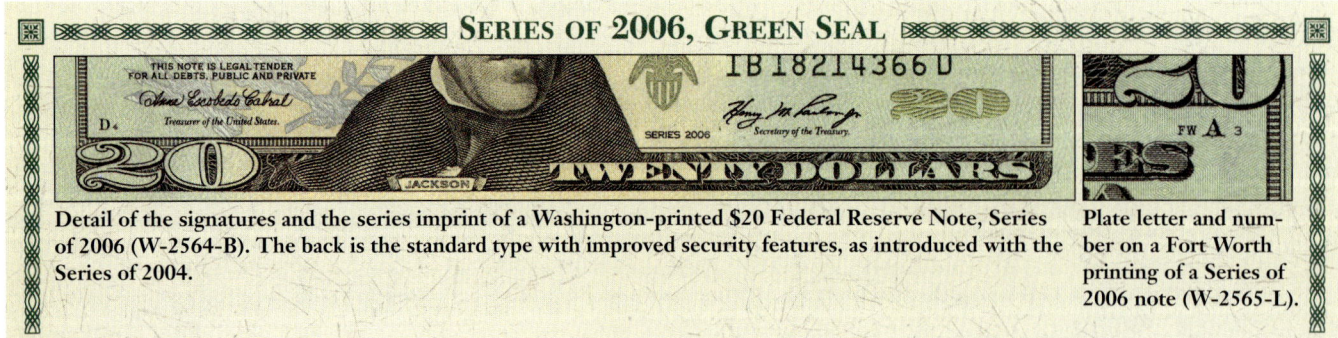

SERIES OF 2006, GREEN SEAL

Detail of the signatures and the series imprint of a Washington-printed $20 Federal Reserve Note, Series of 2006 (W-2564-B). The back is the standard type with improved security features, as introduced with the Series of 2004.

Plate letter and number on a Fort Worth printing of a Series of 2006 note (W-2565-L).

11

$50 NOTES

LARGE SIZE

Large-size $50 notes generally range from scarce to rare. In fact, some of the earlier issues, such as Interest-Bearing Notes, Compound Interest Treasury Notes, and the first Legal Tender Notes, range upward from rare to extremely rare to unobtainable or nonexistent. Although varieties, such as imprint dates on those yielding interest, are interesting to contemplate, so few exist that the best that even the most advanced specialist can hope for is to assemble a few scattered representative examples. As is true of all other large-size federal notes, there was no numismatic interest in collecting them at the time they were issued. Their high face value discouraged people from saving them as souvenirs.

Generally all issues from the 1870s through the 1890s are scarce, punctuated with many rarities. Types from the 20th century become more collectible, such as the 1922 Gold Certificates and the 1914 Blue Seal Federal Reserve Notes, though varieties still range from elusive to extremely rare. The $50 denomination is the largest of the Federal Reserve Bank Note series, issued only in St. Louis. This particular variety has been well known for a long time and has an interesting story to go with it.

Large-size $50 National Bank Notes are likewise elusive. Even for the more available states, such as New York, Pennsylvania, and Massachusetts, certain cities can range from rare to virtually impossible. The poster example of rarity is the 1882 Value Back note, issued by only two institutions: the Winters National Bank of Dayton and the Canal-Commercial National Bank of New Orleans. Today only a few are known of both combined.

National Gold Bank Notes also are numbered among the rarest of the rare, with fewer than a dozen known to remain from only a few thousand issued.

INTEREST-BEARING NOTES

Issued under various authorizations from the act of March 2, 1861, through the Act of March 3, 1865, $50 Interest-Bearing Notes exist in six different design and signature combinations. The first listing was authorized March 2, 1861, with an imprint of the National Bank Note Co. and "for the" added in ink. Other early issues bear the imprints of the National Bank Note Co. and the Treasury department (in an era preceding the Bureau of Engraving and Printing). Plate imprints and other characteristics have not

been fully documented due to the extreme rarity of these notes. From this denomination upward, most numismatic interest is more of an academic than a collecting nature.

March 2, 1861, 6% Interest, 60 Days

The Union needed funds, and the Act of March 2, 1861, provided for notes or bonds (both terms were used) to be issued to borrow money. The shortest term was 60 days, issued in denominations of $50, $100, and $500. No circulated examples are known, but proofs exist. Information regarding these notes is sparse, though we know that $10 million was authorized, and $12,896,350 in these 60-day bonds was eventually issued and quickly redeemed in their entirety.

The $50 notes bear at the top center a signed vignette by Freeman Rawdon (a principal of the erstwhile Rawdon, Wright, Hatch & Edson that in 1858 was merged into the new ABNCo.). The illustration is of Mercury presenting coins in a cornucopia to Ceres, while at the left a griffin stands on a strongbox. Mercury is seated to the left. To the right Justice is standing with a particularly patriotic eagle, wearing a medallion of George Washington; this vignette is also seen on the $100 notes of this series. Denomination counters are at each corner. These same vignettes were used on notes for state-chartered banks produced by RWH&E and ABNCo. The notes measured about 20.5 centimeters by 10.5 centimeters.

W-2590 • F-195b • Unknown

March 2, 1861, 6% Interest, 2 Years

The face of this note (illus. on p. 542) depicts Justice seated at the center, her left hand holding balanced scales. At the lower left is a standard portrait of Andrew Jackson, engraved by Charles Burt. Ironically, an *identical* portrait of Jackson was used in March 1861 by National on its $1,000 "Montgomery Notes," printed for the Confederate States of America. To the right is the portrait of Salmon Chase. To the upper left and right are counters with the denomination 50 at the center, surrounded by overlapping petals (sometimes called a *kaleidograph counter* in Treasury records), each printed with UNITED STATES FIFTY TREASURY. To the left and right of Justice is a cycloidal overprint. PATENTED APRIL 23d 1860 (patent issued to James MacDonough) is printed in

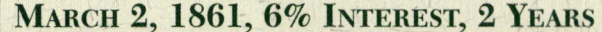

MARCH 2, 1861, 6% INTEREST, 2 YEARS

$50 Interest-Bearing Note, March 2, 1861, 6% Interest, 2 Years (W-2600). The inked date is August 9, 1861. On the illustrated note a Treasury clerk, G. Luff, signed "for the" (in ink) register of the United States. At the right is the inked signature of F.E. Spinner, Treasurer of the United States.

Part of the orange cycloidal configuration (vertically at the center of this image), a National Bank Note Company patented technique, here accompanied by the firm's well-known kaleidograph-style counter.

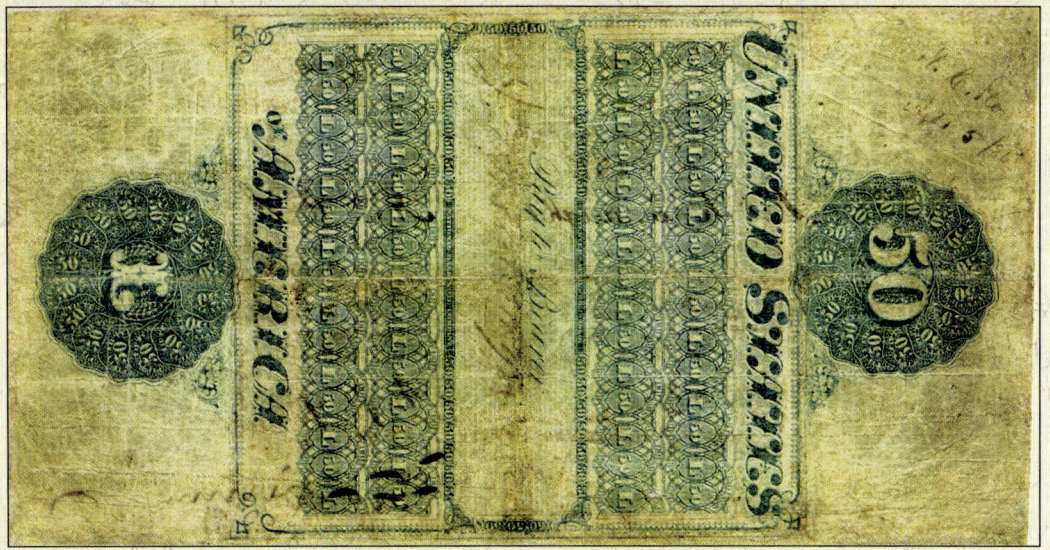

Back of the $50 Interest-Bearing Note, March 2, 1861, 6% Interest, 2 Years (W-2600). The imprint of the National Bank Note Company appears twice, vertically near the center. The ink on the illustrated note is bluish green.

the orange border at the lower left, and NATIONAL BANK NOTE COMPANY in the border at the lower right. Spaces are provided for the autographed signatures of the register of the Treasury and the Treasurer of the United States.

The back is printed in blue with cycloidal configurations. PAY TO BEARER is printed vertically at the center, below which is a space for the holder of the note to sign. NATIONAL BANK NOTE COMPANY and its cycloidal

1860 patent date are printed vertically in a border surrounding the center. Each note measures about 19.5 centimeters by 10 centimeters.

Bills of this authorization and denomination bore interest at the rate of 6% per annum for two years, reflecting that the credit of the Union stood higher than that of the Confederacy, which paid 8% on its notes. At the time of issue they were sold at a discount from face value to reflect the interest to be earned for two years. At the end of this period, nearly all were redeemed. Federal or Union bills in denominations of $100, $500, and $1,000 were also issued under the Act of March 2, 1861, and bore interest at a rate of 6% for two years. As can be said for the 1861 Confederate Notes issued in precisely the same denominations, the Interest-Bearing federal notes can also be considered bonds. In fact, they were widely advertised as such by Jay Cooke & Co.

At first Francis E. Spinner personally autographed such notes. Later, clerks were trained to imitate his signature. The imprint is of the National Bank Note Company. Notes such as this were mainly bought as investments by banks and did not circulate in general commerce.

Although thousands of these notes were issued, only two are known. Likely, there were plate varieties made of which we are not aware today.

W-2600 • F-202a • Chittenden-Spinner (1861–1864) • "for the" handwritten • 46,076
Recorded population: 2 • *Highest graded:* F-12 • *Commentary:* By 1869 only 37 remained outstanding. One is held by the Bureau of the Public Debt. Fine, canceled. • *Selected information:* CAA (5/2001), 17662/C, Fine, $605,000; later seen in CAA (2/2005), $368,000.

W-2610 • F-202a • "for the" printed • Part of W-2600 printage

July 17, 1861, 7.3% Interest, 3 Years

A particularly bold perched eagle dominates the center of the note's face (illus. on p. 544). Counters are to the left and right. These were printed by the American Bank Note Company with three notes to each sheet. Green printing is on the lower face of the note, and the border is in green, composed of L counters. AMERICAN BANK NOTE CO. NEW YORK is on a label at the lower center. The back is in green, with imprints. These were issued with five coupons attached to the right end of the note. The interest on the $50 note was at the rate of one cent per day.

W-2620 • F-207 • Chittenden-Spinner (1861–1864) • *Printed on plate:* AUGUST 19, 1861 • Red serial numbers
Recorded population: 1 • *Graded:* VF-25 • *Selected information:* CAA (2/2005), 4048/A, VF, $172,500.

W-2625 • F-207 • *Printed on plate:* OCTOBER 1, 1861 • Unknown

W-2630 • F-207 • Blue serial numbers • Unknown

March 3, 1863, 5% Interest, 1 Year

On the left of the face (illus. on p. 545) is the vignette *Loyalty* (a.k.a. *Liberty;* the goddess, with her right hand resting on a Bible and the Constitution, was engraved by Alfred Jones). To the lower right is a portrait of Alexander Hamilton. "Will pay to the bearer FIFTY DOLLARS with Five per cent. interest" is lettered under the heavy green overprint at the center and is not easy to discern at quick glance. At the top right of the face is ENGRAVED AND PRINTED AT THE TREASURY DEPARTMENT imprint, a product of the National Currency Bureau. This imprint reflects that the *plates* were made in Washington, using transfer rolls supplied by the National Bank Note Company. These were sold at a discount to reflect the interest, and redeemed at face value upon maturity.

W-2650 • F-198 • Chittenden-Spinner (1861–1864) • 164,800
Recorded population: 3 • *Highest graded:* EF-45 • *Commentary:* Various dates were printed on the plate, including March 15, 1864 and April 11, 1864. • *Selected information:* Knight (3/2006), 8525/D, VG, extensive restoration, $25,070. CAA (2/2005), 35145/A, VF, $92,000; 38161/D, Good, repaired, $21,850.

March 3, 1863, 5% Interest, 2 Years

To the left of the face (illus. on p. 546) is a seated woman, a vignette by John W. Casilear titled *Caduceus*, referring to a winged staff with two intertwined snakes in her hand, a popular motif of the era (not particularly associated with medicine then, as it is today). At the center is *Justice with Shield*, also known simply as *Justice*, engraved by Charles Burt. To the right is *Loyalty*, as used on the March 3, 1863, 5% Interest, 1 Year notes described above. Near the top border left of center is AMERICAN BANK NOTE COMPANY, NEW YORK.

Some were issued with three coupons attached vertically to the right side and have interest payable semi-annually while others were issued without coupons and were payable at maturity. The last were sold at a discount from face value at the time they were issued, with the bearer earning interest by obtaining full face value upon expiration of the term. Various red overprint dates were added to signify the starting time for interest calculation. Most, if not all, were spaced one week apart.

W-2660 • F-203 • Chittenden-Spinner (1861–1864) • Payable at maturity • 136,000
Recorded population: 8 • *Highest graded:* VF-35 • *Commentary:* Various dates are printed on the plates, including April 1 and April 22, 1864. The Smithsonian Institution has a VF–EF in its collection. • *Selected information:* CAA (5/2005), 20575/B, VF–EF, $37,375. Knight (3/2008), 26198/B, VG–F, $54,625.

W-2670 • F-203 • Payable semi-annually; issued with three coupons • 118,112
Recorded population: 1 • *Commentary:* Various dates are presumed to be printed on the plate. The only known example is dated May 27, 1864.

JULY 17, 1861, 7.3% INTEREST, 3 YEARS

$50 Interest-Bearing Note, July 17, 1861, 7.3% Interest, 3 Years (W-2620). Interest commenced on August 19, 1861, and continued for three years. The illustrated note is signed by two Treasury clerks on behalf of the register and the Treasurer of the United States and was purchased by firearms maker Samuel Colt. Two original coupons are still attached.

Detail of the face showing signatures by clerks and Samuel Colt as payee.

Detail of the coupons (image rotated 90 degrees). Each bears the serial number of the note. These could be clipped and individually redeemed.

Back of W-2620 with Samuel Colt's name vertically to left of the center.

June 30, 1864, 7.3% Interest, 3 Years

At the center of the face (illus. on p. 547) is a perched eagle, the same later used on the Series of 1869 $10 "Jackass Note" and its successors. This eagle, when inverted, has the appearance of that animal. These notes were issued with attached coupons. INTEREST ONE CENT PER DAY is

MARCH 3, 1863, 5% INTEREST, 1 YEAR

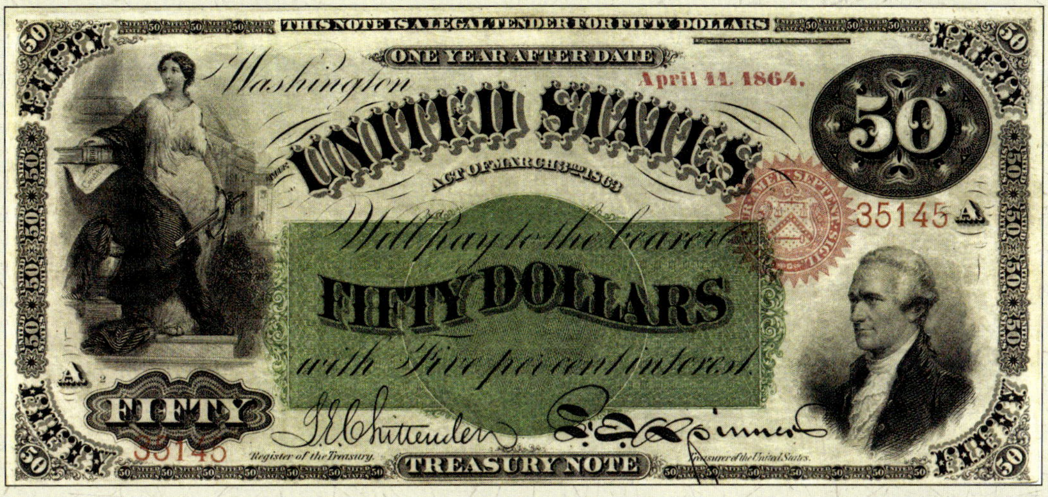

$50 Interest-Bearing Note, March 3, 1863, 5% Interest, 1 Year (W-2650). This note is dated April 11, 1864. Plate A2.

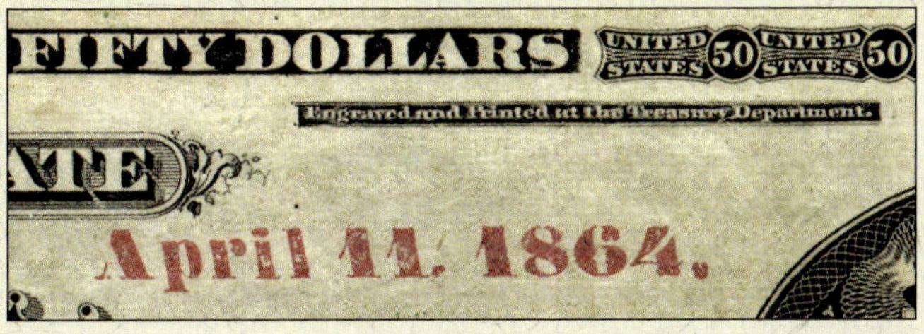

Detail of the interest-starting date and of the Treasury imprint at the upper right of the face.

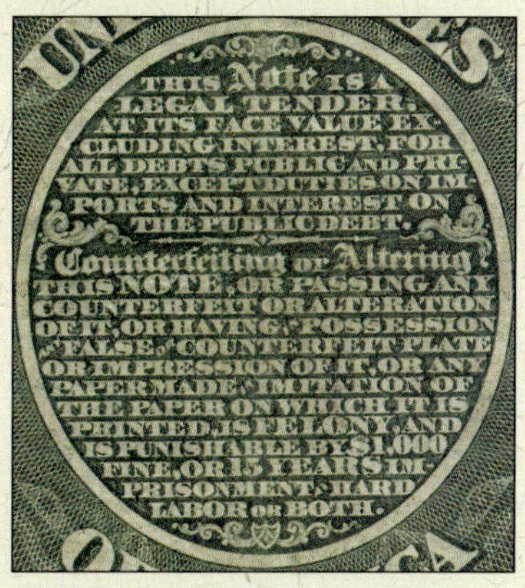

Detail of the center back with the redemption provision and a warning to those who dared to counterfeit or alter the note.

Back of the $50 Interest-Bearing Note, March 3, 1863, 5% Interest, 1 Year (W-2650), printed in rich green.

printed above the eagle, easy enough for a holder of the note to comprehend. TREASURY DEPARTMENT is printed above the bottom border with the coupon information below. The date, AUGUST 15TH 1864, is printed above Spinner's name at the lower right.

The redemption provision on the back allows the holder to receive payment, at his or her option, in 20-year bonds with interest payable in coin after August 15, 1867. The Treasury anticipated that gold and silver coins, trading at a sharp premium when this note was issued, would be readily available at par by the summer of 1867. Reality proved otherwise. Silver coins did not achieve parity with paper until April 20, 1876, and gold not until December 17, 1879. Accordingly, to honor earlier interest payments, the Treasury had to pay an unexpected premium.

W-2680 • F-212 • Colby-Spinner (1864–1867) • 363,952

Recorded population: 7 • *Highest graded:* VF-30 • *Commentary:* Known dates are August 15, 1864, and March 3, 1865. •

MARCH 3, 1863, 5% INTEREST, 2 YEARS

$50 Interest-Bearing Note, March 3, 1863, 5% Interest, 2 Years (W-2660). The April 1, 1864 date marks the commencement of interest. Payable at maturity.

Back of the $50 Interest-Bearing Note, March 3, 1863, 5% Interest, 2 Years (W-2660), with rich green vignette, including redemption and counterfeiting notices.

Selected information: Knight (6/2006), 24346/A, VG+, $74,750. Heritage (1/2007), 65433/C, VF-30 (PMG), $138,000. CAA (2/2005), 111383/B, F–VF, repaired, $51,750.

March 3, 1865, 7.3% Interest, 3 Years

Some have a vertical red overprint at the left end that reads, "The Government reserves the right of paying in COIN, all interest on this Note at the rate of six per cent. per annum" (a superfluous statement as coins were worth about twice as much as an equivalent amount in paper money at the time!). All are convertible into 20-year bonds, per a notice on the back, with interest payable in coin (see description of preceding type for details). The date (June 15, 1865, or July 15, 1865) is printed above Spinner's name at the lower right. All were issued with five coupons attached, and all have a red Treasury seal with a spiked border. (Illus. on p. 548.)

The back of the notes with the June 15, 1865, date is the same as on the preceding type. The back of the July 15, 1865, notes has the denomination in large numerals overprinted in bronzing powder.

W-2690 • F-212d • Colby-Spinner (1864–1867) • *Printed on plate:* JUNE 15, 1865 • Blue serial numbers • 182,926

Recorded population: 1 • *Graded:* VF-20 • *Selected information:* Knight (12/1998), 89959/C VF-20, no coupons, $35,200; later seen in CAA (2/2005), $36,800.

W-2695 • F-212d • *Printed on plate:* JULY 15, 1865 • Red serial numbers • Without COIN overprint on face • Bronze overprint, 50, on back • 343,320

Recorded population: 6 • *Highest graded:* VF–EF • *Selected information:* Existing examples include 57224/D, Fine, sold in a Heritage auction (5/2005) for $41,400; 126378/B, VF–EF, part of the Smithsonian Institution collection; 142143/C, VF–EF, repaired, no coupons, sold in a CAA auction (1/2004) for $66,125; 142145/A, Fine, part of the Smithsonian Institution collection; 161643/C, VF, repaired, no coupons, sold in a Knight auction (10/2005) for $92,000; and 196081/A, VF–EF, 5 coupons, sold in a CAA auction (2/2005) for $172,500.

JUNE 30, 1864, 7.3% INTEREST, 3 YEARS

$50 Interest-Bearing Note, June 30, 1864, 7.3% Interest, 3 Years (W-2680). Large eagle at center. Dated August 15, 1864. Three-year term at 7.3%. Red serial numbers. Treasury department imprint. Red serial numbers. "Payable to the order of Mrs. Charlotte Wales" (the name added in ink). This note has two of the original five coupons still attached. Plate B, serial 111383.

Detail of note recipient's inked name.

Detail of Treasury imprint and coupon information on face.

Detail of the attached coupons (image rotated 90 degrees).

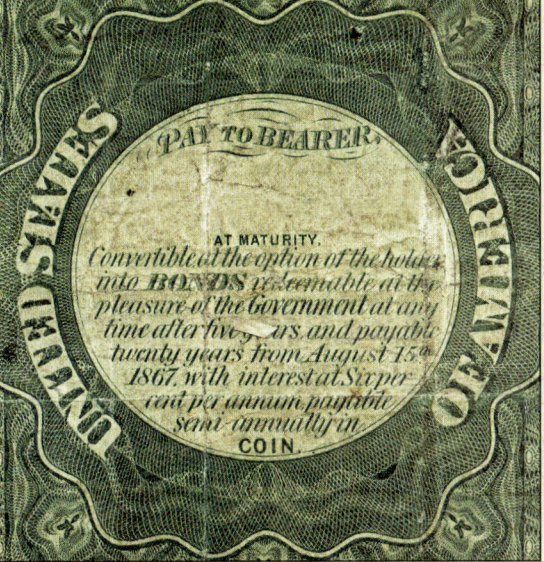

Redemption provision on the back of the note (image rotated 90 degrees).

Back of the $50 Interest-Bearing Note, June 30, 1864, 7.3% Interest, 3 Years (W-2680), also used on the following type.

MARCH 3, 1865, 7.3% INTEREST, 3 YEARS

$50 Interest-Bearing Note, March 3, 1865, 7.3% Interest, 3 Years (W-2690). Coupons used and no longer present. Large eagle at center, design similar to the preceding. Blue serial numbers. Treasury department imprint. The back is the same as the prior note.

$50 Interest-Bearing Note, March 3, 1865, 7.3% Interest, 3 Years (W-2695). Coupons attached. Red serial numbers. Treasury department imprint.

W-2700 • F-212d • Printed on plate: JULY 15, 1865 • With COIN overprint on face • Bronze overprint, 50, on back • Part of W-2695 printage

Estimated population: Included as part of W-2695 • *Highest graded:* Included as part of W-2695 • *Selected information:* Included as part of W-2695.

COMPOUND INTEREST TREASURY NOTES

$50 Compound Interest Treasury Notes bear the imprint TREASURY DEPARTMENT and were printed by the National Currency Bureau. Bronzing powder was applied to create prominent bronze lettering on the face, considered to be a deterrent to counterfeiting. This was the first step in the printing process and was done on blank sheets.

Fortunate (and well-financed) is the collector who can secure even a single example to illustrate the type. When seen, such notes are apt to be well circulated. Fewer than 20 examples are known today across the different varieties.

Series of 1863 and 1864

Compound Interest Treasury Notes of the $50 denomination were issued under the Acts of March 3, 1863, and June 30, 1864. These notes bore interest at the rate of 6% per year for three years.

The face is similar in motifs to the one-year Interest-Bearing Notes of March 3, 1863, with *Loyalty* to the left and the Hamilton portrait to the right but lacking the green overprint, and with the imprint 50 COMPOUND INTEREST TREASURY NOTE in bronzing powder. The highest-issued *provable* printage can be calculated by multiplying the highest known serial number by four.[1]

The back, in green, has an interest table that gives the value of the note for six-month periods up to three years after issue. These were popular investments for banks and well-to-do individuals who were attracted by the high interest rate.

W-2720 • F-192 • Chittenden-Spinner (1861–1864) • Printed on plate: ACT OF MARCH 3D 1863 • Red overprint: JUNE 10, 1864 • 1,216,480

SERIES OF 1863 AND 1864

$50 Compound Interest Treasury Note, Act of June 30, 1864 (W-2740). Plate D5, serial 181988. The same type was used for notes issued under the Act of March 3, 1863.

Detail of the bronzing powder printing. This was applied as the first operation on a blank sheet in a special room in the Treasury department.

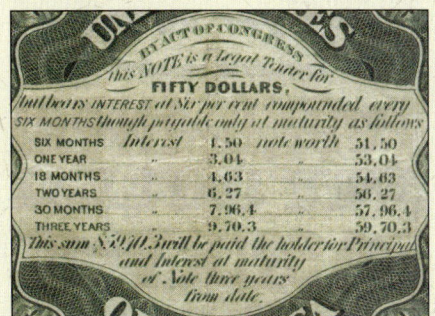

Interest schedule on the back of W-2740.

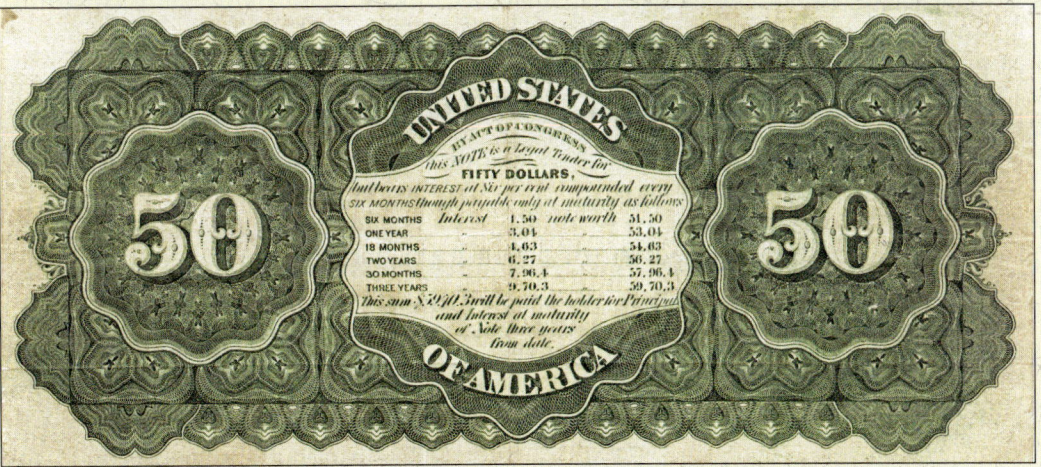

Back of the note. The same type was used for notes issued under the Act of March 3, 1863.

Recorded population: 2 • *Highest graded:* G-4 • *Selected information:* Brigandi Coin Co. (8/1997), 919/C, Good. Kagin's (6/1979), 7049/D, Poor, $2,500.

W-2730 • F-unlisted • *Printed on plate:* ACT OF JULY 2D 1864 (error date) • *Part of W-2720 printage*

Commentary: 15,000,000 of these are said to have been printed, but none are known today. For related $10 notes, see W-1234; $20 notes may also have been printed. The $50 notes were the subject of an article in the *New York Times*

datelined Washington, July 7, 1885, "A Mistake in the Date Annoying the Older Treasury Officials."[2]

W-2740 • F-192b • Colby-Spinner • *Printed on plate:* ACT OF JUNE 30TH 1864 • *Part of W-2720 printage*

Estimated population: 14 • *Highest graded:* AU-50 • *Commentary:* Red overprint dates reported include Aug. 15, 1864; Oct. 15, 1864; Dec. 15, 1864; May 15, 1865; and Sept. 15, 1865.

VG-8	F-12	VF-20	EF-40	AU-50
$19,000	$40,000	—	—	—

LEGAL TENDER NOTES
(Also Known as United States Notes)

Legal Tender or United States $50 notes were first issued in 1862 and 1863, from plates by the National Bank Note Co.—some with just the National imprint, and some with the imprints of both the National and American companies. First Obligation and Second Obligation backs were made, each with slightly different wording as to the redemption or use of the notes. Though they were issued in large quantities at the time, surviving examples are scarce, as nearly all were redeemed. The typical note is well circulated.

Series of 1862, First Obligation

These "greenbacks" exist in several varieties. The face, back, and tint plates for the $50 Series of 1862 and 1863 Legal Tender Notes were engraved by the National Bank Note Company. National printed most (if not all) of the First Obligation notes. American and National shared the printing for the Second Obligation notes.[3] Treasury signatures of Chittenden and Spinner were printed on the face by using a separate plate and a special ink. The numbering was done in "series," starting with SERIES 1, serial number 1.

First Obligation: This wording, with different typography on various denominations, states the note is exchangeable for bonds (a provision dropped from the Second Obligation): "This note is a Legal Tender for all debts public and private, except duties on imports and interest on public debt, and is exchangeable for U.S. six percent twenty years bonds, redeemable at the pleasure of the United States after five years." These notes, called "6-20" bonds, were bought by many banks in an era when stock market shares had an uncertain future.

All bear the address of the Treasury department in Washington, D.C., and have a small red Treasury seal (hues vary among different notes).

W-2771 • F-148 • Chittenden-Spinner (1861–1864) • NATIONAL BANK NOTE COMPANY in top border • Treasury seal without inner border of radial parallel lines • Series 1 to 3 • 280,000 (est.)

Estimated population: 10 to 15 • *Highest graded:* Unc.

VG-8	F-12	VF-20	EF-40	AU-50	Unc-60
$11,500	$23,500	$40,000	—	—	—

SERIES OF 1862, FIRST OBLIGATION

$50 Legal Tender Note, Series of 1862 (W-2771). Portrait of Alexander Hamilton. Imprint of the National Bank Note Company. SERIES 1 imprint, serial 1814, plate B1. At the upper left, above the plate letter, is printed PATENTED 30 JUNE 1857, for the American Bank Note Company's "Patent Green Tint." NATIONAL BANK NOTE COMPANY imprint is in the top border.

Detail of the upper left with the green-tint patent, plate letter and number, and other features. Doug Murray suggests that the green tint was also used by National in the shared printing of notes, and that the patent information does not necessarily indicate that the face was printed by the American Bank Note Company.

Detail of the upper right.

W-2772 • F-148 • Treasury seal with inner border of radial parallel lines • Series 3 to 5 • 153,600 (est.)

Estimated population: 15 to 20 • *Highest graded:* Unc.

VG-8	F-12	VF-20	EF-40	AU-50	Unc-60
$11,500	$23,500	$40,000	—	—	—

Series of 1863, Second Obligation

The basic face design (illus. on p. 552ff.) is similar to the foregoing, but now with NEW SERIES on the face. All have the printed signatures of Chittenden and Spinner. A patent date is printed at the upper left.

Second Obligation: "This note is a Legal Tender for all debts public and private, except duties on imports and interest on public debt, and is receivable in payment of all loans made to the United States." This wording, with different typography for each denomination, does not mention exchanging the notes for 6-20 bonds and thus is different from the First Obligation.

Some have the patent date of April 28th 1863, for Asahel K. Eaton's patent for "improvement in ink for printing bank notes," which replaced the 1857 "Patent Green Tint."

W-2773 • F-150 • Chittenden-Spinner (1861–1864) • Patent date: 30 June 1857 • NATIONAL BANK NOTE COMPANY at top border • Second Obligation back • New Series 1 • 32,000

Estimated population: 9 or 10 • *Highest graded:* Unc • *Selected information:* Existing examples include serials 13308/D, Unc, part of the ANA Museum collection; 13310/B, Unc; 13313/A, EF-40 (PMG), sold in a Heritage auction (1/2008) for $299,000; 13314/B, AU, sold in a CAA auction (9/2004) for $57,500; 13315/C, EF, problems, sold in a Knight auction (10/2005) for $103,500; 13316/D, AU, sold in a Kagin's auction (8/1983) for $7,500; 14518/B, VG–F, sold in a Kosoff auction (8/1966) for $420; and 16790/B, VG, sold in a Kreisberg & Schulman auction (3/1965) for $550.

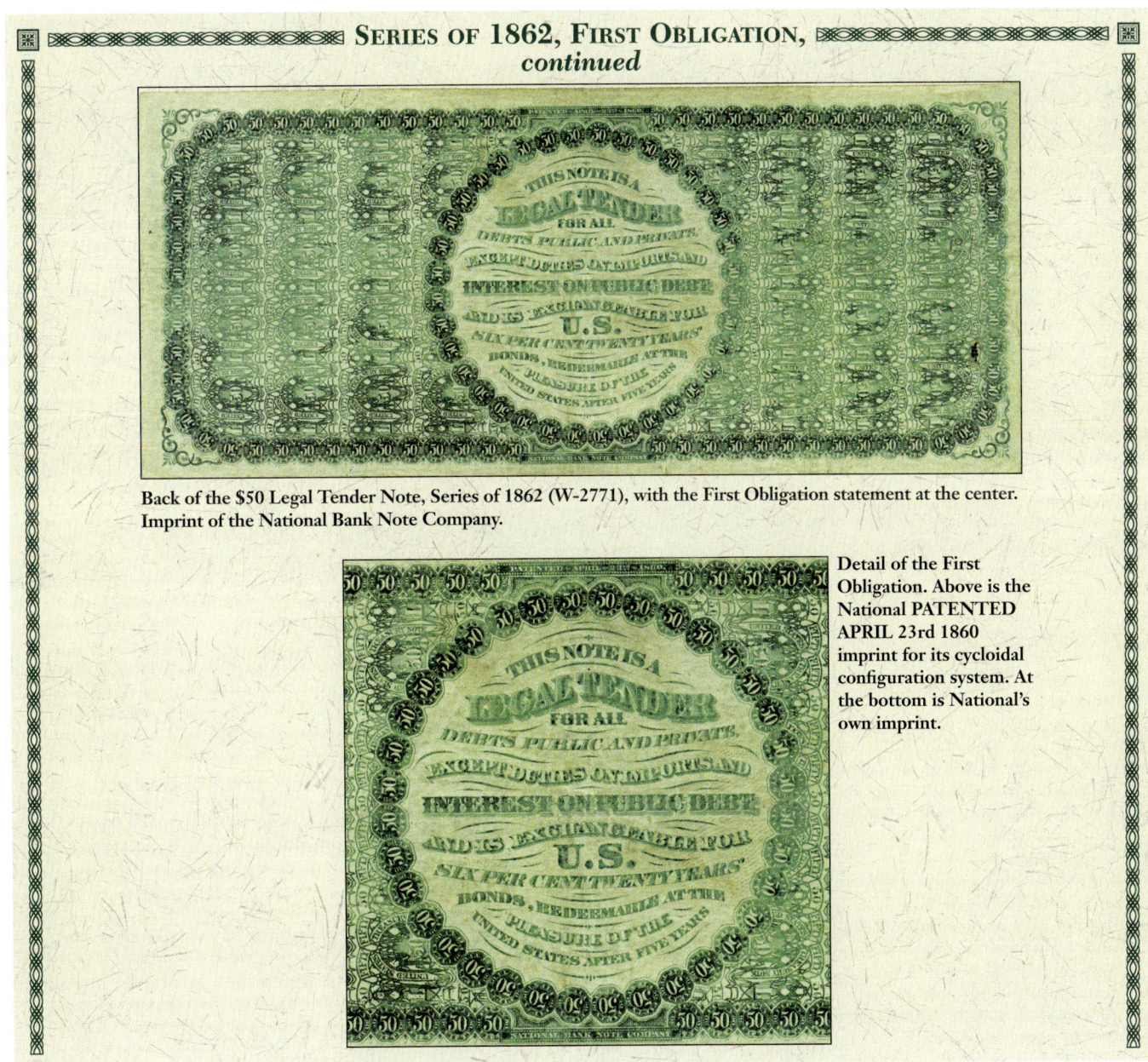

SERIES OF 1862, FIRST OBLIGATION, *continued*

Back of the $50 Legal Tender Note, Series of 1862 (W-2771), with the First Obligation statement at the center. Imprint of the National Bank Note Company.

Detail of the First Obligation. Above is the National PATENTED APRIL 23rd 1860 imprint for its cycloidal configuration system. At the bottom is National's own imprint.

SERIES OF 1863, SECOND OBLIGATION

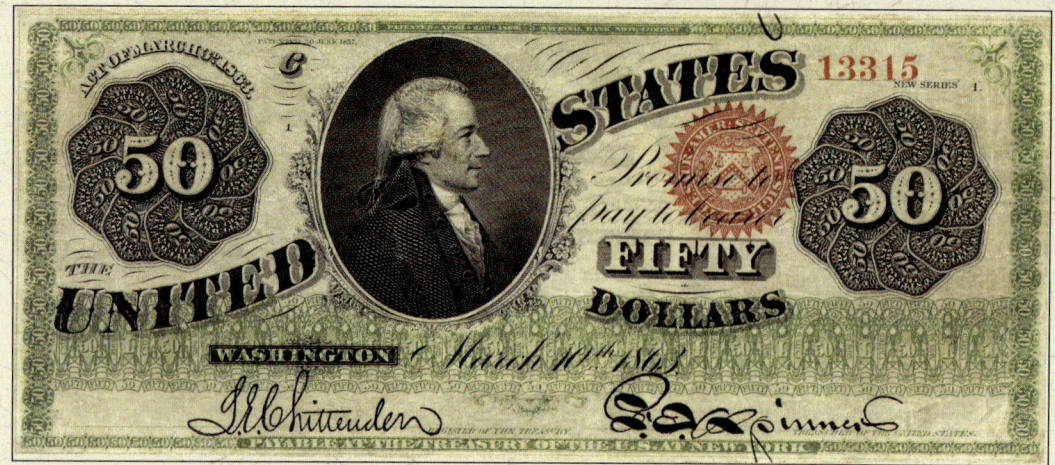

$50 Legal Tender Note, Series of 1863 (W-2773). Design as preceding, with portrait of Alexander Hamilton. New Series 1, serial 13315, plate C.

Detail of National Bank Note Company's imprint in the top border (to right) and, to the left, the 1857 patent date. W-2773.

Detail of W-2776 showing PATENTED APRIL 28TH 1863 below the top border to the left, the 1860 patent date and NATIONAL BANK NOTE COMPANY in the border, and AMERICAN BANK NOTE CO. NEW YORK below the border.

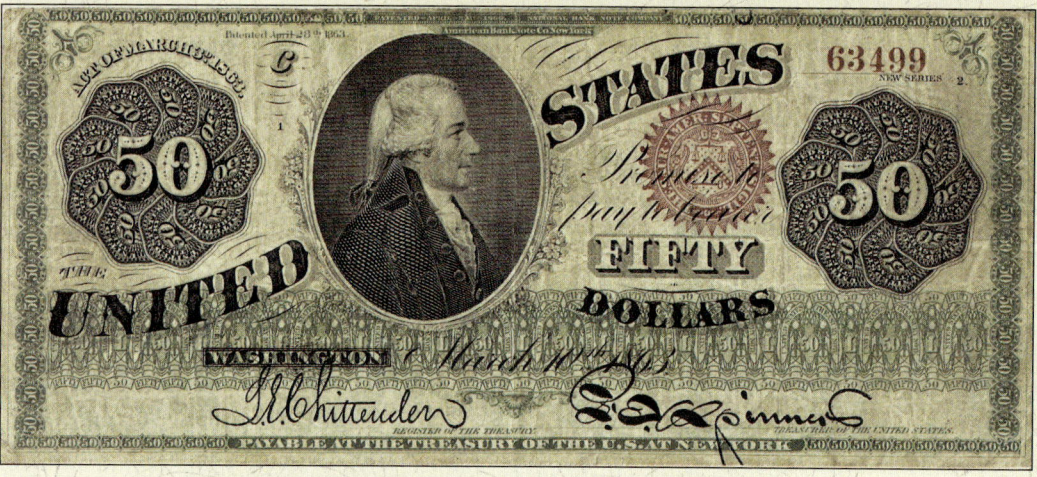

W-2776 with 1863 patent date in the top border. New Series 2, serial 63499, plate C.

W-2775 • F-150a • NATIONAL BANK NOTE COMPANY in the top border and AMERICAN BANK NOTE CO. N.Y. below the top border • New Series 1 to 2 • 70,504

Recorded population: 1.

W-2776 • F-150a • Patent date: April 28th 1863 • New Series 2 • 65,000

Estimated population: 10 to 12 • *Highest graded:* Unc.

VG-8	F-12	VF-20	EF-40	AU-50	Unc-60
$11,500	$23,500	$40,000	—	—	—

Series of 1869

To the left on the face (illus. on p. 554) is the vignette *Return of Peace*, engraved by Charles Smith. The standing woman holds a branch (presumably olive) in her right hand and a small statuette of Mercury in her left. At her feet are the fruits of harvest and a sheep, while a nautical scene is in the distance. At the lower right is a portrait of Henry Clay, engraved by Alfred Seeley. A pink Treasury seal and some embellishments are seen. Serial numbers are in blue, prefaced by Y, and ending with a decorative star. Blue-tinted paper was used.

SERIES OF 1863, SECOND OBLIGATION, *continued*

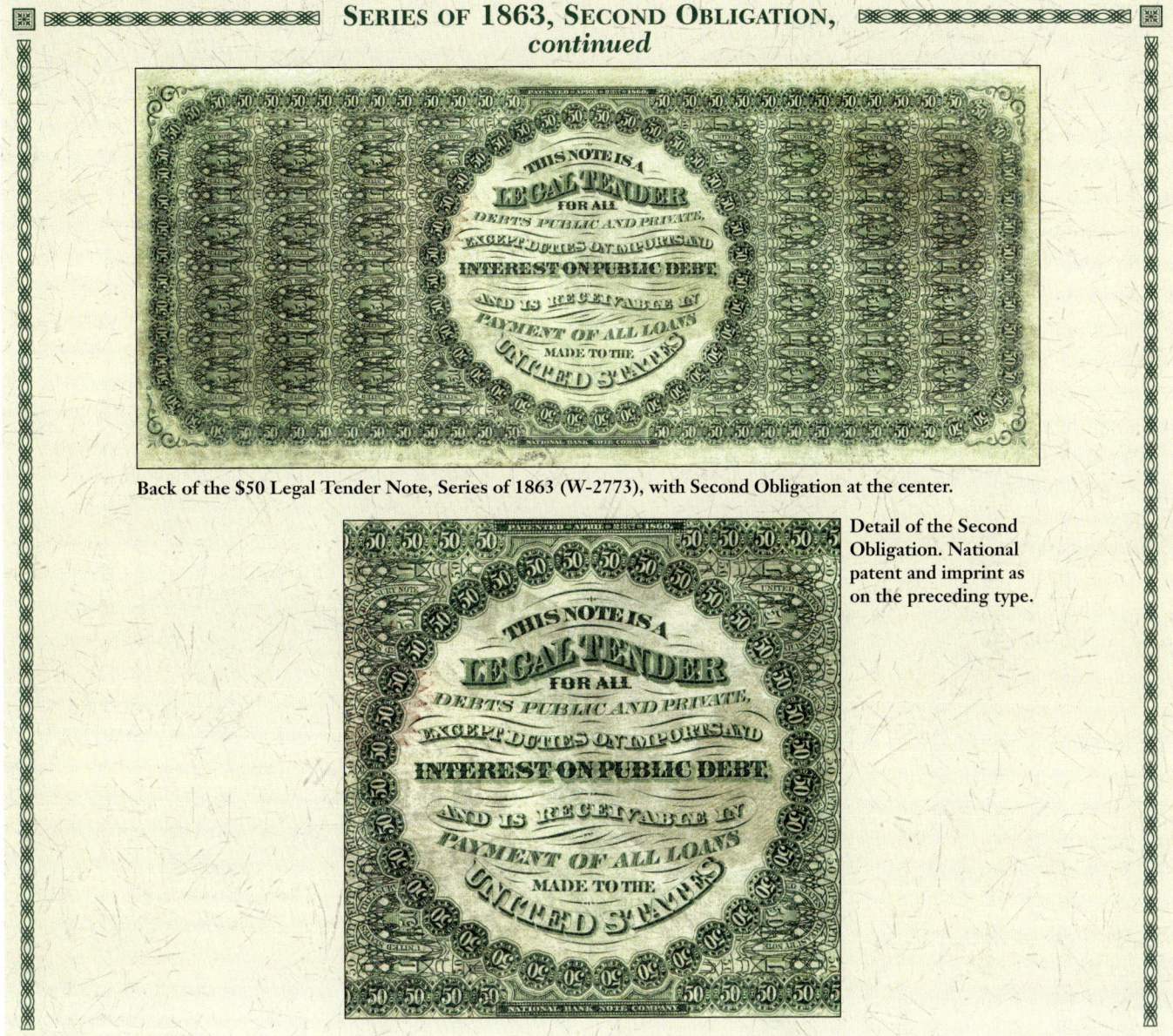

Back of the $50 Legal Tender Note, Series of 1863 (W-2773), with Second Obligation at the center.

Detail of the Second Obligation. National patent and imprint as on the preceding type.

The back is ornately engraved, with the counterfeiting and redemption clauses printed at the left and right. AMERICAN BANK NOTE COMPANY, NEW YORK is printed in the top and bottom border, above and below the designs.

For the Series of 1869 notes, 604,000 were printed, but fewer than 100 are known today. As is true of many of the higher-denomination bills, when examples are encountered they are expensive, reflecting their rarity. Series of 1869 notes were issued from October 19, 1869, to July 25, 1874.

W-2800 • F-151 • Allison-Spinner (1869–1875) • Large red seal • 604,000

Estimated population: 70 to 80 • *Highest graded:* Unc.

VG-8	F-12	VF-20	EF-40	AU-50	Unc-60
$10,000	$17,000	$32,500	—	—	—

Series of 1874

Both the face and back of the new series (illus. on p. 555) are different from the Series of 1869, a departure from the practice of lower denominations to continue the face motifs and change only the back in each series. To the left is a portrait of Benjamin Franklin. To the right is America, a determined-looking woman wearing a crown and holding a sword. At the center the denomination is expressed several ways, including L in a counter and an ornate pink L to each side. The signatures of the Treasurer of the United States and the register of the Treasury are transposed.

On the back, COLUMBIAN BANK NOTE CO. WASHINGTON, D.C. is in the bottom border. As a class, Series of 1874 notes were issued from July 13, 1874, to September 13, 1875.

W-2801 • F-152 • Spinner-Allison (signatures transposed) (1869–1875) • Small reddish seal with spiked border • 489,200

Estimated population: 60 to 70 • *Highest graded:* Unc.

VG-8	F-12	VF-20	EF-40	AU-50	Unc-60	Unc-63
$4,000	$6,500	$10,000	$18,000	$25,000	$31,000	$40,000

SERIES OF 1869

$50 Legal Tender Note, Series of 1869 (W-2800). At the left, *Return of Peace* features a goddess holding a statuette. To the right is a portrait of Henry Clay. Blue-tinted paper. The star at the serial number is an ornament. Serial 196130, plate B2.

Back of the Series of 1869 $50 Legal Tender Note, a design used only here. The imprint of the American Bank Note Company appears twice.

Series of 1875

This note (illus. on p. 556) continues the general style of the preceding. On the back, COLUMBIAN BANK NOTE CO. WASHINGTON, D.C. is in the bottom border (the same as used on Series of 1874 notes). Series of 1875 notes were issued from July 20, 1875, to June 20, 1879. Plate 1 (one of several used to print W-2801) was reentered (altered) to create plate 1 to print the W-3802 notes, now with different, not transposed, signatures.[4]

W-2802 • F-unlisted[5] • Allison-Wyman (1876–1877) • Small reddish seal with spiked border • 40,000

Recorded population: 4 • *Highest graded:* EF-40 • *Selected information:* Existing examples include serials A3295/C, F-12 (PMG), sold in a Stack's auction (11/2007) for $276,000; A13268/D, AU, pinholes, part of the ANA Museum collection; 16513/A, EF, owned by the Federal Reserve Bank of Chicago; and A20197/A, Fine, problems, sold in a CAA auction (10/1998) for $60,500.

Series of 1878

This note (illus. on p. 556) continues the general style of the preceding. The back now bears the added notation

PRINTED AT THE BUREAU ENGRAVING & PRINTING below the Columbian Bank Note Co. imprint. On this series the signatures are transposed.

W-2803 • F-154 • Gilfillan-Allison (signatures transposed) (1877–1878) • Small reddish seal with spiked border • 210,000

Estimated population: 21 to 25 • *Highest graded:* Unc.

VG-8	F-12	VF-20	EF-40	AU-50	Unc-60	Unc-63
$4,000	$6,500	$10,000	$25,000	$40,000	$57,500	$75,000

Series of 1880

The face motifs (illus. on p. 557) are similar to the preceding, but now without the large L counters. Various Treasury seals were used. The signatures of the Treasurer of the United States and the register of the Treasury are transposed on this series through and including W-2810.

Back imprint varieties exist. W-2805 and W-2806 continue the preceding style. Beginning with W-2807 there is no mention of the Columbian Bank Note Company. Notes have only BUREAU ENGRAVING & PRINTING WASHINGTON, D.C. in the bottom border, and SERIES 1880 vertically within the open space at the right.

SERIES OF 1874

$50 Legal Tender Note, Series of 1874 (W-2801). This type has a large pink L to each side of the center. Serial numbers begin with E and end with a cross ornament. Signatures are transposed as Spinner-Allison.

Microprint notice of Geo. W. Casilear's patent under the serial number at the lower left. This had to do with printing the serial on an engraved background, said to offer more security.

Detail of the imprint at the bottom center of the back.

$50 Legal Tender Note, Series of 1874 (W-2801), with the counterfeiting clause at the left and redemption information at the center.

W-2804 • F-155 • Gilfillan-Bruce (signatures transposed) (1881–1883) • Large brown seal • 80,000

Estimated population: 9 or 10 • *Highest graded:* Unc • *Commentary:* CAA (9/2002), 1255/C, Unc, $28,750. CAA (9/2006), Z9020/D, AU-50 (PCGS), $46,000. Heritage (9/2007), Z70388/D, EF-40 (PMG), $29,900.

W-2805 • F-156 • Wyman-Bruce (signatures transposed) (1883–1885) • 160,000

Estimated population: 19 to 22 • *Highest graded:* EF-40.

VG-8	F-12	VF-20	EF-40
$4,000	$6,500	$15,000	$32,500

W-2806 • F-157 • Jordan-Rosecrans (signatures transposed) (1885–1887) • Large red seal with plain border • 80,000

Estimated population: 12 to 14 • *Highest graded:* EF-40.

VG-8	F-12	VF-20	EF-40
$4,250	$6,500	$18,000	$32,500

W-2807 • F-158 • Hyatt-Rosecrans (signatures transposed) (1887–1889) • 20,000

Recorded population: 8 • *Highest graded:* Unc • *Selected information:* Existing examples include serials A80824/D, VF, problems, sold in a Heritage auction (1/2007) for $9,200; A87403/C, Uncirculated, problems, sold in a CAA auction

SERIES OF 1875

$50 Legal Tender Note, Series of 1875 (W-2802). Serial A3295, plate 1C. The back is the same as used on Series of 1874.

SERIES OF 1878

$50 Legal Tender Note, Series of 1878 (W-2803). Serial A49919, plate C2. (ANA Edward C. Rochette Money Museum)

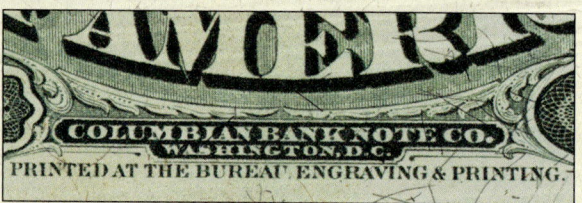

Detail of the imprint at the bottom center of the back.

Back of the $50 Legal Tender Note, Series of 1878 (W-2803).

SERIES OF 1880

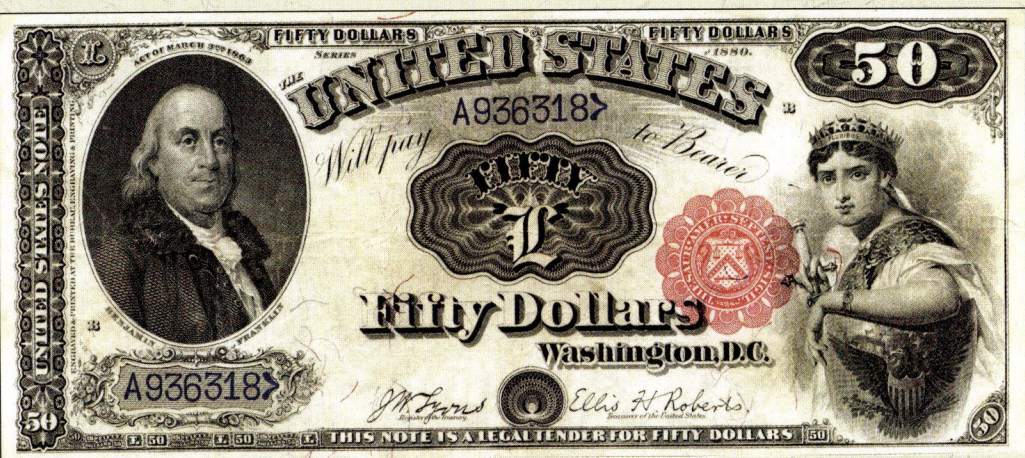

$50 Legal Tender Note, Series of 1880 (W-2813). Similar to the preceding but without the large L's to each side of the center. On this variety the Treasury signatures are in the usual order, Lyons-Roberts. The back is similar to the preceding series except for the imprint.

Detail of the transposed signatures on W-2804.

Detail of the transposed signatures on W-2805.

Detail of the transposed signatures on W-2806.

Detail of the transposed signatures on W-2807.

Detail of the transposed signatures on W-2810.

Back of the $50 Legal Tender Note, Series of 1880 (W-2813).

(1/2001) for $13,200; A87404/D, Uncirculated, owned by the Federal Reserve Bank of Richmond (Charlotte branch); A87405/A, Uncirculated, part of the ANA Museum collection; A87406/B, Unc-65 (PCGS), sold in a Knight auction (10/2005) for $74,750; A87407/C, AU, sold in a Knight auction (8/2003) for $34,500; A87408/D, Uncirculated, sold in a Knight auction (8/2005) for $86,250; and A87409/A, AU-58 (PCGS), sold in a CAA auction (9/2006) for $57,500.

W-2808 • F-159 • Hyatt-Rosecrans (signatures transposed) (1887–1889) • Large red seal with spiked border • 220,000

Estimated population: 20 to 23 • *Highest graded:* AU-55.

VG-8	F-12	VF-20	EF-40	AU-50
$3,750	$6,000	$15,000	$32,500	—

W-2809 • F-160 • Huston-Rosecrans (signatures transposed) (1889–1891) • 80,000

Estimated population: 18 to 20 • *Highest graded:* EF-40.

VG-8	F-12	VF-20	EF-40
$4,250	$6,250	$15,000	$32,500

W-2810 • F-161 • Large brown seal • 100,000

Estimated population: 70 to 80 • *Highest graded:* Unc.

VG-8	F-12	VF-20	EF-40	AU-50	Unc-60	Unc-63
$2,750	$4,500	$8,000	$12,500	$15,000	$17,500	$20,000

W-2811 • F-162 • Tillman-Morgan (regular signature arrangement resumed) (1893–1897) • Small red seal with scalloped border • 212,000

Estimated population: 26 to 30 • *Highest graded:* AU-50.

VG-8	F-12	VF-20	EF-40	AU-50
$3,500	$5,500	$12,000	$20,000	—

W-2812 • F-163 • Bruce-Roberts (1897–1898) • 28,000

Recorded population: 5 • *Highest graded:* Unc • *Selected information:* Existing examples include serials A723512/D, VF, owned by the Federal Reserve Bank of San Francisco; A723583/C, EF, sold in a Knight auction (6/2006) for $34,500; A726554/B, Uncirculated, sold in a Knight auction (8/2005) for $80,500; A727211/C, EF, owned by the Federal Reserve Bank of New York; and A734352/D, F-12 (PMG), sold in a Heritage auction (1/2008) for $69,000.

W-2813 • F-164 • Lyons-Roberts (1898–1905) • 300,000

Estimated population: 220 to 230 • *Highest graded:* Unc.

VG-8	F-12	VF-20	EF-40	AU-50	Unc-60	Unc-63
$2,500	$4,000	$5,750	$7,200	$11,500	$15,750	$20,000

NATIONAL BANK NOTES

Original Series
(Authorized Issue 1863 to 1875)

Notes of this denomination were printed by the American Bank Note Company (whose imprint appears at the bottom border). The contract, dated July 20, 1863, specified the designs for each side of the $20, $50, and $100 denominations, the price for the work, and other matters.[6] These were usually printed in two-subject sheets of $50-$100 with plate letter A for both notes, although there were other sheet layouts. All have a small red Treasury seal with a spiked border. On early notes the Treasury serial number at the upper right is in blue (though it was soon changed to red); on all notes the bank serial number at the lower left is in red. The Act of June 20, 1874, provided for imprinting the bank's charter number, usually twice but on some notes just once. The notes with one charter number have it horizontally on the right.

The face of this note was designed by J.P. Major. At the left is *Washington Crossing the Delaware*, engraved by Alfred Jones after the 1851 painting by Emmanuel Gottlieb Leutze (American artist, 1816–1868), which today hangs in the Metropolitan Museum of Art in New York City. The scene shows Washington and his men rowing from Pennsylvania through drifting ice in the Delaware River on Christmas night 1776 to reach the New Jersey shore. Soldiers of the Continental

Army regrouped and went to defeat British troops and Hessian mercenaries in the battles of Trenton and Princeton, a turning point in the Revolutionary War. The right side of the face of the note has a vignette, *Prayer for Victory* (per the ABNCo contract), also called *Washington at Prayer.* A kneeling officer is shown with three goddesses and a banner inscribed VICTORY above. Louis Delnoce is said to have used his three daughters as models to engrave this scene.

The back illustrates the *Embarkation of the Pilgrims*, engraved by W.W. Rice, of the American Bank Note Co., from a mural by Robert W. Weir. Depicted are emigrants aboard the *Speedwell* (as lettered on a plank). Similar to other back vignettes used on National Bank Notes in this series, under the title is the notation ENGD. BY THE AMERICAN BANK NOTE CO. N.Y. This motif was also used on the $10,000 Federal Reserve Note of 1918, but with the credit line omitted. On the left side is a state seal representing the issuing location of the bank, and to the right is an eagle (on some notes issued in territories an eagle is at both ends).

All $50 notes in this series are very rare. The highest grade listed is a single Extremely Fine–About Uncirculated, followed by an Extremely Fine. Any note in any grade is a numismatic landmark. The opportunity to buy is often more important than the price paid. Market offerings are few and far between.

Banks of Issue and Rarity of Notes

Based upon census information from Don C. Kelly and James M. Kelly (*National Bank Note Census*, Version 4.0) and with some information from other sources, this listing gives each location, the number of banks issuing this series of notes within each, and a commentary.[7]

The Kelly survey records only 23 Original Series $50 notes, including nine from Massachusetts and four from Ohio. None are Uncirculated, and there are no serial number 1 notes.

Alabama • 4 banks of issue • No notes reported.

Colorado Territory • 1 bank of issue • No notes reported.

Connecticut • 48 banks of issue • No notes reported.

Delaware • 4 banks of issue • No notes reported.

District of Columbia • 5 banks of issue • No notes reported.

Georgia • 5 banks of issue • 1 note reported • Merchants National Bank of Savannah (Fair). Even though the grade is low, this note or any similar rare note would merit an extensive description in an auction catalog.

Illinois • 15 banks of issue • No notes reported.

Indiana • 20 banks of issue • 1 note reported • National State Bank of Lafayette (F).

Iowa • 5 banks of issue • No notes reported.

Kentucky • 21 banks of issue • 1 note reported • Citizens National Bank of Winchester (F).

Louisiana • 10 banks of issue • No notes reported.

Maine • 25 banks of issue • 1 note reported • First National Bank of Portland (VG).

Maryland • 20 banks of issue • 1 note reported • Third National Bank of Baltimore (EF).

ORIGINAL SERIES

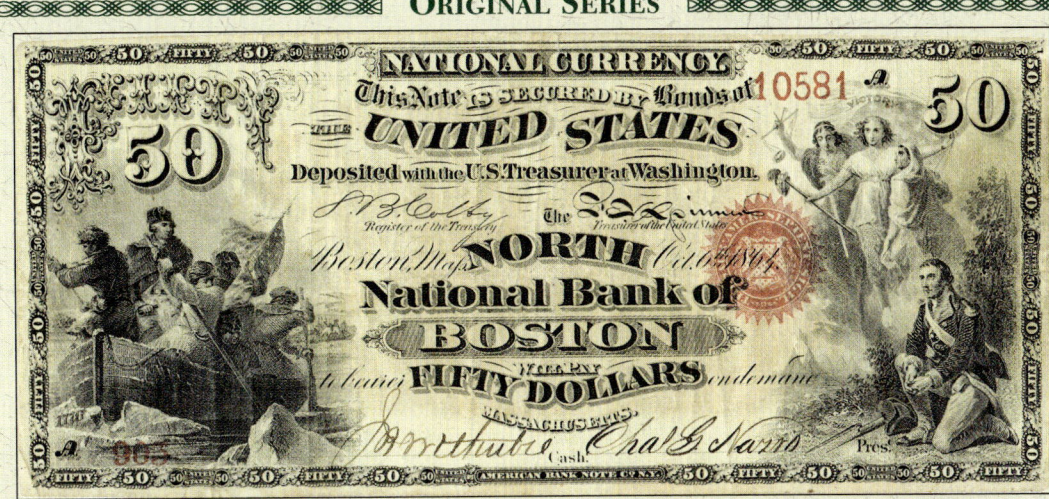

$50 National Bank Note, Original Series (W-2821). North National Bank of Boston, Massachusetts. Chartered as number 525 on October 5, 1864, the bank had an authorized capital of $2,000,000, but began business with half that amount. This note is signed by J.B. Witherbee as cashier and Chas. G. Nazro as president, the first officers of the new institution. This note is from one of 4,700 $20-$20-$50-$100 sheets delivered, an unusual layout. Bank serial 905, plate A, federal serial 10581.

Back of the $50 National Bank Note, Original Series (W-2821), also used on the $50 National Bank Note, Series of 1875. *Embarkation of the Pilgrims* is at the center, and the state seal of Massachusetts is at the left.

Massachusetts • 187 banks of issue • 9 notes reported • Circulated notes from various banks. An EF–AU from the Provincetown National Bank is the finest known from any state.

Michigan • 4 banks of issue • No notes reported.

Minnesota • 2 banks of issue • No notes reported.

Missouri • 5 banks of issue • 1 note reported • National Bank of the State of Missouri, St. Louis (VG–F).

Montana Territory • 1 bank of issue • No notes reported.

Nebraska Territory • 1 bank of issue • No notes reported.

New Hampshire • 20 banks of issue • No notes reported.

New Jersey • 25 banks of issue • No notes reported.

New York • 127 banks of issue • 1 note reported[8] • First National Bank of Rhinebeck (F).

North Carolina • 1 bank of issue • No notes reported.

Ohio • 23 banks of issue • 4 notes reported • Circulated notes from as many banks.

Pennsylvania • 82 banks of issue • 2 notes reported • Third National Bank of Pittsburgh (VG–F) and the Government National Bank of Pottsville (VF).

Rhode Island • 41 banks of issue • No notes reported.

South Carolina • 3 banks of issue • No notes reported.

Tennessee • 8 banks of issue • 1 note reported • Mechanics National Bank of Nashville (VG–F).

Texas • 5 banks of issue • No notes reported.

Utah Territory • 4 banks of issue • No notes reported.

Vermont • 16 banks of issue • No notes reported.

Virginia • 9 banks of issue • No notes reported.

Generic prices for a typical note, although all are rare:

VG-8	F-12	VF-20	EF-40
$15,000	$18,000	$20,000	$35,000

W-2820 • F-440 • Chittenden-Spinner (1861–1864)

Estimated population: 9 or 10 • *Highest graded:* VF-25 • *Selected information:* B&M (11/2002), 4074-472524/A, First

NB of Boston, MA, Good, damaged, $2,070. Smythe (private sale, 6/2001), 1365-37393/A, Third NB of Cincinnati, OH, VG+, $6,600. Stack's (1/2002), 9220-V171566/922A, First NB of Geneva, OH, VG, $4,887.50. Knight (11/2002), 308-70410/A, Third NB of Pittsburgh, PA, VG–F, $6,325.

W-2821 • F-442 • Colby-Spinner (1864–1867)
Estimated population: 12 to 14 • *Highest graded:* EF-40.

VG-8	F-12	VF-20	EF-40
$15,000	$18,000	$20,000	$35,000

W-2822 • F-443 • Allison-Spinner (1869–1875)
Recorded population: 3 • *Highest graded:* F-12 • *Selected information:* B&M (11/2002), 167-P13127/A, NB of the State of Missouri in St. Louis, MO, VG, problems, $41,400. Kreisberg & Schulman (3/1965), 528-47535/A, Mechanics NB of Nashville, TN (only known note on this bank), VG–F, $575.

National Gold Bank Notes, Original Series

The $50 National Gold Bank Note is the rarest denomination in the series, edging out the $100 note by a small margin. Similar to other National Gold Bank Notes, the $50 bills were redeemable at face value in United States gold coins at a time when other federal currency traded at a deep discount in relation to coins. These traded mostly on the West Coast, although they could be redeemed anywhere.

The face of the $50 note has the vignettes *Washington Crossing the Delaware* and *Prayer for Victory*, as found on this denomination's regular National Bank Notes of the Original Series and Series of 1875. Most were printed on yellow-tinted paper, except for some (but not all) of the First National Gold Bank of San Francisco notes.

National Gold Bank Notes of the $50 denomination were issued by banks in California in the cities of Oakland, Petaluma, Sacramento, San Francisco, San Jose, and Santa Barbara. All are rare, with only six Original Series (all but one from the First National Gold Bank of San Francisco) and just one Series of 1875 known today. Fine is the highest grade listed in the Kelly census, and there is just one at that level.

The Kidder National Gold Bank of Boston was the first institution chartered. On March 11, 1871, the Treasury sent 50 sheets of $50-$100 notes. None were ever paid out. On December 4, 1871, all were returned to the Treasury department.[9]

All have the printed signatures of Allison and Spinner and the autographed signatures of the bank cashier and president.

$50 National Gold Bank Note, Original Series (W-2831). Farmers National Gold Bank of San Jose, California.

Back of a $50 National Gold Bank Note. The same montage of gold was used on National Gold Bank Notes of other denominations.

W-2825 • F-1160 • Dated 1870 • San Francisco • First National Gold Bank • 2,000

Recorded population: 5 • *Highest graded:* VF-20 • *Commentary:* Formerly six known, but one was destroyed when an attempt was made to remove it from a laminated seal. One is in the ANA Museum collection. No recent sales.

W-2826 • F-1161b • Dated 1872 • Sacramento • National Gold Bank of D.O. Mills & Co. • 604 • Unknown

W-2827 • F-1161a • San Francisco • National Gold Bank and Trust Co. • 2,856 • Unknown

W-2828 • F-1161d • Dated 1873 • Santa Barbara • First National Gold Bank • 200 • Unknown

W-2829 • F-1161c • Stockton • First National Gold Bank • 867 • Unknown

W-2830 • F-1161e • Dated 1874 • Petaluma • First National Gold Bank • 100 • Unknown

W-2831 • F-1161 • San Jose • Farmers National Gold Bank • 400

Recorded population: 1 • *Graded:* VG-8 • *Commentary:* Harley L. Freeman sold to B. Max Mehl in 1953; acquired by Amon Carter Jr. Private collection.

W-2832 • F-1161f • Dated 1873 • Oakland • Union National Gold Bank • 620 • Unknown

W-2834 • F-unlisted • Dated 1870 • Boston • Kidder National Gold Bank • 50 • None issued

Series of 1875
(Authorized Issue 1875 to 1902)

The Series of 1875 $50 notes continued the use of plates signed by American Bank Note Company. Under the top border at the upper left is PRINTED AT THE BUREAU OF ENGRAVING & PRINTING, U.S. TREASURY DEPT. For some banks for which there had been no Original Series plates made, the Bureau made new plates with BUREAU OF ENGRAVING & PRINTING TREASURY DEPt. at the bottom border, and no additional imprint or mention of the American Bank Note Company. These are exceedingly rare, although scant notice has been taken of them.

The small red Treasury seal now has a scalloped rather than a spiked border. All have SERIES 1875 imprinted vertically in red to the left of center, near the bank charter number. The Treasury and bank serial numbers and two charter numbers are also in red. A small percentage of these notes are printed on paper with a vertical, blue-tinted streak of the type most familiarly used on the Legal Tender Notes beginning with the Series of 1869 (paper made under the James M. Willcox patent of July 24, 1866). These are especially colorful and attractive.

Any Series of 1875 $50 note is a rarity, although not to the degree of the Originals. Just three Uncirculated notes are recorded. Most notes show extensive evidence of circulation, but average grades are higher than on the Original Series notes.

Banks of Issue and Rarity of Notes

Based upon census information from Don C. Kelly and James M. Kelly (*National Bank Note Census*, Version 4.0) and with some information from other sources, this listing gives each location, the number of banks issuing this series of notes within each, and a commentary.[10]

The Kelly survey records 63 Series of 1875 notes, or nearly three times the Original Series bills. The only serial number 1 note is from Illinois, and the only three Uncirculated notes are also from Illinois.

Alabama • 4 banks of issue • 1 note reported • National Commercial Bank of Mobile (F).

California • 1 bank of issue • 2 notes reported • First National Bank of San Francisco (not graded).

Colorado Territory • 1 bank of issue • 1 note reported • First National Bank of Denver (VG).

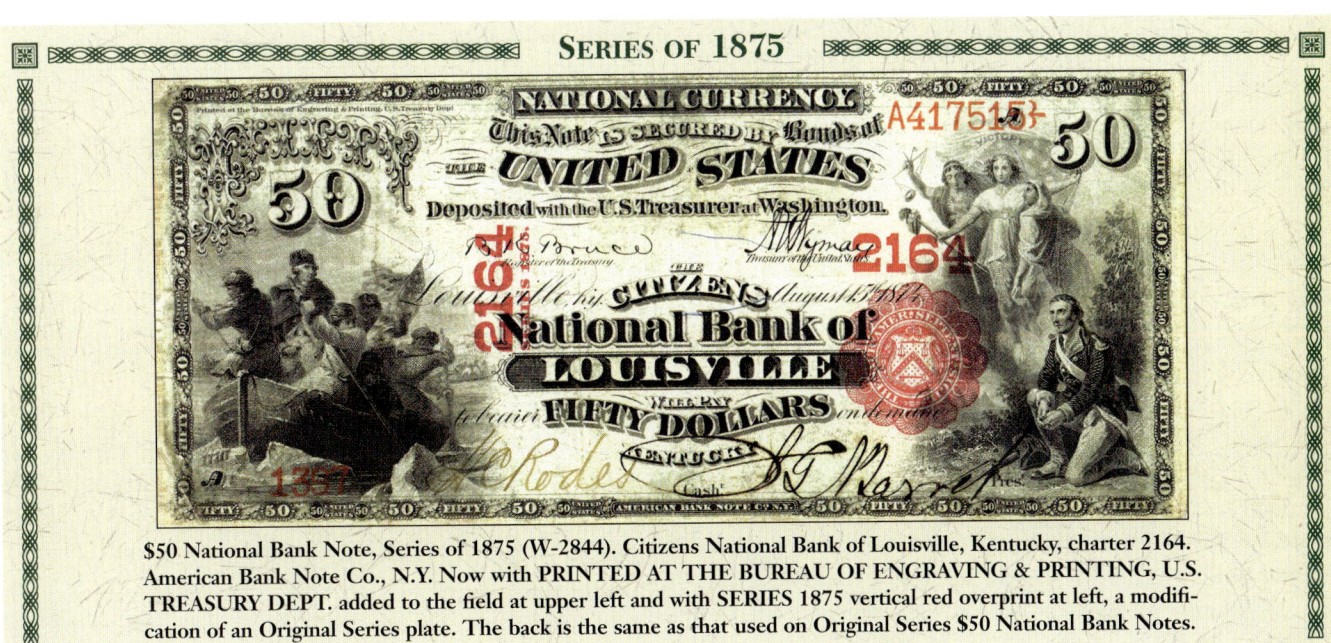

$50 National Bank Note, Series of 1875 (W-2844). Citizens National Bank of Louisville, Kentucky, charter 2164. American Bank Note Co., N.Y. Now with PRINTED AT THE BUREAU OF ENGRAVING & PRINTING, U.S. TREASURY DEPT. added to the field at upper left and with SERIES 1875 vertical red overprint at left, a modification of an Original Series plate. The back is the same as that used on Original Series $50 National Bank Notes.

Colorado • 1 bank of issue • No notes reported.

Connecticut • 32 banks of issue • No notes reported.

Delaware • 3 banks of issue • No notes reported.

Georgia • 4 banks of issue • No notes reported.

Illinois • 11 banks of issue • 7 notes reported • Three Unc, from the Second National Bank of Danville (one) and the Streator National Bank (two). The only Series of 1875 serial number 1 note from any state is from the First National Bank of Lincoln (VF).

Indiana • 14 banks of issue • 1 note reported • Evansville National Bank (EF).

Iowa • 5 banks of issue • 1 note reported • First National Bank of Villisca (EF).

Kansas • 1 bank of issue • 1 note reported • Exchange National Bank of Atchison (not graded).

Kentucky • 21 banks of issue • 5 notes reported • Kentucky National Bank of Louisville (VF); and Citizens National Bank of Louisville (two VF, one VF–EF), and Citizens National Bank of Winchester (VF).

Louisiana • 6 banks of issue • 1 note reported • New Orleans National Bank (not graded).

Maine • 18 banks of issue • 1 note reported • National Traders Bank of Portland (VF).

Maryland • 18 banks of issue • 2 notes reported • National Exchange Bank of Baltimore (not graded) and National Bank of Baltimore (VG).

Massachusetts • 132 banks of issue • 4 notes reported • Circulated notes from as many banks.

Michigan • 3 banks of issue • No notes reported.

Minnesota • 2 banks of issue • 1 note reported • Manistee National Bank (F).

Mississippi • 1 bank of issue • No notes reported.

Missouri • 3 banks of issue • No notes reported.

Nebraska • 3 banks of issue • No notes reported.

New Hampshire • 7 banks of issue • 2 notes reported • Mechanicks National Bank of Concord (F) and National Granite State Bank of Exeter (G).

New Jersey • 15 banks of issue • 2 notes reported • German National Bank of the City of Newark (G) and Mechanics National Bank of Trenton (EF).

New Mexico Territory • 2 banks of issue • No notes reported.

New York • 78 banks of issue • 8 notes reported • Circulated notes from six banks.

Ohio • 24 banks of issue • 3 notes reported • National LaFayette Bank of Cincinnati (VG), First National Bank of Cleveland (AU), and the Commercial National Bank of Cleveland (F).

Pennsylvania • 81 banks of issue • 11 notes reported • Circulated notes from as many different banks, an unusual amount of diversity.

Rhode Island • 20 banks of issue • No notes reported.

South Carolina • 3 banks of issue • No notes reported.

Tennessee • 5 banks of issue • 5 notes reported • Circulated notes from three banks.

Texas • 4 banks of issue • No notes reported.

Utah Territory • 1 bank of issue • 1 note reported • Deseret National Bank of Salt Lake City (F).

Vermont • 10 banks of issue • No notes reported.

Virginia • 7 banks of issue • No notes reported.

Wisconsin • 1 bank of issue • 1 note reported • Second National Bank of Beloit (VF).

Generic prices for a typical note, although all are rare:

VG-8	F-12	VF-20	EF-40
$15,000	$18,000	$20,000	$35,000

W-2839 • F-444 • Allison-New (1875–1876)

Estimated population: 24 to 28 • Highest graded: AU-53.

VG-8	F-12	VF-20	EF-40	AU-50
$15,000	$18,000	$20,000	$35,000	—

W-2840 • F-444a • Allison-Wyman (1876–1877)

Recorded population: 4 • Highest graded: EF-40 • Selected information: Knight (6/2000), 612-A14706/A, State NB of Memphis, TN, EF, $16,500.

W-2841 • F-445 • Allison-Gilfillan (1877–1878)

Recorded population: 5 • Highest graded: EF-40 • Selected information: Knight (9/2005), 2014-A389988/A, Deseret NB of Salt Lake City, Utah Territory, Fine, $94,875. Price is mainly based on its value as a territorial note.

W-2842 • F-446 • Scofield-Gilfillan (1878–1881)

Estimated population: 9 or 10 • Highest graded: AU-50 • Selected information: CAA (1/2004), 290-A18036/290/A, Market NB of Boston, MA, F–VF, pinholes, $19,550. CAA (5/2002), 113-A311775/A, Mechanics NB of Boston, MA, VF, $7,705. Spink (7/2007), 3143-A394041/A, Exchange NB of Pittsburgh, PA, Fine, $37,000.

W-2843 • F-447 • Bruce-Gilfillan (1881–1883)

Estimated population: 12 to 14 • Highest graded: Unc.

VG-8	F-12	VF-20	EF-40	AU-50	Unc-60
$15,000	$18,000	$20,000	$35,000	—	—

W-2844 • F-448 • Bruce-Wyman (1883–1885)

Recorded population: 5 • Highest graded: VF-20 • Selected information: Stack's (3/1990), 4224-A423716/A, First NB of San Francisco, CA, VF–EF, $9,350. Knight (6/2002), 276-A352648/A, Citizens NB of Louisville, KY, VF–EF, $12,650. CAA (1/2006), 1397-A417515/A, Citizens NB of Louisville, KY, VF, $23,000.

W-2845 • F-449 • Rosecrans-Huston (1889–1891)

Recorded population: 1 • Graded: VF-25 • Selected information: Stack's (5/1992), 1-A430837/A, First NB of Lincoln, IL, VF, $8,000. The serial number 1 adds importance to this classic.

W-2846 • F-450 • Rosecrans-Nebeker (1891–1893)

Recorded population: 1 • Graded: VF-25 • Selected information: The known note is serial 1343-A449040/A, VF, from the Millerton National Bank in New York.

W-2847 • F-451 • Tillman-Morgan (1893–1897)

Recorded population: 2 • Highest graded: Unc • Selected information: CAA (5/2000), 1314-A459648/A, Second NB of Danville, IL, Unc, $93,500.

National Gold Bank Notes, Series of 1875

All have the printed signatures of Allison and Spinner and the autographed signatures of the bank cashier and president. Some notes probably were printed on white instead of yellow paper. Only one is known today, graded Fine in the Kelly census.

W-2850 • F-1160a • Dated 1870 • San Francisco • First National Gold Bank • 620

Recorded population: 1 • Selected information: The known note is serial 20-A338681/A, F–VF, ex Wade, Bebee, presently in the ANA Museum collection.

Series of 1882, Brown Back
(Authorized Issue 1882 to 1908)

This series (illus. on p. 565) was the result of the expirations of the earliest national banks' charters and the formation of new chartered banks, as provided by the Act of July 11, 1882.

To create distinctively new notes, the backs of the $10, $20, $50, and $100 notes were changed, while many of the earlier face plates created by the American Bank Note Company for the Original Series and Series of 1875 were retained. This was accomplished by either leaving the American Bank Note Company imprint at the bottom of the face and adding a printed notice in the field that this was a BEP product, or by reentering the Bureau of Engraving and Printing name where the American imprint had been. In still other instances new plates were created using the old designs. The decorative border of the notes was changed to include the bank's charter number six times, said to have been of use if a fragment of a note was sent to the Treasury department for redemption.

Plates were typically laid out as $50-$100, with plate letter A for both notes. Charter numbers were overprinted in brown on the face from the outset, vertically to left of center on the $10 to $100 issues. The Treasury seal is in brown as well. Beginning in September 1890, the position was changed to horizontal at the upper right. Peter Huntoon states that less than 14% of the plates had the vertical position, and as these were earlier printings, an even smaller percentage survives today. Regional letters N, E, M, S, W, and P were overprinted twice in brown on the face of notes starting with shipments received on March 17, 1902.

The reverse side was completely redesigned to create the Brown Back style printed in ink of that color. On the left is a state or territorial seal representing the issuing bank's location, as on earlier series. This necessitated making a set of plates for each state or territory. On the right is a perched eagle. At the center is a greenish-blue impression of the bank's charter number in large figures, enabling the bills to be easily sorted when they were redeemed.

These bills were first issued in 1882. Any bank with its charter extended from mid-1882 to 1902 and any new bank chartered during that period received notes of this type, and continued to receive them for up to 20 years, even though during that time the new Series of 1902 notes were introduced. Series of 1882 Brown Backs were printed into March 1908, at which time the Aldrich-Vreeland Act mandated new wording, and production stopped.

These notes are very scarce. Most are in circulated grades, but enough scattered Uncirculated examples appear that finding one for a type set will not be a problem.

Banks of Issue and Rarity of Notes

Based upon census information from Don C. Kelly and James M. Kelly (*National Bank Note Census*, Version 4.0) and with some information from other sources, this listing gives each location, the number of banks issuing this series of notes within each, and a commentary.[11]

The Kelly survey records 312 of these. Only four serial number 1 notes are recorded; these are listed below.

Alabama • 10 banks of issue • 2 notes reported • City National Bank of Birmingham (VF) and the City National Bank of Selma (VF).

Arizona Territory • 2 banks of issue • No notes reported.

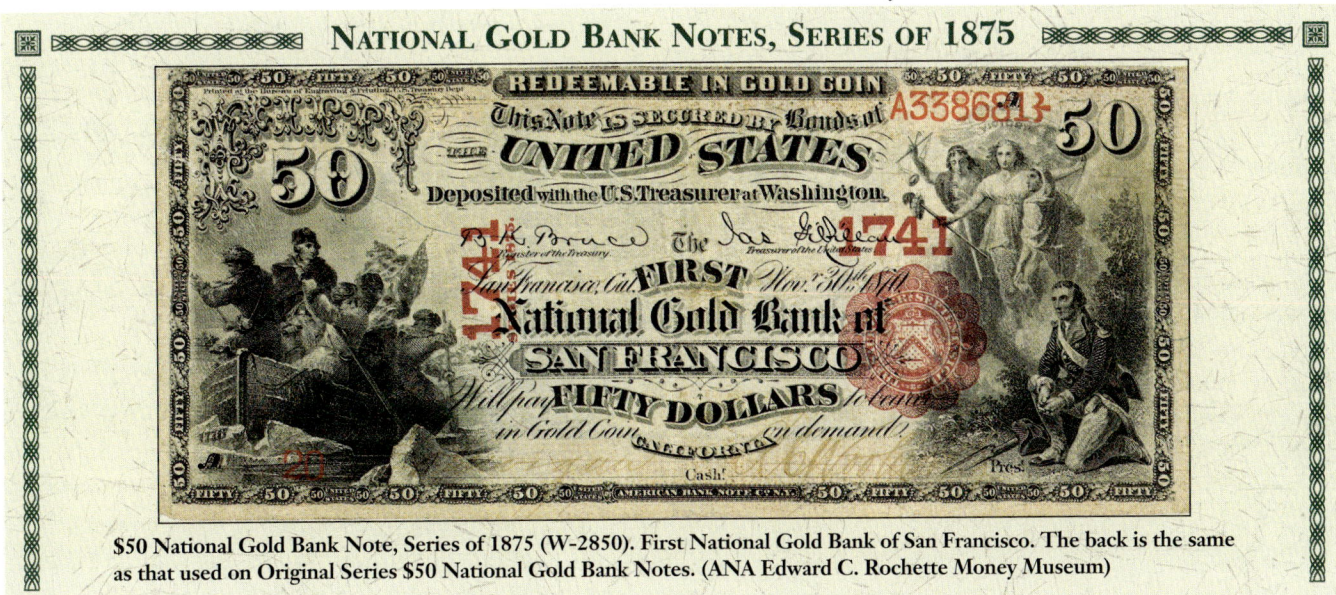

$50 National Gold Bank Note, Series of 1875 (W-2850). First National Gold Bank of San Francisco. The back is the same as that used on Original Series $50 National Gold Bank Notes. (ANA Edward C. Rochette Money Museum)

Arkansas • 5 banks of issue • 3 notes reported • Camden National Bank (VF–EF), First National Bank of Fort Smith (F), and the German National Bank of Little Rock (VF).

California • 27 banks of issue • 7 notes reported • Five different banks are represented. Two Unc notes are from the First National Bank of San Francisco and the First National Bank of San Jose.

Colorado • 17 banks of issue • 6 notes reported • From five different banks. The only Unc note is from the Colorado National Bank of Denver.

Connecticut • 8 banks of issue • 1 note reported • Citizens National Bank of Waterbury (F).

Dakota Territory • 2 banks of issue • No notes reported.

Delaware • 8 banks of issue • 2 notes reported • National Bank of Smyrna (VF) and the First National Bank of Wilmington (VG).

District of Columbia • 4 banks of issue • No notes reported.

Florida • 7 banks of issue • 1 note reported • National Bank of Jacksonville (VF).

Georgia • 7 banks of issue • 3 notes reported • First National Bank of Macon (VF) and the First National Bank of Newnan (F–VF, VF–EF).

Hawaii Territory • 1 bank of issue • No notes reported.

Idaho • 3 banks of issue • No notes reported.

Illinois • 64 banks of issue • 42 notes reported • Five Unc notes are listed. The only serial number 1 note is from the First National Bank of Lincoln (AU).

Indian Territory • 5 banks of issue • No notes reported.

Indiana • 27 banks of issue • 10 notes reported • All are circulated.

Iowa • 42 banks of issue • 15 notes reported • The only Unc note is from the First National Bank of Davenport. The only serial number 1 note is from the Live Stock National Bank of Sioux City (not graded).

Kansas • 29 banks of issue • 8 notes reported • All are circulated.

Kentucky • 23 banks of issue • 8 notes reported • All are circulated. Five banks are represented.

Louisiana • 10 banks of issue • 13 notes reported • All are circulated. Four banks are represented.

Maine • 11 banks of issue • No notes reported.

Maryland • 25 banks of issue • 5 notes reported • From three banks. All are circulated.

Massachusetts • 115 banks of issue • 8 notes reported • All are circulated.

Michigan • 9 banks of issue • 3 notes reported • National Bank of Houghton (EF–AU), First National Bank, Lake Linden (VF–EF), and a serial number 1 note from the First National Bank, Lake Linden (not graded).

Minnesota • 12 banks of issue • 11 notes reported • Two banks are represented. Seven Unc notes are from the First National Bank of Wadena, a remarkable cluster.

Mississippi • 4 banks of issue • 1 note reported • First National Bank, Vicksburg (G).

Missouri • 10 banks of issue • 12 notes reported • All are circulated.

Montana • 3 banks of issue • 3 notes reported • All are from the First National Bank of Butte and all are Unc.

Montana Territory • 2 banks of issue • No notes reported.

Nebraska • 25 banks of issue • 8 notes reported • Four different banks are represented. All are circulated.

New Hampshire • 9 banks of issue • No notes reported.

New Jersey • 29 banks of issue • 3 notes reported • Clinton National Bank (not graded) and the Union National Bank, Newark (VG). There is one serial number 1 note from the Bridgeton National Bank (AU).

New Mexico Territory • 1 bank of issue • 2 notes reported • First National Bank of Albuquerque (F, Unc).

New York • 79 banks of issue • 12 notes reported • All are circulated.

North Carolina • 8 banks of issue • 4 notes reported • All are circulated. Three are from the Blue Ridge National Bank of Asheville.

North Dakota • 4 banks of issue • 1 note reported • First National Bank of Grand Forks (not graded).

Ohio • 54 banks of issue • 31 notes reported • Five Unc notes are listed.

Oklahoma • 6 banks of issue • No notes reported.

Oklahoma Territory • 7 banks of issue • No notes reported.

Oregon • 4 banks of issue • 2 notes reported • First National Bank of Heppner (F) and the First National Bank of Portland (F–VF).

Pennsylvania • 128 banks of issue • 47 notes reported • Six Unc notes are listed.

Rhode Island • 9 banks of issue • 1 note reported • Providence National Bank (F–VF).

South Carolina • 3 banks of issue • No notes reported.

South Dakota • 4 banks of issue • No notes reported.

Tennessee • 19 banks of issue • 4 notes reported • From three banks. All are circulated.

Texas • 77 banks of issue • 21 notes reported • Four Unc notes are known.

Utah • 1 bank of issue • No notes reported.

Utah Territory • 3 banks of issue • No notes reported.

Vermont • 7 banks of issue • 4 notes reported • All are circulated. Three are from National Bank of Barre.

Virginia • 9 banks of issue • No notes reported.

Washington • 7 banks of issue • 5 notes reported • All are circulated.

Washington Territory • 1 bank of issue • No notes reported.

West Virginia • 2 banks of issue • No notes reported.

Wisconsin • 7 banks of issue • 3 notes reported • All are circulated, from National Exchange Bank of Milwaukee.

SERIES OF 1882, BROWN BACK

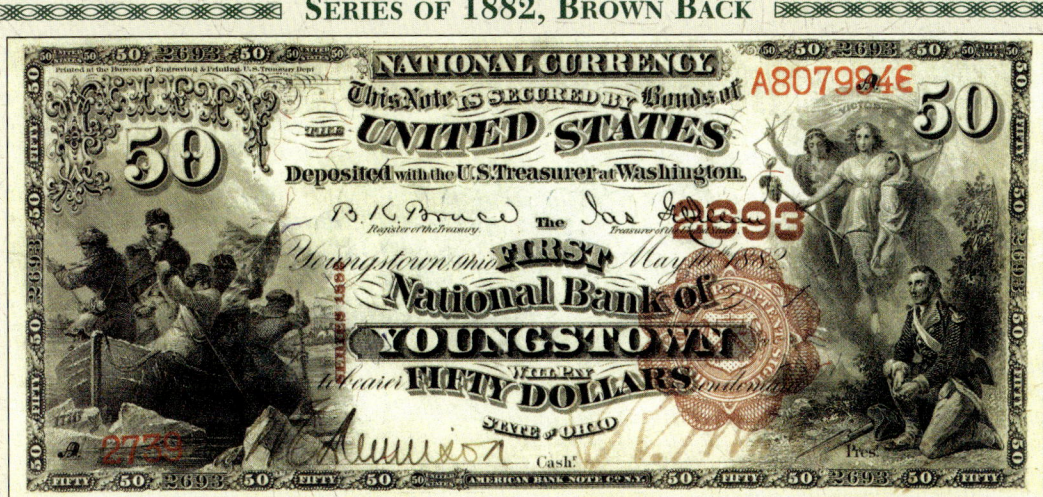

$50 National Bank Note, Series of 1882, Brown Back (W-2855). First National Bank of Youngstown, Ohio, charter 2693. The motifs are similar to Series of 1875, with retained American Bank Note Co. imprint and added PRINTED AT THE BUREAU OF ENGRAVING & PRINTING, U.S. TREASURY DEPT. This indicates the plate was made earlier, then modified slightly for the Series of 1882. SERIES 1882 is printed vertically at the left. Brown Treasury seal.

The distinctive back of the $50 National Bank Note, Series of 1882, Brown Back (W-2855). At the center is the bank's charter number. At the left is the state seal of Ohio, reflecting the location of the issuing bank.

Generic prices for a typical note from a state from which notes range from available to just slightly scarce:

VG-8	F-12	VF-20	EF-40	AU-50	Unc-60	Unc-63
$5,750	$7,500	$9,500	$11,500	$14,000	$17,000	$20,000

W-2855 • F-507 • Bruce-Gilfillan (1881–1883)
Estimated population: 15 to 17 • *Highest graded:* Unc.

VG-8	F-12	VF-20	EF-40	AU-50	Unc-60	Unc-63
$5,750	$7,500	$9,500	$11,000	$14,000	$17,000	$20,000

W-2856 • F-508 • Bruce-Wyman (1883–1885)
Estimated population: 70 to 80 • *Highest graded:* Unc.

VG-8	F-12	VF-20	EF-40	AU-50	Unc-60	Unc-63
$5,750	$7,500	$9,500	$11,000	$14,000	$17,000	$20,000

W-2857 • F-509 • Bruce-Jordan (1885)
Recorded population: 6 • *Highest graded:* VF-25 • *Selected information:* Knight (2/2000), 311-A567454/A, Farmers & Mechanics NB of Frederic, MD, VG–F, pinholes, $6,325.

Smythe (6/2003), B272289/A, Norfolk NB, NE, F–VF, $3,738. Knight (8/1999), 2065-A546674/A, Farmers NB of Amsterdam, NY, VF–EF, $5,225.

W-2858 • F-510 • Rosecrans-Jordan (1885–1887)
Estimated population: 26 to 30 • *Highest graded:* Unc.

VG-8	F-12	VF-20	EF-40	AU-50	Unc-60	Unc-63
$5,750	$7,500	$9,500	$11,000	$14,000	$17,000	$20,000

W-2859 • F-511 • Rosecrans-Hyatt (1887–1889)
Estimated population: 19 to 22 • *Highest graded:* VF-20.

VG-8	F-12	VF-20
$5,750	$7,500	$9,500

W-2860 • F-512 • Rosecrans-Huston (1889–1891)
Estimated population: 36 to 42 • *Highest graded:* Unc.

VG-8	F-12	VF-20	EF-40	AU-50	Unc-60	Unc-63
$5,750	$7,500	$9,500	$11,000	$14,000	$17,000	$20,000

W-2861 • F-513 • Rosecrans-Nebeker (1891–1893)

Estimated population: 42 to 46 • *Highest graded:* Unc.

VG-8	F-12	VF-20	EF-40	AU-50	Unc-60	Unc-63
$5,750	$7,500	$9,500	$11,000	$14,000	$17,000	$20,000

W-2862 • F-514 • Rosecrans-Morgan (1893)

Estimated population: 11 to 13 • *Highest graded:* Unc.

VG-8	F-12	VF-20	EF-40	AU-50	Unc-60	Unc-63
$5,750	$7,500	$9,500	$11,000	$14,000	$17,000	$20,000

W-2863 • F-515 • Tillman-Morgan (1893–1897)

Estimated population: 50 to 60 • *Highest graded:* Unc.

VG-8	F-12	VF-20	EF-40	AU-50	Unc-60	Unc-63
$5,750	$7,500	$9,500	$11,000	$14,000	$17,000	$20,000

W-2864 • F-516 • Tillman-Roberts (1897)

Recorded population: 4 • *Highest graded:* Unc • *Selected information:* Knight (8/2002), 647-B210993/A, First NB of Sequin, TX, AU, $28,750.

W-2865 • F-517 • Bruce-Roberts (1897–1898)

Estimated population: 10 to 12 • *Highest graded:* Unc.

VG-8	F-12	VF-20	EF-40	AU-50	Unc-60	Unc-63
$5,750	$7,500	$9,500	$11,000	$14,000	$17,000	$20,000

W-2866 • F-518 • Lyons-Roberts (1898–1905)

Estimated population: 30 to 35 • *Highest graded:* Unc.

VG-8	F-12	VF-20	EF-40	AU-50	Unc-60	Unc-63
$5,750	$7,500	$9,500	$11,000	$14,000	$17,000	$20,000

W-2867 • F-518a • Vernon-Treat (1906–1909)

Recorded population: 2 • *Highest graded:* VF-25 • *Selected information:* Smythe (9/1997), 2226-B603474/A, Exchange NB of Spokane, WA, VG, damaged, $1,300.

Series of 1882, Date Back
(Authorized Issue 1908 to 1915, Some Through 1922)

This unexpected issue was created to reflect a change in the backing of the notes authorized by the Aldrich-Vreeland Act of May 30, 1908. Notes of the new type were issued beginning in that year. Production of 1882 Brown Backs ceased, and new orders were filled by the Date Back type.

In order to make it easier to fund the notes, banks were allowed to deposit good securities in addition to government bonds, while earlier only U.S. government bonds had been allowed. All have the inscription on the face, "This note is secured by bonds of the United States or other securities." The inscription was often added by altering face plates of the same design used for earlier series. Although the Act expired on June 30, 1915, marking the end of the official use of this imprint and the related back, Peter Huntoon notes that some $50 and $100 plates were continued in use until 1922, while the lower denominations were discontinued in 1916. Logically, the later notes should have been Value Backs. Otherwise the face motifs are the same as on the Series of 1882 Brown Backs (continued from the Original Series and Series

of 1875). The serial numbers, charter number, two regional letters, and the Treasury seal are now all in blue.

The back was redesigned completely. At the center is a large open space with the dates 1882 and 1908, with an ornament between them. Above near the border is the obligation or redemption clause, and below near the border is the counterfeiting clause. To each side are matching heraldic eagles from the reverse of the Great Seal of the United States. Gone are the state and territorial seals previously used, making plate preparation a much easier task.

As a class all 1882 Date Back $50 notes are rarities in any grade. Uncirculated notes are especially hard to find.

Banks of Issue and Rarity of Notes

Based upon census information from Don C. Kelly and James M. Kelly (*National Bank Note Census,* Version 4.0) and with some information from other sources, this listing gives each location, the number of banks issuing this series of notes within each, and a commentary.[12]

The Kelly survey records only 199 of these. Only one number 1 note is listed, from Oklahoma.

Alabama • 1 bank of issue • No notes reported.

Arizona Territory • 1 bank of issue • 1 note reported • National Bank of Tucson (VF).

Arkansas • 1 bank of issue • No notes reported.

California • 16 banks of issue • 25 notes reported • All are circulated.

Colorado • 3 banks of issue • 2 notes reported • First National Bank, Boulder (not graded) and the First National Bank, Trinidad (Fair).

Connecticut • 1 bank of issue • 1 note reported • Manufacturers National Bank, Waterbury (F), serial 131.

Delaware • 2 banks of issue • 1 note reported • First National Bank of Smyrna (F–VF).

District of Columbia • 1 bank of issue • No notes reported.

Florida • 3 banks of issue • No notes reported.

Georgia • 3 banks of issue • No notes reported.

Hawaii Territory • 1 bank of issue • No notes reported.

Idaho • 1 bank of issue • No notes reported.

Illinois • 26 banks of issue • 22 notes reported • Three Unc examples are from the Corn Exchange National Bank, Chicago, Second National Bank of Danville, and the Palmer National Bank of Danville.

Indiana • 12 banks of issue • 8 notes reported • All are circulated.

Iowa • 16 banks of issue • 11 notes reported • The only Unc note is from the Merchants National Bank of Cedar Rapids.

Kansas • 6 banks of issue • 2 notes reported • Baxter National Bank of Baxter Springs (VF) and the National Bank of Seneca (VF).

Kentucky • 8 banks of issue • 6 notes reported • All are circulated.

Maryland • 8 banks of issue • 3 notes reported • National Marine Bank of Baltimore (VF), National Howard Bank of

SERIES OF 1882, DATE BACK

$50 National Bank Note, Series of 1882, Date Back (W-2875). First National Bank of Albuquerque, New Mexico Territory, charter 2614. Imprint of the Bureau of Engraving and Printing as part of lower border, indicating a new plate made for the Series of 1882. Motifs similar to the preceding issue. The W is for West, the bank's location. Territorial imprints are especially desired by numismatists.

The back of the $50 National Bank Note, Series of 1882, Date Back (W-2875), with 1882 and 1908 dates.

Baltimore (F), and the Farmers & Merchants National Bank of Cambridge (VG–F).

Massachusetts • 12 banks of issue • 2 notes reported • Both are circulated and from the National Shawmut Bank of Boston.

Michigan • 3 banks of issue • 4 notes reported • Two Unc notes are from the National Bank of Ionia.

Minnesota • 5 banks of issue • 2 notes reported • National Bank of Glencoe (AU, VG–F).

Missouri • 4 banks of issue • 3 notes reported • State National Bank of Saint Louis (F–VF, AU, EF–AU).

Montana • 1 bank of issue • 7 notes reported • All are circulated and from the First National Bank of Butte.

Nebraska • 4 banks of issue • 3 notes reported • All are circulated.

New Hampshire • 1 bank of issue • No notes reported.

New Jersey • 4 banks of issue • No notes reported.

New Mexico • 1 bank of issue • 5 notes reported • All are circulated.

New Mexico Territory • 1 bank of issue • 2 notes reported • First National Bank of Albuquerque (VG, EF).

New York • 11 banks of issue • 22 notes reported • Seven Unc notes are listed.

North Carolina • 3 banks of issue • 7 notes reported • All are circulated.

North Dakota • 1 bank of issue • 7 notes reported • All are circulated.

Ohio • 21 banks of issue • 11 notes reported • All are circulated.

Oklahoma • 6 banks of issue • 7 notes reported • All are circulated.

Pennsylvania • 28 banks of issue • 14 notes reported • Two Unc notes are from the First National Bank of Parkers Landing.

South Carolina • 1 bank of issue • 1 note reported • City National Bank of Greenville (VF).

Tennessee • 2 banks of issue • 1 note reported • Peoples National Bank of Gallatin (F–VF), serial 250.

Texas • 23 banks of issue • 18 notes reported • All are circulated.

Utah • 1 bank of issue • No notes reported.

Vermont • 2 banks of issue • No notes reported.

Virginia • 3 banks of issue • No notes reported.

Washington • 4 banks of issue • 1 note reported • Exchange National Bank of Spokane (EF), serial 837.

West Virginia • 1 bank of issue • No notes reported.

Generic prices for a typical note

VG-8	F-12	VF-20	EF-40	AU-50	Unc-60	Unc-63
$5,200	$6,750	$8,250	$9,500	$12,250	$14,750	$17,500

W-2870 • F-558 • Rosecrans-Huston (1889–1891)

Recorded population: 7 • *Highest graded:* AU-50 • *Selected information:* Hickman (3/1990), 177-A8157/B, First NB of San Francisco, CA, VF, $2,500. Heritage (4/2008), 4-A74835/B, First NB of Baltimore, OH (low serial), VF, $5,463. Knight (8/2001), 134-A5444/A, American NB of Austin, TX, Fine, $3,080.

W-2871 • F-559 • Rosecrans-Nebeker (1891–1893)

Recorded population: 3 • *Highest graded:* AU • *Selected information:* Heritage (4/2008), 200-A79831/B, Farmers NB of Shelbyville, IN, VF, pinholes, $5,463. CAA 92/2005), 676-A163737/7676/A, Columbia NB of Buffalo, NY, AU, $57,500. Knight (8/2003), 8320-A165381/A, Columbia NB of Buffalo, NY, AU, $5,060.

W-2872 • F-560 • Tillman-Morgan (1893–1897)

Estimated population: 22 to 26 • *Highest graded:* EF-40.

VG-8	F-12	VF-20	EF-40
$5,200	$6,750	$8,250	$9,500

W-2873 • F-561 • Tillman-Roberts (1897)

Estimated population: 18 to 20 • *Highest graded:* Unc.

VG-8	F-12	VF-20	EF-40	AU-50	Unc-60	Unc-63
$5,200	$6,750	$8,250	$9,500	$12,200	$14,750	$17,500

W-2874 • F-562 • Bruce-Roberts (1897–1898)

Estimated population: 10 to 12 • *Highest graded:* Unc • *Selected information:* Smythe (9/1997), 681-A12335/D, Corn Exchange NB of Chicago, IL, Fine, $600. Stack's (3/1995), 1123-A37021/B, Corn Exchange NB of Chicago, IL, Unc, $11,000. Heritage (4/2008), 2790-A67512/D, Corn Exchange NB of Chicago, IL, VF–EF, $5,750. Knight (5/1987), 1928-A37826/B, Corn Exchange NB of Chicago, IL, EF–AU, $1,200.

W-2875 • F-563 • Lyons-Roberts (1898–1905)

Estimated population: 130 to 140 • *Highest graded:* Unc.

VG-8	F-12	VF-20	EF-40	AU-50	Unc-60	Unc-63
$5,200	$6,750	$8,250	$9,500	$12,200	$14,750	$17,500

W-2876 • F-564 • Vernon-Treat (1906–1909)

Recorded population: 7 • *Highest graded:* EF-45 • *Selected information:* CAA (5/2001), 1-A126462/B, First NB of Madill, OK (serial number 1 note), Fine, $19,800. CAA 99/2006), 82-A7182/C, Western NB of Oklahoma City, OK, VF, $13,800.

W-2877 • F-565 • Napier-McClung (1911–1912)

Recorded population: 5 • *Highest graded:* EF-40 • *Selected information:* CAA (9/2005), 1035-A154427/E, First NB of Albuquerque, New Mexico Territory, VF–EF, $4,025; 1996-A167055/E, First NB of Albuquerque, New Mexico Territory, VG, $4,025.

Series of 1882, Value Back
(Authorized Issue 1915+)

When the Aldrich-Vreeland Act expired on June 20, 1915, the BEP created the Value Back, which spelled out the denomination, to replace the Date Back type. The security of the notes reverted to bonds only, as it had been before the implementation of the Aldrich-Vreeland Act of May 30, 1908. Only two banks ordered 1882 $50 Value Back Notes, the Canal-Commercial National Bank of New Orleans and the Winters National Bank of Dayton, Ohio. These were printed on $50-$100 sheets. New face plates were made in the old style used on the Series of 1882 Brown Back notes, without "or other securities." The guarantee reads, "This note is secured by bonds of the United States deposited with the U.S. Treasurer at Washington."

Otherwise the face was similar to that used for the Series of 1882 Date Back, with the serial numbers, charter number, two regional letters, and the Treasury seal all in blue. The back continued the same vignettes as the preceding type, but now with FIFTY DOLLARS in large letters at the center.

Further details are adapted from Peter Huntoon's *United States Large Size National Bank Notes*:

> The Dayton Bank had issued $50 and the $100 Series of 1882 Date Backs earlier, from a $50-$100 plate. This combination had not been used after about November 23, 1910, when the $50-$50-$100 format came into wide use. For the Value Backs the Dayton Bank got 1,800 sheets but the New Orleans Bank got 1,057 sheets. Accordingly, 8,571 of the $50 notes and the 2,857 of the $100 notes were made.

The charter of the Canal-Commercial National Bank of New Orleans was extended on December 12, 1920. By that time just 1,057 of its sheets had been issued. There were 243 other sheets, serials 1058 through 1300, that were cancelled, after which the bank received 1902 Plain Back notes.

This is the rarest National Bank Note type for all denominations from $1 to $50, and it is considered to be a classic. The $100 notes are even rarer. All are circulated.

Banks of Issue and Rarity of Notes

Based upon census information from Don C. Kelly and James M. Kelly (*National Bank Note Census*, 4th edition).[13] The survey records just eight of these, from two different banks. There are no serial number 1 notes and no Uncirculated notes. The $50 notes of this series are closely related to the $100 notes, from the same sheets.

Louisiana • 1 bank of issue • 2 notes reported • Canal-Commercial National Bank of New Orleans (both F).

SERIES OF 1882, VALUE BACK

$50 National Bank Note, Series of 1882, Value Back (W-2878). The Canal-Commercial Bank of New Orleans. Only two banks issued $50 Series of 1882 Value Back notes.

The back of the $50 National Bank Note, Series of 1882, Value Back (W-2878).

Ohio • 1 bank of issue • 6 notes reported • Winters National Bank of Dayton (one VG, two F, two VF, and one VF–EF).

W-2878 • F-586 • Lyons-Roberts (1898–1905) • 8,571

Recorded population: 8 • Highest graded: VF-30 • Selected information: CAA (5/2005), 58-A164727/A, Commercial NB of New Orleans, LA, Fine, $46,000. Knight (8/2003), 783-A170162/B, Commercial NB of New Orleans, LA, VF–EF, $92,000. Heritage, (1/2008), 1008-A170567/C, Commercial NB of New Orleans, LA, Fine, $51,750. Knight (2/2003), 1638-A168557/E, Winters NB of Dayton, OH, Fine, $74,750.

Series of 1902, Red Seal
(Authorized Issue 1902 to 1908)

The Act of April 12, 1902, provided for reputable, established banks to extend their charters for another 20 years and for new banks to gain a 60-year charter. New designs were prepared, known today as 1902 Red Seal notes (illus. on p. 571), though older series were still being issued. All were secured by federal government bonds deposited with the U.S. Treasurer. During the life span of the 1902 Red Seals, certain banks continued to receive Series of 1882 Brown Back notes depending on the date of their charter extension or founding.

The faces and backs were redesigned for the new Series of 1902 notes. These continued to be issued until the Aldrich-Vreeland Act of May 30, 1908, went into effect, when the Red Seals were abruptly replaced by the 1902 to 1908 Date Backs, which were guaranteed in bonds "and other securities." Accordingly, this series was very short-lived.

The face bears the portrait of John Sherman, secretary of the Treasury from 1877 to 1881 and secretary of state from 1897 to 1898. In the early 1860s Sherman, then a senator, conceived the idea of national banks. He was also the author of the Sherman Silver Purchase Act of 1890 that authorized Treasury or Coin Notes. The back bears a vignette designated *Mechanics and Navigation*. At the left a man in ancient garb holds tools, and at the right are a distant ship, a prominent locomotive, and a seated female holding a quill. Both scenes were engraved by G.F.C. Smillie.

These are rare in any grade and are especially difficult to find in Uncirculated grade. Considering the great popularity of Red Seal notes, the $50 note will be a particular challenge to find.

Banks of Issue and Rarity of Notes

Based upon census information from Don C. Kelly and James M. Kelly (*National Bank Note Census*, Version 4.0) and with some information from other sources, this listing gives each location, the number of banks issuing this series of notes within each, and a commentary.[14]

The Kelly survey records only 94 of these. Only five serial number 1 notes are listed; these are specifically listed below.

Alabama • 1 bank of issue • No notes reported.

Arkansas • 1 bank of issue • No notes reported.

California • 20 banks of issue • 2 notes reported • First National Bank of Fresno (VG) and California National Bank of Sacramento (F).

Colorado • 3 banks of issue • 1 note reported • First National Bank of Denver (not graded), serial 1330.

Connecticut • 8 banks of issue • No notes reported.

Delaware • 4 banks of issue • 1 note reported • National Bank of Delaware in Wilmington (VG).

Florida • 2 banks of issue • No notes reported.

Georgia • 4 banks of issue • No notes reported.

Idaho • 3 banks of issue • 1 note reported • Boise City National Bank (VG–F).

Illinois • 15 banks of issue • 11 notes reported • The only Unc note is from the First National Bank of Lacon.

Indian Territory • 1 bank of issue • No notes reported.

Indiana • 14 banks of issue • 2 notes reported • Union National Bank of Richmond (V G–F, F–VF).

Iowa • 8 banks of issue • 2 notes reported • First National Bank of Davenport (VF) and the Merchants National Bank of Grinnell (F).

Kansas • 17 banks of issue • 7 notes reported • All are circulated. The only serial number 1 note is from the Coldwater National Bank (AU).

Kentucky • 4 banks of issue • No notes reported.

Louisiana • 4 banks of issue • 3 notes reported • Whitney-Central National Bank of New Orleans (two Fine) and the German-American National Bank of New Orleans (EF).

Maine • 3 banks of issue • No notes reported.

Maryland • 9 banks of issue • 4 notes reported • All are circulated.

Massachusetts • 30 banks of issue • 2 notes reported • Cape Ann National Bank of Gloucester (VF) and the Central National Bank of Lynn (F).

Michigan • 2 banks of issue • No notes reported.

Minnesota • 5 banks of issue • No notes reported.

Mississippi • 3 banks of issue • No notes reported.

Missouri • 6 banks of issue • 12 notes reported • The only Unc note is from the Third National Bank of Saint Louis.

Montana • 1 bank of issue • No notes reported.

Nebraska • 13 banks of issue • No notes reported.

Nevada • 3 banks of issue • No notes reported.

New Hampshire • 2 banks of issue • No notes reported.

New Jersey • 13 banks of issue • 3 notes reported • The only Unc note is from the Bridgeton National Bank.

New York • 37 banks of issue • 8 notes reported • The only Unc note is from the Manufacturers National Bank of Brooklyn. The only serial number 1 note is from the National Bank of Rochester (AU).

North Carolina • 4 banks of issue • No notes reported.

North Dakota • 1 bank of issue • No notes reported.

Ohio • 22 banks of issue • 5 notes reported • All are circulated. The only serial number 1 note is from the Fairfield National Bank of Lancaster (AU).

Oklahoma • 2 banks of issue • No notes reported.

Oklahoma Territory • 4 banks of issue • No notes reported.

Oregon • 5 banks of issue • 2 notes reported • First National Bank of Portland (VG) and the Merchants National Bank of Portland (G–VG).

Pennsylvania • 70 banks of issue • 8 notes reported • All are circulated.

Porto Rico Territory • 1 bank of issue • 2 notes are from the First National Bank of Porto Rico in San Juan (VG–F, Fair). Spelled *Porto* in the bank title; address: Island of Porto Rico. Called a "territorial" note by numismatists.

Rhode Island • 3 banks of issue • 7 notes reported • Three Unc notes are from the Providence National Bank.

South Dakota • 4 banks of issue • 1 note reported • Citizens National Bank of Watertown (VF).

Tennessee • 8 banks of issue • 2 notes reported • First National Bank of Bristol (EF) and the First National Bank of Nashville (Fair).

Texas • 28 banks of issue • 3 notes reported • Lindsay National Bank of Gainesville (not graded), National Bank of Commerce of San Antonio (not graded), and the Citizens National Bank of Waco (F).

Vermont • 4 banks of issue • No notes reported.

Virginia • 2 banks of issue • 2 notes reported • Virginia National Bank of Petersburg, serial numbers 1 (VF) and 1600 (VG).

Washington • 2 banks of issue • 1 note reported • First National Bank of Seattle (VF).

West Virginia • 1 bank of issue • No notes reported.

Wisconsin • 8 banks of issue • 2 notes reported • Waukesha National Bank (both EF).

Generic prices for a typical note:

VG-8	F-12	VF-20	EF-40	AU-50	Unc-60	Unc-63
$4,000	$6,500	$8,000	$11,000	$13,500	$15,750	$18,000

W-2879 • F-664 • Lyons-Roberts (1898–1905)
Estimated population: 75 to 85 • Highest graded: Unc.

VG-8	F-12	VF-20	EF-40	AU-50	Unc-60	Unc-63
$4,000	$6,500	$8,000	$11,000	$13,500	$15,750	$18,000

SERIES OF 1902, RED SEAL

$50 National Bank Note, Series of 1902, Red Seal (W-2879). Manufacturers National Bank of Brooklyn, New York, charter 1443.

Back of the $50 National Bank Note, Series of 1902, Red Seal (W-2879). Type also used on Series of 1902, Blue Seal, Plain Back notes.

W-2880 • F-665 • Lyons-Treat (1905–1906)

Estimated population: 9 or 10 • *Highest graded:* EF-40 • *Selected information:* Knight (6/2000), 259-A190228/A, Union NB of Richmond, IN, VF, $11,000. CAA (5/2001), 1-A242708/A, NB of Rochester, NY (serial number 1 note), EF, damaged, $33,000. Smythe (6/2003), 720-A384530/A, NB of Rochester, NY, VF–EF, $27,600.

W-2881 • F-666 • Vernon-Treat (1906–1909)

Recorded population: 6 • *Highest graded:* Unc • *Selected information:* Hickman (3/1990), 246-A323638/A, California NB of Sacramento, CA, Fine, $4,900. Smythe (6/2003), 138-A351269/A, Abilene NB, KS, EF, $5,750.

Series of 1902, Blue Seal, Date Back
(Authorized Issue 1908 to 1915, Some Through 1926)

Like the Series of 1882 Date Back type, the unexpected 1902 Blue Seal, Date Back type (illus. on p. 573) was created to reflect a change in the backing of the notes authorized by the Aldrich-Vreeland Act of May 30, 1908. New notes were issued beginning in that year. Production of 1902 Red Seals ceased, and new orders were filled by the Date Back type.

In order to make it easier to fund the notes, banks were allowed to deposit good securities in addition to government bonds, while earlier only U.S. government bonds had been allowed. All have the inscription below the top border on the face, SECURED BY UNITED STATES BONDS OR OTHER SECURITIES. This was often added by altering the face plates of the same design used for the Series of 1902 Red Seal notes. Although the Act expired on June 30, 1915, marking the end of the official use of this imprint and the related back, some plates continued to be used into 1916. Otherwise the face motifs are the same as on the Series of 1902 Red Seals, but now with the serial numbers, two charter numbers, two regional letters, and the Treasury seal in blue. The back is the same as used for the 1902 Red Seals, except that the dates are printed at the top of the field, 1902 to the left of center and 1908 to the right. These were issued in four-subject $50-$50-$50-$100 sheets and in two-subject $50-$100 sheets.

Although the style was obsolete, Date Back notes were delivered as late as 1926. Beginning on March 5, 1924, the regional letter was omitted from newly printed sheets. Beginning on August 22, 1925, new notes omitted the Treasury serial number and had two bank serial numbers.

Accordingly, $50 and $100 notes of this type printed in the 1920s can be in one of three variations:

Overprint Style 1: Two regional letters, a Treasury serial number, and a bank serial number.

Overprint Style 2: No regional letters, a Treasury serial number, and a bank serial number.

Overprint Style 3: No regional letters and no Treasury serial number, but with two bank serial numbers.

These notes are very plentiful in the context of large-size $50 bills. Uncirculated examples are rarities, however.

Banks of Issue and Rarity of Notes

Based upon census information from Don C. Kelly and James M. Kelly (*National Bank Note Census*, Version 4.0) and with some information from other sources, this listing gives each location, the number of banks issuing this series of notes within each, and a commentary.[15]

The Kelly survey records a surprisingly large number of these. The roster of 1,029 is only slightly lower than for Plain Backs. No serial number 1 notes are known. The only territorial note is from Arizona.

Alabama • 2 banks of issue • 1 note reported • City National Bank of Selma (VG).

Arizona Territory • 1 bank of issue • 1 note reported • Consolidated National Bank of Tucson (VF).

Arkansas • 2 banks of issue • No notes reported.

California • 39 banks of issue • 104 notes reported • Three Unc notes are from the Seaboard National Bank of San Francisco.

Colorado • 8 banks of issue • 13 notes reported • The only Unc example is from the First National Bank of Pueblo.

Connecticut • 8 banks of issue • 1 note reported • Stamford National Bank (VF).

Delaware • 4 banks of issue • 1 note reported • First National Bank of Harrington (VF).

Florida • 1 bank of issue • 1 note reported • From Polk County National Bank of Bartow (F), serial number 45.

Georgia • 4 banks of issue • No notes reported.

Idaho • 5 banks of issue • 34 notes reported • The only Unc note is from the Boise City National Bank (Unc).

Illinois • 34 banks of issue • 102 notes reported • Eight Unc notes are listed.

Indiana • 22 banks of issue • 48 notes reported • All are circulated.

Iowa • 20 banks of issue • 64 notes reported • Four Unc notes are known.

Kansas • 20 banks of issue • 32 notes reported • The only Unc note is from the First National Bank of Parsons.

Kentucky • 15 banks of issue • 20 notes reported • All are circulated.

Louisiana • 4 banks of issue • 11 notes reported • All are circulated.

Maine • 3 banks of issue • 2 notes reported • First National Bank of Bangor (Unc) and the Canal National Bank of Portland (VF).

Maryland • 15 banks of issue • 11 notes reported • All are circulated.

Massachusetts • 24 banks of issue • 23 notes reported • The two Unc notes are from the First National Bank of Boston and the Second National Bank of Boston.

Michigan • 7 banks of issue • 12 notes reported • All are circulated.

Minnesota • 5 banks of issue • 3 notes reported • Two are from the Commercial National Bank of Minneapolis (not graded, F), and one is from the First National Bank, Halsted (VG).

Mississippi • 4 banks of issue • 2 notes reported • State National Bank of Jackson (VG) and the Citizens National Bank, Vicksburg (VG–F).

Missouri • 12 banks of issue • 54 notes reported • All are circulated.

Montana • 2 banks of issue • 1 note reported • Silver Bow National Bank of Butte (VG–F).

Nebraska • 18 banks of issue • 60 notes reported • Two Unc notes are from the Omaha National Bank of Omaha.

Nevada • 3 banks of issue • 3 notes reported • Two from the First National Bank of Winnemucca (VG–F, VG) and one from the Nixon National Bank (F).

New Hampshire • 2 banks of issue • 3 notes reported • All are in Fine grade: two from the First National Bank of Concord and one from the National State Capital Bank of Concord.

New Jersey • 16 banks of issue • 2 notes reported • Manufacturers National Bank of Newark (VG) and the Paterson National Bank (F).

New York • 57 banks of issue • 31 notes reported • All are circulated.

North Carolina • 3 banks of issue • 1 note reported • American National Bank of Asheville (F–VF).

North Dakota • 2 banks of issue • No notes reported.

Ohio • 35 banks of issue • 81 notes reported • Two Unc notes are from the Dayton National Bank, and the Lagonda National Bank of Springfield.

Oklahoma • 6 banks of issue • 1 note reported • State National Bank of Ardmore (F).

Oregon • 6 banks of issue • 18 notes reported • All are circulated.

Pennsylvania • 75 banks of issue • 101 notes reported • Eight Unc examples are known.

Porto Rico Territory • 1 bank of issue • No notes reported.

Rhode Island • 3 banks of issue • 11 notes reported • All are circulated.

South Dakota • 7 banks of issue • 18 notes reported • All are circulated.

Tennessee • 10 banks of issue • 15 notes reported • All are circulated.

SERIES OF 1902, BLUE SEAL, DATE BACK

$50 National Bank Note, Series of 1902, Blue Seal, Date Back (W-2890). Merchants-Laclede National Bank of Saint Louis, Missouri. Blue Treasury seal, charter number, serial numbers, and regional letters.

Back of the $50 National Bank Note, Series of 1902, Blue Seal, Date Back (W-2890). The motifs are the same as the preceding, but with the addition of 1902–1908.

Texas • 40 banks of issue • 86 notes reported • Four notes are reported in Unc grade.

Utah • 1 bank of issue • 2 notes reported • National Copper Bank of Salt Lake City (VG, VG–VF).

Vermont • 6 banks of issue • 3 notes reported • Two are from Randolph National Bank (VG, F), and one is from the National Bank of Middlebury (EF).

Virginia • 2 banks of issue • 3 notes reported • Two are from the Virginia National Bank of Petersburg (VG–F, VF), and one is from the Augusta National Bank of Staunton (VG–F).

Washington • 4 banks of issue • 31 notes reported • All are circulated.

Wisconsin • 8 banks of issue • 18 notes reported • The only Unc note is from the First National Bank of Eau Claire.

Generic prices for a typical note from a state from which notes range from available to just slightly scarce:

VG-8	F-12	VF-20	EF-40	AU-50	Unc-60	Unc-63
$1,500	$2,000	$2,850	$3,500	$4,150	$4,850	$5,500

W-2882 • F-667 • Lyons-Roberts (1898–1905)
Estimated population: 340 to 370 • *Highest graded:* Unc.

VG-8	F-12	VF-20	EF-40	AU-50	Unc-60	Unc-63
$1,500	$2,000	$2,850	$3,500	$4,150	$4,850	$5,500

W-2883 • F-668 • Lyons-Treat (1905–1906)
Estimated population: 120 to 130 • *Highest graded:* Unc.

VG-8	F-12	VF-20	EF-40	AU-50	Unc-60	Unc-63
$1,500	$2,000	$2,850	$3,500	$4,150	$4,850	$5,500

W-2884 • F-669 • Vernon-Treat (1906–1909)
Estimated population: 200 to 220 • *Highest graded:* Unc.

VG-8	F-12	VF-20	EF-40	AU-50	Unc-60	Unc-63
$1,500	$2,000	$2,850	$3,500	$4,150	$4,850	$5,500

W-2885 • F-670 • Vernon-McClung (1909–1911)
Estimated population: 145 to 160 • *Highest graded:* Unc.

VG-8	F-12	VF-20	EF-40	AU-50	Unc-60	Unc-63
$1,500	$2,000	$2,850	$3,500	$4,150	$4,850	$5,500

W-2886 • F-671 • Napier-McClung (1911–1912)

Estimated population: 115 to 125 • *Highest graded:* Unc.

VG-8	F-12	VF-20	EF-40	AU-50	Unc-60	Unc-63
$1,500	$2,000	$2,850	$3,500	$4,150	$4,850	$5,500

W-2887 • F-672 • Napier-Thompson (1912–1913)

Estimated population: 24 to 28 • *Highest graded:* Unc.

VG-8	F-12	VF-20	EF-40	AU-50	Unc-60	Unc-63
$1,500	$2,000	$2,850	$3,500	$4,500	$5,750	$6,750

W-2888 • F-673 • Napier-Burke (1913)

Estimated population: 22 to 26 • *Highest graded:* AU-50.

VG-8	F-12	VF-20	EF-40	AU-50
$1,500	$2,000	$2,850	$3,500	$4,150

W-2889 • F-674 • Parker-Burke (1913–1914)

Estimated population: 45 to 50 • *Highest graded:* AU-50.

VG-8	F-12	VF-20	EF-40	AU-50
$1,500	$2,000	$2,850	$3,500	$4,150

W-2890 • F-674a • Teehee-Burke (1915–1919)

Estimated population: 34 to 38 • *Highest graded:* Unc.

VG-8	F-12	VF-20	EF-40	AU-50	Unc-60	Unc-63
$1,500	$2,000	$2,850	$3,500	$4,150	$4,850	$5,500

Series of 1902, Blue Seal, Plain Back
(Authorized Issue 1908 to 1929)

After the Aldrich-Vreeland Act expired on June 30, 1915, the phrase "or other securities" was no longer added to the face of new printing plates. Henceforth, the style reverted to that of years earlier, secured only by U.S. bonds. Old plates remained in use, creating two face plate styles for 1902 Plain Back notes:

> **Plate Style a:** This is the old style of 1902 (used on the face of the Date Backs), with the inscription on part of the top border on the face reading "Secured by United States bonds or other securities."

> **Plate Style b:** This is the new style introduced in 1908, with the inscription on part of the top border on the face reading, "Secured by United States bonds deposited with the Treasurer of the United States of America."

Both Plate Style a and Plate Style b notes had the two regional letters (on certain issues, then deleted), two charter numbers (on all), and serial numbers (on all) in blue. These were issued into 1929.

Moreover, within the two plate styles there are possibilities for three overprint styles:

> **Overprint Style 1:** Two regional letters, a Treasury serial number, and a bank serial number. Printed from 1908 to 1924.

> **Overprint Style 2:** No regional letters, a Treasury serial number, and a bank serial number. Printed in 1924 and 1925.

> **Overprint Style 3:** No regional letters and no Treasury serial number, but with two bank serial numbers. Printed from 1925 to 1929. Notes of this style are very rare as a class.

Within this type, $50 notes are scarce, rare for some states. At present there is little interest in plate styles or overprint varieties, yielding opportunities to acquire rarities while paying no premium—perhaps not important overall, as just about any note is scarce.

Banks of Issue and Rarity of Notes

Based upon census information from Don C. Kelly and James M. Kelly (*National Bank Note Census,* Version 4.0) and with some information from other sources, this listing gives each location, the number of banks issuing this series of notes within each, and a commentary.[16]

The Kelly survey records 1,033 of these. There are seven serial number 1 notes known from four banks in three states. These are specifically listed below.

California • 19 banks of issue • 124 notes reported • The census lists 17 Unc notes, with 15 from the Pacific National Bank of Los Angeles. Five serial number 1 notes are known.

Colorado • 6 banks of issue • 20 notes reported • Five Unc notes are listed.

Connecticut • 3 banks of issue • 6 notes reported • All are circulated and from the First National Bank of Wallingford.

Delaware • 2 banks of issue • 4 notes reported • All are circulated examples, two from the First National Bank of Harrington and two from the National Bank of Smyrna.

District of Columbia • 1 bank of issue • 9 notes reported • All are circulated. Two banks are represented.

Florida • 3 banks of issue • 4 notes reported • All are circulated. Three are from the First National Bank of Lakeland, and one is from the First National Bank of Sanford.

Hawaii Territory • 1 bank of issue • No notes reported.

Idaho • 2 banks of issue • 11 notes reported • All are circulated, from three different banks.

Illinois • 27 banks of issue • 116 notes reported • Nine Unc notes are listed.

Indiana • 13 banks of issue • 25 notes reported • All are circulated.

Iowa • 12 banks of issue • 31 notes reported • The only Unc note is from the First National Bank of Albia.

Kansas • 15 banks of issue • 14 notes reported • The only Unc note is from the First National Bank of Newton.

Kentucky • 12 banks of issue • 31 notes reported • All are circulated.

Louisiana • 3 banks of issue • 29 notes reported • All are circulated.

Maryland • 10 banks of issue • 23 notes reported • All are circulated.

Massachusetts • 7 banks of issue • 4 notes reported • The only Unc note is from the First National Bank of Westfield.

Michigan • 7 banks of issue • 35 notes reported • Six Unc notes are listed.

SERIES OF 1902, BLUE SEAL, PLAIN BACK

$50 National Bank Note, Series of 1902, Blue Seal, Plain Back (W-2896). First National Bank of Forest City, Iowa. With blue charter number, serial numbers, regional letters, and Treasury seal. Plate Style a, secured by bonds or other securities. The president's signature was rubber stamped and has nearly faded away. The back is the same as that used on Series of 1902, Red Seal notes.

Detail of security imprint from Plate Style a.

Detail of security imprint from Plate Style b.

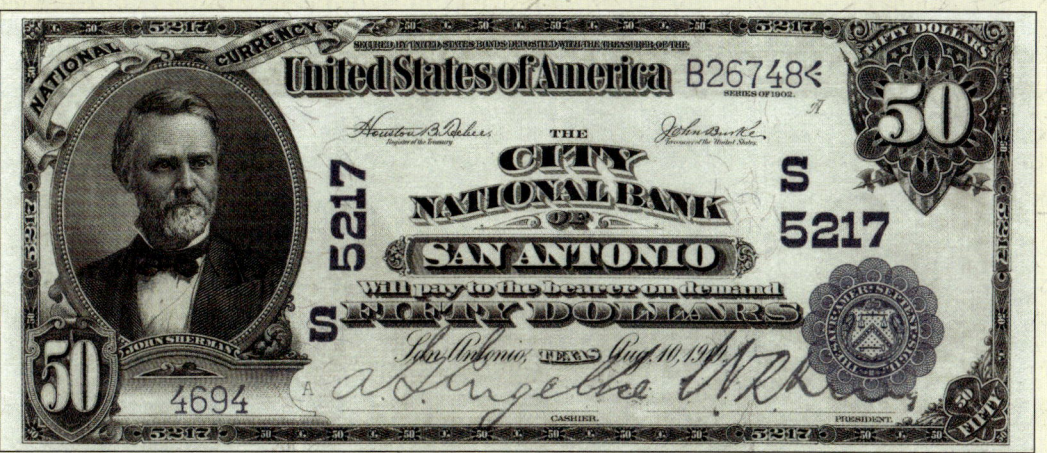

$50 National Bank Note, Series of 1902, Blue Seal, Plain Back (W-2899). City National Bank of San Antonio, Texas. Plate Style b, secured by bonds only.

Minnesota • 3 banks of issue • 1 note reported • First National Bank of Sauk Centre (Fair).

Mississippi • 2 banks of issue • No notes reported.

Missouri • 5 banks of issue • 19 notes reported • The only serial number 1 note is from the National City Bank of Kansas City; this is also the state's only Unc note.

Montana • 1 bank of issue • 3 notes reported • First National Bank of Butte, all circulated.

Nebraska • 8 banks of issue • 21 notes reported • The only Unc note is from the First National Bank of Fairbury.

Nevada • 2 banks of issue • 12 notes reported • The only Unc note is from the Reno National Bank.

New Hampshire • 3 banks of issue • 2 notes reported • First National Bank of Concord (VF) and National State Capital Bank (F).

New Jersey • 9 banks of issue • 22 notes reported • All are circulated.

New York • 12 banks of issue • 31 notes reported • The only Unc example is from the Manufacturers National Bank of Buffalo, and the only serial number 1 note is from the Bank of America NA (VF–EF).

North Carolina • 2 banks of issue • 3 notes reported • American National Bank of Asheville (F, VF, Unc).

North Dakota • 1 bank of issue • 2 notes reported • First National Bank of Fargo (G) and the First National Bank of Lisbon (not graded).

Ohio • 25 banks of issue • 52 notes reported • The only Unc note is from the Winters National Bank of Dayton.

Oklahoma • 7 banks of issue • 68 notes reported • All are circulated.

Oregon • 1 bank of issue • 6 notes reported • All are circulated, from the First National Bank of Baker.

Pennsylvania • 35 banks of issue • 59 notes reported • All are circulated.

Rhode Island • 3 banks of issue • 5 notes reported • All are circulated. Three are from the Mechanics National Bank of Providence.

South Dakota • 7 banks of issue • 3 notes reported • First National Bank of Dakota (VF) and two from the Dakota National Bank of Yankton (both EF).

Tennessee • 2 banks of issue • 7 notes reported • All are circulated. Five are from American National Bank of Nashville.

Texas • 34 banks of issue • 181 notes reported • Seven Unc examples are listed.

Vermont • 5 banks of issue • 5 notes reported • All are circulated; three are from the First National Bank of Vergennes.

Washington • 3 banks of issue • 29 notes reported • Three Unc notes are from the Seattle National Bank.

West Virginia • 1 bank of issue • 8 notes reported • All are from the First Huntington National Bank, and all are circulated.

Wisconsin • 6 banks of issue • 8 notes reported • All are circulated. Four are from the Waukesha National Bank.

Generic prices for a typical note from a state from which notes range from available to just slightly scarce:

VG-8	F-12	VF-20	EF-40	AU-50	Unc-60	Unc-63
$1,500	$2,000	$2,850	$3,500	$4,000	$4,600	$5,250

W-2891 • F-675 • Lyons-Roberts (1898–1905)
Estimated population: 180 to 200 • *Highest graded:* Unc.

VG-8	F-12	VF-20	EF-40	AU-50	Unc-60	Unc-63
$1,500	$2,000	$2,850	$3,500	$4,000	$4,600	$5,250

W-2892 • F-676 • Lyons-Treat (1905–1906)
Estimated population: 55 to 60 • *Highest graded:* EF-40.

VG-8	F-12	VF-20	EF-40
$1,500	$2,000	$2,850	$3,500

W-2893 • F-677 • Vernon-Treat (1906–1909)
Estimated population: 95 to 105 • *Highest graded:* Unc.

VG-8	F-12	VF-20	EF-40	AU-50	Unc-60	Unc-63
$1,500	$2,000	$2,850	$3,500	$4,000	$4,600	$5,250

W-2894 • F-678 • Vernon-McClung (1909–1911)
Estimated population: 165 to 180 • *Highest graded:* Unc.

VG-8	F-12	VF-20	EF-40	AU-50	Unc-60	Unc-63
$1,500	$2,000	$2,850	$3,500	$4,000	$4,600	$5,250

W-2895 • F-679 • Napier-McClung (1911–1912)
Estimated population: 60 to 70 • *Highest graded:* Unc.

VG-8	F-12	VF-20	EF-40	AU-50	Unc-60	Unc-63
$1,500	$2,000	$2,850	$3,500	$4,000	$4,600	$5,250

W-2896 • F-679a • Napier-Thompson (1912–1913)
Estimated population: 35 to 40 • *Highest graded:* AU-50.

VG-8	F-12	VF-20	EF-40	AU-50
$1,500	$2,000	$2,850	$3,500	$4,000

W-2897 • F-680 • Napier-Burke (1913)
Recorded population: 7 • *Highest graded:* AU-50 • *Selected information:* Heritage (6/2008), 2941/B, Lexington City NB, KY, VG–F, $863. Heritage (9/2007), 2987/C, Lexington City NB, KY, Fine (PMG), $920.

W-2898 • F-681 • Parker-Burke (1913–1914)
Estimated population: 38 to 47 • *Highest graded:* Unc.

VG-8	F-12	VF-20	EF-40	AU-50	Unc-60	Unc-63
$1,500	$2,000	$2,850	$3,500	$4,000	$4,600	$5,250

W-2899 • F-682 • Teehee-Burke (1915–1919)
Estimated population: 200 to 220 • *Highest graded:* Unc.

VG-8	F-12	VF-20	EF-40	AU-50	Unc-60	Unc-63
$1,500	$2,000	$2,850	$3,500	$4,000	$4,600	$5,250

W-2900 • F-683 • Elliott-Burke (1919–1921)
Estimated population: 115 to 125 • *Highest graded:* AU-53.

VG-8	F-12	VF-20	EF-40	AU-50
$1,500	$2,000	$2,850	$3,500	$4,000

W-2901 • F-684 • Elliott-White (1921–1922)
Estimated population: 60 to 70 • *Highest graded:* Unc.

VG-8	F-12	VF-20	EF-40	AU-50	Unc-60	Unc-63
$1,500	$2,000	$2,850	$3,500	$4,000	$4,600	$5,250

W-2902 • F-685 • Speelman-White (1922–1927)
Estimated population: 95 to 105 • *Highest graded:* Unc.

VG-8	F-12	VF-20	EF-40	AU-50	Unc-60	Unc-63
$1,500	$2,000	$2,850	$3,500	$4,000	$4,600	$5,250

W-2903 • F-685a • Woods-White (1927–1928)
Recorded population: 2.

SILVER CERTIFICATES

Silver Certificates in the $50 denomination began with the Series of 1878 and continued among large-size designs through the Series of 1891, all payable in silver dollars. Shown on the face is Edward Everett, best known as an orator from Massachusetts, although he held a number of political offices. It was Everett who, at the dedication of the Gettysburg National Battlefield in 1863, gave a two-hour speech before Lincoln made his Gettysburg Address, which the president said would be little remembered. Lincoln's speech became a classic, of course, while what Everett had to say is unknown, except to the most dedicated student of Civil War trivia.

The early $50 issues of the Series of 1878 and 1880 have the word SILVER in large letters across the back—impressive, to say the least. These are known as Silver Certificates of Deposit. All of these early bills range from rare to extremely rare. Those of the Series of 1891, designated as

Silver Certificates, have an open design on the back. These later bills exist in moderate numbers but, due to demand, are expensive when found.

Series of 1878

The Series of 1878 $50 notes are specifically designated CERTIFICATE OF DEPOSIT on the face, SILVER CERTIFICATE on the back. These bear two printed Treasury signatures plus the printed or, in some instances, hand-signed countersignature of another Treasury official. Fewer than 10 are known to exist. Details are scarce regarding the style of countersignature application. All have a large red Treasury seal at top center and FIFTY in ornate pink letters at the lower center. On this seal, for this denomination and other countersigned notes in this series, the key faces to the right (with the handle at the left). These were printed on blue-tinted paper (made under the Willcox patent of 1866). On the back the word SILVER in shingle-style, joined vignettes.

W-2906 • F-323 • New York • *Countersigned:* W.G. White (autographed) • 500 (est.) • Unknown

W-2909 • F-323 • *Countersigned:* J.C. Hopper (autographed) • 7,500 (est.) • Unknown

W-2912 • F-324 • New York • *Countersigned:* Thos. Hillhouse (printed) • 12,000 (est.)
Recorded population: 2 • Highest Graded: VF • Selected information: The known examples are serials A10161/A, VF, repaired, part of the ANA Museum collection, and A12973/A, Fair.

W-2916 • F-324a • San Francisco • *Countersigned:* R.M. Anthony (autographed) • 4,000 (est.)
Recorded population: 1 • Selected information: The known example is serial A461/A, VG, owned by the Federal Reserve Bank of San Francisco.

W-2919 • F-324b • Washington • *Countersigned:* A.U. Wyman (autographed) • 4,000 (est.) • Unknown

$50 Silver Certificate of Deposit, Series of 1878 with printed countersignature of Thos. Hillhouse (W-2912). Backed by silver dollars stored under the supervision of the assistant Treasurer of the United States at the New York Sub-Treasury (the busiest of the Sub-Treasuries). The Scofield-Gilfillan Treasury signatures is on all. Portrait of Edward Everett, who served as secretary of state from 1852 to 1855 and was one of America's best-known orators. (ANA Edward C. Rochette Money Museum)

Back of the $50 Silver Certificate of Deposit, Series of 1878 (W-2912).

W-2922 • F-324c • *Countersigned:* A.U. Wyman (printed) • 60,000 (est.)

Recorded population: 3 • *Highest graded:* VF-20 • *Selected information:* The known examples include serials A12548/D, Fine, owned by the Federal Reserve Bank of San Francisco; A18657/A, VF, sold in a Spink America auction (5/1995) for $46,200; and A40814/B, VG–F, sold in a Knight auction (3/2007) for $230,000.

Series of 1880

The motifs are somewhat similar to the preceding, but with differences in the color printing. A large brown Treasury

$50 Silver Certificate of Deposit, Series of 1880 (W-2927). With large brown Treasury seal and with a roman numeral L denomination counter at the lower center.

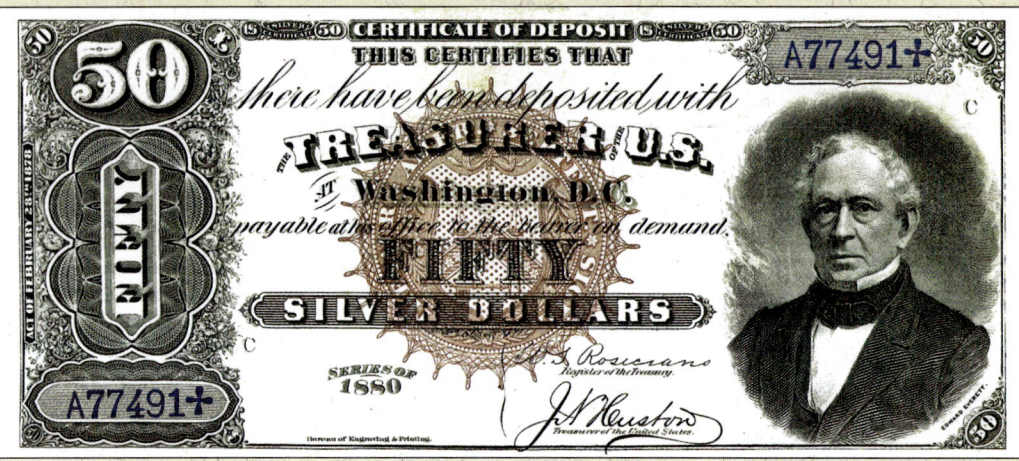

Face of W-2928 with differently styled large brown seal and without the L.

Back of the $50 Silver Certificate of Deposit, Series of 1880 (W-2927).

seal and denomination counter, L, are seen on W-2925 to W-2927. W-2928 and W-2929 lack the large L and have different seals.

W-2925 • F-325 • Scofield-Gilfillan (1878–1881) • Large brown seal • 16,000 (est.)

Recorded population: 1 • *Graded:* Fine • *Selected information:* The known example is serial B15875/C, Fine, part of the Smithsonian Institution collection.

W-2926 • F-326 • Bruce-Gilfillan (1881–1883) • 80,000 (est.)

Recorded population: 5 • *Highest graded:* VF-25 • *Selected information:* Existing examples include serials B43267/C, Fine, from the Amon Carter Jr. collection; B48667/C, VF, owned by the Federal Reserve Bank of San Francisco; B56854/B, VG–F, repaired, sold in a Knight auction (10/2005) for $43,700; B77001/A, Fine, pinholes, sold in a Knight auction (6/2001) for $28,600; and B94616/D, Fine, sold in a CAA auction (1/1996) for $11,550.

W-2927 • F-327 • Bruce-Wyman (1883–1885) • 100,000 (est.)

Estimated population: 11 to 13 • *Highest graded:* Unc.

VG-8	F-12	VF-20	EF-40	AU-50	Unc-60
$17,500	$20,000	$35,000	$80,000	—	—

W-2928 • F-328 • Rosecrans-Huston (1889–1891) • Large brown seal (different border than the preceding) • 100,000

Estimated population: 32 to 35 • *Highest graded:* Unc.

VG-8	F-12	VF-20	EF-40	AU-50	Unc-60	Unc-63
$9,000	$15,000	$25,000	$40,000	$50,000	$76,000	$90,000

W-2929 • F-329 • Rosecrans-Nebeker (1891–1893) • Small red seal with scalloped border • 120,000

Estimated population: 32 to 35 • *Highest graded:* AU-53.

VG-8	F-12	VF-20	EF-40	AU-50
$9,000	$15,000	$25,000	$40,000	$63,000

Series of 1891

The face of the Series of 1891 notes retained the portrait of Edward Everett, but the typography and layout were differently arranged. The back is in an open style, with generous spaces to the left and right of center, in keeping with the belief that this deterred counterfeiting. These and other Silver Certificates of the era were backed by Morgan-design silver dollars stored at various mints and other Treasury facilities, as well as, among emergency measures, at the Philadelphia Post Office.

$50 Silver Certificate, Series of 1891 (W-2933). Portrait of Edward Everett as preceding, but with a different layout of other features.

Back of the $50 Silver Certificate, Series of 1891 (W-2933), introducing the new back design with open spaces.

W-2930 • F-330 • Rosecrans-Nebeker (1891–1893) • Small red seal with scalloped border • 120,000 (est.)

Recorded population: 6 • *Highest graded:* AU-50 • *Selected information:* Existing examples include serials E23682/B, EF-40 (PMG), sold in a Knight auction (6/2008) for $36,800; E71680/D, VG, pinholes, sold in a CAA auction (5/2000) for $5,115; E76864/D, F-15 (PMG), sold in a Knight auction (3/2007) for $29,900; E99938/B, VF, owned by the Federal Reserve Bank of San Francisco; E108906/B, F-12, pinholes (PMG), sold in a CAA auction (1/2005) for $5,750; E112719/C, AU-50 (PMG), sold in a CAA auction (4/2006) for $51,750.

W-2931 • F-331 • Tillman-Morgan (1893–1897) • 380,000 (est.)

Estimated population: 30 to 35 • *Highest graded:* Unc.

VG-8	F-12	VF-20	EF-40	AU-50	Unc-60
$2,400	$3,750	$5,750	$9,000	—	—

W-2932 • F-332 • Bruce-Roberts (1897–1898) • 300,000 (est.)

Estimated population: 24 to 28 • *Highest graded:* VF-20.

VG-8	F-12	VF-20
$2,400	$3,750	$5,750

W-2933 • F-333 • Lyons-Roberts (1898–1905) • 304,000 (est.)

Estimated population: 40 to 44 • *Highest graded:* Unc.

VG-8	F-12	VF-20	EF-40	AU-50	Unc-60
$2,200	$3,500	$7,500	$12,000	—	—

W-2934 • F-334 • Vernon-Treat (1906–1909) • 200,000

Estimated population: 50 to 60 • *Highest graded:* Unc.

VG-8	F-12	VF-20	EF-40	AU-50	Unc-60	Unc-63
$2,000	$3,250	$5,000	$7,500	$13,000	$18,500	$24,000

W-2935 • F-335 • Parker-Burke (1913–1914) • Small blue seal with scalloped border • 812,000

Estimated population: 170 to 185 • *Highest graded:* Unc.

VG-8	F-12	VF-20	EF-40	AU-50	Unc-60	Unc-63
$1,800	$2,900	$4,250	$8,500	$12,000	$15,000	$20,000

TREASURY OR COIN NOTES

The $50 Treasury or Coin Notes do not include the ornate Series of 1890, leaving just the Series of 1891, with open spaces on the back.

$50 Treasury or Coin Note, Series of 1891 (W-2938). Portrait of William Seward, secretary of state from 1860 to 1869.

Back of the $50 Treasury or Coin Note, Series of 1891 (W-2938), with open fields, a style said to deter counterfeiting.

Series of 1891

Depicted on the face of the Treasury or Coin Note, Series of 1891, is a profile portrait of William Henry Seward, secretary of state from 1861 through 1869, best remembered for arranging the purchase of Alaska for $7,200,000—"Seward's Folly," as it was called by his detractors. A decorative star follows the serial number. The back is the open style favored by the Treasury in the early 1890s.

The Treasury printed 80,000 $50 notes, of which 23,500 were distributed, and 25 are said to be outstanding on Treasury records. This figure may be questionable, for Martin Gengerke records 21 different notes in numismatic hands—a number far too high if only 25 have not been redeemed. From time to time the Treasury made adjustments in its numbers, and this may be the explanation.

W-2938 • F-376 • Rosecrans-Nebeker (1891–1893) • Small red seal with scalloped border • 80,000 printed • 23,500 distributed

Recorded population: 21 • *Highest graded:* Unc.

VG-8	F-12	VF-20	EF-40	AU-50	Unc-60
$20,000	$37,500	—	—	—	—

GOLD CERTIFICATES

Series of 1882

Gold Certificates in the $50 denomination began with the Series of 1882. Depicted on the face is Silas Wright, a former U.S. senator and governor of New York. If he had anything particular to do with gold, he is not remembered in this context today. Indeed, he died on August 27, 1847, before the Gold Rush. The face has GOLD in a yellow-gold

SERIES OF 1882

$50 Gold Certificate, Series of 1882 (W-2956). The portrait is of Silas Wright.

Detail of the lower right face of W-2964, as on all, showing an eagle, plate information, and other details.

Back of the $50 Gold Certificate, Series of 1882 (W-2956), with orange-gold printing.

overprint at top and a gold background to the serial numbers. Backed by gold coin, "repayable [unusual word] to the bearer on demand." The Treasury seal, which is found in various hues, adds color. The back is printed entirely in gold-orange and is more distinctly defined than are the backs of some other gold-printed issues, as the orange-gold color tended to fade. Today, notes with a bright back are worth more than those with faded color, regardless of the grade.

Early varieties come with the countersignature of Thomas C. Acton, assistant Treasurer at the New York Sub-Treasury, either autographed or entered into the plate.

W-2940 • F-1189 • Bruce-Gilfillan (1881–1883) • *Countersigned:* Thomas C. Acton (autographed) • Medium-size brown seal with scalloped border • 9,000 • Unknown

W-2942 • F-1189a • *Countersigned:* Thomas C. Acton (printed) • 231,000
Estimated population: 12 to 14 • *Highest graded:* Unc.

VG-8	F-12	VF-20	EF-40	AU-50	Unc-60
$14,000	$18,000	$35,000	—	—	—

W-2944 • F-1188 • No countersignature • 96,000
Recorded population: 8 • *Highest graded:* EF-45 • *Selected information:* Knight (11/2003), A256/D, EF, $27,600. Heritage (1/2008), A8322/B, VG/Fair, $8,625. Knight (8/2005), A39128/D, Fine, stains washed out, tiny edge splits, $17,250. Knight (6/2008), A69922/B, VF-20, repaired (PCGS), $8,625.

W-2948 • F-1190 • Bruce-Wyman (1883–1885) • 40,000
Recorded population: 5 • *Highest graded:* EF-40 • *Selected information:* Existing examples include serials A97616/D, VG, owned by the Federal Reserve Bank of San Francisco; A99018/B, F–VF, sold in a Knight auction (10/2005) for $80,500; A114044/D, VG, repaired, pinholes, sold in a Heritage auction (1/2007) for $17,250; A120969/A, VG+, repaired, pinholes, sold in a NASCA auction (10/1984) for $625.

W-2950 • F-1191 • Rosecrans-Hyatt (1887–1889) • Large red seal • 40,000
Recorded population: 4 • *Highest graded:* EF-40 • *Selected information:* Existing examples include serials C3743/C, VG, owned by the Federal Reserve Bank of San Francisco; C5745/A, VG, pinholes, part of the Smithsonian Institution collection; C8592/D, owned by the Federal Reserve Bank of New York; and C24630/B, EF, pinholes, sold in a Heritage auction (1/2006) for $299,000.

W-2952 • F-1192 • Rosecrans-Huston (1889–1891) • Large brown seal • 99,996 (est.)
Estimated population: 20 to 24 • *Highest graded:* EF-40.

VG-8	F-12	VF-20	EF-40
$12,000	$18,000	$32,500	—

W-2954 • F-1192a • Small red seal with scalloped border • 4 (est.)
Recorded population: 1 • *Selected information:* CAA (4/2006), C128690/B, VF-25 (PMG), "an anomaly; this serial number should have a large brown seal, not small red," $299,000.

W-2956 • F-1193 • Lyons-Roberts (1898–1905) • Blue serial numbers • 1,724,000
Estimated population: 115 to 125 • *Highest graded:* Unc.

VG-8	F-12	VF-20	EF-40	AU-50	Unc-60	Unc-63
$900	$1,750	$3,250	$7,500	$10,250	$15,250	$20,000

W-2958 • F-1194 • Lyons-Treat (1905–1906) • 400,000
Estimated population: 35 to 40 • *Highest graded:* AU-58.

VG-8	F-12	VF-20	EF-40	AU-50
$1,000	$1,950	$5,000	$10,000	—

W-2960 • F-1195 • Vernon-Treat (1906–1909) • 400,000
Estimated population: 55 to 60 • *Highest graded:* Unc.

VG-8	F-12	VF-20	EF-40	AU-50	Unc-60	Unc-63
$1,000	$1,950	$4,500	$8,500	$12,600	$18,750	$25,000

W-2962 • F-1196 • Vernon-McClung (1909–1911) • 400,000
Estimated population: 32 to 35 • *Highest graded:* AU-50.

VG-8	F-12	VF-20	EF-40	AU-50
$1,000	$1,950	$5,000	$10,000	—

W-2964 • F-1197 • Napier-McClung (1911–1912) • 1,204,000
Estimated population: 175 to 185 • *Highest graded:* Unc • *Commentary:* Deliveries began on July 11, 1911, and ended on October 21, 1913.

VG-8	F-12	VF-20	EF-40	AU-50	Unc-60	Unc-63
$900	$1,750	$3,000	$5,500	$7,600	$9,750	$12,000

Series of 1913

Last in the large-size $50 Gold Certificates are the Series of 1913 and 1922, with a portrait of president Ulysses S. Grant. Gold imprints are to the left and right. These notes were backed by gold coins (mostly double eagles) stored by the Treasury department, which regularly published an accounting of them. The reverse was redesigned and printed in gold-orange ink.

These exist in fair numbers today, usually in lower grades, and are affordable. The orange-gold color tended to fade. Today, notes with a bright back are worth more than those with faded color, regardless of the grade.

W-2966 • F-1198 • Parker-Burke (1913–1914) • Small gold seal, gold serial numbers • 400,000
Estimated population: 60 to 65 • *Highest graded:* Unc • *Commentary:* Deliveries began on October 13, 1914, and ended on October 19, 1914.

VG-8	F-12	VF-20	EF-40	AU-50	Unc-60	Unc-63
$900	$1,250	$1,750	$3,250	$4,100	$6,250	$8,500

W-2967 • F-1199 • Teehee-Burke (1915–1919) • 1,224,000
Estimated population: 210 to 230 • *Highest graded:* Unc.

VG-8	F-12	VF-20	EF-40	AU-50	Unc-60	Unc-63
$625	$875	$1,500	$2,750	$4,000	$6,000	$8,000

SERIES OF 1913

$50 Gold Certificate, Series of 1913 (W-2967).

$50 Gold Certificate, Series of 1913 (W-2967); the type also used for Series of 1922 notes.

Series of 1922

The Series of 1922 notes (illus. on p. 584) have an inscription, not present on the earlier issues, in the left field, which reads, "This certificate is a legal tender in the amount thereof in payment of all debts and dues public and private. Acts of March 14, 1900, as amended and December 24, 1919." The back is the same design as the preceding type. The orange-gold color tended to fade. Today, notes with a bright back are worth more than those with faded color, regardless of the grade.

Mules: Back plate numbers can be in one of two locations.[17] Starting May 14, 1921, with the new Elliott-White signature combination, all Legal Tender, Silver Certificate, and Gold Certificate back plates were given numbers beginning with 1 and in a new location, although no notice was given of the change. However, the first use of this on the $50 Gold Certificate was the Speelman-White Series of 1922.

> **Back Plate Location 1** (regular use): W-2966 and W-2967. This was also used to create a mule for W-2968 and W-2969. *All* examples of W-2968 are mules.

> **Back Plate Location 2** (regular use): W-2969 (introduced in 1924 with the Speelman-White combination).

W-2968 Mule • F-1200a • Speelman-White (1922–1927) • Small gold seal, small gold serial numbers • 800,000 • All are mules

Estimated population: 145 to 160 • *Highest graded:* Unc.

VG-8	F-12	VF-20	EF-40	AU-50	Unc-60	Unc-63
$625	$875	$1,400	$2,000	$4,250	$6,500	$9,000

W-2969 • F-1200 • Small gold seal, large gold serial numbers • 4,684,000, or about 90% regular (est.)

Estimated population: 13 to 15 • *Highest graded:* AU-58 • *Selected information:* Knight (6/2008), 6102B/B, VF-30 (PMG), $11,500. CAA (1/2000), 13259B/C, Fine+, $990. Knight (3/2008), 20982B/B, VF-30 (PCGS), $12,075; Knight (11/2007), 30874B/B, VF-20 (PCGS), $8,050.

W-2969★ • F-1200★

Estimated population: 13 to 15 • *Highest graded:* AU-58 • *Commentary:* Current market information not available.

W-2969 Mule • F-1200 • 500,000, or about 10% mules (est.)

Estimated population: 35 to 40 • *Highest graded:* Unc.

VG-8	F-12	VF-20	EF-40	AU-50	Unc-60	Unc-63
$400	$650	$800	$1,550	$2,750	$4,800	$7,500

SERIES OF 1922

$50 Gold Certificate, Series of 1922 (W-2969). The back is the same as that used on $50 Series of 1913 notes.

Redemption statement on the face.

Back Plate Location 1.

Back Plate Location 2.

W-2969 Mule★ • F-1200★

Recorded population: 3 • *Highest graded:* AU • *Selected information:* Knight (11/2003), ★15351B/C, AU, $10,925. Smythe (9/2000), ★20383B/C, F–VF, $2,090.

FEDERAL RESERVE NOTES

Series of 1914, Red Seal

The face bears the portrait of president Ulysses S. Grant, one of the BEP's favorite subjects for paper-money illustration. On the back a goddess representing Panama is standing on land between the Atlantic and Pacific oceans. The Panama Canal opened in 1914. That year the publicity for the forthcoming 1915 Panama-Pacific International Exposition was intense. The event was to celebrate the new canal and also the rebuilding of San Francisco after the 1906 earthquake and fire.

Similar to other denominations, the $50 Federal Reserve Notes, Series of 1914, with Treasury seal and serial numbers in red and the Burke-McAdoo signature combination, are rather simple in their appearance and nearly always are collected singly for the type. A collection of the Federal Reserve Banks is doable, although Boston, Atlanta, and Kansas City are great rarities. As for collecting a and b plates from each Federal Reserve Bank, even coming close to completion would take years and in Uncirculated grade would be impossible. These are considerably scarcer as a group than the Blue Seal notes listed subsequently. Once World War I commenced in Europe in August 1914, the BEP could not import red ink, and so switched to blue after less than a year of printing Red Seals.

In all of the following listings the number (1 to 12) and the large letter (A to L) on the seal at the left indicate the Federal Reserve Bank that issued the note.

Plate Style a (on Red Seals only): In certain of the following listings the small letter a following the Whitman number indicates a large bank district letter and numeral at bottom left and top right. At the upper left is a small plate letter, but no bank district letter and number.

Plate Style b (on Red and Blue Seals): In certain of the following listings the small letter b following the Whitman number indicates a note similar to the preceding, but now with a small bank district letter and number added below the plate letter at the top left and at the lower right.

W-2975-A-a • F-1012A • Boston • 20,000

Recorded population: 4 • *Highest graded:* VF-20 • *Selected information:* Existing examples include serials 644A, VF, damaged; A857A, Fine; A8807A, VG, sold in the Bluestone, Grinnell auction (6/1946) for $67.50; and A14241A, VF, sold in a CAA auction (10/1998) for $1,870, later seen in the Lake Region (1/2003) *Bank Note Reporter* advertisement for $19,750.

W-2975-A-b • F-1012B • 24,000

Recorded population: 5 • *Highest graded:* EF-45 • *Selected information:* Existing examples include serials A22259A, VF, pressed, sold in a Stack's auction (3/1991) for $475; A31536A/D, VG–F, part of the Smithsonian Institution collection; A35134A/B, VF–EF, sold in a CAA auction (5/2003) for $6,038; A38546A/B, VG–F, sold in a Knight auction (2/2004) for $3,163; and A41475A/C, F-15 (PMG), sold in a Heritage auction (4/2008) for $34,500.

W-2975-B-a • F-1013A • New York • 80,000

Estimated population: 10 to 12 • *Highest graded:* AU-50 • *Selected information:* CAA (1/2002), B57324A/D, EF, $3,565. Heritage (4/2008), B59059A/C, VF-25 (PMG), $13,800. CAA (1/2001), B67700A/D, Fine+, $1,540.

SERIES OF 1914, RED SEAL

$50 Federal Reserve Note, Series of 1914, Red Seal. Plate Style a: Face of W-2975-G-a. Federal Reserve Bank of Chicago. With serial G1A, plate A, the very first note. With bank identification 7-G at the lower left and top right (in addition to the Federal Reserve Bank seal).

$50 Federal Reserve Note, Series of 1914, Red Seal. Plate Style b: Face of W-2975-I-b. Federal Reserve Bank of Minneapolis. Similar to Plate Style a, but now with the bank number and letter below the plate letter (in this instance C) at the upper left.

Back of the $50 Federal Reserve Note, Series of 1914, Red Seal, the type also used on Series of 1914 Blue Seal notes. Although some lettering differs, the motifs are the same as used on the Federal Reserve Bank Notes.

W-2975-B-b • F-1013B • 40,000
Estimated population: 13 to 15 • Highest graded: Unc.

VG-8	F-12	VF-20	EF-40	AU-50	Unc-60	Unc-63
$2,700	$3,500	$4,500	$6,500	$10,000	$12,000	$18,000

W-2975-C-a • F-1014A • Philadelphia • 12,000
Estimated population: 16 to 18 • Highest graded: Unc.

VG-8	F-12	VF-20	EF-40	AU-50	Unc-60	Unc-63
$2,700	$3,500	$4,500	$6,500	$10,000	$12,000	$18,000

W-2975-C-b • F-1014B • 40,000

Estimated population: 9 or 10 • *Highest graded:* AU-50 • *Selected information:* Knight (3/2001), C17708A/D, Fine, $1,320. Heritage (1/2007), C24666A/B, Fine, $660. Knight (11/2006), C36264A, EF–AU, $11,500.

W-2975-D-a • F-1015A • Cleveland • 8,000

Recorded population: 5 • *Highest graded:* Unc • *Selected information:* Existing examples include serials D621A/A, VG, sold in a Knight auction (11/2003) for $5,463; D4388A, VF; D4453A, reported by Frank Nowak, grade not stated; D7241A/A, Unc, sold in a CAA auction (9/2000) for $8,800; and D7260A, VG.

W-2975-D-b • F-1015B • 40,000

Estimated population: 9 or 10 • *Highest graded:* Unc • *Selected information:* CAA (1/2001), D8609A/A, Unc, $12,100. Spink (7/2007), D9643A, EF, $24,350. Heritage (4/2008), D47882A/B, VF-35 (PMG), $43,125.

W-2975-E-a • F-1016A • Richmond • 28,000

Recorded population: 8 • *Highest graded:* AU-50 • *Selected information:* CAA (10/1998) E9025A/A, AU, $2,860. Knight (6/2000), E9574A/B, AU, $3,465. Knight (11/2007), E14654A/B, VG–F, $3,737.50. *Bank Note Reporter* (Lake Region 1/2003), E27304A, VF, $7,500.

W-2975-E-b • F-1016B • 40,000

Estimated population: 18 to 20 • *Highest graded:* VF-20.

VG-8	F-12	VF-20
$2,700	$3,500	$4,500

W-2975-F-a • F-1017A • Atlanta • 28,000

Estimated population: 11 to 13 • *Highest graded:* VF-20.

VG-8	F-12	VF-20
$2,800	$3,700	$5,000

W-2975-G-a • F-1018A • Chicago • 20,000

Recorded population: 6 • *Highest graded:* Unc • *Selected information:* Existing examples include serials G1A/A, Uncirculated, owned by the Federal Reserve Bank of San Francisco; G2418A/B, VG–F, part of the Smithsonian Institution collection; G2733A, VG; G6915A/C, VG, damaged, pinholes, sold in a Smythe auction (6/2003) for $1,753.75; G15824A/D, EF-45 (PMG), sold in a Heritage auction (4/2008) for $69,000; and G17273A/A, AU, problems, sold in a Stack's auction (3/1990) for $715.

W-2975-G-b • F-1018B • 40,000

Estimated population: 12 to 14 • *Highest graded:* AU-50.

VG-8	F-12	VF-20	EF-40	AU-50
$2,700	$3,500	$4,500	$8,000	—

W-2975-H-a • F-1019A • St. Louis • 12,000

Estimated population: 11 to 13 • *Highest graded:* EF-40.

VG-8	F-12	VF-20	EF-40
$2,700	$3,500	$4,500	—

W-2975-H-b • F-1019B • 16,000

Estimated population: 16 to 18 • *Highest graded:* Unc.

VG-8	F-12	VF-20	EF-40	AU-50	Unc-60	Unc-63
$2,700	$3,500	$4,500	$8,000	$10,000	$12,000	$18,000

W-2975-I-a • F-1020A • Minneapolis • 8,000

Recorded population: 6 • *Highest graded:* EF-40 • *Selected information:* Existing examples include serials I857A/A, Fine; I1088A/D, VF–EF, part of the Smithsonian Institution collection; I1804A/D, EF, sold in a CAA auction (1/2003) for $3,910; I3852A/D, VG, pinholes; I6103A/C, F–VF, pinholes, sold in a Smythe auction (6/2003) for $1,725; and I6489A/A, VF-25 (PMG), sold in a Heritage auction (4/2008) for $46,000.

W-2975-I-b • F-1020B • 8,000

Estimated population: 18 to 20 • *Highest graded:* Unc.

VG-8	F-12	VF-20	EF-40	AU-50	Unc-60
$2,700	$3,500	$4,500	$8,000	—	—

W-2975-J-a • F-1021A • Kansas City • 8,000

Recorded population: 5 • *Highest graded:* AU-50 • *Selected information:* Existing examples include serials J582A/B, grade not stated, owned by the Federal Reserve Bank of Kansas City; J1271A, AU, owned by the Federal Reserve Bank of San Francisco; J1960A/D, EF, sold in a Stack's auction (3/1991) for $350; J2295A/C, EF, sold by Barney Dean Oakes (5/1990) for $1,200; and J3201A, VG-8 (PMG), sold in a Heritage auction (4/2008) for $17,250.

W-2975-J-b • F-1021B • 8,000

Recorded population: 4 • *Highest graded:* VF-25 • *Selected information:* Existing examples include serials J9962A, Fine, owned by the Federal Reserve Bank of San Francisco; J10041A, Fine, sold in a CAA auction (10/1998) for $1,430; J11571A/C, VF, part of the Smithsonian Institution collection; and J11867A/C, VG, sold in a CAA auction (9/1997) for $440.

W-2975-K-a • F-1022A • Dallas • 28,000

Estimated population: 22 to 26 • *Highest graded:* EF-40.

VG-8	F-12	VF-20	EF-40
$2,700	$3,700	$4,500	$6,500

W-2975-L-a • F-1023A • San Francisco • 8,000

Recorded population: 3 • *Highest graded:* VF-35 • *Selected information:* Existing examples include serials L2582A, VF, sold in a NASCA auction (11/1979) for $400; L5794A/B, VF–EF, reported by Frank Nowak (2/1989) for $375; and L6918A/B, VF, part of the Smithsonian Institution collection.

W-2975-L-b • F-1023B • 24,000

Estimated population: 18 to 20 • *Highest graded:* Unc.

VG-8	F-12	VF-20	EF-40	AU-50	Unc-60	Unc-63
$2,700	$3,500	$4,500	$8,000	$10,000	$12,000	$18,000

Series of 1914, Blue Seal

Series of 1914 Blue Seal $50 notes are much more readily available than those with red seals. These can be collected by Federal Reserve Bank, though signature combinations can be a challenge. As they are not in the mainstream of popularity, scarce and rare varieties are priced lower than might otherwise be the case.

In all of the following listings the number (1 to 12) and the large letter (A to L) on the seal at the left indicates the Federal Reserve Bank that issued the note.

SERIES OF 1914, BLUE SEAL

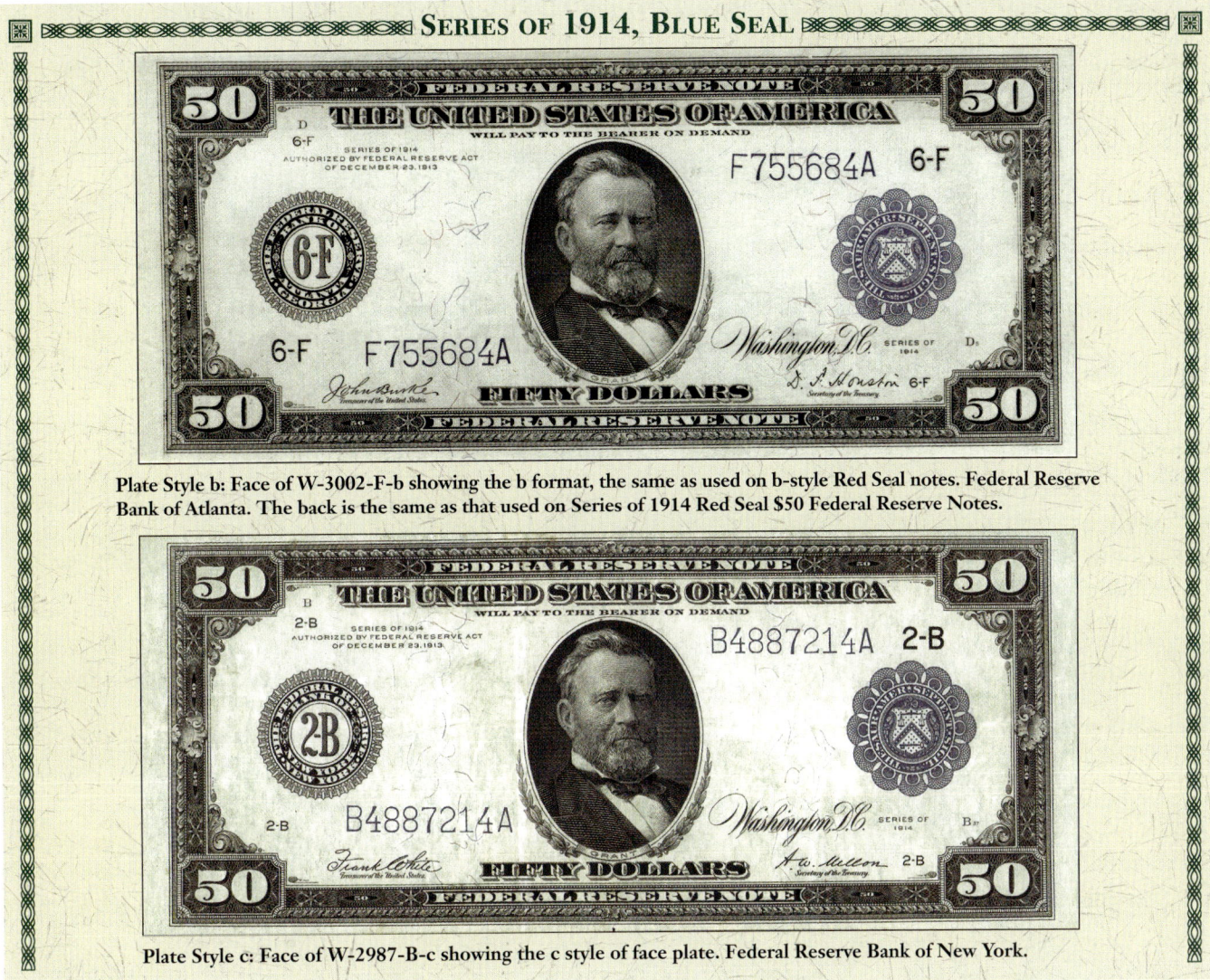

Plate Style b: Face of W-3002-F-b showing the b format, the same as used on b-style Red Seal notes. Federal Reserve Bank of Atlanta. The back is the same as that used on Series of 1914 Red Seal $50 Federal Reserve Notes.

Plate Style c: Face of W-2987-B-c showing the c style of face plate. Federal Reserve Bank of New York.

Plate Style b (on Red and Blue Seals): In certain of the following listings the small letter b following the Whitman number indicates a note in the format of the Style b also used on Red Seal notes. A large district number and letter are at the lower left and top right, and a small bank district letter and number added at the lower right and below the plate letter at the top left. In the Blue Seal series, nearly all Burke-McAdoo, Burke-Glass, and Burke-Houston notes are of this style.

Plate Style c (on Blue Seals only): In certain of the following listings the small letter c following the Whitman number indicates large bank district letter and number at the top right and small district letters and numbers in the other three corners. The letter and number at the upper left corner are below a plate letter. Some late White-Mellon notes are of this style and are very rare.

Plate Style d (on Blue Seals only): This style was not made for the $50 denomination. See smaller denominations for a description.

The following listings include only notes that are known to have been printed. Accordingly, some listings included in other texts are not given here.[18] Research is currently being done for printages from the $100 White-Mellon plates made for Richmond, Chicago, and St. Louis.

W-2980-A-b • F-1024 • Boston • Burke-McAdoo (1913–1918) • 592,000 (est.)

Estimated population: 60 to 70 • *Highest graded:* AU-55.

VG-8	F-12	VF-20	EF-40	AU-50
$250	$300	$500	$800	—

W-2981-A-b • F-1025 • Burke-Glass (1918–1920) • 344,000 (est.)

Estimated population: 35 to 40 • *Highest graded:* Unc.

VG-8	F-12	VF-20	EF-40	AU-50	Unc-60	Unc-63
$250	$300	$500	$800	$1,100	$1,400	$1,750

W-2982-A-b • F-1026 • Burke-Houston (1920–1921) • 92,000 (est.)

Estimated population: 9 or 10 • *Highest graded:* AU-55 • *Selected information:* Knight (3/2005), A1009073A/A, VG, $1,495. CAA (9/2006), A1010940A/D, AU-55 (PMG), $3,002. Heritage (4/2008), A1024110A/B, VF-30 (PMG), $1,093. CAA (5/2000), A1028476A/D, Choice EF, $1,100. CAA (5/2000), A1029721A/A, VF-30 (PMG). Knight (3/2008), A1034448A/D, VF-35 (PCGS), $1,092.50.

W-2984-B-b • F-1028 • New York • Burke-McAdoo (1913–1918) • 2,180,000 (est.)

Estimated population: 75 to 85 • Highest graded: Unc.

VG-8	F-12	VF-20	EF-40	AU-50	Unc-60	Unc-63
$250	$300	$500	$800	$1,100	$1,400	$1,750

W-2985-B-b • F-1029 • Burke-Glass (1918–1920) • 600,000 (est.)

Estimated population: 45 to 50 • Highest graded: Unc.

VG-8	F-12	VF-20	EF-40	AU-50	Unc-60	Unc-63
$350	$500	$750	$1,500	$2,000	$2,500	$3,000

W-2986-B-b • F-1030 • Burke-Houston (1920–1921) • 1,180,000 (est.)

Estimated population: 130 to 145 • Highest graded: Unc.

VG-8	F-12	VF-20	EF-40	AU-50	Unc-60	Unc-63
$250	$300	$500	$800	$1,100	$1,400	$1,750

W-2986-B-b★ • F-1030★

Recorded population: 3 • Highest graded: F-12 • Selected information: CAA (1/2005), B551★/C, Fine, $5,980. CAA (10/1995), B989★/A, VG, $660. Heritage (9/2007), B1189★/A, F-12 (PCGS), $5,750.

W-2987-B-b • F-1031A • White-Mellon (1921–1928) • 528,000 (est.)

Estimated population: 38 to 47 • Highest graded: Unc.

VG-8	F-12	VF-20	EF-40	AU-50	Unc-60
$250	$300	$500	$800	—	—

W-2987-B-c • F-1031B • 656,000 (est.)

Estimated population: 18 to 20 • Highest graded: AU-58.

VG-8	F-12	VF-20	EF-40	AU-50
$350	$500	$750	$1,500	—

W-2988-C-b • F-1032 • Philadelphia • Burke-McAdoo (1913–1918) • 652,000 (est.)

Estimated population: 35 to 40 • Highest graded: Unc.

VG-8	F-12	VF-20	EF-40	AU-50	Unc-60	Unc-63
$250	$300	$500	$800	$1,200	$1,600	$2,000

W-2989-C-b • F-1033 • Burke-Glass (1918–1920) • 244,000 (est.)

Estimated population: 15 to 17 • Highest graded: AU-50.

VG-8	F-12	VF-20	EF-40	AU-50
$350	$450	$500	$1,500	—

W-2990-C-b • F-1034 • Burke-Houston (1920–1921) • 732,000 (est.)

Estimated population: 60 to 65 • Highest graded: Unc.

VG-8	F-12	VF-20	EF-40	AU-50	Unc-60	Unc-63
$250	$300	$500	$800	$1,100	$1,400	$1,750

W-2990-C-b★ • F-1034★

Recorded population: 1 • Graded: EF • Selected information: Stack's (9/1992), C2762★/B, EF, $1,625.

W-2991-C-b • F-1035 • White-Mellon (1921–1928) • 2,040,000 (est.)

Estimated population: 175 to 185 • Highest graded: Unc.

VG-8	F-12	VF-20	EF-40	AU-50	Unc-60	Unc-63
$250	$300	$500	$800	$1,100	$1,400	$1,750

W-2991-C-b★ • F-1035★

Recorded population: 2 • Highest graded: VF-35 • Selected information: Existing examples include serials C4659★/C, Fine, sold in a NASCA auction (5/1977) for $125, and C5992★/D, VF–EF.

W-2992-D-b • F-1036 • Cleveland • Burke-McAdoo (1913–1918) • 1,488,000 (est.)

Estimated population: 95 to 115 • Highest graded: Unc.

VG-8	F-12	VF-20	EF-40	AU-50	Unc-60	Unc-63
$250	$300	$500	$800	$1,100	$1,400	$1,750

W-2993-D-b • F-1037 • Burke-Glass (1918–1920) • 404,000 (est.)

Estimated population: 35 to 45 • Highest graded: AU-50.

VG-8	F-12	VF-20	EF-40	AU-50
$350	$500	$750	—	—

W-2994-D-b • F-1038 • Burke-Houston (1920–1921) • 1,260,000 (est.)

Estimated population: 90 to 100 • Highest graded: AU-50.

VG-8	F-12	VF-20	EF-40	AU-50
$400	$750	$1,000	$14,500	—

W-2995-D-b • F-1039A • White-Mellon (1921–1928) • 2,368,000 (est.)

Estimated population: 170 to 185 • Highest graded: Unc.

VG-8	F-12	VF-20	EF-40	AU-50	Unc-60	Unc-63
$250	$300	$500	$800	$1,100	$1,400	$1,750

W-2995-D-b★ • F-1039A★

Estimated population: 11 to 13 • Highest graded: EF-40 • Selected information: CAA (9/1999), D12007★/C, Fine+, $880. Knight (10/1991), D15954★/B, EF (later "gem Crisp Unc"), $950. Heritage (9/2007), D16025★/A, VG+, problems, $2,300. CAA (10/1998), D23444★/D, VG, $715. CAA (5/1999), D23555★/C, F–VF, $2,090.

W-2995-D-c • F-1039B • 568,000 (est.)

Estimated population: 70 to 80 • Highest graded: Unc.

VG-8	F-12	VF-20	EF-40	AU-50	Unc-60	Unc-63
$250	$300	$500	$800	$1,100	$1,400	$1,750

W-2996-E-b • F-1040 • Richmond • Burke-McAdoo (1913–1918) • 512,000 (est.)

Estimated population: 40 to 45 • Highest graded: Unc.

VG-8	F-12	VF-20	EF-40	AU-50	Unc-60	Unc-63
$250	$300	$500	$800	$1,100	$1,400	$1,750

W-2997-E-b • F-1041 • Burke-Glass (1918–1920) • 160,000 (est.)

Estimated population: 15 to 17 • Highest graded: AU-50.

VG-8	F-12	VF-20	EF-40	AU-50
$350	$500	$750	$1,000	—

W-2998-E-b • F-1042 • Burke-Houston (1920–1921) • 732,000 (est.)

Estimated population: 70 to 80 • *Highest graded:* Unc.

VG-8	F-12	VF-20	EF-40	AU-50	Unc-60	Unc-63
$250	$300	$500	$800	$1,100	$1,400	$1,750

W-2998-E-b★ • F-1042★

Recorded population: 2 • *Highest graded:* VF-25 • *Selected information:* Stack's (5/1978), E195★/C, VF, $260. Heritage (1/2006), E1600★/D, VG–F, $6,325.

W-2999-E-b • F-1043 • White-Mellon (1921–1928) • 196,000 (est.)

Estimated population: 50 to 60 • *Highest graded:* Unc.

VG-8	F-12	VF-20	EF-40	AU-50	Unc-60	Unc-63
$250	$300	$500	$800	$1,100	$1,400	$1,750

W-3000-F-b • F-1044 • Atlanta • Burke-McAdoo (1913–1918) • 312,000 (est.)

Estimated population: 32 to 36 • *Highest graded:* Unc.

VG-8	F-12	VF-20	EF-40	AU-50	Unc-60	Unc-63
$250	$300	$500	$800	$1,100	$1,400	$1,750

W-3001-F-b • F-1045 • Burke-Glass (1918–1920) • 108,000 (est.)

Recorded population: 7 • *Highest graded:* VF-25 • *Selected information:* Existing examples include serials F342860A/D, Fine, sold in a Smythe auction (6/2003) for $2,415; F362943A/C, Fine, problems, sold in a Knight auction (6/2006) for $2,645; F374365A/A, G–VG, sold in a Heritage auction (4/2008) for $460; F380305A, VF, owned by the Federal Reserve Bank of San Francisco; F422335A, Good; F431265A/A, VF-25 (PMG), sold in a Heritage auction (4/2008) for $13,800; and F456635A/C, VF, problems, sold in a Knight auction (8/2002) for $192.

W-3002-F-b • F-1046 • Burke-Houston (1920–1921) • 332,000 (est.)

Estimated population: 95 to 105 • *Highest graded:* Unc.

VG-8	F-12	VF-20	EF-40	AU-50	Unc-60	Unc-63
$250	$300	$500	$800	$1,100	$1,400	$1,750

W-3003-F-b • F-1047 • White-Mellon (1921–1928) • 280,000 (est.)

Estimated population: 19 to 22 • *Highest graded:* Unc.

VG-8	F-12	VF-20	EF-40	AU-50	Unc-60	Unc-63
$325	$450	$750	$1,100	$1,450	$1,800	$2,200

W-3004-G-b • F-1048 • Chicago • Burke-McAdoo (1913–1918) • 1,292,000 (est.)

Estimated population: 90 to 100 • *Highest graded:* Unc.

VG-8	F-12	VF-20	EF-40	AU-50	Unc-60	Unc-63
$250	$300	$500	$800	$1,100	$1,400	$1,750

W-3005-G-b • F-1049 • Burke-Glass (1918–1920) • 288,000 (est.)

Estimated population: 56 to 60 • *Highest graded:* Unc.

VG-8	F-12	VF-20	EF-40	AU-50	Unc-60	Unc-63
$300	$400	$650	$950	$1,350	$1,750	$2,200

W-3005-G-b★ • F-1049★

Recorded population: 1 • *Selected information:* The existing example is serial G309★/A, Fine.

W-3006-G-b • F-1050 • Burke-Houston (1920–1921) • 1,336,000 (est.)

Estimated population: 90 to 95 • *Highest graded:* AU-50.

VG-8	F-12	VF-20	EF-40	AU-50
$250	$300	$500	$800	$1,100

W-3006-G-b★ • F-1050★

Recorded population: 3 • *Highest graded:* EF-45 • *Selected information:* CAA (1/2003), G1128★/D, Good, $748. Knight (11/1997), G2401★/A, VF, $2,600. CAA (1/2000), G7143★/C, EF, $4,125.

W-3007-G-b • F-1051 • White-Mellon (1921–1928) • 1,012,000 (est.)

Estimated population: 75 to 85 • *Highest graded:* Unc.

VG-8	F-12	VF-20	EF-40	AU-50	Unc-60	Unc-63
$250	$300	$500	$800	$1,100	$1,400	$1,750

W-3008-H-b • F-1052 • St. Louis • Burke-McAdoo (1913–1918) • 212,000 (est.)

Estimated population: 33 to 36 • *Highest graded:* Unc.

VG-8	F-12	VF-20	EF-40	AU-50	Unc-60	Unc-63
$250	$300	$500	$800	$1,100	$1,400	$1,750

W-3009-H-b • F-1053 • Burke-Glass (1918–1920) • 192,000 (est.)

Estimated population: 45 to 50 • *Highest graded:* Unc.

VG-8	F-12	VF-20	EF-40	AU-50	Unc-60	Unc-63
$450	$650	$1,000	$1,500	$2,000	$2,500	$3,000

W-3009-H-b★ • F-1053★

Recorded population: 1 • *Graded:* EF • *Selected information:* Smythe (6/2001), H22★/B, EF, $3,740.

W-3010-H-b • F-1054 • Burke-Houston (1920–1921) • 152,000 (est.)

Estimated population: 45 to 50 • *Highest graded:* Unc.

VG-8	F-12	VF-20	EF-40	AU-50	Unc-60	Unc-63
$250	$300	$500	$800	$1,100	$1,400	$1,750

W-3012-I-b • F-1056 • Minneapolis • Burke-McAdoo (1913–1918) • 96,000 (est.)

Estimated population: 45 to 50 • *Highest graded:* Unc.

VG-8	F-12	VF-20	EF-40	AU-50	Unc-60	Unc-63
$250	$300	$500	$800	$1,250	$2,000	$3,500

W-3014-I-b • F-1058 • Burke-Houston (1920–1921) • 32,000 (est.)

Recorded population: 8 • *Highest graded:* AU-50 • *Selected information:* Heritage (4/2008), I121835A/C, VF-30 (PMG), $3,738. Smythe (7/2007), I128739A/C, VF-25 (PCGS), damaged, $1,495. Knight (2/2004), I134970A/B, VF, $1,265. Knight (2/2003), I139492A/D, AU, $3,910.

W-3015-I-b • F-1059 • White-Mellon (1921–1928) • 20,000 (est.)

Recorded population: 3 • *Highest graded:* VF-20 • *Selected information:* Existing examples include serial I144584A/D, F–VF;

I145264A/D, VF-35 (PMG), sold in a Heritage auction (4/2008) for $14,950; and I145950A/B, F–VF, sold in a CAA auction (9/2005) for $978.

W-3016-J-b • F-1060 • Kansas City • Burke-McAdoo (1913–1918) • 308,000 (est.)

Estimated population: 44 to 48 • *Highest graded:* Unc.

VG-8	F-12	VF-20	EF-40	AU-50	Unc-60
$250	$300	$500	$800	—	—

W-3017-J-b★ • F-1060★

Recorded population: 1 • *Selected information:* The existing example is serial J45★/A, owned by the Federal Reserve Bank of Kansas City.

W-3019-J-b • F-1063 • White-Mellon (1921–1928) • 100,000 (est.)

Recorded population: 3 • *Highest graded:* EF-45 • *Selected information:* Existing examples include serials J326574A/B, EF; J334633A, VF-30, damaged, sold in a Heritage auction (1/2008) for $8,625; and J371565A, EF.

W-3020-K-b • F-1064 • Dallas • Burke-McAdoo (1913–1918) • 168,000 (est.)

Estimated population: 32 to 35 • *Highest graded:* Unc.

VG-8	F-12	VF-20	EF-40	AU-50	Unc-60
$300	$450	$700	$1,000	—	—

W-3022-K-b • F-1066 • Burke-Houston (1920–1921) • 44,000 (est.)

Recorded population: 5 • *Highest graded:* EF-40 • *Selected information:* Existing examples include serials K198877A, VF; K199114A/B, F-12 (PMG), sold in a Heritage auction (9/2008) for $3,450; K208616A, Fine; and K209510A, VF-30 (PMG), sold in a Heritage auction (4/2008) for $27,600.

W-3024-L-b • F-1068 • San Francisco • Burke-McAdoo (1913–1918) • 724,000 (est.)

Estimated population: 75 to 80 • *Highest graded:* Unc.

VG-8	F-12	VF-20	EF-40	AU-50	Unc-60
$250	$450	$700	$800	—	—

W-3024-L-b★ • F-1068★

Recorded population: 1 • *Graded:* Fine • *Selected information:* CAA (5/2003), L528★/D, Fine, $8,050.

W-3026-L-b • F-1070 • Burke-Houston (1920–1921) • 292,000 (est.)

Estimated population: 38 to 42 • *Highest graded:* AU-50.

VG-8	F-12	VF-20	EF-40	AU-50
$250	$300	$500	$800	—

W-3026-L-b★ • F-1070★

Recorded population: 1 • *Graded:* Fine • *Selected information:* Smythe (6/2001), L2001★/A, Fine, damaged, $5,280.

W-3027-L-b • F-1071 • White-Mellon (1921–1928) • 308,000 (est.)

Estimated population: 26 to 30 • *Highest graded:* Unc.

VG-8	F-12	VF-20	EF-40	AU-50	Unc-60
$250	$300	$500	$800	—	—

FEDERAL RESERVE BANK NOTES

Series of 1918

For the $50 denomination, the Series of 1918, with the city and bank listed on the face, was issued just in one location, St. Louis, and in only one signature combination. This is a classic for type, with an original distribution of only 4,000 pieces.

Texas collector William A. Philpott Jr., longtime secretary of the Texas Bankers Association, rescued most of these by corresponding with Federal Reserve Banks and alerting employees to his interest. At one time he reported that Treasury records revealed just 33 outstanding, but he later amended that figure to 70. Of the several dozen he found, nearly all showed light circulation. He cleaned them lightly with soap and water, and pressed them to make them brighter and more attractive.[19]

In addition to the St. Louis notes, plates were made for Atlanta, with 40,000 notes printed, and for Boston, for which there is no printage record. The Boston plate has Elliott-Burke and Willett-Morss signatures and was certified on January 11, 1921. The Atlanta plate is listed below.[20]

W-3029 • F-unlisted • Atlanta • Elliott-Burke (1919–1921) • Bell-Wellborn • 40,000 • None issued

W-3030 • F-831 • St. Louis • Teehee-Burke (1915–1919) • Attebery-Wells • 4,000

Recorded population: 54 • *Highest graded:* Unc.

VG-8	F-12	VF-20	EF-40	AU-50	Unc-60	Unc-63
$3,500	$8,000	$10,000	$18,500	$22,500	$28,000	$35,000

SMALL SIZE

All small-size $50 notes have the portrait of Ulysses S. Grant on the face. The portrait is by George F.C. Smillie. The back features a panorama of Washington, D.C., with the U.S. Capitol in the foreground, by Louis S. Schofield. These were used up to the advent of modern security notes.

Early series from the 1920s through the 1940s are generally scarce, especially with regard to specific varieties. Very few numismatists collected them at the time, and scarcely any notice was taken. When collecting did become popular on a wider scale, after the publication of *United States Paper Money* by Robert Friedberg in 1953 and the intense collecting activities of Amon Carter Jr., the face value still precluded more than just scattered notes being saved here and there. Carter, for example, saved "bricks" of 4,000 smaller-denomination small-size notes banded together, as they were shipped from the Federal Reserve Banks, but for $50 notes just a few sufficed. In modern times, the output of small-size $50 Federal Reserve Notes has paralleled those of smaller denominations, with the same series often being issued.

Currently, these bills can be collected by Federal Reserve district as well as by Washington or Fort Worth origin, but it takes a healthy checkbook balance to keep pace with whatever is issued from all 12 Federal Reserve Banks. If the challenge of collecting star notes is added, the search becomes even more difficult. In recent years most printing of $50 notes has been accomplished at the Western Facility in Fort Worth, Texas.

SERIES OF 1918

$50 Federal Reserve Bank Note, Series of 1918 (W-3030). This continues the portrait of President Grant. Notes of this type were only issued by the St. Louis bank.

The back of the $50 Federal Reserve Bank Note, Series of 1918 (W-3030). The design continues the motif of a goddess representing Panama on land between the Atlantic and Pacific oceans. Certain lettering is different.

For all denominations, even including those of $1,000 and above, scattered hoards have been found in bank safe deposit boxes, foreign holdings, and elsewhere, often generating surprise if they are publicized, and, in any event, making the notes more collectible than would otherwise be the case. A few years ago there was a nationwide scare regarding counterfeit $50 notes, prompting retail locations to examine them carefully, often under ultraviolet light, and sometimes to put marks on them to signify that they were good.

NATIONAL BANK NOTES

Series of 1929, Type 1, Brown Seal
Jones-Woods (1929–1933)

Sheets of Type 1 bills each had the same serial number on a given sheet, prefixed by a letter, A through F, such as A000001A to F000001A. This gives six times as many number 1 notes as Series of 1929 Type 2 bills. The signatures of the bank cashier and president were printed directly on each note at the BEP. (Illus. on p. 592.)

The prices listed are for states from which more than just a few notes survive. Notes of this type are rare for many states, for which specialists are grateful to have a single example for type. Colorado and Hawaii Territory have especially strong showings in the Series of 1929, considering their scarcity in earlier National Bank Note series. Typical grades range from Fine to About Uncirculated, and enough Uncirculated bills exist that an example can be readily acquired for type. The value chart shows generic prices for a typical note from a state from which notes range from available to just slightly scarce.

Banks of Issue and Rarity of Notes

Based upon census information from Don C. Kelly and James M. Kelly (*National Bank Note Census*, Version 4.0) and with some information from other sources, this listing gives each location, the number of banks issuing this series of notes within each, and a commentary.[21]

The Kelly survey records 3,836 of these. There are 80 serial number 1 notes, in large part because the first sheet of this type for each bank had six such notes. These are specifically listed below. The territorial notes in this series are all from the same bank in Hawaii.

California • 15 banks of issue • 329 notes reported • The census lists 10 notes in Unc grade. Eight serial number 1 notes are known.

Colorado • 5 banks of issue • 112 notes reported • Seven Unc notes and six serial number 1 notes are known.

Connecticut • 3 banks of issue • 22 notes reported • The only serial number 1 note is from the First National Bank of Wallingford (also the only Unc example reported for the state).

Delaware • 1 bank of issue • 5 notes reported • All are from the First National Bank of Smyrna, all in circulated grades.

Florida • 2 banks of issue • 24 notes reported • Six serial number 1 notes are known, all Unc.

Hawaii • 1 bank of issue • 123 notes reported • All are from Bishop First National Bank of Honolulu, 19 Unc. Hawaii was a territory at the time, but the notes simply say Hawaii.

Idaho • 3 banks of issue • 36 notes reported • All are circulated.

Illinois • 33 banks of issue • 453 notes reported • The census lists 53 Unc notes, including 11 from the Merchants National Bank of Aurora. Seven serial number 1 notes are known, six of them Unc.

Indiana • 13 banks of issue • 133 notes reported • Two Unc examples are from the Citizens National Bank of South Bend.

Iowa • 13 banks of issue • 183 notes reported • The census lists 11 Unc notes. The only serial number 1 note is from the First National Bank of Davenport (Unc).

Kansas • 12 banks of issue • 99 notes reported • Four Unc examples are known. Three serial number 1 notes are known: Howard National Bank (Unc), Farmers National Bank of Salina (VF), and the National Bank of Seneca (Unc).

Kentucky • 4 banks of issue • 34 notes reported • All are circulated.

Louisiana • 2 banks of issue • 46 notes reported • Seven Unc notes are listed. Six serial number 1 notes are known.

Maryland • 8 banks of issue • 55 notes reported • Five Unc notes are listed.

Massachusetts • 7 banks of issue • 40 notes reported • Six Unc notes are listed.

Michigan • 9 banks of issue • 358 notes reported • Most are circulated, but there are many exceptions. The census lists 18 serial number 1 notes, all Unc.

Minnesota • 5 banks of issue • 69 notes reported • Three Unc notes are known, all from the Northern National Bank of Duluth.

Mississippi • 1 bank of issue • 2 notes reported • First National Bank of Jackson, both VF.

Missouri • 4 banks of issue • 61 notes reported • Five Unc notes are listed.

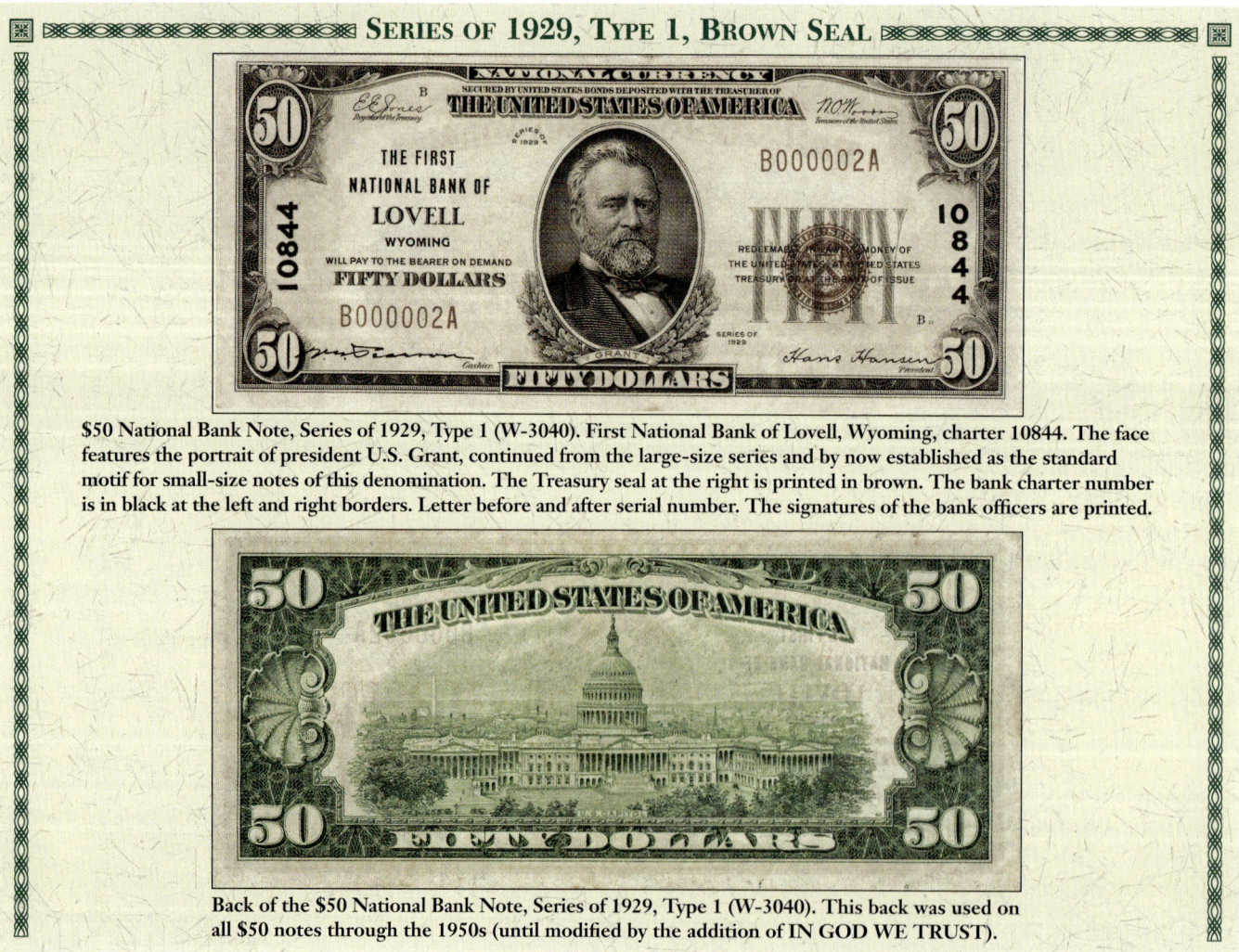

SERIES OF 1929, TYPE 1, BROWN SEAL

$50 National Bank Note, Series of 1929, Type 1 (W-3040). First National Bank of Lovell, Wyoming, charter 10844. The face features the portrait of president U.S. Grant, continued from the large-size series and by now established as the standard motif for small-size notes of this denomination. The Treasury seal at the right is printed in brown. The bank charter number is in black at the left and right borders. Letter before and after serial number. The signatures of the bank officers are printed.

Back of the $50 National Bank Note, Series of 1929, Type 1 (W-3040). This back was used on all $50 notes through the 1950s (until modified by the addition of IN GOD WE TRUST).

Montana • 1 bank of issue • 18 notes reported • All are from the First National Bank of Butte, including the only Unc example.

Nebraska • 6 banks of issue • 122 notes reported • The census lists 12 Unc notes.

Nevada • 1 bank of issue • 23 notes reported • All are from the Reno National Bank; six are Unc.

New Hampshire • 2 banks of issue • 11 notes reported • All are circulated.

New Jersey • 10 banks of issue • 50 notes reported • All are circulated.

New York • 16 banks of issue • 86 notes reported • Six serial number 1 notes are known, all Unc, from the Union National Bank of Troy. These are the only Unc notes from the state, surprising as New York is usually well represented.

North Carolina • 1 bank of issue • 2 notes reported • American National Bank of Asheville (AU, VF).

North Dakota • 1 bank of issue • 8 notes reported • All are from the First National Bank & Trust Company of Fargo, and all are in circulated grades.

Ohio • 17 banks of issue • 211 notes reported • The census lists 20 Unc examples. Six serial number 1 notes are known, five from the First National Bank of Newark, all Unc.

Oklahoma • 7 banks of issue • 165 notes reported • The census lists 14 Unc notes.

Oregon • 3 banks of issue • 10 notes reported • Two Unc notes are from the Citizens National Bank of Portland. The only serial number 1 note is from the Citizens National Bank of Portland (AU).

Pennsylvania • 35 banks of issue • 320 notes reported • The census lists 21 Unc notes. Four serial number 1 notes are known, three from the National Bank of Brookville (all Unc) and one from the Forest County National Bank of Tionesta (not graded).

Rhode Island • 2 banks of issue • 16 notes reported • The only Unc note is from the Mechanics National Bank of Providence.

South Dakota • 2 banks of issue • 21 notes reported • All are circulated. The only serial number 1 note is from the Dakota National Bank of Yankton.

Tennessee • 5 banks of issue • 72 notes reported • Three Unc notes are known, one from the First National Bank of Chattanooga and two from the First National Bank of Memphis.

Texas • 33 banks of issue • 373 notes reported • The census lists 18 Unc notes. Six serial number 1 notes are known.

Utah • 1 bank of issue • 16 notes reported • Four Unc notes are known.

Vermont • 4 banks of issue • 10 notes reported • All are circulated.

Washington • 3 banks of issue • 37 notes reported • The only Unc note is from the National Bank of Commerce, Seattle.

West Virginia • 1 bank of issue • 2 notes reported • First National Bank of Richwood (EF, VF).

Wisconsin • 6 banks of issue • 76 notes reported • The census lists 13 Unc notes.

Wyoming • 1 bank of issue • 3 notes reported • First National Bank of Lovell (AG, VG, VF).

W-3040 • F-1803-1

Estimated population: 4,300 to 4,600 • *Highest graded:* Unc.

VG-8	F-12	VF-20	EF-40	AU-50	Unc-60	Unc-63
$350	$375	$395	$500	$550	$625	$700

Series of 1929, Type 2, Brown Seal
Jones-Woods (1929–1933)

Sheets of Type 2 bills were numbered continuously, with the first sheet from a given bank starting with A000001 and ending with A000006. This yielded a single number 1 note, in contrast to the six on the first Series of 1929 Type 1 sheet. The same numbering system was used on all small-size National Bank Notes. Signatures of the bank cashier and president were printed directly on each note at the BEP. The charter number appears four times on the face, twice in black and twice in brown. (Illus. on p. 594.)

The prices listed are for states from which notes can be readily collected, although the $50 denomination is rare, and patience is needed. Type 2 $50 notes are much rarer than Type 1 notes, and are consequently harder to find in the marketplace. Included are issues of many new banks chartered from 1933 to 1935, often consolidations of two or more banks that experienced difficulties during the Depression. Average grades are the highest for any of the classes of National Bank Notes, generally ranging from Extremely Fine to Uncirculated, though the latter is still a challenge to find in the marketplace. The value chart shows generic prices for a typical note from a state from which notes range from available to just slightly scarce.

Banks of Issue and Rarity of Notes

Based upon census information from Don C. Kelly and James M. Kelly (*National Bank Note Census*, Version 4.0) and with some information from other sources, this listing gives each location, the number of banks issuing this series of notes within each, and a commentary.[22]

The Kelly survey records only 343 of these, or less than a tenth of the Type 1 series. There are just three serial number 1 notes. These are specifically listed below. The territorial notes in this series are all from the same bank in Hawaii.

Arkansas • 1 bank of issue • 1 note reported • First National Bank of Lawrence, Walnut Ridge (VF).

California • 1 bank of issue • 98 notes reported • The only Unc note is from the Bank of America National Bank & Trust Company of San Francisco.

Colorado • 3 banks of issue • 15 notes reported • The only Unc note is from the First National Bank in Boulder.

Hawaii • 1 bank of issue • 8 notes reported • All are circulated and from Bishop National Bank in Honolulu. Hawaii was a territory at the time, but the notes simply say Hawaii.

SERIES OF 1929, TYPE 2, BROWN SEAL

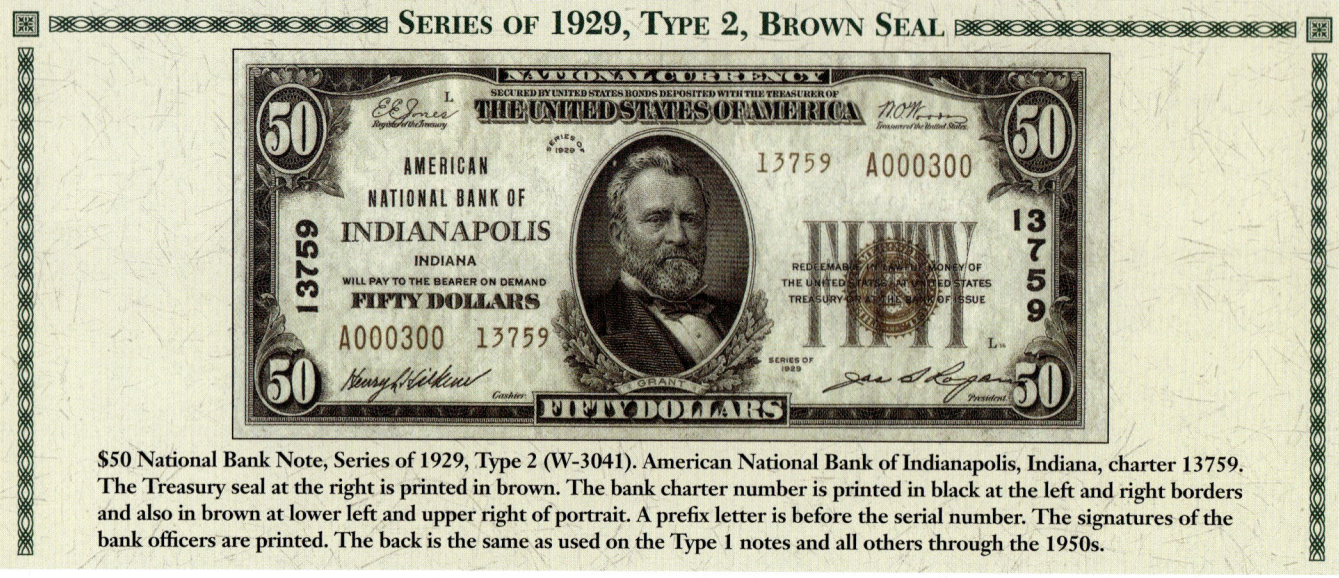

$50 National Bank Note, Series of 1929, Type 2 (W-3041). American National Bank of Indianapolis, Indiana, charter 13759. The Treasury seal at the right is printed in brown. The bank charter number is printed in black at the left and right borders and also in brown at lower left and upper right of portrait. A prefix letter is before the serial number. The signatures of the bank officers are printed. The back is the same as used on the Type 1 notes and all others through the 1950s.

Illinois • 4 banks of issue • 16 notes reported • Five Unc notes are known. Two serial number 1 notes are known, from the Livestock National Bank of Chicago and the Dixon National Bank.

Indiana • 2 banks of issue • 14 notes reported • Five Unc notes are known.

Kansas • 1 bank of issue • No notes reported.

Kentucky • 1 bank of issue • 2 notes reported • Both are from the Citizens National Bank of Covington (F, VF).

Louisiana • 2 banks of issue • 16 notes reported • The only Unc note is from the Hibernia National Bank in New Orleans.

Maryland • 3 banks of issue • 1 note reported • Salisbury National Bank (VF–EF), serial number 13.

Michigan • 2 banks of issue • 11 notes reported • The only Unc note is from the National Bank of Grand Rapids.

Minnesota • 2 banks of issue • 4 notes reported • All are from the Winona National & Savings Bank (unusual to have "Savings" as part of a national bank title) and all are circulated.

Missouri • 1 bank of issue • 2 notes reported • Both are from the First National Bank of Kansas City (VF, VG–F).

Nebraska • 1 bank of issue • 14 notes reported • Six Unc notes are listed. The only serial number 1 note is from the Farmers & Merchants National Bank of Ashland.

New Jersey • 2 banks of issue • 4 notes reported • The only Unc note is from the Allenhurst National Bank & Trust Company.

New York • 3 banks of issue • 26 notes reported • The only Unc note is from the National Bank of Yorkville in New York.

Ohio • 1 bank of issue • No notes reported.

Oklahoma • 3 banks of issue • 26 notes reported • Six Unc notes are known.

Pennsylvania • 4 banks of issue • 27 notes reported • Eight Unc notes are known.

Rhode Island • 1 bank of issue • 5 notes reported • All are from the Rhode Island Hospital National Bank of Providence, and all are circulated.

Tennessee • 1 bank of issue • 5 notes reported • All are from the National Bank of Commerce in Memphis, including one Unc.

Texas • 8 banks of issue • 48 notes reported • Four Unc notes are known.

Virginia • 1 bank of issue • No notes reported.

Wisconsin • 1 bank of issue • No notes reported.

W-3041 • F-1803-2

Estimated population: 375 to 400 • *Highest graded:* Unc.

VG-8	F-12	VF-20	EF-40	AU-50	Unc-60	Unc-63
$350	$500	$750	$900	$1,000	$1,100	$1,200

FEDERAL RESERVE BANK NOTES

Series of 1929, Brown Seal
Jones-Woods (1929–1933)

Small-size Federal Reserve Bank Notes, printed in a hurry in March 1933 to prevent national banks from running out of paper money, were made in large quantities, but the anticipated crisis never happened. Accordingly, relatively few seem to have been distributed at the time. For whatever reason, today notes of the $50 denomination are readily available from the seven (out of 12) districts that issued them. None were printed for Boston, Philadelphia, Richmond, Atlanta, or St. Louis. Although they are hardly common, the various issues can be obtained without great difficulty in Uncirculated grade, an exception to other small-size $50 notes of the late 1920s and early 1930s.

The printed signatures on these and other notes include two of Treasury officials and two of Federal Reserve Bank officials, such as the deputy governor (or assistant deputy governor) and governor, or the cashier and governor. Sometimes CASHIER and always PRESIDENT, already printed on the notes, were blocked out with a black rectangle. Added to the security information already printed at the top center of National Bank Notes was a new line, "or by like deposit of other securities." Sometimes the registration of this added line was careless and caused the printing to slightly overlap the printing of SERIES OF below.

SERIES OF 1929, BROWN SEAL

$50 Federal Reserve Bank Note, Series of 1929 (W-3046-J), Kansas City Federal Reserve Bank.

Detail of a W-3042-B note showing misregistration of the blackout overprint at lower left, inadvertently revealing the earlier CASHIER.

Back of the $50 Federal Reserve Bank Note, Series of 1929 (W-3046-J). This type was used on all small-size $50 notes of the era.

All regular notes are readily collectible, but the Dallas issue is scarcer than the others. Star notes are scarce, rare for Chicago, Minneapolis, and San Francisco. Although 12,000 star notes were printed for Dallas, no examples have been reported by numismatists.

Prices for a typical star note for this series, unless listed otherwise, are as follows:

VG-8	F-12	VF-20	EF-40	AU-50	Unc-60	Unc-63
$350	$500	$650	$1,000	$1,500	$2,400	$3,700

W-3042-B • F-1880B • New York • 636,000

VG-8	F-12	VF-20	EF-40	AU-50	Unc-60	Unc-63
$90	$95	$100	$120	$180	$275	$400

W-3042-B★ • F-1880B★

W-3043-D • F-1880D • Cleveland • 684,000

VG-8	F-12	VF-20	EF-40	AU-50	Unc-60	Unc-63
$90	$95	$100	$120	$175	$250	$350

W-3043-D★ • F-1880D★

W-3044-G • F-1880G • Chicago • 300,000

VG-8	F-12	VF-20	EF-40	AU-50	Unc-60	Unc-63
$90	$95	$100	$120	$160	$225	$375

W-3044-G★ • F-1880G★

W-3045-I • F-1880I • Minneapolis • 276,000

VG-8	F-12	VF-20	EF-40	AU-50	Unc-60	Unc-63
$90	$95	$100	$120	$190	$325	$550

W-3045-I★ • F-1880I★

W-3046-J • F-1880J • Kansas City • 276,000

VG-8	F-12	VF-20	EF-40	AU-50	Unc-60	Unc-63
$90	$95	$100	$120	$175	$250	$350

W-3046-J★ • F-1880J★

W-3047-K • F-1880K • Dallas • 168,000

VG-8	F-12	VF-20	EF-40	AU-50	Unc-60	Unc-63
$200	$350	$550	$1,000	$1,400	$2,200	$3,500

W-3047-K★ • F-1880K★ • Unknown

W-3048-L • F-1880L • San Francisco • 576,000

VG-8	F-12	VF-20	EF-40	AU-50	Unc-60	Unc-63
$100	$120	$150	$250	$325	$410	$525

W-3048-L★ • F-1880L★

GOLD CERTIFICATES

Small-size Gold Certificates were produced in the Series of 1928. Examples are seen with some frequency today and are usually in circulated grades.

Series of 1928, Gold Seal
Woods-Mellon (1929–1932)

The obligation or payable notice reads: "Fifty Dollars in gold coin payable to the bearer on demand." At the left the Treasury seal is overprinted on a more standard commentary, with GOLD above and CERTIFICATE below, with three lines between: "This certificate is a legal tender in the amount thereof in payment of all debts and dues public and private." In addition to the yellow (usually called gold) seal, the serial numbers were printed in yellow.

Circulated notes are readily available in the marketplace. High-quality Uncirculated examples are scarce in relation to the demand for them. Star notes are rare in all grades, extremely so at the Uncirculated level.

W-3050 • F-2404 • 5,520,000

VG-8	F-12	VF-20	EF-40	AU-50	Unc-60	Unc-63
$295	$395	$575	$900	$1,300	$1,750	$2,500

W-3050★ • F-2404★

VG-8	F-12	VF-20	EF-40	AU-50	Unc-60	Unc-63
$1,950	$2,750	$4,250	$9,500	$11,000	$12,500	$14,000

FEDERAL RESERVE NOTES

Series of 1928, Green Seal
Woods-Mellon (1929–1932)

The obligation is printed in four lines in the field at the upper left: "Redeemable in gold on demand at the United States Treasury, or in gold or lawful money at any Federal Reserve Bank." On the Series of 1928 notes, the seal is in the left field and features the number of the issuing Federal Reserve Bank, 1 to 12. For the $50 denomination this layout appears only on Series of 1928 notes. The series imprint appears twice—at the upper left of Grant's portrait and above the plate letter and number at the lower right.

The Boston, Minneapolis, and Dallas notes are scarcer than the others. All star notes are rare, the Boston and Minneapolis issues especially so.

W-3060-A • F-2100A • Boston • 265,200

VG-8	F-12	VF-20	EF-40	AU-50	Unc-60	Unc-63
$125	$170	$300	$500	$1,000	$2,000	$4,000

W-3060-A★ • F-2100A★

VG-8	F-12	VF-20	EF-40	AU-50	Unc-60	Unc-63
$1,250	$2,250	$4,000	$6,000	$8,250	$11,500	$15,000

W-3060-B • F-2100B • New York • 1,351,800

VG-8	F-12	VF-20	EF-40	AU-50	Unc-60	Unc-63
$80	$100	$150	$225	$300	$400	$500

SERIES OF 1928, GOLD SEAL

$50 Gold Certificate, Series of 1928 (W-3050). Portrait of president U.S. Grant.

Detail of the payable notice.

Back of the $50 Gold Certificate, Series of 1928 (W-3050). This type was used on all small-size $50 notes of the era.

W-3060-B★ • F-2100B★

VG-8	F-12	VF-20	EF-40	AU-50	Unc-60	Unc-63
$150	$225	$450	$625	$900	$1,350	$2,000

W-3060-C • F-2100C • Philadelphia • 997,056

VG-8	F-12	VF-20	EF-40	AU-50	Unc-60	Unc-63
$90	$120	$180	$275	$375	$525	$750

W-3060-C★ • F-2100C★

VG-8	F-12	VF-20	EF-40	AU-50	Unc-60	Unc-63
$150	$350	$550	$900	$1,300	$1,900	$2,700

W-3060-D • F-2100D • Cleveland • 1,161,900

VG-8	F-12	VF-20	EF-40	AU-50	Unc-60	Unc-63
$80	$100	$180	$275	$375	$550	$750

W-3060-D★ • F-2100D★

VG-8	F-12	VF-20	EF-40	AU-50	Unc-60	Unc-63
$150	$350	$550	$900	$1,250	$1,750	$2,500

W-3060-E • F-2100E • Richmond • 539,400

VG-8	F-12	VF-20	EF-40	AU-50	Unc-60	Unc-63
$80	$100	$180	$275	$370	$510	$700

W-3060-E★ • F-2100E★

VG-8	F-12	VF-20	EF-40	AU-50	Unc-60	Unc-63
$150	$350	$550	$900	$1,250	$1,800	$2,600

W-3060-F • F-2100F • Atlanta • 538,800

VG-8	F-12	VF-20	EF-40	AU-50	Unc-60	Unc-63
$90	$110	$200	$300	$400	$550	$750

W-3060-F★ • F-2100F★

VG-8	F-12	VF-20	EF-40	AU-50	Unc-60	Unc-63
$150	$350	$550	$950	$1,350	$1,850	$2,600

W-3060-G • F-2100G • Chicago • 1,348,620

VG-8	F-12	VF-20	EF-40	AU-50	Unc-60	Unc-63
$75	$90	$150	$225	$300	$400	$500

W-3060-G★ • F-2100G★

VG-8	F-12	VF-20	EF-40	AU-50	Unc-60	Unc-63
$110	$125	$500	$750	$975	$1,300	$1,750

W-3060-H • F-2100H • St. Louis • 627,300

VG-8	F-12	VF-20	EF-40	AU-50	Unc-60	Unc-63
$80	$100	$160	$275	$370	$500	$700

W-3060-H★ • F-2100H★

VG-8	F-12	VF-20	EF-40	AU-50	Unc-60	Unc-63
$150	$350	$500	$750	$1,150	$1,700	$2,600

W-3060-I • F-2100I • Minneapolis • 106,200

VG-8	F-12	VF-20	EF-40	AU-50	Unc-60	Unc-63
$125	$175	$250	$400	$650	$1,050	$1,750

SERIES OF 1928, GREEN SEAL

$50 Federal Reserve Note, Series of 1928 (W-3060-C). Federal Reserve Bank of Philadelphia.

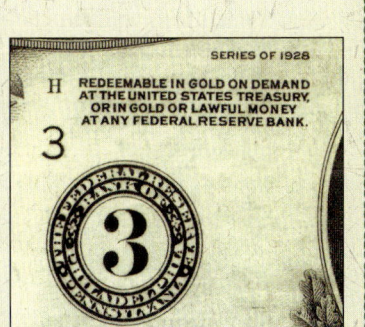

Detail of the payable notice and Federal Reserve seal.

Back of the $50 Federal Reserve Note, Series of 1928 (W-3060-C). This type was used on all small-size $50 notes of the era.

W-3060-I★ • F-2100I★

VG-8	F-12	VF-20	EF-40	AU-50	Unc-60	Unc-63
$500	$1,300	$2,200	$3,500	$4,400	$5,600	$7,000

W-3060-J • F-2100J • Kansas City • 252,600

VG-8	F-12	VF-20	EF-40	AU-50	Unc-60	Unc-63
$80	$125	$200	$275	$400	$575	$850

W-3060-J★ • F-2100J★

VG-8	F-12	VF-20	EF-40	AU-50	Unc-60	Unc-63
$275	$450	$750	$1,300	$1,800	$2,500	$3,400

W-3060-K • F-2100K • Dallas • 109,920

VG-8	F-12	VF-20	EF-40	AU-50	Unc-60	Unc-63
$115	$175	$250	$400	$660	$1,100	$1,850

W-3060-K★ • F-2100K★

VG-8	F-12	VF-20	EF-40	AU-50	Unc-60	Unc-63
$900	$1,400	$2,250	$3,000	$4,100	$5,650	$8,000

W-3060-L • F-2100L • San Francisco • 447,600

VG-8	F-12	VF-20	EF-40	AU-50	Unc-60	Unc-63
$80	$110	$200	$275	$380	$525	$750

W-3060-L★ • F-2100L★

VG-8	F-12	VF-20	EF-40	AU-50	Unc-60	Unc-63
$200	$300	$500	$750	$1,200	$1,975	$3,250

Series of 1928-A, Green Seal
Woods-Mellon (1929–1932)

The obligation in four lines in the field at the upper left is the same as on the preceding series and provides for payment in gold.

On the Series of 1928-A notes, the seal now features the letter (not the number) of the issuing Federal Reserve Bank, A to L. The series imprint appears twice—at the upper left of Grant's portrait and above the plate letter and number at the lower right. The Chicago star note is the only star of this series (including both seal hues) and is a classic rarity.

Prices for a typical note for this series, unless listed otherwise, are as follows:

VG-8	F-12	VF-20	EF-40	AU-50	Unc-60	Unc-63
$65	$70	$80	$90	$140	$190	$285

W-3061-A • F-2101A • Boston • 1,834,989

W-3061-B • F-2101B • New York • 3,392,328

W-3061-C • F-2101C • Philadelphia • 3,078,944

W-3061-D • F-2101D • Cleveland • 2,453,364

W-3061-E • F-2101E • Richmond • 1,516,500

W-3061-F • F-2101F • Atlanta • 338,400

VG-8	F-12	VF-20	EF-40	AU-50	Unc-60	Unc-63
$80	$90	$100	$150	$225	$350	$550

W-3061-G • F-2101G • Chicago • 5,263,956

W-3061-G★ • F-2101G★

F-12	VF-20	EF-40	AU-50
$2,750	$6,750	—	$13,500

W-3061-H • F-2101H • St. Louis • 880,500

W-3061-I • F-2101I • Minneapolis • 780,240

VG-8	F-12	VF-20	EF-40	AU-50	Unc-60	Unc-63
$65	$70	$80	$90	$145	$225	$375

W-3061-J • F-2101J • Kansas City • 791,604

VG-8	F-12	VF-20	EF-40	AU-50	Unc-60	Unc-63
$65	$70	$80	$90	$140	$225	$375

W-3061-K • F-2101K • Dallas • 701,496

VG-8	F-12	VF-20	EF-40	AU-50	Unc-60	Unc-63
$75	$100	$150	$200	$300	$400	$650

W-3061-L • F-2101L • San Francisco • 1,522,620

VG-8	F-12	VF-20	EF-40	AU-50	Unc-60	Unc-63
$65	$70	$80	$90	$140	$200	$350

Series of 1928-A, Light Yellow-Green Seal
Woods-Mellon (1929–1932)

The design is as the preceding issue, but with a different tint to the Treasury seal. This is a brief series with no star notes reported. All are readily available in circulated grades, but are scarce at the Uncirculated level.

W-3062-B • F-2101B • New York • Included in printage above

VG-8	F-12	VF-20	EF-40	AU-50	Unc-60
$120	$145	$240	$350	$450	$700

W-3062-G • F-2101G • Chicago • Included in printage above

VG-8	F-12	VF-20	EF-40	AU-50	Unc-60	Unc-63
$75	$85	$125	$185	$250	$400	$700

SERIES OF 1928-A, GREEN SEAL

Detail of the signatures and the series imprints of a $50 Federal Reserve Note, Series of 1928-A (W-3061-G). Also shown is the revised Federal Reserve seal. The back is the standard type of the era.

W-3062-I • F-2101I • Minneapolis • Included in printage above

VG-8	F-12	VF-20	EF-40	AU-50	Unc-60	Unc-63
$125	$155	$260	$385	$500	$775	$1,200

W-3062-J • F-2101J • Kansas City • Included in printage above

VG-8	F-12	VF-20	EF-40	AU-50	Unc-60	Unc-63
$100	$130	$225	$360	$450	$700	$1,100

W-3062-L • F-2101L • San Francisco • Included in printage above

VG-8	F-12	VF-20	EF-40	AU-50	Unc-60	Unc-63	Unc-65
$80	$100	$180	$250	$375	$550	$1,000	$3,750

Series of 1934, Light Yellow-Green Seal
Julian-Morgenthau (1934–1945)

The Series of 1934 continues the same general configuration as the preceding series, but now with a change in the redemption inscription, eliminating the mention of gold: "This note is legal tender for all debts, public and private, and is redeemable in lawful money at the United States Treasury, or at any Federal Reserve Bank."

All issues are readily collectible, but are scarce at the Uncirculated level. Star notes are elusive.

W-3063-A • F-2102A • Boston • 2,729,400

VG-8	F-12	VF-20	EF-40	AU-50	Unc-60	Unc-63	Unc-65
$65	$70	$80	$110	$165	$225	$325	$500

W-3063-A★ • F-2102A★
Commentary: Current market information not available.

W-3063-B • F-2102B • New York • 17,894,676

VG-8	F-12	VF-20	EF-40	AU-50	Unc-60	Unc-63	Unc-65
$60	$65	$75	$95	$130	$175	$240	$430

W-3063-B★ • F-2102B★
Commentary: Current market information not available.

W-3063-C • F-2102C • Philadelphia • 5,833,200

VG-8	F-12	VF-20	EF-40	AU-50	Unc-60	Unc-63	Unc-65
$60	$65	$75	$90	$130	$175	$230	$525

W-3063-C★ • F-2102C★

VG-8	F-12	VF-20	EF-40
$125	$275	$450	$800

SERIES OF 1928-A, LIGHT YELLOW-GREEN SEAL

$50 Federal Reserve Note, Series of 1928-A (W-3062-I). Light yellow-green Treasury seal. Federal Reserve Bank of Minneapolis. The back is the standard used on all $50 notes through the 1950s.

SERIES OF 1934, LIGHT YELLOW-GREEN SEAL

$50 Federal Reserve Note, Series of 1934 (W-3063-A). Light yellow-green Treasury seal. Federal Reserve Bank of Boston, with the back used on all $50 notes through the 1950s.

Detail of the payable notice.

W-3063-D • F-2102D • Cleveland • 8,817,720

VG-8	F-12	VF-20	EF-40	AU-50	Unc-60	Unc-63	Unc-65
$60	$70	$80	$95	$130	$175	$230	$450

W-3063-D★ • F-2102D★

VG-8	F-12	VF-20	EF-40
$135	$285	$475	$875

W-3063-E • F-2102E • Richmond • 4,826,628

VG-8	F-12	VF-20	EF-40	AU-50	Unc-60	Unc-63	Unc-65
$60	$70	$80	$95	$140	$275	$400	$650

W-3063-E★ • F-2102E★
Commentary: Current market information not available.

W-3063-F • F-2102F • Atlanta • 3,069,348

VG-8	F-12	VF-20	EF-40	AU-50	Unc-60	Unc-63	Unc-65
$60	$70	$80	$95	$135	$185	$245	$450

W-3063-F★ • F-2102F★
Commentary: Current market information not available.

W-3063-G • F-2102G • Chicago • 8,675,940

VG-8	F-12	VF-20	EF-40	AU-50	Unc-60	Unc-63	Unc-65
$60	$65	$75	$90	$130	$165	$210	$325

W-3063-G★ • F-2102G★

VG-8	F-12
$120	$245

W-3063-H • F-2102H • St. Louis • 1,497,144

VG-8	F-12	VF-20	EF-40	AU-50	Unc-60	Unc-63	Unc-65
$60	$65	$75	$90	$120	$160	$210	$340

W-3063-H★ • F-2102H★
Commentary: Current market information not available.

W-3063-I • F-2102I • Minneapolis • 539,700

VG-8	F-12	VF-20	EF-40	AU-50	Unc-60	Unc-63	Unc-65
$70	$75	$85	$120	$165	$265	$500	$1,400

W-3063-I★ • F-2102I★
Commentary: Current market information not available.

W-3063-J • F-2102J • Kansas City • 1,133,520

VG-8	F-12	VF-20	EF-40	AU-50	Unc-60	Unc-63	Unc-65
$60	$70	$85	$110	$140	$190	$265	$475

W-3063-J★ • F-2102J★
Commentary: Current market information not available.

W-3063-K • F-2102K • Dallas • 1,194,876

VG-8	F-12	VF-20	EF-40	AU-50	Unc-60	Unc-63	Unc-65
$80	$90	$105	$135	$175	$225	$375	$550

W-3063-K★ • F-2102K★

VG-8	F-12	VF-20	EF-40	AU-50	Unc-60	Unc-63
$300	$400	$500	$900	$1,350	$1,900	$2,300

W-3063-L • F-2102L • San Francisco • 8,101,200

VG-8	F-12	VF-20	EF-40	AU-50	Unc-60	Unc-63	Unc-65
$65	$75	$85	$95	$135	$175	$285	$525

W-3063-L★ • F-2102L★
Commentary: Current market information not available.

Series of 1934, Green Seal
Julian-Morgenthau (1934–1945)

This series continued the preceding design, with a different hue to the Treasury seal. As a class these are more available than are those with light yellow-green seals.

Prices for a typical note for this series, unless listed otherwise, are as follows:

VG-8	F-12	VF-20	EF-40	AU-50	Unc-60	Unc-63
$55	$60	$65	$80	$110	$135	$175

W-3064-A • F-2102A • Boston • Part of W-3063-A printage

W-3064-A★ • F-2102A★

VG-8	F-12	VF-20	EF-40	AU-50	Unc-60	Unc-63
$90	$100	$150	$190	$315	$450	$900

W-3064-B • F-2102B • New York • Part of W-3063-B printage

SERIES OF 1934, GREEN SEAL

$50 Federal Reserve Note, Series of 1934 (W-3064-J). Dark green Treasury seal. Federal Reserve Bank of Kansas City. The back is the standard used on all $50 notes through the 1950s.

W-3064-B★ • F-2102B★

VG-8	F-12	VF-20	EF-40	AU-50	Unc-60	Unc-63
$90	$100	$150	$190	$300	$425	$750

W-3064-C • F-2102C • Philadelphia • Part of W-3063-C printage

W-3064-C★ • F-2102C★

VG-8	F-12	VF-20	EF-40	AU-50	Unc-60	Unc-63
$90	$100	$150	$190	$315	$525	$1,000

W-3064-D • F-2102D • Cleveland • Part of W-3063-D printage

W-3064-D★ • F-2102D★

VG-8	F-12	VF-20	EF-40	AU-50	Unc-60	Unc-63
$90	$100	$150	$190	$315	$525	$900

W-3064-E • F-2102E • Richmond • Part of W-3063-E printage

VG-8	F-12	VF-20	EF-40	AU-50	Unc-60	Unc-63
$55	$60	$65	$80	$110	$165	$225

W-3064-E★ • F-2102E★

VG-8	F-12	VF-20	EF-40	AU-50	Unc-60	Unc-63
$90	$125	$150	$225	$360	$560	$900

W-3064-F • F-2102F • Atlanta • Part of W-3063-F printage

VG-8	F-12	VF-20	EF-40	AU-50	Unc-60	Unc-63
$55	$60	$65	$80	$110	$155	$200

W-3064-F★ • F-2102F★

VG-8	F-12	VF-20	EF-40	AU-50	Unc-60	Unc-63
$90	$100	$150	$190	$325	$570	$1,000

W-3064-G • F-2102G • Chicago • Part of W-3063-G printage

VG-8	F-12	VF-20	EF-40	AU-50	Unc-60	Unc-63
$55	$60	$65	$80	$100	$115	$135

W-3064-G★ • F-2102G★

VG-8	F-12	VF-20	EF-40	AU-50	Unc-60	Unc-63
$90	$100	$150	$190	$300	$475	$750

W-3064-H • F-2102H • St. Louis • Part of W-3063-H printage

W-3064-H★ • F-2102H★

VG-8	F-12	VF-20	EF-40	AU-50	Unc-60	Unc-63
$90	$100	$150	$190	$325	$570	$1,000

W-3064-I • F-2102I • Minneapolis • Part of W-3063-I printage

VG-8	F-12	VF-20	EF-40	AU-50	Unc-60	Unc-63
$55	$60	$70	$85	$125	$190	$290

W-3064-I★ • F-2102I★

VG-8	F-12	VF-20	EF-40	AU-50	Unc-60	Unc-63
$110	$130	$200	$295	$475	$875	$1,750

W-3064-J • F-2102J • Kansas City • Part of W-3063-J printage

W-3064-J★ • F-2102J★

VG-8	F-12	VF-20	EF-40	AU-50	Unc-60	Unc-63
$90	$100	$150	$190	$325	$525	$750

W-3064-K • F-2102K • Dallas • Part of W-3063-K printage

W-3064-K★ • F-2102K★

VG-8	F-12	VF-20	EF-40	AU-50	Unc-60	Unc-63
$90	$100	$150	$190	$400	$900	$1,850

W-3064-L • F-2102L • San Francisco • Part of W-3063-L printage

W-3064-L★ • F-2102L★

VG-8	F-12	VF-20	EF-40	AU-50	Unc-60	Unc-63
$90	$100	$150	$190	$325	$570	$1,000

Series of 1934-A, Green Seal
Julian-Morgenthau (1934–1945)

This series continued the preceding design.

Mules: From this series through the Series of 1950 are considered mules because they use a "micro"-size plate number on the back, whereas in lower denominations Series of 1934-A changed to "macro"-size plate numbers.

No Philadelphia notes were printed for this series. All are readily available, but Uncirculated notes are in the minority. Star notes are scarce.

W-3065-A • F-2103A • Boston • 406,200

VG-8	F-12	VF-20	EF-40	AU-50	Unc-60	Unc-63
$55	$80	$95	$115	$185	$300	$475

W-3065-A★ • F-2103A★

VG-8	F-12	VF-20	EF-40	AU-50	Unc-60	Unc-63
$125	$175	$375	$575	$800	$1,100	$1,500

Detail of the signatures and the series imprints (at top left and bottom right) of a $50 Federal Reserve Note, Series of 1934-A (W-3065-B). The back is the standard type of the era.

W-3065-B • F-2103B • New York • 4,710,648

VG-8	F-12	VF-20	EF-40	AU-50	Unc-60	Unc-63
$55	$70	$80	$100	$140	$195	$275

W-3065-B★ • F-2103B★

VG-8	F-12	VF-20	EF-40	AU-50	Unc-60	Unc-63
$90	$120	$150	$200	$315	$500	$800

W-3065-D • F-2103D • Cleveland • 864,168

VG-8	F-12	VF-20	EF-40	AU-50	Unc-60	Unc-63
$55	$70	$80	$100	$145	$205	$300

W-3065-D★ • F-2103D★

VG-8	F-12	VF-20	EF-40	AU-50	Unc-60	Unc-63
$150	$225	$425	$650	$850	$1,125	$1,500

W-3065-E • F-2103E • Richmond • 2,235,372

VG-8	F-12	VF-20	EF-40	AU-50	Unc-60	Unc-63
$55	$65	$80	$100	$145	$205	$300

W-3065-E★ • F-2103E★

VG-8	F-12	VF-20	EF-40	AU-50	Unc-60	Unc-63
$150	$225	$425	$650	$800	$1,000	$1,250

W-3065-F • F-2103F • Atlanta • 416,100

VG-8	F-12	VF-20	EF-40	AU-50	Unc-60	Unc-63
$55	$65	$80	$100	$155	$240	$375

W-3065-F★ • F-2103F★

VG-8	F-12	VF-20	EF-40	AU-50	Unc-60	Unc-63
$150	$225	$400	$625	$810	$1,050	$1,400

W-3065-G • F-2103G • Chicago • 1,014,600

VG-8	F-12	VF-20	EF-40	AU-50	Unc-60	Unc-63
$55	$65	$80	$100	$145	$205	$300

W-3065-G★ • F-2103G★

VG-8	F-12	VF-20	EF-40	AU-50	Unc-60	Unc-63
$125	$200	$375	$550	$720	$925	$1,200

W-3065-H • F-2103H • St. Louis • 361,944

VG-8	F-12	VF-20	EF-40	AU-50	Unc-60	Unc-63
$55	$80	$95	$115	$170	$250	$375

W-3065-H★ • F-2103H★

VG-8	F-12	VF-20	EF-40	AU-50	Unc-60	Unc-63
$150	$225	$400	$650	$860	$1,125	$1,500

W-3065-I • F-2103I • Minneapolis • 93,300

VG-8	F-12	VF-20	EF-40	AU-50	Unc-60	Unc-63
$55	$80	$95	$115	$190	$310	$500

W-3065-I★ • F-2103I★

VG-8	F-12	VF-20	EF-40	AU-50	Unc-60	Unc-63
$150	$225	$400	$650	$860	$1,125	$1,500

W-3065-J • F-2103J • Kansas City • 189,300

VG-8	F-12	VF-20	EF-40	AU-50	Unc-60	Unc-63
$55	$80	$95	$115	$190	$310	$500

W-3065-J★ • F-2103J★

VG-8	F-12	VF-20	EF-40	AU-50	Unc-60	Unc-63
$150	$225	$400	$650	$860	$1,125	$1,500

W-3065-K • F-2103K • Dallas • 266,700

VG-8	F-12	VF-20	EF-40	AU-50	Unc-60	Unc-63
$55	$80	$95	$115	$170	$250	$375

W-3065-K★ • F-2103K★

VG-8	F-12	VF-20	EF-40	AU-50	Unc-60	Unc-63
$150	$225	$400	$650	$860	$1,125	$1,500

W-3065-L • F-2103L • San Francisco • 162,000

VG-8	F-12	VF-20	EF-40	AU-50	Unc-60	Unc-63
$55	$80	$95	$115	$170	$250	$375

W-3065-L★ • F-2103L★

VG-8	F-12	VF-20	EF-40	AU-50	Unc-60	Unc-63
$150	$225	$400	$650	$860	$1,125	$1,500

Series of 1934-B, Green Seal
Julian-Vinson (1945–1946)

Beginning with the Series of 1934-B notes there is a change in the wording in the Federal Reserve seal. THE is omitted, giving FEDERAL RESERVE.

All have micro-size plate numbers on the back. All are thus considered mules. All are readily available, but Uncirculated notes are scarcer. All star notes are scarce, and the Philadelphia, Cleveland, Richmond, and Kansas City stars are rare.

W-3066-C • F-2104C • Philadelphia • 509,100

VF-20	EF-40	AU-50	Unc-60	Unc-63
$80	$90	$140	$220	$350

W-3066-C★ • F-2104C★

VF-20	EF-40	AU-50	Unc-60	Unc-63
$1,150	$1,450	$2,050	$2,900	$4,000

W-3066-D • F-2104D • Cleveland • 359,100

VF-20	EF-40	AU-50	Unc-60	Unc-63
$80	$90	$140	$220	$350

W-3066-D★ • F-2104D★

VF-20	EF-40	AU-50	Unc-60	Unc-63
$1,150	$1,450	$2,050	$2,900	$4,000

W-3066-E • F-2104E • Richmond • 596,700

VF-20	EF-40	AU-50	Unc-60	Unc-63
$85	$100	$130	$215	$350

W-3066-E★ • F-2104E★

VF-20	EF-40	AU-50	Unc-60	Unc-63
$1,250	$1,500	$2,100	$2,950	$4,000

W-3066-F • F-2104F • Atlanta • 416,720

VF-20	EF-40	AU-50	Unc-60	Unc-63
$85	$100	$160	$255	$400

W-3066-G • F-2104G • Chicago • 306,000

VF-20	EF-40	AU-50	Unc-60	Unc-63
$80	$90	$150	$245	$400

W-3066-H • F-2104H • St. Louis • 306,000

VF-20	EF-40	AU-50	Unc-60	Unc-63
$85	$100	$160	$255	$400

W-3066-I • F-2104I • Minneapolis • 120,000

VF-20	EF-40	AU-50	Unc-60	Unc-63
$190	$300	$360	$425	$500

W-3066-J • F-2104J • Kansas City • 221,340

VF-20	EF-40	AU-50	Unc-60	Unc-63
$85	$100	$165	$270	$450

W-3066-J★ • F-2104J★ • 2,500

VF-20	EF-40	AU-50	Unc-60	Unc-63
$1,250	$1,600	$2,150	$2,950	$4,000

W-3066-K • F-2104K • Dallas • 120,108

VF-20	EF-40	AU-50	Unc-60	Unc-63
$140	$200	$270	$370	$500

W-3066-L • F-2104L • San Francisco • 441,000

VF-20	EF-40	AU-50	Unc-60	Unc-63
$85	$100	$160	$255	$400

Series of 1934-C, Green Seal
Julian-Snyder (1946–1949)

This series continued the preceding design. All have micro plate numbers on the back. No San Francisco notes were printed for this series. Star notes are scarce in any grade and are more so at the Uncirculated level.

W-3067-A • F-2105A • Boston • 117,600

F-12	VF-20	EF-40	AU-50	Unc-60	Unc-63
$75	$100	$145	$190	$250	$325

W-3067-B • F-2105B • New York • 1,556,400

F-12	VF-20	EF-40	AU-50	Unc-60	Unc-63
$65	$75	$90	$120	$155	$200

W-3067-B★ • F-2105B★

F-12	VF-20	EF-40	AU-50	Unc-60	Unc-63
$200	$375	$600	$820	$1,100	$1,500

W-3067-C • F-2105C • Philadelphia • 107,283

F-12	VF-20	EF-40	AU-50	Unc-60	Unc-63
$75	$100	$145	$190	$250	$325

W-3067-C★ • F-2105C★

F-12	VF-20	EF-40	AU-50	Unc-60	Unc-63
$200	$450	$700	$900	$1,150	$1,500

W-3067-D • F-2105D • Cleveland • 374,400

F-12	VF-20	EF-40	AU-50	Unc-60	Unc-63
$65	$75	$90	$120	$155	$200

W-3067-D★ • F-2105D★

F-12	VF-20	EF-40	AU-50	Unc-60	Unc-63
$200	$450	$700	$900	$1,150	$1,500

W-3067-E • F-2105E • Richmond • 1,821,960

F-12	VF-20	EF-40	AU-50	Unc-60	Unc-63
$70	$85	$120	$155	$200	$250

W-3067-E★ • F-2105E★

F-12	VF-20	EF-40	AU-50	Unc-60	Unc-63
$200	$450	$700	$900	$1,150	$1,500

SERIES OF 1934-B, GREEN SEAL

Detail of the signatures and the series imprints (at top left and bottom right) of a $50 Federal Reserve Note, Series of 1934-B (W-3066-C). The back is the standard type of the era.

Detail of the new Federal Reserve seal.

Detail of the micro plate number 109 on the back of the Philadelphia note. Micro numbers are on *all* notes of this series.

SERIES OF 1934-C, GREEN SEAL

Detail of the signatures and the series imprints (at top left and bottom right) of a $50 Federal Reserve Note, Series of 1934-C (W-3067-D). The back is the standard type of the era.

W-3067-F • F-2105F • Atlanta • 104,640

F-12	VF-20	EF-40	AU-50	Unc-60	Unc-63
$150	$200	$325	$460	$650	$900

W-3067-G • F-2105G • Chicago • 294,432

F-12	VF-20	EF-40	AU-50	Unc-60	Unc-63
$65	$75	$90	$125	$170	$225

W-3067-G★ • F-2105G★

F-12	VF-20	EF-40	AU-50	Unc-60	Unc-63
$200	$375	$600	$800	$1,050	$1,400

W-3067-H • F-2105H • St. Louis • 535,200

F-12	VF-20	EF-40	AU-50	Unc-60	Unc-63
$70	$75	$90	$125	$175	$250

W-3067-I • F-2105I • Minneapolis • 118,800

F-12	VF-20	EF-40	AU-50	Unc-60	Unc-63
$85	$100	$140	$190	$255	$350

W-3067-I★ • F-2105I★

F-12	VF-20	EF-40	AU-50	Unc-60	Unc-63
$225	$450	$700	$900	$1,150	$1,500

W-3067-J • F-2105J • Kansas City • 303,600

F-12	VF-20	EF-40	AU-50	Unc-60	Unc-63
$65	$85	$120	$155	$200	$250

W-3067-K • F-2105K • Dallas • 429,900

F-12	VF-20	EF-40	AU-50	Unc-60	Unc-63
$65	$85	$120	$155	$200	$250

W-3067-K★ • F-2105K★

F-12	VF-20	EF-40	AU-50	Unc-60	Unc-63
$225	$450	$700	$900	$1,150	$1,500

Series of 1934-D, Green Seal
Clark-Snyder (1949–1953)

All notes in this series have micro plate numbers on the back. Not all banks issued this series. Of those that did, the Minneapolis note is the key. Uncirculated notes are quite scarce, despite their modest market values. The explanation is that they are not widely collected by Federal Reserve Bank, and just one will do as a type for many numismatists. All star notes are elusive, particularly in higher grades.

W-3068-A • F-2106A • Boston • 279,600

F-12	VF-20	EF-40	AU-50	Unc-60	Unc-63
$80	$120	$160	$210	$270	$350

W-3068-A★ • F-2106A★

F-12	VF-20	EF-40	AU-50	Unc-60	Unc-63
$700	$1,250	$1,600	$2,150	$2,950	$4,000

W-3068-B • F-2106B • New York • 898,776

F-12	VF-20	EF-40	AU-50	Unc-60	Unc-63
$65	$80	$100	$135	$185	$250

W-3068-B★ • F-2106B★

F-12	VF-20	EF-40	AU-50	Unc-60	Unc-63
$600	$1,000	$1,250	$1,650	$2,250	$3,000

W-3068-C • F-2106C • Philadelphia • 699,000

F-12	VF-20	EF-40	AU-50	Unc-60	Unc-63
$70	$85	$100	$135	$185	$250

W-3068-C★ • F-2106C★

F-12	VF-20	EF-40	AU-50	Unc-60	Unc-63
$700	$1,250	$1,600	$2,100	$2,700	$3,500

W-3068-E • F-2106E • Richmond • 156,000

F-12	VF-20	EF-40	AU-50	Unc-60	Unc-63
$80	$120	$160	$210	$270	$350

W-3068-F • F-2106F • Atlanta • 216,000

F-12	VF-20	EF-40	AU-50	Unc-60	Unc-63
$80	$120	$160	$210	$270	$350

W-3068-F★ • F-2106F★

F-12	VF-20	EF-40	AU-50	Unc-60	Unc-63
$700	$1,250	$1,600	$2,150	$2,950	$4,000

W-3068-G • F-2106G • Chicago • 494,016

F-12	VF-20	EF-40	AU-50	Unc-60	Unc-63
$65	$80	$100	$135	$185	$250

W-3068-G★ • F-2106G★

F-12	VF-20	EF-40	AU-50	Unc-60	Unc-63
$700	$1,250	$1,600	$2,000	$2,450	$3,000

SERIES OF 1934-D, GREEN SEAL

Detail of the signatures and the series imprints (at top left and bottom right) of a $50 Federal Reserve Note, Series of 1934-D (W-3068-K). The back is the standard type of the era.

W-3068-I • F-2106I • Minneapolis

F-12	VF-20
$375	$600

W-3068-K • F-2106K • Dallas • 103,200

F-12	VF-20	EF-40	AU-50	Unc-60	Unc-63
$70	$100	$125	$185	$270	$400

Series of 1950, Green Seal
Clark-Snyder (1949–1953)

The Federal Reserve seal was made smaller and given a spiked border. The payable provision above that seal now appears in three lines of text instead of four. The series designation is at the lower right of the portrait. All have micro plate numbers on the back.

All are readily available, even in Uncirculated grade, but some patience is required to fill in a set. Star notes are in the minority, and the Minneapolis star is a key issue.

Prices for a typical note for this series, unless listed otherwise, are as follows:

VF-20	EF-40	AU-50	Unc-60	Unc-63
$75	$125	$155	$195	$250

W-3069-A • F-2107A • Boston • 1,248,000

W-3069-A★ • F-2107A★

VF-20	EF-40	AU-50	Unc-60	Unc-63
$175	$350	$490	$700	$1,000

W-3069-B • F-2107B • New York • 10,236,000

VF-20	EF-40	AU-50	Unc-60	Unc-63
$75	$125	$150	$185	$225

W-3069-B★ • F-2107B★

VF-20	EF-40	AU-50	Unc-60	Unc-63
$150	$250	$345	$485	$675

W-3069-C • F-2107C • Philadelphia • 2,352,000

VF-20	EF-40	AU-50	Unc-60	Unc-63
$75	$125	$145	$170	$200

W-3069-C★ • F-2107C★

VF-20	EF-40	AU-50	Unc-60	Unc-63
$175	$350	$460	$595	$775

W-3069-D • F-2107D • Cleveland • 6,180,000

W-3069-D★ • F-2107D★

VF-20	EF-40	AU-50	Unc-60	Unc-63
$150	$250	$365	$530	$775

W-3069-E • F-2107E • Richmond • 5,064,000

W-3069-E★ • F-2107E★

VF-20	EF-40	AU-50	Unc-60	Unc-63
$175	$350	$460	$595	$775

W-3069-F • F-2107F • Atlanta • 1,812,000

W-3069-F★ • F-2107F★

VF-20	EF-40	AU-50	Unc-60	Unc-63
$175	$350	$460	$595	$775

W-3069-G • F-2107G • Chicago • 4,212,000

VF-20	EF-40	AU-50	Unc-60	Unc-63
$75	$125	$145	$170	$200

W-3069-G★ • F-2107G★

VF-20	EF-40	AU-50	Unc-60	Unc-63
$150	$250	$325	$425	$550

W-3069-H • F-2107H • St. Louis • 892,000

W-3069-H★ • F-2107H★

VF-20	EF-40	AU-50	Unc-60	Unc-63
$175	$350	$460	$615	$825

W-3069-I • F-2107I • Minneapolis • 384,000

VF-20	EF-40	AU-50	Unc-60	Unc-63
$95	$170	$245	$350	$500

SERIES OF 1950, GREEN SEAL

$50 Federal Reserve Note, Series of 1950 (W-3069-D). Federal Reserve Bank of Cleveland. The back is the standard used on all $50 notes through the 1950s.

W-3069-I★ • F-2107I★

VF-20	EF-40	AU-50	Unc-60	Unc-63
$275	$500	$750	$1,150	$1,750

W-3069-J • F-2107J • Kansas City • 696,000

W-3069-J★ • F-2107J★

VF-20	EF-40	AU-50	Unc-60	Unc-63
$175	$350	$500	$715	$1,000

W-3069-K • F-2107K • Dallas • 1,100,000

W-3069-K★ • F-2107K★

VF-20	EF-40	AU-50	Unc-60	Unc-63
$150	$250	$345	$475	$650

W-3069-L • F-2107L • San Francisco • 3,996,000

W-3069-L★ • F-2107L★

VF-20	EF-40	AU-50	Unc-60	Unc-63
$150	$250	$345	$475	$650

Series of 1950-A, Green Seal
Priest-Humphrey (1953–1957)

This series continued the preceding design. None were issued for Minneapolis. All are readily available, but—as is true for most small-size $50 notes—some searching is needed to track down particular issues, as dealer stocks are often shallow. Star notes are in the minority.

Prices for a typical note for this series, unless listed otherwise, are as follows:

VF-20	EF-40	AU-50	Unc-60	Unc-63
$75	$100	$125	$160	$200

Prices for a typical star note for this series, unless listed otherwise, are as follows:

VF-20	EF-40	AU-50	Unc-60	Unc-63
$100	$200	$280	$390	$550

W-3070-A • F-2108A • Boston • 720,000

VF-20	EF-40	AU-50	Unc-60	Unc-63
$75	$125	$145	$170	$200

W-3070-A★ • F-2108A★

W-3070-B • F-2108B • New York • 6,495,000

W-3070-B★ • F-2108B★

W-3070-C • F-2108C • Philadelphia • 1,728,000

W-3070-C★ • F-2108C★

W-3070-D • F-2108D • Cleveland • 1,872,000

W-3070-D★ • F-2108D★

W-3070-E • F-2108E • Richmond • 2,016,000

W-3070-E★ • F-2108E★

W-3070-F • F-2108F • Atlanta • 288,000

W-3070-F★ • F-2108F★

VF-20	EF-40	AU-50	Unc-60	Unc-63
$100	$200	$295	$435	$650

W-3070-G • F-2108G • Chicago • 2,016,000

W-3070-G★ • F-2108G★

W-3070-H • F-2108H • St. Louis • 576,000

W-3070-H★ • F-2108H★

W-3070-J • F-2108J • Kansas City • 144,000

VF-20	EF-40	AU-50	Unc-60	Unc-63
$85	$110	$145	$190	$250

W-3070-J★ • F-2108J★

W-3070-K • F-2108K • Dallas • 864,000

W-3070-K★ • F-2108K★

W-3070-L • F-2108L • San Francisco • 576,000

W-3070-L★ • F-2108L★

Series of 1950-B, Green Seal
Priest-Anderson (1957–1961)

This series continued the preceding design. Notes in worn grades are inexpensive, and Uncirculated examples are reasonably priced. None are rare, but as dealers' stocks are thin

SERIES OF 1950-A, GREEN SEAL

Signatures and series imprint of a $50 Federal Reserve Note, Series of 1950-A (W-3070-D). The back is the standard type of the era.

SERIES OF 1950-B, GREEN SEAL

Signatures and series imprint of a $50 Federal Reserve Note, Series of 1950-B (W-3071-H). The back is the standard type of the era.

for this denomination, some searching may be needed to find a particular Federal Reserve Bank. Star notes are scarce but readily collectible. No Atlanta or Minneapolis notes were made for this series.

W-3071-A • F-2109A • Boston • 864,000

VF-20	EF-40	AU-50	Unc-60	Unc-63
$60	$80	$100	$125	$150

W-3071-A★ • F-2109A★

VF-20	EF-40	AU-50	Unc-60	Unc-63
$100	$150	$210	$290	$400

W-3071-B • F-2109B • New York • 8,352,000

VF-20	EF-40	AU-50	Unc-60	Unc-63
$55	$75	$90	$105	$125

W-3071-B★ • F-2109B★

VF-20	EF-40	AU-50	Unc-60	Unc-63
$75	$100	$135	$185	$250

W-3071-C • F-2109C • Philadelphia • 2,592,000

VF-20	EF-40	AU-50	Unc-60	Unc-63
$60	$80	$100	$125	$150

W-3071-C★ • F-2109C★

VF-20	EF-40	AU-50	Unc-60	Unc-63
$100	$150	$210	$290	$400

W-3071-D • F-2109D • Cleveland • 1,728,000

VF-20	EF-40	AU-50	Unc-60	Unc-63
$60	$80	$100	$125	$150

W-3071-D★ • F-2109D★

VF-20	EF-40	AU-50	Unc-60	Unc-63
$100	$150	$210	$290	$400

W-3071-E • F-2109E • Richmond • 1,584,000

VF-20	EF-40	AU-50	Unc-60	Unc-63
$60	$80	$100	$125	$150

W-3071-E★ • F-2109E★

VF-20	EF-40	AU-50	Unc-60	Unc-63
$110	$200	$275	$370	$500

W-3071-G • F-2109G • Chicago • 4,320,000

VF-20	EF-40	AU-50	Unc-60	Unc-63
$55	$75	$90	$105	$125

W-3071-G★ • F-2109G★

VF-20	EF-40	AU-50	Unc-60	Unc-63
$100	$150	$210	$290	$400

W-3071-H • F-2109H • St. Louis • 576,000

VF-20	EF-40	AU-50	Unc-60	Unc-63
$70	$90	$110	$140	$175

W-3071-H★ • F-2109H★

VF-20	EF-40	AU-50	Unc-60	Unc-63
$110	$200	$275	$370	$500

W-3071-J • F-2109J • Kansas City • 1,008,000

VF-20	EF-40	AU-50	Unc-60	Unc-63
$60	$80	$100	$125	$150

W-3071-J★ • F-2109J★

VF-20	EF-40	AU-50	Unc-60	Unc-63
$110	$200	$275	$370	$500

W-3071-K • F-2109K • Dallas • 1,008,000

VF-20	EF-40	AU-50	Unc-60	Unc-63
$70	$90	$115	$150	$200

W-3071-K★ • F-2109K★

VF-20	EF-40	AU-50	Unc-60	Unc-63
$110	$200	$275	$370	$500

W-3071-L • F-2109L • San Francisco • 1,872,000

VF-20	EF-40	AU-50	Unc-60	Unc-63
$70	$90	$115	$150	$200

W-3071-L★ • F-2109L★

VF-20	EF-40	AU-50	Unc-60	Unc-63
$110	$200	$275	$370	$500

Series of 1950-C, Green Seal
Smith-Dillon (1961–1962)

This series continued the preceding design. These are easily enough collected, but inventories are shallow. Minneapolis and Kansas City notes are slightly scarcer, as are star notes. None were printed for Atlanta.

Prices for a typical note for this series, unless listed otherwise, are as follows:

VF-20	EF-40	AU-50	Unc-60	Unc-63
$60	$80	$95	$115	$140

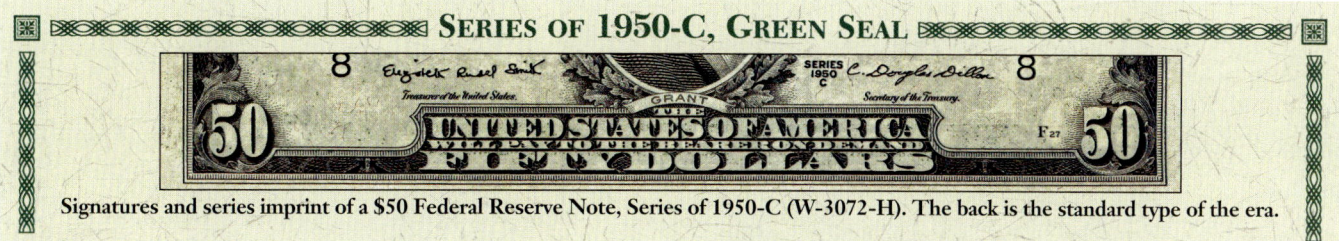

SERIES OF 1950-C, GREEN SEAL

Signatures and series imprint of a $50 Federal Reserve Note, Series of 1950-C (W-3072-H). The back is the standard type of the era.

W-3072-A • F-2110A • Boston • 720,000

W-3072-A★ • F-2110A★

VF-20	EF-40	AU-50	Unc-60	Unc-63
$140	$200	$280	$395	$550

W-3072-B • F-2110B • New York • 5,328,000

VF-20	EF-40	AU-50	Unc-60	Unc-63
$60	$80	$90	$105	$120

W-3072-B★ • F-2110B★

VF-20	EF-40	AU-50	Unc-60	Unc-63
$125	$180	$260	$380	$550

W-3072-C • F-2110C • Philadelphia • 1,296,000

W-3072-C★ • F-2110C★

VF-20	EF-40	AU-50	Unc-60	Unc-63
$140	$200	$295	$435	$650

W-3072-D • F-2110D • Cleveland • 1,296,000

W-3072-D★ • F-2110D★

VF-20	EF-40	AU-50	Unc-60	Unc-63
$125	$180	$260	$380	$550

W-3072-E • F-2110E • Richmond • 1,296,000

W-3072-E★ • F-2110E★

VF-20	EF-40	AU-50	Unc-60	Unc-63
$140	$200	$295	$435	$650

W-3072-G • F-2110G • Chicago • 1,728,000

VF-20	EF-40	AU-50	Unc-60	Unc-63
$60	$100	$125	$160	$200

W-3072-G★ • F-2110G★

VF-20	EF-40	AU-50	Unc-60	Unc-63
$125	$180	$260	$380	$550

W-3072-H • F-2110H • St. Louis • 576,000

W-3072-H★ • F-2110H★

VF-20	EF-40	AU-50	Unc-60	Unc-63
$125	$180	$260	$380	$550

W-3072-I • F-2110I • Minneapolis • 144,000

VF-20	EF-40	AU-50	Unc-60	Unc-63
$70	$115	$160	$220	$300

W-3072-I★ • F-2110I★

VF-20	EF-40	AU-50	Unc-60	Unc-63
$250	$450	$630	$895	$1,250

W-3072-J • F-2110J • Kansas City • 432,000

VF-20	EF-40	AU-50	Unc-60	Unc-63
$70	$100	$135	$185	$250

W-3072-J★ • F-2110J★

VF-20	EF-40	AU-50	Unc-60	Unc-63
$140	$200	$295	$435	$650

W-3072-K • F-2110K • Dallas • 720,000

W-3072-K★ • F-2110K★

VF-20	EF-40	AU-50	Unc-60	Unc-63
$140	$200	$295	$435	$650

W-3072-L • F-2110L • San Francisco • 1,152,000

W-3072-L★ • F-2110L★

VF-20	EF-40	AU-50	Unc-60	Unc-63
$125	$180	$275	$425	$650

Series of 1950-D, Green Seal
Granahan-Dillon (1963–1965)

This series continued the preceding design. All are collectible, but some are slightly scarce, as the prices reflect. Star notes are fairly scarce.

W-3073-A • F-2111A • Boston • 1,728,000

VF-20	EF-40	AU-50	Unc-60	Unc-63
$65	$90	$120	$155	$200

W-3073-A★ • F-2111A★

VF-20	EF-40	AU-50	Unc-60	Unc-63
$100	$150	$230	$355	$550

W-3073-B • F-2111B • New York • 7,200,000

VF-20	EF-40	AU-50	Unc-60	Unc-63
$60	$80	$95	$120	$150

W-3073-B★ • F-2111B★

VF-20	EF-40	AU-50	Unc-60	Unc-63
$100	$150	$215	$310	$450

W-3073-C • F-2111C • Philadelphia • 2,736,000

VF-20	EF-40	AU-50	Unc-60	Unc-63
$60	$80	$95	$120	$150

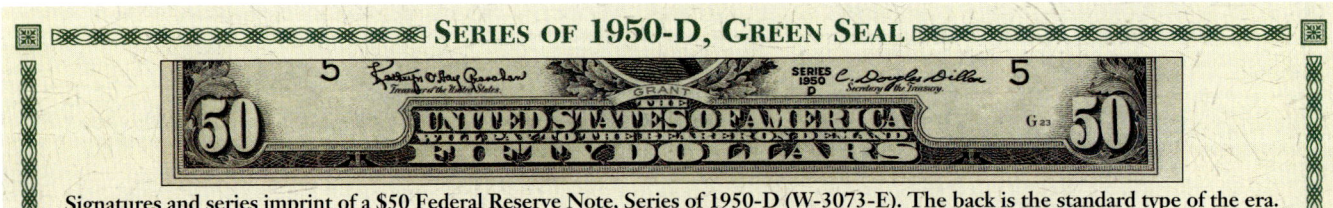

SERIES OF 1950-D, GREEN SEAL

Signatures and series imprint of a $50 Federal Reserve Note, Series of 1950-D (W-3073-E). The back is the standard type of the era.

W-3073-C★ • F-2111C★

VF-20	EF-40	AU-50	Unc-60	Unc-63
$100	$150	$215	$310	$450

W-3073-D • F-2111D • Cleveland • 2,880,000

VF-20	EF-40	AU-50	Unc-60	Unc-63
$60	$80	$95	$110	$130

W-3073-D★ • F-2111D★

VF-20	EF-40	AU-50	Unc-60	Unc-63
$100	$140	$200	$285	$400

W-3073-E • F-2111E • Richmond • 2,616,000

VF-20	EF-40	AU-50	Unc-60	Unc-63
$60	$80	$95	$120	$150

W-3073-E★ • F-2111E★

VF-20	EF-40	AU-50	Unc-60	Unc-63
$100	$150	$215	$310	$450

W-3073-F • F-2111F • Atlanta • 576,000

VF-20	EF-40	AU-50	Unc-60	Unc-63
$60	$80	$95	$110	$130

W-3073-F★ • F-2111F★

VF-20	EF-40	AU-50	Unc-60	Unc-63
$125	$175	$250	$350	$500

W-3073-G • F-2111G • Chicago • 4,176,000

VF-20	EF-40	AU-50	Unc-60	Unc-63
$60	$80	$95	$110	$130

W-3073-G★ • F-2111G★

VF-20	EF-40	AU-50	Unc-60	Unc-63
$100	$140	$200	$280	$400

W-3073-H • F-2111H • St. Louis • 1,440,000

VF-20	EF-40	AU-50	Unc-60	Unc-63
$60	$80	$95	$120	$150

W-3073-H★ • F-2111H★

VF-20	EF-40	AU-50	Unc-60	Unc-63
$100	$140	$200	$280	$400

W-3073-I • F-2111I • Minneapolis • 288,000

VF-20	EF-40	AU-50	Unc-60	Unc-63
$75	$100	$125	$160	$200

W-3073-I★ • F-2111I★

VF-20	EF-40	AU-50	Unc-60	Unc-63
$150	$225	$360	$575	$900

W-3073-J • F-2111J • Kansas City • 720,000

VF-20	EF-40	AU-50	Unc-60	Unc-63
$60	$80	$95	$120	$150

W-3073-J★ • F-2111J★

VF-20	EF-40	AU-50	Unc-60	Unc-63
$100	$140	$200	$280	$400

W-3073-K • F-2111K • Dallas • 1,296,000

VF-20	EF-40	AU-50	Unc-60	Unc-63
$75	$110	$150	$205	$275

W-3073-K★ • F-2111K★

VF-20	EF-40	AU-50	Unc-60	Unc-63
$150	$225	$350	$550	$850

W-3073-L • F-2111L • San Francisco • 2,160,000

VF-20	EF-40	AU-50	Unc-60	Unc-63
$70	$100	$125	$160	$200

W-3073-L★ • F-2111L★

VF-20	EF-40	AU-50	Unc-60	Unc-63
$100	$140	$200	$280	$400

Series of 1950-E, Green Seal
Granahan-Fowler (1965–1966)

This series continued the preceding design. It is the shortest series among modern issues. All are somewhat scarce, and in the context of modern small-size issues, the star notes are rare in Uncirculated grade. When these were issued they were available easily enough, but few dealers stocked them, as the demand was light.

W-3074-B • F-2112B • New York • 3,024,000

VF-20	EF-40	AU-50	Unc-60	Unc-63
$150	$200	$250	$320	$400

W-3074-B★ • F-2112B★

VF-20	EF-40	AU-50	Unc-60	Unc-63
$375	$500	$725	$1,050	$1,500

W-3074-G • F-2112G • Chicago • 1,008,000

VF-20	EF-40	AU-50	Unc-60	Unc-63
$200	$275	$355	$460	$600

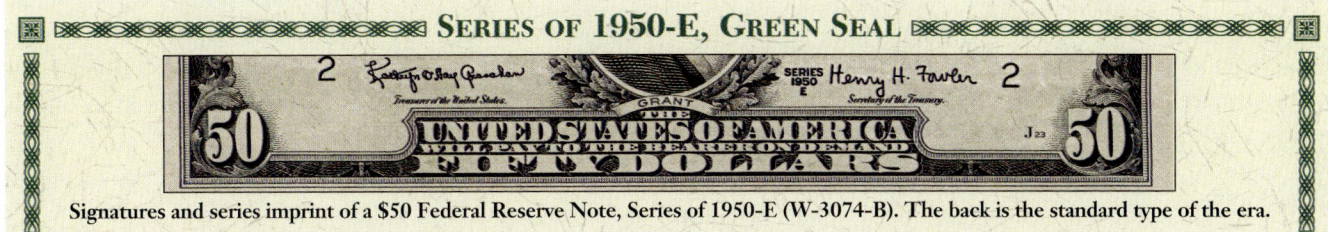

SERIES OF 1950-E, GREEN SEAL

Signatures and series imprint of a $50 Federal Reserve Note, Series of 1950-E (W-3074-B). The back is the standard type of the era.

W-3074-G★ • F-2112G★

VF-20	EF-40	AU-50	Unc-60	Unc-63
$750	$950	$1,400	$2,050	$3,000

W-3074-L • F-2112L • San Francisco • 1,296,000

VF-20	EF-40	AU-50	Unc-60	Unc-63
$175	$200	$250	$320	$400

W-3074-L★ • F-2112L★

VF-20	EF-40	AU-50	Unc-60	Unc-63
$450	$600	$810	$1,100	$1,500

Series of 1963-A, Green Seal
Granahan-Fowler (1965–1966)

The Series of 1963-A (there is no Series of 1963 in the $50 denomination) introduces the motto IN GOD WE TRUST on the back. On the front, a new two-line obligation reads, "This note is legal tender for all debts, public and private."

Although printages vary widely, demand is not strong, yielding the opportunity to acquire scarcer notes at almost generic prices. Star notes are in the minority.

Prices for a typical note for this series, unless listed otherwise, are as follows:

Unc-63
$120

W-3075-A • F-2113A • Boston • 1,536,000

W-3075-A★ • F-2113A★ • 320,000

VF-20	EF-40	AU-50	Unc-60	Unc-63
$125	$150	$250	$350	$450

W-3075-B • F-2113B • New York • 11,008,000

W-3075-B★ • F-2113B★ • 1,408,000

VF-20	EF-40	AU-50	Unc-60	Unc-63
$90	$120	$155	$190	$225

W-3075-C • F-2113C • Philadelphia • 3,328,000

Unc-63
$225

W-3075-C★ • F-2113C★ • 704,000

VF-20	EF-40	AU-50	Unc-60	Unc-63
$100	$125	$215	$305	$400

W-3075-D • F-2113D • Cleveland • 3,584,000

W-3075-D★ • F-2113D★ • 256,000

VF-20	EF-40	AU-50	Unc-60	Unc-63
$100	$125	$215	$305	$400

W-3075-E • F-2113E • Richmond • 3,072,000

W-3075-E★ • F-2113E★ • 704,000

VF-20	EF-40	AU-50	Unc-60	Unc-63
$100	$125	$215	$305	$400

$50 Federal Reserve Note, Series of 1963-A (W-3075-F★). Federal Reserve Bank of Atlanta. Star note.

Back of the $50 Federal Reserve Note, Series of 1963-A (W-3075-F★). The motto IN GOD WE TRUST is added.

W-3075-F • F-2113F • Atlanta • 768,000

Unc-63
$275

W-3075-F★ • F-2113F★ • 384,000

VF-20	EF-40	AU-50	Unc-60	Unc-63
$100	$125	$215	$305	$400

W-3075-G • F-2113G • Chicago • 6,912,000

W-3075-G★ • F-2113G★ • 768,000

VF-20	EF-40	AU-50	Unc-60	Unc-63
$90	$120	$155	$190	$225

W-3075-H • F-2113H • St. Louis • 512,000

W-3075-H★ • F-2113H★ • 128,000

VF-20	EF-40	AU-50	Unc-60	Unc-63
$100	$125	$215	$305	$400

W-3075-I • F-2113I • Minneapolis • 512,000

Unc-63
$225

W-3075-I★ • F-2113I★ • 128,000

VF-20	EF-40	AU-50	Unc-60	Unc-63
$110	$140	$260	$380	$500

W-3075-J • F-2113J • Kansas City • 512,000

W-3075-J★ • F-2113J★ • 64,000

VF-20	EF-40	AU-50	Unc-60	Unc-63
$100	$125	$215	$305	$400

W-3075-K • F-2113K • Dallas • 1,536,000

W-3075-K★ • F-2113K★ • 128,000

VF-20	EF-40	AU-50	Unc-60	Unc-63
$110	$140	$260	$380	$500

W-3075-L • F-2113L • San Francisco • 4,352,000

W-3075-L★ • F-2113L★ • 704,000

VF-20	EF-40	AU-50	Unc-60	Unc-63
$100	$125	$175	$225	$275

Series of 1969, Green Seal
Elston-Kennedy (1969–1970)

The Series of 1969 featured a redesigned Treasury seal, with the inscription THE DEPARTMENT OF THE TREASURY 1789, replacing the earlier style with the Latin wording THESAUR. AMER. SEPTENT. SIGIL. The design in the interior of the seal was modified as well.

This series offers a bit of a challenge, as some of the low-printage issues are elusive, and star notes are scarcer yet. Once again, when they were issued, collectors desiring them were apt to acquire just a single note, and few dealers stocked current bills of this denomination.

W-3076-A • F-2114A • Boston • 2,048,000

Unc-63
$200

W-3076-B • F-2114B • New York • 12,032,000

Unc-63
$125

W-3076-B★ • F-2114B★ • 384,000

VF-20	EF-40	AU-50	Unc-60	Unc-63
$75	$100	$150	$200	$250

W-3076-C • F-2114C • Philadelphia • 3,584,000

Unc-63
$125

W-3076-C★ • F-2114C★ • 128,000

VF-20	EF-40	AU-50	Unc-60	Unc-63
$75	$100	$165	$230	$300

W-3076-D • F-2114D • Cleveland • 3,584,000

Unc-63
$175

W-3076-D★ • F-2114D★ • 192,000

VF-20	EF-40	AU-50	Unc-60	Unc-63
$85	$120	$175	$225	$275

$50 Federal Reserve Note, Series of 1969 (W-3076-D). Federal Reserve Bank of Cleveland. Standard back with motto.

W-3076-E • F-2114E • Richmond • 2,560,000

Unc-63
$175

W-3076-E★ • F-2114E★ • 64,000

VF-20	EF-40	AU-50	Unc-60	Unc-63
$120	$160	$270	$385	$400

W-3076-F • F-2114F • Atlanta • 256,000

Unc-63
$225

W-3076-G • F-2114G • Chicago • 9,728,000

Unc-63
$125

W-3076-G★ • F-2114G★ • 256,000

VF-20	EF-40	AU-50	Unc-60	Unc-63
$75	$100	$150	$200	$250

W-3076-H • F-2114H • St. Louis • 256,000

Unc-63
$225

W-3076-I • F-2114I • Minneapolis • 512,000

Unc-63
$200

W-3076-J • F-2114J • Kansas City • 1,280,000

Unc-63
$175

W-3076-J★ • F-2114J★ • 64,000

VF-20	EF-40	AU-50	Unc-60	Unc-63
$140	$180	$285	$390	$500

W-3076-K • F-2114K • Dallas • 1,536,000

Unc-63
$225

W-3076-K★ • F-2114K★ • 64,000

VF-20	EF-40	AU-50	Unc-60	Unc-63
$140	$180	$285	$390	$500

W-3076-L • F-2114L • San Francisco • 6,912,000

Unc-63
$125

W-3076-L★ • F-2114L★ • 256,000

VF-20	EF-40	AU-50	Unc-60	Unc-63
$120	$160	$205	$250	$300

Series of 1969-A, Green Seal
Kabis-Connally (1971)

Dorothy Andrews Elston married Walter L. Kabis during her term in office, and became Mrs. Kabis.

This series continued the preceding design. The numismatic scenario is similar to that of the preceding issue.

Prices for a typical note for this series, unless listed otherwise, are as follows:

Unc-63
$100

W-3077-A • F-2115A • Boston • 1,536,000

Unc-63
$120

W-3077-A★ • F-2115A★ • 128,000

Unc-63
$225

W-3077-B • F-2115B • New York • 9,728,000

W-3077-B★ • F-2115B★ • 704,000

Unc-63
$225

W-3077-C • F-2115C • Philadelphia • 2,560,000

W-3077-D • F-2115D • Cleveland • 2,816,000

W-3077-E • F-2115E • Richmond • 2,304,000

W-3077-E★ • F-2115E★ • 64,000

VF-20	EF-40	AU-50	Unc-60	Unc-63
$100	$200	$300	$400	$500

W-3077-F • F-2115F • Atlanta • 256,000

Unc-63
$175

W-3077-F★ • F-2115F★ • 64,000

VF-20	EF-40	AU-50	Unc-60	Unc-63
$110	$205	$300	$400	$500

W-3077-G • F-2115G • Chicago • 3,584,000

SERIES OF 1969-A, GREEN SEAL

Signatures and series imprint of a $50 Federal Reserve Note, Series of 1969-A (W-3077-C). The back is the standard type of the era.

W-3077-G★ • F-2115G★ • 192,000

Unc-63
$225

W-3077-H • F-2115H • St. Louis • 256,000

Unc-63
$175

W-3077-I • F-2115I • Minneapolis • 512,000

Unc-63
$150

W-3077-J • F-2115J • Kansas City • 256,000

Unc-63
$175

W-3077-K • F-2115K • Dallas • 1,024,000

W-3077-K★ • F-2115K★ • 64,000

VF-20	EF-40	AU-50	Unc-60	Unc-63
$100	$200	$300	$400	$500

W-3077-L • F-2115L • San Francisco • 5,120,000

W-3077-L★ • F-2115L★ • 256,000

VF-20	EF-40	AU-50	Unc-60	Unc-63
$80	$125	$175	$225	$275

Series of 1969-B, Green Seal
Banuelos-Connally (1971–1972)

This series continued the preceding design. Surprise! Another challenge! This short series, with just seven of the 12 banks issuing notes and star notes issued only from Dallas, is sprinkled with scarce and rare varieties. The reason is simple: not many were saved by numismatists.

W-3078-A • F-2116A • Boston • 1,024,000

VF-20	EF-40	AU-50	Unc-60	Unc-63
$350	$580	$825	$1,050	$1,300

W-3078-B • F-2116B • New York • 2,560,000

VF-20	EF-40	AU-50	Unc-60	Unc-63
$300	$450	$600	$750	$900

W-3078-C • F-2116C • Philadelphia • 2,048,000

VF-20	EF-40	AU-50	Unc-60	Unc-63
$350	$460	$570	$685	$800

W-3078-E • F-2116E • Richmond • 1,536,000

VF-20	EF-40	AU-50	Unc-60	Unc-63
$350	$590	$825	$1,060	$1,300

W-3078-F • F-2116F • Atlanta • 512,000

VF-20	EF-40	AU-50	Unc-60	Unc-63
$450	$660	$875	$1,085	$1,300

W-3078-G • F-2116G • Chicago • 1,024,000

VF-20	EF-40	AU-50	Unc-60	Unc-63
$300	$475	$650	$825	$1,000

W-3078-K • F-2116K • Dallas • 1,024,000

VF-20	EF-40	AU-50	Unc-60	Unc-63
$350	$510	$670	$830	$1,000

W-3078-K★ • F-2116K★ • 128,000

VF-20	EF-40	AU-50	Unc-60	Unc-63
$1,000	$1,375	$1,750	$2,125	$2,500

Series of 1969-C, Green Seal
Banuelos-Shultz (1972–1974)

This series continued the preceding design. The collecting situation changes with this series. All are easily enough found, although the star notes are in the minority.

W-3079-A • F-2117A • Boston • 1,792,000

Unc-63
$110

W-3079-A★ • F-2117A★ • 64,000

Unc-63
$400

W-3079-B • F-2117B • New York • 7,040,000

Unc-63
$90

SERIES OF 1969-B, GREEN SEAL

Signatures and series imprint of a $50 Federal Reserve Note, Series of 1969-B (W-3078-B). The back is the standard type of the era.

SERIES OF 1969-C, GREEN SEAL

Signatures and series imprint of a $50 Federal Reserve Note, Series of 1969-C (W-3079-G). The back is the standard type of the era.

W-3079-B★ • F-2117B★ • 192,000

Unc-63
$300

W-3079-C • F-2117C • Philadelphia • 3,584,000

Unc-63
$100

W-3079-C★ • F-2117C★ • 256,000

Unc-63
$300

W-3079-D • F-2117D • Cleveland • 5,120,000

Unc-63
$100

W-3079-D★ • F-2117D★ • 192,000

Unc-63
$250

W-3079-E • F-2117E • Richmond • 2,304,000

Unc-63
$100

W-3079-E★ • F-2117E★ • 64,000

Unc-63
$400

W-3079-F • F-2117F • Atlanta • 256,000

Unc-63
$125

W-3079-F★ • F-2117F★ • 64,000

Unc-63
$300

W-3079-G • F-2117G • Chicago • 6,784,000

Unc-63
$90

W-3079-G★ • F-2117G★ • 576,000

Unc-63
$200

W-3079-H • F-2117H • St. Louis • 2,688,000

Unc-63
$100

W-3079-H★ • F-2117H★ • 64,000

Unc-63
$400

W-3079-I • F-2117I • Minneapolis • 256,000

Unc-63
$145

W-3079-I★ • F-2117I★ • 64,000

Unc-63
$400

W-3079-J • F-2117J • Kansas City • 1,280,000

Unc-63
$125

W-3079-J★ • F-2117J★ • 128,000

Unc-63
$300

W-3079-K • F-2117K • Dallas • 3,456,000

Unc-63
$125

W-3079-K★ • F-2117K★ • 64,000

Unc-63
$400

W-3079-L • F-2117L • San Francisco • 4,608,000

Unc-63
$100

W-3079-L★ • F-2117L★ • 256,000

Unc-63
$300

Series of 1974, Green Seal
Neff-Simon (1974–1977)

This series continued the preceding design. Although neither this series nor any before it can be called common in the context of, say, $1 notes, they can be collected without difficulty. Patience is still required to track down specific varieties.

W-3080-A • F-2118A • Boston • 3,840,000

Unc-63
$125

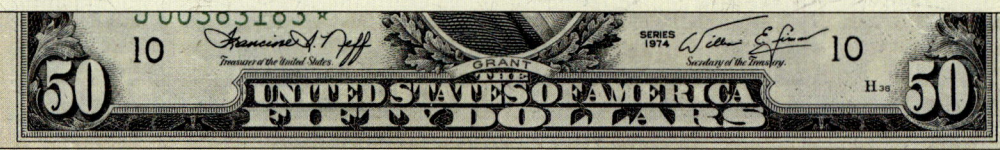

SERIES OF 1974, GREEN SEAL

Signatures and series imprint of a $50 Federal Reserve Note, Series of 1974 (W-3080-J). The back is the standard type of the era.

W-3080-A★ • F-2118A★ • 256,000

Unc-63
$200

W-3080-B • F-2118B • New York • 38,400,000

Unc-63
$100

W-3080-B★ • F-2118B★ • 768,000

Unc-63
$160

W-3080-C • F-2118C • Philadelphia • 7,040,000

Unc-63
$125

W-3080-C★ • F-2118C★ • 192,000

Unc-63
$275

W-3080-D • F-2118D • Cleveland • 21,200,000

Unc-63
$100

W-3080-D★ • F-2118D★ • 640,000

Unc-63
$200

W-3080-E • F-2118E • Richmond • 14,080,000

Unc-63
$125

W-3080-E★ • F-2118E★ • 576,000

Unc-63
$200

W-3080-F • F-2118F • Atlanta • 1,280,000

Unc-63
$125

W-3080-F★ • F-2118F★ • 640,000

Unc-63
$250

W-3080-G • F-2118G • Chicago • 30,720,000

Unc-63
$80

W-3080-G★ • F-2118G★ • 1,536,000

Unc-63
$160

W-3080-H • F-2118H • St. Louis • 1,920,000

Unc-63
$200

W-3080-H★ • F-2118H★ • 128,000

Unc-63
$325

W-3080-I • F-2118I • Minneapolis • 3,200,000

Unc-63
$150

W-3080-I★ • F-2118I★ • 192,000

Unc-63
$400

W-3080-J • F-2118J • Kansas City • 4,480,000

Unc-63
$125

W-3080-J★ • F-2118J★ • 192,000

Unc-63
$400

W-3080-K • F-2118K • Dallas • 8,320,000

Unc-63
$150

W-3080-K★ • F-2118K★ • 128,000

Unc-63
$400

W-3080-L • F-2118L • San Francisco • 7,378,000

Unc-63
$150

W-3080-L★ • F-2118L★ • 64,000

Unc-63
$400

Series of 1977, Green Seal
Morton-Blumenthal (1977–1979)

This series continued the previous design. It is more plentiful than the preceding, but, again, some patience is needed to form a set by varieties.

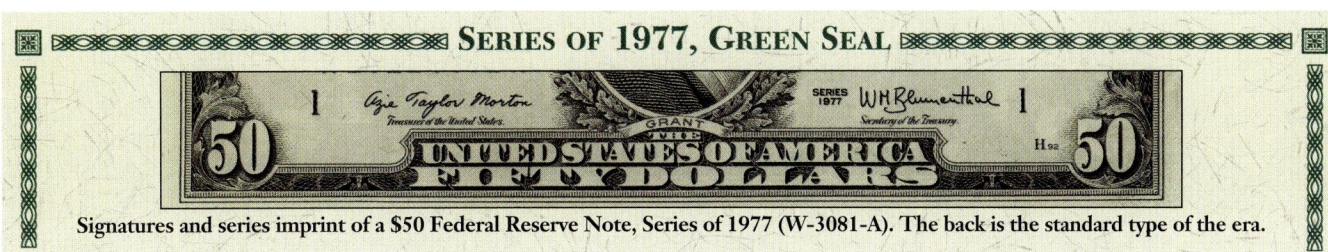

SERIES OF 1977, GREEN SEAL

Signatures and series imprint of a $50 Federal Reserve Note, Series of 1977 (W-3081-A). The back is the standard type of the era.

Prices for a typical note for this series, unless listed otherwise, are as follows:

Unc-63
$80

W-3081-A • F-2119A • Boston • 16,400,000

Unc-63
$100

W-3081-A★ • F-2119A★ • 1,088,000

Unc-63
$200

W-3081-B • F-2119B • New York • 49,920,000

W-3081-B★ • F-2119B★ • 2,112,000

Unc-63
$150

W-3081-C • F-2119C • Philadelphia • 5,120,000

W-3081-C★ • F-2119C★ • 128,000

Unc-63
$300

W-3081-D • F-2119D • Cleveland • 23,040,000

W-3081-D★ • F-2119D★ • 1,024,000

Unc-63
$200

W-3081-E • F-2119E • Richmond • 19,200,000

W-3081-E★ • F-2119E★ • 896,000

Unc-63
$200

W-3081-F • F-2119F • Atlanta • 2,560,000

W-3081-F★ • F-2119F★ • 128,000

Unc-63
$200

W-3081-G • F-2119G • Chicago • 47,360,000

W-3081-G★ • F-2119G★ • 2,304,000

Unc-63
$200

W-3081-H • F-2119H • St. Louis • 3,840,000

Unc-63
$125

W-3081-H★ • F-2119H★ • 512,000

Unc-63
$225

W-3081-I • F-2119I • Minneapolis • 3,840,000

Unc-63
$110

W-3081-I★ • F-2119I★ • 128,000

Unc-63
$325

W-3081-J • F-2119J • Kansas City • 7,680,000

Unc-63
$110

W-3081-J★ • F-2119J★ • 256,000

Unc-63
$300

W-3081-K • F-2119K • Dallas • 14,080,000

Unc-63
$125

W-3081-K★ • F-2119K★ • 576,000

Unc-63
$250

W-3081-L • F-2119L • San Francisco • 19,200,000

W-3081-L★ • F-2119L★ • 768,000

Unc-63
$200

Series of 1981, Green Seal
Buchanan-Regan (1981–1983)

This series continued the previous design. These are slightly scarcer than the preceding, probably as the economy was troubled during the second year of the Reagan administration—interest rates continued to be erratic, and the last thing most people wanted to do was to keep assets in non-producing high-denomination currency.

SERIES OF 1981, GREEN SEAL

Signatures and series imprint of a $50 Federal Reserve Note, Series of 1981 (W-3082-D). The back is the standard type of the era.

Prices for a typical note for this series, unless listed otherwise, are as follows:

Unc-63
$135

W-3082-A • F-2120A • Boston • 18,560,000

W-3082-B • F-2120B • New York • 78,080,000

W-3082-B★ • F-2120B★ • 768,000

Unc-63
$250

W-3082-C • F-2120C • Philadelphia • 1,280,000

W-3082-D • F-2120D • Cleveland • 28,160,000

W-3082-D★ • F-2120D★ • 256,000

Unc-63
$300

W-3082-E • F-2120E • Richmond • 25,600,000

Unc-63
$150

W-3082-F • F-2120F • Atlanta • 4,480,000

Unc-63
$175

W-3082-F★ • F-2120F★ • 768,000

Unc-63
$300

W-3082-G • F-2120G • Chicago • 67,200,000

W-3082-G★ • F-2120G★ • 128,000

Unc-63
$250

W-3082-H • F-2120H • St. Louis • 4,480,000

Unc-63
$175

W-3082-I • F-2120I • Minneapolis • 5,760,000

Unc-63
$150

W-3082-I★ • F-2120I★ • 128,000

Unc-63
$350

W-3082-J • F-2120J • Kansas City • 18,560,000

W-3082-J★ • F-2120J★ • 128,000

Unc-63
$300

W-3082-K • F-2120K • Dallas • 19,840,000

W-3082-L • F-2120L • San Francisco • 35,200,000

W-3082-L★ • F-2120L★ • 256,000

Unc-63
$250

Series of 1981-A, Green Seal
Ortega-Regan (1983–1985)

This series continued the preceding design. With no Philadelphia notes and just three star varieties, this series is easily collectible, but as high denominations are often not stocked by dealers, some searching is required. By the time this issue was released, the economy was improving.

Prices for a typical note for this series, unless listed otherwise, are as follows:

Unc-63
$120

W-3083-A • F-2121A • Boston • 9,600,000

W-3083-B • F-2121B • New York • 28,800,000

Unc-63
$100

W-3083-B★ • F-2121B★ • 3,200,000

Unc-63
$250

W-3083-D • F-2121D • Cleveland • 12,800,000

W-3083-E • F-2121E • Richmond • 704,000

W-3083-E★ • F-2121E★ • 704,000

Unc-63
$300

W-3083-F • F-2121F • Atlanta • 3,200,000

W-3083-G • F-2121G • Chicago • 28,800,000

Unc-63
$100

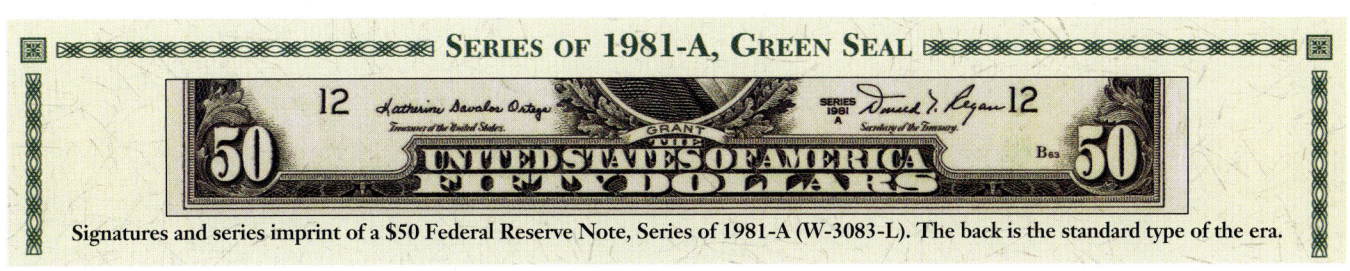

SERIES OF 1981-A, GREEN SEAL

Signatures and series imprint of a $50 Federal Reserve Note, Series of 1981-A (W-3083-L). The back is the standard type of the era.

W-3083-H • F-2121H • St. Louis • 3,200,000

W-3083-I • F-2121I • Minneapolis • 3,200,000

W-3083-J • F-2121J • Kansas City • 6,400,000

W-3083-K • F-2121K • Dallas • 6,400,000

W-3083-L • F-2121L • San Francisco • 22,400,000

W-3083-L★ • F-2121L★ • 640,000

Unc-63
$250

Series of 1985, Green Seal
Ortega-Baker (1985–1988)

This series continued the preceding design. This is an easy series to complete, although the star notes are scarcer than the regular issues.

Prices for a typical note for this series, unless listed otherwise, are as follows:

Unc-63
$90

W-3084-A • F-2122A • Boston • 51,200,000

W-3084-A★ • F-2122A★ • 64,000

Unc-63
$350

W-3084-B • F-2122B • New York • 182,400,000

W-3084-B★ • F-2122B★ • 1,408,000

Unc-63
$200

W-3084-C • F-2122C • Philadelphia • 3,200,000

W-3084-D • F-2122D • Cleveland • 57,600,000

W-3084-D★ • F-2122D★ • 64,000

Unc-63
$350

W-3084-E • F-2122E • Richmond • 54,400,000

W-3084-F • F-2122F • Atlanta • 9,600,000

W-3084-G • F-2122G • Chicago • 112,000,000

W-3084-G★ • F-2122G★ • 1,280,000

Unc-63
$250

W-3084-H • F-2122H • St. Louis • 6,400,000

W-3084-I • F-2122I • Minneapolis • 12,800,000

W-3084-J • F-2122J • Kansas City • 9,600,000

W-3084-K • F-2122K • Dallas • 25,600,000

W-3084-L • F-2122L • San Francisco • 57,600,000

Series of 1988, Green Seal
Ortega-Brady (1988–1989)

This series continued the preceding design. This is a short and sweet series, with just seven banks and one star variety represented. In the context of the era, choice Uncirculated examples are elusive, but when you find them they are not expensive.

Prices for a typical note for this series, unless listed otherwise, are as follows:

Unc-63
$125

W-3085-A • F-2123A • Boston • 9,600,000

W-3085-B • F-2123B • New York • 214,400,000

Unc-63
$100

W-3085-B★ • F-2123B★ • 1,408,000

Unc-63
$275

W-3085-D • F-2123D • Cleveland • 32,000,000

W-3085-E • F-2123E • Richmond • 12,800,000

W-3085-G • F-2123G • Chicago • 80,000,000

Unc-63
$100

W-3085-J • F-2123J • Kansas City • 6,400,000

W-3085-L • F-2123L • San Francisco • 12,800,000

SERIES OF 1985, GREEN SEAL

Signatures and series imprint of a $50 Federal Reserve Note, Series of 1985 (W-3084-D). The back is the standard type of the era.

SERIES OF 1988, GREEN SEAL

Signatures and series imprint of a $50 Federal Reserve Note, Series of 1988 (W-3085-B). The back is the standard type of the era.

Series of 1990, Green Seal
Villalpando-Brady (1989–1993)

New security features were added to this issue. Around the outside of most of the portrait frame THE UNITED STATES OF AMERICA is repeated in micro printing. A security thread was added to the paper. By this time, the counterfeiting of high-denomination federal notes was a large problem, from both the use of color copying machines and clandestine foreign print shops. This series presents no challenge to collect, although once again patience will be required.

Prices for a typical note for this series, unless listed otherwise, are as follows:

Unc-63
$85

W-3086-A • F-2124A • Boston • 28,800,000

W-3086-B • F-2124B • New York • 232,000,000

W-3086-B★ • F-2124B★ • 3,116,000

Unc-63
$125

W-3086-C • F-2124C • Philadelphia • 41,600,000

W-3086-C★ • F-2124C★ • 1,280,000

Unc-63
$125

W-3086-D • F-2124D • Cleveland • 92,800,000

W-3086-E • F-2124E • Richmond • 76,800,000

W-3086-G • F-2124G • Chicago • 108,800,000

W-3086-G★ • F-2124G★ • 1,032,000

Unc-63
$110

W-3086-H • F-2124H • St. Louis • 16,000,000

W-3086-I • F-2124I • Minneapolis • 22,400,000

W-3086-J • F-2124J • Kansas City • 35,200,000

W-3086-J★ • F-2124J★ • 640,000

Unc-63
$150

W-3086-K • F-2124K • Dallas • 16,000,000

W-3086-L • F-2124L • San Francisco • 119,200,000

Series of 1993, Green Seal
Withrow-Bentsen (1994)

This series continued the preceding design. This was a truncated series, with just seven banks and three star varieties. They can be collected easily, although the stars are scarcer than the others.

Prices for a typical note for this series, unless listed otherwise, are as follows:

Unc-63
$85

W-3087-A • F-2125A • Boston • 41,600,000

W-3087-B • F-2125B • New York • 544,000,000

W-3087-B★ • F-2125B★ • 4,224,000

Unc-63
$100

W-3087-D • F-2125D • Cleveland • 60,800,000

W-3087-D★ • F-2125D★ • 1,280,000

Unc-63
$125

SERIES OF 1990, GREEN SEAL

$50 Federal Reserve Note, Series of 1990 (W-3086-D). Federal Reserve Bank of Cleveland. Standard back with motto.

Detail of the microprint text.

SERIES OF 1993, GREEN SEAL

Signatures and series imprint of a $50 Federal Reserve Note, Series of 1993 (W-3087-B). The back is the standard type of the era.

W-3087-E • F-2125E • Richmond • 35,200,000

W-3087-G • F-2125G • Chicago • 144,000,000

W-3087-G★ • F-2125G★ • 1,280,000

Unc-63
$100

W-3087-H • F-2125H • St. Louis • 3,200,000

W-3087-J • F-2125J • Kansas City • 12,800,000

W-3087-K • F-2125K • Dallas • 9,600,000

Series of 1996, Green Seal
Withrow-Rubin (1995–1999)

This issue introduced a modified layout for the face and back, including enhanced security features. On the face the same portrait of Grant is now slightly cropped and is enlarged considerably. There is no microprinting around the portrait frame. At the left is a new Federal Reserve Bank seal. The 12 member banks are no longer identified by name, but have their letter and number at the upper left, below the serial number, from A1 (Boston) to L12 (San Francisco). The denomination counters on each corner have been modified, so that the counter at the lower right is now separate and printed in the field in light green. Other differences are illustrated.

On the back the Capitol is now without the background of Washington seen on earlier issues and is instead viewed from a street-level perspective, head-on. A curved border surrounds the upper part of the vignette. Counters in the corners have been modified; the number 50 at the lower right is especially large and has a plain background.

All of this series were printed in Washington, D.C. Production quantities were generous, even for star notes, resulting in the easy availability of such notes today.

$50 Federal Reserve Note, Series of 1996 (W-3088-L★). Federal Reserve Bank of San Francisco. Star note. Now with modified layout as used through and including the Series of 2001.

Detail of the lower right face showing the B77 plate letter and number, and other features.

Detail of the counter at the lower right of the note back, also showing the plate number 40.

Back of the $50 Federal Reserve Note, Series of 1996 (W-3088-L★). The Capitol motif has been revised and certain other features modified. This back was used on all $50 notes through the Series of 2001.

Prices for a typical note for this series, unless listed otherwise, are as follows:

Unc-63
$65

Prices for a typical star note for this series, unless listed otherwise, are as follows:

Unc-63
$100

W-3088-A • F-2126A • Boston • 54,400,000

Unc-63
$70

W-3088-B • F-2126B • New York • 560,800,000

W-3088-B★ • F-2126B★ • 5,120,000

W-3088-C • F-2126C • Philadelphia • 76,800,000

W-3088-D • F-2126D • Cleveland • 119,200,000

W-3088-E • F-2126E • Richmond • 106,400,000

W-3088-F • F-2126F • Atlanta • 119,200,000

W-3088-G • F-2126G • Chicago • 241,600,000

W-3088-G★ • F-2126G★ • 1,280,000

W-3088-H • F-2126H • St. Louis • 28,800,000

W-3088-I • F-2126I • Minneapolis • 35,200,000

W-3088-J • F-2126J • Kansas City • 57,600,000

W-3088-J★ • F-2126J★ • 1,920,000

W-3088-K • F-2126K • Dallas • 92,800,000

W-3088-L • F-2126L • San Francisco • 219,200,000

W-3088-L★ • F-2126L★ • 3,200,000

Series of 2001, Green Seal
Marin-O'Neill (2001–2002)

This series continued the preceding design. All were printed in Washington, D.C., and are easy enough to collect. The single star note variety receives its share of special attention.

Prices for a typical note for this series, unless listed otherwise, are as follows:

Unc-63
$65

W-3089-A • F-2127A • Boston • 6,400,000

W-3089-B • F-2127B • New York • 54,400,000

W-3089-B★ • F-2127B★ • 320,000

Unc-63
$200

W-3089-C • F-2127C • Philadelphia • 19,200,000

W-3089-D • F-2127D • Cleveland • 16,000,000

W-3089-E • F-2127E • Richmond • 32,000,000

W-3089-E★ • F-2127E★ • 640,000

Unc-63
$175

W-3089-F • F-2127F • Atlanta • 22,800,000

W-3089-G • F-2127G • Chicago • 35,200,000

W-3089-H • F-2127H • St. Louis • 3,200,000

Unc-63
$80

W-3089-I • F-2127I • Minneapolis • 3,200,000

Unc-63
$80

W-3089-J • F-2127J • Kansas City • 3,200,000

Unc-63
$80

W-3089-K • F-2127K • Dallas • 6,400,000

W-3089-L • F-2127L • San Francisco • 32,000,000

Series of 2004, Green Seal, Fort Worth
Marin-Snow (2003)

Both sides of the $50 note were redesigned for the Series of 2004 (illus. on p. 622). Grant's portrait appears without a frame. At the border to the left and right are many microprinted FIFTY notations between horizontal design elements. The left field has stars, and the background is printed in a subtle, light purple-pink-blue mixture of hues. To the right are a blue star and light red flag stripes. The paper includes an embedded security strip. Other changes are depicted.

The new back retains some elements that are familiar, but with extensive changes. The Capitol is no longer within a curved frame and has clouds in the sky in the background. Tiny gold denomination counters are in the fields to the left and right. The background is a subtle, light purple-pink-blue mixture of hues to the left and right sides, away from the center.

SERIES OF 2001, GREEN SEAL

Signatures and series imprint of a $50 Federal Reserve Note, Series of 2001 (W-3089-B). Standard back introduced in 1996.

All notes in this series are available and affordable. Star notes were issued by only three banks—Richmond, Chicago, and Dallas.

Prices for a typical note for this series, unless listed otherwise, are as follows:

Unc-63
$65

W-3090-A • F-2128A • Boston • 9,600,000

W-3090-B • F-2128B • New York • 41,600,000

W-3090-C • F-2128C • Philadelphia • 22,400,000

W-3090-D • F-2128D • Cleveland • 32,000,000

W-3090-E • F-2128E • Richmond • 3,200,000

W-3090-E★ • F-2128E★ • 800,000

Unc-63
$175

W-3090-F • F-2128F • Atlanta • 44,800,000

W-3090-G • F-2128G • Chicago • 115,200,000

W-3090-G★ • F-2128G★ • 3,200,000

Unc-63
$110

W-3090-H • F-2128H • St. Louis • 9,600,000

W-3090-I • F-2128I • Minneapolis • 12,800,000

W-3090-J • F-2128J • Kansas City • 22,400,000

SERIES OF 2004, GREEN SEAL

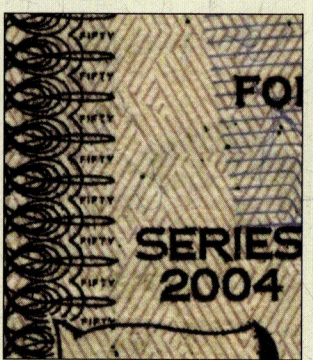

$50 Federal Reserve Note, Series of 2004, printed in Forth Worth (W-3090-I). Federal Reserve Bank of Minneapolis. The layout is similar in style to the preceding, but now with color and other security features added and with a star to the lower right of the portrait.

Closer view showing microprint FIFTY imprints.

Detail of the lower left field.

Detail of the right field, showing the blue star and other elements.

Back of the $50 Federal Reserve Note, Series of 2004 (W-3090-I). Similar in style to the preceding, but with the background of the Capitol revised and now with tiny yellow counters and other security features added. Back used on all Series of 2004 $50 notes to date.

Detail of the lower right of the back, showing plate number 4 and other features including counters in gold.

W-3090-K • F-2128K • Dallas • 32,000,000

W-3090-K★ • F-2128K★ • 3,200,000

Unc-63
$110

W-3090-L • F-2128L • San Francisco • 51,200,000

Series of 2004-A, Green Seal, Fort Worth
Cabral-Snow (2004–2006)

This series continued the preceding design. This is a short series, with only one star variety. As collecting small-size varieties had become very popular by this time, due in no small part to the publication of the *Standard Guide to Small-Size Paper Money 1838 to Date*, by John Schwartz and Scott Lindquist, more examples were saved at the time of issue. Such interest had been building since the 1990s. No valuation charts are provided, as notes in this series can be had in top condition for face value at banks or from dealers (with a nominal handling charge).

W-3091-A • F-2129A • Boston • 16,000,000

W-3091-B • F-2129B • New York • 38,400,000

W-3091-B★ • F-2129B★ • 64,000

W-3091-E • F-2129E • Richmond • 32,000,000

W-3091-E★ • F-2129E★ • 2,560,000

W-3091-F • F-2129F • Atlanta • 51,200,000

W-3091-G • F-2129G • Chicago • 54,400,000

W-3091-J • F-2129J • Kansas City • 19,200,000

W-3091-L • F-2129L • San Francisco • 6,400,000

Series of 2006, Green Seal, Fort Worth
Cabral-Paulson (2006–2009)

This series continued the preceding design. All notes of this series have been printed in Fort Worth. Printing for this series began in December 2006 with Cleveland, Richmond, and St. Louis notes.

The information given here is accurate as of press time. No valuation charts are provided, as notes in this series can be had in top condition for face value at banks or from dealers (with a nominal handling charge).

W-3092-A • F-2130A • Boston

W-3092-A★ • F-2130A★

W-3092-B • F-2130B • New York

W-3092-C • F-2130C • Philadelphia

W-3092-D • F-2130D • Cleveland

W-3092-E • F-2130E • Richmond

W-3092-H • F-2130H • St. Louis

W-3092-I • F-2130I • Minneapolis

W-3092-J • F-2130J • Kansas City

W-3092-K • F-2130K • Dallas

W-3092-L • F-2130L • San Francisco

Series of 2009, Green Seal
Rios-Geithner (2009–)

No printing information as of press time.

SERIES OF 2004-A, GREEN SEAL

Signatures and series imprint of a $50 Federal Reserve Note, Series of 2004-A (W-3091-A). Standard back introduced in 2004.

SERIES OF 2006, GREEN SEAL

Signatures and series imprint of a $50 Federal Reserve Note, Series of 2006 (W-3092-B). Standard back introduced in 2004.

$100 NOTES

LARGE SIZE

The scope and availability of large-size $100 notes closely parallel those of the $50 denomination, but with some important differences.

Interest-Bearing Notes and Compound Interest Treasury Notes were popular in their day, and immense quantities were sold to help finance the Civil War, but no numismatic notice was taken of them at the time. Accordingly, all are exceedingly rare, and some varieties are known only from Treasury records, as no examples survive. Early Legal Tender Notes feature the famous Spread Eagle motif, one of the boldest depictions of the national bird on any paper money. Likewise, all are rare. Certain of these and other large denominations were widely counterfeited in their day—expertly so—with the result that one must be careful when buying uncertified notes; the leading certification services can detect the genuine from the false.

Although the designs are different, Legal Tender Notes, Silver Certificates, and Gold Certificates are similar in characteristics of series, signature combinations, seals, and other aspects to certain $50 notes, and, for that matter, certain other denominations as well. Across the board, the number of varieties of $100 notes is fewer, and the Series of 1915 and 1918 Federal Reserve Bank Notes (issued in denominations from $1 to $50) have no counterpart here.

The $100 Series of 1890 Treasury or Coin Notes are quite popular, famous as "Watermelon Notes" due to the two round, green, and perhaps delicious-appearing digits on the back. Indeed, the appearance of one of these notes in any grade is a matter of publicity and possibly a catalog cover illustration for an auction sale.

Federal Reserve Notes of 1914, Red Seal as well as Blue Seal varieties, were produced in quantity at one time, but were not widely saved. Today, most are fairly scarce, and many varieties are extremely rare. However, numismatists who specialist in them are rare as well, meaning that when a prize item is located, the price is not as high as it might be if it were a comparable rarity in another, more popular series, such Legal Tender Notes, which has more competition at auction.

Large-size $100 National Bank Notes are very rare. Fortunate is the state specialist who is able to have even a single representative of any of the various types and signature combinations from the Original Series down through the Series of 1902, Plain Back. As is true with other values, the Plain Back notes are more available than the others. The $100 denomination was the last to have such an extensive issue of large-size bank notes. Higher denominations, from $500 to $10,000, are much abbreviated in their series and varieties.

INTEREST-BEARING NOTES

Interest-Bearing Notes of all authorizations from 1861 through 1865 are so rare as to be non-collectible. Only a few stray examples exist. The designs are attractive and sometimes complex, but are sometimes known only through viewing proof impressions (one-sided impressions, without serial numbers, made for test or presentation purposes). These were issued in very large quantities, but buyers were clustered, and when the interest period ran out, the notes were redeemed. Each note has an overprinted date of issue, noting the commencement of interest accrual.

March 2, 1861, 6% Interest, 60 Days

The Union was in need of funds, and the Act of March 2, 1861, provided for notes or bonds (both terms were used) to be issued to borrow money. The shortest term was 60 days and was printed in the $50, $100, and $500 denominations. No circulated examples are known, but proofs exist. Information regarding these notes is sparse, though we know that $10 million was authorized, and $12,896,350 in these 60-day bonds was eventually issued and quickly redeemed in its entirety. These were printed in New York City by the American Bank Note Company and bear that firm's imprint, as well as the imprint of Rawdon, Wright & Hatch. These were probably made in a hurry, using old stock vignettes.

At the top center of the face is *Mercury*, a signed vignette by George W. Hatch (principal of the erstwhile Rawdon, Wright, Hatch & Edson, which in 1858 was merged into the new ABNCo.). At the left, a maiden with a cornucopia is seated near a strongbox upon which is a griffin (the mythological guardian of treasure), a vignette designated as *Wealth*. To the right is Justice standing with a particularly patriotic eagle nearby, wearing a medallion of George Washington. Bold denomination counters are at each corner. These same

MARCH 2, 1861, 6% INTEREST, 60 DAYS

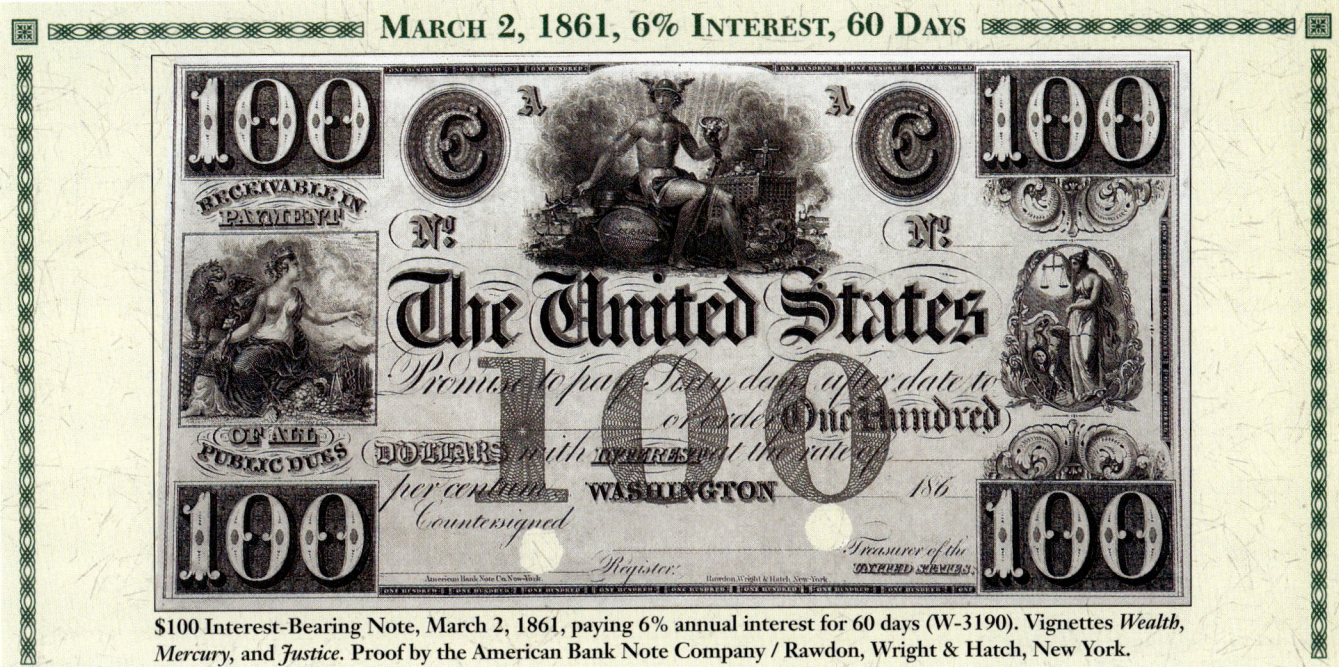

$100 Interest-Bearing Note, March 2, 1861, paying 6% annual interest for 60 days (W-3190). Vignettes *Wealth, Mercury*, and *Justice*. Proof by the American Bank Note Company / Rawdon, Wright & Hatch, New York.

vignettes were used on notes for state-chartered banks produced by RWH&E and ABNCo. The size is about 20.5 centimeters by 10.5 centimeters high.

W-3190 • F-unlisted • Unknown

March 2, 1861, 6% Interest, 2 Years

At the time of issue, these notes (illus. on p. 626) were sold at a discount from face value to reflect the interest that would be earned in two years. Most buyers were banks and brokers, who sold them to wealthy individuals. They did not circulate in commerce, but were held until maturity, then redeemed.

On the left side of the face is Liberty seated, holding a pole and cap, her right arm resting on a pedestal and her left foot on a cornucopia. Below is "Issued in pursuance of an Act of Congress approved March 2d 1861." At the center a perched eagle with wings spread is flanked by two kaleidograph counters with petals lettered UNITED STATES 100 TREASURY. At the upper left border is PATENTED APRIL 23rd 1860 (for the cycloidal configuration) and at the upper right is NATIONAL BANK NOTE COMPANY. An orange security overprint in the cycloidal configuration is on the bottom half of the note. "Interest at Six per Cent payable 1st January and 1st July 1861" is lettered on the plate. The first part of the imprint seems illogical, as this issue was not authorized until March 2, 1861. Perhaps the year 1862 was intended.

The back has ornate engraving, with the printing oriented vertically, and the patent and imprint of the National Bank Note Company. The size is about 19.5 centimeters by 10.5 centimeters.

W-3200 • F-202b • Chittenden-Spinner (1861–1864) • "for the" hand-signed • 44,958 • Unknown
Commentary: By 1869 only 14 remained outstanding.

W-3210 • F-202b • "for the" printed • Included in printage above • Unknown

First Series, July 17, 1861, 7.3% Interest, 3 Years

A portrait of General Winfield Scott, nicknamed "Old Fuss and Feathers," facing to the viewer's left, is at the center, flanked by large C counters. Denomination counters are in each corner, with the roman numeral C printed under the counters at the upper left and right corners. Scott, a hero of the War of 1812, also distinguished himself in the War with Mexico, after which he was designated as lieutenant general, the first person to attain that rank since George Washington. In 1852 he ran for the presidency, but lost to Franklin Pierce.

The back has 100 UNITED STATES of AMERICA 100 at the center and ornate engraving overall, with ample white space at the border. The American Bank Note Company imprint is on each side. These were issued with five coupons attached to the right side and printed in sheets of three notes. Some were numbered in red and some in blue, including duplicate serial numbers, on special request from the Treasury.[1] These were normally numbered by ABNCo, but on September 30, 1861, 50 unnumbered sheets were erroneously sent to the Treasury department, with 100 more on October 3, and 200 more on December 7 of the same year, according to testimony by ABNCo president John Gavit.[2]

Although proof impressions exist, no circulated notes are known.

W-3220 • F-208 • Chittenden-Spinner (1861–1864) • *Printed on plate:* August 19, 1861 • Red serial numbers • Unknown

W-3230 • F-208 • *Printed on plate:* October 1, 1861 • Red serial numbers • Unknown

W-3235 • F-208 • Blue serial numbers • Unknown

MARCH 2, 1861, 6% INTEREST, 2 YEARS

$100 Interest-Bearing Note, March 2, 1861, 6% interest, 2-year term (W-3200). Plate C. With rich orange cycloidal configuration security overprint. Proof impression.

Detail of the patented cycloidal configuration, a National Bank Note Company specialty, which it said was a deterrent to counterfeiting. This claim was ridiculed by competitor W.L. Ormsby, who was a principal in the Continental Bank Note Co. when it was founded in 1862.

This kaleidograph (as it was designated in records) counter, with radiating petals engraved with the denomination, was a National Bank Note Company specialty and was also used on many notes issued by state-chartered banks in the early 1860s. This counter is one of two on the face.

Back of a similar note, proof impression.

March 3, 1863, 5% Interest, 1 Year

On the left of the face is the vignette *Guardian* (also called *Victory* and *Peace* in Treasury records[3]) featuring a woman standing behind a flag-draped cannon, holding a shield, with another nearby shield inscribed, IN GOD IS OUR TRUST. Behind her, to the left, are stacked rifles with bay-

onets. At the top center of the note is the standing figure of George Washington. At the lower right is the vignette *Justice with Shield*, engraved by Charles Burt (this was also used on $50 two-year Interest-Bearing Notes of this date). "Will pay to the bearer with Five per cent interest ONE HUN-DRED DOLLARS" is lettered under the heavy green over-

MARCH 3, 1863, 5% INTEREST, 1 YEAR

$100 Interest-Bearing Note, March 3, 1863, 5%, 1 year (W-3245). Overprinted with issue date, March 25, 1864, for the commencement of interest. Plate A, serial 17148.

Upper right of the face of W-3245, showing details.

Back of the $100 Interest-Bearing Note, March 3, 1863, 5%, 1 year (W-3245), with obligation statement and counterfeiting clause at center.

print at the center and is not easy to discern at quick glance. Red serial numbers are at the upper right and lower left. There is an American Bank Note Company imprint above the bottom center border, largely masked by the rectangular green vignette in that area.

Known red overprint dates include March 25 and April 14, 1864. Likely, such notes were issued more or less continually, with many other dates not presently recorded. These were sold at a discount to reflect the interest, and redeemed at face value upon maturity.

W-3245 • F-199 • Chittenden-Spinner (1861–1864) • Payable at maturity • 136,400

Recorded population: 3 • *Highest graded:* EF-45 • *Commentary:* Red overprint issue date varies. • *Selected information:* Known examples include serials 834/C, VF, sold in a CAA auction (5/2005) for $74,750; 853, EF; and 17148/A, VF, sold in a CAA auction (2/2005) for $126,500.

March 3, 1863, 5% Interest, 2 Years

At the lower left of the face is a vignette, *Farmer and Mechanic*, showing two men seated with a shield between them. At the top center is a small vignette with an angular view of the front of the U.S. Treasury Building (this image was also used on the $1,000 three-year 5% Interest-Bearing Note dated March 2, 1861). To the lower right is a vignette of sailors with two cannons, *In the Turret*, referring to an ironclad (the naval sensation of the day). AMERICAN BANK NOTE CO. NEW YORK and NATIONAL BANK NOTE COMPANY are printed at the bottom border. Below the top border, left of center, is PATENTED APRIL 23rd 1860, the James MacDonough patent for the green cycloidal overprint at bottom center.

These notes had various red dates overprinted on the face to indicate when the note was issued and interest accrual commenced. The known dates are March 25 and April 14, 1864, but others were probably issued. These were issued two ways: (1) they were sold at a discount to reflect the interest and were redeemed at face value upon maturity, or (2) they were sold at face value with redeemable coupons for the interest attached. Each style has slightly different printing.

The back features ornate green engraving with the obligation statement at the left and the counterfeiting clause at the right, both near the center.

MARCH 3, 1863, 5% INTEREST, 2 YEARS

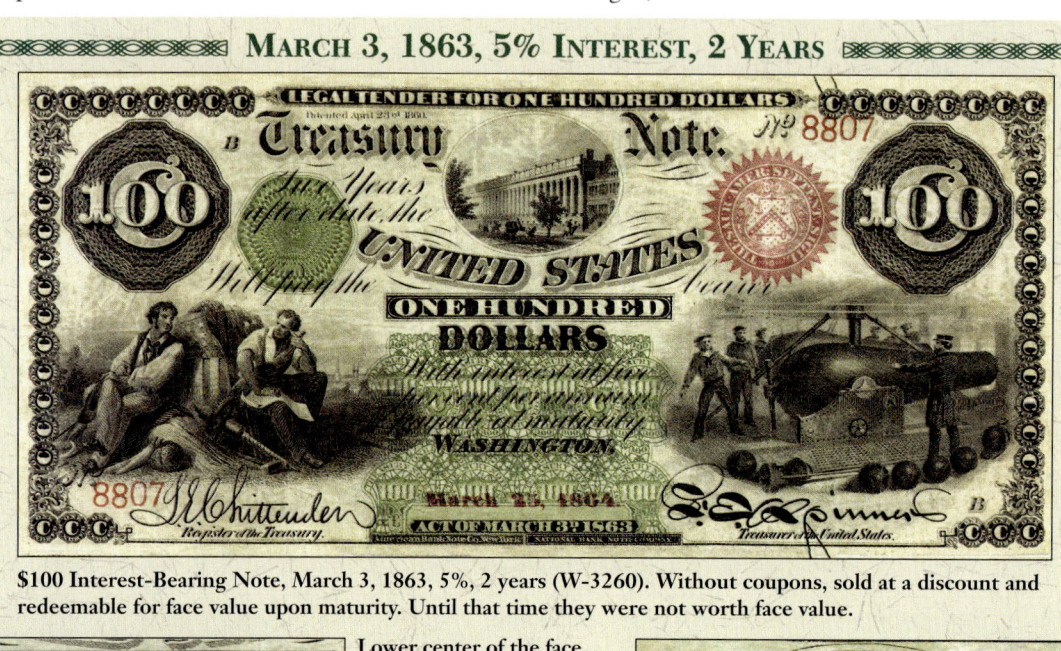

$100 Interest-Bearing Note, March 3, 1863, 5%, 2 years (W-3260). Without coupons, sold at a discount and redeemable for face value upon maturity. Until that time they were not worth face value.

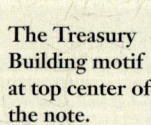

Lower center of the face of the note showing green cycloidal security printing and the red overprint issue date.

The Treasury Building motif at top center of the note.

Back of the same note. To the left and right of the center are the obligation statement and counterfeiting clause.

W-3260 • F-204 • Chittenden-Spinner (1861–1864) • Payable at maturity • 96,800

Recorded population: 2 • Highest graded: VF-35 • Commentary: Red overprint issue date varies. • *Selected information:* The known examples are serials 8807/B, VF–EF, sold in a CAA auction (2/2005) for $299,000, and 18114/A, F, part of the Smithsonian Institution collection.

W-3265 • F-204 • Payable semi-annually; issued with three coupons • 144,844

Commentary: Red overprint issue date varies. No circulation issues located, but proof impressions are known.

June 30, 1864, 7.3% Interest, 3 Years

A portrait of General Winfield Scott, facing to the viewer's right, is at the center, flanked by C counters. Denomination counters are in each corner, with the roman numeral C printed near the counters at the upper left and right corners. TREASURY DEPARTMENT is imprinted at the bottom border. Vertically at the right border is information about the five coupons issued with these notes.

The back is covered with ornate green printing and engraving. The redemption provision on the back allows the holder to receive, at his or her option, payment in 20-year

$100 Interest-Bearing Note, June 30, 1864, 7.3%, 3 years (W-3280). Printed date of August 15, 1864. At the center of this particular note is the inked inscription, "Secretary of the Treasury for redemption." Plate C2, serial 213729.

Detail of the bond purchase option on the back (image rotated 90 degrees).

Back of the same note. Provision is made for the signature of the assignee and for the option of converting the note to a bond with 6% interest payable semi-annually in coin.

bonds with interest payable in coin, after August 15, 1867 (see further comments under $50 notes of this issue).

W-3280 • F-212a • Colby-Spinner (1864–1867) • 566,039

Recorded population: 4 • Highest graded: EF-40 • Commentary: Printed dates vary but known examples include AUGUST 15, 1864, and MARCH 3, 1865. • *Selected information:* Heritage (9/2008), 84752/A, Net VF-20 (PMG), one coupon, $86,250. CAA (2/2005), 213729/C, VF–EF, $97,750. Knight (12/1998), 213731/B, EF, $49,500. Knight (6/2000), 250812/C, F, $35,750.

March 3, 1865, 7.3% Interest, 3 Years

Designs are similar to the preceding, but with differences in the inscriptions. Some have a vertical red overprint at the left end that reads, "The Government reserves the right of paying in COIN, the interest on this Note at the rate of six per cent. per annum." (This was a superfluous statement as coins were worth about twice as much as an equivalent amount in paper money at the time!) Issued with five coupons attached. All are convertible into 20-year bonds, per a notice on the back, with interest payable in coin (see description of the

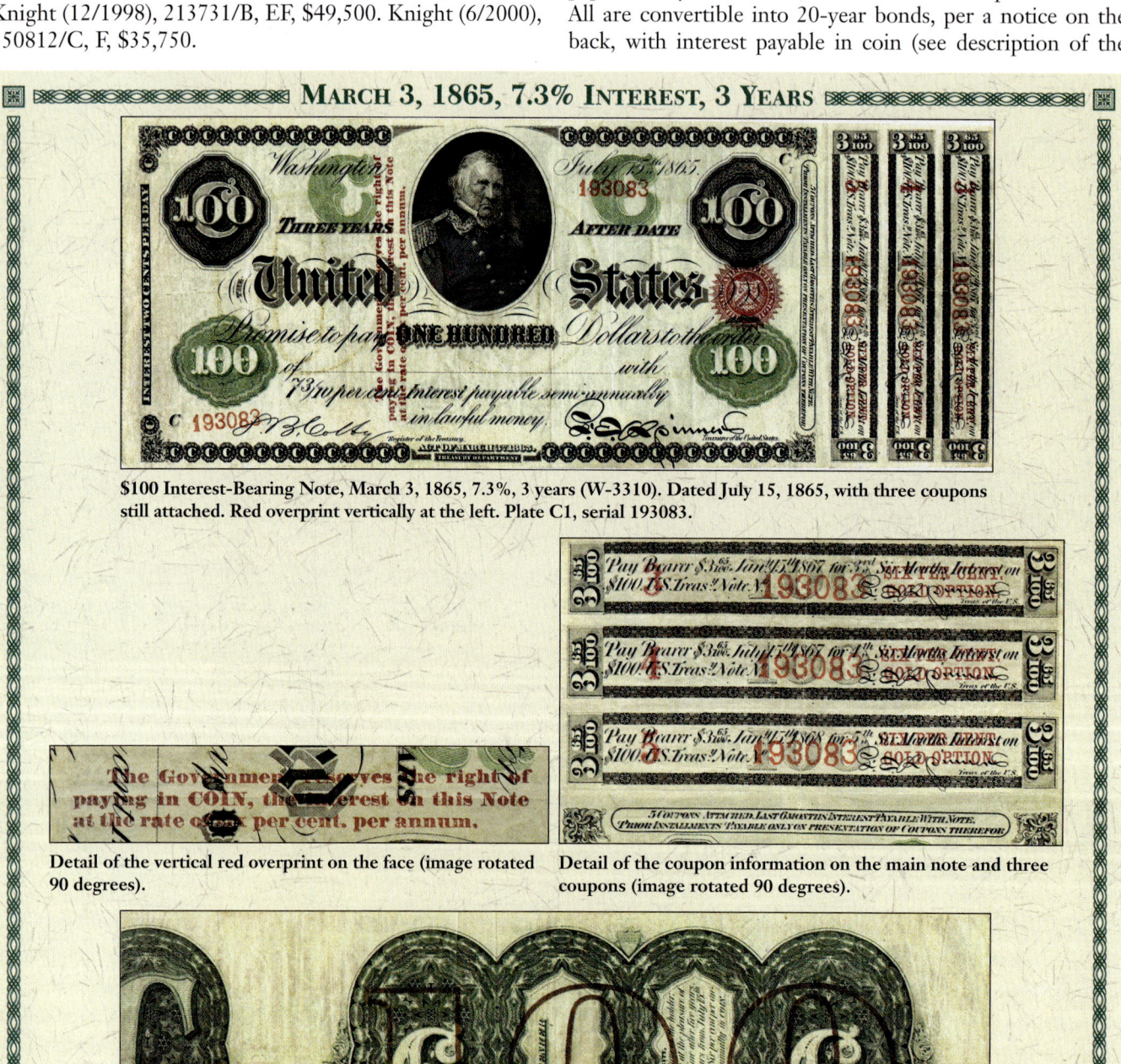

MARCH 3, 1865, 7.3% INTEREST, 3 YEARS

$100 Interest-Bearing Note, March 3, 1865, 7.3%, 3 years (W-3310). Dated July 15, 1865, with three coupons still attached. Red overprint vertically at the left. Plate C1, serial 193083.

Detail of the vertical red overprint on the face (image rotated 90 degrees).

Detail of the coupon information on the main note and three coupons (image rotated 90 degrees).

Back of the $100 Interest-Bearing Note, March 3, 1865, 7.3%, 3 years (W-3310), with large 100 surcharge applied in bronzing powder. The partial vignette to the left is the back side of the remaining three coupons. This note was convertible to bonds at redemption, at the option of the bearer.

related $50 note for details). Printed vertically at the left border is INTEREST TWO CENTS PER DAY. This easy conversion probably helped set the 7.3% interest rate on this and other related Interest-Bearing Notes. Either JUNE 15, 1865, or JULY 15, 1865, is printed at the upper right. All were issued with coupons.

The back of the notes with the June 15, 1865, date is the same as on the preceding type. The back of the July 15, 1865, note has a large counter overprinted in bronzing powder.

W-3300 • F-212e • Colby-Spinner (1864–1867) • *Printed on plate:* JUNE 15, 1865 • Blue serial numbers • 338,227

Recorded population: 1 • *Selected information:* The existing note is serial 272963/C, VF–EF, 1 coupon, part of the Smithsonian Institution collection.

W-3305 • F-unlisted • *Printed on plate:* JULY 15, 1865 • Red serial numbers • Without COIN overprint on face • 100 bronze overprint on back • Not confirmed

W-3310 • F-212e • With COIN overprint on face • 472,080

Recorded population: 2 • *Highest graded:* VF-20 • *Selected information:* The existing notes are serials 193083/C, VF–EF, 3 coupons attached, sold in a CAA auction (2/2005) for $207,000, and 194009/A G–VG, problems, 5 coupons, sold in a CAA auction (5/2003) for $143,750.

COMPOUND INTEREST TREASURY NOTES

The Compound Interest Treasury Notes were authorized under the Acts of March 3, 1863, and June 30, 1864. These bear the imprint TREASURY DEPARTMENT and were printed in the Treasury Building. Bronzing powder was applied as the first operation on blank sheets to create prominent bronze lettering on the face, considered to be a deterrent to counterfeiting. Regardless, these were very extensively counterfeited—so much so that in 1955 a numismatist identified several unrecognized fakes and observed that some experts said they might not have ever seen a genuine one. Counterfeits included those illustrated in popular references and other offerings.[4]

Although $100 notes were issued to the extent of over a half million examples, only about 300 are outstanding on the Treasury books today. Just a handful are known to collectors, and any example is considered to be a first-class rarity.

Series of 1863 and 1864

The $100 Compound Interest Treasury Notes (illus. on p. 632) bore interest at the rate of 6% per year, for three years. The face is similar in motifs to the one-year Interest-Bearing Notes of March 3, 1863, but with different typography and lacking the heavy green printing. A surcharge reading 100 COMPOUND INTEREST TREASURY NOTE is printed in bronzing powder. TREASURY DEPARTMENT is at the upper right. The highest-issued provable printage can be calculated by multiplying the highest-known serial number by four. These are slightly larger than Legal Tender Notes and measure about 3.5 inches by 7.5 inches.

Various red overprints of the dates of issue exist:

W-3350: The date June 10, 1864, has been seen, although others were probably issued.

W-3370: The date June 10, 1864, has been seen, although others were probably issued.

W-3390: The dates August 15 and December 15, 1864, and May 15, August 1, and September 1, 1865 have been seen, although these were issued regularly, and other dates were probably imprinted.

The back, in green, has an interest table that gives the value of the note for six-month periods up to three years after issue. These notes were popular investments for banks and well-to-do individuals who were attracted by the high interest rate.

W-3350 • F-193 • Chittenden-Spinner (1861–1864) • *Printed on plate:* ACT OF MARCH 3d 1863 • Red overprint: JUNE 10, 1864 • 450,944

Recorded population: 2 • *Highest graded:* VF-20 • *Commentary:* Other dates may have been printed. • *Selected information:* The known examples are serials 375/C, F, problems, sold in a Knight auction (6/2006) for $74,750, and 3545/C, VF, sold in a Kagin's auction (8/1977) for $11,000.

W-3370 • F-193a • *Printed on plate:* ACT OF JUNE 30th 1864 • Red overprint: JULY 15, 1864 • Part of W-3350 printage

Recorded population: 1 • *Commentary:* Other dates may have been printed. • *Selected information:* The existing example is serial 879/A, VF, repaired, sold in a CAA auction (2/2005) for $126,500.

W-3390 • F-193b • Colby-Spinner (1864–1867) • Part of W-3350 printage

Estimated population: 12 to 14 • *Highest graded:* EF-40 • *Commentary:* The red overprint features various dates.

VG-8	F-12	VF-20	EF-40
$35,000	—	—	—

LEGAL TENDER NOTES
(Also Known as United States Notes)

Series of 1862, First Obligation

$100 Legal Tender Notes of the Series of 1862 and 1863 (illus. on p. 633) have on the face the famous Spread Eagle motif, engraved by Joseph P. Ourdan, one of the boldest and most compelling designs on any currency of its era. His work was registered in 1862 by the National Currency Bureau, with a microprint (partially visible) attesting to this. The face, back, and tint plates for the $100 Series of 1862 and 1863 Legal Tender Notes were engraved by the National Bank Note Company. American and National shared the printing of notes for both obligations.[5] Treasury signatures of Chittenden and Spinner were printed on the face by using a separate plate and a special ink.

The $100 Series of 1862 notes are imprinted with NATIONAL BANK NOTE COMPANY at the top border and the 1860 patent date for the cycloidal configuration (similar imprints appear on the back). Three ornately

SERIES OF 1863 AND 1864

$100 Compound Interest Treasury Note (W-3390). Red overprint issue date of October 15, 1864, marking the commencement of interest accrual. Serial 4188, plate A.

Detail of the upper right of the face.

Detail of the interest schedule.

Back of the $100 Compound Interest Treasury Note (W-3390).

petaled kaleidograph counters are on the face, two in black and one in green. The word SERIES did not appear on the first run; these notes had the ABNCo monogram. Series 2 and later notes were numbered and did not have the monogram. A red serial number is at the lower right with the word NUMBER curved above it. All bear the address of the Treasury department in Washington, D.C. All have a small red Treasury seal (there are two varieties).

First Obligation: This wording, with different typography on various denominations, states the note is exchangeable for bonds (a provision dropped from the Second Obligation): "This note is a Legal Tender for all debts public and private, except duties on imports and interest on public debt, and is exchangeable for U.S. six percent twenty years' bonds, redeemable at the pleasure of the United States after five years."

Many contemporary counterfeits exist of this issue, and thus purchasing a verified note is essential.

W-3430 • F-165 • Chittenden-Spinner (1861–1864) •
Printed on plate: **ACT OF FEB. 25th 1862 / MARCH 10th**

SERIES OF 1862, FIRST OBLIGATION

$100 Legal Tender Note, Series of 1862 (W-3430), with Spread Eagle motif at left. Plate C, serial 47283.

Detail of the small ABNCo monogram at top left.

Detail of the SERIES 3 imprint on a W-3433 note; the 3 is distant to the right.

Detail of the First Obligation wording.

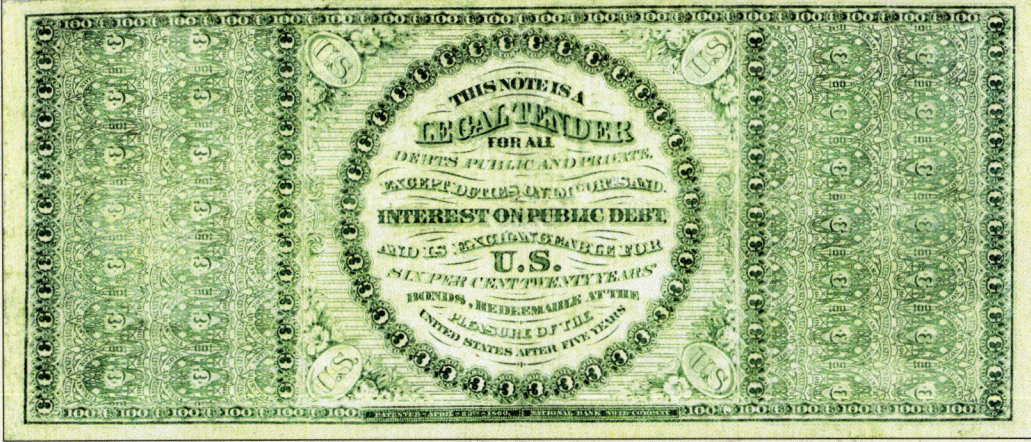

Back of the $100 Legal Tender Note, Series of 1862 (W-3430), with the First Obligation.

1862 • NATIONAL BANK NOTE COMPANY at top border • With ABNCo logotype at upper left border • No SERIES imprint • Treasury seal without inner border of radial parallel lines • 100,000 (est.)

Estimated population: 15 to 17 • *Highest graded:* Unc.

VG-8	F-12	VF-20	EF-40	AU-50	Unc-60
$18,000	$25,000	$45,000	—	—	—

W-3432 • F-165a • Without ABNCo. logotype • Series 2 • 35,000 (est.)

Estimated population: 12 to 14 • *Highest graded:* F-12.

VG-8	F-12
$18,000	$25,000

W-3433 • F-165a • Treasury seal with inner border of radial parallel lines • Series 2 to 3 • 155,000 (est.)

Estimated population: 12 to 14 • *Highest graded:* F-12.

VG-8	F-12
$18,000	$25,000

Series of 1862 and 1863, Second Obligation

The face is the same design as the preceding. The NEW SERIES imprint is on each, followed by a plate number, as on all Second Obligation notes. Each has a small red or pink Treasury seal with a spiked border, the style with radial lines at the inner border.

Second Obligation: "This note is a Legal Tender for all debts public and private, except duties on imports and interest on public debt, and is receivable in payment of all loans made to the United States." This wording, with different typography on the various denominations, does not mention exchanging the notes for 6-20 bonds and thus is different from the First Obligation.

All have ACT OF MARCH 3d 1863 and MARCH 10th 1863 on the plate. All have printed Chittenden-Spinner signatures. There were no $100 Legal Tender Notes printed between October 1863 and November 1868. When printing resumed, two serial numbers were used instead of just one.

W-3434 • F-167b • Chittenden-Spinner (1861–1864) • *Printed on plate:* ACT OF MARCH 3d 1863 / MARCH 10th 1863 • NATIONAL BANK NOTE COMPANY • One serial number • Second Obligation back • New Series 1 • 24,000

Recorded population: 2 • *Selected information:* The known examples are serials 31982/B, VG–F, and 44662/B, VF-25 (PCGS), sold in a CAA auction (9/2006) for $276,000.

W-3435 • F-167 • NATIONAL BANK NOTE COMPANY in the top border and AMERICAN BANK NOTE CO. N.Y. below the top border • 29,440

Recorded population: 2 • *Highest graded:* EF-40 • *Selected information:* The known examples are serials 37284/D, F, owned by the Federal Reserve Bank of San Francisco, and 50986/B, EF, part of the Smithsonian Institution collection.

SERIES OF 1862 AND 1863, SECOND OBLIGATION

$100 Legal Tender Note, Series of 1863 (W-3435). Imprinted NEW SERIES 1, plate B, serial 50986. One serial number. National and American bank-note company imprints.

Face of another variety, W-3436. Imprinted NEW SERIES 1, plate C, serial 92055. Later style with two serial numbers. These were made beginning in 1868.

W-3436 • F-167a • NATIONAL BANK NOTE COMPANY • Two serial numbers • New Series 1 to 2 • 56,560

Estimated population: 27 to 30 • *Highest graded:* Unc • *Commentary:* There were no $100 Legal Tender Notes printed between October 1863 and November 1868; after this double serial numbers commenced.

VG-8	F-12	VF-20	EF-40	AU-50	Unc-60	Unc-63	Unc-65
$12,000	$20,000	$32,500	$55,000	$100,000	$150,000	$200,000	$250,000

Series of 1869

At the upper left of the face (illus. on p. 636) is a portrait of Lincoln, engraved by Charles Burt from a photograph taken by Anthony Berger (of Mathew A. Brady's studio) on February 9, 1864. At the lower center is Miss Liberty wearing a Phrygian cap, a motif also used by the Philadelphia Mint in 1869 as part of the Standard Silver pattern series (where she is depicted in profile). At the lower right the vignette *Reconstruction* shows a woman with a carpenter's square and a child holding a scroll on which the emblems include a pergola. This motif does not logically fit with the use of Lincoln's portrait, as the Great Emancipator was dead by the time that reconstruction of the South began. An immense pink Treasury seal, bright red serial numbers beginning with W and ending with an ornamental star suffix, and blue-tinted paper (Willcox patent of 1866) give the note an attractive appearance.

The back is printed in green, signed AMERICAN BANK NOTE COMPANY, NEW YORK twice, and has at the center the obligation statement and the counterfeiting clause. As a class, Series of 1869 notes were issued from October 19, 1869, to July 25, 1874.

W-3480 • F-168 • Allison-Spinner (1869–1875) • Large red seal • 364,000

Estimated population: 30 to 33 • *Highest graded:* Unc.

VG-8	F-12	VF-20	EF-40	AU-50	Unc-60	Unc-63
$12,500	$22,500	$30,000	$55,000	$85,000	$125,000	$175,000

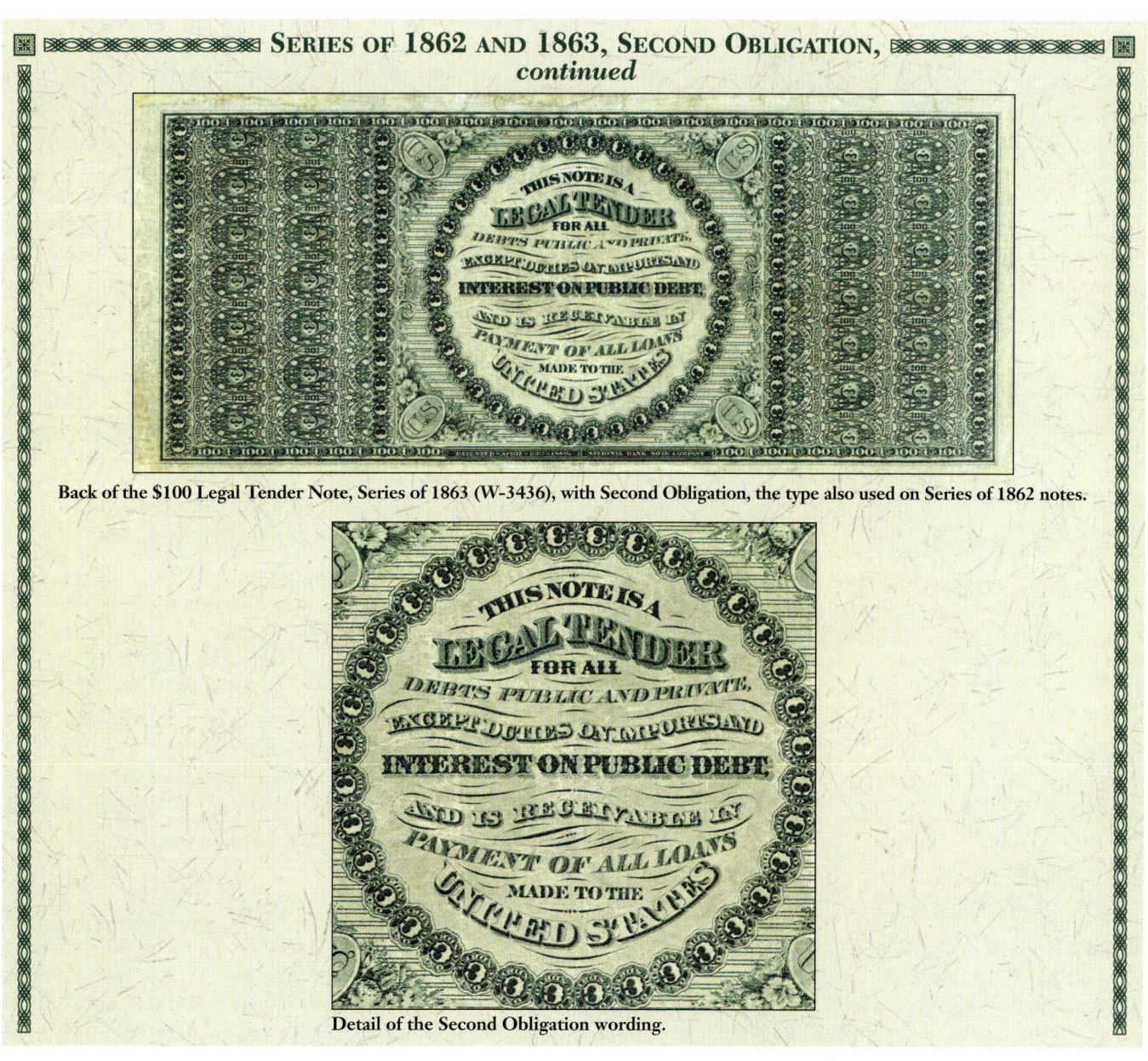

SERIES OF 1862 AND 1863, SECOND OBLIGATION, *continued*

Back of the $100 Legal Tender Note, Series of 1863 (W-3436), with Second Obligation, the type also used on Series of 1862 notes.

Detail of the Second Obligation wording.

SERIES OF 1869

$100 Legal Tender Note, Series of 1869 (W-3480). Serial numbers in red. Printed on special paper with a blue-tinted streak, used on other denominations in this series. The star at the serial number is an ornament. Plate C2, serial W266223.

Detail showing lady with a Phrygian cap at the lower center of the face.

Back of the $100 Legal Tender Note, Series of 1869 (W-3480).

Series of 1875

The faces of the Series of 1875 and Series of 1880 notes have the same basic motifs as the Series of 1869, with Lincoln, a Liberty head, and *Reconstruction*. A decorative pink overprint has been added to the top of the face, and there are other differences. A Maltese cross ornament follows the serial numbers instead of a star. The back has the imprint of the Columbian Bank Note Company. As a class, Series of 1875 notes were issued from July 20, 1875, to June 20, 1879.

W-3481 • F-169 • Allison-New (1875–1876) • SERIES A 1875 imprint in pink • Small red seal with spiked border • 122,000

Estimated population: 13 to 15 • *Highest graded:* Unc.

VG-8	F-12	VF-20	EF-40	AU-50	Unc-60
$10,000	$17,500	$22,500	$50,000	—	—

W-3482 • F-170 • Allison-Wyman (1876–1877) • 40,000

Recorded population: 6 • *Highest graded:* EF-45 • *Selected information:* The known examples include serials A129719/C, EF, owned by the Federal Reserve Bank of Chicago; A140313/A, F–VF; A143371/C, VF-25 (PCGS), sold in a Knight auction

(10/2005) for $27,600; A144963/C, VG, damaged; A145382/B, part of the ANA Museum collection; and A148668/D, F, sold in a Knight auction (3/2007) for $39,100.

Series of 1878

On Series of 1878 notes (illus. on p. 638) PRINTED AT THE BUREAU ENGRAVING AND PRINTING is added to the imprint of the Columbian Bank Note Company.

W-3483 • F-171 • Allison-Gilfillan (1877–1878) • Small red seal with spiked border • 202,000

Estimated population: 22 to 25 • *Highest graded:* Unc.

VG-8	F-12	VF-20	EF-40	AU-50	Unc-60
$7,500	$15,000	$20,000	$30,000	$40,000	—

Series of 1880

The designs (illus. on p. 638) are the same as the preceding. W-3484 and W-3485 have the Columbian Bank Note Company imprint on the back, as used for the Series of 1878. Beginning with W-3486 the Bureau of Engraving and Printing imprint is used.

SERIES OF 1875

$100 Legal Tender Note, Series of 1875 (W-3482). The vignettes are similar to the preceding. Now with UNITED STATES NOTE at bottom border. Treasury imprint in vertical line at left border. Serial numbers in blue. Light pink floral design above UNITED STATES.

Detail of the serial number and micro-print of the Casilear patent date.

Back of the $100 Legal Tender Note, Series of 1875 (W-3482). The type also used on Series of 1878 $100 Legal Tender Notes.

W-3484 • F-172 • Bruce-Gilfillan (1881–1883) • Large brown seal • 60,000

Estimated population: 12 to 14 • *Highest graded:* Unc.

VG-8	F-12	VF-20	EF-40	AU-50	Unc-60	Unc-63	Unc-65
$7,500	$15,000	$20,000	$25,000	$40,000	$60,000	$75,000	$100,000

W-3485 • F-173 • Bruce-Wyman (1883–1885) • 80,000

Estimated population: 10 to 12 • *Highest graded:* EF-45 • *Selected information:* B&M (3/2007), 82880/D, F-12 (PMG), $26,450. Heritage (9/2007), Z96481/A, F-15, repaired (PMG), $25,300. Knight (10/2005), Z115805/A, VG–F, pinholes, $17,250. Knight (11/2005) Z123872/D, Fine, $13,800. Knight (6/2006), Z124178/B, VF–EF, $19,550.

W-3486 • F-174 • Rosecrans-Jordan (1885–1887) • Large red seal with plain border • 80,000

Estimated population: 20 to 23 • *Highest graded:* Unc.

VG-8	F-12	VF-20	EF-40	AU-50	Unc-60
$5,000	$10,000	$17,500	$30,000	$45,000	$60,000

W-3487 • F-175 • Rosecrans-Hyatt (1887–1889) • 20,000

Recorded population: 2 • *Highest graded:* VF-20 • *Selected information:* Known examples are serials A81122/B, F, owned by the Federal Reserve Bank of San Francisco, and A81780/D, VF, part of the Smithsonian Institution collection.

W-3488 • F-176 • Large red seal with spiked border • 80,000

Estimated population: 12 to 14 • *Highest graded:* AU-58.

F-12	VF-20	EF-40	AU-50
$15,000	$25,000	$42,500	$60,000

SERIES OF 1878

$100 Legal Tender Note, Series of 1878 (W-3483). The back is the same as that used on Series of 1875 $100 Legal Tender Notes. (ANA Edward C. Rochette Money Museum)

Detail of the back showing the addition of the bureau imprint.

SERIES OF 1880

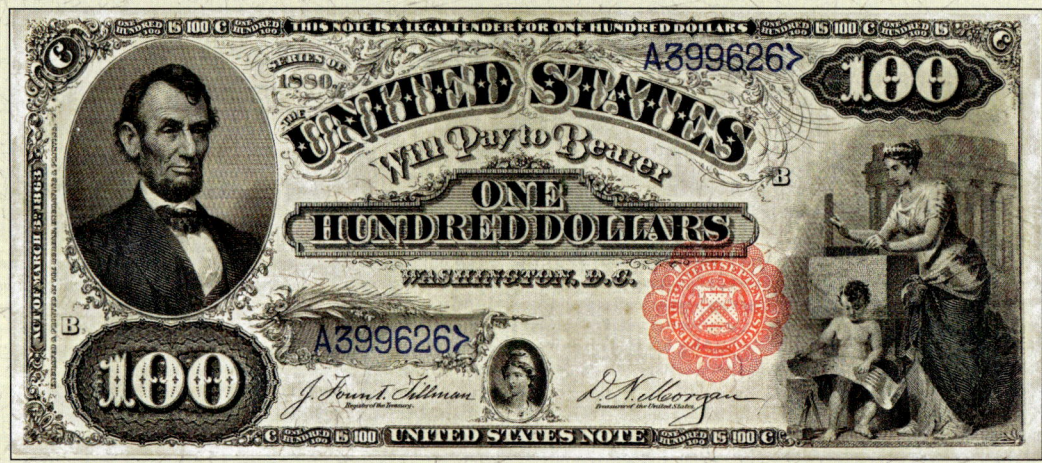

$100 Legal Tender Note, Series of 1880 (W-3491).

Back of the $100 Legal Tender Note, Series of 1880 (W-3491).

W-3489 • F-177 • Rosecrans-Huston (1889–1891) • 80,000

Estimated population: 23 to 26 • *Highest graded:* AU-50.

VG-8	F-12	VF-20	EF-40	AU-50
$5,000	$10,000	$17,500	$25,000	$40,000

W-3490 • F-178 • Large brown seal • 60,000

Estimated population: 18 to 20 • *Highest graded:* Unc.

VG-8	F-12	VF-20	EF-40	AU-50	Unc-60	Unc-63
$6,000	$12,000	$17,500	$32,500	$50,000	$60,000	$75,000

W-3491 • F-179 • Tillman-Morgan (1893–1897) • Small red seal with scalloped border • 172,000

Estimated population: 30 to 35 • *Highest graded:* Unc.

VG-8	F-12	VF-20	EF-40	AU-50	Unc-60	Unc-63
$6,000	$12,000	$17,500	$25,000	$40,000	$60,000	$75,000

W-3492 • F-180 • Bruce-Roberts (1897–1898) • 28,000

Recorded population: 7 • *Highest graded:* EF-40 • *Selected information:* The known examples include serials A492892/D, F+, owned by the Federal Reserve Bank of Richmond; A494598/B, VF, sold in a Knight auction (6/2007) for $36,800; A498033/A, VG, pinholes, sold in a Knight auction (3/2007) for $18,400; A505347/C, F, owned by the Federal Reserve Bank of San Francisco; A510188/D, part of the ANA Museum collection; A514055/C, EF, pinholes, sold in a Spink America auction (5/1995) for $14,300; and A514134/B, G, damaged.

W-3493 • F-181 • Lyons-Roberts (1898–1905) • 176,000

Estimated population: 60 to 70 • *Highest graded:* Unc.

VG-8	F-12	VF-20	EF-40	AU-50	Unc-60	Unc-63
$4,000	$7,500	$12,500	$25,000	$40,000	$60,000	$75,000

W-3494 • F-182 • Napier-McClung (1911–1912) • No evidence of printing[6]

NATIONAL BANK NOTES

Most specialists in National Bank Notes consider themselves fortunate to have a type collection of $100 bills in this class. These notes cannot be systematically collected with any effectiveness, as just about all 19th-century issues range from very rare to extremely rare, and those of the early 20th century are elusive. The Value Back issues are classic rarities, seldom encountered even in the largest collections, as only a few are known. During their time in circulation very few citizens opted to hold them long-term, as gold coins were considered to be of more secure value.

Original Series
(Authorized Issue 1863 to 1875)

The $100 notes (illus. on p. 640) were printed by the American Bank Note Company, whose imprint appears at the bottom border. The contract, dated July 20, 1863, specified the designs for each side of the $20, $50, and $100 denominations and other matters.[7] These were usually printed in two-subject sheets of $50-$100, with plate letter A for each denomination, although there were other sheet layouts. All have a small red Treasury seal with a spiked border. On some early notes the Treasury serial number at the upper right is in blue (most are in red), while on all notes, the bank serial number at the lower left is in red. The Act of June 20, 1874, provided for the imprinting of the bank's charter number. This was done in red ink, one number vertically to the left of center and the other horizontally on the right.

The $100 National Bank Notes of both the Original Series and Series of 1875 depict on the face the vignette *Commodore Perry's Victory* (official title: *A Scene From the Battle of Lake Erie*, but given in the ABNCo contract as *Battle of Lake Erie*) to the left, a scene from the War of 1812, and *The Union*, at the right. The last is dated 1787 (date of the Constitution) and depicts a seated winged figure near a fasces inscribed THE UNION, with the words MAINTAIN IT nearby.

At the center of the back is a panorama of the painting by John Trumbull, *The Declaration of Independence*, engraved by John Girsch. Under the title is printed in tiny letters "Eng'd by the American Bank Note Co. N.Y." This motif was used elsewhere, including a slightly trimmed version (without credit given to ABNCo.) on the modern $2 Federal Reserve Notes. Below the image is the counterfeiting clause. To the left is the seal representing the location of the bank of issue, and to the right is a perched eagle. On the left side is a state seal representing the issuing location of the bank, and to the right is an eagle (on some notes issued in territories, an eagle is at both ends).

Any note is a landmark rarity. Finding a nice note for type from any state is an accomplishment. Very Good to Fine is the average grade in the Kelly census (see below), with Very Fine–Extremely Fine the highest observed, and just one at that level.

Banks of Issue and Rarity of Notes

Based upon census information from Don C. Kelly and James M. Kelly (*National Bank Note Census*, Version 4.0) and with some information from other sources, this listing gives each location, the number of banks issuing this series of notes within each, and a commentary.[8]

The Kelly survey records only 21 Original Series $100 notes, each one a numismatic icon. There are no Uncirculated or serial number 1 notes, although, as in many cases, data reported are incomplete.

Alabama • 4 banks of issue • No notes reported.

Colorado Territory • 1 bank of issue • No notes reported.

Connecticut • 40 banks of issue • 1 note reported • Aetna National Bank of Hartford (VG).

Delaware • 4 banks of issue • No notes reported.

District of Columbia • 5 banks of issue • No notes reported.

Georgia • 5 banks of issue • No notes reported.

Illinois • 8 banks of issue • No notes reported.

Indiana • 18 banks of issue • No notes reported.

Iowa • 5 banks of issue • No notes reported.

Kentucky • 18 banks of issue • No notes reported.

Louisiana • 7 banks of issue • No notes reported.

Maine • 22 banks of issue • No notes reported.

Maryland • 18 banks of issue • No notes reported.

Massachusetts • 180 banks of issue • 6 notes reported[9] • Circulated grades from as many banks.

Michigan • 3 banks of issue • No notes reported.

Minnesota • 3 banks of issue • No notes reported.

Missouri • 3 banks of issue • No notes reported.

Montana Territory • 1 bank of issue • No notes reported.

New Hampshire • 19 banks of issue • No notes reported.

New Jersey • 25 banks of issue • No notes reported.

New York • 81 banks of issue • 6 notes reported[10] • Circulated notes from five banks.

North Carolina • 1 bank of issue • 1 note reported • Raleigh National Bank of North Carolina (VF–EF).

Ohio • 13 banks of issue • 1 note reported[11] • First National Bank of Cincinnati (VG).

Pennsylvania • 73 banks of issue • 4 notes reported • Circulated notes from as many banks.

Rhode Island • 40 banks of issue • No notes reported.

South Carolina • 3 banks of issue • No notes reported.

Tennessee • 8 banks of issue • No notes reported.

Texas • 3 banks of issue • 1 note reported • National Bank of Jefferson (F).

Utah Territory • 3 banks of issue • No notes reported.

Vermont • 14 banks of issue • No notes reported.

Virginia • 6 banks of issue • No notes reported.

Wisconsin • 1 bank of issue • No notes reported.

Generic prices for a typical note:

VG-8	F-12	VF-20	EF-40
$20,000	$30,000	$45,000	$65,000

W-3500 • F-452 • Chittenden-Spinner (1861–1864)

Recorded population: 4 • *Highest graded:* VG-10 • *Selected information:* Hickman & Oakes (4/1976), 423466/A, Bunker Hill NB of Charlestown, MA, VG, problems, $1,575. Spink (7/2007), 6913-173452/A, Fourth NB of the City of New York, NY, VG, $24,350. CAA (1/2004), 2928-N15855/B, First NB of Cincinnati, OH, F, pinholes, $12,075.

W-3501 • F-454 • Colby-Spinner (1864–1867)

Estimated population: 16 to 18 • *Highest graded:* EF.

VG-8	F-12	VF-20	EF-40
$20,000	$30,000	$45,000	$65,000

$100 National Bank Note, Original Series (W-3500). First National Bank of Cincinnati, Ohio, charter 24. Any note is a great rarity.

Back of the $100 National Bank Note, Original Series (W-3500). To the left is the seal of Ohio, reflecting the location of the bank.

W-3502 • F-455 • Allison-Spinner (1869–1875)

Recorded population: 3 • *Highest graded:* VF-20 • *Selected information:* B&M (5/1999), 1105-558957/A, NB of Jefferson, TX (only extant note on the bank), F, damaged, $62,100.

National Gold Bank Notes, Original Series

National Gold Bank $100 bills were issued in California by institutions in Oakland, Petaluma, Sacramento, San Jose, San Francisco, Santa Barbara, and Stockton. Although slightly over 5,000 notes were issued, just 84 are outstanding on Treasury books, and only seven Original Series and two Series of 1875 notes are recorded in the Kelly census today. The highest grade is Very Good.

The Kidder National Gold Bank of Boston was the first such institution chartered. On March 11, 1871, the Treasury sent 50 sheets of $50-$100 notes. None were ever paid out. On December 4, 1871, all were returned to the Treasury department.[12] These notes are styled differently from the others, with NATIONAL GOLD NOTE at the top margin and GOLD in drop-out white letters above the center.

W-3510 • F-1162 • Dated 1870 • San Francisco • First National Gold Bank • 2,000

Recorded population: 3 • *Highest graded:* VG-8 • *Selected information:* Stack's (5/1997), 929-317584/A, G–VG, pressed, $26,400. Knight (undated fixed-price list), 1260-321148/A, G–VG, $14,000. Bluestone/Grinnell (3/1945), 555-321443/A, VG, Fine, $225.

W-3512 • F-1166-II • Dated 1872 • Sacramento • National Gold Bank of D.O. Mills & Co. • 604 • Unknown

W-3514 • F-1166-I • San Francisco • National Gold Bank and Trust Co. • 2,856 • Unknown

W-3516 • F-1164 • Dated 1873 • Santa Barbara • First National Gold Bank • 200

Recorded population: 1 • *Selected information:* The known example is serial 188-375737/A, VG, pinholes, sold in a Stack's auction (10/1990) for $25,300; later seen in Knight (6/2001), part of a larger lot that sold for $231,000.

W-3518 • F-1166 • Dated 1873 • Stockton • First National Gold Bank • 867 • Unknown

W-3520 • F-1165 • Dated 1874 • Petaluma • First National Gold Bank • 400

Recorded population: 2 • *Highest graded:* F-12 • *Selected information:* Stack's (10/1988), 119-476000/A, Fair (but once

NATIONAL GOLD BANK NOTES, ORIGINAL SERIES

$100 National Gold Bank Note, Original Series (W-3510). First National Gold Bank of San Francisco, the most prolific issuer of notes of this type, across the various denominations. Red Treasury seal with spikes.

Back of a $100 National Gold Bank Note, with the same montage of gold coins as on other denominations of National Gold Bank Notes.

graded G–VG), $7,150; later seen in Knight (12/1998), $25,300; later seen in CAA (5/2005), $97,750. B&R (11/1973), 209-497894/A, F, on white paper, $10,500.

W-3522 • F-1166-IV • San Jose • Farmers National Gold Bank • 400 • Unknown

W-3524 • F-1166 • Dated 1875 (but Original Series) • Oakland • Union National Gold Bank • 100

Recorded population: 1 • Graded: *Selected information:* The known example is serial 8-579587/A, ex Grinnell (3/1945) as Fair; later seen in Kagin's (8/1977), $18,000; now graded VG.

W-3526 • F-unlisted • Dated 1870 • Boston • Kidder National Gold Bank • 50 • None issued

Series of 1875
(Authorized Issue 1875 to 1902)

This series continued the use of plates signed by American Bank Note Company. Under the top border at the upper right is PRINTED AT THE BUREAU OF ENGRAVING & PRINTING, U.S. TREASURY DEPT. For some banks for which there had been no Original Series plates made, the Bureau made new plates with BUREAU OF ENGRAVING & PRINTING TREASURY DEPt. at the bottom border, and no additional imprint or mention of the American Bank Note Company. These are exceedingly rare.

The small red Treasury seal now has a scalloped rather than a spiked border. All have SERIES 1875 imprinted vertically in red to the left of center, near the bank charter number. The Treasury and bank serial numbers and two charter numbers are also in red. A small percentage of these notes are printed on paper with a vertical, blue-tinted streak of the type most familiarly used on the Legal Tender Notes beginning with the Series of 1869 (paper made under the James M. Willcox patent of July 24, 1866). These are especially colorful and attractive.

The average grade is higher than on the typical Original Series note, with classifications such as Very Fine and Extremely Fine being more in evidence. All notes are rare, but not in the category of the Original Series issues.

Banks of Issue and Rarity of Notes

Based upon census information from Don C. Kelly and James M. Kelly (*National Bank Note Census*, Version 4.0) and with some information from other sources, this listing gives each location, the number of banks issuing this series of notes within each, and a commentary.[13]

The Kelly survey records 51 $100 notes of the Series of 1875, or about two and a half times the listed Original Series $100 notes. Just one note is graded Uncirculated, from Massachusetts, and only one serial number 1 note is known, from Illinois.

Alabama • 4 banks of issue • 2 notes reported • City National Bank of Selma (one EF, one not graded).

Arkansas • 1 bank of issue • No notes reported.

California • 1 bank of issue • No notes reported.

Colorado • 1 bank of issue • No notes reported.

Colorado Territory • 1 bank of issue • No notes reported.

Connecticut • 25 banks of issue • 2 notes reported • New Haven County National Bank and Yale National Bank, both of New Haven and both VF.

Delaware • 3 banks of issue • No notes reported.

Georgia • 4 banks of issue • No notes reported.

Illinois • 8 banks of issue • 2 notes reported • First National Bank of Lincoln (serial 1, AU) and Streator National Bank (VG–F).

Indiana • 12 banks of issue • 1 note reported • First National Bank of Madison (F–VF).

Iowa • 5 banks of issue • 1 note reported • Des Moines National Bank (EF).

Kansas • 1 bank of issue • No notes reported.

Kentucky • 18 banks of issue • No notes reported.

Louisiana • 5 banks of issue • 1 note reported • Louisiana National Bank of New Orleans (F).

Maine • 16 banks of issue • 1 note reported • Union National Bank of Brunswick (VF–EF).

Maryland • 16 banks of issue • 2 notes reported • First National Bank of Baltimore (VG) and National Bank of Baltimore (AU).

Massachusetts • 125 banks of issue • 4 notes reported • Blackstone National Bank of Boston (F, Unc), National Eagle Bank of Boston (F), and the National Market Bank of Brighton (VG).

Michigan • 3 banks of issue • No notes reported.

Minnesota • 2 banks of issue • No notes reported.

Mississippi • 1 bank of issue • No notes reported.

Missouri • 2 banks of issue • No notes reported.

Nebraska • 2 banks of issue • No notes reported.

New Hampshire • 6 banks of issue • No notes reported.

New Jersey • 14 banks of issue • No notes reported.

New York • 63 banks of issue • 12 notes reported • The census lists 11 circulated and one Unc, the latter from the Garfield National Bank of the City of New York.

Ohio • 17 banks of issue • 11 notes reported • Circulated notes from six banks.

Pennsylvania • 70 banks of issue • 9 notes reported • Circulated notes from six banks.[14]

Rhode Island • 19 banks of issue • 1 note reported • Fifth National Bank of Providence (VF).

South Carolina • 3 banks of issue • 1 note reported • First National Bank of Charleston (VF).

Tennessee • 5 banks of issue • No notes reported.

Texas • 2 banks of issue • No notes reported.

Utah Territory • 1 bank of issue • 1 note reported • Deseret National Bank of Salt Lake City (F).

Vermont • 9 banks of issue • No notes reported.

Virginia • 4 banks of issue • No notes reported.

Wisconsin • 1 bank of issue • No notes reported.

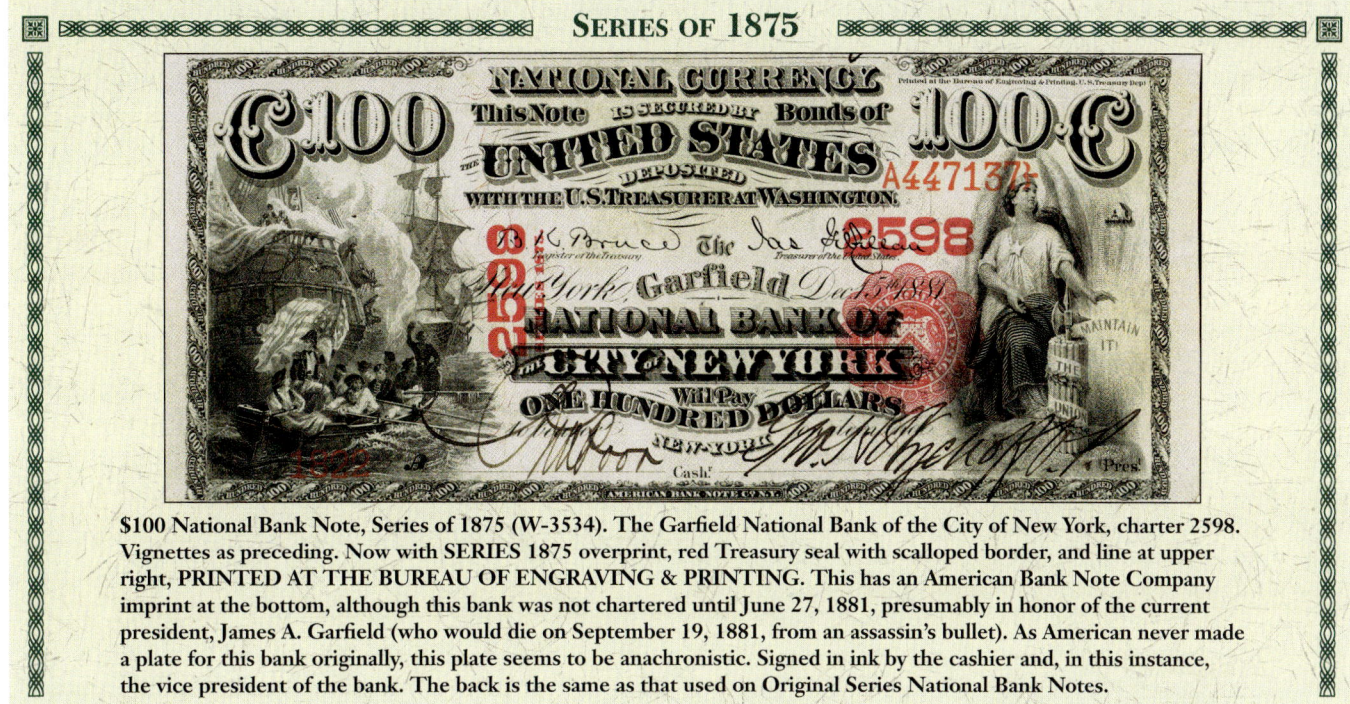

SERIES OF 1875

$100 National Bank Note, Series of 1875 (W-3534). The Garfield National Bank of the City of New York, charter 2598. Vignettes as preceding. Now with SERIES 1875 overprint, red Treasury seal with scalloped border, and line at upper right, PRINTED AT THE BUREAU OF ENGRAVING & PRINTING. This has an American Bank Note Company imprint at the bottom, although this bank was not chartered until June 27, 1881, presumably in honor of the current president, James A. Garfield (who would die on September 19, 1881, from an assassin's bullet). As American never made a plate for this bank originally, this plate seems to be anachronistic. Signed in ink by the cashier and, in this instance, the vice president of the bank. The back is the same as that used on Original Series National Bank Notes.

Generic prices for a typical note from a state from which several or more exist:

VG-8	F-12	VF-20	EF-40
$20,000	$30,000	$45,000	$65,000

W-3530 • F-456 • Allison-New (1875–1876)

Estimated population: 16 to 18 • *Highest graded:* EF-40.

VG-8	F-12	VF-20	EF-40
$20,000	$30,000	$45,000	$65,000

W-3531 • F-457 • Allison-Wyman (1876–1877)

Recorded population: 7 • *Highest graded:* VF-25 • *Selected information:* Kreisberg & Schulman (3/1965), A405020, Yale NB of New Haven, CT, VF, $1,100. Knight (2/1995), 147-A83631/A, First NB of Madison, IN, F–VF, $7,150. Smythe (11/2001), 2259-A134001/A, N Broadway Bank, New York, NY, F, problems, $10,560.

W-3532 • F-458 • Allison-Gilfillan (1877–1878)

Recorded population: 4 • *Highest graded:* VF-25 • *Selected information:* Smythe (11/2001), 7325-A106055/A, Metropolitan NB of New York, NY, Fine, $6,875. CAA (1/2003), 12478-A111832/A, Metropolitan NB of New York, NY, F, $10,063. CAA (5/2000), 418-1362/NY/A91477/A, Flour City NB of Rochester, NY, F, $10,450.

W-3533 • F-459 • Scofield-Gilfillan (1878–1881)

Estimated population: 9 or 10 • *Highest graded:* EF-40 • *Selected information:* Hickman & Oakes (6/1985), 355-A175245/A, N Eagle B of Boston, MA, F, $2,840. Knight (6/1999), 8754-A441914/A, United States NB of New York, NY, VF, $28,600. Knight (10/1991), 2-A449561/A, Merchants NB of Philadelphia, PA (low serial), EF, $7,500. Stack's (5/1997), 414-A358988/A, Fifth NB of Providence, RI, F–VF, pinholes, $5,720.

W-3534 • F-460 • Bruce-Gilfillan (1881–1883)

Recorded population: 7 • *Highest graded:* Unc • *Selected information:* CAA (9/2000), 213-A457391/A, Des Moines NB, IA, EF, $60,500. Spink (7/2007), 439-A295187/A, NB of Commerce in New York, NY, F–VF, problems, $46,200. CAA (6/1994), 233-A9459/B, Metropolitan NB of Cincinnati, OH, AU, $18,150. Smythe (6/2001), 2434-A9160/B, Third NB of Cincinnati, OH, Fair, problems, $1,320.

W-3535 • F-461 • Bruce-Wyman (1883–1885)

Recorded population: 3 • *Highest graded:* EF-40 • *Selected information:* Stack's (3/1989), 33-A405507/A, N New Haven County B of New Haven, CT, VF, pinholes, $2,800. Knight (11/2004), 1948-A43747/A, N LaFayette B of Commerce, Cincinnati, OH, AU, damaged, $4,830. Knight (11/1999), 3029-A444732/A, N LaFayette B of Commerce, Cincinnati, OH, F, pinholes, $12,100.

W-3536 • F-462 • Rosecrans-Huston (1889–1891)

Recorded population: 1 • *Selected information:* CAA (9/2000), 1-A430837/A, First NB of Lincoln, IL (serial number 1), AU, $121,000.

W-3537 • F-462a • Rosecrans-Nebeker (1891–1893)

Recorded population: 1 • *Graded:* Fine.

W-3538 • F-463 • Tillman-Morgan (1893–1897)

Recorded population: 4 • *Highest graded:* VF-25 • *Selected information:* Stack's (9/1996), 153-A452467/A, Citizens NB of Zanesville, OH, F–VF, $4,400. Stack's (5/1978), 227-A452541/A, Citizens NB of Zanesville, OH, VF, pinholes, $5,750.

National Gold Bank Notes, Series of 1875

The First National Gold Bank of San Francisco was the only issuer of this series. The Kelly census records two examples today, in the remarkably high grades of Fine and Extremely Fine.

W-3540 • F-1163 • Dated 1870 • San Francisco • First National Gold Bank • 620

Recorded population: 2 • Selected information: The known examples are serials 232-A338893/A, EF, white paper, and 516-A354442/A, F, white paper, part of the ANA Museum collection.

Series of 1882, Brown Back
(Authorized Issue 1882 to 1908)

This series was the result of the expirations of the earliest national banks' charters and the formation of new chartered banks, as provided by the Act of July 11, 1882. By then the Bureau of Engraving had been printing notes for seven years.

To create distinctively new notes, the backs of the denominations from $10 to $100 were changed, though many of the face plates created by the American Bank Note Company for the Original Series and Series of 1875 were retained. This was accomplished either by leaving the American Bank Note Company imprint at the bottom of the face and adding a printed notice in the field that this was a BEP product, or by reentering the Bureau of Engraving and Printing name where the ABNCo. imprint had been. In other instances new plates were created using the old designs. The decorative border of the notes was changed to include the bank's charter number six times, said to have been useful if a fragment of a note was sent to the Treasury department for redemption. Plates were typically laid out as $50-$100, with plate letter A for each note. Charter numbers were overprinted in brown on the face from the outset, vertically to left of center on the $10 to $100 notes. The Treasury seal is in brown as well. Beginning in September 1890, the position was changed to horizontal at the upper right. Peter Huntoon states that fewer than 14% of the plates had the vertical position, and as these were earlier printings, an even smaller percentage survives today. Regional letters N, E, M, S, W, and P were overprinted twice in brown on the face of notes starting with shipments received on March 17, 1902.

The reverse was completely redesigned to create the Brown Back style printed in ink of that color. To the left is a state or territorial seal representing the issuing bank's location, as on earlier series. This necessitated making sets of plates for each state or territory. On the right is a perched eagle. At the center the bank's charter number was printed in large, greenish-blue figures, enabling the bills to be easily sorted when they were redeemed. These bills were first issued in 1882. Any bank with its charter extended from mid-1882 until the Series of 1902 bills were made, and any new bank chartered during that period, received notes of this type, and continued to receive them for up to 20 years, even though during that time the new Series of 1902 notes were introduced. Series of 1882 Brown Backs were printed until March 1908, at which time the Aldrich-Vreeland Act mandated new wording, and production stopped.

All $100 notes of this series are scarce, and high-quality notes are rare. Brown Backs have always commanded strong market attention.

Banks of Issue and Rarity of Notes

Based upon census information from Don C. Kelly and James M. Kelly (*National Bank Note Census*, Version 4.0) and with some information from other sources, this listing gives each location, the number of banks issuing this series of notes within each, and a commentary.[15]

The Kelly survey records 301 of these notes. Territories account for nine notes, each a numismatic prize. There are two serial number 1 notes as listed below, each a trophy note.

Alabama • 10 banks of issue • 5 notes reported • All are circulated.

Arizona Territory • 2 banks of issue • No notes reported.

Arkansas • 5 banks of issue • No notes reported.

California • 27 banks of issue • 10 notes reported • All are in circulated grades.

Colorado • 17 banks of issue • 3 notes reported • All are circulated, two from the First National Bank of Denver and one from the First National Bank of Pueblo.

Connecticut • 22 banks of issue • No notes reported.

Dakota Territory • 2 banks of issue • No notes reported.

Delaware • 8 banks of issue • 2 notes reported • National Bank of Smyrna (EF) and the National Bank of Delaware in Wilmington (VF).

District of Columbia • 4 banks of issue • No notes reported.

Florida • 7 banks of issue • 3 notes reported • First National Bank of Tallahassee (one Unc).

Georgia • 7 banks of issue • 4 notes reported • All are circulated.

Hawaii Territory • 1 bank of issue • No notes reported.

Idaho • 3 banks of issue • No notes reported.

Illinois • 64 banks of issue • 37 notes reported • Seven notes are known in Unc grade. The only serial number 1 note is from the Canton National Bank (Unc).

Indian Territory • 5 banks of issue • 1 note reported • The only known note is from the Citizens National Bank of Chickasa (G–VG).

Indiana • 27 banks of issue • 8 notes reported • All are circulated.

Iowa • 42 banks of issue • 12 notes reported • Three Unc notes are from the First National Bank of Britt, the Citizens National Bank of Davenport, and the First National Bank of Davenport.

Kansas • 29 banks of issue • 11 notes reported • The only Unc note is from the First National Bank of Manhattan.

Kentucky • 23 banks of issue • 22 notes reported • The only Unc note is from the Louisville City National Bank.

Louisiana • 10 banks of issue • 7 notes reported • Two Unc examples are from the State National Bank of New Orleans.

Maine • 11 banks of issue • 2 notes reported • Biddeford National Bank (EF) and the First National Bank of Brunswick (F–VF).

SERIES OF 1882, BROWN BACK

$100 National Bank Note, Series of 1882, Brown Back (W-3555). The Louisville (Kentucky) National Banking Company, charter 5161. Plate made at the Bureau of Engraving and Printing.

Back of the $100 National Bank Note, Series of 1882, Brown Back (W-3555). To the left is the seal of the state of Kentucky.

Maryland • 25 banks of issue • 6 notes reported • From five different banks. All are circulated.

Massachusetts • 115 banks of issue • 6 notes reported • From five different banks. All are circulated.

Michigan • 9 banks of issue • 1 note reported • National Bank of Houghton (EF).

Minnesota • 12 banks of issue • 3 notes reported • All are circulated, from the First National Bank of Glencoe, the Merchants National Bank of Saint Paul, and the Saint Paul National Bank.

Mississippi • 4 banks of issue • No notes reported.

Missouri • 19 banks of issue • 9 notes reported • All are circulated.

Montana • 3 banks of issue • 4 notes reported • All are from the First National Bank of Butte (two Unc).

Montana Territory • 2 banks of issue • No notes reported.

Nebraska • 25 banks of issue • 4 notes reported • All are circulated.

New Hampshire • 9 banks of issue • 3 notes reported • From the First National Bank of Manchester, all are circulated.

New Jersey • 29 banks of issue • 4 notes reported • All are circulated.

New Mexico Territory • 1 bank of issue • 3 notes reported • First National Bank of Albuquerque (including one Unc).

New York • 79 banks of issue • 7 notes reported • All are circulated.

North Carolina • 8 banks of issue • 4 notes reported • All are circulated and from the Murchison National Bank of Wilmington.

North Dakota • 4 banks of issue • 1 note reported • First National Bank of Grand Forks (EF).

Ohio • 54 banks of issue • 20 notes reported • The only Unc note is from the First National Bank of Ravenna.

Oklahoma • 6 banks of issue • No notes reported.

Oklahoma Territory • 7 banks of issue • 4 notes reported • All are circulated.

Oregon • 4 banks of issue • 1 note reported • First National Bank of Portland (F).

Pennsylvania • 128 banks of issue • 45 notes reported • Eight are Unc.

Rhode Island • 9 banks of issue • The only serial number 1 note is from the Providence National Bank (AU).

South Carolina • 3 banks of issue • 1 note reported • City National Bank of Greenville (VF–EF).

South Dakota • 4 banks of issue • No notes reported.

Tennessee • 19 banks of issue • 3 notes reported • Cleveland National Bank of Cleveland, the Peoples National Bank of Gallatin, and the National Bank of Commerce in Memphis.

Texas • 77 banks of issue • 27 notes reported • Three Unc notes are known, one from the First National Bank of Lockhart and two from the First National Bank of Seguin.

Utah • 1 bank of issue • 1 note reported • Deseret National Bank of Salt Lake City (EF).

Utah Territory • 3 banks of issue • 1 note reported • Deseret National Bank of Salt Lake City (EF).

Vermont • 7 banks of issue • 1 note reported • National Bank of Barre (F–VF).

Virginia • 9 banks of issue • 2 notes reported • National Valley Bank of Staunton (F, not graded).

Washington • 7 banks of issue • 11 notes reported • The only Unc note is from the Exchange National Bank of Spokane.

Washington Territory • 1 bank of issue • No notes reported.

West Virginia • 2 banks of issue • 1 note reported • Farmers & Producers National Bank of Sistersville (F–VF).

Wisconsin • 7 banks of issue • 1 note is reported • From the Waukesha National Bank (VF).

Generic prices for a typical note:

VG-8	F-12	VF-20	EF-40	AU-50	Unc-60	Unc-63
$5,000	$5,500	$7,000	$9,000	$15,000	$17,500	$25,000

W-3544 • F-519 • Bruce-Gilfillan (1881–1883)
Estimated population: 19 to 22 • *Highest graded:* Unc.

VG-8	F-12	VF-20	EF-40	AU-50	Unc-60	Unc-63
$5,000	$5,500	$7,000	$9,000	$15,000	$17,500	$25,000

W-3545 • F-520 • Bruce-Wyman (1883–1885)
Estimated population: 52 to 56 • *Highest graded:* Unc.

VG-8	F-12	VF-20	EF-40	AU-50	Unc-60	Unc-63
$5,000	$5,500	$7,000	$9,000	$15,000	$17,500	$25,000

W-3546 • F-521 • Bruce-Jordan (1885)
Recorded population: 6 • *Highest graded:* AU-50 • *Selected information:* CAA (1/2003), 1757-A528594/A, NB of America, Chicago, IL, F, $5,750. CAA (9/2000), 490-B331104/A, Central NB of Lynn, MA, VF-EF, $5,775. Heritage (9/2007), 3565-A702246/A, N Newark Banking Co., NJ, F+, $13,800.

W-3547 • F-522 • Rosecrans-Jordan (1885–1887)
Estimated population: 32 to 35 • *Highest graded:* Unc.

VG-8	F-12	VF-20	EF-40	AU-50	Unc-60	Unc-63
$5,000	$5,500	$7,000	$9,000	$15,000	$17,500	$25,000

W-3548 • F-523 • Rosecrans-Hyatt (1887–1889)
Estimated population: 10 to 12 • *Highest graded:* Unc • *Selected information:* Stack's (10/1988), 211-B555805/A, Washington

Park NB of Chicago, IL, Unc, $4,675. Heritage (9/2008), 30-A308320/A, Farmers and Mechanics NB of Fort Worth, TX, F, pinholes, $7,475. Knight (2/1997), 3027-B391170/A, Farmers and mechanics NB of Fort Worth, TX, VF, $4,125.

W-3549 • F-524 • Rosecrans-Huston (1889–1891)
Estimated population: 32 to 35 • *Highest graded:* Unc.

VG-8	F-12	VF-20	EF-40	AU-50	Unc-60	Unc-63
$5,000	$5,500	$7,000	$9,000	$15,000	$17,500	$25,000

W-3550 • F-525 • Rosecrans-Nebeker (1891–1893)
Estimated population: 20 to 23 • *Highest graded:* Unc.

VG-8	F-12	VF-20	EF-40	AU-50	Unc-60	Unc-63
$5,000	$5,500	$7,000	$9,000	$15,000	$17,500	$25,000

W-3551 • F-526 • Rosecrans-Morgan (1893)
Recorded population: 7 • *Highest graded:* Unc • *Selected information:* CAA (1/2001), 2189-B287454/A, First NB of Elgin, IL, EF–AU, $15,400. CAA (5/2004), 2697-B347988/A, NB of Lawrence Country at New Castle, PA, EF, $18,400.

W-3552 • F-527 • Tillman-Morgan (1893–1897)
Estimated population: 35 to 40 • *Highest graded:* AU-58.

VG-8	F-12	VF-20	EF-40	AU-50
$5,000	$5,500	$7,000	$9,000	$15,000

W-3553 • F-528 • Tillman-Roberts (1897)
Recorded population: 7 • *Highest graded:* Unc • *Selected information:* Hickman Auctions (3/1990), 1598-B366845/A, San Francisco NB, CA, G–VG, $1,500. Stack's (5/1997), 846-B35114/A, NB of Pottstown, PA, F, $1,100. Knight (8/2002), 647-B210993/A, First NB of Sequin, TX, AU, $43,125.

W-3554 • F-529 • Bruce-Roberts (1897–1898)
Estimated population: 16 to 18 • *Highest graded:* Unc.

VG-8	F-12	VF-20	EF-40	AU-50	Unc-60	Unc-63
$5,000	$5,500	$7,000	$9,000	$15,000	$17,500	$25,000

W-3555 • F-530 • Lyons-Roberts (1898–1905)
Estimated population: 55 to 60 • *Highest graded:* Unc.

VG-8	F-12	VF-20	EF-40	AU-50	Unc-60	Unc-63
$5,000	$5,500	$7,000	$9,000	$15,000	$17,500	$25,000

W-3556 • F-531 • Vernon-Treat (1906–1909)
Estimated population: 10 to 12 • *Highest graded:* AU-50 • *Selected information:* Knight (6/2000), 1584-B602832/A, Exchange NB of Spokane, WA, F, $3,300.

Series of 1882, Date Back
(Authorized Issue 1908 to 1915, Some to 1922)

This issue (illus. on p. 648) was created to reflect a change in the backing of the notes, authorized by the Aldrich-Vreeland Act of May 30, 1908. Notes of the new type were issued beginning in 1908. Production of 1882 Brown Back notes ceased, and new orders were filled by the Date Back type.

In order to make it easier to fund the notes, banks were allowed to deposit good securities in addition to government bonds, while earlier only government bonds had been allowed. All have the inscription on the face, "This Note is Secured by Bonds of the United States or other securities." The last phrase was often added by altering face plates of the same design used for earlier series. Although the Act expired on June 30, 1915, marking the end of the official use of this imprint and the related back, Peter Huntoon notes that some $50 and $100 plates remained in use until 1922, while the lower denominations were discontinued in 1916. Logically, the later notes should have been Value Backs. Otherwise the face motifs are the same as on the Series of 1882 Brown Backs (continued from the Original Series and Series of 1875). The serial numbers, charter number, two regional letters, and the Treasury seal are now all in blue.

The back was redesigned completely. At the center is a large open space with the years 1882 and 1908, with an ornament between them. Above, near the border, is the obligation or redemption clause, and below, near the border, is the counterfeiting clause. At the right is an eagle with wings uplifted, grasping lightning bolts, with a decorative shield. No longer were the state seals used.

All 1882 Date Back $100 notes are rarities, and the Vernon-Treat signature combination is exceedingly rare.

Banks of Issue and Rarity of Notes

Based upon census information from Don C. Kelly and James M. Kelly (*National Bank Note Census*, Version 4.0) and with some information from other sources, this listing gives each location, the number of banks issuing this series of notes within each, and a commentary.[16]

The Kelly survey records only 131 of these. There are two serial number 1 notes as listed below, each a trophy note.

Alabama • 1 bank of issue • 1 note reported • City National Bank of Selma (VF).

Arizona Territory • 1 bank of issue • No notes reported.

Arkansas • 1 bank of issue • No notes reported.

California • 16 banks of issue • 9 notes reported • All are circulated.

Colorado • 3 banks of issue • 2 notes reported • First National Bank of Trinidad, both circulated.

Connecticut • 1 bank of issue • No notes reported.

Delaware • 2 banks of issue • 2 notes reported • National Bank of Smyrna (VG, VG–F).

District of Columbia • 1 bank of issue • No notes reported.

Florida • 3 banks of issue • No notes reported.

Georgia • 3 banks of issue • 1 note reported • First National Bank of Rome (VF).

Hawaii Territory • 1 bank of issue • 1 note reported • First National Bank of Hawaii at Honolulu (VF).

Idaho • 1 bank of issue • No notes reported.

Illinois • 26 banks of issue • 12 notes reported • Three Unc notes are known, from the Second National Bank of Danville, the Palmer National Bank of Danville, and the Grundy County National Bank of Morris.

Indiana • 12 banks of issue • 2 notes reported • Second National Bank of New Albany (VF) and the Farmers National Bank of Shelbyville (VG).

Iowa • 16 banks of issue • 18 notes reported • Four notes are known in Unc grade.

Kansas • 6 banks of issue • 1 note reported • First National Bank of Seneca (VF).

Kentucky • 8 banks of issue • 10 notes reported • All are circulated.

Maryland • 8 banks of issue • 2 notes reported • National Marine Bank of Baltimore (VF–EF) and the Farmers & Merchants National Bank of Cambridge (VF).

Massachusetts • 12 banks of issue • 6 notes reported • Five are from National Shawmut Bank of Boston, all circulated.

Michigan • 3 banks of issue • No notes reported.

Minnesota • 5 banks of issue • 1 note reported • First National Bank of Glencoe (EF).

Missouri • 4 banks of issue • No notes reported.

Montana • 1 bank of issue • 1 note reported • First National Bank of Butte (F).

Nebraska • 4 banks of issue • No notes reported.

New Hampshire • 1 bank of issue • No notes reported.

New Jersey • 4 banks of issue • 1 note reported • Union National Bank of Newark (VF).

New Mexico • 1 bank of issue • 6 notes reported • All are circulated, and all are from the First National Bank of Albuquerque.

New Mexico Territory • 1 bank of issue • No notes reported.

New York • 11 banks of issue • 18 notes reported • The only Unc example is from the Columbia National Bank of Buffalo.

North Carolina • 3 banks of issue • 6 notes reported • All circulated, from the Murchison National Bank of Wilmington.

North Dakota • 1 bank of issue • 2 notes reported • First National Bank of Grand Forks (F, Unc).

Ohio • 21 banks of issue • 3 notes reported • All are circulated, from the Citizens National Bank of Mansfield, the National Exchange Bank of Steubenville, and the Mahoning National Bank of Youngstown.

Oklahoma • 6 banks of issue • 4 notes reported • The only Unc note is from the First National Bank of Chickasha.

Pennsylvania • 28 banks of issue • 5 notes reported • All are circulated.

South Carolina • 1 bank of issue • No notes reported.

Tennessee • 2 banks of issue • No notes reported.

Texas • 23 banks of issue • 13 notes reported • All are circulated.

Utah • 1 bank of issue • No notes reported.

Vermont • 2 banks of issue • 1 note reported • National Bank of Barre (VG).

Virginia • 3 banks of issue • No notes reported.

Washington • 4 banks of issue • 3 notes reported • Two from the Seattle National Bank (EF, ungraded) and one from the Exchange National Bank of Spokane (not graded).

West Virginia • 1 bank of issue • No notes reported.

Generic prices for a typical note:

VG-8	F-12	VF-20	EF-40	AU-50	Unc-60	Unc-63
$4,500	$5,500	$7,000	$10,000	$17,500	$20,000	$30,000

W-3560 • F-566 • Rosecrans-Huston (1889–1891)

Estimated population: 9 or 10 • *Highest graded:* Unc • *Selected information:* CAA 91/2001), 397-A45095/B, City NB of Selma, AL, VF, $26,400. Knight (2/1996), 74-A23640/B, First NB of Sioux City, IA, Unc, $6,600. Stack's (5/1997), 100-A23666/B, First NB of Sioux City, IA, VF, $1,760.

W-3561 • F-567 • Rosecrans-Nebeker (1891–1893)

Estimated population: 13 to 15 • *Highest graded:* AU-50.

VG-8	F-12	VF-20	EF-40	AU-50
$4,500	$5,500	$7,000	$10,000	$17,500

W-3562 • F-568 • Tillman-Morgan (1893–1897)

Estimated population: 30 to 35 • *Highest graded:* Unc.

VG-8	F-12	VF-20	EF-40	AU-50	Unc-60	Unc-63
$4,500	$5,500	$7,000	$10,000	$17,500	$20,000	$30,000

W-3563 • F-569 • Tillman-Roberts (1897)

Estimated population: 12 to 14 • *Highest graded:* VF-25.

VG-8	F-12	VF-20
$4,500	$5,500	$7,000

W-3564 • F-570 • Bruce-Roberts (1897–1898)

Recorded population: 3 • *Highest graded:* VF-25 • *Selected information:* NASCA (10/1984), 199-A35533/C, NB of Smyrna, DE, VG+, pinholes, $1,250.

W-3565 • F-571 • Lyons-Roberts (1898–1905)

Estimated population: 60 to 70 • *Highest graded:* Unc.

VG-8	F-12	VF-20	EF-40	AU-50	Unc-60	Unc-63
$4,500	$5,500	$7,000	$10,000	$17,500	$20,000	$30,000

W-3566 • F-572 • Vernon-Treat (1906–1909)

Recorded population: 3 • *Highest graded:* Unc.

W-3567 • F-572a • Napier-McClung (1911–1912)

Recorded population: 6 • *Highest graded:* VF-25 • *Selected information:* CAA (1/2000), 1007-A154399/C, First NB of Albuquerque, NM, VG–F, damaged, $3,575. Kagin (8/1977),

SERIES OF 1882, DATE BACK

$100 National Bank Note, Series of 1882, Date Back (W-3562). Live Stock National Bank of Sioux City, Iowa, charter 5022, regional letter M. Motifs similar to the preceding.

Back of the $100 National Bank Note, Series of 1882, Date Back (W-3562), with 1882 and 1908 dates.

1290-A154962/C, First NB of Albuquerque, NM, F–VF, $1,800. Knight (8/1997), 1757-A160786/C, First NB of Albuquerque, NM, F–VF, $3,410. Knight (11/2003), 2088-A167147/C, First NB of Albuquerque, NM, F, $10,350.

Series of 1882, Value Back
(Authorized Issue 1915+)

When the Aldrich-Vreeland Act expired on June 20, 1915, the BEP created the Value Back, spelling out the denomination, to replace the Date Back type. The security of the notes reverted to bonds only, as it had been before the implementation of the Aldrich-Vreeland Act of May 30, 1908.

Only two banks ordered $100 Series of 1882 Value Back Notes, the Canal-Commercial National Bank of New Orleans and the Winters National Bank of Dayton, Ohio. These were printed on $50-$50-$50-$100 sheets. The Dayton bank received 1,800 sheets, and the New Orleans bank took 1,057 sheets (out of 1,300 printed for it). The bills were delivered in 1920 and 1921.[17]

New face plates were made, in the old style used on the Series of 1882 Brown Back notes, without "or other securities." The guarantee reads, "This Note is secured by Bonds of the United States deposited with the U.S. Treasurer at Washington."

Otherwise the face was similar to the Series of 1882 Date Back, with the serial numbers, charter number, two regional letters, and the Treasury seal all in blue. The back continued the same vignettes as the preceding type, but now with ONE HUNDRED DOLLARS in two lines at the center.

The face of this denomination has the vignette *Commodore Perry's Victory* (official title), popularly called *The Battle of Lake Erie*, at the left. To the right is a personification of America and liberty, the goddess Union, with the inscription THE UNION on a fasces in the foreground. Union appears with wings on her back, an unusual style for a depiction of the national goddess.

This is the largest denomination in the 1882 Date Back series, which included the $5, $10, $20, and $50 denominations. Only a handful are known today, making this far and away the rarest type in the $100 National Bank Note series (not including the Series of 1875 National Gold Bank Notes).

$100 National Bank Note, Series of 1882, Value Back (W-3569). Canal-Commercial National Bank of New Orleans, charter 5649, regional letter S. Face design similar to the preceding type.

Back of the $100 National Bank Note, Series of 1882, Value Back (W-3569), with value instead of dates.

Banks of Issue and Rarity of Notes

Census information from Don C. Kelly and James M. Kelly (*National Bank Note Census*, Version 4.0)[18] records just five of these notes from two different banks. There are no Uncirculated notes. The $100 notes of this series are closely related to the $50 notes and are from the same sheets.

Louisiana • 1 bank of issue • 2 notes reported • Canal-Commercial National Bank of New Orleans (both F; one is serial number 1).

Ohio • 1 bank of issue • 3 notes reported • Winters National Bank of Dayton (F, F–VF, and VF).

W-3569 • **F-586a** • **Lyons-Roberts (1898–1905)** • **2,857**
Recorded population: 5 • *Highest graded: VF-20* • *Selected information:* Knight (8/2003), 1-A164670/A, Canal-Commercial NB of New Orleans, LA (serial number 1 note), VG, $178,250. Knight (6/1999), 108-A161197C, Winters NB of Dayton, OH, F–VF, $93,500.

Series of 1902, Red Seal
(Authorized Issue From 1902 to 1908)

The Act of April 12, 1902, provided for reputable, established banks to extend their charters for another 40 years and for new banks to gain a 60-year charter. New designs were prepared, known today as 1902 Red Seal notes, though older series were still being issued. During the life span of the 1902 Red Seals, certain banks continued to receive Series of 1882 Brown Back notes, depending on the date of their charter extension or founding. All were secured by federal government bonds deposited with the Treasurer of the United States.

Faces and backs were redesigned for the new Series of 1902 notes. These continued to be issued until the Aldrich-Vreeland Act of May 30, 1908, went into effect, when the Red Seals were abruptly replaced by the 1902 to 1908 Date Backs, which were guaranteed in bonds "and other securities." Accordingly, this series was very short-lived.

The face features John Jay Knox (1828–1891), who served as comptroller of the Currency from 1872 to 1884, in addition to other important positions in government and private finance. Knox was the architect of the Coinage Act of 1873, which created the trade dollar, altered the weights of the dime, quarter, and half dollar, and discontinued the silver dollar. His various Treasury reports are valuable to paper-money researchers. Knox enjoyed collecting coins, participated in auction sales, and was a consummate student of money and finance. In 1900 his *History of Banking* was published posthumously, one of the most authoritative texts on the subject. The back of the note illustrates a shield topped by an eagle, with a man seated to either side.

These notes are rare and in great demand. Not many exist, and of those, very few are Uncirculated.

Banks of Issue and Rarity of Notes

Based upon census information from Don C. Kelly and James M. Kelly (*National Bank Note Census*, Version 4.0) and with some information from other sources, this listing gives each location, the number of banks issuing this series of notes within each, and a commentary.[19]

The Kelly survey records just 119 of these. There are five serial number 1 notes, which are listed below, each a prize. Among the handful of territorial notes is one from Porto Rico (as it was spelled on the notes).

Alabama • 1 bank of issue • No notes reported.

Arkansas • 1 bank of issue • No notes reported.

California • 20 banks of issue • 2 notes reported • Fresno National Bank, Fresno (F–VF) and the Fort Sutter National Bank of Sacramento (VG–F).

Colorado • 3 banks of issue • 5 notes reported • All are circulated. The only number 1 note is from the Carbonate National Bank of Leadville (VF).

Connecticut • 8 banks of issue • 1 note reported • American National Bank of Hartford (F).

Delaware • 4 banks of issue • No notes reported.

Florida • 2 banks of issue • 3 notes reported • All are from the Atlantic National Bank of Jacksonville, and all are circulated.

Georgia • 4 banks of issue • No notes reported.

Idaho • 3 banks of issue • No notes reported.

Illinois • 15 banks of issue • 15 notes reported • The census lists 12 from the Continental National Bank of Chicago; one Unc example is from the same bank.

Indian Territory • 1 bank of issue • No notes reported.

Indiana • 14 banks of issue • 8 notes reported • All are circulated.

Iowa • 8 banks of issue • 9 notes reported • First National Bank of Davenport; two are Unc.

Kansas • 17 banks of issue • 7 notes reported • All are circulated.

Kentucky • 4 banks of issue • No notes reported.

Louisiana • 4 banks of issue • 2 notes reported • Whitney-Central National Bank of New Orleans (VF, VF–EF).

Maine • 3 banks of issue • No notes reported.

Maryland • 9 banks of issue • 1 note reported • National Mechanics Bank of Baltimore (VG).

Massachusetts • 30 banks of issue • 2 notes reported • Merchants National Bank of Boston and the Eliot National Bank of Boston, both Fine.

Michigan • 2 banks of issue • No notes reported.

Minnesota • 5 banks of issue • 1 note reported • National Bank of Commerce, Minneapolis (VG).

Mississippi • 3 banks of issue • 1 note reported • Merchants National Bank of Vicksburg (VF).

Missouri • 6 banks of issue • 12 notes reported • All are circulated.

Montana • 1 bank of issue • No notes reported.

Nebraska • 13 banks of issue • 4 notes reported • All are circulated. The only number 1 note is from the First National Bank of Sargent (not graded).

SERIES OF 1902, RED SEAL

$100 National Bank Note, Series of 1902, Red Seal (W-3570). The Fairfield National Bank of Lancaster, Ohio, charter 7517, regional letter M. Portrait of John J. Knox, comptroller of the Currency, who was also a numismatist and banking historian.

Back of the $100 National Bank Note, Series of 1902, Red Seal (W-3570). The type also used on Series of 1902, Blue Seal, Plain Back, notes.

Nevada • 3 banks of issue • 1 note reported • Nixon National Bank of Reno (F).

New Hampshire • 2 banks of issue • No notes reported.

New Jersey • 13 banks of issue • 1 note reported • Bridgeton National Bank (AU), a serial number 1 note. A spectacular item.

New York • 37 banks of issue • 6 notes reported • All are circulated.

North Carolina • 4 banks of issue • No notes reported.

North Dakota • 1 bank of issue • No notes reported.

Ohio • 22 banks of issue • 5 notes reported • All are circulated. The only number 1 note is from the Fairfield National Bank of Lancaster (AU).

Oklahoma Territory • 4 banks of issue • 3 notes reported • All are circulated, from the National Bank of Commerce in Guthrie; the Oklahoma City National Bank; and the First National Bank, in Verden.

Oklahoma • 2 banks of issue • No notes reported.

Oregon • 5 banks of issue • 1 note reported • Merchants National Bank of Portland (EF).

Pennsylvania • 70 banks of issue • 12 notes reported • Three Uncirculated notes are from the First National Bank of Washington.

Porto Rico Territory • 1 bank of issue • 1 note reported • First National Bank of Porto Rico at San Juan (VF–EF). Spelled *Porto* in the bank title; address: Island of Porto Rico. Called a "territorial" note by numismatists.

Rhode Island • 3 banks of issue • 2 notes reported • Providence National Bank (VG, not graded).

South Dakota • 4 banks of issue • 1 note reported • First National Bank of Huron (AU).

Tennessee • 8 banks of issue • No notes reported.

Texas • 28 banks of issue • 5 notes reported • All are circulated.

Vermont • 4 banks of issue • No notes reported.

Virginia • 2 banks of issue • 4 notes reported • Three from Virginia National Bank at Petersburg. All are circulated.

Washington • 2 banks of issue • No notes reported.

West Virginia • 1 bank of issue • 1 note reported • West Virginia National Bank of Huntington (VF).

Wisconsin • 8 banks of issue • 3 notes reported • Two are from the Germania National Bank of Milwaukee (including a serial number 1), all are circulated.

Generic prices for a typical note:

VG-8	F-12	VF-20	EF-40	AU-50	Unc-60	Unc-63
$5,000	$6,000	$7,000	$8,000	$10,000	$12,500	$17,500

W-3570 • F-686 • Lyons-Roberts (1898–1905)
Estimated population: 95 to 105 • *Highest graded:* Unc.

VG-8	F-12	VF-20	EF-40	AU-50	Unc-60	Unc-63
$5,000	$6,000	$7,000	$8,000	$10,000	$12,500	$17,500

W-3571 • F-687 • Lyons-Treat (1905–1906)
Estimated population: 9 or 10 • *Highest graded:* VF-25 • *Selected information:* Knight (6/2004), 2498-A166360/A, Whitney NB of New Orleans, LA, VF, $12,075. Stack's (11/2007), 364-A197035/A, Omaha NB, NE, VG, damaged, $6,900. Heritage (1/2001), 151-A262314/A, First NB of Corsicana, TX, VF, $16,675.

W-3572 • F-688 • Vernon-Treat (1906–1909)
Recorded population: 6 • *Highest graded:* EF-40 • *Selected information:* Smythe (6/1997), 2061-A320853/A, Central NB of the City of St. Louis, MO, VF–EF, $4,400. Grinnell (c. 1940), 918-A356496/A, Merchants NB of Portland, OR, EF, damaged, $130. Smythe (9/1997), 60-A333453/A, First NB of Granbury, TX, F, pinholes, $4,700.

Series of 1902, Blue Seal, Date Back
(Authorized Issue 1908 to 1915, Some to 1926)

Paralleling the Series of 1882 Date Back notes, the unexpected 1902 Blue Seal, Date Back type was created to reflect a change in the backing of the notes authorized by the Aldrich-Vreeland Act of May 30, 1908. Notes of the new type were issued beginning that year. Production of 1902 Red Seals ceased, and new orders were filled by the Date Back type.

In order to make it easier to fund the notes, banks were allowed to deposit good securities and/or government bonds, while earlier only government bonds had been allowed. All have the inscription as part of the top border on the face, "Secured by United States bonds or other securities." This was often added by altering face plates of the Series of 1902 Red Seal notes. Although the Act expired on June 30, 1915, marking the end of the official use of this imprint and the related back, some plates were continued in use into 1916. The face motifs are the same as on the Series of 1902 Red Seals, but now with the serial numbers, two charter numbers, two regional letters, and the Treasury seal in blue. The back is the same as used for the 1902 Red Seals, except that the dates are printed in the top of the field, 1902 to the left of center and 1908 to the right. These were issued in four-subject $50-$50-$50-$100 sheets and in two-subject $50-$100 sheets.

Although the style was obsolete, Date Back notes were delivered as late as 1926. Beginning on March 5, 1924, the regional letter was omitted from newly printed sheets. Starting August 22, 1925, new notes omitted the Treasury serial

number and had two bank serial numbers. Accordingly, $50 and $100 notes of this type printed in the 1920s can have one of three overprints:

> **Overprint Style 1:** Two regional letters, a Treasury serial number, and a bank serial number.
>
> **Overprint Style 2:** No regional letters, a Treasury serial number, and a bank serial number.
>
> **Overprint Style 3:** No regional letters and no Treasury serial number, but two bank serial numbers.

These are available as a type, but many locations are rare. Nearly all are in circulated grades.

Banks of Issue and Rarity of Notes
Based upon census information from Don C. Kelly and James M. Kelly (*National Bank Note Census*, Version 4.0) and with some information from other sources, this listing gives each location, the number of banks issuing this series of notes within each, and a commentary.[20]

The Kelly survey records 597 of these, more than any other type large-size $100 note. There is just one serial number 1 note, from Nebraska, and one territorial note from Porto (*sic*) Rico.

Alabama • 2 banks of issue • 1 note reported • City National Bank, Selma (VF).

Arizona Territory • 1 bank of issue • No notes reported.

Arkansas • 2 banks of issue • No notes reported.

California • 39 banks of issue • 68 notes reported • All are circulated.

Colorado • 8 banks of issue • 4 notes reported • All are circulated.

Connecticut • 8 banks of issue • 3 notes reported • Aetna National Bank of Hartford, Stamford National Bank of Stamford, and the Waterbury National Bank, all circulated.

Delaware • 4 banks of issue • 1 note reported • National Bank of Delaware at Wilmington (VG).

Florida • 1 bank of issue • 1 note reported • Atlantic National Bank at Jacksonville (VF).

Georgia • 4 banks of issue • 1 note reported • City National Bank of Griffin (EF).

Idaho • 5 banks of issue • 13 notes reported • Two Unc notes are from the First National Bank of Idaho in Boise and the First National Bank of Lewiston.

Illinois • 34 banks of issue • 46 notes reported • Two Unc notes are from the Merchants National Bank of Aurora and the First National Bank of Danville.

Indiana • 22 banks of issue • 24 notes reported • All are circulated.

Iowa • 20 banks of issue • 43 notes reported • Four Unc notes are known.

Kansas • 20 banks of issue • 22 notes reported • Three Unc notes are known, two from the First National Bank of Manhattan and one from the First National Bank of Sedan.

Kentucky • 15 banks of issue • 14 notes reported • All are circulated.

SERIES OF 1902, BLUE SEAL, DATE BACK

$100 National Bank Note, Series of 1902, Blue Seal, Date Back (W-3576). New First National Bank of Columbus, Ohio, charter 4443, regional letter M. Rubber-stamped signatures by the bank officers have completely faded away.

Back of the $100 National Bank Note, Series of 1902, Blue Seal, Date Back (W-3576), showing Date Back style.

Louisiana • 4 banks of issue • 9 notes reported • All are circulated.

Maine • 3 banks of issue • 1 note reported • From the First National Bank of Bangor (EF–AU).

Maryland • 15 banks of issue • 9 notes reported • All are circulated.

Massachusetts • 24 banks of issue • 6 notes reported • All are circulated.

Michigan • 7 banks of issue • 9 notes reported • All are circulated.

Minnesota • 5 banks of issue • No notes reported.

Mississippi • 4 banks of issue • Three notes are reported, from the First National Bank of Jackson (not graded), the Merchants National Bank of Vicksburg (EF), and the Citizens National Bank of Vicksburg (VG).

Missouri • 12 banks of issue • 29 notes reported • All are circulated.

Montana • 2 banks of issue • No notes reported.

Nebraska • 18 banks of issue • 32 notes reported • One note is known in Unc grade, from the First National Bank of Pender. The only serial number 1 note is from the Scottsbluff National Bank (AU).

Nevada • 3 banks of issue • 1 note reported • Nixon National Bank, Reno (VG).

New Hampshire • 2 banks of issue • No notes reported.

New Jersey • 16 banks of issue • 3 notes reported • All are circulated, from the National State Bank of Camden, the Hudson County National Bank of Jersey City, and the Paterson National Bank.

New York • 57 banks of issue • 35 notes reported • All are circulated.

North Carolina • 3 banks of issue • No notes reported.

North Dakota • 2 banks of issue • No notes reported.

Ohio • 35 banks of issue • 50 notes reported • The only Unc note is from the Citizens National Bank of New Philadelphia.

Oklahoma • 6 banks of issue • 3 notes reported • First National Bank of Muskogee, all circulated.

Oregon • 6 banks of issue • 9 notes reported • All are circulated.

Pennsylvania • 75 banks of issue • 51 notes reported • Two Unc notes are known, one each from the Girard National Bank of Philadelphia and the German National Bank of Pittsburgh.

Porto Rico Territory • 1 bank of issue • No notes reported • Spelled *Porto* in the bank title; address: Island of Porto Rico. Called a "territorial" note by numismatists.

Rhode Island • 3 banks of issue • 3 notes reported • Two from the Providence National Bank (F–VF, VF) and one from the Mechanics National Bank of Providence (F–VF).

Vermont • 6 banks of issue • 2 notes reported • Killington National Bank of Rutland (VG, VF).

Virginia • 2 banks of issue • 2 notes reported • Virginia National Bank of Petersburg (G) and the Augusta National Bank of Staunton (VF).

Washington • 4 banks of issue • 16 notes reported • All are circulated.

Wisconsin • 8 banks of issue • 16 notes reported • All are circulated.

South Dakota • 7 banks of issue • 10 notes reported • All are circulated.

Tennessee • 10 banks of issue • 15 notes reported • Seven are Unc.

Texas • 40 banks of issue • 40 notes reported • The only Unc note is from the First National Bank of Houston.

Utah • 1 bank of issue • 1 note reported • National Copper Bank of Salt Lake City (VF).

Generic prices for a typical note from a state from which notes range from available to just slightly scarce:

VG-8	F-12	VF-20	EF-40	AU-50	Unc-60	Unc-63
$1,500	$1,750	$2,000	$3,000	$4,000	$5,000	$6,500

W-3573 • F-689 • Lyons-Roberts (1898–1905)
Estimated population: 260 to 275 • *Highest graded:* Unc.

VG-8	F-12	VF-20	EF-40	AU-50	Unc-60	Unc-63
$1,500	$1,750	$2,000	$3,000	$4,000	$5,000	$6,500

W-3574 • F-690 • Lyons-Treat (1905–1906)
Estimated population: 48 to 54 • *Highest graded:* Unc.

VG-8	F-12	VF-20	EF-40	AU-50	Unc-60
$1,500	$1,750	$2,000	$3,000	$4,000	$5,000

W-3575 • F-691 • Vernon-Treat (1906–1909)
Estimated population: 110 to 120 • *Highest graded:* Unc.

VG-8	F-12	VF-20	EF-40	AU-50	Unc-60	Unc-63
$1,500	$1,750	$2,000	$3,000	$4,000	$5,000	$6,500

W-3576 • F-692 • Vernon-McClung (1909–1911)
Estimated population: 90 to 100 • *Highest graded:* AU-50.

VG-8	F-12	VF-20	EF-40	AU-50
$1,500	$1,750	$2,000	$3,000	$4,000

W-3577 • F-693 • Napier-McClung (1911–1912)
Estimated population: 60 to 65 • *Highest graded:* Unc.

VG-8	F-12	VF-20	EF-40	AU-50	Unc-60	Unc-63
$1,500	$1,750	$2,000	$3,000	$4,000	$5,000	$6,500

W-3578 • F-694 • Napier-Thompson (1912–1913)
Recorded population: 8 • *Highest graded:* EF-40 • *Selected information:* Knight (4/2003), 185A188163/A, City NB of Grif-

fin, GA, VF, $7,475. Heritage (4/2008), 1065-A894147/A, Lagonda NB of Springfield, OH, Fine, repaired, $8,050. Knight (8/1997), 430-A785220/A, First NB of Pittsburg, TX, EF, $3,250.

W-3579 • F-695 • Napier-Burke (1913)
Estimated population: 15 to 17 • *Highest graded:* Unc.

VG-8	F-12	VF-20	EF-40	AU-50	Unc-60	Unc-63
$1,750	$2,250	$3,000	$4,000	$5,000	$6,000	$7,500

W-3580 • F-696 • Parker-Burke (1913–1914)
Estimated population: 18 to 20 • *Highest graded:* Unc.

VG-8	F-12	VF-20	EF-40	AU-50	Unc-60	Unc-63
$1,750	$2,250	$3,000	$4,000	$5,000	$6,000	$7,500

W-3581 • F-697 • Teehee-Burke (1915–1919)
Estimated population: 12 to 14 • *Highest graded:* AU-50.

VG-8	F-12	VF-20	EF-40	AU-50
$1,750	$2,250	$3,000	$4,000	$5,000

Series of 1902, Blue Seal, Plain Back
(Authorized Issue 1908 to 1929)

After the Aldrich-Vreeland Act expired on June 30, 1915, the phrase "or other securities" was no longer added to the face of new printing plates. Henceforth, the style reverted to that of years earlier, secured only by U.S. bonds. Old plates remained in use, creating two face plate styles for 1902 Plain Back notes:

> **Plate Style a:** The old Series of 1902 style (used on the face of the Date Backs), with this inscription as part of the top border on the face: "Secured by United States bonds or other securities."

> **Plate Style b:** The new style introduced in 1908, with the inscription (part of the top border on the face) reading, "Secured by United States bonds deposited with the Treasurer of the United States of America."

For both Plate Style a and Plate Style b notes, the two regional letters (on certain issues, then deleted), two charter numbers (on all), and serial numbers (on all) are in blue. These were issued into 1929.

Moreover, within the two plate styles there are possibilities for three overprint styles:

> **Overprint Style 1:** Two regional letters, a Treasury serial number, and a bank serial number. Printed from 1908 to 1924.

> **Overprint Style 2:** No regional letters, a Treasury serial number, and a bank serial number. Printed in 1924 and 1925.

> **Overprint Style 3:** No regional letters and no Treasury serial number, but with two bank serial numbers. Printed from 1925 to 1929. Notes of this style are very rare as a class.

The $100 notes are elusive. If you are seeking a specific small town or bank, you cannot be choosy as to grade. At present there is little interest in plate styles or overprint

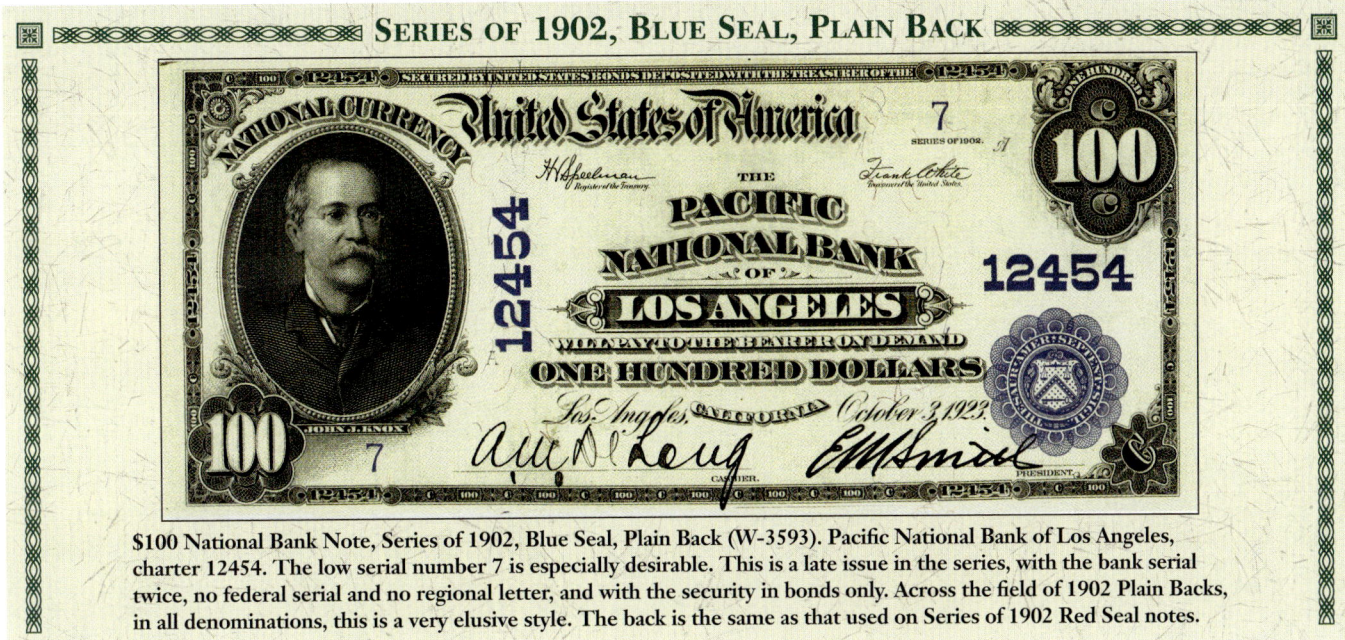

SERIES OF 1902, BLUE SEAL, PLAIN BACK

$100 National Bank Note, Series of 1902, Blue Seal, Plain Back (W-3593). Pacific National Bank of Los Angeles, charter 12454. The low serial number 7 is especially desirable. This is a late issue in the series, with the bank serial twice, no federal serial and no regional letter, and with the security in bonds only. Across the field of 1902 Plain Backs, in all denominations, this is a very elusive style. The back is the same as that used on Series of 1902 Red Seal notes.

varieties, yielding opportunities to acquire rarities while paying no premium, but this is probably moot as these notes are rare overall.

Banks of Issue and Rarity of Notes

Based upon census information from Don C. Kelly and James M. Kelly (*National Bank Note Census*, Version 4.0) and with some information from other sources, this listing gives each location, the number of banks issuing this series of notes within each, and a commentary.[21]

The Kelly survey records 500 of these notes. There are four serial number 1 notes and no territorials.

California • 19 banks of issue • 48 notes reported • Eight Unc notes are listed, and two serial number 1 notes are known, one each from the Pacific National Bank of Los Angeles (Unc) and the Bank of Italy National Trust & Savings Association (AU).

Colorado • 6 banks of issue • 6 notes reported • Two Unc notes are from the First National Bank of Pueblo.

Connecticut • 3 banks of issue • 2 notes reported • First National Bank of Wallingford (VG, Unc).

Delaware • 2 banks of issue • 2 notes reported • First National Bank of Smyrna (F, Unc).

District of Columbia • 1 bank of issue • 6 notes reported • From the Federal-American National Bank. All are circulated.

Florida • 3 banks of issue • No notes reported.

Hawaii Territory • 1 bank of issue • No notes reported.

Idaho • 2 banks of issue • 6 notes reported • All are circulated.

Illinois • 27 banks of issue • 46 notes reported • Three Unc notes are all from the Merchants National Bank of Aurora.

Indiana • 13 banks of issue • 11 notes reported • The only Unc note is from the Union National Bank of Richmond.

Iowa • 12 banks of issue • 30 notes reported • Six Unc notes are known.

Kansas • 15 banks of issue • 4 notes reported • From three different banks. All are circulated.

Kentucky • 12 banks of issue • 12 notes reported • All are circulated.

Louisiana • 3 banks of issue • 14 notes reported • All are circulated.

Maryland • 10 banks of issue • 8 notes reported • The only Unc note is from the Citizens National Bank of Baltimore.

Massachusetts • 7 banks of issue • 3 notes reported • All circulated, from the Fall River National Bank, the Park National Bank of Holyoke, and the Warren National Bank of Peabody.

Michigan • 7 banks of issue • 14 notes reported • Four Unc notes are known, three from the First National Bank in Detroit, and one from Grand Rapids National Bank, Grand Rapids.

Minnesota • 3 banks of issue • No notes reported.

Mississippi • 2 banks of issue • 3 notes reported • First National Bank of Jackson, all circulated.

Missouri • 5 banks of issue • 7 notes reported • The only Unc note is from the National City Bank of Kansas City and is also the only serial number 1 from the state.

Montana • 1 bank of issue • 2 notes reported • First National Bank of Butte (VG, F).

Nebraska • 8 banks of issue • 13 notes reported • All are circulated.

Nevada • 2 banks of issue • 5 notes reported • Reno National Bank (one F, four not graded).

New Hampshire • 3 banks of issue • 3 notes reported • Two are from the National State Capital Bank (VG–F, VG); one is from the First National Bank of Concord (VG–F).

New Jersey • 9 banks of issue • 6 notes reported • All are circulated.

New York • 12 banks of issue • 27 notes reported • All are circulated.

North Carolina • 2 banks of issue • No notes reported.

North Dakota • 1 bank of issue • 2 notes reported • From the First National Bank of Fargo (F) and the First National Bank of Lisbon (not graded).

Ohio • 25 banks of issue • 36 notes reported • Two Unc notes are reported: the First National Bank in Columbus and the Winters National Bank of Dayton.

Oklahoma • 7 banks of issue • 21 notes reported • The only Unc note is from the Exchange National Bank of Ardmore.

Oregon • 1 bank of issue • 4 notes reported • All are circulated, from the First National Bank of Baker.

Pennsylvania • 35 banks of issue • 34 notes reported • The only Unc note is from the United States National Bank of Johnstown.

Rhode Island • 3 banks of issue • 2 notes reported • Both are F, from the First National Bank of Newport and the Mechanics National Bank of Providence.

South Dakota • 7 banks of issue • 5 notes reported • From the Dakota National Bank of Yankton. All are circulated.

Tennessee • 2 banks of issue • 3 notes reported • All are circulated, one from the Clarksville National Bank (VG) and two from the American National Bank of Nashville (not graded, F).

Texas • 34 banks of issue • 83 notes reported • Four notes are reported in Unc grade.

Vermont • 5 banks of issue • 3 notes reported • Two are from the National White River Bank of Bethel (Unc, EF–AU) and National Bank of Middlebury (VG).

Washington • 3 banks of issue • 15 notes reported • Two Unc notes are from the Seattle National Bank.

West Virginia • 1 bank of issue • 2 notes reported • First National Bank of Huntington (both F).

Wisconsin • 6 banks of issue • 12 notes reported • The only Unc note is from the Ashland National Bank.

Generic prices for a typical note from a state from which notes range from available to just slightly scarce:

VG-8	F-12	VF-20	EF-40	AU-50	Unc-60	Unc-63
$1,250	$1,500	$1,750	$2,500	$3,000	$5,000	$6,000

W-3582 • F-698 • Lyons-Roberts (1898–1905)
Estimated population: 120 to 130 • *Highest graded:* Unc.

VG-8	F-12	VF-20	EF-40	AU-50	Unc-60	Unc-63
$1,250	$1,500	$1,750	$2,500	$3,000	$5,000	$6,000

W-3583 • F-699 • Lyons-Treat (1905–1906)
Estimated population: 22 to 25 • *Highest graded:* Unc.

VG-8	F-12	VF-20	EF-40	AU-50	Unc-60	Unc-63
$1,500	$1,750	$2,000	$3,000	$4,000	$5,500	$6,500

W-3584 • F-700 • Vernon-Treat (1906–1909)
Estimated population: 48 to 54 • *Highest graded:* Unc.

VG-8	F-12	VF-20	EF-40	AU-50	Unc-60	Unc-63
$1,250	$1,500	$1,750	$2,500	$3,000	$5,000	$6,000

W-3585 • F-701 • Vernon-McClung (1909–1911)
Estimated population: 70 to 80 • *Highest graded:* Unc.

VG-8	F-12	VF-20	EF-40	AU-50	Unc-60	Unc-63
$1,250	$1,500	$1,750	$2,500	$3,000	$5,000	$6,000

W-3586 • F-702 • Napier-McClung (1911–1912)
Estimated population: 35 to 40 • *Highest graded:* Unc.

VG-8	F-12	VF-20	EF-40	AU-50	Unc-60	Unc-63
$1,250	$1,500	$1,750	$2,500	$3,000	$5,000	$6,000

W-3587 • F-702a • Napier-Thompson (1912–1913)
Estimated population: 19 to 22 • *Highest graded:* EF-40.

VG-8	F-12	VF-20	EF-40
$1,500	$1,750	$2,000	$3,000

W-3588 • F-702b • Napier-Burke (1913) • Unknown

W-3589 • F-703 • Parker-Burke (1913–1914)
Estimated population: 15 to 17 • *Highest graded:* Unc.

VG-8	F-12	VF-20	EF-40	AU-50	Unc-60	Unc-63
$1,500	$1,750	$2,000	$3,000	$4,000	$5,500	$6,500

W-3590 • F-704 • Teehee-Burke (1915–1919)
Estimated population: 75 to 85 • *Highest graded:* Unc.

VG-8	F-12	VF-20	EF-40	AU-50	Unc-60	Unc-63
$1,250	$1,500	$1,750	$2,500	$3,000	$5,000	$6,000

W-3591 • F-705 • Elliott-Burke (1919–1921)
Estimated population: 60 to 70 • *Highest graded:* Unc.

VG-8	F-12	VF-20	EF-40	AU-50	Unc-60	Unc-63
$1,250	$1,500	$1,750	$2,500	$3,000	$5,000	$6,000

W-3592 • F-684 • Elliott-White (1921–1922)
Estimated population: 60 to 70 • *Highest graded:* Unc.

VG-8	F-12	VF-20	EF-40	AU-50	Unc-60	Unc-63
$1,250	$1,500	$1,750	$2,500	$3,000	$5,000	$6,000

W-3593 • F-707 • Speelman-White (1922–1927)
Estimated population: 38 to 47 • *Highest graded:* Unc.

VG-8	F-12	VF-20	EF-40	AU-50	Unc-60	Unc-63
$1,250	$1,500	$1,750	$2,500	$3,000	$5,000	$6,000

W-3594 • F-707a • Woods-White (1927–1928)
Recorded population: 2 • *Highest graded:* F-15 • *Selected information:* Heritage (4/2008), 920/A, B of America NA, New York, NY, F, $25,300. Knight (6/1996), 1800/A, B of America NA, New York, NY, F–VF, $1,760.

SILVER CERTIFICATES

Silver Certificates in the $100 denomination commence with the Series of 1878 and continue in the large size through the Series of 1891. The earlier versions have the word SILVER in large letters across the back, similar to lower denominations, and are known as Silver Certificates of Deposit. For the Series of 1880 and 1891, these were designated simply as Silver Certificates. Depicted at the upper left of each of these notes is the portrait of president James

Monroe. Varieties exist of Treasury seals, signature combinations, and different back designs.

These were printed in relatively small quantities and did not circulate widely in commerce. Interestingly, many were used on the West Coast in the import-export trade with China, a country that preferred silver to gold. Today all notes are very scarce, and those of the Series of 1878 are exceedingly rare.

Series of 1878

Silver Certificates of Deposit commence with the Series of 1878, depicting president James Monroe on the face. These are specifically designated CERTIFICATE OF DEPOSIT on the face, SILVER CERTIFICATE on the back. On the face the inscription SILVER is laid out in a series of patterns,

one for each letter, connected together in a straight row shingle-style, below ONE HUNDRED and above DOLLARS. Below, an ornamental 100 is in red. These notes were printed on blue-tinted paper (Willcox patent of 1866).

Series of 1878 notes bear two printed Treasury signatures of Scofield and Gilfillan plus, on some varieties, the hand-signed countersignature of another Treasury official. This extra signature proved to be a cumbersome idea, and at least one signature, that of A.U. Wyman, was augmented by adding the signature to the printing plate. Possibly, Thos. Hillhouse's signature was added to a plate on these notes, as in other denominations, but no evidence has been found. All have a large red Treasury seal at the top. On this seal, for this denomination and other countersigned notes in this series, the key faces to the right (with the handle at the left).

SERIES OF 1878

$100 Silver Certificate of Deposit, Series of 1878, autographed by R.M. Anthony and datelined San Francisco (W-3604). Serial A292, plate D.

Detail of the autographed signature of W.G. White on a W-3600 note (compare to the Maxwell White signature on W-1466).

Back of the $100 Silver Certificate of Deposit, Series of 1878 (W-3604). Printed on blue-tinted paper, with the tint oriented horizontally (instead of vertically as on certain other series notes). The type also used on Series of 1880 notes.

W-3600 • F-336 • **New York** • *Countersigned:* W.G. White (autographed) • 1,500 (est.)

Recorded population: 1 • *Selected information:* The known example is serial A1362/B, Fair, owned by the Federal Reserve Bank of San Francisco.

W-3604 • F-336a • *Countersigned:* J.C. Hopper (autographed) • 10,500 (est.) • Unknown

W-3608 • F-336a • *Countersigned:* Thos. Hillhouse (printed) • Unknown

W-3612 • F-337 • **San Francisco** • *Countersigned:* R.M. Anthony (autographed) • 4,000 (est.)

Recorded population: 1 • *Selected information:* The known example is serial A392/D, F–VF, pinholes, part of the ANA Museum collection.

W-3614 • F-337a • **Washington** • *Countersigned:* A.U. Wyman (autographed) • 4,000 (est.) • Unknown

W-3616 • F-337b • *Countersigned:* A.U. Wyman (printed) • 36,000 (est.)

Recorded population: 4 • *Highest graded:* VF-25 • *Selected information:* The known examples include serials A8782/B, F–VF, part of the Smithsonian Institution collection; A12467/C, Good, owned by the Federal Reserve Bank of San Francisco; A20438/B, VF, part of the Oat Bin Hoard, sold in a Kagin's auction (10/1976) for $7,000; and A24132/D, F–VF, sold in a Stack's auction (1/1989) for $59,000.

Series of 1880

The motifs are similar to the foregoing, but with differences in the overprints, including the Treasury seal. For the Series of 1880, the idea of countersignatures was dropped entirely.

W-3620 • F-338 • **Scofield-Gilfillan (1878–1881)** • **Large brown seal** • 16,000 (est.) • Unknown

W-3621 • F-339 • **Bruce-Gilfillan (1881–1883)** • 40,000 (est.)

Recorded population: 4 • *Highest graded:* VF-20 • *Selected information:* The known examples include serials B18820/D,

owned by the Federal Reserve Bank of Richmond; B24333/A, VG, owned by the Federal Reserve Bank of San Francisco; B26806/B, F, sold in a Knight auction (10/2006) for $109,250; and B55651/C, VF-20 (PMG), sold in a Knight auction (6/2007) for $149,500.

W-3622 • F-340 • **Bruce-Wyman (1883–1885)** • 80,000
Estimated population: 12 to 14 • *Highest graded:* AU-50.

VG-8	F-12	VF-20	EF-40	AU-50
$15,000	$30,000	$40,000	$100,000	$150,000

W-3623 • F-341 • **Rosecrans-Huston (1889–1891)** • 100,000
Estimated population: 30 to 35 • *Highest graded:* Unc.

VG-8	F-12	VF-20	EF-40	AU-50	Unc-60	Unc-63
$10,000	$15,000	$25,000	$60,000	$100,000	$175,000	$225,000

W-3624 • F-342 • **Rosecrans-Nebeker (1891–1893)** • **Small red seal with scalloped border** • 40,000
Estimated population: 13 to 15 • *Highest graded:* Unc.

VG-8	F-12	VF-20	EF-40	AU-50	Unc-60	Unc-63	Unc-65
$15,000	$30,000	$40,000	$80,000	$125,000	$175,000	$225,000	$250,000

Series of 1891

The Series of 1891 notes are designated as Silver Certificates. The portrait of Monroe is retained, but the typography is different. Silver dollars are now deposited in the Treasury of the United States as backing, no longer with the Treasurer of the United States. The back is completely redesigned and in green, and has large open spaces to the left and right. These were the last Silver Certificates in large-size format.

W-3625 • F-343 • **Rosecrans-Nebeker (1891–1893)** • **Small red seal with scalloped border** • 120,000 (est.)
Estimated population: 23 to 26 • *Highest graded:* Unc.

VG-8	F-12	VF-20	EF-40	AU-50	Unc-60	Unc-63
$7,500	$10,000	$20,000	$45,000	$80,000	$100,000	$150,000

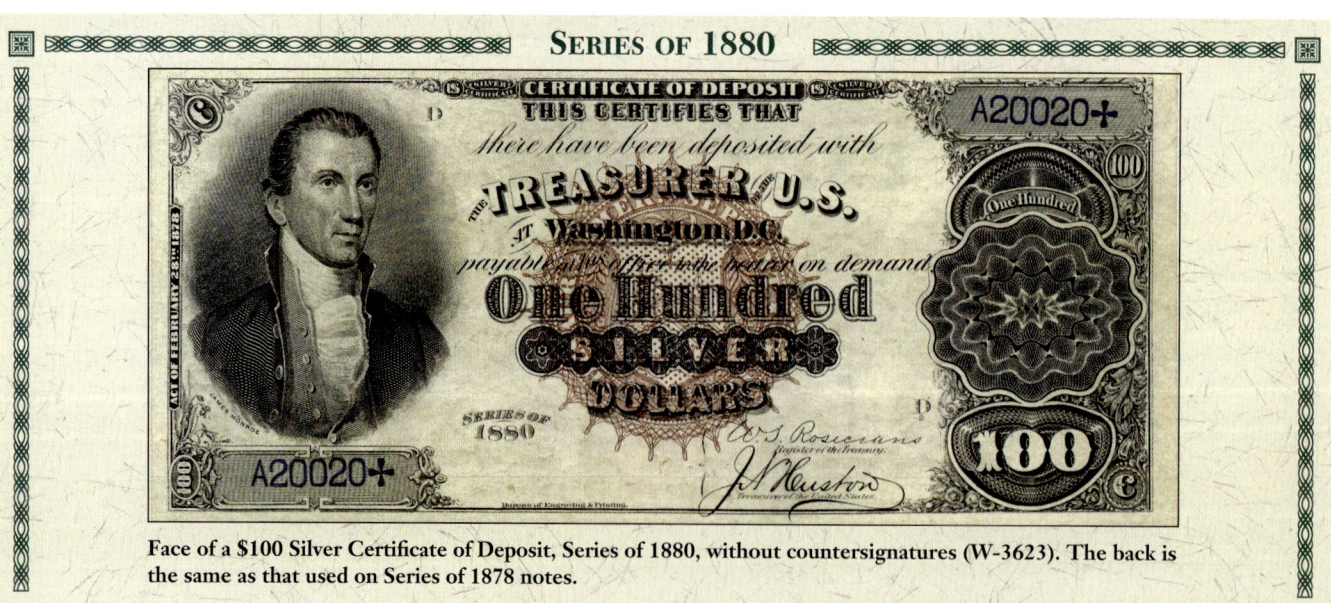

SERIES OF 1880

Face of a $100 Silver Certificate of Deposit, Series of 1880, without countersignatures (W-3623). The back is the same as that used on Series of 1878 notes.

SERIES OF 1891

$100 Silver Certificate, Series of 1891 (W-3625). Differently configured from the earlier type.

Back of the $100 Silver Certificate, Series of 1891 (W-3625).

W-3626 • F-344 • Tillman-Morgan (1893–1897) • 384,000 (est.)

Estimated population: 33 to 36 • *Highest graded:* Unc.

VG-8	F-12	VF-20	EF-40	AU-50	Unc-60	Unc-63
$7,500	$10,000	$20,000	$40,000	$70,000	$85,000	$125,000

TREASURY OR COIN NOTES

Series of 1890

The $100 Treasury Note or Coin Note of 1890 is the famous "Watermelon Note" (illus. on p. 660), designed with the zeros resembling green watermelons. These are famous, rare, and highly desired, one of the great trophy notes of American currency. Depicted on the face is Admiral David G. Farragut. It is the back that gets the attention, though.

The latest edition of *U.S. Paper Money Records* reports that 35 Watermelon Notes are known, of which about nine are in institutional or other holdings viewed as permanent or long term, leaving about two dozen in play on the numismatic market. This is an increase by one note from his previous edition. Although more may be discovered, it is likely that the estimate given below will be on target for quite a few years. The offering of an example is always a high point for the auctioneer as well as for bidders.

W-3630 • F-377 • Rosecrans-Huston (1889–1891) • Large brown seal • 120,000

Estimated population: 37 to 39 • *Highest graded:* Unc.

VG-8	F-12	VF-20	EF-40	AU-50	Unc-60	Unc-63
$40,000	$60,000	$80,000	$175,000	$250,000	$300,000	$400,000

Series of 1891

The Series of 1891 (illus. on p. 661) simplified the reverse and replaced the design with large areas of open field. The Treasury department believed that this deterred counterfeiting. Although the 1891 notes are about three times rarer than those of 1890, they do not bask in the same limelight.

W-3634 • F-378 • Rosecrans-Nebeker (1891–1893) • Small red seal with scalloped border • 80,000

Estimated population: 13 to 15 • *Highest graded:* Unc.

VG-8	F-12	VF-20	EF-40	AU-50	Unc-60
$50,000	$70,000	$125,000	$200,000	—	—

GOLD CERTIFICATES

Gold Certificates issued under the Act of March 3, 1863, are extreme rarities today. Later varieties include issues from the Series of 1870 and 1875. The Series of 1882 Gold Certificates

SERIES OF 1890

$100 Treasury or Coin Note, Series of 1890 (W-3630), with the same motifs as used on the next type. It is the back of this note that gets all of the attention.

Back of the $100 Treasury or Coin Note, Series of 1890 (W-3630)—the famous "Watermelon Note," so called because of the distinctive design of the zeroes. Only three dozen exist.

were made in numerous different Treasury seal styles and signature combinations, and the Series of 1922 ended the class for this denomination. While earlier varieties are rare, the later signature combinations are available on occasion and can be acquired for a type collection. The vast majority of such notes were redeemed in the 1930s after the United States went off the gold standard.

Act of March 3, 1863

The face (illus. on p. 662) is similar to other notes of the same authorization, featuring on the left an eagle perched on a shield with E PLURIBUS UNUM printed faintly above. All were printed by the National Currency Bureau in Washington. At the center is a counter with the numerals in light green. At the bottom center is the head of a woman facing left, wearing a tiara lettered UNION. Multiple counters are at the top and bottom borders. Below the top border is ENGRAVED AND PRINTED AT THE TREASURY DEPARTMENT. At the right is a denomination counter, with the Treasury seal below. Printed signatures include the assistant Treasurer of the United States and Treasurer F.E. Spinner. A proof impression, New York imprint, from plate B1 has the printed signature of assistant United States Treasurer H.H. Van Dyck, while a proof from plate B2 has this area blank so that a countersignature could be added by hand.

The back, printed in gold, is mainly engine-turned vignette work with ONE HUNDRED DOLLARS in the center. Authorized in 1863, notes of this type were issued circa 1865 to 1869. They were obtained by exchanging gold coins at par, and so were valued at a premium over Legal Tender and National Bank Notes. Bills were printed for Boston, New York, Philadelphia, and Washington. Most were issued in New York, with just a tiny fraction in Washington. No record has been found of Boston or Philadelphia notes. At the time, gold coins were worth a strong premium in terms of Legal Tender Notes. These did not circulate hand to hand, but were bought by paying for them in gold coins. Most were used as clearing-house certificates, as gold reserves by banks, or for payment of import duties.[22]

W-3637 • F-1166c • Boston imprint • Colby-Spinner (1864–1867) Autographed countersignature of assistant Treasurer of the United States • Small red seal with spiked border • 20,000 printed • None delivered to Treasurer

W-3639 • F-1166c • New York imprint • Colby-Spinner (1864–1867) • With space for the countersignature of

SERIES OF 1891

$100 Treasury or Coin Note, Series of 1891 (W-3634). Motifs are similar to the Series of 1890 except for the seal and some minor differences.

Back of the $100 Treasury or Coin Note, Series of 1891 (W-3634), featuring an open design, said to deter counterfeiting.

the assistant Treasurer of the United States to add his signature • Small red seal with spiked border • 48,000 (est.[23])

Recorded population: 2 • Selected information: The known examples are serials 11811/C, canceled, ex Schermerhorn, but confiscated and canceled by U.S. Secret Service, now part of the Smithsonian Institution collection, and 46425/A, AU.

W-3640 • F-1166c • With printed signature of H.H. Van Dyck • 72,000 (est.)

Recorded population: 1 • Commentary: The printed signature of H.H. Van Dyck was allowed on $20 and $100 denominations only. • *Selected information:* The known example is serial 112853/A, F, part of the Smithsonian Institution collection.

W-3642 • F-1166c • Philadelphia imprint • Autographed countersignature of assistant Treasurer of the United States • 20,000 printed • None delivered to Treasurer

W-3644 • F-1166c • Washington imprint • 60,000 printed • 32,000 delivered • Unknown

Series of 1870

To the left of the face (illus. on p. 662) is Thomas Hart Benton, a main proponent of the Coinage Act of June 28, 1834, and a long-time adherent of the use of gold. To the right is a counter. To the left above the bottom border is a space for an autographed signature; below is ASSISTANT TREASURER, N.Y. To the right are spaces for two autographed signatures, REGISTER OF THE TREASURY and ASSISTANT TREASURER U.S. At the time the New York Sub-Treasury was the most important repository for gold coins and ingots. These notes were printed on one side only. They did not widely circulate and were available from the Treasury only by exchanging gold coins at par.

W-3646 • F-1166h • Allison and two other Treasury officials (all autographed) • Large red seal with spiked border • 18,000 • Unknown

Series of 1871

The Series of 1871 notes, made only in the $100 denomination, were printed under the act that also authorized Series of 1870 and Series of 1875 Gold Certificates. Doug Murray reports that records indicate that use of the face plate for the Series of 1870 notes, as described above, began on May 18, 1871, and a notation states "Altered to Series 1871" on January 4, 1872. The *Annual Report of the Bureau of Engraving* for 1872 states that 32,000 Series of 1871 notes were printed. No proofs or actual notes have been located.

ACT OF MARCH 3, 1863

$100 Gold Certificate, Act of March 3, 1863 (W-3639). New York imprint, with the autographed countersignature of H.H. Van Dyck. Serial 11811, plate C1. Ink-dated JAN'Y 5, 1866. Marked CANCELED by the Treasury department.

Back of the $100 Gold Certificate, Act of March 3, 1863.

SERIES OF 1870

$100 Gold Certificate, Series of 1870 (W-3646). Proof impression. (Smithsonian Institution)

W-3648 • F-1166h • Allison (autographed) and countersignatures of two clerks • Large red seal with spiked border • 32,000 • Unknown

Series of 1875

The design closely follows that of the Series of 1870. To the left, above the bottom border, is a space for an autographed

SERIES OF 1875

$100 Gold Certificate, Series of 1875 (W-3652). With printed signatures of Treasury officials Allison and New and the autographed signature of assistant Treasurer Maxwell White. Ink-dated JAN'Y 2, 1877.

signature below which is imprinted ASSISTANT TREAS-URER, N.Y. To the right are spaces for two printed signatures, REGISTER OF THE TREASURY and ASSISTANT TREASURER U.S. These notes were printed on one side only. They did not widely circulate and were available from the Treasury only by exchanging gold coins at par. Only a handful exist, each a numismatic landmark.

W-3652 • F-1166m • Allison-New (1875–1876) • Autographed countersignature of Maxwell White • Large pink seal with spiked border • 50,000

Recorded population: 2 • *Highest graded:* VF-25 • *Selected information:* The existing examples are serials B5298/B, canceled, and B13104/D, VF. Both were previously owned by Robert F. Schermerhorn, but confiscated and canceled by the U.S. Secret Service. They are now part of the Smithsonian Institution collection.

W-3656 • F-unlisted • Allison-Gilfillan (1877–1878) • Red seal • 20,000

Recorded population: 1 • *Selected information:* The existing example is serial B56887/C, canceled, owned by the Bureau of the Public Debt in Washington, D.C.

Series of 1882

The face of this note continues the portrait of Missouri senator Thomas Hart Benton to the left and the denomination in two conjoined rosettes at the right. Overprints include GOLD at the top center and backgrounds to the serial numbers in gold-toned ink. These notes were also issued under the Act of March 3, 1863. The back is printed in a rich orange-gold and has an eagle at the center.

After December 17, 1878, gold coins and paper currency were exchangeable at par in general commerce. Accordingly, these are the first of the Gold Certificates that saw wide use. The color tended to fade. Notes with a bright back are worth more than those with faded color, regardless of the grade.

W-3660 • F-1202 • Bruce-Gilfillan (1881–1883) • Autographed countersignature of another Treasury official • Medium-size brown seal with scalloped border • 9,000

Recorded population: 2 • *Selected information:* The known examples are serials A2281/A, VG, part of the Smithsonian Institution collection, and A3386/B, VF, pinholes, sold in a B&M auction (11/2002) for $120,750.

W-3662 • F-1202a • Bruce-Gilfillan (1881–1883) • Engraved countersignature of Thomas C. Acton • 71,000

Recorded population: 3 • *Highest graded:* AU-58 • *Selected information:* The existing examples include serials A12437/A, Fair, damaged, owned by the Federal Reserve Bank of New York; A16180/D, EF, owned by the Federal Reserve Bank of San Francisco; and A20766/B, Ch AU, sold in a Knight auction (12/1998) for $253,000.

W-3664 • F-1201 • Bruce-Gilfillan (1881–1883) • No countersignature • 80,000

Recorded population: 7 • *Highest graded:* VF-25 • *Selected information:* Existing examples include serials A2867/C, VF, pinholes, sold in a Heritage auction (9/2008) for $103,500; A34739/C, F, sold in a Stack's auction (10/1990) for $2,860; A43751/C, owned by the Federal Reserve Bank of Richmond; A46560/D, F, owned by the Federal Reserve Bank of San Francisco; A51784/D, F, sold in a Knight auction (12/1998) for $14,300; A56007/C, owned by the Federal Reserve Bank of Richmond; and A68306/B, VF, owned by the Federal Reserve Bank of San Francisco.

W-3666 • F-1203 • Bruce-Wyman (1883–1885) • 40,000

Recorded population: 3 • *Highest graded:* VF-25 • *Selected information:* The existing examples include serials A104146/B, owned by the Federal Reserve Bank of Richmond; A108124/D, VG–F, sold in a Knight auction (6/2006) for $327,750; and A108237/A, VF, owned by the Federal Reserve Bank of New York.

$100 Gold Certificate, Series of 1882 (W-3686). Notes of the Series of 1882 were issued into the 1920s.

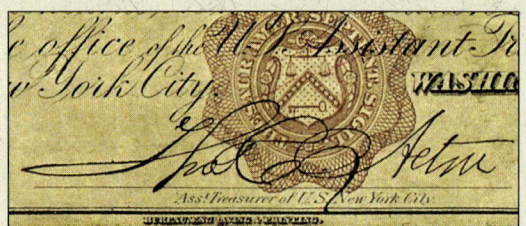

Detail of a W-3662 note with the engraved countersignature of Thomas C. Acton, assistant Treasurer at the New York Sub-Treasury.

Back of the $100 Gold Certificate, Series of 1882 (W-3686), with an eagle perched on fasces. Printed in orange-gold.

W-3668 • F-1204 • Rosecrans-Hyatt (1887–1889) • Large red seal • 40,000

Recorded population: 4 • *Highest graded:* EF-40 • *Selected information:* The existing examples include serials C858/B, VG, owned by the Federal Reserve Bank of San Francisco; C6389/A, VG, part of the Smithsonian Institution collection; C28697/A, EF-40 (PCGS), sold in a CAA auction (1/1999) for $154,000; and C38240/D, F–VF, pinholes, sold in a B&M auction (11/2002) for $48,300.

W-3670 • F-1205 • Rosecrans-Huston (1889–1891) • Large brown seal • 60,000

Recorded population: 8 • *Highest graded:* VF-20 • *Selected information:* The existing examples include serials C61034/B, F, owned by the Federal Reserve Bank of San Francisco; C62962/B, VF–EF, sold in a Knight auction (8/2005) for $63,250; C62965/A, VF, sold in a CAA auction (9/2006) for $120,750; C73783/C, VF, part of the Smithsonian Institu-

tion collection; C79331/C, F, sold in a Knight auction (12/1998) for $23,100; C90018/B, VF-25 (PMG), sold in a Knight auction (6/2007) for $132,250; C92660/D, VF, owned by the Federal Reserve Bank of San Francisco; and C99358/B, F, sold in a CAA auction (1/1999) for $15,400.

W-3672 • F-1206 • Lyons-Roberts (1898–1905) • Small red seal with scalloped border • 1,160,000

Estimated population: 47 to 53 • *Highest graded:* Unc.

VG-8	F-12	VF-20	EF-40	AU-50	Unc-60	Unc-63
$750	$1,250	$2,500	$6,000	$10,000	$12,000	$18,000

W-3674 • F-1207 • Lyons-Treat (1905–1906) • 296,000

Estimated population: 21 to 24 • *Highest graded:* Unc.

VG-8	F-12	VF-20	EF-40	AU-50	Unc-60	Unc-63	Unc-65
$1,250	$2,000	$3,500	$9,000	$12,000	$15,000	$20,000	$25,000

SERIES OF 1922

$100 Gold Certificate, Series of 1922 (W-3690). The back is the same as that used on Series of 1882 notes.

THIS CERTIFICATE IS A LEGAL TENDER IN THE AMOUNT THEREOF IN PAYMENT OF ALL DEBTS AND DUES PUBLIC AND PRIVATE. ACTS OF MARCH 14, 1900, AS AMENDED AND DECEMBER 24, 1919.

Detail of the redemption provision.

W-3676 • F-1208 • Vernon-Treat (1906–1909) • 320,000
Estimated population: 30 to 35 • *Highest graded:* AU-55.

VG-8	F-12	VF-20	EF-40	AU-50
$1,000	$1,750	$3,000	$6,000	$8,500

W-3678 • F-1209 • Vernon-McClung (1909–1911) • 402,000
Estimated population: 52 to 60 • *Highest graded:* Unc • *Commentary:* Deliveries ended on March 3, 1911.

VG-8	F-12	VF-20	EF-40	AU-50	Unc-60	Unc-63
$750	$1,250	$2,500	$3,500	$7,500	$10,000	$15,000

W-3680 • F-1210 • Napier-McClung (1911–1912) • 202,000
Estimated population: 32 to 35 • *Highest graded:* AU-50 • *Commentary:* Deliveries began on November 29, 1911, and ended on December 14, 1911.

VG-8	F-12	VF-20	EF-40	AU-50
$1,000	$1,750	$3,000	$6,000	$12,500

W-3682 • F-1211 • Napier-Thompson (1912–1913) • 198,000
Estimated population: 54 to 58 • *Highest graded:* Unc • *Commentary:* Deliveries began on January 23, 1913, and ended on March 19, 1913.

VG-8	F-12	VF-20	EF-40	AU-50	Unc-60	Unc-63
$750	$1,250	$2,500	$4,500	$9,000	$12,000	$15,000

W-3684 • F-1212 • Napier-Burke (1913) • 200,000
Estimated population: 47 to 53 • *Highest graded:* Unc • *Commentary:* Deliveries began on October 8, 1913, and ended on October 25, 1913.

VG-8	F-12	VF-20	EF-40	AU-50	Unc-60	Unc-63
$750	$1,250	$2,500	$4,500	$9,000	$12,000	$15,000

W-3686 • F-1213 • Parker-Burke (1913–1914) • 200,000
Estimated population: 44 to 48 • *Highest graded:* Unc.

VG-8	F-12	VF-20	EF-40	AU-50	Unc-60	Unc-63
$750	$1,250	$2,500	$4,500	$9,000	$12,000	$15,000

W-3688 • F-1214 • Teehee-Burke (1915–1919) • 1,020,000
Estimated population: 320 to 340 • *Highest graded:* Unc.

VG-8	F-12	VF-20	EF-40	AU-50	Unc-60	Unc-63	Unc-65
$600	$1,000	$2,000	$3,000	$5,000	$7,500	$10,000	$25,000

Series of 1922

Series of 1922 Gold Certificates retain the same motifs, but now with differences in the layout, including the addition of a redemption provision in the lower left field and slightly different positioning of the Treasury signatures. The back is the same design as the preceding. The orange-gold color tended to fade. Today, notes with a bright back are worth more than those with faded color, regardless of the grade.

W-3690 • F-1215 • Speelman-White (1922–1927) • Small red seal with scalloped border • 2,444,000
Estimated population: 750 to 850 • *Highest graded:* Unc.

VG-8	F-12	VF-20	EF-40	AU-50	Unc-60	Unc-63	Unc-65
$550	$800	$1,400	$2,500	$4,000	$5,000	$7,500	$17,500

W-3690★ • F-1215★
Estimated population: 29 to 32 • *Highest graded:* Unc.

VG-8	F-12	VF-20	EF-40	AU-50	Unc-60
$2,500	$5,000	$10,000	$15,000	—	—

FEDERAL RESERVE NOTES

Federal Reserve Notes of the Series of 1914 (both Red Seal and Blue Seal styles) are usually collected as singles to illustrate the types. They can be collected by bank location, but many are so scarce or rare that this is an arduous (but satisfying) task. There are many rare, notable varieties in this class that are surprisingly inexpensive, as the face value and the small supply of available notes preclude wide popularity.

Series of 1914, Red Seal

The face bears the portrait of Benjamin Franklin, who became the subject of choice for the $100 denomination, including all of the small-size issues. On the back are figures, outlined and accented in green to give the impression of bas-relief. The art was done by Kenyon Cox (particularly famous for his Brownies series of books and drawings), and the figures represent Labor, Plenty, America, Peace, and Commerce. The first on the left shows a Romanesque man holding a large sheaf of wheat, while at the far right is Mercury holding a trident and cord-tied package.

Similar to other denominations, the $100 Federal Reserve Notes, Series of 1914, with the Treasury seal and serial numbers in red and with the Burke-McAdoo signature combination, are rather simple in their appearance and nearly always are collected singly. A collection of the Federal Reserve Banks is doable, although Minneapolis is a rarity. As for collecting a and b plates from each Federal Reserve Bank, even coming close to completion would take years and in Uncirculated grade would be impossible. These are considerably scarcer as a group than the Blue Seal notes. After World War I commenced in Europe in 1914, the BEP could not import red ink, so switched to blue after less than a year of printing Red Seals.

In all of the following listings, the number (1 to 12) and the large letter (A to L) on the seal at the left indicate the Federal Reserve Bank that issued the note.

Plate Style a (on Red Seals only): In certain of the following listings, the small letter a following the Whitman number indicates large bank district letter and numeral at bottom left and top right. At the upper left is a small plate letter, but no bank district letter and number.

Plate Style b (on Red and Blue Seals): In certain of the following listings, the small letter b following the Whitman number indicates a note similar to the preceding, but with small bank district letter and numeral added below the plate letter at top left and a small bank district letter and number are at the lower right.

W-3700-A-a • F-1072A • Boston • 16,000

Estimated population: 25 to 28 • *Highest graded:* Unc.

VG-8	F-12	VF-20	EF-40	AU-50	Unc-60	Unc-63	Unc-65
$1,500	$3,000	$4,500	$10,000	$12,000	$15,000	$20,000	$45,000

W-3700-A-b • F-1072B • 28,000

Estimated population: 18 to 20 • *Highest graded:* AU-50.

VG-8	F-12	VF-20	EF-40	AU-50
$2,500	$4,500	$6,000	$10,000	—

W-3700-B-a • F-1073A • New York • 60,000

Estimated population: 16 to 18 • *Highest graded:* Unc.

VG-8	F-12	VF-20	EF-40	AU-50	Unc-60	Unc-63
$2,500	$4,500	$6,000	$10,000	$12,500	$15,000	$20,000

W-3700-B-b • F-1073B • 20,000

Recorded population: 6 • *Highest graded:* EF-45 • *Selected information:* Existing examples include serials B62594A/B, G–VG, pinholes, sold in a CAA auction (9/2000) for $1,870; B68778A/B, F-12 (PMG), sold in a Heritage auction (4/2008) for $6,900; B70167A/C, EF, sold in a Knight auction (8/2003) for $9,200; B73634A, Good; B74657A, VF; and B77905A, VG.

W-3700-C-a • F-1074A • Philadelphia • 12,000

Estimated population: 16 to 18 • *Highest graded:* Unc.

VG-8	F-12	VF-20	EF-40	AU-50	Unc-60	Unc-63
$2,500	$4,500	$6,000	$10,000	$12,500	$15,000	$20,000

W-3700-C-b • F-1074B • 40,000

Estimated population: 25 to 28 • *Highest graded:* Unc.

VG-8	F-12	VF-20	EF-40	AU-50	Unc-60	Unc-63	Unc-65
$1,500	$3,000	$4,500	$10,000	$12,000	$15,000	$18,000	$45,000

W-3700-D-a • F-1075A • Cleveland • 8,000

Recorded population: 6 • *Highest graded:* Unc • *Selected information:* Existing examples include serials D171A, VG, sold in a CAA auction (10/1998) for $412.50; D3138A, G, repaired; D4490A, Good; D6261A/A, EF+, pinholes, sold in a CAA auction (5/2001) for $6,050; D7093A/A, Unc, sold in a CAA auction (1/1998) for $2,420; D7561A, VG–F, sold in a CAA auction (10/1998) for $990.

W-3700-D-b • F-1075B • 40,000

Estimated population: 25 to 28 • *Highest graded:* Unc.

VG-8	F-12	VF-20	EF-40	AU-50	Unc-60	Unc-63
$1,500	$3,000	$4,500	$10,000	$12,000	$15,000	$20,000

W-3700-E-a • F-1076A • Richmond • 16,000

Estimated population: 15 to 17 • *Highest graded:* EF-45.

VG-8	F-12	VF-20	EF-40
$2,500	$4,500	$8,000	$10,000

W-3700-E-b • F-1076B • 8,000

Recorded population: 6 • *Highest graded:* EF-40 • *Selected information:* The existing examples include serials E17709A/A, F–VF, pinholes, sold in a Smythe auction (12/2003) for $1,898; E19307A/C, VF, pinholes, sold in a Smythe auction (6/2003) for $1,955; E21112A/D, EF, sold in a Knight auction (6/1996) for $2,145; E21935A, G–VG, reported by Tom Denly (3/1990); E23404A, VG, reported by Allen's (6/1993); and E23614A/B, VF, part of the Smithsonian Institution collection.

W-3700-F-a • F-1077A • Atlanta • 16,000

Recorded population: 8 • *Highest graded:* Unc • *Selected information:* The existing examples include serials F1138A/B, VF, pinholes (PMG), sold by Stack's (1990) for $1,430; F1973A/A, Unc, sold in a CAA auction (1/2001) for $13,200;

SERIES OF 1914, RED SEAL

Face of a $100 Federal Reserve Note, Series of 1914, Red Seal, with the Plate Style a layout (W-3700-A-a). Federal Reserve Bank of Boston.

Face of a $100 Federal Reserve Note, Series of 1914, Red Seal, with the Plate Style b layout (W-3700-G-b). Federal Reserve Bank of Chicago.

Back of the $100 Federal Reserve Note, Series of 1914, Red Seal. Printed in pale green. The type also used on Series of 1914 Blue Seal $100 Federal Reserve Notes.

F5316A/D, F, problems, sold in a CAA auction (9/1997) for $413; F8126A/B, F, part of the Smithsonian Institution collection; F10542A/B, F–VF, sold in a Knight auction (11/2003) for $1,840; F11443A, Unc; F11619A/C, VF–EF, sold in a Knight auction (8/2003) for $3,738; and F14452A, EF, owned by the Federal Reserve Bank of San Francisco.

W-3700-F-b • F-1077B • 4,000

Recorded population: 2 • Highest graded: EF-45 • Selected information: Knight (6/2001), F17273A/A, F, $3,135. Knight (11/1999), F19120A/D, Ch EF, $4,180.

W-3700-G-a • F-1078A • Chicago • 16,000

Estimated population: 11 to 13 • *Highest graded:* Unc.

VG-8	F-12	VF-20	EF-40	AU-50	Unc-60
$2,500	$4,500	$6,000	$10,000	$12,500	—

W-3700-G-b • F-1078B • 44,000

Estimated population: 32 to 35 • *Highest graded:* Unc.

VG-8	F-12	VF-20	EF-40	AU-50	Unc-60	Unc-63	Unc-65
$1,500	$3,000	$4,500	$6,000	$7,500	$8,000	$12,500	$45,000

W-3700-H-a • F-1079A • St. Louis • 12,000

Estimated population: 11 to 13 • *Highest graded:* AU-58.

VG-8	F-12	VF-20	EF-40	AU-50
$2,500	$4,500	$6,000	$10,000	$15,000

W-3700-H-b • F-1079B • 20,000

Estimated population: 10 to 12 • *Highest graded:* AU-50 • *Selected information:* Knight (10/1999), H12430A, EF–AU, $3,080. Smythe (6/2001), H20580A/D, F, $1,925. Knight (6/1995), H21093A/A, EF–AU, $1,045. Scotsman (5/2005), H23888A, F, $1,121.25.

W-3700-I-a • F-1080A • Minneapolis • 8,000

Recorded population: 3 • *Highest graded:* EF-40 • *Selected information:* The existing examples are serials I2882A, EF, pinholes, part of the Smithsonian Institution collection; I5480A/D, F–VF, pinholes; and I7332A/D, VG-10, problems (PMG), sold in a Heritage auction (4/2008) for $97,750.

W-3700-I-b • F-1080B • 12,000

Estimated population: 9 or 10 • *Highest graded:* EF-45 • *Selected information:* Existing examples include serials I10585A, F, owned by the Federal Reserve Bank of San Francisco; I11908A/D, F, pinholes, sold by Scott Lindquist (1998) for $1,100; I13688A/D, VF, part of the Smithsonian Institution collection; I15384A/D, VF, problems, sold in a Knight auction (4/2003) for $4,888; I16391A/C, VF, sold in a CAA auction (1/2003) for $2,933; I17410A/D, VF, pinholes, sold in a Stack's auction (3/1990) for $2,200; I17922A/B, VF, sold in a B&M auction (3/2002) for $4,140; I18611A/C, EF, sold in a Knight auction (8/2003) for $17,250; and I19262A/B, F, sold in a Knight auction (11/2003) for $2,990.

W-3700-J-a • F-1081A • Kansas City • 8,000

Estimated population: 9 or 10 • *Highest graded:* Unc • *Selected information:* Existing examples include serials J1883A/C, VF, sold in a CAA auction (10/1998) for $1,320; J2073A, F; J3099A/C, Unc, sold in a Stack's auction (9/1996) for $3,300; J3100A/D, VF, owned by the Federal Reserve Bank of Kansas City; J4031A, VF, reported by Tom Denly (9/2006); J4205A/A, Net VF-35 (PMG), sold in a Heritage auction (9/2008) for $18,400; J5651A, VF–EF, reported by Tom Denly (10/2002); J6793A, VG–F, pinholes, reported by Tom Denly (12/1996); and J7365A, G, owned by the Federal Reserve Bank of San Francisco.

W-3700-J-b • F-1081B • 12,000

Estimated population: 18 to 20 • *Highest graded:* AU-58.

VG-8	F-12	VF-20	EF-40	AU-50
$2,500	$4,500	$6,000	$10,000	$15,000

W-3700-K-a • F-1082A • Dallas • 8,000

Recorded population: 6 • *Highest graded:* EF-45 • *Selected information:* Existing examples include serials K1009A, VG; K1576A, VF, owned by the Federal Reserve Bank of San Francisco; K2525A, VF, sold in the Bluestone/Grinnell auction (6/1946) for $130; K6182A/B, VG–F, pinholes, sold in a CAA auction (5/2000) for $825; K6656A/D, F, sold in a Knight auction (8/1998) for $1,650 and later sold in Knight (8/2003) for $3,910; and K7786A/B, EF–AU, sold in a B&M auction (5/1999) for $2,530.

W-3700-K-b • F-1082B • 8,000

Recorded population: 5 • *Highest graded:* EF-45 • *Selected information:* Existing examples include serials K8763A, EF, owned by the Federal Reserve Bank of San Francisco; K11875A/C, VF; K13100A, EF, stained (later Ch AU), sold in a Knight auction (8/1999) for $3,740; K14152A, F-15, stains (PMG), sold in a Heritage auction (4/2008) for $57,500; and K15774A/B, VF–EF, part of the Smithsonian Institution collection.

W-3700-L-a • F-1083A • San Francisco • 8,000

Recorded population: 8 • *Highest graded:* EF-45 • *Selected information:* Existing examples include serials L418A, F–VF, sold in a CAA auction (10/1998) for $1,540; L514A/B, EF, sold in a Knight auction (12/1987) for $375; L4124A, F; L4300A, VG–F; L5216A/D, G, pinholes, sold in a CAA auction (5/2003) for $633; L5871A/C, VG–F; L6057A, VF–EF, sold in a Stack's auction (3/1991) for $575; and L7933A/A, EF–AU (later Ch Unc), sold in a Knight auction (6/1993) for $1,800.

W-3700-L-b • F-1083B • 28,000

Estimated population: 24 to 27 • *Highest graded:* Unc.

VG-8	F-12	VF-20	EF-40	AU-50	Unc-60	Unc-63	Unc-65
$1,500	$3,000	$4,500	$10,000	$12,500	$15,000	$20,000	$45,000

Series of 1914, Blue Seal

The 1914 Blue Seal notes are much more readily available than Red Seal notes and can be easily collected by bank, if not signature combination. As they are not in the mainstream of popularity, scarce and rare varieties are priced lower than might otherwise be the case.

Many counterfeits of this series were made in Russia in the 1920s and distributed widely in the United States. The Secret Service today holds 19 examples from seven Federal Reserve districts, in which all four signature combinations are represented.[24] Examples still surface on the numismatic market, so I recommend that you buy only notes certified by a leading service if you are not familiar with the details of these issues.

In all of the following listings the number (1 to 12) and the large letter (A to L) on the seal at the left indicate the Federal Reserve Bank that issued the note.

Plate Style b (on Red and Blue Seals): All of the 1914 Blue Seal notes are of this plate style (unlike lower denominations, no c and d styles exist). A large district number and letter are at the lower left and top right; at the top left are a small bank district letter and numeral below the plate letter; and a small bank district letter and number are at the lower right.

SERIES OF 1914, BLUE SEAL

$100 Federal Reserve Note, Series of 1914, Blue Seal (W-3713-A). Federal Reserve Bank of Boston. Signatures of White and Mellon. Design similar to the preceding, but with a blue Treasury seal. The back is the same as that used on Series of 1914 Red Seal notes.

The following listings include only notes that are known to have been printed; thus, some listings included in other texts are not given here. Research is currently being done for printages from the $100 White-Mellon plates made for Richmond, Chicago, and St. Louis.

W-3710-A • F-1084 • Boston • Burke-McAdoo (1913–1918) • 296,000 (est.)

Estimated population: 30 to 35 • *Highest graded:* Unc.

VG-8	F-12	VF-20	EF-40	AU-50	Unc-60	Unc-63
$500	$600	$800	$1,500	$2,000	$2,500	$4,000

W-3711-A • F-1085 • Burke-Glass (1918–1920) • 216,000 (est.)

Estimated population: 35 to 40 • *Highest graded:* Unc.

VG-8	F-12	VF-20	EF-40	AU-50	Unc-60	Unc-63
$500	$600	$800	$1,500	$2,000	$2,500	$4,000

W-3713-A • F-1087 • White-Mellon (1921–1928) • 172,000 (est.)

Estimated population: 32 to 35 • *Highest graded:* Unc.

VG-8	F-12	VF-20	EF-40	AU-50	Unc-60	Unc-63	Unc-65
$500	$600	$800	$1,500	$2,000	$2,500	$4,000	$6,000

W-3714-B • F-1088 • New York • Burke-McAdoo (1913–1918) • 2,000,000 (est.)

Estimated population: 160 to 170 • *Highest graded:* Unc.

VG-8	F-12	VF-20	EF-40	AU-50	Unc-60	Unc-63	Unc-65
$400	$500	$700	$1,250	$1,500	$1,750	$2,500	$3,500

W-3714-B★ • F-1088★

Recorded population: 1 • *Selected information:* CAA (1/2005), B241★/A, VF–EF, $12,650.

W-3715-B • F-1089 • Burke-Glass (1918–1920) • 288,000 (est.)

Estimated population: 58 to 63 • *Highest graded:* AU-50.

VG-8	F-12	VF-20	EF-40	AU-50
$500	$750	$1,000	$2,000	$4,000

W-3716-B • F-1090 • Burke-Houston (1920–1921) • 368,000 (est.)

Estimated population: 105 to 115 • *Highest graded:* Unc.

VG-8	F-12	VF-20	EF-40	AU-50	Unc-60	Unc-63
$500	$600	$800	$1,500	$2,000	$2,500	$4,000

W-3716-B★ • F-1090★

Recorded population: 3 • *Highest graded:* AU-50 • *Selected information:* Existing examples include serials B1626★/B, F; B1988★/D, VF, sold in a Knight auction (6/1997) for $1,100; and B353★9/C, AU, sold in a Smythe auction (2/1996) for $4,500.

W-3717-B • F-1091 • White-Mellon (1921–1928) • 348,000 (est.)

Estimated population: 36 to 42 • *Highest graded:* AU-55.

VG-8	F-12	VF-20	EF-40	AU-50
$500	$750	$1,000	$2,000	$4,000

W-3718-C • F-1092 • Philadelphia • Burke-McAdoo (1913–1918) • 548,000 (est.)

Estimated population: 110 to 120 • *Highest graded:* Unc • *Commentary:* For this variety in particular, deceptive Russian counterfeits exist, made in the 1920s. Some have appeared in numismatic auctions. Martin Gengerke in *U.S. Paper Money Records* gives serial numbers. Use extreme caution when contemplating the purchase of this variety. Also see introductory information above.

VG-8	F-12	VF-20	EF-40	AU-50	Unc-60	Unc-63
$500	$600	$800	$1,500	$2,000	$2,500	$4,000

W-3721-C • F-1095 • White-Mellon (1921–1928) • 60,000 (est.)

Recorded population: 5 • *Highest graded:* VF-25 • *Selected information:* Existing examples include serials C602818A, VF; C610044A/D, F-15 (PMG); C611272A/D, VF, sold in a CAA auction (4/2006) for $5,750; C611397A, F-20 (PMG), sold in a Knight auction (6/2008) for $1,380; and C616807A/C, VF, sold in a Knight auction (2/2004) for $2,990.

W-3722-D • F-1096 • Cleveland • Burke-McAdoo (1913–1918) • 188,000 (est.)

Estimated population: 25 to 28 • *Highest graded:* Unc.

VG-8	F-12	VF-20	EF-40	AU-50	Unc-60	Unc-63
$500	$750	$1,000	$2,000	$4,000	$5,000	$7,500

W-3723-D • F-1097 • Burke-Glass (1918–1920) • 68,000 (est.)

Estimated population: 16 to 18 • *Highest graded:* EF-45.

VG-8	F-12	VF-20	EF-40
$750	$1,000	$2,000	$3,500

W-3724-D • F-1098 • Burke-Houston (1920–1921) • 232,000 (est.)

Estimated population: 45 to 50 • *Highest graded:* Unc.

VG-8	F-12	VF-20	EF-40	AU-50	Unc-60	Unc-63	Unc-65
$500	$600	$800	$1,500	$2,000	$2,500	$4,000	$6,000

W-3724-D★ • F-1098★

Recorded population: 1 • *Selected information:* Stack's (3/1991), D6★/B, VF, $1,050.

W-3725-D • F-1099 • White-Mellon (1921–1928) • 132,000 (est.)

Estimated population: 36 to 42 • *Highest graded:* Unc.

VG-8	F-12	VF-20	EF-40	AU-50	Unc-60	Unc-63
$500	$600	$800	$1,500	$2,500	$3,500	$4,500

W-3726-E • F-1100 • Richmond • Burke-McAdoo (1913–1918) • 272,000 (est.)

Estimated population: 48 to 54 • *Highest graded:* Unc.

VG-8	F-12	VF-20	EF-40	AU-50	Unc-60	Unc-63
$500	$600	$800	$1,500	$2,500	$3,500	$4,500

W-3726-E★ • F-1100★

Recorded population: 1 • *Selected information:* CAA (5/2005), E2★/B, G, $13,800.

W-3727-E • F-1101 • Burke-Glass (1918–1920) • 208,000 (est.)

Estimated population: 13 to 15 • *Highest graded:* AU-50.

VG-8	F-12	VF-20	EF-40	AU-50
$750	$1,000	$2,000	$3,500	$5,000

W-3730-F • F-1104 • Atlanta • Burke-McAdoo (1913–1918) • 408,000 (est.)

Estimated population: 215 to 230 • *Highest graded:* Unc.

VG-8	F-12	VF-20	EF-40	AU-50	Unc-60	Unc-63	Unc-65
$400	$500	$700	$1,250	$1,500	$1,750	$2,500	$3,500

W-3730-F★ • F-1104★

Recorded population: 1 • *Selected information:* Stack's (9/1992), F107★/C, VF, $1,900.

W-3732-F • F-1106 • Burke-Houston (1920–1921) • 12,000 (est.)

Recorded population: 7 • *Highest graded:* Unc • *Selected information:* The existing examples include serials F428843A/C, F, stained; F429134A/B, F-12 (PMG), sold in a Heritage auction (4/2008) for $920; F432928A/D, Net VF-20 (PMG); F437754A, F, minute edge tear, sold in a CAA auction (9/2005) for $1,265, and later in Knight (6/2008), graded VF-20 by PMG, for $2,070; and F441329A/A, Unc, changeover pair, only one note of the pair, sold in a CAA auction (5/1998) for $1,540.

W-3733-F • F-1107 • White-Mellon (1921–1928) • 100,000 (est.)

Estimated population: 12 to 14 • *Highest graded:* Unc.

VG-8	F-12	VF-20	EF-40	AU-50	Unc-60	Unc-63	Unc-65
$750	$1,000	$1,500	$2,000	$2,500	$3,000	$4,000	$6,000

W-3734-G • F-1108 • Chicago • Burke-McAdoo (1913–1918) • 596,000 (est.)

Estimated population: 110 to 120 • *Highest graded:* Unc.

VG-8	F-12	VF-20	EF-40	AU-50	Unc-60	Unc-63	Unc-65
$400	$500	$700	$1,250	$1,500	$1,750	$2,500	$3,500

W-3734-G★ • F-1108★

Recorded population: 2 • *Selected information:* The existing examples are serials G28★/D, VG, listed by Doug Murray, and G253★/A, F–VF, sold in a Smythe auction (6/2003) for $6,670.

W-3736-G • F-1110 • Burke-Houston (1920–1921) • 232,000 (est.)

Estimated population: 75 to 85 • *Highest graded:* Unc.

VG-8	F-12	VF-20	EF-40	AU-50	Unc-60	Unc-63	Unc-65
$500	$600	$800	$1,500	$2,000	$2,500	$4,000	$6,000

W-3738-H • F-1112 • St. Louis • Burke-McAdoo (1913–1918) • 156,000 (est.)

Estimated population: 70 to 80 • *Highest graded:* Unc.

VG-8	F-12	VF-20	EF-40	AU-50	Unc-60	Unc-63
$500	$600	$800	$1,500	$2,000	$2,500	$3,500

W-3742-I • F-1116 • Minneapolis • Burke-McAdoo (1913–1918) • 64,000 (est.)

Estimated population: 45 to 50 • *Highest graded:* Unc.

VG-8	F-12	VF-20	EF-40	AU-50	Unc-60	Unc-63
$500	$600	$800	$1,500	$2,000	$2,500	$3,500

W-3745-I • F-1119 • White-Mellon (1921–1928) • 40,000 (est.)

Estimated population: 13 to 15 • *Highest graded:* Unc.

VG-8	F-12	VF-20	EF-40	AU-50	Unc-60	Unc-63	Unc-65
$750	$1,000	$1,500	$2,000	$2,500	$3,000	$4,000	$6,000

W-3746-J • F-1120 • Kansas City • Burke-McAdoo (1913–1918) • 164,000 (est.)

Estimated population: 36 to 42 • *Highest graded:* Unc.

VG-8	F-12	VF-20	EF-40	AU-50	Unc-60	Unc-63	Unc-65
$500	$600	$800	$1,500	$2,000	$2,500	$4,000	$6,000

W-3746-J★ • F-1120★

Recorded population: 4 • *Highest graded:* Unc • *Selected information:* NASCA (11/1979), J9★/A, Unc, $1,750. CAA (10/1995), J118★/B, F, $1,650. Heritage (1/2007), J785★/A, F, $8,050.

W-3749-J • F-1123 • White-Mellon (1921–1928) • 72,000 (est.)

Estimated population: 32 to 35 • *Highest graded:* Unc.

VG-8	F-12	VF-20	EF-40	AU-50	Unc-60	Unc-63	Unc-65
$500	$600	$800	$1,500	$2,000	$2,500	$3,500	$4,500

W-3750-K • F-1124 • Dallas • Burke-McAdoo (1913–1918) • 96,000 (est.)

Estimated population: 40 to 45 • *Highest graded:* Unc.

VG-8	F-12	VF-20	EF-40	AU-50	Unc-60	Unc-63	Unc-65
$500	$600	$800	$1,500	$2,500	$3,500	$4,500	$6,000

W-3750-K★ • F-1124★

Recorded population: 1 • *Selected information:* Hickman & Oakes (6/1988), K97★/A, ex. Amon Carter, VF, $700.

W-3753-K • F-1127 • White-Mellon (1921–1928) • 28,000 (est.)

Recorded population: 4 • *Highest graded:* EF-40 • *Selected information:* The existing examples include serials K115610A, VF, owned by the Federal Reserve Bank of San Francisco; K115798A/B, VF, sold in a Knight auction (11/2001) for $3,960; K117135A/C, VF, sold in a Smythe auction (6/2000) for $4,620; and K122180A/D, EF-40 (PMG), sold in a Heritage auction (4/2008) for $17,250.

W-3754-L • F-1128 • San Francisco • Burke-McAdoo (1913–1918) • 592,000 (est.)

Estimated population: 95 to 105 • *Highest graded:* Unc.

VG-8	F-12	VF-20	EF-40	AU-50	Unc-60	Unc-63	Unc-65
$500	$600	$800	$1,250	$1,500	$1,750	$2,500	$3,500

W-3754-L★ • F-1128★

Recorded population: 1 • *Selected information:* CAA (5/2005), L51★/C, VG, $18,400.

W-3756-L • F-1130 • Burke-Houston (1920–1921) • 196,000 (est.)

Estimated population: 60 to 65 • *Highest graded:* Unc.

VG-8	F-12	VF-20	EF-40	AU-50	Unc-60	Unc-63	Unc-65
$500	$600	$800	$1,250	$1,500	$1,750	$2,500	$3,500

W-3757-L • F-1131 • White-Mellon (1921–1928) • 240,000 (est.)

Estimated population: 40 to 45 • *Highest graded:* Unc.

VG-8	F-12	VF-20	EF-40	AU-50	Unc-60	Unc-63
$600	$800	$1,000	$1,500	$2,000	$3,000	$4,500

SMALL SIZE

All small-size $100 notes have the portrait of Benjamin Franklin, engraved by John Eissler, on the face and a view of Independence Hall, created by Joachim C. Benzing, on the back. These designs were used up to the advent of modern security notes.

Among small-size $100 notes of the late 1920s and early 1930s, National Bank Notes are avidly collected by state and are hard to find in the marketplace. Most other small-size $100 bills are sought only by those desiring a single example of the type. Federal Reserve Notes are still being printed for

and distributed by the 12 different banks, but they are not widely collected by variety. In recent years these have been printed at the Western Facility in Fort Worth, in addition to the regular production at the Bureau of Engraving and Printing in Washington, DC.

Today, the BEP issues more of this denomination, face value, than all others combined, with about two-thirds of the printage circulating in foreign countries. High-quality overseas counterfeits have been a great challenge for the Secret Service in recent years. In popular parlance, modern $100 bills are called "C notes" and "Franklins."

LEGAL TENDER NOTES

Small-size Legal Tender or United States Notes are comprised of the Series of 1966 and 1966-A issues with a red seal. These are the only Legal Tender Note denomination over $5. These were not needed in commerce and were used to redeem in bulk Legal Tender Notes of other denominations, while, for accounting purposes, maintaining the same total face value of Legal Tender bills in Treasury and public hands. This adhered to the Act of May 3, 1878, which limited the total face value of Legal Tender Notes to precisely $346,861,016. By 1996 those held by the Treasury had been destroyed. Single bills are popularly collected for type and are very distinctive in appearance.

Series of 1966
Granahan-Fowler (1965–1966)

Near the end of November 1968, the first Series of 1966 $100 Legal Tender Notes (illus. on p. 662) with the anachronistic signatures of Granahan and Fowler were available at the Treasury department windows in Washington. In early December, the new notes were also available through New York banks. Chuck O'Donnell and others endeavored to round up fancy serial numbers and star notes. The first brick of 4,000 notes was located in Puerto Rico, O'Donnell wrote, and the first pack, with serial numbers 1 to 100 was purchased and offered for sale by a Washington dealer. The second and third packs were found in New York, and several other packs had been paid out over the counter. A search of remaining notes showed fewer than 25 star notes. Brick number four, serials 12,001 to 16,000 produced fewer than 50 star notes. All efforts combined rounded up fewer than 100 stars. Even though 3,450,000 regular notes and 32,000 star notes were printed, they were very difficult to find at the outset.[25]

Today these are readily available on the numismatic market in relation to the demand for them. Their popularity usually causes them to sell quickly from dealers' stocks and to attract many bids at auction. Star notes are scarcer, even though they were printed in unusually large quantities.

W-3800 • F-1550 • 768,000

VF-20	EF-40	AU-50	Unc-60	Unc-63
$165	$195	$250	$325	$500

W-3800★ • F-1550★ • 128,000

VF-20	EF-40	AU-50	Unc-60	Unc-63
$400	$600	$900	$1,200	$1,500

Series of 1966-A
Elston-Kennedy (1969–1970)

This series continued the preceding design. Today these are significantly rarer than the printage suggests. No star notes were made.

W-3801 • F-1551 • 512,000

VF-20	EF-40	AU-50	Unc-60	Unc-63
$225	$350	$525	$700	$950

NATIONAL BANK NOTES

Series of 1929, Type 1, Brown Seal
Jones-Woods (1929–1933)

Type 1 bills each had the same serial number on a given sheet, prefixed by a letter, A through F, such as A000001A to F000001A. For the first sheet of a particular bank, this gave six times more serial number 1 Type 1 notes than Type 2

notes. The signatures of the bank cashier and president were printed directly on each note at the BEP.

The large populations of these notes have stimulated many numismatists to collect as many banks or towns as possible within a given state. Most are in grades of Fine to Very Fine or so, although quite a few Uncirculated notes exist, many of which have low serial numbers. The prices listed are for states from which a large number of notes survive.

Banks of Issue and Rarity of Notes

Based upon census information from Don C. Kelly and James M. Kelly (*National Bank Note Census*, Version 4.0) and with some information from other sources, this listing gives each location, the number of banks issuing this series of notes within each, and a commentary.[26]

The Kelly survey records 2,415 of these. There are 86 serial number 1 notes, as each first sheet had six of these. Hawaii offers quite a few territorial notes.

$100 Legal Tender Note, Series of 1966 (W-3800), with red serial numbers and Treasury seal. These bills were not widely released.

Back of the $100 Legal Tender Note, Series of 1966 (W-3800), with IN GOD WE TRUST above Independence Hall. As Legal Tender Notes of the $100 denomination were not introduced until the late 1960s, they have this late-style back.

SERIES OF 1966-A

Detail of the signatures and the series imprint of a $100 Legal Tender Note, Series of 1966-A (W-3801). The back is the same as used for Series 1966, with Independence Hall and motto.

California • 15 banks of issue • 238 notes reported • The census lists 34 Unc examples. Seven serial number 1 notes are known.

Colorado • 7 banks of issue • 115 notes reported • The census lists 16 Unc notes. Seven serial number 1 notes are known.

Connecticut • 3 banks of issue • 15 notes reported • All are circulated.

Delaware • 1 bank of issue • 2 notes reported • National Bank of Smyrna (EF, not graded).

Florida • 3 banks of issue • 38 notes reported • All are circulated.

Hawaii • 1 bank of issue • 65 notes reported • Two Unc notes; all are from the Bishop First National Bank of Honolulu. Hawaii was a territory at the time, but the notes simply say Hawaii.

Idaho • 3 banks of issue • 30 notes reported • All are circulated.

Illinois • 32 banks of issue • 221 notes reported • The census lists 26 Unc notes. Three serial number 1 notes are known, from the Palmer National Bank of Danville (VF), the Commercial National Bank of Peoria (VF) and the Union National Bank of Streator (not graded).

Indiana • 13 banks of issue • 75 notes reported • The census lists 11 Unc notes. The only serial number 1 note is from the Washington National Bank.

Iowa • 12 banks of issue • 66 notes reported • Seven Unc notes are listed. The only serial number 1 note is from the Merchants National Bank of Cedar Rapids.

Kansas • 12 banks of issue • 39 notes reported • All are circulated. Two serial number 1 notes are known, from the Central National Bank of Junction City (not graded) and the Southwest National Bank of Wichita (VF).

Kentucky • 4 banks of issue • 12 notes reported • All are circulated. The only serial number 1 note is from the First National Bank of Hopkinsville (F).

Louisiana • 2 banks of issue • 27 notes reported • Six serial number 1 notes are from the Commercial National Bank of Shreveport, all Unc.

Maryland • 8 banks of issue • 49 reported • Two Unc examples are known from the Salisbury National Bank, Salisbury.

Massachusetts • 7 banks of issue • 36 notes reported • The only Unc note is from the Webster and Atlas National Bank of Boston. The only serial number 1 note is from the Warren National Bank of Peabody.

SERIES OF 1929, TYPE 1, BROWN SEAL

$100 National Bank Note, Series of 1929, Type 1 (W-3803). Union Planters National Bank & Trust Company of Memphis, Tennessee. The bank charter number, 12249, is in black at the left and right borders. Letters are before and after serial number. The signatures of the bank officers are printed.

Back of the $100 National Bank Note, Series of 1929, Type 1 (W-3803). View of Independence Hall in Philadelphia. This is the basic design used on all $100 notes issued through the 1950s (except for the Series of 1934 Gold Certificates, which were not released).

Michigan • 8 banks of issue • 150 notes reported • The census lists 29 Unc notes, and 19 serial number 1 notes are known.

Minnesota • 5 banks of issue • 36 notes reported • All are circulated examples.

Mississippi • 1 bank of issue • No notes reported.

Missouri • 4 banks of issue • 44 notes reported • The only Unc note is from the Fidelity National Bank & Trust Company, Kansas City. The only serial number 1 note is from the First National Bank of Kansas City (VF).

Montana • 1 bank of issue • 21 notes reported • All are circulated examples from the First National Bank of Butte.

Nebraska • 5 banks of issue • 53 notes reported • All are from the Omaha National Bank of Omaha (including two Unc).

Nevada • 1 bank of issue • 18 notes reported • The only Unc note is from the Reno National Bank, Reno.

New Hampshire • 2 banks of issue • 8 notes reported • All are circulated. Seven are from the National State Capital Bank of Concord.

New Jersey • 9 banks of issue • 50 notes reported • All are circulated. The only serial number 1 note is from the Second National Bank of Paterson (EF–AU).

New York • 14 banks of issue • 45 notes reported • All are circulated.

North Carolina • 1 bank of issue • No notes reported.

North Dakota • 1 bank of issue • 7 notes reported • All are circulated and from the First National Bank & Trust Company of Fargo.

Ohio • 17 banks of issue • 129 notes reported • Six Unc notes are listed. Three serial number 1 notes are from the First National Bank & Trust Company of Findlay (AU), Hocking Valley National Bank, Lancaster (VF), and the Citizens National Bank & Trust Company, Mansfield (VF).

Oklahoma • 6 banks of issue • 92 notes reported • Eight Unc notes are known.

Oregon • 2 banks of issue • 4 notes reported • All circulated, two from Peninsula National Bank of Portland, and two from Citizens National Bank of Portland.

Pennsylvania • 34 banks of issue • 191 notes reported • The census lists 32 Unc notes, and 11 serial number 1 notes are known.

Rhode Island • 2 banks of issue • 10 notes reported • All are circulated.

South Dakota • 2 banks of issue • 5 notes reported • All are circulated.

Tennessee • 5 banks of issue • 205 notes reported • The census lists 92 Unc notes, many from the Union Planters National Bank & Trust Company of Memphis. Eight serial number 1 notes are known.

Texas • 32 banks of issue • 229 notes reported • The census lists 20 Unc notes. Seven serial number 1 notes are known.

Vermont • 4 banks of issue • 10 notes reported • All are circulated. The only serial number 1 note is from the Killington National Bank of Rutland (F).

Washington • 2 banks of issue • 28 notes reported • All are from the National Bank of Commerce, Seattle. Four Unc notes are listed.

West Virginia • 1 bank of issue • No notes reported.

Wisconsin • 6 banks of issue • 52 notes reported • Four Unc examples are reported, and six serial number 1 notes are known.

Wyoming • 1 bank of issue • No notes reported.

W-3803 • F-1804-1

Estimated population: 2,700 to 2,900 • *Highest graded:* Unc.

VF-20	EF-40	AU-50	Unc-60	Unc-63
$450	$500	$600	$700	$800

Series of 1929, Type 2, Brown Seal
Jones-Woods (1929–1933)

Type 2 bills were numbered continuously, with the first sheet from a given bank starting at A000001 and ending A000006. This yielded a single number 1 note, in contrast to six on the first Series of 1929 Type 1 sheet. Signatures of the bank cashier and president were printed directly on each note at the BEP. The charter number appears four times on the face, twice in black and twice in brown.

Type 2 notes are much scarcer than Type 1 notes, and are consequently harder to find in the marketplace. Included are issues of many new banks chartered from 1933 to 1935, often consolidations of two or more banks that experienced difficulties during the Depression. Average grades are the highest for any National Bank Notes, generally from Extremely Fine to Uncirculated. The prices listed are for states from which a large number of notes survive.

Banks of Issue and Rarity of Notes

Based upon census information from Don C. Kelly and James M. Kelly (*National Bank Note Census*, Version 4.0) and with some information from other sources, this listing gives each location, the number of banks issuing this series of notes within each, and a commentary.[27]

The Kelly survey records only 270 of these, with only a single serial number 1 note, from Rhode Island. Hawaii offers territorial notes.

Arkansas • 1 bank of issue • 1 note reported • First National Bank of Lawrence County, Walnut Ridge (VG).

California • 1 bank of issue • 101 notes reported • All are from the Bank of America National Trust and Savings Association of San Francisco. Three Unc notes are reported.

Colorado • 2 banks of issue • 9 notes reported • All are circulated. Eight are from the Exchange National Bank of Colorado Springs.

Hawaii • 1 bank of issue • 3 notes reported • Bishop National Bank of Hawaii at Honolulu (VG, EF–AU, F–VF). Hawaii was a territory at the time, but the notes simply say Hawaii.

Illinois • 3 banks of issue • 41 notes reported • Three Unc notes are known, two from the Livestock National Bank of Chicago and one from the Mount Olive National Bank.

SERIES OF 1929, TYPE 2, BROWN SEAL

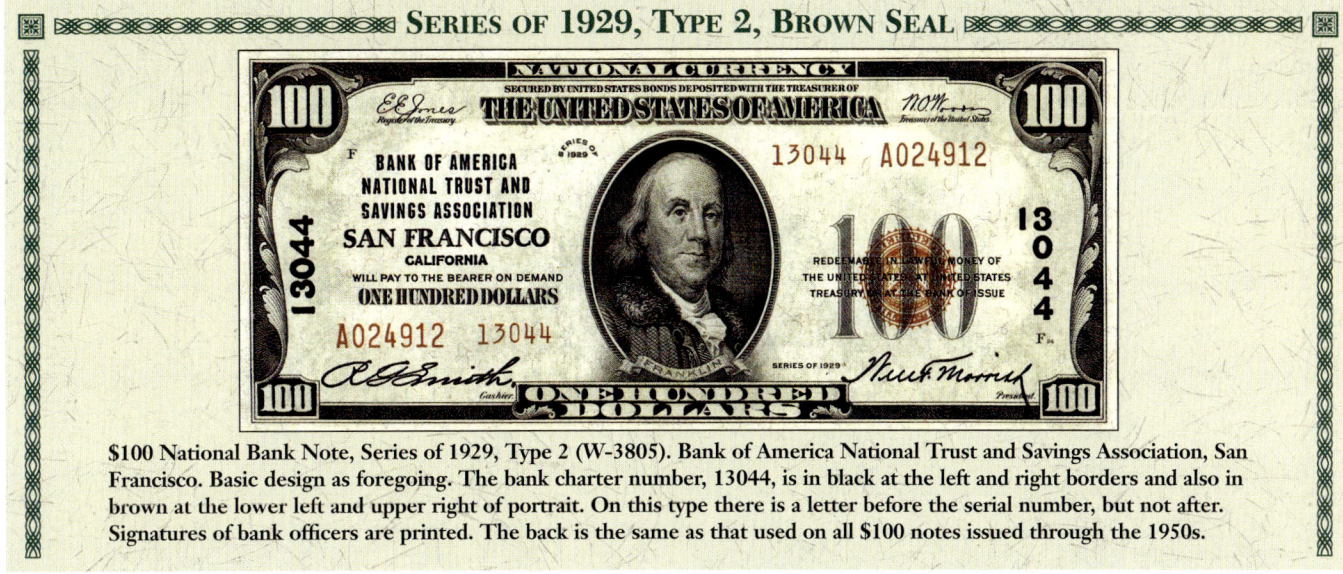

$100 National Bank Note, Series of 1929, Type 2 (W-3805). Bank of America National Trust and Savings Association, San Francisco. Basic design as foregoing. The bank charter number, 13044, is in black at the left and right borders and also in brown at the lower left and upper right of portrait. On this type there is a letter before the serial number, but not after. Signatures of bank officers are printed. The back is the same as that used on all $100 notes issued through the 1950s.

Indiana • 1 bank of issue • 5 notes reported • All are from the American National Bank at Indianapolis, and all are circulated.

Kentucky • 1 bank of issue • 1 note reported • Citizens National Bank of Covington (F).

Louisiana • 2 banks of issue • 10 notes reported • The only Unc note is from the Hibernia National Bank in New Orleans.

Maryland • 3 banks of issue • 2 notes reported • Farmers & Merchants National Bank of Cambridge (VF) and the Salisbury National Bank (F–VF).

Michigan • 2 banks of issue • 3 notes reported • National Bank of Grand Rapids, all circulated.

Minnesota • 1 bank of issue • 9 notes reported • The only Uncirculated example is from the Winona National & Savings Bank.

New Jersey • 2 banks of issue • 2 notes reported • Allenhurst National Bank & Trust Company (VG–F) and the Edgewater National Bank (F).

New York • 2 banks of issue • 1 note reported • First National Bank of Port Jervis (not graded).

Pennsylvania • 3 banks of issue • 17 notes reported • The only Unc example is from the National Bank & Trust Company of Erie.

Rhode Island • 1 bank of issue • 19 notes reported • All are from the Rhode Island Hospital National Bank. Seven Unc notes are listed, including the only serial number 1 note from the state.

Tennessee • 1 bank of issue • No notes reported.

Texas • 8 banks of issue • 45 notes reported • Two Unc notes are from the First National Bank of New Braunfels and Wichita National Bank of Wichita Falls.

Virginia • 2 banks of issue • 1 note reported • First National Bank of Ferrum (VF).

W-3805 • F-1804-2

Estimated population: 300 to 320 • *Highest graded:* Unc.

VF-20	EF-40	AU-50	Unc-60	Unc-63
$500	$700	$800	$900	$1,000

FEDERAL RESERVE BANK NOTES

Series of 1929, Brown Seal
Jones-Woods (1929–1933)

Incomplete sheets intended for National Bank Notes were overprinted with Federal Reserve Bank information to provide paper money in the hope of satisfying what was expected to be a great rush on the banks after the Bank Holiday of March 1933. On these notes (illus. on p. 676) the titles for bank cashier and president have been blacked out and titles for Federal Reserve officers inserted.

The $100 denomination bills are collectible from certain of the banks, but not all. None were printed for Boston, Philadelphia, Atlanta, St. Louis, or San Francisco. Most of the remaining banks are easily collectible today, even in Uncirculated grade, although the Dallas and Kansas City notes are scarcer than the others. All star notes are prime rarities.

W-3810-B • F-1890B • New York • 480,000

VF-20	EF-40	AU-50	Unc-60	Unc-63
$160	$180	$250	$275	$375

W-3810-B★ • F-1890B★

VG-8	F-12	VF-20
$1,100	$1,600	$2,600

W-3811-D • F-1890D • Cleveland • 276,000

VF-20	EF-40	AU-50	Unc-60	Unc-63
$160	$180	$250	$275	$375

W-3811-D★ • F-1890D★

VG-8	F-12	VF-20
$1,150	$1,900	$3,250

W-3812-E • F-1890F • Richmond • 192,000

VF-20	EF-40	AU-50	Unc-60	Unc-63
$165	$200	$285	$325	$400

SERIES OF 1929, BROWN SEAL

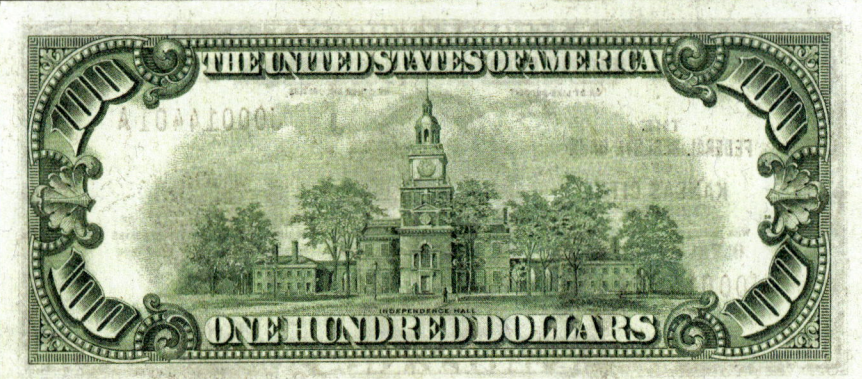

$100 Federal Reserve Bank Note, Series of 1929 (W-3815-J). Federal Reserve Bank of Kansas City.

Back of $100 Federal Reserve Bank Note, Series of 1929 (W-3815-J), the standard design with Independence Hall, without motto, as used through the 1950s.

W-3812-E★ • F-1890F★

VG-8	F-12	VF-20	EF-40	AU-50	Unc-60
$1,750	$2,750	$4,250	—	—	$15,000

W-3813-G • F-1890G • Chicago • 384,000

VF-20	EF-40	AU-50	Unc-60	Unc-63
$160	$180	$250	$275	$325

W-3813-G★ • F-1890G★

VG-8	F-12	VF-20	EF-40
$850	$1,300	$1,900	$2,800

W-3814-I • F-1890I • Minneapolis • 144,000

VF-20	EF-40	AU-50	Unc-60	Unc-63
$165	$200	$275	$325	$475

W-3841-I★ • F-1890I★

VG-8	F-12	VF-20
$3,500	$6,250	$12,500

W-3815-J • F-1890J • Kansas City • 96,000

VF-20	EF-40	AU-50	Unc-60	Unc-63
$155	$180	$250	$300	$425

W-3815-J★ • F-1890J★

VG-8	F-12	VF-20	EF-40	AU-50	Unc-60	Unc-63
$400	$500	$650	$850	$1,050	$1,500	$1,750

W-3816-K • F-1890K • Dallas • 36,000

VG-8	F-12	VF-20	EF-40	AU-50	Unc-60	Unc-63
$425	$600	$800	$950	$1,050	$1,150	$1,750

W-3816-K★ • F-1890K★

Recorded population: 1 • *Selected information:* Heritage (1/2004), raw F, $23,000.

GOLD CERTIFICATES

Small-size Gold Certificates with gold seals were printed for the Series of 1928 and 1934, though the last was not issued. The Series of 1928 bills, with Woods-Mellon signatures, are relatively available today. The Series of 1834, not released, is distinguished by its anachronistic date and by its gold-printed back.

Series of 1928, Gold Seal
Woods-Mellon (1929–1932)

The obligation or payable notice reads, "One hundred dollars in gold coin payable to the bearer on demand." At the left the Treasury seal is overprinted on a more standard commentary, with GOLD above and CERTIFICATE below, with three lines between: "This certificate is a legal tender in the amount thereof in payment of all debts and dues private and public." In addition to the yellow (usually called gold) seal, the serial numbers were printed in yellow. The back is printed in green.

SERIES OF 1928, GOLD SEAL

$100 Gold Certificate, Series of 1929 (W-3818), the design also used for the Series of 1934. Payable in gold.

This series uses the standard back found on all $100 notes issued in commerce through the 1950s.

Circulated examples appear in the market with some frequency, but these are scarce overall. Uncirculated notes are very elusive. Only in recent times has there been a large market differential for higher-grade Uncirculated examples within that category.

W-3818 • F-2405 • 3,240,000

VF-20	EF-40	AU-50	Unc-60	Unc-63
$800	$1,500	$2,250	$3,100	$4,000

W-3818★ • F-2405★ • 12,000

VF-20	EF-40
$4,500	$12,000

Series of 1934, Gold Seal
Julian-Morgenthau (1934–1945)

This anomalous series (illus. on p. 678) was created in 1934, by which time the Treasury was not allowing either gold coins or Gold Certificates into the channels of commerce. The intent was for the notes to be used in banking channels. However, none are known to have been distributed. Unlike all other small-size $100 notes, the back was printed in orange-gold. The same plate, however, was used to print green backs for other series. The obligation is no longer payable in gold *coin* and now reads: "One hundred dollars in gold payable to the bearer as authorized by law."

W-3819 • F-2406 • 120,000 • None in private hands

FEDERAL RESERVE NOTES

Small-size Federal Reserve Notes commenced with the Series of 1928. Since then, $100 notes have been issued for all 12 districts, with various signature combinations and series designations. Not all banks participated in every series. Since the late 1940s these have been the highest-denomination bills produced.

In 1990 a plastic security strip was added to the paper. The design received a makeover for the Series of 1996. The portrait of Franklin was enlarged and various security modifications were made, in view of this denomination being a favorite target for counterfeiters. On the back the image of Independence Hall was retained, but the border was altered. These can be collected by bank and signature combination, although the high face value precludes a wide interest.

Most prices throughout this series are generic, with low-printage issues often selling for little more than issues with quantities five or more times greater. Now and again hoards come on the market, making certain series more available than others. No doubt in time PMG and PCGS reports of the number of notes certified will delineate which are truly rare in high grades. At present, much of the market is a free-for-all, yielding opportunities for cherrypicking.

Series of 1928, Green Seal
Woods-Mellon (1929–1932)

The obligation is in four lines in the field at the upper left: "Redeemable in gold on demand at the United States

Treasury, or in gold or lawful money at any Federal Reserve Bank." On the Series of 1928 notes, the seal is in the left field and features the number of the issuing Federal Reserve Bank, 1 to 12. The series imprint appears twice, at the upper left of Franklin's portrait and in the right field.

Although these are designated as the Series of 1928, these and all other denominations in the series were not released until 1929. Minneapolis and Dallas notes have the lowest printages and are thus the keys to the series. All star notes are rare, especially at the Uncirculated level.

Prices for a typical note for this series, unless listed otherwise, are as follows:

VF-20	EF-40	AU-50	Unc-60	Unc-63
$175	$225	$325	$425	$550

Prices for a typical star note for this series, unless listed otherwise, are as follows:

VF-20	EF-40	AU-50	Unc-60	Unc-63
$750	$1,000	$1,250	$1,500	$1,850

W-3820-A • F-2150A • Boston • 376,000

W-3820-A★ • F-2150A★

VF-20	EF-40	AU-50	Unc-60	Unc-63
$1,000	$2,000	$2,500	$3,250	$4,000

W-3820-B • F-2150B • New York • 755,400

VF-20	EF-40	AU-50	Unc-60	Unc-63
$175	$225	$300	$375	$450

W-3820-B★ • F-2150B★

W-3820-C • F-2150C • Philadelphia • 389,100

W-3820-C★ • F-2150C★

W-3820-D • F-2150D • Cleveland • 542,400

W-3820-D★ • F-2150D★

W-3820-E • F-2150E • Richmond • 364,416

W-3820-E★ • F-2150E★

W-3820-F • F-2150F • Atlanta • 357,000

W-3820-F★ • F-2150F★

W-3820-G • F-2150G • Chicago • 783,300

VF-20	EF-40	AU-50	Unc-60	Unc-63
$175	$225	$300	$375	$475

W-3820-G★ • F-2150G★

W-3820-H • F-2150H • St. Louis • 187,200

W-3820-H★ • F-2150H★

SERIES OF 1934, GOLD SEAL

$100 Gold Certificate, Series of 1934 (W-3819). Serial A00000510A, plate F1. Serially numbered well into a production run.

Detail of the Treasury seal.

Back of the $100 Gold Certificate, Series of 1934 (W-3819), with the standard back as used on other notes of the era, but printed in orange-gold rather than green. (Smithsonian Institution)

Detail of the plate number (29) at the right edge of the field.

W-3820-I • F-2150I • Minneapolis • 102,000

W-3820-I★ • F-2150I★

W-3820-J • F-2150J • Kansas City • 234,612

W-3820-J★ • F-2150J★

VF-20	EF-40	AU-50	Unc-60	Unc-63
$1,500	$2,250	$2,750	$3,250	$4,000

W-3820-K • F-2150K • Dallas • 80,140

VF-20	EF-40	AU-50	Unc-60	Unc-63
$200	$275	$385	$495	$600

W-3820-K★ • F-2150K★

VF-20	EF-40	AU-50	Unc-60	Unc-63
$1,500	$2,250	$2,750	$3,250	$4,000

W-3820-L • F-2150L • San Francisco • 486,000

VF-20	EF-40	AU-50	Unc-60	Unc-63
$175	$225	$300	$375	$475

W-3820-L★ • F-2150L★

VF-20	EF-40	AU-50	Unc-60	Unc-63
$1,500	$2,250	$2,750	$3,250	$4,000

Series of 1928-A, Green Seal
Woods-Mellon (1929–1932)

The Federal Reserve seal was changed beginning with this issue. Instead of a number representing the bank at the center, it has a letter (A to L). A higher quantity was printed of this early issue than the later notes with light yellow-green seals, but this seems to have produced no star notes. All of the Federal Reserve Banks are presented.

SERIES OF 1928, GREEN SEAL

$100 Federal Reserve Note, Series of 1928 (W-3820-A). Federal Reserve Bank of Boston. The face printing notes that the bill is payable "in gold or lawful money."

Back of the $100 Federal Reserve Note, Series of 1928 (W-3820-A), the standard design printed in green, as used on all $100 notes issued in commerce through the 1950s.

SERIES OF 1928-A, GREEN SEAL

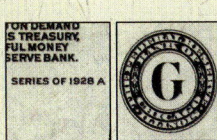

Signatures, series imprints, and Federal Reserve seal (with a letter instead of a numeral) of a $100 Federal Reserve Note, Series of 1928-A (W-3821-G). The back is the standard design printed in green used on all $100 notes issued in commerce through the 1950s.

W-3821-A • F-2151A • Boston • 890,400

F-12	VF-20	EF-40	AU-50	Unc-60	Unc-63	Unc-65
$110	$125	$165	$210	$265	$325	$500

W-3821-B • F-2151B • New York • 2,938,176

F-12	VF-20	EF-40	AU-50	Unc-60	Unc-63	Unc-65
$110	$125	$155	$190	$240	$290	$385

W-3821-C • F-2151C • Philadelphia • 1,496,844

F-12	VF-20	EF-40	AU-50	Unc-60	Unc-63	Unc-65
$110	$125	$165	$200	$265	$325	$525

W-3821-D • F-2151D • Cleveland • 992,436

F-12	VF-20	EF-40	AU-50	Unc-60	Unc-63	Unc-65
$110	$125	$165	$195	$250	$300	$450

W-3821-E • F-2151E • Richmond • 621,364

F-12	VF-20	EF-40	AU-50	Unc-60	Unc-63	Unc-65
$110	$125	$165	$200	$265	$325	$490

W-3821-F • F-2151F • Atlanta • 371,400

F-12	VF-20	EF-40	AU-50	Unc-60	Unc-63	Unc-65
$120	$135	$170	$210	$270	$375	$700

W-3821-G • F-2151G • Chicago • 4,010,424

VF-20	EF-40	AU-50	Unc-60	Unc-63	Unc-65
$115	$145	$175	$220	$250	$350

W-3821-H • F-2151H • St. Louis • 749,544

F-12	VF-20	EF-40	AU-50	Unc-60	Unc-63	Unc-65
$120	$130	$155	$185	$230	$275	$400

W-3821-I • F-2151I • Minneapolis • 503,040

F-12	VF-20	EF-40	AU-50	Unc-60	Unc-63	Unc-65
$130	$145	$180	$220	$275	$370	$675

W-3821-J • F-2151J • Kansas City • 681,804

F-12	VF-20	EF-40	AU-50	Unc-60	Unc-63	Unc-65
$120	$130	$175	$215	$270	$360	$600

W-3821-K • F-2151K • Dallas • 594,456

F-12	VF-20	EF-40	AU-50	Unc-60	Unc-63
$130	$150	$185	$250	$300	—

W-3821-L • F-2151L • San Francisco • 1,228,032

F-12	VF-20	EF-40	AU-50	Unc-60	Unc-63	Unc-65
$115	$125	$165	$195	$250	$300	$450

Series of 1928-A, Light Yellow-Green Seal
Woods-Mellon (1929–1932)

The later notes, with light yellow-green seals, are not known to have been produced for some of the Federal Reserve Banks. Records are not precise, and there is always the possibility for new discoveries. The two star notes in the series are highly prized in any grade.

W-3822-B • F-2151B • New York • Part of W-3821-B printage

VG-8	F-12	VF-20	EF-40	AU-50	Unc-60
$115	$125	$155	$185	$250	—

W-3822-B★ • F-2151B★

VF-20	EF-40	AU-50	Unc-60
$4,000	$7,500	—	—

W-3822-G • F-2151G • Chicago • Part of W-3821-G printage

VG-8	F-12	VF-20	EF-40	AU-50	Unc-60	Unc-63
$110	$120	$150	$170	$325	$425	$625

W-3822-H • F-2151H • St. Louis • Part of W-3821-H printage

VG-8	F-12	VF-20	EF-40	AU-50	Unc-60	Unc-63	Unc-65
$110	$120	$155	$185	$250	$325	$425	$975

W-3822-H★ • F-2151H★

VG-8	F-12	VF-20	EF-40	AU-50	Unc-60	Unc-63	Unc-65
$1,500	$2,500	$3,500	$5,500	$6,500	$7,500	$12,500	$25,000

SERIES OF 1928-A, LIGHT YELLOW-GREEN SEAL

$100 Federal Reserve Note, Series of 1928-A (W-3822-G). Light yellow-green Treasury seal. Federal Reserve Bank of Chicago. The back is the standard design printed in green used on all $100 notes issued in commerce through the 1950s.

W-3822-I • F-2151I • Minneapolis • Part of W-3821-I printage

VG-8	F-12	VF-20	EF-40	AU-50	Unc-60
$115	$135	$165	$200	$375	—

W-3822-J • F-2151J • Kansas City • Part of W-3821-J printage

VG-8	F-12	VF-20	EF-40	AU-50	Unc-60	Unc-63	Unc-65
$115	$130	$160	$190	$300	$375	$500	—

W-3822-L • F-2151L • San Francisco • Part of W-3821-L printage

VG-8	F-12	VF-20	EF-40	AU-50	Unc-60	Unc-63
$115	$125	$155	$175	$335	$415	$600

Series of 1934, Light Yellow-Green Seal
Julian-Morgenthau (1934–1945)

The Series of 1934 continues the same general configuration as the preceding series, but now with a change in the redemption inscription, eliminating the mention of gold: "This note is legal tender for all debts, public and private, and is redeemable in lawful money at the United States Treasury, or at any Federal Reserve Bank." All are readily collectible, but as dealers' stocks are usually thin for this high denomination, some searching will be needed to find certain varieties. All star notes are scarce.

W-3823-A • F-2152A • Boston • 3,710,000

VG-8	F-12	VF-20	EF-40	AU-50	Unc-60	Unc-63	Unc-65
$110	$120	$135	$150	$165	$185	$250	$600

W-3823-A★ • F-2152A★

VG-8	F-12	VF-20	EF-40	AU-50	Unc-60	Unc-63
$200	$300	$450	$750	$850	$975	$1,200

W-3823-B • F-2152B • New York • 3,086,000

VG-8	F-12	VF-20	EF-40	AU-50	Unc-60	Unc-63	Unc-65
$110	$115	$125	$140	$155	$175	$225	$500

W-3823-B★ • F-2152B★

VG-8	F-12	VF-20	EF-40	AU-50	Unc-60	Unc-63
$175	$250	$375	$675	$775	$900	$1,100

W-3823-C • F-2152C • Philadelphia • 2,776,800

VG-8	F-12	VF-20	EF-40	AU-50	Unc-60	Unc-63	Unc-65
$110	$120	$135	$150	$165	$185	$245	$600

W-3823-C★ • F-2152C★

VG-8	F-12	VF-20	EF-40	AU-50	Unc-60	Unc-63
$200	$300	$450	$825	$1,100	$1,300	$2,000

W-3823-D • F-2152D • Cleveland • 3,447,108

VG-8	F-12	VF-20	EF-40	AU-50	Unc-60	Unc-63	Unc-65
$110	$120	$135	$150	$165	$185	$245	$600

W-3823-D★ • F-2152D★

VG-8	F-12	VF-20	EF-40	AU-50	Unc-60	Unc-63
$175	$250	$375	$575	$750	$950	$1,400

W-3823-E • F-2152E • Richmond • 4,317,600

VG-8	F-12	VF-20	EF-40	AU-50	Unc-60	Unc-63	Unc-65
$110	$120	$135	$155	$175	$195	$275	$675

W-3823-E★ • F-2152E★

VG-8	F-12	VF-20	EF-40	AU-50	Unc-60	Unc-63
$225	$325	$500	$850	$1,125	$1,275	$2,000

W-3823-F • F-2152F • Atlanta • 3,264,420

VG-8	F-12	VF-20	EF-40	AU-50	Unc-60	Unc-63	Unc-65
$110	$120	$135	$155	$175	$195	$275	$675

W-3823-F★ • F-2152F★

VG-8	F-12	VF-20	EF-40	AU-50	Unc-60	Unc-63
$225	$325	$500	$850	$1,125	$1,325	$2,000

W-3823-G • F-2152G • Chicago • 7,075,000

VG-8	F-12	VF-20	EF-40	AU-50	Unc-60	Unc-63	Unc-65
$110	$120	$130	$145	$160	$180	$250	$575

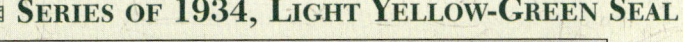

$100 Federal Reserve Note, Series of 1934 (W-3823-B). Light yellow-green Treasury seal. Federal Reserve Bank of New York. The back is the standard design printed in green used on all $100 notes issued in commerce through the 1950s.

Detail of the payable notice.

W-3823-G★ • F-2152G★

VG-8	F-12	VF-20	EF-40	AU-50	Unc-60	Unc-63
$165	$240	$350	$550	$700	$800	$1,050

W-3823-H • F-2152H • St. Louis • 2,106,192

VG-8	F-12	VF-20	EF-40	AU-50	Unc-60	Unc-63	Unc-65
$110	$120	$140	$165	$185	$205	$285	$750

W-3823-H★ • F-2152H★

VG-8	F-12	VF-20	EF-40	AU-50	Unc-60	Unc-63
$225	$325	$500	$850	$1,125	$1,325	$2,000

W-3823-I • F-2152I • Minneapolis • 852,600

VG-8	F-12	VF-20	EF-40	AU-50	Unc-60	Unc-63	Unc-65
$110	$125	$145	$170	$190	$215	$350	$800

W-3823-I★ • F-2152I★

VG-8	F-12	VF-20	EF-40	AU-50	Unc-60	Unc-63
$200	$300	$450	$800	$1,100	$1,300	$2,000

W-3823-J • F-2152J • Kansas City • 1,932,900

VG-8	F-12	VF-20	EF-40	AU-50	Unc-60	Unc-63	Unc-65
$110	$120	$140	$155	$175	$190	$250	$750

W-3823-J★ • F-2152J★

VG-8	F-12	VF-20	EF-40	AU-50	Unc-60	Unc-63
$225	$325	$500	$850	$1,125	$1,350	$2,000

W-3823-K • F-2152K • Dallas • 1,506,516

VG-8	F-12	VF-20	EF-40	AU-50	Unc-60	Unc-63	Unc-65
$110	$125	$145	$170	$190	$215	$350	$800

W-3823-K★ • F-2152K★

VG-8	F-12	VF-20	EF-40	AU-50	Unc-60	Unc-63
$225	$325	$525	$875	$1,150	$1,400	$2,200

W-3823-L • F-2152L • San Francisco • 6,521,940

VG-8	F-12	VF-20	EF-40	AU-50	Unc-60	Unc-63	Unc-65
$110	$125	$135	$145	$175	$235	$400	$850

W-3823-L★ • F-2152L★

VF-20	EF-40	AU-50	Unc-60
$1,100	$2,000	—	—

Series of 1934, Green Seal
Julian-Morgenthau (1934–1945)

This series continued the preceding design. The difference between seal colors of this issue is not great. For best attribution, compare side by side with a note attributed as having a light yellow-green seal.

Mules: Most backs have the plate number in micro letters, but mules have the larger, macro-size serials as used on Series 1934-A (the macro plates have numbers 113 and higher). These are worth a premium. Star note mules are very rare—made for just Richmond, Kansas City, and San Francisco—and are worth considerably more. The San Francisco star is a major rarity. Mitigating this is that the seal color differences are not published in some texts and therefore are not widely known. The essential *Standard Guide to Small-Size U.S. Paper Money 1928 to Date* does treat these and other varieties and is highly recommended for additional information, such as observed serial number ranges.

All within the series are readily collectible, but mules are scarcer. As with most mule varieties, these are not widely known, are not listed in some references, and the number known can only be estimated. Ample opportunity exists for cherrypicking within dealers' stocks. The Kansas City mule star is an extreme rarity.

W-3824-A • F-2152A • Boston • Part of W-3823-A printage

F-12	VF-20	EF-40	AU-50	Unc-60	Unc-63	Unc-65
$105	$125	$135	$145	$160	$185	$250

W-3824-A★ • F-2152A★

VG-8	F-12	VF-20	EF-40	AU-50	Unc-60	Unc-63
$140	$200	$285	$385	$500	$775	$1,350

$100 Federal Reserve Note, Series of 1934 (W-3824-L). Dark green Treasury seal. Federal Reserve Bank of San Francisco. The back is the standard design printed in green used on all $100 notes issued in commerce through the 1950s.

W-3824-A Mule • F-2152A • Part of W-3823-A printage

VG-8	F-12	VF-20	EF-40	AU-50	Unc-60	Unc-63	Unc-65
$120	$130	$145	$155	$170	$190	$325	$675

W-3824-B • F-2152B • New York • Part of W-3823-B printage

F-12	VF-20	EF-40	AU-50	Unc-60	Unc-63	Unc-65
$105	$125	$135	$150	$165	$190	$260

W-3824-B★ • F-2152B★

VG-8	F-12	VF-20	EF-40	AU-50	Unc-60	Unc-63
$140	$200	$285	$385	$450	$675	$1,050

W-3824-C • F-2152C • Philadelphia • Part of W-3823-C printage

F-12	VF-20	EF-40	AU-50	Unc-60	Unc-63	Unc-65
$105	$125	$135	$150	$165	$200	$350

W-3824-C★ • F-2152C★

VG-8	F-12	VF-20	EF-40	AU-50	Unc-60	Unc-63
$140	$200	$285	$385	$450	$750	$1,200

W-3824-C Mule • F-2152C

VG-8	F-12	VF-20	EF-40	AU-50	Unc-60	Unc-63	Unc-65
$120	$130	$145	$155	$170	$190	$325	$675

W-3824-D • F-2152D • Cleveland • Part of W-3823-D printage

F-12	VF-20	EF-40	AU-50	Unc-60	Unc-63	Unc-65
$105	$125	$135	$145	$160	$185	$250

W-3824-D★ • F-2152D★

VG-8	F-12	VF-20	EF-40	AU-50	Unc-60	Unc-63
$150	$225	$335	$425	$525	$825	$1,650

W-3824-D Mule • F-2152D

VG-8	F-12	VF-20	EF-40	AU-50	Unc-60	Unc-63	Unc-65
$120	$130	$145	$155	$170	$190	$325	$675

W-3824-E • F-2152E • Richmond • Part of W-3823-E printage

F-12	VF-20	EF-40	AU-50	Unc-60	Unc-63	Unc-65
$105	$125	$135	$150	$165	$185	$250

W-3824-E★ • F-2152E★

VG-8	F-12	VF-20	EF-40	AU-50	Unc-60	Unc-63
$140	$200	$285	$385	$450	$725	$1,400

W-3824-E Mule★ • F-2152E★

VF-20	EF-40
$1,000	$1,600

W-3824-F • F-2152F • Atlanta • Part of W-3823-F printage

F-12	VF-20	EF-40	AU-50	Unc-60	Unc-63	Unc-65
$105	$125	$135	$150	$165	$185	$275

W-3824-F★ • F-2152F★

VG-8	F-12	VF-20	EF-40	AU-50	Unc-60	Unc-63
$140	$200	$285	$385	$450	$725	$1,300

W-3824-F Mule • F-2152F

VG-8	F-12	VF-20	EF-40	AU-50	Unc-60	Unc-63	Unc-65
$120	$130	$145	$155	$170	$190	$325	$675

W-3824-G • F-2152G • Chicago • Part of W-3823-G printage

F-12	VF-20	EF-40	AU-50	Unc-60	Unc-63	Unc-65
$105	$125	$135	$145	$155	$165	$250

W-3824-G★ • F-2152G★

VG-8	F-12	VF-20	EF-40	AU-50	Unc-60	Unc-63	Unc-65
$135	$185	$265	$360	$425	$575	$950	$1,950

W-3824-G Mule • F-2152G

VG-8	F-12	VF-20	EF-40	AU-50	Unc-60	Unc-63	Unc-65
$115	$125	$140	$150	$160	$180	$290	$625

W-3824-G Mule★ • F-2152G★

VF-20	EF-40
$950	$1,500

W-3824-H • F-2152H • St. Louis • Part of W-3823-H printage

F-12	VF-20	EF-40	AU-50	Unc-60	Unc-63	Unc-65
$105	$125	$135	$150	$165	$225	$375

W-3824-H★ • F-2152H★

VG-8	F-12	VF-20	EF-40	AU-50	Unc-60	Unc-63
$140	$200	$285	$385	$450	$725	$1,300

W-3824-H Mule • F-2152H

VG-8	F-12	VF-20	EF-40	AU-50	Unc-60	Unc-63	Unc-65
$120	$130	$145	$155	$170	$200	$375	$700

W-3824-I • F-2152I • Minneapolis • Part of W-3823-I printage

F-12	VF-20	EF-40	AU-50	Unc-60	Unc-63	Unc-65
$110	$130	$140	$155	$170	$240	$415

W-3824-I★ • F-2152I★

VG-8	F-12	VF-20	EF-40	AU-50	Unc-60	Unc-63
$155	$235	$325	$415	$500	$775	$1,450

W-3824-I Mule • F-2152I

VF-20	EF-40
$2,500	$3,500

W-3824-J • F-2152J • Kansas City • Part of W-3823-J printage

F-12	VF-20	EF-40	AU-50	Unc-60	Unc-63	Unc-65
$105	$125	$135	$150	$165	$200	$300

W-3824-J★ • F-2152J★

VG-8	F-12	VF-20	EF-40	AU-50	Unc-60	Unc-63
$140	$200	$275	$385	$450	$725	$1,200

W-3824-J Mule • F-2152J

VG-8	F-12	VF-20	EF-40	AU-50	Unc-60	Unc-63	Unc-65
$120	$130	$145	$155	$170	$200	$325	$675

W-3824-J Mule★ • F-2152J★

F-12	VF-20
$2,000	$2,900

W-3824-K • F-2152K • Dallas • Part of W-3823-K printage

F-12	VF-20	EF-40	AU-50	Unc-60	Unc-63	Unc-65
$105	$125	$135	$150	$165	$185	$290

W-3824-K★ • F-2152K★

VG-8	F-12	VF-20	EF-40	AU-50	Unc-60	Unc-63	Unc-65
$170	$250	$350	$400	$525	$875	$1,800	$2,900

W-3824-K Mule • F-2152K

VG-8	F-12	VF-20	EF-40	AU-50	Unc-60	Unc-63
$120	$130	$145	$155	$170	$200	$400

W-3824-L • F-2152L • San Francisco • Part of W-3823-L printage

F-12	VF-20	EF-40	AU-50	Unc-60	Unc-63	Unc-65
$105	$125	$135	$145	$170	$220	$275

W-3824-L★ • F-2152L★

VG-8	F-12	VF-20	EF-40	AU-50	Unc-60	Unc-63
$140	$200	$275	$385	$450	$725	$1,100

W-3824-L Mule • F-2152L

Commentary: Current market information not available.

Series of 1934-A, Green Seal
Julian-Morgenthau (1934–1945)

This series continued the preceding design.

Mules: Standard backs for the Series of 1934-A have the plate number in macro numbers, but mules have the smaller, micro-size numbers used on earlier series (the micro plates have numbers 112 and lower).

Mules are generally more available than non-mules for this series. Stars exist only among the mules and are hard to find in higher grades.

Prices for a typical note for this series, unless listed otherwise, are as follows:

VF-20	EF-40	AU-50	Unc-60	Unc-63
$135	$150	$180	$215	$250

W-3825-A • F-2153A • Boston • 102,000

W-3825-A Mule • F-2153A

VG-8	F-12	VF-20	EF-40	AU-50	Unc-60	Unc-63
$120	$130	$140	$150	$160	$200	$350

W-3825-A Mule★ • F-2153A★

VG-8	F-12	VF-20	EF-40	AU-50	Unc-60	Unc-63
$225	$300	$400	$475	$600	$725	$1,350

W-3825-B • F-2153B • New York • 15,278,892

W-3825-B Mule • F-2153B

VF-20	EF-40	AU-50	Unc-60	Unc-63	Unc-65
$120	$130	$140	$150	$225	$375

W-3825-B Mule★ • F-2153B★

VG-8	F-12	VF-20	EF-40	AU-50	Unc-60	Unc-63
$150	$225	$275	$325	$400	$500	$650

W-3825-C • F-2153C • Philadelphia • 588,000

W-3825-C Mule • F-2153C

VG-8	F-12	VF-20	EF-40	AU-50	Unc-60	Unc-63
$110	$120	$130	$140	$150	$200	$350

W-3825-C Mule★ • F-2153C★

VG-8	F-12	VF-20	EF-40	AU-50	Unc-60	Unc-63	Unc-65
$325	$400	$500	$575	$650	$750	$1,500	$3,500

W-3825-D • F-2153D • Cleveland • 645,300

W-3825-D Mule • F-2153D

VF-20	EF-40	AU-50	Unc-60	Unc-63
$120	$130	$140	$150	$235

W-3825-E • F-2153E • Richmond • 770,000

W-3825-E Mule • F-2153E

VF-20	EF-40	AU-50	Unc-60	Unc-63
$130	$150	$160	$200	$350

SERIES OF 1934-A, GREEN SEAL

Detail of the signatures and the series imprints (at top left and bottom right) of a $100 Federal Reserve Note, Series of 1934-A (W-3825-G). The back is the standard design printed in green used on all $100 notes issued in commerce through the 1950s.

W-3825-E Mule★ • F-2153E★

VG-8	F-12	VF-20	EF-40	AU-50	Unc-60	Unc-63
$225	$300	$400	$475	$600	$725	$1,350

W-3825-F • F-2153F • Atlanta • 589,886

W-3825-F Mule • F-2153F

VG-8	F-12	VF-20	EF-40	AU-50	Unc-60	Unc-63
$120	$130	$140	$150	$160	$200	$300

W-3825-F Mule★ • F-2153F★

VG-8	F-12	VF-20	EF-40	AU-50	Unc-60	Unc-63
$225	$300	$400	$475	$600	$725	$1,350

W-3825-G • F-2153G • Chicago • 3,328,800

W-3825-G Mule • F-2153G

VF-20	EF-40	AU-50	Unc-60	Unc-63
$120	$130	$140	$150	$235

W-3825-G Mule★ • F-2153G★

VG-8	F-12	VF-20	EF-40	AU-50	Unc-60	Unc-63
$150	$225	$300	$375	$450	$550	$800

W-3825-H • F-2153H • St. Louis • 434,208

W-3825-H Mule • F-2153H

VF-20	EF-40	AU-50	Unc-60	Unc-63
$130	$140	$150	$160	$275

W-3825-I Mule • F-2153I • Minneapolis • 153,000

VG-8	F-12	VF-20	EF-40	AU-50	Unc-60	Unc-63
$130	$140	$150	$160	$175	$225	$450

W-3825-J • F-2153J • Kansas City • 455,000

W-3825-J Mule • F-2153J

VG-8	F-12	VF-20	EF-40	AU-50	Unc-60	Unc-63
$120	$130	$140	$150	$160	$200	$400

W-3825-J Mule★ • F-2153J★

VG-8	F-12	VF-20	EF-40	AU-50	Unc-60	Unc-63
$325	$400	$500	$575	$650	$750	$1,400

W-3825-K • F-2153K • Dallas • 226,164

W-3825-K Mule • F-2153K

VF-20	EF-40	AU-50	Unc-60	Unc-63	Unc-65
$130	$140	$150	$160	$275	$400

W-3825-L • F-2153L • San Francisco • 1,130,400

W-3825-L Mule • F-2153L

VF-20	EF-40	AU-50	Unc-60	Unc-63
$120	$130	$160	$190	$250

W-3825-L Mule★ • F-2153L★

Commentary: Current market information not available.

Series of 1934-B, Green Seal
Julian-Vinson (1945–1946)

Beginning with the Series of 1934-B notes there is a change in the wording in the Federal Reserve seal. THE is omitted, leaving FEDERAL RESERVE.

Mules: All notes have old-style back plates with micro-size plate numbers, 112 or lower; therefore, all are mules.

Although printages vary widely, prices are mostly generic, as relatively few numismatists collect these by variety. Star notes are rare, and in Uncirculated preservation are particularly so.

Prices for a typical note for this series, unless listed otherwise, are as follows:

VF-20	EF-40	AU-50	Unc-60	Unc-63
$150	$175	$215	$255	$300

Prices for a typical star note for this series, unless listed otherwise, are as follows:

VF-20	EF-40	AU-50	Unc-60	Unc-63
$750	$1,250	$2,000	$2,750	$3,500

W-3826-A • F-2154A • Boston • 41,400

W-3826-C • F-2154C • Philadelphia • 39,600

W-3826-D • F-2154D • Cleveland • 61,200

W-3826-E • F-2154E • Richmond • 977,400

W-3826-E★ • F-2154E★

W-3826-F • F-2154F • Atlanta • 645,000

W-3826-G • F-2154G • Chicago • 396,000

W-3826-H • F-2154H • St. Louis • 676,200

W-3826-H★ • F-2154H★

W-3826-I • F-2154I • Minneapolis • 377,000

W-3826-I★ • F-2154I★

W-3826-J • F-2154J • Kansas City • 364,500

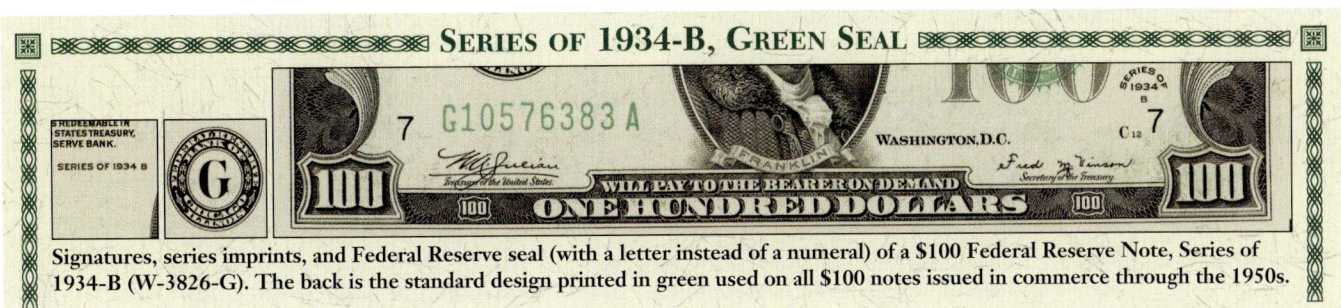

SERIES OF 1934-B, GREEN SEAL

Signatures, series imprints, and Federal Reserve seal (with a letter instead of a numeral) of a $100 Federal Reserve Note, Series of 1934-B (W-3826-G). The back is the standard design printed in green used on all $100 notes issued in commerce through the 1950s.

W-3826-J★ • F-2154J★

W-3826-K • F-2154K • Dallas • 392,700

W-3826-K★ • F-2154K★

Series of 1934-C, Green Seal
Julian-Snyder (1946–1949)

This series continued the preceding design.

Mules: All have old-style back plates with micro-size plate numbers, 112 or lower; therefore, all are mules.

The Federal Reserve Bank of New York did not issue any notes of this series. Again, printages vary widely, but prices are more or less generic. One might think that this is a field ripe for cherrypicking, but it is unlikely that collecting these systematically will become widely popular. Still, rarities are inexpensive in relation to many other areas of currency. In all instances, high-grade star notes are extremely rare.

Prices for a typical note for this series, unless listed otherwise, are as follows:

VF-20	EF-40	AU-50	Unc-60	Unc-63
$150	$175	$200	$225	$250

Prices for a typical star note for this series, unless listed otherwise, are as follows:

VF-20	EF-40	AU-50	Unc-60	Unc-63
$750	$1,500	$2,075	$2,650	$3,250

W-3827-A • F-2155A • Boston • 13,800

W-3827-C • F-2155C • Philadelphia • 13,200

W-3827-D • F-2155D • Cleveland • 1,473,200

W-3827-D★ • F-2155D★

W-3827-E • F-2155E • Richmond • 1,440,000

W-3827-E★ • F-2155E★

W-3827-F • F-2155F • Atlanta • 493,900

W-3827-F★ • F-2155F★

W-3827-G • F-2155G • Chicago • 612,000

W-3827-G★ • F-2155G★

W-3827-H • F-2155H • St. Louis • 957,000

W-3827-H★ • F-2155H★

W-3827-I • F-2155I • Minneapolis • 392,904

W-3827-I★ • F-2155I★

W-3827-J • F-2155J • Kansas City • 401,100

W-3827-K • F-2155K • Dallas • 280,700

W-3827-L • F-2155L • San Francisco • 432,600

W-3827-L★ • F-2155L★

Series of 1934-D, Green Seal
Clark-Snyder (1949–1953)

This series continued the preceding design.

Mules: All have old-style back plates with micro-size plate numbers, 112 or lower; therefore, all are mules.

This was an abbreviated series as the Federal Reserve was well stocked with notes of this denomination. As with other series of this era, most $100 notes are fairly scarce in Uncirculated condition, and star notes are rare. The New York issue has an incredibly low printage of 156, and yet few people know about it.

Prices for a typical note for this series, unless listed otherwise, are as follows:

VF-20	EF-40	AU-50	Unc-60	Unc-63
$250	$325	$365	$405	$450

Prices for a typical star note for this series, unless listed otherwise, are as follows:

VF-20	EF-40	AU-50	Unc-60	Unc-63
$1,500	$2,750	—	—	$4,750

W-3828-B • F-2156B • New York • 156

W-3828-C • F-2156C • Philadelphia • 308,400

W-3828-C★ • F-2156C★

W-3828-F • F-2156F • Atlanta • 260,400

W-3828-F★ • F-2156F★

W-3828-G • F-2156G • Chicago • 78,000

W-3828-G★ • F-2156G★

W-3828-H • F-2156H • St. Louis • 166,800

W-3828-K • F-2156K • Dallas • 66,000

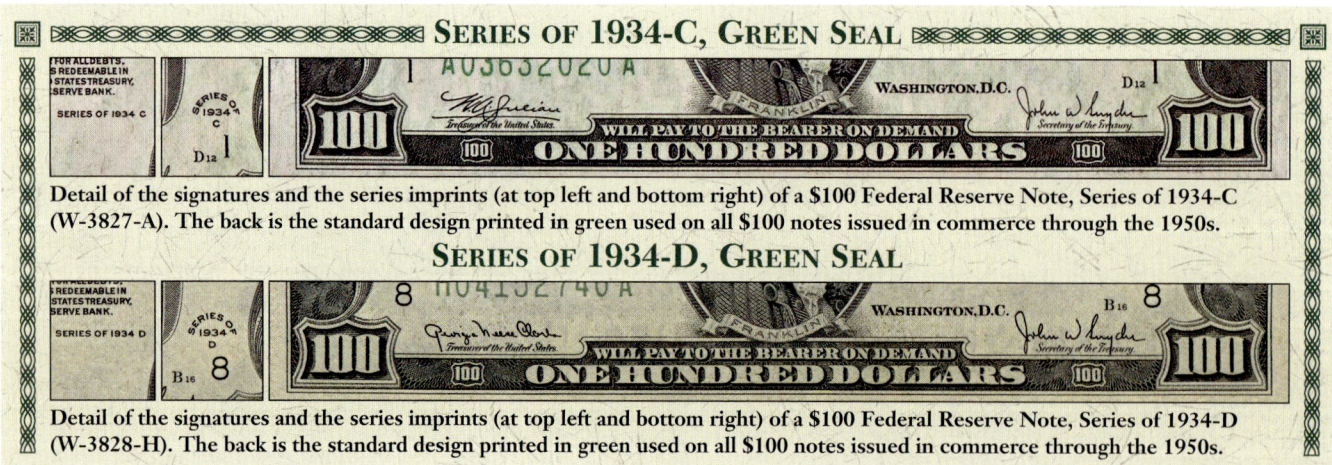

SERIES OF 1934-C, GREEN SEAL

Detail of the signatures and the series imprints (at top left and bottom right) of a $100 Federal Reserve Note, Series of 1934-C (W-3827-A). The back is the standard design printed in green used on all $100 notes issued in commerce through the 1950s.

SERIES OF 1934-D, GREEN SEAL

Detail of the signatures and the series imprints (at top left and bottom right) of a $100 Federal Reserve Note, Series of 1934-D (W-3828-H). The back is the standard design printed in green used on all $100 notes issued in commerce through the 1950s.

Series of 1950, Green Seal
Clark-Snyder (1949–1953)

This series continued the preceding design, but with slight modifications. The Federal Reserve seal was given a spiked border. The payable provision above that seal now appears in three lines of text instead of four. The series designation is at the lower right of the portrait.

Mules: Some have old-style back plates with micro-size plate numbers, 112 or lower, which are considered mules. The Series of 1950 used a mix of old-style and new-style plates.

Although these are hardly common in high grades, prices are generic, and with some perseverance, high-grade examples of just about any variety can be obtained. Star notes are scarcer.

W-3829-A • F-2157A • Boston • 768,000

F-12	VF-20	EF-40	AU-50	Unc-60	Unc-63
$130	$140	$155	$170	$210	$275

W-3829-A★ • F-2157A★

VG-8	F-12	VF-20	EF-40	AU-50	Unc-60	Unc-63
$125	$165	$200	$300	$500	$700	$900

W-3829-A Mule • F-2157A

VG-8	F-12	VF-20	EF-40	AU-50	Unc-60	Unc-63
$115	$125	$135	$150	$165	$200	$325

W-3829-B • F-2157B • New York • 3,908,000

F-12	VF-20	EF-40	AU-50	Unc-60	Unc-63
$130	$140	$150	$160	$175	$200

W-3829-B★ • F-2157B★

VG-8	F-12	VF-20	EF-40	AU-50	Unc-60	Unc-63	Unc-65
$125	$165	$185	$275	$450	$650	$850	$1,750

W-3829-B Mule • F-2157B

VG-8	F-12	VF-20	EF-40	AU-50	Unc-60	Unc-63	Unc-65
$110	$120	$130	$140	$150	$160	$175	$450

W-3829-B Mule★ • F-2157B★

VG-8	F-12	VF-20	EF-40	AU-50	Unc-60	Unc-63
$130	$140	$180	$250	$300	$400	$800

W-3829-C • F-2157C • Philadelphia • 1,332,000

F-12	VF-20	EF-40	AU-50	Unc-60	Unc-63
$130	$140	$155	$170	$200	$250

W-3829-C★ • F-2157C★

VG-8	F-12	VF-20	EF-40	AU-50	Unc-60	Unc-63
$125	$165	$200	$300	$500	$700	$900

W-3829-C Mule • F-2157C

VG-8	F-12	VF-20	EF-40	AU-50	Unc-60	Unc-63
$115	$125	$135	$150	$165	$185	$250

W-3829-C Mule★ • F-2157C★

VG-8	F-12	VF-20	EF-40	AU-50	Unc-60	Unc-63
$125	$150	$240	$300	$375	$475	$1,050

W-3829-D • F-2157D • Cleveland • 1,632,000

VF-20	EF-40	AU-50	Unc-60	Unc-63	Unc-65
$110	$120	$130	$150	$175	$250

W-3829-D★ • F-2157D★

VG-8	F-12	VF-20	EF-40	AU-50	Unc-60	Unc-63
$125	$165	$250	$350	$550	$750	$950

W-3829-D Mule • F-2157D

VG-8	F-12	VF-20	EF-40	AU-50	Unc-60	Unc-63
$115	$125	$135	$150	$165	$175	$250

W-3829-D Mule★ • F-2157D★

VG-8	F-12	VF-20	EF-40	AU-50	Unc-60	Unc-63	Unc-65
$125	$150	$240	$300	$375	$475	$1,050	$2,200

W-3829-E • F-2157E • Richmond • 4,076,000

F-12	VF-20	EF-40	AU-50	Unc-60	Unc-63
$130	$140	$155	$170	$200	$250

$100 Federal Reserve Note, Series of 1950 (W-3829-G). Federal Reserve Bank of Chicago. The back is the standard design printed in green used on all $100 notes issued in commerce through the 1950s.

W-3829-E★ • F-2157E★

VG-8	F-12	VF-20	EF-40	AU-50	Unc-60	Unc-63
$125	$165	$200	$300	$500	$700	$900

W-3829-E Mule • F-2157E

VG-8	F-12	VF-20	EF-40	AU-50	Unc-60	Unc-63
$115	$125	$135	$150	$165	$185	$250

W-3829-E Mule★ • F-2157E★

VG-8	F-12	VF-20	EF-40	AU-50	Unc-60	Unc-63
$130	$140	$180	$250	$300	$400	$800

W-3829-F • F-2157F • Atlanta • 1,824,000

VF-20	EF-40	AU-50	Unc-60	Unc-63
$115	$125	$140	$175	$275

W-3829-F Mule • F-2157F

VG-8	F-12	VF-20	EF-40	AU-50	Unc-60	Unc-63
$110	$120	$130	$140	$150	$160	$175

W-3829-G • F-2157G • Chicago • 4,428,000

VF-20	EF-40	AU-50	Unc-60	Unc-63
$110	$115	$120	$130	$225

W-3829-G Mule • F-2157G

VG-8	F-12	VF-20	EF-40	AU-50	Unc-60	Unc-63
$110	$120	$125	$130	$140	$150	$175

W-3829-G Mule★ • F-2157G★

VG-8	F-12	VF-20	EF-40	AU-50	Unc-60	Unc-63
$130	$140	$180	$250	$300	$375	$700

W-3829-H • F-2157H • St. Louis • 1,284,000

F-12	VF-20	EF-40	AU-50	Unc-60	Unc-63
$130	$140	$155	$170	$185	$275

W-3829-H★ • F-2157H★

VG-8	F-12	VF-20	EF-40	AU-50	Unc-60	Unc-63
$125	$165	$200	$300	$500	$700	$900

W-3829-H Mule • F-2157H

VG-8	F-12	VF-20	EF-40	AU-50	Unc-60	Unc-63
$110	$120	$125	$130	$140	$150	$175

W-3829-H Mule★ • F-2157H★

VG-8	F-12	VF-20	EF-40	AU-50	Unc-60	Unc-63
$125	$150	$240	$300	$375	$475	$1,050

W-3829-I • F-2157I • Minneapolis • 564,000

VG-8	F-12	VF-20	EF-40	AU-50	Unc-60	Unc-63	Unc-65
$120	$130	$140	$160	$175	$215	$350	$450

W-3829-I Mule • F-2157I

VG-8	F-12	VF-20	EF-40	AU-50	Unc-60	Unc-63
$125	$135	$145	$160	$175	$225	$500

W-3829-J • F-2157J • Kansas City • 864,000

VF-20	EF-40	AU-50	Unc-60	Unc-63
$120	$130	$160	$175	$285

W-3829-J★ • F-2157J★

VG-8	F-12	VF-20	EF-40	AU-50	Unc-60	Unc-63
$125	$165	$200	$300	$500	$700	$900

W-3829-J Mule • F-2157J

VG-8	F-12	VF-20	EF-40	AU-50	Unc-60	Unc-63
$115	$125	$140	$150	$165	$200	$350

W-3829-J Mule★ • F-2157J★

VG-8	F-12	VF-20	EF-40	AU-50	Unc-60	Unc-63
$130	$140	$180	$250	$300	$375	$700

W-3829-K • F-2157K • Dallas • 1,216,000

F-12	VF-20	EF-40	AU-50	Unc-60	Unc-63
$130	$140	$155	$170	$190	$275

W-3829-K Mule • F-2157K

VG-8	F-12	VF-20	EF-40	AU-50	Unc-60	Unc-63
$120	$130	$140	$155	$170	$210	$400

W-3829-L • F-2157L • San Francisco • 2,524,000

F-12	VF-20	EF-40	AU-50	Unc-60	Unc-63
$130	$140	$155	$170	$190	$250

W-3829-L★ • F-2157L★

VG-8	F-12	VF-20	EF-40	AU-50	Unc-60	Unc-63
$125	$165	$200	$300	$500	$700	$900

W-3829-L Mule • F-2157L

VG-8	F-12	VF-20	EF-40	AU-50	Unc-60	Unc-63	Unc-65
$110	$120	$125	$130	$140	$150	$175	$250

W-3829-L Mule★ • F-2157L★

VG-8	F-12	VF-20	EF-40	AU-50	Unc-60	Unc-63
$130	$140	$180	$250	$300	$375	$700

Series of 1950-A, Green Seal
Priest-Humphrey (1953–1957)

This series continued the preceding design. Again, prices are generic and do not necessarily reflect the true availability of notes in higher grades. Most dealers do not have even a single Uncirculated note of any variety within this series.

Prices for a typical note for this series, unless listed otherwise, are as follows:

Unc-63
$250

Prices for a typical star note for this series, unless listed otherwise, are as follows:

EF-40	AU-50	Unc-60	Unc-63
$250	$365	$480	$600

W-3830-A • F-2158A • Boston • 1,008,000

W-3830-A★ • F-2158A★

W-3830-B • F-2158B • New York • 2,880,000

W-3830-B★ • F-2158B★

W-3830-C • F-2158C • Philadelphia • 576,000

W-3830-C★ • F-2158C★

W-3830-D • F-2158D • Cleveland • 288,000

W-3830-D★ • F-2158D★

W-3830-E • F-2158E • Richmond • 2,160,000

W-3830-E★ • F-2158E★

W-3830-F • F-2158F • Atlanta • 288,000

W-3830-F★ • F-2158F★

W-3830-G • F-2158G • Chicago • 864,000

W-3830-G★ • F-2158G★

W-3830-H • F-2158H • St. Louis • 432,000

W-3830-H★ • F-2158H★

W-3830-I • F-2158I • Minneapolis • 144,000

W-3830-I★ • F-2158I★

W-3830-J • F-2158J • Kansas City • 288,000

W-3830-J★ • F-2158J★

W-3830-K • F-2158K • Dallas • 432,000

W-3830-K★ • F-2158K★

W-3830-L • F-2158L • San Francisco • 720,000

W-3830-L★ • F-2158L★

Series of 1950-B, Green Seal
Priest-Anderson (1957–1961)

This series continued the preceding design. As with many other $100 notes of this era, prices are generic and typically inexpensive, although in actuality most are scarce in dealers' stocks.

Prices for a typical note for this series, unless listed otherwise, are as follows:

Unc-63
$225

Prices for a typical star note for this series, unless listed otherwise, are as follows:

EF-40	AU-50	Unc-60	Unc-63
$275	$400	$525	$650

W-3831-A • F-2159A • Boston • 720,000

W-3831-B • F-2159B • New York • 6,636,000

W-3831-B★ • F-2159B★

W-3831-C • F-2159C • Philadelphia • 720,000

W-3831-C★ • F-2159C★

W-3831-D • F-2159D • Cleveland • 432,000

W-3831-D★ • F-2159D★

W-3831-E • F-2159E • Richmond • 1,008,000

W-3831-F • F-2159F • Atlanta • 576,000

W-3831-F★ • F-2159F★

W-3831-G • F-2159G • Chicago • 2,592,000

W-3831-G★ • F-2159G★

W-3831-H • F-2159H • St. Louis • 1,152,000

W-3831-H★ • F-2159H★

W-3831-I • F-2159I • Minneapolis • 288,000

W-3831-I★ • F-2159I★

W-3831-J • F-2159J • Kansas City • 720,000

W-3831-J★ • F-2159J★

W-3831-K • F-2159K • Dallas • 1,728,000

W-3831-K★ • F-2159K★

W-3831-L • F-2159L • San Francisco • 2,880,000

W-3831-L★ • F-2159L★

SERIES OF 1950-A, GREEN SEAL

Signatures and series imprint of a $100 Federal Reserve Note, Series of 1950-A (W-3830-H). The back is the standard type of the era.

SERIES OF 1950-B, GREEN SEAL

Signatures and series imprint of a $100 Federal Reserve Note, Series of 1950-B (W-3831-I). The back is the standard type of the era.

Series of 1950-C, Green Seal
Smith-Dillon (1961–1962)

This series continued the preceding design. Printages vary widely, but prices for scarcer varieties are not much above generic levels. Star notes are scarce.

Prices for a typical note for this series, unless listed otherwise, are as follows:

Unc-63
$225

Prices for a typical star note for this series, unless listed otherwise, are as follows:

EF-40	AU-50	Unc-60	Unc-63
$300	$430	$565	$700

W-3832-A • F-2160A • Boston • 864,000

W-3832-A★ • F-2160A★

W-3832-B • F-2160B • New York • 2,448,000

W-3832-B★ • F-2160B★

W-3832-C • F-2160C • Philadelphia • 576,000

W-3832-C★ • F-2160C★

W-3832-D • F-2160D • Cleveland • 576,000

W-3832-D★ • F-2160D★

W-3832-E • F-2160E • Richmond • 1,440,000

W-3832-E★ • F-2160E★

W-3832-F • F-2160F • Atlanta • 1,296,000

W-3832-F★ • F-2160F★

W-3832-G • F-2160G • Chicago • 1,584,000

W-3832-G★ • F-2160G★

W-3832-H • F-2160H • St. Louis • 720,000

W-3832-H★ • F-2160H★

W-3832-I • F-2160I • Minneapolis • 288,000

W-3832-J • F-2160J • Kansas City • 432,000

W-3832-K • F-2160K • Dallas • 720,000

W-3832-K★ • F-2160K★

W-3832-L • F-2160L • San Francisco • 2,160,000

W-3832-L★ • F-2160L★

Series of 1950-D, Green Seal
Granahan-Dillon (1963–1965)

This series continued the preceding design. The printages are generous in most instances, though patience is required when tracking down a specific variety. Star notes are scarce.

Prices for a typical note for this series, unless listed otherwise, are as follows:

Unc-63
$245

Prices for a typical star note for this series, unless listed otherwise, are as follows:

EF-40	AU-50	Unc-60	Unc-63
$300	$415	$530	$650

W-3833-A • F-2161A • Boston • 1,872,000

W-3833-A★ • F-2161A★

W-3833-B • F-2161B • New York • 7,632,000

W-3833-B★ • F-2161B★

W-3833-C • F-2161C • Philadelphia • 1,872,000

W-3833-C★ • F-2161C★

W-3833-D • F-2161D • Cleveland • 1,584,000

W-3833-D★ • F-2161D★

W-3833-E • F-2161E • Richmond • 2,880,000

W-3833-E★ • F-2161E★

W-3833-F • F-2161F • Atlanta • 1,872,000

W-3833-F★ • F-2161F★

W-3833-G • F-2161G • Chicago • 4,608,000

W-3833-G★ • F-2161G★

W-3833-H • F-2161H • St. Louis • 1,440,000

W-3833-H★ • F-2161H★

SERIES OF 1950-C, GREEN SEAL

Signatures and series imprint of a $100 Federal Reserve Note, Series of 1950-C (W-3832-C). The back is the standard type of the era.

SERIES OF 1950-D, GREEN SEAL

Signatures and series imprint of a $100 Federal Reserve Note, Series of 1950-D (W-3833-B). The back is the standard type of the era.

W-3833-I • F-2161I • Minneapolis • 432,000

W-3833-I★ • F-2161I★

W-3833-J • F-2161J • Kansas City • 864,000

W-3833-J★ • F-2161J★

W-3833-K • F-2161K • Dallas • 1,728,000

W-3833-K★ • F-2161K★

W-3833-L • F-2161L • San Francisco • 3,312,000

W-3833-L★ • F-2161L★

Series of 1950-E, Green Seal
Granahan-Fowler (1965–1966)

This series continued the preceding design. This was an abbreviated series, with only a few different issues, which was not generally appreciated at the time. Today, examples are scarce and Uncirculated notes are especially so. An exception to the rule, these are better recognized for their scarcity in the marketplace.

W-3834-B • F-2162B • New York • 3,024,000

EF-40	AU-50	Unc-60	Unc-63
$275	$355	$440	$525

W-3834-B★ • F-2162B★

EF-40	AU-50	Unc-60	Unc-63
$1,000	$1,575	$2,150	$2,750

W-3834-G • F-2162G • Chicago • 576,000

EF-40	AU-50	Unc-60	Unc-63
$300	$415	$530	$650

W-3834-L • F-2162L • San Francisco • 2,736,000

EF-40	AU-50	Unc-60	Unc-63
$275	$355	$440	$525

W-3834-L★ • F-2162L★

EF-40	AU-50	Unc-60	Unc-63
$1,250	$1,825	$2,400	$3,000

Series of 1963-A, Green Seal
Granahan-Fowler (1965–1966)

With this issue, the motto IN GOD WE TRUST was added to the back of the $100 note, the words divided by the top of the cupola on Independence Hall. On the front, a new two-line obligation reads, "This note is legal tender for all debts, public and private." Most are inexpensive and plentiful, but finding a specific note can be challenging.

Prices for a typical note for this series, unless listed otherwise, are as follows:

Unc-63
$200

Prices for a typical star note for this series, unless listed otherwise, are as follows:

EF-40	AU-50	Unc-60	Unc-63
$250	$315	$380	$450

W-3835-A • F-2163A • Boston • 1,536,000

W-3835-A★ • F-2163A★ • 128,000

W-3835-B • F-2163B • New York • 12,544,000

W-3835-B★ • F-2163B★ • 1,536,000

W-3835-C • F-2163C • Philadelphia • 1,792,000

W-3835-C★ • F-2163C★ • 192,000

W-3835-D • F-2163D • Cleveland • 2,304,000

W-3835-D★ • F-2163D★ • 192,000

W-3835-E • F-2163E • Richmond • 2,816,000

W-3835-E★ • F-2163E★ • 192,000

W-3835-F • F-2163F • Atlanta • 1,280,000

W-3835-F★ • F-2163F★ • 128,000

W-3835-G • F-2163G • Chicago • 4,352,000

W-3835-G★ • F-2163G★ • 512,000

W-3835-H • F-2163H • St. Louis • 1,536,000

W-3835-H★ • F-2163H★ • 256,000

W-3835-I • F-2163I • Minneapolis • 512,000

W-3835-I★ • F-2163I★ • 128,000

W-3835-J • F-2163J • Kansas City • 1,024,000

W-3835-J★ • F-2163J★ • 128,000

W-3835-K • F-2163K • Dallas • 1,536,000

W-3835-K★ • F-2163K★ • 192,000

W-3835-L • F-2163L • San Francisco • 6,400,000

W-3835-L★ • F-2163L★ • 832,000

SERIES OF 1950-E, GREEN SEAL

Signatures and series imprint of a $100 Federal Reserve Note, Series of 1950-E (W-3834-B). The back is the standard type of the era.

Series of 1969, Green Seal
Elston-Kennedy (1969–1970)

The Series of 1969 features a redesigned Treasury seal with the inscription THE DEPARTMENT OF THE TREASURY 1789, replacing the earlier style with the Latin wording THESAUR. AMER. SEPTENT. SIGIL. The design in the interior of the seal was modified as well.

Most are priced generically, although printages and actual availability vary. The bottom line is that there are enough to satisfy the relatively small community of specialists, and whether 1,000 Uncirculated examples exist of one variety

and 10,000 of another, for instance, there is an adequate numismatic supply.

Prices for a typical note for this series, unless listed otherwise, are as follows:

Unc-63
$200

Prices for a typical star note for this series, unless listed otherwise, are as follows:

EF-40	AU-50	Unc-60	Unc-63
$225	$280	$340	$400

SERIES OF 1963-A, GREEN SEAL

$100 Series of 1963-A Federal Reserve Note (W-3835-D). Federal Reserve Bank of Cleveland. The design remains the general type as preceding.

Back of the $100 Series of 1963-A Federal Reserve Note (W-3835-D), with the motto IN GOD WE TRUST. This new back was used on all $100 notes from the Series of 1963-A to the Series of 1993.

SERIES OF 1969, GREEN SEAL

$100 Series of 1969 Federal Reserve Note (W-3836-B). Federal Reserve Bank of New York. This series uses the standard back found on all $100 notes from the Series of 1963-A to the Series of 1993.

W-3836-A • F-2164A • Boston • 2,048,000

W-3836-A★ • F-2164A★ • 128,000

W-3836-B • F-2164B • New York • 11,520,000

W-3836-B★ • F-2164B★ • 128,000

W-3836-C • F-2164C • Philadelphia • 2,560,000

W-3836-C★ • F-2164C★ • 128,000

W-3836-D • F-2164D • Cleveland • 768,000

W-3836-D★ • F-2164D★ • 64,000

W-3836-E • F-2164E • Richmond • 2,560,000

W-3836-E★ • F-2164E★ • 192,000

W-3836-F • F-2164F • Atlanta • 2,304,000

W-3836-F★ • F-2164F★ • 128,000

W-3836-G • F-2164G • Chicago • 5,888,000

W-3836-G★ • F-2164G★ • 256,000

W-3836-H • F-2164H • St. Louis • 1,280,000

W-3836-H★ • F-2164H★ • 64,000

W-3836-I • F-2164I • Minneapolis • 512,000

W-3836-I★ • F-2164I★ • 64,000

W-3836-J • F-2164J • Kansas City • 1,792,000

W-3836-J★ • F-2164J★ • 384,000

W-3836-K • F-2164K • Dallas • 2,048,000

W-3836-K★ • F-2164K★ • 128,000

W-3836-L • F-2164L • San Francisco • 7,168,000

W-3836-L★ • F-2164L★ • 320,000

Series of 1969-A, Green Seal
Kabis-Connally (1971)

Dorothy Andrews Elson married Walter L. Kabis during her term in office, and became Mrs. Kabis.

This series continued the preceding design. Printages are generous, but vary widely. The figure of 512,000 for Kansas City is tiny in comparison to 11,254,000 for New York. Still, there seem to be enough of the lower-printage issues to satisfy the demand. Star notes are scarce.

Prices for a typical note for this series, unless listed otherwise, are as follows:

Unc-63
$175

Prices for a typical star note for this series, unless listed otherwise, are as follows:

EF-40	AU-50	Unc-60	Unc-63
$225	$315	$405	$500

W-3837-A • F-2165A • Boston • 1,280,000

W-3837-A★ • F-2165A★ • 320,000

W-3837-B • F-2165B • New York • 11,264,000

W-3837-B★ • F-2165B★ • 640,000

W-3837-C • F-2165C • Philadelphia • 2,048,000

W-3837-C★ • F-2165C★ • 448,000

W-3837-D • F-2165D • Cleveland • 1,280,000

W-3837-D★ • F-2165D★ • 192,000

W-3837-E • F-2165E • Richmond • 2,304,000

W-3837-E★ • F-2165E★ • 192,000

W-3837-F • F-2165F • Atlanta • 2,304,000

W-3837-F★ • F-2165F★ • 64,000

W-3837-G • F-2165G • Chicago • 5,376,000

W-3837-G★ • F-2165G★ • 320,000

W-3837-H • F-2165H • St. Louis • 1,024,000

W-3837-H★ • F-2165H★ • 64,000

W-3837-I • F-2165I • Minneapolis • 1,024,000

W-3837-J • F-2165J • Kansas City • 512,000

W-3837-K • F-2165K • Dallas • 3,328,000

W-3837-K★ • F-2165K★ • 128,000

W-3837-L • F-2165L • San Francisco • 4,352,000

W-3837-L★ • F-2165L★ • 640,000

Series of 1969-C, Green Seal
Banuelos-Shultz (1972–1974)

This series (illus. on p. 694) continued the preceding design. There were no Series of 1969-B $100 notes. The preceding series' comments also apply here.

Prices for a typical note for this series, unless listed otherwise, are as follows:

Unc-63
$200

SERIES OF 1969-A, GREEN SEAL

Detail of the signatures and the series imprint of a $100 Federal Reserve Note, Series of 1969-A (W-3837-H). This series uses the standard back found on all $100 notes from the Series of 1963-A to the Series of 1993.

Prices for a typical star note for this series, unless listed otherwise, are as follows:

EF-40	AU-50	Unc-60	Unc-63
$185	$270	$360	$450

W-3838-A • F-2166A • Boston • 2,048,000

W-3838-A★ • F-2166A★ • 64,000

W-3838-B • F-2166B • New York • 15,616,000

W-3838-B★ • F-2166B★ • 256,000

W-3838-C • F-2166C • Philadelphia • 2,816,000

W-3838-C★ • F-2166C★ • 64,000

W-3838-D • F-2166D • Cleveland • 3,456,000

W-3838-D★ • F-2166D★ • 64,000

W-3838-E • F-2166E • Richmond • 7,296,000

W-3838-E★ • F-2166E★ • 128,000

W-3838-F • F-2166F • Atlanta • 2,432,000

W-3838-F★ • F-2166F★ • 64,000

W-3838-G • F-2166G • Chicago • 6,016,000

W-3838-G★ • F-2166G★ • 320,000

W-3838-H • F-2166H • St. Louis • 5,376,000

W-3838-H★ • F-2166H★ • 64,000

W-3838-I • F-2166I • Minneapolis • 512,000

W-3838-I★ • F-2166I★ • 64,000

W-3838-J • F-2166J • Kansas City • 4,736,000

W-3838-J★ • F-2166J★ • 192,000

W-3838-K • F-2166K • Dallas • 2,944,000

W-3838-K★ • F-2166K★ • 64,000

W-3838-L • F-2166L • San Francisco • 10,240,000

W-3838-L★ • F-2166L★ • 512,000

Series of 1974, Green Seal
Neff-Simon (1974–1977)

This series continued the preceding design. The high printages and their modern status combine to make these available for modest cost, although finding a specific variety may take time.

Prices for a typical note for this series, unless listed otherwise, are as follows:

Unc-63
$175

Prices for a typical star note for this series, unless listed otherwise, are as follows:

EF-40	AU-50	Unc-60	Unc-63
$175	$250	$325	$400

W-3839-A • F-2167A • Boston • 11,520,000

W-3839-A★ • F-2167A★ • 320,000

W-3839-B • F-2167B • New York • 62,720,000

W-3839-B★ • F-2167B★ • 1,728,000

W-3839-C • F-2167C • Philadelphia • 7,680,000

W-3839-C★ • F-2167C★ • 192,000

W-3839-D • F-2167D • Cleveland • 8,320,000

W-3839-D★ • F-2167D★ • 256,000

W-3839-E • F-2167E • Richmond • 11,520,000

W-3839-E★ • F-2167E★ • 256,000

W-3839-F • F-2167F • Atlanta • 4,480,000

W-3839-F★ • F-2167F★ • 128,000

W-3839-G • F-2167G • Chicago • 26,880,000

W-3839-G★ • F-2167G★ • 1,216,000

W-3839-H • F-2167H • St. Louis • 5,760,000

W-3839-H★ • F-2167H★ • 192,000

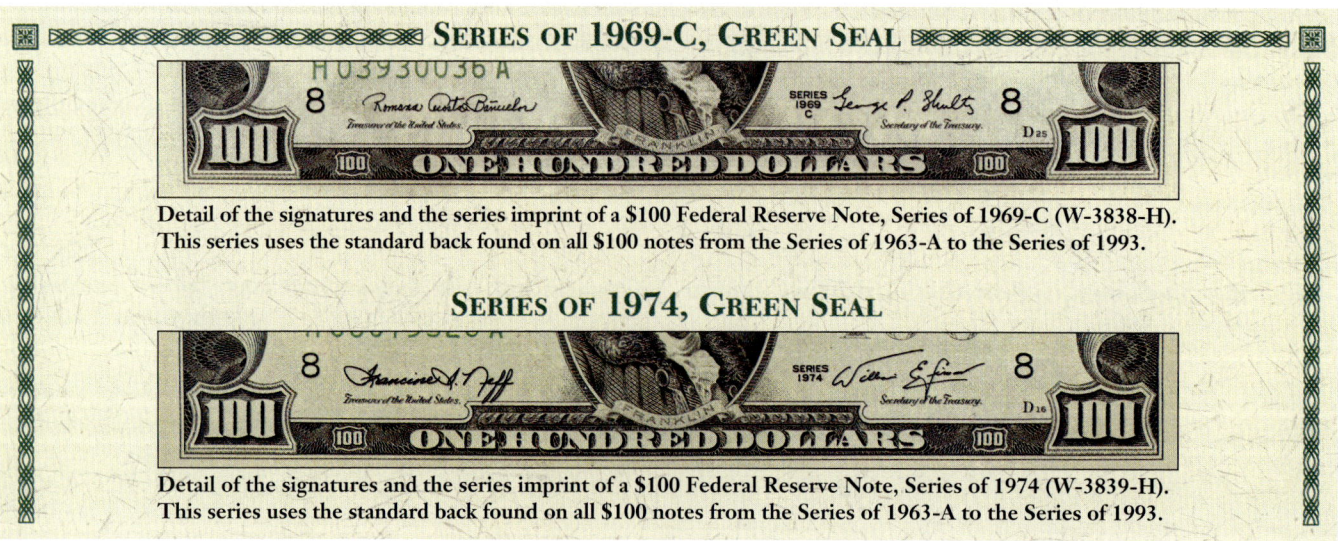

SERIES OF 1969-C, GREEN SEAL

Detail of the signatures and the series imprint of a $100 Federal Reserve Note, Series of 1969-C (W-3838-H). This series uses the standard back found on all $100 notes from the Series of 1963-A to the Series of 1993.

SERIES OF 1974, GREEN SEAL

Detail of the signatures and the series imprint of a $100 Federal Reserve Note, Series of 1974 (W-3839-H). This series uses the standard back found on all $100 notes from the Series of 1963-A to the Series of 1993.

W-3839-I • F-2167I • Minneapolis • 4,480,000

W-3839-I★ • F-2167I★ • 256,000

W-3839-J • F-2167J • Kansas City • 5,760,000

W-3839-J★ • F-2167J★ • 448,000

W-3839-K • F-2167K • Dallas • 10,240,000

W-3839-K★ • F-2167K★ • 192,000

W-3839-L • F-2167L • San Francisco • 29,440,000

W-3839-L★ • F-2167L★ • 896,000

Series of 1977, Green Seal
Morton-Blumenthal (1977–1979)

This series continued the preceding design. The issue is in same situation as the preceding series, except that star notes for Richmond and Chicago are prime rarities.

Prices for a typical note for this series, unless listed otherwise, are as follows:

Unc-63
$175

Prices for a typical star note for this series, unless listed otherwise, are as follows:

Unc-63
$275

W-3840-A • F-2168A • Boston • 19,200,000

W-3840-A★ • F-2168A★ • 320,000

W-3840-B • F-2168B • New York • 166,400,000

W-3840-B★ • F-2168B★ • 1,664,000

W-3840-C • F-2168C • Philadelphia • 5,195,000

W-3840-C★ • F-2168C★ • 128,000

W-3840-D • F-2168D • Cleveland • 16,640,000

W-3840-D★ • F-2168D★ • 192,000

W-3840-E • F-2168E • Richmond • 24,320,000

W-3840-E★ • F-2168E★ • 384,000

W-3840-F • F-2168F • Atlanta • 3,840,000

W-3840-F★ • F-2168F★ • 64,000

W-3840-G • F-2168G • Chicago • 39,680,000

W-3840-G★ • F-2168G★ • 960,000

W-3840-H • F-2168H • St. Louis • 15,360,000

W-3840-H★ • F-2168H★ • 448,000

W-3840-I • F-2168I • Minneapolis • 5,195,000

W-3840-I★ • F-2168I★ • 192,000

W-3840-J • F-2168J • Kansas City • 38,400,000

W-3840-J★ • F-2168J★ • 640,000

W-3840-K • F-2168K • Dallas • 38,400,000

W-3840-K★ • F-2168K★ • 640,000

W-3840-L • F-2168L • San Francisco • 39,680,000

W-3840-L★ • F-2168L★ • 576,000

Series of 1981, Green Seal
Buchanan-Regan (1981–1983)

This series continued the preceding design. No Kansas City notes were printed for this series. Star notes are recorded only for the Federal Reserve Bank of Richmond. As these notes are scarce and also unique as a type, surviving examples are in great demand. Otherwise, generic prices are the rule.

Prices for a typical note for this series, unless listed otherwise, are as follows:

Unc-63
$150

W-3841-A • F-2169A • Boston • 8,960,000

Unc-63
$200

W-3841-B • F-2169B • New York • 105,600,000

W-3841-C • F-2169C • Philadelphia • 12,800,000

W-3841-D • F-2169D • Cleveland • 5,760,000

SERIES OF 1977, GREEN SEAL

Detail of the signatures and the series imprint of a $100 Federal Reserve Note, Series of 1977 (W-3840-B). This series uses the standard back found on all $100 notes from the Series of 1963-A to the Series of 1993.

SERIES OF 1981, GREEN SEAL

Detail of the signatures and the series imprint of a $100 Federal Reserve Note, Series of 1981 (W-3841-D). This series uses the standard back found on all $100 notes from the Series of 1963-A to the Series of 1993.

W-3841-E • F-2169E • Richmond • 23,680,000

W-3841-E★ • F-2169E★ • 640,000

EF-40	AU-50	Unc-60	Unc-63
$500	$630	$760	$900

W-3841-F • F-2169F • Atlanta • 6,400,000

W-3841-G • F-2169G • Chicago • 33,280,000

W-3841-H • F-2169H • St. Louis • 5,760,000

W-3841-I • F-2169I • Minneapolis • 3,200,000

W-3841-J • F-2169J • Kansas City • 23,680,000

W-3841-K • F-2169K • Dallas • 23,680,000

W-3841-L • F-2169L • San Francisco • 24,960,000

Series of 1981-A, Green Seal
Ortega-Regan (1983–1985)

This series continued the preceding design. Star notes are recorded only for the Federal Reserve Bank of San Francisco. The printage was generous, but these stars are elusive. Otherwise, pricing is more or less generic.

Prices for a typical note for this series, unless listed otherwise, are as follows:

Unc-63
$175

W-3842-A • F-2170A • Boston • 16,000,000

W-3842-B • F-2170B • New York • 64,000,000

Unc-63
$150

W-3842-C • F-2170C • Philadelphia • 3,200,000

W-3842-D • F-2170D • Cleveland • 6,400,000

W-3842-E • F-2170E • Richmond • 12,800,000

W-3842-F • F-2170F • Atlanta • 12,800,000

W-3842-G • F-2170G • Chicago • 22,400,000

W-3842-H • F-2170H • St. Louis • 12,800,000

W-3842-I • F-2170I • Minneapolis • 3,200,000

W-3842-K • F-2170K • Dallas • 3,200,000

W-3842-L • F-2170L • San Francisco • 19,200,000

W-3842-L★ • F-2170L★ • 3,200,000

EF-40	AU-50	Unc-60	Unc-63
$225	$280	$340	$400

Series of 1985, Green Seal
Ortega-Baker (1985–1988)

This series continued the preceding design. Although regular notes were produced for each of the 12 Federal Reserve Districts, only three issued star notes. Except for stars, prices are more or less generic.

Prices for a typical note for this series, unless listed otherwise, are as follows:

Unc-63
$175

Prices for a typical star note for this series, unless listed otherwise, are as follows:

EF-40	AU-50	Unc-60	Unc-63
$150	$200	$250	$300

W-3843-A • F-2171A • Boston • 32,000,000

W-3843-B • F-2171B • New York • 259,200,000

W-3843-C • F-2171C • Philadelphia • 19,200,000

W-3843-D • F-2171D • Cleveland • 28,800,000

W-3843-D★ • F-2171D★ • 1,280,000

W-3843-E • F-2171E • Richmond • 54,400,000

W-3843-F • F-2171F • Atlanta • 16,000,000

W-3843-G • F-2171G • Chicago • 64,000,000

W-3843-H • F-2171H • St. Louis • 12,800,000

SERIES OF 1981-A, GREEN SEAL

Detail of the signatures and the series imprint of a $100 Federal Reserve Note, Series of 1981-A (W-3842-H). This series uses the standard back found on all $100 notes from the Series of 1963-A to the Series of 1993.

SERIES OF 1985, GREEN SEAL

Detail of the signatures and the series imprint of a $100 Federal Reserve Note, Series of 1985 (W-3843-D). This series uses the standard back found on all $100 notes from the Series of 1963-A to the Series of 1993.

W-3843-I • F-2171I • Minneapolis • 12,800,000

W-3843-J • F-2171J • Kansas City • 12,800,000

W-3843-J★ • F-2171J★ • 1,280,000

W-3843-K • F-2171K • Dallas • 48,000,000

W-3843-K★ • F-2171K★ • 3,200,000

W-3843-L • F-2171L • San Francisco • 38,400,000

Series of 1988, Green Seal
Ortega-Brady (1988–1989)

This series continued the preceding design. This is a truncated series, with several banks not issuing notes. Generic prices apply, despite wide differences in printage quantities. Star notes were issued only for New York.

Prices for a typical note for this series, unless listed otherwise, are as follows:

Unc-63
$175

W-3844-A • F-2172A • Boston • 9,600,000

W-3844-B • F-2172B • New York • 448,000,000

W-3844-B★ • F-2172B★ • 4,480,000

EF-40	AU-50	Unc-60	Unc-63
$150	$250	$350	$450

W-3844-C • F-2172C • Philadelphia • 9,600,000

W-3844-D • F-2172D • Cleveland • 35,200,000

W-3844-E • F-2172E • Richmond • 19,200,000

W-3844-G • F-2172G • Chicago • 51,200,000

W-3844-H • F-2172H • St. Louis • 9,600,000

W-3844-J • F-2172J • Kansas City • 9,600,000

W-3844-L • F-2172L • San Francisco • 10,200,000

Series of 1990, Green Seal
Villalpando-Brady (1989–1993)

New security features were added to this issue. Around the outside of most of the portrait frame THE UNITED STATES OF AMERICA is repeated in micro printing. A security thread was added to the paper. Printages are very large.

Prices for a typical note for this series, unless listed otherwise, are as follows:

Unc-63
$150

Prices for a typical star note for this series, unless listed otherwise, are as follows:

EF-40	AU-50	Unc-60	Unc-63
$125	$150	$175	$200

W-3845-A • F-2173A • Boston • 76,800,000

W-3845-B • F-2173B • New York • 595,200,000

W-3845-B★ • F-2173B★ • 1,880,000

W-3845-C • F-2173C • Philadelphia • 112,000,000

W-3845-C★ • F-2173C★ • 1,280,000

W-3845-D • F-2173D • Cleveland • 115,200,000

SERIES OF 1988, GREEN SEAL

Detail of the signatures and the series imprint of a $100 Federal Reserve Note, Series of 1988 (W-3844-B). This series uses the standard back found on all $100 notes from the Series of 1963-A to the Series of 1993.

SERIES OF 1990, GREEN SEAL

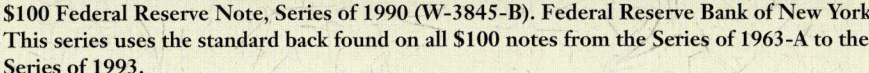

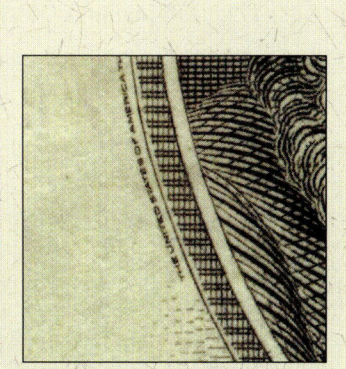

$100 Federal Reserve Note, Series of 1990 (W-3845-B). Federal Reserve Bank of New York. This series uses the standard back found on all $100 notes from the Series of 1963-A to the Series of 1993.   Detail of the microprint text.

W-3845-E • F-2173E • Richmond • 108,800,000

W-3845-F • F-2173F • Atlanta • 64,000,000

W-3845-G • F-2173G • Chicago • 134,400,000

W-3845-G★ • F-2173G★ • 640,000

W-3845-H • F-2173H • St. Louis • 121,600,000

W-3845-I • F-2173I • Minneapolis • 48,000,000

W-3845-J • F-2173J • Kansas City • 76,800,000

W-3845-J★ • F-2173J★ • 3,200,000

W-3845-K • F-2173K • Dallas • 165,400,000

W-3845-K★ • F-2173K★ • 1,920,000

W-3845-L • F-2173L • San Francisco • 147,200,000

W-3845-L★ • F-2173L★ • 3,200,000

Series of 1993, Green Seal
Withrow-Bentsen (1994)

This series continued the preceding design. Prices are generic and stars are scarce.

Prices for a typical note for this series, unless listed otherwise, are as follows:

Unc-63
$150

Prices for a typical star note for this series, unless listed otherwise, are as follows:

EF-40	AU-50	Unc-60	Unc-63
$125	$140	$155	$175

W-3846-A • F-2174A • Boston • 83,200,000

W-3846-B • F-2174B • New York • 288,000,000

W-3846-B★ • F-2174B★ • 2,560,000

W-3846-C • F-2174C • Philadelphia • 41,600,000

W-3846-C★ • F-2174C★ • 1,280,000

W-3846-D • F-2174D • Cleveland • 9,600,000

W-3846-D★ • F-2174D★ • 1,024,000

W-3846-E • F-2174E • Richmond • 64,000,000

W-3846-F • F-2174F • Atlanta • 150,400,000

W-3846-G • F-2174G • Chicago • 44,800,000

W-3846-H • F-2174H • St. Louis • 16,000,000

W-3846-H★ • F-2174H★ • 640,000

W-3846-I • F-2174I • Minneapolis • 9,600,000

W-3846-J • F-2174J • Kansas City • 9,600,000

W-3846-K • F-2174K • Dallas • 51,200,000

W-3846-L • F-2174L • San Francisco • 19,200,000

Series of 1996, Green Seal
Withrow-Rubin (1995–1999)

Both sides of the $100 note were redesigned for the Series of 1996. To the left is a new Federal Reserve seal without any indication of which of the 12 banks issued the note. The letter and number printed below the serial number at the upper left give that information, A1 for Boston, B2 for New York, etc. The obligation or redemption statement is now below a modernized Federal Reserve seal. Franklin's portrait is modified and enlarged. THE UNITED STATES OF AMERICA is in three lines in the upper right field. Other changes are as depicted.

The new back retains some familiar elements, but with extensive changes. A curved frame encloses Independence Hall and a shaded background, with white areas to the left and right. Other changes are illustrated. All were printed in Washington, D.C.

Prices for a typical note for this series, unless listed otherwise, are as follows:

Unc-63
$125

Prices for a typical star note for this series, unless listed otherwise, are as follows:

Unc-63
$165

W-3847-A • F-2175A • Boston • 125,600,000

W-3847-A★ • F-2175A★ • 2,560,000

W-3847-B • F-2175B • New York • 2,325,600,000

W-3847-B★ • F-2175B★ • 17,920,000

W-3847-C • F-2175C • Philadelphia • 86,400,000

W-3847-D • F-2175D • Cleveland • 176,800,000

W-3847-D★ • F-2175D★ • 160,000

W-3847-E • F-2175E • Richmond • 276,800,000

W-3847-E★ • F-2175E★ • 3,200,000

W-3847-F • F-2175F • Atlanta • 222,400,000

W-3847-F★ • F-2175F★ • 2,560,000

SERIES OF 1993, GREEN SEAL

Detail of the signatures and the series imprint of a $100 Federal Reserve Note, Series of 1993 (W-3846-L). This series uses the standard back found on all $100 notes from the Series of 1963-A to the Series of 1993.

W-3847-G • F-2175G • Chicago • 244,800,000

W-3847-G★ • F-2175G★ • 1,920,000

W-3847-H • F-2175H • St. Louis • 112,800,000

W-3847-I • F-2175I • Minneapolis • 32,000,000

W-3847-J • F-2175J • Kansas City • 83,200,000

W-3847-K • F-2175K • Dallas • 144,800,000

W-3847-K★ • F-2175K★ • 1,920,000

W-3847-L • F-2175L • San Francisco • 406,400,000

W-3847-L★ • F-2175L★ • 2,560,000

Series of 1999, Green Seal
Withrow-Summers (1999–2001)

This series continued the preceding design. All were printed in Washington, D.C. Printages vary widely, but prices are generic. Only the Boston and New York banks issued star notes.

Prices for a typical note for this series, unless listed otherwise, are as follows:

Unc-63
$125

Prices for a typical star note for this series, unless listed otherwise, are as follows:

Unc-63
$150

W-3848-A • F-2176A • Boston • 48,000,000

W-3848-A★ • F-2176A★ • 3,520,000

W-3848-B • F-2176B • New York • 172,800,000

W-3848-B★ • F-2176B★ • 3,840,000

W-3848-C • F-2176C • Philadelphia • 3,200,000

W-3848-D • F-2176D • Cleveland • 19,200,000

W-3848-E • F-2176E • Richmond • 60,800,000

SERIES OF 1996, GREEN SEAL

$100 Federal Reserve Note, Series of 1996 (W-3847-A). Federal Reserve Bank of Boston. This illustrates the type introduced with Series 1996. Franklin's portrait is modified, as are other aspects, and security features have been added.

Back of the $100 Federal Reserve Note, Series of 1996 (W-3847-A), showing revisions. The Independence Hall motif is retained, but the features are modified.

SERIES OF 1999, GREEN SEAL

Detail of the signatures and the series imprint of a $100 Federal Reserve Note, Series of 1999 (W-3848-B). This series uses the standard back found on all $100 notes beginning with the Series of 1996.

W-3848-F • F-2176F • Atlanta • 16,000,000

W-3848-G • F-2176G • Chicago • 52,400,000

W-3848-H • F-2176H • St. Louis • 22,400,000

W-3848-I • F-2176I • Minneapolis • 70,400,000

W-3848-J • F-2176J • Kansas City • 25,600,000

W-3848-K • F-2176K • Dallas • 19,200,000

Series of 2001, Green Seal
Marin-O'Neill (2001–2002)

This series continued the preceding design. All were printed in Washington, D.C. Printages are large and the notes are plentiful.

Prices for a typical note for this series, unless listed otherwise, are as follows:

Unc-63
$115

W-3849-A • F-2177A • Boston • 32,000,000

W-3849-B • F-2177B • New York • 579,200,000

W-3849-B★ • F-2177B★ • 320,000

Unc-63	Unc-65
$115	$200

W-3849-C • F-2177C • Philadelphia • 32,000,000

W-3849-D • F-2177D • Cleveland • 19,200,000

W-3849-D★ • F-2177D★ • 1,920,000

Unc-65
$135

W-3849-E • F-2177E • Richmond • 64,000,000

W-3849-E★ • F-2177E★ • 1,920,000

Unc-65
$135

W-3849-F • F-2177F • Atlanta • 99,200,000

W-3849-F★ • F-2177F★ • 1,600,000

Unc-63	Unc-65
$115	$225

W-3849-G • F-2177G • Chicago • 57,600,000

W-3849-H • F-2177H • St. Louis • 25,600,000

W-3849-I • F-2177I • Minneapolis • 9,600,000

Unc-65
$125

W-3849-J • F-2177J • Kansas City • 22,400,000

Unc-65
$120

W-3849-K • F-2177K • Dallas • 60,800,000

W-3849-L • F-2177L • San Francisco • 147,200,000

Series of 2003, Green Seal
Marin-Snow (2003)

This series continued the preceding design. All were printed in Washington, D.C. Printages are large and the notes are plentiful.

W-3850-A • F-2178A • Boston • 35,200,000

Unc-65
$125

W-3850-B • F-2178B • New York • 364,800,000

Unc-65
$115

W-3850-B★ • F-2178B★ • 2,240,000

Unc-65
$135

W-3850-C • F-2178C • Philadelphia • 41,600,000

Unc-65
$125

SERIES OF 2001, GREEN SEAL

Detail of the signatures and the series imprint of a $100 Federal Reserve Note, Series of 2001 (W-3849-L). This series uses the standard back found on all $100 notes beginning with the Series of 1996.

SERIES OF 2003, GREEN SEAL

Detail of the signatures and the series imprint of a $100 Federal Reserve Note, Series of 2003 (W-3850-L). This series uses the standard back found on all $100 notes beginning with the Series of 1996.

W-3850-D • F-2178D • Cleveland • 32,000,000

Unc-65
$125

W-3850-E • F-2178E • Richmond • 86,400,000

Unc-65
$115

W-3850-F • F-2178F • Atlanta • 166,400,000

Unc-65
$115

W-3850-F★ • F-2178F★ • 1,280,000

Unc-65
$135

W-3850-G • F-2178G • Chicago • 80,000,000

Unc-65
$115

W-3850-H • F-2178H • St. Louis • 38,400,000

Unc-65
$125

W-3850-I • F-2178I • Minneapolis • 16,000,000

Unc-65
$130

W-3850-J • F-2178J • Kansas City • 38,400,000

Unc-65
$125

W-3850-K • F-2178K • Dallas • 32,000,000

Unc-65
$125

W-3850-K★ • F-2178K★ • 2,688,000

Unc-65
$175

W-3850-L • F-2178L • San Francisco • 89,600,000

Unc-65
$115

W-3850-L★ • F-2178L★ • 320,000

Unc-65
$150

Series of 2003-A, Green Seal
Cabral-Snow (2004–2006)

This series continued the preceding design. All were printed in Washington, D.C. Printages are large, and the notes are plentiful.

W-3851-A • F-2179A • Boston • 12,800,000

Unc-65
$120

W-3851-B • F-2179B • New York • 316,800,000

Unc-65
$110

W-3851-B★ • F-2179B★ • 1,280,000 (160,000 sheets)

Unc-65
$125

W-3851-C • F-2179C • Philadelphia • 28,800,000

Unc-65
$115

W-3851-D • F-2179D • Cleveland • 12,800,000

Unc-65
$120

W-3851-E • F-2179E • Richmond • 86,400,000

Unc-65
$110

W-3851-F • F-2179F • Atlanta • 140,800,000

Unc-65
$110

W-3851-G • F-2179G • Chicago • 67,200,000

Unc-65
$110

W-3851-G★ • F-2179G★ • 1,920,000

Unc-65
$125

W-3851-H • F-2179H • St. Louis • 32,000,000

Unc-65
$115

SERIES OF 2003-A, GREEN SEAL

Detail of the signatures and the series imprint of a $100 Federal Reserve Note, Series of 2003-A (W-3851-G).
This series uses the standard back found on all $100 notes beginning with the Series of 1996.

W-3851-H★ • F-2179H★

Unc-65
$125

W-3851-I • F-2179I • Minneapolis • 6,400,000

Unc-65
$125

W-3851-J • F-2179J • Kansas City • 28,800,000

Unc-65
$115

W-3851-K • F-2179K • Dallas • 105,600,000

Unc-65
$110

W-3851-L • F-2179L • San Francisco • 249,600,000

Unc-65
$110

W-3851-L★ • F-2179L★ • 1,280,000

Unc-65
$125

Series of 2006, Green Seal, Washington
Cabral-Paulson (2006–2009)

This series continued the preceding design.

The information given here is accurate as of press time. No valuation charts are provided, as notes in this series can be had in top condition for face value at banks or from dealers (with a nominal handling charge).

W-3852-A • F-2180A • Boston

W-3852-B • F-2180B • New York

W-3852-B★ • F-2180B★

W-3852-C • F-2180C • Philadelphia

W-3852-D • F-2180D • Cleveland

W-3852-E • F-2180E • Richmond

W-3852-E★ • F-2180E★

W-3852-F • F-2180F • Atlanta

W-3852-F★ • F-2180F★

W-3852-G • F-2180G • Chicago

W-3852-H • F-2180H • St. Louis

W-3852-I • F-2180I • Minneapolis

W-3852-J • F-2180J • Kansas City

W-3852-K • F-2180K • Dallas

W-3852-L • F-2180L • San Francisco

W-3852-L★ • F-2180L★

Series of 2006, Green Seal, Fort Worth
Cabral-Paulson (2006–2009)

This issue marked the first time the Western Facility in Fort Worth, Texas, was used to print $100 notes. The letters FW appear as part of the face plate designation.

The information given here is accurate as of press time. No valuation charts are provided, as notes in this series can be had in top condition for face value at banks or from dealers (with a nominal handling charge).

W-3853-B • F-2181B • New York

W-3853-C • F-2181C • Philadelphia

W-3853-J • F-2181J • Kansas City

W-3853-K • F-2181K • Dallas

W-3853-K★ • F-2181K★

W-3853-L • F-2181L • San Francisco

W-3853-L★ • F-2181L★

Series of 2009, Green Seal
Rios-Geithner (2009–)

No printing information as of press time.

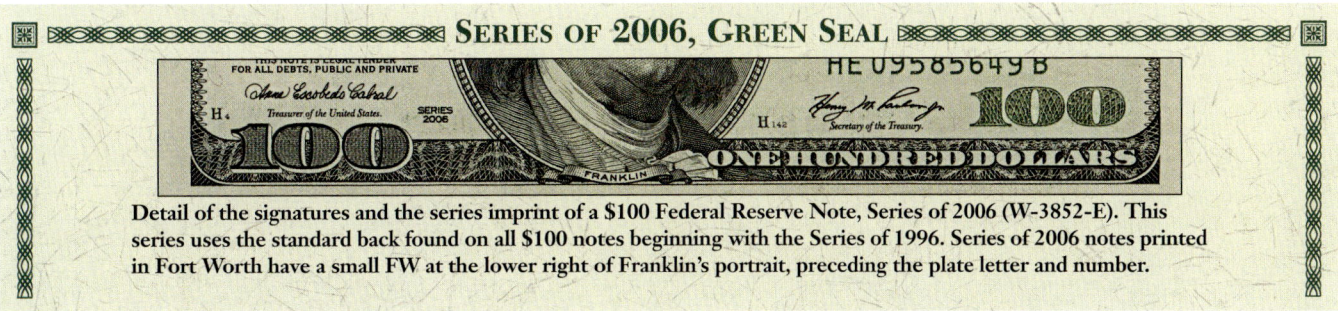

SERIES OF 2006, GREEN SEAL

Detail of the signatures and the series imprint of a $100 Federal Reserve Note, Series of 2006 (W-3852-E). This series uses the standard back found on all $100 notes beginning with the Series of 1996. Series of 2006 notes printed in Fort Worth have a small FW at the lower right of Franklin's portrait, preceding the plate letter and number.

13

$500 NOTES

LARGE SIZE

Large-size notes of the $500 denomination were made in several different series from the 1860s through the 1920s. Early Interest-Bearing Notes were issued as investment securities, not as circulating paper money. Most were bought and held by banks and wealthy individuals. Early issues range from very rare to nonexistent, and most later varieties are elusive. National Bank Notes were made in the Original Series and Series of 1875, but not later. Although these were issued in fairly large numbers, only three examples can be accounted for today.

Legal Tender Note varieties range from rare to extremely rare, with some varieties unknown today. Silver Certificates were made only in the Series of 1878 and 1880 and are so elusive that a single note would be a cause for auction-room excitement.

For Treasury or Coin Notes, it's a case of what might have been, but wasn't. None were made to go with the ornate Series of 1890 bills in other denominations, and although 16,000 of the Series of 1891 notes were printed, none were issued. Gold Certificates of the Series of 1863 were issued, but none are known today. It is not until the Series of 1882 and 1922 that these become collectible. Federal Reserve Notes are collectible by type, but those paid out by certain of the banks are very rare.

Accordingly, selected $500 bills can be acquired as trophy notes, but too few exist to permit forming a collection of varieties, even for the most well-financed buyer.

INTEREST-BEARING NOTES

March 2, 1861, 6% Interest, 60 Days

The Union was in need of funds, and the Act of March 2, 1861, provided for notes or bonds (both terms were used) to be issued to borrow money. The shortest term was 60 days, for the $50, $100, and $500 denominations. No circulated examples are known, but proofs exist. Information regarding these notes is sparse, other than that $10 million was authorized, but $12,896,350 was eventually issued and quickly redeemed in its entirety. These notes were printed in New York City by the American Bank Note Company and bear the imprint of that firm as well as that of Rawdon, Wright, Hatch & Edson.

The $500 notes bear the vignette *Prosperity* at the top center. Two women are seated to either side of an anvil. One holds a cornucopia and the other a mallet. In the distance to the right is a factory building. At the lower left is a portrait of Washington, and to the lower right is a perched eagle. There are denomination counters at each corner. These same vignettes were used on notes for state-chartered banks produced by American Bank Note Company and Rawdon, Wright, Hatch & Edson. The back has three ornate vignettes; the ones at the right and left are counters. The notes are approximately 19.5 centimeters wide by 10 centimeters high.

W-3900 • F-195d • Unknown

March 2, 1861, 6% Interest, 2 Years

At the time of issue these notes (illus. on p. 704) were sold at a discount from face value to reflect the interest to be earned for two years. Most buyers were banks and security houses that retailed them to investors. The notes did not circulate in commerce but were held until maturity, then redeemed at par.

The face depicts a man carrying a bindle stick at the left, a portrait of "Old Fuss and Feathers" General Winfield Scott at the center, and a farmer with a scythe at the right. A green security printing in the cycloidal configuration is at the center. The notes bear the imprint of the National Bank Note Company. The back is printed in brown with center inscriptions oriented vertically. Tiny counters to the left and right are oriented horizontally. There is a D at the center surrounded by ornamental vignettes, again with a National Bank Note Company imprint. Chittenden-Spinner signatures are on all. The notes are approximately 20 centimeters wide by 10 centimeters high.

W-3920 • F-202c • "for the" hand signed • 13,665
Recorded population: 1 • *Commentary:* Supposedly, all were redeemed by 1869 per the *Annual Report*, p. 243. However, one was reported to Martin Gengerke as VF, privately held.[1]

W-3930 • F-202c • "for the" printed • Part of W-3920 printage

$500 Interest-Bearing Note, March 2, 1861, 6% Interest, 2 Years (W-3920). Proof impression.

Back of W-3920, printed in brown with center inscriptions oriented vertically. Proof impression illustrated.

First Series, July 17, 1861, 7.3% Interest, 3 Years

On the face of this note Justice is seated at the left, a portrait of Washington is at the center, and a seated woman with a wagon wheel *(Transportation)* is at the right. There is green security printing, and the notes are signed by Treasury clerks. The back is printed in green with D counters to each side and vertically oriented printing at the center. These were printed by the American Bank Note Company with three notes to each sheet.

W-3950 • F-209 • Issued with coupons

Recorded population: 2 • Selected information: The known serials are 1/A, EF, damaged, canceled, owned by the Bureau of the Public Debt in Washington, D.C., and 15502/A, VF–EF, sold in a CAA auction (2/2005) for $299,000.

March 3, 1863, 5% Interest, 1 Year

These notes have the same design as $500 Compound Interest Treasury Notes and depict the ship *New Ironsides* and the vignette *The Standard Bearer.* The ship engraving has the common artistic error of having the wind blow in one direction and the smoke drift in another (also used on W-3985). At the center of the face is green printing in the cycloidal configuration style, with NATIONAL BANK NOTE COMPANY near the bottom border. Such notes likely were issued more or less continually with various dates printed on the face. These were sold at a discount to reflect the interest and redeemed at face value upon maturity. This would calculate to a $476.12 issue price to an exchange or securities house, which would charge an additional small premium to a customer.

W-3960 • F-200 • Unknown

March 3, 1863, 5% Interest, 2 Years

At the left of the face is a standing woman with a flag in the background, a vignette by Charles Burt titled *Liberty and Union.* At the top center is an eagle on its nest, wings uplifted. D counters are to the left and right of the bottom, and at the center is a deep green overprint making the text somewhat difficult to read. Coupons are attached to the right. Logically,

First Series, July 17, 1861, 7.3% Interest, 3 Years

$500 Interest-Bearing Note, First Series, July 17, 1861 (W-3950). Variety dated October 1, 1861, with red serial numbers.

Back of W-3950, with American Bank Note Company imprint.

in addition to those with three coupons attached, varieties might have been printed without coupons, payable at maturity, as was the procedure of lower denominations in the series. There is no record of this, however, and Gene Hessler's *Comprehensive Catalog* states that all bore coupons.

The back has two large counters, along with inscriptions, ornamental vignettes, and a small red Treasury seal. Three examples are reported outstanding on Treasury books, but none has been located by a numismatist. Proof impressions exist.

W-3970 • F-205 • Issued with three coupons attached • 80,604 • Unknown

at both sides, and an inscription is oriented vertically at the center. The notes were issued with coupons for domestic distribution and without coupons for foreign sales.[2] The notes were printed by the National Currency Bureau.

W-3975 • F-212b • Issued with coupons • *Printed on plate:* AUGUST 15, 1864 • 171,666
Recorded population: 1 • *Graded:* EF-40 • *Commentary:* Ex Philpott Collection. No coupons remain. This note was advertised for $4,500 by Bob Medlar in *The Numismatist* (12/1971). There are no auction records.

W-3976 • F-212b • Issued without coupons • *Printed on plate:* AUGUST 15, 1865 • Unknown

June 30, 1864, 7.3% Interest, 3 Years

The face of this $500 issue has the *Mortar Firing* vignette at the lower left, a portrait of Alexander Hamilton at the center, and a standing figure of Washington at the lower right. The face also shows that it is printed by the Treasury department and has a small red Treasury seal and Colby-Spinner signatures. The back is printed in bright green with large counters

March 3, 1865, 7.3% Interest, 3 Years

The face (illus. on p. 706) is similar to the preceding, with the vignette *Mortar Firing* at the lower left, a portrait of Alexander Hamilton at the center, and a standing figure of Washington at the lower right. The back has two large counters and a vertical inscription. The signatures are of Colby-Spinner, and the small serial numbers are printed in red. The notes were issued with coupons attached to the right side and printed by the National Currency Bureau.

W-3980 • F-212f • *Printed on plate:* JUNE 15, 1865 • 175,682

Recorded population: 1 • Graded: VG-8 • Selected information: This note is dated June 15, 1865, and has one coupon remaining. Punch cancelled. Kreisberg & Schulman (5/1966), $2,600; Stack's (3/1981), $8,500; Knight (6/1981), *Bank Note Reporter* priced offering, $45,000; Knight (12/1998), $71,500; Heritage (2/2005), $115,000; now in a Southern collection.

W-3982 • F-unlisted • *Printed on plate:* JULY 15, 1865 • 108,654 • Unknown

COMPOUND INTEREST TREASURY NOTES

The $500 and other Compound Interest Treasury Notes were authorized under the Acts of March 3, 1863, and June 30, 1864, and bore interest at 6% per year for three years. These bear the imprint TREASURY DEPARTMENT and were printed in the Treasury Building. Bronzing powder was applied to create prominent bronze lettering on the face, which was considered a deterrent to counterfeiting.

Series of 1863 and 1864

The $500 denomination depicts the ship *New Ironsides* and the vignette *The Standard Bearer*. The ship engraving has the common artistic error of having the wind blow in one direction and the smoke drift in another. At the center of the face is a green overprint in the cycloidal configuration, with NATIONAL BANK NOTE COMPANY near the bottom border. No examples are known. Proof impressions exist. These are slightly larger than Legal Tender Notes and measure 3.5 inches by 7.5 inches.

The face is similar in motifs to the one-year Interest-Bearing Notes of March 3, 1863, but with different typography and lacking the heavy green printing. As the first step in production, 100 COMPOUND INTEREST TREASURY NOTE was printed in bronzing powder on a blank sheet. TREASURY DEPARTMENT is partially visible under the seal at the upper right.

Various red overprints stated the dates of issue. Gene Hessler and Carlson Chambliss record June 10 and July 15,

MARCH 3, 1865, 7.3% INTEREST, 3 YEARS

$500 Interest-Bearing Note of March 3, 1865, the only known example (W-3980).

Back of the $500 Interest-Bearing Note of March 3, 1865 (W-3980).

1864, and October 1, 1865. Although 92,000 were issued and Treasury account books show 23 unredeemed, none are known to exist today, although proof impressions survive.

W-3985 • F-194 • Chittenden-Spinner (1861–1864) • 135,692 • Unknown

Commentary: Printed dates include June 10, 1864, and July 15, 1864.

W-3990 • F-194b • Colby-Spinner (1864–1867) • *Printed on plate:* OCTOBER 1, 1865 • Part of W-3985 printage • Unknown

LEGAL TENDER NOTES
(Also Known as United States Notes)

Series of 1862, First Obligation

The $500 Series of 1862 Legal Tender Notes (illus. on p. 708) were no doubt made in multiple varieties, but so few exist that they cannot be studied. Lower-denomination varieties can give an idea of the potential, except that far fewer high-value notes were made. A portrait of secretary of the Treasury Albert Gallatin is at the center. He served from 1801 to 1813 and was very erudite in banking and financial matters.

The face, back, and tint plates for the $500 Series of 1862 and 1863 Legal Tender Notes were engraved by the American Bank Note Company. American also printed most (if not all) of the First Obligation notes. American and National shared the printing for the Second Obligation notes.[3] Treasury signatures of Chittenden and Spinner were printed on the face by using a separate plate and a special ink.

The face bears the imprint AMERICAN BANK NOTE CO. NEW YORK in drop-out white letters on a black strip in the green vignette below the portrait, which is not easy to see. At the left is a red Treasury seal (faded on the one existing note). Below the green vignette to the right is PATENTED 30 JUNE 1857, referring to the "Canada green" said to deter counterfeiting. The serial number is imprinted in red at the upper right. All bear the address of the Sub-Treasury in New York City.

The back is a rich green with counters to the left and right, set against an ornately engraved background. At the center is the obligation text.

First Obligation: This wording, with different typography on the various denominations, states that the note is exchangeable for bonds (a provision dropped from the Second Obligation): "This note is a Legal Tender for all debts public and private, except duties on imports and interest on the public debt, and is exchangeable for U.S. six percent twenty years bonds, redeemable at the pleasure of the U. States after five years." These "6-20" bonds, as they were known, were a popular investment for banks and the public and were widely advertised in their time.

W-4001 • F-183a • *Printed on plate:* ACT OF FEB'Y 25th 1862 / MARCH 10th 1862 • American Bank Note Co. imprint • One serial number • Treasury seal without inner border of radial parallel lines • Series 1 • 26,000
Recorded population: 1 • Highest graded: F-12.

W-4002 • F-183a • Treasury seal with inner border of radial parallel lines • Series 1 • 12,000 • Unknown

Series of 1862 and 1863, Second Obligation

These $500 notes (illus. on p. 709) have the same design as the preceding, but with slightly different typography. The back is the second type.

Second Obligation: "This note is a Legal Tender for all debts public and private, except duties on imports and interest on the public debt, and is receivable in payment of all loans made to the United States." This wording, with different typography on various denominations, does not mention exchanging the notes for bonds and thus is different from the First Obligation.

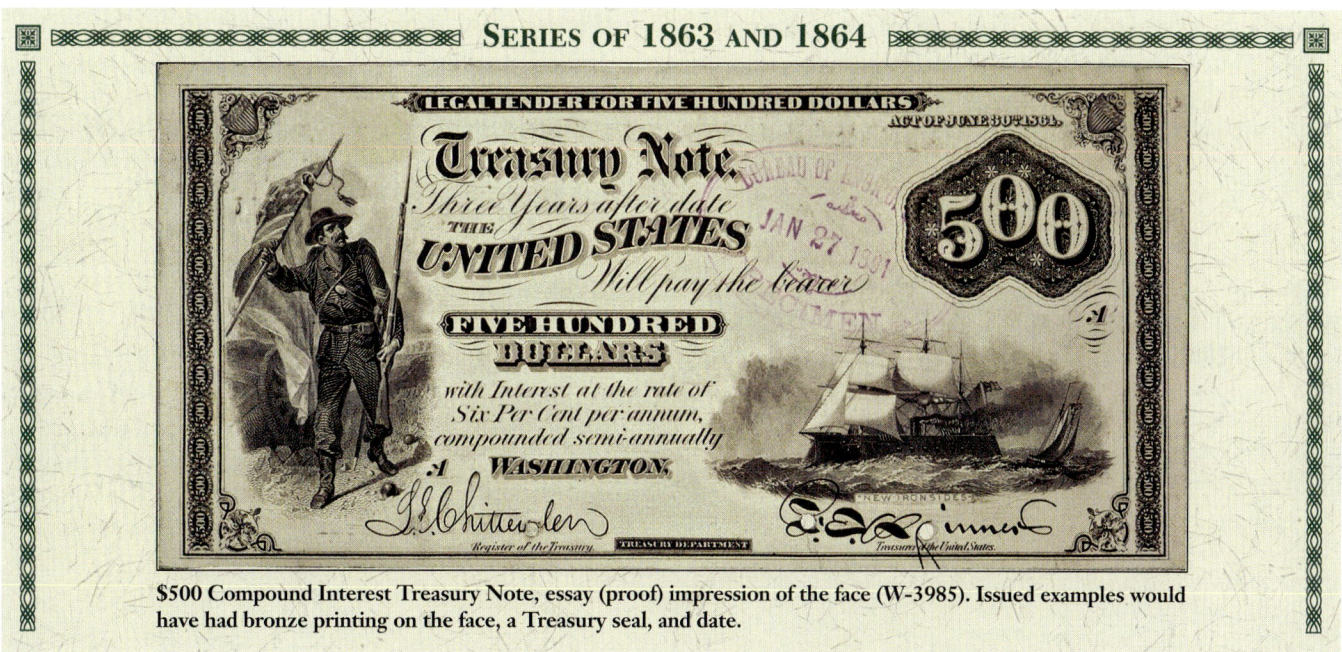

$500 Compound Interest Treasury Note, essay (proof) impression of the face (W-3985). Issued examples would have had bronze printing on the face, a Treasury seal, and date.

SERIES OF 1862, FIRST OBLIGATION

$500 Legal Tender Note, Series of 1862 (W-4001). Imprint of the American Bank Note Co.

Back of the $500 Legal Tender Note, Series of 1862 (W-4001), with First Obligation wording and arrangement at the center.

W-4003 • F-183b • *Printed on plate:* ACT OF FEB'Y 25th 1862 / MARCH 10th 1862 • American Bank Note Co. and National Bank Note Co. imprints • One serial number • Second Obligation back • New Series 1 • 5,000 • Unknown

W-4004 • F-183c • *Printed on plate:* ACT OF MARCH 3d 1863 / MARCH 10th 1862 • 22,828 • Unknown

W-4005 • F-183c • AMERICAN BANK NOTE CO. N.Y. imprint • 22,000

Recorded population: 3 • Highest graded: Unc • Selected information: Known examples include serials 42223/C, Unc, sold in a CAA auction (9/1997) for $233,750; 42227/C, Unc-64 (PCGS), sold in a Knight auction (10/2005) for $621,000; and 49519/C, VG–F, in the Smithsonian Institution collection.

W-4006 • F-183c • *Printed on plate:* ACT OF MARCH 3d 1863 / MARCH 10th 1863 • 8,000

Recorded population: 1 • Selected information: The known note is serial 50239/C, VG–F, damaged, owned by the Federal Reserve Bank of Philadelphia.

W-4007 • F-183d • Two serial numbers • 20,000

Recorded population: 1 • Selected information: The known note is serial 64984/D, VF, damaged, owned by the Federal Reserve Bank of Chicago. The serial numbers are in mismatched fonts.

Series of 1869

The face of the $500 note of this series (illus. on p. 710) bears on the left an engraving of Justice, holding balance scales aloft in her left hand and an upward-pointing sword in her right. At the center the denomination is set against an ornate background. A red serial number is to the lower left, and a large pink Treasury seal is to the right. Near the right border is a portrait of president John Quincy Adams. The back of the note has the denomination to the left and right, and the obligation statement and the counterfeiting clause appear within a circle at the center. As a class, Series of 1869 notes were issued from October 19, 1869, through July 25, 1874.

W-4060 • F-184 • Allison-Spinner (1869–1875) • Large pink seal with spiked border • 89,360

Estimated population: 4 • Commentary: Note N32610/B, EF, once in numismatic circulation, has been condemned as counterfeit. • *Selected information:* The known notes are serials N16035/C, VF, repaired, part of the Smithsonian Institution collection; N16051/C; N31963/C, F, damaged, owned by the Federal Reserve Bank of Chicago; and N48792/D, EF, from the Amon Carter Jr. collection.

SERIES OF 1862 AND 1863, SECOND OBLIGATION

$500 Legal Tender Note, Series of 1863 (W-4006).

Back of the $500 Legal Tender Note, Series of 1863 (W-4006), with Second Obligation wording at the center.

Series of 1874

On the face of this $500 issue (illus. on p. 711) are two vignettes: *Victory* at the left and a portrait of Major General Joseph King Mansfield to the right. Mansfield, little remembered today, was promoted posthumously to the rank of major general after his death on September 17, 1862. During the Mexican-American War in the late 1840s, he distinguished himself and was promoted to colonel. A pink Treasury seal is at the lower left. At the center bottom an ornate counter, D 500 D, is overprinted in pink. The back, a new design, is elaborately engraved and bears the imprint of the Columbian Bank Note Company. As a class, Series of 1874 notes were issued from July 13, 1874, through September 13, 1875.

The $500 Legal Tender Note of this type, made in 14 signature and Treasury seal combinations (see subsequent listings), repeats a scenario familiar to numismatists seeking high-denomination currency. On this series the signatures are transposed, a situation not reflected in certain standard references, but given here.

W-4062 • F-unlisted[4] • **Spinner-Allison (signatures transposed) (1869–1875)** • **Small pink seal with spiked border** • **56,000**

Recorded population: 5 • *Highest graded:* EF-40.

Series of 1875

This series (illus. on p. 711) continues the designs of the preceding, with some small typographical differences on the face. The signatures are in their normal positions (not transposed). Series of 1875 notes were issued from July 20, 1875, through June 20, 1879. Although issued in quantity, these are exceedingly rare today, with just two confirmed to exist.

W-4064 • F-185b • **Allison-New (1875–1876)** • **SERIES A 1875 imprint in pink** • **Small pink seal with spiked border** • **32,000**

Recorded population: 1 • *Selected information:* The known example is serial A20164/D, VF or finer, part of the Smithsonian Institution collection.

W-4066 • F-185c • **Allison-Wyman (1876–1877)** • **24,800**

Recorded population: 1 • *Selected information:* The known example is serial A56900/D, VF or finer, with irregularity at top edge at left, part of the Smithsonian Institution collection.

Series of 1878

Designs for this series are similar to the preceding. Face plate Ao, seen in proof form only, has SERIES OF 1878 on

SERIES OF 1869

$500 Legal Tender Note, Series of 1869 (W-4060). Justice seated to the left. Portrait of John Quincy Adams to the right. Serial N48782, plate d1.

Back of the $500 Legal Tender Note, Series of 1869 (W-4060).

a label near the upper-left border, below ACT OF MARCH 3d 1863. The signatures are in the normal order of Allison and Gilfillan. In face plate B2, which is known to have produced issued notes, SERIES OF 1878 has been removed (although small traces of the left and right sides of the frame remain), and the signatures are transposed as Gilfillan and Allison. Details are illustrated.

The back has PRINTED AT THE BUREAU ENGRAVING & PRINTING added below the Columbian Bank Note Company imprint.

W-4070 • F-unlisted[5] • Gilfillan-Allison (signatures transposed) (1877–1878) • Small pink seal with spiked border • 24,000

Recorded population: 6 • *Highest graded:* EF-40.

Series of 1880

The design of these notes (illus. on p. 713) follows that of the preceding. Based on transpositions among $50 denomination Legal Tender Notes of this series and on known transpositions of Series 1874 and 1878 $500 notes, it seems likely that early listings (but not later) among the Series of 1880 notes may have signatures transposed.

Back varieties exist, the earlier ones (W-4072, if such was made, and W-4074) with the Columbian Bank Note Company imprint and the later (W-4076 to W-4090) with the Bureau of Engraving imprint only.

W-4072 • F-185e • Scofield-Gilfillan (1878–1881) • Large brown seal • No evidence of printing; listed here for the record

W-4074 • F-185f • Bruce-Wyman (1883–1885) • 12,000

Recorded population: 2 • *Selected information:* The known examples are serials 9848/D, VF, owned by the Federal Reserve Bank of New York, and Z11341/A, VF, owned by the Federal Reserve Bank of San Francisco.

W-4076 • F-185g • Rosecrans-Jordan (1885–1887) • Large red seal with plain border • New back style begins • 8,000 • Unknown

W-4078 • F-185h • Rosecrans-Hyatt (1887–1889) • 4,000 • Unknown

W-4080 • F-185i • Rosecrans-Huston (1889–1891) • 16,000

Recorded population: 3 • *Highest graded:* VF-20 • *Selected information:* The known examples are serials A13101/A, F, owned by the Federal Reserve Bank of San Francisco; A13468/D,

SERIES OF 1874

$500 Legal Tender Note, Series of 1874 (W-4062). The face has been redesigned, rather than imitating the Series of 1869 motifs (which was done in certain other Legal Tender Notes of this era). The signatures of the Treasury officials are transposed, as they are on certain subsequent varieties. The same anomaly occurs among $50 Legal Tender Notes of this era.

Detail showing the transposed signatures. Compare to the signatures of the Series of 1869 Legal Tender Note.

Detail of the Columbian Bank Note Company imprint on the back. Here, BANKNOTE is one word or else is too closely spaced. Typography was inconsistent over the years.

Back of the $500 Legal Tender Note, Series of 1874 (W-4062).

SERIES OF 1875

$500 Legal Tender Note, Series of 1875 (W-4064). Allison-New signatures. The back is the same as for the Series of 1874. (Smithsonian Institution)

SERIES OF 1878

$500 Legal Tender Note, Series of 1878 (W-4070). The signatures of the Treasury officials are in normal arrangement as Allison-Gilfillan. Proof impression without overprints. This 1939-made one-subject proof does not reflect the 1878 plate used to print the transposed-signature notes. Date of correction is unknown.

Detail of the Act information, SERIES OF 1878 label, and plate letter and number Ao at the upper left (W-4070). The BEP proofs of 1939 to 1941 all have either A or Ao.

Detail of the Act information and plate letter and number B2 at the upper left (W-4070). Note the vertical remnants of the old SERIES OF 1878 frame under T (ACT) and 8 (1863).

$500 Legal Tender Note, Series of 1878 (W-4070). The signatures of the Treasury officials are transposed.

F–VF, used as the Hessler illustration, part of the Smithsonian Institution collection; and A26456/D, VF, owned by the Federal Reserve Bank of San Francisco.

W-4082 • F-185j • Rosecrans-Nebeker (1891–1893) • Small red seal with scalloped border • 16,000
Recorded population: 2 • Highest graded: VF-35 • Selected information: The known examples are serials A39745/A, VF, owned by the Federal Reserve Bank of Chicago, and A43029/A, VF–EF, part of the Smithsonian Institution collection.

W-4084 • F-185k • Tillman-Morgan (1893–1897) • 20,000
Recorded population: 6 • Highest graded: EF-40 • Selected information: Known examples include serials A48235/C, EF,

stained, part of the Smithsonian Institution collection; A48773/A, F, owned by the Federal Reserve Bank of San Francisco; A59147/C, AU, pinholes, owned by the Federal Reserve Bank of Chicago; A59268/D, F, owned by the Federal Reserve Bank of Richmond; A61569/A, VF, owned by the Federal Reserve Bank of San Francisco; and A62113/A.VG–F, pinholes, sold in a CAA auction (5/2003) for $161,000.

W-4086 • F-185l • Bruce-Roberts (1897–1898) • 12,000
Recorded population: 5 • Highest graded: EF-45 • Selected information: Known examples include serials A68125/A, VF, owned by the Federal Reserve Bank of San Francisco; A69054/B, F, owned by the Federal Reserve Bank of Richmond; A69074/B,

SERIES OF 1878,
continued

Back of the $500 Legal Tender Note, Series of 1878 (W-4070).

Detail of the back showing the added imprint.

SERIES OF 1880

$500 Legal Tender Note, Series of 1880 (W-4088).

Back of the $500 Legal Tender Note, Series of 1880 (W-4088), with later style with the Bureau of Engraving and Printing imprint only.

EF, owned by the Federal Reserve Bank of San Francisco; A69089/A, VF-35 (PMG), sold in a Heritage auction (9/2007) for $690,000; and A75902/B, EF–AU, part of the Smithsonian Institution collection.

W-4088 • F-185m • Lyons-Roberts (1898–1905) • 20,000
Recorded population: 5 • Highest graded: EF-45 • Selected information: Known examples include serials A81758/B, EF, part of the ANA Museum collection; A85034/B, EF-40 (PCGS), sold in a Knight auction (2/2000) for $231,000; A87127/C, AU, repaired, sold in a CAA auction (1/2005) for $281,750; A88070/B, EF–AU, part of the Smithsonian Institution collection; and A88922/B, VF, owned by the Federal Reserve Bank of San Francisco.

W-4090 • F-185n • Napier-McClung (1911–1912) • No evidence of printing

NATIONAL BANK NOTES

Original Series
(Authorized Issue 1863 to 1875)

The Original Series $500 notes were printed by the National Bank Note Company, whose imprint appears at the bottom border.[6] All have a small red Treasury seal with a spiked border. On some early notes the Treasury serial number at the upper right is in blue (but on most it is red), while on all the bank serial number at the lower left is in red. The Act of June 20, 1874, provided for the imprinting of the bank's charter number. Plate arrangements included $500-$1,000 (the usual), $500-$500-$500-$1,000, and $500-$500-$500-$500.

The left of the face shows a standing female figure with a sword, titled *Civilization* by the Treasury department.[7] This is a seemingly satirical illustration, with a cannon in the foreground, a battleship in the offing to the left, and an armed camp in the distance to the right. Perhaps she is dreaming of what civilization *might* be, for above her is a rainbow and, in the far distance, a farmhouse in a bucolic setting. The Friedberg text names this *The Spirit of the Navy*. On the right side is a vignette of a ship, the *Sirius*, arriving in New York City harbor, an event that was important in the news a generation earlier. The first ships to cross the ocean entirely under steam power completed the trip from England together on April 23, 1838. The first of these to arrive, the *Sirius*, took 18 days and 10 hours to make the trip from London, and the second, the *Great Western*, took 15 days traveling from Bristol.

The back of the $500 note features a panoramic scene officially titled *The Surrender of Burgoyne to General Gates at Saratoga* but sometimes expanded in numismatic citations as *The Surrender of General John Burgoyne to General Horatio Gates at Saratoga on October 17, 1777*. The label on the engraving on the note states SURRENDER OF GEN'L BURGOYNE ENG'D BY THE NATIONAL BANK NOTE CO. N.Y. The motif was taken from a painting by John Trumbull. Earlier, this motif was proposed for the face of a $1 note, but it was never used. On the left side a state seal represents the issuing location of the bank, and to the right is an eagle.

Of the Original Series $500 bills, 19,598 were issued (not including National Gold Bank Notes, which are listed separately). The first were sent to the Merchants National Bank of Boston on October 14, 1864, a year after such notes were authorized. Issuance was from October 15, 1864, through June 10, 1875. In 1938 the Treasury department stated that

173 of these notes (without regard to series) remained outstanding.

Only three are believed to exist today, two of them (serials 197 and 206, the former now in the Smithsonian Institution[8]) from the Lowell (Massachusetts) National Bank and one from the Manufacturers National Bank of Philadelphia.

Banks of Issue and Rarity of Notes

Louisiana • 1 bank of issue • 720 printed • Unknown.

Maine • 3 banks of issue • 560 printed • Unknown.

Maryland • 7 banks of issue • 860 printed • Unknown.

Massachusetts • 46 banks of issue • 1,031 printed • 2 known.

New York • 19 banks of issue • 5,767 printed • Unknown.

Pennsylvania • 11 banks of issue • 1,175 printed • 1 known.

Rhode Island • 7 banks of issue • 410 printed • Unknown.

W-4100 • F-464a • Chittenden-Spinner (1861–1864)
Recorded population: 2 • Highest graded: VF-20 • Selected information: Both examples are the same grade.

W-4102 • F-464a • Colby-Spinner (1864–1867)
Recorded population: 1 • Commentary: Reported by Don C. Kelly. Grade and serial are not stated.

W-4104 • F-464a • Allison-Spinner (1869–1875) • Unknown

National Gold Bank Notes, Original Series

Only three California banks issued $500 notes in this series. None are known to exist today. On April 8, 1871, the Treasury sent 75 sheets of $500-$1,000 notes to the Kidder National Gold Bank of Boston. None were ever paid out. All were returned to the Treasury department on December 4, 1871.[9] Of the 610 notes that were issued, none are known today.

W-4110 • F-1166a • Dated 1870 • San Francisco • First National Gold Bank • 300

W-4120 • F-1166a • Dated 1872 • Sacramento • National Gold Bank of D.O. Mills & Co. • 60

W-4125 • F-1166a • San Francisco • National Gold Bank and Trust Co. • 250

W-4130 • F-unlisted • Dated 1870 • Boston • Kidder National Gold Bank • 75 • None issued

Series of 1875
(Authorized Issue 1875 to 1902, Last Issued 1885)

These notes (illus. on p. 716) continued the use of plates signed by American Bank Note Company. Under the top border at the upper left is PRINTED AT THE BUREAU OF ENGRAVING & PRINTING, U.S. TREASURY DEPt. The small red Treasury seal now has a scalloped border. All have SERIES 1875 imprinted vertically in red to the left of center, near the bank charter number. The Treasury and bank serial numbers and two charter numbers are also in red.

Original Series

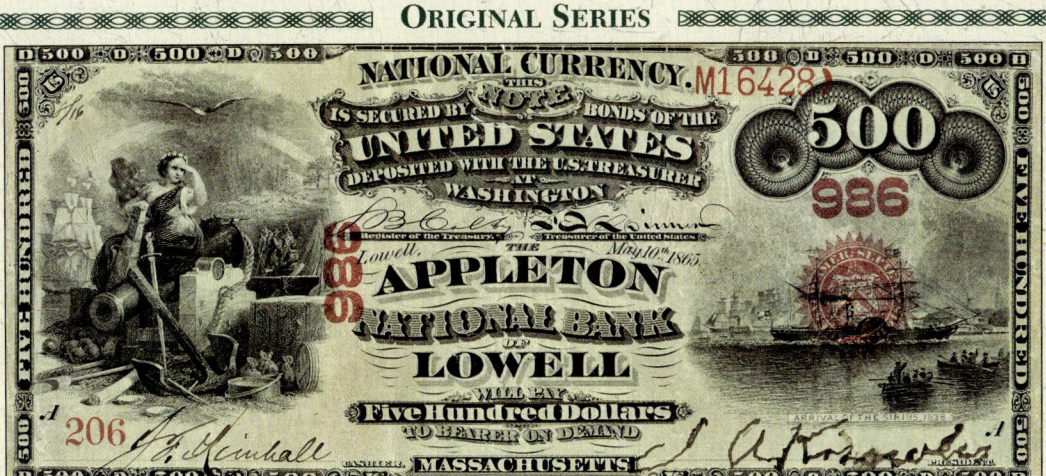

$500 National Bank Note, Original Series (W-4102). Appleton National Bank of Lowell, Massachusetts, charter 986. Bank serial 20. Treasury serial M16428, plate A. Signed by cashier John F. Kimball and president John F. Knowles, who were first in those offices after the bank was chartered on April 7, 1865, with a capital of $200,000 against an authorization of $500,000. (Smithsonian Institution)

Back of the Appleton $500 National Bank Note, Original Series (W-4102), showing the vignette *Surrender of Gen'l Burgoyne* at the center and the Massachusetts state seal at the left.

National Gold Bank Notes, Original Series

$500 National Gold Bank Note, Original Series (W-4130), Kidder National Gold Bank of Boston, specimen impression with Treasury seal, serial numbers, and bank signatures in the plate. (Peter Huntoon / Smithsonian Institution)

The printage for these notes was 4,371. The *last* such notes were sent to the Western National Bank of Baltimore on June 10, 1885.[10]

Only one is known today, on the First National Bank of the City of New York.

Banks of Issue and Rarity of Notes

Alabama • 1 bank of issue • 292 printed • Unknown.

Maine • 1 bank of issue • 9 printed • Unknown.

Maryland • 1 bank of issue • 50 printed • Unknown.

Massachusetts • 12 banks of issue • 842 printed • Unknown.

New York • 6 banks of issue • 2,843 printed • 1 known.

Pennsylvania • 3 banks of issue • 230 printed • Unknown.

Rhode Island • 2 banks of issue • 105 printed • Unknown.

W-4133 • F-464a • Allison-New (1875–1876)
Recorded population: 1 • *Selected information:* This note is graded F, from the First National Bank of the City of New York.

W-4135 • F-464a • Allison-Wyman (1876–1877) • Unknown

W-4137 • F-464a • Scofield-Gilfillan (1878–1881) • Unknown

W-4140 • F-464a • Bruce-Gilfillan (1881–1883) • Unknown

W-4142 • F-464a • Bruce-Wyman (1883–1885) • Unknown

SILVER CERTIFICATES

Series of 1878

Silver Certificates of Deposit of the Series of 1878 and 1880 have a vignette of Charles Sumner on the face, engraved by Charles Burt. Sumner (1811–1874) achieved great distinction as a U.S. senator from Massachusetts. A frightful and famous incident occurred on May 22, 1856, after Sumner delivered his anti-slavery speech, "Crime Against Kansas." Representative Preston Brooks of South Carolina sought him out in his Senate seat and beat him unconscious with a cane, rendering Sumner an invalid for the next several years. This was viewed as great sport by Brooks's friends, who sent him dozens of canes as gifts.

On the face the small word SILVER is done in a series of vignettes, one for each letter, connected together in a straight row. All bear the printed signatures of Scofield and Gilfillan. Series of 1878 notes bear the countersignature of another Treasury official. On earlier notes these are all autographed; certain later notes had the signatures entered in the plate. On the red Treasury seal for this denomination and other countersigned notes in this series, the key faces to the right (with the handle at the left).

On the back the word SILVER is in large, ornate letters at the center. All inscriptions are printed in brown. Presumably, all were printed on blue-tinted paper, this being true for the lower denominations.

Series of 1878 Silver Certificates of Deposit were payable in New York, San Francisco, or Washington. It seems that most of the Series of 1878 and related Series of 1880 Silver Certificates of Deposit, although made in large quantities, were used in import-export trade (under circumstances that are not clear today) and bank-to-bank transactions, rather than in general circulation. Although thousands were printed, only one example is traced today. The listings below are highly conjectural, as it is not known exactly which varieties were made.

W-4150 • F-345a • New York • Countersigned: W.G. White (autographed) • Large pink seal • 500 (est.) • Unknown

W-4153 • F-345a • Countersigned: J.C. Hopper (autographed) • 3,500 (est.) • Unknown

W-4162 • F-345a • San Francisco • Countersigned: R.M. Anthony (autographed) • 2,000 (est.) • Unknown

W-4165 • F-345a • Washington • Countersigned: A.U. Wyman (autographed) • 1 known, in the Smithsonian Institution

W-4168 • F-345a • Countersigned: A.U. Wyman (printed) • 14,000 (est.) • Unknown

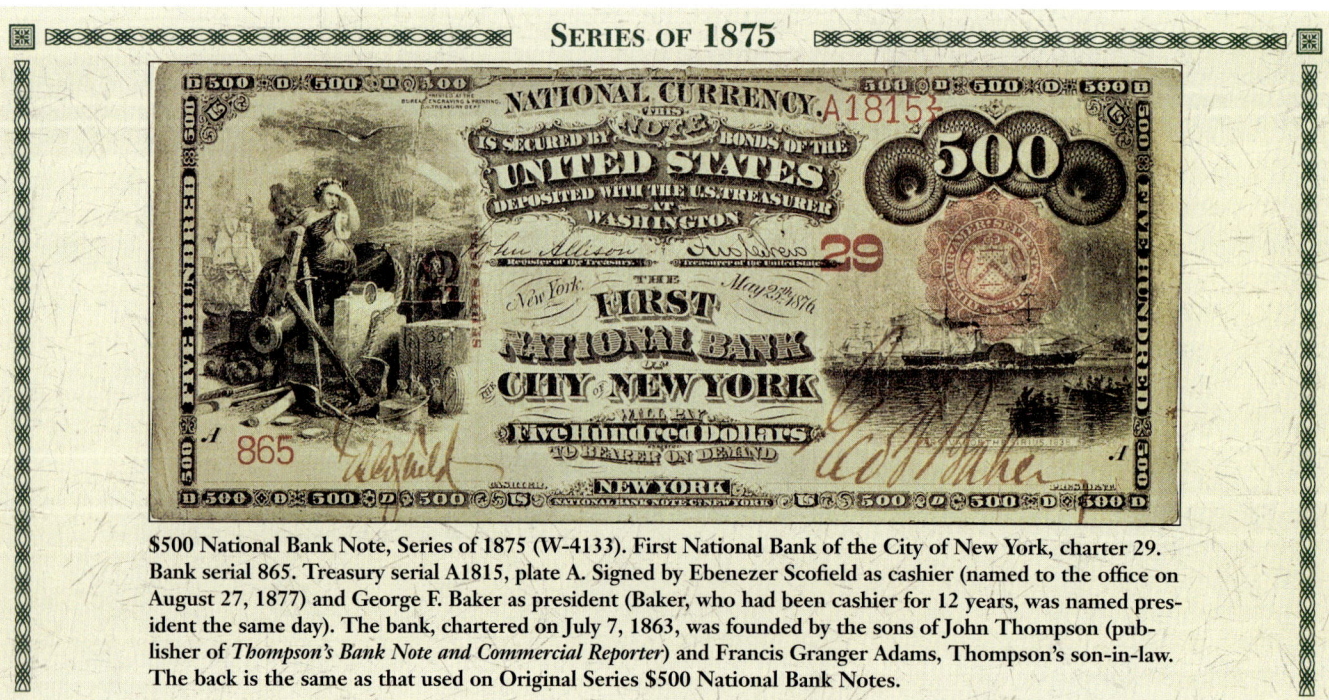

$500 National Bank Note, Series of 1875 (W-4133). First National Bank of the City of New York, charter 29. Bank serial 865. Treasury serial A1815, plate A. Signed by Ebenezer Scofield as cashier (named to the office on August 27, 1877) and George F. Baker as president (Baker, who had been cashier for 12 years, was named president the same day). The bank, chartered on July 7, 1863, was founded by the sons of John Thompson (publisher of *Thompson's Bank Note and Commercial Reporter*) and Francis Granger Adams, Thompson's son-in-law. The back is the same as that used on Original Series $500 National Bank Notes.

Series of 1880

These continue the motifs of the foregoing. There are differences in the typography. At the bottom center the denomination counter is smaller and differently configured. SERIES OF 1880 is to the left of the counter. All are exceedingly rare.

W-4172 • F-345b • Scofield-Gilfillan (1878–1881) • Large brown seal • No evidence of printing[11]

W-4173 • F-345c • Bruce-Gilfillan (1881–1883) • 16,000

Recorded population: 5 • *Highest graded:* VF-35 • *Selected information:* Known examples include serials B259/C, VF, pinholes, sold in a Knight auction (10/2005) for $483,000; B1742/B, VF–EF, part of the Smithsonian Institution collection; B2681/A, VF, part of the ANA Museum collection; B8579/C, VG, pinholes, owned by the Federal Reserve Bank of Chicago; and B13546/B, F–VF, sold by Dean Oakes (1975) for $22,000.

W-4174 • F-345d • Bruce-Wyman (1883–1885) • 8,000

Recorded population: 7 • *Highest graded:* F-12 • *Selected information:* Known examples include serials B18687/C, F, sold in a Knight auction (10/2006) for $776,250; B20545/A, F, owned by the Federal Reserve Bank of San Francisco; B11437/A, VF, from the Amon Carter Jr. collection; B11500/D, VG–F, used as the Friedberg illustration, owned by the Federal Reserve

Bank of San Francisco; B12623/C, VF, sold in a Knight auction (10/2005) for $667,000; B12638/B, AU, pinholes, part of the Smithsonian Institution collection; and B14663/C, EF, owned by the Federal Reserve Bank of Chicago.

TREASURY OR COIN NOTES

Series of 1891

The left side of the face (illus. on p. 718) bears the portrait of General William Tecumseh Sherman, a banker in California during the Gold Rush days who is best known for his Civil War activities, including his devastating march through Georgia. His brother was John Sherman of senatorial and Treasury department renown. Presumably, these notes had small red Treasury seals with a scalloped border. No record has been located of a Series of 1890 Treasury or Coin Note, which, if produced, would have had an ornate back. The Series of 1891 has the open style preferred by the Treasury department at the time, as it was said to be less susceptible to counterfeiting. This series has two vertical banks of distributed fibers in the paper, an additional security measure.

W-4180 • F-379 • Bruce-Roberts (1897–1898) • Small red seal with scalloped border • 16,000 • None are known to have been issued

$500 Silver Certificate of Deposit, Series of 1880 (W-4173).

Back of the $500 Silver Certificate of Deposit, Series of 1880 (W-4173).

GOLD CERTIFICATES

Act of March 3, 1863

Gold Certificates of this and other denominations were issued under the Act of March 3, 1863. ENGRAVED AND PRINTED AT THE TREASURY DEPARTMENT is imprinted below the top border. Presumably, circulating examples of the $500 note were issued with a lacy, green denomination counter overprinted on the face and with a small red Treasury seal with a spiked border—this was the style of known circulating examples in other denominations. At the left of the face is a patriotic depiction of the American eagle on a shield with arrows, an olive branch, and a flag as part of the suite, and E PLURIBUS UNUM lettered above. The note is payable at the New York Sub-Treasury, as are all seen in this series.

The back, printed in orange, has the denomination letter D to each side and FIVE HUNDRED in a circle at the center, with ornate vignettes surrounding.

These were issued only by the New York Sub-Treasury. Most were used as clearing house certificates, as gold reserves by banks, or for payment of import duties.[12] No issued examples are known.

W-4190 • F-1166d • New York imprint only • Colby-Spinner (1864–1867) • Small red seal with spiked border • 80,000 • Unknown

Commentary: An autographed countersignature of an assistant Treasurer of the United States is on all.

Series of 1870

At the upper left is a vignette of Abraham Lincoln. On certain proof impressions, a counter made of an I and backward C is at the right. An issued example has the counter as a more recognizable 500 and may have been altered from the earlier plate. A large pink Treasury seal is at the center, and another denomination counter is at the upper right. There are bright red serial numbers. Register of the Treasury John Allison and two Treasury clerk signatures also appear. The notes are printed on the face only. These were obtainable from the Treasury in exchange for gold coins at par with the notes.

W-4192 • F-unlisted • With counter in right field I and backward C • Not known if any issued

W-4194 • F-1166i • Allison and two other Treasury officials (all autographed) • Large pink seal with spiked border • 40,000

Recorded population: 1 • *Selected information:* This note is serial A25770/B, F, part of the Smithsonian Institution collection.

Face of the $500 Treasury or Coin Note, Series of 1891 (W-4180). Specimen printing without Treasury seal.

Back of the same $500 Treasury or Coin Note variety. Proof impression in black ink.

Series of 1875

These notes (illus. on p. 720), printed on one side only, show Lincoln at the left and a counter at the right. At the bottom center is a large Treasury seal. Gold overprinting is also used. To the left, above the bottom border, is a space for an autographed signature, below which is imprinted ASSISTANT TREASURER, N.Y. To the right are the printed signatures of Allison and New. These were obtainable from the Treasury in exchange for gold coins at par with the notes.

W-4197 • F-1166n • Allison-New (1875–1876) • **Large red seal with spiked border** • 10,400 • Unknown

W-4198 • F-1166n • Allison-Gilfillan (1877–1878) • 4,000 • Unknown

Series of 1882

The Series of 1882 $500 Gold Certificate (illus. on p. 720) features a portrait of Abraham Lincoln engraved by Charles Burt from a photograph taken by Mathew A. Brady. The back has a particularly dynamic motif, *Eagle with Flag*, engraved by George D. Baldwin, who at an earlier time created some of the most elegant artwork seen on notes of state-chartered banks. His *Ocean Telegraph* vignette appears on the back of the $20 Gold Certificate, Series of 1882.

Today, notes of the Series of 1882 are rare in comparison to the demand for them, with slightly more than 100 recorded by Martin Gengerke in *U.S. Paper Money Records*. If the Series of 1922 notes (W-4220, of essentially the same design) are included, then more than 50 notes can be added to the known population. These two series are the only collectible Gold Certificates of the $500 denomination. At the time of issue they were exchangeable at par with Legal Tender Notes, National Bank Notes, and other notes.

As with all Gold Certificates with the back printed in orange-gold, notes that are not faded are worth more, no matter what the grade assigned.

W-4200 • F-1215b • Bruce-Gilfillan (1881–1883) and one countersignature • **Brown seal** • 20,000 • Unknown

$500 Gold Certificate, Act of March 3, 1863 (W-4190), Colby-Spinner Treasury signatures and imprinted space for the addition by hand of a countersignature. Proof impression, plate C. (Smithsonian Institution)

$500 Gold Certificate, Series of 1870 (W-4192). Serial A25770, plate b. Ink dated May 1, 1874. All three signatures, including that of John Allison, are autographed. To the left is the signature of Maxwell White, familiar on certain other notes of the era.

Detail of a proof example with I and backward C counter. (Smithsonian Institution)

W-4202 • F-1215a • Bruce-Gilfillan (1881–1883) • No countersignature • 8,000
Recorded population: 1 • *Selected information:* Smythe (6/2000), A7880/D, VG–F, repaired, $143,000.

W-4204 • F-1215c • Bruce-Wyman (1883–1885) • 20,000
Recorded population: 1 • *Selected information:* The known note is serial A10923/C, VG, owned by the FRB of San Francisco.

W-4206 • F-1215d • Rosecrans-Hyatt (1887–1889) • Large red seal • 16,000
Recorded population: 1 • *Selected information:* The known note is serial C11297/A, EF, owned by the Federal Reserve Bank of San Francisco.

SERIES OF 1875

$500 Gold Certificate, Series of 1875 (W-4197). Proof. (Smithsonian Institution)

SERIES OF 1882

$500 Gold Certificate, Series of 1882 (W-4216). Portrait of Lincoln to the left. Gold overprinting.

Back of the $500 Gold Certificate, Series of 1882 (W-4216). Large D at left. Eagle perched on flag. Printed in gold.

W-4210 • F-1216 • Lyons-Roberts (1898–1905) • Small red seal with scalloped border • 128,000

Estimated population: 28 to 32 • *Highest graded:* EF-45.

VG-8	F-12	VF-20	EF-40
$4,250	$11,000	$27,000	$45,000

W-4214 • F-1216a • Parker-Burke (1913–1914) • 40,000

Estimated population: 38 to 43 • *Highest graded:* AU-58 • *Commentary:* Deliveries began on March 18, 1914, and ended the next day on March 19, 1914.

VG-8	F-12	VF-20	EF-40	AU-50
$4,250	$10,000	$22,000	$40,000	$90,000

W-4216 • F-1216b • Teehee-Burke (1915–1919) • 40,000

Estimated population: 52 to 56 • *Highest graded:* AU-55.

VG-8	F-12	VF-20	EF-40	AU-50
$4,250	$10,000	$20,000	$40,000	$75,000

Series of 1922

The Series of 1922 $500 Gold Certificates are similar in motifs and layout to the Series of 1882, but with some differences, including the addition of this statement in the lower left field: "This certificate is a legal tender in the amount thereof in payment of all debts and dues, public and private Acts of March 14, 1900, as amended and December 24, 1919."

W-4220 • F-1217 • Speelman-White (1922–1927) • Small red seal with scalloped border • 84,000

Estimated population: 60 to 65 • *Highest graded:* AU-58.

VG-8	F-12	VF-20	EF-40	AU-50
$4,250	$11,000	$22,000	$42,000	$75,000

FEDERAL RESERVE NOTES

Series of 1918, Blue Seal

The face (illus. on p. 722) depicts chief justice John Marshall, engraved by Charles Schlecht after a portrait by Henry Inman. The seal to the left has the bank number and letter at the center. To the right is a blue Treasury seal with a scalloped border. The face layout is generic, with the Federal Reserve Bank seal widely spaced from the border and large district numbers and letters in each corner. The back shows *De Soto Discovering the Mississippi*, an engraving by Frederick Girsch. This is a trimmed and slightly altered version of the same engraving used as the back for $10 National Bank Notes of the Original Series and Series of 1875, now with no credit to the American Bank Note Company.

$500 Gold Certificate, Series of 1922 (W-4220).

Back of the $500 Gold Certificate, Series of 1922 (W-4220).

W-4240-A • F-1132A • Boston • Burke-Glass (1918–1920) • 17,600

Recorded population: 4 • *Highest graded:* Unc • *Selected information:* The known notes are serials A290A/B, EF–AU, part of the Smithsonian Institution collection; A6333A/A, Unc, sold in a Mayflower auction (6/1974) $1,600; A6973A/A, VF, sold in a CAA auction (2/2005) for $16,100; and A7133A/A, VF-35 (PCGS), sold in a Knight auction (3/2007) for $43,700.

W-4243-B • F-1132B • New York • 108,000 (est.)

Estimated population: 47 to 52 • *Highest graded:* Unc.

VG-8	F-12	VF-20	EF-40	AU-50	Unc-60
$3,750	$8,000	$16,000	$24,000	$55,000	—

W-4246-B • F-1132b-B • White-Mellon (1921–1928) • 17,600 (est.)

Recorded population: 5 • *Highest graded:* AU-50 • *Selected information:* Known examples include serials B105921A/A, VF–EF, sold in a Stack's auction (5/1997) for $5,225; B105922A/B, EF, sold in a fixed-price list for $1,900; B107739A/C, VG–F, damaged, tear, margin piece missing, sold in a Knight auction (3/2007) for $41,400; B112381A, AU-50 (PMG), sold in a Knight auction (3/2007) for $48,300; and B113822A/B, EF, given by the Federal Reserve Bank of New York to the Federal Reserve Bank of Philadelphia.

W-4249-C • F-1132C • Philadelphia • Burke-Glass (1918–1920) • 24,000

Recorded population: 5 • *Highest graded:* EF-45 • *Selected information:* Known examples include serials C1A/A, EF–AU, part of the Smithsonian Institution collection; C838A/B, G–VG, problems, sold in a Heritage auction (1/2008) for $7,475; C1705A/A, VF-20 (PCGS), sold in a CAA auction (3/2007) for $39,100; C2133A/A, F, sold in a Heritage auction (1/2007) for $25,300; and C2655A/C, VF-25 (PMG), sold in a Heritage auction (4/2008) for $48,875.

W-4252-D • F-1132D • Cleveland • 15,600

Estimated population: 16 to 18 • *Highest graded:* AU-50.

VG-8	F-12	VF-20	EF-40	AU-50
$4,000	$8,500	$17,500	$26,000	$60,000

W-4255-E • F-1132E • Richmond • 23,200 • Unknown

W-4258-F • F-1132F • Atlanta • 30,400

Estimated population: 9 or 10 • *Highest graded:* Unc • *Selected information:* Knight (11/2001), F1509A/A, EF, $10,052. Knight (3/2007), F22726A/B, AU, $74,750. Knight (6/2007), F22727A/C, Unc-67 (CGA), $86,250. Spink America (5/1995), F22730A/B, Unc, problems, $12,650. CAA (2/2005), F26763A/C, AU-50, $48,875.

SERIES OF 1918, BLUE SEAL

$500 Federal Reserve Note, Series of 1918 (W-4282-L). Portrait of chief justice John Marshall. (Federal Reserve Bank of San Francisco Museum)

Back of the $500 Federal Reserve Note, Series of 1918 (W-4282-L), with *De Soto Discovering the Mississippi.*

W-4261-F • F-1132b-F • White-Mellon (1921–1928) • 4,000 • Unknown

W-4264-G • F-1132G • Chicago • Burke-Glass (1918–1920) • 38,000

Estimated population: 44 to 48 • *Highest graded:* Unc.

VG-8	F-12	VF-20	EF-40	AU-50	Unc-60
$4,000	$8,500	$17,500	$26,000	$55,000	—

W-4267-H • F-1132H • St. Louis • 14,400

Estimated population: 5 • *Highest graded:* Unc • *Commentary:* Current market information not available.

W-4270-I • F-1132I • Minneapolis • 7,200

Recorded population: 1 • *Graded:* VG-8 • *Selected information:* CAA (2/2005), 155A/C, VG-8 (PMG), $126,500.

W-4273-J • F-1132J • Kansas City • 15,600

Estimated population: 15 to 17 • *Highest graded:* Unc.

VG-8	F-12	VF-20	EF-40	AU-50	Unc-60
$4,000	$8,500	$17,500	$30,000	$55,000	—

W-4276-J • F-1132-bJ • Kansas City • White-Mellon (1921–1928) • 400 • Unknown

W-4279-K • F-1132K • Dallas • Burke-Glass (1918–1920) • 6,000

Recorded population: 4 • *Highest graded:* Unc • *Selected information:* CAA (1/1998), K2067A/C, Unc, $14,300. Smythe (7/2007), K2717A/A, EF-45 (PMG), $43,700. NASCA (11/1979), K2718A/B, Gem Unc, $8,250; later seen in Stack's (3/1991), EF, $3,740. Heritage (9/2008), K2719A/C, EF-45 (PCGS), $34,500.

W-4282-L • F-1132L • San Francisco • Burke-Glass (1918–1920) • 16,000

Estimated population: 21 to 24 • *Highest graded:* Unc.

VG-8	F-12	VF-20	EF-40	AU-50	Unc-60	Unc-63	Unc-65
$4,000	$8,500	$17,500	$26,000	$55,000	$70,000	—	$115,000

W-4285-L • F-1132a-L • Burke-Houston (1920–1921) • 8,000

Recorded population: 3 • *Highest graded:* EF-45 • *Selected information:* Knight (3/2007), L19867A/C, VF-30 (PMG), $36,800. Stack's (3/1991), L20131A/B, EF, $1,870.

SMALL SIZE

Small-size Federal Reserve Notes and Gold Certificates, each depicting William McKinley on the face (the portrait used earlier on the large-size Series of 1902 $10 National Bank Notes), were issued; these are scarce today. However, enough exist that many varieties can be collected by those who combine the desire and finances to do so. These are very popular as trophy notes.

GOLD CERTIFICATES

Series of 1928, Gold Seal
Woods-Mellon (1929–1932)

The obligation or payable notice reads "Five hundred dollars in gold coin payable to the bearer on demand." At the left the Treasury seal is overprinted on a more standard commentary, with GOLD above, CERTIFICATE below, and three lines between: "This certificate is a legal tender in

SERIES OF 1928, GOLD SEAL

$500 Gold Certificate, Series of 1928 (W-4300).

Back of the $500 Gold Certificate, Series of 1928 (W-4300). This design was standard among $500 notes of the era.

the amount thereof in payment of all debts and dues public and private." In addition to the yellow (usually called gold) seal, the serial numbers were printed in yellow.

The back, printed in green, has a large counter in an ornately engraved panel at the center, with counters at the corners and at the top and bottom borders. The star notes were printed for possible use but were never necessary and are believed to have been destroyed.

W-4300 • F-2407 • 420,000

F-12	VF-20	EF-40	AU-50	Unc-60	Unc-63	Unc-65
$5,000	$11,500	$20,000	$24,000	$26,000	$31,000	$42,500

W-4300★ • F-2407★ • 4,000 • Unknown

FEDERAL RESERVE NOTES

Series of 1928, Green Seal
Woods-Mellon (1929–1932)

The obligation is in four lines in the field at the upper left: "Redeemable in gold on demand at the United States Treasury, or in gold or lawful money at any Federal Reserve Bank." On the Series of 1928 and 1928-A notes, the seal in the left field features the letter of the issuing Federal Reserve Bank (A to L). The series imprint appears twice: at the upper left of McKinley's portrait and below WASHINGTON at the lower right.

These are fairly scarce, but enough exist that a note for this type is easily found. Uncirculated notes are in the minority. Star notes are very rare.

W-4350-A • F-2200A • Boston • 69,120

F-12	VF-20	EF-40	AU-50
$4,500	$6,500	$9,000	$13,500

W-4350-A★ • F-2200A★ • Unknown

W-4350-B • F-2200B • New York • 299,400

VG-8	F-12	VF-20	EF-40	AU-50	Unc-60	Unc-63	Unc-65
$850	$900	$1,150	$1,500	$1,800	$2,400	$2,850	$4,000

W-4350-B★ • F-2200B★ • Unknown

W-4350-C • F-2200C • Philadelphia • 135,120

VG-8	F-12	VF-20	EF-40	AU-50	Unc-60	Unc-63	Unc-65
$850	$900	$1,150	$1,600	$1,900	$2,500	$2,950	$4,200

W-4350-C★ • F-2200C★ • 1 known

W-4350-D • F-2200D • Cleveland • 166,440

VG-8	F-12	VF-20	EF-40	AU-50	Unc-60	Unc-63	Unc-65
$850	$900	$1,150	$1,600	$1,900	$2,500	$2,950	$4,250

W-4350-D★ • F-2200D★ • 1 known

W-4350-E • F-2200E • Richmond • 84,720

VG-8	F-12	VF-20	EF-40	AU-50	Unc-60	Unc-63	Unc-65
$900	$950	$1,200	$1,650	$2,000	$2,600	$3,100	$4,500

W-4350-E★ • F-2200E★ • Unknown

W-4350-F • F-2200F • Atlanta • 69,360

VG-8	F-12	VF-20	EF-40	AU-50	Unc-60	Unc-63	Unc-65
$850	$900	$1,150	$1,600	$1,900	$2,500	$2,950	$4,250

W-4350-F★ • F-2200F★ • Unknown

W-4350-G • F-2200G • Chicago • 573,600

VG-8	F-12	VF-20	EF-40	AU-50	Unc-60	Unc-63	Unc-65
$850	$900	$1,150	$1,500	$1,800	$2,400	$2,850	$4,000

W-4350-G★ • F-2200G★ • 2 known

W-4350-H • F-2200H • St. Louis • 66,180

VG-8	F-12	VF-20	EF-40	AU-50	Unc-60	Unc-63	Unc-65
$850	$900	$1,150	$1,500	$1,800	$2,200	$2,650	$3,800

W-4350-H★ • F-2200H★ • Unknown

W-4350-I • F-2200I • Minneapolis • 34,680

VG-8	F-12	VF-20	EF-40	AU-50	Unc-60
$1,000	$1,250	$1,400	$2,000	$2,800	$4,000

W-4350-I★ • F-2200I★ • Unknown

W-4350-J • F-2200J • Kansas City • 510,720

VG-8	F-12	VF-20	EF-40	AU-50	Unc-60	Unc-63	Unc-65
$900	$950	$1,200	$1,650	$2,000	$2,600	$3,100	$4,500

W-4350-J★ • F-2200J★ • Unknown

W-4350-K • F-2200K • Dallas • 70,560

VG-8	F-12	VF-20	EF-40	AU-50	Unc-60	Unc-63
$1,000	$1,250	$1,500	$2,000	$2,800	$4,000	$7,500

W-4350-K★ • F-2200K★ • Unknown

W-4350-L • F-2200L • San Francisco • 64,080

VG-8	F-12	VF-20	EF-40	AU-50	Unc-60
$1,000	$1,250	$1,400	$2,000	$2,800	$4,000

W-4350-L★ • F-2200L★ • Unknown

Series of 1928, Light Yellow-Green Seal
Woods-Mellon (1929–1932)

This brief series continued the preceding design. Although the seal hue is distinctive, most demand for $500 notes is for the general type.

W-4360-B • F-2200B • New York • Part of W-4350-B printage

EF-40	AU-50	Unc-60	Unc-63	Unc-65
$1,900	$2,300	$3,000	$3,500	$5,500

W-4360-G • F-2200G • Chicago • Part of W-4350-G printage

EF-40	AU-50	Unc-60	Unc-63	Unc-65
$1,900	$2,300	$3,000	$3,500	$5,500

W-4360-J • F-2200J • Kansas City • Part of W-4350-J printage

EF-40	AU-50	Unc-60	Unc-63	Unc-65
$1,900	$2,300	$3,000	$3,500	$5,500

Series of 1934, Light Yellow-Green Seal
Julian-Morgenthau (1934–1945)

The Series of 1934 notes (illus. on p. 726) continued the same general configuration as the preceding series, but now with a change in the obligation that eliminates the mention of gold: "This note is legal tender for all debts, public and private, and is redeemable in lawful money at the United States Treasury, or at any Federal Reserve Bank."

Circulated notes, while scarce in comparison to lower denominations, are seen with some frequency. Uncirculated notes are much scarcer. Star notes are rare.

W-4365-A • F-2201A • Boston • Part of W-4370-A printage

VF-20	EF-40	AU-50	Unc-60	Unc-63
$1,150	$1,300	$1,750	$2,200	$2,750

W-4365-B • F-2201B • New York • Part of W-4370-B printage

VF-20	EF-40	AU-50	Unc-60	Unc-63
$1,150	$1,300	$1,750	$2,200	$2,750

SERIES OF 1928, GREEN SEAL

$500 Federal Reserve Note, Series of 1928 (W-4350-B). Dark green Treasury seal. Federal Reserve Bank of New York.

Back of the $500 Federal Reserve Note, Series of 1928 (W-4350-B). This style was standard among $500 notes of the era.

SERIES OF 1928, LIGHT YELLOW-GREEN SEAL

$500 Federal Reserve Note, Series of 1928 (W-4360-G). Light yellow-green Treasury seal. Federal Reserve Bank of Chicago. Standard back of $500 notes of the era.

W-4365-C • F-2201C • Philadelphia • Part of W-4370-C printage

VF-20	EF-40	AU-50	Unc-60	Unc-63
$1,150	$1,300	$1,750	$2,200	$2,750

W-4365-D • F-2201D • Cleveland • Part of W-4370-D printage

VF-20	EF-40	AU-50	Unc-60	Unc-63
$1,150	$1,300	$1,750	$2,200	$2,750

W-4365-E • F-2201E • Richmond • Part of W-4370-E printage

VF-20	EF-40	AU-50	Unc-60	Unc-63
$1,200	$1,350	$1,900	$2,350	$3,000

W-4365-F • F-2201F • Atlanta • Part of W-4370-F printage

VF-20	EF-40	AU-50	Unc-60	Unc-63
$1,150	$1,300	$1,750	$2,200	$2,750

W-4365-G • F-2201G • Chicago • Part of W-4370-G printage

VF-20	EF-40	AU-50	Unc-60	Unc-63
$1,150	$1,300	$1,750	$2,200	$2,750

W-4365-H • F-2201H • St. Louis • Part of W-4370-H printage

VF-20	EF-40	AU-50	Unc-60	Unc-63
$1,150	$1,300	$1,750	$2,200	$2,750

W-4365-I • F-2201I • Minneapolis • Part of W-4370-I printage

VF-20	EF-40	AU-50	Unc-60	Unc-63
$1,150	$1,450	$2,200	$2,750	$3,250

W-4365-J • F-2201J • Kansas City • Part of W-4370-J printage

VF-20	EF-40	AU-50	Unc-60	Unc-63
$1,150	$1,300	$1,750	$2,200	$2,750

W-4365-K • F-2201K • Dallas • Part of W-4370-K printage

VF-20	EF-40	AU-50	Unc-60	Unc-63
$1,700	$2,250	$2,650	$3,200	$4,250

W-4365-L • F-2201L • San Francisco • Part of W-4370-L printage

VF-20	EF-40	AU-50	Unc-60	Unc-63
$1,200	$1,350	$1,900	$2,350	$3,000

Series of 1934, Green Seal
Julian-Morgenthau (1934–1945)

This series continued the preceding design, but with a different hue to the Treasury seal.

W-4370-A • F-2201A • Boston • 56,628

VG-8	F-12	VF-20	EF-40	AU-50	Unc-60	Unc-63	Unc-65
$775	$900	$975	$1,100	$1,500	$1,800	$2,200	$2,800

W-4370-A★ • F-2201A★

Commentary: Current market information not available.

W-4370-B • F-2201B • New York • 288,000

VG-8	F-12	VF-20	EF-40	AU-50	Unc-60	Unc-63	Unc-65
$750	$860	$920	$1,050	$1,400	$1,650	$2,000	$2,600

W-4370-B★ • F-2201B★

F-12	VF-20	EF-40	AU-50
$3,250	$4,800	$6,000	$8,500

W-4370-C • F-2201C • Philadelphia • 31,200

VG-8	F-12	VF-20	EF-40	AU-50	Unc-60	Unc-63	Unc-65
$775	$900	$975	$1,100	$1,500	$1,800	$2,200	$2,800

W-4370-C★ • F-2201C★

F-12	VF-20	EF-40	AU-50	Unc-60
$3,250	$4,800	$6,000	$8,500	$12,000

$500 Federal Reserve Note, Series of 1934 (W-4365-A). Light yellow-green Treasury seal. Federal Reserve Bank of Boston. The back is the standard type of the era.

W-4370-D • F-2201D • Cleveland • 39,000

VG-8	F-12	VF-20	EF-40	AU-50	Unc-60	Unc-63	Unc-65
$775	$900	$975	$1,100	$1,500	$1,800	$2,200	$2,800

W-4370-D★ • F-2201D★

F-12	VF-20	EF-40	AU-50
$3,750	$6,000	—	$10,000

W-4370-E • F-2201E • Richmond • 40,800

VG-8	F-12	VF-20	EF-40	AU-50	Unc-60	Unc-63
$800	$950	$1,100	$1,350	$1,600	$2,000	$2,400

W-4370-E★ • F-2201E★

VG-8	F-12	VF-20
$3,500	—	$6,750

W-4370-F • F-2201F • Atlanta • 46,200

VG-8	F-12	VF-20	EF-40	AU-50	Unc-60	Unc-63	Unc-65
$775	$900	$975	$1,100	$1,500	$1,800	$2,200	$2,800

W-4370-F★ • F-2201F★

F-12	VF-20	EF-40	AU-50	Unc-60
$3,250	$4,800	$6,000	$8,500	$12,500

W-4370-G • F-2201G • Chicago • 212,400

VG-8	F-12	VF-20	EF-40	AU-50	Unc-60	Unc-63	Unc-65
$750	$860	$920	$1,050	$1,400	$1,650	$2,000	$2,600

W-4370-G★ • F-2201G★

VG-8	F-12	VF-20	EF-40	AU-50	Unc-60
$2,500	$3,250	$4,800	$6,000	$8,500	$12,500

W-4370-H • F-2201H • St. Louis • 24,000

VG-8	F-12	VF-20	EF-40	AU-50	Unc-60	Unc-63	Unc-65
$775	$900	$975	$1,100	$1,500	$1,800	$2,200	$2,800

W-4370-H★ • F-2201H★ • 3 known

W-4370-I • F-2201I • Minneapolis • 24,000

VG-8	F-12	VF-20	EF-40	AU-50	Unc-60	Unc-63	Unc-65
$825	$1,000	$1,250	$1,500	$1,800	$2,250	$3,000	$5,000

W-4370-I★ • F-2201I★ • 2 known

W-4370-J • F-2201J • Kansas City • 40,800

VG-8	F-12	VF-20	EF-40	AU-50	Unc-60	Unc-63	Unc-65
$775	$900	$975	$1,100	$1,500	$1,800	$2,200	$2,800

W-4370-J★ • F-2201J★ • 1 known

W-4370-K • F-2201K • Dallas • 31,200

VG-8	F-12	VF-20	EF-40	AU-50	Unc-60	Unc-63
$825	$1,050	$1,300	$1,600	$2,200	$3,000	$4,000

W-4370-K★ • F-2201K★ • 4 known

W-4370-L • F-2201L • San Francisco • 83,400

VG-8	F-12	VF-20	EF-40	AU-50	Unc-60	Unc-63	Unc-65
$775	$900	$975	$1,100	$1,500	$1,800	$2,200	$2,800

W-4370-L★ • F-2201L★

F-12	VF-20	EF-40	AU-50	Unc-60
$3,250	$4,800	$6,000	$8,500	$12,500

Series of 1934-A, Green Seal
Julian-Morgenthau (1934–1945)

This series (illus. on p. 728) continued the preceding design. All are collectible, but Uncirculated notes are in the minority and are especially desired. Star notes are rare.

W-4375-B • F-2202B • New York • 276,000

VG-8	F-12	VF-20	EF-40	AU-50	Unc-60	Unc-63	Unc-65
$750	$860	$920	$1,050	$1,400	$1,650	$2,000	$2,600

W-4375-B★ • F-2202B★ • 6 known

W-4375-C • F-2202C • Philadelphia • 45,300

VG-8	F-12	VF-20	EF-40	AU-50	Unc-60	Unc-63	Unc-65
$775	$900	$975	$1,100	$1,500	$1,800	$2,200	$2,800

W-4375-D • F-2202D • Cleveland • 28,800

VG-8	F-12	VF-20	EF-40	AU-50	Unc-60	Unc-63	Unc-65
$750	$860	$920	$1,050	$1,400	$1,650	$2,000	$2,600

SERIES OF 1934, GREEN SEAL

$500 Federal Reserve Note, Series of 1934, dark green Treasury seal (W-4370-L). Federal Reserve Bank of San Francisco. The back is the standard type of the era.

W-4375-E • F-2202E • Richmond • 36,000

VG-8	F-12	VF-20	EF-40	AU-50	Unc-60	Unc-63	Unc-65
$775	$900	$975	$1,100	$1,500	$1,800	$2,200	$2,800

W-4375-E★ • F-2202E★ • 3 known

W-4375-F • F-2202F • Atlanta • Part of W-4370-F printage

VG-8	F-12	VF-20	EF-40	AU-50	Unc-60	Unc-63	Unc-65
$750	$860	$920	$1,050	$1,400	$1,650	$2,000	$2,600

W-4375-G • F-2202G • Chicago • 214,800

VG-8	F-12	VF-20	EF-40	AU-50	Unc-60	Unc-63	Unc-65
$750	$860	$920	$1,050	$1,400	$1,650	$2,000	$2,600

W-4375-G★ • F-2202G★ • 7 known

W-4375-H • F-2202H • St. Louis • 57,600

VG-8	F-12	VF-20	EF-40	AU-50	Unc-60	Unc-63	Unc-65
$775	$900	$975	$1,100	$1,500	$1,800	$2,200	$2,800

W-4375-H★ • F-2202H★ • 1 known

W-4375-I • F-2202I • Minneapolis • 14,400

VG-8	F-12	VF-20	EF-40	AU-50	Unc-60	Unc-63
$900	$1,100	$1,450	$1,700	$2,750	$3,750	$5,500

W-4375-J • F-2202J • Kansas City • 55,200

VG-8	F-12	VF-20	EF-40	AU-50	Unc-60	Unc-63	Unc-65
$775	$900	$975	$1,100	$1,500	$1,800	$2,200	$2,800

W-4375-J★ • F-2202J★ • 4 known

W-4375-K • F-2202K • Dallas • 34,800

VG-8	F-12	VF-20	EF-40	AU-50	Unc-60	Unc-63
$875	$1,000	$1,250	$1,500	$2,500	$3,300	$4,800

W-4375-L • F-2202L • San Francisco • 93,000

VG-8	F-12	VF-20	EF-40	AU-50	Unc-60	Unc-63	Unc-65
$755	$900	$975	$1,100	$1,500	$1,800	$2,200	$2,800

W-4375-L★ • F-2202L★

VF-20	EF-40
$4,800	$6,000

Series of 1934-B, Green Seal
Julian-Vinson (1945–1946)

Series of 1934-B notes displayed a change in the wording in the Federal Reserve seal. THE is omitted, leaving FEDERAL RESERVE. This was used across all denominations. These were made only for the Atlanta Federal Reserve Bank. They are not known to have been released.

W-4380-F • F-2203F • Atlanta • Unknown in private hands

Series of 1934-C, Green Seal
Julian-Snyder (1946–1949)

This series continued the preceding design. These are not known to have been released.

W-4385-A • F-2204A • Boston • Unknown in private hands

W-4385-B • F-2204B • New York • Unknown in private hands

SERIES OF 1934-A, GREEN SEAL

Signatures and series imprints of a $500 Federal Reserve Note, Series of 1934-A (W-4375-F). The back is the standard type of the era.

SERIES OF 1934-C, GREEN SEAL

$500 Federal Reserve Note, Series of 1934-C (W-4385-B). Federal Reserve Bank of New York. Specimen note with punch cancellation and ornamental stars. The back is the standard type of the era.

$1,000 NOTES

LARGE SIZE

Large-size notes of the $1,000 denomination were made in several different series from the 1860s through the 1920s. Early Interest-Bearing Notes were issued as investments, not as circulating paper money. Most were bought and held by banks and wealthy individuals. Some early varieties no longer survive, and those that do are exceedingly rare. Most later varieties are elusive. No National Bank Notes of this value are known to exist today, although 5,743 Original Series and 1,636 Series of 1875 notes were printed.

INTEREST-BEARING NOTES

These and related Interest-Bearing Notes were often called bonds in Treasury documents as well as in advertising notices (such as by Jay Cooke & Co., the most important agent). A loss in 1863 of certain of these notes, discovered in 1864, is the subject of this account:

> The loss in the Treasury Department during the past year of one hundred $1,000 Coupon Bonds, amounting to one hundred thousand dollars . . . was discovered in June 1864. The bonds were printed by a New York bank note company and forwarded by mail car to the Loan Branch of the secretary's office, where they were received, counted, and found to agree with the invoice. The package, consisting of six thousand bonds of $1,000 each, numbered from 29301 to 35300, was received from the Loan Branch by this division.[1]

March 2, 1861, 6% Interest, 2 Years

At the left of this design (illus. on p. 730) is a portrait of Washington. At the center, America stands holding a wreath. To the right is a small vignette of the United States Treasury building, also used on the 5% two-year $100 Interest-Bearing Note (March 3, 1863). NATIONAL BANK NOTE COMPANY appears at the bottom border, with an 1860 patent to the left. Green counters are arranged as part of a cycloidal configuration overprint.

The back, printed in reddish brown, is mainly of a geometric nature, with tiny denomination counters in cycloidal configuration, and text oriented vertically. The notes are approximately 20 centimeters wide by 10 centimeters high.

At the time of issue they were sold at a discount from face value to reflect the interest to be earned for two years. They did not circulate in commerce but were held until maturity, and then redeemed.

W-4400 • F-202d • 8,336
Commentary: All were redeemed by 1869.

First Series, July 17, 1861, 7.3% Interest, 3 Years

$1,000 notes of this series (illus. on p. 731) were issued with five coupons attached to the left. The center portrait shows Salmon P. Chase, flanked by two large counters on a green background, and two additional counters are at the upper left and right. AMERICAN BANK NOTE CO. NEW YORK appears between the portrait and the border. The back is mainly a geometric design with counters at the top and bottom center, and text is oriented vertically in a circle between them. These were printed with three notes to each sheet.

W-4410 • F-210 • *Printed on plate:* August 19th 1861 • Unknown

W-4420 • F-210 • *Printed on plate:* OCT. 1, 1861 • Red seal • Unknown

W-4430 • F-210 • Blue seal • Unknown

March 3, 1863, 5% Interest, 1 Year

At the left side of the face (illus. on p. 731) is Justice holding scales and a sword. At the center is *Eagle with Shield*. To the right is the *Standard Bearer*, a standing woman holding a flag and shield. Interest was due upon maturity, and as a result no coupons were attached. The imprint near the bottom border reads CONTINENTAL BANK NOTE Co. NEW YORK. The back design is not known.

Likely, such notes were issued more or less continually with various dates imprinted on the face. These were sold at a discount to reflect the interest and were redeemed at face value upon maturity.

W-4440 • F-201 • *Printed on plate:* OCT. 1st 1863 • Unknown

MARCH 2, 1861, 6% INTEREST, 2 YEARS

$1,000 Interest-Bearing Note, March 2, 1861, 2 years (W-4400). These and related large-denomination notes, often called bonds in their time, did not circulate in commerce, but were held as investments by individuals and financial institutions. Proof impression.

Back of the $1,000 Interest-Bearing Note, March 2, 1861, 2 years (W-4400). Proof impression.

March 3, 1863, 5% Interest, 2 Years

The face of this note (illus. on p. 732) has the *Naval Engagement Between the Guerriere and the Constitution* vignette to the left and *The Discovery of the Mississippi by De Soto* to the right. The explorer seems to be wearing a suit of armor and is astride a caparisoned horse, while a trumpeter brings up the rear. Two Native Americans (Indians) are in the foreground. CONTINENTAL BANK NOTE Co. NEW YORK is on a label below the border at the top center. These were sold at a discount to reflect the interest and were redeemed at face value upon maturity. Although 89,308 such notes are said to be issued, no examples are traced today.

W-4450 • F-206 • Issued with coupons • 89,308 • 25 outstanding in 1869 • Unknown

June 30, 1864, 7.3% Interest, 3 Years

At the center is a small figure of *Justice with Shield*, seated. To the left and right are large counters, with smaller counters at the upper corners. The back has counters and text oriented vertically. These were issued with coupons for domestic distribution and without coupons for foreign sales.[2]

W-4460 • F-212c • Issued with coupons • *Printed on plate:* AUG. 15, 1864 • 118,528 • Unknown

W-4461 • F-212c • Issued without coupons • Part of W-4460 printage • Unknown

March 3, 1865, 7.3% Interest, 3 Years

At the center of this note (illus. on p. 732) is a small figure of *Justice with Shield*, seated. To the left and right are large counters, with smaller counters at the upper corners. The back has counters and text oriented vertically. These were issued with

First Series, July 17, 1861, 7.3% Interest, 3 Years

$1,000 Interest-Bearing Note, July 17, 1861, 7.3%, 3 years (W-4410). The portrait of secretary of the Treasury Salmon P. Chase was a popular vignette on notes of the early 1860s. Patent line at left border, two panels of "Patent Green Tint" flanking portrait. American Bank Note Co. imprint. A proof impression is illustrated.

Back of the $1,000 Interest-Bearing Note, July 17, 1861, 7.3%, 3 years (W-4410). With denomination and vignettes and an American Bank Note Co. imprint. A proof impression is illustrated.

March 3, 1863, 5% Interest, 1 Year

$1,000 Interest-Bearing Note, March 3, 1863, 5%, 1 year (W-4440). Proof impression.

MARCH 3, 1863, 5% INTEREST, 2 YEARS

$1,000 Interest-Bearing Note, March 3, 1863, 5%, 2 years (W-4450). Proof impression of the face.

MARCH 3, 1865, 7.3% INTEREST, 3 YEARS

$1,000 Interest-Bearing Note, March 3, 1865, 7.3%, 3 years (W-4467). Serial 99999, plate A. With red overprint. (Martin Gengerke; Bureau of the Public Debt)

coupons. Some have a vertical red overprint at the left end: "The Government reserves the right of paying in COIN, all interest on this Note at the rate of six per cent. per annum." The notes were printed at the Treasury department.

W-4465 • F-212g • *Printed on plate:* JUNE 15, 1865 • Issued with coupons • 118,528

Recorded population: 2 • *Highest graded:* Unc–EF • *Commentary:* The known examples are serials 68759, grade unknown, New Netherlands Coin Co., part of the Smithsonian Institution collection, "believed lost" (Martin Gengerke); and 102,997/A EF, damaged, cancelled, four coupons, owned by the Bureau of the Public Debt.

W-4467 • F-212g • *Printed on plate:* JULY 15, 1865 • 71,879

Recorded population: 1 • *Highest graded:* Unc • *Commentary:* Punch canceled. The note is property of the Bureau of the Public Debt in Washington, D.C.

COMPOUND INTEREST TREASURY NOTES

June 30, 1864, 6% Interest, 3 Years

The motifs are similar to those of the 5%, one-year $1,000 Interest-Bearing Note (March 3, 1863), except with different wording, including "compounded semi-annually." At the left side of the face is Justice holding scales aloft in her left hand and a sword in her right hand. At the center is *Eagle with Shield*. To the right is the *Standard Bearer*, a standing woman holding a flag and shield. Presumably, the back was similar in style to other Compound Interest Treasury Notes, and presumably bronze printing was used on both sides.

W-4470 • F-195 • Chittenden-Spinner (1861–1864) • Red seal • 39,420 • Unknown

W-4475 • F-195a • Colby-Spinner (1864–1867) • Part of W-4470 printage • Unknown

JUNE 30, 1864, 6% INTEREST, 3 YEARS

$1,000 Compound Interest Treasury Note (W-4475). Proof impression without bronze printing.

LEGAL TENDER NOTES
(Also Known as United States Notes)

Series of 1862, First Obligation

In a green frame at the center is a portrait of Robert Morris, facing forward, engraved by Charles Schlecht. To the left and right the denomination is spelled out against a green background, with additional counters at the upper left and right. The First Obligation note has AMERICAN BANK NOTE CO. NEW YORK vertically in the right border.

The face, back, and tint plates for the $1,000 Series of 1862 and 1863 Legal Tender Notes were engraved by the American Bank Note Company. American also printed most (if not all) of the First Obligation notes. American and National shared the printing for the Second Obligation notes.[3] Treasury signatures of Chittenden and Spinner were printed on the face by using a separate plate and a special ink. All have a small red Treasury seal. On the back is the denomination oriented vertically and the obligation.

First Obligation: This wording, with different typography on various denominations, states that the note is exchangeable for bonds: "This note is a Legal Tender for all debts public and private, except for duties on imports and interest on the public debt, and is exchangeable for U.S. six percent twenty years bonds redeemable at the pleasure of the U. States after five years."

Likely, most such high-denomination notes were used in bank-to-bank transfers and other large exchanges, not carried around by the public. There were some exceptions, including one described in an account of a passenger who perished when the SS *Brother Jonathan* hit a rock and sank off Crescent City, California, on July 30, 1865. The body of a female passenger was found, with "one $1,000 Legal Tender Note; five $20 do.; seven $10 do.; two $100 do.; five $50 do.; one $5 National currency note on the National Bank of Poughkeepsie, New York—in all $1,625."[4]

W-4491 • F-186a • *Printed on plate:* ACT OF FEB'Y 25th 1862 / MARCH 10th 1862 • AMERICAN BANK NOTE CO. imprint • Treasury seal without inner border of radial parallel lines • One serial number • 12,000 • Unknown

W-4492 • F-186a • Treasury seal with inner border of radial parallel lines • 10,000 • Unknown

Series of 1862 and 1863, Second Obligation

The face (illus. on p. 734) is the same design as the preceding. All have the printed signatures of Chittenden and Spinner. The series numbers are prefaced with NEW SERIES, as with Second Obligation bank notes of all denominations.

Second Obligation: "This note is a Legal Tender for all debts public and private, except duties on imports and interest on the public debt, and is receivable in payment of all loans made to the United States." This wording, with different typography on various denominations, does not mention exchanging the notes for 6-20 bonds and thus is different from the First Obligation.

W-4493 • F-186b • *Printed on plate:* ACT OF FEB'Y 25th 1862 / MARCH 10th 1862 • AMERICAN BANK NOTE CO. and NATIONAL BANK NOTE CO. imprints • One serial number • Second Obligation back • New series 1 • 2,500 • Unknown

W-4494 • F-186c • *Printed on plate:* ACT OF MARCH 3d 1863 / MARCH 10th 1862 • 24,904

Recorded population: 1 • *Highest graded:* VG-8 • *Selected information:* This note is serial 15592/D, F, problems. From the Oat Bin Hoard purchased in 1966 by Dr. Howard Carter of Leawood, Kansas. First offered by Dean Oakes in a fixed price list, 1975, for $10,000. Most recently seen in Knight (10/2005), $747,500.

W-4495 • F-186d • AMERICAN BANK NOTE CO. imprint • 22,000 • Unknown

SERIES OF 1862 AND 1863, SECOND OBLIGATION

$1,000 Legal Tender Note, Series of 1862 and 1863, Second Obligation (W-4496). This issue is very distinctive with its bold portrait of Robert Morris at the center with a circular ornamental frame surrounding. One serial number. Imprints of two bank-note companies.

Back of the same note, with the Second Obligation imprint, which does not mention convertibility into bonds.

W-4496 • F-186d • *Printed on plate:* ACT OF MARCH 3d 1863 / MARCH 10th 1863 • New series 1 to 2 • 64,000

Recorded population: 2 • *Highest graded:* AU-50 • *Selected information:* Knight (6/2006), 99202/B, AU, $1,150,000. Hickman & Oakes (6/1985), 99206/B, AU, $30,000.

W-4497 • F-186e • Two serial numbers • New Series 2 • 20,000

Recorded population: 1 • *Selected information:* The known example is serial 23657/A, VF, part of the Smithsonian Institution collection. The serial numbers are in mismatched fonts.

Series of 1869

Depicted on the face are two seemingly unrelated vignettes, which is not particularly unusual for a layout in this period. To the left is *Columbus in His Study*, with a globe on the floor nearby reinforcing his notion that the earth was not flat. At the center is DeWitt Clinton (1769–1828), with the fingers of his right hand touching the side of his head. Perhaps both men were associated with water—Columbus for sailing across the Atlantic Ocean to "discover" America, and Clinton as the driving force behind the Erie Canal, started in 1817 and completed in 1825, which linked the Great Lakes

with the Atlantic. To the right is a large pink Treasury seal. Counters are at the upper-left and upper-right corners.

The back has the denomination expressed as M on the left and the number 1000 on the right, with payment and counterfeiting clauses within a circle at the center. Imprints for the American Bank Note Company are at the top and bottom borders. The back was used only on the Series of 1869 issues. These were printed on paper with a blue-tinted streak (Willcox's 1866 patent). As a class, Series of 1869 notes were issued from October 19, 1869, through July 25, 1874.

W-4510 • F-186f • Allison-Spinner (1869–1875) • Large pink seal • 74,400

Recorded population: 2 • *Highest graded:* EF-40 • *Selected information:* The known examples are serials 29763/C, EF, from the Amon Carter Jr. collection, used on an ANA video program, and Z51324/D, VF+, owned by the Federal Reserve Bank of Chicago.

Series of 1878

The face of this note (illus. on p. 736) continues the motifs of the preceding. The back is redesigned, and has the denomination at the center expressed as "$1000" (the use of dollar

SERIES OF 1869

$1,000 Legal Tender Note, Series of 1869 (W-4510). At the left is Christopher Columbus in his study with a globe. At the center is the portrait of DeWitt Clinton. An ornamental star follows the serial number. Serial Z29763, plate 1C. Small pink 1 to the right of the Treasury seal.

Serial number with microprinting giving patent information below (George W. Casilear's patent for printing a serial number over an engraved background as a security measure). Plate 1C information at the bottom.

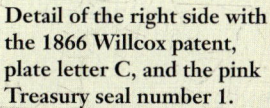

Detail of the right side with the 1866 Willcox patent, plate letter C, and the pink Treasury seal number 1.

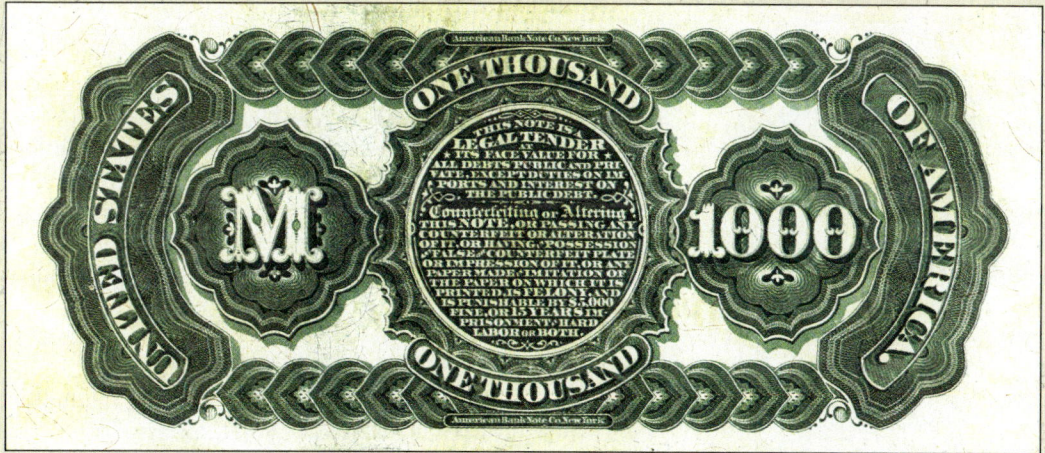

Back of the $1,000 Legal Tender Note, Series of 1869 (W-4510), with an American Bank Note Co. imprint. The redemption and counterfeiting clauses are prominent at the center. These notices were used on many different early types.

signs is highly unusual on American currency), with a vertical M to the left and right, and text at the far left. ENGRAVED & PRINTED AT THE BUREAU, ENGRAVING & PRINTING appears twice in the bottom margin.

W-4512 • F-187a • Allison-Gilfillan (1877–1878) • Small red seal with spiked border • 24,000

Recorded population: 2 • *Highest graded:* EF-40 • *Selected information:* The existing examples are serials A21998/B, EF, part of the Smithsonian Institution collection, and A21999/C, EF, owned by the Federal Reserve Bank of Chicago.

Series of 1880

The face design (illus. on p. 737) continues the preceding, but the back is redesigned. Among other changes, the redemption and counterfeiting clauses are now in smaller type and at the left. There is only one style of back on this series.

W-4513 • F-187b • Bruce-Wyman (1883–1885) • Large brown seal • 12,000

Recorded population: 2 • *Highest graded:* AU with pinholes • *Selected information:* The existing examples are serials

SERIES OF 1878

$1,000 Legal Tender Note, Series of 1878 (W-4512). (Smithsonian Institution)

Back of the $1,000 Legal Tender Note, Series of 1878 (W-4512).

1164/D, AU, pinholes, sold in a Knight auction (6/2006) for $862,500, and Z6498/B, EF, part of the Smithsonian Institution collection.

W-4514 • F-187c • Rosecrans-Jordan (1885–1887) • Large pink seal with plain border • 24,000

Recorded population: 1 • *Selected information:* The existing example is serial A15635/C, VF, owned by the Federal Reserve Bank of San Francisco.

W-4515 • F-187d • Rosecrans-Hyatt (1887–1889) • Large pink seal with spiked border • 4,000

Recorded population: 1 • *Selected information:* The existing example is serial A27395/C, EF, part of the Smithsonian Institution collection.

W-4516 • F-187e • Rosecrans-Huston (1889–1891) • 8,000

Recorded population: 1 • *Selected information:* The existing example is serial A32279/C, VF, owned by the Federal Reserve Bank of San Francisco.

W-4517 • F-187f • Rosecrans-Nebeker (1891–1893) • Large brown seal • 28,000 • Unknown

W-4518 • F-187g • Tillman-Morgan (1893–1897) • Small red seal with scalloped border • 56,000

Recorded population: 1 • *Highest graded:* VF-20 • *Selected information:* The existing example is serial A111488/D, VF, owned by the Federal Reserve Bank of San Francisco.

W-4519 • F-187h • Tillman-Roberts (1897) • Plate made; no evidence of printing

W-4520 • F-187i • Bruce-Roberts (1897–1898) • No evidence a plate was made

W-4521 • F-187j • Lyons-Roberts (1898–1905) • 56,000

Estimated population: 13 to 15 • *Highest graded:* Unc.

VF-20	EF-40	AU-50	Unc-60
$60,000	$125,000	—	—

W-4522 • F-187k • Vernon-Treat (1906–1909) • 20,000

Recorded population: 4 • *Highest graded:* EF-45 • *Selected information:* Existing examples include serials B2425/A, VF, problems, sold in a Knight auction (6/1998) for $38,000, B8407/C, EF-40, restored (PMG), sold in a CAA auction (9/2006) for $517,500; B8800/D, VF, owned by the Federal Reserve Bank of New York; and B10050/B, EF–AU, part of the Smithsonian Institution collection.

SERIES OF 1880

$1,000 Legal Tender Note, Series of 1880 (W-4521).

Back of the $1,000 Legal Tender Note, Series of 1880 (W-4521), with a double imprint at the bottom border: **ENGRAVED & PRINTED AT THE BUREAU, ENGRAVING & PRINTING.**

W-4525 • F-187l • Napier-McClung (1911–1912) • No evidence of printing

NATIONAL BANK NOTES

Original Series
(Authorized Issue 1863 to 1875)

National Bank Notes of the $1,000 denomination (illus. on p. 738) were printed by the National Bank Note Company (whose imprint appears at the bottom border). These were usually printed in two-subject sheets of $500-$1,000 with plate letter A for both notes, although there were other sheet layouts. All had a small red Treasury seal with a spiked border. On some early notes the Treasury serial number at the upper right was in blue (most were red), while on all notes the bank serial number at the lower left was in red. Plate arrangements included a single plate, $500-$1,000, $500-$500-$500-$1,000, and $1,000-$1,000-$1,000-$1,000. The Act of June 20, 1874, provided for the imprinting of the bank's charter number.

On the left side of the face is *General Scott's Entrance into Mexico City*, engraved by Alfred Jones and James D. Smillie, a highlight event in the War with Mexico (1846–1847). On

the right is the United States Capitol. At the center of the back is *Washington Resigning His Commission*, engraved by Louis Delnoce and Frederick Girsch, from a painting by John Trumbull. On the left is a state seal representing the issuing location of the bank, and to the right is an eagle.

From October 15, 1864, to June 10, 1875, 5,818 Original Series $1,000 notes were delivered to 36 different banks in five different states.[5] In 1938 the Treasury department stated that 21 (without regard to series) remained outstanding.

No examples are known to exist today.

Banks of Issue and Rarity of Notes

Maryland • 3 banks of issue • 142 printed • Unknown.

Massachusetts • 9 banks of issue • 1,332 printed • Unknown.

New York • 17 banks of issue • 3,902 printed • Unknown.

Pennsylvania • 5 banks of issue • 237 printed • Unknown.

Rhode Island • 2 banks of issue • 130 printed • Unknown.

W-4530 • F-465 • Chittenden-Spinner (1861–1864) • Unknown

W-4531 • F-465 • Colby-Spinner (1864–1867) • Unknown

W-4532 • F-465 • Allison-Spinner (1869–1875) • Unknown

National Gold Bank Notes, Original Series

The Kidder National Gold Bank of Boston was the first such institution chartered. On April 8, 1871, the Treasury sent 75 sheets of $500-$1,000 notes. None were ever paid out. On December 4, 1871, all were returned to the Treasury department. These were the only $1,000 National Gold Bank Notes printed for any bank.[6]

W-4536 • F-unlisted • Dated 1870 • Boston • Kidder National Gold Bank • 75 • None issued

Series of 1875
(Authorized Issue 1875 to 1902, Last Issued 1884)

The Series of 1875 notes continued the use of plates signed by American Bank Note Company. Although an example has not been seen, there must have been an added notice such as PRINTED AT THE BUREAU OF ENGRAVING & PRINTING, U.S. TREASURY DEPt. We can deduce from related $500 notes that the small red Treasury seal would have a scalloped rather than a spiked border. All have SERIES 1875 imprinted vertically in red left of center near the bank charter number. The Treasury and bank serial numbers and two charter numbers are also in red.

No examples are known to exist today.

Banks of Issue and Rarity of Notes

Massachusetts • 2 banks of issue • 160 printed • Unknown.
New York • 5 banks of issue • 1,465 printed • Unknown.
Pennsylvania • 1 bank of issue • 11 printed • Unknown.

W-4539 • F-unlisted • Allison-New (1875–1876) • Unknown

W-4540 • F-465 • Allison-Wyman (1876–1877) • Unknown

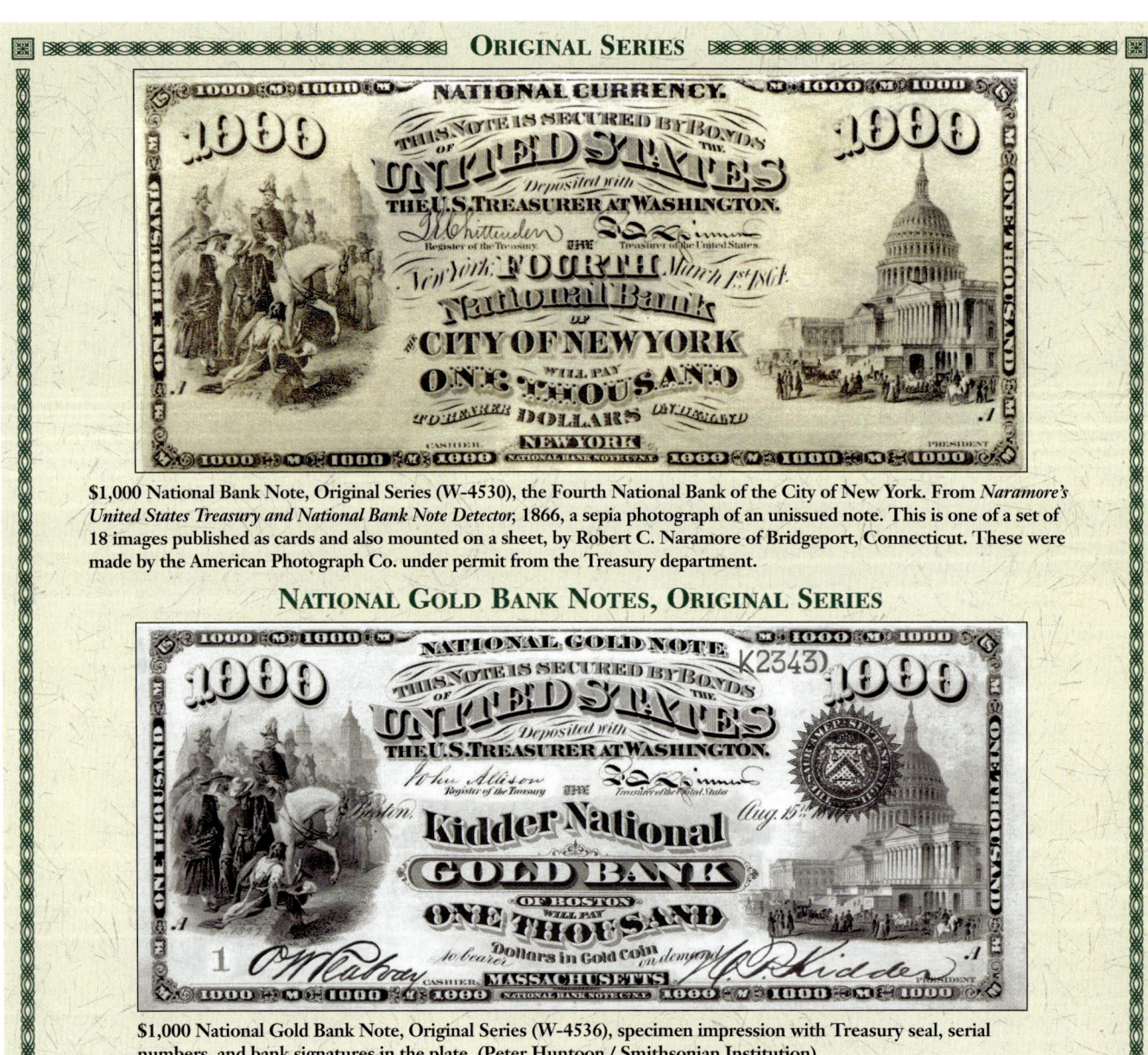

$1,000 National Bank Note, Original Series (W-4530), the Fourth National Bank of the City of New York. From *Naramore's United States Treasury and National Bank Note Detector*, 1866, a sepia photograph of an unissued note. This is one of a set of 18 images published as cards and also mounted on a sheet, by Robert C. Naramore of Bridgeport, Connecticut. These were made by the American Photograph Co. under permit from the Treasury department.

NATIONAL GOLD BANK NOTES, ORIGINAL SERIES

$1,000 National Gold Bank Note, Original Series (W-4536), specimen impression with Treasury seal, serial numbers, and bank signatures in the plate. (Peter Huntoon / Smithsonian Institution)

W-4541 • F-465 • Scofield-Gilfillan (1878–1881) • Unknown

W-4542 • F-465 • Bruce-Gilfillan (1881–1883) • Unknown

SILVER CERTIFICATES

Series of 1878

Silver Certificates of the Series of 1878 bear a portrait of William L. Marcy to the left; a prominent counter, printed 1000 M, to the right; and inscriptions. These have printed Scofield-Gilfillan Treasury signatures and space for a countersignature. On the red Treasury seal, for this denomination and other countersigned notes in this series, the key faces to the right (with the handle at the left). These were printed on paper with a blue-tinted streak. It is not certain which varieties were actually made. The listing is partly conjectural. None are known to exist today.

W-4550 • F-346a • New York • Countersigned: W.G. White (autographed) • 500 (est.) • Unknown

W-4553 • F-346a • Countersigned: J.C. Hopper (autographed) • 3,500 (est.) • Unknown

W-4559 • F-346a • San Francisco • Countersigned: R.M. Anthony • 2,000 (est.) • Unknown

W-4561 • F-346a • Washington • Countersigned: A.U. Wyman (autographed) • 4,000 (est.) • Unknown

W-4562 • F-346a • Countersigned: A.U. Wyman (printed) • 18,000 (est.) • Unknown

Series of 1880

These $1,000 notes (illus. on p. 740) are specifically designated CERTIFICATE OF DEPOSIT on the face and SILVER CERTIFICATE on the back. To the left of the face is William L. Marcy, who among other appointments was charged with managing California Territory during the early days of the Gold Rush. At the center is a Treasury seal with a red 1000 below, and to the right is a counter. The back, printed in brown, has SILVER in small letters and, in contrast to lower denominations, the word CERTIFICATE very large.

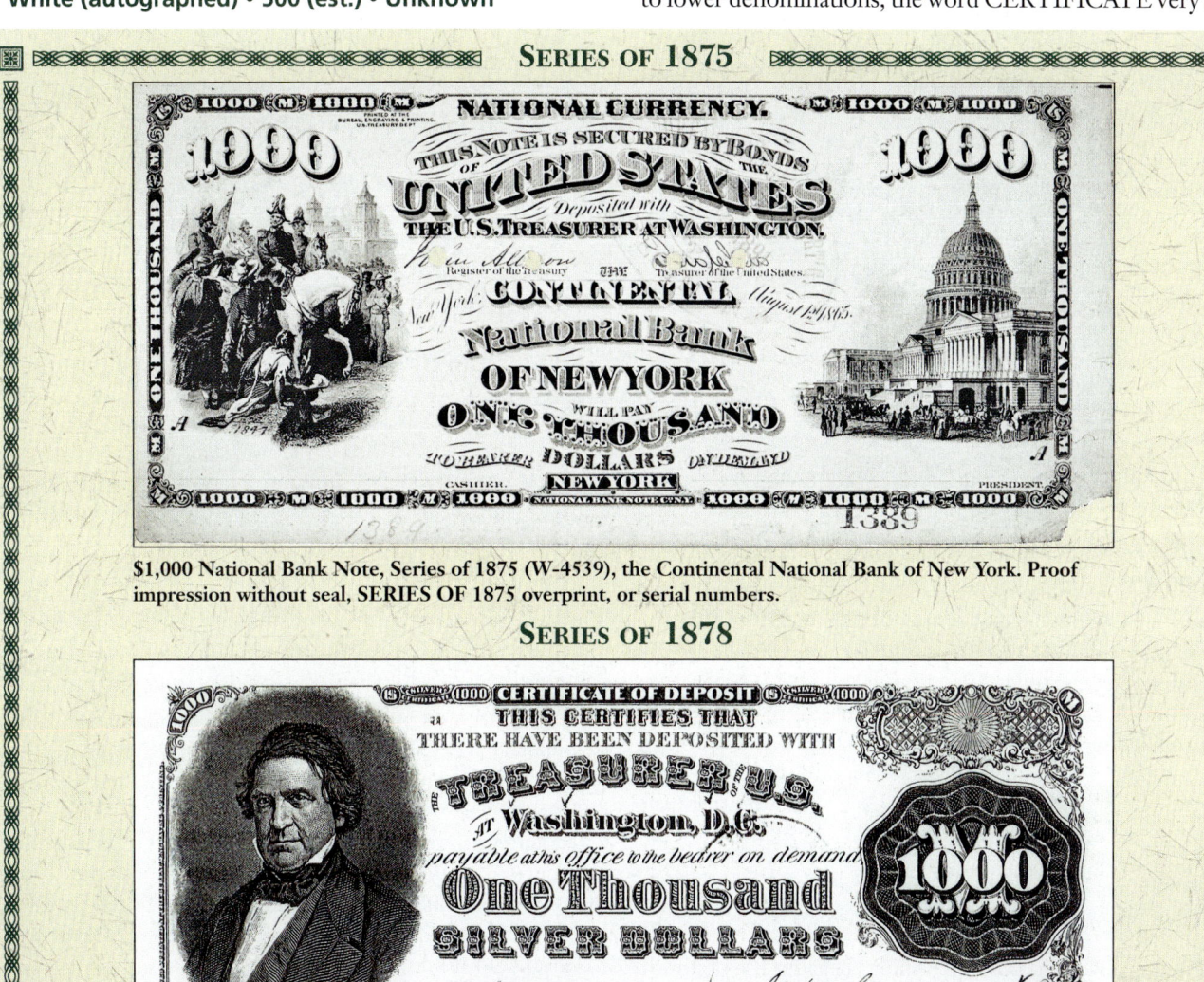

$1,000 National Bank Note, Series of 1875 (W-4539), the Continental National Bank of New York. Proof impression without seal, SERIES OF 1875 overprint, or serial numbers.

$1,000 Silver Certificate of Deposit, Series of 1878 (W-4562), with engraved countersignature of A.U. Wyman, Scofield-Gilfillan signatures. Proof impression. (Smithsonian Institution)

SERIES OF 1880

$1,000 Silver Certificate of Deposit, Series of 1880 (W-4567). Portrait of William L. Marcy.

Back of the $1,000 Silver Certificate of Deposit, Series of 1880 (W-4567).

W-4565 • F-346b • Scofield-Gilfillan (1878–1881) • Large brown seal • No evidence of printing

W-4566 • F-346c • Bruce-Gilfillan (1881–1883) • 8,000 • Unknown

W-4567 • F-346d • Bruce-Wyman (1883–1885) • 8,000
Recorded population: 5 • Highest graded: AU-50 • Selected information: Existing examples include serials B11437/A, VF, formerly part of the Amon Carter Jr. collection; B11500/D, VG–F, owned by the Federal Reserve Bank of San Francisco; B12623/C, VF, sold in a Knight auction (10/2005) for $667,000; B12638/B, AU, pinholes, part of the Smithsonian Institution collection; and B14663/C, EF–AU, owned by the Federal Reserve Bank of Chicago.

Series of 1891

At the left is a woman holding a shield bearing the denomination. To the right is a portrait of William L. Marcy. The back has the denomination in large numerals at the center with ornamental vignettes to the sides that extend to the border, and it is printed in green.

W-4570 • F-346e • Tillman-Morgan (1893–1897) • Small pink seal with scalloped border • 8,000

Recorded population: 2 • Selected information: The existing examples are serials E1/A, Unc, part of the Smithsonian Institution collection, and E1433/A, EF, part of the Amon Carter Jr. collection.

TREASURY OR COIN NOTES

Series of 1890

Called the "Grand Watermelon Note" because of the distinctive shape and color of the zeroes on the back, this type (illus. on p. 741) was voted number one in *100 Greatest American Currency Notes.*

Depicted on the face is General George G. Meade, Civil War hero. The illustrated example was the first note to cross the million-dollar mark at auction. It was offered by Lyn F. Knight at the David Rickey Collection sale in October 2005, where it sold for $1,092,500.

W-4580 • F-379a • Rosecrans-Huston (1889–1891) • Large brown seal • 16,000
Recorded population: 5 • Highest graded: AU-50 • Selected information: Existing examples include serials A3055/C, VF, sold in a Melnick auction (6/1983) for $44,000; A10895/C, VF, owned by the Federal Reserve Bank of San Francisco;

SERIES OF 1891

$1,000 Silver Certificate, Series of 1891 (W-4570). At left is a woman with her left hand resting on a shield. To the right is the portrait of William L. Marcy. Serial E1, plate A. (Smithsonian Institution)

Back of the $1,000 Silver Certificate, Series of 1891 (W-4570).

A11623/C, VF, part of the Smithsonian Institution collection; A13341/A, EF, owned by the Federal Reserve Bank of Chicago; A13343/C, AU-50 (PCGS), sold in a Knight auction (10/2005) for $1,092,500.

W-4581 • F-379b • Rosecrans-Nebeker (1891–1893) • Small red seal with scalloped border • 12,000

Recorded population: 2 • *Highest graded:* AU-50 • *Selected information:* The existing examples are serials A27170/B, AU-50 (CGA), offered in a Parrino fixed-price list (2/2002) for $3,000,000, and A27183/C, EF, owned by the Federal Reserve Bank of San Francisco.

Series of 1891

The Series of 1891 notes (illus. on p. 743) continue the face design of the preceding with minor typographic changes; the back now features an open design said to deter counterfeiting.

W-4585 • F-379d • Rosecrans-Nebeker (1891–1893) • Small red seal with scalloped border • 8,000 • Unknown

W-4586 • F-379c • Tillman-Morgan (1893–1897) • 24,000

Recorded population: 2 • *Selected information:* The existing examples are serials B23792/D, Unc, owned by the Federal

Reserve Bank of San Francisco, and B31973/A, Unc, part of the Smithsonian Institution collection.

GOLD CERTIFICATES

Act of March 3, 1863

Gold Certificates of this and other early denominations were issued under the Act of March 3, 1863. ENGRAVED AND PRINTED AT THE TREASURY DEPARTMENT is imprinted below the top border. At the left of the face (illus. on p. 744) is a patriotic depiction of the American eagle on a shield with arrows, an olive branch, and a flag as part of the suite, and E PLURIBUS UNUM lettered above. The bottom border shows the upper part of Justice holding balance scales. A small red Treasury seal with a spiked border and the number 1000 in a lacy green overprint also appear on the face. The back has two counters printed against an ornately engraved background. These were issued only by the New York Sub-Treasury. Most were used as clearing house certificates, as gold reserves by banks, or for payment of import duties.[7]

W-4590 • F-1166e • New York (only) • Colby-Spinner (1864–1867) • Small red seal with spiked border • 117,000

SERIES OF 1890

$1,000 Treasury or Coin Note, Series of 1890 (W-4580). Portrait is of General George Meade. An ornamental star follows the serial number. The illustrated example is the first note in numismatic history to cross the million-dollar mark at auction.

Back of the famous "Grand Watermelon Note," likely the most famous trophy note in the federal currency series.

Recorded population: 1 • *Commentary:* An autographed countersignature of an assistant Treasurer of the United States is on all. • *Selected information:* The known example is serial 19683/C, canceled, owned by the Bureau of the Public Debt in Washington, D.C.

Series of 1870

Notes in this series (illus. on p. 745) are one-sided. On certain proof impressions, a portrait of Alexander Hamilton is at the left, a large Treasury seal is at the center, and a counter with C, I, and a backward C is at the right. An issued example has the counter as a more recognizable numeral, 1000, and may have been altered from the earlier plate. To the left above the bottom border is a space for an autographed signature, below which is imprinted ASSISTANT TREASURER, N.Y. To the right are spaces for the addition of two autographed signatures, REGISTER OF THE TREASURY and ASSISTANT TREASURER U.S.

W-4598 • F-unlisted • With counter in right field C, I, and backward C • Not known if issued

W-4600 • F-1166j • Allison and two other Treasury officials (all autographed) • Large pink seal with spiked border • 50,000

Recorded population: 1 • *Selected information:* The known example is serial A38887/C, canceled, owned by the Bureau of the Public Debt in Washington D.C.

Series of 1875

Series of 1875 notes (illus. on p. 745) are one-sided. At the left is a portrait of Alexander Hamilton, and at the right is a denomination counter. To the left, above the bottom border, is space for an autographed signature, below which is imprinted ASSISTANT TREASURER, N.Y. To the right are spaces imprinted for the addition of two autographed or printed signatures, REGISTER OF THE TREASURY and ASSISTANT TREASURER U.S.

W-4605 • F-1166o • Allison-New (1875–1876) and an assistant Treasurer (autographed) • Large red seal with spiked border • 10,400 • Unknown

SERIES OF 1891

$1,000 Treasury Note, Series of 1891 (W-4586). The design is as the preceding, with a portrait of General George Meade. An ornamental star is after each of the serial numbers. Although this is a great rarity, its "Grand Watermelon Note" predecessor has captured most of the limelight.

Back of the $1,000 Treasury Note, Series of 1891 (W-4586), with open fields said to deter counterfeiting. Vertically oriented bands of fibers were added as a further precaution.

W-4606 • F-1166o • Allison-Gilfillan (1877–1878) and an assistant Treasurer (autographed) • Large pink seal with spiked border • 10,000 • Unknown

Series of 1882

On the right of this type (illus. on p. 746) is a portrait of Alexander Hamilton, different from the preceding. At the center is a Treasury seal and shield, and at the left is a counter. Early issues have the countersignature of Thomas C. Acton, assistant Treasurer at the New York Sub-Treasury. The back shows an eagle at the center and a large M.

W-4610 • F-1218a • Bruce-Gilfillan (1881–1883) • Countersignature: Thomas C. Acton (autographed) • Medium-size brown seal with scalloped border • 12,000
Recorded population: 2 • *Highest graded:* VF-20 • *Selected information:* The existing examples are serials A10199/C, VF–EF, part of the Smithsonian Institution collection, and A11369/A, F, owned by the Federal Reserve Bank of San Francisco.

W-4612 • F-1218 • Bruce-Gilfillan (1881–1883) • No countersignature • 8,000 • Unknown

W-4614 • F-1218b • Bruce-Wyman (1883–1885) • 20,000
Recorded population: 1 • *Selected information:* The known example is serial A18818/B, VF–EF, part of the Smithsonian Institution collection.

W-4616 • F-1218c • Rosecrans-Hyatt (1887–1889) • Large pink spiked seal • 16,000
Recorded population: 1 • *Selected information:* The known example is serial 6477/A, VF, part of the Smithsonian Institution collection.

W-4618 • F-1218d • Rosecrans-Huston (1889–1891) • Large brown spiked seal • 8,000
Recorded population: 3 • *Highest graded:* AU-50 • *Selected information:* The known examples are serials C22708/D, AU, sold in a Knight auction (6/2006) for $1,092,500; C23727/C, F, owned by the Federal Reserve Bank of San Francisco; and C23847/C, VF, part of the Smithsonian Institution collection.

ACT OF MARCH 3, 1863

$1,000 Gold Certificate, Act of March 3, 1863 (W-4590), Colby-Spinner Treasury signatures and space for the addition by hand of a countersignature. Proof impression, plate B. (Smithsonian Institution)

Back of the $1,000 Gold Certificate, Act of March 3, 1863 (W-4590). Color proof. (Smithsonian Institution)

W-4620 • F-1218e • Rosecrans-Nebeker (1891–1893) • Small red seal with scalloped border • 8,000

Recorded population: 3 • Highest graded: EF-40 • Selected information: The known examples are serials C24623/C, used as the Friedberg illustration; C24675/C, EF, owned by the Federal Reserve Bank of Chicago; and C29156/D, F, owned by the Federal Reserve Bank of San Francisco.

W-4622 • F-1218f • Lyons-Roberts (1898–1905) • 96,000

Estimated population: 9 or 10 • Highest graded: VF-20 • Selected information: Heritage (9/2007), C81906/B, VF-25 (PMG), $97,750. CAA (9/2006), C83210/B, VF-30 (PMG), $195,500. B&M (11/2002), C100258/C, F–VF, pinholes (per Dean Oakes), $97,750. CAA (5/2005), 109771/C, F, $97,750. Knight (12/1998), C119261/A, F, $35,200.

W-4624 • F-1218g • Lyons-Treat (1905–1906) • 16,000

Recorded population: 4 • Highest graded: EF-40 • Selected information: The existing examples are serials D969/A, F, owned by the Federal Reserve Bank of San Francisco; D10213/A, VG, pinholes, sold in a Knight auction (11/2003) for $69,000; D14752/D, VF-30 (CGA, later graded EF-40 by

PCGS), sold in a Knight auction (10/2005) for $264,500; and D15131/C, EF–AU, part of the Smithsonian Institution collection.

Series of 1907

The center of the note (illus. on p. 747) shows Alexander Hamilton, the denomination to the left, and a red Treasury seal to the right. The back, printed in orange-gold, has a heraldic eagle and inscriptions. All have a gold Treasury seal with a scalloped border. For all Gold Certificates, notes with bright unfaded backs are worth more within any given grade.

W-4626 • F-1219 • Vernon-Treat (1906–1909) • 32,000

Recorded population: 6 • Highest graded: EF-40 • Selected information: The existing examples include serials A2258/B, F-12, restoration (PMG); A9050/B, VF, owned by the Federal Reserve Bank of San Francisco; A13296/D, EF–AU, part of the Smithsonian Institution collection; A26707/C, VG, pinholes, sold in a Spink auction (7/2007) for $19,750; A28943/C, VF, reported by Don C. Kelly (1/1995); and A31075/C, F, sold in a CAA auction (1/1999) for $15,400.

SERIES OF 1870

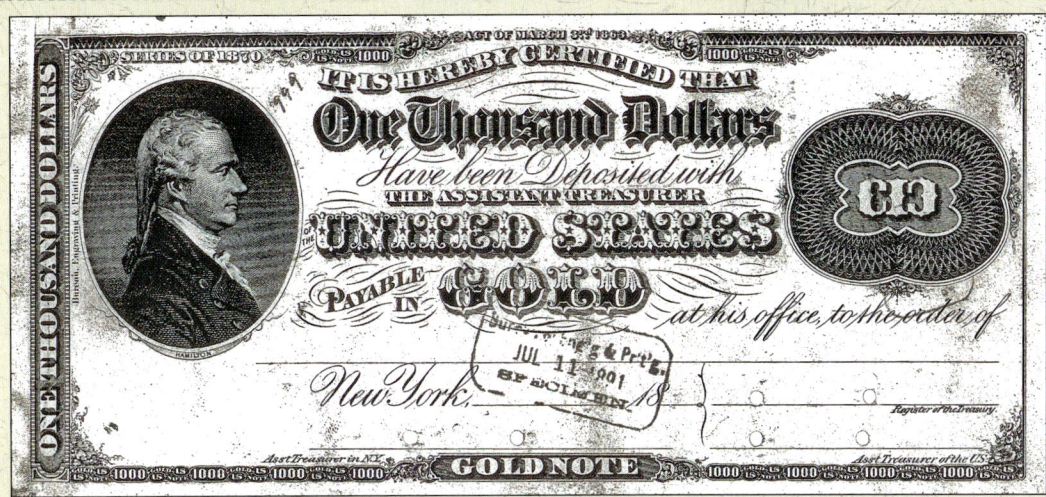

$1,000 Gold Certificate, Series of 1870 (W-4598). Proof impression with the counter as a C, I, and backward C. (Smithsonian Institution)

$1,000 Gold Certificate, Series of 1870 (W-4600). Portrait of Hamilton. All three signatures are autographed. Serial A38887, plate C. A circulated example with the counter as 1000.

SERIES OF 1875

$1,000 Gold Certificate, Series of 1875 (W-4605). Portrait of Hamilton. Space for three autographed signatures. Proof. The Allison-New signatures were likely added to the plate before use. (Smithsonian Institution)

SERIES OF 1882

$1,000 Gold Certificate, Series of 1882 (W-4624). Portrait of Alexander Hamilton to the right. Gold overprinting.

Detail of a W-4610 note with autographed signature of Thomas C. Acton, assistant Treasurer at the New York Sub-Treasury.

Back of the $1,000 Gold Certificate, Series of 1882 (W-4624). Large M denomination counter at the left, perched eagle at the center. Printed in gold.

W-4628 • F-1219a • Vernon-McClung (1909–1911) • 12,000 • Unknown

Commentary: All were delivered on May 17, 1911.

W-4630 • F-1219b • Napier-McClung (1911–1912) • 12,000

Recorded population: 1 • *Commentary:* Deliveries began on April 24, 1912, and ended on three days later, on April 27, 1912. • *Selected information:* Heritage (9/2008), B19908/D, F–VF, pinholes (PMG), $287,500.

W-4632 • F-1219c • Napier-Burke (1913) • 12,000

Recorded population: 4 • *Highest graded:* VF-20 • *Commentary:* All were delivered on August 21, 1913. • *Selected information:* CAA (9/2006), D2616/D, F-15 (PMG), $86,250. Stack's (3/1989), D3953/A, F–VF, problems, $4,840; Stack's (10/1991), D5936/D, Fair, damaged, $1,650. Knight (10/2005), D8776/D, VF-20 (PCGS), $43,125.

W-4634 • F-1219d • Parker-Burke (1913–1914) • 48,000

Estimated population: 9 or 10 • *Highest graded:* AU-50 • *Selected information:* CAA (10/1995), D25100/D, VF, $6,050. Knight (6/2000), D40835/C, AU, $38,500. Knight (11/2003), D40885/A, EF, $29,900. Knight (12/2000), D44933/A, VF, $23,760. CAA (9/2006), D45587/C, F-12 (PMG), $27,600.

W-4636 • F-1219e • Teehee-Burke (1915–1919) • 112,000

Estimated population: 45 to 50 • *Highest graded:* Unc.

VG-8	F-12	VF-20	EF-40	AU-50	Unc-60
$10,500	$20,000	$37,500	—	—	$175,000

Series of 1922

The Series of 1922 notes (illus. on p. 748) continue the preceding design, but now have an inscription in the left field: "This certificate is a legal tender in the amount thereof in

SERIES OF 1907

$1,000 Gold Certificate, Series of 1907 (W-4636).

Back of the $1,000 Gold Certificate, Series of 1907 (W-4636). Great Seal of the United States at center. Printed in gold.

payment of all debts and dues public and private Acts of March 14, 1900, as amended and December 24, 1919."

W-4640 • F-1220 • Speelman-White (1922–1927) • Gold seal with scalloped border • 80,000

Estimated population: 44 to 48 • *Highest graded:* Unc.

VG-8	F-12	VF-20	EF-40	AU-50	Unc-60
$10,500	$20,000	$37,500	$55,000	—	—

FEDERAL RESERVE NOTES

Series of 1918, Blue Seal

At the center is a portrait of Alexander Hamilton. To the left is the Federal Reserve seal with bank identification. A blue Treasury seal is to the right. The face layout has the Federal Reserve seal widely spaced from the border and large district numbers and letters in each corner. (Illus. on p. 749.)

W-4650-A • F-1133A • Boston • Burke-Glass (1918–1920) • 39,600

Recorded population: 3 • *Highest graded:* VF-20 • *Selected information:* The existing examples are serials A10459A/C, VG-8 (PCGS), sold in a Smythe auction (7/2007) for $25,300;

A14880A/D, VF–EF, reported by Tom Denly (6/1992); and A16149A/A, VF–EF, part of the Smithsonian Institution collection.

W-4653-B • F-1133B • New York • 100,000 (est.)

Estimated population: 21 to 24 • *Highest graded:* Unc.

VG-8	F-12	VF-20	EF-40	AU-50	Unc-60	Unc-63
$5,500	$9,000	$13,500	$22,500	—	—	$40,000

W-4656-B • F-1133a-B • Burke-Houston (1920–1921) • 24,800 (est.)

Reported population: 8 or 9 • *Highest graded:* Unc • *Selected information:* Knight (6/2006), B101315A/C, F-15 (PCGS), $19,550. CAA (9/2005), B103739A/C, EF, $23,000. Heritage (1/2006), B104211A/C, F–VF, $20,700. Knight (11/2006), B104316A/D, F, $19,550. Knight (3/2007), B107498A, EF-40 (PCGS), $36,800.

W-4659-C • F-1133C • Philadelphia • Burke-Glass (1918–1920) • 16,400

Estimated population: 13 to 15 • *Highest graded:* Unc.

VG-8	F-12	VF-20	EF-40	AU-50	Unc-60	Unc-63
$5,500	$9,000	$13,500	$22,500	—	—	$40,000

SERIES OF 1922

$1,000 Gold Certificate, Series of 1922 (W-4640).

Back of the $1,000 Gold Certificate, Series of 1922 (W-4640), which continues the preceding design.

W-4662-D • F-1133D • Cleveland • 8,800
Estimated population: 12 to 14 • *Highest graded:* Unc.

VG-8	F-12	VF-20	EF-40	AU-50	Unc-60	Unc-63
$5,500	$9,000	$20,000	$35,000	—	—	$40,000

W-4665-E • F-1133E • Richmond • 17,600 • Unknown

W-4668-F • F-1133F • Atlanta • 26,800
Estimated population: 8 or 9 • *Highest graded:* EF-40 • *Selected information:* Heritage (1/2007), F5682A/B, VG–F, $6,612.50. Heritage (1/2007), F9888A/D, VF-20 (PMG), $12,650. B&M (6/2007), F12144A/D, VF, $20,700. Knight (3/2007), F13064A/D, EF-45 (PCGS), $35,650.

W-4671-F • F-1133b-F • White-Mellon (1921–1928) • 16,400
Recorded population: 5 • *Highest graded:* Unc • *Selected information:* Known examples include serials F27003A/C, Unc-62 (PCGS), sold in a Knight auction (3/2007) for $74,750; F27004A/D, AU, sold in a Stack's auction (3/1991) for $6,050; F28477A/A, EF, part of the Smithsonian Institution collection; F31644A/D, VF, repaired, Frederick J. Bart (5/2000) in a *Bank Note Reporter* advertisement; and F38587A/A, EF.

W-4674-G • F-1133G • Chicago • Burke-Glass (1918–1920) • 23,600
Estimated population: 30 to 35 • *Highest graded:* Unc.

VG-8	F-12	VF-20	EF-40	AU-50	Unc-60	Unc-63
$5,500	$9,000	$17,500	$25,000	—	—	$40,000

W-4677-H • F-1133H • St. Louis • 8,400
Recorded population: 7 • *Highest graded:* VF-20 • *Selected information:* Known examples include serials H1646A/B, F-12 (PMG), sold in a Knight auction (3/2007) for $17,250, and H1998A/B, VF, part of the Smithsonian Institution collection.

W-4680-I • F-1133I • Minneapolis • 7,600
Recorded population: 2 • *Highest graded:* VF-20 • *Selected information:* The known examples are serials I754A/B, VF, sold in a Stack's auction (3/1991) for $5,500; and I1337A/B, reported by Tom Denly (3/1988).

W-4683-J • F-1133J • Kansas City • 13,200
Recorded population: 4 • *Highest graded:* EF-40 • *Selected information:* The known examples include serials J310A/B, F, sold in a Knight auction (3/2007) for $46,000; J3308A/D, EF–

SERIES OF 1918, BLUE SEAL

$1,000 Federal Reserve Note, Series of 1918 (W-4659-C). Federal Reserve Bank of Philadelphia.

Back of the $1,000 Federal Reserve Note, Series of 1918 (W-4659-C). Eagle facing left, perched on flag and arrows.

AU, sold in a CAA auction (2/2005) for $39,100; J3333A, VF–EF, owned by the Federal Reserve Bank of Chicago; and J4319A/C, F-15 (PMG), sold in a Heritage auction (1/2008) for $40,250.

W-4686-J • F-1133b-J • White-Mellon (1921–1928) • 2,000 • Unknown

W-4689-K • F-1133K • Dallas • Burke-Glass (1918–1920) • 6,000
Recorded population: 3 • *Highest graded:* EF-40 • *Selected information:* Knight (3/2007), K528A/D, EF-40 (PMG), $80,500. Kagin's (6/1984), K1767A, VF, $1,500. Knight (3/1982), K2329A/A, VF, $1,400.

W-4692-L • F-1133L • San Francisco • 19,600
Estimated population: 56 to 60 • *Highest graded:* Unc.

VG-8	F-12	VF-20	EF-40	AU-50	Unc-60	Unc-63
$5,500	$9,000	$13,500	$25,000	—	—	$40,000

W-4695-L • F-1133b-L • White-Mellon (1921–1928) • 2,800
Recorded population: 4 • *Highest graded:* Unc • *Selected information:* Heritage (1/2006), L19673A/A, Unc, $48,875. Her-

itage (5/2007), L19961A/A, AU, $74,750. Knight (3/2007), L21025A/A, EF-40 (PCGS), $34,500. Knight (12/1985), L21026A/B, AU, $5,500.

SMALL SIZE

Small-size Federal Reserve Notes and Gold Certificates, each depicting William McKinley on the face (the portrait used earlier on large-size Series of 1902 $10 National Bank Notes), were issued and are scarce today. Enough exist of the Federal Reserve Notes that many varieties can be collected by those who combine the desire and ability to do so.

GOLD CERTIFICATES

The small-size Series of 1928 $1,000 Gold Certificate, featuring the portrait of former president Grover Cleveland, is similar in many design respects to the 1928 small-size Federal Reserve Note. Related Gold Certificates were produced under Series of 1934, by which time they were redundant, in view of president Franklin D. Roosevelt's orders ending the use of gold coins and gold-backed currency in circulation.

Of the Series of 1928 $1,000 Gold Certificates, 288,000 were printed, each with the Treasury signatures of Woods and Mellon. Mellon, who had signed currency earlier as president of the Mellon National Bank, became a controversial figure in the Roosevelt administration amid charges of scandal. Perhaps settling matters in his favor was his endowment of the Mellon Gallery of Art close to the Capitol in Washington, today a storehouse of national treasures. All notes have gold Treasury seals.

Series of 1928, Gold Seal
Woods-Mellon (1929–1932)

The obligation reads "One Thousand Dollars in gold coin payable to the bearer on demand." At the left the Treasury seal is overprinted on a more standard commentary, with GOLD above, CERTIFICATE below, and three lines between: "This certificate is a legal tender in the amount thereof in payment of all debts and dues private and public." In addition to the yellow (usually called gold) seal, the serial numbers were printed in yellow.

W-4800 • F-2408 • 28,800

VG-8	F-12	VF-20	EF-40	AU-50	Unc-60	Unc-63	Unc-65
$5,000	$8,500	$11,000	$17,500	$27,000	$35,000	$45,000	$87,500

W-4800★ • F-2408★
Commentary: Current market information not available.

Series of 1934, Gold Seal
Julian-Morgenthau (1934–1945)

This anomalous series was created in 1934, by which time the Treasury was not paying either gold coins or Gold Certificates into the channels of commerce. It is thought that the notes may have been intended for use in banking channels. The obligation is no longer payable in gold coins and now reads "One Thousand Dollars in gold payable to the bearer as authorized by law." Otherwise, the design is similar to the preceding. The back is printed in gold instead of green. None were released.

W-4805 • F-2409 • 84,000 • None in private hands

FEDERAL RESERVE NOTES

Small-size Federal Reserve Notes of the $1,000 denomination depicted Grover Cleveland, as did Gold Certificates of the era. These Federal Reserve Notes commenced with the Series of 1928 and continued through the Series of 1934-C. Without particular regard to the varieties, collectors eagerly seek these bills, which were last printed in the 1940s. Thousands of examples exist, making them a stock-in-trade item for paper-money dealers.

Every once in a while a cache comes on the market either from some long-hidden private stash or from overseas. In the late 1990s, a group of nearly 2,000 notes was offered, mostly in grades of Very Fine and Extremely Fine. These were said to have been found in Russia. Early in the 21st century a holding of 100 notes was sold. These were mostly

About Uncirculated, although some were improved and later marketed as choice Uncirculated examples.

The various series can be collected by Federal Reserve Bank locations, but only the Series of 1928 is complete with all 12 banks: Boston (designated with the letter A), consecutively through New York, Philadelphia, Cleveland, Richmond, Atlanta, Chicago, St. Louis, Minneapolis, Kansas City, Dallas, and San Francisco (designated with the letter L).

Generally, the Federal Reserve districts with lower populations issued fewer notes. Accordingly, bills imprinted for Boston, New York, Philadelphia, and Chicago are likely to be more available than those from Atlanta and Minneapolis.

Series of 1928, Green Seal
Woods-Mellon (1929–1932)

The obligation on these notes (illus. on p. 752) is in four lines in the field at the upper left: "Redeemable in gold on demand at the United States Treasury, or in gold or lawful money at any Federal Reserve Bank." The seal is in the left field and features the letter of the issuing Federal Reserve Bank (A to L). The series imprint appears twice: near the left border and near the right border.

Most varieties are readily available for those who can afford them. Star notes are very rare.

W-4810-A • F-2210A • Boston • 58,320

VF-20	EF-40	AU-50	Unc-60	Unc-63
$20,000	$25,000	—	—	$52,000

W-4810-A★ • F-2210A★
Commentary: Current market information not available.

W-4810-B • F-2210B • New York • 139,200

VF-20	EF-40	AU-50	Unc-60	Unc-63
$2,300	$2,500	—	—	$4,000

W-4810-B★ • F-2210B★

VF-20	EF-40
$37,500	$65,000

W-4810-C • F-2210C • Philadelphia • 96,708

VF-20	EF-40	AU-50	Unc-60	Unc-63
$2,300	$2,800	—	—	$4,500

W-4810-C★ • F-2210C★

VF-20
$27,500

W-4810-D • F-2210D • Cleveland • 79,680

VF-20	EF-40	AU-50	Unc-60	Unc-63
$2,600	$3,000	—	—	$4,500

W-4810-D★ • F-2210D★

VF-20
$35,000

SERIES OF 1928, GOLD SEAL

$1,000 Gold Certificate, Series of 1928 (W-4800). Portrait of Grover Cleveland.

Back of the $1,000 Gold Certificate, Series of 1928 (W-4800). The type used on all issued small-size $1,000 notes. Printed in green.

SERIES OF 1934, GOLD SEAL

$1,000 Gold Certificate, Series of 1934 (W-4805). Serial A00000001A, plate A2. Serially numbered, but never issued. (Smithsonian Institution)

Detail of the Treasury seal.

Back of the $1,000 Gold Certificate, Series of 1934 (W-4805). Plate 4. Printed in orange-gold. (Smithsonian Institution)

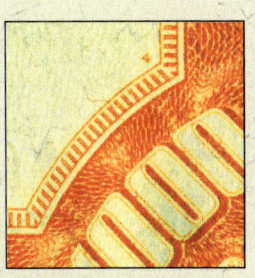

Detail of the plate number (4) at the right edge of the field.

W-4810-E • F-2210E • Richmond • 66,840

VF-20	EF-40	AU-50	Unc-60	Unc-63
$2,300	$2,800	—	—	$4,500

W-4810-E★ • F-2210E★

VF-20
$35,000

W-4810-F • F-2210F • Atlanta • 47,400

VF-20	EF-40	AU-50	Unc-60	Unc-63
$2,300	$2,800	—	—	$5,250

W-4810-F★ • F-2210F★

Commentary: Current market information not available.

W-4810-G • F-2210G • Chicago • 355,800

VF-20	EF-40	AU-50	Unc-60	Unc-63
$2,300	$2,700	—	—	$4,500

W-4810-G★ • F-2210G★

VF-20
$35,000

W-4810-H • F-2210H • St. Louis • 60,000

VF-20	EF-40	AU-50	Unc-60	Unc-63
$2,300	$2,800	—	—	$4,500

W-4810-H★ • F-2210H★

VF-20
$40,000

W-4810-I • F-2210I • Minneapolis • 26,640

VF-20	EF-40	AU-50	Unc-60	Unc-63
$2,500	$3,000	—	—	$6,000

W-4810-I★ • F-2210I★

VF-20
$35,000

W-4810-J • F-2210J • Kansas City • 62,172

VF-20	EF-40	AU-50	Unc-60	Unc-63
$2,300	$2,800	—	—	$5,250

W-4810-J★ • F-2210J★

Commentary: Current market information not available.

W-4810-K • F-2210K • Dallas • 42,960

VF-20	EF-40	AU-50	Unc-60	Unc-63
$2,900	$3,500	—	—	$6,000

W-4810-K★ • F-2210K★

Commentary: Current market information not available.

SERIES OF 1928, GREEN SEAL

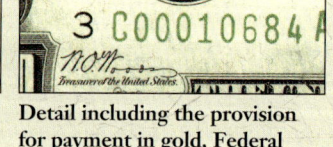

$1,000 Federal Reserve Note, Series of 1928 (W-4810-C), with green Treasury seal. Federal Reserve Bank of Philadelphia. The seal is not as dark as on some other 1928 denominations, but is a deeper shade than the light yellow-green seal.

Detail including the provision for payment in gold, Federal Reserve seal, and other imprints.

Back of the $1,000 Federal Reserve Note, Series of 1928 (W-4810-C), the standard type used on all small-size $1,000 notes.

W-4810-L • F-2210L • San Francisco • 67,920

VF-20	EF-40	AU-50	Unc-60	Unc-63
$2,300	$2,800	—	—	$5,250

W-4810-L★ • F-2210L★
Commentary: Current market information not available.

Series of 1928, Light Yellow-Green Seal
Woods-Mellon (1929–1932)

These notes continued the preceding design, except for the hue of the Treasury seal. As a class these are scarcer than the preceding. There are no star notes with this seal hue.

W-4815-E • F-2210E • Richmond • Part of W-4810-E printage

VG-8	F-12	VF-20	EF-40	AU-50	Unc-60	Unc-63	Unc-65
$1,400	$1,750	$2,400	$2,900	$3,500	$3,900	$6,100	$10,000

W-4815-G • F-2210E • Chicago • Part of W-4810-G printage

VG-8	F-12	VF-20	EF-40	AU-50	Unc-60	Unc-63
$1,350	$1,550	$1,950	$2,650	$3,000	$4,400	$6,500

W-4815-H • F-2210H • St. Louis • Part of W-4810-H printage

VG-8	F-12	VF-20	EF-40	AU-50	Unc-60	Unc-63
$1,350	$1,550	$1,950	$2,200	$2,600	$3,200	$5,000

W-4815-J • F-2210J • Kansas City • Part of W-4810-J printage

VG-8	F-12	VF-20	EF-40	AU-50	Unc-60	Unc-63
$1,400	$1,700	$2,400	$2,900	$3,500	$3,900	$6,250

W-4815-L • F-2210L • San Francisco • Part of W-4810-L printage

VG-8	F-12	VF-20	EF-40	AU-50	Unc-60	Unc-63
$1,375	$1,600	$2,200	$2,800	$3,250	$3,900	$6,250

Series of 1934, Light Yellow-Green Seal
Julian-Morgenthau (1934–1945)

The Series of 1934 continued the same general configuration as the preceding series, but now with a change in the redemption inscription that eliminates the mention of gold: "This note is legal tender for all debts, public and private, and is redeemable in lawful money at the United States Treasury, or at any Federal Reserve Bank."

$1,000 Federal Reserve Note, Series of 1928 (W-4815-G). Light yellow-green Treasury seal. Federal Reserve Bank of Chicago. The back is the standard type used on all small-size $1,000 notes.

Federal Reserve Note, Series of 1934 (W-4820-E). Light yellow-green Treasury seal. Federal Reserve Bank of Richmond. The back is the standard type used on all small-size $1,000 notes.

Examples are readily found and are mostly in circulated grades. There are no star notes with this seal hue.

W-4820-A • F-2211A • Boston • Part of W-4830-A printage

VG-8	F-12	VF-20	EF-40	AU-50	Unc-60	Unc-63	Unc-65
$1,400	$1,550	$1,825	$2,100	$2,450	$3,050	$4,000	$6,500

W-4820-B • F-2211B • New York • Part of W-4830-B printage

VG-8	F-12	VF-20	EF-40	AU-50	Unc-60	Unc-63	Unc-65
$1,350	$1,450	$1,725	$1,950	$2,200	$2,850	$3,700	$5,000

W-4820-C • F-2211C • Philadelphia • Part of W-4830-C printage

VG-8	F-12	VF-20	EF-40	AU-50	Unc-60	Unc-63	Unc-65
$1,375	$1,500	$1,825	$2,100	$2,400	$2,950	$3,800	$5,500

W-4820-D • F-2211D • Cleveland • Part of W-4830-D printage

VG-8	F-12	VF-20	EF-40	AU-50	Unc-60	Unc-63	Unc-65
$1,450	$1,675	$1,925	$2,200	$2,600	$3,250	$3,950	$5,500

W-4820-E • F-2211E • Richmond • Part of W-4830-E printage

VG-8	F-12	VF-20	EF-40	AU-50	Unc-60	Unc-63	Unc-65
$1,575	$1,800	$2,050	$2,400	$2,850	$3,750	$7,500	$13,500

W-4820-F • F-2211F • Atlanta • Part of W-4830-F printage

VG-8	F-12	VF-20	EF-40	AU-50	Unc-60	Unc-63	Unc-65
$1,450	$1,650	$1,875	$2,250	$2,550	$3,100	$3,850	$5,500

W-4820-G • F-2211G • Chicago • Part of W-4830-G printage

VG-8	F-12	VF-20	EF-40	AU-50	Unc-60	Unc-63	Unc-65
$1,350	$1,450	$1,750	$2,000	$2,300	$2,900	$3,750	$5,000

W-4820-H • F-2211H • St. Louis • Part of W-4830-H printage

VG-8	F-12	VF-20	EF-40	AU-50	Unc-60	Unc-63	Unc-65
$1,400	$1,550	$1,825	$2,100	$2,450	$3,050	$3,850	$5,500

W-4820-I • F-2211I • Minneapolis • Part of W-4830-I printage

VG-8	F-12	VF-20	EF-40	AU-50	Unc-60	Unc-63
$1,600	$1,900	$2,100	$2,500	$2,950	$3,750	$8,000

W-4820-J • F-2211J • Kansas City • Part of W-4830-J printage

VG-8	F-12	VF-20	EF-40	AU-50	Unc-60	Unc-63	Unc-65
$1,450	$1,650	$1,875	$2,250	$2,550	$3,100	$3,900	$5,500

W-4820-K • F-2211K • Dallas • Part of W-4830-K printage

VG-8	F-12	VF-20	EF-40	AU-50	Unc-60	Unc-63
$1,600	$1,750	$2,100	$2,500	$2,950	$3,750	$10,500

W-4820-L • F-2211L • San Francisco • Part of W-4830-L printage

VG-8	F-12	VF-20	EF-40	AU-50	Unc-60	Unc-63	Unc-65
$1,450	$1,625	$1,825	$2,250	$2,550	$3,200	$4,050	$6,600

Series of 1934, Green Seal
Julian-Morgenthau (1934–1945)

These continued the preceding design except for the hue of the Treasury seal. Most varieties are readily available for those who can afford them. Star notes range from rare to extremely rare.

W-4830-A • F-2211A • Boston • 46,200

VG-8	F-12	VF-20	EF-40	AU-50	Unc-60	Unc-63
$1,350	$1,500	$1,700	$1,975	$2,300	$2,800	$3,750

W-4830-A★ • F-2211A★

Commentary: Current market information not available.

W-4830-B • F-2211B • New York • 322,784

VG-8	F-12	VF-20	EF-40	AU-50	Unc-60	Unc-63	Unc-65
$1,300	$1,400	$1,650	$1,850	$2,150	$2,600	$3,500	$4,750

W-4830-B★ • F-2211B★

EF-40	AU-50	Unc-60	Unc-63
$20,000	—	$22,000	$25,000

$1,000 Federal Reserve Note, Series of 1934 (W-4830-G). Dark green Treasury seal. Federal Reserve Bank of Chicago. Standard back of $1,000 notes of the era.

W-4830-C • F-2211C • Philadelphia • 33,000

VG-8	F-12	VF-20	EF-40	AU-50	Unc-60	Unc-63
$1,325	$1,450	$1,700	$1,975	$2,300	$2,800	$3,600

W-4830-C★ • F-2211C★

VF-20	EF-40	AU-50	Unc-60	Unc-63	Unc-65
$6,000	$9,500	—	—	—	$35,000

W-4830-D • F-2211D • Cleveland • 35,400

VG-8	F-12	VF-20	EF-40	AU-50	Unc-60	Unc-63
$1,400	$1,600	$1,700	$1,975	$2,350	$2,800	$3,600

W-4830-D★ • F-2211D★

F-12	VF-20	EF-40	AU-50	Unc-60	Unc-63
$3,500	$5,500	$7,750	$12,000	—	$20,000

W-4830-E • F-2211E • Richmond • 19,560

VG-8	F-12	VF-20	EF-40	AU-50	Unc-60	Unc-63
$1,525	$1,700	$1,825	$2,250	$2,550	$3,200	$3,850

W-4830-E★ • F-2211E★

Commentary: Current market information not available.

W-4830-F • F-2211F • Atlanta • 67,800

VG-8	F-12	VF-20	EF-40	AU-50	Unc-60	Unc-63
$1,350	$1,500	$1,700	$1,975	$2,350	$2,800	$3,650

W-4830-F★ • F-2211F★

F-12	VF-20	EF-40
$3,750	$6,000	$9,500

W-4830-G • F-2211G • Chicago • 167,040

VG-8	F-12	VF-20	EF-40	AU-50	Unc-60	Unc-63	Unc-65
$1,300	$1,425	$1,675	$1,875	$2,200	$2,650	$3,550	$4,750

W-4830-G★ • F-2211G★

VG-8	F-12	VF-20	EF-40
$2,500	$3,000	$4,250	$7,000

W-4830-H • F-2211H • St. Louis • 22,400

VG-8	F-12	VF-20	EF-40	AU-50	Unc-60	Unc-63
$1,400	$1,550	$1,700	$1,975	$2,350	$2,800	$3,600

W-4830-H★ • F-2211H★

VF-20	EF-40
$7,000	$12,500

W-4830-I • F-2211I • Minneapolis • 12,000

VG-8	F-12	VF-20	EF-40	AU-50	Unc-60	Unc-63	Unc-65
$1,575	$1,800	$1,950	$2,350	$2,650	$3,300	$4,100	$7,500

W-4830-I★ • F-2211I★

VF-20	EF-40
$12,000	$16,000

W-4830-J • F-2211J • Kansas City • 51,840

VG-8	F-12	VF-20	EF-40	AU-50	Unc-60	Unc-63
$1,400	$1,600	$1,700	$1,975	$2,350	$2,800	$3,600

W-4830-J★ • F-2211J★

VF-20	EF-40
$6,750	$12,000

W-4830-K • F-2211K • Dallas • 46,800

VG-8	F-12	VF-20	EF-40	AU-50	Unc-60	Unc-63
$1,600	$1,900	$2,050	$2,450	$2,750	$3,500	$9,000

W-4830-K★ • F-2211K★

Commentary: Current market information not available.

W-4830-L • F-2211L • San Francisco • 90,600

VG-8	F-12	VF-20	EF-40	AU-50	Unc-60	Unc-63
$1,400	$1,600	$1,750	$1,975	$2,350	$2,800	$3,600

W-4830-L★ • F-2211L★

VF-20	EF-40
$4,750	$9,000

Series of 1934-A, Green Seal
Julian-Morgenthau (1934–1945)

There was no Dallas issue for this series. Most varieties are readily available for those who can afford them. Star notes are great rarities.

W-4835-A • F-2212A • Boston • 30,000

VG-8	F-12	VF-20	EF-40	AU-50	Unc-60	Unc-63
$1,350	$1,500	$1,675	$1,950	$2,300	$3,000	$3,500

W-4835-A★ • F-2212A★

Commentary: Current market information not available.

W-4835-B • F-2212B • New York • 174,348

VG-8	F-12	VF-20	EF-40	AU-50	Unc-60	Unc-63	Unc-65
$1,300	$1,400	$1,600	$1,850	$2,100	$2,600	$3,250	$4,300

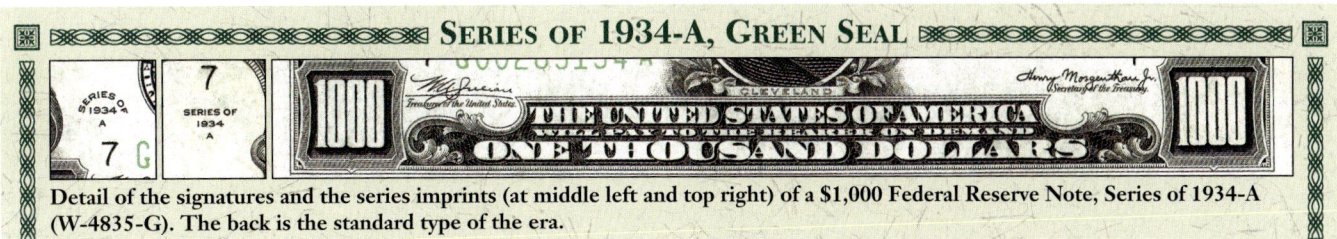

SERIES OF 1934-A, GREEN SEAL

Detail of the signatures and the series imprints (at middle left and top right) of a $1,000 Federal Reserve Note, Series of 1934-A (W-4835-G). The back is the standard type of the era.

W-4835-B★ • F-2212B★

VF-20
$18,500

W-4835-C • F-2212C • Philadelphia • 78,000

VG-8	F-12	VF-20	EF-40	AU-50	Unc-60	Unc-63
$1,350	$1,500	$1,675	$1,950	$2,250	$2,900	$3,450

W-4835-C★ • F-2212C★
Commentary: Current market information not available.

W-4835-D • F-2212D • Cleveland • 28,800

VG-8	F-12	VF-20	EF-40	AU-50	Unc-60	Unc-63
$1,350	$1,500	$1,675	$1,950	$2,300	$3,000	$3,500

W-4835-D★ • F-2212D★
Commentary: Current market information not available.

W-4835-E • F-2212E • Richmond • 16,800

VG-8	F-12	VF-20	EF-40	AU-50	Unc-60	Unc-63	Unc-65
$1,450	$1,600	$1,850	$2,200	$2,500	$3,400	$4,500	$9,500

W-4835-E★ • F-2212E★
Commentary: Current market information not available.

W-4835-F • F-2212F • Atlanta • 80,964

VG-8	F-12	VF-20	EF-40	AU-50	Unc-60	Unc-63
$1,350	$1,500	$1,675	$1,950	$2,250	$2,900	$3,450

W-4835-F★ • F-2212F★
Commentary: Current market information not available.

W-4835-G • F-2212G • Chicago • 134,400

VG-8	F-12	VF-20	EF-40	AU-50	Unc-60	Unc-63	Unc-65
$1,300	$1,400	$1,600	$1,850	$2,100	$2,600	$3,250	$4,400

W-4835-G★ • F-2212G★

VF-20	EF-40	AU-50	Unc-60	Unc-63
$7,000	$12,500	—	—	$19,000

W-4835-H • F-2212H • St. Louis • 39,600

VG-8	F-12	VF-20	EF-40	AU-50	Unc-60	Unc-63
$1,500	$1,650	$1,950	$2,300	$2,650	$3,050	$3,500

W-4835-H★ • F-2212H★
Commentary: Current market information not available.

W-4835-I • F-2212I • Minneapolis • 4,800

VG-8	F-12	VF-20	EF-40	AU-50	Unc-60	Unc-63
$1,700	$1,950	$2,150	$2,900	$4,500	$6,250	$8,000

W-4835-I★ • F-2212I★
Commentary: Current market information not available.

W-4835-J • F-2212J • Kansas City • 21,600

VG-8	F-12	VF-20	EF-40	AU-50	Unc-60	Unc-63
$1,350	$1,500	$1,675	$1,950	$2,300	$3,000	$3,500

W-4835-J★ • F-2212J★
Commentary: Current market information not available.

W-4835-L • F-2212L • San Francisco • 36,600

VG-8	F-12	VF-20	EF-40	AU-50	Unc-60	Unc-63
$1,350	$1,500	$1,675	$1,950	$2,300	$3,000	$3,500

W-4835-L★ • F-2212L★
Commentary: Current market information not available.

Series of 1934-C, Green Seal
Julian-Snyder (1946–1949)

There is no 1934-B series in the $1,000 denomination. Series of 1934-B notes of other denominations display a change in the wording in the Federal Reserve seal: THE is omitted, leaving FEDERAL RESERVE. The Series of 1934-C inaugurated the change for $1,000 notes. The point may be moot, as no examples have been reported to exist today.

W-4840-A • F-2213A • Boston • 1,200 • Unknown

W-4840-B • F-2213B • New York • 168 • Unknown

$1,000 Federal Reserve Note, Series of 1934-C (W-4840-B). Federal Reserve Bank of New York. Unissued specimen note with stars at each end of the serial numbers.

$5,000 NOTES

LARGE SIZE

Large-size notes of the $5,000 denomination were made in several different series from the 1860s through the 1920s. *Rare* is the operative word for all.

Early Interest-Bearing Notes were issued as investments, not as circulating paper money. Most were bought and held by banks and wealthy individuals. Early issues are mainly known to us through proof impressions, and all later varieties range from rare to exceedingly rare. Legal Tender Notes, Gold Certificates, and Federal Reserve Notes are so elusive as to be noncollectible, or nearly so.

INTEREST-BEARING NOTES

First Series, July 17, 1861, 7.3% Interest, 3 Years

On the left of the face is Justice holding scales uplifted in her right hand and a downward-facing sword in her left. At the top center is America in the form of a Native American woman with an eagle, a shield, and a tent in the background. Counters are at the left and right. Below center is an area of "Patent Green Tint" over the spelled-out denomination, with the patent date below. In the top border is AMERICAN BANK NOTE CO. NEW YORK. Five coupons are attached to the right border. The notes were printed three to a sheet by the American Bank Note Company. The back, printed in rich green, has UNITED STATES OF AMERICA as its boldest feature.

W-4900 • F-211 • Chittenden-Spinner (1861–1864) • *Printed on plate:* AUGUST 19, 1861 • Unknown

W-4910 • F-211 • *Printed on plate:* OCT. 1, 1861 • Unknown

March 3, 1863, 5% Interest, 1 Year

At the center of the face (illus. on p. 758) is a seated figure of a woman near an altar depicting George Washington, a vignette variously designated by the Treasury as *America Offering Her Jewels* and *Wealth Offering Up Her Jewels.*[1] A jewel box and pitcher are at her feet. She holds a pendant, which she is about to consign to the flames. Denomination counters are to each side.

Likely, such notes were issued more or less continually with various dates imprinted on the face. These were sold at a discount to reflect the interest and redeemed at face value upon maturity. These were intended to have a wider appeal than coupon-bearing notes and also to be suitable for overseas investors.

W-4920 • F-202 • Chittenden-Spinner (1861–1864) • Unknown

June 30, 1864, 7.3% Interest, 3 Years

The design of this issue is not known. The notes were issued with five coupons attached to the right border.

W-4930 • F-211 • Colby-Spinner (1864–1867) • *Printed on plate:* AUGUST 15, 1864 • 4,166 • Unknown

FIRST SERIES, JULY 17, 1861, 7.3% INTEREST, 3 YEARS

$5,000 Interest-Bearing Note (W-4900). Proof impression.

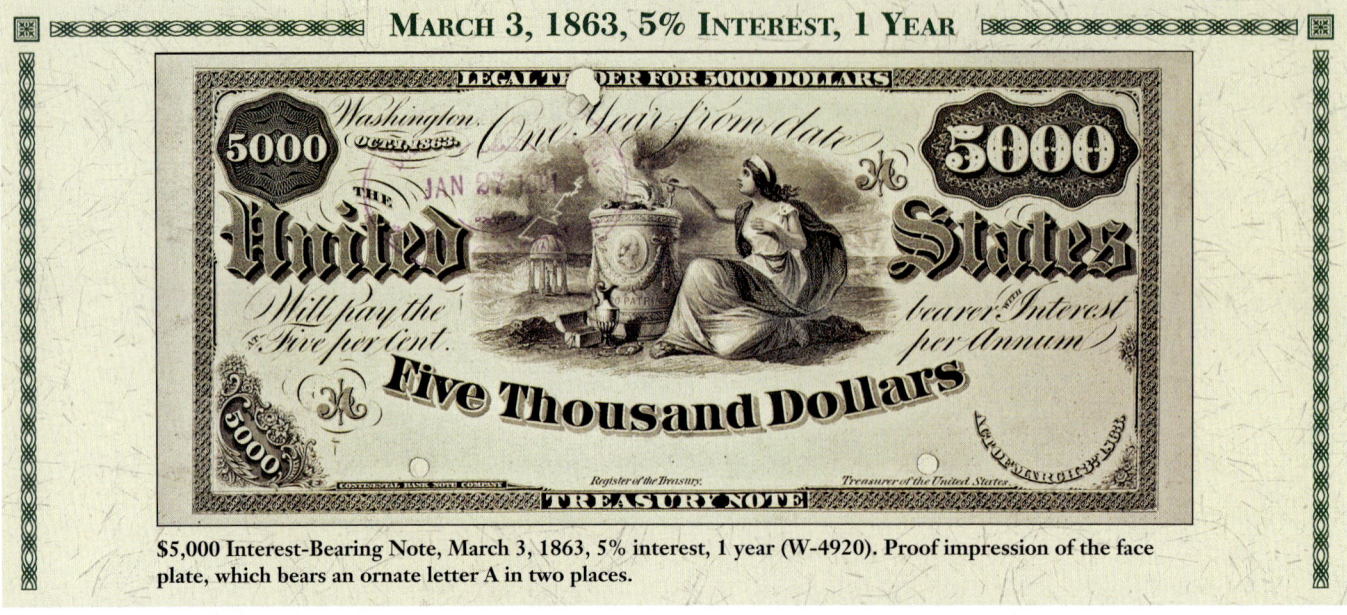

MARCH 3, 1863, 5% INTEREST, 1 YEAR

$5,000 Interest-Bearing Note, March 3, 1863, 5% interest, 1 year (W-4920). Proof impression of the face plate, which bears an ornate letter A in two places.

W-4940 • F-211 • *Printed on plate:* MARCH 3, 1865 • Unknown, if any[2]

March 3, 1865, 7.3% Interest, 3 Years

The design of this issue is not known. The notes were issued with five coupons attached to the right border.

W-4950 • F-211 • Colby-Spinner (1864–1867) • *Printed on plate:* JUNE 15, 1865 • 4,045 • Unknown

W-4960 • F-211 • *Printed on plate:* JULY 15, 1865 • 1,684 • Unknown

LEGAL TENDER NOTES
(Also Known as United States Notes)

Series of 1878

At the left of the face is a portrait of president James Madison. At the center top is a counter in gold, and below it is a large Treasury seal in either brown, pink, or red. At the right is a counter. The gold printing is highly unusual for a Legal Tender Note, as this color is usually associated with Gold Certificates. On the back is an eagle perched on a shield, atop a rock overlooking the sea. There are vertical counters to each side. It is believed the issued notes had Z-prefix serials.

W-4970 • F-188 • Scofield-Gilfillan (1878–1881) • Large brown seal with spiked border • 4,000 • Unknown

W-4973 • F-unlisted • Medium-size pink seal with plain border • Specimen with A prefix and six zeros.

W-4975 • F-unlisted • Large red seal with spiked border • Specimen with serial of three solid stars

GOLD CERTIFICATES

Act of March 3, 1863

Gold Certificates of this and other denominations were issued under the Act of March 3, 1863. These notes (illus. on p. 760) have the standard eagle and shield design, a counter in a lacy green overprint, and a small red Treasury seal with a spiked border at the lower right. ENGRAVED AND PRINTED AT THE TREASURY DEPARTMENT is imprinted below the top border.

At the left of the face is a patriotic depiction of the American eagle on a shield with arrows, an olive branch, and a flag as part of the suite, and E PLURIBUS UNUM lettered above. These were mostly made with the New York Sub-Treasury imprint, but a few were printed for Washington. The New York notes were very popular in their time and were widely held by banks as gold reserves.

W-4980 • F-1166f • New York imprint • Colby-Spinner (1864–1867) • Small red seal with spiked border • 93,400

Recorded population: 1 • *Commentary:* An autographed countersignature of an assistant Treasurer of the United States is on all. • *Selected information:* The known example is serial 42023/C, VF, canceled, ozwned by the Bureau of the Public Debt in Washington, D.C.

W-4982 • F-1166f • Washington imprint • 600 printed • None delivered to Treasurer[3]

Commentary: An autographed countersignature of an assistant Treasurer of the United States is on all (if issued).

Series of 1870

Series of 1870 and 1875 notes have a portrait of James Madison at the left and a large Treasury seal at the center. A proof has as a counter an I and two backward C letters (illus. on p. 761), the meaning of which could not have been clear to the typical viewer. At least some issued notes had the counter in numerals, as 5000, following the style of other Series of 1870 notes, and may have been altered from the earlier plate. These are printed on one side only. To the left above the bottom border is a space for an autographed signature, below which is imprinted ASSISTANT TREAS-URER, N.Y. To the right are spaces imprinted for the addition of two autographed signatures, REGISTER OF THE TREASURY and TREASURER OF THE UNITED

SERIES OF 1878

$5,000 Legal Tender Note, Series of 1878. Portrait of James Madison to the left. Illustrated is a specimen note (with stars in place of serial numbers) with large red seal with spiked border (W-4975).

$5,000 Legal Tender Note as preceding (W-4973). Another specimen note, but with smaller pink seal with plain border.

Back of Legal Tender Note, Series of 1878. Eagle perched on a shield facing right. United States Capitol in distance to the left. Illustrated is a specimen note.

STATES. Certain Series of 1870 notes of the $5,000 and $10,000 denominations were signed by Allison and Gilfillan, although their joint tenure was in the era of the later Series of 1875 notes.

W-4990 • F-unlisted • With counter as an "I" and two backward "C" letters • Unknown, if printed

W-4992 • F-1166k • Allison-Gilfillan (1877–1878) and the assistant Treasurer at New York (all autographed) • Large pink seal with spiked border • Counter as 5000 • 40,000 • Unknown

Series of 1875

These notes continued the preceding design. The numerical counter is used. Assistant Treasurer autographed signature.

W-5000 • F-unlisted • Allison-Gilfillan (1875–1876) • Large pink seal with spiked border • 1,000[4] • Unknown

Series of 1882

A portrait of James Madison is at the upper left of the face, a Treasury seal is at the center, and a counter is at the upper right. The back has UNITED STATES GOLD CERTIFICATE at the center, the number 5000 to the left, and a perched eagle to the right.

The earliest issues have a countersignature of Thomas C. Acton, assistant Treasurer at the United States Sub-Treasury.

W-5005 • F-1221a • Bruce-Gilfillan (1881–1883) • Countersignature: Thomas C. Acton (autographed) • Medium-size brown seal with scalloped border • 4,000 • Unknown

W-5008 • F-1221 • Bruce-Gilfillan (1881–1883) • No countersignature • 500 • Unknown

W-5012 • F-1221b • Bruce-Wyman (1883–1885) • 4,000 • Unknown

W-5015 • F-1221c • Rosecrans-Hyatt (1887–1889) • Large red seal • 4,000 • Unknown

W-5017 • F-1221d • Rosecrans-Nebeker (1891–1893) • Small red seal with scalloped border • 4,000 • Unknown

W-5019 • F-1221e • Lyons-Roberts (1898–1905) • 16,000 • Unknown

W-5022 • F-unlisted • Lyons-Treat (1905–1906) • 4,000 • Unknown

W-5024 • F-1221f • Vernon-Treat (1906–1909) • 4,000 • Unknown

W-5026 • F-1221g • Vernon-McClung (1909–1911) • 4,000 • Unknown

W-5029 • F-1221h • Napier-McClung (1911–1912) • No evidence of printing

W-5031 • F-unlisted • Napier-Thompson (1912–1913) • 4,000 • Unknown

W-5033 • F-1221i • Parker-Burke (1913–1914) • 16,000 • Unknown

W-5036 • F-1221j • Teehee-Burke (1915–1919) • 32,000

Recorded population: 2 • Selected information: The known examples are serials M20625/A, VF, owned by the Federal

$5,000 Gold Certificate, Act of March 3, 1863 (W-4980), issued and later redeemed. With autographed countersignature of the assistant Treasurer at the New York Sub-Treasury, H.H. Van Dyck. Serial 42023/C.

$5,000 Gold Certificate, Act of March 3, 1863 (W-4982), Colby-Spinner Treasury signatures and space for the addition by hand of a countersignature. Washington imprint. Proof impression, plate A. (Smithsonian Institution)

Reserve Bank of San Francisco, and M26080/D, used to illustrate early editions of Friedberg.

Series of 1888

The face of this type (illus. on p. 762) displays a portrait of James Madison to the left and a counter to the right. The cen-

ter is configured slightly differently from the earlier series. Space is provided at the bottom left for the autographed signature of the assistant U.S. Treasurer in New York City. The Series of 1888 notes are overlapped by the preceding in terms of the dates of the Treasury signatories. They were printed by $5,000-$5,000-$5,000 three-subject plates.

SERIES OF 1870

$5,000 Gold Certificate, Series of 1870 (W-4990). Proof with counter as I and two backward C letters. (Smithsonian Institution)

SERIES OF 1882

$5,000 Gold Certificate, Series of 1882 (W-5005), Bruce-Gilfillan Treasury signatures and imprinted space for the addition by hand of a countersignature. Specimen printing without countersignature.

$5,000 Gold Certificate, Series of 1882 (W-5036), Teehee-Burke Treasury signatures. The last variety in the series.

SERIES OF 1888

$5,000 Gold Certificate, Series of 1888 (W-5040). Proof impression. (Smithsonian Institution)

W-5040 • F-1222 • Rosecrans-Hyatt (1887–1889) • Large red seal • B prefix to serial number • 6,000 • Unknown

W-5042 • F-1222 • D prefix to serial number • 7,500 • Unknown

Commentary: Deliveries began on March 19, 1888, and ended on December 19, 1889.

W-5050 • F-1222a • Rosecrans-Nebeker (1891–1893) • Small red seal • B prefix to serial number • 3,000 • Unknown

Commentary: The only delivery was made on November 19, 1891.

FEDERAL RESERVE NOTES

Series of 1918, Blue Seal

The face depicts a James Madison portrait, engraved by Alfred Sealey after a James B. Longacre painting (in the National Portrait Gallery). The face layout is generic, with a Federal Reserve Bank seal widely spaced from the border and large district numbers and letters in each corner. The back is a vignette of *Washington Resigning His Commission*, from a painting by John Trumbull, one of a series depicting scenes from American history. These bills were probably used primarily for bank-to-bank transactions and settlements, not for general circulation.

W-5060-A • F-1134 • Boston • Burke-Glass (1918–1920) • 2,800 • Unknown

W-5065-B • F-1134 • New York • 5,200

Recorded population: 2 • *Commentary:* The known examples are serials B1A/A, Unc, part of the Smithsonian Institution collection, and B2A/B, G, damaged, owned by the Federal Reserve Bank of Chicago.

W-5070-C • F-1134 • Philadelphia • 2,000 • Unknown

W-5075-D • F-1134 • Cleveland • 800

Recorded population: 1 • *Commentary:* The known example is serial D1A/A, Unc, part of the Smithsonian Institution collection.

W-5080-E • F-1134 • Richmond • 1,600 • Unknown

W-5085-F • F-1134 • Atlanta • 400 • Unknown

W-5090-G • F-1134 • Chicago • 2,800

Recorded population: 1 • *Commentary:* The known example is serial G1A/A, Unc, owned by the Federal Reserve Bank of San Francisco.

W-5095-H • F-1134 • St. Louis • 1,200 • Unknown

W-5100-K • F-1134 • Dallas • 1,200 • Unknown

W-5105-L • F-1134 • San Francisco • 3,200

Recorded population: 1 • *Graded:* Unc • *Commentary:* Owned by the Federal Reserve Bank of San Francisco.

W-5110-L • F-1134 • White-Mellon (1921–1928) • 400 • Unknown

SMALL SIZE

Small-size Federal Reserve Notes and Gold Certificates, each depicting James Madison on the face (the same portrait as used on the $5,000 Legal Tender Notes of 1878), were issued. The Gold Certificates are noncollectible, and the Federal Reserve Notes are very elusive today—even scarcer than the higher-denomination $10,000 bills. *Any* example is a first-class trophy note.

GOLD CERTIFICATES

The face of the $5,000 Gold Certificate features a portrait of James Madison. The back has counters prominent in three places and an ample open area at the center. The Treasury seal is at the left and is imprinted in gold, as are the serial numbers.

Series of 1928, Gold Seal
Woods-Mellon (1929–1932)

The obligation or payable notice reads "Five Thousand Dollars in gold coin payable to the bearer on demand." At the left the Treasury seal is overprinted on a more standard commentary, with GOLD above, CERTIFICATE below,

SERIES OF 1918, BLUE SEAL

$5,000 Federal Reserve Note, Series of 1918 (W-5105-L). Federal Reserve Bank of San Francisco (note from the FRBSF museum).

Back of the $5,000 Federal Reserve Note, Series of 1918 (W-5105-L).

and three lines between: "This certificate is a legal tender in the amount thereof in payment of all debts and dues private and public." In addition to the yellow (usually called gold) seal, the serial numbers were printed in yellow.

One verified note, serial 1, is in the Smithsonian Institution.

W-5150 • F-2410 • In the Smithsonian Institution

FEDERAL RESERVE NOTES

The $5,000 Federal Reserve Note has designs similar to the Gold Certificate, but with different face typography. A Federal Reserve Bank seal is at the left, and to the right is a green Treasury seal. This denomination was first made as the Series of 1928, then later as the Series of 1934 (most often seen today), then in limited numbers in Series 1934-A and 1934-B, the last uncertain.

These bear the imprint of the various Federal Reserve Bank districts, with the Series of 1928 notes printed for Boston, New York, Philadelphia, Cleveland, Richmond, Atlanta, Chicago, St. Louis, Dallas, and San Francisco. No star notes were printed.

Today, fewer than a dozen of the Series of 1928 $5,000 notes exist. Series of 1934 notes are great rarities as well. The denomination has great appeal as trophy notes, with great interest when one crosses the auction block.

Series of 1928, Green Seal
Woods-Mellon (1929–1932)

The obligation appears in four lines in the field at the upper left: "Redeemable in gold on demand at the United States Treasury, or in gold or lawful money at any Federal Reserve Bank." On Series of 1928 notes (illus. on p. 764) the seal in the left field features the number of the issuing Federal Reserve Bank (1 to 12). The series imprint appears twice: at the upper left of Madison's portrait and below WASHINGTON at the lower right.

These were made for nine of the 12 Federal Reserve Banks. All are very rare today. No star notes were printed.

W-5204-A • F-2220A • Boston • 1,320

AU-50
$160,000

W-5204-B • F-2220B • New York • Unknown

W-5204-D • F-2220D • Cleveland • Unknown

W-5204-E • F-2220E • Richmond • 3,984

VF-20
$110,000

W-5204-F • F-2220F • Atlanta • 1,440

VF-20	EF-40	AU-50
$100,000	—	$160,000

W-5204-G • F-2220G • Chicago • 3,480

F-12	VF-20	EF-40	AU-50
$90,000	$100,000	—	$160,000

W-5204-J • F-2220J • Kansas City • 720

F-12
$100,000

W-5204-K • F-2220K • Dallas • Unknown

W-5204-L • F-2220L • San Francisco • Unknown

Series of 1934, Light Yellow-Green Seal
Julian-Morgenthau (1934–1945)

The Series of 1934 continued the same general configuration as the preceding series, but now with a change in the redemption inscription that eliminates the mention of gold: "This note is legal tender for all debts, public and private, and is redeemable in lawful money at the United States Treasury, or at any Federal Reserve Bank."

These were made for 11 of the 12 Federal Reserve Banks. Similar to the preceding, the Series of 1934 $5,000 notes are very rare today. No star notes were printed.

W-5206-A • F-2221A • Boston • 9,480

F-12	VF-20	EF-40	AU-50
$65,000	$85,000	$110,000	$130,000

W-5206-B • F-2221B • New York • 11,520

VF-20	EF-40	AU-50
$80,000	$100,000	$120,000

W-5206-C • F-2221C • Philadelphia • 3,000

VF-20	EF-40
$90,000	$120,000

W-5206-D • F-2221D • Cleveland • Unknown

W-5206-E • F-2221E • Richmond • 2,400

VF-20	EF-40	AU-50	Unc-60	Unc-63	Unc-65
$85,000	—	—	—	$175,000	$220,000

W-5206-F • F-2221F • Atlanta • 3,600

F-12	VF-20	EF-40	AU-50
$80,000	—	—	$160,000

W-5206-G • F-2221G • Chicago • 6,600

F-12	VF-20	EF-40	AU-50	Unc-60
$60,000	$75,000	$90,000	$110,000	$120,000

SERIES OF 1928, GREEN SEAL

$5,000 Federal Reserve Note, Series of 1928 (W-5204-A). Federal Reserve Bank of Boston. The face printing notes that the bill is payable "in gold or lawful money."

Back of the $5,000 Federal Reserve Note, Series of 1928 (W-5204-A). The type used on all small-size $5,000 notes.

W-5206-H • F-2221H • St. Louis • 2,400

VF-20	EF-40	AU-50
$80,000	$100,000	$120,000

W-5206-J • F-2221J • Kansas City • 2,400

VF-20	EF-40	AU-50
$80,000	$100,000	$120,000

W-5206-K • F-2221K • Dallas • 2,400

F-12	VF-20	EF-40	AU-50	Unc-60	Unc-63
$60,000	$75,000	$90,000	$110,000	$120,000	$160,000

W-5206-L • F-2221L • San Francisco • 6,000

EF-40
$125,000

Series of 1934-A, Green Seal
Julian-Morgenthau (1934–1945)

This is one of the icons among small-size notes. Only 1,440 were printed. None are known today.

W-5208-H • F-2222H • St. Louis • 1,440 • Unknown

Series of 1934-B, Green Seal
Julian-Vinson (1945–1946)

Series of 1934-B notes display a change in the wording in the Federal Reserve seal: THE is omitted, leaving FEDERAL RESERVE. This was used across all denominations.

The printing of just 12 notes for the Federal Reserve Bank of New York is remarkable. No issued examples from either of the two Federal Reserve Banks are known today.

W-5212-A • F-2223A • Boston • 1,200 • Unknown

W-5212-B • F-2223B • New York • 12 • Unknown

$5,000 Federal Reserve Note, Series of 1934 (W-5206-E). Federal Reserve Bank of Richmond.

$5,000 Federal Reserve Note, Series of 1934-B (W-5212-B). Federal Reserve Bank of New York. Unissued specimen note with stars at each end of the serial numbers.

$10,000 NOTES

LARGE SIZE

Large-size notes of the $10,000 denomination range from nonexistent to extremely rare today. An exception to the rule is the curious 1900 Gold Certificate, printed on one side. These exist by the hundreds today but are of no redemption value, as all are punch-canceled.

LEGAL TENDER NOTES
(Also Known as United States Notes)

Series of 1878

The face has a portrait of president Andrew Jackson at the left and a denomination counter printed "10.000" to the right, a period being used in the place of a comma. The $1,000 and $5,000 notes had neither periods nor commas, but it seems that a visual break was needed for this value. On the back is a perched eagle on a shield atop a rock.

W-5300 • F-189 • Scofield-Gilfillan (1878–1881) • Large brown seal • 4,000 • Unknown

GOLD CERTIFICATES

Act of March 3, 1863

Gold Certificates of this and other denominations were issued under the Act of March 3, 1863. "Engraved and Printed at the Treasury Department" is imprinted above the bottom border to the right of the center. Presumably, circulating examples of the $10,000 note were issued with "10.000" in a lacy green overprint on the face and a small red Treasury seal with a spiked border, as this would be consistent with the other denominations in the series.

At the left of the face is a patriotic depiction of the American eagle on a shield with arrows, an olive branch, and a flag as part of the suite, and E PLURIBUS UNUM lettered above. The note is payable at the New York Sub-Treasury, which at the time was under the direction of John J. Cisco, an entrepreneur who was able to build considerable wealth during this era. The back displays ornate engraving with counters reading "10.000" in each corner. Notes of this denomination were printed only for New York.

W-5310 • F-1166g • New York imprint only • Colby-Spinner (1864–1867) • Small red seal with spiked border • 21,000 • Unknown

Commentary: An autographed countersignature of the assistant Treasurer of the United States is on all.

Series of 1870

The face of the Series of 1870 notes shows Jackson at the left, a large Treasury seal at the center (on issued notes), and a counter at the right with CC, I, and two backward C letters,

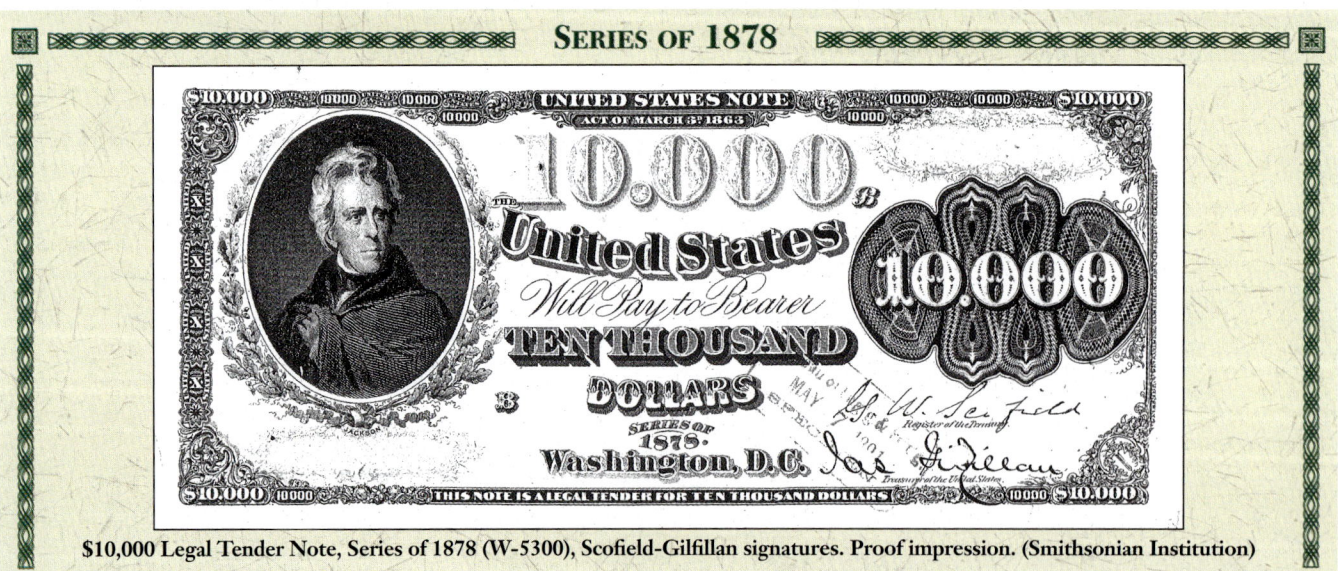

SERIES OF 1878

$10,000 Legal Tender Note, Series of 1878 (W-5300), Scofield-Gilfillan signatures. Proof impression. (Smithsonian Institution)

the meaning of which could not have been clear to the typical viewer. At least some (perhaps all) issued notes had the counter as "10.000" or similar, and may have been altered from the earlier plate. These are printed on one side only. To the left above the bottom border is a space for an autographed signature, below which is imprinted ASSISTANT TREASURER, N.Y. To the right are spaces imprinted for the addition of two autographed signatures, REGISTER OF THE TREASURY and TREASURER OF THE UNITED STATES. Certain Series of 1870 notes of the $5,000 denomination were signed by Allison and Gilfillan, although their joint tenure was in the era of the later Series of 1875 notes.

W-5320 • F-unlisted • With CC, I, and two backward C letters • Unknown, if issued

W-5322 • F-1166l • Allison-Gilfillan (1877–1878) and the assistant Treasurer at New York (all autographed) • Large pink seal with spiked border • 20,000 • Unknown

Series of 1875

The face of the Series of 1875 notes (illus. on p. 768) is similar to that of the Series of 1870, with Jackson at the left and a large Treasury seal at the center. On the Series of 1875 notes the counter is printed "10.000." To the left above the bottom border is a space for an autographed signature, below which is imprinted ASSISTANT TREASURER, N.Y. To the right are the two printed Treasury signatures. These notes are printed on one side only.

W-5330 • F-1166q • Allison-New (1875–1876) and Maxwell White (autographed) • Large pink seal with spiked border • 5,000

Recorded population: 1 • *Selected information:* The known example is serial B3/C, F, punch canceled, owned by the Bureau of the Public Debt in Washington, D.C.

$10,000 Gold Certificate, Act of March 3, 1863 (W-5310), Colby-Spinner Treasury signatures and space for the addition by hand of a countersignature. Proof impression, plate A. (Smithsonian Institution)

$10,000 Gold Certificate, Series of 1870 (W-5322). Proof with counter as CC, I, and two backward C letters. (Smithsonian Institution)

W-5334 • F-1166q • Allison-Wyman (1876–1877) • Red seal • 5,760 • Unknown

W-5336 • F-1166q • Allison-Gilfillan (1877–1878) • 4,000 • Unknown

Series of 1882

A portrait of Jackson is at the left of this note, a Treasury seal is at the center, and there is a counter at the right. The back shows a counter to the left, GOLD in large letters in the

SERIES OF 1875

$10,000 Gold Certificate, Series of 1875 (W-5330). With printed signatures of Treasury officials Allison and New and the autographed signature of assistant Treasurer Maxwell White. Serial B3, plate C. Ink-dated Jan'y 5, 1876. (Martin Gengerke; held by the Bureau of the Public Debt)

SERIES OF 1882

$10,000 Gold Certificate, Series of 1882 (W-5370). Face with portrait of Andrew Jackson to the left. Gold overprint. (Federal Reserve Bank of San Francisco Museum)

Back of the $10,000 Gold Certificate, Series of 1882 (W-5370), with a small perched eagle at right.

bottom center of the field, and the *Eagle of the Capitol*, a familiar motif, at the right.

The earliest notes have the countersignature of Thomas C. Acton, assistant Treasurer at the New York Sub-Treasury.

W-5340 • F-1223a • Bruce-Gilfillan (1881–1883) • Countersignature: Thomas C. Acton (autographed) • Medium-size brown seal with scalloped border • 8,000 • Unknown

W-5344 • F-1223 • Bruce-Gilfillan (1881–1883) • No countersignature • 500 • Unknown

W-5347 • F-1223b • Bruce-Wyman (1883–1885) • 4,000 • Unknown

W-5350 • F-1223c • Rosecrans-Hyatt (1887–1889) • Large red seal • 4,000 • Unknown

W-5354 • F-1223d • Rosecrans-Nebeker (1891–1893) • Small red seal with scalloped border • 4,000 • Unknown

W-5357 • F-1223e • Lyons-Roberts (1898–1905) • 7,000 • Unknown

W-5358 • F-unlisted • Lyons-Treat (1905–1906) • 4,000 • Unknown

W-5360 • F-1223f • Vernon-Treat (1906–1909) • 4,000 • Unknown

W-5363 • F-unlisted • Vernon-McClung (1909–1911) • 4,000 • Unknown

W-5365 • F-unlisted • Napier-Burke (1913) • 4,000 • Unknown

W-5367 • F-unlisted • Parker-Burke (1913–1914) • 12,000 • Unknown

W-5370 • F-1223g • Teehee-Burke (1915–1919) • 108,000
Recorded population: 2 • *Highest graded:* F–VF • *Commentary:* The known examples are serials K31071/A, VF, owned by the Federal Reserve Bank of San Francisco, and K56991/C, EF, used as an illustration in early editions of Friedberg.

Series of 1888

A portrait of Jackson is on the left of the face, and there is a counter printed "10.000" at the upper right. Two Treasury signatures are printed. At the lower left of the bottom is a space for the autographed signature of the assistant U.S. Treasurer at the Sub-Treasury in New York City. These were printed in configurations of $10,000-$10,000-$10,000, on three-subject plates. They are printed on one side only.

W-5380 • F-1224 • Rosecrans-Hyatt (1887–1889) • Large red seal • B prefix to serial number • 6,000 • Unknown

W-5382 • F-1224 • D prefix to serial number • 4,500 • Unknown
Commentary: Deliveries began on February 29, 1888, and ended on December 19, 1889.

W-5385 • F-1224a • Rosecrans-Nebeker (1891–1893) • Small red seal with scalloped border • B prefix to serial number • 3,000 • Unknown
Commentary: The only delivery was made on November 21, 1891. This would have included both B and D prefixes.

W-5387 • F-1224a • D prefix to serial number • 4,500 • Unknown

Series of 1900

Series of 1900 Gold Certificates of the $10,000 denomination (illus. on p. 770) have a portrait of Jackson at the left, a counter at the right, and a small red Treasury seal with a scalloped border at the lower right.

These were printed on one side only, from $10,000-$10,000-$10,000 three-subject plates. The notes were not used in general commerce. They were payable to various financial institutions, as inked on the face, or have printed addresses of Sub-Treasuries in Baltimore, Boston, Chicago, Cincinnati, New Orleans, New York, Philadelphia, St. Louis, San Francisco, and Washington. Production was extensive and amounted to 363,000 notes. By the mid-1930s most, if not all, had been punch-canceled.

$10,000 Gold Certificate, Series of 1888 (W-5385). Proof impression. (Smithsonian Institution)

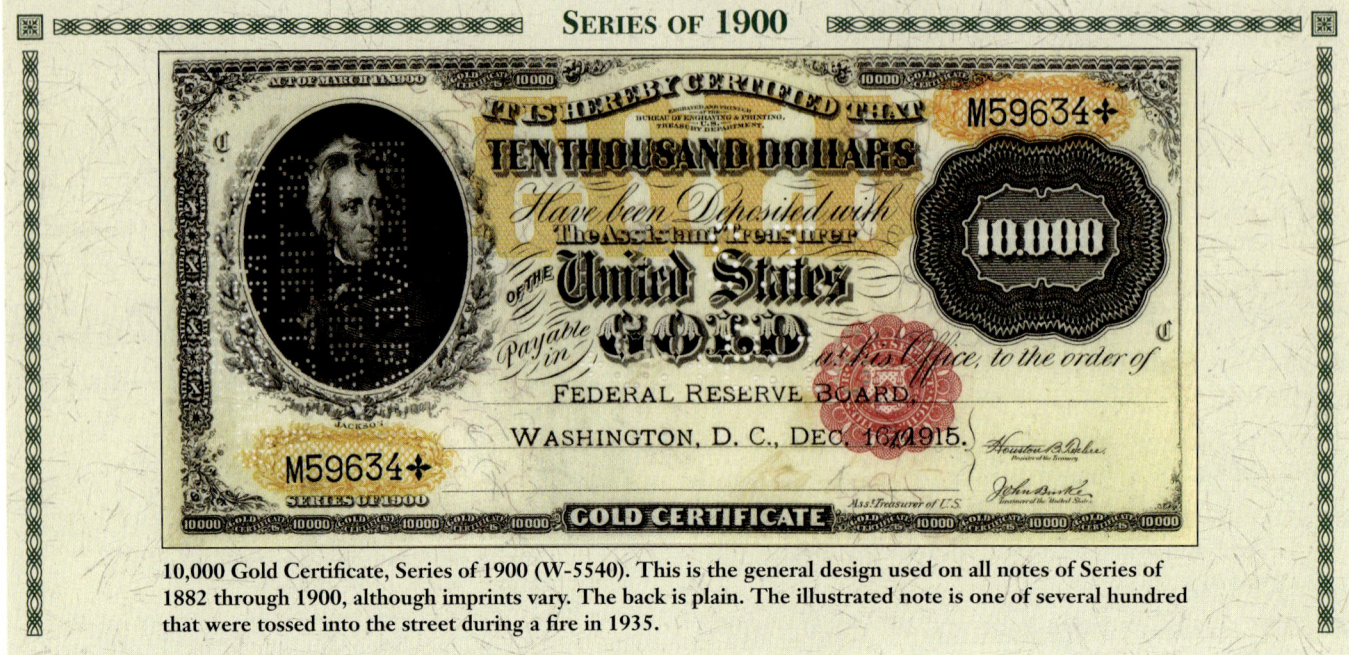

SERIES OF 1900

10,000 Gold Certificate, Series of 1900 (W-5540). This is the general design used on all notes of Series of 1882 through 1900, although imprints vary. The back is plain. The illustrated note is one of several hundred that were tossed into the street during a fire in 1935.

On December 13, 1935, a fire raged within the post office at 13th Street and Pennsylvania Avenue in Washington, D.C., where many canceled notes were in storage. Boxes and cabinets of paper files and documents were thrown out the windows in an effort to save them. Bystanders were amazed and delighted to see hundreds of these $10,000 bills fluttering around on the street. While most were recovered by the government, many were not.

Since that time they have been popular collectibles, although Robert Friedberg's *Paper Money of the United States* observes that "possession is illegal." However, the Treasury department has taken a benign view toward this. Whether the Treasury will remain passive in the future remains to be seen. If the government would "pardon" these bills, their collection would undoubtedly become more widespread.[1] Martin Gengerke's 2008 census listed 365 notes reported to him.

W-5400 • F-1225a • Lyons-Roberts (1898–1905) • Small red seal • 36,000

Recorded population: 4 • *Highest graded:* EF • *Commentary:* Deliveries began on April 7, 1900, and ended on October 16, 1905. Serials E1 to E36000.

F-12	VF-20	EF-40
$900	—	$2,000

W-5420 • F-1225b • Lyons-Treat (1905–1906) • 6,000

Recorded population: 7 • *Highest graded:* EF • *Commentary:* Deliveries began on February 12, 1906, and ended on the next day. Serials H1 to H6000.

W-5440 • F-1225c • Vernon-Treat (1906–1909) • 36,000

Estimated population: 28 to 32 • *Highest graded:* Unc • *Commentary:* Deliveries began on September 25, 1906, and ended on July 2, 1909. Serials H6001 to H42000.

F-12	VF-20	EF-40	AU-50	Unc-60	Unc-63
$650	$1,000	$1,500	$1,800	$2,250	$3,000

W-5460 • F-1225d • Vernon-McClung (1909–1911) • 18,000

Recorded population: 3 • *Highest graded:* VF • *Commentary:* Deliveries began on December 14, 1909, and ended on March 7, 1911. Serials K1 to K18000.

W-5480 • F-1225e • Napier-McClung (1911–1912) • 18,000

Estimated population: 27 to 32 • *Highest graded:* Unc • *Commentary:* Deliveries began on October 5, 1911, and ended on November 6, 1911. Serials K18001 to K36000.

F-12	VF-20	EF-40	AU-50	Unc-60	Unc-63
$650	$1,000	$1,500	$1,800	$2,250	$3,000

W-5500 • F-1225f • Napier-Burke (1913) • 6,000 • Unknown

Commentary: The only delivery was made on December 17, 1913. Serials M1 to M6000.

W-5520 • F-1225g • Parker-Burke (1913–1914) • 30,000

Recorded population: 8 • *Highest graded:* EF • *Commentary:* Deliveries began on February 18, 1914, and ended on March 20, 1915. Serials M6001 to M36000.

W-5540 • F-1225h • Teehee-Burke (1915–1919) • 213,000

Estimated population: 325 to 375 • *Highest graded:* Unc • *Commentary:* Deliveries began on April 24, 1915, and ended on July 16, 1917. Serials M36001 to M249000.

F-12	VF-20	EF-40	AU-50	Unc-60	Unc-63
$500	$800	$1,250	$1,500	$1,900	$2,500

FEDERAL RESERVE NOTES

Series of 1918, Blue Seal

A portrait of Salmon P. Chase is at the center. The face layout is generic, with a Federal Reserve Bank seal widely spaced from the border and large district numbers and letters in each corner.

SERIES OF 1918, BLUE SEAL

$10,000 Federal Reserve Note, Series of 1914 (W-5595-L). Federal Reserve Bank of San Francisco (and courtesy of their collection).

Back of the $10,000 Federal Reserve Note, Series of 1914 (W-5595-L), with the *Embarkation of the Pilgrims* motif.

The back illustrates the *Embarkation of the Pilgrims*, engraved by W.W. Rice of the American Bank Note Company, from a mural by Robert W. Weir. This was created for the $50 Original Series National Bank Note, which had the credit line ENG'D FOR THE AMERICAN BANK NOTE CO. N.Y. below the title.[2] On the $10,000 note this credit is omitted by trimming a slight amount off the bottom of the vignette. Depicted are immigrants aboard the *Speedwell* (as lettered on a plank).

For many varieties that were printed, no examples exist today.[3]

W-5550-A • F-1135A • Boston • Burke-Glass (1918–1920) • 2,000 • Unknown

W-5555-B • F-1135B • New York • 5,600
Recorded population: 2 • *Selected information:* The known examples are serials B1A/A, Unc, part of the Smithsonian Institution collection, and B420A/D, owned by the Federal Reserve Bank of Chicago.

W-5560-C • F-1135C • Philadelphia • 2,400 • Unknown

W-5565-D • F-1135D • Cleveland • 800
Recorded population: 1 • *Selected information:* The known example is serial D1A/A, Unc, part of the Smithsonian Institution collection.

W-5570-E • F-1135D • Richmond • 800 • Unknown

W-5575-F • F-1135E • Atlanta • 400 • Unknown

W-5580-G • F-1135F • Chicago • 1,200 • Unknown

W-5585-H • F-1135G • St. Louis • 1,200 • Unknown

W-5590-K • F-1135H • Dallas • 1,200 • Unknown

W-5595-L • F-1135L • San Francisco • 2,800
Recorded population: 2 • *Selected information:* The known examples are serials L204A/D, F, damaged, and L1957A/A, AU. Both are from the Federal Reserve Bank of San Francisco.

SMALL SIZE

Small-size Federal Reserve Notes and Gold Certificates, each depicting Salmon P. Chase on the face (the same portrait as featured on the $1 Legal Tender Notes of 1862, among several other places), were issued. The Gold Certificates are noncollectible, but enough Federal Reserve Notes exist that they have achieved popularity as trophy notes.

GOLD CERTIFICATES

The $10,000 Gold Certificate depicts Salmon P. Chase, secretary of the Treasury from 1861 to 1864 in the Lincoln administration. After resigning from the Treasury, Chase was appointed chief justice of the Supreme Court. Chase, more than any other person, was responsible for engineering the complex series of currency issues inaugurated in 1861 to raise money to help conduct the Civil War. His image is seen on several different types of currency, the $10,000 being the highest denomination. All have gold Treasury seals.

Series of 1928, Gold Seal
Woods-Mellon (1929–1932)

The obligation or payable notice reads "Ten Thousand Dollars in gold coin payable to the bearer on demand." At the left the Treasury seal is overprinted on a more standard commentary, with GOLD above, CERTIFICATE below, and three lines between: "This certificate is a legal tender in the amount thereof in payment of all debts and dues public and private." In addition to the yellow (usually called gold) seal, the serial numbers were printed in yellow.

Although these notes have Treasury signatures prior to the Roosevelt administration and were intended for use in large transactions, they were never released into general circulation.

W-5650 • F-2411 • None in private hands

Series of 1934, Gold Seal
Julian-Morgenthau (1934–1945)

This anomalous series was created in 1934, by which time the Treasury was not paying either gold coins or Gold Certificates into the channels of commerce. The notes were intended for use in banking channels. The obligation is no longer payable in gold coin and now reads "Ten Thousand Dollars in gold payable to bearer on demand as authorized by law." Otherwise the designs are the same as the preceding, except that the back is printed in gold. None were released.

W-5655 • F-2412 • None in private hands

FEDERAL RESERVE NOTES

The design continued that of the small-size Gold Certificates. From a numismatic viewpoint one might think that $10,000 bills would draw little interest, due to their high face value. However, just the opposite is true. For those who can afford them, these are readily available trophy notes, guaranteed to surprise viewers when displayed.

The late Amon Carter Jr., who collected currency with a passion and acquired many rarities, enjoyed notes of this denomination and often carried some with him as conversation pieces.

SERIES OF 1928, GOLD SEAL

$10,000 Gold Certificate, Series of 1928 (W-5650). Serial A00000001, plate A1. Serially numbered, but never issued. (Smithsonian Institution)

Detail of the Treasury seal.

Back of the $10,000 Gold Certificate, Series of 1928 (W-5650). Plate 1. This standard back was used on other notes of the era.

Detail of the plate number (1) in the lower right corner of the field.

For many years, Binion's Horseshoe Club in Las Vegas had 100 of these $10,000 bills mounted behind glass in a stainless steel frame in the lobby at the entrance of the casino.[4] Visitors could pose in front of the exhibit and have their picture taken. The notes were later sold and, through Jay Parrino and others, went to the numismatic community.

Bills of the Series of 1928 and 1934 bear the imprints of the various Federal Reserve Banks. The 1928 bills were issued by all branches except Philadelphia, and the 1934 bills were not issued by Minneapolis. Today, a particular feat of one-upmanship is to collect $10,000 bills by Federal Reserve cities. No star notes were printed.

Small-size $10,000 notes have not been printed since the 1940s (Series 1934-B with Julian and Vinson signatures), which is rather ironic, as it would seem that these would be more useful than ever today, when the purchasing power of the American dollar is far less than it was then.

Series of 1928, Green Seal
Woods-Mellon (1929–1932)

The obligation appears in four lines in the field at the upper left: "Redeemable in gold on demand at the United States Treasury, or in gold or lawful money at any Federal Reserve Bank." On Series of 1928 notes (illus. on p. 774) the seal in the left field features the letter of the issuing Federal Reserve Bank, A to L. The series imprint appears twice: at the upper left of Chase's portrait and below WASHINGTON at the lower right.

There was no Philadelphia issue in this series. All Series of 1928 notes are great rarities.

W-5670-A • F-2230A • Boston • 1,320 • Unknown

W-5670-B • F-2230B • New York • 4,680 • Government held

W-5670-D • F-2230D • Cleveland • 960

F-12
$125,000

W-5670-E • F-2230E • Richmond • 3,024

Unc-63
$275,000

W-5670-F • F-2230F • Atlanta • 1,440

VF-20	EF-40	AU-50
$150,000	$175,000	$200,000

W-5670-G • F-2230G • Chicago • 1,800 • Unknown

W-5670-H • F-2230H • St. Louis • 480 • Unknown

SERIES OF 1934, GOLD SEAL

$10,000 Gold Certificate, Series of 1934 (W-5655). Serial A00000540A, plate F1. Serially numbered well into a production run. (Smithsonian Institution)

Detail of the Treasury seal.

Back of the $10,000 Gold Certificate, Series of 1928 (W-5655). Plate 1. This standard back was used on other notes of the era, but here is printed in gold rather than green.

Detail of the plate number (1) in the lower right corner of the field.

SERIES OF 1928, GREEN SEAL

$10,000 Federal Reserve Note, Series of 1928 (W-5670-E). Federal Reserve Bank of Richmond.

Back of the $10,000 Federal Reserve Note, Series of 1928 (W-5670-E). Another use of plate 1.
Standard back of small-size $10,000 Federal Reserve Notes.

W-5670-I • F-2230I • Minneapolis • 480 • Unknown

W-5670-J • F-2230J • Kansas City • 480 • Unknown

W-5670-K • F-2230K • Dallas • 360 • Unknown

W-5670-L • F-2230L • San Francisco • 1,824 • Unknown

Series of 1934, Light Yellow-Green Seal
Julian-Morgenthau (1934–1945)

The Series of 1934 continued the same general configuration as the preceding series, but now with a change in the redemption inscription that eliminates the mention of gold: "This note is legal tender for all debts, public and private, and is redeemable in lawful money at the United States Treasury, or at any Federal Reserve Bank."

All range from scarce to rare today, but enough exist that market appearances occur multiple times each year, mainly due to the Binion hoard.

W-5676-A • F-2231A • Boston • 9,720

VF-20	EF-40	AU-50
$85,000	$95,000	$110,000

W-5676-B • F-2231B • New York • 11,520

VG-8	F-12	VF-20	EF-40	AU-50	Unc-60	Unc-63	Unc-65
$50,000	$60,000	$65,000	$75,000	$95,000	$110,000	$125,000	$150,000

W-5676-C • F-2231C • Philadelphia • 6,000

F-12	VF-20	EF-40	AU-50
$75,000	$85,000	—	$120,000

W-5676-D • F-2231D • Cleveland • 1,480 • Unknown

W-5676-E • F-2231E • Richmond • 1,200

AU-50
$140,000

W-5676-F • F-2231F • Atlanta • 2,400

AU-50
$130,000

W-5676-G • F-2231G • Chicago • 3,840

VF-20	EF-40	AU-50	Unc-60	Unc-63
$80,000	$90,000	$100,000	$120,000	$135,000

W-5676-H • F-2231H • St. Louis • 2,040

F-12	VF-20	EF-40	AU-50
$75,000	$85,000	—	$120,000

W-5676-J • F-2231J • Kansas City • 1,200

VF-20	EF-40	AU-50	Unc-60	Unc-63	Unc-65
$85,000	$95,000	$110,000	—	$145,000	$165,000

SERIES OF 1934, LIGHT YELLOW-GREEN SEAL

$10,000 Federal Reserve Note, Series of 1934 (W-5676-A). Light yellow-green seal. Federal Reserve Bank of Boston. (ANA Edward C. Rochette Money Museum)

W-5676-K • F-2231K • Dallas • 1,200

F-12	VF-20	EF-40	AU-50	Unc-60	Unc-63
$70,000	$80,000	$90,000	$100,000	$120,000	$135,000

W-5676-L • F-2231L • San Francisco • 3,600

EF-40	AU-50
$90,000	$120,000

Series of 1934-A, Green Seal
Julian-Morgenthau (1934–1945)

Although these seem to have been issued in their time, the printage was very small, and none are known today.

W-5685-G • F-2232G • Chicago • 1,560 • Unknown

Series of 1934-B, Green Seal
Julian-Vinson (1945–1946)

Series of 1934-B notes display a change in the wording in the Federal Reserve seal: THE is omitted, leaving FEDERAL RESERVE. This was used across all denominations. Only 24 were printed of this issue. None are known to exist today.

W-5690-B • F-2233B • New York • 24 • Unknown

$100,000 Notes

SMALL SIZE

Gold Certificates

Series of 1934, Gold Seal
Julian-Morgenthau (1934–1945)

Small-size notes of the $100,000 denomination were made to facilitate transactions within the Treasury department and the Federal Reserve system. A portrait of Woodrow Wilson is on the face. The back is printed in orange and has the number 100,000 five times and ONE HUNDRED THOUSAND DOLLARS in large letters. These are Series of 1934 Gold Certificates with printed signatures of Julian and Morgenthau. Of the 42,000 printed, several are preserved by the Treasury department and are occasionally displayed. A specimen sheet on loan from the Bureau of Engraving and Printing is displayed at the American Numismatic Association headquarters in Colorado Springs.

W-5800 • F-2413

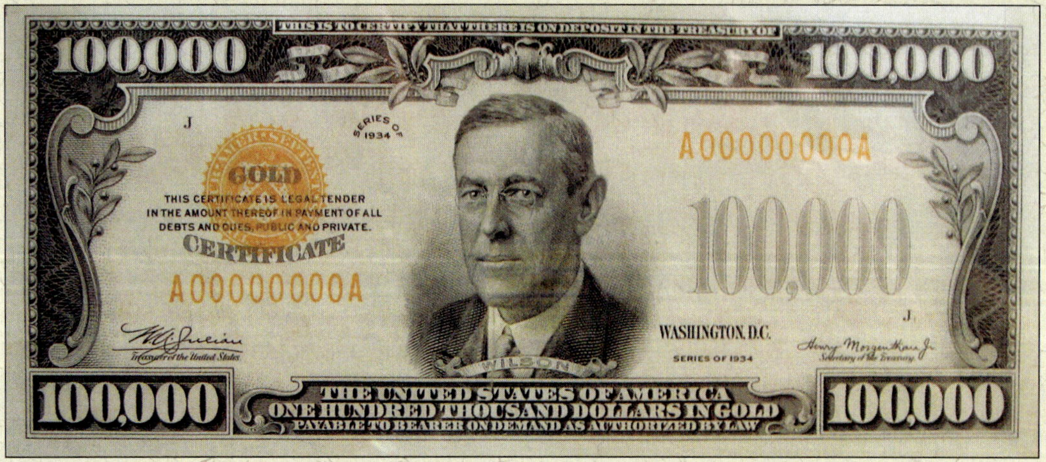

$100,000 Gold Certificate, Series of 1934 (W-5800), with portrait of Woodrow Wilson.

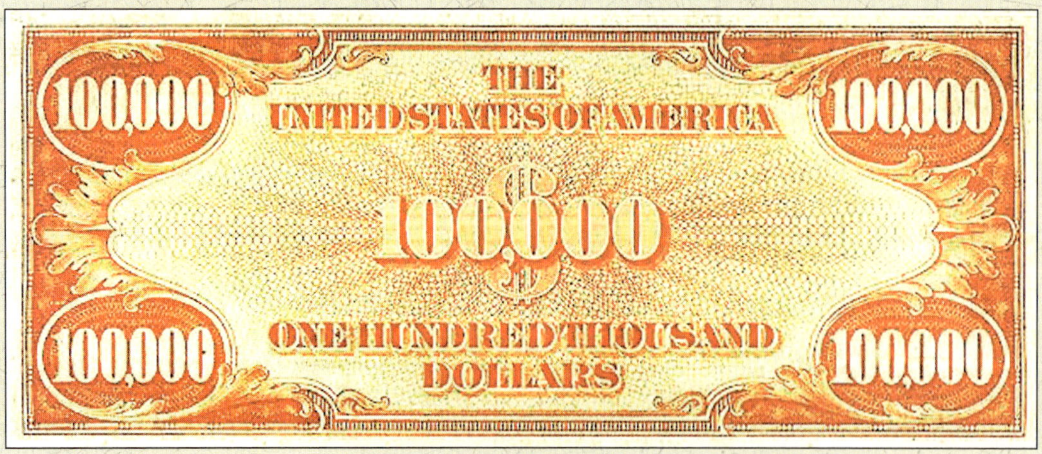

Back of the $100,000 Gold Certificate, Series of 1934 (W-5800). Printed in orange.

18

POSTAGE AND FRACTIONAL CURRENCY, 1862–1876

UNCERTAINTY IN THE EARLY 1860s

In the autumn of 1861 the Union position in the Civil War was becoming increasingly uncertain, and in the South the citizens of the Confederacy were experiencing shortages and other problems.[1] Gold coins disappeared from circulation in late December 1861, as there was fear that they would be replaced with paper money of questionable value. Already, the Demand Notes of July 1861 had met with a nervous reception, even though they were redeemable in gold.

The North's issuance of Legal Tender Notes in the spring of 1862 caused even more concern, as these had no backing whatsoever, other than the good faith and credit of the federal government, and that foundation was anything but certain. Such currency could not be redeemed for gold or silver coins. A $10 Legal Tender Note could be exchanged for two $5 notes, five $2 notes, or some other combination of notes, but for nothing of intrinsic value.

Seeking to preserve the integrity of their money, citizens rushed to hoard silver coins from three-cent pieces to dollars. Soon circulating silver, like gold before it, was all gone. By early summer the only coins in circulation were copper-nickel Flying Eagle and Indian Head cents.

In the meantime, the federal government was issuing more and more paper money. By June 1862, over $100,000,000 in Legal Tender Notes flooded the North. Silver and gold coins sold at increasing premiums, and daily exchange rates were published in the papers. In New York City on July 11, 1862, it took $130 in greenbacks to buy $100 in such federal coins.

THE CURIOUS EVENTS OF JULY 1862

Seeking to grasp *any* money that was metallic, the public next hoarded one-cent pieces. By July 1862 no coins of any kind were to be seen! It was impossible to buy a glass of soda or a newspaper or take a ride in a horse-drawn car.

On July 9 Horace Greeley, proprietor of the *New York Tribune*, suggested that ordinary postage stamps could be used as change, these being conveniently pasted onto the bottom of a small piece of paper with the top folded over.

The idea achieved some popularity, but mostly by putting loose postage stamps into small envelopes imprinted on the front with a value, such as 25¢. Others took postage stamps and pasted them to small pieces of cardboard. The idea caught on, and the Treasury department began experimenting with similar concepts.

STAMPS BECOME MONEY

On July 14, 1862, secretary of the Treasury Salmon P. Chase sent a report to Congress suggesting that government stamps be made official as legal tender for small transactions. In the meantime, Treasurer Francis E. Spinner had pasted postage stamps amounting to 5¢, 10¢, 25¢, and 50¢ onto sheets of Treasury department letterhead paper, cut down and bearing his signature. He contacted the local post office and made an arrangement for damaged stamps that had not been used for postage to be exchanged for new ones.

In response to Chase's request, the Act of July 17, 1862, provided for the use of postage stamps for *monetary* transactions, including the authority that by August 1 stamps would be exchangeable for Legal Tender Notes (greenbacks) at all Treasury offices. They were also receivable for government obligations in amounts under $5, but they were not given official legal tender status, despite Chase's request.

Breaching the gap, many merchants, towns, and others issued tickets imprinted with various values from 1¢ onward. Paper-money scrip notes with 3¢ and 5¢ were the most popular, although values ranged up to a dollar or more. In time, many merchants issued bronze tokens, the size of a cent, which served for that value, and 31 different merchants and products were advertised on encased postage stamps (see chapter 22).

BUSY TIMES AT THE MINT

Indian Head cents, first struck in 1859, were minted at a furious pace in 1862 in an effort to help fill the gap created by the disappearance of silver and gold. As soon as they were put into circulation, they were hoarded. Shopkeepers took them in and did not pay them out. Instead, they gave change in stamps or store credit. Neil Carothers comments in his study *Fractional Money*, "Bus companies, theatres, and

777

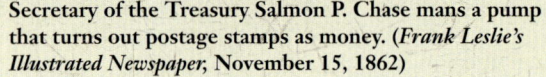

Secretary of the Treasury Salmon P. Chase mans a pump that turns out postage stamps as money. (*Frank Leslie's Illustrated Newspaper,* November 15, 1862)

When stamps served as money, not everyone wanted them. (*Frank Leslie's Illustrated Newspaper,* December 13, 1862)

restaurants accepted these rolls everywhere. A retail store in New York received so many that the floor of the room in which they were stored collapsed."

By July 10, 1862, copper-nickel cents were trading at a 4% premium (in terms of paper money) in New York City, and by July 15 they cost a similar premium in Springfield, Massachusetts. Carothers continues:

> In a vain effort to satisfy the demand [for copper-nickel Indian Head cents] the Mint forced itself into a rate of production even higher than that of 1858. By the end of July the weekly issue amounted to 1,200,000 pieces. One-third of this total was reserved for Philadelphia, the remainder going to the other large cities. No applicant anywhere received more than $5 worth.

> The coinage jumped from 12,000,000 pieces in the [fiscal] year ending June 30, 1862, to 47,800,000 in the following year. Even this extraordinary value in cents, $478,000, was a small sum which contrasted with the $25,000,000 or more in silver coin that had disappeared. The demand for the cent pieces was never satisfied. The conditions in Philadelphia, which were duplicated in other cities, were described in the *Public Ledger* of July 18th:

> "The difficulty among small shopkeepers, provision dealers in the markets and in the city generally, in making change, has caused an extraordinary demand for

cents, and all that can be commanded at the Mint are eagerly bought. . . . Though many of those who desired cents stood in line for hours, waiting an opportunity to get into the Mint, they had to go home without them, as the supply on hand was exhausted before half the applicants were accommodated."

Carothers goes on to note that these cents were in demand because the ownership of a few cents "meant that the owner could ride rather than walk. And, for months after it meant that he could buy a postage stamp without an altercation with the clerk or a cigar without receiving in change a handful of the dealer's own manufactured currency."

The Philadelphia *North American* gave this view of a scene outside of the Mint in July:

> At an early hour in the morning there were not less than 150 boys and men, and 31 young ladies and girls, awaiting a supply of pennies. The boys and men carried shot bags, cigar boxes, baskets, and all sorts of contrivances in which to carry off the much-needed coin. The girls principally carried neat baskets. When the distribution came to be made, the girls were first served, to the intense chagrin of the men, who had been standing on a single foot, alternately, upon the sidewalk for two or three hours. The men and boys were not attended to until the last girl had departed.[2]

THE GOVERNMENT RESPONDS
POSTAGE CURRENCY AND OTHER MONEY

The Treasury department interpreted the Act of July 17, 1862, as a license to create a new type of postage-stamp money of the same designs as stamps, but more convenient. The National Bank Note Company was given a contract to supply sheets of Postage Currency, as it was called. These were small notes of 5¢, 10¢, 25¢, and 50¢ denominations, illustrated with images of current postage stamps. National already had a contract to print 1861-series stamps. National's name was printed near the bottom border of the face of each note. The first Postage Currency issues were printed on sheets perforated between subjects, so that recipients could easily tear them off. Soon, sheets were made without perforations as well, so that scissors or shears would be needed to separate the notes. It seems that for a time, both perforated and imperforated sheets were issued simultaneously.

The backs stated that these were "Receivable in payment of all dues to the U. States less than Five Dollars." Chase's Treasury department had inadvertently recommended to Congress that stamps be lawful in payment of customs, something for which not even Legal Tender Notes were suitable. Only Demand Notes ("Receivable in Payment of All Public Dues," i.e., legally equivalent to gold) and specie itself could otherwise satisfy those obligations.

Postage Currency was first distributed to Army paymasters on August 21, 1862, and to the public in September. When Postage Currency was first paid out, it was popular to cut a sheet so that four 25¢ notes took the place of a $1 bill and four 50¢ notes took the place of a $2 bill, as Legal Tender Notes of these denominations were very scarce in circulation.[3] A lively trade developed in the making and selling of small cardboard and leather wallets for the storage of these little bills. By early 1863 about $100,000 of these notes reached circulation per day, but the demand remained unsatisfied.[4]

The *New York Times* furnishes this chronology:[5]

July 22, 1862: Reported third assistant postmaster general A.N. Zevely's instructions to the New York City postmaster to curtail the run on "postage stamps for currency."

August 1, 1862: Reported that "the new stamps" to be used as money would be printed by the "National Bank Note Co., who are now doing the Treasury ones and twos."

August 3, 1862: Reprinted a July 31 story from the *Washington Republican:* "The designs for the postage stamps to be used as currency were adopted yesterday, and are in the hands of the engraver."

August 5, 1862: Reported that ferry companies and street railroads were "refus[ing] to take postage-stamps."

August 9, 1862: "The stamp currency for change will, like other United States notes, be supplied from the Treasury to disbursing officers. No commissions will be paid to intermediate parties."

August 16, 1862: "Delay in the Issue of the Stamp Currency" headlined an article datelined Washington, August 15th. "The new postage stamp bills for small change were expected to begin arriving from the engravers in New-York to-morrow; but it is understood now that they will not come till about Tuesday next. The Post-office Department turns them over to the Treasury, and it distributes only through regular Treasury depositories. At first no orders will be filled except for small amounts, so as to throw them into as general circulation as [soon as] possible."

August 17, 1862: Reported that the new currency "will be delivered to the public in sheets."

August 22, 1862: Reported that the new postage stamp bills began to be paid out from the Treasury in Washington on August 21. Further: "The currency is delivered in sheets which are perforated like those of postage stamps. The stamps are printed on the best of bank-note paper, and are therefore more difficult of separation than the old stamps. The public must therefore be cautious when separating this currency and not mutilate the notes, as their receipt and redemption by the Treasury Department are subject to the same regulations as now in force for United States notes, namely: if any part of the note is missing a proportionate amount is deducted from the nominal value. For some days Paymasters will absorb a large share of this new currency."

August 29, 1862: Reported that the new stamp money was in circulation in small quantities in the city.

September 5, 1862: Reported that the tardiness in circulating quantities of the new postage stamp currency caused people to return to using regular postage stamps and shinplasters.

As stated, money for small transactions was in short supply. Cent-sized bronze tokens and encased postage stamps eased the shortage slightly, but more effective were the countless printed scrip notes issued by merchants and others. In New Hampshire the *Portsmouth Journal* printed this on September 13:

Private Fractional Bills

When silver change disappeared in July, four of our substantial firms procured the engraving of 25c bills, all of which were signed by such firm as issued them, and were redeemable by either firm in bank bills, whenever four might be presented. For a few days they were frequently returned for redemption.

But after a week or two the matter was well understood to be only for a public accommodation, and without risk. They were then everywhere received like silver, in this and neighboring towns, and up to the time that Congress prohibited the issue, about five thousand, of these bills were issued, and are now still in circulation—those who issued them not having a dollar's worth of them on hand. A premium has in some instances been paid for them.

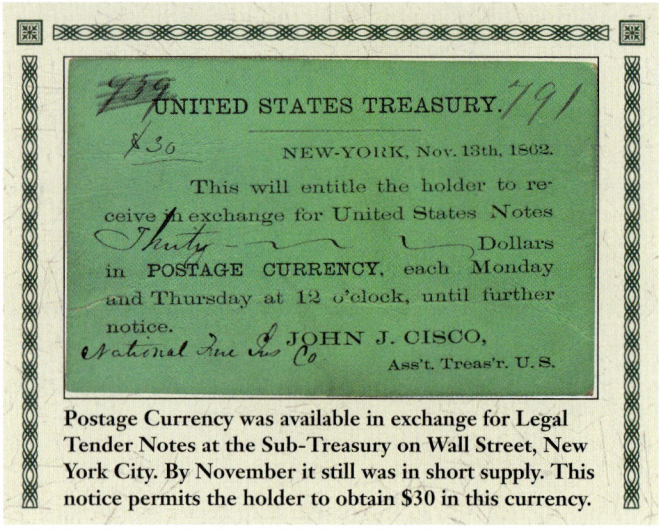

Postage Currency was available in exchange for Legal Tender Notes at the Sub-Treasury on Wall Street, New York City. By November it still was in short supply. This notice permits the holder to obtain $30 in this currency.

One of those who issued them had last week twelve bills presented at this counter. On handing out a three dollar bank bill, the lady replied, "O, I can get that for them anywhere—I thought you paid a premium!"[6]

The American Bank Note Company later obtained part of the contract, after which the ABNCo monogram was added to the backs of the notes. By March 1863 the Treasury department's so-called Postage Currency notes in values of 5¢ to 50¢ had become common in trade and, seemingly, should have alleviated the cent shortage. However, the public still preferred coins, silver and gold remained nowhere to be seen, and attention continued to be focused on the copper-nickel Indian Head cent. On March 9, 1863, the *Public Ledger* reported that in Philadelphia cents were "so scarce as to command a premium of 20%."[7]

Due to the inadvertent redemption clause making them payable for customs duties and all other debts, these notes were hoarded and sold at a premium just like Demand Notes and their coinage counterparts. With the slow printing of the notes by the private bank-note companies and the erratic release by the Treasury, Postage Currency was a sad chapter in finance. Doomed to interrupted circulation, the notes did not prove to be the remedy to the small-change shortage they were hoped to be.

CLARK'S PROPOSALS

Making the matter even more complex, Spencer M. Clark, chief of the newly formed National Currency Bureau, felt that the National and American bank-note companies were charging extortionate prices to produce Postage Currency. He discussed this with secretary of the Treasury Salmon P. Chase, who looked into the situation and found that "though bearing no interest, it was the dearest loan. . . . He directed me to investigate the matter, and if I found that if any economy, with equal security, could be obtained by any other method of production, to report the result of my investigations to him."[8] Clark proposed that this class be replaced with a new "revenue currency" to be made by the Bureau itself, with all denominations (5¢, 10¢, 25¢, and 50¢) to be the same size as the present 10¢ Postage Currency.

It was further proposed that $100,000 per day in new notes be issued in the form of 8,000 sheets (14 inches by 19 inches) of 5¢, or $20,000 face value; 4,000 sheets of the same size of 10¢, or $20,000 face value; 2,000 sheets, 14.5 inches by 16 inches, of 25¢, or $20,000 face value; and 2,000 sheets of the same size of 50¢, or $40,000 face value. Clark recommended that the faces of all notes be printed "in black, and the reverse in four different colors, say fifties in reds, twenty-fives purple, tens green, and fives tan."

Clark said that to print 16,000 sheets per day, with the faces being plate printed and the backs surface printed, would require 30 22-inch copper plate presses, 10 18-inch copper plate presses, and four Gordon presses for surface printing similar to those now being used for bonds.[9] To separate and trim 16,000 sheets per day, there would need to be five trimming and 10 separating machines. These would be powered by steam engines located at a distance in the building and connected by shafts and pulleys.[10]

On October 10, 1862, Secretary Chase approved Clark's designs for revenue currency (later called Fractional Currency). The size of 2.5 inches by 4 inches was recommended by Clark in place of a smaller size the secretary wanted. On October 10 Clark wrote to the secretary stating that the steam-powered plate printing would enable them to use larger plates to print the larger-size notes, and other efficiencies could also be accomplished. Heretofore, all currency had been printed by hand-roller presses. The new arrangement was expected to produce $100,000 face value per day.

Clark, an engineer, thought in terms of efficiency. He rejected the idea of using American Bank Note Company's patented green tint, stating that it provided no security against counterfeiting. He considered the traditional roller presses to be cumbersome, messy, and costly, so he explored methods of dry printing, including hydraulic presses (as discussed in detail in chapter 3).

FRACTIONAL CURRENCY AUTHORIZED

The Act of March 3, 1863, provided for a new small-denomination series designated Fractional Currency, following Clark's proposal. These were receivable in payment for all dues to the United States except customs, thereby correcting an oversight in the wording used on Postage Currency.

The National Currency Bureau set up equipment to produce these notes within the Treasury building. Hydrostatic, or dry-printing, presses were used along with traditional roller presses. The hydrostatic presses were fraught with problems, and roller presses were slow. Accordingly, a large workforce was needed. Special membrane paper was made on the premises by Dr. Stuart Gwynn through early January 1864, after which the operation closed for several months. When it reopened, only regular bank-note paper was made.

By the end of the Mint's fiscal year on June 30, 1863, copper-nickel cents were still being hoarded to such an extent that director James Pollock reported that they were "scarcely to be had" in circulation and that he could not guess "as to the amount of cents that will be required to meet the public demand." Accordingly, Postage Currency, although not in short supply by that time, still filled an important need.

Distribution of the Fractional Currency notes ("Second Issue" in numismatic nomenclature) in the same denominations as Postage Currency began in October 1863. When production was underway, Bureau chief Clark reported:

> The machinery for dry printing is now and has been for some months in successful running order, producing daily a large number of impressions much superior to any impressions by wet printing. Any number of dry-printing presses can be operated simultaneously, without interference with each other, by the peculiar novel adjuncts devised for the purpose.
>
> But ten of them now are in active use, and although a pressure of more than two hundred tons is exerted at each impression, yet an impression can be taken in a few seconds. Experience proves that impressions can be taken as fast as the plates can be inked and put in the press, the process of inking being the same as for wet printing, and this is the only limit to the rapidity of their execution, while every impression is not only perfect in itself, but each is likewise an *exact* counterpart of the originals—a result impossible by any wet printing.
>
> During the last two months not a single imperfect impression has been produced on any one of the dry presses now in use, while by the wet presses, the production of imperfect impressions is daily reckoned by the hundreds.

Finally, by December 1863 the monetary situation eased appreciably. Millions of bronze tokens, more Indian Head cents, and countless privately issued scrip notes permitted commerce to proceed on a nearly normal basis. Still, federal cents remained scarce. As late as June 30, 1864, at the end of the Mint's fiscal year, Director Pollock reported, "Large quantities are hoarded, and thus kept from circulation." Production of Fractional Currency continued apace, although the hydraulic presses were continually bedeviled by breakdowns. Both Clark and Secretary Chase had praised these expensive machines highly and seem to have managed the news about them, often commending their excellent performance when the reality was quite different.

By the late summer of 1864, many if not most of the hoarded one-cent pieces came out of hiding. Not so for silver and gold coins, which remained hoarded for many years thereafter. This situation accelerated the demand for Fractional Currency to take the place of half dimes, quarters, and half dollars.

In late autumn 1864 a new Fractional Currency denomination, the 3¢ note, reached circulation, but it never became popular. In summer 1869 another Fractional Currency denomination, 15¢, was added to the Fractional Currency lineup, but it, too, was never widely used. Face and back colors varied over time, as did the sizes.

Postage Currency and Fractional Currency notes quickly became dirty and tattered and could not be counted easily. The public referred to them derisively as "stamps." By the mid-1870s a new generation of children in the East and Midwest had reached teenage years without ever seeing a Liberty Seated silver coin or a gold piece in pocket change or a store transaction.

In early 1876, production of Fractional Currency ended, just before the April 20 release of large quantities of long-stored silver coins. By that time the value of such coins had achieved parity with Legal Tender Notes (although gold coins continued to trade at a premium).

COLLECTING FRACTIONAL CURRENCY

Fractional Currency has been popular in numismatic circles since it was first issued. In the 1860s, when Postage Currency notes with designs similar to current stamps were introduced, they were immediately attractive to philatelists, this being a widely–spreading, dynamic hobby at the time. Numismatists also caught on quickly. As the varieties proliferated, interest increased. The National Currency Bureau and later the Bureau of Engraving and Printing issued many proof and specimen notes for sale to collectors, especially from 1863 to 1869.

Today, at first glance the numismatic references for the field of Postage Currency and Fractional Currency appear to be very complex. In actuality, it can be simplified, and that effort is made in the present text. There are five different issues, most of which have a single design for a given denomination, although there are exceptions. A basic set of Postage and Fractional Currency would consist of one each of these designs. In instances in which more than one distinctive color printing was used, such as the Third Issue notes with red backs and green backs, each is desired to complete a type set of 29 different notes plus three specimens of the unissued Grant-Sherman 15¢ specimens (face plus two colors of backs).

Beyond these, there are many different surcharges or imprints to be found on the face or back, as well as occasional position numerals and letters; these are prevalent among the Second and Third Issue notes. A specialist delights in such variations, and certain of them have great value.

There are many studies, articles, and listings of this series, the most exhaustive being Milton R. Friedberg's 1978 work, *The Encyclopedia of United States Fractional and Postal Currency*. The bibliography lists others, including a modern *Collector's Guide* by Robert J. Kravitz.

While some enthusiasts may aspire to own varieties with small differences, most opt to acquire major types. To do this, examine the headings and major types as listed. Within the types there are many different varieties. Simply seek a variety that is inexpensive.

As a general rule of thumb, earlier issues, which circulated longer, are likely to be found in lower average condition than those toward the end, such as the Fifth Issues, which were produced from 1874 to 1876. Of the $368,724,079.45 of Postage Currency and Fractional Currency produced, less than $487,000 (about 0.001%) remains outstanding, according to a 1964 Treasury report.[11] For each of the issues, many high-grade examples were preserved by collectors and dealers, furnishing the basis for a large supply today.

For a given note, the centering is important. The face should have full margins, and the back should be reasonably

Face of an uncut sheet of 10¢ Postage Currency stamps.

Back of the sheet.

well centered in relation to the face. Pinholes, folds, stains, and other detractions are often seen, mostly on lower-grade notes. Check any potential purchase carefully, and opt for quality within a given grade. The colors should be crisp and bright. All of the basic types are readily found in high grades, although many of the technical plate and surcharge varieties are rare. Proofs and specimens were made in large quantities for collectors and survive in higher average grades, although some have been unevenly trimmed and others have glue or album marks on their backs.

FIRST ISSUE, POSTAGE CURRENCY

August 21, 1862, to May 27, 1863

5¢, 10¢, 25¢, AND 50¢

The designs for the First Issue copied contemporary postage stamps. Early printings were issued in sheets with perforations between the notes. Afterward, imperforated sheets were distributed. There was overlapping of these two styles, and perforated sheets continued to be issued after the imperforated style was initiated.

The face designs were as follows: 5¢ (with the design of a 5¢ stamp), 10¢ (10¢ stamp), 25¢ (five 5¢ stamps in a row), and 50¢ (five 10¢ stamps in a row). The National Bank Note Company was given the contract to make the dies and plates and do the printing. They already had dies on hand for the stamp designs, as they had printed postage under contract. John Gavit, president of National, later recalled:

> After [printing Postage Currency] for some time ourselves it seemed to be growing in magnitude, and we thought it best to have the backs printed by one company and the faces by another. The paper came to us, we sent it to the American Company, they printed the backs. They sent it back to us, and we printed the faces and sent the packages to Washington.[12]

Spencer M. Clark, chief of the National Currency Bureau, investigated the matter and reported that paper from the New York Bank Note Company cost $22.50 per thousand sheets, but the identical paper could be purchased in the open market for $12. Perceived overcharges and problems prompted secretary of the Treasury Salmon P. Chase to authorize later (Second Issue) notes to be printed in-house by the bureau.

There is no denomination on the First Issue Postage Currency notes except for what appears on the face of the copied postage stamp; nor is there any promise to pay. Notes totaling $20,215,631 face value were produced, according to one source. However, as noted, accounting was not precise. Some were printed on watermarked paper, but little is known about these today.

First Issue Postage Currency notes were distributed from August 21, 1862, to May 27, 1863. Then ensued an interregnum, as the Second Issue of Fractional Currency was not distributed until nearly five months later on October 20. Conditions remained chaotic for small change. A flood of bronze (mostly) tokens helped fill the gap. These were struck by private shops mainly in Cincinnati and New York City, but also in Chicago, Connecticut, and other places. Today, these are the numismatically familiar Civil War tokens, usually divided into "patriotic" and "store card" types. Privately issued scrip notes were commonly used as well, but unlike the tokens, they mainly circulated in and near the towns and cities where they were issued.

FIRST ISSUE, 5¢

The face, printed in brown, depicts a standard 5¢ postage stamp with a portrait of Thomas Jefferson and a counter to each side. At the bottom border is NATIONAL BANK NOTE CO. N.Y. The back has the counter at the center, with an inscription and frame around. The ABNCo monogram appears on the lower right in later printings. The notes are found in two styles: with the face in medium-brown ink printed on yellow paper, and with the face in darker brown ink on orange-yellow paper. *Printage:* 44,857,780 notes. *Size:* 65 mm wide (narrowest in the series), 45 mm high.

W-6101 • F-1229 • Perforated edges • No monogram on back • First issue commencing in August 1862

VG-8	F-12	VF-20	EF-40	AU-50	Unc-60	Unc-63	Unc-65
$45	$75	$100	$150	$225	$290	$500	$850

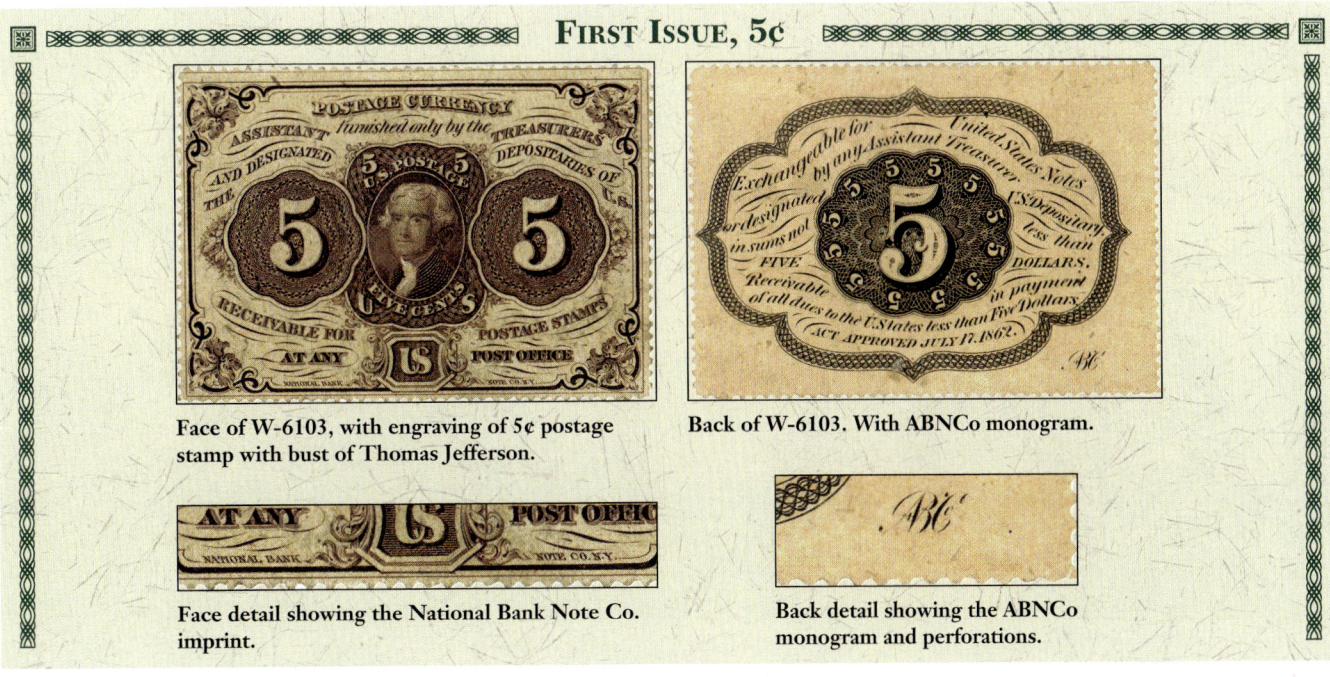

FIRST ISSUE, 5¢

Face of W-6103, with engraving of 5¢ postage stamp with bust of Thomas Jefferson.

Back of W-6103. With ABNCo monogram.

Face detail showing the National Bank Note Co. imprint.

Back detail showing the ABNCo monogram and perforations.

W-6103 • F-1228 • ABNCo monogram on back • Later issue

VG-8	F-12	VF-20	EF-40	AU-50	Unc-60	Unc-63	Unc-65
$35	$60	$80	$125	$195	$250	$425	$750

W-6105 • F-1231 • Straight edges • No monogram on back • Early issue, but not the first

VG-8	F-12	VF-20	EF-40	AU-50	Unc-60	Unc-63	Unc-65
$32	$60	$70	$95	$180	$300	$500	$850

W-6107 • F-1230 • ABNCo monogram on back • Later issue

VG-8	F-12	VF-20	EF-40	AU-50	Unc-60	Unc-63	Unc-65
$25	$32	$42	$65	$85	$110	$200	$375

FIRST ISSUE, 10¢

The face, printed in green, depicts a standard 10¢ postage stamp with a portrait of George Washington and a counter to each side. At the bottom border is NATIONAL BANK NOTE CO. N.Y. The back has the counter at the center, with an inscription and frame around it. The ABNCo monogram appears on the lower right in later printings. The faces of the notes were printed with green ink, and the reverse is in black. Most are on white bond or bank-note paper with visible fibers. Some were printed on grayish-white paper. *Printage:* 41,153,780. *Size:* 65 mm wide (narrowest in the series), 45 mm high.

W-6121 • F-1241 • Perforated edges • No monogram on back • First issue commencing in August 1862

VG-8	F-12	VF-20	EF-40	AU-50	Unc-60	Unc-63
$45	$75	$100	$140	$180	$225	$375

W-6123 • F-1240 • ABNCo monogram on back • Later issue

VG-8	F-12	VF-20	EF-40	AU-50	Unc-60	Unc-63
$40	$65	$90	$125	$150	$190	$275

W-6125 • F-1243 • Straight edges • No monogram on back • Early issue, but not the first

VG-8	F-12	VF-20	EF-40	AU-50	Unc-60	Unc-63	Unc-65
$35	$45	$75	$140	$200	$375	$625	$1,250

W-6127 • F-1242 • ABNCo monogram on back • Later issue

VG-8	F-12	VF-20	EF-40	AU-50	Unc-60	Unc-63	Unc-65
$24	$30	$45	$75	$100	$125	$200	$500

FIRST ISSUE, 25¢

The face, printed in brown, depicts five standard 5¢ postage stamps with portraits of Thomas Jefferson, each slightly overlapped except for the rightmost. At the bottom border to the right is NATIONAL BANK NOTE CO. N.Y. The back has the counter at the center, with an inscription and frame around it. The ABNCo monogram appears on the

Face of W-6123, with engraving of 10¢ postage stamp with bust of George Washington. Perforated edges.

Back of W-6123. With ABNCo monogram at the lower right.

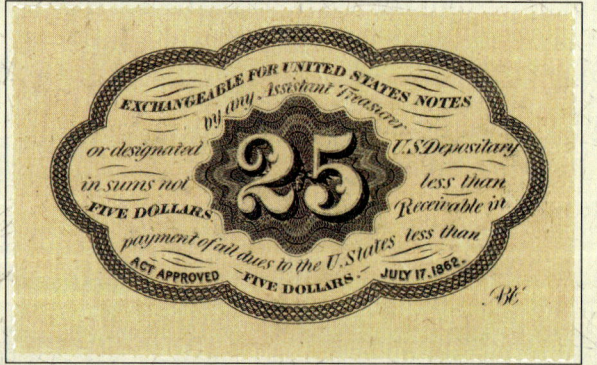

Face of W-6143. Five overlapping 5¢ postage stamps with the portrait of Thomas Jefferson.

Back of W-6143. ABNCo monogram to the lower right.

lower right in later printings. The notes can be found with the face in dark-brown ink on yellow paper, or on orange-yellow paper, or on buff-yellow paper. *Printage: 20,902,768. Size:* 78 mm wide, 48 mm high.

W-6141 • F-1280 • Perforated edges • No monogram on back • First issue commencing in August 1862

VG-8	F-12	VF-20	EF-40	AU-50	Unc-60	Unc-63	Unc-65
$50	$115	$175	$225	$350	$450	$700	$1,300

W-6143 • F-1279 • ABNCo monogram on back • Later issue

VG-8	F-12	VF-20	EF-40	AU-50	Unc-60	Unc-63	Unc-65
$35	$60	$75	$120	$210	$325	$550	$1,050

W-6145 • F-1282 • Straight edges • No monogram on back • Early issue, but not the first

VG-8	F-12	VF-20	EF-40	AU-50	Unc-60	Unc-63	Unc-65
$45	$75	$125	$200	$350	$500	$750	$1,500

W-6147 • F-1281 • ABNCo monogram on back • Later issue

VG-8	F-12	VF-20	EF-40	AU-50	Unc-60	Unc-63	Unc-65
$28	$37	$50	$70	$90	$165	$275	$480

FIRST ISSUE, 50¢

The face, printed in green, depicts five standard 10¢ postage stamps with portraits of George Washington, each slightly overlapped except for the rightmost. At the border at the lower left is NATIONAL BANK NOTE CO. N.Y. The back has the counter at the center, with an inscription and frame around it. The ABNCo monogram appears on the lower right of some notes. These notes were printed with yellow-green ink on white or bank-note paper, dark-green ink on grayish-white paper, and light-green ink on grayish-white paper. *Printage: 17,263,344. Size:* 78 mm wide, 48 mm high.

W-6161 • F-1311 • Perforated edges • No monogram on back • First issue commencing in August 1862

VG-8	F-12	VF-20	EF-40	AU-50	Unc-60	Unc-63	Unc-65
$65	$115	$180	$210	$290	$375	$950	$1,500

W-6162 • F-1310 • Perforated edges, 12 perforations per 20 mm • ABNCo monogram on back • Later issue

VG-8	F-12	VF-20	EF-40	AU-50	Unc-60	Unc-63	Unc-65
$45	$70	$100	$160	$200	$300	$750	$1,250

W-6163 • F-1310a • Perforated edges, 14 perforations per 20 mm • Later issue

VF-20	EF-40	AU-50	Unc-60	Unc-63	Unc-65
$1,500	$2,000	$3,000	$3,500	$4,000	$5,550

W-6165 • F-1313 • Straight edges • No monogram on back • Early issue, but not the first

VG-8	F-12	VF-20	EF-40	AU-50	Unc-60	Unc-63	Unc-65
$55	$100	$180	$225	$320	$410	$1,000	$1,600

W-6167 • F-1312 • ABNCo monogram on back • Later issue

VG-8	F-12	VF-20	EF-40	AU-50	Unc-60	Unc-63	Unc-65
$28	$45	$60	$90	$120	$175	$260	$525

SECOND ISSUE, FRACTIONAL CURRENCY

October 20, 1863, to February 23, 1867
5¢, 10¢, 25¢, AND 50¢

All Second Issue notes have the same scenic vignette and a portrait of Washington within a printed oval frame applied with bronzing powder, a messy process that caused problems in production. At first, a special adhesive ink was printed on the sheets, and female operatives dusted the bronzing powder onto the ink and then brushed away the remainder. This resulted in very dirty, unhealthful conditions. Later, the procedure was simplified, so that the powder was mixed into the ink and then applied, but this was still dirty.

FIRST ISSUE, 50¢

Face of W-6167. Five overlapping 10¢ stamps with portrait of George Washington. Straight edges.

Back of W-6167 with ABNCo monogram at the lower right.

The artwork was reduced photographically as an early step in making the printing plates. These represented the fruition of Spencer M. Clark's plans to have the National Currency Bureau replace the New York City bank-note companies in the printing of fractional notes. Paper was made in the bureau by Dr. Stuart Gwynn and his helpers.

Unlike all other issues, the faces of Second Issue notes are uniform in their basic design and differ only in the denomination imprint. At the bottom is a panorama depicting transportation and commerce, ostensibly by engraver James Duthie (but some Bureau engravers sometimes secretly subcontracted their work during this era). At the left are two steamships tied up on a river with barrels and merchandise on the shore. At the right is a freight wagon with barrels and crates nearby and a locomotive and tender in the distance. At the center of the note is a portrait of George Washington, said to be by Joseph P. Ourdan, with FRACTIONAL CURRENCY above, the denomination spelled out, and numerical counters to each side. All are printed in black. The heavy bronze oval surrounding the portrait was imprinted on paper with bronzing powder as the first step in the printing process. Inscriptions are at the top and bottom borders, including ENGRAVED AND PRINTED AT THE TREASURY DEPARTMENT at the bottom.

George W. Casilear, a New York City engraver who was hired by the bureau and moved to Washington in autumn of 1862, is credited with creating the designs for the backs, each with a shield surmounted by an eagle and inscriptions to the sides. Each of the denominations were of a different color, making them easy to differentiate. The ink was made within the bureau. Casilear also had responsibility for managing the inventory of dies, transfer rolls (cylinder dies), and printing plates.

Second Issue Fractional Currency notes were made by three main methods, the printages for each being given below: (1) on membrane paper using a hydrostatic press, (2) on bank-note paper using a hydrostatic press, and (3) on bank-note paper of various kinds and compositions using a traditional hand-roller press. The last accounted for the overwhelming majority of production. Many different varieties of paper were used, but these are not widely studied by numismatists today. A new heavy "fibrous paper" was introduced about October 1864.

As related in chapter 3, the New York City bank-note companies plotted against Clark and accused him of many improprieties. In January 1864, Gwynn was summarily arrested and locked up in the Old Capitol Prison. No charges were made against him, and a few weeks later he was released, whereupon he resigned in disgust. On May 4, 1864, James A. Garfield, chairman of the Select Committee of the Treasury Department, House of Representatives, led and supervised the questioning of Clark and others, which was also done by other committee members.

Clark related that over $4 million in Fractional Currency had been printed by the Bureau since the summer of 1863, when production began. "I had about half a million dollars printed prior to the arrest of Dr. Gwynn; some of it, however, has been finished and gone into circulation, which was then partly printed." Eventually, the other notes were fin-

ished as well. Paper manufacturing ceased for a short time, and further supplies were purchased on the open market. Afterward, paper production resumed in a large facility in the basement of the Treasury Building.

According to Clark's accounting, the cost for the bureau to print $1,000 face value in 50¢ Fractional Currency was $1.59, as compared to the cost in New York City of $6.97 for Postage Currency of the same denomination. The same face value in 25¢ notes cost $3.08 at the Bureau and $13.94 in New York, while 10¢ notes cost $6.71 at the Bureau and $28.87 in New York, and 5¢ notes cost $13.43 at the Bureau and $55.75 in New York. Of course, the lower denominations required many more notes to achieve the same face value, as 10 sheets of 5¢ notes was equal in value to one sheet of 50¢ notes.

For the wet printing process, the paper needed to be dampened for 12 hours so that it would take the impression better from roller presses. The membrane paper for dry printing took the bronze imprint better in the first step, after which no dampening was needed, and the notes could be printed without delay. However, the hydrostatic presses were poorly constructed and caused no end of problems, with the result that only a few of them were in operation, while dozens remained idle.

Another investigation of Clark and the bureau, commenced in 1867 and published in 1869, revealed that accounting for Fractional Currency was very poorly kept, with little coordination as to the number of sheets of paper made compared to those actually used. In one instance, the issue quantity of Second Issue notes was *larger* than the number posted for the quantity printed. Matters were so disorganized that no correct printage figures will ever be known. When discrepancies were found within the bureau, employees simply altered the figures to make them appear logical. Those given here are from the investigation report, which are probably closer to the truth than are other Treasury figures.[13]

The Second Issue notes were made entirely at the Treasury department from October 10, 1863, through February 23, 1867, with a face value of over $23,000,000. Up to and including October 1, 1864, dry membrane paper had been used to produce $11,587 worth of 5¢ notes, $17,098 of 10¢ notes, $58,689 of 25¢ notes, and $63,300 of 50¢ notes, according to Clark's accounting (later proved to be inaccurate).

Dry bank-note paper, but not of the membrane type, was used to produce $6,500 of the 5¢ type, $9,000 of the 10¢ type, $65,000 of the 25¢ type, and $4,100 of the 50¢ type. Wet bank-note paper was used for the vast majority of production, including $96,004 in 5¢ notes, $1,249,295 of 10¢ notes, $475,846 of 25¢ notes, and $573,375 of 50¢ notes, again according to Clark's contrived figures.

Better and later figures, from the investigation published in 1869, are given in the descriptions below. To summarize, each denomination was made in three major categories: (1) membrane paper printed on hydrostatic presses, (2) other bank-note paper types printed on hydrostatic presses, and (3) bank-note paper types printed on wet roller presses.

Bronze-ink letters and numbers applied to the backs of certain issues, generally referred to as surcharges, likely referred to the type of paper used, although no direct evidence of this has been found as no accounts were kept. On existing notes these imprints are often blurry or otherwise poorly defined. For the numismatic market, some have been altered or faked. Further, some bronze surcharges have flaked away, thus creating a without-surcharges back or some other, unintended variation. Thus, authentication is mandatory for varieties that are particularly scarce or rare.

Size: 66 mm wide, 48 mm high for all denominations.

SECOND ISSUE, 5¢

The face, printed in black, is the same as on other denominations in the series, except for the denomination imprint. At the bottom is a scenic vignette, while at the center is a portrait of Washington surrounded by an oval bronze frame.

The back, printed in brown, is the standard shield design for the Second Issue, with the denomination at the center as part of the vignette and also in a large bronzed overprint. It is seen below that membrane paper issues were in the tiny minority of the printage.

Printage information is as follows.

Hydrostatic press (dry) production:

5¢ membrane paper: sheets printed, 12,207; number of notes printed, 305,186; notes delivered, 298,936

5¢ bank-note paper, dry printing (commenced in March 1864): sheets printed, 57,480; number of notes printed, 1,437,000; notes delivered, 1,437,000

Roller press (wet) production:

5¢ bank-note paper, various weights and compositions, wet printing: sheets printed, 2,198,644 and two-fifths; number of notes printed, 54,966,110 (*sic*); notes delivered, 55,005,910 (*sic*)

W-6201 • F-1232 • No surcharges on the corners of the back

VG-8	F-12	VF-20	EF-40	AU-50	Unc-60	Unc-63	Unc-65
$24	$32	$40	$60	$80	$100	$150	$395

W-6203 • F-1233 • Surcharges 18/63

VG-8	F-12	VF-20	EF-40	AU-50	Unc-60	Unc-63	Unc-65
$25	$34	$42	$65	$90	$115	$175	$450

W-6205 • F-1234 • Surcharges S/18/63

VG-8	F-12	VF-20	EF-40	AU-50	Unc-60	Unc-63	Unc-65
$35	$50	$65	$100	$125	$175	$250	$600

W-6207 • F-1235 • Surcharges R/1/18/63 • Fiber paper

VG-8	F-12	VF-20	EF-40	AU-50	Unc-60	Unc-63	Unc-65
$75	$140	$220	$425	$575	$750	$1,000	$1,750

SECOND ISSUE, 10¢

The face, printed in black, is the same as on other denominations in the series, except for the denomination imprint. At the bottom is a scenic vignette, while at the center is a portrait of Washington surrounded by an oval, bronze frame.

The back, printed in green, is the standard shield design for the Second Issue, with the denomination at the center as part of the vignette and also in a large bronzed overprint. The membrane paper notes were made in relatively small quantities.

Printage information is as follows.

Hydrostatic press (dry) production:

10¢ membrane paper: sheets printed, 21,961; number of notes printed, 549,029; notes delivered, 539,882

10¢ bank-note paper, dry printing (commenced in March 1864): sheets printed, 175,480; number of notes printed, 4,387,000; notes delivered, 4,387,000

Roller press (wet) production:

10¢ bank-note paper, various weights and compositions, wet printing: sheets printed, 2,323,062; number of notes printed, 58,076,550; notes delivered, 58,040,250

SECOND ISSUE, 5¢

Face of W-6201. Head of George Washington in bronze-colored oval frame. Scenic panorama below. This is the general style of all Second Issue Fractional Currency, differing only in the denomination imprints.

Back of W-6201. Printed in brown. Bronze 5 overprint. No surcharges.

Detail of the surcharge 18, in bronzing powder at the lower left corner of the back.

W-6221 • F-1244 • No surcharges on the corners of the back

VG-8	F-12	VF-20	EF-40	AU-50	Unc-60	Unc-63	Unc-65
$20	$29	$35	$50	$70	$90	$180	$350

W-6223 • F-1245 • Surcharges 18/63

VG-8	F-12	VF-20	EF-40	AU-50	Unc-60	Unc-63	Unc-65
$24	$34	$42	$59	$80	$110	$200	$400

W-6225 • F-1246 • Surcharges S/18/63

VG-8	F-12	VF-20	EF-40	AU-50	Unc-60	Unc-63	Unc-65
$30	$40	$65	$90	$125	$165	$300	$550

W-6227 • F-1247 • Surcharges 1/18/63

VG-8	F-12	VF-20	EF-40	AU-50	Unc-60	Unc-63	Unc-65
$55	$80	$115	$180	$270	$350	$500	$950

W-6229 • F-1248 • Surcharges O/63

VG-8	F-12	VF-20	EF-40	AU-50	Unc-60	Unc-63	Unc-65
$750	$850	$1,250	$200	$2,250	$2,500	$2,750	$4,000

W-6231 • F-1249 • Surcharges T/1/18/63 • Fiber paper

VG-8	F-12	VF-20	EF-40	AU-50	Unc-60	Unc-63	Unc-65
$60	$95	$130	$200	$250	$600	$1,000	$2,250

SECOND ISSUE, 25¢

The face, printed in black, is the same as on other denominations in the series, except for the denomination imprint. At the bottom is a scenic vignette, while at the center is a portrait of Washington surrounded by an oval, bronze frame.

The back, printed in various shades of purple and, scarcer, in gray, is the standard shield design for the Second Issue, with the denomination at the center as part of the vignette and also in a large bronzed overprint. Purple was an unusual color and was specifically noticed by a *New York Tribune* reporter who visited the Bureau late in 1863. The membrane paper notes were made in much smaller quantities.

Printage information is as follows.

Hydrostatic press (dry) production:
25¢ membrane paper: sheets printed, 60,649; number of notes printed, 1,212,993; notes delivered, 1,203,353

SECOND ISSUE, 10¢

W-6225. Style as preceding, but 10¢ denomination.

Back of W-6225. Printed in green. With S/18/63 surcharge in corners somewhat blurry, as is often the case with bronze corner overprints. Bronze counter overprinted at the center.

SECOND ISSUE, 25¢

W-6257. Style as preceding, but 25¢ denomination.

Back of W-6257. Printed in purple. With S/18/63 surcharge in corners somewhat blurry as is often the case with bronze corner overprints. Bronze counter overprinted at the center.

25¢ bank-note paper, dry printing (commenced in March 1864): sheets printed, 628,600; number of notes printed, 12,572,000: notes delivered, 12,471,860

Roller press (wet) production:

25¢ bank-note paper, various weights and compositions, wet printing: sheets printed, 917,933; number of notes printed, 18,358,660; notes delivered, 18,236,620

W-6251 • F-1283 • No surcharges on the corners of the back

VG-8	F-12	VF-20	EF-40	AU-50	Unc-60	Unc-63	Unc-65
$28	$45	$65	$95	$125	$200	$300	$500

W-6253 • F-1284 • Surcharges 18/63

VG-8	F-12	VF-20	EF-40	AU-50	Unc-60	Unc-63	Unc-65
$40	$60	$90	$150	$175	$275	$450	$850

W-6255 • F-1285 • Surcharges A/18/63

VG-8	F-12	VF-20	EF-40	AU-50	Unc-60	Unc-63	Unc-65
$32	$52	$75	$110	$145	$275	$450	$850

W-6257 • F-1286 • Surcharges S/18/63

VG-8	F-12	VF-20	EF-40	AU-50	Unc-60	Unc-63	Unc-65
$28	$45	$65	$95	$125	$200	$300	$550

W-6259 • F-1288 • Surcharges 2/18/63

VG-8	F-12	VF-20	EF-40	AU-50	Unc-60	Unc-63	Unc-65
$45	$70	$125	$175	$220	$350	$625	$950

W-6261 • F-1289 • Surcharges T/1/18/63 • Fiber paper

VG-8	F-12	VF-20	EF-40	AU-50	Unc-60	Unc-63	Unc-65
$50	$80	$135	$185	$240	$400	$800	$1,500

W-6263 • F-1290 • Surcharges T/2/18/63 • Fiber paper

VG-8	F-12	VF-20	EF-40	AU-50	Unc-60	Unc-63	Unc-65
$50	$80	$135	$185	$240	$400	$800	$1,500

SECOND ISSUE, 50¢

The face, printed in black, is the same as on other denominations in the series, except for the denomination imprint. At the bottom is a scenic vignette, while at the center is a portrait of Washington surrounded by an oval, bronze frame.

The back, printed in various shades of pink and carmine, is the standard shield design for the Second Issue, with the denomination at the center as part of the vignette and also in a large bronzed overprint. It is thought that *all* of the 50¢ denomination notes were issued with surcharges on the corners of the back. Those that are seen without surcharges are believed to have had the surcharges flaked off or to have been deceptively altered. For this denomination the dry printed notes on bank-note paper are the rarest.

Printage information is as follows.

Hydrostatic press (dry) production:

50¢ membrane paper: sheets printed, 69,851; number of notes printed, 1,397,022; notes delivered, 1,386,233

50¢ bank-note paper, dry printing (commenced in March 1864): sheets printed, 11,600; number of notes printed, 232,000; notes delivered, 232,000

Roller press (wet) production:

50¢ bank-note paper, various weights and compositions, wet printing: sheets printed, 594,749; number of notes printed; 11,894,980; notes delivered, 11,892,320

W-6271 • F-1316 • Surcharges 18/63

VG-8	F-12	VF-20	EF-40	AU-50	Unc-60	Unc-63	Unc-65
$50	$75	$100	$150	$225	$300	$500	$850

W-6273 • F-1317 • Surcharges A/18/63

VG-8	F-12	VF-20	EF-40	AU-50	Unc-60	Unc-63	Unc-65
$34	$50	$70	$95	$150	$250	$375	$650

W-6275 • F-1318 • Surcharges 1/18/63

VG-8	F-12	VF-20	EF-40	AU-50	Unc-60	Unc-63	Unc-65
$34	$50	$70	$110	$200	$300	$450	$800

SECOND ISSUE, 50¢

W-6277. Style as preceding, but 50¢ denomination.

Back of W-6277. Printed in carmine. With O/1/18/63 surcharge in corners somewhat blurry as is often the case with bronze corner overprints. Bronze counter overprinted at the center. Various shades of red exist for this denomination.

W-6277 • F-1320 • Surcharges O/1/18/63 • Fiber paper

VG-8	F-12	VF-20	EF-40	AU-50	Unc-60	Unc-63	Unc-65
$55	$75	$100	$160	$275	$410	$700	$1,500

W-6279 • F-1321 • Surcharges R/2/18/63 • Fiber paper

VG-8	F-12	VF-20	EF-40	AU-50	Unc-60	Unc-63	Unc-65
$70	$125	$175	$275	$350	$750	$1,000	$1,600

W-6281 • F-1322 • Surcharges T/1/18/63 • Fiber paper

VG-8	F-12	VF-20	EF-40	AU-50	Unc-60	Unc-63	Unc-65
$55	$75	$100	$160	$275	$410	$700	$1,000

THIRD ISSUE, FRACTIONAL CURRENCY

December 5, 1864, to August 16, 1869

3¢, 5¢, 10¢, 25¢, AND 50¢

The Third Issue of Fractional Currency is the largest and most complex in the series. Authorized under the Act of June 30, 1864, these notes were made at the request of Spencer M. Clark, who wrote to the secretary of the Treasury in hopes of a remedy for the flood of counterfeits in circulation:

> To protect that portion of the public which will not protect itself by the exercise of ordinary diligence in scrutinizing paper money, the only course in my judgment when a counterfeit gets into the channels of circulation is therefore to make a new issue and withdraw the latter from circulation.

Printing began in November 1864, after which this issue was made concurrently with Second Issue notes until February 1867, this being curious in view of Clark's letter.[14] One might assume that Clark simply wanted to create more varieties, as he appreciated the wide interest that numismatists as well as stamp collectors had in Fractional Currency. The production of such proofs, specimens, and special issues became a very profitable business and resulted in the creation of varieties that would not have been made otherwise. Some special albums and other delicacies were made privately with no records being kept.[15] Printing is said to have ended on April 16, 1869, and comprised over $86,000,000 in notes. By that time, Clark had been forced to leave the bureau. The printages for the Third Issue must be viewed as approximate even though they appear to be precise; as with the Second Issue, record keeping was lax.

The Third Issue has two series. The first includes all denominations and has green backs. The second, with red backs, does not include the 3¢ denomination and also lacks the variety known as the 50¢ Spinner "new style" or open back. The red backs of this issue have autographed signatures. Most were signed by clerks. In addition, authentic sig-

natures of Treasury officials were often applied as a courtesy by the officials themselves, sometimes in different positions. No one rule fits all, as Clark was very aware of interest in special varieties, and little documentation was made.

The 3¢ denomination, introduced with the Third Issue of Fractional Currency, was made for just a short time, as the law of March 3, 1865, which authorized the nickel three-cent coin, prohibited any further issue of notes of this value.

Several types of paper were used for the Third Issue, sometimes classified as parchment, coarse-fiber, fine-fiber, and simply plain bank-note paper. The coarse fiber was printed first and was made within the bureau. The 50¢ red-back note appears only on this paper when bearing the surcharge of S-2-6-4 and the signatures of Colby and Spinner.

Black ink was used on the face of all of the Third Issue, with red on the back of one series and green on the back of another series. Surcharges including S-2-6-4, A-2-6-5, and M-2-6-5 are on the corners of the backs of the 10¢, 25¢, and 50¢ denominations. The 10¢ note has the surcharge on the obverse with the numeral 10 in four quarter sections. The 25¢ and 50¢ notes have surcharges near the end of the face with a label, either solid or outline, with the numerals, but not on all varieties.

Several varieties of the Third Issue have what D.W. Valentine called *location marks*, although others call them plate letters or plate numbers. These other designations are inaccurate according to Valentine, who pointed out that the imprints were given to notes in particular positions on printed sheets. The small letter "a" appears on some 5¢ notes, and the small numeral 1 appears on some 10¢ notes. Some of the 25¢ notes have the letter in different sizes, and 50¢ notes have 1 and a in combination or alone. They are called position letters and numbers in the present text.

Spencer M. Clark had his own portrait placed on the 5¢ note of this issue. When told that the image was of "Clark," most people thought that William Clark, of 1804–1806 Lewis and Clark Expedition fame, was the one being honored. This curious 5¢ note inspired the Act of April 7, 1866, which specified, "No portrait or likeness of any living person hereafter engraved, shall be placed upon any of the bonds, securities, notes, fractional or postal currency of the United States."

The Act of May 17, 1866, provided for the coinage of the nickel five-cent piece and eliminated the issuance of any Fractional Currency bill of a denomination less than 10¢. Accordingly, the 5¢ notes were produced only for a short time. These were printed with red and green backs.

The 10¢ note, or at least what was intended to be so, simply says "10," with no mention of CENTS—a numismatic precursor to the famous 1883 CENTS-less Liberty Head nickel. These were printed with red and green backs.

Prior to the Act of April 7, 1866, the Bureau had essays of 15¢ notes with pictures of Grant and Sherman in preparation, but these could not be issued under the new law because both men were very much alive. Accordingly, these exist only on specimen impressions, with face and back impressions printed separately. These have been particularly popular with collectors ever since they were made. These are listed separately here under "Essays, Proofs, Specimens and Other Special Issues."

The 25¢ denomination depicts William P. Fessenden, then-current secretary of the Treasury. These were printed with red and green backs and with plate and surcharge varieties.

Two face designs and two back designs were made of the 50¢ denomination, issued in three combinations and with green and red backs. The green backs were printed first and were designated as First Series by D.W. Valentine and F.C.C. Boyd. The red backs, made in much smaller quantities, are the Second Series. A large number of plate and surcharge varieties characterize the issues. As a class, these were issued from December 5, 1864, through April 16, 1869. Although no *new* plates were made depicting living persons, old plates with such motifs were continued in use after the act prohibiting them.

THIRD ISSUE, 3¢

The 3¢ denomination is unique to the Third Series. These notes were made for only a few months, until production was forbidden under the Act of March 3, 1865, which provided for the coinage of nickel coins of the same value.

The face depicts George Washington with a curtain or drapery in the background. The curtain is usually light, but some notes have it slightly darker. The difference is not dramatic and can best be appreciated when two are viewed side by side. The back of both varieties is printed in green. These were printed in sheets of 25 notes, arranged five notes across and five down. All were printed on standard white bank-note paper. *Printage:* 20,064,130. *Size:* 67 mm wide, 42 mm high (shortest in the series).

W-6301 • F-1226 • Light curtain to portrait

VG-8	F-12	VF-20	EF-40	AU-50	Unc-60	Unc-63	Unc-65
$25	$45	$55	$80	$95	$175	$225	$375

W-6303 • F-1227 • Dark curtain to portrait

VG-8	F-12	VF-20	EF-40	AU-50	Unc-60	Unc-63	Unc-65
$35	$55	$70	$100	$125	$225	$350	$650

THIRD ISSUE, 5¢

The face depicts Spencer M. Clark, chief of the National Currency Bureau, in the famous usage that precipitated the Act of April 7, 1866, which prohibited the use of portraits of any living person on federal paper money or bonds (but not on coins). At the lower left is a caduceus, and at the lower right a scythe. The printed signatures of Colby and Spinner are near the border. Some notes have a tiny position letter (sometimes called a plate letter) "a" on the face above the caduceus. The backs were printed in green (First Series) and red (Second Series). The notes were arranged 20 to a sheet, with five across and four down. The four in the left margin have the "a" position letter. All were printed on standard white bank-note paper. *Printage:* 13,140,055. *Size:* 67 mm wide, 48 mm high.

Green Back (First Series)

W-6311 • F-1238 • Green back (or First Series) • No "a" on face

VG-8	F-12	VF-20	EF-40	AU-50	Unc-60	Unc-63	Unc-65
$27	$40	$50	$80	$100	$140	$185	$400

W-6313 • F-1239 • With "a" on face

VG-8	F-12	VF-20	EF-40	AU-50	Unc-60	Unc-63	Unc-65
$40	$55	$70	$100	$125	$175	$250	$300

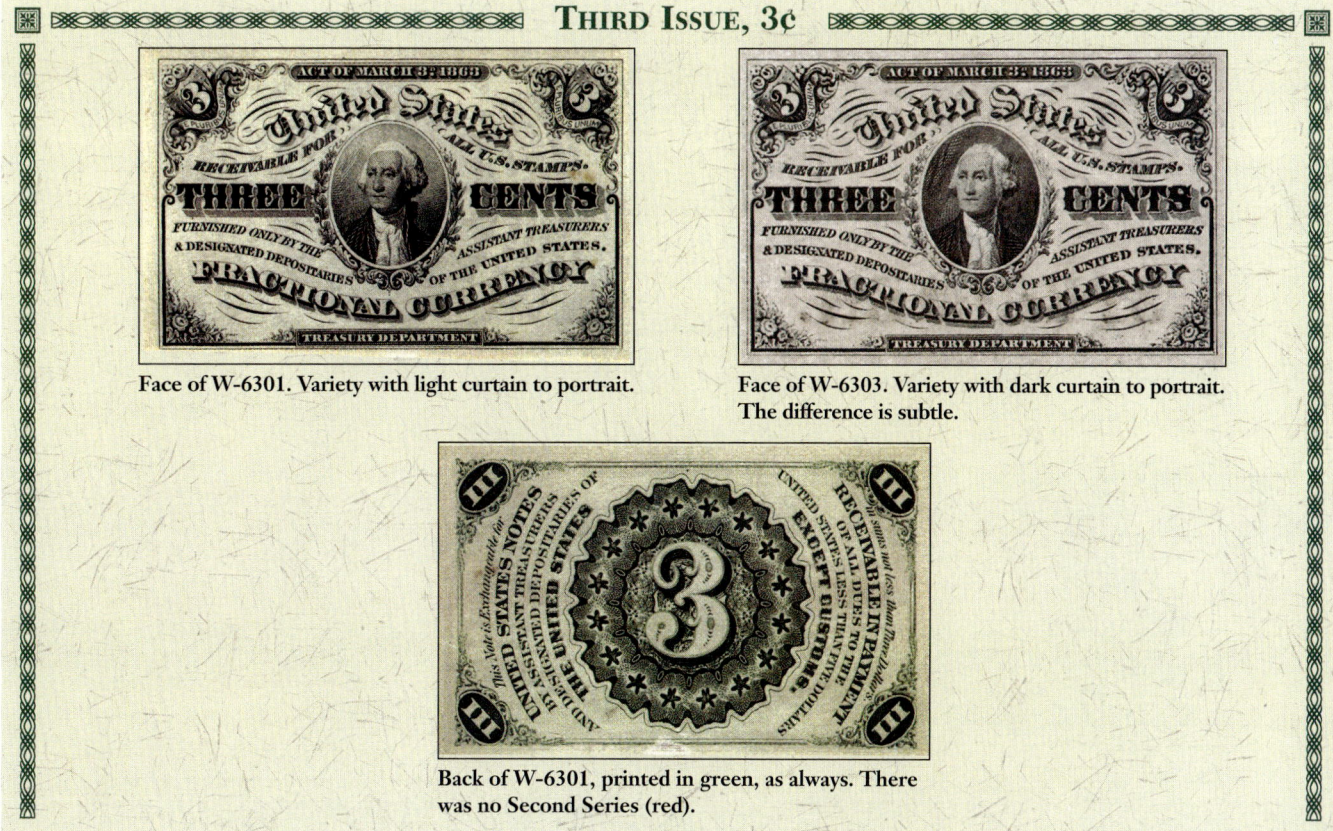

THIRD ISSUE, 3¢

Face of W-6301. Variety with light curtain to portrait.

Face of W-6303. Variety with dark curtain to portrait. The difference is subtle.

Back of W-6301, printed in green, as always. There was no Second Series (red).

Red Back (Second Series)

W-6315 • F-1236 • Red back (or Second Series) • No position letter "a" on face

VG-8	F-12	VF-20	EF-40	AU-50	Unc-60	Unc-63	Unc-65
$30	$50	$70	$115	$175	$250	$300	$600

W-6317 • F-1237 • With "a" on face

VG-8	F-12	VF-20	EF-40	AU-50	Unc-60	Unc-63	Unc-65
$40	$60	$90	$140	$230	$300	$500	$850

THIRD ISSUE, 10¢

The face has a portrait of George Washington at the center, a different image from that used on the Third Series 3¢ notes. Counters are printed to the left and right and are also in bronze ink at the four corners. The word CENTS does not appear on either side, apparently an oversight. A tiny "1" position numeral appears centered inside of the left border on the face of some notes. These notes were printed in sheets of 16 notes, arranged four notes across and four down. The four notes in the left margin each have the "1" numeral. Accordingly, they are about three times rarer than the variety without the "1." Some notes have inked signatures of Colby and Spinner or Jeffries and Spinner, called "autographed," but typically signed by clerks. The backs were printed in red and green. All were printed on standard white bank-note paper. *Printage:* 169,761,345. *Size:* 84 mm wide, 48 mm high.

Green Back (First Series)

W-6331 • F-1255 • Green back • No "1" on face • Printed signatures of Colby and Spinner

VG-8	F-12	VF-20	EF-40	AU-50	Unc-60	Unc-63	Unc-65
$22	$32	$45	$60	$80	$105	$160	$400

W-6333 • F-1255a • Inked signatures of Colby and Spinner

Recorded population: 3 • *Commentary:* Autographed notes were signed using ink with high iron content, which turns the signatures brownish. Signatures that are fully black are usually printed.

W-6335 • F-1256 • With "1" on face • Printed signatures of Colby and Spinner

VG-8	F-12	VF-20	EF-40	AU-50	Unc-60	Unc-63	Unc-65
$25	$36	$50	$75	$100	$130	$210	$500

Red Back (Second Series)

W-6337 • F-1251 • Red back • No design number "1" on face • Printed signatures of Colby and Spinner

VG-8	F-12	VF-20	EF-40	AU-50	Unc-60	Unc-63	Unc-65
$30	$50	$75	$115	$140	$170	$200	$400

THIRD ISSUE, 5¢

W-6315. Portrait of Spencer M. Clark, chief of the National Currency Bureau. With printed signatures of Colby and Spinner. No "a" on face.

Detail showing the tiny position letter "a" near the left edge on W-6313.

Back of W-6311, printed in green. First Series.

Back of W-6315, printed in red. Second Series.

W-6339 • F-1253 • Inked signatures of Colby and Spinner

VG-8	F-12	VF-20	EF-40	AU-50	Unc-60	Unc-63	Unc-65
$75	$110	$150	$250	$300	$400	$600	$900

W-6341 • F-1254 • Inked signatures of Jeffries and Spinner

VG-8	F-12	VF-20	EF-40	AU-50	Unc-60	Unc-63	Unc-65
$75	$120	$160	$270	$320	$450	$700	$1,250

W-6343 • F-1252 • With "1" on face • Printed signatures of Colby and Spinner

VG-8	F-12	VF-20	EF-40	AU-50	Unc-60	Unc-63	Unc-65
$40	$60	$75	$125	$150	$225	$350	$550

THIRD ISSUE, 25¢

The face of the Third Issue 25¢ note has the bust of William P. Fessenden at the center. He served as a senator until tapped to be the 26th secretary of the Treasury in 1864, a position he held until returning to the Senate in March 1865, which post he held until his death in 1869. There are counter surcharges, oriented vertically with the bases of the numerals toward the portrait, to the left and right, but these are not bold due to the heavy black printing in the same areas. Early issues have them in outline form, with ornate flourishes surrounding. Later issues have a solid, heavy background with a counter in drop-out white.

Sheets of 12 notes were arranged with four across and three down. The three at the left margin had a position letter "a" at the lower left of the face. This letter is found in several different sizes. The back, printed in either green (First Series) or red (Second Series), has a large, outlined 25 bronze surcharge at the center. Most 25¢ notes are on thick fiber paper. Those with the face surcharge in drop-out white are on thinner paper of a different kind. All have printed signatures of Colby and Spinner.

Gene Hessler suggests that about 124,570,000 Third Series 25¢ notes were printed, of which only about 16,000 were red backs. The last would seem to have been made primarily for numismatic purposes. *Printage:* 124,572,755. *Size:* 98 mm wide, 48 mm high.

Green Back (First Series)

W-6351 • F-1294 • Green back • No position letter "a" on face • Outline "25" in bronze on face

VG-8	F-12	VF-20	EF-40	AU-50	Unc-60	Unc-63	Unc-65
$24	$40	$50	$75	$100	$125	$200	$450

W-6353 • F-1295 • With small position letter "a" on face in Position 1

VG-8	F-12	VF-20	EF-40	AU-50	Unc-60	Unc-63	Unc-65
$26	$45	$55	$80	$110	$145	$225	$500

THIRD ISSUE, 10¢

W-6331, with portrait of George Washington.

Detail of the tiny position numeral "1" near the left edge of W-6335.

Back of W-6331. First Series, printed in green.

Back of W-6339. Second Series, printed in red.

W-6355 • F-1296 • Position letter "a" on face in Position 2, located about 7 mm to the lower right of the position used the Position 1 "a" • Outline "25" in bronze on face

VG-8	F-12	VF-20	EF-40	AU-50	Unc-60	Unc-63	Unc-65
$700	$1,000	$1,550	$1,750	$2,000	$2,250	$3,000	$4,500

W-6357 • F-1297 • No position letter "a" on face • Surcharge M/2/6/5 on back • Thick fiber paper

VG-8	F-12	VF-20	EF-40	AU-50	Unc-60	Unc-63	Unc-65
$40	$60	$75	$110	$190	$300	$600	$1,000

W-6359 • F-1298 • With small position letter "a" on face in Position 1

VG-8	F-12	VF-20	EF-40	AU-50	Unc-60	Unc-63	Unc-65
$65	$85	$110	$150	$250	$400	$700	$1,250

W-6361 • F-1299 • No position letter "a" on face • Drop-out white "25" in bronze on face

VG-8	F-12	VF-20	EF-40	AU-50	Unc-60	Unc-63	Unc-65
$350	$650	$1,000	$1,500	$2,000	$2,250	$3,200	$4,500

W-6363 • F-1300 • With small position letter "a" on face

VG-8	F-12	VF-20	EF-40	AU-50	Unc-60	Unc-63
$600	$1,300	$2,000	$3,000	$4,000	$4,500	$6,500

Red Back (Second Series)

W-6365 • F-1291 • Red back • No position letter "a" on face • Thin white paper

VG-8	F-12	VF-20	EF-40	AU-50	Unc-60	Unc-63	Unc-65
$40	$60	$75	$110	$175	$250	$500	$750

THIRD ISSUE, 25¢

Face of W-6357. Portrait of secretary of the Treasury William P. Fessenden (1864–1865).

Plate letter "a" in Position 1.

Plate letter "a" in Position 2.

First Series back, printed in green.

Second Series back, printed in red.

W-6366 • F-1292 • Small position letter "a" on face

VG-8	F-12	VF-20	EF-40	AU-50	Unc-60	Unc-63	Unc-65
$50	$75	$100	$150	$225	$350	$700	$950

THIRD ISSUE, 50¢

The Third Issue 50¢ notes are the most extensive and complex in the Fractional Currency series. These were made with two basic face designs and two back designs.

Spinner Face: The face has the portrait of Treasurer of the United States Francis E. Spinner (who served in that post from 1861 to 1875), whose florid signature is the best known in the paper-money field. Heavy bronze imprints with FIFTY in drop-out white are to the left and right. This is the *only* instance in which a Treasury official appears on the same note as his signature.

Justice Face: The face has the seated figure of Justice with scales in her left hand and her right arm resting on a shield. Heavy bronze imprints with FIFTY in drop-out white are to the left and right. Justice notes had approximately 1/16 to 3/32 of an inch of space between notes on a sheet. As a result, when trimmed from sheets, most notes have two or three sides with margins while the remaining sides are trimmed into the engraving. As such, Justice notes with four margins are highly prized by collectors.[16]

Text Back: The center has a panel filled with horizontal text. To each side is a vertical counter.

Fifty Cents Back: The center has FIFTY 50 CENTS on a lobed vignette.

Backs are in green (First Series) and red (Second Series). A large, outlined bronze counter is at the center.

The Third Issue 50¢ notes were printed 12 to a sheet, arranged four across and three down. Six of these notes had no position letter or numeral. Two had the position letter "a." Three had the position numeral "1." One had both a letter "a" and a numeral "1." These combinations, plus back surcharges create many different varieties within this issue.

All have printed signatures of Colby and Spinner except as otherwise designated. Some with inked signatures were created for the numismatic and philatelic trade, including some after the Third Issue had officially ended. *Printage:* 73,470,853 total: 50¢ Spinner with Text Back, 52,866,690 notes; Spinner with Fifty Cents Back, 10,868,028; Justice, 9,737,135. *Size:* 115 mm wide (widest in the series), 49 mm high.

Spinner Face, Red Text Back
Back Surcharge A/2/6/5

W-6371 • F-1324 • No position letter or numeral on face • Printed signatures of Colby and Spinner

VG-8	F-12	VF-20	EF-40	AU-50	Unc-60	Unc-63	Unc-65
$80	$100	$140	$200	$260	$380	$575	$900

W-6373 • F-1328 • Inked signatures of Colby and Spinner (1864–1867)

VG-8	F-12	VF-20	EF-40	AU-50	Unc-60	Unc-63	Unc-65
$80	$115	$150	$200	$270	$400	$600	$850

W-6375 • F-1329 • Inked signatures of Allison and Spinner (1869–1875)

VG-8	F-12	VF-20	EF-40	AU-50	Unc-60	Unc-63	Unc-65
$100	$140	$200	$275	$400	$575	$900	$1,325

W-6377 • F-1330 • Inked signatures of Allison and New (1875–1876)

VG-8	F-12	VF-20	EF-40	AU-50	Unc-60	Unc-63	Unc-65
$1,000	$1,250	$1,900	$2,300	$2,900	$3,500	$5,000	$7,500

W-6379 • F-1327 • Design letter "a" on face

VG-8	F-12	VF-20	EF-40	AU-50	Unc-60	Unc-63	Unc-65
$95	$125	$175	$240	$300	$450	$675	$1,100

W-6381 • F-1326 • Position numeral "1" on face

VG-8	F-12	VF-20	EF-40	AU-50	Unc-60	Unc-63	Unc-65
$90	$120	$160	$225	$280	$425	$625	$1,000

W-6383 • F-1325 • Both "a" and "1" on face

VG-8	F-12	VF-20	EF-40	AU-50	Unc-60	Unc-63	Unc-65
$225	$290	$400	$575	$700	$1,000	$1,300	$2,100

Spinner Face, Green Text Back
No Back Surcharge

W-6391 • F-1331 • No position letter or numeral on face

VG-8	F-12	VF-20	EF-40	AU-50	Unc-60	Unc-63	Unc-65
$60	$80	$100	$140	$210	$325	$500	$700

W-6393 • F-1334 • Design letter "a" on face

VG-8	F-12	VF-20	EF-40	AU-50	Unc-60	Unc-63	Unc-65
$65	$85	$115	$190	$250	$380	$600	$900

W-6395 • F-1333 • Position numeral "1" on face

VG-8	F-12	VF-20	EF-40	AU-50	Unc-60	Unc-63	Unc-65
$65	$85	$110	$175	$235	$360	$550	$800

W-6397 • F-1332 • Both "a" and "1" on face

VG-8	F-12	VF-20	EF-40	AU-50	Unc-60	Unc-63	Unc-65
$75	$100	$130	$195	$275	$400	$675	$1,000

Spinner Face, Green Text Back
Back Surcharge A/2/6/5

W-6399 • F-1335 • No position letter or numeral on face

VG-8	F-12	VF-20	EF-40	AU-50	Unc-60	Unc-63	Unc-65
$100	$125	$150	$175	$275	$400	$650	$1,000

W-6401 • F-1338 • Design letter "a" on face

VG-8	F-12	VF-20	EF-40	AU-50	Unc-60	Unc-63	Unc-65
$125	$165	$200	$250	$350	$550	$850	$1,500

W-6403 • F-1337 • Position numeral "1" on face

VG-8	F-12	VF-20	EF-40	AU-50	Unc-60	Unc-63	Unc-65
$125	$165	$200	$250	$350	$550	$850	$1,500

THIRD ISSUE, 50¢, SPINNER FACE

Detail showing position numeral "1" near left border (to the left of the second F in "FIFTY" and position letter "a" near bottom border below the first F.

W-6383. With "a" and "1" on face. Bust of United States Treasurer F.E. Spinner.

Red Text Back of W-6383. Surcharge A/2/6/5.

Green Text Back.

Green Fifty Cents Back.

W-6405 • F-1336 • Both "a" and "1" on face

VG-8	F-12	VF-20	EF-40	AU-50	Unc-60	Unc-63	Unc-65
$500	$850	$1,100	$1,700	$2,100	$2,600	$3,700	$5,000

Spinner Face, Green Fifty Cents Back
No Back Surcharge

W-6407 • F-1339 • No position letter or numeral on face

VG-8	F-12	VF-20	EF-40	AU-50	Unc-60	Unc-63	Unc-65
$50	$70	$115	$160	$225	$290	$350	$600

W-6409 • F-1342 • Design letter "a" on face

VG-8	F-12	VF-20	EF-40	AU-50	Unc-60	Unc-63	Unc-65
$60	$85	$130	$185	$320	$400	$600	$900

W-6411 • F-1341 • Position numeral "1" on face

VG-8	F-12	VF-20	EF-40	AU-50	Unc-60	Unc-63	Unc-65
$60	$85	$130	$185	$275	$340	$500	$750

W-6413 • F-1340 • Both "a" and "1" on face

VG-8	F-12	VF-20	EF-40	AU-50	Unc-60	Unc-63	Unc-65
$75	$130	$200	$275	$450	$750	$1,000	$1,600

Justice Face, Red Text Back
No Back Surcharge

W-6415 • F-1343 • No position letter or numeral on face
• Printed signatures of Colby and Spinner

VG-8	F-12	VF-20	EF-40	AU-50	Unc-60	Unc-63	Unc-65
$50	$75	$130	$185	$275	$375	$600	$850

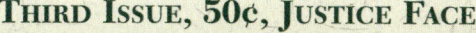

THIRD ISSUE, 50¢, JUSTICE FACE

W-6421. Justice seated with arm on shield.

Red Text Back of note W-6421.

Green Text Back of note W-6445.

THIRD ISSUE, 50¢, JUSTICE FACE, *continued*

Back of W-6467 showing corner bronze surcharges close to margins.

Back of W-6473 showing corner bronze surcharges distant from margins and on part of the design.

W-6417 • F-1355 • Inked signatures of Colby and Spinner

VG-8	F-12	VF-20	EF-40	AU-50	Unc-60	Unc-63	Unc-65
$75	$100	$150	$240	$325	$400	$600	$1,000

W-6419 • F-1346 • Design letter "a" on face • Printed signatures of Colby and Spinner

VG-8	F-12	VF-20	EF-40	AU-50	Unc-60	Unc-63	Unc-65
$55	$80	$145	$200	$325	$450	$700	$1,050

W-6421 • F-1345 • With position numeral "1" on face

VG-8	F-12	VF-20	EF-40	AU-50	Unc-60	Unc-63	Unc-65
$55	$80	$145	$200	$300	$425	$675	$975

W-6423 • F-1344 • Both "a" and "1" on face

VG-8	F-12	VF-20	EF-40	AU-50	Unc-60	Unc-63	Unc-65
$350	$500	$700	$1,000	$1,750	$2,500	$3,000	$4,250

W-6427 • F-1356 • Inked signatures of Colby and Spinner

VG-8	F-12	VF-20	EF-40	AU-50	Unc-60	Unc-63	Unc-65
$100	$150	$225	$350	$450	$550	$700	$1,150

W-6429 • F-1350 • Design letter "a" on face • Printed signatures of Colby and Spinner

VG-8	F-12	VF-20	EF-40	AU-50	Unc-60	Unc-63	Unc-65
$75	$120	$200	$350	$500	$750	$950	$1,550

W-6431 • F-1349 • With position numeral "1" on face

VG-8	F-12	VF-20	EF-40	AU-50	Unc-60	Unc-63	Unc-65
$75	$100	$175	$275	$380	$525	$750	$1,400

W-6433 • F-1348 • Both "a" and "1" on face

VG-8	F-12	VF-20	EF-40	AU-50	Unc-60	Unc-63	Unc-65
$450	$600	$800	$1,100	$2,000	$2,500	$3,500	$5,000

Justice Face, Red Text Back
Back Surcharge A/2/6/5

W-6425 • F-1347 • No position letter or numeral on face • Printed signatures of Colby and Spinner

VG-8	F-12	VF-20	EF-40	AU-50	Unc-60	Unc-63	Unc-65
$50	$75	$130	$185	$275	$350	$575	$800

Justice Face, Red Text Back
Back Surcharge S/2/6/4, Fiber Paper

W-6435 • F-1351 • No position letter or numeral on face • Printed signatures of Colby and Spinner

VG-8	F-12	VF-20	EF-40	AU-50	Unc-60	Unc-63
$2,500	$5,000	$6,500	$9,000	$12,500	$15,000	$25,000

W-6437 • F-1357 • Inked signatures of Colby and Spinner

VG-8	F-12	VF-20	EF-40	AU-50	Unc-60	Unc-63	Unc-65
$250	$350	$500	$700	$1,300	$2,000	$3,000	$5,000

W-6439 • F-1354 • With position letter "a" on face • Printed signatures of Colby and Spinner

VG-8	F-12	VF-20	EF-40	AU-50	Unc-60
$3,250	$6,750	$10,000	$14,000	$20,000	$32,500

W-6441 • F-1353 • With position numeral "1" on face

VG-8	F-12	VF-20	EF-40	AU-50	Unc-60
$3,000	$6,000	$8,000	$12,500	$15,000	$25,000

W-6443 • F-1352 • Both "a" and "1" on face

F-12	VF-20
$55,000	$100,000

Justice Face, Green Text Back
No Back Surcharge

W-6445 • F-1358 • No position letter or numeral on face

VG-8	F-12	VF-20	EF-40	AU-50	Unc-60	Unc-63	Unc-65
$65	$90	$125	$190	$245	$400	$650	$1,000

W-6447 • F-1361 • Design letter "a" on face

VG-8	F-12	VF-20	EF-40	AU-50	Unc-60	Unc-63	Unc-65
$75	$110	$150	$225	$300	$525	$875	$1,400

W-6449 • F-1360 • Position numeral "1" on face

VG-8	F-12	VF-20	EF-40	AU-50	Unc-60	Unc-63	Unc-65
$75	$100	$140	$200	$275	$475	$800	$1,200

W-6451 • F-1359 • Both "a" and "1" on face

VG-8	F-12	VF-20	EF-40	AU-50	Unc-60	Unc-63	Unc-65
$375	$575	$1,000	$1,600	$1,900	$2,250	$3,500	$6,000

Justice Face, Green Text Back
Back Surcharge A/2/6/5 Close to Margins, Bank-Note Paper

W-6453 • F-1366 • No position letter or numeral on face

VG-8	F-12	VF-20	EF-40	AU-50	Unc-60	Unc-63	Unc-65
$80	$125	$190	$275	$375	$500	$750	$1,200

W-6455 • F-1369 • Design letter "a" on face

VG-8	F-12	VF-20	EF-40	AU-50	Unc-60	Unc-63	Unc-65
$150	$300	$475	$600	$725	$850	$1,350	$2,200

W-6457 • F-1368 • Position numeral "1" on face

VG-8	F-12	VF-20	EF-40	AU-50	Unc-60	Unc-63	Unc-65
$90	$175	$325	$425	$600	$750	$1,500	$2,600

W-6459 • F-1367 • Both "a" and "1" on face (similar in location to the Spinner issue)

VG-8	F-12	VF-20	EF-40	AU-50	Unc-60	Unc-63
$750	$1,250	$1,750	$2,250	$3,000	$4,500	$7,500

Justice Face, Green Text Back
Back Surcharge A/2/6/5 Close to Margins, Fiber Paper

W-6461 • F-1370 • No position letter or numeral on face

VG-8	F-12	VF-20	EF-40	AU-50	Unc-60	Unc-63	Unc-65
$100	$180	$270	$350	$450	$750	$1,100	$1,750

W-6463 • F-1373 • Design letter "a" on face

VG-8	F-12	VF-20	EF-40	AU-50	Unc-60	Unc-63	Unc-65
$130	$200	$275	$390	$700	$900	$2,000	$3,500

W-6465 • F-1372 • Position numeral "1" on face

VG-8	F-12	VF-20	EF-40	AU-50	Unc-60	Unc-63	Unc-65
$125	$195	$260	$360	$650	$825	$1,750	$3,000

W-6467 • F-1371 • Both "a" and "1" on face

VG-8	F-12	VF-20	EF-40	AU-50	Unc-60	Unc-63	Unc-65
$600	$1,050	$1,500	$1,800	$2,600	$3,800	$6,000	$15,000

Justice Face, Green Text Back
Back Surcharge A/2/6/4 Close to Margins, Fiber Paper

W-6469 • F-1373a • No position letter or numeral on face

VG-8	F-12	VF-20	EF-40	AU-50
$7,500	$12,500	$20,000	$37,500	$50,000

Justice Face, Green Text Back
Back Surcharge A/2/6/5 Distant from Margins, Bank-Note Paper

W-6471 • F-1362 • No position letter or numeral on face

VG-8	F-12	VF-20	EF-40	AU-50	Unc-60	Unc-63	Unc-65
$65	$90	$125	$190	$245	$400	$600	$1,000

W-6473 • F-1365 • Design letter "a" on face

VG-8	F-12	VF-20	EF-40	AU-50	Unc-60	Unc-63	Unc-65
$75	$100	$145	$215	$300	$500	$750	$1,200

W-6475 • F-1364 • Position numeral "1" on face

VG-8	F-12	VF-20	EF-40	AU-50	Unc-60	Unc-63	Unc-65
$70	$95	$135	$200	$275	$475	$700	$1,100

W-6477 • F-1363 • Both "a" and "1" on face

VG-8	F-12	VF-20	EF-40	AU-50	Unc-60	Unc-63	Unc-65
$130	$200	$295	$400	$600	$800	$1,100	$1,500

FOURTH ISSUE, FRACTIONAL CURRENCY

July 14, 1869, to February 16, 1875
10¢, 15¢, 25¢, AND 50¢

This series included the 15¢ denomination, which was never popular, and was also the first to have the Treasury seal imprinted. Three designs were made of the 50¢ note, each of a different size. Some Fourth Issue bills were printed on paper with blue tinting from the tiny colored fibers under the Willcox patent of 1866. This tinting is also seen on certain National Bank, Legal Tender, and other bills of the era, giving them a special elegance.

With Spencer M. Clark gone from the National Currency Bureau, contract printing of Fractional Currency was resumed by the American Bank Note Company and National Bank Note Company in New York (printers of Postage Currency in 1862 and 1863).

Beginning with the Fourth Issue, the Treasury seal is used for the first time and appears on all varieties. The seal is very large on the 10¢, 15¢, 25¢, and Lincoln 50¢ notes. The 50¢ notes were made in three types—depicting Abraham Lincoln, Edwin M. Stanton, and Samuel Dexter—each with a different face and back and each with a different style of Treasury seal. The Dexter notes have plate numbers and letters. The backs of all are printed in green.

All Fourth Issue notes have the printed signatures of Allison and Spinner. The bronze printing no longer appears, and the paper is of a better quality. Various types of paper were used including plain, watermarked, blue-tinted, coarse-fiber, and tiny-fiber forms.

Watermarks appear on certain of the regular issues, as noted. In addition, "they are on 'specimens' of earlier issues which were probably printed at a later date than the regular issues of those series," as D.W. Valentine observed.

This issue began on July 14, 1869, and continued until February 16, 1875, and amounted to $166,000,000.

Fractional Currency continued to be in strong demand by collectors. In July 1871, this notice was included in the *American Journal of Numismatics:* "Those of our friends who desire to obtain complete sets of the varieties and denominations of this currency, as originally issued by the Treasury Department, can do so by remitting $8.65 to the 'Currency Bureau, Treasury Department, Washington, D.C.' A complete set consists of 32 pieces."

FOURTH ISSUE, 10¢

The Fourth Issue 10¢ note is the only one that is RECEIVABLE FOR ALL UNITED STATES STAMPS. The Liberty portrait is said to have been modeled by Mary Hull and was engraved by Charles Burt. AMERICAN BANK NOTE

CO. N.Y. is in the top border. The back, printed in green, has NATIONAL BANK NOTE COMPANY NEW YORK in the bottom margin. The large red Treasury seal adds a vivid splash of color. The seal is found in two diameters: 40 mm, which slightly overlaps the border, and 38 mm, which barely fits within the border.

Sheets of 16 notes were arranged four across and four down. On uncut sheets a red plate number for the Treasury seal appears at the intersection between the four notes in the upper left corner. The typical note is on watermarked paper with silk fibers. *Printage:* 349,409,600. *Size:* 80 mm wide, 47 mm high.

W-6601 • F-1257 • 40 mm Treasury seal • Watermarked paper

VG-8	F-12	VF-20	EF-40	AU-50	Unc-60	Unc-63	Unc-65
$22	$32	$50	$65	$90	$120	$210	$300

W-6603 • F-1258 • White paper with fibers • No watermark

VG-8	F-12	VF-20	EF-40	AU-50	Unc-60	Unc-63	Unc-65
$25	$36	$55	$85	$110	$160	$210	$300

W-6605 • F-1259 • Paper with blue-tinted streak

VG-8	F-12	VF-20	EF-40	AU-50	Unc-60	Unc-63	Unc-65
$22	$32	$50	$65	$100	$140	$210	$400

W-6607 • F-1261 • 38 mm Treasury seal

VG-8	F-12	VF-20	EF-40	AU-50	Unc-60	Unc-63	Unc-65
$25	$36	$55	$85	$110	$160	$210	$300

FOURTH ISSUE, 15¢

The Fourth Issue was the only 15¢ denomination note made for regular commerce (notes of this denomination in the Third Issue were made in essay form only). At the left of the face is a classical bust of Columbia in a feathered headdress with eagle head, created by Douglas C. Romerson and engraved by Charles Burt. It resembles the Liberty used on certain pattern coins of the 1860s and elsewhere. Below the portrait is a horizontal fasces with part of the motto showing as PLURIBUS UNUM.

A large red Treasury seal (in 40 mm and 38 mm variations) is at the center, and a counter is at the upper right. The back is richly engraved and has counters vertically at each end. The National Bank Note Company imprint appears on the face, and that of the American Bank Note Company appears on the back. The varieties closely follow those of the 10¢ denomination.

Sheets of 12 notes were arranged four across and three down. On uncut sheets a red plate number for the Treasury seal appears at the intersection between the four notes in the upper left. *Printage:* 35,361,440. *Size:* 90 mm wide, 48 mm high.

W-6611 • F-1267 • 40 mm Treasury seal • Watermarked paper

VG-8	F-12	VF-20	EF-40	AU-50	Unc-60	Unc-63	Unc-65
$50	$60	$75	$105	$140	$185	$300	$600

FOURTH ISSUE, 10¢

 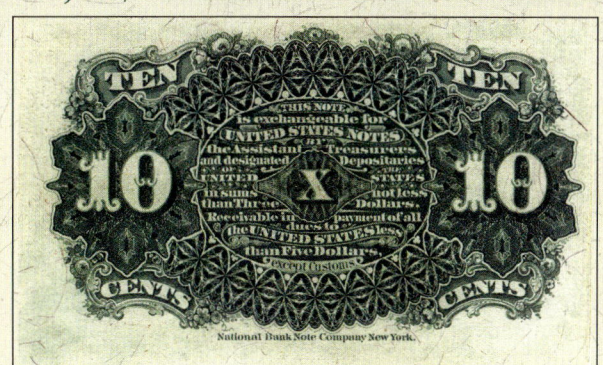

W-6603. Portrait of Liberty. This is the only Fourth Issue denomination that mentions stamps.

Back of W-6603.

FOURTH ISSUE, 15¢

W-6611. Bust of Columbia in oval frame of leaves above a horizontal fasces. This motif is especially artistic. 40 mm Treasury seal touches the borders. This is the only 15¢ issue made for circulation.

W-6617 with 39 mm Treasury seal.

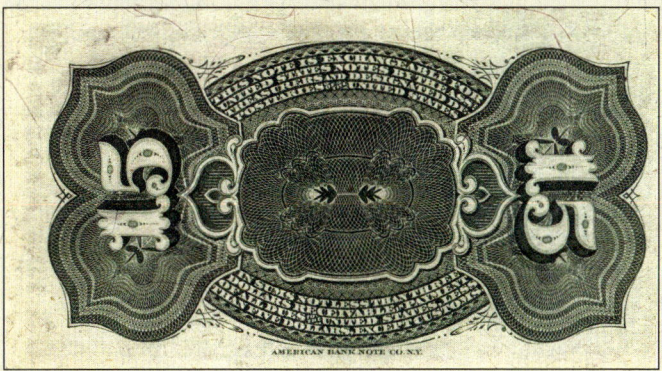

Back of W-6611.

W-6613 • F-1268 • White paper with fibers • No watermark

Unc-60	Unc-63	Unc-65
$1,500	$2,000	$3,000

W-6615 • F-1269 • Paper with blue-tinted streak

VG-8	F-12	VF-20	EF-40	AU-50	Unc-60	Unc-63	Unc-65
$50	$60	$75	$105	$140	$200	$320	$650

W-6617 • F-1271 • 38 mm Treasury seal

VG-8	F-12	VF-20	EF-40	AU-50	Unc-60	Unc-63	Unc-65
$50	$60	$85	$120	$160	$215	$320	$650

FOURTH ISSUE, 25¢

The Fourth Issue 25¢ note has the Stuart portrait of Washington to the left, a large red Treasury Seal (in 40 mm and 38 mm varieties) at the center, and a "25" counter to the right. The back is ornately engraved with a counter in drop-out white at the center. The National Bank Note Company imprint appears on the face, and that of the American Bank Note Company appears on the back. The Treasury seal and paper variations follow those of the 10¢ and 15¢ denominations.

Sheets of 12 notes were arranged four across and three down. On uncut sheets a red plate number for the Treasury seal appears at the intersection between the four notes in the upper left. *Printage:* 235,689,024. *Size:* 97 mm wide, 47 mm high.

W-6621 • F-1301 • 40 mm Treasury seal • Watermarked paper

VG-8	F-12	VF-20	EF-40	AU-50	Unc-60	Unc-63	Unc-65
$22	$35	$50	$80	$100	$120	$225	$400

W-6623 • F-1302 • White paper with fibers • No watermark

VG-8	F-12	VF-20	EF-40	AU-50	Unc-60	Unc-63	Unc-65
$24	$40	$60	$90	$135	$160	$275	$475

W-6625 • F-1303 • Paper with blue-tinted streak

VG-8	F-12	VF-20	EF-40	AU-50	Unc-60	Unc-63	Unc-65
$22	$35	$50	$90	$200	$300	$425	$700

W-6627 • F-1307 • 38 mm Treasury seal

VG-8	F-12	VF-20	EF-40	AU-50	Unc-60	Unc-63	Unc-65
$24	$40	$60	$90	$150	$180	$300	$575

FOURTH ISSUE, 50¢

The Fourth Issue 50¢ notes are of three distinct types:

Lincoln: The face has a portrait of Abraham Lincoln engraved by Charles Burt from a photograph by Anthony Berger. A large red Treasury seal is slightly left of the center. The back is heavily and richly engraved. These are typically on white bank-note paper. Sheets of 12 notes were arranged four across and three down. On uncut sheets a red plate number for the Treasury seal appears at the intersection between the four notes in the upper left. *Printage:* 19,152,000. *Size:* 106 mm wide, 47 mm high.

Stanton: The face has a portrait of Edwin M. Stanton, secretary of war in Lincoln's cabinet. Stanton was with Lincoln after the president's mortal wounding. Stanton died on December 24, 1869. Notes with his visage were issued soon afterward, in December 1870. A small red Treasury seal is to the lower right of the portrait. The back has the counter 50 CENTS in an ellipse at the right. The left and center are mostly open, with light lettering. These are typically on paper with a blue-tinted streak and coarse fibers. *Printage:* 86,048,000. *Size:* 103 mm wide, 47 mm high.

Dexter: Samuel Dexter, secretary of the Treasury and secretary of war (1800–1802), is depicted to the left. At the center is a Treasury seal in green with a scalloped border. The back has the counter in a circle with a scalloped border at the right. The left and center are mostly open, with light lettering. These are typically on paper with a blue-tinted streak and coarse fibers. *Printage:* 49,599,200. *Size:* 96 mm wide, 55 mm high (tallest in the series).

The American Bank Note Company made the plates for the face of the Lincoln type and for the back of the Stanton type. The National Bank Note Company made the plates for the backs of the Lincoln and Dexter types. The Bureau of Engraving and Printing made the plates for the faces of the Stanton and Dexter types.

Lincoln Face

W-6631 • F-1374 • Lincoln portrait • Large red Treasury seal • Watermarked paper

VG-8	F-12	VF-20	EF-40	AU-50	Unc-60	Unc-63	Unc-65
$60	$110	$170	$280	$450	$600	$900	$1,300

Stanton Face

W-6635 • F-1376 • Stanton portrait • Small red Treasury seal • Paper with blue-tinted streak

VG-8	F-12	VF-20	EF-40	AU-50	Unc-60	Unc-63	Unc-65
$25	$40	$65	$115	$150	$225	$400	$725

Dexter Face

W-6639 • F-1379 • Dexter portrait • Small green Treasury seal with scalloped border • Paper with blue-tinted streak

VG-8	F-12	VF-20	EF-40	AU-50	Unc-60	Unc-63	Unc-65
$25	$35	$60	$100	$135	$195	$300	$525

FOURTH ISSUE, 25¢

W-6621, with bust of George Washington.

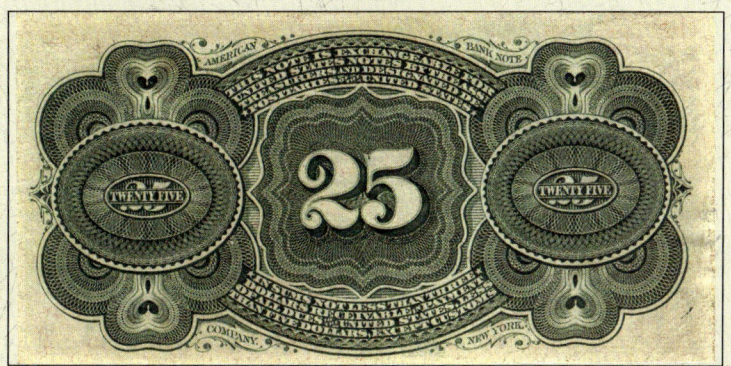

Back of W-6621.

FOURTH ISSUE, 50¢, LINCOLN FACE

W-6631, with portrait of Abraham Lincoln.

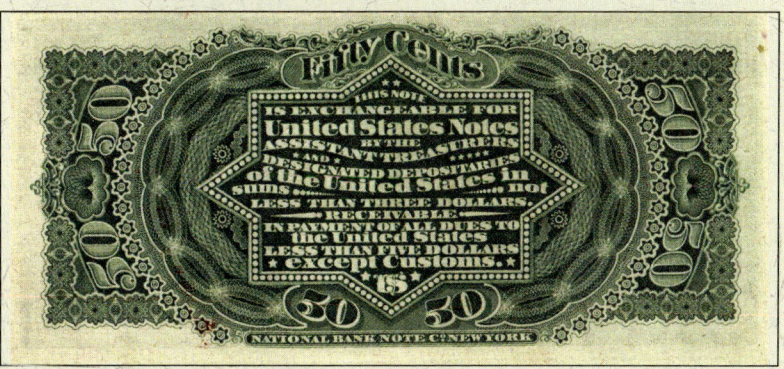

Back of W-6631.

FOURTH ISSUE, 50¢, STANTON FACE

W-6635, with bust of secretary of war Edwin M. Stanton.

Back of W-6635.

FOURTH ISSUE, 50¢, DEXTER FACE

W-6639, with bust of Samuel Dexter.

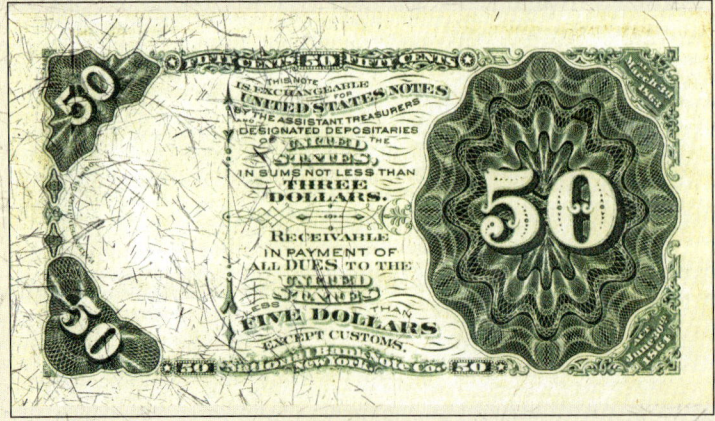

Back of W-6639.

FIFTH ISSUE, FRACTIONAL CURRENCY

February 26, 1874, to February 15, 1876
10¢, 25¢, AND 50¢

The Fifth Issue of Fractional Currency spanned just two years and came to an end when the Act of April 17, 1876, provided for the resumption of payment at par of silver coins. Such coins had been absent from commerce since the spring of 1862. Actual resumption began on a large scale on April 20.

Notes were produced in three denominations and were issued from February 26, 1874, to February 15, 1876. This was in the twilight era of this class of paper money, and many undistributed pieces were sold by banks to dealers, as the collecting of such bills had become popular.

Certain issues have variations in the Treasury seal, described as Thin Key and Thick Key (both keys are the same length), but there are other differences as well. Notes of the Fifth Issue have a face plate letter and number.

FIFTH ISSUE, 10¢

The 10¢ note has an unflattering portrait of William M. Meredith by Thomas Knollwood, engraved by Charles

Burt. Meredith, of Pennsylvania, was appointed secretary of the Treasury on March 7, 1849, and retired on July 10, 1850. The Treasury seal is found in green or red, and in Thin and Thick Key varieties. The face plates were made by the Bureau of Engraving and Printing, and the backs by the Columbian Bank Note Company of Washington, D.C.

Many of these notes went into the hands of coin and stamp dealers, often in little bundles wrapped with paper strips, and were seen in quantity for years afterward. *Printage:* 199,899,000. *Size:* 84 mm wide, 53 mm high.

W-6651 • F-1264 • Green Treasury seal • Thin Key

VG-8	F-12	VF-20	EF-40	AU-50	Unc-60	Unc-63	Unc-65
$40	$55	$70	$80	$100	$150	$200	$350

W-6653 • F-1265 • Red Treasury seal

VG-8	F-12	VF-20	EF-40	AU-50	Unc-60	Unc-63	Unc-65
$22	$32	$40	$50	$60	$75	$100	$225

W-6655 • F-1266 • Thick Key

VG-8	F-12	VF-20	EF-40	AU-50	Unc-60	Unc-63	Unc-65
$22	$32	$40	$50	$60	$75	$100	$225

FIFTH ISSUE, 25¢

The 25¢ note has the bust of Robert J. Walker, who served as secretary of the Treasury from March 5, 1845, until he retired in March 1849 with the change of administration. Similar to the arrangement for the 10¢ notes of the Fifth

FIFTH ISSUE, 10¢

W-6651, with bust of Treasury secretary William M. Meredith. Green Treasury seal with Thin Key.

Back of W-6651.

Detail of Treasury seal with Thin Key.

Detail of Treasury seal with Thick Key.

FIFTH ISSUE, 25¢

W-6663, with bust of Treasury secretary Robert J. Walker.

Back of W-6663.

Issue, the face plates for the 25¢ notes were made by the Bureau of Engraving and Printing, and the backs by the Columbian Bank Note Company of Washington, D.C. Thin and Thick Key varieties are seen in the Treasury seal. *Printage:* 144,368,000. *Size:* 91 mm wide, 53 mm high.

W-6661 • F-1308 • Red Treasury seal • Thin key

VG-8	F-12	VF-20	EF-40	AU-50	Unc-60	Unc-63	Unc-65
$22	$31	$40	$50	$60	$75	$125	$270

W-6663 • F-1309 • Thick key

VG-8	F-12	VF-20	EF-40	AU-50	Unc-60	Unc-63	Unc-65
$22	$31	$40	$50	$60	$75	$125	$270

FIFTH ISSUE, 50¢

The 50¢ note depicts William H. Crawford, who was appointed secretary of the Treasury on November 5, 1816, and served until March 6, 1825, when he retired as the administration changed. Simultaneously, he was secretary of war.

The face plates were made by the Bureau of Engraving and Printing, and the backs by Joseph B. Carpenter of Philadelphia. *Printage:* 13,160,000. *Size:* 112 mm wide, 53 mm high.

W-6667 • F-1381 • Small red Treasury seal

VG-8	F-12	VF-20	EF-40	AU-50	Unc-60	Unc-63	Unc-65
$29	$37	$50	$75	$100	$125	$200	$400

ESSAYS, PROOFS, SPECIMENS AND OTHER SPECIAL ISSUES

FRACTIONAL CURRENCY SHIELDS

To aid in the identification of counterfeits and to provide bills for display to banks and others interested, the Treasury department created Fractional Currency Shields. These consisted of a shield outline printed in gray (although a few are in green or pink, which are much rarer) surmounted by an eagle and stars. On the shield, 39 specimens of Fractional Currency, consisting of 20 faces and 19 backs, were pasted by hand. These were of the First, Second, and Third Issues.

These shields were sold for $4.50 each, beginning in 1867. In January 1868, Philadelphia dealer E.L. Mason Jr. offered them for $6 each, stating that they had just been released. Purchasers mounted many of them under glass in a wooden frame with a gilt inner frame next to the glass, and backed by thin wooden slats.

In 1869 Treasurer Francis E. Spinner stated that the remaining examples in Washington had been destroyed. Spinner, a man of unimpeachable integrity, must have been misinformed at the time. It seems that a few were kept on

FIFTH ISSUE, 50¢

W-6667, with bust of Treasury secretary William H. Crawford.

Back of W-6667.

hand and later augmented with a few later Fractional Currency notes, sometimes with a postage stamp or two and even with a courtesy autograph of Spinner himself. As to how many were issued, no records have been found, but the figure was certainly in the high hundreds, or perhaps even far more than a thousand. Gene Hessler comments, "About 4,500 Shields are believed to have been prepared, but only about 300 are known to collectors today."[17]

Among all the numismatic items produced in American history, the Fractional Currency Shield is no doubt the most displayable in its original form. Indeed, this is one of only a few such 19th-century items originally intended for this purpose.

Most of these have slight water stains along the bottom (especially to the right) from flooding in the Treasury department's basement, where they were stored. Best prices are for framed shields in Very Fine to Extremely Fine preservation, with minimal stains, good color to the notes, and backgrounds intact. Shields with trimmed backgrounds or with other problems sell for far less.

W-6801 • F-1382 • **Fractional Currency Shield with gray background** • 300 to 400 estimated to exist today • Price in VF to EF: $5,000 to $6,500

W-6803 • F-1383 • **Fractional Currency Shield with pink background** • About 20 estimated to exist today • Price in VF to EF: $10,000 to $15,000

W-6805 • F-1383a • **Fractional Currency Shield with green background** • About 10 estimated to exist today • Price in VF to EF: $16,000 to $24,000

SPECIMENS AND PROOFS

Special printings of Fractional Currency can be divided into essays, proofs, specimens, and experimental notes.

An essay is a printed impression of an artist's design or a proposed plate that is made for study and review. Sometimes essays are adopted, and the design becomes a regular issue. Other times, the design is abandoned. Some essays have certain imprints, vignettes, or other features that were deleted on regular issues. The only essay specifically studied here is the Third Issue 15¢ note with the portraits of Grant and Sherman. The face and back designs were accepted, but the notes were never issued for circulation. Specimens, essays, and proofs are usually, but not always, printed on one side only.

The demarcation between a specimen and a proof note is muddied in this series. Strictly speaking, a proof (not usually capitalized) note is an impression of the face or back that is carefully printed to show the motif to government officials, artists, and others before such notes are made in quantity for commerce. A specimen note is an imprint made of one side or another, for observation, souvenir, or numismatic purposes, even though the design may be in use for circulating notes. Some Fractional Currency specimens have SPECIMEN stamped on them, while others do not. Some have thin-lined frames printed outside of the engraving to represent the border or edge of a note or to showcase the engraving.

Specimen and proof impressions of Fractional Currency bills were made in narrow-margin and wide-margin styles. Many if not most narrow-margin specimens were cut from

FRACTIONAL CURRENCY SHIELD

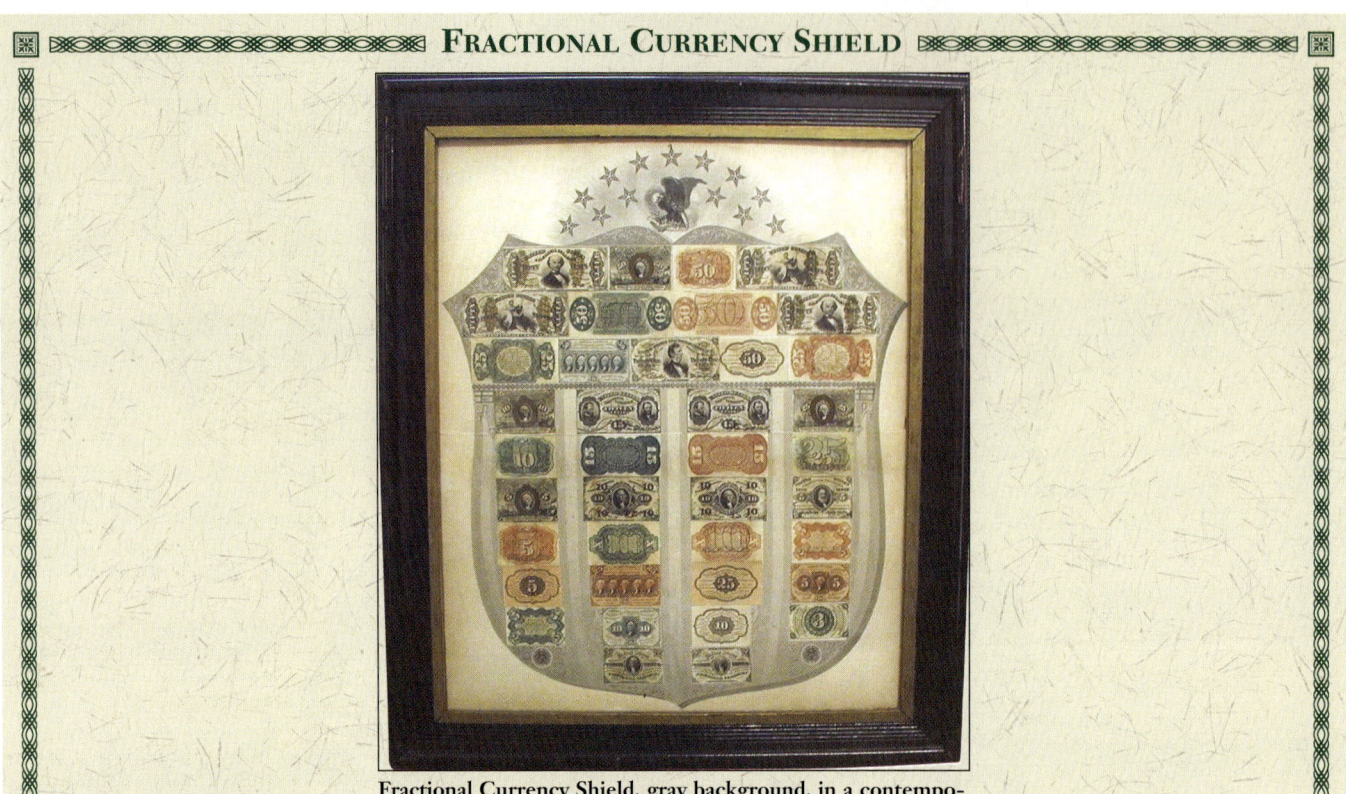

Fractional Currency Shield, gray background, in a contemporary wooden frame with a gilt liner.

printed sheets. Many of these were intended to be pasted on Fractional Currency Shields. Others on the market today have been removed from shields and typically show signs of glue or mounting on the back. In still other instances, collectors trimmed wide-margin notes to make them more convenient for display.

Wide-margin specimens were printed one at a time on single sheets of paper larger than a normal note, giving a broad border. These are much scarcer as a class.

D.W. Valentine notes that as many as 10 different types of paper were used for such proofs within a single series. A Mr. Phelps, in writing to dealer David Proskey, called pieces printed in purple ink "specimen" notes, and those with a semi-circular punch near the end, "experimental pieces." Other variations occur in the absence or presence of bronze printing. Some are stamped "specimens" and others are not. In addition to the foregoing, the paper can be thick or thin.

From time to time the Treasury department reported the number of specimen notes printed. In addition, Spencer M. Clark printed others for which no accounting was kept.[18]

Among the more interesting of the specimens are those autographed by clerks, bearing the inked signatures of Treasury officials Spinner, Colby, Jeffries, and Allison. Although no doubt some were actually signed as a courtesy by these men, most were the work of employees. In addition, some unsigned notes were later given fantasy signatures of Treasury officials for the numismatic trade.

It is a curious sidelight on the collecting of United States paper money that in the 1860s and 1870s the acquisition of regular and specimen Fractional Currency notes was a passion for many, and all dealers with storefront shops maintained good stocks of them. Stamp collectors and dealers

avidly sought them as well, this in an era in which there was absolutely no interest in collecting regular federal notes such as Legal Tender and National Bank issues.

During this time the Treasury tapped into collector interest for Fractional Currency and issued various notices, this being representative:

> Specimen Currency: The Treasury Department is now ready to supply applicants with sets of specimen Fractional Currency of all the descriptions ever issued, including two varieties of fifty-cent notes and one of the ten-cent notes, which are signed by the Register and Treasurer. The sets of full notes may be purchased for $5.75, while a set of half notes, or those having the face and back separate, will be sold for $4. The latter variety will be printed on Confederate bank-note paper, bearing the letters C.S.A. in watermark, which was manufactured in London for the Treasury Department of the Confederate States, so-called, and was found on board a blockade runner captured by one of the vessels composing the blockade squadron. A large quantity was obtained and sent to the Treasury Department, where it has been used for various purposes.

This paper had been seized on April 27, 1862, from the *Bermuda*, which was on her way back from England. A million sheets were purchased by the National Currency Bureau.[19]

On October 27, 1868, U.S. Treasurer Francis E. Spinner reported, "There has been sold at full face-value of Fractional Currency, for specimens, with faces and backs printed separately, and little, if any, of which will ever be returned for payment, $20,317.05."

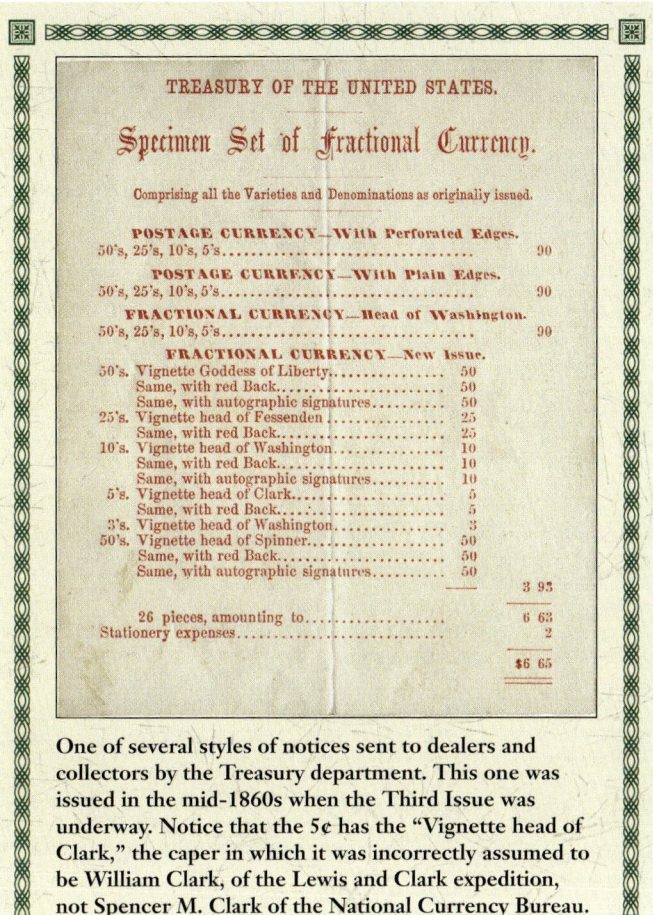

TREASURY OF THE UNITED STATES.

Specimen Set of Fractional Currency.

Comprising all the Varieties and Denominations as originally issued.

POSTAGE CURRENCY—With Perforated Edges.
50's, 25's, 10's, 5's... 90

POSTAGE CURRENCY—With Plain Edges.
50's, 25's, 5's.. 90

FRACTIONAL CURRENCY—Head of Washington.
50's, 10's, 5's.. 90

FRACTIONAL CURRENCY—New Issue.
50's. Vignette Goddess of Liberty,................ 50
     Same, with red Back....................... 50
     Same, with autographic signatures.......... 50
25's. Vignette head of Fessenden 25
     Same, with red Back....................... 25
10's. Vignette head of Washington............... 10
     Same, with red Back....................... 10
     Same, with autographic signatures.......... 10
5's. Vignette head of Clark..................... 5
     Same, with red Back....................... 5
3's. Vignette head of Washington................ 3
50's. Vignette head of Spinner.................. 50
     Same, with red Back....................... 50
     Same, with autographic signatures.......... 50
                              3 95

26 pieces, amounting to................... 6 63
Stationery expenses....................... 2
                              $6 65

One of several styles of notices sent to dealers and collectors by the Treasury department. This one was issued in the mid-1860s when the Third Issue was underway. Notice that the 5¢ has the "Vignette head of Clark," the caper in which it was incorrectly assumed to be William Clark, of the Lewis and Clark expedition, not Spencer M. Clark of the National Currency Bureau.

The CSA-watermarked paper was used extensively to make specimen notes of the Second Issue and Third Issue. Little numismatic account has been kept of the specific varieties involved.

First Issue, Postage Currency
August 21, 1862, to May 27, 1863

First Issue, 5¢

Printage (faces and backs count as separate notes): 43,560.

W-7001 • Related to regular issue W-6105 • F-1231-SP • Face • Straight edges • Narrow margins

EF-40	AU-50	Unc-60	Unc-63	Unc-65
$40	$75	$125	$200	$395

W-7003 • F-1231-SP • Wide margins

EF-40	AU-50	Unc-60	Unc-63	Unc-65
$100	$175	$30	$450	$750

W-7005 • F-1231-SP • Back • Straight edges, no ABNCo monogram • Narrow margins

EF-40	AU-50	Unc-60	Unc-63	Unc-65
$40	$75	$125	$200	$395

W-7008 • F-1231-SP • Wide margins, with line frame around

EF-40	AU-50	Unc-60	Unc-63	Unc-65
$100	$175	$300	$450	$650

First Issue, 10¢

Printage (faces and backs count as separate notes): 67,560.

W-7011 • Related to regular issue W-6125 • F-1243-SP • Face • Straight edges • Narrow margins

EF-40	AU-50	Unc-60	Unc-63	Unc-65
$40	$75	$125	$200	$395

W-7013 • F-1243-SP • Wide margins

EF-40	AU-50	Unc-60	Unc-63	Unc-65
$100	$175	$300	$450	$650

W-7015 • F-1243-SP • Back • Straight edges, no ABNCo monogram • Narrow margins

EF-40	AU-50	Unc-60	Unc-63	Unc-65
$40	$75	$125	$200	$395

W-7018 • F-1243-SP • Wide margins, with line frame around

EF-40	AU-50	Unc-60	Unc-63	Unc-65
$80	$175	$300	$450	$650

First Issue, 25¢

Printage (faces and backs count as separate notes): 62,688.

W-7021 • Related to regular issue W-6143 • F-1282-SP • Face • Straight edges • Narrow margins

EF-40	AU-50	Unc-60	Unc-63	Unc-65
$40	$75	$125	$200	$395

W-7023 • F-1282-SP • Wide margins

EF-40	AU-50	Unc-60	Unc-63	Unc-65
$80	$175	$300	$450	$650

W-7025 • F-1282-SP • Back • Straight edges, no ABNCo monogram • Narrow margins

EF-40	AU-50	Unc-60	Unc-63	Unc-65
$40	$75	$125	$200	$395

W-7027 • F-1282-SP • Wide margins, no line frame around • None known

W-7028 • F-1282-SP • Wide margins, with line frame around

EF-40	AU-50	Unc-60	Unc-63	Unc-65
$80	$175	$300	$450	$650

First Issue, 50¢

Printage (faces and backs count as separate notes): 43,488.

W-7031 • Related to regular issue W-6165 • F-1313-SP • Face • Straight edges • Narrow margins

EF-40	AU-50	Unc-60	Unc-63	Unc-65
$40	$75	$125	$200	$395

W-7033 • F-1313-SP • Wide margins

EF-40	AU-50	Unc-60	Unc-63	Unc-65
$100	$225	$425	$600	$950

W-7035 • F-1313-SP • Back • Straight edges, no ABNCo monogram • Narrow margins

EF-40	AU-50	Unc-60	Unc-63	Unc-65
$40	$75	$125	$200	$395

W-7038 • F-1313-SP • Wide margins, with line frame around

EF-40	AU-50	Unc-60	Unc-63	Unc-65
$100	$175	$300	$550	$900

Second Issue, Fractional Currency
OCTOBER 20, 1863, TO FEBRUARY 23, 1867

SECOND ISSUE, 5¢

Printage (faces and backs count as separate notes): 18,000.

W-7101 • Related to regular issue W-6201 • F-1232-SP • Face • Narrow margins

EF-40	AU-50	Unc-60	Unc-63	Unc-65
$40	$75	$175	$200	$395

W-7103 • F-1232-SP • Wide margins

EF-40	AU-50	Unc-60	Unc-63	Unc-65
$100	$175	$300	$450	$650

W-7105 • F-1232-SP • Back • Narrow margins

EF-40	AU-50	Unc-60	Unc-63	Unc-65
$40	$75	$175	$200	$395

W-7107 • F-1232-SP • Wide margins

EF-40	AU-50	Unc-60	Unc-63	Unc-65
$100	$175	$300	$450	$650

SECOND ISSUE, 10¢

Printage (faces and backs count as separate notes): 18,000.

W-7111 • Related to regular issue W-6221 • F-1244-SP • Face • Narrow margins

EF-40	AU-50	Unc-60	Unc-63	Unc-65
$40	$75	$125	$200	$395

W-7113 • F-1244-SP • Wide margins

EF-40	AU-50	Unc-60	Unc-63	Unc-65
$100	$175	$300	$450	$650

W-7115 • F-1244-SP • Back • Narrow margins

EF-40	AU-50	Unc-60	Unc-63	Unc-65
$40	$75	$125	$200	$395

W-7117 • F-1244-SP • Wide margins

EF-40	AU-50	Unc-60	Unc-63	Unc-65
$100	$175	$300	$450	$650

SECOND ISSUE, 25¢

Printage (faces and backs count as separate notes): 18,000.

W-7121 • Related to regular issue W-6251 • F-1283-SP • Face • Narrow margins

EF-40	AU-50	Unc-60	Unc-63	Unc-65
$40	$75	$125	$200	$395

W-7123 • F-1283-SP • Wide margins

EF-40	AU-50	Unc-60	Unc-63	Unc-65
$100	$175	$300	$450	$650

W-7125 • F-1283-SP • Back • Purple • Narrow margins

EF-40	AU-50	Unc-60	Unc-63	Unc-65
$40	$75	$125	$200	$395

W-7127 • F-1283-SP • Wide margins

EF-40	AU-50	Unc-60	Unc-63	Unc-65
$100	$175	$300	$450	$700

SECOND ISSUE, 50¢

Printage (faces and backs count as separate notes): 18,000.

W-7131 • Related to regular issue W-6271 • F-1314-SP • Face • Narrow margins

EF-40	AU-50	Unc-60	Unc-63	Unc-65
$40	$75	$125	$200	$395

W-7133 • F-1314-SP • Wide margins

EF-40	AU-50	Unc-60	Unc-63	Unc-65
$100	$200	$350	$500	$700

W-7135 • F-1314-SP • Back • Narrow margins

EF-40	AU-50	Unc-60	Unc-63	Unc-65
$40	$75	$125	$200	$395

W-7137 • F-1314-SP • Wide margins

EF-40	AU-50	Unc-60	Unc-63	Unc-65
$170	$300	$500	$700	$900

Third Issue, Fractional Currency
DECEMBER 5, 1864, TO AUGUST 16, 1869

THIRD ISSUE, 3¢

Printage (faces and backs count as separate notes): 21,000.

W-7201 • Related to regular issue W-6301 • F-1226-SP • Face • Light curtain or background • Narrow margins

EF-40	AU-50	Unc-60	Unc-63	Unc-65
$40	$75	$125	$200	$400

W-7203 • F-1226-SP • Wide margins

EF-40	AU-50	Unc-60	Unc-63	Unc-65
$2,250	$5,000	$7,000	$9,000	$10,000

W-7205 • Related to regular issue W-6303 • F-1227-SP • Dark curtain or background • Narrow margins

EF-40	AU-50	Unc-60	Unc-63	Unc-65
$40	$75	$125	$200	$400

W-7207 • F-1227-SP • Wide margins

EF-40	AU-50	Unc-60	Unc-63	Unc-65
$100	$175	$450	$500	$800

W-7209 • F-1227-SP • Back • Narrow margins

EF-40	AU-50	Unc-60	Unc-63	Unc-65
$45	$100	$195	$250	$400

W-7211 • F-1227-SP • Wide margins

EF-40	AU-50	Unc-60	Unc-63	Unc-65
$140	$250	$350	$450	$650

THIRD ISSUE, 5¢

Printage (faces and backs count as separate notes): 31,500.

W-7231 • Related to regular issue W-6311 • F-1238-SP • Face • Narrow margins

EF-40	AU-50	Unc-60	Unc-63	Unc-65
$45	$100	$195	$250	$400

W-7233 • F-1238-SP • Wide margins

EF-40	AU-50	Unc-60	Unc-63	Unc-65
$140	$250	$350	$450	$700

W-7235 • F-1238-SP • Green back • Narrow margins

EF-40	AU-50	Unc-60	Unc-63	Unc-65
$45	$100	$125	$250	$400

W-7237 • F-1238-SP • Wide margins

EF-40	AU-50	Unc-60	Unc-63	Unc-65
$100	$195	$300	$400	$700

W-7239 • F-1236-SP • Red back • Narrow margins

EF-40	AU-50	Unc-60	Unc-63	Unc-65
$45	$100	$195	$250	$400

W-7241 • F-1236-SP • Wide margins

EF-40	AU-50	Unc-60	Unc-63	Unc-65
$100	$200	$400	$550	$750

THIRD ISSUE, 10¢

Printage (faces and backs count as separate notes): 54,250.

W-7251 • Related to regular issue W-6337 • F-1251-SP • Face • Printed signatures of Colby-Spinner (1864–1867) • Narrow margins

EF-40	AU-50	Unc-60	Unc-63	Unc-65
$45	$100	$125	$250	$400

W-7253 • F-1251-SP • Wide margins

EF-40	AU-50	Unc-60	Unc-63	Unc-65
$100	$225	$325	$450	$700

W-7255 • Related to regular issue W-6339 • F-1253-SP • Inked signatures of Colby-Spinner (1864–1867) • Narrow margins

EF-40	AU-50	Unc-60	Unc-63	Unc-65
$45	$100	$190	$295	$450

W-7257 • F-1253-SP • Wide margins

EF-40	AU-50	Unc-60	Unc-63	Unc-65
$125	$250	$500	$700	$900

W-7259 • Related to regular issue W-6341 • F-1254-SP • Inked signatures of Jeffries-Spinner (1867–1869) • Narrow margins

EF-40	AU-50	Unc-60	Unc-63	Unc-65
$160	$300	$400	$500	$750

W-7261 • F-1254-SP • Wide margins

EF-40	AU-50	Unc-60	Unc-63	Unc-65
$1,800	$3,000	$4,000	$5,000	$9,000

W-7263 • Related to regular issue W-6331 • F-1255-SP • Green back • Narrow margins

EF-40	AU-50	Unc-60	Unc-63	Unc-65
$45	$100	$150	$250	$400

W-7265 • F-1255-SP • Wide margins

EF-40	AU-50	Unc-60	Unc-63	Unc-65
$100	$200	$325	$450	$700

W-7267 • Related to regular issue W-6337 • F-1251-SP • Red back • Narrow margins

EF-40	AU-50	Unc-60	Unc-63	Unc-65
$45	$100	$150	$250	$400

W-7269 • F-1251-SP • Wide margins

EF-40	AU-50	Unc-60	Unc-63	Unc-65
$150	$300	$400	$500	$750

THIRD ISSUE, 15¢ (GRANT AND SHERMAN ESSAYS)

The 15¢ denomination was proposed for the Third Series, and essays were prepared with the portraits of Civil War generals Ulysses S. Grant and William T. Sherman. However, the Act of April 7, 1866, which prohibited using the portrait of any living person on federal paper money or bonds, intervened, and no examples were ever made for general circulation.

These essays proved to be very popular with numismatists as well as stamp collectors, and many thousands were made, often accompanied by separate essays of the backs in either red or green. From inception through June 30, 1869, some 9,016 face impressions were sold. *Printage* (faces and backs

GRANT AND SHERMAN ESSAYS

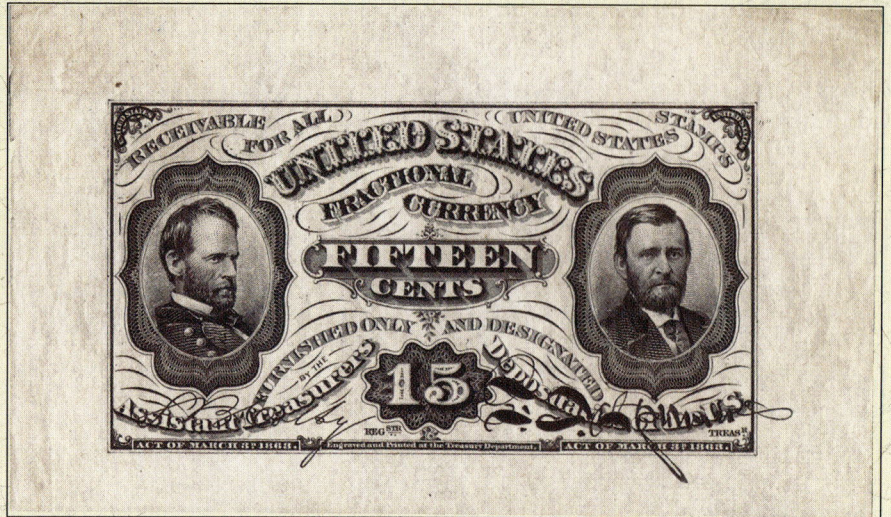

Face of W-7285. Printed signatures of Colby and Spinner.

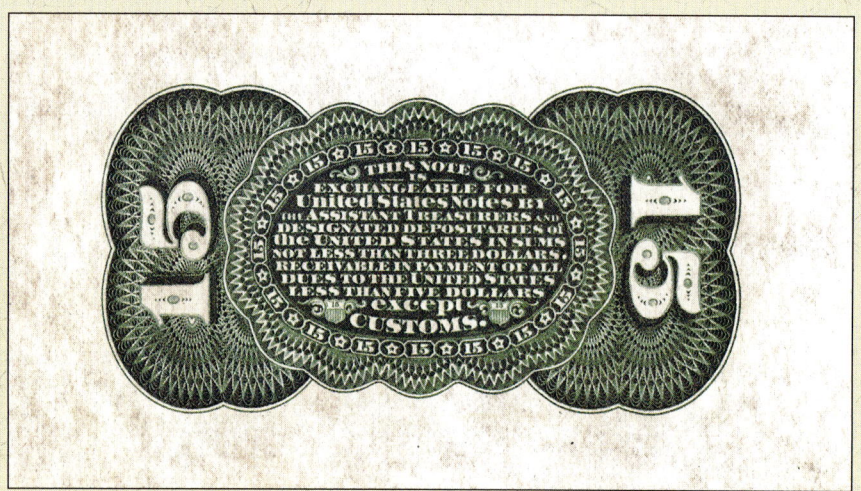

Green back of the type.

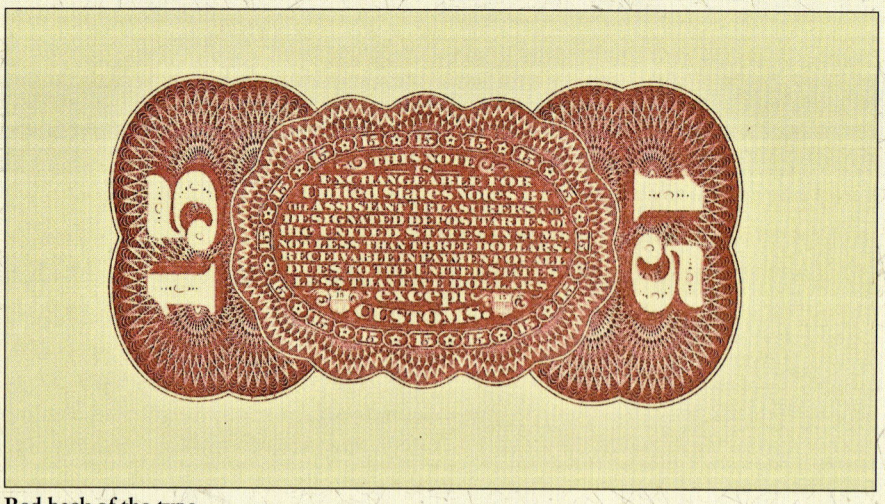

Red back of the type.

count as separate notes): 25,800. *Size of engraving on face:* 90 mm wide, 47 mm high. *Size of engraving on back:* 87 mm wide, 43 mm high.

W-7281 • F-1276-SP • Face • Without signatures • Narrow margins • Unique

W-7285 • F-1272-SP • Printed signatures of Colby-Spinner (1864–1867)

F-12	VF-20	EF-40	AU-50	Unc-60	Unc-63	Unc-65
$125	$200	$300	$375	$750	$1,100	$1,600

W-7287 • F-1272-SP • Wide margins

F-12	VF-20	EF-40	AU-50	Unc-60	Unc-63	Unc-65
$200	$375	$500	$600	$750	$2,000	$3,000

W-7289 • F-1273-SP • Inked signatures of Colby-Spinner (1864–1867) • Narrow margins

F-12	VF-20	EF-40	AU-50	Unc-60	Unc-63	Unc-65
$500	$700	$900	$1,400	$2,500	$3,600	$6,000

W-7293 • F-1274-SP • Inked signatures of Jeffries-Spinner (1867–1869)

VF-20	EF-40	AU-50	Unc-60	Unc-63	Unc-65
$190	$275	$350	$500	$1,200	$2,000

W-7295 • F-1274-SP • Wide margins

F-12	VF-20	EF-40	AU-50	Unc-60	Unc-63	Unc-65
$200	$325	$500	$700	$900	$2,250	$3,200

W-7297 • F-1275-SP • Inked signatures of Allison-Spinner (1869–1875) • Narrow margins

F-12	VF-20	EF-40	AU-50	Unc-60	Unc-63	Unc-65
$100	$175	$300	$500	$700	$1,100	$2,000

W-7299 • F-1275-SP • Wide margins

F-12	VF-20	EF-40	AU-50	Unc-60	Unc-63	Unc-65
$225	$350	$550	$800	$1,000	$2,600	$3,500

W-7301 • F-1272-SP • Green back • Narrow margins

EF-40	AU-50	Unc-60	Unc-63	Unc-65
$125	$200	$300	$450	$600

W-7303 • F-1272-SP • Wide margins

EF-40	AU-50	Unc-60	Unc-63	Unc-65
$250	$375	$425	$750	$1,000

W-7305 • F-1274-SP • Red back • Narrow margins

EF-40	AU-50	Unc-60	Unc-63	Unc-65
$200	$250	$400	$450	$700

W-7307 • F-1274-SP • Wide margins

EF-40	AU-50	Unc-60	Unc-63	Unc-65
$350	$900	$1,800	$2,300	$2,700

THIRD ISSUE, 25¢

Printage: not known, but probably in the range of 50,000.

W-7321 • Related to regular issue W-6351 • F-1294-SP • Face • Narrow margins

EF-40	AU-50	Unc-60	Unc-63	Unc-65
$45	$100	$125	$250	$400

W-7323 • F-1294-SP • Wide margins

EF-40	AU-50	Unc-60	Unc-63	Unc-65
$100	$225	$325	$500	$700

W-7325 • F-1294-SP • Green back • Narrow margins

EF-40	AU-50	Unc-60	Unc-63	Unc-65
$45	$100	$125	$250	$400

W-7327 • F-1294-SP • Wide margins

EF-40	AU-50	Unc-60	Unc-63	Unc-65
$100	$225	$350	$550	$750

W-7329 • Related to regular issue W-6365 • F-1291-SP • Red back • Narrow margins

EF-40	AU-50	Unc-60	Unc-63	Unc-65
$55	$110	$150	$275	$425

W-7331 • F-1291-SP • Wide margins

EF-40	AU-50	Unc-60	Unc-63	Unc-65
$100	$225	$350	$550	$750

THIRD ISSUE, 50¢

Printage (faces and backs count as separate notes): 50,584.

W-7351 • Related to regular issue W-6391 • F-1324-SP • Spinner Face • Printed signatures of Colby-Spinner (1864–1867) • Narrow margins

EF-40	AU-50	Unc-60	Unc-63	Unc-65
$45	$100	$200	$300	$400

W-7353 • F-1324-SP • Wide margins

EF-40	AU-50	Unc-60	Unc-63	Unc-65
$100	$225	$350	$450	$700

W-7355 • Related to regular issue W-6393 • F-1328-SP • Inked signatures of Colby-Spinner (1864–1867) • Narrow margins

EF-40	AU-50	Unc-60	Unc-63	Unc-65
$80	$150	$300	$500	$750

W-7357 • F-1328-SP • Wide margins

EF-40	AU-50	Unc-60	Unc-63	Unc-65
$190	$350	$700	$900	$1,200

W-7359 • No circulation-issue counterpart • F-1330a-SP • Spinner Face • Inked signatures of Jeffries-Spinner (1867–1869) • Narrow margins

EF-40	AU-50	Unc-60	Unc-63	Unc-65
$140	$250	$400	$550	$700

W-7361 • F-1330a-SP • Wide margins

EF-40	AU-50	Unc-60	Unc-63
$2,000	$3,500	$7,000	$9,000

W-7363 • Related to regular issue W-6395 • F-1329-SP • Inked signatures of Allison-Spinner (1869–1875) • Narrow margins

EF-40	AU-50	Unc-60	Unc-63
$1,750	$3,000	$4,500	$6,000

W-7365 • F-1329-SP • Wide margins

EF-40	AU-50	Unc-60	Unc-63
$5,000	$9,000	$14,500	$17,500

W-7367 • Related to regular issue W-6481 • F-1343-SP • Justice Face • Printed signatures of Colby-Spinner (1864–1867) • Narrow margins

EF-40	AU-50	Unc-60	Unc-63	Unc-65
$45	$100	$125	$250	$400

W-7369 • F-1343-SP • Wide margins

EF-40	AU-50	Unc-60	Unc-63	Unc-65
$125	$225	$350	$550	$750

W-7371 • Related to regular issue W-6483 • F-1355-SP • Inked signatures of Colby-Spinner (1864–1867) • Narrow margins

EF-40	AU-50	Unc-60	Unc-63	Unc-65
$140	$250	$350	$500	$900

W-7373 • F-1355-SP • Wide margins

EF-40	AU-50	Unc-60	Unc-63	Unc-65
$300	$500	$700	$900	$1,200

W-7375 • No circulation-issue counterpart • F-1357a-SP • Inked signatures of Jeffries-Spinner (1867–1869) • Narrow margins

EF-40	AU-50	Unc-60	Unc-63	Unc-65
$175	$300	$500	$700	$900

W-7377 • F-1357a-SP • Wide margins

EF-40	AU-50	Unc-60	Unc-63
$4,500	$6,000	$9,000	$12,000

W-7379 • Related to regular issue W-6371 • F-1331-SP • Green Text Back • Narrow margins

EF-40	AU-50	Unc-60	Unc-63	Unc-65
$45	$100	$125	$250	$400

W-7381 • F-1331-SP • Wide margins

EF-40	AU-50	Unc-60	Unc-63	Unc-65
$125	$225	$350	$550	$750

W-7383 • Related to regular issue W-6411 • F-1339-SP • Green 50 Cents Back • Narrow margins

EF-40	AU-50	Unc-60	Unc-63	Unc-65
$1,750	$3,000	$4,500	$6,000	$9,000

W-7385 • F-1339-SP • Wide margins

EF-40	AU-50	Unc-60	Unc-63	Unc-65
$2,500	$4,500	$5,500	$8,000	$10,000

W-7387 • Related to regular issue W-6391 • F-1324-SP • Red Text Back • Narrow margins

EF-40	AU-50	Unc-60	Unc-63	Unc-65
$45	$100	$125	$250	$400

W-7389 • F-1324-SP • Wide margins

EF-40	AU-50	Unc-60	Unc-63	Unc-65
$100	$275	$350	$550	$750

PAPER-MONEY ERRORS

Although errors have occurred in all sizes and types of U.S. currency since the nation first started printing paper money, collecting error notes has historically been a very limited pursuit. In the past 30 years, however, errors have grown into a widely collected part of the hobby.

Error notes can be inexpensive or very costly, depending on what you collect. A double-denomination note (the "king of errors" in the bank-note field) is the rarest of the rare and is worth many thousands of dollars. Other errors can be easily obtained for $10 to $15 over face value.

The following discussion includes price estimates for errors on small-size notes. Mistakes on large-size notes are mostly very rare. Errors have also been found on National Bank Notes but are extremely rare.

The following are just a few examples of different types of paper-money errors.

GUTTER FOLDS OR CREASES

A gutter fold occurs when the paper is creased during printing, resulting in a blank area when the note is smoothed. The value of such an error will depend on the size and severity: for a minor crease, the note will be worth about $15 more than face value in Very Fine condition, or $25 over face value in Uncirculated. A larger or more severe crease increases the value to $25 over face value in Very Fine, or $100 or more in Uncirculated.

OFFSET TRANSFERS

A note that exhibits the face design on the back will bring prices according to how bold the transfer is. A partial or faint image will bring $25 over face value in Very Fine or $50 in Uncirculated. If the transfer is complete and strong, collectors will pay $200 and $500 over face value in Very Fine and Uncirculated.

A complete and dark view of the back design on the note's face will increase its value by $150 to $200 in grades ranging from Very Fine to Uncirculated.

INK SMEARS

A minor ink smear (from the printing process, not from a leaky fountain pen!) will increase a note's worth by $20 over face value in Very Fine, or $50 in Uncirculated.

SHIFTS OR MISALIGNED OVERPRINTS

While minor shifts are easily found in circulation, major displacements are more rare and thus more valuable to collectors. A shifted overprint will fetch $50 to $100 over face value, depending on the grade (Very Fine or Uncirculated). A shifted overprint appearing on a star note (a replacement for a damaged note or an error caught in the production process) is more valuable.

OFFSET TRANSFERS

$20 Federal Reserve Note, Series of 1981-A (W-2545-B), with the back design showing on the face.

MISMATCHED SERIAL NUMBERS

These mistakes are much sought after by collectors of error notes. A Series of 1969 $1 note with mismatched digits in the serial number sold for $230 in Very Fine in 2007. For a Series of 1976 $2 note with mismatched prefix, a collector in 2009 would pay $275 in Very Fine or $450 in Gem Uncirculated.

INVERTED SERIAL NUMBERS AND SEALS

A note printed with upside-down serial numbers and seals is worth $250 to $750 over face value in grades ranging from Very Fine to Uncirculated.

INVERTED FACE

A typical note has its face and back aligned in the same up-down position. With the face printed upside down, a note's value generally increases to $350 in Very Fine and $1,500 in Uncirculated.

THIRD PRINTING ON BACK

With its seals and serial numbers printed on the back instead of the face, a modern small-size note would bring $150 (Very Fine) to $350 (Gem Uncirculated) from a collector. If they were also printed upside down, the value would increase to $200 and $800, respectively.

MISSING PRINTING

SECOND PRINTING MISSING

A $1 note that is missing its second printing—that bears its serial numbers and seals, but is otherwise missing the front design—is worth $300 (Very Fine) to $750 (Uncirculated) to a collector. A $100 note of this type is worth $600 in Very Fine or $1,250 in Uncirculated.

THIRD PRINTING MISSING

A $20 note with its seals and serial numbers missing is worth $140 in Very Fine and $425 in Uncirculated.

PRINTED FOLDS

A small-size $20 note with a large, attractively printed-over fold runs $500 in Very Fine or $900 in Uncirculated.

BLANK BACK

A note with a blank back gives a collector only half the design, while increasing its value considerably—a good example of "less is more." A $20 note made this way is worth $150 in Very Fine or $350 in Uncirculated.

DOUBLE DENOMINATION

The most famous and desirable type of error is the double-denomination note, which has one value on the face and another on the back. These were produced in two main ways, as described below.

For small-size bills, a sheet first printed on one side, with $5 designs and information, was then mistakenly put with one-sided $10 bills and imprinted on the other side with $10 information. A famous Series of 1934-D Silver Certificate, printed circa 1960, is of this type, with a $5 face and $10 back. Nearly a dozen of these were found by dealer Aubrey Bebee of Omaha, Nebraska. Today an example is worth about $25,000 in Very Fine and $40,000 in Uncirculated.

For large-size bills with more than one denomination per sheet, this could occur when the correct sheet was printed on the back, but upside down. A $50-$100 two-subject sheet might be printed correctly on one side, then printed on the other with the sheet misaligned so as to give the $50 note the imprint intended for the $100 note, and vice versa.

In March 1909, *The Numismatist* reported on a batch of misprinted notes from the First National Bank of Albuquerque, New Mexico. One of these notes was mentioned in a story that made the rounds of the American Bankers' Association convention held in Denver the preceding autumn. A hotel cashier (who was working overtime because of the convention) counted his cash, turned it over to count it again, and found a $50 discrepancy. According to the story, three more days (!) were spent counting the cash, driving the cashier to the point of distraction. Finally the bill with the $100-$50 combination was found.

SECOND PRINTING MISSING

L 19602764 G

$1 Federal Reserve Note from San Francisco, series unknown, with the second printing (the main front design) missing.

20

CONTINENTAL CURRENCY, 1775–1779

On May 10, 1775, the Continental Congress—the provisional national government organized among the colonies—authorized the issuance of paper money. The seeds of the American Revolution had been sown in recent years, from resistance to the Stamp Act to the Boston Tea Party and other protests against British rule. The armed encounter between American patriots and British troops at Lexington and Concord, Massachusetts, on April 19 brought to the fore the hostility that had been felt by American patriots for a long time and launched the Revolutionary War. The conflict would drag on until the surrender of British forces at Yorktown, Virginia, in 1781. In the meantime, the outcome was uncertain, British troops occupied New York City for several years, and General George Washington's Continental Army endured many hardships.

The members of the Continental Congress had high hopes, but no reserve of precious metal or coins to provide backing for the authorized paper money. Still, the program went forward. Other currency authorizations followed, through 1779, with bills denominated in "Spanish milled dollars, or the value thereof in gold or silver." In reality, the bills could be exchanged for other Continental Currency denominations, but not at face value for much else. The notes were given out as soldiers' pay and used in commerce by those who would accept them. In later times, this was always at a discount. Bills were denominated in dollars and had printed values from 1/6 of a dollar to $80. These related to Spanish milled dollars—silver coins worth eight reals struck at Spanish mints from Mexico to South America. At the time there were no federal dollars (the first U.S. silver dollars would not be struck until years later, in 1794).

Early Continental Currency issues bore the imprint "United Colonies." Beginning with the authorization of May 20, 1777, the imprint was changed to "United States." The $20 note of the first issue was printed on paper ordered in France by Benjamin Franklin and is of unusual dimensions and appearance, with one end printed in colored marbling. All others were on paper made in the United States. This stock was heavy, almost like thin cardboard, and included tiny flakes of mica that were intended to deter counterfeiting.

All the bills were printed by Hall and Sellers of Philadelphia, a firm also well known for producing state-issued currency. Certain of the backs featured imprints of tree leaves made by a process called nature printing, which used a single leaf to create part of a printing plate. (This technique, also used on some earlier colonial bills, was an invention of Benjamin Franklin's.) This was another deterrent to counterfeiting, as the veins and other small features of each leaf were unique and not easily copied.

Continental Currency was printed in sheets with multiple bills of different denominations. These were signed in ink and then cut apart for distribution. Each bill with a face value of $1 or more bore two authorized signatures. Some were signed by men who also signed the Articles of Confederation, Declaration of Independence, Bill of Rights, or other important early documents. This lends particular interest and value to such bills today.

In addition to regular issues, impressions of certain Continental Currency issues were printed on blue-tinted paper. Unsigned, these were distributed to aid in the detection of counterfeits but had no value in commerce. Examples are occasionally seen in the marketplace today.

As time went on and the financial strength of the Continental Congress became weaker and weaker, the notes depreciated to the point at which they were nearly valueless by 1791. The first issue, authorized by the session of May 10, 1775, held its value fairly well, as did the next several releases. By January 1, 1777, it took the equivalent of $1.05 in paper to buy $1.00 in Spanish-American silver coins, and this raised to $1.07 in the next month. By January 1778, the value had slipped to the point at which $3.25 was required, and then $7.42 by January 1779. The last Continental Currency issue was authorized by the session of January 14, 1779, and included the record-high denomination of $80. The exchange rate inflated to $29.34 by January 1780, then to $74.00 by January 1781. In the next month the rate was $75.00, at which time trading in such bills virtually ended in the Northern states, with notes being worth about 1/75 of their face value. The bills continued to trade in parts of Virginia and North Carolina for about another year, to the point where they depreciated to 1/1,000 of face value.

Extensive losses were sustained by anyone who held such money for any length of time, even if acquired at a discount.

Although such currency no longer had value in commerce, speculators who hoped that the government would eventually redeem it bought quantities at deep discounts, down to 1/1,000 of face value or even lower. Wise buyers profited greatly when an act of Congress, passed August 4, 1790, provided that Continental paper money would be received at the Treasury until September 1, 1791, at the rate of $100 in bills to $1 in gold or silver coins. One such speculator is said to have been "Lord" Timothy Dexter of Newburyport, Massachusetts, who used his fortune to build a mansion that remains prominent in that town today. The Act of May 8, 1791, extended the redemption period to March 7, 1792, after which time the bills were repudiated, the status they retain today.

ASPECTS OF COLLECTING

The Continental Congress authorized and issued paper money in 11 different series dated from May 10, 1775, to January 14, 1779. Today, all are highly collectible. Considered to be the key issue is the previously mentioned $20 note of May 10, 1775, printed on the thin French paper with a marbled end that was imported by Benjamin Franklin. As noted, in addition to regular issues, thick rag paper with mica flakes and blue fibers (to deter counterfeiting) was used for all other issues. The bills dated April 11, 1778, are imprinted "Yorktown," having been authorized when the Continental Congress was in session in York, Pennsylvania. This particular series was extensively counterfeited, resulting in many being called in and replaced with other notes. As a result, the Yorktown bills, which were issued in denominations from $4 to $40, are especially scarce today. As time went on and the bills depreciated in value, lower denominations were dropped from new issues and higher values were added, up to $80.

The typical Continental Currency note found today will show evidence of circulation, sometimes extensive. The earlier the issue, the more likely it is to have extensive wear. A high-grade, especially desirable note might be called Extremely Fine or better, but should have these characteristics:

- The borders should be full, although perhaps closely trimmed (as notes were spaced closely on sheets), with no trimming cutting into the frame or design.
- The signatures, applied in ink, should all be visible, but not necessarily bold. Some inks, especially those of red hues, faded more than others. Certain certification services do not take the clarity of signatures into consideration. Therefore, cherry-picking is needed to be sure signatures are clearly visible.
- The printing and designs should be clear.
- The body of the note should be solid, not easily bendable on a fold or crease.
- The corners should be fairly sharp, not worn or rounded.

Although such a note is ideal, there is an active market for lower grades, including examples that are trimmed into the borders or have faded signatures or other deficiencies. The trade-off is that these often sell for much lower prices.

Forming a set of Continental Currency paper money requires patience and care. Even in lower grades, many of the notes are elusive and come on the market only at widely separated intervals. A combination of auctions and inquiries to specialist dealers is the best way to build a collection. Buy carefully, as a note that is "just right" within a given grade will certainly come along sooner or later. The easiest route is to acquire one note of each denomination, as this will include each motto and design. An expanded collection might include one of each date and denomination within that date. A collection can be formed by autograph combinations and varieties, of which there are multiples within given dates and denominations. This path is rarely followed by collectors, however.

Illustrated auction catalogs of the past several decades provide a rich source of images that are useful for learning about border trimming, the clarity of printing, and related characteristics. Counterfeits of Continental Currency bills, described as such, are collected by many numismatists. The masterwork to consult for historical and other information is Eric P. Newman's *Early Paper Money of America.*

BLUE- AND PINK-TINTED ANTICOUNTERFEITING NOTES

The Continental Congress issued sheets of certain series for use in counterfeit detection. These were typically printed on blue-tinted paper, with a few exceedingly rare examples being printed on pink paper. Detector notes were not signed; nor did they have any exchange or redemption value. These are occasionally seen in the marketplace today, but infrequently. Thus they have no standard values, but are not worth as much as high-grade circulated, signed notes of the same types.

INTERESTING CHARACTERISTICS

Studying and collecting the signatures of members of the Continental Congress is an interesting pursuit. So is researching to connect these bills to the history of the Revolutionary War. Only one signer of the Declaration of Independence also inked his name on Continental Currency: James Wilson. Some Wilson signatures were done by an amanuensis (or ghost-signer), so authentication is necessary if this aspect is important to you.

The border engravings are attributed to David Rittenhouse, who was appointed first director of the U.S. Mint years later in 1792. Continental Currency notes were printed with a wide variety of interesting emblems and mottoes, which are fascinating to study today. Each denomination had its own design. Surrounding a motif was an inscription in Latin. Examples are given on the pages following, with translations adapted from Wayte Raymond's *Standard Catalogue of Paper Money* (1940).

Listings begin on page 830.

REPRESENTATIVE CONTINENTAL CURRENCY NOTES

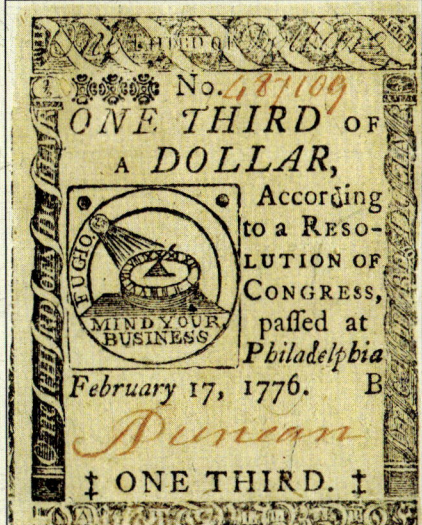

$1/6, $1/3, $1/2, and $2/3 • *FUGIO. MIND YOUR BUSINESS* • *Translation:* I fly [therefore] mind your business • *Motif:* Sundial. This motif was also used on the 1776 Continental dollar coin and the 1787 Fugio copper.

$1 • *DEPRESSA RESURGIT* • *Translation:* Though pressed down it rises again • *Motif:* A thistle with a heavy board on its blossom. The allegory is to the subjugation of the colonies by England.

REPRESENTATIVE CONTINENTAL CURRENCY NOTES,
continued

$2 • *TRIBULATIO DITAT* • *Translation:* Affliction enriches • *Motif:* Hand holding tool, a flail. The allegory is that the American people, at war with England, are undergoing travails, but this can be beneficial in a way.

$3 • *EXITUS IN DUBIO EST* • *Translation:* The end is in doubt • *Motif:* Birds of prey fighting, the lower bird on its back. The allegory is to the conflict between the United States and England.

REPRESENTATIVE CONTINENTAL CURRENCY NOTES,
continued

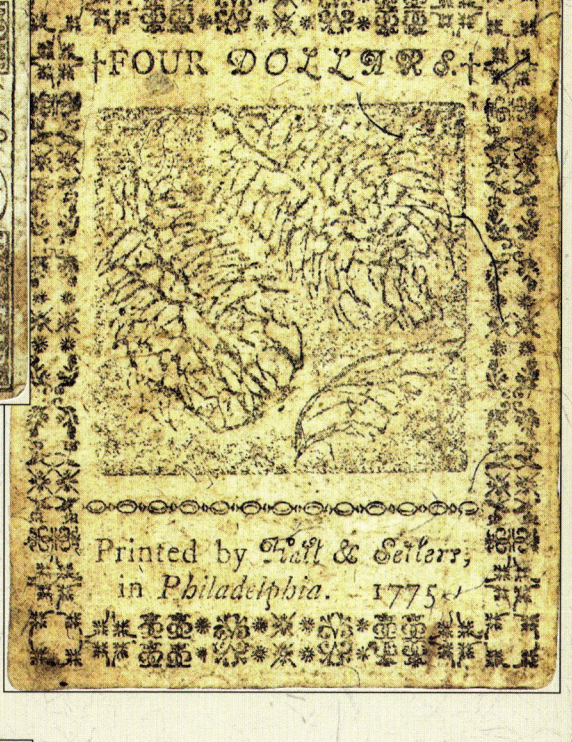

$4 • *AUT MORS AUT VITA DECORA* • *Translation:* Either death or an honorable life • *Motif:* A running boar about to impale itself on a spear.

$5 • *SUSTINE VEL ABSTINE* • *Translation:* Sustain or abstain • *Motif:* Hand caressing growing bush. Either help nourish a movement, such as the independence of America, or abstain.

REPRESENTATIVE CONTINENTAL CURRENCY NOTES,
continued

$6 • *PERSEVERANDO* • *Translation:* By persevering • *Motif:* Beaver gnawing a tree. By persevering the beaver slowly eats away at the tree trunk until the tree (England) collapses.

$7 • *SERENABIT* • *Translation:* It will clear up • *Motif:* Storm clouds and rain over a landscape. The allegory is that war, now in progress, will eventually end.

REPRESENTATIVE CONTINENTAL CURRENCY NOTES,
continued

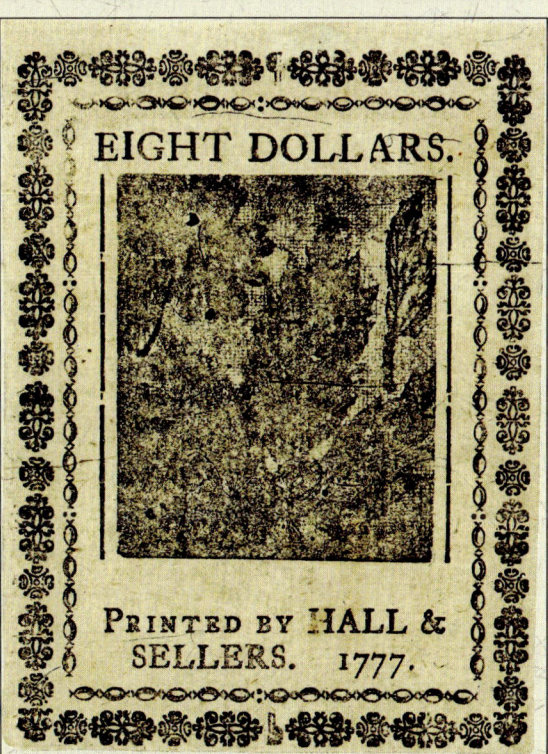

$8 • *MAJORA MINORIBUS CONSONANT* • *Translation:*
The greater ones sound in harmony with the smaller • *Motif:*
An ornate harp with 13 strings. The allegory is that all states,
large and small, are in harmony with each other.

REPRESENTATIVE CONTINENTAL CURRENCY NOTES, *continued*

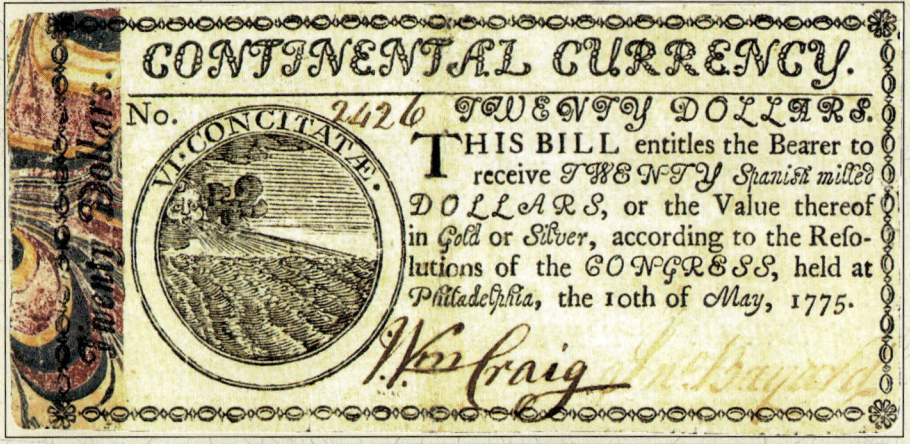

$20, May 10, 1775 • Face of note: *VI CONCITATÆ* • *Translation:* Driven by force • *Motif:* The wind raises waves on the sea, meaning turbulent forces have stirred the nation. • Back of note: *CESSANTE VENTO CONQUIESCEMUS* • *Translation:* When the storm ceases we will rest • *Motif:* The sun shining on a still sea where ships lie becalmed, referring to the peace that will come after the war. • French paper with marbling at the left end of the face.

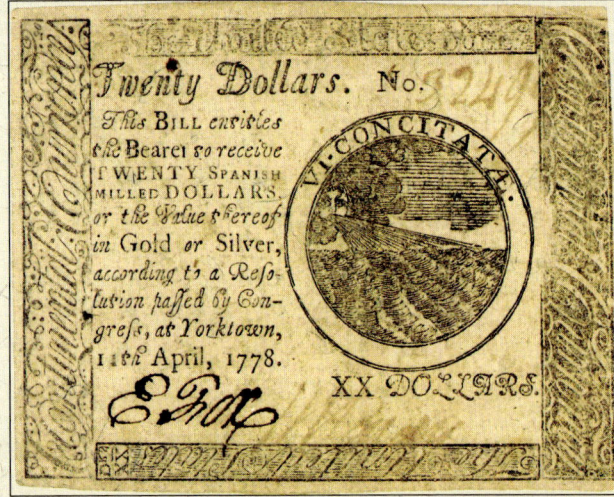

$20, April 11, 1778 • Legend and motif as on face of May 10, 1775, issue.

REPRESENTATIVE CONTINENTAL CURRENCY NOTES,
continued

$30 • *SI RECTE FACIES* • *Translation:* If thou shalt do well • *Motif:* Laurel wreath on pedestal. The allegory is that those who do well are recognized.

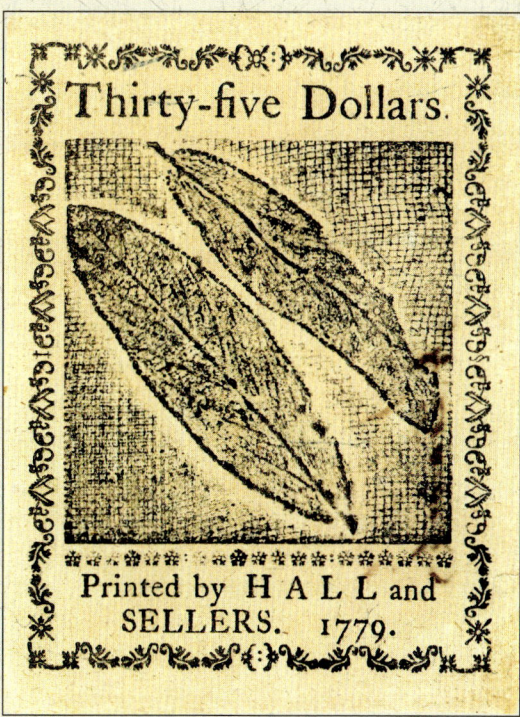

$35 • *HINC OPES* • *Translation:* Hence our wealth • *Motif:* A plow in a field. Symbolic of agriculture being the strength of America.

REPRESENTATIVE CONTINENTAL CURRENCY NOTES,
continued

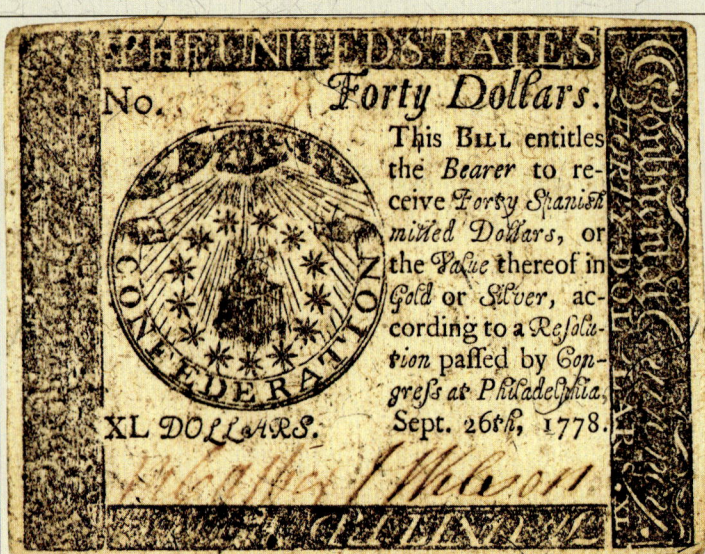

$40 • *CONFEDERATION* • *Motif:* All-seeing eye with 13 stars. Represents the confederation of the states.

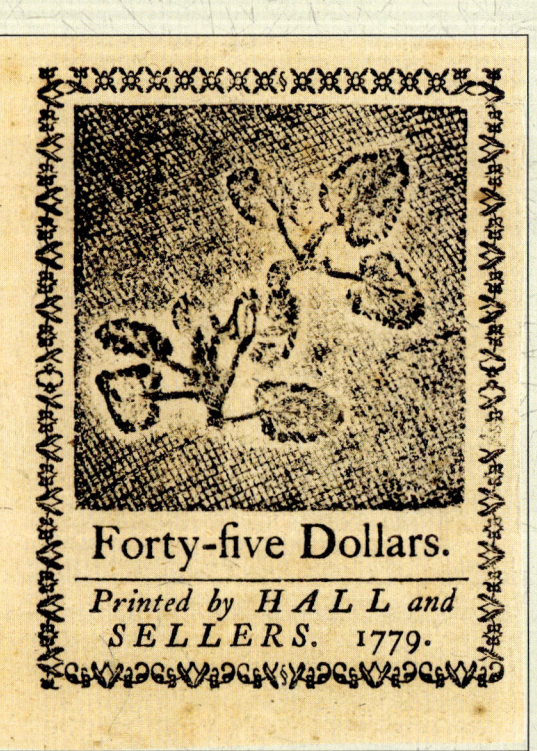

$45 • *SIC FLORET RESPUBLICA* • *Translation:* Thus flourishes the Republic • *Motif:* Two skep-type beehives under cover, with bees flying nearby. The allegory is that industry and activity sustain the republic.

REPRESENTATIVE CONTINENTAL CURRENCY NOTES, *continued*

$50 • *PERENNIS* • *Translation:* Everlasting • *Motif:* Illustration of a step pyramid, representing durability.

$55 • *POST NUBILA PHOEBUS* • *Translation:* After the clouds comes the sun • *Motif:* Landscape with clouds on the left departing and with the sun, on the right, bathing trees and ground in light. The allegory is that after the war there will be peace.

REPRESENTATIVE CONTINENTAL CURRENCY NOTES, *continued*

$60 • *DEUS REGNAT EXULTET TERRA* • *Translation:* The Lord reigneth, let the world rejoice • *Motif:* Illustration of a globe in space, representing the earth.

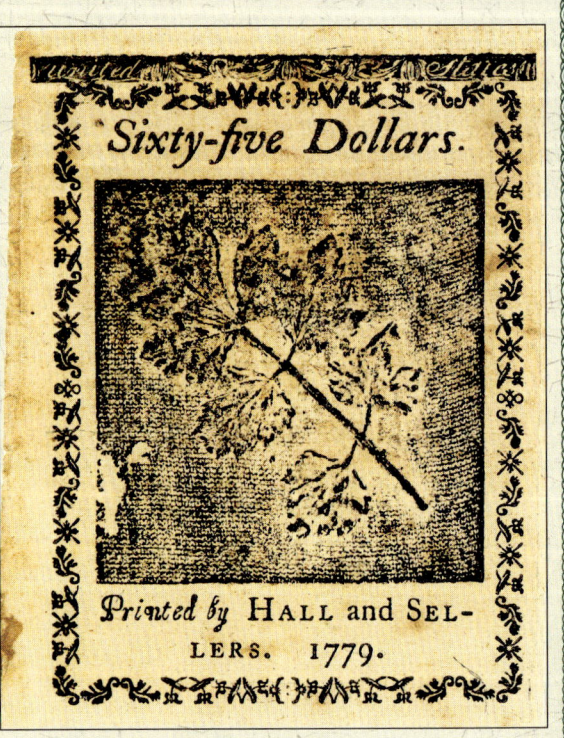

$65 • *FIAT JUSTITIA* • *Translation:* Let justice be done • *Motif:* A hand holding scales of justice. In the conflict justice will eventually prevail.

REPRESENTATIVE CONTINENTAL CURRENCY NOTES,
continued

$70 • *VIM PROCELLARUM QUADRENNIUM SUSTI-NUIT* • *Translation:* For four years it has withstood the force of the gales • *Motif:* A leafy tree flourishing on a hillside, apparently with sunny skies. The allegory is that after being tossed by wind and rain (four years of war), the tree at last flourishes.

$80 • *ET IN SECULA SECULORUM FLORESCEBIT* • *Translation:* It will flourish forever and ever • *Motif:* Sturdy oak tree on solid ground. The allegory is that America, the oak, will be ever enduring.

May 10, 1775
Authorized Amount: $3,000,000

The $20 of this date is of the special French paper issue.

Prices for a typical note for this issue (without signatures of great historical significance), unless listed otherwise, are as follows:

VG-8	F-12	VF-20	EF-40	AU-50	Unc-63	Unc-65
$75	$125	$200	$300	$450	$1,000	$2,000

W-8501 • $1 • 49,000

VG-8	F-12	VF-20	EF-40	AU-50	Unc-63	Unc-65
$100	$175	$300	$450	$650	$1,200	$1,750

W-8502 • $2 • 49,000

W-8503 • $3 • 49,000

W-8504 • $4 • 49,000

W-8505 • $5 • 49,000

W-8506 • $6 • 49,000

W-8507 • $7 • 49,000

W-8508 • $8 • 49,000

W-8509 • $20 • 11,800

VG-8	F-12	VF-20	EF-40	AU-50
$800	$2,000	$4,000	$8,000	$12,000

W-8510 • $30 • 33,333

VG-8	F-12	VF-20	EF-40	AU-50	Unc-63	Unc-65
$100	$175	$400	$500	$700	$1,200	$2,500

November 29, 1775
Authorized Amount: $3,000,000, Plus an Additional $10,000

Bills of this date are serially numbered in red ink to differentiate them at a glance from the preceding.

Prices for a typical note for this issue (without signatures of great historical significance), unless listed otherwise, are as follows:

VG-8	F-12	VF-20	EF-40	AU-50	Unc-63	Unc-65
$80	$125	$200	$300	$450	$950	$1,750

W-8511 • $1 • 83,611

W-8512 • $2 • 83,611

W-8513 • $3 • 83,611

W-8514 • $4 • 83,611

W-8515 • $5 • 83,611

W-8516 • $6 • 83,611

W-8517 • $7 • 83,611

W-8518 • $8 • 83,611

February 17, 1776
Authorized Amount: $4,000,000, Including $1,000,000 in Fractional Bills

The fractional bills, issued only in this series, each have the sundial–linked rings design similar to that used on the 1776 pewter Continental Currency dollar and later adapted for the 1787 Fugio copper cent. Note the misspelling in $1/6 CURRENCEY. Fractional bills bear one signature instead of the two used on larger denominations.

Prices for a typical note for this issue (without signatures of great historical significance), unless listed otherwise, are as follows:

VG-8	F-12	VF-20	EF-40	AU-50	Unc-63	Unc-65
$90	$125	$225	$375	$450	$1,000	$1,950

W-8519 • $1/6 • 600,000

VG-8	F-12	VF-20	EF-40	AU-50	Unc-63	Unc-65
$100	$200	$350	$550	$850	$1,800	$3,000

W-8520 • $1/3 • 600,000

VG-8	F-12	VF-20	EF-40	AU-50	Unc-63	Unc-65
$100	$200	$350	$550	$850	$1,800	$3,000

W-8521 • $1/2 • 600,000

VG-8	F-12	VF-20	EF-40	AU-50	Unc-63	Unc-65
$100	$200	$350	$550	$850	$1,800	$3,000

W-8522 • $2/3 • 600,000

VG-8	F-12	VF-20	EF-40	AU-50	Unc-63	Unc-65
$100	$200	$350	$550	$850	$1,800	$3,000

W-8523 • $1 • 130,436

W-8524 • $2 • 130,437

W-8525 • $3 • 130,436

W-8526 • $4 • 130,435

W-8527 • $5 • 65,217

W-8528 • $6 • 65,217

W-8529 • $7 • 65,217

W-8530 • $8 • 65,217

May 9, 1776
Authorized Amount: $5,000,000

Prices for a typical note for this issue (without signatures of great historical significance), unless listed otherwise, are as follows:

VG-8	F-12	VF-20	EF-40	AU-50	Unc-63	Unc-65
$90	$150	$250	$350	$450	$1,000	$1,650

W-8531 • $1 • 138,889

W-8532 • $2 • 138,889

W-8533 • $3 • 138,889

W-8534 • $4 • 138,889

W-8535 • $5 • 138,889

W-8536 • $6 • 138,889

W-8537 • $7 • 138,889

W-8538 • $8 • 138,889

July 22, 1776
Authorized Amount: $5,000,000

These bills were authorized on two dates, July 22 and August 13, 1776, but the bills are all imprinted July 22, 1776.

Prices for a typical note for this issue (without signatures of great historical significance), unless listed otherwise, are as follows:

VG-8	F-12	VF-20	EF-40	AU-50	Unc-63	Unc-65
$100	$195	$275	$350	$450	$1,200	$2,000

W-8539 • $2 • 76,923

W-8540 • $3 • 76,923

W-8541 • $4 • 76,923

W-8542 • $5 • 76,923

W-8543 • $6 • 76,923

W-8544 • $7 • 76,923

W-8545 • $8 • 76,923

W-8546 • $30 • 76,923

VG-8	F-12	VF-20	EF-40	AU-50	Unc-63	Unc-65
$125	$225	$300	$450	$600	$1,500	$2,750

November 2, 1776
Authorized Amount: $5,000,000, Plus $500,000 for Fractional Bills (Never Issued)

These bills were authorized on two dates, November 2 and December 28, 1776, but the bills are all imprinted November 2, 1776.

Prices for a typical note for this issue (without signatures of great historical significance), unless listed otherwise, are as follows:

VG-8	F-12	VF-20	EF-40	AU-50	Unc-63	Unc-65
$90	$165	$265	$350	$450	$1,200	$2,000

W-8547 • $2 • 76,923

W-8548 • $3 • 76,923

W-8549 • $4 • 76,923

W-8550 • $5 • 76,923

W-8551 • $6 • 76,923

W-8552 • $7 • 76,923

W-8553 • $8 • 76,923

W-8554 • $30 • 76,923

February 26, 1777
Authorized Amount: $5,000,000

This resolution was passed in Baltimore, where the Continental Congress met by necessity because the British occupied Philadelphia from December 20, 1776, until February 27, 1777.

Prices for a typical note for this issue (without signatures of great historical significance), unless listed otherwise, are as follows:

VG-8	F-12	VF-20	EF-40	AU-50	Unc-63	Unc-65
$100	$175	$250	$375	$475	$1,200	$1,900

W-8555 • $2 • 76,923

W-8556 • $3 • 76,923

W-8557 • $4 • 76,923

W-8558 • $5 • 76,923

W-8559 • $6 • 76,923

W-8560 • $7 • 76,923

W-8561 • $8 • 76,923

W-8562 • $30 • 76,923

VG-8	F-12	VF-20	EF-40	AU-50	Unc-63	Unc-65
$125	$200	$300	$450	$525	$1,500	$2,250

May 20, 1777
Authorized Amount: $16,500,000

Although the bills are all dated May 20, 1777, the large amount was authorized in 10 separate resolutions extending to April 18, 1778. From this issue onward the bills were imprinted with "United States" instead of "United Colonies." This issue was extensively counterfeited. Many bills were called in and exchanged.

Prices for a typical note for this issue (without signatures of great historical significance), unless listed otherwise, are as follows:

VG-8	F-12	VF-20	EF-40	AU-50	Unc-63	Unc-65
$150	$300	$600	$900	$1,250	$2,800	$3,500

W-8563 • $2 • 253,850

W-8564 • $3 • 253,839

W-8565 • $4 • 253,839

W-8566 • $5 • 253,840

W-8567 • $6 • 253,839

W-8568 • $7 • 253,840

W-8569 • $8 • 253,851

W-8570 • $30 • 253,850

VG-8	F-12	VF-20	EF-40	AU-50	Unc-63	Unc-65
$200	$350	$700	$1,000	$1,500	$3,450	$4,500

April 11, 1778
Authorized Amount: $25,000,000

These bills were authorized by multiple acts in York ("York-town" on the bills), Pennsylvania, on April 11 and other dates, as well as in Philadelphia, but all are imprinted April 11, 1778. As a class, currency of this series is rarer than any other issue, as many were called back to be replaced with other bills, in view of widespread counterfeiting.

Prices for a typical note for this issue (without signatures of great historical significance), unless listed otherwise, are as follows:

VG-8	F-12	VF-20	EF-40	AU-50	Unc-63
$275	$450	$750	$1,200	$2,000	$4,000

W-8571 • $4 • 208,335

W-8572 • $5 • 208,330

W-8573 • $6 • 208,335

W-8574 • $7 • 208,330

W-8575 • $8 • 208,330

W-8576 • $20 • 208,330

W-8577 • $30 • 208,335

W-8578 • $40 • 208,335

September 26, 1778
Authorized Amount: $75,001,080

These bills were issued under nine different resolutions but are all dated September 26, 1778. This authorization was for a greater amount of money than all previous issues combined.

Prices for a typical note for this issue (without signatures of great historical significance), unless listed otherwise, are as follows:

VG-8	F-12	VF-20	EF-40	AU-50	Unc-63	Unc-65
$80	$125	$175	$275	$350	$800	$1,300

W-8579 • $5 • 340,914

W-8580 • $7 • 340,914

W-8581 • $8 • 340,914

W-8582 • $20 • 340,914

W-8583 • $30 • 340,914

W-8584 • $40 • 340,914

W-8585 • $50 • 340,914

W-8586 • $60 • 340,914

January 14, 1779
Authorized Amount: $95,051,695

These bills were authorized by nine different resolutions, but all are dated January 14, 1779. This is the final series and also the most extensive in terms of different denominations. Generally, notes of this series are found in relatively higher grades as they did not circulate for a long time.

Prices for a typical note for this issue (without signatures of great historical significance), unless listed otherwise, are as follows:

VG-8	F-12	VF-20	EF-40	AU-50	Unc-63	Unc-65
$70	$85	$150	$200	$275	$625	$1,250

W-8587 • $1 • 139,811

VG-8	F-12	VF-20	EF-40	AU-50	Unc-63	Unc-65
$80	$100	$175	$240	$350	$950	$1,600

W-8588 • $2 • 139,811

W-8589 • $3 • 139,811

W-8590 • $4 • 139,811

W-8591 • $5 • 139,811

W-8592 • $20 • 139,811

W-8593 • $30 • 182,070

W-8594 • $35 • 182,070

VG-8	F-12	VF-20	EF-40	AU-50	Unc-63	Unc-65
$90	$115	$200	$275	$375	$750	$1,500

W-8595 • $40 • 182,070

W-8596 • $45 • 182,070

VG-8	F-12	VF-20	EF-40	AU-50	Unc-63	Unc-65
$90	$115	$200	$275	$375	$750	$1,500

W-8597 • $50 • 182,070

W-8598 • $55 • 182,070

VG-8	F-12	VF-20	EF-40	AU-50	Unc-63	Unc-65
$90	$115	$200	$275	$375	$750	$1,500

W-8599 • $60 • 182,071

W-8600 • $65 • 182,070

VG-8	F-12	VF-20	EF-40	AU-50	Unc-63	Unc-65
$90	$115	$150	$200	$275	$750	$1,500

W-8601 • $70 • 139,811

VG-8	F-12	VF-20	EF-40	AU-50	Unc-63	Unc-65
$100	$150	$200	$300	$450	$1,000	$2,000

W-8602 • $80 • 139,811

VG-8	F-12	VF-20	EF-40	AU-50	Unc-63	Unc-65
$125	$175	$250	$400	$600	$1,500	$2,500

EARLY 19TH-CENTURY TREASURY NOTES

After the collapse in value of Continental Currency notes in the 1780s, any new issue of paper money by the United States of America would have met with a poor reception. In the meantime, various state-chartered banks started issuing their own paper money. By 1861, when federal Demand Notes were issued, several thousand banks had issued currency with their own imprints. Known today as *obsolete bank notes*, these were made in many different varieties. Many banks were soundly operated, while others failed or were fraudulent from the beginning. Accordingly, while many if not most bills could be exchanged at par for gold or silver coins, others were worthless. The subject is large and forms a dynamic specialty in numismatics.

The first Bank of the United States—privately owned, but with the federal government as a significant stockholder—operated from 1791 until its 20-year charter expired in 1811. It was not renewed. Officers, directors, and shareholders of state-chartered banks deeply resented the Bank of the United States as they considered it to be unfair competition. They wielded considerable political influence, making the bank controversial.

In 1816, at a time of financial uncertainty, the second Bank of the United States opened, again with a 20-year charter. Branches were established in different cities. While it seems to have acquitted itself satisfactorily, again it was resented by private interests. Whether the charter should be renewed in 1836 was a key political issue beginning in 1829, after Andrew Jackson was inaugurated as president. In 1832 Congress sought to resolve the matter in advance by renewing the charter. Jackson vetoed it, and the death knell was sounded. During the next several years the second Bank of the United States wound down its operations, and funds were transferred to designated state-chartered banks, called "pet banks" by Jackson's detractors.

In the meantime, there was great prosperity fueled by the opening of public lands in the West, the building of railroads, and growth in manufacturing. In 1835 the Treasury declared a surplus and distributed funds to the states, unprecedented before and not seen since. The matter of whether Jackson's veto of the bank charter was beneficial for the United States, or was a disaster, is still debated among historians. In any event, as his successor Martin Van Buren entered the White House, the country was plunged into the Panic of 1837. On May 10, most banks stopped redeeming their paper money with coins. The Hard Times era, as it was called, extended into 1843.

FEDERAL LOANS

During the early 19th century the federal government was in need of funds on several occasions. In 1810, secretary of the Treasury Albert Gallatin proposed interest-bearing Treasury Notes as a resource for raising government revenue. An issue was authorized by Congress on June 30, 1812. A total of $15,000,000 in denominations of $100 and $1,000 was authorized and by December 1812 was fully subscribed by banks and securities dealers. The notes bore interest at 5.4% annually (expressed as 5 and 2/5%) or one-half cent per day per $100.

Later needs for money included financing the War of 1812, which lasted into early 1815, and the War with Mexico in 1846 and 1847. Various issues of interest-bearing bonds were authorized.

These never circulated as paper money in commerce, although that had been the intent for the last of the War of 1812 issues. Buyers continued to be banks and securities brokers who bought them as an investment, not as a circulating medium. These bonds were typically held until maturity and then redeemed. Today, examples are seen now and again on the market, but they are nearly always in the form of unissued remainders or proof impressions. *United States Notes*, by John J. Knox, and *An Illustrated History of U.S. Loans 1775–1898*, by Gene Hessler, are the standard references on these issues. Knox's text is historical, while Hessler's is both historical and numismatic.

TREASURY NOTES OF THE WAR OF 1812

War was declared against Great Britain on June 18, 1812. The conflict was built upon years of interference in American maritime trade by British ships. The ill-conceived Embargo Act of 1807 sought partially to solve the dilemma by restricting American ships to coastwise trade, forbidding them to travel to Europe, the Caribbean, and other ports.

Commerce along the East Coast suffered greatly. Treasury reserves were depleted because tariffs on imported goods were the main source of revenue. The secretary of the Treasury estimated that there would be a deficit of $19 million for the year 1813.

Congress authorized $16 million of this amount to be obtained by loans, without stating that the bonds should be sold at par or specifically giving the interest rate. From the outset there was much opposition. One argument was that people would not accept them; and even if they did, the bonds would simply depreciate in the manner of the old Continental Currency—memories of which still lingered in the minds of citizens. In addition, the moneyed class of America, prime candidates for buying the notes, were generally against the war, as government policies had been a disaster for commerce. Supporters of the loan said that the bonds were backed by the government and could be exchanged for silver or gold coins, while in the meantime they drew interest, making them even better to hold than the coins themselves. In actuality, federal reserves of gold and silver were low.

On June 26, 1812, an act authorizing the bonds passed the House of Representatives 85 to 14, and then the Senate on June 27, and was signed into law on June 30.

While the government did not set aside any reserves to redeem the 1812 notes, they were receivable for duties and taxes, as well as for purchases of public land, and therefore had value, even if not backing. They were not legal tender. The notes were individually signed by people authorized by the president of the United States, who were paid $1.25 for each 100 notes they autographed. These were to be countersigned by the commissioners of the loans in the states for which the notes were made payable. When the notes were paid to revenue collectors and receivers of public money, the interest stopped on that particular day. Various records had to be kept by those paying out and receiving them.

There was great difficulty in selling the bonds. Because of this, a bill was introduced in the House of Representatives on January 27, 1813, to issue more Treasury Notes. The arguments for and against were the same as before. The new act became law on February 25, 1813. No more than $5 million of these notes were to be outstanding at any given time. They were all to be redeemed by the first quarter of the calendar year 1815, but at the close of that quarter, only $1,483,900 had been redeemed. The remainder were not finally paid until 1820.

The Act of March 4, 1814, authorized a further $5 million of Treasury Notes that, if issued, was to be considered part of a stock loan. On March 24, 1814, a loan for $25 million was authorized, but notes could be sold only at a large discount from face value, raising the interest costs higher than that imprinted on the notes.

On August 31, 1814, specie payments were suspended by banks, except in New England. By that time $10,649,800 in Treasury notes was outstanding. Secretary of the Treasury Thomas Crawford was succeeded in October 1814 by Alexander J. Dallas. In his report of October 17, 1814, the new secretary said that as silver and gold coins were not available, and banks had increased the issue of their own paper money, there were great difficulties in marketing government securities. He suggested that a national bank be established to provide stability. By that time the first Bank of the United States, which came close to being a national bank, was defunct.

The Treasury Notes continued to be poorly received. On October 12, 1814, Representative Bolling Hall, of Georgia, introduced a series of five resolutions to bolster the credit of the Treasury Notes. He suggested that these should be Legal Tender between citizens and between citizens and foreigners, instead of just payments to the government. Nothing happened to these or other proposals.

On December 26, 1814, an act was passed that authorized the issue of $7,500,000 of Treasury Notes to replace parts of the loans of March 24 and November 15, 1814, that were not sold, plus $3 million more for expenses of the war department. Some $8,318,400 of notes were issued, some in denominations of $20 and $50.

In the meantime, the treaty of peace ending the War of 1812 was signed in Ghent, Belgium, on December 14, 1814, but the news did not reach the United States until early 1815. The Battle of New Orleans was fought in January 1815 without knowledge that the war was over.

The Act of February 15, 1815, the last in the series, provided for up to $25,000,000 to be issued in $100 notes bearing 5.4% interest and "small Treasury Notes" of values of $3, $5, $10, $20, and $50 convertible into 7% United States "stock" (bonds). $4,969,400 of the $100 notes was issued, and $3,992,994 of the smaller values.

In his report for 1815, the secretary of the Treasury said that the notes issued prior to February 24, 1815, were for the most part too high in denomination to serve as a medium of exchange. Furthermore, although the small Treasury Notes, fundable at interest of 7%, were convenient for common use, they were usually converted into stock as soon as they were issued and served no circulating purpose at all.

SYNOPSIS OF THE 1812–1815 TREASURY NOTES

In summary, these notes were issued in five series from 1812 to 1815, in denominations ranging from $3 to $1,000.

The large-denomination notes measure 7.375 inches by 3.875 inches. Notes of denominations less than $100, called small Treasury Notes in government records, were payable to the bearer, carried no interest, and measure 6.5 inches by 3 inches.

The total issue of the Treasury bills was as follows:

Act of June 30, 1812: $5,000,000

Act of February 25, 1813: $5,000,000

Act of March 4, 1814: $10,000,000

Act of December 26, 1814: $8,318,400.

Act of February 24, 1815: $100 notes, $4,969,400.

Act of February 24, 1815: small Treasury Notes less than $100, $3,392,994.

The total amount issued was $36,680,794.

All Treasury Notes were printed by Murray, Draper, Fairman and Company in Philadelphia and are one-sided. The first two issues were signed by Timothy Matlock and Charles Biddle, while the last three were signed by Edward Fox and Samuel Clarke. The last issue was alternately signed by F.W. McGeary and C.A. Colville. Some were countersigned by William White (first two issues), T.D.T. Tucker (last two issues), or Joseph Nourse (the register on the last issue only).

ACT OF JUNE 30, 1812

One-year notes of this issue bore interest at 5.4%. Denominations of $100 and $1,000 were printed. Total face value was $5,000,000, all issued. These notes were receivable by the government for money due it, but were not legal tender. All were redeemed by the end of 1814.

$100 Treasury Notes, June 30, 1812

W-8650 • F-TN-2 • 15,000 issued • Remainder notes • 5 known

VF-20	Unc-63
$17,500	$30,000

$1,000 Treasury Notes, June 30, 1812

W-8653 • F-TN-1 • 2,000 issued • Remainder notes • 3 known

VF-20	Unc-63
$25,000	$40,000

$100 Treasury Note, June 30, 1812 (W-8650). This and all others printed by Murray, Draper, Fairman and Company, Philadelphia. Eagle on branch at upper right. Shield and cannon at lower center. Unsigned remainder.

$1,000 Treasury Note, June 30, 1812 (W-8653). Unsigned remainder.

ACT OF FEBRUARY 25, 1813

One-year notes of this issue bore interest at 5.4%. Denominations of $100 and $1,000 were printed. Total face value was $5,000,000, all issued. These notes were receivable by the government for money due it, but were not legal tender.

$100 Treasury Notes, February 25, 1813

W-8658 • F-TN-3 • 4,000 issued • Unknown

$1,000 Treasury Notes, February 25, 1813

W-8662 • F-TN-4 • 4,000 issued • Unknown

ACT OF MARCH 4, 1814

One-year notes of this issue bore interest at 5.4%. Denominations of $20, $100, and $1,000 were printed. Total face value was $10,000,000, all issued. These notes were receivable by the government for money due it, but were not legal tender.

$20 Treasury Notes, March 4, 1814

W-8666 • F-TN-7 • 8,000 (est.) • Unknown

$100 Treasury Notes, March 4, 1814

W-8668 • F-TN-6a • 24,000 (est.) • Remainder notes • 3 known

VF-20	Unc-63
$20,000	$30,000

$1,000 Treasury Notes, March 4, 1814

W-8670 • F-TN-5 • 6,000 (est.) issued • Unknown

ACT OF DECEMBER 26, 1814

One-year notes of this issue bore interest at 5.4%. Denominations of $20 and $100 were printed. Total face value of $10,500,000 was authorized, but only $8,318,400 was issued. These notes were receivable by the government for money due it, but were not legal tender.

$20 Treasury Notes, December 26, 1814

W-8675 • F-TN-9, 9a, 9p • 8,000 (est.) • Unknown

$100 Treasury Notes, December 26, 1814

W-8678 • F-TN-8, 8a, 8p • 24,000 (est.) • Remainder notes • 3 known

VF-20	Unc-63
$15,000	$20,000

ACT OF FEBRUARY 24, 1815

This issue included denominations from $3 to $100. Total face value of $25,000,000 was authorized, but only $3,392,444 was issued. These were receivable by the government for money due it, but were not legal tender. These small-denomination notes were fundable into 7% stock (taking up part of the $9,070,386 issued of this stock). This made them popular, and some of them were sold at a premium of 4%, and others at a premium of 2.5%. Nearly all were used in this manner. None served as paper money in general commerce or circulation. The balance, $100 notes bearing 5.4% interest, sold better, but still below expectations.

$3 Treasury Notes, February 24, 1815

W-8683 • F-TN-16, 16a, 16b • Mostly remainder notes as priced here

Commentary: One signed issued note is known; it sold for $52,500 in the Stack's 2004 sale of the John J. Ford Jr. collection.

VF-20	Unc-63
$7,000	$12,000

$5 Treasury Notes, February 24, 1815

W-8686 • F-TN-15, 15a, 15p • Remainder notes

VF-20	Unc-63
$6,500	$11,000

$10 Treasury Notes, February 24, 1815

W-8689 • F-TN-13, 13a • Text vertical in right border: "Receivable everywhere by the United States . . ." • Remainder notes

VF-20	Unc-63
$8,500	$12,500

W-8691 • F-TN-14, 14a, 14b, 14p • Text vertical in right border: "TEN DOLLARS" • Remainder notes

VF-20	Unc-63
$6,500	$8,500

$20 Treasury Notes, February 24, 1815

W-8696 • F-TN-12, 12a, 12p • Remainder notes

VF-20	Unc-63
$6,500	$10,000

$50 Treasury Notes, February 24, 1815

W-8700 • F-TN-11, 11a, 11b, 11p • Remainder notes

VF-20	Unc-63
$8,500	$12,500

Act of December 26, 1814

$20 Treasury Note, December 26, 1814 (W-8675). Spread eagle on shield at upper left; 20 surrounded by cornucopia at the lower center.

$100 Treasury Note, December 26, 1814 (W-8678). Spread eagle on shield at upper right; shield and military regalia at the lower center.

$100 Treasury Notes, February 24, 1815

W-8705 • F-TN-10, 10a, 10p • Remainder notes

VF-20	Unc-63
$8,000	$12,500

Treasury Notes 1837 to 1860

Many other Treasury Notes were issued under legislation from 1837 to 1860. These were bonds bearing interest and were not intended to circulate as paper money. They were made by Rawdon, Wright & Hatch, of New York City; its successor firm, Rawdon, Wright, Hatch & Edson; and then the American Bank Note Company. Gene Hessler's *An Illustrated History of U.S. Loans 1775–1898* gives extensive information on these. The John J. Ford Jr. Collection, Part VI, Stack's, October 12, 2004, offered a wide selection of such notes.

ACT OF FEBRUARY 24, 1815

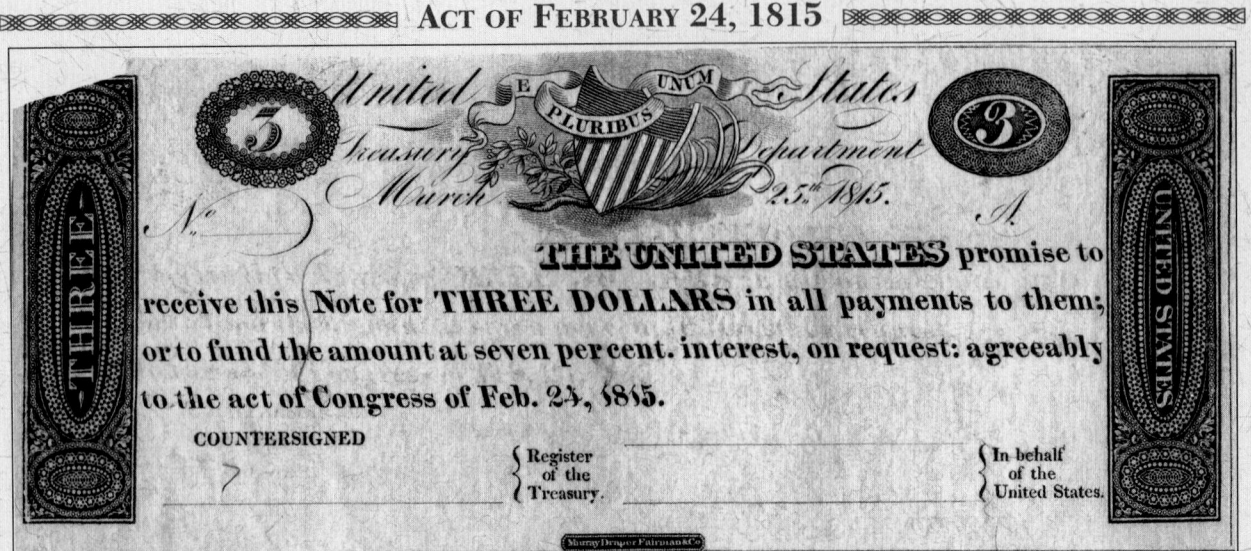

$3 Treasury Note, February 24, 1815 (W-8683). Shield with motto at the upper center.

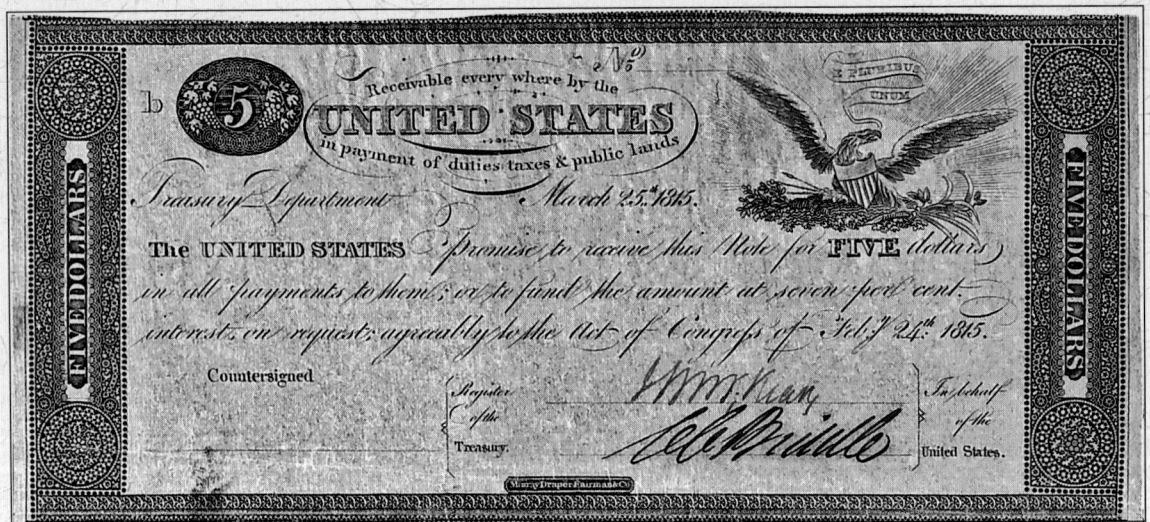

$5 Treasury Note, February 24, 1815 (W-8686). Remainder partially signed by F.W. McGeary and C.C. Biddle.

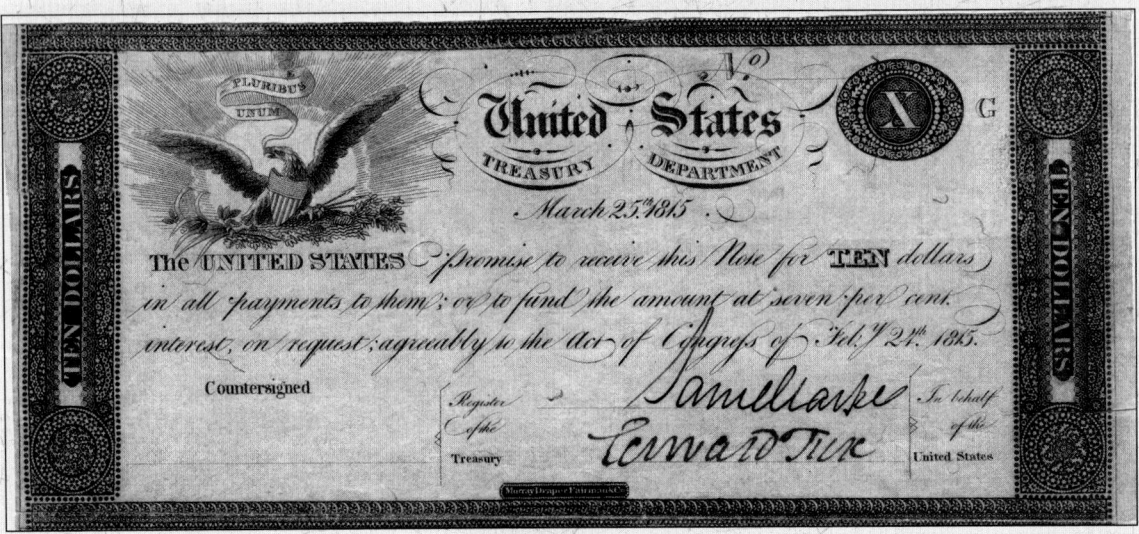

$10 Treasury Note, February 24, 1815 (W-8691). Similar to the preceding, but with TEN DOLLARS vertically at right, Remainder partially signed by Samuel Clarke and Edward Fox.

ACT OF FEBRUARY 24, 1815,
continued

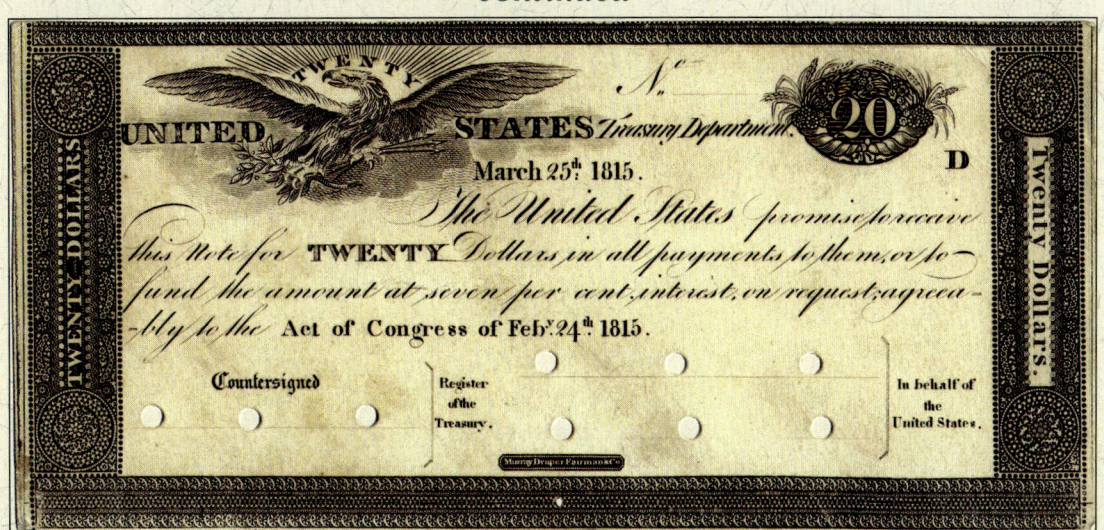

$20 Treasury Note, February 24, 1815 (W-8696). Spread eagle on branch at upper left.

$50 Treasury Note, February 24, 1815 (W-8700). Spread eagle on branch at upper right. Signed by F.W. McGeary and C.C. Biddle; countersigned by Joseph Nourse.

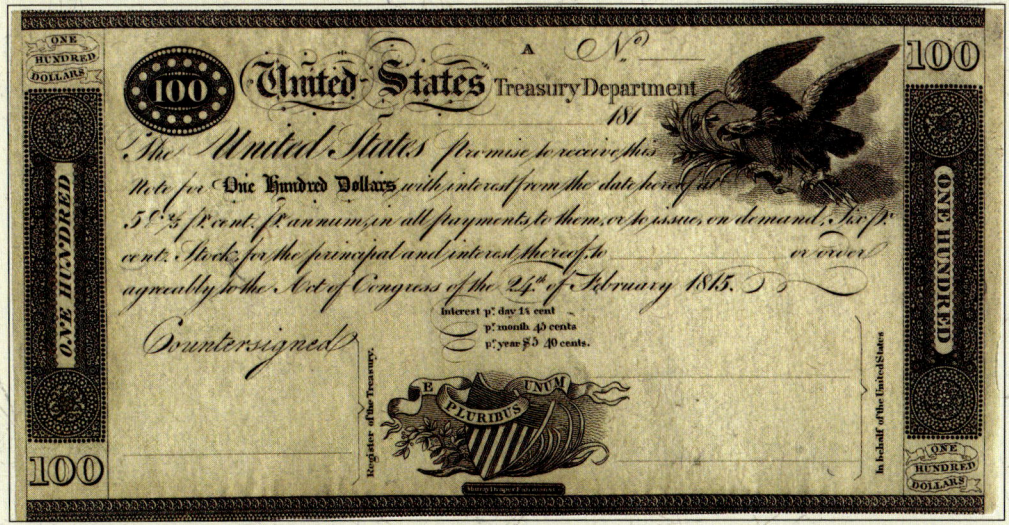

$100 Treasury Note, February 24, 1815 (W-8705). Eagle on branch at upper right; shield at lower center. This denomination bore 5.4% interest.

TREASURY NOTES OF 1837 TO 1860

$100 Treasury Note ink-dated April 16, 1838, with interest inked in at 5%. Signed, issued, redeemed, and canceled. At the top is Mercury, at the left Wealth, and at the right Justice. By Rawdon, Wright & Hatch, New York City.

$1,000 Treasury Note, Act of January 28, 1847. 2 years, 6%, or convertible at the option of the holder into 6% U.S. stock, redeemable after 1867. Portraits of Albert Gallatin and Alexander Dallas at the left, eagle and ships at the top center, Liberty as a Native American maiden at the right. Proof by Toppan, Carpenter & Co., but not imprinted.

Treasury Notes of 1837 to 1860,
continued

$1,000 1857 Interest-Bearing Note. Pictured at the lower right is James Buchanan, the sitting president. Proof by Rawdon, Wright, Hatch & Edson, New York City. At the bottom border is the imprint PATENTED 30 JUNE 1857, referring to the special green tint that RWH&E and later, the American Bank Note Company, promoted.

22

ENCASED POSTAGE STAMPS OF 1862

Among the entrepreneurs with an eye to profiting from the extreme shortage of coins in the summer of 1862 was John Gault of Boston, who in the same year relocated to New York City. Born in Baltimore in 1831, he had moved with his family to Boston around 1840. In 1850 he headed for California, one year too late to be a forty-niner, but still in time to be a part of the action. He remained there until 1855, although he did not make his pile, as the term went. Few others did either.

In 1855 he came back to Boston and went to work in a machine shop. Possessing an inventive mind, he developed several gadgets and improvements, including an illuminated coal-hole cover, an improved lockstitch device for the sewing machine (then wildly popular on the American market), and a sharpener for erasers. By that time he had a business in Boston at 5 Water Street. It was there that he worked on military improvements and crafted three different variations of artillery shrapnel rounds. Sometime early in 1862 he moved to New York City, in time to become engaged in the encased-postage-stamp enterprise that arose in response to the coin shortage (see chapter 3).

During the coin shortage, stamps provided a convenient alternative, with unused examples exchanged at face value to buy newspapers, food, and more. Soon, the government made stamps official for use as money.

Recognizing that stamps glued to paper or cardboard would soon become discolored or damaged and that those in envelopes would be clumsy to inspect and also might become damaged, Gault felt that encased postage stamps would serve a need. Basically, the unit consisted of a multiple-part arrangement displayed in an encasement made of brass.

The back part could be blank or bear simply the name of Gault, or it could be sold as an advertising medium, which became the usual style. Within the frame was a small piece of cardboard padding, then a regular postage stamp with its corners folded down, then a thin sheet of clear mica, and then a top frame to fit around the back frame, in the manner that might be used to make a brass button. The result was a colorful and attractive token, about the size of a quarter dollar, that had a clear view of a particular postage stamp and was usable in circulation at that value. Businesses warmed to the idea of advertising, and most encased postage stamps

Enlarged view of a typical encased postage stamp, this being W-9548, issued by White the Hatter. On the face is a 1¢ stamp mounted at a slight angle in the frame. On the back is White's advertisement and location, and at the bottom border, Gault's patent information.

Barnum's American Museum on lower Broadway in the early 1860s, flying a flag, the era when White had his hat store on the bottom level of the building. The Astor House, the city's finest hotel, is to the right. New York City was the location of John Gault and his encased-postage-stamp business and also where many of his customers were located.

bore commercial messages, such as for Ayer's Sarsaparilla, Brown's Bronchial Troches, Joseph Bates's Fancy Goods, or the name of a hotel or hat manufacturer—there were over 30 variations. Lord & Taylor, a name still familiar today, was among Gault's customers.

The exact time of Gault's production is not known, but it commenced sometime after his patent (no. 1627) was granted on August 2, 1862, and certainly lasted through spring 1863, at which time Postage Currency notes issued by the Treasury department flooded circulation. The encased postage stamps were made by the Scovill Manufacturing Company of Waterbury, Connecticut, long established as a maker of buttons, tokens (including in the Hard Times era), and other small metal goods.

By 1863 millions of privately issued copper tokens were also available, these containing less than one cent's worth of metal and thus yielding a nice profit for those who made them and those who used them for advertisements. These pieces, called Civil War tokens today, probably lessened the demand for Gault's product. The situation remains something of a mystery, for the leading advertisers on encased postage stamps did not advertise on Civil War tokens. Whatever the reasons, by the summer of 1863 there were so many tokens and Postal Currency notes in circulation, plus a flood of privately printed scrip notes, that the encased postage stamps no longer filled a critical need. It is likely that existing encased postage stamps circulated occasionally for a year or two afterward, as some in existence today show extensive wear in the form of dents on the cases or cracks or breaks in the mica. The glory period of encased postage was probably less than a year.

THE PANORAMA OF ENCASED POSTAGE STAMPS

During this time 31 different merchants signed up to advertise on encased postage stamps. Today, the collecting of encased postage stamps is a vital specialty in American numismatics. As a class all varieties are so scarce or rare that if interest were to become widespread there simply would not be enough to go around, even of certain issues that are viewed as plentiful within the series.

Postage-stamp denominations used included these:

1¢ blue. Franklin portrait. August 17, 1861. Scott catalog number 63.

3¢ rose. Washington portrait. 1861. S-65.

5¢ red-brown. Jefferson portrait. January 2, 1862. S-75.

10¢ yellow-green. Washington portrait. August 20, 1861. S-68.

12¢ black. Washington portrait. After August 20, 1861. S-69. This is a very scarce denomination today.

24¢ red-lilac. Washington portrait. January 7, 1862. S-70. Also very scarce.

30¢ orange. Franklin portrait. August 20, 1861. S-71. Seldom seen in the marketplace.

90¢ blue. Washington portrait. After November 1861. S-72. The rarest of all encased postage denominations.

Occasionally a two-cent stamp with the Jackson portrait is offered on the market as an encased postage stamp, as it may be, but the only one believed to have been issued by Gault is W-9283. The position of a stamp within an encasement can vary. While most are oriented vertically, many are tilted one way or the other or are off center. In some rare instances a few edge perforations are visible.

Some varieties of stamps were issued with the brass panel at the back tinned (sometimes called silvered). Most encased postage stamps have plain tabs on the front of the case—the projections extending from left to right. A few varieties have ribbed frames with ridges. Plain Frame and Ribbed Frame are often capitalized in numismatic usage.

Around the back border there is raised beading on all varieties except Brown's Bronchial Troches, Hunt & Nash (which have a plain inner rim), and J. Gault. The Gault encasement is unique with its circle of recessed (incuse) dots and recessed lettering.

Various deceptions exist among encased postage stamps in numismatic hands today, including fabrications of supposed rarities and new varieties made by opening the cases and substituting a more valuable high-denomination stamp for a lower one, or by inserting stamps not used originally in the series or varieties of denominations made after 1863. An extensive discussion of such impostures is given in the *Standard Catalogue of Encased Postage Stamps* by Michael Hodder and Q. David Bowers (1989). A detailed description of the issuers of encased postage stamps may also be found in the Hodder-Bowers book, as well as in Fred L. Reed's *Civil War Encased Stamps* (1995).

The encased postage stamps are arranged by Whitman numbers, cross-referenced to HB (Hodder-Bowers) numbers, EP (Friedberg) numbers, and alphanumeric (Reed) numbers.

Detail of a Plain Frame and a Ribbed Frame as used on encased postage stamps.

GRADING ENCASED POSTAGE STAMPS

Grading encased postage stamps presents some problems unique to the series. Each encasement was composed of several separate items, including the stamp and its backing, the mica facing, and the two-part case fitted together containing the other components.

Each item was, and is, subject to its own types of change over time, through wear or simple aging. Accordingly, grading encased postage stamps must take into account the conditions of the major constituents of each piece: the stamp, the mica, and the case. Stamps can be bright or faded, intact or torn, wrinkled or smooth, water stained or not, and so on. Similarly, the mica can be clear or crazed, cracked or sound, laminated or not, and so on. Most stamps were probably issued with the mica either clear or with only tiny laminations, as occur in nature. In its turn, the case may be dark or bright; dented, bent, or both; and so on. Some varieties were issued with tinning on the back, which today may be fully (rare) or partially present.

Any description of an encased postage stamp should accurately convey to the potential collector the individual conditions of each of the three major components just described. Finally, summing up the conditions of the stamp, mica, and case, an overall adjectival grade can be assigned to the specimen that represents the overall eye appeal and condition of the piece. In the descriptions that follow, varieties are valued under three grade columns. While these grades are an approximate guide, specific descriptions of an encasement are always desirable as a supplement.

Uncirculated-60 and finer: Mica intact with no laminations, stamp bright, case pristine and with luster to the brass and tinning (if present).

About Uncirculated-50: A bright brass, nearly as new encasement with no more than microscopic flaws to the mica. Tinning (silvering), if present, will be silvery and lustrous, although usually not complete. This grade is more theoretical than practical. Only a few varieties exist so fine.

Extremely Fine-40: Mica intact with no more than minor flaking or lamination. Stamp bright. A prime grade for the specialist, a reasonable objective for the advanced collector.

Very Fine-20: Mica intact, but may have laminations, flaking, or small cracks, but with a clear view of the stamp. Stamp bright or only slightly faded. Brass case may be slightly oxidized or dark, but will have no major problems. This is a typical nice-quality encasement, attractive and without major problems except for mica.

Low Grades, Damaged, and Impaired: Encased postage stamps with pieces of the mica broken out, parts of the stamp missing, the stamp severely faded, or a bent, damaged, or obviously tampered-with frame are worth fractions of the prices listed for Very Fine. At best, they can be used as fillers. If the back of the case is well preserved, it will be more valuable than if it is damaged, as it can be collected for a merchant or product that might otherwise be rare.

Accordingly, a Claflin or Miles encasement, even with damaged mica or an impaired stamp, will have significant value. In contrast, an Ayer's encasement would be of little worth. Encasements with severe problems have relatively little added value even if they enclose a damaged high-denomination stamp such as 24¢ or 90¢.

MARKET VALUES

The prime determinant of market value is the rarity of the encased postage stamp as a basic type. Accordingly, examples from such issuers as B.F. Miles, Sands's Ale, and Arthur M. Claflin will elevate the temperature in an auction room. This reflects the fact that the preponderance of numismatists desire just one of each issuer. High-denomination stamps also add significant value, such as the 12¢, with importance increasing through the 24¢, 30¢, and in particular the 90¢ stamps. Of less importance in terms of value are rare frame or lettering varieties of otherwise plentiful issues, although these varieties do have their own audience.

Values are given in several grades as described. The prices of the more elusive issues are likely to vary widely at auction and private sale, and it is not unusual to see a Very Fine example priced at $2,000 in one place and $3,000 or even $4,000 in another. Pedigree and eye appeal are factors as well. Uncirculated examples should be studied carefully, as grading can vary widely in the marketplace. These are valued at 50 percent to 100 percent or more above the About Uncirculated listings. As more data become available, we anticipate listing specific Uncirculated values in future editions.[1]

Aërated Bread Company
New York City

The Aërated Bread Company was located on the corner of Lafayette Place and Fourth Street in New York City. Aërated bread was developed by Stephen F. Ambler of Brooklyn, New York. By injecting the dough with carbonated gas, Ambler gave his bread a light texture and consistency that were very different from the usual loaves sold in New York. Ambler received his patent on August 12, 1862, the same day John Gault's patent for encasements was granted. Ambler's process was at first successful as a novelty item. By 1864, however, the business failed for lack of customers.

This is one of the rarer issues. The 5¢ value is unique. All are of the Plain Frame style.

W-9000 • 1¢ • EP-1, HB-1, AB01 • Plain Frame
Commentary: An AU example sold for $4,887 in the 2007 Heritage sale of the Frederick Mayer collection.

VF-20	EF-40
$2,500	$4,000

W-9004 • 5¢ • EP-59a, HB-2, AB05

Recorded population: 1 • *Commentary:* The unique example, graded EF, sold for $14,375 in the 2007 Heritage sale of the Frederick Mayer collection.

Ayer's Cathartic Pills
Lowell, Massachusetts

The firm of James C. Ayer and Company was Gault's biggest single customer, advertising three different patent medicine products on the encasements as described below. Between 1855 and 1870 Ayer became the king of the patent medicine industry. Ayer's nostrums were little different from many others available at the time. What made Ayer's venture successful was his understanding of the power of advertising. Today, trade cards, almanacs, bottles, and other ephemera are easily collected as go-withs for encased postage stamps.

The Ayer's Cathartic Pills encasement exists with two styles of arrows on the reverse: Short Arrows and Long Arrows. As a class the Short Arrows issues are common and the Long Arrows issues are scarce. The pills were advertised as an aid to digestion, with the reverse inscription THE CURRENCY TO PASS perhaps being a punning reference to elimination. All are of the Plain Frame style.

W-9016 • 1¢ • EP-2, HB-3, AC01SA • Short Arrows • Plain Frame

VF-20	EF-40	AU-50
$250	$350	$500

W-9017 • 1¢ • HB-4, AC01LA • Long Arrows • Unique

W-9019 • 3¢ • EP-32, HB-5, AC03SA • Short Arrows

VF-20	EF-40	AU-50
$200	$300	$525

W-9020 • 3¢ • EP-32a, HB-6, AC03LA • Long Arrows

VF-20	EF-40	AU-50
$375	$500	$700

W-9022 • 5¢ • EP-60, HB-7, AC05SA • Short Arrows

VF-20	EF-40
$700	$1,000

W-9023 • 5¢ • EP-60a, HB-8, AC05LA • Long Arrows

VF-20	EF-40	AU-50
$800	$1,500	$2,200

W-9025 • 10¢ • EP-96, HB-9, AC10SA • Short Arrows

Commentary: An AU example sold for $2,530 in the 2007 Heritage sale of the Frederick Mayer collection.

VF-20	EF-40
$650	$1,200

W-9026 • 10¢ • EP-96a, HB-10, AC10LA • Long Arrows

VF-20	EF-40
$750	$1,250

W-9028 • 12¢ • EP-135, HB-11, AC12SA • Short Arrows

Commentary: An EF example sold for $2,760 in the 2007 Heritage sale of the Frederick Mayer collection.

VF-20
$1,500

W-9029 • 12¢ • HB-12, AC12LA • Long Arrows

Commentary: An EF example sold for $2,070 in the 2007 Heritage sale of the Frederick Mayer collection.

VF-20
$1,700

W-9031 • 24¢ • EP-159b, HB-13, AC24SA • Short Arrows

VF-20	EF-40
$2,700	$3,500

W-9032 • 24¢ • HB-14, AC24LA • Long Arrows

Commentary: Current market information not available.

W-9034 • 30¢ • EP-172b, HB-15, AC30SA • Short Arrows

Recorded population: 1 • *Commentary:* The unique example, graded EF, sold for $6,900 in the 2007 Heritage sale of the Frederick Mayer collection.

W-9035 • 30¢ • HB-16, AC30LA • Long Arrows

Commentary: Current market information not available.

"Take Ayer's Pills"
Lowell, Massachusetts

Issued in large quantities, these encasements are among the most plentiful today. Plain Frame (usual) and Ribbed Frame (rare) styles exist. The lettering font on this issue is the largest in the series. Patent information on the back is in two lines curved along the bottom border, an unusual configuration.

W-9038 • 1¢ • EP- 3, HB-17, AP01 • Plain Frame

VF-20	EF-40	AU-50
$475	$600	$800

W-9040 • 3¢ • EP-33, HB-18, AP03

VF-20	EF-40	AU-50
$300	$400	$600

W-9042 • 5¢ • EP-61, HB-19, AP05

VF-20	EF-40
$750	$1,250

W-9043 • 5¢ • EP-62, HB-20, AP05RB • Ribbed Frame
Commentary: An EF example sold for $5,750 in the 2007 Heritage sale of the Frederick Mayer collection.

VF-20
$3,200

W-9045 • 10¢ • EP-97, HB-21, AP10 • Plain Frame
Commentary: An AU example sold for $1,610 in the 2007 Heritage sale of the Frederick Mayer collection.

VF-20	EF-40
$800	$1,500

W-9046 • 10¢ • EP-97a, HB-22, AP10RB • Ribbed Frame
Recorded population: 1 • *Commentary:* The unique example sold for $4,888 in the 2004 Stack's sale of the John J. Ford Jr. collection, and for $4,600 in the 2007 Heritage sale of the Frederick Mayer collection.

W-9048 • 12¢ • EP-136, HB-23, AP12 • Plain Frame
Commentary: An AU example sold for $3,737 in the 2007 Heritage sale of the Frederick Mayer collection.

VF-20
$1,200

W-9050 • 24¢ • EP-159C, HB-24, AP24
Commentary: Current market information not available.

W-9052 • 30¢ • HB-25, AP30
Commentary: An example sold for $5,750 in the 2007 Heritage sale of the Frederick Mayer collection.

W-9054 • 90¢ • EP-183a, HB-26, AP90
Commentary: Current market information not available.

Ayer's Sarsaparilla
Lowell, Massachusetts

This encasement exists with the word AYER'S either small, medium, or large and of the Plain Frame or Ribbed Frame style. Not all combinations are known today, perhaps providing the opportunity for discoveries in the future.

W-9056 • 1¢ • EP-4, HB-27, AS01SM • Small AYER'S, Plain Frame

VF-20	EF-40	AU-50
$600	$900	$1,200

W-9057 • 1¢ • EP-4a, HB-28, AS01MD • Medium AYER'S

VF-20	EF-40	AU-50
$300	$400	$650

W-9059 • 3¢ • EP-34, HB-29, AS03SM • Small AYER'S

VF-20	EF-40	AU-50
$600	$800	$1,200

W-9060 • 3¢ • EP-34a, HB-30, AS03MD • Medium AYER'S

VF-20	EF-40
$300	$400

W-9061 • 3¢ • EP-35, HB-31, AS03MDRB • Medium AYER'S, Ribbed Frame
Commentary: An EF example sold for $2,875 in the 2007 Heritage sale of the Frederick Mayer collection.

VF-20
$2,000

W-9062 • 3¢ • EP-34b, HB-32, AS03LG • Large AYER'S, Plain Frame

VF-20	EF-40	AU-50
$350	$450	$700

W-9064 • 5¢ • EP-63, HB-33, AS05MD • Medium AYER'S

VF-20	EF-40	AU-50
$375	$475	$650

W-9065 • 5¢ • EP-63a, HB-34, AS05LG • Large AYER'S
Commentary: An EF example sold for $3,737 in the 2007 Heritage sale of the Frederick Mayer collection.

VF-20
$2,200

W-9067 • 10¢ • EP-98, HB-35, AS10SM • Small AYER'S

VF-20	EF-40
$2,000	$2,500

W-9068 • 10¢ • EP-98a, HB-36, AS10MD • Medium AYER'S

VF-20	EF-40	AU-50
$450	$625	$900

W-9069 • 10¢ • EP-99, HB-37, AS10MDRB • Medium AYER'S, Ribbed Frame
Commentary: A VF example sold for $2,760 in the 2007 Heritage sale of the Frederick Mayer collection.

VF-20
$3,750

W-9070 • 10¢ • EP-98b, HB-38, AS10LG • Large AYER'S, Plain Frame

Commentary: An EF example sold for $2,530 in the 2007 Heritage sale of the Frederick Mayer collection.

VF-20	EF-40	AU-50
$1,500	—	$3,200

W-9072 • 12¢ • EP-137a, HB-39, AS12SM • Small AYER'S

VF-20	EF-40	AU-50
$3,000	$4,000	$5,500

W-9073 • 12¢ • EP-137, HB-40, AS12MD • Medium AYER'S

VF-20	EF-40	AU-50
$3,000	$4,000	$6,000

W-9074 • 12¢ • HB-41, AS12LG • Large AYER'S

Recorded population: 2 • Commentary: An example graded EF sold for $6,326 in the 2007 Heritage sale of the Frederick Mayer collection.

W-9078 • 30¢ • EP-173, HB-42, AS30MD • Medium AYER'S

Recorded population: 1 • Commentary: The unique example, graded AU, sold for $7,475 in the 2007 Heritage sale of the Frederick Mayer collection.

W-9080 • 90¢ • EP-183b, HB-43, AS90MD • Medium AYER'S

VF-20	EF-40	AU-50
$12,000	$14,000	$18,000

Bailey & Company
Philadelphia, Pennsylvania

Bailey & Company was founded in 1832 under the name of Bailey & Kitchen. It is thought that partner Andrew Boyd Kitchen was a numismatist. The Dr. Lewis Roper collection was acquired by him as collateral and sold at auction in 1851, the first truly notable rare coin sale to be held in the United States. In 1859 the business moved to the address found on its encasements, 819 Chestnut Street (misspelled as Chesnut Street). At the time they commissioned their encasements, Bailey & Company could claim to be the largest jewelry firm in the United States, contesting Tiffany's for that honor. Their relations with the U.S. Mint were close: at times they shared the services of the same engravers. In 1861 an agent for the government of the Confederate States of America approached the company, proposing that it strike cents for the Confederacy. Bailey & Company commissioned Robert Lovett Jr., a well-known local die sinker, to cut the dies.

Encasements of this issuer are fairly scarce. All are of the Plain Frame style.

W-9083 • 1¢ • EP-5, HB-44, BC01 • Plain Frame

VF-20	EF-40	AU-50
$1,000	$1,500	$2,000

W-9085 • 3¢ • EP-36, HB-45, BC03

VF-20	EF-40	AU-50
$900	$1,400	$1,900

W-9087 • 5¢ • EP-64, HB-46, BC05

VF-20	EF-40	AU-50
$750	$1,800	$2,600

W-9089 • 10¢ • EP-100, HB-47, BC10

VF-20	EF-40	AU-50
$750	$1,800	$2,600

W-9091 • 12¢ • EP-138, HB-48, BC12

Commentary: Current market information not available.

Joseph L. Bates
Boston, Massachusetts

Joseph L. Bates started in business in 1828 as a maker of musical instruments at 44 Market Street, Boston. In 1846 he expanded his product line to include umbrellas. In 1847 he dropped musical instruments in favor of "fancy goods" and moved to larger premises in a more fashionable part of Boston. His new location, 129 Washington Street, was near Faneuil Hall and adjoined Tichnor's bookstore, a meeting place for New England's avant-garde literary artists. This new address was the one that later appeared on his encasements. He carried a wide selection of luxury items for the carriage trade and was a pioneer in the selling of stereographic viewers and cards.

Encasements are found with two reverse varieties: FANCY GOODS as two words (normal) and run together as FANCYGOODS.

W-9095 • 1¢ • EP-6a, HB-49, BA01FG • FANCYGOODS, Plain Frame

VF-20	EF-40	AU-50
$650	$900	$1,200

W-9096 • 1¢ • EP-6, HB-50, BA01F/G • FANCY GOODS

VF-20	EF-40	AU-50
$650	$1,000	$1,400

W-9098 • 3¢ • EP-37a, HB-51, BA03FG • FANCYGOODS
Commentary: Current market information not available.

W-9099 • 3¢ • EP-37, HB-52, BA03F/G • FANCY GOODS

VF-20	EF-40	AU-50
$1,000	$1,500	$2,600

W-9101 • 5¢ • EP-66a, HB-53, BA05FG • FANCYGOODS
Commentary: Current market information not available.

W-9102 • 5¢ • EP-65, HB-54, BA05F/G • FANCY GOODS
Commentary: An EF example sold for $3,450 in the 2007 Heritage sale of the Frederick Mayer collection.

VF-20
$3,250

W-9103 • 5¢ • EP-66, HB-55, BA05FGRB • FANCYGOODS, Ribbed Frame
Commentary: An EF example sold for $3,737 in the 2007 Heritage sale of the Frederick Mayer collection.

VF-20
$2,200

W-9105 • 10¢ • EP-102a, HB-56, BA10FG • FANCYGOODS, Plain Frame

VF-20	EF-40	AU-50
$1,200	$1,750	$2,600

W-9106 • 10¢ • EP-101, HB-57, BA10F/G • FANCY GOODS

VF-20	EF-40	AU-50
$950	$1,500	$2,200

W-9107 • 10¢ • EP-102, HB-58, BA10F/GRB • FANCY GOODS, Ribbed Frame
Commentary: An EF example sold for $3,450 in the 2007 Heritage sale of the Frederick Mayer collection.

VF-20
$3,000

W-9109 • 12¢ • HB-59, EP-139, BA12F/G • FANCY GOODS, Plain Frame

VF-20	EF-40	AU-50
$3,000	$3,500	$4,000

W-9111 • 24¢ • HB-60, BA24F/G • FANCY GOODS • Unique

W-9114 • 90¢ • HB-61, BA90F/G • FANCY GOODS • Unique

Brown's Bronchial Troches
Boston, Massachusetts

John I. Brown reaped profits from patent medicines, including Bronchial Troches advertised on encased postage, and the opium-laced Mrs. Winslow's Soothing Syrup. The syrup was advertised as a remedy for colicky infants, but each bottle contained a large dose of laudanum, an opium solution. During the debate over passage of the Pure Food and Drug Act (1906), it was reported that hundreds of children had died after being given the syrup, undoubtedly the result of inadvertent overdoses. The testimony helped the legislation gain passage. Like Ayer and Drake's Plantation Bitters, Brown issued a yearly almanac to promote his products.

These encasements are among the more plentiful in the series. All are of the Plain Frame style. The back is one of just two (the other is Hunt & Nash) in the series without beading or dots around the border.

W-9116 • 1¢ • EP-7, HB-62, BT01 • Plain Frame
Commentary: An AU example sold for $3,220 in the 2007 Heritage sale of the Frederick Mayer collection.

VF-20	EF-40
$1,500	$2,000

W-9118 • 3¢ • EP-38, HB-63, BT03

VF-20	EF-40	AU-50
$400	$600	$900

W-9120 • 5¢ • EP-67, HB-64, BT05

VF-20	EF-40	AU-50
$450	$650	$1,000

W-9122 • 10¢ • EP-103, HB-65, BT10

VF-20	EF-40	AU-50
$950	$1,300	$1,700

W-9124 • 12¢ • EP-140, HB-66, BT12
Commentary: An AU example sold for $2,127 in the 2007 Heritage sale of the Frederick Mayer collection.

VF-20	EF-40
$1,500	$2,000

F. Buhl and Company
Detroit, Michigan

F. (Frederick) Buhl and Company were dealers in hats and furs and were the only Detroit-based company that commissioned encasements from Gault. The company made men's and women's hats of all kinds, primarily from felt, beaver skins, and other furs. Located across the strait from Windsor, Ontario, Buhl was well placed to buy his furs from the Hudson's Bay Company depot there.

Buhl encasements range from scarce to rare. All are of the Plain Frame style.

W-9130 • 1¢ • EP-8, HB-67, BU01 • Plain Frame

VF-20	EF-40	AU-50
$2,500	$3,000	$4,000

W-9132 • 3¢ • EP-38a, HB-68, BU03
Commentary: An AU example sold for $9,200 in the 2004 Stack's sale of the John J. Ford Jr. collection.

W-9134 • 5¢ • EP-68, HB-69, BU05

VF-20	EF-40	AU-50
$2,000	$2,500	$3,200

W-9136 • 10¢ • EP-104, HB-70, BU10

VF-20	EF-40	AU-50
$2,000	$2,500	$2,750

W-9138 • 12¢ • EP-141, HB-71, BU12
Commentary: An AU example sold for $6,031 in the 2004 Stack's sale of the John J. Ford Jr. collection.

W-9140 • 24¢ • EP-162, HB-72, BU24
Commentary: Current market information not available.

Burnett's Cocoaine Kalliston
Boston, Massachusetts

Joseph Burnett (1820–1894) studied medicine and styled himself "doctor" even though he never practiced. At an early age he left home and moved to Boston. Shortly afterward, at the age of 17, he founded a perfumery and extracts business that would make his fortune. In 1854 he sold this business and founded Joseph Burnett & Co. with the proceeds. The new firm marketed goods in the same line, with his flavoring extracts in particular enjoying a wide sale.

This encasement advertised three personal-care products made by Burnett's company: Cocoaine, Kalliston, and toilet sets. Cocoaine was a coconut oil–based hair tonic that had nothing to do with the nearly eponymous drug cocaine. It was advertised as capable of restoring hair to a bald man's head and was favored both by men and women as a hair-care product. Kalliston was a diluted skin cream said to remove dandruff as well as improve the appearance of the skin. Its name came from the Greek word *kalli*, meaning beauty.

Issued in large numbers, these are plentiful today. All are of the Plain Frame style.

W-9145 • 1¢ • EP-9, HB-73, BK01 • Plain Frame

VF-20	EF-40	AU-50
$650	$900	$1,300

W-9147 • 3¢ • EP-39, HB-74, BK03

VF-20	EF-40	AU-50
$425	$550	$800

W-9149 • 5¢ • EP-69, HB-75, BK05

VF-20	EF-40	AU-50
$425	$550	$900

W-9151 • 10¢ • EP-105, HB-76, BK10

VF-20	EF-40	AU-50
$425	$550	$800

W-9153 • 12¢ • EP-142, HB-77, BK12
Commentary: A VF example sold for $2,070 in the 2007 Heritage sale of the Frederick Mayer collection.

EF-40
$2,800

W-9155 • 24¢ • EP-163, HB-78, BK24
Commentary: An EF example sold for $4,000 in the 2004 Stack's sale of the John J. Ford Jr. collection.

W-9157 • 30¢ • EP-175, HB-79, BK30
Commentary: An EF example sold for $4,600 in the 2007 Heritage sale of the Frederick Mayer collection.

W-9159 • 90¢ • EP-184, HB-80, BK90
Commentary: Current market information not available.

Burnett's Standard Cooking Extracts
Boston, Massachusetts

Burnett's company manufactured a line of 12 different flavorings for use in cooking. These included such familiar additives as vanilla extract, attar of roses, and almond, peach, orange, and apple flavorings. The extracts were sold to distributors and the public in rectangular aqua-colored bottles with cork stoppers, examples of which are easily located today (minus their labels and contents).

Issued in large numbers, these are plentiful today. All except W-9168 are of the Plain Frame style.

W-9161 • 1¢ • EP-10, HB-81, BE01 • Plain Frame

VF-20	EF-40	AU-50
$550	$650	$900

W-9163 • 3¢ • EP-40, HB-82, BE03

VF-20	EF-40	AU-50
$375	$550	$850

W-9165 • 5¢ • EP-70, HB-83, BE05

Commentary: An AU example sold for $1,610 in the 2007 Heritage sale of the Frederick Mayer collection.

VF-20	EF-40
$600	$900

W-9167 • 10¢ • EP-106, HB-84, BE10

VF-20	EF-40	AU-50
$700	$1,000	$1,700

W-9168 • 10¢ • EP-107, HB-85, BE10RB • Ribbed Frame

Commentary: An AU example sold for $4,025 in the 2004 Stack's sale of the John J. Ford Jr. collection.

W-9170 • 12¢ • EP-143, HB-86, BE12 • Plain Frame

Commentary: An AU example sold for $2,760 in the 2007 Heritage sale of the Frederick Mayer collection.

AU-50
$4,000

W-9172 • 24¢ • EP-164, HB-87, BE24

Commentary: An AU example sold for $8,625 in the 2007 Heritage sale of the Frederick Mayer collection.

VF-20	EF-40
$3,000	$4,500

W-9174 • 30¢ • EP-176, HB-88, BE30

Commentary: An AU example sold for $6,325 in the 2007 Heritage sale of the Frederick Mayer collection.

VF-20	EF-40
$3,000	$4,000

W-9176 • 90¢ • EP-184a, HB-89a, BE90

Recorded population: 1 • *Commentary:* The unique example sold for $13,800 in the 2007 Heritage sale of the Frederick Mayer collection.

Arthur M. Claflin
Hopkinton, Massachusetts

In the mid-1850s Arthur M. Claflin tried his hand at merchandising in Sumner (today, Atchison), Kansas, where he set up a small general store. Soon he returned to his native Massachusetts and opened a clothing store in Hopkinton and, among other activities, issued a modest quantity of encased postage stamps. In 1870 he returned to Kansas, where he became a well-known citizen.

The Claflin encasement is among the top several rarest in the series. Examples come on the market infrequently, usually when specialized collections are dispersed. All are of the Plain Frame style. Patent information on the back is in two lines curved along the bottom border, an unusual configuration.

W-9178 • 1¢ • EP-11, HB-89, CL01 • Plain Frame

Commentary: An AU example sold for $17,250 in the 2007 Heritage sale of the Frederick Mayer collection.

W-9180 • 3¢ • EP-40a, HB-90, CL03

Commentary: Current market information not available.

W-9182 • 5¢ • EP-71, HB-91, CL05

Commentary: An EF example sold for $14,950 in the 2004 Stack's sale of the John J. Ford Jr. collection, and an AU example sold for $21,850 in the 2007 Heritage sale of the Frederick Mayer collection.

W-9184 • 10¢ • EP-108a, HB-92, CL10

Commentary: A VF example sold for $12,650 in the 2007 Heritage sale of the Frederick Mayer collection.

W-9186 • 12¢ • EP-144, HB-93, CL12

Commentary: An EF example sold for $20,700 in the 2007 Heritage sale of the Frederick Mayer collection.

H.A. Cook
Evansville, Indiana

H.A. Cook emigrated with his family from New York City to Evansville, Indiana, shortly before the outbreak of the Civil War. His father opened a grocery business there called the Eureka Bazaar. The elder Cook is said to have carved a business niche for himself by offering free home delivery of orders. Following his father's death a few years later, Cook expanded the business, making it more of a general store than it had been before. In addition to the fruit, vegetables, and minor household goods already carried, the younger Cook stocked live poultry, axle grease, brooms, and brushes. A line of luxury consumer goods was also added, and customers could choose from a selection that included such exotic items as bottled English ales, Brazilian coffee, and French figs.

Cook encasements are among the rarer issues. All are of the Plain Frame style.

W-9194 • 5¢ • EP-72, HB-94, CO05 • Plain Frame

VF-20	EF-40
$1,600	$2,500

W-9196 • 10¢ • EP-108, HB-95, CO10

VF-20	EF-40
$2,800	$4,000

Dougan the Hatter
New York City

Dougan's hat store was located on the corner of Nassau and Ann streets in downtown Manhattan. That area of the city, today part of the financial district, was then a warren of narrow streets populated by small establishments like Dougan's. Grocers, tailors, booksellers, chandlers, tallow makers, lawyers, and other businesspeople all crowded together, the more important ones on the street level with store fronts open to walk-in trade. The streets were crowded and noisy. Men who could afford it seldom went hatless. No doubt Dougan's emporium was popular in its time.

Dougan encasements are rare. This is the only issue with an icon of a product, in this case a hat. All are of the Plain Frame style.

W-9203 • 1¢ • EP-12, HB-96, DO01 • Plain Frame
Commentary: An EF example sold for $3,450 in the 2007 Heritage sale of the Frederick Mayer collection.

VF-20	EF-40	AU-50
$2,200	—	$4,200

W-9205 • 3¢ • EP-41, HB-97, DO03

VF-20	EF-40
$2,500	$3,800

W-9207 • 5¢ • EP-73, HB-98, DO05

VF-20	EF-40
$2,500	$3,800

W-9209 • 10¢ • EP-109, HB-99, DO10
Commentary: A VF example sold for $3,737 in the 2007 Heritage sale of the Frederick Mayer collection.

EF-40
$5,000

Drake's Plantation Bitters
New York City

Colonel Patrick H. Drake started his patent medicine business in the 1850s with a product he named Catawba Bitters. In 1860 Drake slightly altered the ingredients and renamed the beverage Plantation Bitters. The chief constituent of the drink was West Indian rum, nearly 100 proof; the flavorings included Angostura bitters, chamomile, cardamom, orange, and raisins. In an era when alcohol was taxed but bitters were not since they were classed as medicine, and when temperance societies frowned on drinking liquor but overlooked the use of such "medicines," Drake's bitters found a ready market. The secret to Drake's meteoric success was his skill in advertising. The enigmatic cryptogram that appears on the backs of his encasements, S.T.1860.X, was a popular topic of conversation. Many suggested he Started Trade in 1860 with X dollars (the Roman numeral for 10). However, the 1871 edition of the company's almanac, *Morning, Noon, and Night*, explained that S.T. stood for Saint, 1860 for Croi, and X for itself, the whole meaning thus being St. Croix, the source of the company's rum. Drake's Plantation Bitters, packaged in bottles shaped like log cabins, were advertised as able to "create an appetite, cure weakness, dullness, constipation, dyspepsia, sour stomach, diarrhea, general debility, etc." At nearly 100 proof, some of these claims were certainly true! Interestingly, the bitters were also claimed as a cure for hangovers!

This encasement has a particularly rich history and is one of the most plentiful types. They are of the Plain Frame style except for W-9222 and W-9225, which are Ribbed Frame. Patent information on the back is in two lines along the bottom border, one curved, one straight.

W-9217 • 1¢ • EP-13, HB-100, DR01 • Plain Frame

VF-20	EF-40	AU-50
$350	$500	$800

W-9219 • 3¢ • EP-42, HB-101, DR03
Commentary: An Unc example sold for $2,760 in the 2007 Heritage sale of the Frederick Mayer collection.

VF-20	EF-40	AU-50
$350	$500	$800

W-9221 • 5¢ • EP-74, HB-102, DR05

VF-20	EF-40	AU-50
$400	$600	$1,000

W-9222 • 5¢ • EP-75, HB-103, DR05RB • Ribbed Frame
Commentary: An AU example sold for $3,220 in the 2007 Heritage sale of the Frederick Mayer collection.

W-9224 • 10¢ • EP-110, HB-104, DR10 • Plain Frame

VF-20	EF-40	AU-50
$600	$1,000	$1,500

W-9225 • 10¢ • EP-111, HB-105, DR10RB • Ribbed Frame
Commentary: An EF example sold for $2,875 in the 2004 Stack's sale of the John J. Ford Jr. collection, and an AU example sold for $4,312 in the 2007 Heritage sale of the Frederick Mayer collection.

W-9227 • 12¢ • EP-145, HB-106, DR12 • Plain Frame
Commentary: An EF example sold for $4,312 in the 2007 Heritage sale of the Frederick Mayer collection.

VF-20
$2,500

W-9229 • 24¢ • EP-165, HB-107, DR24
Commentary: An EF example sold for $3,737 in the 2007 Heritage sale of the Frederick Mayer collection.

VF-20
$3,000

W-9231 • 30¢ • EP-177, HB-108, DR30

VF-20	EF-40
$2,900	$3,500

W-9233 • 90¢ • EP-185, HB-109, DR90
Commentary: A VF example sold for $7,475 in the 2007 Heritage sale of the Frederick Mayer collection.

EF-40
$12,000

Ellis, McAlpin & Company
Cincinnati, Ohio

George Washington McAlpin was born in 1827. In 1843, at the age of 16, he was employed by John Taylor in the latter's wholesale dry goods business located in Cincinnati. John Washington Ellis was born in 1817. In 1840 he moved to Cincinnati, where he worked as a trader to the Western frontier. By 1850 he joined Taylor's firm, and two years later Ellis and McAlpin bought the business from Taylor, renaming it John W. Ellis & Company. Partners in the new company included McAlpin, M.V. Barkalow of Cincinnati, and James E. Polk of New York City. Polk may have been the financier of the new venture, for in 1861 the company's name was again changed, this time to the form found on their encasements. Polk's name did not appear, but he was still listed as a partner in 1865. The firm dealt in wholesale dry goods in the busiest port on the bustling Ohio River.

All encasements of this issuer are scarce, although examples come on the market with some regularity. All are of the Plain Frame style. The patent information on the back is in two lines below the center of the frame and not at the border, a unique configuration.

W-9235 • 1¢ • EP-13a, HB-110, EM01 • Plain Frame
Commentary: Current market information not available.

W-9237 • 3¢ • EP-43, HB-111, EM03
Commentary: A VF example sold for $1,840 in the 2004 Stack's sale of the John J. Ford Jr. collection, and an EF

example sold for $2,070 in the 2007 Heritage sale of the Frederick Mayer collection.

W-9239 • 5¢ • EP-76, HB-112, EM05
Commentary: An EF example sold for $2,990 in the 2007 Heritage sale of the Frederick Mayer collection.

VF-20
$2,000

W-9241 • 10¢ • EP-112, HB-113, EM10
Commentary: An EF example sold for $2,990 in the 2007 Heritage sale of the Frederick Mayer collection.

VF-20	EF-40	AU-50
$2,000	—	$3,900

W-9243 • 12¢ • EP-146, HB-114, EM12
Commentary: An AU example sold for $3,450 in the 2007 Heritage sale of the Frederick Mayer collection.

VF-20	EF-40
$3,050	$3,450

W-9245 • 24¢ • EP-166, HB-115, EM24
Commentary: A VF example sold for $3,737 in the 2007 Heritage sale of the Frederick Mayer collection.

EF-40
$4,500

G.G. Evans
Philadelphia, Pennsylvania

George G. Evans opened his Gift Book Store (later called the Original Gift Book Store after competition arose) in Philadelphia in 1854 and through skillful promotion methods managed to sell hundreds of thousands of dollars in books annually. Sales were promoted by giving away free gifts with each book purchased, such as a watch, a pen, other books, and so on. His book business prospered and enabled him to open branches in New York City and Boston. Evans also distributed wines from California, as advertised on the backs of his encasements. His wines were claimed to be "Absolutely Pure" in contrast to the watered-down vintages sometimes shipped to the East. The Civil War made Evans successful in a big way. He marketed products to soldiers, such as strap cases, abdominal supports (in which valuables could be hidden), albums, stationery, books, and more. Evans's best-selling title was aimed at the newly drafted soldier or disillusioned volunteer; it claimed to offer foolproof methods for obtaining an early discharge from the army or navy. Years later Evans published the *Illustrated History of the United States Mint* in annual editions from 1885 to 1898 (save for 1895), with a further edition dated 1901.

Evans's encasements are the only ones in the series that do not bear Gault's notice of patent at the base of the back. They are also somewhat different in fabric from the encasements made for Gault by Scovill Manufacturing Company. Their backs are concave, with wider, rounded rims. The mica covering the stamps is usually concave, with a pushed-in appearance, suggesting a lack of a filler or a thinner cardboard backing than that found on the Scovill products. Today, some specialists believe that Evans's encasements were made in violation of Gault's patent, possibly just after Gault ceased making encasements. Facts are elusive.

Evans's encasements are quite scarce. They play to a wide audience of numismatic historians who appreciate the issuer's later *Illustrated History*. All are of the Plain Frame style.

W-9250 • 1¢ • EP-14, HB-116, EV01 • Plain Frame
Commentary: An AU example sold for $2,530 in the 2007 Heritage sale of the Frederick Mayer collection.

VF-20	EF-40
$1,250	$2,000

W-9252 • 3¢ • EP-44, HB-117, EV03

VF-20	EF-40	AU-50
$1,250	$1,800	$2,500

W-9254 • 5¢ • EP-76a, HB-118, EV05
Commentary: An EF example sold for $4,887 in the 2007 Heritage sale of the Frederick Mayer collection.

VF-20
$3,400

W-9256 • 10¢ • EP-113, HB-119, EV10
Commentary: An AU example sold for $7,188 in the 2004 Stack's sale of the John J. Ford Jr. collection, and an EF example sold for $6,325 in the 2007 Heritage sale of the Frederick Mayer collection.

Gage Brother & Drake (Tremont House)
Chicago, Illinois

The Tremont House Hotel opened for business in Chicago in 1850. The five-story hostelry was viewed as the grandest and most resplendent Western hotel of its day. The establishment became the watering hole of choice for Chicago's wealthy and socially prominent citizens. In 1853 it was purchased by David and George Gage, who later advertised on encased postage stamps that they commissioned from Gault. They styled the partnership as Gage Brother (no final "s") & Drake, which to modern eyes may look like a misspelling. Two years later John B. Drake bought a 25 percent interest in the hotel, creating the partnership whose name is found on their encasements. The new partnership lasted until 1863,

when David Gage surrendered his share in the hotel for an unspecified amount. Five years afterward George Gage sold his interest in the Tremont House to Drake, who managed the hotel until its destruction in the Chicago fire of 1871. "Tremont House" was a popular name for stopping places, and earlier, similarly designated hotels were in Boston and Galveston.

As a class these encasements are slightly scarce. This variety is sometimes alphabetized under Tremont. All are of the Plain Frame style except W-9272, which is Ribbed Frame.

W-9265 • 1¢ • EP-15, HB-120, TH01 • Plain Frame

VF-20	EF-40	AU-50
$900	$1,200	$1,500

W-9267 • 3¢ • EP-45, HB-121, TH03

VF-20	EF-40	AU-50
$650	$900	$1,100

W-9269 • 5¢ • EP-77, HB-122, TH05
Commentary: An AU example sold for $2,070 in the 2007 Heritage sale of the Frederick Mayer collection.

VF-20	EF-40
$800	$1,100

W-9271 • 10¢ • EP-114, HB-123, TH10

VF-20	EF-40	AU-50
$550	$700	$800

W-9272 • 10¢ • EP-115, HB-124, TH10RB • Ribbed Frame
Commentary: An EF example sold for $4,600 in the 2007 Heritage sale of the Frederick Mayer collection.

VF-20
$3,500

W-9274 • 12¢ • EP-147, HB-125, TH12 • Plain Frame
Commentary: An EF example sold for $3,737 in the 2007 Heritage sale of the Frederick Mayer collection.

VF-20
$2,500

John Gault
Boston and New York City

John Gault, whose biography is featured in the introduction to this chapter, issued his own encased postage stamps in the summer of 1862, before he became a partner in Kirkpatrick & Gault (see listing below). These encasements were used as currency on their own and must have circulated widely, for examples are readily located today.

Encasements of this issuer are among the most common. Varieties exist with Plain Frame and Ribbed Frame styles.

W-9280 • 1¢ • EP-16, HB-126, JG01 • Plain Frame

VF-20	EF-40	AU-50
$550	$900	$1,500

W-9281 • 1¢ • EP-17, HB-127, JG01RB • Ribbed Frame

Commentary: An AU example sold for $8,625 in the 2007 Heritage sale of the Frederick Mayer collection.

VF-20	EF-40
$4,500	$6,000

W-9283 • 2¢ • EP-31, HB-128, JG02 • Plain Frame • Not a circulation issue

Commentary: An EF example sold for $13,900 in the 2007 Heritage sale of the Frederick Mayer collection.

VF-20
$9,000

W-9285 • 3¢ • EP-46, HB-129, JG03

Commentary: An AU example sold for $1,495 in the 2007 Heritage sale of the Frederick Mayer collection.

VF-20	EF-40
$600	$800

W-9286 • 3¢ • EP-47, HB-130, JG03RB • Ribbed Frame

Commentary: An AU example sold for $2,070 in the 2007 Heritage sale of the Frederick Mayer collection.

VF-20	EF-40
$1,500	$2,000

W-9288 • 5¢ • EP-78, HB-131, JG05 • Plain Frame

Commentary: An AU example sold for $1,495 in the 2007 Heritage sale of the Frederick Mayer collection.

VF-20	EF-40
$400	$650

W-9289 • 5¢ • EP-79, HB-132, JG05RB • Ribbed Frame

VF-20	EF-40	AU-50
$450	$600	$800

W-9291 • 10¢ • EP-116, HB-133, JG10 • Plain Frame

VF-20	EF-40	AU-50
$500	$650	$1,000

W-9292 • 10¢ • EP-117, HB-134, JG10RB • Ribbed Frame

VF-20	EF-40	AU-50
$400	$550	$800

W-9294 • 12¢ • EP-148, HB-135, JG12 • Plain Frame

VF-20	EF-40	AU-50
$850	$950	$1,200

W-9295 • 12¢ • EP-149, HB-136, JG12RB • Ribbed Frame

Commentary: An AU example sold for $1,725 in the 2007 Heritage sale of the Frederick Mayer collection.

VF-20	EF-40
$1,500	$2,000

W-9297 • 24¢ • EP-167, HB-137, JG24 • Plain Frame

Commentary: An AU example sold for $4,887 in the 2007 Heritage sale of the Frederick Mayer collection.

VF-20
$1,800

W-9298 • 24¢ • EP-168, HB-138, JG24RB • Ribbed Frame

VF-20	EF-40	AU-50
$2,500	$3,000	$4,000

W-9300 • 30¢ • EP-178, HB-139, JG30 • Plain Frame

Commentary: An EF example sold for $4,312 in the 2007 Heritage sale of the Frederick Mayer collection.

VF-20	EF-40	AU-50
$3,000	—	$5,000

W-9301 • 30¢ • EP-179, HB-140, JG30RB • Ribbed Frame

VF-20	EF-40	AU-50
$4,000	$5,000	$6,000

W-9303 • 90¢ • EP-186, HB-141, JG90 • Plain Frame

Commentary: An EF example sold for $12,650 in the 2007 Heritage sale of the Frederick Mayer collection.

VF-20
$8,500

W-9304 • 90¢ • HB-142, JG90RB • Ribbed Frame

Commentary: Current market information not available.

L.C. Hopkins & Co.
Cincinnati, Ohio

Lewis C. Hopkins was born in Massachusetts and moved with his family to Cincinnati at the age of 16. There he married the daughter of G.M. Wood, who conducted an active wholesale and retail dry goods business at Fifth and Vine streets. Hopkins became a partner in the firm in 1857 and the sole owner four years later. During the Civil War he landed large contracts to supply the Union army with uniforms and other goods through quartermasters. This caused him to neglect other aspects of his business, and he found himself in declining circumstances after the conflict ended. Unable to regain the public trade the company enjoyed before the war, Hopkins drifted downward. The firm failed in the early 1870s. He left Cincinnati, went to Indianapolis, and then settled in New York City, where he was successful in a new line: the insurance business.

Hopkins encasements are rare and seldom offered for sale. All are of the Plain Frame style.

W-9306 • 1¢ • EP-17a, HB-143, HO01 • Plain Frame
Commentary: Current market information not available.

W-9308 • 3¢ • EP-48, HB-144, HO03
Commentary: An EF example sold for $2,990 in the 2007 Heritage sale of the Frederick Mayer collection.

VF-20	EF-40	AU-50
$2,750	—	$5,500

W-9310 • 5¢ • EP-80, HB-145, HO05
Commentary: An AU example sold for $8,050 in the 2007 Heritage sale of the Frederick Mayer collection.

VF-20	EF-40
$4,250	$5,500

W-9312 • 10¢ • EP-117a, HB-146, HO10
Commentary: An EF example sold for $7,475 in the 2007 Heritage sale of the Frederick Mayer collection.

Hunt & Nash (Irving House)
New York City

The Irving House was located at the corner of Broadway and 12th Street, a fashionable address on New York City's main thoroughfare. The hotel was named for Washington Irving and earlier had been graced by the "Swedish Nightingale" Jenny Lind, who stayed there in 1850 during her triumphant American tour under the aegis of P.T. Barnum. The Irving House advertised on its encasements that it offered its guests the "European Plan." Under this arrangement, the hotel charged its customers a flat rate for their rooms, and all other services were at an additional charge. George W. Hunt was the proprietor, and he oversaw the hotel's daily operations. The Hunt & Nash partnership lasted until 1863, when Nash left to open a restaurant. Hunt stayed on until 1869, when he sold his interest to George Harlow. By that time, however, Irving House's glory days were over. The hub of New York's social scene had moved farther north along Broadway, leaving 12th Street and the Irving House behind.

As a class the Hunt & Nash encasements are among the most common. Plain Frame and Ribbed Frame varieties exist. This issuer is sometimes alphabetized under Irving House (retaining the same place in the order of issuers, however). Patent information on the back is in two lines: one straight and the other curved along the bottom border, as on the Drake issues. The back is one of just two in the series (the other is Brown's Bronchial Troches) without beading or dots around the border.

W-9320 • 1¢ • EP-18, HB-147, IH01 • Plain Frame
Commentary: Current market information not available.

W-9321 • 1¢ • HB-148, IH01RB • Ribbed Frame
Commentary: Current market information not available.

W-9323 • 3¢ • EP-49, HB-149, IH03 • Plain Frame
Commentary: An AU example sold for $3,737 in the 2007 Heritage sale of the Frederick Mayer collection.

VF-20	EF-40
$2,000	$3,000

W-9324 • 3¢ • EP-49a, HB-150, IH03RB • Ribbed Frame
Commentary: An AU example sold for $2,415 in the 2007 Heritage sale of the Frederick Mayer collection.

W-9326 • 5¢ • EP-81, HB-151, IH05 • Plain Frame
Commentary: A VF example sold for $1,840 in the 2007 Heritage sale of the Frederick Mayer collection.

EF-40	AU-50
$3,000	$4,000

W-9327 • 5¢ • EP-82, HB-152, IH05RB • Ribbed Frame

VF-20	EF-40	AU-50
$500	$700	$1,000

W-9329 • 10¢ • EP-118, HB-153, IH10 • Plain Frame
Commentary: A VF example sold for $3,737 in the 2007 Heritage sale of the Frederick Mayer collection.

EF-40
$4,500

W-9330 • 10¢ • EP-119, HB-154, IH10RB • Ribbed Frame

VF-20	EF-40	AU-50
$475	$650	$1,100

W-9332 • 12¢ • EP-150, HB-155, IH12 • Plain Frame
Commentary: An EF example sold for $1,495 in the 2007 Heritage sale of the Frederick Mayer collection.

VF-20	EF-40	AU-50
$1,800	—	$2,750

W-9333 • 12¢ • EP-151, HB-156, IH12RB • Ribbed Frame

VF-20	EF-40	AU-50
$3,000	$3,750	$4,250

W-9335 • 24¢ • EP-169, HB-157, IH24 • Plain Frame

VF-20	EF-40
$3,000	$3,500

W-9336 • 24¢ • EP-170, HB-158, IH24RB • Ribbed Frame
Commentary: Current market information not available.

W-9338 • 30¢ • EP-180, HB-159, IH30 • Plain Frame
Commentary: An EF example sold for $8,625 in the 2007 Heritage sale of the Frederick Mayer collection.

VF-20
$4,500

Kirkpatrick & Gault
New York City

John Gault moved from Boston to New York City sometime before July 1, 1862. Shortly after his arrival, but probably after he had issued his first encasements, Gault entered into partnership with Joseph Kirkpatrick, a wholesale jobber of anything for which he could find a market. The exact business relationship between the two is unknown. Kirkpatrick was a small-scale entrepreneur. In 1861 he imported rifled muskets from England, which he sold to the Union army. He also ran a small express-forwarding company, located in the same building at 1 Park Place in which he and Gault later kept offices. Kirkpatrick's role in the partnership seems to have been that of business manager and general expediter. After 1865 Kirkpatrick fades from the historical record.

Encasements of this issuer are slightly scarcer than the preceding John Gault pieces. They are known only with the Plain Frame style, whereas Gault issues come with both Plain and Ribbed Frame styles, suggesting that Ribbed Frame varieties were issued earlier. The patent date, but not the name of J. Gault, is given high in the field among the inscriptions.

W-9341 • 1¢ • EP-19, HB-160, KG01 • Plain Frame

VF-20	EF-40
$1,600	$2,300

W-9343 • 3¢ • EP-50, HB-161, KG03
Commentary: An AU example sold for $1,840 in the 2007 Heritage sale of the Frederick Mayer collection.

W-9345 • 5¢ • EP-83, HB-162, KG05

VF-20	EF-40	AU-50
$500	$850	$1,000

W-9347 • 10¢ • EP-120, HB-163, KG10

VF-20	EF-40	AU-50
$500	$900	$1,200

W-9349 • 12¢ • EP-152, HB-164, KG12

VF-20	EF-40	AU-50
$1,200	$1,800	$2,400

W-9351 • 24¢ • EP-171, HB-165, KG24

VF-20	EF-40	AU-50
$1,800	$2,200	$3,000

W-9353 • 30¢ • EP-181, HB-166, KG30

VF-20	EF-40	AU-50
$2,500	$3,000	$4,500

W-9355 • 90¢ • EP-187, HB-167, KG90
Commentary: An AU example sold for $13,800 in the 2007 Heritage sale of the Frederick Mayer collection.

VF-20	EF-40
$8,000	$10,000

Lord & Taylor
New York City

In the 1830s a newly arrived English immigrant, Samuel Lord, borrowed $1,000 from John Taylor, his wife's uncle, and started a small dry goods business in New York's Greenwich Village. Sometime later, Taylor's son, George Washington Taylor, joined the venture. By 1853 Lord & Taylor had "departmentalized" their dry goods store, creating America's first department store. By 1862, when the firm commissioned encasements from Gault, Lord & Taylor had three business locations. The first was at 255–261 Grand Street; a second was located slightly north, at 47–49 Catherine Street; and the flagship store was at 461–467 Broadway, then New York's most fashionable thoroughfare. The firm's headquarters was described at the time as "more like an Italian palace than a place for the sale of broadcloth." After the end of the Civil War both Lord and Taylor retired to England, leaving the management of their affairs to relatives. The firm is notable among Gault's clients as still being in business today.

Encasements of Lord & Taylor are slightly scarce. They enjoy a special popularity as the issuer is well known in fashion circles today. All are of the Plain Frame style.

W-9357 • 1¢ • EP-20, HB-168, LT01 • Plain Frame

VF-20	EF-40	AU-50
$1,500	$2,400	$3,000

W-9359 • 3¢ • EP-51, HB-169, LT03

VF-20	EF-40	AU-50
$1,200	$2,000	$3,000

W-9361 • 5¢ • EP-84, HB-170, LT05
Commentary: An EF example sold for $1,955 in the 2007 Heritage sale of the Frederick Mayer collection.

VF-20
$1,500

W-9363 • 10¢ • EP-121, HB-171, LT10

VF-20	EF-40
$1,500	$2,000

W-9365 • 12¢ • EP-153, HB-172, LT12
Commentary: A VF example sold for $4,600 in the 2007 Heritage sale of the Frederick Mayer collection.

EF-40
$5,500

W-9367 • 24¢ • EP-172, HB-173, LT24

VF-20	EF-40
$3,250	$4,000

W-9369 • 30¢ • EP-182, HB-174, LT30
Commentary: An AU example sold for $4,312 in the 2007 Heritage sale of the Frederick Mayer collection.

VF-20	EF-40
$3,500	$4,400

W-9371 • 90¢ • EP-188, HB-175, LT90
Commentary: An AU example sold for $18,400 in the 2007 Heritage sale of the Frederick Mayer collection.

Mendum's Family Wine Emporium
New York City

George Mendum started a wine and foodstuff business in New York City in the 1850s. His first store was in the Wall Street area and catered to seamen and employees of local businesses. By 1861 he had moved north to the corner of Broadway and Cedar Street, the address found on his encasements. Mendum's establishment was more than just a saloon. Besides a full line of wines, ales, and liquors, he stocked pickles, sauces, condiments, and cheeses. Alcoholic beverages were consumed on the premises, however, so his business was a hybrid between the German-style delicatessen with which New Yorkers had become familiar by the 1860s and the traditional type of saloon so common on New York City's streets. Mendum cannily named his business a "family" emporium in the hopes of lessening some of the stigma attached to the sale and consumption of alcohol. In this he was successful, for his establishment actually became a tourist attraction during the Civil War years. By 1865 Mendum had opened two other emporia in the city. He died the following year, however, so he did not harvest the fruits of his labor.

Mendum's encasements are slightly scarce. All are of the Plain Frame style except W-9380, which is Ribbed Frame. The patent information is given low in the field in two straight lines, a rare configuration.

W-9373 • 1¢ • EP-21, HB-176, ME01 • Plain Frame

VF-20	EF-40	AU-50
$775	$1,000	$1,400

W-9375 • 3¢ • EP-52, HB-177, ME03
Commentary: Current market information not available.

W-9377 • 5¢ • EP-85, HB-178, ME05

VF-20	EF-40	AU-50
$700	$900	$1,200

W-9379 • 10¢ • EP-122, HB-179, ME10
Commentary: An AU example sold for $2,070 in the 2007 Heritage sale of the Frederick Mayer collection.

VF-20	EF-40
$800	$1,200

W-9380 • 10¢ • EP-123, HB-180, ME10RB • Ribbed Frame
Commentary: An AU example sold for $4,600 in the 2007 Heritage sale of the Frederick Mayer collection.

VF-20	EF-40
$2,500	$3,500

W-9382 • 12¢ • EP-154, HB-181, ME12 • Plain Frame

VF-20	EF-40
$2,750	$3,250

B.F. Miles
Peoria, Illinois

Benjamin Franklin Miles was born in Pennsylvania, where his father was a well-known trial lawyer in the 1840s. His mother wrote short stories and poetry that were well received in their day. Despite being a qualified physician, Miles decided that following the Hippocratic oath was not for him, at least not for the present. After working as a route surveyor for the Pennsylvania Railroad, he signed up as a ship's doctor and sailed for England. On his return to America he practiced medicine for a time in New Jersey. In 1853 Miles left the East to settle in Peoria, Illinois, where he joined a local drug firm for a short time. Soon he started his own wholesale and retail drug business. He also sold paints, different grades of lubricating oil, and glassware. His shop, located in Rouse's Block, became a center for the city's social life. Miles's business prospered through the Civil War years. In later life Miles changed careers once again, becoming an insurance agent. He died in 1899 from Bright's disease, the same illness that killed Gault shortly afterward.

The Miles encasement is generally considered to be the very rarest of the issues—the key to a collection. Examples come on the market only at widely spaced intervals, usually when specialized collections are sold. All are of the Plain Frame style.

W-9389 • 1¢ • EP-22, HB-182, MI01 • Plain Frame
Commentary: An AU example sold for $34,500 in the 2007 Heritage sale of the Frederick Mayer collection.

W-9391 • 5¢ • EP-86, HB-183, MI05
Commentary: An AU example sold for $27,600 in the 2007 Heritage sale of the Frederick Mayer collection.

EF-40
$23,000

John W. Norris
Chicago, Illinois

John W. Norris began in business before 1860, selling books, local newspapers, and Eastern magazines. By 1860 he had expanded his line to include Eastern newspapers as well as papers and magazines imported from Europe. His North-western Newsdealers' Emporium, located at 102 Madison Street, was advertised as "The oldest and most reliable dealer west of New York." To a growing local trade Norris added a distributorship that serviced the needs of newsdealers in other Western cities and towns. In addition, by 1862 his emporium stocked diaries, song books, and stationery. To attract even more business he advertised a custom want-finding service, which promised to locate any desired item requested by his clientele.

Norris encasements are among the rarer issues in the series. All are of the Plain Frame style. The patent information is given low in the field in two straight lines, a rare configuration.

W-9401 • 1¢ • EP-23, HB-184, NO01 • Plain Frame
Commentary: An AU example sold for $3,450 in the 2007 Heritage sale of the Frederick Mayer collection.

VF-20	EF-40
$1,750	$3,250

W-9403 • 3¢ • EP-52a, HB-185, NO03

VF-20	EF-40	AU-50
$2,200	$3,000	$4,000

W-9405 • 5¢ • EP-87, HB-186, NO05
Commentary: An EF example sold for $4,025 in the 2007 Heritage sale of the Frederick Mayer collection.

VF-20
$2,800

W-9407 • 10¢ • EP-124, HB-187, NO10
Commentary: An EF example sold for $3,737 in the 2007 Heritage sale of the Frederick Mayer collection.

VF-20
$2,500

North America Life Insurance Company
New York City

The North America Life Insurance Company was founded in 1862 by Nathan Dennison Morgan, a successful insurance broker. With offices at 63 William Street in New York City, the firm was in a district with many other insurance houses. The firm prospered during the Civil War by writing life and property insurance policies for Northern soldiers. In the postwar boom of 1865–1871 the company engaged in real estate speculation in the New York City market. This proved to be its downfall, for in the Panic of 1873 it found itself unable to meet all its obligations. The company collapsed with the real estate market, and Morgan disappeared from the pages of history.

These encasements exist with two reverse types: INSURANCE straight and with patent information curved along the bottom border, and with INSURANCE lettered in a curve and with the patent information in one straight line and one curved line at the bottom. Plain Frame and Ribbed Frame varieties exist of each, making the series unusually extensive within the various denominations.

W-9418 • 1¢ • EP-24, HB-188, NA01ST • INSURANCE straight, Plain Frame

VF-20	EF-40	AU-50
$450	$600	$1,000

W-9419 • 1¢ • EP-24a, HB-189, NA01CU • INSURANCE curved

VF-20	EF-40	AU-50
$600	$900	$1,500

W-9421 • 3¢ • EP-53, HB-190, NA03ST • INSURANCE straight

VF-20	EF-40	AU-50
$575	$750	$1,200

W-9422 • 3¢ • EP-53a, HB-191, NA03CU • INSURANCE curved
Commentary: A VF example sold for $1,725 in the 2004 Stack's sale of the John J. Ford Jr. collection, and an EF example sold for $3,070 in the 2007 Heritage sale of the Frederick Mayer collection.

W-9424 • 5¢ • EP-88, HB-192, NA05ST • INSURANCE straight

Commentary: An AU example sold for $3,450 in the 2007 Heritage sale of the Frederick Mayer collection.

VF-20	EF-40
$1,800	$2,750

W-9425 • 5¢ • EP88b, HB-193, NA05CU • INSURANCE curved

Commentary: An AU example sold for $4,600 in the 2007 Heritage sale of the Frederick Mayer collection.

VF-20
$2,200

W-9426 • 5¢ • EP-88a, HB-194, NA05STRB • INSURANCE straight, Ribbed Frame

Commentary: Current market information not available.

W-9428 • 10¢ • EP-125, HB-195, NA10ST • INSURANCE straight, Plain Frame

VF-20	EF-40	AU-50
$1,000	$1,750	$2,100

W-9429 • 10¢ • EP-125a, HB-196, NA10CU • INSURANCE curved

VF-20	EF-40	AU-50
$1,200	$1,750	$2,250

W-9430 • 10¢ • HB-197, NA10STRB • INSURANCE straight, Ribbed Frame

Commentary: An EF example sold for $3,220 in the 2004 Stack's sale of the John J. Ford Jr. collection.

VF-20
$2,500

W-9431 • 10¢ • EP-126, HB-198, NA10CURB • INSURANCE curved

VF-20	EF-40
$2,750	$3,500

W-9433 • 12¢ • EP-155, HB-199, NA12ST • INSURANCE straight, Plain Frame

Commentary: An AU example sold for $4,025 in the 2007 Heritage sale of the Frederick Mayer collection.

VF-20	EF-40
$2,500	$3,000

W-9434 • 12¢ • HB-200, NA12CU • INSURANCE curved

Commentary: A VF example sold for $3,450 in the 2004 Stack's sale of the John J. Ford Jr. collection.

Pearce, Tolle, & Holton
Cincinnati, Ohio

Pearce, Tolle, & Holton was formed in Cincinnati in the early 1860s. Partners were William B. Pearce, Alexander M. Holton, and Thomas Porter Jr., all of Cincinnati, and W.B. Tolle of New York City. Tolle appears to have been the firm's New York buying agent, a role similar to that played by William Barkalow for Ellis, McAlpin & Company, also of Cincinnati. The firm of Pearce, Tolle, & Holton was engaged in the wholesale dry goods business. Most of the company's business products were shipped down the Ohio River to the Mississippi River for transshipment into the interior. Pearce left the company in 1872, and five years later the remaining partners dissolved the firm. The die cutter who punched the advertising message onto the back of these encasements made a mistake, incorrectly spelling TOLLE as TOOLE. When the error was noticed, an L was punched over the erroneous O. This error can be seen on all of Pearce, Tolle, & Holton's encasements.

Encasements of this issuer are rare. All are of the Plain Frame style.

W-9442 • 1¢ • EP-24b, HB-201, PE01 • Plain Frame

Commentary: A VF example sold for $3,220 in the 2004 Stack's sale of the John J. Ford Jr. collection, and an EF example sold for $3,737 in the 2007 Heritage sale of the Frederick Mayer collection.

W-9444 • 3¢ • EP-54, HB-202, PE03

Commentary: An EF example sold for $1,840 in the 2007 Heritage sale of the Frederick Mayer collection.

VF-20	EF-40	AU-50
$1,900	—	$3,500

W-9446 • 5¢ • EP-89, HB-203, PE05

Commentary: An EF example sold for $3,450 in the 2007 Heritage sale of the Frederick Mayer collection.

VF-20	EF-40	AU-50
$2,400	—	$4,500

W-9448 • 10¢ • EP-127, HB-204, PE10

Commentary: An AU example sold for $13,800 in the 2007 Heritage sale of the Frederick Mayer collection.

VF-20	EF-40
$6,000	$8,000

W-9450 • 12¢ • EP-156, HB-205, PE12

Commentary: An AU example sold for $7,475 in the 2007 Heritage sale of the Frederick Mayer collection.

VF-20	EF-40
$4,000	$5,000

W-9452 • 24¢ • EP-172a, HB-206, PE24
Commentary: Current market information not available.

Sands' Ale
Milwaukee, Wisconsin

Josiah J. Sands was a Chicago brewer of ales who developed a lager-making process that gave his products a longer shelf life than his competitors' ales. Since ale spoiled at room temperature, most brewers' products of the time had only local popularity. Sands's process allowed him to ship his ales as far south as New Orleans. With a wider market for his product, the increased sales led to business expansion. In 1859 Sands sent his brothers to Milwaukee, where they purchased a brewery already in operation and renovated it to their own specifications. The two breweries together produced the improved ale. During the Civil War years Sands's company enjoyed increased success. His ale was even advertised as a healthy drink for ladies and infants! There was no end to hyperbole for most liquid products advertised on encasements. By 1867, however, the Milwaukee brewery was sold.

Sands's encasements are among the top several rarest in the series. Examples are infrequently offered and create attention when they are sold. The record is $18,400 for the EF Homren specimen in 2006. All are of the Plain Frame style.

W-9460 • 5¢ • EP-90, HB-207, SA05 • Plain Frame

VF-20	EF-40
$8,000	$13,000

W-9462 • 10¢ • EP-128, HB-208, SA10

VF-20	EF-40
$10,000	$16,000

W-9464 • 12¢ • EP-156a, HB-209, SA12
Commentary: Current market information not available.

W-9468 • 30¢ • EP-183, HB-210, SA30
Commentary: Current market information not available.

Schapker & Bussing
Evansville, Indiana

This company, which sold dry goods, millinery, and carpets, was the second of Gault's clients in Evansville, Indiana. Like the other (Cook), Schapker & Bussing was also located on Main Street. Bernard Schapker was born in Germany in 1834. When he was nine his family emigrated to America. In 1850 Schapker moved to Evansville, where he clerked in Samuel Embich's dry goods store for the next eight years. In 1858 Embich took the young man into the business as a junior partner, and when Embich died two years later, Schapker assumed his benefactor's mantle. John W. Bussing was also a German emigrant. His family came to Cincinnati in 1844 but moved to Evansville the following year. Sometime later Bussing was also hired by Embich as a clerk, and there he met Schapker. Their friendship led to their partnership in 1860. Schapker & Bussing continued in business until the Panic of 1873, which hit the company hard and led to its dissolution.

Encasements of Schapker & Bussing are fairly plentiful. All are of the Plain Frame style.

W-9471 • 1¢ • EP-25, HB-211, SB01 • Plain Frame
Commentary: An EF example sold for $2,990 in the 2007 Heritage sale of the Frederick Mayer collection.

VF-20	EF-40	AU-50
$1,900	—	$3,400

W-9473 • 3¢ • EP-55, HB-212, SB03

VF-20	EF-40	AU-50
$900	$1,100	$1,500

W-9475 • 5¢ • EP-91, HB-213, SB05

VF-20	EF-40
$800	$1,100

W-9477 • 10¢ • EP-129, HB-214, SB10

VF-20	EF-40	AU-50
$850	$975	$1,200

W-9479 • 12¢ • EP-157, HB-215, SB12
Recorded population: 1 • *Commentary:* The unique example, graded AU, sold for $8,050 in the 2007 Heritage sale of the Frederick Mayer collection.

John Shillito & Co.
Cincinnati, Ohio

Founded in 1830 by John Shillito, the company bearing his name remained in the Shillito family until its sale in 1928, after which it was still called Shillito's. John Shillito began merchandising in 1817, at the age of nine! Until 1830 he was a clerk, but in that year he formed a partnership with William McLaughlin. The new partnership was soon dissolved, but Shillito retained the store and stock of goods. By 1837 his dry goods store could boast that it was the largest such establishment west of the Delaware River (a boundary that conveniently excluded New York City and Boston from comparison), as well as the oldest. In 1857 Shillito built the store he later advertised on his encasements, an emporium that was locally famous for many years.

Encasements of John Shillito are fairly plentiful. All are of the Plain Frame style.

W-9486 • 1¢ • EP-26, HB-216, SH01 • Plain Frame

VF-20	EF-40	AU-50
$1,700	$2,000	$2,500

W-9488 • 3¢ • EP-56, HB-217, SH03

VF-20	EF-40	AU-50
$475	$700	$1,400

W-9490 • 5¢ • EP-92, HB-218, SH05

VF-20	EF-40	AU-50
$450	$600	$1,200

W-9492 • 10¢ • EP-130, HB-219, SH10

Commentary: An AU example sold for $1,035 in the 2007 Heritage sale of the Frederick Mayer collection.

VF-20	EF-40
$700	$900

W-9494 • 12¢ • EP-158, HB-220, SH12

Commentary: An EF example sold for $6,900 in the 2007 Heritage sale of the Frederick Mayer collection.

VF-20
$4,000

S. Steinfeld
New York City

Simon Steinfeld began in business in New York City as a hatter. In 1855 he opened a confectionery store at 70 Nassau Street that sold candies and sweets imported from Europe. Before the end of that year Steinfeld secured the agency for French Cognac Bitters, which he subsequently advertised on his encasements. Steinfeld renovated the candy store to become a saloon and entered a period of thriving sales. French Cognac Bitters had a very high alcohol content. The product took advantage of the law that allowed the sale of so-called medicinal alcohol. His advertisements claimed that his bitters were so beneficial that he would give them away free of charge to anyone unable to pay for them. No fool, Steinfeld made sure that such claims were only printed in newspapers located far away from New York! Steinfeld remained at the Nassau Street address until 1868, after which he moved several times to different locations in New York City.

Steinfeld is one of the rarer issuers. When examples are seen, they are nearly always of the 1¢ denomination. All are of the Plain Frame style.

W-9500 • 1¢ • EP-27, HB-221, ST01 • Plain Frame

Commentary: An AU example sold for $2,990 in the 2007 Heritage sale of the Frederick Mayer collection.

VF-20	EF-40
$1,900	$2,800

W-9504 • 5¢ • EP-93, HB-222, ST05

Commentary: An AU example sold for $10,350 in the 2007 Heritage sale of the Frederick Mayer collection.

VF-20	EF-40
$6,000	$8,000

W-9506 • 10¢ • EP-131, HB-223, ST10

Commentary: An AU example sold for $9,200 in the 2007 Heritage sale of the Frederick Mayer collection.

VF-20
$4,500

W-9508 • 12¢ • EP-159, HB-224, ST12

Commentary: Current market information not available.

N.G. Taylor & Co.
Philadelphia, Pennsylvania

N.G. Taylor & Company was a long-established metals merchant in Philadelphia when the firm commissioned encasements from John Gault. The company had been in business since as early as 1810, when it was known for its wire, files, and tinned metal sheeting. Later, its product line was expanded as new technology became available and included such diverse metal products as sheet iron and copper, machine tools, tin cans, milk cans, and lead products. It owned copper mines in Wales and had several warehouse locations in Philadelphia, as well as docks and storage facilities. During the 1876 Centennial Exhibition, held in Philadelphia, N.G. Taylor & Company had four different booths exhibiting four different products and manufacturing processes. N.G. Taylor & Company was one of only four of Gault's clients who also advertised on metal tokens.

Taylor encasements are among the rarer issues. All are of the Plain Frame style.

W-9516 • 1¢ • EP-28, HB-225, TA01 • Plain Frame

VF-20	EF-40	AU-50
$2,250	$3,250	$4,500

W-9518 • 3¢ • EP-57, HB-226, TA03

VF-20	EF-40	AU-50
$2,000	$3,500	$4,750

W-9520 • 5¢ • EP-93a, HB-227, TA05
Commentary: Current market information not available.

W-9522 • 10¢ • EP-132, HB-228, TA10
Commentary: Current market information not available.

W-9524 • 12¢ • EP-159a, HB-229, TA12
Commentary: An EF example sold for $5,750 in the 2007 Heritage sale of the Frederick Mayer collection.

VF-20	EF-40	AU-50
$5,000	—	$8,500

Weir & Larminie
Montreal, Canada

Located in Montreal, Canada, the banking, exchange, and bullion-dealing firm of Weir & Larminie was Gault's sole foreign client. Why a Canadian firm would order U.S. postage stamps remains an unanswered question. William Weir came to Canada from Scotland in 1842. At first a teacher in the public schools, he later became a broker in Montreal. Shortly before the Civil War, he founded a private banking firm with G.H. Larminie as his partner. He also obtained a Canadian charter. Unfortunately, Weir was not a careful manager. After a teller was caught stealing, a run began on Weir's Banque Ville Marie; when the auditors finished their work, it was found that Weir had issued fraudulent statements about the soundness of his operations and had made dubious loans. Weir was indicted, tried for fraud, and convicted. After serving his prison term, Weir died, broken in body and spirit. Nothing is known of Larminie, save that he was Weir's partner.

Weir & Larminie encasements are among the rarer issues. All are of the Plain Frame style.

W-9530 • 1¢ • EP-29, HB-230, WL01 • Plain Frame

VF-20	EF-40	AU-50
$1,950	$2,700	$3,700

W-9532 • 3¢ • EP-58, HB-231, WL03
Commentary: An AU example sold for $14,950 in the 2007 Heritage sale of the Frederick Mayer collection.

VF-20	EF-40
$9,000	$12,000

W-9534 • 5¢ • EP-94, HB-232, WL05
Commentary: Current market information not available.

W-9536 • 10¢ • EP-133, HB-233, WL10

VF-20	EF-40	AU-50
$2,750	$3,500	$4,250

White the Hatter
New York City

George W. White was in the hat-making business by 1850 in New York City's Greenwich Village. White made hats, muffs, capes, and other fur items. In 1855 he relocated to the ground floor of 216 Broadway, the same building that housed P.T. Barnum's famous American Museum, the most popular tourist attraction in the city. With the continual throng of the curious passing by Barnum's establishment, White's choice of location augured well for his success. Unfortunately for White, the fame of Barnum's museum also attracted notice in the Confederacy. On Thanksgiving Day 1864, a Confederate raider attempted to set fire to the building. The blaze was soon extinguished, but smoke damage to White's stock was severe. Slightly less than one year later a more serious fire broke out in Barnum's museum and consumed the structure, although most of Barnum's animals were saved. White reopened at a new location. Between 1865 and 1872 he had expanded his business to include a clothing store, two woolen goods stores, and a "fancy goods emporium." During 1863 White commissioned a series of Civil War tokens; these are very plentiful in numismatic circles today.

White the Hatter issues are rare. All are of the Plain Frame style.

W-9548 • 1¢ • EP-30, HB-234, WH01 • Plain Frame

VF-20	EF-40	AU-50
$1,800	$2,750	$3,750

W-9550 • 3¢ • EP-59, HB-235, WH03
Commentary: An AU example sold for $3,450 in the 2007 Heritage sale of the Frederick Mayer collection.

VF-20	EF-40
$2,500	$3,250

W-9552 • 5¢ • EP-95, HB-236, WH05
Commentary: An AU example sold for $4,312 in the 2007 Heritage sale of the Frederick Mayer collection.

VF-20	EF-40
$3,000	$4,000

W-9554 • 10¢ • EP-134, HB-237, WH10
Commentary: A VF example sold for $6,325 in the 2007 Heritage sale of the Frederick Mayer collection.

APPENDIX A
Signatures on U.S. Currency, 1861 to Date

The following information relates to the Treasury officials whose signatures appeared on various federal currency. It was often the case that plates bearing certain signatures or combinations of signatures were used to print notes after the individuals had left office and were succeeded by others. Accordingly, a short combined term of office does not necessarily indicate that notes with these signatures are scarce or rare. Actual printages are more important.

REGISTER OF THE TREASURY AND TREASURER

April 17, 1861, to August 10, 1864 • Register of the Treasury: Lucius E. Chittenden • Treasurer: F.E. Spinner • *In office together:* 3 years, 113 days

August 11, 1864, to September 21, 1867 • Register of the Treasury: S.B. Colby • Treasurer: F.E. Spinner • *In office together:* 3 years, 40 days

October 5, 1867, to March 15, 1869 • Register of the Treasury: Noah L. Jeffries • Treasurer: F.E. Spinner • *In office together:* 1 year, 160 days

April 3, 1869, to March 23, 1875 • Register of the Treasury: John Allison • Treasurer: F.E. Spinner • *In office together:* 5 years, 350 days

June 30, 1875, to July 1, 1876 • Register of the Treasury: John Allison • Treasurer: John C. New • *In office together:* 1 year, 1 day

July 1, 1876, to June 30, 1877 • Register of the Treasury: John Allison • Treasurer: A.U. Wyman • *In office together:* 11 months, 29 days

July 1, 1877, to March 23, 1878 • Register of the Treasury: John Allison • Treasurer: James Gilfillan • *In office together:* 264 days

April 1, 1878, to May 20, 1881 • Register of the Treasury: Glenni W. Scofield • Treasurer: James Gilfillan • *In office together:* 3 years, 50 days

May 21, 1881, to March 31, 1883 • Register of the Treasury: Blanche K. Bruce • James Gilfillan • *In office together:* 1 year, 310 days

April 1, 1883, to April 30, 1885 • Register of the Treasury: Blanche K. Bruce • Treasurer: A.U. Wyman • *In office together:* 2 years, 29 days

May 1, 1885, to June 5, 1885 • Register of the Treasury: Blanche K. Bruce • Treasurer: Conrad N. Jordan • *In office together:* 36 days

June 8, 1885, to March 23, 1887 • Register of the Treasury: William S. Rosecrans • Treasurer: Conrad N. Jordan • *In office together:* 1 year, 285 days

May 24, 1887, to May 10, 1889 • Register of the Treasury: William S. Rosecrans • Treasurer: James W. Hyatt • *In office together:* 1 year, 346 days

May 11, 1889, to April 24, 1891 • Register of the Treasury: William S. Rosecrans • Treasurer: J.N. Huston • *In office together:* 1 year, 344 days

April 25, 1891, to May 31, 1893 • Register of the Treasury: William S. Rosecrans • Treasurer: Enos H. Nebeker • *In office together:* 2 years, 36 days

June 1, 1893, to June 19, 1893 • Register of the Treasury: William S. Rosecrans • Treasurer: Daniel N. Morgan • *In office together:* 19 days

July 1, 1893, to June 30, 1897 • Register of the Treasury: James F. Tillman • Treasurer: Daniel N. Morgan • *In office together:* 3 years, 364 days

July 1, 1897, to December 2, 1897 • Register of the Treasury: James F. Tillman • Ellis H. Roberts • *In office together:* 155 days

December 3, 1897, to March 17, 1898 • Register of the Treasury: Blanche K. Bruce • Treasurer: Ellis H. Roberts • *In office together:* 104 days

April 7, 1898, to June 30, 1905 • Register of the Treasury: Judson W. Lyons • Treasurer: Ellis H. Roberts • *In office together:* 7 years, 84 days

July 1, 1905, to April 1, 1906 • Register of the Treasury: Judson W. Lyons • Treasurer: Charles H. Treat • *In office together:* 274 days

June 12, 1906, to October 30, 1909 • Register of the Treasury: William T. Vernon • Treasurer: Charles H. Treat • *In office together:* 3 years, 140 days

November 1, 1909, to March 14, 1911 • Register of the Treasury: William T. Vernon • Treasurer: Lee McClung • *In office together:* 1 year, 133 days

March 15, 1911, to November 21, 1912 • Register of the Treasury: James C. Napier • Treasurer: Lee McClung • *In office together:* 1 year, 266 days

November 22, 1912, to March 31, 1913 • Register of Treasury: James C. Napier • Treasurer: Carmi A. Thompson • *In office together:* 129 days

April 1, 1913, to September 30, 1913 • Register of the Treasury: James C. Napier • Treasurer: John Burke • *In office together:* 183 days

October 1, 1913, to December 31, 1914 • Register of the Treasury: Gabe E. Parker • Treasurer: John Burke • *In office together:* 1 year, 92 days

March 24, 1915, to November 20, 1919 • Register of the Treasury: Houston B. Teehee • Treasurer: John Burke • *In office together:* 4 years, 242 days

November 21, 1919, to January, 1921 • Register of the Treasury: William S. Elliott • Treasurer: John Burke • *In office together:* 1 year, 45 days

May 2, 1921, to January 24, 1922 • Register of the Treasury: William S. Elliott • Treasurer: Frank White • *In office together:* 268 days

January 25, 1922, to September 30, 1927 • Register of the Treasury: Harley V. Speelman • Treasurer: Frank White • *In office together:* 5 years, 247 days

October 1, 1927, to May 1, 1928 • Register of the Treasury: Walter O. Woods • Treasurer: Frank White • *In office together:* 214 days

May 31, 1928, to January 17, 1929 • Register of the Treasury: Walter O. Woods • Treasurer: H.T. Tate • *In office together:* 235 days

January 22, 1929, to May 31, 1933 • Register of the Treasury: Edward E. Jones • Treasurer: Walter O. Woods • *In office together:* 4 years, 129 days

TREASURER AND SECRETARY OF THE TREASURY

March 6, 1913, to December 15, 1918 • Treasurer: John Burke • Secretary of the Treasury: William G. McAdoo • *In office together:* 5 years, 285 days

December 16, 1918, to February 1, 1920 • Treasurer: John Burke • Secretary of the Treasury: Carter Glass • *In office together:* 1 year, 47 days

February 2, 1920, to March 3, 1921 • Treasurer: John Burke • Secretary of the Treasury: D.F. Houston • *In office together:* 395 days

May 2, 1921, to May 1, 1928 • Treasurer: Frank White • Secretary of the Treasury: A.W. Mellon • *In office together:* 6 years, 333 days

May 31, 1928, to January 17, 1929 • Treasurer: H.T. Tate • Secretary of the Treasury: A.W. Mellon • *In office together:* 232 days

January 18, 1929, to February 12, 1932 • Treasurer: Walter O. Woods • Secretary of the Treasury: A.W. Mellon • *In office together:* 3 years, 25 days

February 13, 1932, to March 3, 1933 • Treasurer: Walter O. Woods • Secretary of the Treasury: Ogden L. Mills • *In office together:* 1 year, 18 days

March 5, 1933, to May 31, 1933 • Treasurer: Walter O. Woods • Secretary of the Treasury: W.H. Woodin • *In office together:* 87 days

June 1, 1933, to December 31, 1933 • Treasurer: W.A. Julian • Secretary of the Treasury: W.H. Woodin • *In office together:* 215 days

January 1, 1934, to July 22, 1945 • Treasurer: W.A. Julian • Secretary of the Treasury: Henry Morgenthau Jr. • *In office together:* 11 years, 203 days

July 23, 1945, to June 23, 1946 • Treasurer: W.A. Julian • Secretary of the Treasury: Fred M. Vinson • *In office together:* 308 days

June 25, 1946, to May 29, 1949 • Treasurer: W.A. Julian • Secretary of the Treasury: John W. Snyder • *In office together:* 2 years, 338 days

June 21, 1949, to January 20, 1953 • Treasurer: Georgia Neese Clark • Secretary of the Treasury: John W. Snyder • *In office together:* 3 years, 214 days

January 28, 1953, to July 28, 1957 • Treasurer: Ivy Baker Priest • Secretary of the Treasury: George M. Humphrey • *In office together:* 4 years, 181 days

July 29, 1957, to January 20, 1961 • Treasurer: Ivy Baker Priest • Secretary of the Treasury: Robert B. Anderson • *In office together:* 3 years, 176 days

January 30, 1961, to April 13, 1962 • Treasurer: Elizabeth Rudel Smith • Secretary of the Treasury: C. Douglas Dillon • *In office together:* 1 year, 73 days

January 3, 1963, to March 31, 1965 • Treasurer: Kathryn O'Hay Granahan • Secretary of the Treasury: C. Douglas Dillon • *In office together:* 2 years, 87 days

April 1, 1965, to November 22, 1966 • Treasurer: Kathryn O'Hay Granahan • Secretary of the Treasury: Henry Fowler • *In office together:* 1 year, 236 days

December 21, 1968, to January 20, 1969 • Treasurer: Kathryn O'Hay Granahan • Secretary of the Treasury: Joseph W. Barr • *In office together:* 30 days

May 8, 1969, to September 16, 1970 • Treasurer: Dorothy Andrews Elston • Secretary of the Treasury: David Kennedy • *In office together:* 1 year, 131 days

September 17, 1970, to February 1, 1971 • Treasurer: Dorothy Andrews Kabis (married name of the former Dorothy Andrews Elston) • Secretary of the Treasury: David Kennedy • *In office together under the Kabis surname:* 138 days

February 11, 1971, to July 3, 1971 • Treasurer: Dorothy Andrews Kabis • Secretary of the Treasury: John B. Connally • *In office together:* 142 days

December 17, 1971, to June 12, 1972 • Treasurer: Romana Acosta Banuelos • Secretary of the Treasury: John B. Connally • *In office together:* 177 days

June 12, 1972, to February 14, 1974 • Treasurer: Romana Acosta Banuelos • Secretary of the Treasury: George P. Shultz • *In office together:* 1 year, 247 days

June 21, 1974, to January 19, 1977 • Treasurer: Francine I. Neff • Secretary of the Treasury: William E. Simon • *In office together:* 2 years, 212 days

September 12, 1977, to August 4, 1979 • Treasurer: Azie Taylor Morton • Secretary of the Treasury: W. Michael Blumenthal • *In office together:* 1 year, 298 days

August 7, 1979, to January 20, 1981 • Treasurer: Azie Taylor Morton • Secretary of the Treasury: G. William Miller • *In office together:* 1 year, 166 days

March 17, 1981, to July 5, 1983 • Treasurer: Angela Marie Buchanan • Secretary of the Treasury: Donald T. Regan • *In office together:* 2 years, 110 days

September 22, 1983, to February 1, 1985 • Treasurer: Katherine Davalos Ortega • Secretary of the Treasury: Donald T. Regan • *In office together:* 1 year, 132 days

February 4, 1985, to August 17, 1988 • Treasurer: Katherine Davalos Ortega • Secretary of the Treasury: James A. Baker • *In office together:* 3 years, 194 days

September 15, 1988, to June 30, 1989 • Treasurer: Katherine Davalos Ortega • Secretary of the Treasury: Nicholas F. Brady • *In office together:* 260 days

November 20, 1989, to January 17, 1993 • Treasurer: Catalina Vasquez Villalpando • Secretary of the Treasury: Nicholas F. Brady • *In office together:* 3 years, 58 days

March 1, 1994, to December 22, 1994 • Treasurer: Mary Ellen Withrow • Secretary of the Treasury: Lloyd M. Bentsen • *In office together:* 297 days

October 1, 1995, to July 2, 1999 • Treasurer: Mary Ellen Withrow • Secretary of the Treasury: Robert E. Rubin • *In office together:* 3 years, 275 days

July 2, 1999, to January 20, 2001 • Treasurer: Mary Ellen Withrow • Secretary of the Treasury: Lawrence F. Summers • *In office together:* 1 year, 202 days

August 16, 2001, to December 31, 2002 • Treasurer: Rosario Marin • Secretary of the Treasury: Paul H. O'Neil • *In office together:* 1 year, 137 days

February 3, 2003, to June 30, 2003 • Treasurer: Rosario Marin • Secretary of the Treasury: John W. Snow • *In office together:* 147 days

December 13, 2004, to June 29, 2006 • Treasurer: Anna Escobedo Cabral • Secretary of the Treasury: John W. Snow • *In office together:* 1 year, 199 days

July 10, 2006, to January 20, 2009 • Treasurer: Anna Escobedo Cabral • Secretary of the Treasury: John W. Snow • *In office together:* 1 year, 199 days

July 10, 2006, to January 20, 2009 • Treasurer: Anna Escobedo Cabral • Secretary of the Treasury: Henry Merritt Paulson Jr. • *In office together:* 2 years, 163 days

APPENDIX B

Terms of Service of Treasury Officials, 1913 to Date

John Burke served as Treasurer from April 1, 1913, to January 5, 1921.

William G. McAdoo served as secretary from March 6, 1913, to December 15, 1918.

Carter Glass served as secretary from December 16, 1918, to February 1, 1920.

D.F. Houston served as secretary from February 2, 1920, to March 3, 1921.

Frank White served as Treasurer from May 2, 1921, to May 1, 1928.

A.W. Mellon served as secretary from March 4, 1921, to February 12, 1932.

H.T. Tate served as Treasurer from May 31, 1928, to January 17, 1929.

Walter O. Woods served as Treasurer from January 18, 1929, to May 31, 1933.

Ogden L. Mills served as secretary from February 13, 1932, to March 3, 1933.

W.H. Woodin served as secretary from March 4, 1933, to December 31, 1933.

W.A. Julian served as Treasurer from June 1, 1933, to May 29, 1949.

Henry Morgenthau Jr. served as secretary from January 1, 1934, to July 22, 1945.

Fred M. Vinson served as secretary from July 23, 1945, to June 23, 1946.

John W. Snyder served as secretary from June 25, 1946, to January 20, 1953.

Georgia Neese Clark served as Treasurer from June 21, 1949, to January 27, 1953.

Ivy Baker Priest served as Treasurer from January 28, 1953, to January 20, 1961.

George M. Humphrey served as secretary from January 21, 1953, to July 29, 1957.

Robert B. Anderson served as secretary from July 29, 1957, to January 20, 1961.

Elizabeth Rudel Smith served as Treasurer from January 31, 1961, to April 13, 1962.

C. Douglas Dillon served as secretary from January 21, 1961, to April 1, 1965.

Kathryn O'Hay Granahan served as Treasurer from January 9, 1963, to October 13, 1966.

Henry H. Fowler served as secretary from April 1, 1965, to December 20, 1968.

Joseph W. Barr served as secretary from December 21, 1968, to January 20, 1969.

Dorothy Andrews Elston served as Treasurer from May 8, 1969, to July 3, 1971.

David Kennedy served as secretary from January 22, 1969, to February 11, 1971.

John B. Connally served as secretary from February 11, 1971, to June 12, 1972.

Romana Acosta Banuelos served as Treasurer from December 17, 1971, to February 14, 1974.

George P. Shultz served as secretary from June 12, 1972, to May 8, 1974.

Francine I. Neff served as Treasurer from June 21, 1974, to January 19, 1977.

William E. Simon served as secretary from May 8, 1974, to January 20, 1977.

Azie Taylor Morton served as Treasurer from September 12, 1977, to January 20, 1981.

W. Michael Blumenthal served as secretary from January 23, 1977, to August 4, 1979.

G. William Miller served as secretary from August 6, 1979, to January 20, 1981.

Ronald Reagan served as acting Treasurer from January 20, 1981, to March 17, 1981.

Angela Marie Buchanan served as Treasurer from March 20, 1981, to July 5, 1983.

Donald T. Regan served as secretary from January 22, 1981, to February 2, 1985.

Ronald Reagan served as acting Treasurer from July 5, 1983, to September 22, 1983.

Katherine Davolas Ortega served as Treasurer from September 26, 1983, to July 1, 1989.

James A. Baker served as secretary from February 3, 1985, to August 17, 1988.

Nicholas F. Brady served as secretary from September 16, 1988, to January 17, 1993.

George H.W. Bush served as acting Treasurer from July 1, 1989, to November 20, 1989.

Catalina Vasquez Villalpando served as Treasurer from December 11, 1989, to January 20, 1993.

Mary Ellen Withrow served as Treasurer from March 1, 1994, to January 20, 2001.

Lloyd M. Bentsen served as secretary from January 22, 1993, to December 22, 1994.

Frank Newman (undersecretary of the Treasury for domestic finance) served as acting secretary from December 22, 1994, to January 11, 1995.

Robert E. Rubin served as secretary from January 10, 1995, to July 2, 1999.

Lawrence F. Summers served as secretary from July 2, 1999, to January 20, 2001.

George W. Bush served as acting Treasurer from January 20, 2001, to August 16, 2001.

Rosario Marin served as Treasurer from August 16, 2001, to June 30, 2003.

Paul H. O'Neil served as secretary from January 30, 2001, to December 31, 2002.

Kenneth W. Dam (deputy secretary of the Treasury) served as acting secretary from December 31, 2002, to February 3, 2003.

John W. Snow served as secretary from February 3, 2003, to June 29, 2006.

George W. Bush served as acting secretary from June 30, 2003, to December 13, 2004.

Anna Escobedo Cabral served as Treasurer from January 19, 2005, to August 8, 2009.

Robert Kimmitt (deputy secretary of the Treasury) served as acting secretary from June 30, 2006 to July 9, 2006.

Timothy F. Geithner was sworn in as secretary of the Treasury on January 26, 2009.

Rosa Gumataotao Rios was sworn in as Treasurer on August 8, 2009.

GLOSSARY

American Bank Note Company (ABNCo). Firm founded in 1858 in New York City. Provider, by contract, of certain federal currency and Fractional Currency notes in the 1860s through the mid-1870s. The ABNCo monogram appears on certain Fractional Currency and early federal notes of the 1860s.

autographed signature. A signature handwritten in ink by a Treasury Department or other official. In contrast, an *inked* signature may appear to be by a Treasury official, such as F.E. Spinner, but was done by a clerk.

back (of a note). The reverse side of a note; the paper-money equivalent of *reverse* used for coins. The other side of a note is called the *face*. In Treasury records, obverse and reverse are sometimes used, but *face* and *back* are preferred by numismatists today.

Bank Note Reporter. A newspaper issued monthly by F+W Publications (Iola, Wisc.) and devoted to the collecting of paper money.

bank-note reporter. Generic term for a 19th-century newspaper or magazine that listed the exchange rates for notes issued by state-chartered banks, described counterfeits, and gave news of insolvencies and other problems. After the mid-1860s bank-note reporters emphasized counterfeits of federal notes.

Battleship Note. Nickname for a Series of 1918 $2 Federal Reserve Bank Note with a battleship printed in green on the back.

bill. A piece of paper money with a face value of $1 or higher. *Synonym:* note.

Bison Note. Nickname for the $10 Series of 1901 Legal Tender Notes depicting such an animal. Modeled either by Pablo or by a stuffed animal; not the same bison shown on the 1913 "Buffalo" nickel.

black charter. A rare variety of $5 National Bank Note issued in the 1870s, from plates originally made by the Continental Bank Note Company and with the bank charter number printed in black (instead of the normal red) as part of the printing plate.

Black Eagle Note. Nickname for the $1 Series of 1899 Silver Certificates depicting a bold eagle printed in black on the center of the face of the note (official name of vignette: *Eagle of the Capitol*).

bronzing; bronze surcharge. The National Currency Bureau's process of applying a bronzing powder to note-sheets in the form of lettering or designs; used mostly on Compound Interest Treasury Notes and certain Fractional Currency.

bond. Financial certificate with a stated face value, interest rate, and maturity, issued to raise funds. Includes certain items that are collected as currency—including Interest-Bearing Notes, Compound Interest Treasury Notes, and 1879 $10 Refunding Certificates.

Bureau of Engraving and Printing (BEP). Federal bureau in charge of printing paper money and certain other security items. Successor to the National Currency Bureau, although the BEP name was used as early as 1864.

C-note. Nickname for a $100 bill.

Canada green. See *patent green tint.*

certified note. A note graded and placed in a sealed holder by a commercial grading service.

charter number. Number given to each of thousands of National Banks that, beginning in 1863, were chartered by the Treasury Department; usually printed on the face of each note issued by the bank, along with the note's serial number. Sometimes retained when a bank changed its name or even its geographical location.

circulation (of a National Bank). The total face value of a given National Bank's bills in circulation in commerce (not including notes held in the bank's vault or not yet issued).

Coin Note. Note of a denomination from $1 to $1,000 issued in the Series of 1890 and 1891, redeemable in coins (silver or gold, at the option of the Treasury Department, though in practice the bearer could make the selection). Also called Treasury Notes.

colorized note. Multi-colored printing on modern federal paper money initiated in the early 21st century. Consists of various hues and shades, some subtle, with tiny color denomination counters and other security techniques.

color-shifting ink. An ink that changes color when a note is viewed from different angles; used on modern notes to help deter counterfeiting.

Columbian Bank Note Company. Firm located in Washington, D.C., that undertook contract printing for the backs of certain currency in the 1870s.

Compound Interest Treasury Note. Note of a denomination from $10 to $1,000 issued in the early 1860s, that yielded interest to the bearer. One of several distinct U.S. currency series.

comptroller of the Currency. Treasury Department–appointed official in charge of paper-money distribution, the granting of National Bank charters, and related matters.

Continental Bank Note Company. Firm founded in January 1863 in New York City. Provider, by contract, of certain federal currency in the 1860s through the mid-1870s.

counter. Technical name for the part of a note showing the denomination in a separate vignette, as either an arabic (5, 10, 20, etc.) or a roman numeral (V, X, M, etc.).

counterfeit. A bill in imitation of an original design, but printed from false plates by someone not authorized by the Treasury Department.

Crane paper. Currency paper produced by Crane & Co. of Dalton, Massachusetts; varieties since 1890 have included red and/or blue threads that run the length of the note, individual red and blue fibers scattered throughout the note, and bands with red and blue fibers distributed throughout.

cycloid work; cycloid counter. See *kaleidograph counter.*

cycloidal configuration. Term used by the National Bank Note Company to describe a latticework pattern printed on notes, usually in colored ink, with arcs and inscriptions; said to deter counterfeiting. Based on James McDonough's patent of March 23, 1860, in which an engraving included the name of the issuer and the denomination with geometric, cycloidal, and rosette work to prevent alteration or counterfeiting of bank notes.

cylinder die. See *transfer roll.*

Date Back. Certain Series of 1882 National Bank Notes with the dates 1882–1908 printed prominently on the back, or certain Blue Seal Series of 1902 National Bank Notes with the dates 1902 and 1908 printed on the back (in addition to other motifs).

Demand Note. Note of a denomination from $5 to $20 issued in 1861 and early 1862, redeemable in gold coins on demand.

denomination. A bill's face or stated value (i.e., the amount for which the bill could be redeemed in specie or exchanged for other bills). In U.S. currency, may be whole dollar amounts or fractions of a dollar (as with Postage and Fractional Currency).

deuce. Nickname for a $2 bill.

Educational Note. Name for any one of the $1, $2, and $5 Series of 1896 Silver Certificates with ornately engraved designs, among the most famous of all U.S. currency issues.

embossing. Refers to the raised printing on a note caused when damp paper is pressed into the recesses of a printing plate.

encased postage stamp. A regular federal postage stamp of a denomination from 1¢ to 90¢, enclosed within a brass frame with clear mica face; usually with the name of an advertiser embossed on the back. Patented by John Gault, and popular as a money substitute in 1862 and 1863. Often capitalized in numismatic usage. *Synonym:* encasement.

essay. An experimental impression of a partial or complete note printed to test the design or evaluate a concept; the paper-money equivalent of a pattern or trial coin.

face (of a note). The front side of a note; the paper-money equivalent of *obverse* used for coins. The other side of a note is called the *back*. In Treasury records, obverse and reverse are sometimes used, but *face* and *back* are preferred by numismatists today.

Federal Reserve Bank Note. Note of a denomination from $1 to $50 (Series of 1915 and 1918, large-size) or $5 to $100 (Series of 1929, small-size). Each bears the name of a Federal Reserve Bank (boldly imprinted across the center of the face on large-size notes) and a letter designating its district.

Federal Reserve Note. Note of a denomination from $1 to $10,000, issued in large-size and small-size formats, Series of 1914 to the present day; the standard imprint on all of today's notes. Each bears the name of a Federal Reserve Bank and a letter and number designating its district.

First Charter Note. Nickname, with no basis in Treasury documents, for Original Series and Series of 1875 National Bank Notes.

First Obligation. Wording on the back of a Legal Tender Note of the early 1860s stating its redemption status ("This note is a Legal Tender for all debts public and private, except for duties on imports and interest on the public debt, and is exchangeable for U.S. six percent twenty years bonds redeemable at the pleasure of the U. States after five years.") Called *convertible backs* at ABNCo. Also see *Second Obligation*.

Fort Worth (Western Facility). Branch currency facility of the Bureau of Engraving and Printing established in Fort Worth, Texas, in the late 19th century. Bills made there are imprinted FW at the face-plate number.

Fractional Currency. Federal bills made in denominations of 3¢, 5¢, 10¢, 15¢, 25¢, and 50¢, and issued under the Act of March 3, 1863, continuing into 1876, succeeding Postage Currency notes.

Franklin. Nickname for a small-size $100 bill, derived from the portrait depicted thereon.

Gold Certificate. Note of a denomination from $10 to $10,000 issued in large-size and small-size formats, redeemable in gold coins. The backs of large-size notes were printed in gold color; the backs of small-size notes in were printed in green.

grade. Designation assigned by numismatists to signify the amount of wear or circulation a note has experienced and its condition today. Can be expressed by adjectives such as Good, Extremely Fine, and Uncirculated, or by abbreviations in combination with numbers from 1 to 70 (adapted from the ANA coin-grading system), such as EF-40 or Unc-63.

Grand Watermelon Note. Nickname for the $1,000 Series of 1890 Treasury Notes (Coin Notes), with three zeros on the back in the form, fancifully, of watermelons. Also see *Watermelon Note*.

Green Eagle Note. Nickname for a $1 Series of 1918 Federal Reserve Bank Note with an eagle printed in green on the back.

green tint. See *patent green tint*.

greenback. Piece of paper money with a face value of $1 or higher and with the back printed in green. Unofficial popular term for U.S. paper money in general; popularized in reference to the Legal Tender Notes of the 1860s with their green backs (though these were not the first to be printed in this color), and widely used since.

Gwynn membrane paper. Paper made from 1862 to 1864 within the National Currency Bureau, in at least 10 variations; mostly used for Fractional Currency. Named for Dr. Stuart Gwynn, upon whose resignation manufacturing ceased.

Hawaii Note. Nickname for certain $1 Silver Certificates and $5, $10, and $20 Federal Reserve Notes with brown seals and HAWAII overprinted on both sides, issued in Hawaii during World War II.

Indian Chief Note. Nickname for the $5 Series of 1899 Silver Certificates depicting Chief Running Antelope on the face.

inked signature. A handwritten signature, often of a Treasury official, applied by a clerk. Distinct from *autographed* signatures, which are applied personally by the person named.

Interest-Bearing Note. Note of a denomination from $10 to $10,000 issued in the early 1860s, and yielding interest to the bearer.

Jackass Note. Nickname for the $10 Series of 1869 Legal Tender Notes showing an eagle that, if turned upside down, resembles a jackass.

kaleidograph counter. Treasury Department name for a counter or denomination vignette with a repeated, petal-like border imprinted with the denomination or other information. *Synonyms:* cycloid work; cycloid counter.

launder. Term, often used in a derogatory sense, referring to the cleaning of paper money to enhance its appearance. In the early 20th century the Treasury Department added several machines to launder soiled paper money, after which the reconditioned notes were again placed into circulation.

Lazy 2; Lazy Deuce. Nicknames for a $2 Original Series or Series of 1875 National Bank Note with a large 2 placed horizontally in a resting, or "lazy," position.

Legal Tender Note. Note of a denomination from $1 to $10,000, issued in large-size and small-size formats. The basic mainstay of the federal paper-money system for many years. *Synonym:* United States Note.

legal-tender status. Information given in the lettered inscriptions on the back of a note, and describing its exchangeability (e.g., on certain early Legal Tender Notes, "This note is a legal tender for all debts, public and private, except duties on imports and interest on the public debt, and is receivable in payment of all loans made to the United States"). *Synonym:* obligation.

margin. The blank area or white strip at the border of a note beyond the design or printed information.

Martha Washington Note; Martha Note. Nickname for the $1 Series of 1886 and 1891 Silver Certificates depicting the first of the nation's first ladies.

microprinting. Nearly microscopic lettering added to a note (e.g., UNITED STATES OF AMERICA added to the frame of a $5 Federal Reserve Note) to deter copying and counterfeiting. Introduced by the BEP in the 1990s.

mule. Note that incorporates an older feature, such as a larger or smaller plate-number left over from the past, in a series in which a newer feature is standard; also, an older-series note face combined with a later back.

National Bank. Commercial bank incorporated under the laws of the federal government and given a federal charter number pursuant to the National Banking Act of 1863 and its amendments. Regulated by the comptroller of the currency, an officer of the Treasury Department.

National Bank Note. Note bearing the imprint of a specific National Bank and its location, plus the signatures of bank officers, in addition to federal signatures and information; denominations: large-size

Original Series and Series of 1875 ("First Charter") notes, $1 to $1,000; large-size Series of 1882 ("Second Charter") notes, $5 to $100; large-size Series of 1902 ("Third Charter"), $5 to $100; small-size Series of 1929 notes, $5 to $100 (types 1 and 2).

National Bank Note Company. Firm founded in 1859 in New York City; a provider, by contract, of certain federal and Fractional Currency notes in the 1860s through the mid-1870s.

National Bank Note regional letter. Large capital letter printed on the face of National Bank Notes from about March 17, 1902, to March 5, 1924, to designate the regions in which they were issued; intended to help Treasury personnel sort the notes when they were redeemed at a later date. Letters used: N (Northeast banks), E (East), S (South), M (Midwest), W (West), and P (Pacific district).

National Currency Bureau, First Division. Government office that began operations in 1862 in part of the Treasury Building; activities included adding Treasury seals to bills printed by private contractors, the printing of certain Fractional Currency, and eventually, the printing of currency of all denominations. Succeeded in name by the Bureau of Engraving and Printing in the 1870s.

National Gold Bank Note. Note bearing the imprint of a specific National Bank and its location, plus the signatures of bank officers, in addition to federal signatures and information; redeemable in gold coins. Issued in the early 1870s (in denominations of $5 to $100) by National Gold Banks located in the state of California. The reverse bore an image (the same one for all denominations) of various gold coins.

nature printing. Anti-counterfeiting technique devised by Benjamin Franklin, who noticed that leaves of plants not only differed from each other but had complex veins of diminishing thickness toward the edges. Impressions were taken of the leaves; from these impressions a metal plate segment, suitable for printing, was made.

notaphily. Term proposed by Kenneth R. Lake to describe the study and appreciation of paper money.

note. A piece of paper money of with a face value of $1 or higher. *Synonym:* bill.

obligation. See *legal-tender status.* Also see *First Obligation; Second Obligation.*

obverse. The face or front of a note or printing plate. Although the term is widely used in Treasury Department data and reports prior to the mid-1870s, and in certain 20th-century numismatic texts, for most numismatists *face* is preferred.

overprint. Extra printing or information added to a note after the main printing. *Synonym:* surcharge.

paper (for currency). Fiber-based material imprinted as currency by the National Currency Bureau and the Bureau of Engraving and Printing from 1861 to date. Also see *Crane paper; Gwynn membrane paper; Willcox blue-tint fiber paper.*

Paper Money magazine. A publication issued six times per year by the nonprofit Society of Paper Money Collectors.

patent green tint; green tint; "Canada green." Green imprint (usually called an *overprint*) of lacy green, said to be a deterrent against counterfeiting. Except for paper-money sheets that required bronzing, the adding of a green tint was the first printing operation on a blank sheet.

pinhole. Tiny perforation in a currency note caused by the 19th-century practice of stitching several notes together for safekeeping, for hiding within a coat's lining, or for storing in a small pile.

Plain Back. A description of certain blue-seal Series of 1902 National Bank Notes *without* the dates 1902 and 1908 printed on the back, introduced in 1908 and issued through early 1929.

Poker Chip Note. Nickname for the Series of 1923 $10 Legal Tender Note with the denomination surrounded by a round frame.

Porthole Note. Nickname for the $5 Series of 1923 Silver Certificate with the portrait of Abraham Lincoln in a heavy, fanciful frame that resembles a ship's porthole.

Postage Currency. Federal fractional bills made in denominations of 5¢, 10¢, 25¢, and 50¢, and first issued in August 1862 to help alleviate a coin shortage.

printage. Quantity of notes printed, or an estimate thereof.

Professional Currency Dealers Association (PCDA). A trade group composed of paper-money dealers.

proof note. An impression made from a complete or partially complete plate, to illustrate its appearance. Usually bears no serial numbers, or else just zeroes, and may be missing other elements, such as the Treasury seal and signatures. Usually printed on only one side. Also see *Specimen note.*

ragpicker. Old-time nickname, less common today, for a collector of paper money.

Rainbow Note. Nickname for any $1, $2, $5, or $10 Series of 1869 Legal Tender Note, derived from the colorful face, which includes a green overprint.

re-entry. Mechanical process whereby new information is engraved or transferred into

an existing currency printing plate. Done to strengthen worn vignettes, change wording, replace Treasury signatures, or add new information.

Refunding Certificate. Interest-bearing $10 certificate, not a currency note, issued in 1879.

regional letter. See *National Bank Note regional letter.*

reverse. A term referring to the back of a note or printing plate, and widely used in early Treasury Department data and reports and in occasional numismatic listings (today *back* is preferred).

roll; roller die. See *transfer roll.*

Second Charter Note. Nickname, with no basis in Treasury documents, for Series of 1882 National Bank Notes.

Second Obligation. Wording on the back of a Legal Tender Note of the early 1860s stating its redemption status ("This note is a Legal Tender for all debts public and private, except for duties on imports and interest on the public debt, and is receivable in payment of all loans made to the United States"). Also see *First Obligation.*

security features. Aspects of the design or printing of a note intended to deter copying and counterfeiting. In early times, consisted of minute design elements expertly engraved, as well as printing on special paper (often with silk fibers embedded); recent features have included watermark designs, color-shifting ink, micro-printing, and the embedding of plastic strips.

selvage. Unused space on a sheet of paper money beyond the normal trim borders of the individual notes.

series. A type or class of currency. Typically signifies a change in authorization or design, for large-size notes; or a change in signature combinations, for small-size notes.

series number. Part of a numbering system printed on the face of certain early federal currency notes to ensure that each note received a unique identification number. Serial numbers from 1 to 100,000 were applied to the notes; each time the counter was reset to 1, a new *series* number was added to the face (e.g., the note numbered Series 17, serial number 100,000, was followed by a note numbered Series 18, serial number 1).

sheet. An uncut group of notes, as printed. For large-size notes of 1861–1929, four subjects; for small-size notes of the late 1920s and early 1930s, twelve subjects (cut apart into two six-subject sheets); for modern small-size notes, 36 subjects.

shinplaster. Derogatory 19th-century nickname for a scrip note or bank note that had no monetary value, such as an issue of the Hard Times era. Derived from the practice of using a hardening substance to affix sheets of paper to a person's shins to relieve pain, the implication being that the note might be good for this but little else.

signatures on notes. Handwritten, rubber-stamped, or mechanically printed autographs of bank officials (e.g., U.S. treasurer and register, Federal Reserve Bank cashier and governor, etc.), the selection of which varies by note type and series.

Silver Certificate. Note of a denomination from $1 to $1,000 that was redeemable first in silver dollars, and later in silver bullion; issued in large-size and small-size formats.

Silver Dollar Note. Nickname for the $5 Series of 1886 Silver Certificates depicting five Morgan silver dollars printed in green in a row on the back of the note.

Society of Paper Money Collectors (SPMC). A nonprofit organization, founded in 1961, devoted to the study and appreciation of currency; publisher of the periodical *Paper Money*.

Specimen note. A printed impression of a note, usually one side only, of a type currently in production. Most were made for presentation purposes, for inclusion in albums, or for the numismatic trade. Also see *proof note*.

stamp. Derisive nickname used by the public in the 1860s and 1870s for Postage Currency and Fractional Currency notes.

star note. Beginning with Silver Certificates of 1910, a note with a star next to the serial number to indicate that it is a replacement note, printed as a substitute for a defective note that was subsequently destroyed. The star serial number does not match that of any note being replaced. Prior to 1910, stars added to serial numbers were purely decorative.

surcharge. Extra printing or information added to a note after the main printing was finished. Also widely applied to bronze printing on certain Fractional Currency and Compound Interest Treasury Notes, such being the *first* imprint on a blank sheet of paper. *Synonym:* overprint.

Technicolor Note. Nickname (since the 1930s) for the Series of 1905 large-size Gold Certificates, the faces of which have part of the inscription in gold ink, a gold tint to part of the paper, and a red Treasury seal and serial numbers.

Third Charter Note. A nickname, with no basis in Treasury documents, for Series of 1902 National Bank Notes.

tinted paper. Currency paper with color embedded in the material rather than applied to the surface during printing. Notes printed on tinted paper include Series of 1869 Legal Tender "Rainbow Notes," Fractional Currency, National Gold Bank Notes of the early 1870s, and Series of 1905 Gold Certificates, among others. Also see *Willcox blue-tint fiber paper*.

Tombstone Note. Nickname for the $1 Series of 1886, 1891, and 1908 Silver Certificates with the portrait of the recently (1885) deceased vice president, Thomas A. Hendricks, in a frame that, whether intentionally or not, resembles the outline of a tombstone.

transfer roll. Hard steel cylinder, with a hole at the center for the shaft, on the outside face of which is a *raised* design, vignette, counter, or other element used in bank-note printing. Used to imprint a design into a printing plate by the siderographic process. *Synonyms:* cylinder die, roll, roller die.

Treasury Department. Branch of the U.S. government that operates the Bureau of Engraving and Printing, the Federal Reserve System, the Secret Service, the coinage mints, and other monetary bureaus.

Treasury Note. Another name for a Coin Note.

Treasury seal. Emblem of the Treasury Department; circular, sometimes with an ornate border, and varying in size and color, as used on the face of all federal currency denominated $1 and up from 1862 to the present, as well as on the fourth and fifth issues of Fractional Currency. The basic motif is a pair of scales above and a key below, with inscription surrounding.

United States Note. Another name for a Legal Tender Note.

Value Back. Describes certain Series of 1882 National Bank Notes on which the denomination is spelled out (as FIVE DOLLARS, TEN DOLLARS, etc.) in green on the back.

vignette. An ornamental or illustrative design element, such as a portrait, allegorical scene, or motif from history (e.g., the scene depicting two men, a shield, and an eagle on the back of the $100 Series of 1902 National Bank Note).

Watermelon Note. Nickname for the $100 Series of 1890 Treasury Notes (Coin Notes) with two zeros on the back in the form, fancifully, of watermelons. Also see *Grand Watermelon Note*.

Western Facility. Bureau of Engraving and Printing branch currency facility established in Fort Worth, Texas, in the late 19th century, and using the imprint FW on the face plate for all bills it prints.

Willcox blue-tint fiber paper. Paper printed by the James M. Willcox Paper Company with a wide stripe of "blue tint," with fibers, across white stock; used extensively for notes from Fractional Currency to large-denomination notes from 1869 to 1880.

BIBLIOGRAPHY

While there are dozens of books, past and present, on federal currency, the following are some of the basic texts used in connection with the present work. These are also recommended for addition to any numismatic library. In addition, certain auction catalogs by Bowers and Merena Galleries, Currency Auctions of America (Heritage), William P. Donlon, Ira and Larry Goldberg, Hickman and Oakes, Lyn F. Knight, R.M. Smythe & Co., Stack's, and Superior Galleries have yielded much useful information. Useful periodicals include the *Bank Note Reporter* (Krause Publications), *Currency Dealer Newsletter,* and *Essay-Proof Journal.*

Acts of Congress Relating to Loans in the Currency, From 1790 to 1867. Washington, DC: Government Printing Office, 1867.

American Cyclopaedia, The. New York: D. Appleton and Company. Various volumes and editions, 1860–1875. Alternate title: *The American Encyclopedia.*

American State Papers—Finance. Vols. III–V. Washington, DC: Gales & Seaton, 1834–1861. Reprinted by William S. Hein Co.

Ames, Mary Clemmer. *Ten Years in Washington: Life and Scenes in the National Capital, as a Woman Sees Them.* Chicago: A.D. Worthington and Co., 1873.

Baker, L(afayette) C. *History of the United States Secret Service.* Philadelphia: Author, 1867.

Ball, Farlin Q. *The Law of National Banks Containing the National Bank Act, as Amended.* Chicago: Callaghan and Company, 1881.

Bankers' Magazine and Statistical Register, The. Various issues, 1846–1880s.

Blaine, James G. *Twenty Years of Congress.* Norwich, CT: Henry Bill, 1884.

Blake, George H. "A Paper by J.E. Ralph, Director of the Bureau of Engraving and Printing, Read Before The New York Numismatic Club, February 10, 1911." *The Numismatist,* April 1911 and May 1911.

———. *United States Paper Money: A Reference List of Paper Money, Including Fractional Currency, Issued Since 1861.* New York: George H. Blake, 1908.

Bolin, Benny. "Civil War Blockade Leads to a Currency Variety." *Paper Money,* March–April 1988.

———. "Spencer M. Clark, Cornerstone of the Bureau of Engraving and Printing." *Paper Money,* May–June 1988.

Bowers, Q. David. *Harry W. Bass Jr. Collection, Part I: Currency.* Wolfeboro, NH: Bowers and Merena Galleries, 1999.

Bowles, Samuel. *Across the Continent: A Summer's Journey to the Rocky Mountains, the Mormons, and the Pacific States, With Speaker Colfax.* Springfield, MA: Samuel Bowles and Co., 1865.

Breen, Walter. "Chasing Rainbows and Other Colorful Notes." *Paper Money,* March–April 1977.

Bronson, S.A. *John Sherman: What He Has Said and Done.* Columbus, OH: H.W. Derby and Co., 1880.

Buckingham, J.S. *America, Historical, Statistic, and Descriptive.* Vols. I–III. London: Fisher, Son and Co., 1841.

Burnham, George P. *American Counterfeits: How Detected, and How Avoided.* Springfield, MA: W.J. Holland, 1875.

Chase, S(almon) P(ortland). *Report of the Secretary of the Treasury on the State of the Finances, the Year Ending June 30, 1863.* Washington, DC: Government Printing Office, 1863.

Childs, C.F. *Concerning U.S. Government Securities: A Condensed Review of the Nation's Currency, Public Debt, and the Market for Representative United States Government Loans 1635–1945.* Chicago: R.H. Donnelley and Sons, 1947.

Clark, S(pencer) M(orton). *Report to the Secretary of the Treasury from the First Division National Currency Bureau, Showing Its Origin, Growth, and Present Condition, with Details of Work Done, &c.* No imprint, November 26, 1864. Published separately in November 1864; also as part of *Letter from the Secretary of the Treasury in Answer to a resolution of the House of January 24, in regard to the Printing Bureau of the Treasury Department,* February 4, 1865, 38th Cong., 2nd sess., House of Representatives, Ex. doc. no. 50.

Cochran, Bob. "None Outstanding, All Redeemed, Not So!" *Paper Money,* September–October 1997.

———. "Process Notes." *Paper Money,* March–April 1995.

Coombs, Leslie S. "National Bank Notes—First Charter Period." *The Numismatist,* September 1951.

Cross, Ira B. *Financing an Empire: History of Banking in California.* Vol. I, *Chicago and other cities.* S.J. Clarke, 1927.

Cruse, Guy A. "The Grading Game." *Paper Money* 9, no. 1 (1970).

Daniel, Forrest W. "The Paper Money Laundry." *Paper Money,* March–April 1967.

———. "Rules for Redemption Reveal Coupon Note Issue." *Paper Money* 7, no. 4 (1968).

———. "Running Antelope—Misnamed Onepapa." *Paper Money* 8, no. 29 (1969): 4ff.

Dean, Charles A. "Those Lazy Twos." *Paper Money* 16 (1977): 234ff.

Dean, Charles A., and Don C. Kelly. "What the Deuce!" *Paper Money,* January–February 1988 and March–April 1988.

Dillistin, William H. *Bank Note Reporters and Counterfeit Detectors 1826–1866.* Numismatic Notes and Monographs no. 114. New York: American Numismatic Society, 1949.

———. *A Descriptive History of National Bank Notes, 1863–1935.* Paterson, NJ: Author, 1956.

———. "National Bank Notes in the Early Years." *The Numismatist,* December 1948.

———. "National Gold Banks and Bank Notes." *The Numismatist,* March 1950.

Donlon, William P. *Hewitt-Donlon Catalog of United States Small Size Paper Money.* 13th ed. Chicago: Hewitt Numismatic Publications, 1977.

———. *United States Large Size Paper Money 1861 to 1923.* 6th ed. Iola, WI: Krause Publications, 1979.

Doty, Richard. *America's Money, America's Story.* 2nd ed. Atlanta: Whitman Publishing, 2008.

Drowne, Henry Russell. "U.S. Postage Stamps as Necessity War Money." *American Journal of Numismatics* 52 (1918).

Ellis, John B. *The Sights and Secrets of the National Capital.* New York: United States, 1869.

Friedberg, Arthur L., and Ira S. Friedberg. *A Guide Book of United States Paper Money.* 2nd ed. Atlanta: Whitman Publishing, 2008.

———. *Paper Money of the United States.* 18th ed. Clifton, NJ: Coin & Currency Institute, 2006.

Friedberg, Milton R. *The Encyclopedia of United States Fractional & Postal Currency.* Rockville Centre, NY: NASCA, 1978.

———. "New Information on Fractional Currency." *Paper Money* 7, no. 4 (1968).

Gengerke, Martin. *U.S. Paper Money Records.* CD-ROM. 2008.

Goldstein, Nathan, II. "Collecting Current Paper Money." *Paper Money* 5, no. 1 (1966).

———. "Rotary Press Currency." *Paper Money* 5, no. 3 (1966).

———. "Sheet Twelve National Currency." *Paper Money* 6, no. 2 (1967).

Goodman, Leon J., John L. Schwartz, and Chuck O'Donnell. *The Standard Handbook of Modern U.S. Paper Money.* New York: Authors, 1967.

Griffiths, William H. *The Story of American Bank Note Company.* New York: American Bank Note Company, 1959.

Hepburn, A. Barton. *A History of Currency in the United States and the Perennial Contest for Sound Money.* New York: Macmillan, 1903.

———. *A History of Currency in the United States.* Rev. ed. New York: Macmillan, 1924.

Hessler, Gene. "The Educational Note Designers: Blashfield, Low & Shirlaw." *Paper Money* 23, nos. 112–114 (1984).

———. *The Engraver's Line.* Portage, OH: BNR Press, 1993.

———. *An Illustrated History of U.S. Loans 1775–1898.* Port Clinton, OH: BNR Press, 1988.

———. "Notes that Might Have Been: A Sequel." *Paper Money,* March–April 1991.

———. "Signatures Out of Sequence on Gold Certificate Proofs." *Paper Money,* January–February, 1986.

———. "Unissued Circulating Notes of 1873." *The Numismatist,* February 1985.

———. *U.S. Essay, Proof and Specimen Notes.* Portage, OH: BNR Press, 1979.

———. "Walter Shirlaw and His Work." *Paper Money,* September–October 1984.

———. "Will Low and His Work." *Paper Money,* November–December 1984.

Hessler, Gene, and Carlson Chambliss. *Comprehensive Catalog of U.S. Paper Money.* 7th ed. Port Clinton, OH: BNR Press, 2006.

Hickman, John D., and Dean Oakes. *Standard Catalog of National Bank Notes.* Iola, WI: Krause Publications, 1983.

Horstman, Ronald L. "The First Greenbacks of the Civil War: The $100 Two-Year Treasury Notes of March 2, 1861." *Paper Money,* May–June 1988.

Hughes, Brent H. "Development of the Spinner Signature." *Paper Money* 14 (1974): 236ff.

———. "The Hidden Engraving on the Fractional Currency Shield." *Paper Money* 11 (1972): 23ff.

Huntoon, Peter. "The Binion $10,000 Notes of Las Vegas, Nevada." *Paper Money* 38 (1999): 85ff.

———. "The Doctored Note—A Menace to Legitimate Collecting." *Paper Money,* July 1974.

———. "$50 FRBN Series of 1918 St. Louis Note." Manuscript.

———. "The Kidder National Gold Bank of Boston, Massachusetts." *Paper Money,* November–December 2007.

———. "Small Issue Sheets of Large Notes a Rarity." *Bank Note Reporter,* September 2008.

———. "Small Note Mules, a Fifty Year Retrospective." *Paper Money,* January–February 1988.

———. "Small Note Mules: New Data for the Fifty-Year Retrospective." *Paper Money,* November–December 1988.

———. *Territorials: A Guide to U.S. Territorial National Bank Notes.* N.p.: Society of Paper Money Collectors, Inc., 1980.

———. "The $2 Legal Tender Series 1928C and 1928D Mules." *Paper Money,* September–October 1992.

———. "The United States $500 & $1,000 National Bank Notes." *Paper Money,* July–August 1988.

———. *United States Large Size National Bank Notes.* Laramie, WY: Society of Paper Money Collectors, 1995.

Huntoon, Peter, and James Hodgson. "The Transition from Wide to Narrow Designs on U.S. Small Size Notes." *Paper Money,* September–October 2006.

Hutchins, Frank H. "Unrecognized Varieties in the Later Large Size Notes." *Paper Money,* May–June 1981.

Instructions of the Comptroller of the Currency Relative to the Organization and Powers of National Banks. Washington, DC: Government Printing Office, 1923.

Isted, John R. "The 1899 and 1908 Silver Certificates." *The Numismatist,* August 1983.

———. "Signature Combinations on Untied States Currency 1888–1929." *The Numismatist,* July 1979.

Kane, Thomas P. *The Romance and Tragedy of Banking.* New York: Bankers, 1922.

Kelly, Don C. *National Bank Notes.* 6th ed. Oxford, OH: Paper Money Institute, 2008.

Kelly, Don C., and James M. Kelly. *National Bank Note Census.* Supplement to the 6th edition of *National Bank Notes.* Oxford, OH: Paper Money Institute, 2008.

Kemm, Theodore. "Assistant Treasurer of the United States $10 Silver Certificate." *Paper Money* 6, no. 4 (1967).

Klaes, Francis X. "Series 1995 $1 'B' Star Notes with Duplicate Serial Numbers." *Paper Money,* July–August 2005.

Klein, David H. "The Last $1 Silver Certificates." *Paper Money,* January–February 1986.

Knebl, Tom. "Postage Due." *Paper Money,* September–October 1979.

Knox, John J. *History of Banking.* New York: Bradford Rhodes & Company, 1900.

———. *United States Notes: A History of the Various Issues of Paper Money by the Government of the United States.* 2nd ed. New York: Charles Scribner's Sons, 1885.

———. *Reports of the Comptroller of the Currency and Commissioner of Internal Revenue.* 2nd sess., 45th Cong., 1877–1878, vol. 12. Washington, DC: Government Printing Office.

Koster, William P. "Some Thoughts on Grading." *Paper Money,* January–February 1977.

———. "A Superb Counterfeit: The $100 Compound Interest Note." *Paper Money,* January–February 1955.

Kravitz, Robert J. *A Collector's Guide to Postage and Fractional Currency.* San Francisco, CA: Arkives Press, n.d. [2003?].

Kvederas, Bob, Sr., and Bob Kvederas Jr. "Varieties of Series 1993 $1 Web Notes." *Paper Money,* September–October 1997.

———. "Varieties of Series 1995 $1 Web Notes." *Paper Money,* May–June 1998.

Linderman, Henry R. *Money and Legal Tender of the United States.* New York: G.P. Putnam's Sons, 1877.

Lloyd, Robert H. "The Unfortunate Series 1902–1908." *Paper Money* 26 (1987): 129.

Logan, Mrs. John A. *Thirty Years in Washington.* Hartford, CT: A.D. Worthington and Company, 1901.

Lowe, Ken. "The Little Known First ANS Paper Money Exhibition in ANS's First Meeting Devoted Exclusively to Paper Money." *Paper Money*, September–October 1995.

McCulloch, Hugh. *Men and Measures of Half a Century*. New York: Charles Scribner's Sons, 1900.

McCurdy, Bob. "The 1942 Issue of Federal Reserve Bank Notes." *Paper Money* 10, no. 2.

Morris, Thomas F. "The Events of 1863: The First U.S. National Bank Notes." *Essay-Proof Journal* 20, no. 3 (1963).

———. "U.S. Silver Certificates, Series of 1896." *The Numismatist*, June 1934.

Murray, Doug. *Complete Catalog of U.S. Large Size Star Notes 1910–1929*. 3rd ed. Clifton, N.J.: Coin & Currency Institute, 2007.

———. "Paper money grading firms now designate 'mule' notes." *Coin World*, October 3, 2005.

Newman, Eric P. *The Early Paper Money of America*. 5th ed. Iola, WI: Krause Publications, 2008.

O'Donnell, Chuck. "$100 Red Seal—A New Gem for Your Collection." *Paper Money* 8, no. 1 (1969).

Ormsby, W.L. *Bank Note Engraving*. New York: Author, 1852.

———. *Cycloidal Configurations, or the Harvest of Counterfeiters*. New York: Author, 1862.

Perlmutter, Morey. "The Quintessential Quintet." *Paper Money*, March 1974.

———. "Territorial National Bank Notes." *Paper Money* 8, no. 3 (1969).

Persichetti, Joseph. "Portraits and Vignettes on Modern Size Paper Currency." *Paper Money*, first quarter 1968.

Philpott, William A., Jr. "Choosing Type Faces for National Bank Titles." *Paper Money* 10, no. 38 (1971): 62ff.

———. "Federal Reserve Bank Notes, Series 1915–1918." *The Numismatist*, July 1951.

———. "Federal Reserve Bank Notes, Series of 1914." *The Numismatist*, November 1952.

———. "National Currency, Series of 1929: Why Number One Sheets Are Not Too Rare." *Paper Money* 10, no. 1 (1971).

———. "National Gold Bank Notes." *The Numismatist*, November 1934.

———. "One U.S. $50 Note of Amazing Rarity." *The Numismatist*, April 1969.

———. "Rare Signatures on Large Size U.S. Currency." *Paper Money* 8, no. 3 (1969).

———. "Red Seals Are Rare!" *The Numismatist*, July 1971.

———. "Replacement (Star) Notes Used in Connection with U.S. Paper Money." *The Numismatist*, September 1967.

Price, Bonamy. *Currency and Banking*. New York: D. Appleton and Company, 1876.

Raguet, Condy. *A Treatise on Currency & Banking*. 2nd edition. Philadelphia, PA: Grigg and Elliot, 1840.

Ralph, J.E. "The Production of Paper Money." *The Numismatist*, April 1911.

Raymond, Wayte. *The Standard Paper Money Catalogue*. New York: Wayte Raymond, 1940.

Reed, Fred L., III. *Civil War Encased Stamps, the Issuers and Their Times*. Port Clinton, OH: BNR Press, 1995.

———. "Shades of the Blue and Gray: Feds Look to Second Anti-Photographic Ink." *Bank Note Reporter*, October 2008.

Reinfeld, Fred. *A Simplified Guide to Collecting American Paper Money*. Garden City, NY: Hanover House, 1960.

Rules and Regulations for the Bureau of Engraving and Printing. Washington, DC: Government Printing Office, 1880.

Schmeckebier, Laurence F. *The Bureau of Engraving and Printing: Its History, Activities and Organization*. Service Monographs of the United States Government no. 56. Baltimore: The Johns Hopkins Press, 1929.

Schwartz, John, and Scott Lindquist. *Standard Guide to Small-Size U.S. Paper Money 1928 to Date*. 8th ed. Iola, WI: Krause Publications, 2007.

Schuckers, J.W. *The Life and Public Services of Salmon Portland Chase, United States Senator and Governor of Ohio, Secretary of the Treasury, and Chief Justice of the United States*. New York: D. Appleton and Company, 1874.

Slabaugh, Arlie. *Encased Postage Stamps, U.S. and Foreign*. Chicago: Hewitt Brothers, 1967.

Smedley, Glenn B. "Walter Shirlaw: Paper Money Designer." *Paper Money*, March–April 1999.

Stauffer, David McNeely. *American Engravers Upon Copper and Steel*. New York: The Grolier Club of the City of New York, 1907.

Stiff, James. "Conversation Pieces of Large Size U.S. Paper Money." *Paper Money* 7, no. 4 (1968).

Stratton, Michael V. "'Misplaced' Back Plate Numbers." *Paper Money*, July–August 2002.

Talks, R. Logan. "A Study of $1 1928 United States Notes." *Paper Money*, September–October 1980.

Ton, Graeme M., Jr. "Please: A Little Respect for the Gem CU!" *Paper Money*, November–December 1980.

Turner, Craig J. "Early Engravings of Andrew Jackson and Their Bank Note and Stamp Applications." *Paper Money* 21, no. 101 (1982): 203ff.

Uhler, Frank. "Bureau of Engraving and Printing Modernization Program." *The Numismatist*, January 1966.

U.S. Congress. House. *Journal of Proceedings of Select Committee of the Treasury Department*. 38th Cong., April 30, 1864.

———. *Money Paid to Bank-Note Companies, Etc.: Letter from the Secretary of the Treasury in Answer to a Resolution of the House of January 17, 1870, on the Above Subject*. 41st Cong., 2nd sess., Ex. doc. no. 188. Washington, DC: Government Printing Office, 1870.

U.S. Congress. Senate. *Report of the Joint Committee on Retrenchment*. 40th Cong., 3rd sess., S. Rep. 273, March 3, 1869.

———. *Testimony taken [in 1897] by the Committee appointed to Investigate the Bureau of Engraving and Printing*. 55th Cong., 3rd sess., doc. 109, part II, March 3, 1899.

U.S. Department of Commerce, Bureau of the Census. *Historical Statistics of the United States: Colonial Times to 1970*. Washington, DC: Government Printing Office, 1975.

Valentine, D.W. *United States Fractional Currency*. New York: F.C.C. Boyd, 1924.

Waszilycsak, Bob. "Incomplete Observations About the Faded Backs of $1 Federal Reserve Notes." *Paper Money*, January–February 1990.

Van Belkum, Louis. *National Bank Notes of the Note Issuing Period, 1863–1935*. Chicago: Hewitt Brothers Numismatic Publications, 1968.

———. "New Information on Seldom Seen Notes." *Paper Money* 7, no. 1 (1969).

Yakes, Jamie. "An Update on $5 Silver Certificate Series of 1934C Narrow Faces: New Data and Information." *Paper Money*, November–December 2008.

NOTES

Chapter 2

1. Doug Murray, *Complete Catalog of U.S. Large Size Star Notes 1910–1929*, third edition (Coin & Currency Institute, 2007), 18–19, illustrates certain variations and their standardization.

2. Testimony of Fitch Shepard, president of the National Bank Note Company, in U.S. Congress, Senate, *Report of the Joint Committee on Retrenchment*, 40th Cong., 3rd sess., S. Rep. 273, March 3, 1869, 182.

3. William A. Philpott Jr., "Replacement (Star) Notes Used in Connection with Issuance Of U.S. Paper Currency," *The Numismatist* 80 (September 1967). Beyond this, the article contains some inaccurate information, as determined later by careful research by Doug Murray ($10 star notes were not delivered on June 20, 1910, for example).

4. Letter acquired by the author. "Money is returning on them rapidly" refers to paper money issued by a state-chartered bank being returned to the bank in exchange for gold coins, while the bank wanted to keep the bills in circulation.

5. Retrospective in *Banker's Magazine*, December 1874. Although such figures appear to be precise, in fact they are an estimate.

6. John Sherman, *Recollections of Forty Years in the House, Senate and Cabinet* (1895), 253–255.

7. U.S. Congress, Senate, *Report of the Joint Committee on Retrenchment*, passim.

8. J.W. Schuckers, *The Life and Public Services of Salmon Portland Chase* (1874), 218.

9. Forrest W. Daniel, "Rules for Redemption Reveal Coupon Note Issue," *Paper Money* 7, no. 4 (1968), gives additional information.

10. U.S. Congress, Senate, *Report of the Joint Committee on Retrenchment*, 210.

11. Schuckers, *The Life and Public Services of Salmon Portland Chase*, 229–230.

12. Ibid., 225–226.

13. No numismatic roster of the clerks has ever been made. Treasury reports of the era often include complete rosters of everyone employed in Washington, so the identification of certain of the signatures is a possibility for anyone interested.

14. Letter from Tracy R. Edson, president, to John J. Cisco, July 11, 1862, noting in part: "The one-dollar, two-dollar, and three-dollar plates would have been finished 10th instant had it not been for the change required in the legal tender clause. If no further changes are required they will be finished by Tuesday next."

15. Examination of ABNCo and NBNCo ledgers by Doug Murray, in some cases yielding information superseding that published in the *Report of the Joint Committee on Retrenchment*.

16. In Washington an enterprise thought to have been fraudulent, the Bullion Bank, put out its own paper money dated July 4, 1862, payable in Demand Notes issued by the United States and, at the same time, another issue payable in Legal Tender Notes. Likely, their significance is moot as there is no evidence of their having been used in this matter. These notes are easily found today in the numismatic marketplace.

17. *Reports of the Comptroller of the Currency and Commissioner of Internal Revenue*, 45th Cong., 2nd sess., December 3, 1877.

18. U.S. Congress, Senate, *Report of the Joint Committee on Retrenchment*, 182.

19. Langley's *San Francisco Directory*, 1864–5, 17.

20. United States Patent Office, James M. Willcox, of Glen Mills, Pennsylvania, "Safety-Paper," Letters Patent number 56,650, dated July 24, 1866 (courtesy of Fred L. Reed III).

21. United States Patent Office, George W. Casilear, of Washington, District of Columbia, "Method of Preventing the Alteration of Numbers on Bonds, Notes, and Other Securities," Letters Patent number 84,341, dated Nov. 24, 1868 (courtesy of Fred L. Reed III).

22. His brother was General William Tecumseh Sherman, famous (or infamous) for his Civil War march through Georgia.

23. The use of the terms *obverse* and *reverse* was common in Treasury correspondence and documents, but in numismatics, *face* and *back* are preferred.

24. Peter Huntoon's *United States Large Size National Bank Notes* is the prime source for technical and detailed historical information concerning the notes, including variations in bank titles and printing formats. Don C. Kelly's *National Bank Notes* and the *National Bank Note Census*, by Don C. Kelly and James M. Kelly, are essential references for quantities printed and distributed by over 13,000 banks.

25. Gene Hessler, "Unissued National Bank Circulating Notes of 1873," *The Numismatist* 98 (February 1985).

26. From the diary of Touro Robertson, a Continental employee, as cited by Thomas F. Morris in "Our First National Bank Notes," *The Numismatist*

51 (July 1938). Dunbar of the firm had been a private coiner of gold half eagles in San Francisco during the Gold Rush.

27. *Reports of the Comptroller of the Currency and Commissioner of Internal Revenue*, 45th Cong., 2nd sess., December 3, 1877.

28. Peter Huntoon, *United States Large Size National Bank Notes*.

29. Samuel Bowles, *Across the Continent* (1865), 342–344.

30. John J. Knox, *United States Notes*, 115.

31. Schuckers, *The Life and Public Services of Salmon Portland Chase*, 361.

32. *Investigation into the Causes of the Gold Panic: Report of the Majority of the Committee on Banking and Currency*, March 1, 1870, passim.

33. A detailed account of one such unfortunate seizure is given in *The Numismatist* of August 1959. Separately, Texas currency specialist Robert Schermerhorn had Gold Certificates seized, after which the Treasury kept them (later transferring them to the Smithsonian Institution, where they can be studied today).

34. U.S. Congress, Senate, *Testimony taken by the Committee appointed to Investigate the Bureau of Engraving and Printing*, 55th Cong., 3rd sess., Doc. 109, pt. 2, March 3, 1899.

35. Certain information is from W.A. Philpott Jr., "Federal Reserve Bank Notes, Series 1915–1918," *The Numismatist* 64 (August 1951).

36. W.A. Philpott Jr., "Federal Reserve Bank Notes, Series 1915–1918."

37. Notes with questionable signatures that may have been applied later by numismatists can be checked, to a degree, by reviewing the serial number ranges in the Martin Gengerke census, although there are some slight overlaps.

38. *History of the Bureau of Engraving and Printing* (1962), 117. Bob McCurdy, in "The 1942 Issue of Federal Reserve Bank Notes" (*Paper Money* 10, no. 2), stated that about $360 million in these notes was issued in 1933, with the remainder (about $600 million) issued in 1942. Estimates were given as to the number released stating that 14% of the $50 notes were released in 1933 and 21% of the $100 notes, the rest in 1942. Most were released of the $5 notes, 51% in 1933 and 49% in 1942. The notes were still seen in circulation at that time (1971).

39. W.A. Philpott Jr., "Federal Reserve Notes—Series of 1914," *The Numismatist* 65 (November 1952). Also by the same author and more specific is "Red

Seals Are Rare!" in *The Numismatist* 84 (July 1971).

40. Nathan Goldstein II, "Collecting Current Paper Money," *Paper Money* 5, no. 1 (1966).

Chapter 3

1. *Annual Report of the Secretary of the Treasury*, 1861, 7. The precise nature of the estimate arose from Chase adding together estimates received from various departments and not rounding them off.

2. John Sherman, *John Sherman's Recollections* (Werner, 1895), 278–283, includes this and many other comments about paper money.

3. Hugh McCulloch, *Men and Measures of Half a Century* (Scribner, 1889), 160–161.

4. In December 1860, Cobb left his post and decamped to his home in the South, later gaining a post with the Confederate government. In 1861 New York engraver George H. Lovett inscribed his name as part of a list on his "traitors' medal."

5. Thomas F. Morris II, "The Events of 1863: The First U.S. National Bank Notes," *Essay-Proof Journal* 20, no. 3 (1963), 99–103.

6. Leslie S. Coombs, "National Bank Notes —First Charter Period," *The Numismatist* 64 (September 1951).

7. *History of the Bureau of Engraving and Printing* (BEP, 1962), 21.

8. *Statutes at Large*, vol. 12, 313.

9. Ibid., 346.

10. S.M. Clark, *Report to the Secretary of the Treasury*, November 26, 1864. In July 1885 the *American Journal of Numismatics* article "About Greenbacks" gave a highly dramatized version of this report, without crediting the source.

11. *History of the Bureau of Engraving and Printing*, 22–23.

12. In early 1862, Stuart Gwynn boarded at the Parker House Hotel in Boston and had an office as a consulting engineer in the Phoenix Building. With Herman Haupt and Edward Hamilton he had recently organized the Pneumatic Drill Company, with an authorized capital of $250,000, the charter of which had been approved by the Massachusetts General Court on February 28, 1862. Apparently, little was done further in this connection. Haupt, with the rank of colonel, joined the staff of General Irvin MacDowell on April 21, and in July participated in the Battle of Bull Run. Later, he became a brigadier general.

13. *History of the Bureau of Engraving and Printing*, 35–37. The use of Gwynn's paper created varieties on certain currency printed by the Bureau, but scant notice of these differences has been taken by numismatists.

14. Ibid.

15. Clark, *Report to the Secretary of the Treasury*, 6.

16. S.M. Clark, testimony to Congress, May 4, 1864.

17. Clark, *Report to the Secretary of the Treasury*, 6.

18. Duthie, born in England, was skilled as a painter and engraver. In 1849 and 1850 he was a partner in with John E. Gavit in Gavit & Duthie, bank-note engravers and printers, Exchange Building, in Albany, New York. Later, he was on the staff of Rawdon, Wright, Hatch & Edson, New York City, which in 1858 was the most important of the eight firms that merged to combine as the American Bank Note Company.

19. *History of the Bureau of Engraving and Printing*, 3.

20. Ourdan was born in New York circa 1813, and by the late 1830s was a professional engraver in Albany, New York, afterward working with several firms in New York City and Philadelphia. In 1859 he was one of the first engravers hired by the newly formed National Bank Note Company. His father, Joseph James Prosper Ourdan, learned engraving from his son, and worked at the National Currency Bureau from 1866 until his death in 1874.

21. *History of the Bureau of Engraving and Printing*, 6, citing an 1880 memorandum by O.H. Irish, then chief of the bureau.

22. Clark, *Report to the Secretary of the Treasury*, 7.

23. *History of the Bureau of Engraving and Printing*, 7; other sources.

24. Hugh McCulloch, *Men and Measures of Half a Century*, 166–167. Spencer M. Clark is not even mentioned in his autobiography, which was published many years later in 1900. McCulloch hired John Burroughs as a clerk in 1864; he would go on to become an important author on nature, in the footsteps of Henry David Thoreau.

25. Hopper later moved to the New York Sub-Treasury, where he countersigned Silver Certificates of the Series of 1878. In July 1889 he was made chief bookkeeper there at a salary of $2,000 per year.

26. John Joy Edson later became prominent in financial circles, including serving as president of the Washington Loan & Trust Company.

27. Quoted from Salmon P. Chase, *Report of the Secretary of the Treasury on the State of the Finances, the Year Ending June 30, 1863*, 59.

28. *History of the Bureau of Engraving and Printing*, 11.

29. He later became involved in railroading in the West. The Cisco name was attached to a town in Texas, to the "Cisco Kid," and to today's Cisco Systems in the computer field. No serious study has ever been done on Cisco.

30. Although Wilson said that the prostitution raid had been a sensational event and had been widely reported in newspapers, he was unable to produce any specific accounts.

31. The investigation of him was inconclusive, but it was learned that he had received "gifts" from those with whom the government did business.

32. Detailed in the *38th Congressional Report, Select Committee of the Treasury Department, House of Representatives, April 30, 1864*.

33. The deceased was Miss Laura Duvall, one of the ladies from whom Baker extracted a coerced statement. She had worked at the Treasury since November 18, 1863, and had been hired on the recommendation of Mayor Richard Wallach of the city.

34. McCulloch, *Men and Measures of Half a Century*, 16; a detailed story of the scandal is in the same book. Similar to the situation for John J. Cisco, a well-researched book on Baker would make interesting reading. Among other things, in 1856 Baker was in San Francisco where he was a member of the Committee of Vigilance. He later conducted the Mercantile Agency in the same city, until 1861, when he returned to the East.

35. Some of this paper, intended for the Confederate States of America, had CSA watermarks and was later used by Clark to print Fractional Currency, including specimen notes. Other of the paper was cut into strips and used for banding bundles of redeemed notes slated for burning.

36. A statement from Captain W.A. Wright of the schooner *J.P. Augur* noted that the first shipment was of 16 presses weighing 11,000 pounds each. The freight bill at $8 per ton was $704.

37. *History of the Bureau of Engraving and Printing*, 20.

38. U.S. Congress, Senate, *Report of the Joint Committee on Retrenchment*. This report contains testimony concerning these presses, including widely varying reports of how many sheets could be printed in a day.

39. Schuckers, *The Life and Public Services of Salmon Portland Chase*, 294.

40. *New-York Daily Tribune*, October 13, 1864; continued November 11, 1864.

41. Also with the exception of Legal Tender Notes, which continued to be printed

by the American and National bank note companies in New York.

42. This would seem to date the introduction of heavy fiber paper, following a year of making Fractional Currency on other paper within the Department.

43. "Department issues" refers to notes printed within the National Currency Bureau, as opposed to those made by contractors in New York.

44. Tichenor had worked with geometric lathes since the 1830s. He later joined the staff of the BEP.

45. The process of transferring via roller dies (or cylinder dies) is known as siderography. Siderographers were among the highest-paid employees of the private bank note companies.

46. At this time the Bureau was printing no low-denomination bills (except Fractional Currency). Sheets of $1 and $2 notes, and other Legal Tender Notes made under contract in New York City, were sent to the Bureau to be sealed, trimmed, and cut.

47. U.S. Congress, Senate, *Report of the Joint Committee on Retrenchment*, 195–196 (testimony of October 11, 1867, by three employees of James Conner's Sons (Frank L. Bower, Charles H. Quail, and Gustave H. Schauppner); in Treasury reports the firm is also referred to as James Conner & Sons; see also pp. 367–368, of Charles Neale, chief of the Bureau of Redemption within the Treasury, and earlier a plate printer.

48. The *Report of the Joint Committee on Retrenchment* gives details.

49. Ibid., 109, 131.

50. U.S. Congress, Senate, *Report of the Joint Committee on Retrenchment*, 329–340 (on paper making), 383 (on space occupied).

51. The blue-tinted paper was used for certain Fourth and Fifth issue Fractional Currency, Series of 1875 National Bank Notes, Legal Tender Notes of the series of 1869 and 1878, Silver Certificates of the Series of 1878, and Series of 1879 $10 Refunding Certificates.

52. *History of the Bureau of Engraving and Printing*, 37.

53. Quoted text has been slightly edited.

54. The mention of correcting misnumbered sheets is interesting, an aspect not otherwise recorded in any text seen.

55. 19th Stat. L., 152. This provision proved to be an easy compliance, as contracts nearly always cost more than work done in-house by the Treasury.

56. Terms popularized by Doug Walcutt and Peter Huntoon.

57. 24 Stat. L. 227.

58. *Rules and Regulations for the Bureau of Engraving and Printing* (BEP, 1880), 43n.

59. Patent 180,490, granted August 1, 1876.

60. *History of the Bureau of Engraving and Printing*, 30–35.

61. This was Charles A. Williams, a founder and director of the Second National Bank of Nashua, New Hampshire.

62. Clara Belle Rouse, *Iowa Leaves* (Illinois Printing, 1891); R.L. Polk & Co.'s *Northwestern Gazetteer and Business Directory* 20 (1916–1917); *History of the Counties of Woodbury and Plymouth, Iowa, Including an Extended Sketch of Sioux City* (Chicago: Werner & Co., 1891).

63. "Monetary Stringency of 1890," *Annual Report of the Comptroller of the Currency*, December 7, 1891, 9.

64. "Morgan Talks with Cleveland," *New York Herald Tribune*, February 6, 1895.

65. Although de facto the United States had issued gold coins worth full face value for a long time, it did not officially go to a strict gold standard until 1900.

66. Thomas F. Morris, "U.S. Silver Certificates, Series of 1896," *The Numismatist* 47 (June 1934).

67. Ibid.

68. "Testimony taken [in 1897] by the Committee appointed to Investigate the Bureau of Engraving and Printing," 55th Cong., 3rd sess., Senate, document 109, part II, March 3, 1899.

69. The building is located where the Empire State Building is today.

70. Peter Huntoon's *United States Large Size National Bank Notes* gives details.

71. Doug Murray, *Complete Catalog of U.S. Large Size Star Notes 1910–1929*, third edition (Clifton, New Jersey: Coin & Currency Institute, 2007), 9ff.

72. Huntoon, *United States Large Size National Bank Notes*, revised manuscript.

73. Lee Lofthus, "Redemption Errors. Treasury ledgers found to be inaccurate," *Bank Note Reporter* 35, no. 9 (September 2008).

74. Per testimony in the 1897 congressional investigation of the BEP.

75. *History of the Bureau of Engraving and Printing*, 108.

76. Ibid., 110–114; see also various articles in *The Numismatist*, the most important of which is Robert H. Lloyd's "The New Currency in Review" (July 1929).

77. *History of the Bureau of Engraving and Printing*, 115.

78. Henry left numismatics. Julius remained and was important in the Westchester County (New York) Coin Club when in 1938 it sponsored the New Rochelle commemorative half dollar. In the 1950s I spoke with him in New York City.

79. Losses to depositors and shareholders were about $2.5 billion. This includes National Banks as well as other banks. N. Gregory Minkiw, "But Have We Learned Enough?" *New York Times*, October 26, 2008.

80. *History of the Bureau of Engraving and Printing*, 164–165.

81. Grover Criswell, "From Your President," *The Numismatist* 89 (October 1977).

82. From "U.S. Government's Tryst with a Plastic Substrate for Currency," Robert J. Leuver's address to the Chicago Coin Club, July 9, 2008, published online by the club. Perhaps some were distributed as souvenirs, as Leuver asked the audience, "Does anyone have any of the U.S. Tyvek notes?"

Chapter 4

1. William P. Koster, "Some Thoughts on Grading," *Paper Money* 67 (January–February 1977).

2. Sometimes large-size notes will be encountered that are obviously Uncirculated but have some tiny pinholes. This is perfectly acceptable. It was customary in the old days to spindle or pin new notes together, and that is why so many Uncirculated notes show tiny pinholes.

Chapter 5

1. Largely through the research and contributions of Doug Murray.

2. Certain of the following hoards are discussed in detail in my 1997 book, *American Coin Treasures and Hoards* (Zyrus Press).

3. Details of the bank's evolution and mergers over the years and quantities of notes issued may be found in John Hickman and Dean Oakes, *Standard Catalogue of National Bank Notes* (Krause, 1990), 283.

4. Adapted from an interview with Dean Oakes in Denver, Colorado, August 12, 1996.

5. Information is also from "Storied 'Oat Bin' Nationals Go To Auction," *Bank Note Reporter*, November 1979, 1. Citation furnished by David Harper.

Chapter 6

1. Information compiled by Doug Murray based upon examination of the ABNCo and NBNCo ledgers, the Senate's *Report of the Joint Committee on Retrenchment*, and other sources.

2. Information from Doug Murray.

3. Per *Bank Note Reporter*, October 2006, and Doug Murray.

4. William H. Dillistin, "National Bank Notes in the Early Years," *The Numismatist* 60 (December 1948); Huntoon,

United States Large Size National Bank Notes, 59.

5. Kelly census information as of August 2008. Subject to change or modification as new information is obtained.

6. This state may be proportionally over-reported due to extensive research by the author and David M. Sundman in the New Hampshire Currency Project.

7. Imprinting of the two charter numbers on $1-$1-$1-$2 sheets actually began on May 14, 1874, before the legislation was passed. On some early impressions the red charter number on the right appears above the Treasury seal instead of the normal (later) position below it. Normally positioned, the Treasury seal has the space above it occupied by the bank serial number. The first two deliveries with the charter numbers seem to have been the Wickford (Rhode Island) National Bank, charter 1592; and the First National Bank of Bennington, Vermont, charter 130. Information from Doug Walcutt provided by Peter Huntoon.

8. Huntoon, *United States Large Size National Bank Notes*.

9. James M. Kelly and Don C. Kelly, *National Bank Note Census*, information as of August 2008. Subject to change or modification as new information is obtained.

10. Thomas F. Morris (Jr.) was an avid numismatist and historian. In particular, he contributed much to the pages of the *Essay-Proof Journal*. His 1934 article in *The Numismatist* stated that the first notes had a word in the Constitution spelled as TRANQUILLITY, instead of TRANQUILITY, as it is on the original document. "While none of these notes were recalled, the plate was re-engraved to the correct spelling and the later notes indicate that the error does not occur." This is fiction, as plate 1, still in existence, does not have the variant spelling.

11. Information from Doug Murray.

12. *The Numismatist* 22 (April 1910).

13. R. Logan Talks, "A Study of $1 1928 United States Notes," *Paper Money* 19 (September–October 1980).

14. Louis S. Werner, "Small-Size Silver Certificate Experimental Issues," *Paper Money* 9, no. 2 (1970).

15. See Graeme M. Ton Jr., "The $1 Silver Certificate Mules," *Paper Money* 23 (May–June 1984); only four mule stars were known to him.

16. David H. Klein, "The Last $1 Silver Certificates," *Paper Money* 25 (January–February 1986).

17. Ibid.

18. Authorized under H.R. 5389, sent to President John F. Kennedy for his signature on May 23, 1963.

19. Bob Waszilycsak, "Incomplete Observations about the Faded Backs of $1 Federal Reserve Notes," *Paper Money* 29 (January–February 1990).

20. Michael V. Stratton, "'Misplaced' Back Plate Numbers," *Paper Money* 41 (July–August 2002).

21. Waszilycsak, "Incomplete Observations about the Faded Backs of $1 Federal Reserve Notes."

22. "Ceremonies for first Regan/Ortega FR Notes," *Paper Money* 23 (March 1984).

23. Stratton, "'Misplaced' Back Plate Numbers."

24. Bob Kvederas Sr. and Bob Kvederas Jr., "Varieties of Series 1993 $1 Web Notes," *Paper Money* 36 (September–October 1997).

25. Stratton, "'Misplaced' Back Plate Numbers."

26. Bob Kvederas Sr. and Bob Kvederas Jr., "Varieties of Series 1995 $1 Web Notes," *Paper Money* 37 (May–June 1998).

Chapter 7

1. Robert H. Lloyd, "The Two-Dollar Bill," *The Numismatist* 41 (June 1928).

2. Information compiled by Doug Murray based upon examination of the ABNCo and NBNCo ledgers, the Senate's *Report of the Joint Committee on Retrenchment*, 40th Cong., 3rd sess., Rep. Com. no. 273, March 3, 1869, and other sources.

3. Doug Murray, communication, November 23, 2008.

4. Information from Doug Murray.

5. Information from Doug Murray.

6. Information from Doug Murray.

7. Dillistin, "National Bank Notes in the Early Years"; Huntoon, *United States Large Size National Bank Notes*, 59.

8. Kelly census information as of August 2008. Subject to change or modification as new information is obtained.

9. Although this comment is not necessarily relevant to the Paola note, the Kelly census gives information as reported by the owners of notes and observers, in addition to those submitted by experienced collectors, dealers, and in auction listings. Accordingly, actual grades of certain notes may differ from those listed.

10. This state may be proportionally over-reported due to extensive research by David M. Sundman and me in the New Hampshire Currency Project.

11. Not including 25 notes listed as counterfeit (see Kelly database for details).

12. Kelly census information as of August 2008. Subject to change or modification as new information is obtained.

13. Not including one note listed as counterfeit (see Kelly database for bank and serial of this).

14. Frank DeWitt in *The Numismatist* 53 (July 1940).

15. By that time, in 1896, he had so strongly protested the three Series of 1896 designs that he felt he was in danger of being fired by bureau chief Claude M. Johnson. Among the criticisms was that large portraits of people belonged on the face of notes, not the back.

16. U.S. Congress, *Testimony taken (in 1897) by the Committee appointed to Investigate the Bureau of Engraving and Printing*, 55th Cong., 3rd sess., document 109, part II, March 3, 1899.

17. Information from Doug Murray.

18. Featured by Peter Huntoon in "The $2 Legal Tender Series 1928-C and 1928-D Mules," *Paper Money* 31 (September–October 1992).

19. *The Numismatist* 95 (July 1982).

20. As reported by the BEP. Neither 9,999 nor 1,280,000 divides evenly to indicate the normal 36-subject sheets, so some notes must have been removed from distribution.

Chapter 8

1. Information compiled by Doug Murray based upon examination of the ABNCo and NBNCo ledgers, the Senate's *Report of the Joint Committee on Retrenchment*, 40th Cong., 3rd sess., Rep. Com. no. 273, March 3, 1869, and other sources.

2. James Stiff, "Conversation Pieces of Large Size U.S. Paper Money," *Paper Money* 7, no. 4 (1968), is an early mention of the PCBLIC error.

3. Information from Doug Murray.

4. S.M. Clark, *Report to the Secretary of the Treasury*, November 26, 1864. The contract specified the vignettes to be used on $5 and also $10 notes.

5. Ibid.

6. Dillistin, "National Bank Notes in the Early Years."

7. Imprinting of the two charter numbers on $5-$5-$5-$25 sheets actually began on May 13, 1874, before the legislation was passed (information from Doug Walcutt provided by Peter Huntoon).

8. President of this bank was Henry Cooke, brother of Jay Cooke of Jay Cooke & Co., Philadelphia, which controlled the bank, the most important dealer in government securities, accounting for the honor given to the bank to have the first release. Both the bank and Jay Cooke & Co. collapsed in the Panic of 1873. The plate position A, serial number 1 note, illustrated here, was discovered by Littleton Coin Company in 2000 and was the subject of a front-page article by

William T. Gibbs in *Coin World* on January 15, 2001.

9. Peter Huntoon, correspondence, September 29, 2008.

10. Certain banks in this charter number sequence (2131, 2133, 2134, 2140) were newly formed and ordered plates for the first time. No notes have been located by Peter Huntoon.

11. Peter Huntoon writes: "In what is a remarkable coincidence given the size of Pennsylvania, and the abundance of banks in the state, these three (Black Charter) banks are located within eleven 11 miles of each other some 25 miles northwest of the heart of Philadelphia."

12. Census information is accurate as of August 2008. The information given here is subject to change or modification as new information is obtained.

13. Not including 13 listed as counterfeit (see Kelly database for details).

14. Lot 13487 in Heritage sale of September 18, 2008, graded as given in the catalog. Earlier this note was listed as Fine–Very Fine in the Kelly census.

15. Not including five listed as counterfeit (see Kelly database for details).

16. Not including three listed as counterfeit (see Kelly database for details).

17. Not including one listed as counterfeit (see Kelly database for bank and serial).

18. Not including three listed as counterfeit (see Kelly database for details).

19. Certain banks in this charter number sequence (2131, 2133, 2134) were newly formed and ordered plates for the first time. No notes have been located by Peter Huntoon.

20. See note 12.

21. In the collection of the Federal Reserve Bank of Kansas City (cf. Don C. Kelly, *National Bank Notes*).

22. Grades reported by Peter Huntoon (correspondence).

23. Information from the New Hampshire Currency Project.

24. Serial 3095 plate D in the Kelly census. Not verified by Peter Huntoon.

25. None in the Kelly census. Gene Hessler and Carlson Chambliss report one, bank title not given, in the *Complete Catalog of U.S. Paper Money*.

26. *United States Large Size National Bank Notes*, chapter 14.

27. See note 12.

28. Not including five listed as counterfeit (see Kelly database for details).

29. See note 12.

30. See note 12.

31. See note 12.

32. See note 12.

33. See note 12.

34. U.S. Congress, Senate, *Testimony taken (in 1897) by the Committee appointed to Investigate the Bureau of Engraving and Printing*, in 55th Cong., 3rd sess., document 109, part II, March 3, 1899.

35. Information from Doug Murray.

36. Per archival research by Doug Murray. Serial numbers range from A90716001A to A92008000A.

37. See note 12.

38. See note 12.

39. For additional information concerning these and other mules the essential reference is the *Standard Guide to Small-Size U.S. Paper Money 1928 to Date*, by John Schwartz and Scott Lindquist.

40. Communication, November 17, 2008.

41. Jamie Yakes, communication, November 17, 2008.

Chapter 9

1. Dies and documentation were found in the American Bank Note Company Archives.

2. S.M. Clark, *Report to the Secretary of the Treasury*, November 26, 1864.

3. Ibid.

4. Gene Hessler, "Compound Interest Treasury Notes with the Incorrect Act Date, a second look," *Paper Money* 34 (January–February 1995).

5. Information compiled by Doug Murray based upon examination of the ABNCo and NBNCo ledgers, the *Report of the Joint Committee on Retrenchment*, 40th Congress, 3rd Session, Senate, Rep. Com. No. 273, March 3, 1869, and other sources.

6. Per Tom Koch, papermoneyworld.net website, September 14, 2005; sources included William Cox, associate archivist at the Smithsonian Institution.

7. Dillistin, "National Bank Notes in the Early Years."

8. Leslie S. Coombs, "National Bank Notes—First Charter Period," *The Numismatist* 63 (September 1951).

9. Census information is accurate as of August 2008. The information given here is subject to change or modification as new information is obtained.

10. Not including three listed as counterfeit (see Kelly database for details).

11. Not including 18 listed as counterfeit (see Kelly database for details).

12. Not including three listed as counterfeit (see Kelly database for details).

13. Information from Peter Huntoon.

14. See note 9.

15. Not including one listed as counterfeit (see Kelly database for details).

16. The rarer style seems to have been used on plates made from September 1885 to part way through August 1893. Some of the plates have the American Bank Note Company name at the bottom, while others have the Bureau of Engraving and Printing imprint. Information from Peter Huntoon.

17. See note 9.

18. The rarer style seems to have been used on plates made from September 1885 to part way through August 1893, later reentered. Per communication with Peter Huntoon, October 24, 2008.

19. Peter Huntoon, "Small Issue Sheets of Large Notes a Rarity," *Bank Note Reporter*, September 2008. Across the entire spectrum of large-size notes only *four* National Banks ever received just a single sheet of a particular issue.

20. See note 9.

21. The rarer style seems to have been used on plates made from September 1885 to part way through August 1893, later reentered. Per communication with Peter Huntoon, October 24, 2008.

22. See note 9.

23. Mortally wounded, McKinley lingered in seclusion for eight days, while news of his condition was telegraphed to the world by a young man, Thomas L. Elder, who later achieved fame as a professional numismatist. McKinley was also honored on several coins, including the 1903 Louisiana Purchase gold dollar and on the 1916 and 1917 McKinley gold dollar, the last two depicting the McKinley Memorial at Niles, Ohio, where he was born in 1843.

24. Huntoon, "Small Issue Sheets of Large Notes a Rarity." See note 19.

25. See note 9.

26. Information from Peter Huntoon.

27. Huntoon, "Small Issue Sheets of Large Notes a Rarity." See note 19.

28. See note 9.

29. See note 9.

30. Friedberg lists W.G. White for the $10, but probably meant the White we mention here (whose identity was discovered during research for this book).

31. My consultants and I have not been able to confirm the existence of F-284a with an *autographed* signature of Hillhouse (who held the position of assistant Treasurer in New York from 1870 to 1881).

32. *The Numismatist* 19 (August 1907).

33. Information from Doug Murray.

34. See note 9.

35. See note 9.

Chapter 10

1. Gene Hessler and Carlson Chambliss, *Comprehensive Catalog of U.S. Paper Money*.

2. S.M. Clark, *Report to the Secretary of the Treasury*, November 26, 1864. A scrubbing woman was suspected and the theft

"clearly proven," but no charges were filed.

3. Information compiled by Doug Murray based upon examination of the ABNCo and NBNCo ledgers; the *Report of the Joint Committee on Retrenchment*; and other sources.

4. Letter located in the National Archives by Doug Murray.

5. Information from Doug Murray.

6. S.M. Clark, *Report to the Secretary of the Treasury*, November 26, 1864.

7. Dillistin, "National Bank Notes in the Early Years."

8. Visitors to the ABNCo offices in New York City in the early 1860s could view an exhibit of Darley's art and bank notes featuring his motifs, these being issues of state-chartered banks before the National Bank era.

9. Census information is accurate as of August 2008. The information given here is subject to change or modification as new information is obtained.

10. Not including five listed as counterfeit (see Kelly database for details).

11. Not including two listed as counterfeit (see Kelly database for details).

12. See note 9.
13. See note 9.
14. See note 9.
15. See note 9.
16. See note 9.
17. See note 9.
18. See note 9.

19. Information and illustrations from Doug Murray.

20. Information from Doug Murray.

21. Printages except for New York are from the *Report of the Joint Committee on Retrenchment*, 123–124.

22. Estimates for New York derived by Doug Murray and the author from the 1869 *Annual Report*. Printages of Gold Certificates vary in different reports.

23. The Atlantic cable celebration spawned several medals, most notably by New York City engraver George H. Lovett. These were well received and launched a numismatic medal craze that extended into 1860 and saw many interesting varieties depicting notable events in American history, prominent figures, and other topics.

24. "The Submarine Cable," *Scientific American*, July 25, 1896, and other sources.

25. Technicolor, in development since 1912, was first successfully used with red and green colors in the 1926 Douglas Fairbanks film *The Black Pirate*. Three-color Technicolor films were not produced until the 1930s.

26. Information from Doug Murray.

27. Per archival research by Doug Murray.

28. Per archival research by Doug Murray.
29. See note 9.
30. See note 9.
31. *The Numismatist* 60 (August 1948).

Chapter 11

1. The F-192a variety with Chittenden-Spinner signatures and ACT OF JUNE 30TH 1864 has been adjudged as counterfeit by Martin Gengerke. No authentic examples are known to have been printed. Accordingly, it is not listed here.

2. Gene Hessler, "Compound Interest Treasury Notes with the Incorrect Act Date, a Second Look," *Paper Money* 34 (January–February 1995).

3. Information compiled by Doug Murray, based upon examination of the ABNCo and NBNCo ledgers, the *Report of the Joint Committee on Retrenchment*, and other sources.

4. Doug Murray, personal communication, October 11, 2008.

5. F-153 *is* listed, with transposed signatures as Wyman-Allison, which may have been intended as this note. Otherwise, F-153 has not been seen.

6. S.M. Clark, *Report to the Secretary of the Treasury*, November 26, 1864.

7. Census information is accurate as of August 2008. The information given here is subject to change or modification as new information is obtained.

8. Not including one listed as counterfeit (see Kelly database for details).

9. Information from Peter Huntoon.

10. See note 7.
11. See note 7.
12. See note 7.
13. See note 7.
14. See note 7.
15. See note 7.
16. See note 7.

17. Information from Doug Murray.

18. Information from Doug Murray.

19. Personal conversation with Mr. Philpott in the late 1950s.

20. Peter Huntoon, unpublished manuscript, "$50 FRBN Series of 1918 St. Louis Note."

21. See note 7.
22. See note 7.

Chapter 12

1. U.S. Congress, Senate, *Report of the Joint Committee on Retrenchment*, 192. Testimony of C.L. Van Zandt, secretary of ABNCo.

2. Ibid., 174.

3. S.M. Clark, *Report to the Secretary of the Treasury*, November 26, 1864.

4. William P. Koster, "A Superb Counterfeit: The $100 Compound Interest Note," *Paper Money*, January–February 1955.

5. Information compiled by Doug Murray based upon examination of the ABNCo and NBNCo ledgers, the *Report of the Joint Committee on Retrenchment*, and other sources.

6. Information from Doug Murray.

7. S.M. Clark, *Report to the Secretary of the Treasury*, November 26, 1864.

8. Census information is accurate as of August 2008. The information given here is subject to change or modification as new information is obtained.

9. Not including one listed as counterfeit (see Kelly database for details).

10. Not including four listed as counterfeit (see Kelly database for details).

11. Not including five listed as counterfeit (see Kelly database for details).

12. Information from Peter Huntoon.

13. See note 8.

14. Not including one listed as counterfeit (see Kelly database for details).

15. See note 8.
16. See note 8.

17. The niche occupied by the curious and rare Series of 1882 $50 and $100 Value Back bills is the subject of chapter 19 of Peter Huntoon's *United States Large Size National Bank Notes*, an essential volume for any serious student of paper money.

18. See note 8.
19. See note 8.
20. See note 8.
21. See note 8.

22. Printages except for New York are from the *Report of the Joint Committee on Retrenchment*, 123–124.

23. Estimates for New York derived by Doug Murray and the author from the 1869 *Annual Report*. Printages of Gold Certificates vary in different reports.

24. Communication from Doug Murray, October 31, 2008. A feature story about them, "When Stalin Counterfeited Dollars," by W.G. Krivitsky, which appeared in the *Saturday Evening Post*, September 30, 1939, speculated on their origin but contained no numismatic information. See Hessler and Chambliss, page 234, for expanded discussion and illustrations.

25. Chuck O'Donnell, "$100 Red Seal—A New Gem for Your Collection," *Paper Money* 8, no. 1 (1969).

26. See note 8.
27. See note 8.

Chapter 13

1. Communication to the author, November 10, 2008.

2. S.M. Clark, *Report to the Secretary of the Treasury*, November 26, 1864.

3. Information compiled by Doug Murray based upon examination of the ABNCo and NBNCo ledgers, the *Report of the*

Joint Committee on Retrenchment, and other sources.

4. Listed by Hessler and Chambliss as their CH-1371.

5. Listed by Hessler and Chambliss as their CH-1374.

6. Peter W. Huntoon, "The United States $500 and $1,000 National Bank Notes," *United States Large Size National Bank Notes*, 87–111, gives a detailed study of these two denominations.

7. So titled in a Treasury-issued volume of vignettes.

8. Serial 206 was reported by Fred Reinfeld, a popular writer on numismatics and chess, in 1960, giving its location as the BEP. Peter Huntoon notes that there seems to be no record of it there.

9. Information from Peter Huntoon.

10. This does not include 695 National Gold Bank Notes, listed separately in this text. This and certain other information from Peter Huntoon and Don C. Kelly.

11. Although this variety is listed in various texts, Doug Murray has located no record of its ever having been printed.

12. Printages except for New York are from the *Report of the Joint Committee on Retrenchment*, 123–124.

Chapter 14

1. S.M. Clark, *Report to the Secretary of the Treasury*. Apparently, the loss was never recovered. Clark further commented that it took place outside of his National Currency Bureau, where he maintained that security was very tight.

2. Ibid.

3. Information compiled by Doug Murray based upon examination of the ABNCo and NBNCo ledgers, the *Report of the Joint Committee on Retrenchment*, and other sources.

4. The only National Bank in that New York town to issue notes was the City National Bank of Poughkeepsie, chartered on June 19, 1865. It would seem that the $5 note found on this luckless passenger was among the very first issued by that institution.

5. Huntoon, *United States Large Size National Bank Notes*, manuscript notes.

6. Ibid.

7. Printages except for New York are from the *Report of the Joint Committee on Retrenchment*, 123–124.

Chapter 15

1. S.M. Clark, *Report to the Secretary of the Treasury*.

2. This issue is not listed in the recapitulation of this series in the 1868 *Report to the Secretary of the Treasury*.

3. *Report of the Joint Committee on Retrenchment*, 123–124, for Washington (but not New York) printage.

4. Hessler and Chambliss, in *Comprehensive Catalog of U.S. Paper Money*, 7th edition, give the issued amount as 5,977. BEP annual reports show that only 1,000 notes were printed (fiscal year 1878) with this signature combination.

Chapter 16

1. See Hessler and Chambliss, *Comprehensive Catalog of U.S. Paper Money*, 283–284, which also has a detailed discussion of varieties. In his 6th edition Gene Hessler stated that over 100 Uncirculated notes entered the market in 1995, with no action taken toward them regarding legality.

2. It would be an interesting exercise to delineate the motifs made by or for the private bank-note companies and used without credit on new currency designs created by the BEP after 1880.

3. Information from Doug Murray.

4. Also on exhibit was a stuffed bear, labeled "Helen **Waite**, Credit Manager," and the comment: "If you want credit here, go to Helen Waite" (think about it). For a list of serial numbers of the notes and other information, see Peter Huntoon, "The Binion $10,000 Notes of Las **Vegas**, Nevada," *Paper Money* 38 (1999).

Chapter 18

1. Certain remarks are adapted from my introduction to part of the John J. Ford Jr. sale of encased postage stamps (Stack's, 2004).

2. As quoted in *The Bankers' Magazine and Statistical Register*, November 1862.

3. John J. Knox, *United States Notes*, 104.

4. Neil Carothers, *Fractional Money*, 177–178.

5. Compiled by Fred L. Reed.

6. Citation contributed by Richard Winslow III.

7. Carothers, *Fractional Money*, 189.

8. S.M. Clark, *Report to the Secretary of the Treasury*, 17.

9. The Gordon Press, also called the Franklin Press (although other types of presses also used that name), was the invention of George Phineas Gordon, of New York. Powered by either a foot treadle or by connection to an engine, the device featured a platen mounted at a 45-degree angle and multiple ink rolls. It could produce printed sheets much faster than a typical handpress used in commercial print shops. Among other duties, the Gordon Press was used to apply bronzing ink to certain security paper at the Bureau.

10. Clark, *Report to the Secretary of the Treasury*, 16–17.

11. The total amount of these notes originally produced will never be known, as record keeping was poor and incomplete for the Second and Third Issues. Certain accounts of the late 1870s place the amount at about $347,000,000. Later, "precision" seems to have been added.

12. U.S. Congress, Senate, *Report of the Joint Committee on Retrenchment*, 183.

13. Ibid., 107–116, 167 (summary), and others.

14. Ibid., 115; commencement date, this being earlier than the December 5, 1864, date given in some numismatic texts.

15. Ibid., 394.

16. Comment added at the suggestion of Jerry Fochtman.

17. *Complete Catalog of U.S. Paper Money*, 286–287.

18. *Report of the Joint Committee on Retrenchment*, 394.

19. Ibid., 158.

Chapter 22

1. The two most comprehensive auction offerings of encased postage stamps have been the John J. Ford Jr. Collection (Stack's, 2004) and the Frederick Mayer Collection (Heritage, 2007). Meyer had been a large buyer in the Ford sale.

INDEX

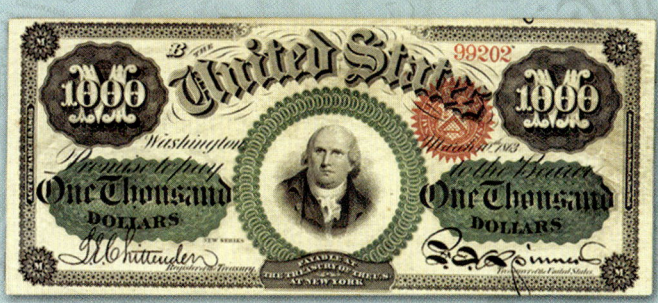

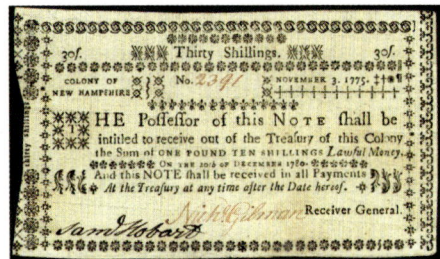
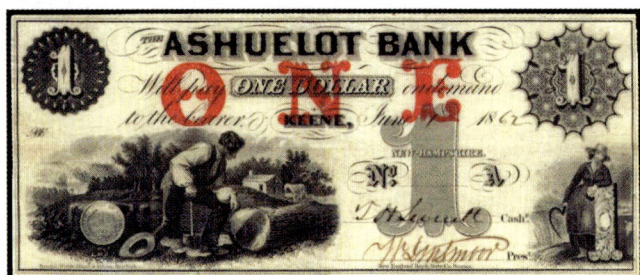

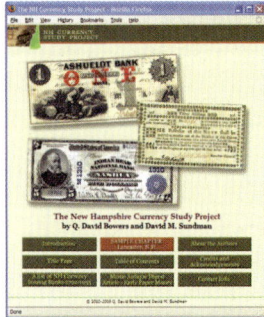

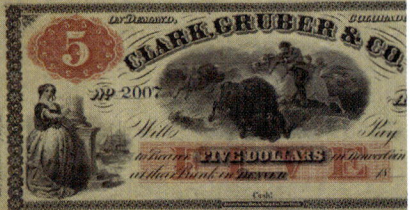

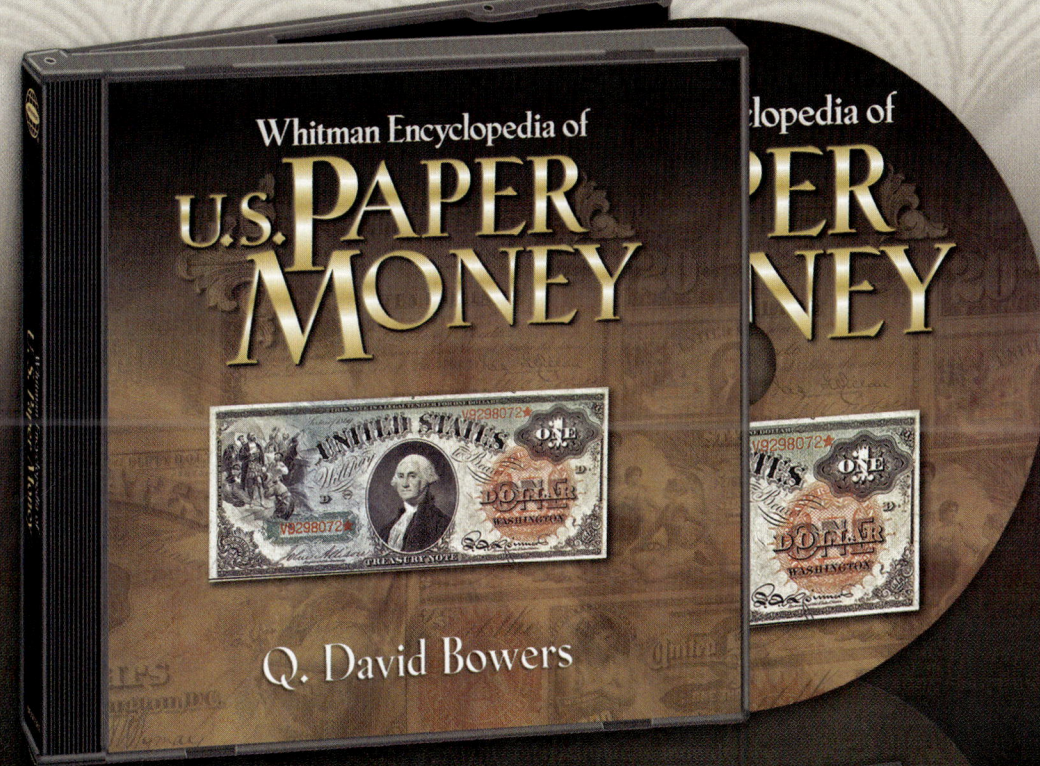